Contents

The MILEPOST®
All-The-North Travel Guide®

Introduction

Major Attractions

Ins

Highways

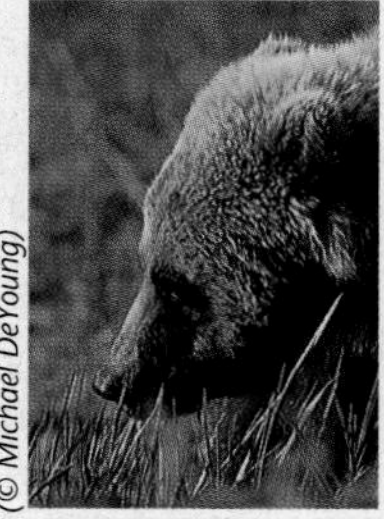

(© Michael DeYoung)

Railroads

Marine Access Routes

Travel Planning

General Information

The MILEPOST®

EDITORIAL AND ADVERTISING SALES OFFICES:
619 E. Ship Creek Ave, Suite 329
Anchorage, AK 99501
Phone (907) 272-6070; fax (907) 258-5360

To order *THE MILEPOST®* and related products, phone 1-800-726-4707; e-mail books@themilepost.com; or visit our book catalog at www.themilepost.com

The MILEPOST® is an annual publication of Morris Communications Corporation, 735 Broad Street, Augusta, GA 30901.

ISSN 0361-1361 ISBN 1-892154-02-1
Key title: The Milepost Printed in U.S.A.

Photography credits: Cover—RV on Alaska's Seward Highway. (Steven Nourse/Ken Graham Agency). **Insets**—Tour boat at Hole-in-the-Wall waterfall, Tracy Arm Fjord. (© Beth Davidow). Brown bear with red salmon. (© Roy Corral)
Column insets: Deborah Bernard, page 475; Gladys Blyth, pages 214, 224, 228; Alisha A. Brown, page 723; Earl L. Brown, pages 45, 49, 76, 77, 81, 83, 90, 91, 97, 98, 101, 106, 107, 114, 116, 117, 119, 120, 122, 125, 126, 138, 142, 143, 153, 154, 158, 163, 169, 170, 172, 175, 177, 197, 203, 213, 243, 248, 249, 250, 253, 258, 260, 261, 262, 698, 701, 706, 711, 734, 735; Perry E. Brown, page 260; Chuck Dell, page 442; Laurent Dick; page 196; Edmonton Tourism, pages 38, 44; Kris Graef, pages 1, 70, 179–182, 184, 189, 203, 264, 266–269, 274, 275, 319, 320, 328, 344, 348, 356, 357, 363, 369, 377, 387, 388, 416, 417, 471, 489, 490, 492, 495, 499–501, 508, 511, 538, 544, 548, 552, 563, 566, 569–572, 583, 586, 596; Lyn Hancock, pages 707, 743; Blake Hanna, pages 38, 39, 41, 44, 64, 68, 69, 71, 210, 218, 235; Leslie Leong, pages 740, 742, 744, 745; Sheryl L. Mills, page 203; Judy Parkin, pages 59, 60, 68, 74, 75, 204, 213, 219, 236; Tom Parkin, page 221; Roger Pickenpaugh, pages 737, 738; Rollo Pool, pages 1, 726; David Ranta, pages 480, 481; Jill Shepherd, page 286; Scottie Creek Services, page 179; Wolf Song of Alaska, page 330.

Photo submissions: Copies of photo submission guidelines *must* be requested before submitting photos. Send request and postpaid return envelope to the Editor. *The MILEPOST®* assumes no responsibility for unsolicited materials.

A PUBLICATION OF THE MAGAZINE DIVISION
OF MORRIS COMMUNICATIONS CORPORATION

Advertising and Editorial Policy: *The MILEPOST®* does not endorse or guarantee any advertised service or facility. A sincere effort is made to give complete, accurate and annually up-to-date travel information for this immense segment of North America. However, between the time of our field surveys and the time of the readers' trip, many things may change. In all such cases, the publisher will not be held responsible.

Thank you: *The MILEPOST®* appreciates the assistance of the many individuals, agencies and associations that help provide up-to-date information each year.

Key to Highways in *The MILEPOST*®

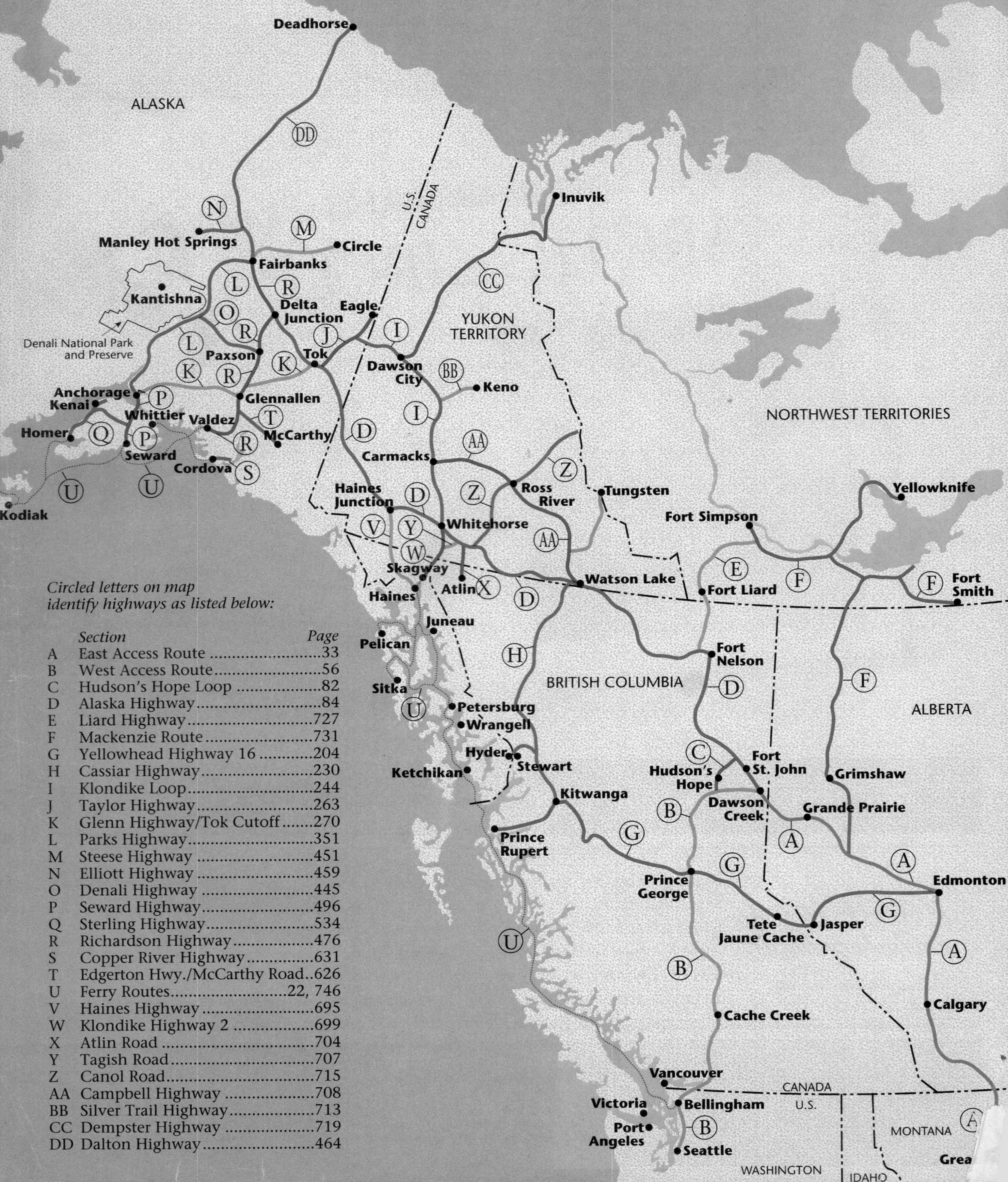

Circled letters on map identify highways as listed below:

How to Use The MILEPOST®

The MILEPOST® provides mile-by-mile descriptions of all major highways and roads in Alaska and northwestern Canada; detailed information on all major destinations (cities, communities, national parks and other attractions) in the North; and how-to help for various modes of transportation (air, ferry, railroads, etc.). Refer to the Contents page and Index for subjects and destinations.

The MILEPOST® will work for you regardless of how you plan to travel—whether by car, by plane, on a tour bus, or by bicycle. It will help you plan your trip, as well as acting as a valuable guide during your trip.

The backbone of *The MILEPOST®* is the highway logs. The Key to Highways map on the opposite page shows you what highways are covered in *The MILEPOST®*. In these mile-by-mile descriptions of the highways and byways of the North, you will find campgrounds; businesses offering food, lodging, gas and other services; attractions; fishing spots; road conditions; descriptions of the geography and history of the land and communities; and much more.

To the right is an abbreviated version of part of the Parks Highway log, keyed to help you understand how to read all highway logs in *The MILEPOST®*.

1. A boldface paragraph appears at the beginning of each highway log in *The MILEPOST®* that explains what beginning and ending destinations are used, and what boldface letters represent those destinations. In this log **A** represents **Anchorage**, F is **Fairbanks.**

2. The boldface numbers represent the distance in miles from the beginning and ending destinations, and the lightface numbers are the metric equivalent in kilometers (unless otherwise noted). For example, the entrance to Denali National Park and Preserve is 237.3 miles, or 381.9 kilometers, from Anchorage.

3. **Junctions** with other logged roads are indented and color-coded.And the cross-referenced section is always uppercased. In this example, the DENALI NATIONAL PARK section is referenced. Refer to the Contents page to quickly find other sections.

4. "Log" advertisements are classified-type advertisements that appear in the text. These are identified by the boldface name of the business at the beginning of the entry and "[ADVERTISEMENT]" at the end. These log advertisements are written by the advertisers.

5. Display advertisements are keyed in the log by a boldface entry at their highway locations, followed by the words "See display ad." Their advertisement will appear near this entry or a page or section will be referenced.

It may also help you to know how our field editors log the highways. *The MILEPOST®* field editors drive each highway, taking notes on facilities, features and attractions along the way and noting the mile at which they appear. Mileages are measured from the beginning of the highway, which is generally at a junction or the city limits, to the end of the highway, also usually a junction or city limits. Most highways in *The MILEPOST®* are logged either south to north or east to west. If you are traveling the opposite direction of the log, you will read the log back to front.

To determine driving distance between 2 points, simply subtract the first mileage figures. For example, the distance from Crabb's Crossing at **Milepost A 231.3** to the park entrance at **Milepost A 237.3** is 6 miles.

Look for these symbols throughout *The MILEPOST®*:

▲ Campground ♿ Wheelchair accessible
Fishing

Parks Highway Log

Distance from Anchorage (A) is followed by distance from Fairbanks (F). ❶

ALASKA ROUTE 1

A 231.3 (372.2 km) **F 126.7** (203.9 km) Crabb's Crossing, second bridge northbound over the Nenana River. Boundary of Denali National Park and Preserve.

A 234.1 (376.7 km) **F 123.9** (199.4 km) Double-ended turnout with litter barrels to east; scenic viewpoint.

A 235.1 (378.4 km) **F 122.9** (197.8 km) *CAUTION: Railroad crossing.*

A 237.2 (381.7 km) **F 120.8** (194.4 km) Riley Creek bridge.

❷ **A 237.3** (381.9 km) **F 120.7** (194.2 km) Turnoff to east for entrance to **DENALI NATIONAL PARK AND PRESERVE** (formerly Mount McKinley National Park) to west. Visitor Center is 0.5 mile/0.8 km from the highway junction.

Junction with Park Road. See DENALI NATIONAL PARK section for log of Park Road and details on the park. ❸

Clusters of highway businesses north and south of the park entrance offer a variety of services to the highway traveler and park visitor.

A 238 (383 km) **F 120** (193.4 km) Third bridge northbound over the Nenana River.

❹ **A 238.1** (383.2 km) **F 119.9** (193 km) **Denali Raft Adventures.** Come with the original Nenana River rafters! Paddleboats too! Age 5 or older welcome, 7 departures daily. Whitewater or scenic floats. Get away to untouched wilderness! 2-hour, 4-hour, full-day and overnight trips are available. See display ad in DENALI NATIONAL PARK section. Phone (907) 683-2234. Internet: www.alaskaone.com/denraft. VISA, Master Card accepted. [ADVERTISMENT]

A 238.4 (383.6 km) **F 119.6** (192.5 km) **Denali Bluffs Hotel.** See display ad this section. ❺

The introduction to each highway logged in *The MILEPOST®* includes a chart of mileages between major points (see below).

Maps also accompany each highway logged in *The MILEPOST®*. Consult the map key for an explanation of abbreviations (see example at bottom). Mileage boxes at communities and junctions on the highway map reflect the rounded off mileage in the highway log at the corresponding point.

	Anchorage	Denali Park	Fairbanks	Talkeetna	Wasilla
Anchorage		237	358	113	42
Denali Park	237		121	153	195
Fairbanks	358	121		245	316
Talkeetna	113	153	245		71
Wasilla	42	195	316	71	

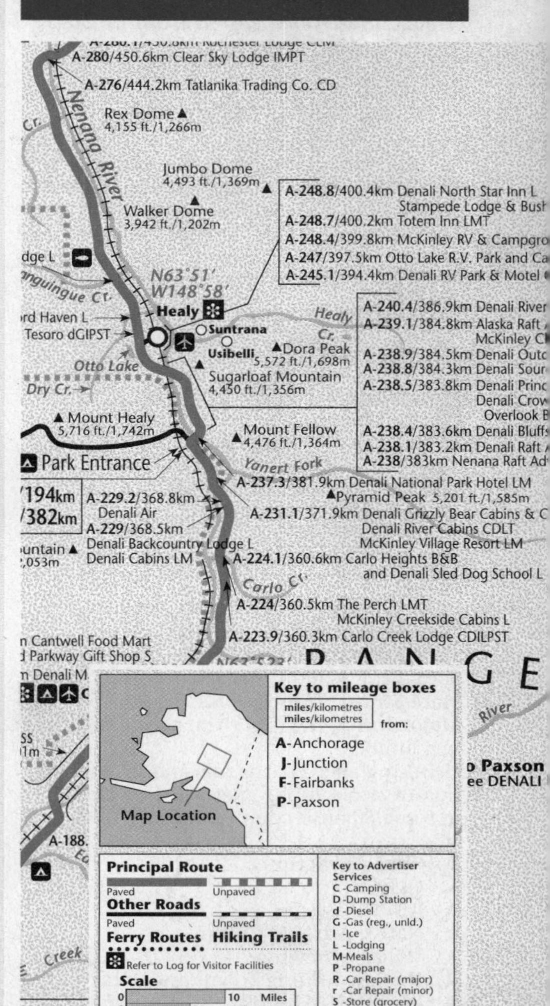

Welcome to the North Country

Hiker and Dall sheep in front of 20,320-foot Mount McKinley (Denali). (© Mike Jones)

The North Country is the land north of 51° 16' latitude. Geographically, it encompasses Alaska, Yukon Territory, Northwest Territories, northern British Columbia and Alberta. Following are some facts and figures about each of these areas.

Alaska

Population: 621,400
Capital: Juneau
Largest City: Anchorage
Area: 587,878 square miles/ 1,522,486 square km
Coastline: 33,904 miles/ 54,562 km
Highest Point: Mount McKinley, 20,320 feet/6,194m
Lowest Point: Pacific Ocean, sea level
State Flower: Forget-me-not
State Tree: Sitka spruce
State Bird: Willow ptarmigan
State Motto: "North to the Future"
Major Industries: Tourism, petroleum, fishing, lumber
Drinking age: 21. The sale and/or importation of alcoholic beverages is prohibited in some 50 bush communities.

Top Ten Attractions:

1. Glaciers
2. Inside Passage
3. Native Arts and Culture
4. Wildlife Viewing
5. Historic Mining Towns and Areas
6. Museums
7. Sportfishing
8. Trans-Alaska Pipeline
9. Russian Heritage
10. National Parks and Monuments

Fish & Game: Alaska Dept. of Fish and Game, Box 25526, Juneau, AK 99802; phone (907) 465-4180, fax (907) 465-2772; Internet www.state.ak.us/local/akpages/FISH.GAME/adfghome.htm
Visitor Information: Alaska Division of Tourism, Box 110801, Juneau, AK 99811-0801; phone (907) 465-2010; Internet www.travelalaska.com and www.state.ak.us/tourism

Alaska was purchased by the U.S. from Russia in 1867. It became the 49th state on January 3, 1959. Alaska is the largest state in the union in area (twice the size of Texas), but ranks 49th in population, based on the 1990 census. (Only Wyoming has fewer residents.) Approximately 15 percent of the population is Native: Eskimo, Aleut and Indian (Athabascan, Tlingit, Haida, Tsimshian).

Alaska has 17 of the 20 highest mountains in the United States, including the highest peak in North America—Mount McKinley (Denali). Geographically, the state falls into roughly 6 distinct natural regions: Southeastern, Southcentral, the Interior, Southwestern, Western and the Brooks Range/Arctic.

Southeastern Alaska is a moist, luxuriantly forested panhandle extending some 500 miles/805 km from Dixon Entrance south of Ketchikan to Icy Bay on the Gulf of Alaska coast. This narrow strip of coast, separated from the mainland and Canada by the Coast Mountains and the hundreds of islands of the Alexander Archipelago, form the Inside Passage water route used by ships and ferries. Cruise ships bring thousands of passengers through the Inside Passage each summer.

The Southcentral region of Alaska curves 650 miles/1,046 km north and west from the Gulf of Alaska coast to the Alaska Range. This region's tremendous geographic variety includes the Matanuska–Susitna river valleys, the Chugach and Wrangell–St. Elias mountain ranges, the Kenai Peninsula and the glaciers of Prince William Sound. Anchorage, the state's largest city, is the hub of Southcentral.

Interior Alaska lies cradled between the Brooks Range to the north and the Alaska Range to the south, a vast area that drains the Yukon River and its tributaries. It is a climate of extremes, holding both the record high (100°F at Fort Yukon) and the record low (-80°F at Prospect Creek). Fairbanks is the hub of the Interior and a jump-off point for bush communities in both the Interior and Arctic.

Southwestern Alaska takes in Kodiak Island, the Alaska Peninsula and Aleutian Islands. Kodiak, less than an hour's flight from Anchorage and about 10 hours by ferry from Homer, is the largest island in Alaska. Kodiak was Russian Alaska's first capital city. Brown bear viewing is an attraction on Kodiak and at Katmai National Park and Preserve near King Salmon. The Southwest ferry system provides service from Kodiak to Unalaska/ Dutch Harbor.

Western Alaska stretches from the head of Bristol Bay north along the Bering Sea coast to the Seward Peninsula near the Arctic Circle. This region extends inland from the coast to encompass the Yukon–Kuskokwim Delta. Nome is one of the best known destinations in Western Alaska.

Arctic Alaska lies above the Arctic Circle (latitude 66°33'), between the Brooks Range to the south and the Arctic sea coast to the north, and from the Canadian border to the east westward to Kotzebue. Day and overnight trips to Kotzebue, Barrow and Prudhoe Bay are popular packages offered out of both Anchorage and Fairbanks.

If you include the Marine Highway, all regions of Alaska are connected by highway with the exception of Western Alaska. And that region's hub cities—Bethel and Nome—are less than 2 hours from Anchorage by air.

Yukon Territory

Population: 31,768
Capital: Whitehorse
Largest City: Whitehorse
Area: 186,661 square miles/ 483,414 square km
Highest Point: Mount Logan, 19,545 feet/5,957m
Lowest Point: Beaufort Sea, sea level
Territorial Flower: Fireweed
Territorial Bird: Raven
Drinking age: 19. Packaged liquor, beer and wine are sold in government liquor stores.
Major Industries: Tourism, mining

Midnight sun lights clouds over the Yukon River near Carmacks, YT. (© Paul Souders)

Top Ten Attractions:
1. SS *Klondike,* Whitehorse
2. MacBride Museum, Whitehorse
3. Northern Lights Centre, Watson Lake
4. Diamond Tooth Gerties, Dawson City
5. Palace Grand Theatre, Dawson City
6. Beringia Interpretive Centre, Whitehorse
7. Dredge #4, Dawson City
8. Kluane National Park
9. Whitehorse Fish Ladder
10. Robert Service Cabin, Dawson City

Fish & Game: Yukon Government, Dept. of Renewable Resources, Fish and Wildlife Branch, Box 2703, Whitehorse, YT Y1A 2C6, phone (867) 667-5221
Visitor Information: Tourism Yukon, Box 2703, Whitehorse, YT Y1A 2C6; phone (867) 667-5340; Internet www.touryukon.com; E-mail info@touryukon.com

Shaped somewhat like a right triangle, Yukon Territory is bordered on the west by Alaska at 141° longitude; on the north by the Beaufort Sea/Arctic Ocean; on the south by British Columbia at latitude 60°; and on the east by the western Northwest Territories.

Yukon Territory is larger than all the New England states combined. Canada's highest peak, Mount Logan (elev. 19,545 feet/5,957m), is located in Yukon's St. Elias Mountains.

First Nations peoples of the Yukon belong to the Athabascan and Tlingit language families. These are Gwitchin, Han, Northern Tutchone, Southern Tutchone, Kaska, Tagish, Tlingit and Upper Tanana.

The Yukon was made a district of the Northwest Territories in 1895, and became a separate territory in June of 1898. The territory's first capital was Dawson City, site of the great Klondike gold rush, which brought thousands of gold seekers to the Yukon and Alaska in 1897–98. The Klondike gold rush began celebrating its centennial in 1996—marking the discovery of gold on Bonanza Creek on August 16, 1896—and continued the celebration through 1998.

At the height of the gold rush, an estimated 40,000 people lived in Dawson City. By 1903, as other gold stampedes drew off much of Dawson's population, the city's

Mount Minto is reflected in Atlin Lake. (© Ralph & Leonor Barrett, Four Corners Imaging)

boom days were over, although mining continued to support the community for many years. On March 31, 1953, Whitehorse—on the railway and the highway, with a large airport—replaced Dawson City as capital.

Yukon Territory's parklands include Kluane National Park, a UNESCO World Heritage Site, accessible from the Haines Highway. The undeveloped Ivvavik and Vuntut national parks are in the remote northwestern corner of the territory. Klondike Gold Rush International Historical Park encompasses the Canadian portions of the Chilkoot and White Pass gold rush trails from Skagway.

Northwest Territories

Population: 41,807
Capital: Yellowknife
Largest City: Yellowknife
Area: 550,000 square miles/1.4 million square km
Highest Point: Cirque of the Unclimbables Mountain, 9,062 feet/2,762m
Lowest Point: Beaufort Sea, sea level
Territorial Flower: Mountain avens
Drinking age: 19. Packaged liquor, beer and wine are sold in government liquor stores. Sale and possession of alcohol is prohibited in several communities.
Major Industries: Mining, manufacturing, fishing, tourism

Top Ten Attractions:
1. Nahanni National Park Reserve
2. Wood Buffalo National Park
3. Canol Heritage Trail Park Reserve
4. Dempster Highway
5. Pingos (cone-shaped hills) of the Tuktoyaktuk Peninsula
6. Roman Catholic "Igloo" Church, Inuvik
7. Twin Falls Gorge Territorial Park
8. Prince of Wales Northern Heritage Center, Yellowknife
9. Northwest Territories Legislative Assembly Building, Yellowknife
10. Old Town, Yellowknife

Fish & Game: Dept. of Resources, Wildlife & Economic, Tourism Development and Marketing, Box 1320, Yellowknife, NT X1A 2L9; phone (800) 661-0788
Visitor Information: NWTAT (MP), Box 610, Yellowknife, NT X1A 2N5; phone (800) 661-0788; Internet www.nwttravel.nt.ca

On April 1, 1999, Northwest Territories was divided into 2 territories. Passed by popular vote in 1982 and approved by the Canadian Parliament in 1993, this division created Nunavut and its capital, Iqaluit on Baffin Island, in what was the eastern half of the old Northwest Territories.

The new Northwest Territories comprises a sixth of Canada and is about the size of Alaska. Northwest Territories' Wood Buffalo National Park is the second largest national park in the world.

A majority of the population of Northwest Territories is Native. Aboriginal groups are the Dene, Inuvialuit, Inuit, Gwich'in, Dogrib and Metis.

Access to Northwest Territories is from Alberta via the Mackenzie Highway system, from British Columbia via the Liard Highway, and from Yukon Territory via the Dempster Highway. A major road-building project in the 1960s constructed most of the highway system in western Northwest Territories. Road improvement is ongoing, with most roads now paved.

British Columbia

Population: 3,900,000
Capital: Victoria
Largest City: Vancouver
Area: 365,900 square miles/947,608 square km
Highest Point: Mount Fairweather, 15,295 feet/4,662m
Lowest Point: Pacific Ocean, sea level
Provincial Flower: Pacific dogwood
Provincial Tree: Western red cedar
Provincial Bird: Settler's jay
Provincial Motto: *Splendor Sine Occasu* (Splendour Without Diminishment)
Drinking age: 19. Packaged liquor, beer and wine are sold in government liquor stores.
Major Industries: Forestry, mining and energy, tourism, agriculture, seafood products, food

Top Attractions:
1. Royal BC Museum, Victoria
2. Butchart Gardens, Victoria
3. Vancouver Aquarium

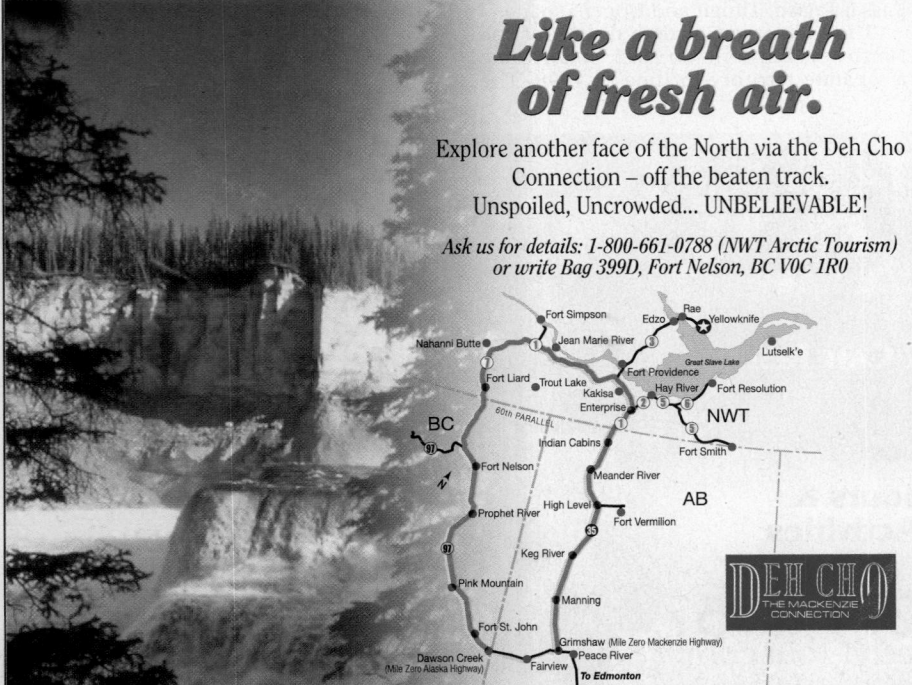

4. Capilano Suspension Bridge, North Vancouver
5. Barkerville Historic Town
6. Fort Steele Heritage Town
7. Grist Mill and Gardens, Keremeos
8. Grouse Mountain, North Vancouver
9. Ksan Historical Indian Village Museum, Hazelton

Fish & Game: Fish and Wildlife Branch, Ministry of Environment, Parliament Buildings, Victoria, BC V8V 1X4
Visitor Information: Tourism British Columbia, Dept. TG, Box 9830, Stn. Prov. Govt., Victoria, B.C. V8W 9W5 Canada; phone (800) 663-6000; Internet www.travel.bc.ca

Canada's most westerly—and 3rd largest—province, British Columbia stretches 813 miles/1,300 km from its southern border with the United States to the northern boundary with Yukon Territory. It is bounded on the east by Alberta and on the west by the Pacific Ocean. The province encompasses the Queen Charlotte Islands and Vancouver Island, site of the capital city of Victoria. Approximately half the province's population resides in the Victoria–Vancouver area.

British Columbia entered the Dominion of Canada on July 20, 1871, as the 6th province. The region was important in early fur trade, and expansion of the province came with the 1860s Cariboo gold rush, followed by the completion of Canada's first transcontinental railway—the Canadian Pacific.

Vancouver and Victoria are popular tourist areas, as are Vancouver Island and the Gulf and San Juan island groups. The Sunshine Coast, along the shores of British Columbia facing Vancouver Island, is popular for its scenic drives, parks and beaches. The region's national parks, including Glacier, Mt. Revelstoke, Kootenay and Yoho, are among the most spectacular in North America.

Mile Zero of the Alaska Highway is located in Dawson Creek, BC (not to be confused with Dawson City, YT), in the northeastern corner of the province.

Alberta

Population: 2,774,512
Capital: Edmonton
Largest City: Calgary
Area: 255,287 square miles/661,142 square km
Highest Point: Mount Columbia, 12,293 feet/3,747m
Lowest Point: Salt River at the border with Northwest Territories, 600 feet/183m
Drinking age: 18. Liquor, beer and wine are sold in private liquor stores.
Major Industries: Petrochemicals, plastics, forest products, computer and business services, processed foods, electronics, tourism

Top Ten Attractions:
1. West Edmonton Mall
2. Calgary Zoo
3. Glenbow Museum, Calgary
4. Heritage Park, Calgary
5. Alberta Legislature Building, Edmonton
6. Fort Edmonton Park, Edmonton
7. Muttart Conservatory, Edmonton
8. Provincial Museum of Alberta, Edmonton
9. Royal Tyrrell Museum of Palaeontology, Drumheller
10. Edmonton Space and Science Centre

Fish & Game: Environmental Protection Branch, Information Centre, 9920 108 St., Edmonton, AB T5K 2M4
Visitor Information: Travel Alberta, 3rd floor, Commerce Place, 10155 102 St., Edmonton, AB T5J 4G8; phone (800) 661-8888; Internet www.atp.ab.ca

The Province of Alberta is bounded to the west by British Columbia, to the south by Montana, to the east by Saskatchewan and to the north by the Northwest Territories. Among the dramatic features of this geographically fascinating area are a stretch of the Rocky Mountains and the Columbia Icefield—source of the Athabasca, Columbia and Saskatchewan glaciers—along the British Columbia border, and the bizarre rock formations of the badlands to the west along the Red Deer River.

Native inhabitants included Assiniboine, Blackfoot, Cree and Sarcee Indians. The first European settlers—fur traders—arrived in the mid-18th century. In 1875 Alberta became a province of Canada. Discoveries of oil and natural gas deposits in the 1930s caused economic growth, and in the 1970s and 1980s these same deposits brought new industries to the area and a resulting rise in population.

Edmonton in central Alberta and Calgary to the south are popular areas. The national parks—Banff and Jasper along the British Columbia border, Waterton Lakes in the southwest corner and Wood Buffalo far in the north—are also major attractions.

Travel Planning

Historic Manley Roadhouse in Manley Hot Springs. (© Kris Graef, staff)

Accommodations

Accommodations in the North—as anywhere else—can range from luxurious to utilitarian to downright funky. You'll find lodging in fine lodges and major-chain hotels/motels; in bed and breakfasts; in hostels; in rustic log cabins; and in mobile homes. Considering the remoteness of many communities, and the seasonal nature of Northern travel, visitors are often surprised at the wide variety of lodging available.

The larger cities (Anchorage, Fairbanks, etc.) have more to choose from than the smaller, more remote communities. But in midsummer, even those locations with greater numbers of rooms available can fill up quickly. You should consider making reservations ahead of time during the busy summer season, whether your destination is a major city or a small highway community.

Some facilities along highways of the North may be a bit on the rustic side compared to what you're used to. This is, after all, the Last Frontier. You'll also find some first-class establishments in surprisingly remote locations. Sometimes the frills of city travel may be missing, but the hospitality of the North more than makes up for it.

We do not rate accommodations. In our experience, you can have a 5-star experience in a 1-star hotel (or vice versa), and sometimes the remote location and lack of choices in lodging make it moot anyway. Paid advertisements for accommodations appearing in *The MILEPOST*®—whether display ads or "log ads" placed in the highway log—are written by the advertisers themselves. We do not endorse or guarantee any of these facilities or services, although we trust the advertisers will live up to their promises. If they don't, please write us, phone us or e-mail us. We do not mediate disputes, but if we get enough complaints about a business not living up to their advertisement, we will ask the advertiser to do a reality check. Keep in mind that businesses may close, ownership may change, and rates may increase. As rates often change, it's a good idea to contact the particular lodging you are interested in and inquire about their current rates.

Air Travel

Slightly more than half of all visitors to Alaska arrive by air. Air travel is also one of the most common forms of transportation in the North. You can fly just about anywhere. If there is no scheduled service, you can charter a plane. Besides offering transportation from one place to another, many flying services also offer—or specialize in—flightseeing. For a fixed fee, you can fly around mountains or go looking for wildlife.

About 10 domestic airlines and 2 dozen small scheduled carriers provide scheduled passenger service within Alaska. There are more than 200 certified charter/air taxi operators in Alaska.

Check the advertisements for scheduled and charter air service in the communities covered in *The MILEPOST*®. There are many to choose from.

Air taxi operators conduct their business from a specific base of operations, primarily through the charter of aircraft, and offer a wide variety of options: drop-off and pickup for hunters, sport fisherman and river runners; photo safaris to see wildlife or glaciers; round-trip flights to remote communities which may include an overnight.

Air taxi rates may vary from carrier to carrier. Most operators charge an hourly rate either per plane load or per passenger; others may charge on a per-mile basis. Flightseeing trips to area attractions are often available at a fixed price per passenger.

Sample per-hour fares for charter planes with varied wheel, float and ski capabilities (luggage space limited and dependent on number of passengers): Piper Archer (3 passengers), $175; Piper Cherokee 6 (5 passengers), $230; Islander (9 passengers), $430; Chieftain (9 passengers), $650.

Any pilot flying for hire is required to

FLIGHT TIMES BETWEEN SELECTED CITIES

Between	Time	Between	Time	Between	Time
Anchorage—Bethel	1 hr. 15 min.	Anchorage—Valdez	40 min.	Juneau—Haines	35 min.
Anchorage—Cordova	45 min.	Anchorage—Wrangell	2 hrs. 20 min.	Juneau—Ketchikan	50 min.
Anchorage—Dutch Harbor	2 hrs. 5 min.	Fairbanks—Barrow	1 hr. 20 min.	Juneau—Seattle, WA	2 hrs. 10 min.
Anchorage—Fairbanks	50 min.	Fairbanks—Delta Junction	35 min.	Juneau—Sitka	35 min.
Anchorage—Juneau	1 hr. 35 min.	Fairbanks—Kotzebue	2 hrs. 10 min.	Juneau—Skagway	45 min.
Anchorage—King Salmon	1 hr.	Fairbanks—Nome	2 hrs. 20 min.	Juneau—Whitehorse, YT	1 hr.
Anchorage—Kodiak	55 min.	Fairbanks—Northway	1 hr.	Juneau—Yakutat	45 min.
Anchorage—Kotzebue	1 hr. 30 min.	Fairbanks—Prudhoe Bay	1 hr. 25 min.	Ketchikan—Sitka	50 min.
Anchorage—Nome	1 hr. 30 min.	Fairbanks—Whitehorse, YT (1 stop in Dawson City)	3 hrs. 35 min.	Nome—Kotzebue	40 min.
Anchorage—Petersburg	2 hrs.			Whitehorse—Dawson City	1 hr. 40 min.
Anchorage—Seattle, WA	3 hrs. 15 min.	Juneau—Glacier Bay	25 min.	Yakutat—Cordova	45 min.

hold a commercial or airline transport pilot certificate. The customer can and should be protected by having the pilot show his/her credentials. A pilot with the necessary credentials will be glad to show them. Do not fly with a pilot who cannot produce certification.

The MILEPOST® highway logs include the location of most airstrips along the highways and in the communities in Alaska and northwestern Canada. Aircraft symbols corresponding to airstrip locations are included on the highway strip maps. The map symbol (✈) is the same for airports with scheduled service, as for airstrips with no scheduled service and limited facilities.

Private aircraft information in these logs includes only the name and location of the airstrip, the elevation, length and surface material of the longest runway and the availability of fuel. Many Northland pilots fly jet craft. Jet and other fuel is available at many airports. Fuel sold in Alaska and Canada is almost exclusively 100LL; 80 octane fuel is no longer available, though some airports offer car gasoline. *NOTE: The brief description of airstrips given in* The MILEPOST® *is in no way intended as a guide.* Pilots should have a current copy of the *Alaska Supplement*. For a packet of free brochures including *Flight Tips for Pilots in Alaska*, write the Federal Aviation Administration, 222 W. 7th Ave., Anchorage, AK 99513.

Pilots may also get in touch with the Alaska Airmen's Assoc., Inc., P.O. Box 241185, Anchorage, AK 99524-1184, phone (907) 245-1251, fax (907) 245-1259, to order a copy of the *Alaska Airmen's Logbook for Alaska, Northwest Canada and Russia*.

Two free Canadian publications of interest are *Air Tourist Information—Canada* (TP771) and *Flying the Alaska Highway in Canada* (TP2168). Both are available from the Civil Aviation Publications Office, phone (800) 305-2059.

Boating

Boating is a big subject in the North, where it might mean a half-day sightseeing cruise on a chartered yacht; a 1-day fishing charter in an offshore heated-cabin boat; a 2-hour river raft trip; a narrated cruise tour plus lunch on a sightseeing vessel with walk-around decks; or an independent trip by sea kayak or canoe.

The North offers thousands of miles of scenic waterways, and a variety of ways to experience them.

Scheduled Day Cruises

There are dozens of opportunities to experience a day cruise along the rivers, lakes and coastline of the North.

Some of Alaska's most famous glaciers and glaciated areas are tidewater glaciers and thus viewed from the sea. The opportunity to observe birds and sea mammals is also a major attraction on these salt-water day cruises. Species include sea otters, Steller sea lions, dolphins, harbor seals, Dall porpoises, whales (minke, gray, fin, humpback), puffins, eagles, black-legged kittiwakes, common murres, cormorants, parakeet and rhinoceros auklets, etc. These cruises are often combined with motorcoach service, railway service or flying, either out of necessity or to enhance the travel experience.

If you are interested in Alaska's glaciated coastline and/or marine wildlife, consider one of the following destinations (ports are shown in parentheses): Misty Fiords National Monument (Ketchikan); Tracy Arm Fjord/Sawyer Glacier Cruise (Juneau); Icy Strait (Juneau, Gustavus), Glacier Bay National Park (Juneau, Haines and Skagway); Prince William Sound (Whittier, Valdez); Kenai Fjords National Park, Chiswell Islands (Seward); Kachemak Bay, Barren Islands (Homer).

Opportunities for scheduled day cruises on rivers and lakes in the North—offering a different view of the natural history of the region—include the following: Yukon River (Dawson City, YT, Eagle, AK); Portage Lake (Portage Glacier, AK); Susitna, Talkeetna and Chulitna rivers (Talkeetna, AK); Chena and Tanana Rivers (Fairbanks, AK); Great Slave Lake (Yellowknife, NWT).

Sea Kayaking

Rentals and/or guided kayak tours are available out of the following ports in Alaska: Homer (for Kachemak Bay); Seward (Resurrection Bay, Kenai Fjords National Park); Valdez and Whittier (Prince William Sound); and in Southeastern Alaska out of Juneau, Sitka and Ketchikan.

Southeast Alaska has hundreds of miles of sheltered waterways that are ideal for sea kayaking. Favorite destinations (and ports of origin) include: Gastineau Channel and Tracy Arm (Juneau); Seymour Canal on Admiralty Island (Juneau); Glacier Bay National Park and Preserve; Point Adolphus in Icy Strait (Hoonah); Misty Fiords

(Ketchikan); Sitka Sound and Outer Chichagof Island (Sitka); Tebenkof Bay and Kuiu Island (Kake); Yakutat Bay and Russell Fiord (Yakutat); west coast of Prince of Wales Island (Craig).

River Running

Guided float trips can be arranged for almost any major runnable river in the North. Some of the more popular runnable rivers along the road system have outfitters offering daily scheduled departures, and many of these operators advertise in *The MILEPOST®*. Scheduled float trips include the following: Kenai River (Cooper Landing, AK); Nenana River (Denali Park, AK); Matanuska River (Chickaloon, AK); Six-Mile Creek (Hope, AK); Mendenhall River (Juneau, AK); Yukon River/Miles Canyon (Whitehorse, YT); Tatshenhsini River (Haines Junction, YT.

For the independent river runner, there are an even greater number of opportunities. The Bureau of Land Management maintains 6 rivers that are part of the National Wild and Scenic Rivers System: Birch Creek, Beaver Creek, Fortymile River, Delta River, Gulkana River and Unalakleet River. These rivers offer a variety of float trips. The Fortymile River is accessible from the Taylor Highway; the Gulkana River is accessible from the Richardson and the Denali highways. The BLM offers brochures on the river trails, including access points, portages and scale of difficulty. Write the Bureau of Land Management, 1150 University Ave., Fairbanks, AK 99709-3899; phone (907) 474-2251.

Canoeing

Several rivers and lakes are especially popular with canoeists. The Kenai Peninsula's Swan Lake and Swanson River canoe trails, accessible from Swanson River Road off the Sterling Highway, are 2 such destinations (see page 548). In the Interior, Yukon–Charley Rivers National Preserve is a popular summer float between Eagle and Circle (canoe rentals are available in Eagle).

In Southcentral Alaska, Kepler-Bradley Lakes State Recreation Area, at **Milepost A 36.4** on the Glenn Highway, is a popular canoeing area. Nancy Lake Recreation Area, at **Milepost A 67.2** Parks Highway, offers an extensive system of canoeing lakes, portages and public-use cabins.

Canoe trails have been established on Prince of Wales Island along the Honker Divide and at Sarkar Lakes. Contact Craig Ranger District, Tongass National Forest, Box 145, Craig, AK 99921, phone (907) 826-3271. For maps and information contact the Thorne Bay Ranger District, Tongass National Forest, Box 19001, Thorne Bay, AK 99919, phone (907) 828-3304.

Bus Lines

Travelers who are able to achieve their goals by using the bus systems find them a comfortable and economical way to get around, but independent travelers generally find that routes and services within Alaska and Yukon Territory are far more limited than in the Lower 48. Most scheduled bus service in the North is seasonal and, although available within Alaska and the Yukon, is not feasible from the Lower 48 unless you join an escorted motorcoach tour. If your schedule permits, you can get to Alaska via public bus service by using several carriers. The larger cities of the North offer city-wide transit service. Shuttle lines provide intrastate service, incorporating stops at popular National Parks in their schedules. Charter buses are available, and various lines such as Gray Line of Alaska, Princess Tours and Alaska Sightseeing rely on bus connections as links in their tour schedules. Contact the following companies for current schedules:

Alaska Direct Bus Line, P.O. Box 100501, Anchorage, AK 99510. (907) 277-6652 or (800) 770-6652 or (867) 668-4833. Service from Anchorage to Fairbanks, Tok, Whitehorse, Dawson City, Skagway and Denali.

Alaska Sightseeing/Cruise West, 513 W. 4th Ave., Anchorage, AK 99501. (907) 276-1305 or (800) 426-7702. Motorcoach trips connect Anchorage and Denali National Park.

Alaskon Express/Gray Line of Alaska, 745 W. 4th Ave., Anchorage, AK 99501. (907) 277-5581 or (800) 544-2206 or fax (206) 281-0621. Scheduled service to Anchorage, Fairbanks, Skagway, Whitehorse, Haines and most communities en route. Motorcoach tours to Anchorage, Denali National Park, Fairbanks, Prudhoe Bay, Prince William Sound, Seward and Portage Glacier.

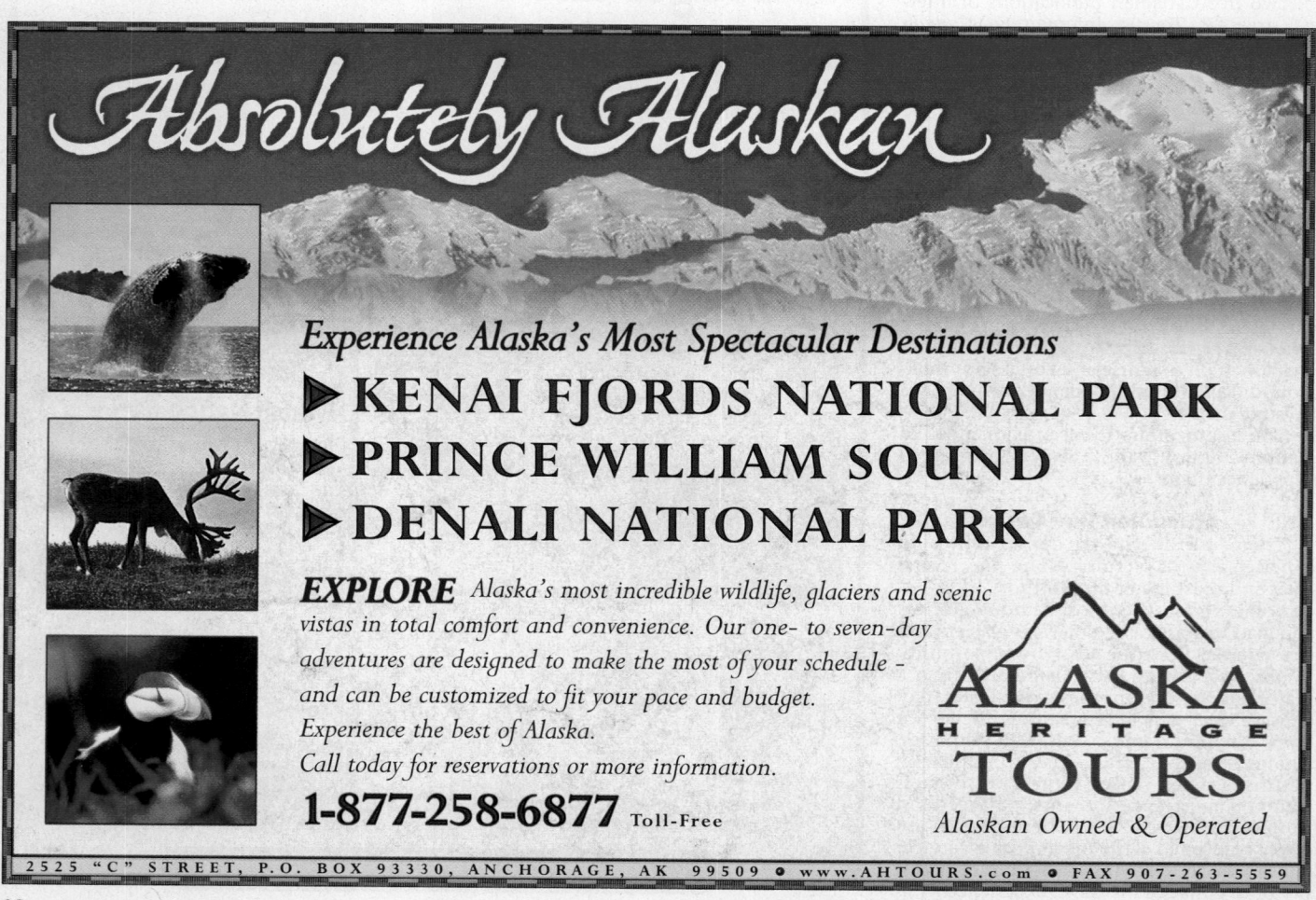

The View From The Bus

Lots of take-out coffees are being consumed as passengers gather by the Fairbanks visitor center. Our bus is already waiting. No one is moving very fast, no one is talkative, although it's nearly 9 A.M. This is Alaskan summer, after all, when most people stay up late to take advantage of round-the-clock daylight, and the A.M. hours are for slow starts.

Gear stowed in the efficient rooftop carrier, seats selected, we start off through Fairbanks' still-sleepy streets. The driver has outlined safety features and the rules of the road. Most passengers find a comfortable position and resume their interrupted sleep.

We head south along the birch-lined Parks Highway. At a vantage point overlooking the broad Tanana Valley, we catch a glimpse of Denali on the southwest horizon, a sight that bodes well for spectacular views farther down the highway.

Some 120 miles out of Fairbanks we stop at the busy mini-city of hotels, cabins and businesses crowding the highway just north of the entrance to Denali National Park. Here we disembark to buy snacks, use restrooms, stretch our legs. People are waking up, as most soon will be getting off at the park.

We stop for about half an hour at the park visitor center. No hardship, as it's a hub of energy and activity, with a film to watch, a gift shop, a fascinating cross-section of tourists and hostellers to share stories with, and crowds seeking information and reservations for park facilities. The hikers, campers and backpackers among us sort out their gear. Many more of same prepare to board the bus for the trip to Anchorage, and our driver skillfully arranges their belongings atop the bus.

These travellers usually have been in the park for several days, often in rainy weather. The backpacks, duffle bags and their owners all look weathered. As we reboard and settle down, many of these adventurers promptly fall asleep. The driver counts heads so as not to leave anyone behind. "If you're not here, speak up," he quips as latecomers rush aboard.

We drift around the Riley Creek campground, on the lookout for a camper who has reserved bus space by phone earlier in the week. It's a long search, but our driver persists. At last the lost is found—a lone young man who's been camping for a long time and has the gear to prove it: a tent, stove, collapsible kayak, bicycle, numerous duffles, equipment that seems sufficient to outfit several others just like himself. Passengers make humorous wagers about fitting all this stuff in, but somehow the driver finds a place for everything, the camper takes the last empty seat, and away we go.

Several newcomers mention that during their days in the park they have yet to see Denali. "Will we see the mountain?" one asks wistfully. She is counseled to be patient just a little longer; we know what lies ahead.

A short ride to Cantwell (with rewarding sights of a caribou and two moose) where we have a good rest stop and a chance to feed our faces with something more substantial than fast food. The bus is gassed up for the next long haul. We are almost halfway to Anchorage now. The weather is perfect. The passengers who are awake are rehashing their experiences in the park, comparing notes, sharing tips about gear and hostels. We talk with a family from Germany, an Australian woman, an Israeli couple.

South of Cantwell, we round a bend in the road and THERE IT IS! The mountain, totally clear, its 20,320-foot summit sharp against a cloudless sky. A collective gasp goes up. Passengers root in their packs for cameras. The driver stops the bus, everyone pours out, a dozen cameras click repeatedly, excited voices rise. Some are silent, awed by the majesty of the scene and the moment.

Several more photo stops along the next hundred miles. Nature has put her best foot forward for us. The mountain dominates the skyline at many viewing points. A stop at McKinley View Lodge lets everyone experience Denali about as up close and personal as one can get short of climbing it.

We're now south of the Alaska Range. More moose along the road near the Talkeetna turnoff. We wish we could stop at that unique little town that "owns" such an incomparable view of Denali, but it is 12 miles off the main road, and there is a schedule to keep. Soon we see evidence of approaching civilization: traffic increases noticeably by the time we reach Willow. We leave a young couple and their gear off on the road to Nancy Lake. When we pass the fireworks stands near Big Lake, we know our wilderness drive is fast winding down.

Loading up luggage at Denali Park.

(© Carol A. Phillips)

"What are those mountains?" asks a passenger, impressed by the jagged peaks of the Chugach Range punctuating the skyline before us. The driver supplies another informative description as we hit the traffic light at Wasilla, the first such light in about 300 miles.

From here on it's heavy traffic speeding along the Glenn Highway. People are talking about where they need to get off, what hostel or hotel they're booked into, what plane they have to catch. Entering downtown Anchorage at rush hour after our long day's drive through the heart of Alaska creates a strangely surreal sensation. It's deeply satisfying to look northward and see Denali's unmistakable profile on the horizon. It's still there. It'll be there the next time we make this trip. We can't wait to do it again.

Backcountry Connection, Inc., Glennallen, AK. (907) 822-5292 or (800) 478-5292. Service from Glennallen to Chitina and down McCarthy Rd. for access to Wrangell-St. Elias National Park and Kennicott/McCarthy.

Capital City Transit. Juneau city bus system. (907) 789-6901.

Cruise Bus Alaska. Charter service out of Seward. (907) 224-7239 or (888) 371-7234.

Denali Express Alaska Tours, 405 L St., Anchorage, AK 99501, phone (907) 274-0696. Service between Anchorage and Denali Park; group tours and special itineraries.

Denali Shuttle. (907) 277-0401 or (888) 666-9676. Daily round-trip service between Anchorage and Denali National Park.

Greyhound Lines of Canada, 2191 2nd Ave., Whitehorse, YT Y1A 3T8, phone (867) 667-2223, fax (867) 633-6858. Scheduled service to Whitehorse from all U.S.–Canada border crossings; also the Whitehorse depot has carriers to Dawson City and Alaska destinations.

Homer Stage Line, P.O. Box 1912, Homer, AK 99603. (907) 235-7009 or (907) 272-8644. Service between Anchorage, Seward & Homer.

Metropolitan Area Commuter System (MACS). 3175 Peger Rd., Fairbanks, AK 99709. (907) 459-1002

Norline Coaches (Yukon) Ltd., 34 MacDonald Rd., Whitehorse, YT Y1A 4I2, phone (867) 668-3355 for scheduled service, (867) 633-3864 for charter lines. Service between Whitehorse, Mayo, Carmacks and Dawson City. Daily service to Skagway.

Parks Highway Express, Box 82884, Fairbanks, AK 99708, phone (907) 479-3065, (888) 600-6001. Service between Anchorage, Denali Park , Fairbanks, Valdez and Dawson City.

People Mover. Anchorage municipal bus service. (907) 343-6543.

Princess Tours®, 2815 2nd Ave., Suite 400, Seattle, WA 98121, phone 1-800-835-8907. Motorcoach tours include the Klondike in Canada's Yukon, Anchorage, the Kenai Peninsula, Denali National Park, Fairbanks and Prudhoe Bay.

Seward Bus Line, Box 1338, Seward, AK 99664, phone (907) 224-3608 or (907) 563-0800. Daily, year-round service between Anchorage and Seward.

Talkeetna Shuttle Service, P.O. Box 468, Talkeetna, AK 99676. (888) 288-6009. Daily round-trip service between Anchorage and Talkeetna.

The Park Connection. Alaska Tour and Travel, P.O. Box 221011, Anchorage, AK 99522. (907) 245-0200 or (800) 208-0200 toll free. Daily coach service between Denali, Talkeetna, Anchorage and Seward.

Calendar of Events

Following are some of the major events in the North by month and by place. Also check the current Calendar of Events on www.themilepost.com.

January

Seward—Polar Bear Jump-Off Festival.

February

Anchorage—Fur Rendezvous. **Anchor Point**—Snow Rondi. **Cordova**—Iceworm Festival. **Fairbanks/Whitehorse, YT**—Yukon Quest Sled Dog Race; Yukon Sourdough Rendezvous. **Homer**—Winter Carnival. **Whitehorse, YT**—Sourdough Rendezvous. **Willow**—Winter Carnival. **Wrangell**—Tent City Festival.

March

Anchorage—Iditarod Trail Sled Dog Race. **Bethel**—Camai Native Dance Festival. **Dawson City, YT**—Thaw-Di-Graw Spring Carnival. **Fairbanks**—Winter Carnival; North American Sled Dog Championships. **Kodiak**—Pillar Mountain Golf Classic. **Nenana**—Tripod Raising. **Nome**—Bering Sea Ice Classic Golf Tournament; month of Iditarod events. **North Pole**—Winter Carnival. **Skagway**—Windfest; Buckwheat Ski Classic. **Valdez**—Winterfest.

April

Anchorage—Great Alaska Sportsman Show. **Cordova**—Copper Days Celebration. **Girdwood**—Alyeska Spring Carnival. **Juneau**—Alaska Folk Festival. **Skagway**—Mini Folk Festival. **Summit Lake (Richardson Highway)**—Arctic Man Ski and Snow Go Classic. **Valdez**—Extreme Skiing Championships; Mountain Man Snowmachine Hill Climb. **Whitehorse, YT**—Rotary Music Festival. **Wrangell**—Garnet Festival.

May

This month is a busy one for fishing derbies for halibut (Homer, Seldovia and Valdez) and salmon (Ketchikan, Petersburg, Seldovia and Sitka). **Cordova**—Copper River Delta Shorebird Festival. **Dawson City, YT**—International Gold Show. **Delta Junction**—Buffalo Wallow Square Dance Jamboree. **Haines**—Great Alaska Craft Beer & Homebrew Festival. **Haines Junction, YT**—Kluane Mountain Festival. **Homer**—Kachemak Bay Shorebird Festival. **Kodiak**—Crab Festival. **Nome**—Polar Bear Swim. **Petersburg**—Little Norway Festival.

June

Anchorage—Mayor's Midnight Sun Marathon. **Anchor Point**— Kids All-American Fishing Derby. **Cordova**—Annual Salmon & Seafood Festival. **Fairbanks**—Midnight Sun Baseball Game. **Fairbanks/Galena**—Yukon 800. **Haines Junction, YT**—Alsek Music Festival; Kluane Chilkat Bike Relay to **Haines, AK. Juneau**—Gold Rush Days. **Nome**—Midnight Sun Festival. **Palmer**—Colony Days. **Sitka**—Summer Music Festival. **Skagway**—"Golden Spike" Centennial; International Softball Tournament.. **Whitehorse, YT**—Yukon International Storytelling Festival.

July

Anderson—Bluegrass Festival. **Chugiak/ Eagle River**—Bear Paw Festival. **Dawson City, YT**—Canadian Airlines International Midnight Dome Race; Dawson City Music Festival; Yukon Gold Panning Championships. **Delta Junction**—Deltana Fair. **Fairbanks**—Golden Days; World Eskimo-Indian Olympics. **Girdwood**—Forest Fair. **Haines Junction, YT**—Canada Day celebration; Pine Lake Regatta. **Seward**—Mount Marathon Race. **Skagway**—International Softball Tournament; Ducky Derby; Soapy Smith's Wake. **Soldotna**—Progress Days. **Stewart-Hyder**—International Rodeo. **Talkeetna**—Moose Dropping Festival. **Watson Lake, YT**—Watson Lake Rodeo.

August

Dawson City and Watson Lake, YT—Discovery Days. **Fairbanks**—Tanana Valley State Fair. **Haines**—Southeast Alaska State Fair; Bald Eagle Music Fest. **Ketchikan**—Blueberry Arts Festival. **Kodiak**—State Fair and Rodeo. **Ninilchik**—Kenai Peninsula State Fair. **Palmer**—Alaska State Fair. **Seward**—Silver Salmon Derby. **Skagway**—Flower & Garden Show. **Talkeetna**—Bluegrass Festival. **Whitehorse/ Dawson City, YT**—Annual Sourdough Rendezvous Bathtub Race; Klondyke Harvest Fair.

September

Dawson City, YT—Great Klondike Outhouse Race and Bathroom Wall Limerick Contest. **Fairbanks**—Equinox Marathon. **Nome**—Great Bathtub Race. **Skagway/ Whitehorse**—Klondike Trail of '98 Road Relay.

October

Anchorage—Oktoberfest. **Kodiak**—Oktoberfest. **Sitka**—Alaska Day Festival.

November

Anchorage—Carrs/Safeway Great Alaska Shootout. **Fairbanks**—Athabascan Old-Time Fiddling Festival; Top of the World Classic . **Haines**—Bald Eagle Festival. **Ketchikan**—Winter Arts Fair.

December

Cordova—Community Tree Lighting. **Fairbanks**—Winter Solstice Festival. **North Pole**—Candle-lighting. **Talkeetna**—Winterfest.

Camping

Alaska and Canada have both government and private campgrounds. With few exceptions, government and private campgrounds are located along the road system and most roadside campgrounds accommodate both tents and RVs. Wilderness camping is also available in most state, federal and provincial parklands. *The MILEPOST®* logs all public roadside campgrounds and includes facilities (water, firewood, etc.) and camping fees, length of vehicle or length of stay limits. *The MILEPOST®* highway logs also include private campgrounds. Keep in mind that government campgrounds generally do not offer hookups or other amenities, and often cannot accommodate large RVs and 5th-wheelers. Season dates for most campgrounds in the North depend on weather.

NOTE: Campers are urged to use established campgrounds. Overnighting in rest areas and turnouts is illegal unless otherwise posted, and may be unsafe.

Two special passes for federal campgrounds are available to U.S. citizens. The Golden Age Passport is for persons 62 and older and costs a one-time fee of $10. The Golden Access Passport is free for persons with blindness or other permanent disability. Both provide lifetime admittance to federally operated parks, monuments, historic sites, recreation areas and wildlife refuges that charge entrance fees.

The MILEPOST® indicates both private and public campgrounds with ▲ tent symbols in the highway logs and on the strip maps.

Alaska

Federal agencies offering recreational campsites are the Bureau of Land Management (BLM), the National Park Service (NPS), the U.S. Forest Service (USFS) and the U.S. Fish and Wildlife Service (USF&WS). Alaska State Parks, the largest state park system in the United States, maintains more than 3,000 campsites within its 120-unit park system.

State Parks. Camping is available at 40 state recreation sites, 5 state parks (Chugach, Denali, Chilkat, Kachemak Bay and Wood-Tikchik), 14 state recreation sites and a state historic park. Reservations are not accepted at any state campgrounds. Camping rates (subject to change) range from $6 to $15. An annual pass, good for unlimited camping in

Camping at Captain Cook State Park on the Kenai Peninsula. (© David L. Ranta, staff)

a calendar year, is available for $75 for Alaska residents only. The pass is a windshield decal and is not transferable. There is a day-use parking fee of $3 or $5 per vehicle at a small number of state park facilities, including some picnic sites, trailheads and fishing access sites. Residents may also purchase a full-year parking pass for $25. To obtain resident camping or parking passes, send check or money order payable to the State of Alaska. Mail to Alaska Camping Pass, 550 W. 7th Ave., Ste. 1260, Anchorage, AK 99501.

BLM maintains about 12 campgrounds; fees are charged at some. Unless otherwise posted, all undeveloped BLM public lands are open to free camping, usually for a maximum of 14 days per stay. Write the Bureau of Land Management, 1150 University Ave., Fairbanks, AK 99709-3899, phone (907) 474-2251.

The **National Park Service** maintains 7 campgrounds in Denali National Park and Preserve (see DENALI NATIONAL PARK section). There are established hike-in campgrounds at Glacier Bay and Katmai national parks and preserves, and wilderness camping in other national parks and preserves in Alaska. For more information, contact any of the Alaska Public Lands Information Centers or access on-line information for the national parks (see "National Parks" on page 764).

U.S. Forest Service campgrounds are available in Alaska's 2 national forests: Tongass and Chugach. Most USFS campgrounds charge a fee of under $10 per night depending on facilities. There is a 14-day limit at most campgrounds; this regulation is enforced. For further information write the Office of Information, USDA Forest Service, Box 21628, Juneau, AK 99802. Campgrounds in the Chugach National Forest are operated under permit by Alaska Recreational Management, Inc. For information phone (907) 522-8368; fax: (907) 522-8383.

U.S. Fish & Wildlife Service manages camping areas along Skilak Road and Swanson River/Swan Lake Roads within Kenai National Wildlife Refuge. Contact the Refuge Manager, Kenai National Wildlife Refuge, Box 2139, Soldotna, AK 99669, phone (907) 262-7021.

Canada

Territorial campgrounds in Northwest Territories charge $12 or $15 per night, depending upon the site, in attended campgrounds and parks with facilities. Campground-use firewood is available for a fee.

Yukon Territory has 43 Yukon government campgrounds located along its road system. These well-maintained campgrounds often have kitchen shelters (which may not be used as sleeping accommodations) and free firewood for use at the campground. There is a 14-day limit. A camping permit ($8/night) is required for nonresidents to camp in Yukon government campgrounds. These camping permits may be purchased at Visitor Reception Centres and at many highway businesses in the Yukon. In a pinch, campers without a permit can purchase one from campground attendants or officers. Permits are transferable.

Provincial park campgrounds and private campgrounds are readily available along Alaska Highway connecting routes in British Columbia and Alberta. Provincial park camping fees range from $10 to $20 a night depending on facilities.

National park campgrounds in Canada generally have a per-night fee ranging from $12 for a tent site to $25 for a full-hookup site. A park motor-license sticker is required for motorists staying overnight in the national parks. Electrical service is standard 60 cycle. Wood for campfires is supplied free to all camping and picnicking grounds. Bring your own ax to split kindling. "Serviced" campgrounds have caretakers.

Crossing the Border

Travel between the United States and Canada is usually a fairly straightforward procedure. However, travelers are reminded that all persons and their vehicles are subject to search and seizure at the border according to the laws of whichever country they are entering. Vehicles may be searched at the discretion of the customs officials, whether or not the traveler feels that he or she has complied with customs requirements.

Customs agents in both Canada and the U.S. are charged with enforcing a daunting number of regulations pertaining to agricultural products, commercial goods, alcohol, tobacco and firearms. Canada vigorously enforces its firearms importation laws, and border officials may—at their discretion—search any vehicle for handguns.

Certain items, mainly crafts and souvenirs made from parts of wild animals, have caused some problems for travelers to the North in recent years. An item which may be purchased legally in Alaska, for example carved ivory, can be brought back into the Lower 48 but may not be permitted transit through Canada without a permit. Some items which may be purchased legally in parts of Canada may not be allowed into the United States. For example, a seal-fur doll purchased in Inuvik, NWYT, would be confiscated by the U.S. Fish and Wildlife Service or U.S. customs because the import of seal products is prohibited except by special permit.

For information on Canadian customs, contact Customs Border Services, Regional Information Unit, 333 Dunsmuir St., Main Floor, Vancouver, BC V6B 5R4; phone (604) 666-0545.

For further U.S. customs information, contact the nearest U.S. customs office or write U.S. Customs Service, P.O. Box 7407, Washington, DC 20044. In Seattle, WA, phone (206) 553-4676. Also try the internet at www.customs.ustreas.gov/

Entry into Canada from the U.S. (non-residents)

Identification: Citizens or permanent residents of the United States do not require passports or visas to enter Canada. However, native-born U.S. citizens should carry some identifying paper that shows their citizenship, in case they are asked for it. This could include a driver's license and voter's registration (together), passport with photo, or some employment cards with description and photo. Social security cards or driver's licenses alone are not positive identification. Birth certificates of children are sometimes required. Proof of residence may also be required. Naturalized U.S. citizens should carry a naturalization certificate or some other evidence of citizenship. Permanent residents of the United States who are not U.S. citizens are advised to have their Resident Alien Card (U.S. Form 1-151 or Form 1-551).

Officials at Canadian customs are concerned about child abductions. If you are traveling with children, remember to bring identification for them. A divorced parent traveling with his or her young child, *without the other parent,* should be able to present a notarized statement of custody; a copy of divorce/custody papers is recommended. When traveling with children who are not your own, have proper identification *and* written permission from a parent or guardian.

Persons under 18 years of age who are not accompanied by an adult should bring a letter with them from a parent or guardian giving them permission to travel into Canada. Proof of sufficient funds to travel within—and back out of—Canada may be required.

Motorists: U.S. motorists are advised to obtain a Canadian Nonresident Interprovincial Motor Vehicle Liability Insurance Card, which provides evidence of financial responsibility. This card is available only in the United States through U.S. insurance companies or their agents. All provinces in Canada require visiting motorists to produce evidence of financial responsibility should they be involved in an accident. Financial responsibility limits vary by province.

All national driver's licenses are valid in Canada. (See also Driving Information this section.)

Entry by private boat or plane: Report to Canada Customs by phoning (888) 226-7277. Provide the names, dates of birth and citizenships of all people on board, the purpose of trip, and declare any firearms or other goods. You will then be given a reporting number for your records. Upon arriving at the designated customs reporting site, you must call Canada Customs a second time to be advised either to wait for a customs officer or to proceed with your travels.

Baggage: The necessary wearing apparel and personal effects in use by the visitor are admitted free of duty. Up to 50 cigars, 200 cigarettes (1 carton) and 14 ounces of manufactured tobacco, 200 tobacco sticks, and up to 40 ounces of spiritous liquor or wine or 24 12-ounce cans or bottles of beer or ale may be allowed entry in this manner. Additional quantities of alcoholic beverages up to a maximum of 2 gallons may be imported into Canada (except the Northwest Territories) on payment of duty and taxes plus charges for a provincial permit at port of entry. To import tobacco products a person must be 18 years of age or over, and to import alcoholic beverages the importer must have reached the legal age established by authorities of the province or territory into which the alcoholic beverages are being entered.

Gifts: Be prepared to provide receipts for gifts, in case you are asked to show the dollar value. Gifts are duty- and tax-free when each gift is valued at $60 (Canadian) or less. If the value of a gift exceeds $60, you may have to pay duties and taxes on the excess amount.

Firearms: Firearms are divided into 3 categories—prohibited, restricted and long guns. The *only* category of gun a U.S. visitor may bring into Canada is a long gun, which is a regular hunting rifle or shotgun with a barrel at least 18½ inches/47 cm, and an overall length of 26 inches/66 cm, and which does not fall into the category of a prohibited or restricted firearm. Non-restricted firearms may be imported only for sporting or hunting use while in Canada, for use in competitons, for in-transit movement through Canada or for a person's protection against wildlife in remote regions of Canada (excluding national parks) as long as the customs officer is satisfied that the circumstances warrent the importation of the firearm. Restricted weapons may only be imported for the purpose of attending an approved shooting competition in Canada. A temporary permit to carry is required.

Nonresidents arriving at a Canada customs port must declare all their firearms, including long guns. Anyone who illegally carries a firearm into Canada is subject to a number of penalties, including seizure of the weapon and the vehicle in which it is carried. It is against the law for visitors to bring handguns into Canada. Personal protection devices such as stun-guns, mace or pepper spray are also prohibited. Specific questions on importing guns should be directed to the Regional Information Unit; phone (604) 666-0545.

Plants, fruit and vegetables: House plants may be imported without a permit. Some fruits and vegetables may be restricted or prohibited entry into Canada and all are subject to inspection at the border.

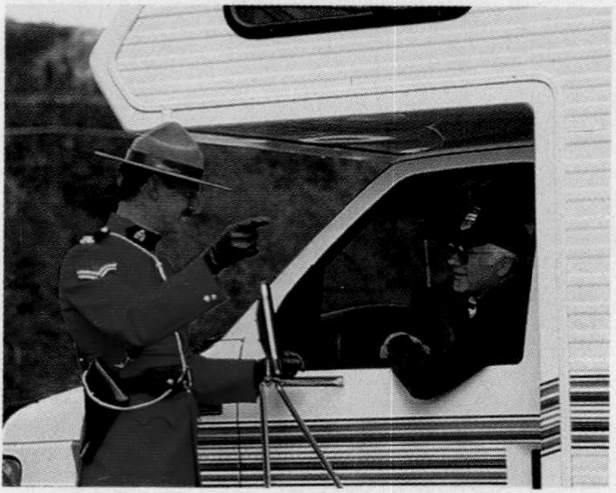

Canada law enforcement includes the RCMP as well as local police.

(© Tourism Yukon Photo)

Meat and dairy products: You can import some meat and dairy products from the United States. There are limits on the quantity or dollar value of certain food products you can bring into Canada at the low rates of duty or that you can include in your personal exemption. If you bring in quanitities of these products over and above the limits, you will have to pay a high rate of duty (from 150 to 350 percent). You may also need an agricultural inspection certificate.

Animals: Dogs and cats (over 3 months of age) from the United States must be accompanied by a certificate issued by a licensed veterinarian of Canada or the United States certifying that the animal has been vaccinated against rabies during the preceding 36 months; such a certificate shall describe the animal and date of vaccination and shall be initialed by inspectors and returned to the owner.

Up to 2 pet birds per family may be imported into Canada. Birds of the parrot family and song birds may be admitted when accompanied by the owner, if the owner certifies in writing that, upon entering the country, the birds have not been in contact with any other birds during the preceding 90 days and have been in the owner's possession for the entire period. All birds of the parrot family, except budgies, cockatiels and Rose-ringed parakeets, are on the CITES endangered species list and require special permits.

GST Refund: You can claim a Goods and Services Tax (GST) refund of the GST paid on most goods and on accommodation of less than one month. For more information, phone (800) 668-4748 when in Canada.

Re-entry into the U.S. (residents)

It is the responsibility of the traveler to satisfy U.S. immigration authorities of his right to re-enter the United States. Canadian immigration officers may caution persons entering from the United States if they may have difficulty in returning.

Re-entry to the United States can be simplified if you list all your purchases before you reach the border; have sales receipts and invoices; and pack purchases separately.

Within 48 hours: Residents of the United States visiting Canada for less than 48 hours may bring in for personal or household use merchandise to the fair retail value of $200, free of U.S. duty and tax. Any or all of the following may be included, as long as the total value does not exceed $200: 50 cigarettes, 10 cigars (non-Cuban in origin), 4 ounces/150 ml of alcoholic beverages or alcoholic perfume.

If any article brought back is subject to duty or tax, or if the total value of all articles exceeds $200, no article may be exempted from duty or tax. Members of a family household are not permitted to combine the value of their purchases under this exception.

Persons crossing the international boundary at one point and re-entering the United States in order to travel to another part of Canada should inquire at U.S. customs regarding special exemption requirements.

After more than 48 hours: Residents may bring back, once every 30 days, merchandise for personal or household use to the value of $400 free of U.S. duty and tax. The exemption will be based on the fair retail value of the article acquired and goods must accompany the resident upon arrival in the United States. Members of a family household traveling together may combine their personal exemptions—thus a family of 5 could be entitled to a total exemption of $2,000. Up to 100 cigars (non-Cuban in origin) per person may be imported into the United States by U.S. residents, and up to 200 cigarettes, and 1 liter of alcoholic beverages if the resident has reached the age of 21 years.

Animals: Your pets, including those taken out of the country and being returned, must have a valid veterinarian health certificate. Particularly, dogs must have proof of rabies vaccination. If you are traveling with pet birds, check with customs about specific requirements. Wildlife and fish are subject to certain import and export restrictions, prohibitions, permits or certificates, and quarantine requirments. Endangered species of wildlife and products made from them are generally prohibited from being imported or exported.

Trademarked items: Foreign-made trademarked items may be limited as to the quantity which can be brought into the U.S. The types of items usually of interest to tourists are lenses, cameras, binoculars, optical goods, tape recorders, musical instruments, jewelry, precious metal-ware, perfumes, watches and clocks. Returning residents are allowed an exemption, usually one article of a type bearing a protected trademark. The item must be for your personal use and not for sale.

Plants: Plants, cuttings, seeds, unprocessed plant products and certain endangered species either require an import permit or are prohibited from entering the U.S. Every single plant or plant product must be declared to the customs officer. Call Quarantines at (303) 436-8645 for information on current plants and import permits.

Entry into the U.S. from Canada (non-residents)

(Notice from U.S. Dept. of Justice, Immigration and Naturalization Service, to Foreign Visitors Needing a Passport to Enter the U.S.A.: If you are entering the U.S. for the first time on this trip, you are required to pay a land border user fee of $6.00 U.S. per person. This fee is payable in U.S. currency or U.S. travelers cheques only. Please have U.S. funds prior to arriving at the U.S. border. NOTE: This notice does not apply to citizens of Canada.)

Exemptions: Non-residents of the U.S. may bring in for personal or household use merchandise to the fair retail value of $200, free of U.S. duty and tax. In addition to $200 in items, some articles may be brought in free of duty and tax. They must be for your personal use and not for others or for sale. These exemptions include personal effects (wearing apparel, articles of personal adornment, toilet articles, hunting, fishing and photographic equipment); one liter of alcoholic beverages (wine, beer or liquor) if you are an adult nonresident; 200 cigarettes, or 50 cigars, or 2 kilograms (4.4 lb.) of smoking tobacco, or proportionate amounts of each; and vehicles for personal use if imported in connection with your arrival.

Gifts: Articles up to $100 in total value for use as bona fide gifts to other persons may be brought in free of duty and tax, if you will be in the U.S. for at least 72 hours and have not claimed this gift exemption in the past 6 months. This gift exemption may include up to 100 cigars.

Restricted or Prohibited Items: Some items must meet certain requirements, require a license or permit, or may be prohibited entry. Among these are: liquor-filled candy (prohibited); fruits, plants and endangered species of plants, vegetables and their products; firearms and ammunition, if not intended for legitimate hunting or lawful sporting purposes; hazardous articles (fireworks, dangerous toys, toxic or poisonous substances); lottery tickets; meats, poultry and products (sausage, pate); narcotics and dangerous drugs; pets (cats, dogs and birds); pornographic articles and publications; switchblade knives; trademarked items (certain cameras, watches, perfumes, musical instruments, jewelry and metal flatware); vehicles and motorcycles not equipped to comply with U.S. safety or clean air emission standards if your visit is for more than one year; wildlife (birds, fish, mammals, animals) and endangered species, including any part or product (pheasants, articles from reptile skins, whalebone or ivory, mounted specimens and trophies, feathers or skins of wild birds).

If you require medicine containing habit-forming drugs, carry only the quantity normally needed and properly identified, and have a prescription or written statement from your personal physician that the medicine is necessary for your physical well-being. Other pharmaceuticals and/or medicinal devices other than for the personal use of the traveler must be approved by the U.S. Food and Drug Administration.

Re-entry into Canada (residents

When returning to Canada, residents must declare all of the goods they acquired abroad and are bringing back, as purchases, gifts, prizes or awards. Residents need to include goods still in their possession that they bought at a Canadian or foreign duty-free shop. They must also declare any repairs or modifications made to their vehicle, vessel or aircraft while they were out of the country. If unsure about whether an article is admissible or if it should be declared, residents should always declare it first and then ask a customs officer.

(NOTE: Residents of Canada should be aware that they may not import U.S. rental vehicles into Canada. These conveyances are not admissable under customs regulations for touring purposes or for other leisure activities, nor is any local use permitted. The only time a U.S. conveyance may be entered into Canada by a Canadian resident is if there is an emergency situation involving the Canadian resident, and he/she has no other means of getting back to Canada. If a U.S. vehicle is found in Canada and driven or rented by a Canadian resident, the vehicle is subject to customs seizure.)

Absence of 24 hours or more: Residents can claim goods worth up to $50 as a personal exemption. This does not apply to tobacco products and alcoholic beverages. Residents may have to make a written declaration. If the goods they bring in are worth more than $50, they cannot claim this exemption and must pay duties on the full value.

Absence of 48 hours or more: Residents can claim goods worth up to $200 in total. These goods can include tobacco products and alcoholic beverages. They may have to make written declaration.

After any trip of 48 hours or longer, you are entitled to a special duty rate on goods worth up to $300 more than your personal exemption. The current special duty rate under the United States Tariff treatment, when combined with GST, is 8 percent.

Absence of 7 days or more: Residents can claim goods up to $500 in total. These goods can include tobacco products and alcoholic beverages. Residents may have to make a written declaration.

To claim tobacco products and alcoholic beverages, residents must meet the age requirements set by the province or territory where they enter Canada. Tobacco products may include up to 200 cigarettes, 50 cigars or cigarillos, 200 tobacco sticks and 200 grams of manufactured tobacco. Alcoholic beverages may include up to 1.14 litres (40 ounces) of wine or liquor, or 24 355 ml (12-ounce) cans or bottles (8.5 liters) of beer or ale. If you bring in more than the free allowance, the cost may be high, since you will have to pay both customs and provincial or territorial assessments.

Gifts: Under certain conditions, residents may send gifts from outside Canada duty- and tax-free to friends in Canada. Each gift must be worth $60 or less and cannot be an alcoholic beverage, a tobacco product or advertising matter. If the gift is worth more than $60, the recipient will have to pay regular duties on the excess amount. It is always a good idea to include a gift card to avoid any misunderstanding. Gifts brought back with the resident do not qualify for the gift exemption.

In most cases, you have to pay regular duties on prizes and awards you receive outside Canada. ♿

Cruise Ship Travel

If a poll were conducted to determine the most comfortable, luxurious and desirable mode of travel, there's little doubt that cruise ships would win hands down. Cruises to Alaska are primarily available from May through September on board more than 30 ships—ranging from large luxury cruise ships to small explorer-class ships. Most ships depart from Vancouver, BC (some from San Francisco and Seattle) and cruise to Alaska via the Inside Passage.

The Inside Passage is the route north along the coast of British Columbia and through southeastern Alaska that uses the protected waterways between the islands and the mainland. (Inside Passage is also commonly used to refer to Southeast Alaska and its communities, which are the ports of call for the cruise ships.) The water passage travels along hundreds of miles of forested coastline, passing deep fjords and the steep, snow-capped peaks of the Coast Range.

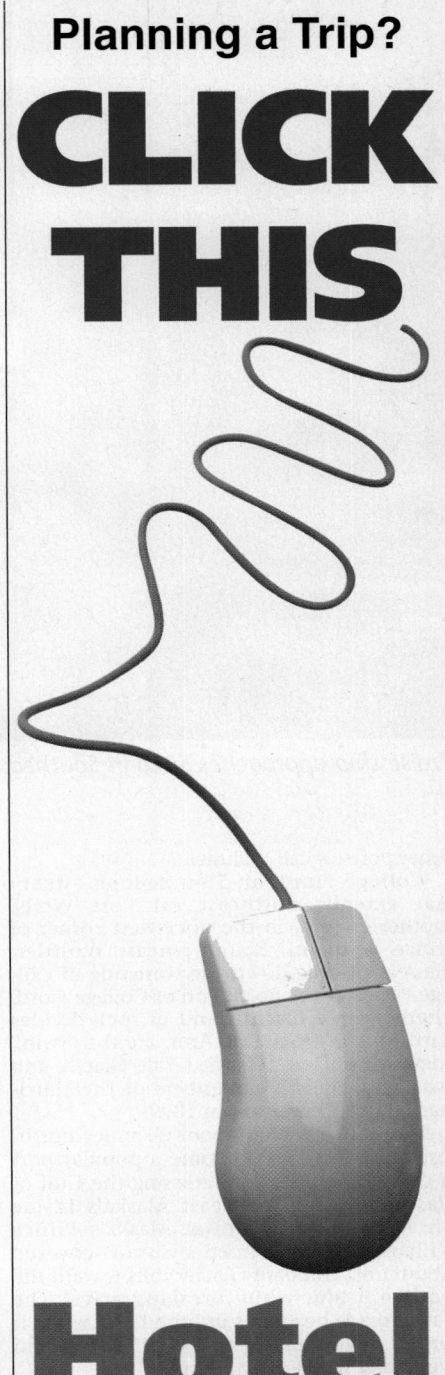

Cruise ship approaches Sitka in Southeast Alaska. (© Loren Taft, Alaskan Images))

Other ports of call include:

College Fjord, an 18-mile-long estuary that extends northeast off Port Wells, another estuary, in the northwest corner of Prince William Sound, near Whittier. Glaciers cascade down the west side of College Fjord. At the north end of College Fjord, where a large black island of rock divides Harvard Arm from Yale Arm, are the "twin" tidewater glaciers— named Yale Glacier and Harvard Glacier by members of the Harriman Alaska Expedition in 1899.

Hubbard Glacier, about 34 miles northeast of Yakutat, has become a popular port of call with cruise ships crossing the Gulf of Alaska between Southeast Alaska's Inside Passage and Southcentral Alaska's Prince William Sound. Framed by snow-covered mountains, Hubbard Glacier rolls toward the sea like a blue-white breaking wave. The glacier made headlines in June 1986, when it surged, damming Russell Fiord. The ice dam eventually weakened and broke.

Misty Fiords, a national monument encompassing more than 2 million acres of Southeast Alaska. Large cruise ships sail Behm Canal, a more than 100-mile-long, deepwater canal that is the major waterway through the monument. The scenery is dramatic: thick rainforest, vertical granite cliffs and snowy peaks. Waterfalls plunge to salt water along the steep-walled waterways, fed by lakes and streams which absorb an annual rainfall in excess of 14 feet.

Tracy Arm, and adjoining *Endicott Arm*, both long, deep, narrow fjords that extend more than 30 miles into the heavily glaciated Coast Mountain Range, about 50 miles southeast of Juneau. At the head of each arm are active tidewater glaciers, which continually calve icebergs into the fjords: Sawyer and South Sawyer glaciers at the head of Tracy Arm; Dawes Glacier at the head of Endicott Arm.

One cruise line (Society Expeditions) offers a new cruise in 2000 to western Alaska, the Bering Sea, the Pribilofs and the Aleutians, a tour of special interest to those in search of new territory to see and explore.

Cruise Lines

Following is a list of cruise lines serving Alaska in 2000. Included are the names of the line's ships (passenger capacity is shown in parentheses) and proposed Alaska ports of call. Not all ships have the same itinerary. Contact the cruise line directly or your travel agent for more details.

There's a bewildering array of travel options connected with cruise ship travel. Both round-trip and one-way cruises are available, or a cruise may be sold as part of a packaged tour that includes air, rail and/or motorcoach transportation. Various shore excursions may be included in the cruise price or offered to passengers for added cost. Ports of call may depend on length of cruise, which ship you choose, time of sailing or debarkation point. Because of the wide variety of cruise trips available, it is wise to work with your travel agent.

Alaska's Glacier Bay Tours & Cruises, 226 2nd Ave. W, Seattle, WA 98119; phone 1-800-451-5952 or (206) 623-2417; fax (206) 623-7809; web: www.glacierbaytours.com. *Executive Explorer* (49 passengers), *Wilderness Discoverer* (86 passengers), *Wilderness Explorer* (36 passengers) and the *Wilderness Adventure* (74 passengers). Glacier Bay, Haines, Juneau, Kake, Ketchikan, Misty Fiords, Tracy Arm, Sitka, Skagway.

Carnival Cruise Line, Carnival Place, 3655 NW 87th Ave., Miami, FL 33178-2428; phone (305) 599-2600. *Jubilee* (1,486 passengers). Ports of call: College Fjord, Haines, Hubbard Glacier, Juneau, Ketchikan, Seward, Sitka, Skagway, Tracy Arm, Valdez.

Celebrity Cruises, Inc., 5201 Blue Lagoon Dr., Miami, FL 33126; phone (305) 262-6677. *Mercury* (1,870 passengers) and *Galaxy* (1,870 passengers). Ports of call: College Fjord, Glacier Bay, Haines, Hubbard Glacier, Inside Passage, Juneau, Ketchikan, Misty Fiords, Seward, Sitka, Skagway, Valdez.

Clipper Cruise Lines, Windsor Bldg., 7711 Bonhomme Ave., St. Louis, MO 63105-1956; phone 1-800-325-0010 or (314) 727-2929, fax (314) 727-6576. *Yorktown Clipper* (138 passengers). Ports of call: Glacier Bay, Haines, Juneau, Ketchikan, Misty Fiords, Petersburg, Sitka, Skagway, Tracy Arm, Wrangell.

Cruise West, 4th & Battery Bldg., Suite 700, Seattle, WA 98121-1438; phone 1-800-426-7702 or (206) 441-8687, fax (206) 441-4757. *Spirit of Glacier Bay* (52 passengers); *Spirit of Alaska* (78 passengers); *Spirit of Discovery* (84 passengers); *Spirit of '98* (96 passengers); *Spirit of Endeavor* (102 passengers); and *Spirit of Columbia* (78 passengers); *Sheltered Seas* (70 passengers). Ports of call: Anchorage, Cordova, Glacier Bay, Haines, Juneau, Ketchikan, Misty Fiords, Petersburg, Sitka, Skagway, Tracy Arm, Valdez, Wrangell.

Crystal Cruises, 2121 Avenue of the Stars, Los Angeles, CA 90067; phone 1-800-446-6620, (310) 785-9300. *Crystal Harmony (*940 passengers*)*. Ports of call: Glacier Bay, Hubbard Glacier, Juneau, Ketchikan, Misty Fiords, Seward, Sitka, Skagway, Tracy Arm.

Holland America Line Westours, Inc., 300 Elliot Ave. W., Seattle, WA 98119; phone (206) 281-3535, fax (206) 281-0351; Internet: www.hollandamerica.com. *Statendam* (1,266 passengers); *Nieuw Amsterdam* (1,214 passengers); *Ryndam* (1,266 passengers); *Westerdam* (1,494 passengers); and *Veendam* (1,266 passengers). Ports of call: College Fjord, Glacier Bay, Hubbard Glacier, Skagway, Juneau, Ketchikan, Seward, Sitka, Valdez.

Lindblad Special Expeditions, 50 Mount Bethel Rd., Warren NJ 07059 or 1415 Western Ave., Suite 700, Seattle, WA 98101; (908) 222-8800 or 1-800-397-3348. *Sea Bird* and *Sea Lion* (70 passengers each). Ports of call: Althorp Rocks, Glacier Bay, Haines, Juneau, Ketchikan, Le Conte Bay, Point Adolphus, Sitka, Tracy Arm, Petersburg.

Norwegian Cruise Lines, 7665 Corporate Center Dr., Miami, FL 33126; phone 1-800-327-7030, (305) 436-0866. *Norwegian Sky* (2,002 passengers); *Norwegian Wind* (1,748 passengers). Ports of call: Glacier Bay, Haines, Hubbard Glacier, Juneau, Ketchikan, Prince William Sound, Seward, Sitka, Skagway.

Princess Cruises, 10100 Santa Monica Blvd., Los Angeles, CA 90067; phone (310) 553-1770, fax (310) 277-6175. *Regal Princess* and *Crown Princess* (1,590 passengers); *Dawn Princess* and *Sea Princess* (2,000 passengers); *Sky Princess* (1,200 passengers); *Sun Princess* (1,950 passengers). Ports of call: College Fjord, Glacier Bay, Hubbard Glacier, Juneau, Ketchikan, Seward, Sitka, Skagway.

Royal Caribbean Cruise Line, 1050 Caribbean Way, Miami, FL 33132; phone 1-800-327-6700. *Rhapsody of the Seas* (2,400 passengers); *Vision of the Seas* (passenger capacity not available). Ports of call: Haines, Hubbard Glacier, Glacier Bay, Juneau, Ketchikan, Misty Fiords, Skagway.

Society Expeditions, 2001 Western Ave., Suite 710, Seattle, WA 98121; phone 1-800-548-8669. *World Discoverer* (138 passengers). Ports of call: College Fjord, Hubbard Glacier, Misty Fiords, Seward, Sitka, Tracy Arm; Little Diomede, St. Lawrence, St. Matthew, Pribilof Islands, Aleutian Islands..

World Explorer Cruises, 555 Montgomery St., Suite 1400, San Francisco, CA

A bicycle-laden RV is coated with mud after driving the Dalton Highway.

(© Rich Reid)

94111; phone 1-800-854-3835, (415) 393-1565. *Universe Explorer* (550 passengers). Ports of call: Glacier Bay, Hubbard Glacier, Juneau, Ketchikan, Seward, Sitka, Skagway, Valdez, Wrangell.

Daylight Hours

An advantage to Northern summer travel are the long hours of daylight at these latitudes. Following are sunrise and sunset times for June 21, 2000 (summer solstice) and December 21, 2000 (winter solstice), representing the longest and shortest days in the North in Anchorage, Fairbanks, Barrow and Juneau. You can get sunrise and sunset times for any location, for any day or year, from the U.S. Naval Observatory website at www. usno.navy.mil

Summer Maximum Daylight
(June 21, 2000)

	Sunrise	Sunset
Anchorage	4:20 A.M.	11:42 P.M.
Barrow	sun does not set	
Fairbanks	2:59 A.M.	12:47 A.M. following day
Juneau	3:51 A.M.	10:08 P.M.

Winter Minimum Daylight
(December 21, 2000)

	Sunrise	Sunset
Anchorage	10:14 A.M.	3:42 P.M.
Barrow	sun does not rise	
Fairbanks	10:58 A.M.	2:41 P.M.
Juneau	8:45 A.M.	3:07 P.M.

Driving North

Driving to the North is no longer the ordeal it was in the early days. Those old images of the Alaska Highway with vehicles stuck in mud up to their hubcaps are far removed from the asphalt-surfaced Alaska Highway of today.

Motorists can still expect road construction and some rough road, but have patience! Ongoing projects are helping to improve severely deteriorated sections of road.

Roads in the North range from multi-lane freeways to 1-lane dirt and gravel roads. The more remote roads are gravel. Motorists are much farther from assistance and more preparation is required for these roads.

Major highways in Alaska are paved with the exception of the following highways that are at least partially gravel: Steese Highway (Alaska Route 6), Taylor Highway (Alaska Route 5), Elliott Highway (Alaska Route 2), Dalton Highway (Alaska Route 11) and Denali Highway (Alaska Route 8).

In Yukon Territory, the Alaska Highway, the Haines Highway and the Klondike Highway from Skagway to Dawson City are asphalt-surfaced. All other roads are gravel.

Major routes through Alberta and British Columbia are paved, with the exception of the Cassiar Highway (BC Highway 37).

Highways within western Northwest Territories are mostly gravel roads, although paving continues on many routes. Paving is almost completed on NWT Highway 3 to Yellowknife, and NWT Highway 1 is paved from its junction with Highway 3 to the Alberta border.

RV owners should be aware of the height of their vehicles in metric measurements, as bridge heights in Canada are noted in meters.

Know your vehicle and its limitations. Some Northern roads may not be suitable for a large motorhome or trailer, but most roads will present no problem to a motorist who allots adequate time and uses common sense.

Also safeguard against theft while at campgrounds, rest stops or in the cities. Always lock your vehicle, be sure valuables are out of sight in an unattended vehicle and report any thefts to the authorities.

NOTE: Driving with the headlights on at all times is the law in Yukon Territory and recommended on roads in Alaska.

Road Conditions

General road conditions are noted in the introduction to each highway in *The MILEPOST*®. Specific areas of concern are also called out in the log. Current seasonal road conditions provided by government agencies are posted on www.themilepost.com. You may also contact the following:

Alaska road conditions: For summer road construction advisories, phone 24-hour recorded daily reports hot line (907) 273-6037 in Anchorage for Southcentral Alaska; phone (907) 456-7623 for Fairbanks, Tok and Valdez areas; or (907) 456-7623 for the Steese Highway. Or toll-free (in Alaska) 1-800-478-7675. Or visit the home page of the Alaska Dept. of Transportation at www.dot.state.ak.us for both summer construction advisories and winter road conditions. "Navigator" reports on road construction are available from visitor centers; also check local newspapers.

Yukon road conditions: For year-round daily recorded updates, phone (867) 456-7623; toll free in YT only 1-877-456-7623. Internet: www.gov.yk.ca/depts/cts/highways/report.html.

British Columbia road conditions: Province-wide operator information (604)

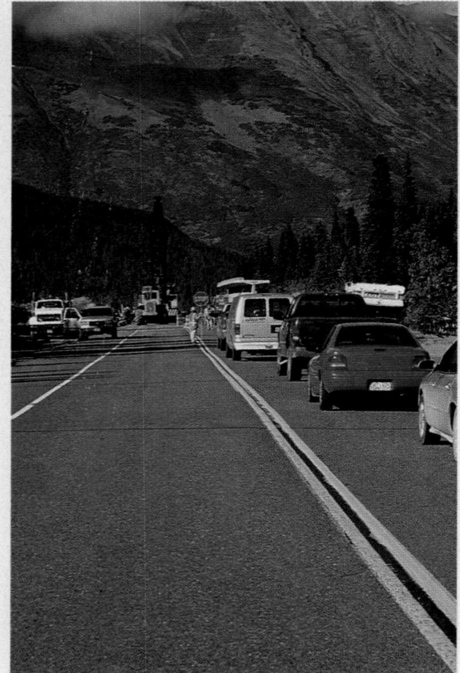

Traffic delays for road construction are a fact of life along northern highways in summer.

(© Kay McElrath Johnson)

660-9770; province-wide recorded information, 75¢/minute (VISA or Mastercard) 1-800-550-4997; province-wide recorded information, 75¢/min. (900) 565-4997; Vancouver-area recorded information, 75¢/min. (604) 420-4997; province-wide recorded information from the U.S., $1/min. (900) 288-4997. Free cellular call at *4997. Or call Talking Yellow Pages in Victoria (250) 953-9000 ext. 7623; Vancouver (604) 299-9000 ext. 7623. Internet address: www.th.gov.bc.ca/bchighways/jump3.htm.

Northwest Territories road conditions: For the South Mackenzie, phone 1-800-661-0751 in NWT; for the North Mackenzie, 1-800-661-0750 in NWT. For reports on condition of the Dempster Highway, call 1-800-661-0752.

Alberta road conditions: 1-800-642-3810 (in Alberta).

Keep in mind the variable nature of road conditions. Some sections of road may be in poor condition because of current construction or recent bad weather. Other highways—particularly gravel roads closed in winter—may be very rough or very smooth, depending on when maintenance crews last worked on the road.

Asphalt surfacing for most Northern roads is Bituminous Surface Treatment (BST), an alternative to hot-mix pavement which involves application of aggregates and emulsified asphalt. Also known as "chip seal," recently applied or repaired BST is as smooth as any Lower 48 superhighway. However, weather and other factors can lead to failures in the surfacing which include potholes and loss of aggregate.

Also watch for "frost heaves" caused by subsidence of the ground under the road.

Many gravel roads in the North (such as the Dalton Highway) are treated with calcium chloride as a dust-control measure. Because calcium chloride tends to eat into paint and metal parts on your vehicle, be sure to thoroughly wash your vehicle.

Gravel road is treated with calcium chloride to keep the dust down. This substance corrodes paint and metal; Wash your vehicle as soon as possible. In heavy rains, calcium chloride and mud combine to make a very slippery road surface; drive carefully! Keep in mind that many highways in the Yukon and some highways in Alaska are gravel.

Planning your trip

Depending on where you want to stop and how much time you have to spend, you can count on driving anywhere from 150 to 500 miles a day. On most roads in the North, you can figure on comfortably driving 250 to 300 miles a day.

In the individual highway sections, log mileages are keyed on the highway strip maps which accompany each highway section in *The MILEPOST*®. You may also use the mileage boxes on these maps to calculate mileages between points, or refer to the mileage box at the beginning of the highway as well. Also use the Mileage Chart on the back of the Plan-A-Trip Map.

Once you have figured the number of driving miles in your itinerary, you can calculate approximate gas cost using the Gas Price Averages chart. (Keep in mind that year 2000 prices will vary from 1999 summer averages.) U.S. motorists factor in the exchange rate for Canadian prices using the accompanying conversion chart.

Normally, May through October is the best time to drive to Alaska. A severe winter or wet spring may affect road conditions and there may be some rough road until road maintenance crews get out to upgrade and repair. Motels, hotels, gas stations and restaurants are open year-round in the cities and on many highways. On more remote

GAS PRICE AVERAGES SUMMER 1999

Alaska Location	Per Gallon U.S. Funds	Canada Location	Per Liter Canadian Funds*
Anchorage	$1.25	Atlin, BC	$.79
Coldfoot	2.05	Contact Creek, BC	.68
Denali Park	1.54	Dawson City, YT	.81
Eagle	1.64	Dawson Creek, BC	.60
Fairbanks	1.37	Destruction Bay, YT	.74
Glennallen	1.62	Fort Nelson, BC	.71
Soldotna	1.44	Fort St. John, BC	.62
Tok	1.58	Grande Prairie, AB	.58
		Watson Lake, YT	.70
		Whitehorse, YT	.69

*See chart below for equivalent cost in U.S. funds for 1 gallon

GAS COST IN U.S. FUNDS PER GALLON

f the Canadian Exchange rate is: $1.00 U.S. equals Canadian funds:		30% $1.30	35% $1.35	40% $1.40	45% $1.45	50% $1.50
	.58	1.69	1.63	1.57	1.51	1.46
	.59	1.72	1.65	1.60	1.54	1.49
	.60	1.75	1.68	1.62	1.57	1.51
Canadian	.61	1.78	1.71	1.65	1.59	1.54
Price	.62	1.81	1.74	1.68	1.62	1.56
Per Liter	.63	1.83	1.77	1.70	1.64	1.59
	.64	1.86	1.79	1.73	1.67	1.62
	.65	1.89	1.82	1.76	1.70	1.64
	.66	1.92	1.85	1.78	1.72	1.67
	.67	1.95	1.88	1.81	1.75	1.69
	.68	1.98	1.91	1.84	1.78	1.72
	.69	2.01	1.93	1.87	1.80	1.74
	.70	2.04	1.96	1.89	1.83	1.77
	.72	2.10	2.02	1.95	1.88	1.82
	.75	2.18	2.10	2.03	1.96	1.83

For example: If gas costs $0.60 Canadian per liter and the current exchange rate is 30% ($1.00 U.S. equals $1.30 Canadian), using the above chart, the equivalent to 1 U.S. gallon of gas costs $1.75 U.S. Or cost per liter X 3.785 divided by exchange rate (1.30)=U.S. cost per gallon.

LITERS TO U.S. GALLONS

Liters	Gallons	Liters	Gallons	Liters	Gallons
1	.3	21	5.5	41	10.8
2	.5	22	5.8	42	11.1
3	.8	23	6.1	43	11.4
4	1.1	24	6.3	44	11.6
5	1.3	25	6.6	45	11.9
6	1.6	26	6.9	46	12.2
7	1.8	27	7.1	47	12.4
8	2.1	28	7.4	48	12.7
9	2.4	29	7.7	49	12.9
10	2.6	30	7.9	50	13.2
11	2.9	31	8.2	51	13.5
12	3.2	32	8.5	52	13.7
13	3.4	33	8.7	53	14.0
14	3.7	34	9.0	54	14.3
15	4.0	35	9.2	55	14.5
16	4.2	36	9.5	56	14.8
17	4.5	37	9.8	57	15.0
18	4.8	38	10.0	58	15.3
19	5.0	39	10.3	59	15.6
20	5.3	40	10.6	60	15.9

For more precise conversion: 1 liter equals .2642 gallons; 1 gallon equals 3.785 liters.

routes, such as the Cassiar Highway, not all businesses are open year-round. Check ahead for accommodations and gas if traveling these roads in winter.

Vehicle Preparation

There are some simple preparations before your trip North that will make driving easier and more trouble-free. First make sure your vehicle and tires are in good condition. An inexpensive and widely available item to include is a set of clear plastic headlight covers (or black metal matte screens). These protect your headlights from flying rocks and gravel. You might also consider a wire-mesh screen across the front of your vehicle to protect paint, grill and radiator from flying rocks. The finer the mesh, the more protection from flying gravel. For those hauling trailers, a piece of quarter-inch plywood fitted over the front of your trailer offers protection. There is no practical way to protect the windshield.

Crankcases are seldom damaged, but gas tanks can be harmed on rough gravel roads. Sometimes rocks work their way in between the plate and gas tank, wearing a hole in the tank. However, drivers maintaining safe speeds should have no problems with punctured gas tanks. A high vehicle clearance is best for some of the rougher gravel roads.

Also keep in mind the simple precautions that make driving easier. A visor or tinted glass helps when you're driving into the sun. Good windshield wipers and a full windshield washer (or a bottle of wash and a squeegee) make life easier. Many motorists also find bug screens to be a wise investment.

Dust and mud are generally not a major problem on northern roads, though you may run into both. Heavy rains combined with a gravel road or roadbed torn up for construction make mud. Mud flaps are suggested. Dust can seep into everything and it's difficult if not impossible to keep it out. Remember to close the windows on your trailer or camper when on a dusty road. It also helps to keep clothes, food and bedding in sealed plastic bags. Also check your air filter periodically.

Driving at slow, safe speeds not only keeps down the dust for drivers behind you, it also helps prevent you from spraying other vehicles with gravel.

Drive with your headlights on at all times. This allows you to be seen more easily, especially in dusty conditions, or when approaching vehicles are driving into the sun. It is also the law in the Yukon and posted roads in Alaska.

NOTE: If driving on a paved surface, it is still necessary to observe "Loose Gravel" signs. Drive slowly.

Although auto shops in Northern communities are generally well-stocked with parts, carry the following for emergencies and on-the-spot repairs: flares; first-aid kit; trailer bearings; bumper jack with lug wrench; electrician's tape; assortment of nuts and bolts; fan belt; 1 or 2 spare tires (2 spares for remote roads); and a tool set including crescent wrenches, socket and/or open-end wrenches, hammer, screwdrivers, pliers, wire, and prybar for changing the fan belt.

If you are driving a vehicle which may require parts not readily available up North, add whatever you think necessary. You may wish to carry an extra few gallons of gas, water, and fluid for brakes, power steering and automatic transmissions.

If your vehicle should break down on the highway and tow truck service is needed, normally you will be able to flag down a passing motorist. Travelers in the North are generally helpful in such situations (traditionally, the etiquette of the country requires one to stop and provide assistance). If you are the only person traveling in the disabled vehicle, be sure to leave a note on your windshield indicating when you left the vehicle and in what direction you planned to travel.

Gasoline

Unleaded gas is widely available in Alaska and is the rule in Canada. Diesel fuel is also commonly available. Good advice for Northern travelers: gas-up whenever possible.

In the North, as elsewhere, gas prices vary (see chart opposite page). Generally, gas prices are slightly higher in Canada and Alaska than the Lower 48, but this is not a hard and fast rule. You may find gas in Anchorage or elsewhere at the same price—or even lower—than at home. A general rule of thumb is the more remote the gas station, the higher the price. Gas prices may vary considerably from service station to service station within the same community.

It is a good idea to carry cash, since some gas stations in Alaska are independents and do not accept credit cards. Most Chevron, Texaco and Tesoro stations will accept VISA or MasterCard. Also watch for posted gas prices that are for *cash,* but not noted as such. Besides double-checking the posted price before filling up, also ask the attendant which pump is for unleaded, regular or diesel, depending on what you want.

Keep in mind that Canadian gas stations have converted to the metric system; quantity and price are based on liters (see Gas

Cost in U.S. Funds Per Gallon chart opposite page). There are 3.785 liters per U.S. gallon, 4.5 liters per imperial gallon. See also Liters to U.S. Gallons conversion chart opposite.

Insurance

Auto insurance is mandatory in Alaska and all Canadian provinces and territories. Drivers should carry adequate car insurance before entering the country. Visiting motorists are required to produce evidence of financial responsibility should they be involved in an accident. There is an automatic fine if visitors are involved in an accident and found to be uninsured. Your car could be impounded for this. Your insurance company should be able to provide you with proof of insurance coverage (request a Canadian Nonresident Interprovincial Motor Vehicle Liability Insurance Card) that would be accepted as evidence of financial responsibility.

The minimum liability insurance requirement in Canada is $200,000 Canadian, except in the Province of Quebec where the limit is $50,000 Canadian. Further information regarding automobile insurance in Canada may be obtained from The Insurance Bureau of Canada, 151 Young St., 18th floor, Toronto, ON M5C 2W7; phone (416) 362-2031 or fax (416) 361-5952.

Alaska state ferry E.L. Bartlett *at Whittier.* (© Tom Culkin)

Tires

On gravel, the faster you drive, the faster your tires will wear out. So take it easy and you should have no tire problems, provided you have the right size for your vehicle, with the right pressure, not overloaded, and not already overly worn. Belted bias or radial ply tires are recommended for gravel roads.

Carry 1 good spare. Consider 2 spares if you are traveling remote gravel roads such as the Dempster or Dalton highways. The space-saver doughnut spare tires found in some passenger cars are not adequate for travel on gravel roads.

Winter Driving

In addition to the usual precautions taken when driving in winter, such as keeping the windshield clear of ice, checking antifreeze and reducing driving speeds on icy pavement, equip your vehicle with the following survival gear: traction material (ashes, kitty litter, wood chips); chains (even with snow tires); first-aid kit; shovel, ice scraper, flashlight, flares; fire extinguisher; extra warm clothing (including gloves and extra socks), blankets or sleeping bags; food; tools; and an extension cord to plug car into block heater. Other items which may be added to your survival gear are a tow rope or cable, ax, jumper cables and extra gas.

Extremely low temperatures occur in the North. A motorist may start out in -35° to -40°F weather and hit cold pockets along the road where temperatures drop to -60°F or more. If you do become stranded in weather like this, do not leave your vehicle; wait for aid. DO NOT attempt to drive unmaintained secondary roads or highways in winter (i.e. Denali Highway, Top of the World Highway), even if the roads look clear of snow.

Call ahead for road conditions and weather reports.

Ferry Travel

Ferry travel to and within Alaska is provided by the Alaska Marine Highway, which is the name of the Alaska state ferry system and also refers to the water route the ferries follow from Bellingham, WA, up the Inside Passage to Skagway, AK.

The Inside Passage is the route north along the coast of British Columbia and through southeastern Alaska that uses the protected waterways between the islands and the mainland. (Inside Passage is also commonly used to refer to Southeast Alaska and its communities.)

BC Ferries also serves the Inside Passage, providing marine transportation for passengers and vehicles between Port Hardy and Prince Rupert, BC. Port Hardy is located at the north end of Vancouver Island. Prince Rupert is the western terminus of Yellowhead Highway 16 and the southern port for 3 Alaska state ferries serving southeastern Alaska. Prince Rupert is also the farthest north of the 46 ports served by BC Ferries.

If traveling to Alaska by ferry, visitors may make their way up the Inside Passage to any Southeast Alaska community via the Inside Passage/Southeast ferry system. Motorists often use the Alaska Marine Highway northbound or southbound as an alternative to driving all of the Alaska Highway and its access routes. By using the Alaska state ferry one way to transport themselves and their vehicles between Bellingham or Prince Rupert and Skagway or Haines, travelers can eliminate between 700 and 1,700 miles of highway driving (depending on their itinerary), avoid covering the same ground twice, and have the opportunity to take in the magnificent scenery and picturesque communities of the Inside Passage.

The MV *Kennicott's* Southeast/Southwest Inter-Tie Trips between Juneau, Valdez and Seward save additional highway mileage.

The Alaska Marine Highway also provides marine access for passengers and vehicles to various communities in Southcentral/Southwest Alaska. Complete details on the Alaska state ferry system are given here. See also the ALASKA STATE FERRY SCHEDULES beginning on page 746.

Alaska State Ferries

The main office of the Alaska Marine Highway is in Juneau. Write 1591 Glacier

FERRY ROUTES *Washington and British Columbia from Puget Sound to Hecate Strait*

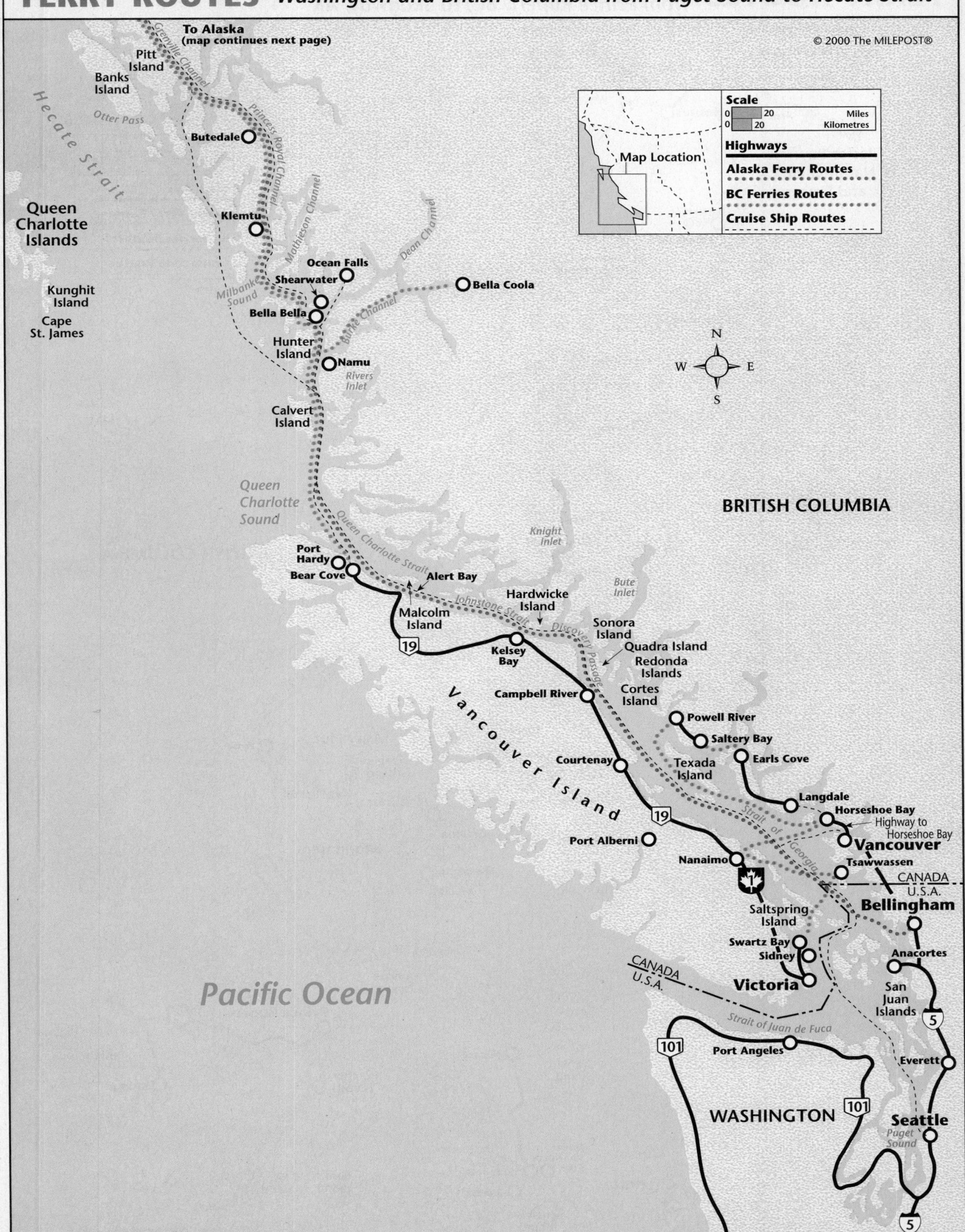

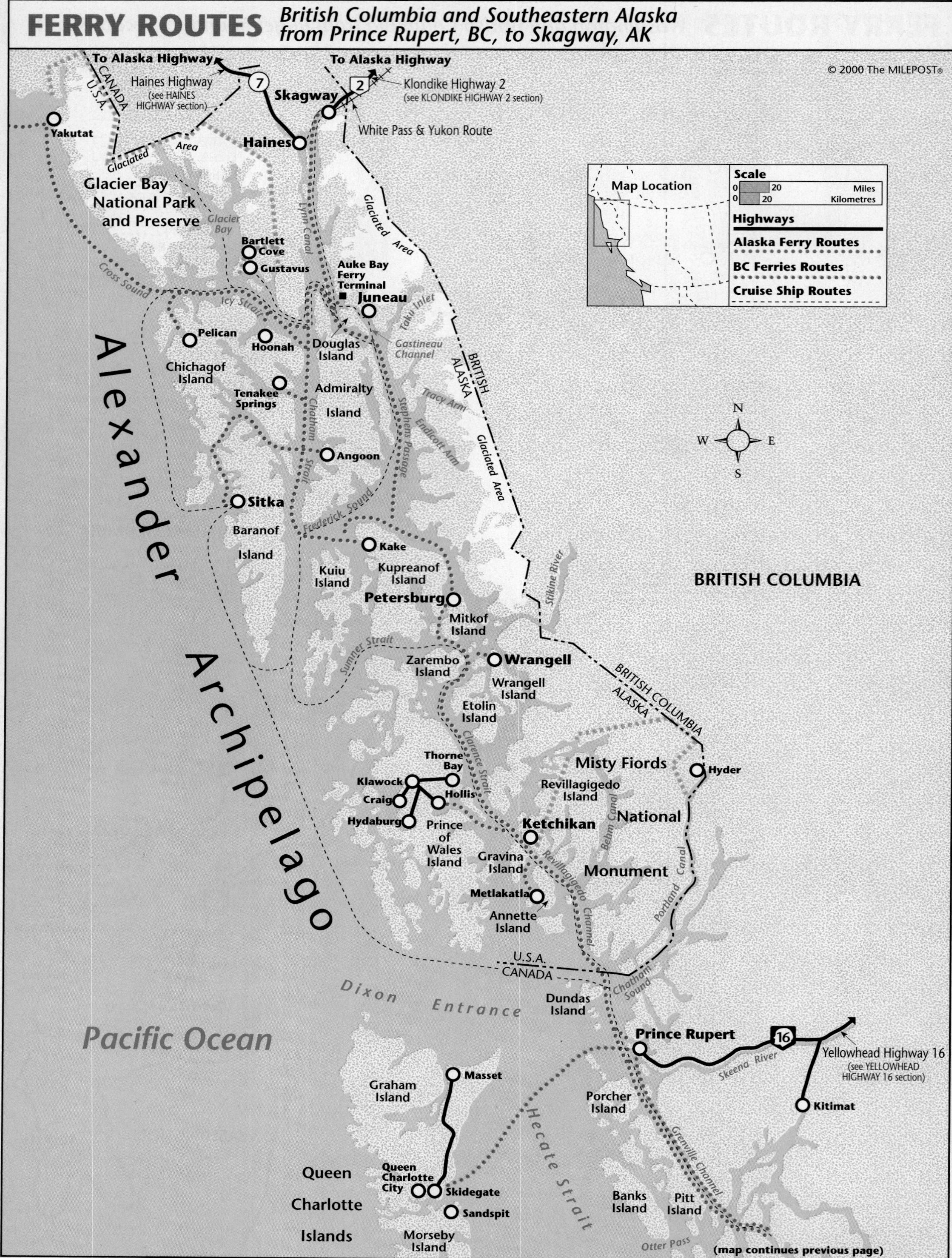
FERRY ROUTES
British Columbia and Southeastern Alaska from Prince Rupert, BC, to Skagway, AK
© 2000 The MILEPOST®
To Alaska Highway
To Alaska Highway
Haines Highway (see HAINES HIGHWAY section)
Klondike Highway 2 (see KLONDIKE HIGHWAY 2 section)
White Pass & Yukon Route
CANADA
U.S.A.
Skagway
Haines
Yakutat
Glaciated Area
Glacier Bay National Park and Preserve
Glacier Bay
Bartlett Cove
Gustavus
Lynn Canal
Glaciated Area
Auke Bay Ferry Terminal
Juneau
Taku Inlet
Cross Sound
Icy Strait
Pelican
Hoonah
Douglas Island
Gastineau Channel
Chichagof Island
Tenakee Springs
Admiralty Island
Chatham Strait
Stephens Passage
Tracy Arm
Endicott Arm
BRITISH COLUMBIA
ALASKA
Glaciated Area
Angoon
Sitka
Baranof Island
Frederick Sound
Kake
Kupreanof Island
Kuiu Island
Petersburg
Mitkof Island
Stikine River
Alexander Archipelago
Sumner Strait
Zarembo Island
Wrangell
Wrangell Island
Etolin Island
BRITISH COLUMBIA
ALASKA
Clarence Strait
Thorne Bay
Klawock
Craig
Hollis
Hydaburg
Prince of Wales Island
Misty Fiords National Monument
Revillagigedo Island
Behm Canal
Hyder
Ketchikan
Gravina Island
Revillagigedo Channel
Metlakatla
Annette Island
Portland Canal
U.S.A.
CANADA
Dixon Entrance
Dundas Island
Chatham Sound
Pacific Ocean
Prince Rupert
16
Skeena River
Yellowhead Highway 16 (see YELLOWHEAD HIGHWAY 16 section)
Kitimat
Masset
Graham Island
Porcher Island
Hecate Strait
Grenville Channel
Queen Charlotte Islands
Queen Charlotte City
Skidegate
Sandspit
Morseby Island
Banks Island
Pitt Island
Otter Pass
(map continues previous page)
Map Location
Scale
0 20 Miles
0 20 Kilometres
Highways
Alaska Ferry Routes
BC Ferries Routes
Cruise Ship Routes
N
S
E
W
BRITISH COLUMBIA

SOUTHCENTRAL/SOUTHWEST FERRY ROUTES

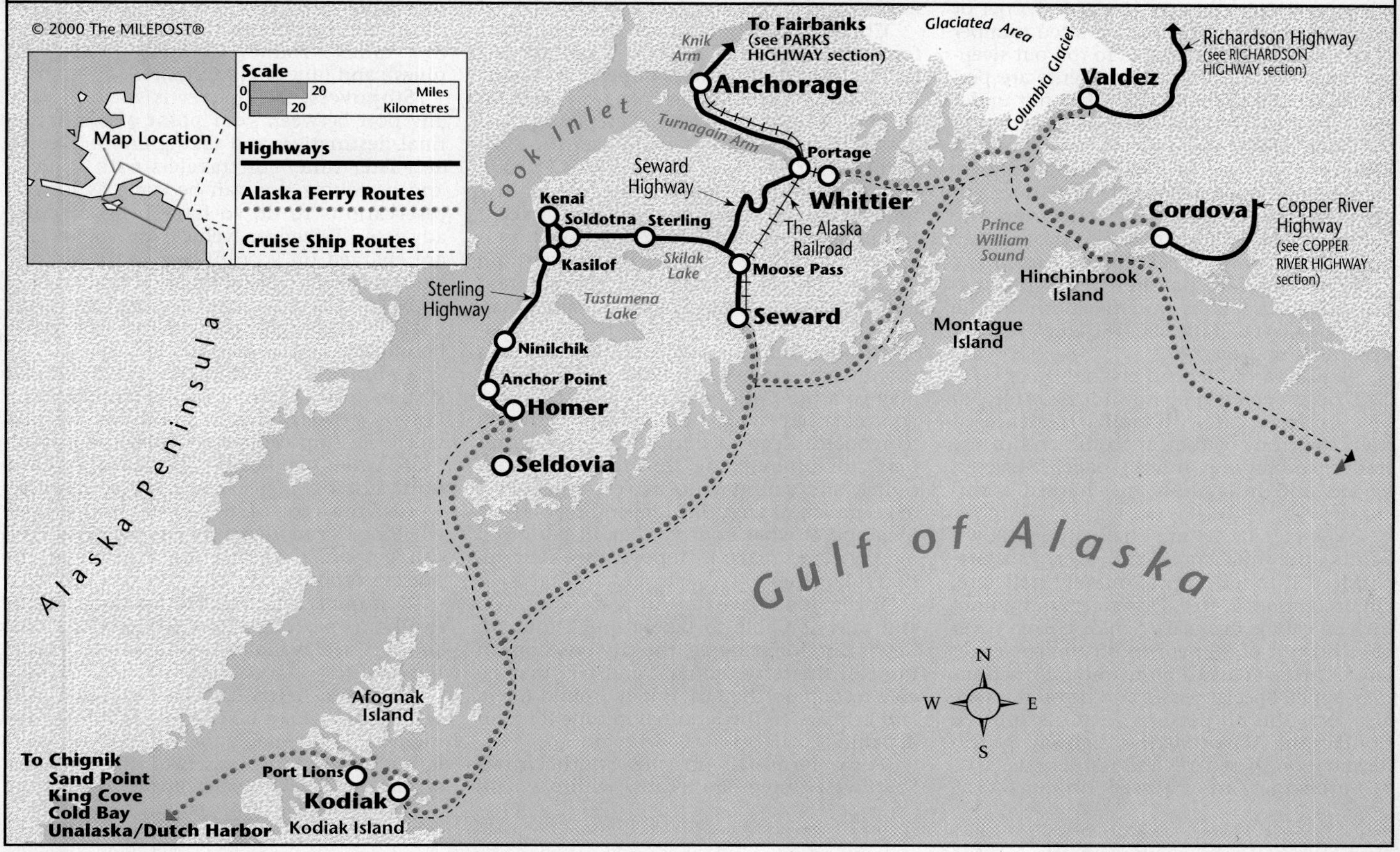

Ave., Juneau, AK 99801-1427; phone toll free 1-800-642-0066, TDD 1-800-764-3779; fax (907) 277-4829. Or via the Internet: www.dot.state.ak.us/amhshome.html.

Local ferry reservation numbers are: Juneau (907) 465-3941 and Anchorage (907) 272-7116.

The Alaska Marine Highway actually operates 2 ferry systems, one in Southeast Alaska and one in Southcentral/Southwest Alaska. The MV *Kennicott* connects the 2 systems with a once-a-month round-trip between Juneau, Valdez and Seward in summer. (See the MV *Kennicott* Southeast/Southwest Inter-Tie Trips schedule.)

The Alaska state ferries on the Southeast system depart from Bellingham, WA (85 miles north of Seattle on Interstate 5, Exit 250), or Prince Rupert, BC (450 miles/724 km west of Prince George, BC, or approximately 1,000 miles/1,609 km by highway from Seattle, WA) for Southeast Alaska communities.

Bellingham is accessible by Amtrak and bus. Fairhaven Station transportation center, next to the Bellingham Cruise Terminal at 401 Harris Ave. in south Bellingham, provides a central location for rail, bus, airporter, taxi and ferry services.

Motorists should keep in mind that only 2 major Southeast communities are connected to the Alaska Highway: Haines, via the Haines Highway; and Skagway, via Klondike Highway 2. (See the HAINES HIGHWAY and KLONDIKE HIGHWAY 2 sections.)

The Southeast system also includes feeder service between Ketchikan and Hollis; Ketchikan and Metlakatla; and Juneau and Pelican. See Inside Passage/Southeast Alaska schedules in the ALASKA STATE FERRY SCHEDULES section beginning on page 748.

The Southcentral/Southwest ferry system of the Alaska Marine Highway serves coastal communities from Prince William Sound to the Aleutian Islands. Southcentral communities on the ferry system that are also accessible by highway are Valdez, Seward and Homer. Southcentral communities accessible only by ferry are Cordova, Seldovia and Kodiak. Until the Whittier Access Road opens in June 2000, access is only via shuttle train (see "Railroads" this section). All communities on the Southwest system are accessible only by ferry or by air.

Travel on the Alaska state ferries is at a leisurely pace, with observation decks, food service (hot meals, snacks and beverages) and vehicle decks on all ferries. Cabins are available only on 5 Southeast ferries (the *Columbia, Malaspina, Matanuska, Taku* and *Kennicott*) and 1 Southwest ferry (the *Tustumena*).

Keep in mind that the state ferries are not cruise ships: They do not have beauty salons, gift shops, deck games, telephones and the like. The small stores on the larger ferries are open limited hours and sell a limited selection of items.

It's a good idea to bring your own books, games and toiletries, since these are not always available on board.

Season: The Alaska ferry system has 2 seasons—May 1 to Sept. 30 (summer), when sailings are most frequent, and Oct. 1 to April 30 (fall/winter/spring). Summer schedules for 2000 appear in the ALASKA STATE FERRY SCHEDULES section beginning on page 746.

Contact the Alaska Marine Highway office for fall/winter/spring schedules, fares and information. In winter, departures are somewhat less frequent on the Inside Passage/Southeast Alaska routes. On the Southcentral system, the MV *Bartlett* is out of service from mid-September through March, resuming sailings between Cordova and Valdez in April. The port of Whittier is not on the winter schedule. The MV *Tustumena* continues service in winter to Seldovia, Homer, Kodiak, Seward, Cordova, Valdez and the Aleutian Chain. The MV *Kennicott* has limited sailings in winter.

Reservations: Required on all vessels for passengers, vehicles and cabins. For reservations write the Alaska Marine Highway,1591 Glacier Ave., Juneau, AK 99801-1427; phone toll free 1-800-642-0066, or fax (907) 277-4829; TDD 1-800-764-3779. Or via the Internet: www.dot.state.ak.us/amhshome.html.

Local ferry reservation numbers are: Juneau (907) 465-3941; and Anchorage (907) 272-7116.

The Alaska state ferries are very popular in summer. Reservations should be made as far in advance as possible to get the sailing dates you wish. Cabin space on summer sailings is often sold out quickly on the Bellingham sailings. Requests for space are accepted year-round and held until reservations open. (See also "Call or Fax Reservations" and "Getting on our Waitlist" on page 746–747.

Deck Passage: If cabin space is filled, or

you do not want a cabin, you may go deck passage. This means you'll be sleeping in one of the reclining lounge chairs or rolling out your sleeping bag in an empty corner or even out on deck. There is a limited number of recliner chairs and spaces to roll out sleeping bags. Small, free-standing tents are permitted on the solarium deck (but not under the heated covered area) and on the stern of the cabin deck if space allows (except on the *Kennicott*). Beware of wind; some campers duct-tape their tents to the deck. Pillows and blankets are available for rent from the purser on most sailings. Public showers are available on all vessels except the *Bartlett*.

Fares and fare payment: See information regarding fares and payment in the ALASKA STATE FERRY SCHEDULES section beginning on page 746.

Vehicle tariffs depend on the size of vehicle. You are charged by how much space you take up, so a car with trailer is measured from the front of the car to the end of the trailer, including hitch space. Bicycles, kayaks and inflatables are charged a surcharge.

Passenger tariffs are charged as follows: adults and children 12 and over, full fare; children 2 to 11, approximately half fare; children under 2, free. Passenger fares do not include cabins or meals. Senior citizen (over 65) discount of 50 percent off the passenger fare between Alaskan ports only; restrictions may apply. Special passes and travel rates are also available to persons with disabilities. Contact the Alaska Marine Highway System for more on these fares and restrictions.

Surcharges are assessed on pets ($25 to/from Bellingham, $10 to/from Prince Rupert) and unattended vehicles ($50 to/from Bellingham, $20 to/from Prince Rupert, and $10 to/from other ports).

Check-in times: Summer check-in times for reserved vehicles prior to departure are: Bellingham and Prince Rupert, 3 hours; Ketchikan, Juneau, Haines, Skagway, Homer, Seward, Kodiak, 2 hours; Petersburg, 1½ hours; all other ports, 1 hour. Call the Sitka terminal for check-in time (907/747-3300). Passengers without vehicles must check in 1 hour prior to departure at all ports except Bellingham, where check-in is 2 hours prior to departure. For MV *Bartlett* departures from Whittier, check-in time at the Portage train loading ramp is 1 hour prior to train departure.

In-port time: In-port time on all vessels is only long enough to unload and load. You may go ashore while the ferry is in port, but you must have your ticket receipt with you to reboard. Keep in mind that ferry terminals are often some distance from city center, and you may not have enough time to see much of anything, depending on how long and at what hour you are in port. You may want to make a stopover (see description following).

If you don't have time for a stopover, you still may be able to take a quick tour. In Ketchikan, for example, the city bus stops in front of the ferry terminal and you may be able to hop on the bus, ride it around town, and get back to the terminal in time for your depature.

Ferry terminals in the Southcentral/Southwest system are located within a half-mile of city centers. In Southeast, ferry terminals close to city center include Wrangell and Skagway. Terminals more distant from city center (from nearest to farthest) are: Petersburg (0.9 mile); Ketchikan (2.5 miles); Haines (5 miles); Sitka (7.1 miles); and Juneau (14 miles).

Stopovers: A stopover is getting off at any port between your point of origin and final destination and taking another vessel at a later time. For travelers with vehicles and/or cabins this can be done as long as reservations to do so have been made in advance. Passenger, vehicle and cabin fares are charged on a point-to-point basis, and stopovers will increase the total ticket cost.

NOTE: Check the schedules carefully. Ferries do *NOT* stop at all ports daily, and northbound and southbound routes vary.

Cabins: Most cabins on the Southeast system ferries have a toilet and shower. Linens (towels, sheets, blankets) are provided. Pick up cabin keys from the purser's office when you board. Cabins are sold as a unit, not on a per berth basis. In other words, the cost of the cabin is the same whether 1 or more passengers occupy it. You can get on a waitlist for a cabin at the purser's office.

Restrooms are available for deck-passage (walk-on) passengers on all vessels. Public showers are available on all vessels except the *Bartlett*.

Vehicles: Reservations are required. Any vehicle that may be driven legally on the highway is acceptable for transport on the 4 larger vessels. Most vessels on the Southeast system can load vehicles up to 70 feet/21m long with special arrangements. Maximum length on the *Tustumena* is 40 feet/12m. Vehicle fares are determined by the overall length and width of the vehicle. Vehicles from 8½ to 9 feet wide are charged 125 percent of the fare listed for the vehicle length. Vehicles over 9 feet in width are charged 150 percent of the fare listed for vehicle length.

Once you are on the vehicle deck of the vessel, a crew member will direct you to your parking location. Park, set your hand brake, lock your vehicle, take the personal possessions you will need and proceed to a passageway leading to the passenger areas. If the vehicle you are putting on board will not be accompanied, lock the vehicle and leave the keys with the loading officer.. RVs cannot be used as dining or sleeping facilities while on the ferries.

Hazardous materials may not be transported on the ferries. The valves on propane or similar type tanks must be turned off and sealed by a ferry system employee. If this has not been done by the time you board, notify the purser when surrendering your ticket for boarding. Portable containers of fuel are permitted but must be stored with vessel personnel while en route.

The state assumes no responsibility for the loading and unloading of unattended vehicles.

Food Service: Food service varies from vessel to vessel. There's dining room service on the *Columbia*, *Tustumena* and *Bartlett*. Cafeteria service is available on all ferries except the *Bartlett*. Alcoholic beverages are available on some vessels. The cost of meals is not included in passenger, cabin or vehicle fares. Tipping is prohibited.

Luggage: You are responsible for your own luggage! Foot passengers may bring hand luggage only (not to exceed 100 lbs.). There is no limit on luggage carried in a vehicle. Coin-operated storage lockers are available aboard most ships, and baggage carts are furnished on the car deck. Baggage handling is NOT provided by the Marine Highway.

Vehicle deck restrictions: Periodic "car-deck calls" are made 3 times a day between Bellingham and Ketchikan. These are announced over the loudspeaker and allow passengers approximately 15 minutes to visit the car deck and walk pets, retrieve items from cars, etc. North of Ketchikan, car deck visits are allowed only when the ferry is in port.

Pet policy: Dogs and other pets are not allowed in cabins and must be transported on the vehicle deck only—*NO EXCEPTIONS.* (There are special accommodations for animals aiding disabled passengers. Proper paperwork is required.) Animals and pets are to be transported inside a vehicle or in suitable containers furnished by the passenger. Animals and pets must be cared for by the owner. Passengers who must visit pets or animals en route should apply to the purser's office for an escort to the vehicle deck. (On long sailings the purser periodically announces "car-deck calls.") You may walk your pet at port stops. Keep in mind that some port stops are very brief and that sailing time between some ports will be as long as 36 hours (Bellingham to Ketchikan).

BC Ferries

BC Ferries provides year-round service on 25 routes throughout coastal British Columbia, with a fleet of 40 passenger- and vehicle-carrying ferries. BC Ferries' "Inside Passage" service between Port Hardy and Prince Rupert offers Alaska-bound travelers a convenient connection with the Alaska Marine Highway at Prince Rupert.

Traveling the Inside Passage aboard B.C. Ferries. (© Lyn Hancock)

Port Hardy is approximately 307 miles/494 km north of Victoria via Trans-Canada Highway 1 and BC Highway 19. From Nanaimo it is 236 miles/380 km—or about 5 hours' driving time—to Port Hardy. If you are driving from Victoria, allow at least 8 hours (the route is almost all 2-lane highway between Victoria and Campbell River). The Port Hardy ferry terminal is located at Bear Cove, 4 miles/7 km south of downtown Port Hardy.

Prince Rupert is located 450 miles/724 km west of Prince George via the Yellowhead Highway (see YELLOWHEAD HIGHWAY 16 section).

Summer service between Port Hardy and Prince Rupert is aboard the *Queen of the North,* which carries 750 passengers and 157 vehicles. The ferry has a cafeteria, buffet dining room, news/gift shop, elevator, facilities for passengers with special needs, video arcade, licensed and view lounges, children's playroom, day cabins and staterooms (for round-trip use). Summer service (May 16 to Oct. 14, 2000) on this route is during daylight hours to make the most of the scenery, so cabins are not necessary. Fall/winter/spring service is an overnight trip on the *Queen of Prince Rupert.*

Or travel the Discovery Coast Passage between Port Hardy and Bella Coola. Summer service only from June 13 to Sept. 11, 2000. The *Queen of Chilliwack* features a cafeteria, gift shop, licensed lounge, reclining seats, showers and a lively atmosphere.

Reservations: Strongly recommended for passengers and required for vehicles on the Inside Passage and Discovery Coast Passage routes. For reservations (7 A.M. to 10 P.M. daily) and recorded schedule information (24-hours) phone (250) 386-3431 in Victoria, or long distance from outside B.C.; or 1-888-223-3779 in British Columbia outside the Victoria dialing area. Or fax (250) 381-5452. Reservations may also be made on-line at www.bcferries.bc.ca. The Internet site also has rates, schedules and fleet profiles. Or contact BC Ferries at 1112 Fort St., Victoria, BC V8V 4V2.

Schedules and fares: The 2000 Inside Passage sailing schedule is shown here. Schedules are subject to change without notice. Rates current at time of printing (subject to change) are as follows (1-way, in Canadian funds): Adult passenger, $106; child (5 to 11 years), $53; car, $218; camper/RV (up to 20 feet in length, over 6 feet 8 inches in height), $362; additional length, $18.10 per foot; motorcycle, $109; bicycle, $6.50. Service during the fall, winter and spring is less frequent and fares are reduced. Contact BC Ferries for details.

Check-in time is 1 hour before sailing. Cancellations made less than 30 days prior to departure are subject to a cancellation fee

BC FERRIES 2000 INSIDE PASSAGE SCHEDULE

Port Hardy to Prince Rupert • May 16 – October 14, 2000

NORTHBOUND

Departs: Port Hardy 7:30 A.M.

Arrives: Prince Rupert 10:30 P.M.

Dates: May 16, 18, 20, 22, 24, 26, 28, 30 only.

June, July, September (odd-numbered days)

August (even-numbered days)

October 1, 3, 5, 7, 9, 11, 13 only.

SOUTHBOUND

Departs: Prince Rupert 7:30 A.M.

Arrives: Port Hardy 10:30 P.M.

Dates: May 17, 19, 21, 23, 25, 27, 29, 31 only.

June, July, September (even-numbered days)

August (odd-numbered days)

October 2, 4, 6, 8, 10, 12, 14 only

Relaxing at Billie's Backpackers Hostel in Fairbanks. (© Carol A. Phillips)

Hostels

During the past decade bed-and-breakfasts proliferated to meet a growing need for alternative lodging, and recently, as more and more people seek ways to achieve their travel goals without breaking the bank, we have seen a dramatic increase in the number of hostels in Alaska. Once considered the province of the young (indicated by the original designation: "youth hostels"), these reasonably priced, generally plain but comfortable accommodations have gained wide acceptance and popularity. No longer is there such a thing as a typical hosteller, as this approach to travel draws all ages and all nationalities, with special appeal to the energetic and independent. The cost of overnight stays varies between $8 and $50, depending upon the type of quarters (bunkhouse or more private sleeping arrangements). Kitchens, baths, laundries, living areas and other amenities are shared. Accommodations run from rustic to relatively luxurious.

Some hostels are affiliated with national/international hostelling groups; many Alaska hostels, not surprisingly, are independent operations. Both types have their benefits, and house rules vary from hostel to hostel. For individuals or groups searching for an economical way to experience Alaska, for the hiker, backpacker, bicyclist, the loner, the sociable, the young, not-so-young, and the young-at-heart, hostelling offers a realistic, practical and enjoyable answer to the question: "How can we afford to spend a vacation in Alaska?"

Not so long ago we knew of fewer than a dozen hostels; today we list 35 and still counting. If you know of others, please share the information with us so that we may include them in future editions of *The MILEPOST®*.

Anchorage & Area

Alyeska Home Hostel, P.O. Box 953, Girdwood, AK 99587.

Anchorage Guest House, 2001 Hillcrest Dr., Anchorage, AK 99517.

HI-Anchorage, 700 H St., Anchorage, AK 99501.

International Backpackers Inn/Hostel, 3601 Peterkin Ave., Anchorage, AK 99508.

Spenard Hostel International, 2845 West 42nd Pl., Anchorage, AK 99517.

Wasilla Backpackers, 3950 Carefree Dr., Wasilla, AK 99654.

Denali Park & Area

Alaskan Retreat B&B, Box 38, Nenana, AK 99760.

Byers Creek Station, Milepost A 144 Parks Highway.

Denali Hostel (Healy), P.O. Box 801, Denali Park, AK 99755.

K-2 Climbers Bunkhouse, P.O. Box 545, Talkeetna, AK 99676.

Mt. McKinley Gold Camp, P.O. Box 149, Denali Park, AK 99755.

Talkeetna Hostel International, P.O. Box 952, Talkeetna, AK 99676.

Fairbanks & Area

Alaska Heritage Inn, 1018 22nd Ave., P.O. Box 74877, Fairbanks, AK 99707.

Arctic Circle Hot Springs Resort, P.O. Box 30069, Central, AK 99730.

Billie's Backpackers Hostel, 2895 Mack Rd., Fairbanks, AK 99709.

Boyle's Hostel, 310 18th Ave., Fairbanks, AK 99701.

Chandalar Ranch, Mile 18.6 Chena Hot Springs Rd., P.O. Box 74877, Fairbanks, AK 99707.

Fairbanks Shelter & Shower, 248 Madcap Lane, Fairbanks, AK 99709.

Grandma Shirley's Hostel, 510 Dunbar St., P.O. Box 73661, Fairbanks, AK 99707.

North Woods Lodge, Chena Hills Dr., P.O. Box 83615, Fairbanks, AK 99708.

Glenn Highway

HI-Tok, P.O. Box 532, Tok, AK 99780.

Hi-Sheep Mountain Lodge, Milepost A 113.5 Glenn Highway, HC 03, Box 8490, Palmer, AK 99645.

Huck Hobbit's Homestead Retreat & Campground, Nabesna Road, Box 420, Slana, AK 99586.

Kenai Peninsula

HI-Ninilchik, The Eagle Watch, Box 39083, Ninilchik, AK 99639.

Moby Dick Hostel, P.O. box 624, Seward, AK 99664.

Moose Range Hostel, P.O. Box 501, Sterling, AK 99672.

Seaside Farms Hostel, 40904 Seaside Farm Dr., Homer, AK 99607.

Prince William Sound & Area

Valdez Hostel, P.O. Box 3101, Valdez, AK 99686.

Kennicott River Lodge & Hostel, McCarthy, AK 99588.

Southeast Alaska

Bear Creek Cabins & International Hostel, P.O. Box 908, Haines, AK 99827.

HI-Juneau, 614 Harris St., Juneau, AK 99801.

HI-Ketchikan, 400 Main St., P.O. Box 8515, Ketchikan, AK 99901.

HI-Sitka, P.O. Box 2645, Sitka, AK 99835.

Presbyterian Church Hostel, P.O. Box 439, Wrangell, AK 99929.

Skagway Home Hostel, Box 231, Skagway, AK 99840.

And for hostellers coming in from Canada, be sure to stop at **Dawson City River Hostel**, Box 32, Dawson City, Yukon Y0B 1G0, Canada. We have heard many good things about it.

Railroads

Although no railroads connect Alaska or the Yukon with the Lower 48, there are 2 railroads in the North: the Alaska Railroad and the White Pass & Yukon Route.

The Alaska Railroad

The Alaska Railroad operates year-round passenger and freight service between Anchorage, Fairbanks, Portage and Whittier. In summer, passenger service is available daily between Anchorage and Fairbanks via Talkeetna and Denali Park; Portage and Whittier; Anchorage and Whittier; and between Anchorage and Seward. For more information on the Alaska Railroad, write Passenger Services Dept., Box 107500, Anchorage 99510. Phone 1-800-544-0552 or (907) 265-2494; fax 265-2323; e-mail reservations@akrr.com. Homepage: http://www.alaska.net/~akrr.

Construction of the railroad began in 1915 under Pres. Woodrow Wilson. On July 15, 1923, Pres. Warren G. Harding drove the golden spike at Nenana, signifying completion of the railroad. The main line extends from Seward to Fairbanks, approximately 470 miles/756 km.

The Alaska Railroad accommodates visitors with disabilities. Six coaches feature wheelchair lifts. Coaches have provisions for occupied wheelchairs, and restrooms are accessible. With advance notice, sign language interpreters are available. ♿

Following are services, schedules and fares available on Alaska Railroad routes. Keep in mind that schedules and fares are subject to change without notice.

Anchorage–Talkeetna–Denali–Fairbanks: Passenger service between Anchorage, Talkeetna, Denali Park and Fairbanks is offered daily on the *Denali Star* from May 13 to Sept. 23, 2000. The express service operates with full-service dining, a vista-dome for all passengers to share and coaches with comfortable reclining seats. Travel along the 350-mile/563-km route between Anchorage and Fairbanks at a leisurely pace with comfortable window seats and good views of the countryside. Packages including sightseeing tours, hotels, river rafting, hiking and flightseeing are available in Talkeetna, Denali, Fairbanks and Anchorage from Alaska Railroad Scenic Tours.

Luxury railcars are available on the Anchorage–Denali Park–Fairbanks route through Gray Line of Alaska (Holland America Lines/Westours) and Princess Tours. These tour companies operate (respectively) the *McKinley Explorer* and *Midnight Sun Express.* These luxury railcars, which are coupled onto the end of the regular Alaska Railroad train, are glass-domed and offer gourmet cuisine along with other amenities. Tickets are priced higher than those for the regular Alaska Railroad cars, and are sold on a space-available basis. Packages with a Denali Park overnight are also available. Phone Princess Tours at (800) 835-8907, or Gray Line of Alaska at (800) 544-2206 for details.

During the summer, northbound express trains depart Anchorage at 8:15 A.M., arrive Talkeetna at 11:25 A.M., arrive Denali Park at 3:45 P.M., and arrive Fairbanks at 8:15 P.M. Southbound express trains depart Fairbanks at 8:15 A.M., arrive Denali Park at noon, and arrive Anchorage at 8:15 P.M.

One-way fares are as follows: Anchorage–Denali Park, $120; Anchorage–Talkeetna, $70; Fairbanks–Denali Park, $48; Anchorage–Fairbanks, $160. Children ages 2 through 11 ride for 50 percent of adult fare; under 2 ride free.

During fall, winter and spring, weekend-only rail service is provided between Anchorage and Fairbanks on the *Aurora*. The train travels from Anchorage to Fairbanks on Saturday and returns on Sunday. The *Aurora* is a "flag stop" train and will stop wherever people want to get on or off.

Reservations should be made more than 40 days prior to travel. Include the dates you plan to travel, points of departure and destination, the number of people in your party and your home phone number. Tickets may be purchased in advance by mail if you desire. Checks, Visa, MasterCard, Discover and Diners Club are accepted.

Each adult is allowed 2 pieces of luggage with a maximum combined weight of 100 lbs. Children are allowed 2 pieces of baggage with a maximum combined weight of 75 lbs. One carry-on is allowed per passenger. Excess baggage may be checked for a nominal fee. Bicycles are accepted for a charge of $20 per station, on a space-available basis on the day of travel. Keep in mind that baggage, including backpacks, must be checked before boarding, and it is not accessible during the trip. Canoes, motors, motorcycles, items weighing over 150 lbs., etc., are not accepted for transportation on passenger trains. These items are shipped via freight train.

Local Service: Local rural service between Talkeetna and Hurricane Gulch operates Thursday, Friday, Saturday and Sunday each week between May 13 and Sept. 23, 2000. This 1-day trip aboard the *Hurricane* takes you past breathtaking views of Mount McKinley (weather permitting), into some remote areas and provides an opportunity to meet local residents who use the train for access. Local service uses self-propelled rail diesel cars and provides vending-machine snacks. The *Hurricane* is a "flag stop" train and will stop wherever people want to get on or off.

Portage–Whittier: The Portage–Whittier shuttle train carries passengers and vehicles between Portage on the Seward Highway and Whittier on Prince William Sound. Portage, which has no facilities other than the railroad's vehicle loading ramp, is 47 miles/76 km south of Anchorage at **Milepost S 80.3** on the Seward Highway. Whittier, on Prince William Sound, is port to the Alaska Marine Highway's ferry MV *Bartlett,* which provides passenger and vehicle service to Cordova and Valdez. The Portage–Whittier railway line is 12.4 miles/20 km long, includes 2 tunnels (one 13,090 feet/3,990m long, the other 4,910 feet/1,497m long). Called the Whittier Cutoff, the line was constructed in 1942–43 as a safeguard for the flow of military supplies. It is a 35-minute train ride.

The shuttle makes several round trips daily between Portage and Whittier, from mid-May through mid-September, connecting with Alaska Marine Highway ferry sailings and other vessels which operate between Whittier and Valdez. (Remember that ferry tickets are purchased separately from train tickets.)

Train tickets for the Whittier shuttle may be purchased from ticket sellers at Portage. Reservations are not accepted for the shuttle train, although passengers with confirmed ferry connections are given priority boarding on the 1:20 P.M. shuttle between Portage and Whittier, if vehicles are at Portage by no later than 12:30 P.M. Standard vehicles under 23 feet/7m in length are charged $50, round-trip, between Portage and Whittier; this includes driver fare. Other adult passengers in the vehicle, $10 round-trip; children (2—11 years of age), $5 round-trip. Vehicle rates are based on length. Some height and width restrictions apply.

During fall, winter and spring, service to Whittier is provided on Wednesday, Friday, Saturday and Sunday.

NOTE: The Whittier access road is scheduled to open in June 2000. When the road opens to vehicle traffic, the Alaska Railroad will suspend shuttle service for vehicles. For current information on passenger service or vehicle shuttle service to Whittier, contact (907) 265-2607 or (907) 472-2532.

Anchorage–Seward: Rail passenger service between Anchorage and Seward operates daily on the *Coastal Classic* between May 13 and Sept. 10, 2000. The 230-mile/370-km round-trip excursion follows Turnagain Arm south from Anchorage and passes through some of the most beautiful scenery to be found along the railroad. Travel is aboard classic passenger coaches. Food service is available in the bar/deli car. Departs Anchorage at 6:45 A.M., arrives Seward at 11:05 A.M. The return trip departs Seward at 6 P.M., arriving Anchorage at 10:25 P.M. Reservations are recommended. The round-trip fare is $86 for adults; 50 percent fare for children 2 through 11. Overnight tours which include hotel and Resurrection Bay boat excursions, Exit Glacier and Alaska SeaLife Center are available from the railroad ticket office.

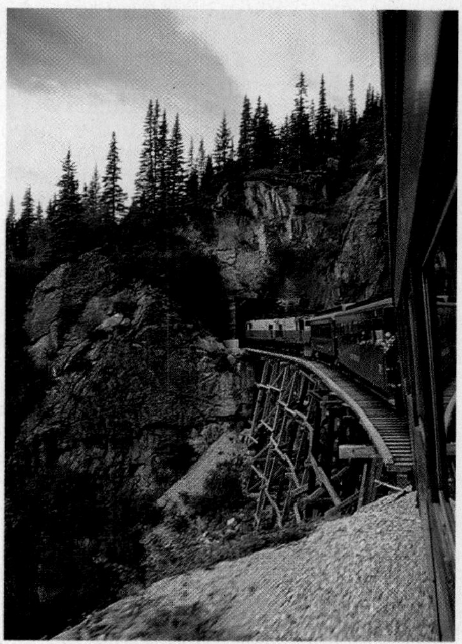

The White Pass & Yukon Route Railway out of Skagway. (© Stephanie Sater)

Anchorage–Whittier: Rail passenger service between Anchorage and Whittier operates daily on the *Glacier Discovery* between May 13 and Sept. 10, 2000. The 50-mile/80-km excursion follows the Turnagain Arm of the Cook Inlet, passes through 2 tunnels, and arrives in Whittier, located on the Prince William Sound. Food service is available in the bar/deli car. Departs Anchorage at 10 A.M. and arrives Whittier at 12:30 A.M. The return trip departs Whittier at 6:45 P.M. and arrives Anchorage at 9:45 P.M. Reservations are recommended. The round-trip fare is $52 for adults; children ages 2-11 pay 50 percent of adult fare. Tours are available, including one-day connecting cruises of Prince William Sound and cruises offering overnight accommodations.

White Pass & Yukon Route

The White Pass & Yukon Route (WP&YR) is a narrow-gauge (36-inch) privately owned railroad built in 1898 at the height of the Klondike Gold Rush. Between 1900 and 1982, the WP&YR provided passenger and freight service between Skagway, AK, and Whitehorse, YT. The WP&YR no longer offers scheduled rail service the entire way to Whitehorse.

The WP&YR now operates a 3-hour round-trip train excursion between Skagway and the White Pass Summit, an 8-hour steam excursion between Skagway and Lake Bennett, and a combination train and bus trip between Skagway and Whitehorse, as well as other special trips.

Construction of the WP&YR began in May 1898. The railroad reached White Pass in February 1899 and Whitehorse in July 1900. It was the first railroad in Alaska and at the time the most northern of any railroad in North America. The White Pass & Yukon Route was declared an International Historic Civil Engineering Landmark, one of only 22 in the world, in 1994.

The railroad follows the old White Pass trail. The upper section of the old "Deadhorse" trail near the summit (Mile 19 on the WP&YR railway) is visible beside the tracks. During the Klondike Gold Rush, thousands of men took the 40-mile/64-km White Pass trail from Skagway to Lake Bennett, where they built boats to float down the Yukon River to Dawson City and the goldfields.

The WP&YR has one of the steepest railroad grades in North America. From sea level at Skagway the railroad climbs to 2,885 feet/879m at White Pass in only 20 miles/32 km of track. Currently, the railroad offers daily train service between Skagway and Fraser, BC, mid-May to mid-September, and a limited number of rail trips to Carcross and steam trips to Lake Bennett in summer.

Following are services, schedules and fares (U.S. funds) for White Pass & Yukon Route in 2000. All times indicated in schedules are local times (Skagway is on Alaska Time, which is 1 hour earlier than Whitehorse, which is on Pacific Time.) Children 12 and under ride for half fare when accompanied by an adult. Children under 2 years ride free if not occupying a seat; half fare for separate seat. Reservations are required. (Tuesdays, Wednesdays and Thursdays are especially busy days.) For reservations and information, contact the White Pass & Yukon Route, Box 435, Skagway, AK 99840. Phone toll free in the U.S. and Canada (800) 343-7373 or (907) 983-2217 in Skagway. E-mail: info@whitepassrailroad.com. Internet: www.whitepassrailroad.com.

Summit Excursion: This approximately 3-hour round-trip excursion features the most spectacular part of the WP&YR railway, including the steep climb (3000 feet in 20 miles) to White Pass Summit, Bridal Veil Falls, Inspiration Point and Dead Horse Gulch. Offered twice daily from May 9 to Sept. 21, 2000; the morning train departs Skagway at 8:30 A.M. and returns at 11:45 A.M.; the afternoon train departs Skagway at 1 P.M. and returns at 4:15 P.M. On Tuesdays and Wednesdays another trip departs Skagway at 4:30 P.M. and returns at 7:30 P.M. Fares are $78 for adults and $39 for children 12 and under.

Skagway to Whitehorse: Through-service between Skagway, AK, and Whitehorse, YT, is offered daily from May 12 to Sept. 12, 2000. Through passengers travel 28 miles/45 km by train between Skagway, AK, and Fraser, BC, and then 87 miles/140 km by bus between Fraser and Whitehorse, YT. The train portion of this trip takes passengers over historic White Pass Summit. Northbound service departs Skagway at 8 A.M. Alaska time. Southbound service departs Whitehorse at 1:30 P.M. Yukon time. One-way fares are $95 for adults and $47.50 for children 12 and under.

Special Steam Excursions: Steam travel returns to the White Pass & Yukon Route with Saturday excursions to beautiful Lake Bennett. This 80-mile/128.7-km round-trip takes 8 hours and includes a layover at a restored 1903 station. Steam trips are scheduled for Saturdays in June, July and August, 2000. Departs Skagway at 8 A.M. Fares are $156 for adults and $78 for children 12 and under; includes lunch.

Lake Bennett Adventure: Travel 20 miles/32 km beyond the Summit to historic Bennett, BC, the end of the Chilkoot Trail. A two-hour layover allows time to explore the area, participate in a walking tour with a Park Historian and tour historic displays in the restored 1903 station. The 8 1/2-hour, 80-mile/129 km round-trip is on Sundays, Mondays and Fridays in June, July and August, departing Skagway at 8 A.M.. Fares are $128 for adults and $64 for children 12 and under; includes lunch.

Chilkoot Trail Hikers Service: Service between Bennett and Fraser, BC, offered daily in June, July and August. Hikers who have completed the 33-mile/53 km Chilkoot Trail can be picked up at Lake Bennett and transported back to Skagway, or with bus connections on to Whitehorse. $25 to Fraser, BC; $65 to Skagway.

Most excursions are escorted out of Skagway by a restored 1947 Baldwin steam locomotive. You'll ride in comfort aboard an 1890s parlor car, viewing scenes of incredible beauty through wide panoramic windows. Cruise ship passengers will find ample space has been reserved for excursions on the WP&YR and should purchase excursion tickets on board their cruise vessel.

Two Canadian railways provide connections for travelers heading for Prince Rupert and on to Alaska:

1. VIA Rail's "Skeena" goes from Jasper, Alberta to Prince George, where it overnights and then continues on to Prince Rupert for connection to the Alaska Marine Highway. Phone toll free 1-800-561-8630.

2. BC Rail's "Cariboo Prospector" runs from Vancouver to Prince George and connects with VIA Rail's train to Prince Rupert. Phone 1-800-339-8752.

Renting An RV

An increasingly popular way to explore Alaska and northwestern Canada is through the big, wide windows of an RV. The good news is you don't have to own an RV to take an RV vacation. You can rent one!

Across the North, dealers offer every type of rig, from modest tent trailers to top-of-the-line, self-contained motorhomes. In between, you have a choice of trailers, converted vans or truck campers. Amenities vary from luxurious to utilitarian, and some dealers have specially-equipped wheelchair-accessible units. Many RV rental companies advertise in *The MILEPOST®*. Check advertisements in Anchorage, Fairbanks and other cities.

How do you decide what to rent? The most popular are Class C units, measuring 20 to 29 feet in length. Laura Bly of "USA Today," in an article on her RV rental experience, wrote: "When estimating how much space you'll need, err on the liberal side. In our case, a 29-footer for a family of 3. What had initially seemed like a palace grew smaller with each passing mile, and I was grateful we didn't need to fold the dinette table into an extra bed each evening." And she and her family were gone only 3 nights.

Further evidence of that point comes from the Recreational Vehicle Renters Association (www.rvamerica.com): "Most families will want the space and comfort of a full-size motorhome. Smaller units are ideal for smaller parties or those who want to 'rough it'."

Inside a Class C, you'll find almost every convenience of home. Some larger units include 2 queen-size beds, air conditioning, a microwave, dinette seating 4, even a bathroom with a shower stall. On the other hand, you can choose a trimmed-down RV for much less money and still have your shower by using the campground facilities.

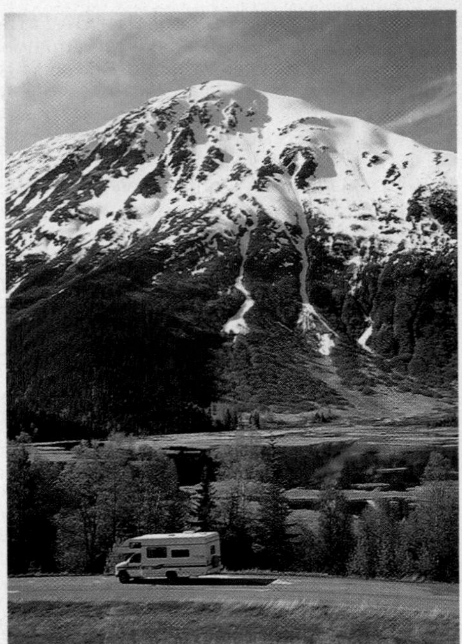

An RV on the Seward Highway at Tern Lake. (© Susan Cole Kelly)

What will it cost? The basic rule is: The more space, privacy and comfort you want, the more the RV costs to rent. How much depends on the size of the RV you rent and the length of your vacation. Depending on the season, motorhomes generally rent from about $70 to $170 per day plus mileage. Truck campers and travel trailers average $50 to $120 per day. Weekly rates offer a savings over daily rates. Keep in mind that some RVs come fully equipped with all the necessities so you need only your own personal items. Others provide linens and kitchen gear, but for an additional charge. Or you can pack your own bedding (sleeping bags work well) and cooking supplies. Ask what your RV rental includes.

The "early bird gets the worm" adage applies here, so make reservations as soon as possible. That way you will get exactly the model and size you want. One experienced renter suggests getting the reservation in writing, so you won't encounter any last-minute disappointments. With nothing on paper to prove confirmation, you might end up with a smaller unit than the one you requested.

What's more, you need to know exactly what's inside the unit before you confirm. Are kitchen supplies (cookware, dinnerware, utensils) included? Bed and bath linens? Maps? Are airport transfers provided? At a charge or no charge? Be sure to know the fee for dropping the RV at a destination other than your pick-up point. Fees can be extremely high.

If you see a sign that states a small unit sleeps 6, be advised that even the larger ones claim sleeping room for no more than 6 or 7 people. Also find out when seasonal rates change. You could save a significant amount of money or rent a larger vehicle for about the same price just by scheduling your trip to coincide with the off-season. Many consider May off-season, June peak time, which means mid-to-late May could be an ideal time for your holiday.

A deposit of about $200 holds your reservation. The majority of rental agencies accept major credit cards, cash or traveler's checks. As a rule, they don't take personal checks. The reservationist will inform you of payment options.

You don't need a special license to rent an RV, yet it is a bit more complicated than renting a car. Most dealers include comprehensive insurance coverage, but with a high deductible. To lower it, some offer a waiver for a daily fee. Talk to your own insurance agent; your policy may or may not cover rentals.

You may be eager to get on the road right away, but take the advice of some renters who regretted they didn't learn more about their new traveling companion before driving off. Here are some things to remember:

When the dealer demonstrates how to operate the rental, pay close attention. This is for your safety and convenience. Ask questions. For example, how to extinguish the propane pilot light (necessary when you add gas) and how to re-ignite it. Critical areas are maintenance and operation: filling fresh water tanks, emptying waste, using appliances, hooking up. The more you know about your home on wheels, the more likely you'll enjoy a trouble-free trip.

On your rental agreement, note any dents, rips or other damage you see in or on the RV. Keep a log of anything that goes wrong with the RV which is not your fault.

Make a backup set of keys if the dealer doesn't give you one.

Ask for a written statement about the fee structure. Will your reservation deposit be applied to your total charges? Are you required to prepay the rental including mileage charges? Does the rental agency require a security deposit? Is it refundable? Is there a prep charge? Are you required to fill the gas tank to avoid additional charges? Propane? How much do additional days and miles cost? Will you be charged if you don't clean the interior and/or wash the exterior?

Know exactly what procedures to follow if you encounter mechanical problems or an emergency. What if you get a ding in the windshield? Is the unit equipped with a spare tire? Write down emergency phone numbers and be sure you have a thorough understanding of all of the agency's policies.

Ask the dealer about any restrictions for RV travel due to the size or weight of the vehicle, or conditions of the roads you plan to travel. Don't overload the RV. Factor in full gas, water and waste tanks to allowable load.

Be sure you understand the papers required should you cross the border between Alaska and Canada.

Know what time the vehicle must be returned to avoid another day's charge.

Shipping

Whether you are moving to Alaska, or plan to ship your vehicle North rather than drive one or both ways, there is a shipper to accommodate your needs.

Vehicles: Carriers that will ship cars, campers, trailers and motorhomes from Anchorage to Seattle include: Alaska Railroad, Box 107500, Anchorage, AK 99510-7500, phone (907) 265-2490; Alaska Vehicle Transport, Inc., phone 1-800-422-7925; Sea–Land Freight Service, Inc., 1717 Tidewater Ave., Anchorage, AK 99501, phone 1-800-478-2671 or (907) 274-2671; and Totem Ocean Trailer Express (TOTE), 2511 Tidewater, Anchorage, AK 99501, phone (907) 276-5868 or toll free 1-800-234-8683.

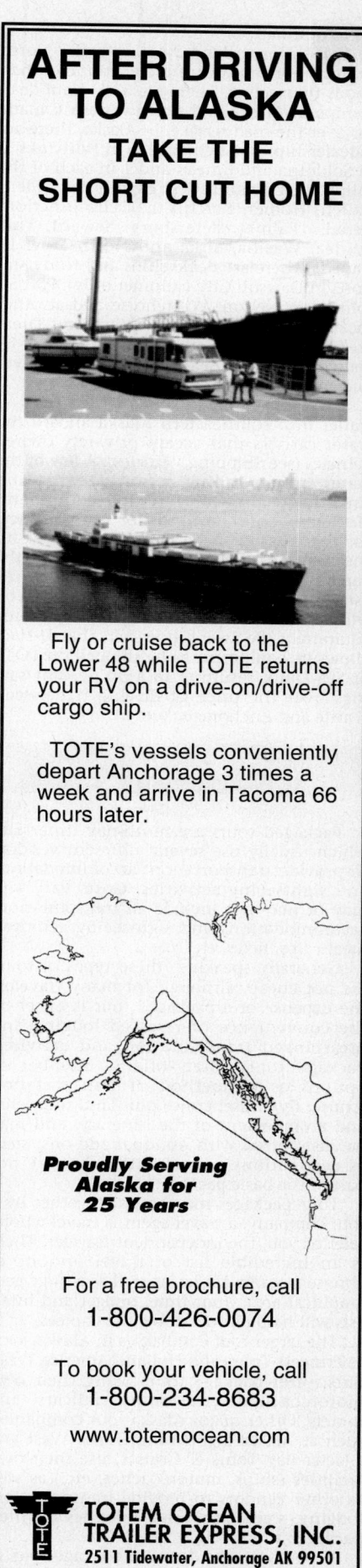

In the Seattle, WA, area, contact A.A.D.A. Systems, Box 2323, Auburn 98071, phone (206) 762-7840 or 1-800-929-2773; Alaska Railroad, 2203 Airport Way S., Suite 215, Seattle, WA 98134, phone (206) 624-4234; Sea–Land Service, Inc., 3600 Port of Tacoma Road, 4th floor, Tacoma, WA 98424, phone (206) 593-8100 or 1-800-426-4512 (outside the Tacoma area); or Totem Ocean Trailer Express (TOTE), 500 Alexander Ave., Tacoma, WA 98421, phone (206) 628-9280 or 1-800-426-0074.

Vehicle shipment between southeastern Alaska and Seattle is provided by Alaska Marine Lines, 5615 W. Marginal Way SW, Seattle, WA 98106, phone (206) 763-4244 or toll free (800) 950-4AML or (800) 326-8346 (direct service to Ketchikan, Wrangell, Prince of Wales Island, Kake, Petersburg, Sitka, Juneau, Haines, Skagway, Yakutat, Excursion Inlet and Hawk Inlet). Boyer Alaska Barge Line, 7318 4th Ave. S., Seattle, WA 98108, phone (206) 763-8575 (serves Ketchikan, Metlakatla, Prince of Wales Island and Wrangell).

Persons shipping vehicles between Seattle/Tacoma and Anchorage are advised to shop around for the carrier that offers the services and rates most suited to the shipper's needs. Not every carrier offers year-round service, and freight charges vary greatly depending upon the carrier and the length and height of the vehicle. Rates increase frequently and the potential shipper is cautioned to call carriers' rate departments for those rates in effect at shipping time. An approximate sample fare from Seattle/ Tacoma to Anchorage to ship a 4-door sedan one-way is $1,200; for a truck, you might pay $1,400. From Anchorage to Seattle/Tacoma, it is approximately $750 for a vehicle and $950 to ship a truck.

Not all carriers accept rented moving trucks and trailers, and a few of those that do, require authorization from the rental company to carry its equipment to Alaska. Check with the carrier and your rental company before booking service.

Book your reservation at least 2 weeks in advance and 3 weeks during summer months, and prepare to have the vehicle at the carrier's loading facility 2 days prior to sailing. Carriers differ on what non-vehicle items they allow to travel inside, from nothing at all to goods packaged and addressed separately. Coast Guard regulations forbid the transport of vehicles holding more than one-quarter tank of gas, and none of the carriers listed above allow owners to accompany their vehicles in transit. Remember to have fresh antifreeze installed in your car or truck prior to sailing!

Household Goods and Personal Effects: Most moving van lines have service to and from Alaska through their agency connections in most Alaska and Lower 48 cities. To initiate service contact the van line agents nearest your origin point.

Northbound goods are shipped to Seattle and transferred through a port agent to a water vessel for carriage to Alaska. Few shipments go over the road to Alaska. Southbound shipments are processed in a like manner through Alaska ports to Seattle, then on to destination.

U-Haul provides service into the North Country for those who prefer to move their goods themselves. There are 53 U-Haul dealerships in Alaska and northwestern Canada for over-the-road service. In Alaska, there are 8 dealerships in Anchorage, 6 in Fairbanks, 2 in Soldotna and Juneau and 1 in each of the following communities: Eagle River, Glennallen, Homer, Ketchikan, Delta Junction, Kenai, Palmer, Petersburg, Seward, Tok, Valdez, Wasilla, Sitka and North Pole. In Canada, there are dealerships and ready stations in Dawson City (summer only), Fort St. John, Fort Nelson, Whitehorse and at other locations along the Alaska Highway. There are also breakdown stations for service of U-Haul vehicles in Beaver Creek, Swift River and the Kluane Wilderness Area.

It's also possible to ship a rented truck or trailer into southeastern Alaska aboard the water carriers that accept privately owned vehicles (see Shipping Vehicles). A few of the water carriers sailing between Seattle and Anchorage also carry rented equipment. However, shop around for this service, for this has not been common practice in the past, and rates can be very high if the carrier does not yet have a specific tariff established for this type of shipment. You will not be allowed to accompany the rented equipment. Be aware, however, that U-Haul allows its equipment to be shipped on TOTE or Sea-Land, resulting in a 30 percent savings over the price of driving it between Seattle and Anchorage.

Tours

Packaged tours are multi-day itineraries which usually use several different vendors to provide transportation, accommodations and sightseeing/activities. Costs vary and may or may not include all transportation, accommodations and sightseeing/activites, meals, tips, taxes, etc.

Generally speaking, these types of tours are not cheap, although for many travelers the expense of a packaged tour is offset by the convenience of reserved lodging and prearranged transportation and activites. Package tours often offer a number of options as to method of transportation (cruise; fly/cruise; cruise plus land tour; etc.) and arrangement of the itinerary, and may be customized with optional add-ons, such as destinations and activities that are not part of the basic package.

Tour packages may be put together by a tour company, a travel agent, a travel wholesaler or you, the independent traveler. There is an incredible list of travel options to choose from in Alaska, as well as a huge geographical area. Your time, budget and interests will help narrow down the choices.

The larger tour companies in Alaska, such as Princess Tours and Holland America Westours, offer package tours using their own motorcoaches, cruiseships, railcars and motels. Other major Alaska tour companies, such as Alaska Sightseeing/Cruise West and Glacier Bay Tours & Cruises, use their own facilities (ships, motorcoaches, etc.) as well as other vendors to provide transportation, lodging, sightseeing and activities on their packaged tours.

If you are considering a package tour to Alaska from the Lower 49, start by reviewing the list of cruise lines offering all-inclusive cruisetours to Alaska this summer. Also look at the advertisements appearing throughout *The MILEPOST®*. Your travel agent or any of the travel agents in Alaska can also acquaint you with what package tours are available and their cost.

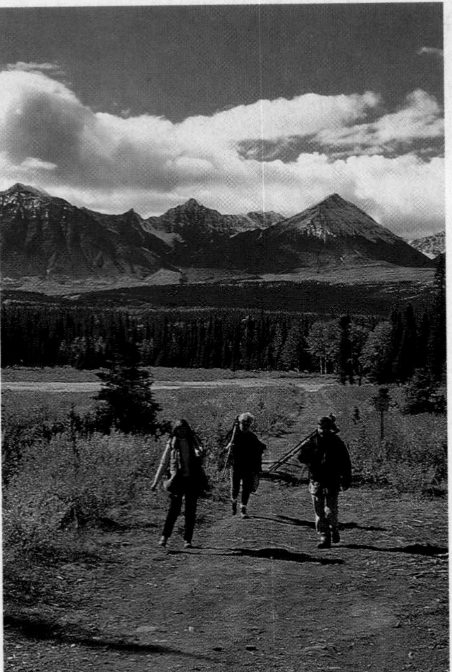

Photo tours are extremely popular in Alaska. (© George Wuerthner)

Travelers who don't wish to join a large tour may customize their own package tour, either with the help of a travel agent or just with the help of *The MILEPOST®*.

Read through the descriptions of major destinations in Alaska, such as Southeast/Inside Passage, Prince William Sound, Denali National Park, Kenai Peninsula, Anchorage, Fairbanks, etc. Everything from half-day motorcoach trips, sightseeing cruises or fly-in bear viewing to overnights on islands or on the North Slope, are covered in both the editorial and in the advertising.

As a travel agent or travel wholesaler would do, independent travelers can book any tour that might interest them, but they may also have to make arrangements for additional lodging and transportation. For example, a visitor might make independent arrangements for a flight to Anchorage and lodging for a night, then book a tour to Denali Park or Barrow or some other destination that would include transportation and lodging. The options are almost limitless. You can even purchase portions of the packaged tours (if space is available), such as the land tour portion of a cruise/tour.

When to go

One of the most often asked questions is "when is the best time to travel?" The high season is June through August, generally the warmest and sunniest months in the North, although July is often one of the wettest months in some regions. The weather is as variable and unpredictable in the North as anywhere else. Go prepared for sunny hot days and cold rainy days. Waterproof footwear is always a good idea, as are a warm coat and rain gear. Generally, dress is casual. Comfortable shoes and easy-care clothes are best. There are stores in the North—just like at home—where you can buy whatever you forgot to bring along. There are laundromats (some with showers) in most communities and dry cleaners in the major cities and some smaller towns.

Because most people travel in the summer, filling up hotels, motels, campgrounds and ferries, you might consider an early spring (April or May) or fall (late August into October) trip. There's usually more room at the lodges and campgrounds and on the ferries in these shoulder seasons. The weather can also be quite beautiful in early spring and in the fall. Keep in mind that some tours, attractions, lodges and other businesses operate seasonally. Check the advertisements in *The MILEPOST®* for details on months of operation or call ahead if in doubt.

While June through August are the warmest months, weather can be really beautiful—clear, sunny and mild—in spring and fall. (Record highs for summer are generally in the 90s with record winter lows to minus 60 degrees.) Precipitation is normally heaviest in August and September in Anchorage; July and August in Fairbanks; and September and October in Juneau. But it can be a dry or a wet summer, depending on El Niño and other variable factors.

The landscape "greens up" in late May, and June has the longest days (21 hours and 49 minutes of daylight on June 21 in Fairbanks). Wildflowers peak in July. The trees and tundra are especially colorful in the fall; they start turning in late August. The days are short in winter (3 hours and 42 minutes of daylight is the winter solstice minimum in Fairbanks), but people who choose to live in the North feel that the winter has a special beauty all its own, and there are many popular events in winter (Fur Rendezvous and the Iditarod, for example).

The following numbers provide recorded weather information: Anchorage, phone (907) 936-2525; Fairbanks, phone (907) 452-3553; Alaska Highway in BC, phone (250) 774-6461; Alaska Highway in Yukon Territory, phone (867) 668-6061; Dawson Creek, BC, phone (250) 784-2244.

The Alaska region National Weather Service Internet address is www.alaska.net/~nwsar/. To view weather conditions at various airports in Alaska, go to the FAA web site at www.akweathercams.com. Another web site—www.alaskacam.com—ties in to the FAA weather cams as well as cameras in Valdez, Fairbanks, Juneau and Alyeska/Girdwood.

Alaska Highway via

EAST ACCESS ROUTE

15 2 3 4 43

Connects: Great Falls, MT, to Dawson Creek, BC **Length:** 866 miles
Road Surface: Paved **Season:** Open all year
Major Attractions: Waterton Lakes National Park, Head-Smashed-In Buffalo Jump, Royal Tyrrell Museum, Fort Edmonton Park

(See maps, pages 34–35)

	Calgary	Dawson Creek	Edmonton	Great Falls	Lethbridge	Valleyview
Calgary		548	181	318	140	395
Dawson Creek	548		367	866	688	153
Edmonton	181	367		499	321	214
Great Falls	318	866	499		178	713
Lethbridge	140	688	321	178		535
Valleyview	395	153	214	713	535	

Bright yellow flowers of canola fields brighten the scenery along highways in northern Alberta. (© Blake Hanna, staff)

The East Access Route is logged in *The MILEPOST®* as one of the 2 major access routes (the other is the West Access Route) to the Alaska Highway. When the Alaska Highway opened to civilian traffic in 1948, this was the only access route to Dawson Creek, BC, the start of the highway.

Highways on this route are all paved primary routes, with visitor services available along the way. Total driving distance from Great Falls, MT, to Dawson Creek, BC, is 867 miles/1,394 km.

The East Access Route log is divided into 3 sections: Great Falls to Sweetgrass, MT, at the Canadian border; Coutts, AB, at the Canadian border to Edmonton; and Edmonton to Dawson Creek, BC.

East Access Route Log

This section of the log shows distance from Great Falls (GF) followed by distance from Sweetgrass (SG). Physical mileposts and exit numbers reflect distance from Idaho–Montana border.

INTERSTATE HIGHWAY 15

GF 0 SG 117.5 (189 km) Exit 280 to **GREAT FALLS** (pop. 55,100; elev. 3,333 feet/1,016m), Montana's second largest city, located at the confluence of the Sun and Missouri rivers, Great Falls is home to the Charles M. Russell Museum. Giant Springs State Park on the north edge of the city has one of the largest springs in the world. The Roe River, which flows out of the springs, is 201 feet long and recognized by the Guinness Book of Records as the world's shortest river.

GF 10.5 (16.9 km) **SG 107** (172.2 km) Exit 290 west to U.S. Highway 89/Choteau.

GF 33.5 (53.9 km) **SG 84** (135.2 km) **Junction** with MT Highway 221 and exit 313 to Dutton; services.

GF 38.5 (61.9 km) **SG 79** (127.1 km) Rest areas near Teton River bridge.

GF 47 (75.6 km) **SG 70.5** (113.4 km) Exit 328 to Brady; services.

GF 54.5 (87.7 km) **SG 63** (101.4 km) Exit 335 to Midway Road.

GF 58.5 (94.1 km) **SG 59** (94.9 km) Exit 339 to **CONRAD** (pop. 3,074); 3 motels, 2 private campgrounds. ▲

GF 68.5 (110.2 km) **SG 49** (78.9 km) Exit 348 to **junction** with MT Highway 44 west to Valier and Lake Frances Recreation Area.

GF 73.5 (118.3 km) **SG 44** (70.8 km) Exit 352 to Bullhead Road and Marias River picnic area.

GF 81.5 (131.2 km) **SG 36** (57.9 km) Exit 363 to **SHELBY** (pop. 3,000); all visitor services available, including several private campgrounds. Marias Museum of History and Art located across from city park. ▲

Junction with U.S. Highway 2 to Cut Bank and Glacier National Park.

GF 83 (133.6 km) SG 34.5 (55.5 KM) EXIT 364 to Shelby; access to Lewis & Clark RV Park.

Lewis & Clark RV Park. See display ad this section. ▲

GF 98.5 (158.5 km) **SG 19** (30.5 km) Exit 379 to Kevin/MT Highway 215 and Oilmont/MT Highway 343; services.

GF 109.5 (176.2 km) **SG 8** (12.9 km) Exit 389 to **SUNBURST** (pop. 520); all services.

GF 117.5 (189 km) **SG 0** Exit 397 to rest area at **SWEETGRASS** at U.S.–Canada border; food, gas, and lodging. Duty-free shop. Customs and immigration open 24 hours a day.

(Continues on page 36)

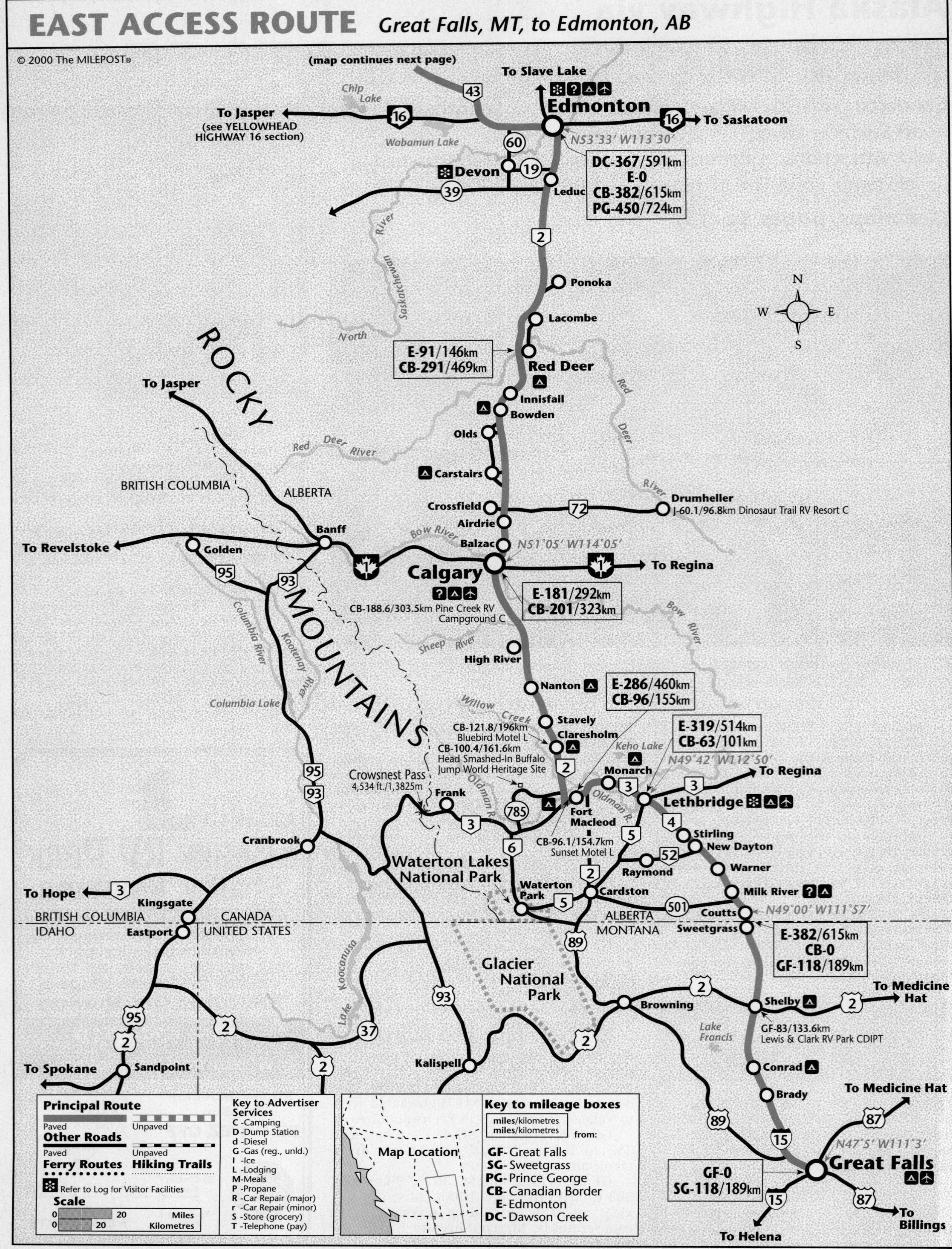
EAST ACCESS ROUTE Great Falls, MT, to Edmonton, AB
© 2000 The MILEPOST®
(map continues next page)
To Slave Lake
Edmonton
N53°33' W113°30'
To Jasper
(see YELLOWHEAD HIGHWAY 16 section)
To Saskatoon
Chip Lake
Wabamun Lake
Devon
Leduc
DC-367/591km
E-0
CB-382/615km
PG-450/724km
North Saskatchewan River
Ponoka
Lacombe
E-91/146km
CB-291/469km
Red Deer
Innisfail
Bowden
Olds
Carstairs
Crossfield
Airdrie
Balzac
N51°05' W114°05'
Drumheller
J-60.1/96.8km Dinosaur Trail RV Resort C
Red Deer River
ROCKY MOUNTAINS
To Jasper
BRITISH COLUMBIA
ALBERTA
Banff
Bow River
To Revelstoke
Golden
Calgary
To Regina
E-181/292km
CB-201/323km
CB-188.6/303.5km Pine Creek RV Campground C
Columbia River
Kootenay River
Sheep River
High River
Nanton
E-286/460km
CB-96/155km
Columbia Lake
Willow Creek
Stavely
Claresholm
CB-121.8/196km Bluebird Motel L
CB-100.4/161.6km Head Smashed-In Buffalo Jump World Heritage Site
Keho Lake
E-319/514km
CB-63/101km
N49°42' W112°50'
Monarch
To Regina
Crowsnest Pass
4,534 ft./1,3825m
Frank
Oldman R.
Fort Macleod
Lethbridge
CB-96.1/154.7km Sunset Motel L
Stirling
New Dayton
Cranbrook
Waterton Lakes National Park
Raymond
Warner
Waterton Park
Cardston
Milk River
To Hope
Kingsgate
BRITISH COLUMBIA
CANADA
ALBERTA
Coutts
N49°00' W111°57'
IDAHO
Eastport
UNITED STATES
MONTANA
Sweetgrass
E-382/615km
CB-0
GF-118/189km
Lake Koocanusa
Glacier National Park
To Medicine Hat
Browning
Shelby
Lake Francis
GF-83/133.6km Lewis & Clark RV Park CDIPT
To Spokane
Sandpoint
Kalispell
Conrad
Brady
To Medicine Hat
N47°5' W111°3'
Great Falls
GF-0
SG-118/189km
To Helena
To Billings
N W E S
Principal Route
Paved
Unpaved
Other Roads
Paved
Unpaved
Ferry Routes
Hiking Trails
Refer to Log for Visitor Facilities
Scale
0 20 Miles
0 20 Kilometres
Key to Advertiser Services
C -Camping
D -Dump Station
d -Diesel
G -Gas (reg., unld.)
I -Ice
L -Lodging
M -Meals
P -Propane
R -Car Repair (major)
r -Car Repair (minor)
S -Store (grocery)
T -Telephone (pay)
Map Location
Key to mileage boxes
miles/kilometres
miles/kilometres
from:
GF- Great Falls
SG- Sweetgrass
PG- Prince George
CB- Canadian Border
E- Edmonton
DC- Dawson Creek

EAST ACCESS ROUTE *Edmonton, AB, to Dawson Creek, BC*

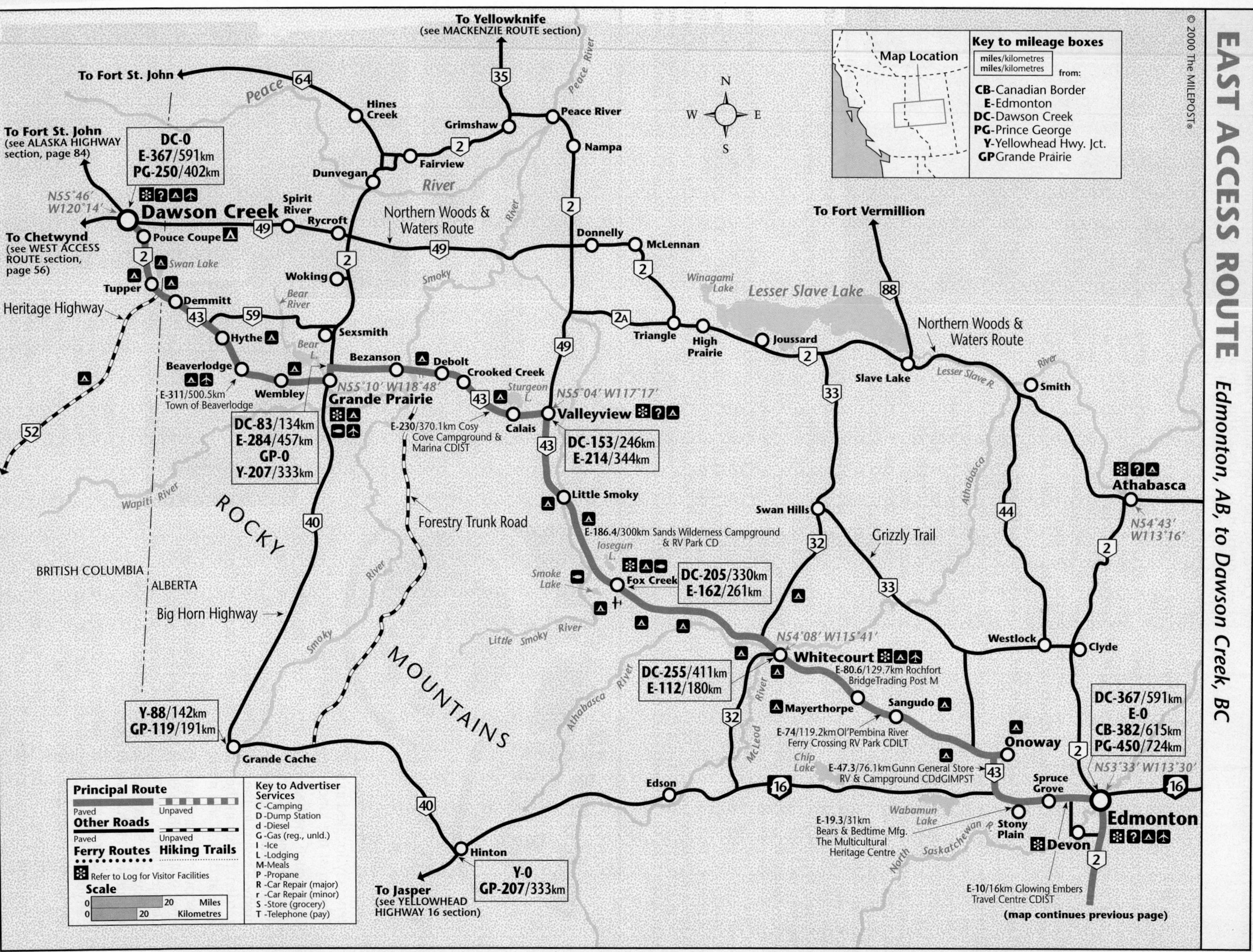

(Continued from page 33)

This section of the log shows distance from the Canadian border (CB) followed by distance from Edmonton (E).

ALBERTA HIGHWAY 4

CB 0 E 382.2 (615 km) U.S.–Canada border, **COUTTS** border crossing; customs and immigration open 24 hours a day. Food, gas and lodging at border. Duty-free shop.

NOTE: Watch for road construction at the border in 2000.

CB 9.9 (15.9 km) **E 372.3** (599.1 km) **Junction** with Secondary Road 501, which leads west 67 miles/108 km to **CARDSTON** (pop. 3,502), located at the **junction** of Highways 2, 5 and 501. Established in 1887 by Mormon pioneers from Utah, Cardston's **Remington–Alberta Carriage Centre** features one of the world's foremost collections of horse-drawn vehicles.

Waterton Park, 25 miles/40.2 km west of Cardston, is the tourist centre for **Waterton Lakes National Park**. Known for its dramatic lake and mountain scenery, Waterton Lakes is actually one large lake broken into 3 sections—Lower, Middle and Upper Waterton lakes. Lower Waterton Lake extends down into Montana. Park adjoins Glacier National Park in Montana, and the 2 parks together are known as the Waterton–Glacier International Peace Park. Both parks are also noted for their grand old hotels. The Prince of Wales Hotel, just north of the townsite, was built in 1927 by the Great Northern Railway.

CB 10.4 (16.7 km) **E 371.8** (598.3 km) Turnout with litter barrels.

CB 11.9 (19.1 km) **E 370.3** (595.9 km) Milk River Travel Information and Interpretive Centre; picnic tables, dump station and travel information. The large dinosaur model on display here makes a good photo subject. Advanced bookings for Alberta adventures and attractions available here, open mid-May to Labour Day weekend for tickets.

CB 13 (21 km) **E 369.2** (594.1 km) **MILK RIVER** (pop. 926) has food, gas, stores, lodging and a small public campground (6 informal sites; no hookups). The 8 flags flying over the campground represent 7 countries and the Hudson's Bay Co., all of which once laid claim to the Milk River area. Grain elevators are on the west side of the highway, services are on the east side.▲

CB 13.5 (21.7 km) **E 368.7** (593.3 km) **Junction** with Secondary Road 501 east to **Writing-on-Stone Provincial Park**, 26 miles/42 km; camping, Indian petroglyphs.

CB 23.6 (38 km) **E 358.6** (577.1 km) Road west to **WARNER** (pop. 434); store, gas, restaurant. Warner is the gateway to **Devil's Coulee Dinosaur Egg Site**, where dinosaur eggs, and fossilized fish and reptiles were discovered in 1987. Guided tours of Devil's Coulee are available through the Devil's Coulee Heritage Museum in Warner from mid-May to mid-September.

CB 23.8 (38.3 km) **E 358.4** (576.8 km) **Junction** with Highway 36A north to Taber, centre of Alberta's sugar beet industry.

CB 36.3 (58.5 km) **E 345.9** (556.6 km) Small community of New Dayton.

CB 41 (66 km) **E 341.2** (549.1 km) **Junction** at Craddock elevators with Highway 52 west to Raymond (10 miles/16 km), site of the annual Stampede and Heritage Days; Magrath (20 miles/32 km); Cardston (46 miles/74 km); and Waterton Lakes Natic Park (74 miles/119 km).

View from beneath High Level Bridge Lethbridge. (© Blake Hanna, staff)

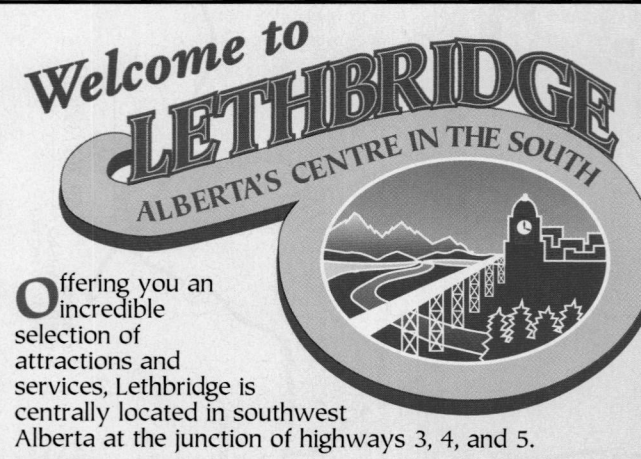

CB 44.4 (71.4 km) **E 337.8** (543.6 l Small community of Stirling to west; mu ipal campground with 15 sites, some w power and water, dump station, showers tennis court. Grain elevators and rail ya

alongside highway. Stirling is the oldest, best-preserved Mormon settlement in Canada and a National Historic Site. ▲

CB 46.1 (74.2 km) **E 336.1** (540.9 km) **Junction** with Highway 61 east to Cypress Hills.

CB 62.7 (100.9 km) **E 319.5** (514.2 km) **Junction** with Highway 5 south to Cardston (48 miles/77 km south) and Waterton Park (81 miles/131 km). Mayor Magrath Drive to north provides access to Lethbridge motels, hotels and Henderson Lake Park (see city description following). Continue west on Scenic Drive for access to Indian Battle Park (via Whoop-Up Drive) and junction with Crowsnest Highway 3.

Chinook Country Tourist Information Centre, on the north side of the intersection of Highways 4, 5 and Mayor Magrath Drive, has RV parking, restrooms, picnic shelter, dump station and dumpster; open year-round.

Lethbridge

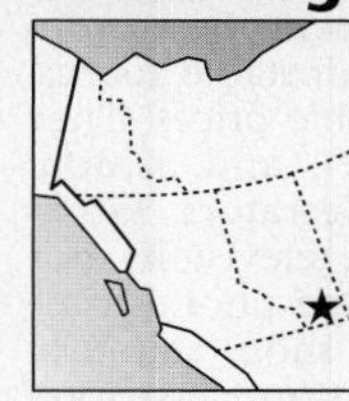

CB 63 (101.4 km) **E 319.2** (513.7 km) At junction of Highways 3, 4 and 5. **Population:** 68,000. **Elevation:** 3,048 feet/929m. **Emergency Services:** Phone 911 for police, ambulance and fire department. **Hospital:** Lethbridge Regional Hospital, phone (403) 382-6111.

Visitor Information: Chinook Country Tourist Association, on the north side of the intersection of Highways 4, 5 and Mayor Magrath Drive, has souvenirs, RV parking, restrooms, picnic shelter, dump station and dumpster; open year-round. Phone (800) 661-1222 and ask for operator 48 (while in the area call 320-1222) for information on attractions and facilities in southwest Alberta. A tourist information centre is also located off Highway 3 at the Scenic Drive South enrance to the city, next to the Brewery Gardens; open March 1 to Oct. 31. **Newspaper:** *The Lethbridge Herald* (daily).

Private Aircraft: Airport 4 miles/6.4 km southeast; elev. 3,047 feet/929m; length 6,500 feet/1,981m; paved, fuel 100, jet. FSS.

Description

The Lethbridge region was home to 3 Indian nations: the Sik-si-kah (Blackfoot), Kai'nah (Many Chiefs, now called Bloods), and Pi-ku'ni (Scabby Robes, now called Peigans). Collectively, they formed the Sow-ki'tapi (Prairie People). Because European fur traders along the North Saskatchewan River first came into contact with the Blackfoot, that tribal name came to be applied to the entire confederacy.

In 1869, the American Army decided to stop trade in alcohol with Indians on reservations across Montana. In December 1869, 2 American traders, John Jerome Healy and Alfred Baker Hamilton, built a trading post at the junction of the St. Mary and Belly (now Oldman) rivers, near the future site of Lethbridge. The post became known as Fort Whoop-Up, the most notorious of some 44 trading posts built in southern Alberta from 1869 to 1874. An important trade commodity was "whiskey," a concoction of 9 parts river water to 1 part pure alcohol, to which was added a plug of chewing tobacco for colour and a can of lye for more taste. The mixture was boiled to bring out its full flavour, and well deserved the Indian name "firewater."

Alarmed by the activities of the whiskey traders, Prime Minister Sir John A. Macdonald formed the North West Mounted Police (NWMP), now the Royal Canadian Mounted Police, to bring law and order to the West. The NWMP reached Fort Whoop-Up on Oct. 9, 1874, and immediately put a stop to the whiskey trade.

Early development of Lethbridge commenced in 1874 with the arrival of Nicholas Sheran in search of gold. The gold, in fact, turned out to be black gold—coal—and by the late 1870s a steady coal market and permanent settlement had developed. Elliot Galt, working with his father, Sir Alexander Galt, helped pioneer coal shipments on the Oldman River and later a narrow-gauge railway that connected to the mainline of the Canadian Pacific Railway.

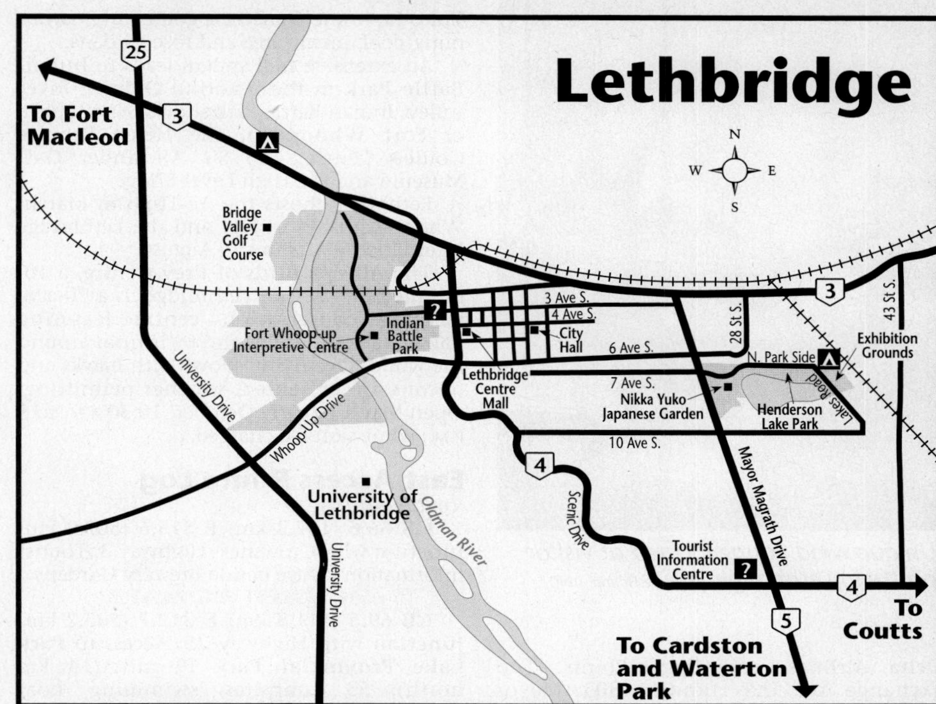

The climax of the early development of Lethbridge came with the CPR construction in 1909 of the high level rail bridge that today carries freight shipments by rail westward through Crowsnest Pass to Vancouver, and onward by ship to the Pacific Rim. The "Bridge"—with a mile-long span and 300-foot elevation—is still the longest and highest bridge of its kind in the world.

Today, Lethbridge is Alberta's third largest city. It has a strong agricultural economy. In late June and early July, bright yellow fields of canola surround the highways leading into the city. Other fields, both irrigated and dryland, produce wheat, sugar beets, potatoes, corn and a variety of other crops.

Lodging & Services

Lethbridge is southwest Alberta's service and shopping centre, with several malls and a variety of retail businesses. There is a wide choice of restaurants, hotel/motel accommodations, and bed and breakfasts.

Best Western Heidelberg Inn offering 66 immaculate rooms in modern 9-story building. On-site facilities include J.B.'s Restaurant, Hi Pub, sauna and fitness room. AAA Three Diamond rating. Awards points for: Gold Crown Club, Alaska Airlines, America West, American Advantage, Canadian Plus,

LETHBRIDGE ADVERTISERS

Chinook Country Tourist Assoc. ....Ph. (800) 661-1222
Best Western Heidelberg Inn ....Ph. (800) 791-8488
Days Inn Lethbridge ....Ph. (403) 327-6000
Lethbridge R.V. Parks ....2 locations—see ad

Unique wind gauge located at visitor centre in Lethbridge. (© Blake Hanna, staff)

Camping

There are 2 campgrounds in the city: Henderson Lake campground and Bridgeview campground. ▲

Attractions

Henderson Lake Park also holds several of the city's attractions, including the **Nikka Yuko Japanese Garden**, a golf course, swimming pool, picnic area and rose gardens.

An extensive trail system leads to **Indian Battle Park** in the beautiful Oldman River valley. Indian Battle Park showcases a replica of **Fort Whoop-Up**, the Helen Schuler Coulee Centre, the Sir Alexander Galt Museum and the High Level Bridge.

Lethbridge hosts the Ag–Expo in March, Whoop-Up Days in July and the Lethbridge International Airshow in August.

The Alberta Birds of Prey Centre, a 10-minute drive east of Lethbridge, is a 70-acre working conservation centre featuring hawks, falcons, eagles and owls from around the world. Live flying shows with hawks and falcons are presented, weather permitting. Open May 1 to early October, 10:30 A.M. to 5 P.M.; admission fee charged.

East Access Route Log

(continued)

CB 66.6 (107.2 km) **E 315.6** (507.9 km) **Junction** with Crowsnest Highway 3. Tourist information centre beside Brewery Gardens.

CROWSNEST HIGHWAY 3

CB 69.5 (111.8 km) **E 312.7** (503.2 km) **Junction** with Highway 25. Access to **Park Lake Provincial Park** (9 miles/14 km north); 53 campsites, swimming, boat launch, fishing, playground. ▲

CB 71.9 (115.7 km) **E 310.3** (499.4 km) Rest area with litter barrels and historical information sign about Coalhurst.

CB 72.4 (116.5 km) **E 309.8** (498.6 km) Community of Coalhurst just north of highway; gas station.

CB 73.8 (118.9 km) **E 308.4** (496.3 km) CPR marshalling yards at Kipp.

CB 77.5 (124.7 km) E 304.7 (490.3 km) Large turnout with litter barrels for northbound traffic.

CB 78.8 (126.8 km) **E 303.4** (488.3 km) **Junction** with Highway 23 north. Continue west on Highway 3 for Fort Macleod.

CB 81.5 (131.2 km) **E 300.7** (483.9 km) Westbound, the highway enters Oldman River valley. Good view west of the Rockies on a clear day.

CB 81.7 (131.5 km) **E 300.5** (483.6 km) Oldman River.

CB 82.9 (133.4 km) **E 299.3** (481.7 km) **Junction** with Highway 3A.

CB 95.7 (154 km) **E 286.5** (461.1 km) **Junction** with Highway 2 south to Cardston and the U.S. border, with access to Waterton Lakes and Glacier national parks. Continue on Highway 3.

Fort Macleod

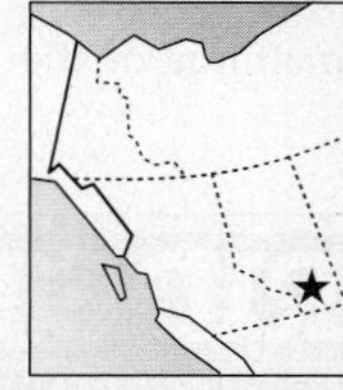

CB 96.1 (154.7 km) **E 286.1** (460.4 km) Turn south for tourist services and town centre. **Population:** 3,100. **Elevation:** 3,300 feet/1,006m. **Visitor Information:** The tourist office is located at the east entrance to town.

There are several hotels and motels, campgrounds, restaurants, shopping facilities and gas stations. This community's Main Street is a designated historic site; walking tours are offered.

The main attraction in Fort Macleod is the **Fort Macleod Museum**, a replica of Fort Macleod, which features the history of the Mounted Police, local Native cultures and early pioneers, in a fort setting. The original fort, named for Colonel J.F. Macleod, was built in 1874 and was the first outpost of the North West Mounted Police (later the RCMP) in western Canada.

During July and August, the museum features a local re-creation of the official RCMP Musical Ride: Youth in NWMP uniforms execute drills on horseback in a colorful display. The museum is open daily from May to mid-October; open weekdays the rest of the year (closed Dec. 24 to March 1). ▲

East Access Route Log

(continued)

CB 99 (159.4 km) **E 283.2** (455.8 km) **Junction** with Highway 2 north to Calgary and Edmonton. Highway 3 (Crowsnest) continues 600 miles/965.6 km west to Hope, BC. The highway takes its name from Crowsnest Pass (elev. 4,534 feet/1,382m), one of the lowest passes in the Rockies, which Highway 3 crosses 65.5 miles/105.5 km west of here.

ALBERTA HIGHWAY 2

CB 100 (160.8 km) **E 282.2** (454.1 km) **Oldman River** bridge. Alberta government campground to southwest with 40 campsites, dump station, playground, fishing and swimming. North of the river is the largest turkey farm in Alberta. ▲

CB 100.4 (161.6 km) **E 281.8** (453.5 km) **Junction** with Highway 785, which leads 10 miles/16 km to **Head-Smashed-In Buffalo Jump**, a UNESCO World Heritage Site. The 1,000-foot/305-m-long cliff, where Plains peoples stampeded buffalo to their deaths for nearly 6,000 years, is one of the world's oldest, largest and best-preserved buffalo jumps. The site was named, according to

legend, for a young brave whose skull was crushed when he tried to watch the stampede from under a protective ledge which gave way. An interpretive centre houses artifacts and displays describing the buffalo hunting culture. First Nations interpretive guides available on site. Guided walks available twice daily during July and August. Open daily year-round; 9 A.M. to 7 P.M., May 15 to Labour Day; 9 A.M. to 5 P.M., Labour Day to May; closed major holidays. Admission fee charged.

Head-Smashed-In Buffalo Jump. See display ad this section.

CB 111.2 (179 km) **E 271** (436.1 km) **Junction** with Highway 519 east to small settlement of **GRANUM.** Private RV park with 27 campsites. ▲

CB 116.2 (187 km) **E 266** (428 km) Community of Woodhouse.

CB 121.8 (196 km) **E 260.4** (419.1 km) **CLARESHOLM** (pop. 3,427), a prosperous ranching centre with all visitor facilities.

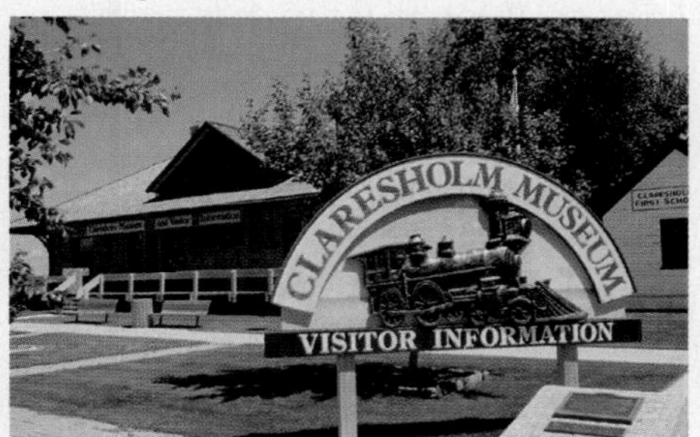

The old railway station houses a museum and tourist infocentre. Camping at Centennial Park; 17 sites, dump station, playground. ▲

Bluebird Motel. Winner of 8 Provincial Housekeeping awards. 23 meticulously clean, quiet units, each with its own unique charm. Choose between 1-, 2-, and 3-room suites or pamper yourself in a heritage room decorated in antiques. Kitchenettes available. Large-screen cable TVs, free movie channels, fridges, in-room coffee, air-conditioning, laundry service. Pets welcome. Fair U.S. exchange, off-season rates. Don't be disappointed—call ahead. (403) 625-3395 or 1-800-661-4891 (Alberta only). [ADVERTISEMENT]

CB 125.5 (201.9 km) **E 256.7** (413.1 km) Turnout with litter cans.

CB 131.3 (211.3 km) **E 250.9** (403.8 km) Community of Stavely to the east.

CB 132.1 (212.6 km) **E 250.1** (402.5 km) Access road west to **Willow Creek** Provincial Park; 150 campsites, swimming, fishing. ▲

CB 138.4 (222.8 km) **E 243.8** (392.3 km) Small settlement of Parkland.

CB 146.8 (236.3 km) **E 235.4** (378.8 km) **NANTON** (pop. 1,665); all visitor facilities.

Southern Alberta's "happy farm." (© Blake Hanna, staff)

Nanton is famous for its springwater, which is piped from Big Spring in the Porcupine Hills, 6 miles/10 km west of town, to a large tap located in town centre. Springwater tap operates mid-May to September. WWII Lancaster bomber on display at **Lancaster Air Museum** on Highway 2 South.

CB 147.7 (237.8 km) **E 234.5** (377.4 km) Nanton campground (75 sites) at **junction** with Secondary Road 533, which leads west to Chain Lakes Provincial Park. ▲

CB 151.1 (243.2 km) **E 231.1** (371.9 km) **Junction** with Highway 2A, which parallels Highway 2 northbound.

CB 162.8 (262 km) **E 219.4** (353.1 km) **Junction** with Highway 23 west to **HIGH RIVER** (pop. 6,893) located on Highway 2A. All visitor facilities. Once the centre of a harness-making industry, High River has elegant sandstone buildings and the Museum of the Highwood (open in summer).

CB 164 (264 km) **E 218.2** (351.1 km) Stop of interest commemorating Spitzee Post, built in 1869.

CB 171.6 (276.1 km) **E 210.6** (338.9 km) **Junction** at Aldersyde with Highways 2A and 7 to Okotoks, Black Diamond and Turner Valley (18.5 miles/30 km). Stop of interest commemorating the Turner Valley oil fields.

CB 173.3 (278.9 km) **E 208.9** (336.2 km) Sheep Creek bridge. **Sheep Creek** Provincial Park has a picnic area, playground, swimming and fishing.

CB 183 (294.5 km) **E 199.2** (320.6 km) **Junction** with Highway 2A to **OKOTOKS** (5 miles/8 km west); all visitor services. Visitor information at "The Station", which also has a local history display and an art exhibit in summer. Open daily, May to Labour Day; Tuesdays through Saturdays, September to May.

CB 184.6 (297.2 km) **E 197.6** (318 km) Restaurant and gas station with diesel and propane to east.

CB 188.6 (303.5 km) **E 193.6** (311.6 km) Calgary southern city limits; access to Pine Creek RV park to east. Priddis/Deerfoot Trail to Highway 2 North exit northbound. ▲

Pine Creek R.V. Campground. See display ad this section. ▲

NOTE: To bypass downtown Calgary, take 22X exit; keep right, follow Highway 2 north.

CB 190.6 (306.8 km) **E 191.6** (308.3 km) Access to **Spruce Meadows Equestrian Center,** which hosts the International Horse Show, June to September; phone (403) 974-4200.

CB 196.5 (316.2 km) **E 185.7** (298.8 km) Exit for Glenmore Trail, the southwest bypass route that connects with Trans-Canada Highway 1 west to Banff and Vancouver, BC.

Calgary

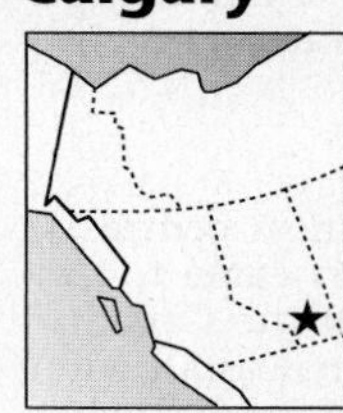

CB 200.8 (323.1 km) **E 181.4** (291.9 km) Located at the confluence of the Bow and Elbow rivers. **Population:** 820,000. **Elevation:** 3,440 feet/1,049m. **Emergency Services:** Phone 911 for emergency services. **Hospitals:** Alberta Children's Hospital, Richmond Rd. SW; Rockyview, 7007 14th St. SW; Peter Lougheed Center, 3500 26th Ave. NE.

Visitor Information: In the downtown area at the base of Calgary Tower, and at the Calgary Airport; both are open year-round. A visitor centre at Canada Olympic Park is open in summer only. Or call Calgary Convention & Visitors Bureau at (403) 263-8510 or (800) 661-1678 (toll-free in North America); or visit www.tourismcalgary.com.

Private Aircraft: Calgary International Airport, 4 miles/6.4 km northeast; elev. 3,557 feet/1,084m; 3 runways. See Canadian Flight Supplement.

This bustling city is one of Alberta's 2

Side Trip to Alberta's Badlands

Alberta Highways 72 and 9 lead 60 miles/97 km east to Drumheller in Alberta's Badlands—a region characterized by scanty vegetation and intricate erosional features. Besides its fantastic scenery, the Badlands is also famous for its dinosaurs. It is one of the best places in the world to recover the fossilized remains of dinosaurs, many of which are displayed at the world-famous Royal Tyrrell Museum in Drumheller.

Distance from Highway 2 junction (J) is shown.

J 0 Junction with Alberta Highway 2 at **Milepost CB 224.9** (approximately 25 miles/40 km north of Calgary).

J 7.5 (12.1 km) **Junction** with Highway 791, which leads to the Fairview Colony.

J 13.8 (22.2 km) Rosebud River.

J 14 (22.6 km) Beiseker Colony.

J 20.7 (33.4 km) **BEISEKER** (pop. 640); all services available. Small community campground. Highway 72 becomes Highway 9 eastbound. ▲

J 33.2 (53.5 km) **Junction** with Highway 21 to Three Hills and Trans-Canada Highway 1.

J 37.3 (60.1 km) **Junction** with Highway 836. Food and gas available.

J 45.1 (72.6 km) **Junction** with Highway 840 to Rosebud and Standard.

J 50.6 (81.5 km) Horseshoe Canyon Viewpoint; restrooms and picnic tables. Canyon tours available.

J 60.1 (96.8 km) **DRUMHELLER** (pop. 7,489); all visitor facilities available, including bed and breakfasts, motels, campgrounds, restaurants and gas. **Visitor Information:** Drumheller Regional Chamber of Development and Tourism, Box 999, Alberta T0J 0Y0; phone (403) 823-8100.

The first dinosaur fossil found in the badlands was an Albertosaurus (a slightly smaller version of the Tyrannosaurus), unearthed in 1884 by Joseph Burr Tyrrell pronounceds TEER-ell), just east of what is today Drumheller. The "Great Canadian Dinosaur Rush" followed, as famous fossil hunters Barnum Brown, Joseph Sternberg and others vied for trophies. Today, the major attraction in Drumheller is the **Royal Tyrrell Museum**, located in Midland Provincial Park just outside the town limits. The museum boasts an outstanding fossil collection presented in stunning displays. More than 30 complete dinosaur skeletons, as well as flying reptiles, prehistoric mammals and marine invertebrates, are displayed in a huge walk-through diorama exhibit. A tropical plant conservatory with more than 100 species of plants simulates the botanical world of the dinosaurs. A viewing window in the main laboratory allows visitors to watch scientists at work. Park rangers lead visitors on 90-minute interpretive hikes into the badlands around the museum, and there are special programs for children. The museum has a restaurant and gift shop. Summer hours are 9 A.M. to 9 P.M. daily. Admission fee charged. For more information, contact the museum at Box 7500, Drumheller, AB T0J 0Y0; phone (403) 823-7707; www.tyrrellmuseum.com.

Youngsters enjoy posing with dinosaur outside the Royal Tyrrell Museum in Drumheller. (© Blake Hanna, staff)

An annual event in Drumheller is the Canadian Badlands Passion Play, presented in a natural bowl amphitheatre each summer. Phone (403) 823-7750 for dates.

**Return to Milepost CB 224.9
East Access Route**

major population and business centres. A great influx of homesteaders came to Calgary with the completion of the Canadian Pacific Railway in 1883. It grew as a trading centre for surrounding farms and ranches. Oil and gas discovered south of the city in 1914 contributed to more growth.

Calgary has large shopping malls, department stores, restaurants, and many hotels and motels. Most lodging is downtown or on Highway 2 south (Macleod Trail), Trans-Canada Highway 1 north (16th Avenue) and Alternate 1A (Motel Village). There are several campgrounds in and around the city. ▲

Major attractions in Calgary include: **Calgary Science Centre**, 11th Street and 7th Avenue; the Glenbow Museum, which presents a lively journey into the heritage of the Canadian West, 130 9th Avenue SE; **Calgary Zoo Botanical Garden and Prehistoric Park**, off Memorial Drive, featuring a prehistoric park with life-sized replicas of dinosaurs; and **Heritage Park**, west of 14th Street and Heritage Drive SW, a re-creation of Calgary's pioneer eras.

The city's best-known event is the annual **Calgary Stampede**, which takes place at the Exhibition Grounds, July 7–16, 2000. The 10-day event includes a parade and daily rodeo; phone (800) 661-1260 for Stampede information and tickets.

East Access Route Log

(continued)

CB 211.3 (340 km) **E 170.9** (275 km) Calgary northern city limits.

Highway 2 from Calgary to Edmonton bypasses most communities. Except for a few service centres built specially for freeway traffic, motorists must exit the freeway for communities and gas, food or lodging.

CB 212.8 (342.6 km) **E 169.4** (272.6 km) Exit to community of **BALZAC**. Private RV park with dump station. ▲

CB 214.2 (344.8 km) **E 168** (270.4 km) Pay phone at vehicle inspection site.

CB 216.9 (349.1 km) **E 165.3** (266 km) Road west to **AIRDRIE** (pop. 14,506). Visitor facilities include hotels and motels.

CB 224.5 (361.4 km) **E 157.7** (253.8 km) Dickson–Stephensson Stopping House on Old Calgary Trail; rest area and tourist information on west side of highway.

CB 224.9 (361.9 km) **E 157.3** (253.1 km)

Junction with Highway 2A west to Crossfield and Highway 72 east to Drumheller, 60 miles/97 km, site of Alberta's Badlands. See Side Trip to Alberta's Badlands above for log of this route.

The Badlands are famous for the dinosaur fossils found there. Fossil displays at world-renowned Royal Tyrrell Museum in Drumheller.

CB 226.8 (365.1 km) **E 155.4** (250.1 km) Gas and restaurant at turnout.

CB 231.2 (372 km) **E 151** (243 km) Exit to **CROSSFIELD**; gas, hotel, food.

CB 237 (381.5 km) **E 145.2** (233.7 km) Exit west for **CARSTAIRS** (pop. 1,796), a farm and service community with tourist information centre and campground. The campground has 28 sites, electric hookups, hot showers and dump station. Services here include groceries, liquor store, banks, a motel, propane and gas stations. ▲

CB 253.7 (408.3 km) **E 128.5** (206.8 km) **Junction** with Highway 27 west to **OLDS** (pop. 5,542); all visitor facilities, museum and information booth.

CB 258.2 (415.6 km) **E 124** (199.5 km) Turnout with litter barrels.

CB 263.6 (424.2 km) **E 118.6** (190.9 km) **Junction** with highway west to Bowden and Red Lodge Provincial Park (8.5 miles/14 km); 110 campsites, playground, swimming and fishing. **BOWDEN** (pop. 936) is the site of a large oil refinery and Alberta Nurseries and Seeds Ltd., a major employer. Most visitor services available. Heritage rest area with 24 campsites, dump station and tourist information booth at junction. ▲

CB 271 (436.2km) **E 111.2** (179 km) **Junction** with Highway 54 west to **INNISFAIL** (pop. 6,064); all visitor facilities. South of Innisfail 3 miles/5 km is the RCMP Dog Training Centre, the only one in Canada; open to the public daily year-round from 9 A.M. to 4 P.M.

CB 273 (440.7 km) **E 109.2** (175.7 km) Turnout with pay phone and litter cans.

CB 285.5 (459.5 km) **E 96.7** (155.6 km) Tourist service area with gas stations and restaurants.

CB 286.6 (461.3 km) **E 95.6** (153.8 km) **Junction** with Highway 2A (Gaetz Avenue) east to **RED DEER** (pop. 59,834). **Emergency Services:** Phone 911. **Visitor Information:** At Heritage Ranch, adjacent Highway 2 (watch for signs). Heritage Ranch has a staffed visitor centre (open daily year-round) with a gift shop and snack bar, ample parking and access to Waskasoo Park. Phone (800) 215-8946.

Red Deer has all visitor facilities, including major chain motels and retail outlets. Camping at Lions Municipal Campground on Riverside Drive; from Highway 2 exit to 67th Street or 32nd Street. Open May to September. ▲

CB 289.3 (465.6 km) **E 92.9** (149.5 km) Large turnout with pay phone and litter barrels.

CB 291.6 (469.3 km) **E 90.6** (145.8 km) **Junction** with Highway 11 west to Sylvan Lake (10 miles/16 km), a popular watersports destination for Red Deer residents, with swimming beach and marina. **Sylvan Lake Provincial Park** has picnicking and swimming. Private campgrounds and waterslide nearby. ▲

CB 304 (489.6 km) **E 78.2** (125.8 km) **Junction** with Highway 12. Exit east for **LACOMBE** (pop. 7,580); all visitor facilities. Camping at Michener Park; 21 sites. Site of the Federal Agricultural Research Station; open to the public weekdays, 8 A.M. to 4:30 P.M. Exit west on Highway 12 for **Aspen Beach Provincial Park** at Gull Lake (6 miles/10 km); camping, swimming. ▲

CB 321.3 (517.1 km) **E 60.9** (98 km) **Junction** with Highway 53 east to **PONOKA** (pop. 5,861); all visitor facilities. Camping at Ponoka Stampede Trailer Park, May to October. Ponoka's Stampede is held June 29 to July 3 at Stampede Park. ▲

CB 325.4 (523.7 km) **E 56.8** (91.4 km) Turnout with pay phone.

CB 336.7 (541.8 km) **E 455** (73.2 km) Northbound-only access to Wetaskiwin rest area with picnic tables and information centre (open May to September); restrooms, gas service, dump station and groceries.

CB 340.5 (548 km) **E 41.7** (67.1 km) **Junction** of Highway 13 east to Wetaskiwin, site of the Reynolds–Alberta Museum and Canada's Aviation Hall of Fame.

CB 351.2 (565.2 km) **E 31** (49.9 km) Turnout to east with litter barrels and pay phone.

CB 362.4 (583.2 km) **E 19.8** (31.9 km) Exit to **LEDUC** (pop. 14,117); all visitor facilities. Founded and named for the Leduc oil field. The 200-million barrel Leduc oil field was the first in a series of post-war oil and natural gas finds that changed the economy of Alberta.

CB 367.4 (591.3 km) **E 14.8** (23.8 km)

Junction with Highway 19 west and Edmonton Bypass route (see DEVONIAN WAY BYPASS ROUTE on pages 41-42 this section).

Devonian Way Bypass

This bypass route circles the southwest edge of Edmonton, connecting Highway 2 and Highway 16 via Secondary Highway 19 (Devonian Way) and Highway 60. **Distance from Highway 2 and Devonian Way junction (J) is shown.**

J 0 Junction with Highway 19, Devonian Way, at **Milepost CB 367.4**. Follow Devonian Way west.

J 0.4 (0.7 km) Rest area to south.

J 2.1 (3.4 km) Capital Raceway to south, Amerlea Meadows equestrian facility to north.

J 5.2 (8.3 km) Rabbit Hill Ski area to west.

J 8.2 (13.2 km) **Junction** with Highway 60 (Edmonton truck bypass). Turn north on Highway 60 for Devon and Yellowhead Highway; turn south at intersection and drive 0.6 mile/1 km for **Leduc No. 1 Well Historic Site** and Canadian Petroleum Interpretive Centre.

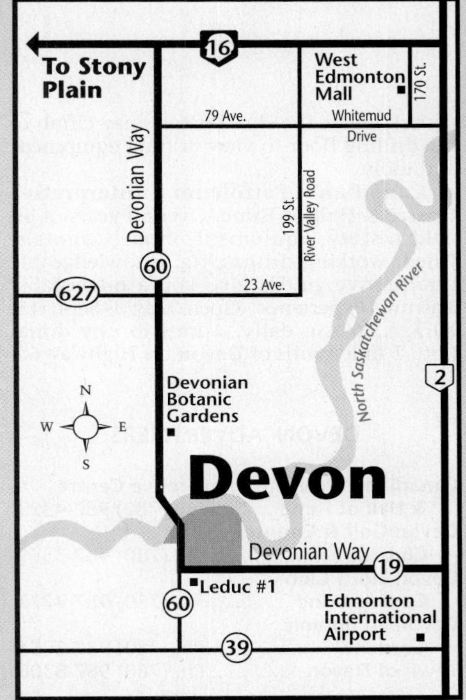

The Leduc Well was drilled on Feb. 13, 1947, before an invited asssembly of businesspeople, government officials and reporters. It was the 134th try for Imperial Oil after drilling 133 dry wells, and it was wildly successful, making Edmonton the "Oil Capital of Canada." A 174-foot/53-m

(Continues on page 42)

Devonian Way Bypass *(continued)*

derrick marks the site. Visitors may climb to the drilling floor to view drilling equipment and tools.

Canadian Petroleum Interpretive Centre & Hall of Fame. Over 50 years of oil field history. Equipment, models, murals, video, working drilling rig. Knowledgeable interpretive guides give you a memorable learning experience. Open May 1–Sept. 15. 10 A.M.–6 P.M. daily. Admission by donation. 1 mile south of Devon on Highway 60.

Phone (780) 987-4323; www.c-pic.org. [ADVERTISEMENT]

J 9.2 (14.8 km) Dump station.

J 10.2 (16.4 km) Turn east on Athabasca Avenue for downtown **DEVON** (pop. 4,900). This small, relaxed community has all visitor services, including accommodations, restaurants, fast-food outlets, gas stations, grocery stores and an 18-hole golf course. It's an easy 20-minute drive from here to West Edmonton Mall.

Camping at Devon Lions Club Campground, 180 sites on North Saskatchewan River; follow signs for Patrick O'Brien Memorial Park. The campground is adjacent to Devon Golf & Country Club. ▲

J 10.6 (17 km) Bridge over North Saskatchewan River.

J 13.8 (22.2 km) **University of Alberta Devonian Botanic Garden**; alpine garden, orchid house, 5-acre Kurimoto Japanese Garden, and other special collections gardens set in natural landscape. Live exotic butterfly showhouse with 30 species of butterflies. Open daily, 10 A.M. to 7 P.M. in summer, shorter hours rest of year. Fee charged.

J 16.9 (27.2 km) **Junction** with Secondary Highway 627; turn east for Edmonton.

J 22.7 (36.6 km) **Junction** with Yellowhead Highway 16; turn to **Milepost E 10.**

Return to Milepost E 10 (page 47) or CB 367.4 (page 41) East Access Route

Access to Leduc No. 1 well historic site.

NOTE: Northbound motorists wishing to avoid heavy traffic through Edmonton may exit west on Highway 19 (Devonian Way) for Devon Bypass route. Drive 8.2 miles/13.2 km west on Highway 19, then 14.5 miles/23.3 km north on Highway 60 to junction with Yellowhead Highway 16, 10 miles/16 km west of Edmonton (see Milepost E 10 on page 47 this section for continuation of East Access Route northbound log).

Highway 2 northbound becomes Calgary Trail. Access to Edmonton Airport.

CB 377.2 (607.1 km) **E 5** (8 km) Edmonton Tourism's Gateway Park Visitor InfoCentre, open year-round; pay phones, restrooms, dump station.

CB 377.9 (608.2 km) **E 4.3** (6.9 km) Stoplight at Ellerslie. Access to golf course and private campground; follow Ellerslie west to 127th and turn south to 41st Avenue SW. ▲

CB 382.2 (615 km) **E 0 Junction** with Whitemud Drive/Highway 2. Whitemud Drive west continues as Highway 2, crossing the North Saskatchewan River, then turns north to become 170th Street. Access to West Edmonton Mall on 170th Street. Turn west for Highway 2 north to Highway 16A West and continuation of East Access Route to the Alaska Highway for northbound travelers (log continues on page 47). Or follow Highway 2 north to Athabasca and the Northern Woods and Waters Route (see HISTORIC ATHABASCA ROUTE TO THE ALASKA HIGHWAY pages 45-47). Access west to Whitemud Park's Rainbow Valley Campground. ▲

Edmonton

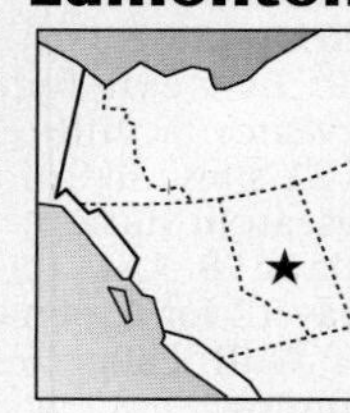

E 0 DC 367 (590.6 km) Capital of Alberta, 1,853 miles/2,982 km from Fairbanks, AK. **Population:** 648,284; area 900,000. **Elevation:** 2,182 feet/668m. **Emergency Services:** Phone 911 for all emergency services. **Hospitals:** Grey Nuns Community Health Centre, 3015–62 St., phone (780) 450-7000; Misericordia, 16940 87th Ave., phone (780) 930-5611; Royal Alexandra, 10240 Kingsway Ave., phone (780) 477-4111; University, 8440–112 St., phone (780) 407-8822.

Visitor Information: Edmonton Tourism operates visitor information centres downtown and on Highway 2 south. Or contact Edmonton Tourism, 9797 Jasper Ave., Edmonton, AB T5J 1N9; phone (780) 496-8400 or (800) 463-4667; web site www.tourism.ede.org.

Private Aircraft: Edmonton International Airport (phone 780/890-8382) 14 miles/22.5 km southwest and Edmonton City Centre Airport (780/496-2836) north side of downtown. See Canadian Flight Supplement.

There are 100 hotels and motels in Edmonton and some 2,000 restaurants. Within the Edmonton vicinity there is camping at Rainbow Campground on White-

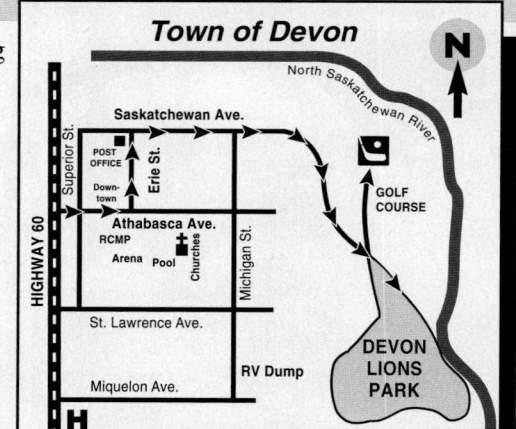

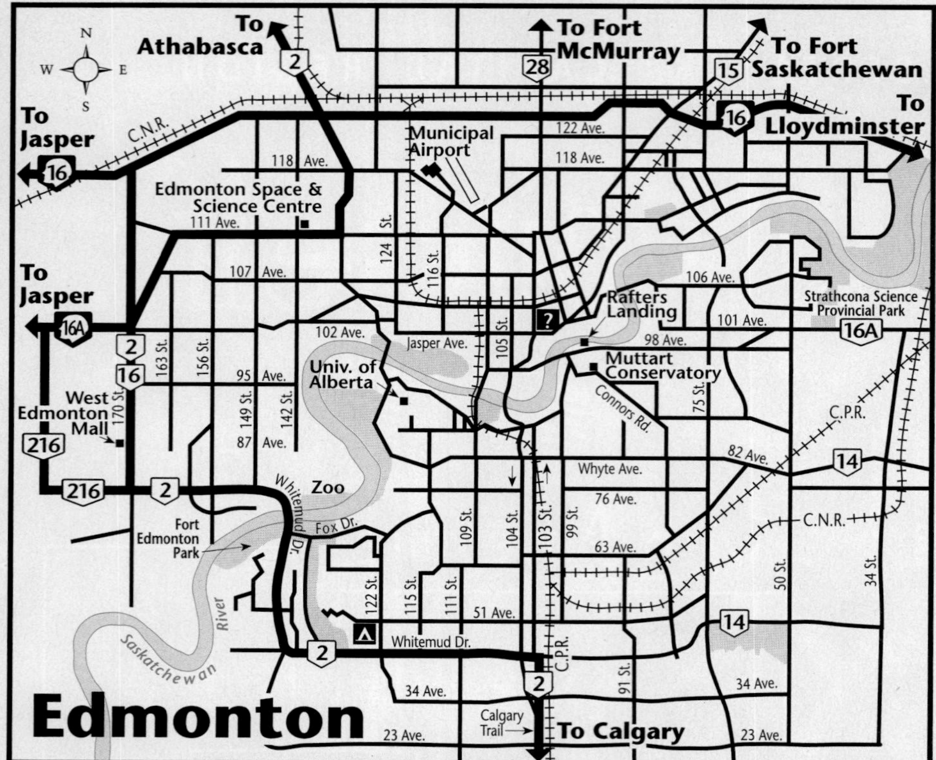

mud Drive, and at Glowing Embers Travel Centre, at the Devon Overpass. ▲

The North Saskatchewan River winds through the centre of Edmonton, its banks lined with 22 public parks. It is the largest stretch of urban parkland in North America. William Hawrelak Park on the river has the Heritage Amphitheatre, which hosts the Heritage Festival (Aug. 5–7, 2000), Symphony Under the Sky (Aug. 31–Sept. 4, 2000), and Shakespeare in the Park (TBA).

Riverboat tours aboard the *Edmonton Queen* (424-2628) depart from Rafter's Landing, located on 98th Avenue, across from Muttart Conservatory.

The 4 spectacular glass pyramids of **Muttart Conservatory** showcase plants from the temperate, tropical and arid climates of the world; cafe and gift shop. Located at 9626 96 A Street, phone (780) 496-8755; open daily.

Also located along the river's parkland are Kinsmen Sports Centre, a top fitness and recreation facility, and Victoria Golf Course, the oldest (1907) municipal golf course in Canada.

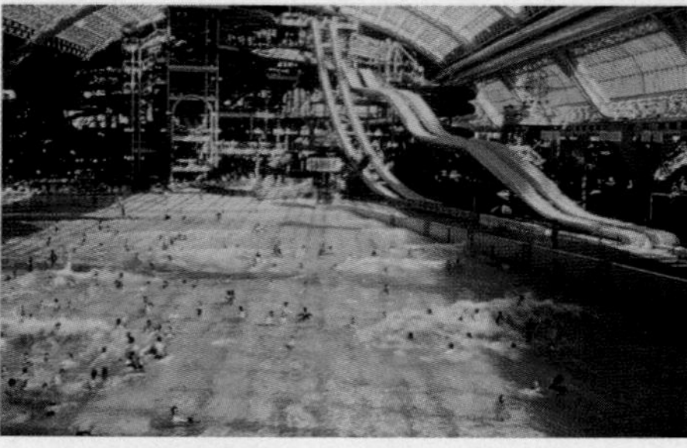

Top of the list of major attractions for visitors to Edmonton is the world's largest shopping mall—**West Edmonton Mall**. The mall features some 800 stores and 100 restaurants, as well as a water park, ice skating rink, mini-golf, submarine rides, dolphin theatre, a spa and roof-top driving range. Also located in the mall are Palace Casino, Galaxyland Amusement Park, Sea Life Caverns and IMAX Theatre. Located on 87 Avenue at 170 Street, the shopping mall is open 7 days a week; www.westedmontonmall.com.

Other major attractions in Edmonton include the **Edmonton Space & Science Centre**, which has the largest planetarium dome in North America and an IMAX theatre, at 11121–142 St., phone 451-3344 (www.edmontonscience.com); the architectural highlight of the city, the **Alberta Legislature Building**, at 10800–97 Ave.,

phone 427-7362 (www.assembly.ab.ca); and the **Alberta Aviation Museum**, 11410 Kingsway Ave., phone 453-1078.

The **Provincial Museum of Alberta**, at 12845–102 Avenue, features the Syncrude

(Continues on page 47)

Historic Athabasca Route to Alaska Highway

When the Alaska Highway opened to civilian traffic in 1948, the original access route from Edmonton to Dawson Creek, BC, was north 91 miles/147 km via Highway 2 to the historic fur-trading post of Athabasca. Motorists then headed west along what is today the Northern Woods & Waters Route to High Prairie, then turned south to Grande Prairie, AB. In late 1955, Highway 43 was completed connecting Edmonton and Valleyview via Whitecourt.

Distance from Edmonton (E) is shown.

ALBERTA HIGHWAY 2

E 0 Junction with Whitemud Drive/Highway 2. Turn west for Highway 16A West (see YELLOWHEAD HIGHWAY 16 section) and for continuation of Highway 2 north to Athabasca and the Northern Woods and Waters Route.

E 3.5 (5.6 km) **ST. ALBERT** (pop. 50,000); all visitor services.

E 10.5 (17 km) **Junction** with Highway 37 west to Onoway and east to Fort Saskatchewan.

E 17.2 (27.7 km) Turnoff to Morinville to east.

E 18.8 (30.3 km) Divided highway ends northbound. Canola fields along side highway are a brilliant yellow in early summer.

E 28.1 (45.3 km) Gas station.

E 28.3 (45.5 km) **Junction** with Highway 651. Turnoff to east for town of Legal (1.8 miles/3 km).

E 43.2 (69.6 km) **Junction** with Highway 18 west to Highway 44.

E 43.9 (70.7 km) Gas station.

E 62.3 (100.3 km) Turnoff to east for Rochester (2.5 miles/4 km) and junction with Secondary Road 661.

E 80.5 (129.6 km) **Cross Lake Provincial Park** 27 miles/44 km; camping, boat launch, fishing, hiking, swimming.

E 83.3 (134 km) Motel and gas station.

E 87.4 (140.7 km) Turnout to west.

E 91.4 (147 km) **ATHABASCA** (pop. 2,313). **Visitor Information:** Tourist information booth along the Athabasca River in an old train caboose. Open during the summer months only.

Visitor facilities include 2 hotels, 3 motels, a full-service RV park, a campground, restaurants, retail and grocery outlets, public library, hockey and curling rink, tennis courts and a swimming pool. A 9-hole golf course is 1.2 miles/2 km north on Highway 813. The course has a clubhouse, driving range and grass greens.

Athabasca Landing was founded by the Hudson's Bay Co. in 1874, when the

ATHABASCA ADVERTISERS

Athabasca Hillside Motel..Ph. (780) 675-5111
Athabasca Lodge Motel.....Ph.(780) 675-2266
Best Western Athabasca Inn...............................Ph. (800) 567-5718
Blueberry Hill RV Park ......Ph. (800) 859-9452
Town of Athabasca...........Ph. (780) 675-2063

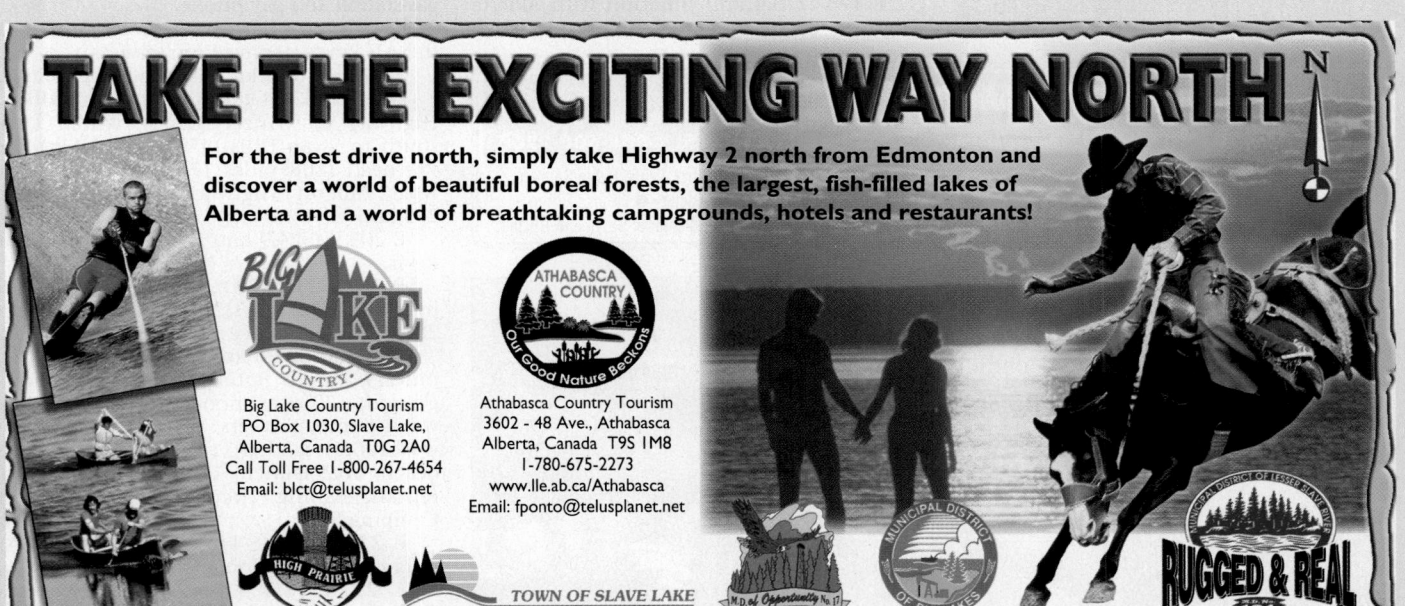

Historic Athabasca Route *(continued)*

Athabasca Landing Trail was established and a trading post was constructed. In its early years, Athabasca was a busy transshipment point for freight movement in northwestern Canada. The Athabasca Landing Trail, running from Athabasca south 99 miles/160 km to Edmonton, became in 1880 the first registered highway in Alberta. The railroad arrived in Athabasca in 1912.

The Athabasca Landing Trail, a 76-mile/121-km corridor from Gibbons to Athabasca, runs roughly parallel to Highway 2 and served the Indians long before the arrival of the Europeans. It became the overland route connecting the Athabasca and north Saskatchewan rivers. The Hudson's Bay Co. developed the trail in 1875, and for the next 35 years it played a vital role in the development of the North. The first part of the old trail has been lost to the plough, and today the trail begins 24 miles/40 km north of Edmonton.

E 91.5 (147.2 km) Bridge over Muskeg Creek.

E 105.7 (170.1 km) Access road east 2.5 miles/4 km and then north 5 miles/8 km to Island Lake Recreation Campground, open mid-May to mid-September; 11 sites, water pump, fishing, boat launch. Camping fee. Chain Lakes Provincial Recreation Area Campground, located another 7 miles/12 km north, has 20 sites, water pump, fishing and boat launch. Electric motors only. Camping fee.

E 107 (172.2 km) Community of Island Lake South.

E 107.8 (173.5 km) North entrance east into Island Lake Recreation Area (see **Milepost E 105.7**).

E 108.4 (174.4 km) **ISLAND LAKE** (pop. 126) store and gas station to east.

E 109.6 (176.4 km) Access road east 12 miles/20 km to Chain Lakes Provincial Recreation Area (see **Milepost E 105.7**).

E 120.1 (193.3 km) **Lawrence Lake Provincial Recreation Area** Campground to west; 27 sites, picnic shelter, water pump, fishing, boat launch. Camping fee.

E 127.5 (205.2 km) Secondary side road north 14 miles/23 km to Smith.

E 132.5 (213.2 km) Secondary side road north 5.5 miles/9 km to Hondo.

E 136.6 (219.8 km) **Junction** with Alberta Highway 44 south 66 miles/105 km to Westlock and to Alberta Highway 18.

E 137.2 (220.8 km) Roadside turnout for large trucks on both sides of highway.

E 138.7 (223.2 km) **Junction** with Highway 2A north 1.8 miles/3 km to Hondo (no services) and 9 miles/15 km to **SMITH** (pop. 250). Smith has a hotel, restaurant, small store and service station with minor-repair facilities. A secondary road continues north and west out of Smith, along the Slave River, and rejoins the highway at **Milepost E 162.5**. **Fawcett Lake**, 20 miles/32 km northeast of Smith, has fishing and boating. Camping and boat launch at private resort and at provincial recreation area.

E 140.5 (226.1 km) Bridge over the Athabasca River.

E 149.2 (240.1 km) Bridge over the Saulteaux River.

E 156.8 (252.3 km) Bridge over the Otauwau River.

E 161.9 (260.5 km) Divided highway begins westbound.

E 162.5 (261.5 km) **Junction** with loop road from Smith. **Lesser Slave River** is 5.5 miles/9 km north on the return road; fishing.

E 165.9 (267 km) **Mitsue Lake**; fishing.

E 173 (278.4 km) **Junction** with Alberta Highway 88 (Bicentennial Highway), which leads north to Lesser Slave Lake Provincial Park (see description following); 105 miles/168 km to the community of Red Earth Creek; and 255 miles/410 km to Fort Vermilion. Highway 88 is paved to Red Earth Creek; the remainder of the road to Fort Vermilion is gravel and in poor condition.

Lesser Slave Lake Provincial Park, along the east shore of Lesser Slave Lake, is divided into 3 different recreational areas. Devonshire Beach day-use area is 3.6 miles/6 km north on Highway 88. Northshore day-use area, 7 miles/11 km north on Highway 88, has 14 picnic sites, shelter, water pump and a fish-cleaning stand. Marten River Campground, 18 miles/30 km north on Highway 88, has 113 sites, dump station, flush toilets, showers, playground, public phone, ski trails, hiking trails, swimming, fishing.

E 173.8 (279.7km) **SLAVE LAKE** (pop. 6,553) located on the southeast shore of Lesser Slave Lake. Visitor facilities include motels, restaurants and fast-food outlets, numerous stores, service stations with major-repair facilities and car washes. **Visitor Information:** In a small building on the service road just off Highway 2, phone 849-4611. Open mid-May to mid-September. The town office is located at 328 2nd St. NE, phone 849-3606.

Originally known as Sawridge when it was founded in the 1880s, Slave Lake was an important jumping-off point for steamboat traffic that carried prospectors bound for the Yukon and the Klondike gold rushes. Early settlers included the Metis and Cree Indians. Today, their descendants contribute to the rich cultural heritage of this well-integrated community.

E 174.6 (281 km) **Sawridge Recreation Area** Campground to north; 35-site campground, electrical hookups, water pump, showers, picnic tables, picnic shelter, swimming, fishing and hiking trails.

E 179.5 (288.9 km) Turnout with litter barrels to north.

E 185.5 (298.5 km) Access road north 0.6 mile/1 km to **WIDEWATER** (pop. 203); small store, gas station and pay phone.

E 187.6 (301.9 km) **CANYON CREEK** (pop. 164) to north has a hotel, grocery store, gas station and pay phone.

E 192 (309 km) Access road north 1.8 miles/3 km to Assineau (no services).

E 192.5 (309.8 km) Assineau River bridge.

E 199.7 (321.4 km) **Junction** with Alberta Highway 33 (Grizzly Trail), which leads south to Swan Hills (45 miles/72 km) and Barrhead (108 miles/174 km) to junction with Alberta Highway 43 (136 miles/219 km).

E 201.9 (324.9 km) Bridge over the Swan River.

E 202.2 (325.4 km) **Junction** with side road north 1.2 miles/2 km to **KINUSO** (pop. 282); cafe and service station.

E 204.8 (329.6 km) Access road north 5 miles/9 km to Spruce Point Park Campground; 120 sites, hookups, dump station, water pump, showers, wheelchair-accessible washroom, shelter, store, public phone, beach, boat launch, 100-boat marina, boat rentals, fishing, fireplaces and firewood. Camping fee.

E 210.4 (338.6 km) **FAUST** (pop. 344); restaurant, gas station and camping.

E 217.7 (350.3 km) Bridge over the Driftpile River.

E 222.4 (357.9 km) Turnouts with litter

barrels on both sides of highway.

E 224.4 (361.1 km) **JOUSSARD** (pop. 269) to north has a store and service station. Joussard Lakeshore Campground, located on the south shore of **Lesser Slave Lake**, has 39 sites, full hookups, dump station, tap water, showers, picnic tables, firewood, fishing and boat launch. Camping fee.

E 234.7 (377.7 km) Small cafe and gas station to north.

E 235.4 (378.8 km) Turnout to north with litter barrels and historical point of interest.

E 235.7 (379.3 km) **Junction** with Highway 750 northeast to Alberta Highway 88 (Bicentennial Highway), 103 miles/165 km. Highway 750 also provides access to **GROUARD**, 13 miles/21 km north, site of St. Bernard Mission Church and the Native Cultural Arts Museum. **Hilliard's Bay Provincial Park**, 5 miles/8 km east of Grouard on Lesser Slave Lake, has 189 sites, tap water, hookups, dump station, showers, playground, phone, beach and fishing.

E 236.2 (380.1 km) Small store and gas to north.

E 238.8 (384.3 km) **ENILDA** (pop. 128); gas station and private RV park.

E 239.9 (386.1 km) East Prairie settlement and sawmill to south. Turnouts on both sides of highway.

E 240.1 (386.4 km) Bridge over the East Prairie River.

E 244.6 (393.6 km) High Prairie Lions Campground to north; 16 sites, hookups, tap water, flush toilets, showers, picnic tables, picnic shelter and firewood. Camping fee.

E 246 (395.9 km) **HIGH PRAIRIE** (pop. 2,932) has motels, restaurants, retail and grocery stores, and service stations with major-repair facilities. **Visitor Information**: Tourist information centre in the centre of town on the north side of Highway 2. Open summer months only.

The High Prairie District Museum, part of the library complex located on Highway 2, features pioneer artifacts.

While the High Prairie area was being settled by homesteaders in the late 19th century, the arrival of the railroad in 1914 heralded the beginning of High Prairie as a town. A busy agricultural center, this picturesque community serves the surrounding forest and oil field industries.

E 246.1 (396 km) **Junction** with Highway 749. Highway 749 North from High Prairie becomes Highway 679, which leads west 18 miles/30 km to rejoin Highway 2. **Winagami Lake Provincial Park**, 20 miles/32 km northwest of High Prairie off Highway 679, has 63 campsites (one site for disabled use), day-use area, dump station, fishing, boat launch, wading pool, paved trails, bird-viewing platforms with scopes, fireplaces, firewood, shelter and tap water.

Heart River Dam Provincial Recreation Area, 24 miles/40 km northwest of High Prairie, is a day-use area with picnic tables, beach, fishing and boat launch.

E 246.6 (396.8 km) Bridge over the West Prairie River.

E 255.2 (410.7 km) **Junction** with Alberta Spur Highway 2A west to Highway 49 and Highway 2 north to McLennan. In the early days of Alaska Highway travel, this intersection was known as Triangle. From here, motorists either turned left on what was then Highway 34 (today's Highway 2A) and drove 100 miles to Grande Prairie via Valleyview, or turned right on Highway 2 to McLennan and Peace River.

(Continued from page 44)

Gallery of Aboriginal Culture, the Natural History Gallery, the Bug Room and the Habitat Gallery. Also special exhibits, gift shop, cafe and a 400-seat theatre. Open daily; phone 453-9100, or visit www.pma.edmonton.ab.ca.

Fort Edmonton Park, Canada's largest living history park, features more than 70 period buildings and a fort on 158 acres. Join the costumed interpreters and experience life as it was at the 1846 fort and on the streets of 1885, 1905 and 1920. There are activities for all ages: pioneer children's games; learning to bead at the Native encampment; taking aim at the shooting gallery; and playing 1920s-style miniature golf. Period restaurants and retail shops, Steam train and streetcar rides are included in the admission price. Open 10 A.M. daily, May to September; special events year-round. Located at Fox Drive and Whitemud Drive. For more information, phone (780) 496-8787 or visit www.gov.edmonton.ab.ca/fort.

Skyreach Centre is home to the Edmonton Oilers NHL hockey team. The Edmonton Trappers baseball team play at Telus Field.

Northlands Spectrum features live harness raciing and thoroughbred racing March through December. There are 6 casinos operating in the Greater Edmonton Area. Casinos in Alberta are run in support of charitable groups.

Known as Canada's Festival City, Edmonton hosts a number of events throughout the year. These events include Jazz City International Music Festival (June 23–July 2, 2000); International Street Performers Festival (July 7–16, 2000); Klondike Days (July 20–29, 2000); Edmonton Folk Music Festival (Aug. 10–13, 2000); and the Fringe Theatre Event (Aug. 17–27, 2000).

Two area attractions are **Elk Island National Park** and the **Ukrainian Cultural Heritage Village**, both a 45-minute drive east of Edmonton on Yellowhead Highway 16. Elk Island National Park, open year-round, has more than 40 species of mammals roaming freely on its 194 square km. The Ukrainian Cultural Heritage Village offers guided tours through its farmsteads and townsite. Open 10 to 6 mid-May to Labour Day, 10 to 4 Labour Day to Thanksgiving.

East Access Route Log

(continued)

This section of the log shows distance from Edmonton (E) followed by distance from Dawson Creek (DC).

HIGHWAY 16A WEST

E 0 DC 367 (590.6 km) Downtown Edmonton. Jasper Avenue westbound (becomes Yellowhead 16A.

E 10 (16 km) **DC 357** (574.5 km) **Junction** of Highways 16A West and 60 (Devon Overpass); access to Glowing Embers campground.

Glowing Embers Travel Center. See display ad this section.

NOTE: Southbound travelers may bypass Edmonton by taking Highway 60 south, then Highway 19 east to Highway 2 (see DEVONIAN WAY BYPASS log beginning on page 41).

E 16 (26 km) **DC 351** (564.9 km) **SPRUCE GROVE** (pop. 15,069). All visitor facilities including motels, restaurants, gas and service stations, grocery stores, farmer's market, shopping malls and all emergency services. Recreational facilities include a golf course, swimming pool, skating and curling rinks, parks, and extensive walking and cycling trails. The chamber of commerce tourist information booth, located on Highway 16A, is open year-round; phone (780) 962-2561.

E 19.3 (31 km) **DC 347.7** (559.5 km) **STONY PLAIN** (pop. 7,405). All visitor facilities including hotels, restaurants, supermarkets, shopping mall and gas stations with major repair service; RCMP and hospital; outdoor swimming pool, tennis courts and 18-hole golf course. The Multicultural Heritage Centre here has historical archives, a craft shop and home-cooked meals. Other attractions include 16 outdoor murals; Oppertshauser Art Gallery; the Andrew Wolf Winery; and the Pioneer Museum at Exhibition Park. Visitor information centre at Rotary Park rest area. Camping at Lions RV Park and Campground; 26 sites.

Bears and Bedtime Mfg. features handmade, limited-edition collectible teddy bears, largest selection of bear-making supplies in Canada, Cherished Teddies,

Trinity Lutheran church at Rochfort Bridge. (© Judy Parkin)

Boyd's Bearstones, Beanie Babies and gift items. Hours: Monday–Friday 9 A.M.–6 P.M., Saturday 10 A.M.–6 P.M.. Visit our website at www.bearsandbedtime.com. Phone 1-800-461-BEAR(2327). See ad in the YELLOWHEAD HIGHWAY section. [ADVERTISEMENT]

The Multicultural Heritage Centre features a regional museum, unique restaurant, a public art gallery featuring Canadian artists, as well as both local and imported craft shops. Award-winning grounds and historically significant buildings complete this rewarding experience. Open Monday to Saturday 10 A.M. to 4 P.M., Sunday 10 A.M. to 6:30 P.M.. Phone (780) 963-2777. Address: 5411–51 St. [ADVERTISEMENT]

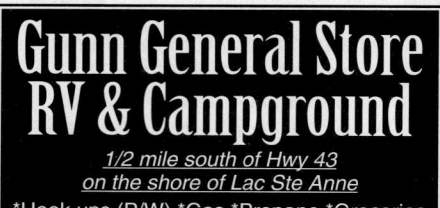

E **23.9** (38.5 km) **DC 343.1** (552.1 km) Edmonton Beach turnoff to south; campground. ▲

E **24.2** (39.4 km) **DC 342.8** (551.7 km) Hubbles Lake turnoff to north.

E **25.5** (41.1 km) **DC 341.5** (549.6 km) Restaurant, gas station and store to north.

E **29.8** (47.9 km) **DC 337.2** (542.6 km)

Junction of Yellowhead Highway 16 and Highway 43. If you are continuing west on Yellowhead Highway 16 for Prince George or Prince Rupert, BC, turn to **Milepost E 25** in the YELLOWHEAD HIGHWAY section.

Turn north onto Highway 43 and continue with this log for Dawson Creek, BC.

HIGHWAY 43

E **31.7** (51 km) **DC 335.3** (539.6 km) Turnout to east with litter barrel and historical information sign about construction of the Alaska Highway.

E **33.7** (54.3 km) **DC 333.3** (536.4 km) Gas station to east.

E **38** (61.1 km) **DC 329** (529.5 km) Highway 633 west to Alberta Beach Recreation Area on Lac Ste. Anne. Facilities include a municipal campground (open May 15 to Sept. 15) with 115 sites. ▲

E **40.7** (65.5 km) **DC 326.3** (525.1 km) **ONOWAY** (pop. 788) has a medical clinic, dentist and veterinary clinic. Other services include gas, propane, banks and bank machine, grocery stores, laundromat, restaurants, motel, car wash, post office, pharmacy and a sani-dump with potable water. Elks campground with 8 sites (no hookups). ▲

E **46.8** (75.3 km) **DC 320.2** (515.3 km) **Junction** of Highways 43 and 33 (Grizzly Trail). Continue on Highway 43.

Alberta government campground with dump station, water, toilets and stoves. ▲

E **47.3** (76.1 km) **DC 319.7** (514.5 km) Restaurant and gas station. Campground south on **Lac Ste. Anne**; fishing. ▲

Gunn General Store & Campground. See display ad this section. ▲

E **49.1** (79 km) **DC 317.9** (511.6 km) **Lessard Lake** county campground; water, stoves, boat launch, fishing for pike and perch. Golf course to west. ▲

E **72.7** (117 km) **DC 294.3** (473.6 km) **SANGUDO** (pop. 405) is on a 0.3-mile/0.4-km side road. Restaurants, motel and hotel accommodations; gas station with garage open 7 days a week; grocery, clothing and liquor stores; antique shop; banks, post office, pharmacy, laundromat and car wash. Oval race car track with racing in summer; shale baseball diamonds; elk farm tours. A public campground (supervised) is located at the sportsgrounds nestled along the Pembina River. ▲

E **73.1** (117.7 km) **DC 293.9** (473 km) Pembina River bridge.

E **74** (119.2 km) **DC 293** (471.5. km) **Ol' Pembina River Ferry Crossing RV Park.** "Peaceful camping along the Pembina River, where history surrounds the RV park." Spacious sites on 5 landscaped acres in the Pembina River Valley. Water and electric sites, pull-through sites, day camping and tenting, showers and flush toilets, cozy motel unit, coin washer and dryer. Dump station. Telephone. Walking/history trails. Private museum, featuring 1928 REO Truck and Model A Ford car. Pioneer cabin with local artifacts. 1 km off Highway 43, turn south at RV park sign, flying 3 flags. Phone (780) 785-2379 with answering machine. [ADVERTISEMENT] ▲

E **74.1** (119.3 km) **DC 292.9** (471.3 km) Gas station and restaurant to south.

E **78.3** (126 km) **DC 288.7** (464.6 km) Second longest wooden railway trestle in the world crosses highway and Paddle River. The C.N.R. Rochfort Bridge trestle is 2,414 feet/736m long and was originally built in 1914.

E **80.6** (129.7 km) **DC 286.4** (460.9 km) **ROCHFORT BRIDGE.** Trading post (open daily, year-round) with gas, convenience store, gift shop, restaurant and Lac Ste. Anne Pioneer Museum. Camping. ▲

Rochfort Bridge Trading Post—A fun stop. Fresh bread and pies baked from scratch: rhubarb, blueberries, sour-cream and raisin pies, and more. Home-style meals. Licensed. Verandah. One of the largest all-Canadian gift stores. Distinctive items, including rare First Nations art: birch bark biting, fish scale art and moose tufting. Par 3 golf course with rentals. And you can photograph our cute donkeys. See display ad this section. [ADVERTISEMENT]

E **83.1** (133.7 km) **DC 283.9** (456.1 km) Paved turnouts with litter barrels both sides of highway.

E **85** (136.8 km) **DC 282** (453.8 km) **MAYERTHORPE** (pop. 1,692). One mile/1.6 km from the highway on a paved access road. Hotel, motel, restaurant, grocery store, gas stations with repair service, car wash, hospital, laundromat, post office, RCMP and banks. A public campground with 30 sites (no hookups, pit toilets) and 9-hole golf course are located 1 mile/1.6 km south of town. Airstrip located 2 miles/3.2 km southwest of town; no services. (Most northbound air travelers use Whitecourt airport, which has fuel.) ▲

E **87** (140 km) **DC 280** (450.6 km) Gas station and restaurant at junction with Highway 658 north to Goose Lake.

E **109** (175.4 km) **DC 258** (415.2 km) **Lions Club Campground**; 74 sites, flush toilets, showers, water, tables, dump station, firewood and firepits. Fee charged. ▲

Whitecourt

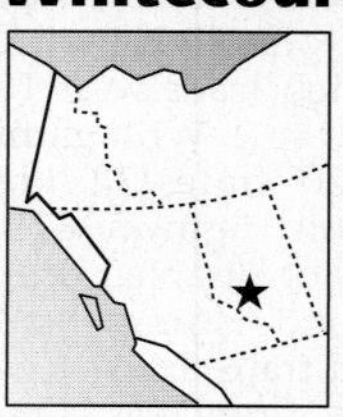

E **111.8** (179.9 km) **DC 255.2** (410.7 km). Located two hours from Edmonton. **Population:** 7,800. **Emergency Services: Police,** phone (780) 778-5454. **Fire Department,** phone (780) 778-2311. **Hospital** located on Hilltop, phone (780) 778-2285. Ambulance service available.

Visitor Information: Tourist information in the Forest Interpretive Centre at the

WHITECOURT ADVERTISERS

Forest Interpretive Centre & Heritage Park ....Ph. (780) 778-2214
Gateway Esso....................................Hwy. 43
Glenview Motel ....Ph. (780) 778-2276
Sagitawah Tourist Park.....Ph. (780) 778-3734
White Kaps Motel & RV Parking ....Ph. (780) 778-2246
Whitecourt Lions Club Campground ....Ph. (780) 778-6782

east end of town off Highway 43. Open daily, 9 A.M. to 6 P.M., July 1 to Sept. 1; weekdays, 9 A.M. to 5 P.M., rest of year.

Elevation: 2,567 feet/782m. **Radio:** 96.7 CJYR-FM, 107.5 SKUA-FM. **Television:** 10 channels. **Newspaper:** *Whitecourt Star* (weekly); *Community Classifieds* (weekly).

Private Aircraft: Airport 4 miles/6.4 km south on Highway 32; elev. 2,567 feet/782m; length 5,800 feet/1,768m; paved; fuel 80, 100, jet (24-hour, self-serve). Aircraft maintenance, 24-hour flight service station, all-weather facility.

Transportation: Air—Local charter air service available; helicopter and fixed-wing aircraft. **Bus**—Greyhound service to Edmonton, Grande Prairie, Peace River and points north.

Located at the junction of Highways 43 and 32, Whitecourt dubs itself the "Gateway to the Alaska Highway and the fabulous North." Established as a small trading, trapping and forestry centre, Whitecourt became an important stop for Alaska Highway travelers when a 106-mile section of Highway 43 connecting Whitecourt and Valleyview was completed in October 1955. This new route was 72 miles shorter than the old Edmonton to Dawson Creek route via Slave Lake.

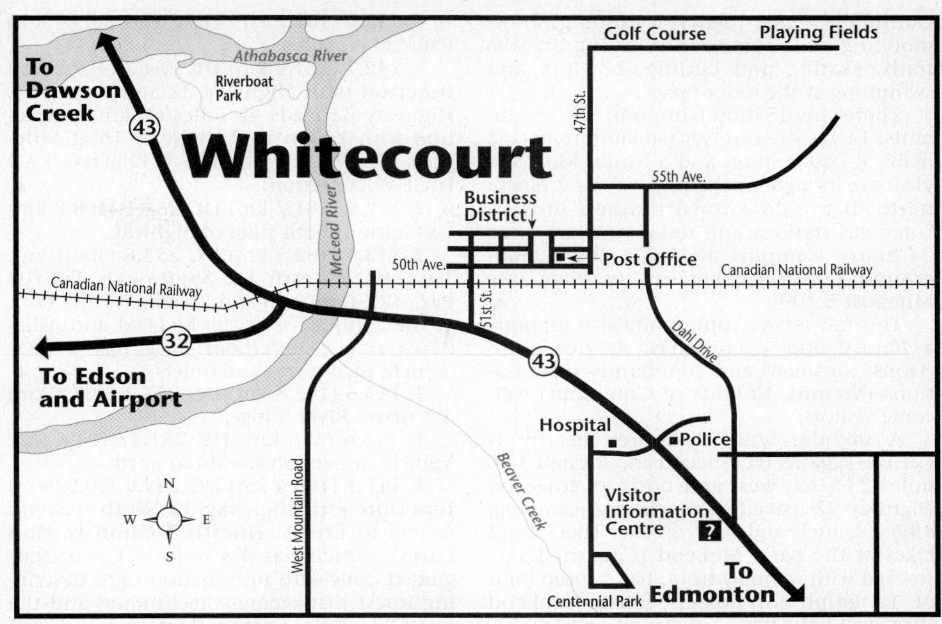

Several major forest industries operating in and around Whitecourt offer tours. Visitors may observe state-of-the-art technologies at sawmills, medium-density fiberboard production and pulp plants. For tour times, check with the tourist information booth or chamber of commerce (778-5363).

Tbe new Whitecourt & District Forest Interpretive Centre and Heritage Park at the east end of town celebrates Alberta's forest industry through artifacts, audio-visual displays and exhibits.

Recreational activities include an excellent 18-hole public golf course and fishing in area creeks, rivers and lakes (boat rentals at Carson–Pegasus Provincial Park). Swimming, in-line skating, tennis, gold panning, walking trails, beach volleyball and river boating are also enjoyed in summer. In the fall, big game hunting is very popular.

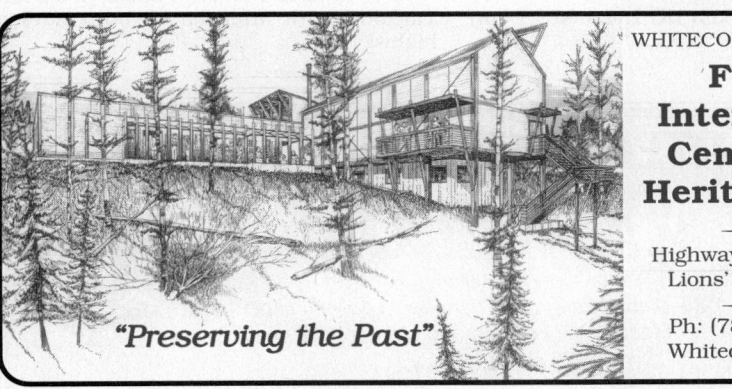

During the winter there is ice fishing, snowmobiling and cross-country skiing on area trails, skating and curling, bowling and swimming at the indoor pool.

There are 15 hotels/motels, 23 restaurants, 14 gas stations, several laundromats, 2 malls, 6 liquor stores and 5 banks. Most services are located on the highway or 2 blocks north in the downtown business district. Some gas stations and restaurants are open 24 hours. Camping at Lion's Club Campground 1 mile/1.6 km east of town (see **Milepost E 109**). ▲

This full-service community also supports a library and 7 churches. Service clubs (Lions, Kinsmen) and community organizations (Masons, Knights of Columbus) welcome visitors.

A popular wilderness area nearby is Carson–Pegasus Provincial Park, located 14.6 miles/23.5 km west and north of town on Highway 32 (paved). The park has camping, a boat launch and boat rentals. There are 2 lakes at the park: **McLeod (Carson) Lake**, stocked with rainbow trout, has a speed limit of 12 kmph for boaters; **Little McLeod (Pegasus) Lake** has northern pike and whitefish; electric motors and canoes only. ▲

East Access Route Log

(continued)

E 111.9 (180.1 km) **DC 255.1** (410.5 km) Beaver Creek bridge.

CAUTION: The highway between Whitecourt and Valleyview is known locally as "Moose Row" and "Moose Alley." Several moose–vehicle accidents occur yearly. Northbound travelers, watch for moose on road, especially at dusk and at night.

E 112.4 (180.9 km) **DC 254.6** (409.7 km) McLeod River.

E 112.6 (181.2 km) **DC 254.4** (409.4 km) Railroad crossing.

E 112.7 (181.4 km) **DC 254.3** (409.2 km) **Junction** with Highway 32 South (paved). Highway 32 leads 42 miles/68 km to junction with Yellowhead Highway 16 at **Milepost E 97.5** (see the YELLOWHEAD HIGHWAY section). ▲

E 112.9 (181.7 km) **DC 254.1** (408.9 km) Gas stations both sides of highway.

E 113.4 (182.5 km) **DC 253.6** (408.1 km) Turnoff to north for **Sagitawah Tourist Park** (RV camping) and Riverboat Park, both at the confluence of the McLeod and Athabasca rivers. Riverboat Park has a boat launch, picnic area and toilets. ▲

E 113.6 (182.8 km) **DC 253.4** (407.8 km) Athabasca River bridge.

E 115.6 (186 km) **DC 251.4** (404.6 km) Vehicle inspection station to north.

E 117.1 (188.4 km) **DC 249.9** (402.2 km) **Junction** with Highway 32 North (paved). Access to **Eric S. Huestis Demonstration Forest**, which has 4.3 miles/7 km of self-guided trails with information signs describing forest management techniques and the forest life-cycle. **Carson–Pegasus Provincial Park**, 9.3 miles/15 km north, has 182 campsites, electrical hookups, tables, flush toilets, showers, water, dump station, firewood and playground. Boat launch, boat rentals and rainbow trout fishing are available. ▲

E 117.6 (189.2 km) **DC 249.4** (401.4 km) Alberta Newsprint Co. to south.

E 122 (196.3 km) **DC 245** (394.3 km) Turnout with litter barrel.

E 124.3 (200 km) **DC 242.7** (390.6 km) Chickadee Creek.

E 131.8 (212.1 km) **DC 235.2** (378.5 km) Turnouts with litter barrels both sides of highway.

Drilling rig on display at Rig Earth Resource Park in Fox Creek.

(© Earl L. Brown, staff)

E 140.5 (226.1 km) **DC 226.5** (364.5 km) Two Creeks government campground; 8 campsites, pit toilets, water, picnic tables and firepits. ▲

E 142.5 (229.3 km) **DC 224.5** (361.3 km) Turnout with litter barrel to south.

E 143 (230.1 km) **DC 224** (360.5 km) Turnout with litter barrel to north.

E 152 (244.6 km) **DC 215** (346 km) Iosegun Creek government campground; 12 sites, pit toilets, water, tables and firepits. ▲

E 159 (255.9 km) **DC 208** (334.7 km) Fox Creek airport.

Fox Creek

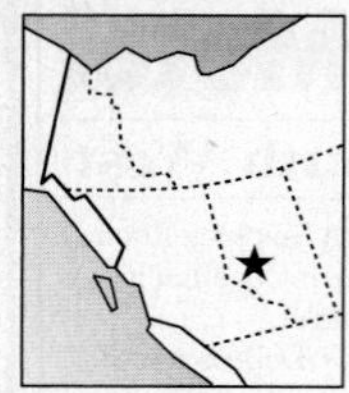

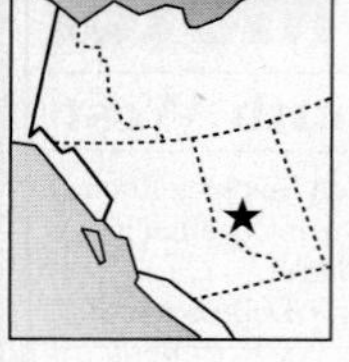

E 162 (260.7 km) **DC 205** (329.9 km) **Population:** 2,600. **Elevation:** 2,800 feet/853m. **Emergency Services: RCMP**, phone (780) 622-3740. **Ambulance**, phone (780) 622-3000. **Hospital**, phone (780) 622-3545.

FOX CREEK ADVERTISERS

Alaskan Motel, The..........Ph. (780) 622-3073
Fox Creek R.V. Campground..............Ph. (780) 622-3896

Visitor Information: Tourist Information Centre at the Rig Earth Resource Park, open in summer; gift shop, coffee area and selection of informational videos to view; phone (780) 622-2000. Off-season contact the Town Office at (780) 622-3896 for information.

Private Aircraft: Fox Creek airport, 3 miles/4.8 km south on Highway 43; elev. 2,840 feet/866m; length, 2,950 feet/899m; paved; no fuel. Unattended.

Fox Creek is in the centre of oil and gas exploration and production. (A Jomax 4, 150-foot/46m drilling rig is on display at Rig Earth Resource Park.) North America's largest known natural gas field is here.

All visitor facilities including 2 hotels, 3 motels and gas stations with repair service. Grocery store open daily until midnight. Convenience stores, pharmacy, laundromats, liquor stores, restaurants and banks.

Fox Creek R.V. Campground, located near the visitor information centre, is a municipal campground with 17 sites, full hookups, showers and dump station ▲

Fox Creek is also a popular outdoor recreation area. Two local lakes popular with residents and visitors are **Iosegun** and **Smoke lakes**, which are located within 10 miles/16 km on either side of the townsite on good gravel road. Camping, boat launch and fishing for northern pike, perch and pickerel are favorites for this area. ▲

East Access Route Log

(continued)

E 167 (268.7 km) **DC 200** (321.9 km) Turnout with litter barrel.

E 169.5 (272.8 km) **DC 197.5** (317.8 km) Turnouts with litter barrels both sides of highway.

E 182.1 (293 km) **DC 184.9** (297.6 km) Turnout with litter barrel.

E 186.4 (300 km) **DC 180.6** (290.6 km Turnoff for RV park.

E 192 (309 km) **DC 175** (281.6 km) **LITTLE SMOKY** (pop. about 50). Motel, RV park, antique shop, gift shop, pay phone, propane, grocery store, service station and post office. ▲

E 192.2 (309.3 km) **DC 174.8** (281.3 km) Little Smoky River bridge.

E 193.5 (311.4 km) **DC 173.5** (279.2 km) Waskahigan (House) River bridge at confluence with Smoky River. Government campground with 24 sites, pit toilets, tables and firepits. ▲

E 197 (317 km) **DC 170** (273.6 km) Turnout.

E 206.7 (332.6 km) **DC 160.3** (258 km) Turnout with litter barrel.

E 208.5 (335.5 km) **DC 158.5** (255.1 km) Peace pipeline storage tanks.

E 210.8 (339.2 km) **DC 156.2** (251.4 km) Valleyview Riverside golf course.

E 213.2 (343.1 km) **DC 153.8** (247.5 km) Valleyview & District Chamber of Commerce Visitor Information Centre (phone 780/524-2410) has local, regional, provincial and Canada-wide travel information; pay phone, postal service, souvenir gift shop, picnic tables, water, flush toilets, dump station. Open daily in summer, 8 A.M. to 8 P.M.

E 213.4 (343.4 km) **DC 153.6** (247.2 km) Valleyview airport to west.

Private Aircraft: Valleyview airport; elev. 2,434 feet/742m; length, 3,300 feet/1,006m; paved; no fuel. Unattended.

CAUTION: The highway between Valleyview and Whitecourt is known locally as "Moose Row" and "Moose Alley." Several moose–vehicle accidents occur yearly. Southbound travelers, watch for moose on road, especially at dusk and at night.

Valleyview

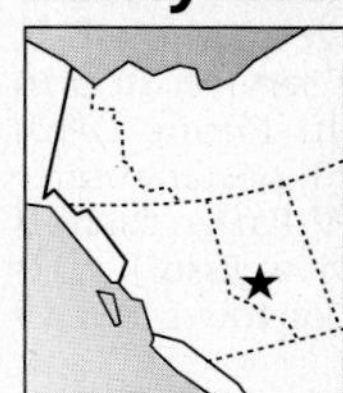

E 214.1 (344.4 km) **DC 152.9** (246.1 km) Approximately 4 hours drive time from Edmonton. **Population:** 1,944. **Emergency Services:** Phone 911 for all emergency services. **RCMP**, phone (780) 524-3343. **Hospital**, Valleyview General, 45 beds, phone (780) 524-3356.

VALLEYVIEW ADVERTISERS

Horizon Motel & Restaurant ....Ph. (780) 524-3904
Sherk's R.V. Park ....Ph. (780) 524-4949
Town of Valleyview ....Ph. (780) 524-5150
Valleyview Esso Service ....Ph. (780) 524-3504

Visitor Information: Major tourist information centre and rest stop located 0.9 mile/1.5 km south of Valleyview on Highway 43. Open daily, 8 A.M. to 8 P.M. from May through Labour Day weekend; phone (780) 524-2410, fax (780) 524-2727, e-mail valvadm@vvw-TEQ.Net. Postal service, souvenirs and refreshments, as well as regional travel and community events and services information. For information on small business opportunities, contact the Valleyview Regional Economic Development Board office at (780) 524-5051.

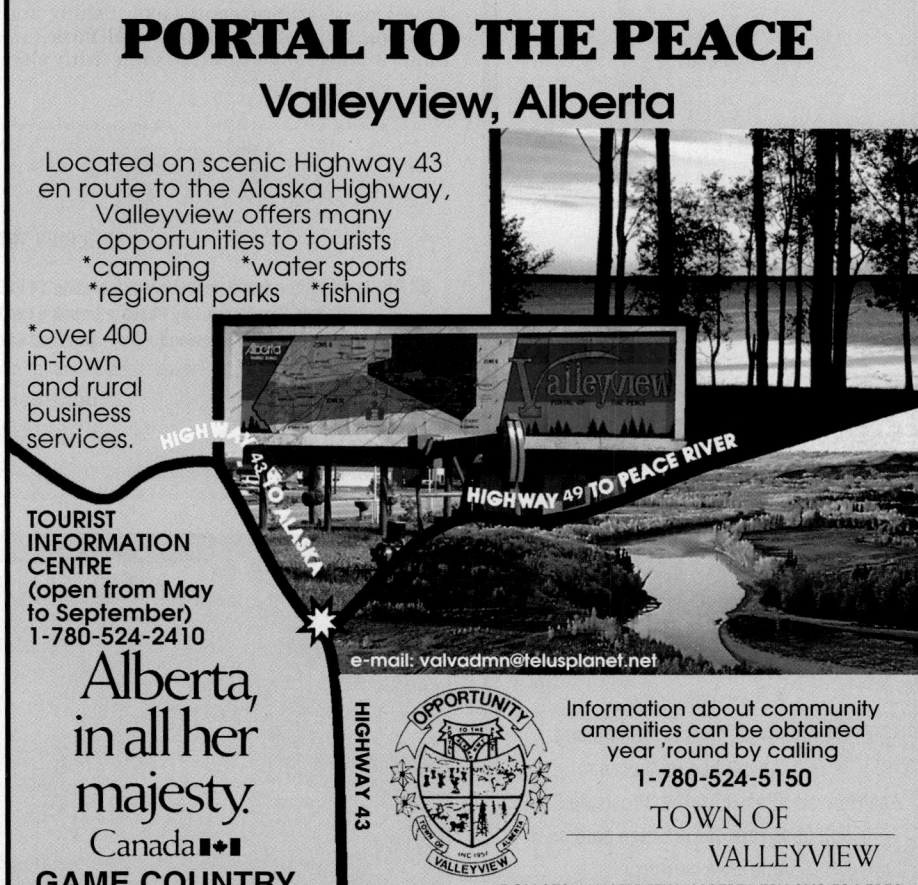

Elevation: 2,400 feet/732m. **Newspaper:** *Valley Views* (weekly). **Transportation: Air—** Airport 0.7 mile/1.1 km south (see **Milepost E 213.4**). **Bus**—Greyhound.

Valleyview, known as the "Portal to the Peace Country" of northwestern Alberta, is located at the junction of Highways 43 and 49. From Valleyview, Highway 43 continues west to Grande Prairie and Dawson Creek. Highway 49 leads north to connect with Highway 2 east to Athabasca and north to Peace River. From Peace River, travelers may follow the Mackenzie Highway to Northwest Territories (see the MACKENZIE ROUTE section for details).

Originally called Red Willow Creek when it was homesteaded in 1916, Valleyview boomed with the discovery of oil and gas in the 1950s, and services grew along with the population. Today, Valleyview's economy has diversified to include the oil and gas industry, forestry, tourism, agriculture and government services. Farming consists mainly of grain, oilseed, beef cattle and forage production.

The community has a full range of services including banks, automatic teller machines, post office, a library, several churches and a veterinary clinic.

All visitor facilities available, including 5 motels and hotels, several restaurants, gas stations (many with major repair service, propane and diesel), laundromat, grocery, liquor store, clothing and hardware stores, gift shops and a golf course. Some gas stations and restaurants open 24 hours a day.

The area boasts many lakes and streams, abundant wildlife, and lush vegetation, including berries. Summer travelers can take advantage of the long summer days here by attending local rodeos, fairs and festivals; playing a round of golf on one of the local golf courses; visiting one of the provincial parks along Sturgeon Lake; taking a dip in the outdoor swimming pool in town; or exploring the wilderness by all-terrain vehicle, horse, canoe or hiking trail.

Horizon Motel & Restaurant. At the Horizon, we have built our business on loyalty and customer satisfaction. An Alberta Best property, clean, well-appointed rooms, several nonsmoking and deluxe family suites available, reasonable rates. Our Westside Cafe, "where to turn when you simply must have a good meal...," tastefully decorated, featuring Western and Chinese menu. Open daily 6 A.M. to 10 P.M. Tour buses welcome. Bank rate of exchange paid on U.S. funds. We take pride in our service; stop in and experience for yourself! Phone (780) 524-3904. Fax (780) 524-4223. [ADVERTISEMENT]

Camping at Sherk's RV Park; turnoff Highway 43 West at Valleyview Esso. Lion's Den Campground, west end of town, has 19 sites. ▲

East Access Route Log

(continued)

E 216 (347.6 km) **DC 151** (243 km) Highways 49/2 lead north 86 miles/138.4 km to Peace River and **junction** with the Mackenzie Highway 12 miles/19 km west of Peace River. See the MACKENZIE ROUTE section for a description of Peace River and the log of the Mackenzie Highway to western Northwest Territories.

Continue on Highway 43 west for Dawson Creek.

E 222.6 (358.2 km) **DC 144.4** (232.4 km) 24-hour convenience store and gas.

E 224.7 (361.6 km) **DC 142.3** (229 km) Access north to **Sturgeon Lake**; fishing and camping. **Williamson Provincial Park** (1.2 miles/2 km); 60 campsites (some with electrical hookups), boat launch, dump station. Fishing for perch, pickerel, northern pike and whitefish. ◄▲

E 227 (365.3 km) **DC 140** (225.3 km) **CALAIS** (pop. about 550); post office and grocery store.

E 230 (370.1 km) **DC 137** (220.5 km) Private campground and marina on **Sturgeon Lake**; hookups, laundry, dump station, fishing, boat rentals. ◄▲

Cosy Cove Campground & Marina. See display ad this section. ▲

E 232 (373.3 km) **DC 135** (217.3 km) Sturgeon Heights. Turnoff for **Youngs Point Provincial Park**, 6 miles/10 km northeast; 97 campsites, boat launch, fishing in **Sturgeon Lake.** ◄▲

E 235 (378.2 km) **DC 132** (212.4 km) Turnouts both sides of highway; historic marker.

E 240 (386.2 km) **DC 127** (204.4 km) **CROOKED CREEK** (pop. 10); gas station, grocery, ice cream store (with giant cones), post office and pay phone.

E 246 (395.9 km) **DC 121** (194.7 km) **DeBOLT**, a small farming community north of highway with a general store and district museum. Garage with gas on highway.

E 253.8 (408.7 km) **DC 113.2** (181.9 km) **Junction.** Forestry Trunk Road leads 632 miles/1,017 km south, intersecting Yellowhead Highway 16 and Trans-Canada Highway 1, to Highway 3.

E 255.2 (410.7 km) **DC 111.8** (179.9 km) Microwave towers to east.

E 259.5 (417.6 km) **DC 107.5** (173 km) Smoky River bridge and government campground; 30 sites, shelter, firepits, firewood, tables, pit toilets, water pump and boat launch. ▲

E 264 (424.9 km) **DC 103** (165.7 km) **BEZANSON.** Post office, gas station with diesel, cafe, liquor store, grocery, general store, propane.

E 269 (432.9 km) **DC 98** (157.7 km)

Kleskun Hills Park to north 3 miles/5 km. The park features an ancient sea bottom with fossils of dinosaurs and marine life.

E 270.6 (435.5 km) **DC 96.4** (155.1 km) Turnout to north with historical sign about the Kleskun Hills.

E 283.5 (456.2 km) **DC 83.5** (134.4 km) Weigh scales to north.

E 283.8 (456.7 km) **DC 83.2** (133.9 km) Railroad crossing.

E 284 (457 km) **DC 83** (133.6 km) **Junction** with Highway 2. Dawson Creek-bound travelers continue on Highway 43. Access to Country Roads R.V. Park.

Turn north on Highway 2 for Sexsmith (8.5 miles/13.7 km) and Grimshaw (105 miles/169 km), Mile 0 of the Mackenzie Highway to Northwest Territories (see MACKENZIE ROUTE section).

To reach Grande Prairie city centre, keep straight ahead on Highway 43 (Clairmont Road) as it becomes 100th Street and follow it downtown. To skirt the downtown area, take the Highway 43 Bypass. Highway 43 becomes 100th Avenue (Richmond Avenue) on the west side of Grande Prairie.

To reach the Bighorn Highway, follow Wapiti Road (108th Street) south from Highway 43 on the west side of Grande Prairie. Bighorn Highway 40 (paved) connects Grande Prairie with Grande Cache (119 miles/191 km) and Yellowhead Highway 16 (207 miles/333 km). If you are headed south on the Big Horn Highway, fuel up in Grande Prairie, because there is no gas available southbound until Grande Cache.

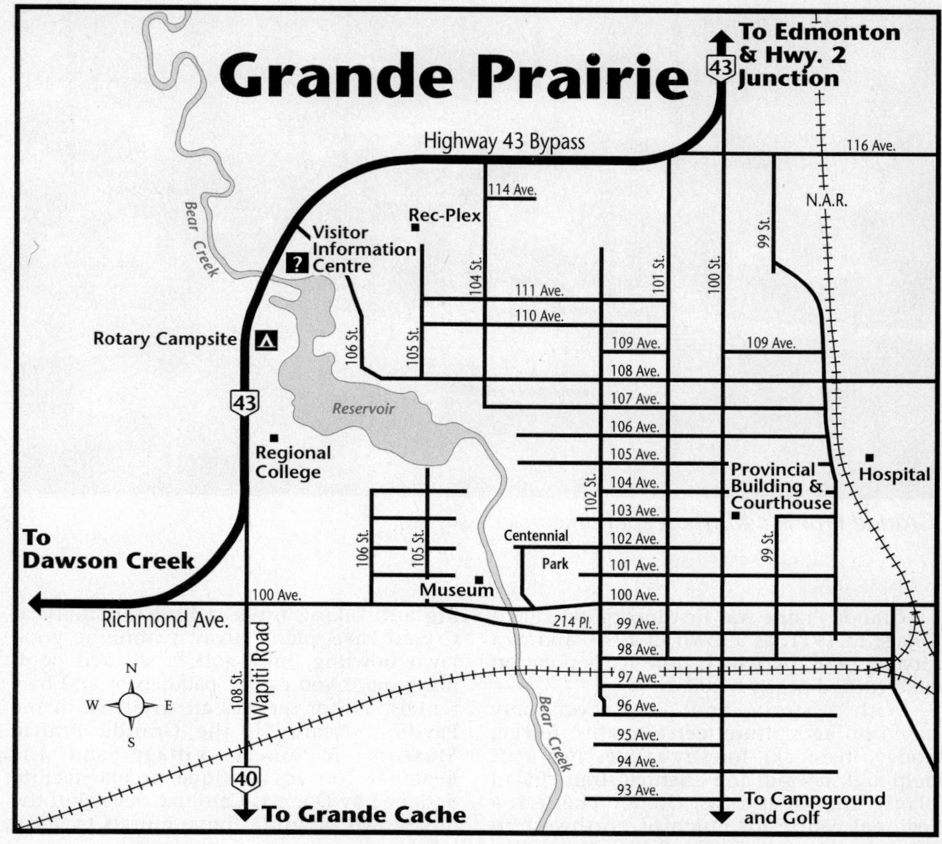

Grande Prairie

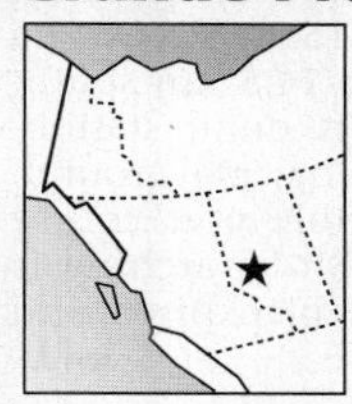

E 288 (463.5 km) **DC 79** (127.1 km). Located at **junction** of Highways 43 and 40. **Population:** 33,500. **Emergency Services: RCMP**, phone (780) 538-5700. **Fire Department**, phone (780) 532-2100. **Ambulance**, phone (780) 532-9511. **Hospital**, Queen Elizabeth, 10409 98th St., phone (780) 538-7100.

Visitor Information: Chamber of Commerce office at 10632 102nd Ave, T8V 6J8; open weekdays 8:30 A.M. to 4:30 P.M. Visitor service center located off Highway 43 Bypass on 106th Street at Bear Creek Reservoir; phone (780) 539-7688. Open 8:30 A.M. to 8:30 P.M., May to Labour Day; shorter hours in September. The Grande Prairie Rotary Club operates a free bus tour of the city Monday, Tuesday and Thursday at 7 P.M. Check with the infocentre for details.

Private Aircraft: Airport 3 miles/4.8 km west; elev. 2,195 feet/669m; length 6,500 feet/1,981m; paved; fuel 80, 100, jet. 24-hour flight service station.

Elevation: 2,198 feet/670m. **Transportation: Air**—Scheduled air service to Vancouver, BC, Edmonton, Calgary, and points north. **Bus**—Greyhound.

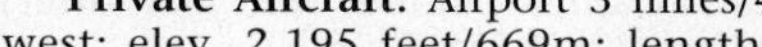

Welcome to the North Country!

Grande Prairie's Muskoseepi Park. (© Earl L. Brown, staff)

Grande Prairie was first incorporated as a village in 1911, as a town in 1919, and as a city in 1958, by which time its population had reached nearly 8,000.

With a strong and diverse economy based on agriculture (cereal grains, fescue, honey, livestock), forestry (a bleached kraft pulp mill, sawmill and oriented strand board plant), and oil and gas, Grande Prairie is a regional centre for much of northwestern Alberta and northeastern British Columbia. The trumpeter swan is the symbol of Grande Prairie and is featured throughout the city.

A variety of shopping is available at a major mall, several strip malls and a well-developed downtown area. Visitor facilities include several restaurants, hotels, motels, and bed and breakfasts. Recreation facilities include 2 swimming pools, 3 18-hole golf courses, a par 3 golf course, ball diamonds, amusement park, tennis courts, public library, a public art gallery and 3 private galleries. Churches representing almost every denomination are located in Grande Prairie. There are several public schools and a regional college.

Area attractions include Muskoseepi Park, which follows the Bear Creek corridor. The park includes 9 miles/15 km of paved walking and biking trails, a bird sanctuary at Crystal Lake, picnic areas, swimming pool, lawn bowling, mini-golf, a stocked pool, playground and canoe, paddleboat and bike rentals. Visitor services are available in the Pavilion. Nearby is the **Grande Prairie Museum & Pioneer Village** and the Regional College, a unique circular facility designed by Douglas Cardinal. Several of the downtown buildings have murals by local artists.

Weyerhaeuser offers tours of their pulp mill and sawmill in summer; phone (780) 539-8213. Canfor Lumber Mill also offers tours; phone (780) 538-7756.

The area has prime hunting for both migratory birds and big game. Area lakes are the nesting sites of the trumpeter swan. Hiking, camping and fishing are popular outdoor activities.

Annual events include the Stompede the first weekend in June, several smaller rodeos, Highland Games, pari-mutuel racing during July, Heritage Day and the Dinosaur Festival. Contact the visitor information centre for more information.

Camping within the city limits at Rotary Park public campground, located off the Highway 43 Bypass at the northwest edge of town near the college; Country Roads R.V. Park near the junction of Highway 43 and 2; and Camp Tamerack RV Park south on Highway 40. ▲

East Access Route Log

(continued)

E 298 (479.6 km) **DC 69** (111 km) **Saskatoon Island Provincial Park** is 1.9 miles/3 km north on park road; 96 campsites, dump station, boat launch, swimming, playground; Saskatoon berry picking in July; game preserve for trumpeter swans. ▲

E 299 (481.2 km) **DC 68** (109.4 km) **WEMBLEY** (pop. 1,463) has a hotel (banking service and liquor store at hotel), post office, grocery store, gas stop, car wash and restaurants. Picnicking and camping at Sunset Lake Park in town (dump station). Camping May 1 to Oct. 15 at Pipestone Creek County Park, 9 miles/14.5 km south; 99 sites, showers, flush toilets, dump station, boat launch, firewood, fishing, playground, fossil display and an 18-hole golf course with grass greens nearby. Bird watching is good here for red-winged blackbirds and yellow-headed blackbirds.

Beaverlodge

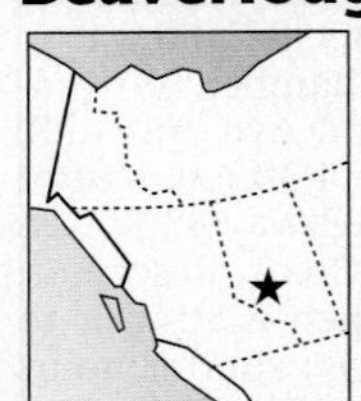

E 311 (500.5 km) **DC 56** (90.1 km) **Population:** 1,997. **Elevation:** 2,419 feet/737m. **Emergency Services: RCMP,** phone 911. **Ambulance,** phone 911. **Hospital,** Beaverlodge Municipal Hospital, phone (780) 354-2136.

Visitor Information: Located in the restored Lower Beaver Lodge School at Pio-

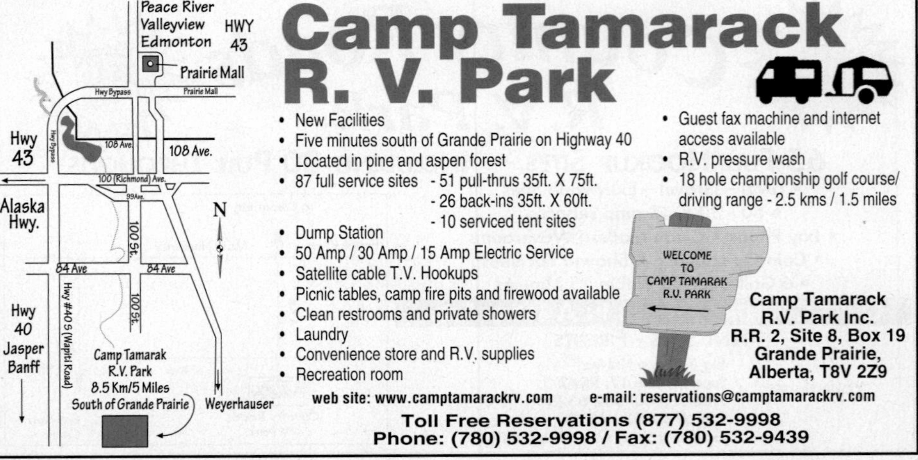

neer Campsite on the north side of Highway 43 at the west end of town.

Private Aircraft: DeWit Airpark 2 miles/3.2 km south; elev. 2,289 feet/1,698m; length 3,000 feet/914m; paved; no fuel.

Beaverlodge is a service centre for the area with RCMP, hospital, medical and dental clinic. There are 9 churches, schools, a swimming pool and tennis courts.

Visitor services include 3 motels, 8 restaurants and gas stations. There are supermarkets, banks, a drugstore, car wash and sporting goods store. **Beaverlodge Area Cultural Centre**, at the south end of town, features local arts and crafts as well as a tea room. South Peace Centennial Museum is west of town (see **Milepost E 312**). Camping is available at **Pioneer Campsite**, a municipal campground with 19 sites, showers, dump station, electrical hookups, tourist information. The Beaverlodge Airpark, 2 miles/3.2 km south of town, is becoming a popular stopover on the flying route to Alaska. ▲

Beaverlodge is the gateway to Monkman Pass and Kinuseo Falls. Beaverlodge is also home to Canada's most northerly Agricultural Research Station (open to the public), and serves as regional centre for grain transportation, seed cleaning and seed production. Cereal grains, such as wheat, barley and oats, are the main crops in the area. The PRT Alberta Inc. reforestation nursery here, visible from the highway as you enter town, grows about 8 million seedlings a year. Tours are available; phone (780) 354-2288.

Town of Beaverlodge. See display ad this section.

East Access Route Log

(continued)

E 312 (502.1 km) **DC 55** (88.5 km) **South Peace Centennial Museum** to east, open daily in summer; phone (780) 354-8869. Well worth a stop, the museum features vintage vehicles and working steam-powered farm equipment from the early 1900s. Open 10 A.M. to 8 P.M., mid-May through mid-October. The annual Pioneer Day celebration, held here the third Sunday in July, attracts several thousand visitors.

E 312.4 (502.7 km) **DC 54.6** (87.9 km) Turnoff for Driftwood Ranch Wildlife Haven, 14.3 miles/23 km west, a private collection of exotic and endangered animals. Opens May 1 for season; phone (780) 356-3769 for more information.

E 314.3 (505.8 km) **DC 52.6** (84.8 km) Golf course. This joint project of Hythe and Beaverlodge residents has a clubhouse that was once an NAR station. The 9-hole par 35 course has grass greens. Visitors are welcome; rentals available.

E 320 (515 km) **DC 47** (75.6 km) **HYTHE** (pop. 623) is an agricultural service community and processing center for fruit and berry crops, especially saskatoon berries. Canola is also a major crop. There's also bison ranching is this region; inquire locally for directions to Riverside Bison Ranch.

Visitor Information: Located between the highway and railroad tracks in an old 1910 tack shop, staffed by volunteers in summer. The town has a motel, a bed and breakfast, restaurant, laundromat, gas station, tire repair, car wash, outdoor covered heated swimming pool, complete shopping facilities and a hospital. Municipal campground in town with 17 sites, showers, dump station and playground. ▲

E 329 (529.4 km) **DC 38** (61.1 km) **Junction** with Highway 59 east to Sexsmith.

E 337 (542.3 km) **DC 30** (48.3 km) **DEMMITT**, an older settlement with postal service, cafe and gas.

E 340 (547.2 km) **DC 27** (43.4 km) Railway crossing.

E 341 (548.8 km) **DC 26** (41.8 km) Public campground to east; 15 sites, shelter, firewood, tables, pit toilets, pump water and playground. ▲

E 341.3 (549.2 km) **DC 25.7** (41.3 km) Vehicle inspection station to west.

E 342 (550.4 km) **DC 25** (40.2 km) Gas, diesel and convenience store.

E 343.3 (552.5 km) **DC 23.7** (38.1 km) Alberta–British Columbia border. Turnout with litter barrels and pay phone.

TIME ZONE CHANGE: Alberta is on Mountain time; most of British Columbia is on Pacific time.

E 345.1 (555.4 km) **DC 21.9** (35.2 km) **Junction** with Heritage Highway 52 (gravel surface) which leads 18.5 miles/30 km south to **One Island Lake Provincial Park** (30 campsites, fee charged, rainbow and brook trout fishing) and 92 miles/148 km southwest from Highway 2 to Tumbler Ridge townsite, built in conjunction with the North East Coal development. Monkman Provincial Park, site of spectacular Kinuseo Falls, lies south of Tumbler Ridge. A campground with viewing platform of falls is accessible via a 25-mile/40-km road from Tumbler Ridge. Heritage Highway loops north 59.5 miles/96 km from Tumbler Ridge to join Highway 97 just west of Dawson Creek (see **Milepost PG 237.7** in the WEST ACCESS ROUTE section).

E 345.7 (556.3 km) **DC 21.3** (34.3 km) Tupper Creek bridge.

E 347 (558.5 km) **DC 20** (32.1 km) Swan Lake Provincial Park, with 41 campsites, picnic area, playground and boat launch, is 1.2 miles/2 km north of the tiny hamlet of **TUPPER**, which has a general store. ▲

E 347.9 (559.9 km) **DC 19.1** (30.7 km) Sudeten Provincial Park day-use area; 8 picnic tables. Plaque tells of immigration to this valley of displaced residents of Sudetenland in 1938–39.

E 348.9 (561.5 km) **DC 18.1** (29.1 km) Tate Creek bridge.

E 349.7 (562.7 km) **DC 17.3** (27.8 km) Side road west to community of Tomslake.

E 356.3 (573.4 km) **DC 10.7** (17.2 km) Turnout to east with litter barrel.

E 358 (576.1 km) **DC 9** (14.5 km) Historic sign tells of Pouce Coupe Prairie.

E 359.4 (578.4 km) **7.6** (12.2 km) Railway crossing.

E 360 (579.3 km) **DC 7** (11.2 km) Weigh scales to east.

Farmland near Dawson Creek, BC.

(© Earl L. Brown, staff)

E 360.4 (580 km) **DC 6.6** (10.6 km) Bissett Creek bridge. Regional park located at south end of bridge.

E 361 (581 km) **DC 6** (9.6 km) **POUCE COUPE** (pop. 904; elev. 2,118 feet/646m). **Visitor Information:** Tourist Bureau Office located in Pouce Coupe Museum, 5006 49th Ave. (1 block south of Highway 2). Open 8 A.M. to 5 P.M., May to August. Phone (250) 786-5555.

The Pouce Coupe area was first settled in 1898 by a French Canadian, Hector Tremblay, who set up a trading post in 1908. The Edson Trail, completed in 1911, brought in the main influx of settlers from Edmonton in 1912. Historical artifacts are displayed at the **Pouce Coupe Museum**, located in the old NAR railroad station.

The village has a motel, hotel, restaurant, post office, gas station, dump station, car wash, municipal office, library, schools and food store. Camping at Regional Park, open May to September; hookups. ▲

E 364.5 (586.6 km) **DC 2.5** (4 km) Dawson Creek airport.

E 367 (590.6 km) **DC 0 DAWSON CREEK**, the beginning of the Alaska Highway.

Turn to the ALASKA HIGHWAY section, page 84, for description of Dawson Creek and log of the Alaska Highway.

Alaska Highway via

WEST ACCESS ROUTE

5 1 97

Connects: Seattle, WA, to Dawson Creek, BC **Length:** 817 miles
Road Surface: Paved **Season:** Open all year
Highest Summit: Pine Pass, 3,068 feet
Major Attractions: Fraser River Canyon/Hell's Gate, Barkerville

(See maps, pages 57–58)

	Cache Creek	Dawson Creek	Prince George	Seattle
Cache Creek		527	277	290
Dawson Creek	527		250	817
Prince George	277	250		567
Seattle	290	817	567	

Motorists on Trans-Canada Highway 1 between Lytton and Spences Bridge.

(© Judy Parkin)

The West Access Route links Interstate 5, Trans-Canada Highway 1 and BC Highway 97 to form the most direct route to Dawson Creek, BC, for West Coast motorists. This has been the major western route to the start of the Alaska Highway since 1952, when the John Hart Highway connecting Prince George and Dawson Creek was completed.

Travelers may also continue on I-5 to the international border at Blaine (22 miles/35.4 km beyond Exit 256), the more direct route if you are bound for Vancouver, BC.

The West Access Route junctions with Yellowhead Highway 16 at Prince George. This east–west highway connects with the Alaska State Ferry System and BC Ferries at Prince Rupert, and with the East Access Route to the Alaska Highway at Edmonton. Turn to the YELLOWHEAD HIGHWAY 16 section for a complete log of that route.

Distances via this 817-mile route between Seattle, WA, and Dawson Creek, BC, are: Seattle to Abbotsford, 120 miles; Abbotsford to Cache Creek, 170 miles; Cache Creek to Prince George, 277 miles; and Prince George to Dawson Creek, 250 miles.

The West Access Route log is divided into 4 sections: Seattle to the Canadian border; Abbotsford to Cache Creek; Cache Creek to Prince George; and Prince George to Dawson Creek.

West Access Route Log

This section of the log shows distance from Seattle (S) followed by distance from the Canadian border (CB) at Sumas.

INTERSTATE HIGHWAY 5

S 0 CB 116 (186.7 km) Exit 165 northbound (165B southbound) to downtown **SEATTLE** (pop. 532,900), the Alaska gateway city since the Klondike Gold Rush days, when it became the major staging and departure point for most of the gold seekers.

S 12 (19.3 km) **CB 104** (167.4 km) Exit 177 east to **LAKE FOREST PARK** (pop. 3,402) and west 4.5 miles to **EDMONDS** (pop. 30,341). Food, gas, diesel east off exit.

S 28 (45 km) **CB 88** (141.6 km) Exit 193 to **EVERETT** (pop. 76,685); all services.

S 34 (54.7 km) **CB 82** (132 km) Exit 199 to **MARYSVILLE** (pop. 11,714); food, gas and lodging either side of freeway.

S 41 (66 km) **CB 75** (120.7 km) Exit 206 to Twin Lakes Park day-use area 1 mile west, Wenberg State Park 6.2 miles west. Arlington Airport 2.3 miles east. 24-hour gas, food and shopping east off exit.

S 42 (67.6 km) **CB 74** (119.1 km) Rest area northbound.

S 43 (69.2 km) **CB 73** (117.5 km) Exit 208; food, 24-gas and diesel east off exit.

S 56 (90.1 km) **CB 60** (96.5 km) Exit 221 to **La CONNER** (pop. 751), 11 miles northwest; gas station east off exit.

S 61 (98.2 km) **CB 55** (88.5 km) Exit 226 to **MOUNT VERNON** (pop. 20,680); all services.

S 65 (104.6 km) **CB 51** (82 km) Exit 230 to **BURLINGTON** (pop. 4,854) to east, and **ANACORTES** (pop. 12,871, 16 miles/20 km west. Food, gas and lodging at exit.

S 66 (106.2 km) **CB 50** (80.5 km) Exit 231 to Chuckanut Drive scenic route and access to Bay View State Park.

S 67 (107.8 km) **CB 49** (78.9 km) Exit 232 to diesel, 24-hour gas, food and camping.

S 73 (117.5 km) **CB 43** (69.2 km) Rest area.

S 81 (130.3 km) **CB 35** (56.3 km) Exit to North Lake Samish and Lake Padden Recreation Area; diesel, gas and groceries west off exit.

S 85 (136.8 km) **CB 31** (50 km) Exit 250 to **Bellingham's Fairhaven Transportation Center** and **Bellingham Cruise Terminal**, departure point for Alaska State Ferries.

S 88 (141.6 km) **CB 28** (45.1 km) Exit 253 to **BELLINGHAM** (pop. 57,830); all services.

S 91 (146.4 km) **CB 25** (40.2 km) Exit 256 to Washington Highway 539 north to Lynden and the Canadian border; access to Bellis Fair Mall parkway, food, gas and lodging at this exit. *The MILEPOST® log exits here to cross the border at Sumas.* (Travelers may continue north on I-5 to cross the international border at Blaine.)

Follow Highway 539 North 12 miles to **junction** with Highway 546. Continue on Highway 546 for 13 miles to **junction** with Highway 9.

S 116 (186.7 km) **CB 0** U.S.–Canada International border at Sumas, WA. The Sumas, WA–Huntingdon, BC, border crossing is open 24-hours.

Follow BC Highway 11 north 4 miles/6.4 km to Abbotsford.

This section of the log shows distance from Abbotsford (A) followed by distance from Cache Creek (CC).

TRANS-CANADA HIGHWAY 1

A 0 CC 170 (273.6 km) Exit 92. **Junction** of Trans-Canada Highway 1 and Highway 11

(Continues on page 59)

WEST ACCESS ROUTE *Seattle, WA, to Lac La Hache, BC*

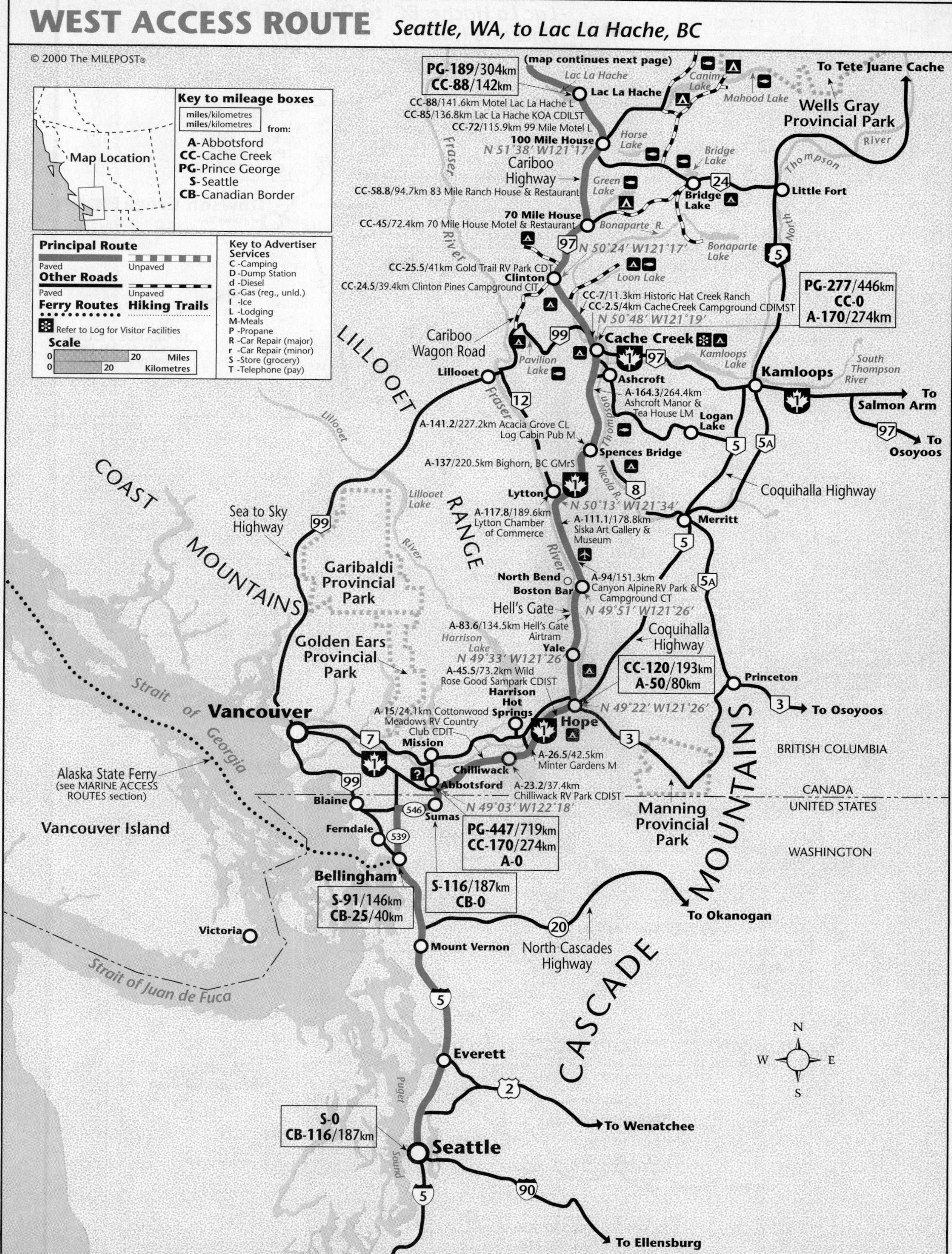

WEST ACCESS ROUTE

Lac La Hache, BC, to Dawson Creek, BC (includes Hudson's Hope Loop)

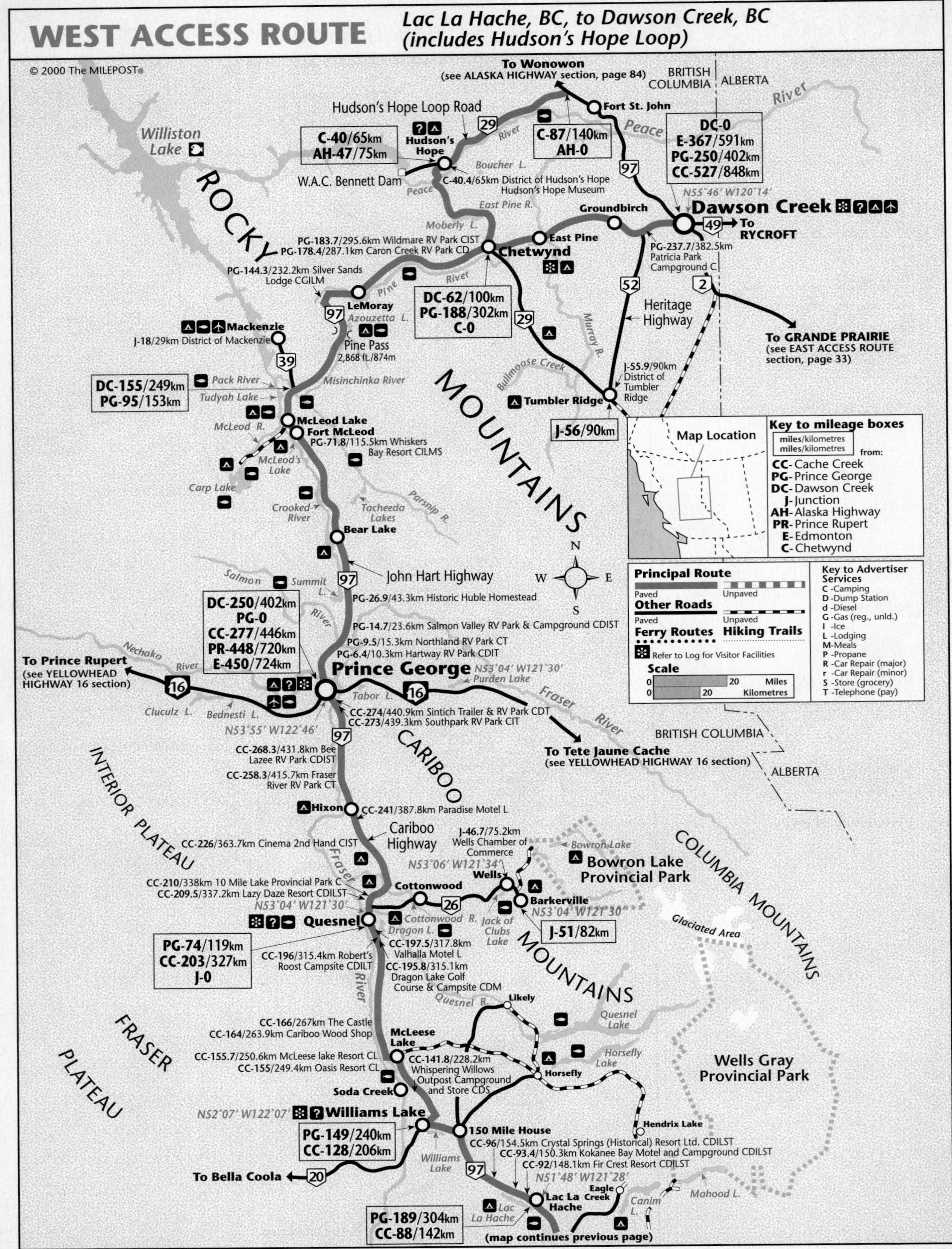

(Continued from page 56)
south to the international border crossing at Sumas–Huntingdon. Highway 11 north to **ABBOTSFORD** (pop. 105,403), all visitor services. Abbotsford is the "Raspberry Capital of Canada" and is the home of the Abbotsford International Airshow in August. **Visitor Information:** Abbotsford Chamber of Commerce, 2462 McCallum Road; phone (604) 859-9651.

Highway 11 north crosses the bridge over the Fraser River to Mission (7.2 miles/11.9 km north), and connects with Highway 7 to Harrison Hot Springs (41 miles/66 km). This 2-lane highway traverses the rural farmland on the north side of the Fraser River, rejoining Trans-Canada Highway 1 at Hope (56 miles/90 km).

A 1.9 (3 km) **CC 168.1** (270.5 km) Exit 95 to Whatcom Road and westbound exit to Sumas River rest area. Access to Sumas Mountain Provincial Park; hiking.

A 5.3 (8.5 km) **CC 164.7** (265.1 km) Exit 99 to Sumas River rest area (eastbound only); tables, toilet, pay phones.

A 8.8 (14.2 km) **CC 161.2** (259.4 km) Exit 104 to small farming community of Yarrow and road to Cultus Lake. The Lower Fraser Valley is prime agricultural land.

CAUTION: Watch for farm vehicles crossing freeway.

A 15 (24.1 km) **CC 155** (249.4 km) Exit 116 to Lickman Road; access south to Visitor Infocentre, open daily in summer, and Cottonwood Meadows RV park. Chilliwack Antique Powerland museum located behind the infocentre. ▲

Cottonwood Meadows RV Country Club. Exit 116. Highly rated and recommended by Good Sam, Woodalls, Tourism B.C. New, secure, clean, well-maintained, full service park. Easy access, electronic gates, well lit and well managed. Lazy stream, full hookups (15/30/50 amp), cable TV, wide level sites, paved roadways. Nicest washrooms, laundromat, clubhouse, Jacuzzi, pay phone. Near U.S. border crossing, shopping centers, golf courses. Pets on leash only. Open end of March to early November. VISA, MasterCard. 44280 Luckakuk Way, Chilliwack, BC V2R 4A7. Phone (604) 824-PARK (7275). E-mail: camping@cottonwoodRVpark.com. Web site: www.cottonwoodRVpark.com. [ADVERTISEMENT] ▲

A 16.8 (27.1 km) **CC 153.2** (246.5 km) Highway 119B to Chilliwack Airport.

A 17 (27.4 km) **CC 153** (246.2 km) Exit 119 north to Chilliwack (all services, description follows) and south to Sardis (all services) and Cultus Lake Provincial Park.

Cultus Lake Provincial Park has 300 campsites; water, flush and pit toilets, showers, firewood, water, boat launch, swimming, fishing, canoeing, kayaking, and hiking and walking trails. Cultus Lake resort area also offers water slides, go-carts and other activities. ▲

CHILLIWACK (pop. 60,186) has motels, restaurants, shopping malls, banks, gas stations, RV parks and other services. There are a library, 2 movie theatres and an arts centre. Recreational attractions include golf and the popular Cultus Lake area with water park, boat rentals, horseback riding and camping. **Visitor Information:** Visitor Information Centre, 44150 Luckakuck Way; phone (604) 858-8121. ▲

A 18 (29 km) **CC 152** (244.6 km) Exit 123 Prest Road north to Rosedale, south to Ryder Lake.

A 23.2 (37.4 km) **CC 146.8** (236.2 km) Exit 129 for Annis Road and RV park. ▲

Chilliwack RV Park & Campground. See display ad this section. ▲

A 26.5 (42.5 km) **CC 143.5** (230.9 km) Exit 135 to Highway 9 east to Harrison Hot Springs and alternate route Highway 7 to Hope and Vancouver. Westbound exit for **Bridal Veil Falls.** Also exit here for access to **Minter Gardens**, which rivals Victoria's famous Butchart Gardens for beauty. The 27 acres of floral displays feature 11 themed gardens, topiary figures and a rare collection of Chinese Penjing Rock Bonsai. Opens 9 A.M. daily, April to mid-October. Entertainment is scheduled Sundays and holidays, weather permitting. Internet: www.minter.org.

Exit north for Cheam Lake Wetlands Regional Park. Once mined for its marl deposits, Cheam Lake is now a wildlife habitat; interpretive trails, good bird watching.

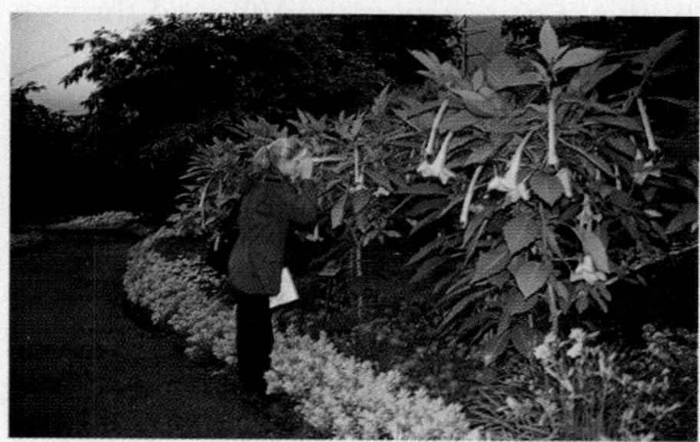

Minter Gardens. See display ad this section.

A 27.3 (43.9 km) **CC 142.7** (229.6 km) Exit 138 to Popkum Road. Eastbound access to **Bridal Veil Falls Provincial Park** to south; picnicking, trail to base of falls. Also access to small community of Popkum and various roadside attractions, including water slide, Sandstone Gallery rock and gem museum, and prehistoric-themed amusement park. Food, gas and lodging.

A 34.5 (55.5 km) **CC 135.5** (218.1 km) Exit 146 Herrling Island, a cottonwood tree farm (no access or services), visible from highway.

A 40.5 (65.2 km) **CC 129.5** (208.4 km) Exit 153 to Laidlaw and access to Jones (Wahleach) Lake. Country store in Laidlaw.

A 42.5 (68.4 km) **CC 127.5** (205.2 km) Truck weigh scales; public phone.

A 44.7 (71.9 km) **CC 125.3** (201.6 km) Exit 160 to Hunter Creek rest area; tables, toilet, pay phone, information kiosk.

A 45.5 (73.2 km) **CC 124.5** (200.4 km) Exit 165 to Flood–Hope Road (eastbound); access to Wild Rose RV park. ▲

Wild Rose Good Sampark.. See display ad this section. ▲

A 48.5 (78.1 km) **CC 121.5** (195.5 km) Exit 168 to Flood–Hope Road (westbound); access to Wild Rose RV park, Skagit Valley and Silver Lake provincial parks. ▲

A 48.7 (78.4 km) **CC 121.3** (195.2 km) Silver Creek, Flood–Hope Road exit.

A 50 (80.5 km) **CC 120** (193.1 km) **Junction** of Trans-Canada Highway 1, Highway 3 (Crowsnest Highway) and Highway 5 (Coquihalla Highway). Use Exit 170 northbound for Trans-Canada Highway 1 to Hope.

Hope

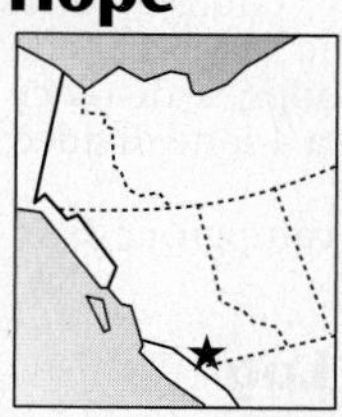

A 50.2 (80.8 km) **CC 119.8** (192.8 km) Located on the Fraser River near Mount Hope (elev. 6,000 feet/1,289m). **Population:** 6,247. **Elevation:** 140 feet/43m. **Emergency Services: RCMP, Fire Department, Ambulance,** phone 911. **Hospital,** 1275 7th Ave., phone (604) 869-5656. **Visitor Information:** Visitor Info-Centre and museum building, corner of Hudson Bay Street and Water Avenue, on the right northbound as you enter town. Open daily 8 A.M. to 8 P.M. in July and August, 9 A.M. to 5 P.M. in May, June and September; weekdays only, 10 A.M. to 4 P.M., rest of the year. Chamber of Commerce web site: www.hopechamber.bc.ca.

Hope is known as the "Chainsaw Carving Capital" of Canada, with more than 20 large wood carvings in the downtown area. Hope is a convenient tourist stop with complete services. About 30 motels and resorts are in Hope or just outside town on Trans-Canada

Highway 1 and on Highway 3.

The major attraction in the Hope area is the Coquihalla Canyon Provincial Recreation Area, the focus of which is the Othello Quintette Tunnels. The 4 rock tunnels which cut through the tortuous canyon were part of the Kettle Valley Railway. This stretch of railway has been restored as a walking trail through the tunnels and across bridges. The tunnels are accessible from downtown Hope via Kawkawa Lake Road and Othello Road, about a 10-minute drive.

The Coquihalla Highway, completed in 1986, connects Hope with the Trans-Canada Highway just west of Kamloops, a distance of 118 miles/190 km. This is a 4-lane divided highway; toll charged.

There are several private campgrounds in Hope. ▲

West Access Route Log

(continued)

A 50.7 (81.6 km) **CC 119.3** (191.9 km) Bridge over Fraser River. Turnout at north end, access to pedestrian bridge across the Fraser.

A 51.5 (82.8 km) **CC 118.5** (190.7 km) **Junction** with Highway 7, which leads west to Harrison Hot Springs (22.5 miles/36 km) and Vancouver.

A 53.1 (85.5 km) **CC 116.9** (188.1 km) Rest area (westbound access only) with picnic tables to west by Lake of the Woods.

A 60.8 (97.8 km) **CC 109.2** (175.7 km) Easy-to-miss turnoff (watch for sign 1,320 feet/400m before turn) for Emory Creek Provincial Park east of highway; 34 level gravel sites in trees, water, fire rings, picnic tables, firewood, flush and pit toilets, and litter barrels. Camping fee April to October. Hiking and walking trails. Gold panning and fishing in **Fraser River.** ▲

Very much in evidence between Hope and Cache Creek are the tracks of the Canadian National and Canadian Pacific railways. Construction of the CPR—Canada's first transcontinental railway—played a significant role in the history of the Fraser and Thompson river valleys. Begun in 1880, the CPR line between Kamloops and Port Moody was contracted to Andrew Onderdonk.

A 64.8 (104.3 km) **CC 105.2** (169.3 km) **YALE** (pop. 500; elev. 250 feet/76m). **Emergency Services: Police, Fire Department, Ambulance,** phone 911. **Visitor Information:** In the museum, phone (604) 863-2324. Visitor facilities include motels, store, gas station and restaurant.

Yale is a popular starting point for river rafters on the Fraser River. Historically, Yale was the head of navigation for the Lower Fraser River and the beginning of the overland gold rush trail to British Columbia's goldfields. The Anglican Church of Saint John the Divine here was built for the miners in 1859 and is the oldest church still on its original foundation in mainland British Columbia. Next to the church is Yale Museum and a bronze plaque honouring Chinese construction workers who helped build the Canadian Pacific Railway. Walking around town, look for the several plaques relating Yale's history. Daily guided walking tours of historic Yale are offered in summer; fee charged, includes admission to museum and church. Phone (604) 863-2324 for more information.

A 65.6 (105.5 km) **CC 104.5** (168.2 km) Entering **Fraser Canyon** northbound. The Fraser River and canyon were named for Simon Fraser (1776–1862), the first white man to descend the river in 1808. This is the dry forest region of British Columbia, and it can be a hot drive in summer. The scenic Fraser Canyon travelers drive through today was a formidable obstacle for railroad engineers in 1881.

A 66 (106.2 km) **CC 104** (167.4 km) Yale Tunnel, first of several northbound through the Fraser Canyon.

A 67.3 (108.3 km) **CC 102.7** (165.2 km) Turnout to east with plaque (missing in 1999) about the Cariboo Wagon Road, which connected Yale with the Cariboo goldfields near Barkerville. Built between 1861 and 1863 by the Royal Engineers, it replaced an earlier route to the goldfields—also called the Cariboo Wagon Road—which started from Lillooet.

A 68.4 (110.1 km) **CC 101.6** (163.5 km) Saddle Rock Tunnel. This 480-foot-/146-m-long tunnel was constructed from 1957–58.

A 72.1 (116 km) **CC 97.9** (157.5 km) Private campground. ▲

A 72.3 (116.3 km) **CC 97.7** (157.2 km) Sailor Bar Tunnel, nearly 984 feet/300m long. There were dozens of bar claims along the Fraser River in the 1850s bearing colourful names such as Sailor Bar.

A 76.5 (123.1 km) **CC 93.5** (150.5 km) Spuzzum (unincorporated), gas station and food.

A 77.1 (124.1 km) **CC 92.9** (149.5 km) Stop of interest at south end of Alexandra Bridge, built in 1962, the second largest fixed arch span in the world at more than 1,640 feet/500m in length.

A 77.5 (124.8 km) **CC 92.5** (148.9 km) **Alexandra Bridge Provincial Park,** picnic areas and interpretive displays on both sides of highway. Hiking trail down to the old Alexandra Bridge, still intact. This suspension bridge was built in 1926, replacing the original built in 1863.

A 77.8 (125.2 km) **CC 92.2** (148.4 km) Historic Alexandra Lodge (closed), is the last surviving original roadhouse on the Cariboo Waggon Road.

A 79.5 (128 km) **CC 90.5** (145.6 km) Alexandra Tunnel.

A 80.5 (129.5 km) **CC 89.5** (144 km) Turnout to east.

A 82.6 (133 km) **CC 87.4** (140.7 km) Hells Gate Tunnel (328 feet/100m long).

A 83.3 (134 km) **CC 86.7** (139.5 km) Ferrabee Tunnel (328 feet/100m long).

A 83.6 (134.5 km) **CC 86.4** (139 km) **Hells Gate**, the narrowest point on the Fraser River and a popular attraction. (Northbound traffic park at lot immediately south of attraction on east side of road; southbound traffic park on west side of road at attraction.) Two 25-passenger airtrams take visitors some 500 feet down across the river to a restaurant and shop complex. Footbridge across river to view fishways through which some 2 million salmon pass each year. A display details the life cycle of the salmon, the construction of the International Fishways and the history of Hells Gate. From the footbridge, visitors may also see rafters running Hells Gate. The trams operate daily, March 30 to Oct. 28, 2000. There is also a steep trail down to the fishways; strenuous hike.

Hells Gate was well named. It was by far the most difficult terrain for construction of both the highway and the railway. To haul supplies for the railway upstream of Hells Gate, Andrew Onderdonk built the sternwheel steamer *Skuzzy*. The *Skuzzy* made its way upstream through Hells Gate in 1882, hauled by ropes attached to the canyon walls by bolts.

Hell's Gate Airtram. See display ad this section.

A 83.8 (134.9 km) **CC 86.2** (138.7 km) Hells Gate turnaround for travelers who miss the Hells Gate parking lot.

A 85.7 (137.9 km) **CC 84.3** (135.7 km) China Bar Tunnel, built in 1960. It is almost 2,300 feet/700m long, one of the longest tunnels in North America. Point of interest sign at south end about Simon Fraser.

A 91 (146.5 km) **CC 79** (127.1 km) **BOSTON BAR** (pop. 885; elev. 400 feet/122m). **Emergency Services:** Phone 911. Services include gas stations, cafes, grocery store, motels and private RV parks. Site of the J.S. Jones Timber Mill; tours may be available in summer, phone (604) 867-9214 for information. Boston Bar was the southern landing for the steamer *Skuzzy,* which plied the Fraser River between here and Lytton during construction of the CPR.

North Bend, located across the river from Boston Bar, is a former railway community. Old cable cage from the aerial car ferry that once served North Bend is on display at the CN station in Boston Bar.

North Bend is the access point for the Nahatlatch River and lakes via a logging road. River rafting trips are available on the Nahatlatch River.

A 94 (151.3 km) **CC 76** (122.3 km) **Canyon Alpine RV Park & Campground.** Still the best-kept secret in the Fraser Canyon, but quickly being discovered and described as "...one of the nicest parks on the Alaskan route." Secure RV parking and tenting 3 miles north of Boston Bar. 31 level, pull-through sites, fully serviced with 30 amp, water, sewer and cable TV. Easy access

Lytton is located at the confluence of the Thompson and Fraser rivers.
(© Judy Parkin)

and turnarounds for rigs over 35 feet. 14-foot entrance gate clearance. Away from traffic noise and railroads. Clean washrooms. Hot showers. Shaded sites. Fire rings. Firewood. 50 yards south of restaurant, store, laundromat and telephones. Pets on leash welcome. 10 minutes from world-famous Hell's Gate Airtram. Open April 15 to Oct. 15. 50490 Trans-Canada Highway. Toll free (800) 644-PARK. Your friendly hosts, Jay and Maggie. See display ad this section. [ADVERTISEMENT] ▲

A 101 (162.5 km) **CC 69** (111 km) Turnoff for Blue Lake, 0.6 mile/1 km gravel road. Access to private campground. ▲

A 111.1 (178.8 km) **CC 58.9** (94.8 km) **Siska Art Gallery & Museum.** See display ad this section.

A 112.8 (181.5 km) **CC 57.2** (92.1 km) Viewpoint to west overlooking the Fraser River.

A 113.6 (182.9 km) **CC 56.4** (90.7 km) Canadian National and Canadian Pacific railways cross over the Fraser River here; a favorite spot for photos. Gravel turnout to east.

A 114.6 (184.5 km) **CC 55.4** (89.2 km) Skupper rest area (northbound only); toilets, tables, litter barrels.

A 117.8 (189.6 km) **CC 52.2** (84 km) **Junction** with Highway 12 to Lillooet (see description at **Milepost CC 7**). Turn west here for community of Lytton (description follows).

LYTTON (pop. 322; elev. 561 feet/171m). **Emergency Services: RCMP**, phone (250) 455-2225. **Fire Department**, phone (250) 455-2333. **Ambulance**, phone (250) 374-5937. **Hospital**, St. Bartholomew's, phone (250) 455-2221. **Visitor Information**: Visitor Infocentre, 400 Fraser St., phone (250) 455-2523. Located at the confluence of the Thompson and Fraser rivers, Lytton acts as headquarters for river raft trips. All visitor facilities are available. Sand bars at Lytton yielded much gold, and river frontage has been set aside for recreational gold panning. Lytton has recorded the highest temperature in British Columbia, 111°F/44°C.

Lytton. Rafting capital of British Columbia. Whitewater on the Thompson, and Hells Gate on the Fraser. Hiking is great in our interior dry climate, amid beautiful scenery. Enjoy the Stein Valley, Native and Gold Rush history in our museums. Sawmill tours arranged at the Visitor Infocentre, 400 Fraser St., phone (250) 455-2523, fax (250) 455-6669. [ADVERTISEMENT]

A 122.8 (197.6 km) **CC 47.2** (76 km) **Skihist Provincial Park** to east; 58 campsites on east side of highway with water, flush and pit toilets, firewood and dump station. Picnic area on west side of highway (good place to watch the trains go by); wheelchair-accessible restrooms.

A 134.7 (216.8 km) **CC 35.3** (56.8 km) **Goldpan Provincial Park** to west alongside river; 14 campsites, picnic area, water, firewood, canoeing, kayaking, fishing.

A 136 (218.9 km) **CC 34** (54.7 km) In summer, watch for fruit stands selling locally grown produce along the highway. Watch for bighorn sheep on the hillsides in the fall.

A 137 (220.5 km) **CC 33** (53.1 km) **BIG HORN**; trading post, fuel, tire shop and 24-hour towing.

Big Horn, BC. Bring your binoculars! Depending on month and season, you may see eagles, osprey, bears, deer or bighorn sheep on our mountain face. Large viewing windows in our cafe. Enjoy our extra-deep-dish pies, custom burgers. We also sell fishing tackle, fishing licenses. Fresh fruit (June–September), local rocks and minerals, fireworks, souvenirs. Trading post. Fuel. 24-hour towing BCAA. Tire shop. Family operated. Box 98, Spences Bridge, BC V0K 2L0. (250) 458-2333. [ADVERTISEMENT]

A 140 (225.3 km) **CC 30** (48.3 km) **Junction** with Highway 8 to Merritt and south access to Spences Bridge. Plaque here about the great landslide of 1905.

A 141.2 (227.2 km) **CC 28.8** (46.3 km) North access to **SPENCES BRIDGE** (pop. 300; elev. 760 feet/231m) located at the confluence of the Thompson and Nicola rivers. Services include lodging, camping, restaurant, pub and grocery with tackle and fishing licenses. A record 30-lb., 5-oz. steelhead was caught in the Thompson River in 1984. Look for an osprey nest atop the hydroelectric pole on the east side of the river.

Acacia Grove. One block off Highway 1. RV park, cabins with kitchen units, tenting. Serene river valley setting overlooking the Thompson River, famous for steelhead, salmon, rainbow trout fishing and rafting. Visit with the mountain sheep August to May. Horseshoes, croquet, darts, walking trails to river. Pull-throughs, full service, laundromat, free hot showers, flush toilets, groceries and gift shop. Your hosts Ed and Gayleen Streifel. Phone/fax (250) 458-2227. Box 69, Spences Bridge, BC V0K 2L0. [ADVERTISEMENT]

Log Cabin Pub. You will appreciate this unique log structure. The logs were specially selected and prepared locally, some spanning 50 feet. This pub combines the rustic charm of a turn-of-the-century roadhouse with all the amenities of a neighborhood pub. Excellent food and hospitality by your hosts John and Laurie Kingston. [ADVERTISEMENT]

A 153.4 (246.9 km) **CC 16.6** (26.7 km) Viewpoint overlooking Thompson River with plaque about the Canadian Northern Pacific (now the Canadian National Railway), Canada's third transcontinental railway, completed in 1915.

A 158.4 (255 km) **CC 11.6** (18.7 km) Red Hill rest area to east; tables, toilets, litter barrels, pay phone.

A 164.3 (264.4 km) **CC 5.7** (9.2 km) Stop of interest sign to east describes **Ashcroft Manor Historic Site**, a roadhouse on the Cariboo Waggon Road. Small museum (no charge).

Ashcroft Manor & Tea House. See display ad this section.

Summer temperatures in this dry and desert-like region typically reach the high 80s and 90s (26°C to 32°C). Fields under black plastic mesh tarps—which may be seen as the highway descends northbound—are ginseng, an Asian medicinal root crop. The world supply of North American ginseng, which takes 4 years to mature, is grown in the southern Cariboo.

A 164.5 (264.7 km) **CC 5.5** (8.9 km) **Junction** with road to **ASHCROFT**, a small village on the Thompson River with full tourist facilities just east of the highway. Historic Ashcroft supplanted Yale as gateway to the Cariboo with the arrival of the Canadian Pacific Railway in 1885. There are a number of original buildings with distinctive architectural details. Ashcroft Museum houses a fine collection of artifacts tracing the history of the region. Logan Lake, east of Ashcroft, is the site of the second largest open-pit copper mine in North America (tours available).

Also **junction** with Highway 97C to Logan Lake and Merritt.

A 168.2 (270.7 km) **CC 1.8** (2.9 km) Second turnoff northbound for Ashcroft and road to Logan Lake.

Cache Creek

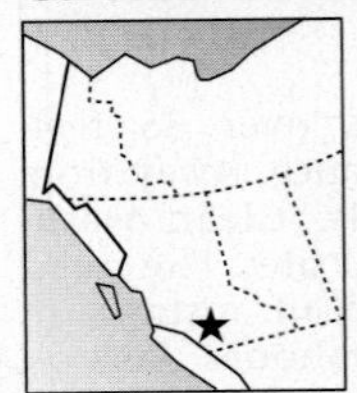

A 170 (273.6 km) **PG 277** (445.8 km) Located at the junction of Trans-Canada Highway 1 and Highway 97. **Population:** 1,115. **Elevation:** 1,508 feet/460m. **Emergency Services: RCMP,** phone (250) 453-2216. **Ambulance,** phone (250)-374-5937. **Hospital,** phone (250) 453-5306.

Visitor Information: Write Box 460, Cache Creek, BC V0K 1H0; fax (250) 457-

CACHE CREEK ADVERTISERS

Bonaparte Motel	Ph. (250) 457-9693
Bear's Claw Lodge	Ph. (250) 457-9705
Brookside Campsite	Ph. (250) 457-6633
Cariboo Jade Shoppe	Ph. (250) 457-9566
Cache Creek Campground	Ph. (250) 457-6414
Desert Motel	Ph. (250) 457-6226
Good Knight Inn, The	Ph. (250) 457-9500
Tumbleweed Motel	Ph. (800) 667-1501
Wander-Inn Restaurant	Ph. (250) 457-6511

Rafting the Thompson River between Lytton and Spences Bridge. (© Judy Parkin)

9669 or phone toll-free (877) 453-9467.

Cache Creek has ample facilities for the traveler (most located on or just off the main highways), including motels, restaurants, service stations and grocery store. Private campgrounds are available east of Cache Creek on Trans-Canada Highway 1 (across from the golf course) and just north of town on Highway 97.

A post office and bus depot are on Todd Road. Nearby, Cariboo Jade Shoppe offers free stone-cutting demonstrations in summer. On display out front is a 2,850-lb. jade boulder. Public park and swimming pool on the Bonaparte River, east off Highway 97 at the north edge of town.

The settlement grew up around the confluence of the creek and the Bonaparte River. The Hudson's Bay Co. opened a store here, and Cache Creek became a major supply point on the Cariboo Waggon Road. Today, hay and cattle ranching, ginseng farming, mining, logging and tourism support the community. Area soils are dry but fertile. Residents claim that with irrigation nearly anything can be grown here.

From the junction, Highway 97 leads north 277 miles/445.8 km to Prince George. Kamloops is 52 miles/83.7 km east via Trans-Canada Highway 1. Traveling north from Cache Creek the highway generally follows the historic route to the Cariboo goldfields.

Brookside Campsite. 1 km east of Cache Creek on Highway 1, full (30 amp) and partial hookups, pull-throughs, tent sites, super-clean heated wash and laundry rooms, free showers, sani-stations, store, playground, nature path, heated pool, golf course adjacent, pets on leash, pay phones. VISA, MasterCard, C.P. two days. Box 737, Cache Creek, BC V0K 1H0. Phone/fax: (250) 457-6633. [ADVERTISEMENT] ♿▲

West Access Route Log

(continued)

This section of the log shows distance from Cache Creek (CC) followed by distance from Prince George (PG).

BC HIGHWAY 97

CC 0 PG 277 (445.8 km) Cache Creek, **junction** of Trans-Canada Highway 1 and Highway 97.

CC 2.5 (4 km) **PG 274.5** (441.8 km) **Cache Creek Campground**, 3 km north of Cache Creek on Highway 97 north. Full hookups, pull-throughs and tenting, sani-station, store, country kitchen restaurant, laundromat, coin showers, heated washrooms. Outdoor pool and whirlpool (no charge). 18-hole mini-golf, horseshoes, seasonal river swimming and fishing. P.O. Box 127, Cache Creek, BC V0K 1H0. For reservations, phone (250) 457-6414. See display ad this section. [ADVERTISEMENT] ▲

CC 7 (11.3 km) **PG 270** (434.5 km) **Junction** with Highway 99 to Hat Creek Ranch, Marble Canyon Provincial Park (descriptions follow) and to **LILLOOET** (pop. 2,984), a 46.5-mile/75-km drive west from here. Lillooet boasts high summer temperatures, rockhounding, gold panning and 15 historic points of interest from the gold rush days.

Drive 0.4 mile/0.7 km west on Highway 99 for Hat Creek Heritage Ranch, a restored Cariboo Trail roadhouse and farm with reconstructed barn, working blacksmith shop, wagon and trail rides and tours.

Historic Hat Creek Ranch. Explore the history of this 326-acre attraction. Tour the 1861 travelers' roadhouse, over 25 rooms each with a unqiue story to share. Visit the native Shuswap Vilage. See their summer and winter homes. Learn about the foods they ate, the games they played and the life they led. Relax in the heritage apple orchard. Cool off in the air-conditioned gift shop and coffee shop. Open daily 10 A.M. to 6 P.M. June to September. 1-800-782-0922. [ADVERTISEMENT]

Marble Canyon Provincial Park, 17.5 miles/28 km west on Highway 99, has 34 campsites, picnicking, swimming and hiking trails. ▲

This route, formerly Highway 12, was designated as part of Highway 99 when the logging road between Lillooet and Pemberton was paved, making it possible to drive to the Cariboo from Vancouver (209 miles/336.5 km from here) via Whistler and Blackcombe ski areas. Highway 99, promoted as the "Sea to Sky Highway," is a scenic route with many winding sections and steep (to 13 percent) grades. Sea to Sky Highway is logged in *Northwest Mileposts®*.

CC 10 (16 km) **PG 267** (430 km) Gravel turnout with plaque about the BX stagecoaches that once served Barkerville. Formally known as the BC Express Company, the BX served the Cariboo for 50 years.

CC 13.6 (21.9 km) **PG 263.4** (423.9 km) Paved road leads east to Loon Lake, rainbow fishing, boat launch. Camping at **Loon Lake Provincial Park** (16 miles/26 km); 14 sites, water, pit toilets, firewood. ▲

CC 16.6 (26.7 km) **PG 260.4** (419.1 km) Carguile rest area.

CC 24.5 (39.4 km) **PG 252.5** (406.3 km)

Clinton Pines Campground. New 20-acre facility. Easy access. Large shady sites, pull-throughs. Full and partial hookups. Free hot showers. Laundromat. Open year-round. Situated on the original Gold Rush Trail. Beautiful scenery, nature trails. Bike rentals, horseshoes, communal firepits. Pets welcome. Credit cards/Interac accepted. Owner operated. Located 0.5 mile south of Clinton on the east side of Highway 97. Phone (250) 459-0030; e-mail clinton pines@goldcountry.bc.ca. [ADVERTISEMENT] ▲

CC 25 (40.2 km) **PG 252** (405.5 km) **Junction** with Pavilion Mountain Road west to Pavilion via Kelly Lake. Camping at **Downing Provincial Park** (11 miles/18 km); 25 sites, swimming, fishing. ▲

CC 25.5 (41 km) **PG 251.5** (404.7 km) **CLINTON** (pop. 729, area 4,000; elev. 2,911 feet/887m). **Visitor Information**: Available at various local businesses; look for signs. All visitor facilities are available, including 3 motels, campgrounds, gas stations, 24-hour towing and stores. Originally the site of 47 Mile Roadhouse, a gold-rush settlement on the Cariboo Wagon Road from Lillooet, today Clinton is called the "guest ranch capital of British Columbia." The museum, housed in a building of local, handmade red brick that once served as a courthouse, has fine displays of pioneer tools and items from the gold rush days, and a scale model of the Clinton Hotel. Clinton pioneer cemetery just north of town. Clinton boasts the oldest continuously held event in the province, the Clinton Ball (in May the weekend following Victoria Day), an annual event since 1868.

Clinton has its own sign forest. Visitors may sign a wooden slab (donated by the local sawmill) and add it to the sign forest.

Gold Trail RV Park. Fully serviced sites, 30-amp power. Pull-throughs. Immaculate. Washrooms with flush toilets, handicap-equipped. Free hot showers for guests. On highway in town; easy walking to all amenities. Well-lit level sites. Grassed and landscaped. Sani-station. 1640 Cariboo Highway North, Clinton, BC V0K 1K0. Phone (250) 459-2519. [ADVERTISEMENT] ♿▲

CC 31 (49.9 km) **PG 246** (395.9 km) Dirt and gravel road leads 21 miles/34 km west to **Big Bar Lake Provincial Park**; 33 campsites, water, pit toilets, firewood, swimming, fishing and boat launch. ▲

Clinton Lookout and Big Bar rest area to east just north of turnoff; toilets, tables, litter barrels.

CC 35 (56.3 km) **PG 242** (389.5 km) Loop road leads east 3 miles/5 km to Painted Chasm geological site and **Chasm Provincial Park** picnic area. This 1-mile/1.6-km-long bedrock box canyon was cut by glacial meltwaters.

CC 45 (72.4 km) **PG 232** (373.4 km) **70 MILE HOUSE** (unincorporated), originally a stage stop named for its distance from Lillooet, Mile 0. General store, post office, restaurant, motel, gas station with diesel and bus depot.

70-Mile House Motel & Restaurant. Sleeping units and kitchenettes. No pets; one no-smoking room. Motel open all year. Overnight parking for RVs. Restaurant open April 1 to November 1, from 7 A.M. to 3 P.M., closed Wednesdays. Home-cooked German and Canadian cuisine, specializing in breakfast and lunch. Home of the Buffalo Burger. Phone (250) 456-7500. [ADVERTISEMENT]

North Bonaparte Road leads east 7.5 miles/12 km to **Green Lake Provincial Park**; 121 campsites, water, toilets, firewood, dump station, swimming and boat launch. Rainbow and kokanee fishing at Green Lake. Paved road leads north to Watch Lake, east to Bonaparte Lake, and northeast to join Highway 24 at Bridge Lake. ▲

CC 58.8 (94.7 km) **PG 218.2** (351.1 km) **83 MILE HOUSE**; restaurant, gas, propane, store, public phone. Turnoff for Green Lake (7 miles/11 km).

83-Mile Ranch House & Restaurant. Home-style cooking. Specializing in Canadian and European cuisine. One of the best breakfasts along the highway. Try our delicious wiener schnitzel. Licensed premises. Enjoy our 1860 Rustic Historic site. Convenience store. Gas and diesel. RV parking $6 per night. Tenting sites available. Phone (250) 395-4372. [ADVERTISEMENT] ▲

CC 60 (96 km) **PG 217** (347.2 km) Lookout Road to forestry tower on summit of Mount Begbie (elev. 4,186 feet/1,276m); great views.

CC 66 (106.2 km) **PG 211** (339.6 km) **Junction** with Highway 24 East to Lone Butte Bridge Lake and Little Fort (60 miles/96.5 km) on Yellowhead Highway 5. Highway 24 provides access to numerous fishing lakes and resorts, including **Bridge Lake Provincial Park** (31 miles/50 km east) with 20 campsites. ▲

100 Mile House

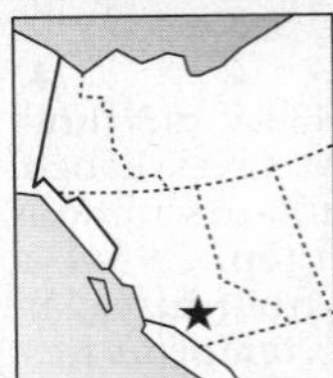

CC 72 (115.9 km) PG 205 (329.9 km) **Population:** 2,600. **Elevation:** 3,050 feet/930m. **Emergency Services: Police**, phone (250) 395-2456. **Ambulance**, phone (250) 395-3288. **Hospital**, phone (250) 395-2202. **Visitor Information:** At the log cabin by 100 Mile House Marsh (a bird sanctuary at the south edge of town); phone (250) 395-5353, fax 395-4085. Look for the 39-foot-/12-m-long skis! Contact the South Cariboo Chamber of Commerce, Box 2312, 100 Mile House, BC V0K 2E0; phone (250) 395-5353; Internet www.100mile.com/visitors; e-mail cham ber@bc.internet.net or visitors@bc.internet .net. Or visit www.cariboolinks.com/visitors guide/index.html.

This large, bustling town was once a stop for fur traders and later a post house on the Cariboo Wagon Road to the goldfields. In 1930, the Marquess of Exeter established the 15,000-acre Bridge Creek Ranch here. Today, 100 Mile House is the site of 2 lumber mills, and an extensive log home building industry.

Visitor services include restaurants, motels, a campground, gas stations with repair service, stores, a post office, 2 golf courses, a government liquor store, 2 supermarkets and banks. Shopping malls and the downtown area are located east of the highway. Centennial Park in town has picnic sites and walking trails. ▲

Horse Lake Road leads east from 100 Mile House to **Horse Lake** (kokanee) and other fishing lakes of the high plateau.

99 Mile Motel. Air-conditioned sleeping and housekeeping units. Fridges in all units, housekeeping units with microwave ovens. DD touchtone phones, remote control cable TV, super channel and TSN, courtesy in-room coffee and tea. Carports, winter plug-ins, freezer available for guests, bowling, legion; supermarket and cross-country ski trails. Senior citizens discount, commercial rates, partially wheelchair accessible, small dogs only. Highway 97, 100 Mile House, BC V0K 2E0. (250) 395-2255 (call collect), or fax (250) 395-2243. [ADVERTISEMENT] ♿

Lac La Hache offers lakeshore resorts and campgrounds, and fishing and swimming. (© Blake Hanna, staff)

West Access Route Log

(continued)

CC 74 (119 km) **PG 203** (326.7 km) **Junction** with road east to **Ruth, Canim** and **Mahood lakes**; resorts and fishing. Camping at **Canim Beach Provincial Park** (27 miles/43 km); 16 sites, water, pit toilets, swimming. Access to Canim Falls. ▲

CC 78.2 (125.8 km) **PG 198.8** (319.9 km) **108 Mile Ranch**, a recreational community built in the 1970s, was once a cattle ranch. Motel and golf course.

CC 80.5 (129.5 km) **PG 196.5** (316.2 km) Rest area to west beside 108 Mile Lake. Alongside is **108 Heritage Site** with some of the original log buildings from 108 Mile Ranch, and others relocated from 105 Mile. Guided tours; open May to early September.

CC 85 (136.8 km) **PG 192** (309 km) **Lac La Hache KOA.** Located on 60 acres of rolling ranchland 3 miles south of Lac La Hache on Highway 97. Heated swimming pool, free showers, store, laundromat, games room. Extra-long shady pull-throughs; shaded grassy tent sites; camping cabin. Full hookup facilities, sani-dump, phone. Pets welcome. VISA, MasterCard. (250) 396-4181. Box 68, Lac La Hache, BC V0K 1T0. [ADVERTISEMENT] ▲

CC 88 (141.6 km) PG 189 (304.2 km) LAC LA HACHE (pop. 400; elev. 2,749 feet/838m); motels, stores, gas stations and a museum. The community holds a fishing derby in July and a winter carnival in mid-February. Lac La Hache is French for "Ax Lake." There are many stories of how the lake got its name, but local historian Molly Forbes says it was named by a French–Canadian *coureur de bois* (voyageur) "because of a small ax he found on its shores."

Motel Lac La Hache. Motel is located directly on the lake. Each unit has a view and private access to the lake. Garden chairs, picnic tables and outside deck. Walking distance to restaurants and amenities. Kitchen units, non-smoking rooms. Cable TV. Four RV sites with full hookups. Phone or fax (250) 396-4422. Lac La Hache, BC V0K 1T0. [ADVERTISEMENT] ▲

Lac La Hache, lake char, rainbow and kokanee; good fishing summer and winter (great ice fishing).

CC 92 (148.1 km) **PG 185** (297.7 km) **Fir Crest Resort**. Open all year. Quiet park-like setting on the lakeshore, just 2 minutes from Highway 97, but away from traffic noise. Full hookups, pull-throughs, 50 amp, immaculate washrooms. Sandy beaches, swimming, groceries, sani-dump, laundry. Full marina with boat, motor, canoe, tackle rentals. *MILEPOST®* discount 10 percent. Phone (250) 396-7337. [ADVERTISEMENT] ▲

CC 93.4 (150.3 km) **PG 183.6** (295.4 km) **Kokanee Bay Motel and Campground.** Relaxation at its finest right on the lake-shore. Fish for kokanee and char or take a refreshing dip. We have a modern, comfortable motel, cabins. Full trailer hookups, grassy tenting area, hot showers, laundromat. Aquabike, boat and canoe rentals. Fishing tackle and ice. Phone (250) 396-7345. Fax (250) 396-4990. [ADVERTISEMENT] ▲

CC 96 (154.5 km) **PG 181** (291.3 km) **Crystal Springs (Historical) Resort Ltd.** Visit the Cariboo's best. We honour Good Sam, AAA and are a Good Neighbor Park. Ask about senior rates. 8 miles north of Lac La Hache. Parklike setting on lakeshore. Showers, flush toilets, laundromat, full (20- and 30-amp pull-throughs) and partial hookups, boat rentals. New chalets. Groceries, tackle, camping supplies, handicrafts. Games room, playground, picnic shelter. Pets on leash. Public beach and boat launch adjacent, fishing. Your hosts, Doug and Lorraine Whitesell. Phone (250) 396-4497. [ADVERTISEMENT] ♿▲

CC 96 (154.5 km) **PG 181** (291.3 km) **Lac La Hache Provincial Park**; 83 campsites, lakeshore picnic area, water, flush and pit toilets, firewood, dump station, boat launch, swimming, hiking trail and fishing. Camping on east side of highway, picnicking and boat launch on west side of highway. ▲

CC 97 (156.1 km) **PG 180** (289.7 km) San Jose River parallels highway to west. Canadian artist A.Y. Jackson painted in this valley.

CC 104.4 (168 km) **PG 172.6** (277.7 km) Stop of interest sign commemorating the miners, traders and adventurers who came this way to the Cariboo goldfields in the 1860s.

CC 116.6 (187.6 km) **PG 160.4** (258.1 km) 148 Mile Ducks Unlimited conservation area. This is an important waterfowl breeding area in Canada and offers good bird watching for bald eagles, osprey, great horned owls, American kestrels and pileated woodpeckers.

CC 118.5 (190.7 km) **PG 158.5** (255.1 km) **150 MILE HOUSE,** so named because it was 150 miles from Lillooet on the old Cariboo Waggon Road. The post office, which serves about 1,200 people in the area, was established in 1871. Hotel, restaurant, pub, gas station with repair service and a store open daily. Hunting and fishing licenses available at the store.

CC 119.1 (191.7 km) **PG 157.9** (254.1 km) **Junction** with road to Quesnel and Horsefly lakes. **Horsefly Lake Provincial Park** (40 miles/65 km) has 22 campsites. Fishing for rainbow and lake trout. ▲

Williams Lake

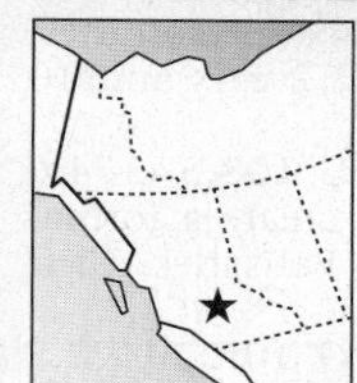

CC 128 (206 km) PG 149 (239.8 km) Located at the junction of Highway 97 and Highway 20 to Bella Coola. **Population:** 12,000. **Elevation:** 1,922 feet/586m. **Emergency Services: Police,** phone (250) 392-6211. **Hospital,** phone (250) 392-4411. **Ambulance,** phone (250) 392-5402.

Visitor Information: Visitor Infocentre located on east side of highway just south of the junction of Highways 97 and 20, open year-round; phone (250) 392-5025, fax (250) 392-4214. Write the Williams Lake Chamber of Commerce, 1148 S. Broadway, Williams Lake, BC V2G 1A2; e-mail wldcc@stardate.bc.ca. Or contact the Cariboo Chilcotin Coast Tourism Assoc., 266 Oliver St., Williams Lake, BC V2G 1M1; phone toll free (800) 663-5885.

WILLIAMS LAKE ADVERTISERS

Jamboree Motel .... Ph. (250) 398-8208
Super 8 Motel .... Ph. (800) 800-8000

Williams Lake has complete services, including hotels/motels, restaurants, an 18-hole golf course and par-3 golf course, a twin sheet arena and pool complex. Highway 97 northbound bypasses the business and shopping districts of downtown Williams Lake, which are situated to the west of the highway. Motels, gas stations and fast-food restaurants are located on frontage roads paralleling Highway 97 on the south side of town.

The famous **Williams Lake Stampede**, British Columbia's premier rodeo, is held here annually on the July 1 holiday. The 4-day event draws contestants from all over Canada and the United States. The rodeo grounds are located in the city.

At the north end of Williams Lake is Scout Island Nature Center. This island is reached by a causeway, with boardwalks providing access to the marshes. A nature house is open May to August.

Located on the shore of the lake of the same name, the town was named for Shuswap Indian Chief Willyum. It grew rapidly with the advent of the Pacific Great Eastern Railway (now B.C. Railway) in 1919, to become a major cattle marketing and shipping centre for the Cariboo–Chilcotin.

Highway 20, the Chilcotin Highway, heads west from Williams Lake 282 miles/454 km (paved and gravel) to Bella Coola. Highway 20 is logged in *Northwest Mileposts®*.

West Access Route Log

(continued)

CC 136.4 (219.5 km) **PG 140.6** (226.3 km) Wildwood Road; gas station, store, access to private campground. ▲

C 141.3 (227.3 km) **PG 135.7** (218.4 km) Turnout with litter barrel.

CC 141.8 (228.2 km) **PG 135.2** (217.6 km) **Whispering Willows Outpost Campground and Store**. RV pull-throughs, sani-dump. Power and water hookups, free hot showers, flush toilets. Level, spacious treed area for camping. Safe firepits, wood available. Play area. Confectionary store. Pets and horse trailers welcome, corrals available. Deep Creek runs by Whispering Willows Campground. RR 4, Site 12, Comp. 46, Williams Lake, BC V2G 4M8. Phone (250) 989-0359. [ADVERTISEMENT] ▲

CC 145.3 (233.9 km) **PG 131.7** (211.9 km) Turnout with litter barrel.

CC 147.8 (237.9 km) **PG 129.2** (207.9 km) Replica of a turn-of-the-century roadhouse (current status of services unknown) at junction with side road which leads west 2.5 miles/4.5km to the tiny settlement of **SODA CREEK**. The original wagon road to the goldfields ended here and miners went

the rest of the way to Quesnel by river steamboats. Soda Creek became an important transfer point for men and supplies until the railway went through in 1920. Soda Creek was so named because the creek bed is carbonate of lime and the water bubbles like soda water.

CC 155 (249.4 km) PG 122 (196.4 km) **McLEESE LAKE**, small community with gas stations, cafe, post office, store, pub, private campground and motel on McLeese Lake. The lake was named for a Fraser River steamboat skipper. **McLeese Lake**, rainbow to 2 lbs., troll using a flasher, worms or flatfish lure.

Oasis Resort. Lakefront resort overlooking beautiful McLeese Lake. Kitchenettes and sleeping units. Covered patio deck with tables and chairs. Double occupancy from $40. Serviced RV parking and camping on lakeshore. Firepits, washrooms, coin showers. Boat launch and rentals. Private dock. 6557 Highway 97, McLeese Lake, BC. Phone (250) 297-6447. Fax (250) 297-6279. [ADVERTISEMENT]

Junction with road to Beaver Lake and on to Likely. Historic **Quesnelle Forks**, a heritage site with a Forestry campsite, is located near Likely. Travelers may continue north from Likely to Barkerville and rejoin Highway 97 at Quesnel.

CC 155.5 (250.2 km) PG 121.5 (195.5 km) Rest area to west overlooking McLeese Lake.

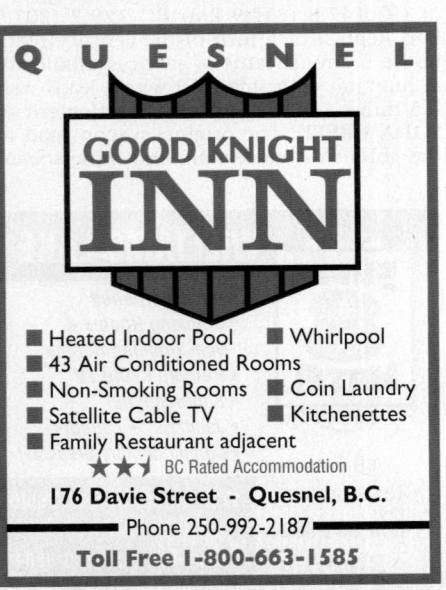

CC 155.7 (250.6 km) PG 121.3 (195.2 km) **McLeese Lake Resort.** Camping on the lake! Newly renovated lakefront sleeping and housekeeping units. Satellite TV. Lakeside camping. Full hookup and pull-through, group sites; coin showers, firepits, large lawns, horseshoes, swimming, fishing, boat rental/launch, ice, major credit cards, pets, internet access. Rex and Maj Sutherland. Phone (250) 297-6525. Fax (250) 297-6531. [ADVERTISEMENT]

CC 160 (257.5 km) PG 117 (188.3 km) Turnout with litter barrel to west with plaque about Fraser River paddle-wheelers.

CC 164 (263.9 km) PG 113 (181.8 km) **Cariboo Wood Shop.** A gift shop you must stop at. We specialize in Canadian-made gifts and souvenirs. Our woodshop produces quality furniture and accessories. Also many other great gifts—pottery, wheat weaving, art calendars, note pads, easy listening music on tapes and CDs—to name a few. Best of all our famous homemade fudge. 20 flavors to choose from: Maple nut, amaretto, Heavenly Goo and many more! Ask for a free taste. 16 flavors of sugar-free candy. Come in for a visit and treat yourself to a relaxing atmosphere and friendly staff. Easy access drive-through loop for every size of RV. Open 7 days a week 8:30 A.M.–5:30 P.M. Groups welcome. Phone (800) 986-WOOD. [ADVERTISEMENT]

CC 166 (267 km) PG 111 (178.6 km) Glass sculpture museum and rock shop.

the Castle. See display ad this section.

CC 166.5 (267.9 km) PG 110.5 (177.8 km) Marguerite rest area. View upriver to Marguerite reaction cable ferry across the Fraser River. Ferry crossing takes 10 minutes, operates 7 A.M. to 6:45 P.M.; 2 cars and 10 passengers, no charge.

CC 168.5 (271.2 km) PG 108.5 (174.6 km) Basalt columns to east create a formation known as the Devil's Palisades. Cliff swallows nest in the columns.

CC 169.8 (273.2 km) PG 107.2 (172.5 km) Stone cairn commemorates **Fort Alexandria**, the last North West Co. fur-trading post established west of the Rockies, built in 1821. The actual site of the fort is across the river. Cairn also marks the approximate farthest point reached by Alexander Mackenzie in his descent of the Fraser in 1793.

CC 180 (289.7 km) PG 97 (156.1 km) Australian rest area to west with toilets, tables and litter barrels. Private campground to east.

CC 188.5 (303.4 km) PG 88.5 (142.4 km) Kersley (unincorporated), gas and food.

CC 188.6 (303.6 km) PG 88.4 (142.3 km) Restaurant, gas and private campground.

CC 195.8 (315.1 km) PG 81.2 (130.6 km) **Dragon Lake Golf Course & Campsite.** Situated on edge of Dragon Lake. RV and campsites at $10 per night. Flush toilets, showers, sani-dump, wharf, trout fishing. Located off Hwy 97 just 10 minutes south of city centre. 9-hole golf course with driving range. Snack bar, lounge. Campers register at golf club pro shop. Phone (250) 747-1358. 1692 Flint Avenue, Quesnel, BC, V2J 4R8. [ADVERTISEMENT]

CC 196 (315.4 km) PG 81 (130.4 km) South end of loop road east to **Dragon Lake**, a small, shallow lake popular with Quesnel families. Camping and fishing for rainbow.

CC 196 (315.4 km) PG 81 (130.4 km) **Robert's Roost Campsite** located 6 km south of Quesnel and 2 km east of Highway 97 in a parklike setting on beautiful Dragon Lake. Partial and fully serviced. 15- and 30-amp service. Sani-dump, fishing, boat rental, swimming, horseshoes, playground, shower$, flush toilets and laundromat. E-mail access. Can accommodate any length unit. Limited accommodation. Approved by Tourism BC. Close to golfing. Hosts: Bob and Vivian Wurm, 3121 Gook Road, Quesnel, BC V2J 4K7. Phone (250) 747-2015 or (888) 227-8877; RobertsRoost@bcadventure.com. [ADVERTISEMENT]

CC 197.5 (317.8 km) PG 79.5 (127.9 km) **Valhalla Motel.** Quietly situated at the top of Dragon Hill. All rooms have air conditioning, individual electric heat, colour televisions, direct dial telephones, queen beds, refrigerators. Nonsmoking rooms available. Complimentary coffee. Guest laundry. Winter plug-ins. Close to fairgrounds, recreation centre, racing oval, shopping centre. Senior discount. Pets welcome. Major credit cards. 2010 Valhalla Rd., Quesnel, BC V2J 4C1. Toll-free 1-888-843-8922, or e-mail Valhalla@quesnelbc.com. See display ad this section. [ADVERTISEMENT]

Quesnel

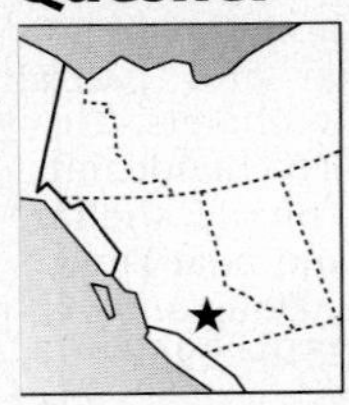

CC 203 (326.7 km) PG 74 (119.1 km). Located at the confluence of the Fraser and Quesnel rivers. **Population:** 10,000. **Elevation:** 1,789 feet/545m. **Emergency Services:** Emergency only, phone 911. **RCMP**, phone (250) 992-9211. **Ambulance**, phone (250) 992-3211. **Hospital**, phone (250) 992-2181.

Visitor Information: Located on the west side of the highway just north of Quesnel River bridge, in LeBourdais Park. Open year-round. Write Quesnel Visitor Infocentre, Stn. A, 703 Carson Ave., Quesnel, BC V2J 2B6; phone (250) 992-8716, or toll free (800) 992-4922. For information on the Cariboo Tourist Region, contact the Cariboo Tourist Assoc., P.O. Box 4900, Williams

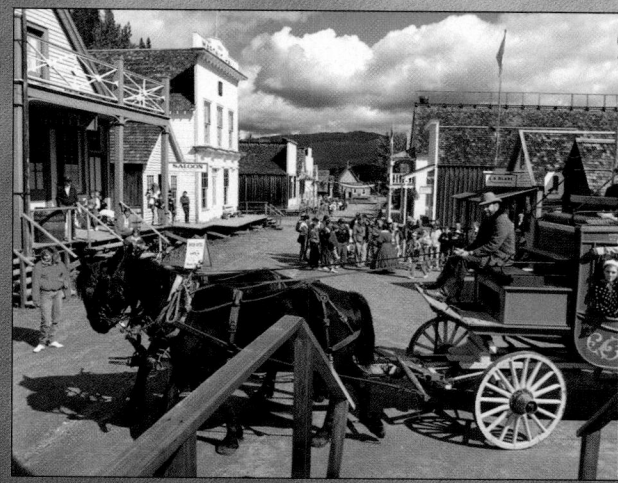

Highway 26 to Barkerville

This 51-mile/82-km paved road leads to Barkerville Historic Town in the Cariboo gold fields (active mining under way). Gas available in Wells.

The Barkerville gold strike was made in 1861. Today, Highway 16 follows the route of the original Cariboo wagon road built to serve the boom towns.

Distance from Highway 97 junction (J) is shown.

J 0 Junction with Highway 97 at **Milepost CC 206.** Visitor Infocentre on southeast side of junction.

J 0.8 (1.3 km) Barlow Creek residential area; grocery, food and fuel. Eastbound, Highway 26 accesses local roads. Watch for deer.

J 13 (21 km) Rest area and interpretive trails to south. Wooden rail "snake" and wire fences with wooden top rail allow deer and moose to safely jump them, while penning domestic livestock.

J 15.2 (24.5 km) Cottonwood River bridge. The river is named for the black cottonwood trees growing alongside it.

J 16.7 (26.9 km) **Cottonwood House Historic Site**, a restored and furnished log roadhouse built in 1864. Gift shop, coffee shop, picnicking and guided tours by costumed docents. Open May to September.

J 20.1 (32.4 km) Swift River Forest Road leads 0.2 mile/0.3 km to Lightning Creek Forest Service recreation site (first turn on left); free camping, 14-day limit. *CAUTION: Active logging road, drive with headlights on.* ▲

J 21.4 (34.5 km) Lover's Leap viewpoint and Mexican Hill Summit, one of the steepest grades on the original Cariboo Waggon Road, to the south.

J 27.1 (43.6 km) Historical stop of interest marker for Charles Morgan Blessing's grave. Blessing, from Ohio, was murdered on his way to Barkerville in 1866. His killer, John Barry, was caught when he gave Blessing's keepsake gold nugget stickpin, in the shape of a skull, to a Barkerville dance-hall girl. John Barry was the only white man hanged in the Cariboo during the gold rush.

J 37.3 (60.1 km) Stanley Road and Boulder Gold Mines (active claim). Stanley Road is a 1.9-mile/3-km loop road that leads past the gold-rush ghost towns of Stanley and Van-Winkle, the old Lightning Hotel, and gold rush-era gravesites. A worthwhile sidetrip.

J 38.6 (62.2 km) Stanley (Loop) Road, Chisholm Creek. Remnants of Stanley townsite and cemetery dating back to 1800's. The authentic Stanley Trail leads from the townsite through the remnants of Van Winkle, ending at the Richfield Courthouse in Barkerville.

J 40.2 (64.7 km) Devil's Canyon paved turnout to south. This was the highest point on the Cariboo Waggon Road.

J 42.9 (69 km) Slough Creek, site of much hydraulic mining activity after Joe Shaw discovered gold here in 1870.

J 44.9 (72.2 km) Paved turnout to litter barrel to south. **Jack o' Clubs Lake**; fishing for rainbows, lake trout and Dolly Varden.

J 45.2 (72.7 km) Rest area on peninsula to south with picnic tables, pit toilets and boat launch.

J 45.7 (73.6 km) Paved turnout with litter barrels to south.

J 46.1 (74.2 km) Lakeshore turnout with area information sign.

J 46.7 (75.2 km) **WELLS** (pop. 300, elevation 4,200 feet/1280m) was built in the 1930s when the Cariboo Gold Quartz Mine, promoted and developed by Fred Wells, brought hundreds of workers to this valley. The mine closed in 1967, but this quaint town has continued as a service centre and attraction for tourists, with numerous art galleries and gift shops, some housed in refurbished buildings from the 1930's.

Guided and self-guided tours of the town are available. Shuttle bus service is available to nearby Barkerville Historic Town and to Quesnel. The local museum has displays of local mining history and visitor information; it's open daily from June to September.

Recreation in the area is centered around an extensive system of marked trails leading into alpine country. Adventure tour operators in Wells offer guided trips into the backcountry. Summer activities include fishing, hiking historical trails, mountain biking and gold panning. In winter, trails are groomed for skiing, snowmobiling and dogsledding. A snowmobile hill climb is held in March at Mount Agnes, a popular spot for extreme sports enthusiasts.

J 49.6 (79.8 km) Barkerville Provincial Park Forest Rose Campground to north. Lowhee Campground to south; 170 campsites, picnic areas and dump stations. ▲

J 50 (80.5 km) Gravel road leads north 18 miles/29 km to **Bowron Lakes Provincial Park**, noted for its interconnecting chain of

lakes and the resulting 72-mile/116-km canoe circuit which takes from 7 to 10 days to complete. Visitor information available at registration centre next to main parking lot where canoeists must register and pay circuit fees. Reservations recommended in July and August (required for 7 or more people); phone (250) 992-3111.

Airfield at junction, 2,500-foot/762-m paved runway, elev. 4,180 feet/1,274m.

There are 2 private lodges at the north end of the lake with restaurants, camping, a general store and canoe rentals. Provincial park campground has 25 sites, water, pit toilets, firewood and a boat launch. Swimming, fishing, canoeing, kayaking and hiking.

J 50.1 (80.7 km) Entrance to Barkerville; admission charged. Price for a 2-day pass: Adults $7.50; seniors $5; youth $4.50; children $2; and families $17.

J 50.3 (81.7 km) Former site of Cameronton, named for John A. "Cariboo" Cameron who found gold in this area. Also in this area is Williams Creek, the richest gold-producing creek during the gold rush.

J 50.9 (81.9 km) Turnoff on 1.8-mile/2.9-km side road for gold rush cemetery and Government Hill Campground (0.2 mile/0.4 km), New Barkerville (0.4 mile/0.7 km) and Grubstake Store (0.7 mile/1.1 km).

J 51 (82.1 km) **BARKERVILLE**, a provincial historic town; open year-round, phone (250) 994-3302. Visitor information at Reception Centre.

Barkerville was named for miner Billy Barker, who struck gold on Williams Creek. The resulting gold rush in 1862 created Barkerville. Virtually a ghost town when the provincial government began restoration in 1958, today Barkerville's buildings and boardwalks are faithful restorations or reconstructions from the town's heyday. Visitors can pan for gold, shop at the old-time general store, watch a blacksmith at work, or take in a show at the Theatre Royal. Restaurants and food service available. It is best to visit between June 1 and Labour Day, when the Theatre Royal offers performances and all exhibits are open.

The Theatre Royal is extremely popular with visitors. The hour-long show plays daily except Fridays in summer at 1 P.M.. Admission is charged.

History comes alive at Barkerville thanks to interpreters and street performers who represent actual citizens of the town in 1870, discuss "current" events with visitors, conduct tours and stage daily dramas throughout the summer.

Beyond Main Street, the Cariboo Waggon Road leads on (for pedestrians only) to Richfield, 1 mile/1.6 km, to the courthouse of "Hanging" Judge Begbie.

Return to Milepost CC 206
West Access Route

Lake, BC V2G 2V8; phone toll free (800) 663-5885.

Quesnel (kwe NEL) began as a supply town for the miners in the gold rush of the 1860s. The city was named after the Quesnel River, which in turn was named after fur trader Jules Maurice Quesnel, a member of Simon Fraser's 1808 expedition down the Fraser River and later a political figure in Quebec. Today, forestry is the dominant economic force in Quesnel, with 2 pulp mills, a plywood plant, and 5 sawmills and planer mills. Check with the Tourist Infocentre about tours.

Accommodations include 4 hotels, 15 motels, 5 bed and breakfasts and 8 campgrounds. There are gas stations (with diesel and propane), 2 shopping malls and 45 restaurants offering everything from fast food to fine dining. Golf and a recreation centre with pool are available.

QUESNEL ADVERTISERS

Billy Barker Casino Hotel	Ph. (888) 992-4255
City of Quesnel	Ph. (800) 992-4922
Country Haven Family Restaurant	Ph. (250) 992-9654
Good Knight Inn, The	Ph. (250) 992-2187
Quesnel & District Museum and Archives	Adjacent Infocentre
Ramada Limited	Ph. (800) 663-1581
Talisman Inn	Ph. (250) 992-7247
Tower Inn	Ph. (800) 663-2009
Valhalla Motel	Ph. (250) 747-1111

Visitors can take a walking tour of the city along the **Riverfront Park** trail system. The 3.1-mile/5-km north Quesnel trail starts at Ceal Tingley Park at the confluence of the Fraser and Quesnel rivers. The west Quesnel trail is a 2.7-mile/4.3-km walk through a residential area. Trail information is available at the Visitor Infocentre.

There are some interesting hoodoo formations and scenic canyon views at nearby **Pinnacles Provincial Park**, 5 miles/8 km west of Highway 97; picnicking. It is a 1.1-mile/1.8-km walk round-trip from the parking area to the pinnacle viewpoints.

Quesnel offers gold panning tours, guided hiking tours and Voyager canoe trips on the Fraser River. Boat tours are also available on other area rivers. Contact the Visitor Infocentre for more information.

A worthwhile side trip is Highway 26, which intersects Highway 97 at **Milepost CC 206** (see facing page). This paved highway leads to Wells, Bowron Lake and **Barkerville**

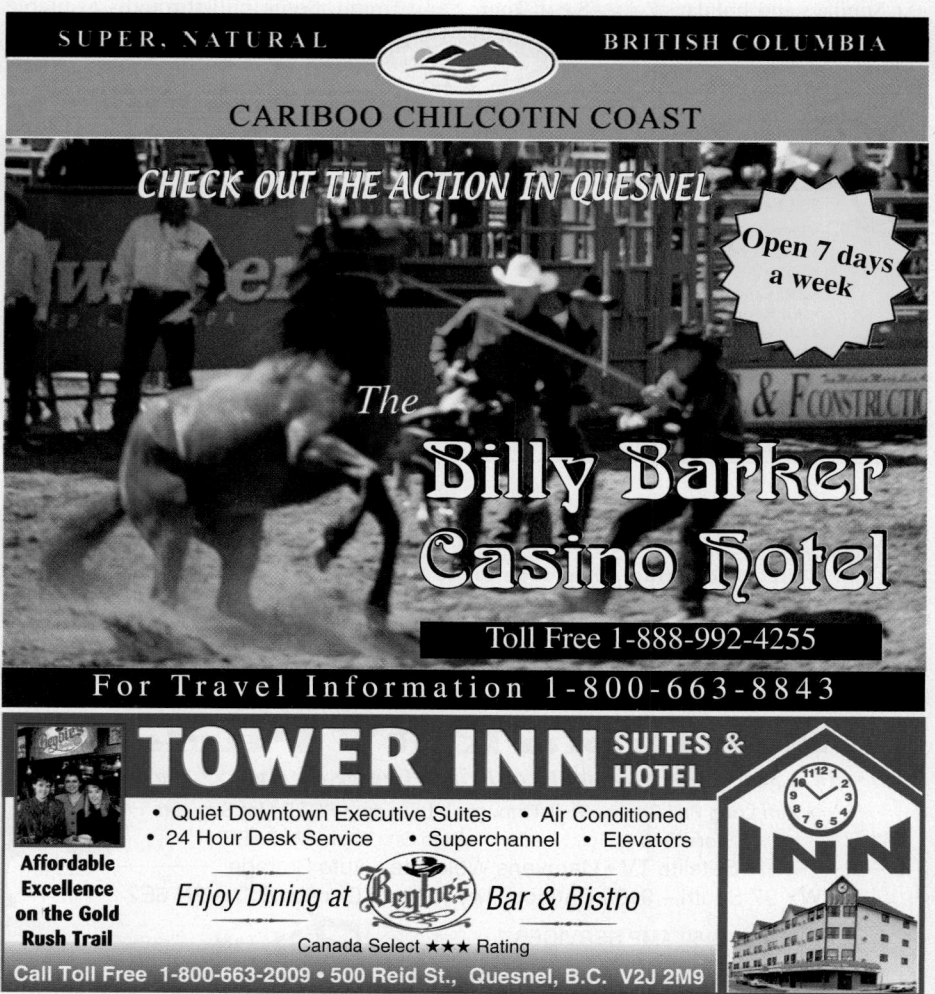

Provincial Historic Park, a reconstructed and restored Cariboo gold rush town. Gold Pan City Stage Lines offers charter and scheduled tours of Barkerville and surrounding area from Quesnel.

Billy Barker Days, a 4-day event held the third full weekend in July, commemorates the discovery of gold at Barkerville in 1862. Held in conjunction with the Quesnel Rodeo, Billy Barker Days is the third largest outdoor family festival in the province. For more information, write Box 4441, Quesnel, BC V2J 3J4.

Quesnel & District Museum and Archives. The best-kept secret in the Cariboo. Exhibits from farming, logging and mining. Artifacts used by our pioneers in their homes. Coins from all over the world; 1911 White car; a famous Centennial quilt. First Nations exhibit and a collection of some of the rarest Chinese artifacts found in western Canada. Mystery surrounds our museum with Mandy, our "haunted doll," and for a chuckle and a smile see the 80-year-old prophylactic. Considered one of the top 10 British Columbia museums! Admission fee $2 per person; 12 and under free. Located across from BC Rail amongst the famous rose garden and adjacent to the Tourist Information Centre on Highway 97. Open year-round. Phone 1-250-992-9580. [ADVERTISEMENT]

Country Haven Family Restaurant. Home-style cooking. Breakfast served all day. Fully licensed. Located 1/2-block from Quesnel Tourist Infocentre on Highway 97 North (490 Carson Ave.). Open year-round. Summer hours Monday–Saturday 6 A.M.–9 P.M. Sundays and holidays 7 A.M.–8 P.M. Tour groups welcome. Please phone ahead. (250) 992-9654. [ADVERTISEMENT]

Mary's Gifts. Unique collectibles. Canadian pottery and hand-crafted gifts, linens. Official Bradford exchange dealer. Aston Drake Dolls, Canadian Seagull Pewter. Licensed Ty dealer. Beanie Babies. Jewellery. Music boxes, cards and stationery. Framed prints. bath products, candles and accessories. Easy access; parking lot adjacent. Located in the heart of downtown Quesnel. #102–246 St. Laurent Ave. (250) 992-2959. [ADVERTISEMENT]

West Access Route Log

(continued)

CC 206 (331.5 km) **PG 71** (114.3 km) Quesnel airport.

Junction with Highway 26 to Wells, Barkerville and Bowron Lake. See HIGHWAY 26 TO BARKERVILLE beginning on page 68.

CC 209.5 (337.2 km) **PG 67.5** (108.6 km) **Lazy Daze Resort.** RV sites, cabins and tenting only 3 minutes off highway. Pull-throughs, hookups. 30 amp service. Free hot showers for guests. Located on Ten Mile Lake; boat rentals, convenience store, laundry, play area and picnic shelter. (250) 992-3282. RR8, Box 29, Best site, Quesnel, BC, V2J 5E6. [ADVERTISEMENT] ▲

CC 210 (338 km) **PG 67** (107.8 km) Paved side road leads 0.6 mile/1 km 10 Mile Lake Provincial Park (description follows).

10 Mile Lake Provincial Park. Clean, friendly park, on paved kilometer from Highway 97. Quiet, treed sites with table and firepit. Some pull-throughs available. Coin-operated hot showers. Security gates closed 11 P.M.–7 A.M. 30 kms of hiking and maintained mountain bike trails. Playground. Only one hour to Barkerville. [ADVERTISEMENT] ▲

Good fishing for rainbow to 3 lbs.

CC 214.2 (344.7 km) **PG 62.8** (101.1 km) Cottonwood River bridge. Turnout with litter barrels and stop-of-interest sign at south end of bridge describing railway bridge seen upriver.

CC 218.7 (352 km) **PG 58.3** (93.8 km) Hush Lake rest area to west; toilets, tables, litter barrels.

CC 226 (363.7 km) **PG 51** (82 km) **Cinema 2nd Hand.** General store, groceries. Movie rentals, souvenirs. Local artwork, circle drive. 9 A.M.–9 P.M. every day. Free camping, picnic tables, firepits and wood, toilet, some long pull-throughs, some shady sites, fireworks, phone. Welcome to friendly Cinema, BC. Vic and Theresa Olson, RR 1 Box 1, Site 10, Hixon, BC V0K 1S0. (250) 998-4774. [ADVERTISEMENT] ▲

CC 229.6 (369.5 km) **PG 47.4** (76.3 km) Strathnaver (unincorporated), no services.

CC 241 (387.8 km) **PG 36** (58 km) **HIXON** (pop. 1,500) has a post office, 2 motels, gas stations, grocery stores, 2 restaurants (1 with licensed premises), a pub and private campground. Hixon is the Cariboo's most northerly community. Extensive placer mining took place here in the early 1900s. Southbound motorists watch for roadside display about points of interest in the Cariboo region located just north of Hixon. ▲

Paradise Motel. Sleeping and kitchenette units. Combination baths. Satellite TV. Quiet creekside setting. Near stores and food services. Singles from $38; doubles from $45. Ask about our senior and off-season rates. Major credit cards. Pets welcome. Phone (250) 998-4685. 270 Colgrove Road, Box 456, Hixon, BC V0K 1S0. [ADVERTISEMENT]

CC 247.6 (398.5 km) **PG 29.4** (47.3 km) Woodpecker rest area to west; toilets, tables, litter barrels.

CC 257.7 (414.7 km) **PG 19.3** (31 km) Stoner (unincorporated), no services.

CC 258.3 (415.7 km) **PG 18.7** (30.1 km) **Fraser River RV Park.** See display ad this

section. ▲

CC 261.8 (421.3 km) **PG 15.2** (24.5 km) Red Rock (unincorporated); ice; gas station with diesel; pay phone.

CC 268.3 (431.8 km) **PG 8.7** (14 km) **Bee Lazee RV Park, Campground & Honey Farm.** See display ad this section. ▲

CC 270.6 (435.5 km) **PG 6.4** (10.3 km) **Junction** with bypass road to Yellowhead 16 East. Keep left for Prince George; continue straight ahead for Jasper and Edmonton. If you are headed east on Yellowhead Highway 16 for Jasper or Edmonton, turn to **Milepost E 450** in the YELLOWHEAD HIGHWAY 16 section and read the log back to front.

CC 273 (439.3 km) **PG 4** (6.4 km) **Southpark RV Park.** See display ad this section. ▲

CC 273.4 (440 km) **PG 3.6** (5.8 km) Access to Prince George airport to east.

CC 274 (440.9 km) **PG 3** (4.8 km) **Sintich Trailer Park.** See display ad this section. ▲

CC 275.2 (442.8 km) **PG 1.8** (2.8 km) Bridge over the Fraser River. Turn right at north end of bridge then left at stop sign for city centre via Queensway. This is the easiest access for Fort George Park; follow Queensway to 20th Avenue and turn east.

Continue straight ahead for Highway 16 entrance to city.

CC 276 (444.1 km) **PG 1** (1.6 km) **Junction** of Highway 97 with Yellowhead 16 West. Description of Prince George follows.

If you are headed west on Yellowhead Highway 16 for Prince Rupert, turn to **Milepost PG 0** in the YELLOWHEAD HIGHWAY 16 section. Prince Rupert is port of call for Alaska state ferries and BC Ferries.

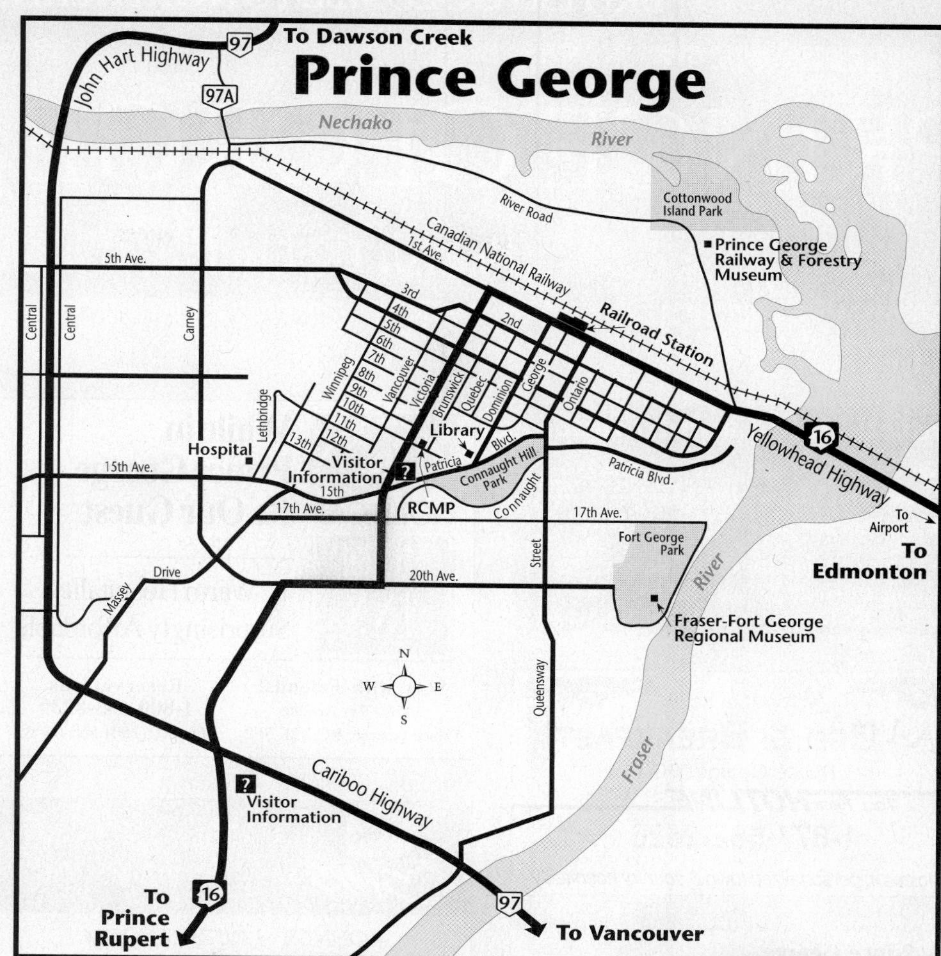

Prince George

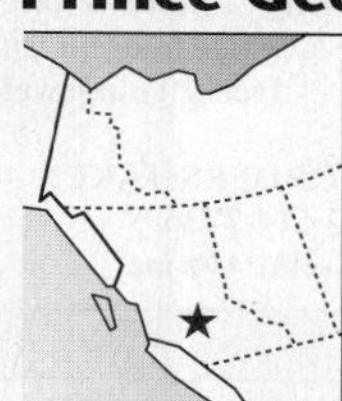

CC 277 (445.8 km) **Population:** 76,500, area 160,000. **Emergency Services: RCMP**, phone (250) 562-3371, emergency only, phone 911. **Fire Department**, phone 911. **Ambulance**, 24-hour service, phone 911. **Poison Control Centre**, phone (250) 565-2442. **Hospital**, Prince George Regional, phone (250) 565-2000; emergency, phone (250) 565-2444.

Visitor Information: Tourism Prince George & Area, Dept. MP, 1198 Victoria St., phone (250) 562-3700 or fax 563-3584, or toll free (800) 668-7646. Open year-round, 8:30 A.M. to 5 P.M. weekdays Monday through Saturday. Visitor centre, junction Yellowhead 16 and Highway 97; open daily late-May to Labour Day, phone (250) 563-5493.

Elevation: 1,868 feet/569m. **Climate:** The inland location is tempered by the protection of mountains. The average annual frost-free period is 85 days, with 1,793 hours of bright sunshine. Dry in summer; chinooks off and on during winter which, accompanied by a western flow of air, break up the cold weather. Summer temperatures average 72°F/22°C with lows to 46°F/8°C. **Radio:** CKPG 550, CJCI 620, BC-FM 94.3, CBC-FM 91.5, C-101 FM. **Television:** 36 channels via cable. **Newspaper:** *The Citizen* (daily except Sunday); *Prince George This Week* (Sunday and Thursday); *Free Press* (Thursday and Sunday).

Description

Prince George is located at the confluence of the Nechako and Fraser rivers, near the geographical centre of British Columbia. It is the fourth largest city in British Columbia. Hub of the trade and travel routes of the province, Prince George is located at the junction of Yellowhead Highway 16—linking Prince Rupert on the west coast with

PRINCE GEORGE & AREA

British Columbia, Canada

Dutch Maid Laundromat

- Shower
- 100% Soft Water
- Drop Off Laundry Service
- Open 8 am: last wash @ 8:45 pm

2930 5th Avenue (5th & Harper)
Prince George, BC Phone 564-1260
(3 BLOCKS OFF Highway 97 on 5th Ave.)

A-1 BED & BREAKFAST

Prince George, BC

TOLL FREE **HOTLINE**

1-877-562-2626

Choices in personalized town & country hospitality

Prince George Railway & Forestry Museum

Enjoy a "Hands-on" All Aboard Experience

See Vintage Railway Cars and Locomotives, Fire Engines, Forestry and Industrial Heritage and more.

• Park Setting • Visitor Centre • Gift Shop
• Family Picnic Area • Ample Parking

850 River Road, Prince George, BC
Ph: (250) 563-7351 Fax: (250) 563-7337
Visit us at www.pgrfm.bc.ca

Experience It!

Local, Regional & National Artists

2820 15th Avenue
(250) 563-6447 or 1-888-221-1155

While in Prince George Be Our Guest

Warm Hospitality
Surprisingly Affordable

Stay with Friends!
1458 - 7th Avenue
Prince George, BC V2L 3P2

Reservations
1-800-663-8239
Phone: (250) 563-0666

Esther's INN

A Tropical Oasis in Northern BC

LOUNGE • DINING ROOM
COFFEE GARDEN • SWIMMING POOL

Jacuzzis • Sauna • Waterslides
132 Air Conditioned Units
Health and Fitness Club • In-House Movies

1151 Commercial Drive
Prince George, BC V2M 6W6
Toll Free 1-800-663-6844
Ph: 250-562-4131 Fax: 250-562-4145

Grama's Inn Ltd.

An Annex to Esther's Inn

- 60 air conditioned units
- 40 completely renovated
- New Lobby and Hospitality Room

Reservations for Grama's New Warmth & Comfort
toll-free 1-877-563-7174
Ph: (250) 563-7174 / Fax: (250) 563-7147
901 Central Street, Prince George, BC V2M 3C8

Centrally located at 10th Ave off Highway 97

RESTAURANT & BREWPUB

Located in one of Prince George's Landmark Heritage Buildings

LUNCH • BRUNCH • DINNER
For Reservations Call - 564-7100
Brunswick St. & 6th. Downtown, near major hotels

Prince George Native Art Gallery

TRADITIONAL & CONTEMPORARY NATIVE ARTS

carvings - prints & original works of art - handcrafted leather work - silver & gold jewellery

- CUSTOM ORDERS TAKEN -
250-614-7726
1600 - 3rd Avenue

BALDY HUGHES ADVENTURELAND

Open 7 days a week, year round

• Pub/Restaurant • Rooms • Gas • Diesel
• Store • Campground • Showers
• Laundromat • Hiking • Fishing • Much More

Located 27 kms west off Hwy 16 on Blackwater Rd, Prince George, BC

Phone: 250-964-3137 or 250-964-0766
Fax: 250-964-3137
www.baldyhughes.com
baldyhughes-lifestyles@telus.net

ANCO MOTEL

- 65 comfortable rooms
- kitchenettes • affordable rates
- free phones • Cable TV
- heated pool (seasonal)
- movie channels • laundry

Call (250) 563-3671
1-800-663-3290 (BC only)

1630 Central Street
(on Hwy 97)

DOWNTOWN MOTEL

• 45 Comfortable Rooms • Air Conditioning
• Cable TV W/Remote • Movies
• Direct Dial Phones • Winter Plug-ins
Phone (250) 563-9241
BC Toll Free 1-800-663-5729
650 Dominion St., Prince George, BC V2L 1T8

Econo Lodge

1915 Third Avenue,
Prince George, BC V2M 1G6
Phone: 250-563-7106
Fax: 250-561-7216
1-888-566-6333

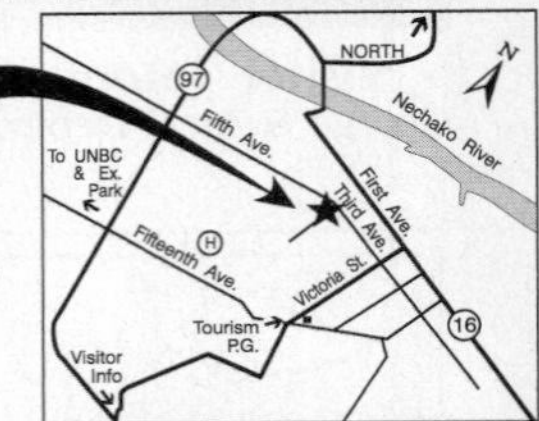

For Information Contact: Tourism Prince George & Area, 1198 Victoria Street, Prince George, BC V2L 2L2
Phone: (250) 562-3700 Fax: (250) 563-3584 1-800-668-7646 e-mail: information@tourismpg.bc.ca

Connaught Hill Park offers flower gardens and a view of Prince George. (© Earl L. Brown, staff)

the Interior of Canada—and Highway 97, which runs south to Vancouver and north to Dawson Creek.

In the early 1800s, Simon Fraser of the North West Trading Co. erected a post here which he named Fort George in honour of the reigning English monarch. In 1906, survey parties for the transcontinental Grand Trunk Pacific Railway (later Canadian National Railways) passed through the area, and with the building of the railroad a great land boom took place. The city was incorporated in 1915 under the name Prince George. Old Fort George is now a park and picnic spot and the site of Fort George Museum.

Prince George is primarily an industrial centre, fairly dependent on the lumber industry, with 3 pulp mills, sawmills, planers, dry kilns, a plywood plant and 2 chemical plants to serve the pulp mills. Oil refining, mining and heavy construction are other major area industries. The Prince George Forest Region is the largest in the province.

Prince George is the focal point of the central Interior for financial and professional services, equipment and wholesale firms, machine shops and many services for the timber industry. One of Canada's newest universities opened here in the fall of 1994. The campus of the University of Northern British Columbia is located at the top of Cranbrook Hill.

Agriculture in central British Columbia is basically a forage-livestock business, for which the climate and soils are well suited. Dairying and beef are the major livestock enterprises, with minor production in sheep and poultry.

Lodging & Services

Prince George offers 5 hotels, 17 motels, 9 RV parks, and more than 3 dozen bed and breakfasts. Most accommodations are within easy reach of the business district. There are more than 80 restaurants in the city. Most stores are open 7 days a week. The usual hours of operation are: Sunday, noon to 5 P.M.; Saturday and Monday through Wednesday, 9:30 A.M. to 6 P.M.; Thursday and Friday, 9:30 A.M. to 9 P.M.

Transportation

Air: Prince George airport is southeast of the city, serviced by Canadian Airlines International, Air BC and Central Mountain Air. Limousine service to and from the airport.

Railroad: VIA Rail connects Prince George with Prince Rupert and Jasper, AB. Passenger service south to Vancouver via British Columbia Railway.

Bus: Greyhound. City bus service by Prince George Transit & Charter Ltd.

Attractions

City Landmarks: Centennial Fountain at the corner of 7th Avenue and Dominion

Prince George Railway Museum features 50 pieces of rolling stock. (© Blake Hanna, staff)

Street depicts the early history of Prince George in mosaic tile. A cairn at Fort George Park commemorates Sir Alexander Mackenzie.

Connaught Hill Park offers colorful flower gardens and a panoramic view of the city. Follow Connaught Drive to the park.

The Prince George Art Gallery showcases local, regional and national artists. Prince George's foremost cultural attraction will occupy a new location downtown in the Civic Centre Plaza in July 2000.

Fraser Fort George Regional Museum. Located in Fort George Park at 333 20th Avenue, the museum includes an explorations gallery focusing on the region's natural history and environment. A history hall provides an overview of the area's developmental history and includes an interactive multimedia film display. Open daily in summer, 10 A.M. to 5 P.M. Wheelchair accessible. Admission fee charged. For more information phone (250) 562-1612. ♿

Giscome Portage Regional Park, next to the scenic Fraser River, includes the Huble Homestead, which dates from 1912. These original and reconstructed buildings are surrounded by grazing land and forest. Picnic tables and snackbar. Guided interpretive tours during peak season; admission free. Located north of Prince George on Highway 97; turn east off the highway at **Milepost PG 26.9** and drive 3.7 miles/ 6 km.

Fort George Park is the largest park in Prince George and a good stop for travelers with its playgrounds, picnic tables, barbecue facilities and museum. The Fort George Railway operates on weekends and holidays at the park from a railway building patterned after the original Grand Trunk Pacific stations.

Cottonwood Island Park, located on the Nechako River (see city map), has picnic facilities and extensive nature trails.

Prince George Railway and Forestry Museum features a dozen original railway buildings, including 2 stations. Among the 50 pieces of rolling stock are 5 locomotives, a 1903 snow plow, a 1913 100-ton steam wrecking crane and a 90-foot 100-ton turntable. Items from 8 past and present railway companies are displayed. There is also a small collection of forestry, mining and agricultural machinery. Located at 850 River Road next to Cottonwood Island Nature Park. Open May to September daily from 9:30 A.M. to 5 P.M. For more information phone (250) 563-7351.

Golf Courses. Aspen Grove Golf Club is 9 miles/14.5 km south of the city; Yellowhead Grove Golf Club, Pine Valley Golf Club, and Prince George Golf and Curling Club are on Yellowhead Highway 16 West. Aberdeen Glen Golf Club, Prince George's newest golf course, is on Highway 97 North.

Swimming. Four Seasons Swimming Pool at the corner of 7th Avenue and Dominion Street has a pool, water slide, diving tank and fitness centre. Open to the public afternoons and evenings. Or check out the new Aquatic Centre at 1770 Munroe Street. It's equipped with a leisure-style wave pool and a 10-metre diving tower.

Rockhounding. The hills and river valleys in the area provide abundant caches of Omineca agate and Schmoos. For more information, contact Prince George Rock and Gem Club, phone (250) 562-4526; or Spruce City Rock and Gem Club, phone (250) 562-1013.

Tennis Courts. A total of 20 courts currently available to the public at 3 places: 20th Avenue near the entrance to Fort George Park; at Massey Drive in Carrie Jane Gray Park; and on Ospika Boulevard in the Lakewood Secondary School complex.

Industrial Tours are available from mid-May through August by contacting Tourism Prince George at (250) 562-3700. Tours, which are on weekdays only, include Northwood Pulp and Timber, Prince George Sawmill and North Central Plywoods. Tours of Prince George Pulp and Intercon Pulp are available June–August, Monday–Friday; reservations required.

Tours of the Pacific Western Brewery are available; reservations required. Phone (250) 562-2424 or (800) 663-8002, Monday through Friday.

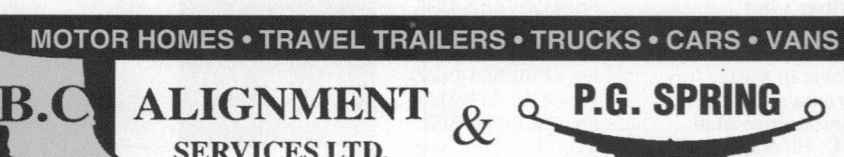

Special Events: Elks May Day celebration; Forest Expo in May (even years); rodeo in June; Canada Day (July 1) celebration, Fort George Park; Ol' Sawmill Bluegrass Jamboree in July; Annual Sandblast Skiing, Prince George Exhibition and Summerfest in August; Oktoberfest in October; Studio Fair in November; and Mardi Gras Winter Festival in February. Details on these and other events are available from Tourism Prince George & Area; phone (250) 562-3700.

Side Trips: Prince George is the starting point for some of the finest holiday country in the province. There are numerous lakes and resorts nearby, among them: Bednesti Lake, 30 miles/48 km west of Prince George; Cluculz Lake, 44 miles/71 km west; Purden Lake, 42 miles/68 km east; and Tabor Lake, 6 miles/10 km east.

AREA FISHING: Highways 16 and 97 are the ideal routes for the sportsman, with year-round fishing and easy access to lakes and rivers. Hunters and fishermen stop over in Prince George as the jumping-off place for some of North America's finest big game hunting and fishing. For more information contact Fish & Wildlife at (250) 565-6145, or Tourism Prince George & Area, phone (250) 562-3700.

West Access Route Log

(continued)

The John Hart Highway, completed in 1952, was named for the former B.C. premier who sponsored its construction. The highway is a 2-lane paved highway with both straight stretches and winding stretches.

This section of the log shows distance from Prince George (PG) followed by distance from Dawson Creek (DC).

BC HIGHWAY 97/HART HIGHWAY

PG 0 DC 250 (402.3 km) John Hart Bridge over the Nechako River. The 4-lane highway extends 6.5 miles/10.5 km northbound through the commercial and residential suburbs of Prince George.

PG 1.5 (2.4 km) **DC 248.5** (399.9 km) Truck weigh scales. 24-hour gas station with diesel and propane; lube and oil service.

PG 2.5 (4 km) **DC 247.5** (398.3 km) RV service centre.

PG 6.4 (10.3 km) **DC 243.6** (392 km) **Hartway RV Park**. Shaded, fully-serviced sites. Pull-throughs. Free hot showers, laundromat, 30-amp, cable TV. Modern, friendly. Groceries nearby. Phone. On-site antique

and gift shop. On south Kelly Road adjacent to highway. Access at stop light (Handlen Road Junction); south of RV park. 7729 South Kelly Rd., Prince George, BC V2K 3H5. Phone (250) 962-9724. [ADVERTISEMENT]

PG 6.5 (10.5 km) **DC 243.5** (391.9 km) Two-lane highway (with passing lanes) begins abruptly northbound.

PG 9.5 (15.3 km) **DC 240.5** (387 km) **Northland RV Park.** See display ad this section.

PG 14.6 (23.5 km) **DC 235.4** (378.8 km) Salmon River bridge. Litter barrel and river access to west at north end of bridge.

PG 14.7 (23.6 km) **DC 235.3** (378.7 km) **Salmon Valley RV Park and Campground** and convenience store, on over 27 acres along the scenic Salmon River. All facilities are wheelchair accessible, including showers. 50 treed sites, 12 pull-throughs, all with fire

rings, tables, laundry. Limited water and power 15–30 amp. Swimming and camping on the Salmon that's second to none. Fair fishing for rainbows, grayling and spring salmon. "Home of the Happy Camper." Phone (250) 971-2212. Fax (250) 971-2212. Good Sam discounts. [ADVERTISEMENT]

PG 16.4 (26.4 km) **DC 233.6** (375.9 km) Highway overpass crosses railroad tracks.

PG 22 (35.4 km) **DC 228** (366.9 km) Gravel turnouts both sides of highway.

PG 26.5 (42.6 km) **DC 223.5** (359.7 km) Paved turnout to east with litter barrels and point-of-interest sign about Crooked River Forest Recreation Area.

PG 26.9 (43.3 km) **DC 223.1** (359 km) Access east 3.7 miles/6 km to Giscome Portage regional park via Mitchell Road. Site of historic Huble Homestead; guided tours, picnicking. Free admission.

Historic Huble Homestead. Northern BC Pioneer Homestead and Fraser River Trading Post. Scenic riverfront location. Original furnished log buildings, including the Huble House—oldest home in the region. Guided interpretive tours. farm animals, picnic areas, general store. Admission by donation. Just 6 km east off Highway 97. Phone (250) 960-4400. [ADVERTISEMENT]

PG 28.2 (45.4 km) **DC 221.8** (356.9 km) Turnoff to west for **Summit Lake,** a resort area popular with Prince George residents; lake char and rainbow fishing spring and fall.

PG 29.3 (47.2 km) **DC 220.7** (355.2 km) Westcoast Energy compressor station.

PG 30.7 (49.4 km) **DC 219.3** (352.9 km) Second turnoff to west for Summit Lake.

PG 36.6 (58.9 km) **DC 213.4** (343.4 km) Cottonwood Creek.

PG 38.8 (62.4 km) **DC 211.2** (339.9 km) Paved turnout with litter barrel.

PG 40.6 (65.3 km) **DC 209.4** (337 km) Railroad crossing.

PG 42 (67.6 km) **DC 208** (334.7 km) Slow down for sharp turn across railroad tracks.

PG 43.9 (70.6 km) **DC 206.1** (331.7 km) Turnoff to west for **Crooked River Provincial Park**; 90 campsites, picnic area, flush toilets, tables, firepits, dump station. Camping fee charged. Also horseshoe pits, volleyball, playground, trails, swimming, picnic shelter and paddleboat rentals. Powerboats prohibited. Crooked River and area lakes have fair fishing for rainbow, Dolly Varden, grayling and whitefish.

Highway 97 follows the Crooked River north to McLeod Lake.

PG 44.8 (72.1 km) **DC 205.2** (330.1 km) **BEAR LAKE** (unincorporated). Population 300; gas, diesel, propane, grocery, restaurant, motel, RV park, gift shop, post office and ambulance station. Highway maintenance camp.

The 2 lumber mills in town are the main industry of the area, employing approximately two-thirds of the community. Information on area fishing, hiking, hunting and swimming may be obtained from the Bear Lake Community Commission; phone (250) 972-4488, or write general delivery, Bear Lake, BC V0J 3G0.

PG 50.7 (81.6 km) **DC 199.3** (320.7 km) Angusmac Creek.

PG 54.2 (87.2 km) **DC 195.8** (315.1 km) Tumbler Ridge branch line British Columbia Railway connects Tumbler Ridge with the B.C. Railway and Canadian National Railway, allowing for shipments of coal from Tumbler Ridge to Ridley Island near Prince Rupert.

PG 55.6 (89.5 km) **DC 194.4** (312.8 km) Large gravel turnout with litter barrel to west.

PG 56.1 (90.3 km) **DC 193.9** (312 km) Large gravel turnout with litter barrel to west.

PG 57 (91.7 km) **DC 193** (310.6 km) Large gravel turnout with litter barrel to west.

PG 60.8 (97.8 km) **DC 189.2** (304.5 km) Turnout with litter barrel to east.

PG 62.4 (100.4 km) **DC 187.6** (301.9 km) Large gravel turnout with litter barrel to east.

PG 65.2 (104.9 km) **DC 184.8** (297.4 km) Lomas Creek.

PG 67.9 (109.3 km) **DC 182.1** (293 km) Large, double-ended, paved rest area to west beside small lake; litter barrels, picnic tables and pit toilets.

PG 68.8 (110.7 km) **DC 181.2** (291.6 km) 42 Mile Creek.

PG 71.8 (115.5 km) **DC 178.2** (286.8 km) **Whiskers Bay Resort** has beautiful lakeside camping spots on a quiet bay, some with electricity and water. Hot showers. Cabins with showers, fridges and cooking facilities. Fishing is right off our dock or in the many surrounding lakes. Sunsets are sensational and hummingbirds are bountiful. The cafe

offers breakfast, lunch, wonderful burgers, homemade pies, soups, the best coffee on the highway and real northern hospitality. Come visit us! [ADVERTISEMENT] ▲

PG 76.6 (123.3 km) **DC 173.4** (279.1 km) First view northbound of McLeod Lake and view of Whisker's Point.

PG 77.7 (125 km) **DC 172.3** (277.3 km) Turnoff to west for **Whisker's Point Provincial Park** on McLeod Lake. This is an exceptionally nice campground with a paved loop road, 69 level gravel sites, a dump station, tap water, flush toilets, boat ramp, fire rings, firewood and picnic tables. Also horseshoe pits, volleyball, playground and picnic shelter. Camping fee charged. Boat launch, swimming, sandy beach and fishing. ▲

McLeod Lake has fair fishing for rainbow, lake char and Dolly Varden, spring and fall, trolling is best.

PG 84 (135.2 km) **DC 166** (267.1 km) Food, gas, camping and lodging. ▲

PG 84.5 (136 km) **DC 165.5** (266.3 km) **FORT McLEOD** (unincorporated) has a gas station, grocery, motel and cafe. A monument here commemorates the founding of Fort McLeod, oldest permanent settlement west of the Rockies and north of San Francisco. Founded in 1805 by Simon Fraser as a trading post for the North West Trading Co., the post was named by Fraser for Archie McLeod.

PG 84.7 (136.3 km) **DC 165.3** (266 km) **McLEOD LAKE** (unincorporated), post office, store and liquor store.

PG 84.8 (136.5 km) **DC 165.2** (265.8 km) McLeod lake Lodge; food, gas, lodging.

PG 85 (136.8 km) **DC 165** (265.5 km) Turnoff for **Carp Lake Provincial Park**, 20 miles/32 km west via a gravel road; 105 campsites on Carp and War lakes, limited island camping, picnic tables, firepits, boat launch, fishing and swimming. Also tap water, dump station, horseshoe pits, playground and picnic shelter. Ten-minute walk to scenic War Falls. Camping fee charged. Park access road follows the McLeod River to Carp Lake. Carp Lake, rainbow June through September; special restrictions in effect, check current posted information. **McLeod River**, rainbow from July, fly-fishing only. ▲

PG 85.6 (137.8 km) **DC 164.4** (264.6 km) Paved turnout with litter barrel to west.

PG 87.6 (141 km) **DC 162.4** (261.4 km)

Westcoast Energy compressor station and McLeod Lake school.

PG 89.8 (144.5 km) **DC 160.2** (257.8 km) Turnoff to west for **Tudyah Lake Provincial Park**; 36 campsites, picnic tables, fire rings, firewood, pit toilets, drinking water. Also swimming, boat ramp, fishing. Camping fee charged. ▲

Tudyah Lake, shore access, rainbow, Dolly Varden and some grayling in summer and late fall. **Pack River** (flows into Tudyah Lake), fishing for grayling (catch-and-release only), June 1 to July 1; rainbow, June 10 to November; large Dolly Varden, Sept. 15 to Oct. 10, spinning.

PG 89.9 (144.7 km) **DC 160.1** (257.6 km) Bear Creek bridge.

PG 93.9 (151.1 km) **DC 156.1** (251.2 km) Gas, food and lodging (open year-round).

PG 94.7 (152.4 km) **DC 155.3** (249.9 km) Parsnip River bridge. This is the Rocky Mountain Trench, marking the western boundary of the Rocky Mountains. Northbound motorists begin gradual climb through the Misinchinka then Hart ranges of the Rocky Mountains.

Parsnip River, good fishing for grayling and Dolly Varden, some rainbow, best from August to October; a boat is necessary.

PG 95.2 (153.2 km) **DC 154.8** (249.1 km)

Junction with Highway 39 (paved), which leads 18 miles/29 km to the community of Mackenzie (see HIGHWAY 39 TO MACKENZIE on facing page).

Food, gas, lodging, camping and **tourist information caboose** at junction.

PG 95.5 (153.7 km) **DC 154.5** (248.6 km) Highway crosses railroad tracks.

PG 98.9 (158.2 km) **DC 151.1** (243.2 km) Gravel turnout with litter barrel to east.

PG 106 (170.6 km) **DC 144** (231.7 km) Turnout with litter barrel to east.

PG 108.4 (174.4 km) **DC 141.6** (227.9 km) Highway maintenance yard.

PG 108.5 (174.6 km) **DC 141.5** (227.7 km) Bridge over Honeymoon Creek.

Improved road northbound to Dawson Creek.

PG 109.6 (176.4 km) **DC 140.4** (225.9 km) Powerlines crossing highway carry electricity south from hydro dams in the Hudson's Hope area (see **Milepost PG 187.9**).

PG 110.5 (177.8 km) **DC 139.5** (224.5 km) Slow down for sharp curve across railroad tracks.

PG 112.3 (180.7 km) **DC 137.7** (221.6 km) Bridge over Rolston Creek; dirt turnout by small falls to west.

PG 115.3 (185.6 km) **DC 134.7** (216.8 km) **Bijoux Falls Provincial Park**; pleasant stop on west side of highway to view the falls and spot Steller's jays. Good photo opportunities. Paved parking area; no facilities.

Misinchinka River, southeast of the highway; fishing for grayling, whitefish and Dolly Varden.

Bijoux Falls at Milepost PG 115.3.
(© Earl L. Brown, staff)

PG 116.3 (187.2 km) **DC 133.7** (215.2 km) Highway crosses under railroad.

PG 119.3 (191.8 km) **DC 130.8** (210.5 km) Crossing **Pine Pass** (elev. 2,868 feet/874m), the highest point on the John Hart-Peace River Highway, and the lowest pass breaching the Rocky Mountains in Canada. Beautiful view of the Rockies to the northeast. Good highway over pass; steep grade southbound.

PG 119.4 (192.2 km) **DC 130.6** (210.2 km) Turnoff to Powder King Ski Village. Skiing November to late April; chalet with ski shop, cafeteria, restaurant and lounge, hostel-style hotel. This area receives an annual average snowfall of 495 inches.

PG 121.4 (195.4 km) **DC 128.6** (207 km) Paved viewpoint to east with point-of-interest sign about Pine Pass and view of Azouzetta Lake. Pit toilet and litter barrels.

PG 122.4 (197 km) **DC 127.6** (205.3 km) Pine Valley Park, open year-round; cafe, lodge, campground on **Azouzetta Lake.** Very scenic spot. Spectacular hiking on Murray Mountain Trail; inquire at lodge for details. A scuba diving school operates at Azouzetta Lake in summer. Fishing for rainbow (stocked lake) to 1½ lbs., flies or lures, July to October. Boat launch. ▲

PG 125.5 (202 km) **DC 124.5** (200.3 km) Microwave station and receiving dish to west.

PG 125.7 (202.3 km) **DC 124.3** (200 km) Westcoast Energy compressor station.

PG 128.7 (207.1 km) **DC 121.3** (195.2 km) Power lines cross highway.

PG 131.1 (211 km) **DC 118.9** (191.3 km) Turnout with litter barrel. Watch for moose northbound.

PG 140.6 (226.3 km) **DC 109.4** (176.1 km) Bridge over Link Creek.

PG 141.4 (227.5 km) **DC 108.6** (174.8

(Continues on page 78)

Highway 39 to Mackenzie

Highway 39 is a paved road which leads 18 miles/29 km northwest from the John Hart Highway 97 to the community of Mackenzie. Signed trailheads along Highway 39 are part of the Mackenzie Demonstration Forest. There are 8 self-guiding trails in the demonstration forest, each focusing on an aspect of forest management. Interpretive signs are posted along each trail.

Mackenzie

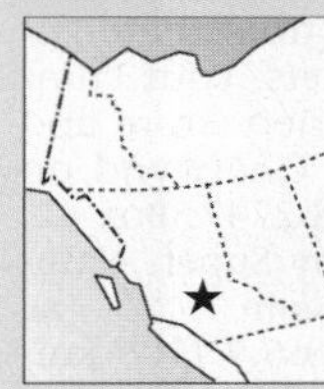

J 18 (29 km) Located 18 miles/29 km northwest of the John Hart Highway 97 via Highway 39. **Population:** 6,000. **Emergency Services:** Emergency only, phone 911. **RCMP**, phone (250) 997-3288. **Hospital**, 12 beds. **Ambulance**, phone 911.

Visitor Information: Visitor/tourist information booth in the railway caboose located at the junction of Highways 97 and 39. Or write the Chamber of Commerce, Box 880, Mackenzie, BC V0J 2C0; phone (250) 997-5459.

Elevation: 2,300 feet/701m. **Radio:** CKMK 1240, CKPG 1240; CBC-FM 990. **Television:** Channels 3, 13 and cable.

A large, modern, planned community, Mackenzie was built in 1965. The city was named after Alexander Mackenzie, early explorer. It lies at the south end of Williston Lake, the largest man-made reservoir on the continent. Construction of the new town in what had been just wilderness was sparked by the Peace River Dam project and the need to attract skilled employees for industrial growth. Mackenzie was incorporated in May 1966 under "instant town" legislation; the first residents moved here in July 1966. Industry here includes mining and forestry, with 4 sawmills, a paper mill and 2 pulp mills. Inquire about mill tours at the Infocentre.

On display in Mackenzie is the "world's largest tree crusher." The 56-foot-long electrically powered Le Tourneau G175 tree crusher was used in clearing land at the Peace River Power Project in the mid-1960s.

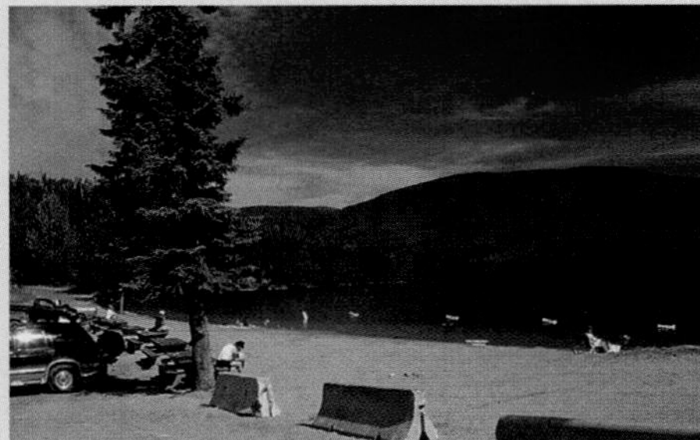

Attractions include swimming, waterskiing, fishing and boating at **Morfee Lake**, a 10-minute walk from town. There are boat launches on both Morfee Lake and Williston Lake reservoir. Good view of Mackenzie and Williston Lake reservoir from the top of Morfee Mountain (elev. 5,961 feet/1,817m); check with Infocentre for directions. There are self-guided hiking trails at John Dahl Regional Park, located behind the recreation centre. Check at the infocentre for additional hiking information. A local business offers llama trekking.

The Mackenzie and District Museum, located at the Ernie Bodin Community Centre, offers exhibits on early settlers, area wildlife and lakes, and the birth of the town; phone (250) 997-3021. Local artists are displayed monthly at the Mountain Gifts and Gallery (250/997-5818), located in the Ernie Bodin Bldg.

Mackenzie has all visitor facilities, including motels, restaurants, shopping malls, gas stations, swimming pool, tennis courts, 9-hole golf course and other recreation facilities. There is also a paved 5,000-foot/1,524-m airstrip.

There is a municipal RV park with 20 sites, flush toilets, showers and sani-dump. Fee only for electrical hookups ($10–$16). Fishing for rainbow, Dolly Varden, arctic char and grayling in **Williston Lake.**

District of Mackenzie. See display ad this section.

Return to Milepost PG 95.2
West Access Route

(Continued from page 76)
km) Gravel turnout with litter barrels.

PG 142.3 (229 km) **DC 107.7** (173.3 km) Bridge over West Pine River.

PG 142.8 (229.8 km) **DC 107.2** (172.5 km) Bridge over West Pine River.

PG 143 (230.1 km) **DC 107** (172.2 km) Large, double-ended paved rest area with picnic tables, litter barrels and pit toilets beside Pine River. Across the road is **Heart Lake** Forestry campground with toilets, picnic tables, firepits and garbage containers; fishing for stocked trout. ▲

PG 143.4 (230.8 km) **DC 106.6** (171.6 km) Bridge over West Pine River, B.C. Railway overpass. Private RV park. ▲

PG 144.3 (232.2 km) **DC 105.7** (170.1 km) Food, gas, towing, lodging and camping; phone (250) 788-0800. ▲

Silver Sands Lodge. See display ad on page 76. ▲

PG 146.1 (235.1 km) **DC 103.9** (167.2 km) Cairns Creek.

PG 146.9 (236.4 km) **DC 103.1** (165.9 km) Gravel access road to Pine River to south.

PG 148.2 (238.5 km) **DC 101.8** (163.8 km) LeMoray (unincorporated). Highway maintenance camp.

PG 148.3 (238.7 km) **DC 101.7** (163.7 km) Gravel turnout to south.

PG 148.8 (239.5 km) **DC 101.2** (162.9 km) Lillico Creek.

PG 149.7 (240.9 km) **DC 100.3** (161.4 km) Marten Creek.

PG 150.4 (242 km) **DC 99.6** (160.3 km) Big Boulder Creek.

PG 156.2 (251.4 km) **DC 93.8** (151 km) Fisher Creek.

PG 156.9 (252.5 km) **DC 93.1** (149.8 km) Large gravel turnout with litter barrel to south beside Pine River.

PG 159.9 (257.3 km) **DC 90.1** (145 km) Crassier Creek. Watch for moose and deer in area, especially at dusk and night.

PG 161.7 (260.2 km) **DC 88.3** (142.1 km) Westcoast Energy compressor station.

PG 163.6 (263.3 km) **DC 86.4** (139 km) Pull-off to south.

PG 169.5 (272.8 km) **DC 80.5** (129.5 km) Turnout with picnic tables, pit toilets and litter barrel to south at Jack Pine Point overlooking the beautiful Pine River valley. Chetwynd area map.

PG 172.4 (277.4 km) **DC 77.6** (124.9 km) Westcoast Energy (natural gas), Pine River plant. View of the Rocky Mountain foothills to the south and west.

PG 177.4 (285.5 km) **DC 72.6** (116.8 km) Turnout with litter barrel.

PG 178.4 (287.1 km) **DC 71.6** (115.2 km) **Caron Creek RV Park.** See display ad this section. ▲

PG 181.9 (292.7 km) **DC 68.1** (109.6 km) Bissett Creek.

PG 183.6 (295.5 km) **DC 66.4** (106.9 km) Turnout with litter barrels at Wildmare Creek.

PG 183.7 (295.6 km) **DC 66.3** (106.7 km) **Wildmare RV Park.** 50 sites. 32 long pull-throughs, back-ins, tent sites, full hookups,

firepits and picnic tables. Quiet, beautifully treed with easy access to and from the highway. Hot showers, flush toilets, coin laundry. Excellent water; ice; variety store and pay phone. 3 miles west of Chetwynd on Highway 97. Phone (250) 788-2747. Box 42, Chetwynd, BC V0C 1J0. Enjoy Super, Natural Scenic Adventure. [ADVERTISEMENT] ▲

PG 184.1 (296.3 km) **DC 65.9** (106 km) Truck stop; gas, diesel, food and lodging.

PG 187 (300.9 km) **DC 63** (101.4 km) Forestry Interpretive Centre. Trailhead for 50-mile/80-km Chetwynd area hiking and biking trail system.

PG 187.2 (301.3 km) **DC 62.8** (101.1 km) **Little Prairie Heritage Museum.** Features the region's pioneer days, and is well worth a visit. The museum is open from the first Tuesday in July to the last Saturday in August. Phone (250) 788-3358.

Chetwynd

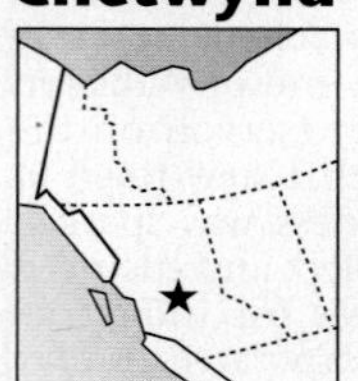

PG 187.6 (301.9 km) **DC 62.4** (100.4 km) Located on Highway 97 at the junction with Highway 29 north to the Alaska Highway via Hudson's Hope, and south to Tumbler Ridge. **Population:** 3,200, area 8,000. **Emergency Services:** RCMP, phone (250) 788-9221. **Hospital, Poison Control Centre** and **Ambulance,** phone (250) 788-3522. **Fire Department,** phone (250) 788-2345.

Visitor Information: Chamber of Commerce, open 8 A.M. to 5 P.M. in summer, 9 A.M. to 4 P.M. weekdays rest of year. Write Box 1000, Chetwynd V0C 1J0, or phone (250) 788-3345 or 788-3655; fax 788-7843.

CHETWYND ADVERTISERS

District of Chetwynd ....Ph. (250) 788-2281
Pine Cone Motor Inn ....Ph. (800) 663-8082
Swiss Inn
Restaurant, The ....Ph. (250) 788-2566
Westwind RV Park ....Ph. (250) 788-2190

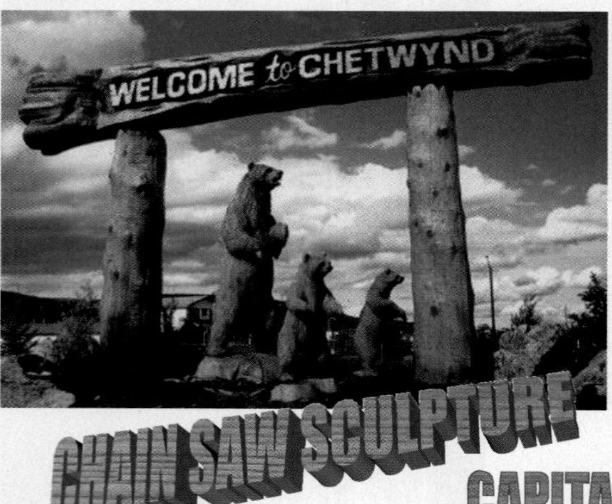

Chetwynd's Little Prairie Heritage Museum. (© Earl L. Brown, staff)

Elevation: 2,017 feet/615m. **Radio:** CFGP 105, CISN-FM 103.9, CJDC 890, CKNL 560, CBC 1170, CFMI-FM 102, CHET-FM 94.5. **Television:** 7 channels (includes CBC, BCTV, ABC, CBS and NBC) plus pay cable.

The town, formerly known as Little Prairie, is a division point on the British Columbia Railway. The name was changed to honour the late British Columbia Minister of Railways, Ralph Chetwynd, who was instrumental in the northward extension of the province-owned railway.

In recent years, Chetwynd's collection of chain saw sculptures has earned it the title, "Chain Saw Sculpture Capital of the World." The Infocentre has a map showing locations of the 2 dozen sculptures in town.

Chetwynd lies at the northern end of one of the largest known coal deposits on earth. Access from Chetwynd south to Tumbler Ridge and the resource development known as the North East Coal is via Highway 29 south, a 56-mile/90-km paved road (see HIGHWAY 29 SOUTH side road log this section). Forestry, mining, natural gas processing, ranching and farming are the main industries in Chetwynd. Louisiana Pacific has a modern non-polluting pulp mill here.

Chetwynd is a fast-growing community with several large motels, fast-food outlets, restaurants, banks and 4 bank machines, post office, 2 laundromats, gas stations, supermarkets and 2 9-hole golf courses. Good traveler's stop with easy access to all services. (Heavy commercial and industrial traffic often fill up local motels and campgrounds; reserve ahead.)

Recreation includes a skate park, hockey arena, curling rink and ball diamonds. Chetwynd & District Leisure Pool has a wave machine, whirlpool, sauna and weight room; open daily 6 A.M. to 10 P.M., visitors welcome.

There's a dump station at the 51st Avenue car/truck wash. There are private RV parks in town and on Highway 97. **Moberly Lake Provincial Park** is 12 miles/19.3 km north of Chetwynd via Highway 29 north (see **Milepost PG 187.9**) and 1.9 miles/3 km west via a gravel road. The park has 109 campsites, beach, picnic area, playground, nature trail, boat launch and a private marina next door with boat rental and concession. There's good swimming at huge Moberly Lake on a warm summer day. Worth the drive. ▲

Westwind RV Park. Good Sam. Area's newest and most modern. On Highway 97 North towards Dawson Creek. 50 large pull-through sites with full hookups. New, immaculate restrooms and showers. Laundry facility. Wheelchair access. Walking distance to leisure pool and hiking trails. Your perfect stopping point for your Northern travels ... ask about our area attractions. Your hosts, David and Laurie Gayse. Phone (250) 788-2190, fax (250) 788-2086. See our display ad for more. [ADVERTISEMENT] ♿▲

West Access Route Log

(continued)

PG 187.8 (302.2 km) **DC 62.2** (100.1 km) Highway crosses railroad tracks.

PG 187.9 (302.4 km) **DC 62.1** (99.9 km)

> **Junction** with Highway 29 north to Moberly Lake, Peace River Provincial Recreation Area and Peace Canyon Dam and Hudson's Hope. Highway 29 north connects with the Alaska Highway 53.7 miles/86.4 km north of Dawson Creek. Turn to HUDSON'S HOPE LOOP section on page 82 for log of this route.

Highway climbs next 12 miles/19 km for Dawson Creek-bound motorists.

PG 189.4 (304.8 km) **DC 60.6** (97.5 km)

> **Junction** with Highway 29 (paved) south to Gwillim Lake and Tumbler Ridge (see TUMBLER RIDGE LOOP beginning on page 80).

Tumbler Ridge is also accessible from **Milepost PG 237.7** via the Heritage Highway.

District of Tumbler Ridge. See display ad this section.

PG 199.3 (320.7 km) **DC 50.7** (81.6 km) Gravel turnouts with litter barrels both sides of highway.

PG 201.2 (323.8 km) **DC 48.8** (78.5 km) Slow down for sharp curve across railroad tracks.

PG 204.3 (328.8km) **DC 45.7** (73.5km) Access to Louisiana Pacific Pulp Mill to north.

PG 205.6 (330.9 km) **DC 44.4** (71.5 km) Turnout with litter barrel and view of the East Pine River valley to the south.

PG 206.5 (332.3 km) **DC 43.5** (70 km) Sharp curves approximately next 2 miles/3.2 km as highway descends toward Dawson Creek. View of Table Mountain.

PG 207.9 (334.6 km) **DC 42.1** (67.7 km) Highway crosses under railroad.

PG 208.1 (334.9 km) **DC 41.9** (67.4 km) East Pine River bridge.

Sharp turn to south at west end of bridge for **East Pine Provincial Park** (0.5 mile on gravel road); boat launch on Pine River. Turnout with litter barrel at park entrance.

From East Pine Provincial Park, canoeists may make a 2-day canoe trip down the Pine River to the Peace River; take-out at Taylor Landing Provincial Park (at **Milepost DC 34**

(Continues on page 81)

Tumbler Ridge Loop

Travelers can make a loop trip south from Highway 97 by taking Highway 29 south from **Milepost PG 189.4** just east of Chetwynd, to the town of Tumbler Ridge, and returning to Highway 97 via Highway 52 (the Heritage Highway).

Highway 29 South is a paved road that leads 55.9 miles/90 km from **Milepost PG 189.4** to the community of Tumbler Ridge. Highway 52, the Heritage Highway, is also a paved road that leads 59.6 miles/96 km from Tumbler Ridge to junction with Highway 97 at **Milepost PG 237.7**, just west of Dawson Creek Highway 52 has many rolling hills, some 8 percent grades and several S curves.

Distance from Highway 97 junction at Milepost PG 189.4 (J) is shown.

HIGHWAY 29 SOUTH

J 0 Junction with Highway 97 at **Milepost PG 189.4.**

J 0.1 (0.2 km) Turnout with litter barrels to east.

Highway 29 climbs next 2.3 miles/3.7 km southbound.

J 1.9 (3.1 km) Distance marker indicates Tumbler Ridge 88 km.

J 2.8 (4.5 km) Sign: Trucks check brakes, steep hill ahead.

J 3 (4.8 km) Large gravel turnouts with litter barrels both sides of highway.

J 5.5 (8.8 km) Twidwell Bend bridge.

J 5.6 (9 km) Access road east to Long Prairie (8 miles/12.9 km).

J 6.6 (10.6 km) Highway parallels Sukunka River to west.

J 8.2 (13.2 km) Zonnebeke Creek.

J 8.5 (13.7 km) Natural Springs Resort; 9-hole golf course.

J 9 (14.5 km) Kilometrepost 15.

J 10.6 (17 km) Bridge over Dickebush Creek.

J 11 (17.7 km) Sanctuary River.

J 13.7 (22 km) **Junction** with Sukunka Forest Road, which leads west 11 miles/17.7 km to Sukunka Falls. *NOTE: Radio-controlled road, travelers must monitor channel 151.325 MHz.*

J 13.8 (22.2 km) Highway climbs next 3 miles/4.8 km southbound.

J 16.7 (26.9 km) Turnouts with litter barrels both sides of highway.

J 21.6 (34.8 km) Turnout with litter barrels to east.

J 26.9 (43.3 km) Turnouts with litter barrels both sides of highway.

J 28.4 (45.7 km) Paved road leads east 1.2 miles/1.9 km to **Gwillim Lake Provincial Park** (gate closed 11 P.M. to 7 A.M.); 49 campsites, picnic tables, firewood and firepits. Day-use area and boat launch. Fishing for lake trout, grayling and pike. Camping fee $7 to $12. ▲

J 40.8 (65.6 km) Access road leads west 9 miles/14.5 km to Bullmoose Mountain and mine.

J 41.1 (66.1 km) Turnout to east.

J 41.5 (66.8 km) Bridge over Bullmoose Flats River.

J 46.1 (74.2 km) Turnout with litter barrels to east. Phillips Way Summit, elev. 3,695 feet/1,126m.

J 51.4 (82.7 km) Bullmoose Creek bridge.

J 52.6 (84.3 km) Wolverine River bridge.

J 54.1 (87 km) Murray River bridge.

J 54.8 (88.2 km) Flatbed Creek bridge.

J 54.9 (88.3 km) Flatbed Creek Campground; 28 sites, hookups, water, flush toilets, showers, dump station, picnic tables and playground. Camping fee $10. ▲

J 55.9 (90 km) Turnoff for community of Tumbler Ridge (description follows).

Tumbler Ridge

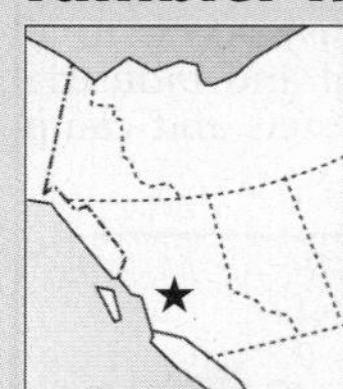

Located 116.5 miles/187.5 km southwest of Dawson Creek via Highways 97 and 29. **Population**: 3,775. **Emergency Services: RCMP**, phone (250) 242-5252. **Medical Centre**, phone (250) 242-5271. **Ambulance**, phone (800) 461-9911. **Fire Department**, phone (250) 242-5555.

Visitor Information: Located in town at Southgate Road and Front Street, across from the hospital. Open year-round. Free slide presentation on Tumbler Ridge history and development. Write the Chamber of Commerce, Box 606, Tumbler Ridge, BC V0C 2W0, or phone (250) 242-4702, fax 242-5159.

Elevation: 3,000 feet/914m. **Private Air-**

Kinuseo Falls, located in Monkman Provincial Park, is accessible from Tumbler Ridge via gravel road. (© Earl L. Brown, staff)

craft: 9 miles/15 km south; elev. 3,150 feet/960m, length 4,000 feet/ 1,218m; asphalt; fuel 80, 100, Jet B.

Tumbler Ridge was built in conjunction with development of the North East Coal resource. Construction of the townsite began in 1981. It is British Columbia's newest community, incorporated June 1, 1984.

The Quintette Mine south of town is the world's largest computerized open pit mine. Bullmoose Mine is located 9 miles/14.5 km west of **Milepost J 40.8** on Highway 29.

Visitor facilities include a motel, restaurants, retail and grocery outlets, service stations with major repairs and propane and a car wash. Camping at Flatbed Creek Campground just outside of town and at Monkman RV Park in town. Recreational facilities include a community centre with arena, curling rink, weight room, indoor pool and a library. Outdoor facilities include tennis courts and a 9-hole golf course. ▲

Major attraction in the area is Monkman Provincial Park, site of spectacular 225-foot/69-m Kinuseo (keh-NEW-see-oh or Keh-NEW-soh) Falls. The falls and a 42-site campground are accessible from Tumbler Ridge via a 37-mile/60-km gravel road (watch for trucks) south from town. Viewing platform of falls is a short walk from the campground. For more information on the park, contact BC Parks in Fort St. John, phone (250) 787-3407.

District of Tumbler Ridge. See display ad this section.

Distance from Tumbler Ridge (T) is shown.

HIGHWAY 52 NORTH

T 0 Town of Tumbler Ridge.

T 2.9 (4.7 km) Small turnout to west with litter barrels.

T 4.8 (7.7 km) Recreation area turnout to west.

T 9.9 (16 km) Large turnout to west with view of Murray River Valley and Rocky Mountains.

T 10.3 (19.6 km) **Heritage Highway Summit**, elev. 4,150 foot/1,265m.

T 15.9 (25.7 km) Recreation area turnout to west.

T 17.6 (28.8 km) Gravel pit turnout to west.

T 25.4 (41 km) Small turnout to west.

T 29.3 (47.2 km) *CAUTION: Pavement breaks and dips in road; reduce speed*. Slide area.

T 33.3 (53.7 km) Large turnout to west with litter barrels.

T 35.6 (57.5 km) Salt Creek Valley.

T 43.1 (69.5 km) Brassey Creek.

T 43.3 (69.7 km) Large turnout to east with litter barrels.

T 45.9 (74 km) Salt Ridge Hills.

T 46.9 (75.5 km) *CAUTION: Watch for livestock.*

T 47.8 (77 km) Patched pavement. Slide area.

T 50.7 (81.6 km) Kiskatinaw River Valley.

T 51.1 (82.3 km) Turnoff for **Upper Cutbank** (unincorporated).

T 52.3 (84.3 km) *CAUTION: Watch for trucks turning at logging road.*

T 53.1 (85.5 km) Puggins Mountain Road.

T 53.2 (85.7 km) Fellers Heights.

T 54.9 (88.8 km) Cutbank Community Hall.

T 58.2 (93.7 km) Turnoff for **Arras** (unincorporated).

T 58.5 (94.2 km) Small turnout to east.

T 59.6 (96 km) **Junction** with Highway 97 at **Milepost PG 237.7**.

Return to Milepost PG 237.7 or 189.4 West Access Route

(Continued from page 79)
on the Alaska Highway.

PG 208.2 (335.1 km) **DC 41.8** (67.3 km) Bridge across East Pine River. Railroad also crosses river here.

PG 208.3 (335.2 km) **DC 41.7** (67.1 km) Turnout with litter barrel to south.

PG 209.8 (337.6 km) **DC 40.2** (64.7 km) East Pine (unincorporated) has a store and gas station.

Watch for good views of East Pine River bridges next mile northbound.

PG 211.7 (340.7 km) **DC 38.3** (61.6 km) Turnout with litter barrel to north. Westbound brake-check area.

PG 221.5 (356.5 km) **DC 28.5** (45.9 km) Turnouts with litter barrels both sides of highway.

PG 222 (357.3 km) **DC 28** (45 km) **Groundbirch** (unincorporated); store, liquor outlet, gas, propane, diesel, post office and camping.

PG 237.7 (382.5 km) **DC 12.3** (19.8 km) **Junction** with Heritage Highway (Highway 52), which leads 59.6 miles/96 km south to the community of Tumbler Ridge. (See TUMBLER RIDGE LOOP this section.)

Patricia Park Campground. See display ad this section. ▲

From Tumbler Ridge, the Heritage Highway continues 92 miles/148 km east and north to connect with Highway 2 southeast of Dawson Creek. Inquire locally about road conditions.

PG 238 (383 km) **DC 12** (19.3 km) Kiskatinaw River bridge.

PG 240.7 (387.4 km) **DC 9.3** (15 km) Arras (unincorporated), cafe and gas station.

PG 247.9 (398.9 km) **DC 2.1** (3.4 km) Small turnout with litter barrel and point of interest sign to south.

PG 248 (399.1 km) **DC 2** (3.2 km) Private RV Park. ▲

PG 249.9 (402.2 km) **DC 0.1** (0.2 km) Entering Dawson Creek. Private campground on south side of highway; Rotary Lake Park and camping on north side of highway. ▲

PG 250 (402.3 km) **DC 0 Junction** of the Hart Highway and Alaska Highway; turn right for downtown Dawson Creek, Mile Zero of the Alaska Highway.

Turn to the ALASKA HIGHWAY section on page 84 for description of Dawson Creek and log of the Alaska Highway.

HUDSON'S HOPE LOOP

29

Connects: Chetwynd, BC, to Alaska Hwy. **Length:** 87 miles
Road Surface: Paved **Season:** Open all year
Steepest Grade: 10 percent
Major Attraction: W.A.C. Bennett and Peace Canyon Dams

(See map, page 58)

	Alaska Hwy	Chetwynd	Hudson's Hope
Alaska Hwy		87	47
Chetwynd	87		40
Hudson's Hope	47	40	

View from Highway 29 of fertile Peace River valley. (© Earl L. Brown, staff)

The Hudson's Hope Loop links the John Hart Highway (Highway 97) with the Alaska Highway (also Highway 97). This 86.9-mile/139.8-km paved loop road provides year-round access to the town of Hudson's Hope, W.A.C. Bennett Dam, Peace Canyon Dam and Moberly Lake. As a shortcut bypassing Dawson Creek, the Hudson's Hope Loop saves 28.9 miles/46.5 km. Highway 29 is a good, scenic 2-lane road but is steep and winding in places.

Hudson's Hope Loop Log

Distance from Chetwynd (C) is followed by distance from Alaska Highway junction (AH).

BC HIGHWAY 29

C 0 AH 86.9 (139.8 km) **Junction** of Highways 29 and 97 at Chetwynd.

Turn to **Milepost PG 187.6** in the WEST ACCESS ROUTE section for description of Chetwynd and log of BC Highway 97.

C 0.5 (0.8 km) **AH 86.4** (139 km) Truck weigh scales to west. Highway climbs next 4.3 miles/7 km westbound.

C 2.3 (3.7 km) **AH 84.6** (136.1 km) Jackfish Road to east.

C 5 (8 km) **AH 81.9** (131.8 km) Turnout with litter barrel to west.

C 12 (19.3 km) **AH 74.9** (120.5 km) Gravel access road leads 2 miles/3.2 km west to **Moberly Lake Provincial Park** on south shore; 109 campsites, swimming, waterskiing, picnicking, drinking water, dump station, boat launch, $9.50 camping fee. This beautiful 9-mile-/14.5-km-long lake drains at its east end into Moberly River, which in turn runs into the Peace River. Fishing for lake trout, Dolly Varden and whitefish. ▲

C 12.2 (19.6 km) **AH 74.7** (120.2 km) Moberly River bridge; parking area with litter barrel at south end.

C 15.9 (25.6 km) **AH 71** (114.3 km) Highway cairn is memorial to John Moberly, fur trader and explorer who first landed here in 1865.

C 16.4 (26.4 km) **AH 70.5** (113.5 km) Spencer Tuck Regional Park; picnic tables, swimming, fishing and boat launch.

C 17.4 (28 km) **AH 69.5** (111.8 km) Camping resort. ▲

C 18.3 (29.5 km) **AH 68.6** (110.4 km) **MOBERLY LAKE.** Post office, cafe, store and pay phone.

C 18.5 (29.8 km) **AH 68.4** (110.1 km) Moberly Lake and District Golf Club, 0.7 mile/1.1 km from highway; 9 holes, grass greens, rentals, clubhouse, licensed lounge. Open May to September.

C 25.4 (40.9 km) **AH 61.5** (99 km) Cameron Lake camping area; tables, water, toilets, firewood, playground, horseshoe pits, boat launch (no motorboats) and swimming. Camping fee by donation. ▲

C 30.7 (49.4 km) **AH 56.2** (90.4 km) Gravel turnout with litter barrel to east. Highway descends northbound to Hudson's Hope.

C 35.9 (57.8 km) **AH 51** (82.1 km) Suspension bridge over Peace River; paved turnouts at both ends of bridge with concrete totem pole sculptures. View of Peace Canyon Dam.

C 36.5 (58.7 km) **AH 50.4** (81.1 km) Turnoff to west for Dinosaur Lake Campground and B.C. Hydro **Peace Canyon Dam**. The dam's visitor centre, 0.6 mile/1 km on paved access road, is open from 8 A.M. to 4 P.M. daily from late May through Labour Day; Monday through Friday the rest of the year (closed holidays). Self-guided tour includes a full-scale model of duck-billed dinosaurs and a tableau portraying Alexander Mackenzie's discovery of the Peace River canyon. A pictorial display traces the construction of the Peace Canyon Dam. Phone (250) 783-5211 for a guided tour (groups of 8 or more).

Dinosaur Lake Campground, on Dinosaur Lake, has 30 campsites with firepits, water, toilets and tables. Boat launch and swimming area. Camping fee by donation. ▲

C 38.3 (61.6 km) **AH 48.6** (78.2 km) Alwin Holland Memorial Park (0.5 mile/0.8 km east of highway) is named for the first teacher in Hudson's Hope, who willed his property, known locally as The Glen, to be used as a public park. There are 17 campsites, picnic grounds, barbecues and water. Camping fee by donation. ▲

C 39 (62.8 km) **AH 47.9** (77.1 km) King Gething Park; small campground with 15 grassy sites, picnic tables, cookhouse, flush toilets, showers and dump station east side of highway. Camping fee by donation. ▲

Hudson's Hope

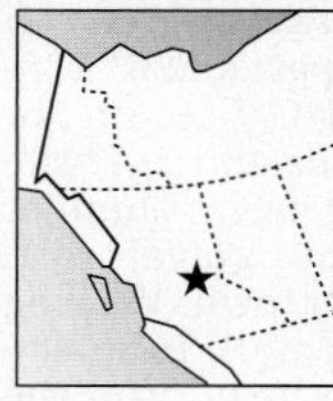

C 40.4 (65 km) AH 46.5 (74.8 km) **Population:** 1,122. **Emergency Services: RCMP**, phone (250) 783-5241. **Fire Department**, phone (250) 783-5700. **Ambulance**, phone (800) 461-9911. **Medical Clinic**, phone (250) 783-9991.

Visitor Information: A log building houses the tourist information booth at Beattie Park. Open daily mid-May to the end of August, hours are 8 A.M. to 5:30 P.M.

Phone (250) 783-9154 or write Box 330, Hudson's Hope, BC V0C 1V0. (Off-season, phone the District Office at 250/783-9901.)

Elevation: 1,707 feet/520m. **Climate:** Summer temperatures range from 60°F/16°C to 90°F/32°C, with an average of 135 frost-free days annually. **Radio:** CBC, CKNL 560, CJDC 870. **Television:** Channels 2, 5, 8, 11 and cable.

Private Aircraft: Hudson's Hope airstrip, 3.7 miles/6 km west; elev. 2,200 feet/671m; length 5,200 feet/1,585m; asphalt.

Visitor services in Hudson's Hope include a motel, hotel, 2 bed and breakfasts, 3 restaurants, 2 service stations, a laundromat, bank, post office, supermarket, bakery, and convenience and hardware stores.

Hudson's Hope is the third oldest permanently settled community in British Columbia. The site was first visited in 1793 by Alexander Mackenzie. In 1805 a Hudson's Bay trading post was established here by Simon Fraser. In 1916, after the fur-trading days were over, a major influx of settlers arrived in the area. It was the head of navigation for steamboats on the lower Peace River until 1936, the year of the last scheduled steamboat run. Area coal mines supplied Alaska Highway maintenance camps during the 1940s.

Modern development of Hudson's Hope was spurred by construction of the Peace Power project in the 1960s. Today the area's principal claim to fame is the 600-foot-/183-m-high **W.A.C. Bennett Dam** at the

upper end of the Peace River canyon, 15 miles/24.1 km west of Hudson's Hope. The 100-million-ton dam is one of the largest earth-fill structures in the world, and Williston Lake, behind it, is the largest body of fresh water in British Columbia. The dam provides about 20 percent of British Columbia's hydroelectricity. Tours of the Gordon M. Shrum generating station are available daily from mid-May to the end of September, weekdays only the remainder of the year (closed holidays). Phone (250) 783-5211 for information. Tours are available each hour on the half hour from 9:30 A.M. to 4:30 P.M.

Also of interest is the Hudson's Hope Museum on Highway 29 in town. The museum has a fine collection of artifacts and dinosaur fossils from the Peace District. It offers hands-on paleontology and dinosaur activities, and is well worth a visit. Souvenir shop in the museum; (250) 783-5735; admission by donation. The historic log **St. Peter's Anglican United Church**

is next door to the museum

District of Hudson's Hope. See display ad this section.

Hudson's Hope Museum. See display ad this section.

Hudson's Hope Loop Log

(continued)

C 41.2 (66.3 km) **AH 45.7** (73.5 km) Turnout to north with Hudson's Hope visitor map.

CAUTION: Watch for deer between here and the Alaska Highway, especially at dusk and at night.

C 44 (70.8 km) **AH 42.9** (69 km) Lynx Creek bridge.

C 48.4 (77.9 km) **AH 38.5** (62 km) Turnout to south for view of the Peace River.

C 50.9 (81.9 km) **AH 36** (57.9 km) Farrell Creek bridge and picnic site.

C 56.6 (91.1 km) **AH 30.3** (48.8 km) Pull-through turnout with litter barrels. View of Peace River valley.

CAUTION: Watch for frost heaves and rough spots next 10 miles/16 km.

C 57.1 (91.9 km) **AH 29.8** (48 km) Turnout to south with litter barrels and view of Peace River valley.

C 59.3 (95.4 km) **AH 27.6** (44.4 km) Turnout to south with litter barrels.

C 64.7 (104.1 km) **AH 22.2** (35.7 km) Halfway River.

C 67.2 (108.1 km) **AH 19.7** (31.7 km) Rest area to south with point of interest sign, litter barrel and toilet. A slide occurred here on May 26, 1973, involving an estimated 10 million to 15 million cubic yards of overburden. Slide debris completely blocked the river channel for some 12 hours, backing up the river an estimated 24 feet/7.3m above normal level.

C 71.1 (114.4 km) **AH 15.8** (25.4 km) Turnout to north.

C 73.5 (118.3 km) **AH 13.4** (21.6 km) Beaver dam to north.

C 74.6 (120.1 km) **AH 12.3** (19.8 km) Cache Creek 1-lane bridge. Turnout to north at east end of bridge for picnic area with litter barrels.

C 76.6 (123.3 km) **AH 10.3** (16.6 km) Turnout with litter barrel to north overlooking Bear Flat in the Peace River valley. Highway begins climb eastbound. *CAUTION: Switchbacks.*

C 78.1 (125.7 km) **AH 8.8** (14.2 km) Highest point on Highway 29 (2,750 feet/838m) overlooking Peace River Plateau. Highway descends on a 10 percent grade westbound. *CAUTION: Switchbacks.*

C 86.9 (139.8 km) **AH 0** Truck stop at junction with gas, diesel, propane, tire repair, restaurant and convenience store.

Junction with the Alaska Highway, 6.7 miles/10.8 km north of Fort St. John; turn to **Milepost DC 53.7** in the ALASKA HIGHWAY section for log.

CAUTION: Watch for deer on the highway between here and Hudson's Hope, especially at dusk and at night.

ALASKA HIGHWAY 97  

Connects: Dawson Creek, BC, to Delta Junction, AK **Length:** 1,390 miles
Road Surface: Paved **Season:** Open all year
Highest Summit: Summit Lake 4,250 feet
Major Attractions: Muncho Lake, Liard Hotsprings, Watson Lake Signforest, SS *Klondike*, Kluane Lake, Trans-Alaska Pipeline Crossing

(See maps, pages 85–89)

	Dawson Cr.	Delta Jct.	Fairbanks	Ft. Nelson	Haines Jct.	Tok	Watson Lk.	Whitehorse
Dawson Cr.		1390	1488	283	985	1282	613	895
Delta Jct.	1390		98	1107	405	108	777	495
Fairbanks	1488	98		1205	593	206	875	593
Ft. Nelson	283	1107	1205		702	999	330	612
Haines Jct.	985	405	593	702		297	372	90
Tok	1282	108	206	999	297		669	387
Watson Lk.	613	777	875	330	372	669		282
Whitehorse	895	495	593	612	90	387	282	

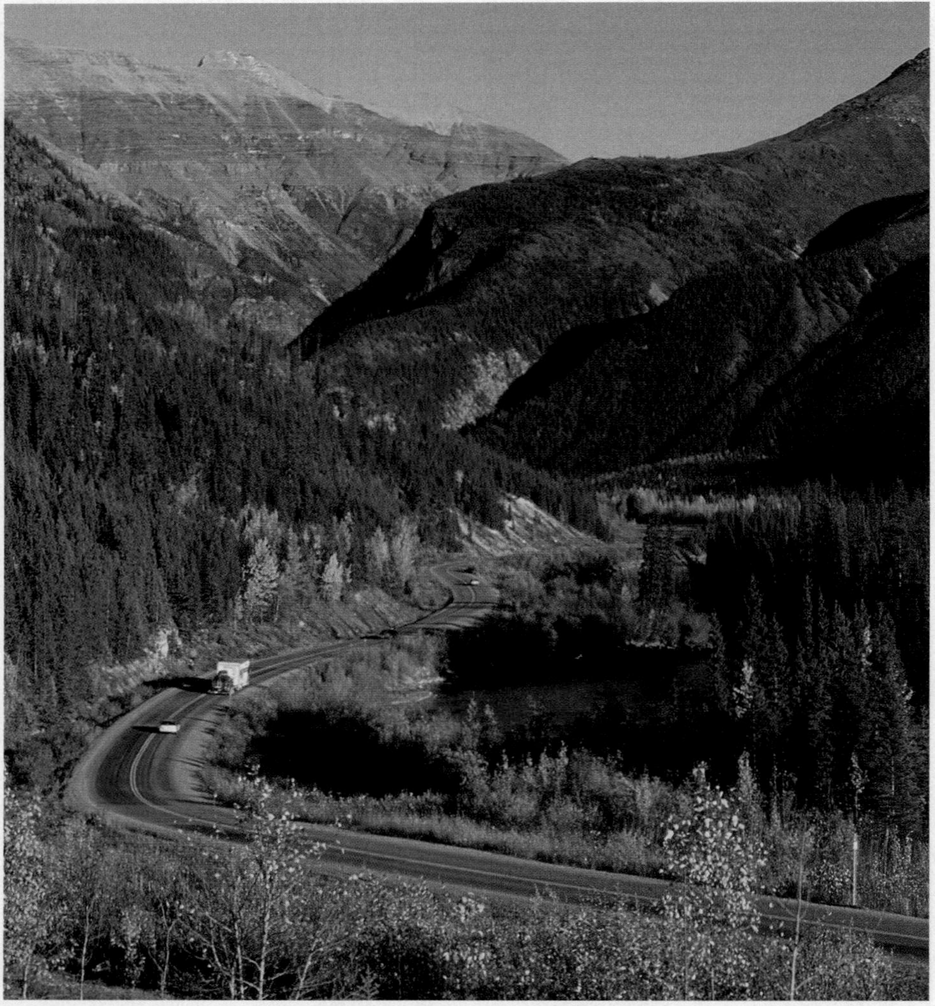

Alaska Highway follows the Toad River near Milepost DC 421. (© Earl L. Brown, staff)

The Alaska Highway begins as BC Highway 97 at **Mile 0** in Dawson Creek, BC. The Alaska Highway then travels 613 miles/987 km in a northwesterly direction from Dawson Creek to the Yukon Territory border near Watson Lake, YT, **Historical Mile 635**, where it becomes Yukon Highway 1. The highway then crosses 577 miles/929 km of Yukon Territory to Port Alcan on the Alaska border, entering Alaska at **Historical Mile 1221.8**, where it becomes Alaska Route 2. From this international border, it is 200 miles/322 km to Delta Junction, AK, **Historical Mile 1422**, the official end of the Alaska Highway.

From Delta Junction to Fairbanks, a distance of 98 miles/158 km, travelers will be on the Richardson Highway, Alaska Route 4. Although often treated as a natural extension of the Alaska Highway (and logged as such in previous editions of *The MILEPOST®*), the highway between Delta Junction and Fairbanks is designated as Alaska Route 4, the Richardson Highway. Originally known as the Richardson Trail, this route predates construction of the Alaska Highway by some 50 years. (Turn to the RICHARDSON HIGHWAY section for a log of that route.)

Road Conditions

All of the Alaska Highway is asphalt surfaced. Repaving and highway improvement are ongoing. Surfacing of the Alaska Highway ranges from poor to excellent.

There are still some stretches of poor surfacing with many chuckholes, gravel breaks (sections of gravel ranging from a few feet to several miles), hardtop with loose gravel, deteriorated shoulders and bumps.

CAUTION: Loose gravel patches are common on the Alaska Highway and are often signed. Slow down for loose gravel! Excessive speeds can lead to loss of control of your vehicle.

Surfacing on much of the highway is fair, with older patched pavement and a minimum of gravel breaks and chuckholes. There are also sections of excellent surfacing where highway maintenance crews have recently upgraded the road.

On the northern portion of the highway—in Yukon Territory and on into Alaska—watch for frost heaves. This rippling effect in the pavement is caused by the freezing and thawing of the ground. Drive slowly in sections of frost heaves to avoid breaking an axle or trailer hitch.

Keep in mind that road conditions are subject to change! Weather and traffic may cause deterioration of newer pavement, while construction may improve older sections. Always be alert for bumps and holes in the road and for abrupt changes in highway surfacing. There are stretches of narrow, winding road without shoulders. Also watch for soft shoulders. Dust and mud are generally only a problem in construction areas.

Always watch for construction crews along the Alaska Highway. Extensive road construction may require a detour, or travelers may be delayed while waiting for a pilot car to guide them through the construction. Motorists may encounter rough driving at construction areas, and muddy roadway if there are heavy rains while the roadbed is torn up.

For current road conditions, see Road Condition Report sources listed under Driving Information in the TRAVEL PLANNING section of this book.

Detailed weather information for the Canadian portion of the Alaska Highway is available from Atmospheric Environment

(Continues on page 90)

ALASKA HIGHWAY *Dawson Creek, BC, to Milepost DC 409*

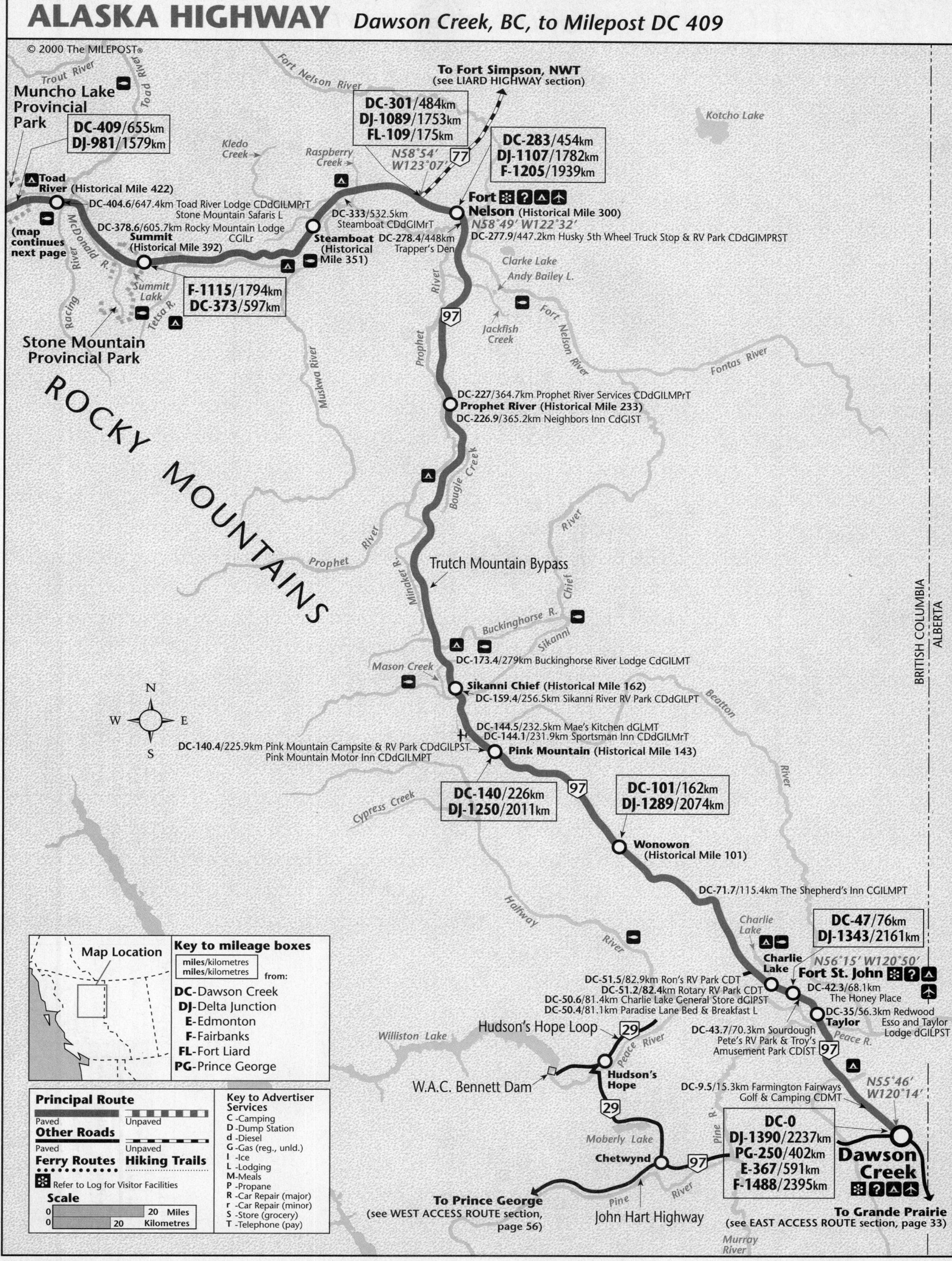

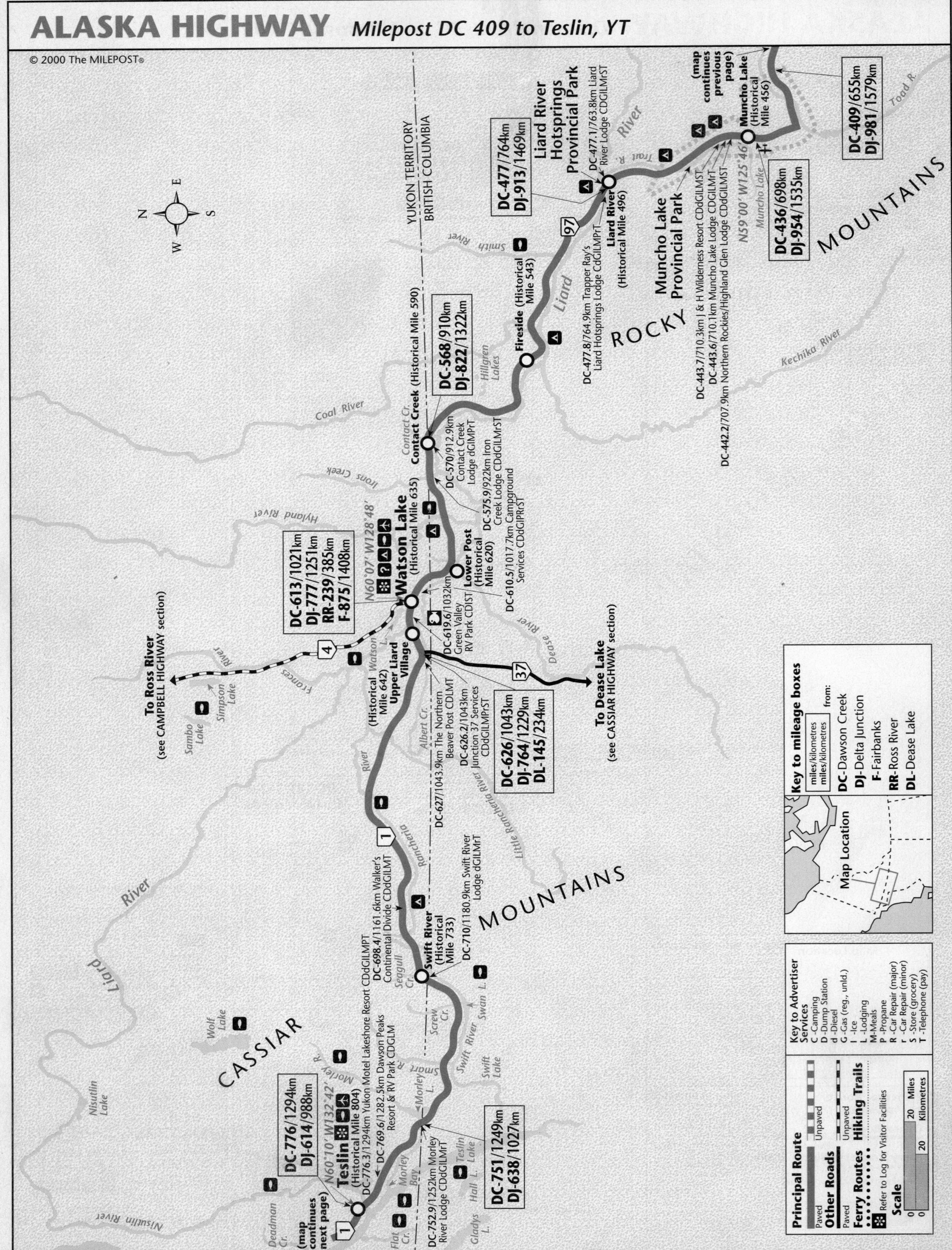
ALASKA HIGHWAY Milepost DC 409 to Teslin, YT
© 2000 The MILEPOST®
YUKON TERRITORY
BRITISH COLUMBIA
(map continues previous page)
Muncho Lake (Historical Mile 456)
DC-409/655km
DJ-981/1579km
Toad R.
N59°00' W125°46'
Muncho Lake
DC-436/698km
DJ-954/1535km
MOUNTAINS
Muncho Lake Provincial Park
DC-443.7/710.3km J & H Wilderness Resort CDdGILMrST
DC-443.6/710.1km Muncho Lake Lodge CDdGILMrT
DC-442.2/707.9km Northern Rockies/Highland Glen Lodge CDdGILMST
Trout R.
River
Liard River Hotsprings Provincial Park
DC-477.1/763.8km Liard River Lodge CDGILMrST
DC-477/764km
DJ-913/1469km
Liard River (Historical Mile 496)
DC-477.8/764.9km Trapper Ray's Liard Hotsprings Lodge CDdGILMPrT
97
Smith River
Fireside (Historical Mile 543)
Liard
ROCKY
Kechika River
DC-568/910km
DJ-822/1322km
Contact Creek (Historical Mile 590)
Contact Cr.
Hillgren Lakes
Coal River
DC-570/912.9km Contact Creek Lodge dGIMPrT
DC-575.9/922km Iron Creek Lodge CDdGILMrST
DC-610.5/1017.7km Campground Services CDdGIPRrST
Irons Creek
Hyland River
Lower Post (Historical Mile 620)
Watson Lake (Historical Mile 635)
N60°07' W128°48'
DC-613/1021km
DJ-777/1251km
RR-239/385km
F-875/1408km
DC-619.6/1032km Green Valley RV Park CDIST
Dease River
Upper Liard Village (Historical Mile 642)
Watson L.
4
To Ross River (see CAMPBELL HIGHWAY section)
Frances River
Simpson Lake
Sambo Lake
37
To Dease Lake (see CASSIAR HIGHWAY section)
DC-627/1043.9km The Northern Beaver Post CDLMT
DC-626.2/1043km Junction 37 Services CDdGILMPrST
DC-626/1043km
DJ-764/1229km
DL-145/234km
Albert Cr.
Little Rancheria River
River
1
Rancheria
MOUNTAINS
DC-698.4/1161.6km Walker's Continental Divide CDdGILMT
Swift River (Historical Mile 733)
DC-710/1180.9km Swift River Lodge dGILMrT
Seagull Cr.
Swan L.
Screw Cr.
Swift River
Swift Lake
Smart R.
Morley L.
Liard
River
Wolf Lake
CASSIAR
Morley R.
Nisutlin Lake
DC-776.3/1294km Yukon Motel Lakeshore Resort CDdGILMPT
DC-769.6/1282.5km Dawson Peaks Resort & RV Park CDGILM
DC-776/1294km
DJ-614/988km
Teslin (Historical Mile 804)
N60°10' W132°42'
DC-752.9/1252km Morley River Lodge CDdGILMrT
Morley Bay
Teslin Lake
DC-751/1249km
DJ-638/1027km
Hall L.
Gladys L.
Flat Cr.
Deadman Cr.
Nisutlin River
(map continues next page)
Map Location
Key to mileage boxes
miles/kilometres
miles/kilometres from:
DC-Dawson Creek
DJ-Delta Junction
F-Fairbanks
RR-Ross River
DL-Dease Lake
Principal Route
Paved
Other Roads
Paved
Unpaved
Unpaved
Ferry Routes
Hiking Trails
Refer to Log for Visitor Facilities
Scale
0 20 Miles
0 20 Kilometres
Key to Advertiser Services
C -Camping
D -Dump Station
d -Diesel
G -Gas (reg., unld.)
I -Ice
L -Lodging
M -Meals
P -Propane
R -Car Repair (major)
r -Car Repair (minor)
S -Store (grocery)
T -Telephone (pay)

ALASKA HIGHWAY *Teslin, YT, to Milepost DC 1136*

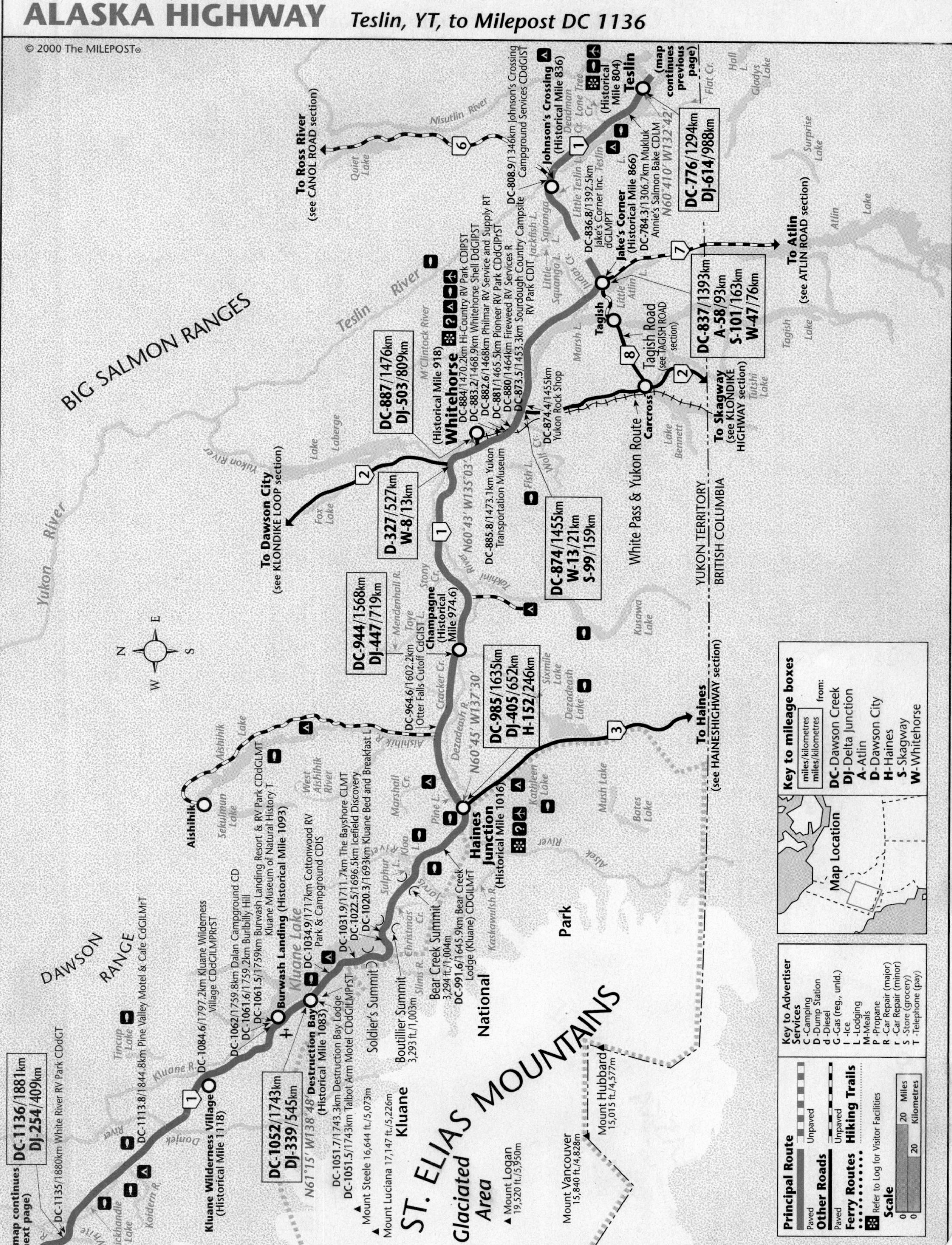

ALASKA HIGHWAY *Milepost DC 1136 to Milepost DC 1380*

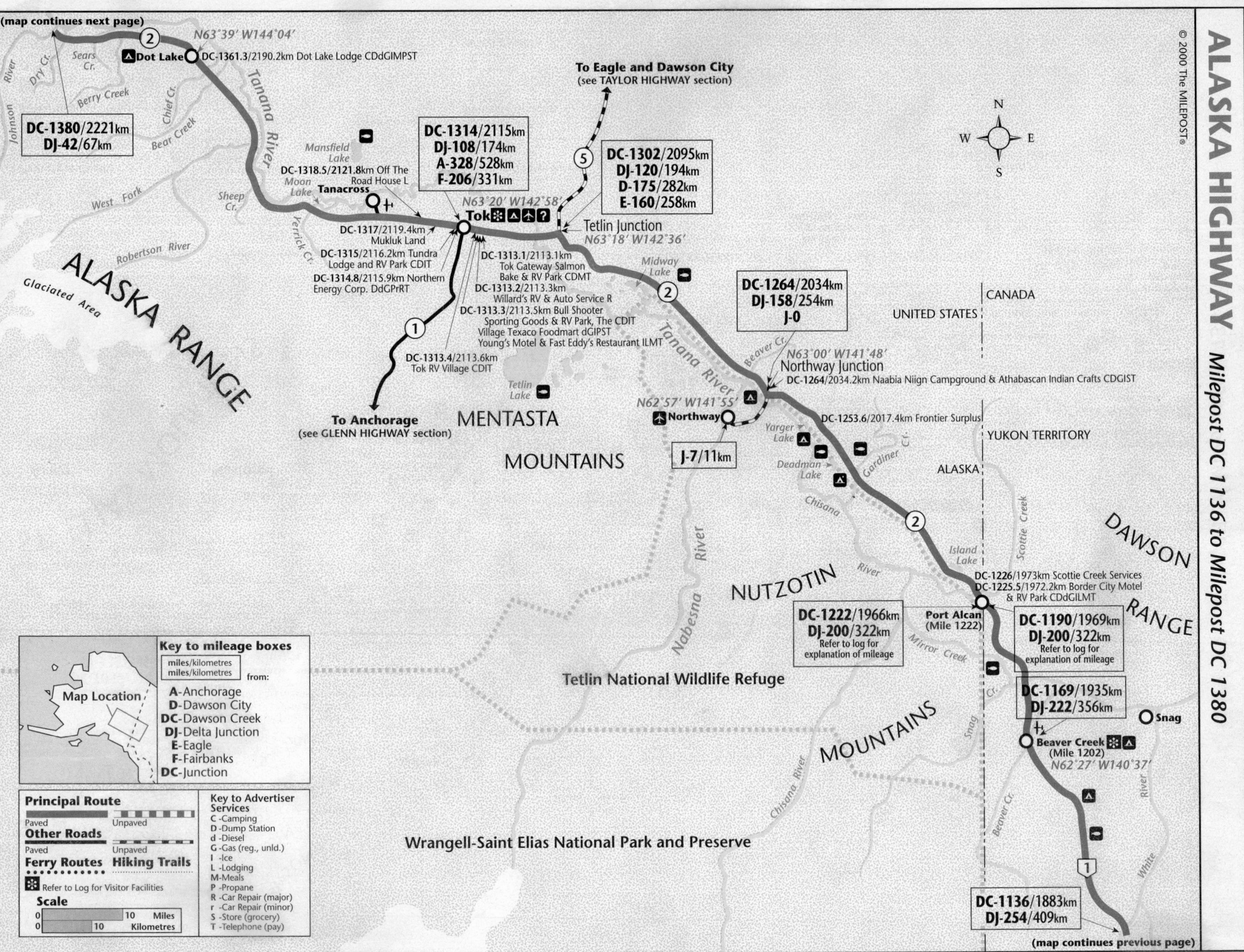

vided construction materials along the route.

A massive mobilization of men and equipment began. Regiments of the U.S. Army Corps of Engineers were moved north to work on the highway. By June, more than 10,000 American troops had poured into the Canadian North. The Public Roads Administration tackled the task of organizing civilian engineers and equipment. Trucks, road-building equipment, office furniture, food, tents and other supplies all had to be located and then shipped north.

Road work began in April, with crews working out of the 2 largest construction camps, Whitehorse and Fort St. John. The highway followed existing winter roads, old Indian trails, rivers and, on occasion, "sight" engineering.

For the soldiers and civilian workers, it was a hard life. Working 7 days a week, they endured mosquitoes and black flies in summer, and below zero temperatures in winter. Weeks would pass with no communication between headquarters and field parties. According to one senior officer with the Public Roads Administration, "Equipment was always a critical problem. There never was enough."

In June 1942, the Japanese invaded Attu and Kiska islands in the Aleutians, adding a new sense of urgency to completion of the road. Crews working from east and west connected at Contact Creek on Sept. 25. By October, it was possible for vehicles to travel the entire length of the highway. The official opening of the Alaska Highway was a ribbon-cutting ceremony held Nov. 20, 1942, on Soldier's Summit at Kluane Lake. (A rededication ceremony was held Nov. 20, 1992, as part of the 50th anniversary celebration of the Alaska Highway.) The Alaska Highway was named an International Historical Engineering Landmark in 1996.

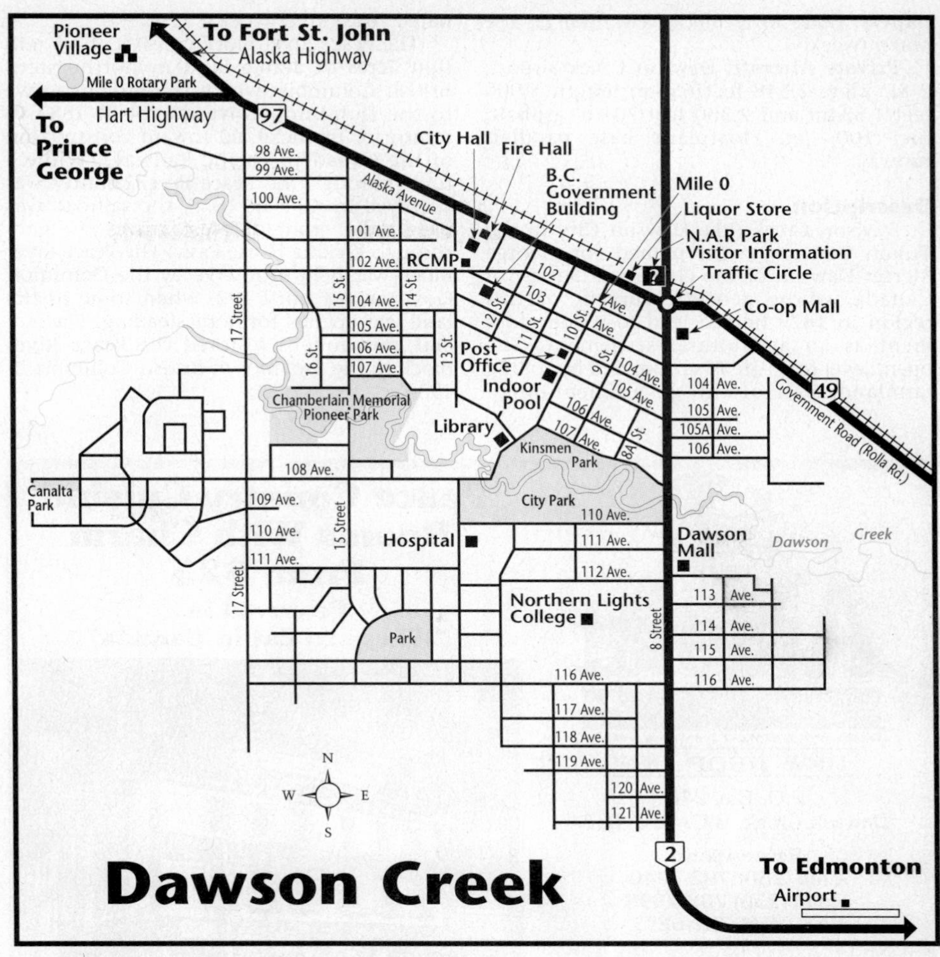

Dawson Creek

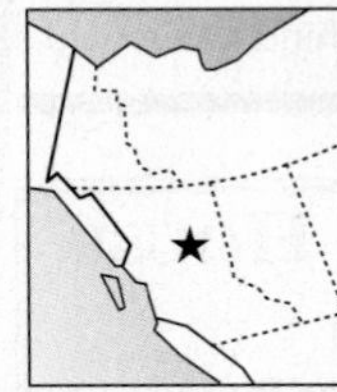

Milepost 0 of the Alaska Highway; 367 miles/591 km northwest of Edmonton, AB; 250 miles/402 km northeast of Prince George, BC. **Population:** 11,125, area 27,000. **Emergency Services: RCMP**, phone (250) 782-5211. **Fire Department**, phone (250) 782-5000. **Ambulance**, phone (250) 782-2211. **Hospital and Poison Centre**, Dawson Creek and District Hospital, 11000 13th St., phone (250) 782-8501.

Visitor Information: At NAR (Northern Alberta Railway) Park on Alaska Avenue at 10th Street (one block west of the traffic circle), in the building behind the railway car. Open year-round, 8 A.M. to 7 P.M. daily in summer, 10 A.M. to 4 P.M. Tuesday through Saturday in winter. Phone (250) 782-9595, or e-mail dawsoncrk@pris.bc.ca. Trained visitor-information counselors can answer questions about weather and road conditions, local events and attractions. Plenty of public parking in front of the refurbished grain elevator that houses the Dawson Creek Art Gallery and Museum.

Elevation: 2,186 feet/666m. **Climate**: Average temperature in January is 0°F/-18°C; in July it is 60°F/15°C. The average annual snowfall is 72 inches with the average depth of snow in midwinter at 19.7 inches. Frost-free days total 97, with the first frost of the year occurring about the first week of September. **Radio**: CJDC 890. **Television**: 13 channels via cable including pay TV. **News-**

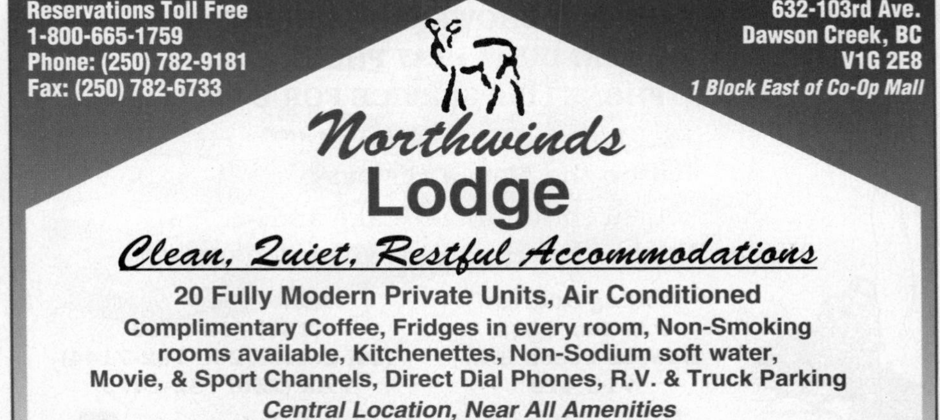

papers: *Peace River Block News* (daily); *The Mirror* (weekly).

Private Aircraft: Dawson Creek airport, 2 SE; elev. 2,148 feet/655m; length 5,000 feet/1,524m and 2,300 feet/701m; asphalt; fuel 100, jet. Floatplane base parallels runway.

Description

Dawson Creek (like Dawson City in the Yukon Territory) was named for George Mercer Dawson of the Geological Survey of Canada, whose geodetic surveys of this region in 1879 helped lead to its development as an agricultural settlement. The open, level townsite is surrounded by rolling farmland, part of the government-designated Peace River Block.

The Peace River Block consists of 3.5 million acres of arable land in northeastern British Columbia, which the province gave to the Dominion Government in 1883 in return for financial aid toward construction of the Canadian Pacific Railway. (While a route through the Peace River country was surveyed by CPR in 1878, the railroad was eventually routed west from Calgary through Kicking Horse Pass.) The Peace River Block was held in reserve by the Dominion Government until 192, when some of the land was opened for homesteading. The federal government restored the Peace River Block to the province of British Columbia in 1930.

Today, agriculture is an important part of this area's economy. The fields of bright yellow flowers (in season) in the area are canola, a hybrid of rapeseed that was developed as a low cholesterol oil seed. Raw seed is processed in Alberta and Japan. The Peace River region also produces most of the province's cereal grain, along with fodder, cattle and dairy cattle. Other industries include the production of honey, hogs, eggs and poultry. Some potato and vegetable farming is also done here.

On the British Columbia Railway line and the western terminus of the Northern

DAWSON CREEK ADVERTISERS

Alahart RV Park................Ph. (250) 782-4702
Alaska Hotel Cafe & Dew Drop Inn Pub ....55 paces south of Mile 0 Post
Dawson Creek Art Gallery ....NAR Park
Dawson Creek Coin Laundry Ltd.........5 blocks S. of traffic circle
Dawson Creek Visitor Information Bureau.....Ph. (250) 782-9595
Joy Propane......................Ph. (888) 782-6008
King Koin Laundromat .....Ph. (250) 782-2395
Lodge Motor Inn & Cafe, The ....Ph. (250) 782-4837
Mile "0" Gifts ....10109 10th St.
Mile "0" RV Park & Campground ....Adjacent Walter Wright Pioneer Village
Northern Lights RV Park Ltd.........1 mile from Alaska Hwy. Jct. on Hwy. 97 S
Northern Treasures Gift Shop....................................NAR Park
Northwinds Lodge.........1 block E. Co-op Mall
Organic Farms Bakery.......Ph. (250) 782-6533
Peace Villa Motel..................1641 Alaska Ave.
Rowland House Bed & Breakfast...........Ph. (250) 782-5654
Super 8 Motel ....Ph. (250) 782-8899
Trail Inn..............................Ph. (250) 782-8595
Tubby's RV Park.....................1913 Hart Hwy.
United Spring & Brake Ltd.........Directly behind McDonald's

Alberta Railway (now Canadian National Railway), Dawson Creek is also the hub of four major highways: the John Hart Highway (Highway 97 South) to Prince George; the Alaska Highway (Highway 97 North); Highway 2, which leads east to Grande Prairie, AB; and Highway 49, which leads east to Spirit River and Donnelly.

The Northern Alberta Railway reached Dawson Creek in 1931. As a railhead, Dawson Creek was an important funnel for supplies and equipment during construction of the Alaska Highway in 1942. Some 600 carloads arrived by rail within a period of five weeks in preparation for the construction program, according to a report by the Public Roads Administration in 1942. A "rutted provincial road" linked Dawson Creek with Fort St. John, affording the only approach to the southern base of operations. Field headquarters were established at Fort St. John and Whitehorse. Meanwhile, men and machines continued to arrive at Dawson Creek. By May of 1942, 4,720 carloads of equipment had arrived by rail at Dawson Creek for dispersement to troops and civilian engineers to the north.

With the completion of the Alaska Highway in 1942 (and opening to the public in 1948) and the John Hart Highway in 1952, Dawson Creek expanded both as a distribution centre and tourist destination. Dawson Creek was incorporated as a city in 1958.

The development of oil and natural gas exploration in northeastern British Columbia, and related industries such as pipeline construction and oil storage, has contributed to the economic expansion of Dawson Creek. The city is also one of the major supply centres for the massive resource development known as North East Coal, southwest of Dawson Creek. Access to the coal development and the town of Tumbler Ridge is via the Heritage Highway, which branches off the John Hart Highway just west of Dawson Creek and also branches off Highway 2 southeast of the city. Highway 29 extends south from Chetwynd to Tumbler Ridge.

Provincial government offices and social services for the South Peace region are located in Dawson Creek. City Hall is located on Ben Heppner Way, a street recently renamed in honor of the famous opera tenor, who comes from this area.

The city has a modern 100-bed hospital, a public library and a college (Northern Lights, associated with the University of Northern BC in Prince George). There are also an indoor swimming pool, 2 skating arenas, a curling rink, bowling alley, golf

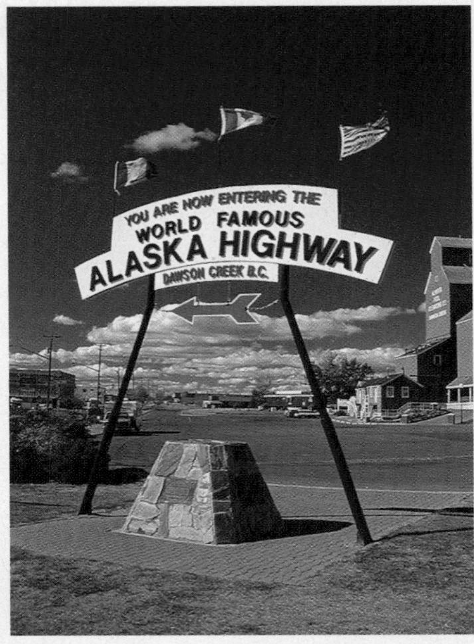

Alaska Highway monument near N.A.R. Park. Milepost 0 is located downtown on 10th St. (© Earl L. Brown, staff)

course, art gallery, museum, tennis and racquetball courts. There are numerous churches in Dawson Creek. (Check at the Visitor Infocentre for location and hours of worship.)

Lodging & Services

There are 14 hotels/motels, several bed and breakfasts, and dozens of restaurants. Department stores, banks, grocery, an organic bakery, drug and hardware stores, antique shop and other specialty shops. Shopping is downtown and in the 2 shopping centres, Co-op Mall and Dawson Mall. Visitors will also find laundromats, car washes, gas stations and automotive repair shops. The liquor store is adjacent the NAR Visitor Infocentre on Alaska Avenue.

The Alaska Hotel Cafe & Dew Drop Inn Pub combines the spirit of Northern Adventure with Old World charm. Where to Eat in Canada, which lists the 500 top restaurants, suggests, "It is a good idea to start out on the Alaska Highway with a good meal under your belt, and there's no better place than the Alaska Cafe." The cafe also holds membership in World Famous Restaurants International. The pub features live entertainment nightly, a hot spot in town. The building, having 15 "rooms with charm," provides a perfect backdrop for the Kux-Kardos collection of antiques and works of art (tours available). At the Alaska, our philosophy is Deluxe Evolutionary ... "Always changing for the better." Phone (250) 782-7998 to reserve. Pets welcome. Located 55 paces south of the mile "0" post. A definite must to experience. [ADVERTISEMENT]

Organic Farms Bakery. Using grain crops from our family farm, 100 percent certified organic stoneground flour. Specializing in German-style rye, spelt and whole wheat breads, buns, pretzels and delicious pastries. Flours and spelt pastas. Taste the difference! 1425 97th Ave., Dawson Creek (look for our colourful bakery), just off Alaska Ave. Phone (250) 782-6533. [ADVERTISEMENT]

Camping

There are 4 campgrounds in Dawson Creek, 2 located on either side of the Hart Highway at its junction with the Alaska Highway and 2 located on Alaska Avenue. There is a private campground on the Hart Highway, 2 miles/3.2 km west from the Alaska Highway junction. There are also campgrounds (both private and provincial) north of Dawson Creek on the Alaska Highway. ▲

Northern Lights RV Park welcomes you! Enjoy peaceful surroundings just 1.5 miles from Dawson Creek. Check out our souvenir shop or try fly fishing in our trout pond. Or, just sit back and relax while we pamper you and your rig to prepare you for your Alaska Highway adventure! Your hosts—the Bates Family. Phone (250) 782-9433. E-mail: lbates@pris.bc.ca. Internet address: www.pris.bc.ca\rvpark\. [ADVERTISEMENT] ▲

Rotary Park pool is a popular spot on hot summer days. (© Earl L. Brown, staff)

Transportation

Air: Scheduled service from Dawson Creek airport to Prince George, Vancouver, Edmonton, Grande Prairie and Calgary via Air BC. The airport is located 2 miles/3.2 km south of the Alaska Avenue traffic circle via 8th Street/Highway 2; there is a small terminal at the airport. There is also a floatplane base.

Railroad: Canadian National Railroad and British Columbia Railway provide freight service only. B.C. Railway provides passenger service from Vancouver to Prince George.

Bus: Greyhound service to Prince George and Vancouver, BC; Edmonton, AB; and Whitehorse, YT. Dawson Creek also has a city bus transit system.

Attractions

NAR Park, on Alaska Avenue at 10th Street (near the traffic circle), is the site of the Visitor Infocentre, which is housed in a restored railway station; phone (250) 782-9595. The Visitor Infocentre offers a self-guided historical walking tour with descriptions of Dawson Creek in the early 1940s during construction of the Alaska Highway.

Also at the station is the **Dawson Creek Station Museum**, operated by the South Peace Historical Society, which contains pioneer artifacts and wildlife displays, including a collection of more than 50 birds' eggs from this area. Be sure to leave enough time to view the hour-long video about the building of the Alaska Highway. Souvenirs and restrooms at the museum.

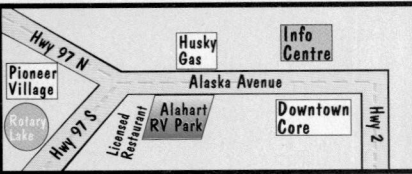

In front of the station is a 1903 railway car, called "The Blue Goose Caboose." Adjacent to the station is a huge wooden grain elevator, which has been refurbished; its annex now houses an art gallery with art shows throughout the summer; admission by donation. Good display of Alaska Highway construction photos; restroom, gift shop. The last of Dawson Creek's old elevators, it was bought and moved to its present location through the efforts of community organizations. Every Saturday in summer there is an outdoor farmer's market featuring flowers, produce, baked goods and crafts for sale.

Inquire at the Visitor Infocentre for the location of Bear Mountain Community Forest. This Ministry of Forests recreation area features interpretive trails on the flora and fauna of the area. It is located 6 miles/10 km south of the city.

Recreational facilities in Dawson Creek include a bowling alley, miniature golf, indoor pool, 2 ice arenas, curling rink, 18-hole golf course, tennis courts and an outdoor pool at Rotary Lake Park.

Walter Wright Pioneer Village and Mile 0 Rotary Park. The entrance to the village is highlighted by Gardens North, consisting of 9 separate gardens, including a memorial rose garden. Bring a camera to capture the amazing variety of perennials and annuals that grow in the North. The pioneer village contains an impressive collection of local pioneer buildings, including a teahouse; antiques and collectibles shop; and a general store. Souvenirs and Gardens North seeds are available. Admission is $1. Food service available at the Mile 1 Cafe. Check at the infocentre for summer tours of the gardens.

Adjacent to the village is the Sudeten Memorial Hall. "A Mile Zero Welcome," a presentation about Dawson Creek, then and now, by Marilyn Croutch, is held either in Sudeten Hall or the old Dawson School in summer; phone (250) 782-7144. Check with the Visitor Infocentre for details on entertainment offerings. Also located here is Rotary Lake, an outdoor man-made swimming facility; restrooms and picnic areas are found throughout Rotary Park.

Dawson Creek Walking Path, a community project to restore the creek, provides a peaceful path for travelers to stretch their legs and take in some local scenery. When complete, the path will connect Rotary Park with Kinsmen Park on 8th Street. Pick up a brochure at the visitor centre.

Special Events. Mile Zero Celebration Days held in May. July 4th festivities take place at Sudeten Hall. The Fall Fair and Stampede in August features the largest amateur rodeo in North America.

Tumbler Ridge Side Trip. Tumbler Ridge is the townsite for Quintette Coal Limited's large-scale surface mines, and also serves workers of the Bullmoose Mine. Tours of Quintette and Bullmoose mines are available; inquire at the Visitor Infocentre in Tumbler Ridge. The huge coal processing plant and overhead conveyor are visible from the road. Monkman Provincial Park, site of spectacular 225-foot/69-m Kinuseo (Keh-NEW-see-oh) Falls, lies south of Tumbler Ridge. Contact Tumbler Ridge Infocentre (250/242-4702) for more information. See "Tumbler Ridge Loop" on page 80 in the WEST ACCESS ROUTE section for more information.

Alaska Highway Log

Distance from Dawson Creek (DC) is followed by distance from Delta Junction (DJ). Original mileposts are indicated in the text as Historical Mile.

In Canada, mileages from Dawson Creek are based on actual driving distance, not historical mileposts, and kilometres are based on physical kilometreposts. Mileages from Delta Junction are also based on actual driving distance, not historical mileposts, but are followed by the metric conversion to kilometres.

BC HIGHWAY 97

DC 0 DJ 1390 (2236.9 km) **Mile 0** marker of the Alaska Highway on 10th Street in downtown Dawson Creek.

Northbound: Good pavement approximately next 284 miles/457 km (through Fort Nelson). Watch for road construction and surface changes from Pink Mountain north.

DC 1.2 (1.9 km) DJ 1388.8 (2235 km) **Junction** of the Alaska Highway and John Hart Highway.

Prince George-bound travelers turn to the end of the WEST ACCESS ROUTE section and read log back to front. Alaska-bound travelers continue with this log.

DC 1.5 (2.4 km) **DJ 1388.5** (2234.5 km) Mile 0 Rotary Park (picnicking and swimming), Walter Wright Pioneer Village and Mile 0 Campground to west. ▲

DC 1.7 (2.7 km) **DJ 1388.3** (2234.2 km) **Historic Milepost 2**. Sign about Cantel Repeater Station. Cantel telephone–teletype lines stretched from Alberta to Fairbanks, AK, making it one of the world's longest open-wire toll circuits at the time.

DC 2 (3.2 km) **DJ 1388** (2233.7 km) Recreation centre and golf course to west. Louisiana Pacific waferboard plant to east.

DC 2.7 (4.3 km) **DJ 1387.3** (2232.6 km) Truck scales and public phone to east. Truck stop to west; gas, cafe.

DC 2.9 (4.7 km) **DJ 1387.1** (2232.3 km) Northern Alberta Railway (NAR) tracks.

DC 3.3 (5.3 km) **DC 1386.7** (2231.6 km) Turnout with litter barrel to east. **Historic Milepost 3**; historic sign marks Curan & Briggs Ltd. Construction Camp, U.S. Army Traffic Control Centre.

DC 3.4 (5.5 km) **DJ 1386.6** (2231.4 km) **Historical Mile 3**. The Trading Post to east.

DC 9.5 (15.3 km) **DJ 1380.5** (2221.6 km) Golf course, driving range and RV park. ▲

Farmington Fairways Golf and Camping. See display ad this section. ▲

DC 11.2 (18 km) **DJ 1378.8** (2218.9 km) Turnout with litter barrels to west.

Winter view across the Peace River to Taylor, BC. (© Earl L. Brown, staff)

DC 11.5 (18.5 km) **DJ 1378.5** (2218.4 km) Turnout with litter barrels to east.

DC 14.8 (24 km) **DJ 1375.2** (2213.1 km) Farmington (unincorporated).

DC 15.8 (25.4 km) **DJ 1374.2** (2211.5 km) Farmington store to west; gas, groceries, phone.

DC 17.3 (27.8 km) **DJ 1372.7** (2209.1 km) Exit east for loop road to **Kiskatinaw Provincial Park**. Follow good 2-lane paved road (old Alaska Highway) 2.5 miles/4 km for provincial park; 28 campsites, drinking water, firewood, picnic tables, fire rings, outhouses and garbage containers. Camping fee $12. ▲

This interesting side road gives travelers the opportunity to drive the original old Alaska Highway and to cross the historic curved wooden **Kiskatinaw River Bridge**. A sign at the bridge notes that this 531-foot-/162-m-long structure is the only original timber bridge built along the Alaska Highway that is still in use today.

DC 17.5 (28.2 km) **DJ 1372.5** (2208.8 km) Distance marker indicates Fort St. John 29 miles/47 km.

CAUTION: Watch for deer.

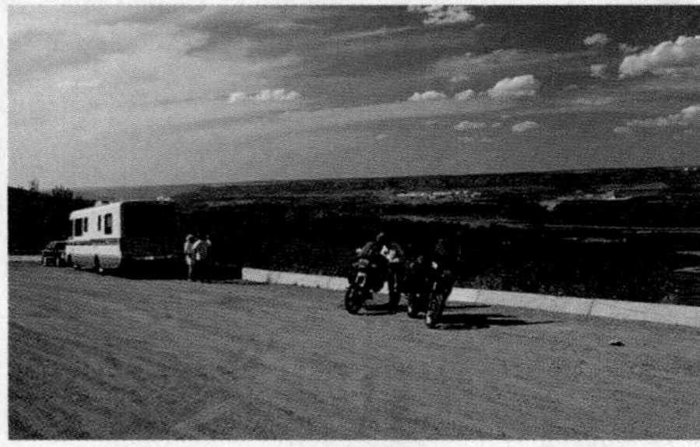

DC 19.4 (31.2 km) **DJ 1370.6** (2205.7 km) Large turnout to east.

DC 19.8 (31.9 km) **DJ 1370.2** (2205.1 km) Highway descends northbound to Kiskatinaw River.

DC 20.9 (33.6 km) **DJ 1369.1** (2203.3 km) Kiskatinaw River bridge.

CAUTION: Strong crosswinds on bridge.

Turnout with litter barrel and picnic tables to east at north end of bridge. View of unique bridge support.

DC 21.6 (34.5 km) **DJ 1368.4** (2202.2 km) Loop road to Kiskatinaw Provincial Park and Kiskatinaw River bridge (see **Milepost DC 17.3**).

DC 25.4 (41 km) **DJ 1364.6** (2196.1 km) NorthwesTel microwave tower to east. Alaska Highway travelers will be seeing many of these towers as they drive north. The Northwest Communications System was constructed by the U.S. Army in 1942–43. This land line was replaced in 1963 with the construction of 42 microwave relay stations by Canadian National Telecommunications (Cantel, now NorthwesTel) between Grande Prairie, AB, and the YT–AK border.

DC 30.5 (49.1 km) **DJ 1359.5** (2187.8 km) Turnout to east with litter barrels. Turnout to west with litter barrels, pit toilet and historical marker about explorer Alexander Mackenzie.

Highway begins steep winding descent northbound to the Peace River bridge. Good views to northeast of Peace River valley and industrial community of Taylor. Some wide gravel shoulder next 4 miles/6.4 km for northbound traffic to pull off.

CAUTION: Trucks check your brakes.

DC 32.1 (51.6 km) **DJ 1357.9** (2185.3 km) Large turnout with litter barrels.

DC 33.8 (54.4 km) **DJ 1356.2** (2182.5 km) Pingle Creek.

DC 34 (54.7 km) **DJ 1356** (2182.2 km) Access to **Taylor Landing Provincial Park**; boat launch, parking and fishing. Jet boat outfitter. Also access to Peace Island Regional Park, 0.5 mile/0.8 km west of the highway, situated on an island in the **Peace River** connected to the south shore by a causeway. Peace Island has 35 shaded campsites with gravel pads, firewood, fire rings, picnic tables, picnic shelter, toilets, potable water, playground and horseshoe pits. There are also 4 large picnic areas and a tenting area. Camping fee. Open Memorial Day to Labour Day. Nature trail, good bird watching and good fishing in clear water. Boaters should use caution on the Peace River since both parks are downstream from the W.A.C. Bennett and Peace Canyon dams and water levels may fluctuate rapidly. ▲

DC 34.4 (55.4 km) **DJ 1355.6** (2181.6 km) **Peace River Bridge**. Bridging the Peace was one of the first goals of Alaska Highway engineers in 1942. Traffic moving north from Dawson Creek was limited by the Peace River crossing, where 2 ferries with a capacity of 10 trucks per hour were operating in May. Three different pile trestles were constructed across the Peace River, only to be washed out by high water. Work on the permanent 2,130-foot suspension bridge began in December 1942 and was completed in July 1943. One of 2 suspension bridges on the Alaska Highway, the Peace River bridge collapsed in 1957 after erosion undermined the north anchor block of the bridge. The cantilever and truss-type bridge that crosses the Peace River today was completed in 1960.

Gas pipeline bridge visible to east.

DC 35 (56.3 km) **DJ 1355** (2180.6 km) **Historic Milepost 35** at **TAYLOR** (pop. 1,031; elev. 1,804 feet/550m), located on the north bank of the Peace River. **Visitor Information**: On left northbound (10114 100 St.); phone (250) 789-9015. Inquire here about industrial tours of Canadian Forest Products, Fiberco Pulpmill and Greenhouse Complex. Taylor is an industrial community clustered around a Westcoast Energy Inc. gas-processing plant and large sawmill. Established in 1955 with the discovery and development of a natural gas field in the area, Taylor is the site of a pulp mill and plants that handle sulfur processing, gas compressing, high-octane aviation gas production and other byproducts of natural gas. The Westcoast Energy natural gas pipeline reaches from here to Vancouver, BC, with a branch to western Washington.

The fertile Taylor Flats area has several market gardens and roadside stands in summer. A hotel, motels, cafes, grocery store, private RV park, gas station and post office are located here. Free municipal dump station and potable water located behind the North Taylor Inn. Recreation facilities include a championship 18-hole golf course, a motorcross track and a recreation complex with swimming pool, curling rink and district ice centre for skating (open year-round). Gold Panning Championship held in August. ▲

Redwood Esso and Taylor Lodge. See display ad this section.

DC 36.3 (58.4 km) **DJ 1353.7** (2178.5 km) Railroad tracks.

DC 40 (64.5 km) **DJ 1350** (2172.6 km) **Historical Mile 41**. Post office.

DC 40.3 (64.9 km) **DJ 1349.7** (2172.1 km) Exit east for Fort St. John airport.

DC 40.4 (65 km) **DJ 1349.6** (2171.9 km) B.C. Railway overhead tracks.

DC 40.9 (65.8 km) **DJ 1349.1** (2171.1 km) **Historic Milepost 42** Access Road to Fort St. John Airport.

DC 42.3 (68.1 km) **DJ 1347.7** (2168.9 km) World's largest glass beehive at the Honey Place to west. Well worth a visit. The Peace Country produces several tons of high quality honey annually.

The Honey Place. See display ad this section.

DC 43.7 (70.3 km) **DJ 1346.3** (2166.6 km) **Historical Mile 44**. Miniature golf, driving range and RV park. ▲

Sourdough Pete's RV Park and Troy's Amusement Park. See display ad this section. ▲

DC 44.6 (71.7 km) **DJ 1345.4** (2165.2 km) Access to Fort St. John via 86th Street.

DC 45.7 (73.5 km) **DJ 1344.3** (2163.4 km) **Historic Milepost 47**, Fort St. John/"Camp Alcan" sign. In 1942, Fort St. John "exploded." What had been home to 200 became a temporary base for more than 6,000.

DC 45.8 (73.7 km) **DJ 1344.2** (2163.2 km) South access to Fort St. John via 100th Street. Exit east for Visitor Infocentre and downtown Fort St. John.

DC 47 (75.6 km) **DJ 1343** (2161.3 km) **Historical Mile 48**. North access to Fort St. John via 100th Avenue to downtown. Truck stop with 24-hour gas and food.

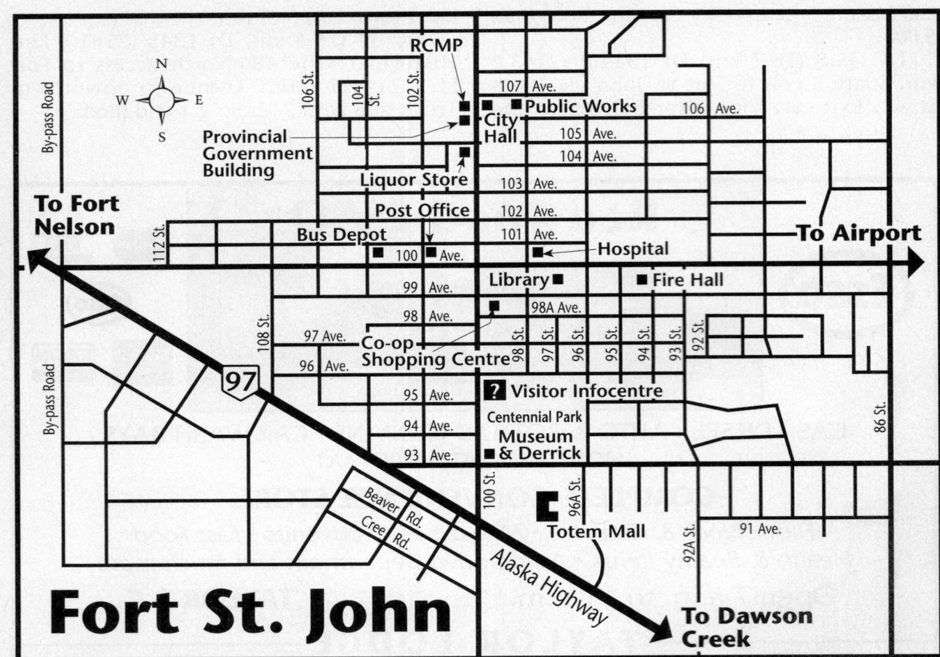

The 136-foot-high oil derrick at Centennial Park stands outside Fort St. John's museum. (© Earl L. Brown, staff)

Fort St. John

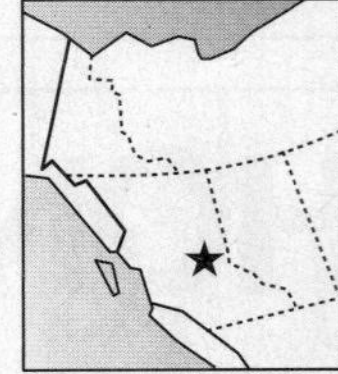

DC 47 (75.6 km) **DJ 1343** (2161.3 km) Located approximately 236 miles/380 km south of Fort Nelson. **Population:** 16,021; area 55,000. **Emergency Services: RCMP**, phone (250) 787-8100. **Fire Department**, phone (250) 785-2323. **Ambulance**, phone (250) 785-2079. **Hospital**, on 100th Avenue and 96th Street, phone (250) 785-6611.

Visitor Information: Visitor Information Centre is located at 9923–96th Ave., corner of 100th St. and 96th Ave.; phone (250) 785-3033. It is in the same building as the chamber of commerce and the Northern Rockies Alaska Highway Tourism Assoc. Open year-round; regular hours are 9 A.M. to 5 P.M.; extended hours in summer. Write Chamber of Commerce, 9923 96th Ave., Fort St. John, BC V1J 4K9; phone (250) 785-6037, fax (250) 785-7181, e-mail fsjchofcom@awink.com; web site www.gbsweb.net/fortstjohnchamber.

Visitors may also contact the following agencies for information on wilderness hiking and camping opportunities: BC Parks, #150, 10003–110th Ave., Fort St. John, BC V1J 6M7, phone (250) 787-3407; and Ministry of Forests, 8808–72nd St., Fort St. John, BC V1J 6M2, phone (250) 787-5600.

Direct hunting and fishing queries to the Ministry of Environment, #400, 10003–110th Ave., Fort St. John, BC V1J 6M7; phone (250) 787-3411.

Elevation: 2,280 feet/695m. **Climate**: Average high temperature in July, 73°F/23°C, average low 50°F/10°C. In January, average high is 12°F/-11°C; low is -2°F/-19°C. **Radio**: CKNL 560, CHRX Energy 98.5 FM, CBC 88.3. **Television**: Cable. **Newspaper**: *Alaska Highway News* (daily), *The Northerner* (weekly).

Private Aircraft: Fort St. John airport, 3.8 E; elev. 2,280 feet/695m; length 6,900 feet/2,103m and 6,700 feet/2,042m; asphalt; fuel 100, Jet. Charlie Lake airstrip, 6.7 NW; elev. 2,680 feet/817m; length 1,800 feet/549m; gravel; fuel 100.

FORT ST. JOHN ADVERTISERS

Best Western Coachman Inn.............Ph. (250) 787-0651
City of Fort St. John..........Ph. (250) 785-6037
Fort St. John–North Peace Museum................1 blk. N. of Alaska Hwy.
Four Seasons Motor Inn...Ph. (250) 785-6647
Husky Car and Truck Wash.....................Across from McDonald's
Northgate Inn..................Ph. (250) 787-8475
Petro-Canada Truck Stop.............Alaska Hwy.
Tirecraft...........................Ph. (250) 785-2411

View of the fertile Peace River valley near Fort St. John. (© Earl L. Brown, staff)

Description

Fort St. John is set in the low, rolling hills of the Peace River Valley. The original Fort St. John was established as Rocky Mountain Fort in 1794, making Fort St. John the oldest white settlement in mainland British Columbia.

The Peace region was homesteaded in the early 1900s. The town's early commercial development centered around a store established by settler C.M. Finch. His stepson, Clement Brooks, carried on Finch's entrepreneurship, starting several businesses in Fort St. John after WWII.

In 1942, Fort St. John became field headquarters for U.S. Army troops and civilian engineers working on construction of the Alaska Highway in the eastern sector. It was the largest camp, along with Whitehorse (headquarters for the western sector), of the dozen or so construction camps along the highway. Much of the field housing, road building equipment and even office supplies were scrounged from old Civilian Conservation Corps camps and the Work Projects Administration.

The Alaska Highway was opened to the traveling public in 1948, attracting vacationers and homesteaders. An immense natural oil and gas field discovered in 1955 made Fort St. John the oil capital of British Columbia. "Energetic City," referring to the natural energy resources and the city's potential for positive growth, became the slogan for the region.

An extension of the Pacific Great Eastern Railway, now called British Columbia Railway, from Prince George in 1958 (continued to Fort Nelson in 1971), gave Fort St. John a link with the rail yards and docks at North Vancouver.

Today, Fort St. John's economy is based primarily on oil and gas exploration, forestry a nd agriculture, tourism, hydro-electric power generation, and consumer and public services.

Transportation

Air: Served by Canadian Regional Airlines and Central Mountain Air. Connecting flights to Fort Nelson, Whitehorse, Vancouver, Grande Prairie, Edmonton and Prince George. **Bus:** Coachways service to Prince George, Vancouver, Edmonton and Whitehorse; depot at 10355 101st Ave., phone (250) 785-6695.

Lodging & Services

Visitor services are located just off the Alaska Highway and in the city centre, several blocks north of the highway.

Numerous major motels, hotels, restaurants, fast-food outlets and full-service gas stations are located on the Alaska Highway and in town. Other services include 5 supermarkets, laundromats, several banks (automatic teller machines at Totem Mall and downtown at Charter Banks), car washes and shops. There is a shopping mall on the Alaska Highway.

North Peace Recreation Centre, located behind Centennial Park at 98th and 96th Ave., has tennis, skating and curling. A Farmer's Market is held in the centre lobby on Saturdays, 9 A.M. to 4 P.M., May through December. North Peace Leisure Pool, next to the centre, has a waterslide, wave pool, lap pool, swirl pool, sauna and steam rooms; phone (250) 787-8178.

Camping

A private campground (Sourdough Pete's RV Park) is located south of town at **Milepost DC 43.7**. North of town at Charlie Lake is Rotary R.V. Park, **Milepost DC 51.2**, and Ron's R.V. Park, **Milepost DC 51.5**. Camping at Beatton Provincial Park, 5 miles east of **Milepost DC 49.5**, and at Charlie Lake Provincial Park, **Milepost DC 53.7**.

Fresh water fill-up and dump station located at the northwest corner of 86th Street and the Alaska Highway. ▲

Attractions

Centennial Park, located on 100th Street, is home to the Visitor Information Centre, North Peace Museum and **North Peace Recreation Centre and Leisure Pool**.

The park offers a curling rink, tennis courts, skateboard park, horseshoe pits and grassy picnic area.

Fort St. John–North Peace Museum features more than 6,000 artifacts from the region, including items from Finch's Store, an 1806 Fort St. John post, a trapper's cabin and early-day schoolroom. The museum gift

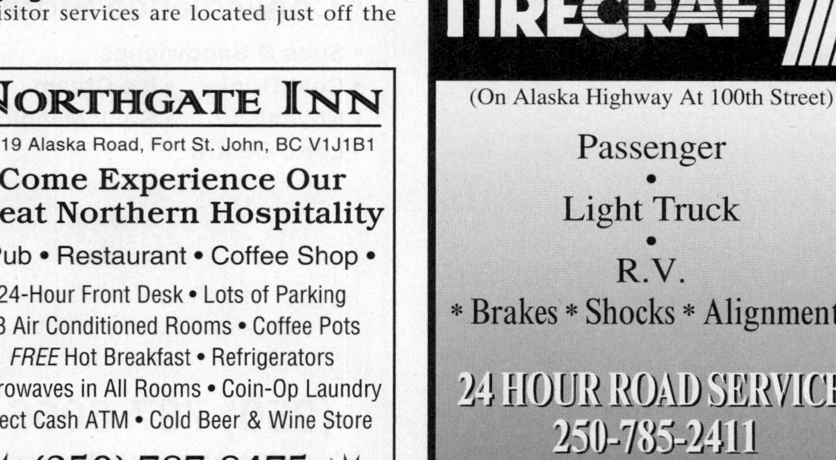

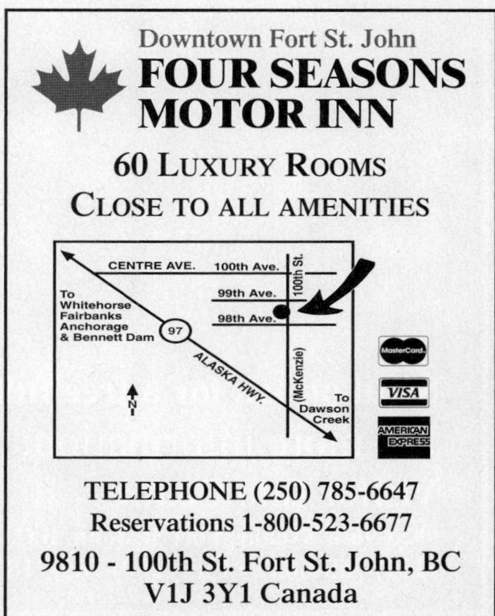

shop offers a good selection of local and Northwest books. The museum is open year-round; phone (250) 787-0430.

Outside the museum is a 136-foot-high oil derrick, presented to the North Peace Historical Society and the people of Fort St. John.

A granite monument in Centennial Park commemorates Sir Alexander Mackenzie's stop here on his journey west to the Pacific Ocean in 1793.

North Peace Cultural Centre, at 10015 100th Ave., has a library, a 413-seat theatre, an art gallery, cafe and gift shop. Phone (250) 785-1992.

Play golf. Fort St. John's only in-town golf course is Links Golf Course, just off the Bypass Road at 86 Street; 9 holes, pro shop and lounge. Phone (250) 785-9995. The Lakepoint Golf Course, on Golf Course Road at Charlie Lake, is rated one of the nicest courses in British Columbia. Open 8 A.M. to 9 P.M. daily; 18 holes, pro shop, lounge and restaurant. Phone (250) 785-5566.

Industry and agriculture of the area are showcased for the public at various places. Check with the Infocentre for directions and details. Visitors can register for Canada Forest Products (Canfor) tours at the visitor centres in Fort St. John or Taylor. The Honey Place, just south of town on the Alaska Highway, offers guided tours, fresh honey for sale, and the world's largest glass beehive for viewing year-round; phone (250) 785-4808.

Fish Creek Community Forest, adjacent to Northern Lights College, has 3 interpretive trails to view forest management activities and learn more about the forest. Cross-country ski trails in winter. From the Alaska Highway follow 100th Street north 1.2 miles/2 km and turn right on the Bypass Road just before the railway tracks. Take the first left and park behind Northern Lights College.

W.A.C. Bennett Dam is a major attraction in the area. For an interesting side trip, drive north from Fort St. John on the Alaska Highway to **Milepost DC 53.7** and take Highway 29 west 46.5 miles/74.8 km to Hudson's Hope. Highway 29 follows the original Canadian government telegraph trail of 1918. Hudson's Hope, formerly a pioneer community established in 1805 by explorer Simon Fraser, grew with construction of the W.A.C. Bennett Dam, which is located 13.5 miles/21.7 km west of town. B.C. Hydro's Peace Canyon dam is located approximately 4 miles/6.4 km south of Hudson's Hope. Turn to the HUDSON'S HOPE LOOP section for more information.

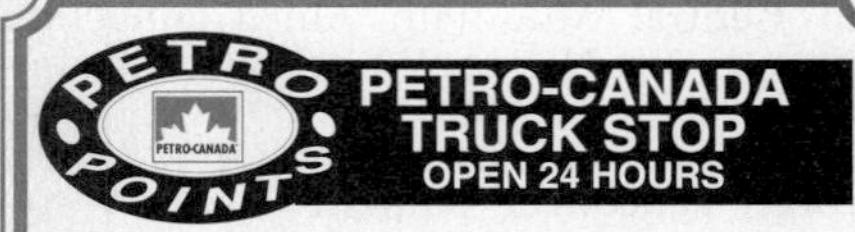

Alaska Highway Log

(continued)

Distance from Dawson Creek (DC) is followed by distance from Delta Junction (DJ). Original mileposts are indicated in the text as Historical Mile.

In Canada, mileages from Dawson Creek are based on actual driving distance, not historical mileposts, and kilometres are based on physical kilometreposts. Mileages from Delta Junction are also based on actual driving distance, not historical mileposts, but are followed by the metric conversion to kilometres.

Watch for deer and other wildlife along the Alaska Highway. (© Earl L. Brown, staff)

DC 45.8 (73.7 km) **DJ 1344.2** (2163.2 km) South access to Fort St. John via 100th Street.

DC 47 (75.6 km) **DJ 1343** (2161.3 km) **Historical Mile 48**. North access to Fort St. John via 100th Avenue.

DC 48.6 (78.2 km) **DJ 1341.4** (2157.3 km) **Historic Milepost 49** commemorates "Camp Alcan."

DC 49.5 (79.6 km) **DJ 1340.5** (2157.3 km) Exit for **Beatton Provincial Park**, 5 miles/8 km east via paved road; 37 campsites, picnic shelter, wood stove, horseshoe pits, volleyball net, playground, baseball field, sandy beach, swimming and boat launch. Camping fee $12. Fishing for northern pike, walleye (July best) and yellow perch in **Charlie Lake**. ▲

DC 50.4 (81.1 km) **DJ 1339.6** (2155.8 km) **Paradise Lane Bed and Breakfast**. See display ad this section.

DC 50.6 (81.4 km) **DJ 1339.4** (2155.5 km) **CHARLIE LAKE** (unincorporated), gas, diesel and propane, grocery, pub, post office, bed and breakfast, private RV parks and Ministry of Energy, Mines and Petroleum. Access to lakeshore east side of highway; boat launch, no parking. At one time during construction of the Alaska Highway, Charlie Lake was designated Mile 0, as there was already a road between the railhead at Dawson Creek and Fort St. John, the eastern sector headquarters for troops and engineers.

Charlie Lake General Store. See display ad this section.

DC 51.2 (82.4 km) **DJ 1338.8** (2154.5 km) **Historic Milepost 52**.. Turnoff for Rotary R.V. Park and restaurant and pub.

Rotary R.V. Park. See display ad this section. ♿▲

Historical Mile 52 was Charlie Lake Mile 0 of the Army Tote Road during construction of the Alaska Highway. It was also the site of a major distribution camp for workers and supplies heading north. 12 American soldiers drowned here in 1942 while crossing the lake aboard pontoon barges.

DC 51.5 (82.9 km) **DJ 1338.5** (2154 km) **Ron's R.V. Park. Historical Mile 52.** Treed sites with complete RV hookups, shaded lawned tenting areas, picnic tables, firepits, firewood provided. Walking trails, playground, flush toilets, hot showers, laundromat, pay phone, ice. Shaded full-hookup pull-throughs, good drinking water. Large boat launching facilities nearby. Quiet location away from hectic city confusion. Post office, golf course, fishing licenses. Charlie Lake, world famous for walleye and northern pike fishing. Phone (250) 787-1569. [ADVERTISEMENT] ▲

DC 52 (83.7 km) **DJ 1338** (2153.2 km) Exit east on Charlie Lake Road for lakeshore picnicking.

DC 53.6 (86.3 km) **DJ 1336.4** (2150.7 km) Truck weigh scales east side of highway.

DC 53.7 (86.4 km) **DJ 1336.3** (2150.5 km) Truck stop with restaurant, gas and diesel (open year-round).

Junction with Highway 29, which leads west 47 miles/75.6 km to Hudson's Hope and the W.A.C. Bennett Dam, then south to connect with the Hart Highway at Chetwynd (see HUDSON'S HOPE LOOP section).

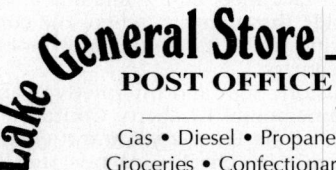

Turn east for **Charlie Lake Provincial Park**, just off highway; paved loop road (with speed bumps) leads through campground. There are 58 shaded sites, picnic tables, kitchen shelter with wood stove, firepits, firewood, outhouses, dump station, water and garbage containers. Level gravel sites, some will accommodate 2 large RVs. Camping fee $12. Playfield, playground, horseshoe pits, volleyball net and a 1.2-mile/2-km hiking trail down to lake. Watch for wildflowers. Because of the wide variety of plants here, including some that may not be seen elsewhere along the Alaska Highway, Verna E. Pratt's *Wildflowers Along the Alaska Highway* includes a special list of species for this park. Fishing in Charlie Lake for walleye, northern pike and yellow perch. Access to the lake for vehicles and boats is from the Alaska Highway just east of the park entrance. Boat launch and picnic area at lake. ▲

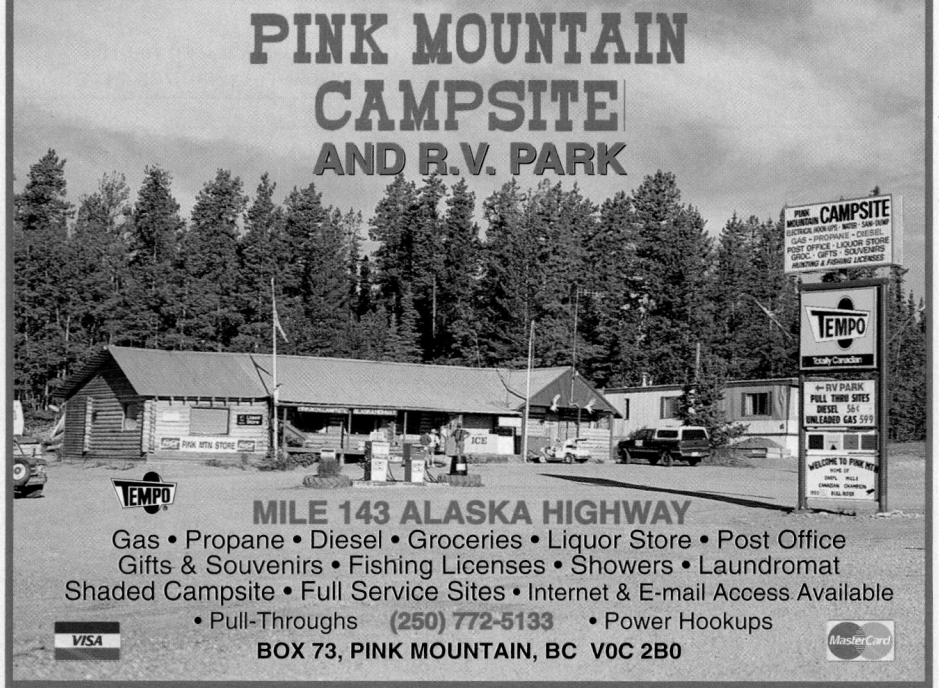

DC 62.4 (100.4 km) **DJ 1327.6** (2136.5 km) A 30-foot/9-m statue of a lumberjack marks Clarke Sawmill to west. (The statue wears a Santa suit at Christmas.)

DC 63.6 (102 km) **DJ 1326.4** (2134.6 km) Microwave tower to east.

DC 65.4 (105 km) **DJ 1324.6** (2131.7 km) Turnout with litter barrel to west.

DC 71.7 (115.4 km) **DJ 1318.3** (2121.5 km) **Historical Mile 72**. Food, gas, camping, lodging and crafts store. ▲

The Shepherd's Inn. We specialize in making folks at home, offering regular and breakfast specials, complete lunch and dinner menu. Low-fat buffalo burgers. Our specialties: homemade soups, home-baked sweet rolls, cinnamon rolls, blueberry and bran muffins, bread, biscuits and trappers bannock. Delicious desserts, rhubarb-strawberry, Dutch apple and chocolate dream pie, cherry and strawberry cheesecake. Hard ice cream. Refreshing fruit drinks from local fruits: blueberry and raspberry coolers. Caravaners and bus tours ... a convenient and delightful stop on your Alaska Highway adventure! You may reserve your stop–break with us. Full RV hookups, motel service 24 hours. NOTE: Highway 29 traffic from Hudson's Hope northbound entering Alaska Highway ... your first motel stop. Southbound ... your last motel selection. Quality Husky products. Your "Husky Buck" is a great traveling idea. Phone (250) 827-3676. An oasis on the Alcan at Mile 72. [ADVERTISEMENT] ▲

DC 72.7 (117 km) **DJ 1317.3** (2119.9 km) Cafe and private campground. ▲

DC 72.8 (117.1 km) **DJ 1317.2** (2119.8 km) **Historic Milepost 73** commemorates Beatton River Flight Strip, 1 of 4 gravel airstrips built for American military aircraft during WWII. Road to Prespetu and Buick Creek.

DC 79.1 (127.3 km) **DJ 1310.9** (2109.6 km) **Historical Mile 80** paved rest area to west with litter barrels, picnic tables, water and flush toilets. Information panel on Alaska Highway parks.

DC 91.4 (147.1 km) **DJ 1298.6** (2089.8 km) **Historical Mile 92**. Westcoast Energy compressor station to west.

DC 94.6 (152.2 km) **DJ 1295.4** (2084.7 km) Oil pump east of highway behind trees.

DC 95 (152.9 km) **DJ 1295** (2084 km) Access west to Crystal Springs Ranch (32 miles/52 km).

DC 101 (161.7 km) **DJ 1289** (2074.4 km) **Historic Milepost 101. WONOWON** (pop. 150), unincorporated, has 3 gas stations (gas, diesel, propane), 2 restaurants, 2 motels, camping, a food store, pub and post office. Formerly known as Blueberry, Wonowon was the site of an official traffic control gate during WWII. Wonowon Horse Club holds an annual race meet and gymkhana at the track beside the highway, where the community club holds its annual snowmobile rally in February. ▲

The historic sign and interpretive panel here commemorate Blueberry Control Station, "site of the Blueberry Control Gate, a 24-hour military checkpoint operated by U.S. Army personnel through the war years."

The Alaska Highway follows the Blueberry and Prophet river drainages north to Fort Nelson. The Blueberry River, not visible from the highway, lies a few miles east of Wonowon.

DC 101.5 (163.3 km) **DJ 1288.5** (2073.6 km) Food, diesel, gas, camping and lodging to east; open year-round. ▲

DC 103.5 (166.5 km) **DJ 1244** (2002 km) **Historic Milepost 104** marks start of Adolphson, Huseth, Layer & Welch contract during Alaska Highway construction.

DC 114 (183.2 km) **DJ 1276** (2053.5 km) Paved turnout with litter barrel to east.

DC 122.9 (197.8 km) **DJ 1267.1** (2039.1 km) Townsend Creek.

DC 124.1 (199.7 km) **DJ 1265.9** (2037.2 km) Turnout to east with dumpster.

DC 124.3 (200 km) **DJ 1265.7** (2036.9 km) The Cut (highway goes through a small rock cut). Relatively few rock cuts were necessary during construction of the Alaska Highway in 1942–43. However, rock excavation was often made outside of the roadway to obtain gravel fill for the new roadbed.

DC 135.3 (217.7 km) **DJ 1254.7** (2019.2 km) Gravel turnout to east.

CAUTION: Northbound travelers watch for moose next 15 miles/24 km, especially at dusk and at night.

DC 140.4 (225.9 km) **DJ 1249.6** (2011 km) **Historical Mile 143. PINK MOUNTAIN** (pop. 99, area 300; elev. 3,600 feet/1,097m). Post office, grocery, motels, restaurant, campgrounds, gas stations (gas, diesel, propane) with minor repair service. Bus depot at Pink Mountain Motor Inn east side of highway. Pink Mountain is home to Darryl Mills, Canadian champion bullrider. ▲

According to local resident Ron Tyerman, Pink Mountain gets its name from the local fall foliage, when red-barked willows give the mountain a pink colour in the morning sun. Another source attributes the pink color of the mountain—and thus the name—to concentrations of feldspar.

Pink Mountain Campsite & R.V. Park, on the left northbound. Take it easy folks, you've arrived at one of the nicest campgrounds on the highway ... coffee's always on. Unleaded Tempo gas, diesel, metered propane for RVs and auto. Fuel discount for overnight guests. Post office, general store, liquor store, fishing and hunting licenses.

Souvenirs—you'll like our prices. Shaded campsites, picnic tables, firepits and free firewood. Tents and RVs welcome. Full hookups, power hookups, water and sani-dump. Pull-throughs. Something for everyone. Cabins starting at $20 (weekly rates available). Laundromat and clean showers. Open year-round. VISA and MasterCard. Phone and fax (250) 772-5133. [ADVERTISEMENT] ▲

Pink Mountain Motor Inn. Mile 143, a welcome stopping point for all travelers. 34 rooms, gift shop, and licensed restaurant with pies and pastries and home-cooked meals. The perfect lunch break stop for bus tours. For RVs, electric hookups, gravel sites. Treed camping and picnic tables. Water, hot showers, laundromat. Dump station. Caravans welcome, reservations recommended. Full line of Esso products. Fax (250) 774-1071. Phone (250) 772-3234. Your hosts, Jimmy and Grace. [ADVERTISEMENT] ▲

DC 144.1 (231.9 km) **DJ 1245.9** (2005 km) **Historical Mile 147**. Food, gas, diesel, lodging and camping. ▲

Sportsman Inn. See display ad this section. ▲

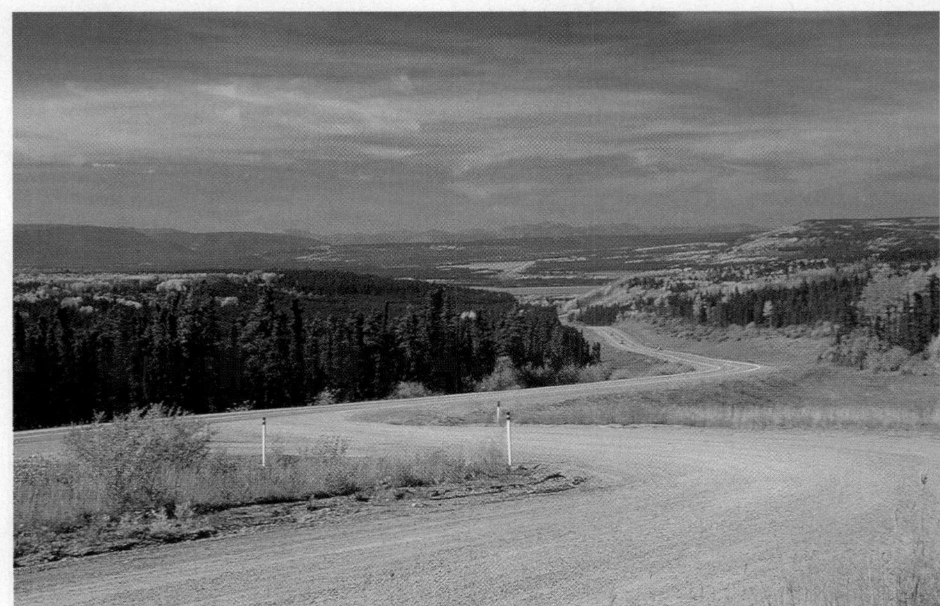
View of the Alaska Highway from Pink Mountain. (© Earl L. Brown, staff)

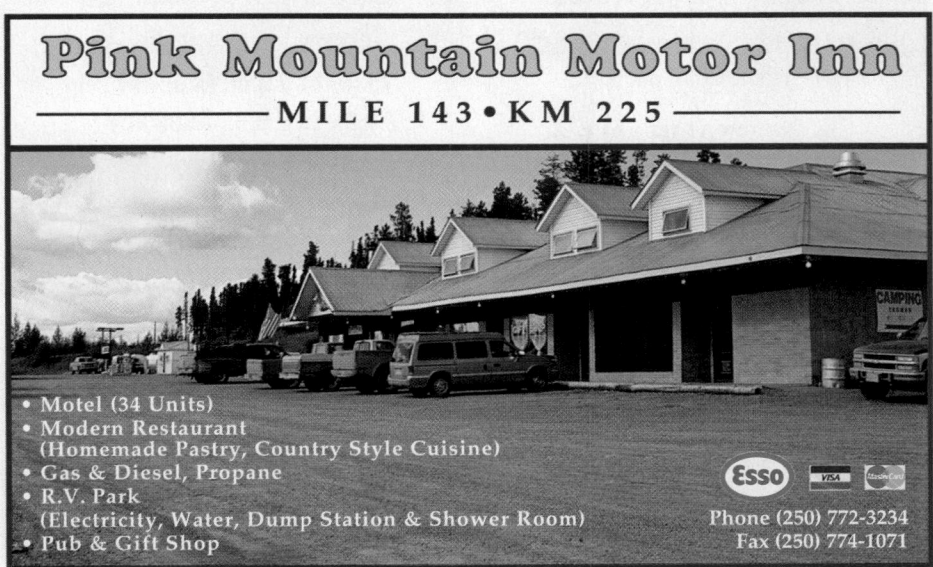

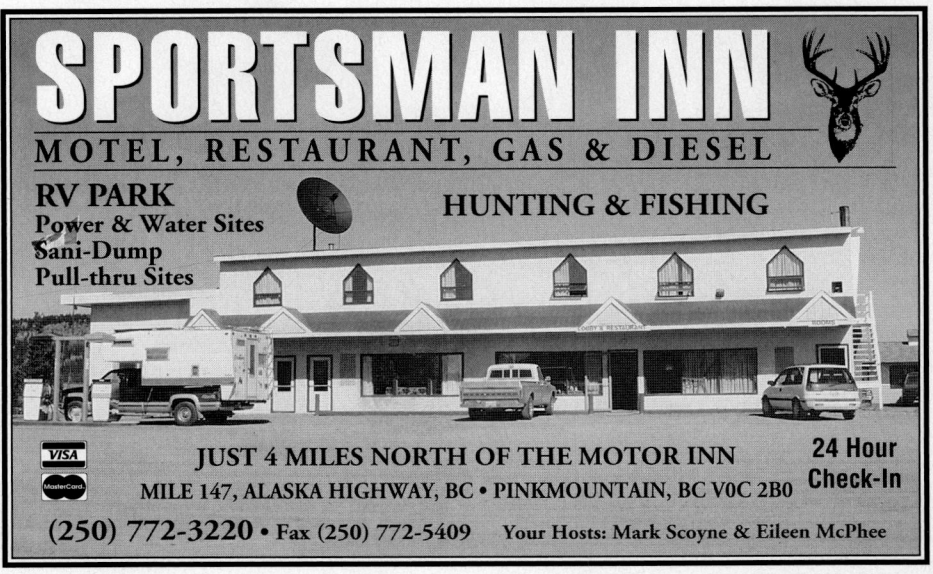

DC 144.5 (232.5 km) **DJ 1245.5** (2004.4 km) **Historical Mile 147**. Mae's Kitchen restaurant, motel, gas and diesel; open year-round, closed Sundays.

Mae's Kitchen. See display ad this section.

DC 144.7 (232.9 km) **DJ 1245.3** (2004. km) **Historic Milepost 148** commemorates **Suicide Hill**, one of the most treacherous hills on the original highway, noted for its ominous greeting: "Prepare to meet thy maker."

Beatton River bridge. The Beatton River was named for Frank Beatton, a Hudson's Bay Co. employee. The Beatton River flows east and then south into the Peace River system.

DC 146 (234 km) **DJ 1244** (2002 km) **Private Aircraft**: Sikanni Chief flight strip to east; elev. 3,258 feet/993m; length, 6,000 feet/1,829m; gravel, current status unknown. Well-known local pilot Jimmy "Midnight" Anderson used the Sikanni Chief airstrip, which was the southernmost airfield in the Northwest Staging Route used during WWII.

DC 150.3 (241.9 km) **DJ 1239.7** (1995 km) *CAUTION: Southbound travelers watch for moose next 15 miles/24 km, especially at dusk and at night.*

DC 155.6 (250.4 km) **DJ 1234.4** (1986.5 km) Large double-ended, gravel turnout with litter barrels. *CAUTION: Slow down! Watch for loose gravel.*

DC 156.6 (252 km) **DJ 1233.4** (1984.9km) Sikanni Hill. *CAUTION: Slow down for hill.*

DC 159.2 (256.2 km) **DJ 1230.8** (1980.9 km) Sikanni Chief River bridge (elev. 2,662 feet/811m). To the west you may see steel stanchions, all that remains of the historic wooden Sikanni bridge, which was destroyed by arson July 10, 1992. The original timber truss bridge built across the Sikanni Chief River in the spring of 1943 was the first permanent structure completed on the Alaska Highway. Highway construction crews rerouted much of the pioneer road built in 1942 and replaced temporary bridges with permanent structures in 1943. The Sikanni Chief River flows east and then north into the Fort Nelson River, which flows into the Liard River and on to the Mackenzie River, which empties into the Arctic Ocean. Check at the lodge for information on Sikanni River Falls (see **Milepost DC 168.5**).

Sikanni Chief River, fair fishing at mouth of tributaries in summer for pike; grayling to $2^{1}/_{2}$ lbs.; whitefish to 2 lbs.

DC 159.4 (256.5 km) **DJ 1230.6** (1980.4 km) **Historical Mile 162. SIKANNI CHIEF**. Food, gas, lodging and camping.

Sikanni River RV Park. See display ad this section.

DC 160 (257.5 km) **DJ 1230** (1979.4 km) "Drunken forest" on hillside to west is shallow-rooted black spruce trees growing in unstable clay-based soil that is subject to slide activity in wet weather.

DC 160.4 (258.1 km) **DJ 1229.6** (1978.8 km) Section of the old Alaska Highway is visible to east; no access.

DC 168.5 (271.2 km) **DJ 1221.5** (1965.7 km) Gravel road west to Sikanni River Falls. This private road is signed "Travel at own risk." Drive in 10.5 miles/16.9 km to parking area with picnic tables at B.C. Forest Service trailhead; 10-minute hike in on well-marked trail to view falls. Gravel access road has some steep hills and a single-lane bridge. *CAUTION: Do not travel in wet weather. Not recommended for vehicles with trailers.*

*IMPORTANT: Watch for moose on highway northbound to **Milepost DC 200**, especially at dusk. Drive carefully!*

DC 172.5 (277.6 km) **DJ 1217.5** (1959.3 km) Polka Dot Creek.

DC 173.1 (278.6 km) **DJ 1216.9** (1958.3 km) Buckinghorse River bridge; access to river at north end of bridge.

DC 173.2 (278.7 km) **DJ 1216.8** (1958.2 km) **Historical Mile 175**. Inn with gas and camping to east at north end of bridge. Also turnoff east for **Buckinghorse River Provin-**

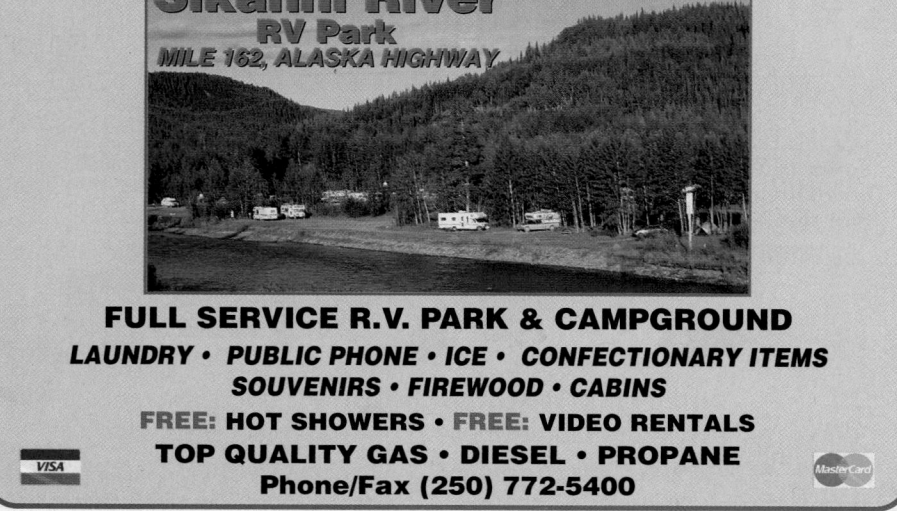

cial Park. Follow the narrow gravel road past the gravel pit 0.7 mile/1.1 km along river to camping and picnic area. The park has 30 picnic tables, side-by-side camper parking, fire rings, water pump, outhouses and garbage containers; user-maintained, no camping fee. ▲

Fishing for grayling in **Buckinghorse River**. Swimming in downstream pools.

DC 173.4 (279 km) **DJ 1216.6** (1957.9 km) **Historical Mile 175. Buckinghorse River Lodge**, on left northbound. Motel, cafe with home cooking, ice cream and ice cream novelties. Bed and breakfast available. Service station, large parking area, free camping. Pets welcome, corrals available. Look forward to our friendly atmosphere. Picnic tables and beautiful scenery. A great spot to take a break for fishing or walking. Phone (250) 773-6468. [ADVERTISEMENT] ▲

DC 176 (283.2 km) **DJ 1214** (1953.7 km) South end of 27-mile/43-km **Trutch Mountain Bypass**. Completed in 1987, this section of road rerouted the Alaska Highway around Trutch Mountain, eliminating the steep, winding climb up to Trutch Summit (and the views). Named for Joseph W. Trutch, civil engineer and first governor of British Columbia, Trutch Mountain was the second highest summit on the Alaska Highway, with an elevation of 4,134 feet/1,260m. The new roadbed cuts a wide swath through the flat Minnaker River valley. The river, not visible to motorists, is west of the highway; it was named for local trapper George Minnaker. Trutch Mountain is to the east of the highway. Motorists can see part of the old highway on Trutch Mountain.

DC 182.8 (294.2 km) **DJ 1207.2** (1942.7 km) Large gravel turnout to west with dumpster.

DC 199.1 (320 km) **DJ 1190.9** (1916.5 km) Large gravel turnout with litter barrels.

DC 202.5 (325.5 km) **DJ 1187.5** (1911 km) Turnout with dumpster at north end of Trutch Mountain bypass (see **Milepost DC 176**).

CAUTION: Southbound travelers watch for moose on highway, especially at dusk, to Sikanni Chief. Drive carefully!

DC 204.2 (328 km) **DJ 1185.8** (1908.3 km) **Beaver Creek**; fishing for grayling to 2½ lbs.

DC 217.2 (349.3 km) **DJ 1172.8** (1887.4 km) Turnoff to west for **Prophet River Wayside Provincial Park**. Drive in 0.4 mile/0.6 km via gravel road; side-by-side camper parking (12 sites, some pull-throughs), picnic tables, fire rings, water pump, outhouses and garbage containers. User-maintained; no camping fee. The park access road crosses an airstrip (originally an emergency airstrip on the Northwest Air Staging Route) and part of the old Alaska Highway (the Alcan). Trembling aspen stands and mature white spruce. ▲

The Alaska Highway roughly parallels the Prophet River from here north to the Muskwa River south of Fort Nelson.

Private Aircraft: Prophet River emergency airstrip; elev. 1,954 feet/596m; length 6,000 feet/1,829m; gravel; no services.

DC 218.2 (350.7 km) **DJ 1171.8** (1885.8 km) View of Prophet River to west.

DC 222.3 (357.2 km) **DJ 1167.7** (1879.2 km) Bougie Creek bridge; turnout with litter barrel beside creek at south end of bridge. Note the typical climax white spruce stand and trees of a variety of ages.

CAUTION: Watch for rough road approaching Bougie Creek bridge from either direction.

DC 224.8 (360.6 km) **DJ 1165.2** (1875.2 km) Microwave tower to east.

DC 226.2 (363.4 km) **DJ 1163.8** (1872.9 km) Prophet River Indian Reserve to east.

DC 226.5 (363.9 km) **DJ 1163.5** (1872.4 km) St. Paul's Roman Catholic Church to east.

DC 226.9 (365.2 km) **DJ 1163.1** (1871.8 km) Gas, diesel, food and camping to east at Neighbors Inn.

Neighbors Inn. See display ad this section. ▲

DC 227 (364.7 km) **DJ 1163** (1871.6 km) **Historical Mile 233. PROPHET RIVER**, gas, diesel, propane, food, camping and lodging. ▲

Prophet River Services. See display ad this section. ▲

Southbound travelers note: Next service 68 miles/109 km.

DC 227.6 (366.3 km) **DJ 1162.4** (1870.6 km) **Historic Milepost 234**, Adsett Creek Highway Realignment. This major rerouting eliminated 132 curves on the stretch of highway that originally ran between Miles 234 and 275. Double-ended turnout with dumpster.

The Alaska Highway south of Fort Nelson. (© Earl L. Brown, staff)

DC 227.7 (366.4 km) **DJ 1162.3** (1870.5 km) Adsett Creek.

DC 230.7 (371.3 km) **DJ 1159.3** (1865.7 km) Natural gas pipeline crosses beneath highway.

DC 232.9 (374.8 km) **DJ 1157.1** (1862.1 km) Turnout to west with dumpster.

DC 235.5 (378.4 km) **DJ 1154.5** (1857.9 km) Mesa-like topography to the east is Mount Yakatchie.

DC 241.5 (388 km) **DJ 1148.5** (1848.3 km) Parker Creek.

DC 245.9 (395.7 km) **DJ 1144.1** (1841.2 km) Gravel turnout with dumpster.

DC 261.1 (420.2 km) **DJ 1128.9** (1816.7 km) Turnout to east with dumpster.

DC 264.6 (425.2 km) **DJ 1125.4** (1811.1 km) Jackfish Creek bridge. Note the variety of trembling aspen stands and the white spruce seedlings under them.

DC 265.5 (426.5 km) **DJ 1124.5** (18.09.6 km) Turnoff to east for **Andy Bailey Lake Provincial Park** via 6.8-mile/11-km dirt and gravel access road. (Large RVs and trailers note: only turnaround space on access road is approximately halfway in.) The park is located on Andy Bailey Lake (formerly Jackfish Lake); 6 campsites, picnic sites, picnic tables, fire rings, firewood, water, outhouses, garbage containers, boat launch (no powerboats), swimming and fair fishing for northern pike. Bring insect repellent! ▲

DC 270.8 (435.1 km) **DJ 1119.2** (1801.1 km) Sulphur gas pipeline crosses highway overhead.

DC 271 (435.4 km) **DJ 1119** (1800.8 km) Westcoast Energy gas processing plant to east. Sulfur processing to west.

DC 276.2 (443.8 km) **DJ 1113.8** (1792.4 km) Rodeo grounds to west. The rodeo is held in August.

DC 276.7 (444.6 km) **DJ 1113.3** (1791.6 km) Railroad tracks. Microwave tower.

DC 277.5 (446.2 km) **DJ 1112.5** (1790.3 km) **Muskwa Heights** (unincorporated), an industrial area with rail yard, plywood plant, sawmill and bulk fuel outlet.

DC 277.9 (447.2 km) **DJ 1112.1** (1789.7 km) 24-hour truck stop with gas, diesel, propane, major repair, grocery, restaurant and RV campground. ▲

Husky 5th Wheel Truck Stop and RV Park. See display ad this section. ▲

DC 278.1 (447.5 km) **DJ 1111.9** (1789.4 km) Truck scales to west.

DC 278.4 (448 km) **DJ 1111.6** (1788.9 km) **Trapper's Den. Historic Mile 293.** Owned and operated by a local trapping family. Moose horns, diamond willow, Northern novelties, books, artwork. Fur hats, headbands, earmuffs. Birchbark baskets,

moose-hair tuftings. Mukluks, moccasins, mits and gloves. Professionally tanned furs. See our "Muskwa River Pearls." Photographers welcome. Located 1/2 mile north of Husky 5th Wheel RV Park on the Alaska Highway. VISA, MasterCard. Mail orders. Open 10 A.M. to 6 P.M. daily or phone for appointment. John, Cindy and Mandy Wells. Box 1164, Fort Nelson, BC V0C 1R0. (250) 774-3400. Recommended. [ADVERTISEMENT]

DC 279 (448.6 km) **DJ 1111** (1787.9 km) Site of oriented strand board plant processing aspen and balsam poplar. This 400,000-square-foot building is the largest industrial building of its kind in the province.

DC 281 (451.4 km) **DJ 1109** (1784.7 km) **Muskwa River** bridge, lowest point on the Alaska Highway (elev. 1,000 feet/305m). The Muskwa River flows to the Fort Nelson River.

Fair fishing at the mouth of tributaries for northern pike; some goldeye. The Fort Nelson River is too muddy for fishing. The Muskwa River valley exhibits typical river-bottom balsam poplar and white spruce stands.

The Alaska Highway swings west at Fort Nelson above the Muskwa River, winding southwest then northwest through the Canadian Rockies.

DC 283 (454.3 km) **DJ 1107** (1781.5 km) Entering Fort Nelson northbound. Fort Nelson's central business district extends along the highway from the private campground at the east end of the town to the private campground at the west end. Businesses and services are located both north and south of the highway.

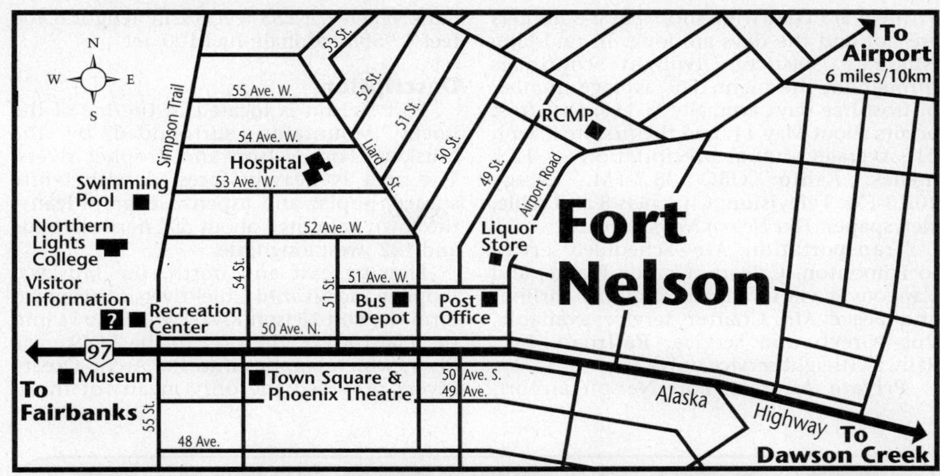

Fort Nelson

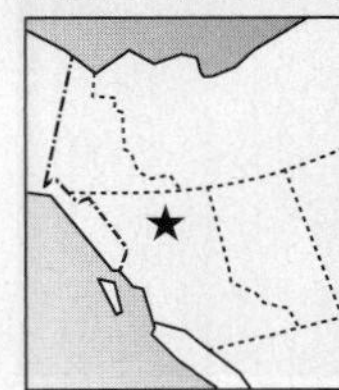

DC 283 (454.3 km) **DJ 1107** (1781.5 km) **Historical Mile 300. Population:** 4,401; area 6,000. **Emergency Services: RCMP**, phone (250) 774-2777. **Fire Department,** phone (250) 774-2222. **Hospital**, 35 beds, phone (250) 774-6916. **Ambulance**, phone (250) 774-2344. Medical, dental and optometric clinics. Visiting veterinarians and chiropractors.

Visitor Information: Located in the Recreation Centre at the west end of town, open 8 A.M. to 8 P.M. Inquire here about local attractions, industrial tours and information about the Liard Highway. Fort Nelson Heritage Museum across the highway from the Infocentre. Contact the Town of Fort Nelson by writing Bag Service 399M, Fort Nelson, BC V0C 1R0; phone (250) 774-6400, ext. 241 or (250) 774-2541; e-mail ecdev@pris.bc.ca.

Elevation: 1,383 feet/422m. **Climate**:

Winters are cold with short days. Summers are hot and the days are long. In mid-June (summer solstice), twilight continues throughout the night. The average number of frost-free days annually is 116. Last frost occurs about May 11, and the first frost Sept. 21. Average annual precipitation of 17.7 inches. **Radio**: CBC 88.3-FM, Energy 102.3-FM. **Television**: Channels 8 and cable. **Newspaper**: *Fort Nelson News* (weekly).

Transportation: **Air**—Scheduled service to Edmonton, Calgary, Grande Prairie, and Vancouver via Canadian Regional Airlines and Peace Air. Charter service available. **Bus**—Greyhound service. **Railroad**—B.C. Railway (freight service only).

Private Aircraft: Fort Nelson airport, 3.8 ENE; elev. 1,253 feet/382m; length 6,400 feet/1,950m; asphalt; fuel 100, Jet.

Description

Fort Nelson is located in the lee of the Rocky Mountains, surrounded by the Muskwa, Fort Nelson and Prophet rivers. The area is heavily forested with white spruce, poplar and aspen. Geographically, the town is located about 59° north latitude and 122° west longitude.

Flowing east and north, the Muskwa, Prophet and Sikanni Chief rivers converge to form the Fort Nelson River, which flows into the Liard River, then on to the Mackenzie River, which empties into the Arctic Ocean. Rivers provided the only means of transportation in both summer and winter in this isolated region until 1922, when the Godsell Trail opened, connecting Fort Nelson with Fort St. John. The Alaska Highway linked Fort Nelson with the Outside in 1942.

In the spring, the Muskwa River frequently floods the low country around Fort Nelson and can rise more than 20 feet/6m. At an elevation of 1,000 feet/305m, the Muskwa (which means "bear") is the lowest point on the Alaska Highway. There was a danger of the Muskwa River bridge washing out every June during spring runoff until 1970, when a higher bridge—with piers arranged to prevent log jams—was built.

Fort Nelson's existence was originally based on the fur trade. In the 1920s, trapping was the main business in this isolated pioneer community populated with less than 200 Indians and a few white men.

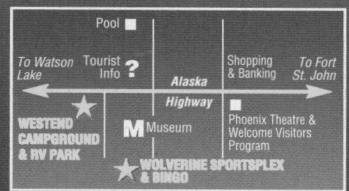

Aerial view from west of the Alaska Highway as it cuts through Fort Nelson. (© Earl L. Brown, staff)

Trappers still harvest beaver, wolverine, weasel, wolf, fox, lynx, mink, muskrat and marten. Other area wildlife includes black bear, which are plentiful, some deer, caribou and a few grizzly bears. Moose remains an important food source for the Indians.

Fort Nelson aboriginal people are mostly Dene, who arrived here about 1775 from the Great Slave Lake area and speak an Athabascan dialect.

Fort Nelson was first established in 1805 by the North West Fur Trading Co. The post, believed to have been located about 80 miles/129 km south of Nelson Forks, was named for Lord Horatio Nelson, the English admiral who won the Battle of Trafalgar.

A second Fort Nelson was later located south of the first fort, but was destroyed by fire in 1813 after Indians massacred its 8 residents. A third Fort Nelson was established in 1865 on the Fort Nelson River's west bank (1 mile from the present Fort Nelson airport) by W. Cornwallis King, a Hudson's Bay Co. clerk. This trading post was built to keep out the free traders who were filtering in from the Mackenzie River and Fort St. John areas. The free traders' higher fur prices were a threat to the Hudson's Bay Co., which in 1821 had absorbed the rival North West Fur Trading Co. and gained a monopoly on the fur trade in Canada.

This Hudson's Bay Co. trading post was destroyed by a flood in 1890 and a fourth Fort Nelson was established on higher ground upstream and across the river, which is now known as Old Fort Nelson. The present town of Fort Nelson is the fifth site.

Marl Brown shows off Fort Nelson Museum's antique car. (© Earl L. Brown, staff)

Fort Nelson saw its first mail service in 1936. Scheduled air service to Fort Nelson—by ski- and floatplane—also was begun in the 1930s by Yukon Southern Air (which was later absorbed by CPAir, now Canadian Airlines International and Canadian Regional Airlines). The Canadian government began construction of an airport in 1941 as part of the Northwest Air Staging Route, and this was followed by perhaps the biggest boom to Fort Nelson—the construction of the Alaska Highway in 1942. About 2,000 soldiers were bivouacked in Fort Nelson, which they referred to as Zero, as it was the beginning of a road to Whitehorse and another road to Fort Simpson. Later Dawson Creek became Mile 0 and Fort Nelson Mile 300.

Fort Nelson expanded in the 1940s and 1950s as people came here to work for the government or to start their own small businesses: trucking, barging, aviation, construction, garages, stores, cafes, motels and sawmills. It is surprising to consider that as recently as the 1950s Fort Nelson was still a pioneer community without power, phones, running water, refrigerators or doctors. Interesting recollections of Fort Nelson's early days may be found in Gerri Young's book *The Fort Nelson Story*, available at the museum.

Fort Nelson was an unorganized territory until 1957 when it was declared an Improvement District. Fort Nelson took on village status in 1971 and town status in 1987.

Forestry is a major industry here with a veneer plant, plywood plant, oriented strand board plant and sawmill complex. Check with the Infocentre about scheduled industrial tours.

Forestry products are shipped south by truck and rail. Fort Nelson became a railhead in 1971 with the completion of a 250-mile extension of the Pacific Great Eastern Railway (now British Columbia Railway) from Fort St. John.

Agriculture is under development here with the establishment of the 55,000-acre McConachie Creek agricultural subdivision.

Northeastern British Columbia is the only sedimentary area in the province currently producing oil and gas. Oil seeps in the Fort Nelson area were noted by early residents. Major gas discoveries were made in

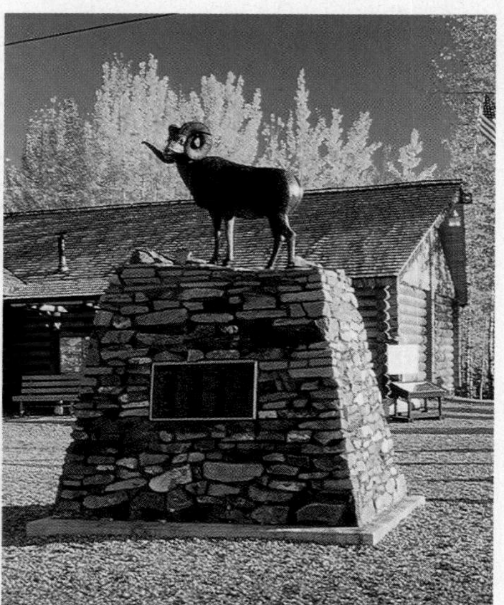

Chadwick Ram bronze sculpture is outside the Fort Nelson Heritage Museum. (© Earl L. Brown, staff)

the 1960s when the Clarke Lake, Yoyo/Kotcho, Beaver River and Pointed Mountain gas reserves were developed. The Westcoast Energy natural gas processing plant at Fort Nelson, the largest in North America, was constructed in 1964. This plant purifies the gas before sending it south through the 800-mile-long pipeline that connects the Fort Nelson area with the British Columbia lower mainland. Sulfur, a byproduct of natural gas processing, is processed in a recovery plant and shipped to outside markets in pellet form.

In 1997, the BC government set aside more than 4.4 million hectares of Northern Rockies wilderness near Fort Nelson. The Muskwa–Kechika area preserves critical wildlife habitat while allowing logging, mining, oil and gas exploration, and is designed to balance resource management with conservation. For more information contact the Land Use Coordination Office; phone (250) 953-3471, www.luco.gov.bc.ca.

Lodging & Services

Fort Nelson has 9 hotels/motels, 4 bed and breakfasts, several gas stations and restaurants, a pub, fast food, deli and health food outlets; laundromat; an auto supply store, department stores and other services, most located north and south just off the Alaska Highway. The post office and liquor store are on Airport Drive. There are 2 banks, both with ATMs, on the business frontage road north of the highway. Fresh water fill-up and free municipal dump station adjacent to the blue chalet near the museum. Inquire at the Infocentre for location of local churches and their hours of worship.

Ardendale Bed & Breakfast. Welcome to our large log home. Comfortable rooms, spa, cable TV, guest lounge. Excellent breakfast of your choice. Sleigh, buggy and wagon rides available. Close to the golf course and cross-country skiing. Laundry facilities. Smoking outdoors on deck. Phone (250) 774-2433. Fax (250) 774-2436. VISA. Frank and Gail Parker, Box 427, Fort Nelson, BC V0C 1R0. [ADVERTISEMENT]

Camping

Fort Nelson has 2 campgrounds: one is located at the north (or west) end of town near the museum; the other is at Muskwa Heights south of Fort Nelson. ▲

Westend RV Campground welcomes RVs, caravans and tenters. Located in town next to the Museum, only a few minutes from stores and downtown. Over 140 sites, lots of shade, full hookups, pull-throughs. Town water, coin-op showers and laundry, playground. Free RV wash and firewood. Open April 1–Nov. 1. We hope you enjoy our Northern hospitality. VISA, MasterCard, American Express. Cash accepted with iden-

tification. Under new management. Phone (250) 774-2340. [ADVERTISEMENT] ▲

Attractions

Fort Nelson offers travelers a free "Welcome Visitor Program" on summer evenings at the Phoenix Theatre. These interesting and entertaining presentations are put on by local residents and range from slide shows to talks on items of local interest. Check with the Visitor Infocentre or at the Town Square for details.

The **Fort Nelson Heritage Museum**, across the highway from the Travel Infocentre, has excellent displays of pioneer artifacts, Alaska Highway history, wildlife (including a white moose), a spruce bark canoe, and souvenirs and books for sale. Outside the museum is the Chadwick Ram, a bronze sculpture by Rick Taylor. The statue commemorates the world record stone sheep taken in the Muskwa Valley area in 1936. This nonprofit museum charges a modest admission fee. Native crafts are displayed at the Fort Nelson–Liard Native Friendship Centre, located on 49th Avenue.

The **Fort Nelson Recreation Centre**, across from the museum, has tennis courts; hockey and curling arena for winter sports. Swimming pool, swirl pool, sauna and gym located in the Aqua Centre on Simpson Trail.

For golfers, the **Poplar Hills Golf and Country Club**, just north of town on the Old Alaska Highway, has grass greens; open daily.

A community demonstration forest is open to the public. There is a forest trail (0.6 mile/1 km, half-hour walk), a silviculture trail (1.9 miles/3 km, 45-minute walk) and a Native trail. Located off the Simpson Trail via Mountainview Drive; check at the Infocentre for trail guide.

Fort Nelson hosts a number of annual benefits, dances, tournaments and exhibits.

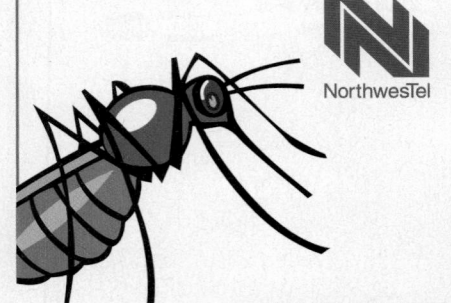

Check locally for details and dates on all events. Summer events include the Canada Day celebration, various ball and golf tournaments, and a rodeo in August. Winter events include a big cash prize curling bon spiel in February and the Canadian Open Sled Dog Races in December (with local racers from the well-known Streeper Kennels). Terry Streeper is a four-time World Champion (Anchorage) and also an Open North American Champion (Fairbanks) sled dog racer, and won more than 30 major races in 6 countries during the 1990s. Streeper Kennels is located on Radar Road.

The Northern Rockies Toastmasters Club meets at Town Square every second Thursday (check with the Visitor Infocentre). Travelling Toastmasters are welcome to join the meeting, according to Earl Brown, *The MILEPOST®* field editor and president of the local club.

Alaska Highway Log

(continued)

Distance from Dawson Creek (DC) is followed by distance from Delta Junction (DJ). Original mileposts are indicated in the text as Historical Mile.

In Canada, mileages from Dawson Creek are based on actual driving distance, not historical mileposts, and kilometres are based on physical kilometreposts. Mileages from Delta Junction are also based on actual driving distance, not historical mileposts, but are followed by the metric conversion to kilometres.

DC 284 (456.4 km) **DJ 1106** (1779.9 km) **Historic Milepost 300**, historic sign and interpretive panel at west end of Fort Nelson. Visitor information in the Recreation Centre north side of highway, log museum south side of highway. Private campground adjacent museum. ▲

Northbound: Watch for sections of rough, narrow, winding road and breaks in surfacing between Fort Nelson and the BC–YT border (approximately next 321 miles/516.5 km).

Southbound: Good pavement, wider road, next 284 miles/457 km (to Dawson Creek).

DC 284.5 (457.5 km) **DJ 1105.5** (1779.1 km) Fort Nelson Forest District Office to north.

Farmland next 15 miles/24 km northbound.

DC 284.7 (458.2 km) **DJ 1105.3** (1778.8 km) **Junction** with south end of Old Alaska Highway (**Mile 301–308**). The Muskwa Valley bypass between Mile 301 and 308 opened in 1992.

DC 287.9 (462.6 km) **DJ 1102.1** (1773.6 km) Access to Poplar Hills Golf and Country Club, located on Old Alaska Highway; 9-hole golf course, driving range, grass greens, clubhouse (licensed), golf club rentals. Open 8 A.M. to dusk, May to October.

DC 288.7 (463.9 km) **DJ 1101.3** (1772.3) Watch for bison ranches on your right northbound.

DC 291 (467.6 km) **DJ 1099** (1768.6 km) Parker Lake Road. **Junction** with north end of Old Alaska Highway (**Mile 308–301**).

DC 292 (469.9 km) **DJ 1098** (1767 km) Private airstrip alongside highway; status unknown.

DC 301 (483.5 km) **DJ 1089** (1752.5 km)

Junction with Liard Highway (BC Highway 77) north to Fort Liard, Fort Simpson and other Northwest Territories destinations. See LIARD HIGHWAY section.

DC 304.1 (489.4 km) **DJ 1085.9** (1747.4 km) **Historic Milepost 320**. Sign marks start of Reese & Olson contract during construction of the Alaska Highway.

DC 308.2 (495.3 km) **DJ 1081.8** (1740.9 km) Raspberry Creek. Turnout with dumpster to south.

DC 316.6 (506.2 km) **DJ 1073.4** (1727.4 km) Turnout with dumpster to south.

DC 318.4 (509.1 km) **DJ 1071.6** (1724.5 km) Kledo Creek bridge. The Kledo River is a tributary of the Muskwa River. This is a popular hunting area in the fall.

DC 318.7 (509.5 km) **DJ 1071.3** (1724 km) Kledo Creek wayside rest area to north (unmaintained).

DC 322.7 (516 km) **DJ 1067.3** (1717.6 km) Steamboat Creek bridge. *NOTE: Improved highway begins climb northbound up Steamboat Mountain; winding road, some 10 percent grades.*

DC 329 (526.1 km) **DJ 1061** (1707.5 km) Pull-through turnout with dumpster to south.

DC 333 (532.5 km) **DJ 1057** (1701 km) **Historic Milepost 351. STEAMBOAT** (unincorporated), lodge with food, gas, diesel and camping to south. Historical sign marks start of Curran & Briggs Ltd. contract during construction of the Alaska Highway. ▲

Steamboat at **Historical Mile 351**. Cafe serving breakfast, homemade bread and pies. Husky gas, diesel and oil products. Full-hookup pull-throughs, RV parking with a view. Store, confectionary, movie rentals. Public phone. Picnic area (pets on a leash, please). Ice, souvenirs and handicrafts. Your hosts, Ed and Carol Paynter. Phone (250) 774-3388. [ADVERTISEMENT] ▲

DC 333.7 (533.5 km) **DJ 1056.3** (1699.9 km) Winding road ascends Steamboat Mountain westbound. Views of the Muskwa River valley and Rocky Mountains to the southwest from summit of 3,500-foot/1,067-m Steamboat Mountain, named because of its resemblance to a steamship.

DC 334.3 (534.5 km) **DJ 1055.7** (1698.9 km) Turnout with view and dumpster to south.

DC 336.7 (538.5 km) **DJ 1053.3** (1695.1

km) Large turnouts both sides of highway with dumpsters, payphones and toilets.

Highway descends for westbound travelers. NOTE: Recent road reconstruction has improved and shortened the highway in this area. Kilometreposts and driving distances have not been recalibrated in The MILEPOST® log.

DC 342.8 (548 km) **DJ 1047.2** (1685.2 km) Turnout with dumpster and point of interest sign to south. View of **Indian Head Mountain**, a high crag resembling the classic Indian profile. *IMPORTANT: DO NOT FEED BEARS!*

DC 345 (551.5 km) **DJ 1045** (1681.7 km) **Teetering Rock** viewpoint with dumpster and outhouses to north. Teetering Rock is in the distance on the horizon. (*MILEPOST®* field editor Earl Brown used a 500mm lens to get this shot.)

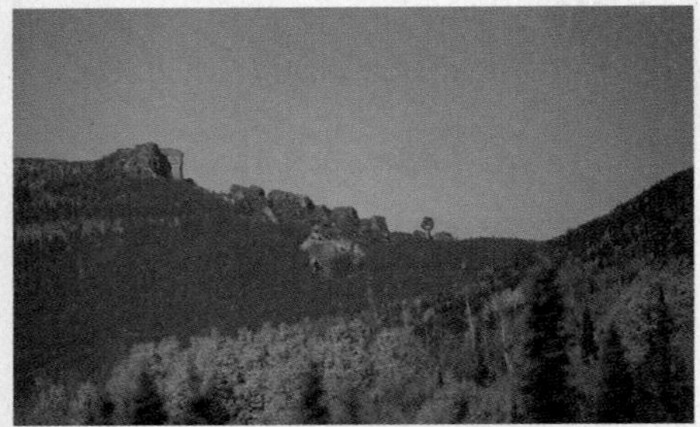

Fort Nelson Forest District (phone 250/774-5511) has developed a 7.6-mile-/12.3-km-long trail to Teetering Rock; steep climbs. Stay on well-marked trails, keep pets on leash; it is easy to get lost in this country.

DC 346.4 (553.9 km) **DJ 1043.6** (1679.5 km) Mill Creek, which flows into the Tetsa River. The highway follows the Tetsa River westbound. The Tetsa heads near Summit

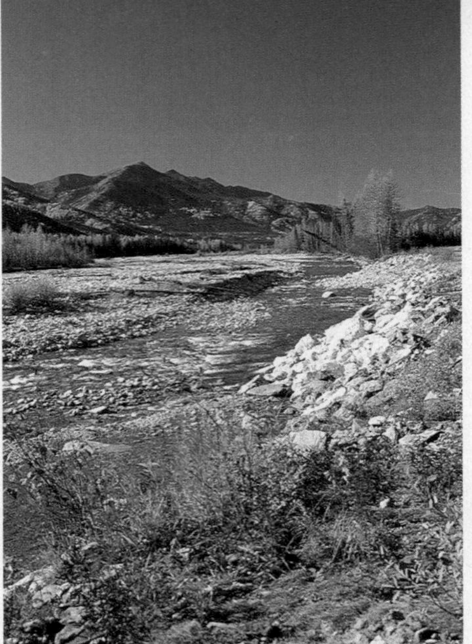

Tetsa River flows alongside the Alaska Highway. The river offers good fishing for grayling. (© Earl L. Brown, staff)

Lake in the northern Canadian Rockies.

Tetsa River, good fishing for grayling to 4 lbs., average 1½ lbs., flies or spin cast with lures; Dolly Varden to 7 lbs., average 3 lbs., spin cast or black gnat, coachman, Red Devils, flies; whitefish, small but plentiful, use flies or eggs, summer.

DC 346.5 (554 km) **DJ 1043.5** (1679.3 km) Turnoff to south for **Tetsa River Provincial Park**, 1.2 miles/1.9 km via gravel road. Grass tenting area, 25 level gravel sites in trees, picnic tables, fire rings, firewood, outhouses, water and garbage containers. Camping fee $12. ▲

DC 351 (561.2 km) **DJ 1039** (1672.1 km) *CAUTION: Slow down, dangerous curve! Watch for road construction next 2 miles/3.2 km northbound in 2000.*

DC 357.5 (571.5 km) **DJ 1032.5** (1661.6 km) **Historical Mile 375**. Gas, store, cabins and private campground. ▲

DC 358.6 (573.3 km) **DJ 1031.4** (1659.8 km) Highway follows Tetsa River westbound. Turnouts next 0.2 mile/0.3 km south to river.

DC 360.2 (575.9 km) **DJ 1029.8** (1657.2 km) Turnout with dumpster, picnic site. Note the aspen-dominated slopes on the north side of the Tetsa River, and the white spruce on the south side.

DC 364.4 (582.6 km) **DJ 1025.6** (1650.5 km) Gravel turnout to south.

DC 365.6 (584.6 km) **DJ 1024.4** (1648.6 km) Tetsa River bridge No. 1, clearance 17 feet/5.2m.

DC 366 (585.4 km) **DJ 1024** (1647.9 km) Pull-through turnout with dumpster to north.

DC 366.1 (585.6 km) **DJ 1023.9** (1647.7 km) Beaver dam to north.

DC 367.3 (587.3 km) **DJ 1022.7** (1645.8 km) Tetsa River bridge No. 2.

The high bare peaks of the central Canadian Rockies are visible ahead westbound.

DC 371.5 (594.2 km) **DJ 1018.5** (1639.1 km) East boundary of **Stone Mountain Provincial Park**. Stone Mountain Park encompasses the Summit Pass area and extends south to include Wokkpash Protected Area. Access is via MacDonald Creek hiking trail and by 4-wheel drive from 113 Creek (see **Milepost DC 382.2**) to Wokkpash Creek trail. Contact BC Parks District Office in Fort St. John; phone (250) 787-3407.

Stone sheep are frequently sighted in this area. *PLEASE REDUCE YOUR SPEED.*

Stone sheep are indigenous to the mountains of northern British Columbia and southern Yukon Territory. They are darker and somewhat slighter than the bighorn sheep found in the Rocky Mountains. Dall or white sheep are found in the mountains of Yukon, Alaska and Northwest Territories.

CAUTION: Northbound, watch for caribou and Stone sheep along the highway. DO NOT FEED WILDLIFE. DO NOT STOP VEHICLES ON THE HIGHWAY TO TAKE PHOTOS; use shoulders or turnouts. You are now in bear country ... a fed bear is a dead bear—don't feed bears!

DC 372.2 (595.2 km) **DJ 1017.8** (1637.9 km) **Historical Mile 390.** North Tetsa River flows under road thorugh large culverts.

DC 372.7 (596 km) **DJ 1017.3** (1637.1 km) Pull-through turnout with dumpster to north. Steep access to Tetsa River canyon.

DC 373.3 (597 km) **DJ 1016.7** (1636.2 km) **Historical Mile 392. SUMMIT LAKE** (unincorporated), lodge with gas, diesel, propane, cafe, camping and lodging. The peak behind Summit Lake is Mount St. George (elev. 7,419 feet/2,261m) in the Stone Mountain range. The Summit area is known for dramatic and sudden weather changes. ▲

DC 373.5 (597.4 km) **DJ 1016.5** (1635.9 km) Rough gravel side road (closed to vehicles) leads 1.5 miles/2.5 km to Flower Springs Lake trailhead, 4.3 miles/7 km to microwave tower viewpoint.

DC 373.6 (597.6 km) **DJ 1016.4** (1635.7 km) **Historic Milepost 392 Summit Pass** (elev. 4,250 feet/ 1,295m); gravel turnout, sign and interpretive panel at the highest summit on the Alaska Highway. A very beautiful area of bare rocky peaks (which can be snow-covered any time of the year). Summit Lake provincial campground to south at east end of lake; 28 level gravel sites; camping fee $12; picnic tables; water and garbage containers; information shelter; boat launch. Hiking trails to Flower Springs Lake and Summit Peak. Fair fishing for lake trout, whitefish and rainbows. ▲

DC 375.6 (600.8 km) **DJ 1014.4** (1632.5 km) Turnout to north.

DC 375.9 (601.3 km) **DJ 1014.1** (1632 km) Picnic site to south with tables and dumpster on Rocky Crest Lake. Nice spot for photos; good reflections in lake when calm.

DC 376 (601.5 km) **DJ 1014** (1631.8 km) Erosion pillars (hoodoos) north of highway (0.6-mile/1-km hike north); watch for caribou. Northbound, the highway winds through a rocky limestone gorge before descending into the wide and picturesque MacDonald River valley.

Turnouts next 2.5 miles/4 km northbound with views of the valley. Watch for Stone sheep along the rock cut; they are frequently sighted along this stretch of road.

DC 378.2 (605.1) **DJ 1011.8** (1628.3 km) Baba Canyon to north. Popular with hikers (strenuous).

DC 378.6 (605.7 km) **DJ 1011.4** (1627.6 km) **Historical Mile 397.** Rocky Mountain Lodge to south; food, gas, lodging and camping. A map in the lodge shows Wokkpash hiking trails. ▲

Rocky Mountain Lodge. See display ad this section. ▲

DC 379.7 (607.4 km) **DJ 1010.3** (1625.9 km) Turnout to south.

DC 380.7 (609 km) **DJ 1009.3** (1624.3 km) West boundary of **Stone Mountain Provincial Park** (see description at the east boundary of the park at Milepost **DC 371.5**).

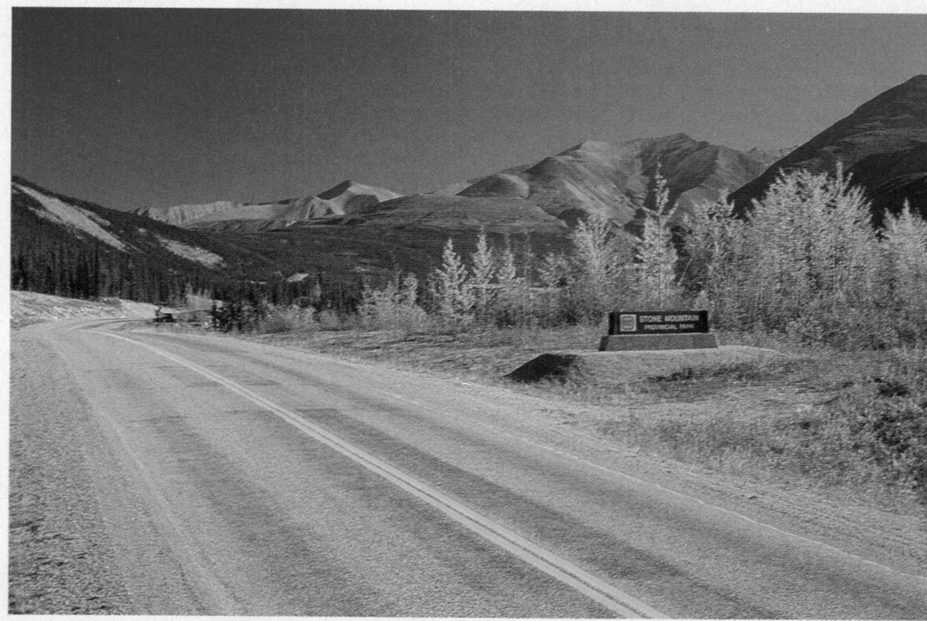

West boundary of Stone Mountain Provincial Park. (© Earl L. Brown, staff)

CAUTION: Southbound, watch for wildlife alongside and on the road. DO NOT FEED WILDLIFE.

DC 381.2 (611.2 km) **DJ 1008.8** (1623.5 km) Highway winds along above the wide rocky valley of MacDonald Creek. MacDonald Creek and river were named for Charlie MacDonald, a Cree Indian credited with helping Alaska Highway survey crews locate the best route for the pioneer road.

DC 382.2 (612.8 km) **DJ 1007.8** (1621.8km) Trail access via abandoned Churchill Copper Mine Road (4-wheel drive only beyond river) to **Wokkpash Protected Area**, located 12 miles/20 km south of the highway, which adjoins the southwest boundary of Stone Mountain Provincial Park. This remote area features extensive hoodoos (erosion pillars) in Wokkpash Gorge, and the scenic Forlorn Gorge and Stepped Lakes. Wokkpash Creek hiking trail follows Wokkpash Creek to Wokkpash Lake: 9 miles/15 km. Contact BC Parks District Office in Fort St. John before venturing into this area; phone (250) 787-3407.

DC 383.3 (614.6 km) **DJ 1006.7** (1620.1 km) 113 Creek. The creek was named during construction of the Alaska Highway for its distance from Mile 0 at Fort Nelson. While Dawson Creek was to become Mile 0 on the completed pioneer road, clearing crews began their work at Fort Nelson, since a rough winter road already existed between Dawson Creek and Fort Nelson. Stone Range to the northeast and Muskwa Ranges of the Rocky Mountains to the west.

DC 384.2 (615.4 km) **DJ 1005.8** (1618.6 km) 115 Creek provincial campground to southwest, adjacent highway; double-ended entrance. Side-by-side camper parking (8 sites), water, garbage containers, picnic tables. User-maintained, no camping fee. Access to the riverbank of 115 Creek and **MacDonald Creek.** Beaver dams nearby. Fishing for grayling and Dolly Varden. ▲

DC 385.4 (616.6 km) **DJ 1004.6** (1616.7 km) 115 Creek bridge. Turnout to south at east end of bridge with tables and dumpster. Like 113 Creek, 115 Creek was named during construction of the Alaska Highway for its distance from Fort Nelson, Mile 0 for clearing crews.

DC 390.5 (624.8 km) **DJ 999.5** (1608.5 km) **Historical Mile 408.** MacDonald River Services (closed for many years).

DC 392.5 (627.8 km) **DJ 997.5** (1605.3 km) MacDonald River bridge, clearance 17 feet/ 5.2m. Highway winds through narrow valley.

MacDonald River, fair fishing from May to July for Dolly Varden and grayling.

DC 394.8 (631.8 km) **DJ 995.2** (1601.6 km) Turnout with litter barrel to east.

DC 396.1 (633.8 km) **DJ 993.9** (1599.5 km) Folding rock formations on mountain face to west. The Racing River forms the boundary between the Sentinel Range and the Stone Range, both of which are composed of folded and sedimentary rock.

DC 399.1 (638.6 km) **DJ 990.9** (1594.7 km) Stringer Creek.

DC 400.7 (641.1 km) **DJ 989.3** (1592.1 km) Racing River bridge, clearance 17 feet/5.2m. River access to north at east end of bridge.

Note the open south-facing slopes on the north side of the river that are used as winter range by stone sheep, elk and deer. Periodic controlled burns encourage the growth of forage grasses and shrubs, and also allow chinook winds to clear snow from grazing grounds in winter. *CAUTION: Watch for horses.*

Racing River, grayling to 16 inches; Dolly Varden to 2 lbs., use flies, July through September.

DC 404.1 (646.6 km) **DJ 985.9** (1586.6 km) Welcome to Toad River.

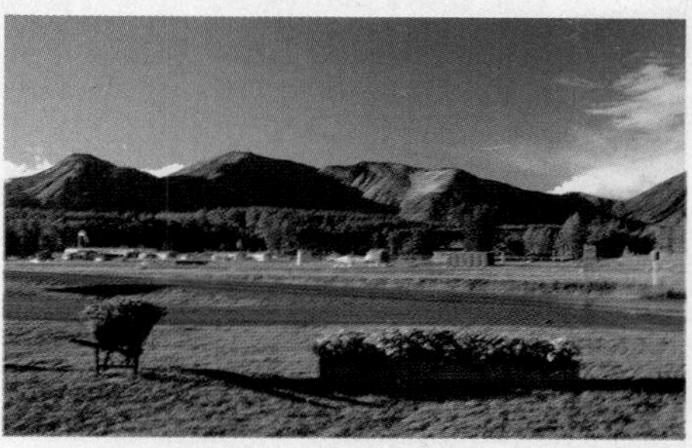

DC 404.6 (647.4 km) **DJ 985.4** (1585.8 km) **Historical Mile 422. TOAD RIVER** (unincorporated), situated in a picturesque valley. Popular artist Trish Croal makes her home here. Highway maintenance camp, school and private residences on north side of highway.

Toad River Lodge. See display ad on page 118. ▲

Toad River Lodge on south side of highway with cafe, gas, tire repair, propane, camping and lodging. Ambulance service. Toad River Lodge is open year-round. The lodge is known for its collection of hats, which numbers more than 4,800. Also, inquire at the lodge about good wildlife viewing locations nearby. ▲

Private Aircraft: Toad River airstrip; elev. 2,400 feet/732m; length 3,000 feet/914m. Unattended; no fuel; prior permission to land required.

DC 405.5 (648.8 km) **DJ 984.5** (1584.4 km) Turnout to south with **Historic Milepost 422.** Sign and interpretive panel commemorate Toad River/Camp 138 Jupp Construction.

DC 406.3 (650.1 km) **DJ 983.7** (1583.1 km) Turnout with dumpster to north.

DC 406.9 (651.1 km) **DJ 983.1** (1582.1 km) 141 Creek.

DC 407.5 (652 km) **DJ 982.5** (1581.1 km) **Historical Mile 426.** Food, gas, lodging and camping south side of highway. ▲

DC 409.2 (654.6 km) **DJ 980.8** (1578.4 km) South boundary of **Muncho Lake Provincial Park.** (The north boundary is at **Milepost DC 460.7** on the highway.) Muncho Lake Park straddles the Alaska Highway, encompassing the alpine peaks and valleys surrounding Muncho Lake. There are no signed trails. Guides and outfitters offers trips into the backcountry.

DC 410.2 (656.4 km) **DJ 979.8** (1576.8 km) **Stone Mountain Safaris.** New 4-bedroom cedar log lodge with queen and single beds per room. Two shared baths. Hot tub, snooker table, wildlife displays, horseback riding, wildlife viewing and adventure trips available. Private scenic ranch setting. From Toad River go west 6 miles on Alaska Highway and turn right at sign for 1 mile, then right again for 2 miles. Reservations required. Your hosts Dave and Ellie Wiens, Box 7870, Toad River, BC V0C 2X0. Phone (250) 232-5469; fax (250) 232-5801. [ADVERTISEMENT]

A look at just some of the 4,800 hats adorning the ceiling and walls of Toad River Lodge. (© Earl L. Brown, staff)

DC 410.6 (656.8 km) **DJ 979.4** (1576.1 km) Turnout with information panel on area geology. Impressive rock folding formation on mountain face, known as Folded Mountain.

DC 411 (657.4 km) **DJ 979** (1575.5 km) Beautiful turquoise-coloured Toad River to north. The highway now follows the Toad River westbound.

Toad River, grayling to 16 inches; Dolly Varden to 10 lbs., use flies, July through September.

DC 415.5 (664.7 km) **DJ 974.5** (1568.3 km) 150 Creek bridge. Creek access to south at east end of bridge.

DC 416.9 (667.1 km) **DJ 973.1** (1566 km) 151 Creek culvert.

DC 417.6 (668.2 km) **DJ 972.4** (1564.9 km) Centennial Falls to south. (Waterfall dries up in summer, unless it is raining.)

DC 419.8 (671.7 km) **DJ 970.2** (1561.3 km) **Toad River** bridge. Turnout with dumpster to south at west end of bridge; fishing.

DC 422.6 (676.2 km) **DJ 967.4** (1556.8 km) Watch for moose in pond to north; morning or evening best.

DC 423 (676.8 km) **DJ 967** (1556.2 km) Double-ended turnout with dumpster to north. Excellent wildlife viewing area; watch for Stone sheep, caribou, bear and moose.

CAUTION: Watch for Stone sheep along the highway (or standing in the middle of the highway). DO NOT FEED WILDLIFE. Do not stop vehicles on the highway to take photos; use shoulders or turnouts.

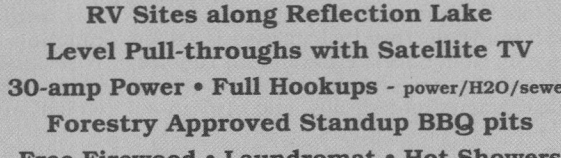

DC 423.1 (677 km) **DJ 966.9** (1556 km) The highway swings north for Alaska-bound travelers. Highway climbs next 6 miles/9.7 km northbound. For Dawson Creek-bound

travelers, the highway follows an easterly direction.

DC 424.1 (678.7 km) **DJ 965.9** (1554.4 km) **Historic Milepost 443** at Peterson Creek No. 1 bridge. The creek was named for local trapper Pete Peterson, who helped Alaska Highway construction crews select a route through this area. Historic sign marks start of Campbell Construction Co. Ltd. contract during construction of the Alaska Highway.

DC 424.3 (679 km) **DJ 965.7** (1554.1 km) The Village (closed).

DC 429.5 (688.9 km) **DJ 960.5** (1545.7 km) Viewpoint to east with information shelter and dumpster. Information panel on geology of "Sawtooth Mountains."

DC 436.5 (698.5 km) **DJ 953.5** (1534.5 km) **Historic Milepost 456.** Entering **MUNCHO LAKE** (pop. 29; elev. 2,700 feet/823m). Muncho Lake businesses extend from here north along the east shore of Muncho Lake to approximately **Milepost DC 443.7**. Businesses in Muncho Lake include 4 lodges, gas stations with repair, restaurants, cafes and campgrounds. The post office is located at Double G Service; open year-round. ▲

A historic sign and interpretive panel mark Muncho Lake/Refueling Stop, Checkpoint during Alaska Highway construction. The road around the lake was a particular challenge. Workers had to cut their way through the lake's rocky banks. Horses were used to haul away the rock.

The Muncho Lake area offers hiking in the summer and cross-country skiing in the winter. Boat rentals are available from J&H Wilderness Resort and Northern Rockies Lodge. MV *Sandpiper* boat tours of the lake available from Double G Service. Flightseeing and fly-in fishing service available at Northern Rockies Lodge with Liard Air Ltd. and at J&H Wilderness Resort with Duke Air Services Ltd. An annual lake trout derby is held in June; inquire locally for dates.

CAUTION: Watch for Stone sheep and caribou on the highway north of here. Please DO NOT FEED WILDLIFE. Please do not stop on the highway to take photos; use shoulders or turnouts.

DC 436.6 (698.7 km) **DJ 953.4** (1534.3 km) Double G Service; post office, gas, diesel, food and lodging.

DC 436.9 (699.2 km) **DJ 953.1** (1533.8 km) Gravel airstrip to west; length 1,200 feet/366m. View of Muncho Lake ahead northbound. The highway along Muncho Lake required considerable rock excavation by the Army in 1942. The original route went along the top of the cliffs, which proved particularly hazardous. (Portions of this hair-raising road can be seen high above the lake; local residents use it for mountain biking.) The Army relocated the road by benching into the cliffs a few feet above lake level.

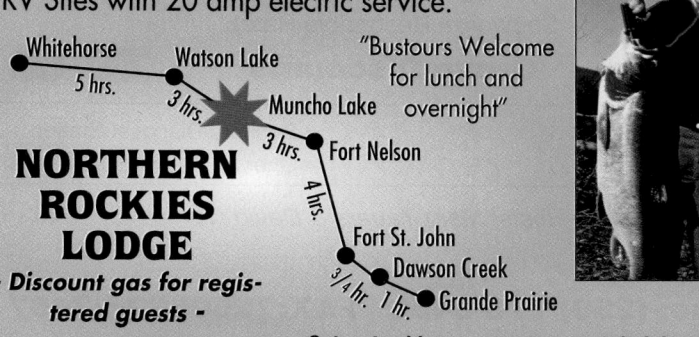

Muncho Lake, known for its beautiful deep green and blue waters, is 7 miles/11

km in length, and 1 mile/1.6 km in width; elevation of the lake is 2,680 feet/817m. The colours are attributed to copper oxide leaching into the lake. Deepest point has been reported to be 730 feet/223m, although

recent government tests have not located any point deeper than 400 feet/122m. The lake drains the Sentinel Range to the east and the Terminal Range to the west, feeding the raging Trout River in its 1,000-foot/305-m drop to the mighty Liard River. The mountains surrounding the lake are approximately 7,000 feet/2,134m high.

For fishermen, Muncho Lake offers Dolly Varden; some grayling; rainbow trout; whitefish to 12 inches; and lake trout. The lake trout quota is 3 trout per person, minimum size 15¾ inches; use spoons, spinners, diving plug or weighted spoons; June and July best. A 40-lb. lake trout was landed here in summer 1999; record is 50 lbs. Make sure you have a current British Columbia fishing license and a copy of the current regulations.

DC 437.7 (700.5 km) **DJ 952.3** (1532.5 km) Strawberry Flats Campground, Muncho Lake Provincial Park; 15 sites on rocky lakeshore, picnic tables, outhouses, garbage containers. Camping fee $12. ▲

CAUTION: Watch for bears in area.

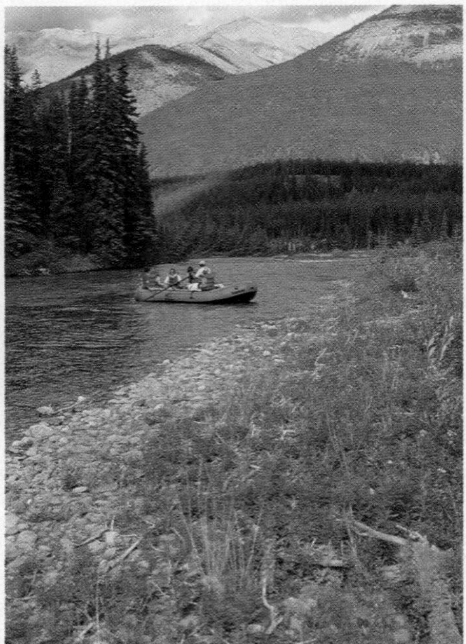

Rafting the Trout River between Muncho Lake and Trout River bridge.

(© Earl L. Brown, staff)

DC 442.2 (707.9 km) **DJ 947.8** (1525.3 km) **Historical Mile 462.** Northern Rockies/Highland Glen Lodge (open year-round) with lodging, restaurant, gas and camping west side of highway. Flying service for sightseeing and fly-in fishing. ▲

DC 442.9 (709 km) **DJ 947.1** (1524.2 km) Turnoff to west for MacDonald campground, Muncho Lake Provincial Park; 15 level gravel sites, firewood, picnic tables, outhouses, boat launch, information shelter, pump water, on Muncho Lake. Camping fee $12. *CAUTION: Watch for bears in area.* ▲

DC 443.6 (710.1 km) **DJ 946.4** (1523 km) **Historical Mile 463.** Muncho Lake Lodge; gas, food, camping and lodging. ▲

Muncho Lake Lodge. See display ad this section. ▲

DC 443.7 (710.3 km) **DJ 946.3** (1522.9 km) **Historical Mile 463.1.** J&H Wilderness Resort; food, gas, lodging, camping, store, boat rentals, tackle, flightseeing and rafting trips available. Muncho Lake businesses extend south to **Milepost DC 436.5.** ▲

J&H Wilderness Resort. See display ad this section. ▲

DC 444.9 (712.2 km) **DJ 945.1** (1520.9 km) Muncho Lake viewpoint to west with information panel, large parking area, picnic tables, dumpster and outhouses. View of Peterson Mountain at south end of lake. The island you see is Honeymoon Island.

CAUTION: Watch for Stone sheep on highway next 10 miles/16 km northbound.

DC 453.3 (725.6 km) **DJ 936.7** (1507.4 km) Turnout with dumpster to east.

DC 454 (726.7 km) **DJ 936** (1506.3 km) Mineral lick; watch for Stone sheep. There is a trailhead 0.2 mile/0.3 km off the highway; a 5- to 10-minute loop hike takes you to viewpoints overlooking the Trout River valley and the steep mineral-laden banks frequented by sheep, goats, caribou and elk. Good photo opportunities, early morning best. *CAUTION: Steep banks, slippery when wet. Bring insect repellent.*

DC 455.5 (729.2 km) **DJ 934.5** (1503.9 km) Turnout with dumpster and message board to west.

DC 457.7 (732.7 km) **DJ 932.3** (1500.4 km) Trout River bridge. The Trout River drains into the Liard River. The Trout River offers rafting: Grade II from Muncho Lake to the bridge here; Grade III to Liard River. Inquire locally for river conditions.

The highway follows the Trout River north for several miles.

Trout River, grayling to 18 inches; whitefish to 12 inches, flies, spinners, May, June and August best.

DC 458.9 (734.6 km) **DJ 931.1** (1498.4 km) Gravel turnout to east.

DC 460.7 (737.4 km) **DJ 929.3** (1495.5 km) Prochniak Creek bridge. The creek was named for a member of Company A, 648th Engineers Topographic Battalion, during construction of the Alaska Highway. North boundary of Muncho Lake Provincial Park.

DC 463.3 (741.6 km) **DJ 926.7** (1491.3 km) Watch for curves next 0.6 mile/1 km northbound.

DC 465.6 (745.3 km) **DJ 924.4** (1487.6 km) Turnout with dumpster to east.

DC 466.3 (746.3 km) **DJ 923.7** (1486.5 km) *CAUTION: Dangerous curves next 3 miles/5 km northbound. Watch for road construction between Kilometreposts 750 and 762 in 2000.*

DC 468.9 (749.5 km) **DJ 921.1** (1482.3 km) Pull-through turnout with dumpster to east. A fire in 1959 swept across the valley bottom here. Lodgepole pine, trembling aspen and paper birch are the dominant species that re-established this area.

DC 471 (754.1 km) **DJ 919** (1478.9 km) First glimpse of the mighty Liard River for northbound travelers. Named by French-Canadian voyageurs for the poplar ("liard") that line the banks of the lower river. The Alaska Highway parallels the Liard River from here north to Watson Lake. The river offered engineers a natural line to follow during routing and construction of the Alaska Highway in 1942.

DC 472.2 (756 km) **DJ 917.8** (1477 km) Washout Creek.

DC 474.3 (759.5 km) **DJ 915.7** (1473.6 km) Turnout with dumpster to west.

DC 476.7 (763 km) **DJ 913.3** (1469.8 km) Lower Liard River bridge (elev. 1,400 feet/427m). This is the only remaining suspension bridge on the Alaska Highway. The 1,143-foot suspension bridge was built by the American Bridge Co. and McNamara Construction Co. of Toronto in 1943.

The **Liard River** flows eastward toward the Fort Nelson River and parallels the Alaska Highway from the Lower Liard River bridge to the BC–YT border. The scenic Grand Canyon of the Liard is to the east and not visible from the highway. Many early fur traders lost their lives negotiating the wild waters of the Liard. The river offers good fishing for Dolly Varden, grayling, northern pike and whitefish.

DC 477.1 (763.8 km) **DJ 912.9** (1469.1 km) **Historical Mile 496. LIARD RIVER** (unincorporated), lodge with gas, store, pay phone, food, camping and lodging to west; open year-round. ▲

Liard River Lodge. See display ad on page 122. ▲

DC 477.7 (764.7 km) **DJ 912.3** (1468.2 km) **Historic Milepost 496.** Turnoff to north for **Liard River Hotsprings Provincial Park**, long a favorite stop for Alaska Highway travelers. The park has become so popular in recent years that the campground fills up very early each day in summer. Overflow day-parking area across highway from park entrance. The park is open year-round. This well-developed provincial park has 53 large, shaded, level gravel sites (some will accommodate 2 RVs), picnic tables, picnic shelter, water pump, garbage containers, firewood, fire rings, playground and restrooms at the hot springs with wheelchair-accessible toilet. Camping fees to $15. There is no fee to use the hot springs. Pay phone at park entrance. Park gate closes at 11 P.M. and opens at 6 A.M.. ♿▲

Excellent interpretive programs and nature walks in summer; check schedule posted at park entrance and at information shelter near trailhead. Emergency phone at

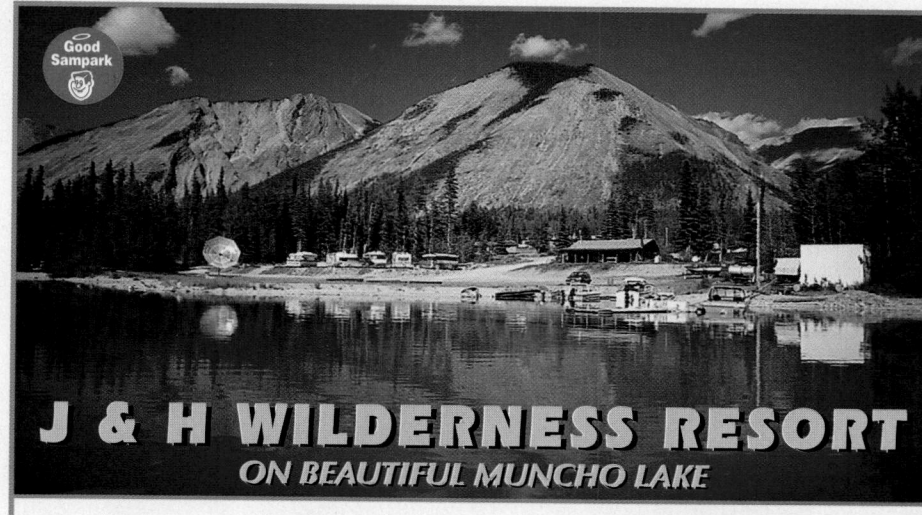

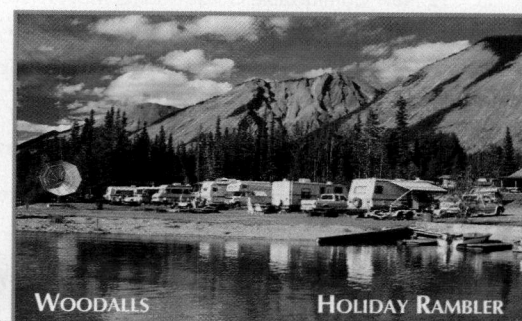

park headquarters. *CAUTION: BEWARE OF BEARS!*

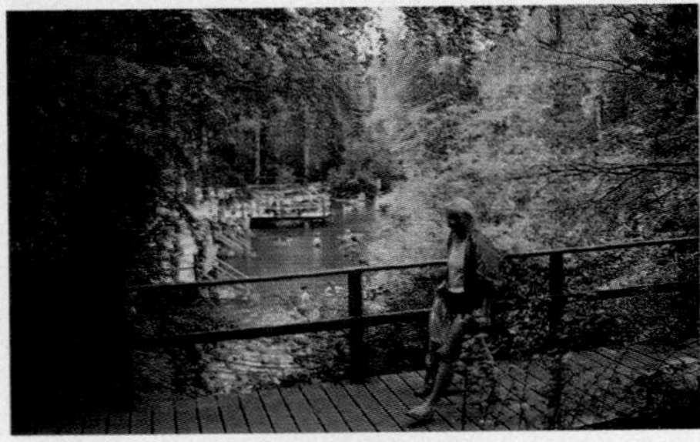

A short walk leads to the pools. The boardwalk trail crosses a wetlands environment that supports more than 250 boreal forest plants, including 14 orchid species and 14 plants that survive at this latitude because of the hot springs. Watch for moose feeding in the wetlands. There are 2 hot springs pools with water temperatures ranging from 108° to 126°F/42° to 52°C. Nearest is the Alpha pool with a children's wading area. Beyond the Alpha pool is Beta pool, which is larger and deeper. Both have changing rooms. Beta pool is about a 0.4-mile/0.6-km walk. Plenty of parking at trailhead. *NOTE: No pets on boardwalk trail.*

DC 477.8 (764.9 km) **DJ 912.2** (1468 km) **Historical Mile 497.** Liard Hotsprings Lodge (open year-round) with food, gas, lodging and camping. Fishing, sightseeing charter trips and jetboat tours available.

Trapper Ray's Liard Hotsprings Lodge. See display ad this section.

NOTE Highway narrows nothbound.

DC 482.8 (772.9 km) **DJ 907.2** (1460 km) Teeter Creek. A footpath leads upstream; 10-minute walk to falls. Grayling fishing.

DC 485.4 (777 km) **DJ 904.6** (1455.8 km) Small turnout overlooking the Liard River.

DC 489 (783.6 km) **DJ 901** (1450 km) **Private Aircraft:** Liard River airstrip; elev. 1,400 feet/427m; length 4,000 feet/1,219m; gravel; no fuel.

DC 495 (792.3 km) **DJ 895** (1440.3 km) **Historic Milepost 514.** Smith River bridge, clearance 17 feet/5.2m. The historic sign here commemorates Smith River Airport Road. The old airstrip, part of the Northwest Staging Route, is located in a burned-over area about 25 miles/40 km from the highway (accessible by 4-wheel drive only).

Access to **Smith River Falls** via 1.6-mile/2.6-km gravel road; not recommended for large RVs or trailers or in wet weather. There is a hiking trail down to 2-tiered Smith River Falls from the parking area. Grayling fishing.

DC 509.4 (815.6 km) **DJ 880.6** (1417.1 km) Large turnout with dumpster to east.

DC 513.9 (822.8 km) **DJ 876.1** (1409.9 km) **Historical Mile 533. COAL RIVER.** Lodge was closed in 1999; current status unknown.

DC 514.2 (823.2 km) **DJ 875.8** (1409.4 km) **Historical Mile 533.2.** Coal River bridge. The Coal River flows into the Liard River south of the bridge.

DC 519.5 (831.4 km) **DJ 870.5** (1400.9 km) Sharp easy-to-miss turnoff to west for undeveloped "do-it-yourself campsite" (watch for sign). Small gravel parking area with outhouse, dumpster, and beautiful view of the Liard River (not visible from the highway). Although signed "Whirlpool Canyon," this scenic stretch of the Liard River has been identified by one astute reader as **Mountain Portage Rapids**, with Whirlpool Canyon being located farther downriver.

DC 524.2 (839.2 km) **DJ 865.8** (1393 km) **Historical Mile 543. FIRESIDE** (unincorporated). This community was partially destroyed by fire in the summer of 1982. Evidence of the fire can still be seen from south of Fireside north to Lower Post. The 1982 burn, known as the Eg fire, was the second largest fire in British Columbia history, destroying more than 400,000 acres.

Highway maintenance camp and truck stop; gas and seervices.

DC 524.7 (840 km) **DJ 865.3** (1392.5 km) Good view of Liard River and Cranberry

Rapids to west.

DC 530 (848.7 km) **DJ 860** (1384 km) Gravel turnout with dumpster to south.

DC 540.4 (865.3 km) **DJ 849.6** (1367.3 km) North end of rerouting of Alaska Highway (see **Milepost DC 527.7**).

DC 545.9 (874.2 km) **DJ 844.1** (1358.4 km) Turnout with litter barrel to west overlooking the Liard River.

DC 550.9 (882.2 km) **DJ 839.1** (1350.4 km) **Historical Mile 570, Allen's Lookout.** Very large pull-through turnout with picnic tables, outhouse and dumpster to west overlooking the Liard River. Goat Mountain to west. Legend has it that a band of outlaws took advantage of this sweeping view of the Liard River to attack and rob riverboats.

DC 555 (888.8 km) **DJ 835** (1343.8 km) Good berry picking in July among roadside raspberry bushes; watch for bears.

DC 556 (890.4 km) **DJ 834** (1342.2 km) Highway swings west for Alaska-bound travelers.

NOTE: Watch for road construction between Kilometreposts 895 and 906 in 2000.

DC 562.5 (900.8 km) **DJ 827.5** (1331.7 km) Large gravel turnout with dumpster.

DC 567.9 (909.4 km) **DJ 822.1** (1323 km) **Historic Milepost 588, Contact Creek.** (Contact Creek Bridge was replaced by a culvert in 1999.) Turnout with historic sign and interpretive panel. Contact Creek was named by soldiers of the 35th Regiment from the south and the 340th Regiment from the north who met here Sept. 24, 1942, completing the southern sector of the Alaska Highway. A personal reminiscence about the work of A Company 35th Combat Engineers is found in Chester Russell's "Tales of a Catskinner."

DC 568.3 (910.2 km) **DJ 821.7** (1322.4 km) First of 7 crossings of the BC–YT border. Large gravel turnout to north. Point of interest sign (missing in 1999): "The Yukon Territory takes its name from the Indian word *Youcon,* meaning 'big river.' It was first explored in the 1840s by the Hudson's Bay Co., which established several trading posts. The territory, which was then considered a district of the Northwest Territories, remained largely untouched until the Klondike Gold Rush, when thousands of people flooded into the country and communities sprang up almost overnight. This sudden expansion led to the official formation of the Yukon Territory on June 13, 1898."

DC 570 (912.9 km) **DJ 820** (1319.6 km) **Historical Mile 590. CONTACT CREEK.** Contact Creek Lodge is open year-round; food, gas, diesel, car repair, 24-hour towing and pay phone.

Contact Creek Lodge. See display ad this section.

DC 573.9 (918.9 km) **DJ 816.1** (1313.3 km) Iron Creek culvert, completed in 1998, is the largest culvert in the world at 25 feet high, 135 feet long and 62 feet wide. Turnout with litter barrel.

According to the folks at Iron Creek Lodge, Iron Creek was named during construction of the Alaska Highway for the trucks that stopped here to put on tire irons (chains) in order to make it up the hill.

DC 575.9 (922 km) **DJ 814.1** (1310.1 km) **Historical Mile 596.** Iron Creek Lodge; food, gas, diesel, lodging, camping and dump station. Fishing at private stocked lake.

Iron Creek Lodge. See display ad this section.

DC 582 (931.8 km) **DJ 808** (1300.3 km) NorthwesTel microwave tower.

DC 585 (937 km) **DJ 805** (1295.5 km) **Hyland River** bridge; good fishing for rainbow, Dolly Varden and grayling.

NOTE: Watch for logging trucks northbound to Watson Lake.

DC 585.3 (937.2 km) **DJ 804.7** (1295 km) **Historical Mile 605.9.** Hyland River bridge. The Hyland River is a tributary of the Liard River. The river was named for Frank Hyland, an early-day trader at Telegraph Creek on the Stikine River. Hyland operated trading posts throughout northern British Columbia, competing successfully with the Hudson's Bay Co., and at one time printing his own currency.

DC 595 (951.5 km) **DC 795** (1279.4 km) *CAUTION: Watch for horses.*

DC 598.7 (957.5 km) **DJ 791.3** (1273.4 km) Access to Lower Post (unincorporated), at **Historical Mile 620**, via short gravel road.

DC 605.1 (967.6 km) **DJ 784.9** (1263.1 km) **Historic Milepost 627** marks official BC–YT border; Welcome to the Yukon sign.

Monitor CB Channel 9 for police. The Alaska Highway (Yukon Highway 1) dips back into British Columbia several times before making its final crossing into the Yukon Territory near Morley Lake (**Milepost DC 751.5**).

NOTE: Kilometreposts on the British Columbia portion of the highway reflect actual driving distance. Kilometreposts on the Yukon Territory portion of the highway reflect historical mileposts. There is approximately a 40-kilometre difference at the BC–YT border between these measurements. A recalibration of kilometres is possible in 2000 or 2001.

Northbound: Good paved highway with wide shoulders next 380 miles/611.5 km to Haines Junction, with the exception of some short sections of narrow road and occasional gravel breaks.

Southbound: Good sections of reconstructed road. Watch for more construction and rough, narrow, winding road and breaks in surfacing between border and Fort Nelson (approximately 321 miles/516.6 km).

DC 606.9 (1012 km) **DJ 783.1** (1260.2 km) **Lucky Lake** picnic area and **Liard Canyon Overlook** to south; ball diamond and 1.4-mile/2.2-km hiking trail through mature pine and spruce forest down to observation platform overlooking the Liard

River. Information panels on natural features of the area. Allow at least an hour for hike. Watch for gray jays, Northern flickers and black-capped and boreal chickadees.

Lucky Lake is a popular local swimming hole for Watson Lake residents, who installed a water slide here. Relatively shallow, the lake warms up quickly in summer, making it one of the few area lakes where swimming is possible. Stocked with rainbow trout.

According to R. Coutts in *Yukon Places & Names*, Lucky Lake was named by American Army Engineer troops working on construction of the Alaska Highway in 1942: "A young woman set up a tent business and clients there referred to transactions as 'a change of luck.'"

DC 609.2 (1015.5 km) **DJ 780.8** (1256.5 km) Paved drive-through rest area to north

with litter barrel, outhouses and Watson Lake community map.

DC 610.4 (1017.5 km) **DJ 779.6** (1254.6 km) Weigh station.

DC 610.5 (1017.7 km) **DJ 779.5** (1254.4 km) **Mile 632.5. Campground Services** at Mile 632.5 is the largest and best equipped RV park in Watson Lake, the gateway to the Yukon. The park features 140 full or partial hookups and pull-throughs, tent sites, playground, firepits and a screened kitchen. Coin-op showers, laundry and car wash. Good Sam Park. A food market stocks groceries, convenience items, movie rentals,

fishing tackle, licenses and ice. Gasoline and diesel and ICG propane are available at the self-serve pumps. A licensed mechanic is available for repairs, alignments, tire changes, etc. Open for business year-round, serving the traveler's needs for over 25 years! Phone (867) 536-7448. [ADVERTISEMENT] ▲

Watson Lake

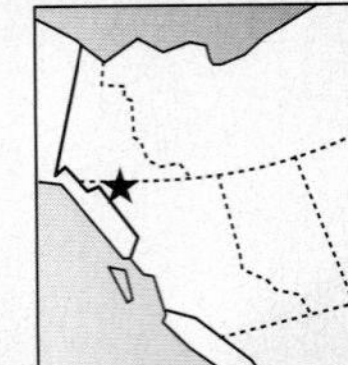

DC 612.9 (1021 km) **DJ 777.1** (1250.6 km) **Historic Milepost 635.** "Gateway to the Yukon," located 330 miles/531 km from Fort Nelson, 275 miles/443 km from Whitehorse. **Population:** 1,794. **Emergency Services: RCMP**, phone (867) 536-5555 (if no answer call 867/667-5555). **Fire Department**, phone (867) 536-2222. **Ambulance**, phone (867) 536-4444. **Hospital**, phone (867) 536-4444.

Visitor Information: Located in the Alaska Highway Interpretive Centre behind the Signpost Forest, north of the Alaska Highway; access to the centre is from the Campbell Highway. Open 8 A.M. to 8 P.M. daily, mid-May to September. Phone (867) 536-7469; fax (867) 536-2003.

Inquire here about Yukon Government campground permits. One permit ($8) pays for one night of camping. These permits are sold at visitor centres, lodges, stores and other vendors and may also be purchased from campground attendants. Permits are transferable. **Elevation:** 2,265 feet/690m. **Climate:** Average temperature in January is -16°F/-27°C, in July 59°F/15°C. Record high temperature 93°F/34°C in June 1950, record low -74°F/-59°C in January 1947. Annual snowfall is 90.6 inches. Driest month is April, wettest month is September. Average date of last spring frost is June 2; average date of first fall frost is Sept. 14. **Radio:** CBC 990. **Television:** Channel 8 and cable.

Private Aircraft: Watson Lake airport, 8 miles/12.9 km north on Campbell Highway; elev. 2,262 feet/689m; length 5,500 feet/1,676m and 3,530 feet/1,076m; asphalt; fuel 100, jet. Heliport and floatplane bases also located here. The Watson Lake airport terminal building was built in 1942. The log structure has been designated a Heritage Building.

Watson Lake is an important service stop on the Alaska and Campbell highways (Campbell Highway travelers, fill your gas tanks here!); a communication and distribution centre for the southern Yukon; a base for trappers, hunters and fishermen; and a supply point for area mining and mineral exploration.

Watson Lake businesses are located along

WATSON LAKE ADVERTISERS

Bee Jay's Cafe	Ph. (867) 536-2335
Bee Jay's Services	Ph. (867) 536-2335
Belvedere Motor Hotel	Ph. (867) 536-7712
Big Horn Hotel	Ph. (867) 536-2020
Campground Services	E. edge of town
Cedar Lodge Motel	Ph. (867) 536-7406
Downtown R.V. Park	Ph. (867) 536-2646
Gateway Motor Inn	Ph. (867) 536-7744
Green Valley RV Park	Kmpost 1032 Alaska Hwy.
Greenway's Greens	Ph. (867) 536-2477
Hougen's Department Store	Ph. (867) 536-7475
Northern Lights Centre	Ph. (867) 536-7817
Napa Auto Parts	Ph. (867) 536-2521
Northwestel	See ad
Rudy's Towing	Ph. (867) 536-2123
Watson Lake Hotel	Ph. (867) 536-7781
Watson Lake Motors	Across from Signpost Forest

Welcome to North 60° Country!

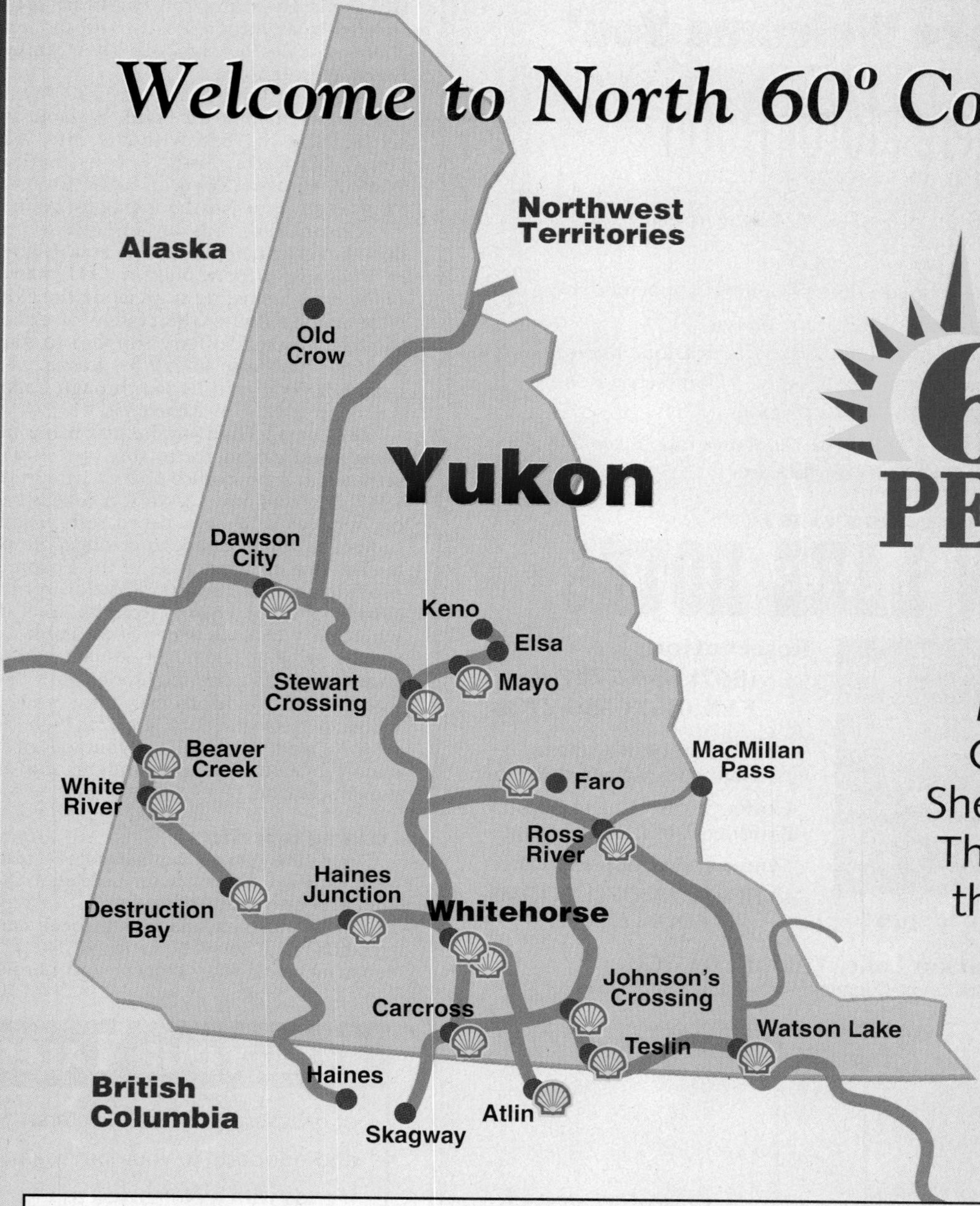

Northwest Territories
Alaska
Old Crow
Yukon
Dawson City
Keno
Elsa
Mayo
Stewart Crossing
Beaver Creek
White River
Faro
MacMillan Pass
Ross River
Haines Junction
Whitehorse
Destruction Bay
Johnson's Crossing
Carcross
Watson Lake
Teslin
Haines
British Columbia
Atlin
Skagway

NORTH 60° PETRO

Your Mileage Guide to Shell Stations Throughout the Yukon

Shell products are distributed by North 60° Petro at the following stations:

Alaska Hwy.

KM	MI	
1022	635	Watson Lake Shell
1294	804	Teslin Lake Motors
1345	836	Johnson's Crossing Lodge
1464	910	McCrae Shell
1465	911	Pioneer RV Park
1469	913	Whitehorse Shell
1477	918	Second Ave. Shell
		Yukon Tire Centre
		Granger Shell
1635	1016	Haines Junction
1743	1083	Talbot Arm Motel
1879	1168	White River Lodge
1931	1202	1202 Motor Inn

Atlin Road

KM	MI	
98	61	Pine Tree Services

Robert Campbell Hwy.

KM	MI	
427	258	Faro Shell
364	220	Ross River

Silver Trail Hwy.

KM	MI	
53	33	Heartland Services–Mayo

Klondike Hwy.

KM	MI	
105	65	Montana Services
116	73	Spirit Lake Resort
538	334	Stewart Crossing Shell
720	447	Dominion Shell

1-867-633-8820

FINE FUELS. SUPER SERVICE.
QUALITY LUBRICANTS.

either side of the Alaska Highway. The lake itself is not visible from the Alaska Highway. Access to the lake, airport, hospital and Ski Hill is via the Campbell Highway (locally referred to as Airport Road). The ski area is about 4 miles/6.4 km out the Campbell Highway from town.

Originally known as Fish Lake, Watson Lake was renamed for Frank Watson, who settled here in 1898 with his wife, Adela Stone, of Kaska First Nations heritage. Watson, who was born in Tahoe City, California, had come North looking for gold.

Watson Lake was an important point during construction of the Alaska Highway in 1942. The airport, built in 1941, was one of the major refueling stops along the Northwest Staging Route, the system of airfields through Canada to ferry supplies to Alaska and later lend-lease aircraft to Russia. Of the nearly 8,000 aircraft ferried through Canada, 2,618 were Bell P–39 Airacobras.

The Alaska Highway helped bring both people and commerce to this once isolated settlement. A post office opened here in July 1942. The economy of Watson Lake is based on services and also the forest products industry. White spruce and lodgepole pine are the two principal trees of the Yukon and provide a forest industry for the territory. White spruce grows straight and fast wherever adequate water is available, and it will grow to extreme old age without showing decay. The lodgepole pine developed from the northern pine and can withstand extreme cold, grow at high elevations and take full advantage of the almost 24-hour summer sunlight of a short growing season.

Lodging & Services

There are several hotels/motels, restaurants and gas stations with unleaded, diesel and propane, automotive and tire repair. Dump stations available at local campgrounds and service stations. There are department, variety, grocery and hardware stores. The RCMP office is east of town centre on the Alaska Highway. There is 1 bank in Watson Lake—Canadian Imperial Bank of Commerce; it is open Monday through Thursday from 10 a.m. to 3 p.m., Friday 10 a.m. to 6 p.m., closed holidays. ATM available 24 hours.

Check at the Visitor Information Centre for locations of local churches. Dennis Ball Memorial Swimming Pool is open weekdays in summer. Lucky Lake waterslide is open on weekends in summer from 1–4 P.M.

Belvedere Motor Hotel, located in the centre of town, is Watson Lake's newest and finest hotel. It offers such luxuries as Jacuzzi tubs in the rooms, Internet access, in-room coffee, cable TV, and all at competitive prices. Dining is excellent, whether you decide to try the superb dining room menu or the coffee shop menu. Our Birchwood Tours offers travel planning and a complimentary activity list for the Yukon. Phone (867) 536-7712, fax (867) 536-7563. [ADVERTISEMENT]

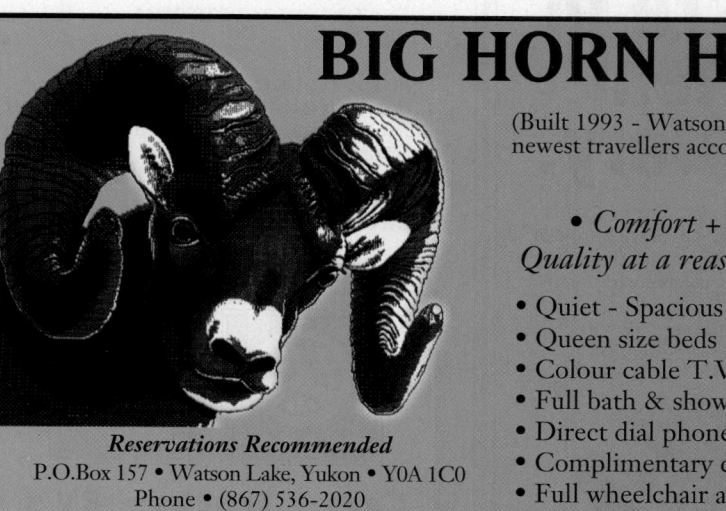

Big Horn Hotel. New in 1993. 29 beautiful rooms. Centrally located on the Alaska Highway in downtown Watson Lake, YT. Our rooms are quiet, spacious, clean and they boast queen-size beds and complimentary coffee. You get quality at a reasonable price. Available to you are king-size motionless waterbeds, Jacuzzi rooms, kitchenette suites. We know you'll enjoy staying with us. Book ahead. Phone (867) 536-2020, fax (867) 536-2021. [ADVERTISEMENT]

Watson Lake Hotel. The historic Watson Lake Hotel. We're right in the heart of Watson Lake's historical Signpost Forest. Enjoy northern hospitality at its finest. Ample parking on our 6 acres of property. Quiet outside modern units, boardwalk gift shops. Senior, government, military and corporate discounts. Phone for reservations (867) 536-7781; fax (867) 536-2724. [ADVERTISEMENT]

Aerial view of Watson Lake's Wye Lake Park. (© Earl L. Brown, staff)

Camping

The turnoff for Watson Lake Yukon government campground is 2.4 miles/3.9 km west of the Signpost Forest via the Alaska Highway; see description at **Milepost DC 615.3.** There is a private campground at **Milepost DC 619.6**, 4.3 miles/6.9 km past

Watson Lake's best known landmark is the Signpost Forest. (© Earl L. Brown, staff)

the turnoff for the government campground; a private campground 2.4 miles/3.9 km east of the Signpost Forest on the Alaska Highway (see **Milepost DC 610.5**); and an RV park located downtown. ▲

Downtown R.V. Park, situated in the centre of town. 71 full-hookup stalls, 19 with pull-through parking; showers; laundromat. Town water. Free truck/trailer, motorhome wash with overnight stay. Easy walking distance to stores, garages, hotels, restaurants, liquor store, banking, churches, information centre and the world-famous Signpost Forest. Just across the street from Wye Lake Park. Excellent hiking trails. Phone (867) 536-2646 in summer, phone/fax (867) 536-2224 in winter. [ADVERTISEMENT] ▲

Transportation

Air: No scheduled service. Helicopter charters available from Frontier Helicopters and Trans North Helicopters.

Bus: Scheduled service to Edmonton and Whitehorse via Coachways.

Taxi and **Car Rental:** Available.

Attractions

The **Alaska Highway Interpretive Centre**, operated by Tourism Yukon, is well worth a visit. Located behind the Signpost Forest, north of the Alaska Highway, the centre offers a video on Yukon history and the Alaska Highway. Excellent slide presentation and displays, including photographs taken in the mid-1940s showing the construction of the Alaska Highway in this area. The centre is open daily, May to mid-September. Free admission. Phone (867) 536-7469.

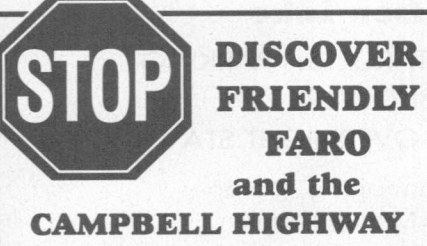

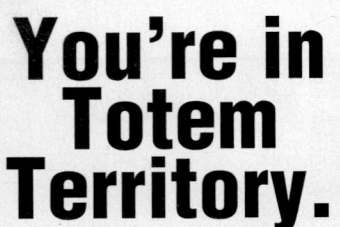

Northern Lights Centre. The only planetarium in North America featuring the myth and science of the northern lights. Using advanced video and laser technology, the centre offers 2 different presentations on the aurora borealis inside a 110-seat "Electric Sky" theatre environment. Also interactive displays. Afternoon and evening showings daily from May to September. Admission charged. Located across from the Signpost Forest. Get your Yukon Explorer's Passport stamped here. Phone (867) 536-STAR; Internet www.yukon.net/northernlights.

The Watson Lake Signpost Forest, seen at the north end of town at the junction of the Alaska and Robert Campbell highways, was started by Carl K. Lindley of Danville, IL, a U.S. Army soldier in Company D, 341st Engineers, working on the construction of the Alaska Highway in 1942. Travelers are still adding signs to the collection, which numbered 42,000 in September 1999. Visitors are encouraged to add a sign to the Signpost Forest. **Historic Milepost 635** is located at the Signpost Forest.

Special Events. The annual Watson Lake Rodeo (NRA-approved) is held in July. A parade, 8 main events and junior events are featured.

Wye Lake Park offers a picnic area, a bandshell, kitchen shelter and wheelchair-accessible restrooms. A 1-mile/1.5-km trail winds around First Wye Lake. Interpretive panels along the trail present information on Yukon wildflowers and local birds. The lake attracts both migrating birds (spring and fall) and resident species, such as nesting red-necked grebes. Also watch for tree swallows, violet-green swallows, mountain bluebirds and white-throated sparrows. The development of this park was initiated by a local citizens group. ♿

St. John the Baptist Anglican Church has a memorial stained-glass window designed by Yukon artist Kathy Spalding. Titled "Our Land of Plenty," the window features a scene just north of Watson Lake off the Campbell Highway.

Drive the Campbell Highway. This good gravel road offers an excellent wilderness highway experience. Motorists can travel the entire 373 miles/600 km of the Campbell Highway, stopping at Ross River and Faro en route, to junction with the Klondike Highway at Carmacks. Or drive north 52 miles/83 km from Watson Lake to Simpson Lake for picnicking, fishing and camping. (See CAMPBELL HIGHWAY section for details.)

Play golf at Greenway's Greens outside Upper Liard Village at **Milepost DC 620.3** Alaska Highway. The 9-hole, par-35 course has grass greens and is open daily May through September. Phone (867) 536-2477.

Explore the area. Take time to fish, canoe a lake, take a wilderness trek or sightsee by helicopter. Outfitters in the area offer guided fishing trips to area lakes. Trips can be arranged by the day or by the week. Check with the visitor information centre.

AREA FISHING: Watson Lake has grayling, trout and pike. **McKinnon Lake** (walk-in only), 20 miles/32 km west of Watson Lake, pike 5 to 10 lbs. **Toobally Lake**, string of lakes 14 miles/23 km long, 90 air miles/145 km east, lake trout 8 to 10 lbs.; pike 5 to 10 lbs.; grayling 1 to 3 lbs. **Stewart Lake**, 45 air miles/72 km north northeast; lake trout, grayling.

Alaska Highway Log

(continued)

Distance* from Dawson Creek (DC) is followed by distance from Delta Junction (DJ). Original mileposts are indicated in the text as Historical Mile.

*In Canada, mileages from Dawson Creek are based on actual driving distance, not historical mileposts, and kilometres are based on physical kilometreposts. Mileages from Delta Junction are also based on actual driving distance, not historical mileposts, but are followed by the metric conversion to kilometres.

YUKON HIGHWAY 1

DC 612.9 (1021 km) **DJ 777.1** (1250.6 km) Watson Lake Signpost Forest at the **junction** of the Campbell Highway (Yukon Route 4) and Alaska Highway. The first 6 miles/9.7 km of the Campbell Highway is known locally as Airport Road; turn here for access to visitor information (in the Alaska Highway Interpretive Centre), airport, hospital and ski hill.

The Campbell Highway leads north to Ross River and Faro (see CAMPBELL HIGHWAY section), to junction with the Klondike Highway to Dawson City. Campbell Highway travelers should fill gas tanks in Watson Lake.

DC 615.3 (1025 km) **DJ 774.7** (1246.7 km) Turnoff to north for **Watson Lake Recreation Park.** Drive in 1 mile/1.5 km for Watson Lake Yukon government campground; 55 gravel sites, most level, some pull-through, drinking water, kitchen shelters, outhouses, firepits, firewood and litter barrels. Camping permit ($8/night). ▲

There is a separate group camping area and also a day-use area (boat launch, swimming, picnicking at Watson Lake). Follow signs at fork in access road. Trails connect all areas.

DC 618.5 (1030 km) **DJ 771.5** (1241.6 km) Watch for livestock.

DC 619.6 (1032 km) **DJ 770.4** (1239.8 km) **Green Valley R.V. Park.** Phone (867) 536-2276. Just 7 miles west of Watson Lake, quiet greenbelt area along Liard River. Friendly service, clean facilities. Pay phone. Serviced and unserviced sites, dump station, grassy tent sites, riverside camping, firepits, laundry, showers, grocery, coffee, pastries, ice, souvenirs, free gold panning, game room, fishing licenses and tackle. Fish for grayling and dollies. Pick wild strawberries and raspberries in season. Cold beer and off sales. Bikers welcome. Your hosts: Ralph and Marion Bjorkman. [ADVERTISEMENT] ▲

DC 620 (1032.4 km) **DJ 770** (1239.2 km) Upper Liard River bridge. The Liard River heads in the St. Cyr Range in southcentral Yukon Territory and flows southeast into British Columbia, then turns east and north to join the Mackenzie River at Fort Simpson, NWT.

Liard River, grayling, lake trout, whitefish and northern pike.

DC 620.2 (1032.7 km) **DJ 769.8** (1238.8 km) **Historical Mile 642. UPPER LIARD VILLAGE**, site of **Our Lady of the Yukon Church.** Food, lodging and camping. ▲

DC 620.3 (1033 km) **DJ 769.7** (1238.7 km) Greenway's Greens golf course to south with 9 holes, par 35, grass greens, clubhouse, club rentals, putting green, pro shop, power and pull carts. Open daily in summer; tee times not required.

DC 620.8 (1033.7 km) **DJ 769.2** (1237.9

km) Albert Creek bridge. Turnout with litter barrel to north at east end of bridge. A sign near here marks the first tree planting project in the Yukon. Approximately 200,000 white spruce seedlings were planted in the Albert Creek area in 1993.

White spruce is the most common conifer in the Yukon, and the most widely distributed. Mature trees are 23 to 66 feet tall. An average mature spruce can produce 8,000 cones in a good year. Each cone has 140 seeds. The seed cones are about 2 inches/5 cm long and slender in shape. The pollen cones are small and pale red in colour.

DC 625.5 (1041.9 km) **DJ 764.5** (1230.3 km) Ratlin Lake access road.

DC 626.2 (1043 km) **DJ 763.8** (1229.2 km) **Historic Milepost 649. Junction 37 Services.** See display ad this section.

Services here include gas, store with souvenirs, propane, car repair, car wash, laundromat, cafe, camping and lodging. ▲

Junction with the Cassiar Highway, which leads south to Yellowhead Highway 16. See CASSIAR HIGHWAY section.

DC 627 (1043.9 km) **DJ 763** (1227.9 km) **Historic Mile 650. The Northern Beaver Post and Wolf It Down Restaurant.** As with trading posts of the past, The Northern Beaver Post is an essential stop for any traveler. Here you will find quality 90 percent Canadian-made gifts and souvenirs which are as useful as they are decorative. In the friendly atmosphere of the Post, discover the largest inventoried family gift shop on the Alaska Highway. Mention this ad to save $5 on your purchase of our family's "Rivers of Gold" autographed book ... complete with gold nugget! Enjoy Native and Eskimo arts

and crafts, porcelain dolls, furs, wildflower books, cards and stamps. Licensed Beanie Baby dealer and Bradford plate dealer. Present this ad to receive a 10 percent discount on regular priced Ts and sweatshirts. Shipping available. Caravans and buses call for special early morning openings. 7 days a week, April–Jan., extended summer hours. Winter 9-8. Limited free RV parking. New, clean, nonsmoking cabins with private washrooms and separate laundry facilities. (Ask about our new Jacuzzi suites). Great food next door at newly built Wolf It Down Restaurant. On-site bakery; fresh breads and pastries. Homemade, full-course meals (just like Gramma's). Ice cream, espresso, lattes, cappuccino. Licensed dining room and deck. Liquor to go. Ice. Clean washrooms. Caravans and bus tours welcome (reservations requested). For all your souvenir wolf collections. Also, Baby Nuggett RV Park Inc. currently being constructed. Peaceful, quiet and level 60–100 foot treed pull-through sites. Dry parking available in the beginning of the season. Some fully-serviced sites avail-

Alaska Highway winds through Rancheria River Valley. (© Earl L. Brown, staff)

able later in the season. Phone for progress report (867) 536-2307; (867) 536-7666 after hours. [ADVERTISEMENT] ▲

DC 627.3 (1044.5 km) **DJ 762.7** (1227.4 km) Large double-ended gravel turnout and rest area with litter barrels, pit toilets and Watson Lake community map.

DC 630 (1050.8 km) **DJ 760** (1223.1 km) Several hundred rock messages are spelled out along the highway here. The rock messages were started in summer 1990 by a Fort Nelson swim team.

DC 633 (1055.6 km) **DJ 757** (1218.2 km) Gravel turnout to north.

DC 637.8 (1063.3 km) **DJ 752.2** (1210.5 km) Microwave tower access road.

DC 639.8 (1066.5 km) **DJ 750.2** (1207.3 km) *NOTE: Hill and sharp curve.*

DC 647.2 (1078.5 km) **DJ 742.8** (1195.4 km) Turnout with litter barrel on Little Rancheria Creek to north.

DC 647.4 (1079 km) **DJ 742.6** (1195.1 km) Little Rancheria Creek bridge. Northbound winter travelers put on chains here.

DC 650.6 (1084 km) **DJ 739.4** (1189.9 km) Highway descends westbound to Big Creek.

DC 651.1 (1084.8 km) **DJ 738.9** (1189.1 km) Big Creek bridge, clearance 17.7 feet/5.4m. Turnout at east end of bridge.

DC 651.2 (1085 km) **DJ 738.8** (1189 km) Turnoff to north for Big Creek Yukon government day-use area, adjacent highway on Big Creek; gravel loop road, outhouses, firewood, kitchen shelter, litter barrels, picnic tables, water pump.

DC 652.5 (1087.3 km) **DJ 737.5** (1186.8 km) Sign reads: "Northbound winter travelers chains may be removed."

DC 658.4 (1096.7 km) **DJ 731.6** (1177.4 km) Pull-through turnout south side of highway.

DC 662.3 (1102.9 km) **DJ 727.7** (1171.1 km) NorthwesTel microwave tower road to north.

NOTE: Recent highway reconstruction and straightening in this area has resulted in the displacement of many kilometreposts.

DC 664.1 (1105.8 km) **DJ 725.9** (1168.2 km) Double-ended turnout to north to Lower Rancheria River.

DC 664.3 (1106.2 km) **DJ 725.7** (1167.9 km) Bridge over Lower Rancheria River. For northbound travelers, the highway closely follows the Rancheria River west from here to the Swift River. Northern bush pilot Les Cook was credited with helping find the best route for the Alaska Highway between Watson Lake and Whitehorse. Cook's Rancheria River route saved engineers hundreds of miles of highway construction.

Rancheria River, fishing for Dolly Varden and grayling.

DC 665.1 (1110.4 km) **DJ 724.9** (1166.6 km) Scenic viewpoint.

DC 667.2 (1113.7 km) **DJ 722.8** (1163.2 km) Turnout to south.

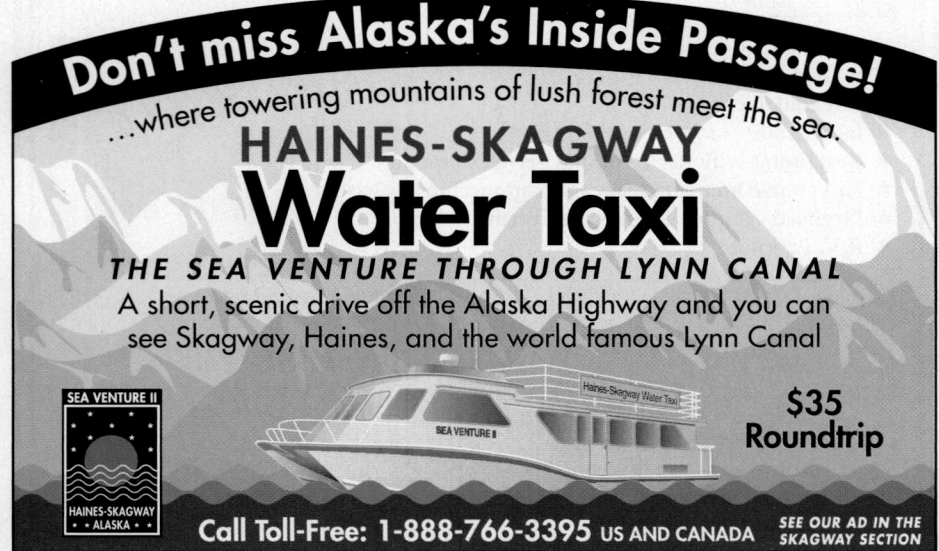

DC 667.6 (1114.3 km) **DJ 722.4** (1162.5 km) Large double-ended turnout with litter barrel to south.

DC 671.9 (1118.7 km) **DJ 718.1** (1155.6 km) Spencer Creek.

DC 673.4 (1121 km) **DJ 716.6** (1153.2 km) Improved highway and view of Cassiar Mountains westbound.

DC 677 (1126.9 km) **DJ 713** (1147.4 km) Turnout with litter barrel to south overlooking the Rancheria River. Trail down to river.

According to R.C. Coutts, author of *Yukon: Places & Names,* the Rancheria River was named by Cassiar miners working Sayyea Creek in 1875, site of a minor gold rush at the time. Rancheria is an old Californian or Mexican miners' term from the Spanish, meaning a native village or settlement. It is pronounced Ran-che-RI-ah.

DC 678.5 (1129.3 km) **DJ 711.5** (1145 km) George's Gorge, culvert.

DC 683.2 (1137 km) **DJ 706.8** (1137.4 km) NorthwesTel microwave tower to south.

DC 684 (1138.4 km) **DJ 706** (1136.2 km) Turnout with litter barrel overlooking Rancheria River. *CAUTION: Watch for livestock on or near highway in this area.*

DC 687.2 (1143.8 km) **DJ 702.8** (1131 km) **Historic Milepost 710.** Rancheria Hotel–Motel to south; gas, food, camping and lodging. Historic sign and interpretive panel on highway lodges. ▲

DC 687.4 (1143.9 km) **DJ 702.6** (1130.7 km) Turnoff to south for private campground (formerly Rancheria Yukon government campground) adjacent highway overlooking Rancheria River. The Rancheria is a tributary of the Liard River. ▲

DC 689.2 (1146.6 km) **DJ 700.8** (1127.8 km) Canyon Creek.

DC 690 (1148 km) **DJ 700** (1126.5 km) Highway follows the Rancheria River.

DC 692.5 (1152 km) **DJ 697.5** (1122.5 km) Young Creek.

DC 694.2 (1155 km) **DJ 695.8** (1119.7 km) **Historical Mile 717.5.** Abandoned building.

DC 695.2 (1156.5 km) **DJ 694.8** (1118.1 km) **Rancheria Falls Recreation Site** has a good gravel and boardwalk trail through boreal forest to the picturesque falls; easy 10-minute walk. Large parking area with toilets and litter barrels at trailhead.

DC 696 (1156.8 km) **DJ 694** (1116.8 km) Porcupine Creek.

DC 697.4 (1160 km) **DJ 692.6** (1114.6 km) Beautiful view of the Cassiar Mountains.

DC 698.4 (1161.6 km) **DJ 691.6** (1113 km) **Historical Mile 721.** Walker's Continental Divide; gas, food, camping and lodging. ▲

Walker's Continental Divide. Fresh baking daily, mouth-watering cinnamon rolls, rhubarb pie, muffins and tarts. Breakfast served all day—try our sourdough pancakes. Gift shop, hard ice cream. New motel, clean, comfortable, cozy rooms (nonsmoking rooms available). RV park with water and power hookups, pull-throughs, showers and trailer dump. Clean washrooms. Hospitality spoken here, free of charge. Phone/fax (867) 851-6451. [ADVERTISEMENT] ▲

DC 698.7 (1162 km) **DJ 691.3** (1112.5 km) Upper Rancheria River bridge, clearance 17.7 feet/5.4m. For northbound travelers, the highway leaves the Rancheria River.

DC 699.1 (1162.8 km) **DJ 690.9** (1111.9 km) Large gravel turnout to north with outhouses, litter barrels and p;oint of interest signs.

Continental Divide sign reads: "This height of land divides 2 of the largest drainage systems in North America—the Yukon River and Mackenzie River watersheds. Water draining west from this point forms the Swift River. This river drains into the Yukon River and continues a northwest journey of 3,680 kilometres (2,300 miles) to the Bering Sea (Pacific Ocean). Water that drains to the east forms the Rancheria River which flows into the Liard River then the Mackenzie River. These waters flow northward and empty into the Beaufort Sea (Arctic Ocean) after a journey of 4,200 kilometres (2,650 miles).

All rivers crossed by the Alaska Highway between here and Fairbanks, AK, drain into the Yukon River system.

DC 699.6 (1163.3 km) **DJ 690.4** (1111.1 km) **Historic Milepost 722. Private Aircraft:** Pine Lake airstrip 3 miles/4.8 km north; deserted WWII emergency airstrip; elev. 3,250 feet/991m; length 6,000 feet/1,829m; gravel, status unknown.

DC 702.2 (1168 km) **DJ 687.8** (1106.9 km) Swift River bridge. For northbound travelers, the highway now follows the Swift River west to the Morley River.

View of Simpson Peak from turnout at Milepost DC 719.6. (© Earl L. Brown, staff)

DC 706.2 (1174.5 km) **DJ 683.8** (1100.4 km) *Steep hill for westbound travelers.*

DC 709.5 (1180 km) **DJ 680.5** (1095.1 km) Seagull Creek.

DC 709.8 (1180.9 km) **DJ 680.2** (1094.6 km) **Historic Milepost 733, SWIFT RIVER.** Lodge with food, gas, lodging, car repair, pay phone and highway maintenance camp. Open year-round.

Swift River Lodge. Friendly haven in a beautiful mountain valley. Tasty cooking with a plentiful supply of coffee. Mouth-watering homemade pies and pastries fresh daily. Wrecker service, welding and repairs. Reasonable rates. Gas and diesel at some of the best prices on the highway. Clean restrooms; gifts; and public phone. [ADVERTISEMENT]

DC 710.3 (1181.5 km) **DJ 679.7** (1093.8 km) **Historical Mile 733.5.** The highway re-enters British Columbia for approximately 42 miles/68 km northbound.

DC 712.7 (1185 km) **DJ 677.3** (1090 km) Partridge Creek.

DC 716 (1190.3 km) **DJ 674** (1084.7 km) Gravel turnout with litter barrels.

DC 718.5 (1194.2 km) **DJ 671.5** (1080.6 km) Screw Creek.

DC 719.6 (1196 km) **DJ 670.4** (1078.9 km) **Historical Mile 743.** Turnout with litter barrel to south on **Swan Lake.** Fishing for trout and whitefish. The pyramid-shaped mountain to south is Simpson Peak.

DC 724.2 (1203.7 km) **DJ 665.8** (1071.5

km) Pull-through turnout to south.

DC 727.9 (1209.5 km) **DJ 662.1** (1065.5 km) Logjam Creek.

DC 735.8 (1222.5 km) **DJ 654.2** (1052.8 km) Smart River bridge. The **Smart River** flows south into the Cassiar Mountains in British Columbia. The river was originally called Smarch, after the Tlingit family of that name who lived and trapped in this area. The Smarch family currently includes well-known artist Keith Wolfe Smarch, whose carvings are found in collections around the world.

DC 741.4 (1231.7 km) **DJ 648.6** (1043.8 km) Microwave tower access road to north.

DC 744.1 (1236 km) **DJ 645.9** (1039.4 km) Upper Hazel Creek.

DC 745.2 (1238 km) **DJ 644.8** (1037.7 km) Lower Hazel Creek.

DC 746.9 (1240.7 km) **DJ 643.1** (1034.9 km) Turnouts both sides of highway; litter barrel at south turnout.

DC 749 (1245 km) **DJ 641** (1031.5 km) Andrew Creek.

DC 751.5 (1249.2 km) **DJ 638.5** (1027.5 km) Morley Lake to north. The Alaska Highway re-enters the Yukon Territory northbound. This is the last of 7 crossings of the YT–BC border.

DC 752 (1250 km) **DJ 638** (1026.7 km) Sharp turnoff to north for **Morley River** Yukon government day-use area; large gravel parking area, picnic tables, kitchen shelter, water, litter barrels and outhouses. Fishing.

DC 752.3 (1251 km) **DJ 637.7** (1026.2 km) Morley River bridge; turnout with litter barrel to north at east end of bridge. Morley River flows into the southeast corner of Teslin Lake. The river, lake and Morley Bay (on Teslin Lake) were named for W. Morley Ogilvie, assistant to Arthur St. Cyr on the 1897 survey of the Telegraph Creek–Teslin Lake route.

Morley Bay and **River**, good fishing near mouth of river for northern pike 6 to 8 lbs., best June to August, use small Red Devils; grayling 3 to 5 lbs., in May and August, use small spinner; lake trout 6 to 8 lbs., June to August, use large spoon.

DC 752.9 (1252 km) **DJ 637.1** (1025.3 km) **Historic Milepost 777.7.** Morley River Lodge, food, gas, diesel, towing, tires, camping and lodging. Open year-round. ▲

Morley River Lodge. See display ad this section. ▲

DC 754.8 (1256 km) **DJ 635.2** (1022.2 km) *CAUTION: Watch for livestock on highway.*

DC 757.9 (1261 km) **DJ 632.1** (1017.2 km) Small marker to south (no turnout) reads: "In memory of Max Richardson 39163467, Corporal Co. F 340th Eng. Army of the United States; born Oct. 10, 1918, died Oct. 17, 1942. Faith is the victory."

DC 761.5 (1267.9 km) **DJ 628.5** (1011.4 km) Strawberry Creek.

DC 764.1 (1273.7 km) **DJ 625.9** (1007.3 km) Hayes Creek.

DC 769.6 (1282.5 km) **DJ 620.4** (998.4 km) **Historical Mile 797.** Food, lodging and camping. ▲

Dawson Peaks Resort & RV Park. Slow down folks! No need to drive any farther. Fishing's good, coffee's on, camping is easy and the rhubarb pie can't be beat. Couple that with our renowned Yukon hospitality and you'll have one of the best experiences on your trip. We're looking forward to seeing you this summer. [ADVERTISEMENT] ▲

DC 769.9 (1283 km) **DJ 620.1** (997.9 km) Gas bar.

DC 776 (1292 km) **DJ 614** (988.1 km) **Nisutlin Bay Bridge,** longest water span on the Alaska Highway at 1,917 feet/584m. The Nisutlin River forms the "bay" as it flows into Teslin Lake here. Put-in for canoeing the Nisutlin River is at Mile 42 on the South Canol Road.

Good view northbound of the village of Teslin and Teslin Lake. **Teslin Lake** straddles the BC–YT border; it is 86 miles/138 km long, averages 2 miles/3.2 km across, and has an average depth of 194 feet/59m. The name is taken from the Indian name for the lake—Teslintoo ("long, narrow water").

Turnout with litter barrel and point of interest sign at south end of bridge, east side of highway.

Historic Milepost 804 at the north end of the bridge, west side of the highway; historic sign and interpretive panel, parking area, marina and day-use area with picnic tables and boat ramp.Turn west on side road here for access to Teslin village (description follows).

The Nisutlin Delta National Wildlife Area is an important waterfowl migration stopover for trumpeter and tundra swans, Canada and white-fronted geese, Northern pintail and Barrow's goldeneye.

DC 776.3 (1294 km) **DJ 613.7** (987.6 km) Entering Teslin **(Historic Milepost 804)** at north end of bridge. Gas, food, camping and lodging along highway.

Yukon Motel Lakeshore Resort, just right (northbound) on the north side of Nisutlin Bridge. An excellent stop for a fresh lake trout dinner (or full menu), accompanied by good and friendly service topped off with a piece of fantastic rhubarb and strawberry pie (lots of fresh baking). Ice cream. New in 1998 ... visit our Yukon wildlife display. Five satellite TV channels. Open year-round, summer hours 6 A.M.–11 P.M. New lakeshore RV park (mosquito control area), 70 sites, full and partial hookups, 40 pull-throughs. "Good Sam Park"—washhouse rated TL 9.5. A real home away from home on the shore of beautiful Nisutlin Bay. Phone (867) 390-2575. [ADVERTISEMENT] ▲

Teslin

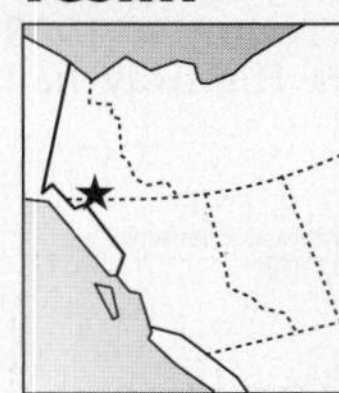

Located at **Historic Milepost 804,** 111 miles/179 km southeast of Whitehorse, 163 miles/263 km northwest of Watson Lake. **Population:** 482. **Emergency Services: RCMP,** phone (867) 390-5555 (if no answer call 867/667-5555). **Fire Department,** phone (867) 390-2222. **Nurse,** phone (867) 390-4444.

Elevation: 2,239 feet/682.4m. **Climate:** Average temperature in January, -7°F/-22°C, in July 57°F/14°C. Annual snowfall 66.2 inches/168.2 cm. Driest month April, wettest month July. Average date of last spring frost is June 19; first fall frost Aug. 19. **Radio:** CBC 940; CHONFM 90.5; CKRW 98.7. **Television:** Channel 13.

The village of Teslin, situated on a point of land at the confluence of the Nisutlin River and Teslin Lake, began as a trading post in 1903. Today the community consists of a trading post, Catholic church, health centre and post office. There is a 3-sheet regulation curling rink and a skating rink. A Native heritage centre is under development.

Teslin has one of the largest Native populations in Yukon Territory and much of the community's livelihood revolves around traditional hunting, trapping and fishing. In addition, some Tlingit (Klink-it) residents are involved in the development of Native woodworking crafts (canoes, snowshoes and sleds); traditional sewn art and craft items (moccasins, mitts, moose hair tufting, gun cases); and the tanning of moose hides

George Johnston Museum is located on the left side of the highway heading north. The museum, operated by the Teslin Historical Museum Society (phone 867/390-2550), is open daily, 9 A.M. to 7 P.M. in summer; minimal admission fee, wheelchair accessible. Get your Yukon Explorer's Passport stamped here. The museum displays items from gold rush days and the pioneer mode of living, Indian artifacts and many items of Tlingit culture. Website: www/yukon web.com/community/teslin/museum. ♿

A Tlingit Indian, George Johnston (1884–1972) was an innovative individual, known for his trapping as well as his pho-

tography. With his camera he captured the life of the inland Tlingit people of Teslin and Atlin between 1910 and 1940. Johnston also brought the first car to Teslin, a 1928 Chevrolet. Since the Alaska Highway had not been built yet, George built a 3-mile road for his "Teslin taxi." In winter, he put chains on the car and drove it on frozen Teslin Lake. The '28 Chevy has been restored and is now on permanent display at the museum.

The Yukon Motel has an impressive display of Yukon wildlife.

Teslin is located west of the Alaska Highway, accessible via a short side road from the north end of Nisutlin Bay bridge. Nisutlin Trading Post in the village has groceries and general merchandise. Gas, diesel and propane, car repair, gift shop, restaurants and motels are found along the Alaska Highway. The Teslin area has boat rentals, houseboat tours and an air charter service. Canoeists can fly into Wolf Lake for a 5- to 6-day trip down the Wolf River and Nisutlin River to Teslin Lake.

Nisutlin Trading Post, on short loop road, left northbound in Teslin Village. A pioneer store established in 1928, and located on the shore of Nisutlin Bay, an "arm" of Teslin Lake. This store handles a complete line of groceries, general merchandise including clothing, hardware, fishing tackle and licenses. Lottery tickets. Open all year 9 A.M. to 5:30 P.M. Closed Sunday. Founded by the late R. McCleery, Teslin pioneer, the trading post is now operated by Mr. and Mrs. Bob Hassard. Phone (867) 390-2521, fax 390-2103. [ADVERTISEMENT]

AREA FISHING: Guides and boats are available at Nisutlin Bay Marina. **Teslin Lake's Nisutlin Bay** (at the confluence of the Nisutlin River and Teslin Lake), troll the

TESLIN ADVERTISERS

George Johnston Museum......................Ph. (867) 390-2550
Nisutlin Trading Post.......Ph. (867) 390-2521
Yukon Motel Lakeshore Resort..........................Ph. (867) 390-2575

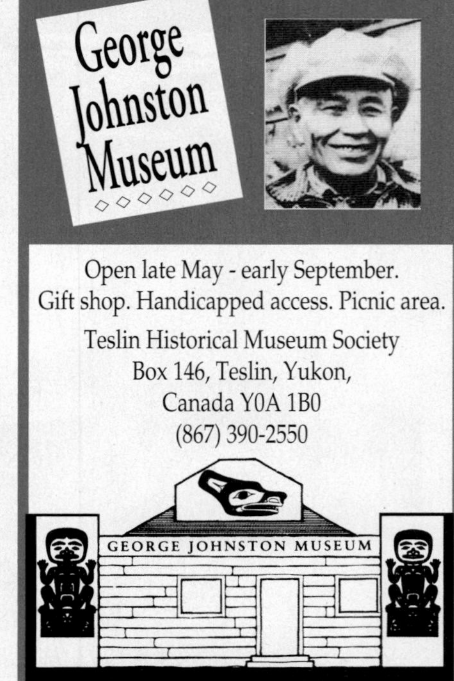

mud line in May and June for lake trout up to 25 lbs.; **Eagle Bay**, casting close to shore for northern pike to 15 lbs.; **Morley Bay**, excellent fishing for lake trout at south end of the bay's mouth, good fishing at the bay's shallow east side for northern pike to 10 lbs. **Morley River**, excellent fly fishing for grayling to 4 lbs. near river mouth and upriver several miles (by boat), fish deep water.

Alaska Highway Log

(continued)

Distance* from Dawson Creek (DC) is followed by distance from Delta Junction (DJ). Original mileposts are indicated in the text as Historical Mile.

*In Canada, mileages from Dawson Creek are based on actual driving distance, not historical mileposts, and kilometres are based on physical kilometreposts. Mileages from Delta Junction are also based on actual driving distance, not historical mileposts, but are followed by the metric conversion to kilometres.

Cow moose photographed along the shore of Teslin River. (© Earl L. Brown, staff)

DC 777 (1295 km) **DJ 613** (986.5 km) **Historic Milepost 805. Private Aircraft:** Teslin airstrip to east; elev. 2,313 feet/705m; length 5,500 feet/1,676m; gravel; fuel 100, jet. Runway may be unusable during spring breakup.

DC 778 (1296.6 km) **DJ 612** (984.9 km) Teslin Lake Viewing Platform at **Historic Milepost 806**, west side of highway, overlooks Teslin Lake. Interpretive panels, outhouses and parking.

DC 779.1 (1298.4 km) **DJ 610.9** (983.1 kim) Halsteads (closed)

DC 779.5 (1299 km) **DJ 610.5** (982.5 km) Fox Creek.

DC 784.3 (1306.7 km) **DJ 605.7** (974.7 km) **Historical Mile 812.** Mukluk Annie's; food, lodging and camping.

Mukluk Annie's Salmon Bake. See display ad this section.

DC 785.2 (1308 km) **DJ 604.8** (973.3 km) **Historical Mile 813.** Teslin Lake Yukon government campground to west; 27 sites (some level) in trees on **Teslin Lake**, water pump, litter barrels, kitchen shelter, firewood, firepits, picnic tables. Camping permit ($8/night). Fishing. Boat launch 0.3 mile/0.5 km north of campground.

DC 785.3 (1308.2 km) **DJ 604.7** (973.1 km) Tenmile Creek.

DC 788.9 (1314 km) **DJ 601.1** (967.3 km) Lone Tree Creek.

DC 794.6 (1323 km) **DJ 595.4** (958.2 km) Deadman's Creek.

DC 800.8 (1333.3 km) **DJ 589.2** (948.2 km) Robertson Creek.

DC 801.6 (1334.4 km) **DJ 588.4** (946.9 km) **Historic Milepost 829.** Brooks' Brook. According to R.C. Coutts in *Yukon: Places & Names,* this stream was named by black Army engineers, who completed this section of road in 1942, for their company officer, Lieutenant Brooks.

DC 808.2 (1345 km) **DJ 581.8** (936.3 km)

Junction with the Canol Road (Yukon Highway 6) which leads northeast to the Campbell Highway. See the CANOL ROAD section for details.

Historic sign and interpretive panel about the Canol Project at junction. The Canol (Canadian Oil) Road was built in 1942–44 to provide access to oil fields at Norman Wells, NWT. Conceived by the U.S. War Dept., the $134 million project was abandoned soon after the war ended in 1945. Canol truck "graveyard" nearby.

DC 808.6 (1345.6 km) **DJ 581.4** (935.6 km) **Teslin River Bridge**, third longest water span on the highway (1,770 feet/539m), was constructed with a very high clearance above the river to permit steamers of the British Yukon Navigation Co. to pass under it en route from Whitehorse to Teslin. River steamers ceased operation on the Teslin River in 1942. Before the construction of the Alaska Highway, all freight and supplies for Teslin traveled this water route from Whitehorse.

DC 808.9 (1346 km) **DJ 581.11** (935.2 km) **Historic Milepost 836. JOHNSON'S CROSSING** to east at north end of bridge; store, food, lodging and camping. One of the original lodges on the Alaska Highway, the history of Johnson's Crossing is related in Ellen Davignon's *The Cinnamon Mine.* Access to Teslin River; boat launch, no camping on riverbank. The bridge is home to a large colony of cliff swallows.

Teslin River, excellent grayling fishing from spring to late fall, 10 to 15 inches, use spinner or red-and-white spoons for spinning or black gnat for fly-fishing. King salmon in August.

Canoeists report that the Teslin River is wide and slow, but with gravel, rocks and weeds. Adequate camping sites on numerous sand bars; boil drinking water. Abundant wildlife—muskrat, porcupine, moose, eagles and wolves—also bugs and rain. Watch for bear. The Teslin enters the Yukon River at Hootalinqua, an old steamboat landing and supply point (under restoration). Roaring Bull rapids: choppy water. Pullout at Carmacks. Inquire locally about river conditions before setting out.

DC 809.1 (1346.5 km) **DJ 580.9** (934.8 km) Access road east to the Teslin River. The Big Salmon Range, also to the east, parallels the Teslin. For Alaska-bound travelers, the highway now swings west.

DC 812.8 (1352.5 km) **DJ 577.2** (928.9 km) Little Teslin Lake on south side of highway.

DC 819.8 (1364 km) **DJ 570.2** (917.6 km) In mid-June, the roadside is a profusion of purple Jacob's ladder and yellow dandelions.

DC 820.3 (1364.8 km) **DJ 569.7** (916.8 km) Seaforth Creek bridge.

DC 820.4 (1365 km) **DJ 569.6** (916.6 km) Large turnout to south; picnic area.

DC 820.6 (1365.3 km) **DJ 569.4** (916.3 km) Squanga Lake to northwest. The Tagish name for Squanga Lake is Desgwaage Mene, "whitefish lake", referring to the rare Squanga Pygmy whitefish found in these waters.

A pair of osprey make their nest on top of a nearby tower. Osprey feed on fish and may be observed perched on top of the poles along the highway here.

Historic Milepost 843 and sign about

Steamers once traveled the Teslin River from Whitehorse to Teslin. (© Earl L. Brown, staff)

Squanga Lake flightstrip.

Private Aircraft: Squanga Lake airstrip, 1 N; elev. 2,630 feet/802m; length 6,000 feet/965m; gravel, summer only, current status unknown; no services.

DC 821 (1366 km) **DJ 569** (915.7 km) Turnoff to northwest to **Squanga Lake** Yukon government campground: 16 sites, kitchen shelter, drinking water, camping permit ($8/night). Small boat launch. Fishing for northern pike, grayling, whitefish, rainbow and burbot.

DC 827.5 (1376.8 km) **DJ 562.5** (905.2 km) White Mountain, to the southeast, was named by William Ogilvie during his 1887 survey, for Thomas White, then Minister of the Interior. The Yukon government introduced mountain goats to this area in 1981.

DC 836.8 (1392.5 km) **F 651.2** (1048 km) **Historic Milepost 866. Junction,** commonly known as **JAKE'S CORNER;** gas, food and lodging. There's also a large collection on the premises of artifacts from the Canol Project, Alaska Highway construction, and the gold rush and other antiques, including 2 fine old Model T's. Cliff swallows nest on the specially-designed bird houses outside the service station. This is also the only known location of the black arctic ground squirrel.

Jake's Corner Inc. See display ad this section.

Junction with Yukon Highway 7 south to Atlin, a very scenic spot that is well worth a side trip (see ATLIN ROAD section). This turnoff also provides access to Yukon Highway 8 to Carcross and Klondike Highway 2 to Skagway, AK (see TAGISH ROAD and KLONDIKE HIGHWAY 2 sections for details).

There are 2 versions of how Jake's Corner got its name. In 1942, the U.S. Army Corps of Engineers set up a construction camp here to build this section of the Alcan Highway and the Tagish Road cutoff to Carcross for the Canol pipeline. (The highway south to Atlin, BC, was not constructed until 1949–50.) The camp was under the command of Captain Jacobson, thus Jake's Corner. However, another version that predates the Alcan construction is that Jake's Corner was named for Jake Jackson, a Teslin Indian who camped in this area on his way to Carcross. Roman "Jake" Chaykowsky (1900–1995) operated Jake's Corner Service here for many years. It was known locally as The Crystal Palace, after the first lodge Chaykowsky had owned at Judas Creek, just up the road.

DC 843.2 (1402.7 km) **DJ 546.8** (880 km) Judas Creek bridge.

DC 850 (1413.5 km) **DJ 540** (869 km) Turnoff for Marsh Lake resort; boating and excellent fishing for grayling and northern pike.

DC 851.6 (1416 km) **DJ 538.4** (866.4 km) Several access roads along here which lead to summer cottages. Marsh Lake is a popular recreation area for Whitehorse residents.

DC 852.7 (1417.8 km) **DJ 537.3** (864.7 km) Good view of **Marsh Lake** to west. The highway parallels this beautiful lake for several miles. Marsh Lake (elev. 2,152 feet/656m) is part of the Yukon River system. It is approximately 20 miles/32 km long and was named in 1883 by Lt. Frederick Schwatka, U.S. Army, for Yale professor Othniel Charles Marsh.

DC 854.4 (1421 km) **DJ 535.6** (861.9 km) **Historic Milepost 883,** Marsh Lake Camp historic sign. Boat ramp turnoff to west.

DC 854.8 (1421.2 km) **DJ 535.2** (861.3 km) Caribou Road leads northwest to Airplane Lake; hiking trail, good skiing and snowmachining in winter. This road was bulldozed out to get men and equipment into a small lake where an airplane had made an emergency landing.

DC 859.9 (1430 km) **DJ 530.1** (853.1 km) **Historical Mile 890.** Turnoff to west for Marsh Lake Yukon government campground via 0.4-mile/0.6-km gravel loop road: 41 sites, most level, some pull-through; outhouses, firewood, firepits, litter barrels, picnic tables, kitchen shelter, water pump. Camping permit ($8).

For group camping and day-use area, follow signs near campground entrance. Day-use area includes sandy beach, change house, picnic area, playground, kitchen shelter and boat launch.

DC 861.1 (1433.9 km) **DJ 528.9** (851.2 km) **M'Clintock River** bridge. Boat ramp turnoff to west at north end of bridge. This boat launch is a popular put-in spot for canoe trips down the M'Clintock River to M'Clintock Bay, at the north end of Marsh Lake, where the river flows into the lake. M'Clintock Bay is a critical habitat for migrating waterfowl in spring; see **Milepost DC 861.3.**

The M'Clintock River is narrow, winding and silty with thick brush along the shoreline. However, it is a good river for boat trips, especially in late fall.

The river was named by Lieutenant Schwatka for Arctic explorer Sir Francis M'Clintock.

DC 861.3 (1434 km) **DJ 528.7** (850.8 km) Swan Haven Interpretive Centre overlooking

M'Clintock Bay. The centre is staffed from early April to mid-May, when thousands of migrating tundra and trumpeter swans stopover here. The annual Celebration of Swans is held at the centre the third week of April.

DC 864.3 (1437 km) **DJ 525.7** (846 km) Bridge over Kettley's Canyon.

DC 867.3 (1441.8 km) **DJ 522.7** (841.2 km) **Historic Milepost 897.** Yukon River bridge (elev. 2,150 feet/645m). Turnout to north for day-use area and boat launch on **Yukon River** at Marsh Lake bridge near Northern Canada Power Commission (NCPC) control gate. Point of interest sign and litter barrels. New (1999) viewing platform on hillside overlooks Lewes River Marsh (accessible by canoe from M'Clintock River bridge boat launch). Good fishing for grayling, jackfish and some trout.

From here, the Yukon River flows 1,980 miles/3,186 km to the Bering Sea.

DC 873.5 (1453.3 km) **DJ 516.5** (831.2 km) **Historical Mile 904. Sourdough Country Campsite RV Park**, just 15 minutes from downtown Whitehorse. Good Sam. If you're looking for privacy and relaxation, then this is your destination! Many treed sites, marked walking trails—pets welcome. Our spacious pull-through sites have water, 15/30 amp power and cable TV. Laundromat, car wash and dump station. *Clean private washrooms*. From our guests: "After over a month on the road, the best showers/washrooms we encountered were at Sourdough Country Campsite. We'll be back!" (A. and A. Brown). We invite you to see for yourself! Phone (867) 668-2961. [ADVERTISEMENT] ▲

DC 874.4 (1455 km) **DJ 515.6** (829.7 km) **Historical Mile 905.** Restaurant, convenience store, gas, diesel, propane, car repair and rock shop here.

Yukon Rock Shop. See display ad this section.

Junction with Klondike Highway 2 (Carcross Road) which leads south to Carcross and Skagway. See KLONDIKE HIGHWAY 2 section.

DC 874.6 (1455.3 km) **DJ 515.4** (829.4 km) Whitehorse city limits. Incorporated June 1, 1950, Whitehorse expanded in 1974 from its original 2.7 square miles/6.9 square kilometres to 162 square miles/421 square kilometres.

DC 875.6 (1456.9 km) **DJ 514.4** (827.8 km) Kara Speedway to west.

DC 875.9 (1457.4 km) **DJ 514.1** (827.3 km) Cowley Creek.

DC 876.8 (1459 km) **DJ 513.2** (825.9 km) **Historical Mile 906. Wolf Creek** Yukon government campground to east. An 0.8-mile/1.3-km gravel loop road leads through this campground: 40 sites, most level, some pull-through; kitchen shelters, water pumps, picnic tables, firepits, firewood, outhouses, litter barrels, playground; camping permit ($8). A 1.2-mile/2-km nature loop trail winds through boreal forest to an overlook of the Yukon River and returns along Wolf Creek. Interpretive brochure at trailhead and information panels at campground entrance. Fishing in Wolf Creek for grayling. ▲

DC 878 (1461 km) **DJ 512** (824 km) Meadow Lakes Golf and Country Club, 9-hole, par 36 course; cart rentals, club rentals, licensed clubhouse.

DC 879.4 (1463 km) **DJ 510.6** (821.7 km) Highway crosses abandoned railroad tracks of the White Pass & Yukon Route (WP&YR) narrow-gauge railroad. Construction of the WP&YR began in May 1898 at the height of the Klondike Gold Rush. Completion of the railway in 1900 linked the port of Skagway, AK, with Whitehorse, YT, providing passenger and freight service for thousands of gold seekers. The WP&YR ceased operation in 1982, but started limited service again in 1988 between Skagway and Fraser. (See Railroads in the TRAVEL PLANNING section for current schedule.)

DC 879.6 (1463.3 km) **DJ 510.4** (821.4 km) Point of interest sign about 135th meridian to east; small turnout. Gas station.

DC 879.8 (1463.7 km) **DJ 510.2** (821.1 km) **Historic Milepost 910.** Historic sign reads: "McCrae originated in 1900 as a flag stop on the newly-constructed White Pass & Yukon Railway. During WWII, this area served as a major service and supply depot, a major construction camp and a recreation centre." McCrae truck stop to east.

DC 880 (1464 km) **DJ 510** (820.7 km) **Historical Mile 910.5. Fireweed R.V. Services.** See display ad this section.

DC 880.4 (1464.5 km) **DJ 509.6** (820.1 km) Turnoff to west for Whitehorse Copper Mines (closed). Road to east leads to Yukon River.

DC 881 (1465.5 km) **DJ 509** (819.1 km) **Historic Milepost 911.** Site of Utah Construction Co. Camp. Campground to east.

Pioneer R.V. Park. See display ad this section. ▲

DC 881.3 (1466 km) **DJ 508.7** (818.6 km) White Pass & Yukon Route's Utah siding to east. This was also the site of an Army

Fireweed is the territorial flower of the Yukon. (© Earl L. Brown, staff)

camp where thousands of soldiers were stationed during construction of the Alaska Highway.

DC 881.7 (1466.6 km) **DJ 508.3** (818 km) Sharp turnoff to east (watch for camera viewpoint sign) to see **Miles Canyon**. Drive down side road 0.3 mile/0.5 km to fork. The right fork leads to Miles Canyon parking lot. From the parking area it is a short walk to the Miles Canyon bridge; good photo spot. Cross bridge for easy hiking trails overlooking Yukon River.

Wildlife to watch for include least chipmunks and arctic ground squirrels along south-facing slopes; violet-green, cliff and bank swallows; belted kingfishers; and Townsend's solitaires in the forest on the far side of the bridge.

A 1.1-mile/1.7-km hiking trail from the bridge leads to the historic site of **Canyon City**, a gold rush settlement that existed from 1897 to 1900 as a portage point around Miles Canyon and Whitehorse Rapids. Two tramways, each several miles long, transported goods along the east and west sides of the river. Completion of the White Pass & Yukon Route in 1900 made the trams obsolete, and the settlement was abandoned. Interpreters on site daily in July and most of August. Contact the Yukon Conservation Society (867/668-5678) for more information. No restrooms or litter barrels available at site; plan accordingly.

The left fork on this side road leads to Schwatka Lake Road, which follows the lake and intersects the South Access Road into Whitehorse. Turnouts along road overlook Miles Canyon.

DC 881.9 (1466.9 km) **DJ 508.1** (817.7 km) Riding stable with daily trail rides in summer.

DC 882.6 (1468 km) **DJ 507.4** (816.5 km) **Historical Mile 912. Philmar RV Service and Supply.** See display ad this section.

DC 883.2 (1468.9 km) **DJ 506.8** (815.6 km) **Historical Mile 913. Whitehorse Shell**. See display ad this section.

DC 883.7 (1469.7 km) **DJ 506.3** (814.8 km) Turnout to east with litter barrel, outhouses and information sign.

DC 884 (1470.2 km) **DJ 506** (814.3 km) **Hi-Country R.V. Park.** Good Sam. First-class facilities to serve the traveler. Large wooded sites, full hookups, 30-amp power, cable TV, dump station, new clean hot showers, coin-op pressurized vehicle wash. Picnic tables

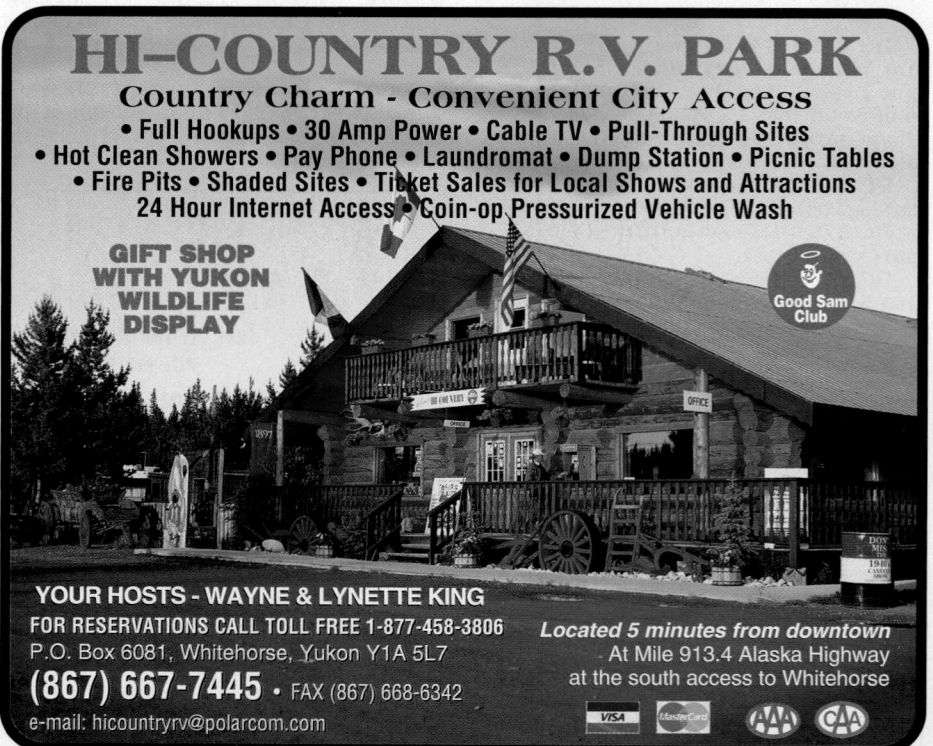

and firepits, gift shop. 24-hour e-mail/Internet access. Conveniently located on the highway at the south access to Whitehorse. Just 2 minutes by vehicle to Miles Canyon, the Beringia Centre and the Transportation Museum. Mile 913.4 Alaska Highway. P.O. Box 6081, Whitehorse, YT Y1A 5L7; phone (867) 667-7445, fax (867) 668-6342. Toll-free reservations 1-877-458-3806. See display ad this section. [ADVERTISEMENT] ▲

DC 884 (1470.2 km) **DJ 506** (814.3 km). First exit northbound for Whitehorse. Exit east for Robert Service Way (also known as South Access Road) to Whitehorse via 4th Avenue and 2nd Avenue. At Mile 1.4/2.3 km on this access road is the side road to Miles Canyon and Schwatka Lake; at Mile 1.6/2.6 km is Robert Service Campground (tent camping only) with a picnic area for day use; at Mile 2.6/4.2 km is the SS *Klondike* National Historic Site, turn left for downtown Whitehorse. ▲

DC 884.5 (1471.1 km) **DJ 505.5** (813.5 km) Government weigh scale and vehicle inspection station to west.

DC 885.3 (1472.3 km) **DJ 504.7** (812.2 km) Entrance to Yukon Beringian Centre (see description next milepost).

DC 885.7 (1472.9 km) **DJ 504.3** (811.6 km) **Yukon Beringia Interpretive Centre** traces the Ice Age in Yukon, which unlike

the rest of Canada, was ice-free. The Blue Fish Caves near Old Crow reputedly hold the earliest evidence of humans in the New World. Displays at the centre trace the science and myth of an Ice Age subcontinent inhabited by great woolly mammoths, giant short-faced bears, lions, scimitar cats, camels and Jefferson's Ground Sloth. Ice Age artifacts include a cast of the largest woolly mammoth skeleton ever recovered. Open 8 A.M. to 8 P.M. daily, mid-May to mid-September. Theatre, gift shop and cafe. Phone (867) 667-8855, fax (867) 667-8844.

DC 885.8 (1473.1 km) **DJ 504.2** (811.4 km) Yukon Transportation Museum features exhibits on all forms of transportation in the North (see Attractions in description of Whitehorse following for more details). A mural on the front of the museum depicts the methods of transportation used in construction of the Alaska Highway in 1942. The 16-by-60-foot/5-by-8-m mural was painted by members of the Yukon Art Society. Open 10 A.M. to 6 P.M., mid-May to mid-September. Admission fee.

Cairns in front of the museum commemorate 18 years of service on the Alaska Highway (1946–64) by the Corps of Royal Canadian Engineers. Near this site, the U.S. Army officially handed over the Alaska Highway to the Canadian Army on April 1, 1946.

Yukon Transportation Museum. See display ad this section.

DC 886.2 (1473.8 km) **DJ 503.8** (810.7 km) Turnoff to east for Whitehorse International Airport. Built for and used by both U.S. and Canadian forces during WWII.

Mural adorns the outside of Yukon Transportation Museum. (© Earl L. Brown, staff)

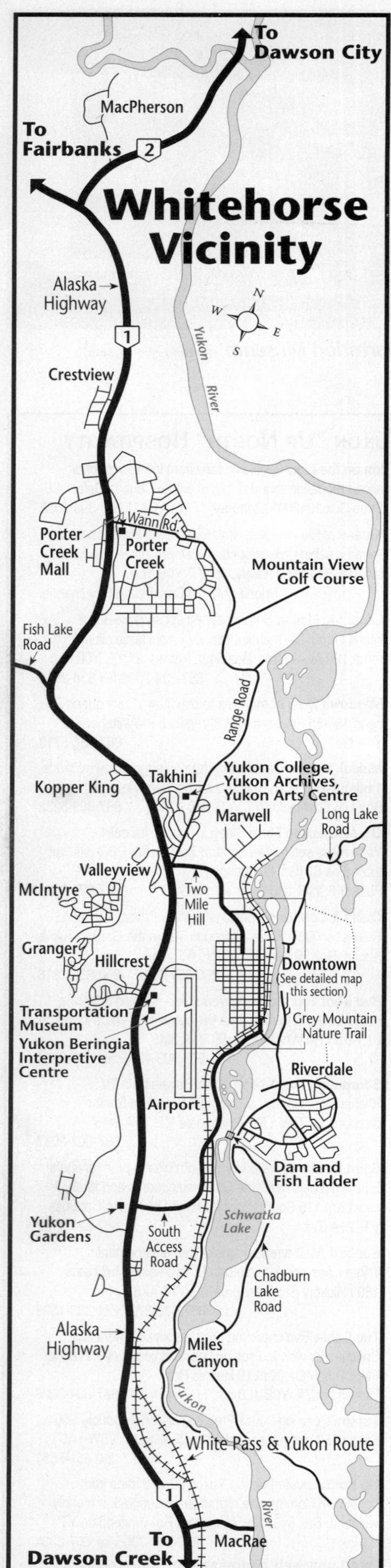

View of Whitehorse, capital of Yukon Territory. (© Earl L. Brown, staff)

Watch for the DC–3 weathervane (see Attractions in description of Whitehorse following for more details).

DC 887.4 (1475.6 km) **DJ 502.6** (808.8 km) Second (and last) exit northbound for Whitehorse. North access road to Whitehorse (exit east) is via Two-Mile Hill and 4th Avenue. Access to private RV park. At Mile 1.2/1.9 km on this access road is Qwanlin Mall.

Alaska Highway log continues on page 161. Description of Whitehorse follows.

Whitehorse

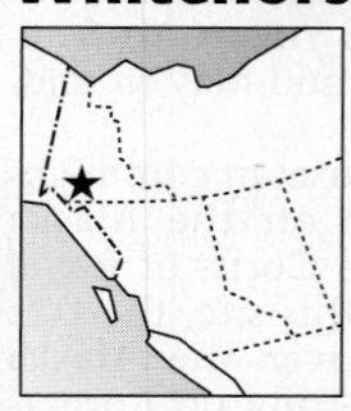

Historic Milepost 918. Located on the upper reaches of the Yukon River in Canada's subarctic at latitude 61°N. Whitehorse is 100 miles/160 km from Haines Junction; 109 miles/175 km from Skagway, AK; 250 miles/241 km from Haines, AK; and 396 miles/637 km from Tok, AK. **Population:** 23,474. **Emergency Services: RCMP, Fire Department, Ambulance, Hospital,** phone 911.

Visitor Information: Tourism Yukon's Visitor Reception Centre is located next to the Yukon Territorial Government Building on 2nd Avenue. Visitor guides and touch-screen terminals are available; 15-minute film on the Yukon; daily updated information on accommodations, weather and road conditions; printout information on attractions, restaurants or events in Whitehorse. The centre is open mid-May to mid-September daily 8 A.M. to 8 P.M.; phone (867) 667-2915. Or contact Tourism Yukon, Box 2703, Whitehorse, YT Y1A 2C6; phone (867) 667-5340; fax (867) 667-3546; Internet www.touryukon.com.

The city of Whitehorse offers year-round visitor information through their Tourism Coordinator; phone (867) 668-8687. Through the year 2000, Whitehorse is celebrating many gold rush anniversaries; their Anniversary Coordinator can be reached at (867) 668-8665. Phone either of these numbers for information or write: Tourism Coordinator, City of Whitehorse, 2121 Second Avenue, Whitehorse, YT Y1A 1C2. Access up-to-date information on events, accommodations and attractions on the City of Whitehorse Internet web page at www.city.whitehorse.yk.ca.

Elevation: 2,305 feet/703m. **Climate:** Wide variations are the theme here with no two winters alike. The lowest recorded temperature is -62°F/-52°C and the warmest 94°F/35°C. Mean temperature for month of January is -6°F/-21°C and for July 57°F/14°C. Annual precipitation is 10.3 inches, equal parts snow and rain. On June 21 Whitehorse enjoys 19 hours, 11 minutes of daylight and on Dec. 21 only 5 hours, 37 minutes. **Radio:** CFWH 570, CBC network with repeaters throughout territory; CBC Montreal; CKRW 610, local; CHON-FM 98.1. **Television:** CBC–TV live, colour via ANIK satellite, Canadian network; WHTV, NADR (First Nation issues), local cable; CanCom stations via satellite, many channels. **Newspapers:**

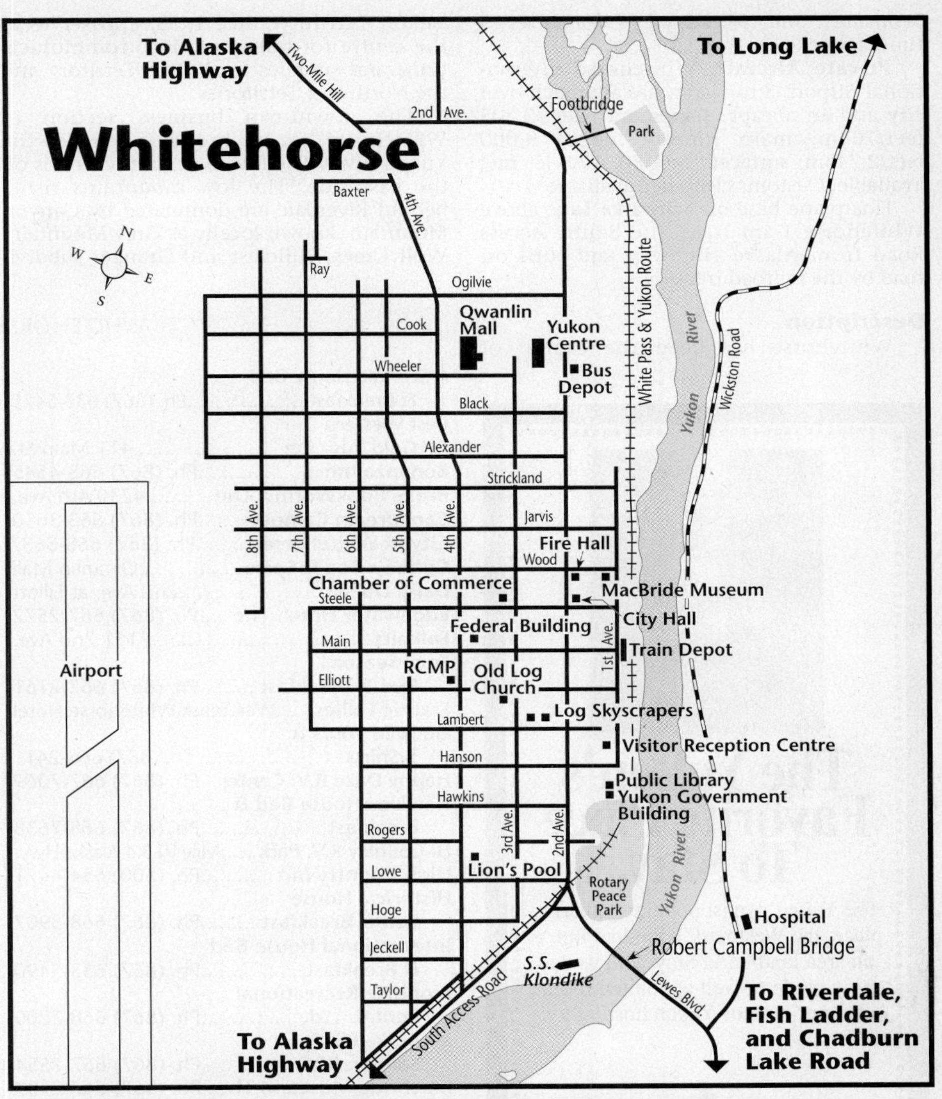

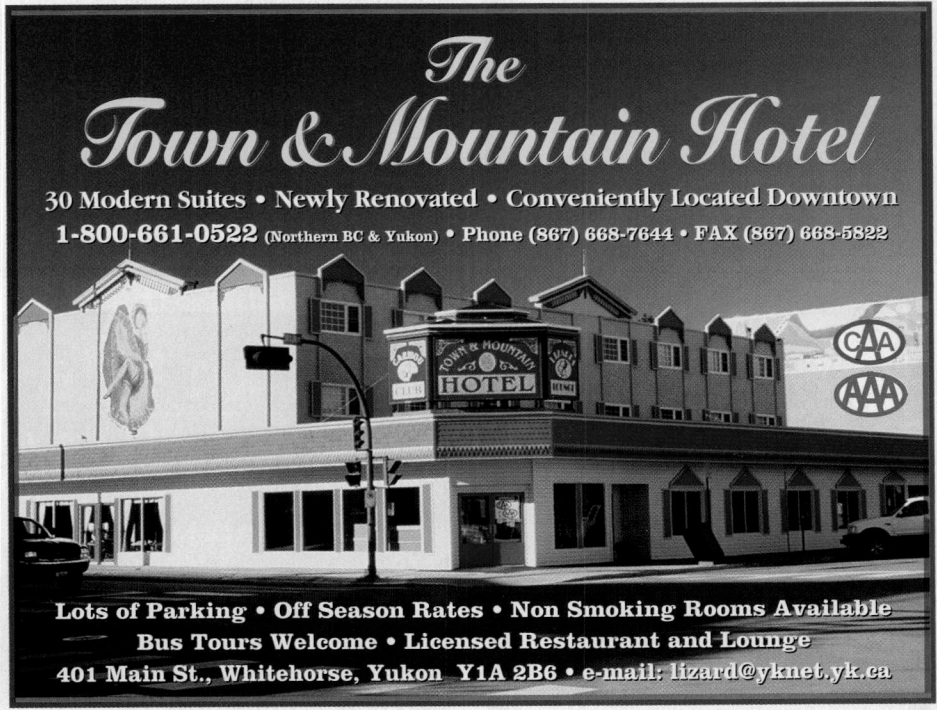

In Canada, 1 gallon of gas equals 3.785 liters and 1 mile equals 1.6 kilometres

Whitehorse Star (weekdays); *Yukon News* (3 times a week).

Private Aircraft: Whitehorse International Airport, 3 runways; has approach over city and an abrupt escarpment; elev. 2,305 feet/703m; main runway length 9,000 feet/2,743m; surfaced; fuel 80, 100, jet fuel available. Customs clearance available.

Floatplane base on Schwatka Lake above Whitehorse Dam (take the South Access Road from Alaska Highway and turn on road by the railroad tracks).

Description

Whitehorse has been the capital of Yukon Territory since 1953, and serves as the centre for transportation, communications and supplies for Yukon Territory and the Northwest Territories.

The downtown business section of Whitehorse lies on the west bank of the Yukon River. The Riverdale subdivision is on the east side. The low mountains rising behind Riverdale are dominated by Canyon Mountain, known locally as Grey Mountain. Wolf Creek, Hillcrest and Granger subdivisions lie south of the city; McIntyre subdivision is to the west; and Porter Creek, Takhini and Crestview subdivisions are north of the city. The Takhini area is the location of the Yukon College campus.

Downtown Whitehorse is flat and marked at its western limit by a rising escarpment dominated by the Whitehorse International Airport. Originally a woodcutter's lot, the airstrip was first cleared in 1920 to accommodate 4 U.S. Army planes on a

WHITEHORSE ADVERTISERS

- **A Scandia House Bed & Breakfast** .... Ph. (867) 633-5421
- **Best Western Gold Rush Inn** .... 411 Main St.
- **Bonanza Inn** .... Ph. (867) 668-4545
- **Broke BookWorms, The** .... 4230 4th Ave.
- **Canadream Campers** .... Ph. (867) 668-3610
- **City of Whitehorse** .... Ph. (867) 668-8687
- **Coffee • Tea & Spice** .... Qwanlin Mall
- **Dairy Queen** .... 2nd Ave. at Elliott
- **Edgewater Hotel, The** .... Ph. (867) 667-2572
- **Folknits** .... 2151 2nd Ave.
- **Four Seasons Bed & Breakfast** .... Ph. (867) 667-2161
- **Frantic Follies** .... Westmark Whitehorse Hotel
- **Go Wild Tours & T-Shirts** .... Ph. (867) 668-2411
- **Happy Daze R.V. Center** .... Ph. (867) 667-7069
- **Hawkins House Bed & Breakfast** .... Ph. (867) 668-7638
- **Hi-Country R.V. Park** .... Mile 913.4 Alaska Hwy.
- **High Country Inn** .... Ph. (800) 554-4471
- **Historical House Bed & Breakfast** .... Ph. (867) 668-3907
- **International House Bed & Breakfast** .... Ph. (867) 633-5490
- **Klondike Recreational Rentals Ltd.** .... Ph. (867) 668-2200
- **Klondike Rib & Salmon BBQ** .... Ph. (867) 667-7554
- **MacBride Museum, The** .... Ph. (867) 667-2709
- **MacKenzie's RV Park** .... Km 1484 Alaska Hwy.
- **Mac's Fireweed Books** .... 203 Main St.
- **Main Man, The** .... Ph. (867) 633-6139
- **Midnight Sun Gallery & Gifts** .... 205C Main St.
- **Murdoch's** .... 207 Main St.
- **North End Gallery** .... Ph. (867) 393-3590
- **NorthwesTel** .... See ad for location
- **Parks Canada** .... Ph. (867) 667-3910
- **Pioneer RV Park** .... Ph. (867) 668-5944
- **Pot O' Gold** .... 4th Ave. & Wood
- **Qwanlin Mall, The** .... 4th Ave. & Ogilvie
- **River View Hotel** .... Ph. (867) 677-7801
- **Sam N Andy's** .... Ph. (867) 668-6994
- **Sandor's** .... Ph. (867) 667-6171
- **Select Reservations** .... Ph. (867) 667-2161
- **Sourdough Country Campsite** .... Ph. (867) 668-2961
- **Special Discoveries** .... Ph. (867) 667-6765
- **Spring Shop, The** .... Mile 922 Alaska Hwy.
- **S.S. *Klondike* National Historical Site** .... Ph. (867) 667-3910
- **Stop In Family Hotel** .... Ph. (867) 668-5558
- **Stratford Motel** .... Ph. (867) 668-4243
- **Takhini Hot Springs** .... Takhini Hot Springs Rd.
- **Tea Garden Soups & Sweets** .... Ph. (867) 393-8000
- **Three Beans Natural Foods** .... Ph. (867) 668-4908
- **Totem Oil** .... See ad for locations
- **Town & Mountain Hotel, The** .... Ph. (867) 668-7644
- **Trail of '98 RV Park** .... Ph. (867) 668-3768
- **Trails North Car & Truck Stop Ltd.** .... Mile 922 Alaska Hwy.
- **Up North Boat & Canoe Rentals, Bed & Breakfast,** .... Ph. (867) 667-7905
- **Wharf On Fourth, The** .... Ph. (867) 667-7473
- **Westmark Klondike Inn** .... Ph. (867) 668-4747
- **Westmark Whitehorse** .... Ph. (867) 393-9700
- **Whitehorse General Store** .... 205 Main St.
- **Whitehorse Performance Centre** .... 4th Ave. at Jarvis
- **Whitehorse Shell** .... Mile 913 Alaska Hwy.
- **White Pass & Yukon Route** .... Ph. (800) 343-7373
- **Yukon Brewing Co.** .... Ph. (867) 668-4183
- **Yukon Inn** .... 4220 4th Ave.
- **Yukon Mining Company** .... Ph. (867) 667-4471
- **Yukon Tire Centre** .... 107 Industrial Rd.
- **Yukon Transportation Museum** .... Ph. (867) 668-4792

test flight from New York to Nome. Access to the city is by Two-Mile Hill from the north and by Robert Service Way (South Access Road) from the south; both connect with the Alaska Highway.

In 1974, the city limits of Whitehorse were expanded from the original 2.7 square miles/6.9 square kilometres to 162 square miles/421 square kilometres, making Whitehorse at one time the largest metropolitan area in Canada. More than two-thirds of the population of Yukon Territory live in the city. Whitehorse is the hub of a network of about 2,664 miles/4,287 km of all-weather roads serving Yukon Territory.

History & Economy

When the White Pass & Yukon Route railway was completed in July 1900, connecting Skagway with the Yukon River, Whitehorse came into being as the northern terminus. Here the famed river steamers connected the railhead to Dawson City, and some of these boats made the trip all the way to St. Michael, a small outfitting point on Alaska's Bering Sea coast.

Klondike stampeders landed at White-

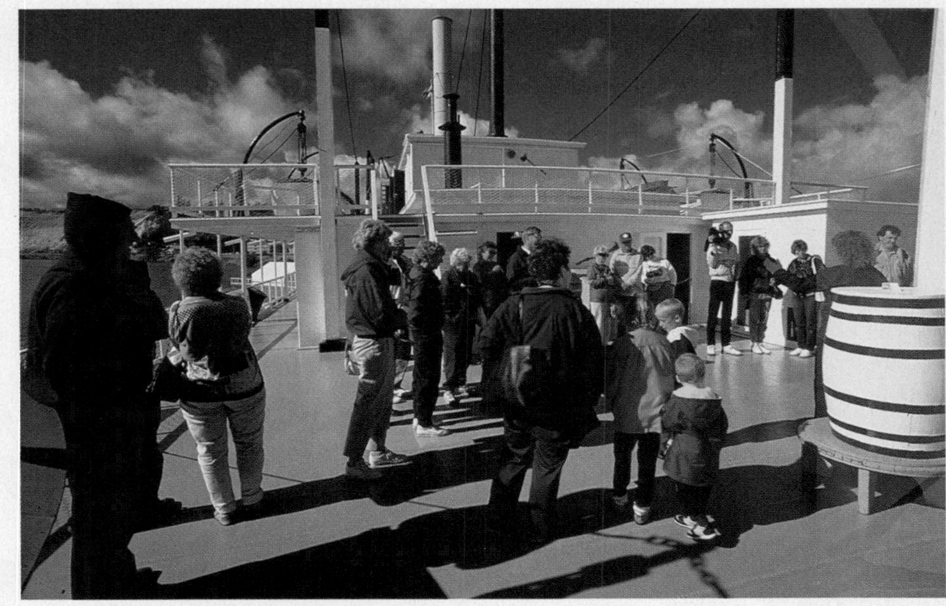

Visitors tour the S.S. Klondike *National Historic Site.* (© Earl. L. Brown, staff)

Whitehorse Welcomes you!

This is your year to visit the Yukon!

Summer Events

May 5-7
Yukon Trade Show

June
City of Whitehorse 50th Birthday

Midnight Sun Golf Tournament.

June 2-4
Yukon International Storytelling Festival.

June 5-10
Moose Conference.

June 7
Yukon River Quest Canoe Race.

June 10-11

June 16-18
Extreme Fest.

June 17
Kluane Chilkat International Bike Relay.

June 21-24
Quilts Under the Midnight Sun. Downtown Whitehorse

June 24
St.-Jean Baptiste Day. Francophone Culture & Language

June 23-25
Gathering of Scottish Clans & Celtic Festival.

July
Sister Cities/Special Olympics Golf Tournament.

July 1
Canada Day Celebrations organized by Sourdough Rendezvous Society.

July 1-2
Kluane Lake Fishing Derby.

July 7-9
Commissioner's Potlatch.

July 7-9
Whitehorse Rodeo.

July 13-16
Annual Dustball Int'l Slowpitch Tournament

July 14-16
Annual Horse Show.

August 18-21
9th Annual NMI Mobility Yukon River Bathtub Race.Whitehorse-Dawson City.

August 26-27
Klondike Harvest Fair, Rotary Peace Park.

September 8-9
Klondike Trail of '98 International Road

Whitehorse welcomes visitors travelling the Alaska Highway. Take time to stay in the Capital of Yukon and enjoy some of our warm Yukon hospitality. There is lots to see and do in Whitehorse and the surrounding areas: great Fishing, beautiful Hotsprings, trips on the historic Yukon River, a walking tour of our downtown, great shopping, exciting entertainment from Vaudeville to Bach, an interpreted River Walk, Golf under the midnight sun, wildlife viewing, restaurants both casual and chic, tons of summer events and a gorgeous new Visitor Reception Centre with easy access RV Parking.

Whitehorse provides RV Parking, at the waterfront and throughout the city core. We have some of the best RV Campgrounds surrounding us, with the nicest hosts you would wish to meet. Please take your time to enjoy us for a few days. Stop in at the City Hall for more information, sign our guest book and collect your city pin.

Call or write ahead to
Tourism,
City of Whitehorse,
2121, 2nd Avenue
Whitehorse, Yukon
(867) 668-8687
F(867)668-8384
www.city.whitehorse.yk.ca

Places to see

SS Klondike Sternwheeler
MacBride Museum
Yukon Transportation Museum
Yukon Arts Centre Gallery
Yukon Berengia Interpretive Centre
Miles Canyon
Canyon City
Whitehorse Fishway
Old Log Church
LePage Park, Heritage walking tour
The Visitor Reception Centre and film
The Yukon River by boat
All the great nightly entertainment

Day Trips

Skagway and the Whitepass and Yukon Route Railway, Kookatsoon Lake, the Hot Springs, Ibex Valley, Marsh Lake and Swan Haven wildlife viewing, Atlin, Fox Lake, Carcross and the smallest dessert in the world, flightseeing over the Chilkoot Trail or Kluane Park.

City of Whitehorse

horse to dry out and repack their supplies after running the famous Whitehorse Rapids. (The name Whitehorse was in common use by the late 1800s; it is believed that the first miners in the area thought that the foaming rapids resembled white horses' manes and so named the river rapids.) The rapids are no longer visible since construction of the Yukon Energy Corporation's hydroelectric dam on the river. This dam created man-made Schwatka Lake, named in honour of U.S. Army Lt. Frederick Schwatka, who named many of the points along the Yukon River during his 1883 exploration of the region.

The gold rush brought stampeders and the railroad. The community grew as a transportation centre and trans-shipment point for freight from the Skagway–Whitehorse railroad and the stern-wheelers plying the Yukon River to Dawson City. The river was the only highway until WWII, when military expediency built the Alaska Highway in 1942.

Whitehorse was headquarters for the western sector during construction of the Alaska Highway. Fort St. John was headquarters for the eastern sector. Both were the largest construction camps on the highway.

The first survey parties of U.S. Army engineers reached Whitehorse in April of 1942. By the end of August, they had constructed a pioneer road from Whitehorse west to White River, largely by following an existing winter trail between Whitehorse and Kluane Lake. November brought the final breakthrough on the western end of the highway, marking completion of the pioneer road.

During the height of the construction of

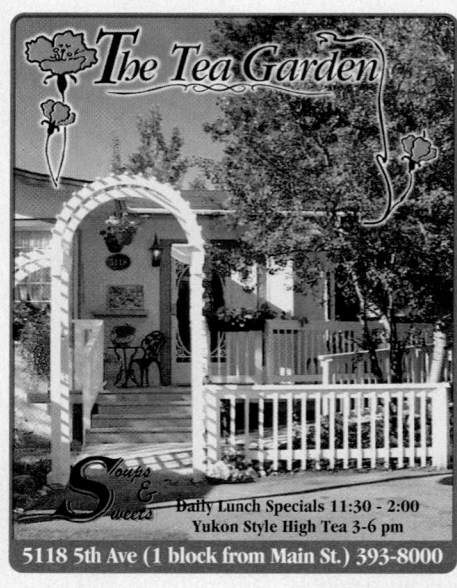

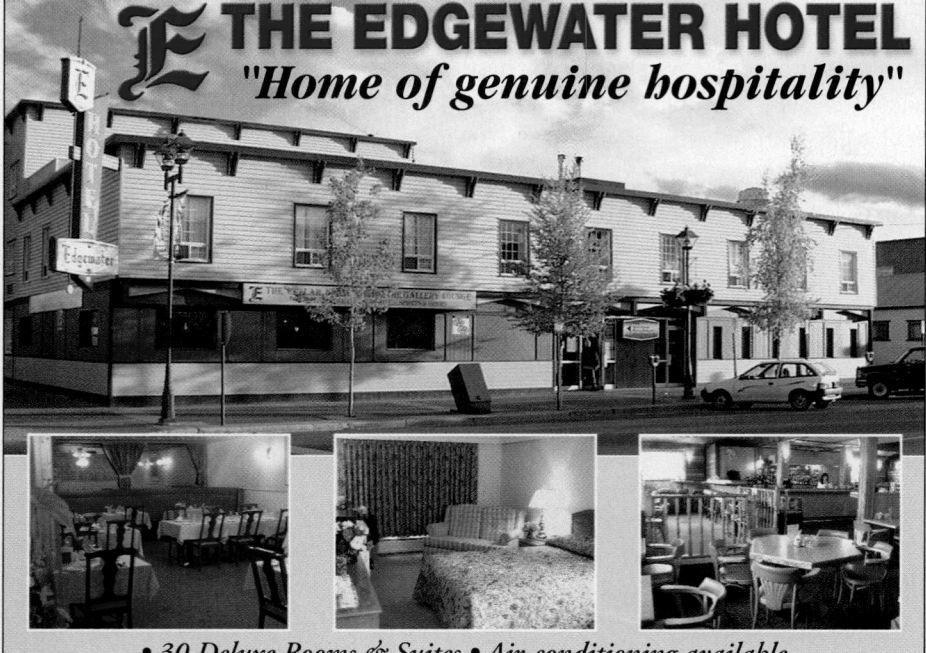

the Alaska Highway, thousands of American military and civilian workers were employed in the Canadian North. It was the second boom period for Whitehorse.

There was an economic lull following the war, but the new highway was then opened to civilian travel, encouraging new development. Mineral exploration and the development of new mines had a profound effect on the economy of the region, as did the steady growth of tourism. The Whitehorse Copper Mine, located a few miles south of the city in the historic Whitehorse copper belt, is now closed. The Grum Mine site north of Faro produced lead, silver and zinc concentrates for Cyprus–Anvil (1969– 1982), Curragh Resources (1986–1992) and Anvil Range Mining Corp. (1994–1998). Stop by the Yukon Chamber of Mines office at 3rd and Strickland for information on mining and rockhounding in Yukon Territory. There is an excellent Yukon mineral display at the entrance to the Visitor Reception Centre downtown.

Because of its accessibility, Whitehorse became capital of the Yukon Territory (replacing Dawson City in that role) on March 31, 1953.

Bridges built along the highway to Dawson City, after Whitehorse became capital of the territory, were too low to accommodate the old river steamers, and by 1955 all steamers had been beached. After her last run in 1960, the SS *Keno* was berthed on the riverbank in Dawson City where she became a national historic site in 1962. The SS *Klondike* was moved through the streets of Whitehorse in 1966 to its final resting place as a riverboat museum beside the Robert Campbell bridge.

Lodging & Services

Whitehorse offers 22 hotels and motels for a total of about 840 rooms. Several hotels include conference facilities; most have cocktail lounges, licensed dining rooms and taverns. Bed-and-breakfast accommodations are also available.

The city has 31 restaurants downtown and in surrounding residential subdivisions that serve meals ranging from French cuisine to fast food; 14 have liquor licenses.

Whitehorse has a downtown shopping district stretching along Main Street. The Qwanlin Mall at 4th Avenue and Ogilvie has a supermarket and a variety of shops. The Yukon Centre Mall on 2nd Avenue has a liquor store. The Riverdale Mall is located on the east side of the river in the Riverdale subdivision. Another shopping mall is located in the Porter Creek subdivision north of the city on the Alaska Highway.

In addition to numerous supermarkets, garages and service stations, there are churches, movie houses, beauty salons and a

Klondike Harvest Fair takes place in Rotary Peace Park in August. (© Earl L. Brown, staff)

covered swimming pool. Whitehorse also has several banks with ATMs. (Many businesses in Whitehorse participate in the Fair Exchange Program, which guarantees an exchange rate within 4 percent of the bank rate set once a week on Mondays. Participating businesses display the Fair Exchange logo.)

NOTE: There is no central post office in Whitehorse. Postal services are available in Qwanlin Mall at Coffee • Tea & Spice; The Hougen Centre on Main Street (lower floor below Shoppers Drugs); and in Riverdale and Porter Creek subdivisions. Stamps are available at several locations. General delivery pickup at corner of 3rd and Wood.

Specialty stores include gold nugget and ivory shops where distinctive jewelry is manufactured, and Indian craft shops specializing in moose hide jackets, parkas, vests, moccasins, slippers, mukluks and gauntlets. Inuit and Indian handicrafts from Canada's Arctic regions are featured in some stores. Whitehorse area maps are available at Mac's Fireweed Bookstore at 203 Main Street; phone (867) 668-2434.

A Scandia House Bed and Breakast. Hospitality, comfort and beautiful view of the Yukon River Valley. Breakfast of gourmet sourdough delights. Queen beds, Jacuzzi room, private bath and 2 shared bathrooms, 2-bedroom suite. Guest lounge. Kitchenette with fridge, microwave and cable TV. Smoke-free. Minutes from downtown—families welcome. (2-story log cabin available at Tagish Lake.) Phone (867) 633-5421. Cell (867) 668-1432. E-mail scandia@yukon.net; website www.yukonalaska.com/scandia. 89 Ponderosa Dr., Whitehorse, YT Y1A 5E7. [ADVERTISEMENT]

Hawkins House Bed & Breakfast. Enjoy the Yukon's most luxurious accommodations in our Victorian home in downtown Whitehorse. Turn-of-the-century charm includes a grand foyer, guest parlor, high ceilings, balconies, hardwood floors, and historical and cultural themes. 5 star rating Canada Select. Rates $100–$175. Phone (867) 668-7638, fax (867) 668-7632, or write 303 Hawkins St., Whitehorse, YT, Canada Y1A 1X5. www.hawkinshouse.yk.ca. [ADVERTISEMENT]

High Country Inn. During your stay in Whitehorse, relax and enjoy "Country Inn" atmosphere and great Northern hospitality. We offer 100 rooms from executive and Jacuzzi suites to deluxe double rooms. Located downtown, great views, elevators, guest laundry, exercise room, colour TV, coffee maker, etc. AAA approved (3 stars, reservations recommended). Phone (800) 554-4471 or (867) 667-4471, fax (867) 667-6457. See our display ad. [ADVERTISEMENT]

Historical House Bed and Breakfast. Sleep in Sam McGee's house! Built for the real "Sam McGee" in 1907 by the "Cyr" brothers, Historical House offers our guests comfort and friendliness in authentic heritage surroundings. Convenient downtown location. Complimentary fax, phone and e-mail. Continental breakfast. VISA/MasterCard. 5128 Fifth Ave., Whitehorse, YT Y1A 1L6. Phone/fax (867) 668-3907. Web site:

www.yukongold.com; e-mail pam.phillips@yt.sympatico.ca. [ADVERTISEMENT]

Klondike Rib & Salmon BBQ. Located in 2 of the oldest buildings in Whitehorse at Second and Steele, across from the Frantic Follies and Westmark Hotel. Delicious fresh Alaskan halibut and salmon BBQ, Texas BBQ ribs, English-style fish and chips, and specialty northern food like caribou, musk-ox, arctic char and fresh bannock. Just some of the mouthwatering fare served in a unique historic Klondike Airways building with historical exhibits as part of the fascinating decor. Indoor and outdoor seating. Beer and wine licensed. Free parking after 5 P.M. across the street. Phone (867) 667-7554. [ADVERTISEMENT]

Yukon Mining Company. Join us for "Barbecue" on the deck at the most popular 'Eatery' in Whitehorse. Fresh Alaska halibut, king salmon, wild game, including buffalo and caribou steaks and burgers, chicken, ribs, pasta and local brewed beer, including our very own "Grizzly Beer"—the best beer in the North! Meet local folk, enjoy great food and the friendliest staff in the north. (See High Country Inn display ad for more detail.) [ADVERTISEMENT]

Camping

Tent camping only is available at Robert Service Park on Robert Service Way (South Access Road). There are 4 private campgrounds south of downtown Whitehorse on the Alaska Highway (see **Mileposts DC 873.5, 881, 882.9** and **883.7** in the highway log), and 1 private campground 6 miles/9.6 km north of the city on the highway (see **Milepost DC 891.9**). Wolf Creek Yukon government campground is 7 miles/11 km south of Whitehorse on the Alaska Highway. A private campground and Yukon government campground are located at Marsh Lake. Takhini Hot Springs on the Klondike Loop is also a popular camping spot (1/2-hour drive from Whitehorse). ▲

IMPORTANT: RV caravans should contact private campground operators well in advance of arrival regarding camping arrangements. At our press time, there was no designated RV parking in downtown Whitehorse.

Transportation

Air: Service by Canadian Airlines International to major cities and Yukon communities. Air North to Dawson City, Old Crow, Juneau and Fairbanks, AK. Whitehorse International Airport is reached from the Alaska Highway.

Seaplane dock on Schwatka Lake just above the Whitehorse Dam (take Robert Service Way from Alaska Highway and turn right on road by the railroad tracks to reach the base). Flightseeing tours available.

Trans North Air offers helicopter sightseeing tours from the airport.

Bus: Whitehorse Transit offers downtown and rural service. See also Bus Lines in the TRAVEL PLANNING section.

Railroad: Arrangements for White Pass & Yukon Route rail trips may be made by phoning WP&YR in Skagway at (800) 343-7373, or contacting local travel agencies.

Car, Truck, Motorhome and Camper Rentals: Several local and national agencies are located in Whitehorse.

Attractions

The **SS *Klondike* National Historic Site** is hard to miss. This grand old stern-wheeler sits beside the Yukon River near the Robert Campbell bridge. After carrying cargo and passengers between Whitehorse and Dawson

City from 1937 until the 1950s, the SS *Klondike* went into permanent retirement on the bank of the Yukon River, donated to the people of Canada by the White Pass & Yukon Route. It is administered by Parks Canada and open to the public for tours. In addition to the regular tours of the SS *Klondike* in summer 2000, visitors will have the opportunity to see shipbuilding in action as workers restore the original hull of the vessel. All aspects of the restoration project (which is expected to last several years) are included in the interpretive tour.

Built by British Yukon Navigation Co., the SS *Klondike* is 210 feet/64m long and 41.9 feet/12.5m wide. Interpretive centre, gift shop and public parking at the site. A film on the history of riverboats is shown continuously in a tent theatre adjacent the boat. Tours of the stern-wheeler leave on the half hour. The 20-minute film is shown prior to each tour. Admission fee charged. Large groups are advised to book tours in advance. Contact Parks Canada, 205–300 Main St., Whitehorse, YT Y1A 2B5; phone (867) 667-3910, fax (867) 398-6701; toll-free 1-800-661-0486. The SS *Klondike* is open from mid-May to mid-September.

Special Events. The Yukon International

Storytelling Festival, held June 2–4, 2000, features storytellers, musicians and theatre groups from around the world. Other events in June include the Yukon River Quest Canoe Race, June 7, 2000, and Kids Day in the Park June 10–11, 2000. July 1st is Canada Day, and it's celebrated with events and entertainment for the whole family. The Annual Sourdough Yukon Bathtub Race, scheduled for Aug. 18-21, 2000, is the longest and toughest bathtub race in the world; it runs on the Yukon River from Whitehorse to Dawson City. The Klondike Trail of '98 International Road Relay, Sept. 8–9, 2000, is the 18th annual running of the road relay from Skagway, AK, to Whitehorse, YK; it attracted more than 1,300 runners last year. See Summer Events calendar on page 148.

Live Shows. Frantic Follies, a very popular vaudeville stage show, is held nightly mid-May through mid-September at the Westmark Whitehorse Hotel. 2000 marks the 31st season for this 1½-hour show which features a chorus line, rousing music and hilarious skits from Robert W. Service ballads. Visitors are advised to get tickets in advance; available at the box office in the Westmark or phone (867) 668-2042. Tickets are also available at most area RV parks.

North End Gallery features art created in Canada's "North End." Original works, Inuit sculpture, First Nation masks and made-in Yukon crafts such as antler sculpture, moosehair tufting, pottery, baskets and burl woodwork, are a specialty. Klondike jewellery—gold nugget, mastodon ivory, trade bead—is available, as is a wide selection of Yukon and illustrated children's books. We ship worldwide! Located on First Avenue across from the MacBride Museum, at the north end of Horwood's Mall. [ADVERTISEMENT]

Yukon Arts Centre Gallery, at 300 College Drive, is the Yukon's only public art museum. The Arts Centre has new shows every 6 to 10 weeks featuring international, national and regional artists. Phone (867) 667-8578 for hours; admission by donation.

Historical walking tours of Whitehorse are conducted by the Yukon Historical & Museums Association. Tour guides wear period costumes for these walks that take in the city's heritage buildings. Meet at the Donnenworth House, 3126 3rd Ave.; phone 667-4704. Fee charged. There are tours Monday through Saturday from June to the end of August. For self-guided tours, *Exploring Old Whitehorse* is available from local stores or from the Yukon Historical & Museums Assoc., Box 4357, Whitehorse, YT Y1A 3T5.

The MacBride Museum, on 1st Avenue between Steele and Wood streets, showcases Yukon's cultural and natural history in 4 indoor galleries featuring gold rush exhibits and outdoor displays featuring Sam McGee's cabin. The Museum Shop features books, local arts and crafts and northern souvenirs. Admission charged. Open daily, 10 A.M. to 6 P.M., June, July and August; phone for seasonal hours, (867) 667-2709, fax 633-6607 or write Box 4037, Whitehorse, YT Y1A 3S9. Phone for winter hours. ♿

Old Log Church Museum, 1 block off Main on Elliott at 3rd. Built in 1900 by Rev. R.J. Bowen for the Church of England, this recently restored log church and rectory have been declared the first territorial historic sites in the Yukon. The museum, located in the log church, displays relics of pioneer northern missions. Open to the public June to September; admission fee.

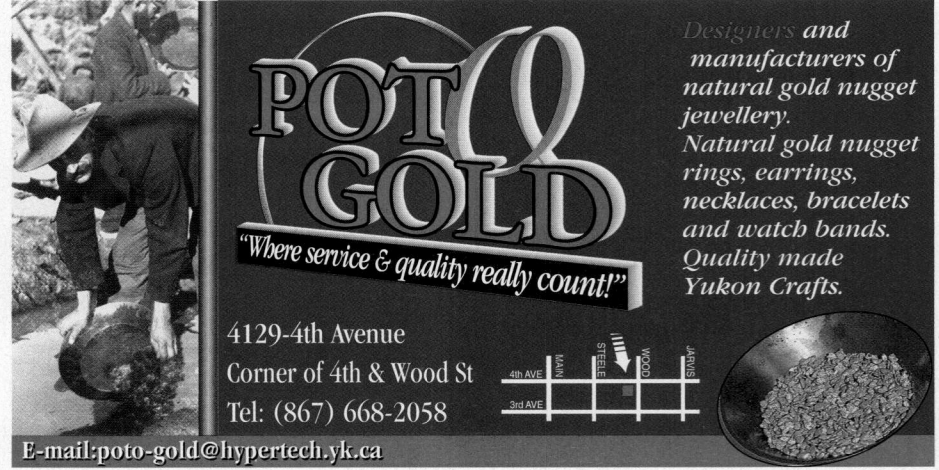

Yukon Government Building, 2nd Avenue and Hawkins, open 9 A.M. to 5 P.M. Administrative and Legislative headquarters of Yukon Territory, the building contains some notable artworks. On the main floor mall is an acrylic resin mural, 120 feet/37m long, which portrays the historical evolution of the Yukon. The 24 panels, each measuring 4 by 5 feet/1.2 by 1.5m, highlight events such as the arrival of Sir John Franklin at Herschel Island in 1825, the Klondike Gold Rush, and the coming of the automobile. The mural was created by Vancouver, BC, artist David MacLagen.

In the Legislative Chamber, an 18-by-12-foot/5-by-4m tapestry is an abstraction of the fireweed plant, Yukon's floral emblem. The Yukon Women's Tapestry, 5 panels each 7-by-13-feet/2-by-4m, hangs in the legislative library lounge. The wool panels portray the role of women in the development of the territory, depicting the 5 seasons of the North; spring, summer, autumn, winter and "survival," the cold gray season between winter and spring and fall and winter. Begun by the Whitehorse Branch of the Canadian Federation of Business and Professional Women in 1976 to mark International Women's Year, the wall hangings were stitched by some 2,500 Yukoners.

Whitehorse Rapids Fishway. Located at the end of Nisutlin Drive in the Riverdale suburb. The fish ladder was built in 1959 to provide access for chinook (king) salmon and other species above the Yukon Energy Corporation hydroelectric dam. It is the longest wooden fish ladder in the world. The fish ladder is flowing from mid-July to early September during salmon-spawning season. Interpretive displays and viewing decks; open daily.

Take a hike. In July and August, the Yukon Conservation Society (YCS) offers free guided nature walks, ranging in difficulty from easy to strenuous. Trips are 2 to 6 hours in length and informative guides explain the local flora, fauna, geology and history along the trails. The YCS conducts interpretive walks at Canyon City (see **Milepost DC 881.7**) during the summer. For a schedule of hikes, contact the Yukon Conservation Society at 302 Hawkins St.; phone (867) 668-5678.

The Boreal Worlds Trail starts at the end of the student parking lot at Yukon College. The trail leads through an aspen grove, past a beaver pond, and through an area dense with lichen. Free interpretive brochure available at the bookstore.

Grey Mountain Nature Trail, east of downtown and the Riverdale subdivision, offers views of the Upper Yukon River valley.

Chadburn Lake Recreation Area is accessed via a gravel side road just before reaching the Whitehorse Rapids and Fish Ladder at the end of Nisutlin Drive. Several small lakes with trails, picnic sites and boat launches, make up the recreation area. Bird watching for yellow warblers, ruby-crowned kinglets, Northern waterthrush and Swainson's thrush.

World's largest weathervane. Located in front of the Whitehorse International Airport is the world's largest weathervane—a Douglas DC–3. This vintage plane (registration number CF–CPY) flew for several Yukon airlines from 1946 until 1970, when it blew an engine during takeoff. The plane was restored by Joe Muff with the help of the Yukon Flying Club and the Whitehorse community. It is now owned and managed by the Yukon Transportation Museum. The restored plane was mounted on a rotating pedestal in 1981 and now acts as a weathervane, pointing its nose into the wind.

The Yukon Transportation Museum, located on the Alaska Highway adjacent to the Whitehorse Airport (see **Milepost DC 885.8**), features exhibits on all forms of transportation in the North. Displays inside include the full-size replica of the *Queen of the Yukon* Ryan monoplane, sister ship to Lindbergh's *Spirit of St. Louis;* railway rolling stock; Alaska Highway vintage vehicles, dogsleds and stagecoaches. Also featured are the Chilkoot Trail, the Canol Highway and bush pilots of the North. The museum includes video theatres and a gift shop. Plenty of parking. Admission charged. Open daily, 10 A.M. to 6 P.M., mid-May to mid-September. Write P.O. Box 5867, Whitehorse, YT Y1A 5L6 or phone (867) 668-4792, fax 633-5547.

Play Golf. Mountain View Public Golf Course is accessible via the Porter Creek exit off the Alaska Highway or from Range Road; 18 holes, grass greens; green fees. Meadow Lakes Golf and Country Club, 5 minutes south of Whitehorse at **Milepost DC 878**, has a 9-hole par 36 course, clubhouse, cart and club rentals; phone (867) 668-4653.

Picnic in a Park. Lepage Park, located across from the Yukon Theatre, is open to everyone for daily lunches, Monday to Friday, in summer. Picnic facilities are also available at Robert Service Campground, located on Robert Service Way into Whitehorse. Rotary Peace Park is central to downtown and a popular picnic spot.

Whitehorse Public Library, part of the Yukon Government Building on 2nd Avenue, has a room with art displays and books about the Yukon and the gold rush. It features a large stone and copper double fireplace, comfortable chairs, tables and helpful staff. Open 10 A.M. to 9 P.M. weekdays, 10 A.M. to 6 P.M. Saturday, 1 to 9 P.M. Sunday; closed holidays. Phone (867) 667-5239.

Yukon Archives is located adjacent Yukon College at Yukon Place. The archives was established in 1972 to acquire, preserve and make available the documented history of the Yukon. The holdings, dating from 1845, include government records, private manuscripts, corporate records, photographs, maps, newspapers (most are on microfilm), sound recordings, university theses, books, pamphlets and periodicals. Visitors are welcome. Phone (867) 667-5321 for hours, or write Box 2703, Whitehorse, YT Y1A 2C6, for more information.

North West Mounted Police Patrol Cabin. This re-creation of an early NWMP Patrol Cabin was built in 1995 as part of the 100th anniversary of the RCMP. It is located next to the RCMP building at 4th Avenue and Elliott. Whitehorse became the territo-

Welcome to the North!

Northern residents depend on Totem Oil every day for the finest fuel, diesel, automobile repair and convenience store items. Visitors will discover the same level of service and quality throughout the north. Our 21 Totem Oil service stations will help energize your northern adventure.

Call 1-800-661-0550

Delta Western
Totem Oil

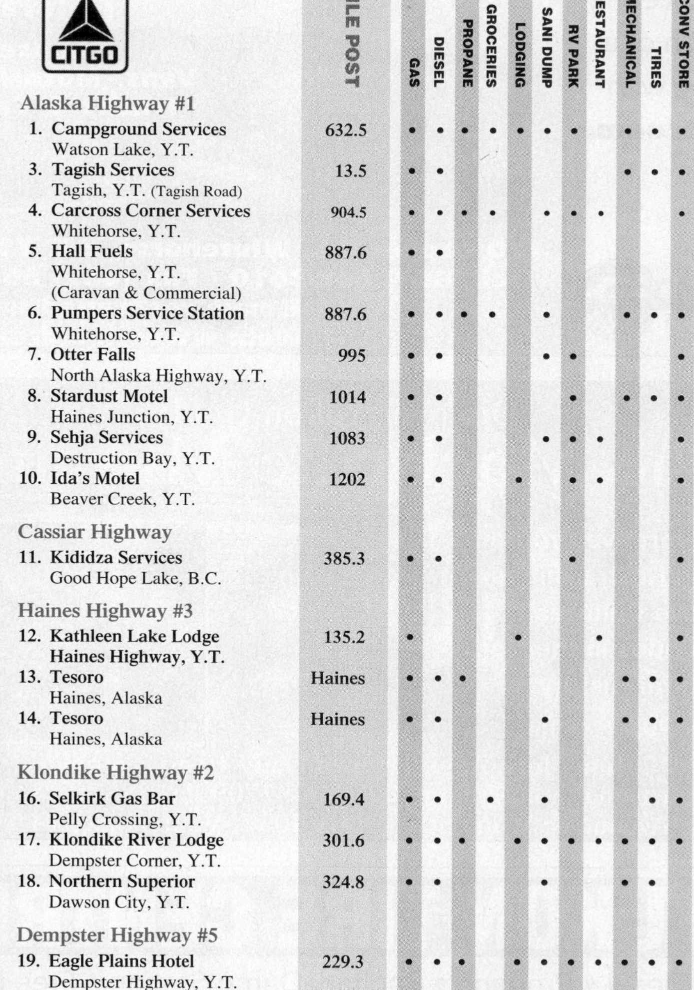

CITGO

	MILE POST	GAS	DIESEL	PROPANE	GROCERIES	LODGING	SANI DUMP	RV PARK	RESTAURANT	MECHANICAL	TIRES	CONV STORE
Alaska Highway #1												
1. **Campground Services** Watson Lake, Y.T.	632.5	•	•	•	•	•	•	•		•	•	•
3. **Tagish Services** Tagish, Y.T. (Tagish Road)	13.5	•	•							•	•	•
4. **Carcross Corner Services** Whitehorse, Y.T.	904.5	•	•	•	•		•	•	•			•
5. **Hall Fuels** Whitehorse, Y.T. (Caravan & Commercial)	887.6	•	•									
6. **Pumpers Service Station** Whitehorse, Y.T.	887.6	•	•	•	•		•			•	•	•
7. **Otter Falls** North Alaska Highway, Y.T.	995	•	•				•	•				•
8. **Stardust Motel** Haines Junction, Y.T.	1014	•	•					•		•	•	•
9. **Sehja Services** Destruction Bay, Y.T.	1083	•	•				•	•	•			•
10. **Ida's Motel** Beaver Creek, Y.T.	1202	•	•			•		•	•			•
Cassiar Highway												
11. **Kididza Services** Good Hope Lake, B.C.	385.3	•	•					•				•
Haines Highway #3												
12. **Kathleen Lake Lodge Haines Highway, Y.T.**	135.2	•				•			•			•
13. **Tesoro** Haines, Alaska	Haines	•	•	•						•	•	•
14. **Tesoro** Haines, Alaska	Haines	•	•				•			•	•	•
Klondike Highway #2												
16. **Selkirk Gas Bar** Pelly Crossing, Y.T.	169.4	•	•		•		•				•	•
17. **Klondike River Lodge** Dempster Corner, Y.T.	301.6	•	•	•		•	•	•	•	•	•	•
18. **Northern Superior** Dawson City, Y.T.	324.8	•	•				•			•	•	
Dempster Highway #5												
19. **Eagle Plains Hotel** Dempster Highway, Y.T.	229.3	•	•	•		•	•	•	•	•	•	•

A FUEL COMPANY DEDICATED TO SERVICE

Old Crow
(Fort McPherson, N.W.T.)
19
YUKON TERRITORY
ALASKA
Dawson City
18
17
Sixtymile
Elsa
Keno
Mayo
16 Pelly Crossing
Faro
Ross River
NORTHWEST TERRITORIES
Beaver Creek 10
Carmacks
Burwash Landing
Aishihik
9
7
Champagne
Whitehorse
4-6
Destruction Bay
Haines Junction
8
Johnson's Crossing
3
Tagish
Teslin
Upper Liard Village
Watson Lake
1
Klukshu
Carcross
Jake's Corner
Dalton Post
12
BRITISH COLUMBIA
13-14 (Haines, Alaska)
Good Hope Lake 11

rial headquarters of the NWMP in 1900. The NWMP were bestowed the title "Royal" in 1904, and in 1920, became the Royal Canadian Mounted Police. The Patrol Cabin is dedicated each year to a famous figure in 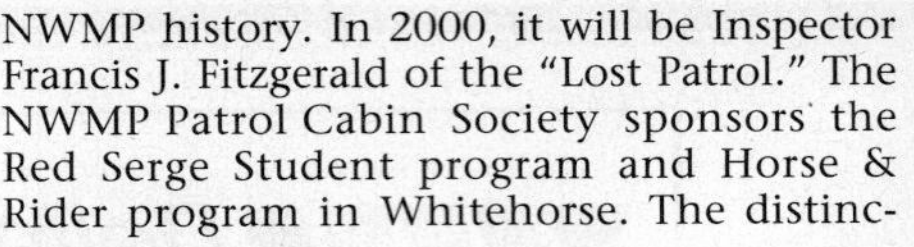NWMP history. In 2000, it will be Inspector Francis J. Fitzgerald of the "Lost Patrol." The NWMP Patrol Cabin Society sponsors the Red Serge Student program and Horse & Rider program in Whitehorse. The distinctive red serge of the modern review order of the RCMP is now worn only at formal occasions or for special programs. The red cloth tunic was first worn by the NWMP in 1897.

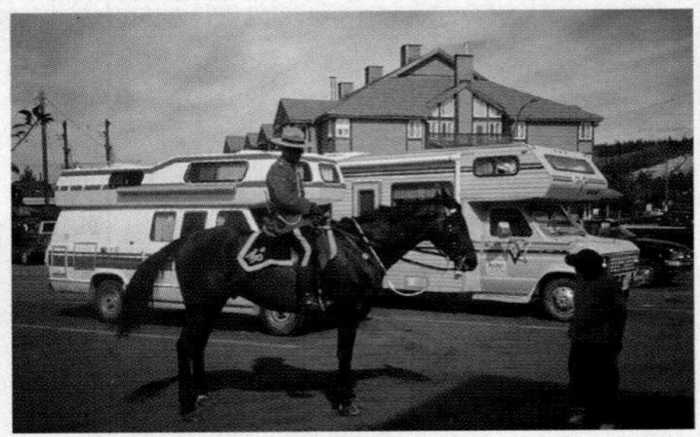

Day trips from Whitehorse. Marsh Lake, 24 miles/39 km south of Whitehorse on the Alaska Highway, and Takhini Hot Springs, 17 miles/27 km north of town via the Alaska and Klondike highways, are within easy driving distance of Whitehorse.

Drive south on the Alaska Highway to turnoff for Marsh Lake Yukon Government Recreation Site, a scenic 30-minute drive from Whitehorse city centre. The recreation area offers an excellent day-use area and campground at Army Beach on Marsh Lake. In the winter, trails originating from this recreation site are used for cross-country skiing and snowmobiling. In spring, this is a popular swan migration viewing area. Swan Haven Interpretive Centre at **Milepost DC 861.3**, overlooking M'Clintock Bay, is staffed from early April to mid-May, when thousands of migrating tundra and trumpeter swans stopover here. The annual Celebration of Swans is held at the centre the third week of April.

Go north on the Alaska Highway to **Milepost DC 894.8** and turn off onto Klondike Highway 2 (the road to Dawson City) and drive just 3.8 miles/6.1 km from the junction to reach Takhini Hot Springs. The resort offers swimming, horseback riding and camping. See **Milepost J 3.8** in the KLONDIKE LOOP section for more information on Takhini Hot Springs and other attractions on the North Klondike Highway.

Longer trips (which you may want to extend to an overnight) are to Atlin, about 2½ hours by car, and Skagway, 3 hours by car. Skagway is an old gold rush town and port of call for both the Alaska state ferries and cruise ships. Skagway is also home to the famed White Pass & Yukon Route Railway, said to be the most scenic railway in the world as it climbs through beautiful mountain terrain to White Pass summit. Book ahead for the trip. Complete your Skagway visit with a trip to Dyea, a short drive from downtown, to see the start of the Chilkoot Trail and a gold rush graveyard. Atlin, which also dates from 1898, is known for its spectacular scenery. Visitors heading for Skagway should call ahead for accommodations if they expect to overnight. You may make a circle tour, driving down to Skagway then turning off onto the Tagish Road on your way back and continuing on to Atlin via the Atlin Road.

Rockhounding and Mining. A wide variety of minerals can be found in the Whitehorse area. Sources of information for rock hounds and gold panners include the Yukon Rock Shop, at the junction of the Alaska Highway and Klondike Highway 2 (Carcross Road), which has mineral samples, gold pans and nuggets, and Murdoch's gem shop on Main Street, which displays gold nugget jewellery and gold rush artifacts and photos.

The following rockhounding location is suggested by Fred Dorward of the Whitehorse Gem & Mineral Club (26 Sunset Dr. N., Whitehorse, YT Y1A 4M8). Drive north on the Alaska Highway to the Fish Lake Road turnoff (**Milepost DC 889.4**), located 2 miles/3.2 km from the north entrance to Whitehorse. About 0.5 mile/0.8 km in on Fish Lake Road, park and walk across McIntyre Creek to the old Copper

King mine workings. Excellent but small specimens of brown garnet, also serpentine. *IMPORTANT: Rock hounds should exercise extreme caution when exploring. Do not enter old mine workings. Please respect No Trespassing signs.*

Canoe, Raft or Boat the Yukon River. Canoe rentals by the day, week or month, and guide services are available in Whitehorse. From Whitehorse to Dawson City it is 467 miles/752 km by river, and can take from 14 to 21 days to travel. There is a boat launch at Rotary Peace Park, behind the Yukon Government Bldg. You may also launch at Deep Creek Campground on Lake Laberge. Contact Up North Canoe Rentals, phone (867) 667-7905.

Boat tours are offered of the Yukon River and scenic Miles Canyon. Inquire locally for tour operators. Miles Canyon is accessible by road: take Schwatka Lake Road off Robert Service Way (South Access Road) into Whitehorse, or turn off the Alaska Highway (see **Milepost DC 881.7**); follow signs.

Hike the Chilkoot Trail. The 33-mile/53-km trail begins near Skagway, AK, and climbs Chilkoot Pass (elev. 3,739 feet/1,140m) to Lake Bennett, following the historic route of the gold seekers of 1897–98. Hikers should check with Parks Canada in the Federal Building at 4th and Main; phone (867) 667-3910 or 1-800-661-0486. The Chilkoot Trail fee is $35 for adults ($17.50 for children under 14).

Mount McIntyre Recreation Centre, 0.9 mile/1.5 km west of the Alaska Highway (see **Milepost DC 887.6**), has 70 kilometres of groomed cross-country ski trails (open for hiking, running and mountain biking in summer). Contact Whitehorse Cross-Country Ski Club, P.O. Box 4639, Whitehorse, YT Y1A 3Y7.

Sportsmen can obtain complete information on fishing and hunting in the Whitehorse area by writing Tourism Yukon, Box

Canada's highest peak, Mount Logan (elev. 19,545 feet), is located in the Yukon.

2703, Whitehorse, YT Y1A 2C6. They will provide lists of guides and advise what licenses are required.

AREA FISHING: Fish for rainbow and coho salmon in the following lakes: **Hidden, Scout, Long, Jackson** and **McLean.** Inquire locally for directions. Nearby fly-in fishing lakes are accessible by charter plane; see advertisements in this section. **Yukon River,** fish for grayling below the dam and bridge. Fishing below the dam prohibited in August during the salmon run.

Alaska Highway Log

(continued from page 138)

Distance* from Dawson Creek (DC) is followed by distance from Delta Junction (DJ). Original mileposts are indicated in the text as Historical Mile.

*In Canada, mileages from Dawson Creek are based on actual driving distance, not historical mileposts, and kilometres are based on physical kilometreposts *as they occurred in summer 1999*. Mileages from Delta Junction are also based on actual driving distance, not historical mileposts, but are followed by the metric conversion to kilometres.

DC 887.4 (1475.6 km) **DJ 502.6** (808.8 km) First exit southbound for Whitehorse. North access road to Whitehorse (exit east) is via Two-Mile Hill and 4th Avenue.

DC 887.6 (1476 km) **DJ 502.4** (808.5 km) Turnoff to west on Hamilton Boulevard for Mount McIntyre Recreation Centre (0.9 mile/1.5 km); 70 kilometres of cross-country ski trails (summer hiking and biking).

DC 888.6 (1477.5 km) **DJ 501.4** (806.9 km) **Historical Mile 918.3**. Gas, store, food.

DC 889.3 (1478.6 km) **DJ 500.7** (805.8 km) McIntyre Creek.

DC 889.4 (1478.8 km) **DJ 500.6** (805.6 km) Fish Lake Road to west. Located only 9.3 miles/15 km from Whitehorse, Fish Lake and adjacent Bonneville Lakes were the site of a Kwanlin Dun First Nations archaeology project documenting the long history of habita-

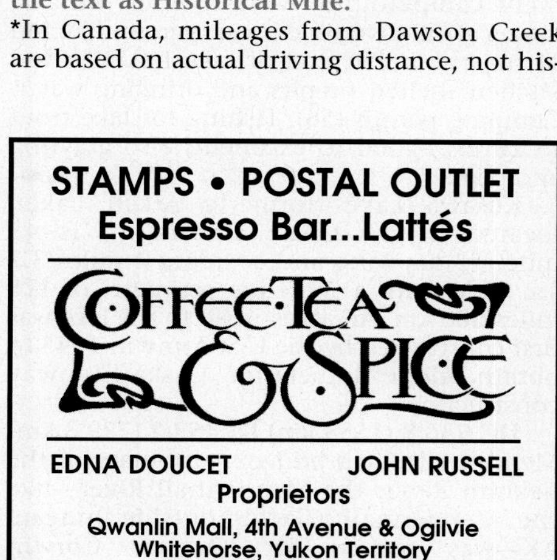

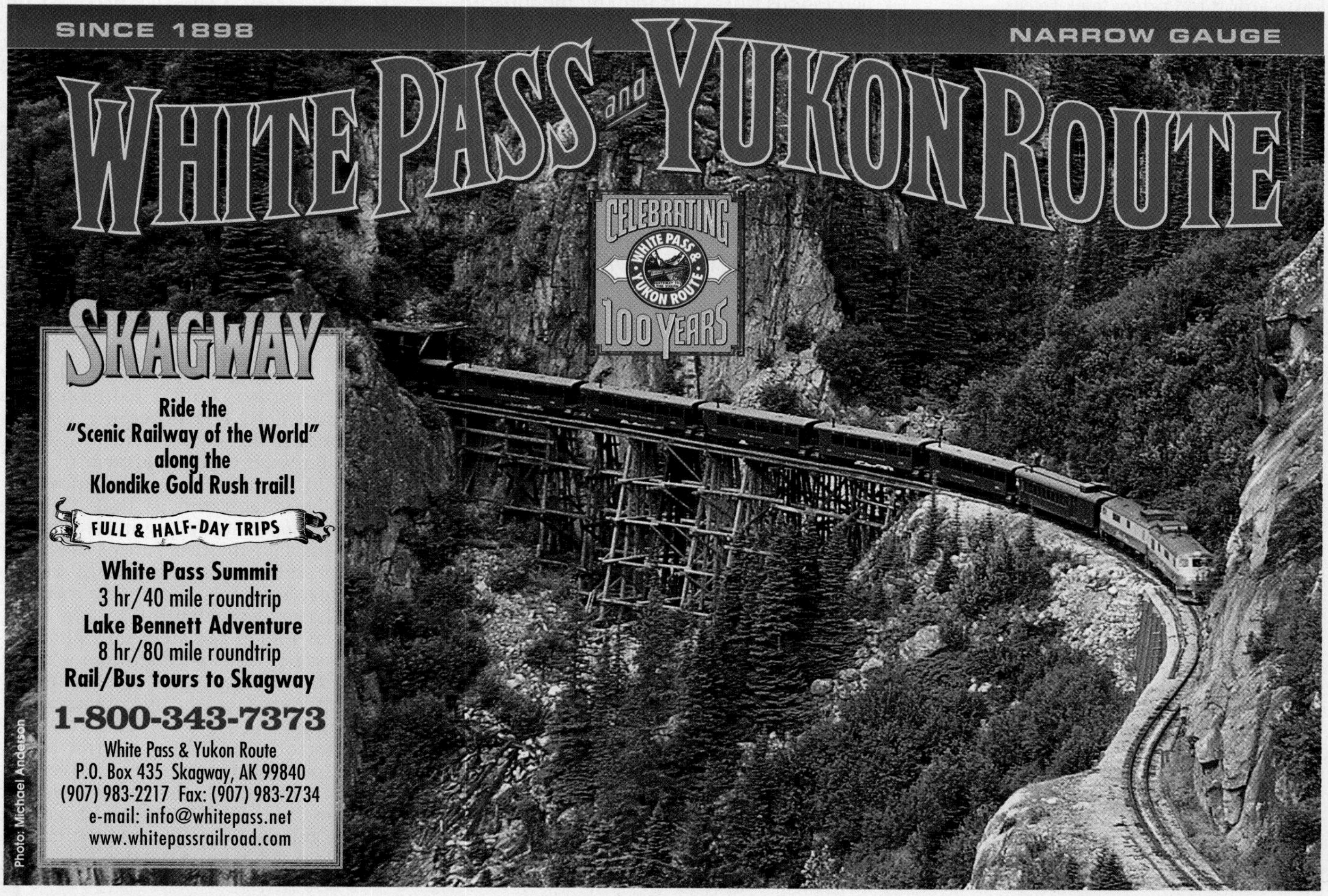

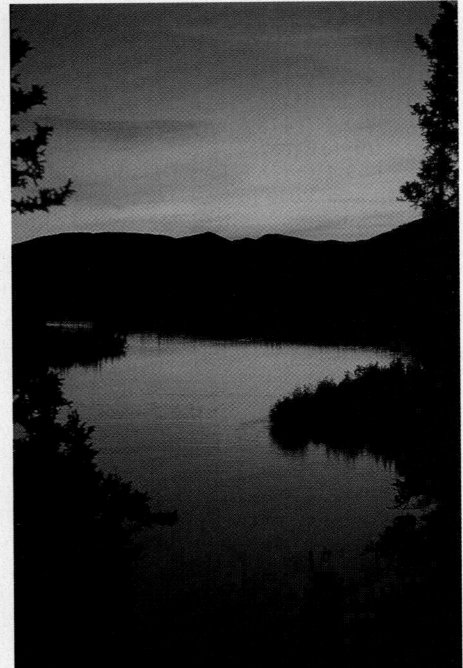

Sunset over the Takhini River north of Whitehorse.

(© Earl L. Brown, staff)

tion in this area.

DC 890.1 (1479.9 km) **DJ 499.9** (804.5 km) Rabbit's Foot Canyon.

DC 890.5 (1480.6 km) **DJ 499.5** (803.8 km) Turnoff to Porter Creek to east.

DC 891 (1481.4 km) **DJ 499** (803 km) Porter Creek grocery.

DC 891.3 (1482 km) **DJ 498.7** (802.6 km) **Historical Mile 921,** laundromat, gas and other businesses.

DC 891.5 (1482.3 km) **DJ 498.5** (802.2 km) Clyde Wann Road and Porter Creek subdivision, a residential suburb of Whitehorse. Access to Range Road and Mountain View Golf Course (18 holes).

DC 891.6 (1482.4 km) **DJ 498.4** (802 km) **Historical Mile 922**. Trails North Car & Truck Stop.

DC 891.8 (1482.5 km) **DJ 498.2** (801.7 km) MacDonald Road to north.

DC 891.9 (1484 km) **DJ 498.1** (801.6 km) **Historical Mile 922.5.** Azure Road. Access to MacKenzie's RV Park. ▲

DC 894.3 (1486.4 km) **DJ 495.7** (797.7 km) Turnoff east to Cousins dirt airstrip.

DC 894.5 (1486.7 km) **DJ 495.5** (797.4 km) Rest area to west with litter barrels, outhouses, information sign and pay phone.

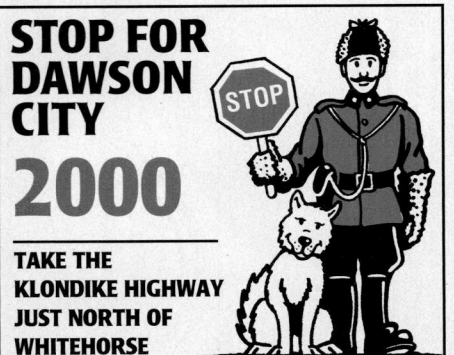

DC 894.8 (1487.2 km) **DJ 495.2** (796.9 km) For Alaska-bound travelers, the highway now swings west. Turn off to north on Klondike Highway 2 for Takhini Hot Springs (swimming, camping), 3.8 miles/6.1 km north. ▲

Junction with Klondike Highway 2 to Dawson City. See KLONDIKE LOOP section page 244 for log of that route.

DC 895.5 (1488.3 km) **DJ 494.5** (795.8 km) Turnoff to south for Haeckel Hill. Not recommended for hiking as this area is used for target practice.

DC 899.1 (1495.4 km) **DJ 490.9** (790 km) Turnoff for 3-mile/4.8-km loop drive on old section of Alaska Highway. Access to stocked lake.

DC 901.6 (1499.3 km) **DJ 488.4** (786 km) Turnoff to north to sled dog track.

DC 905.4 (1507.1 km) **DJ 484.6** (779.9 km) **Historic Milepost 937.** Camera viewpoint turnout to north with point of interest sign about the old Dawson Trail. There were at least 50 stopping places along the old Dawson Trail winter stagecoach route between Whitehorse and Dawson City, and from 1 to 3 roadhouses at each stop. At this point, the stagecoach route crossed the Takhini River. This route was discontinued in 1950 when the Mayo–Dawson Road (now Klondike Highway 2) was constructed.

DC 908.7 (1512.4 km) **DJ 481.3** (774.5 km) Private farm and windmill; good example of Yukon agriculture. Facilities for overnighting large livestock.

DC 914 (1524 km) **DJ 476** (766 km) **Takhini Salt Flats**, a series of bowl-shaped depressions where salts form on the surface as water brought up from underground springs evaporates. Although alkaline flats are not uncommon in the Yukon, this one is notable for the size of its salt crystals as well as the variety of salt-loving plants that thrive here, such as the distinctive red sea asparagus.

DC 914.7 (1525 km) **DJ 475.3** (764.9 km) **Takhini River** bridge. According to R. Coutts in *Yukon: Places & Names,* the name Takhini derives from the Tagish Indian *tahk,* meaning mosquito, and *heena,* meaning river.

DC 918 (1530.6 km) **DJ 472** (759.5 km) Turnoff to north for Blue Kennels and Dog Sled Trips (0.5 miles/0.8 km) from highway, operated by Yukon Quest musher.

DC 922.7 (1535 km) **DJ 467.3** (752 km) *CAUTION: Watch for horses and other livestock grazing on open range near highway.*

DC 924.5 (1538.4 km) **DJ 465.5** (749.1 km) Stoney Creek.

DC 924.7 (1538.7 km) **DJ 465.3** (748.8 km) View of Mount Bratnober, elev. 6,313 feet/1,924m. According to R. Coutts in *Yukon: Places & Names,* the mountain was named in 1897 by J.J. McArthur, Canadian government surveyor, for Henry Bratnober, who along with Jack Dalton was assisting in a cursory survey of the Dalton Trail.

DC 926 (1540.8 km) **DJ 464** (746.7 km) **Takhini River Valley Viewpoint.** Turnout to south with litter barrels and viewing platform with information panels on wildlife found in the Takhini River Valley. Point of interest sign about 1958 Takhini Burn. More than 1.5 million acres/629,058 hectares of Yukon forest lands were burned in 1958. Campfires were responsible for most of these fires.

Watch for free-ranging elk often seen near the highway here. Introduced in 1951–1954 from Elk Island National Park, the elk moved into this area following the 1958 burn. The elk population numbered around 60 animals in 1999.

DC 927.3 (1542.9 km) **DJ 462.7** (744.6 km) Turnoff to south for **Kusawa Lake** access road, a narrow, winding gravel side road that leads 15 miles;/24 km to the lake. The road is slippery when wet and not recommended for large RVs or trailers. At Mile 1.9/3 km on Kusawa Lake Road there is a viewpoint at Mendenhall Landing, which was a freight transfer point in the early 1900s for goods shipped up the Yukon and Takhini rivers. From the landing, goods were loaded onto wagons headed for Kluane mining operations. At Mile 9/15 km on the side road is Takhini River Yukon government campground, with 13 sites. Kusawa Lake Yukon government campground at end of road at north end of lake has 48 sites, kitchen shelter, firepits and drinking water. Camping permit ($8). Fishing for lake trout to 20 lbs., good to excellent; also grayling and pike. ▲

Kusawa Lake (formerly Arkell Lake), located in the Coast Mountains, is 45 miles/72 km long and averages 2 miles/3.2 km wide, with a shoreline perimeter of 125 miles/200 km. An access road to the lake was first constructed by the U.S. Army in 1945 to obtain bridge timbers for Alaska Highway construction.

DC 936.8 (1558 km) **DJ 453.2** (729.3 km) Mendenhall River bridge. A tributary of the Takhini River, the Mendenhall River—like the Mendenhall Glacier outside Juneau, AK—was named for Thomas Corwin Mendenhall (1841–1924), superintendent of the U.S. Coast & Geodetic Survey.

DC 939.5 (1562.3 km) **DJ 450.5** (725 km) View of 3 prominent mountains northbound (from left to right): Mount Kelvin; center mountain unnamed; and Mount Bratnober.

DC 942.2 (1565.5 km) **DJ 447.8** (720.6 km) Native traditional camp, **Kwaday Dan Kenji**, featuring a replica traditional First Nation camp interpretive site. Fee charged.

DC 942.8 (1567.6 km) **DJ 447.2** (719.7 km) NorthwesTel microwave tower to south.

DC 943.5 (1568.5 km) **DJ 446.5** (718.5 km) **Historic Milepost 974.** Historic sign and interpretive panel about **CHAMPAGNE;** snack bar.

Originally a camping spot on the Dalton Trail to Dawson City, established by Jack Dalton in the late 1800s. In 1902, Harlow "Shorty" Chambers built a roadhouse and trading post here, and it became a supply centre for first the Bullion Creek rush and later the Burwash Creek gold rush in 1904. The origin of the name is uncertain, although one account is that Dalton's men—after successfully negotiating a herd of cattle through the first part of the trail—celebrated here with a bottle of French champagne. Today, it is home to members of the Champagne–Aishihik Indian Band. There is an Indian cemetery on right westbound, just past the log cabin homes; a sign there reads: "This cemetery is not a tourist attraction. Please respect our privacy as we respect yours."

For northbound travelers, the Alaska Highway parallels the Dezadeash River (out of view to the south) from here west to Haines Junction. The Dezadeash Range is to the south and the Ruby Range to the north.

DC 944.4 (1570 km) **DJ 445.6** (717.1 km) Gravel turnout with litter barrel.

DC 955.8 (1588 km) **DJ 434.2** (698.7 km) First glimpse northbound of Kluane Range.

DC 957 (1590 km) **DJ 433** (696.8 km) **Historic Milepost 987.** Cracker Creek. Former roadhouse site on old stagecoach trail. Watch for "Old Man Mountain" on right northbound (the rocky crags look like a face, particularly in evening light).

DC 964.6 (1602.2 km) **DJ 425.4** (684.6 km) **Historical Mile 995. Otter Falls Cutoff, junction** with Aishihik Road. Gas station, store and camping to south, Bird-watching trails. Aishihik Road turnoff to north (description follows). ▲

Otter Falls Cutoff. See display ad this section. ▲

Aishihik Road leads north 26.1 miles/42.2 km to Aishihik Lake campground and 84 miles/135 km to the old Indian village of Aishihik (AYSH-ee-ak, means high place). This is a narrow, winding gravel road, maintained for summer travel only to the government campground at the lake. There are some steep hills and single-lane bridges. Aishihik Road is not recommended for large RVs and trailers. It is a scenic drive, and visitors have a good chance of seeing bison. *CAUTION: Watch for bison. Bears in area.*

At Mile 17.6/28.4 km is the **Otter Falls** viewpoint and day-use area with outhouse and information panels. Otter Falls

was once pictured on the back of the Canadian five-dollar bill, but in 1975 the Aishihik Power Plant diverted water from the falls. The 32-megawatt dam was built by Northern Canada Power Commission to supply power principally to the mining industry. Some water is still released over the falls during the summer. Flow hours for Otter Falls are given at the start of Aishihik Road. An interpretive sign here describes the reintroduction of the wood bison.

At Mile 26.1/42.2 km is the turnoff for Aishihik Lake Yukon government campground, located at the south end of the lake; 13 sites, drinking water, picnic tables, firepits, kitchen shelter, boat launch and playground. Camping permit ($8). ▲

Aishihik Lake, fishing for lake trout and grayling. As with most large Yukon lakes, ice is not out until late June. Low water levels may make boat launching difficult. *WARNING: Winds can come up suddenly on this lake.* **Pole Cat Lake,** just before the Aishihik weather station; fishing for pike.

DC 965.6 (1603.8 km) **DJ 424.4** (683 km) **Historic Milepost 996.** Turnoff to north at east end of Aishihik River bridge (watch for camera viewpoint sign) to see **Canyon Creek Bridge**. The original bridge was built about 1920 by the Jacquot brothers to move freight and passengers across the Aishihik River to Silver City on Kluane Lake, and from there by boat to Burwash Landing. The bridge was reconstructed in 1942 by Army Corps of Engineers during

construction of the Alaska Highway. It was rebuilt again in 1987 by the Yukon government.

DC 965.7 (1604 km) **DJ 424.3** (682.8 km) Aishihik River bridge.

DC 966.3 (1605 km) **DJ 423.7** (618.9 km) View of impressive Kluane Range ice fields straight ahead northbound between Kilometreposts 1604 and 1616.

DC 974.9 (1619 km) **DJ 415.1** (668 km) Turnout to south on Marshall Creek.

DC 977.1 (1622.4 km) **DJ 421.9** (664.5 km) The rugged snowcapped peaks of the Kluane Icefield Ranges and the outer portion of the St. Elias Mountains are visible to the west, straight ahead northbound.

The Kluane National Park Icefield Ranges are Canada's highest and the world's largest nonpolar alpine ice field, forming the interior wilderness of the park. In clear weather, Mount Kennedy and Mount Hubbard, 2 peaks that are twice as high as the front ranges seen before you, are visible from here.

DC 979.3 (1626 km) **DJ 410.7** (660.9 km) Between Kilometreposts 1626 and 1628, look for the NorthwesTel microwave repeater station on top of Paint Mountain. The station was installed with the aid of helicopters and supplied by the tramline carried by high towers, which is also visible from here.

DC 980.8 (1628.4 km) **DJ 409.2** (658.5 km) Turnoff to north for Yukon government **Pine Lake Recreation Park**. Day-use area with sandy beach, boat launch and dock, group firepits, drinking water and 7 tent sites near beach.The campground, adjacent

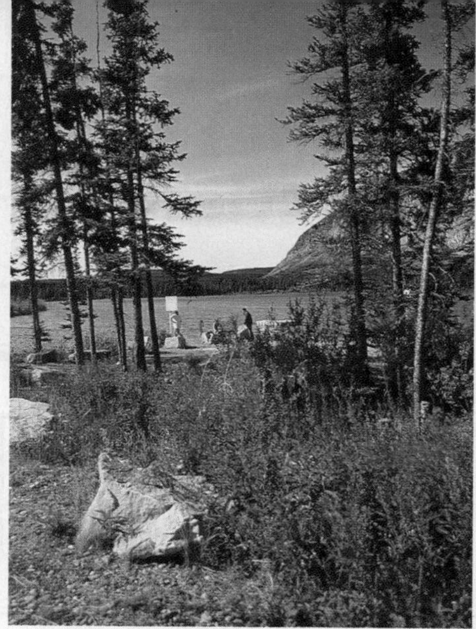

Pine Lake Recreation Park at Milepost DC 980.8 has a walking and biking trail to Haines Junction. (© Earl L. Brown, staff)

Pine Lake with a view of the St. Elias Mountains, has 42 sites, outhouses, firewood, litter barrels, kitchen shelter, playground and drinking water. Camping permit ($8). Fishing is good for lake trout, northern pike and grayling. *CAUTION: Bears in area.* ▲

A short nature trail winds through the boreal forest from the beach to the campground. Panels along the trail interpret the lake's aquatic habitats and marl formations. The white sediment marl is a form of calcium carbonate, and the marl beds intensify the blue and green reflections of the lake on a sunny day. Forest dwellers to watch for on the trail include: gray jays, ruby-crowned kinglets, boreal chickadees and red squirrels.

A 3.5-mile/6-km walking and biking trail begins at the campground entrance and ends at Haines Junction.

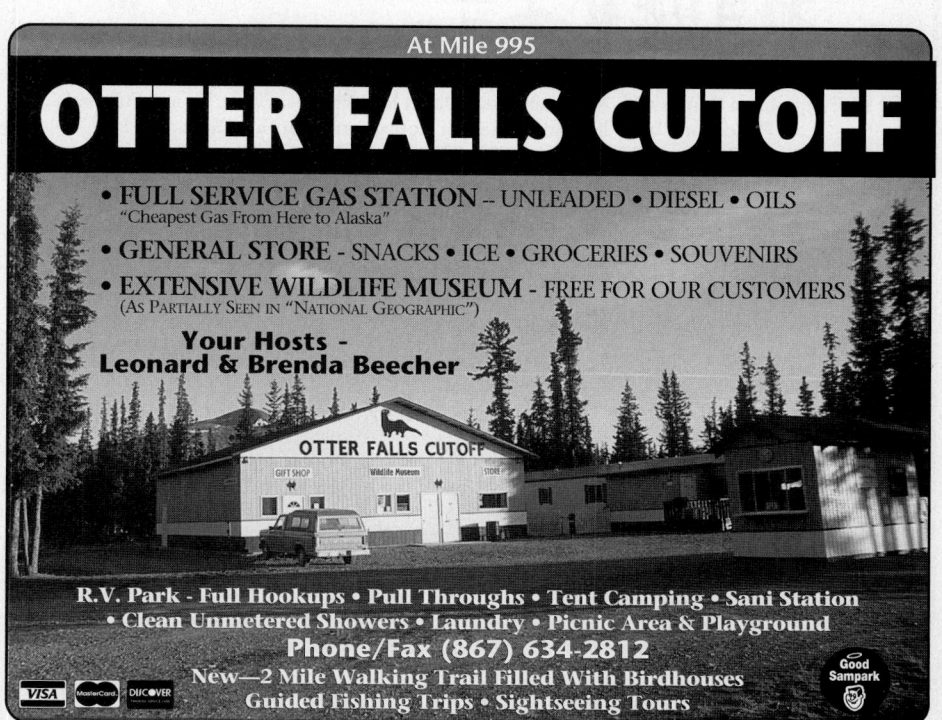

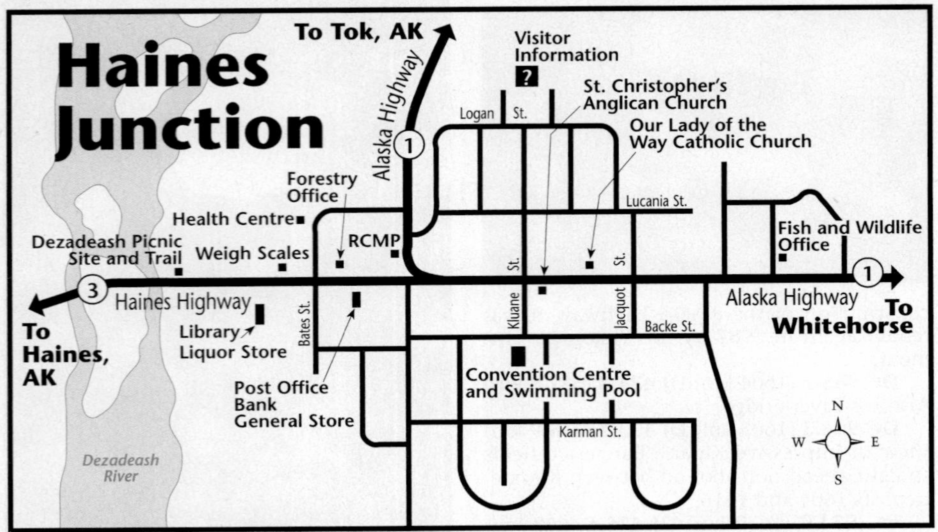

Yukon is on Pacific Time, Alaska is on Alaska Time (1 hour earlier)

DC 980.9 (1628.5 km) **DJ 409.1** (658.4 km) Access road to floatplane dock.

DC 982.2 (1630.8 km) **DJ 407.8** (656.3 km) Turnoff to north for Haines Junction airport. Flightseeing tours of glaciers, fly-in fishing and air charters available; fixed-wing aircraft or helicopters.

Private Aircraft: Haines Junction airstrip; elev. 2,150 feet/655m; length 5,500 feet/ 1,676m; gravel. Fuel sales (100L) from Sifton Air.

Highway swings to south for last few miles into Haines Junction, offering a panoramic, close-up view of the Auriol Range straight ahead.

DC 984.8 (1635 km) **DJ 405.2** (652.1 km) Northbound travelers turn right (southbound travelers turn left) on Kluane Street for Kluane National Park Visitor Centre.

DC 985 (1635.3 km) **DJ 405** (651.8 km) **Historic Milepost 1016.** *IMPORTANT: THIS JUNCTION CAN BE CONFUSING; CHOOSE YOUR ROUTE CAREFULLY! Fairbanks- and Anchorage-bound travelers TURN NORTH at this junction for continuation of Alaska Highway (Yukon 1). Alaska Highway log continues on page 169.* (Haines-bound motorists note: It is a good idea fill up with gas in Haines Junction.)

Junction of Alaska Highway and Haines Highway (Haines Road). Head west on the Haines Highway (Yukon Highway 3) for port of Haines, AK. See HAINES HIGHWAY section.

Haines Junction

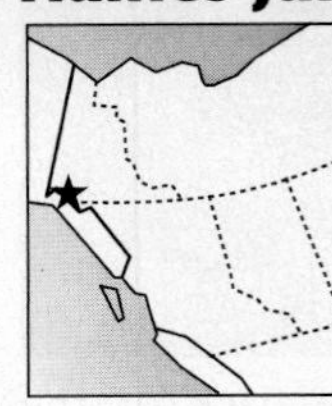

DC 985 (1635.3 km) **DJ 405** (651.8 km) **Historic Milepost 1016**, at the **junction** of the Alaska Highway (Yukon Highway 1) and the Haines Highway (Yukon Highway 3, also known as the Haines Road). Driving distance to Whitehorse, 100 miles/161 km; YT–AK border, 205 miles/330 km; Tok, 296 miles/ 476 km; and Haines, 150.5 miles/242 km. **Population:** 811. **Elevation:** 1,956 feet/ 596m. **Emergency Services: RCMP,** phone (867) 634-5555 or (867) 667-5555 **Fire Department**, phone (867) 634-2222. **Nursing Centre**, phone (867) 634-4444.

Visitor Information: At the Yukon Government and **Kluane National Park Visitor Information Centre**, 0.2 mile/0.3 km east of the junction just off the Alaska Highway. Phone (867) 634-2345. Interpretive exhibits, displays and a multi-image slide presentation on Yukon national parks and historic sites (fee charged). The centre is open 8 A.M. to 8 P.M. daily from May to September; 10 A.M. to 4 P.M., Monday through Friday, the rest of the year.

Private Aircraft: The airport is located on the Alaska Highway just east of town; see description at **Milepost DC 982.2. Radio:** 106.1 FM, 103.5 FM, CKRW 98.7 FM, CHON 90.5 FM.

Haines Junction was established in 1942 during construction of the Alaska Highway. The first buildings here were Army barracks for the U.S. Army Corps of Engineers. The engineers were to build a new branch road connecting the Alaska Highway with the port of Haines on Lynn Canal. The branch road—today's Haines Highway—was completed in 1943.

Haines Junction is still an important stop for travelers on the Alaska and Haines highways. Services are located along both highways, and clustered around Village Square at the junction, where the 24-foot **Village Monument** depicts area wildlife.

Haines Junction is on the eastern bound-

Village Monument in Haines Junction depicts area wildlife. (© Earl L. Brown, staff)

ary of Kluane (pronounced kloo-WA-nee) National Park and Reserve. The park was first suggested in 1942, and in 1943 land was set aside and designated the Kluane Game Sanctuary. A formal park region was established in 1972 and the national park and reserve boundaries were official in 1976. In 1980, Kluane National Park Reserve, along with Wrangell–St. Elias National Park in Alaska, became a joint UNESCO World Heritage Site. Kluane National Park and Reserve encompasses extensive ice fields, mountains and wilderness, and has become a world-class wilderness destination among outdoor recreation enthusiasts.

Lodging & Services

Haines Junction offers an excellent range of accommodations and also has a convention centre. Visitor services include motels, 4 bed and breakfasts, restaurants, gas stations, garage services, groceries, souvenirs and a bakery. Gourmet dining at The Raven. There is a full-facility indoor heated swimming pool with showers available; open daily from May to late-August, fee charged. Also here are a RCMP office, Lands and Forest District Office and health centre. The post office and bank are located in Madley's General Store. (Banking service weekday afternoons; extended hours on Fridays.) The Commissioner James Smith Administration Building, at Kilometre 255.6 Haines Road, 0.2 mile/0.3 km south from the Alaska Highway junction, contains the government liquor store and public library.

The Glacier View Inn offers the traveler complete services in one stop. The motel has direct dial phones with data ports as well as satellite TV with all of your favorite channels from home. The restaurant is family-style, with a wide variety of menu items; fresh baking; and licensed dining. Best of all, it is priced with your budget in mind! We also offer regular, supreme and diesel fuel for your convenience. Phone (867) 634-2646. [ADVERTISEMENT]

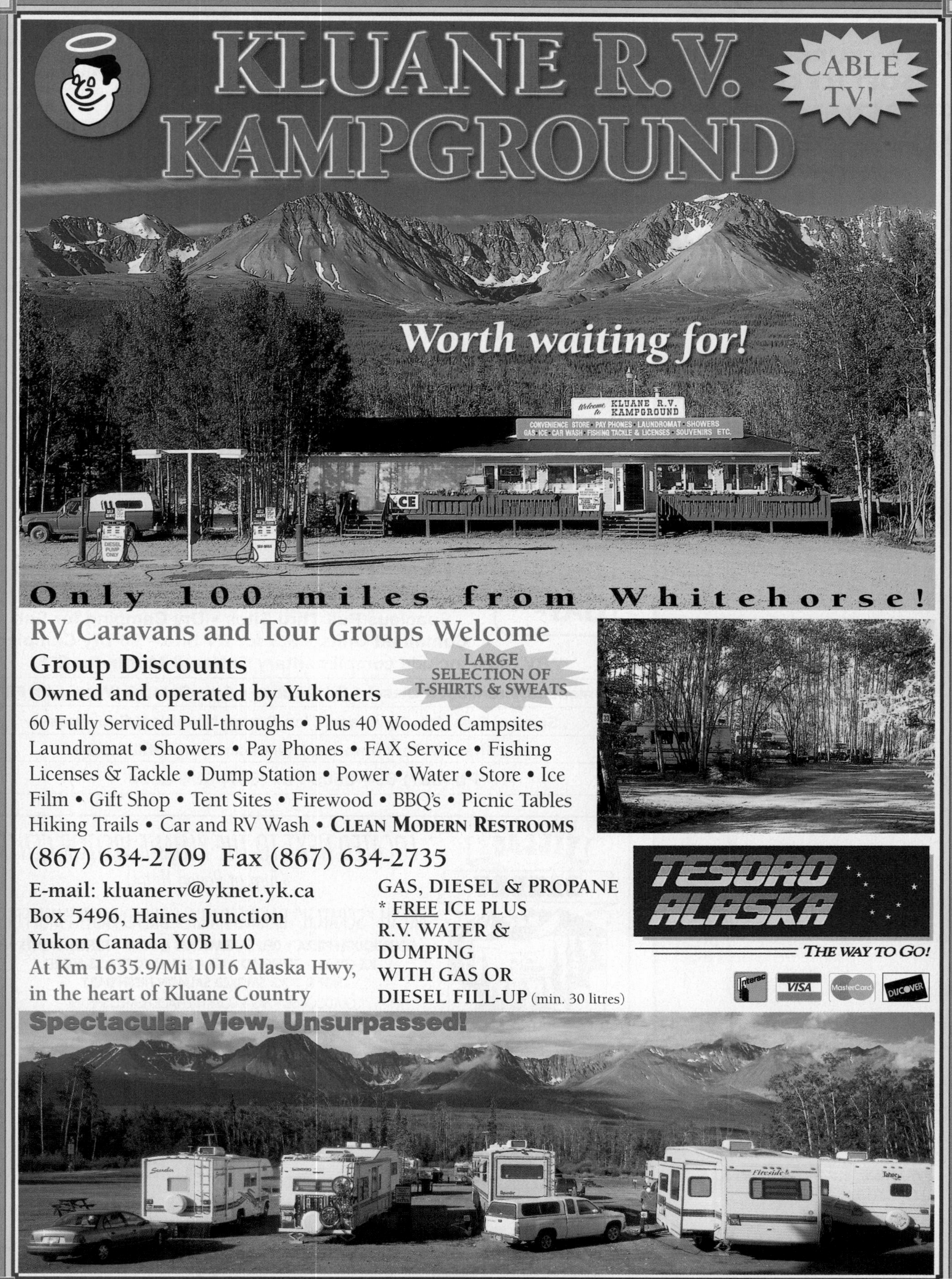
KLUANE R.V.
KAMPGROUND
CABLE TV!
Worth waiting for!
Welcome to KLUANE R.V. KAMPGROUND
CONVENIENCE STORE · PAY PHONES · LAUNDROMAT · SHOWERS
GAS · ICE · CAR WASH · FISHING TACKLE & LICENSES · SOUVENIRS ETC.
ICE
Only 100 miles from Whitehorse!
RV Caravans and Tour Groups Welcome
Group Discounts
Owned and operated by Yukoners
LARGE SELECTION OF T-SHIRTS & SWEATS
60 Fully Serviced Pull-throughs • Plus 40 Wooded Campsites
Laundromat • Showers • Pay Phones • FAX Service • Fishing
Licenses & Tackle • Dump Station • Power • Water • Store • Ice
Film • Gift Shop • Tent Sites • Firewood • BBQ's • Picnic Tables
Hiking Trails • Car and RV Wash • CLEAN MODERN RESTROOMS
(867) 634-2709 Fax (867) 634-2735
E-mail: kluanerv@yknet.yk.ca
Box 5496, Haines Junction
Yukon Canada Y0B 1L0
At Km 1635.9/Mi 1016 Alaska Hwy,
in the heart of Kluane Country
GAS, DIESEL & PROPANE
* FREE ICE PLUS
R.V. WATER &
DUMPING
WITH GAS OR
DIESEL FILL-UP (min. 30 litres)
TESORO ALASKA
THE WAY TO GO!
Interac
VISA
MasterCard
DISCOVER
Spectacular View, Unsurpassed!

Camping

RV camping available at several campgrounds in and near town; see advertisements this section. Dump stations and water are also available at local service station and campgrounds. Yukon government campground located 4.2 miles/6.7 km east of junction on the Alaska Highway at Pine Lake. Kluane National Park has one campground, Kathleen Lake, located 16 miles/27 km south of town on the Haines Highway ▲

Attractions

Kluane National Park Visitor Centre has natural history exhibits and a slide presentation (shown on the hour and half hour, fee charged). Also check at the visitor centre for details on the park's numerous hiking trails and for a schedule of guided hikes, walks and campfire talks. (Hikers note: There is mandatory registration for overnight trips into the park. Nightly or annual wilderness permits may be purchased. Bear resistant food canisters are mandatory on some overnight hikes; a $150 deposit is required). Interpretive programs are available daily from the third week in June through August; fee charged. Contact Kluane National Park at Box 5495, Haines Junction, YT Y0B 1L0, or phone (867) 634-7207, fax (867) 634-7208.

Flightseeing Kluane National Park by fixed-wing aircraft or helicopter from Haines Junction is a popular way to see the spectacular mountain scenery. Check with charter services at the airport.

Tatshenshini–Alsek Wilderness Park. Created in 1993, the park protects the magnificent Tatshenshini and Alsek rivers area in Canada, where the 2 rivers join and flow (as the Alsek) to the Gulf of Alaska at Dry Bay. Known to river runners as "the Tat," the Tatshenshini is famous for its whitewater rafting, stunning scenery and wildlife. Due to a dramatic increase in river traffic in recent years, permits are required from the park agencies (the National Park Service in Alaska and B.C. Parks in Canada). For more information about the park, contact BC Parks, Tatshenshini Office, Box 5544, Haines Junction, YT Y0B 1L0; phone (867) 634-7043, fax (867) 634-7208.

The **Dezadeash River** offers a relaxed rafting experience. Picnicking and hiking trail are available at a day-use area on the river at the west edge of town on the Haines Highway.

Our Lady of the Way Catholic Mission is a local landmark and visitor attraction. It was built in 1954, using parts from an old Army hut left from highway construction days.

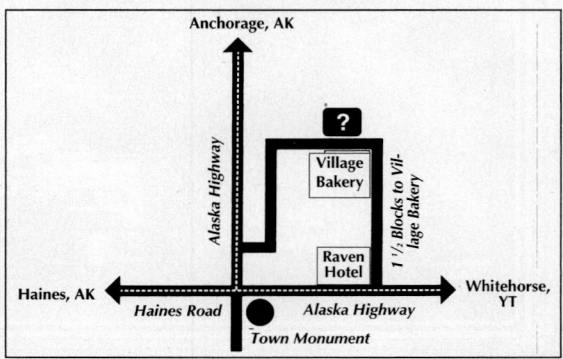

Special events in Haines Junction include the Alsek Music Festival held June 9–11, 2000, and Canada Day (the anniversary of Canada's confederation), celebrated on July 1st with parades, barbecue and flags.

Bicycling offers several events, including the Trail of '42 Road Race (May 27, 2000) and the Kluane to Chilkat International Bike Relay (June 17, 2000). *IMPORTANT: Watch for cyclists on the Alaska and Haines highways during these events.*

Alaska Highway Log

(continued)

Distance* from Dawson Creek (DC) is followed by distance from Delta Junction (DJ). Original mileposts are indicated in the text as Historical Mile.

**In Canada, mileages from Dawson Creek are based on actual driving distance, not historical mileposts, and kilometres are based on physical kilometreposts *as they occurred in summer 1999*. Mileages from Delta Junction are also based on actual driving distance, not historical mileposts, but are followed by the metric conversion to kilometres.

DC 985 (1635.3 km) **F 503** (809.5 km) **Junction** of the Alaska Highway (Yukon Highway 1) and the Haines Highway (Yukon Highway 3).

NOTE: This junction can be confusing; choose your route carefully! Whitehorse-bound travelers turn east at junction for continuation of Alaska Highway (Yukon Highway 1). Turn west for the Haines Highway (Yukon Highway 3) to the port of Haines, AK, 152 miles/246 km from here.

See the HAINES HIGHWAY section for log of that route. (Haines-bound motorists note: It is a good idea to fill up with gas in Haines Junction.)

Northbound: Markers indicate distance to Destruction Bay 67 miles/108 km, Beaver Creek 186 miles/299 km. From Haines Junction to the YT–AK border, the Alaska Highway is in fair to good condition but narrow, often without shoulders. Watch for frost heaves north from Destruction Bay to Beaver Creek.

Southbound: Good paved highway with wide shoulders next 380 miles/611.5 km (from here to Watson Lake) with the exception of some short sections of narrow road and occasional gravel breaks.

DC 985.3 (1635.9 km) **DJ 404.7** (651.3 km) Kluane RV Kampground; RV and tent camping, gas, diesel, dump station, pay phone. ▲

DC 985.8 (1636.5 km) **DJ 404.2** (650.2 km) **Historical Mile 1017.** Source Motors; gas, diesel, propane, auto repair, towing, snowmachine, ATV and watercraft rentals and repairs. Open daily, year-round.

DC 985.9 (1636.7 km) **DJ 404.1** (650.3 km) Stardust Motel and Triple S Service Station.

DC 986.6 (1637.8 km) **DJ 403.4** (649.2 km) Highway follows the Kluane Ranges which are to the west.

DC 987.8 (1639.8 km) **DJ 402.2** (647.3 km) **Historical Mile 1019.** Kluane National Park warden headquarters. (Visitor information in Haines Junction at the visitor centre.)

DC 988.3 (1640.6 km) **DJ 401.7** (646.4 km) Rest area to west with pit toilets.

DC 991.4 (1645.6 km) **DJ 398.6** (641.5 km) Highway climbs next 9 miles/14.5 km northbound to Bear Creek Summit.

DC 991.6 (1646 km) **DJ 398.4** (641.1 km) **Historic Milepost 1022**, Mackintosh Trading Post historic sign. Bear Creek Lodge to east; food, gas, lodging and camping. Corral for overnighting horses. Trailhead to west for Alsek Pass trail; 18 miles/29 km long, suitable for shorter day hikes, mountain bikes permitted. ▲

Bear Creek Lodge See display ad this section. ▲

DC 999 (1653.2 km) **DJ 391** (629.2 km) Turnout with 1-mile/1.7-km **Spruce Beetle Interpretive Trail.** This easy loop interpretive trail examines the life of the spruce bark beetle and its effect on the forests of the area. Allow 35 to 45 minutes for walk. (The spruce beetle has also infested areas of Alaska, particularly around Anchorage and on the Kenai Peninsula.)

DC 1000.1 (1660 km) **DJ 389.9** (627.5 km) **Bear Creek Summit** (elev. 3,294 feet/1,004m), highest point on the Alaska Highway between Whitehorse and Fairbanks.

Glimpse of Kloo Lake to north of highway between Kilometreposts 1660 and 1662.

DC 1003.5 (1665.4 km) **DJ 386.5** (622 km) Jarvis River.

DC 1003.6 (1665.6 km) **DJ 386.4** (621.8 km) **Historic Milepost 1035.** Turnout to west just north of crossing Jarvis River. Pretty spot for a picnic. Poor to fair fishing for grayling 8 to 16 inches all summer; Dolly Varden 8 to 10 inches, early summer.

DC 1006 (1671 km) **DJ 384** (238.6 km) Turnout to north at **Sulphur Lake;** canoeing, birdwatching. Thousands of birds use the lake, mostly in late summer, for moulting.

DC 1013.6 (1682 km) **DJ 376.4** (605.7 km) Beautiful view to west of the snow-covered **Kluane Ranges.** The Alaska Highway parallels the Kluane Ranges from Haines Junction to Koidern, presenting a nearly unbroken chain of mountains to 8,000-feet/2,438-m interrupted by only a few large valleys cut by glacier-fed rivers and streams. West of the Kluane Ranges is the Duke Depression, a narrow trough separating the Kluane Ranges from the St. Elias Mountains. Major peaks in the St. Elias (not visible from the highway) are: Mount Logan, Canada's highest peak, at 19,545 feet/ 5,959m; Mount St. Elias, 18,008 feet/5,489m; Mount Lucania, 17,147 feet/5,226m; King Peak, 16,971 feet/5,173m; and Mounts Wood, Vancouver, Hubbard and Steele, all over 15,000 feet/4,572m. Mount Steele (16,664 feet/ 5,079m) was named for Superintendent Sam Steele of the North West Mounted Police. As commanding officer of the NWMP in the Yukon in 1898, Steele established permanent detachments at the summits of the White and Chilkoot passes to ensure not only that gold stampeders obeyed Canadian laws, but also had sufficient supplies to carry them through to the gold fields.

DC 1016.5 (1686.7 km) **DJ 373.5** (601.1 km) Large gravel turnout to west with view of Kluane Ranges.

DC 1017.2 (1687.8 km) **DJ 372.8** (599.9 km) Christmas Creek.

DC 1019 (1689 km) **DJ 371** (597 km) Highway climbs northbound.

DC 1019.8 (1692 km) **DJ 370.2** (595.7 km) First glimpse of Kluane Lake for northbound travelers at **Boutillier Summit** (elev. 3,293 feet/1,003m), second highest point on the highway between Whitehorse and Fairbanks.

DC 1020 (1692.5 km) **DJ 370** (595.4 km) Double-ended photo viewpoint to east with information plaques on area history and geography.

DC 1020.3 (1693 km) **DJ 369.7** (595km) **Historic Milepost 1053.** Historic sign and

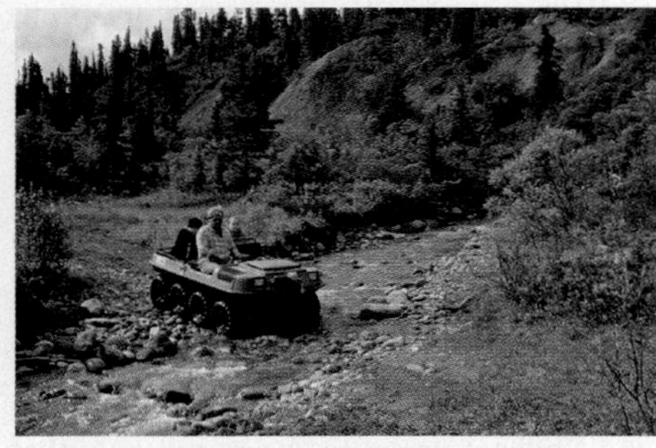

interpretive panel at turnoff for **Silver City**. Kluane Bed and Breakfast. Follow dirt and gravel road east 3.1 miles/5 km to ruins of Silver City. Silver City was the site of a trading post, roadhouse and North West Mounted Police barracks. It served traffic traveling the wagon road from Whitehorse to the placer goldfields of the Kluane Lake district from 1904 to 1924. Silver City's picturesque old buildings offer good photo opportunities. Kluane Bed and Breakfast offers ATV tours.

Kluane Bed and Breakfast. Just 3 miles off the highway at historical Silver City on the shore of Kluane Lake. Private, heated, A-frame cabins on lakeshore with mountain view, cooking and shower facilities, full family-style breakfast. Mountain bike rentals, high-country Alpine Argo (8-wheel ATV) trips. Your hosts—The Sias Family, a sixth generation Yukon family. Contact mobile operator, Destruction Bay channel 2M 3924. Reservations recommended. Mailing address: c/o Box 5459, Haines Junction, YT Y0B 1L0. [ADVERTISEMENT]

DC 1020.9 (1694 km) **DJ 369.1** (594 km) Silver Creek.

DC 1022.5 (1696.5 km) **DJ 367.5** (591.4 km) Turnoff to east for Icefield Discovery tours and Kluane Lake Research Station. Research station and airstrip are 0.9 mile/1.4 km via a straight gravel road. This research station is sponsored by the Arctic Institute of North America, University of Calgary.

Icefield Discovery offers full package trips to Mount Logan, Canada's highest mountain. Packages include spectacular glacier flights, accommodation in heated polar lodge, glacier clothing, meals and the friendly company of our on-site interpreters. Flights depart from the Silver City airstrip on the shore of Kluane Lake., Watch for the Icefield Discovery sign and drop in for more information; or call (867) 668-6744; e-mail icefields@yukon.net. Check out our great web site: www.icefields.com. [ADVERTISEMENT]

Private Aircraft: Silver City airstrip; elev. 2,570 feet/783m; length 3,000 feet/914m; gravel; no services.

Highway follows west shore of Kluane Lake next 39 miles/63 km northbound to Burwash Landing.

DC 1023.7 (1698.5 km) **DJ 366.3** (589.5 km) **Historical Mile 1056** (**Historical milepost 1055**). Kluane Camp commemorative plaque. Kluane Lake Lodge (closed).

DC 1024.6 (1700 km) **DJ 365.4** (588 km) Informal gravel turnout on Kluane Lake; access to beach.

DC 1026.8 (1703.4 km) **DJ 363.2** (584.5 km) Slim's River East trail turnoff (2-mile/3.3-km access road, not recommended for motorhomes); parking at trailhead. This 12.4-mile/20-km trail is rated "easy" by the *Kluane Hiking Guide*. NOTE: Hikers must register for overnight hikes in Kluane National Park at either the Sheep Mountain or Haines Junction visitor centres.

DC 1027.8 (1705 km) **DJ 362.2** (582.9 km) Slim's River bridge (clearance 17.7 feet/5.4m). Slim's River, which flows into Kluane Lake, was named for a packhorse that drowned here during the 1903 Kluane gold rush. Sheep Mountain is directly ahead for northbound travelers. The highway winds along Kluane Lake: Drive carefully!

DC 1028.8 (1706.6 km) **DJ 361.2** (581.3 km) **Sheep Mountain Visitor Information Centre**. Excellent interpretive programs, laser disc information videos, parking and outhouses are available. Open mid-May to early September. Hours are 9 A.M. to 5 P.M. Stop here for information on Kluane National Park's flora and fauna. A viewing telescope is set up to look for sheep on Sheep Mountain. This is the sheep's winter range; best chance to see them is late August and September, good chance in late May to early June. Register at the Sheep Mountain Centre for hiking in the park. NOTE: The face of Sheep Mountain has been designated a special preservation zone. Check with the centre for designated hiking areas, trail conditions and bear activity.

DC 1029 (1706.9 km) **DJ 361** (581 km) Slim's River West trail; trailhead adjacent visitor information centre.

The small white cross on the side of Sheep Mountain marks the grave of Alexander Clark Fisher, a prospector who came into this area about 1906.

DC 1030.7 (1709.5 km) **DJ 359.3** (578.2 km) **Historic Milepost 1061.** Large gravel turnouts both sides of highway at **Soldier's Summit**. The Alaska Canada Military Highway was officially opened with a ribbon-cutting ceremony here on blizzardy Nov. 20, 1942. A rededication ceremony was held Nov. 20, 1992, commemorating the 50th anniversary of the highway. A trail leads up to the original dedication site from the parking area.

Several turnouts overlooking **Kluane Lake** next mile northbound. This beautiful lake is the largest in Yukon Territory, covering approximately 154 square miles/400 square km. The Ruby Range lies on the east side of the lake. Boat rentals are available at Destruction Bay and Burwash Landing. Excellent fishing for lake trout, northern pike and grayling.

DC 1031.9 (1711.7 km) **DJ 358.1** (576.3 km) **Historical Mile 1064. The Bayshore.**

See display ad this section.

DC 1034.5 (1715.8 km) **DJ 355.5** (572.1 km) Williscroft Creek. Named for Walt Williscroft, Superintendent of Highway maintenance for the southern part of the Alaska Highway from 1950 to 1970.

DC 1034.9 (1717 km) **DJ 355.1** (571.5 km) **Historical Mile 1067. Cottonwood RV Park and Campground.** See display ad this section. ▲

DC 1039.9 (1725 km) **DJ 350.1** (563.4 km) **Historical Mile 1072.** Turnoff to east for **Congdon Creek** Yukon government campground on Kluane Lake. Drive in 0.4 mile/0.6 km via gravel loop road; tenting area, 81 level sites (some pull-through), outhouses, kitchen shelters, water pump, firewood, firepits, picnic tables, sandy beach, interpretive talks, playground, boat launch. Camping permit ($8). ▲

DC 1040.4 (1725.6 km) **DJ 349.6** (562.6 km) Congdon Creek. According to R. Coutts, *Yukon: Places & Names,* Congdon Creek is believed to have been named by a miner after Frederick Tennyson Congdon. A lawyer from Nova Scotia, Congdon came to the Yukon in 1898 and held various political posts until 1911.

DC 1040.6 (1726 km) **DJ 349.4** (562.3 km) *NOTE: Hills next 1.2 miles/2 km northbound; winding 2-lane road, no shoulders, informal gravel turnouts.*

DC 1046.9 (1735.3 km) **DJ 343.1** (552.1 km) Nines Creek. Turnout to east.

DC 1047.3 (1736.2 km) **DJ 342.7** (551.5 km) Mines Creek.

DC 1048.9 (1739 km) **DJ 341.1** (548.9 km) Bock's Brook.

DC 1051.5 (1743 km) **DJ 338.5** (544.7 km) **DESTRUCTION BAY** at **Historic Milepost 1083. Population:** 100. **Emergency Services: Health clinic**, phone (867) 841-4444; **Ambulance**, phone (867) 841-3333; **Fire Department**, phone (867) 841-3331.

Located on the shore of Kluane Lake, Destruction Bay is one of several towns that grew out of the building of the Alaska Highway. It earned its name when a storm destroyed buildings and materials here. Destruction Bay was one of the many relay stations spaced at 100-mile intervals to give truck drivers a break and a chance to repair their vehicles. Historic sign adjacent historic milepost. A highway maintenance camp is located here.

Destruction Bay has camping, boat launch, boat rentals and guided fishing tours. The **Kluane Lake Fishing Derby** is scheduled for July 1–2, 2000. Food, gas, camping and lodging available at the Talbot Arm (open year-round). ▲

Talbot Arm Motel. See display ad on page 172.

DC 1051.7 (1743.3 km) **DJ 338.3** (544.4 km) Gas, meals, lodging and camping. ▲

Destruction Bay Lodge. See display ad this section.

DC 1051.9 (1743.6 km) **DJ 338.1** (544.1 km) Rest area with litter barrels and toilet.

DC 1054.5 (1747.8 km) **DJ 335.5** (539.9 km) Evidence of June 1999 fire from here north to **Milepost DC 1066.2**. The human-caused fire closed the Alaska Highway and destroyed 5 homes in Burwash Landing (the town was evacuated). Some 8,000 acres were burned before fire crews were able to contain the fire. Fireweed, as its name implies, will be one of the first plants to reestablish itself in the burned area.

DC 1055.1 (1748.8 km) **DJ 334.9** (539 km) Lewes Creek.

Sheep Mountain Visitor Centre at Milepost DC 1028.8. (© Earl L. Brown, staff)

DC 1058.3 (1753.9 km) **DJ 331.7** (533.8 km) Halfbreed (Copper Joe) Creek trailhead.

DC 1061.3 (1758.7 km) **DJ 328.7** (529 km) Store.

DC 1061.5 (1759 km) **DJ 328.5** (528.6 km) **Historic Milepost 1093.** Kluane Museum and turnoff to east for **BURWASH LANDING,** (pop. 84). **Emergency Services: Ambulance**, phone (867) 841-333; **Fire Department**, phone (867) 841-2221.

Burwash Landing has a post office, community hall, church and gas, food, camping and lodging on Kluane Lake. Boat rentals and Kluane Lake fishing trips available. Flightseeing trips of Kluane National Park are also available out of Burwash Landing.

Burwash Landing is known for its black spruce burl bowls. Burls start as an irritation in the spruce. The tree sends extra sap as healant, which creates a growth or burl. Burls are either "green," harvested from live trees in the spring, or they are "dry burls," taken from dead burl trees. Burls are peeled of their bark and used in their natural form as fenceposts, for example, or they may be shaped and finished into a variety of objects, such as bowls. Check out Burlbilly Hill at **Milepost DC 1061.6.**

The highly recommended **Kluane Museum of Natural History** is located on the east side of the highway at the turnoff; open 9 A.M. to 9 P.M. in summer; phone (867) 841-5561. The museum features displays of wildlife in natural habitats; Native (First Nations) clothing and artifacts, including a moose skin boat; minerals exhibit; and videos. Modest admission is charged. Get your Yukon Explorer's Passport stamped here. Next to the museum is the world's largest gold pan, measuring 28 feet/8m high.

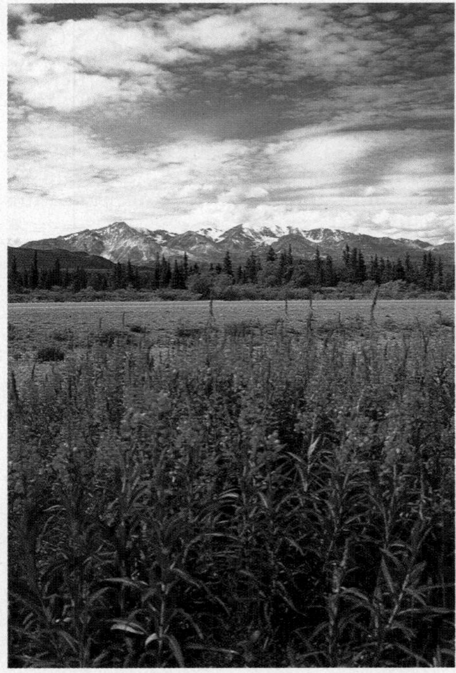

Fireweed loses its flowers progressively over the summer, making it the North's harbinger of fall . (© Earl L. Brown, staff)

Burwash Landing was settled in 1904 by the Jacquot brothers, Louis and Eugene, as a supply centre for local miners. The log **Our Lady of the Holy Rosary Mission**, was built

in 1944. Sign reads: "This was the first church northwest of Whitehorse on the new Alcan Highway. Father Morrisset, then auxiliary chaplain to the U.S. Army at the road construction camps, was asked by the local residents to start a mission and day school. Land was donated by Eugene Jacquot, trading post owner. Building materials came from the Duke River camp site and included an unfinished U.S. Army mess hall and a log cabin, which form the 2 arms of the complex. The day school closed in 1952. The church opened with Christmas eve mass in 1944 and is still in use today."

Burwash Landing Resort & RV Park. See display ad this section. ▲

Kluane Museum of Natural History. See display ad this section.

DC 1061.6 (1759.2 km) **DJ 328.4** (528.5 km) **Burlbilly Hill.** The most unique stop at Mile 1093 is "Burlbilly Hill," 200 feet north of the museum. The visitor will see rows of "burly logs" on the hill. Another surprise is a small woodshop with its variety of finely finished burl products, "burl bowls" and "diamond willow canes." Come and watch Obie and Karin at work. Wir sprechen deutsch! Phone (867) 841-4607. [ADVERTISEMENT]

DC 1062 (1759.8 km) **DJ 328** (527.8 km) Dalan Campground to north. ▲

Dalan Campground. Turn off north, to Dalan Campground, 1 km off the Alaska Highway on the shores of beautiful Kluane Lake, "largest lake in the Yukon." Owned and operated by Kluane First Nation, this campground offers 25 individual private campsites, RVs welcome! Firewood, water pump, picnic tables, firepits and dump station are available., For additional infor-

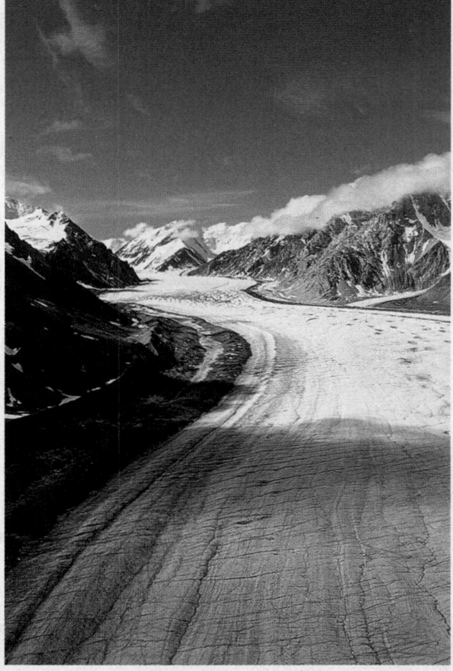
Flightseeing gives a good look at Kluane Icefield. (© Earl L. Brown, staff)

mation, call (867) 841-4274. [ADVERTISEMENT] ▲

DC 1062.7 (1761 km) **DJ 327.3** (526.7 km) **Historic Milepost 1094. Private Aircraft:** Burwash Yukon government airstrip to north; elev. 2,643 feet/806m; length 6,000 feet/1,829m; gravel, no fuel.

DC 1066.2 (1767.5 km) **DJ 323.8** (521.1 km) First evidence southbound of June 1999 Burwash Landing fire (see **Milepost DC 1054.5**).

DC 1067 (1768.8 km) **DJ 323** (519.8 km) **Duke River** bridge (clearance 17.7 feet/5.4m). The Duke River flows into Kluane Lake; named for George Duke, an early prospector.

DC 1071.9 (1776.5 km) **DJ 318.1** (511.9 km) Turnout to north. Burwash Creek, named for Lachlin Taylor Burwash, a mining recorder at Silver City in 1903.

DC 1076.7 (1784.1 km) **DJ 313.3** (504.2 km) Sakiw Creek.

DC 1077.3 (1785.1 km) **DJ 312.7** (503.2 km) **Kluane River Overlook.** Rest area with information panels and observation platform overlooking Kluane River. Interpretive

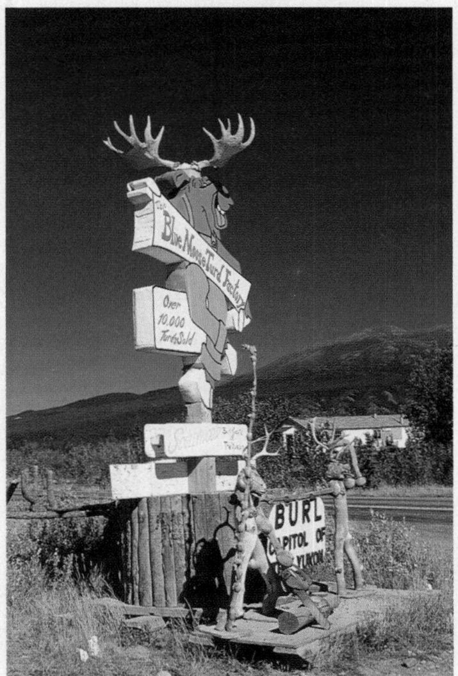

Roadside sign at Kluane Wilderness Village, "Burl Capital of the Yukon."

(© Earl L. Brown, staff)

panels describe the life cycle of the chum salmon that come to spawn in this river in August and September.

DC 1078.5 (1787 km) **DJ 311.5** (501.3 km) Buildings to west belong to Hudson Bay Mining and Smelting Co.'s Wellgreen Nickel Mines, named for Wellington Bridgeman Green, the prospector who discovered the mineral showing in 1952. During the mine's operation, from May 1972 to July 1973, three shiploads of concentrates (averaging 13,000 tons each) were trucked to Haines, AK. The material proved to be too insufficient to be economical. No facilities or services.

NOTE: Watch for road construction between Kilomeptreposts 1787 and 1800 in summer of 2000.

DC 1079.4 (1788.5 km) **DJ 310.6** (499.8 km) Quill Creek.

DC 1080.9 (1791 km) **DJ 309.1** (497.4 km) Glacier Creek. Kluane River to east of highway.

DC 1083.5 (1795.5 km) **DJ 306.5** (493.2 km) **Historic Milepost 1117.** Photo viewpoint turnout. Sign commemorates 1st Lt. Roland Small, of the 18th Engineers Regiment, who died in a jeep accident near this site during construction of the Alaska Highway in 1942. Short road to Kluane River; no turnaround.

DC 1084.6 (1797.2 km) **DJ 305.4** (491.5 km) **Historical Mile 1118, Kluane Wilderness Village** (unincorporated). Lodge complex with gas, restaurant, bar; camping and lodging. Open year-round. Scully, "Burl King of the North," resides here. His work can be seen across the highway from Kluane Wilderness Village, as well as in the saloon (which has a burl bar). Viewing platform of Mount Kennedy, Mount Logan and Mount Lucania. Halfway mark between Whitehorse and Tok. ▲

Kluane Wilderness Village offers all amenities to modern day travelers. 24-hour service station. Full-menu restaurant, "Scully's Saloon" and comfortable accommodation. Our Good Sam R.V. Park (with direct Satellite TV) is the ideal resting location halfway between Whitehorse and Tok, nestled in the beautiful Kluane Mountains. See our display ad on facing page for more. Phone/fax (867) 841-4141. [ADVERTISEMENT] ▲

DC 1086.6 (1799.5 km) **DJ 303.4** (488.3 km) Swede Johnson Creek. Turnout to east.

DC 1091.3 (1808 km) **DJ 298.7** (480.7 km) Buildings to east are a dormant pump station once used to pressure up fuel being transferred from Haines to Fairbanks.

DC 1095 (1814 km) **DJ 295** (474.7 km) NorthwesTel microwave tower visible ahead northbound.

Improved highway northbound.

DC 1095.4 (1814.6 km) **DJ 294.6** (474.1 km) Abandoned Mountain View Lodge. View of Donjek River Valley.

Alaska Highway workers faced one of their toughest construction jobs during completion of the Alaska Highway in 1943 from the Donjek River to the Alaska border. Swampy ground underlain by permafrost, numerous creeks, lakes and rivers, plus a thick insulating ground cover made this section particularly difficult for road builders.

In recent years, this same section of highway has been the object of a massive, ongoing reconstruction known as the Shakwak Highway project.

DC 1096.3 (1816 km) **DJ 293.7** (472.6 km) Turnout to west with view of **Donjek River Valley** and the Icefield Ranges of the St. Elias Mountains. Interpretive display.

DC 1099.7 (1819.5 km) **DJ 290.3** (467.2 km) **Historic Milepost 1130.** Turnout with interpretive panel on the Donjek River bridge. Sign reads: "Glacial rivers, like the Donjek, posed a unique problem for the builders of the Alaska Highway. These braided mountain streams would flood after a heavy rainfall or rapid glacial melt, altering the waters' course and often leaving bridges crossing dry ground."

DC 1100 (1820 km) **DJ 290** (466.7 km) **Donjek River** bridge (clearance 17.4 feet/5.3m). Access to river at north end of bridge on west side of highway. This wide silty river is a major tributary of the White River. According to R. Coutts, *Yukon: Places & Names,* the Donjek is believed to have been named by Charles Willard Hayes in 1891 from the Indian word for a peavine that grows in the area.

DC 1101.2 (1822 km) **DJ 288.8** (464.8 km) *NOTE: Watch for road construction between Kilometreposts 1822 and 1830 in summer 2000.*

DC 1108.7 (1834 km) **DJ 381.3** (613.6 km) *CAUTION: Loose gravel next 5 miles/8 km northbound; narrow, winding road, no shoulders. Road conditions alternate between excellent surface and wide road with gravel shoulders, to narrow road with loose gravel and no shoulders, northbound to Beaver Creek. Good highway begins northbound at Beaver Creek Highway Maintenance section and continues to the border.*

DC 1113.5 (1844.4 km) **DJ 276.5** (445 km) **Edith Creek** bridge, turnout to west. Try your hand at gold panning here; "colours" have been found. Grayling fishing, June through September.

DC 1113.8 (1844.8 km) **DJ 276.2** (444.5 km) **Historical Mile 1147. Pine Valley Motel and Cafe.** Hi! Thanks to all our customers for your patronage from your host Carmen and our staff. Open 24 hours. We have unleaded and diesel available (seniors gas discount). Minor repairs. RV park and campground, pull-throughs, power, picnic tables, free showers included. Free coffee included with any overnight stay. Good fishing stream nearby. Rooms, cabins with TV, bath, showers. Lounge and cafe with full menu bakery featuring hearty soups, homemade breads, pies, pastries—all made here.

Enjoy a scenic view while our friendly morning cook prepares you up a mean breakfast, or sink your teeth into Carmen's wonderful sweet rolls. We have cold beer and spirits for take-out, or sit and relax in our lounge. Pay phone, cubed ice, fishing license and tackle, souvenirs. Book exchange. Harleys welcome. Corral for overnighting horses. MasterCard and VISA. Interac direct payment. Enjoy your drive through Kluane National Park and keep it clean and green. Thanks! Phone/fax (867) 862-7407. [ADVERTISEMENT] ▲

DC 1118.3 (1852.2 km) **DJ 271.7** (437.2 km) Koidern River bridge No. 1.

DC 1118.8 (1853 km) **DJ 271.2** (436.4 km) **Historical Mile 1152. Lake Creek** Yukon government campground just west of highway; 27 large level sites (6 pull-through), water pump, litter barrels, firewood, firepits, picnic tables, kitchen shelter and outhouses. Camping permit ($8). ▲

DC 1122.7 (1859.5 km) **DJ 267.3** (430.2 km) **Historical Mile 1156.** Longs Creek.

DC 1125 (1863.5 km) **DJ 265** (426.5 km) Turnout to east with litter barrel.

DC 1125.7 (1864.7 km) **DJ 264.3** (425.3 km) **Pickhandle Lake** to west; interpretive panels on Native trading routes, pond life and muskrats. Good fishing from boat for northern pike all summer; also grayling, whitefish and lingcod.

DC 1128 (1868.4 km) **DJ 262** (421.6 km) Aptly named Reflection Lake to west mirrors the Kluane Range. The highway parallels this range between Koidern and Haines Junction.

NOTE: Watch for B.S.T. surfacing under way between Kilomereposts 1868 and 1872 in 2000.

DC 1130.6 (1872.6 km) **DJ 259.4** (417.4 km) **Historical Mile 1164.** Lodge.

DC 1130.7 (1872.8 km) **DJ 259.3** (417.3 km) Koidern River bridge No. 2.

DC 1133.7 (1877.6 km) **DJ 256.3** (412.5 km) **Historic Milepost 1167.** Bear Flats Lodge (closed in 1999, current status unknown).

DC 1135 (1880 km) **DJ 255** (410.4 km) **Historical Mile 1169**, Food, gas, diesel, dump station and camping. ▲

White River RV Park. See display ad this section. ▲

DC 1135.6 (1881 km) **DJ 254.4** (409.4 km) **White River** bridge. The White River, a major tributary of the Yukon River, was named by Hudson's Bay Co. explorer Robert Campbell for its white colour, caused by the volcanic ash in the water. *NOTE: This river is considered very dangerous; not recommended for boating.*

DC 1141.5 (1890.5 km) **DJ 248.5** (399.9 km) **Moose Lake** to west, grayling to 18 inches, use dry flies and small spinners, midsummer. Boat needed for lake.

DC 1144.3 (1895 km) **DJ 245.7** (395.4 km) Sanpete Creek, named by an early prospector after Sanpete County in Utah.

DC 1147.5 (1900.3 km) **DJ 242.5** (390.2 km) Dry Creek No. 1. Turnout to east.

DC 1150.3 (1904.5 km) **DJ 239.7** (385.7 km) **Historical Mile 1184.** Dry Creek No. 2. Historical marker to west about the Chrisna gold rush.

DC 1155 (1911.8 km) **DJ 235** (378.2 km) Small Lake to east.

DC 1155.2 (1913 km) **234.8** (377.9 km) **Historical Mile 1188.** Turnoff for **Snag Junction** Yukon government campground, 0.4 mile/0.6 km in on gravel loop road. There are 15 tent and vehicle sites (some level), a kitchen shelter, outhouses, picnic tables, firewood, firepits and litter barrels. Camping permit ($8). Small-boat launch. Swimming in Small Lake. ▲

A dirt road (status unknown) connects the Alaska Highway here with the abandoned airfield and Indian village at **Snag** to the northeast. Snag's claim to fame is the lowest recorded temperature in Canada: -83° F/-63° C on Feb. 3, 1947.

DC 1162.1 (1924.5 km) **DJ 227.9** (366.7 km) Inger Creek.

DC 1165.7 (1930 km) **DJ 224.3** (361 km) View of Nutzotin Mountains to northwest, Kluane Ranges to southwest. On a clear day you should be able to see the snow-clad Wrangell Mountains in the distance to the west.

DC 1167.2 (1932.4 km) **DJ 222.8** (358.5 km) Beaver Creek plank bridge, clearance 17.1 feet/5.2m.

Beaver Creek

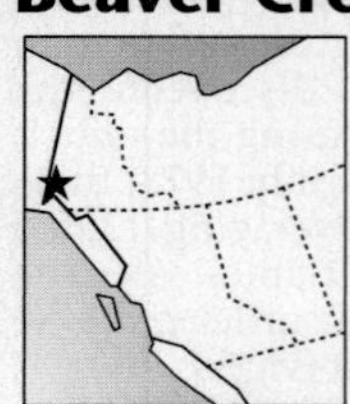

DC 1168.5 (1934.5 km) **DJ 221.5** (356.4 km) **Historic Milepost 1202.** Driving distance to Haines Junction, 184 miles/295 km; to Tok, 113 miles/182 km; to Haines, 334 miles/ 538. km. **Population:** 112. **Emergency Services: RCMP**, phone (867) 862-5555. **Ambulance**, phone (867) 862-3333. **Nursing Station:** (867) 862-4444.

Visitor Information: Yukon government Visitor Reception Centre, open daily late May through mid-September. Phone (867) 862-7321. The visitor centre has a book of dried Yukon wildflowers for those interested in the flora of the territory.

Private Aircraft: Beaver Creek Yukon government airstrip 1 NW; see description at **Milepost DC 1170.3**.

Site of the old Canadian customs station. Local residents were pleased to see customs relocated north of town in 1983, having long endured the flashing lights and screaming sirens set off whenever a tourist forgot to stop.

Beaver Creek is 1 of 2 sites where Alaska Highway construction crews working from

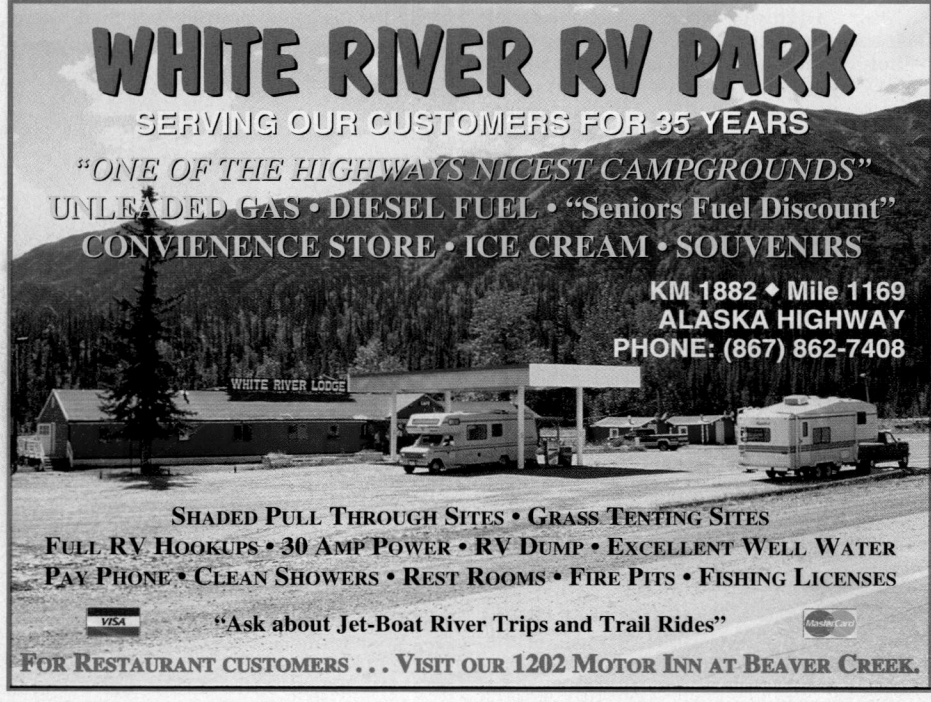

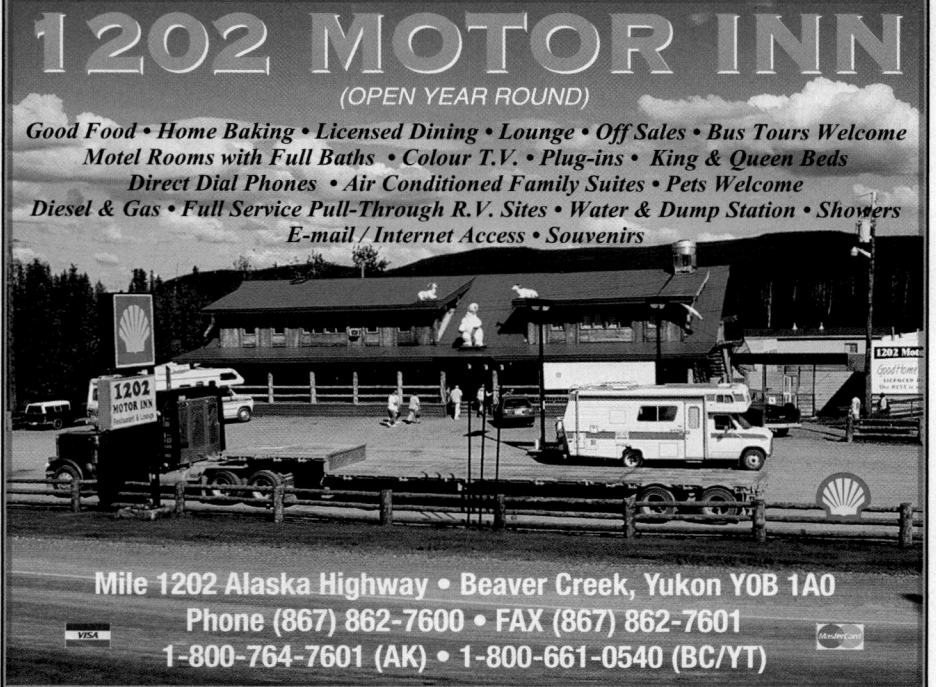

BEAVER CREEK ADVERTISERS

Ida's Motel & Restaurant ....Ph. (867) 862-7223
1202 Motor Inn ....Ph. (867) 862-7600
Westmark Inn Beaver Creek................Ph. (867) 862-7501

opposite directions connected the highway. In October 1942, Alaska Highway construction operations were being rushed to conclusion as winter set in. Eastern and western sector construction crews (the 97th and 18th Engineers) pushed through to meet at a junction on Beaver Creek on Oct. 28., thus making it possible for the first time for vehicles to travel the entire length of the highway. East–west crews had connected at Contact Creek on Sept. 24, 1942.

Motels, gas stations with repair service, mini-mart and licensed restaurants are located here. (Beaver Creek is an overnight stop for bus travelers.) A hostel operated here in 1999; inquire locally. There is a post office; a bank, open 2 days a week, located in the post office building; community library; and public swimming pool beside the community club. RV park with hookups, hot showers, store, laundry and dump station at the Westmark. ▲

The interesting looking church here is **Our Lady of Grace mission**. Built in 1961 from a salvaged quonset hut left over from highway construction days, it is 1 of 3 Catholic missions on the north Alaska Highway (the others are in Burwash Landing and Haines Junction). **St. Columba's Anglican Church** in Beaver Creek was prefabricated in Whitehorse and constructed in one week in 1975.

Stretch your legs on 1 of 2 walking paths (both 1.2 miles/2 km in length) at either end of town. One goes east to the Beaver Creek bridge; the other west to Canada Customs.

Yukon Centennial Gold Rush figurines and displays are located just west of How Far West Plaza. The plaza—at town centre—features information panels on wildlife and a map of Beaver Creek.

Check with the information centre about the live stage show at the Westmark Inn, evenings in summer; admission charged. The Westmark also has a wildlife display and mini-golf.

Alaska Highway Log

(continued)

Distance* from Dawson Creek (DC) is followed by distance from Delta Junction (DJ). Original mileposts are indicated in the text as Historical Mile.

*In Canada, mileages from Dawson Creek are based on actual driving distance, not historical mileposts, and kilometres are based on physical kilometreposts *as they occurred in summer 1999*. Mileages from Delta Junction are also based on actual driving distance, not historical mileposts, but are followed by the metric conversion to kilometres.

DC 1169.7 (1936.3 km) **DJ 220.3** (354.5 km) Rest area to west with litter barrels, picnic tables and outhouses.

DC 1170.3 (1937.3 km) **DJ 219.7** (353.6km) **Private Aircraft:** Beaver Creek Yukon government airstrip; elev. 2,129 feet/649m; length 3,740 feet/1,140m; gravel; no fuel. Airport of entry for Canada customs.

DC 1170.5 (1937.6 km) **DJ 219.5** (353.2 km) **Beaver Creek Canada Customs** station; phone (403) 862-7230. Open 24 hours a day year-round. All traffic entering Canada must stop here for clearance.

DC 1175.4 (1945.5 km) **DJ 214.8** (345.7 km) Snag Creek plank bridge.

DC 1176.3 (1946.9 km) **DJ 213.7** (343.9 km) Mirror Creek.

DC 1177 (1950 km) **DJ 213** (342.8 km) **Swan Lake**, east side of highway, is home to a nesting pair of trumpeter swans. Also look for shorebirds and migratory waterfowl.

DC 1178.3 (1952 km) **DJ 211.7** (340.7 km) Lake to east, turnout to west.

DC 1186 (1963 km) **DJ 204** (328.3 km) Little Scottie Creek.

DC 1189.5 (1967.5 km) **DJ 200.5** (322.7 km) **Historic Milepost 1221.** Turnout with plaque and other markers at **Canada–U.S. International Border**. Litter barrels. From the viewing decks, note the narrow clearing marking the border. This is part of the 20-foot-/6-m-wide swath cut by surveyors from 1904 to 1920 along the 141st meridian (from Demarcation Point on the Arctic Ocean south 600 miles/966 km to Mount St.

Elias in the Wrangell Mountains) to mark the Alaska–Canada border. This swath continues south to mark the boundary between southeastern Alaska and Canada. Portions of the swath are cleared periodically by the International Boundary Commission.

TIME ZONE CHANGE: Alaska observes Alaska time; Yukon Territory observes Pacific time. Alaska Time is 1 hour earlier than Pacific Time.

DC 1189.8 (1968 km) **DJ 200.2** (322.2 km) **Historical Mile 1221.8.** U.S. customs border station.

IMPORTANT: The MILEPOST® log now switches to physical mileposts for northbound travelers. For southbound travelers, the log is based on actual driving distance. The Alaska Highway is approximately 32 miles/51 km shorter than the traditional figure of 1,221.8 miles between Dawson Creek and the YT–AK border. Please read the information on Mileposts and Kilometreposts in the introduction to the Alaska Highway.

Northbound: Fair to good pavement to Fairbanks. Watch for frost heaves, potholes and pavement breaks next 40 miles/64 km.

Southbound: Narrow, winding road to Haines Junction. Improved highway to Beaver Creek, fair to good pavement to Haines Junction. Watch for rough spots, gravel breaks and road construction.

ALASKA ROUTE 2
Distance* from Dawson Creek (DC) is followed by distance from Delta Junction (DJ).
*Mileages from Dawson Creek and Fairbanks are based on physical mileposts in Alaska. Kilometres given are the metric equivalents of these mileages.

DC 1221.8 (1966.3 km) **DJ 200.2** (322.2 km) **Port Alcan** U.S. Customs and Immigration Service border station, open 24 hours a day year-round; pay phone (credit card and collect calls only) and restrooms. All traffic entering Alaska must stop for clearance. Phone (907) 774-2242; emergencies, (907) 774-2252.

Border Branch U.S. post office is located here (ZIP 99764); ask for directions at the customs office.

DC 1222.5 (1967.4 km) **DJ 199.5** (321.1 km) **Tetlin National Wildlife Refuge** boundary sign to west. Established in 1980, the 730,000-acre refuge stretches south from the Alaska Highway and west from the Canadian border. The major physical features include rolling hills, hundreds of small lakes and 2 glacial rivers, the Nabesna and Chisana), which combine to form the Tanana River. The refuge has a very high density of nesting waterfowl. Annual duck production in favorable years exceeds 50,000. Among the larger birds using the refuge are trumpeter swans, sandhill cranes, Pacific and common loons, osprey, bald eagles and ptarmigan. Other wildlife includes moose, black and grizzly bear, wolf, coyote, beaver, red fox, lynx and caribou. Activities allowed on the refuge include wildlife observation, hunting, fishing, camping, hiking and trapping. Check with refuge personnel in Tok prior to your visit for more detailed information. Write Refuge Manager, Tetlin National Wildlife Refuge, Box 779, Tok, AK 99780; or phone (907) 883-5312. Information on the refuge is also available at the Tetlin National Wildlife Visitor Center at **Milepost DC 1229** on the Alaska Highway.

DC 1223.4 (1968.9 km) **DJ 198.6** (319.6 km) Scottie Creek bridge. Old cabins to west.

DC 1224.6 (1970.7 km) **DJ 197.4** (317.7 km) Double-ended gravel turnout to southwest at Highway Lake with interpretive sign on wetlands; beaver lodges.

DC 1225.4 (1972 km) **DJ 196.6** (316.4 km) Tetlin NWR Desper Creek parking area and canoe launch.

DC 1225.5 (1972.2 km) **DJ 196.5** (316.2 km) Border City Motel & RV Park west side of highway.

Border City Motel & RV Park. See display ad this section. ▲

DC 1226 (1973 km) **DJ 196** (315.4 km) Scottie Creek Services east side of highway.

Scottie Creek Services. See display ad this section.

The old cabin adjacent Scottie Creek Services was identified in summer 1999 as the "Original Historic Canadian Customs Log

Cabin (1946–1952)". It was built by Pete Ecklund and Bill Blair of Beaver Creek, YT. Originally it stood at Milepost 1220, but it was purchased by an unknown party in the early 1960s and moved to its present location. The cabin is being restored.

DC 1227.8 (1975.9 km) **DJ 194.2** (312.5 km) Large double-ended paved parking area to west with interpretive sign on migratory birds and area geography. Good view to south of lakes in Chisana (SHOE-sanna) River valley. The Nutzotin Mountains are to the west.

DC 1229 (1977.8 km) **DJ 193** (310.6 km) **Tetlin National Wildlife Refuge Visitor Center** west side of highway. Viewing deck with telescopes, displays on wildlife and other subjects. Nature videos shown on

request. Free audio tour tape available for travelers headed towards Tok (return tape to Public Lands Information Center in Tok). Restrooms (wheelchair accessible). Freshwater hose located beneath cache. The visitor center is open 8 A.M. to 4:30 P.M. May 25 to September 5. Current highway conditions and fishing information posted on outside message boards. ♿

DC 1230.9 (1980.9 km) **DJ 200.1** (322 km) View of Island Lake.

DC 1233.3 (1984.7 km) **DJ 188.7** (303.7 km) Long paved double-ended parking area to northeast on old alignment.

DC 1237 (1990.7 km) **DJ 185** (297.7 km) Trail to **Hidden Lake** (1 mile/1.6 km); rainbow fishing. Interpretive signs on rainbow trout and permafrost.

DC 1240 (1995.5 km) **DJ 182** (292.9 km) Turnout to west; no easy turnaround. Walk-in access to **Willow Lake** for fishing (stocked with trout every other year).

DC 1240.3 (1996 km) **DJ 181.7** (292.4 km) Waist-high vertical corrugated metal culverts topped with cone-shaped "hats" seen on either side of highway are an experiment to keep ground from thawing and thus prevent frost heaves.

DC 1241.9 (1998.6 km) **DJ 180.1** (289.8 km) Tetlin NWR boundary marker southbound.

DC 1243 (2000.4 km) **DJ 179** (288.1 km) Good examples of sand dune road cut and rock graffiti typical along this stretch of highway.

DC 1243.6 (2001.3 km) **DJ 178.4** (287.1 km) Scenic viewpoint to south on loop road has interpretive signs on fire management and the effects of forest fires on the natural history of area. Sand dunes.

DC 1246.6 (2006.1 km) **DJ 175.4** (282.3 km) **Gardiner Creek** bridge; parking to west at south end of bridge. Grayling fishing.

DC 1247.6 (2007.8 km) **DJ 174.4** (280.7 km) Paved double-ended viewpoint to east.

DC 1249.3 (2010.5 km) **DJ 172.7** (277.9 km) **Historic Milepost 1254.** Sharp turn west for **Deadman Lake Campground** (Tetlin NWR), 1.2 miles/1.9 km in on narrow dirt and gravel access road. Turnout at highway junction with campground access road. The campground has 18 sites in spruce forest along the loop road; firepits, toilets, picnic tables, no drinking water, boat ramp, interpretive signs, information board and self-guided nature trail. Evening naturalist programs offered Monday through Friday in

summer. Wheelchair accessible. Scenic spot. Swimming and fishing. Northern pike average 2 feet, but skinny (local residents call them "snakes"); use wobbling lures or spinners. ♿▲

DC 1250.1 (2011.8 km) **DJ 171.9** (276.6 km) Rest area to west is a double-ended paved parking area with picnic tables and concrete fireplaces. No water or toilets.

DC 1252.2 (2015.2 km) **169.8** (273.2 km) Double-ended dirt turnout on hill to southwest with interpretive sign on solar basins (warm ponds and shallow marshes) and scenic viewpoint.

DC 1253.6 (2017.4 km) DJ 168.4 (271 km) Turn up hill to southwest for Frontier Surplus.

Frontier Surplus. Military surplus goods. Clothing, sleeping bags, extreme cold weather "bunny boots," military tents, ammunition, tanned furs. Alaska T-shirts and caps. Local crafts, shed moose and caribou antlers. Antler products, belt buckles, bolo ties, hat racks, handmade ulus. "Moosquitoes," diamond willow lamps and canes, finished or unfinished. Used Alaska

license plates, cold pop. Open late every day. Motorhome and RV loop. Phone (907) 778-2274. [ADVERTISEMENT]

DC 1254 (2018.1 km) **DJ 168** (270.4 km) Views of lakes and muskeg in Chisana River valley.

DC 1256.3 (2021.7 km) **DJ 165.7** (266.7 km) Northway state highway maintenance camp; no services.

DC 1256.7 (2022.5 km) **DJ 165.3** (266 km) Turnoff to west for **Lakeview Campground** (Tetlin NWR), 0.2 mile from highway via a narrow, bumpy access road. There are 8 sites on a small loop next to beautiful

Yarger Lake; tables, toilets, firepits, firewood, garbage container, no drinking water. Wheelchair accessible. Interpretive signs. *NOTE: Not recommended for trailers, 5th wheels or RVs over 30 feet.* ♿▲

This is a good place to view ducks and loons. Look for the Nutzotin Mountains to the south and Mentasta Mountains to the west. These 2 mountain masses form the eastern end of the Alaska Range.

Roadside wildflowers include sweet pea, pale yellow Indian paintbrush, yarrow and Labrador tea.

DC 1260.2 (2028 km) **DJ 161.8** (260.4 km) 1260 Inn roadhouse (closed).

DC 1263 (2032.5 km) **DJ 159** (255.9 km) Wrangell View Truck Stop; current status unknown.

DC 1263.5 (2033.4 km) **DJ 158.5** (255.1 km) Chisana River parallels the highway to the southwest. This is the land of a thousand ponds, most unnamed. Good trapping country. In early June, travelers may note numerous cottony white seeds blowing in the wind; these seeds are from willow and poplars.

DC 1264 (2034.2 km) **DJ 158** (254.3 km) **Northway Junction.** Campground, gas, laundromat, store, and Native arts and crafts shop located at junction. An Alaska State Trooper office is located on the east side of the highway. ▲

Naabia Niign Campground & Athabascan Indian Crafts. See display ad this section. ▲

Junction with 9-mile-long Northway Road (paved), which leads south across the Chisana River bridge to Northway Airport and village (see description facing page).

DC 1265 (2035.8 km) **DJ 154.6** (248.8 km) Northbound, the highway cuts through several sand dunes stabilized by aspen and

Perhaps the most commonly seen animal in the North is the Arctic ground squirrel. (© Beth Davidow)

spruce trees. *CAUTION: Watch for loose gravel and rough road.*

DC 1267.3 (2039.5 km) **DJ 154.7** (249 km) Wonderful view of the Tanana River at Beaver Slide. The Tanana River is largest tributary of the Yukon River.

DC 1268.1 (2040.8 km) **DJ 153.9** (247.7 km) Beaver Creek bridge. The tea-colored water flowing in the creek is the result of tannins absorbed by the water as it flows through muskeg. This phenomenon may be observed in other Northern creeks.

DC 1269 (2042.2 km) **DJ 153** (246.2 km) **Historic Milepost 1271.** Scenic viewpoint. Double-ended gravel turnout to west has a litter barrel and Gold Rush Centennial sign about the short-lived Chisana Gold Rush. The 1913 gold discovery on the north side of the Wrangell Mountains triggered the last major rush of the Gold Rush era. Some 2,000 stampeders reached the Chisana diggings, but most left disappointed: only a few creeks had gold and the area was remote and expensive to supply. The boom lasted little more than a year.

DC 1272.7 (2048.2 km) **DJ 149.3** (240.3 km) Scenic viewpoint to west is a double-ended paved turnout with interpretive sign on pond ecology and mosquitoes.

To the northwest the Tanana River flows near the highway; beyond, the Kalukna River snakes its way through plain and marshland. Mentasta Mountains are visible to the southwest.

DC 1274 (2050.2 km) **DJ 148** (238.2 km) Paved parking area to west.

In June, wild sweet peas create thick borders along the highway. This is rolling country, with aspen, birch, cottonwood, willow and white spruce.

DC 1284 (2066.3 km) **DJ 138** (222.1 km) Distance marker shows Tok 30 miles, Fairbanks 235 miles, Anchorage 365 miles.

DC 1284.6 (2067.3 km) **DJ 137.4** (221.1 km) Long double-ended turnout to east.

DC 1285.7 (2069.1 km) **DJ 136.3** (219.3 km) Granite intrusion in older metamorphosed rock is exposed by road cut.

DC 1289 (2074.4 km) **DJ 133** (214 km) First view northbound of 3.4-mile-/5.5-km-long Midway Lake.

DC 1289.4 (2075 km) **DJ 132.6** (213.4 km) **Historic Milepost 1292.** Turnout uphill on east side of highway. *NOTE: Difficult access for large vehicles and trailers, easier access from southbound lane.* View of Midway Lake and the Wrangell Mountains. Interpretive signs on Wrangell–St. Elias National Park and Native peoples.

DC 1290 (2076 km) **DJ 132** (212.4 km) Beautiful view of Midway Lake southbound.

DC 1291 (2077.6 km) **DJ 131** (210.8 km) Burn area from 1998 fire.

DC 1292.4 (2079.8 km) **DJ 129.6** (208.5 km) Paved turnout west side.

DC 1293.7 (2081.9 km) **DJ 128.3** (206.5 km) Paved turnout west side.

DC 1294 (2082.4 km) **DJ 128** (206 km) Distance marker shows Tok 20 miles, Fairbanks 225 miles, Anchorage 355 miles.

DC 1301.7 (2094.8 km) **DJ 120.3** (193.6 km) **Historic Milepost 1306 Tetlin Junction.** 40 Mile Roadhouse (closed, current status unknown).

Junction of the Alaska Highway with the Taylor Highway (Alaska Route 5), which leads northeast 160.3 miles to Eagle on the Yukon River (see TAYLOR HIGHWAY section page 263). The Taylor Highway junctions with Yukon Highway 9 (Top of the World Highway) to Dawson City. See KLONDIKE LOOP section page 244 for log of Yukon Highway 9 (Top of the World Highway) and description of Dawson City.

NOTE: If you are traveling to Dawson City, keep in mind that both the Canada and U.S. customs stations are closed at night; you CANNOT cross the border unless customs stations are open. Customs hours in summer have been 8 A.M. to 8 P.M. Alaska time, 9 A.M. to 9 P.M. Pacific time on the Canadian side. Travelers are advised to check for current information at Alaska Public Lands Information Center in Tok.

DC 1302.7 (2096.4 km) **DJ 119.3** (192 km) Scenic viewpoint to southwest is a paved turnout with Gold Rush Centennial signs on Alaska's Gold Rush era and the gold

Northway

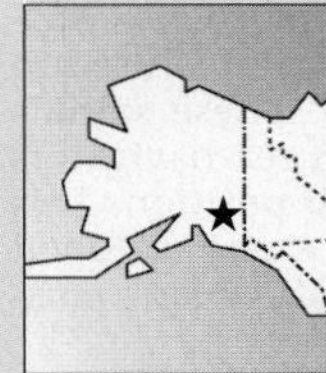

Located south of the Alaska Highway on Northway Road. **Population:** 351 (area). **Emergency Services: Alaska State Troopers,** phone (907) 778-2245. **EMS,** phone (907) 778-2211. **Clinic,** phone (907) 778-2283.

Elevation: 1,710 feet/521m. **Climate:** Mean monthly temperature in July, 58.5°F/15°C; average high, 69°F/21°C. Mean monthly temperature in January, -21°F/-30°C; average low -27°F/-33°C. Record high 91°F/33°C in June 1969; record low-72°F/-58°C in January 1952. Average annual precipitation, 10 inches; snowfall 30 inches.

Private Aircraft: Northway airport, adjacent south; elev. 1,716 feet; length 5,130 feet; asphalt; fuel 100LL, Jet, MOGAS; customs available. Floatplanes use Yarger Lake 8 nm E.

Northway consists of 3 dispersed settlements: Northway Junction at **Milepost DC 1264** on the Alaska Highway; Northway at the airport, 6.5 miles south of Northway Junction on Northway Road; and the Native Village of Northway, 2 miles beyond the airport on the spur road. Northway has a community hall, post office, school. FAA station and customs office. Visitor services include a motel, cafe and bar at the airport.

Northway is the aviation entry point into Alaska for most private planes. According to customs agent Thomas Teasdale, some 700 planes clear customs each year here, most arriving between May and September.

Northway's airport was built in the 1940s as part of the Northwest Staging Route. This cooperative project of the United States and Canada was a chain of air bases from Edmonton, AB, through Whitehorse, YT, to Fairbanks. This chain of air bases helped build up and supply Alaska defense during WWII and also was used during construction of the Alcan and the Canol project. Lend-lease aircraft bound for Russia were flown up this route to Ladd Field (now Fort Wainwright) in Fairbanks. A propeller from one of these lend-lease planes (a P-39 Bell Aerocobra) that crashed in a nearby marsh in 1944, is on display outside the Northwest Airport Lodge.

Historically occupied by Athabascan Indians, Northway was named to honor the village chief who adopted the name of a riverboat captain in the early 1900s. (Chief Walter Northway died in 1993. He was thought to be 117 years old.) The rich Athabascan traditions of dancing, crafts, and hunting and trapping continue today in Northway Village. Local Athabascan handicrafts available for purchase include birchbark baskets, beadwork accessories, and moose hide and fur items such as moccasins, mukluks, mittens and hats.

Confluence of Moose Creek and Chisana River, about 0.8 mile/1.3 km downstream from Chisana River bridge on Northway Road, south side of river, northern pike to 15 lbs., use red-and-white spoon, spring or fall. Look for rivers on the Chisana River. **Chisana River,** downstream from bridge, lingcod (burbot) to 8 lbs., use chunks of liver or meat, spring. **Nabesna Slough,** south end of runway, grayling to 3 lbs., use spinner or gold flies, late May.

Although lynx range throughout Alaska, few people see them in the wild. These shy cats prowl mostly at night. Their primary prey is snowshoe hare.
(© Rich Reid, Color of Nature)

strike on the Fortymile River in 1886.

Distance marker northbound shows Tok 12 miles, Fairbanks 217 miles, Anchorage 347 miles.

DC 1303.4 (2097.5 km) **DJ 118.6** (190.9 km) Tanana River bridge.

DC 1303.6 (2097.9 km) **DJ 118.4** (190.5 km) Informal parking area and boat launch to east at north end of bridge. Tanana (TAN-uh-naw), an Indian name, was first reported by the Western Union Telegraph Expedition of 1886. According to William Henry Dall, chief scientist of the expedition, the name means "mountain river."

From here the highway parallels the Tanana River to Fairbanks. The Alaska Range looms in the distance.

DC 1304.6 (2099.5 km) **DJ 117.4** (188.9 km) Evidence of burn from here north to Tok. The Tok River fire occurred in July of 1990 and burned more than 100,000 acres. The fire closed the Alaska Highway and Tok Cutoff and threatened to engulf the town of Tok. Tok was evacuated as firefighters' efforts to stop the fire appeared to be in vain. A "miracle wind" diverted the fire from town at the last minute.

DC 1308.5 (2105.7 km) **DJ 113.5** (182.6 km) Weigh station; phone. Turnoff to U.S. Coast Guard Loran-C station and signal towers.

This Loran (Long Range Aids to Navigation) station is 1 of 7 in Alaska. It was constructed by the U.S. Coast Guard in 1976. A series of four 700-foot/213-m towers suspends a multi-element wire antenna used to transmit navigation signals. These signals may be used by air, land and sea navigators as an aid in determining their position. This station is located here as necessary for good geometry with 2 Gulf of Alaska loran transmitting stations.

DC 1308.8 (2106.3 km) **DJ 113.2** (182.2 km) Paved turnout to south.

DC 1309.2 (2106.9 km) **DJ 112.8** (181.5 km) Turnoff to north for **Tok River State Recreation Site**; 43 campsites (maximum vehicle length 60 feet) located along a good loop road beside the Tok River; campground

host, tables, firepits, toilets (wheelchair accessible), litter barrels, nature trail, boat launch and pay phone. Check bulletin board for schedule of interpretive programs. Camping fee $10/night. *CAUTION: Swift water.* ♿▲

DC 1309.4 (2107.2 km) **DJ 112.6** (181.2 km) Tok River bridge.

DC 1312.7 (2112.5 km) **DJ 109.3** (175.9 km) Tok community limits. Mountain views ahead northbound.

DC 1312.8 (2112.7 km) **DJ 109.2** (175.7 km) Tok Dog Mushers Assoc. track and buildings. Paved bike trail from Tok ends here.

DC 1313 (2113 km) **DJ 109** (175.4 km) Tok Junction airstrip. See Private Aircraft information in Tok section. Entering Tok (northbound), description follows.

Southbound travelers: Driving distance from Tok to Beaver Creek is 113 miles/182 km; Haines Junction 296 miles/476 km; Haines (departure point for Alaska state ferries) 446.5 miles/718.5 km; and Whitehorse 396 miles/637 km.

CAUTION: Watch for and slow down for sections of rough road with loose gravel and road construction southbound to border.

DC 1313.1 (2113.1 km) **DJ 108.9** (175.3 km) **Tok Gateway Salmon Bake and RV Park.** Rated, *Alaska's Best Places*, Tok's Gateway Salmon Bake, features outdoor flame-

grilled Alaska king salmon, halibut, ribs and reindeer sausage. Buffalo burgers. Chowder. Good food, friendly people; casual dining at its best. Open 11 A.M. to 9 P.M., except Sunday 4 P.M. to 9 P.M. Free shuttle bus service from local hotels and RV parks. Wooded RV and tent sites with tables, clean restrooms, dump station and water. Showers available. Free dry camping with dinner. Phone/fax (907) 883-5555. Winter phone (520) 685-2687. Internet www.tokalaska.com/toksamon.shtml. [ADVERTISEMENT] ▲

DC 1313.2 (2113.3 km) **DJ 108.8** (175.1 km) **Willard's RV & Auto Service.** See display ad this section.

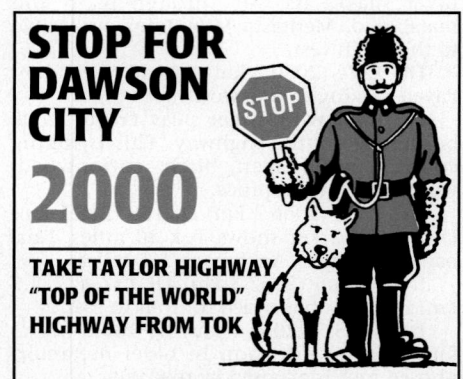

DC 1313.3 (2113.5 km) **DJ 108.7** (174.9 km) **Village Texaco Foodmart.** Filtered unleaded and premium gas and diesel. Lubricants and propane. Automatic teller machine, laundromat, phone cards, pay phones and clean restrooms. Deli chicken, burritos, mojos, snacks, pop, ice, milk shakes, ice cream and espresso. RV supplies. Alaskan souvenirs. Across highway from Tok RV Village. See display ad this section. [ADVERTISEMENT]

DC 1313.3 (2113.5 km) **DJ 108.7** (174.9 km) **Young's Motel and Fast Eddy's Restaurant.** A touch of Alaskana in a modern

setting. Affordable, clean and spacious. We cater to the independent highway traveler. Open year-round with all the amenities: telephones, private baths, satellite TV, ample parking. Nonsmoking rooms available. Check in at Fast Eddy's full-service restaurant, open 6 A.M. to midnight. Reserve early! P.O. Box 482, Tok, AK 99780. (907) 883-4411; fax (907) 883-5023; e-mail edyoung@ptinet.com. [ADVERTISEMENT]

DC 1313.3 (2113.5 km) **DJ 108.7** (174.9 km) **The Bull Shooter Sporting Goods & RV Park.** Fishing and hunting licenses and supplies. Stay at the Bull Shooter's RV park. 30 spaces, 24 pull-throughs. Full or partial hookups, 30-amp electric, dump station. Non-metered showers, ice, phone. VISA, MasterCard. On the left coming into Tok. P.O. Box 553, Tok, AK 99780. Reservations: (907) 883-5625. See display ad in Tok section. [ADVERTISEMENT] ▲

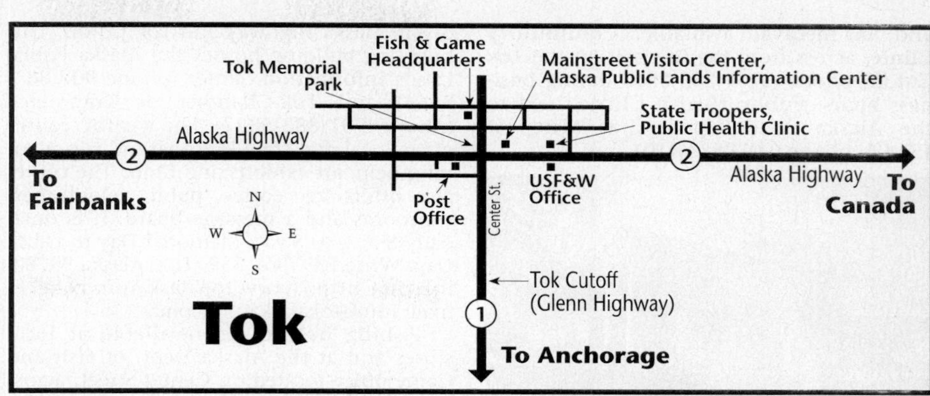

DC 1313.4 (2113.6 km) **DJ 108.6** (174.8 km) **Tok RV Village.** Alaska's finest. Good Sam or KOA cards honored. Convenient pull-through spaces with 20-30-50 amp. Full and partial hookups, clean restrooms and showers, dump station, laundry, vehicle wash, picnic tables, public phones, e-mail terminals. Gift shop. RV supplies, ice. MasterCard, VISA and Discover. Located across highway from Village Texaco Foodmart. Restaurants, liquor store, night club, hardware store, oil change and lube service nearby. See display ad this section. [ADVERTISEMENT] ▲

DC 1314.1 (2114.8 km) **DJ 107.9** (173.6 km) U.S. Fish and Wildlife Office to west; State Troopers to east.

DC 1314.2 (2115 km) **DJ 107.8** (173.5 km) **Tok Junction.** Tok Mainstreet Visitor Center and Tok Memorial Park (picnicking) to east at intersection with Alaska Route 1. See description of Tok following.

Junction of the Alaska Highway (Alaska Route 2) and the Tok Cutoff to the Glenn Highway (Alaska Route 1), which leads 328 miles to Anchorage. Turn to the GLENN HIGHWAY section on page 270 for log of that route.

Tok

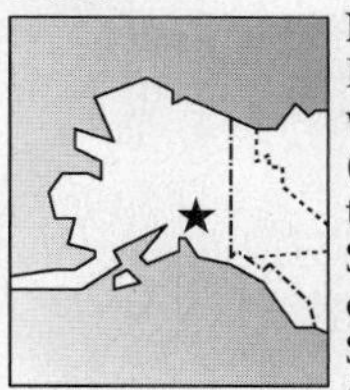

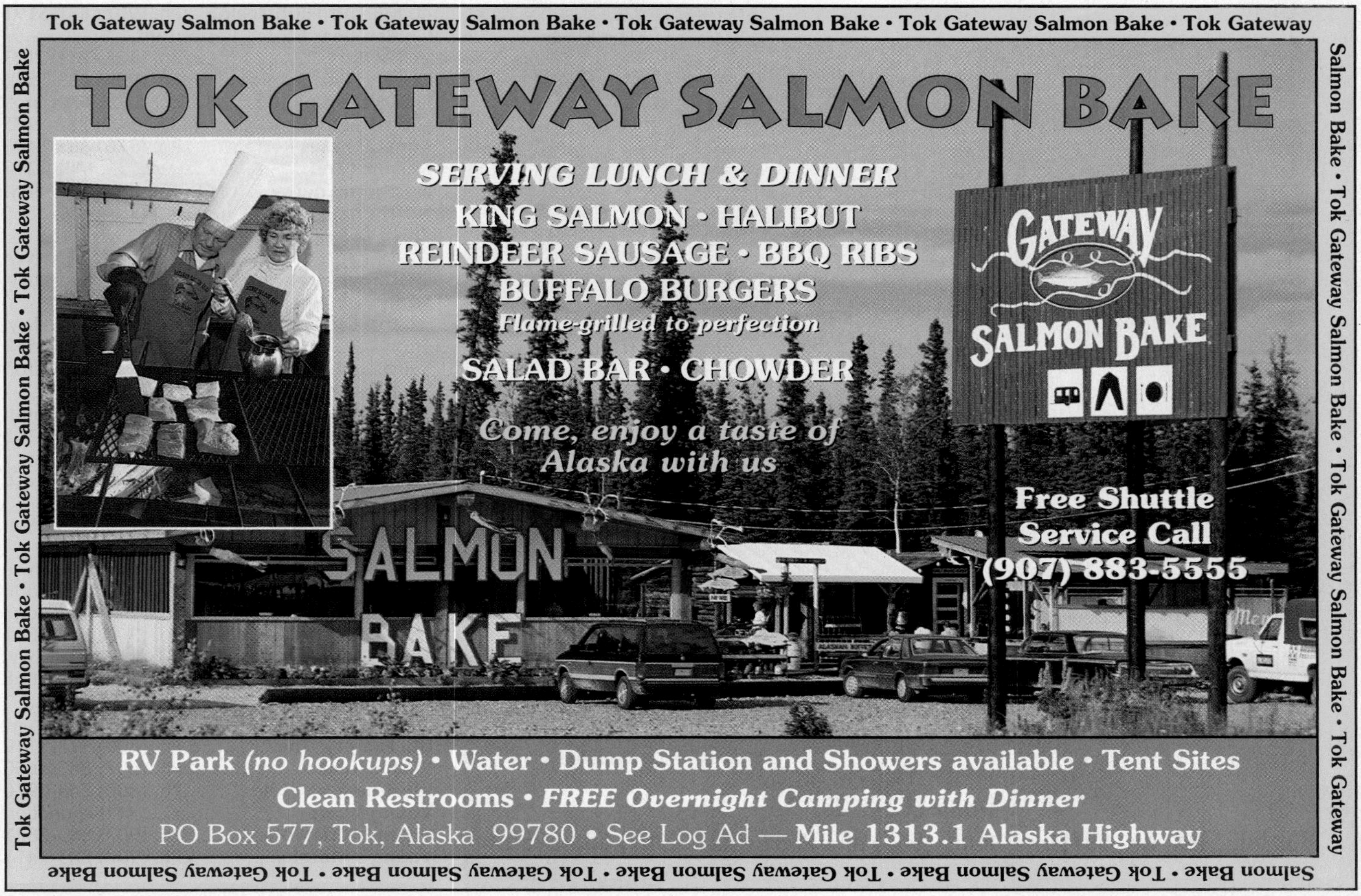

Milepost 1314.2 Alaska Highway, at the junction with the Tok Cutoff (Glenn Highway). **Population:** 1,214. **Emergency Services:** Phone 911 for emergency services. **Alaska State Troopers**, phone (907) 883-5111. **Fire Department**, phone (907) 883-2333. **Ambulance**, phone (907) 883-2301. EMT squad and air medivac available. **Community Clinic**, across from the fire hall on the Tok Cutoff, phone (907) 883-5855 during business hours. **Public Health Clinic**, next to the Alaska State Troopers at **Milepost 1314.1**, phone (907) 883-4101.

Visitor Information: Tok Mainstreet Visitiors Center, is located at the junction of the Alaska Highway and Tok Cutoff. This huge log building houses the Alaska Public Lands Information Center (phone 907/883-5666) and Tok Chamber of Commerce (phone 907/883-5887) The visitor center offers local and state information, trip planning help, art exhibits and films. The center also offers free coffee, public telephones, restrooms and a message board. It is open daily 8 A.M. to 8 P.M. Memorial Day to Labor Day. Write P.O. Box 359, Tok, Alaska 99780; internet http://www.tokalaskainfo.com. E-mail: info@tokalaskainfo.com.

Fishing licenses are available at local stores and at the Alaska Dept. of Fish and Game office located on Center Street, across from Tok Mainstreet Visitor Center at **Milepost DC 1314.2**. Contact ADF&G, Box 305, Tok, AK 99780; Phone (907) 883-2971.

The U.S. Fish & Wildlife Service office is located at **Milepost DC 1314.1** next to the grocery store, directly across the highway from the State Troopers. Visitors are welcome. Stop in for information regarding Tetlin National Wildlife Refuge and wildlife import/export permits. Office hours are 7:30 A.M. to 5 P.M., weekdays. Or write U.S. Fish & Wildlife Service, Box 155, Tok, AK 99780; phone (907) 883-5312.

Elevation: 1,635 feet/498m. **Climate:** Mean monthly temperature in January is -19° F/-29°C; average low is -32°F/-36°C. Mean monthly temperature in July is 59°F/14°C; average high is 72°F/22°C. Record low was -71°F/-57°C (January 1965); record high, 99°F/37°C. **Radio:** FM stations are 90.5, 91.1 (KUAC-FM, University of Alaska–Fairbanks) and 101.5. **Television:** Satellite channel 13. **Newspaper:** *Mukluk News* (twice monthly).

Private Aircraft: Tok Junction, 1 E; elev. 1,630 feet; length 2,510 feet; asphalt; fuel 100LL; unattended. Tok airstrip, on Tok

(Continues on page 188)

TOK ADVERTISERS

"A Tent in Tok" ............P.O. Box 110
A WinterCabin B&B ....Ph. (907) 883-5655
All Alaska Gifts & Crafts..........N. corner of junction
Bull Shooter Sporting Goods, The ....Ph. (907) 883-5625
Bull Shooter RV Park, The ....Mile 1313.3 Alaska Hwy.
Burnt Paw ....Adjacent post office
Cabins Outback B&B ....Ph. (907) 883-4121
Cleft of the Rock B&B..........Ph. (800) 478-5646
Faith Chapel..........First & Center
Fast Eddy's Restaurant..........Mile 1313.3 Alaska Hwy.
40 Mile Air Flightseeing ...Ph. (907) 883-5191
Golden Bear Motel, Restaurant, RV Park ....Ph. (888) 252-2123
Grizzly Auto Service ....Ph. (907) 883-5514
Jack Wade Gold Co. ......1 block S. on Tok Cutoff
Mainstreet Visitors Center..Ph. (907) 883-5775
Mineral Lakes Retreat..........Ph. (970) 883-5498
Mukluk Land ....Mile 1317
Northern Energy ....Mile 1314.8 Alaska Hwy.
Northern Explorer Tours ..Ph. (907) 883-3866
Rita's Campground/ RV Park..........Mile 1315.7 Alaska Hwy.
Shamrock Hardware..Mile 1313.3 Alaska Hwy.
Snowshoe Fine Arts and Gifts..........Mile 1314 Alaska Hwy.
Snowshoe Motel..........Ph. (907) 883-4511
Sourdough Campground ...Mile 1.7 Tok Cutoff
Sourdough Campground's Pancake Breakfast ....Mile 1.7 Tok Cutoff
Stage Stop, The ....Ph. (907) 883-5338
Texaco Fast Lube & R.V. Service..........Next to Village Texaco
Tok Chamber of Commerce ....Next to Public Lands Info Center
Tok Gateway Salmon Bake..........Mile 1313.1 Alaska Hwy.
Tok Line Camp B&B..........Ph. (907) 883-5506
Tok Liquor Mini-Mart ....Adjacent Tok Lodge
Tok Lodge ....Ph. (907) 883-2851
Tok RV Village ....Mile 1313.4 Alaska Hwy.
Toklat Auto Parts ....Ph. (907) 883-5858
Tundra Lodge & RV Park..........Mile 1315 Alaska Hwy.
Ulu Factory, The..........Ph. (800) 478-3119
Village Texaco..........Ph. (907) 883-4660
Westmark Inn Tok ....Ph. (800) 544-0970
Young's Cafe ....At the junction
Young's Chevron ....Ph. (907) 883-2821
Young's Motel ....Ph. (907) 883-4411

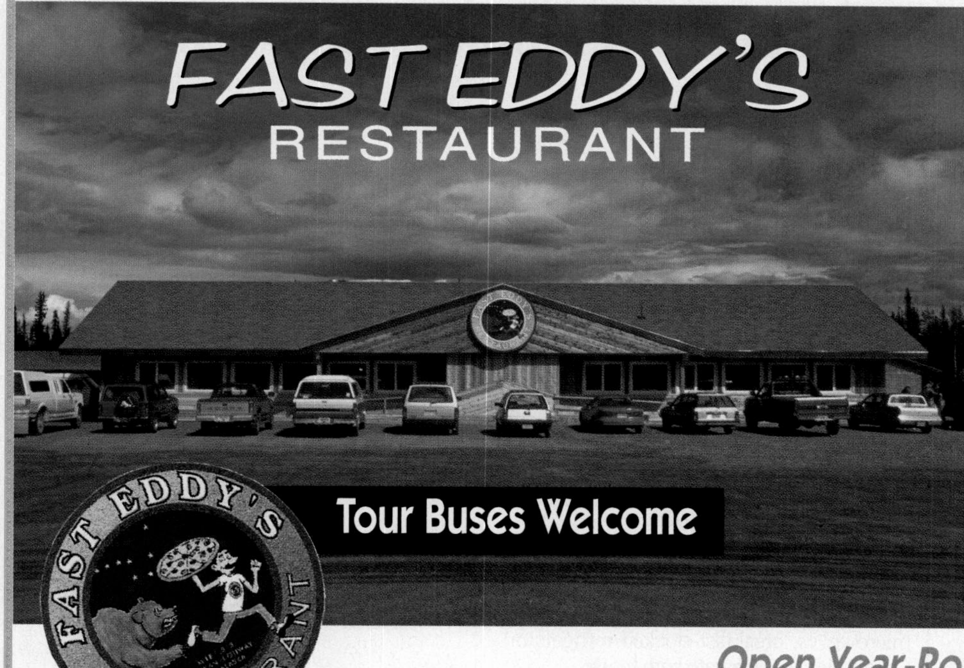

(907) 883-4411

Breakfast • Lunch • Dinner
Steaks • Seafood
Pasta • Burgers
• Sandwiches •
Fresh Salad Bar
Pies • Ice Cream
Milk Shakes

Entire Menu Available To Go

Open Year-Round • 6am to Midnight

(907) 883-4411

43 Large,
Clean, Modern Rooms
Non-Smoking Rooms
Private Baths
with Tubs & Showers
Satellite TV • Private,
In-Room Telephones

YOUNG'S MOTEL
TOK, ALASKA

When You Visit Tok, Enjoy the Comfort!

VISA

Office and Motel Check-In Inside Fast Eddy's Restaurant

(907) 883-4411 • fax (907) 883-5023
e-mail: edyoung@ptinet.com
Box 482, Tok, Alaska 99780
See our log ad at Mile 1313.3 Alaska Highway • 3/4 mile from the Junction

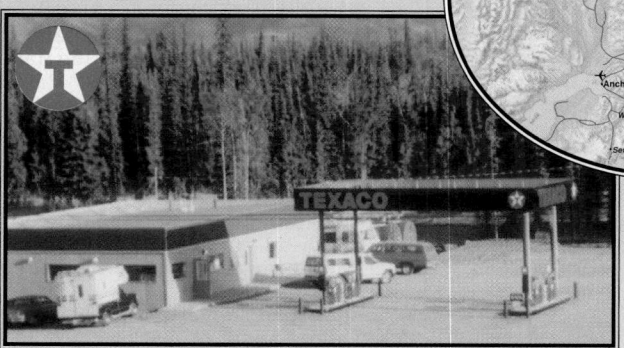

Flowers brighten visitor center sign in Tok. (© Kris Graef, staff)

(Continued from page 184)
Cutoff, 2 S; elev. 1,670 feet; length 3,000 feet; gravel; no fuel, unattended.

Description

Tok had its beginnings as a construction camp on the Alcan Highway in 1942. Highway engineer C.G. Polk was sent to Fairbanks in May of 1942 to take charge of Alaskan construction and start work on the road between Tok Junction and Big Delta. Work was also under way on the Gulkana–Slana–Tok Junction road (now the Tok Cutoff on the Glenn Highway to Anchorage). But on June 7, 1942, a Japanese task force invaded Attu and Kiska islands in the Aleutians, and the Alcan took priority over the Slana cutoff.

The name Tok (rhymes with poke) was long believed to be derived from Tokyo Camp, patriotically shortened during WWII to Tok. There exist at least three other versions of how Tok got its name. According to local author Donna Blasor–Bernhardt in *Tok, the Real Story* (1996), Tok was named for a young husky pup during construction of the Alaska Highway in 1942.

Because Tok is the major overland point of entry to Alaska, it is primarily a trade and service center for all types of transportation, especially for summer travelers coming up the Alaska Highway. A stopover here is a good opportunity to meet other travelers and swap experiences. Tok is the only town in Alaska that the highway traveler must pass through twice—once when arriving in the state and again on leaving the state. The governor proclaimed Tok "Mainstreet Alaska" in 1991. Townspeople are proud of this designation and work hard to make visitors happy.

Tok's central business district is at the junction of the Alaska Highway and Tok Cutoff. From the junction, homes and businesses spread out along both highways on flat terrain dotted with densely timbered stands of black spruce.

Tok has 13 churches, a public library, an elementary school, a 4-year accredited high school and a University of Alaska extension program. Local clubs include the Lions, Disabled American Veterans, Veterans of Foreign Wars and Chamber of Commerce.

Lodging & Services

There are 8 hotels/motels, bed and breakfast, restaurants and gas stations in the Tok area, located along both the Alaska Highway and Tok Cutoff. Tok AYH youth hostel is located on Pringle Road, 0.8 mile/1.3 km south of **Milepost DC 1322.6**; phone (907) 883-3745.

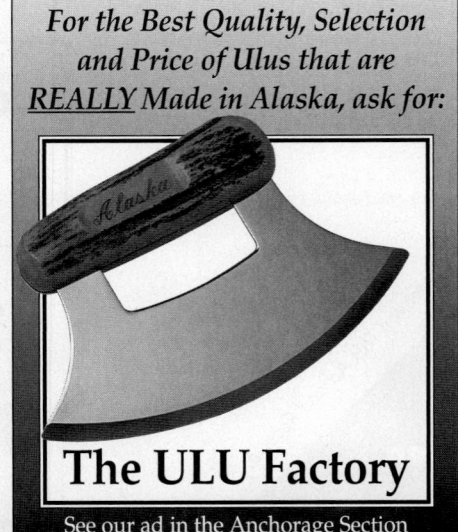

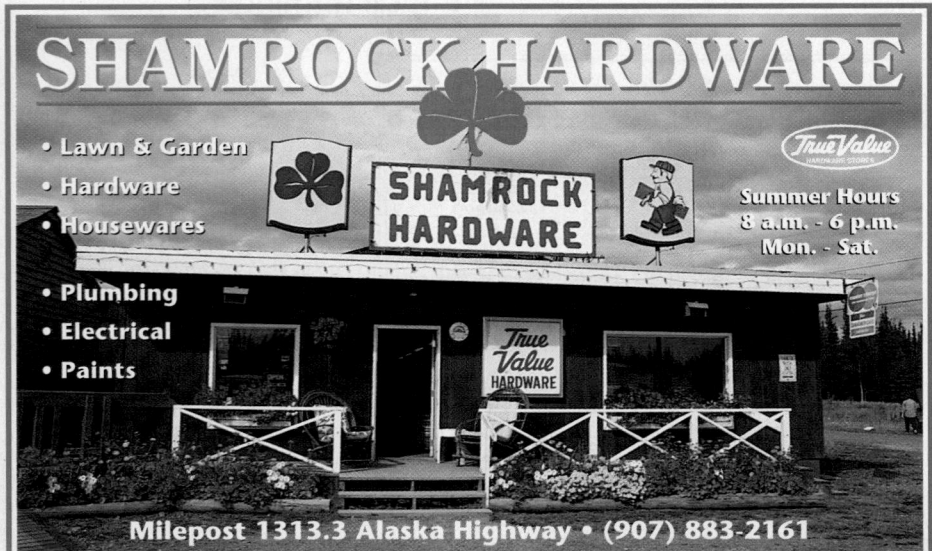

The post office is located between the Westmark and Burnt Paw gift shop on the west side of the Alaska Highway. Grocery, hardware and sporting goods stores, beauty shop, gift shops, liquor stores, auto repair and auto parts stores, wrecker service and laundromats are available. The bank is located across the highway from the Public Lands Information Center. There is an ATM at Village Texaco. Parking, playground and picnic shelters are available at Tok Memorial Park, across from the Tok Main Street Visitor Center

A WinterCabin Bed & Breakfast. New, individual log cabins each with peaceful surroundings, sun porch, picnic table, barbecue, microwave, breakfast-stocked refrigerator, excellent beds, fully carpeted. Special feature: Alaskan-size tub/shower in modern, separate, shared bath house. No pets. Non-smoking. Reservations advised. Built on original site of the "Tent In Tok." Reservations/brochure—P.O. Box 61, Tok, AK 99780. Phone (907) 883-5655. Internet: http://www.ptialaska.net/~wntrcabn/cabin.html. E-mail: wntrcabn@ptialaska.net. [ADVERTISEMENT]

Snowshoe Motel. 24 units with private baths. Excellent accommodations for families or 2 couples traveling together. In-room phones, satellite TV. Free continental breakfast served summers only. Our guests are invited to enjoy panoramic mountain views and sunsets from our upstairs porch. (800) 478-4511 or (907) 883-4511. [ADVERTISEMENT]

Tok Lodge, located on Glenn Highway, 1 block from junction. Alcan Room serves buses, leaving full-service restaurant open for car traffic. 36 new motel rooms. Common comments are "nicest rooms on the highway" and "best meal since leaving home." Locally owned by Pam and Bud Johnson for 22 years. Mini-Mart and liquor store located on premises. Internet: www.alaskan.com/toklodge. E-mail: toklodge@polarnet.com. See display ad this section. [ADVERTISEMENT]

Camping

There are several full-service private RV parks in Tok (see ads this section), located along the Alaska Highway and Tok Cutoff.

Nearby state campgrounds include: Tok River State Recreation Site, 5 miles south of Tok on the Alaska Highway at **Milepost DC 1309.2**; Moon Lake State Recreation Site, 17.7 miles north of Tok at **Milepost DC 1331.9** Alaska Highway; and Eagle Trail State Recreation Site, 16 miles west of Tok at **Milepost GJ 109.3** Tok Cutoff. ▲

Sourdough Campground's Pancake

Maintaining sod-roofed Burnt Paw shop requires a lawnmower and hose.
(© Kris Graef, staff)

Breakfast, served 7–11 A.M. (June, July, August). Genuine "Sourdough!" Full and partial RV hookups. Dry campsites. Showers included. Guaranteed clean restrooms. High-pressure car wash. Open-air museum with gold rush memorabilia. Free evening video program. Located 1.7 miles from the junction toward Anchorage on Tok Cutoff (Glenn Highway). See display ad this section. [ADVERTISEMENT] ▲

Tundra Lodge & RV Park. Spacious, tree-shaded camping sites. Full and partial hookups; 20-, 30-, 50-amp power. Tent sites. Pull-throughs. Clean restrooms and showers included in price. Picnic tables, fire rings and wood. Dump station. Laundromat. Vehicle wash. Pay phone. Ice. Cocktail lounge and meeting room. E-mail access: tundrarv@pti.net. See display ad **Milepost 1315** Alaska Highway. [ADVERTISEMENT] ▲

Transportation

Air: Charter air service available; inquire at Tok state airstrip (**Milepost DC 1313**). Charter flightseeing and fly-in fishing trips available. Scheduled passenger and freight service between Tok, Delta Junction and Fairbanks 4 days a week via 40-Mile Air.

Bus: Alaska Direct Busline.

Attractions

Tok Mainstreet Visitors Center. Located at the junction of the Tok Cutoff and the Alaska Highway, this 7,000-square-foot building houses the Tok Mainstreet Visitor Center, the Alaska Public Lands Information Center and the Tok Community Library. Huge natural spruce logs support an open-beamed, cathedral ceiling. Large picture windows frame the Alaska Range. Displays include: the gold rush; rock, gems and fossils; Alaskan wildlife; waterfowl; and Alaska Highway memorabilia. The Alaska Public Lands Information Center offers videos on Alaska destinations and trip-planning services. Alaska Marine Highway reservations may be booked here. Restrooms, pay phone and message board.

Tok Memorial Park, at the Alaska Highway and Tok Cutoff intersection (across

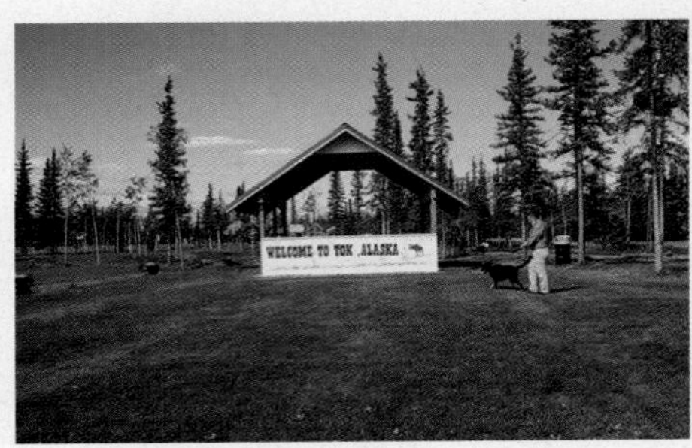

from Tok Mainstreet Visitors Center), has day parking, a picnic shelter and playground.

Local Events: There is a variety of things to do in Tok, thanks to local individuals, businesses and clubs. Local campgrounds offer slide shows, movies, gold panning, a salmon bake, miniature golf and sourdough pancake breakfasts. Sled dog demonstrations are given at Burnt Paw gift shop.

Other local events include bingo games and softball games at the local field. Visitors are welcome at the senior citizens center.

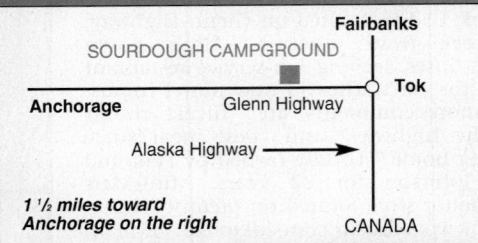

The Tok Triathlon (12 miles of biking, 10 of canoeing and 5 of jogging) and Tok Trot are both held annually. Tok's Fourth of July celebration is a major event, complete with a parade, picnic and games. Check at the Mainstreet Visitor Center for more information on these local events.

Bike Trail: A wide paved bike trail extends southeast from Tok on the Alaska Highway as far east as the Dog Mushers Assoc. track, and as far west as Tanacross Junction; approximate length is 13.2 miles/21.2 km. You may also bike out the Tok Cutoff past Sourdough Campground. Travelers may park their vehicles in and around Tok and find a bike trail nearby leading into or out of Tok.

Native Crafts: Tok is a trade center for the Athabascan Native villages of Tanacross, Northway, Tetlin, Mentasta, Dot Lake and Eagle. Several of the Native women make birch baskets, beaded moccasins, boots and beaded necklaces. Examples of Native work may be seen at the Native-operated gift shop at Northway junction and at several gift shops and other outlets in Tok.

The state of Alaska has a crafts identification program which identifies authentic

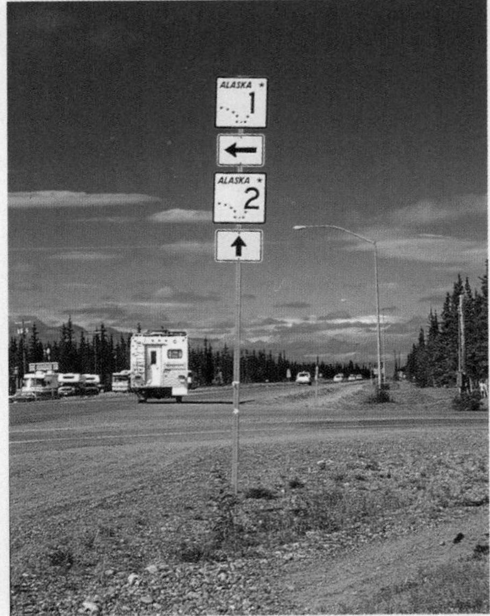

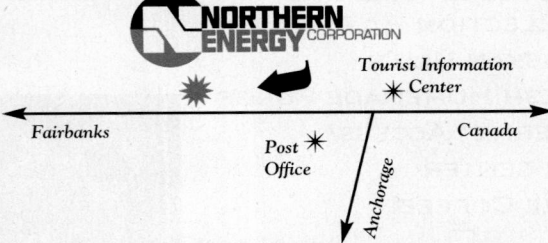

Tok is at the junction of the Alaska Highway and Tok Cutoff.
(© Kris Graef, staff)

Native and Alaskan handicrafts. This symbol is of a polar bear.

Birch baskets were once used in the Native camps and villages. Traditionally they had folded corners, which held water, and were even used for cooking by dropping heated stones into the liquid in the baskets. The baskets are made by peeling the bark from the birch trees, usually in the early summer months. The bark is easiest to work with when moist and pliable. It is cut into shape and sewn together with strips of spruce root dug out of the ground and split. If the root is too dry it is soaked until it is manageable. Holes are put in the birch bark with a punch or screwdriver, and the spruce root is laced in and out. Native women dye the spruce root with food coloring, watercolors or berry juice. A few Natives also make birch canoes and birch baby carriers.

Many of the moccasins and mukluks for sale in Tok are made with moose hide that has the "Native tan." This means moose hide tanned by the Native. First the excess fat and meat is scraped off the hide, then it is soaked in a soap solution (some use a mixture of brains and ashes). After soaking, all the moisture is taken out by constant scraping with a dull knife or scraper. The hide is then scraped again and rubbed together to soften it. Next it is often smoke-cured in rotted spruce wood smoke. The tanning process takes from a few days to a week.

Beading can be a slow and tedious process. Most women say if they work steadily all day they can put the beading on one moccasin, but usually they do their beadwork over a period of several days, alternating it with other activities.

Sled Dog Breeding and Training: Dog mushing is Alaska's official state sport, and Tok has become known as the "Sled Dog Capital of Alaska," with at least 1 out of every 3 people in town involved in some way with raising dogs. Kennels range in size from 100 dogs to a single family pet. Visitors who come to Tok seeking either a pet or a racing sled dog will probably find what they are looking for here.

The Siberian husky is the most popular sled dog and oftentimes has distinctive blue eyes. The Alaskan malamute is much larger than the Siberian and is used for hauling heavy loads at a slower pace. Both breeds are AKC recognized. The Alaskan husky (or husky) is a catchall term for any of the arctic breeds or northern types of dogs and is usually a cross. Sled dogs may be any registered breed or crossbreed, since mushers look for conformation, attitude and speed when putting together a working team rather than pedigrees. Common strains in racing dogs have included Irish setter, Labrador and wolf, among others.

Sled Dog Trails and Races: Tok boasts a well-known and long-established dog mushing trail, which draws many world-class and recreational mushers. The 20.5-mile/33-km trail begins at the rustic log Tok Dog Mushers Assoc. building at **Milepost DC 1312.8**

Sled dogs and sled dog racing are popular in Tok. (© Kris Graef, staff)

on the Alaska Highway. The trail is a favorite with spectators because it affords many miles of viewing from along the Alaska Highway.

Racing begins in late November and extends through the end of March. Junior mushers include 1-, 2-, 3- and 5-dog classes; junior adult mushers include 5- and 8-dog classes. Open (unlimited) classes can run as many as 16 dogs.

The biggest race of the season in Tok is the Race of Champions, held in late March, which also has the largest entry of any sprint race in Alaska. Begun in 1954 as a bet between 2 roadhouse proprietors, today the Race of Champions includes over 100 teams in 3 classes competing for prize money and trophies. It is considered to be the third leg of sled dog racing's "triple crown," following the Fur Rendezvous in Anchorage and the Fairbanks North American Championship. Visitors are also welcome to attend the Tok Native Assoc.'s potlatch, held the same weekend as the race, in the Tok school gym.

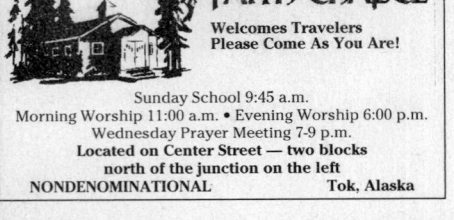

AREA FISHING: Fly-in fishing to area lakes for northern pike, grayling and lake trout; inquire at Tok state airstrip. There are 43 lakes in the Delta–Tok area that are stocked by the Alaska Dept. of Fish and Game. Lakes are stocked primarily with rainbow trout; other stocked species include arctic grayling, lake trout, arctic char and king salmon. Most of these lakes are located close to the road system, but there are walk-in lakes available as well. Most easily accessible are **North Twin**, **South Twin** and **Mark lakes.** There is a trailhead 0.5 mile/0.8 km east of the Gerstle River bridge for **Big Donna Lake** (3.5-mile/5.6-km hike) and **Little Donna Lake** (4.5 miles/7.2 km). **Quartz Lake**, north of Delta Junction, is a popular spot for rainbow trout and silver salmon. Consult ADF&G offices in Tok or Delta Junction for other locations.

Alaska Highway Log

(continued)

DC 1314.8 (2115.9 km) **DJ 107.2** (172.5 km) Gas, diesel, tire repair and car wash.

Northern Energy Corp. See display ad this section.

DC 1315 (2116.2 km) **DJ 107** (172.2 km) **Tundra Lodge and RV Park.** See display ad this section.

DC 1315.7 (2117.3 km) **DJ 106.3** (171 km) Rita's Campground RV Park.

DC 1316.6 (2118.8 km) **DJ 105.4** (169.6 km) Scoby Road, Sundog Trail. Access to bed and breakfasts.

DC 1317 (2119.4 km) **DJ 105** (169 km) **Mukluk Land.** See display ad this section.

DC 1318.5 (2121.8 km) **DJ 103.5** (166.6 km) **Off The Road House.** See display ad this section.

DC 1322.6 (2128.5 km) **DJ 99.4** (160 km) Pringle Road. Tok youth hostel, housed in a wall tent, is located 0.8 mile/1.3 km south; 10 beds, tent space available.

DC 1324.6 (2131.7 km) **DJ 97.4** (156.7

km) Alaska Dept. of Natural Resources **Tanacross Air Tanker Base.** Gravel access road leads 1.6 miles/2.6 km northeast to Tanacross airstrip. The airfield was built in the 1930s, with assistance from local Tanacross Natives, and was used by the U.S. Army in WWII as part of the Russia–America Lend Lease Program. (The Lend Lease Program send war planes to Russia, a U.S. ally, to use in fighting Nazi Germany.) The Tanacross Airfield was the sixth largest city in Alaska in 1944, housing more than 8,000 troops. After WWII, the airfield was used for specialized arctic operations and maneuvers until 1970, when the BLM acquired the property because of the strategic location of its paved runway for refueling air tankers fighting forest fires. Alaska DNR now controls the air tanker operations at the airfield.

Private Aircraft: Tanacross airstrip; elev. 1,549 feet; 2 runways, length 5,000 feet and 5,100 feet; asphalt; unattended. *CAUTION: Forest fire aviation support may be in progress.*

DC 1325.6 (2133.3 km) **DJ 96.4** (155.1 km) End of paved bike trail from Tok and main access road north to Tanacross. Drive past "store" signs 1.2 miles/1.9 km on gravel road to "Y" intersection; turn right for airstrip (see **Milepost DC 1324.6**), turn left for loop road through Native village of **TANACROSS** (pop. 99), home of the once numerous Denn daey, Athabascan Indians. Tanacross has a community store.

DC 1325.7 (2133.4 km) **DJ 96.3** (155 km) **Historic Milepost 1328.**

DC 1327.4 (2136.2 km) **DJ 94.6** (152.2 km) Informal turnout by small lake to north.

DC 1330.1 (2140.5 km) **DJ 91.9** (147.9 km) Scenic viewpoint to north is a paved turnout.

DC 1331.9 (2143.5 km) **DJ 90.1** (145 km) **Moon Lake State Recreation Site**, 0.2 mile/0.3 km north off highway; 15 campsites, picnic area, toilets, tables, water, firepits, boat launch, sandy beach, swimming (watch for floatplanes). Camping fee $10/night. ▲

DC 1333.6 (2146.2 km) **DJ 88.4** (142.3 km) **Historic Milepost 1339.** Yerrick Creek bridge.

DC 1338.2 (2153.5 km) **DJ 83.8** (134.8 km) Highway crosses Cathedral Creek 3 times between here and **Milepost DC 1339.**

DC 1342.2 (2160 km) **DJ 79.8** (128.4 km) Sheep Creek culvert.

DC 1344.5 (2163.8 km) **DJ 77.5** (124.7 km) **Historic Milepost 1352.** Paved parking area to north. Interpretive panel on the "father of the international highway," Donald MacDonald. Alaska Range to the south. Good photo stop.

DC 1347.2 (2168 km) **DJ 74.8** (120.4 km) **Forest Lake** trailhead (not signed in 1999); 6 mile/9.6 km ATV trail (not easy access) to lake stocked with rainbow trout.

DC 1347.3 (2168.2 km) **DJ 74.7** (120.2 km) Entering Game Management Unit 20D westbound, Unit 12 eastbound.

DC 1347.5 (2168.5 km) **DJ 74.5** (119.9 km) Robertson River bridge. The river was named by Lt. Henry T. Allen for a member of his 1885 expedition. The Robertson River heads at the terminus of Robertson Glacier in the Alaska Range and flows 33 miles northeast to the Tanana River.

DC 1348 (2169.3 km) **DJ 74** (119.1 km) *CAUTION: Watch for loose gravel northbound.*

DC 1348.1 (2169.5 km) **DJ 73.9** (118.9 km) Side road west to public fishing access; parking. Hike in 0.3 mile/0.5 km for **Robertson No. 2 Lake**; rainbow fishing (stocked by ADF&G).

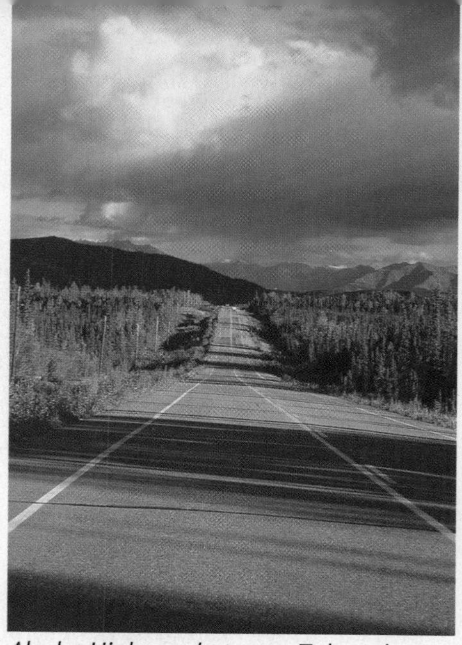

Alaska Highway between Tok and Delta Junction. (© Kris Graef, staff)

DC 1350.5 (2173.3 km) **DJ 71.5** (115.1 km) Double-ended paved turnout to west. *Rough road next 1.5 miles westbound.*

DC 1353.6 (2178.3 km) **DJ 68.3** (109.9 km) Jan Lake Road to south; public fishing access. Drive in 0.5 mile/0.8 km to parking area with boat launch and toilets. No overnight camping, carry out garbage. **Jan Lake** is stocked by ADF&G with rainbow; use spinners, flies, or salmon eggs with bobber. Dot Lake Native Corp. land, limited public access.

DC 1357.3 (2184.4 km) **DJ 64.7** (104.1 km) Bear Creek bridge. Paved parking area to south at west end of bridge.

DC 1358.7 (2186.6 km) **DJ 63.3** (101.9 km) Chief Creek bridge. Paved parking area to south at west end of bridge.

DC 1361 (2190.2 km) **DJ 60.4** (97.2 km) Dot Lake School.

DC 1361.3 (2190.7 km) **DJ 60.7** (97.7 km) **DOT LAKE** (pop. 70). Lodge with gas, groceries, restaurant, car wash, motel, camping and post office. Headquarters for the Dot Lake (Athabascan) Indian Corp. Homesteaded in the 1940s, a school was established here in 1952. Dot Lake's historic chapel was built in 1949. ▲

Dot Lake Lodge. See display ad this section. ▲

DC 1361.5 (2191.1 km) **DJ 60.5** (97.4km) **Historic Milepost 1368.** *CAUTION: Rough road westbound; watch for gravel breaks.*

DC 1370.2 (2205.1 km) **DJ 51.8** (83.4 km) Double-ended paved scenic viewpoint to north.

DC 1370.8 (2206 km) **DJ 57.8** (83.4 km) Entering **Tanana Valley State Forest** westbound. Established as the first unit of Alaska's state forest system in 1983, Tanana Valley State Forest encompasses 1.81 million acres and lies almost entirely within the Tanana River Basin. The forest extends 265 miles from near the Canadian border to Manley Hot Springs. Almost 90 percent of the state forest is forested. Principal tree species are paper birch, quaking aspen, balsam poplar, black spruce, white spruce and tamarack. Almost 7 percent of the forest is shrubland, chiefly willow. The forest is managed by the Dept. of Natural Resources.

DC 1371.5 (2207.2 km) **DJ 50.5** (81.3 km) Berry Creek bridge. Parking area to south at west end of bridge.

DC 1374.3 (2211.7 km) **DJ 47.7** (76.8 km) Sears Creek bridge. Parking area to south at west end of bridge.

DC 1376.5 (2215.2 km) **DJ 45.5** (73.2 km) Entering Tanana Valley State Forest eastbound.

DC 1378 (2217.6 km) **DJ 44** (70.8 km) Bridge over Dry Creek.

DC 1379 (2219.2 km) **DJ 43** (69.2 km) Double-ended paved parking area with mountain views to south. Pay phone.

DC 1380.5 (2221.6 km) **DJ 41.5** (66.8 km) Johnson River bridge (clearance 15′ 6″). A tributary of the Tanana River, the Johnson River was named by Lt. Henry T. Allen in 1887 for Peder Johnson, a Swedish miner and member of his party.

Moose hunters: Antler restriction area.

DC 1381.1 (2222.6 km) **DJ 40.9** (65.8 km) Paved parking area to south. Hiking trail to **Lisa Lake** (stocked).

DC 1382.6 (2225 km) **DJ 39.4** (63,4 km) Sign: $1,000 fine for littering.

DC 1383.8 (2226.9 km) **DJ 38.2** (61.5 km) **Craig Lake** access west side of highway via 0.5-mile/0.8-km trail; rainbow trout fishing.

DC 1385 (2228.9 km) **DJ 37** (59.5 km) Paved parking area to north with Gold Rush Centennial sign about the effect of the Gold Rush era on Tanana Valley Natives. Access to Tanana River.

DC 1386 (2230.5 km) **DJ 36** (57.9 km) *Improved (1999) wide road westbound to Milepost DC 1398.*

DC 1388.4 (2234.4 km) **DJ 33.6** (54.7 km) Parking area to south.

DC 1388.5 (2234.5 km) **DJ 33.5** (53.9 km) Little Gerstle River bridge.

DC 1391.9 (2240 km) **DJ 30.1** (48.4 km) Parking area to south; public fishing access. **Big Donna Lake**, 3.5 miles/5.6 km, and **Little Donna Lake**, 4.5 miles/7.2 km; stocked with rainbow.

DC 1392.7 (2241.3 km) **DJ 29.3** (47.2 km) Gerstle River Black Veterans Recognition bridge. The river was named for Lewis Gerstle, president of the Alaska Commercial Co., by Lt. Henry T. Allen, whose 1885 expedition explored the Copper, Tanana and Koyukuk river regions for the U.S. Army Dept. of the Columbia.

DC 1393 (2241.8 km) **DJ 29** (46.7 km) Rest area to south at west end of bridge.

DC 1400.9 (2254.5 km) **DJ 21.1** (33.9 km) Double-ended paved parking area to northeast.

DC 1398 (2250 km) **DJ 24** (38.6 km) *Improved (1999) wide road eastbound to Milepost DC 1386.*

DC 1403.3 (2258.3 km) **DJ 18.7** (30.1 km) Sawmill Creek Road to northeast. This rough gravel road goes through the heart of the Delta barley fields. A sign just off the highway explains the barley project. Visiting farmers are welcome to talk with local farmers along the road, except during planting (May) and harvesting (August or September) when they are too busy. Commercial farm tours available from Farm Tours on Sawmill Creek Road; phone (907) 895-4715.

DC 1403.6 (2258.8 km) **DJ 18.4** (29.6 km) Sawmill Creek.

DC 1404 (2259.5 km) **DJ 18** (29 km) Sawmill Creek Lodge.

DC 1404.3 (2259.9 km) **DJ 17.7** (28.5 km) Watch for buffalo sign. On the southwest side of the Alaska Highway approaching Delta Junction is the Bison Sanctuary. This range provides the bison herd with autumn and winter grazing on over 3,000 acres of grassland. It was developed to reduce agricultural crop depredation by bison.

DC 1408 (2265.9 km) **DJ 14** (22.5 km) Knight Lane. Access to University of Alaska Agricultural and Forestry Experiment Station. Major research at this facility concentrates on agricultural cropping, fertilization and tillage management.

DC 1410 (2269.1 km) **DJ 12** (19.3 km) Spruce Road. Access road north to Delta barley project.

DC 1411.7 (2271.8 km) **DJ 10.3** (16.6 km) Paved double-ended scenic viewpoint of Alaska Range to south.

DC 1412.5 (2273.1 km) **DJ 9.5** (15.3 km) Food, lodging, camping and phone to south.

Cherokee Lodge and RV Park. See display ad this section. ▲

DC 1413.3 (2274.4 km) **DJ 8.7** (14 km) Grain storage facility to south.

DC 1413.4 (2274.6 km) **DJ 8.6** (13.8 km) Delta Meat & Sausage Co. to south.

DC 1414.8 (2276.8 km) **DJ 7.2** (11.6 km) Clearwater Road leads north past farmlands to **Clearwater State Recreation Site** campground and junctions with Remington Road. Stay on pavement leading to Jack Warren Road, which goes west to the Richardson Highway at **Milepost V 268.3**. Good opportunity to see area agriculture; see Delta Vicinity map this page.

To reach the state campground, follow Clearwater Road 5.2 miles/8.4 km north to junction with Remington Road; turn right and drive 2.8 miles/4.5 km east for Clearwater state campground, situated on the bank of Clearwater Creek. There are 15 campsites, toilets, tables, firepits, water and boat ramp. Camping fee $8/night. ▲

Delta–Clearwater River (local reference; stream is actually Clearwater Creek, which flows northwest to the Tanana River), boat needed for best fishing; beautiful spring-fed stream; grayling and whitefish; silver salmon spawn here in October. **Goodpaster River,** accessible by boat via Delta–Clearwater and Tanana rivers; excellent grayling fishing.

DC 1415.4 (2277.8 km) **DJ 6.6** (10.6 km) Dorshorst Road; access to homestead farm and private museum, open to public June 1 to Sept. 15, admission charged. Guided tours of an authentic Alaska homestead farm. There's also a large collection of historical farming equipment. Open daily 10 A.M. to 7 P.M.

DC 1420.7 (2286.3 km) **DJ 1.3** (2.1 km) Alaska State Troopers and veterinary to south.

DC 1422 (2288.4 km) **DJ 0 V 266** (428.1

km) End of the Alaska highway at Delta Junction (description follows); visitor center.

Junction of the Alaska Highway (Alaska Route 2) and the Richardson Highway (Alaska Route 4). Turn to **Milepost V 266** in the RICHARDSON HIGHWAY section for log of the highway north to Fairbanks (98 miles/158 km), and south to Paxson (81 miles/130 km) and Valdez (266 miles/428 km).

Delta Junction

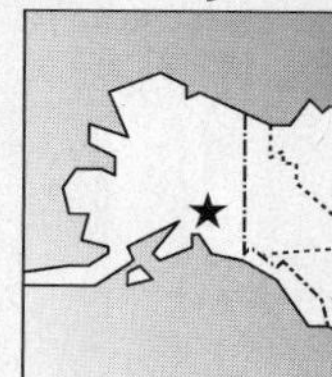

Junction of the Alaska and Richardson highways: **Milepost DC 1422** Alaska Highway, **Milepost V 266** Richardson Highway. **Population:** 884. **Emergency Services:** Phone 911 for all emergency services. **Alaska State Troopers,** in the Jarvis Office Center at **Milepost DC 1420.7**, phone (907) 895-4800. **Fire Department** and **Ambulance**, Delta Rescue Squad/EMS at **Milepost V 265.2** Richardson Highway, phone (907) 8995-4656. **Clinic,** Family Medical Center (1 doctor); 2 dentists in private practice.

Visitor Information: Visitor Center at junction of Alaska and Richardson highways, open daily 8 A.M. to 7:30 P.M., May to mid-September; phone (907) 895-5068, fax (907) 895-5141. The visitor center has historical and wildflower displays and a pay phone. Highway information, phone (907) 451-2207. Dept. of Fish and Game at north edge of town; phone (907) 895-4844.

City Hall and the Delta Junction Library, located at **Milepost V 266.5**, are also good sources of information. City Hall, open 9 A.M. to 5 P.M. weekdays, has a pay phone, public restrooms, and can give local directions. The library has a free paperback book and magazine exchange, Anchorage newspaper, public fax and copier service. The library, open Wednesdays and Saturdays, also offers free Alaska video programs to any traveler waiting for vehicle repairs in Delta (ask at the circulation desk).

Elevation: 1,180 feet. **Climate:** Mean monthly temperature in January, -15° F/-26°C; in July 58°F/14°C. Record low was -66°F/-54°C in January 1989; record high was 88°F/31°C in August 1990. Mean monthly precipitation in July, 2.57 inches/6.5cm. **Radio:** KUAC-FM 91.7 broadcasts from University of Alaska, Fairbanks; Fort Greely broadcasts on 90.5 FM and 93.5 FM. **Television:** Three channels from Fairbanks.

Private Aircraft: Delta Junction (former BLM) airstrip, 1 mile north; elev. 1,150 feet; length 2,400 feet, gravel; length 1,600 feet, dirt; no fuel; unattended.

Description

Delta Junction is the end of the Alaska Highway. From here, the Richardson Highway leads to Fairbanks. The Richardson Highway, connecting Valdez at tidewater with Fairbanks in the Interior, predates the Alaska Highway by 20 years. The Richardson was already a wagon road in 1910, and was updated to automobile standards in the 1920s by the Alaska Road Commission (ARC).

Named after the nearby Delta River, Delta Junction began as a construction camp on the Richardson Highway in 1919. (It was first known as Buffalo Center because of the American bison that were transplanted here in the 1920s.)

Since the late 1970s, the state has encouraged development of the agricultural industry in the Delta area. They have conducted local land disposal programs involving more than 112,000 acres. These programs generated 37 farms averaging 2,310 acres and 169 small farms averaging 161 acres.

In 1996, nearly 40,000 acres were in some form of agricultural use (including production of barley, oats, wheat, forage, pasture, grass seed, canola, potatoes, field peas, forage brassicas) and conservation use. Barley is the major feed grain grown in Delta. It is an excellent energy feed for cattle, hogs and sheep. Production acreages are determined by the anticipated in-state demand for barley.

Delta barley is stored on farms or in a local co-op elevator, sold on the open market or used to feed livestock. Small-scale farming of vegetables, 3 commercial potato farms, 5 active dairies, a dairy processing center, 6 beef producers, 2 beef feedlots, 3 swine producers, 3 bison ranches, 1 red-meat processing plant and 4 commercial greenhouses all contribute to Delta Junction's agriculture.

(Continues on page 203)

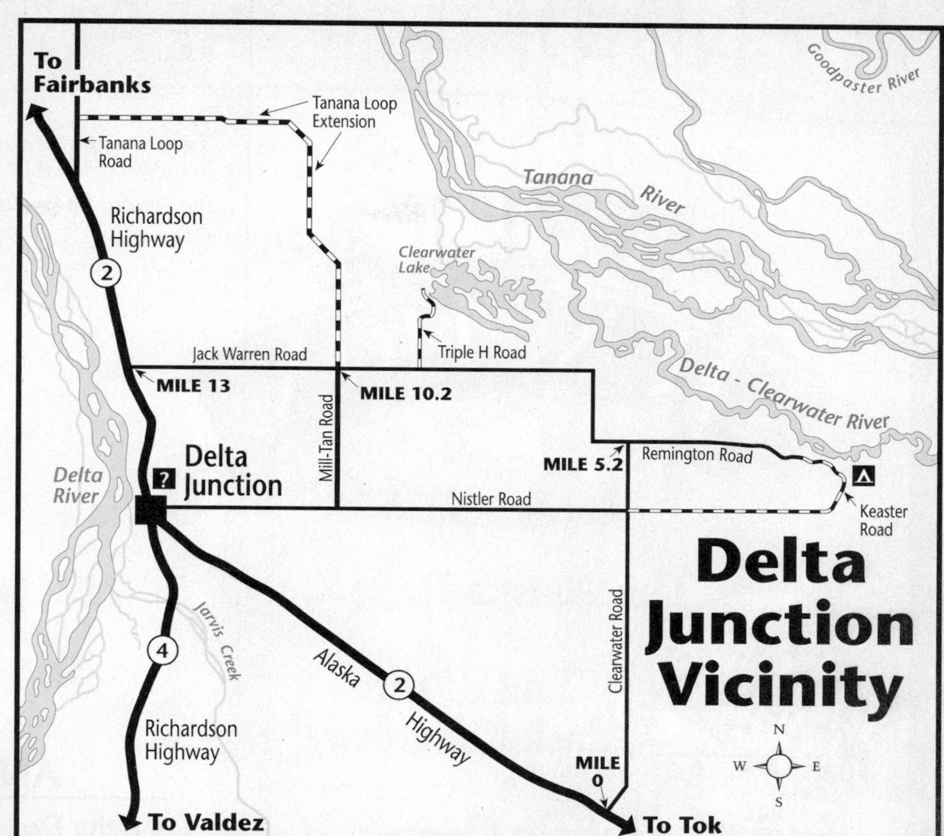

Delta Junction, Alaska

(Continued from page 197)

Lodging & Services

Delta Junction has 3 motels, several bed and breakfasts, restaurants, gas stations, a coin-operated car wash, a shopping center, post office, gift shops, RV parks, bank with ATM and other businesses. There are several churches. Delta Community Park, on Kimball Street one block off the highway, has softball and soccer fields and playground.

Camping

A private RV park, Smith's Green Acres, is just north of town. There are 3 public campgrounds in the area: Delta state campground, 1.1 miles north at **Milepost V 267.1** Richardson Highway; Quartz Lake Recreation Area, 10.7 miles north via the Richardson Highway to **Milepost V 277.7** and 2.5 miles east on a side road; and Clearwater state campground on Remington Road, accessible from **Milepost DC 1414.9** Alaska Highway or **V 268.3** Richardson Highway (see Delta Vicinity map on page 197). ▲

Transportation

Air: Scheduled service via 40-Mile Air from Tok to Fairbanks; Delta stop on request. Local air service available.

Attractions

Delta Junction Visitor Center. Have your picture taken with the monument in front of the visitor center that marks the highway's end. The chamber of commerce visitor center also has free brochures describing area businesses and attractions, and displays of Alaska wildflowers, mounted animals and furs to touch. Travelers may also purchase certificates here, certifying that they have reached the end of the Alaska Highway. There is also an interesting display of pipe used in 3 Alaska pipeline projects outside the visitor center.

See the Pipeline Crossing. Delta Junction is the first view of the trans-Alaska pipeline for travelers coming up the Alaska Highway from Canada. A good spot to see and photograph the pipeline is at **Milepost V 275.4** Richardson Highway, 9.5 miles/15.3 km north of town, where the pipeline crosses the Tanana River.

Visit Pump Station No. 9. Located 7.7 miles/12.4 km south of Delta Junction at **Milepost V 258.3** Richardson Highway, the pump station has several 1-hour tours in summer. Tours limited to 10 people; children must be at least 9 years old. Reservations recommended. Phone (907) 895-5069 or inquire at the visitor center in Delta Junction for tour times.

Buffalo Herd. American bison were transplanted into the Delta Junction area in the 1920s. Because the bison have become costly pests to many farmers in the Delta area, the 90,000-acre Delta Bison Sanctuary was created south of the Alaska Highway in 1980. However, keeping the bison on their refuge and out of the barley fields is a continuing problem. Summer visitors who wish to look at the bison are advised to visit the viewpoint at **Milepost V 241.3** on the Richardson Highway; use binoculars. The herd contained 482 bison in 1992 when the last census was taken by the ADF&G.

Rika's Roadhouse. Located north of town about 8 miles/12.9 km at Milepost V 275 Richardson Highway at Big Delta State Historical Park, this restored roadhouse was built in 1910. Open daily in summer. There are a number of other historic outbuildings, a gift shop and restaurant.

Special Events: The Deltana Fair is held in late July. The fair includes a barbecue, Lions' pancake breakfast, local handicrafts, horse show, livestock display and show, games, concessions, contests and a parade. A highlight of the fair is the Great Alaska Outhouse Race, held on Sunday, in which 4 pushers and 1 sitter compete for the coveted "Golden Throne" award. The Alaska Farm Bureau and Alaska Cooperative Extension sponsor an annual Farm Tour the second Wednesday in August. Phone (907) 895-4215 for more information.

An annual Winter Carnival is held in December; check with the Chamber of Commerce for dates; phone (907) 895-5068.

A Festival of Lights is held each February in Delta Junction. This special event, designed to break up the monotony of long winter nights, features a parade of lights where the local citizenry builds and decorates floats with lights. There are also dog races, fireworks, square dancing, ice sculpting and more.

Winter is also celebrated in Delta with the Deep Freeze Classic, a lottery based on guessing the exact time when the thermometer will hit its lowest point for the winter. Results aren't final until early spring. Winning time and temperature in 1999 was 9:24 P.M. February 3, with a low of –57.4°F.

Sullivan Roadhouse, relocated across from the visitor center, was originally built

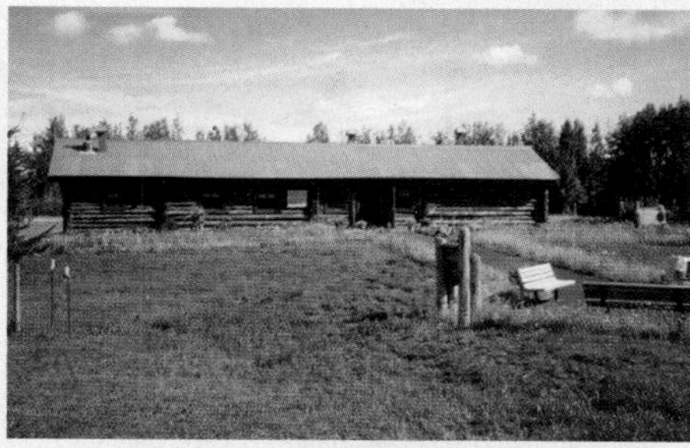

in 1906. It is one of the last remaining roadhouses from the Valdez to Fairbanks Trail. Open daily in summer as a walk-through museum.

Tour the agriculture of the area by driving Sawmill Creek Road (turn off at **Milepost DC 1403.6** Alaska Highway) and Clearwater Road (see **Milepost DC 1414.9**). Sawmill Creek Road goes through the heart of the grain-producing Delta Ag Project. Along Clearwater and Remington roads you may view the older farms, which produce forage crops and livestock. Tanana Loop Road (**Milepost V 271.7**), Tanana Loop Extension and Mill–Tan Road also go past many farms. The visitor information center in downtown Delta Junction can answer many questions on local agriculture and has information about local tours.

Delta's barley fields are a popular migration stop for 150,000 to 200,000 sandhill cranes. In 1998, a common crane was sighted among a flock of lesser sandhill cranes. It was only the sixth sighting of a common crane—classified as a Eurasian species—in North America. Delta–Clearwater Creek is a good place to see spring and fall migrations of sandhill cranes, geese and other waterfowl.

AREA FISHING: **Delta–Clearwater River** (local name for Clearwater Creek), grayling and whitefish; silver salmon spawn here in October. Access via Clearwater Road or Jack Warren Road (see map). **Goodpaster River**, accessible by boat via Delta–Clearwater and Tanana rivers; excellent grayling fishing.

There are 43 lakes in the Delta–Tok area that are stocked by the ADF&G. Lakes are stocked primarily with rainbow trout, and also with arctic grayling, lake trout, arctic char and king salmon. Lakes are located along the road or reached by trail. **Quartz Lake**, at **Milepost V 277.7** north of Delta Junction, one of the most popular fishing lakes in the Delta area, is also the largest and most easily accessed of area lakes; angler success is excellent. Consult ADF&G offices in Delta or Tok for other locations.

YELLOWHEAD HIGHWAY 16

Connects: Edmonton, AB, to Prince Rupert, BC **Length:** 898 miles
Road Surface: Paved **Season:** Open all year
Highest Summit: Obed Summit, 3,819 feet
Major Attractions: Jasper National Park, Mt. Robson, North Pacific National Historic Site

(See maps, pages 205–207)

	Edmonton	Jasper	Prince George	Prince Rupert	Terrace
Edmonton		216	450	898	807
Jasper	216		234	682	591
Prince George	450	234		448	357
Prince Rupert	898	682	448		91
Terrace	807	591	357	91	

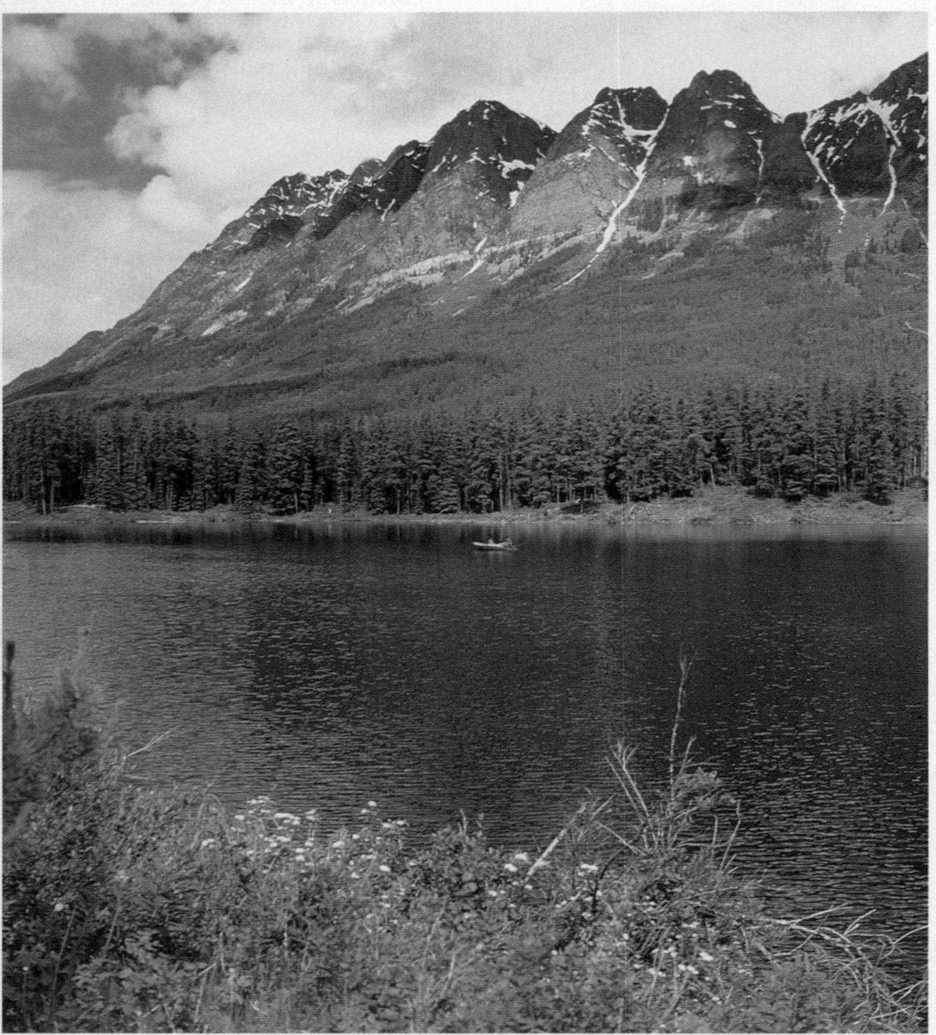

Lake and mountain scenery on the Yellowhead Highway. *(© Blake Hanna, staff)*

Yellowhead Highway 16 is a paved trans-Canada highway extending from Winnipeg, MB, through Saskatchewan, Alberta, and British Columbia to the coastal city of Prince Rupert. (The highway connecting Masset and Queen Charlotte on Graham Island has also been designated as part of Yellowhead Highway 16.) *The MILEPOST®* logs Yellowhead Highway 16 from Edmonton, AB, to Prince Rupert, BC, a distance of 898 miles/1,444 km.

Yellowhead Highway 16 terminates at Prince Rupert, BC, where you may connect with the Alaska Marine Highway System to southeastern Alaska cities, and the British Columbia ferry system to Port Hardy on Vancouver Island and Skidegate in the Queen Charlotte Islands.

This is a major east–west route, providing access to a number of attractions in Alberta and British Columbia. Yellowhead Highway 16 is also a very scenic highway, passing through mountains, forest and farmland. Visitor services are readily available in towns along the way, and campsites may be found in towns and along the highway at both private and provincial park campgrounds. (It is unsafe and illegal to overnight in rest areas.)

Yellowhead Highway 16 Log

This section of the log shows distance from Edmonton (E) followed by distance from Prince George (PG).

The Yellowhead Highway log is divided into 2 sections: Edmonton to Prince George, and Prince George to Prince Rupert.

Kilometreposts on Yellowhead reflect distances within highway maintenance districts; The MILEPOST® periodically notes these physical posts as reference points.

HIGHWAY 16

E 0 PG 450 (724.2 km) **EDMONTON** city limit. See page 42 in the EAST ACCESS ROUTE section for description of city.

E 4 (6.4 km) **PG 446** (717.8 km) **Junction** of Highways 16 West and 60 (Devon Overpass); access to Glowing Embers Travel Centre campground (273 sites) via Devfon exit. ▲

E 12 (19.3 km) **PG 438** (704.9 km) **SPRUCE GROVE** (pop. 13,076). All visitor facilities including motels, restaurants, gas and service stations, grocery stores, farmer's market, shopping malls and all emergency services. Recreational facilities include a golf course, swimming pool, 2 ice skating rinks, a curling rink, and extensive walking and cycling trails. The chamber of commerce tourist information booth, located on Highway 16, is open year-round; phone (780) 962-2561.

E 18.1 (29.1 km) **PG 431.9** (695.1 km) **STONY PLAIN** (pop. 7,800). All visitor facilities including hotels, restaurants, supermarkets, shopping mall and gas stations with major repair service; RCMP and hospital; outdoor swimming pool and 18-hole

YELLOWHEAD HIGHWAY 16 *Edmonton, AB, to Prince George, BC*

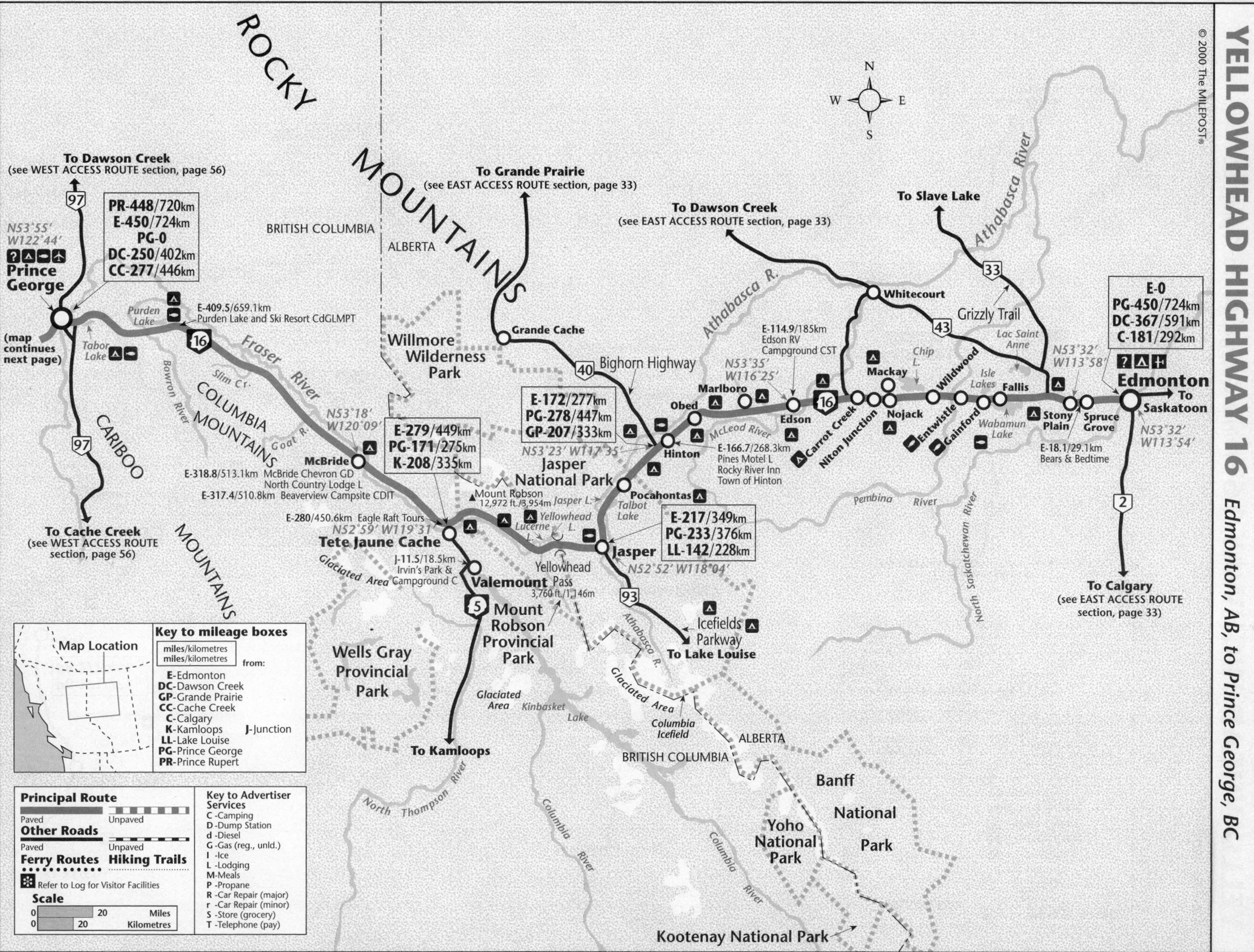

YELLOWHEAD HIGHWAY 16 *Prince George, BC, to Topley, BC*

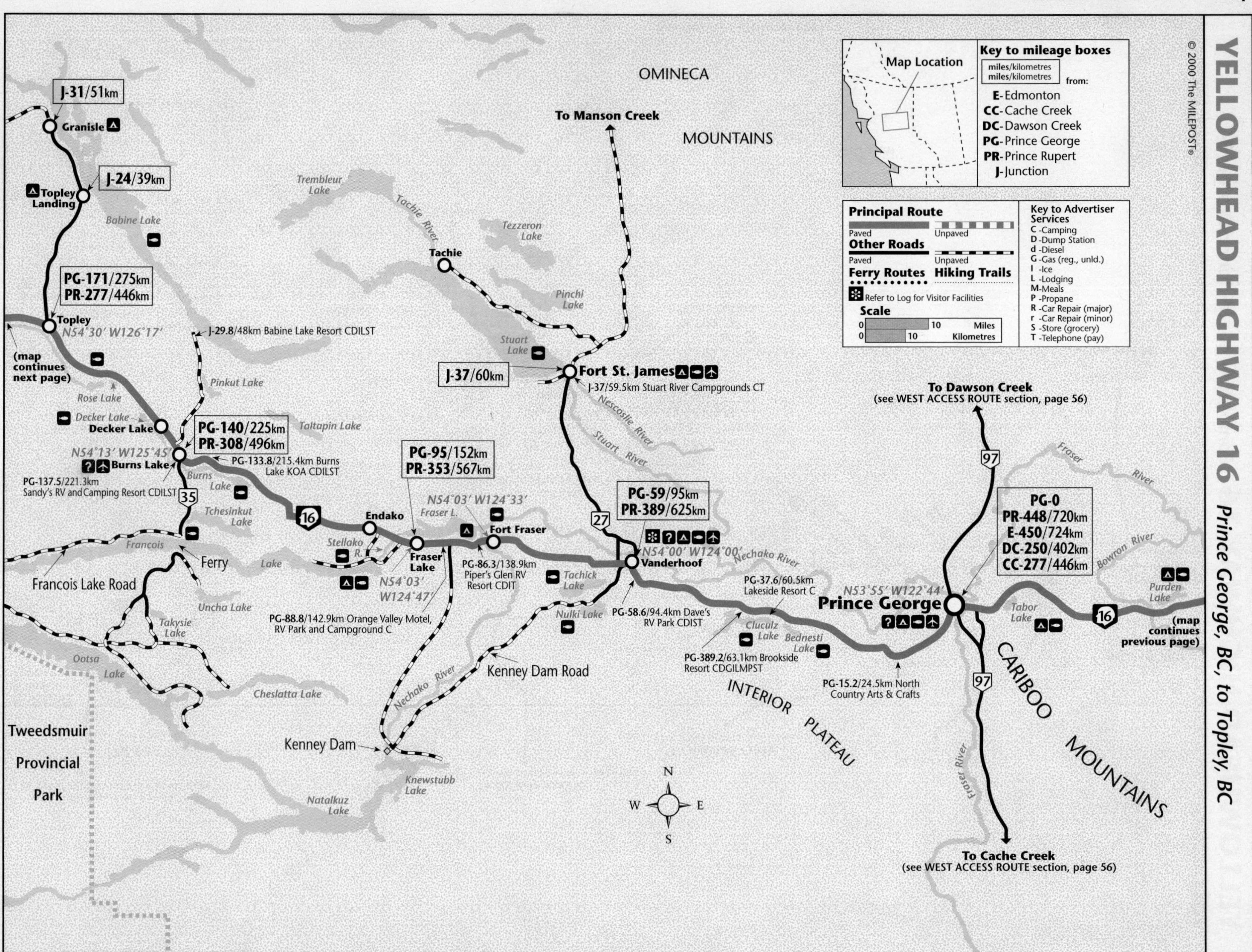

YELLOWHEAD HIGHWAY 16 *Topley, BC, to Prince Rupert, BC*

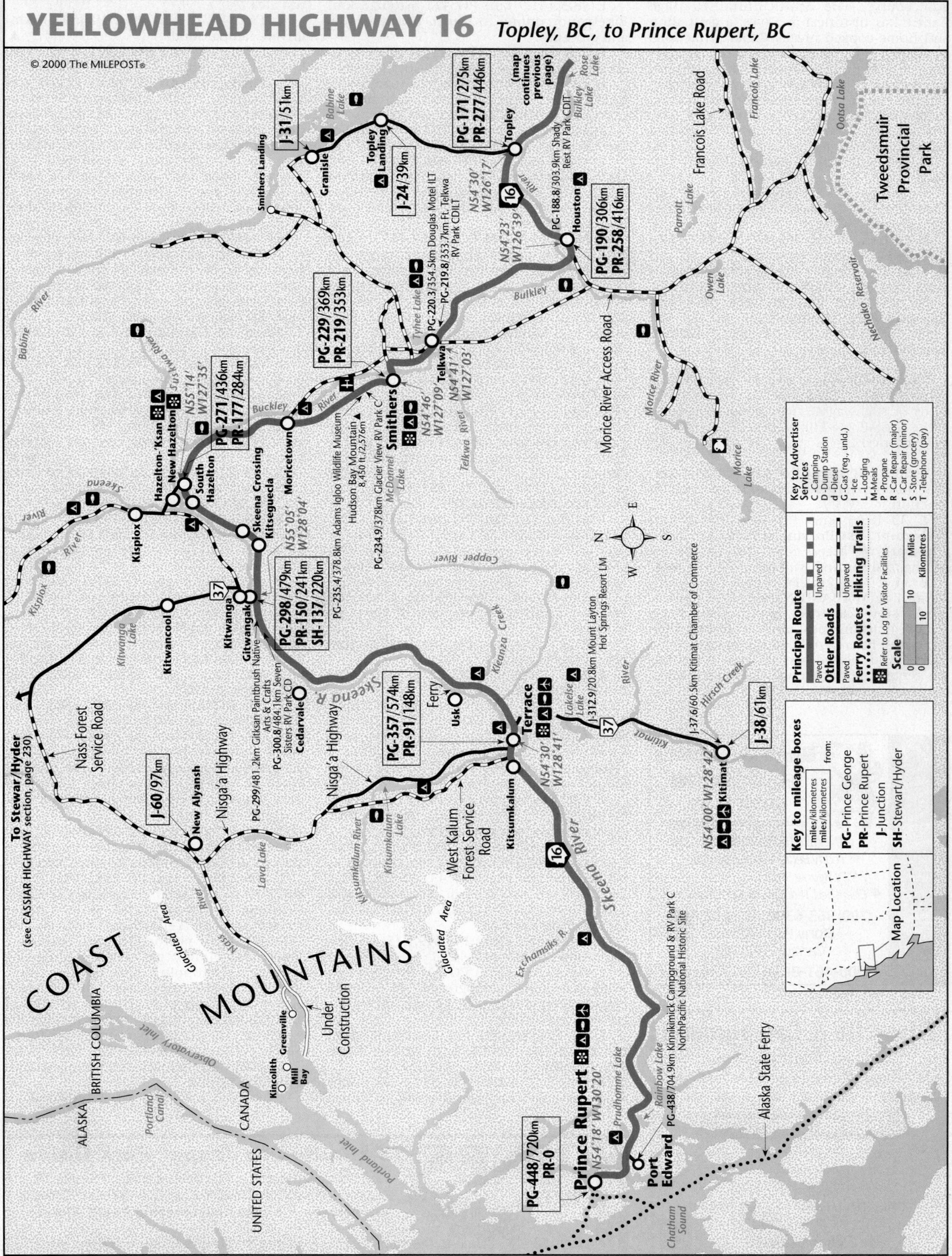

golf course. The Multicultural Heritage Centre has historical archives, a craft shop and home-cooked meals. Other attractions include 19 outdoor murals; a farmer's market; a teahouse; Oppertshauser House; the Andrew Wolf Winery (visitors welcome); and the Pioneer Museum at Exhibition Park. Visitor information centres at Rotary Park and rest area. Camping at Lions RV Park and Campground; 26 sites.

Bears & Bedtime. See display ad this section.

E 19.6 (31.5 km) **PG 430.4** (692.7 km) Turnoff to south for Edmonton Beach and campground.

E 20.1 (32.3 km) **PG 429.9** (691.9 km) Hubbles Lake turnoff to north.

E 21.2 (34.1 km) **PG 428.8** (690.1 km) Restaurant, gas station and store to north.

E 25 (40.2 km) **PG 425** (684 km) **Junction** with Highway 43 to Dawson Creek, BC (337 miles/543 km). Continue west for Prince George.

Turn to **Milepost E 29.8** on page 48 in the EAST ACCESS ROUTE section for log of Highway 43, which also accesses the Mackenzie Highway to Northwest Territories.

E 30.3 (48.8 km) **PG 419.7** (675.4 km) Gas and groceries south side of road at junction.

E 33 (53.1 km) **PG 417** (671.1 km) **Wabamun Lake Provincial Park**, 1 mile/1.6 km south on access road; 288 campsites, fishing, boating and swimming.

E 34.7 (55.9 km) **PG 415.3** (668.3 km) Village of **WABAMUN** with gas, convenience store, car wash, laundromat, dump station, hotel and post office. Park with shelter, tables, litter barrels, washroom and flush toilets. Also located here is Trans Alta Utilities generating station, which generates electricity from coal.

E 38.5 (61.9 km) **PG 411.5** (662.3 km) Emergency phone to south. Propane, fuel and groceries.

E 393 (63.3 kmO) **PG 410.7** (660.9 km) Strip mining for coal north side of highway.

E 42.5 (68.4 km) **PG 407.5** (655.8 km) **FALLIS** (pop. 190); no services. Strip mining of coal on north side of highway.

E 46.2 (74.4 km) **PG 403.8** (649.8 km) Private campground.

E 48.7 (78.3 km) **PG 401.3** (645.9 km) **GAINFORD** (pop. 205). Cafe, hotel and post office. Free public campground at west end of town with 8 sites, firewood, tables, pit toilets and water.

E 56.6 (91.1 km) **PG 393.4** (633.1 km) **ENTWISTLE** (pop. 477). Restaurants, gas station, 2 motels, post office, swimming pool and grocery store. **Pembina River Provincial Park**, 1.9 miles/3.1 km north; 132 campsites, tables, showers, flush toilets, water and dump station. Open all year; camping fee $11 to $16. Fishing, swimming, playground and phone.

E 66.2 (106.5 km) **PG 383.8** (617.7 km) **WILDWOOD** (pop. 375), the "Bingo Capital of Canada." Post office, hotel, gas station, restaurants and shops. Campground at **Chip Lake** with 14 sites, tables, firewood, pit toilets, water, fishing, swimming and boat launch.

E 68.7 (110.6 km) **PG 381.3** (613.6 km) View of Chip Lake to north.

E 81.5 (131.1 km) **PG 368.5** (593.1 km) **NOJACK** and **MACKAY** (pop. 250). Grocery, post office, restaurant and gas station with towing, diesel and major repair service. Mackay is 1.9 miles/3.1 km north of Nojack on a gravel road. Campgrounds 1 mile/1.6 km and 3 miles/4.8 km west of town on Highway 16.

E 81.6 (131.4 km) **PG 368.4** (592.8 km) Emergency phone.

E 84.6 (136.1 km) **PG 365.4** (588.1 km) Private campground to north.

E 89.5 (144 km) **PG 360.5** (580.2 km) **NITON JUNCTION.** Hamlet has 2 gas stations with tires and parts, diesel, propane, car wash, pay phone, groceries, post office, 2 restaurants, lounge, motel. Private campground with full hookups.

E 93.7 (150.8 km) **PG 356.3** (573.4 km) **CARROT CREEK.** Post office, grocery store, gas station, car wash and phone.

E 97.5 (157 km) **PG 352.5** (567.2 km) **Junction** with Highway 32 which leads to Whitecourt and Highway 43, 42 miles/67.6 km north on paved road. (See **Milepost E 112.7** in the EAST ACCESS ROUTE section for log of Highway 43.)

E 100.9 (162.4 km) **PG 349.1** (561.5 km) Turnout with litter barrels.

E 102.1 (164.4 km) **PG 347.9** (559.8 km) Wolf Lake public campground, 33 miles/53 km south on gravel road; 14 sites, pit toilets, tables, litter barrels.

E 105 (169 km) **PG 345** (555.2 km) Edson rest area to south with flush toilets, water, tables, shelter, phone and sani-dump.

E 106 (170.6 km) **PG 344** (553.6 km) Rosevear Road; eastbound access to Edson rest area.

E 110 (177.1 km) **PG 340** (547.1 km) Private campground.

E 113.1 (182 km) **PG 336.9** (542.2 km) McLeod River bridge.

E 114.9 (185 km) **PG 335.1** (539.2 km) **EDSON** (pop. 7,400). **Emergency Services: Hospital** and RCMP post **Visitor Information:** South on 55th Street. Edson's economy is based on coal mining, forestry, oil, natural gas and manufacturing. Edson is a large highway community with 16 motels, many restaurants and gas stations; 18-hole golf course and driving range; and an indoor pool.

RV camping at Edson RV Campground, located at the east end of Edson, south of Highway 16 on the road to the golf course. The nearest public campgrounds are Lions Park Campground east of town and Willmore Recreation Park south of town.

Edson RV Campground. See display ad this section.

E 123.2 (198.3 km) **PG 326.8** (525.9 km) Food, gas, lodging and phone.

E 128 (206 km) **PG 322** (518.2 km) Hornbeck Creek government campground to north adjacent to highway; 33 sites, picnic area, firewood, water pump, stream fishing.

E 133 (214 km) **PG 317** (510.2 km) Small community of Marlboro to north. First view of Canadian Rockies westbound.

E 140.8 (226.6 km) **PG 309.2** (497.6 km) Westbound-only turnout with picnic tables, pit toilets and litter barrels; generous, paved parking area.

E 142.7 (229.6 km) **PG 307.3** (494.6 km) Eastbound-only turnout with litter barrels.

E 148.1 (238.3 km) **PG 301.9** (485.9 km) **Obed Lake** government campground to north; 8 sites, picnic area, firewood, pit toilets, boat launch, beach area. Fishing for rainbows, brown and eastern brook trout, and yellow perch.

E 150.3 (241.9 km) **PG 299.7** (482.3 km) **OBED**. Phone, gas and groceries.

E 156.4 (251.8 km) **PG 293.6** (472.4 km) **Obed Summit**, highest elevation on the Yellowhead Highway at 3,819 feet/1,164m. Paved turnout with picnic tables, toilets and litter barrels; good view of the Rockies, weather permitting.

E 157.7 (253.9 km) **PG 292.3** (470.3 km) Treed roadside turnout; generous parking area, picnic tables, toilets and litter barrels.

E 166.7 (268.3 km) **PG 283.3** (455.9 km) **HINTON** (pop. 10,000). **Emergency services: Hospital**, dentist and RCMP post. A major service stop on Yellowhead Highway 16, Hinton has all visitor facilities, including hotels and motels; gas stations; shopping centres and shopping mall; bowling alley, curling rink, golf course and recreation complex with indoor pool. Hinton is only 18 miles/28 km east of Jasper National Park gate.

There are 3 campgrounds in town. Nearby William A. Switzer Provincial Park on Highway 40 encompasses 5 campgrounds and offers fishing.

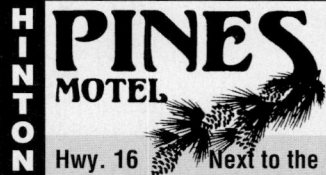

Hinton is the site of Weldwood of

Canada Ltd. pulp mill; tours of the mill complex may be arranged. Hinton began in the 1900s as a construction camp for railroad, coal mining and logging crews. The commmunity grew dramatically after construction of the pump mill in 1955. The subsequent addition of 3 major coal mining operations and a sawmill further increased the population.

Pines Motel. See display ad this section.

Rocky River Inn. See display ad this section.

Town of Hinton. See display ad this section.

E 171 (275.3 km) **PG 279** (448.9 km) South **junction** with Highway 40.

E 172.2 (277.1 km) **PG 277.8** (447.1 km) **Junction** with Bighorn Highway 40 (paved), which leads north 88 miles/142 km to Grande Cache then another 117 miles/188 km to Grande Prairie.

William A. Switzer Provincial Park 16.8 miles/27 km north on Big Horn Highway 40; camping, picnicking, fishing. ▲

E 176.8 (284.5 km) **PG 273.2** (439.7 km) Maskuta Creek picnic area with tables, shelter, toilets and litter barrels.

E 177.8 (286.2 km) **PG 272.2** (438 km) Weigh scales and pay phone.

E 179 (288.1 km) **PG 271** (436.1 km) Public campground 3.1 miles/5 km north. ▲

E 181.5 (292.2 km) **PG 268.5** (432 km) Private campground, pay phone. ▲

E 182.4 (293.6 km) **PG 267.6** (430.6 km) Turnout to north with litter barrels and point of interest sign about Athabasca River.

E 182.9 (294.4 km) **PG 267.1** (429.8 km) Resort with lodging and camping to north. ▲

E 184.2 (296.5 km) **PG 265.8** (427.7 km) **Jasper National Park, East Entrance.** Park fees are charged on a per-person basis and must be paid by all visitors using facilities in Rocky Mountain national parks. Public phones.

Alberta's Jasper National Park is part of the Canadian Rocky Mountains World Heritage Site. It is the largest of Canada's Rocky Mountain parks, covering 4,200 square miles/20,878 square kms. It adjoins Banff National Park to the south. Most visitors sightsee Jasper's (and Banff's) spectacular mountain scenery from Highway 93 (Icefields Parkway).

E 185.6 (298.8 km) **PG 264.4** (425.4 km) Fiddle River bridge.

E 189 (304.2 km) **PG 261** (420 km) **POCAHONTAS** has a motel with cabins, swimming pool and restaurant; and grocery.

Junction with Miette Hot Springs Road. Self-guiding interpretive trail 0.2 mile/0.3 km south on Miette Road; Park Service campground (140 sites) 0.6 mile/1 km south; and **Miette Hot Springs** resort 11 miles/17.7 km south. The resort has a motel and cafe; 2 thermal pools and one cool pool (towels and bathing suits for rent, admission fee). Beautiful setting, look for mountain sheep and black bear. ▲

E 192 (309 km) **PG 258** (415.2 km) Turnout with cairn to south. Mineral lick here is frequented by goats and sheep. Watch for wildlife, especially at dawn and dusk.

Highway 16 has restricted speed zones where wildlife sightings are frequent. Drive carefully and watch out for moose, elk, white-tailed and mule deer, mountain goats, bighorn sheep, and black and grizzly bears. *NOTE: It is illegal to feed, touch, disturb or hunt wildlife in the national park. All plants and natural objects are also protected and may not be removed or destroyed.*

Blooming dandelions and a black bear on the Yellowhead Highway. (© Blake Hanna, staff)

Many turnouts next 25 miles/40 km westbound.

E 193 (310.6 km) **PG 257** (413.6 km) First Rocky River bridge westbound.

E 194.3 (312.7 km) **PG 255.7** (411.5 km) Second Rocky River bridge westbound.

E 203 (326.7 km) **PG 247** (397.5 km) Two bridges spanning the Athabasca River. Raft trips down the Athabasca may be arranged in Jasper. Watch for elk and bighorn sheep.

E 205.1 (330.1 km) **PG 244.9** (394.1 km) Snaring River bridge.

E 206.7 (332.7 km) **PG 243.3** (391.5 km) Jasper airfield to south.

E 208.1 (335 km) **PG 241.9** (389.2 km) Snaring overflow camping south. ▲

E 208.4 (335.4 km) **PG 241.6** (388.8 km) Snaring rest area to south.

E 208.8 (336 km) **PG 241.2** (388.2 km) Palisades picnic area.

E 212.9 (342.6 km) **PG 237.1** (381.6 km) Access road to Jasper Park Lodge (lodging, restaurant, golf, etc.), Maligne Canyon and **Maligne Lake.** Glacier-fed Maligne Lake (35 miles/56 km south) is one of Jasper's premier attractions; scheduled boat tours.

E 215.8 (347.3 km) **PG 234.2** (376.9 km) **Junction** with Highway 93A. Lodging and restaurant to south.

E 216.6 (348.6 km) **PG 233.4** (375.6 km)

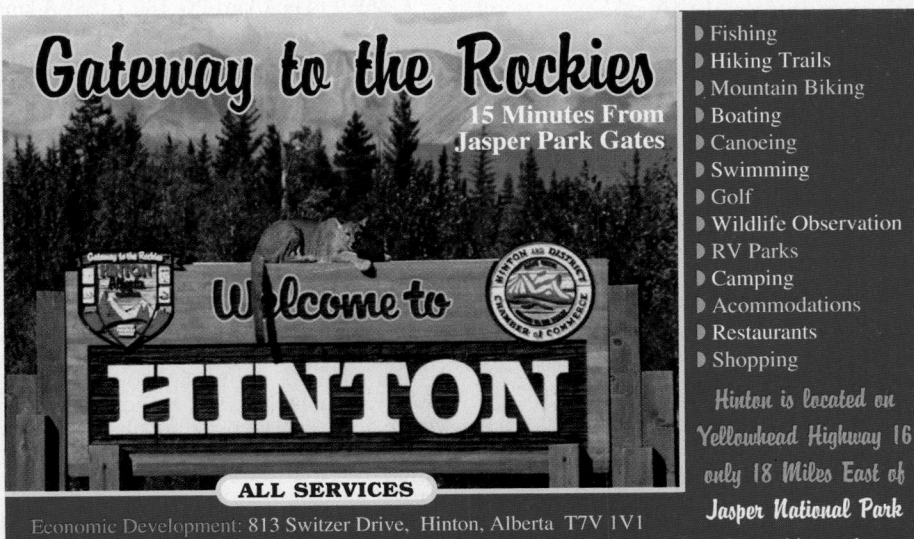

Access to **JASPER** (pop. 4,800), townsite for Jasper National Park. **Visitor Information:** At park headquarters in town.

All visitor services available downtown along Connaught Blvd. Jasper has a local museum, recreation centre with indoor pool and summer interpretive programs.

Junction with Highway 93, the scenic Icefields Parkway, south to junction with Trans-Canada Highway 1 (140 miles/225 km), providing access to Columbia Icefield, Lake Louise and Banff.

NOTE: No fuel next 62.5 miles/100.6 km westbound on Highway 16.

E 217.1 (349.5 km) **PG 232.9** (374.7 km) Miette River.

E 222.2 (357.6 km) **PG 227.8** (366.6 km) Paved turnout to north with outhouses, litter barrels and interpretive sign about Yellowhead Pass. Many turnouts next 25 miles/40 km eastbound.

E 223.2 (359.3 km) **PG 226.8** (364.9 km) Meadow Creek.

E 223.4 (359.5 km) **PG 226.6** (364.7 km) Trailhead for Virl Lake, Dorothy Lake and Christine Lake.

E 226.1 (363.9 km) **PG 223.9** (360.3 km) Clairvaux Creek.

E 229.4 (369.3 km) **PG 220.6** (354.9 km) **Jasper National Park, West Entrance.** Park fee must be paid by all visitors using facilities in Rocky Mountain national parks.

E 231.6 (372.7 km) **PG 218.4** (351.5 km) **Yellowhead Pass** (elev. 3,760 feet/1,146m), Alberta–British Columbia border. Named for an Iroquois trapper and guide who worked for the Hudson's Bay Co. in the early 1800s. His light-colored hair earned him the name Tete Jaune ("yellow head") from the French voyageurs.

Mount Robson Provincial Park, East Entrance. Portal Lake picnic area with tables, toilets, information board and hiking trail.

TIME ZONE CHANGE: Alberta observes Mountain standard time. Most of British Columbia observes Pacific standard time. Both observe daylight saving time.

E 232.8 (374.7 km) **PG 217.2** (349.5 km) Kilometrepost 75. Kilometreposts on Yellowhead Highway 16 reflect distances within highway maintenance districts; *The MILEPOST®* periodically notes these physical posts as reference points.

E 235.8 (379.6 km) **PG 214.2** (344.6 km) Rockingham Creek.

E 236.2 (380.1 km) **PG 213.8** (344.1 km) **Yellowhead Lake**; picnic tables, viewpoint, boat launch and fishing.

E 238 (383 km) **PG 212** (341.2 km) Lucerne Campground; 32 sites, picnic tables, drinking water, firewood and swimming; camping fee charged. ▲

E 239.3 (385.2 km) **PG 210.7** (339 km) Fraser Crossing rest area to south; litter barrels and toilets.

E 239.4 (385.3 km) **PG 210.6** (338.9 km) Fraser River bridge No. 1.

E 242.4 (390.1 km) **PG 207.6** (334.1 km) Fraser River bridge No. 2.

E 245.2 (394.6 km) **PG 204.8** (329.6 km) Kilometrepost 55.

E 246.2 (396.2 km) **PG 203.8** (328 km) Grant Brook Creek.

E 249 (400.8 km) **PG 201** (323.4 km) Moose Creek bridge.

E 251.1 (404.2 km) **PG 198.9** (320 km) Turnout at east end of Moose Lake; information kiosk, tables, litter barrels, toilet and boat launch.

E 255.5 (411.2 km) **PG 194.5** (313 km) Turnout with litter barrels.

E 257.5 (414.4 km) **PG 192.5** (309.8 km) Kilometrepost 35.

E 263.7 (424.4 km) **PG 186.3** (299.8 km) Paved turnout with litter barrels.

E 268 (431.3 km) **PG 182** (292.9 km) **Overlander Falls** rest area to south; pit toilets and litter barrels. Hiking trail to Overlander Falls, about 30 minutes round-trip.

E 268.8 (432.7 km) **PG 181.2** (291.4 km) Viewpoint of **Mount Robson** (elev. 12,972 feet/3,954m), highest peak in the Canadian Rockies, and Visitor Infocentre. Parking, picnic tables, restrooms, litter barrels, gas and restaurant. Berg Lake trailhead; hike-in campgrounds. Private campground north of highway. Robson Meadows government campground south of highway with 125 sites, dump station, showers, pay phone, interpretive programs, tables, firewood, flush toilets, water and horseshoe pits; group camping; camping fee charged. ▲

E 269.4 (433.6 km) **PG 180.6** (290.6 km) Robson River government campground to north with 19 sites (some wheelchair-accessible), tables, firewood, pit toilets, showers, water and horseshoe pits; camping fee charged. ♿▲

E 269.8 (434.3 km) **PG 180.2** (289.9 km) Kilometrepost 15.

E 269.9 (434.4 km) **PG 180.1** (289.8 km) Robson River bridge. Look for Indian paintbrush June through August. The bracts are orange-red while the petals are green.

E 270.3 (435.1 km) **PG 179.7** (289.1 km) West entrance to Mount Robson Provincial Park. Turnout with litter barrels and statue.

E 270.5 (435.3 km) **PG 179.5** (288.9 km) Gravel turnout to south.

E 271.4 (436.8 km) **PG 178.6** (287.4 km) Swift Current Creek.

E 274.4 (441.7 km) **PG 175.6** (282.5 km) **Mount Terry Fox Provincial Park** picnic area with tables, restrooms and viewing telescope. The information board here points out the location of Mount Terry Fox in the Selwyn Range of the Rocky Mountains. The peak was named in 1981 to honour cancer victim Terry Fox, who, before his death from the disease, raised some $25 million for cancer research during his attempt to run across Canada.

E 276.3 (444.7 km) **PG 173.7** (280.5 km) Gravel turnout to north with Yellowhead Highway information sign.

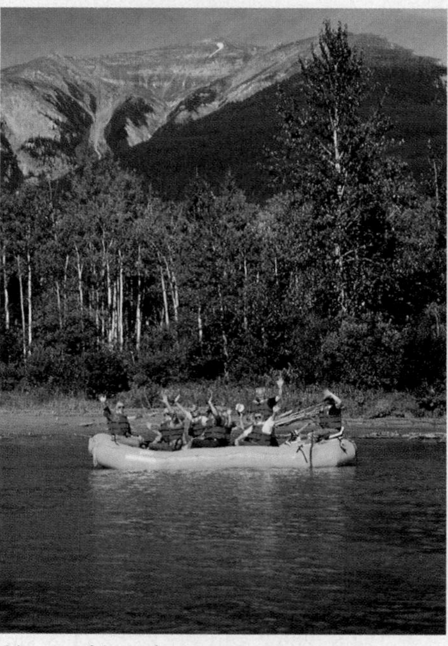

River rafting the Fraser River near Valemount. (Photo courtesy of Eagle Raft Tours)

E 276.4 (444.9 km) **PG 173.6** (280.3 km) **Rearguard Falls Provincial Park** picnic area. Easy half-hour round-trip to falls viewpoint. Upper limit of 800-mile/1,300-km migration of Pacific salmon; look for chinook in late summer.

E 277.8 (447.1 km) **PG 172.2** (277.1 km) Gravel turnout to south overlooking Fraser River.

E 278.2 (447.8 km) **PG 171.8** (276.4 km) Weigh scales.

E 278.7 (448.6 km) **PG 171.3** (275.6 km) Tete Jaune Cache rest area with tables, litter barrels and toilets.

E 279 (449.1 km) **PG 171** (275.1 km) **Junction** with Yellowhead Highway 5 south to the small community of **TETE JAUNE CACHE**, 1/2 mile (store and gas), and to **VALEMOUNT** (pop. 1,200), 12 miles/20 km; tourist information office and all visitor facilities. Yellowhead Highway 5 junctions with Trans Canada Highway 1 at Kamloops, 208 miles/335 km from here.

Irvin's Park & Campground. See display ad this section. ▲

E 279.1 (449.2 km) **PG 170.9** (275 km) Turnoff for gas, general store and deli, camping and lodging.

NOTE: No fuel eastbound next 62.5 miles/100.6 km.

E 279.6 (450.1 km) **PG 170.4** (274.1 km) Private lodging, restaurants.

E 280 (450.6 km) **PG 170** (273.6 km) **Eagle Raft Tours.** Gentle float trip on the majestic Fraser River with an old-fashioned barbecue on the deck of our historic log cabin overlooking the river. Depending on the season, you can view bald eagles, golden eagles, bears, beaver or watch spawning chinook salmon. This beautiful, scenic, wilderness tour is suitable for all ages. RV accessible. Phone (250) 566-9194; fax (250) 566-9927; www.eagleraft.com. [ADVERTISEMENT]

E 283.1 (455.7 km) **PG 166.9** (268.5 km) Spittal Creek Interpretive Forest; hiking trails, tables, litter barrels and toilets. Kilometrepost 140.

E **288.2** (463.8 km) **PG 161.8** (260.4 km) Private resort. Lodging, restaurant.

E **289.1** (465.3 km) **PG 160.9** (258.9 km) Small River rest area by stream with tables, toilets and litter barrels.

E **293.6** (472.5 km) **PG 156.4** (251.7 km) Horsey Creek.

E **295.4** (475.5 km) **PG 154.6** (248.7 km) Kilometrepost 120.

E **300** (482.9 km) **PG 150** (241.3 km) Turnoff to south for settlement of Dunster; gas and general store.

E **303.8** (489 km) **PG 146.2** (235.2 km) Holiday Creek rest area with toilets, picnic tables, litter barrel and hiking trails.

E **304.3** (489.7 km) **PG 145.7** (234.5 km) Baker Creek rest area with tables, litter barrels and toilets.

E **308.5** (496.6 km) **PG 141.5** (227.6 km) Kilometrepost 100.

E **308.9** (497.2 km) **PG 141.1** (227 km) Nevin Creek.

E **312** (502.1 km) **PG 138** (222.1 km) Turnouts at both ends of Holmes River bridge.

E **317.4** (510.8 km) **PG 132.6** (213.4 km) **Beaverview Campsite**. See display ad this section. ▲

E **317.9** (511.6 km) **PG 132.1** (212.6 km) Fraser River bridge.

E **318.2** (512.1 km) **PG 131.8** (212.1 km) Turnout to north with litter barrels.

E **318.8** (513.1 km) **PG 131.2** (211.1 km) **McBRIDE** (pop. 700; elev. 2,369 feet/722.1m), located in the Robson Valley by the Fraser River. The Park Ranges of the Rocky Mountains are to the northeast and the Cariboo Mountains are to the southeast. A road leads to Teare Mountain lookout for a spectacular view of countryside. The village of McBride was established in 1913 as a divisional point on the railroad and was named for Richard McBride, then premier of British Columbia. Forest products are a major industry here today.

Visitor Information: Visitor Infocentre located in railcar on south side of Highway 16. Look for the carved grizzly bear family in front. When the Infocentre isn't open, try the McBride Village Office. Located beside the railcar in the same parking lot, it is open 9 A.M. to 5 P.M.

McBride has all visitor facilities, including 5 hotels/motels, 2 bed and breakfasts, 2 supermarkets, 2 convenience/video stores, clothing stores, restaurants, pharmacy, hospital and gas stations. A library, museum and neighborhood pub are 1.9 miles/3 km from town. There is a private campground just east of town. Dump station located at the gas station. ▲

While in McBride, watch wood ducks, scoters, teals and more at the Horseshoe Lake Bird Watch. In late summer, see the salmon run in the Holmes River. In winter, go cross-country skiing on developed trails and snowmobiling in the backcountry. Helicopter service available for fly-in skiing and hiking.

McBride Chevron. See display ad this section.

North Country Lodge. See display ad this section.

NOTE: Next gas westbound is 90.7 miles/146 km from here (Purden Lake).

E **321.9** (518.1 km) **PG 128.1** (206.1 km) Dore River bridge.

E **326.7** (525.8 km) **PG 123.3** (198.4 km) Macintosh Creek.

E **328.8** (529.2 km) **PG 121.2** (195 km) Clyde Creek.

E **333.1** (536.2 km) **PG 116.9** (188 km) Kilometrepost 60.

E **336.9** (542.3 km) **PG 113.1** (181.9 km) West Twin Creek bridge.

E **343.6** (553.1 km) **PG 106.4** (171.1 km) Goat River bridge. Paved rest area to north with tables, toilets and litter barrels.

E **346.7** (558 km) **PG 103.3** (166.2 km) Little LaSalle Recreation Area and BC Forest Service site. Small lake, small wharf, toilet.

E **351.2** (565.2 km) **PG 98.8** (159 km) Snowshoe Creek.

E **351.8** (566.2 km) **PG 98.2** (158 km) Kilometrepost 30.

E **354.9** (571.2 km) **PG 95.1** (153 km) Catfish Creek.

E **360.7** (580.6 km) **PG 89.3** (143.6 km) Ptarmigan Creek bridge.

E **363.8** (585.6 km) **PG 86.2** (138.6 km) Turnout with litter barrels to north.

E **369.2** (594.1 km) **PG 80.8** (130.1 km) Dome Creek.

E **371.5** (597.9 km) **PG 78.5** (126.3 km) Food, phone.

E **373.3** (600.8 km) **PG 76.7** (123.4 km) Slim Creek paved rest area to south with information kiosk, tables, playground, litter barrels and wheelchair-accessible toilets. Watch for bears. ♿

E **373.4** (601 km) **PG 76.6** (123.2 km) Ministry of Highways camp.

E **374.1** (602.1 km) **PG 75.9** (122.1 km) Slim Creek bridge.

E **382.5** (615.6 km) **PG 67.5** (108.6 km) Kilometrepost 100.

E **385.6** (620.7 km) **PG 64.4** (103.5 km) Driscol Creek.

E **386.4** (621.9 km) **PG 63.6** (102.3 km) Forests in this area have been destroyed by the hemlock looper, an insect which has killed or damaged over 45.9 million cubic feet/1.3 million cubic metres of wood in British Columbia.

E **387.6** (623.9 km) **PG 62.4** (100.3 km) Gravel turnout with litter barrel to north.

E **388.9** (626 km) **PG 61.1** (98.2 km) Lunate Creek.

E **391.8** (630.6 km) **PG 58.2** (93.6 km) Grizzly hiking trail to south.

E **392** (630.9 km) **PG 58** (93.3 km) Hungary Creek. Watch for Ministry of Forests signs indicating the year in which a logged area was replanted. Wildflowers include fireweed, mid-July through August.

E **395.8** (637 km) **PG 54.2** (87.2 km) Sugarbowl Creek.

E **400.5** (644.6 km) **PG 49.5** (79.6 km) Paved turnout with litter barrel to north.

E **408.2** (657 km) **PG 41.8** (67.2 km) Kenneth Creek.

E **408.4** (657.4 km) **PG 41.6** (66.8 km) Purden Mountain ski resort.

E **409.5** (659.1 km) **PG 40.5** (65.1 km) Purden Lake resort with gas, phone, lodging and camping. ▲

NOTE: Next gas eastbound is 90.7miles/146 km from here (McBride).

E **411.2** (661.9 km) **PG 38.8** (62.3 km) **Purden Lake Provincial Park**, 1.9 miles/3 km from highway; 78 campsites, 48 picnic tables, water, dump station, firewood, playground and horseshoe pits. This recreation area offers a sandy beach, change houses, swimming, walking trails, waterskiing and boat launch. Good rainbow fishing to 4 lbs. Camping fee charged. ▲

E **412.6** (664.1 km) **PG 37.4** (60.1 km) Bowron River bridge. Paved rest area to north beside river, on west side of bridge; toilets, tables and litter barrels. Entrance on curve; use care. Turnaround space.

E **420.7** (677.1 km) **PG 29.3** (47.1 km) Kilometrepost 40.

E **421** (677.6 km) **PG 29** (46.6 km) Vama Vama Creek.

E **424** (682.4 km) **PG 26** (41.8 km) Wansa Creek.

E **427.1** (687.4 km) **PG 22.9** (36.8 km) Willow River bridge. Rest area at west end of bridge beside river; tables, litter barrels, toilets and nature trail. The 1.2-mile-/1.9-km-long Willow River Forest Interpretation Trail is an easy 45-minute walk.

E **429.5** (691.3 km) **PG 20.5** (32.9 km) Bowes Creek.

E **429.7** (691.6 km) **PG 20.3** (32.6 km) Turnout to north with litter barrels and information board on 1961 forest fire and moose habitat. Circle trail to moose observation site.

E **433** (697 km) **PG 17** (27.2 km) Kilome-

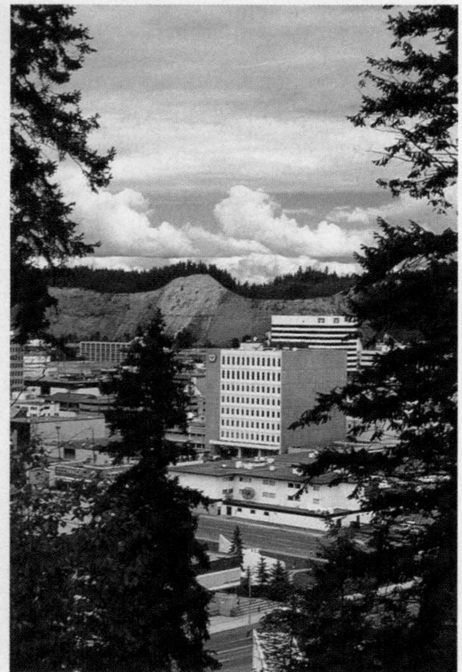

Prince George lies at the junction of Yellowhead Highway 16 and Highway 97. (© Judy Parkin)

trepost 20.

E 435.2 (700.5 km) **PG 14.8** (23.7 km) Tabor Mountain ski hill.

E 435.4 (700.8 km) **PG 14.6** (23.4 km) Gravel turnout to north with litter barrels.

E 437.6 (704.3 km) **PG 12.4** (19.9 km) Access to **Tabor Lake**; good fishing for rainbow in spring. ▲

E 444.8 (715.9 km) **PG 5.2** (8.3 km) **Junction** of Highway 16B with Highway 97 south bypass. Turn to page 71 in the WEST ACCESS ROUTE section for log of Highway 97 South to Cache Creek.

E 450 (724.2 km) **PG 0 PRINCE GEORGE** (see description on pages 71–75). Continue west on Yellowhead Highway 16 for Prince Rupert (log follows).

Junction with Highway 97 north to Dawson Creek and the beginning of the Alaska Highway. Turn to page 75 in the WEST ACCESS ROUTE section for the log of Highway 97 North.

This section of the log shows distance from Prince George (PG) followed by distance from Prince Rupert (PR).

NOTE: Physical kilometreposts west from here are up along Highway 16 about every 5 km and reflect distance from Prince Rupert. Because the posts do not always accurately reflect driving distance, mileages from Prince Rupert are based on actual driving distance while the kilometre conversion is based on physical kilometreposts as they occurred in summer 1999.

PG 0 PR 447.7 (720 km) **Junction** of Highways 16 and 97 (Central Avenue/Cariboo Highway) in Prince George. **Visitor Information:** Visitor centre at southeast corner of intersection (look for Mr. P.G. mascot); open daily in summer.

From Prince George to Prince Rupert, Highway 16 is a 2-lane highway with 3-lane passing stretches. Fairly straight, with no high summits, the highway follows the valleys of the Nechako, Bulkley and Skeena rivers, paralleling the Canadian National Railway route. There are few services between towns.

PG 0.2 (0.4 km) **PR 447.5** (719.6 km) Prince George Golf and Curling Club.

PG 0.6 (1 km) **PR 447.1** (719 km) Ferry Avenue.

PG 1.2 (1.9 km) **PR 446.5** (718.1 km) Tyner/Domano Blvd.; access to the University of Northern B.C.

PG 3.8(6.2 km) **PR 443.9** (714.4 km) Blue Spruce RV Park and Campground to north.▲

PG 5.7 (9.2 km) **PR 442** (711.3 km) Blackwater Road. Access to Baldy Hughes Adventure Land with camping, restaurant and pub. ▲

West Lake Provincial Park 8 miles/12.9 km south; day-use area with picnic shelter, swimming, fishing and boat launch.

PG 7.3 (11.8 km) **PR 440.4** (708.7 km) Western Road.

PG 12.5 (20.2 km) **PR 435.2** (700.4 km) Chilko River.

PG 15.2 (24.5 km) **PR 432.5** (696 km) **North Country Arts & Crafts.** See display ad this section.

PG 28.2 (45.4 km) **PR 419.5** (675.1 km) Tamarac Lake to south.

PG 37.6 (60.5 km) **PR 410.1** (660 km) **Lakeside Resort**. See display ad this section. ▲

Access to lakeside resort and fishing at **Cluculz Lake** (not visible from highway). Rainbow to 3 3/4 lbs. by trolling, use snell hook and worms; kokanee to 1 1/2 lbs., troll with snell hook and worms in spring; char to 57 lbs., use large flatfish, spoons, plugs and weights, early spring and late fall; whitefish to 5 lbs., year-round. Very good fishing in spring; ice goes out about the first week of May. Good ice fishing December to March. In September kokanee are at their peak. *Lake gets rough when windy.* ▲

PG 38.7 (62.4 km) **PR 409** (658.2 km) Cluculz rest area to south with flush toilets (summer only), picnic tables and litter barrels.

PG 39.2 (63.1 km) **PR 408.5** (657.4 km) **Brookside Resort.** Stay in a quiet pine forest next to Cluculz Creek. Serviced and unser-

viced sites. 30-amp spacious, shaded, level pull-throughs. Tent and camper sites with tables. Clean washrooms. Free showers and firewood for registered guests. Sani-dump, laundromat, grocery store, sleeping cabins. Ice, propane, gasoline, diesel, boat gas. Phone. VISA and MasterCard. R.R. #1, Site 16, Comp 75, Vanderhoof, BC V0J 3A0. (250) 441-0035. [ADVERTISEMENT] ▲

PG 58.6 (94.4 km) **PR 389.1** (626.2 km) **Dave's R.V. Park**. 2 miles east of Vanderhoof, 1/2 mile down Derksen Road. Clean, quiet, rural setting. 56 sites, long pull-throughs, full hookups (30 amp), partial hookups or no hookups on regular sites. Tent sites. Sani-dump. Limited groceries and RV supplies. Member of BCMRCA, FMCA. Pets on leash. VISA, MasterCard, Interac. Phone (250) 567-3161; fax (250) 567-5461. See ad this section. [ADVERTISEMENT] ▲

Vanderhoof

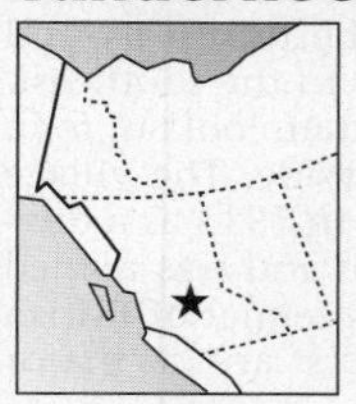

PG 58.7 (94.5 km) **PR 389** (624.8 km). Stoplight at junction with Highway 27; turnoff to downtown Vanderhoof. **Population:** 4,400; area 12,000. **Emergency Services: Police,** phone (250) 567-2222. **Fire Department**, phone (250) 567-2345. **Ambulance**, phone (800) 461-9911. **Hospital**, St. John's, Northside District, phone (250) 567-2211.

Visitor Information: Visitor Infocentre downtown on Burrard Avenue, 1 block off Highway 16. Write Vanderhoof & District Chamber of Commerce, Box 126-MP, Vanderhoof, BC V0J 3A0; phone (250) 567-2124.

Elevation: 2,225 feet/667.5m. **Radio:** CJCI 620, CFPR-FM 96.7, CKPG 550, CIVH

VANDERHOOF ADVERTISERS

Dave's R.V. Park	Ph. (250) 567-3161
Riverside Campsite	Ph. (250) 567-4710
Siesta Motel	Ph. (250) 567-2365

1340, CIRX-FM 95.9. **Television:** Channels 2, 4, 5, 6, 8. **Newspapers:** *Omineca Express–Bugle* (weekly). **Transportation: Air**—Vanderhoof airport, 2 miles/3.2 km from intersection of Highways 16 and 27; 5,000-foot/1,524-m paved runway. Seaplane landings on Nechako River at corner of View Street and Boundary Avenue. **Railroad**—VIA Rail, station at 2222 Church Ave. **Bus**—Greyhound.

Vanderhoof is the geographical centre of British Columbia. The city was named for Chicago publisher Herbert Vanderhoof, who founded the village in 1914 when he was associated with the Grand Trunk Development Co. Today, Vanderhoof is the supply and distribution centre for a large agricultural, lumbering and mining area.

The community's history is preserved at **Vanderhoof Heritage Village Museum**, just

off Highway 16. Relocated pioneer structures furnished with period artifacts recall the early days of the Nechako Valley.

Located on the Nechako River, Vanderhoof is a stopping place in April and September for thousands of migrating waterfowl. The river flats upstream of the bridge are a bird sanctuary. Pelicans have been spotted feeding at Tachick Lake south of town.

There are 7 hotels and motels and 17 restaurants in the town. All shopping facilities and several gas stations. An 18-hole golf course is located 1.9 miles/3.1 km north of town. Dump station at Dave's R.V. Park at **Milepost PG 58.6** and at Riverside Campsite (municipal campground) on Burrard Avenue. ▲

Fort St. James

Fort St. James

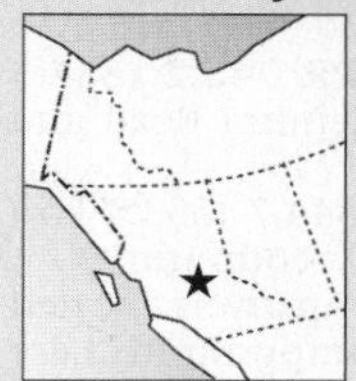

Located 37 miles/59.5 km north of Vanderhoof on Highway 27. **Population:** 2,146. **Emergency Services: Police**, phone (250) 996-8269. **Ambulance:** phone 1-562-7241. **Elevation:** 2,208 feet/ 673m. **Radio:** CKPG 550, CJCI 1480; CBC-FM 107.0. **Visitor Information:** At the Visitor Infocentre.

Fort St. James is located on Stuart Lake. Named for John Stuart, the man who succeeded Simon Fraser as head of the New Caledonia district, the 59-mile-/95-km-long lake is the southernmost in a 3-lake chain which provides hundreds of miles of boating and fishing. Fort St. James also boasts the Nation Lakes, a chain of 4 lakes (Tsayta, Indata, Tchentlo and Chuchi) connected by the Nation River.

Fort St. James has several hotel/motels, restaurants, gas station, private campgrounds, dump stations and 2 shopping centres. Picnicking and swimming at Cottonwood Park on Stuart Lake. A 9-hole golf course overlooks Stuart Lake; rentals available. ▲

Camping is also available at **Paarens Beach Provincial Park**, located 6.8 miles/10.9 km off Highway 27 on Sowchea Bay Road; 36 campsites, picnic shelter, picnic tables, toilets, water, firepits, firewood, boat launch and swimming; camping fee. **Sowchea Bay Provincial Park**, located 10.6 miles/17.1 km off Highway 27 on Sowchea Bay Road, has 30 campsites, camping fee, picnic tables, toilets, water, firepits, firewood, boat launch and swimming. ▲

Attractions include the Our Lady of Good Hope Catholic Church and the Chief Kwah burial site. The recently renovated church is one of the oldest in British Columbia. Chief Kwah was one of the first Carrier Indian chiefs to confront early white explorers. His burial site is located on the Nak'azdli Indian Reserve at the mouth of the Stuart River. At Cottonwood Park on the shore of Lake Stuart, look for a model of a Junkers airplane, which depicts the Fort's major role in early bush flying in Northern British Columbia.

Fort St. James is the home of **Fort St. James National Historic Site.** Established in 1806 by Simon Fraser as a fur trading post for the Northwest Co., Fort St. James served throughout the 19th century as headquarters for the Hudson's Bay Co.'s New Caledonia fur trade district. The fur warehouse, fish cache, men's house, officers' dwelling and trade store have been restored in 1896-style. The site is open from mid-May to September. Admission is charged.

Good fishing in **Stuart Lake** for rainbow and char (to trophy size), kokanee and Dolly Varden.

Return to Milepost PG 58.7 or PG 63.2 Yellowhead Highway 16

Yellowhead Highway 16 Log

(continued)

PG 58.7 (94.5 km) **PR 389** (624.8 km)

Junction with Highway 27 north 37 miles/60 km to Fort St. James. Ssee description this section.

PG 59.2 (95.2 km) **PR 388.5** (624.1 km) Vanderhoof Heritage Museum to south.

PG 63.2 (101.7 km) **PR 384.5** (617.6 km) Second **junction** westbound with Highway 27 (see description at **Milepost PG 58.7**). This route skirts Vanderhoof. Truck weigh scales to north.

PG 72.3 (116.3 km) **PR 375.4** (602.9 km) Plateau Division Sawmill to south.

PG 81.5 (131.1 km) **PR 366.2** (588 km) Turnout to south with view of Nechako River. The Grand Trunk Pacific Railway was completed near this site in 1914. The railroad (later the Canadian National) linked Prince Rupert, a deep-water port, with interior British Columbia. Entering Lakes District. This high country has over 300 freshwater lakes.

PG 81.8 (131.6 km) **PR 365.9** (587.5 km) **FORT FRASER** (pop. 600). **Radio:** CBC-FM 102.9. Small community with food, gas, propane, lodging and first-aid station. Gas station with hot showers, convenience store and restaurant. Named for Simon Fraser, who established a trading post here in 1806. Now a supply centre for surrounding farms and sawmills. The last spike of the Grand Trunk Railway was driven here on April 7, 1914.

PG 82.6 (133 km) **PR 365.1** (586.1 km) Nechako River bridge. Turnout to south with parking, litter barrels and access to **Nechako River;** fishing for rainbow and Dolly Varden, June to fall. At the east end of Fraser Lake, the Nautley River—less than a mile long—drains into the Nechako River.

PG 84.1 (135.4 km) **PR 363.6** (583.7 km) Nautley Road. **Beaumont Provincial Park**, on beautiful **Fraser Lake,** north side of highway; site of original Fort Fraser. Boat launch, swimming, hiking, fishing, 49 campsites, picnic tables, firewood, flush toilets, water, playground, horseshoe pits, dump station. Fishing for rainbow and lake trout, burbot, sturgeon and Dolly Varden. ▲

PG 85.9 (138.3 km) **PR 361.8** (580.8 km) View of Fraser Lake to north.

PG 86.3 (138.9 km) **PR 361.7** (580.5 km) Access to private campground on Fraser

Lake; chainsaw sculpture.

Pipers Glen RV Resort. See display ad this section. ▲

PG 88.8 (142.9 km) **PR 358.9** (577.4 km) **Orange Valley Motel, RV Park and Campground.** Easy access featuring level sites, large, pull-throughs, electricity, water, some with sewer. Free showers, flush toilets, sani-dump, treed shaded sites with picnic tables. Firepits, firewood available; freezer space available. Quiet relaxed setting. Pay phone, hiking trails, beaver dam. Phone (250) 699-6350. [ADVERTISEMENT] ▲

PG 87.9 (141.4 km) **PR 359.8** (578 km) Dry William Lake rest area to south with picnic tables, toilets and litter barrels.

PG 89.7 (144.4 km) **PR 358** (575 km) View of Mouse Mountain to northwest.

PG 90.9 (146.3 km) **PR 356.8** (573 km) Fraser Lake sawmill to north.

PG 91.3 (147 km) **PR 356.4** (572.3 km) Gas and diesel.

PG 94.5 (152.1 km) **PR 353.2** (567.2 km) **FRASER LAKE** (pop. 1,400; elev. 2,580 feet/786m). **Visitor Information:** Fraser Lake Museum and Visitor Infocentre in log building. **Radio:** CJCI 1450. Small community with all facilities. Created by Endako Mines Ltd. in 1964 on an older townsite; named after the explorer Simon Fraser. Endako Mines Ltd. began operating in 1965 and was Canada's largest molybdenum mine until production slowed in 1982. Mining resumed in 1986. Mine tours are available on Wednesdays; check with the Visitor Infocentre for reservations. Also located here is Fraser Lake Sawmills, the town's largest employer.

PG 96.9 (156 km) **PR 350.8** (563.3 km) **Junction** with main access road south to scenic Francois Lake; also accessible via roads from Burns Lake to Houston. Francois Lake Road (chip seal surfacing) leads south 7 miles/11 km to the east end of Francois Lake (where the Stellako River flows from the lake) and back to Highway 16 at Endako. (It does *not* link up to the Francois Lake Ferry, south of Burns Lake.) Golf course and several resorts with camping, cabins and boats are located on this scenic rural road along the lake through the Glenannan area. ▲

Francois Lake, good fishing for rainbow to 5 lbs., May to October; kokanee to 3/4 lb., use flashers, willow leaf, flashers with worms, flatfish or spinners, August and September; char to 30 lbs., use large flatfish or spoon, June and July. **Stellako River** is considered one of British Columbia's better fly-fishing streams with rainbow over 2 lbs., all summer; whitefish averaging 1 lb., year-round.

Welcome to the North Country!

PG 97.6 (157.1 km) **PR 350.1** (562.2 km) Bridge over Stellako River. Highway passes through the Stellako Indian Reserve. Slenyah Indian village to north.

PG 102.5 (164.9 km) **PR 345.2** (554.3 km) Endako Mine (molybdenum) Road and Four Mile Creek.

PG 103 (165.8 km) **PR 344.7** (553.4 km) **ENDAKO**, a small highway community. A log home construction company is located here. Several private campgrounds are located along Francois Lake Road to the south in the Glenannan area. ▲

PG 103.8 (167.1 km) **PR 343.9** (552 km) CNR Bunkhouse.

Watch for moose next 10 miles/16 km westbound.

PG 105.5 (169.8 km) **PR 342.2** (549.3 km) Endako River bridge.

PG 109.1 (175.6 km) **PR 338.6** (543.5 km) Savory rest area with picnic tables and litter barrels to north beside Watskin Creek.

PG 109.5 (176.2 km) **PR 338.2** (543.8 km) Turnout.

PG 109.8 (176.8 km) **PR 337.9** (542.3 km) Restaurant to north.

PG 112 (180.3 km) **PR 335.7** (538.8 km) Ross Creek.

PG 112.9 (181.7 km) **PR 334.8** (537.4 km) Tschinkut Creek and moose flats.

PG 120.4 (193.8 km) **PR 327.3** (525.2 km) Moose meadow to south.

PG 121 (194.7 km) **PR 326.6** (524.3 km) Paved turnout to south with litter barrel.

PG 125 (201.1 km) **PR 322.7** (517.8 km) Babine Forest Products sawmill to south.

PG 128.3 (206.4 km) **PR 319.4** (512.5 km) View of Burns Lake to south.

PG 130.1 (209.4 km) **PR 317.6** (509.5 km) Tintagel Creek.

PG 130.2 (209.6 km) **PR 317.5** (509.3 km) Rest area to south with toilet, tables, litter barrels and Tintagel Cairn point of interest.

PG 133.8 (215.4 km) **PR 313.8** (503.4 km) **Burns Lake K.O.A.**, a day's drive from Prince Rupert ferry. Cabins, tenting to full hookups, store, heated showers, laundromat, game room, playground. Lake swimming. Open May 1 to Sept. 30. Pay phone. Your host, Ed Brown, Box 491, Burns Lake, BC V0J 1E0. Phone (250) 692-3105, (800) 562-0905. [ADVERTISEMENT] ▲

PG 136.7 (220 km) **PR 311** (498.9 km) Motel.

PG 137.5 (221.3 km) **PR 310.2** (497.5 km) Welcome to Burns Lake sign.

Junction with scenic Highway 35 (paved) south 18 miles/29 km past **Tchesinkut Lake** to **Francois Lake Ferry** landing. A free 36-car ferry departs from the south shore on the hour, from the north shore on the half-hour. From the south shore of Francois Lake, Highway 35 continues to **Takysie Lake** and **Ootsa Lake**, with access to a number of other fishing lakes. Another of the Yellowhead's popular fishing areas with a variety of family-owned camping and cabin resorts. Gas stations, stores and food service are also available. ▲

Sandy's RV and Camping Resort. Over 50 full-service, easy-access sites along the shores of Francois Lake. Hot showers, laundromat, boat rentals, launch, marina, cabins and more. Enjoy northern hospitality; only 18 paved miles south of Burns Lake on Highway 35; located on a true fishing lake. Rainbow, kokanee and lake trout. Pets welcome. VISA, MasterCard. May 15–Oct. 1. Phone/fax (250) 695-6321. Box 42, Burns Lake, BC V0J 1E0. [ADVERTISEMENT] ▲

Burns Lake

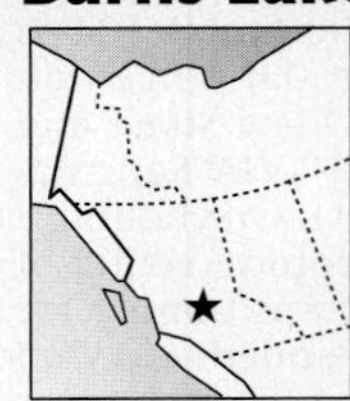

PG 139.9 (225.1 km) **PR 307.8** (496.3 km) **Junction** with road to Babine Lake. **Population:** 2,500; area 10,000. **Visitor Information:** On Highway 16 in the **Burns Lake Heritage Centre**. The former Old Forestry Home, built in 1919, the Heritage Centre also houses the Lakes District Museum.. Or contact the Chamber of Commerce, Box 339, Burns Lake, BC V0J 1E0; phone (250) 692-3773; fax (250) 692-3493.

Elevation: 2,320 feet/707m. **Radio:** CFLD 760, CJFW-FM 92.9 or 105.5, CBC-FM 99.1. **Transportation:** Greyhound Bus, VIA Rail.

The village of Burns Lake had its modest beginnings in 1911, as the site of railway construction. Forestry is the mainstay of the economy, along with ranching and tourism.

Burns Lake has 4 motels, a hotel, 7 bed and breakfasts, 16 restaurants, 3 shopping centres and a golf course. Overnight camping is available at the municipal campground at Radley Beach; washrooms, playground, picnic tables and swimming area. ▲

Burns Lake is situated in the heart of the Lakes District, which boasts "3000 miles of fishing." Species include kokanee, rainbow trout, char and salmon. Small family-owned campgrounds and fishing resorts, offering lodging, camping and boat rentals, are tucked along these lakes.

From Burns Lake, a side road leads north to **Babine Lake**, the longest natural lake in the province. One of British Columbia's most important salmon producing lakes, Babine Lake drains into the Skeena River. Excellent fishing for char and trout in summer. At Mile 15/Km 24.1 on this road is **Ethel F. Wilson Provincial Park** on **Pinkut Lake**; 10 campsites, fishing, swimming, water pump, toilets, firewood, picnic tables, boat launch. Tours of nearby Pinkut Fish Hatchery available. Look for pictographs on cliffs across from hatchery. **Pendleton Bay Provincial Park** on Babine Lake, open May to October, offers 20 campsites, picnic tables, water pump, fishing, swimming and boat launch. Resort with cabins and camping on Babine Lake. ▲

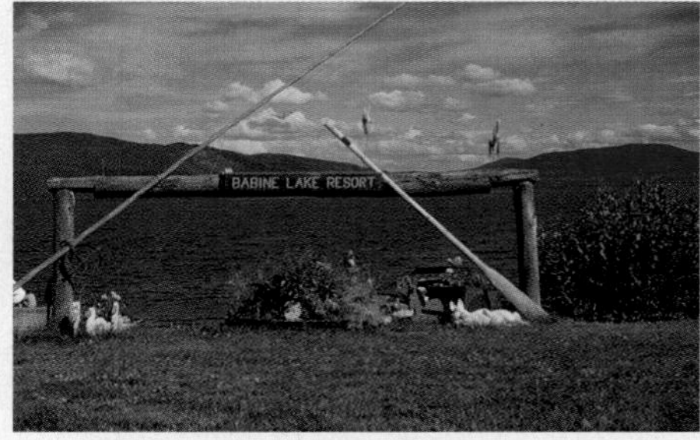

Babine Lake Resort, 29.8 miles/48 km from Burns Lake. British Columbia's largest natural body of water. Good fishing. Photographer's dream. Self-contained cabins, power, water hookups, showers, tenting, boats, smokehouses, store, licensed dining by reservation only. Ausserdem sprechen wir deutsch. Accepting VISA. Bill and Traude Hoff welcome you. Box 528, Burns Lake.

(250) 964-4692 or Burns Lake channel N696674. [ADVERTISEMENT] ▲

Yellowhead Highway 16 Log

(continued)

PG 140.3 (225.3 km) **PR 307.4** (494.7 km) Turnout with map and information sign to south.

PG 143.9 (231.5 km) **PR 303.8** (489.9 km) Small community of **DECKER LAKE.**

Decker Lake, good char and trout fishing; fly-fishing in **Endako River**, which joins Decker and Burns lakes.

PG 149.3 (240.3 km) **PR 298.4** (481.2 km) Golf course.

PG 150.9 (242.8 km) **PR 296.8** (478.7 km) Palling rest area with picnic tables, toilets and litter barrels.

PG 153.2 (246.5 km) **PR 294.5** (475 km) Baker Lake airstrip to south is used by fire-fighting tankers. Weather station. Emergency telephone.

PG 158 (254.2 km) **PR 289.7** (467.3 km) Rose Lake to south.

PG 161.7 (260.3 km) **PR 286** (461.2 km) **Broman Lake**, rainbow and char to 4 lbs., use white-winged flies, spring and summer. Dyncan Lake Indian band. Broman Lake Fuel.

PG 164.7 (265.1 km) **PR 283** (456.4 km) Six Mile Summit (elev. 4,669 feet/1,423m) to west. China Nose Mountain, with steep west-facing cliff, is visible to the south.

PG 165 (265.5 km) **PR 282.7** (456 km) Turnout with litter barrel to south.

PG 166.3 (267.7 km) **PR 281.4** (453.7 km) Turnout to south.

PG 171 (275.3 km) **PR 276.7** (446.1 km) Large turnout to north with information sign on Lakes District. Entering **TOPLEY** (pop. 300) westbound; grocery, post office, cafe, motel and gas station.

Turn north for **Babine Lake Recreation Area**. This paved side road leads north to Topley Landing and Granisle on Babine Lake (descriptions follow). From its junction with the highway at Topley, mileages are as follows: Mile 23.6/38 km, private lodge; Mile 24.4/39.3 km, turnoff to village of Topley Landing; Mile 28.8/46.3 km, Fulton River spawning channel; Mile 28/45.1 km, **Red Bluff Provincial Park** with 43 campsites, picnicking and day-use facilities, boat launch, drinking water, toilets, firewood, swimming, fishing and hiking; Mile 30.6/49 km, Lions Beach Park with 16 campsites, picnicking and day-use facilities, boat launch, dock, toilets, firewood, swimming and fishing; Mile 31.4/50.5 km, Granisle; Mile 33.4/53.8 km, begin 16-mile/25.7-km gravel road to Smithers Landing Road, which connects Smithers Landing and Smithers. *CAUTION: Watch for moose along road.* ▲

TOPLEY LANDING has several resorts and an unmaintained provincial park. It is also the home of the restored, historic Church of Angels; open June through September. This rustic log church has a collage of angels, a museum and gift shop.

The government-operated **Fulton River spawning channel** has 2 major spawning channels on the river that connect Fulton Lake and Babine Lake. Babine Lake, which flows into the Skeena River, is one of the largest freshwater habitats for sockeye salmon. The salmon enhancement project at Fulton River produces about 95 million sockeye fry annually. The sockeye run takes place in August and September. Tours may be available at hatchery office.

GRANISLE (pop. 400) was established in 1965 as a company town for the Granisle Copper Mine. In 1972, Noranda Bell Mines Copper Division went into operation. Granisle Copper was closed in 1982 and the Noranda mine was closed in 1992. During mining excavations, a mammoth skeleton was unearthed. The fossilized remains were donated to the Museum of Civilization in Ottawa–Hull. Granisle has become a retirement community and remains a resort area for fishing, boating, waterskiing and camping on Babine Lake. Facilities at Granisle include a convenience store and liquor outlet; resort condominiums and area lakefront wilderness resorts; post office, museum; boat rentals, marina and tackle shop. Dump station, showers, laundromat and fresh water available at the Visitor Infocentre. ▲

Babine Lake, rainbow 6 to 8 lbs.; lake trout to 40 lbs., use spoons, flashers and red-and-white spoons, May through November. When fishing early in the year, use a short troll.

PG 172.3 (277.3 km) **PR 275.4** (444 km) Rest area to south with toilets and view of mountains.

PG 176.9 (284.7 km) **PR 270.8** (437.8 km) Byman Creek.

PG 178.7 (287.6 km) **PR 269** (434.9 km) Motel and laundromat.

PG 180.1 (289.9 km) **PR 267.6** (432.5 km) Turnout to north.

PG 184.1 (295.7 km) **PR 263.6** (424.3 km) Golf course to south.

PG 186.5 (300.1 km) **PR 261.2** (422.2 km) Golf course to south.

PG 188.8 (303.9 km) **PR 258.9** (418.4 km) **Shady Rest RV Park**. See display ad this section. ▲

Houston

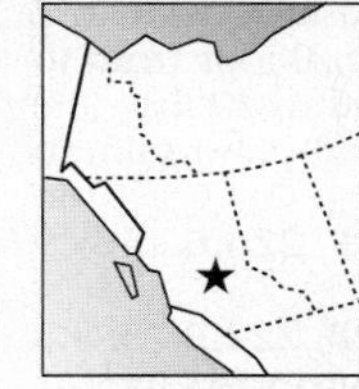

PG 190.1 (305.9 km) **PR 257.6** (416.4 km) Houston Infocentre. **Population:** 4,343. **Emergency Services: Police**, phone (250) 845-2204. **Ambulance**, phone (250) 845-2900. **Visitor Information:** Visitor Infocentre in log building on Highway 16 across from the mall and next to Steelhead Park (look for the fish fountain); open year-round. Write Houston Visitor Infocentre, Box 396, Houston, BC V0J 1Z0, or phone (250) 845-7640.

The World's Largest Fly Fishing Rod is on display at the Visitor Infocentre. The 60-foot-long anodized aluminum fly rod was designed by a local avid fly fisherman and built by local volunteers. (The 21-inch fly is a fluorescent "Skykomish Sunrise.")

Elevation: 1,926 feet/587m. **Climate:** Average temperature in summer, 71°F/21°C; in winter, 19°F/-7°C. **Radio:** CFBV 1450, CFPR-FM 102.1, CJFW-FM 105.5. **Newspaper:** *The Houston Today*. **Transportation:** Greyhound bus, VIA Rail.

Established in the early 1900s, Houston was a tie-cutting centre during construction of the Grand Trunk Pacific Railway in 1912. It was named for Prince Rupert newspaperman John Houston, the former mayor of Nelson, BC. Logging continued to support the local economy with the rapid growth of mills and planer mills in the 1940s and 1950s. Houston was incorporated as a village in 1957.

The Equity Silver Mine began production in 1980. Production ceased in January 1994 and equipment was dismantled.

World's Largest Fly Fishing Rod is on display at Houston's Visitor Infocentre. (© Blake Hanna, staff)

Today, the main industry in Houston is forest products. The 2 large sawmills here, Houston Forest Products and Northwood Pulp and Timber, offer forestry-awareness tours. The Chamber of Commerce and Visitor Infocentre arrange tours of the sawmills and also offer a day-long tour through the area's forests to provide a first-hand look at the forest industry.

Hunting, canoeing and sportfishing are major attractions here. Special events include Pleasant Valley Days in May and Houston Days in August.

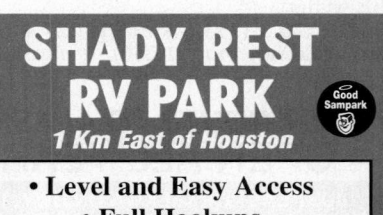

Houston has all visitor facilities, including motels, campgrounds, restaurants, gas stations, a shopping centre and golf courses. ▲

Yellowhead Highway 16 Log

(continued)

PG 192.6 (310 km) **PR 255.1** (412.2 km) **Junction** with the Morice River access road which extends 52 miles/84 km south to Morice Lake. Approximately 20 miles/32 km along the Morice River Road you can turn east on a gravel road which leads past Owen Lake and Nadina River Road to Francois Lake. From Francois Lake ferry landing Highway 35 leads north to Burns Lake.

The 2 famous salmon and steelhead streams, **Morice** and **Bulkley**, unite near Houston, and it is possible to fish scores of pools all along the Morice River. Fishing for resident rainbow, cutthroat and Dolly Varden; steelhead and salmon (chinook, coho) in season. *NOTE: Special requirements apply to fishing these streams; check with Fish and Game office.*

PG 193 (310.7 km) **PR 254.7** (411.5 km) Bulkley River bridge and rest area; tables, litter barrel and toilets.

PG 196.7 (316.5 km) **PR 251** (405.7 km) Barrett Station Airport. View of Barrett's Hat northbound.

PG 200.5 (322.6 km) **PR 247.2** (399.6 km) **Hungry Hill Summit** (elev. 2,769 feet/844m). To the north are the snow-capped peaks of the Babine Mountains, to the west is the Hudson Bay Range.

PG 203.3 (327.2 km) **PR 244.4** (394.9 km) Bulkley View paved rest area with picnic tables, toilets and litter barrels.

PG 208.1 (334.9 km) **PR 239.6** (387 km) Deep Creek.

PG 210.4 (338.7 km) **PR 237.2** (383.2 km) Quick Road East. Original telegraph cabin.

PG 211.4 (340.2 km) **PR 236.3** (381.7 km) Garage.

PG 213.3 (343.3 km) **PR 234.4** (378.6 km) Quick Road West.

PG 216.8 (348.9 km) **PR 230.9** (373 km) Bulkley field and river.

PG 217.1 (349.4 km) **PR 230.6** (372.5 km) Large rest area to west with toilets and litter barrels overlooking the Bulkley River.

PG 219.8 (353.7 km) **PR 227.9** (368.1 km) **Ft. Telkwa R.V. Park.** See display ad this section. ▲

PG 220.3 (354.5 km) **PR 227.4** (367.3 km) **TELKWA** (pop. 1,250). A pleasant village at the confluence of the Telkwa and Bulkley rivers (you can fish from Riverside Street or the riverbanks). Visitor Infocentre at the village office and museum. Facilities include a grocery, post office, a gas station with auto repair, and some unique shops. Lodging at Douglas Motel, dining at 5 restaurants.

Fishing and hunting information, licenses and supplies available at the general store. Kinsmen Barbecue is held over Labour Day weekend; games, contests and demolition derby. Eddy Park, on the western edge of town beside the Bulkley River, is a good spot for picnicking (look for the wishing well). St. Stephen's Anglican Church was built in 1911 and the bell and English gate added in 1921. Other Heritage buildings date back to 1908.

PG 220.7 (355.3 km) **PR 227** (366.5 km) Turnoff to north for **Tyhee Lake Provincial Park**; 55 campsites, 20 picnic tables, dump station, hiking trails, fishing, swimming, boat launch. Seaplane base at lake; charter fly-in fishing. ▲

Also turnoff here on the Telkwa High Road, which intersects with Babine Lake access road (gravel), which leads 46 miles/74 km north to Smithers Landing on Babine Lake and 56 miles/90 km to Granisle.

Tyhee Lake, rainbow and lake trout to 2 lbs., June through August; Kamloops trout to 2 lbs. **Babine River**, steelhead to 40 lbs., late fall. **Telkwa River**, spring and coho salmon to 24 lbs., summer to fall.

PG 221.1 (355.9 km) **PR 226.6** (365.9 km) Gas station.

PG 225.5 (362.9 km) **PR 222.2** (358.8 km) Second turnoff westbound for Babine Lake.

PG 227.2 (365.7 km) **PR 220.5** (356 km) Riverside Recreation Centre; golf, restaurant and campground. ▲

PG 227.5 (366.1 km) **PR 220.2** (355.7 km) Turnoff to north on gravel road for **Driftwood Canyon Provincial Park**; picnic area and toilets. Fossil beds in shale outcroppings along creekbank. *(Please do not remove fossils.)* This gravel side road continues north to Smithers Landing.

PG 227.7 (366.4 km) **PR 220** (355.3 km) Bridge over Bulkley River.

Smithers

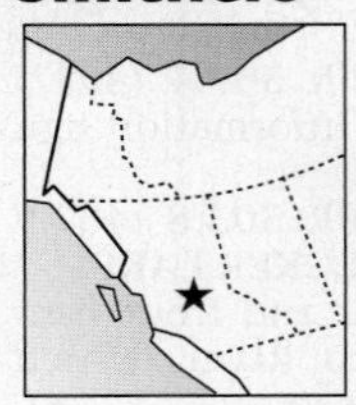

PG 229.2 (368.8 km) **PR 218.5** (352.6 km). Smithers infocentre. **Population:** 6,000; area 30,000. **Emergency Services: Police**, phone (250)847-3233. **Hospital** and **Poison Centre**, 3950 8th Ave., phone (250) 847-2611. **Ambulance**, phone 1-562-7241.

Visitor Information: Visitor Infocentre and Chamber of Commerce are located adjacent to the Central Park Bldg., which houses the museum and art gallery; open year-round. Contact P.O. Box 2379, Smithers, BC V0J 2N0; phone (800) 542-6673; www.bulkley.net/~smicham.

Elevation: 1,621 feet/494m. **Climate:** Relatively warmer and drier than mountainous areas to the west; average temperature in July is 58°F/14°C, in January 14°F/-10°C; annual precipitation, 13 inches. **Radio:** CFBV 870, CJFW-FM 92.9 or 105.5, CBC -FM 97.5. **Television:** Channels 5, 13 and cable. **Newspaper:** *Interior News* (weekly).

Transportation: Air—Scheduled service via Canadian Regional Airlines and Central Mountain Air. **Railroad**—VIA Rail. **Bus**—Greyhound. **Car Rentals**—Available.

Sitting amidst rugged mountains, the town has been enhanced by Swiss-style storefronts that have been added to many of the buildings. Reconstructed in 1979, Main Street offers many shops and restaurants. Incorporated as a village in 1921, Smithers officially became a town in Canada's centennial year, 1967. The original site was chosen in 1913 by construction crews working on the Grand Trunk Pacific Railway (the town was named for one-time chairman of the railway A.W. Smithers). Today it is a distri-

Smithers is the largest town in the Bulkley Valley. (© Judy Parkin)

bution and supply centre for farms, mills and mines in the area.

Smithers is the largest town in the Bulkley Valley and the site of Hudson Bay Mountain, a popular ski area (skiing from November to mid-April).

Smithers has several motels, gas stations, restaurants, laundromat/car wash and good shopping. Government liquor store located on Queen Street at Broadway Avenue. There are 2 18-hole golf courses, both with rentals and clubhouses.

There is a municipal campground with security and firewood (no hookups) at Riverside Park on the Bulkley River; turn north at the museum across from Main Street and drive up the hill about a mile and watch for sign. There are private campgrounds located east and west of town; see highway log. ▲

Special events include the Bulkley Valley Fall Fair, held on the last weekend in August each year, one of the largest agricultural exhibitions in the province. The Midsummer Music Festival in June features local, regional and national artists.

Smithers offers a number of scenic drives. Hudson Bay Mountain (elev. 8,700 feet/2,652m) is a 14-mile/23-km drive from Highway 16; the plateau above timberline at the ski area is a good spot for summer hikes. In the winter months, Smithers boasts one of the largest ski hills in northern British Columbia. A 6,000-foot/1,829-m triple chair and 2 T-bars climb the 1,750-foot/533-m vertical, offering skiers 18 different runs.

Fossil enthusiasts should drive to Driftwood Canyon Provincial Park; turn off Highway 16 just east of the Bulkley River bridge (travelers are advised to stop first at the Visitor Infocentre in town for a map and directions). A display at the park illustrates the fossils, such as metasequoia, a type of redwood which occurs in the shale formation. BC Parks ask visitors to refrain from removing any fossils.

Adams Igloo Wildlife Museum, just west of town on Highway 16, has an excellent display of mammals found in British Columbia.

A beautiful spot not to be missed is Twin Falls and Glacier Gulch. Take the 4-mile-/6.4-km-long gravel road (steep in places) from Highway 16 on the western edge of town.

A 2.2-mile-/3.5-km-long interpretive nature trail with native wildlife and plant species is 10 miles/16 km west of Smithers on the Hudson Bay Mountain Ski Hill road in Smithers Community Forest. This trail can also be used in winter for cross-country skiing, and connects to other cross-country ski trails. Detailed maps of the area showing all hiking trails are available at the infocentre.

An extensive list of lake and river fishing spots in the area, with information on boat launches and boat rentals, is available from the Smithers District Chamber of Commerce, Box 2379, Smithers, BC V0J 2N0; phone (250) 847-5092; or ask at the Visitor Infocentre.

Moose, mule deer, grizzly and black bears, mountain goats and caribou are found in the area, and guides and outfitters are available locally. All species of grouse can be hunted in the Bulkley Valley during the fall. Information is available from the Fish and Wildlife Branch office in Smithers.

Yellowhead Highway 16 Log

(continued)

PG 230.6 (371.1 km) **PR 217.1** (350.1 km) Smithers golf club.

PG 231.7 (372.8 km) **PR 216** (348.4 km) Paved access road to Lake Kathlyn. There is a municipal park with small beach and boat launch located here. Powerboats not permitted. Closed to waterfowl hunting. Side road continues 4 miles/6.4 km (gravel) to Twin Falls and Glacier Gulch.

PG 232.7 (374.5 km) **PR 215** (346.7 km) Road to north leads to Smithers airport.

PG 234 (376.6 km) **PR 213.7** (344.6 km) Lake Kathlyn Road to west.

PG 234.9 (378 km) **PR 212.8** (343.6 km) **Glacier View RV Park.** Wake up to a panoramic view of the Hudson Bay Glacier. Eight level gravel sites with 15-/30-amp service and water hookups. Dry pull-throughs up to 55 feet. Pit toilets. Walking distance to Wildlife Museum. Easy access. Reservations: RR 1, S 9 C 31, Smithers, BC V0J 2N0, (250) 847-3961. [ADVERTISEMENT] ▲

PG 235.1 (378.3 km) **PR 212.6** (342.9 km) Hudson Bay rest area to west with picnic tables, toilets and litter barrels. Beautiful view of Hudson Bay Mountain.

PG 235.4 (378.8 km) **PR 212.3** (342.4 km) **Adams Igloo Wildlife Museum.** The finest collection of big game animals, furbearers and birds native to British Columbia, mounted life-size and displayed in their natural habitat. The inside mural, painted by leading wildlife artist Tom Sander, gives a 3-dimensional impression for realism. Stop at the White Dome, 7 miles west of Smithers beside one of the highway's most beautiful viewpoints. Fur rugs and souvenirs for sale. Ted Moon, Curator. [ADVERTISEMENT]

PG 238.4 (383.6 km) **PR 209.3** (337.6 km) Tobaggan Creek Fish Hatchery.

PG 243.1 (391.3 km) **PR 204.6** (329.8 km) Trout Creek bridge. Store with groceries, post office and phone; fishing licenses available.

PG 248.7 (400.3 km) **PR 199** (320.7 km) Turnout to north with picnic tables and view of Bulkley River and Moricetown Canyon; good photo stop.

PG 248.9 (400.6 km) **PR 198.8** (320.4 km) Telkwa High Road is a short side road on the north side of the highway leading to **Moricetown Canyon and Falls** on the Bulk-

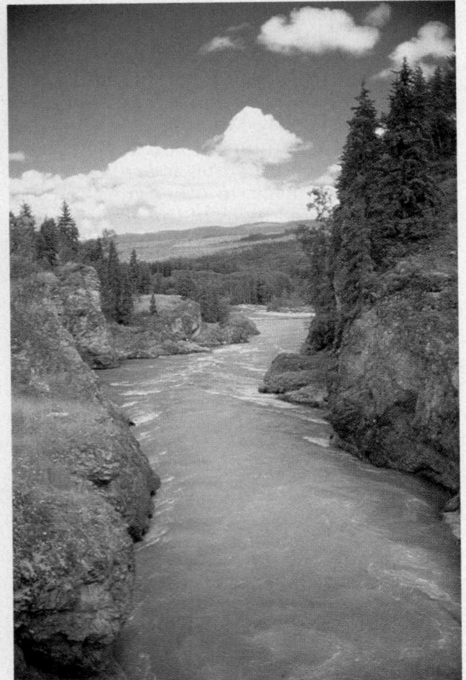
Bulkley River flows through scenic Moricetown Canyon west of Smithers. (© Blake Hanna, staff)

ley River and Moricetown campground. For centuries a famous First Nation's fishing spot, Aboriginal people may still be seen here netting salmon in July and August. A worthwhile stop. ▲

PG 249.2 (401.1 km) **PR 198.5** (319.9 km) **MORICETOWN** (pop. 680; elev. 1,341 feet/409m). **Radio:** CBC-FM 96.5. Moricetown has a gas station with minor repair service and diesel fuel. There is a handicraft store. A campground is located in Moricetown Canyon (turnoff at **Milepost PG 255.7**). Moricetown is a First Nations reserve and village, the oldest settlement in the Bulkley Valley. Traditionally, the Native people (Wet'su-wet'en) took advantage of the narrow canyon to trap salmon. The centuries-old settlement ('Kyah Wiget) is now named after Father A.G. Morice, a Roman Catholic missionary. Born in France, Father Morice came to British Columbia in 1880 and worked with the Aboriginals of northern British Columbia from 1885 to 1904. He achieved world recognition for his writings in anthropology, ethnology and history.

PG 253.8 (408.5 km) **PR 193.9** (312.4 km) Chicken Creek.

PG 255.9 (411.9 km) **PR 191.8** (306.6 km) East Boulder Creek.

PG 258.9 (416.6 km) **PR 188.8** (304.3 km) Paved turnout.

PG 260.7 (419.5 km) **PR 187** (301.4 km) Paved turnout with picnic tables and litter barrels.

PG 260.9 (419.9 km) **PR 186.8** (300.9 km) View of Bulkley River.

PG 261.5 (420.9 km) **PR 186.2** (299.9 km) Paved turnout.

PG 263.9 (424.8 km) **PR 183.8** (296 km) Turnoff to north for Forest Service campsite (7.5 miles/12.1 km) with pit toilets, tables and litter barrels. Fishing in **Suskwa River;** coho salmon to 10 lbs., use tee-spinners in July; steelhead to 20 lbs., use Kitamat #32 and soft bobbers in late fall.

PG 269.1 (433.1 km) **PR 178.6** (287.6 km) Turnoff to north for **Ross Lake Provincial Park;** 25 picnic sites, boat launch (no powerboats), swimming. Fishing for rainbow to 4 lbs.

PG 270.5 (435.3 km) **PR 177.2** (285.4 km) Entering New Hazelton, the first of 3 communities westbound sharing the name Hazelton (the others are Hazelton and South Hazelton), known collectively as The Hazeltons; description follows.

New Hazelton

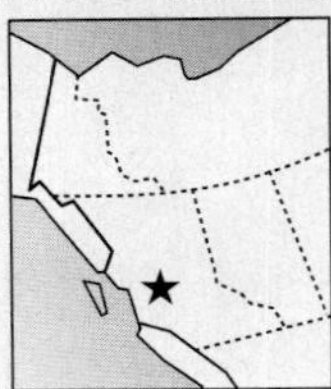

PG 271.1 (436.3 km) **PR 176.6** (284.4 km) **Junction** of Highway 16 with Highway 62 to Hazelton, 'Ksan and Kispiox (descriptions follow). The turnoff for Highway 62 is located just west of the railway overpass in New Hazelton. The turn is on the north side (right for westbound travelers) of Highway 16 between the overpass and the Visitor Infocentre at the base of the hill. **Population:** area 6,500. **Emergency Services: Police,** phone (250) 842-5244.

Visitor Information: Visitor Infocentre in 2-story log building at the junction; museum, restrooms, free sani-dump, potable water, picnic tables. Look for the 3 statues representing the gold rush packer Cataline, the Northwest miner, and the Upper Skeena logger.

Elevation: 1,150 feet/351m. **Radio:** CBC 1170. **Transportation:** VIA Rail. Greyhound bus and regional transit system.

This small highway community has gas stations, major auto repair, restaurants, cafes, post office, general store, a hotel and a motel. Laundromat, propane, sporting goods, and hunting and fishing licenses available in town. ATMs located at the Chevron station in New Hazelton and at Bulkley Valley Credit Union in the mall on Highway 16.

Attractions here include historic Hazelton, the Indian village of 'Ksan and sportfishing the Bulkley and Kispiox rivers (descriptions follow). Mount Rocher Deboule, elev. 8,000 feet/2,438m, towers behind the town.

HAZELTON. Situated at the confluence of the Skeena and Bulkley rivers, Hazelton grew up at "The Forks" as a trans-shipping point at the head of navigation on the Skeena and a wintering place for miners and prospectors from the rigorous Interior. Thomas Hankin established a Hudson's Bay Co. trading post here in 1868. The name Hazelton comes from the numerous hazelnut bushes growing on the flats.

Cataline, famous pioneer packer and traveler, is buried near here in an unmarked grave at Pioneer Cemetery. Jean Caux (his real name) was a Basque who, from 1852 to 1912, with loaded mules, supplied mining and construction camps from Yale and Ashcroft northward through Hazelton, where he often wintered.

For some years, before the arrival of the railroad and highways, supplies for trading posts at Bear and Babine lakes and the Omineca goldfields moved by riverboat from the coast to Hazelton and from there over trails to the backcountry. Some of the Yukon gold rushers passed through Hazelton on their way to the Klondike, pack trains having made the trip from Hazelton to Telegraph Creek over the old Telegraph Trail as early as 1874.

"Old" Hazelton has been reconstructed to look much like it did in the 1890s. Look for the antique machinery downtown. The history of the Hazelton area can be traced by car on the Hand of History tour. Pick up a brochure from the Visitor Infocentre showing the location of the 19 historic sites on the driving tour.

'KSAN HISTORICAL VILLAGE and Museum, a replica Gitksan Indian village, is 4.5 miles/7.2 km from Highway 16. It is a reconstruction of the traditional Gitksan Village, which has stood at this site for centuries. It is located at the confluence of the Bulkley and Skeena rivers by the 'Ksan Assoc. There are 7 communal houses, totem poles and dugout canoes. At the carving shed, carvers produce First Nation's arts and

St. Peter's Anglican Church in Old Hazelton is a heritage landmark.
(© Judy Parkin)

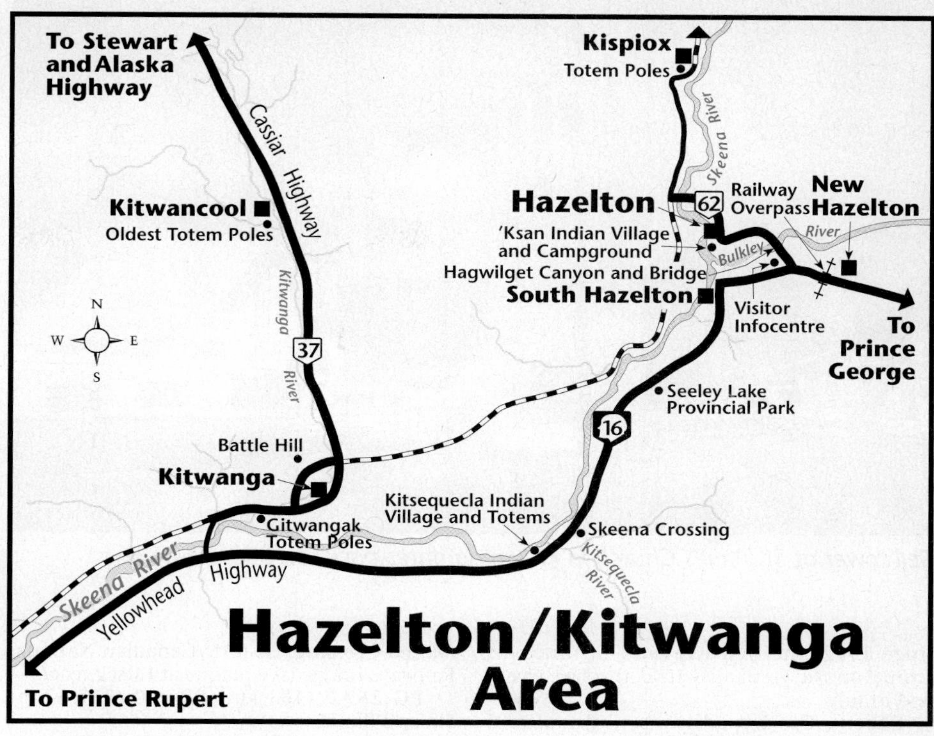

crafts which can be purchased. Food service is available on site.

For a nominal charge from May to September, you can join a guided tour of the communal houses. Performances of traditional song and dance are presented every

Friday evening during July and August in the Wolf House. Admission to grounds is $2, children under 6 are free. Guided tours of the grounds run $8 for adults, $6.50 for students and seniors. The site is open year-round, hours vary. Open daily April 15–Oct. 15. Tours are available mid-April to late September. Phone (250) 842-5544.

A well-maintained full-service trailer park and campground on the banks of the Skeena and Bulkley rivers is operated by the Gitanmaax Band. ▲

KISPIOX (pop. 825) Indian village and 3 fishing resorts are 20 miles/32 km north on a good paved road at the confluence of the Skeena and Kispiox rivers. Kispiox is noted for its stand of totems close to the river. There is a market garden (fresh vegetables) located approximately 7 miles/11 km north on the Kispiox Road (about 2 miles/ 3.2 km before the Kispiox totem poles). Camping, cabins and fishing at lodges and campgrounds in the valley. Valley residents host the Kispiox Rodeo, which has run annually

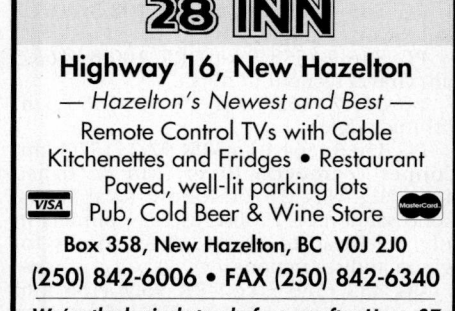

Bell tower at St. Paul's Church in Kitwanga dates back to 1893. (© Gladys Blyth)

since 1952, the first weekend of June. An annual music festival is held the last weekend in July

Skeena Eco-Expeditions. Cultural and outdoor adventures. We offer a variety of exciting outdoor opportunities. Totem pole interpretive tours, river drifting, river rafting, fishing, canoe rentals, guided hiking trips with an experienced Native guide. Book your trip at the Kispiox Band office, Monday–Friday from 8 A.M. to 4 P.M., or call us at (250) 842-5248 or toll free at 1-877-842-5911. [ADVERTISEMENT]

Bulkley River, Dolly Varden to 5 lbs.; spring salmon, mid-July to mid-August; coho salmon 4 to 12 lbs., Aug. 15 through September, flies, spoons and spinners; steelhead to 20 lbs., July through November, flies, Kitamats, weighted spoons and soft bobbers. **Kispiox River** is famous for its trophy-sized steelhead. Check on regulations and obtain a fishing license before your arrival. Fishing is done with single-hook only, with catch-release for steelhead between Aug. 15 and Sept. 30. Season is July 1 to Nov. 30 for salmon, trout and steelhead. Excellent fly-fishing waters: spring salmon, July to early August; coho salmon, late August to early September; steelhead from September until freezeup. Sizable Dolly Vardens and cutthroat. Steelhead average 20 lbs., with some catches over 30 lbs.

Yellowhead Highway 16 Log

(continued)

PG 273.3 (439.9 km) **PR 174.4** (280.8 km) Turnoff to north for 2-mile/3.2-km loop road through small community of **SOUTH HAZELTON**; restaurant, general store, lodging.

PG 277.1 (445.9 km) **PR 170.6** (274.8 km) **Seeley Lake Provincial Park**; 20 campsites, drinking water, pit toilets, firewood, sani-dump, day-use area with picnic tables, swimming, fishing.

PG 282.4 (454.5 km) **PR 165.3** (266.1 km) Carnaby Sawmill; tours available, phone (250) 842-5399.

PG 286.6 (461.2 km) **PR 161.1** (259.3 km) **KITSEGUECLA,** First Nation's village. Totem poles throughout village are classic examples, still in original locations. Historical plaque about Skeena Crossing.

PG 287.4 (462.5 km) **PR 160.3** (258 km) Skeena Crossing. Historic Canadian National Railways bridge (see plaque at Kitseguecla).

PG 287.7 (463 km) **PR 160** (257.6 km) Sheep's Rapids.

PG 292.5 (470.7 km) **PR 155.2** (250 km) Road winds along edge of river.

CAUTION: Watch for falling rock next 32 miles/51.5 km.

PG 297.7 (479.1 km) **PR 150** (241.4 km) Gas station and cafe at Cassiar Highway turnoff. **GITWANGAK,** 0.2 mile/0.4 km north, has many fine old totems and St. Paul's church and bell tower..

Junction with Cassiar Highway (BC Highway 37). Bridge across Skeena River to Kitwanga and Cassiar Highway to Stewart, Hyder, AK, and Alaska Highway. See CASSIAR HIGHWAY section on page 230.

Westbound, the Yellowhead Highway passes Seven Sisters peaks; the highest is 9,140 feet/2,786m.

PG 299 (481.2 km) **PR 148.7** (239.4 km) **Gitksan Paintbrush Native Arts & Crafts.** Silver and gold jewelry: rings, earrings, bracelets. BC jade. Limited edition prints and originals. Smoked moosehide moccasins, beaded leatherwork. Wood carvings, cedar baskets. Clothing and souvenirs. Quality merchandise, most from local artists. Excellent prices. Easy access. Summer hours 9 A.M.–7 P.M. P.O. Box 97, Kitwanga, BC V0J 2A0. Phone or fax (250) 849-5085. [ADVERTISEMENT]

PG 300.8 (484.1 km) **PR 146.9** (236.5 km) **Seven Sisters RV Park and Campground.** Outstanding value. Beautiful park-like setting. Many treed sites. Fresh water, sani-dump, picnic tables at every site, flush toilets, shower, firepits with free firewood, all for $9. Excellent salmon fishing close by. Tenters and cyclists welcome. (250) 849-5489 for reservations. Box 338, Kitwanga, BC V0J 2A0. [ADVERTISEMENT]

PG 303.4 (488.2 km) **PR 144.3** (232.4 km) Boulder Creek rest area; parking for large vehicles; toilets, litter barrels and picnic tables.

PG 306.6 (493.4 km) **PR 141.1** (227.3 km) Whiskey Creek.

PG 307.6 (495 km) **PR 140.1** (225.8 km) Gravel turnout to north with litter barrel.

PG 308 (495.6 km) **PR 139.7** (225.2 km) Gull Creek.

PG 309.1 (497.4 km) **PR 138.6** (223.4 km) **CEDARVALE,** cafe. Loop road through rural setting. Historical plaque about Holy City.

PG 309.2 (497.6 km) **PR 138.5** (223.2 km) Hand of History sign about "Holy City."

Watch for bears fishing the river for salmon in late July and early August.

PG 312.5 (502.9 km) **PR 135.2** (218 km) Gravel turnout to north with litter barrel.

PG 313.6 (504.6 km) **PR 134.1** (216.4 km) Watch for fallen rock on this stretch of highway.

PG 315.3 (507.4 km) **PR 132.4** (213.6 km) Flint Creek.

PG 318.5 (512.6 km) **PR 129.2** (208.5 km) Turnout with historical plaque about Skeena River Boats: "From 1889, sternwheelers and smaller craft fought their way through the Coast Mountains, churning past such awesome places as 'The Devil's Elbow' and 'The Hornet's Nest.' Men and supplies were freighted upstream, furs and gold downstream. A quarter century of colour and excitement began to fade in 1912, as the Grand Trunk Pacific neared completion."

PG 322.4 (518.8 km) **PR 125.2** (202.4 km) Gravel turnout to north.

PG 323.2 (520.1 km) **PR 124.5** (201.1 km) Gravel turnout to south with litter barrel.

PG 332 (534.3 km) **PR 115.7** (187.3 km) Legate Creek.

PG 335.7 (540.2 km) **PR 112** (181.5 km) Rest area on river with water pump, picnic tables, toilets and litter barrels.

PG 336 (540.7 km) **PR 111.7** (181 km) Skeena Cellulose bridge (private) crosses Skeena River to access tree farms on north side.

PG 336.9 (542.1 km) **PR 110.8** (179.6 km) St. Croix Creek.

PG 340.3 (547.7 km) **PR 107.4** (173.9 km) Chindemash Creek.

PG 342.8 (551.6 km) **PR 104.9** (170 km) Tiny chapel to south serves small community of **USK**; the village is reached via the reaction ferry seen to north. The nondenominational chapel is a replica of the pioneer church that stood in Usk until 1936, when the Skeena River flooded, sweeping away the village and the church. The only item from the church to survive was the Bible, which was found floating atop a small pine table.

PG 345 (555.2 km) **PR 102.7** (166.4 km) Entrance to Kitselas Canyon (1 mile/1.6 km).

PG 345.2 (555.6 km) **PR 102.4** (166 km) Side road leads 0.5 mile/0.8 km south to **Kleanza Creek Provincial Park**; 21 campsites, 25 picnic sites, fishing, drinking water, toilets, firewood, wheelchair access. Short trail to remains from Cassiar Hydraulic Mining Co. gold-sluicing operations here (1911–14).

PG 345.4 (555.9 km) **PR 102.3** (165.7 km) Kleanza Bridge.

PG 346.9 (558.3 km) **PR 100.8** (163.3 km) Gravel turnout to north.

PG 349.7 (562.8 km) **PR 98** (158.7 km) Fishing lodge.

PG 350.5 (564.1 km) **PR 97.2** (157.4 km) **Copper (Zymoetz) River,** can be fished from Highway 16 or follow local maps. Coho salmon to 10 lbs., use tee-spinners in July; steelhead to 20 lbs., check locally for season and restrictions.

PG 352 (566.5 km) **PR 95.7** (155 km) Turnout to north with tourist information sign and area map.

Highway 37 South Log

Distance is measured from the junction with Yellowhead Highway 16 (J).

J 0 Junction with Yellowhead Highway 16 at **Milepost PG 354.7** (east exit to Terrace).

J 0.9 (1.4 km) Krumm Road. Turn east for golf course.

J 3.1 (5 km) Terrace–Kitimat airport access road.

J 7.9 (12.7 km) Lakelse Lake Provincial Park parking area and trail to Gruchy's Beach.

J 8.7 (14 km) Lakelse Lake Provincial Park parking areas and picnic area; tables, toilets, showers, changehouses and beach. Park headquarters located here.

J 10.6 (17.1 km) Waterlily Bay; food, lodging, boat launch.

J 11.4 (18.3 km) **Lakelse Lake Provincial Park** Furlong Bay campground and picnic area; 156 vehicle and tent campsites, nature trails, swimming, sandy beach, flush toilets, showers, dump station, boat launch, drinking water, wheelchair access, firewood and interpretive programs.

J 12.9 (20.8 km) **Mount Layton Hot Springs Resort.** See display ad this section.

J 13.8 (22.2 km) Onion Lake hiking and ski trails to west.

J 20.6 (33.2 km) Access to Kitimat River.

J 27.4 (44.1 km) Kitimat Airpark landing strip for small planes.

J 34.8 (56 km) Hirsch Creek Park to west; picnic area, camping, fishing and hiking.

J 35 (56.3 km) Hirsch Creek bridge.

J 35.8 (57.6 km) Kitimat Travel Infocentre to east.

J 36.2 (58.3 km) Minette Bay Road leads east to MK Bay Marina.

J 36.6 (58.9 km) Viewpoint of Douglas Channel and city map. Picnic tables, garden.

Kitimat

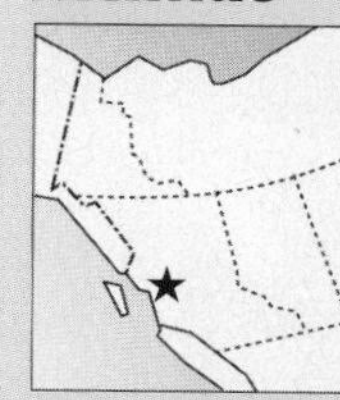

J 37.6 (60.5 km) Located at the head of Douglas Channel. **Population:** 12,000. **Emergency Services: RCMP**, phone (250) 632-7111. **Fire Department**, phone (250) 639-9111. **Ambulance**, phone (250) 632-5433. **Hospital**, phone (250) 632-2121.

Visitor Information: A free visitor coupon book and information on local attractions are available from the Visitor Information Centre., Box 214, Kitimat, BC V8C 2G7; phone (800) 664-6554 or (250) 632-6294; fax (250) 632-4685; e-mail kchamber@sno.net; www.sno.net/kcoc.

Radio: CKTK 1230; CBC-FM 101.1, CJFW-FM 103.1. **Newspaper:** *The News Advertiser* (weekly); *Northern Sentinel* (weekly).

This community was planned and built in the early 1950s when the B.C. government attracted Alcan (Aluminum Co. of Canada) to establish a smelter here. Today, Kitimat is a major port and home to several industries. Free tours are available (primarily in summer, reservations recommended) at Alcan, (250) 639-8259; Eurocan Pulp and Paper, (250) 639-3597; Methanex Corp., (250) 639-9292; and Kitimat fish hatchery, (250) 639-9616. Tour Mike's Wildlife Museum to see over 100 mounts; admission fee; (250) 632-7083.

Kitimat's location at the head of Douglas Channel makes it a popular boating, fishing and scuba diving destination. There are several charter operators.

Kitimat has all visitor facilities, including a modern shopping mall, restaurants and motels; library, theatre, swimming pool and gym; and an 18-hole golf course. Many scenic hiking trails are available. A free guide to area day hikes is available at the Visitor Infocentre. The Centennial Museum is located at city centre.

Camping at Radley Park in town; electrical hookups, showers, fishing, toilets, playground and dump station. (Radley Park—on the other side of the river—is also the site of a 500-year-old, 165-foot/50-m Sitka spruce, one of the largest of its kind in the province.) There is also camping at Hirsch Creek Park on the edge of town and private campgrounds.

Local fishermen line the banks of the **Kitimat River** in May for the steelhead run. Chinook salmon run in June and July. Coho run from August into September.

Kitimat also offers many winter activities, including cross-country skiing and indoor ice rinks. Downhill skiing at nearby Terrace and Smithers.

Kitimat Chamber of Commerce. See display ad this section.

Return to Milepost PG 354.7
Yellowhead Highway 16

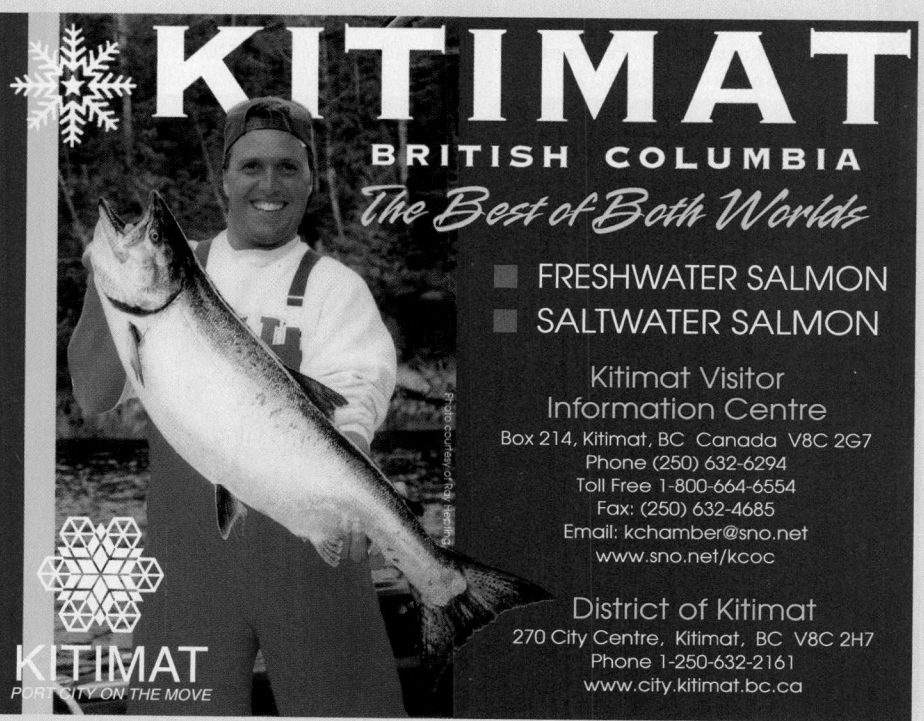

PG 352.2 (566.8 km) **PR 95.5** (154.7 km) Motel and gas.

PG 352.9 (568 km) **PR 94.8** (153.5 km) Motel.

PG 354.3 (570.2 km) **PR 93.4** (151.3 km) Old Lakelse Lake Road; access to Terrace golf course.

PG 354.7 (570.8 km) **PR 93** (150.7 km) Four-way stop. For access to downtown Terrace, turn north here and continue over 1-lane bridge. For west access to Terrace and continuation of Yellowhead Highway 16 westbound, go straight at intersection. Turn off for Kitimat, 37 miles/60 km south via Highway 37. Kitimat is a major port and home to several industries.

Junction with Highway 37 South to Kitimat. Log of HIGHWAY 37 SOUTH begins on page 221.

PG 354.9 (571.1 km) **PR 92.8** (150.4 km) First bridge westbound over **Skeena River.** "Skeen" means "River of the mist" in First Nation's language.

PG 355.2 (571.7 km) **PR 92.5** (149.8 km) Ferry Island municipal campground; 68 sites, some electrical hookups. Covered picnic shelters, barbecues, walking trails and a fishing bar are also available.

PG 355.3 (571.8 km) **PR 92.4** (149.7 km) Second westbound Skeena River Bridge.

PG 355.7 (572.4 km) **PR 92** (149.1 km) Terrace Chamber of Commerce Visitor Infocentre.

PG 356.6 (573.8 km) **PR 91.1** (147.7 km) Stoplight; west access to Terrace. Turn north at intersection for downtown.

Continue through intersection on Highway 16 westbound for Prince Rupert, eastbound for Prince George.

CAUTION: No gas or services available between Terrace and Prince Rupert.

Terrace

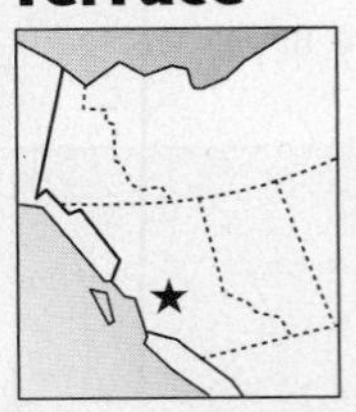

Located on the Skeena River. City centre is located north of Highway 16: Exit at **PG 356.6** or at Highway 37 junction (**PG 354.7**). **Population:** 13,000; area 21,500. **Emergency Services:** Police, fire and ambulance located at intersection of Eby Street and Highway 16. **Police,** phone (250) 635-4911. **Fire Department,** phone (250) 638-8121. **Ambulance,** phone (250) 638-1102. **Hospital,** phone (250) 635-2211.

Visitor Information: Visitor Infocentre located in the chamber of commerce log building at **Milepost PG 355.7** Open daily in summer, 9 A.M. to 8 P.M.; weekdays in winter, 8 A.M. to 4:30 P.M. Write 4511 Keith Ave, Terrace, BC V8G 1K1; phone (250) 635-2063. Information also available from

Pioneer log buildings in Terrace's Heritage Park. (© Judy Parkin)

Municipal Hall, #5-3215 Eby St.; open weekdays, phone (250) 635-6311.

Elevation: 220 feet/67m. **Climate:** Average summer temperature is 69°F/21°C; average annual rainfall 44 inches/112 cm, snowfall 129 inches/327 cm. **Radio:** CFTK 590; CFPR-FM 95.3, CFNR 92.1. **Television:** 13 channels (cable). **Newspapers:** *Terrace Standard* (weekly) *Terrace Times* (weekly).

Transportation: Air—Canadian Airlines International, Air BC and Central Mountain Air from Terrace-Kitimat airport on Highway 37 South. **Railroad**—VIA Rail, 4531 Railway Ave. **Bus**—Farwest Bus Lines, Greyhound and Seaport Limousine with connection between Terrace and Stewart/Hyder. **Car Rentals**—Available.

Terrace was once a port of call for Skeena River stern-wheelers. The first farmer in the area, George Little, gave land to the community that became a port of call and post office in 1905. Originally it was known as Little Town, and later was named Terrace because of the natural terraces cut by the river. The village site was laid out in 1910 and the Grand Trunk Pacific Railway reached Terrace in 1914. The municipality was incorporated in 1927.

There are 17 motels/hotels, 35 restaurants and 2 shopping centres. The government liquor store is at 3250 Eby St. There are 5 laundromats. The community has a library and art gallery, indoor swimming pool, tennis courts, a golf course, bingo parlor, bowling alley, theatre and billiards.

Terrace has private campgrounds (see advertisements this section) and a public campground located at Ferry Island (see **Milepost PG 355.2**). Lakelse Lake Provincial Park at Furlong Bay, 11.4 miles/18.3 km south of Highway 16 on Highway 37, offers campsites and day-use facilities, restrooms, changing rooms, showers, boat launch, sandy beaches, swimming, nature trails and interpretive forestry programs. ▲

Major attractions in Terrace include **Heritage Park**, a collection of original log buildings from this region. Chosen to represent both the different aspects of pioneer life as well as different log building techniques, the structures include a trapper's cabin, miner's cabin and lineman's cabin. The 9 structures also house artifacts from the period. Managed by the Terrace Regional Museum Society; guided tours available in summer, admission charged.

Recreation includes hiking, biking, rock-climbing, canoeing, kayaking and snowmobiling. Hiking trails in the Terrace area range from easy to moderate. Terrace Mountain Nature Trail is a 3.2-mile/5.1-km uphill hike which offers good views of the area; it begins at Halliwell and Anderson streets. Check with the Visitor Infocentre for details on other area trails.

Special events in Terrace include the Skeena Valley Fall Fair, Labour Day weekend; River Boat Days, B.C. Day weekend; and the Terrace Trade Show in late April.

Nisga'a Lava Memorial Park lava beds are 42 miles/67 km north of Terrace via the Nisga'a Highway (see description at **Milepost PG 357.5**). Limited picnic spots; limited camping; interesting hikes. Canada's youngest volcano last erupted approximately 250 years ago, burying 2 Indian villages. Guided hikes into the cones are available; phone (250) 798-2277.

Terrace is ideally situated for sportfishing, with easy access to the **Skeena, Copper, Kalum, Kitimat** and **Lakelse rivers.** Cutthroat, Dolly Varden and rainbow are found in all lakes and streams; salmon (king and coho) from May to late autumn. Kings average 40 to 70 lbs.; coho 14 to 20 lbs. Check locally for season and restrictions on steelhead. Information and fishing licenses are available from B.C. Government Access Centre, 3220 Eby St., Terrace (phone 250/638-6515), and at most sporting goods stores.

Yellowhead Highway 16 Log

(continued)

PG 356.6 (573.8 km) **PR 91.1** (147.7 km) Stoplight; west access to Terrace. Turn north at intersection for downtown. Continue through intersection eastbound for Prince George, westbound for Prince Rupert.

PG 357.5 (575.4 km) **PR 90.2** (146.1 km) **Junction** with Nisga'a Highway (Kalum Lake Road). The **Nisga'a Highway/Nass Forest Service Road** travels north to New Aiyansh and then east to join the Cassiar Highway. Total driving distance is 98.6 miles/158.7 km and the first 39.3 miles/63.2 km are paved; the remainder is gravel. Beyond the Nass Road junction, the Nisga'a Highway is narrow and used by logging trucks. Services along this route are limited.

The southern boundary of **Nisga'a Memorial Lava Bed Park** is at Mile 42.2/67.9 km on the Nisga'a Highway. This lava flow is thought to be the most recent volcanic eruption in Canada (approximately 250 years ago). It covers an area approximately 6.3 miles/10 km long and 1.8 miles/3 km wide and was created by a volcano less than 361 feet/100m high. The eruption produced little ash or cinder, but large quantities of basalt. The eruption destroyed 2 villages and killed more than 2,000 people.

Principal access to the Cassiar Highway is from Kitwanga at **Milepost PG 306.6** Yellowhead Highway.

PG 357.9 (576 km) **PR 89.8** (145.5 km) West Fraser Sawmill.

PG 359 (377.8 km) **PR 88.7** (143.7 km) Kalum Bridge.

PG 359.2 (578 km) **PR 88.5** (143.5 km) Access road to boat launch (fee charged) on the Kitsumkalum River downstream from Highway 16 bridge; RV parking.

Leaving Terrace, Highway 16 is in good condition westbound although the few straightaways are interrupted by some amazing 70-degree zigzags as the highway crosses the railroad tracks. The highway along the Skeena River is spectacular, with waterfalls cascading down the steep rock faces.

PG 359.3 (578.2 km) **PR 88.4** (143.3 km) **KITSUMKALUM.** Grocery store and Native craft centre. House of Sim-oi-Ghets handles only authentic arts and crafts such as totem poles, leather goods and local carvings.

This is also the **junction** with West Kalum Forest Service Road, which leads north to **Kitsumkalum Provincial Park** (15 miles/24 km), with 20 campsites, and to Red Sand Demonstration Forest, with 14 campsites. West Kalum Road junctions with the Nisga'a Highway. ▲

PG 359.7 (578.8 km) **PR 88** (142.7 km) Turnout to south.

PG 360 (579.4 km) **PR 87.7** (142.1 km) Paved turnout to south.

PG 363.1 (584.4 km) **PR 84.6** (137 km) Zimacord Bridge.

PG 366.1 (589.2 km) **PR 81.6** (132.1 km) Turnout to south.

PG 368.7 (589.2 km) **PR 79** (127.9 km) Delta Creek.

PG 371.3 (597.5 km) **PR 76.4** (123.7 km) Shames River.

PG 371.4 (597.7 km) **PR 76.3** (123.5 km) Shames Mountain Ski Area.

PG 377.2 (607.1 km) **PR 70.5** (113.8 km) Rest area on left westbound with picnic tables, toilets and water pump.

PG 378 (607.7 km) **PR 69.7** (112.3 km) Boat launch.

PG 378.2 (608.7 km) **PR 69.5** (112.4 km) Exstew River.

PG 381.7 (613.7 km) **PR 66** (106.3 km) Boat launch.

PG 383 (616.4 km) **PR 64.7** (104.9 km) *CAUTION! Highway turns sharply across rail-*

road tracks.

PG 385.3 (620.1 km) **PR 62.4** (100.9 km) *CAUTION: Carwash Rock overhangs highway. Water cascades down mountain and onto highway during heavy rains.*

PG 385.8 (620.8 km) **PR 61.9** (100.2 km) Sharp curves and falling rocks approximately next mile westbound. *CAUTION: Slow down for sharp curve and steep grade.*

PG 389.6 (627 km) **PR 58.1** (94 km) **Exchamsiks River Provincial Park**; 20 campsites and 20 picnic sites among old-growth Sitka spruce. Open May to October, camping fee, water and pit toilets. Good salmon fishing in Exchamsiks River. Access to Gitnadoix River canoeing area across Skeena River.

PG 389.8 (627.3 km) **PR 57.9** (93.7 km) Very pleasant rest area north side of road at west end of Exchamsiks bridge; boat launch on Exchamsiks River. Toilets, tables and litter barrels.

PG 390 (627.7 km) **PR 57.7** (93.3 km) Boat launch.

PG 390.2 (628 km) **PR 57.5** (93 km) *CAUTION: Very narrow road next to railway.*

PG 391.3 (629.7 km) **PR 56.4** (91.3 km) Conspicuous example of Sitka spruce on north side of highway. Aboriginal people ate its inner bark fresh or dried in cakes, served with berries. As you travel west, the vegetation becomes increasingly influenced by the maritime climate.

PG 394.1 (634.2 km) **PR 53.6** (86.8 km) Kasiks River and view of mountains.

PG 394.8 (635.3 km) **PR 52.9** (85.7 km) Kasiks River; boat launch.

PG 394.9 (635.5 km) **PR 52.8** (85.5 km) River access at the west end of bridge.

PG 396 (637.3 km) **PR 51.7** (83.7 km) Bridal Falls.

PG 399.9 (643.5 km) **PR 47.8** (77.4 km) Boat launch.

PG 401.1 (645.6 km) **PR 46.6** (75.3 km) Hanging Valley and Blackwater Creek.

PG 404.8 (651.4 km) **PR 42.9** (69.5 km) Kwinitsa River bridge and boat launch. No public moorage.

PG 409.3 (658.7 km) **PR 38.4** (62.1 km) Telegraph Point rest area to south on bank of Skeena River; paved turnout with outhouses, picnic tables, litter barrels and water pump. Watch for seals and sea lions in spring and during salmon season.

PG 413.3 (665.1 km) **PR 34.4** (55.7 km) Paved turnout with litter barrel.

PG 415.5 (668.7 km) **PR 32.2** (52.1 km) Basalt Creek rest area to south with picnic tables.

PG 416.3 (669.9 km) **PR 31.4** (50.8 km) Khyex River bridge. Remains of old sawmill visible at west end of bridge to south.

PG 420.2 (676.2 km) **PR 27.5** (44.5 km) Turnout to south.

PG 422.5 (680 km) **PR 25.2** (39.8 km) Watch for pictograph, visible from the road for eastbound traffic only, possibly a boundary marker for Chief Legaic over 150 years ago. It was rediscovered in the early 1950s by Dan Lippett of Prince Rupert.

PG 423.7 (681.8 km) **PR 24** (38 km) **Skeena River Viewpoint** to south with litter barrels and historical plaque about the Skeena River. Highway leaves Skeena River westbound. Abandoned townsite of Port Essington visible on opposite side of river.

PG 424.3 (682.3 km) **PR 23.4** (37.7 km) Large turnout.

PG 424.6 (683.3 km) **PR 23.1** (37.4 km) Green River Forest Service road.

PG 427.5 (688 km) **PR 20.2** (32.7 km) **Rainbow Summit**, elev. 528 feet/161m.

PG 429.1 (690.1 km) **PR 18.6** (29.9 km) Large paved turnout.

PG 430 (692 km) **PR 17.7** (28.7 km) Side road south to Rainbow Lake Reservoir; boat launch. The reservoir water is used by the pulp mill on Watson Island.

PG 432.5 (695.9 km) **PR 15.2** (24.7 km) **Prudhomme Lake Provincial Park**; 24 campsites, well water, toilets, firewood, fishing, camping fee.

PG 432.9 (696.6 km) **PR 14.8** (24 km) Paved turnout to north with litter barrel.

PG 433.4 (697.5 km) **PR 14.3** (23.1 km) Turnoff for **Diana Lake Provincial Park**, 1.5 miles/2.4 km south via single-lane gravel road (use turnouts). Day-use facility. Very pleasant grassy picnic area on lakeshore with 50 picnic tables, kitchen shelter, firewood, grills, wheelchair access, outhouses, water pump and garbage cans. Parking for 229 vehicles. The only freshwater swimming beach in the Prince Rupert area. Fish viewing at Diana Creek on the way into the lake; 2 hiking trails.

PG 438 (704.9 km) **PR 9.7** (15.6 km) **Junction.** Turnoff for **PORT EDWARD**, pulp mill and historic cannery. The **North Pacific Historic Fishing Village** at Port Edward is open daily in summer. Built in 1889, this is the oldest cannery village on the north coast. Phone (250) 628-3538 for more information.

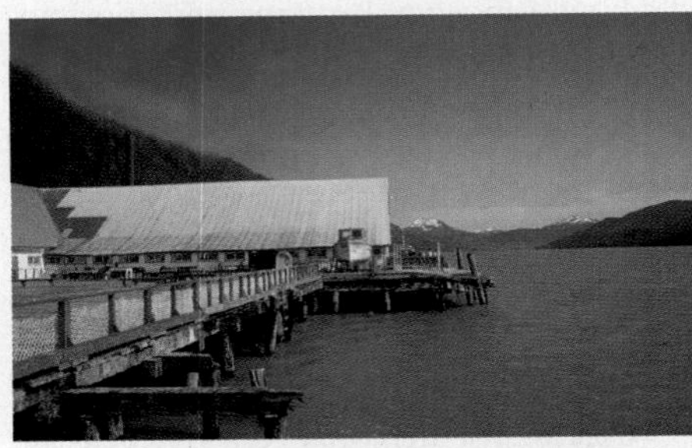

PG 438.3 (705.3 km) **PR 9.4** (15.2 km) Galloway Rapids rest area to south with litter barrels, picnic tables and visitor information sign. View of Watson Island pulp mill.

PG 439.1 (706.6 km) **PR 8.6** (13.9 km) Miller Bay Hill campground.

PG 439.5 (707.3 km) **PR 8.2** (13.2 km) Ridley Island access road. Ridley Island is the site of terminals used for the transfer of coal and grain—from, respectively, the North East Coal resource near Dawson Creek and Canada's prairies—to ships

PG 440.2 (708.5 km) **PR 7.5** (12 km) Oliver Lake rest area to south just off highway; picnic tables, grills, firewood. Point of interest sign about bogs.

PG 441.2 (710 km) **PR 6.5** (10.5 km) Shoe Tree or Tree of Lost Soles to east. Tongue-in-cheek local attraction which has grown over years. Worn-out footwear is hung from trees in this local shrine to shoes.

PG 442.3 (711.8 km) **PR 5.4** (8.7 km) **Butze Rapids** viewpoint and trail. The current flowing over these rapids changes direction with the tide. The phenomenon is called a reversing tidal rapid, and the effect is most dramatic about half an hour after high tide. Easy, fairly level hiking on well-maintained, chip-covered trail.

PG 442.7 (712.4 km) **PR 5** (8.1 km) Prince Rupert industrial park on the outskirts of Prince Rupert. Yellowhead Highway 16 becomes McBride Street as you enter the city centre.

PG 443.4 (713.7 km) **PR 4.2** (6.8 km) Frederick Street junction.

PG 447 (719.3 km) **PR 0.7** (1.2 km) Park Avenue campground.

PG 447.7 (720 km) **PR 0** Ferry terminal for B.C. Ferries and Alaska state ferries. Airport ferry terminal. End of Highway 16.

CAUTION: No gas or services available eastbound between Prince Rupert and Terrace.

Prince Rupert

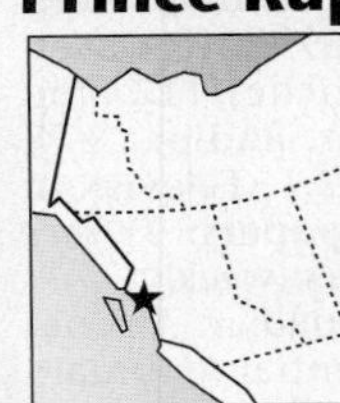

Located on Kaien Island near the mouth of the Skeena River, 90 miles/145 km by air or water (6-hour ferry ride) south of Ketchikan, AK. **Population:** 17,500; area 25,000. **Emergency Services:** Phone 911 for **Police, Ambulance** and **Fire Department. RCMP,** 6th Avenue and McBride Street, non-emergency phone (250) 627-0700. **Hospital,** Prince Rupert Regional, phone (250) 624-2171.

Visitor Information: Visitor Infocentre at 100 1st Avenue West (at McBride Street); open daily in summer, 9 A.M. to 8 P.M. Travel information is also available at the Park Avenue Campground; open daily in summer, 9 A.M. to 9 P.M., and until midnight for B.C. Ferry arrivals. Write the Prince Rupert Visitor Information Centre at Box 669-MP, Prince Rupert, BC V8J 3S1, phone (800) 667-1994 and (250) 624-5637, fax (250) 627-8009; e-mail pr.info@citytel.net; web site at http://city.prince-rupert.bc.ca. Also check with the Visitor Infocentre about guided tours, or pick up a brochure for a self-guided tour.

Elevation: Sea level. **Climate:** Temperate with mild winters. Annual precipitation 95.4

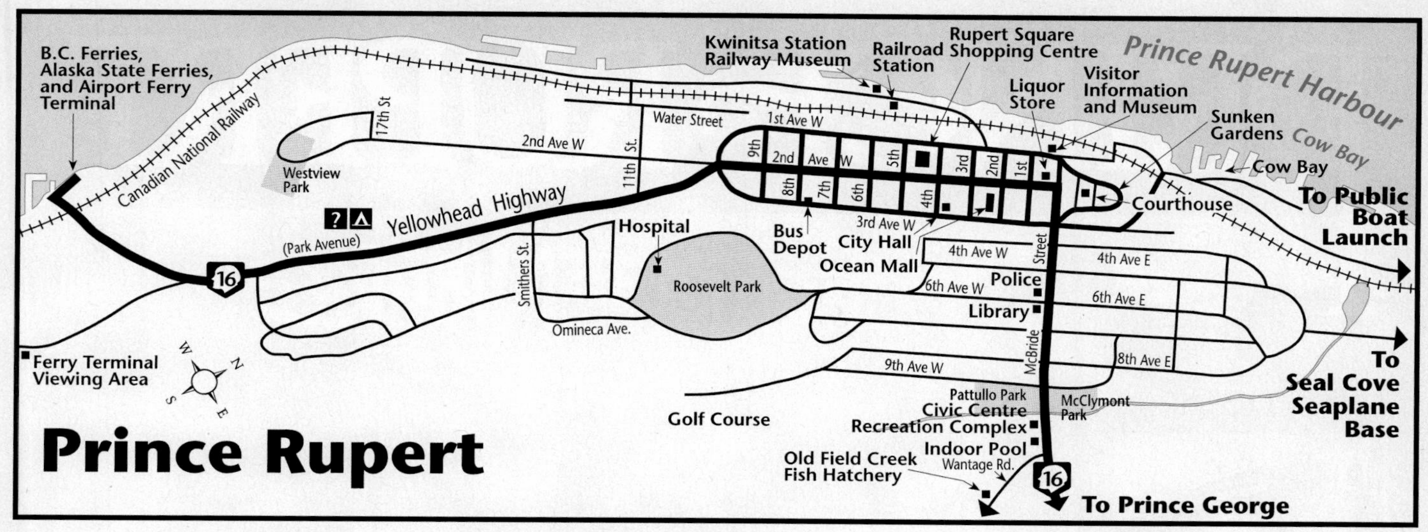

inches. **Radio:** CHTK 560, CBC 860; CJFW-FM 101.9. **Television:** 31 channels, cable. **Newspaper:** *The Prince Rupert Daily News, Prince Rupert This Week* (weekly).

Description

Prince Rupert, "Gateway to Alaska," was surveyed prior to 1905 by the Grand Trunk Pacific Railway (later Canadian National Railways) as the terminus for Canada's second transcontinental railroad.

Twelve thousand miles/19,300 km of survey lines were studied before a final route along the Skeena River was chosen. Some 833 miles/1,340 km had to be blasted from solid rock, 50 men drowned and costs rose to $105,000 a mile (the final cost of $300 million was comparable to Panama Canal construction) before the last spike was driven near Fraser Lake on April 7, 1914. Financial problems continued to plague the company, forcing it to amalgamate to become part of the Canadian National Railways system in 1923.

Charles M. Hays, president of the company, was an enthusiastic promoter of the new terminus, which was named by competition from 12,000 entries. While "Port Rupert" had been submitted by two contestants, "Prince Rupert" (from Miss Eleanor M. Macdonald of Winnipeg) called to mind the dashing soldier–explorer, cousin to Charles II of England and first governor of the Hudson's Bay Co., who had traded on the coast rivers for years. Three first prizes of $250 were awarded and Prince Rupert was officially named in 1906.

Prince Rupert's proposed port and adjacent waters were surveyed by G. Blanchard Dodge of the Hydrographic branch of the Marine Dept. in 1906, and in May the little steamer *Constance* carried settlers from the village of Metlakatla to clear the first ground on Kaien Island. Its post office opened Nov. 23, 1906, and Prince Rupert, with a tent-town population of 200, began an association with communities on the Queen Charlotte Islands, with Stewart served by Union steamships and Canadian Pacific Railways boats, and with Hazelton 200 miles/322 km up the Skeena River on which the stern-wheelers of the Grand Trunk Pacific and the Hudson's Bay Co. traveled.

Incorporated as a city March 10, 1910, Prince Rupert attracted settlers responding to the enthusiasm of Hays, with his dreams of a population of 50,000 and world markets supplied by his railroad. Both the city and the railway suffered a great loss with the death of Charles M. Hays when the *Titanic* went down in April 1912. Even so, work went ahead on the Grand Trunk Pacific. Two years later the first train arrived at Prince Rupert, linking the western port with the rest of Canada. Since then, the city has progressed through 2 world wars and economic ups and downs to its present period of growth and expansion, not only as a busy port but as a visitor centre.

During WWII, more than a million tons of freight and 73,000 people, both military and civilian, passed through Prince Rupert on their way to military operations in Alaska and the South Pacific.

Construction of the pulp operations on Watson Island in 1951 greatly increased the economic and industrial potential of the

PRINCE RUPERT'S COW BAY

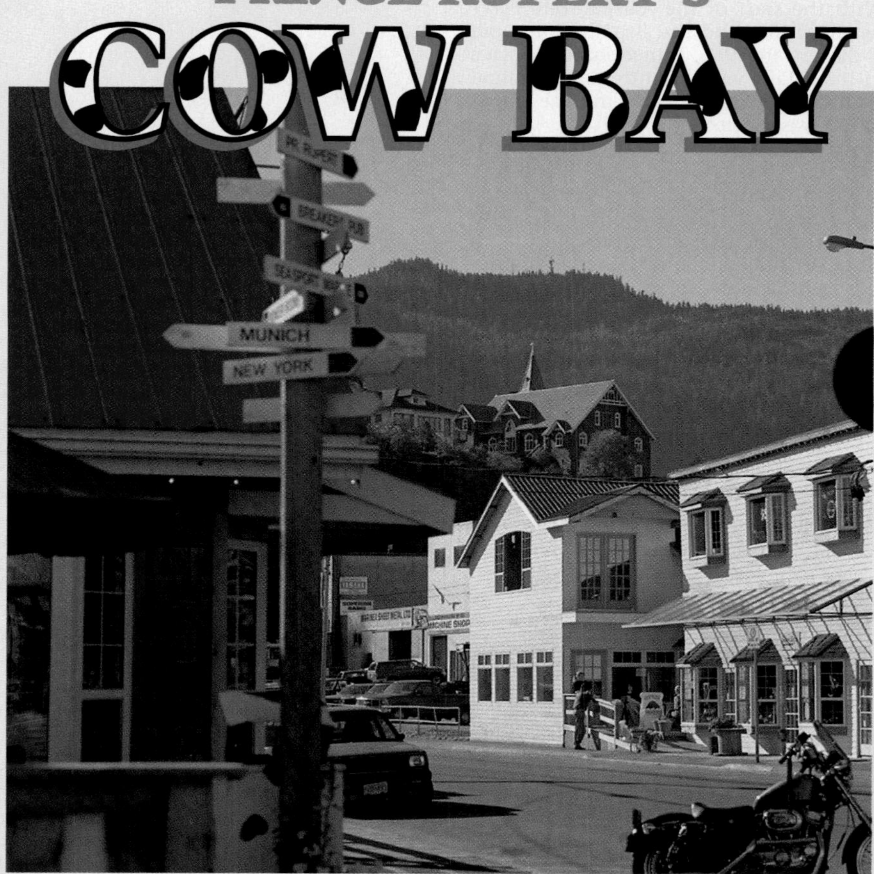

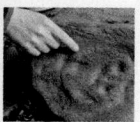

area. The operations include a pulp mill and a kraft mill.

With the start of the Alaska State Ferry System in 1963, and the British Columbia Ferry System in 1966, Prince Rupert's place as an important visitor centre and terminal point for highway, rail and marine transportation was assured.

Prince Rupert is the second major deep-sea port on Canada's west coast, exporting grain, pulp, lumber and other resources to Europe and Asia. Prince Rupert has also become a major coal and grain port with facilities on Ridley Island. Other industries include fishing and fish processing, and the manufacture of forest products.

Promenade overlooks Prince Rupert Harbor. (© Blake Hanna, staff)

Prince Rupert is underlaid by muskeg (a deep bog common to Northwest Canada and Alaska) over solid rock, which makes for a difficult foundation to build on. Many sites are economically unfeasible for development as they would require pilings 70 feet/21m or more into the muskeg to provide a firm foundation. Some of the older buildings have sagged slightly as a result of unstable foundations.

Lodging & Services

More than a dozen hotels and motels accommodate the influx of ferry passengers each summer. Many restaurants feature fresh local seafood in season.

Modern supermarkets and shopping centres are available. Government liquor store is at the corner of 2nd Avenue and Highway 16. There are 5 main banks and 2 laundromats.

The Civic Centre Recreation Complex, located on McBride Street, has a fitness gym, squash, basketball and volleyball; ice skating and roller skating rinks; phone (250) 624-6707 for more information. Earl Mah Aquatic Centre nextdoor has an indoor swimming pool, tot pool, weight room, saunas, showers, whirlpool, slides and diving boards. Access for persons with disabilities. Phone (250) 627-7946. Admission charged. ♿

The golf course includes 18-hole course, resident pro, equipment rental, clubhouse and restaurant. Entrance on 9th Avenue W.

Camping

Park Avenue Campground on Highway 16 in the city has 87 campsites with hookups, unserviced sites, restrooms with hot showers, coin-operated laundry facilities, children's play area and picnic shelters. There are 24 campsites at Prudhomme Lake Provincial Park, 12.5 miles/20.1 km east on Highway 16. A private RV park on McBride Street offers camper and trailer parking. ▲

Transportation

Air: Harbour Air and Inland Air Charter to outlying villages and Queen Charlotte Islands; Canadian Airlines offer daily jet service to Vancouver.

Prince Rupert airport is located on Digby Island, which is connected by city-operated ferry to Prince Rupert. There is a small terminal at the airport. The airport ferry leaves from the Fairview dock, next to the Alaska state ferry dock; fare is charged for the 20-minute ride. Bus service to airport from Rupert Mall downtown.

There is a seaplane base at Seal Cove with airline and helicopter charter services.

Ferries: British Columbia Ferry System, Fairview dock, phone (250) 624-9627, provides automobile and passenger service from Prince Rupert to Port Hardy, and between Prince Rupert and Skidegate in the Queen Charlotte Islands.

Alaska Marine Highway System, Fairview dock, phone (250) 627-1744 or (800) 642-0066, provides automobile and passenger service to southeastern Alaska.

NOTE: Vehicle storage is available; inquire at the Information Centre.

Car Rentals: Tilden, phone (250) 624-5318, and Budget, phone (250) 627-7400.

Taxi: Available. Prince Rupert taxi cabs are powered by LNG (liquefied natural gas); phone (250) 624-2185.

Railroad: VIA Rail, in British Columbia, phone (800) 561-8630 (from Manitoba west to British Columbia) or (800) 561-3949 (from the United States).

Bus: PR Transit System, phone (250) 624-3343. Greyhound, phone (250) 624-5090. Farwest Bus Lines, phone (250) 624-6400. Charter sightseeing tours available.

Attractions

Totem Pole Tour. Scattered throughout the city are 18 large cedar totem poles, each with its own story. Most are reproductions by Native craftsmen of the original Tsimshian (SHIM shian) poles from the mainland and the Haida (HI duh) carvings from the Queen Charlotte Islands. The originals are now in the British Columbia Provincial Museum in Victoria. Several totem poles may be seen at Totem Park near the hospital. Maps are available at the Visitor Infocentre.

City Parks. Mariner's Park, overlooking the harbour, has memorials to those who have been lost at sea. Roosevelt Park honours Prince Rupert's wartime history. Service Park overlooks downtown Prince Rupert.

And Kinsmen's Linear Park takes you from one end of town to the other via a system of trails. Sunken Gardens, located behind the Provincial Courthouse, is a public garden planted in the excavations for an earlier court building. Maps are available at the Visitor Infocentre.

New Museum of Northern British Columbia/Art Gallery, situated in an award-winning Chatham Village Longhouse, displays an outstanding collection of artifacts depicting the settlement history of British Columbia's north coast. Traveling art collections are displayed in the gallery, and works by local artists are available for purchase. Centrally located at 1st Avenue and McBride Street, marked by several tall totem poles. Summer hours 9 A.M. to 8 P.M. Monday through Saturday; 9 A.M. to 5 P.M. Sunday. Winter hours 10 A.M. to 5 P.M. Monday through Saturday. Phone (250) 624-3207. Admission charged.

Pike Island Guided Tours. Knowledgeable First Nations' guides conduct excursions of Pike Island, site of 3 ancient Tsimshian village sites. Pike Island is accessible by 40-minute water taxi from Prince Rupert Harbour. The walking tour also explores the natural history of this tiny island. Tour tickets may be purchased at the museum, which is also the departure point for the tours. Daily departures at 11 A.M.. in summer. The 5-hour tour includes transportation, lunch and guide services.

Kwinitsa Station Railway Museum. Built in 1911, Kwinitsa Station is one of the few surviving stations of the nearly 400 built along the Grand Trunk Pacific Railway line. In 1985 the station was moved to the Prince Rupert waterfront park. Restored rooms, exhibits and videos tell the story of early Prince Rupert and the role the railroad played in the city's development. Open daily in summer.

Performing Arts Centre offers both professional and amateur theatre, with productions for children, and classical and contemporary plays presented. The 700-seat facility may be toured in summer; phone (250) 627-8888.

Special Events. Seafest is a 4-day celebration, held the second weekend in June, which includes a parade and water-jousting competition. Indian Culture Days, a 2-day event held during Seafest, features Native food, traditional dance, and arts and crafts. The All Native Basketball Tournament, held in February, is the largest event of its kind in Canada.

Watch the Seaplanes. From McBride Street, head north on 6th Avenue E. (watch for signs to seaplane base); drive a few miles to Solly's Pub, then turn right to Seal Cove seaplane base. Visitors can spend a fascinating hour here watching seaplanes loading, taking off and landing. Helicopter and seaplane tours of the area are available at Seal Cove.

Cow Bay. Located along the waterfront northeast of downtown, this revitalized area boasts numerous boutiques, cafes, a popular pub and 2 bed-and-breakfasts. The ambience is historic (antique phone booths, old-fashioned lampposts), but the theme is bovine, with businesses and buildings bearing cow names (like Cowpuccinos, a coffee house) or cow colors (black and white pattern).

North Pacific Village Museum at Port Edward, located east of Prince Rupert on the Yellowhead Highway ((turnoff at **Milepost PG 438**), was built in 1889. This restored heritage site has dozens of displays on this once-major regional industry. A live performance highlights the history of the cannery. Open daily in summer, closed Mondays and Tuesdays October through April; admission charged. Phone (250) 628-3538.

Butz Rapids. This reversing tidal rapid, most dramatic about half an hour after high tide, can be seen from a viewpoint 5.4 miles;/8.7 km east from the ferry terminal in Prince Rupert at **Milepost PG 442.3** Yellowhead Highway. From the parking area, an easy trail takes you past Grassy Bay to the rapids.

Swim at Diana Lake. This provincial park, about 13 miles/21 km from downtown on Highway 16, offers the only freshwater swimming in the Prince Rupert area. Picnic tables, kitchen shelter, parking and beach.

Visit the Queen Charlotte Islands. Ferry service is available between Prince Rupert and Skidegate on Graham Island, largest of the 150 islands and islets that form the Queen Charlotte Islands. Located west of Prince Rupert—a 6- to 8-hour ferry ride—Graham Island's paved road system connects Skidegate with Masset, the largest town in the Queen Charlottes. Scheduled flights from Prince Rupert to Sandspit and Masset are available. Island attractions include wild beaches, Haida culture, flora and fauna. For more information, contact the Visitor Infocentre in Queen Charlotte; phone (250) 559-8316.

Go Fishing. Numerous freshwater fishing areas are available near Prince Rupert. For information on bait, locations, regulations and licensing, contact local sporting goods stores or the Visitor Infocentre. This area abounds in all species of salmon, steelhead, crab and shrimp. Public boat launch facility is located at Rushbrook Public Floats at the north end of the waterfront. Public floats are also available at Fairview, past the Alaska state ferry terminal near the breakwater.

Harbour Tours and Fishing Charters are available. For information, contact the Prince Rupert Infocentre at (800) 667-1994.

Sunken Gardens are located behind the Provincial Courthouse.

(© Blake Hanna, staff)

CASSIAR HIGHWAY 

Connects: Yellowhead Hwy. 16 to Alaska Hwy. **Length:** 446 miles
Road Surface: 75% paved, 25% gravel **Season:** Open all year
Highest Summit: Gnat Pass 4,072 feet
Major Attractions: Bear and Salmon glaciers, Stikine River

(See map, page 231)

	Alaska Hwy.	Dease Lake	Iskut	Stewart/Hyder	Yellowhead Hwy.	Watson Lake
Alaska Hwy.		145	196	390	446	14
Dease Lake	145		51	245	301	159
Iskut	196	51		194	250	210
Stewart/Hyder	390	245	194		136	404
Yellowhead Hwy.	446	301	250	136		460
Watson Lake	14	159	210	404	460	

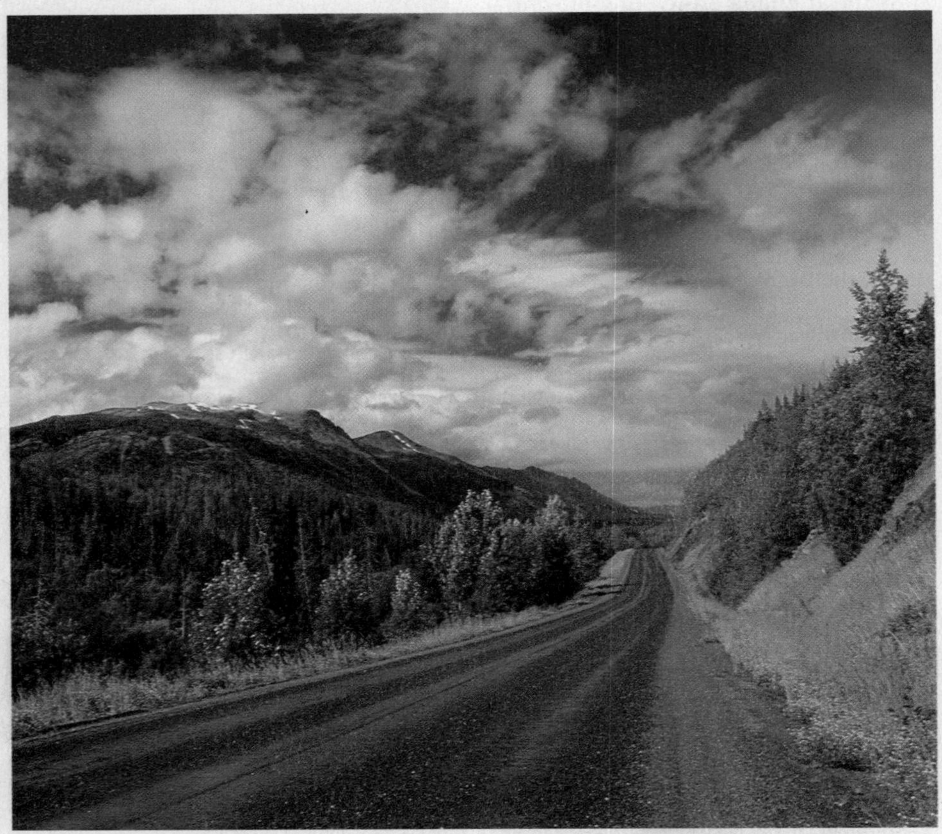

Much of the Cassiar Highway has been chip-sealed. (© Gladys Blyth)

The Cassiar Highway junctions with Yellowhead Highway 16 at the Skeena River bridge (**Milepost PG 297.7** in the YELLOWHEAD HIGHWAY 16 section) and travels north to the Stewart, BC–Hyder, AK, access road, Telegraph Creek access road and Dease Lake, ending at the Alaska Highway 13.3 miles/21.4 km west of Watson Lake, YT. Total driving distance is 446.1 miles/718 km.

Travelers driving between Prince George and the junction of the Alaska and Cassiar highways will save 132.4 miles/213 km by taking the Cassiar Highway. (Yellowhead–Cassiar route is 743.8 miles/1,197 km; Alaska Highway route is 876.2 miles/1,410.1 km.) The Cassiar Highway, which was completed in 1972, is a somewhat rougher road than the Alaska Highway, and has fewer (but sufficient) fuel and service stops along the way. The Cassiar also offers outstanding scenery.

Although much of the highway is asphalt-surfaced, keep in mind that seal coat is subject to deterioration from weather and traffic. Also, a few bridges are still single lane. Watch for potholes at bridge ends and slippery bridge decks. There are several 8 percent grades. Drive with your headlights on at all times. On gravel stretches of highway watch for washboard and potholes. Gravel road may be dusty in dry weather and muddy in wet weather. The calcium chloride, which is used for dust control and to stabilize the road base, results in the road surface becoming muddy and rough in wet weather. (Wash calcium chloride off your vehicle as soon as possible.)

Watch for logging and freight trucks on the highway. *WARNING: Exercise extreme caution when passing or being passed by these trucks; reduce speed and allow trucks adequate clearance.*

The Cassiar also provides access to Hyder and Stewart. These communities are described in detail in this section beginning on page 234. Watch for bears with cubs along the highway (especially in spring); cariboo at Gnat Pass (spring and fall); and Dall sheep south of Good Hope.

Food, gas and lodging are available along the Cassiar Highway, but check the highway log for distances between services. Be sure your vehicle is mechanically sound with good tires and carry a spare. It is a good idea to carry extra fuel in the off-season. In case of emergency, motorists are advised to flag down trucks to radio for help. *NOTE: It is unlawful to camp overnight in turnouts and rest areas unless otherwise posted.* Camp at private campgrounds or in provincial park campgrounds.

According to the Ministry of Highways, litter barrels on the Cassiar Highway are often moved to areas which are being used more frequently. Litter barrels may not be in the same location from season to season.

Cassiar Highway Log

Distance from junction with the Yellowhead Highway (J) is followed by distance from Alaska Highway (AH).
Kilometreposts are along the Cassiar Highway every 5 km. Because the posts do not always accurately reflect driving distance, mileages from the Yellowhead Highway 16 junction are based on actual driving distance while the kilometre conversion is based on physical kilometreposts as they occurred in summer 1999.

BC HIGHWAY 37

J 0 AH 446.1 (718 km) Gas station. Bridge across Skeena River from Yellowhead Highway 16 to start of Cassiar Highway.

Junction with Yellowhead Highway 16 (see **Milepost PG 297.7** in the YELLOWHEAD HIGHWAY 16 section).

J 0.2 (0.4 km) **AH 445.9** (717.6 km) Turn east on side road to view totem poles of **GITWANGAK.** The Native reserve of Gitwangak was renamed after sharing the name Kitwanga with the adjacent white settlement. Gitwangak has some of the finest authentic totem poles in the area. Also here is St. Paul's Anglican Church (the original old bell tower standing beside the church dates back to 1893) and one of the last existing Grand Trunk Pacific railway stations.

J 2.5 (4 km) **AH 443.6** (714 km) Kitwanga post office, a private RV park, and a bed and breakfast. ▲

CASSIAR HIGHWAY

Yellowhead Highway Junction to Alaska Highway Junction

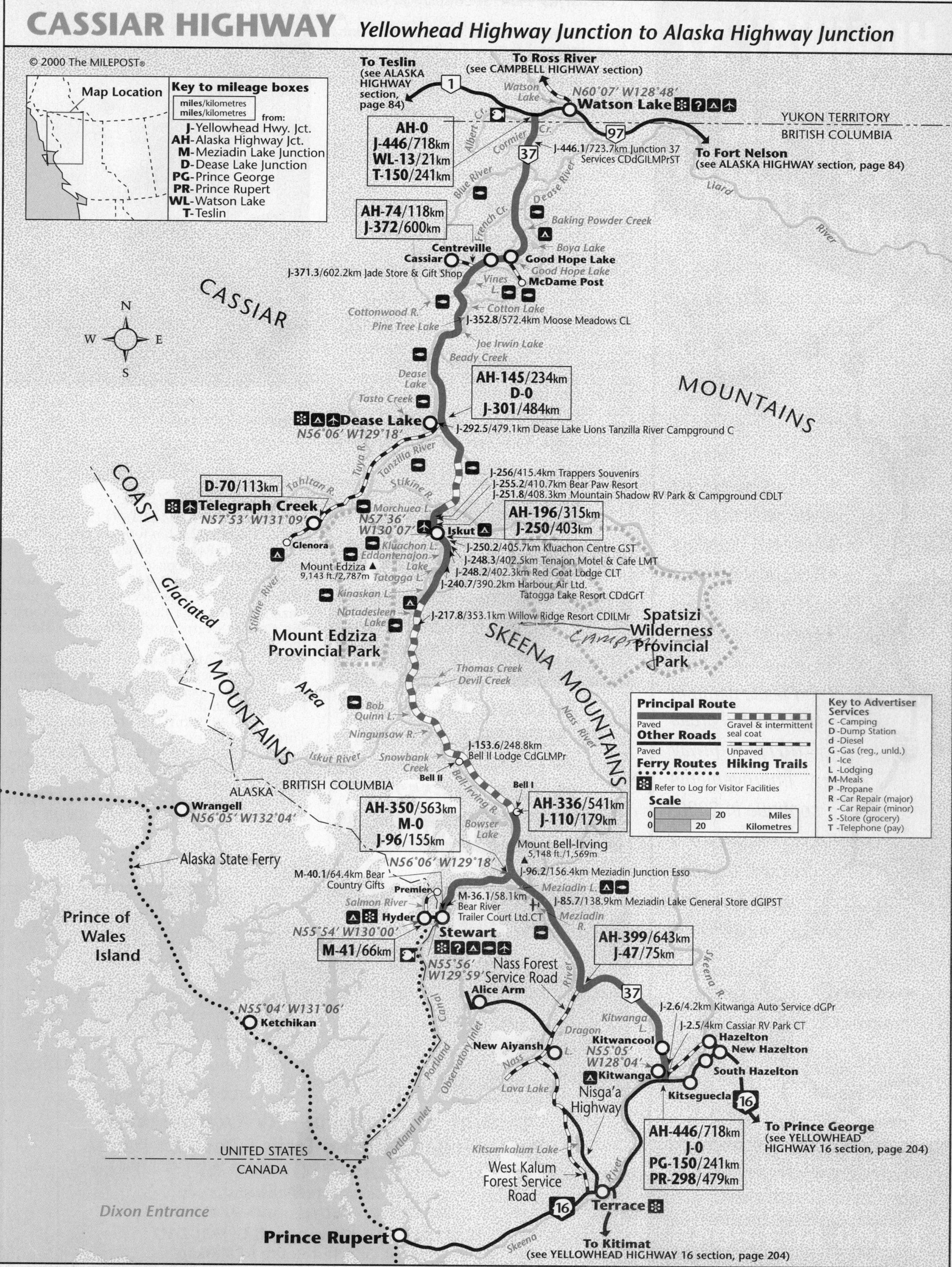

© 2000 The MILEPOST®
Map Location
Key to mileage boxes
miles/kilometres
miles/kilometres
from:
J-Yellowhead Hwy. Jct.
AH-Alaska Highway Jct.
M-Meziadin Lake Junction
D-Dease Lake Junction
PG-Prince George
PR-Prince Rupert
WL-Watson Lake
T-Teslin
To Teslin (see ALASKA HIGHWAY section, page 84)
To Ross River (see CAMPBELL HIGHWAY section)
N60°07' W128°48'
Watson Lake
YUKON TERRITORY
BRITISH COLUMBIA
AH-0
J-446/718km
WL-13/21km
T-150/241km
J-446.1/723.7km Junction 37 Services CDdGILMPrST
To Fort Nelson (see ALASKA HIGHWAY section, page 84)
Liard River
Blue River
Dease River
Baking Powder Creek
AH-74/118km
J-372/600km
Centreville
Cassiar
Good Hope Lake
Boya Lake
J-371.3/602.2km Jade Store & Gift Shop
McDame Post
CASSIAR
Cotton Lake
Cottonwood R.
Pine Tree Lake
J-352.8/572.4km Moose Meadows CL
Joe Irwin Lake
Beady Creek
Dease Lake
Tasto Creek
AH-145/234km
D-0
J-301/484km
MOUNTAINS
Dease Lake
N56°06' W129°18'
J-292.5/479.1km Dease Lake Lions Tanzilla River Campground C
COAST
Tanzilla River
Stikine R.
D-70/113km
Tahltan R.
Tuya R.
J-256/415.4km Trappers Souvenirs
J-255.2/410.7km Bear Paw Resort
J-251.8/408.3km Mountain Shadow RV Park & Campground CDLT
Telegraph Creek
N57°53' W131°09'
Morchuea L.
N57°36' W130°07'
Iskut
AH-196/315km
J-250/403km
Glenora
Kluachon L.
Eddontenajon Lake
J-250.2/405.7km Kluachon Centre GST
J-248.3/402.5km Tenajon Motel & Cafe LMT
J-248.2/402.3km Red Goat Lodge CLT
Mount Edziza 9,143 ft./2,787m
Tatogga L.
J-240.7/390.2km Harbour Air Ltd. Tatogga Lake Resort CDdGrT
Kinaskan L.
Glaciated
Stikine River
Natadesleen Lake
J-217.8/353.1km Willow Ridge Resort CDILMr
Spatsizi Wilderness Provincial Park
Mount Edziza Provincial Park
SKEENA MOUNTAINS
Thomas Creek
Devil Creek
MOUNTAINS
Area
Bob Quinn L.
Ningunsaw R.
Nass River
Principal Route
Paved
Gravel & intermittent seal coat
Other Roads
Paved
Unpaved
Ferry Routes
Hiking Trails
Refer to Log for Visitor Facilities
Scale
Miles
Kilometres
Key to Advertiser Services
C -Camping
D -Dump Station
d -Diesel
G -Gas (reg., unld.)
I -Ice
L -Lodging
M -Meals
P -Propane
R -Car Repair (major)
r -Car Repair (minor)
S -Store (grocery)
T -Telephone (pay)
Iskut River
Snowbank Creek
J-153.6/248.8km Bell II Lodge CdGLMPr
Bell II
Bell-Irving R.
Bell I
BRITISH COLUMBIA
ALASKA
Wrangell
N56°05' W132°04'
AH-350/563km
M-0
J-96/155km
AH-336/541km
J-110/179km
Bowser Lake
Mount Bell-Irving 5,148 ft./1,569m
Alaska State Ferry
N56°06' W129°18'
J-96.2/156.4km Meziadin Junction Esso
M-40.1/64.4km Bear Country Gifts
Premier
Meziadin L.
Salmon River
M-36.1/58.1km Bear River Trailer Court Ltd. CT
J-85.7/138.9km Meziadin Lake General Store dGIPST
Prince of Wales Island
Hyder
Stewart
N55°54' W130°00'
Meziadin R.
M-41/66km
AH-399/643km
J-47/75km
N55°56' W129°59'
Nass Forest Service Road
Alice Arm
Skeena R.
N55°04' W131°06'
Ketchikan
J-2.6/4.2km Kitwanga Auto Service dGPr
Kitwanga L.
J-2.5/4km Cassiar RV Park CT
Dragon L.
Kitwancool
Hazelton
New Hazelton
New Aiyansh
N55°05' W128°04'
Kitwanga
South Hazelton
Portland Canal
Observatory Inlet
Lava Lake
Nisga'a Highway
Kitseguecla
Portland Inlet
AH-446/718km
J-0
PG-150/241km
PR-298/479km
To Prince George (see YELLOWHEAD HIGHWAY 16 section, page 204)
UNITED STATES
CANADA
Kitsumkalum Lake
West Kalum Forest Service Road
Dixon Entrance
Terrace
Prince Rupert
Skeena
To Kitimat (see YELLOWHEAD HIGHWAY 16 section, page 204)

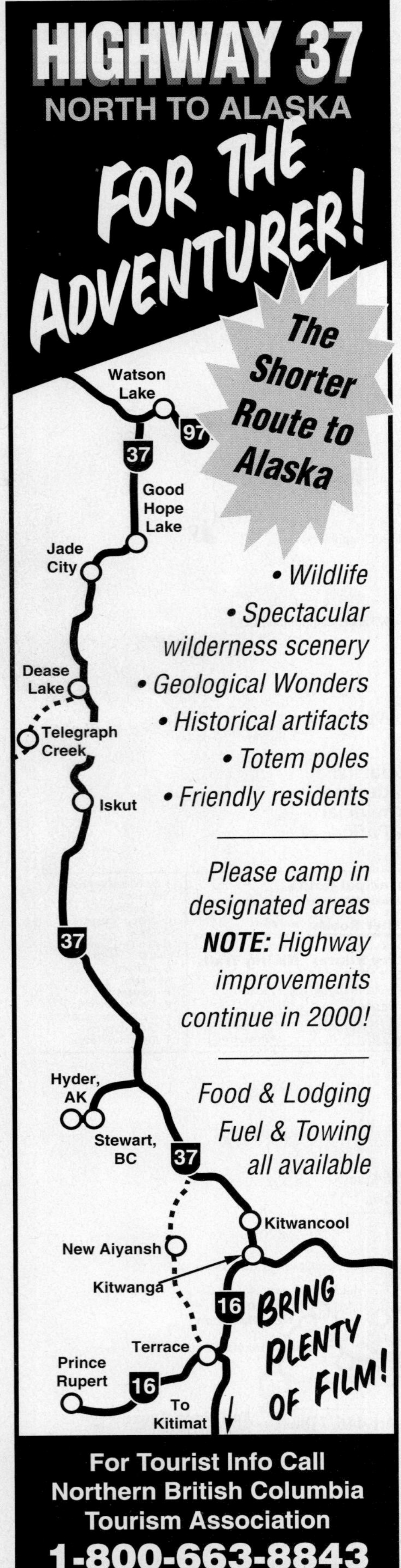

Cassiar RV Park. See display ad this section. ▲

J 2.6 (4.2 km) **AH 443.5** (713.8 km) South end of 1.6-mile/2.5-km loop access road which leads to **KITWANGA** (pop. 1,200). **Radio:** CBC 630 AM. **Emergency Services:** Ambulance. Gas station, towing, car wash, a general store and small restaurant. There is a free public campground across from the gas station. (Donations for campground upkeep gratefully accepted at the Kitwanga Tempo service station.) ▲

Kitwanga is at the crossroads of the old upper Skeena "grease trail" trade. The "grease" was eulachon (candlefish) oil, which was a trading staple among tribes of the Coast and Interior. The grease trails are believed to have extended north to the Bering Sea.

A paved turnout with litter barrel and sign on the Kitwanga access road mark **Kitwanga Fort National Historic Site**, where a wooden fortress and palisade once crowned the large rounded hill here. Seven interpretive panels along the trail up Battle Hill explain the history of the site. Kitwanga Fort was the first major western Canadian Native site commemorated by Parks Canada.

Kitwanga Auto Service. See display ad this section.

Kitwancool has many fine replicas of original totem poles.
(© Judy Parkin)

J 4 (6.5 km) **AH 442.1** (711.5 km) North end of 1.6-mile/2.6-km loop access road (Kitwanga North Road) to Kitwanga; see description preceding milepost.

J 4.1 (6.6 km) **AH 442** (711.4 km) **Junction** with alternate access route (signed Hazelton–Kitwanga Road) from Hazelton to the Cassiar Highway via the north side of the Skeena River.

J 5 (8 km) **AH 441.1** (710 km) The mountain chain of Seven Sisters is visible to southwest (weather permitting) next 4 miles/6.4 km northbound.

J 12.5 (20.2 km) **AH 433.6** (697.9 km) Turnout with litter barrels to west.

J 12.6 (20.3 km) **AH 433.5** (697.7 km) Highway follows Kitwanga River and former grease trail route.

J 13 (21 km) **AH 433.1** (697.1 km) South access to **KITWANCOOL** (2 miles/3.3 km from highway), a small Indian village; gas

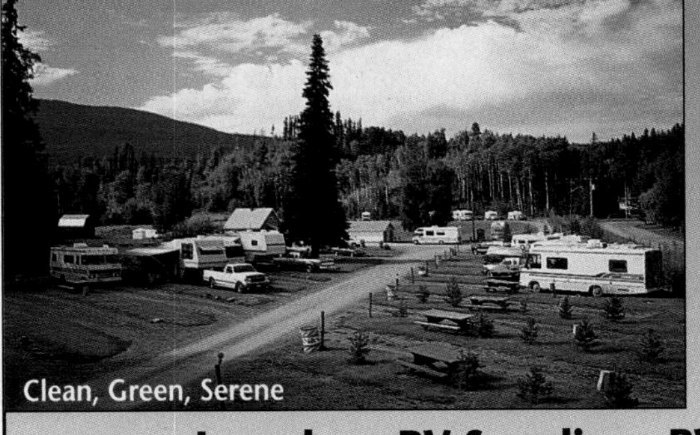

available. Kitwancool has many fine old and restored totems. Guided tours of the totem poles may be available; inquire at the Visitor Infocentre. A Native craft shop in the village sells local art. The village of Kitwancool was originally called Gitanyow, meaning place of many people, but was renamed Kitwancool, meaning place of reduced number, after many of its inhabitants were killed in raids.

J 16.1 (26.1 km) **AH 430** (692.1 km) North access to Kitwancool.

J 18.8 (30.4 km) **AH 427.3** (687.8 km) Bridge over Moonlit Creek.

J 18.9 (30.7 km) **AH 427.2** (687.5 km) Rest area north of creek, east of road, with tables, toilets and litter barrels. Road west is the old highway and access to **Kitwanga Lake.** Fishing, camping and boat launch spots on lake. Old highway may be in poor condition; drive carefully. It rejoins the main highway at Mile 24.1. Access to the lake is strictly from the old highway.

J 19.9 (32.2 km) **AH 426.2** (686 km) Access to Kitwanga Lake.

J 21.3 (34.5 km) **AH 424.8** (683.7 km) Good views of Kitwanga Lake to west; old highway visible, below west, winding along lakeshore.

J 26.1 (42.2 km) **AH 420** (676 km) Kitwancool Forest Road to west.

J 38.8 (62.9 km) **AH 407.3** (655.5 km) **Cranberry River** bridge No. 1. A favorite salmon stream in summer; consult fishing regulations.

J 46.5 (75.3 km) **AH 399.6** (643.2 km) Paved turnout to west.

J 46.8 (75.9 km) **AH 399.3** (642.6 km) **Junction** with the Nass Forest Service Road/Nisga'a Highway to New Aiyansh (38 miles/62 km) and Terrace (99 miles/159 km).

J 47.1 (76.3 km) **AH 399** (642.2 km) Cranberry River bridge No. 2. Turnout with toilets, tables and litter barrels.

J 53.1 (86 km) **AH 393** (632.6 km) BC Hydro power line crosses and parallels highway. Completed in 1990, this line links Stewart to the BC Hydro power grid. Previously, Stewart's power was generated by diesel fuel.

Entering Kalum Forest District northbound. Watch for signs telling dates of logging activity, and observe patterns of regrowth.

J 58.6 (94.9 km) **AH 387.5** (623.7 km) Kelly Lake rest area at north end of lake on west side of highway, with tables, toilet and litter barrels. First view northbound of Nass River.

J 64.1 (103.8 km) **AH 382** (614.9 km) Paved turnout.

J 65.6 (106.4 km) **AH 380.5** (612.4 km) View of Nass River to west. The Nass River is one of the province's prime producers of sockeye salmon.

J 66.4 (107.7 km) **AH 379.7** (611.1 km) Views northbound (weather permitting) of the Coast Mountains to the west. Cambrian ice field to west.

J 70.1 (113.6 km) **AH 376** (605.2 km) Paved turnout with litter barrel to west.

J 78.7 (127.4 km) **AH 367.4** (591.3 km) Paved turnout with litter barrel.

J 85 (137.8 km) **AH 361.1** (581.2 km) Paved turnout with litter barrels to west.

J 85.7 (138.9 km)**AH 360.4** (580.1 km) Elsworth logging camp and Meziadin Lake General Store (VanDyke Camp Services), open to public; fuel, groceries, dump station, hunting and fishing licenses, emergency phone. Private airstrip.

Meziadin Lake General Store. See display ad this section.

J 87.9 (142.4 km) **AH 358.2** (576.6 km) *CAUTION: 1-lane bridge over Nass River.* Paved rest area with picnic tables, toilets and litter barrel to east at south end of bridge. A plaque at the north end commemorates bridge opening in 1972 that joined roads to form Highway 37. The gorge is almost 400 feet/122m wide; main span of bridge is 1feet/57m. Bridge decking is 130 feet/40m above the riverbed.

J 89.4 (145 km) **AH 356.7** (574.1 km) Tintina Logging Road.

J 93.1 (151 km) **AH 353** (568.1 km) Tintina Creek. Along with Hanna Creek, this stream produces 40 percent of the sockeye salmon spawning in the Meziadin Lake watershed.

J 94.3 (152.8 km) **AH 351.8** (566.3 km) Large gravel turnout to west with litter barrels.

J 94.4 (153 km) **AH 351.7** (566 km) Bridge over Hanna Creek South. Sockeye salmon spawn here in autumn and can be observed from creek banks and bridge deck. It is illegal to fish for or harass these fish. *CAUTION: Watch for bears.*

J 95.6 (155.3 km) **AH 350.5** (564.2 km) **Meziadin** (Mezy-AD-in) **Lake Provincial Park**; 46 campsites (many on lake), drinking water, toilets, wheelchair access, swimming, firewood, bear-proof garbage containers, boat launch. The lake has a significant fish population, including rainbow trout, mountain whitefish and Dolly Varden Fishing is especially good at the mouths of small streams draining into Meziadin Lake.

Four species of salmon spawn in the lake. This is one of only 3 areas in the province where salmon spawn in the bays and inlets of a lake. *CAUTION: Watch for bears. The hills around the lake are prime bear habitat.*

J 96.2 (156.4 km) **AH 349.9** (563.1 km) **Meziadin Junction.** Fuel, minor car repair, food, laundry, RV parking and dump station at turnoff for Stewart/Hyder. *NOTE: This junction can be confusing. Choose your route carefully.*

Meziadin Junction Esso. See display ad this section.

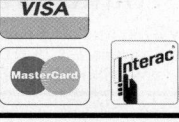

Junction with the access road to Stewart, BC, and Hyder, AK. See STEWART, BC–HYDER, AK, ACCESS ROAD beginning on page 234.

J 97.5 (158.5 km) **AH 348.6** (561.1 km) Travelers will notice large areas of clear-cut

(Continues on page 236)

Stewart, BC–Hyder, AK, Access Road Log

HIGHWAY 37A
Distance is measured from Meziadin Lake Junction (M).

M 0 Junction with Cassiar Highway at **Milepost J 96.2.** Visitor information cabin, status unconfirmed at press time.

M 7.7 (12.4 km) Surprise Creek bridge.

M 10.1 (16.3 km) Turnout to north with view of hanging glaciers.

M 10.4 (16.7 km) Turnout to south with view of hanging glaciers.

M 11.5 (18.5 km) Windy Point bridge.

M 12.5 (20.1 km) Cornice Creek bridge.

M 13.5 (21.7 km) Strohn Creek bridge.

M 14.4 (23.2 km) Rest area with litter barrels, view of Bear Glacier.

M 15.4 (24.8 km) Turnouts along lake into which **Bear Glacier** calves its icebergs. Watch for falling rock from slopes above road in spring. Morning light is best for photographing spectacular Bear Glacier. At one time the glacier reached this side of the valley; the old highway can be seen hundreds of feet above the present road.

M 17.5 (28.8 km) Cullen River bridge.

M 19.8 (31.9 km) Huge delta of accumulated avalanche snow. Little shoulder; no stopping.

M 21 (33.8 km) Argyle Creek.

M 22.4 (36.1 km) Narrow, steep-walled Bear River canyon. Watch for rocks on road.

M 23.9 (38.5 km) Turnout with litter barrel to north.

M 28.9 (46.5 km) Turnout with litter barrel to south.

M 29.4 (47.4 km) Bitter Creek bridge.

M 31.8 (51.2 km) Wards Pass cemetery. The straight stretch of road along here is the former railbed from Stewart.

M 36.1 (58.1 km) Bear River bridge and welcome portal to Stewart.

Bear River Trailer Court Ltd. See display ad this section. ▲

M 37.8 (60.8 km) Highway joins main street of Stewart (description follows).

M 40.1 (64.4 km) **U.S.–Canada Border.** Hyder (description follows). *TIME ZONE CHANGE: Stewart observes Pacific time, Hyder observes Alaska time.*

Bear Country Gifts. See display ad this section.

Stewart, BC–Hyder, AK

Stewart is at the head of Portland Canal on the AK–BC border. **Hyder** is 2.3 miles/3.7 km beyond Stewart. **Population: Stewart** 650; **Hyder** 102. **Emergency Services:** In Stewart, **RCMP**, phone (250) 636-2233. EMS personnel and Medivac helicopter in Hyder. **Fire Department**, phone (250) 636-2345. **Hospital** and **Ambulance**, Stewart Health Care Facility (10 beds), phone (250) 636-2221.

Visitor Information: Stewart Visitor Infocentre (Box 306, Stewart, BC V0T 1W0), located in Chamber of Commerce/ Infocentre Building on 5th Avenue; phone (250) 636-9224, toll-free 1-888-366-5999, or fax (250) 636-2199. Limited off-season hours. Hyder Information Center and Museum is located in the Hyder Community Association Bldg.

Elevation: Sea level. **Climate:** Maritime, with warm winters and cool rainy summers. Summer temperatures range from 50°F/11°C to 68°F/20°C; winter temperatures range from 25°F/-4°C to 43°F/6°C. Average temperature in January is 27°F/-3°C; in July, 67°F/19°C. Reported record high 89°F/32°C, record low -18°F/-28°C. Slightly less summer rain than other Northwest communities, but heavy snowfall in winter. **Radio:** CFPR 1450, CJFW-FM 92.9, CFMI-FM 101. **Television:** Cable, 15 channels.

Private Aircraft: Stewart airport, on 5th Street; elev. 10 feet/3m; length 3,900 feet/1,189m; asphalt; fuel 80, 100.

Description

Stewart and Hyder are on a spur of the Cassiar Highway, at the head of Portland Canal, a narrow saltwater fjord approximately 90 miles/145 km long. The fjord forms a natural boundary between Alaska and Canada. Stewart has a deep harbour and boasts of being Canada's most northerly ice-free port.

Prior to the coming of the white man, Nass River Indians knew the head of Portland Canal as *Skam-A-Kounst,* meaning safe place, probably referring to the place as a retreat from the harassment of the coastal Haidas. The Nass came here annually to hunt birds and pick berries. Little evidence of their presence remains.

In 1896, Captain D.D. Gaillard (after whom the Gaillard Cut in the Panama Canal was later named) explored Portland Canal for the U.S. Army Corps of Engineers. Two years after Gaillard's visit, the first prospectors and settlers arrived. Among them was D.J. Raine, for whom a creek and mountain in the area were named. The Stewart brothers arrived in 1902 and in 1905 Robert M. Stewart, the first postmaster, named the town Stewart. Hyder was first called Portland City. It was then renamed Hyder, after Canadian mining engineer Frederick B. Hyder, when the U.S. Postal Authority told residents there were already too many cities named Portland.

Gold and silver mining dominated the early economy. Hyder boomed with the discovery of rich silver veins in the upper Salmon River basin in 1917–18. Hundreds of pilings, which supported structures during

Bitter Creek Cafe in downtown Stewart, BC. (© Blake Hanna, staff)

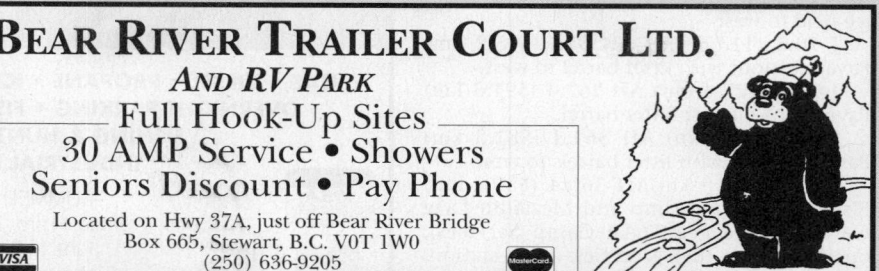

this boom period, are visible on the tidal flats at Hyder.

Hyder became an access and supply point for the mines, while Stewart served as the centre for Canadian mining activity. Mining ceased in 1956, with the exception of the Granduc copper mine, which operated until 1984. Today the economy is driven by forestry, mining and tourism.

Lodging & Services

Stewart: 2 hotels/motels, 4 restaurants, a grocery store, 4 churches, service stations, laundromat, pharmacy, post office, a bank (open Monday, Wednesday and Friday), ATM, liquor store and other shops. Camping at 2 campgrounds/RV parks with washrooms, showers and hookups. ▲

Hyder: 2 groceries, 4 gift shops, a post office, 2 cafes, a Baptist church, 2 motels and 2 bars. Boat launch at salt water, tenting area and RV park with TV reception. Visitor info-centre and museum. Laundromat, public restroom and showers. There is no bank in Hyder. There is an ATM in Stewart.. ▲

Transportation

Bus: Limousine service to Terrace with connections to Greyhound and airlines. **Ferry:** Service between Ketchikan and Hyder. *IMPORTANT: Check ferry departure times carefully!*

Attractions

Historic Buildings: In Stewart, the former fire hall at 6th and Columbia streets built in 1910, which now houses the Historical Society Museum; the Empress Hotel on 4th Street; and St. Mark's Church (built in 1910) on 9th Street at Columbia. On the border at Eagle Point is the stone storehouse built by Captain D.D. Gaillard of the U.S. Army Corps of Engineers in 1896. This is the oldest masonry building in Alaska. Originally 4 of these buildings were built to hold exploration supplies. This one was subsequently used as a cobbler shop and jail. Storehouses Nos. 3 and 4 are included on the (U.S.) National Register of Historic Places.

Stewart Historical Society Museum, in the fire hall, has a wildlife exhibit on the main floor and an exhibit of historical items on the top floor. Included is a display on movies filmed here: "Bear Island" (1978), John Carpenter's "The Thing" (1981), "The Ice Man" (1982) and "Leaving Normal."

Toaster Museum. Stewart's unique

Toaster Museum has more than 500 different toasters on display.

Hyder's night life is well-known, and has helped Hyder earn the reputation and town motto of "The Friendliest Little Ghost Town in Alaska."

Recreation in Stewart includes winter sports at the indoor skating rink; an outdoor tennis court; ball parks; hiking trails; and a self-guided historical walking tour.

Downtown Hyder, Alaska. (© Paul Souders)

Salmon Glacier Road. Guided sightseeing tours are available or check with the

Stewart Info Centre for self-guided auto tours out Salmon Glacier Road. This narrow winding road connected Stewart with mining interests to the north. Extended from Premier Mine to Grand Duc in 1965, the road now offers visitors the opportunity to take in active and abandoned mine sites, such as Granduc, and spectacular **Salmon Glacier;** the toe of Salmon Glacier is seen at Mile

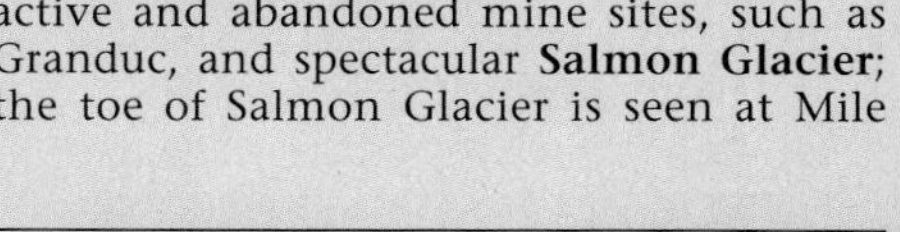

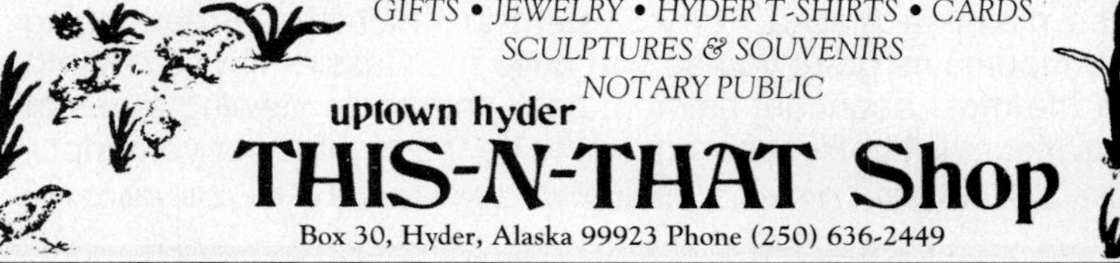

Stewart–Hyder Access Road Log *(continued)*

17.2/27.7 km on the self-guided auto tour from Stewart. Summit Viewpoint at Mile 22.9/37 km provides a spectacular view of the glacier.

Other sights include nearby **Fish Creek Wildlife Viewing Area** at Mile 6/9.6 km. Chum and pink salmon are seen in their spawning colors in Fish Creek from July to September; they ascend the streams and rivers in great numbers to spawn. Visitors from all over the world come to photograph bald eagles and black bears which are drawn to the streams by the salmon.

International Days. Fourth of July begins July 1 as Stewart and Hyder celebrate Canada Day and Independence Day. Parade and fireworks.

International Rodeo. The Stewart–Hyder International Rodeo is held the second weekend in June.

Charter trips by small boat on Portland Canal and vicinity available for sightseeing and fishing. Flightseeing air tours available.

AREA FISHING: Portland Canal, salmon to 50 lbs., use herring, spring and late fall; coho to 12 lbs. in fall, fly-fishing. (NOTE: Alaska or British Columbia fishing license required, depending on whether you fish U.S. or Canadian waters in Portland Canal.) Excellent fishing for salmon and Dolly Varden at mouth of **Salmon River**. Up the Salmon River road from Hyder, Fish Creek has Dolly Varden 2 to 3 lbs., use salmon eggs and lures, best in summer. **Fish Creek** is a spawning ground for some of the world's largest chum salmon, mid-summer to fall; it is illegal to kill chum in fresh water in British Columbia. It is legal to harvest chum from both salt and fresh water in Alaska.

Return to Milepost J 96.2 on the Cassiar Highway

HYDER ADVERTISERS

(Continued from page 233)

along the southern half of the Cassiar Highway. Bark beetle infestation necessitated the harvest of timber along this particular stretch of highway. After logging, it was reforested.

J 100.8 (164.8 km) **AH 345.3** (555.8 km) Hanna Creek North river and bridge. Gravel turnout at north end of bridge on west side of road with litter barrel.

J 104.1 (169.2 km) **AH 342** (550.5 km) Large turnout to west with litter barrels.

J 116 (189.2 km) **AH 330.1** (531.3 km) **Bell I Crossing** of Bell-Irving River. Rest area at north end of Bell–Irving bridge with picnic tables, pit toilets and litter barrels.

J 118.2 (192.2 km) **AH 327.9** (527.7 km) Spruce Creek bridge.

J 122.8 (198.9 km) **AH 323.3** (520.3 km) Bell–Irving River parallels highway.

J 125.1 (202.5 km) **AH 321** (516.7 km) Cousins Creek.

J 126.7 (205.2 km) **AH 319.4** (514.1 km) Ritchie Creek bridge, wooden-decked, slippery when wet.

J 130.4 (211.2 km) **AH 315.7** (508.1 km) Taft Creek bridge, wooden-decked, slippery when wet.

J 136.1 (220.4 km) **AH 310** (499 km) **Deltaic Creek.** *Pavement ends, gravel begins, northbound.*

J 141.5 (229.2 km) **AH 304.6** (490.3 km) Glacier Creek.

J 142 (230 km) **AH 304.1** (489.5 km) *Seal coat begins, gravel ends northbound.*

J 143.6 (232.7 km) **AH 302.5** (486.8 km) Skowill Creek Bridge.

J 145.1 (235 km) **AH 301** (484.5 km) Large gravel turnout with litter barrels.

J 148.1 (239.8 km) **AH 298** (479.7 km) Oweegee Creek.

J 152.1 (246.2 km) **AH 294** (473.2 km) Provincial rest area by **Hodder Lake;** information kiosk, tables, litter barrels, pit toilets, cartop boat launch. Fly or troll for small rainbows.

J 153.6 (248.8 km) **AH 292.5** (470.7 km) **Bell II Crossing;** food, gas, diesel, propane, pay phone and lodging just south of second crossing (northbound) of Bell-Irving River.

J 153.8 (249.3 km) **AH 292.3** (470.5 km) Bridge crosses Bell–Irving River.

J 156.8 (254.2 km) **AH 289.3** (465.6 km) Large gravel turnout with litter barrel.

J 159.2 (258.1 km) **AH 286.9** (461.7 km) Snowbank Creek.

J 161.2 (261.1 km) **AH 284.9** (458.6 km) *CAUTION: Avalanche area northbound to Ningunsaw Pass; no stopping in winter or spring.* Avalanche chutes are visible on slopes to west in summer. Highway serves as emergency airstrip. Watch for aircraft landing or taking off; keep to side of road!

J 161.6 (261.8 km) **AH 284.5** (457.9 km) Redflat Creek.

J 164.1 (266 km) **AH 282** (453.8 km) Revision Creek.

J 165.1 (267.6 km) **AH 281** (452.2 km) Fan Creek.

J 167.3 (271 km) **AH 278.8** (448.7 km) Avalanche area. No stopping.

J 168.7 (273.2 km) **AH 277.4** (446.5 km) Turnout with litter barrels to east overlooking large moose pasture, beaver lodge.

J 169.6 (274.9 km) **AH 276.5** (445 km) **Ningunsaw Pass** (elev. 1,530 feet/466m). Nass–Stikine water divide; turnout with litter barrels to west beside **Ningunsaw River**. Mountain whitefish and Dolly Varden. The highway parallels the Ningunsaw northbound. Watch for fallen rock on road through the canyon. The Ningunsaw is a tributary of the Stikine watershed.

J 169.9 (275.4 km) **AH 276.2** (444.5 km) Beaverpond Creek Bridge.

J 170.3 (276 km) **AH 275.8** (443.9 km) Liz Creek Bridge.

J 172.7 (279.9 km) **AH 273.4** (440 km) Alger Creek. The massive piles of logs and debris in this creek are from a 1989 avalanche. Avalanche chutes visible to west.

J 173 (280.3 km) **AH 273.1** (439.5 km) Large gravel turnout to east with litter barrel.

J 174.8 (283.2 km) **AH 271.3** (436.7 km) Bend Creek.

J 175.6 (284.5 km) **AH 270.5** (435.4 km) Gamma Creek.

J 176.9 (286.9 km) **AH 269.2** (433.2 km) Ogilvie Creek.

J 177.8 (288.2 km) **AH 268.3** (431.9 km) Point of interest sign about Yukon Telegraph line. The 1,900-mile/3,057-km Dominion Telegraph line linked Dawson City with Vancouver. Built from 1899–1901, the line was a route for prospectors and trappers headed to Atlin, BC; it was replaced by radio in the 1930s.

J 178 (288.6 km) **AH 268.1** (431.5 km) Echo Lake. Flooded telegraph cabins are visible in the lake below. Good view of Coast Mountains to west. Spectacular cliffs seen to the east are part of the Skeena Mountains (Bowser Basin).

J 181 (293.7 km) **AH 265.1** (426.6 km) Bob Quinn Forest Service Road, under construction as the Iskut Mining Road, will provide year-round access to goldfields west of the Ningunsaw River. The road will follow the Iskut River Valley toward the Stikine River, with a side branch to Eskay Creek gold deposit. *CAUTION: Watch for turning trucks.*

J 181.5 (294.4 km) **AH 264.6** (425.9 km) **Little Bob Quinn Lake**, rainbow and Dolly Varden, summer and fall. Access to Bob Quinn Lake at **Milepost J 183.3.**

J 182.2 (295.3 km) **AH 263.9** (424.7 km) Bob Quinn flight airstrip. This is a staging site for supplies headed for the Stikine/Iskut goldfields. Paved rest area with litter barrels, picnic tables and toilet.

J 183.3 (297 km) **AH 262.8** (423 km) Bob Quinn highway maintenance camp; helicopter base. Emergency assistance. Access to Bob Quinn Lake; toilet, picnic table, cartop boat launch.

J 187 (303.1 km) **AH 259.1** (417 km) Gravel turnout with litter barrels on both sides of road.

J 188.3 (305.2 km) **AH 257.8** (415 km) Old kilometrepost 150, which reflects distance from Meziadin Junction.

J 190.2 (308.4 km) **AH 255.9** (411.8 km) Devil Creek Canyon bridge.

J 191.1 (309.7 km) **AH 255** (410.5 km) Gravel turnout with litter barrel to west.

J 191.6 (310.7 km) **AH 254.5** (409.6 km) Devil Creek Forest Service Road.

J 193.6 (313.9 km) **AH 252.5** (406.4 km) Thomas Creek and Thomas Creek Forest Service Road.

Highway passes through Iskut burn, where fire destroyed 78,000 acres in 1958. This is also British Columbia's largest huckleberry patch.

Northbound, the vegetation begins to change to northern boreal white and black spruce. This zone has cold, long winters and low forest productivity. Look for trembling aspen and lodgepole pine.

Southbound, the vegetation changes to become part of the interior cedar–hemlock zone. Cool wet winters and long dry summers produce a variety of tree species including western hemlock and red cedar, hybrid white spruce and subalpine fir.

CAUTION: Watch for turning trucks.

J 196.3 (318.1 km) **AH 249.8** (402 km) Large gravel turnout with litter barrel to west.

J 197.3 (319.6 km) **AH 248.8** (400.5 km) Slate Creek.

J 198.4 (321.5 km) **AH 247.7** (398.6 km) Gravel turnout with litter barrels to east.

J 199 (322.6 km) **AH 247.1** (397.7 km) Brake-check pullout.

J 199.7 (323.7 km) **AH 246.4** (396.6 km) Durham Creek.

J 203.7 (330.2 km) **AH 242.4** (390.1 km) *Gravel begins, seal coat ends northbound. NOTE: Watch for road construction next 21 miles/34 km northbound to Kinaskan Lake in summer 2000.*

J 204 (330.6 km) **AH 242.1** (389.7 km) Gravel turnout with litter barrels to west.

J 205.1 (332.4 km) **AH 241** (387.9 km) Single-lane bridge crosses Burrage River, northbound traffic yields. Note the rock pinnacle upstream to east.

J 205.5 (333 km) **AH 240.6** (387.2 km) Iskut River to west.

J 206.8 (335 km) **AH 239.3** (385.2 km) Gravel turnout to west.

J 207.8 (336.6 km) **AH 238.3** (383.6 km) Emergency airstrip crosses road; no stopping, watch for aircraft.

J 213 (345.4 km) **AH 233.1** (375.1 km) Rest area by Eastman Creek; picnic tables, outhouses, litter barrels, and information sign with map and list of services in Iskut Lakes Recreation Area. The creek was named for George Eastman (of Eastman Kodak fame), who hunted big game in this area before the highway was built.

J 216 (350.2 km) **AH 230.1** (370.3 km) Slow down for 1-lane bridge across **Rescue Creek**, northbound traffic yields. *NOTE: New 2-lane bridge planned for spring 2000.*

J 217.8 (353.1 km) **AH 228.3** (367.4 km) **Willow Ridge Resort**. See display ad this section.

J 217.9 (353.2 km) **AH 228.2** (367.2 km) New (1998) 2-lane bridge over Willow Creek.

J 218.3 (353.9 km) **AH 227.8** (366.6 km) Willow Creek Forest Service Road. *CAUTION: Watch for turning trucks.*

J 219.9 (356.6 km) **AH 226.2** (364 km) Gravel turnout with litter barrels to east.

J 220.6 (357.7 km) **AH 225.5** (362.9 km) Natadesleen Lake trailhead to west; toilets and litter barrel. Hike 0.6 mile/1 km west to lake.

J 222.6 (360.9 km) **AH 223.5** (359.7 km) Gravel turnout to west.

J 223.9 (362.9 km) **AH 222.2** (357.7 km) Snapper Creek.

J 225.1 (365 km) **AH 221** (355.7 km) Entrance to Kinaskan campground with 50 sites, outhouses, firewood, picnic and day-use area, wheelchair access, swimming, 2 hiking trails, drinking water and boat launch on **Kinaskan Lake**; rainbow fishing, July and August. Start of 15-mile/24.1-km hiking trail to Mowdade Lake in Mount Edziza Provincial Park.

NOTE: Watch for road construction next 21

miles/34 km southbound in summer 2000.

J 230.1 (373.1 km) **AH 216** (347.6 km) Turnout with litter barrel and view of Kinaskan Lake to west.

J 231.1 (374.6 km) **AH 215** (346.1 km) Small lake to east.

J 233.1 (377.9 km) **AH 213** (342.8 km) Gravel turnout with litter barrels to east.

J 233.4 (378.4 km) **AH 212.7** (342.3 km) Todagin Creek 1-lane bridge, northbound traffic yields. *NOTE: New 2-lane bridge proposed for 2000.*

J 239.4 (388.1 km) **AH 206.7** (332.7 km) Gravel turnout to west.

J 240.7 (390.2 km) **AH 205.4** (330.6 km) Resort with gas, diesel, food, lodging, camping and air charter service.

Harbour Air Ltd. See display ad this section.

Tatogga Lake Resort. See display ad this section.

J 241.3 (391.1 km) **AH 204.8** (329.7 km) Coyote Creek.

J 241.9 (392.1 km) **AH 204.2** (328.7 km) **Ealue Lake** (EE-lu-eh) turnoff. Small B.C. Forest Service recreation area, 7.5 miles/12 km off highway on gravel access road. Rustic sites, picnic tables, rock fire rings (bring own firewood), user-maintained, no fee. ▲

J 244.5 (396.4 km) **AH 201.6** (324.5 km) Turnout with litter barrel.

J 244.6 (396.6 km) **AH 201.5** (324.3 km) Turnout beside **Eddontenajon Lake** (Eddon-TEN-ajon); picnic tables, litter barrels, toilets and boat launch. It is unlawful to camp overnight at turnouts. People drink from the lake; be careful not to contaminate it. Use dump stations. Spatsizi trailhead to east. Lake breaks up in late May; freezeup is early November. Rainbow fishing July and August.

J 248.2 (402.3 km) **AH 197.9** (318.6 km) **Red Goat Lodge.** Lovely treed lakeshore setting with power and water hookups for RVs. Bed and Breakfast with unparalleled reputation. Coin showers, laundry, phone. Canoe and rowboat rentals. Fishing is excellent from shore. Choose Red Goat for a special vacation experience. AAA approved and undoubtedly one of the finest facilities on Highway 37. Open year-round. Your hosts, Jacquie and Mitch. Phone/fax (250) 234-3261. [ADVERTISEMENT] ▲

J 248.3 (402.5 km) **AH 197.8** (318.4 km) **Tenajon Motel & Cafe**. See display ad this section.

J 250 (405.4 km) **AH 196.1** (315.6 km) Zetu Creek. B.C. Hydro generating plant, supplies power for Iskut area.

J 250.2 (405.7 km) **AH 195.9** (315.3 km) **ISKUT** (pop. 300). **Clinic**: Phone (250) 234-3511. Small Tahltan Native community with post office in the Kluachon Centre on the highway, grocery store, public phone, motel and gas station. Quality leather goods available locally. Camping and cabins available at local lodges and guest ranches. Horse trips, canoe rentals and river rafting may be available; inquire at local lodges and resorts. ▲

Kluachon Centre. See display ad this section.

Private Aircraft: Eddontenajon airstrip, 0.6 mile/1 km north of Iskut; elev. 3,100 feet/945m; length 3,000 feet/914m; gravel; fuel available at Trans-Provincial Airlines base south on Eddontenajon Lake.

J 251.8 (408.3 km) **AH 194.3** (312.7 km) **Mountain Shadow RV Park & Campground.** Quiet, secluded, park-like setting with spectacular mountain vistas and lake views. Away from highway noise for a restful stopover or extended stay. Short nature walk to Kluachon Lake with excellent fishing. Wilderness trails, bird and wildlife viewing. A unique and breathtaking wilderness setting. [ADVERTISEMENT] ▲

J 255.2 (410.7 km) **AH 190.9** (307.2 km) **Bear Paw Resort**. See display ad this section.

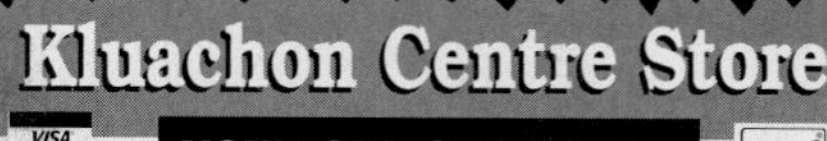

J 256 (415.4 km) **AH 190.1** (306 km) **Trapper's Souvenirs.** See display ad this section.

J 257.6 (418 km) **AH 188.5** (303.4 km) Tsaybahe Creek. Watch for beaver lodges which are visible from the highway.

J 260.6 (423 km) **AH 185.5** (298.5 km) Turnout with litter barrels to west. From here the dormant volcano of **Mount Edziza** (elev. 9,143 feet/2,787m) and its adjunct cinder cone can be seen to the southwest. The park, not accessible by road, is a rugged wilderness with a glacier, cinder cones, craters and lava flows. Panoramic view of Skeena and Cassiar mountains for next several miles northbound. Information signs.

J 261.8 (424.9 km) **AH 184.3** (296.6 km) Turnoff to Morchuea Lake B.C. Forest Service campsite. Rustic, some tables, rock fire rings (bring firewood), no fee. ▲

J 264 (428.4 km) **AH 182.1** (293.1 km) Entering Stikine River Recreation Area.

J 266.3 (432.1 km) **AH 179.8** (289.4 km) *Steep grade. Winding road next 1.2 miles/2 km northbound.*

J 267.2 (433.6 km) **AH 178.9** (287.9 km) *Hairpin turn: Keep to right. Highway descends to Stikine River in switchbacks.*

J 269 (436.6 km) **AH 177.1** (285 km) Turnout with litter barrels and toilets to south. Tourist map and services directory for area located here.

J 269.5 (437.3 km) **AH 176.6** (284.3 km) Stikine River bridge. Turnout at north end of bridge.

J 271.3 (440.2 km) **AH 174.8** (281.4 km) Turnout to east with litter barrel.

J 273.4 (443.6 km) **AH 172.7** (278 km) Leaving Stikine River Recreation Area northbound.

J 277.3 (450 km) **AH 168.8** (271.6 km) Turnout on **Upper Gnat Lake**; tables, toilets, litter barrels. Long scar across Gnat Pass valley to east is grading preparation for B.C. Railway's proposed Dease Lake extension from Prince George. Construction was halted in 1977. Grade is visible for several miles northbound.

J 279 (452.7 km) **AH 167.1** (268.9 km) Large gravel turnout with litter barrel to east at Tees Creek.

J 282 (457.6 km) **AH 164.1** (264.1 km) Gravel turnout with litter barrel to east.

J 283.9 (460.7 km) **AH 162.2** (261.1 km) Gravel turnout to east.

Trapper's Den Gift Shoppe in Dease Lake. (© Blake Hanna, staff)

J 284.2 (461.3 km) **AH 161.9** (260.5 km) Upper Gnat Rest Area.

J 284.5 (461.7 km) **AH 161.6** (260.1 km) Wilderness trail rides.

J 285.8 (463.8 km) **AH 160.3** (258 km) Turnout overlooking **Lower Gnat Lake**, abundant rainbow.

J 287.9 (467.1 km) **AH 158.2** (254.7 km) Turnout with litter barrel.

J 290.6 (467.7 km) **AH 155.5** (250.2 km) **Gnat Pass Summit**, elev. 4,072 feet/1,241m. Watch for cariboo in spring.

J 291.7 (473.3 km) **AH 154.4** (248.5 km) Steep grade, 8 percent downhill.

J 295.2 (479.1 km) **AH 150.9** (242.8 km) **Tanzilla River** bridge. Pleasant rest area with picnic tables and outhouses at north end of bridge beside river. Fishing for grayling to 16 inches, June and July; use flies.

J 296.5 (481.2 km) **AH 149.6** (240.7 km) Dalby Creek.

J 298.4 (484.1 km) **AH 147.7** (237.8 km) Turnout with litter barrel to west.

J 300.2 (487.1 km) **AH 145.9** (234.9 km) Divide (elev. 2,690 feet/820m) between Pacific and Arctic ocean watersheds.

J 300.9 (488.3 km) **AH 145.2** (233.7 km) **Dease Lake Junction.** Access west to Dease Lake (description follows) and Telegraph Creek.

Junction with Telegraph Creek Road. See TELEGRAPH CREEK ROAD on pages 240–241.

Dease Lake

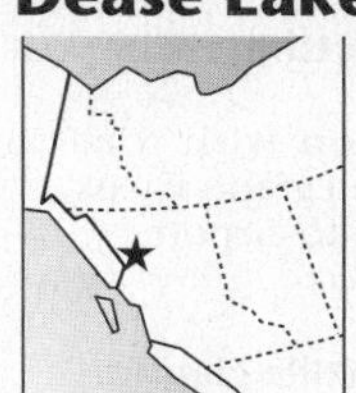

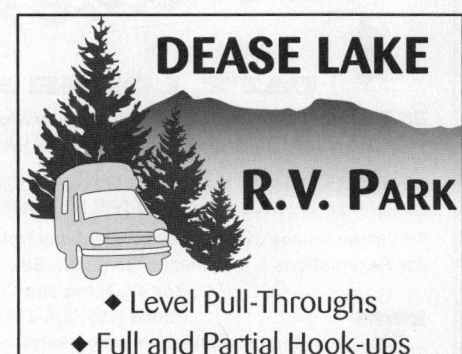

Located just west of the Cassiar Highway. **Emergency Services: RCMP** detachment. **Private Aircraft:** Dease Lake airstrip, 1.5 miles/2.4 km south; elev. 2,600 feet/792m; length 6,000 feet/1,829m; asphalt; fuel JP4, 100. **Visitor Information:** Write Dease Lake and

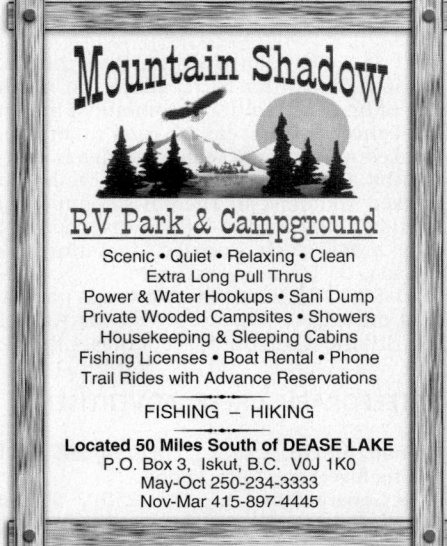

Telegraph Creek Road Log

Built in 1922, this was the first road in the Cassiar area of northern British Columbia. The scenery is remarkable and the town of Telegraph Creek is a picture from the turn of the century. Many of the original buildings remain from the gold rush days.

CAUTION: Telegraph Creek Road has some steep narrow sections and several sets of steep switchbacks; it is not recommended for trailers or large RVs. Car and camper drivers who are familiar with mountain driving should have no difficulty, although some motorists consider it a challenging drive even for the experienced. DRIVE CAREFULLY! Use caution when road is wet or icy. Watch for rocks and mud. There are no visitor facilities en route. Allow a minimum of 2 hours driving time with good conditions. Check road conditions at highway maintenance camp or RCMP office in Dease Lake before starting the 70.1 miles/112.8 km to Telegraph Creek. Phone the Stikine RiverSong Cafe (250) 235-3196 for weather and road conditions.

Distance from Dease Lake junction (D) on the Cassiar Highway is shown.

Stikine River canyon extends for some 50 miles/80 kms. (© Judy Parkin)

D 0 Dease Lake junction, Milepost J 300.9 Cassiar Highway.

D 0.9 (1.4 km) **Junction** with road to Dease Lake. Turn left for Telegraph Creek.

D 1.4 (2.3 km) Entrance to airport.

D 3.1 (5 km) *Pavement ends, gravel begins westbound.*

D 5 (8 km) Entering Tanzilla Plateau.

D 7.2 (11.6 km) Tatsho Creek (Eightmile).

D 15.9 (25.6 km) 16 Mile Creek.

D 17.1 (27.5 km) Augustchilde Creek, 1-lane bridge.

D 18.8 (30.3 km) 19 Mile Creek.

D 20.2 (32.5 km) 22 Mile Creek. Turnout with litter barrels south.

D 22.4 (36 km) Tanzilla River to south.

D 35.7 (57.5 km) Cariboo Meadows. Entering old burn area for 12 miles/19.3 km.

D 36.7 (59.1 km) Entering **Stikine River Recreation Area.** Tuya River valley viewpoint to north; turnout with litter barrels. Short walk uphill for good views and photographs.

D 37.7 (60.6 km) Approximate halfway point to Telegraph Creek from Dease Lake. Turnout with litter barrels to north. Excellent view of Mount Edziza on clear days.

D 45.5 (73.2 km) *CAUTTION: Begin 18 percent grade as road descends canyon; steep and narrow with switchbacks.*

D 46 (74.1 km) Turnout with litter barrels to south.

D 47.2 (76 km) Tuya River bridge.

D 47.7 (76.8 km) End of burn area.

D 49 (78.9 km) Y–intersection. Old road to left; keep right for newer section.

D 50.4 (81.1 km) Old road rejoins newer road.

D 50.8 (81.7 km) Golden Bear Mine access road. Private.

D 51.1 (82.2 km) *CAUTION: 20 percent downhill grade for approximately 0.6 mile/1 km.* Day's Ranch on left.

D 54.2 (87.3 km) Rest area with table, toilet and litter barrel; overlooks river gorge.

D 55.7 (89.7 km) Road runs through lava beds, on narrow promontory about 150 feet/51m wide, dropping 400 feet/122m on each side to Tahltan and Stikine rivers. Excellent views of the **Grand Canyon of the Stikine** and Tahltan Canyon can be seen by walking a short distance across lava beds to promontory point. Best views of the river canyon are by flightseeing trip. The Stikine River canyon is only 8 feet/2.4m wide at its narrowest point.

D 56.1 (90.3 km) *CAUTION: Sudden 180-degree right turn begins 18 percent downhill grade to Tahltan River and Indian fishing camps.*

D 56.5 (90.9 km) **Tahltan River** bridge. Turnout with litter barrel south, on north side of bridge. Traditional communal Indian smokehouses adjacent to road at bridge. Smokehouse on north side of bridge is operated by a commercial fisherman; fresh and smoked salmon sold. There is a commercial inland fishery on the Stikine River, one of only a few such licensed operations in Canada.

D 57.5 (92.6 km) Start of very narrow road on ledge rising steeply up the wall of the Stikine Canyon for 3 miles/4.8 km,

TELEGRAPH CREEK ADVERTISERS

Graham Air Ltd. ....Ph. (250) 235-3701
Stikine RiverSong Cafe, Lodge & General Store...........Ph. (250) 235-3196

rising to 400 feet/122m above the river.

D 60 (96.6 km) Ninemile Creek.

D 60.1 (96.7 km) Old **Tahltan** Indian community above road. *Private property: No trespassing!* Former home of Tahltan bear dogs. The Tahltan bear dog, believed to be extinct, was only about a foot high and weighed about 15 pounds. Short-haired, with oversize ears and shaving-brush tail, the breed was recognized by the Canadian Kennel Club. First seen by explorer Samuel Black in 1824, the dogs were used to hunt bears.

D 61.8 (99.5 km) Eightmile Creek bridge. Spectacular falls into canyon on left below. Opposite the gravel pit at the top of the hill there is a trailhead and parking on the west side of the creek.

D 63.1 (101.5 km) Turnout. Good photos of Stikine Canyon to east.

D 69.1 (111.2 km) Indian community. Road follows steep winding descent into old town, crossing a deep narrow canyon via a short bridge. Excellent picture spot 0.2 mile/0.3 km from bridge.

Glenora Road junction; 12-mile/19.3-km road leads west to Glenora, site of attempted railroad route to the Yukon and limit of larger riverboat navigation. There are 2 primitive B.C. Forest Service campsites and a full-service private campground on the road to Glenora. Several spur roads lead to the Stikine River and to Native fish camps. ▲

D 70.1 (112.8 km) **TELEGRAPH CREEK** (pop. 300; elev. 1,100 feet/335m). Former head of navigation on the Stikine and once a telegraph communication terminal. During the gold rush, an estimated 5,000 stampeders set off from Telegraph Creek to attempt the Stikine–Teslin Trail to the goldfields in Atlin and the Klondike.

There are a cafe, lodge, general store, post office, and a public school and nursing station here. Gas, minor auto and tire repair are available. Stikine River trips and charter flights are available. Anglican church services held weekly; Roman Catholic services held every other week.

Residents make their living fishing commercially for salmon, doing local construction work and guiding visitors on hunting, fishing and river trips. Telegraph Creek is becoming a jumping-off point for wilderness hikers headed for Mount Edziza Provincial Park.

The scenic view along the main street bordering the river has scarcely changed since gold rush days. The 1898 Hudson's Bay Co. post, which now houses the RiverSong Cafe, is a recognized Heritage Building. Historic St. Aidan's Church (Anglican) and several other buildings pre-dating 1930 are also located here.

Return to Milepost J 300.9
Cassiar Highway

Dease Lake has fishing for lake trout. (© Gladys Blyth)

Tahltan District Chamber of Commerce, Box 338, Dease Lake, BC V0C 1L0; phone (250) 771-3900.

Dease Lake has motels, gas stations (with regular, unleaded, diesel, propane and minor repairs), food stores, restaurant, a post office, hardware/sporting goods, highway maintenance centre and government offices. Charter flights and regular air service to Terrace and Smithers with interprovincial connections. Information kiosks at south entrance to town. ▲

A Hudson's Bay Co. post was established by Robert Campbell at Dease Lake in 1838, but abandoned a year later. The lake was named in 1834 by John McLeod of the Hudson's Bay Co. for Chief Factor Peter Warren Dease. Laketon, on the west side of the lake (see **Milepost J 327.7**), was a centre for boat building during the Cassiar gold rush of 1872–80. In 1874, William Moore, following an old Indian trail, cut a trail from Telegraph Creek on the Stikine River to the gold rush settlement on Dease Lake. This trail became Telegraph Creek Road, which was used in 1941 to haul supplies for Alaska Highway construction and Watson Lake Airport to Dease Lake. The supplies were then ferried down the Dease River.

Today, Dease Lake is a government centre and supply point for the district. The community has dubbed itself the "jade capital of the world." Jade is available locally. It is a popular point from which to fly-in, hike-in, or pack-in by horse to Mount Edziza and Spatsizi wilderness parks.

Cassiar Highway Log

(continued)

J 300.9 (488.3 km) **AH 145.2** (233.7 km) **Dease Lake Junction**. Access west to Dease Lake and Telegraph Creek.

Junction with Telegraph Creek Road. See TELEGRAPH CREEK ROAD on pages 240–241.

J 301.7 (489.6 km) **AH 144.4** (232.4 km) Hotel Creek.

J 308.8 (501.3 km) **AH 137.3** (220.9 km) Turnout with litter barrel to west.

J 309.6 (502.5 km) **AH 136.5** (219.7 km) Serpentine Creek.

J 313.5 (508.7 km) **AH 132.6** (213.5 km) Gravel turnout to west with litter barrel.

J 314.1 (509.8 km) **AH 132** (212.4 km) Good views of Dease Lake, limited access to lakeshore.

J 315.7 (512.3 km) **AH 130.4** (209.9 km) Gravel turnout to west.

J 316.3 (513.3 km) **AH 129.8** (208.9 km) Halfmoon Creek.

J 318.8 (517.4 km) **AH 127.3** (204.9 km) Rabid Grizzly rest area with picnic tables, travel information signs, litter barrels and outhouses. View of Dease Lake.

J 322.1 (522.8 km) **AH 124** (199.5 km) Gravel turnout to west.

J 324.2 (526.1 km) **AH 121.9** (196.2 km) Black Creek.

J 326.3 (529.5 km) **AH 119.8** (192.8 km) Sawmill Point Recreation Site to west; side road leads to **Dease Lake** for fishing. Lake trout to 30 lbs., use spoons, plugs, spinners, June to October, deep trolling in summer, spin casting in fall.

J 327.2 (531.2 km) **AH 118.9** (191.4 km) Dorothy Creek.

J 327.7 (532 km) **AH 118.4** (190.5 km) The site of the ghost town **Laketon** lies across the lake at the mouth of Dease Creek. Laketon was the administrative centre for the district during the Cassiar gold rush (1872–80). Boat building was a major activity along the lake during the gold rush years, with miners heading up various creeks and rivers off the lake in search of gold. Today's miners ford the lake when the water is low to reach claims on the northwest side.

J 330.2 (535.9 km) **AH 115.9** (186.5 km) Beady Creek. Entering the Cassiar Mountains northbound.

J 333.5 (541.1 km) **AH 112.6** (181.3 km) Turnout to west with litter barrels.

J 333.8 (541.7 km) **AH 112.3** (180.7 km) Turnout with litter barrel to west. **Dease River** parallels the highway. Grayling to 17 inches; Dolly Varden and lake trout to 15 lbs.; northern pike 8 to 10 lbs., May through September.

Marshy areas to west; good moose pasture. Watch for wildlife, especially at dawn and dusk.

J 334.4 (542.7 km) **AH 111.7** (179.7 km) Packer Tom Creek, named for a well-known Indian who lived in this area.

J 336.1 (545.4 km) **AH 110** (177 km) Elbow Lake.

J 342 (554.7 km) **AH 104.1** (167.5 km) Pyramid Creek.

J 342.4 (555.6 km) **AH 103.7** (166.9 km) Dease River 2-lane concrete bridge.

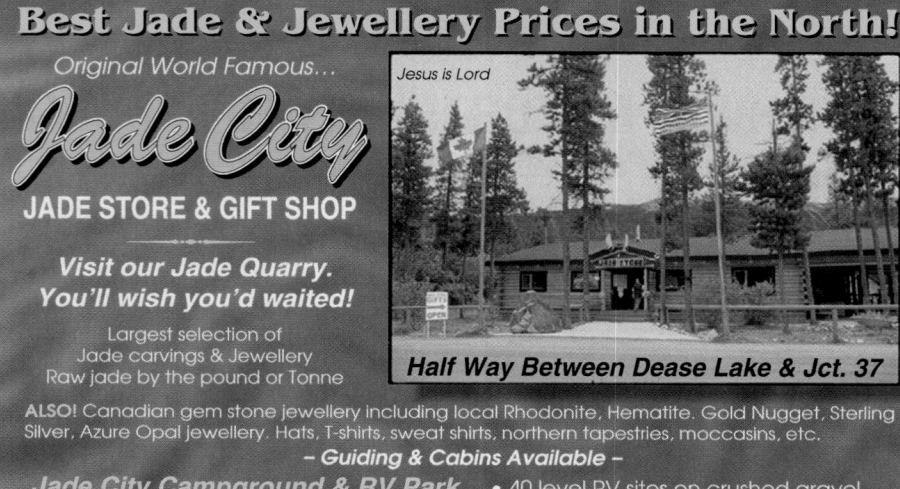

Close-up of jade boulder, photographed at Jade City.

(© Gladys Blyth)

J 343.9 (558 km) **AH 102.2** (164.5 km) Beale Creek.

J 350.9 (563.4 km) **AH 95.2** (153.2 km) Turnout beside **Pine Tree Lake.** Good grayling and lake char fishing.

J 351 (569.5 km) **AH 95.1** (153.1 km) Burn area. An abandoned campfire started the fire in July 1982.

J 352.8 (572.4 km) **AH 93.3** (150.2 km) **Moose Meadows**.

J 353.7 (573.9 km) **AH 92.4** (148.7 km) Gravel turnout with litter barrels to east. Views of **Needlenose Mountain** southbound.

J 357.9 (580.9 km) **AH 88.2** (141.9 km) **Cottonwood River** bridge; rest area 0.4 mile/0.6 km west on old highway on south side of river. Fishing for grayling and whitefish. Early summer runs of Dolly Varden.

J 358.7 (582 km) **AH 87.4** (140.7 km) Cottonwood River rest area No. 2 is 0.5 mile/0.8 km west on old highway on north side of river.

J 363.6 (589.8 km) **AH 82.5** (132.8 km) Large turnout to west beside **Simmons Lake;** information kiosk, picnic tables, picnic shelter, toilets, small beach and dock. Fishing for lake trout.

J 365.3 (592.7 km) **AH 80.8** (130 km) Road runs on causeway between Twin Lakes.

J 365.8 (593.5 km) **AH 80.3** (129.2 km) **Vines Lake,** named for bush pilot Lionel Vines; fishing for lake trout.

J 366.9 (595.3 km) **AH 79.2** (127.4 km) Limestone Creek.

J 367.3 (595.9 km) **AH 78.8** (126.8 km) Lang Lake and creek. Needlepoint Mountain visible straight ahead southbound.

J 369.8 (599.9 km) **AH 76.3** (122.8 km) Cusak gold mine visible on slopes to east. Gold mined on the far side of the mountain is processed in the mill here.

J 370.1 (600.3 km) **AH 76** (122.3 km) Side road east leads to McDame Lake.

J 370.9 (601.6 km) **AH 75.2** (121 km) Trout Line Creek.

J 371.1 (601.9 km) **AH 75** (120.7 km) **JADE CITY** (pop. 12); fuel available. Named for the jade deposits found to the east of the highway community. The huge jade boulders that visitors can see being cut here are from the Princess Jade Mine, 82 miles/132 km east, one of the largest jade claims in the world.

J 371.3 (602.2 km) **AH 74.8** (120.4 km) **Jade Store & Gift Shop**. World famous jade capital. Extensive selection of raw jade, jade jewellery and carvings crafted from local Cassiar jade. Best jade and jewellery prices in the North. Rock hounds will appreciate the extensive selection of raw Canadian gemstones and jewellery. See display ad this section. Jesus is Lord. [ADVERTISEMENT]

J 372.5 (604.1 km) **AH 73.6** (118.5 km) **Cassiar junction.** Cassiar Road to west leads 9.7 miles/15.6 km to the former Cassiar townsite and Cassiar Asbestos Mine. Continue straight ahead for Alaska Highway.

CASSIAR (pop. 25) was the company town of Cassiar Mining Corp. Much of the world's high-grade chrysotile asbestos came from Cassiar. The mine closed in March 1992, and the site is closed to visitors. It is now the site of a B.C. Chrysotile Corp. reclamation project. No services available.

J 372.7 (604.4 km) **AH 73.4** (118.2 km) Snow Creek.

J 372.8 (605.6 km) **AH 73.3** (117.9 km) Gravel turnout with litter barrel to east.

J 373.5 (606.1 km) **AH 72.6** (116.8 km) Deep Creek.

J 377.4 (612.2 km) **AH 68.7** (110.6 km) No. 3 North Fork Creek.

J 378.4 (613.9 km) **AH 67.7** (108.9 km) No. 2 North Fork Creek. Small gold mining operations may be visible to east.

J 381 (618 km) **AH 65.1** (104.7 km) Historic plaque about Cassiar gold.

CENTREVILLE (pop. 2; elev. 2,600 feet/792m), a former gold rush town of 3,000. The only evidence of Centreville along the highway today is the town name painted on an old piece of mining equipment parked on the east side of the road. Centreville was founded and named by miners for its central location between Sylvester's Landing (later McDame Post) at the junction of McDame Creek with the Dease River, and Quartzrock Creek, the upstream limit of pay gravel on McDame Creek. A miner named Alfred Freeman washed out the biggest all-gold (no quartz) nugget ever found in British Columbia on a claim near Centreville in 1877; it weighed 72 ounces. Active mining in area.

J 381.1 (618.2 km) **AH 65** (104.6 km) No. 1 North Fork Creek.

J 383 (621.3 km) **AH 63.1** (101.5 km) Watch for Dall sheep in this area.

J 385.2 (625 km) **AH 60.9** (98 km) **GOOD HOPE LAKE** (pop. 100), Indian village with limited services; fuel may be available.

Turn east on Bush Road and drive 9 miles/14.5 km for **McDAME POST**, an early Hudson's Bay post, at the **confluence of Dease River and McDame Creek.** Good fishing and hunting here.

J 386.9 (627.7 km) **AH 59.2** (95.3 km) Turnout to east alongside Aeroplane Lake.

J 387.7 (629 km) **AH 58.4** (94 km) Dry Creek. Old cabin.

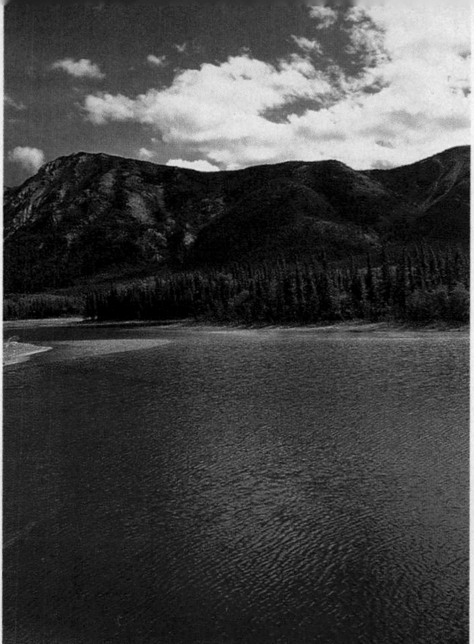

Good Hope Lake. The Indian village of Good Hope Lake is located at Milepost J 385.2. (© Gladys Blyth)

J 389.5 (631.9 km) **AH 56.6** (91.1 km) Mud Lake to east.

J 393.6 (638.5 km) **AH 52.5** (84.5 km) Turnout with litter barrels at entrance to **Boya Lake Provincial Park**. The park is 1.6 miles/2.6 km east of highway; 45 campsites, picnic area on lakeshore, boat launch, toilets, wheelchair access, walking trails, drinking water, firewood and swimming. Fishing for lake char, whitefish and burbot. Attendant on duty during summer.

J 393.7 (638.6 km) **AH 52.4** (84.4 km) Turnout. Horseranch Range may be seen on the eastern horizon northbound. These mountains date back to the Cambrian period, or earlier, and are the oldest in northern British Columbia. According to the Canadian Geological Survey, this area contains numerous permatites with crystals of tourmaline, garnet, feldspar, quartz and beryl. Road crosses Baking Powder Creek and then follows Dease River.

J 397.9 (645.4 km) **AH 48.2** (77.6 km) Camp Creek.

J 399.4 (648 km) **AH 46.7** (75.1 km) Beaver Dam Creek.

J 400.3 (649.4 km) **AH 45.8** (73.7 km) Beaver Dam rest area with visitor information sign to west.

J 400.6 (649.8 km) **AH 45.5** (73.3 km) Leaving Cassiar Mountains, entering Yukon Plateau, northbound.

J 402.5 (652.9 km) **AH 43.6** (70.2 km) Baking Powder Creek.

J 410.9 (666.5km) **AH 35.2** (56.7 km) Gravel access road to French Creek B.C. Forest Service campsite 0.6 miles/1 km from highway. Rustic. Tables, rock fire ring (bring firewood), small boat launch into Dease River, no fee.

J 411.2 (667 km) **AH 34.9** (56.1 km) French Creek 2-lane concrete bridge.

J 417.5 (677.2 km) **AH 28.6** (46.1 km) Twentyeight Mile Creek. Cassiar Mountains rise to south.

J 420.2 (681.8 km) **AH 25.9** (41.6 km) Wheeler Lake to west.

J 422.9 (686.1 km) **AH 23.2** (37.3 km) Blue River Forest Service Road to east.

J 426.3 (691.5 km) **AH 19.8** (31.9 km) Blue River 2-lane concrete bridge.

J 429.7 (697.1 km) **AH 16.4** (26.4 km) Turnout at **Blue Lakes**; litter barrels, picnic tables and fishing for pike and grayling.

J 431.5 (700 km) **AH 14.6** (23.5 km) Mud Hill Creek.

J 436 707.4 km) **AH 10.1** (16.2 km) Old Faddy Forest Service Road.

J 440.1 (714 km) **AH 6** (9.6 km) Turnout with litter barrels beside Cormier Creek.

J 441.3 (718.5 km) **AH 4.8** (7.7 km) High Lake to east.

J 444 (720.3 km) **AH 2.1** (3.4 km) Turnout to west at **BC–YT Border**, 60th parallel. Information sign.

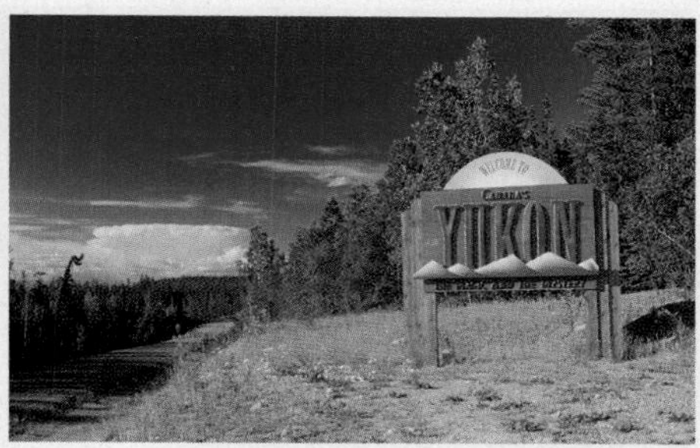

Yukon Territory's flag consists of 3 vertical panels of colour: blue, representing the rivers and lakes; green symbolizing forests; and white signifying snow. The Yukon coat of arms appears on the central panel, framed by 2 stems of fireweed, the territory's floral emblem. The flag was chosen from a design competition sponsored in 1967. Yukon Territory was made a district of Northwest Territories in 1895 and became a separate territory in June 1898, at the height of the Klondike Gold Rush.

NOTE: Drive with headlights on at all times in Yukon Territory.

J 445.3 (722.5 km) **AH 0.8** (1.2 km) **Albert Creek.** Good grayling fishing. Yukon Territory fishing license required.

J 446.1 (723.7 km) **AH 0 Junction** of Cassiar Highway with Alaska Highway. Gas, store, campground and RV park, cafe, souvenirs, laundromat, camp-style motel, saloon, propane, towing and car repair at junction. Turn left for Whitehorse, right for Watson Lake, 13.3 miles/21.4 km southeast. Watson Lake is the nearest major community.

Junction 37 Services. See display ad this section.

Turn to **Milepost DC 626.2** on page 133 in the ALASKA HIGHWAY section for log of Alaska Highway from this junction.

KLONDIKE LOOP  9

Connects: Alaska Hwy. to Taylor Hwy. **Length:** 406 miles
Road Surface: Paved to Dawson City; seal coat and gravel to Taylor Highway junction
Season: Hwy. 2 open all year, Hwy. 9 closed in winter
Major Attraction: Dawson City

(See maps, pages 245–246)

	Alaska Hwy. Jct.	Carmacks	Dawson City	Taylor Hwy Jct.	Whitehorse
Alaska Hwy Jct.		103	327	406	10
Carmacks	103		225	303	113
Dawson City	327	225		79	337
Taylor Hwy Jct.	406	303	79		416
Whitehorse	10	113	337	416	

Motorhomes cross the Top of the World Highway into Alaska. (© Earl L. Brown, staff)

The "Klondike Loop" refers to the 327-mile/527-km-long stretch of Yukon Highway 2 (the North Klondike Highway, also sometimes called the "Mayo Road"), from its junction with the Alaska Highway north of Whitehorse to Dawson City; the 79-mile/127-km Top of the World Highway (Yukon Highway 9); and the 96 miles/154 kms of the Taylor Highway (Alaska Route 5) that connect with the Alaska Highway near Tok. The North Klondike Highway and Top of the World Highway are logged in this section. The Taylor Highway is logged in the TAYLOR HIGHWAY section following.

Alaska-bound motorists turn off the Alaska Highway north of Whitehorse (**Milepost DC 894.8**); follow the Klondike Highway to Dawson City; ferry from there across the Yukon River; drive west via the Top of the World Highway into Alaska; then take the Taylor Highway south back to the Alaska Highway near Tok (**Milepost DC 1301.7**). Total driving distance is 501 miles/806 km. (Driving distance from Whitehorse to Tok via the Alaska Highway is approximately 396 miles/637 km.)

All of the Klondike Highway between the Alaska Highway junction and Dawson City is asphalt-surfaced. The Top of the World Highway—a truly scenic route—is seal-coated on the Canadian portion with some hills. It is gravel on the U.S. side with some steep grades and winding sections that can be slippery in wet weather. Check with the Dawson City Visitor Centre for current road and weather conditions; phone (867) 993-5566.

The Taylor Highway is a narrow gravel road with some steep, winding sections and washboard (see the TAYLOR HIGHWAY section). Both the Taylor and Top of the World highways are not maintained from mid-October to April and the arrival of snow effectively closes the roads for winter. Yukon Highway 2 is open year-round. *Drive with your headlights on at all times.*

Travelers should be aware that the Top of the World Highway (reached by ferry from Dawson City) may not open until late spring. In heavy traffic, there may be a wait as long as 3 hours for the Yukon River ferry at Dawson City during peak hours. Customs stations are open in summer only, 12 hours a day: 9 A.M. to 9 P.M. (Pacific time), 8 A.M. to 8 P.M. (Alaska time). There are no restrooms, services or currency exchanges available at the border.

The highway between Skagway and the Alaska Highway, sometimes referred to as the South Klondike, is also designated Klondike Highway 2 (see KLONDIKE HIGHWAY 2 section for log of that road).

Kilometreposts along the highway to Dawson City reflect distance from Skagway. Our log's driving distances were measured in miles from the junction of the Alaska Highway to Dawson City by our field editor. These mileages were converted into kilometres with the exception of the kilometre distance following Skagway (S). That figure reflects the physical location of the kilometrepost and is not necessarily an accurate conversion of the mileage figure.

The route from Whitehorse to Dawson City began as a trail, used first by Natives, trappers and prospectors, and then by stampeders during the Klondike Gold Rush of 1897–98. Steamships also provided passenger service between Whitehorse and Dawson City. A road was built connecting the Alaska Highway with the United Keno Hill Mine at Mayo in 1950. By 1955, the Mayo Road had been upgraded for automobile traffic and extended to Dawson City. In 1960, the last of 3 steel bridges, crossing the Yukon, Pelly and Stewart rivers, was completed. The only ferry crossing remaining is the Yukon River crossing at Dawson City. Mayo Road (Yukon Highway 11) from Stewart Crossing to Mayo, Elsa and Keno was redesignated the Silver Trail in 1985 (see SILVER TRAIL section for road log).

Emergency Medical Services: On Yukon Highway 2 from **Milepost J 0** to **J 55.6** (Whitehorse to Braeburn Lodge), phone Whitehorse Ambulance toll free 1-667-3333 or RCMP 1-667-3333. From **Milepost J 55.6** to **J 169.4** (Braeburn Lodge to Pelly Crossing), phone Carmacks Medical Emergency (867) 863-4444 or RCMP (867) 863-5555. From **Milepost J 169.4** to **J 242.9** (Pelly Crossing to McQuesten River Lodge), phone Mayo Medical Emergency (867) 996-4444 or RCMP (867) 996-5555. From **Milepost J 242.9** to **J 327.2** and on Yukon Highway 9 from **Milepost D 0** to **D 66.1** (McQuesten River Lodge to Dawson City to Alaska border), phone Dawson City Medical Emergency (867) 993-4444 or RCMP (867) 993-5555. From **Milepost D 66.1** to **D 78.8** (Alaska border to Taylor Highway), phone Tok Area EMS at 911 or (907) 883-5111.

Klondike Loop Log

This section of the log shows distance from junction with the Alaska Highway (J) followed by distance from Dawson City (D) and distance from Skagway (S). Physical kilometreposts show distance from Skagway.

YUKON HIGHWAY 2

J 0 D 327.2 (526.6 km) **S 119.2** (191.8 km) **Junction** with the Alaska Highway

KLONDIKE LOOP *Milepost J 0 to Milepost J 296 (includes Silver Trail)*

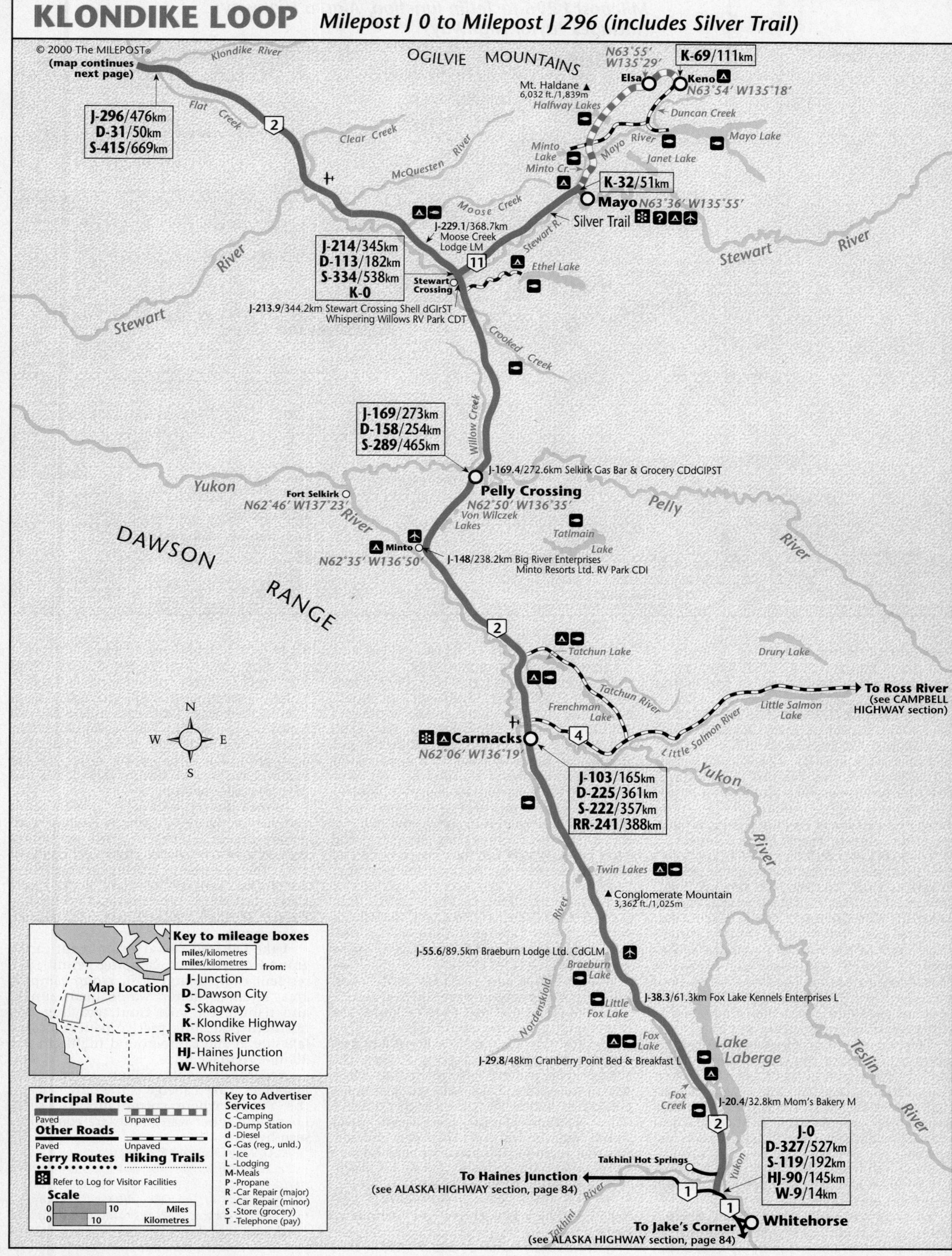

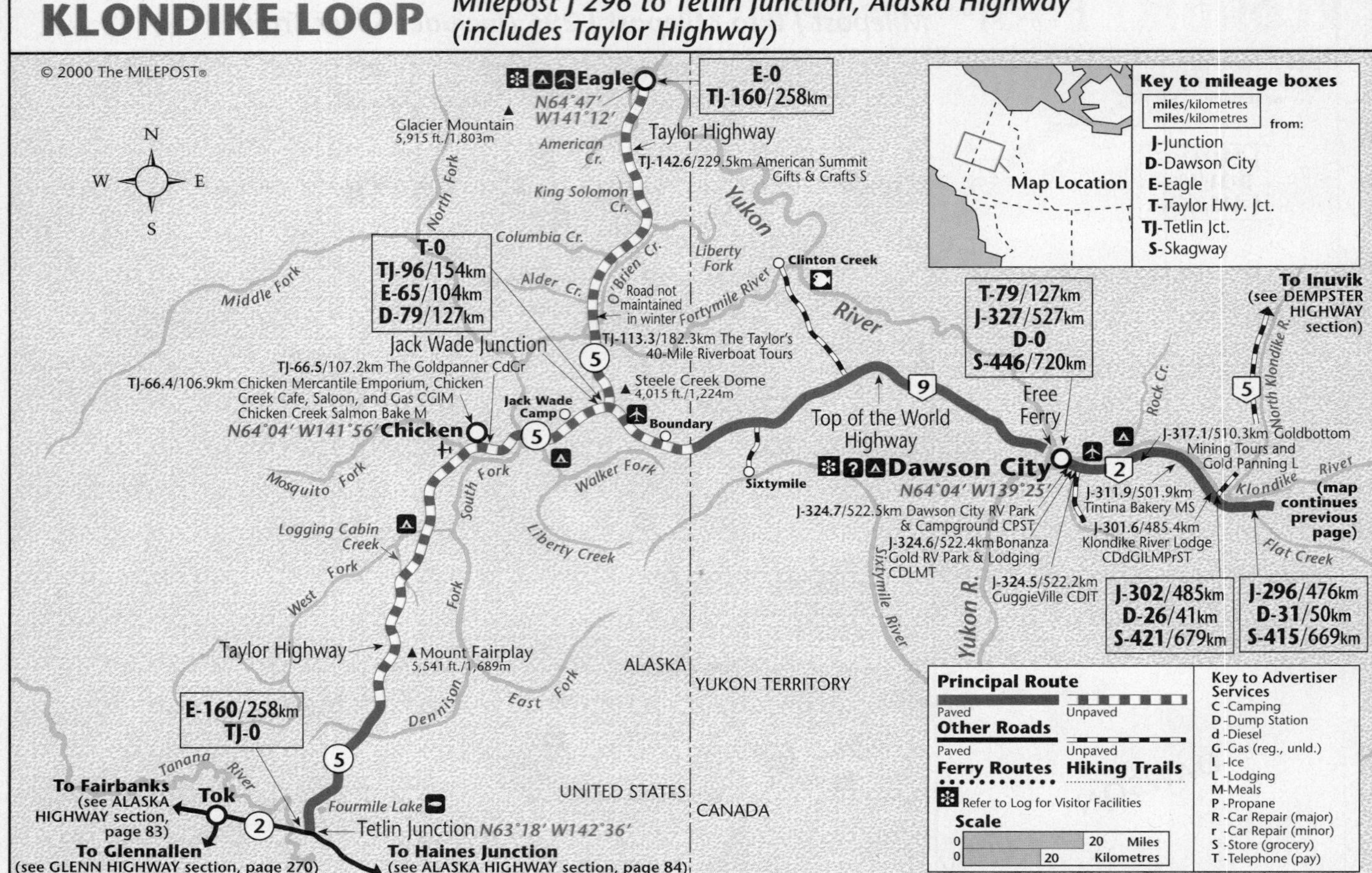

(**Milepost DC 894.8**).

J 0.6 (1 km) **D 326.6** (525.6 km) **S 119.8** (192.8 km) Road west leads to McPherson subdivision.

J 1 (1.6 km) **D 326.2** (525 km) **S 120.2** (193.4 km) Ranches, farms and livestock next 20 miles/32 km northbound.

J 2.3 (3.7 km) **D 324.9** (522.9 km) **S 121.5** (195.5 km) Takhini River bridge. The Takhini flows into the Yukon River. The name is Tagish Indian, *tahk* meaning mosquito and *heena* meaning river, according to R. Coutts in *Yukon: Places & Names*.

J 3.8 (6.1 km) **D 323.4** (520.4 km) **S 123** (197.9 km) Gas bar and convenience store at **junction** with Takhini Hot Springs Road. Drive west 6 miles/9.7 km via paved road for **Takhini Hot Springs**, open year-round; camping, cafe, trail rides, ski trails in winter. The source of the springs maintains a constant 117°F/47°C temperature and flows at 86 gallons a minute. The hot springs pool averages 100°F/38°C year-round. The water contains no sulfur. The chief minerals present are calcium, magnesium and iron. ▲

Trappers and Indians used these springs around the turn of the century, arriving by way of the Takhini River or the old Dawson Trail. During construction of the Alaska Highway in the early 1940s, the U.S. Army maintained greenhouses in the area and reported remarkable growth regardless of the season.

J 6.7 (10.8 km) **D 320.5** (515.8 km) **S 125.9** (202.6 km) Start odometer test section next 5 km northbound.

J 7 (11.3 km) **D 320.2** (515.3 km) **S 126.2** (203.1 km) Whitehorse rodeo grounds to west. The Yukon Rodeo takes July x–x, 2000.

J 9.4 (15.1 km) **D 317.8** (511.4 km) **S 128.6** (207 km) Sawmill to west.

J 10.7 (17.2 km) **D 316.5** (509.3 km) **S 129.9** (209 km) **Shallow Bay** Road. According to Yukon's Renewable Resources Wildlife Viewing Program, a trail 300 feet/100m north of this side road on the east side of the highway leads to a good waterfowl viewing site at Shallow Bay on Lake Laberge. Northern pintail, Barrow's goldeneye, and tundra and trumpeter swans stage here by the thousands in spring and fall. It is also a hot spot for migrating shorebirds and song birds. Watch for short-eared owls and northern harriers in the open fields around Shallow Bay.

J 12.7 (20.4 km) **D 314.5** (506.1 km) **S 131.9** (212.2 km) Horse Creek Road leads east to Lower Laberge Indian village and lakeshore cottages. **Horse Creek**; good grayling fishing from road.

J 15.8 (25.4 km) **D 311.4** (501.1 km) **S 135** (217.2 km) Microwave site near road.

J 16.8 (27 km) **D 310.4** (499.5 km) **S 136** (219.1 km) Large turnout to west.

J 17.4 (28 km) **D 309.8** (498.6 km) **S 136.6** (220 km) Lake Laberge to east. The Yukon River widens to form this 40-mile-/64-km-long lake. Lake Laberge was made famous by Robert W. Service with the lines: "The Northern Lights have seen queer sights. But the queerest they ever did see, was that night on the marge of Lake Lebarge I cremated Sam McGee," (from his poem "The Cremation of Sam McGee").

J 18.2 (29.3 km) **D 309** (497.3 km) **S 137.4** (221.1 km) Gravel pit turnout to east.

J 20.3 (32.7 km) **D 306.9** (493.9 km) **S 139.5** (224.5 km) Deep Creek.

J 20.4 (32.8 km) **D 306.8** (493.7 km) **S 139.6** (224.6 km) Turnoff for Lake Laberge Yukon government campground. Campground road leads past residential area with a small store, Mom's Bakery, canoe rentals, emergency phone and message post. The campground is situated 1.8 miles/2.9 km east on Lake Laberge next to Deep Creek (see description following).

Lake Laberge Yukon government campground has 16 sites, camping permit ($8), resident campground host, group camping area, kitchen shelter, water, boat launch, and fishing for lake trout, grayling and northern pike. Interpretive panels located lakeside at the campground highlight the 30-mile Heritage River. ▲

According to Yukon Renewable Resources, Lake Laberge is the only place in the Yukon where cormorants are seen. Loons and other water brids are commonly seen here.

CAUTION: Storms can blow up quickly and without warning on Lake Laberge, as on other northern lakes. Canoes and small craft stay to the west side of the lake, where the shoreline offers safe refuges. The east side of the lake is lined with high rocky bluffs, and there are few places to pull out. Small craft should not navigate the middle of the lake.

J 20.9 (33.6 km) **D 306.3** (492.9 km) **S 140.1** (225.5 km) View of Lake Laberge for southbound travelers.

J 21.2 (34.1 km) **D 306** (492.4 km) **S 140.4** (225.9 km) Northbound the highway enters the Miners Range, plateau country of the Yukon, an immense wilderness of forested dome-shaped mountains and high ridges, dotted with lakes and traversed by tributaries of the Yukon River. To the west, Pilot Mountain in the Miners Range (elev. 6,739 feet/2,054m) is visible.

J 22.8 (36.7 km) **D 304.4** (489.9 km) **S 142** (228.5 km) **Fox Creek**; grayling, excellent in June and July.

J 23.5 (37.8 km) **D 303.7** (488.7 km) **S 142.7** (229.8 km) Marker shows distance to Dawson City 486 km.

J 26.9 (43.3 km) **D 300.3** (483.3 km) **S 146.1** (235.1 km) Gravel pit turnout to east.

J 28.8 (46.3 km) **D 298.4** (480.2 km) **S 148** (238.2 km) Highway now follows the east shoreline of **Fox Lake** northbound. Fox Lake is a waterfowl stop during spring migration. Muskrats also feed here: muskrat "push-ups" can be seen dotting the frozen surface of the lake in the winter and spring.

J 29.4 (47.3 km) **D 297.8** (479.2 km) **S 148.6** (239.1 km) Turnout to west on Fox Lake. Sign reads: "In 1883, U.S. Army Lt. Frederick Schwatka completed a survey of the entire length of the Yukon River. One of many geographical features that he named was Fox Lake, which he called Richthofen Lake, after geographer Freiherr Von Richthofen. Known locally as Fox Lake, the name was adopted in 1957. The Miners Range to the west was named by geologist/explorer George Mercer Dawson in 1887 'for the miners met by us along the river.'"

J 29.8 (48 km) **D 297.4** (478.6 km) **S 149** (239.8 km) **Cranberry Point Bed & Breakfast.** Open year-round. Charming and rustic with a touch of elegance on peaceful scenic Fox Lake. Be pampered as you enjoy the sauna, hot gravity showers, oil lamps, private lakefront cabins and sanitized outhouses—all lovingly detailed for your comfort. Old-time woodstove cooking, full breakfast, other great meals by arrangement. Radio phone Whitehorse mobile operator JJ39257 Fox Lake Channel. Km 240 Klondike Hwy., P.O. Box 20091, Whitehorse, YT Y1A 7A7. [ADVERTISEMENT]

J 34.8 (56 km) **D 292.4** (470.6 km) **S 154** (247.8 km) Turnoff west for **Fox Lake** Yukon government campground; 30 RV and 3 tent-only sites, camping permit ($8), kitchen shelter, drinking water and boat launch. Good fishing for lake trout and burbot from the shore at the campground; excellent grayling year-round.

J 35.2 (56.6 km) **D 292** (469.9 km) **S 154.4** (248.5 km) Turnout with view of Fox Lake. Good photo spot.

J 38.3 (23.8 km) **D 288.9** (464.9 km) **S 157.5** (253.4 km) **Fox Lake Kennels Enterprises.** Open year-round. Vacations, Bed and breakfast, canoe and kayak rentals and guided tours, sled dog adventures and snowmobiling. Comfortable log guesthouse with fireplace, 4 bedrooms (3 with lake view, 2 have private bath), sauna. Beautiful setting on Fox Lake. Good fishing! Radio phone Whitehorse mobile operator 2M3128 Fox Lake Channel or voice mail and fax (867) 393-4364. Box 5338, Whitehore, YT Y1A 4Z2. [ADVERTISEMENT]

J 39.8 (64.1 km) **D 287.4** (462.5 km) **S 159** (255.8 km) North end of Fox Lake.

There was a major forest fire in this area in summer 1998; burn areas on both sides of road should have some spectacular fireweed displays in the next couple of years.

J 42 (67.6 km) **D 285.2** (459 km) **S 161.2** (259.4 km) **Little Fox Lake** to west; lake trout 3 to 8 lbs., fish the islands.

J 43.8 (70.5 km) **D 283.4** (456.1 km) **S 163** (262.1 km) Double-ended turnout with litter barrel to west beside Little Fox Lake. Small boat launch.

J 47.3 (76.2 km) **D 279.9** (450.4 km) **S 166.5** (267.9 km) **Boreal Fire Interpretive Site** turnout with outhouses, litter barrels and interpretive panels on fire and the boreal forest ecosystem.

J 49.5 (79.7 km) **D 277.7** (446.9 km) **S 168.7** (271.5 km) Large turnout to west.

J 50.1 (80.6 km) **D 277.1** (445.9 km) **S 169.3** (272.4 km) First glimpse of Braeburn Lake for northbound travelers.

J 52.5 (84.5 km) **D 274.7** (442.1 km) **S 171.7** (276.3 km) Gravel pit turnout to east. According to Renewable Resources Wildlife Viewing Program, about 50 elk live here year-round. They are most commonly seen in winter and spring. Look for their distinctive white rumps on the exposed south-facing slopes. Elk are a protected species in the Yukon. Grizzly bears feed on roadside vegetation (and also elk) in this area in spring and summer.

CAUTION: Watch for elk along highway.

J 55.6 (89.5 km) **D 271.6** (437.1 km) **S 174.8** (281.5 km) Braeburn Lodge to west; food, gas, lodging and minor car repairs. One Braeburn Lodge cinnamon bun will feed 4 people. The lodge is also home of the 200-mile/320-km "Cinnamon Bun" Dog Sled Race, held the first weekend in February.

Braeburn Lodge. See display ad this section.

Private Aircraft: Braeburn airstrip to east, dubbed Cinnamon Bun Strip; elev. 2,350 feet/716m; length 3,000 feet/914m; dirt strip; wind sock.

J 55.8 (89.8 km) **D 271.4** (436.8 km) **S 175.1** (281.8 km) Side road to Braeburn Lake.

J 66.3 (106.7 km) **D 260.9** (419.9 km) **S 185.5** (298.5 km) Photo stop; pull-through turnout on east side of highway with information sign about **Conglomerate Mountain** (elev. 3,361 feet/1,024m). Sign reads: "The Laberge Series was formed at the leading edge of volcanic mud flows some 185 million years ago (Early Jurassic). These flows solidified into sheets several kilometres long and about 1 km wide and 100m thick. This particular series of sheets stretches from Atlin, BC, to north of Carmacks, a distance of about 350 km. Other conglomerates of this series form Five Finger Rapids."

Rock hounds can find pieces of conglomerate in almost any borrow pit along this stretch of highway.

J 71.6 (115.2 km) **D 255.6** (411.3 km) **S 190.8** (307 km) Turnouts on both sides of highway between Twin Lakes. These 2 small lakes, 1 on either side of the road, are known for their beauty and colour.

J 72.3 (116.4 km) **D 254.9** (410.2 km) **S 191.5** (308.2 km) Turnoff to west for **Twin Lakes** Yukon government campground; 18 sites, camping permit ($8), drinking water, boat launch. Lake is stocked. Large parking area with informational panels on the Nordenskiold River. Enjoyable fishing for lake trout, grayling and pike. Good swimming for the *hardy!*

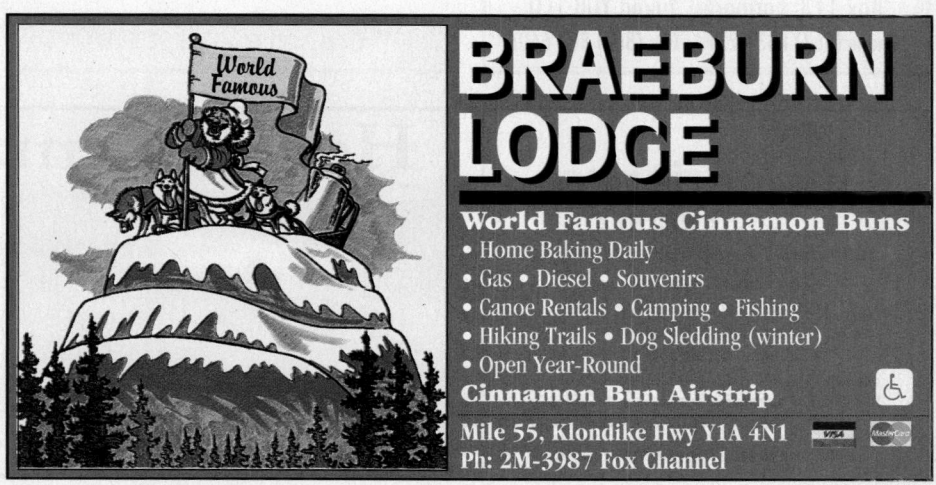

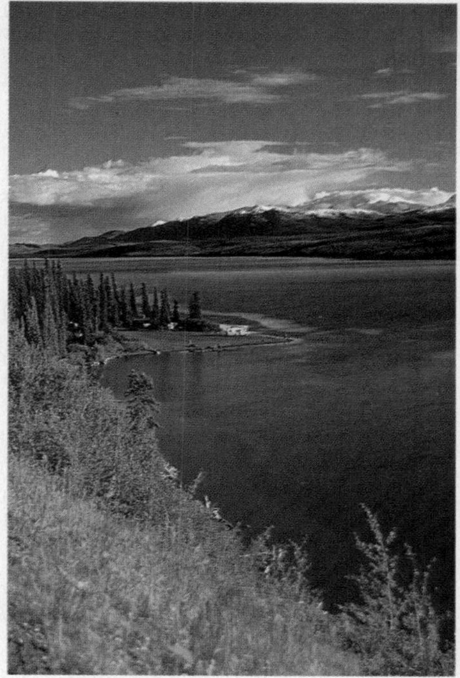

Klondike Highway follows shoreline of Fox Lake, a waterfowl stop in spring.

(© Earl L. Brown, staff)

J 81.4 (131 km) **D 245.8** (395.6 km) **S 200.6** (323 km) Large turnout with litter barrel to east at remains of **Montague House**, a typical early-day roadhouse which offered lodging and meals on the stagecoach route between Whitehorse and Dawson City. A total of 52 stopping places along this route were listed in the Jan. 16, 1901, edition of the *Whitehorse Star* under "On the Winter Trail between White Horse and Dawson Good Accommodations for Travellers." Montague House was listed at Mile 99. Good photo stop.

J 87.4 (140.7 km) **D 239.8** (385.9 km) **S 206.6** (332.5 km) Small lake to west.

J 93.7 (150.8 km) **D 233.5** (375.8 km) **S 212.9** (343.9 km) Plume Trail Agate Road to east, information sign about agate deposits.

J 100.1 (161.1 km) **D 227.1** (365.5 km) **S 219.3** (352.9 km) Carmacks town limits.

J 101.3 (163 km) **D 225.9** (363.5 km) **S 220.5** (354.8 km) Wetlands to west are part of the **Nordenskiold River** system. Waterfowl stage here during spring and fall migrations. Watch for trumpeter swans and ruddy ducks. Other area wildlife include beaver, muskrat, moose, mink and fox.

The Nordenskiold was named by Lt. Frederick Schwatka, U.S. Army, for Swedish arctic explorer Erik Nordenskiold. This river, which parallels the highway for several miles, flows into the Yukon River at Carmacks. Good grayling and pike fishing all summer.

J 101.5 (163.3 km) **D 225.7** (363.2 km) **S 220.7** (355.2 km) Pull-through rest area to east with large mural of *Moment at Tantalus Butte*. Litter barrels and outhouses.

Carmacks

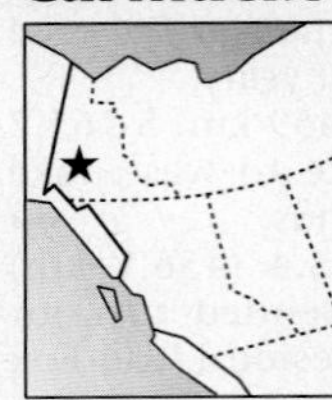

J 102.7 (165.3 km) **D 224.5** (361.3 km) **S 221.9** (357.1 km). Located on the banks of the Yukon River, Carmacks is the only highway crossing of the Yukon River between Whitehorse and Dawson City. **Population:** 489.

Emergency Services: RCMP, phone (867) 863-5555. **Fire Department**, phone (867) 863-2222. **Nurse**, phone (867) 863-4444. **Ambulance**, phone (867) 863-4444. **Forest Fire Control**, (867) 863-5271.

Visitor Information: Located in the Old Telegraph Office. Write Village of Carmacks, P.O. 113, Carmacks, YT Y0B 1C0; phone (867) 863-6271, fax (867) 883-6606.

Private Aircraft: Carmacks airstrip; elev. 1,770 feet/539m; length 5,200 feet/1,585m; gravel; no fuel.

Carmacks was once an important stop for Yukon River steamers traveling between Dawson City and Whitehorse, and it continues as a supply point today for modern river travelers. Carmacks has survived—while other river ports have not—as a service centre for highway traffic and mining interests. Carmacks was also a major stopping point on the old Whitehorse to Dawson Trail.

Carmacks was named for George Carmack, who established a trading post here in the 1890s. Carmack had come North in 1885, hoping to strike it rich. He spent the next 10 years prospecting without success. In 1896, when the trading post went bankrupt, Carmack moved his family to Fortymile, where he could fish to eat and cut timber to sell. That summer, Carmack's remarkable persistence paid off—he unearthed a 5-dollar pan of coarse gold, during a time when a 10-cent pan was considered a good find. That same winter, he extracted more than a ton of gold from the creek, which he renamed Bonanza Creek, and its tributary, Eldorado. When word of Carmack's discovery reached the outside world the following spring, it set off the Klondike Gold Rush.

Traveler facilities include a hotel, motel, bed and breakfast, the village-operated Tantalus Campground on the bank of the Yukon River; restaurant, gas bar, general store (with groceries, bakery and hardware) and laundromat at Hotel Carmacks; post office and bank (both with limited hours), general store at Northern Tutchone Trading Post. The trading post also has some Native crafts for sale. There are also churches, a school, swimming pool, service centre, cafe and a community library.

A 1.2-mile/2-km interpretive boardwalk makes it possible to enjoy a stroll along the Yukon River; beautiful view of countryside and Tantalus Butte, gazebo and park at end of trail. Wheelchair accessible.

The Northern Tutchone First Nations Tage Cho Hudan Interpretive Centre features archaeological displays on Native life in a series of indoor and outdoor exhibits, and marked interpretive trails. The centre also features a mammoth snare diorama and has an arts and crafts store. Phone (867) 863-5830, fax (867) 863-5710.

Carmacks is also an excellent area for rock hounds. There are 5 agate trails in the area, which can double as good, short hiking trails.

Check locally for boat tours to Five Finger and Rink rapids and Fort Selkirk. Fort Selkirk was an important trading post and subsequent RCMP post (see **Milepost J 148.6**). Helicopter service and local canoe

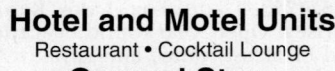

CARMACKS ADVERTISERS

Experience Yukon Inc. ....ph. (867) 863-6021
Hotel Carmacks................Ph. (867) 863-5221
Tantalus Campground........Ph. (867) 863-6271

and hiking tours available. Abundant fishing in area rivers and lakes: salmon, grayling, northern pike, lake and rainbow trout, whitefish and ling cod.

Klondike Loop Log

(continued)

J 103.2 (166.1 km) **D 224** (360.5 km) **S 222.4** (357.9 km) Yukon River bridge. Turnout and parking area at south end of bridge; 2.3-mile-/3.7-km-long trail to Coal Mine Lake.

J 103.3 (166.2 km) **D 223.9** (360.3 km) **S 222.5** (358.1 km) Northern Tutchone Trading Post with store and post office at north end of Yukon River bridge. Fishing tackle and licenses available. Tage Cho Hudan Interpretive Centre.

J 104.4 (168 km) **D 222.8** (358.6 km) **S 223.6** (359.8 km) Turnoff to east for Campbell Highway, also known as Watson Lake–Carmacks Road, which leads south to Faro (107 miles/173 km), Ross River (141 miles/226 km) and Watson Lake (373 miles/600 km).

Junction with Campbell Highway (Yukon Highway 4). Turn to end of CAMPBELL HIGHWAY section and read log back to front.

J 105.1 (169.1 km) **D 222.1** (357.4 km) **S 224.3** (361 km) Side road east to Tantalus Butte Coal Mine; the coal was used in Cyprus Anvil Mine's mill near Faro for drying concentrates. The butte was named by Lt. Frederick Schwatka because it is seen many times before it is actually reached.

J 105.4 (169.6 km) **D 221.8** (356.9 km) **S 224.6** (361.4 km) Turnout to west with litter barrels, information sign, view of Yukon River Valley.

J 108 (173.8 km) **D 219.2** (352.8 km) **S 227.2** (365.3 km) Side road west to agate site for rock hounds.

J 110 (177 km) **D 217.2** (349.5 km) **S 229.2** (368.8 km) Small lake to west.

J 117.5 (189.1 km) **D 209.7** (337.5 km) **S 236.7** (378.5 km) Large double-ended rest area to west with toilets, litter barrels and viewing platform for **Five Finger Rapids**.

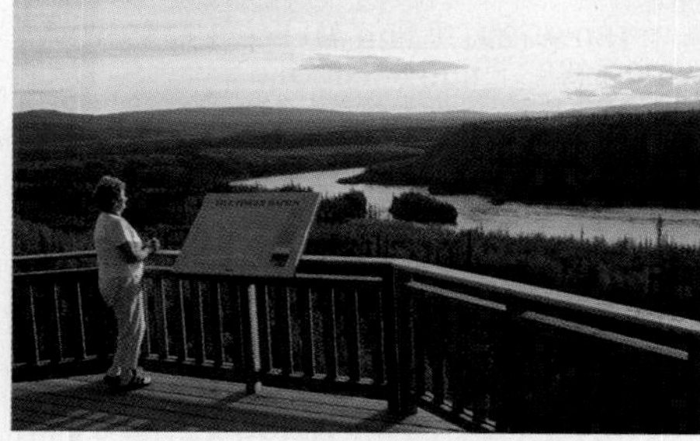

Information sign here reads: "Five Finger Rapids named by early miners for the 5 channels, or fingers, formed by the rock pillars. They are a navigational hazard. The safest passage is through the nearest, or east, passage." Stairs (219 steps) and a trail lead down to rapids. Flora includes prairie crocus, kinnikinnick, common juniper and sage. Watch for white-crowned sparrows and American tree sparrows. Interpretive panels.

J 118.9 (191.3 km) **D 208.3** (335.2 km) **S 238.1** (380.6 km) Tatchun Creek.

J 119 (191.5 km) **D 208.2** (335.1 km) **S 238.2** (380.8 km) First turnoff (northbound) to east for **Tatchun Creek** Yukon government campground; 12 sites, camping permit ($8), kitchen shelter and drinking water. Good fishing for grayling, June through September; salmon, July through August.

J 119.1 (191.7 km) **D 208.1** (334.9 km) **S 238.3** (380.9 km) Second turnoff (northbound) east for Tatchun Creek Yukon government campground.

J 119.6 (192.5 km) **D 207.6** (334.1 km) **S 238.8** (381.8 km) Side road leads east to **Tatchun Lake.** Follow side road 4.3 miles/6.9 km east to boat launch and pit toilets. Continue past boat launch 1.1 miles/1.8 km for Tatchun Lake Yukon government campground with 20 sites, camping permit ($8), pit toilets, firewood, litter barrels and picnic tables. Fishing for northern pike, best in spring or fall.

This maintained side road continues east past Tatchun Lake to Frenchman Lake, then loops south to the Campbell Highway, approximately 25 miles/40 km distance. The main access to Frenchman Lake is from the Campbell Highway.

J 121.8 (196 km) **D 205.4** (330.6 km) **S 241** (388 km) Tatchun Hill.

J 126.6 (203.7 km) **D 200.6** (322.8 km) **S 245.8** (395.8 km) Large turnout overlooking Yukon River. Good photo stop.

J 126.9 (204.2 km) **D 200.3** (322.3 km) **S 246.1** (396.3 km) Highway descends hill, northbound. Watch for falling rocks.

J 132 (212.4 km) **D 195.2** (314.1 km) **S 251.2** (404.5 km) McGregor Creek.

J 135 (217.3 km) **D 192.2** (309.3 km) **S 254.2** (409.4 km) Northbound, first evidence of 1995 burn. The fire consumed 325,000 acres of forest. Dramatic summer fireweed displays here in recent years.

J 136.6 (219.8 km) **D 190.6** (306.7 km) **S 255.8** (411.9 km) Good representation of White River ash layer for approximately one mile northbound. About 1,250 years ago a layer of white volcanic ash coated a third of the southern Yukon, or some 125,000 square miles/323,725 square km, and it is easily visible along many roadcuts. This distinct line conveniently provides a division used by archaeologists for dating artifacts: Materials found below this major stratigraphic marker are considered to have been deposited before A.D. 700, while those found above the ash layer are postdated A.D. 700. The small amount of data available does not support volcanic activity in the White River area during the same period. One theory is that the ash could have spewn forth from a single violent volcanic eruption. The source may be buried under the Klutlan Glacier in the St. Elias Mountains in eastern Alaska.

J 144 (231.7 km) **D 183.2** (294.8 km) **S 263.2** (423.8 km) McCabe Creek.

J 148 (238.2 km) **D 179.2** (288.4 km) **S 267.2** (430.4 km) Private RV park and boat tours to Fort Selkirk. Trees along this portion of highway were burned in a 1995 forest fire. Amazingly, the businesses in the immediate surrounding area were spared.

Big River Enterprises. See display ad this section.

Minto Resorts Ltd. R.V. Park. 1,400-foot Yukon River frontage. Halfway between Whitehorse and Dawson City on the Old Stage Road, Minto was once a steamboat landing and trading post. 27 sites, wide easy access, picnic tables, firepits, souvenirs, fishing licenses, ice, snacks, pop. Coin-op showers and laundry, clean restrooms, dump station and water. Bus tour buffet, reservation only. Caravans welcome. Wildlife viewing opportunities. Try fishing the river. Owned and operated by Yukoners. Come and visit us! See display ad this section. [ADVERTISEMENT]

J 148.6 (239.1 km) **D 178.6** (287.4 km) **S 267.8** (431.4 km) Minto Road, a short loop road, leads west to location of the former riverboat landing and trading post of **MINTO.** Check with Big River Enterprises about river tours to Sheep Mountain and Fort Selkirk leaving daily from Minto Resorts.

FORT SELKIRK, 25 river miles/40 km from here, was established by Robert Campbell in 1848 for the Hudson's Bay Co. In 1852, the fort was destroyed by Chilkat Indians, who had dominated the fur trade of central Yukon—trading here with the Northern Tutchone people (Selkirk First Nation), who used the area as a seasonal home and exchanged furs for the Chilkats' coastal goods—until the arrival of the Hudson's Bay Co. The site was occupied sporadically by traders, missionaries and the RCMP until the 1950s. About 40 buildings—dating from 1892 to 1940—still stand in good repair. A river trip to Fort Selkirk lets travelers see the fort virtually unchanged since the turn of the century. A highly recommended side trip, if time permits. Government preservation and interpretation staff are available on site.

Private Aircraft: Minto airstrip; elev. 1,550 feet/472m; length 5,000 feet/1,524m; gravel.

J 160.3 (258 km) **D 166.9** (268.6 km) **S 279.5** (450.5 km) Side road east to **L'hutsaw Wetlands (Von Wilczek Lakes)**,

Fort Selkirk historic site on the Yukon River is accessible by tour boat. (© Lyn Hancock)

now a protected area; an important wetlands for duck staging, nesting and moulting.

J 162.8 (262 km) **D 164.4** (264.6 km) **S 282** (454.5 km) Northern limits of 1995 burn. Fireweed displays southbound in July.

J 163.4 (263 km) **D 163.8** (263.6 km) **S 282.6** (455.5 km) **Tthi Ndu Mun Lake (Rock Island Lake)** to east. Water lilies and other seldom seen aquatic wildflowers bloom in the shallow areas of the lake. American coots, rarely seen in the Yukon, nest in the area.

J 164.2 (264.2 km) **D 163** (262.3 km) **S 283.4** (456.8 km) Turnout by **Meadow Lake** to west. This shallow lake is an athalassic or inland salt lake. Note the white salts deposted on old stumps along the lakeshore. Look for American coots and horned grebes.

J 168.7 (271.5 km) **D 158.5** (255.1 km) **S 287.9** (464 km) Road west to garbage dump.

J 169.4 (272.6 km) **D 157.8** (253.9 km) **S 288.6** (465 km) Side road to **PELLY CROSSING** (pop. about 350). **Emergency Services:** RCMP, phone (867) 537-5555; Nurse, phone (867) 537-4444. Located on the banks of the Pelly River, traveler facilities include take-out food, grocery store, gas and diesel (24-hour access with MasterCared or Visa), minor vehicle repairs, campground, post office and a bank. There is a school, curling rink, baseball field, swimming pool, church and craft shop. ▲

Private Aircraft: Pelly Airstrip, elev. 1,870 feet/570m; length 3,000 feet/914m; gravel; no services.

Pelly Crossing became a settlement when the Klondike Highway was put through in 1950. A ferry transported people and vehicles across the Pelly River, where the road eventually continued to Dawson City. Most inhabitants of Pelly Crossing came from historic Fort Selkirk. Today, the restored Fort Selkirk can be visited by boat from Pelly Crossing.

This Selkirk Indian community attracted residents from Minto when the highway to Dawson City was built. School, mission and sawmill located near the big bridge. The local economy is based on hunting, trapping, fishing and guiding. The Selkirk Indian Band has erected signs near the bridge on the history and culture of the Selkirk people.

The **Selkirk Heritage Centre**, located adjacent to the Selkirk Gas Bar, is a replica of the Big Jonathon House at Fort Selkirk. The centre offers self-guided tours of First Nation heritage.

Selkirk Gas Bar & Grocery. See display ad this section. ▲

J 169.7 (273.1 km) **D 157.5** (253.5 km) **S 288.9** (465.5 km) Pelly River bridge.

J 170.4 (274.2 km) **D 156.8** (252.3 km) **S 289.6** (467 km) Turnout with litter barrel to east. View of Pelly Crossing and river valley. A historical marker here honours the Canadian Centennial (1867–1967). The Pelly River was named in 1840 by explorer Robert Campbell for Sir John Henry Pelly, governor of the Hudson's Bay Co. The Pelly heads near the Northwest Territories border and flows approximately 375 miles/603 km to the Yukon River.

J 171.5 (276 km) **D 155.7** (250.6 km) **S 290.7** (468.6 km) **Private Aircraft:** Airstrip to east; elev. 1,870 feet/570m; length 3,000 feet/914m; gravel. No services.

J 179.6 (289 km) **D 147.6** (237.5 km) **S 298.8** (481.7 km) Pull-through turnout to east.

J 180.9 (291.1 km) **D 146.3** (235.4 km) **S 300.1** (483.8 km) Small lake to west.

J 183.8 (295.8 km) **D 143.4** (230.8 km) **S 303** (488.6 km) Large turnout to west. Bridge over Willow Creek.

J 185.5 (298.5 km) **D 141.7** (228 km) **S 304.7** (491.3 km) Side road west to Jackfish Lake.

J 195.6 (314.8 km) **D 131.6** (211.8 km) **S 314.8** (506.6 km) Access road west to **Wrong Lake** (stocked); fishing.

J 197.4 (317.7 km) **D 129.8** (208.9 km) **S 316.6** (511 km) Turnout with litter barrel to west. Winding descent begins for northbound traffic.

J 203.6 (327.7 km) **D 123.6** (198.9 km) **S 322.8** (521 km) Pull-through turnout to east.

J 205.9 (331.4 km) **D 121.3** (195.2 km) **S 325.1** (524.6 km) **Crooked Creek** comprises the southern boundary of Ddhaw Gro Special Management Area (formerly McArthur Wildlife Sanctuary). Pike; grayling, use flies, summer best.

Grey Hunter Peak and surrounding hillsides support many species of wildlife, including Fannin sheep.

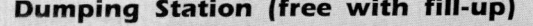

J 207.2 (333.4 km) **D 120** (193.1 km) **S 326.4** (526.7 km) Pull-through turnout with litter barrel to east at turnoff for **Ethel Lake** Yukon government campground. Drive in 16.6 miles/26.7 km on narrow and winding side road (not recommended for large RVs) for campground; 12 sites, boat launch, fishing. Camping permit ($8).

J 213.8 (344.1 km) **D 113.4** (182.5 km) **S 333** (537.3 km) Stewart Crossing government maintenance camp to east.

J 213.9 (344.2 km) **D 113.3** (182.3 km) **S 333.1** (537.5 km) Stewart Crossing; private RV park and campground, and gas station with towing, tires and minor repair, east side of highway. Turnout with information sign west side of highway; Silver Trail information booth (unmanned) contains information on the Silver Trail, or listen to a 5-minute message on the radio at 93.3 FM.

In 1886 **STEWART CROSSING** was the site of a trading post established by Arthur Harper, Alfred Mayo and Jack McQuesten to support gold mining in the area. Later a roadhouse was built here as part of the Whitehorse to Dawson overland stage route. Stewart Crossing also functioned as a fuel stop for the riverboats and during the 1930s was a transfer point for the silver ore barges from Mayo. Harper, Mayo and McQuesten are 3 prominent names in Yukon history. Harper, an Irish immigrant, was one of the first white men to prospect in the Yukon, although he never struck it rich. He died in 1898 in Arizona. (His son, Walter Harper, was on the first complete ascent of Mount McKinley in 1913. Walter died in 1918 in the SS *Princess Sophia* disaster off Juneau.)

Mayo, a native of Maine, explored, prospected and traded in the Yukon until his death in 1924.

McQuesten, like Harper, worked his way north from the California goldfields. Often referred to as the "Father of the Yukon" and a founding member of the Yukon order of Pioneers, Jack Leroy Napoleon McQuesten ended his trading and prospecting days in 1898 when he moved to California. He died in 1909 while in Seattle for the Alaska–Yukon–Pacific Exposition.

Stewart Crossing Shell. See display ad this section.

J 214.3 (344.9 km) **D 112.9** (181.7 km) **S 333.5** (538 km) Stewart River bridge. The Stewart River flows into the Yukon River upstream from Dawson City.

J 214.4 (345 km) **D 112.8** (181.5 km) **S 333.6** (538.2 km) **Silver Trail (Stewart Crossing)**; turnoff for Mayo and Keno City at north end of Stewart River bridge. Marker shows distance to Dawson 182 km.

Silver Trail Tourism Association. See display ad this section.

Junction with the Silver Trail (Yukon Highway 11) which leads northeast to Mayo, Elsa and Keno; see SILVER TRAIL section.

J 214.8 (345.7 km) **D 112.4** (180.9 km) **S 334** (538.8 km) View to west of Stewart River and mountains as highway climbs northbound.

J 220.8 (355.3 km) **D 106.4** (171.2 km) **S 340** (545.1 km) Dry Creek.

J 224.4 (361.1 km) **D 102.8** (165.4 km) **S 343.6** (556.2 km) Access to Stewart River to west. Historical information sign about Stewart River. A major tributary of the Yukon River, the Stewart River was named for James G. Stewart, who discovered it in 1849. Stewart was assistant to Robert Campbell of the Hudson's Bay Co.

J 229.1 (368.7 km) **D 98.1** (157.9 km) **S 348.3** (561.9 km)

J 229.2 (368.9 km) **D 98** (157.7 km) **S 348.4** (562 km) Moose Creek bridge.

J 229.5 (369.3 km) **D 97.7** (157.2 km) **S 348.7** (562.4 km) Turnout to west at turnoff for Moose Creek Yukon government campground adjacent to **Moose Creek** and Stewart River; good picnic spot. There are 30 RV sites, 6 tent-only sites, kitchen shelter, playground and playfield. Camping permit ($8). Good fishing for grayling, 1 to 1¼ lbs. Short trail to Stewart River is a 30-minute walk through boreal forest along Moose Creek. Note the change of habitat from dry spruce forest to floodplain willow. Listen for Northern waterthrush, Wilson's warbler and common yellowthroat.

J 242.7 (390.6 km) **D 84.5** (136 km) **S 361.9** (583.7 km) McQuesten River, a tributary of the Stewart River, named for Jack (Leroy Napoleon) McQuesten.

J 242.9 (390.9 km) **D 84.3** (135.7 km) **S 362.1** (584 km) McQuesten, a lodge with cafe, cabins and RV sites. Site of Old McQuesten River Lodge to east.

J 247.5 (398.3 km) **D 79.7** (128.3 km) **S 366.7** (590.1 km) Partridge Creek Farm.

J 249.3 (401.2 km) **D 77.9** (125.4 km) **S 368.5** (594 km) **Private Aircraft:** McQuesten airstrip 1.2 miles/1.9 km west; elev. 1,500 feet/457m; length 5,000 feet/1,524m; gravel and turf. No services.

J 251.3 (404.4 km) **D 75.9** (122.1 km)

Canoes make their way down the Yukon River to Dawson City. (© Lyn Hancock)

S 370.5 (596.5 km) Clear Creek, access via side road west.

J 260.4 (419.1 km) D 66.8 (107.5 km) S 379.6 (612 km) Barlow Lake, access via 0.6-mile-/1-km-long side road west.

J 263.7 (424.4 km) D 63.5 (102.2 km) S 382.9 (617.2 km) Beaver Dam Creek.

J 266 (428.1 km) D 61.2 (98.5 km) S 385.2 (621 km) Willow Creek.

J 268.5 (432.1 km) D 58.7 (94.5 km) S 387.7 (625 km) Flat Hill.

J 268.8 (432.6 km) D 58.4 (94 km) S 388 (625.5 km) Turnout to east at **Gravel Lake**, an important wetland for migratory birds in spring and fall. Just north of the turnout a dirt road leads to the lake. Because of its location on the Tintina Trench corridor, unusual birds are sometimes seen here, including ruddy ducks, black scoters and the most northerly sightings of American coots. (See also **Milepost J 289.3**.)

J 272.1 (437.9 km) D 55.1 (88.7 km) S 391.3 (630.8 km) Meadow Creek.

J 272.5 (438.5 km) D 54.7 (88 km) S 391.7 (631.4 km) Rest area with litter barrel to south.

J 276.5 (445 km) D 50.7 (81.6 km) S 395.7 (637.9 km) French Creek.

J 279.7 (450.1 km) D 47.5 (76.4 km) S 398.9 (643.1 km) Stone Boat Creek.

J 288.9 (464.9 km) D 38.3 (61.6 km) S 408.1 (657.9 km) Rest area.

J 289.3 (465.6 km) D 37.9 (61 km) S 408.5 (658.5 km) **Tintina Trench Viewpoint**. Large gravel turnout to east overlooking Tintina Trench. This geologic feature, which extends hundreds of miles across Yukon and Alaska, is the largest fault in North America and 1 of 2 major bird migration corridors in the Yukon (the other is the Shakwak Trench).

J 295.1 (474.9 km) D 32.1 (51.7 km) S 414.3 (667.8 km) Flat Creek.

J 295.9 (476.2 km) D 31.3 (50.4 km) S 415.1 (669 km) Klondike River to east.

J 297.6 (478.9 km) D 29.6 (47.6 km) S 416.8 (671.9 km) Large turnout to east with historic sign about Klondike River and information sign on Dempster Highway.

J 298 (479.6 km) D 29.2 (47 km) S 417.2 (672.5 km) Watch for livestock.

J 301.6 (485.4 km) D 25.6 (41.2 km) S 420.8 (678.5 km) **Dempster Corner**; Klondike River Lodge east side of highway just north of the junction; open year-round, food, lodging, camping, gas, diesel and propane. ▲

Klondike River Lodge. See display ad this section.

Junction of Klondike Highway and the Dempster Highway (Yukon Highway 5), which leads northeast to Inuvik, NWT. See DEMPSTER HIGHWAY section for log of that road.

J 307.3 (494.5 km) D 19.9 (32 km) S 426.5 (687.4 km) Goring Creek.

J 308.4 (496.3 km) D 18.8 (30.3 km) S 427.6 (689.2 km) Turnout to north for Rock Creek subdivision and Klondike River access.

J 311.9 (501.9) D 15.3 (24.6 km) S 431.7 (694.8 km) **Tintina Bakery**. Great news, folks, you've arrived at the favourite little bakery in the Klondike. All our baked goods made from scratch ... bread (including sourdough), buns, butter tarts, sweets, Danish pastry, cinnamon rolls. Tasty meat pies. Coffee, cold sodas and juice, and a limited supply of groceries and dairy. Open daily, Thursday and Friday until 9 P.M.. Phone (867) 993-5558. [ADVERTISEMENT]

J 315.2 (507.3 km) D 12 (19.3 km) S 434.4 (700 km) Turnoff to north for **Klondike River** Yukon government campground, located on Rock Creek near the Klondike River; 38 sites, kitchen shelter, drinking water, playground. Camping permit ($8). A nature trail leads to the river. Flora includes Labrador tea, highbush cranberry, prickly rose, Arctic bearberry and horsetails. ▲

J 315.7 (508.1 km) D 11.5 (18.5 km) S 434.9 (700.8 km) Dawson City airport to south. **Private Aircraft:** Runway 02-20; elev. 1,211 feet/369m; length 5,000 feet/1,524m; gravel; fuel 80 (in drums at Dawson City), 100, JP4. Flightseeing trips and air charters available.

J 317.1 (510.3 km) D 10.1 (16.3 km) S 436.3 (703.4 km) Hunker Creek Road to south. Hunker Creek Road (gravel) connects with Upper Bonanza Creek Road and loops back to the Klondike Highway via Bonanza Creek Road.

Access to Goldbottom Mining Tours, 9 miles/15 km south, a family-run placer mine offering tours and gold panning; fee charged.

Goldbottom Mining Tours and Gold Panning. See display ad this section.

J 318.4 (512.4 km) D 8.8 (14.2 km) S 437.6 (705.4 km) Turnout to south with point of interest sign about Hunker Creek. Albert Hunker staked the first claim on Hunker Creek Sept. 11, 1896. George Carmack made the big discovery on Bonanza Creek on Aug. 17, 1896. Hunker Creek is 16 miles/26 km long, of which 13 miles/21 km was dredged between 1906 and 1966.

J 318.9 (513.2 km) D 8.3 (13.4 km) S 438.1 (706.1 km) Bear Creek Road leads to subdivision.

J 319.6 (514.3 km) D 7.6 (12.2 km)

S 438.8 (707.2 km) Turnout with historic sign about the Yukon Ditch and tailings to north. To the south is **Bear Creek Historical Site**, operated by Parks Canada. This 62-acre compound of the Yukon Consolidated Gold Corp. features blacksmith and machinery shops and Gold Room. Open daily in summer, with tours twice daily from the end of May to early September. Admission charged.

J 321.3 (517.1 km) **D 5.9** (9.5 km) **S 441.1** (709.9 km)Welcome to Dawson City information kiosk, across from government highway works yard.

J 323.3 (520.3 km) **D 3.9** (6.3 km) **S 442.5** (712 km) Callison industrial area; charter helicopter service, mini-storage, bulk fuel plant and heavy equipment repairs. Access to Ridge Road Heritage Trail lower trailhead (see Attractions in Dawson City).

J 324.5 (522.2 km) **D 2.7** (4.3 km) **S 443.7** (714 km) Commercial RV park and gold panning at **junction** with **Bonanza Creek Road**; access to Dredge No. 4 (7.8 miles/12.3 km) and Discovery Claim (9.3 milew/14.8 km). Bonanza Creek Road is maintained for 11 miles/18 km. It connects with Upper Bonanza Creek Road (gravel), which provides access to Ridge Road Heritage Trail and loops back to the Klondike Highway via Hunker Creek Road. ▲

GuggieVille. Good Sam. This clean, attractive campground is built on dredge

tailings at the former site of the Guggenheim's mining camp. 72 RV sites with water and electricity (15- and 30-amp), 28 unserviced sites, public showers ($2 each). Car wash, dump station and laundromat are available. E-mail access. A mining display is open to the public free of charge. Gold panning discount for those staying at GuggieVille. Phone (867) 993-5008. Fax (867) 993-5006. Off-season phone/fax (867) 993-5319. [ADVERTISEMENT] ▲

Dredge No. 4 is the largest wooden hull dredge in North America. Interpretive

centre at dredge site; scheduled tours and a 10-minute video on the restoration of this historic site are offered daily, end of May through August. Admission: $5 adults, $2.50 youth, $12.50 family, or Parks Pass.

Marked by a plaque, **Discovery Claim** was the first gold claim on Bonanza Creek and the one that started the Klondike Stampede of 1898. Visitors are welcome to try gold panning for free at Klondike Visitor Association's **Claim No. 6**, located above Discovery at Mile 9/Km 14 Bonanza Creek Road. Bring your own gold pan.

J 324.6 (522.4 km) **D 2.6** (4.2 km) **S 443.8** (714.2 km) **Bonanza Gold R.V. Park & Lodging**. See display ad this section. ▲

J 324.7 (522.5 km) **D 2.5** (4 km) **S 443.9** (715.3 km) **Dawson City R.V. Park & Campground**. See display ad this section. ▲

J 324.8 (522.7 km) **D 2.4** (3.9 km) **S 444** (715.5 km) Klondike River bridge.

J 325.3 (523.5 km) **D 1.9** (3.1 km) **S 444.5** (716.4 km) Large turnout with information sign and map.

J 325.8 (524.3 km) **D 1.4** (2.3 km) **S 445** (717.2 km) Dome Road (chip-sealed) to north leads 4.5 miles/7.2 km to **Dome Mountain** (elev. 2,911 feet/887m), which offers views of Dawson City, the Yukon and Klondike rivers, Bonanza Creek and the Ogilvie Mountains.

J 325.8 (524.3 km) **D 1.4** (2.3 km) **S 445** (716.1 km) Rock face on right northbound is known locally as **Crocus Bluff**. Short (0.3 mile/0.4 km) interpretive foot trail leads to viewpoint overlooking Klondike River and Dawson City; interpretive panels. Trailhead is located near the cemetery on Dome Road.

J 326.1 (524.8 km) **D 1.1** (1.8 km) **S 445.3** (717.7 km) Fifth Avenue. Turnout with sign about the Klondike River to south: "With headwaters in the Ogilvie Mountains, the Klondike River and its tributaries gave birth to the world's greatest gold rush—the Klondike Gold Rush of '98."

J 327.2 (526.6 km) **D 0 S 446.4** (719.5 km) Dawson City, ferry at Yukon River. *Description of Dawson City follows. Log of Klondike Loop continues on page 262.*

Dawson City

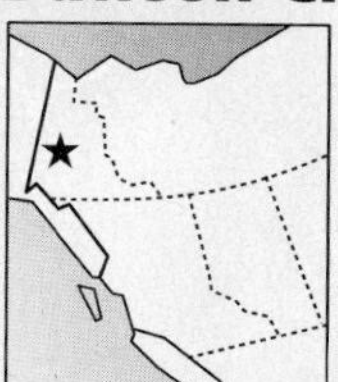

J 327.2 (526.6 km) **D 0 S 446.4** (719.5 km) Located 165 miles/266 km south of the Arctic Circle on the Yukon River at its junction with the Klondike River. **Population:** 2,019. **Emergency Services: RCMP**, 1st Avenue S., phone (867) 993-5555. **Fire Department**, phone (867) 993-2222. **Nursing station**, phone (867) 993-4444. **Ambulance**, phone (867) 993-4444.

Visitor Information: Visitor Reception Centre, operated by Tourism Yukon and Parks Canada, at Front and King streets, is housed in a replica of the 1897 Alaska Commercial Co. store. Accommodation informa-

(Continues on page 258)

ACCOMMODATIONS

ACCOMMODATIONS • RV PARKS

For Information, Contact
The Visitors Reception Centre
(867) 993-5566

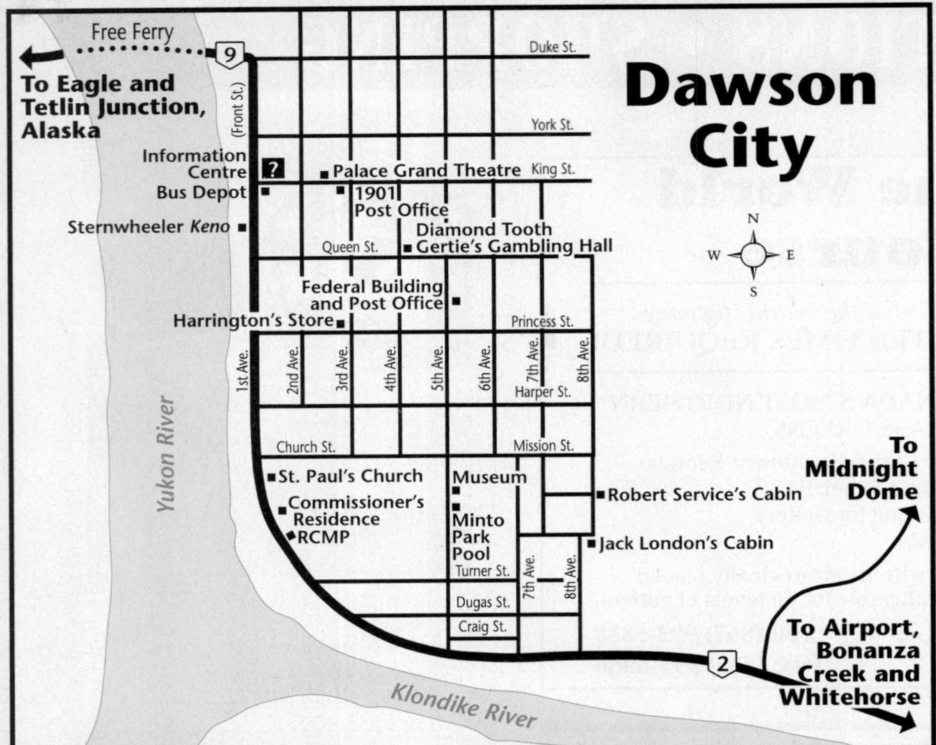

(Continued from page 253)
tion, schedule of daily events and a Dawson City street map are available. Three continuous films/videos on Dawson history. Walking tours are part of the daily schedule (fee charged). Open daily, 8 A.M. to 8 P.M. mid-May to mid-September, phone (867) 993-5566, fax (867) 993-6449; web site www.dawsoncity.org. Dawson City has lots to do and see. If you want to take it all in, plan for 3 days to cover most of the attractions. Ask about a Parks Pass, which entitles

you to admission to 5 Parks Canada sites for $15 (normally $5 each).

The Dempster Highway and Northwest Territories Information Centre is located in the B.Y.N. (British Yukon Navigation) Building on Front Street, across from the Yukon visitor centre; open 9 A.M. to 8 P.M., June to September. Information on Northwest Territories and the Dempster Highway. Phone (867) 993-6167, fax 993-6334.

Elevation: 1,050 feet/320m. **Climate:** There are 20.9 hours of daylight June 21, 3.8 hours of daylight on Dec. 21. Mean high in July, 72°F/22.2°C. Mean low in January, -30.5°F/ -34.7°C. First fall frost end of August, last spring frost end of May. Annual snowfall 59.8 inches. **Radio:** CBC 560 AM and 104.9-FM. **Television:** Cable channels include 2 (ABC), 4 (ITV), 7 (CBC), 13 (BCTV), 28 (TBS), 31 (CNN) and others. **Newspaper:** *Klondike Sun* (semi-monthly).

Private Aircraft: Dawson City airport located 11.5 miles/18.5 km southeast (see **Milepost J 315.7**). Customs available.

Description

Dawson City sits at the confluence of the Klondike and Yukon rivers, at what was once a summer fish camp of the Han people. With the discovery of gold on a Klondike River tributary (Rabbit Creek, renamed Bonanza Creek) in 1896, the Han were soon displaced by the influx of whites and the boom town built to serve them.

Most of the prospectors who staked claims on Klondike creeks were already in the North before the big strike, many working claims in the Fortymile area. The men coming North in the great gold rush the following year found most of the gold-bearing streams already staked.

Dawson City was Yukon's first capital, when the Yukon became a separate territory in 1898. But by 1953, Whitehorse—on the railway and the highway, and with a large airport—was so much the hub of activity that the federal government moved the capital from Dawson City, along with 800 civil servants, and years of tradition and pride. Some recompense was offered in the form of a road linking Whitehorse with the mining at Mayo and Dawson City. With its completion, White Pass trucks replaced White Pass river steamers.

New government buildings were built in Dawson, including a fire hall. In 1962 the federal government reconstructed the Palace Grand Theatre for a gold rush festival that

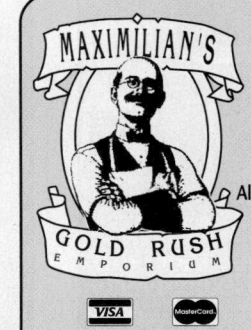

View of Dawson City from across the Yukon River on Highway 9. (© Earl L. Brown, staff)

featured the Broadway musical *Foxy,* with Bert Lahr. A museum was established in the Administration Building and tours and entertainments were begun.

Dawson City was declared a national historic site in the early 1960s. Parks Canada is currently involved with 35 properties in Dawson City. Many buildings have been restored, some reconstructed and others stabilized. Parks Canada offers an interpretive program each summer for visitors to this historic city.

Dawson City is hosting a "Decade of Centennials" to 2002. For further information on events, contact the Klondike Centennial Society, Bag 1996, Dawson City, YT Y0B 1G0.

DAWSON CITY ADVERTISERS

Ancient Voices Wilderness Camp.........Ph. (867) 993-5605
Art's Gallery......................Ph. (867) 993-6967
Aurora Inn, The................Ph. (867) 993-6860
Bear Creek Bed & Bannock...........Ph. (867) 993-6765
Bombay Peggy's Victorian Inn & Lounge...............2nd Ave. & Princess St.
Bonanza Gold Motel........Ph. (867) 993-6789
Bonanza Gold RV Park...1 mi. from city centre
Bonanza Market..........2nd Ave. & Princess St.
Cruise the Yukon River.....Ph. (867) 993-5599
Dawson City Museum...5th Ave. & Church St.
Diamond Tooth Gerties....Ph. (867) 993-5566
Downtown Hotel.............Ph. (867) 993-5346
Eldorado Hotel, The.........Ph. (867) 993-5451
5th Avenue Bed and Breakfast.......Ph. (867) 993-5941
Gold City Tours................Ph. (867) 993-5175
Gold City Travel...............Ph. (867) 993-6424
Gold Claim, The...............................3rd Ave.
Gold Rush Campground RV Park.........................5th Ave. & York St.
Guggieville.......................Ph. (867) 993-5008
Klondike Kate's Cabins and Restaurant...........Ph. (867) 993-6527
Klondike Nugget & Ivory Shop..................Ph. (867) 993-5432
Klondike Visitor's Association..................Ph. (867) 993-5575
Maximillian's Gold Rush Emporium...........Ph. (867) 993-5486
Midnight Sun Hotel..........Ph. (867) 993-5495
Northwestel..See ad
Peabody's Photo Parlour..Ph. (867) 993-5209
Raven's Nook................2nd Ave. & Queen St.
Top of the World Golf Course.................Ph. (867) 993-5888
Triple J Hotel....................Ph. (867) 993-5323
Tr'ondek Hwech'in Cultural Centre..Front St.
Versatile Welding & Mechanical Repairs......Ph. (867) 993-5072
Westmark Inn Dawson City................Ph. (867) 993-5542
White Ram Manor Bed & Breakfast..........Ph. (867) 993-5772
Whitehorse Motel............Ph. (867) 993-5576

Lodging & Services

Accustomed to a summer influx of visitors, Dawson has modern hotels and motels (rates average $75 and up) and several bed and breakfasts. The community has a bank, ATM (cash advances on MasterCard and VISA are also available at Diamond Tooth Gertie's Casino), restaurants, 4 laundromats (with showers), a grocery store with bakery, a deli/grocery store, general stores, souvenir shops, churches, art gallery, post office, government offices, government liquor store, nursing station and doctor services, information centre, hostel, swimming pool, tennis, basketball and plenty of entertainment. Many Dawson City merchants abide by the Fair Exchange Policy, offering travelers an exchange rate within 4 percent of the banks'. Dawson City's hotels and motels fill up early, especially at times of special events. Reservations are a must from June through August.

Bonanza Gold Motel. Dawson City's newest accommodation. Queen rooms, Jacuzzi suites, handicap suite, non-smoking available. Cable TV, direct dial phones. Fax

and e-mail service. Hungry? Restaurant on site. Just minutes from downtown; look for the gold entrance arch past Bonanza Road on your way into Dawson. Full RV facilities at Bonanza Gold RV Park. Phone (867) 993-6789, toll-free 1-888-993-6789. Fax (867) 993-6777. Bag 5000, Dawson City, Yukon Y0B 1G0l E-mail: accommodations@dawsoncity.net. [ADVERTISEMENT]

5th Avenue Bed and Breakfast. Located adjacent to the museum overlooking Victory Gardens. A modern home with a historic

finish, serving a hearty, healthy, all-you-can-eat breakfast. We guarantee comfort, cleanliness and courteous service along with the most convenient location in town. VISA, MasterCard. Call or write Larry and Pat Vezina, Box 722, Dawson City, YT Y0B 1G0. Phone/fax (867) 993-5941; e-mail: 5thave@dawson.net. [ADVERTISEMENT]

Klondike Kate's Cabins and Restaurant. We offer you charming, clean and affordable accommodations with private bath. Located near all major attractions. Enjoy the friendly atmosphere of our restaurant, set in a 1904 historic building. Dine inside or on our outdoor patio. Full-service, fully licensed restaurant with Canadian and ethnic foods. Espresso coffees. Special $4.99 breakfast. Box 417, Dawson City, YT Y0B 1G0. Phone (867) 993-6527. Fax (867) 993-6044. E-mail klondikekates@yknet.yk.ca. [ADVERTISEMENT]

White Ram Manor Bed & Breakfast. Look for the pink house at 7th and Harper. Centrally located. A clean, comfortable, friendly home-away-from-home. Full breakfast. Laundry. Guest kitchen. Barbecue/picnic sun deck area. Hot tub. Also, for Dawson's newest motel accommodation, consider our Bonanza Gold Motel & RV Park (see our display ad for more). Our guarantee:

If there is a room in Dawson, we'll find it for you. (Reservations recommended.) VISA, MasterCard. Box 515, Dawson City, YT Y0B 1G0. Phone (867) 993-5772. Fax (867) 993-

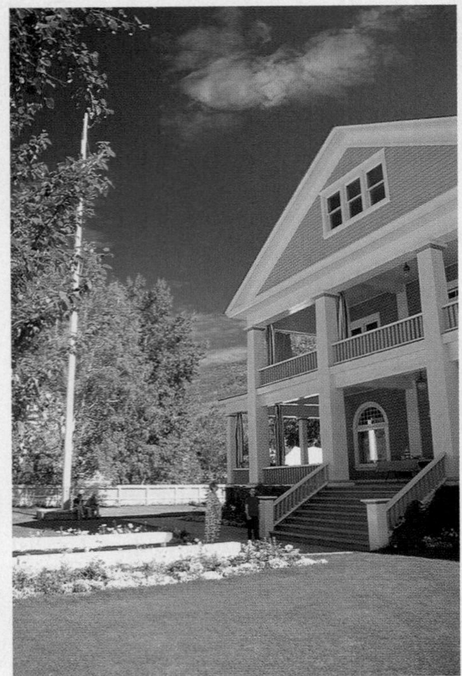

Afternoon tea with "Martha Black" is served on the verandah of the Commissioner's Residence.

(© Earl L. Brown, staff)

6509. Internet: www.dawson.net/ whiteram.. [ADVERTISEMENT]

Bear Creek Bed & Bannock. "A touch of First Nation culture" is offered in this 4 bedroom, full facility bed and breakfast. We provide a self-serve continental breakfast with baked goods. Group and family house rates available as well as senior and extended stay discounts. Located in historic Bear Creek, just 7 minutes from downtown Dawson City. Handicap accessible. Reservations recommended. (867) 993-6765 or 993-5605. [ADVERTISEMENT] ♿

Bombay Peggy's Victorian Inn & Lounge. Centrally located heritage house boasting a past as a house of ill-fame. Victorian-style rooms with private baths and modern amenities for the discerning traveler. Open year-round. 2nd Ave. and Princess Street. Box 411, Dawson City, YT Y0B 1G0. Phone (867) 933-6969; fax 993-6199. [ADVERTISEMENT]

Whitehorse Motel. Enjoy comfortable and clean accommodations with a picturesque riverfront view. Quaint units with kitchenettes, televisions and full baths at affordable rates. Our turn-of-the-century buildings provide a quiet and rustic setting within walking distance from town. Located at the north end of Front Street. Contact us at Bag 2020, Dawson City, YT Y0B 1G0; phone (867) 993-5576. e-mail: dougc@dawson.net. [ADVERTISEMENT]

Camping

There are 2 Yukon government (YTG) campgrounds in the Dawson area. Yukon River YTG campground is across the Yukon River (by ferry) from town, adjacent to the west-side ferry approach (see **Milepost D 0.2** on Top of the World Highway log, following Dawson City section). Klondike River YTG campground is southeast of town near the airport (see **Milepost J 315.2**). Private RV parks in the Dawson area include Gold Rush Campground, downtown at 5th and York; GuggieVille, east of town at **Milepost J 324.5**; Bonanza Gold RV Park at **Milepost J 324.6**; and Dawson City R.V. Park and Campground at **Milepost J 324.7.** ▲

Transportation

Air: Dawson City airport is 11.5 miles/18.5 km southeast of the city. Air North connects Dawson City with Whitehorse (daily service in summer); with Inuvik, NWT, Old Crow and Juneau (3 times weekly in summer); and Fairbanks (4 times weekly in summer). Charter service from Alkan Air. Charter and flightseeing tours available.

Ferry: The Yukon government operates a free ferry, the *George Black,* across the Yukon from about the third week in May to mid-October (depending upon breakup and freezeup). The ferry operates 24 hours a day (except for Wednesdays, 5–7 A.M. when it is shut down for servicing), and departs Dawson City on demand. It carries vehicles and passengers across to the public campground and is the only connection to the Top of the World Highway (Yukon Highway 9). Be prepared to wait as long as 3 hours during peak traffic periods (7–11 A.M. and 4–7 P.M. daily). Shut off all propane appliances and follow directions from ferry personnel when loading/unloading. Tour bus traffic has priority 6–9 A.M. and 5–9 P.M.; fuel truck traffic has priority 7 P.M. to 6 A.M. Phone (867) 993-5441 or 993-5344 for more information.

Bus: Service between Whitehorse and Dawson City by Dawson City Taxi, 6 days a week year-round; phone (867) 993-6787. Service between Inuvik, NWT, and Dawson City available by charter only, contact Gold City Tours. Service from Whitehorse via Dawson City to Tok, AK, by Alaska Direct Buslines; weekly. Phone (800) 770-6652. Service between Fairbanks and Dawson City by Parks Highway Express, phone 1-888-600-6001.

Taxi: Airport taxi service available from downtown hotels and bed and breakfasts. Scheduled and charter limo service available from Gold City Tours.

Rental Car: Car and truck rentals at Norcan, located in the Northern Superior Bldg., and Budget Rent-A-Car, located on Craig Street.

Attractions

Take a Walking Tour. Town-core tours leave the Visitor Reception Centre daily in summer. The 1½ hour guided walk highlights the history and charters of Dawson City. Audio tapes also available. Fee charged.

The Commissioner's Residence on Front Street was once the residence of Hon. George Black, M.P., Speaker of the House of Commons, and his famous wife, Martha Louise, who walked to Dawson City via the Trail of '98 and stayed to become the First Lady of the Yukon. A 1-hour tour, is given 2 times daily in summer. Admission is $5 adult, $2.50 youth, $12.50 family.

Take a Bus Tour. Motorcoach and van tours of Klondike creeks, goldfields and Dawson City are available; inquire at Gold City Tours (ask about step-on guide service, too). For a panoramic view of Dawson City, the Klondike River, Bonanza Creek and Yukon River, take the bus or drive the 5 miles/8 km to the top of Dome Mountain (elev. 2,911 feet/887m).

Take a River Tour: Fishwheel Charter offers guided 2-hour river tours 2 times a day; tickets at the Han Cultural Centre. Westours (Grayline Yukon) operates the *Yukon Queen II* on the Yukon River between Dawson City and Eagle, AK; check with the Grayline Yukon office about tickets. One-way and round-trip passage is sold on a space-available basis. The trip takes 4 hours downstream to Eagle, and 6 hours back to Dawson. Ancient Voices Wilderness Camp transports their guests via *River Dancer* boat to their camp on the Yukon River. Canoe rentals available from Dawson Trading Post and at the hostel across the river.

Ancient Voices Wilderness Camp. Let your adventurous spirit soar as you discover nature's splendor in an authentic First Nation's camp. Three northern Native cultures share their traditional way of life in a wilderness setting along the banks of the mighty Yukon River. Rustic cabins, wall tents, meals and cultural activities provided. Experience our highly acclaimed, personalized evening salmon barbecue feast. Day, overnight or package trips also available from Dawson City, transportation provided via our Ancient Voices "*River Dancer*" boats. Tickets sold locally at the Trading Post on 5th Ave. Canoe travelers from Whitehorse to Dawson have enthusiastically remarked, "We have discovered an oasis in the Yukon!" Group discounts. VISA, MasterCard accepted. Mailing address: Box 679, Dawson City, YK Y0B 1G0. Phone (867) 993-5605. Fax (867) 993-6532. Internet: www.yukon.net/avwcamp. [ADVERTISEMENT]

Cruise the Yukon River. Cruise from Dawson City down the famous Yukon River to Eagle, Alaska, aboard the MV *Yukon Queen II*. Retrace the old stern-wheeler route of this historic Gold Rush area as you cruise past abandoned settlements among the forested hills. A hearty prospector's meal is included. Daily departures. Roundtrip fare is $196 U.S. per person. Prices subject to change. Phone (867) 993-5599. [ADVERTISEMENT]

Diamond Tooth Gertie's Casino, open daily 7 P.M. to 2 A.M. mid-May to mid-September, has Klondike gambling tables

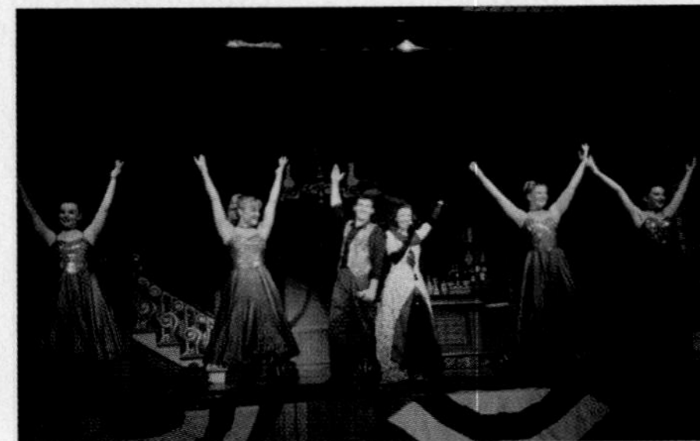

(specially licensed in Yukon), 56 "Vegas-style" slot machines, bar service and floor shows nightly. You may have a soft drink if you prefer, and still see the cancan girls present their floor show. Persons under 19 not admitted. Gertie's hosts Yukon Talent Night in September.

Dawson City Museum. Housed in the renovated Territorial Administration Building on 5th Avenue, the museum is open daily from 10 A.M. to 6 P.M., mid-May through early September; by appointment year-round. Admission fees: $4 adults, $3 senior or youth, $10 family.

Featured are the Kings of the Klondike and City Life Galleries, hourly audiovisual and dramatic presentations, and the museum's collection of narrow-gauge locomotives, including a Vauclain-type Baldwin engine, the last one in existence in Canada. Weekly lecture series during summer; check for schedule. The films "City of Gold" and "The Yukoner" are shown daily. A selection of silent film serials, news and documentary reels from 1903 to 1929 is shown in the gallery. Also take part in the "Meet a Klondike Character" show and explore the "Klondike Gold" CD Rom.

The museum has a gift shop, wheelchair ramp, resource library, genealogy service and an extensive photography collection. For more information write the museum at Box 303, Dawson City, YT Y0B 1G0; phone (867) 993-5291, fax 993-5839. ♿

Visit the Palace Grand Theatre. This magnificently reconstructed theatre, now a national historic site, is home to the "Gaslight Follies," a turn-of-the-century entertainment. Performances nightly from mid-May to mid-September. Arizona Charlie Meadows opened the Palace Grand in 1899, and today's visitors, sitting in the curtained boxes around the balcony, will succumb to the charm of this beautiful theatre. Tours of the building are conducted once daily by Parks Canada, from the end of May through early September. Films and presentations daily in summer. Admission charged or Parks Pass.

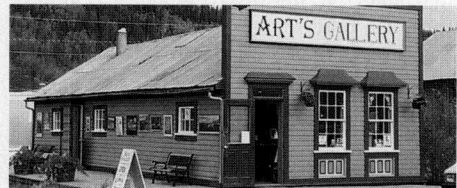

SS *Keno* National Historic Site. The SS *Keno* was the last steamer to run the Yukon River when she sailed from Whitehorse in 1960 to her present berth on the riverbank next to the bank. Under restoration in 1999. An interpretive display is set up beside the site.

Visit Robert Service's Cabin. Highly recommended. On the hillside on 8th Avenue, the author–bank clerk's cabin has been restored by Parks Canada. Stories and poetry

recitals are offered daily in summer. Photographers are welcomed, but no videotaping. Visitors come from every part of the world to sign the guest book on the rickety desk where Service wrote his famous poems, including "The Shooting of Dan McGrew" and "The Cremation of Sam McGee." Open daily. Admission: $6 adult, $3 youth.

Visit the Historic Post Office, where you may buy stamps; all first-class mail sent from here receives the old hand-cancellation stamp. Open daily.

Fire Fighters Museum, located at the fire hall at 5th Avenue and King Street, is open Monday to Saturday, 12:30 to 5:30 P.M. Admission: Donation.

Tr'ondek Hwech'in (Han) Cultural Centre, at Front and York streets overlooking the Yukon River, presents the culture and history of the Han First Nation people. The centre has a theatre, arts and crafts shop, art exhibit area and barbecue and picnic facilities.

Visit the Jack London Interpretive Centre at the corner of 8th Avenue and Firth Street. The centre features a log cabin built with some of the original logs from the cabin where London stayed in 1897. (Original logs were also used to build a second replica cabin located in Jack London Square in Oakland, CA.) Also at the site are a cache and a museum with a collection of photos tracing London's journe;y to the Klondike during the Gold Rush. Interpretations daily mid-May to September. Jack London was the author of *The Call of the Wild* and *White Fang*.

Pierre Berton Residence, located on 8th Avenue, was once home of the famous Canadian author. Now used for a writer-in-residence program. View the grounds and interpretive signage placed by the Klondike Visitors Association.

Special Events. Dawson City hosts a number of unique celebrations during the year. In May, there's the Dawson City International Gold Show; phone (867) 993-6720 for dates. Klondike Slo-Pitch Tournament is scheduled for May 26–28, 2000.

The Commissioner's Ball is held June 3, 2000. This gala event, commemorating Yukon becoming a territory in 1898, features turn-of-the-century fashion. The Yukon Gold Panning Championship is held July 1 each year in Dawson City, along with a celebration of Canada Day. The Annual Dawson City Music Festival, July 21–23, 2000, features entertainers and artists from Canada and the United States, free workshops, dances and dinners. Tickets and information from the Music Festival Assoc., phone (867) 993-5584, fax (867) 993-5510.

If you are near Dawson Aug. 18–21, 2000, be sure to join the Discovery Days Festival fun when Yukon Order of Pioneers stages its annual parade. This event is a Yukon holiday commemorating the Klondike gold discovery of Aug. 17, 1896.

The Great Klondike International Outhouse Race, held the Sunday of Labour Day weekend (Sept. 3, 2000), is a race of decorated outhouses on wheels over a 1.9 mile/3-km course through the streets of Dawson City. The Mixed Slo-Pitch Tournament, Sept. 1–4, 2000, draws teams from the Yukon and Alaska. And at Yukon Talent Night, Sept. 22, 2000, local stars and visitors take to the stage at Diamond Tooth Gertie's Casino to perform songs, skits and comedy.

See the Midnight Sun: If you are in Dawson City on June 21, be sure to make it to the top of the Dome by midnight, when the sun barely dips behind the 6,000-foot/1,829-m Ogilvie Mountains to the north—the picture of a lifetime. There's quite a local celebration on the Dome on June 21, so for those who don't like crowds, a visit before or after summer solstice will also afford fine views and photos. Turnoff for Dome Mountain is at **Milepost J 325.8**; it's about a 5-mile/8-km drive.

Pan for Gold. The chief attraction for many visitors is panning for gold. There are several mining operations set up to permit you to actually pan for your own "colours" under friendly guidance. The Klondike Visitors Assoc. sponsors a public panning area at No. 6 above Discovery, 13 miles/21 km from Dawson City on Bonanza Creek Road. Check with the Visitor Reception Centre for more information.

Dredge No. 4. Built in 1912 for the Canadian Klondike Mining Co.'s claim on Bonanza Creek, this historic dredge is the largest wooden hull bucket-line dredge in North America. Scheduled 1-hour tours several times daily June through August. Admission charged, or Parks Pass. To reach the dredge, take Bonanza Creek Road from **Milepost J 324.5** 7.8 miles/12.3 km up famous Bonanza Creek, to Dredge No. 4. Continue up Bonanza Creek Road for Discovery Claim and to see miles of gravel tailings worked over 2 and 3 times in the continuing search for gold.

Bear Creek Camp, (see **Milepost J 319.6** on the Klondike Highway), was operated by Yukon Consolidated Gold Corp. until 1966.

Tours are conducted by Parks Canada interpreters; check with the Visitor Reception Centre for current tour schedule. The compound features the Gold Room, where the gold was melted and poured into bricks, complete blacksmith and machinery shops, and other well-preserved structures. Open 9:30 A.M. to 5 P.M. from mid-June to late August. Admission charged, or Parks Pass.

Ridge Road Heritage Trail. Originally built in 1899 to move mining supplies along Bonanza Creek, the Ridge Road was abandoned by 1902. The road was reopened in 1996 as a 20-mile/32-km heritage trail. Travel time is 1½ to 2 days by foot (or 4–6 hours by mountain bike). Interpretive signs and building remnants are along the route, which winds along the high ground between Bonanza and Hunker creeks. Short walks possible from the Upper Trailhead (outhouses) on Upper Bonanza Road to Soda Station on the abandoned Klondike Mines Railway line, and from Jackson Gulch (Lower) Trailhead behind Callison subdivision to the Yukon Ditch (Trail Gulch diversion). There are 2 tent campgrounds on the trail: 11-Mile at Mile 7/11.3 km, and 15-Mile at Mile 12.2/19.2; outhouses, firepits and water pump.

Klondike Loop Log

(continued from page 253)

The **Top of the World Highway** (Yukon Highway 9) connects Dawson City with the Taylor Highway (Alaska Route 5). The Alaska Highway is 174.5 miles/280.8 km from here; Eagle, AK, is 143.4 miles/230.8 km from here. Yukon Highway 9 and the Taylor Highway (Alaska Route 5) in Alaska are not maintained from mid-October to April, and the arrival of snow effectively closes the roads for winter. *CAUTION: Allow plenty of time for this drive; average speed for this road is 25 to 40 mph/40 to 64 kmph. DRIVE WITH YOUR HEADLIGHTS ON! The Canadian portion of the highway is seal coated; the Alaska side is gravel. Check with the Dawson City Visitor Reception Centre for current road and weather conditions; phone (867) 993-5566.*

This section of the log shows distance from Dawson City (D) followed by distance from junction with the Taylor Highway (T) at Jack Wade Junction. Physical kilometreposts show distance from Dawson City.

TOP OF THE WORLD HIGHWAY
YUKON HIGHWAY 9

D 0 T 78.8 (126.8 km) **DAWSON CITY.** A free ferry carries passengers and vehicles from Dawson City across the Yukon River to the beginning of the Top of the World Highway in summer. *NOTE: The ferry wait in heavy traffic may be as long as 3 hours during peak times.*

D 0.2 (0.3 km) **T 78.6** (126.5 km) **Yukon River** government campground on riverbank opposite Dawson City; 74 RV sites, 24 tent-only sites, 2 kitchen shelters, playground and drinking water. Camping permit ($8). Within walking distance of sternwheeler graveyard. Put in and takeout spot for Yukon River travelers. Deck overlooks the Yukon River. A family of peregrine falcons nest in the cliffs across the river during the summer. ▲

D 2.7 (4.4 km) **T 76.1** (122.5 km) Access to 9-hole golf course via 3.2-mile/5.1-km gravel road; rentals.

D 2.9 (4.6 km) **T 75.9** (122.1 km) Turnout for viewpoint overlooking Dawson City and the Yukon and Klondike rivers.

D 3.2 (5 km) **T 75.6** (121.7 km) Turnout with good view of Yukon River and river valley farms.

D 9 (12.4 km) **T 69.8** (112.3 km) Large rest area with toilets, picnic tables, litter barrels. A short trail leads to a deck overlooking the Yukon River valley. Interpretive displays about the Fortymile caribou herd and and the history of the people of this area. Welcome to Dawson City information kiosk.

D 11 (15.6 km) **T 67.8** (109.1 km) "Top of the world" view as highway climbs above tree line.

D 16.4 (26.2 km) **T 62.4** (100.4 km) Snow fence along highway next 8 miles/13 km westbound.

D 18.4 (29.4 km) **T 60.4** (97.2 km) Turnout to south.

D 29.2 (47 km) **T 49.6** (79.8 km) Evidence of 1989 burn.

D 32.1 (51.2 km) **T 46.7** (75.2 km) First outcropping (westbound) of Castle Rock. Turnout to south with panoramic view of countryside.

D 33.1 (52.8 km) **T 45.7** (73.5 km) Distance marker shows customs 52 km, Dawson City 53 km.

D 35.2 (56 km) **T 43.6** (70.2 km) Main outcropping of Castle Rock; lesser formations are also found along this stretch. Centuries of erosion have created these formations. Turnout to south.

D 37.4 (59 km) **T 41.4** (66.6 km) Unmaintained road leads 25 miles/40 km to the former settlement of Clinton Creek, which served the Cassiar Asbestos Mine from 1967–79. There are no facilities or services available there. Distance marker shows U.S. border 43 km.

The confluence of the Yukon and Fortymile rivers is 3 miles/4.8 km below the former townsite of Clinton Creek. Clinton Creek bridge is an access point on the Fortymile River National Wild and Scenic River system, managed by the Bureau of Land Management. The Fortymile River offers intermediate and advanced canoeists over 100 miles/160 km of challenging water.

Yukon River, near Clinton Creek, grayling to 3 lbs. in April; chum salmon to 12 lbs. in August; king salmon to 40 lbs., July and August. **Fortymile River,** near Clinton Creek, grayling to 3 lbs. during spring breakup and fall freezeup; inconnu (sheefish) to 10 lbs. in July and August.

D 54 (85.6 km) **T 24.8** (39.9 km) Rest stop with outhouses near adjacent old sod-roofed cabin to north. This was originally a supply and stopping place for the McCormick Transportation Co.

D 54.3 (86.1 km) **T 24.5** (39.4 km) Road forks south to old mine workings at Sixtymile, which have been reactivated by Cogasa Mining Co. Keep to right for Alaska. The road winds above timberline for many miles. The lack of fuel for warmth and shelter made this a perilous trip for the early sourdoughs.

D 64.1(101.9 km) **T 14.7** (23.7 km) Large gravel turnout. Information sign about Top of the World Highway viewpoint.

D 65.2 (103.7 km) **T 13.6** (21.9 km) Pull-through rest area with toilet and litter barrels; good viewpoint. Just across the highway, short hike to cairn, excellent viewpoint. Highest point on Top of the World Highway (elev. 4,515 feet/1,376 m).

D 66.1 (105.1 km) **T 12.7** (20.4 km) **U.S.–Canada Border** (elev. 4,127 feet/1,258m). Customs only; no public facilities available. *IMPORTANT: U.S. and Canada customs are open from about May 15 to Sept. 15. In summer 1999, customs was open 7 days a week, 9 A.M. to 9 P.M. (Pacific time) on the Canadian side; 8 A.M. to 8 P.M. (Alaska time) on the U.S. side. Customs hours of operation subject to change. Check with the RCMP or Visitor Reception Centre in Dawson City to make certain the border crossing will be open. Serious fines are levied for crossing the border without clearing customs! There are no restrooms, services or currency exchanges available here.*

Canada Customs and Immigration Little Gold Creek. All traffic entering Canada must stop here.

The **U.S. Poker Creek Border Station** office, just west of the Canadian station. All traffic entering the United States must stop here. A short hike up the hill behind U.S. border station provides good viewpoint.

TIME ZONE CHANGE: Alaska observes Alaska time; Yukon Territory observes Pacific time.

D 67.1 (108 km) **T 11.7** (18.8 km) Large double-ended turnout to north with viewing platform, toilet, litter barrel. Welcome to Alaska and Fortymile River interpretive signs.

D 69.2 (111.4 km) **T 9.6** (15.4 km) **BOUNDARY.** Boundary Lodge was one of the first roadhouses in Alaska; food, gas, lodging, diesel, tire repair, emergency phone.

Watch your gas supply. Between here and Tetlin Junction on the Alaska Highway, gas is available again only at Chicken, **Milepost TJ 66.5.** From here to Eagle, gas may be available at O'Brien Creek Lodge, **Milepost TJ 125.4.** Gas is available in Eagle.

Private Aircraft: Boundary airstrip; elev. 2,940 feet/896m; length 2,100 feet/640m; earth and gravel; fuel 80; unattended.

D 78 (125.6 km) **T 0.8** (1.3 km) Viewpoint.

D 78.8 (126.9 km) **T 0 Jack Wade Junction**. *CAUTION: Watch for cross traffic at this intersection.*

Junction with the Taylor Highway (Alaska Route 5), which leads north 64.6 miles/104 km to Eagle, AK, or south 95.7 miles/154 km to Tetlin Junction, just east of Tok, on the Alaska Highway. Turn to page 267 **Milepost TJ 95.7** in the TAYLOR HIGHWAY section.

TAYLOR HIGHWAY (5)

Connects: Alaska Hwy. (Tetlin Jct.) to Eagle, AK **Length:** 160 miles
Road Surface: 85% gravel, 15% paved **Season:** Closed in winter
Steepest Grade: 9 percent
Major Attraction: Fort Egbert

(See map, page 246)

	Chicken	Dawson City	Eagle	Tok
Chicken		109	94	78
Dawson City	109		144	187
Eagle	94	144		172
Tok	78	187	172	

The gravel Taylor Highway winds across mountains to Eagle. (© Kris Graef, staff)

The 160.3-mile/258-km Taylor Highway (Alaska Route 5) begins at Tetlin Junction on the Alaska Highway and ends at the small town of Eagle on the Yukon River. The Taylor Highway also forms part of the Klondike Loop for traffic coming from (or going to) Canada via the Top of the World Highway (Yukon Highway 9). The Ta;ylor Highway splits at **Milepost TJ 95.7** (Jack Wade Junction) with one fork going east towards the border and the other north to Eagle.

This is a beautiful "top of the world" drive, and Eagle is well worth a visit. Construction of the Taylor Highway began in 1946, and was completed to Eagle in late 1953, providing access to the historic Fortymile Mining District.

Gas is available in Chicken (**Milepost TJ 66**); at O'Brien Creek Lodge (**Milepost TJ 125.4**) en route to Eagle; and in Boundary, en route to Canada (Top of the World Highway, **Milepost D 69.2**). Gas is also available in Tok, which is located approximately 11 miles northwest of Tetlin Junction on the Alaska Highway.

The Taylor Highway is a narrow, winding, mountain road with many steep hills and some hairpin curves. Allow plenty of time to drive its length. Watch for pilot cars accompanying tour buses on the very narrow stretch of highway between Chicken and Eagle. *NOTE: Large RVs and trailers especially should use caution in driving this road.*

The first 24 miles/39 km of the highway are seal coated, the rest is gravel. Between 20 and 40 more miles of road are scheduled to be chip-sealed in 2000. The gravel portion of highway has sporadic soft spots during breakup or after heavy rains. Road surface ranges from good to poor depending on maintenance. Shoulders are narrow and may be unstable.

The Taylor Highway is not maintained from mid-October to April. The arrival of snow effectively closes the road to vehicle traffic for the winter, although it is open to snowmobiles. (Trek Over The Top is an organized snowmobile ride to Dawson City held in February. An adventure for the hardy.)

The highway provides river runners with access to the Fortymile River National Wild and Scenic River system. A brochure on access points and float times is available from the Bureau of Land Management, P.O. Box 309, Tok AK 99780; phone (907) 883-5121.

The Taylor is the shortest route to Dawson City, YT, from Alaska. Drive 95.7 miles/154 km north on the Taylor Highway to Jack Wade Junction, and turn east on the Top of the World Highway (Yukon Highway 9) for Dawson City. (See end of KLONDIKE LOOP section for log of Yukon Highway 9.)

Dawson City-bound travelers keep in mind that the U.S. and Canadian customs offices at the border are open from about mid-May to mid-September. Customs hours for summer 1999 were 8 A.M. to 8 P.M. Alaska time; 9 A.M. to 9 P.M. Pacific time on the Canadian side. Check for current information with Alaska Public Lands Information Center in Tok; phone (907) 883-5667. There are no restrooms, services or currency exchanges available at the border.

IMPORTANT: You cannot cross the border unless the customs office for the country you are entering is open. Severe fines are levied for crossing without clearing customs. Officials at Canadian customs are concerned about child abductions. If you are traveling with children, remember to bring identification for them.

NOTE: All gold-bearing ground in area is claimed. Do not pan in streams.

Emergency medical services: Between Tetlin Junction and O'Brien Creek bridge at **Milepost TJ 113.2**, phone the Tok Area EMS at 911 or (907) 883-5111. Between O'Brien Creek bridge and Eagle, phone the Eagle EMS at (907) 547-2300 or (907) 547-2211. Use CB channel 21.

Taylor Highway Log

Distance from Tetlin Junction (TJ) is followed by distance from Eagle (E).

ALASKA ROUTE 5

TJ 0 E 160.3 (258 km) **Tetlin Junction.** 40 Mile Roadhouse (closed in 1999). Highway begins long, winding climb (up and down grades to 7 percent) out of the Tanana River valley. The first 23.6 miles/38 km of the Taylor Highway are seal coated. Distance marker shows Chicken 66 miles, Boundary 104 miles, Eagle 160 miles.

Chicken post office at Milepost TJ 66.3. (© Kris Graef, staff)

Junction with the Alaska Highway. Turn to **Milepost DC 1301.7** on page 182 in the ALASKA HIGHWAY section for log of that route.

Note stabilized sand dunes first 5 miles/8 km.

TJ 0.9 (1.4 km) **E 159.4** (256.5 km) Double-ended parking area to east.

TJ 2.7 (4.3 km) **E 157.6** (253.6 km) Double-ended parking area to east.

TJ 4.5 (7.2 km) **E 155.8** (250.7 km) Large double-ended gravel turnout to east. A 0.7-mile/1.1-km trail leads to **Four Mile Lake;** rainbow trout and sheefish.

TJ 5.7 (9.2 km) **E 154.6** (248.8 km) Entering Tok Management Area, **Tanana Valley State Forest**, northbound. Established as the first unit of Alaska's state forest system in 1983, Tanana Valley State Forest encompasses 1.81 million acres and lies almost entirely within the Tanana River Basin. The forest extends 265 miles from near the Canadian border to Manley Hot Springs. Almost 90 percent of the state forest is forested. Principal tree species are paper birch, quaking aspen, balsam poplar, black spruce, white spruce and tamarack. Almost 7 percent of the forest is shrubland, chiefly willow. The forest is managed by the Dept. of Natural Resources.

Evidence of 1990 forest fire known as the Porcupine burn.

TJ 6 (9.7 km) **E 154.3** (248.3 km) Turnout to east.

TJ 9.3 (15 km) **E 151** (243 km) Entering Game Management Unit 20E northbound; entering GMU 12 southbound. Road begins gradual climb of Mount Fairplay for northbound travelers.

TJ 10.1 (16.2 km) **E 150.2** (241.7 km) Parking area to east.

TJ 12.1 (19.5 km) **E 148.2** (238.5 km) Entering Tok Management Area, Tanana State Forest, southbound.

TJ 12.4 (20 km) **E 147.9** (238 km) Turnout to east.

TJ 15.6 (25.1 km) **E 144.7** (232.9 km) Turnout.

TJ 21.2 (34.1 km) **E 139.1** (223.9 km) Long descent (7 percent grade) northbound from true summit of Mount Fairplay.

TJ 21.4 (34.4 km) **E 138.9** (223.5 km) Turnout to west.

TJ 22.1 (35.4 km) **E 138.2** (221.1 km) Double-ended parking area to east. Information panels on Fortymile region and caribou herd. The Fortymile Mining District is home range for the Fortymile caribou herd. Once a massive herd of 500,000 animals, the herd is now stable at about 23,000 caribou. The herd moves east across the highway in late fall for the winter, and returns again in spring for calving. During the summer, small bands of caribou can sometimes be seen in the high country above timberline.

TJ 23 (37 km) **E 137.3** (219.4 km) Scenic views; Alaska Range visible to west on clear days.

TJ 23.6 (38 km) **E 136.7** (220 km) *NOTE: Pavement ends, gravel begins and road surface deteriorates, northbound. Watch for road consturction next 20 miles in 2000 as highway is chip-sealed to Logging Cabin Creek.*

TJ 28.4 (45.7 km) **E 131.9** (212.3 km) Turnout with view of mountains to west.

TJ 32.8 (52.8 km) **E 127.5** (205.2 km) Rough informal turnout to west.

TJ 34.4 (55.4 km) **E 125.9** (202.6 km) Large double-ended turnout with view to west.

TJ 35.1 (56.5 km) **E 125.2** (201.5 km) Large double-ended turnout to east near summit of **Mount Fairplay** (elev. 5,541 feet/1,689m). Interpretive sign, viewing platform, litter barrels, aluminum recycling, outhouse, wheelchair accessible.

NOTE: 9 percent downgrade northbound. Southbound, the road descends for the next 25 miles/40 km from Mount Fairplay's summit, winding through heavily forested terrain. Panoramic views of the Fortymile River forks' valleys. Views of the Alaska Range to the southwest.

Entering **Fortymile Mining District** northbound. The second-oldest mining district in Alaska, it first yielded gold in 1886. Claims were filed in both Canada and Alaska due to boundary uncertainties.

TJ 39 (62.8 km) **E 121.3** (195.2 km) *CAUTION: Slow for narrow road and sharp curve.*

TJ 43 (69.2 km) **E 117.3** (188.8 km) **Logging Cabin Creek** bridge (abrupt edge on bridge). Side road to creek. This is the south end of the Fortymile River National Wild and Scenic River system managed by BLM.

Evidence of old forest fire.

NOTE: Watch for road construction next 20 miles southbound in 2000 as more of the Taylor Highway is chip-sealed. Also be prepared for possible paving from here north to Chicken.

TJ 49 (78.9 km) **E 111.3** (179.1 km) Loop road through **West Fork Campground** (Forty Mile River BLM Recreation Management); 25 sites, mostly level back-in and some pull-through sites; garbarge container, outhouses, well water; tables, firepits; camping fee $8.

TJ 49.3 (79.3 km) **E 111** (178.6 km) Bridge over **West Fork of the Dennison Fork of the Fortymile River**. Access point for Fortymile River National Wild and Scenic River system. Fishing for grayling and lingcod.

TJ 50.5 (81.3 km) **E 109.8** (176.7 km) Taylor Creek bridge. Watch for potholes and rough road at bridge approaches (abrupt edge on bridge). All-terrain vehicle trail to Taylor and Kechumstuk mountains; heavily used in hunting season.

TJ 57 (91.7 km) **E 103.3** (166.2 km) Scenic view from turnout to east; no easy turnaround for trailers.

TJ 58.9 (94.8 km) **E 101.4** (163.2 km) Scenic viewpoint turnout to east.

TJ 62.5 (100.6 km) **E 97.8** (157.4 km) Large turnout to west.

TJ 63.2 (101.7 km) **E 97.1** (156.3 km) View of Chicken northbound.

TJ 50.1 (80.6 km) **E 110.2** (177.3 km) Federal Subsistence Hunting Area boundary. These areas allow local residents earlier hunting seasons for subsistence hunting of moose and caribou. There are several of these signs along the Taylor Highway.

TJ 64.1 (103.2 km) **E 96.2** (154.8 km) Well-traveled road leads to private buildings, not into Chicken.

TJ 64.3 (103.5 km) **E 96** (154.5 km) Bridge over Mosquito Fork of the Fortymile River. **BLM Mosquito Fork Bridge River Access** to west; day-use area with parking, picnic table, outhouse and litter barrel to

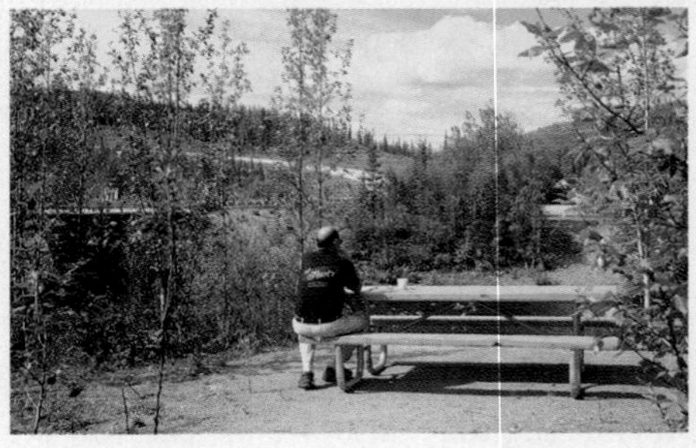

west at north end of bridge. A nice picnic spot overlooking the river. The Mosquito Fork is a favorite access point for the Fortymile National Wild and Scenic River system, according to the BLM.

TJ 66 (106.2 km) **E 94.3** (151.8 km) Welcome to Chicken sign. *Driving distance between **Mileposts TJ 66** and **67** is 0.7 mile.*

TJ 66.3 (106.7 km) **E 94** (151.3 km) Chicken post office (ZIP code 99732), located up hill to west of road, was establishede in 1903 along with the mining camp. **CHICKEN** (pop. 37) was supposedly named by early miners who wanted to name their camp ptarmigan, but were unable to spell it and settled instead for chicken, the common name in the North for ptarmigan. Today, Chicken consists of 2 commerical establishments: Beautiful Downtown Chicken and The Goldpanner.

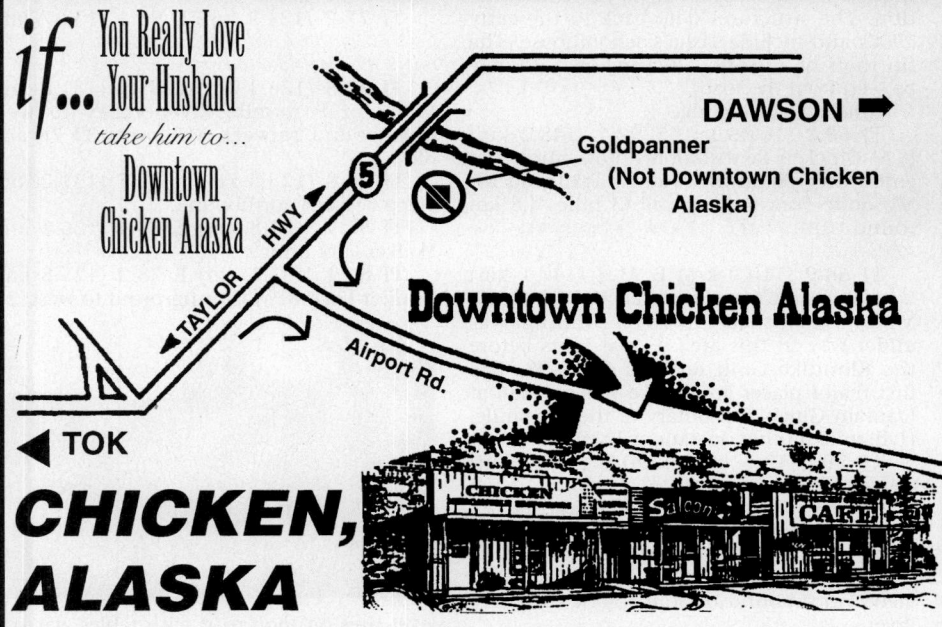

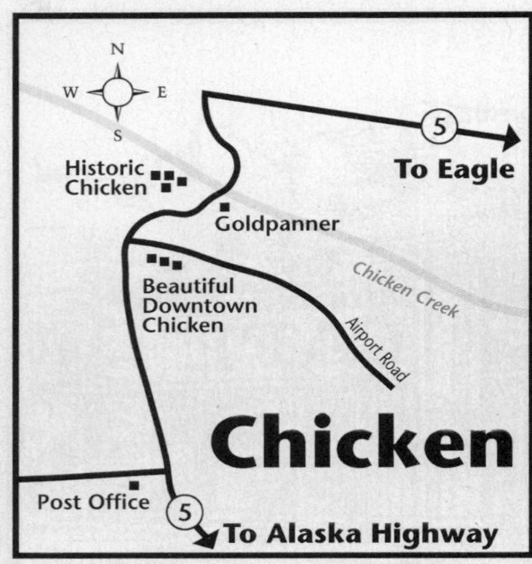

Chicken is perhaps best known as the home of the late Ann Purdy, whose book *Tisha* was based on her experiences as a young schoolteacher in the Bush.

TJ 66.4 (106.9 km) **E 93.9** (151.1 km) Airport Road to east provides access to Beautiful Downtown Chicken—a combination store, restaurant, bar and gas station—and to Chicken airstrip. Access point for the Fortymile River canoe trail is below Chicken airstrip.

Private Aircraft: Chicken airstrip, adjacent southwest; elev. 1,640 feet/500m; length 2,500 feet/762m; gravel; maintained year-round.

The Chicken Creek Salmon Bake uses only wild Alaska–Yukon king salmon. Besides salmon, we also feature halibut, barbecue chicken, buffalo and halibut burgers, our famous potato salad and chowder. All are offered daily from 4 P.M. to 8 P.M. Another good reason to visit Beautiful Downtown Chicken, Alaska! [ADVERTISEMENT]

Downtown Chicken Mercantile Emporium, Chicken Creek Cafe, Saloon and Gas. Unfortunately, as too often happens, the main road bypasses the most interesting part of Chicken. If it's modern facilities you are looking for, original Chicken is not for you. The Chicken Creek Saloon and Cafe are some of the last remnants of the old frontier Alaska. It is a trading post where local miners (some straight out of Jack London and Robert Service) trade gold for supplies and drink. It's also possible to purchase an autographed copy of *Tisha* at the Chicken Mercantile Emporium. A wealth of gifts abound in the Chicken Mercantile Emporium, and the cafe is famous throughout Alaska for its excellent food, homemade pies, pastries and cinnamon buns. For a bird's-eye view of this spectacular country and fantastic photo opportunities, check out the local flightseeing service, Chicken Air. Chicken Creek Saloon, Cafe and Mercantile Emporium are a rare treat for those with the courage to stray just a few hundred yards from the beaten path. Major credit cards accepted. Note: The Goldpanner, located on the main road, is not the same as "Beautiful Downtown Chicken, Alaska." [ADVERTISEMENT]

TJ 66.6 (107.2 km) **E 93.7** (150.8 km) Private access to Historic Chicken across from turnoff to The Goldpanner. The Goldpanner offers gas, diesel, propane, RV camping, gold panning in Chicken Creek; and gift shop. Travelers may drop-off trailers here for the drive to Eagle (inquire at The Goldpanner). View of Pedro Dredge, which has been moved down behind The Goldpanner.

The Goldpanner. See display ad this section.

The dozen or so old buildings that comprise **Historic Chicken** are on private property; access restricted to guided tours only. Inquire at the Goldpanner for more information. The structures date back to the early 1900s and include Tisha's schoolhouse. The tin roofs of Historic Chicken townsite may be seen from the road.

Chicken Creek bridge.

TJ 68.2 (109.8 km) **E 92.1** (148.2 km) BLM Chicken field station; information and emergency communications. Trailhead for Mosquito Fork Dredge trail (3 miles/4.8 km round-trip). *NOTE: Watch for potholes and soft spots.*

TJ 68.9 (110.9 km) **E 91.4** (147.1 km) Lost Chicken Creek. Site of Lost Chicken Hill Mine, established in 1895. Mining was under way in this area several years before the Klondike Gold Rush of 1897–98. The first major placer gold strike was in 1886 at Franklin Gulch, a tributary of the Fortymile. Hydraulic mining operations in the creek.

TJ 70 (112.7 km) **E 90.3** (145.3 km) *CAUTION: Road narrows, road surface deteriorates northbound. Watch for hairpin curves.*

TJ 72 (115.9 km) **E 88.3** (142.1 km) *NOTE: Slow for steep descent northbound as road switchbacks down to South Fork.* Good views northbound of South Fork Fortymile River.

TJ 74.4 (119.7 km) **E 85.9** (138.2 km) South Fork River access.

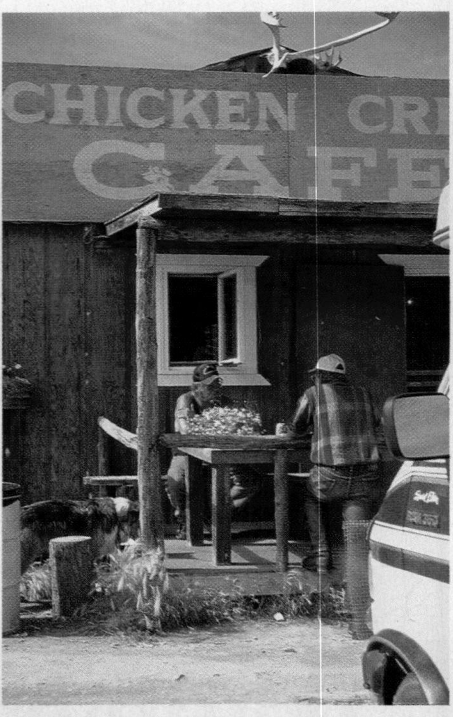

Taylor Highway travelers take a break in Chicken.

(© Kris Graef, staff)

TJ 74.5 (119.9 km) **E 85.8** (138.1 km) South Fork DOT/PF state highway maintenance station.

TJ 75.3 (121.2 km) **E 85** (136.8 km) South Fork Fortymile River bridge. **BLM South Fork River Access** to west at south end of bridge; day-use area with outhouse and garbarge container. Access point for the Fortymile River National Wild and Scenic River system.

The muddy, bumpy road leading into the brush is used by miners.

TJ 76.8 (123.6 km) **E 83.5** (134.4 km) Turnout to west. View of oxbow lakes in South Fork valley.

TJ 77.2 (124.2 km) **E 83.1** (133.7 km) *CAUTION: Slow for sharp turns and watch for rough road northbound.*

TJ 78.5 (126.3 km) **E 81.8** (131.6 km) Views of Fortymile River valley to west northbound between **Mileposts TJ 78** and **82.**

TJ 78.8 (126.8 km) **E 81.5** (131.2 km) Steep descent northbound.

TJ 81.9 (131.8 km) **E 78.4** (126.2 km) Walker Fork bridge.

TJ 82.1 (132.1 km) **E 78.2** (125.8 km) **Walker Fork BLM Campground** to west; 21

level sites on loop road with tables, garbage container, outhouses; $8 camping fee. Picnic area. Old road grader on display at campground entrance. ▲

TJ 86.1 (138.6 km) **E 74.2** (119.4 km) Old **Jack Wade No. 1 dredge** in creek next to

road. Turnout to east. This is actually the Butte Creek Dredge, installed in 1934 below the mouth of Butte Creek and eventually moved to Wade Creek. This was one of the first bucketline dredges used in the area, according to the BLM.

TJ 88.3 (142.1 km) **E 72** (115.9 km) Mining claims and active mining under way next 4 miles northbound. *Do not trespass on mining claims.*

NOTE: Road width varies from here to Eagle. Large vehicles use turnouts when meeting oncoming vehicles.

TJ 90 (144.8 km) **E 70.3** (113.1 km) Jack Wade, an old mining camp that operated until 1940, to west.

TJ 91.9 (147.9 km) **E 68.4** (110.1 km) Rough turnout to east; primitive campsite by stream.

TJ 93 (149.7 km) **E 67.3** (108.3 km) *Slow down for hairpin curves Steep climb northbound as highway ascends Jack Wade Hill.*

TJ 94.1 (151.4 km) **E 66.2** (106.5 km) Turnout to west.

TJ 95.7 (154 km) **E 64.6** (104 km) **Jack Wade Junction**. Northbound travelers turn left (north) for Eagle; keep right for Canadian border to east. *CAUTION: Watch for oncoming traffic when turning here.*

Junction with the Top of the World Highway (Yukon Highway 9) east to Boundary Lodge, the Alaska–Canada border and Dawson City, YT (78.8 miles/126.8 km). Turn to the end of the KLONDIKE LOOP section on page 262 and read the Top of the World Highway log back to front.

TJ 96.2 (154.8 km) **E 64.1** (103.2 km) Large turnout to west. Fireweed displays. Lupine and chiming bells bloom in June. Views northbound of Canada's Ogilvie Mountains in the distance to the north-northeast.

TJ 99.5 (160.1 km) **E 60.8** (97.8 km) Road winds around the summit of Steele Creek Dome (elev. 4,015 feet/1,224m) visible directly above the road to the east. *CAUTION: Rough road, slippery when wet.*

TJ 105.5 (169.8 km) **E 54.8** (88.2 km) Turnout to east. Scenic views of mountains on horizon as road descends next 7 miles northbound to the valley of the Fortymile River, so named because its mouth was 40 miles below Fort Reliance, an old trading post near the confluence of the Yukon and Klondike rivers.

TJ 108 (173.8 km) **E 52.3** (84.2 km) *CAUTION: Steep, narrow, winding road northbound. Slippery when wet. Slow down for hairpin curves.*

Frequent small turnouts and breathtaking views to north and west. Watch for arctic poppies and lupine along the highway in June.

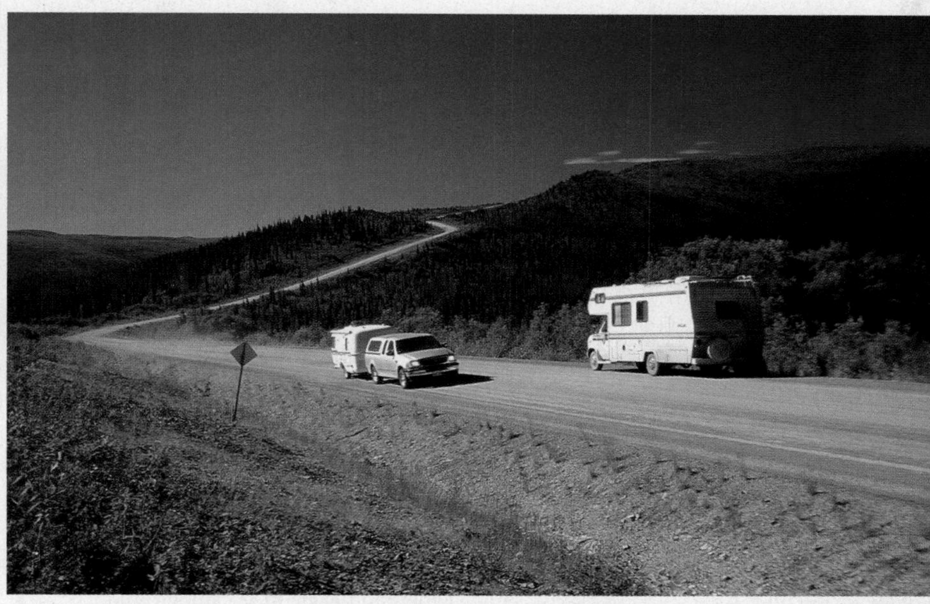

Taylor Highway becomes part of Top of the World route at Jack Wade Junction.
(© Earl L. Brown, staff)

TJ 112.5 (181 km) **E 47.8** (76.9 km) Fortymile River bridge; parking area at south end of bridge, toilet, canoe launch, trash cans. No camping. Active mining in area. Nearly vertical beds of white marble can be seen on the northeast side of the river. Access to the Fortymile River National Wild and Scenic River system.

TJ 113.1 (182 km) **E 47.2** (76 km) O'Brien Creek DOT/PF state highway maintenance camp located here.

TJ 113.2 (182.2 km) **E 47.1** (75.8 km) O'Brien Creek bridge.

CAUTION: Watch for small aircraft using road as runway.

TJ 113.3 (182.3 km) **E 47** (75.6 km) Sign and flags mark entrance to Lary and June Taylor's residence; riverboat tours.

TJ 114.4 (184.1 km) **E 45.9** (73.9 km) *Road narrows to 1-lane northbound.* Slide area: Watch for falling rock next 1.5 miles/2.4 km northbound. Highway parallels O'Brien Creek to Liberty Fork; several turnouts.

TJ 117.2 (188.6 km) **E 43.1** (69.4 km) Alder Creek bridge.

TJ 119.2 (191.8 km) **E 41.1** (66.1 km) "Slide area" sign, watch for rocks northbound.

TJ 119.7 (192.6 km) **E 40.6** (65.3 km) "End slide area" sign northbound. Turnout to east.

TJ 121.1 (194.9 km) **E 39.2** (63.1 km) Large turnout at gravel pit to west.

TJ 122.4 (197 km) **E 37.9** (61 km) *CAUTION: Slow down for hairpin curves northbound.*

TJ 123.2 (198.3 km) **E 37.1** (59.7 km) Turnout to east.

TJ 124.6 (200.5 km) **E 35.7** (57.5 km) Columbia Creek bridge.

TJ 125.4 (201.8 km) **E 34.9** (56.2 km) O'Brien Creek Lodge; cafe, gas.

TJ 130.5 (208.8 km) **E 29.8** (47.7 km) Turnout to east.

Tj 131.5 (211.6 km) **E 28.8** (46.3 km) Turnout. Federal subsistence land boundary.

TJ 131.6 (211.8 km) **E 28.7** (46.2 km) King Solomon Creek bridge. (The creek has a tributary named Queen of Sheba.) Private homestead to east at north end of bridge.

TJ 134.6 (216.6 km) **E 25.7** (41.3 km) Turnout to west.

TJ 135.8 (218.5 km) **E 24.5** (39.4 km) North Fork Solomon Creek bridge. *Road narrows northbound.*

TJ 141 (226.9 km) **E 19.3** (31.1 km) Glacier Mountain management area; walk-in hunting only. Top of the world views to west.

TJ 142.6 (229.5 km) **E 17.7** (28.5 km) **American Summit.** Snack shop, gifts, crafts and liquor store.

American Summit Gifts & Crafts. See display ad this section.

TJ 143.2 (230.5 km) **E 17.1** (27.5 km) Turnout on American Summit. Top of the world views. Road begins winding descent northbound to Yukon River.

TJ 148 (236.8 km) **E 12.3** (19.7 km) Two small turnouts.

TJ 149.1 (239.9 km) **E 11.2** (18 km) Bridge over Discovery Fork Creek.

TJ 150.7 (242.5 km) **E 9.6** (15.4 km) Old cabin by creek to west is a local landmark.

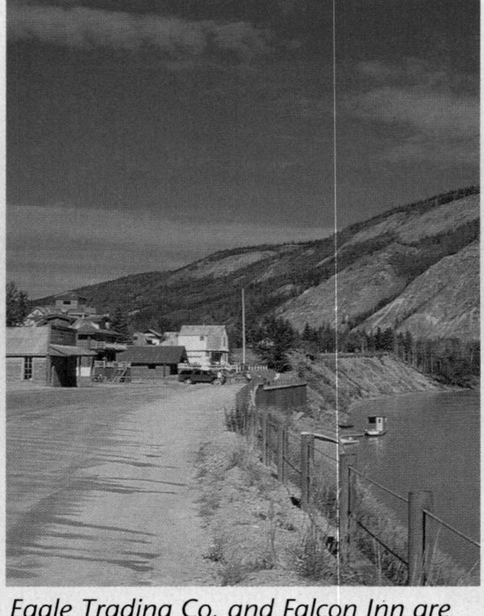

Eagle Trading Co. and Falcon Inn are located on Front Street.

(© Kris Graef, staff)

Private property.

TJ 151.8 (244.3 km) **E 8.5** (13.7 km) American Fork Creek bridge No. 1. Turnout to east at north end of bridge. Narrow winding road through American Creek Canyon. Outcroppings of asbestos, greenish or gray with white, and serpentine along roadcut. Doyon Ltd. claims ownership of surface and mineral estates on these lands; do not trespass.

TJ 152.5 (245.4 km) **E 7.8** (12.6 km) Bridge No. 2 over American Creek. Turnout to west at north end of bridge.

TJ 153.2 (246.5 km) **E 7.1** (11.4 km) Small turnout. Springwater piped to road.

TJ 153.6 (247.2 km) **E 6.7** (10.8 km) Small turnout. Springwater piped to road.

TJ 156.3 (251.5 km) **E 4** (6.4 km) *Slow for rough road.*

TJ 159.3 (256.4 km) **E 1** (1.6 km) Telegraph Hill Services; gas and tire repair. Telegraph Hill is visible from the road.

TJ 159.4 (256.5 km) **E 0.9** (1.4 km) Access to Eagle BLM campground.

TJ 159.7 (257 km) **E 0.6** (1 km) Historical sign about the settlement of Eagle.

TJ 160.3 (258 km) **E 0** Taylor Highway becomes Amundsen Avenue as it enters Eagle (description follows). Eagle school to east. Turn west on 4th Avenue for Fort Egbert and Eagle BLM campground. ▲

Eagle

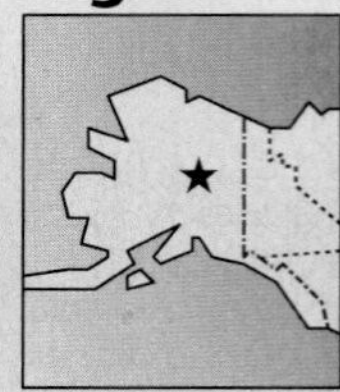

Population: 152. **Emergency Services:** Eagle EMS/Ambulance, phone (907) 547-2256; Eagle Village Health Clinic, phone (907) 547-2243. **Visitor Information:** Contact the Eagle Historical Society and Museums, Box 23, Eagle, AK 99738; phone 907/547-2325; fax 907/547-2232; e-mail ehsmuseums@aol.com.

The National Park Service office, headquarters for Yukon–Charley Rivers National Preserve, is located along the Yukon River at the end of the grass airstrip. The National Park Service Visitor Center has a reference library and maps and books for sale. Also a video on the preserve is shown on request. Informal talks and interpretive programs available. Visitor center hours are 8 A.M. to 5 P.M. daily in summer (Memorial Day weekend through Labor Day weekend). Write Box 167, Eagle, AK 99738, or phone (907) 547-2233.

Elevation: 820 feet/250m. **Climate:** Mean monthly temperature in July 59°F/15°C; in January -13°F/-25°C. Record low -71°F/-57°C in January 1952; record high 95°F/35°C in July 1925. July also has the greatest mean number of days (21) with temperatures above 70°F/21°C. Mean precipitation in July, 1.94 inches; in December, 10.1 inches. Record snow depth 42 inches in April 1948.

Transportation: By road via the Taylor Highway (closed by snow October to April);

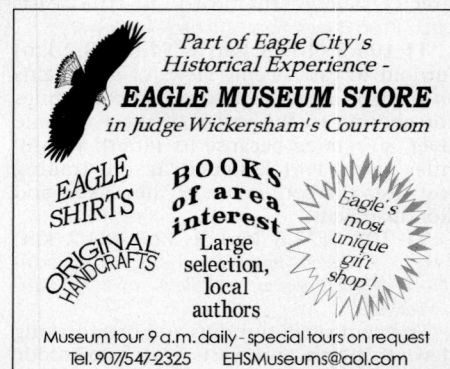

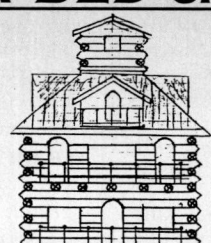

air taxi, scheduled air service; dog team and snow machine in winter. Eagle is also accessible via the Yukon River. U.S. customs available for persons entering Alaska via the Yukon River or by air.

Private Aircraft: Eagle airstrip, 1.2 miles east on First Avenue, then 0.3 miles on airport access road; elev. 880 feet; length 4,500 feet; gravel; unattended. Floatplanes land on the Yukon River.

Visitor services in Eagle include 2 gas stations, a cafe, grocery store, gift shops, museum store, post office, shower, laundromat and mechanic shop with tire repair. Overnight accommodations at the motel, rental cabins and bed and breakfast. Camping at Eagle BLM campground just outside town (take 4th Avenue to Fort Egbert and follow signs). The BLM campground has 13 sites, outhouses, water, campground host, $8 camping fee. ▲

This small community was once the supply and transportation center for miners working the upper Yukon and its tributaries. Francois Mercier established his Belle Isle trading post here in 1874. Eagle City was founded in 1897 and became the commercial, military and judicial center for the Upper Yukon. By 1898, Eagle's population was 1,700.

Fort Egbert was established in 1899 adjacent to the city, and became a key communications center for Alaska when the 1,506-mile-long Washington-Alaska Military Cable and Telelgraph System (WAMCATS) was completed in June 1903.

On July 15, 1900, Judge James Wickersham arrived to establish the first federal court in the Interior of Alaska. In 1901, Eagle became the first incorporated city in the Interior of Alaska. But by 1910, the population had dwindled to 178, as gold strikes in Fairbanks and Nome lured away many of Eagle's residents. With the conversion of telegraph communication to the wireless, the U.S. Army left Fort Egbert in 1911.

Eagle is perched on the south bank of the Yukon River below Eagle Bluff (elev. 1000 feet/305m). It remains relatively untouched, with many of the town's original structures still standing.

EAGLE VILLAGE (pop. 32) a traditional Han Kutchin Indian settlement, is located 3 miles east of Eagle (follow First Avenue out of town) overlooking the Yukon River. Some village residents have relocated to housing near the road end at Mile 7.8 due to erosion and seasonal flooding on the Yukon River. There are no visitor facilities at Eagle Village.

Daily walking tours of downtown Eagle historic sites are offered by the historical society from Memorial Day through mid-September; fee charged. Special tours may be arranged. For more information, contact the Eagle Historical Society and Museums, Box 23, Eagle 99738; phone (907) 547-2325; fax (907) 547-2232.

Two of Eagle's best known sites are the **Wickersham Courthouse**, built in 1901 for Judge James Wickersham, and the windmill and wellhouse (hand-dug in 1903). The well still provides water for over half the town's population. Other original structures include the church (1901), the Waterfront Customs House (1900), and the schoolhouse (1903).

Fort Egbert, which celebrated its centennial in 1999, is comprised of 5 original structures which were stabilized and restored by the BLM between 1974 and 1979. The BLM and Eagle Historical Society and Museums manage the Fort Egbert National Historic Landmark, which includes the Quartermaster Storehouse (1899), the Mule Barn (1900), the Water Wagon Shed, the Granary (1903), and the NCO quarters (1900). The Granary has an interpretive exhibit and photo display showing the stages of reconstruction.

View of Eagle from boat landing on the Yukon River. (© Kris Graef, staff)

Historically an important riverboat landing, Eagle is still a popular jumping-off point for Yukon River travelers. Breakup on the Yukon is in May; freezeup in October. Most popular is a summer float trip from Eagle downriver through the **Yukon-Charley Rivers National Preserve** to Circle. Length of the Eagle–Circle trip is 154 river miles/248 km, with most trips averaging 5 to 10 days. Float trips may also be made from Dawson City, YT, to Circle (252 miles/406 km, 7 to 10 days) with a halfway stop at Eagle. Boaters also often float the Fortymile River to the Yukon River, then continue to the boat landing at Eagle to take out. For details on weather, gear and precautions, contact the National Park Service, Box 167, Eagle 99738; phone (907) 547-2233.

Commercial boat trips are also available on the Yukon. The *Yukon Queen* makes round trips daily between Eagle and Dawson City, YT.

Eagle Canoe Rentals. Canoe and raft rentals on the Yukon River between Dawson City, Yukon Territory; Eagle City, Alaska; and Circle City. Brochures available, or call for details. From April to October: Dawson City River Hostel, Dieter Reinmuth, Box 32, Dawson City, YT Y0B 1G0, (867) 993-6823; or Eagle Canoe Rentals, Mike Sager, Box 4, Eagle, AK 99738; phone/fax (907) 547-2203. [ADVERTISEMENT]

Special events in Eagle include a Memorial Day Service and an old-fashioned 4th of July celebration

GLENN HIGHWAY/TOK CUTOFF ① ④

Connects: Tok to Anchorage, AK **Length:** 328 miles
Road Surface: Paved **Season:** Open all year
Highest Summit: Eureka Summit 3,322 feet
Major Attractions: Matanuska Glacier, Palmer State Fair

(See maps, pages 271-272)

	Anchorage	Glennallen	Palmer	Tok	Valdez
Anchorage		189	42	328	304
Glennallen	189		147	139	115
Palmer	42	147		286	262
Tok	328	139	286		254
Valdez	304	115	262	254	

View down the Glenn Highway of Mount Drum. (© Rich Reid, Colors of Nature)

The Glenn Highway/Tok Cutoff (Alaska Route 1) is the principal access route from the Alaska Highway west to Anchorage, a distance of 328 miles/527.8 km. This route includes the 125-mile/201-km Tok Cutoff, between Tok and the Richardson Highway junction; a 14-mile/22.5-km link via the Richardson Highway; and the 189-mile/304-km Glenn Highway, between the Richardson Highway and Anchorage.

It is a full day's drive between Tok and Anchorage on this paved all-weather highway. There is some spectacular scenery along the Glenn Highway with mountain peaks to the north and south. Road conditions are generally good. The highway between Tok and Glennallen has a few very narrow sections with no shoulders. There is also winding road without shoulders between Matanuska Glacier and Palmer. Watch for frost heaves and pavement breaks along the entire highway. Slow down at signs saying Bump—they mean it!

Four major side roads are logged in this section: the Nabesna Road, which also provides access to Wrangell–St. Elias National Park and Preserve; Lake Louise Road to Lake Louise Recreation Area; the Hatcher Pass Road, connecting the Glenn and Parks highways to Independence Mine State Historical Park; and the Old Glenn Highway, an alternate route between Palmer and Anchorage.

Emergency medical services: Between Tok and Duffy's Roadhouse at **Milepost GJ 63**, phone the Alaska State Troopers at 911 or (907) 883-5111. Between Duffy's and Gakona Junction, phone the Copper River EMS at Glennallen at (907) 822-3203 or 911. From Gakona Junction to Anchorage phone 911. CB channel 9 between **Milepost A 30.8** and Anchorage.

Tok Cutoff Log

Distance from Gakona Junction (GJ) is followed by distance from Anchorage (A) and distance from Tok (T).
*Physical mileposts read from **Milepost 125** at Tok to **Milepost 0** at Gakona Junction, the north junction with the Richardson Highway.*

ALASKA ROUTE 1

GJ 125 (201.2 km) **A 328** (527.8 km) **T 0 TOK.**

Junction of the Glenn Highway (Alaska Route 1) and the Alaska Highway (Alaska Route 2) at Tok. Turn to page 183 in the ALASKA HIGHWAY section for log of the Alaska Highway southeast to the Canadian border or northwest to Delta Junction.

GJ 124.2 (199.9 km) **A 327.2** (526.6 km) **T 0.8** (1.3 km) Tok Community Center.

GLENN HIGHWAY *Tok Cutoff (GJ-125 to GJ-0) to Milepost A 160*

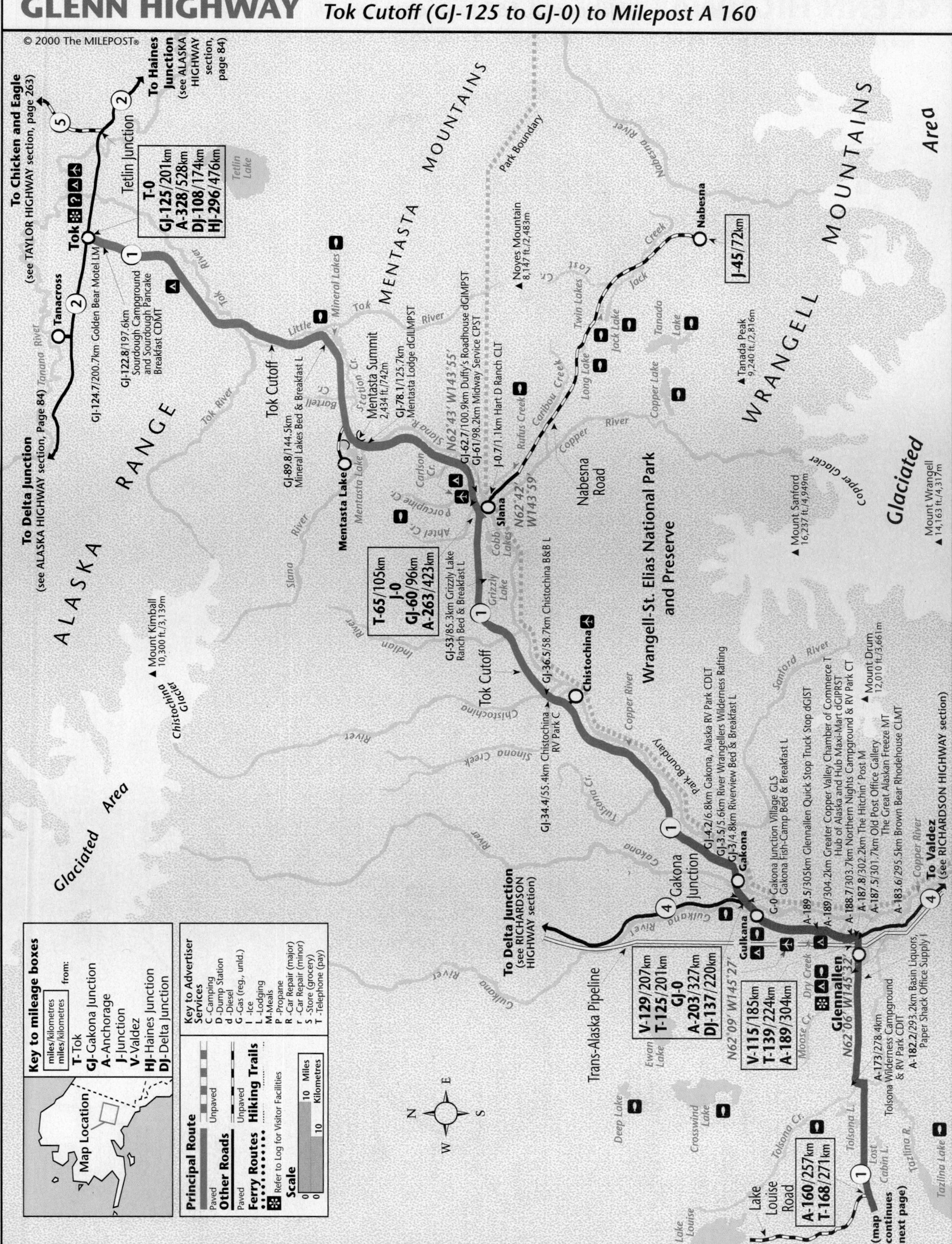

GLENN HIGHWAY *Milepost A 160 to Anchorage, AK*

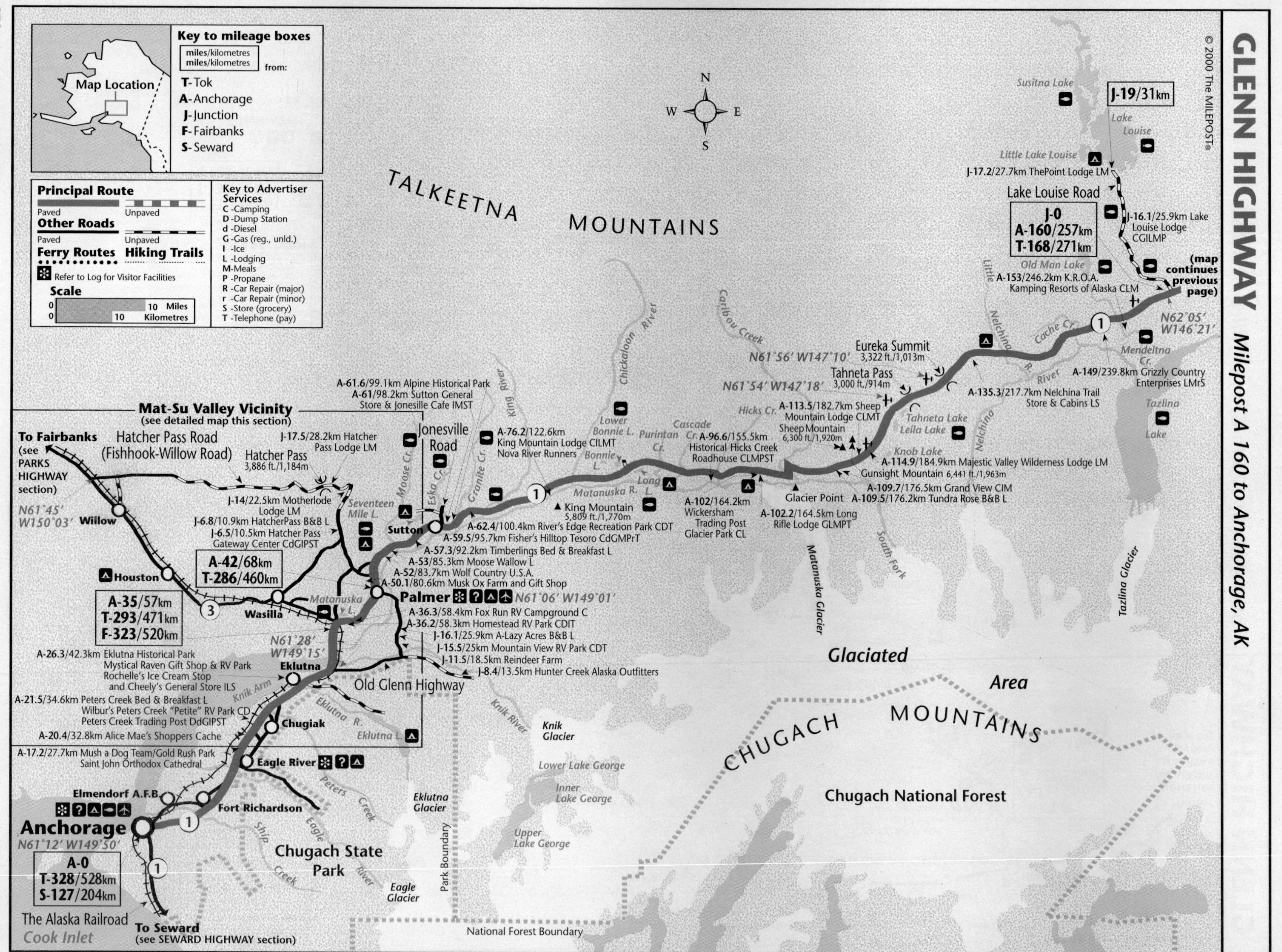

GJ 124.1 (199.7 km) **A 327.1** (526.4 km) **T 0.9** (1.4 km) Tok Community Clinic, Tok Fire Station.

GJ 124 (199.6 km) **A 327** (526.2 km) **T 1** (1.6 km) Dept. of Natural Resources.

GJ 123.9 (199.4 km) **A 326.9** (526.1 km) **T 1.1** (1.8 km) Dept. of Transportation and Public Facilities, Tok Station.

GJ 123.7 (199.1 km) **A 326.7** (525.8 km) **T 1.3** (2.1 km) Borealis Avenue.

CAUTION: Road narrows westbound; no shoulders.

GJ 123.3 (198.4 km) **A 326.3** (525.1 km) **T 1.7** (2.7 km) Trading post to northwest.

GJ 122.8 (197.6 km) **A 325.8** (524.3 km) **T 2.2** (3.5 km) Campground to northwest.

GJ 122.6 (197.3 km) **A 325.6** (524 km) **T 2.4** (3.9 km) Paved bike trail from Tok ends here.

Private Aircraft: Tok airstrip to southeast; elev. 1,670 feet/509m; length 1,700 feet/518m; gravel; unattended. No services. Private airfield across the highway.

GJ 116.7 (187.8 km) **A 319.7** (514.5 km) **T 8.3** (13.4 km) Entering Tok Management Area, **Tanana Valley State Forest**, westbound. Established as the first unit of Alaska's state forest system in 1983, Tanana Valley Sate Forest encompasses 1.81 million acres and lies almost entirely within the Tanana River Basin. The forest extends 265 miles from near the Canadian border to Manley Hot Springs. Almost 90 percent of the state forest is forested. Principal tree species are paper birch, quaking aspen, balsam poplar, black spruce, white spruce and tamarack. Almost 7 percent of the forest is shrubland, chiefly willow. The forest is managed by the Dept. of Natural Resources.

GJ 114 (183.5 km) **A 317** (510.1 km) **T 11** (17.7 km) *CAUTION: Watch for rough, patched pavement in construction areas and frost heaves westbound.*

GJ 110 (177 km) **A 313** (503.7 km) **T 15** (24.1 km) Flashing lights to north are from U.S. Coast Guard loran station at **Milepost DC 1308.5** on the Alaska Highway.

GJ 109.5 (176.2 km) **A 312.5** (502.9 km) **T 15.5** (24.9 km) **Eagle Trail State Recreation Site** to north; 40 campsites, 15-day limit, 4 picnic sites, water, toilets, firepits, pay phone, picnic pavilion, Clearwater Creek. Camping fee $10/night or resident pass. The access road is designed with several loops to aid larger vehicles. Valdez to Eagle Trail (Old Slana Highway and WAMCATS); 1 mile nature rail or 2.5 mile trail to overview of Tok River Valley. ▲

NOTE: Highway widens westbound. Road narrows eastbound; no shoulders.

GJ 104.5 (168.2 km) **A 307.5** (494.9 km) **T 20.5** (33 km) Extra wide shoulders to north for pulling off highway. **Little Tok River** overflow runs under highway in culvert; fishing for grayling and Dolly Varden.

GJ 104 (167.4 km) **A 307** (494 km) **T 21** (33.8 km) Bridge over **Tok River**, side road north to riverbank and boat launch. The Tok River heads at Tok Glacier in the Alaska Range and flows northeast 60 miles to the Tanana River. Tok-bound travelers are in the Tok River Valley, although the river is out of sight to the southeast most of the time.

Good view of the Tok River at Milepost GJ 104. (© Kris Graef, staff)

GJ 103.5 (166.6 km) **A 306.5** (493.3 km) **T 21.5** (34.6 km) Paved turnout to north. **Little Tok River** overflow; fishing for grayling and Dolly Varden.

GJ 102.4 (164.8 km) **A 305.4** (491.5 km) **T 22.6** (36.4 km) Entering Tok Management Area, Tanana Valley State Forest, eastbound. (See **Milepost GJ 116.7**.)

GJ 99.3 (159.8 km) **A 302.3** (486.5 km) **T 25.7** (41.4 km) Rest area; paved double-ended turnout to north. Cranberries may be found in late summer.

GJ 98 (157.7 km) **A 301** (484.4 km) **T 27** (43.5 km) Bridge over **Little Tok River**, which parallels highway. Parking at west end of bridge. The Little Tok River heads at a glacier terminus in the Mentasta Mountains and flows north 32 miles to the Tok River.

GJ 91 (146.4 km) **A 294** (473.1 km) **T 34** (54.7 km) Side road south to **Little Tok River** bridge (weight limit 20 tons); good fishing for grayling, 12 to 14 inches, use small spinner.

GJ 90 (144.8 km) **A 293** (471.5 km) **T 35** (56.3 km) Paved turnout to south.

GJ 89.8 (144.5 km) **A 292.8** (471.2 km) **T 35.2** (56.6 km)

GJ 89.5 (144 km) **A 292.5** (470.7 km) **T 35.5** (57.1 km) **Mineral Lakes.** Watch for moose and birds in ponds to southeast between **Mileposts A 89.5** and **86.** These are sloughs of the Little Tok River and provide both moose habitat and a breeding place for waterfowl. Good fishing for northern pike and grayling.

GJ 89 (143.2 km) **A 292** (469.9 km) **T 36** (57.9 km) Turnout to south.

GJ 85.7 (137.9 km) **A 288.7** (464.6 km) **T 39.3** (63.2 km) Turnout to north.

GJ 83.2 (133.9 km) **A 286.2** (460.6 km) **T 41.8** (67.3 km) Bridge over Bartell Creek. Just beyond is the divide between the drainage of the Tanana River, tributary of the Yukon River system flowing into the Bering Sea, and the Copper River system, emptying into the North Pacific near Cordova.

GJ 81 (130.4 km) **A 284** (457 km) **T 44** (70.8 km) Access road leads north 7 miles/11.3 km to **MENTASTA LAKE** (pop. 125), a primarily Athabascan community, unincorporated.

GJ 79.4 (127.8 km) **A 282.4** (454.5 km) **T 45.6** (73.4 km) **Mentasta Summit** (elev. 2,434 feet/742m). The U.S. Army Signal Corps established a telegraph station here in 1902. The Mentasta Mountains rise to about 6,000 feet on either side of the highway. The 40-mile-long, 25-mile-wide Mentasta Range is bounded on the north by the Alaska Range. Watch for Dall sheep on mountainsides.

Boundary between Game Management Units 12 and 13C and Sportfish Management Units 8 and 2.

GJ 78.1 (125.7 km) **A 281.1** (452.4 km) **T 46.9** (75.5 km) Mentasta Lodge to south with cafe, motel, gas, diesel, laundromat, showers, bar and liquor store.

Mentasta Lodge. See display this section.

GJ 78 (125.5 km) **A 281** (452.2 km) **T 47** (75.6 km) View for westbound traffic of snow-covered Mount Sanford (elev. 16,237 feet/4,949m).

GJ 77.9 (125.4 km) **A 280.9** (452.1 km) **T 47.1** (75.8 km) Paved turnout to north by Slana Slough; salmon spawning area in August. Watch for beavers.

GJ 76.3 (122.8 km) **A 279.3** (449.5 km) **T 48.7** (78.4 km) Bridge over Mable Creek. Mastodon flowers (marsh fleabane) in late July; very large (to 4 feet) with showy seed heads.

GJ 76 (122.3 km) **A 279** (449 km) **T 49** (78.8 km) Bridge over Slana Slough.

GJ 75.6 (121.7 km) **A 278.6** (448.3 km) **T 49.4** (79.5 km) Bridge over **Slana River**. This river flows from its source glaciers some 55 miles/88.5 km to the Copper River.

Parking area with outhouse to south at west end of bridge.

GJ 74 (119.1 km) **A 277** (445.8 km) **T 51** (82.1 km) Large scenic viewpoint to south overlooking Slana River.

GJ 68 (109.4 km) **A 271** (436.1 km) **T 57** (91.7 km) Carlson Creek bridge.

Good views of Mount Sanford westbound.

GJ 65.5 (105.4 km) **A 268.5** (432.1 km) **T 59.5** (95.8 km) Paved turnout to south by mail boxes has magnificent views (weather permitting) of the Wrangell mountains. Dominant peak is **Mount Sanford**, elev. 16,237 feet/4,949m.

GJ 64.2 (103.3 km) **A 267.2** (430 km) **T 60.8** (97.8 km) Sharp turn to north at east end of Porcupine Creek bridge for

Porcupine Creek State Recreation Site 0.2 mile/0.3 km from highway; 12 forested campsites on loop road, 15-day limit, $10 nightly fee or resident pass, water pump, firepits, outhouses, picnic tables and fishing. Hiking trails up Porcupine Creek to Carlson Lake and Bear Valley (trails are poorly marked, carry topo map). Wood and charcoal available from concessionaire at Hart D Ranch, Mile 0.7 Nabesna Road. Lowbush cranberries in fall. *CAUTION: Watch for bears.*

Bridge over Porcupine Creek.

GJ 63 (101.4 km) **A 266** (428 km) **T 62** (99.8 km) Scenic viewpoint with view of Wrangell Mountains. The dominant peak to the southwest is Mount Sanford, a dormant volcano; the pinnacles of Capital Mountain can be seen against its lower slopes. Mount Jarvis (elev. 13,421 feet/4,091m) is visible to the south behind Mount Sanford; Tanada Peak (elev. 9,240 feet/2,816m) is more to the south. (Tanada Peak is sometimes mistaken for Noyes Mountain.)

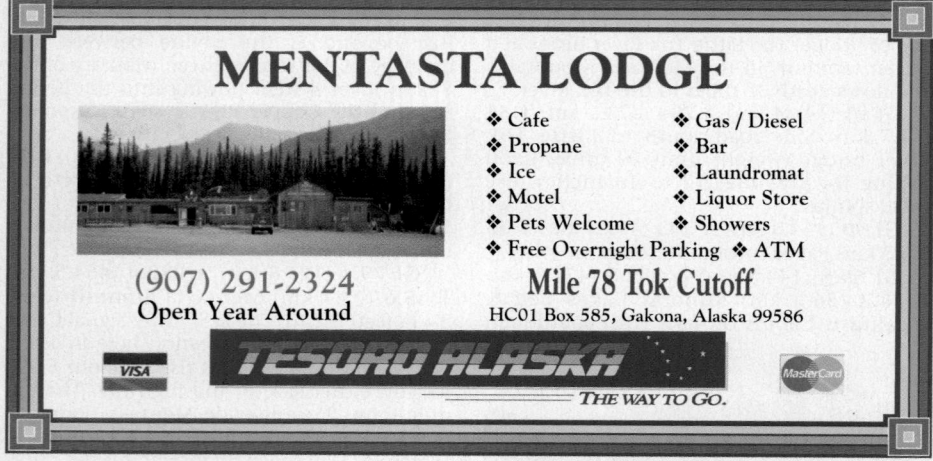

Walk up the gravel hill to view Noyes Mountain (elev. 8,147 feet/2,483m), named for U.S. Army Brig. Gen. John Rutherford Noyes, a one-time commissioner of roads in the territory of Alaska. Appointed adjutant general of the Alaska National Guard in 1953, he died in 1956 from injuries and frostbite after his plane crashed near Nome.

GJ 62.7 (100.9 km) **A 265.7** (427.6 km) **T 62.3** (100.3 km) Duffy's Roadhouse to southeast; food, gas, diesel, propane, groceries, gif shop. Open daily year-round.

Duffy's Roadhouse. See display ad this section.

GJ 61.8 (99.4 km) **A 264.8** (426.1 km) **T 63.2** (101.7 km) *NOTE: 7 percent downhill grade westbound.*

GJ 61 (98.2 km) **A 264** (424.9 km) **T 64** (103 km) Midway Service to northwest; grocery store, fishing and hunting licenses, showers, laundromat and campground.

Midway Service. See display ad this section.

NOTE: 7 percent uphill grade eastbound.

GJ 60.8 (97.8 km) **A 263.8** (424.6 km) **T 64.2** (103.3 km) Bridge over **Ahtell Creek**; grayling. Parking area to north at east end of bridge. This stream drains a mountain area of igneous rock, where several gold and silver-lead claims are located.

GJ 59.8 (96.2 km) **A 262.8** (422.9 km) **T 65.2** (104.9 km) Gas, post office and services south on Nabesna Road.

Junction with Nabesna Road. See NABESNA ROAD log facing page.

GJ 59.4 (95.6 km) **A 262.4** (422.3 km) **T 65.6** (105.6 km) Distance marker westbound shows Glennallen 76 miles; Valdez

Nabesna Road Log

Nabesna Road leads 45 miles/72.4 km southeast from **Milepost GJ 59.8** on the Tok Cutoff to the old Nabesna Mine. The road crosses the northwest corner of Wrangell–St. Elias National Park and Preserve. Stop at the ranger station at **Milepost J 0.2** for current road conditions and information on backcountry travel in the park.

There are no formal public campgrounds on this side road, but there are plenty of spots to camp and a private campground at Mile 0.7. The area offers good fishing and several hiking trails. Horses are permitted on all trails. Off-road vehicles must have permits from the National Park Service.

The first 4 miles of road are paved. The remainder is gravel, in fair condition to **Milepost J 30.6** (Lost Creek crossing) in summer 1999. Beyond the road becomes rough and crosses several creeks which may be difficult to ford. Vehicles are not recommended beyond Mile 42, where state road maintainence ends.

Distance is measured from the junction with the Tok Cutoff (J).

J 0 Junction with the Tok Cutoff.

J 0.2 (0.3 km) Turnoff to right southbound for access to state DOT station and Slana NPS ranger station. Information on road conditions and on Wrangell–St. Elias National Park and Preserve at ranger station; open 8 A.M. to 5 P.M. daily, June 1 through September. USGS maps and natural history books for sale. Phone (907) 882-5238.

J 0.7 (1.1 km) Slana post office and Hart D Ranch complex. The picturesque ranch is the home and studio of sculptor Mary Frances DeHart. The ranch offers RV and tent camping, an art gallery, bed and breakfast accommodations, pay phone and dog kennels (DeHart raises Affenpincscher dogs).

Hart D Ranch. See display ad this section.

J 1 (1.6 km) Slana elementary school. **SLANA** (pop. 55; unincorporated), once an Indian village on the north bank of the Slana River, now refers to this general area, much of which was homesteaded in the 1980s. Besides the Indian settlement, Slana boasted a popular roadhouse, now a private home.

J 1.5 (2.4 km) Slana River Bridge; undeveloped camping area. Boundary between Game Management Units 11 and 13C.

J 3.8 (6.1 km) Entering Wrangell–St. Elias National Park and Preserve.

J 4 (6.4 km) Four Mile Road. Hostel: Huck Hobbit's Homestead Retreat & Campground.

Pavement ends, gravel begins, southbound.

J 7 (11.3 km) Road crosses **Rufus Creek** culvert. Private homes. Fishing in creek for Dolly Varden to 8 inches, June to October. Watch for bears, especially during berry season.

J 11.1 (17.8 km) Gravel pit parking area to west. Walk back to Suslota Lake trailhead on east side of road.

J 12.1 (19.5 km) Turnout to east; picnic table, primitive campsite. **Copper Lake** trailhead; fishing for lake trout, grayling and burbot.

J 16.5 (26.5 km) Primitive campsite with picnic table to west.

Beautiful views of Kettle Lake, Mount Sanford, Capital Mountain, Mount Wrangell, Mount Zanetti and Tanada Peak in the Wrangell Mountains to the southwest.

J 17.7 (28.5 km) **Dead Dog Hill** rest area; picnic table, outhouse, garbage container. Camping. View of Noyes Mountain (elev. 8,235 feet) in the highly mineralized Mentasta Mountains to the north.

J 18.3 (29.4 km) Caribou Creek culvert.

J 18.5 (29.8 km) Milepost 19.

J 18.8 (30.2 km) Gravel pit parking area to east.

J 19.1 (30.7 km) Caribou Creek trailhead, multi-use trail first 3 miles. Park at **Milepost J 18.8.**

J 19.7 (31.7 km) Parking areas both sides of road.

J 20.5 (33 km) Milepost 21.

J 20.6 (33.2 km) Parking area.

J 21.7 (34.9 km) Rock Lake rest area; picnic table, outhouse, garbage container. Camping.

J 22.7 (36.5 km) **Long Lake**; grayling fishing.

J 23.7 (38.1 km) Turnout.

J 23.9 (38.5 km) **Tanada Lake** trailhead; parking to west. Multi-use trail. Fishing for grayling and lake trout.

J 24.6 (39.6 km) Watershed divide (elev. 3,320 feet) between streams draining into the Copper River watershed and into the Gulf of Alaska, and those entering the Yukon River watershed which drains into the Bering Sea. Boundary between Sportfish Areas C and K, and Game Management Areas 11 and 12.

J 24.8 (39.9 km) Lodge. Glimpse of Tanada Lake beneath Tanada Peak to the south.

J 25.2 (40.5 km) Little Jack Creek.

J 27.5 (44.3 km) Turnout.

J 27.6 (44.4 km) Horse crossing.

J 27.7 (44.6 km) **Twin Lakes** rest area; picnic table, outhouse, garbage container, camping. Good place to observe waterfowl. Fishing for grayling 10 to 18 inches, mid-May to October, flies or small spinner; also burbot and lake trout. Wildflowers in June include Lapland rosebay, lupine and 8-petalled mountain avens.

J 27.9 (44.9 km) Sportsmen Paradise Lodge.

J 28.9 (46.5 km) Trail Creek crossing and trailhead. Changing water levels may require high clearance or 4-wheel-drive vehicle.

J 30.6 (49.2 km) Lost Creek crossing, a very wide expanse of water in spring; may remain difficult to cross well into summer.

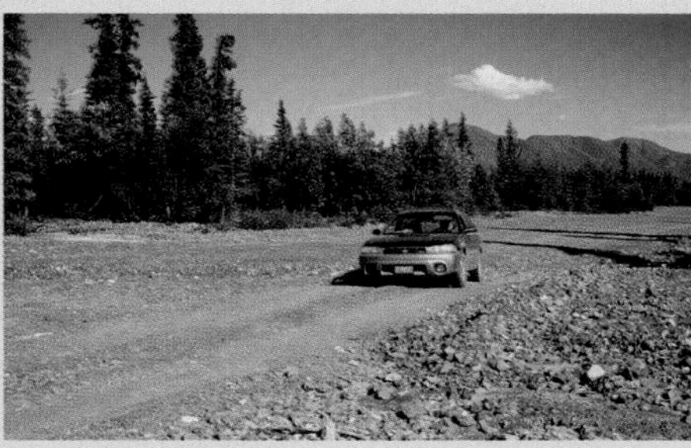

The road deteriorates beyond this point and you may have to ford several more creeks beyond here. Inquire at lodge here or Slana Ranger Station about road conditions.

J 31 (49.9 km) Lost Creek Trailhead, a multi-use trail with access to Big Grayling Lake, Soda Creek, Platinum Creek, Mineral Springs and Soda Lake.

J 34.3 (55.2 km) Boyden Creek crossing.

J 35.3 (56.8 km) **Jack Creek** bridge and rest area; picnic tables, outhouse, garbage container, camping. Grayling fishing.

J 36.2 (58.2 km) Skookum Volcano trailhead.

J 40.2 (64.7 km) Nabesna River trailhead. A marked trail, approximately 5 miles/8 km long, leads to Nabesna River and old Reeves Field airstrip, once used to fly gold out of and supplies in to mining camps. View of Devil's Mountain to the east.

J 42 (67.6 km) State-maintained road ends. Hiking only recommended beyond this point. Lodge (private property) charges for parking here.

J 45 (72.4 km) **NABESNA** (area pop. less than 25; elev. 3,000 feet). No visitor services. Nasbena Mine operated here from 1923 until the late 1940s, mining primarily for gold as well as other minerals. This region has copper reserves, as well as silver, molybdenum and iron ore deposits. Tailings deposits here are closed to the public.

Return to Milepost GJ 59.8 Tok Cutoff

Flagger directs traffic around bridge repair site on the Tok Cutoff. (© Kris Graef, staff)

189 miles; Anchorage 263 miles.

GJ 59 (94.9 km) **A 262** (421.6 km) **T 66** (106.2 km) *SIGN: $1,000 fine for littering.*

GJ 58.6 (94.3 km) **A 261.6** (421 km) **T 66.4** (106.9 km) Ahtell Creek trailhead.

NOTE: Hill; 6 percent downgrade eastbound.

GJ 56.5 (90.9 km) **A 259.5** (417.6 km) **T 68.5** (110.2 km) Narrow double-ended turnout to south is a scenic viewpoint overlooking Cobb Lakes. View of Tanada Peak, Mount Sanford, Mount Blackburn and Mount Drum to the south and southwest. The Mentasta Mountains are to the east.

Gold Rush Centennial sign on Lieutenant Henry T. Allen, who led one of America's epic journeys of exploration in 1885. In 5 months, his expedition crossed 1,500 miles of largely unexplored territory including this valley. Ordered to investigate the unmapped Copper and Tanana river valleys, Allen started up the Copper River in March 1885 and passed this point 2 months later, reaching the headwaters of the Copper River and entering the Tanana Valley. Allen descended the Tanana River and trekked from the Yukon to the headwaters of the Koyukuk River.

GJ 55.2 (88.8 km) **A 258.2** (415.5 km) **T 69.8** (112.3 km) Tanada Peak viewpoint; gravel turnout to south.

CAUTION: Watch for horses on road.

GJ 53 (85.3 km) **A 256** (412 km) **T 72** (115.9 km) Grizzly Lake; lodging, camping, trail rides.

Grizzly Lake Ranch Bed & Breakfast. See display ad this section. ▲

GJ 47 (75.6 km) **A 250** (402.3 km) **T 78** (125.5 km) Indian Creek trailhead to north.

GJ 44.6 (71.8 km) **A 247.6** (398.5 km) **T 80.4** (129.4 km) Long doublel-ended parking area to north. Eagle Trail access.

GJ 43.8 (70.5 km) **A 246.8** (397.1 km) **T 81.2** (130.6 km) Bridge over Indian River. This is a salmon spawning stream, usually late-June through July. Turnout to south at west end of bridge.

GJ 39 (62.8 km) **A 242** (389.5 km) **T 86** (138.4 km) Views of the Copper River valley and Wrangell Mountains. Looking south, peak on left is Mount Sanford and on right is Mount Drum (elev. 12,010 feet/3,661m).

GJ 38.8 (62.4 km) **A 241.8** (389.1 km) **T 86.2** (138.7 km) Turnout to northwest.

GJ 38 (61.2 km) **A 241** (387.8 km) **T 87** (140 km) *CAUTION: Road narrows westbound. Road widens eastbound.*

GJ 36.5 (58.7 km) **A 239.5** (385.4 km) **T 88.5** (142.4 km) **Chistochina Bed and Breakfast** is open all year. Located in Interior Alaska, an easy day's drive to Valdez, Anchorage or Haines Junction, Canada. Clean, comfortable rooms available in the main house. Private cabin with kitchen and bath available. Wrangell-St. Elias Park enrance 25 miles. Quiet, rural, scenic location. Doyle and Norma Traw, Mile 36.5 Tok Cutoff, Box 288, Gakona, AK 99586. Phone (907) 822-3989. [ADVERTISEMENT]

GJ 35.5 (57.1 km) **A 238.5** (383.8 km) **T 89.5** (144 km) Chistochina River Bridge No. 2. Mount Sanford is first large mountain to the southeast, then Mount Drum.

GJ 35.4 (57 km) **A 238.4** (383.7 km) **T 89.6** (144.2 km) **Chistochina River** Bridge No. 1; parking at west end. Chistochina River trailhead. This river heads in the Chistochina Glacier on Mount Kimball (elev. 10,300 feet/3,139m) in the Alaska Range and flows south 48 miles to the Copper River, which is just south of the highway here. The Tok Cutoff parallels the Copper River from here southeast to the Richardson Highway. Chistochina is thought to mean marmot creek.

GJ 34.7 (55.8 km) **A 237.7** (382.5 km) **T 90.3** (145.3 km) Sinona Creek Trading Post (closed in 1999; current status unknown).

GJ 34.6 (55.7 km) **A 237.6** (382.4 km) **T 90.4** (145.5 km) Bridge over Sinona Creek. Sinona is said to mean place of the many burls, and there are indeed many burls on area spruce trees.

GJ 34.4 (55.4 km) **A 237.4** (382 km) **T 90.6** (145.8 km) **Chistochina RV Park.** See display ad this section. ▲

GJ 34.1 (54.9 km) **A 237.1** (381.6 km) **T 90.9** (146.3 km) Chistochina ball fields.

GJ 32.9 (52.9 km) **A 235.9** (379.6 km) **T 92.1** (148.2 km) Chistochina school. Road access to **CHISTOCHINA** (pop. 52, unincorporated), a traditional Copper River Athabascan Indian village.

GJ 32.8 (52.8 km) **A 235.8** (379.5 km) **T 92.2** (148.4 km) Chistochina Lodge to southeast, a National Historic Site, burned to the ground in November 1999. Built in the early 1900s, the original roadhouse served foot and sled traffic on the Valdez to Eagle Trail (later the Valdez to Fairbanks Trail). The owners plan to rebuild.

Private Aircraft: Chistochina airstrip, adjacent south; elev. 1,850 feet; length 2,060 feet; turf and gravel; autogas.

GJ 30.3 (48.4 km) **A 233.1** (375.1 km) **T 94.7** (152.4 km) *CAUTION: Road narrows Tok-bound; no shoulders. Road widens for Anchorage-bound motorists.*

GJ 28.1 (45.2 km) **A 231.1** (371.9 km) **T 96.9** (155.9 km) Double-ended paved parking area to south with a marker on the Alaska Road Commission. The ARC was established in 1905, the same year the first automobile arrived in Alaska at Skagway. The ARC operated for 51 years, building roads, airfields, trails and other transportation facilities. It was replaced by the Bureau of Public Roads (referred to by some Alaskans at the time as the Bureau of Parallel Ruts) in 1956. In 1960 the Bureau of Public Roads was replaced by the Dept. of Public Works.

GJ 24 (38.6 km) **A 227** (365.3 km) **T 101**

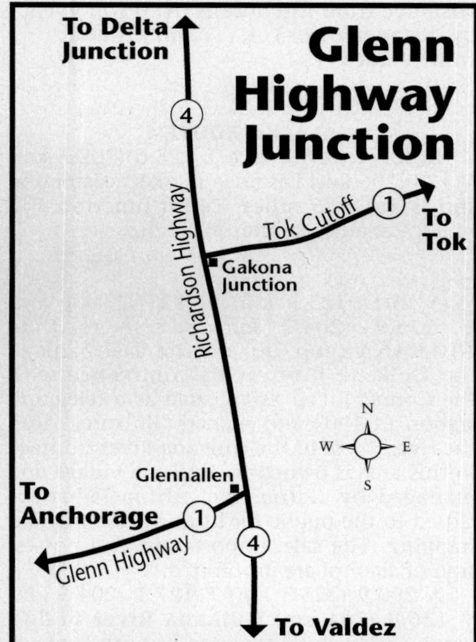

(162.5 km) Large rest area to south with paved double-ended parking area, toilets, picnic tables and firepits. Gold Rush Centennial sign on Discovering Gold on the Chistochina. During the Klondike Gold Rush of 1898, a few stampeders heard of a gold discovery in the upper Copper River and actually found gold in the headwaters of the Chistochina River north of here.

Paths from parking area lead to the **Copper River**. The Copper River heads on the north side of the Wrangell Mountains and flows 250 miles to the Gulf of Alaska. The river parallels Nabesna Road then the Tok Cutoff and finally the Richardson Highway.

View of Mount Sanford is to the southeast, Mount Drum to the south.

GJ 17.5 (28.2 km) **A 220.5** (354.8 km) **T 107.5** (173 km) **Tulsona Creek** bridge. Good grayling fishing.

GJ 12.9 (20.7 km) **T 112.1** (180.4 km) **A 215.9** (347.4 km) Turnout to north.

GJ 11.8 (19 km) **T 113.2** (182.2 km) **A 214.8** (345.7 km) Distance marker westbound shows Glennallen 28 miles, Anchorage 215 miles.

GJ 11.6 (18.7 km) **A 214.6** (345.4 km) **T 113.4** (182.5 km) Yellow pond lily *(Nuphar polysepalum)* in ponds north of highway.

GJ 11.3 (18.2 km) **A 214.3** (344.9 km) **T 113.7** (183 km) **HAARP** (High frequency Active Auroral Research Program) to north of highway. This is a major Dept. of Defense Arctic facility for upper atmospheric and solar-terrestrial research. Principal elements include a high power, high frequency phased array radio transmitter—known as the Ionospheric Research Instrument (IRI)—and an ultra-high frequency incoherent scatter radar (IST). An annual open house is held in August. Approximate coordinates are N62º 23.5′ W145º 8.8′.

GJ 9.4 (15.1 km) **A 212.4** (341.8 km) **T 115.6** (186 km) Fox Lake BLM trailhead.

GJ 8.8 (14.2 km) **A 211.8** (340.8 km) **T 116.2** (187 km) Paved turnout to north. BLM trailhead.

GJ 6.4 (10.3 km) **T 118.6** (190.9 km) **A 209.4** (337 km) Turnout to south.

GJ 6 (9.7 km) **A 209** (336.3 km) **T 119** (191.5 km) View opens up westbound as highway descends to Gakona River.

GJ 4.2 (6.8 km) **A 207.2** (333.4 km) **T 120.8** (194.4 km) **Gakona Alaska R.V. Park.** See display ad this section. ▲

GJ 3.5 (5.6 km) **A 206.5** (332.3 km) **T 121.5** (195.5 km) **River Wrangellers Wilderness Rafting**. See display ad this section.

GJ 3 (4.8 km) **A 206** (331.5 km) **T 122** (196.3 km) **Riverview Bed & Breakfast** to south. See display ad this section.

GJ 2.7 (4.3 km) **A 205.7** (331 km) **T 122.3** (196.8 km) Post office to south serves **GAKONA** (pop. 22). Originally a Native wood and fish camp., and then a permanent village of the Ahtna Indians, Gakona is located at the confluence of the Gakona and Copper rivers. (Gakona is Athabascan for rabbit.) The community has a commercial district, a non-Native residential area, and a Native village.

GJ 2 (3.2 km) **A 205** (330 km) **T 123** (198 km) Gakona Lodge, entered on the National Register of Historic Places in 1977, was built in 1929. It replaced an earlier roadhouse built in 1904 known as Doyle's. Located at the jujnction of the Valdez to Eagle and Valdez to Fairbanks trails, this was an essential stopping point for travelers.

GJ 1.8 (2.9 km) **A 204.8** (329.6 km) **T 123.2** (198.3 km) Bridge over **Gakona River**, which flows 64 miles south from Gakona Glacier in the Alaska Range to join the Copper River here. Fine view of the many channels where the Gakona and Copper rivers join.

Entering Game Management Unit 13B westbound and 13C eastbound.

GJ 1 (1.6 km) **A 204** (328.3 km) **T 124** (200 km) Paved viewpoint to south overlooks the valley of the Gakona and Copper rivers; picnic tables. View of Mount Drum and Mount Sanford. Good photo stop.

Gold Rush Centennial sign about Alaska's first telegraph, known as the Washington-Alaska Military Cable and Telegraph System (WAMCATS), built to assist communication between U.S. Army posts during the Gold Rush. Crews completed the 1,506-mile line in 1903. Although a military line, WAMCATS carried more civilian than military messages, as it assisted commerce and safe travel between gold camps and brought in news of the outside world. By the late 1920s, radio technology made WAMCATS obsolete.

GJ 0 A 203 (326.7 km) **T 125** (201.2 km) **Gakona Junction**; food, gas, lodging, fishing guides. Stop sign westbound at **junction** of Tok Cutoff (Alaska Route 1) and Richardson Highway (Alaska Route 4). The 2 roads share a common alignment for the next 14 miles/22.5 km westbound. Turn north here for Delta Junction. Turn south for Anchorage or Valdez. *NOTE: This junction can be confusing. Choose your route carefully.*

Gakona Junction Village. See display ad on page 278.

Gakona Fish-Camp Bed and Breakfast. Clean, comfortable rooms for budge-minded travelers. Rooms from $59.95 (including breakfast), lowest in Copper Valley. Gakona

Stop 'n Shop, Gakona Texaco and Gulkana Fish Guides, at the same location, provide one-stop shopping for highway visitors. Reservations: Phone (907) 822-3664, toll-free 1-800-462-3221; fax (907) 822-3696; email:gakona@alaska.net. Internet connection: www.alaskaone.com/coppervalley. [ADVERTISEMENT]

Distance marker shows Paxson 56 miles, Delta Junction 137 miles; Fairbanks 235 miles.

Delta Junction-bound travelers turn to **Milepost V 128.6** in the RICHARDSON HIGHWAY section for log of that route.

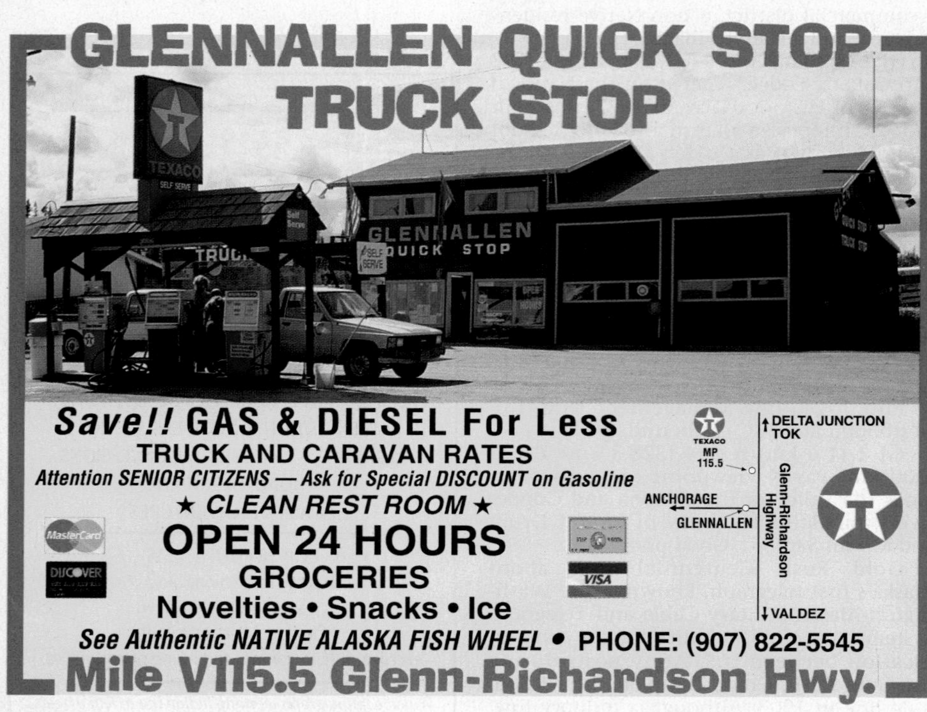

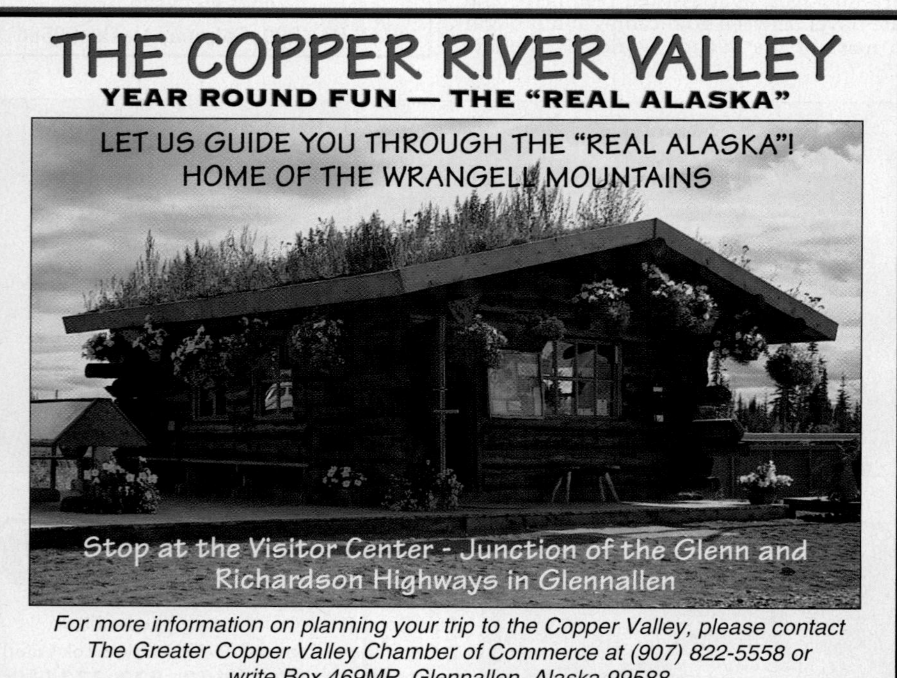

Distance from Anchorage (A) is followed by distance from Tok (T) and distance from Valdez (V).

Physical mileposts for the next 14 miles/22.5 km southbound give distance from Valdez.

ALASKA ROUTE 4

A 202.4 (325.7 km) **T 125.6** (202.1 km) **V 128** (206 km) Distance markers eastbound shows Tok 125 miles; Tetlin Junction 137 miles; Canadian border 210 miles.

CAUTION: Slow down for frost heaves and rough road Anchorage-bound..

A 201 (323.5 km) **T 127** (204.4 km) **V 126.9** (204.2 km) Access road to **GULKANA** (pop. 90) on the east bank of the Gulkana River at its confluence with the Copper River. Established as a telegraph station in 1903 and named "Kulkana" after the river. Most of the Gulkana River frontage in this area is owned by Gulkana village and managed by Ahtna, Inc. Ahtna lands are closed to the public for hunting, fishing and trapping. The sale, importation and possession of alcohol are prohibited.

A 200.9 (323.3 km) **T 127.1** (204.5 km) **V 126.8** (204 km) **Gulkana River** bridge. Large gravel parking areas at both ends of bridge provide access to river. Camping permitted. Grayling fishing and good king and sockeye salmon fishing (June and July). The Gulkana River flows 60 miles from the Gulkana Glacier in the Alaska Range to the Copper River. ▲

Entering Game Management Unit 13B eastbound, 13A westbound.

A 200.3 (322.3 km) **T 127.7** (205.5 km) **V 126.2** (203.1 km) Bear Creek Inn.

A 200.1 (322 km) **T 127.9** (205.8 km) **V 126** (202.8 km) Paved double-ended turnout to west.

A 197.3 (317.5 km) **T 130.7** (210.3 km) **V 123.2** (198.3 km) Large paved turnout to east.

CAUTION: Slow down for frost heaves and rough road Tok-bound.

A 192.1 (309.1 km) **T 135.9** (218.7 km) **V 118.1** (190 km) **Private Aircraft:** Gulkana airstrip; elev. 1,579 feet/481m; length 5,000 feet/1,524m; asphalt; fuel 100LL. Flying service located here.

A 192 (309 km) **T 136** (218.9 km) **V 118** (189.9 km) **Dry Creek State Recreation Site;** 58 campsites, 15-day limit, $10 nightly fee or resident pass, 4 picnic sites, toilets, picnic shelter. Bring mosquito repellent! ▲

A 189.5 (305 km) **T 138.5** (222.9 km) **V 115.5** (185.9 km) **Glennallen Quick Stop Truck Stop.** Stop for friendly family service, gas, diesel, convenience store with ice, pop, snacks, postcards, ice cream, specialty items, pay phone and free coffee. Truck, caravan, senior citizen discounts. Several interesting items on display, including an authentic Native Alaskan fish wheel. Full-service restaurant adjacent. See display ad this section. [ADVERTISEMENT]

A 189 (304.2 km) **T 139** (223.7 km) **V 115** (185.1 km) Greater Copper Valley Chamber of Commerce Visitor Center in log cabin; open 8 A.M. to 7 P.M. daily in summer. There's also a convenience grocery and a gas station (with diesel) at junction.

The Greater Copper Valley Chamber of Commerce. See display ad this section.

The Hub of Alaska and **Hub Maxi-Mart.** See display ad this section.

NOTE: This junction can be confusing. Choose your route carefully. Continue west on the Glenn Highway for Anchorage. Turn south here on the Richardson Highway for Valdez.

Junction of the Richardson Highway (Alaska Route 4) with the Glenn Highway (Alaska Route 1). Turn to **Milepost V 115** in the RICHARDSON HIGHWAY section for log of highway to Valdez.

Caribou are not uncommon along the Glenn Highway. The Nelchina herd crosses the highway near Milepost A 127 in the late fall. (© Craig Brandt)

Distance from Anchorage (A) is followed by distance from Tok (T).
Physical mileposts between Glennallen and Anchorage show distance from Anchorage.

ALASKA ROUTE 1

A 188.7 (303.7 km) **T 139.3** (224.2 km) **Northern Nights Campground & RV Park.** See display ad this section. ▲

A 188.5 (303.3 km) **T 139.9** (225.1 km) Glennallen Community Chapel.

A 188.3 (303 km) **T 139.7** (224.8 km) Trans–Alaska pipeline passes under the highway.

A 187.8 (302.2 km) **T 140.2** (225.6 km) **The Hitchin' Post.** Serving breakfast, lunch and dinner. Open at 6 A.M. It's *THE* place for breakfast among locals, with a $2.99 special! Quaint dining room, drive-through window and clean outdoor tables. Hand-scooped gourmet ice creams, famous fries, Mexican fare, old-fashioned burgers. Look for the yellow place across from the car wash! [ADVERTISEMENT]

A 187.5 (301.7 km) **T 140.5** (226.1 km) **The Great Alaskan Freeze** (formerly the Glennallen Tastee–Freez). This popular spot features an excellent menu of fast food, including breakfast, with some of the lowest prices on the highway. We satisfy appetites of all sizes, from a quick taco to double cheeseburgers, cooked fresh and fast. All our burgers are homemade and our ice cream desserts can't be beat. Plan to stop! [ADVERTISEMENT]

Old Post Office Gallery. Owner and resident artist Jean Rene´ invites you to explore an appealing array of fine art and one-of-a-kind gifts. Here you will find original paintings, limited edition prints, Alaska Native crafts, photography, Alaskan books and more. Stop by for a memorable experience. See display ad this section. [ADVERTISEMENT]

A 187.2 (301.3 km) **T 140.8** (226.6 km) National Bank of Alaska; ATM. Post office a block north of highway. Description of Glennallen follows.

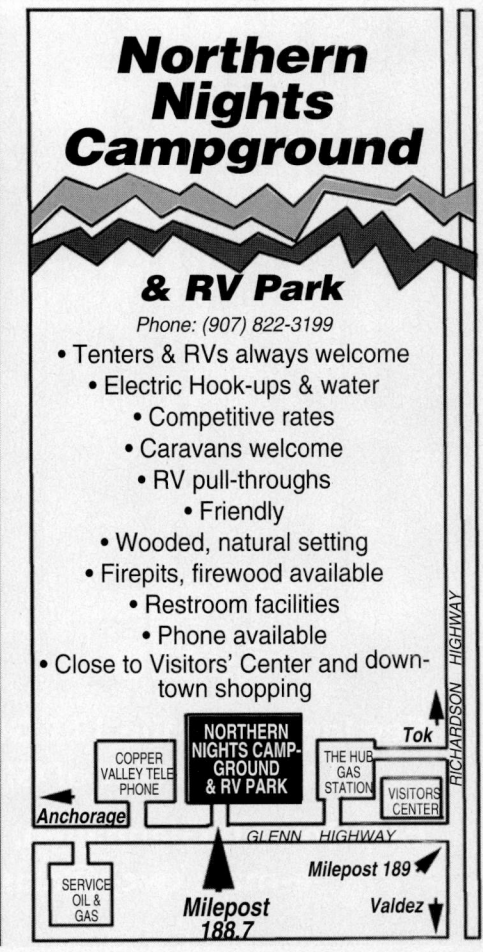

Glennallen

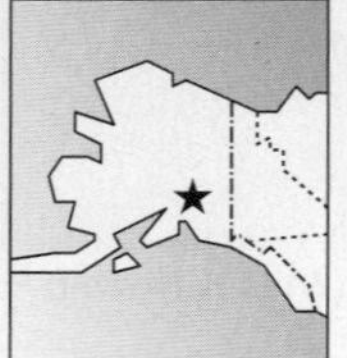

A 187 (300.9 km) **T 141** (226.9 km) Near the south junction of Glenn and Richardson highways. **Population:** 494. **Emergency Services: Alaska State Troopers, Milepost A 189**, phone (907) 822-3263. **Fire Department**, phone 911. **Ambulance**, Copper River EMS, phone (907) 822-3203 or 911. **Clinic, Milepost A 186.6**, phone (907) 822-3203.

Visitor Information: The Greater Copper Valley Chamber of Commerce Visitor Center is located in the log cabin at the junction of the Glenn and Richardson highways. **Milepost A 189**; open 8 A.M. to 7 P.M. daily in summer, phone (907) 822-5555 or write Box 469MP, Glennallen, AK 99588. The Alaska Dept. of Fish and Game office is located at **Milepost A 186.3** on the Glenn Highway, open weekdays 8 A.M. to 5 P.M.; phone (907) 822-3309.

Elevation: 1,460 feet/445m. **Climate:** Mean monthly temperature in January, -10°F/-23°C; in July, 56°F/13°C. Record low was -61°F/-52°C in January 1975; record high, 90°F/32°C in June 1969. Mean precipitation in July, 1.53 inches/3.9cm. Mean precipitation (snow/sleet) in December, 11.4 inches/29cm. **Radio:** KCAM 790, KOOL 107.1, KUAC-FM 92.1. **Television:** KYUK (Bethel) and Wrangell Mountain TV Club via satellite; Public Broadcasting System.

Private Aircraft: Gulkana airstrip, northeast of Glennallen at **Milepost A 192.1**; elev. 1,579 feet/481m; length 5,000 feet/1,524m;

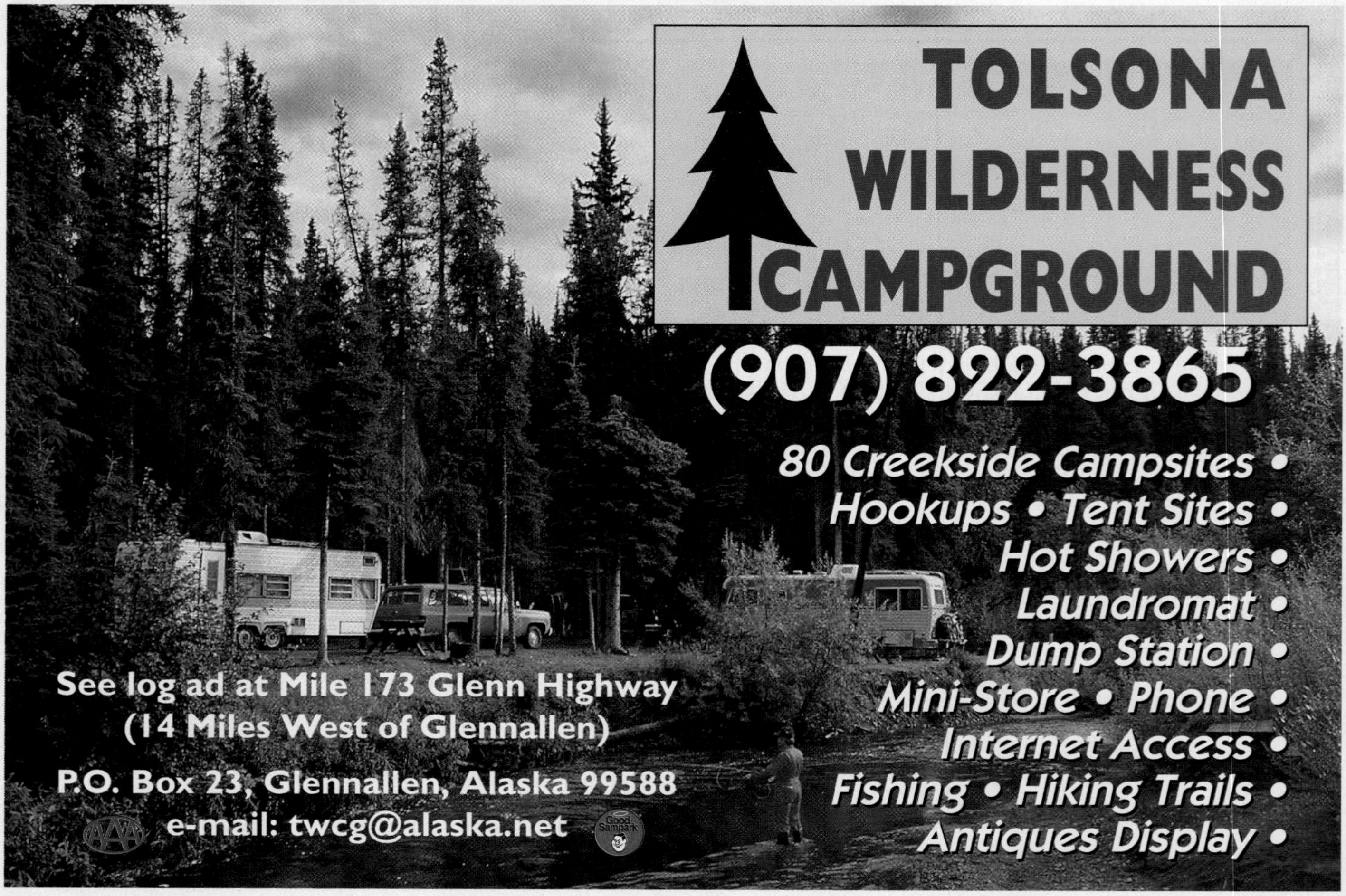

asphalt; fuel 100LL. Parking with tie downs. Mechanic available.

The name Glennallen is derived from the combined last names of Capt. Edwin F. Glenn and Lt. Henry T. Allen, both leaders in the early exploration of the Copper River region.

Glennallen lies at the western edge of the huge Wrangell–St. Elias National Park and Preserve. It is a gateway to the Wrangell Mountains and the service center for the Copper River basin. Glennallen is also a fly-in base for several guides and outfitters.

Four prominent peaks of the majestic Wrangell Mountains are to the east; from left they are Mounts Sanford, Drum, Wrangell and Blackburn. The best views are on crisp winter days at sunset. The rest of the countryside is relatively flat.

Towering above the town is an AT&T Alascom microwave tower. AT&T Alascom owns and operates 180 communications towers throughout the state of Alaska. The towers are also located along the Alaska, Parks, Richardson, Dalton and Sterling highways, as well as on mountaintops in Southeast Alaska and in remote locations such as Nome. With heights ranging from 100 to over 300 feet, they are often used as landmarks, but their primary purpose is to carry digital or analog microwave signals for the transmission of long-distance voice and data messages and, in some cases, 2-way radio communications.

The main business district is 1.5 miles/2.4 km west of the south junction of the Glenn and Richardson highways. There are also several businesses located at the south junction. About two-thirds of the area's residents are employed by trade/service firms; the balance hold various government positions. Offices for the Bureau of Land Management, the Alaska State Troopers and Dept. of Fish and Game are located here. There are several small farms in the area. There is a substantial Native population in the area, and the Native-owned Ahtna Corp. has its headquarters in Glennallen at the junction of the Glenn and Richardson highways.

Also headquartered here is KCAM radio, which broadcasts on station 790. KCAM broadcasts area road condition reports daily and also airs the popular "Caribou Clatter," which will broadcast personal messages. Radio messages are still a popular form of communication in Alaska and a necessary one in the Bush. Similar radio programs throughout the state are KJNP's "Trapline Chatter"; KYAK's "Bush Pipeline"; KHAR's "Northwinds"; and KIAK's "Pipeline of the North."

Lodging & Services

Because of its strategic location, most traveler services are available. During summer months reservations are advised for visitor accommodations. Glennallen has several lodges and motels and a variety of restaurants. Auto parts, groceries, gift shops, clothing, propane, sporting goods and other supplies are available at local stores. Services include a bank and ATM, a dentist, several churches, a chiropractic center, a laundromat, gas stations and major auto repair.

New Caribou Hotel, Gift Shop and Restaurant. The New Caribou Hotel in

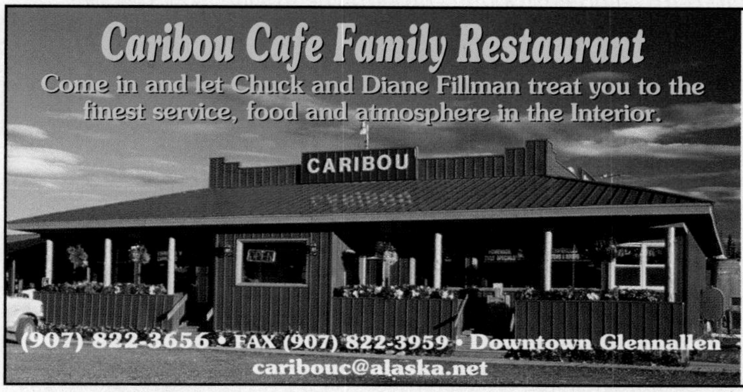

GLENNALLEN ADVERTISERS

Ahtna Inc. .... Ph. (907) 822-3476
Brown Bear Rhodehouse .... Mile 183.6 Glenn Hwy.
Caribou Cafe Family Restaurant .... Downtown
Glennallen Chevron .... Ph. (907) 822-3303
Great Alaskan Freeze ... Mile 187.5 Glenn Hwy.
KCAM Radio .... Ph. (907) 822-3434
Mechanix Warehouse Auto Parts .... Ph. (907) 822-3444
New Caribou Hotel, Gift Shop and Restaurant .... Ph. (907) 822-3302
Northern Nights Campground & RV Park .... Ph. (907) 822-3199
Old Post Office Gallery .. Adjacent Tastee-Freez
Tolsona Wilderness Campground .... Mile 173 Glenn Hwy.

View of Mount Sanford traveling eastbound through Glennallen. (© Kris Graef, staff)

downtown Glennallen, on the edge of the largest national park in America, was completed fall of 1990. This 55-unit modern facility features custom-built furniture, state-of-the-art color coordinated Alaskan decor, 6 rooms with 2-person whirlpool baths, 2-bedroom, fully furnished suites with kitchens and cooking facilities. Alaskan art, handicap facilities, conference rooms, phones and fax lines, satellite TV. Large full menu restaurant with banquet room, unique Alaskan gift shop (a must stop in your travels). All major credit cards accepted. Tour buses welcome. Airport transportation. Ask us for travel and visitor information. Open year-round. Phone (907) 822-3302. Toll free in Alaska phone (800) 478-3302, fax (907) 822-3711. Web site: www.alaskan.com/caribouhotel/. [ADVERTISEMENT]

There are private campgrounds west of town on the Glenn Highway (see **Milepost A 183.6, A 173** and **A 170.5**) and east of town at **Milepost A 188.7**. There are 2 private RV parks in Glennallen and at **Milepost V 110.5** Richardson Highway (4.5 m/7.2 km south of the junction). Northeast of Glennallen 5 miles/8 km is Dry Creek state campground (see **Milepost A 192**). ▲

Transportation

Bus: Scheduled service between Anchorage and Whitehorse via Glennallen. Bus service between Glennallen and McCarthy via Copper Center and Chitina in summer.

Attractions

Fourth of July weekend is a major event in Glennallen. Activities include the Ahtna Arts and Crafts Fair, a music festival, raft race, parade and salmon bake.

Recreational opportunities in the Glennallen area include hiking, flightseeing, hunting, river running, bird watching and fishing. According to the ADF&G, approximately 50 lakes in the Glennallen area are stocked with grayling, rainbow trout and coho salmon. A complete list of lakes, locations and species is available at the Copper River Valley Visitor Center at **Milepost A 189**, or from the ADF&G office at **Milepost A 186.3**. Locally, there is good grayling fishing in **Moose Creek; Tulsona Creek** to the east at **Milepost GJ 17.5;** west on the Glenn Highway at **Tolsona Creek, Milepost A 173;** and **Mendeltna Creek, Milepost A 152.8. Lake Louise**, approximately 27 miles/43 km west and 16 miles/25.7 km north from Glennallen, offers excellent grayling and lake trout fishing.

Many fly-in lakes are located in the Copper River basin and Chugach Mountains near Glennallen. **Crosswind Lake**, large lake trout, whitefish and grayling, early June to early July. **Deep Lake**, all summer for lake trout to 30 inches. **High Lake**, lake trout to 22 inches, June and early July with small spoons; some rainbow, fly-fishing; cabin, boat and motor rental. **Tebay Lakes**, excellent rainbow fishing, 12 to 15 inches, all summer, small spinners; cabin, boat and motor rental. **Jan Lake**, 12- to 14-inch silver salmon, June, spinners; also rainbow. **Hanagita Lake**, excellent grayling fishing all summer; also lake trout and steelhead in September. **Minnesota Lake**, lake trout to 30 inches, all summer; boat only, no cabins.

Glenn Highway Log

(continued)

A 186.6 (300.3 km) **T 141.4** (227.6 km) Cross Road Medical Center clinic; EMS. Alaska Bible College, the state's only accredited resident 4-year Bible college, is located behind the clinic.

A 186.4 (300 km) **T 141.6** (227.9 km) Bureau of Land Management district office; phone (907) 822-3217.

A 186.3 (299.8 km) **T 141.7** (228 km) Alaska State Dept. of Fish and Game; phone (907) 822-3309.

A 186 (299.3 km) **T 142** (228.5 km) Moose Creek culvert. Copper Valley library.

A 185.5 (298.5 km) **T 142.5** (229.3 km) *NOTE: Speed zone eastbound, 40 mph. Improved highway westbound.*

A 183.6 (295.5 km) **T 144.4** (232.4 km) Lodge restaurant to north.

A 182.2 (293.2 km) **T 145.8** (234.6 km) Liquor and office supply store to south has some interesting topiary done in native shrubs like willow and birch.

A 176.6 (284.2 km) **T 151.4** (243.6 km) Paved historical viewpoint to south with interpretive sign about the Wrangell Mountains and view southeast across the Copper River valley to Mount Drum. Northeast of Mount Drum is Mount Sanford and southeast is Mount Wrangell (elev. 14,163 feet/4,317m), a semiactive volcano. Mount Wrangell last erupted in 1912 when lava flowed to its base and ash fell as far west as this point.

Wildflowers growing along the roadside include lupine, cinquefoil, oxytrope, Jacob's ladder and sweet pea.

A 174.5 (280.8 km) **T 153.5** (247 km) Double-ended paved turnout to south.

Great views of Mount Sanford directly ahead for eastbound travelers.

A 173 (278.4 km) **T 155** (249.4 km) Turnoff to north for RV park and campground with dump station and laundromat.

A 172.9 (278.2 km) **T 155.1** (249.7 km) Ranch House Lodge.

A 172.8 (278.1 km) **T 155.2** (249.8 km) Bridge over **Tolsona Creek**, grayling to 16 inches, use mosquito flies in still, clear pools behind obstructions, June, July and August. Best fishing 1.5 miles/2.4 km upstream from highway.

A 170.5 (274.4 km) **T 157.5** (253.5 km) Tolsona Lake Road to north. **Tolsona** and **Moose lakes**, rainbow trout, burbot, grayling to 16 inches, all summer; good ice fishing for burbot in winter.

A 169.3 (272.3 km) **T 158.7** (255.4 km) Paved double-ended turnout to south. Long narrow **Mae West Lake**, fed by Little Woods Creek, is a little less than 1 mile/1.6 km away. Grayling fishing.

A 168 (270.4 km) **T 160** (257.5 km) Soup Lake to north. Trumpeter swans can sometimes be seen in lakes and ponds along this section of highway. Watch for moose. In June and July look for wildflowers such as sweet pea, fireweed, lupine, cinquefoil, oxytrope, Jacob's ladder and milk-vetch.

A 166.1 (267.3 km) **T 161.9** (260.5 km) **Atlasta House**, a local landmark, was named by the homesteader who was happy to have a real house at last.

A 166 (267.2 km) **T 162** (260.7 km) Paved double-ended turnout to south and 2-mile/3.2-km hiking trail to **Lost Cabin Lake**; grayling fishing.

Tolsona Mountain (elev. 2,974 feet/906m), a prominent ridge just north of highway, is a landmark for miles in both directions. This area is popular with berry-pickers in late summer and early fall. Varieties of wild berries include blueberries, lowbush cranberries and raspberries.

A 164 (263.9 km) **T 164** (263.9 km) First glimpse westbound of Tazlina Glacier and lake to south. Half-way point between Tok and Anchorage.

A 162.3 (261.2 km) **T 165.7** (266.7 km) Paved turnout to south.

A 162 (260.7 km) **T 166** (267.1 km) Turnout to north; access to **Tex Smith Lake** to north; stocked with rainbow.

NOTE: Watch for horses.

A 160 (257.5 km) **T 168** (270.4 km) **TOLSONA** (sign).

A 159.8 (257.2 km) **T 168.2** (270.7 km)

Junction with 19.3-mile/31-km Lake Louise Road (gravel) to Lake Louise Recreation Area. See LAKE LOUISE ROAD log on page 284.

A 159.6 (256.8 km) **T 168.4** (271 km) **Little Junction Lake** fishing access, 0.3-mile/0.4-km hike south; grayling.

A 157 (252.7 km) **T 171** (275.2 km) Distance marker shows Palmer 109 miles, Anchorage 157 miles.

CAUTION: Slow down for severe frost heaves.

A 156.9 (252.5 km) **T 171.1** (275.3 km) Trails to south to **DJ Lake** 0.5 mile/0.8 km (rainbow fishing) and **Sucker Lake** 4 miles/6.4 km (grayling and burbot).

A 156.4 (251.7 km) **T 171.6** (276.1 km) Good view (weather permitting) of **Tazlina Glacier** to the south. The glacier feeds into 20-mile/32-km-long **Tazlina Lake** at its foot.

A 156.3 (251.5 km) **T 171.7** (276.3 km) **Buffalo Lake**; stocked with rainbow.

A 156.2 (251.4 km) **T 171.8** (276.5 km) Tazlina Glacier Lodge.

A 156 (251 km) **T 172** (276.8 km) Tazlina airstrip; elev. 2,450 feet/747m; length 1,200 feet/366m; gravel. Not recommended for use.

A 155.8 (250.7 km) **T 172.2** (277.2 km) **Arizona Lake** to south; fishing for

Lake Louise Road Log

This wide gravel road leads north 19.3 miles/31 km from **Milepost A 159.8** Glenn Highway to Lake Louise Recreation Area. The road is state-maintained and open year-round. Lake Louise is known for its lake trout and grayling fishing; lodges, dining, boat rentals and fishing charters at lake. Views of Tazlina Glacier and Lake; berry picking for wild strawberries and blueberries (July and August), and cranberries (September). Excellent cross-country skiing and snowmobiling in winter.

Distance is measured from the junction with the Glenn Highway (J).

Glassy waters of Lake Louise on a calm day. (© Alan D. Musy/ADM PhotoGraphics)

J 0 Junction with Glenn Highway at **Milepost A 154.8.**

J 0.2 (0.3 km) **Junction Lake** to east; grayling fishing.

J 1.1 (1.8 km) Turnout.

J 1.2 (1.9 km) Double-ended turnout to west with view of Tazlina Glacier.

Just north is the road west to Little **Crater Lake.** There are a number of small lakes along the road with good fishing for grayling.

J 5.2 (8.4 km) **Old Road Lake and Round Lake** to east (1/4 mile); rainbow fishing.

J 6.7 (10.8 km) **Mendeltna Creek** to west 5 miles); grayling fishing.

J 7 (11.2 km) **Forgotten Lake** to east (0.1 mile/0.2 km); grayling fishing.

J 9.4 (15.1 km) Parking area to west with view of pothole lakes. First view of Lake Louise northbound.

J 10.5 (16.9 km) Hill; use low-gear. Good view on clear days of the Alaska Range and Susitna River valley.

J 11.5 (18.5 km) Road west to **Caribou Lake;** grayling fishing. Turnout to east by Elbow Lake.

J 14 (22.5 km) Boundary of Matanuska–Susitna Borough.

J 15.5 (24.9 km) Gas station.

J 15.9 (25.6 km) Parking rea to east.

J 16 (25.7 km) **North and South Jan's Lakes** to east (7 miles); fishing.

J 16.1 (25.9 km) Turnoff for Lake Louise Lodge (0.9 miles/1.4 km).

Lake Louise Lodge. See display ad this section.

J 16.5 (26.6 km) Turnoff for Evergreen Lodge (0.3 miles/0.5 km).

J 16.8 (27 km) **Conner Lake,** rainbow and grayling fishing.

J 17.2 (27.7 km) Side road leads northeast to The Point Lodge (0.9 miles) and **Lake Louise State Recreation Area.** Drive 0.4 miles to "T"; turn left for The Point Lodge (0.5 mile) and Lake Louise Campground (0.3 mile); turn right for Army Point Campground (0.7 mile). Army Point and Lake Louise campgrounds have 52 campsites on loop roads, firepits, water pumps, toilets (wheelchair accessible), covered picnic tables, picnic shelter, walking trail and a boat launch. Camping fee $10/night or annual pass. Swimming in Lake Louise. Winter ski trail access.

The Point Lodge. See display ad this section.

J 18.8 (30.3 km) **Private Aircraft:** Lake Louise airstrip is closed. Seaplane landing and docking at all lodges. No avgas available.

J 19.3 (31 km) Road ends. Parking and boat launch to west on Dinty Lake. Side road east to Lake Louise rest area; picnic tables, fireplaces, toilets.

Lake Louise, grayling and lake trout fishing good year-round, best spring through July, then again in the fall; early season use herring or whitefish bait, cast from boat; later (warmer water) troll with #16 red-and-white spoon, silver Alaskan plug or large silver flatfish; for grayling, casting flies or small spinners, June, July and August; in winter jig for lake trout. Check ADF&G regulations for Lake Louise area.

Susitna Lake can be reached by boat across Lake Louise (narrow channel; watch for signs); burbot, lake trout and grayling fishing. *Both lakes can be rough; under-powered boats not recommended.* **Dinty Lake,** launch from public launch at Mile 19.3; grayling and lake trout fishing.

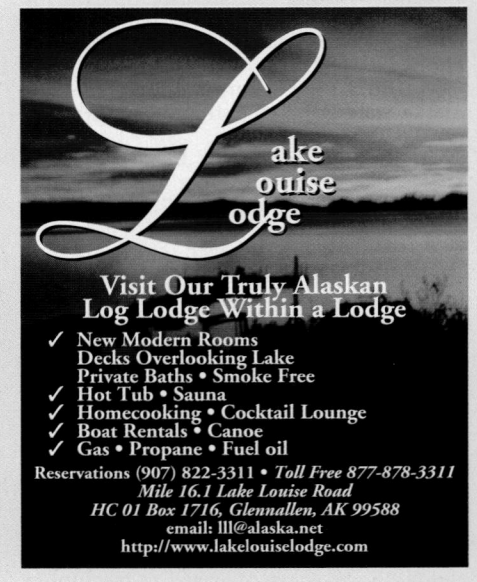

Return to Milepost A 159.8 Glenn Highway

grayling.

A **155.6** (250.4 km) **T 172.4** (277.4 km) Paved turnout to south.

A **155.2** (249.8 km) **T 172.8** (278.1 km) **Gergie Lake** 1/4 mile to south; fishing for grayling and rainbow.

CAUTION: Slow down for frost heaves.

A **154** (247.8 km) **T 174** (280 km) **MENDELTNA** (pop. 80) sign. This unincorporated community includes the large RV campground (K.R.O.A.), the state highway maintenance station and general store at Nelchina, and Eureka Lodge. The area was originally a stop used by Natives traveling from Lake Tyone to Tazlina Lake. Gold brought prospectors into the area in the 1800s.

A **153.7** (247.3 km) **T 174.3** (280.5 km) Community chapel.

A **153** (246.2 km) **T 175** (281.6 km) Lodge-type restaurant, bar, campground, liquor store, cabins and gas to south.

A **152.8** (245.9 km) **T 175.2** (282 km) **Mendeltna Creek** bridge. Watch for spawning salmon in August. (The Mendeltna Creek drainage is closed to the taking of salmon.) Excellent fishing for grayling to 17 1/2 inches and whitefish to 16 inches, May to November, use spinners and flies. Walk or boat away from the bridge. Good fishing north to Old Man Lake; watch for bears.

A **152.5** (245.4 km) **T 175.5** (282.4 km) Paved double-ended turnout to north.

A **150.4** (242 km) **T 177.6** (285.8 km) **NELCHINA** (sign).

A **150** (241.4 km) **T 178** (286.4 km) Distance marker westbound shows Sutton 89 miles, Palmer 103 miles.

Eastbound view of Mount Sanford and Mount Drum straight ahead.

A **149.1** (239.9 km) **T 178.9** (287.9 km) **Ryan Lake** public fishing access; grayling and rainbow.

A **149** (239.8 km) **T 179** (288.1 km) Food, lodging and towing service on south side of highway.

Grizzly Country Enterprises. See display ad this section.

A **144.9** (233.2 km) **T 183.1** (294.7 km) Lottie Sparks (Nelchina) Elementary School.

A **141.2** (227.2 km) **T 186.8** (300.6 km) Nelchina state highway maintenance station. Slide Mountain trailhead located behind station.

A **139.9** (225.1 km) **T 188.1** (302.7 km) *CAUTION: Rough road.*

A **138.5** (222.9 km) **T 189.5** (305 km) **NELCHINA** (sign).

A **137.6** (221.4 km) **T 190.4** (306.4 km) **Little Nelchina State Recreation Site** 0.3 mile/0.5 km north from highway; 11 campsites, 15-day limit, no camping fee, no drinking water, tables, firepits, toilet, boat launch. Watch for moose and bear. ▲

A **137.5** (221.3 km) **T 190.5** (306.6 km) Little Nelchina River bridge.

NOTE: Eastbound, highway curves uphill from bridge. Westbound to summit it is good paved straightaway with passing lanes.

A **137** (220.5 km) **T 191** (307.4 km) Boundary of Matanuska–Susitna Borough. Good views to south of glaciers in the Chugach Mountains.

A **135.8** (218.5 km) **T 192.2** (309.3 km) Paved turnout to north.

Truck lane begins westbound.

A **135.3** (217.7 km) **T 192.7** (310.1 km) Store and cabins to south.

Nelchina Trail Store & Cabins. See display ad this section.

A **135** (217.3 km) **T 193** (310.6 km) *CAUTION: Watch for moose.*

A **134** (215.6 km) **T 194** (312.2 km) Gravel turnout to south.

A **133** (214 km) **T 195** (313.8 km) Paved turnout to north.

Truck lane ends westbound.

A **132.1** (212.6 km) **T 195.9** (315.2 km) Gravel turnout to north.

Great views to south of Nelchina Glacier. View of snow-covered Mount Sanford eastbound.

A **130.5** (201 km) **T 197.5** (317.8 km) Large gravel parking area to north used by hunters and hikers. Old Man Creek trailhead. (Old Man Creek 2 miles/3 km; Crooked Creek 9 miles/14.5 km; Nelchina Town 14.5 miles/23 km.) Established trails west from here to Palmer are part of the Chickaloon–Knik–Nelchina trail system.

A **129.5** (208.4 km) **T 198.5** (319.4 km) **Eureka Summit** (elev. 3,322 feet/1,013m), highest point on the Glenn Highway. Turnout to south with unobstructed views of the Chugach Mountains. Snow poles along roadside guide snow plows in winter. Truck lane ends westbound.

Gold Rush Centennial sign about Captain Edwin F. Glenn, who passed near here on his way from Cook Inlet to the Tanana River in 1898. Glenn led one of 3 teams, the Cook Inlet Exploring Expedition.

His orders were to locate the most practical route from Prince William Sound through Cook Inlet to the Tanana River. The Glenn Highway is named in his honor.

The Nelchina Glacier winds downward through a cleft in the mountains. To the northwest are the peaks of the Talkeetnas, and to the west the highway descends through river valleys which separate these 2 mountain ranges. This is the divide of 3 big river systems: Susitna, Matanuska and Copper.

A 128 (206 km) **T 200** (321.9 km) Food, gas, diesel, lodging, bar and liquor store at the Eureka Lodge. The first lodge on the Glenn Highway, it was opened in 1937 by Paul Waverly and has operated continuously ever since. The original log building (Eureka Roadhouse) is next to Eureka Lodge.

Private Aircraft: Eureka (Skelton) airstrip, one of the highest in the state; elev. 3,289 feet/1,002m; length 2,400 feet/732m; gravel; fuel autogas; unattended. Runway narrows to 15 feet.

A 127 (204.4 km) **T 201** (323.4 km) *CAUTION: Watch for caribou.* Caribou crossing. The Nelchina caribou herd travels through here October through November.

A 126.4 (203.4 km) **T 201.6** (324.4 km) Watch for turnout to south to Belanger Creek–Nelchina River trailhead parking. (Eureka Creek 1.5 miles/2.4 km; Goober Lake 8 miles/13 km; Nelchina River 9 miles/14.5 km.)

A 125 (201.2 km) **T 203** (326.7 km) **Gunsight Mountain** (elev. 6,441 feet/1,963m) is visible to the west for the next few miles to those approaching from Glennallen.The notch or "gunsight" is plain if one looks closely. Eastbound views of snow-covered Mount Sanford (weather permitting), Mount Drum, Mount Wrangell and Mount Blackburn.

A 123.3 (198.4 km) **T 204.7** (329.4 km) Belanger Pass trailhead to north on Martin Road. Part of a network of ATV trails and mining roads around Syncline Mountain, leading to Belanger Pass (elev. 4,350 feet), 3 miles; Alfred Creek, 6.5 miles; and Albert Creek, 8 miles.

A 123.1 (198.1 km) **T 204.9** (329.8 km) Old Tahneta Inn to south (closed).

A 122.9 (197.8 km) **T 205.1** (330 km) Gunsight Mountain Lodge to north (closed in 1999; current status unknown).

A 122 (196.3 km) **T 206** (331.5 km) **Tahneta Pass** (elev. 3,000 feet). Double-ended paved turnout to north.

Leila Lake trailhead (unsigned) on old alignment to north; grayling 8 to 14 inches abundant through summer, best fishing June and July. Burbot, success spotty for 12 to 18 inches in fall and winter.

A 121.4 (195.4 km) **T 206.6** (332.5 km) Signed trailhead to north; small parking area.

NOTE: Improved highway westbound to ***Milepost A 109.***

A 120.8 (194.4 km) **T 207.2** (333.4 km) Boundary of Sportfish Management Area 2 and Sheep Mountain Closed Area.

A 120 (193.4 km) **T 207.8** (334.4 km) Scenic viewpoint to south (double-ended paved turnout). The largest lake is Leila Lake; in the distance is Tahneta Lake.

A 119.2 (191.8 km) **T 208.8** (336 km) Turnout to south with beautiful view of Chugach Mountains and lakes (weather permitting).

A 118.6 (190.9 km) T 209.4 (337 km) Trailhead Road turnoff to north leads to large parking area with outhouses, picnic tables, viewing telescope and Gold Rush Centennial signs. Nice stop, good views.

Trailhead for the Chickaloon-Knik-Nelchina Trail System.

A 118.5 (190.7 km) **T 209.5** (337.1 km) Alascom Road to south.

A 118.4 (190.5 km) **T 209.6** (337.3 km) Trail Creek.

A 118 (189.9 km) **T 210** (338 km) Truck lane ends eastbound and begins westbound.

A 117.8 (189.5 km) **T 210.2** (338.2 km) Turnout with viewpoint to south. Tip of Powell Glacier can be seen coming down the canyon of the South Fork Matanuska River. Knob Lake and the "knob" (elev. 3,000 feet/914m), topped by microwave tower, marks entrance to Chickaloon Pass for small planes.

A 117.6 (189.3 km) **T 210.4** (338.6 km) Large parking area to north at Squaw Creek trailhead. (Squaw Creek 3.5 miles/5.6 km; Caribou Creek 9.5 miles/15 km; Alfred Creek 13 miles/21 km; Sheep Creek 15 miles/24

km.)

A 117.2 (188.6 km) **T 210.8** (339.2 km) Paved turnout to south with view of Chugach Mountains. Signed Camp Creek Trail Trailhead.

A 117.1 (188.4 km) **T 210.9** (339.4 km) Camp Creek.

A 116.1 (186.8 km) **T 211.9** (341 km) Truck lane begins eastbound.

A 115.6 (186 km) **T 212.4** (341.8 km) Large paved turnout to south with view of Chugach Mountains.

A 115 (185 km) **T 213** (342.8 km) Double-ended paved turnout to north. Look for sheep on mineralized Sheep Mountain.

A 114.9 (184.9 km) **T 213.1** (342.9 km) Majestic Valley Lodge to south. Watch for sheep on mountainside.

Majestic Valley Lodge combines the rustic charm of a quaint mountain lodge with all modern conveniences. In the 3,000-foot Tahneta Pass area, enjoy hiking treks, Dall sheep and other wildlife, blueberry picking, glacier walks, cross-country skiing and snowmobiling. Gourmet meals (advance reservation required). Sauna and the spectacular view top off a day in the mountains. Rooms include private baths and use of the large viewing lounge and Alaskan library. Phone (907) 746-2930; fax (907) 746-2931; Web site: www.majesticvalleylodge.com. [ADVERTISEMENT]

A 114.6 (184.4 km) **T 213.4** (343.4 km) Truck lane ends eastbound.

For Anchorage-bound travelers a vista of incomparable beauty as the road descends in a long straightaway toward Glacier Point, also known as the **Lion Head**, an oddly formed rocky dome.

A 114.4 (184.1 km) **T 213.6** (343.7 km) Glacial Fan Creek (sign).

A 113.5 (182.7 km) **T 214.5** (345.2 km) Truck lane begins eastbound. Sheep Mountain Lodge on north side of highway.

Wonderful views to north of **Sheep Mountain** (elev. 6,300 feet/1,920m). Sheep are often seen high up these slopes. The area surrounding Sheep Mountain is closed to the taking of mountain sheep.

Sheep Mountain Lodge. Our charming log lodge, established in 1946, has been serving travelers for half a century. We're famous for our wholesome homemade food, fresh baked breads, pastries and desserts. Our comfortable guest cabins, all with private bathrooms, boast spectacular mountain views. We also have RV hookups, full bar, liquor store and Alaskan gifts. You can watch Dall Sheep through our telescope and relax in the hot tub or sauna after a day of traveling or hiking. HC03 Box 8490, Palmer, AK 99645. Phone (907) 745-5121; fax (907) 745-5120. E-mail: sheepmtl@alaska.net. Internet: www.alaska.net/~sheepmtl. See display ad this section. [ADVERTISEMENT] ▲

Private Aircraft: Sheep Mountain airstrip; elev. 2,750 feet/838m; length 2,300 feet/701m; gravel/dirt; unattended.

A 113.5 (182.7 km) **T 214.5** (345.2 km) As the highway descends westbound into the valley of the Matanuska River, there is a view of the great glacier which is the main headwater source and gives the water its milky color.

A 113 (181.9 km) **T 215** (346 km) Turnoff for Sheep Mountain airstrip to north.

A 112.7 (181.4 km) **T 215.3** (346.5 km) Large paved turnout to south with picnic table; good camera viewpoint for Sheep Mountain to north and Chugach Mountains to south.

Mineralized Sheep Mountain in the Talkeetna Range. (© Jill Shepherd, staff)

A 112.5 (181 km) **T 215.5** (346.8 km) Truck lane ends eastbound.

A 112.1 (180.4 km) **T 215.9** (347.4 km) Gypsum Creek (sign).

A 111.2 (179 km) **T 216.8** (348.9 km) Bug Lake (sign).

A 111.6 (179.6 km) **T 216.4** (348.2 km) Truck lane begins eastbound.

A 110.9 (178.5 km) **T 217.1** (349.4 km) Truck lane ends eastbound.

A 110.5 (177.8 km) **T 217.5** (350 km) Truck lane begins eastbound.

A 109.7 (176.5 km) **T 218.3** (351.3 km) Log building to south. Good views westbound of Matanuska Glacier.

Grand View. Enjoy spectacular mountain views while viewing Dall sheep or an occasional bear in their natural habitat. Stop for espresso, pastries, deli-style sandwiches and more, in our handicap-accessible log reception area. Spend the night with us in one of our RV campsites. Easy access to pull-through sites offer 30–50 amp electric, water and sewer. Showers. Ice. The Dietrich family assures a clean, friendly atmosphere for our guests! Open May 20–September 15. E-mail: tundrose@alaska.net. [ADVERTISEMENT] ♿▲

A 109.5 (176.2 km) **T 218.5** (351.6 km) Access to bed and breakfast.

Tundra Rose Bed & Breakfast. "Alaska Hideaway with a Glacier View," writes the *San Francisco Examiner*. Quiet, relaxed setting. Private log cottage or 2-bedroom suite offer kitchenettes, private baths and spectacular views of Matanuska Glacier and sur-

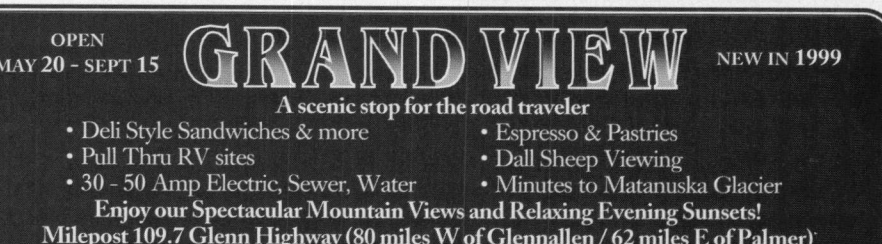

View of Matanuska Glacier in the Chugach Mountains. (© Jill Shepherd, staff)

rounding mountains. View Dall sheep from our yard. Continental breakfast. http://www.alaska.net/~tundrose. [ADVERTISEMENT]

A 107.8 (173.5 km) **T 220.2** (354.4 km) Slide area. Exceptional views of Glacier Point (Lion Head) and Matanuska Glacier.

A 107.5 (173 km) **T 220.5** (354.9 km) Gravel turnouts to south along highway with views of Matanuska Glacier to southwest.

A 106.8 (171.9 km) **T 221.2** (356 km) Caribou Creek Bridge.

Fortress Ridge (elev. 5,000 feet/1,524m) above the highway to the north. Sheep Mountain reserve boundary.

NOTE: Highway makes a steep, winding descent (from both directions) down to Caribou Creek.

A 106 (170.6 km) **T 222** (357.3 km) Large gravel parking area for **Caribou Creek Recreational Gold Mining Area** (Dept. of Natural Resources); outhouse. Steep trail leads from parking area down to creek (pedestrians only, no ATVs). Recreational gold panning, mineral prospecting or mining using light portable field equipment (e.g. hand-operated pick, backpack power drill, etc.) allowed in designated recreational mining area on state lands without mining claims below the ordinary high water mark of Caribou Creek, its tributaries and the Matanuska River. Suction dredging requires a permit from the ADF&G. Contact Dept. of Natural Resources Public Information Center in Anchorage for more information; phone (907) 269-8400.

A 105.8 (170.3 km) **T 222.2** (357.6 km) Road (closed to public) to FAA station on flank of Glacier Point. Mountain sheep occasionally are seen on the upper slopes.

A 105.5 (169.8 km) **T 222.5** (358.1 km) Gravel turnout to south.

A 105.3 (169.4 km) **T 222.7** (358.4 km) Turnout to south. FAA station on Glacier Point.

Great views of Matanuska Glacier from the highway westbound.

A 104.1 (167.5 km) **T 223.9** (360.3 km) Access to Glacier View School, which overlooks Matanuska Glacier.

A 103.2 (166.1 km) **T 224.8** (361.8 km) Majestic View RV Park.

A 102.8 (165.4 km) **T 225.2** (362.4 km) Paved turnout to south with view of Matanuska Glacier.

A 102.2 (164.5 km) **T 225.8** (363.4 km) Long Rifle Lodge to south.

Long Rifle Lodge. Welcome to Alaska's most fabulous dining view of the Matanuska Glacier. We offer a complete breakfast, lunch and dinner menu, specializing in home-cooked meals. Twenty-five wildlife mounts make our lodge a "must see" for all ages. Numerous hiking, cross-country skiing and snowmobile trails surround the area. In addition, we have motel rooms, gasoline, 24-hour wrecker service, gift shop and a full-service lounge. Phone (800) 770-5151. Fax (907) 745-5153. E-mail: lrl@matnet.com. See display ad this section. [ADVERTISEMENT]

A 102 (164.2 km) **T 226** (363.7 km) Access to foot of Matanuska Glacier via Glacier Park Resort to south. Admission fee charged.

Glacier Park. We invite you to experience the Matanuska Glacier through a private park at the terminus of the Matanuska Glacier. Our location to the glacier allows us to offer a most unique glacier tour. From our parking area it is about a 15-minute hike to the white ice.

Offering a variety of guided tours on the white ice June 1–September 7. Off-season reservations required. This is where the locals bring their guests for an Alaska experience. The most common remark is "I never dreamed we could walk out on a glacier like this." Group and per person rates. Access at Milepost 102 Glenn Highway. HC03 Box 8449, Palmer, AK 99645. Phone (907) 745-2534.[ADVERTISEMENT] ▲

Wickersham Trading Post. See display ad this section.

A 101.7 (163.7 km) **T 226.3** (364.2 km) Paved turnout with good view of **Matanuska Glacier**, which heads in the Chugach Mountains and trends northwest 27 miles. Some 18,000 years ago the glacier reached all the way to the Palmer area. The glacier's average width is 2 miles; at its terminus it is 4 miles wide. The glacier has remained fairly stable the past 400 years. At the glacier terminus meltwater drains into a stream which flows into the Matanuska River.

A 101 (162.5 km) **T 227** (365.3 km) **Matanuska Glacier State Recreation Site**; 12 campsites on loop drive, 15-day limit, $10 nightly fee or resident pass, wheelchair accessible, water and toilets. *Park may be closed for repairs in summer 2000.* Excellent views of the glacier from hiking trails along the bluff. (Use caution when walking near edge of bluff.) Wildflowers here in late July include fireweed, yarrow and sweet peas. ♿▲

A 100.4 (161.6 km) **T 227.6** (366.3 km) Pinochle Hill.

A 99.9 (160.8 km) **T 228.1** (367.1 km) *NOTE: Highway narrows eastbound.*

A 99.5 (160.1 km) **T 228.5** (367.7 km) Scenic viewpoint to north. Good view of Matanuska Glacier from highway.

A 99.1 (159.5 km) **T 228.9** (368.4 km) Truck lane begins westbound.

A 98.6 (158.6 km) **T 229.4** (369.2 km) Truck lane ends eastbound.

A 98.3 (158.2 km) **T 229.7** (369.6 km) Truck lane ends westbound.

A 97.1 (156.3 km) **T 230.9** (371.6 km) Truck lane begins eastbound.

A 96.6 (155.5 km) **T 231.4** (372.4 km) Private campground, lodge and store. Hicks Creek was named by Captain Glenn in 1898 for H.H. Hicks, the guide of his expedition. A highway construction camp was set up here in the early 1940s, as the rough, narrow Glenn Highway was pushed through to connect with the Tok Cutoff, connecting it to the Alaska Highway in 1945.

Anthracite Ridge to the north.

Historical Hicks Creek Roadhouse. See display ad this section. ▲

A 96.5 (155.3 km) **T 231.5** (372.6 km) Bridge over Hicks Creek.

More winding road westbound as highway climbs above the Matanuska River.

A 95 (152.9 km) **T 233** (375 km) Beautiful views to south of Matanuska River and peaks and glaciers in the Chugach Range. The **Chugach Mountains** arc 250 miles from Bering Glacier on the Gulf of Alaska to the east to Turnagain Arm south of Anchorage. They are bounded on the north by the Matanuska, Copper and Chitina Rivers, and on the south by the gulf and Prince William Sound.

A 94.6 (152.2 km) **T 233.4** (375.6 km) Victory Road to Spring Creek Bible Church.

A 93.2 (150 km) **T 234.8** (377.9 km) Cascade state highway maintenance station.

A 90.5 (145.6 km) **T 237.5** (382.2 km) Trailhead parking.

A 89 (143.2 km) **T 239** (384.6 km) Purinton Creek bridge; turnout to north at west end of bridge. The stream heads on Anthracite Ridge and flows into the Matanuska River.

Westbound, watch for moose.

A 88 (141.6 km) **T 240** (386.2 km) *CAUTION: Slide areas, winding road, westbound to **Milepost A 84**. Gravel turnouts on south side of highway to **Milepost A 78**.*

A 87.5 (140.8 km) **T 240.5** (387 km) **Weiner Lake** (stocked) to south; public access. Fishing for rainbow and grayling.

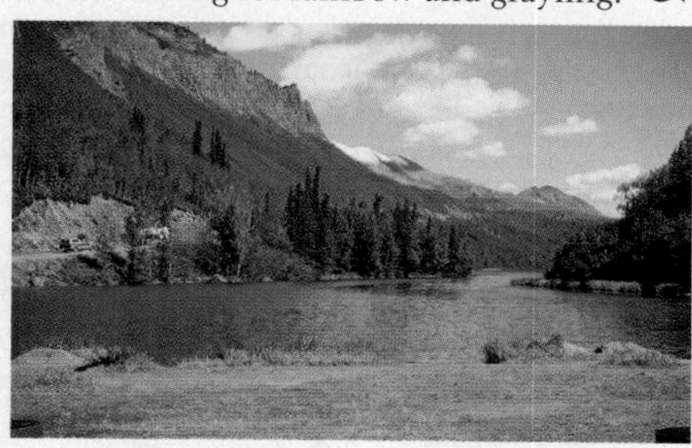

A 85.3 (137.3 km) **T 242.7** (390.6 km) **Long Lake State Recreation Site**; 9 campsites, 15-day limit, no camping fee, no water, no garbage; tables, firepits and toilets. Long Lake is a favorite fishing spot for Anchorage residents. Fair for grayling to 18 inches, spring through fall; fish deeper as the water warms in summer. Good ice fishing in winter for burbot, average 12 inches. ▲

A 84.1 (135.3 km) **T 243.9** (392.5 km) Large gravel turnout to southeast.

A 84 (135.2 km) **T 244** (392.7 km) *CAUTION: Slide areas, winding road, eastbound to **Milepost A 88**.*

Great views of Matanuska River and Chugach Mountains to south as highway descends eastbound.

A 83.2 (133.9 km) **T 244.8** (394 km) Narrow gravel road (unsigned) leads north to Ravine and Lower Bonnie lakes. Drive in 0.8 mile/1.3 km on side road to reach **Ravine Lake**; fishing from shore for rainbow. Lower Bonnie Lake is a 2-mile/3.2-km drive from the highway; no public access. *NOTE: This steep and winding road is signed as unsafe and closed to motorhomes, large vehicles or trailers. All travel is at owner's risk. During rainy season this side road is not recommended for any vehicle.*

A 82 (132 km) **T 246** (395.9 km) Distinctive pyramid shape of **King Mountain** (elev. 5,809 feet/1,770m) to the southeast.

A 80.8 (130 km) **T 247.2** (397.8 km) Eastern boundary of Matanuska Valley Moose Range. Turnout to south.

A 80.5 (129.5 km) **T 247.5** (398.3 km) Distance marker westbound shows Glennallen 107 miles, Tok 224 miles, Valdez 248 miles.

A 78.3 (126 km) **T 249.7** (401.8 km) Gravel turnout to south with view of King Mountain and Matanuska River.

*NOTE: Highway climbs steeply eastbound to **Milepost A 84**. Gravel turnouts to south of highway to **Milepost A 88**.*

A 77.7 (125 km) **T 250.3** (402.8 km) Chickaloon River bridge. Gravel turnout to south at east end of bridge. Boundary between Game Management Units 13 and 14.

At west end of bridge is turnoff to north for **Chickaloon River Road** (gravel; state road maintenance ends 1.2 miles from highway). No trespassing and private property signs are posted along this road.

A 77.5 (124.7 km) **T 250.5** (403.1 km) Gravel turnout to south. Highway closely parallels the **Matanuska River** westbound to

Palmer. Nova River Runners in Chickaloon offers scenic floats and whitewater trips on the river. The Matanuska River is formed by its East and South Forks and flows southwest

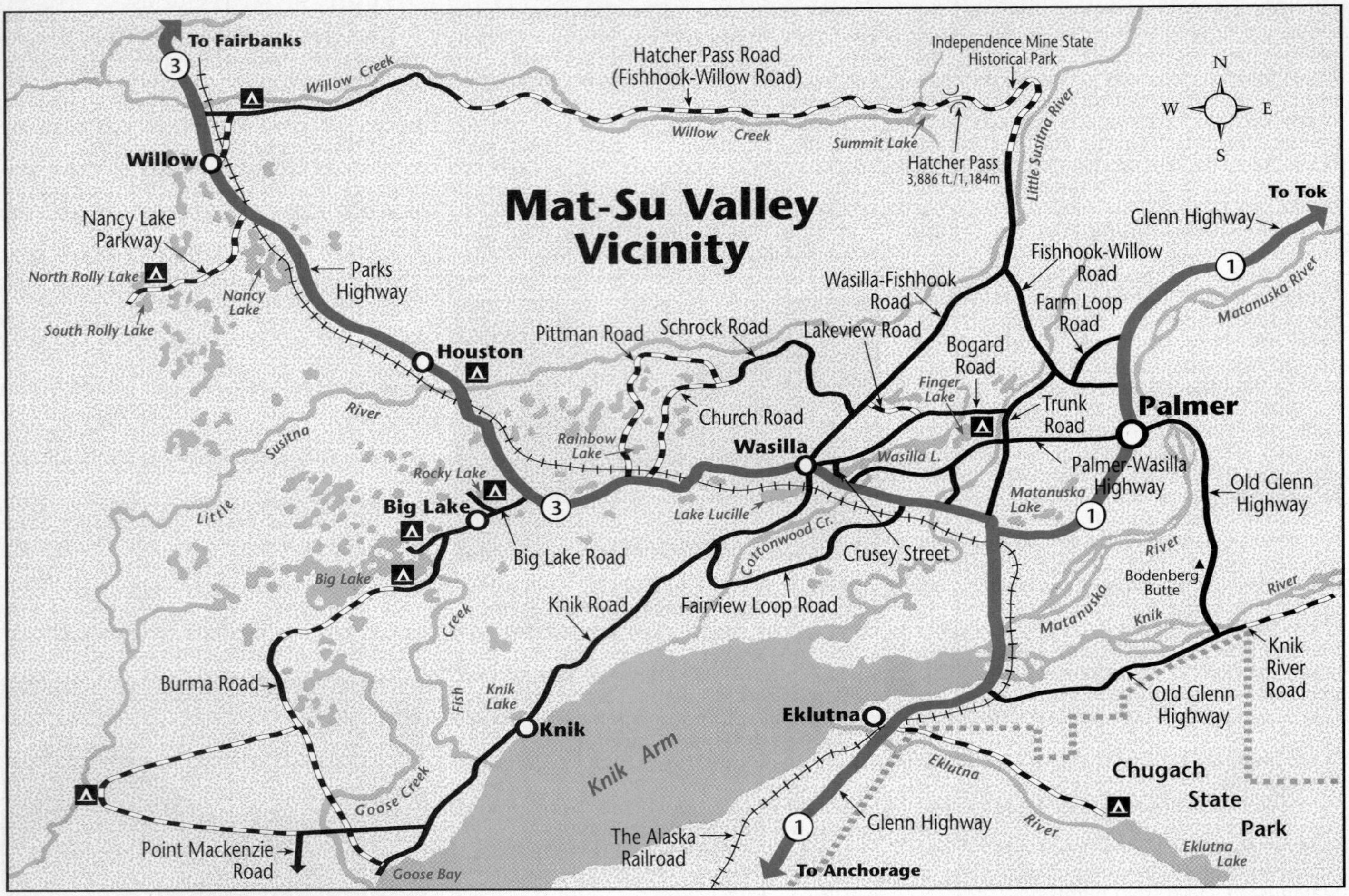

Mat-Su Valley Vicinity

75 miles to the Knik Arm of Cook Inlet.

*NOTE: Slide areas, gravel turnouts to south, westbound to **Milepost A 68**.*

A 76.2 (122.6 km) **T 251.8** (405.2 km) **CHICKALOON** (pop. 212); post office, lodge, cafe, cabins, camping, general store, gas station and river rafting office. Chickaloon was established around 1916 as the terminus of an Alaska Railroad spur. ▲

Nova River Runners. See display ad this section.

King Mountain Lodge, established 1947, oldest continuously operated lodge on the Glenn Highway, with its own resident ghost. Authentic Alaskan atmosphere in the plank-floor bar ("Chickaloon Performing Arts Center") dates from coal mining days. Stay in a real miner's cabin or camp free along the Matanuska River. All cooking from scratch. Famous sausage gravy, musk ox or buffalo burgers. Home of the King Mountain Burger, the most bodacious burger of all. [ADVERTISEMENT] ▲

A 76.1 (122.5 km) **T 251.9** (405.4 km) **King Mountain State Recreation Site**. Pleasant campground on the banks of the Matanuska River *(Danger: Swift current)*: 22 campsites, picnic shelter, campground host, fireplaces, picnic tables, water, toilets. Camping fee $10/night or resident pass; 15-day limit. King Mountain to the southeast. ▲

A 73.7 (118.6 km) **T 254.3** (409.2 km) *"Hill"; winding descent eastbound.*

A 72.9 (117.3 km) **A 255.1** (410.5 km) Fish Lake Road. Ida Lake (sign).

A 72.8 (117.2 km) **T 255.2** (410.7 km) Ida Lake.

A 70.6 (113.6 km) **T 257.4** (414.2 km) Access to Matanuska River to south.

A 68 (109.4 km) **T 260** (418.4 km) *NOTE: Slide areas, gravel turnouts to south, eastbound to **Milepost A 77.5** as highway winds along bank of the Matanuska River.*

Pinnacle Mountain (elev. 4,541 feet/1,384m) rises directly southeast of the highway—easy to identify by its unusual top. Cottonwoods and aspen along the highway. Talkeetna Mountains to the north.

A 66.4 (106.8 km) **T 261.6** (421 km) **King River** bridge. Turnout to north at east end of bridge. King River Trail; King River Crossing 5 miles/8 km. Fishing for trout, early summer best, use eggs.

A 65.9 (106.1 km) **T 262.1** (421.8 km) *CAUTION: Watch for moose.*

A 62.8 (101 km) **T 265.2** (426.8 km) Large gravel turnout with interpretive sign to south along Matanuska River. Dwarf fireweed and sweet pea in June.

A 62.4 (100.4 km) **T 265.6** (427.4 km) **Granite Creek** bridge. Fishing for small Dolly Varden and trout, spring or early summer, use flies or single eggs.

A 62.5 (100.6 km) **T 265.5** (427.3 km) **River's Edge Recreation Park.** Campground greeting, highway travelers! Camping in Alaska should include woods; wildflowers; clear, rushing streams; privacy; quiet; and wildlife. River's Edge Recreation Park offers that and more. As lifelong Alaskans, we value all the natural beauty in our 18-acre facility and try to maintain that natural splendor for our guests. Our campsites are perfect for tents and RVs. We have

(Continues on page 292)

Hatcher Pass Road Log

The 49-mile-long Hatcher Pass Road leads northwest from **Milepost A 49.5** on the Glenn Highway (as Palmer-Fishhook Road) over Hatcher Pass (elev. 3,886 feet) and connects with the Parks Highway at **Milepost A 71.2** (as Fishhook-Willow Road). (See Mat-Su Valley Vicinity map on page 290.) This is a mostly gravel road, not recommended for large RVs or trailers beyond **Milepost J 14**. *NOTE: Watch for road paving between Milepost J 8.7 and 13.7 in summer 2000. Also, Independence Mine State Historical Park may be closed due to restoration projects at the park.* The portion of the road over the pass usually does not open until late June or early July, and snow may close the pass in September. The road stays open to the historical park and to Hatcher Pass Lodge, a popular winter sports area for snowmobiling and cross-country skiing, in winter.

Distance from junction with the Glenn Highway (J) is followed by distance from junction with the Parks Highway (P).

View from Independence Mine State Historical Park. (© Susan Cole Kelly)

J 0 P 49.1 (79 km) **Junction** with the Glenn Highway at **Milepost A 49.5**. Fishhook–Willow Road heads west through farm country.

J 1.4 (2.3 km) **P 47.7** (76.8 km) **Junction** with Farm Loop Road.

J 2.4 (3.9 km) **P 46.7** (75.2 km) **Junction** with Trunk Road.

J 6.5 (10.5 km) **P 42.5** (68.4 km) Tesoro gas station with diesel, propane, grocery, ice, liquor store, laundromat and showers; overnight RV parking.

Hatcher Pass Gateway Center. See display ad this section.

J 6.8 (10.9 km) **P 42.3** (68.1 km) **Junction** with Wasilla–Fishhook Road. Access to bed and breakfast.

Hatcher Pass Bed and Breakfast. Experience our authentic Alaskan log cabins located at the base of beautiful Hatcher Pass, yet only minutes from Palmer and Wasilla. Cozy, comfortable, and private with all the modern amenities—come enjoy a peaceful getaway! Phone (907) 745-6788, fax (907) 745-6787. Web site www.AlaskaOutdoors.com/HPBB. [ADVERTISEMENT]

J 8.1 (13 km) **P 41** (66 km) Hatcher Pass Management Area boundary.

J 8.5 (13.7 km) **P 40.6** (65.3 km) **Little Susitna River** bridge. Large double-ended paved turnout at north end of bridge. Road parallels river. This scenic mountain stream heads at Mint Glacier in the Talkeetna Mountains and flows 110 miles to Cook Inlet. This is a gold-bearing stream.

J 8.7 (14 km) **P 40.4** (65 km) Pavement ends, gravel begins, northbound. Road parallels river. *NOTE: Paving may be under way to Milepost J 13.7 in summer 2000.*

J 9 (14.5 km) **P 40.1** (64.5 km) Gravel loop turnout and sign; entering Hatcher Pass public-use area westbound. No flower picking or plant removal without a permit.

J 9.2 (14.8 km) **P 39.9** (64.2 km) Graffiti Rock.

J 9.3 (15 km) **P 39.8** (64.1 km) Turnout; distance marker shows Independence Mine State Historical Park 10 miles.

J 9.4 (15.1 km) **P 39.7** (63.9 km) Dirt pull-out by river.

J 9.7 (15.6 km) **P 39.4** (63.4 km) This area open to all recreational mining (sign).

J 9.8 (15.8 km) **P 39.3** (63.2 km) Turnout and sign on pass status.

J 10.7 (17.2 km) **P 39.7** (63.9 km) Long loop turnout.

J 11.7 (18.8 km) **P 37.4** (60.2 km) **Milepost 12.** Large turnout.

J 12.6 (20.3 km) **P 36.5** (58.7 km)

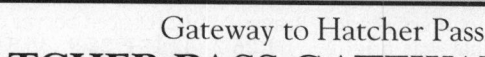

Hatcher Pass Road Log (continued)

Turnout

J 13 (20.9 km) **P 36.1** (58.1 km) Turnout.

J 13.7 (22 km) **P 35.4** (57 km) **Milepost 14.** Motherlode Lodge; food and lodging.

Large parking area with restrooms. Trailhead for Gold Mint Trail. A very popular hiking area. Naturalist programs here in summer. Phone (907) 745-2827 or (907) 745-3975 for current information.

CAUTION: Westbound, Hatcher Pass Road makes a sharp turn and begins a very steep climb to Hatcher Pass via a series of switchbacks.

J 14.6 (23.5 km) **P 34.5** (55.5 km) Archangel Road (very rough road) leads 4 miles up Archangel Valley and ends at Fern Mine (private property, do not trespass). Reed Lakes Trail access. Parking area.

J 16.4 (26.4 km) **P 32.7** (52.6 km) Parking lot to east; Fishhook trailhead, outhouse Hiking in summer; snowmobiling in winter.

J 17 (27.3 km) **P 32.1** (51.6 km) Sharp turn through gates to continue westbound on Hatcher Pass Road, or turn on access road for Hatcher Pass Lodge and Independence Mine State Historical Park (1.2 miles/1.9 km).

Hatcher Pass Lodge. See display ad this section.

The 271-acre **INDEPENDENCE MINE STATE HISTORICAL PARK** includes several buildings and old mining machinery. Park visitor center is housed in what was originally the mine manager's home, built in 1939. Alaska Pacific Consolidated Mine Co., one of the largest gold producers in the Willow Creek mining district, operated here from 1938 through 1941. The Gold Cord Mine buildings (private property) are visible on the hill above and to the north of Independence Mine.

IMPORTANT: Due to construction of visitor facilities and restoration at this site, the park may be closed in summer 2000; phone Alaska State Park's Mat-Su office at (907) 745-3975 for current status.

Snowmobiling is prohibited in the park.

CAUTION: Very steep and potholed road westbound, with many switchbacks.

J 18.7 (30.1 km) **P 30.4** (48.9 km) Entering Summit Lake State Recreation Site westbound; no camping or ground fires permitted. Watch for parasailer; many launch from a spot known as "Nixon's Nose."

J 19.2 (30.9 km) **P 29.8** (48 km) **Hatcher Pass Summit** (elev. 3,886 feet/1,184m); parking area, hiking trails.

J 19.4 (31.2 km) **P 29.7** (47.8 km) Parking area at Summit Lake, headwaters of Willow Creek. Summit Lake State Recreation Site under development.

Westbound, the road descends following Willow Creek from here to the Parks Highway.

J 20.4 (32.8 km) **P 28.6** (46 km) Gates. Upper Willow Creek Valley Road to mine (private).

J 23.8 (38.3 km) **P 25.3** (40.7 km) Craigie Creek Trail (very rough) leads to mine sites. Remains of historic Lucky Shot and War

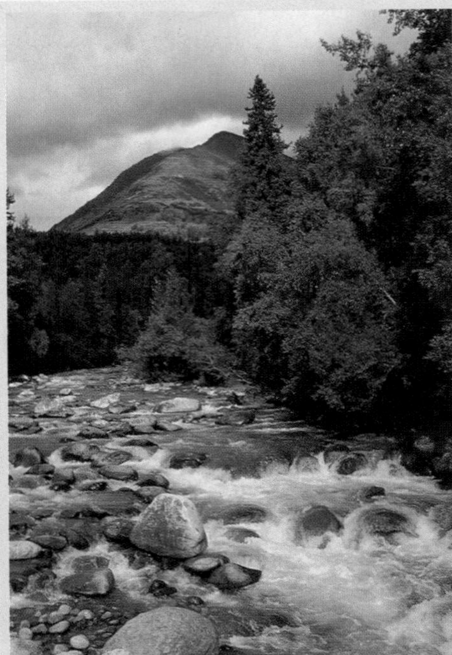

Little Susitna River photographed from the bridge at Milepost J 8.5 Hatcher Pass Road. (© Kris Graef, staff)

Baby mines on hillside are visible on hillside ahead westbound.

J 24.3 (39.1 km) **P 24.8** (39.9 km) Beaver lodges and dams.

J 27.3 (43.9 km) **P 21.8** (35.1 km) View of Beaver Ponds; terraced beaver dams.

J 26.2 (42.1) **P 22.9** (36.8 km) Turnout. Road begins descent westbound into Little Willow Creek valley; numerous turnouts.

J 30.3 (48.8 km) **P 18.7** (30.1 km) Leaving Hatcher Pass public-use area westbound.

J 31.1 (50 km) **P 18** (29 km) Pull-out by river; informal campsite.

J 31.7 (51 km) **P 17.4** (28 km) Dave Churchill Memorial Trail.

J 32.9 (52.9 km) **P 16.2** (26.1 km) Last Chance Coffee House.

J 34.2 (55 km) **P 14.9** (24 km) Little Willow Creek bridge; large parking area.

J 38.1 (61.3 km) **P 11** (17.7 km) *Gravel ends, pavement begins, westbound.*

J 38.5 (62 km) **P 10.6** (17.1 km) Public Safety Building; ***Emergency Phone 911.***

J 41.7 (67.1 km) **P 7.4** (11.9 km) Coyote Gardens (private).

J 47.4 (76.3 km) **P 1.7** (2.7 km) Anchorage to Fairbanks Intertie, a 345KV Transmission Line constructed in 1983-84 (Alaska Power Authority).

J 47.7 (76.7 km) **P 1.4** (2.3 km) **Deception Creek State Campground**; 7 campsites, 15-day limit, $10 nightly fee per vehicle or resident pass, covered picnic tables, water, toilets (wheelchair accessible) Bumpy access road. ♿▲

J 47.8 (76.9 km) **P 1.3** (2.1 km) Deception Creek bridge; turnout at east end.

J 49.1 (79 km) **P 0 Junction** with Parks Highway at **Milepost A 71.2.** (Turn to the PARKS HIGHWAY section.)

Return to Milepost A 49.5 Glenn Highway or Milepost A 71.2 Parks Highway

(Continued from page 290)

electrical hookups, 6 pull-through sites, dump station, drinking water, and very clean shower facilities. You'll find quality for your camp fee at River's Edge. Overnight and electrical fees include water and dump station. Showers are an extra charge and include towels, shampoo and soap in a private dressing room cleaned after each use. We have 27 sites. Looking for a wilderness setting for your camp tonight? Drive on in. Mid-May to mid-September. Phone (907) 746-2267. [ADVERTISEMENT] ♿▲

A 61.6 (99.1 km) **T 266.4** (428.7 km) Turnoff on Chickaloon Way for post office and entrance to Alpine Historical Park, an open-air museum featuring the concrete ruins of the Sutton Coal Washery (1920–22). Donations accepted.

Alpine Historical Park. See display ad this section.

A 61 (98.2 km) **T 267** (429.7 km) **SUTTON** (pop. 470) was established as a railroad siding in about 1918 for the once-flourishing coal industry and is now a small highway community. Sutton has a fire department, library, general store, post office and gas station. Fossilized shells and leaves can be found in this area 1.7 miles/2.7 km up the Jonesville Road. Inquire locally for directions.

Private Aircraft: Jonesville Mine airstrip, 2 NW; elev. 870 feet; length 1,400 feet; gravel; unattended.

Sutton General Store and Jonesville Cafe. Full line menu, good food, homemade pies, orders to go. We supply all your camping, fishing and cooking needs. Groceries,

snacks, ice cream, ice, general merchandise. Clean restrooms, shower, washers and dryers, phone and propane. Tour buses welcome. Stop by and see us! (907) 746-7461 and (907) 746-7561. [ADVERTISEMENT]

*NOTE: Improved highway (1999) westbound to **Milepost A 56**. Driving distances may vary from log.*

A 60.9 (98 km) **T 267.1** (429.8 km) Jonesville Road. Access to Seventeenmile Lake (for recommended access see **Milepost A 57.9**). Drive north 1.7 miles/2.7 km to end of pavement; continue straight ahead for residential area and old Jonesville and Eska coal mines; turn left where pavement ends for Seventeenmile Lake (3.1 miles/5 km via a rough dirt road).

A 60.8 (97.8 km) **T 267.2** (430 km) Eska Creek bridge.

A 59.5 (95.7 km) **T 268.5** (430.5 km) Gas station to south.

A 57.9 (93.2 km) **T 270.1** (434.7 km) Access to Palmer Correctional Center. 58 Mile Road north to **Seventeenmile Lake**; day-use area, fishing for small grayling, early spring, use flies or spinners; trout, early spring, use eggs.

A 56.7 (91.2 km) **T 271.3** (436.6 km) Western boundary of Matanuska Valley Moose Range.

*NOTE: Improved highway (1999) eastbound to **Milepost A 61**. Driving distances may vary from log.*

A 54.6 (87.9 km) **T 273.4** (440 km) Bridge over **Moose Creek**. Fishing for trout and Dolly Varden, summer, use eggs.

A 54 (86.9 km) **T 274** (440.9 km) Truck lane starts westbound.

A 53.4 (85.9 km) **T 274.6** (441.9 km) Truck lane ends westbound.

A 53 (85.3 km) **T 275** (442.6 km) **Buffalo Mine Road** to north; cabins at Mile 2.9. Access to Wishbone Lake 4-wheel-drive trail.

Moose Wallow B&B, Mile 2.9 Buffalo Mine Road. Relax, put your feet up, enjoy the cozy fireplace while staying in one of our wonderful cabins. If you like adventure, we have many trails for summer and winter activities. Pets welcome. Visit our unique gift shop and hair salon. Phone (907) 745-7777; Fax (907) 745-7727. [ADVERTISEMENT]

A 52.3 (84.2 km) **T 275.7** (443.7 km) Soapstone Road.

A 52 (83.7 km) **T 276** (444.2 km) **Wolf Country U.S.A.** See display ad this section.

A 51.2 (82.4 km) **T 276.8** (445.5 km) Fire station.

A 50.9 (81.9 km) **T 277.1** (445.9 km) Farm Loop Road, a 3-mile/4.8-km loop road connecting with Fishhook–Willow Road.

A 50.1 (80.6 km) **T 277.9** (447.2 km) Sharp turn north (watch for signs) for the Musk Ox Farm. Well worth a stop.

Musk Ox Farm and Gift Shop. The world's only domestic musk-oxen farm. The animals are combed for the precious qiviut, which is then hand-knit by Eskimos in isolated villages, aiding the Arctic economy. During the farm tours in the summer, you can see these shaggy ice age survivors romping in beautiful pastures with Pioneer Peak as a backdrop. Open May to September. Phone (907) 745-4151. P.O. Box 587, Palmer, AK 99645. [ADVERTISEMENT]

A 50 (80.5 km) **T 278** (447.4 km) Matanuska River viewpoint to south is a double-ended turnout with a short pedestrian walkway up to a fenced viewing area.

A 49.5 (79.7 km) **T 278.5** (448.2 km)

Junction with Hatcher Pass (Fishhook–Willow) Road which leads west and north over Hatcher Pass to connect with the Parks Highway at **Milepost A 71.2** north of Willow. See HATCHER PASS ROAD log this section.

A 49 (78.9 km) **T 279** (449 km) Cedar Hills subdivision to north. Entering Palmer, which extends to **Milepost A 41.** (Actual driving distance between **Milepost 49** and **42** is 1 mile.) Good view westbound of the farms and homes of one of Alaska's major agricultural areas.

NOTE: Speed zone begins westbound, 45 mph speed limit.

A 42.1 (67.8 km) **T 285.9** (460.1 km) West Arctic Avenue (see Palmer map). Access to Palmer High School to north at this junction. Turn south for downtown Palmer and for the **Old Glenn Highway**, a

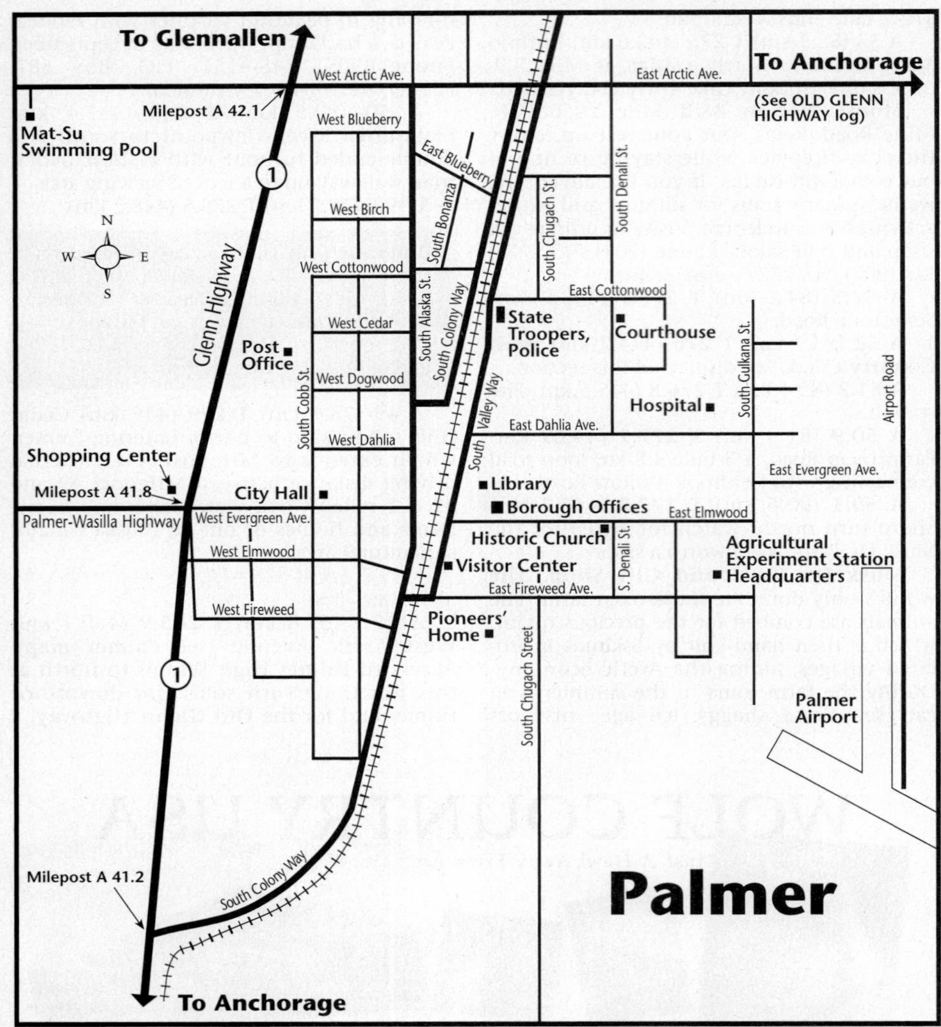

scenic alternate route to Anchorage that rejoins the Glenn Highway at **Milepost A 29.6.** Highlights along the old Glenn Highway include the original Matanuska Colony Farms and a reindeer farm.

Turn to OLD GLENN HIGHWAY log on page 297 for log. (Anchorage-bound travelers read log back to front.)

Palmer

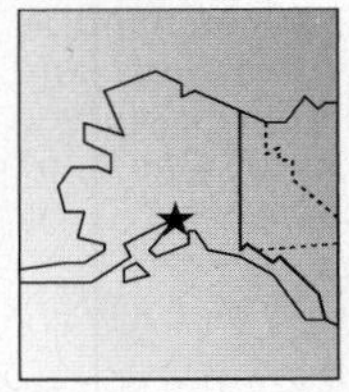

A 42 (67.6 km) T 286 (460.3 km) In the Matanuska Valley northeast of Anchorage. **Population:** 4,151. **Emergency Services:** Phone 911. **Alaska State Troopers,** phone (907) 745-2131. **City Police,** phone (907) 745-4811. **Fire Department** and **Ambulance,** phone (907) 745-3271. **Valley Hospital,** Valley Hospital, 515 E. Dahlia, phone (907) 745-4813.

Visitor Information: Visitor center in log cabin across the railroad tracks on South Valley Way at East Fireweed Avenue. Pick up a brochure and map of downtown Palmer's historic buildings. Open daily 8 A.M. to 7 P.M. May to Sept. 15; weekdays 9 A.M. to 4 P.M. mid-September to May. Pay phone. Small museum in basement; Alaskan-made gifts may be for sale on main floor. Mailing address: Chamber of Commerce, P.O. Box 45, Palmer, AK 99645. Matanuska Valley

PALMER ADVERTISERS

Alaska's Mat-Su Bed & Breakfast Assoc. ....Ph. (800) 401-7444
Alaskan Sampler Bed & Breakfast ....Ph. (907) 745-7829
Colony Inn ....325 Elmwood St.
Fairview Motel & Restaurant ....Ph. (907) 745-1505
Gold Miner's Hotel ....Ph. (800) 725-2752
Iditarod House Bed & Breakfast ....Ph. (907) 745-4348
Motherlode Lodge ....Ph. (907) 746-1464
Mountain View RV Park ....Off Old Glenn Hwy.
Musk Ox Farm & Gift Shop ....Mile 50.1 Glenn Hwy.
Pioneer Motel & Apt. ....Ph. (907) 745-3425
Rose Ridge Bed & Breakfast ....Ph. (907) 745-8604
Tara Dells Bed & Breakfast ....Ph. (907) 745-0407
Valley Hotel ....Ph. (907) 745-3330
Wash Day Too ....Ph. (907) 746-4141

Agricultural Showcase adjacent visitor center features flower and vegetable gardens.

Excellent local library, located at 655 S. Valley Way; open Monday through Saturday. Paperback and magazine exchange. Wheelchair accessible. ♿

Elevation: 240 feet/74m. **Climate:** Temperatures range from 4° to 21°F/-16° to -6°C in January and December, with a mean monthly snowfall of 8 to 10 inches. Record low was -40°F/-40°C in January 1975. Temperatures range from 44° to 68°F/7° to 20°C in June and July, with a mean monthly precipitation of 2 inches. Record high was 89°F/32°C in June 1969. Mean annual rainfall is 15.5 inches, with 50.7 inches of snow. **Radio:** Anchorage stations; KMBQ (Wasilla). **Television:** Anchorage channels and cable. **Newspaper:** *The Frontiersman* (twice weekly).

Private Aircraft: Palmer Municipal Airport, 1 nm SE; elev. 232 feet; length 6,000 feet and 3,616 feet; asphalt; fuel 100LL, Jet. FSS and full services.

Planting potatoes in the Matanuska Valley. (© Loren Taft/Alaskan Images)

Description

This appealing community is both a bit of pioneer Alaska as well as a modern-day commercial center for the Matanuska and Susitna valleys (collectively referred to as the Mat–Su valleys). Take time to explore the small downtown area off the highway.

Palmer was established about 1916 as a railway station on the Matanuska branch of the Alaska Railroad.

In 1935, Palmer became the site of one of the most unusual experiments in American history: the Matanuska Valley Colony. The Federal Emergency Relief Administration, one of the many New Deal relief agencies created during Franklin Roosevelt's first year in office, planned an agricultural colony in Alaska to utilize the great agricultural potential in the Matanuska–Susitna valleys, and to get some American farm families—struck by first the dust bowl, then the Great Depression—off the dole. Social workers picked 203 families, mostly from the northern counties of Michigan, Wisconsin and Minnesota, to join the colony, because it was thought that the many hardy farmers of Scandinavian descent in those 3 states would have a natural advantage over other ethnic groups. The colonists arrived in Palmer in the early summer of 1935, and though the failure rate was high, many of their descendants still live in the Matanuska Valley. Palmer gradually became the unofficial capital of the Matanuska Valley, acting as headquarters for a farmers cooperative marketing organization and as the business and social center for the state's most productive farming region.

Palmer is Alaska's only community that developed primarily from an agricultural economy. (Real estate now takes a close second to agriculture.) The growing season averages 80 to 110 days a year, with long hours of sunshine. Fresh vegetables from Valley farms are popular with Anchorage residents, many of whom drive out to pick up "Valley peas" and other favorites in season. Local produce is available at roadside stands and is marketed in local stores.

The University of Alaska–Fairbanks has an Agricultural and Forestry Experiment Station Office and a district Cooperative Extension Service Office here. The university also operates its Matanuska Research Farm, located on Trunk Road off the Parks Highway, about a 7-mile/11.3-km drive from Palmer. The university farm conducts research in agronomy, horticulture, soil science and animal science.

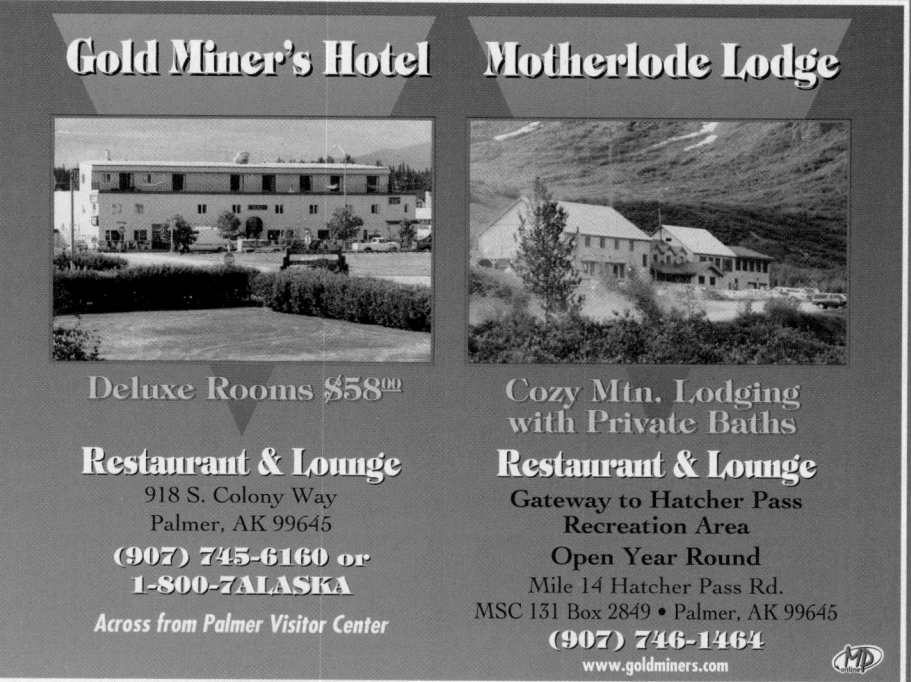

The community has a hospital, the Mat–Su College (University of Alaska), a library, banks, the Mat–Su Borough offices, borough school district, and several other state and federal agency offices. Palmer has churches representing most denominations. The United Protestant Church in Palmer, the **Church of a Thousand Logs**, dates from Matanuska Colony days and is one of the oldest churches in Alaska still holding services. It is included in the National Register of Historic Places.

Lodging & Services

Palmer has all visitor facilities including 3 hotels, 2 motels, bed and breakfasts, gas stations, grocery stores, laundromat, auto repair and parts, and shopping. The Matanuska Valley region has several lake resorts offering boat rentals, golf, fly-in fishing, hunting and horseback riding.

Alaska's Mat-Su Bed & Breakfast Association offers a variety of clean, quality lodging throughout the Mat-Su Valley. Check us out on the internet at http://alaska.net/~akhosts. While traveling, check our vacancy listings at local visitor centers in Palmer and Wasilla. Alaska's Mat-Su Bed & Breakfast Association serving you in Southcentral Alaska. [ADVERTISEMENT]

Alaskan Sampler Bed & Breakfast. Located 40 minutes outside Anchorage on the way to Valdez, Denali Park or Hatcher

Pass. Luxury accommodations on a 3-acre estate with incredible mountain views. Two private entrance suites with private baths, full kitchen, laundry facility. Located at 8300 Regents Road, Palmer. (907) 745-7829 or toll-free (877) 228-7829. [ADVERTISEMENT]

Iditarod House Bed and Breakfast. Hosted by 2-time Iditarod musher and 1980 Iditarod "Rookie of the Year" Donna (Gentry) Massay. Conveniently

located country acreage with scenic mountain views. Queen beds, private baths, private entrance. Wheelchair accessible. Open year-round. Reasonable rates. Great

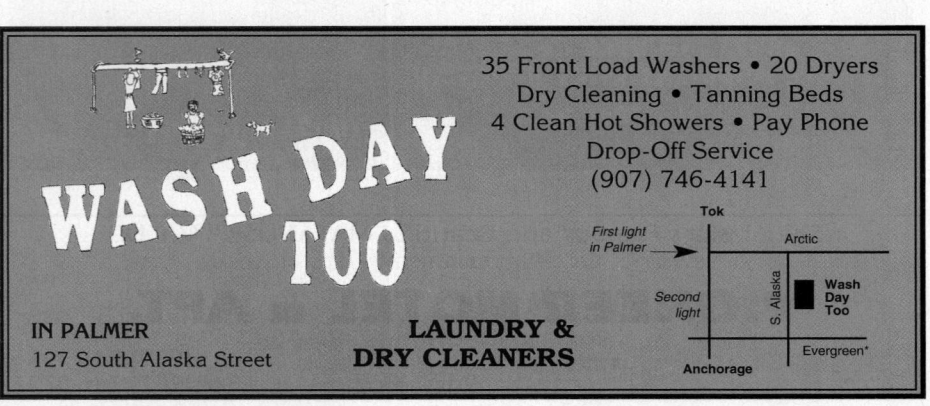

Children enjoy the rides at the Alaska State Fair in Palmer. (© David L. Ranta, staff)

location for exploring the Mat-Su Valley and Anchorage. P.O. Box 3096, Palmer, AK 99645. Phone (907) 745-4348; www.matnet.com/iditabed. [ADVERTISEMENT]

Camping

There is a private RV park on Smith Road off the Old Glenn Highway. There are also private campgrounds on the Glenn Highway a few miles west of Palmer. The Mat–Su Borough operates **Matanuska River Park**, located 1.1 miles south of town at Mile 17.5 Old Glenn Highway; 80 campsites for tents or RVs, picnic area, water, dump station (fee charged), firewood for sale, flush toilets, hot showers, camping fee. **Finger Lake State Recreation Site** (see PALMER-WASILLA HIGHWAY log this section), has 69 campsites, 7-day limit, toilets, water, trails, boating and fishing; camping fee $10/night. ▲

Mountain View RV Park offers breathtaking views of the Matanuska mountains.

Watch wildlife from your door. Full hookups, hot showers included. New bathrooms and laundromat, dump station. Good Sam Park. Half-day scenic airboat tours on Knik River. Call (907) 745-5747 for reservations. Mail forwarding. Write P.O. Box 2521, Palmer, AK 99745. From Mile A 42.1 Glenn Highway (Arctic), follow Old Glenn Highway 2.8 miles. Turn east on Smith Road, drive 0.6 mile, turn right (0.3 mile). We're 3.7 miles from the Glenn Highway. See display ad this section. [ADVERTISEMENT] ♿▲

Transportation

Air: No scheduled service, but the local airport has a number of charter operators.

Bus: Mat-Su Community Transit connects Palmer, Wasilla, Eagle River and Anchorage.

Attractions

Go Swimming: The 80 foot/25m swimming pool is open to the public weekdays (closed weekends). Fees are: $4.25 for adults, $3 youth and seniors. Showers available. The pool is located at Palmer High School on West Arctic Avenue; phone (907) 745-5091.

Get Acquainted: Stop at the visitor information center, a log building just off the "main drag" (across the railroad tracks at the intersection of East Fireweed Avenue and South Valley Way). The center includes a museum, artifacts, a gift shop and agricultural showcase garden.

Visit the Musk Ox Farm. Located east of Palmer on the Glenn Highway at **Milepost 50.1**, the Musk Ox Farm is the only place in the world where these exotic animals are raised domestically. Hunted to near extinction in Alaska in 1865, the species was reintroduced in the 1930s. The farm is open May to September; admission is charged.

Visit a Reindeer Farm, located 8.1 miles/11.5 km south of Palmer via the Old Glenn Highway to Bodenburg Loop Road. This commercial reindeer farm is open daily in summer; admission is charged.

Play Golf in the spectacular Matanuska Valley. The Palmer Golf Course has 18 holes (par 72, USGA rated), rental carts and clubs, driving range, pro shop, practice green and snack bar. Phone (907) 745-4653.

Enjoy Water Sports. Fishing, boating, waterskiing and other water sports are

(Continues on page 298)

Old Glenn Highway (Palmer Alternate) Log

This 18.6-mile/29.9-km paved road (2 lanes, 45 mph curves) is a scenic alternate route between Palmer and Anchorage, exiting the Glenn Highway at **Milepost A 29.6** and rejoining the Glenn Highway at **Milepost A 42.1**. The Old Glenn Highway goes through the heart of the original Matanuska Colony agricultural lands.

Distance from south junction with the Glenn Highway (J) is followed by distance from Palmer (P).

Original Matanuska Colony farm on Bodenburg Butte Road. (© Loren Taft/Alaskan Images)

J 0 P 18.6 (29.9 km) Exit from Glenn Highway at **Milepost A 29.6**.

J 4 (6.4 km) **P 14.6** (23.5 km) Eklutna Power Plant (Alaska Power Administration) uses water from Eklutna Lake to provide power to Anchorage and the Mat-Su Valley.

J 6 (9.6 km) **P 12.6** (20.3 km) Goat Creek Bridge.

J 7.2 (11.6 km) **P 11.4** (18.3 km) View of Bodenburg Butte across Knik River.

J 8.7 (14 km) **P 9.9** (15.9 km) **Junction** with **Knik River Road.** Road dead ends 11.2 miles east of here. Knik River Road is a mostly flat road that is bordered by private property (do not trespass). The first 9.8 miles are paved. The only public access to the Knik River is at Mile 1.4. Of interest: **Pioneer Falls** (a waterfall) at Mile 1.2 *(CAUTION: Black bears)*; Pioneer Ridge-Knik River trailhead at Mile 3.8; and a view of Knik Glacier at about Mile 7. The glacier is best viewed from the river. An airboat outfitter at Mile 8.4 offers trips to the glacier face. Shuttle bus service available.

Knik Glacier Visitor Center, Mile 8.4 Knik River Road. Log cabin surrounded by breathtaking scenery. Inside has photos and historic video of the area's largest glacier. Park has RV and tent sites. Hiking trails with glacier views. Airboat and flightseeing tours depart daily to our wilderness camp at the face of this spectacular glacier. Camping equipment and kayak rentals. Reservations phone (907) 745-1577. www.huntercreekoutfitters.com. [ADVERTISEMENT]

J 8.8 (14.2 km) **P 9.8** (15.8 km) Knik River bridge; pedestrian bridge adjacent highway bridge.

J 9 (14.5 km) **P 9.6** (15.4 km) Access to river and pedestrian bridge at east end of Knik River bridge.

J 10 (16 km) **P 8.6** (13.8 km) Pioneer Peak dominates the skyline southbound.

J 10.4 (10.7 km) **P 8.2** (13.1 km) Alaska Raceway Park turnoff.

J 11.5 (18.5 km) **P 7.1** (11.4 km) Gas station at **junction** of Bodenburg Loop Road and Plumley Road.

The 5.8-mile/9.3-km Bodenburg Butte Road rejoins the Old Glenn Highway opposite Dack Acres Road (**Milepost J 12.5**). From this junction it is 0.6 mile to **Bodenburg Butte** trailhead and 0.7 mile to reindeer farm (visitors welcome, fee charged) and trail rides. The Bodenburg Butte area has original Matanuska Colony farms.

Reindeer Farm. Bodenburg Loop Road 0.8 mile off Old Glenn Highway (turn at **Mile J 11.5** at the flashing light). Hand feed reindeer. View moose, black-tailed deer and elk. Bring camera. Hours 10 A.M.–6 P.M. daily. Fee charged. Guided horseback trail rides by appointment. (907) 745-4000; e-mail reindeer@core.com.net; Internet site: www.core.com.net/~reindeer/tours.htm. [ADVERTISEMENT]

J 11.7 (18.8 km) **P 6.9** (11.1 km) **BUTTE** (pop. 2,654); fire and ambulance service station #21; emergency phone 911. Fire permits May 1 to Sept. 30. Area map.

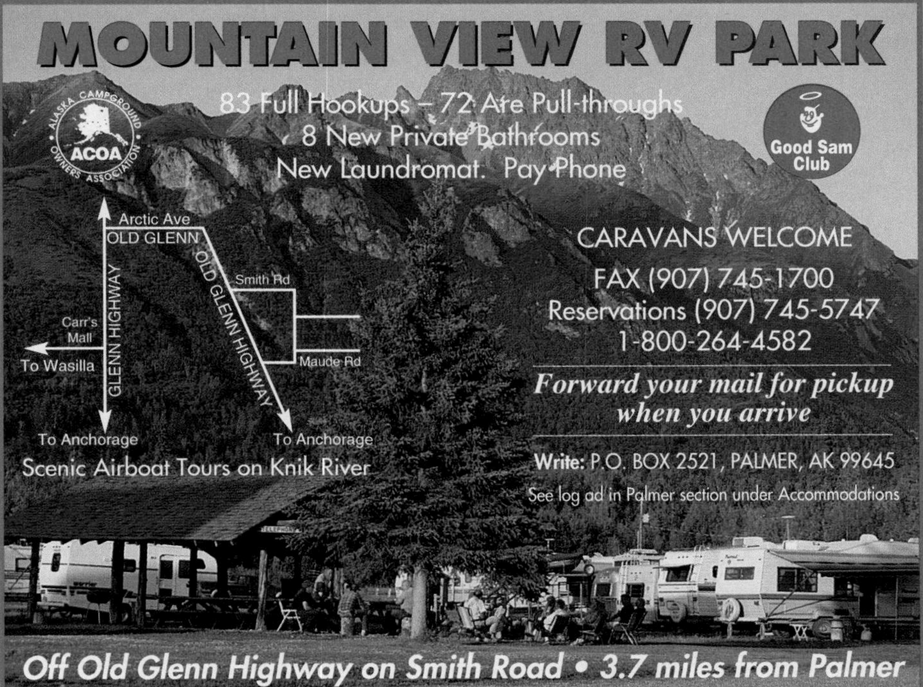

Old Glenn Highway Log (continued)

J 12 (19.3 km) **P 6.6** (10.6 km) Store and post office. Marilyn Road.

J 12.5 (20.1 km) **P 6.1** (9.8 km) **Junction** with Dack Acres Road, north end of Bodenburg Butte Loop Road (see **Milepost J 11.5**).

J 15.5 (25 km) **P 3.1** (5 km) **Junction** with Smith Road. Access to private campground (0.8 mile/1.3 km). Turn east on Smith Road and drive 1.5 miles/2.4 km for Matanuska Peak trailhead.

Mountain View RV Park. See display ad this section. ▲

J 16.1 (25.9 km) **P 2.5** (4 km) Clark–Wolverine Road; access bed and breakfast and to **Lazy Mountain Recreation Area**. For recreation area, drive in 0.7 mile; turn right on Huntley Road at T; drive 1 mile on gravel road and take right fork to recreation area and overlook. Popular 2.5-mile trail to summit of Lazy Mountain (elev. 3,720 feet); steep and strenuous.

A Lazy Acres Bed and Breakfast is quiet and secluded on 10 acres. 15 minutes from Palmer. Two comfortable rooms with private baths, smoke-free home. Call (907) 745-6340; fax (907) 745-8664. Or write P.O. Box 4013, Palmer, AK 99645 for rates and reservations. Helen Muñoz, hostess. [ADVERTISEMENT]

J 16.7 (26.9 km) **P 1.9** (3.1 km) Paved loop road down to Matanuska River photo viewpoint.

J 17 (27.4 km) **P 1.6** (2.5 km) Matanuska River bridge. Photo viewpoint to east at north end of bridge on old alignment; access to pedestrian bridge.

J 17.5 (28.2 km) **P 1.1** (1.8 km) Turnoff for **Matanuska River Park** (Mat-Su Borough Parks & Recreation) camping and day-use areas; 80 level tent/RV sites with picnic tables on gravel loop road. Day-use area has playground and picnic pavilions. Facilities include some pull-through sites, water, fireplaces, dump station, flush toilets, hot showers, softball fields and hiking trails. Camping, shower and dump station fees charged. Phone (907) 745-9631 for more information. ▲

J 17.7 (28.5 km) **P 0.9** (1.4 km) Palmer municipal airport. Pioneer cemetery.

J 18.6 (29.9 km) **P 0 Junction** of Old Glenn Highway (West Arctic Avenue) at Palmer, **Milepost A 42.1** Glenn Highway.

Return to Milepost A 42.1 or A 29.6 Glenn Highway

Produce from the Matanuska Valley on sale at the Alaska State Fair in Palmer. (© Barb Willard)

popular in summer at Finger Lake west of Palmer. Kepler–Bradley Lakes State Recreation Area on Matanuska Lake has canoe rentals; turn off the Glenn Highway at **Milepost A 36.4.**

Special events include **Colony Days** (June 9, 2000), the **Palmer Pride Picnic** (July 22, 2000) and the **Alaska State Fair** (Aug. 25–Sept. 4, 2000). The 11-day state fair, ending on Labor Day, has agricultural exhibits from farms throughout Alaska. There are also food booths, games, pony rides and midway rides. This is a very popular event, and fairgoers from Anchorage can tie up traffic. But it's worth the drive just to see the huge vegetables. Phone (907) 745-4827.

Visit Scenic Hatcher Pass: A 6- to 8-hour drive from **Milepost A 49.5** near Palmer that climbs through the beautiful Hatcher Pass Recreation Area and connects with the Parks Highway at **Milepost A 71.2.** Access to Independence Mine State Historical Park. See HATCHER PASS ROAD this section.

See the Matanuska Glacier: Drive 50 miles/80 km east on the Glenn Highway from Palmer to visit this spectacular 27-mile/43.5-km-long glacier, one of the few you can drive to and explore on foot. Access to the foot of the glacier is through a private campground at **Milepost A 102**; admission charged. If you're not interested in getting close, there are several vantage points along the highway and from trails at Matanuska Glacier Campground, **Milepost A 101.**

Glenn Highway Log

(continued)

A 41.8 (67.3 km) **T 286.2** (460.6 km) West Evergreen Avenue access to downtown Palmer. Gas station, fast food and Carrs Pioneer Square shopping mall (24-hour supermarket) north side of highway. A bronze sculpture by Jacques and Mary Regat dedicated to the Matanuska Valley pioneers is located at the mall.

Junction with Palmer–Wasilla Highway which leads northwest 10 miles/16 km to the Parks Highway at Wasilla. See the PALMER–WASILLA HIGHWAY LOG on facing page.

A 41.6 (66.9 km) **T 286.4** (460.9 km) Gas station and fast-food south side of highway.

A 41.2 (66.3 km) **T 286.8** (461.5 km) First access eastbound to Palmer business district via South Colony Way.

A 40.5 (65.2 km) **T 287.5** (462.7 km) Fairview Motel & Restaurant.

A 40.2 (64.7 km) **T 287.8** (463.2 km) Main entrance to fairgrounds (site of Alaska State Fair) and Herman Field (home of the Mat–Su Miners baseball team). Alaska State Fair is held the end of August through the first week in September (heavy traffic during the fair; drive carefully!).

A 39.2 (63.1 km) **T 288.8** (464.8 km) Outer Springer Loop. Gift shop. Short, steep trail to **Meier Lake**; grayling fishing.

A 37.4 (60.2 km) **T 290.6** (467.7 km) Kepler Drive; access to private campground and lake. ▲

A 37.2 (59.9 km) **T 290.8** (468 km) **Echo Lake** turnout; parking and trail to lake. Fishing for landlocked salmon and rainbow.

A 37 (59.5 km) **T 291** (468.3 km) Echo Lake Road.

A 36.4 (58.6 km) **T 291.6** (469.3 km) **Kepler–Bradley Lakes State Recreation Area** to north on Matanuska Lake; day-use area with water, toilets, parking, picnic tables, canoe rentals, hiking trails and fishing. ADF&G stocks lakes with rainbow trout, grayling and silver salmon. Wheelchair-accessible trail to lake. The lakes are Kepler, Bradley, Matanuska, Canoe, Irene, Long, Claire and Victor.

A 36.3 (58.4 km) **T 291.7** (469.4 km) **Fox Run RV Campground** sits on Matanuska Lake with a fantastic view of the Chugach Mountains. We offer full hookups, pull-throughs, tents sites, clean restrooms and showers (handicapped access), laundry,

Palmer-Wasilla Highway Log

This 10.1 mile road connects the Glenn and Parks highways (Alaska Routes 1 and 3). There is a bike path along this highway. **Distance from Palmer (P) is followed by distance from Wasilla (W).**

P 0 W 10.1 (16.3 km) **Junction** with Glenn Highway at **Milepost A 41.8** in Palmer; Carrs Mall (24-hour supermarket) and McDonalds.

P 0.4 (0.6 km) **W 9.7** (15.6 km) NOAA Alaska Tsunami Warning Center; phone (907) 745-4212.

P 0.5 (0.8 km) **W 9.6** (15.4 km) South end of Irwin Loop; access to Iditarod House B&B (0.7 mile).

P 0.8 (1.3 km) **W 9.3** (15 km) North end Irwin Loop.

P 0.9 (1.4 km) **W 9.2** (14.8 km) Hemmer Road.

P 1.5 (2.4 km) **W 8.6** (13.8 km) Equestrian Acres subdivision.

P 2 (3.1 km) **W 8.1** (13.2 km) Loma Prieta Drive. Access to **Crevasse–Moraine Trail**; 0.7 mile south to trailhead parking. This loop trail system is used for cross-country skiing in winter and hiking, mountain biking and horseback riding in summer.

P 2.3 (3.7 km) **W 7.8** (12.6 km) Trinity Barn Plaza.

P 2.8 (4.5 km) **W 7.3** (11.7 km) North 49th/State Street intersection. Stoplight.

P 3.4 (5.5 km) **W 6.7** (10.8 km) Midtown Community Business Park; pizza.

P 3.6 (5.8 km) **W 6.5** (10.5 km) The Highlands subdivision.

P 3.9 (6.2 km) **W 6.2** (10 km) **Four Corners junction.** Tesoro gas station and grocery at **junction** with Trunk Road. Turn north for access to Bogard Road and **Finger Lake State Recreation Site**; go north on Trunk Road 1 mile to Bogard Road; turn west and drive 0.8 mile to park entrance; drive in 0.3 mile on gravel road. A scenic spot with 41 campsites, wheelchair-accessible toilets, picnic tables, water, hiking trails and boat launch, $10 camping fee, 7-day limit. Use the life jackets provided! Finger Lake is on the **7-Mile Canoe Trail.** Public access to canoe trail also from Wasilla and Cottonwood lakes. ♿▲

P 4.2 (6.7 km) **W 5.9** (9.5 km) Wasilla Creek. Cache Camper.

P 6.3 (10.1 km) **W 3.8** (6.1 km) The Frontiersman newspaper office.

P 6.9 (11.1 km) **W 3.2** (5.1 km) Brentwood Plaza.

P 7 (11.3 km) **W 3.1** (5 km) Hatcherview Business Park.

P 7.2 (11.6 km) **W 2.9** (4.7 km) Alaskan Agate Inn bed and breakfast.

P 8.2 (13.2 km) **W 1.9** (3.1 km) Fire station and gas station at **junction** with Seward Meridian Road, which connects to Parks Highway at **Milepost A 39.4.**

P 9 (14.5 km) **W 1.1** (1.8 km) Country Lakes Bed and Breakfast.

P 9.6 (15.4 km) **W 0.5** (0.8 km) Gas station.

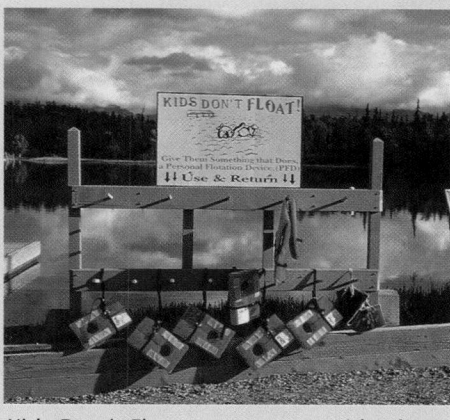

Kids Don't Float program provides free life-jackets for use at area lakes.

(© Kris Graef, staff)

P 9.4 (15.1 km) **W 0.7** (1.1 km) Cottonwood Creek; fish viewing platform; spawning salmon.

P 10.1 (16.3 km) **W 0 Junction** with Parks Highway at **Milepost A 41.1**; Safeway, Fred Meyer store and other businesses.

Return to Milepost A 41.8 Glenn Highway or A 41.1 Parks Highway

e-mail, phone. Hiking, fishing, swimming and boating. Open May 15–September 15. E-mail: foxrun@alaska.net. Web site: www.foxrun.freeservers.com. Phone (907) 745-6120. [ADVERTISEMENT] ♿▲

A 36.2 (58.3 km) **T 291.8** (469.6 km) **The Homestead RV Park.** Beautiful, wooded setting overlooking the scenic Matanuska Valley. Good Sam, AAA, 64 sites, pull-throughs to 70 feet. Very clean restrooms and showers. Electric and water hookups; dump station; also on-site portable dumping. Laundry. Picnic tables, pay phone. Enclosed pavilion and Matanuska Amphitheatre, home of the musical narrative "Cream Puff Pioneers." Evening entertainment. Square dancing Thursday nights. Walking and jogging trails, trout fishing nearby. Modern, friendly. Handicap access. Commuting distance to Anchorage. Caravans welcome. Phone (907) 745-6005. Toll free in Alaska (800) 478-3570. See display ad this section. [ADVERTISEMENT] ♿▲

A 35.3 (56.8 km) **T 292.7** (471.1 km) Traffic signal at busy junction with Parks Highway. *NOTE: Expect major road constructions at this highway junction in summer 2000.*

Junction of the Glenn Highway (Alaska Route 1) with the Parks Highway (Alaska Route 3) to Denali Park and Fairbanks. See the PARKS HIGHWAY section for log.

A 34.9 (56.2 km) **T 293.1** (471.7 km) *CAUTION: Alaska Railroad crossing.*

A 34 (54.7 km) **T 294** (473.1 km) Exit to espresso stop; access to Rabbit Slough, a tributary of the Matanuska River, and Nelson Road.

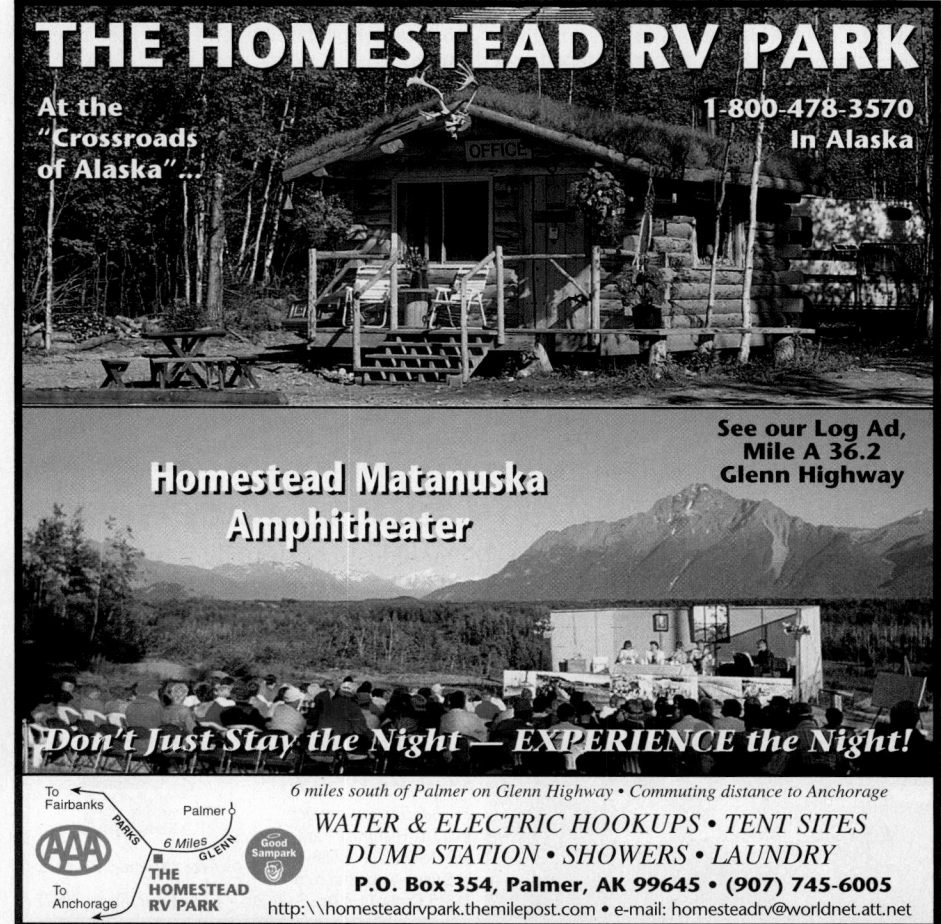

Eklutna Lake is a 10-mile drive from the Eklutna exit. (© Kris Graef, staff)

A 32.4 (52.1 km) **T 295.6** (475.7 km) **Palmer Hay Flats State Game Refuge.** According to the ADF&G, this is the most heavily utilized waterfowl hunting area in Alaska. Access to the refuge is via Fairview Loop Road off the Parks Highway. Moose winter in this area, and the cows and calves may be seen early in the morning and in the evening as late as early July.

CAUTION: Watch for moose.

A 31.5 (50.7 km) **T 296.5** (477.2 km) Bridge over the Matanuska River, which is fed by the Matanuska Glacier.

A 30.8 (49.6 km) **T 297.5** (478.8 km) Knik River bridge. The **Knik River** comes down from the Knik Glacier to the east and splits into several branches as it approaches Knik Arm. Knik Arm is a 3-mile-wide estuary that extends 40 miles southeast to Cook Inlet.

Game Management Unit 14C boundary. Also boundary of Matanuska–Susitna Borough.

A 30.6 (49.2 km) **T 297.4** (478.6 km) Knik River Access; exits both sides of highway lead west to parkin area next to Knik River via short potholed road.

A 30.3 (48.7 km) **T 297.7** (479 km) Kinik River bridge. Entering Game Management Unit 15A northbound.

A 29.6 (47.6 km) **T 298.4** (480.2 km) Exit to the Old Glenn Highway (Palmer Alternate).

Junction with Old Glenn Highway. See OLD GLENN HIGHWAY log on page 297.

A 27.3 (43.9 km) **T 300.7** (483.9 km) The highway crosses a swampy area known locally as Eklutna Flats. These flats are a protected wildflower area (picking flowers is strictly prohibited). Look for wild iris, shooting star, chocolate lily and wild rose in early June.

A 26.3 (42.3 km) **T 301.7** (485.5 km) Eklutna exit. Exit east for private RV park, Eklutna Lake Road (descriptions follow). This exit is also the southbound access to Thunderbird Falls (see **Milepost A 25.2** for description).

 ▲

Exit west for **EKLUTNA** (pop. 434), a residential community and Athabascan village, and for **Eklutna Historical Park.** The historical park, just west of the highway, preserves the heritage and traditions of the Athabascan Alaska Natives. Attractions include the Eklutna Heritage Museum, the historic St. Nicholas Russian Orthodox Church and a hand-built Siberian prayer chapel. Admission fee charged. Open daily mid-May to mid-September. The bright little grave houses or spirit houses in the cemetery are painted in the family's traditional colors.

Eklutna Historical Park. See display ad this section.

From the overpass, follow Eklutna Lake signs east 10 miles/16.1 km for **Eklutna Lake Recreation Area** in Chugach State Park. The access road is paved to Mile 2.2, and then dirt and gravel to road end at Mile 10. Rochelle's Ice Cream Stop and Cheely's General Store at Mile 9. The recreation area has 50 campsites in the trees; 23 picnic sites, also in the trees; water pumps, picnic tables, firepits, outhouses; campground host in residence; ranger station; overflow camping area; and hiking trails. Camping fee $10/night or resident pass; 15-day limit. The trailhead parking lot offers easy access to the lake and will accommodate 80 cars. It also acts as a boat launch for hand-carried boats. Three trails branch off the trailhead: Twin Peaks, Lakeside and Bold Ridge. The Lakeside trail skirts Eklutna Lake and gives access to Eklutna Glacier (12.7 miles/20.4 km).

Eklutna Lake is the largest lake in Chugach State Park, measuring approximately 7 miles long by a mile wide. The lake is used to generate power at the Eklutna Plant, and is also a water source for Anchorage. Fed by Eklutna Glacier, Eklutna Lake offers fair fishing for Dolly Varden. *CAUTION: High winds can make this lake dangerous for boaters.* Interpretive displays on wildlife and a viewing telescope are located at the trailhead.

A 25.2 (40.5 km) **T 302.8** (487.3 km) **Thunderbird Falls** exit (northbound traffic only) and northbound access to Eklutna Road (see **Milepost A 26.3** for description). Drive 0.4 mile to parking area just before Eklutna River bridge (follow signs). Thunderbird Falls is a 2-mile round-trip hike from the trailhead. This easy family walk is along

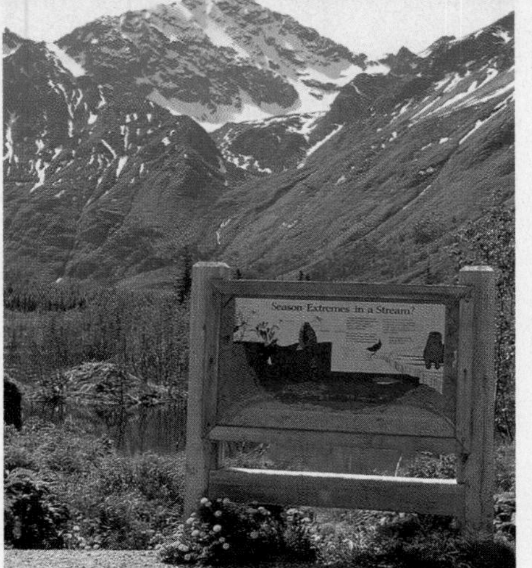

Eagle River Nature Center offers beautiful mountain views and nature programs. (© Kris Graef, staff)

a wide, scenic trail. The trail forks at end: right fork leads to view of falls, left fork leads down to Thunderbird Creek. The falls are just upstream. *CAUTION: Do NOT venture beyond the end of the trail to climb the steep cliffs overhanging the falls!*

A 24.5 (39.4 km) **T 303.5** (488.4 km) Southbound-only exit to Edmonds Lake residential area and Mirror Lake picnic wayside. The shallow 73-acre **Mirror Lake** is located at the foot of Mount Eklutna; rainbow.

A 23.6 (38 km) **T 304.4** (489.9 km) Northbound-only exit to Mirror Lake picnic wayside and Edmonds Lake.

A 23 (37 km) **T 305** (490.8 km) Exit to North Peters Creek Business Loop (use next exit at **Milepost A 21.9** for more direct access to services).

A 21.9 (35.2 km) **T 306.1** (492.6 km) South Peters Creek exit to **PETERS CREEK** services; gas stations, grocery, car wash, body repair shop and restaurant.

Peters Creek Bed & Breakfast. Located on the north shore of Peters Creek only 0.8 mile from exit. Wheelchair accessible; open year-round. Rooms have private baths, cable TV, VCR, refrigerator; full Alaskan breakfast. Lovely new home, wooded setting, smoke-free environment, major credit cards accepted. Phone (888) 688-3465, (907) 688-3465, fax (907) 688-3466. [ADVERTISEMENT]

Peters Creek "Petite" RV Park. See display ad this section. ▲

Peters Creek Trading Post. See display ad this section.

A 20.9 (33.6 km) **T 306.9** (493.9 km) North Birchwood Loop Road exits both sides of highway. Turn east for community of **CHUGIAK.** Chugiak post office, senior center, convenience store with gas, diesel, showers and laundromat on Old Glenn Highway.

Alice Maes Shoppers Cache. See display ad this section.

A 17.2 (27.7 km) **T 310.8** (500.2 km) South Birchwood Loop Road exits both sides of highway. Access west to Chugiak High School and Mush A Dog sled dog demonstrations; exit east for to St. John Orthodox Cathedral (on Monastery Drive) and Old Glenn Highway.

Mush A Dog Team/Gold Rush Park. Ride Gold Tram pulled by Iditarod sled dogs. Outdoor pioneer museum. Gold panning on creek. Gift shop. Tent/RV camping. Open daily. Turn at South Birchwood exit. Drive west past the school 3/4 mile. Sign on left. Phone (907) 688-1391. [ADVERTISEMENT] ▲

Saint John Orthodox Cathedral. Take a peaceful break from your travels. Visit this unique, geodesic-dome cathedral with birch ceiling and beautiful icons. Discover how this church connects to the early church and how Christianity came to Alaska 200 years ago. Bookstore. Monastery Drive off Old Glenn. (907) 696-2002. [ADVERTISEMENT]

A 15.3 (24.6 km) **T 312.7** (503.2 km) Exit to North Eagle River, Terrace Lane. Access to Eagle River Car Wash and Duck Pond at Mile 15.5 Old Glenn Highway.

A 13.4 (21.6 km) **T 314.6** (506.3 km) Eagle River exit east to community of Eagle River via Artillery Road; all visitor services (description follows). Also access to Eagle River Road to Eagle River Nature Center in Chugach State Park (see Eagle River Road description above).

Eagle River Road

Eagle River Road leads 12.3 miles east from the community of Eagle River through a rural residential area to Eagle River Nature Center in Chugach State Park. It is a good paved 2-lane road, with older patched pavement beginning about Mile 5.4. Speed limits are 40 mph on winding grades, 55 mph on straightaways. *Note: Watch for driveway traffic, school bus stops and pedestrians.*

Distance from junction (J) with Old Glenn Highway is shown.

J 0 Junction with Old Glenn Highway (Artillery Road).

J 0.3 Fire station. VFW Road; access to Hidden Haven RV Park. ▲

J 1.5 Junction with Eagle River Loop Road.

J 2.8 P & M Garden Services (a nursery).

J 3.5 Milepost 4.

J 4.5 Milepost 5.

J 7.6 Mile 7.4 North Fork Put-In. Short, bumpy, gravel road south to **North Fork Eagle River** access for kayaks, rafts and canoes; large gravel parking area, outhouse. Day-use area only, no camping. No fires; carry out trash. Hiking trail from parking area to main stem of river. The Eagle River offers class II, III and IV float trips. Fishing for rainbow trout, Dolly Varden and a limited king salmon fishery. Cross-country skiing and snow machining in winter. Check with Chugach State Park ranger (345-5014) for information on river conditions.

J 8.8 Mile 9 Moose Pond Put-In; small gravel parking area at boat access for Eagle River floats.

J 11.4 Rough gravel turnout to south; abrupt pavement edge.

J 12.3 Eagle River Nature Center; operated by the non-profit Friends of Eagle River Nature Center to provide educational and interpretive opportunities to Chugach State Park visitors. Beautiful views of the Chugach Mountains, viewing telescope, self-guiding nature trails. Also the trailhead for the Old Iditarod–Crow Pass trail. Guided nature hikes are offered daily in summer and there are regularly scheduled nature programs. The center has a pay phone and restrooms. Public-use yurt and cabin available for rent; reserve in advance with the Nature Center. The center is open daily in summer from 10 A.M. to 5 P.M.; $5 parking fee. (Overnight hikers use designated parking space; $5 for 3 nights.) Phone (907) 694-2108 for activities schedule, cabin reservations and winter hours; 694-6391 recorded message; 345-5014 Chugach State Park ranger.

Return to Milepost A 13.4 Glenn Highway

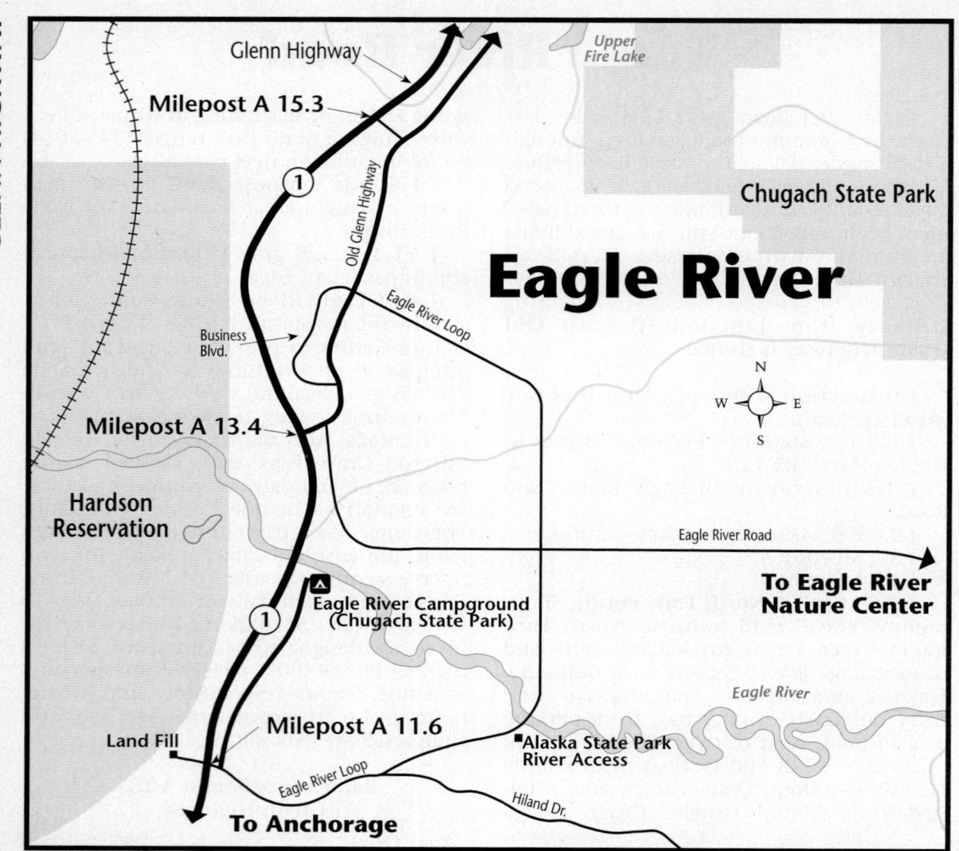

Eagle River

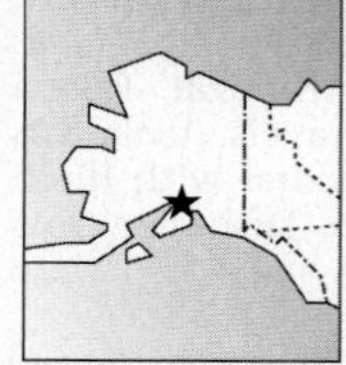

A 13.4 (21.6 km) **T 314.6** (506.3 km) **Population:** Area 18,040. **Emergency Services: Police**, Anchorage Police Dept., phone (907) 786-8500. **Alaska State Troopers**, phone (907) 269-5711. **Ambulance**, phone 911. **Fire Department**, phone 911.

Visitor Information: At the Alaska Museum of Natural History in the Parkgate Building at 11723 Old Glenn Highway. The North Anchorage Visitor Information Center brochure racks (unmanned) are located at the entrance to the museum. For information on Eagle River/Chugiak, contact the Chugiak–Eagle River Chamber of Commerce, P.O. Box 770353, Eagle River, AK 99577; phone (907) 694-4702. You can also visit the Chamber office at 11401 Old Glenn Highway, #105, in the Eagle River Shopping Center.

The Chugiak–Eagle River area was homesteaded after WWII when the new Glenn Highway opened this rural area northeast of Anchorage. Today, Eagle River is a fast-growing residential area with a full range of businesses, most located along the Old Glenn Highway east off the Glenn Highway.

Lodging & Services

Visitor services include fast-food restaurants, supermarkets, banks, laundromat, post office, gas stations and shopping centers.

Eagle River Car Wash and Duck Pond. Facilities available for washing cars, campers, trucks, boats and travel homes. Vacuums available. A duck pond on the premises is open to the public and features cedar viewing decks for observing some of the natural wild Alaskan waterfowl in their natural habitat. Mile 15.5 Old Glenn Highway. Turn off at North Eagle River access for car wash. See display ad this section. [ADVERTISEMENT]

Three Olde Ladies B&B. This cozy home, located 11 miles north of Anchorage off the Glenn Highway, offers a beautifully decorated suite with private bath, featherbed, sitting room with TV/VCR and a private hot tub room. Hearty continental breakfast delivered to your suite each morning. Open year-round. Reasonable rates. Military discount. All major credit cards accepted. Hosts, military retired and antique shop owners, Alyce and Jon Cavanaugh. 18720 Danny Drive, Eagle, River, AK 99577. Phone (907) 696-7951. E-mail: threeoldeladies@gci.net. [ADVERTISEMENT]

Camping

The nearest public campground is Eagle River Campground, at **Milepost A 11.6**. Local directions are "take the exit to the dump and turn at the prison." Nearby private campgrounds include Hidden Haven RV Park on Eagle River Road; Gold Rush Park on South Birchwood Loop; and Peters Creek Petite RV Park (South Peters Creek exit).

Attractions

There is a summer **Farmer's Market** at Chief Alex Park (in 1999 hours were 3–7 P.M. Tuesdays). Boondock Sporting Goods store on Eagle River Loop Road rents fishing tackle. Bonndock's also has an antique gun display.

Special events include the Alaskan Scottish Highland Games (June 17, 2000); fireworks and a parade (July 3–4); and the Bear

EAGLE RIVER ADVERTISERS

Alaska Museum of Natural History ....Ph. (907) 694-0819
Eagle River Car Wash and Duck Pond ....Old Glenn Hwy.
Eagle River Motel........Ph. (907) 694-5000
Hidden Haven RV Park.....Ph. (907) 694-7275
Laundry Basket, The........Business Blvd.
South Fork B&B........Ph. (907) 694-4255
Three Olde Ladies B&B.....Ph. (907) 696-7951
Tips Bar & Cafe........Old Glenn Hwy.

Paw Festival and parade (July 6–9, 2000).

The **Alaska Museum of Natural History** is located in the Parkgate Building across from McDonald's at the corner of Easy Street and the Old Glenn Highway. Although relatively small in square-footage (a larger facility is in the planning stages), the museum manages to house a great variety of small but comprehensive displays, including the largest exhibit of rocks and minerals on display in

Alaska; a pollen and spores photo display; dioramas of local ecosystem; mining history; Ice Age animals; and Alaska's Dinosaur Discoveries of the 90s. This last small exhibit features casts of "Lizzie's toes." Lizzie is a 90-million year-old duck-billed dinosaur found in the Talkeetna Mountains in 1994. (Lizzie's surviving bones are currently stored at the University of Alaska Fairbanks.) See also www.alaska.net/~nathist/webed/dinosaurs/. Phone (907) 694-0819 for museum hours.

The 4.5 mile **Eagle River Loop** (see map) provides access to Eagle River residential and business areas. Eagle Pointe (follow signs from Hiland Road intersection) is a good example of one of Anchorage's newer suburban subdivisions. Alaska State parks maintains a day-use area and river access at Mile 1.7 Eagle River Loop (eastbound access only). Boaters are advised that a permit is required for boating Eagle River on Fort Richardson Military Reservation; phone (907) 384-2072.

Glenn Highway Log

(continued)

A 12.8 (20.6 km) **T 315.2** (507.3 km) Eagle River Bridge.

A 11.6 (18.7 km) **T 316.4** (509.2 km) Exit to Hiland Drive/Eagle River Loop; access to Anchorage Municipal Landfill (343-6298); state correctional center (follow signs); and state campground (description follows). The 4.5-mile Eagle River Loop provides access to Alaska State Parks River Access (1.7 miles); Eagle River Road (2.5 miles); and downtown Eagle River. Also access this exit for Eagle Pointe subdivision.

For **Eagle River Campground** (Chugach State Park) follow signs 1.4 miles/2.3 km from the highway, has 58 campsites, walk-in tent camping, a 4-day camping limit, picnic shelter (may be reserved in advance), dump station, pay phones, flush toilets and drinking water. Camping fee $15/night. Day-use

fee $3. Dump station $5. Canoe/kayak staging area. This is one of the most popular campgrounds in the state. Phone the state park office at (907) 345-5014 for information. ▲

A 10.6 (17.1 km) **T 317.4** (510.8 km) Truck weigh stations on both sides of highway. Pay phones.

The last 9 miles/14.5 km of the Glenn Highway has been designated the **Veterans' Memorial Parkway**.

A 7.5 (12.1 km) **T 320.5** (515.8 km) Exit west for main gate to **FORT RICHARDSON**, home of "America's Arctic Warriors." Exit east for southbound access to Arctic Valley Road (see description next milepost).

NOTE: A driver's license, proof of insurance and vehicle registration or rental agreement are required for civilians visiting the base.

A 6.1 (9.8 km) **T 321.9** (518 km) Northbound only exit to Arctic Valley Road and access to Fort Richardson Army base (2 miles from exit). **Arctic Valley Road** leads 1 mile to **Moose Run military golf course**; 18-holes, clubhouse, public welcome, phone (907) 428-0056. This photo was taken at the close of golf season in mid-October.

It is 7.5 miles to Arctic Valley Ski Area. (Steep and winding road, not recommended for large vehicles.) Spectacular views of Anchorage and Cook Inlet. Alpine wildflowers in spring, good berry picking in late summer.

A 5.1 (8.2 km) **T 322.9** (519.6 km) *CAUTION: Watch for moose.*

A 4.4 (7.1 km) **T 323.6** (520.8 km) Muldoon Road overpass. Exit north for new **Alaska Native Heritage Center**, a 26-acre site featuring 5 traditional village sites along a walking path around a 2-acre lake. Cultural presentations, food and crafts in the dramatic Welcoming House. Admission fee charged. U.S. Air Force Hospital and Bartlett High School also to the north.

Exit south for **Centennial Park** municipal campground (follow signs), and to connect with Seward Highway via Muldoon and Tudor roads bypass. ▲

There is a bicycle trail from Muldoon Road to Mirror Lake, **Milepost A 23.6**.

A 3.7 (5.9 km) **T 324.3** (521.9 km) Turpin Road (eastbound exit only).

A 3 (4.8 km) **T 325** (523 km) Boniface Parkway. Exit south for businesses and Russian Jack Springs city campground on Boniface Parkway just north of DeBarr.

Exit north 0.5 mile for Boniface Gate **ELMENDORF AFB**, 3rd Wing. *NOTE: Visitor and vehicle passes required to get on base. Visitors must have current vehicle registration or rental car agreement; current driver's license; name, location and phone numnber of sponsor on base.*

A 1.9 (3 km) **T 326.1** (524.8 km) Bragaw Street.

A 1.2 (1.9 km) **T 326.8** (525.9 km) Welcome to Anchorage sign. Airport Heights Drive to south; access to Northway Mall, Merrill Field and hospital. Mountain View Drive to north.

A 0 T 328 (527.9 km) Glenn Highway forks at Blue Star Highway Memorial and becomes 5th Avenue (one-way westbound) to downtown Anchorage, 6th Avenue (one-way eastbound) from downtown. Turn south at Gambell Street (one-way southbound) for the Seward Highway to the Kenai Peninsula (see SEWARD HIGHWAY section). See ANCHORAGE section following for description of city.

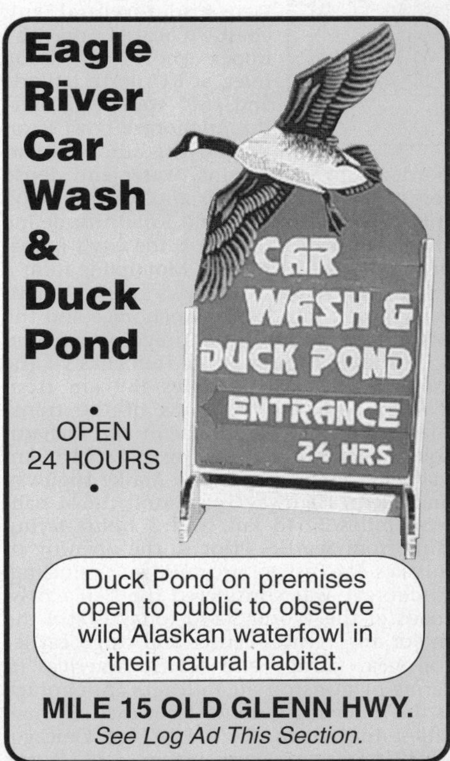

ANCHORAGE

(See maps, pages 305, 312 and 321)

Anchorage skyline in summer as seen from Earthquake Park. (© Mike Jones)

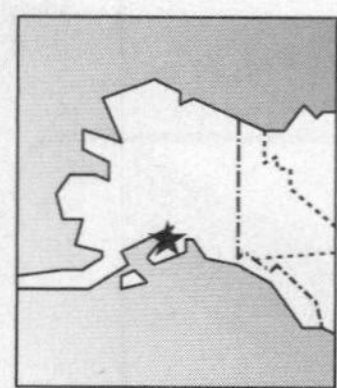

Anchorage, Alaska's largest city, is in the heart of the state's southcentral gulf coast. Located on the upper shores of Cook Inlet, at 61° north latitude and 150° west longitude, the Anchorage bowl is on a low-lying alluvial plain bordered by mountains, water and dense forests for spruce, birch and aspen. Cook Inlet's Turnagain Arm and Knik Arm define the broad peninsula that is the city's home, and the rugged Chugach Mountains form a striking backdrop. Of Alaska's 621,400 citizens, nearly half live in Anchorage and the Matanuska region. Anchorage is situated 358 miles/576 km south of Fairbanks via the Parks Highway; 304 miles/489 km from Valdez, southern terminus of the trans-Alaska pipeline, via the Glenn and Richardson highways; 2,459 driving miles/3,957 km via the West Access Route, Alaska Highway and Glenn Highway/Tok Cutoff; 1,644 nautical miles/2,646 km, and 3 hours flying time from Seattle. Prior to the opening of Russia's Far East to air traffic and refueling, Anchorage was considered the "Air Crossroads of the World," and today is still the major air logistics center and cargo carrier for Asia, Europe and North America. In terms of nonstop air mileages, Anchorage is the following distance from each of these cities: Amsterdam, 4,475/7,202 km; Chicago, 2,839/4,569 km; Copenhagen, 4,313/6,941 km; Hamburg, 4,430/7,129 km; Honolulu, 2,780/4,474 km; London, 4,487/7,221 km; Paris, 4,683/7,536 km; San Francisco, 2,015/3,243 km; Seattle, 1,445/2,325 km; Tokyo, 3,460/5,568 km.

Population: Anchorage Municipality, 259,391. **Emergency Services: Police, Fire Department, Ambulance** and **Search & Rescue**, phone 911, CB Channel 9. **Police**, phone (907) 786-8500. **Alaska State Troopers**, phone (907) 269-5511. **Alaska Department of Public Safety**, web site: www.dps.state.ak.us. **Hospitals:** Alaska Regional Hospital, phone (907) 276-1131; Alaska Native Medical Center, phone (907) 563-2662; Providence, Alaska Medical Center, phone (907) 562-2211; Elmendorf Air Force Base emergency room, phone (907) 552-5555. **Dental Emergencies**, phone (907) 279-9144 (24-hour service). **Emergency Management**, phone (907) 267-4904 or 1-800-478-8999. **Suicide Intervention**, phone (907) 563-3200 (24-hour service). **Rape & Assault**, phone (907) 276-7273 (24-hour service). **Battered Women**, phone (907) 272-0100. **Pet Emergency**, phone (907) 274-5636. **Poison Control**, phone (907) 261-3193. **Road Conditions**, statewide, phone (800) 478-7675 or (907) 273-6037.

Visitor Information: Log Cabin Visitor Information Center, operated by the Anchorage Convention and Visitors Bureau, is at 4th Avenue and F Street; open daily, year-round. Hours are 7:30 A.M. to 7 P.M. June through August; 8 A.M. to 6 P.M. in May and September; and 9 A.M. to 4 P.M. the remainder of the year; closed only on Thanksgiving, Christmas and New Year's Day. The cabin offers a wide assortment of free brochures and maps. Write 524 W. 4th Ave., Anchorage 99501; phone (907) 274-3531; Internet: www.anchorage.net. E-mail: info@anchorage.net. The bureau also operates a year-round visitor information phone with a recorded message of the day's special events and attractions, including films, plays, sports events and gallery openings, and it produces several publications including 2 visitor guides, a restaurant directory, a fall/winter discount book and a monthly calendar of events; phone (907) 276-3200. Additional visitor information centers are open daily at Anchorage International Airport, one on the lower level for passengers arriving on domestic flights; another in the customs-secured area of the international concourse; and a third in the lobby of the international terminal. The North Anchorage Visitor Information Center is located in the Parkgate Building, just off the Glenn Highway at 11723 Old Glenn Highway in Eagle River. The Anchorage Convention and Visitors Bureau offers information on community events, phone (907) 276-4118.

The Alaska Public Lands Information Center, 605 W. 4th, in the historic Old Federal Building, has extensive displays and information on outdoor recreation lands in Alaska; phone (907) 271-2737. (See detailed description under Attractions, this section.)

Elevation: 38 to 120 feet/16 to 37m. **Climate:** Anchorage has a climate resembling that of the Rocky Mountains area, tempered by proximity to the Pacific Ocean. Shielded from excess ocean moisture by the Kenai Mountains to the south, the city has an annual average of only 15.9 inches of precipitation. Winter snowfall averages about 70 inches per year, with snow on the ground typically from October to April. Anchorage is in a transition zone between the moderating influence of the Pacific and the extreme temperatures found in interior Alaska. The average temperature in January (coldest month) is 15°F/-9°C; in July (warmest month), 58°F/14°C. A record 40 days of 70°F/21°C temperatures or higher was set in 1936, according to the National Weather Service. The record high was 85°F/29°C in June of 1969. The record low was -34°F/-37°C in January 1975. The growing season of 100 to 120 days typically extends from late May to early September. Anchorage has a daily maximum of 19 hours, 21 minutes of daylight in summer, and 5 hours, 28 minutes in winter. Prevailing wind direction is north.

Radio: AM stations: KTZN 550 (Sports Radio); KHAR 590 (Easy Listening); KENI 650 (News, Talk, Sports); KBYR 700 (News, Talk, Sports); KFQD 750 (News, Talk); KAXX 1020 (Sports Radio); KASH 1080 (Business/financial news, talk, BBC); FM stations: KRUA 88.1

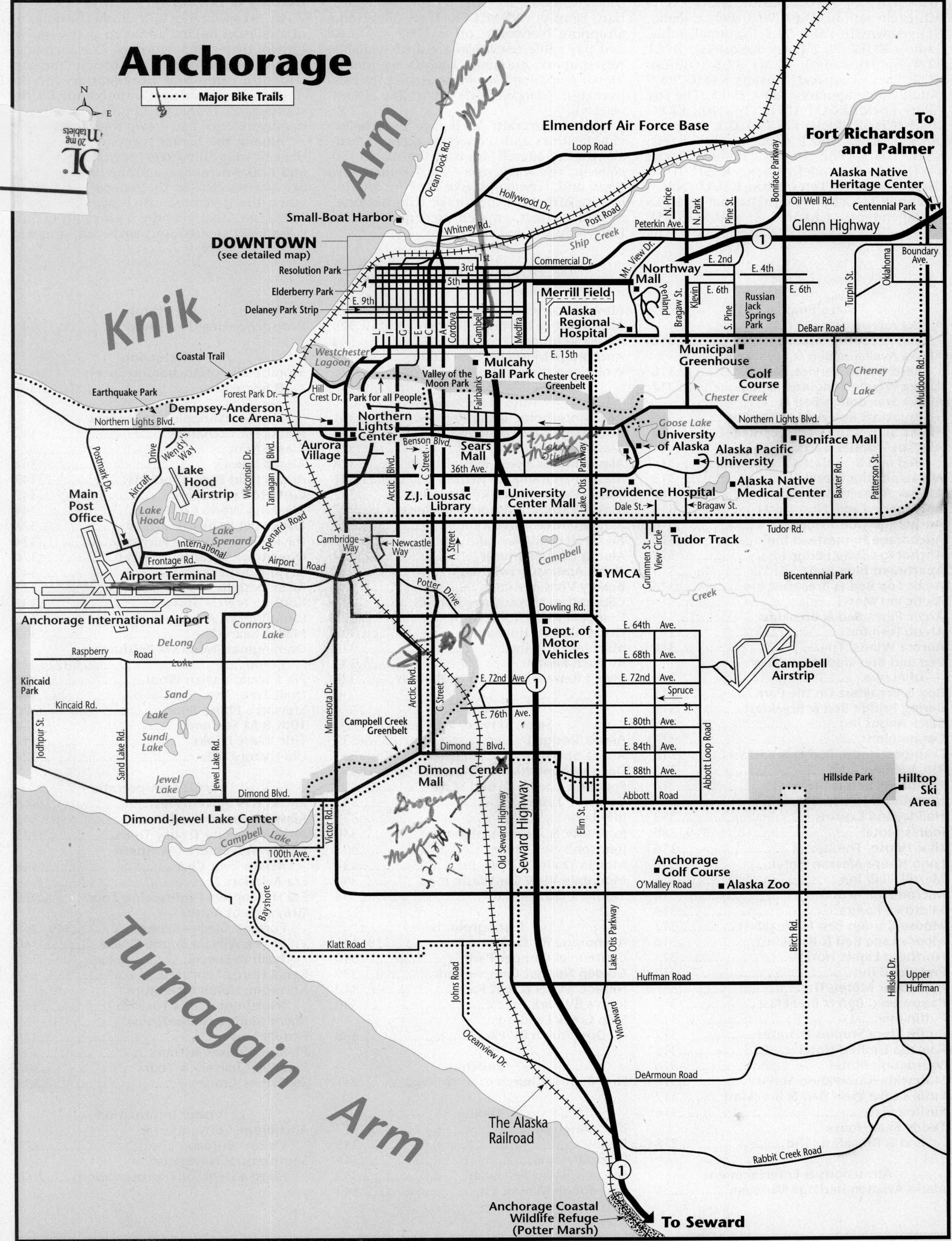
Anchorage
Major Bike Trails
Knik
Arm
Turnagain
Arm
Elmendorf Air Force Base
To Fort Richardson and Palmer
Alaska Native Heritage Center
Centennial Park
Glenn Highway
Small-Boat Harbor
DOWNTOWN (see detailed map)
Resolution Park
Elderberry Park
Delaney Park Strip
Coastal Trail
Earthquake Park
Westchester Lagoon
Merrill Field
Alaska Regional Hospital
Northway Mall
Municipal Greenhouse
Russian Jack Springs Park
Golf Course
Cheney Lake
Mulcahy Ball Park
Chester Creek Greenbelt
Valley of the Moon Park
Park for all People
Dempsey-Anderson Ice Arena
Northern Lights Center
Aurora Village
Sears Mall
University of Alaska
Alaska Pacific University
Boniface Mall
Alaska Native Medical Center
Providence Hospital
University Center Mall
Z.J. Loussac Library
Lake Hood Airstrip
Main Post Office
Airport Terminal
Anchorage International Airport
Tudor Track
YMCA
Bicentennial Park
Campbell Airstrip
Dept. of Motor Vehicles
Kincaid Park
Campbell Creek Greenbelt
Dimond Center Mall
Dimond-Jewel Lake Center
Hillside Park
Hilltop Ski Area
Anchorage Golf Course
Alaska Zoo
Seward Highway
The Alaska Railroad
Anchorage Coastal Wildlife Refuge (Potter Marsh)
To Seward

(University of Alaska station); KATB 89.3 (Christian radio); KNBA 90.3 (Public Radio, Native-owned); KSKA 91.1 (National Public Radio); KQEZ 92.1 (Easy Favorites); KFAT 92.9 (Sports Radio); KEAG 97.3 (Oldies); KLEF 98.1 (Classical Music); KYMG 98.9 (Adult Contemporary); KBFX 100.5 (The Fox - Pure Rock); KGOT 101.3 (Top 40); KKRO 102.1 (Classic Rock); KMXS 103.1 (Contemporary); KBRJ 104.1 (Country Favorites); KNIK 105.3 (The Breeze - Smooth Jazz); KWHL 106.5 (Modern Rock); KASH 107.5 (New Country). **Television:** KTUU (NBC), Channel 2; KTBY (Fox), Channel 4; KYES (Independent), Channel 5; KAKM (PBS), Channel 7; KTVA (CBS), Channel 11; KIMO (ABC), Channel 13; KCFT TV UHF 20 (Christian Family); KDMD TV UHF 33 (Home Shopping Network); other UHF channels and pay cable television are also available. **Newspapers:** *Anchorage Daily News* (daily); *Alaska Journal of Commerce, Anchorage Press* (weekly); *Chugiak-Eagle River Star* (semi-weekly).

Private Aircraft: Anchorage airports provide facilities and services to accommodate all types of aircraft. Consult the *Alaska Supplement*, the *Anchorage VFR Terminal Area Chart* and *Terminal Alaska Book* for the following airports: Anchorage International, Merrill Field, Campbell airstrip and Lake Hood seaplane and strip.

History & Economy

In 1914 Congress authorized the building of a railroad linking an ocean port with the interior river shipping routes. The anchorage at the mouth of Ship Creek became the construction camp and headquarters for the Alaskan Engineering Commission. By the summer of 1915 the population, housed mainly in tents, had grown to about 2,000.

Among the names suggested for the settlement were Ship Creek, Spenard, Woodrow and Knik Anchorage, and the name Anchorage was selected by the federal government when the first post office opened in May 1915. Later that year the bluff south of Ship Creek was cleared and surveyed, and 655

Downtown Anchorage in February. (© Tom Bol Photography)

lots, on 347 acres, were auctioned off by the General Land Office for $148,000. The center of the business district was the 4th Avenue and C Street intersection. Anchorage prospered and was incorporated in 1920.

Anchorage's growth has been in spurts, spurred by: (1) construction of the Alaska Railroad and the transfer of its headquarters from Seward to Anchorage in 1917; (2) colonization of the Matanuska Valley, a farming region 45 miles to the north, in 1935; (3) construction of Fort Richardson and Elmendorf Field (now Elmendorf Air Force Base) in 1940; (4) discovery of oil in Cook Inlet between 1957 and 1961; and (5) the development of North Slope/Prudhoe Bay oil fields and the construction of the trans-Alaska pipeline—all since 1968.

The current population of 259,391 includes diverse racial and cultural groups, with about 78 percent white, 8 percent Native Alaskan, and between 6 and 7 percent African-American, Asian-Pacific Islander and Hispanic groups. Government jobs, including the military, account for about one-quarter of the employment picture; service industries for another-quarter. The oil, gas and mining industries employ roughly 3 percent. Other fields of work are similar to those in other American cities of this size (in the classified section of the Anchorage phone directory, 78 pages are devoted to attorneys and law firms).

The Good Friday earthquake of March 27, 1964, the most powerful quake (9.2 on the Richter scale) ever recorded in North America, caused more than $300 million in damage throughout southcentral Alaska. In Anchorage most losses resulted from landslides caused by changes in the composition of the clay underlying much of the city. Government Hill, downtown neighborhoods and the Turnagain area now known as Earthquake Park suffered the most extensive damage, losing many homes and other buildings. Considering the severity of the disaster, the number of casualties (131) was miraculously low. Relief funds in the form of federal Small Business Administration loans helped many rebuild, and from the devastation a distinctly new Anchorage emerged.

In the 1970s and 1980s, Anchorage experienced a population and construction boom related to oil production. Major oil companies set up corporate headquarters, and Anchorage's first 20-story buildings punctuated the skyline. Declining oil prices in the 1980s and 1990s triggered a slowdown in the economic climate, but business prospects are upbeat today, and the number of new building starts is high. The advent of several national retail chains during the past decade has resulted in the closure of many smaller, family-owned businesses. Mergers, malls and megastores are the order of the day here as in the Lower 48. With its strategic location and modern facilities, Anchorage's key role as the center of commerce and distribution for the rest of Alaska is assured

Description

Covering approximately 2,000 square miles/5,180 sq.km, Anchorage lies between the Chugach Mountains on the east and Knik Arm of Cook Inlet on the west. The surrounding mountain ranges--the Chugach, the Kenais, the Talkeetnas, the icy peaks of the Alaska Peninsula's mountains and volcanoes, and the dramatic peaks of the Alaska Range (with Mount McKinley visible on the northern horizon, weather permitting)--encompass the city in a setting of scenic splendor.

Perched on the edge of Alaska's vast, varied expanse of forests, mountains, rivers, taiga and tundra, Anchorage has sometimes been described as "half an hour from Alaska." Its similarities to other medium-sized American cities increase steadily, but, although it is true that a half-hour trip in any direction from the city offers an abundance of wilderness experiences, this modern metropolis still possesses many features that mark it as uniquely Alaskan. Combining cosmopolitan amenities with the creative enthusiasm of a young, progressive state has made Anchorage a spirited city and an exciting destination.

Among the many buildings erected during Project 80s, the largest construction program in the city's history, funded by millions of dollars allocated by the legislature, is the **Alaska Center for the Performing Arts** on 5th Avenue and F Street. During its 11 years the center has hosted a wide range of productions, from Broadway shows, world-renowned performers and Anchorage's own symphony orchestra to local productions of choral, theatrical and dance groups. Fences were added on the center's steep-pitched roof to prevent snow from sliding off onto unsuspecting pedestrians below. Other completed projects include the George M. Sullivan Sports Arena, William A. Egan Civic and Convention Center, Z.J. Loussac Public Library, and a major expansion and renovation of the Anchorage Museum of History and Art.

With its distinctive mixture of old frontier and jet age, Anchorage is a truly unique city. It is noted for the profusion of flowers and hanging baskets that decorate homes and businesses during summer months: parks, street medians and lamp posts are vibrant with the colors of millions of flowers. As shadows lengthen with winter's approach in October, residents are encouraged to follow the lead of municipal agencies in displaying strings of miniature white lights on homes, trees and office buildings, brightening the entire city "until the last Iditarod racer makes it to Nome" in March. The summertime City of Flowers becomes the wintertime City of Lights.

Anchorage is also the City of Moose, sharing its streets and yards with these largest members of the deer family, especially when winter's deep snows drive the moose toward easier browsing in settled areas where cultivated trees and shrubs abound. Frequent summertime sightings attest to the steady increase of the moose population.

CAUTION: Do not attempt to approach or intercept moose at any time, whether for purposes of photography or to satisfy curiosity. Unpredictable and aggressive, moose are huge wild animals that can be extremely dangerous. This applies also to bears that occasionally wander into the city.

In profile, Anchorage has:

• About 88 schools, including special education and alternative public programs, a number of privately operated schools, both secular and parochial; also the University of Alaska, Alaska Pacific University and Charter College, a computer-oriented, "career-building" technical school; also rehabilitation/training schools for the blind and the deaf.

• More than 200 churches and temples.

• Z.J. Loussac Public Library, plus 5 branch libraries, and the Alaska Public Resources and Information Services (ARLIS), which comprises 9 natural and cultural resource libraries; the National Bank of Alaska Heritage Library Museum, Alaska State Library Services for the Blind and the University of Alaska Library.

• Municipal bus service, 4 major taxi companies and various shuttle bus services.

• In the arts—**Dance:** Alaska Center for the Performing Arts; Alaska Dance Theatre; Anchorage Concert Assoc.; Anchorage Opera; Ballet Alaska. **Music:** Alaska Airlines Autumn Classics; Anchorage Concert Chorus; Anchorage Community Concert Band; Anchorage Concert Assoc.; Anchorage Children's Choir; Anchorage Symphony Orchestra; Anchorage

(Continues on page 313)

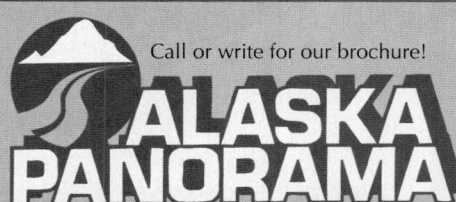

Anchorage City Center

The Alaska Railroad
Ship Creek
Whitney Rd.
Ship Creek Salmon Viewing Platform
The MILEPOST® Office
E. Ship Creek Ave.
Post Road
Alaska Railroad Depot
Nesbett Courthouse
Christensen
Knik Arm
Oscar Anderson House
Resolution Park
Elderberry Park
State Court Bldg.
Old Federal Bldg.
Sunshine Mall
Post Office Mall
Log Cabin Visitor Center
Old City Hall
Convention Center
5th Ave. Mall
Center for the Performing Arts
Bus Accommodation Center
City Hall
Police
Fire
Federal Bldg.
Anchorage Museum of History and Art
Hostel
City Cemetery
Pioneer Schoolhouse
Mile 0 Glenn Highway
Neighborhood Health Center
Delaney Park Strip
W. 1st, W. 2nd, W. 3rd, W. 4th, W. 5th, W. 6th, W. 7th, W. 8th, W. 9th, W. 10th, W. 11th, W. 12th, W. 13th, W. 14th, W. 15th, W. 15th Ter., W. 16th
E. 1st, E. 2nd, E. 2nd Ct., E. 3rd, E. 4th, E. 5th, E. 6th, E. 7th, E. 8th, E. 9th, E. 10th, E. 11th, E. 12th, E. 13th, E. 14th, E. 15th, E. 15th Ter., E. 16th, E. 16th Ter.
P Street, O St., N St., M St., L Street, K Street, I Street, H Street, G Street, F Street, E Street, D Street, C Street, B Street, A Street
Inlet Pl., Coffey Ln., Virginia Ct., L Street
Barrow St., Cordova St., Denali St., Eagle St., Fairbanks St., Gambell St., Hyder St., Ingra St., Juneau St., Karluk St., Latouche St., Medfra St., Nelchina St., Orca St.
McHugh Ln.
Avenues West / Avenues East
George M. Sullivan Sports Arena
Begin/End New Seward Highway
Ben Boeke Arena
Mulcahy Ball Park
1

(Continued from page 308)
Festival of Music; Sweet Adelines (Sourdough, Cheechako and Top of the World choruses); University of Alaska Anchorage Singers; Young People's Concerts.

• **Theater:** Alaska Community Theatre; Alaska Festival Theatre; Alaska Junior Theater; Alaska Stage Company; Alaska Theatre of Youth; Cyrano's Off Center Playhouse; Out North Theater Company; UAA Theatre; Valley Performing Arts. **Art:** About 25 art galleries.

• A total of 259 miles of trails for hiking, biking, jogging, skiing and dog mushing, including 120 miles of paved trails and 105 miles of maintained ski trails.

Lodging & Services

There are more than 70 motels and hotels in the Anchorage area with prices for a double room ranging from $50 to $70 and up. Reservations are a must. Bed-and-breakfast accommodations are also available in more than 100 private residences, prices ranging from $60-$100.

Comfortable, low-cost accommodations are available for hostellers and other budget-conscious travelers:

Anchorage Guest House welcomes hostellers. Located at 2001 Hillcrest Drive, Anchorage, AK 99517, phone (907) 274-0408.

Hosteling International–Anchorage is located at 700 H St., 1 block from the People Mover Transit Center in downtown Anchorage. The hostel is open 7:30 A.M. to noon and 1 P.M. to 11 P.M. June through October; 8 A.M. to noon, 1 P.M. to 3 P.M. and 5 P.M. to 11 P.M., October through May. Common

Anchorage is known as the City of Flowers in summer.

Statue of Capt. James Cook at Resolution Park, located at the end of 3rd Avenue. (© Kris Graef, staff)

areas open all day. Cost for members: $16 per night, nonmembers: $19. AYH cards available at hostel or by mail. Dormitory rooms with bunkbeds, kitchen facilities, common rooms, laundry room and TV room. Additional, private accommodations available in an historic house located near the hostel. For information or reservations no less than 1 day in advance with VISA or MasterCard, phone (907) 276-3635, or write for reservations (prepayment required): 700 H St., Anchorage, AK 99501.

International Backpackers Hostel is located in the Mountain View section of Anchorage and offers a homelike setting, kitchen and laundry facilities, cable TV, and other amenities. 3601 Peterkin Avenue, Anchorage, AK 99508; phone (907) 274-3870.

Spenard Hostel International is a non-affiliated hostel on the bus line at 2845 W. 42nd Place, Anchorage, AK. For reservations phone (907) 248-5036; fax (907) 248-5063; e-mail: spenrdhstl@alaskalife.net; web site: http://www.alaskalife.net/spenrdhstl/hostel.html.

Restaurants number more than 600, with many major fast-food chains, formal dining rooms and specialty establishments including Italian, Japanese, Korean, Chinese (Cantonese and Mandarin), Mexican, Polynesian, Greek, German, Sicilian, Thai, soul food, seafood, smorgasbord and vegetarian.

Phone 844 in Anchorage for the time and current temperature. Phone 276-3200 for a recorded list of current events in Anchorage.

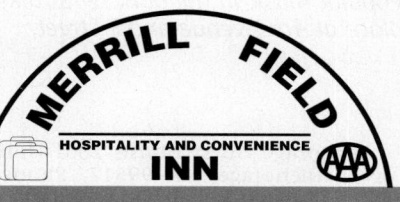

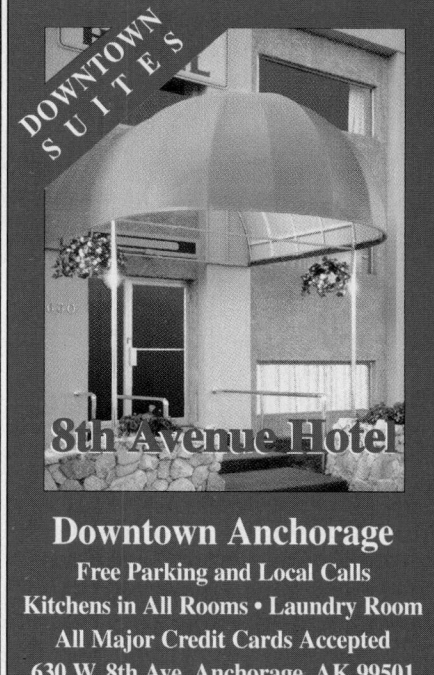

Popular music in the park series takes place at 4th Avenue and E Street.
(© Kris Graef, staff)

Anchorage Guest House. 2001 Hillcrest Drive, Anchorage, AK 99517. Phone/fax (907) 274-0408; E-mail: house@alaska.net; web page: www.alaska.net/~house. Large friendly house on Coastal Trail, close to downtown and Westchester Lagoon. Single beds and private rooms for low rates. Continental breakfast served. Groups up to 10 persons. Internet, laundry, bike rentals. Open year-round. [ADVERTISEMENT]

Anchorage Homestead Inn. (907) 561-3138; toll free: (888) 488-1800. E-mail: homesteadinn@corecom.net. Clean, comfortable rooms conveniently located near airport and Lake Hood. Low rates. Open year-round. Free HBO, coffee, phone use. Kitchen, laundry and freezer facilities available. Walking distance from restaurants. 4215 Spenard Rd., Anchorage, AK 99517. [ADVERTISEMENT]

Arctic Fox Bed & Breakfast Inn. 326 E. 2nd Ct., Anchorage, AK 99501. Phone (907) 272-4818, fax 272-4819. Quiet downtown location with some inlet views. Tastefully decorated rooms and suites with moderate summer rates, low winter rates. Near downtown hotels, restaurants, museum, bike trail, train and Ship Creek. Laundry. Private baths, TV and phone in room. [ADVERTISEMENT]

Aurora Winds, The. Anchorage's exceptional bed and breakfast resort is situated on 2 meticulously landscaped acres and features 5 suites, all with private bath, TV, VCR and phone. The "McKinley Suite" also has a fireplace, wide-screen TV, double Jacuzzi and a habitat-environment chamber. The atmosphere is one of quiet elegance: contemporary, with an Alaskan home-style atmosphere where breakfast is a gourmet delight, and the staff strives to satisfy your every need. Take advantage of the full gym, billiard room, sauna, theater room, 10-person outdoor hot tub, or one of the 4 fireplaces. "Our recommendation for Anchorage's best bed and breakfast, the Aurora Winds B & B Resort." For information, phone (907) 347-2533, e-mail: awbnb@alaska.net or web page: www.aurorawinds.com. [ADVERTISEMENT]

Bed and Breakfast Association of

Alaska. Stay where real Alaskans stay, in their homes! A new directory is available representing our members throughout Alaska. All types of accommodations, from homestays to inns, from luxurious B&B's to cabins, from cities to the bush. Licensed, insured and many inspected. BBAA, P.O. Box 202663, Anchorage, AK 99501; phone (907) 566-2627 or fax (907) 272-1899. [ADVERTISEMENT]

Caribou Inn. 501 L Street, Anchorage, AK 99501. Clean, comfortable rooms in an excellent downtown Anchorage location. Shared or private bath, some with kitchenettes. Major credit cards accepted. Free shuttle to airport and train station. (907) 272-0444 or fax (907) 274-4828. Toll free (800) 272-5878. E-mail: caribou@alaska.net. Web site: http://www.alaska.net/~caribou. [ADVERTISEMENT]

Puffin Inn. Experience comfortable, quality accommodations and exceptional service at reasonable rates. Our friendly Alaskan hospitality includes complimentary coffee, muffin and daily newspaper. Located near Lake Hood floatplane airport with courtesy airport shuttle, nonsmoking rooms, cable TV and freezer space for your hunting and fishing needs. Handicap accessible. 4400 Spenard Rd., Anchorage, AK 99517. Phone (907) 243-4044. Fax (907) 248-6853. (800) 4PU-FFIN. [ADVERTISEMENT] ♿

Puffin Place Studios & Suites. Relax and enjoy 1 of our 38 attractively furnished studios and 1-bedroom suites featuring fully equipped kitchens with microwaves. Within walking distance of restaurants, shopping and Tony Knowles Coastal Trail. Our amenities include: courtesy airport shuttle, nonsmoking rooms, laundry facility, freezer space, cable TV. Weekly and monthly rates offered October–May. 1058 W. 27th, Anchorage, AK 99503, (907) 279-1058. Fax (907) 257-9595. (800) 71-PLACE. [ADVERTISEMENT]

Susie's Lake View Bed & Breakfast. Enjoy the quiet setting overlooking scenic Campbell Lake. Unwind with a leisure tour of our quaint garden setting. The large deck areas offer comfortable privacy for an individual but are big enough for a family barbe-

cue. Start or end your day with a steamy hot tub—available 24 hours a day and located where it should be ... outside. Continental or traditional breakfast. Business travelers welcome. Located only 11 minutes from the airport. VISA and MasterCard accepted. 9256 Campbell Terrace, Anchorage, AK 99515. Phone (907) 243-4624. [ADVERTISEMENT]

The Teddy Bear House Bed & Breakfast. Experience a traditional home stay in our uniquely decorated home in a quiet south Anchorage neighborhood, 15 minutes from airport and downtown. Close to Anchorage Zoo and shopping. Twin or queen beds. Private and shared bath. Continental or traditional breakfast. Large deck for your relaxation. Open year-round. No smoking. P.O. Box 190265, Anchorage, AK 99519; (907) 344-3111, e-mail: tbearbb@alaska.net. [ADVERTISEMENT]

Camping

Anchorage has several private campgrounds; see ads this section.

Anchorage has 2 public campgrounds: Centennial Park, open from May through September, and Lions Camper Park, open July and part of August on an as-needed basis. Fees are $13 for non-Alaskans and $11 for Alaska residents. To reach Centennial Park, take the Muldoon Road exit south off the Glenn Highway, take the first left onto Boundary, take the next left and follow the signs. Lions Camper Park is located at 5800 Boniface Parkway, half a mile south of the Glenn Highway. Centennial, recommended for large RVs, has 90 RV sites and 40 tent sites. Lions has 50 tent sites. Both feature barracks-type showers, flush toilets, water and dump stations and no hookups. Between May and September, phone (907) 333-9711 for details on either park. In the off-season, phone (907) 343-6397.

Chugach State Park has campgrounds located near Anchorage at Bird Creek (Seward Highway), and at Eagle River and Eklutna Lake (Glenn Highway). The Anchorage Ski Club rents space to RVs at its Alpenglow Lodge parking lot from June 15-September 1; mile 7 Arctic Valley Road; phone (907) 346-4098. ▲

Anchorage RV Park. Experience Alaska's premier RV park located in a quiet wooded setting just 10 minutes from downtown Anchorage and just across from the new Alaska Native Heritage Center. Fully equipped with all the essentials plus much more including: cable TV connections, laundry, showers, and work station with modem port in our comfortable main lodge. The park has 195 spaces with 78 pull-throughs and access to a network of bike trails. Open mid-May through mid-Sept. Enjoy Alaska's premier RV park. Call today for reservations 800-400-7275 or (907) 338-7275. GPS: N61° 13.81' W149° 44.46'. 7300 Oilwell Rd., Anchorage, AK 99506. See display ad this section. [ADVERTISEMENT] ▲

Transportation

Air: More than a dozen international and domestic air carriers and numerous intrastate airlines serve Anchorage International Airport, located 6.5 miles km from downtown.

Ferry: The nearest ferry port to Anchorage is Whittier on Prince William Sound, served by Alaska state ferry from Cordova and Valdez. Whittier is accessible by train from either Anchorage or Portage on the Seward Highway.

Railroad: The Alaska Railroad offers daily passenger service in summer from Anchorage to Seward and to Fairbanks via Denali National Park. Reduced service in winter. Summer rail service is also available between Anchorage and Whittier, with optional connections to Prince William Sound cruises. In addition, a shuttle train for foot passengers and vehicles operates daily in summer between Portage and Whittier, connecting with the state ferry to Valdez and Cordova. Contact Passenger Services Dept., Box 107500, Anchorage 99510-7500; phone (800) 544-0552 or (907) 265-2494, fax 265-2323 or 265-2509.

The **Alaska Railroad Depot** is located on 1st Avenue, within easy walking distance of downtown.

Bus: Local service via People Mover, serving most of the Anchorage bowl from Peters Creek to Oceanview. Fares are $1 for adults, 50¢ for youth 5 to 18, 25¢ for senior citizens and disabled citizens with transit identification. Monthly passes are sold at the Transit Center (6th Avenue and H Street), the Dimond Transit Center, municipal libraries and Cook Inlet Book Co. on 5th Ave. downtown; monthly commuter pass $30. Day passes are also available for $2.50 at the Transit Center, Dimond Transit Center and Tesoro 2 Go stores. For bus route information, phone the Rideline at (907) 343-6543. (See display ad this section.)

Taxi: There are 4 major taxi companies, as well as various shuttle services. Consult the yellow pages under Taxicabs.

Car and Camper Rentals: There are dozens of car rental agencies located at the airport and downtown, as well as several RV rental agencies (see advertisements this section).

RV Parking: The Anchorage Parking Authority offers a lot with spaces for oversized vehicles (motorcoaches, campers, large trucks) at 3rd Avenue, north of the Holiday Inn, between A and C streets. Parking is $5 per space, per day. For more information, phone (907) 276-PARK or (800) 770-ACAR.

Highway: Anchorage can be reached via the Glenn Highway and the Seward Highway. See GLENN HIGHWAY and SEWARD HIGHWAY sections for details.

Attractions

Get Acquainted: Stop by the Log Cabin Visitor Information Center at 4th Avenue and F Street, open 7:30 A.M. to 7 P.M. June through August; 8 A.M. to 6 P.M. in May and September; and 9 A.M. to 4 P.M. the remainder of the year; phone (907) 274-3531. Free visitor guidebooks.

Take a Historic Walking Tour: Start at the Log Cabin Visitor Information Center at 4th Avenue and F Street. The Anchorage Convention and Visitors Bureau's *Anchorage Visitors Guide* suggests an excellent downtown walking tour.

The Alaska Public Lands Information Center, located in the historic Old Federal Building on 4th Avenue and F Street, offers a wide variety of exhibits, movies, special programs and information on all of Alaska's state and federal parks, forests and wildlife refuges. Natural history exhibits, cultural exhibits, a GIS computer and self-help trip-planning area provide an enjoyable way to obtain knowledge and information necessary for a safe and exhilarating Alaskan adventure whether you are a cruise passen-

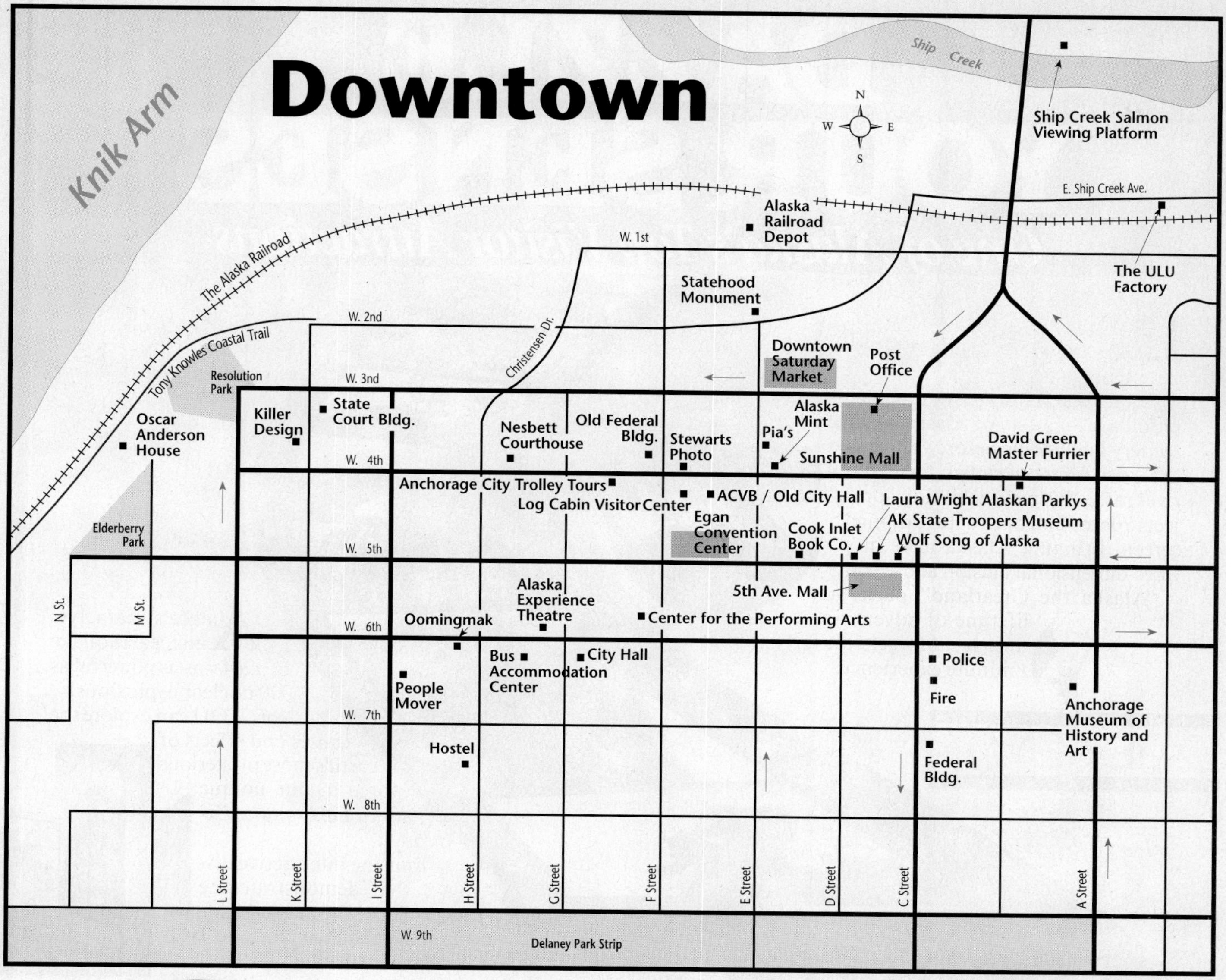

Downtown

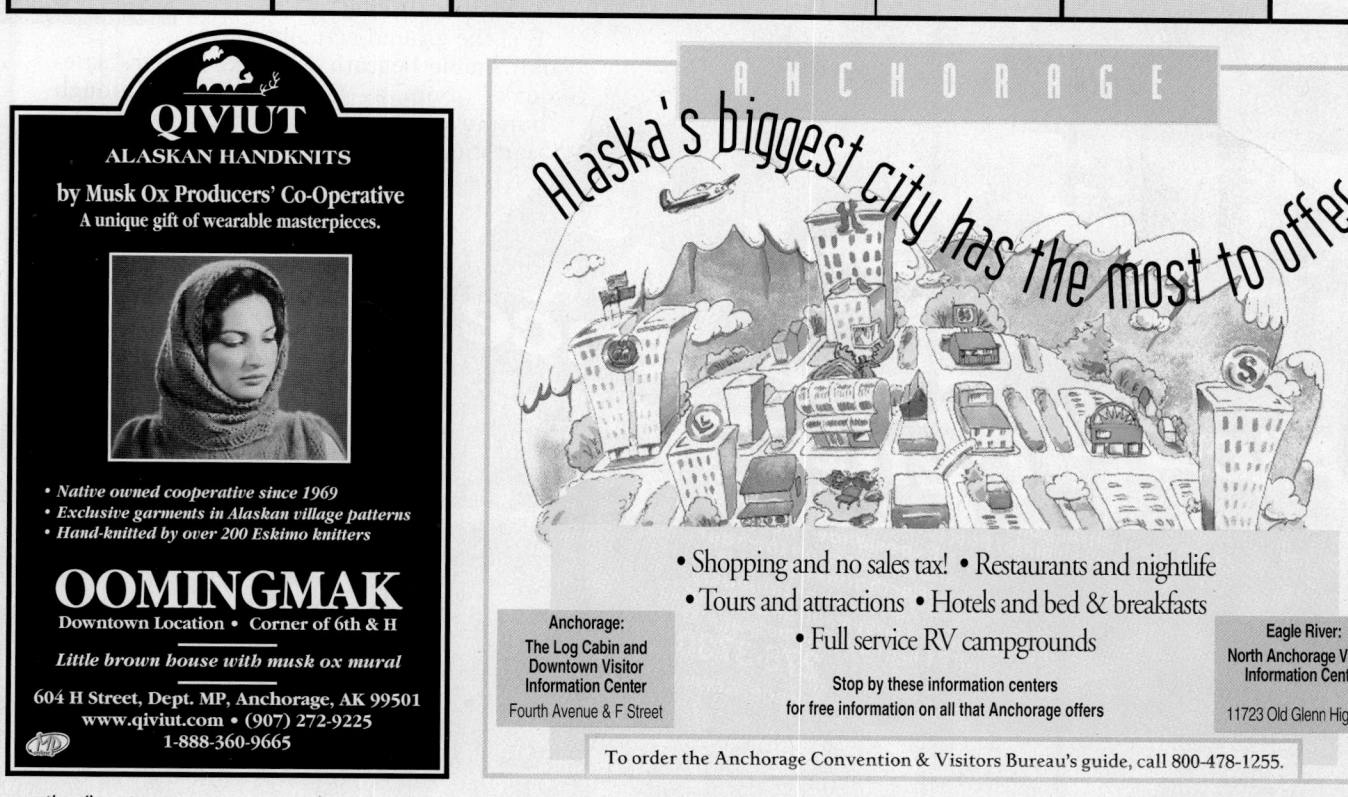

Knik Arm
Ship Creek
N
W
E
S
Ship Creek Salmon Viewing Platform
E. Ship Creek Ave.
Alaska Railroad Depot
The ULU Factory
W. 1st
The Alaska Railroad
Statehood Monument
Tony Knowles Coastal Trail
W. 2nd
Christensen Dr.
Resolution Park
W. 3rd
Downtown Saturday Market
Post Office
Alaska Mint
Oscar Anderson House
Killer Design
State Court Bldg.
Nesbett Courthouse
Old Federal Bldg.
Stewarts Photo
Pia's
Sunshine Mall
David Green Master Furrier
W. 4th
Anchorage City Trolley Tours
Log Cabin Visitor Center
ACVB / Old City Hall
Laura Wright Alaskan Parkys
Egan Convention Center
Cook Inlet Book Co.
AK State Troopers Museum
Wolf Song of Alaska
Elderberry Park
W. 5th
5th Ave. Mall
Alaska Experience Theatre
Oomingmak
Center for the Performing Arts
N St.
M St.
W. 6th
Bus Accommodation Center
City Hall
Police
People Mover
Fire
Anchorage Museum of History and Art
W. 7th
Hostel
Federal Bldg.
W. 8th
L Street
K Street
I Street
H Street
G Street
F Street
E Street
D Street
C Street
A Street
W. 9th
Delaney Park Strip

DAZZLE YOUR SENSES

One of Alaska's Top Visitor Attractions

Explore with us "Alaska the Greatland" in a dazzling OMNI THEATER motion picture experience.

Our unique 180-degree wrap-around screen unfolds the majesty of Alaska's wildlife, scenery and people before your eyes.

Filmed from helicopters, trains and river rafts, this new technology projects 70mm film onto a huge domed screen, bringing Alaska alive in a three-dimensional illusion above you!

"Alaska the Greatland" packs a lifetime of adventure into an unforgettable forty-minute experience.

Alaska's cataclysmic earthquake of 1964 was as powerful as 2,000 nuclear explosions.

Now, YOU can explore the causes and effects of earth's most mysterious force in our unique *Alaska Earthquake Exhibit.*

Tour the inter-active displays that demonstrate the Richter Scale, the massive slide of Earthquake Park and the Tsunami Warning Center.

Feel the ground actually shake and rumble beneath your feet in our "safe-quake" room, as you relive history through our movie presentation of the great Alaska earthquake!

It's an experience you won't soon forget.

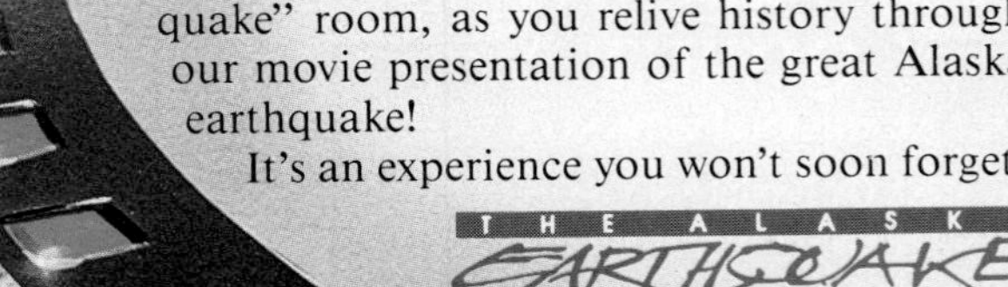

The Alaska Experience Center

TWO great attractions at ONE convenient downtown location near all major hotels — corner of 6th and G.

Alaska Experience Theatre — shows begin on the hour

Earthquake Exhibit — shows continuously

For admission prices and showtimes call 24-hr. recorded message at

276-3730

Anchorage, Alaska

Gift Shop

Don't miss Alaska's finest gift shop in our lobby. Featuring more than 150 T-shirt styles, plus an outstanding selection of Alaskan souvenirs and gifts.

ger or an avid hiker. Expert staff provide additional assistance and supply maps, brochures and other aids. Federal passports (Golden Age, Eagle and Access) and state park passes are available. Live animal demonstrations occur every Thursday at 2 P.M. in the summer. Call for current schedule. Museum scavenger hunts are a popular activity enjoyed by young and old alike. The center is open year-round. Summer hours (Memorial Day to Labor Day) are 9 A.M. to 5:30 P.M. Monday through Friday; closed weekends and holidays. Phone (907) 271-2737, write the center at 605 W. 4th Ave., Suite 105, Anchorage 99501, or visit the web at www.nps.gov/aplic for more information.

The Anchorage Museum of History and Art, located at 121 W. 7th Ave., is a must stop. One of the most visited attractions in Anchorage, this world-class museum features permanent displays of Alaska's cultural heritage and artifacts from its history. The 15,000-square-foot Alaska Gallery on the second floor is the museum's showcase, presenting Alaska Native cultures—Aleut, Eskimo and Indian—and displays about the Russians, New England whalers, as well as gold rush, WWII, statehood and Alaska today. Displays include full-scale dwellings and detailed miniature dioramas. The gallery contains some 300 photographs, more than 1,000 artifacts, 33 maps, and specially made ship and aircraft models. The main floor of the museum consists of 6 connecting galleries displaying Alaska art, such as works by Sydney Laurence. Also on the 1st floor are a Children's Gallery and 3 temporary exhibition galleries. The museum has a reference library and archives, a free film series and public tours (daily in summer), the Museum Shop and a cafe in the atrium. Admission is $5 for adults, $4.50 for seniors, under 18 free. Mid-May to mid-September, open 9 A.M. to 9 P.M. Sunday through Friday; 9 a.m. to 6 p.m. Saturdays. Mid-September to mid-May, open 10 A.M. to 6 P.M. Tuesday through Saturday, and 1–5 P.M. Sunday (closed Mondays and on Thanksgiving, Christmas and New Year's Day). Phone (907) 343-6173 for recorded information about special shows, or (907) 343-4326 during business hours for more information.

Killer Designs. The working studio of artist Tam Johannes. A downtown destination for the bead and glass art enthusiast, the studio features one of a kind fused wearable glass, lampworked and trade beads and "jewelry to die for." Located at 401 K Street between 3rd and 4th avenue. (907) 258-5933. [ADVERTISEMENT]

Anchorage City Trolley Tours. It's fun. It's 1-hour. It's only $10. A lively, informative tour of Alaska's largest city. Located at

612 W. 4th Ave. between F and G streets. Departs hourly. 9 A.M.–6 P.M. P.O. Box 102299, Anchorage, AK 99510. Phone (907) 276-5603. [ADVERTISEMENT]

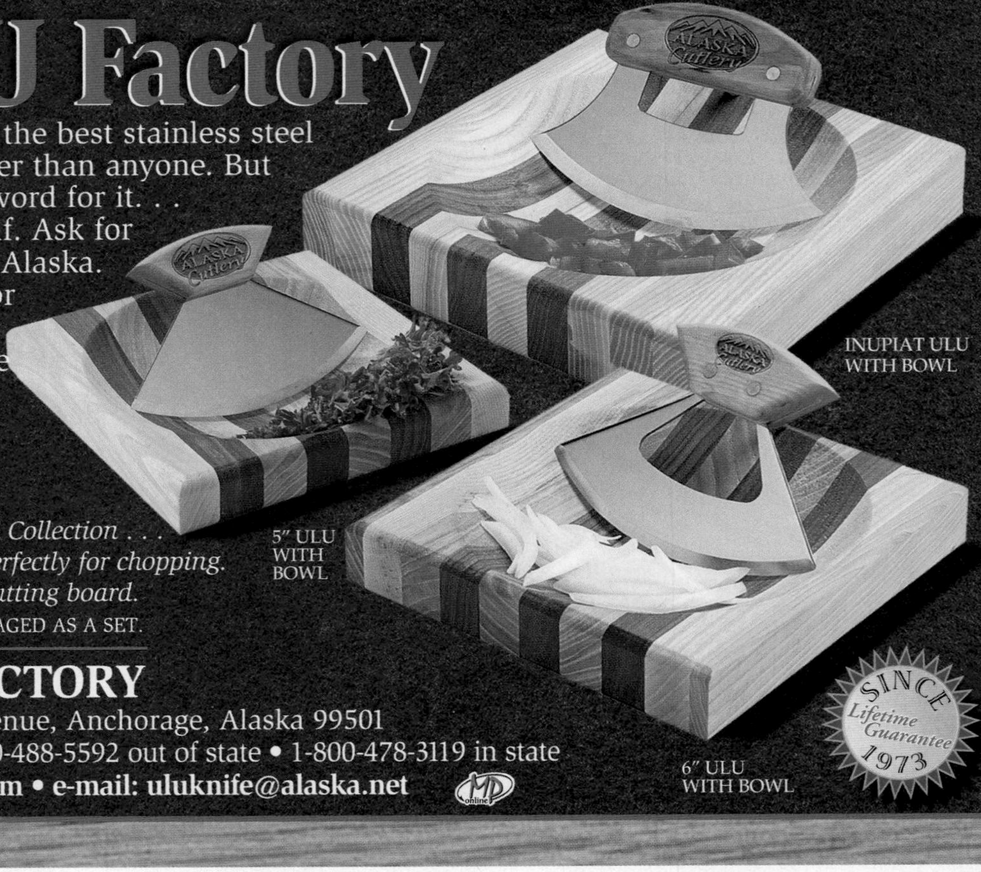

Laura Wright Alaskan Parkys. Known worldwide for beautiful Eskimo-style summer and winter parkas. Off the rack or custom-made. Started by Laura Wright in Fairbanks in 1947; continuing the tradition is granddaughter Sheila Ezelle. Purchase "Wearable Alaskan Art" for the whole family at 343 W. 5th Ave., Anchorage, AK 99501. Phone (907) 274-4215. Bank cards welcome. Mail and phone orders accepted. We airmail worldwide. [ADVERTISEMENT]

Visit the Oscar Anderson House Museum, one of the city's first wood-frame houses. Built in 1915, it was home to Oscar Anderson, a Swedish immigrant and early Anchorage pioneer and businessman. Now on the National Register of Historic Places, it has been beautifully restored and is well worth a visit. Located in the north corner of Elderberry Park, at the west end of 5th Avenue, 420 M St. Open June to mid-September for guided tours. Hours are 11 A.M. to 4 P.M., Tuesday through Saturday. Swedish Christmas tours, first 2 weekends in December. Adults, $3; children 5 to 12, $1. Group tours (maximum 10 participants per group) must be arranged in advance. Phone (907) 274-2336; fax (907) 274-3600.

Oomingmak, Musk Ox Producers' Co-operative, is a Native-owned co-operative specializing in knitted masterpieces. Using Qiviut, the soft and rare fiber from the arctic Musk Oxen, our 250 Native Alaskan knitters create hats and scarves in a variety of traditional patterns from their culture. Since

1969, this co-operative organization has provided the opportunity for Native women to earn a supplementary income while still pursuing their subsistence lifestyle. For over 25 years, the exquisite items the co-op members make on their knitting needles have been worn with pride and enjoyment by satisfied customers from around the world. We invite you to visit us in downtown Anchorage at the little brown house with the Musk Ox mural on the corner of 6th and H streets. (907) 272-9225, 604 H Street, Anchorage, AK 99501. [ADVERTISEMENT]

Exercise Your Imagination: Visit the Imaginarium, 737 W. 5th Ave., Suite G (across from the Westmark Hotel), a hands-on science discovery center offering unique insights into the wonders of nature, science and technology. Open daily year-round Monday through Saturday 10 A.M. to 6 P.M., Sunday noon to 5 P.M., closed on major holidays. Adults, $5; seniors, $4; children 2 to 12, $4. Wheelchair accessible. Phone (907) 276-3179. ♿

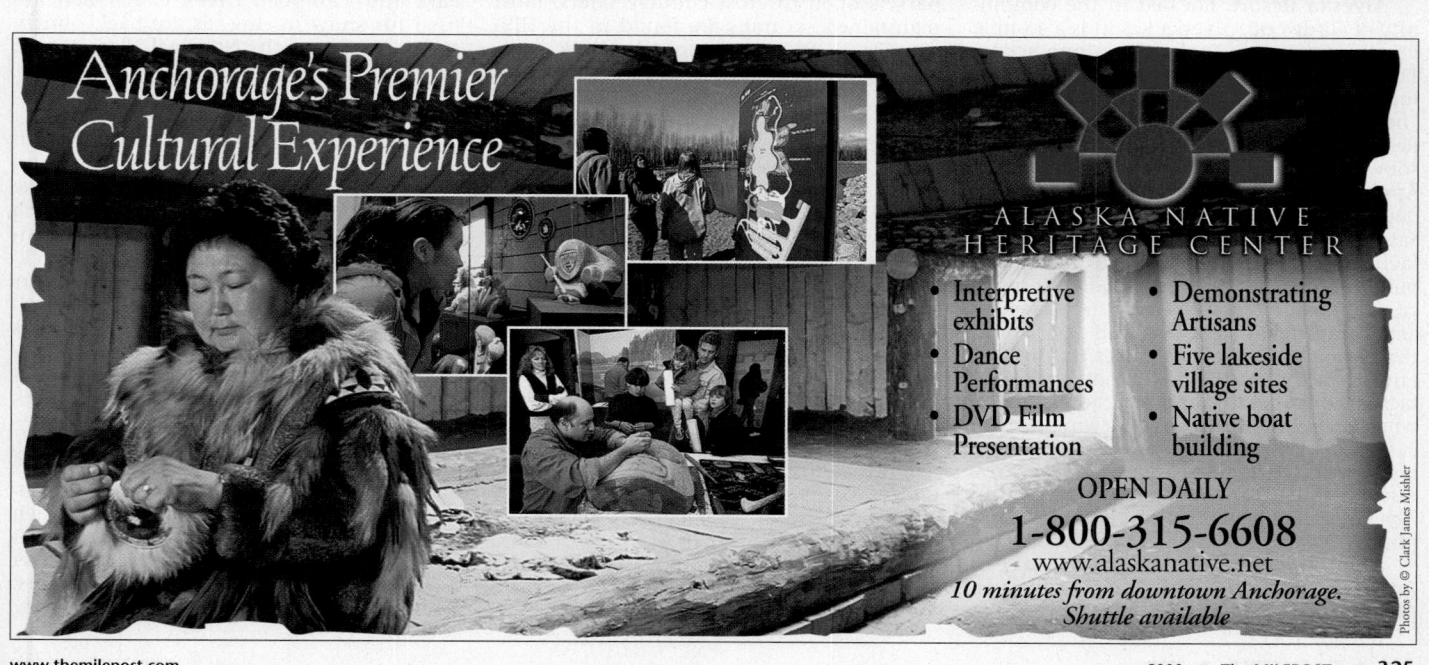

See an Old Schoolhouse: The Pioneer Schoolhouse at 3rd Avenue and Eagle Street is a 2-story memorial to the late Ben Crawford, an Anchorage banker. This was the first

Winter Attractions

Winter Events

Anchorage Fur Rendezvous: The major event of the winter season in Anchorage. Billed as the "Mardi Gras of the North," this elaborate winter festival attracts thousands of celebrants each February.

The 10-day-long celebration dates from 1936 when it began primarily as a fur auction where trappers could bring their pelts to town and sell them to buyers from around the world. Trappers still bring the pelts, and the fur auction still attracts many buyers.

Alaskans shake off cabin fever during "Rondy" (the local term for the Fur Rendezvous).as they enjoy arts and crafts exhibits, a parade, the Miners' and Trappers' Ball, a carnival, an ice and snow sculpturing contest and a home-brew competition.

Highlights of the Fur Rendezvous include the Annual World Championship Dog Weight Pulling Contest and the World Championship Sled Dog Race. The race attracts dozens of mushers from Alaska, Canada and the Lower 48. Spectators line the 25-mile race course, which begins and ends on 4th Avenue in downtown Anchorage. The women's and junior world championship sled dog races are held at Tozier Track the first weekend of the Fur Rendezvous. For more information, phone (907) 277-8615.

The Iditarod Trail Sled Dog Race begins on 4th Avenue in downtown Anchorage in early March. Mushers can be seen on the trail along the Glenn Highway to Eagle River. The racers then pack up and head to Wasilla for the restart of the race the following day, an event which also draws crowds.

Winter Basketball. Anchorage hosts 2 major collegiate basketball events. Carrs/Safeway Great Alaska Shootout, held Thanksgiving weekend, features 8 major college basketball teams in this well-known invitational tournament. The Northern Lights Invitational showcases women's collegiate basketball with 8 teams in a 3-day playoff the last weekend in February.

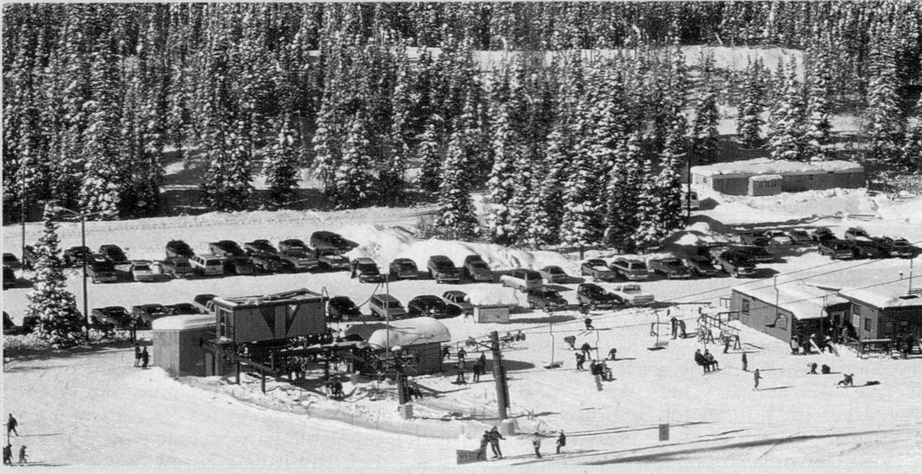

Hilltop Ski Area is just 15 minutes from downtown Anchorage. (© Tom Bol Photography)

Downhill Skiing

Alyeska Resort. Located in the community of Girdwood, Alyeska Resort is a 45-mile drive south from Anchorage along scenic Turnagain Arm via the Seward Highway. Judged by *Conde Nast Traveler* as having the "best view" of any U.S. ski resort, Alyeska Resort is Alaska's largest ski resort, with snow from early November to the middle of April. Night skiing is available during holiday periods in December and on Fridays and Saturdays from January through March. Ski facilities include a high-speed detachable bubble quad, 2 fixed grip quads, 3 double chair lifts and 2 pony tows. A 60-passenger aerial tram takes sightseers and skiers from the mountain's base at 250 feet to a mountaintop facility at the 2,300-foot level. This facility, open year-round and accessible by wheelchair, features a large viewing deck, a cafeteria-style restaurant and a fine dining restaurant and lounge. Centerpiece for the resort is the 307-room, chateau-style Westin Alyeska Prince Hotel. For more information, phone (907) 754-1111 or (800) 880-3880. ♿

Alpenglow at Arctic Valley. East of Anchorage in the Chugach Mountains, Alpenglow Ski Area has a 2,800-foot T-bar platter lift combination and a 700-foot rope tow for beginners. Day lodge with full cafeteria and ski shop. Cross-country skiing available, but trails are not maintained. The ski area operates from about late October to early May. Drive northeast from downtown on the Glenn Highway to Arctic Valley Road and follow the road 7.5 miles to the ski area. For more information, phone (907) 428-1208.

Hilltop Ski Area: Located 15 minutes from downtown Anchorage, 4 miles east of the Seward Highway off Abbott Road, Hilltop has 2 miles of lighted slopes classified as beginner to intermediate. Ski facilities include a double chair lift; a beginner rope tow; 15m, 40m and 60m jumps; and certified snowboard half-pipe. Ski rentals (Alpine, Nordic and snowboards), ski school, gift shop and restaurant. Open daily with complete night lighting. For more information, phone (907) 346-2167 or 346-1446.

Cross-Country Skiing

Chugach State Park: Although the entire park is open to cross-country skiers, most maintained ski trails are found in the Hillside Trail System/Campbell Creek area, accessible via Upper Huffman Road and Upper O'Malley Road. Skiers are encouraged to use established trails as most of Chugach State Park is prime avalanche country.

Ski trail maps are available at the trailheads or from the park office, phone (907) 345-5014.

The Municipality of Anchorage maintains ski trails throughout the city park system. City parks or city-maintained trails include: Russian Jack Springs, DeBarr Road and Boniface Parkway;. Far North Bicentennial/Hillside Parks, access via Hilltop Ski Area on Abbott Road; Campbell Creek Green Belt; Centennial Park, located near Glenn Highway and Muldoon Road.; Chester Creek Green Belt, located in the heart of Anchorage; Kincaid Park, access is from the west end of Raspberry Road. Ski trail maps are available at Anchorage Sports & Recreation, phone (907) 343-4474; or Kincaid Park, phone (907) 343-6397. Ski trail maps are available from Anchorage Sports & Recreation, phone (907) 343-4474.

Ice Skating & Hockey

There are 3 municipal rinks: Ben Boeke Ice Arena (334 E. 16th Ave.), Harry J. McDonald Center (Mile 2.2 Old Glenn Highway, Eagle River) and Dempsey-Anderson Ice Arena (1741 W. Northern Lights). City-maintained outdoor ice-skating lakes include Cheney Lake, Westchester Lagoon, Goose Lake, Jewel Lake, Spenard Lake and Delong Lake. The municipality also maintains outdoor areas for both skating and hockey at Tikishla Park, Chester Creek Sports Complex, Delaney Park Strip and Wendler Jr. High.

Private facilities include Dimond Ice Chalet in the Diamond Mall; Bonnie Cusack Rink on Abbott Loop, and the South Anchorage ice rink.

Sledding & Snowshoeing

Popular sledding hills are at Balto Seppala Park, Centennial Park, Conifer Park, Kincaid Park, Nunaka Valley Park, Sitka Street Park, Sunset Park, Service High School and Alaska Pacific University.

Muldoon Park, Far North Bicentennial Park and Campbell Creek Green Belt are used for snowshoeing, as are backcountry areas of Chugach National Forest and Chugach State Park.

Snowmobiling

Chugach State Park: Five major areas in the park are open to snowmobiling when snow levels are deep enough: Eklutna Lake Valley, reached from the Glenn Highway via Eklutna Road; Eagle River valley, also accessible from the Glenn Highway; Bird Creek, **Milepost S 101.2** Seward Highway; Peters Creek Valley and Little Peters Creek, accessible from the Glenn Highway; and portions of the Hillside/Campbell Creek area, accessible from Upper Huffman Road. Snowmobiling information is available from the park office; phone (907) 345-5014.

Turnagain Pass: On the Seward Highway, about 59 miles south of downtown Anchorage. Turnagain Pass (elev. 988 feet) is a popular winter recreation area in the Chugach National Forest. The west side of the pass is open to snowmobiling as soon as snow cover permits; the east side is reserved for skiers. Snow depths in this pass often exceed 12 feet.

Welcome to the North Country!

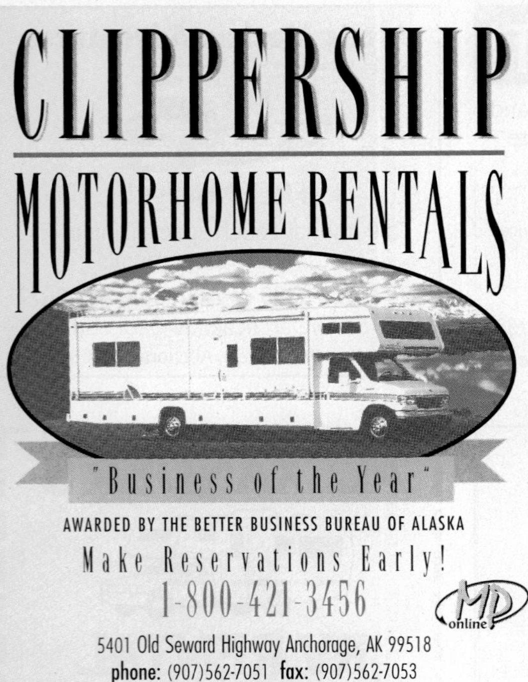

The Alaska State Fair takes place August 25–September 4, 2000, at the state fairgrounds in Palmer, a 40-mile drive from downtown Anchorage.

school in Anchorage. The interior is not open to the public.

"Whaling Wall": Stop by D Street between 5th and 6th avenues for a view of the 400-foot long, 5-story airbrushed mural of beluga whales, bowhead whales and seals by artist Wyland covering the west wall of the J.C. Penney store.

Visit the City Hall, Federal Building, Post Office: The city hall offices are at 6th Avenue and G Street. The Federal Building, located at 7th Avenue and C Street, is one of the largest and most modern office buildings in Anchorage. The lobby features a multimedia collection of artwork, and the cafeteria is open to the public. In downtown Anchorage, the U.S. Post Office is located on the lower level of the Post Office Mall at 4th Avenue and D Street. (The main post office is located near the airport and open 24 hours a day. Smaller postal stations are located throughout the city.)

Wolf Song of Alaska is at the corner of 6th Avenue and C Street in downtown Anchorage. Visitors enter the world of the wolf at this internationally acclaimed wolf

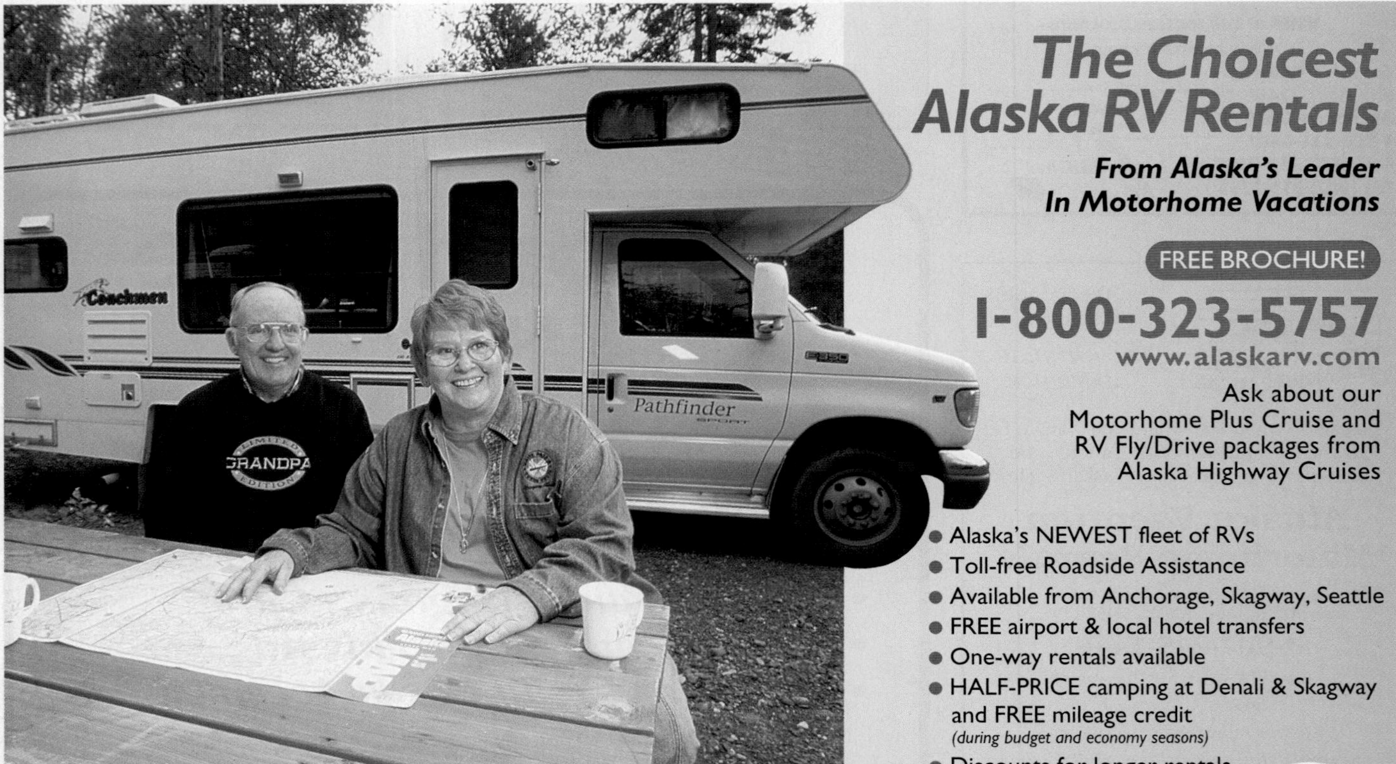

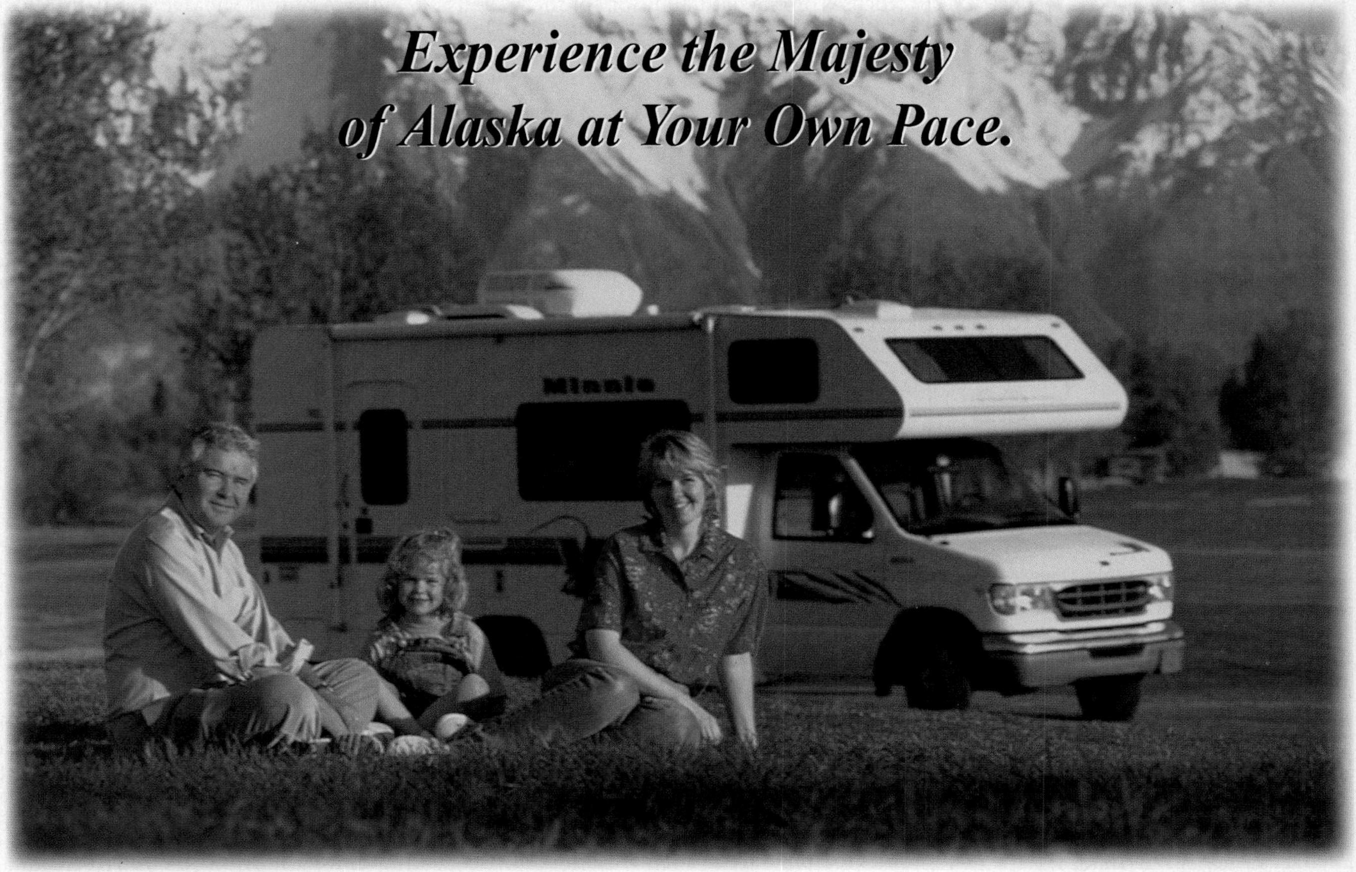

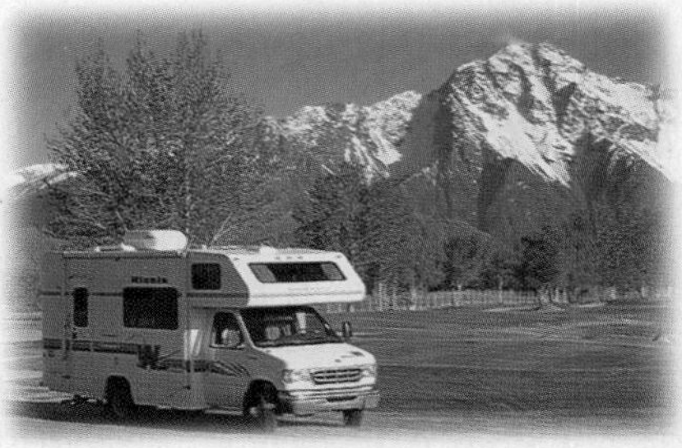

Welcome to Alaska

Sweet Retreat is a family-owned and operated business serving Alaskan visitors since 1983. We take personal pride in our motorhomes and thoroughly detail and mechanically maintian each one because *your safety and comfort is our number one concern!* Price includes complete insurance coverage

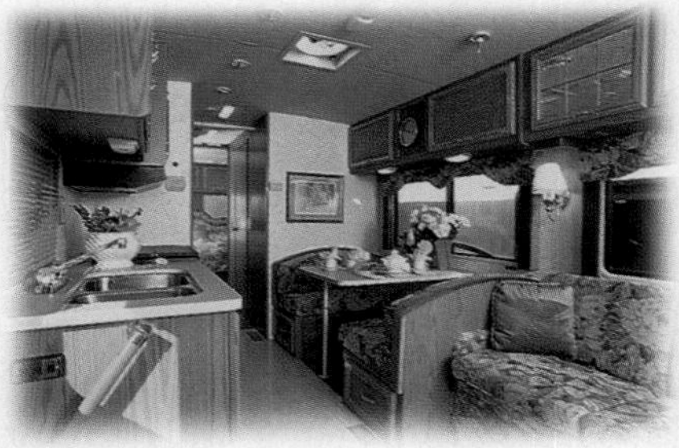

Rent a fully equipped motorhome

- ❖ Several sizes
- ❖ Fully self-contained including microwave & generator
- ❖ Trip planning and fishing gear available
- ❖ Free airport & hotel transfers
- ❖ No cleanup fees
- ❖ New model Winnebagos
- ❖ Unlimited mileage available
- ❖ Linens & dishes stocked at no fee

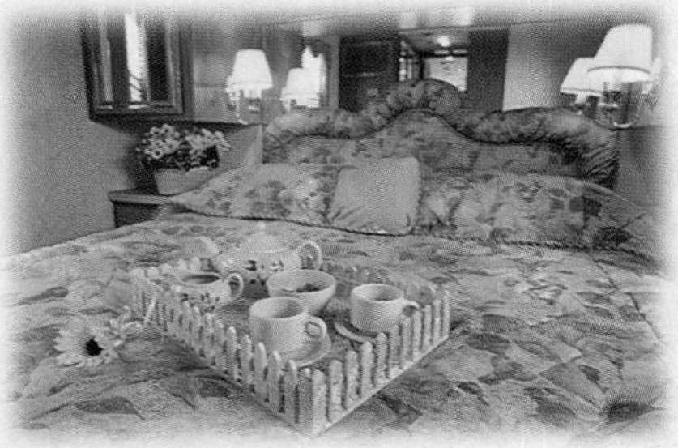

SWEET RETREAT INC
MOTORHOME RENTALS

Call or write for a free brochure: 1-800-759-4861
6820 Arctic Blvd. Anchorage, AK 99518
(907) 344-9155 Fax (907) 344-8279

Home Page: http://www.sweetretreat.com   E-mail- sweetretreat@customcpu.com

MD online   Anchorage Convention & Visitors Bureau   BBB   AVA

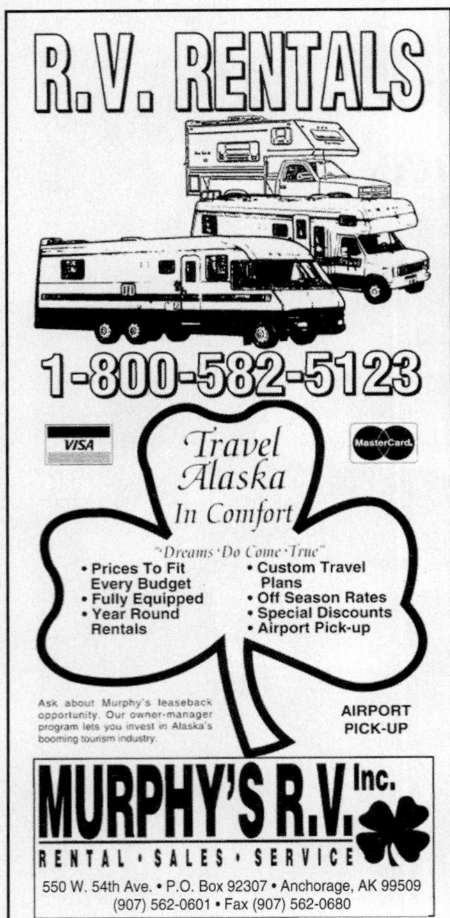

exhibit and education center. This wolf's lair focuses on the natural history of the wolf, its historical relation to humans, and its role as a major symbol in human folklore, art and religion. Wildlife dioramas and interactive displays enhance this unique, one-of-a-kind experience. The expansive gift shop offers a plethora of wolf art, photography and educational materials as well as traditional wolf gifts and collectibles. A nonprofit organization, the exhibit is open daily in summer; hours vary in winter. Parking is available on the street and at garages at 6th Avenue and E Street or 5th Avenue and C Street. RV parking available 3 blocks north at 3rd Avenue and C Street. For more information, phone (907) 274-9653 or (907) 346-3073. E-mail: wolfsong@alaska.net. Web site: www.wolfsongalaska.org.

Alaska State Troopers Museum. This unique little museum, next door to Wolf Song of Alaska, presents the history of law enforcement in the Territory and State of Alaska, with displays of photos and exhibits of historic police equipment. Gifts and memorabilia are available. Admission free. 6th Avenue near C Street. (907) 279-5050.

4th Avenue Theatre. Built in 1947 by Alaska millionaire "Cap" Lathrop, this Anchorage landmark has been refurbished and now includes a gift shop, city trolley tours, cafe, museum exhibit and special events center. Much of the original art-deco design has been preserved and the trademarks of the theater have been restored, including the bas-relief gold leaf murals and the ceiling lights marking the Big Dipper. There is no admission fee to the theater. The 4th Avenue Theatre is located a half block from the visitor center. Open year-round 8 A.M.–10 P.M. summers, 10 A.M.–6 P.M. Tuesday–Saturday winters. For more information phone (907) 257-5635.

Visit the Downtown Saturday Market. This popular outdoor market operates each Saturday May 20 through September 16, 10 A.M. to 6 P.M. The festivities are held on 4th Avenue and in the parking lot at 3rd Avenue between C and E streets. There is no admission fee. Over 320 booths sell a variety of Alaska-made and Alaska-grown products as well as handmade and imported home and novelty items of all types. Local entertainment and community groups add to the fun. For more information contact Webb's Consulting & Management Services, Inc. at (907) 272-5634.

Take in an Alaska Film: Alaska films can be seen at the Anchorage Museum of History and Art, 121 W. 7th Ave., at 3 P.M., daily during summer. Alaska Experience Center, located at 6th Avenue and G Street, offers "Alaska the Great Land," a 70mm film presented on a 180-degree domed screen, and a film and exhibit on the 1964 earthquake.

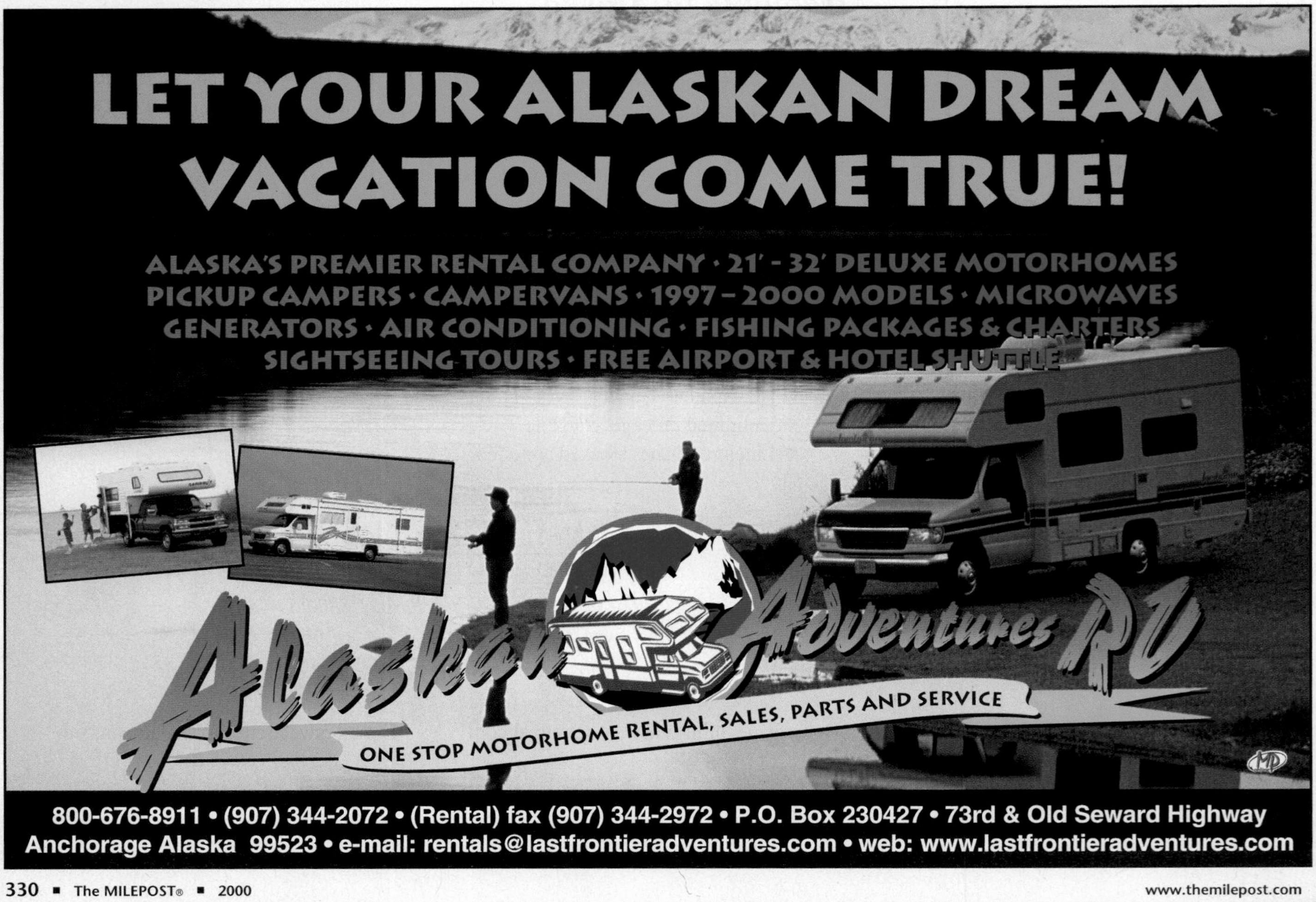

Admission fee charged; open year-round. Call (907) 276-3730 for recorded information.

Visit the Port of Anchorage: The Anchorage waterfront, with its huge cargo cranes off-loading supplies from container ships, makes an interesting stop, especially in winter when ice floes drift eerily past the dock on the fast-moving tide. Visitors may watch activity on the dock from a viewing platform on the 3rd floor of the port office building. To get there, drive north from the downtown area on A Street, take the Port off-ramp and follow Ocean Dock Road to the office about 1.5 miles/2.4 km from downtown. **The Sea Services Veterans Memorial Park**, at the mouth of Ship Creek near the small-boat harbor, is dedicated to veterans of the Navy, Marine Corps, Coast Guard and Merchant Marine. This park offers good whale watching when belugas are in the inlet. A good viewpoint of the port for downtown walkers is at the northeast corner of 3rd Avenue and Christensen Drive.

Alaska Statehood Monument. Located at the corner of 2nd Avenue and E Street (just a block down from the Hilton), a plaque and bronze bust of President Eisenhower commemorates the Alaska Statehood Act making Alaska the 49th state on January 3, 1959.

Heritage Library Museum, in the National Bank of Alaska, Northern Lights Boulevard and C Street, has an excellent collection of historical artifacts, Native tools, clothing and weapons, paintings by Alaskan artists and a research library. Free admission. Open weekdays noon to 5 P.M. between Memorial Day and Labor Day, noon to 4 P.M. at other times of the year. Phone (907) 265-2834. ♿

Moose are a common sight in the Anchorage Bowl. They are also a traffic hazard. (© Bruce M. Herman)

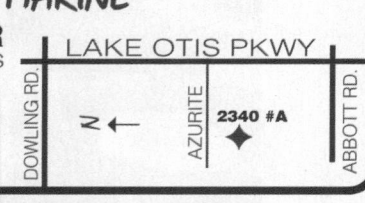

Knitting Frenzy Store, The. Best source for yarn, fiber, books, patterns, supplies for use in knitting, crochet, tatting, cross stitch and needlepoint. Largest Alaskan inventory. Choose a project for the road! Open Monday through Saturday 10-6. Day phone (907) 563-2717 or toll free (800) 478-8322. 4240 Old Seward Hwy. #18, corner of Old Seward and Tudor. Fax (907) 563-1081. E-mail:

frenzy@alaska.net. [ADVERTISEMENT]

Enjoy the Parks: Anchorage is rich in parks, and the parks are rich in the range of activities they offer. More than 190 designated parks have something for everyone's taste, from small "pocket parks" perfect for relaxing or picnicking to vast tracts set aside for skiing, hiking and bicycling; from Government Hill's appealing 1.3-acre rest area, renamed in 1998 in memory of a noted local journalist, to Kincaid Park's 1,516 acres of hills, forests and trails. Many parks are ideal for family picnics and outings. The **Chester Creek Greenbelt**, which stretches from Westchester Lagoon to Goose Lake, contains several parks, and a paved bike trail (also popular with joggers) runs the length of the greenbelt. The greenbelt is accessible from several streets: Spenard Road leads to Westchester Lagoon, and E Street leads to **Valley of the Moon Park**, with a large playground. Other attractive sites, with colorful, modern playground equipment, are David Green Park on 36th Avenue between the Seward Highway and Lake Otis Parkway; Campbell Creek Park on Lake Otis Parkway near Tudor Road.

Downtown Anchorage parks include **Delaney Park Strip**, from A to P streets between 9th and 10th avenues, which has ball fields, tennis courts and **Engine No. 556** at 9th and E Street, a real locomotive for children to explore. To make reservations to use picnic facilities, phone (907) 343-4474. Sports & Recreation publishes a complete listing of all parts and trails, $2. Municipality of Anchorage Web page: www.ci.anchorage.ak.us. **Elderberry Park**, at the foot of 5th Avenue, faces Knik Arm. And **Resolution Park**, at 3rd Avenue and L Street, where the statue of Capt. James Cook overlooks Knik Arm of the inlet which bears his name. The statue was dedicated in 1976 as a bicentennial project.

Go to the Libraries. The modern **Z.J. Loussac Public Library**, located at 36th Avenue and Denali Street, is headquarters for the Anchorage library system. Branch libraries include Chugiak-Eagle River, Mountain View, Muldoon, Samson-Dimond and the Scott & Wesley Gerrish branch in Girdwood. Call (907) 343-2975 for information and hours of operation. **The Alaska Resources Library and Information Services (ARLIS)** is a partnership of 9 natural and cultural resource libraries and information centers, including: U.S. Fish & Wildlife Service Library, State of Alaska Dept. of Fish & Game Habitat Library; U.S. Bureau of Land Management Alaska Resources Library, U.S. Minerals Management Service Library, U.S. National Park Service Library, U.S. Geological Survey Library, Arctic Environmental Information and Data Center Library, Oil Spill Public Information Center, and the Joint Pipeline Office, in conjunction with the University of Alaska Anchorage. Hours are 8 A.M.-5 P. M. Monday-Friday. 3150 C Street, Suite 100, Anchorage, AK 99503. Phone (907) 271-4742.

Visit the Alaska Native Heritage Center: Just 12 minutes north of downtown, the Alaska Native Heritage Center is Anchorage's newest attraction. Visitors have an opportunity to view, in one facility, all of Alaska's Native cultures. Located on a 26-acre parcel of wooded land at Heritage Center Drive at the intersection of Muldoon Road and the Glenn Highway, the center includes a 26,000-square-foot Welcome House, five traditional village settings, a 2-acre lake and walking trails. Programs and exhibits in the Welcome House demonstrate how Alaska Natives live their culture today. A 95-seat theater offers a film introduction, and Native performers and storytellers share through stories, song and dance at the Gathering Place. Artists and tradition bearers share their harmony with the land as visitors walk through the Hall of Cultures. The Village Store provides an outlet for authentic Native arts and crafts. In the summer months an outdoor walk offers a glimpse into rural Alaska as Native artisans use traditional techniques for fishing, hunting, building kayaks and constructing dwellings. Hours are from 9 A.M. to 9 P.M. daily. Adults, $20; Children (5-12), $15; group discounts and family rates are available. Phone (907) 263-5150.

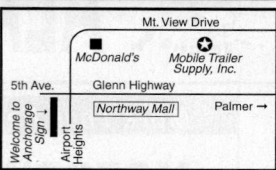

Stroll through Alaska Botanical Garden. The 110-acre garden, located off Campbell Airstrip Road across from the Benny Benson School in East Anchorage, showcases perennials hardy to southcentral Alaska in several large display gardens, a pergola-enclosed herb garden and a rock garden. Interpretive signs guide visitors and identify plants. Paths provide easy walking through a native spruce and birch forest with wildflowers adding seasonal interest. A 1.2-mile nature trail offers views of Campbell Creek, the Chugach Mountains and a natural wetland. Many of the garden beds and trails are maintained by volunteers. Open year-round. Call for recorded information on hours, special events and guided tours; phone (907) 265-3165. Admission by donation.

Enjoy the Public Gardens. In addition to the Municipal Greenhouses and the Alaska Botanical Gardens, many sites around the city are beautified with a variety of plants and flowers for the pleasure of both residents and visitors. In the downtown area the Town Square, the Log Cabin Visitor's Center and the Anchorage Museum of History and Art all blaze with spectacular color during summer months. Numerous hanging baskets transform the core area of downtown Anchorage, and thematic arrangements highlight the well-maintained flower beds lining the city's walkways. The Centennial Rose Garden is the centerpiece of the Delaney Park Strip at 9th and N Streets, and at 15th and L Streets a floral graphic "surprise" greets the public eye each summer. Many neighborhood plots and highway medians are planted and maintained throughout the city by community volunteers .

Alaska Zoo's Ahpun and Oreo are a popular attraction. (© Paul Souders)

See Alaskan Wildlife: Fort Richardson Alaskan Fish and Wildlife Center has been closed for extensive renovation, and its reopening date is indefinite. The operator at the base can provide information for those interested in visiting this exhibit of approximately 250 mounts and trophies of Alaska sport fish, birds and mammals, located in Building 600 on the military reservation. Call (907) 384-1110. Elmendorf Air Force Base Wildlife Museum is open year-round Monday–Thursday 3 P.M.–4:45 P.M.; Friday noon–5 P.M.; Saturday 3 P.M.–4:45 P.M.; and closed on Sunday. Displays include more than 200 native Alaskan species, from big game to small birds and fish, displayed in groupings of forest, tundra, wetlands, mountains and coastal habitat. Wheelchair access but not to restroom. Enter the base from the intersection of Boniface Parkway and the Glenn Highway. Ask guards for directions to Building 4-803. Phone (907) 552-2282 for details. ♿

Charter a Plane: Dozens of air taxi operators are based in Anchorage. Fixed-wheel (skis in winter) planes or floatplanes may be chartered for flightseeing trips to Mount McKinley and Prince William Sound, for fly-in hunting and fishing or just for transportation. Scheduled flightseeing trips by helicopter are also available. Consult the yellow pages of the Anchorage phone book.

Watch Small Planes: Drive out to Merrill Field, Lake Hood or Lake Spenard for an afternoon of plane watching. Lake Hood is the world's largest and busiest seaplane base, with more than 800 takeoffs and landings on a peak summer day. Easy access to lakes Hood and Spenard off International Airport Road (follow signs).

Merrill Field, named for early Alaska aviator, Russell Hyde Merriill, ranked 96th busiest light-plane airport in the nation in 1997, with 187,190 takeoffs and landings. Follow 15th Street East to light at Lake Otis Parkway and turn north on Merrill Field Drive. This route takes you under the approach to one of the runways. Merrill Field is also accessible off the Glenn Highway and from Airport Heights Drive (across from Northway Mall).

Alaska Aviation Heritage Museum, 4721 Aircraft Dr. on the south shore of Lake Hood, preserves the colorful history of Alaska's pioneer bush pilots. Rare historical films and extensive photo exhibit. The museum features a collection of 26 Alaska bush planes. RV parking. Open year-round, May 15 to Sept. 15, 9 A.M. to 6 P.M. daily; Sept. 15 to May 15, 10 A.M. to 4 P.M. Tuesday through Saturday; phone (907) 248-5325. Adults $7.00, seniors and active military, $5.00, children 7 to 12, $2.75, children under 7 free. Wheelchair accessible. ♿

Elmendorf Air Force Base presents an annual, day-long **Open House** on the base, a summer event featuring aerial shows, aircraft displays, ground demonstrations, booths and more. A tour of the base has been offered on Fridays during summer months in years past, but depends on availability of personnel. For more information, phone 3rd Wing Public Affairs (907) 552-8151.

Take a Tour: Several tour operators offer local and area sightseeing tours. These range from a 1-hour narrated trolley tour of Anchorage to full-day tours of area attrac-

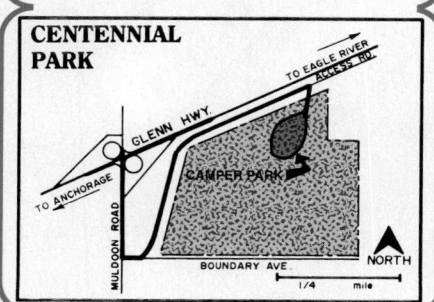

Canada 1-800-544-0529, (907) 276-8023 or phillips@alaskanet.com. [ADVERTISEMENT]

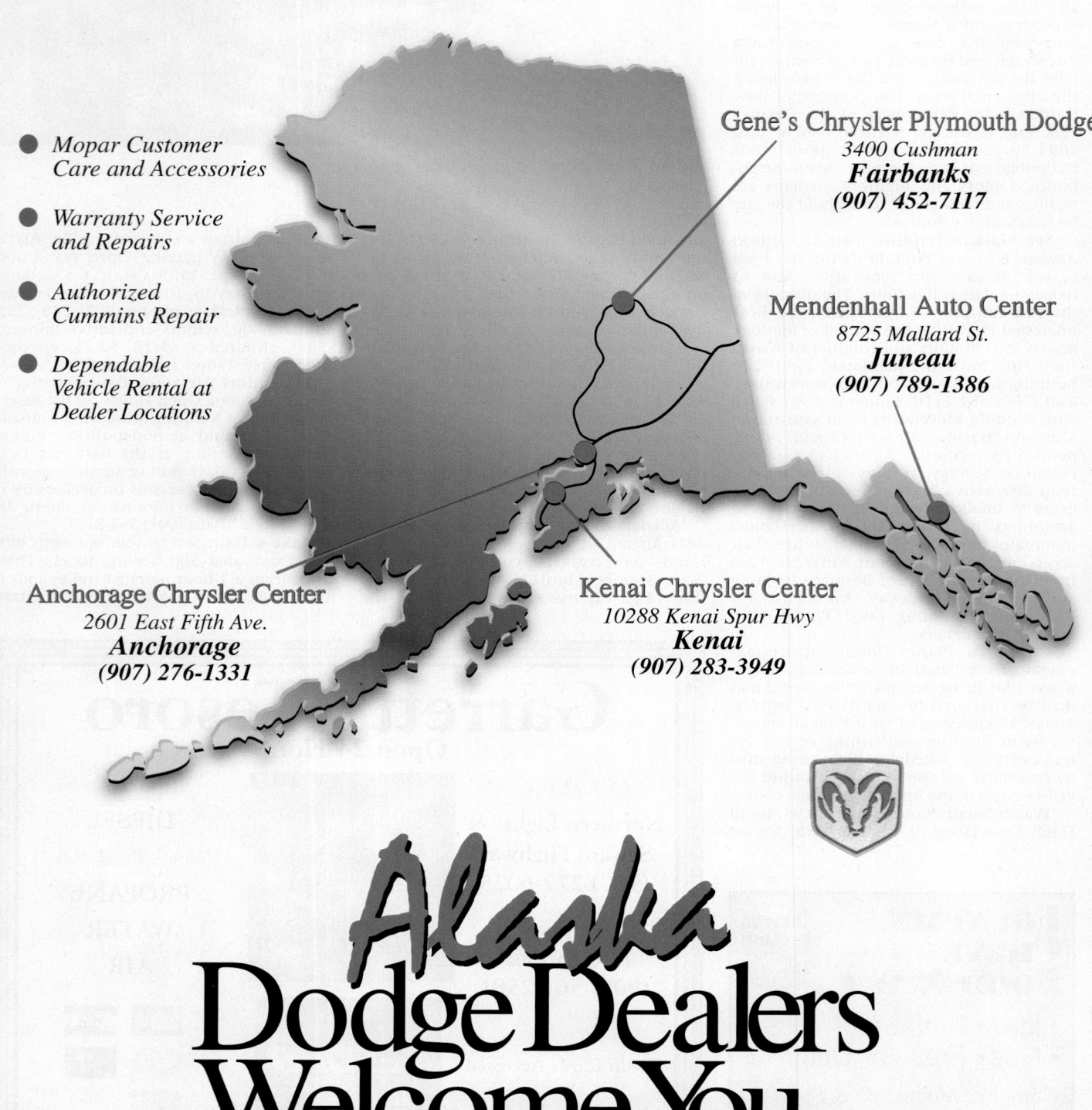

Portage Glacier Cruise. See Alaska's most popular attraction, up close from the deck of the MV *Ptarmigan*. This Gray Line of Alaska cruise takes you right to the face of imposing 10-story-high Portage Glacier. An incredible experience. Tours depart Anchorage twice daily or you may drive to Portage Glacier and board the MV *Ptarmigan* for the cruise-only portion. Tour price is $62 per person; cruise-only price is $25 per person. Prices subject to change. Phone (907) 277-5581. [ADVERTISEMENT]

Prince William Sound Cruise. Experience the spectacular beauty of Prince William Sound aboard the *MV Nunatak*. This Gray Line of Alaska tour cruises past Columbia Glacier, the largest glacier in Prince William Sound. Watch for abundant marine life as you travel to picturesque Valdez. Return to Anchorage via the scenic Matanuska Valley. Two days, 1 night from $289 ppdo. Prices subject to change. Tour departs Anchorage daily. Phone (907) 277-5581. [ADVERTISEMENT]

Train to Denali. Ride the luxurious private, domed railcars of the *McKinley Explorer* to Denali National Park from either Anchorage or Fairbanks. Overnight packages in Denali with roundtrip train service available from $415-$519 ppdo. for 3 days/2 nights, overnight in Anchorage or Fairbanks included. Prices subject to change. Phone Gray Line of Alaska at (907) 277-5581 for train and package tour options. [ADVERTISEMENT]

Tour a Campus: Two colleges are located in Anchorage: the University of Alaska Anchorage at 3211 Providence Dr. and Alaska Pacific (formerly Alaska Methodist) University at 4101 University Dr.

Eskimo dance demonstration at Alaska Native Heritage Center.

(© Loren Taft/Alaskan Images)

Alaska Pacific University was dedicated

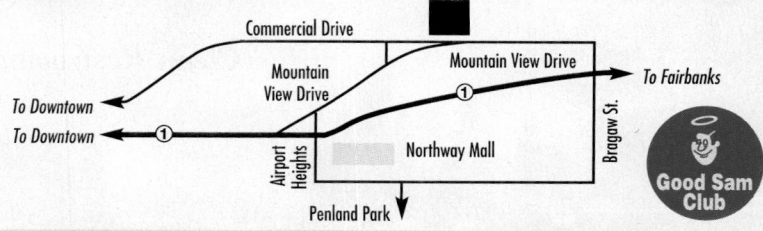

tions such as Portage Glacier and Alyeska Resort. Two-day or longer excursions by motorcoach, rail, ferry and air to nearby attractions such as Prince William Sound or remote areas are also available. Inquire at your hotel, see ads this section, or contact a travel agent.

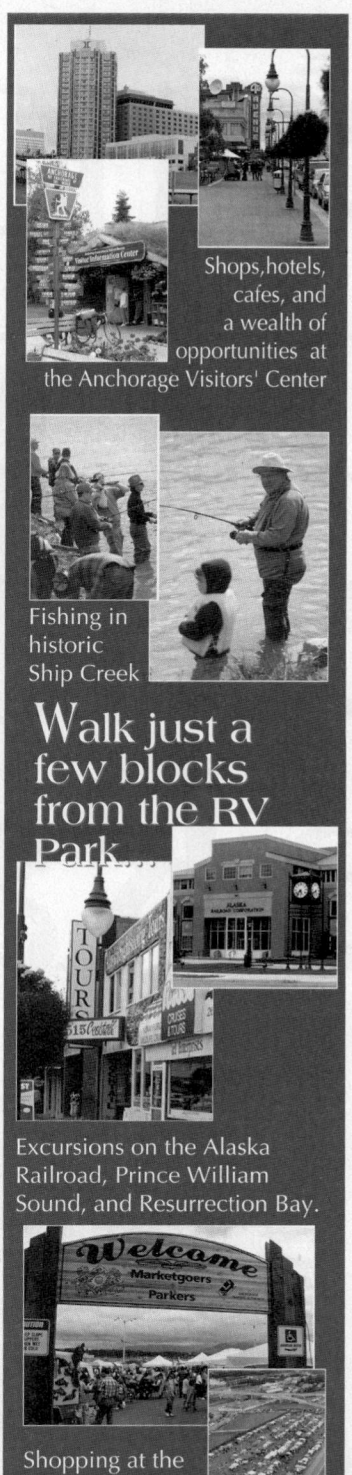

Era Aviation (Alaska Airlines Partnership Service). Over 50 years of experience in Alaska. Scheduled airlines service from Anchorage to Cordova, Homer, Iliamna, Kenai, Kodiak, Valdez and Whitehorse. Seventeen southwest villages served from Bethel hub. Charter service 18-50 seats available. Contact us at 6160 Carl Brady Dr., Anchorage, AK 99502. 800-866-8394. On the web at www.eraaviation.com. [ADVERTISEMENT]

Era Helicopters Flightseeing Tours. 6160 Carl Brady Drive. 50-minute and 2-hour tours available of Anchorage and the Chugach Mountain Range. Experience the natural beauty of Alaska's glaciers and view wildlife in its natural habitat. Other tours available in Denali Park, Juneau and Valdez. Phone (907) 266-8351 locally or 1-800-843-1947. [ADVERTISEMENT]

Kenai Fjords Tours. Don't miss Kenai Fjords National Park with its abundant wildlife and glaciers. "Alaska's #1 Wildlife and Glacier Cruise" departs daily from Seward and has a convenient reservation office in downtown Anchorage. Located at 513 W. 4th Ave. Phone (970) 276-6249 or (800) 468-8068. Convenient one-day transportation packages are available from Anchorage aboard our Wildlife Express private dome car. This is the original Kenai Fjords National Park cruise you've been looking for. [ADVERTISEMENT]

Major Marine Glacier Tours. At Major Marine Tours, we don't try to see every glacier in Prince William Sound...just the best glaciers. As an added bonus to our guests, every cruise is hosted by a uniformed National Forests Ranger —a Major Marine Tours exclusive. Our relaxing, 5-1/2-hour cruise takes you to see the many active tidewater glaciers in Blackstone Bay. We stop the boat, turn off the engines and drift in front of the glaciers, watching the wildlife and spectacular calving. Every passenger on board is assigned table seating in our comfortable heated cabin. Our outside viewing decks are perfect for spotting otters, eagles, seals and the large bird colonies on our route. A freshly prepared all-you-can-eat salmon and prime rib buffet is available for only $10. The food is consistently rated as the best of any day-cruise company. Complete tours cost only $99 and depart daily from Whittier's boat harbor early May to mid-September. Convenient rail and bus packages are available from Anchorage. Why rush around Prince William Sound when you can relax and see the best of Alaska at a more leisurely pace? Major Marine Tours...always your best value in Prince William Sound. For reservations or a free brochure, call (800) 764-7300 or (907) 274-7300. Major Marine Tours, 411 W. 4th, Anchorage, AK 99501. Internet: www.majormarine.com. [ADVERTISEMENT]

26 Glacier Cruise. Cruise the calm, protected waters of Prince William Sound and come face to face with tidewater glaciers plus an amazing array of wildlife on the fastest, largest and most luxurious high-speed catamaran in Alaska. See our full-page ad in the Anchorage section. Our year-round sales office is located at 519 W. 4th Ave., Anchorage, AK 99501. Toll free from USA and

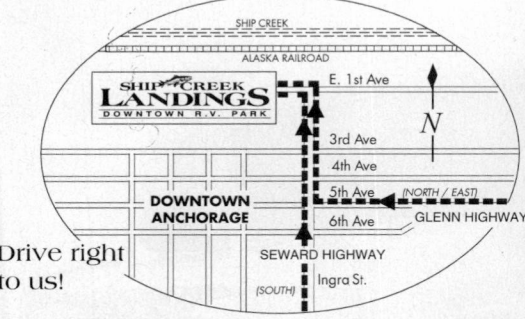

June 29, 1959, the same year that Alaska became the 49th state, and is now the state's largest private 4-year university. APU's first students were enrolled in the fall of 1960. The university offers liberal arts-based educational programs for all ages, including an annual Elderhostel. The APU campus is located on 170 forested acres, featuring the 3-tiered Atwood Fountain, Waldron Carillon Bell Tower and the Jim Mahaffey Trail System for skiers, runners, hikers and mountain bikers. Phone (907) 564-8248 or (800) 252-7528 for tours or information about university programs, or access the university on the Internet at www.alaskapacific.edu.

The University of Alaska Anchorage is 1 of 3 regional institutions in the state's university system (the others are in Fairbanks and Southeast Alaska). For information on tours of the UA campus in Anchorage, phone (907) 786-1529.

Go to the Zoo: The Alaska Zoo is located on 25 acres of wooded land and displays more than 85 species of Arctic wildlife, including glacier bears, polar bears, brown (grizzly) and black bears, reindeer, moose, Dall sheep, otters, wolves, foxes, musk-oxen and wolverines, as well as non-Alaskan species such as Bactrian camels, Siberian tigers and an elephant.. Be sure to stop in at the gift shop, located on your right as you enter. The zoo is open 9 A.M. to 6 P.M. daily from May 1 to Oct. 1; 10 A.M. to 4:30 P.M. the remainder of the year. Drive south from the downtown area on the Seward Highway to **Milepost S 120.8.** Take O'Malley exit, turn left on O'Malley Road and proceed 2 miles km to the zoo, which will be on your left. Admission $7 for adults, $6 for seniors, $5 for students 13 to 18, and $4 for children 3 to 12. Family passes $50. Free admission for children under 3. Handicap parking, wheelchair accessible. Phone (907) 346-3242 for details. ♿

Visit the Greenhouses: The municipality maintains the extensive Mann Leiser greenhouses at Russian Jack Park, 5200 DeBarr Road, where myriad plantings supply local parks and public gardens with summer's colorful flowers. Visitors enjoy the displays of tropical plants, the fish pond and the aviary where finches, cockatiels and tropical birds enliven an attractive area popular for small weddings and school tours. Open year-round, 8 A.M. to 3 P.M., the greenhouses are closed only on a few specific holidays. Phone (907) 343-4717 for additional information.

Watch the Tide Come In: With frequent tidal ranges of 30 feet within 6 hours, and many approaching 40 feet, one of Anchorage's best nature shows is the action of the tides in both the Knik and Turnagain arms of upper Cook Inlet. Vantage points along Knik Arm are Earthquake Park, Elderberry Park (west end of 5th Avenue), Resolution Park (near corner of 3rd Avenue and L Street) and the Anchorage small-boat harbor.

Turnagain Arm has the second highest tides in North America, rising to a maximum high of 42 feet, exceeded only by the Bay of Fundy in eastern Canada. A good overlook for Turnagain tides is Bird Creek State Recreation Site south of Anchorage at **Milepost S 101.2** on the Seward Highway. With careful timing you might see a tidal bore, an interesting phenomenon rarely seen elsewhere. A bore tide is a foaming wall of tidal water, up to 6 feet in height, formed by a flood tide surging into a constricted inlet such as Knik or Turnagain Arm.

CAUTION: In many places the mud flats of

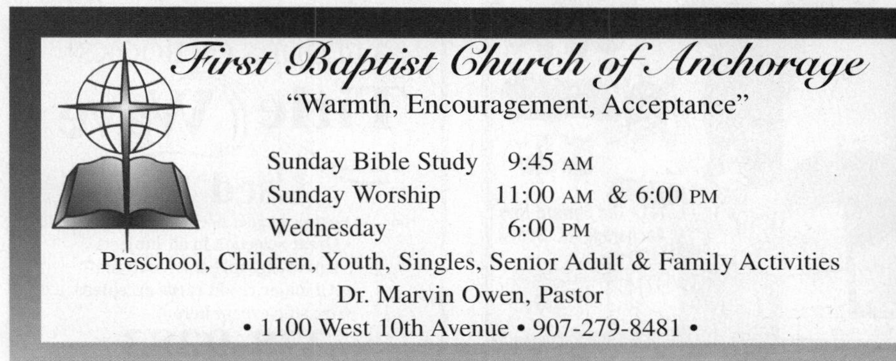

Fishermen line the banks of Ship Creek in downtown Anchorage. *(Kris Graef, staff)*

Knik and Turnagain arms are like quicksand. Don't go wading!

Play Golf: The Municipality of Anchorage maintains a 9-hole golf course at Russian Jack Springs Park, Debarr Road and Boniface Parkway, featuring artificial turf greens. It is open from mid-May through September; phone (907) 333-8338 or (907) 343-4474 off-season (October–April). Alyeska Resort maintains the Anchorage Golf Course, 3651 O'Malley Road, an all-grass, 18-hole course open from mid-May through mid-September; phone (907) 522-3363 for more information. Two military courses are open to civilians. Eagle Glen Golf Course, an 18-hole par-72 course, is located on Elmendorf Air Force Base, near the Post Road gate. Open mid-May through September. Phone (907) 552-2773 for tee times; rentals available. Fort Richardson's 18-hole Moose Run Golf Course is the oldest golf course in Alaska. The course is accessible from Arctic Valley Road (**Milepost A 6.1** on the Glenn Highway) and is open May through September. Rentals available. Phone (907) 428-0056 for tee times. All golf course hours depend on the amount of sunlight.

Play Tennis: The Municipality of Anchorage maintains more than 55 tennis courts, including those in Eagle River and Girdwood. In addition, private clubs offer year-round indoor courts.

Run: Few summer weeks pass in Anchorage without at least one scheduled race for every cause, interest and level of ability imaginable. Sports & Recreation, phone (907) 343-4474, issues a complete schedule of these events, from 5k runs/walks to marathons and triathlons. Great for spectators and participants alike.

Summer Solstice. Alaskans celebrate the longest day of the year with a variety of special events. In Anchorage, there's the annual Mayor's Midnight Sun Marathon, a 26-mile, 385-yard run through the city, as well as two other runs: a half-marathon and a 5-miler. These events are usually scheduled on the Saturday nearest summer solstice (June 20 or 21).

Tour Anchorage by Bicycle: The municipality has about 120 miles of paved bike trails (including trails in Eagle River and

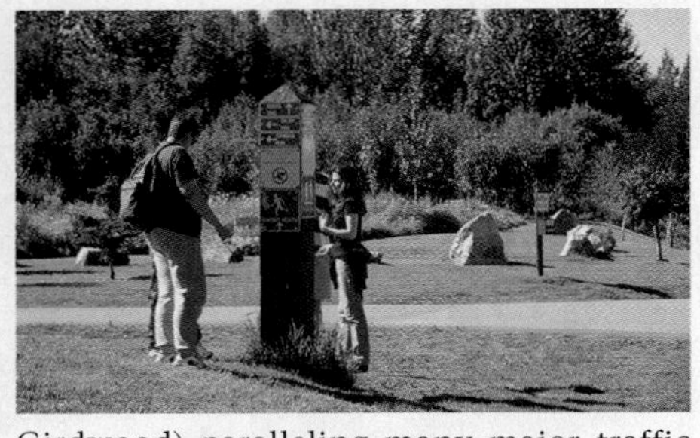

Girdwood) paralleling many major traffic arteries and also passing through some of the city's beautiful greenbelt areas. Maps of the trail system are available at Anchorage Sports & Recreation, 120 South Bragaw St. Offering an especially unique experience is the 11-mile **Tony Knowles Coastal Trail**, which begins at 3rd Avenue and Christensen Drive, and follows the coast around Point Woronzof to Point Campbell and Kincaid Park. This is one of the most popular trails in the city with bicyclists, joggers and walkers, who are treated to close-up views of Knik Arm (watch for beluga whales) and on clear days a beautiful view of the Alaska Range.

Another popular bike route for families is the Chester Creek Bike Trail from Westchester Lagoon, at 15th Avenue and U Street, to Russian Jack Springs Park. The 6.5-mile trail traverses the heart of Anchorage, following Chester Creek past Goose Lake, a favorite summer swimming beach.

Watch Birds: Excellent bird-watching opportunities are abundant within the city limits. Lakes Hood and Spenard, for example, are teeming with seaplanes but also, during the summer, are nesting areas for grebes and arctic loons. Also seen are widgeons, arctic terns, mew gulls, green-winged teals and sandpipers.

Huge flocks of Canada geese nest and raise their young during the summer. It is not unusual to see traffic at a standstill as a pair of geese, followed by a tandem procession of goslings, cross the city's highways.

Another great spot is the **Potter Point State Game** Refuge, south of downtown on the Seward Highway at **Milepost S 117.4.** Early July evenings are best, according to local bird watchers. Forests surrounding Anchorage also are good for warblers, juncos, robins, white-crowned sparrows, varied thrushes and other species.

At the Park for All People on W. 19th Avenue near Spenard Road in the Chester Creek Greenbelt, a nature trail winds through a bird-nesting area.

Go for a Hike. Hiking trails in the Anchorage area are found in Chugach State Park and in Municipality of Anchorage parks. Three popular hikes in Chugach State Park's Hillside Trail System, accessed from the Glen Alps trailhead, are Flattop Mountain, Powerline Trail and Williwaw Lakes. To reach the trailhead, take the Seward Highway south to the O'Malley exit and go east 4 miles to Hillside Drive; take a right on Hillside, go about 1.5 miles to the intersection of Hillside and Upper Huffman. Turn left on Upper Huffman and continue 4 miles to the Glen Alps trailhead and take a left turn to parking lot. The hike up Flattop Mountain begins here; elevation gain is 1,550 feet in 3.5 miles, hiking time is 3 to 5 hours. Also accessible from Glen Alps is the Powerline trail; total length 11 miles, elevation gain 1,300 feet. Williwaw Lakes trail branches off

Powerline trail to several small alpine lakes; round-trip is 13 miles with a 742-foot elevation gain. For more information phone Chugach State Park at (907) 345-5014.

Hilltop Ski Area, 4 miles east of the Seward Highway at Dimond, is the trailhead for summer hiking, biking and horseback riding on trails in Bicentennial and Hillside municipal parks. The trails range in length from an easy mile walk to a strenuous 16-mile hike. For more information phone Hilltop Ski Area at (907) 346-1446.

Other Anchorage parks offering hiking, jogging or biking include Kincaid Park, Russian Jack Springs Park and Far North Bicentennial Park. For more information phone Anchorage Sports and Recreation at (907) 343-4474.

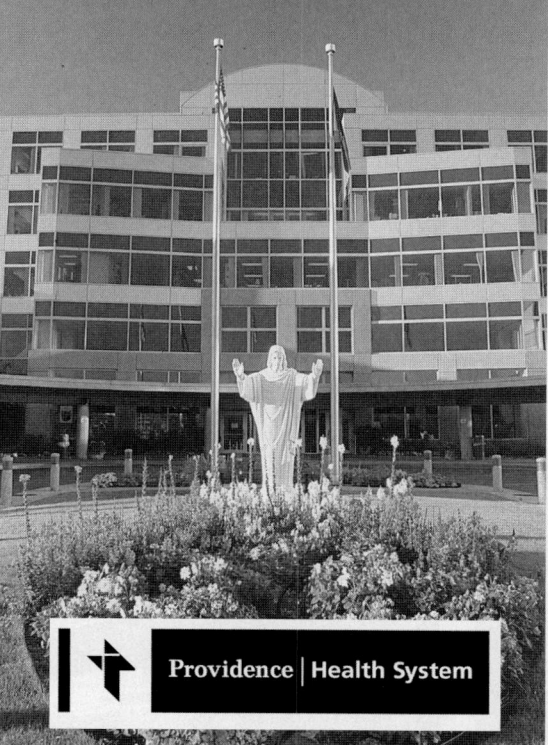

See a Baseball Game: Some fine semi-pro baseball is played in Anchorage. Every summer some of the nation's top college players (among past notables are Tom Seaver and 1998 home-run king Mark McGwire) play for the Anchorage Glacier Pilots and Anchorage Bucs, the Peninsula Oilers, the Mat–Su Miners and the Fairbanks Goldpanners. Anchorage games are played at Mulcahy Ball Park, Cordova Street and E. 16th Avenue. Check local newspapers for schedules or call the Anchorage Bucs, (907) 561-2827, or the Glacier Pilots, (907) 344-5444.

Watch Salmon: King, coho, pink and a few chum salmon swim up Ship Creek and can be seen jumping a spillway in the dam just east of Ocean Dock Road. Watch for kings from early June until mid-July and for other species from mid-August until September. A fine wooden platform, with handicapped access, was completed on Ship Creek last year to make salmon watching and/or fishing easier and more enjoyable. It is named for Sarah Bidwell, an avid fisher and long-time Salmon Derby volunteer.

Watch an Equestrian Event. The William Clark Chamberlin Equestrian Center in 530-acre Ruth Arcand Park hosts a variety of equestrian events every weekend from late-May through August. This public facility is open from 11 A.M. to 9 P.M. Phone (907) 522-1552. The Eaton Equestrian Center at 5801 Moose Meadow on the Hillside offers riding lessons and special events. Phone (907) 346-3745 for more information.

Kayaking, Canoeing, Rafting: All are available in or near Anchorage. Guided tours from 1-14 days run on several rivers within 100 miles of Anchorage, including the Chulitna, Susitna, Little Susitna, Matanuska and Kenai rivers. Information on guided raft and canoe trips is available through travel agencies, local sporting goods stores and in the free *Visitors Guide* available from the Log Cabin Visitor Information Center.

Several flying services provide unguided float trips. The service flies customers to a remote river, then picks them up at a predetermined time and place downriver.

Several area streams offer excellent canoeing and kayaking. Information on the Swanson River and Swan Lake canoe trails on the Kenai Peninsula is available from the Kenai National Wildlife Refuge Manager, Box 2139, Soldotna, AK 99669-2139; phone (907) 262-7021. Nancy Lake State Recreation Area, 67 miles north of Anchorage, offers a popular canoe trail system. Contact the Alaska State Parks, Mat–Su/Valdez–Copper River Area, H.C. 32, Box 6706, Wasilla, AK 99654-9719; phone (907) 745-3975.

Sailing in the Anchorage area is limited to freshwater lakes and lagoons (usually ice free by May).

Mirror Lake, 24.5 miles north of Anchorage on the Glenn Highway, and Big Lake, 52.3 miles north of Anchorage on the Parks Highway, are popular spots for small sailboats.

Motorboating: Big Lake and Lake Lucille along the Parks Highway offer motorboating. Several rivers, including the Susitna, offer riverboating, but the shallowness and silty, shifting beds of most Alaska rivers

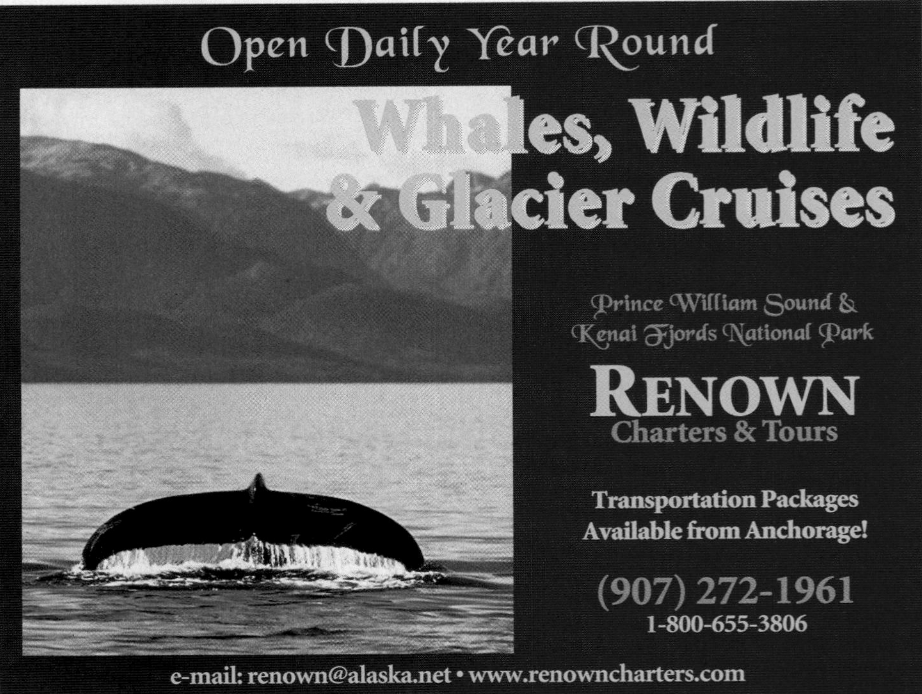

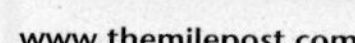

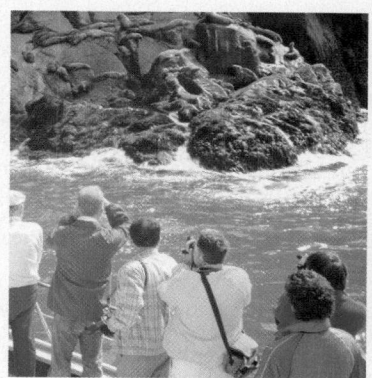

Day Trips From Anchorage

Anchorage is the hub for Southcentral Alaska: You can get anywhere in the state from here, traveling by car, plane or train. Here are just a few driving trips you can make, ranging from a few hours to all day, that take in Native culture, glaciers and wildlife.

53 Miles Round Trip

You can easily visit 2 interesting Native cultural sites in a day. Drive out the Glenn Highway 4.4 miles from downtown and exit north on Muldoon Road for the **Alaska Native Heritage Center**, a 26-acre site featuring 5 traditional village sites along a walking path around a 2-acre lake. Cultural presentations, food and crafts in the dramatic Welcoming House.

Back on the Glenn Highway, continue east to the Eklutna exit at **Milepost A 26.3** for **Eklutna Historical Park**. Attractions include the Eklutna Heritage Museum, the historic St. Nicholas Russian Orthodox Church and a hand-built Siberian prayer chapel. Admission fee charged. Open daily mid-May to mid-September. The bright little grave houses or spirit houses in the cemetery are painted in the family's traditional colors. (See pages 300-303 in the GLENN HIGHWAY section.)

55 Miles Round Trip

If natural history and mountain scenery are your interest, this short drive out to Eagle River offers both. Drive out the Glenn Highway and exit east to Eagle River at **Milepost A 13.4**. Turn on Eagle River Road and drive 12 miles for **Eagle River Nature Center.** The center has beautiful views of the Chugach Mountains; viewing telescope; and self-guiding nature trails. It is also the trailhead for the Old Iditarod–Crow Pass trail. Guided nature hikes are offered daily in summer and there are regularly scheduled nature programs.

Return to downtown Eagle River and stop by the **Alaska Museum of Natural History**, located in the Parkgate Building across from McDonald's at the corner of Easy Street and Old Glenn Highway. Although relatively small in square-footage, the museum manages to house a great variety of small but comprehensive displays, including the largest exhibit of rocks and minerals on display in Alaska. (See pages 301-303 in the GLENN HIGHWAY section.)

88 Miles Round Trip

Drive south on the Seward Highway to **Milepost S 90** (37 miles from Anchorage) and turn off on the Alyeska Highway. About 2 miles up this road, a gravel road forks to the left and leads 3.1 miles to **Crow Creek Mine**, a historic 1898 mining camp where visitors can tour the camp's old buildings and pan for gold. Returning from the mine to the main road, continue to the small town of Girdwood, where the **Girdwood Forest Fair** takes place in July. It's then a short drive up to the Alyeska Prince Hotel at the base of Mt. Alyeska, Alaska's largest ski resort. The 60-passenger **Alyeska Aerial Tramway** carries summer sightseers (and winter skiers) from the hotel to a mountaintop complex featuring the Seven Glaciers restaurant. The tram ride offers wonderful views of Turnagain Arm. (See SEWARD HIGHWAY section.)

101 Miles Round Trip

Drive out on the Glenn Highway from downtown Anchorage to Palmer, heart of the Matanuska-Susitna Valley, for a look at Alaska agriculture and some very different wild animals in captivity. The **Musk Ox Farm**, at **Milepost A 50.1**, is home to a number of these shaggy, ice age survivors. Tours through their fenced pastures are given May to September. Just beyond the Musk Ox Farm turnoff is **Wolf Country USA**, at **Milepost A 52**, home to several wolves. (For more information about wolves, visit Wolf Song of Alaska in Anchorage.) Return to Anchorage via the Old Glenn Highway alternate route and stop by the **Reindeer Farm**, where you can hand feed reindeer, moose, black-tailed deer and elk. Nearby is a picturesque original homestead farm. (See pages 293 and 297 in the GLENN HIGHWAY section.)

107 Miles Round Trip

Drive south on the Seward Highway to **Milepost S 78.9** (48.1 miles from Anchorage) to junction with the 5.5-mile access road east to **Portage Glacier**. On the drive in, watch for salmon spawning at Williwaw Creek and look for the hanging Explorer Glacier. The Begich, Boggs Visitor Center at Portage Glacier has interpretive displays on glaciers, regular showings of films of interest and Forest Service naturalists available to answer your questions. You can stand on the shore of Portage Lake or take a tour boat for a close-up view of Portage Glacier. (See SEWARD HIGHWAY section.)

Returning to the Seward Highway for the drive back to Anchorage, stop by **Big Game Alaska**, just north of the junction (on the west side of the road) at **Milepost S 79**, for a drive-through tour of this wild animal park. Big Game Alaska is home to Mattie the Moose, an orphaned moose who has starred in many commericals.

122 Miles Round Trip

Dogs, dog mushing and Alaska history highlight this day trip. Drive out the Glenn to the Parks Highway and continue north to Wasilla at **Milepost A 42.2.** Turn left for Knik Road; turn right for Wasilla's Main Street. Take a right turn for the Dorothy Page Museum and Historical Townsite in downtown Wasilla. The museum features local history and is the site of a Farmer's Market on Wednesdays.

Turn left on Knik Road for **Iditarod Trail Sled Dog Race Headquarters** at Mile 2.2, which doubles as a visitor center, with displays of race memorabilia, films on dog mushing and Iditarod souvenirs. Continue on Knik Road to Mile 13.9 for the **Knik Museum Mushers' Hall of Fame** for more Iditarod Race history.

Back at the highway, drive north to **Milepost A 47** for the **Museum of Alaska Transportation and Industry**, featuring historic aircraft, railroad equipment and old farm machinery. (See pages 357-362 in the PARKS HIGHWAY section.)

require jet-equipped, flat-bottomed boards for maximum safety.

Cruises on larger boats are available from Whittier into Prince William Sound, from Homer Spit into Kachemak Bay and Cook Inlet, and from Seward into Resurrection Bay and Kenai Fjords National Park. Venturing into those areas in small boats without a knowledgeable local guide is dangerous and should not be attempted.

Cook Inlet waters around Anchorage are only for the experienced because of powerful bore tides, unpredictable weather, dangerous mud flats and icy, silty waters. Turnagain Arm is strictly off-limits for any boat, and Knik Arm and most of the north end of Cook Inlet is the domain of large ships and experienced skiff and dory operators.

Swimming: Anchorage Sports & Recreation can answer questions about aquatics; phone (907) 343-4476.

Goose Lake is open daily, June through August, from 10:30 A.M. to 5:30 P.M.; lifeguards, bathhouse and picnic area. It is located 3 miles east from downtown Anchorage on UAA Drive.

Jewel Lake, 6.5 miles from downtown Anchorage on W. 88th Avenue off Jewel Lake Road, is open daily June through August, from 10:30 A.M. to 5:30 P.M.; lifeguards, restrooms and covered picnic area.

Spenard Lake is open daily, June through August, from 10:30 A.M. to 5:30 P.M.; lifeguards, restrooms, picnic area. Located 3 miles southwest of downtown Anchorage on Spenard Road, then west on Wisconsin Street to Lakeshore Drive.

CAUTION: Do not even consider swimming in Cook Inlet! Soft mud, swift tides and icy water make these waters extremely dangerous!

The YMCA, 5353 Lake Otis Parkway, offers discounts to outside members with YMCA identification. Phone (907) 563-3211 for pool schedule and more information.

The following pools, operated by Sports & Recreation, are open to the public: Service High School pool, 5577 Abbott Road, phone (907) 346-3040; Bartlett High School pool, 25-500 Muldoon Road, phone (907) 337-6375; West High School pool (with a water slide, new in 1999), 1700 Hillcrest Dr., phone (907) 274-5161; East High School pool, 4025 E. 24th Ave., phone (907) 278-9761; Dimond High School pool, 2909 W. 88th Ave., phone (907) 249-0355; general information phone (907) 343-4476; Chugiak High School pool, operated by Eagle River Parks & Recreation, is located off South Birchwood Loop Road, off the Glenn Highway north of Anchorage, phone (907) 696-2010; and University of Alaska pool, Providence Drive, phone (907) 786-1233.

Charter Boats: Visitors must drive south

Chugach State Park

This 495,000-acre park, flanking Anchorage to the north, east and south, offers wilderness opportunities for all seasons: hiking, wildlife viewing, camping, berry picking, skiing and snowmobiling. Information about the park is available from Chugach State Park, H.C. 52, Box 8999, Indian, AK 99540; phone (907) 345-5014. The Chugach State Park office, located in Potter Section House on the Seward Highway, has maps showing access to the park's recreation areas.

Between June and September, park staff offer guided nature walks and more strenuous hikes on the weekends to various points of interest in the park. The nature walks, which last about 2 hours, focus on some aspect of natural history, such as wildflower identification or bird watching. The longer hikes last approximately 4 hours. Phone (907) 694-6391 for a recorded message.

The park's hillside trailheads may be reached by driving south from downtown to the O'Malley Road exit at **Milepost S 120.8** on the Seward Highway. Follow O'Malley Road east for 4 miles to Hillside Drive; turn right on Hillside and proceed about 1.5 miles to the intersection of Upper Huffman and Hillside Drive. Turn left on Upper Huffman and continue 4 miles to the Glen Alps trailhead and parking lot. This is the trailhead for several popular trails, including **Powerline** and **Flattop**, the most popular hiking trail in the state. Flattop is a fairly easy hike with great views of Anchorage.

There are several access points to Chugach State Park attractions from the Glenn Highway. Take the Eklutna Road exit (**Milepost A 26.3**) and drive in 10 miles to reach **Eklutna Lake Recreation Area**. Eklutna Lake is the largest lake in Chugach State Park. The recreation area has a campground, picnic area and hiking trails. (See page 300.)

From the Eagle River exit off the Glenn Highway (**Milepost A 13.4**) follow Eagle River Road 12.7 miles to reach **Eagle River Nature Center**, a beautiful spot with views

Ptarmigan Lake in Chugach State Park. (© Bruce M. Herman)

of the Chugach Mountains. Excellent wildlife displays, a nature trail and a year-round program of naturalist led hikes and talks make this a worthwhile stop. Phone (907) 694-2108 for more information. (See page 301.)

Arctic Valley is another park area easily accessible from the Glenn Highway via Arctic Valley Road exit at **Milepost A 6.1**. Drive in 7.5 miles for spectacular views of Anchorage and Cook Inlet. Good berry picking and hiking in summer; downhill and cross-country skiing in winter.

The Seward Highway south from Anchorage also gives access to several Chugach State Park hiking trails. See the SEWARD HIGHWAY section for details.

to the Kenai Peninsula for charter boats. Sightseeing and fishing charters are available at Whittier, Seward and Homer.

Fishing: The Alaska Dept. of Fish and Game annually stocks about 28 lakes in the Anchorage area with rainbow trout, landlocked chinook (king) salmon, grayling and arctic char. Approximately 103,000 6- to 8-inch rainbow trout are released each year along with about 50,000 salmon. All lakes are open to the public. In addition, salmon-viewing areas and limited salmon fishing are available in the immediate Anchorage area. For specific information, check the Alaska fishing regulations book, call the agency at (907) 267-2218, or phone (907) 349-4687 for a recorded message. Urban salmon fisheries have been developed by the Alaska Dept. of Fish and Game in several Anchorage-area streams. King and coho (silver) salmon can be caught in **Ship Creek** in downtown Anchorage through July as well as in **Eagle River** just north of town. Coho salmon fisheries are found in **Campbell Creek** in Anchorage and at **Bird Creek** just north of Girdwood on the Seward Highway.

In winter, lakes in the Anchorage and the Matanuska–Susitna Valley offer excellent ice fishing. Ice fishing is especially good in the early winter in Southcentral.

Several excellent fishing spots are within a day's drive of Anchorage. The Kenai Peninsula offers streams where king, red, silver, pink and chum salmon may be caught during the season. Dolly Varden and steelhead also run in peninsula streams. Several lakes contain trout and landlocked salmon. In-season saltwater fishing for halibut, rockfish and several species of salmon is excellent at many spots along the peninsula and out of Whittier, Homer and Seward. For specific fishing spots both north and south of Anchorage see the Seward, Sterling, Glenn and Parks highways sections. Because of the importance of fishing to Alaska both commercially and for sport, regulations are strictly enforced. Regulations are updated yearly by the state, often after *The MILEPOST®* deadline, so it is wise to obtain a current regulations book. Check the ADF&G's home page at www.state.ak.us.

PARKS HIGHWAY ① ③

Connects: Anchorage to Fairbanks, AK **Length:** 358 miles
Road Surface: Paved **Season:** Open all year
Highest Summit: Broad Pass 2,400 feet
Major Attraction: Denali National Park

(See maps, pages 352–353)

	Anchorage	Denali Park	Fairbanks	Talkeetna	Wasilla
Anchorage		237	358	113	42
Denali Park	237		121	153	195
Fairbanks	358	121		245	316
Talkeetna	113	153	245		71
Wasilla	42	195	316	71	

Parks Highway at Milepost A 201 near Broad Pass summit. (© Kris Graef, staff)

The Parks Highway was called the Anchorage–Fairbanks Highway after its completion in 1971, and renamed in July 1975 in honor of George A. Parks (1883–1984), the territorial governor from 1925 to 1933. The Parks Highway (Alaska Route 3) junctions with the Glenn Highway (Alaska Route 1) 35 miles from Anchorage and leads 323 miles north to Fairbanks. Together, these highways connect Alaska's largest population centers.

The entire route runs 358 miles through some of the grandest scenery that Alaska has to offer. Highest summit on the Parks Highway is at Broad Pass (see **Milepost A 195**), at approximately 2,400 feet. Motorists can see current weather conditions at Broad Pass by checking the FAA videocam at Summit airport at www.akweathercams.com.

The Parks Highway is a good 2-lane paved road, but with few passing lanes. Several sections of moderate S-curves and heavy foliage reduce sight distance: Pass with care. *CAUTION: Drive with headlights on at all times. Watch for moose. Watch for local cross traffic.* Motorists who plan to drive the highway during the winter should check highway conditions before proceeding.

The Parks Highway provides the most direct highway access to Denali National Park and Preserve (formerly Mount McKinley National Park) from either Anchorage or Fairbanks. Driving distance to the park entrance is 237.3 miles from Anchorage and 120.7 miles from Fairbanks. Mount McKinley—also called Denali—(elev. 20,320 feet) is visible from the highway, weather permitting, and there are several viewing turnouts. Best scenic viewpoints of the mountain (on a clear day) are at **Milepost A 135.2** and **162.4**. See DENALI NATIONAL PARK section for details on the park.

Emergency medical services: Between the Glenn Highway junction and **Milepost A 202.1**, phone 911. Between **Milepost A 174** at Hurricane Gulch bridge and **Milepost A 224** at Carlo Creek bridge, phone the Cantwell ambulance at 768-2982 or the state troopers at 768-2202. Between **Milepost A 224** and Fairbanks, phone 911.

Parks Highway Log

Distance from Anchorage (A) is followed by distance from Fairbanks (F).
Mileposts along the Parks Highway indicate distance from Anchorage.

ALASKA ROUTE 1

A 0 F 358 (576.1 km) ANCHORAGE.

Follow the Glenn Highway (Alaska Route 1) north 35 miles/56.3 km to junction with the Parks Highway. (Turn to the end of the GLENN HIGHWAY section on page 303 and read log back to front from Anchorage to junction with the Parks Highway.)

A 35.3 (56.8 km) **F 322.7** (519.3 km) Traffic light at intersection of Glenn and Parks highways; Fairbanks-bound travelers turn on Parks Highway. *NOTE: Expect major road construction at this junction in summer 2000.*

Homestead RV Park. See display ad this section. ▲

Junction of the Parks Highway (Alaska Route 3) and the Glenn Highway (Alaska Route 1). Turn to **Milepost A 35.3** in the GLENN HIGHWAY section for log of highway to Anchorage or Tok.

Fairbanks-bound travelers continue with this log. Begin truck lane northbound next 1.1 miles/1.8 km.

ALASKA ROUTE 3

A 35.4 (57 km) **F 322.6** (519.2 km) **Junction** with Trunk Road. **Trunk Road** leads northeast 0.7 mile/1.1 km to University of Alaska Fairbanks' Matanuska agricultural research farm (no tours). Also access via Trunk Road to Mat-Su College (1.8 miles/2.9 km); Palmer-Wasilla Highway (3.1 miles/5

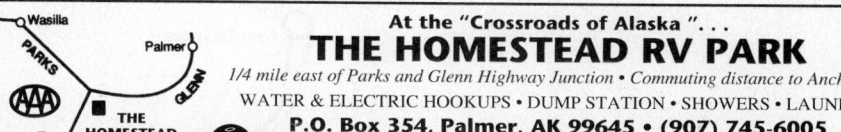

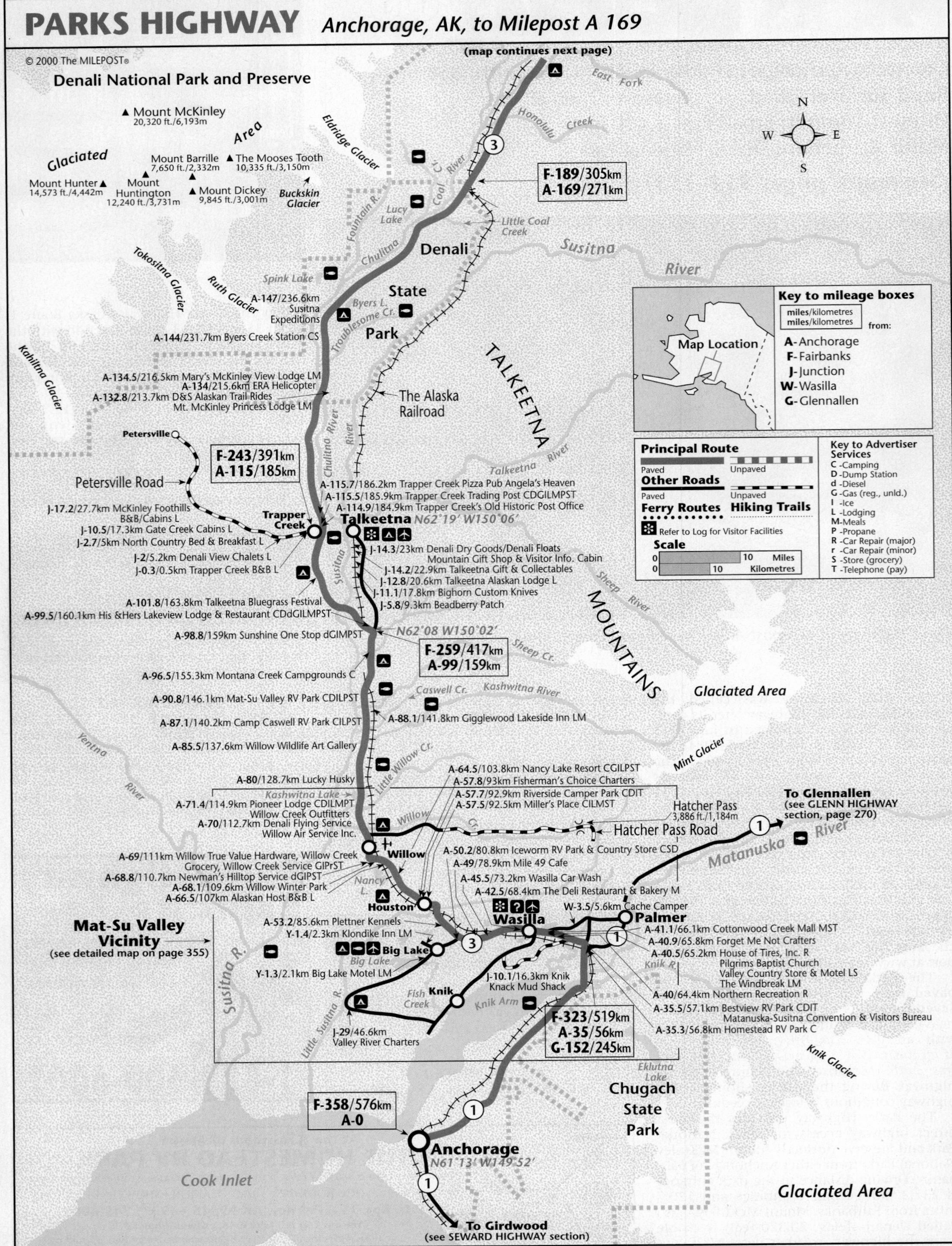

PARKS HIGHWAY Anchorage, AK, to Milepost A 169
© 2000 The MILEPOST®
(map continues next page)
Denali National Park and Preserve
Mount McKinley 20,320 ft./6,193m
Glaciated Area
Mount Barrille 7,650 ft./2,332m
The Mooses Tooth 10,335 ft./3,150m
Mount Hunter 14,573 ft./4,442m
Mount Huntington 12,240 ft./3,731m
Mount Dickey 9,845 ft./3,001m
Buckskin Glacier
Eldridge Glacier
East Fork
Honolulu Creek
F-189/305km
A-169/271km
Coal Cr.
River
Lucy Lake
Fountain R.
Little Coal Creek
Susitna River
Chulitna
Denali
State
Park
Tokositna Glacier
Ruth Glacier
Spink Lake
A-147/236.6km Susitna Expeditions
Byers L.
Troublesome Cr.
A-144/231.7km Byers Creek Station CS
Kahiltna Glacier
TALKEETNA
MOUNTAINS
A-134.5/216.5km Mary's McKinley View Lodge LM
A-134/215.6km ERA Helicopter
A-132.8/213.7km D&S Alaskan Trail Rides
Mt. McKinley Princess Lodge LM
The Alaska Railroad
Petersville
Petersville Road
F-243/391km
A-115/185km
Chulitna River
River
Talkeetna River
A-115.7/186.2km Trapper Creek Pizza Pub Angela's Heaven
A-115.5/185.9km Trapper Creek Trading Post CDGILMPST
A-114.9/184.9km Trapper Creek's Old Historic Post Office
J-17.2/27.7km McKinley Foothills B&B/Cabins L
J-10.5/17.3km Gate Creek Cabins L
J-2.7/5km North Country Bed & Breakfast L
J-2/5.2km Denali View Chalets L
J-0.3/0.5km Trapper Creek B&B L
Trapper Creek
Talkeetna N62°19' W150°06'
J-14.3/23km Denali Dry Goods/Denali Floats
Mountain Gift Shop & Visitor Info. Cabin
J-14.2/22.9km Talkeetna Gift & Collectables
J-12.8/20.6km Talkeetna Alaskan Lodge L
J-11.1/17.8km Bighorn Custom Knives
J-5.8/9.3km Beadberry Patch
Susitna
A-101.8/163.8km Talkeetna Bluegrass Festival
A-99.5/160.1km His &Hers Lakeview Lodge & Restaurant CDdGILMPST
A-98.8/159km Sunshine One Stop dGIMPST
N62°08' W150°02'
F-259/417km
A-99/159km
Sheep River
Sheep Cr.
A-96.5/155.3km Montana Creek Campgrounds C
A-90.8/146.1km Mat-Su Valley RV Park CDILPST
Caswell Cr.
Kashwitna River
Glaciated Area
A-87.1/140.2km Camp Caswell RV Park CILPST
A-88.1/141.8km Gigglewood Lakeside Inn LM
A-85.5/137.6km Willow Wildlife Art Gallery
Yentna River
Little Willow Cr.
Mint Glacier
A-80/128.7km Lucky Husky
A-64.5/103.8km Nancy Lake Resort CGILPST
A-57.8/93km Fisherman's Choice Charters
A-57.7/92.9km Riverside Camper Park CDIT
A-57.5/92.5km Miller's Place CILMST
Kashwitna Lake
A-71.4/114.9km Pioneer Lodge CDILMPT
Willow Creek Outfitters
A-70/112.7km Denali Flying Service
Willow Air Service Inc.
Willow Cr.
Hatcher Pass 3,886 ft./1,184m
Hatcher Pass Road
To Glennallen (see GLENN HIGHWAY section, page 270)
Matanuska River
A-69/111km Willow True Value Hardware, Willow Creek Grocery, Willow Creek Service GIPrST
Willow
A-68.8/110.7km Newman's Hilltop Service dGIPST
A-68.1/109.6km Willow Winter Park
A-66.5/107km Alaskan Host B&B L
A-50.2/80.8km Iceworm RV Park & Country Store CSD
A-49/78.9km Mile 49 Cafe
A-45.5/73.2km Wasilla Car Wash
A-42.5/68.4km The Deli Restaurant & Bakery M
Nancy L.
Houston
W-3.5/5.6km Cache Camper
Mat-Su Valley Vicinity (see detailed map on page 355)
A-53.2/85.6km Plettner Kennels
Y-1.4/2.3km Klondike Inn LM
Wasilla
Palmer
A-41.1/66.1km Cottonwood Creek Mall MST
A-40.9/65.8km Forget Me Not Crafters
A-40.5/65.2km House of Tires, Inc. R
Pilgrims Baptist Church
Valley Country Store & Motel LS
The Windbreak LM
Big Lake
Y-1.3/2.1km Big Lake Motel LM
Susitna R.
Knik R.
J-10.1/16.3km Knik Knack Mud Shack
A-40/64.4km Northern Recreation R
A-35.5/57.1km Bestview RV Park CDIT
Matanuska-Susitna Convention & Visitors Bureau
A-35.3/56.8km Homestead RV Park C
Fish Creek
Knik
Knik Arm
F-323/519km
A-35/56km
G-152/245km
Little Susitna R.
J-29/46.6km Valley River Charters
Knik Glacier
Eklutna Lake
Chugach State Park
F-358/576km
A-0
Anchorage N61°13' W149°52'
Cook Inlet
Glaciated Area
To Girdwood (see SEWARD HIGHWAY section)
N W E S
Key to mileage boxes
miles/kilometres
from:
A-Anchorage
F-Fairbanks
J-Junction
W-Wasilla
G-Glennallen
Map Location
Principal Route
Paved
Unpaved
Other Roads
Paved
Unpaved
Ferry Routes
Hiking Trails
Refer to Log for Visitor Facilities
Scale
0 10 Miles
0 10 Kilometres
Key to Advertiser Services
C -Camping
D -Dump Station
d -Diesel
G -Gas (reg., unld.)
I -Ice
L -Lodging
M-Meals
P -Propane
R -Car Repair (major)
r -Car Repair (minor)
S -Store (grocery)
T -Telephone (pay)

PARKS HIGHWAY *Milepost A 169 to Fairbanks, AK*

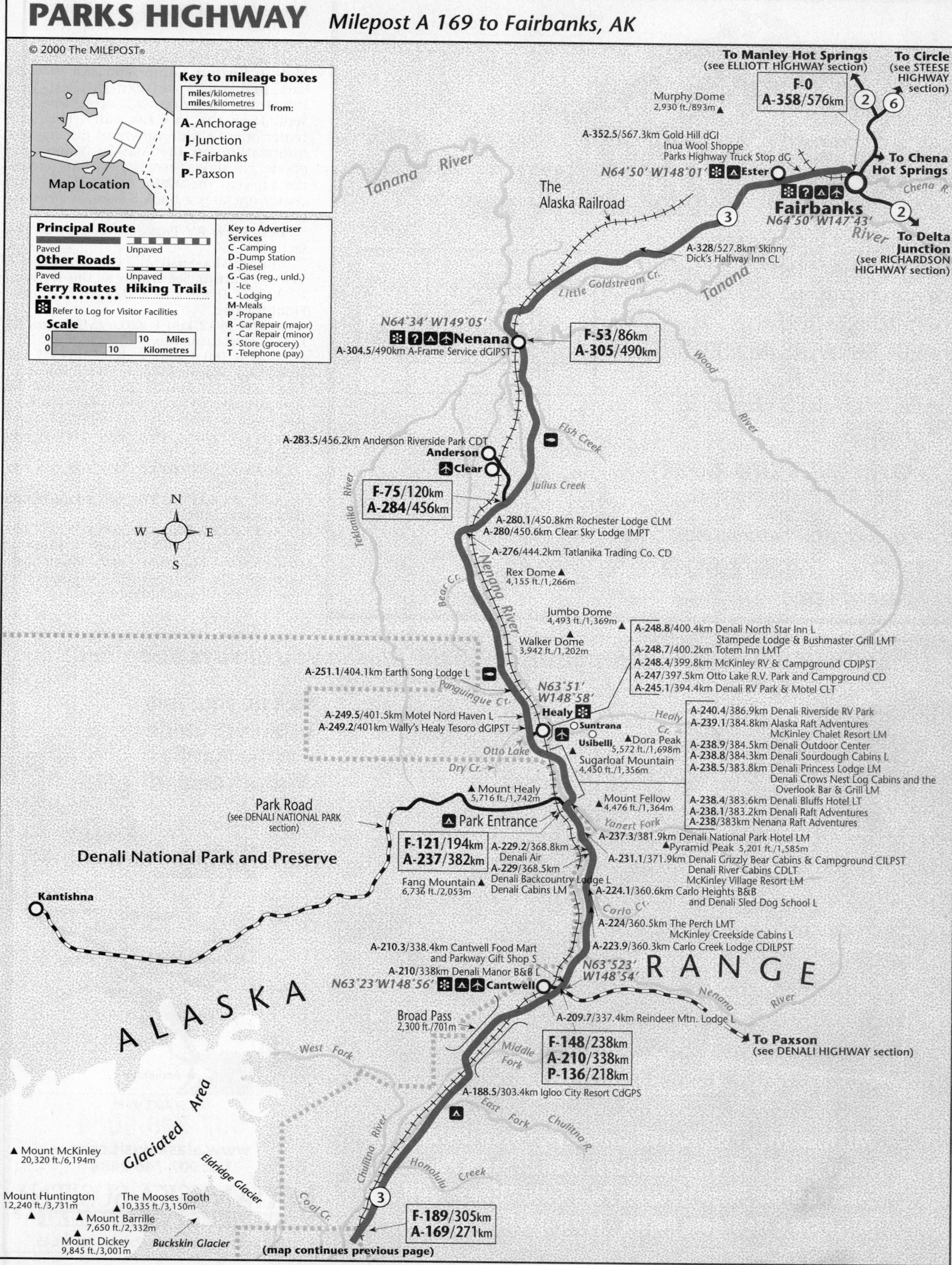

km); Bogard Road (4.2 miles/6.8 km); and Palmer-Fishhook Road (6.5 miles/10.5 km).

NOTE: Watch for road construction northbound next 2 miles in summer 2000.

A 35.5 (57.1 km) **F 322.5** (519 km) **Mat–Su Visitors Center** and Best View RV Park (0.6 mile/1 km east on Best View Drive). The visitor center is open May 15 to Sept. 15, 8 A.M. to 6 P.M. daily. This large center offers a wide variety of displays and information on the Mat–Su Valley; pay phone, gift shop. There is a veterans' memorial adjacent the visitor center. The visitor center operates a booking and reservation service; phone (907) 746-5000.

Best View RV Park. See display ad this section. ▲

Matanuska–Susitna Convention & Visitors Bureau. See display ad this section.

A 36.7 (59.1 km) **F 321.3** (517.1 km) Pioneer Drive.

A 37.4 (60.2 km) **F 320.6** (515.9 km) Air Lane; access to airstrip.

A 37.8 (60.8 km) **F 320.2** (515.3 km) Hyer Road. Wasilla Creek bridge. Turnout.

A 38 (61.2 km) **F 320** (515 km) Gas station/foodmart at turnoff to Fairview Loop Road west to Knik Road (11 miles/17.7 km). Access to Palmer Hay Flats State Game Refuge.

A 38.3 (61.6 km) **F 319.7** (514.5 km) Pioneer Plaza.

A 39 (62.8 km) **F 319** (513.4 km) Wasilla Backpackers Hostel.

A 39.4 (63.4 km) **F 318.6** (512.7 km) Shopping center and RV park at **junction** with Seward Meridian Road, which junctions with the Palmer–Wasilla Highway. (See Mat-Su Vicinity map this section.)

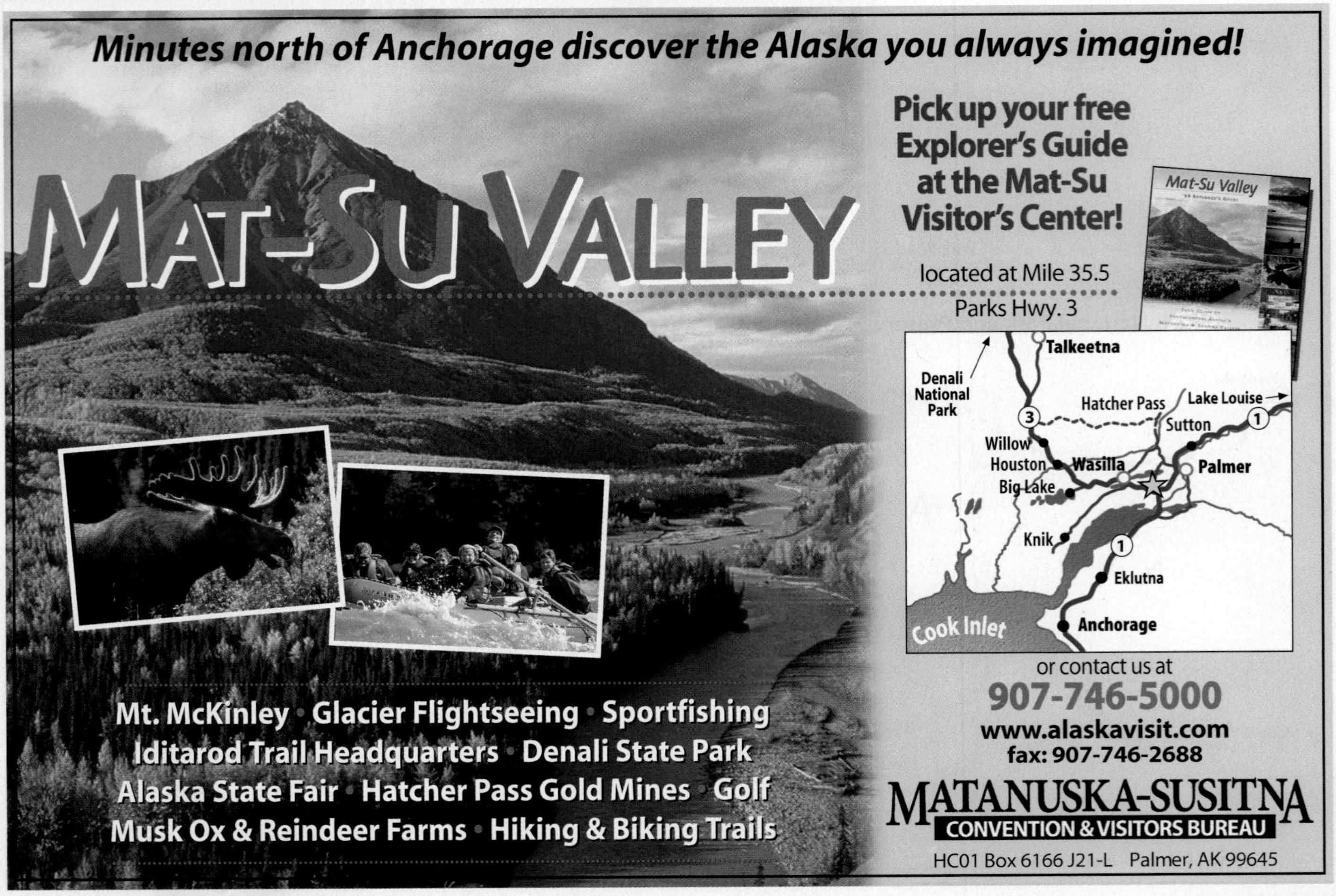

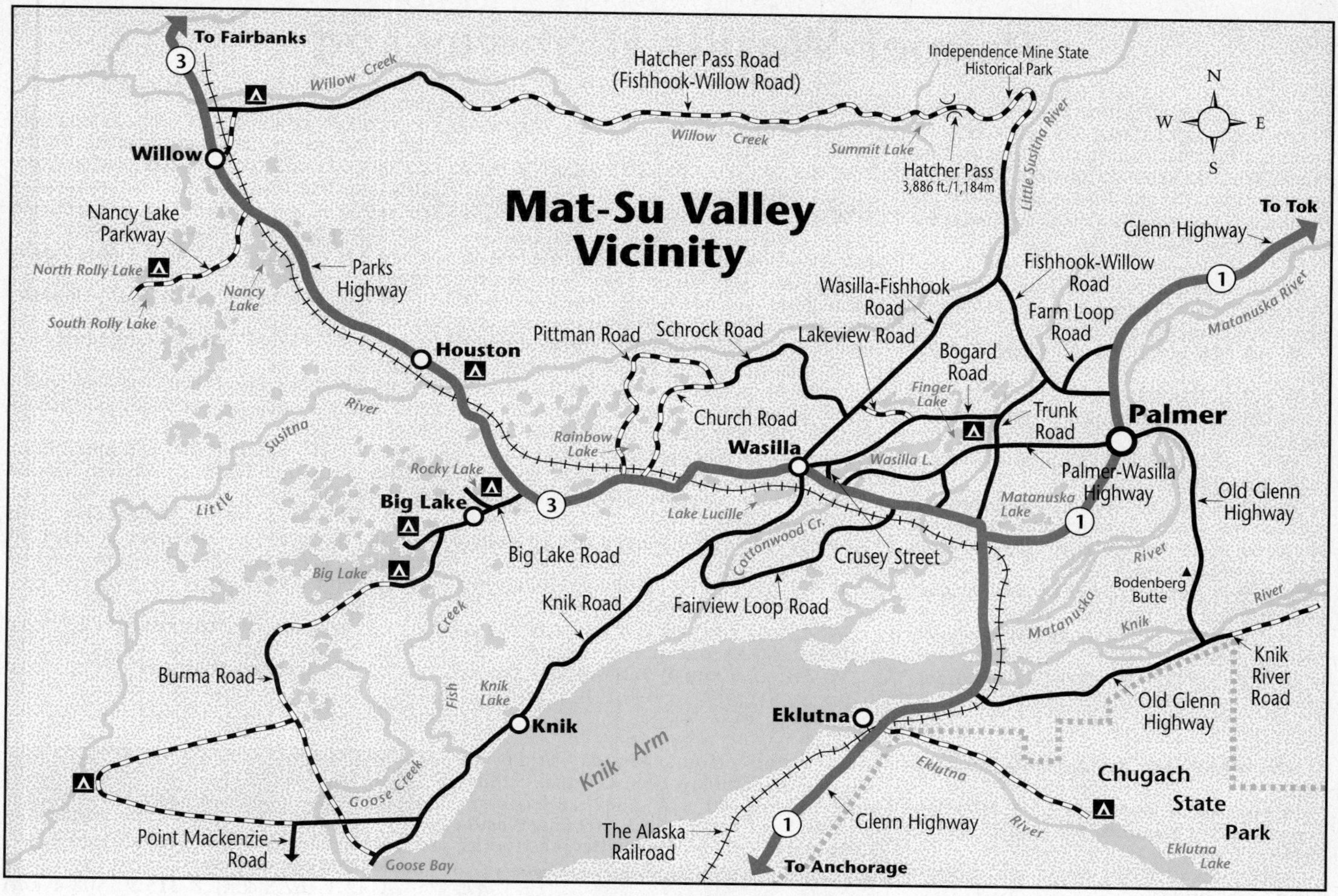

Mat-Su Valley Vicinity

To Fairbanks
Hatcher Pass Road (Fishhook-Willow Road)
Independence Mine State Historical Park
Willow Creek
Summit Lake
Hatcher Pass 3,886 ft./1,184m
Little Susitna River
Willow
Nancy Lake Parkway
North Rolly Lake
South Rolly Lake
Nancy Lake
Parks Highway
To Tok
Glenn Highway
Fishhook-Willow Road
Wasilla-Fishhook Road
Farm Loop Road
Matanuska River
Houston
Pittman Road
Schrock Road
Lakeview Road
Bogard Road
Finger Lake
Trunk Road
Palmer
Susitna River
Rainbow Lake
Church Road
Wasilla
Wasilla L.
Palmer-Wasilla Highway
Old Glenn Highway
Rocky Lake
Big Lake
Little
Lake Lucille
Matanuska Lake
Big Lake Road
Cottonwood Cr.
Crusey Street
Big Lake
Knik Road
Fairview Loop Road
Bodenberg Butte
Creek
Burma Road
Fish
Knik Lake
Knik
Eklutna
Knik River Road
Old Glenn Highway
Knik Arm
Eklutna River
Chugach State Park
Goose Creek
Point Mackenzie Road
Goose Bay
The Alaska Railroad
Glenn Highway
To Anchorage
Eklutna Lake

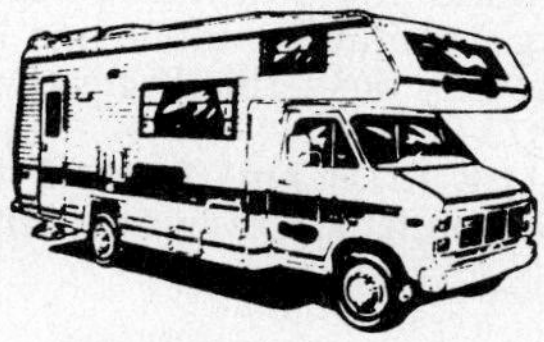

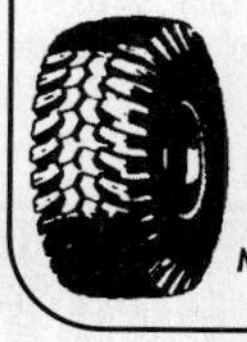

A 39.5 (63.6 km) **F 318.5** (512.6 km) Wasilla city limits; medical clinic (phone 376-1276). Wasilla shopping, services and attractions are located along the highway (from here north to **Milepost A 45**) and at Main Street in Wasilla city center.

A 40 (64.4 km) **F 318** (511.8 km) Herman Road. Gas station with diesel. Turnoff for RV service and supplies.

Northern Recreation. See display ad this section.

A 40.5 (65.2 km) **F 317.5** (511 km) Tire and auto repair, church, hotel, cafe and lounge.

House of Tires, Inc. See display ad this section.

Pilgrims Baptist Church. See display ad this section.

Valley Country Store & Motel. See display ad this section.

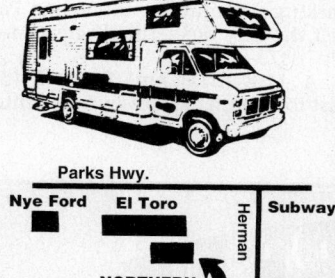

Palmer-Wasilla Highway Log

This 10.1 mile road connects the Parks and Glenn highways (Alaska Routes 3 and 1). There is a bike path along the highway. The Palmer-Wasilla Highway provides access to a number of Wasilla and Palmer businesses. **Distance from Wasilla (W) is followed by distance from Palmer (P).**

W 0 P 10.1 (16.3 km) **Junction** with Parks Highway at **Milepost A 41.1**; Safeway, Fred Meyer and other businesses.

W 0.5 (0.8 km) **P 9.6** (15.4 km) Gas station.

W 0.7 (1.1 km) **P 9.4** (15.1 km) Cottonwood Creek; fish viewing platform; spawning salmon.

W 1.1 (1.8 km) **P 9** (14.5 km) Country Lakes Bed and Breakfast.

W 1.9 (3.1 km) **P 8.2** (13.2 km) Fire station and gas station at **junction** with Seward Meridian Road, which connects to Parks Highway at **Milepost A 39.4**.

W 2.9 (4.7 km) **P 7.2** (11.6 km) Alaskan Agate Inn bed and breakfast.

W 3.1 (5 km) **P 7** (11.3 km) Hatcherview Business Park.

W 3.2 (5.1 km) **P 6.9** (11.1 km) Brentwood Plaza.

W 3.8 (6.1 km) **P 6.3** (10.1 km) The Frontiersman newspaper office.

W 5.9 (9.5 km) **P 4.2** (6.7 km) Wasilla Creek. Cache Camper.

W 6.2 (10 km) **P 3.9** (6.2 km) Tesoro gas station and grocery at **Four Corner junction** with Trunk Road. Turn north for access to Bogard Road and **Finger Lake State Recreation Site**; go north on Trunk Road 1 mile/1.6 km to Bogard Road; turn west and drive 0.8 mile/1.3 km to park entrance; drive in 0.3 mile/0.5 km on gravel road. A scenic spot with 41 campsites, wheelchair-accessible toilets, picnic tables, water, hiking trails and boat launch, $10 camping fee, 7-day limit. Use the life jackets provided! Finger Lake is on the **7-Mile Canoe Trail**. Public access to the canoe trail is also from Wasilla Lake and Cottonwood Lake. ♿▲

W 6.5 (10.5 km) **P 3.6** (5.8 km) The Highlands subdivision.

W 6.7 (10.8 km) **P 3.4** (5.5 km) Midtown Community Business Park; pizza.

W 7.3 (11.7 km) **P 2.8** (4.5 km) North 49th/State Street intersection; stoplight.

W 7.8 (12.6 km) **P 2.3** (3.7 km) Trinity Barn Plaza.

W 8.1 (13.2 km) **P 2** (3.1 km) Loma Prieta Drive. Access to **Crevasse–Moraine Trails;** 0.7 miles/1.1 km south to trailhead parking. This loop trail system is used for cross-country skiing in winter and hiking, mountain biking and horseback riding in summer.

W 8.6 (13.8 km) **P 1.5** (2.4 km) Equestrian Acres subdivision.

W 9.2 (14.8 km) **P 0.9** (1.4 km) Hemmer Road.

W 9.3 (15 km) **P 0.8** (1.3 km) North end Irwin Loop.

W 9.6 (15.4 km) **P 0.5** (0.8 km) South end of Irwin Loop; access to Iditarod House B&B (0.7 mile).

W 9.7 (15.6 km) **P 0.4** (0.6 km) NOAA Alaska Tsunami Warning Center; phone (907) 745-4212.

W 10.1 (16.3 km) **P 0 Junction** with Glenn Highway at **Milepost A 41.8** in Palmer; Carrs Mall (24-hour supermarket) and McDonalds.

Return to Milepost A 41.1 Parks Highway or A 41.8 Glenn Highway

---

The Windbreak. See display ad this section.

A 40.9 (65.8 km) **F 317.1** (510.3 km) **Forget-Me-Not Crafters.** See display ad this section.

A 41 (66 km) **F 317** (510.1 km) Cottonwood Creek bridge.

A 41.1 (66.1 km) **F 316.9** (510 km) Cottonwood Mall, 24-hour supermarket and gas station at turnoff.

Junction with Palmer–Wasilla Highway, which leads east 10 miles/16 km to the Glenn Highway at Palmer. See PALMER–WASILLA HIGHWAY side road log above.

Cottonwood Creek Mall. "We Do What We Do For You"! The area's only enclosed mall is located in Wasilla with ample parking—RVs welcome! Offering 24-hour grocery, Alaskan gifts, banking, family apparel and shoes, hair and nail salons, health store, family dining, free entertainment events. Hours Monday–Friday 10 A.M.–6 P.M.; Saturday 10 A.M.–6 P.M.; Sunday noon to 5 P.M. (907) 376-6802. [ADVERTISEMENT]

A 41.7 (67 km) **F 316.3** (509 km) **Wasilla Lake Park** with picnic shelter, restrooms,

playground and swimming beach; limited parking. Monument to George Parks. Contact the City of Wasilla Recreational Services (907) 373-9053.

A 41.8 (67.3 km) **F 316.2** (508.9 km) Fast food outlet at Crusey Street intersection.

Junction with Bogard Road. See BOGARD ROAD log on page 357.

A 42 (67.6 km) **F 316** (508.5 km) Supermarket and gas stations.

A 42.1 (67.8 km) **F 315.9** (508.4 km) Boundary Street, directional signs for Lake Lucille Park.

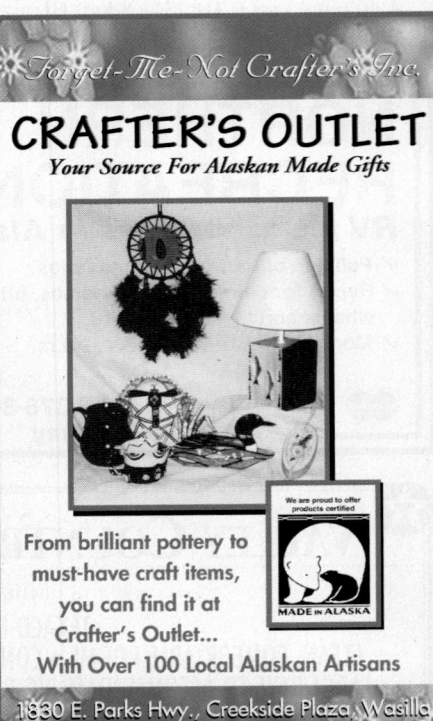

A 42.2 (67.9 km) **F 315.8** (508.2 km) Wasilla's Main Street; visitor center and museum 1 block north; post office 2 blocks north (ZIP code 99687). Access to Hatcher

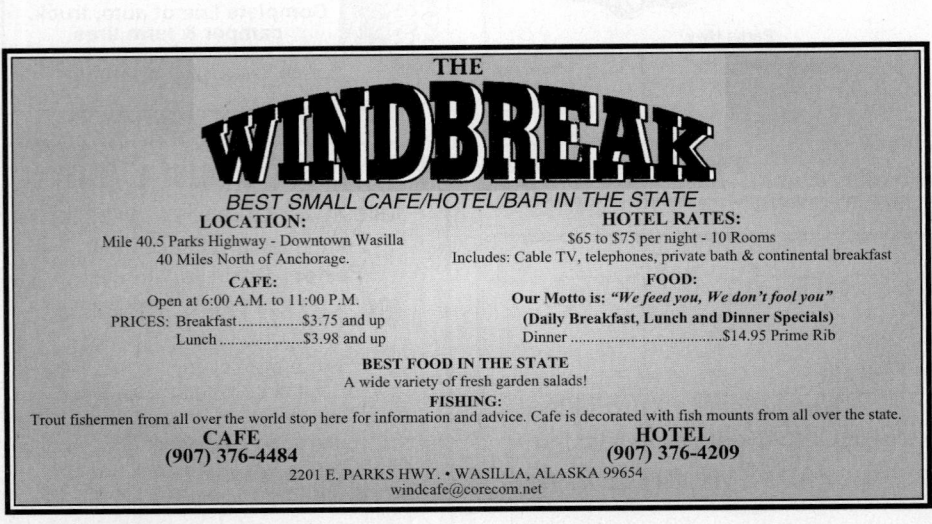

Pass and Knik from this intersection. Turn south across railroad tracks for Knik Road to Knik (see KNIK ROAD log on page 358). Turn north on Wasilla's Main Street for downtown Wasilla and Hatcher Pass. Description of Wasilla follows.

Wasilla–Fishhook Road leads northeast about 10 miles to junction with the Hatcher Pass (Fishhook–Willow) Road to Independence Mine State Historical Park; see the map on page 355. (The Hatcher Pass Road is logged on page 291 in the GLENN HIGHWAY section.)

Wasilla

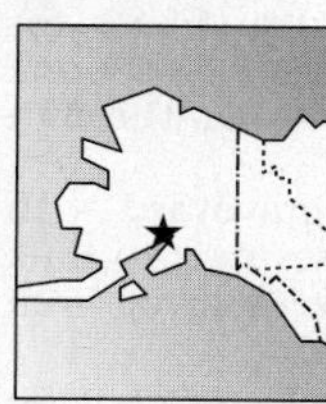

A 42.2 (67.9 km) **F 315.8** (508.2 km). Located between Wasilla and Lucille lakes in the Susitna Valley, about an hour's drive from Anchorage. **Population:** 5,213. **Emergency Services: Police,** phone (907) 745-2131, emergency only phone 911. **Fire Department** and **Ambulance,** phone 911. **Hospital,** in Palmer.

Visitor Information: At the Dorothy Page Museum and Historical Townsite on Main Street just off the Parks Highway, phone (907) 373-9071, fax 373-9072. Or contact the chamber of commerce, Box 871826, Wasilla 99687, phone (907) 376-1299. Mat–Su Visitors Center at **Milepost A 35.5,** write Mat–Su Convention & Visitors Bureau, HC 01, Box 6166J21-MP, Palmer, AK 99645; phone (907) 746-5000.

Radio and **Television** via Anchorage stations; KNBZ-FM 99.7. **Newspapers:** *The*

(Continues on page 359)

Bogard Road Log

This 7.2 mile road provides access to Wasilla businesses and Finger Lake State Recreation Site.

Distance from junction with Parks Highway (J) is shown.

J 0 Junction with Parks Highwat at Crusey Street intersection, **Milepost A 41.8;** fast-food outlets. Turn east on Crusey Street for Bogard Road.

J 0.5 (0.8 km) Wasilla High School; turn southeast on Bogard Road. Turn west for entrance to swimming pool.

J 0.6 (1 km) Phillips Plaza.

J 1.5 (2.4 km) Turnoff for **Mat-Su Resort** on Wasilla Lake; dining and lodging.

J 1.6 (2.6 km) **Special Feet Studio** of Alaskan artist Sabine Becker.

J 2 (3.2 km) Lake Haven subdivision.

J 2.8 (4.5 km) **Junction** with Seward–Meridian Road.

J 4.2 (6.7 km) Country store, Texaco gas station.

J 4.3 (6.9 km) Intersection with E. Selden Road; *Bogard Road turns.*

J 4.5 (7.2 km) West Cottonwood Drive.

J 5.6 (9 km) Cottonwood Creek.

J 6.4 (10.3 km) **Finger Lake State Recreation Site;** drive in 0.3 mile/0.5 km on gravel road. A scenic spot with 41 campsites, wheelchair-accessible toilets, picnic tables,

water, hiking trails and boat launch, $10 camping fee, 7-day limit. Use the life jackets provided! Finger Lake is on the **7-Mile Canoe Trail.** Public access to the canoe trail is also from Wasilla and Cottonwood Lakes. ♿▲

J 6.7 (10.8 km) Bogard Safety Station. *Emergency phone.*

J 7.2 (11.6 km) **Junction** with Trunk Road, which leads south 1 mile to Palmer–Wasilla Highway and north 2.3 miles to Palmer-Fishhook Road.

Return to Milepost A 41.8 Parks Highway

WASILLA ADVERTISER

Knik Road Log

Distance is measured from the junction (J) with Parks Highway.

J 0 Junction with Parks Highway at **Milepost A 42.2**, Main Street, Wasilla.

J 0.1 (0.2 km) *CAUTION: Road crosses railroad tracks.*

J 0.2 (0.3 km) VFW Post No. 9365.

J 0.7 (1.1 km) Glenwood Avenue, senior center.

J 1.5 (2.4 km) Gas station.

J 2 (3.2 km) Smith ball fields.

J 2.2 (3.5 km) Turnoff for **Iditarod Trail Sled Dog Race® headquarters** and visitor center; historical displays, films, dogs and musher, souvenir shop. Open 8 A.M. to 5 P.M., daily in summer, weekdays the rest of the year. .

J 2.3 (3.7 km) **Lake Lucille Park** (Mat–Su Borough) campground and day-use area 0.6 mile/1 km north via gravel road just past Iditarod headquarters parking lot. There are 64 campsites in a heavily wooded area on a gravel loop road; picnic pavilions; firewood, firepits, rest- rooms. Camping fee charged. Fishing for landlocked silver salmon. Boardwalk trail to lake (non-motorized access only).

J 4.1 (6.6 km) **Junction** with Fairview Loop Road, which joins the Parks Highway at **Milepost A 38**; access to Palmer Hay Flats State Game Refuge. Shopping center with gas and groceries at this junction.

J 7 (11.3 km) Knik fire hall.

J 8 (12.9 km) **Settlers Bay**, a residential development built around the 18-hole Settlers Bay Golf Course (phone 907/376-5466); 4-star Legends at Settlers Bay restaurant with scenic view; airstrip.

J 10.1 (16.3 km) Turnoff for **Homestead Museum**, with a large collection of early Alaskan memorabilia, and gift shop.

Knik Knack Mud Shack. See display ad this section.

J 11.1 (17.9 km) Laurence airport.

J 13 (20.9 km) Knik Kennels.

J 13.3 (21.4 km) KNIK (pop. 483) on **Knik Lake.** There is a bar here with a pay phone, a liquor store, gas station and private campground. Lake fishing for rainbow; inquire at the Knik Bar. Knik is a checkpoint on the Iditarod Trail Sled Dog Race® route and is often called the "Dog Mushing Center of the World"; many famous Alaskan dog mushers live in this area.

J 13.9 (22.4 km) **Knik Museum and Sled Dog Mushers' Hall of Fame**, open noon to 6 P.M. Wednesday through Sunday, from June 1 through Aug. 31. The museum is housed in 1 of 2 buildings remaining from Knik's gold rush era (1898–1916). Regional memorabilia, artifacts, archives, dog mushing equipment, mushers' portraits and historical displays on the Iditarod Trail. Admission fee $2 for adults, $1.50 for seniors, free for children under 18. Phone (907) 376-7755, from September through May call 376-2005.

Traditional Athabascan graveyard with fenced graves and spirit houses next to Knik Museum. The gravesite can be observed from the Iditarod Trail.

J 16.1 (25.9 km) **Fish Creek** bridge; parking, fishing for silver salmon.

J 17.2 (27.7 km) Goose Bay Point Road to Little Susitna River public-use facility at **Susitna Flats State Game Refuge** (12 miles); 83 parking spaces, 65 campsites, boat ramps, dump station, water, tables, toilets. Also access to Point Mackenzie. Daily parking $5; boat launch, $5 (includes parking); overnight camping, $10. For more information phone (907) 745-3975.

J 18.5 (29.8 km) Pavement ends at small bar beside road. Road continues into rural area.

Return to Milepost A 42.2 Parks Highway

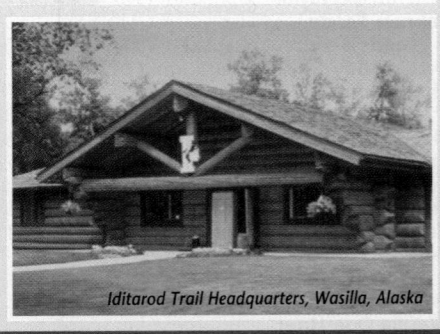

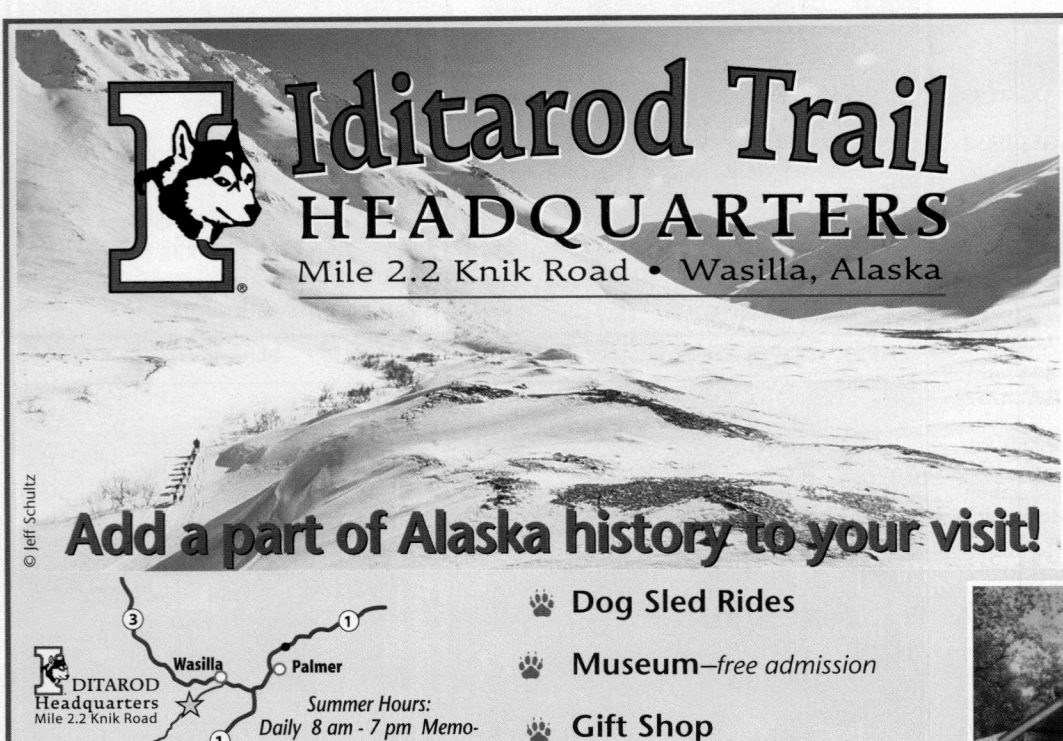

Valley Sun (weekly); *The Frontiersman* (semi-weekly). **Transportation: Air**—Charter service available. **Railroad**—Alaska Railroad. **Bus**—Mat-Su Community Transit, service between Mat-Su locations and Anchorage; phone (907) 376-5000.

Private Aircraft: Wasilla municipal airport, 4.8 miles north on Neuser Drive; elev. 348 feet; length 3,700 feet; asphalt; unattended. Wasilla Lake seaplane base, 0.9 mile east; elev. 330 feet. Numerous private airstrips and lakes in vicinity.

Wasilla is one of the Matanuska–Susitna Valley's pioneer communities, supplying mines and farms in the area. Long before the Parks Highway was built, local residents and visitors bound for Lake Lucille, Wasilla Lake, Big Lake and Knik drove over the valley roads from Palmer to the village of Wasilla. Wasilla became a station on the Alaska Railroad about 1916.

Today, Wasilla is the largest community on the Parks Highway between Anchorage and Fairbanks. Shopping malls and businesses here offer a wide assortment of services. The Mat-Su Valley Federal Credit Union, 501 N. Main St. in Wasilla, also has branches at Big Lake (East Lake Mall) and in Willow; ATM services are available at various locations noted in the log..

Iditarod restart at Wasilla takes place the day after the race starts in Anchorage.
(© Tom Bol Photography)

Lodging & Services

All visitor facilities are available here, including sporting goods stores, post office, gas stations, tire and RV repair, laundromats and other services. The Brett Memorial Ice Arena, at Bogard Road and Crusey Street, has ice skating, picnic area and fitness court. Wasilla High School has a pool and showers.

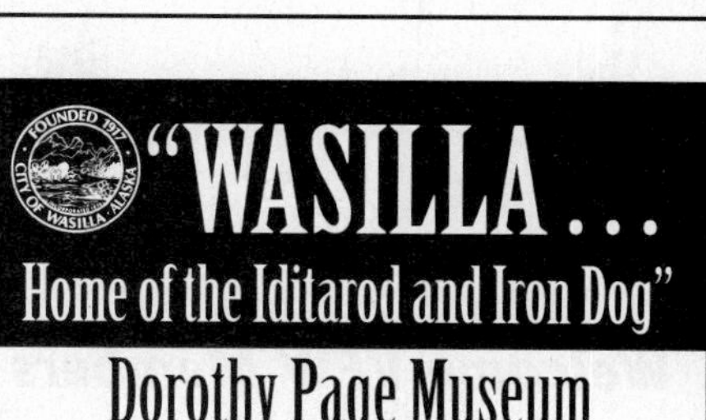

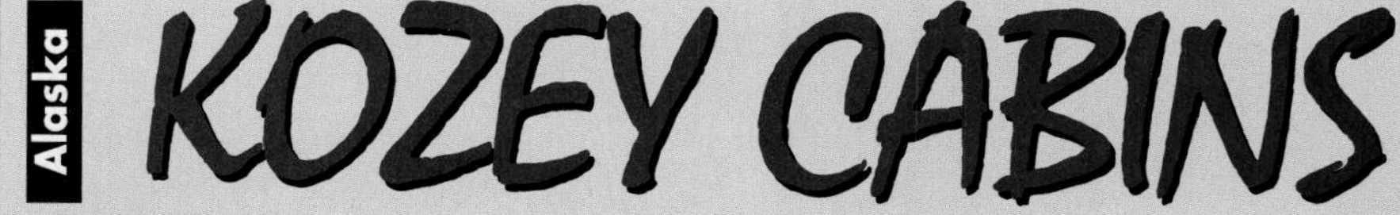

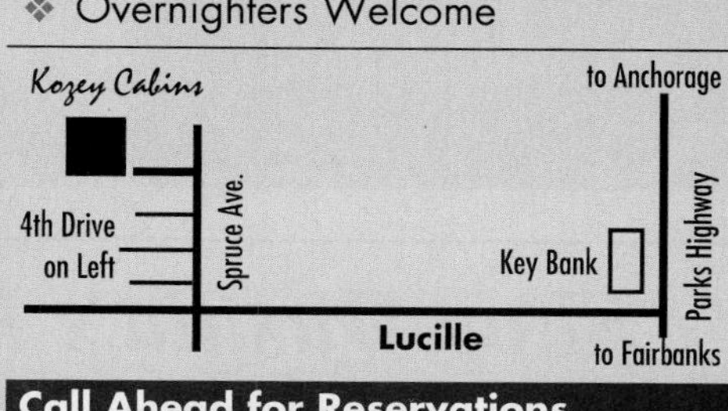

Alaska's Lake Lucille Bed & Breakfast. Our central Wasilla location is ideal for exploring the Matanuska-Susitna Valley. Premier setting, private entrance, fireplace, laundry. We offer a 1st-class lakeside retreat with great mountain views and we're close to everything! Call toll free 888-353-0352 ... you'll be glad you did! www.lakelucillebnb.com. [ADVERTISEMENT]

Alaska's Mat-Su Bed & Breakfast Association offers a variety of clean, quality lodging throughout the Mat-Su Valley. Check us out on the internet at http://alaska.net/~akhosts. While traveling, check our vacancy listings at local visitor centers in Palmer and Wasilla. Alaska's Mat-Su Bed & Breakfast Association serving you in Southcentral Alaska. 1-800-401-7444. [ADVERTISEMENT]

Lake Lucille Inn. Located 45 miles north of Anchorage on the shores of beautiful Lake Lucille. 54 deluxe rooms, suites with Jacuzzi, health club with sauna and hot tub. Boat and float plane dock, water craft rentals and lighted gazebo. Winter activities include lighted ice rink. Fine dining restaurant and lounge with pristine view. Convention and meeting facilities. See display ad this section. [ADVERTISEMENT]

Country Lakes B&B. These cozy accommodations nestled on the shores of Lake Wasilla, 40 miles east of Anchorage, include

a hearty homemade breakfast prepared by 35-year Alaska resident, Louise Carswell. Conveniently located for fishing, hiking and Mount Denali flightseeing. Laundry facilities and freezer space available. Families welcome. Reasonable rates. Special requests accommodated. The coffee is on...we look forward to meeting you! P.O. Box 876694, Wasilla, AK 99687. Toll-free 1-877-373-5868. Web site: lakesbnb@alaska.net. [ADVERTISEMENT]

Sleepy Dog B&B. Alaskan comfort with English hospitality. Spacious cedar home, less than 5 minutes from the Parks Highway. Midway between the Kenai Peninsula and Denali. Offers mountain view ideal for

Children enjoy Wasilla Lake beach on a summer's day. *(© Kris Graef, staff)*

aurora viewing. 3 custom-decorated non-smoking rooms, shared bath. Convenient self-service breakfast. Friendly atmosphere. Open year-round. Pets welcome. Garry & Caroline Buell, P.O. Box 871526, Wasilla, AK 99687. Phone (907) 373-0305. Web site: www.alaskasleepydog.com. [ADVERTISEMENT]

Special Feet Studio. A must-see on your way to Denali. Meet foot artist Sabine Becker in her studio and gift shop. Right in front of you she will create her famous Alaskan spirit dolls. Born without arms, Sabine uses her feet to create her artwork. Open from Memorial Day to Labor Day, 10 A.M.–6 P.M. Tuesday through Sunday. Take Crusey Street off Parks Highway to Bogard Road; turn right. Gift shop 1.2 miles on left. Phone (907) 376-5397. [ADVERTISEMENT]

Attractions

On the town's Main Street, north of the Parks Highway, are the **Dorothy Page Museum and Historical Townsite**, the library and the post office. The museum and historical townsite are open daily year-round, 10 A.M. to 6 P.M. in summer, 8 A.M. to 5 P.M. in winter; admission fees are $3 adults, $2.50 senior citizens; under 18 years free. Picnic tables and museum shop on site. Local Farmer's Market on Wednesdays in summer. The historical park has 7 renovated buildings from before, during and after Wasilla's pioneer days, including Wasilla's first schoolhouse (built in 1917). Adjacent to the park is the Herning/Teeland Country Store, which is currently under restoration. The log museum building, school, store and nearby railroad depot are on the National Register of Historic Sites.

Wasilla is home to the **Iditarod Trail Sled Dog Race® Headquarters**. The internationally known 1,150-mile Iditarod Trail Sled Dog Race® between Anchorage and Nome takes place in March. The Iditarod Headquarters and Visitors Center is located at Mile 2.2 Knik Road. The center has historical displays on the Iditarod, videos, an Iditarod musher and dog team, and a gift shop with unique souvenirs. Open daily in summer, weekdays in winter. Large tours are welcome, phone (907) 376-5155 in advance. Circular drive for buses and motor-homes, camping at adjacent Lake Lucille campground. No fee for museum or film. Fee charged for rides on wheeled dogsled.

Historical displays on Alaskan mushers and sled-dog trails can be found at the Knik Museum at Mile 13.9 Knik Road (see KNIK ROAD log this section). The museum is open from noon to 6 P.M. daily except Monday and Tuesday in summer. Admission fee $2 adults.

Iditarod Days is held in conjunction with the Iditarod Race in March. Other area winter events include ice golf at Mat–Su Resort and ice bowling at Big Lake. Check with the chamber of commerce about summer events.

Town Square Art Gallery. Representing the best of Alaskan and national artists—prints and originals distinctively custom framed. Local jewelry, pottery, unique gifts, porcelain collectibles, plates, books, cards. Open Monday–Friday 10 A.M.–6 P.M., Saturday 10 A.M.–5 P.M., seasonally Sundays

Veteran's Memorial at Mat-Su Visitors Center in Wasilla. (© Harry M. Walker Photo)

12–4 P.M. We pack and ship. We welcome credit cards. Carrs Mall. (907) 376-0123.
[ADVERTISEMENT]

Please support our MILEPOST® advertisers.

Parks Highway Log
(continued)

A 42.5 (68.4 km) **F 315.5** (507.7 km) **The Deli Restaurant & Bakery.** See display ad this section.

A 42.7 (68.7 km) **F 315.3** (507.4 km) Shoprite Mall, Wasilla Shopping Center.

A 43.5 (70 km) **F 314.5** (506.1 km) Lucas Road; Hallea Lane access to Lake Lucille. Best Western Lake Lucille Inn.

A 44.2 (71.1 km) **F 313.8** (505 km) Deskas Road. Divided highway ends northbound.

A 44.4 (71.4 km) **F 313.6** (504.7 km) Church Road. Access to Bumpus ball fields.

CAUTION: Moose Danger Zone. Watch for moose next 12.7 miles northbound. According to the Alaska DOT, this section of highway has the greatest number of moose-related vehicle accidents in the state.

A 45.5 (73.2 km) **F 312.5** (502.9 km) **Wasilla Car Wash.** See display ad this section.

A 45.4 (73.1 km) **F 312.6** (503.1 km) Welcome to Meadow Lakes Community signed (incorporated).

A 47 (75.6 km) **F 311** (500.5 km) Neuser Drive. Turnoff for Wasilla municipal airport and the **Museum of Alaska Transportation and Industry**. The museum features historic aircraft, railroad equipment, old farm machinery and heavy equipment. Steam train rides on selected Saturdays. Admission fees in summer are $5 adults, $12 families. Group tours by arrangement.

A 48.8 (78.5 km) **F 309.2** (497.6 km) Tesoro/7-Eleven at **junction** with Pittman Road to Rainbow Lake.

A 49 (78.9 km) **F 309** (497.3 km) Meadow Lakes Road **junction**. B&J Center; Mile 49 Cafe.

Mile 49 Cafe. See display ad this section.

A 50.1 (80.6 km) **F 307.9** (495.5 km) Sheele Road.

Big Lake

Big Lake has been a resort destination for Alaskans since the 1940s. Summer recreation includes swimming, camping, boating, fishing and jet skiing. Winter sports include snow machining, cross-country skiing and ice fishing.

Access is via North Big Lake Road to the Y; and then North Shore Drive and South Big Lake Road. There is a bike trail along these roads.

NORTH BIG LAKE ROAD

Distance is measured from the junction (J) with the Parks Highway.

J 0 Junction with Parks Highway. Meadowood Mall. Alaska State Troopers office inside mall. *Emergency phone* on outside of mall at Napa entrance.

J 1.3 (2.1) Houston High School and senior center.

J 1.7 (2.7 km) Entering **BIG LAKE** (pop. 2,162) sign. Evidence of the June 1996 Miller's Reach wildfire, which destroyed some 37,500 acres and 433 buildings and homes, is visible along Big Lake Road. Willow, birch and aspen trees are growing among the charred spruce killed by the fire. New groundcover includes Labrador tea, moss and yarrow.

J 3.4 (5.5 km) Beaver Lake Road turnoff. Turn north and drive 0.3 mile to turnoff on gravel access road (Rocky Street) for **Rocky Lake State Recreation Site**; 10 campsites on bumpy loop road through birch trees, $10 nightly fee or resident pass, outhouses, firepits, water pump and boat launch. Rocky Lake is closed to jet skis, jet boats and airboats. ▲

J 3.5 (5.6 km) 24-hour gas station, ATM.

J 3.6 (5.8 km) **Fisher's Y**; Big Lake post office (ZIP code 99652). Big Lake Road forks here: Keep to right southbound for North Shore Drive access to resorts and state recreation site (description follows); keep to left for South Big Lake Road businesses (see log following).

NORTH SHORE DRIVE

Distance is measured from the Y (Y).

Y 0 Fisher's Y.

Y 1.4 (2.3 km) Turnoff for Kondike Inn; restaurant and lodging on Big Lake. The Klondike Inn hosts several of the major events during the Big Lake Regatta held in June.

Klondike Inn. See display ad this section.

Big Lake is connected with smaller lakes by dredged waterways. It is possible to boat for several miles in the complex. Fish in Big Lake include lake trout, Dolly Varden, rainbow, red and coho salmon, and burbot.

Y 1.6 (2.6 km) North Shore Drive ends at of South Big Lake Road and Marion and Susitna Streets.

Jet skiing is a popular water sport at Big Lake in summer. (© Barb Willard)

Big Lake North State Recreation Site; 60 campsites, walk--in tent sites, picnicking, $10 nightly fee per vehicle or resident pass, water, outhouses, dumpsters. Boat launch $5 fee, day-use parking $5. Pay phone. ▲

SOUTH BIG LAKE ROAD

Distance is measured from the Y (Y).

Y 0 Fisher's Y.

Y 0.1 (0.2 km) East Lake Mall; food mart, pizza, art gallery, restaurant, liquor store, laundromat and other businesses.

Y 0.2 (0.3 km) Library. Edward "Bud" Beech Firehall. *Emergency phone*.

Y 0.9 (1.4 km) Elementary school.

Y 1 (1.6 km) Aero drive to Big Lake airport. Big Lake is a 15-minute flight from Anchorage.

Private Aircraft: 1 mile southeast; elev. 150 feet; length 2,400 feet; gravel; fuel 100LL.

Y 1.3 (2.1 km) **Big Lake Motel.** See display ad this section.

Y 1.4 (2.2 km) **Fish Creek Park**, a day-use area with access to Fish Creek, salmon spawning observation deck, picnic area, restroom, playground, parking and open lawn area. End bike lane.

Bridge over Fish Creek.

Y 1.5 (2.4 km) Big Lake Chapel. Lakeview Drive

Y 1.6 (2.6 km) **Big Lake South State Recreation Site**; day-use area with parking, outhouses, water, dumpsters, boat ramp ($5 fee). Day-use fee $5.

Y 1.8 (2.9 km) Double-ended turnout; overflow parking area and picnic site.

Y 1.9 (3 km) Turnoff for **South Port Marina**; food, phone, snowmachine, ATV, watercarft rentals and repair service; boat launch, gas, propane.

Y 2.1 (3.4 km) Sunset View condominiums.

Y 3.2 (5.1 km) Begin winding road southbound; steep grades.

Y 4.5 (7.2 km) State road maintenance ends (sign); turnout.

Y 4.8 (7.7 km) Alaska State Forestry DNR Mat-Su area headquarters. Alaska Sailing Club (sign); contact P.O. Box 873023, Wasilla, AK 99687.

Y 5 (8 km) Turnout.

Y 5.5 (8.8 km) Stop sign at intersection

Y 5.6 (9 km) Pavement ends, gravel begins. Burma Road continues into rural area, providing access to the south Big Lake area, former Point MacKenzie dairy project and the Little Susitna River public-use facility at Susitna Flats State Game Refuge (also accessible via Knik Road); parking, camping, boat ramps. Fee charged, state parks annual pass not accepted. See description and fee schedule at **Milepost J 17.2** Knik Road this section.

Return to Milepost A 52.3 Parks Highway

A 50.2 (80.8 km) **F 307.8** (495.3 km) **Ice Worm RV Park & Country Store.** See display ad this section. ▲

A 51 (82 km) **F 307** (494 km) Veterinary hospital.

A 52.3 (84.2 km) **F 305.7** (492 km) Meadowood shopping mall, service station, hardware store, ATM, grocery and emergency phone (dial 911) at Big Lake turnoff.

Junction with Big Lake Road. See BIG LAKE road log on page 363.

Houston city limits; fireworks outlets. Begin bike trail next 4.6 miles/7.4 km northbound. (The bike trail also extends down Big Lake Road.)

A 53.2 (85.6 km) **F 304.8** (490.6 km) Turnoff for Houston High School, Wasilla Senior Center and Plettner sled dog kennels.

Plettner Sled Dog Kennels. We are a full-service Iditarod sled dog training facility. Come play with puppies; summer and winter sled rides, sled shop. Learn to mush. Mile 53 Parks Highway, Houston school turn-off. Phone (907) 892-6944, Fax (907) 892-6945. E-mail: plettner@mtaonline.net. [ADVERTISEMENT]

A 54.1 (87.1 km) **F 303.9** (489.1 km) Truck lane begins northbound.

A 55.4 (89.2 km) **F 302.6** (487 km) Truck lane ends northbound.

A 56.1 (90.3 km) **F 301.9** (485.8 km) Miller's Reach Road. Alaska's most destructive wildfire began here in June 1996. The Big Lake wildfire burned some 37,500 acres and 433 buildings and homes.

A 56.4 (90.8 km) **F 301.6** (485.4 km) Alaska Railroad overpass.

A 56.6 (91.1 km) **F 301.4** (485 km) King Arthur Road; public access to Bear Paw, Loon lakes to east (no camping).

A 56.8 (91.4 km) **F 301.2** (484.7 km) Bike route ends northbound.

CAUTION: Moose Danger Zone. Watch for moose next 12.7 miles southbound.

A 57.1 (91.9 km) **F 300.9** (484.2 km) Bridge over the **Little Susitna River**; a very popular fishing and camping area.

The Little Susitna River has a tremendous king salmon run and one of the largest silver salmon runs in southcentral Alaska. Kings to 30 lbs. enter the river in late May and June; use large red spinners or salmon eggs. Silvers to 15 lbs. come in late July and August, with the biggest run in August; use small weighted spoons or fresh salmon roe. Artificials are required during the early weeks of the fishery in the first part of August. Also red salmon to 10 lbs.; in mid-July, use coho flies or salmon eggs. Charter boats nearby. This river heads at Mint Glacier in the Talkeetna Mountains to the northeast and flows 110 miles/177 km into Upper Cook Inlet.

A 57.3 (92.4 km) **F 300.7** (483.9 km) Turnoff to east to Houston City Hall, fire station, emergency phone and city-operated **Little Susitna River Campground** (follow signs). Large, well-maintained campground with 86 sites (many wide, level gravel sites); picnic tables, firepits; restrooms, water pump, playground large covered picnic area; 10-day limit, camping fee charged. Off-road parking lot near river with access to river. Follow signs to camping and river. Day-use area with water and toilets west side of highway. ▲

A 57.5 (92.5 km) **F 300.5** (483.6 km) **HOUSTON** (pop. 836) has a grocery store, restaurant (open daily), laundromat, gift shop, inn with food, lodging and pay phone, a campground and gas station. Post office located in the grocery store. Fishing charter operators and marine service are located here. Emergency phone at Houston fire station. ▲

Homesteaded in the 1950s, incorporated as a city in 1966. Houston is a popular fishing center for anglers on the Little Susitna River.

Miller's Place. Don't miss this stop! Groceries, post office, laundry, RV parking, cabin rentals, tenting on riverbank. Gift shop, fishing tackle and licenses, fresh salmon eggs. Ice, sporting goods sales and rental, pay phone. Fishing charters available; full day only $45. Probably the best soft ice cream and hamburgers in Alaska. Clean restrooms. Visitor information experts. Family-run Christian business. Gary and Debbie Miller. (907) 892-6129. [ADVERTISEMENT] ▲

A 57.7 (92.9 km) **F 300.3** (483.3 km) **Riverside Camper Park.** See display ad this section. ▲

A 57.8 (93 km) **F 300.2** (483.1 km) **Fisherman's Choice Charters.** We know where the fish are; we go where the fish are. Trophy kings, silvers, sockeye and trout. We fish the Little Susitna, Deshka and Talkeetna Rivers giving us over 200 miles of fishing

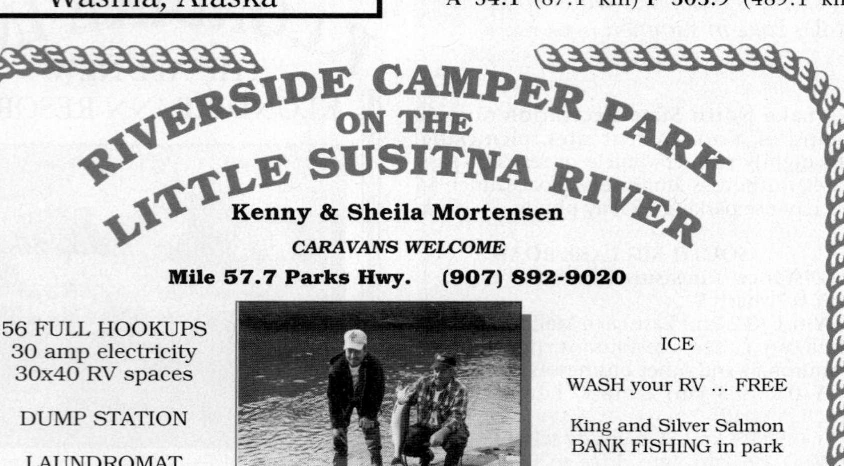

Prickly devil's club at Nancy Lake Recreation Area. (© Susan Cole Kelly)

waters to choose from and a better than 90 percent succcess rate! 1-800-980-8707. P.O. Box 940276, Houston, AK 99694. E-mail: info@akfishermanschoice.com. Internet: www.akfishermanschoice.com. See display ad. [ADVERTISEMENT]

A 64.5 (103.8 km) F 293.5 (472.3 km) Turnoff to west for Nancy Lake Resort.

Nancy Lake Resort. See display ad this section.

A 64.7 (104.1 km) F 293.3 (472 km) *NOTE: No passing; drive with headlights on.*

A 66.5 (107 km) F 291.5 (469.1 km) **Alaskan Host Bed & Breakfast.** See display ad this section.

A 66.7 (107.3 km) F 291.3 (468.8 km) Highway crosses Alaska Railroad tracks. Turnoff for **Nancy Lake State Recreation Site**; 30 campsites, 30 picnic sites, toilets, boat launch, horseshoe pits. Camping fee $10/night or resident pass. ▲

Nancy Lake Road mileages: Mile 2.5 Tulik Nature Trail, toilets and parking area; Mile 4.7 Tanaina Lake canoe trail, canoe launch, toilet and parking area; Mile 5.1 Rhein Lake trailhead; Mile 6.2 South Rolly Lake Overlook day-use area with barbecues, picnic tables, litter barrels and toilets; Mile 6.6 **South Rolly Lake** Campground, 106 campsites, firepits, toilets, water, canoe rental (phone Tippecanoe Rentals 907/495-6688) and boat launch; firewood sometimes is provided. Camping fee $10/night or resident pass. South Rolly Lake has a small population of rainbow, 12 to 14 inches. ▲

A 68.1 (109.6 km) F 289.9 (466.5 km) **Willow Winter Park Bed & Breakfast.** See display ad this section.

A 68.8 (110.7 km) F 289.2 (465.4 km) Miner's Last Stand Museum of Hatcher Pass, gas, diesel and gift shop.

Newman's Hilltop Service. See display ad this section.

A 69 (111 km) F 289 (465.1 km) Entering Willow, northbound. Gas station, grocery and hardware store to west. Willow extends about 2.5 miles north along the Parks Highway.

Willow True Value Hardware, Willow Creek Grocery and **Willow Creek Service.** See display ad this section.

A 69.2 (111.4 km) F 288.8 (464.8 km) Long Lake Road.

A 69.4 (111.7 km) F 288.6 (464.4 km) Gas station, convenience store. Willow elementary school.

A 69.5 (111.8 km) 288.5 (464.3 km) Turnoff to east on Willow Station Road for

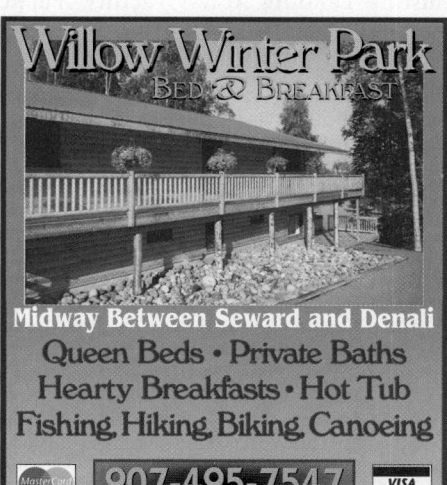

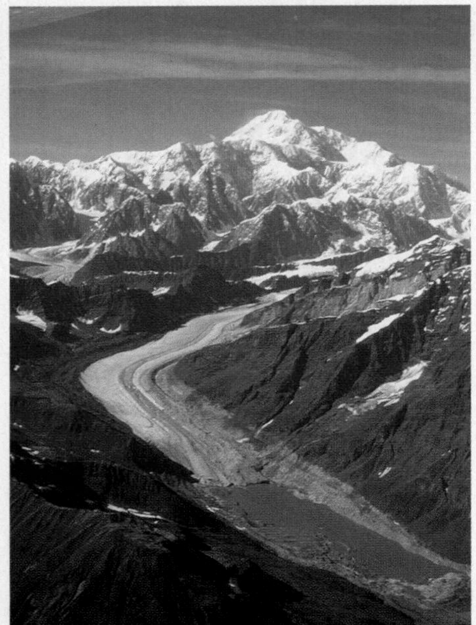

Flightseeing trips can be arranged to see Mount McKinley and the Alaska Range. (© Jill Kaniut, staff)

WILLOW (pop. 507) post office, trading post with cabins and camper spaces, Alaska Railroad depot and access to Ruth Lake Lodge.

Willow had its start about 1897, when gold was discovered in the area. In the early 1940s, mining in the nearby Talkeetna Mountains slacked off, leaving Willow a virtual ghost town. The community made a comeback upon completion of the Parks Highway in 1972. In 1976, Alaska voters selected the Willow area for their new capital site. However, funding for the capital move from Juneau to Willow was defeated in the November 1982 election.

The community is also a stop on the Alaska Railroad. The Willow civic organization sponsors an annual Winter Carnival in January. ▲

A 69.7 (112.2 km) **F 288.3** (464 km) Willow Community Center, open daily, has a large parking area, commercial kitchen, showers, covered picnic pavilion, grills, ball court, boat launch and pay phone. (Available for rent to groups, 500-person capacity; phone 907/495-6633). Willow library.

A 69.9 (112.5 km) **F 288.1** (463.6 km) Fire station.

A 70 (112.7 km) **F 288** (463.5 km) **Private Aircraft:** Willow airport; elev. 220 feet; length 4,400 feet; gravel; fuel 100LL. Unattended.

Denali Flying Service. See display ad this section.

Willow Air Service Inc. See display ad this section.

A 70.8 (113.9 km) **F 287.2** (462.2 km) Willow Creek Parkway (Susitna River access road) west 4 miles to **Willow Creek State Recreation Area**; camping $10/night, parking, litter barrels, water, toilets, dump station, trail to mouth of creek. Access to **Deshka Landing** boat launch facility off Willow Creek Parkway. Fishing for king and silver salmon, rainbow trout. The Susitna River heads at Susitna Glacier in the Alaska Range to the northeast and flows west then south for 260 miles to Cook Inlet. The Deshka River, a tributary of the Susitna River about 6 miles downstream from Deshka Landing, is one of Southcentral Alaska's best king salmon fisheries. ▲

A 71 (114.3 km) **F 287** (461.9 km) Willow DOT/PF highway maintenance station.

A 71.2 (114.6 km) **F 286.8** (461.5 km) Turnoff to **Deception Creek** state campground, located 1.4 miles east on Hatcher Pass Road; 7 campsites, tables, firepits and outhouses. Camping fee $10/night or resident pass. ▲

Junction with Hatcher Pass (Fishhook–Willow) Road, which leads east and south across Hatcher Pass 49 miles/79 km to junction with the Glenn Highway. Independence Mine State Historical Park is 31.8 miles from here. Turn to the Hatcher Pass Road Log on page 291 in the GLENN HIGHWAY section and read log back to front.)

A 71.4 (114.9 km) **F 286.6** (461.2 km) Pioneer Lodge to west on south side of **Willow Creek** bridge; Food, camping, lodging. Excellent king salmon fishing; also silvers, rainbow. Inquire at either lodge or resort for information.

Entering Game Management Subunit 14B northbound, 14A southbound.

Pioneer Lodge and **Willow Creek Outfitters**. See display ad this section. ▲

A 71.5 (115.1 km) **F 286.5** (461.1 km) Willow Island campground resort to west on north side of Willow Creek bridge. Willow Creek heads in Summit Lake, west of Hatcher Pass on the Hatcher Pass Road. It is a favorite launch site for airboat enthusiasts.

A 74.7 (120.2 km) **F 283.3** (455.9 km) Bridge over **Little Willow Creek**. Parking on either side of creek; fishing for salmon and trout.

A 75.2 (121 km) **F 282.8** (455.1 km) Speedway Inn.

A 76.4 (122.9 km) **F 281.6** (453.2 km) Paved double-ended turnout to west by **Kashwitna Lake.** Stocked with rainbow trout. Small planes land on lake. Private floatplane base on east shore. Good camera viewpoints of lake and Mount McKinley (weather permitting).

A 76.6 (123.3 km) **F 281.4** (452.9 km) Air service.

A 78 (125.5 km) **F 280** (450.6 km) Great view of Mount McKinley northbound, weather permitting. From here to Denali National Park and Preserve watch for views of the Alaska Range to the east of the highway.

A 80 (128.7 km) **F 278** (447.4 km) **Lucky Husky**. Year-round "dog-gone" fun! Take an exciting summer dogsled ride! Tour the kennel and meet the Lucky Husky family. Get dressed in original musher's clothes at the Iditarod checkpoint display. Wir sprechen Deutsch. May 24–September 3:

Open Wednesday–Saturday, 9 A.M.–5 P.M. August 4–October 15: Half-hour rides by reservation only. November–March: Mushing adventures/Drive your own dogteam; reservation required. Phone (907) 495-6470. Fax (907) 495-6471, E-mail: info@luckyhusky.com. Web: www.luckyhusky.com. Write: HC 89, Box 256, Willow, AK 99688. [ADVERTISEMENT]

A 81.3 (130.8 km) **F 276.7** (445.3 km) **Grey's Creek**, gravel turnouts both sides of highway. Fishing for salmon and trout.

A 82.5 (132.8 km) **F 275.5** (443.4 km) **Susitna Landing Access Facility**, Public Boat Launch (open year-round); 1 mile west via gravel road. Concessionaire-operated (ADF&G land) boat launch on **Kashwitna River**, just upstream of the **Susitna River;** access to both rivers from Susitna Landing. Camping ($8), boat launch ($14), daily parking ($6), firewood ($3). Wheelchair-accessible restrooms, bank fishing. Ron's Riverboat Service. ♿▲

A 83.2 (133.9 km) **F 274.8** (442.2 km) Bridge over the **Kashwitna River**; public parking area at north end of bridge. Salmon and trout fishing. The river heads in a glacier in the Talkeetna Mountains and flows westward 60 miles/ 96.5 km to enter the Susitna River 12 miles/19 km north of Willow.

A 84 (135.2 km) **F 274** (440.9 km) Gravel turnout to west. Public access (walk-in) for fishing at **Caswell Creek**; kings, silvers, pinks and rainbow.

A 85.1 (137 km) **F 272.9** (439.2 km) Caswell Creek.

A 85.5 (137.6 km) **F 272.5** (438.5 km) Gift shop and art gallery east side of highway.

Willow Wildlife Art Gallery. Features Alaskan wildlife and sled dog art, as well as locally handcrafted gifts. Meet artist Dave

Totten in his home studio/gallery. "From Anchorage to Fairbanks ... best gallery," Jerry Griswold, *L.A. Times,* Aug. 1, 1993. Free coffee and wildberry muffins. Phone (907) 495-1090. Open all year. [ADVERTISEMENT]

A 86 (138.4 km) **F 272** (437.7 km) **Bluffs Boat Launch** public access. Drive 1.3 miles west to mouth of Sheep Creek public boat launch and Bluffs on Susitna. **Sheep Creek** has parking, toilets, dumpster and wheelchair-accessible trail to mouth of creek; fishing for kings, silvers, pinks and rainbow. ♿

A 87.5 (140.8 km) **F 270.5** (435.3 km) Campground to east.

Camp Caswell RV Park. Open year-round. Located in the heart of Alaska's finest fishing and winter sports. We offer 15/30-amp pull-throughs, clean showers, laundromat, dump station, cabins, tent sites, propane, groceries, campwood, fishing tackle and game tags, licenses, phone and information. Free coffee and Alaska friendly! Phone/fax: (907) 495-7829. P.O. Box 333, Willow, AK 99688. E-mail: campcaswell@2webtv.net. [ADVERTISEMENT]

A 88.1 (141.8 km) **F 269.9** (434.4 km) Signed turnoff for Gigglewood Lakeside Inn.

Gigglewood Lakeside Inn. See display ad this section.

A 88.2 (142 km) **F 269.8** (434.2 km) Sheep Creek Lodge.

A 88.5 (142.4 km) **F 269.5** (433.7 km) Bridge over **Sheep Creek.** Turnout on west side at north end of bridge. Fishing for salmon and trout.

A 89 (143.2 km) **F 269** (432.9 km) Rough gravel turnouts both sides of highway.

A 90.8 (146.1 km) **F 267.2** (430 km) **Mat-Su Valley RV Park.** Clean full-service RV park conveniently located 1 block off the Parks Highway between Willow and Talkeetna junction. Good Sam's approved. Level pull-through gravel spaces, water, sewer and electric hookups. Picnic and secluded grassy tent sites. Store offers groceries, ice, propane, hot showers, laundromat, and fishing tackle. Fishing licenses sold on premises. We offer guided fishing charters on the Talkeetna and Susitna rivers. Open May–Sept. Modem friendly. Phone (907) 495-6300; Fax (907) 495-5550; www.matsurvpark.com. See display ad this section. [ADVERTISEMENT]

A 91.2 (146.7 km) **F 266.8** (429.4 km) Turnoff to west for dog tours.

A 91.7 (147.6 km) **F 266.3** (428.5 km) *CAUTION: Railroad crossing.*

A 92.2 (148.4 km) **F 265.8** (427.7 km) Gravel turnout to east. Distance marker northbound shows Talkeetna Junction 7 miles, McKinley Park 135 miles, Fairbanks 267 miles.

A 93.4 (150.3 km) **F 264.6** (425.8 km) Gravel turnouts both sides of highway.

A 93.5 (150.5 km) **F 264.5** (425.7 km) **Goose Creek** culvert; gravel turnout. Fishing.

A 93.6 (150.6 km) **F 264.4** (425.5 km) Goose Creek community center to west; park pavilion, picnic tables, grills, litter barrels.

A 95.1 (153 km) **F 262.9** (423.1 km) **Private Aircraft:** Montana Creek airstrip (private); elev. 250 feet; length 2,300 feet; dirt/gravel; no fuel. Current status unknown.

A 96 (154.5 km) **F 262** (421.6 km) Turnout to east.

A 96.3 (155 km) **F 261.7** (421.1 km) Montana Creek Road. **MONTANA CREEK** (pop. about 200) was settled by homesteaders in the 1950s.

A 96.5 (155.3 km) **F 261.5** (420.8 km) **Montana Creek Campground**. See display ad this section.

A 96.6 (155.5 km) **F 261.4** (420.7 km) Bridge over **Montana Creek**. Camping and picnic areas on both sides of Montana Creek (operated by concessionaire). Water and parking. Excellent king salmon fishing, also silvers, pinks (even-numbered years), grayling, rainbow and Dolly Varden.

A 97.8 (157.4 km) **F 260.2** (418.7 km) Alaska State Troopers post (phone 907/733-2556 or 911 for emergencies).

A 98.4 (158.3 km) **F 259.6** (417.8 km) Turnoff to west for Susitna Valley High School; 3.1-mile/5-km trail for running in summer, cross-country skiing in winter. Senior Center.

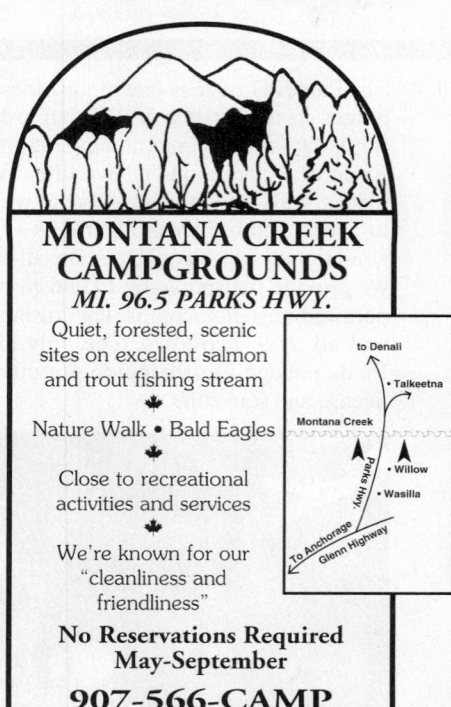

A 98.7 (158.8 km) **F 259.3** (417.3 km) **Talkeetna Y.** Access to hardware, lumber and feed store with ATM. Turn east on paved spur road for Talkeetna, an interesting side trip. Talkeetna/Denali Visitor Center at junction with information on area attractions and lodging; restrooms, picnic area. Tesoro gas station just north of junction.

Junction with Talkeetna Spur Road. See TALKEETNA SPUR ROAD log beginning on page 370.

Downtown Talkeetna is just 14 miles/23 km northeast of the Parks Highway via a paved spur road.

A 98.8 (159 km) **F 259.2** (417.1 km) Sunshine Restaurant and Tesoro truck stop at Talkeetna Y; food, gas, diesel, propane, store, pay phone.

Sunshine One Stop. See display ad this section.

A 99.3 (159.8 km) **F 258.7** (416.3 km) **Montana and Little Montana lakes** on opposite sides of highway, stocked with rainbow. Watch for floatplanes. Public access to west.

A 99.5 (160.1 km) **F 258.5** (416 km) **His & Hers Lakeview Lounge & Restaurant.** See display ad this section.

A 100.4 (161.6 km) **F 257.6** (414.6 km) *CAUTION: Railroad crossing.*

A 101.8 (163.8 km) **F 256.2** (412.3 km) **Talkeetna Blue Grass Festival**, Aug. 3, 4, 5, 6, 2000. Alaska's greatest musicians, arts, crafts and food. Good roads, outhouses, RV parking, no hookups. Great family weekend camping. Bring camping gear and cushions. $30 fee includes camping. Showers available, DEC-approved drinking water. Seniors and children 12 and under are free. No carry-in alcohol please. For information, phone (907) 495-6718. [ADVERTISEMENT]

A 102.2 (164.5 km) **F 255.8** (411.6 km) Large, paved double-ended turnout to east. Lakes both sides of highway.

A 102.6 (165.1 km) **F 255.4** (411 km) Turnout at Sunshine Road; access to **Sunshine Creek** for fishing via dirt road.

A 104 (167.4 km) **F 254** (408.8 km) Big Su Lodge to east.

A 104.2 (167.7 km) **F 253.8** (408.4 km) Entering Game Management Unit 16A, northbound, Unit 14B southbound. Bridge over Big Susitna River. State rest area to west on south bank of river; loop road, parking area, tables, firepits, toilets, no drinking water.

This area is noted for its fiddlehead ferns. Lady fern, ostrich fern and shield fern are harvested in the spring, when their young shoots are tightly coiled, resembling a fiddle's head.

A 104.6 (168.3 km) **F 253.4** (407.8 km) Rabideux Creek access; parking, 0.3 mile trail to mouth of creek. Watch for seasonal flooding.

A 104.8 (168.7 km) **F 253.2** (407.5 km) Large dirt and gravel turnout to west.

A 105.9 (170.4 km) **F 252.1** (405.7 km) Rabideux Creek.

A 107.6 (173.2 km) **F 250.4** (403 km) View of Mount McKinley (weather permitting) for northbound travelers.

(Continues on page 375)

View of Mount McKinley from Talkeetna Alaskan Lodge on the Spur Road.
(© Barb Willard)

Talkeetna Spur Road Log

Distance from Parks Highway junction (J) at Milepost A 98.7 is shown.

J 0 Junction with the Parks Highway at **Milepost A 98.7. Talkeetna/Denali Visitor Center** has information on area activities and services; phone (800) 660-2688 or (907) 733-2688.

J 1 (1.6 km) Mary Carey's Fiddlehead Fern Farm.

J 2.2 (3.5 km) Gold Pan Bed and Breakfast.

J 3.1 (5 km) Turn west on Jubilee Road. Turn east on Yoder Road for Benka Lake (private).

J 4.4 (7 km) Sunshine Community Medical Center.

J 5.8 (9.3 km) **Beadberry Patch.** See display ad this section.

J 7.1 (11.4 km) Question Lake.

J 7.8 (12.6 km) Paradise Cabins turnoff.

J 9.2 (14.8 km) Fish Lake private floatplane base.

J 11.1 (17.8 km) **Little Bighorn Custom Knives.** Custom knives, scrimshaw, jewelry, leatherwork, antler carving and fine art collectibles. Hand-crafted knives made in Alaska using only the finest steels, native Alaskan and other specialty materials. Owner John "Dancing Bear" Saily has over 10 years experience specializing in custom designs. Open year-round. Highlighting original designs as well as restorations and repair. A proud sponsor of the Made in Alaska program. VISA, MasterCard and American Express welcome. Phone (907) 733-4424. Email: littlebighorn@gci.net. [ADVERTISEMENT]

J 12 (19.3 km) Comsat Road (paved) leads east 0.8 mile to X-Y Lakes (public access) and 3.4 miles to Bartlett Earth Station/AT&T Alascom at road end. The dish-shaped antenna stands 98 feet/32m and can rotate 1 degree per second to receive satellite signals. No tours available.

J 12.8 (20.6 km) Entrance to Talkeetna Lodge, 0.3 mile east.

Talkeetna Alaskan Lodge. Conveniently located at Mile 12.8 Talkeetna Spur Road, just 2 hours north of Anchorage, the Talkeetna Alaskan Lodge offers 98 deluxe rooms, full-service restaurant and lounge, and great room—all with unsurpassed views of Mt. McKinley. Relax by a roaring fire in our great room featuring a 45-foot river rock fireplace. Many activities available including nature trails, flightseeing, riverboat excursions and more. For reservations call 888-959-9590; in Talkeetna (907) 733-9500, or visit us on the web at www.talkeetnalodge.com. [ADVERTISEMENT]

J 13 (20.9 km) Large paved double-ended turnout with interpretive sign and viewpoint to west. Splendid views of Mount McKinley, Mount Foraker and the Alaska Range above the Susitna River. A must photo stop when the mountains are out.

J 13.3 (21.4 km) *CAUTION: Alaska Railroad crossing.*

J 13.5 (21.7 km) Talkeetna public library.

J 13.8 (22.2 km) Restaurant and motel. VFW Post No. 3836 is 2 blocks west.

J 14 (22.5 km) East Talkeetna Road leads to state airport (Hudson Air, Doug Geeting and other air services), Talkeetna Hostel, Swiss Alaska Inn, Mahay's Riverboat Service, McKinley Jetboat Safaris, campground and public boat launch.

J 14.2 (22.9 km) Talkeetna post office (ZIP code 99676).

Talkeetna Gifts & Collectables. "One of the nicest and most complete gift shops in Alaska," located in a spacious log building with handmade keepsakes, souvenirs, jewelry, books, Alaskana, birch bowls, quilts and other treasures. Fur slippers/accessories, beautiful sweatshirts, sweaters, plush toys, puppets and huggable Eskimo dolls. Alaskan foods and sourdough. Suzy's exclusive "Alaska Map" cross-stitch pattern. Quality merchandise with friendly service. We mail purchases. Goldpanning, with gold guaranteed! Open daily year-round. Main Street, Talkeetna. (907) 733-2710. [ADVERTISEMENT]

J 14.3 (23 km) "Welcome to Beautiful Downtown Talkeetna" sign and Talkeetna Historical Society visitor center log cabin; walking tour brochures available. Public parking at Village Park.

Denali Dry Goods/Denali Floats. See display ad.

Museum of Northern Adventure. Highlighting Alaska's exciting history in 24 realistic dioramas, featuring life-sized figures and sounds. Entertaining and educational for all ages. Meander through the historic railroad building, experiencing Alaskana at every turn: homesteading, prospecting, wildlife, famous characters and more. Open daily year-round with special group/family rates. Clean restrooms. Gift shop featuring Eskimo dolls and totems. Carved grizzly and prospector outside to greet you. Main Street, Talkeetna. (907) 733-3999. Handicap accessible. [ADVERTISEMENT]

J 14.5 (23.3 km) Talkeetna Spur Road ends at Talkeetna River Park (camping). (Description of Talkeetna follows.)

Talkeetna

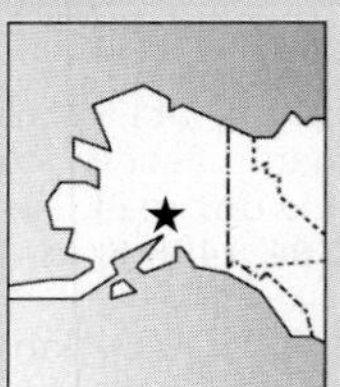

Located on a spur road, north of **Milepost A 98.7** Parks Highway. **Population:** 363. **Emergency Services: Alaska State Troopers, Fire Department** and **Ambulance,** phone 911 or (907) 733-2256. Sunshine Community Medical Center, Mile 4.4 Spur Road, phone (907) 733-2273.

Visitor Information: Stop by the **Talkeetna Historical Society Visitor Information Center** cabin on entering Talkeetna. Or write the Chamber of Commerce, P.O. Box 334, Talkeetna, AK 99676.

The National Park Service maintains a

Downtown Talkeetna has restaurants, shops and services. (© Barb Willard)

ranger station that is staffed full time from mid-April through mid-September and intermittently during the winter. Mountaineering rangers provide information on Denali National Park and climbing within the Alaska Range. A reference library and video program are available to climbers. Mountaineering regulations and information may be obtained from Talkeetna Ranger Station, P.O. Box 588, Talkeetna, AK 99676; phone (907) 733-2231.

Elevation: 346 feet/105m. **Radio:** KSKA-FM (PBS), local KTNA 88.5-FM. **Television:** Channels 2, 4, 5, 7 & 13.

Private Aircraft: Talkeetna state airport, adjacent east; elev. 358 feet; length 3,500 feet; paved; fuel 100LL, Jet B.

A "Welcome to Beautiful Downtown Talkeetna" sign is posted at the town park as you enter Talkeetna's old-fashioned Main Street, the only paved street in town. Log cabins and clapboard homes and businesses line Main Street, which dead-ends at the Susitna River.

There are a certain few places which, by virtue of sometimes undefinable elements, possess an innate charisma. Talkeetna is such a place, but in the case of this town it is not difficult to explain its charm. Few other locations are blessed with such fortunate geography. How many towns own such breathtaking views of Denali and the Alaska Range and look out over a broad valley where 3 rivers meet? This spectacular setting combines with a highly creative citizenry, imaginative shops and businesses, the mystique of the mountain-climbing community, unique celebrations such as the Moose Dropping Festival and the Bachelors' Auction. Small wonder this is a popular destination

TALKEETNA ADVERTISERS

Denali Dry Goods..............................Main St.
Denali Floats.....................Ph. (907) 733-2384
Doug Geeting Aviation.......................Ph. (907) 733-2366
Doug Geeting's Peak Dodger Flight Tours.............Main St.
Gold Pan Bed & Breakfast....Mile 2.2 Spur Rd.
Hudson Air Service, Inc...................................Airport
K2 Aviation.......................Ph. (800) 764-2291
Mahay's McKinley Jetboat Safari...........................Ph. (800) 736-2210
Mahay's Riverboat Service.........................Ph. (800) 736-2210
McKinley Air Service............................Airport
Museum of Northern Adventure...................................Main St.
Paradise Lodge & Cabins..Ph. (907) 733-1471
Ptarmigan View Cabins..........Beaver Loop Rd.
Swiss–Alaska Inn...............Ph. (907) 733-2424
Talkeetna Air Taxi.............Ph. (907) 733-2218
Talkeetna Gifts and Collectables.................................Main St.
Talkeetna Cabins..............Ph. (907) 733-2227
Talkeetna Alaskan Lodge..Ph. (888) 959-9590
Talkeetna River Adventures..................Ph. (907) 733-2604
Talkeetna River Guides......................Main St.
Talkeetna Riverboat Service.........................Ph. (907) 733-3336
Talkeetna Roadhouse........................Main St.
Three Rivers Tesoro...........................Main St.

Talkeetna Spur (continued)

for tourists as well as Alaskans.

Talkeetna is the jumping-off point for many climbing expeditions to Mount McKinley (Denali). Most expeditions use the West Buttress route, pioneered by Bradford

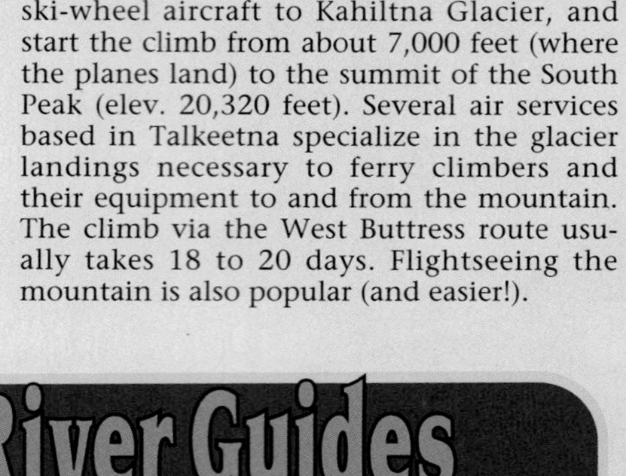

Washburn. They fly in specially equipped ski-wheel aircraft to Kahiltna Glacier, and start the climb from about 7,000 feet (where the planes land) to the summit of the South Peak (elev. 20,320 feet). Several air services based in Talkeetna specialize in the glacier landings necessary to ferry climbers and their equipment to and from the mountain. The climb via the West Buttress route usually takes 18 to 20 days. Flightseeing the mountain is also popular (and easier!).

Lodging & Services

Talkeetna has 5 motels/hotels, a hostel, several bed and breakfasts, 9 restaurants, 1 gas station, a laundromat, gift and clothing shops, grocery stores, canoe and bike rentals. A dump station is located at Three Rivers Tesoro.

Paradise Lodge & Cabins. Enjoy the panoramic view of Mt. McKinley, Mt. Hunter, Mt. Foraker, and privacy of Fish Lake. The beautifully appointed unique log cabins are situated on 10 acres of beautiful birch and pine forest. Each cabin has a completely equipped kitchenette. New and complete shower facilities are available. Open year-round. Reservations: Phone (907) 733-1471. [ADVERTISEMENT]

Talkeetna Roadhouse. Located on the edge of wilderness in a living pioneer village, the Talkeetna Roadhouse (Frank Lee cabin, circa 1917) has served the territory since early gold rush days. Still family owned and operated, this historic restaurant, lodge and bakery featuring 1902 sourdough is known worldwide for its fine

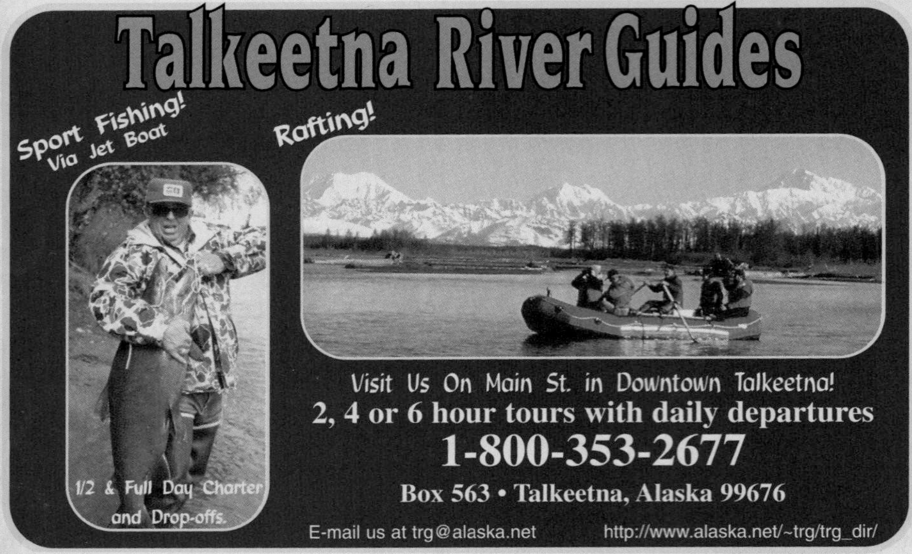

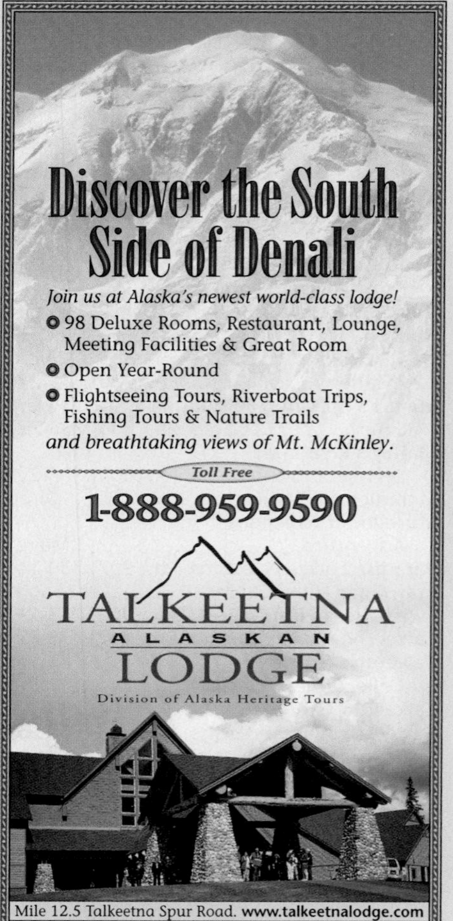

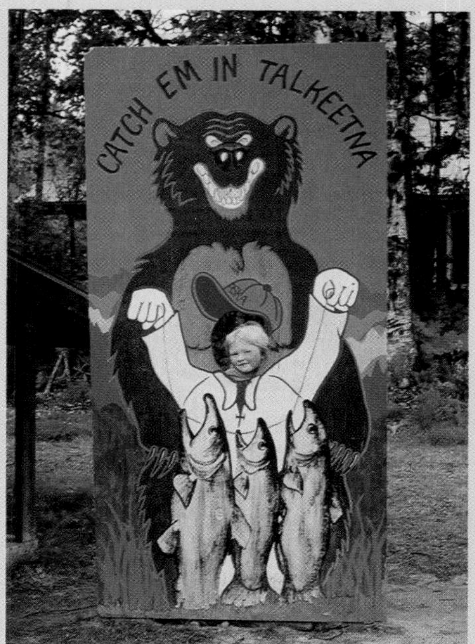

Talkeetna provides photo opportunities for visitors. (© Kris Graef, staff)

home-style cooking, cinnamon rolls, and frontier hospitality. Slow down to "Talkeetna time," relax amidst the rustic charm and listen to the stories these old walls have to tell! Rooms start at $45, bunk spaces $21. Restaurant features classic roadhouse breakfast, daily soup and sandwich menu. Serving family-style supper by reservation. Phone (907) 733-1351, fax (907) 733-1353. E-mail: rdhouse@alaska.net. Internet: www.alaska.net/~rdhouse. [ADVERTISEMENT]

Camping

RV and tent camping at River Park (located at the end of main street); hosted campground, $8 camping fee. Camping is also available at the ADF&G concessionaire-operated public boat launch in East Talkeetna near the Swiss Alaska Inn; camping fee $12, collected at Talkeetna River Adventures. ▲

Transportation

Air: There are several air taxi services in Talkeetna. Charter service, flightseeing and glacier landings are available. See ads this section.

Railroad: The Alaska Railroad provides daily passenger service.

Highway: At the end of a 14.5-mile-long spur road off the Parks Highway (Alaska Route 3).

Attractions

The Talkeetna Historical Society Museum is located 1 block off Main Street opposite the Fairview Inn. The original 1-room schoolhouse, built in 1936, exhibits historical items, local art, a historical library and a display on the late Don Sheldon, famous Alaskan bush pilot. In the Railroad Section House see the impressive 12-foot-by-12-foot scale model of Mount McKinley (Denali) with photographs by Bradford

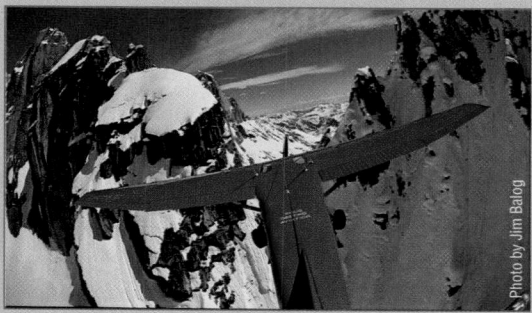

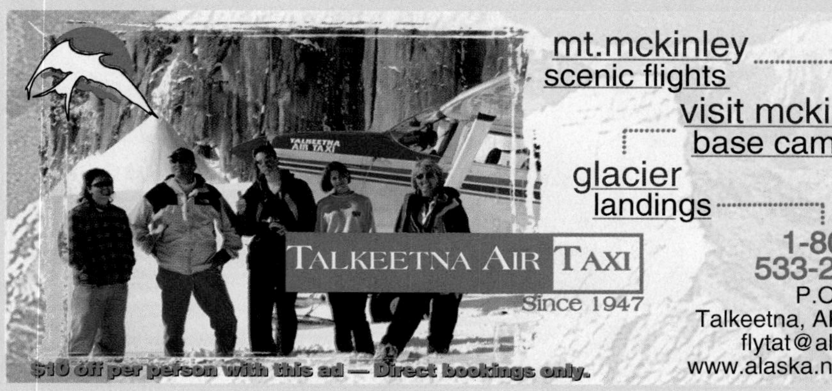

Talkeetna Spur *(continued)*

Washburn. A mountaineering display features pioneer and recent climbs of Mount McKinley. The Ole Dahl cabin, an early trapper/miner's cabin located on the museum grounds, is furnished with period items. Admission: $1 adult, under 12 free. Pick up a walking tour map of Talkeetna's historic sites here. Picnic area adjacent museum. Museum buildings open 10 A.M. to 5 P.M. daily in summer. Reduced hours other seasons. Phone (907) 733-2487. Privately operated guided history tours.

Annual Moose Dropping Festival is held the second Saturday in July as a fund-raising project for the museum. Activities include a 5-km run and walk, a parade, entertainment, music, barbecue, food and game booths, and, of course, a moose dropping throwing contest.

Annual Talkeetna Bachelor Festival takes place on a Saturday in early winter and features a Wilderness Woman's contest and the Bachelor Ball and Auction benefit.

Riverboat tours up Talkeetna Canyon, Devils Canyon, Chulitna River and Tokositna River are available. Several guides also offer riverboat fishing trips from Talkeetna. Commercial float trips and raft tours offer another popular way of exploring the roadless wilderness. Talkeetna is located at the confluence of the Susitna, Talkeetna and Chulitna rivers. Inquire locally for details and see ads this section.

Mahay's McKinley Jetboat Safari. The safari offers opportunities to view nesting bald eagles, beaver activity, moose and black bear in their natural habitat. Be sure to bring your camera so you can capture this unforgettable adventure. Please dress warmly and wear comfortable walking shoes for the leisurely 1/4-mile nature walk. Phone (800) 736-2210. www.alaskan.com/mahays. [ADVERTISEMENT]

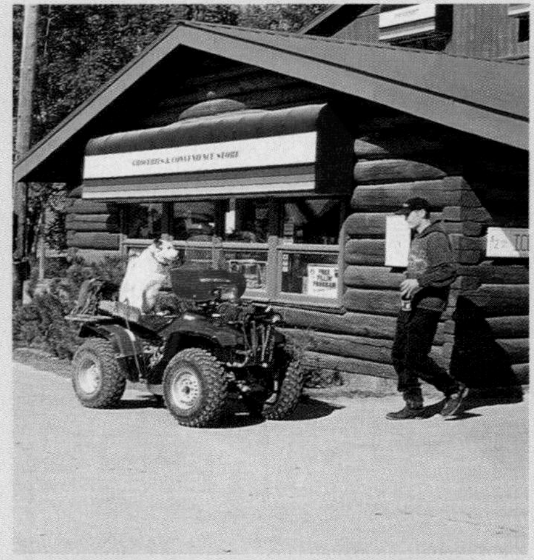

An assortment of dogs and vehicles are found along Talkeetna's Main Street.

(© David L. Ranta, staff)

Mahay's Riverboat Service. Fish clear-water streams for all 5 species of Pacific salmon and trout. Custom-designed jet boats allow access to over 200 miles of prime fishing territory. Guided fishing charters include all equipment needed. Fishing packages are also available that include accommodations, meals and all the "extras." Drop-off fishing also available at reasonable rates. Phone (800) 736-2210. www.alaskan.com/mahays. [ADVERTISEMENT]

Talkeetna River Guides. Fish with a recognized leader for salmon and trout in our exciting area streams and rivers. Guided

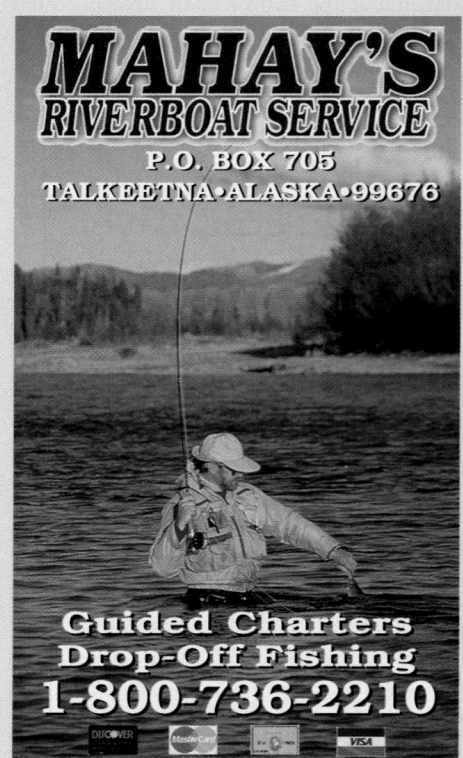

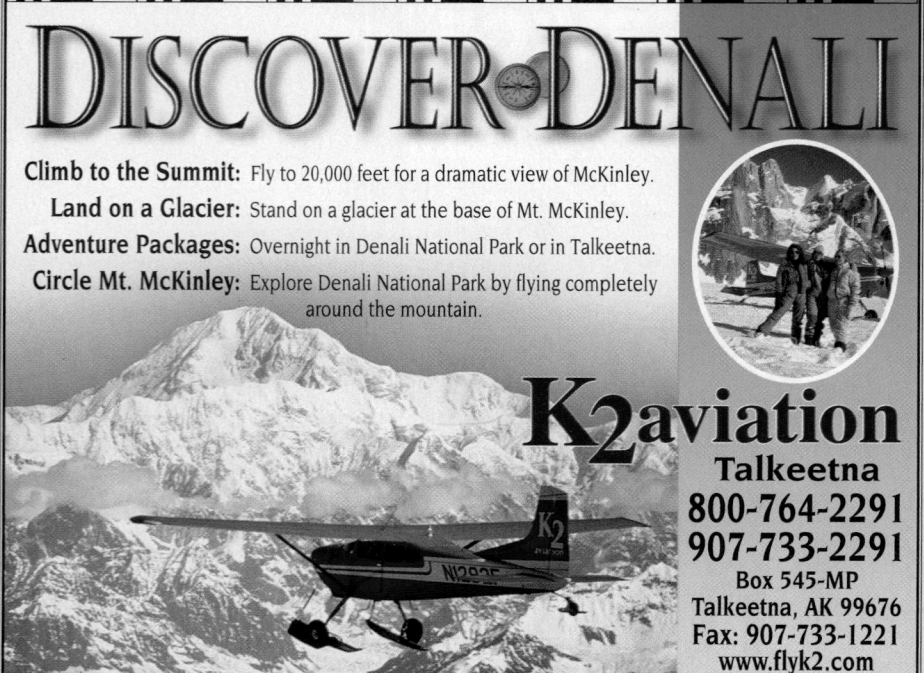

charters available and include all equipment and use of our specialized jet boats. Drop-off fishing available as well. Also, join us on a wildlife, natural history float trip. 2-, 4-, and 6-hour tours available daily. 1-800-353-2677. See display ad. [ADVERTISEMENT]

Fishing. The **Susitna River** basin offers many top fishing streams and lakes, either accessible by road, plane or riverboat.

Doug Geeting's Peak Dodger Flight Tours. Take flight with world renowned Doug Geeting Aviation. Look up at 14,000-foot rock and ice walls and land on a glacier—an Alaskan adventure highlight

that will astound even the most experienced world traveler! We hold an NPS concession for Mount McKinley glacier landings, available only from the Talkeetna State Airport. Planes are intercom equipped. Group rates available. Over-night accommodations available. For prices and reservations: Doug Geeting Aviation, P.O. Box 42MP, Talkeetna, AK 99676; (800) 770-2366. Fax (907) 733-1000. E-mail: airtours@alaska.net. Web: alaskaairtours.com. See display ad this section. [ADVERTISEMENT]

Hudson Air Service, Inc. is Talkeetna's "senior" air taxi; 50 years of experience and knowledge of Mount McKinley will make your flightseeing tour the highlight of your Alaskan adventure! Visit with pioneer aviator Cliff Hudson and fly with second generation Hudson pilots as you tour Denali National Park while enjoying narratives on the natural and local history. Fly over the Kahiltna Glacier and view base camp as climbers from all over the world prepare to ascend "The Great One." Include a landing on either the Ruth or Kahiltna Glacier for an

experience you will never forget. We offer flights around the mountain, wildlife tours (bear, moose, caribou and sheep) and remote drop-off hunting/fishing. Open year-round. Hudson Air Service Inc. is a National Park Service concessionaire. Office at Talkeetna State Airport. P.O. Box 648, Talkeetna, AK 99676. Phone (907) 733-2321, fax (907) 733-2333, e-mail: hasi@customcpu.com. Web site: www.alaskan.com/hudsonair/. See display ad in DENALI NATIONAL PARK section. [ADVERTISEMENT]

Talkeetna Air Taxi. View Denali's most spectacular peaks and glaciers. Circle McKinley and land on a glacier, starting at $90. Anchorage–Denali Park–Talkeetna packages: Fly–Rail–Bus. Leave the logistics to us. Since 1947. Call 1-800-533-2219 or (907) 733-2218. http://www,alaska.net/~flytat. See display ad. [ADVERTISEMENT]

Return to Milepost A 98.7 Parks Highway

(Continued from page 369)

A 114 (183.5 km) **F 244** (392.7 km) *NOTE: Slow for 55 mph speed zone northbound.*

A 114.7 (184.6 km) **F 243.3** (391.5 km) *Emergency phone* to west.

A 114.8 (184.7 km) **F 243.2** (391.4 km) **TRAPPER CREEK** (pop. 344); post office. **Emergency services: Ambulance**, phone 911. Miners built the Petersville Road in the 1920s, and federal homesteading began here in 1948. Today, a cluster of businesses around the junction with Petersville Road serve highway travelers. Accommodations are also available along Petersville Road.

A 114.9 (184.9 km) **F 243.1** (391.2 km)

Junction with Petersville Road, which leads west 18.7 miles. See PETERSVILLE ROAD log page 376.

Historic Trapper Creek post office (ZIP code 99683) at junction on east side of Parks Highway.

Trapper Creek's Old Historic Post Office. See display ad this section.

A 115.2 (185.4 km) **F 242.8** (390.7 km) Trapper Creek community park.

A 115.5 (185.9 km) **F 243** (391 km) Trapper Creek trading Post and Texaco gas station east side of highway; cafe, gas, diesel, grocery, cabins, campground. ▲

Trapper Creek Trading Post. See display ad this section. ▲

A 115.6 (186 km) **F 242.4** (390.1 km) Highway crosses Trapper Creek.

Excellent views of Mount McKinley (weather permitting) northbound.

A 115.7 (186.2 km) **F 242.3** (389.9 km) **Trapper Creek Pizza Pub–Angela's Heaven** Enjoy delicious homemade pizza, fresh salads, great sandwiches (hot and cold) in a friendly atmosphere. If you like tasty, dark bread, call 1 day ahead to order a loaf or two of Angela's famous German Beer Bread—made according to a very old family recipe. By the way: We also speak German! Phone (907) 733-3344. [ADVERTISEMENT]

A 119 (191.5 km) **F 239** (384.6 km) Distance marker northbound shows Cantwell 82 miles, McKinley Park 103 miles, Fairbanks 240 miles.

A 121.1 (194.9 km) **F 236.9** (381.2 km) Chulitna highway maintenance camp to west.

A 121.5 (195.5 km) **F 236.5** (380.6 km) Large paved double-ended rest area to east with tables, firepits, drinking water, toilet

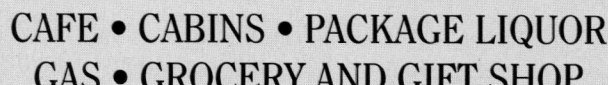

Petersville Road Log

Miners built the Petersville Road in the 1920s and federal homesteading began here in 1948, with settlement continuing through the 1950s and 1960s. Petersville Road leads west and north from Trapper Creek through a homestead and gold mining area that also contains some new subdivisions. Berry picking in season. *Please respect private property.*

Distance from junction with the Parks Highway (J) is shown.

J 0 **Junction** with Parks Highway at **Milepost A 114.9.**

J 0.3 (0.5 km) **Trapper Creek B & B.** You will enjoy your stay with hosts Jim and Susan in their 3-bedroom, shared bathroom, Alaskan home. The rooms are clean, showers hot, and a hearty homemade breakfasts daily with affordable rates. Flightseeing trips of Mt. McKinley and rafting trips can be arranged. Open all year at the southern gateway to Denali National Park. Phone (907) 733-2234. E-mail: trappercreekbnb@matnet.com. [ADVERTISEMENT]

J 0.7 (1.1 km) Trapper Creek Museum and Gifts. Gold Rush Centennial sign.

J 2 (3.2 km) Denali View Chalets. Private, secluded, modern chalets with spectacular views of Mount McKinley and the Alaska Range. Open year-round with access by paved road. Fullyfurnished with kitchenettes, microwave, gas grills and 2 twin

and 2 double beds. Lots of area activities. The wildernessat your doorstep. Reasonable rates. E-mail address: denalivw@ptialaska.net. Homepage address: http://www.denaliviewchalets.com. P.O. Box 13245, Trapper Creek, AK 99683. Phone (907) 733-1333. [ADVERTISEMENT]

J 2.7 (4.3 km) Trapper Creek elementary school to south, bed and breakfast to north.

North Country Bed and Breakfast. Nestled on a lake with a spectacular view of Mount McKinley. Five first-class rooms with private bathrooms and private entries. Mount McKinley flightseeing trips available at the lake by appointment. Bird watching, wildlife, paddleboating and horseshoes available. Open year-round. Your hosts—Mike and Sheryl Uher. Phone (907) 733-3981. See display ad this section. [ADVERTISEMENT]

J 3.1 (5 km) Pavement ends, gravel begins, westbound.

J 7 (11.3 km) Moose Creek. Road narrows and climbs westbound.

J 10.5 (16.9 km) **Gate Creek Cabins** modern 1, 2 and 3-bedroom log cabins. Located at Mile 10.5 on historic Petersville Road, with year-round access. Furnished

with linens, dishes, utensils, stove, refrigerator, TV, VCR, showers, sauna, barbecue grill. Mountain viewing, hiking, biking, photography, fishing, berry picking. Free canoeing and paddleboating on our small lake; mountain bike and 4-wheeler rentals; snowmachine rentals in winter. Children 12 and under free. Weekly rate, 6th and 7th nights free. Family pets welcome. Your hosts, Gary and Dorothy Rawie. Reservations (907) 733-1393 or e-mail: gRawie@worldnet.att.net. Web page: alaskan.com/gatecreekcabins/. [ADVERTISEMENT]

J 13.4 (21.6 km) Steep grade and switchback.

J 13.9 (22.4 km) Kroto Creek. Narrow road climbs westbound. Slow down for some washboard.

J 17.2 (27.7 km) Turnoff for McKinley Foothills B&B (2.6 miles/4.2 km south).

McKinley Foothills B&B/Cabins. Off Mile 17.2 Petersville Road. Furnished, rustic log cabins, kitchenettes. Full breakfast. Great food, Alaskan hospitality.Great

Mount McKinley views. Summer: gold panning tours, fishing nearby, birding, hiking, mountain biking. Winter: skiing, snow machining, dog mushing tours. Major credit cards. Homepage: www.matnet.com/~mckinley. E-mail: mckinley@matnet.com. Phone/ fax (907) 733-1454. P.O. Box 13089, Trapper Creek, AK 99683. [ADVERTISEMENT]

J 18.7 (30.1 km) Forks Roadhouse; food and lodging. Petersville Road forks here. Turn down the right fork for the former mining camp of Petersville (4-wheel drive only). The left fork leads 0.2 mile to **Peters Creek**; fishing for salmon and trout.

Return to Milepost A 114.9 Parks Highway

and interpretive bulletin board. Shade trees; cow parsnip grows lush here.

A 126.6 (203.7 km) **F 231.4** (371.7 km) Large paved parking area to east.

A 127 (204.4 km) **F 231** (372.1 km) Large unpaved turnout to west.

A 128.4 (206.6 km) **F 229.6** (369.5 km) Undeveloped parking area to east below highway on south side of creek.

A 132 (212.4 km) **F 226** (363.7 km) Boundary of Denali State Park (see description next milepost).

A 132.3 (212.9 km) **F 225.7** (363.2 km) **Denali State Park** entrance sign northbound. This 325,460-acre state park has 48 miles of hiking trails. Camping at Troublesome Creek (**Milepost A 137.3**), Byers Lake (**Milepost A 147**) and Denali View North (**Milepost A 162.7**). Hunting is permitted in the park, but discharge of firearms is prohibited within 0.3 mile of highway, 0.5 mile of a developed facility or 0.5 mile of trail around Byers Lake.

A 132.8 (213.7 km) **F 225.2** (362.4 km) Middle of the **Chulitna River** bridge. Fishing for grayling, rainbow.

Entering Game Management Subunit 13E, leaving unit 16A, northbound.

A 132.9 (213.9 km) **F 225.1** (362.2 km) Intersection with **Mt. McKinley View Drive** at north end of bridge. Turn east uphill and follow paved road 0.4 mile for turnout with view and 1 mile for Mt. McKinley Princess Lodge. D & S Trail Rides is located on this road just before the lodge.

D & S Alaskan Trail Rides. Open mid-May through mid-September, offers 1 1/2- to 8-hour adventurous trail rides on seasoned trails with majestic views of Mount McKinley. Ride into the wilderness to experience

the serenity of the forest and all that nature has to offer. It's a ride that the entire family can enjoy! Also available: pack trips or horse-drawn wagon rides. Outback coats, cowboy hats and helmets are provided. Summer phone (907) 733-2205; winter (907) 745-2207. www.alaskantrailrides.com. [ADVERTISEMENT]

Mt. McKinley Princess Lodge. A stylish, cozy riverside retreat bordering the south side of Denali National Park featuring incredible views of Mount McKinley and the Alaska Range, expansive main lodge, finely appointed guest rooms, array of dining options, tour desk, gift shop. Open mid-May through mid-September. Reservations (800) 426-0500 year round. [ADVERTISEMENT]

A 134 (215.6 km) **F 224** (360.5 km) Helicopter sightseeing service; private airstrip.

ERA Helicopters Flightseeing Tours. See Mt. McKinley up close. Explore the south side of Denali and see numerous glaciers, spectacular mountain peaks, and the majestic Mt. McKinley. Located at Milepost 134. May to September. For reservations phone (800) 843-1947. Tours also available in Anchorage, Denali Park, Juneau and Valdez. [ADVERTISEMENT]

From here northbound for many miles there are views of glaciers on the southern slopes of the Alaska Range to the west. Ruth, Buckskin and Eldridge glaciers are the most conspicuous. Ruth Glacier trends southeast through the Great Gorge for 31 miles/50 km. The glacier was named in 1903 by F.A. Cook for his daughter. The Great Gorge was named by mountain climbers in the late 1940s. Peaks on either side of the gorge tower up to 5,000 feet/1,500m above Ruth Glacier. The gorge, nicknamed the Grand Canyon of Alaska, opens into Don Sheldon Amphitheater at the head of Ruth Glacier, where the Don Sheldon mountain house sits. Donald E. Sheldon (1921–75) was a well-known bush pilot who helped map, patrol, and aid search and rescue efforts in this area.

Flightseeing trips can be arranged that take you close to Mount McKinley, into the Don Sheldon Amphitheater, through the Great Gorge and beneath the peak of The Mooses Tooth. Inquire with flightseeing oeprators along the Parks Highway and in the national park.

A 134.5 (216.5 km) **F 223.5** (359.7 km) **Mary's McKinley View Lodge.** Located on Mary Carey's original homestead. Spectacular view of McKinley from every room, especially the glass-walled restaurant. Mary, famous for Alaskan books, homesteaded before the state park was created. She fought for highway completion to share her magnificent view with travelers. Now a movie is being filmed about her life. Enjoy dining, browse the gift shop or spend a pleasant night in the modern rooms. Call (907) 733-1555. See display ad this page. [ADVERTISEMENT]

A 135.2 (217.6 km) **F 222.8** (358.6 km) **Denali Viewpoint** (Denali State Park) is a large paved turnout overlooking the Chulitna River; toilet. A display board here points out peaks. View of 20,320-foot Mount McKinley. Peaks to be sighted, south to north, along the next 20 miles to the west are: Mount Hunter (elev. 14,573 feet); Mount Huntington (12,240 feet); Mount Barrille (7,650 feet); and Mount Dickey (9,845 feet).

A 137.3 (221 km) **F 220.7** (355.1 km) **Lower Troublesome Creek State Recreation Site** to west has 10 campsites, $6/night camping fee per vehicle or annual pass, day-use area with sheltered picnic sites, toilets, water and litter barrels. Lower Troublesome Creek trailhead. This is usually a clear runoff stream, not silted by glacial flour. The stream heads in a lake and flows 14 miles to the Chulitna River.

Troublesome Creek bridge. Troublesome Creek, rainbow, grayling and salmon (king salmon fishing prohibited); June through September.

A 137.6 (221.4 km) **F 220.4** (354.7 km) Upper Troublesome Creek trailhead and parking area. Trails to Byers Lake (15 miles) and Tarn Point, elev. 2,881 feet (10.8 miles). *NOTE: Trailhead and trail to Mile 5.5 closed from mid-July to Sept. 1 due to the high concentration of bears feeding on spawning salmon.*

A 139.9 (225.1 km) **F 218.1** (351 km) Paved turnout to west.

A 143.9 (231.6 km) **F 214.1** (344.6 km) Bridge over Byers Creek.

A 144 (231.7 km) **F 214** (344.4 km) **Byers Creek Station.** Mile 144 Parks Highway on crystal-clear Byers Creek. Complete general store and gift shop. Stay in our RV/camp sites, backpackers bunkhouse or private cabins in a pristine setting with clean comfortable beds, laundry and showers. Fishing, hiking, canoeing, gold panning and tours available! Reservations (907) 457-3224. [ADVERTISEMENT]

A 145.7 (234.5 km) **F 212.3** (341.6 km) Paved turnout to west.

A 147 (236.6 km) **F 211** (339.6 km) **Byers Lake Campground** (Denali State Park) to east with 66 sites, $12/night camping fee or resident pass, picnic tables, firepits, water, toilets (wheelchair accessible) and access to Byers Lake (electric motors permitted). Fishing for grayling, burbot, rainbow, lake trout and whitefish. Remote campsite 1.8-mile hike from campground (see directions posted on bulletin board). Hiking trail to Curry Ridge and south to Troublesome Creek. *CAUTION: Bears frequent campground. Keep a clean camp.*

Susitna Expeditions offers canoe, kayak and boat rentals in Denali State Park. We also offer guided hiking, kayak and mountain bike tours, firewood bundles and visitor information. Experience Alaska with lifelong Alaskans Kay and Toby Riddell. Our office is located at Byers Lake Campground. Phone (800) 891-6916. [ADVERTISEMENT]

A 147.2 (236.9 km) **F 210.8** (339.2 km) **Alaska Veterans Memorial rest area** to east; large parking area, pet walk, picnic tables, visitor information center, garbage containers, outhouses, interpretive kiosk, and spotting scopes. Wheelchair accessible. The

concrete memorial honors the armed forces. The visitor center/store is open daily in summer. Camping is permitted at this rest area only "after 8 P.M. if Byers Lake Campground is full. You must pay the $12 camping fee at the campground."

A 156.2 (251.4 km) **F 201.8** (324.8 km) Wolf Park Lodge; gas.

A 156.5 (251.9 km) **F 201.5** (324.3 km) Large gravel turnout to east.

A 157.6 (253.6 km) **F 200.4** (322.5 km) Small paved turnout to west.

A 159.4 (256.5 km) **F 198.6** (319.6 km) Double-ended paved turnout to west.

A 159.8 (257.2 km) **F 198.2** (319 km) Creek (signed).

A 161 (259.1 km) **F 197** (317 km) Large gravel turnout to east.

A 162.4 (261.4 km) **F 195.6** (314.8 km) **Denali Viewpoint** (Denali State Park); large paved turnout to west with a view of Mount McKinley.

A 162.7 (261.8 km) **F 195.3** (314.3 km) **Denali View North Campground** (Denali State Park) to west; 20 sites, $10/night, day-use parking, toilets (wheelchair accessible), water, interpretive kiosks, spotting scope, short loop trail. Overlooks Chulitna River. Views of Denali, Mooses Tooth, Mount Huntington and Alaska Range peaks above Hidden River valley.

A 163.1 (262.5 km) **F 194.9** (313.6 km) Large double-ended paved turnout to west.

A 163.2 (262.6 km) **F 194.8** (313.5 km) Bridge over Little Coal Creek.

Coal Creek; rainbow, grayling and salmon, July through September.

A 163.8 (263.6 km) **F 194.2** (312.5 km) **Little Coal Creek Trailhead** (Denali State Park); parking area. According to park rangers, this trail offers easy access ($1^1/_2$-hour

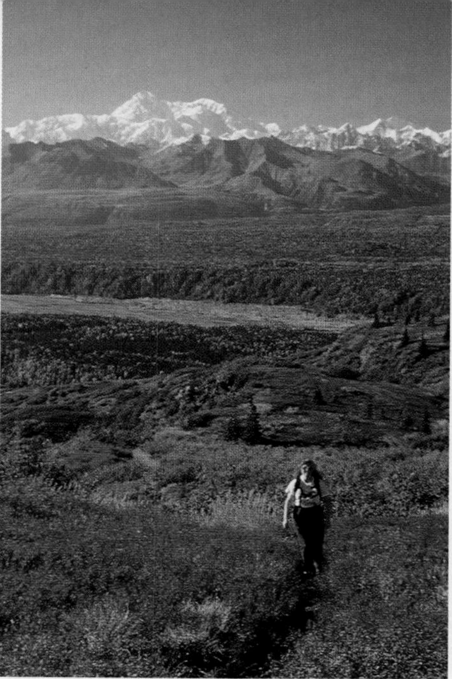

Hiking Little Coal Creek Trail along Curry Ridge in Denali State Park.
(© Bruce M. Herman)

hike) to alpine country. It is a 27-mile/43.5-km hike to Byers Lake via Kesugi Ridge.

A 165.6 (266.5 km) **F 192.4** (309.6 km) Paved turnouts on both sides of highway. Good berry picking in the fall.

A 169 (272 km) **F 189** (304.2 km) *CAUTION: Railroad crossing.* A solar collector here helps power the warning signals.

Denali State Park boundary (leaving park northbound, entering park southbound).

A 170 (273.6 km) **F 188** (302.5 km) Extra-wide shoulders west side of highway provide parking area.

A 174 (280 km) **F 184** (296.1 km) **Hurricane Gulch Bridge.** Parking areas at both ends of bridge. From the south end of the bridge, scramble through alders up the east bank of the gulch to find photographers' trail (unmarked). A 0.3-mile trail along edge of Hurricane Gulch offers good views of the bridge span and gulch. A pleasant walk, good berry picking in the fall. *Do not go too near the edge.*

Construction costs for the bridge were approximately $1.2 million. The 550-foot/deck of the bridge is 260 feet above Hurricane Creek, not as high as the railroad bridge that spans the gulch near the Chulitna River. From this bridge the highway begins a gradual descent northbound to Honolulu Creek.

A 176 (283.2 km) **F 182** (292.9 km) Paved turnout to east.

NOTE: Slow for curves northbound as highway descends long grade.

A 176.5 (284 km) **F 181.5** (292.1 km) Rough, narrow, double-ended gravel turnout to west with view of the Alaska Range.

A 177 (284.8 km) **F 181** (291.3 km) Gravel pit parking to west.

A 177.8 (286.1 km) **F 180.2** (290 km) Paved turnout to east. View of eroded bluffs to west.

A 178.1 (286.6 km) **F 179.9** (289.5 km) Bridge over Honolulu Creek. The highway begins a gradual ascent northbound to Broad Pass, the gap in the Alaska Range crossed by both the railroad and highway. Undeveloped parking areas below highway on the creek (narrow and bumpy access road).

A 179.7 (289.2 km) **F 178.3** (286.9 km) Paved turnout to west by small lake. In early September blueberries are plentiful for the next 25 miles.

A 180 (289.7 km) **F 178** (286.5 km) Narrow double-ended paved turnout to west by small lake. Short trail to **Mile 180 Lake,** stocked with grayling.

A 183.2 (294.8 km) **F 174.8** (281.3 km) Double-ended turnout to west of highway. Look to the west across the Chulitna River for dramatic view of the Alaska Range (weather permitting).

A 184.5 (296.9 km) **F 173.5** (279.2 km) Paved turnout to west.

A 185 (297.7 km) **F 173** (278.4 km) East Fork DOT/PF highway maintenance station.

A 185.1 (297.9 km) **F 172.9** (278.3 km) Bridge over East Fork Chulitna River.

A 185.6 (298.7 km) **F 172.4** (277.4 km) East Fork rest area (no sign at turnoff) on right northbound. A 0.5-mile paved loop gives access to a gravel picnic area with overnight parking, 23 tables, concrete fireplaces and picnic shelter. The rest area is in a bend of the East Fork Chulitna River amid a healthy growth of Alaskan spruce and birch. Cut wood is often available. ▲

A 186.3 (299.8 km) **F 171.7** (276.3 km) Small turnout to east; view of eroded bluffs.

A 187.5 (301.8 km) **F 170.5** (274.4 km) Paved double-ended turnout to west; small paved turnout east side of highway.

A 188.5 (303.3 km) **F 169.5** (272.8 km) **Igloo City**, an Alaskan landmark, 50 miles south of entrance to Denali National Park. New ownership. Unleaded, regular and diesel fuels, propane. Ask for 5-cent discount for cash fill-ups. Caravan discounts. Espresso, postcards, candy, snacks, soft drinks, ice, pay phone. Camping, lodging. Unique Alaskan art, gifts and souvenirs not seen elsewhere. Open 24 hours year-round. Phone (907) 768-2622. See display ad. [ADVERTISEMENT]

A 189.9 (305.6 km) **F 168.1** (270.5 km) Unmaintained, narrow gravel double-ended turnout to west.

A 191 (307.4 km) **F 167** (268.8 km) Large paved parking area to west. Look for cotton grass. There are 14 species of cotton grass in Alaska.

A 192.9 (310.4 km) **F 165.1** (265.7 km) Bed and breakfast 0.2 mile west.

A 194.3 (312.7 km) **F 163.7** (263.4 km) *CAUTION: Highway curves and crosses railroad tracks.*

A 194.5 (313 km) **F 163.5** (263.1 km) Bridge over Middle Fork Chulitna River. Rough gravel parking area at north end.

CAUTION: Windy area through Broad Pass.

A 195 (313.8 km) **F 163** (262.3 km) Entering **Broad Pass** northbound. Broad Pass is one of the most beautiful areas on the Parks Highway. A mountain valley, bare in some places, dotted with scrub spruce in others, and surrounded by mountain peaks, it provides a top-of-the-world feeling for the traveler, although it is one of the lowest summits along the North American mountain system. Named in 1898 by George Eldridge and Robert Muldrow, the 2,400-foot pass, sometimes called Caribou Pass, marks the divide between the drainage of rivers and streams that empty into Cook Inlet and those that empty into the Yukon River.

A 195.9 (315.3 km) **F 162.1** (260.9 km) Large paved turnout east; mountain views.

A 199 (320.3 km) **F 159** (255.9 km) Summit Lake (1.3 miles long) to east.

A 201 (323.5 km) **F 157** (252.7 km) Large paved parking area to east with mountain view.

A 201.4 (324.1 km) **F 156.6** (252 km) **Broad Pass summit** (not signed), 2,409 feet. Summit airport to west. According to Ray Atkins (Atkins Guiding and Flying Service in Cantwell), Summit airstrip was built at the start of WWII. Its location was considered to be far enough inland to make it invulnerable to carrier-based enemy aircraft. It was used as a P51 Mustang fighter base, and was supplied by the railroad (since the highway had not yet been built).

Also visible is the abandoned weather service station. The FAA maintains a remote weather reporting service and video camera here (www.akweathercams.com).

Private Aircraft: Summit airstrip; elev. 2,409 feet; length 3,800 feet; gravel; unmaintained.

A 201.9 (324.9 km) **F 156.1** (251.2 km) Small green-roofed white cabins at south end of Mirror Lake to east are privately-owned; no road access.

A 202.1 (325.2 km) **F 155.9** (250.9 km) Boundary of Matanuska–Susitna and Denali boroughs.

A 203.2 (327 km) **F 154.8** (249.1 km) *CAUTION: Railroad crossing.*

A 203.6 (327.7 km) **F 154.4** (248.5 km) Paved parking area with view to east.

A 208 (334.7 km) **F 150** (241.4 km) Small turnout to west at end of bridge over Pass Creek; blueberries in season.

A 209.5 (337.1 km) **F 148.5** (239 km) Bridge over Jack River.

A 209.9 (337.8 km) **F 148.1** (238.3 km) **Junction** of Parks and Denali highways. Turn west for Backwoods Lodge, Cantwell RV Park (0.3 mile), Cantwell Lodge (2 miles), Atkins Guiding & Flying Service (2.2 miles) and other Cantwell businesses (see description facing page). Turn east for Denali Highway.

Junction of the Parks Highway and the Denali Highway (Alaska Route 8). Turn west for Cantwell; see description this page. Turn east for Denali Highway; see the DENALI HIGHWAY section for log.

Cantwell

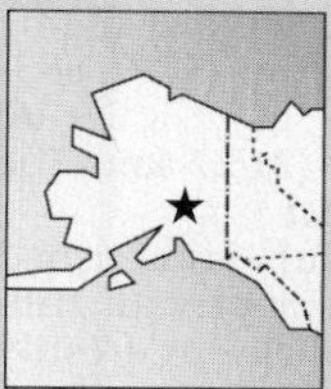

Located 1.8 miles west of Parks Highway, end of the Denali Highway. **Population:** 166. **Emergency Services: Alaska State Troopers**, business phone (907) 768-2202. **Fire Department**, emergency only phone (907) 768-2240. **Ambulance**, phone (907) 768-2982.

Elevation: 2,190 feet/668m. **Private Aircraft:** Cantwell airport, adjacent north; elev. 2,190 feet/668m; length 2,100 feet/640m; gravel, dirt; fuel 100LL.

Cantwell began as a railroad flag stop on the Alaska Railroad. The village was named for the Cantwell River, the original name of the Nenana River, which was named by Lt. Allen in 1885 for Lt. John C. Cantwell of the Revenue-Cutter Service, who explored the Kobuk River region.

Many of Cantwell's businesses are clustered around the intersection of the Denali and Parks highways or on the way into downtown Cantwell. Services include food, gas, lodging and camping.

Cantwell began as a flag stop on the Alaska Railroad. (© Bruce M. Herman)

Return to Milepost A 209.9 Parks Highway

CANTWELL ADVERTISERS

Atkins Guiding & Flying Service	Ph. (907) 768-2143
Backwoods Lodge	Ph. (907) 768-2232
Cantwell Lodge	Ph. (907) 768-2300
Cantwell RV Park	Ph. (907) 768-2210
Denali Manor Bed and Breakfast	Ph. (800) 378-5990

Beaver occur throughout most of Alaska. Adults can weigh up to 80 lbs.

(© Paul Souders)

A 210 (338 km) **F 148** (238.2 km) Cantwell post office (ZIP code 99729) west side of highway.

Denali Manor B&B. Welcome to Denali, where you can view Mount McKinley. Close access to Denali Highway. Full breakfast every morning: fresh golden brown potatoes, ham and bacon or Alaska sausage and bacon, scrambled eggs, pancakes or french toast, fruits and juices—"I won't let you go away hungry!" Call 1-800-378-5990 for reservations. [ADVERTISEMENT]

A 210.3 (338.4 km) **F 147.7** (237.7 km) Gas station (diesel), food mart and gift shop.

Cantwell Food Mart and Parkway Gift Shop. See display ad this section.

A 212 (341.2 km) **F 146** (235 km) Slide area northbound.

A 213.9 (344.2 km) **F 144.1** (231.9 km) Paved double-ended parking area to west among tall white spruce and fireweed.

A 215.3 (346.5 km) **F 142.7** (229.6 km) Access road on west side of highway to Nenana River; staging area for river boats. The Nenana River parallels the highway northbound.

A 215.7 (347.1 km) **F 142.3** (229 km) First bridge northbound over the Nenana River. Highway narrows northbound.

A 216.2 (347.9 km) **F 141.8** (228.2 km) Entering Game Management Unit 20A and leaving unit 13E northbound.

A 216.3 (348.1 km) **F 141.7** (228 km) Paved double-ended turnout to west. Good spot for photos of **Panorama Mountain** (elev. 5,778 feet), the prominent peak in the Alaska Range visible to the east.

A 218.5 (351.6 km) **F 139.5** (224.5 km) Paved double-ended turnout to west with beautiful view of Nenana River.

A 219 (352.4 km) **F 139** (223.7 km) Slide area: Watch for rocks next 0.4 mile/0.6 km northbound.

A 219.8 (353.7 km) **F 138.2** (222.4 km) Paved double-ended parking area to west overlooking Nenana River.

A 220.6 (355 km) **F 137.4** (221.1 km) Long, paved, double-ended turnout to west (old highway alignment) along the Nenana River.

A 222.2 (357.6 km) **F 135.8** (218.5 km) Large paved double-ended turnout to west beside Nenana River.

A 222.5 (358.1 km) **F 135.5** (218.1 km) Snow poles beside roadway guide snowplows in winter.

A 223.9 (360.3 km) **F 134.1** (215.8 km) Carlo Creek Lodge to west.

Carlo Creek Lodge. Located 12 miles south of Denali Park entrance. 32 wooded acres bordered by beautiful Carlo Creek, the Nenana River and Denali National Park. Cozy creekside log cabins with own bathroom, showers. RV park, dump station, potable water, propane. Clean bathroom, showers. Dishwashing facility. Individual sheltered tent sites each with picnic table and firepit. Unique gift shop. Small store. Information. Pay phone. You won't be disappointed. It's a beautiful place to be. HC 2, Box 1530, Healy, AK 99743. Summer phone (907) 683-2576; winter phone (907) 683-2573. [ADVERTISEMENT] ▲

A 224 (360.5 km) **F 134** (215.7 km) The Perch Restaurant uphill to east.

The Perch. A beautiful, established restaurant-bar perched on a private hill. Spectacular dining, specializes in freshly

baked bread, seafood and steaks. Also, take-out giant cinnamon rolls. Breakfast 6 A.M. to 11:30 A.M.; dinner 5 P.M. to 10 P.M., open year-round. 10 new cabins. Sleeping cabins with central bath, some with private baths, beside Carlo Creek. Owners/operators, Duane and Leslie Watters. Phone (907) 683-2523. P.O. Box 53, Denali Park, AK 99755. See display ad in the DENALI NATIONAL PARK section. [ADVERTISEMENT]

A 224 (360.5 km) **F 134** (215.7 km) Bridge over Carlo Creek. McKinley Creekside Cabins to east at north end of bridge.

McKinley Creekside Cabins. Scenic, peaceful setting on the banks of Carlo Creek. All cabins have private bath. Home-style cafe and bakery, gourmet espresso bar, tour desk, gift shop, barbecue area. Reservations: (888) 5-DENALI, or (907) 683-2277. Fax (907) 683-1558. P.O. Box 89, Denali National Park, AK 99755. Web: www.mckinleycabins.com. [ADVERTISEMENT]

A 224.1 (360.6 km) **F 133.9** (215.5 km) **Carlo Heights Bed & Breakfast and Denali Sled Dog School.** Share seclusion and spectacular views. Located on bluff overlooking Nenana River and Alaska Range. Accommodations include 2 double rooms, a private suite, and full kitchen. Open year-round. Reservations recommended during summertime and required during off-season. Sled dog school offers dog mushing courses and tours. Box 86, Denali Park, AK 99755. (907) 683-5212; www.alaskabest.net; carloheights @alaskabest.net.

A 225 (362.1 km) **F 133** (214 km) Beautiful mountain views southbound.

A 226 (363.7 km) **F 132** (212.4 km) Fang Mountain (elev. 6,736 feet/2,053m) may be visible to the west through the slash in the mountains.

A 229 (368.5 km) **F 129** (207.6 km) Lodge and cabins to east.

Denali Backcountry Lodge. Stop at Denali Cabins (located at **Milepost 229**) and visit the sales office for Denali Backcountry Lodge. The wilderness vacation lodge is for those who want to escape the park's crowded entrance and immerse themselves deep within Denali National Park for a few days. Located at the end of the 95-mile park road, Denali Backcountry Lodge features full-service accommodations, dining room and lounge. One- to 4-night stays include round-trip transportation from the train depot, all meals and lodging, guided hikes, wildlife viewing, bicycling, photography and natural history programs. Many famous naturalists are found staying

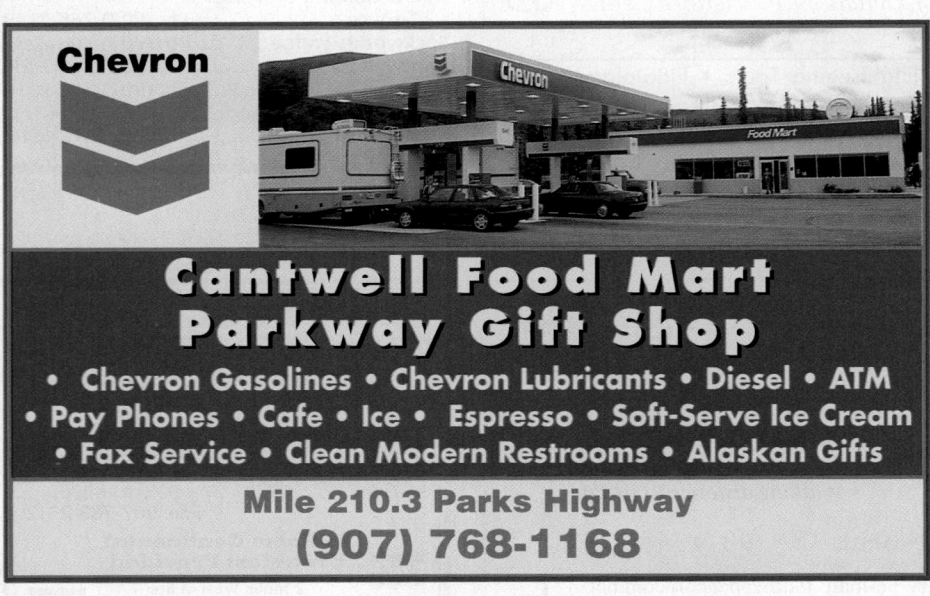

Peak times for seeing aurora displays are March–April and September–October.

at the lodge and occasionally they conduct special presentations. Credit cards accepted and discounts given for last-minute bookings if space is available. P.O. Box 189, Denali National Park, AK 99755. Internet: www.denalilodge.com/mp. Phone (800) 841-0692. [ADVERTISEMENT]

Denali Cabins. Private cabins with bath, outdoor hot tubs, complimentary coffee and extensive information about Denali National Park. Restaurant on premises. Seasonal service mid-May through

mid-September. Toll free (888) 560-2489. Brochure: 200 W. 34th Ave., #362, Anchorage, AK 99503. Fax (907) 243-2062 or summer (907) 683-2595. Web: www.alaskan.com/denalicabins. See display ad in the DENALI NATIONAL PARK section. [ADVERTISEMENT]

A 229.2 (368.8 km) **F 128.8** (207.3 km) Private airstrip. Flightseeing service.

Denali Air, Inc. Fly closer to Denali's beauty on our 1-hour aerial tour of Mount McKinley/Denali National Park. Our private airstrip is the closest to Denali Park hotels

and the Alaska Range, offering the best tour and value. A pioneer service with the most experienced pilots. Two person minimum. Reservations: (907) 683-2261. See display ad in the DENALI NATIONAL PARK section. [ADVERTISEMENT]

A 229.7 (369.7 km) **F 128.3** (206.5 km) Double-ended paved turnout to west.

A 230.5 (370.9 km) **F 127.5** (205.2 km) *Highway descends 6 percent grade northbound.*

A 231.1 (371.9 km) **F 126.9** (204.2 km) **McKinley Village Resort** in Denali is nestled in the trees on the banks of the Nenana River at Milepost 231.3 and boasts 150 comfortable rooms, rustic lobby and fireplace, casual dining room, lounge, shopping and full-service tour and activities desk. Call 1-800-276-7234. In Anchorage (907) 276-7234. Or visit www.denalinationalpark.com. [ADVERTISEMENT]

Denali Grizzly Bear Cabins & Campground. South boundary Denali National Park. Denali's only AAA-approved campground. Drive directly to your individual kitchen, sleeping or tent cabin with its old-time Alaskan atmosphere overlooking scenic Nenana River. Two conveniently located buildings with toilets, sinks, coin-operated hot showers. Advance reservations suggested. Tenting and RV campsite available in peaceful wooded areas. Hookups. Propane, laundromat. Caravans welcome! Coffee and rolls, ice cream, snacks, groceries, ice, liquor store, Alaskan gifts, tour desk. VISA, MasterCard, Discover accepted. Owned and operated by pioneer Alaskan family. Reservations (907) 683-2696 (summer); (907) 683-1337 (winter). Internet: www.alaskaone.com/dengrzly/index.htm. See display ad this section and the DENALI NATIONAL PARK section. [ADVERTISEMENT] ▲

Denali River Cabins. Located on the banks of the Nenana River near the entrance to Denali National Park, our cedar cabins offer the ideal base for your Denali Park experience. Cozy cedar cabins are fully furnished, with private baths. Some front directly on the river. Restaurant and bar services are a short walk from the cabins, near to our gift shop, bookstore and Alaskana library. We feature 3 large sun decks for picnicking or just relaxing on the river, and a Finnish-style sauna for guest use. Complete tour desk and information service is available for our guests planning excursions around and into Denali Park. Phone 1-800-230-7275 year-round for reservations. E-mail us at: drcriver@mtaonline.net. See our web site at: www.denalirivercabins.com. [ADVERTISEMENT]

A 231.3 (372.2 km) **F 126.7** (203.9 km) **Crabb's Crossing**, second bridge northbound over the Nenana River. Small paved turnout with wide shoulders west side of highway.

At the north end of this bridge is the boundary of Denali National Park and Preserve. From here north for 6.8 miles/10.9 km the Parks Highway is within the boundaries of the park and travelers must abide by park rules. No discharge of firearms permitted.

A 233 (375 km) **F 125** (201.2 km) Gravel turnout to east.

A 234.1 (376.7 km) **F 123.9** (199.4 km) Double-ended scenic viewpoint with litter barrels to east. No overnight parking or camping. Mount Fellows (elev. 4,476 feet/1,364m) to the east. The constantly changing shadows make this an excellent camera subject. Exceptionally beautiful in the evening. To the southeast stands Pyramid Peak (elev. 5,201 feet/1,585m).

A 235.1 (378.4 km) **F 122.9** (197.8 km) *CAUTION: Railroad crossing.* Solar panels and wind generators provide power for crossing signals. Travel information tune to 1610 radio (sign).

A 236 (379.8 km) **F 122** (196.3 km) Begin 55 mph/86 kmph speed zone northbound.

A 236.7 (380.9 km) **F 121.3** (195.2 km) Alaska Railroad crosses over highway.

NOTE: Highway begins 6 percent downgrade northbound.

A 237.2 (381.7 km) **F 120.8** (194.4 km)

One of the clusters of businesses along the Parks Highway near the park entrance.

(© Kris Graef, staff)

Riley Creek bridge.

A 237.3 (381.9 km) **F 120.7** (194.2 km) Turnoff for **Denali National Park and Preserve**. The park visitor center is a half-mile west of the highway junction on the Park Road.

Junction with Park Road. See DENALI NATIONAL PARK section on page 427 for Park Road log and details on the park.

McKINLEY PARK (pop. 169 in summer), refers to the community that has developed around the national park, providing services and seasonal workers for the Park Service. Businesses clustered around the park entrance along the Parks Highway here offer a variety of services to the highway traveler and park visitor, including river running, gift shops, accommodations, gas stations, foodmarts, and restaurants. Most are open in summer only.

Denali National Park Hotel offers the only accommodations inside the park and is the center for visitor activities. A short walk from the train depot and adjacent walking and hiking trails, the hotel features dining, gifts, a snack shop, grocery store and unique railcar lounge. The auditorium hosts National Park Service programs. Tours and activities can be arranged at the front desk. Call 1-800-276-7234. In Anchorage (907) 276-7234. Or visit www.denalinationalpark.com. [ADVERTISEMENT]

A 238 (383 km) **F 120** (193.4 km) Third bridge northbound over the Nenana River. Staging area for raft trips on the Nenana River.

Nenana Raft Adventures. Raft Denali with the first raft company in Alaska to

outfit every client in a full drysuit. Day trips as well as multi-day expeditions on the Talkeetna River. Oar rafts and paddle rafting both available. Our riverfront office is directly next door to ERA Helicopters. Phone 1-800-7899-RAFT; in Denali (907) 683-RAFT. [ADVERTISEMENT]

Dall sheep are regularly sighted in the early and late summer months on Sugarloaf Mountain (elev. 4,450 feet), to the east (closed to hunting). Mount Healy (elev. 5,716 feet) is to the west.

Southbound for 6.8 miles the Parks Highway is within the boundaries of Denali National Park and Preserve and travelers must abide by park rules. No discharge of firearms.

A 238.1 (383.2 km) **F 119.9** (193 km) Public access to Nenana River. **A 238.3** (383.5 km) **F 119.7** (192.6 km) Kingfisher Creek.

Denali Raft Adventures. Come with the original Nenana River rafters! Paddleboats

too! Age 5 or older welcome. 7 departures daily. Whitewater or scenic floats. Get away to untouched wilderness! 2-hour, 4-hour, full-day and overnight trips available. See display ad in DENALI NATIONAL PARK section. Phone (907) 683-2234. Internet: www.denaliraft.com. E-mail: denraft@mtaonline.net. VISA, Mastercard accepted. [ADVERTISEMENT]

A 238.4 (383.6 km) **F 119.6** (192.5 km) **Denali Bluffs Hotel.** AAA approved. The newest and closest hotel to the Denali National Park and Preserve entrance. 112 rooms; each room features 2 double beds, TVs, phones, refrigerators, in-room coffee, cafe. Spectacular views of the Alaska Range. The lodge features a large stone fireplace and cathedral ceilings. There are comfortable sitting areas inside the lodge or outside on the deck to enjoy the panoramic views. Gift shop and coin-operated laundry. Shuttle service to all area facilities. Complete tour and activity desk. Wheelchair accessible. Open mid-May through mid-September. Credit cards accepted. P.O. Box 72460, Fairbanks, AK 99707. Phone (907) 683-7000. Fax (907) 683-7500. E-mail: denali@denalibluffs.com. Internet: wwwdenalibluffs.com. See display ad in the DENALI NATIONAL PARK section. ♿ [ADVERTISEMENT]

A 238.5 (383.8 km) **F 119.5** (192.3 km) Alaska flag display in front of Denali Princess Lodge (west side of highway) features a 10-by-15-foot/3-by-5-m state flag and plaques detailing history of flag design and song. Denali Crow's Nest to east of highway.

Denali Princess Lodge. Riverside lodging near the entrance to Denali National Park featuring spectacular park and Nenana River views, several dining options including dinner theatre, tour desk, gift shop, complimentary shuttle to rail depot and park activities. Open mid-May through mid-September. Reservations (800) 426-0500 year-round. [ADVERTISEMENT]

Denali Crow's Nest Log Cabins and The Overlook Bar & Grill. Open mid-May to mid-September, offering the finest view in the area. Close to park entrance. Authentic Alaska log cabins with hotel comforts; all rooms with private bath. Courtesy transportation. Hot tub, tour bookings. Dine on

steaks, seafood, burgers, salmon and halibut indoors or on the deck at The Overlook Bar & Grill. 76 varieties of beer, 9 draft beers; meals 11 A.M. to 11 P.M. Bar open till midnight. For restaurant's courtesy shuttle from all local hotels, call (907) 683-2723; fax (907) 683-2323; Out-of-state toll-free reservations (888) 917-8130. See display ad in DENALI NATIONAL PARK section. [ADVERTISEMENT]

A 238.8 (384.3 km) **F 119.2** (191.8 km) **Denali Sourdough Cabins.** Enjoy the beauty of Denali National Park from your individual cabin set in a spruce forest one mile from the park. The cabins offer comfortable accommodations in a warm atmosphere, all with private bath and within walking distance to all services. Courtesy transportation available. May to September. Phone (907) 683-2773, 1-800-354-6020; fax (907) 683-2357. www.denalisourdoughcabins.com. VISA, MasterCard, American Express accepted. See display ad in DENALI NATIONAL PARK section. [ADVERTISEMENT] ▲

A 238.9 (384.5 km) **F 119.1** (191.7 km) **Denali Outdoor Center.** Denali's most diversified river outfitter! Oar rafts, paddle rafts, inflatable kayak tours and mountain bike rentals. 2-hour, 4-hour, and 1/2-day guided whitewater and scenic wilderness river trips. Custom "drysuits," professional guides and exceptional equipment provided. Ages 5 and up. Call for reservations (888) 303-1925 or (907) 683-1925. Major credit cards accepted. [ADVERTISEMENT]

A 239.1 (384.8 km) **F 118.9** (191.3 km) **McKinley Chalet Resort** in Denali features over 300 comfortable rooms and mini-suites and provides the most convenient access to Denali Park Tours, river rafting, gold panning and walking trails. Home of the famous Alaska Cabin Nite Dinner Theater and featuring the Chalet Center Cafe and

Nenana View Restaurant with private deck overlooking the river. Call 1-800-276-7234. In Anchorage (907) 276-7234. Or visit www.denalinationalpark.com. [ADVERTISEMENT]

Alaska Raft Adventures in Denali offers river rafting with experienced guides. Float through a glacial valley along the Park boundary on the Wilderness Run, or take on exciting whitewater on the Canyon Run. Free transportation available between area hotels and train depot. Visit the tour desks at McKinley Chalet or McKinley Village resorts. (907)276-7234. [ADVERTISEMENT]

A 240 (386.2 km) **F 118** (189.9 km) Bridge over Iceworm Gulch.

CAUTION: Sharp curves, rock slide area, northbound. Do not park along the highway. Use the many parking areas provided. High winds in the Nenana Canyon can make this stretch of road dangerous for campers and motorhomes.The 4.8 miles of road and 7 bridges in the rugged Nenana Canyon cost $7.7 million to build.

A 240.3 (386.7 km) **F 117.7** (189.4 km) Turnout to west.

A 240.4 (386.9 km) **F 117.6** (189.2 km) Entrance to Denali Riverside RV Park to west. ▲

Denali Riverside RV Park. Two miles from park entrance. 100 sites, 20 to 50 amp, pull-throughs, dry and tent camping. Shoulder season discount and 25 percent off third night. Handicapped-accessible restrooms, pay showers, laundry, propane, gift shop, tours. Caravans and groups welcome. Reservations: P.O. Box 158, Denali National Park, AK 99755; phone (888) 778-8800; alaskarv@aol.com; www.alaskarv.com. [ADVERTISEMENT] ▲

A 240.7 (387.3 km) **F 117.3** (188.8 km) Paved double-ended turnout to west beside river.

A 241.6 (388.8 km) **F 116.4** (187.3 km) Large gravel turnout to west.

A 242.1 (389.6 km) **F 115.9** (186.5 km) Paved parking area to west.

A 242.3 (389.9 km) **F 115.7** (186.2 km) Paved double-ended turnout to west.

A 242.4 (390.1 km) **F 115.6** (186) Dragonfly Creek bridge.

A 242.7 (390.6 km) **F 115.3** (185.5 km) Paved double-ended turnout to west.

CAUTION: Windy area next mile northbound. Wind sock mid-span.

A 242.9 (390.9 km) **F 115.1** (185.2 km) Moody Bridge. This 4th bridge northbound over the Nenana River measures 174 feet/53m from its deck to the bottom of the canyon. Dall sheep can be spotted from the bridge. Entering Game Management Unit 20A northbound, 20C southbound.

A 243.5 (391.9 km) **F 114.5** (184.3 km) Bridge over Bison Gulch. Sharp turn at north end to east for paved viewpoint.

A 244.1 (392.8 km) **F 113.9** (183.3 km) Large gravel turnout to east; abrupt edge.

A 244.5 (393.5 km) **F 113.5** (182.6 km) Bridge over Antler Creek.

NOTE: Watch for bumpy, patched pavement and frost heaves northbound.

A 245.1 (394.4 km) **F 112.9** (181.7 km) **Denali RV Park & Motel.** 90 full and partial RV hookups, 30-amp electric, pull-throughs, level sites, easy access. RV rates $15–$26 (20 percent off extra RV nights). Caravans welcome! Private restrooms with pay showers, dump station. 14 motel rooms. Double with bath $74; family units with full kitchen and TV $119. Laundry, pay phones, outdoor cooking area, covered meeting area. Gift shop, tour booking, information. Beautiful panoramic mountain views, hiking trails. E-mail access line available. VISA/ Mastercard/Discover. Web address: www.denaliRVpark.com. E-mail: stay@denaliRVpark.com. Located 8 miles north of park entrance. Box 155, Denali National Park, AK 99755. (800) 478-1501, (907) 683-1500. See dislay ad in the DENALI NATIONAL PARK section. [ADVERTISEMENT] ▲

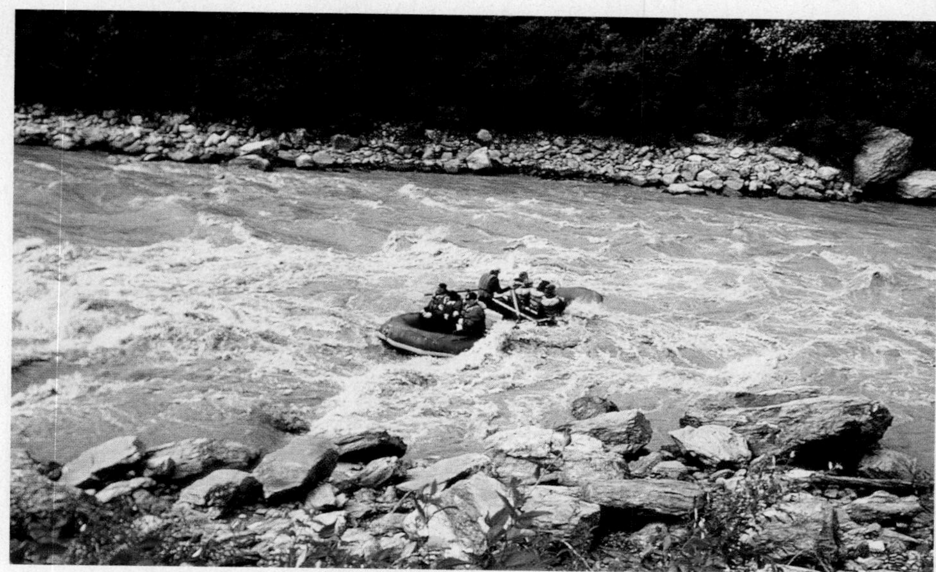

Rafting the Nenana River at Denali National Park. (© Loren Taft/Alaskan Images)

A 246.8 (397.2 km) **F 111.2** (179 km) Paved turnout to east.

A 247 (397.5 km) **F 111** (178.6 km) Side road leads 1 mile to **Otto Lake**, 5 miles to Black Diamond Coal Mine. Access to Denali hostel, bed and breakfasts, golf driving range and RV park. Primitive parking area on lakeshore (0.8-mile drive in) with toilet, litter barrels, shallow boat launch. Stocked with rainbow and coho. ▲

Otto Lake R.V. Park and Campground. Beautiful mountain views from wooded lakeside RV and tent sites, 1/2 mile west of Parks Highway on Otto Lake Road. Spacious and secluded sites with picnic tables, firepits, firewood, potable water, toilets, dump station and pay phone. Boat rentals. Family camping at its best, not a gravel strip. Located 9.7 miles north of Denali National Park entrance. Phone (907) 683-2603 (winter); (907) 683-2100 (summer); Fax (907) 683-1230; E-mail: ottolake@mtaonline.net. Web site: www.ottolakealaska.com. [ADVERTISEMENT] ▲

A 248 (399.1 km) **F 110** (177 km) *Speed zone begins 45 mph northbound.*

A 248.2 (399.4 km) **F 109.8** (176.7 km) Gas station.

A 248.3 (399.6 km) **F 109.7** (176.5 km) Auto and truck repair and parts.

A 248.4 (399.8 km) **F 109.6** (176.4 km) Gas station. RV park.

McKinley RV & Campground. See display ad this section. ▲

A 248.5 (399.9 km) **F 109.5** (176.2 km) Paved

Healy

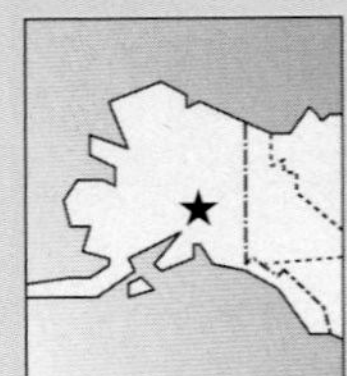

Located on a spur road just east of the Parks Highway. **Population:** 646. **Emergency Services: Alaska State Troopers,** phone (907) 683-2232. **Fire Department,** Tri–Valley Volunteer Fire Dept., phone 911 or (907) 683-2223. **Clinic,** Healy Clinic, located on 2nd floor of Tri–Valley Community Center at Mile 0.5 Healy Spur Road, phone (907) 683-2211 or 911 (open 24 hours).

Visitor Information: Available at the Healy Senior Center, located on Healy Spur Road behind the grocery store. Open 11 A.M. to 7 P.M., year-round; phone (907) 683-1317.

Elevation: 1,294 feet. **Radio:** KUAC-FM 101.7. **Private Aircraft:** Healy River airstrip adjacent north; length 2,800 feet; paved; unattended.

Burls on spruce trees are harvested for wood crafts. (© Susan Cole Kelly)

Healy's power plant has the distinction of being the largest coal-fired steam plant in Alaska, as well as the only mine-mouth power plant. This plant is part of the Golden Valley Electric Assoc., which furnishes electric power for Fairbanks and vicinity. The Fairbanks–Tanana Valley area uses primarily coal and also oil to meet its electrical needs.

Across the Nenana River lie the mining settlements of Suntrana and Usibelli. Dry Creek, Healy and Nenana river valleys comprise the area referred to as Tri–Valley. Coal mining began here in 1918 and has grown to become Alaska's largest coal mining operation. Usibelli Coal Mine, the state's only commercial coal mine, mines about 800,000 tons of coal a year, supplying South Korea, the University of Alaska, the military and other Fairbanks-area utilities.

From the highway, you may see a 33-cubic-yard walking dragline (named Ace in the Hole by local schoolchildren in a contest) removing the soil, or overburden, to expose the coal seams. This 4,275,000-lb. machine, erected in 1978, moves an average of 24,000 cubic yards each 24 hours. Private vehicles are not allowed into the mining area and no tours are available.

Denali Suites. Located 15 minutes north of entrance to Denali National Park on Healy Spur Road. Units include 2 or 3 bedrooms, kitchen and dining area, living room with queen-sized hide-a-bed, TV and VCR, and private baths. Coin-operated laundry facilities. Clean, comfortable, affordable. Each unit accommodates up to 6 people, one accommodates 8, with 2 private baths; families welcome. VISA, MasterCard, Discover. Open all year. Call (907) 683-2848 or write Box 393, Healy, AK 99743. E-mail: bharris@mail.denali.k12.ak.us. Internet: www.alaskaone.com/densuites. See display ad in the DENALI NATIONAL PARK section. [ADVERTISEMENT]

Greyfox Manor, located at Mile 0.75 Healy Spur Road, is a comfortable, spacious, smoke-free home with a family atmosphere, conveniently situated near Denali National Park. Offering a peaceful respite for weary travelers. Full breakfast served daily. Early continental breakfasts available. Open year-round. Credit cards accepted. Phone (907) 683-2419 for reservations. [ADVERTISEMENT]

Return to Milepost A 248.7 Parks Highway

HEALY ADVERTISERS

Denali North Star Inn	Mile 248.8 Parks Hwy.
Denali Suites	Ph. (907) 683-2848
Earth Song Lodge	Mile 251.1 Parks Hwy.
Greyfox Manor	Ph. (907) 683-2419
Motel Nord Haven	Mile 249.5 Parks Hwy.
Pat & Windell's Bed and Breakfast	Ph. (800) 683-2472
Stampede Lodge	Mile 248.8 Parks Hwy.
Totem Inn	Ph. (907) 683-2384

turnout to east.

A 248.7 (400.2 km) **F 109.3** (175.9 km)

Junction with spur road to community of Healy (see description this page).

Homes and businesses of Healy are dispersed along the highway from here north to **Milepost A 249.6** and in the first mile east along the spur road toward the Nenana River. Hotel and motel accommodations are available at the highway junction, and several bed and breakfasts are located along the spur road.

Totem Inn. Full-service facility year-round. Deluxe, mid-range and economy rooms, restaurant, lounge and gift shop. Satellite TV and laundry facilities for guests. 24-hour access to pay telephones. Good food, reasonable rates, Alaskan hospitality. MasterCard/VISA/Discover. Restaurant (907) 683-2420. Motel (907) 683-2384. Fax (907) 683-2432. [ADVERTISEMENT]

A 248.8 (400.4 km) **F 109.2** (175.7 km) North side of Healy Spur Road intersection.

Denali North Star Inn is a full-service year-round hotel located in Healy, 10 miles north of Denali National Park at Milepost 248.8 George Parks Highway (Route 3). Amenities offered to our guests include comfortable, reasonably priced rooms; finest food and cocktail lounge in the Denali Park area. Alaskan gifts, self-service laundry, hair salon, and recreation and exercise areas with tanning beds and saunas. Information and reservations for Denali Park tours and other activities; courtesy shuttle service. (8800) 684-1560. [ADVERTISEMENT]

Stampede Lodge and Bushmaster Grill. Historic Alaskan lodge and restaurant recently remodeled. Warm, comfortable atmosphere, located 10 minutes from the park entrance. Private baths and phones in all rooms. Free train station pickup. Restaurant open 6 A.M.–10 P.M. Denali's best value—all rooms $79–89. Phone (800) 478-2370, fax (907) 683-2243. [ADVERTISEMENT]

A 249 (400.7 km) **F 109** (175.4 km) Suntrana Road, post office and Tri–Valley School.

A 249.2 (401 km) **F 108.8** (175.1 km) Gas station.

Wally's Healy Tesoro. See display ad this section.

A 249.3 (401.2 km) **F 108.7** (174.9 km) Dry Creek Bridge No. 1.

A 249.5 (401.5 km) **F 108.5** (174.6 km) **Motel Nord Haven.** Meticulously kept family-owned inn. 24 large rooms, all non-smoking, feature queen beds, TVs, telephones, private baths, and Alaskan art. Let us pack your lunch for your Denali Park visit! Peaceful location away from the crowds and only a 15-minute drive from park entrance. Open year-round. Phone 1-800-683-4501. Fax (907) 683-4503. E-mail: nordhaven@ptialaska.net. Web site: www.ptialaska.net/~nordhavn/. [ADVERTISEMENT]

A 249.8 (402 km) **F 108.2** (174.1 km) Dry Creek Bridge No. 2. Good berry picking area first part of August.

Speed zone begins 45 mph southbound.

A 251.1 (404.1 km) **F 106.9** (172 km) Stampede Road to west. Lignite Road to east.

Earth Song Lodge, Denali's natural retreat. Enjoy the Denali Park area without the crowds. Ten charming log cabins with private baths. Evening programs by staff naturalist at comfortable central lodge. Dog sled demonstrations and rides. Continental breakfast available. Located on scenic and historic Stampede Road, just north of the

park. Wonderful views of Denali and wildlife. Open year-round. Phone/fax (907) 683-2863. P.O. Box 89-MP, Healy, AK 99743. Internet: www.earthsonglodge.com. E-mail: earthsong@mail.denali.k12.ak.us. See display ad in the DENALI NATIONAL PARK section.
[ADVERTISEMENT]

A 251.2 (404.3 km) **F 106.8** (171.9 km) Paved turnout to west. Coal seams visible in bluff to east.

A 252.4 (406.2 km) **F 105.6** (169.9 km) Gravel turnout to west.

A 252.5 (406.4 km) **F 105.5** (169.8 km) Bridge over **Panguingue Creek**. Moderate success fishing for grayling. This stream, which flows 8 miles/13 km to the Nenana River, was named for a Philippine card game.

A 254 (408.7 km) **F 104** (167.4 km) *Watch for rough road (bumps, dips, loose gravel, patched pavement) northbound to Nenana.*

A 259.4 (417.5 km) **F 98.6** (158.7 km) Large paved turnout to east. Views of Rex Dome to the northeast. Walker and Jumbo domes to the east. Liberty Bell mining area lies between the peaks and highway.

A 260.9 (419.8 km) **F 97.1** (156.3 km) Gravel turnout to east. Look for bank swallows, small brown birds that nest in clay and sand banks near streams and along highways. Pond with beaver dam to west.

A 262.7 (422.8 km) **F 95.3** (153.4 km) Large gravel turnout to east.

A 264.5 (425.7 km) **F 93.5** (150.5 km) Paved turnout to west.

A 268 (431.3 km) **F 90** (144.8 km) *CAUTION: Frost heaves.*

A 269 (432.9 km) **F 89** (143.2 km) June Creek rest area and picnic spot to east; large gravel parking area. Gravel road leads down to lower parking area on June Creek (trailers and large RVs check turnaround space before driving down). Wooden stairs lead up to the picnic spot and a view of the Nenana River. There are picnic tables, fireplaces, toilets, a litter bin and a sheltered table. Cut wood may be available.

A 269.4 (433.5 km) **F 88.6** (142.6 km) Gravel turnout to east. Bridge over Bear Creek.

A 271.5 (436.9 km) **F 86.5** (139.2 km) Paved turnout to west.

A 272 (437.7 km) **F 86** (138.4 km) Extra-wide shoulders provide parking area next mile northbound.

A 275.6 (443.5 km) **F 82.4** (132.6 km) Entering Game Management Unit 20A northbound, 20C southbound.

A 275.8 (443.9 km) **F 82.2** (132.3 km) Rex Bridge over Nenana River.

A 276 (444.2 km) **F 82** (132 km) **Tatlanika Trading Co.** Located in a beautiful pristine wilderness setting. Tent sites and RV parking with electricity, water, dump station, showers. 39 miles from Denali National Park on the Nenana River. Our gift shop features a gathering of handmade art/crafts/artifacts from various villages. See the rare Samson fox, along with relics and antiques

Watch for moose along the Parks Highway. (© Robin Brandt)

from Alaska's colorful past in a museum atmosphere. Many historical and educational displays. Nothing sold from overseas. Visitor information. Coffee, pop, juice, snacks. Clean restrooms. This is a must stop. See display ad this section. [ADVERTISEMENT] ▲

A 276.4 (444.8 km) **F 81.6** (131.3 km) *CAUTION: Railroad crossing.*

A 280 (450.6 km) **F 78** (125.5 km) Lodge with dining and a cafe/grocery.

Clear Sky Lodge. See display ad this section.

A 280.1 (451.8 km) **F 77.9** (125.4 km) **Rochester Lodge.** See display ad this section.

A 282.3 (454.3 km) **F 75.7** (121.8 km) Denali Borough Landfill.

CAUTION: Moose Danger Zone next 22 miles northbound. Watch for moose!

A 283.5 (456.2 km) **F 74.5** (119.9 km) Access road leads west 1 mile to **Clear Air Force Station** (ballistic missile early warning site) and 6 miles to **ANDERSON** (pop. 517). Clear is a military installation; sign at turnoff states it is unlawful to enter without permission. However, you can drive into Anderson without permission.

Anderson, named for homesteader Arthur Anderson, was settled in the late 1950s and was incorporated in 1962. **Visitor information:** Contact the city office at (907) 582-2500. **Emergency services:** Anderson Fire Dept./EMS Ambulance, phone 911. Anderson has a city campground with 40 sites on the Nenana River. The community also has churches, a restaurant, softball fields and shooting range. ▲

Anderson Riverside Park. Come enjoy our city's 616 beautiful acres located along the bank of the Nenana River! Featuring restrooms, showers, RV dump station, electrical hookups. Riverside campsites, rustic campsites with barbecue pits, picnic area with covered pavilion, fireplace. Shooting range, bandstand, telephone. Home of the annual Anderson Bluegrass Festival, held the last weekend in July. City of Anderson, P.O. Box 3100, Anderson, AK 99744. Phone (907) 582-2500; fax (907) 582-2496. [ADVERTISEMENT] ▲

Private Aircraft: Clear Airport, 3 nm SE; elev. 552 feet; length 4,000 feet; asphalt; unattended. Clear Sky Lodge airstrip, 4 nm S; elev. 650 feet; length 2,500 feet; gravel, earth.

A 284.2 (457.4 km) **F 73.8** (118.8 km) AT&T/Alascom tower to west.

A 285.7 (459.8 km) **F 72.3** (116.3 km) Julius Creek bridge.

A 286.3 (460.7 km) **F 71.7** (115.4 km) View of Mount McKinley southbound.

A 286.8 (461.5 km) **F 71.2** (114.6 km) Large double-ended paved parking area to east.

A 288.3 (463.9 km) **F 69.7** (112.2 km) Denali Borough boundary.

A 288.7 (464.6 km) **F 69.3** (111.5 km) Roadhouse.

A 296.7 (477.5 km) **F 61.3** (98.7 km) Bridge over **Fish Creek.** Small gravel turnout with litter barrels by creek. Access to creek at south end of bridge; moderate success fishing for grayling.

A 298 (479.6 km) **F 60** (96.5 km) Tamarack Inn. Emergency phone.

A 301.4 (485 km) **F 56.6** (91.1 km) Nenana city limits.

A 302.9 (487.4 km) **F 55.1** (88.7 km) Nenana municipal rifle range.

A 303 (487.6 km) **F 55** (88.5 km) *Begin 45 mph speed zone northbound.*

A 303.7 (488.7 km) **F 54.3** (87.4 km) Nenana airport (see Private Aircraft information in Nenana).

A 304.5 (490 km) **F 53.5** (86.1 km) Chevron gas station, diesel, food mart to west.

A Frame Service. See display ad this section.

CAUTION: Moose Danger Zone next 22 miles southbound. Watch for moose!

Nenana

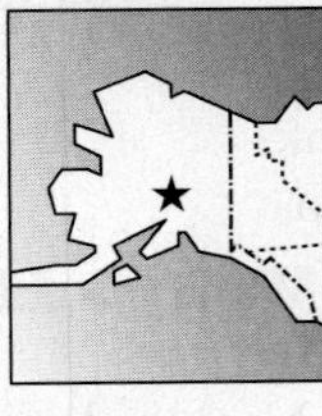

A 304.5 (490 km) **F 53.5** (86.1 km) Located at the confluence of the Tanana and Nenana rivers. **Population:** 348. **Emergency Services:** Emergency only (fire, police, ambulance), phone 911. **Fire Department/EMT**, phone (907) 832-5632.

Visitor Information: In the sod-roofed log cabin at the junction of the highway and A Street. Open 8 A.M. to 6 P.M., 7 days a week, Memorial Day to Labor Day; phone (907) 832-9953. Pay phone. Ice Classic tick-

ets may be purchased here. Picnic tables and restrooms are beside the restored *Taku Chief,* located behind the visitor information center. This proud little tugboat plied the waters of the Tanana, Yukon and Koyukuk rivers for many years.

Elevation: 400 feet/122m. **Radio:** KIAM 630, KUAC-FM 91.1. **Transportation: Air**—Nenana maintains an FAA-approved airport. **Railroad**—The Alaska Railroad.

Private Aircraft: Nenana Municipal Airport, 0.9 mile/1.4 km south; elev. 362 feet/110m; length 5,000 feet/1,524m; asphalt; fuel 100, Jet B. Floatplane and skiplane strip.

Nenana has an auto repair shop, radio station, several churches, a library, restaurants, a cultural center, a laundromat, a seniors' social center and senior housing units, gift shops, and Coghill's, a grocery/general store that has served the community for 83 years. Accommodations are available at motel, hostel, inn and bed and breakfast. RV park with hookups. ▲

The town was first known as Tortella, a white man's interpretation of the Athabascan word *Toghottele.* A 1902 map indicates a village spelled Tortilli on the north bank of the Tanana River, on the side of the hill still known as Tortella. In the same year Jim Duke built a roadhouse and trading post, supplying river travelers with goods and lodging. The settlement became known as

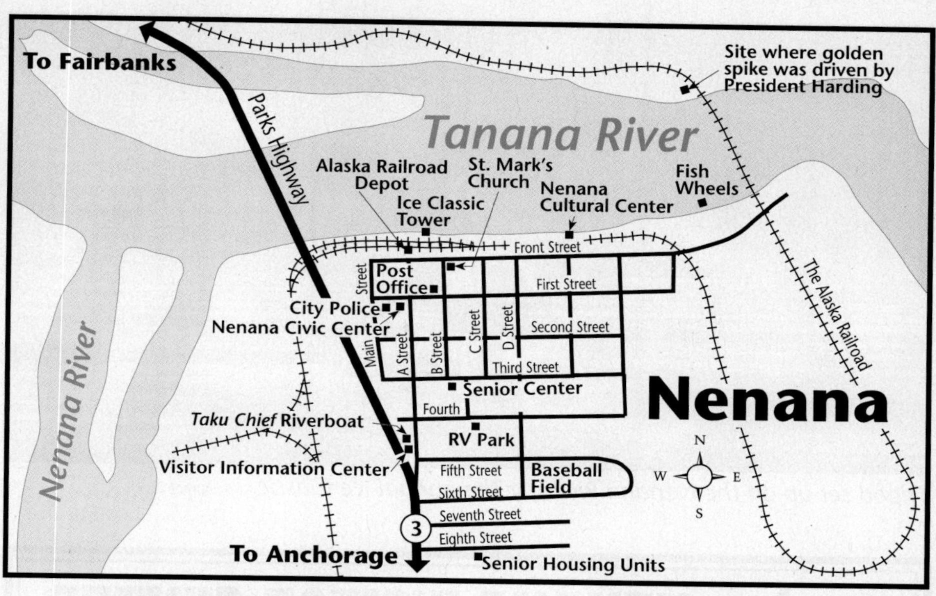

NENANA ADVERTISERS

Moose are the largest member of the deer family. Alaska moose are the largest of their species.

Tripod set up on the Nenana River for the annual Ice Classic. (© Laurent Dick)

Nenana, an Athabascan word meaning, "a good place to camp between the rivers." The town thrived as a trading center for Natives of the region and travelers on the vast network of interior rivers.

Nenana boomed during the early 1920s as a construction base for the Alaska Railroad. On July 15, 1923, Pres. Warren G. Harding drove the golden spike at Nenana signifying the completion of the railroad. The depot, located at the end of Main Street, is on the National Register of Historic Places. Built in 1923 and renovated in 1988, the depot houses the state's **Alaska Railroad Museum**, open 9 A.M. to 6 P.M. daily.

The location "where rail and river meet" led to—in addition to occasional seasonal flooding—the town's vital role in the tugboat/barge shipping industry that traverses the rivers of the interior, providing goods to numerous villages. Tons of fuel, freight and supplies move from the docks at Nenana from late May through September each year. Because the rivers are shallow and silt-laden, the barges move about 12 mph downstream and 5 mph upstream. The dock area is to the right of the highway northbound.

One block from the depot is **St. Mark's Mission Church**. In 1905 the Episcopal Church founded a boarding home and school upriver from the town. Many Native children from interior villages lived and were educated at the mission. Erosion of the riverbank threatened and in some cases destroyed mission buildings, and the church was relocated. The school and boarding home closed in the 1950s. The church, still serving a small but active cóngregation, is all that remains today of the once extensive mission property. The little log building, sometimes open to the public, is graced with hand-hewn pews and a raised altar decorated with Native beaded moosehide frontal and dossal hangings.

Nenana is perhaps best known for the **Nenana Ice Classic**, an annual event that awards cash prizes to the lucky winners who guess the exact minute of the ice breakup on the Tanana River. Ice Classic festivities begin the last weekend in February with the Tripod Raising Festival and culminate at breakup time (late April or May) when the surging ice on the Tanana River dislodges the tripod. A line attached to the tripod stops a clock, recording the official breakup time. The contest has been a spring highlight throughout the state since 1917.

The famous serum race in 1925, when the city of Nome was threatened with a diphtheria epidemic, started in Nenana when the serum was delivered by the Alaska Railroad to the first of the mushers who relayed the package by dog teams 600 miles to the stricken city on Norton Sound in western Alaska. (The sled dog "Balto"—featured in a popular animated film—led the final relay into Nome.) The achievement was re-enacted in a 1995-1996 Nenana-to-Nome relay. The annual Iditarod Trail Sled Dog Race between Anchorage and Nome also commemorates the event. Nenana celebrates River Daze the first weekend in June, welcoming summer's activities. The main event is "The Annihilator," the toughest 10-km footrace in Alaska, over Tortella Hill.

Nenana's train depot is on the National Register of Historic Places.
(© Kris Graef, staff)

Parks Highway Log

(continued)

A 305.1 (491 km) **F 52.9** (85.1 km) **Tanana River** bridge. Large paved turnout to west at north end of bridge. The Tanana is formed by the joining of the Chisana and the Nabesna rivers near Northway and flows 440 miles/708 km westward to the Yukon River. From the bridge, watch for freight-laden river barges bound for the Yukon River. North of this bridge, fish wheels may sometimes be seen in action and occasionally fish may be purchased from the owners of the wheels.

Entering Game Management Unit 20B northbound, 20A southbound.

A 305.5 (491.6 km) **F 52.5** (84.5 km) Turnout to east and to west by Tanana River.

A 305.6 (491.8 km) **F 52.4** (84.3 km) Paved turnout to west overlooking Tanana River.

A 305.9 (492.3 km) **F 52.1** (83.8 km) Double-ended gravel turnout to east. Paved turnout to west.

A 308.7 (496.8 km) **F 49.3** (79.3 km) *CAUTION: Railroad crossing.*

A 308.9 (497.1 km) **F 49.1** (79 km) Restaurant.

A 314.6 (506.3 km) **F 43.4** (69.8 km) Paved double-ended turnout to west.

A 314.8 (506.6 km) **F 43.2** (69.5 km) Bridge over Little Goldstream Creek.

A 315.4 (507.6 km) **F 42.6** (68.6 km) Truck lanes next 4 miles/6.4 km northbound to **Milepost A 319.5**.

A 318.8 (513 km) **F 39.2** (63.1 km) Paved double-ended scenic viewpoint to west. The view is mostly of bogs, small lakes and creeks, with names like Hard Luck Creek, Fortune Creek, All Hand Help Lake and Wooden Canoe Lake.

Southbound travelers will see the Tanana River on both sides of the highway. It follows a horseshoe-shaped course, the top of the closed end being the bridge at Nenana.

A 321 (516.6 km) **F 37** (59.5 km) *NOTE: Long winding grades and intermittent truck lanes northbound to Fairbanks.*

A 324.7 (522.5 km) **F 33.3** (53.6 km) **Purvis Lookout**; a double-ended turnout to east along an on old highway alignment.

A 325 (523 km) **F 33** (53.1 km) This stretch of highway is often called Skyline Drive; views to west. Downgrade northbound; truck lane southbound.

A 325.7 (524.1 km) **F 32.3** (52 km) Entering Fairbanks North Star Borough northbound.

A 328 (527.8 km) **F 30** (48.3 km) **Skinny Dick's Halfway Inn.** See display ad this section.

A 328.3 (528.3 km) **F 29.7** (47.8 km) Emergency parking west side of highway. Truck lane next 3 miles southbound.

A 331.6 (533.6 km) **F 26.4** (42.5 km) South end of long double-ended turnout to east on old alignment. (North end at **Milepost A 331.9**.)

A 335.5 (539.9 km) **F 22.5** (36.2 km) South end of long double-ended turnout to west on old alignment. (North end at **Milepost A 335.9**.)

A 338.5 (544.7 km) **F 19.5** (31.4 km) Expansive views to southeast of Tanana River. To west, look for Murphy Dome (elev. 2,930 feet/893m), with white communication installations on summit.

A 339.9 (547 km) **F 18.1** (29.1 km) Turnoff (unmarked) for Bonanza Experimental Forest via 1-mile/1.6-km loop road east; scenic viewpoint.

A 341 (548.8 km) **F 17** (27.3 km) Long double-ended gravel turnout to west.

A 342.2 (550.7 km) **F 15.8** (25.4 km) Rosie Creek Road to east.

A 342.4 (551 km) **F 15.6** (25.1 km) Old Nenana Highway to west.

A 344.2 (553.9 km) **F 13.8** (22.2 km) Viewpoint to east with view of Tanana River; good photo opportunity. Monument in honor of George Alexander Parks (1883-1984) the territorial governor of Alaska from 1925 to 1933, for whom the Parks Highway is named. Also here is a Blue Star Memorial highway plaque honoring the armed forces.

A 346 (556.8 km) **F 12** (19.3 km) Long downhill northbound to **Milepost A 350.**

A 349 (561.6 km) **F 9** (14.5 km) Cripple Creek Road to south, Park Ridge Road to north. Truck lane next 4.2 miles southbound.

NOTE: Watch for rough road and dips.

A 350 (563.3 km) **F 8** (12.9 km) Alder Creek.

A 350.1 (563.4 km) **F 7.9** (12.7 km) Welcome to Fairbanks North Star Borough sign.

Long uphill southbound to **Milepost A 346.**

A 351.2 (565.2 km) **F 6.8** (10.9 km) Old gold dredges visible to the east.

Ester

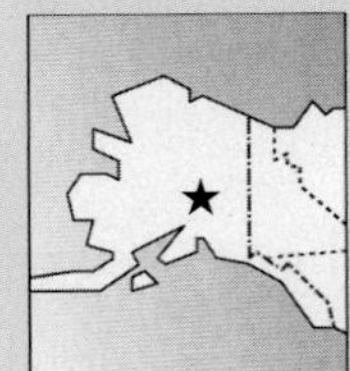

Located 0.6 mile west of highway. **Population:** 240. **Emergency Services:** Emergency only, phone 911. **Fire Department,** phone (907) 479-6858. A former gold mining camp and current visitor attraction, Ester has a hotel, RV camping, 2 saloons, 3 gift shops and a post office. A village sign on Main Street locates these services.

Ester was a raucous mining camp in 1906, with a population of some 5,000 miners. Today a quiet bedroom community of Fairbanks, Ester's heydays are relived in music, song and dance at the Malemute Saloon. Active gold mining is still under way in the area. One of the best preserved gold dredges from the gold rush days can be seen from **Milepost A 351.2**.

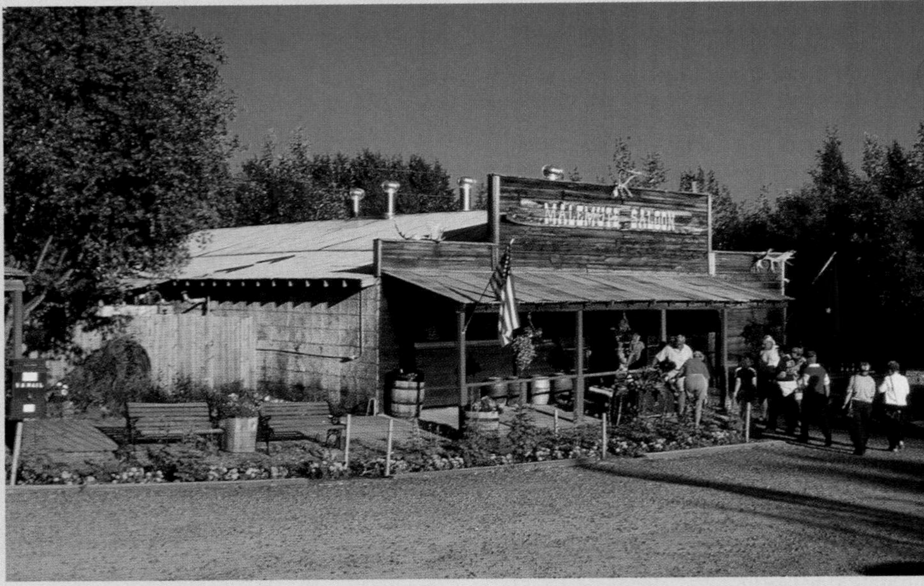

Ester's Malemute Saloon offers entertainment during the summer months.

(© Kris Graef, staff)

Ester Gold Camp. At the turn of century, discovery of gold in the Ester region drew hundreds of prospectors to seek their fortunes. In 1936, the Fairbanks Exploration Company built Ester Camp to support a large-scale gold dredge operation. After 20 years of operation, the camp was closed. It opened again in 1958, but this time as a summer visitor attraction. Today, Ester Gold Camp, on the National Register of Historic Places, provides services for another kind of prospector: those seeking accommodations, excellent food and a fun-filled night of entertainment. Open late May through early September. See display ad in FAIRBANKS section. [ADVERTISEMENT] ▲

Ester Hatworks. Inspired by 3 decades of living in Alaska's Interior, Judy Stauffer handcrafts headgear suitable for every weather extreme. Classic, fun, practical designs are available at her shop nestled beneath the birches, next to Ester Gold Camp Hotel. Open daily, May 28–Sept. 4, 5–9 P.M.; year-round by appointment. Phone/fax (907) 479-5525. Brochure available; P.O. Box 146, Ester, AK 99725. [ADVERTISEMENT]

Judie Gumm Designs. Noted for her sculptural interpretations of northern images, her work has been featured in many national publications. Priced moderately; easy to pack—her jewelry makes a perfect remembrance of your adventure North. Follow the signs in Ester. Weekdays 10-6; Saturdays 12-5. Catalog available. P.O. Box 169, Ester, AK 99725. Phone (907) 479-4568. See display ad this section. [ADVERTISEMENT]

Return to Milepost A 351.7 Parks Highway

ESTER ADVERTISERS

Ester Gold Camp...............Ph. (907) 479-2500
Ester Hatworks...................Ph. (907) 479-5525
Judie Gumm Design..........Ph. (907) 479-4568

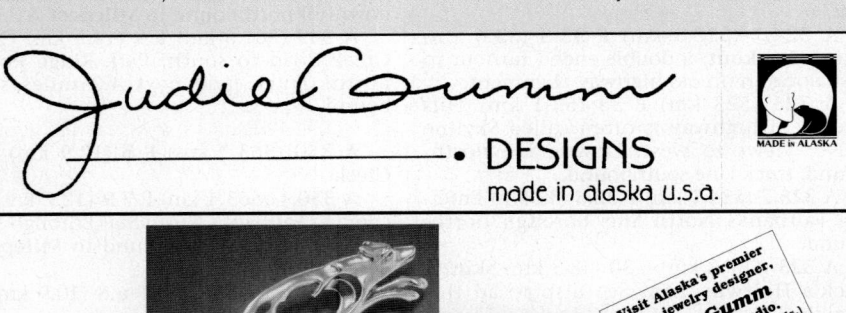

Alaska became the 49th state on Jan. 3, 1959, under President Dwight D. Eisenhower.

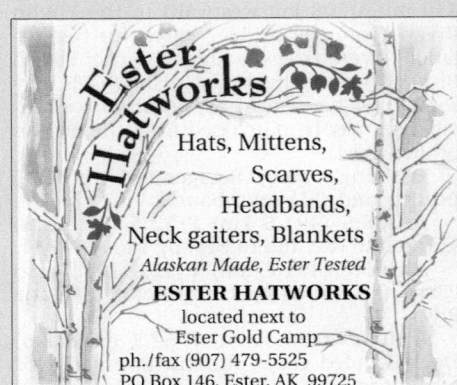

A 351.7 (566 km) **F 6.3** (10.1 km) Turnoff for Ester; fire station.

Junction with side road west to Ester; see description facing page.

A 351.8 (566.2 km) **F 6.2** (10 km) Weigh stations. Yellow Eagle Gold Mine; tours available. This is a working gold mining operation, averaging about 100 oz. of gold daily from the property.

A 352.5 (567.3 km) **F 5.5** (8.8 km) Gold Hill Road. Gas stations, truck stop; diesel, groceries, liquor. Access to Inua Wool Shoppe.

The U.S. Smelting, Refining and Mining Co. mined some 126,000 ounces of gold from Gold Hill between 1953 and 1957.

Gold Hill. See display ad this section.

Parks Highway Truck Stop. See display ad this section.

Inua Wool Shoppe. Turn on Gold Hill Road, go 0.3 mile left to Henderson, 1 mile to 202 Henderson Road. Inua Wool Shoppe is Interior Alaska's most complete knitting shoppe. Fabulous selection of qiviuq and other fine wool yarns. Large selection of Alaskan, Norwegian and American patterns, needlepoints, buttons, books and needles. Come enjoy a unique knitting shoppe. Open 10–5 Monday–Saturday. (907) 479-5830 (Alaska 1-800-478-9848). VISA and MasterCard welcome. See display ad this section. ADVERTISEMENT]

A 353.5 (568.9 km) **F 4.5** (7.2 km) Burton Road, Permafrost Reserve.

The Climatic Change Permafrost Reserve, dedicated in 1999, commemorates the work of University of Alaska professor Troy L. Pewe, head of the geology department from 1958 to 1965. This permanent scientific research site records geological and climatic history to about 3 million years ago.

A 355.8 (572.6 km) **F 2.2** (3.5 km) Sheep Creek Road and Tanana Drive. Road to Murphy Dome (a restricted military site).

A 356.8 (574.2 km) **F 1.2** (1.9 km) Geist Road/Chena Pump Road Exit. Access to University of Alaska, Geist Road, Chena Ridge Loop and Chena Pump Road to Chena Pump House Historical Site (restaurant).

A 357.6 (575.5 km) **F 0.4** (0.6 km) Bridge over Chena River.

A 357.7 (575.6 km) **F 0.3** (0.5 km) West Airport Way exit to Fairbanks International Airport and access to *Discovery* sternwheeler.

A 358 (576.1 km) **F 0** East Airport Way exit to River's Edge RV Park and University Avenue to Chena River State Recreation Site; access to Johansen Expressway. Parks Highway (Alaska Route 3) continues through Fairbanks as the Mitchell Expressway. See FAIRBANKS section following for description of city and Fairbanks Vicinity map.

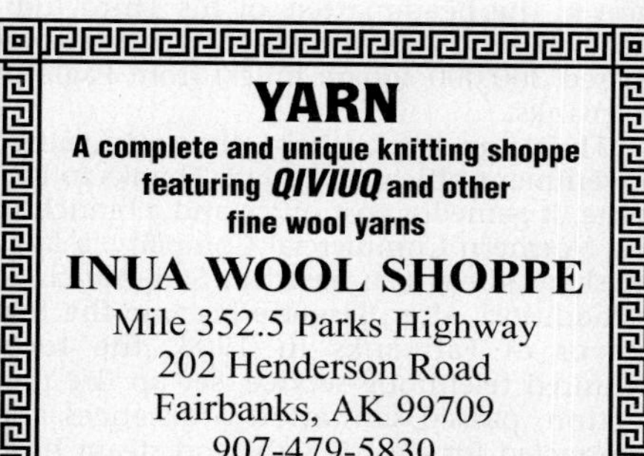

Parks Highway crosses the Chena River on the way into Fairbanks. The Chena River is used by boaters, floatplanes and fishermen. (© Kris Graef, staff)

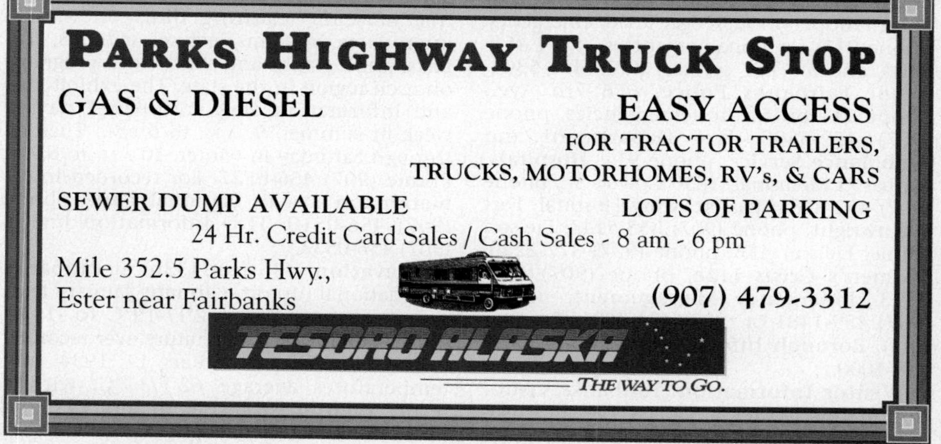

FAIRBANKS

(See maps, page 398)

Aerial view of Fairbanks. (© Laurent Dick)

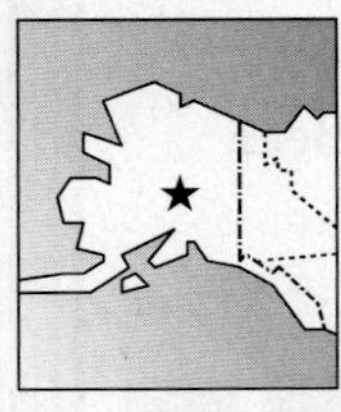

Located in the heart of Alaska's Great Interior country. By highway,it is approximately 1,488 miles/2,395 km north of Dawson Creek, BC, the start of the Alaska Highway (traditional milepost distance is 1,523 miles); 98 miles/158 km from Delta Junction (official end of the Alaska Highway); 358 miles/576 km from Anchorage via the Parks Highway; and 2,305 miles/3,709 km from Seattle.

Population: Fairbanks–North Star Borough, 83,773. **Emergency Services: Alaska State Troopers**, 1979 Peger Road, emergency phone 911; for nonemergencies, (907) 451-5100, and for TTY service, (907) 451-5344. phone **Fairbanks Police**, 656 7th Ave., phone 911 or, for nonemergencies, phone (907) 459-6500. **Fire Department** and **Ambulance Service**, phone 911. **Hospitals**, Fairbanks Memorial, 1650 Cowles St., phone (907) 452-8181; Bassett Army Hospital, Fort Wainwright, phone (907) 353-5143; Eielson Clinic, Eielson AFB, phone (907) 377-2259. **Women's Crisis Line**, phone (907) 452-2293. **Emergency Management**, phone (907) 459-1481 or (907) 474-7721 (24-hour line). **Borough Information**, phone (907) 459-1000.

Visitor Information: Fairbanks Visitor Information Center at 550 1st Ave. (at Cushman Street, where a riverside marker reads "Mile 1523, Official End of the Alaska Highway"); phone (907) 456-5774 or 1-800-327-5774. In summer, open 8 A.M. to 8 P.M. daily; in winter, open 8 A.M. to 5 P.M. weekdays, closed weekends. Phone (907) 456-INFO for current events and activities.

Visitor information is also available at Fairbanks International Airport in the baggage claim area and at the Alaska Railroad depot.

For information on Alaska's state parks, national parks, national forests, wildlife refuges and other outdoor recreational sites, visit the Alaska Public Lands Information Center downstairs in historic Courthouse Square at 250 N. Cushman St. The center is a free museum featuring films on Alaska, interpretive programs, lectures, exhibits, artifacts, photographs and short video programs on each region in the state. The exhibit area and information desk are open 7 days a week in summer, 9. A.M. to 6 P.M.; Tuesday through Saturday in winter, 10 A.M. to 6 P.M. Phone (907) 456-0527. For recorded information on Denali National Park, phone (907) 456-0510. TDD information line is (907) 456-0532.

Elevation: 436 feet/133m at Fairbanks International Airport. **Climate:** January temperatures range from -2°F/-19°C to -19°F/-28°C. The lowest temperature ever recorded was -66°F/-54°C on January 14, 1934. July temperatures average 62°F/17°C, with a record high of 99°F/37°C in July 1919. In June and early July daylight lasts 21 hours—and the nights are really only twilight. Annual precipitation is 10.9 inches, with an annual average snowfall of 65 inches. The record for snowfall is 147.3 inches, set the winter of 1990–91. **Radio:** KSUA-FM, KFAR, KCBF, KAKQ, KWLF-FM, KIAK, KIAK-FM, KJNP-AM and FM (North Pole), KUAC-FM 104.7. **Television:** Channels 2, 4, 7, 9, 11, 13 and cable. **Newspapers:** *Fairbanks Daily News–Miner*.

Private Aircraft: Facilities for all types of aircraft. Consult the *Alaska Supplement* for information on the following airports: Eielson AFB, Fairbanks International, Fairbanks International Seaplane, Chena Marina Air Field and Fort Wainwright. For more information phone the Fairbanks Flight Service Station at (907) 474-0137.

History

In 1901, Captain E.T. Barnette set out from St. Michael on the stern-wheeler *Lavelle Young*, traveling up the Yukon River with supplies for his trading post, which he proposed to set up at Tanana Crossing (Tanacross), the halfway point on the Valdez–Eagle trail. But the stern-wheeler could not navigate the fast-moving, shallow Tanana River beyond the mouth of the Chena River. The stern-wheeler's captain dropped off Barnette on the Chena near the present site of 1st Avenue and Cushman Street. A year later, Felix Pedro, an Italian prospector,discovered gold about 16 miles/26 km north of Barnette's temporary trading post. The opportunistic Barnette quickly abandoned his original plan to continue on to Tanana Crossing.

In September 1902, Barnette convinced the 25 or so miners in the area to use the name "Fairbanks" for the town that he expected would grow up around his trading post. The name had been suggested that summer by Court District Judge James Wickersham, who admired Charles W. Fairbanks, the senior senator from Indiana. The senator later became vice president of the United States under Theodore Roosevelt.

The town grew, largely due to Barnette's promotion of gold prospects and discoveries in the area, and in 1903 Judge Wickersham moved the headquarters of his Third Judicial District Court (a district which encompassed 300,000 square miles) from Eagle to Fairbanks.

Thanks to Wickersham, the town gained government offices and a jail. Thanks to Barnette, it gained a post office and a branch of the Northern Commercial Company, a large Alaska trading firm based in San Francisco. In addition, after Barnette became the first mayor of Fairbanks in 1903, the town acquired telephone service, set up fire protection, passed sanitation ordinances and contracted for electric light and steam heat. In 1904, Barnette started a bank.

The town of "Fairbanks" first appeared in

(Continues on page 399)

RIVERBOAT DISCOVERY • A most memorable adventure

The Riverboat Discovery is the one adventure you won't want to miss when you travel to Fairbanks. Owned and operated by the Binkley family, whose river boating experience in Alaska spans four generations and more than 100 years, the Riverboat Discovery tour has been rated the top boating attraction in North America in Travel Weekly Magazine. Captain Jim Binkley and his crew of children, grandchildren and native Alaskans takes you back to the heyday of sternwheelers, to an era when prospectors, fur traders and Native people of the Interior relied on rivers as their only link to the outside world.

Passengers relax in the comfort of glass enclosed or open decks as the Discovery III winds its way down the Chena and Tanana Rivers. Drawing on their knowledge of Alaskan history, the Binkley family entertains listeners with witty descriptions of Alaskan life during the four hour narrated cruise. The Discovery makes a brief stop at the river front home of veteran Iditarod Dog Musher Susan Butcher, where visitors hear tales of Susan's Iditarod adventures and are introduced to her champion sled dogs.

One of the highlights of the trip is a stop ashore at the Old Chena Indian Village. Here passengers disembark for a guided tour. Alaskan Natives share their culture as they recount how their ancestors hunted, fished, sewed clothing and built shelters to survive for centuries in the harsh Alaskan wilderness. At the village a dog mushing distance racing team gives passengers a "close-up" view of an actual mushing kennel.

The Discovery departs Steamboat Landing, off Dale Road, daily at 8:45 AM and 2:00 PM mid-May through mid-September. Reservations are required. For further information call 907-479-6673.

Before or after your cruise step into the past at Steamboat Landing, one of the finest gift stores in Alaska. Stroll along the picturesque boardwalk beside the Chena River and enter any of four turn-of-the-century shops. Discovery Trading Post offers unique Alaskan gifts at great low prices. The Susan Butcher Dog Mushing gallery features mementos of the Iditarod champion's lifestyle and an exclusive line of sportswear. Susan's winning Iditarod dogsled and Iditarod trophies are conveniently located so you can take photos you'll always treasure. The Binkley and Barrington Gift Shop offers Alaskan made products, and the Pioneer Hotel is replica of Fairbanks' first luxury hotel featuring authentic Native handicrafts. Be sure not to miss this cultural treat between Discovery III departures - you'll find an impressive selection of gifts at some of the best prices in Alaska. Open 7 days a week.

EL DORADO GOLD MINE • Gold Mining History

PAN for GOLD
You're guaranteed to find it!

Pan for gold at the El Dorado Gold Mine. Join the Binkley family for another Alaskan experience that can't be missed! El Dorado Gold Mine is an exciting hands-on adventure for the whole family. Visitors learn about the history of mining in Alaska, experience a modern day mining operation and pan for gold, while enjoying El Dorado Gold Mine's famous Alaskan hospitality.

The two hour tour to a working gold mine begins when passengers board the Tanana Valley Railroad for a narrated trip through the original gold fields of the Interior that were once part of Alaska's richest mining district on record.

Passengers ride the narrow gauge rails through a permafrost tunnel where miners with head lamps and pick-axes seek out the rich gold veins, reminiscent of mining days gone by. Winding through the valley, the train comes to a halt as a prospector crouches down to dip his gold pan into cold, clear waters of Fox Creek in search of the sparkle of gold.

At El Dorado Camp, local miners "Yukon Yonda" and her husband Dexter Clark are on hand to conduct a guided tour through a working gold mine. Visitors gather around to watch the operation of a modern day sluice box and enjoy stories about life in Alaskan mining camps.

A crash course in gold panning is followed by the real thing. Visitors grab a poke filled with pay dirt right from the sluice box and try their hand at panning for gold. And when they strike it rich, they keep the gold!

The next stop is the assay office where visitors, while enjoying complimentary homemade cookies and coffee, weigh their gold and assay its market value. The "all aboard" call gathers everyone onto the train for the short ride back to the station.

Daily tours for the El Dorado Gold Mine depart from the old train station at 1.3 mile Elliott Highway, just past Fox, Alaska, nine miles north of Fairbanks. For reservations call 907-479-7613.

Visit our web site
www.riverboatdiscovery.com
E-mail: reservations@riverboatdiscovery.com

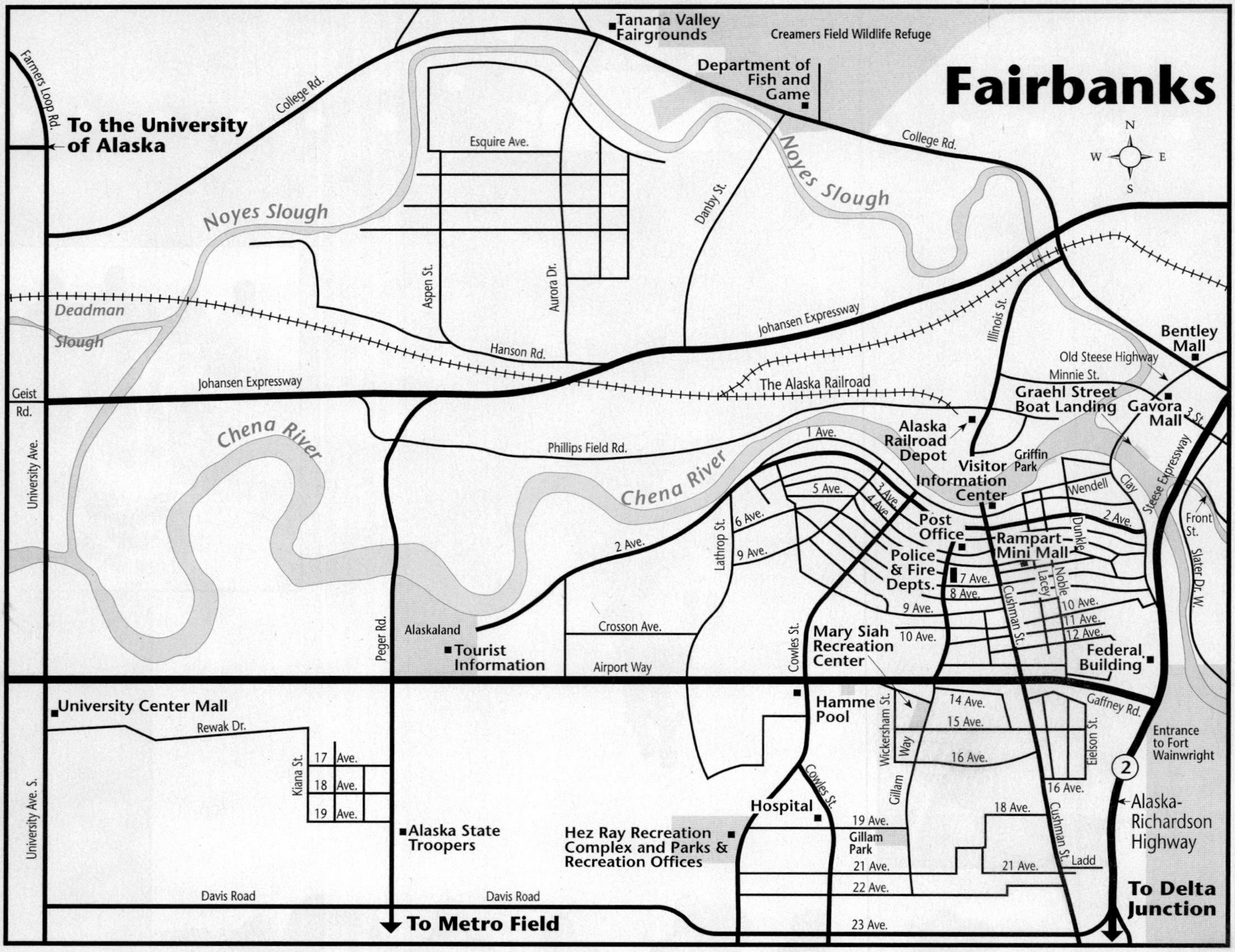

Fairbanks

N
W E
S

Tanana Valley Fairgrounds
Creamers Field Wildlife Refuge
Department of Fish and Game
Farmers Loop Rd.
To the University of Alaska
College Rd.
Esquire Ave.
College Rd.
Noyes Slough
Noyes Slough
Danby St.
Aspen St.
Aurora Dr.
Deadman Slough
Hanson Rd.
Johansen Expressway
Illinois St.
Bentley Mall
Old Steese Highway
Minnie St.
Geist Rd.
Johansen Expressway
The Alaska Railroad
Graehl Street Boat Landing
Gavora Mall
3 St.
Chena River
Alaska Railroad Depot
1 Ave.
Phillips Field Rd.
Visitor Information Center
Griffin Park
Steese Expressway
University Ave.
Chena River
5 Ave.
3 Ave.
4 Ave.
Wendell
Clay
Front St.
6 Ave.
Post Office
2 Ave.
2 Ave.
Rampart Mini Mall
Dunkle
Lathrop St.
9 Ave.
Police & Fire Depts.
7 Ave.
8 Ave.
Noble
Lacey
Slater Dr. W.
9 Ave.
10 Ave.
11 Ave.
12 Ave.
Cushman St.
Peger Rd.
Alaskaland
Crosson Ave.
Cowles St.
Mary Siah Recreation Center
10 Ave.
Tourist Information
Airport Way
Federal Building
University Center Mall
Hamme Pool
Wickersham St.
14 Ave.
Gaffney Rd.
Rewak Dr.
15 Ave.
Eielson St.
Entrance to Fort Wainwright
Way
16 Ave.
Kiana St.
17 Ave.
18 Ave.
19 Ave.
2
Cowles St.
Gillam
16 Ave.
Hospital
18 Ave.
Alaska-Richardson Highway
University Ave. S.
Alaska State Troopers
Hez Ray Recreation Complex and Parks & Recreation Offices
19 Ave.
Gillam Park
Cushman St.
21 Ave.
21 Ave.
Ladd
Davis Road
Davis Road
22 Ave.
To Delta Junction
To Metro Field
23 Ave.

Fairbanks and Vicinity

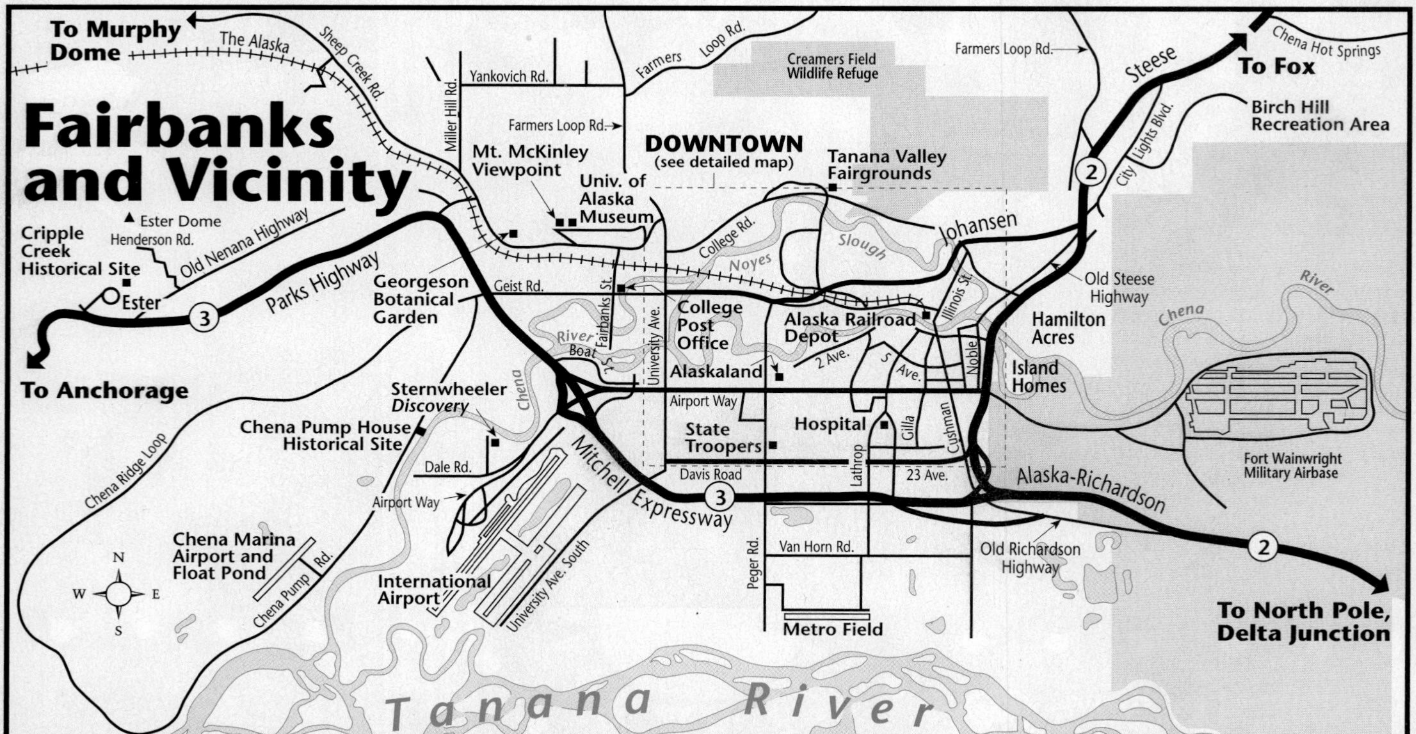

To Murphy Dome
The Alaska
Sheep Creek Rd.
Farmers Loop Rd.
Farmers
Loop Rd.
Creamers Field Wildlife Refuge
Farmers Loop Rd.
Chena Hot Springs
To Fox
Steese
Yankovich Rd.
Miller Hill Rd.
Birch Hill Recreation Area
Farmers Loop Rd.
DOWNTOWN (see detailed map)
Tanana Valley Fairgrounds
City Lights Blvd.
2
Mt. McKinley Viewpoint
Univ. of Alaska Museum
Ester Dome
Henderson Rd.
Old Nenana Highway
Cripple Creek Historical Site
College Rd.
Slough
Johansen
Noyes
Old Steese Highway
River
Geist Rd.
Ester
Parks Highway
Georgeson Botanical Garden
3
Fairbanks St.
University Ave.
College Post Office
Alaska Railroad Depot
Illinois St.
Hamilton Acres
Chena
River Boat
2 Ave.
S Ave.
Noble
Island Homes
To Anchorage
Alaskaland
Chena
Airport Way
Sternwheeler *Discovery*
Gilla
Cushman
Chena Pump House Historical Site
Hospital
State Troopers
Fort Wainwright Military Airbase
Chena Ridge Loop
Dale Rd.
Mitchell Expressway
Lathrop
Davis Road
3
23 Ave.
Alaska-Richardson
Airport Way
N
W E
S
Chena Marina Airport and Float Pond
Rd.
Chena Pump
Peger Rd.
Van Horn Rd.
Old Richardson Highway
2
International Airport
University Ave. South
To North Pole, Delta Junction
Metro Field
Tanana River

(Continued from page 392)
the U.S. Census in 1910 with a population of 3,541. Miners living beside their claims on creeks north of town brought the area population figure to about 11,000.

Barnette stayed in Fairbanks until late 1910, when he resigned the presidency of the Washington–Alaska Bank and moved to California. When the bank collapsed early in 1911, the people of Fairbanks blamed Barnette. The tale of the "most hated man in Fairbanks" is told in *E.T. Barnette, The Strange Story of the Man Who Founded Fairbanks.*

Economy

The city's economy is linked to its role as a service and supply point for Interior and Arctic industrial activities. Fairbanks played a key role during construction of the trans-Alaska pipeline in the 1970s. The Dalton Highway (formerly the North Slope Haul Road) to Prudhoe Bay begins about 75 miles/121 km north of town. Extractive industries such as oil and mining continue to play a major role in the economy.

Government employment contributes significantly to the Fairbanks economy. Including military jobs, 50 percent of employment in Fairbanks is through the government. Fort Wainwright (formerly Ladd Field) was the first Army airfield in Alaska, established in 1938. The fort currently employs 4,600 soldiers and 1,600 civilians, and it houses 6,200 family members. Fort Wainwright also provides emergency services by assisting with search and rescue operations. Eielson Air Force Base, located 25 miles/40 km southeast of Fairbanks on the Richardson–Alaska Highway, also has a strong economic impact on the city. Eielson has about 2,700 military personnel and approximately 4,200 family members assigned, with about 1,200 military personnel and family members living off base.

Also boosting the Fairbanks economy are the University of Alaska Fairbanks, and trade and service industries such as retail sales and tourism.

Description

Alaska's second largest city and the administrative capital of the Interior, Fairbanks lies on the flat valley floor of the Tanana River on the banks of the Chena River. Good views of the valley are available from Chena Ridge Road to the west and Farmers Loop Road to the north.

The city is a blend of old and new: Modern hotels and shopping strips stand beside log cabins and historic wooden buildings.

Fairbanks is bounded to the north, east and west by low rolling hills of birch and white spruce. To the south is the Alaska Range and Denali National Park, about a 2½-hour drive via the Parks Highway. The Steese and Elliott highways lead north to the White Mountains.

Lodging & Services

Fairbanks has more than 100 restaurants, about 2 dozen hotels and motels, 6 hostels and more than 100 bed and breakfasts. Many are open year-round. Rates vary widely, from a low of about $40 for a single to a high of $150 for a double (hostels are considerably cheaper). Reservations for all accommodations are suggested during the busy summer months.

Ah, Rose Marie Downtown Bed and Breakfast. Historic 1928 Fairbanks home. Very centrally located. Full hearty breakfasts.

Visitors relax and enjoy the view from Discovery *sternwheeler.* (© Joanne McCubrey)

Friendly cat. Outdoor smoking areas. Singles, couples, triples, families welcomed. Open year-round. Extraordinary hospitality. Single $50 up, doubles $65 up. Wow! John E. Davis, 302 Cowles St., Fairbanks, AK 99701. Phone (907) 456-2040; fax (907) 456-6193; website: www.akpub.com/akbbrv/ahrose.html. [ADVERTISEMENT]

A-1 Yankovich Inn Bed & Breakfast. Located on a 2-acre estate bordering musk-ox farm. Warm, relaxing atmosphere. Queen Beautyrest beds, rollaway for extra person. Alaska Blueberry Waffles, house specialty. Hiking/skiing trails, aurora viewing. $75 double, $65 single. 2268 Yankovich Rd., Fairbanks, AK 99709. Phone (907) 479-2861. Toll free: 1-888-801-2861. [ADVERTISEMENT]

Bridgewater Hotel. Located in the heart of the city, the Bridgewater is centrally located and absolutely charming! It's known for its quaint, personal atmosphere, contemporary, fresh decor and consistent, friendly service. We offer very competitive, great rates! Call 800-528-4916 or (907) 452-6661.

FAIRBANKS ADVERTISERS

Accommodations

Attractions and Entertainment

Auto & RV Gas, Rentals, Service and Supplies

Campgrounds/RV Parks

Dining

Shopping and Services

Tours and Transportation

Visitor Information

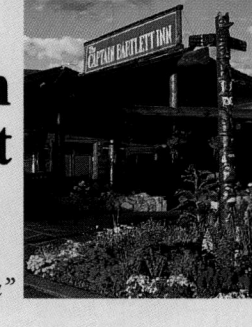

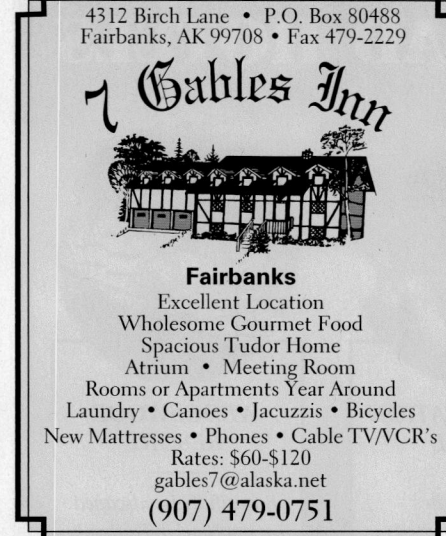

On summer solstice (June 21, 2000), sunrise will be at 2:59 A.M. and sunset will be at 12:47 , the following day. That's almost 22 hours of daylight.

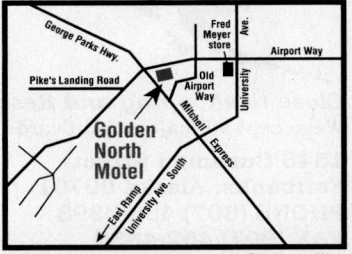

October 18th is Alaska Day. This official state holiday marks the anniversary of the formal transfer of Alaska from Russia to the United States in 1867.

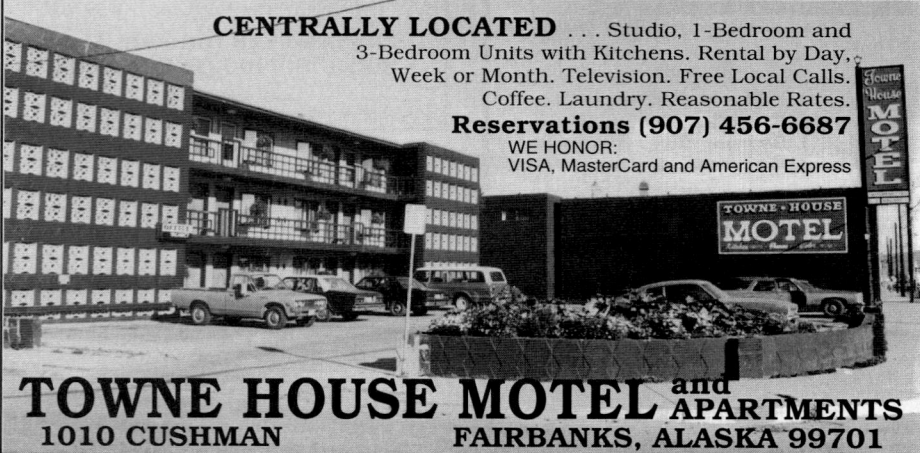

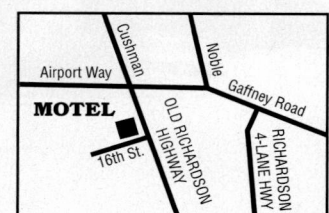

Write 723 First Avenue, Fairbanks, AK 99701. Internet: www.fountainheadhotels.com. [ADVERTISEMENT]

Country Comforts Bed and Breakfast. Stay free! Ask how! Quiet spacious home located near Birch Hill recreation area 5 minutes from downtown. Alaskan art. Queen/twin beds, Jacuzzi, sauna, full breakfasts. Hosts Audrey and Ken Dunshie, 30-year residents. Open year-round. (907) 457-6867; toll free (888) 401-3232; pin 1761. 174 Crest Dr., Fairbanks 99712. Web site: www.bbhost./countrycomforts. [ADVERTISEMENT]

Eleanor's Northern Lights Bed and Breakfast: Conveniently located, a 5-minute walk from downtown Fairbanks. Hearty, full, all-you-can-eat "home cooked breakfasts," a selection of six clean rooms, very reasonable rates. Energetic and bright hosts—Stella and Mike—have created a warm, cozy "home away from home." 360 State St. (corner of 4th Ave. and State St.), Fairbanks, AK 99701. Phone: (907) 452-2598, or 1-800-467-4167; fax: (907) 452-7247; e-mail: nlightsb@eagle.ptialaska.net; web page: www.akpub.com/akbbrv/elean.html. [ADVERTISEMENT]

Fairbanks Bed and Breakfast. Barbara Neubauer, hostess and 26-year resident, has many bear and gold mining tales. The quiet historical neighborhood is walking distance to town on bus route. Our home has many interesting ivory artifacts and Alaskan art. Private bath, large yard and deck. Deck smoking. Hearty breakfast and laundry facilities for fee plus ample parking. 902 Kellum Street. (907) 452-4967, fax (907) 451-6955. [ADVERTISEMENT]

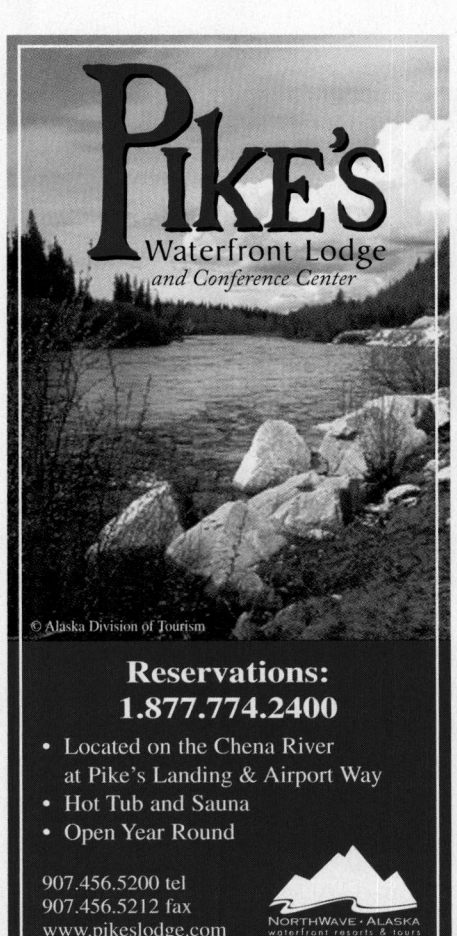

Fairbanks Princess Hotel. Interior Alaska's finest accommodations located on the Chena River. Featuring an array of dining options, lounge, terraced riverside deck, tour desk, gift shop, health club with steam rooms, complimentary airport shuttle, meeting facilities for groups up to 435. Open year-round. Phone (800) 426-0500 for reservations. [ADVERTISEMENT]

Fairbanks Private Vacation Homes Network. Peaceful, quiet, wooded settings, all within 12 minutes of city center. All have clean and modern kitchens and bathrooms, phones, TV/VCRs and stock breakfast fixings. Smoking outdoors. Reasonable rates. Brochures available. *Beth's Vacation Home, 1 bedroom house sleeps four, 1000 Bennett Road., Fairbanks, AK 99712, (907) 457-2725; e-mail:jimsamp@mosquitonet.com. *Cedar Creek Vacation Home, custom-built 2-story, $2\frac{1}{2}$ bedrooms, pets on approval, P.O. Box 10355, Fairbanks, AK 99710, (907) 457-3392; within Alaska 1-800-764-3392; fax (907) 457-3332; e-mail: appleinn@ mosquitonet. com. Web site: http://www.akpub.com/ak. bbrv/apple.html. *Gram's Cabin, on 3 river-front acres, pets on approval. P.O. Box 58034, Fairbanks, AK 99711, phone (907) 488-6513; fax: (907) 488-6593; e-mail: braniff@mosquitonet.com. Web site: http://www.mosquitonet.com/~braniff. [ADVERTISEMENT]

Fountainhead Hotels. Three of Fairbanks' most popular hotels: Sophie Station, Wedge-

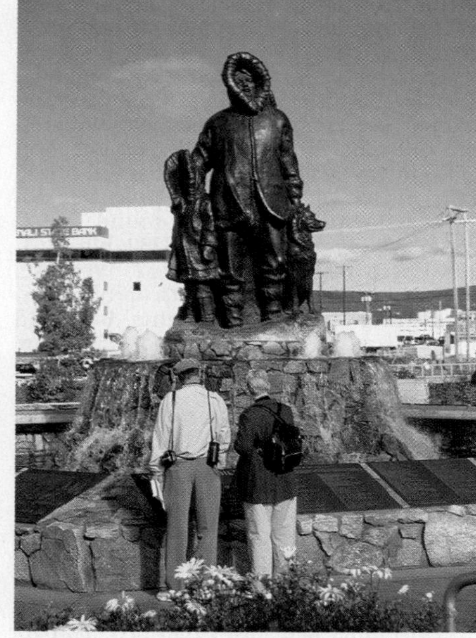

Unknown First Family *statue in Golden Heart Park adjacent the Fairbanks Visitor Information Center.* (© Kris Graef, staff)

wood Resort, and the Bridgewater Hotel. Each property varies in design, personality and location, assuring you that we have exactly what you're looking for, including great rates! Call (800) 528-4916, or write us at 1501 Queens Way, Fairbanks, Alaska 99701. [ADVERTISEMENT]

Geni's Bed & Breakfast. Country hospitality May to September. Large bedroom, private bath. Two bedrooms with queen-sized beds, shared full bath. No pets, smoking on deck only. Glassroom dining, full breakfast. Affordable accommodations in woodland setting 15 minutes from Fairbanks at Mile 5.3 Chena Hot Springs Road. Handmade Alaska crafts available. George and Nila Lyle, P.O. Box 10352, Fairbanks, AK 99710; phone (907) 488-4136; E-mail: genisbb@mosquitonet.com. [ADVERTISEMENT]

Grizzly Lodge & Dog Mushing. Enjoy staying in an Alpine chalet with Swiss hospitality. Located near the pipeline and 15 min. from downtown. 12 spacious rooms with private bath and balcony. No pets. Dog mushing tours during the winter. Free kennel tours. We speak German, French,

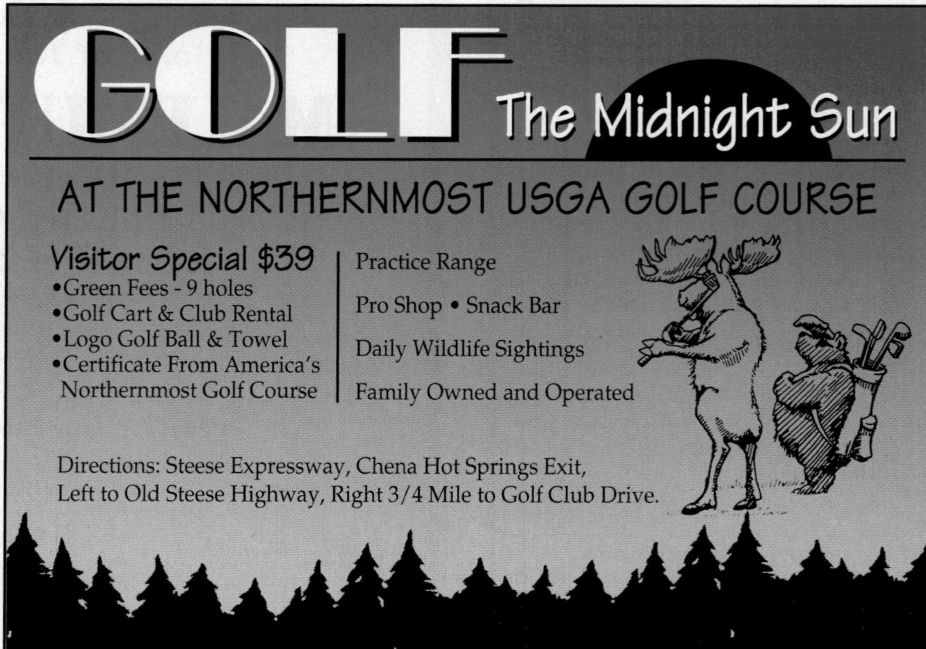

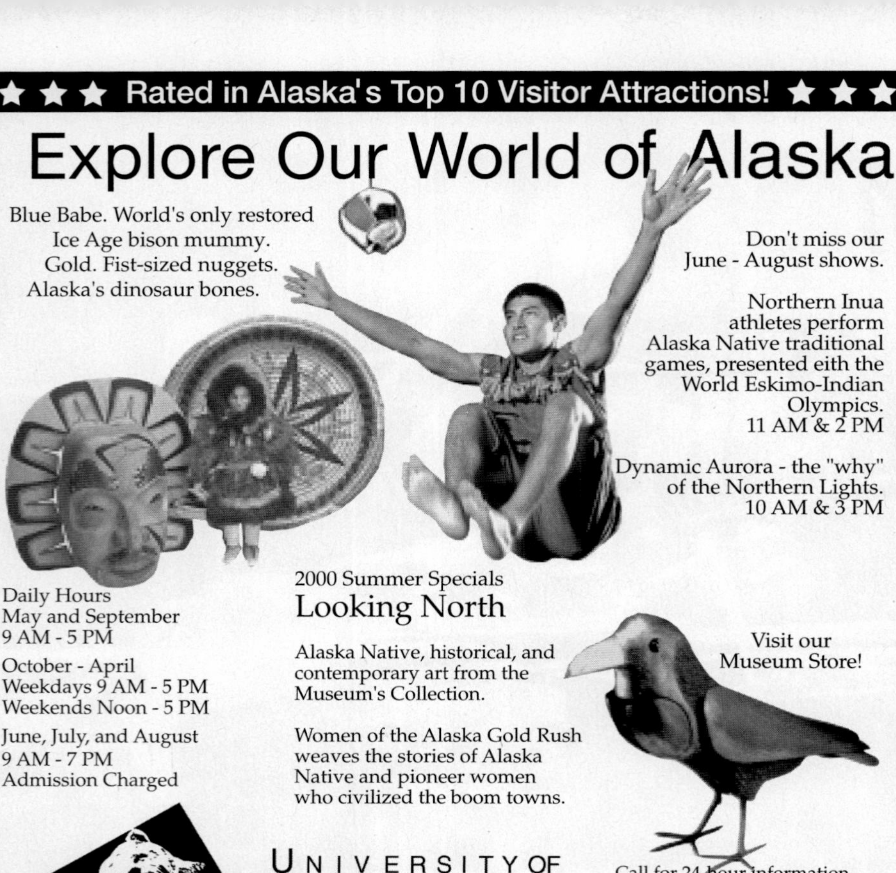
★ ★ ★ Rated in Alaska's Top 10 Visitor Attractions! ★ ★ ★
Explore Our World of Alaska
Blue Babe. World's only restored Ice Age bison mummy. Gold. Fist-sized nuggets. Alaska's dinosaur bones.
Don't miss our June - August shows.
Northern Inua athletes perform Alaska Native traditional games, presented eith the World Eskimo-Indian Olympics. 11 AM & 2 PM
Dynamic Aurora - the "why" of the Northern Lights. 10 AM & 3 PM
Daily Hours
May and September 9 AM - 5 PM
October - April Weekdays 9 AM - 5 PM Weekends Noon - 5 PM
June, July, and August 9 AM - 7 PM Admission Charged
2000 Summer Specials
Looking North
Alaska Native, historical, and contemporary art from the Museum's Collection.
Women of the Alaska Gold Rush weaves the stories of Alaska Native and pioneer women who civilized the boom towns.
Visit our Museum Store!
university of alaska Museum
UNIVERSITY OF ALASKA MUSEUM
Call for 24-hour information (907) 474-7505
907 YUKON DRIVE PO BOX 756960 FAIRBANKS, AK 99775-6960
Visit our web site: http://www.uaf.edu/museum

Italian. http://www.ptialaska.net/~grizzlyf. Phone: (907) 488-9605; fax: (907) 490-0378. [ADVERTISEMENT]

Pike's Waterfront Lodge and Conference Center. New for 2000—a comfortable waterfront lodge on the Chena River, located in Fairbanks with convenient airport access, in one of Alaska's most historic areas and gateway to the Arctic. Pike's Waterfont Lodge, featuring a hot tub, sauna and a comfortable lobby with fireplace. The 180-plus room lodge offers delicious dining at its own restaurant and at the famous Pike's Landing Restaurant next door. Open year-round. Check our web site: www.pikeslodge.com for rates; E-mail: denali@polarnet.com; phone 1-877-774-2400. If planning a trip to Seward and Kenai Fjords National Park, inquire about Hotel Edgewater in Seward. [ADVERTISEMENT

7 Gables Inn. Central to major attractions, this remodeled fraternity house is between the University campus and the airport. The spacious Tudor-style house features a floral solarium, stained-glass foyer with indoor waterfall, cathedral ceilings, banquet/conference facilities. Gourmet breakfast served daily. Cable TV, VCR, phone in each room, laundry, bikes, canoes and skis. Rates \$50–\$120; 4312 Birch Lane, Fairbanks, AK 99709. Phone (907) 479-0751. [ADVERTISEMENT]

The Aurora Borealis

While the aurora borealis may be viewed in the Northern sky from many places, both scientists and tourists alike have found Fairbanks to be the city of choice for aurora watchers, regardless of the differences in their appreciation of this event.

"Oh," thinks the scientist as he witnesses a vivid display of the aurora, "there's a high-vacuum electrical discharge, powered by the sun's energy and causing interaction between the solar wind and earth's magnetic field."

"Ooh," sighs another observer, unconcerned with scientific explanations, "I've never seen anything so incredibly awesome."

Scientist and layman both stand transfixed by the celestial light show. With all his knowledge, the scientist still appreciates the patterns and motions and colors of the undulating lights. The layman, engrossed in the aesthetics of the sight, still shakes his head in wonder over the miracles and mysteries that combine to create such a soul-satisfying phenomenon.

Scientific research has solved the mysteries of the aurora. Books and articles abound to explain it. We know the causes, the peak times for its occurrence (March–April, September–October). We know it is all happening about 50 miles above the earth. We know that the varying colors are related to gases in the upper atmosphere: oxygen causing green and red, nitrogen responsible for blue, purple and red. We know that capturing the aurora on film is a challenge to any photographer. We have read about—and, with luck, have seen—the myriad forms assumed by the aurora: the fluorescent ribbons that explore the heavens, the drapery-like waves of rayed arcs, the late-night phantom lights that seem to blink and pulsate.

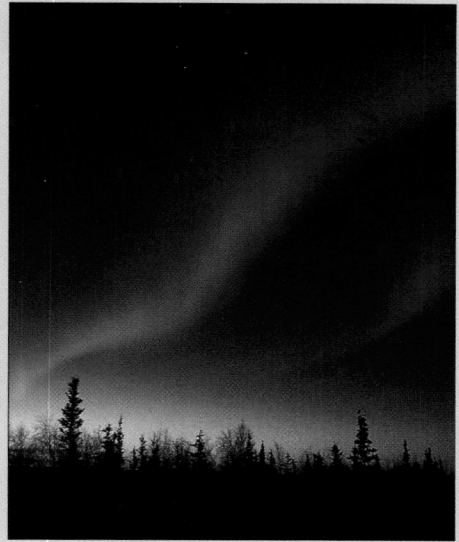

The Northern Lights are a constantly changing light show. (© Nancy Faville)

One mystery always in contention is whether the northern lights emit any sort of sound. Although scientists agree that sound from auroral displays is "highly unlikely," Dr. C.T. Elvey, an Auroral Research professor at University of Alaska Fairbanks, writing in 1962, conceded that "there might be high-frequency sounds." Individuals who have stood in reverential silence beneath the northern lights miles out on a frozen, uninhabited tundra, with no interference from streetlights or extraneous noises, sometimes tell another story of rustling and whispering emanating from the overhead wonder.

Above and beyond all the questions and explanations, one fact is undeniable: among the many rewards of living in the North, the opportunity to experience the northern lights ranks high. As George Cresswell of the University of Alaska's Geophysical Institute said in 1968: "Without a doubt, the aurora must be one of the most beautiful natural events that can be observed by man."

The Geophysical Institute at the University of Alaska Fairbanks has been providing aurora forecasts since 1994. Professor Emeritus Charles Deehr is the aurora forecaster. Regular forecasts of auroral activity over Alaska are available on the Internet when the nights are dark enough to observe them (from about September through April). These forecasts, as well as answers to the most frequently asked questions about auroras, may be found on the Internet at http://www.gi.alaska.edu. Or for more information contact the Geophysical Insitute information office by phoning (907) 474-7558.

Fairbanks' Aurora Borealis Monument is located on the road leaving Fairbanks International Airport. The *Solar Borealis* sculpture is made of laser light reflective material so that it changes colors as you drive under it.

Sophie Station Hotel. Exceptional service and accommodations combined with a warm, upscale atmosphere! Guest rooms feature a full kitchen, living area with private balcony, separate bedroom with dressing alcove, and a full bath—all of this at a great rate! Call 800-528-4916 or (907) 479-3650. Write 1717 University Avenue, Fairbanks, AK 99709. [ADVERTISEMENT]

Uebernachtung und Fruehstueck, Bed & Breakfast. English and German speaking with German hospitality. Pets in house. Queen beds, private and shared bath, full breakfast. German TV. Robert and Sylvia Harris, 2402 Cowles St., Fairbanks, Alaska 99701. Phone (907) 455-7958, Fax (907) 452-7958, e-mail: 103707.2401@Compuserve. [ADVERTISEMENT]

Wedgewood Resort. This beautifully landscaped property site on 27 acres, between the University and downtown. Each spacious suite features a full kitchen, living and dining area, separate bedroom, full bath and a balcony, offering a comfortable, home-like atmosphere. Great rates! Call 800-528-4916 or (907) 452-1442. Write 212 Wedgewood Drive, Fairbanks, AK 99701. [ADVERTISEMENT]

Camping

There are several private campgrounds in the Fairbanks area. Chena River recreation site, a state campground, is located on University Avenue by the Chena River bridge. The campground has 57 sites, tables, firepits, toilets, water and a dump station. Camping

fee are $15/night or resident pass; $3 for use of dump station; and $5 for use of boat launch. There is overnight camping at Alaskaland for self-contained RVs only with a 4-night limit, $12 fee and use of the borough dump station on 2nd Avenue. ▲

Chena Marina RV Park guests speak: "RV having fun? Yes—Thanks to folks like you!...'Dankeschon' services really special... One of the best—location, spacious, landscaped...First-rate." Extra-wide, long pull-throughs (slide-outs welcome). Free Klondinental breakfast; on floatplane pond (fishing); laundry, free guest showers, electric, water, TV, dump, tour tickets, free RV/car wash. Mile 3.1 Chena Pump Road, watch for signs. (907) 479-GOLD (4653), 1145 Shypoke Dr., Fairbanks, AK 99709. See map in display ad for directions. Open May 1. [ADVERTISEMENT] ▲

River's Edge RV Park & Campground. Beautiful setting on the Chena River and within walking distance of major shopping centers. 180 spacious wooded sites. Wide pull-throughs; 30-amp electric; dump station; full and partial hookups; free showers; gifts; free shuttle to Riverboat *Discovery* and Alaskaland Salmon Bake. Tour arrangements featuring Point Barrow and Arctic Circle. Immaculate facilities. [ADVERTISEMENT] ▲

Riverview RV Park & Cookout is one of the top-rated RV parks in Alaska. It is situated on 20 acres adjoining the beautiful Chena River. Total atmosphere and only 10 minutes from downtown Fairbanks. It is the only RV park with cable TV in the Fairbanks area. Call Riverview RV Park (888) 488-6392 or (907) 488-6281. Telephones and e-mail. See display ad. [ADVERTISEMENT] ▲

Farmers Market on College Road offers home-grown vegetables and crafts.
(© Laurent Dick)

Transportation

Air: Several international, interstate and intra-Alaska carriers serve Fairbanks.

Air charter services are available for flightseeing; fly-in fishing, hunting and hiking, and trips to bush villages; see ads.

Railroad: Alaska Railroad passenger depot at 280 N. Cushman St. in the downtown area. Daily passenger service in summer between Fairbanks and Anchorage with stopovers at Denali National Park; less frequent service in winter. For details, phone (800) 544-0552.

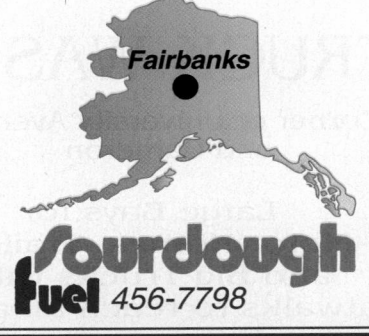

Train to Denali (Gray Line of Alaska). Ride the luxurious private-domed railcars of the *McKinley Explorer* to Denali National Park from either Anchorage or Fairbanks. Overnight packages in Denali with round-trip train service are available from $415 for

3 days/2 nights, ppdo. Pre-overnight in either Anchorage or Fairbanks is included. Prices subject to change. Call Gray Line of Alaska at (907) 451-6835 for train and package tour options. [ADVERTISEMENT]

Bus: Local daily bus service is provided by the Metropolitan Area Commuter System (MACS). MACS service is available from Fairbanks to the University of Alaska, North Pole, Hamilton Acres, Davis Road and the International Airport daily Monday through Saturday (limited scheduled on Saturdays); no service on Sundays and six major holidays. Drivers do not carry change so exact change or tokens must be used. Fares: $1.50 or 1 token for adults; grade K-12, senior citizens or disabled, $0.75. All-day passes are $3, purchased from the drivers. Tokens are available at Transit Park, UAF Wood Center, Fred Meyer West, Bentley Mall and North Pole Plaza. Information is available via the Transit Hotline at (907) 459-1011 or from MACS office at 3175 Peger Road, phone (907) 459-1002 or on the internet at www.co.fairbanks.ak.us/transit/ transit.htm. Shuttle buses serve the highway areas (see Buse Lines in TRAVEL PLANNING section).

Tours: Local and area sightseeing tours are available from several companies; see ads in this section.

Taxi: At least 10 cab companies.

Car and Camper Rentals: Several companies rent cars, campers and trailers; see ads in this section.

Attractions

Get Acquainted: A good place to start is the Visitor Information Center at 550 1st Ave., where you'll find free brochures, maps and tips on what to see and how to get there. Phone (907) 456-5774 or 1-800-327-5774. For a recording of current daily events phone (907) 456-INFO.

Next to the Visitor Information Center log cabin is **Golden Heart Park**, site of the 18-foot/5-m bronze monument, "Unknown First Family." The statue, by sculptor Malcolm Alexander, and park were dedicated in July 1986 to celebrate Fairbanks' history and heritage.

Fairbanks has a number of public parks that make good stops for a picnic. **Graehl Park** has a boat launch and is a good place to watch traffic on the river.

Alaska Bird Observatory at Creamer's

Refuge. Observe bird research, obtain local birding information, or enjoy a guided walk. Bird banding demonstrations are every half-hour from 10 A.M. to noon (July 16-August 31). Donation requested. Field guides, bird song tapes, and T-shirts available. For more information, phone (907) 451-7059 or birds@alaskabird.org. [ADVERTISEMENT]

The Alaska Public Lands Information Center, located in the lower level of historic Courthouse Square at 3rd Avenue and Cushman Street, is a free museum and information center featuring Alaska's natural history, cultural artifacts and recreational opportunities. In addition to detailed information on outdoor recreation in the state, the center offers films, interpretive programs, lectures and a book shop.

Tour the University of Alaska Fairbanks. Situated on a 2,250-acre ridge overlooking Fairbanks and the Alaska Range, UAF has the best view in town! With all the amenities of a small town, including a fire station, post office, radio and TV stations, medical clinic and a concert hall, it boasts a world-class faculty and a unique blend of students from around the world.

UAF is a land-, sea- and space-grant university and serves 170 communities statewide through distance delivery of instruction, public service and research activities. With an enrollment of over 8,000 students each year, it is America's only arctic university and is center stage for researching global climate change and arctic phenomena.

UAF offers special tours and programs from June through August. Free guided walking tours of campus are offered Monday through Friday at 10 A.M. Tours begin at the UA Museum and last about 2 hours. Several other summer tours are available across campus, including a musk-oxen and caribou farm, rocket range, botanical garden and supercomputing center. Call (907) 474-7581 for information on any tour; or visit our web site: www.uaf.edu/univrel/Tour.

Consider UAF when you or someone you know is thinking about college. Guided tours of campus for prospective students can be arranged throughout the year by calling the Office of Admissions, (907) 474-7500 or (800) 478-1823.

The University of Alaska Museum is a "must-stop" for Fairbanks visitors. The museum features cultural and natural history displays from all the state's regions. The 5 galleries explore Alaska's history, Native culture, art, natural phenomena, wildlife, birds, geology and prehistoric past. Highlights include a 36,000-year-old Steppe bison mummy, the state's largest gold display, the trans-Alaska pipeline story and a special section on the northern lights. The museum grounds hold sculptures, totem poles, a Russian blockhouse and a nature trail with signs identifying local vegetation.

Northern Inua dance performance at University of Alaska Museum.

(© Robin Brandt)

The museum's special summer exhibit in 2000 is called "Looking North," showing contemporary, historical and Alaska Native art from the museum's collection. Free summer programs include presentations on natural and cultural history topics discussing traditional and contemporary lifestyles. Summer shows include "Northern Inua," a 50-minute show of northern athletic games, dance and creation stories, produced in conjunction with the World Eskimo Indian Olympics (daily, 11 A.M. and 2 P.M.), and "Dynamic Aurora," a 50-minute show on the scientific understanding of the northern lights (daily, 10 A.M. and 3 P.M.). Admission is charged for these shows.

Museum hours: May and September, 9 A.M.–5 P.M.; June through August, 9 A.M.–7 P.M.; October through April, weekdays, 9 A.M.–5 P.M., weekends, noon to 5 P.M. Museum admission fees: adults, $5; seniors, $4.50; youth (7–17), $3; children under 6, free. For 24-hour information, call (907) 474-7505, or check our web site: www.uaf.edu/museum.

The UAF Summer Fine Arts Camp will be held on the UAF campus from June 16–July 15, 2000. Students in grades 7–12 study visual arts, theatre, music, dance and creative writing. Supervised dormitory housing is available. Evening concerts, arts exhibits and fully staged theatrical productions are open to the public. Call (907) 474-6837 or E-mail: fysfac@uaf.edu for more information, or visit their web site at: www.uaf.edu/music/artscamp/.

See Gold Displays. In addition to the large gold display at the university museum, visitors will find many exotic gemstones, a knowledgeable gemologist and staff, and rock specimens from around the world at Taylor's Gold-N-Stones on Cushman Street in downtown Fairbanks. A combination museum and old-fashioned working jewelry store, where skilled goldsmiths create gold-

Georgeson Botanical Garden on University of Alaska campus.

(© Harry M. Walker Photo)

nugget and other jewelry, Taylor's is a fascinating stop for rockhounds.

Celebrate Summer Solstice: Fairbanks has several unique summer celebrations associated with summer solstice in June, when residents celebrate the longest day of the year (summer solstice is June 21). The Midnight Sun Baseball Game will be played at 10:30 P.M. on June 21, 2000, without artificial lights. For details, phone (907) 451-0095. The Midnight Sun 10K Fun Run begins at 10 P.M. on June 17, 2000; phone (907) 452-7211 for further information.

The World Ice Art Championships, scheduled for March 1–12, 2000, draws thousands of people to admire ice sculptures created by artists from around the world. An ice castle, an ice chapel and all-ice children's play area are popular features.

The World Eskimo and Indian Olympics , with Native competition in such events as the high kick, greased pole walk, stick pull, fish cutting, parka contest and muktuk-eating contest will be held July 12–15, 2000. Phone (907) 452-6646.

The Fairbanks Summer Arts Festival, 2 weeks of workshops and concerts including music from jazz to classics, dance, theater and the visual arts, will be held July 21–Aug. 6, 2000 on the University of Alaska Fairbanks campus. Phone (907) 474-8869 for more information.

Golden Days, when Fairbanksans turn out in turn-of-the-century dress and celebrate the gold rush, is July 13–23, 2000. Golden Days starts off with a Felix Pedro look-alike taking his gold to the bank and includes a parade and rededication of the Pedro Monument honoring the man who started it all when he discovered gold in the Tanana Hills. Other events include pancake breakfasts, a dance, canoe and raft races, and free outdoor concerts. For additional information, phone (907) 452-1105.

The Tanana Valley State Fair will be

Day Trips From Fairbanks

125 Miles Round Trip

Drive north about 5 miles from Fairbanks via the Steese Expressway and exit west on Chena Hot Springs Road. This good all-weather paved road leads 56.5 miles east to Chena Hot Springs, a private resort (open daily year-round) offering an indoor hot springs pool, ATV rentals, trail rides and other activities.

Chena Hot Springs Road passes through the middle of Chena River Recreation Area, a year-round recreation area with many places to stop and fish for grayling, picnic or camp. See CHENA HOT SPRINGS ROAD log on pages 453–454.

130 Miles Round Trip

For some gold rush history, head out the Steese Expressway to Fox, 11 miles north, to see Gold Dredge Number 8, a 5-deck, 250-foot dredge built in 1928. Now privately owned, tours and gold panning are available.

After visiting the dredge, drive out the Steese Highway 57.3 miles to see another piece of gold mining history at the **Davidson Ditch Historical Site**. This large pipe was built in 1925 by the Fairbanks Exploration Co. to carry water to float gold dredges. If you are feeling adventurous, U.S. Creek Road (steep, gravel) winds up and over the hills from the Davidson Ditch site 7 miles to Nome Creek Gold Panning Area in the White Mountains National Recreation Area.

See the STEESE HIGHWAY section beginning on page 451 for more details.

40 to 50 Miles Round Trip

Drive 17.3 miles southeast of Fairbanks on the Richardson Highway to the turnoff for **Chena Lake Recreation Area**. Operated by the Fairbanks North Star Borough, this recreation area is built around the Chena

Flood Project constructed by the Army Corps of Engineers. Drive 5.5 miles from the highway on the main road along Moose Creek Dike to the visitor kiosk below the damsite. You can also bike out to the dam on the 5-mile-long Moose Creek Dam Bikeway. (There's a park-and-ride lot less than a mile from the Richardson Highway.) From the Main Road, turn on Lake Park Road for 250-acre Chena Lake. There's a swimming beach, play area, picnic tables, fishing dock and boat ramp. Chena Lake Bike Trail begins at Chena Lake swim beach and intersects with the Moose Creek Dam Bikeway. Day-use fee is $3 per vehicle between Memorial Day and Labor Day.

You can combine this destination with a tour of Eielson Air Force Base if you call ahead. A tour of the base is offered every Friday during the summer months from 10:30 A.M. to noon; phone the public affairs office at (907) 377-2116 for reservations and more information.

Eielson Air Force Base, about 6 miles southeast of the Chena Lakes turnoff, was built in 1943. Originally a satellite base to Ladd Field (now Fort Wainwright) and called Mile 26, it served as a storage site for aircraft on their way to the Soviet Union under the WWII Lend–Lease program. Closed after WWII, the base was reactivated in 1946 and renamed Eielson AFB, after Carl Ben Eielson, the first man to fly from Alaska over the North Pole to Greenland.

On your way back to town, stop in North Pole to visit Santa Claus and get a head-start on your Christmas shopping.

289 Miles Round Trip

For a good look at the Trans-Alaska pipeline, and a taste of the Dalton Highway, consider this long day trip. Drive out the Steese Expressway from Fairbanks, stopping first at the Trans-Alaska Pipeline Viewpoint just outside Fairbanks at **Milepost F 8.4**. Here you'll get a close-up look at the pipeline. Drive north a few more miles to the end of the Steese Expressway and then continue north on the Elliott Highway 73 miles to the junction with the Dalton Highway. This stretch of the Elliott Highway is paved for its first 30 miles, the rest is good gravel highway. Turn off onto the Dalton Highway and drive 55.6 miles north to the Yukon River bridge. The pipeline parallels the route much of the way, although there is no public access, so you'll get good views but no close-ups.

From the Yukon River crossing it is another 59.7 miles to the **Arctic Circle BLM Wayside**, with interpretive display and picnic area, at N 66°33′ W 150°48′. At this latitude, the sun does not set on summer solstice (June 20 or 21) and it does not rise on winter solstice (December 21 or 22).

See the ELLIOTT HIGHWAY section (page 459) and the DALTON HIGHWAY section (page 464) for more details on this trip.

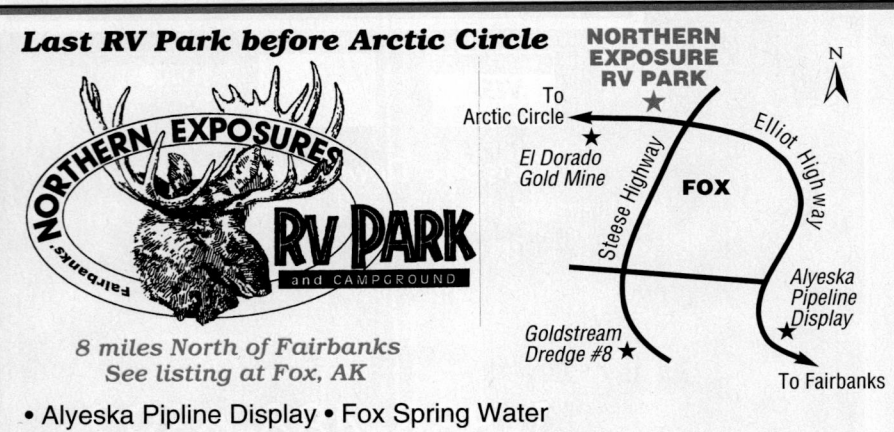

held Aug. 4–12, 2000. Alaska's oldest state fair, the Tanana Valley State Fair features agricultural exhibits, arts and crafts, food booths, a rodeo and other entertainment. Phone (907) 452-3750 for more information.

Check with the Fairbanks visitor information center for more information on all local events.

Besides these special events, summer visitors can take in a semipro baseball game at Growden Park where the Alaska Goldpanners take on other Alaska league teams.

Visit Creamer's Field. Follow the flocks of waterfowl to Creamer's Field Migratory Waterfowl Refuge. Located 1 mile from downtown Fairbanks, this 1,800-acre refuge managed by the Alaska Dept. of Fish and Game offers opportunities to observe large concentrations of ducks, geese, shorebirds and cranes in the spring and fall. Throughout the summer, sandhill cranes eat in the planted barley fields.

Explore the 2-mile/3.2-km self-guided

nature trail and the renovated historic farmhouse that serves as a visitor center. Stop at 1300 College Road to find the trailhead, viewing areas and brochures on Creamer's Field. For more information, phone (907) 452-5162.

Creamer's Field Migratory Waterfowl Refuge—where nature is at its best. Summer visitor center hours, 10 A.M. to 5 P.M., closed Sunday and Monday. June through August, guided walks begin at Farmhouse Visitor Center Tuesday and Thursday at 7 P.M.; Wednesday and Saturday at 9 A.M. No charge and the refuge is always open. Phone (907) 452-5162. [ADVERTISEMENT]

See the Pipeline: Drive about 10 miles north from downtown on the Steese Expressway to the Trans–Alaska Pipeline

Viewpoint. You can walk along a portion of the pipeline and see a real "pig"—a device used to clean the pipeline. Excellent opportunity for pipeline photos. Alyeska Pipeline Service Co. visitor center at the site is open daily from May to September. Free literature and information; phone (907) 456-9391.

Tanana Valley Farmers Market. Visit Alaska's premier Farmers Market, located next to the Fairgrounds on College Road, open from mid-May to mid-September. Vendors offer "thousands of miles fresher" Alaska grown vegetables; blue-ribbon florals; Alaskan meats, fish, honey, jams and syrups; made-in-Alaska handcrafts and baked goods. Look for our brochure at local Visitor's Centers. Market hours are Wednesdays 11 A.M. to 4 P.M. and Saturdays 9 A.M. to 4 P.M.; there's plenty of parking. Stop by the Market and enjoy Alaska made and grown products. "Meet You At The Market!" [ADVERTISEMENT]

The Alaska Rag Co. A must-see for Fairbanks travelers. This unique Alaskan gift shop manufactures beautiful handwoven rag rugs from 100 percent recycled clothing. The store also features works from 70-plus Alaskan artists. Items include jewelry, pottery, mittens, Polar fleece, dreamcatchers, native dolls, cards and much more. Downtown Fairbanks. Phone (907) 451-4401. ("A part of FCMHC's vocational unit.") [ADVERTISEMENT]

On December 25, 2000, sunrise is at 10:59 A.M. and sunset is at 2:44 P.M.

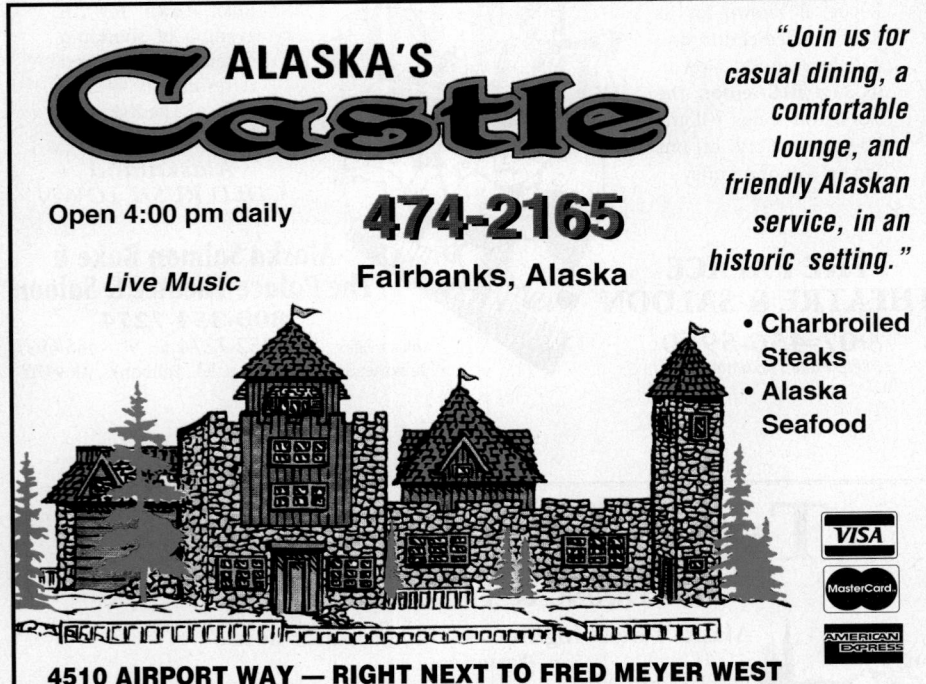

Chena Pump House National Historic Site. Built in 1931–33 by the Fairbanks Exploration Co. to pump water from the Chena River to dredging operations at Cripple Creek, the pump house was remodeled in 1978 and now houses a restaurant and saloon. The sheet metal cladding, interior roof and some equipment (such as the intake ditch) are from the original pump house, which shut down in 1958 when the F.E. Co. ceased its Cripple Creek dredging operations. The pump house is located at Mile 1.3 Chena Pump Road.

See Bank Displays: Key Bank, at 1st Avenue and Cushman Street, has a display of gold nuggets and several trophy animals. Mount McKinley Mutual Savings Bank features a display of McKinley prints and the original cannonball safe used when the bank opened. The bank is at 531 3rd Ave.

Visit Historic Churches: St. Matthew's Episcopal Church, 1029 1st Ave., was originally built in 1905, but burned in 1947 and was rebuilt the following year. Of special interest is the church's intricately carved altar, made in 1906 of Interior Alaska birch and saved from the fire. **Immaculate Conception Church,** on the Chena River at Cushman Street bridge, was drawn by horses to its present location in the winter of 1911 from its original site at 1st Avenue and Dunkel Street.

View Mount McKinley: The best spot to see Mount McKinley is from the University of Alaska Fairbanks campus (on Yukon Drive, between Talkeetna and Sheenjek streets) where a turnout and marker define the horizon view of Mount Hayes (elev. 13,832 feet/4,216m); Hess Mountain (elev. 11,940 feet/3,639m); Mount Deborah (elev. 12,339 feet/3,761m); and Mount McKinley (elev. 20,320 feet/6,194m). Distant foothills are part of the Wood River Butte.

Cruise Aboard the Riverboat *Discovery*: Every day at 8:45 A.M. and 2 P.M. in summer, the riverboat *Discovery* departs for a half-day cruise on the Chena and Tanana rivers. Drive out Airport Road, turn south at Dale Road and continue 0.5 mile/0.8 km on Dale to Discovery Drive. Reservations are required, as this is one of the most popular attractions in town. For the first leg of the trip, the *Discovery* winds its way down the meandering Chena River, its banks lined by old homesteads, modern homes and bush planes. The Chena River also joins with Cripple Creek, the Interior's richest gold rush stream. Passengers have the opportunity to see Susan Butcher's Iditarod-champion dog team in action at her home along the river. On the Tanana River, fish wheels turn in the swift glacial water, scooping up salmon to be dried and smoked for winter food. Returning up the Tanana, the boat stops at Old Chena Indian Village where passengers disembark for a tour. Guides from the *Discovery*, who are of Indian or Eskimo heritage, are on hand to explain past and present Native culture. For more information on the riverboat *Discovery*, contact Alaska Riverways, Inc., 1975 Discovery Dr., Fairbanks, AK 99709; phone (907) 479-6673, fax 479-4613.

Play Tennis: There are 6 outdoor asphalt courts at the Mary Siah Recreation Center, 805 14th Ave. No fees or reservations. For more information phone (907) 459-1082.

Play Golf: Maintaining a scenic 9-hole course with natural greens, the Fairbanks Golf and Country Club (public is invited) is west of the downtown area at 1735 Farmers

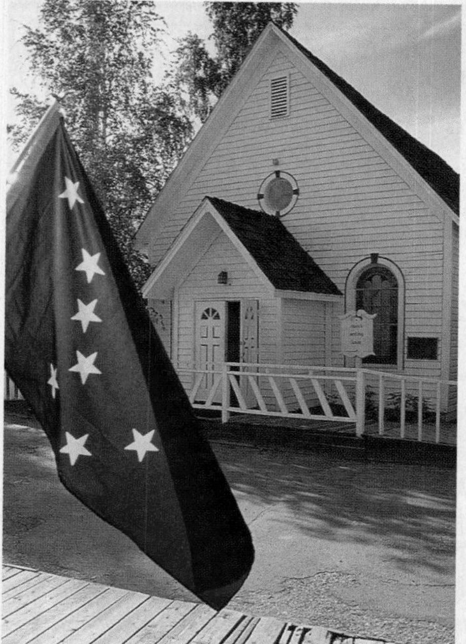

Alaskaland has many pioneer Fairbanks buildings.

(© Ralph & Leonor Barrett, Four Corners Imaging)

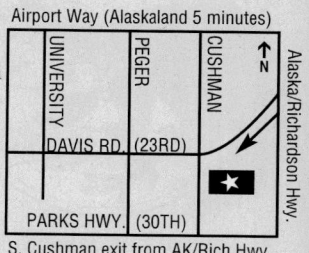

Loop Road; phone (907) 479-6555 for information and reservations. The 18-hole Chena Bend Golf Course is located on Fort Wainwright, open to the public; phone (907) 353-6223. North Star Golf Club, located 10 minutes north of downtown on the Old Steese Highway, offers a regulation 9-hole course;, open to the public; phone (907) 457-4653 or (907) 452-2104.

Ride Bikes Around Fairbanks: There are many day-touring choices in Fairbanks. A round-trip tour of the city, the University of Alaska and the College area can be made by leaving town on Airport Way and returning on College Road. The Farmers Loop Road or a ride out the Old Steese Highway toward Fox are easy tours.

Visit Alaskaland Pioneer Park. Visitors will find a relaxed atmosphere at Alaskaland, a pleasant park with historic buildings, small shops, food, entertainment, playgrounds and 4 covered picnic shelters. The park— which has no admission fee—is open year-round.

To drive to Alaskaland (at Airport Way and Peger Road), take Airport Way to Wilbur, turn north onto Wilbur, then immediately west onto access road, which leads to Alaskaland enclosure.

The 44-acre historic park was created in 1967 as the Alaska Centennial Park to commemorate the 100th anniversary of U.S. territorial status and provide a taste of Interior Alaska history. Visitors may begin their visit at the information center, which is located just inside the park's main gate. Walk through Gold Rush Town, a narrow, winding street of authentic old buildings that once graced downtown Fairbanks and now house gift shops. Here you will find the Kitty Hensley and Judge Wickersham houses, furnished with turn-of-the-century items; the First Presbyterian Church, constructed in 1906; and the Pioneers of Alaska Museum, dedicated to those who braved frontier life to found Fairbanks. Free guided historical

Totem poles are a product of Tlingit and Haida cultures.

Please support our MILEPOST® advertisers.

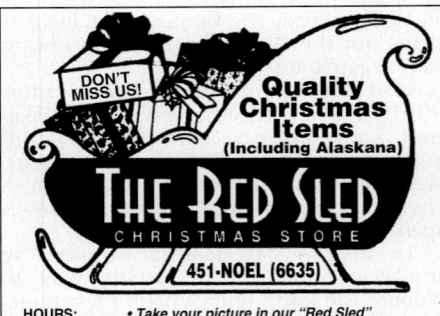

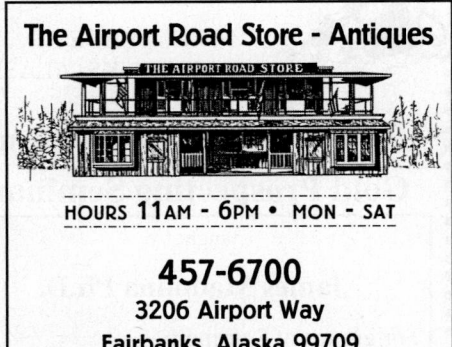

walking tours take place each afternoon.

The park is home to the newly renovated SS *Nenana,* a national landmark. Cared for by the Fairbanks Historical Preservation Foundation, the *Nenana* is the largest sternwheeler ever built west of the Mississippi, and the second largest wooden vessel in existence. The Foundation also displays a 300-foot/91-m diorama of life along the Tanana and Yukon rivers in the early 1900s.

The top level of the Civic Center houses an art gallery featuring rotating contemporary exhibits and paintings; 11 A.M. to 9 P.M. daily, Memorial Day through Labor Day; noon to 8 P.M. daily, except Monday, during the rest of the year.

Behind the Civic Center, you'll find the Pioneer Air Museum, which features antique aircraft and stories of their Alaskan pilots, with displays from 1913–48. Phone (907) 451-0037, Memorial Day through Labor Day, for information. Admission is $1.

At the rear of the park is the Native Village Museum and Kashims with Native wares, artifacts and crafts. Across from the Native Village is Mining Valley, with displays of gold-mining equipment. The Alaska Salmon Bake, with both outdoor and heated indoor seating areas, is also part of Mining Valley. A popular feature, the Alaska Salmon Bake is open daily for lunch from noon to 2 P.M. (June 10 to Aug. 15), and for dinner from 5–9 P.M. (end of May to mid-September). Salmon, barbecued ribs, halibut and 18-oz. porterhouse steaks are served, rain or shine.

There's entertainment 7 nights a week starting at 8 P.M. at the Palace Theatre & Saloon, featuring a musical comedy review about life in Fairbanks titled "Golden Heart Revue." The Big Stampede show in Gold Rush Town is a theater in the round, presenting the paintings of Rusty Heurlin, depicting the trail of '98; narrative by Ruben Gaines.

The Crooked Creek & Whiskey Island Railroad, a 30-gauge train, takes passengers for a 12-minute ride around the park. Other types of recreational activities available at Alaskaland include miniature golf, an antique carousel and picnicking in covered shelters. A public dock is located on the Chena River at the rear of the park.

Visitors are welcome to take part in square and round dances year-round at the Alaskaland Dance Center. Phone (907) 452-5699 evenings for calendar of events. For more information about Alaskaland, phone (907) 459-1087.

Historic Gold Dredge No. 8 (Gray Line of Alaska). Gold Dredge No. 8 is a monument to the miners who used the machinery to produce more than 7.5 million ounces of

Sandhill cranes at Creamer's Field in Fairbanks. (© Robin Brandt)

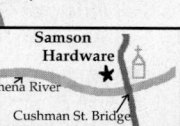

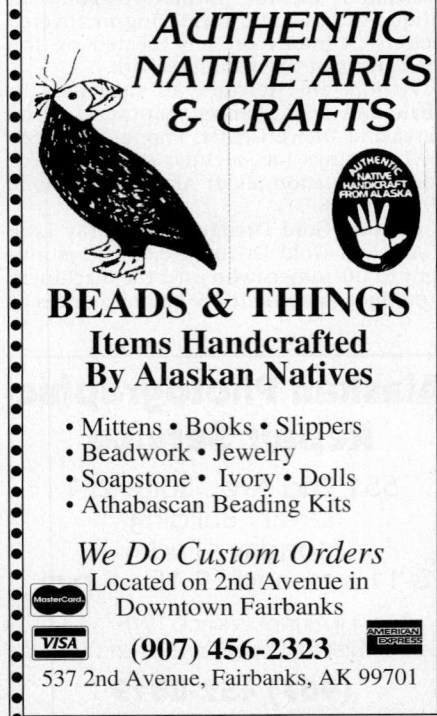

gold, and to the engineers who built it. Visitors tour the only dredge in Alaska open to the public. Gold panning and a Miner's lunch are also available at this national historic site. See advertisement on page 407 in this section. [ADVERTISEMENT]

Go Swimming. Fairbanks North Star Borough Parks and Recreation Dept. offers 3 pools: Mary Siah Recreation Center, 805 14th Ave., phone (907) 459-1082; Robert Hamme Memorial Pool, 901 Airport Way, phone (907) 459-1086; and Robert Wescott Memorial Pool, 8th Avenue in North Pole, phone (907) 488-9402.

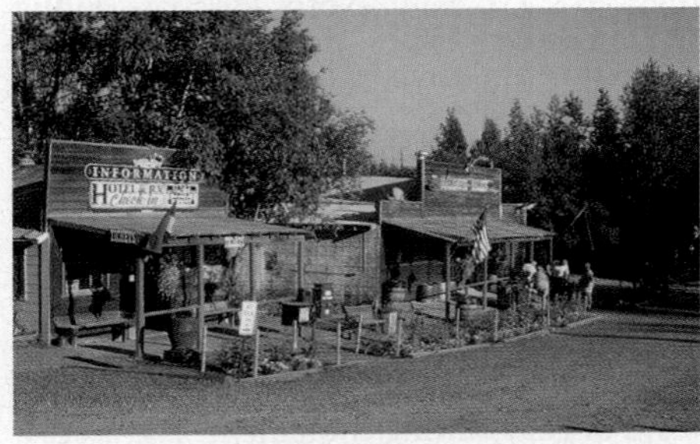

Ester Gold Camp. Ester was a raucous mining camp in 1906, with a population of some 5,000 miners. Today a much quieter community just 7 miles west of Fairbanks, Ester's heydays are relived in music, song and dance at the Malemute Saloon, a popular stop with tourists in summer and always a good family show. The Northern Lights Show, a slide show about the aurora borealis, also receives rave reviews.

Visit a Gold Mine. No matter the price of gold, you'll find gold mining in the Fairbanks area. Gold mines (both commercial and industrial) offering tours include El Dorado Gold Mine, north of Fairbanks via the Steese Expressway, and Yellow Eagle Mine, west of Fairbanks on the Parks Highway near the Ester turnoff.

El Dorado Gold Mine. Travel professionals describe this tour at the El Dorado Gold

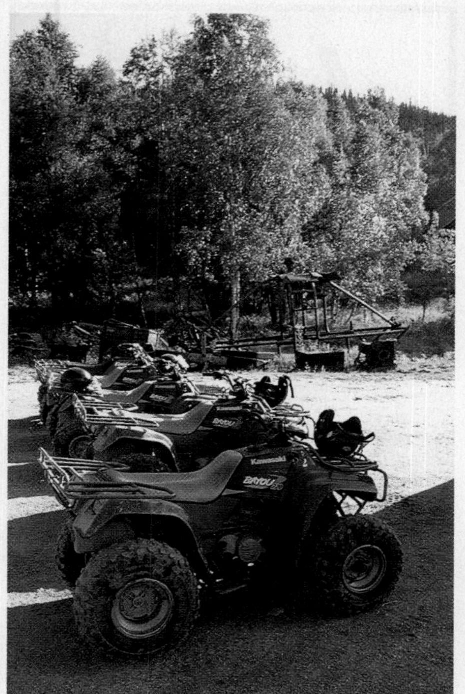

Rental ATVs at Chena Hot Springs Resort at the end of Chena Hot Springs Road. (© Kris Graef, staff)

Mine, which was featured nationally on NBC television, as "the best 2 hours you will spend in the State." The tour begins with a ride on the Tanana Valley Railroad and takes you through the gold fields of Interior Alaska. Along the way you'll see demonstrations of early mining techniques, including a stop in a permafrost tunnel where underground mining is explained. Upon arrival at the camp, Alaskan gold miners give you a brief but informative course in mining, and then you receive your own "poke" of paydirt to pan. The experienced crew will help you

pan your own gold—and they guarantee that everyone finds gold. This interesting and entertaining tour is great fun for the whole family. It's a "must do" for everyone who visits Fairbanks. Tours depart daily at 9:45 A.M. and 3 P.M. in summer, *except* for Saturday and Monday, when there are afternoon tours only. Reservations are required (907) 479-7613. Take the Steese Expresswway to Fox (about 10 miles north of Fairbanks) and then continue straight ahead on the Elliott Highway for 1.3 miles. Ask about our free shuttle. [ADVERTISEMENT]

Go Skiing: Fairbanks has several downhill ski areas: Cleary Summit, **Milepost F 20.3** Steese Highway; Skiland, **Milepost F 20.9** Steese Highway; Eielson AFB, Fort Wainwright ski hills and Moose Mountain

The Arctic Circle lies at approximately 66°33'N latitude. Fairbanks lies at 64°50'N.

Seward's Day, an Alaska state holiday, is celebrated the last Monday in March. William Henry Seward negotiated the 1867 purchase of Alaska from Russia for $7.2 million.

Ski Resort, Spinach Creek Road on Murphy Dome.

Chena Hot Springs Resort at **Milepost J 56.5** Chena Hot Springs Road has over 20 miles of cross-country ski trails, as well as cross-country ski rentals. Other cross-country ski trails are at Birch Hill Recreation Area; drive 2.8 miles/4.5 km north of Fairbanks via Steese Expressway to a well-marked turnoff, then drive in 2.3 miles/3.7 km. University of Alaska–Fairbanks has 26 miles/42 km of cross-country ski trails. The trail system is quite extensive: you may ski out to Ester Dome.

Sled Dog Racing. The Alaska Dog Mushers' Assoc. (ADMA) hosts a series of dog races from December to March, ending with the Open North American Championship, a 3-day event with 3 heats (of 20, 20 and 30 miles). The "Open" is considered by many to be the "granddaddy of dog races." Fairbanks also hosts the 1,000-mile/1,609-km Yukon Quest Sled Dog Race between Fairbanks and Whitehorse, YT, with the start in Fairbanks in 2000. For more information, contact the ADMA at (907) 457-MUSH, or the Yukon Quest office at (907) 452-7954. The ADMA has a Mushers Hall at 4 mile Farmers Loop Road where people can see dog teams train and race.

Go Fishing: There are several streams and lakes within driving distance of Fairbanks, and local fishing guides are available. **Chena Lake**, about 20 miles/32 km southeast of the city via the Richardson–Alaska Highway at Chena Lakes Recreation Area, is stocked with rainbow trout, silver salmon and arctic char. The **Chena River** and its tributaries offer fishing for sheefish, whitefish, northern pike and burbot. The Chena River flows through Fairbanks. Grayling fishing in the upper Chena is very good, with some large fish. Grayling fishing in the Chena is restricted to catch-and-release year-round. Chena Hot Springs Road off the Steese Highway provides access to fisheries in the Chena River Recreation Area (see the STEESE HIGHWAY section). The Steese Highway also offers access to the **Chatanika River.** Special regulations apply in these waters for grayling and salmon fishing. Phone the ADF&G Division of Sport Fish office at (907) 459-7207.

Air taxi operators and guides in Fairbanks offer short trips from the city for rainbow trout, grayling, northern pike, lake trout and sheefish in lakes and streams of the Tanana and Yukon river drainages. Some operators have camps set up for overnight trips while others specialize in day trips. The air taxi

Fishing for rainbow in a stocked pond along the Steese Highway.

(© Kris Graef, staff)

operators usually provide a boat and motor for their angling visitors. Rates are reasonable and vary according to the distance from town and type of facilities offered.

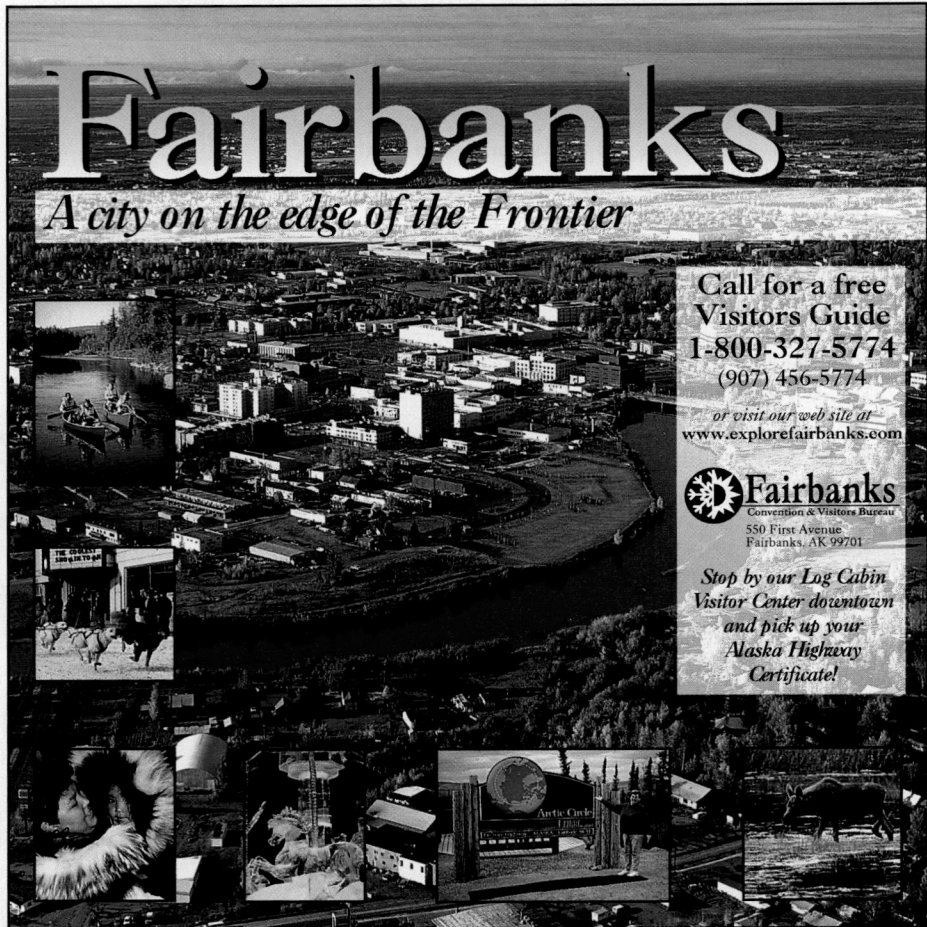

DENALI NATIONAL PARK

(formerly Mount McKinley National Park)

Includes log of Park Road

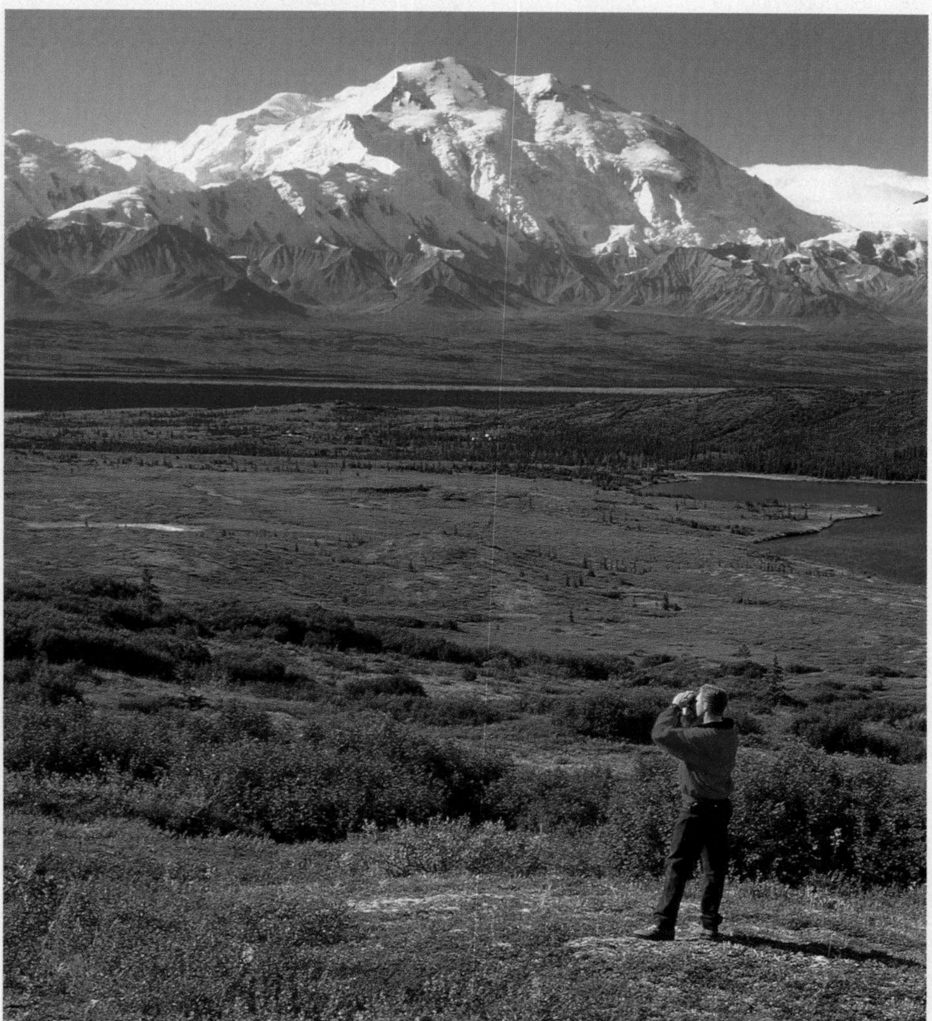

Hiker scans the tundra for wildlife at Wonder Lake. (© Tom Bol Photography)

Denali National Park and Preserve lies on the north flank of the Alaska Range, 250 miles/402 km south of the Arctic Circle. The park entrance, accessible by highway, railroad and aircraft, is 237 highway miles/381 km north of Anchorage, and about half that distance from Fairbanks.

An admission fee of $5 per person (between the ages of 17 and 62; children under 17 are exempt from the fee; $10 per vehicle/family) is charged to visitors traveling the park road. The fee is collected when visitors obtain shuttle bus tickets, campground permits or stop at the Visitor Center. U.S. citizens 62 and older may purchase a $10 lifetime Golden Age Passport. (A $20 annual park pass and the $50 Golden Eagle Pass are valid for admission.)

For detailed information about the park, write Denali National Park and Preserve, Box 9, Denali Park, AK 99755; winter phone (907) 683-2294, summer phone (907) 683-1266 or 1267. The park's web site (www.nps.gov/dena) has current information and reservation forms.

The park is open year-round to visitors, although the hotel, most campgrounds, and food and shuttle bus service within the park are available only from late May or early June to mid-September. Opening dates for facilities and activities for the summer season are announced in the spring by the Park Service and depend mainly on snow conditions in May. Closing dates for facilities and activities at the park are announced in the fall. Most park campgrounds close for the season in early September.

When you arrive be sure to stop at the Visitor Center, near the park entrance. The center offers information and limited reservations for campgrounds in the park; maps, brochures and schedules of events; details on ranger talks, hikes, nature walks, sled dog demonstrations and wildlife tours; and shuttle bus schedules and ticket reservations. Also available are National Park entrance passes. The center is open daily in summer, generally from early morning into the evening.

Parking space is limited at the Visitor Center. Day parking is available at Riley Creek Campground (walk or mini-shuttle to Visitor Center).

Lodging and camping are available outside the park on the Parks Highway, and there are many activities—river rafting, hikes and ranger programs—to enjoy. Check with operators outside the park and with personnel at the Visitor Center about programs and activities.

First-time visitors should be particularly aware of the controlled-access system for Park Road use. Private vehicle traffic on the 92-mile/148-km road into the park is restricted beyond the Savage River check station (**Milepost J 14.8**) to registered campers. Campers may reserve campsites by phone or at the Visitor Center. The shuttle bus system and concessionaire-operated tours are available to allow visitors a means of viewing the park without disturbing the wildlife. See Accommodations/Visitor Services this section for details on the shuttle bus service and campsite reservations system.

There is no policy restricting access by bicycle on the Park Road, although cyclists must stay on the road and overnight at one of the established campgrounds.

In an effort to preserve wildlife viewing opportunities for the public, the National Park Service has set road traffic limits. Traffic will be held to the 1986 averages. Consequently, there are limited bus seats available. When planning trips to the park, visitors should reserve shuttle bus tickets in advance by phone or plan activities in the entrance area—such as attending ranger-led interpretive programs—for the first 1 or 2 days, until bus seats can be obtained.

Each summer the park issues permits to a limited number of individuals, selected by lottery, to drive their vehicles through the park on one day of a specific weekend in early September. It is not unusual for these late-season visitors, the majority of whom are Alaskans, to have their tour curtailed because of early snows within the park. Information on how to apply for this popular lottery appears during the summer in local newspapers.

The crown jewel among the park's attractions is Mount McKinley, North America's highest mountain at 20,320 feet/6,194m. On a clear day, Mount McKinley is visible from Anchorage and many points along the Parks Highway; however, summer's often overcast

DENALI NATIONAL PARK AND PRESERVE

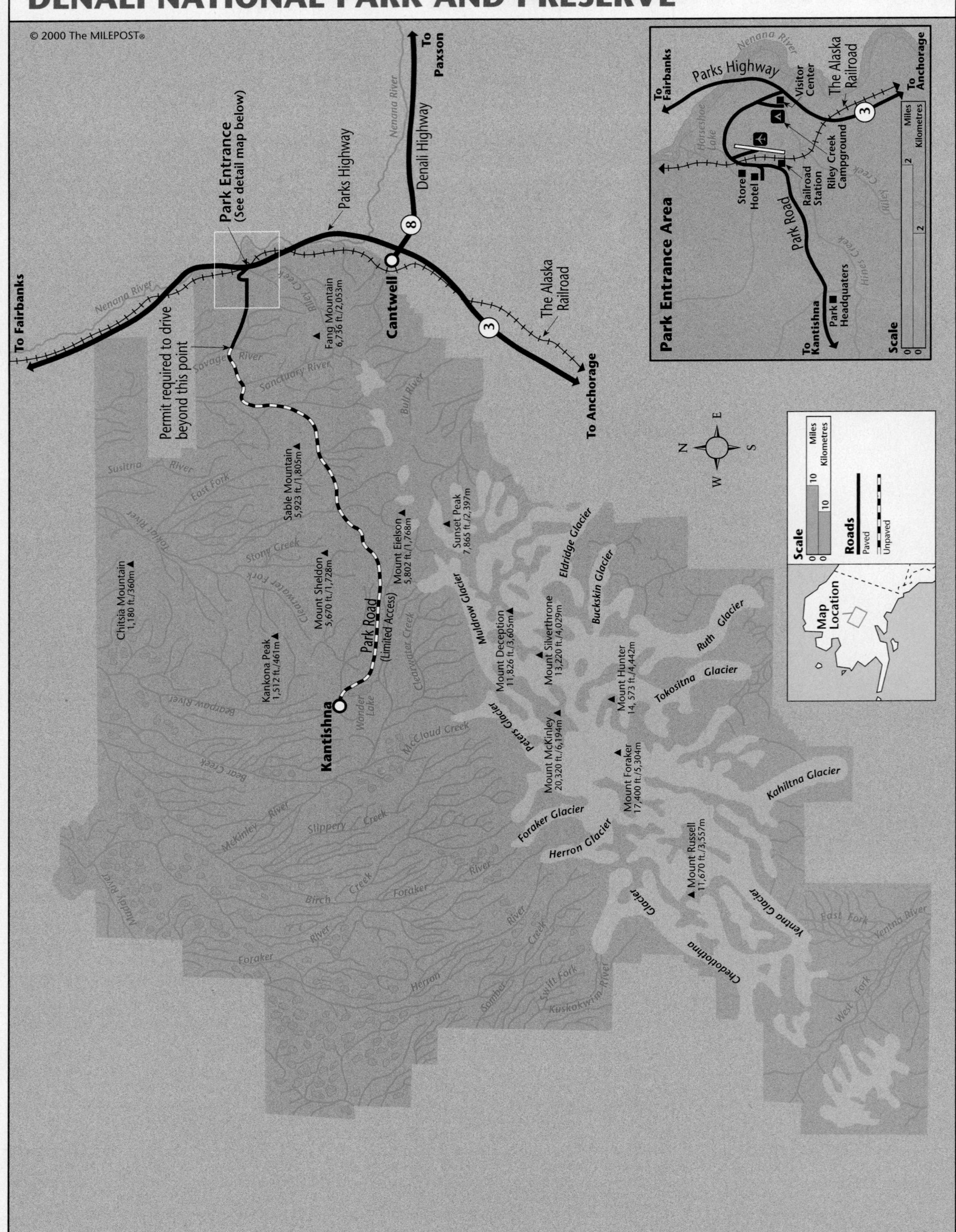
© 2000 The MILEPOST®
To Fairbanks
To Paxson
To Anchorage
Parks Highway
Denali Highway
The Alaska Railroad
Park Entrance
(See detail map below)
Permit required to drive beyond this point
Cantwell
Kantishna
Park Road
(Limited Access)
Nenana River
Savage River
Sanctuary River
Riley Creek
Bull River
Susitna River
East Fork
Toklat River
Stony Creek
Clearwater Fork
Clearwater Creek
Bearpaw River
Wonder Lake
McCloud Creek
Bear Creek
McKinley River
Slippery Creek
Muddy River
Birch Creek
Foraker River
Herron River
Somber Creek
Swift Fork
Kuskokwim River
Fang Mountain
6,736 ft./2,053m
Sable Mountain
5,923 ft./1,805m
Mount Eielson
5,802 ft./1,768m
Sunset Peak
7,865 ft./2,397m
Mount Sheldon
5,670 ft./1,728m
Chitsia Mountain
1,180 ft./360m
Kankona Peak
1,512 ft./461m
Mount Deception
11,826 ft./3,605m
Mount Silverthrone
13,220 ft./4,029m
Mount Hunter
14, 573 ft./4,442m
Mount McKinley
20,320 ft./6,194m
Mount Foraker
17,400 ft./5,304m
Mount Russell
11,670 ft./3,557m
Muldrow Glacier
Eldridge Glacier
Buckskin Glacier
Ruth Glacier
Tokositna Glacier
Peters Glacier
Kahiltna Glacier
Foraker Glacier
Herron Glacier
Chedotlothna Glacier
Yentna Glacier
East Fork
Yentna River
West Fork
N
E
S
W
Park Entrance Area
Parks Highway
Nenana River
Visitor Center
The Alaska Railroad
Horseshoe Lake
Riley Creek Campground
Railroad Station
Store
Hotel
Park Road
Park Headquaters
Hines Creek
Riley Creek
To Kantishna
Scale
0 2 Miles
0 2 Kilometres
Scale
0 10 Miles
0 10 Kilometres
Roads
Paved
Unpaved
Map Location

or rainy weather frequently obscures the mountain, and travelers have about a 30 percent chance of seeing it in summer.

First mention of "the mountain" was in 1794, when English explorer Capt. George Vancouver spotted a "stupendous snow mountain" from Cook Inlet. Early Russian explorers and traders called the peak *Bolshaia Gora,* or "Big Mountain." The Athabascan Indian name for the mountain is *Denali,* "the High One." In 1896 a prospector named William A. Dickey named the mountain for presidential nominee William McKinley of Ohio, although McKinley had no connection with Alaska. Even today, the mountain is known by two names: Mount McKinley according to USGS maps, and Denali according to the state Geographic Names Board.

The history of climbs on McKinley is as intriguing as its names. In 1903, Judge James Wickersham and party climbed to an estimated 8,000 feet/2,438m, while the Dr. Frederick A. Cook party reached the 11,000-foot/3,353-m level. In 1906, Cook returned to the mountain and made 2 attempts at the summit—the first unsuccessful, the second (according to Cook) successful. Cook's vague description of his ascent route and a questionable summit photo led many to doubt his claim. The exhaustive research of McKinley expert Bradford Washburn has proven quite conclusively the exaggeration of Cook's claims. Tom Lloyd, of the 1910 Sourdough Party (which included Charles McGonagall, Pete Anderson and Billy Taylor), claimed they had reached both summits (north and south peaks) but could not provide any photographic evidence. (Much later it was verified that they had reached the summit of the lower north peak.) The first complete and well documented ascent of the true summit of Mount McKinley was made in June 1913 by the Rev. Hudson Stuck, Episcopal archdeacon of the Yukon, accompanied by Harry Karstens, Robert Tatum and Walter Harper. Harper, a Native Athabascan, was the first person to set foot on the higher south peak. The story of their achievement was colorfully recorded in Stuck's book, *The Ascent of Denali.* Out of respect for the Native people among whom he lived and worked, Stuck refused to refer

Two adult Dall sheep rams in Denali National Park. (© Mike Jones)

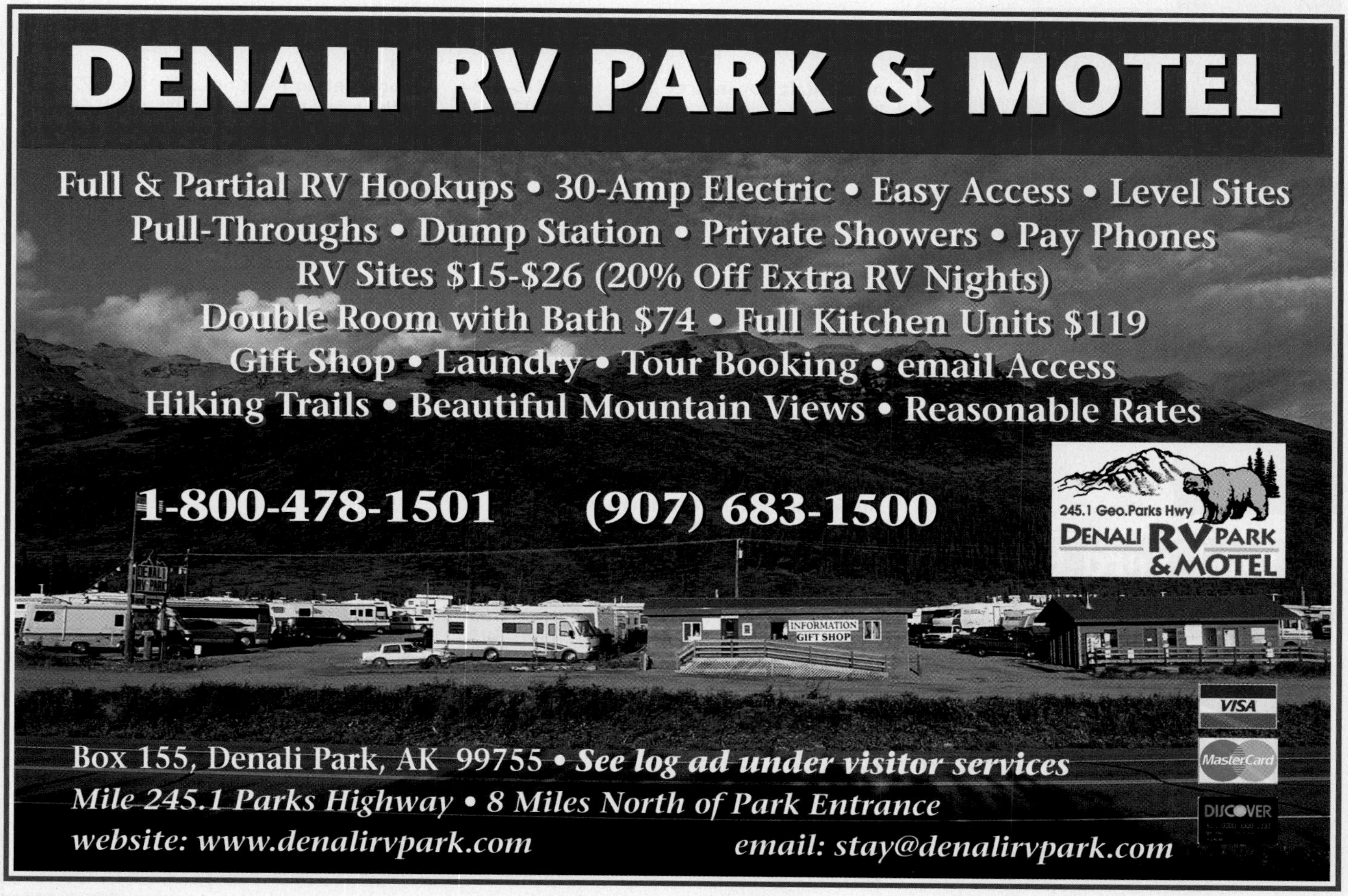

Historic cabin at Kantishna at the end of the Park Road. (© Tom Bol Photography)

to the mountain as McKinley.

Today, more than a thousand people attempt to climb Mount McKinley each year between April and June, most flying in to base camp at 7,000 feet/2,134m. (The first airplane landing on the mountain was flown in 1932 by Joe Crosson.) Geographic features of McKinley and its sister peaks bear the names of many early explorers: Eldridge and Muldrow glaciers, after George Eldridge and Robert Muldrow of the U.S. Geographic Service who determined the peak's altitude in 1898; Wickersham Wall; Karstens Ridge; Harper Icefall; and Mount Carpe and Mount Koven, named for Allen Carpe and Theodore Koven, both killed in a 1932 climb.

The National Park Service maintains a ranger station in Talkeetna that is staffed full time from mid-April through mid-September and intermittently during the winter. Mountaineering rangers provide information on climbing within the Alaska Range. A reference library and slide/tape program are available for climbers. Mountaineering regulations and information may be obtained from Talkeetna Ranger Station, P.O. Box 588, Talkeetna, AK 99676; phone (907) 733-2231.

Timberline in the park is at 2,700 feet/823m. The landscape below timberline in this subarctic wilderness is called taiga, a term of Russian origin that describes the scant tree growth. Black and white spruce, willow, dwarf birch and aspen grow at lower elevations. The uplands of alpine tundra are carpeted with lichens, mosses, wildflowers and low-growing shrubs. Wildflowers bloom in spring, usually peaking by early July.

Denali National Park is one of the last intact ecosystems in the world, according to the National Park Service. Here visitors have the opportunity to observe the natural behavior of wild animals. Grizzly bears, caribou, wolves and red foxes wander freely over the tundra. Moose wade through streams and lake shallows. Lynx pursue snowshoe hare in taiga forests. Marmots, pikas and Dall sheep inhabit high, rocky areas. The arctic ground squirrel's sharp warning call is heard throughout the park.

DENALI PARK AREA ADVERTISERS

Alaska Raft Adventures.....Ph. (907) 276-7234
Backwoods Lodge.............Ph. (800) 292-2232
Black Diamond Golf..........Ph. (907) 683-2427
Cantwell RV Park..............Ph. (907) 768-2210
Carlo Creek Lodge............Ph. (907) 683-2576
Carlo Heights Bed & Breakfast & Sled Dog School.....Ph. (907) 683-5212
Crow's Nest.......................Ph. (907) 683-2723
Denali Air..........................Ph. (907) 683-2261
Denali Backcountry Lodge..........................Ph. (800) 841-0692
Denali Bluffs Hotel............Ph. (907) 683-7000
Denali Cabins Alaska........Ph. (888) 560-2489
Denali Dome Home Bed & Breakfast...........Ph. (907) 683-1239
Denali Grizzly Bear Cabins & Campground.............Mi. 231.1 Parks Hwy.
Denali Hostel...................Ph. (907) 683-1295
Denali Park Hotel.............Ph. (800) 276-7234
Denali National Park Wilderness Centers–Camp Denali..Ph. (907) 683-2290
Denali National Park Wilderness Centers–North Face Lodge...................Ph. (907) 683-2290
Denali North Star Inn.......Ph. (800) 684-1560
Denali Outdoor Center.....Ph. (907) 683-1925
Denali Princess Lodge......Ph. (800) 426-0500
Denali Raft Adventures.....Ph. (907) 683-2234
Denali River Cabins...........Ph. (800) 239-7275
Denali Riverside RV Park...Ph. (888) 778-7700
Denali RV Park & Motel....Mi. 245.1 Parks Hwy.
Denali Sourdough Cabins........................Mi. 238.8 Parks Hwy.
Denali Suites..................Mi. 248.8 Parks Hwy.
Denali West Lodge...........Ph. (907) 674-3112
Denali Wilderness Lodge..Ph. (800) 541-9979
Doug Geeting Aviation.....Ph. (800) 770-2366
Earth Song Lodge.............Ph. (907) 683-2863
Era Helicopters Flight-seeing Tours................Ph. (800) 843-1947
Evan Industries, Inc.......Mi. 247.3 Parks Hwy.
Healy Heights Family Cabins..........................Ph. (907) 683-2639
Kantishna Roadhouse.......Ph. (800) 942-7420
Kantishna Wilderness Trails............................Ph. (800) 942-7420
K2 Aviation.......................Ph. (907) 733-2291
Lynx Creek Pizza............Mi. 238.6 Parks Hwy.
McKinley Air Service.........Ph. (800) 564-1765
McKinley Chalet Resort....Ph. (800) 276-7234
McKinley Creekside Cabins..........................Ph. (888) 5-DENALI
McKinley RV & Campground.............Mi. 248.4 Parks Hwy.
McKinley Village Resort..............................Ph. (800) 276-7234
Midnight Sun Express®.....Ph. (800) 835-8907
Motel Nord Haven............Ph. (800) 683-4501
Mt. McKinley Princess Lodge............Ph. (800) 426-0500
Nenana Raft Adventures..................Ph. (800) 789-RAFT
Otto Lake RV Park.............Mi. 247 Parks Hwy.
Perch, The.........................Mi. 224 Parks Hwy.
Pere Air............................Ph. (877) 683-6033
Ridgetop Cabins.............Mi. 253.3 Parks Hwy.
Stampede Lodge..............Ph. (800) 478-2370
Talkeetna Air Taxi.............Ph. (907) 733-2218
Totem Inn.........................Ph. (907) 683-2420
Valley Vista Bed & Breakfast...........Ph. (877) 683-2841
White Moose Lodge.........Ph. (800) 481-1232

There are 3 types of bears found in Alaska: the black bear, brown/grizzly bear and the polar bear.

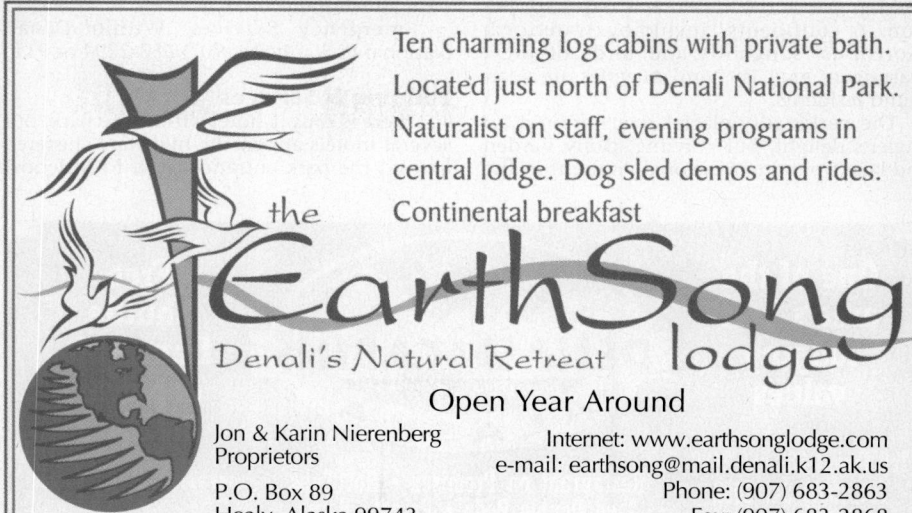

Migratory bird life encompasses species from 6 continents, including waterfowl, shorebirds, songbirds and birds of prey. Ptarmigan, gray jays and magpies are year-round residents.

The park's silty glacial rivers are not an angler's delight, but grayling, Dolly Varden and lake trout are occasionally caught in the clear streams and small lakes.

Emergency Services: Within Denali National Park, phone (907) 683-2294 or 911.

Lodging & Services

There is only 1 hotel within the park, but several motels are on the highway, clustered around the park entrance (turn to **Milepost A 237.3** in the PARKS HIGHWAY section). Private accommodations are also available in the Kantishna area. *NOTE: Visitors should make reservations for lodging far in advance.* The park hotel and area motels are often filled during the summer. Visitors must book their own accommodations. See ads for accommodations this section. For area accommodations, also turn to pages 379–384 in the PARKS HIGHWAY section.

Visitor services are available from late May to mid-September, depending on weather. The Denali National Park Hotel has a gift shop, restaurant, snack bar and saloon. Limited groceries and showers are available at a small store near the hotel. Gas is no longer available inside the park. Gas service 1 mile/1.6 km north of the Park Road junction, May to mid-September. The post office is near the hotel.

NOTE: There are no food services in the park after you leave the headquarters entrance area.

Shuttle bus: The National Park Service concessionaire (Denali Park Resorts) provides shuttle bus service from the Visitor Center to Toklat, Eielson Visitor Center and Wonder Lake. During peak season, bus tickets for the next day's shuttles are generally gone by mid-morning. Up to 8 tickets may be reserved in advance; see Reservation System following. Shuttle buses pick up and drop off passengers along the Park Road on a space-available basis, and stop for scenic and wildlife viewing as schedules permit. The buses generally depart the Visitor Center between 5:15 A.M. and 3 P.M., May 27 to Sept. 11..

Ticket prices are $12.50 adult, $6.25 youth (13–16 years) to Toklat; $21 adult, $10.50 youth to Wonder Lake; and $31 adult, $15.50 youth to Kantishna. Children 12 and under are free.

A round-trip between the Visitor Center and Eielson Visitor Center takes approximately 8 hours. The round-trip to Wonder Lake takes about 11 hours. Bring a lunch, camera, binoculars, extra film, warm clothes and rain gear. Buses run daily from about Memorial Day through Labor Day, weather permitting.

Reservation System: Park shuttle bus tickets and campsites may be reserved through a nationwide, toll-free number, 1-800-622-7275 (PARK). Advance reservations (more than 2 days before departure) are available for 65 percent of the bus tickets and campsites. Two days prior to departure the remaining 35 percent can be reserved by phone. The day of departure tickets must be purchased at the Visitor Center only. 100 percent of campsites: Riley Creek, Savage River, Teklanika River and Wonder Lake) can be reserved in advance. Anchorage residents and residents of foreign countries phone (907) 272-7275 for reservations. The phone-in reservation system opens in February. The call center is open 7 A.M. to 5 P.M. (Alaska time), 7 days a week. A maximum of 8 shuttle bus tickets may be requested with each call. Shuttle bus and campsite reservations may also be faxed (907/264-4684) or mailed to Denali Park Resorts, Visitor Transportation System, 241 W. Ship Creek Ave., Anchorage, AK 99501, between Dec. 1 and Sept. 1. Mail-in requests must include a check or credit card number with expiration date, and must be received by Denali Park Resorts 30 days prior to your scheduled departure. Tickets that have been requested and paid for prior to the date of departure can be picked up at a dedicated window at

Shuttle buses stop for photos of grizzly bears crossing the Park Road near Highway Pass. (© Michael DeYoung)

the park visitor center. For travel up to 7 A.M. each day, unclaimed, prepaid reserved tickets will be in the possession of the bus drivers. During peak season, campgrounds fill up by midmorning for the following day and, on occasion, the day after. *NOTE: This reservation system may be revised in 2000.*

Black Diamond Golf invites you to enjoy a unique golf experience. Your adventure at our rugged course includes a sweeping view of the Alaska Range, a serene mountain lake, and the midnight sun! All golfing essentials are available to buy in our Pro Shop or rent for your use. We also offer a great cafe with fresh entrees, cold drinks, and reasonable prices! The kids will love our 18-hole Alaskan Tundra Mini Golf. We are located just off the Parks Highway at **Milepost A 247**. For tee times, call (907) 683-GOLF. Midnight golfing available. www.blackdiamondgolf.com. [ADVERTISEMENT]

Carlo Heights Bed & Breakfast and Denali Sled Dog School. Share seclusion and spectacular views. Located on bluff overlooking Nenana River and Alaska Range. Accommodations include 2 double-rooms, a private suite, and full kitchen. Open year-round, reservations recommended during summertime and required during off-season. Sled dog school offers dog mushing courses and tours. Box 86, Denali Park, AK 99755. (907) 683-5212. www.alaskasbest.net; carloheights@alaskasbest.net. [ADVERTISEMENT]

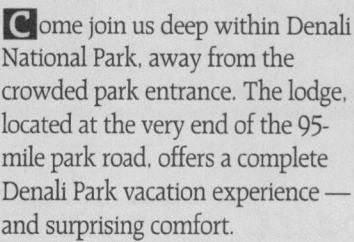

Denali Backcountry Lodge. Don't pass up a visit to this lodge if you want to escape the park's crowded east entrance and immerse yourself deep within Denali National Park for a few days. The lodge is located at the end of the 95-mile park road. Full service accommodations feature a comfortable wilderness vacation lodge, cozy cedar cabins, dining room and lounge. One to 4-night stays include round-trip transportation from the train depot, all meals and lodging, guided hikes, wildlife viewing, bicycling, photography and natural history programs. Many famous naturalists are found staying at the lodge, and occasionally they conduct special presentations. Credit cards accepted. P.O. Box 189, Denali National Park, Alaska 99755. www.denalilodge.com/mp. Phone (800) 841-0692. [ADVERTISEMENT]

Denali Dome Home Bed, Breakfast and Hospitality is the longest established B&B in Denali and is rated 3-diamond from AAA. Denali Dome is a 7,200-foot geodesic home, run year-round by the Miller Family and is located one turn and 12 miles north of Denali National Park. Denali Dome has 7 bedrooms with private baths, sauna, jacuzzi, fireplaces, decks and large paved, off-street parking on 5 wooded acres. Full, Alaskan breakfasts served. Millers are happy to arrange your Alaskan vacation. Super clean with best rates! Major cards accepted. Call (907) 683-1239 or write Box 262, Healy, AK 99734. E-mail: info@denalidomehome.com. [ADVERTISEMENT]

Denali Wilderness Lodge is Alaska's classic fly-in adventure lodge. Located in the pristine Wood River valley, it's accessible only by a spectacular bush-plane flight. Itineraries can be tailored to your needs. Comfortable accommodations, delicious meals, naturalist programs, flightseeing, horseback riding, nature/photo hikes, gold panning, and fascinating relaxation. 24 log buildings, hand-hewn over decades, offer an enticing glimpse into Alaska's trapping, hunting, and gold mining history. Exciting day excursions are available, but stay from one to four nights for the full experience. 800-541-9979 for brochure, or visit: www.denaliwildernesslodge.com. See display ad this section. [ADVERTISEMENT]

Denali National Park Hotel offers the only accommodations inside the Park and is the center for visitor activities. A short walk from the train depot and adjacent walking and hiking trails, the hotel features dining, gifts, a snack shop, grocery store and unique railcar lounge. The auditorium hosts National Park Service programs. Tours and activities can be arranged at the front desk. Call 1-800-276-7234. In Anchorage (907) 276-7234. Or visit www.denalinational park.com. [ADVERTISEMENT]

Denali National Park Wilderness Centers—Camp Denali. Since 1951, Alaska's premier small wilderness lodge and active learning center. Log cabin lodging with unparalleled views of Mount McKinley. Natural history emphasis, guided backcountry hiking, wildlife observation, canoeing, biking. Special Emphasis series with guest lecturers. Three- and 4-night stays or longer include lodging, all meals and activities, round-trip transportation from park entrance. Brochure: P.O. Box 67, Denali National Park, AK 99755. (907) 683-2290. E-mail: dnpwild@alaska.net. Web site: www.gorp.com/dnpwild. [ADVERTISEMENT]

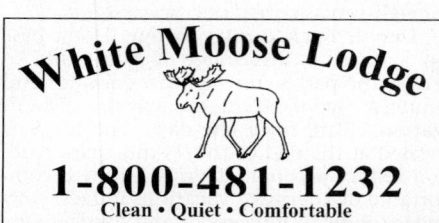

There Are No Roads to the Real Alaska

Denali National Park is high on the agenda of all Alaska visitors, and rightfully so. Can a half-million travelers each year be wrong? But arrival at the congested park entrance may lead to a bit of disappointment. After watching the crowds head west down the busy park road into the well-managed wilderness beyond, savvy travelers look at a map and wonder, "Surely natural beauty doesn't stop at a park boundary. What lies over our shoulder, away from the park, in that vast roadless area?"

The answer: a rare opportunity.

Here, amid two thousand square miles of true wilderness, lie only a couple of frontier cabins. . .and Denali Wilderness Lodge. The short but spectacular flight from the park entrance, a once-in-a-lifetime flightseeing experience, leads to one of the world's classic getaways, and a real taste of the Alaskan bush.

Once there you're greeted with great hospitality and comfort, at what has long been called "the world's most remote hotel." Hand-crafted over decades as a distinguished hunting lodge, today this great history is carried on by a knowledgeable, friendly staff. These days however, only photos are shot; the emphasis is on adventurous exploration.

A wide range of activities is available for every type of visitor. Guided hikes range from challenging treks up nearby rugged peaks to casual walks along the beautiful Wood River. Thousands of acres of alpine tundra are there for roaming, along with placid ponds and stands of spruce and cottonwood. Well-trained horses led by experienced wranglers make that roaming even more enjoyable. Wildlife, including caribou, moose, Dall sheep, wolves, and grizzlies call the valley home as well, and lodge naturalists are expert at interpreting their behavior and signs.

Although civilization has been left behind, its comforts have not. Whether relaxing in your own heated cabin (each with private bath), the modern atrium dining room, or "The Logs" lounge, the atmosphere is warmly Alaskan. And importantly after a full Alaskan day, the food is plentiful and delicious.

Denali Wilderness Lodge offers an excellent addition -- or alternative -- to a visit to one of America's great, but busy, national parks.

Call for more information, or a free brochure.

1-800-541-9779

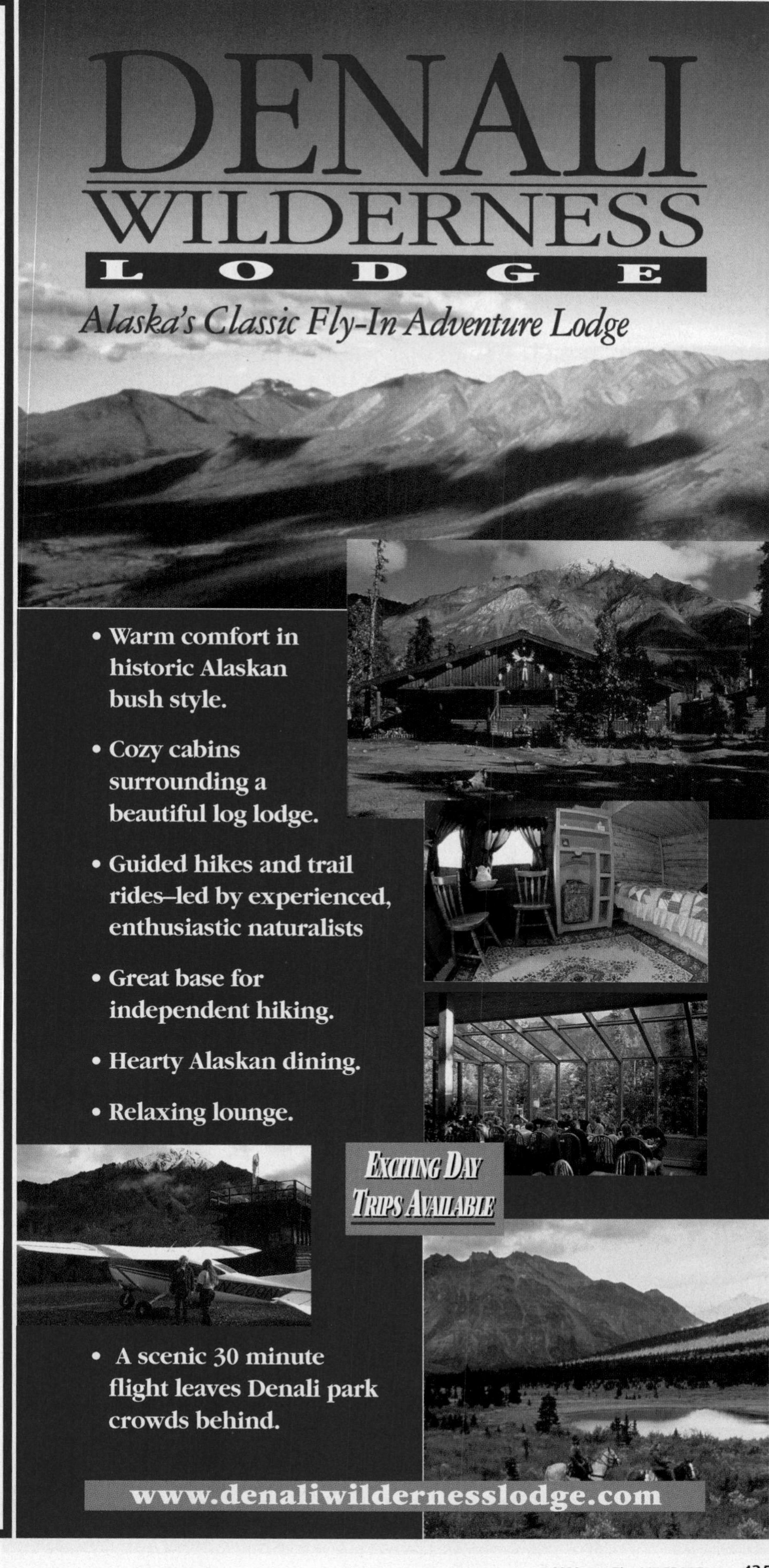

DENALI
WILDERNESS
LODGE
Alaska's Classic Fly-In Adventure Lodge
• Warm comfort in historic Alaskan bush style.
• Cozy cabins surrounding a beautiful log lodge.
• Guided hikes and trail rides–led by experienced, enthusiastic naturalists
• Great base for independent hiking.
• Hearty Alaskan dining.
• Relaxing lounge.
EXCITING DAY TRIPS AVAILABLE
• A scenic 30 minute flight leaves Denali park crowds behind.
www.denaliwildernesslodge.com

Tour buses stop at Stony Hill overlook and a clear view of Mount McKinley (Denali). (© Michael DeYoung)

Denali National Park Wilderness Centers—North Face Lodge. Small, well-appointed inn and active learning center with spectacular Mount McKinley view. Located in the remote heart of the park near the end of the 90-mile park road. Natural history emphasis, guided backcountry hiking, wildlife observation, canoeing, biking. Three- and four-night stays or longer include lodging, all meals and activities, round-trip transportation from park entrance. Brochure: P.O. Box 67, Denali National Park, AK 99755. (907) 683-2290. E-mail: dnpwild@alaska.net. Web site: www.gorp.com/dnpwild. [ADVERTISEMENT]

Denali Princess Lodge. Riverside lodging near the entrance to Denali National Park featuring spectacular park and Nenana River views, several dining options including dinner theatre, tour desk, gift shop, complimentary shuttle to rail depot and park activities. Open mid-May through mid-September. Reservations (800) 426-0500 year-round. [ADVERTISEMENT]

Kantishna Roadhouse. Premier wilderness lodge located at the quiet west end of Denali National Park offers opportunities to view, photograph and explore the park. Packages include comfortable log cabins with private baths, guided hiking, gold panning, horses, fishing, fine meals and Alaskan hospitality. P.O. Box 130, Denali Park, AK 99755. Phone (800) 942-7420. E-mail: kantshna@polarnet.com. Internet address: www.alaskaone.com/krhouse/. [ADVERTISEMENT]

Lynx Creek Pizza in Denali features "the best handmade pizza in Alaska" along with fine selections of beer, wine, even hand-dipped ice cream. A locals' favorite for years with frequent live entertainment. Located 1 mile north of the Park entrance, Mile 238.6, adjacent to McKinley Chalet Resort (907) 683-2547. [ADVERTISEMENT]

McKinley Chalet Resort in Denali features over 300 comfortable rooms and mini-

Denali Park experiences about 20 hours of daylight a day in mid-June.

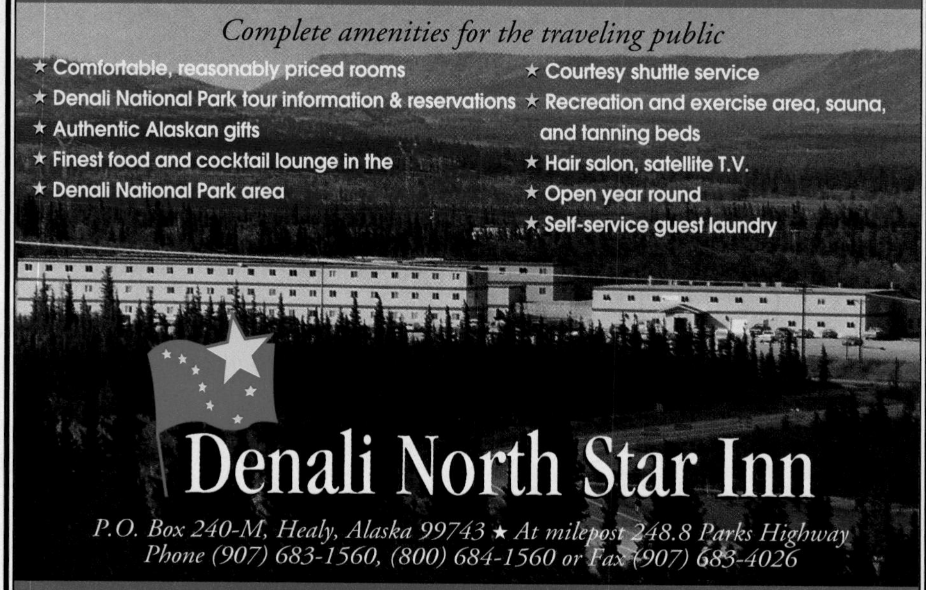

Collared pikas—members of the rabbit family—grow to 6–8 inches. They inhabit rock slides and store dried plants for winter. *(© Susan Cole Kelly)*

suites and provides the most convenient access to Denali Park Tours, river rafting, gold panning and walking trails. Home of the famous Alaska Cabin Nite Dinner Theater and featuring the Chalet Center Cafe and Nenana View Restaurant with private deck overlooking the river. Call 1-800-276-7234. In Anchorage (907) 276-7234. Or visit www.denalinationalpark.com. [ADVERTISEMENT]

McKinley Village Resort in Denali is nestled in the trees on the banks of the Nenana River at Milepost 231.3 and boasts 150 comfortable rooms, rustic lobby and fireplace, casual dining room, lounge, shopping and full-service tour and activities desk. Call 1-800-276-7234. In Anchorage (907) 276-7234. Or visit www.denalinational park.com. [ADVERTISEMENT]

Camping

There are 7 campgrounds in the park along the 92-mile Park Road (see log of Park Road in this section for most locations). Wonder Lake, Sanctuary River and Igloo Creek campgrounds are tent camping only and accessible only by shuttle bus. Riley Creek, Savage River and Teklanika are available for both RV and tent camping. Morino is only for those without vehicles and is not on the reservation system. ▲

The campgrounds are open from about late May to early September, except for Riley Creek, which is open year-round (snow-covered and no water, flush toilets or dump station in winter). There is a fee and a 14-day limit at all campgrounds in summer. Reservations for campsites at Riley Creek, Teklanika River and Savage River campgrounds are available; see Reservation

Campground	Spaces	Tent	Trailer	Pit toilets	Flush toilets	Tap water	Fee
Morino	60	•		•			$12
Riley Creek	102	•	•		•	•	$12
Savage River	33	•	•		•	•	$12
Sanctuary River	7	•		•		•	$12
Teklanika River	50	•	•	•		•	$12
Igloo Creek	7	•		•		•	$12
Wonder Lake	28	•			•	•	$12

System information on page 432. There is a 3-night minimum stay requirement at Teklanika River Campground, and also a limit of one round-trip to this campground for registered campers with vehicles. Additional travel to and from Teklanika is by shuttle bus. See chart for facilities at each campground. (NOTE: Campground fees are subject to change!)

Several private campgrounds are located outside the park along the George Parks Highway. See display ads this section.

Campers should bring rain gear and a tent or waterproof shelter because of frequent rains; also a gasoline or propane stove, or be prepared to purchase firewood from concessionaire.

Transportation

Highway: Access via the Parks Highway or the Denali Highway.

The Park Road runs westward 92 miles from the park's east boundary to Kantishna. The road is paved only to Savage River (**Milepost J 14.7**). Private vehicle travel is restricted beyond the Savage River checkpoint at Mile 14.8. Mount McKinley is first visible at about **Milepost J 9** Park Road, but the best views begin at about **Milepost J 60** and continue with few interruptions to Wonder Lake. At the closest point, the summit of the mountain is 27 miles/43.5 km from the road. See log this section.

Air: Charter flights are available from most nearby towns with airfields, and flightseeing tours of the park are offered by operators from the park area or out of Talkeetna, Anchorage or Fairbanks. A round-trip air tour of the park from Anchorage takes 3 to 4 hours. See ads this section.

Era Helicopters Flightseeing Tours. Enjoy the beautiful habitat of Denali on a personally guided heli-hiking adventure. Experience our new Glacier Expedition tour featuring a walk on a glacier. Narrated tours of Mt. McKinley also available. Free transportation provided from area hotels. May–September. Located at Milepost 238. Phone (907) 683-2574 locally or 1-800-843-1947. [ADVERTISEMENT]

Pere Air. Air tours the way they should be! Flightseeing with Pere Air may be your most memorable vacation highlight. Specializing in around the mountain and to the top of Mount McKinley tours. Soar among massive mountain peaks while classical music plays in the background. Two-way headsets

Grizzly bear photographed near Highway Pass on the Park Road.
(© Michael DeYoung)

allow communication between the pilot and passengers. Record both the sights and sounds of Denali with our modified intercom system for video cameras. Pere Air also offers charter services around the state, dinner tours and fly-in backpacking and biking tours. Twenty years accident-free flying in the Alaskan wilderness. Toll free reservations: 1-877-683-6033. Visit our web site: www.pereair.com. E-mail: pereair@rmci.net. [ADVERTISEMENT]

Railroad: The Alaska Railroad offers daily northbound and southbound trains between Anchorage and Fairbanks, with stops at Denali Park Station, during the summer season. For reservations and information, phone (800) 544-0552.

Midnight Sun Express®. Ultra Domes feature glass-domed ceilings, meals freshly prepared by on-board chefs, and exclusive outdoor viewing platforms. Daily service between Anchorage, Talkeetna, Denali National Park and Fairbanks. Rail packages include overnights at the new Mt. McKinley Princess Lodge and/or Denali Princess Lodge, May through September. Phone (800) 835-8907. [ADVERTISEMENT]

Bus: Daily bus service to the park is available from Anchorage and Fairbanks, and special sightseeing tours are offered throughout the summer months. A 6- to 8-hour guided bus tour of the park is offered by the park concessionaire. Tickets and information are available in the hotel lobby at the front desk tour window. For details on the park shuttle bus system, see Accommodations/Visitor Services this section.

Tours by plane, bus and van are available. See ads this section.

Caribou are called the "nomads of the North."

Attractions

Ranger-led activites. Organized activities put on by the Park Service include nature hikes; sled dog demonstrations at park headquarters; campfire programs at Riley Creek, Savage River, Teklanika River and Wonder Lake campgrounds; and interpretive programs at the hotel and Visitor Center. Information on ranger-led hikes and other activities is available at the Visitor Center near the park entrance.

Hiking. There are few established trails in the park, but there is plenty of terrain for cross-country hiking. Free permits are required for any overnight hikes.

Alaska Raft Adventures in Denali offers river rafting with experienced guides. Float through a glacial valley along the Park boundary on the Wilderness Run, or take on exciting whitewater on the Canyon Run. Free transportation available between area hotels and train depot. Visit the tour desks at McKinley Chalet or McKinley Village resorts. (907) 276-7234. [ADVERTISEMENT]

Kantishna Wilderness Trails. The ultimate tour through Denali National Park. 95 miles each way with breathtaking mountain vistas and the likelihood of seeing some of Denali's wildlife en route. Arrive at the Kantishna Roadhouse in time for lunch in the dining room, followed by gold panning or an interpretive program. For reservations phone (800) 942-7420; e-mail: kantshna@polarnet.com. [ADVERTISEMENT]

Park Road Log

Distance from the junction (J) with Parks Highway is shown.

J 0 Junction. Turn west off the Parks Highway (Alaska Route 3) at **Milepost A 237.3** onto the Park Road. The Park Road is paved to the Savage River bridge.

J 0.2 (0.3 km) Turnoff for **Riley Creek Campground** and overflow parking area. Make sure you get all necessary supplies before proceeding to campgrounds west of the checkpoint. ▲

J 0.5 (0.8 km) **Visitor Center** has information on all visitor activities as well as shuttle bus tickets and camping and overnight hiking permits. A park orientation program is available in the theater. The center is open daily. This is also the shuttle bus departure point.

J 1.2 (1.9 km) Alaska Railroad crossing. Horseshoe Lake trailhead; length, 1.5 miles/2.4 km round trip, allow about 1 hour..

J 1.4 (2.3 km) Convenience store, showers.

J 1.5 (2.4 km) Denali Park Hotel; post office. Taiga Loop Trail begins and ends at

Special Notes for Visitors

The 1980 federal legislation creating a much larger Denali National Park and Preserve also changed some rules and regulations normally followed in most parks. The following list of park rules and regulations apply in the Denali Wilderness Unit—the part of the park that most people visit. Contact the Park Superintendent (Box 9, Denali Park, AK 99755) for regulations governing the use of aircraft, firearms, snow machines and motorboats in the park additions and in the national preserve units.

For those driving: The Park Road was built for scenic enjoyment and not for high speed. Maximum speed is 35 mph/56 kmph except where lower limits are posted.

Your pets and wildlife don't mix. Pets are allowed only on roadways and in campgrounds and must be leashed or in a vehicle at all times. Pets are not allowed on shuttle buses, trails or in the backcountry.

Backcountry camping permits are required for hikers who stay overnight and can be obtained only at the Visitor Center, no more than 1 day in advance. A camper bus pass ($15.50) must be purchased in order to reach most backcountry camping units.

Professional photographer permits are available to qualified applicants. Contact the Chief Ranger at (907) 683-2294.

Mountaineering expeditions are required to acquire a permit and pay a $150 fee before climbing Mount McKinley or Mount Foraker. Permit applications must be received at least 60 days prior to the start of the expedition. Contact the Talkeetna Ranger Station, Box 588, Talkeetna, AK 99676; phone (907) 733-2231.

Natural features: The park was established to protect a natural ecosystem. Destroying, defacing or collecting plants, rocks and other features is prohibited. Capturing, molesting, feeding or killing any animal is prohibited.

Firearms and hunting are not allowed in the wilderness area.

Fishing licenses are not required in the wilderness area; state law is applicable on all other lands. Limits for each person per day are: lake trout—2 fish; grayling and other fish—10 fish or 10 lbs. and 1 fish. Fishing is poor because most rivers are silty and ponds are shallow.

Motor vehicles of any type, including trail bikes, motorcycles and mopeds, may not leave the Park Road.

Feeding wildlife is prohibited. Wild animals need wild food; your food will not help them.

hotel parking lot; length 1.3 miles/2.1 km, allow 1-hour round trip.

J 1.6 (2.6 km) Denali Park Station (elev. 1,730 feet/527m), where visitors can make train connections to Anchorage and Fairbanks; daily service during the summer. Denali Park Hotel is across from the depot. *NOTE: No commercial traffic allowed without permit beyond this point.*

Private Aircraft: McKinley Park airstrip, 1.7 miles northeast of park headquarters; elev. 1,720 feet; length 3,000 feet; gravel; unattended.

J 3.5 (5.6 km) Park headquarters. This is the administration area for Denali National Park and Preserve. In winter, information on all visitor activities can be obtained here. Report accidents and emergencies to the rangers; phone (907) 683-9100 or 911, or outside Alaska (907) 474-7722. *NOTE: There are no telephones west of this point.*

J 5.5 (8.9 km) Paved turnout with litter barrel. Sweeping view of countryside. There are numerous small turnouts along the Park

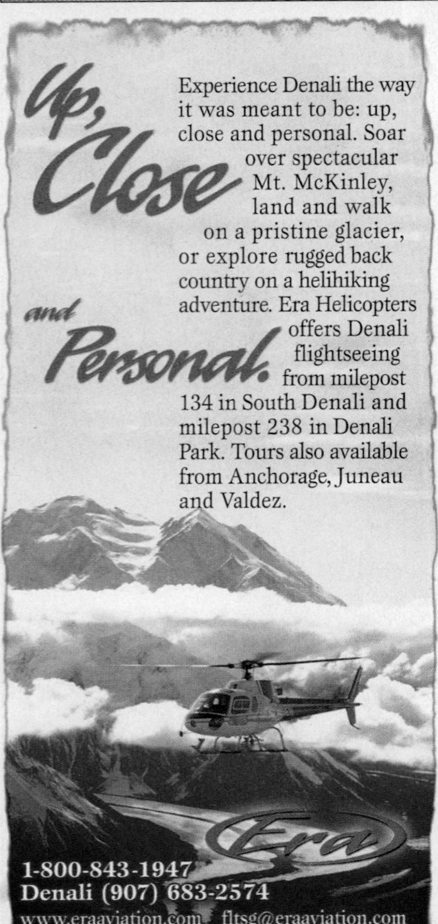

Road.

J 12.8 (20.6 km) **Savage River Campground** (elev. 2,780 feet); 3 group tent sites (9 to 20 people each); 33 sites (8 people each); advance reservations required. ▲

J 14.7 (23.7 km) Bridge over the Savage River. Blacktop pavement ends. Access to river, toilet and picnic tables at east end of bridge.

J 14.8 (23.8 km) Savage River check station. PERMIT OR SHUTTLE/BUS TICKET REQUIRED BEYOND THIS POINT.

NOTE: Road travel permits for access to the Kantishna area are issued at park headquarters only under special conditions; however, the road may be open to all vehicles to Milepost 30 in early May and late September, weather permitting.

J 17.3 (27.8 km) Viewpoint of the Alaska Range and tundra.

J 21.3 (34.3 km) Hogan Creek bridge.

J 22 (35.4 km) Sanctuary River bridge, ranger station and **Sanctuary River Campground** (tents only). Sanctuary available by shuttle bus only. ▲

J 29.1 (46.8 km) **Teklanika River Campground**, elev. 2,580 feet; 3-night minimum stay. Grizzly bears may sometimes be seen on the gravel bars nearby. ▲

J 30.7 (49.4 km) Rest area with chemical toilets.

J 31.3 (50.4 km) Bridge over Teklanika River. Habitat closure at bridge.

J 34.1 (54.9 km) **Igloo Creek Campground** (tents only); accessible by shuttle bus only. ▲

J 37 (59.5 km) Igloo Creek bridge. *NOTE: The area within 1 mile of each side of the Park Road from **Milepost J 38.3** to **J 42.9** is closed to all off-road foot travel as a special wildlife protection area.* Toklat grizzlies are often seen in the area.

J 39.1 (62.9 km) **Sable Pass** (elev. 3,900 feet).

J 43.4 (69.8 km) Bridge over East Fork Toklat River. Views of Polychrome Mountain, the Alaska Range and several glaciers are visible along the East Fork from open country south of the road.

J 45.9 (73.9 km) Summit of **Polychrome Pass** (elev. 3,700 feet); rest stop with toilets. The broad valley of the Toklat River is visible below to the south. Good hiking in alpine tundra above the road.

J 53.1 (85.5 km) Bridge over the Toklat River. The Toklat and all other streams crossed by the Park Road drain into the Tanana River, a tributary of the Yukon River.

J 53.7 (86.4 km) Ranger station.

J 58.3 (93.8 km) Summit of **Highway Pass** (elev. 3,980 feet). This is the highest point on the Park Road.

J 61 (98.2 km) **Stony Hill Overlook** (elev. 4,508 feet). A good view of Mount McKinley and the Alaska Range on clear days.

J 62 (99.8 km) Viewpoint.

J 64.5 (103.8 km) **Thorofare Pass** (elev. 3,900 feet/1,189m).

J 66 (106.2 km) **Eielson Visitor Center**. Ranger-led hikes, nature programs, displays, restrooms and drinking water. Film, maps and natural history publications for sale. Report accidents and emergencies here.

Excellent Mount McKinley viewpoint. On clear days the north and south peaks of Mount McKinley are visible to the southwest. The impressive glacier, which drops from the mountain and spreads out over the valley floor at this point, is the Muldrow.

For several miles beyond the visitor center the road cut drops about 300 feet/91m to the valley below, paralleling the McKinley River.

J 84.6 (136.1 km) Access road leads left, westbound, to **Wonder Lake Campground** (elev. 2,090 feet/637m). Tents only; campground access by shuttle bus only. An excellent Mount McKinley viewpoint. ▲

The road continues to Wonder Lake, where rafting and canoeing are permitted (no rental boats available).

J 85.6 (137.8 km) Reflection Pond, a kettle lake formed by a glacier.

J 86.6 (139.4 km) Wonder Lake ranger station.

J 87.7 (141.1 km) Moose Creek bridge.

J 88 (141.6 km) North Face Lodge.

J 88.2 (141.9 km) Camp Denali.

J 91 (146.4 km) **KANTISHNA** (pop. 135 in summer, 0 in winter; elev. 1,750 feet). Established in 1905 as a mining camp at the junction of Eureka and Moose creeks. Most of the area around Kantishna is private property and there may be active mining on area creeks in summer. Kantishna Roadhouse, which consists of a dozen log guest cabins and a dining hall, comprises the townsite of Kantishna.

Private Aircraft: Kantishna airstrip, 1.3 miles northwest; elev. 1,575 feet; length 1,850 feet; gravel; unattended, no regular maintenance.

J 91.8 (147.7 km) Mt. McKinley Gold Camp.

J 92 (148.1 km) Denali Backcountry Lodge.

DENALI HIGHWAY ⑧

Connects: Paxson to Cantwell, AK **Length:** 136 miles
Road Surface: Gravel **Season:** Closed in winter
Highest Summit: Maclaren Summit 4,086 feet
Major Attraction: Tangle Lakes–Delta River Canoe Trail

(See map, page 446)

	Cantwell	Delta Junction	Denali Park	Paxson
Cantwell		217	27	136
Delta Junction	217		244	81
Denali Park	27	244		163
Paxson	136	81	163	

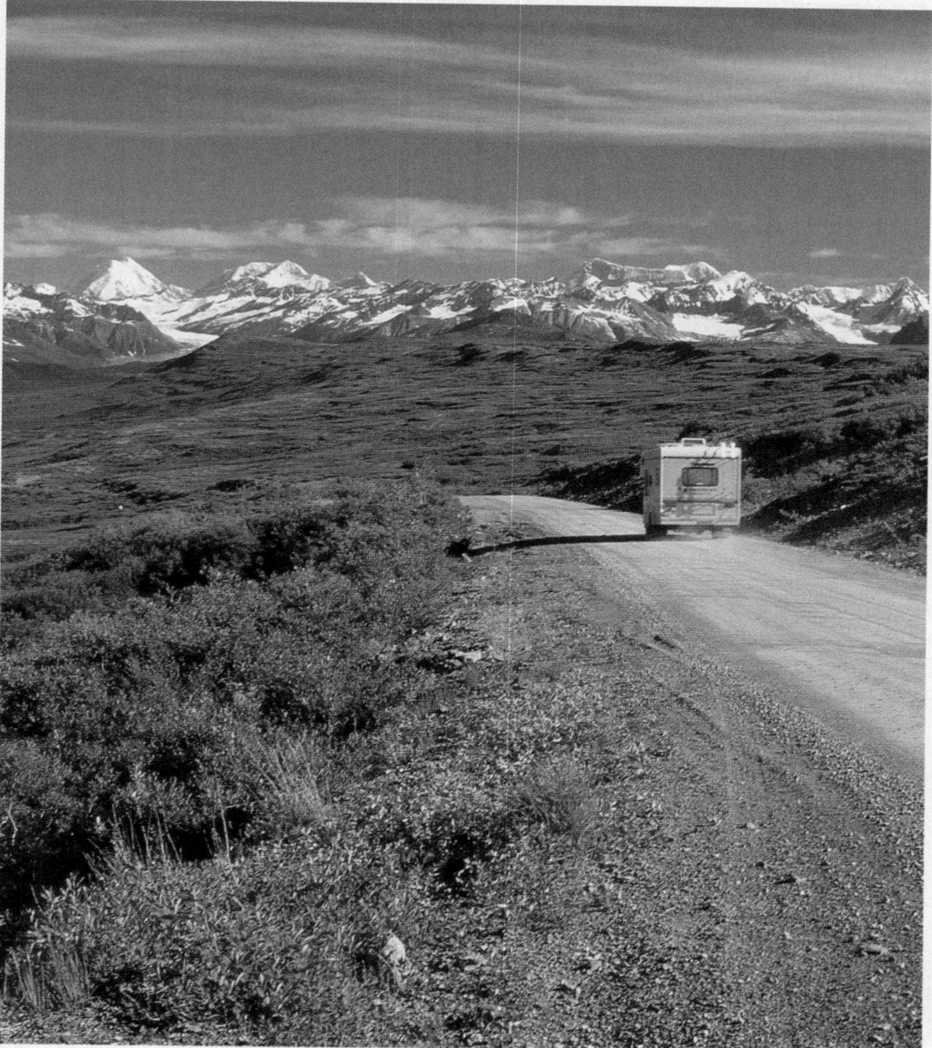

Most of the Denali Highway is still gravel. (© Mike Jones)

The Denali Highway extends 135.5 miles from Paxson at **Milepost V 185.5** on the Richardson Highway to Cantwell, about 2 miles west of **Milepost A 209.9** on the Parks Highway. The first 21 miles from Paxson and the last 4 miles into Cantwell are paved and the rest is gravel. *NOTE: Watch for paving in summer 2000.* The highway is closed from October to mid-May. Do not attempt to drive this highway in the off-season.

The Denali Highway was the only road link to Denali National Park and Preserve (then Mount McKinley National Park) prior to completion of the Parks Highway in 1972. Before the Denali Highway opened in 1957, the national park was accessible only via the Alaska Railroad.

The condition of the gravel portion of the highway varies, depending on highway maintenance, weather and the opinion of the driver. The road surface is rough; washboard can develop quickly. Much of the road is in need of gravel, but the roadbed is solid. This can be a dusty and bumpy drive in dry weather. Watch for potholes in wet weather. The Denali Highway becomes progressively narrower and more winding from east to west.

The Denali Highway has very beautiful scenery and some interesting geography. Glacier-formed features visible from the road include: moraines (drift deposited by glaciers); kames (conical hills or terraces of gravel and sand); kettle lakes (holes formed by blocks of ice melting); and eskers (ridges of gravel formed by streams flowing under glaciers).

There are dozens of primitive campsites and turnouts along the highway which are heavily used by hunters during caribou and moose seasons. Excellent fishing in lakes and streams accessible on foot or via designated off-road vehicle trails. There are also many unmarked trails leading off into the Bush. Inquire locally and carry a good topographic map when hiking off the highway. Highway access to the Delta River canoe trail through the Tangle Lakes, headwaters of the Delta National Wild, Scenic and Recreational River System, is at **Milepost P 21.5**. The Denali Highway is also popular with mountain bikers.

Off-road vehicles are permitted, although some restrictions may apply on private and federal lands. Check at the lodges along the Denali Highway and at the Bureau of Land Management office in Glennallen, phone (907) 822-3217.

Emergency medical services: Between Paxson and **Milepost P 77.5** (Susitna Lodge), phone 911 or the state troopers at (907) 822-3263. Between **Milepost P 77.5** and Cantwell, phone the Cantwell ambulance at (907) 768-2982 or the state troopers at (907) 768-2202.

Denali Highway Log

Distance from Paxson (P) is followed by distance from Cantwell (C).

ALASKA ROUTE 8

P 0 C 135.5 (218.1 km) **PAXSON** (pop. 30; elev. 2,650 feet), at **Milepost V 185.5** on the Richardson highway, began in 1906 when Alvin Paxson established a roadhouse at Mile 192. He later built a larger roadhouse at Mile 191. Today, services here include lodging at Paxson Inn & Lodge (with restaurant) and Paxson Alpine Cabins, a gas station and post office.

Junction of the Richardson Highway (Alaska Route 4) with the Denali Highway (Alaska Route 8). Turn to **Milepost V 185.5** on page 486 in the RICHARDSON HIGHWAY section for log.

Private Aircraft: Paxson airstrip, adjacent south; elev. 2,653 feet; length 2,800

DENALI HIGHWAY *Paxson, AK, to Cantwell, AK*

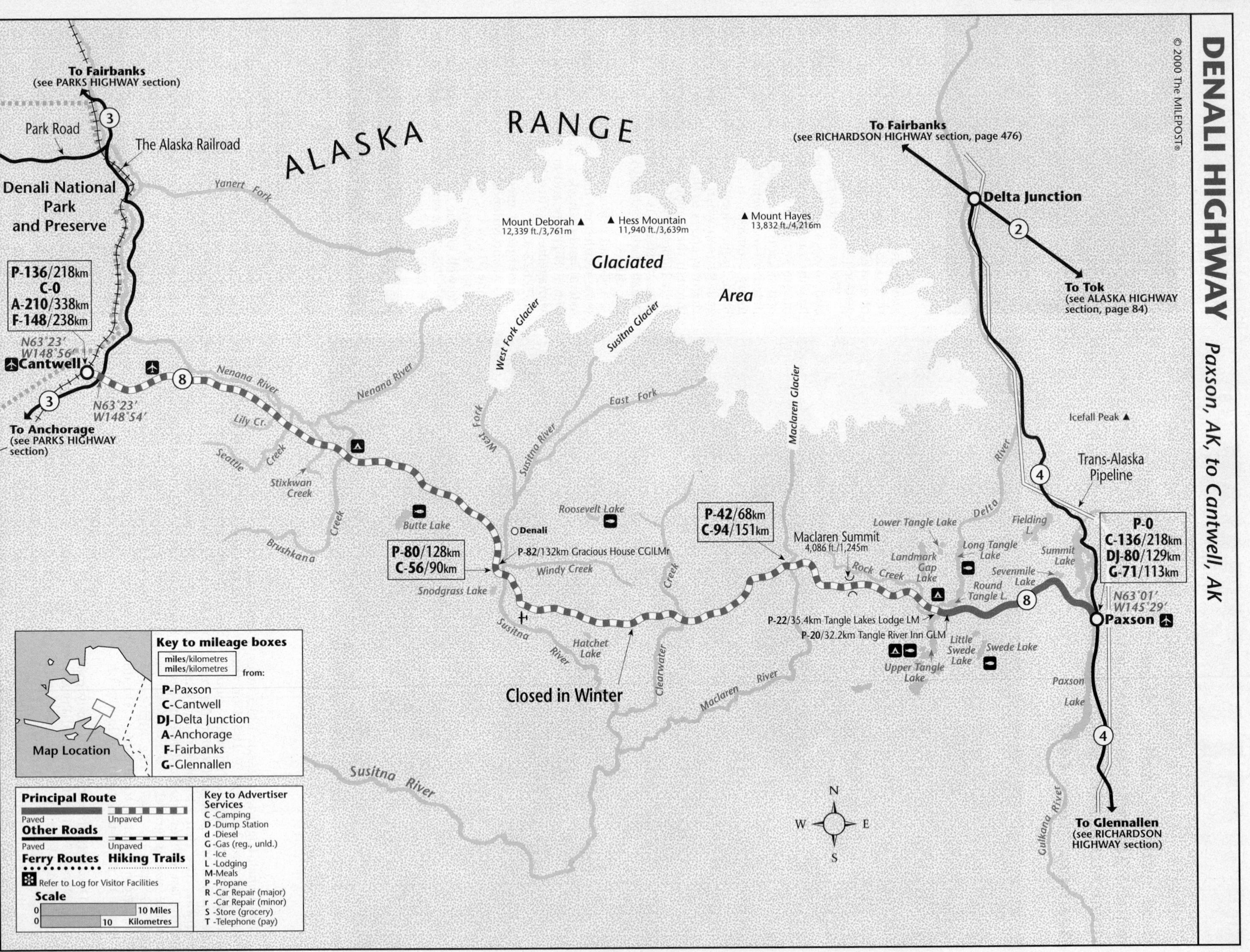

© 2000 The MILEPOST®
To Fairbanks (see PARKS HIGHWAY section)
Park Road
The Alaska Railroad
ALASKA RANGE
Denali National Park and Preserve
Yanert Fork
Mount Deborah 12,339 ft./3,761m
Hess Mountain 11,940 ft./3,639m
Mount Hayes 13,832 ft./4,216m
Glaciated Area
To Fairbanks (see RICHARDSON HIGHWAY section, page 476)
Delta Junction
To Tok (see ALASKA HIGHWAY section, page 84)
P-136/218km C-0 A-210/338km F-148/238km
N63°23' W148°56'
Cantwell
N63°23' W148°54'
To Anchorage (see PARKS HIGHWAY section)
Nenana River
Lily Cr.
Seattle Creek
Stixkwan Creek
Creek
Brushkana
West Fork Glacier
Susitna Glacier
West Fork
Susitna River
East Fork
Maclaren Glacier
Icefall Peak
Trans-Alaska Pipeline
Delta River
Butte Lake
Denali
Roosevelt Lake
P-80/128km C-56/90km
P-82/132km Gracious House CGILMr
Windy Creek
Snodgrass Lake
Creek
P-42/68km C-94/151km
Maclaren Summit 4,086 ft./1,245m
Lower Tangle Lake
Fielding L.
Long Tangle Lake
Landmark Gap Lake
Rock Creek
Summit Lake
Sevenmile Lake
Round Tangle L.
P-0 C-136/218km DJ-80/129km G-71/113km
N63°01' W145°29'
Paxson
P-22/35.4km Tangle Lakes Lodge LM
P-20/32.2km Tangle River Inn GLM
Little Swede Lake
Swede Lake
Upper Tangle Lake
Susitna River
Hatchet Lake
Clearwater
Closed in Winter
Maclaren River
Paxson Lake
Gulkana River
To Glennallen (see RICHARDSON HIGHWAY section)
Key to mileage boxes
miles/kilometres miles/kilometres from:
P-Paxson
C-Cantwell
DJ-Delta Junction
A-Anchorage
F-Fairbanks
G-Glennallen
Map Location
Principal Route
Paved
Unpaved
Other Roads
Paved
Unpaved
Ferry Routes
Hiking Trails
Refer to Log for Visitor Facilities
Scale
0 10 Miles
0 10 Kilometres
Key to Advertiser Services
C -Camping
D -Dump Station
d -Diesel
G -Gas (reg., unld.)
I -Ice
L -Lodging
M -Meals
P -Propane
R -Car Repair (major)
r -Car Repair (minor)
S -Store (grocery)
T -Telephone (pay)
N W E S

feet; gravel; emergency fuel; attended.

P 0.2 (0.3 km) **C 135.3** (217.7 km) Entrance to Paxson Alpine Cabins.

Gulkana River bridge; parking at west end. In season, spawning salmon may be seen here. This portion of the Gulkana River is off-limits to salmon fishing.

P 0.3 (0.5 km) **C 135.2** (217.6 km) Entering Paxson Closed Area westbound. This area is closed to the taking of all big game. Side road leads south to Mud Lake.

Westbound, there are many long steep upgrades and many turnouts the next 21 miles. Wildflowers carpet the tundra in the spring and summer. Watch for nesting swans.

P 0.7 (1.1 km) **C 134.8** (216.9 km) Large paved turnout to south.

P 1.1 (1.8 km) **C 134.4** (216.3 km) **Mud Lake** below highway; early grayling fishing.

P 1.5 (2.4 km) **C 134** (215.6 km) Large paved turnout to south.

P 2.2 (3.5 km) **C 133.3** (214.5 km) Large paved turnout to south.

P 3.6 (5.8 km) **C 131.9** (212.3 km) Paved turnout to south. Several more turnouts next 3 miles westbound with views of Summit Lake to the north, Gakona Glacier to the northeast, Icefall Peak and Gulkana Glacier west of Icefall Peak, all in the **Alaska Range**. The 650-mile-long range, which extends across southcentral Alaska from the Canadian border southwest to Iliamna Lake, also contains Mount McKinley (Denali), the highest peak in North America.

P 6.8 (10.9 km) **C 128.7** (207.1 km) Access to **Sevenmile Lake** 0.8 mile/1.3 km north; excellent fishing for lake trout in summer.

P 7.1 (11.4 km) **C 128.4** (206.6 km) Paved turnout to south.

P 7.3 (11.7 km) **C 128.2** (206.3 km) Gravel turnout overlooking Sevenmile Lake. Two Bit Lake is the large lake to the north; Summit Lake is to the northeast.

P 7.5 (12.1 km) **C 128** (206 km) Paved turnout to north overlooking Sevenmile Lake. Summit Lake visible to east.

P 8.7 (14 km) **C 126.8** (204.1 km) Entering BLM lands westbound; federal hunting regulations apply.

P 9 (14.5 km) **C 126.5** (203.6 km) Gravel turnout. Entering BLM public lands westbound.

P 10.1 (16.3 km) **C 125.4** (201.8 km) Paved turnout to south overlooking **Ten Mile Lake**. Short hike downhill to outlet. Fishing for lake trout, grayling and burbot in summer.

P 10.6 (17.1 km) **C 124.9** (201 km) Paved turnout overlooking **Teardrop Lake** to south. Short hike down steep hill to lake; lake trout, grayling and burbot in summer.

For the next 4 miles westbound, there are wide-open spaces with magnificent views of the great Denali country. Look for kettle lakes and kames.

P 11.1 (17.9 km) **C 124.4** (200.2 km) Paved turnout and trail to **Octopus Lake** 0.3 mile/0.5 km south; lake trout, grayling, whitefish.

P 11.8 (19 km) **C 123.7** (199.1 km) Paved turnout to south.

P 12 (19.3 km) **C 123.5** (198.7 km) Paved turnout to south.

P 12.6 (20.3 km) **C 122.9** (197.8 km) Paved turnout to south.

P 13.1 (21.1 km) **C 122.4** (197 km) Viewpoint at summit of Wrangell Mountains to the southeast; interpretive plaque. Mount Sanford (16,237 feet) is on the left; Mount Drum (12,000 feet) is on the right; and Mount Wrangell (14,163 feet) is in the center.

In the spring from this spot a traveler can count at least 40 kettle lakes. Kettles are circular depressions left by melting glafcial ice. Highway begins descent westbound to Tangle Lakes area. Lupine blooms alongside the road in late June.

P 14.5 (23.3 km) **C 121** (194.7 km) Paved turnout and small lakes to north.

P 14.9 (24 km) **C 120.6** (194.1 km) Turnout to south.

P 15 (24.1 km) **C 120.5** (193.9 km) Swede Lake trail, 3 miles/4.8 km long, to south; **Little Swede Lake**, 2 miles/3.2 km. This trail connects with the Middle Fork Gulkana River branch trail (access to Dickey Lake and Meier Lake trail) and the Alphabet Hills trail. **Big Swede Lake** has excellent fishing for lake trout, grayling, whitefish and burbot. Little Swede Lake is excellent for lake trout. Inquire at Tangle River Inn for directions.

P 15.7 (25.3 km) **C 119.8** (192.8 km) Paved turnout to south.

P 16.5 (26.6 km) **C 119** (191.5 km) Entering BLM **Tangle Lakes Archaeological District** westbound. Within this 226,000-acre area, more than 400 archaeological sites chronicle man's seasonal exploitation of the local natural resources. For more than 10,000 years, hunter-gatherers have dug roots, picked berries, fished and hunted big game (primarily caribou) in this area. You may hike along the same high, gravel ridges once used by prehistoric people and used today by modern hunters, anglers and berry pickers.

P 16.8 (27 km) **C 118.7** (191 km) **16.8 Mile Lake** to north (walk up creek 200 yards); lake trout and grayling. **Rusty Lake**, 0.5 mile/0.8 km northwest of 16.8 Mile Lake; lake trout and grayling.

P 17 (27.4 km) **C 118.5** (190.7 km) **17 Mile Lake** to north, turnout at west end of lake; lake trout and grayling fishing.

In summer, look for blueberries along the Denali Highway.

(© Mike Jones)

P 17.3 (27.8 km) **C 118.1** (190.2 km) Paved turnout to south.

P 17.7 (28.5 km) **C 117.8** (189.6 km) Paved turnouts both sides of highway.

P 18.1 (29.1 km) **C 117.4** (188.9 km) Paved turnouts both sides of highway.

P 18.2 (29.3 km) **C 117.3** (188.8 km) Paved turnout with lake access on both sides of highway.

P 18.4 (29.6 km) **C 117.1** (188.4 km) Gravel turnout by **Denali–Clearwater Creek**; grayling fishing.

P 18.8 (30.2 km) **C 116.7** (187.8 km) Paved turnout to north.

P 19.6 (31.5 km) **C 115.9** (186.5 km) Paved turnout to south.

P 20 (32.2 km) **C 115.5** (185.9 km) **Tangle River Inn**, known for our cleanliness and warm atmosphere. Restaurant with full menu featuring delicious home-style cook-

RVs camped along the Denali Highway during hunting season. (© Tom Bol Photography)

ing. Karaoke bar, liquor store, game room. Cozy cabins, log cabin with 5 rooms, 10 beds and private bath—wonderful for groups or families. Newly remodeled rooms with bathrooms. Great fishing, hunting, hiking, berry picking and bird watching. Jack and Naidine Johnson, original owners for over 29 years. Come, meet our friendly crew that's been here for years—a memorable experience. See display ad. [ADVERTISEMENT]

P 20.1 (32.3 km) **C 115.4** (185.7 km) Large paved turnout to north overlooking lake.

P 20.6 (33.2 km) **C 114.9** (184.9 km) Paved parking area with toilet to north.

P 21 (33.8 km) **C 114.5** (184.3 km) The Nelchina caribou herd travels through this area, usually around the end of August or early in September.

P 21.3 (34.3 km) **C 114.2** (183.8 km) *NOTE: Pavement ends, gravel begins westbound. Watch for road paving westbound in summer 2000.*

P 21.4 (34.4 km) **C 114.1** (183.6 km) One-lane bridge over Tangle River.

P 21.5 (34.6 km) **C 114** (183.5 km) Tangle Lakes BLM campground and wayside, 0.7 mile north from highway on shore of Round Tangle Lake; 13 sites, toilets, boat launch, picnicking, hiking (no thick brush, good views). Blueberry picking in August. ▲

Easy access to boat launch for Delta River canoe trail, which goes north through Tangle Lakes to the Delta River. The 2- to 3-day float to the take-out point on the Richardson Highway requires 1 portage. The Delta National Wild, Scenic and Recreational River system is managed by the BLM. For details on this river trail or the Gulkana River trail, contact the BLM, Box 147, Glennallen, AK 99588; phone (907) 822-3217.

Watershed divide. The Gulkana River joins the Copper River, which flows into Prince William Sound. The Delta River joins the Tanana River, which flows into the Yukon River. The Yukon flows into the Bering Sea.

P 21.7 (34.9 km) **C 113.8** (183.1 km) Tangle River BLM campground to south; toilets, water pump, boat launch. Watch for caribou on surrounding hills. Watch for arctic warblers nesting along the Tangle River. ▲

The name Tangle is a descriptive term for the maze of lakes and feeder streams contained in this drainage system. Access to Upper Tangle Lakes canoe trail, which goes south through Tangle Lakes (portages required) to Dickey Lake, then follows the Middle Fork to the main Gulkana River.

AREA FISHING: Tangle Lakes system north and south of the highway (**Long Tangle**, **Round Tangle**, **Upper Tangle** and **Lower Tangle Lake**). Good grayling, burbot and lake trout fishing. Fishing begins as soon as the ice goes out, usually in early June, and continues into September. Good trolling, and some fish are taken from the banks. Early in season, trout are hungry and feed on snails in the shallows at the outlet. Inquire at Tangle Lakes Lodge or Tangle River Inn for information and assistance in getting to where the fish are.

P 22 (35.4 km) **C 113.5** (182.6 km) **Tangle Lakes Lodge.** Now the newest and oldest lodge on the Denali Highway! After a devastating fire in 1998, which destroyed the main lodge building, Tangle Lakes Lodge is back. Featuring an all new kitchen (many say the finest food around), dining room, lounge, observation deck and patio. The place for up-to-date accurate birding information and daily birding tours. (Specialty birds of the area include Smith's longspur, arctic warbler, long-tailed jaeger and gyr falcon.) Guided fishing and local information. Lakeside log cabins and canoe rental. Special this year is a cabin and canoe for $85. All located on the banks of a nationally designated Wild and Scenic Waterway. You will discover the real Alaska at Tangle Lakes Lodge. [ADVERTISEMENT]

P 22.3 (35.9 km) **C 113.2** (182.2 km) Trail to south along esker.

P 24.8 (39.9 km) **C 110.7** (178.1 km) Double-ended turnout to south. **Landmark Gap**, the cut in the mountains to the north, is visible from the highway. It is used by caribou during migration.

Landmark Gap BLM trail to north open to ORVs to **Landmark Gap Lake**. Grayling in stream at trail end; trout in main lake. Mountain biking is also popular on this trail.

P 24.9 (40.1 km) **C 110.6** (178 km) **Rock Creek** 1-lane bridge; parking and informal campsites at both ends of bridge. Fair grayling fishing. Landmark Gap Lake lies north of highway between the noticeable gap in the mountains (a caribou migration route).

P 25.5 (41 km) **C 110** (177 km) Informal campsite to south.

P 27.7 (44.6 km) **C 107.8** (173.5 km) Turnout to north.

P 28.1 (45.2 km) **C 107.4** (172.8 km) Rough turnout and Downwind Lake north side of road.

P 29.3 (47.1 km) **C 106.2** (170.9 km) Informal campsite beside small lake to south.

P 30.6 (49.2 km) **C 104.9** (168.8 km) Cat trail leads 2 miles/3.2 km north to **Glacier Lake**; lake trout, grayling.

P 30.7 (49.4 km) **C 104.8** (168.6 km) Rough turnouts both sides of highway.

P 32 (51.5 km) **C 103.5** (166.6 km) Amphitheater Mountains rise above High Valley to the north. Glacier Lake is visible in the gap in these mountains. Turnout to north.

P 32.1 (51.6 km) **C 103.4** (166.4 km) Rough side road to turnout to north.

P 33.7 (54.2 km) **C 101.8** (163.8 km) Doubled-ended parking area to south.

P 35.2 (56.6 km) **C 100.3** (161.4 km) Gravel turnout. Wildflowers here include: various heaths, frigid shooting star, dwarf fireweed.

P 36 (57.9 km) **C 99.5** (160.1 km) **36 Mile Lake** 0.5-mile hike north; lake trout and grayling.

P 36.4 (58.6 km) **C 99.1** (159.5 km) Entering Clearwater Creek controlled-use area westbound. Closed to motorized hunting. Small turnouts to north and south.

P 36.6 (58.9 km) **C 98.9** (159.2 km) Osar Lake ORV trail leads 5 miles south toward the Alphabet Hills. Osar Lake was first named Asar Lake, the Scandinavian word for esker. (An esker is a ridge of sand and gravel marking the former stream channel of a glacier.) A profusion of black currant berries in season.

P 36.9 (59.4 km) C 98.6 (158.7 km) Maclaren Summit trail leads 3 miles/4.8 km north to good view of Alaska Range; mountain biking.

P 37 (59.5 km) **C 98.5** (158.5 km) **Maclaren Summit** (elev. 4,086 feet). Second highest highway pass in Alaska (after 4,800-foot Atigun Pass on the Dalton Highway). Turnout with view of Susitna River valley, Mount Hayes (13,382 feet) and the Alaska Range.

P 37.8 (60.8 km) **C 97.7** (157.2 km) Leaving Tangle Lakes Archaeological District westbound (see description at **Milepost P 16.5**).

P 39.8 (64.1 km) **C 95.7** (154 km) Sevenmile Lake ORV trail to north; 6.5 miles long, parallels Boulder Creek, crosses peat bog.

P 40.3 (64.8 km) **C 95.2** (153.2 km) Double-ended turnout to south.

P 41.3 (66.5 km) **C 94.2** (151.6 km) Double-ended turnout to south.

P 41.4 (66.6 km) **C 94.1** (151.4 km) Turnout to north.

P 42 (67.6 km) **C 93.5** (150.5 km) **Maclaren River Bridge**, a 364-foot multiple span crossing this tributary of the Susitna River. Parking and litter barrels. Maclaren River Lodge to south on west side of bridge; boat launch (pay fee at lodge). Look for cliff swallows nesting under bridge.

P 43.3 (69.7 km) **C 92.2** (148.4 km) Maclaren River Road to north leads 12 miles to Maclaren Glacier; mountain biking. *NOTE: This side road may not be driveable beyond the river crossing at Mile 4.5.*

Maclaren River trailhead to south. The Maclaren River rises in the glaciers surrounding Mount Hayes. For the next 60 miles westbound, the highest peaks of this portion of the mighty Alaska Range are visible, weather permitting, to the north. From east to west: Mount Hayes, Hess Mountain (11,940 feet) and Mount Deborah (12,339 feet). Mount Hayes, first climbed in August 1941, is named after Charles Hayes, an early member of the U.S. Geological Survey. Mount Deborah, first climbed in August 1954, was named in 1907 by Judge Wickersham after his wife.

P 44.6 (71.8 km) **C 90.9** (146.3 km) Highway crosses **Crazy Notch**, a gap in the glacial moraine cut by a glacial stream.

P 46.9 (75.5 km) **C 88.6** (142.6 km) Road north to **46.9 Mile Lake**; fishing for grayling in lake and outlet stream.

P 47 (75.6 km) **C 88.5** (142.4 km) Beaver dam. Excellent grayling fishing in **Crooked Creek**, which parallels the highway.

P 48.6 (78.2 km) **C 86.9** (139.8 km) Informal campsite by small lake.

P 49 (78.8 km) **C 86.5** (139.2 km) The road follows an esker between 4 lakes. Parts of the highway are built on eskers. Watch for ducks, geese, grebes and shorebirds in lakes, as well as bald eagles, moose, caribou, beaver and fox in the vicinity. Look for a pingo (earth-covered ice hill) at lakeshore.

P 49.6 (79.8 km) **C 85.9** (138.2 km) Turnout to north.

P 49.7 (80 km) **C 85.8** (138.1 km) Turnout to north overlooks 50 Mile lake. Interpretive plaque on glacial topography and wildlife, including trumpeter swans and loons. Road access to north.

P 51.8 (83.4 km) **C 83.7** (134.7 km) Private hunting camp to south. Trail to north.

P 56 (90.1 km) **C 79.5** (127.9 km) **Clearwater Creek** 1-lane bridge. Rest area with toilet west side of bridge; informal camping. Grayling fishing in summer.

P 57.8 (93 km) **C 77.7** (125 km) Clearwater Creek walk-in (no motorized vehicles) hunting area north of highway.

P 58.8 (94.6 km) **C 76.7** (123.4 km) Road winds atop an esker flanked by kames and kettle lakes. Watch for moose.

P 59 (94.9 km) **C 76.5** (123.1 km) Turnout to north.

P 59.3 (95.4 km) **C 76.2** (122.6 km) Long turnout to north.

P 60 (96.5 km) **C 75.5** (121.5 km) Hunting trail to south.

P 61 (98.2 km) **C 74.5** (119.9 km) *CAUTION: Slow for potholes between Mileposts P 61 and 64.*

P 63.8 (102.7 km) **C 71.7** (115.4 km) Double-ended turnouts both sides of highway.

P 64 (103 km) **C 71.5** (115.1 km) Road descends westbound into Susitna Valley. Highest elevation of mountains seen to north is 5,670 feet.

The Denali Highway winds through the McClaren River valley. (© Mike Jones)

P 70 (112.6 km) **C 65.5** (105.4 km) Great view westbound of Susitna Valley.

P 74 (119.1 km) **C 61.5** (99 km) Side road north to lakes; informal camping.

P 75 (120.7 km) **C 60.5** (97.4 km) Clearwater Mountains to north; watch for bears on slopes. View of Susitna River in valley below.

P 77 (123.9 km) **C 58.5** (94.1 km) **Private Aircraft:** Private airstrip, adjacent west; elev. 2,675 feet; length 2,000 feet; gravel.

P 77.5 (124.7 km) **C 58** (93.3 km) Lodge; current status of services unknown.

P 78.3 (126 km) **C 57.2** (92 km) Short (0.1 mile) access road south to scenic viewpoint overlooking Susitna River.

P 78.8 (126.8 km) **C 56.7** (91.2 km) Valdez Creek Road. Former mining camp of Denali, about 6 miles north of the highway via a gravel road, was first established in 1907 after the 1903 discovery of gold in the Clearwater Mountains. The **Valdez Creek Mine** operated at this site from 1990 to 1995, producing 495,000 ozs. of gold. The mine pit was converted into a lake in 1996 as part of a reclamation project. Area mining equipment was donated to the Museum of Transportation and Industry (see **Milepost A 47** in the PARKS HIGHWAY section). *Do not trespass on private mining claims.*

Fair fishing reported in **Roosevelt Lake** and area creeks. Watch for bears.

P 79.3 (127.6 km) **C 56.2** (90.4 km) **Susitna River Bridge** (1-lane), a combination multiple span and deck truss, 1,036 feet/316m long. Butte Creek trailhead.

The Susitna River heads at Susitna Glacier in the Alaska Range (between Mounts Hess and Hayes) and flows southwest 260 miles/418 km to Cook Inlet. Downstream through Devil's Canyon it is considered unfloatable. The river's Tanaina Indian name, said to mean "sandy river," first appeared in 1847 on a Russian chart.

Entering Game Management Unit 13E westbound, leaving unit 13B eastbound.

P 80 (128.7 km) **C 55.5** (89.3 km) Gravel pit; parking.

P 80.3 (129.2 km) **C 55.2** (88.8 km) Turnouts both sides of highway (used by hunters in season; watch for ATVs on road).

P 80.5 (129.5 km) **C 55** (88.5 km) Double-ended turnout to south.

P 81 (130.4 km) **C 54.5** (87.7 km) Gracious House campground on lake to north.

P 82 (132 km) **C 53.5** (86.1 km) **Gracious House.** Centrally located on the shortest, most scenic route to Denali National Park. 27 modern units including a large den with adjoining rooms for groups, most with pri-

Grayling fishing along the Denali Highway. (© Robin Brandt)

P 111.5 (179.4 km) **C 24** (38.6 km) Turnout with vista.

P 112 (180.2 km) **C 23.5** (37.8 km) Lily Creek. Matanuska–Susitna Borough boundary.

P 113.2 (182.2 km) **C 22.3** (35.9 km) View to east of the Alaska Range and extensive rolling hills grazed by caribou.

P 115.7 (186.2 km) **C 19.8** (31.9 km) Large gravel turnout with beautiful view of the Nenana River area.

P 116 (186.7 km) **C 19.5** (31.4 km) Turnout with interpretive sign. The Denali Highway parallels the Nenana River westbound. The Nenana River heads in Nenana Glacier and flows into the Tanana River, a tributary of the Yukon River, which empties into the Bering Sea. The Nenana is popular with professional river rafters—particularly the stretch of river along the Parks Highway near the Denali Park entrance—but it is not good for fishing, due to heavy glacial silt.

Steep downgrade westbound.

P 117.5 (189.1 km) **C 18** (29 km) Leaving BLM public lands westbound.

P 120.6 (194.1 km) **C 14.9** (24 km) Large gravel turnout.

P 121 (194.7 km) **C 14.5** (23.3 km) Turnout at gravel pit.

P 122.3 (196.8 km) **C 11.3** (18.2 km) Views westbound (weather permitting) of Mount McKinley.

P 125.7 (202.3 km) **C 9.8** (15.8 km) **Joe Lake,** about 0.5 mile/0.8 km long (large enough for floatplane), is south of highway. **Jerry Lake** is about 0.2 mile north of the highway. Two small turnouts provide room for campers and fishermen. Both lakes have grayling.

P 128.1 (206.2 km) **C 7.4** (11.9 km) Fish Creek bridge. Access to creek and informal campsite at east end of bridge.

Beautiful view (weather permitting) of Talkeetna Mountains to the south.

P 129.8 (208.9 km) **C 5.7** (9.2 km) Double-ended turnout to south.

P 131.1 (211 km) **C 4.4** (7.1 km) Large turnout to north.

NOTE: Gravel ends, pavement begins, westbound.

P 132 (212.4 km) **C 3.5** (5.6 km) Good grayling fishing in stream beside road. Large turnouts in slide area.

P 132.8 (213.7 km) **C 2.7** (4.3 km) Large gravel turnout to south.

P 133 (214 km) **C 2.5** (4 km) Cantwell Station highway maintenance camp.

P 133.1 (214.2 km) **C 2.4** (3.9 km) **Junction** with old Anchorage–Fairbanks Highway; turn right westbound for Alaska State Troopers complex located approximately 0.2 mile north on left side of road.

P 133.7 (215.2 km) **C 1.8** (2.9 km) Cantwell post office and school, a lodge, rental cabins, RV park with hookups, 2 restaurants, mini-grocery, gas stations and gift shop are clustered around this intersection with the Parks Highway. Continue straight ahead 1.8 miles for the original town of Cantwell.

Junction of Denali and Parks highways (Alaska Routes 8 and 3). See **Milepost A 209.9** in the PARKS HIGHWAY section on page 378 for log.

P 134.5 (216.5 km) **C 1** (1.6 km) Jack River bridge.

P 135.5 (218.1 km) **C 0 CANTWELL.** See description on page 379 in the PARKS HIGHWAY section.

P 83 (133.6 km) **C 52.5** (84.5 km) Visible across the Susitna River is Valdez Creek Mine at the old Denali townsite. See description at **Milepost P 78.8.**

P 84 (135.2 km) **C 51.5** (82.9 km) **Stevenson's Lake** 0.5 mile/0.8 km south; grayling fishing.

P 85.1 (137 km) **C 50.4** (81.1 km) There are numerous informal campsites used by hunters the next 7.9 miles westbound.

P 90.5 (145.6 km) **C 45** (72.4 km) A major water drainage divide occurs near here. East of the divide, the tributary river system of the Susitna flows south to Cook Inlet. West of the divide, the Nenana River system flows north to the Yukon River, which empties into the Bering Sea.

P 93.8 (151 km) **C 41.7** (67.1 km) **Butte Lake,** 5 miles/8 km south of highway. Motorized access by all-terrain vehicle from lodge at **Milepost P 99.5**. Best fishing June through September. Lake trout to 30 lbs., troll with red-and-white spoons or grayling remains; grayling to 20 inches, small flies or spinners; burbot to 12 lbs., use bait on bottom.

P 94.3 (151.8 km) **C 41.2** (66.3 km) Short road north leads to parking area above pond. View of Monahan Flat and Alaska Range to the north. Interpretive plaque on earthquakes.

P 94.8 (152.6 km) **C 40.7** (65.5 km) Bridge over Canyon Creek.

P 95.4 (153.5 km) **C 40.1** (64.5 km) Turnout to north.

P 95.8 (154.2 km) **C 39.7** (63.9 km) Turnout to north.

P 96.3 (155 km) **C 39.2** (63.1 km) Rough narow side road north up to viewpoint of the West Fork Glacier. Looking north up the face of this glacier, Mount Deborah is to the left and Hess Mountain is in the center.

P 97 (156.1 km) **C 38.5** (62 km) Looking at the Alaska Range to the north, Mount Deborah, Hess Mountain and Mount Hayes are the highest peaks to your right; to the left are the lower peaks of the Alaska Range and Nenana Mountain.

P 99.5 (160.1 km) **C 36** (57.9 km) Adventures Unlimited Lodge.

P 100 (160.9 km) **C 35.5** (57.1 km) Residents of this area say it is a wonderful place for picking cranberries and blueberries in August. Numerous turnouts and some patches of rough road next 3 miles westbound.

P 103.2 (166 km) **C 32.3** (52 km) Turnout to north.

Highway is built on an esker between kettle lakes.

P 104.6 (168.3 km) **C 30.9** (49.7 km) **Brushkana River** Bridge. BLM campground to north at west end of bridge; 12 sites beside river, tables, firepits, toilets, litter barrels and water. Fishing for grayling and Dolly Varden. Watch for moose.

P 106.6 (171.6 km) **C 28.9** (46.5 km) **Canyon Creek,** grayling fishing.

P 107.1 (172.3 km) **C 28.4** (45.7 km) Gravel side road north to informal campsite.

P 107.2 (172.5 km) **C 28.3** (45.5 km) **Stixkwan Creek** flows under highway in culvert. Grayling.

P 110.5 (177.8 km) **C 25** (40.2 km) *CAUTION: Steep downgrade westbound; trucks use low gear.*

P 111.2 (179 km) **C 24.3** (39.1 km) **Seattle Creek** 1-lane bridge. Fishing for grayling and Dolly Varden.

STEESE HIGHWAY 

Connects: Fairbanks to Circle, AK **Length:** 162 miles
Road Surface: 30% paved, 70% gravel **Season:** Open all year
Highest Summit: Eagle Summit, 3,624 feet
Major Attractions: Hot Springs, Gold Dredge No. 8, Pipeline Viewpoint, Davidson Ditch, White Mountains NRA

(See map, page 452)

	Central	Chena Hot Springs	Circle	Circle Hot Springs	Fairbanks
Central		180	35	8	128
Chena Hot Springs	180		214	188	61
Circle	35	214		43	162
Circle Hot Springs	8	188	43		136
Fairbanks	128	61	162	136	

The Steese Highway follows the Chatanika River. (© Kris Graef, staff)

The Steese Highway connects Fairbanks with Chena Hot Springs (61 miles) via Chena Hot Springs Road; the town of Central (128 miles); Circle Hot Springs (136 miles) via Circle Hot Springs Road; and with Circle, a small settlement 162 miles to the northeast on the Yukon River and 50 miles south of the Arctic Circle. The scenery alone makes this a worthwhile drive.

The first 44 miles of the Steese Highway are paved. *NOTE: Watch for resurfacing under way between Mileposts 22 and 35.2 in summer 2000.* From the pavement end, it is a wide gravel road into Central, where there is a stretch of paved road. From Central to Circle, the highway is a narrow, winding road with gravel surface.

The highway is open year-round; check with the Dept. of Transportation in Fairbanks regarding winter road conditions. The Steese Highway was completed in 1927 and named for Gen. James G. Steese, U.S. Army, former president of the Alaska Road Commission.

Among the attractions along the Steese are Eagle Summit, highest pass on the highway, where there is an unobstructed view of the midnight sun at summer solstice (June 21); the Chatanika River and Chena River recreation areas; and Chena and Circle Hot Springs.

Emergency medical services: Between Fairbanks and Circle, phone the state troopers at 911 or (907) 452-1313. Use CB Channels 2, 19, 22.

Steese Highway Log

Distance from Fairbanks (F) is followed by distance from Circle (C).

ALASKA ROUTE 2

F 0 C 162 (260.7 km) **FAIRBANKS. Junction** of Airport Way, Richardson–Alaska Highway and the Steese Expressway. Follow the 4-lane Steese Expressway north.

F 0.4 (0.6 km) **C 161.6** (260.1 km) Tenth Avenue exit.

F 0.6 (1 km) **C 161.4** (259.7 km) Expressway crosses Chena River.

F 0.9 (1.4 km) **C 161.1** (259.3 km) Third Street exit.

F 1 (1.6 km) **C 161** (259.1 km) College Road exit to west and access to Bentley Mall and University of Alaska.

F 1.4 (2.3 km) **C 160.6** (258.5 km) Trainor Gate Road; access to Fort Wainright.

F 2 (3.2 km) **C 160** (257.5 km) Johansen Expressway (Old Steese Highway) to west; access to Fairbanks shopping. City Lights Boulevard to east.

F 2.8 (4.5 km) **C 159.2** (256.2 km) Gas station (diesel, unleaded) with foodmart at junction of Farmers Loop Road (to west) and Fairhill Road (to east).

Exit east for **Birch Hill Recreation Area,** 2 miles from the highway via paved road (follow signs). This Fairbanks North Star Borough recreation area has nordic skiing in winter on trails maintained by the Nordic Ski Club (phone 474-4242), and is used in summer by mountain bikers and cross-country runners. Outdoor theatre productions of Shakespeare evenings in July.

F 4.9 (7.9 km) **C 157.1** (252.8 km) **Junction** with Chena Hot Springs Road; exits both sides of highway. Ambulance east off exit; gas station west off exit. Turn east at exit for Chena Hot Springs Road.

See CHENA HOT SPRINGS ROAD log beginning on page 453.

F 6.4 (10.3 km) **C 155.6** (250.4 km) Steele Creek Road. Exit for Bennett Road, Hagelbarger Avenue, Old Steese Highway and Gilmore Trail. Exit to left northbound on Hagelbarger for scenic viewpont of Fairbanks a short distance west of expressway.

F 7 (11.3 km) **C 155** (249.4 km) View northbound of pipeline from top of hill.

F 8 (12.9 km) **C 154** (247.8 km) End 4-lane divided highway, begin 2 lanes, northbound. *CAUTION: Watch for moose.*

F 8.4 (13.5 km) **C 153.6** (247.2 km) **Trans–Alaska Pipeline Viewpoint** with interpretive displays. Excellent opportunity for pipeline photos. Alyeska Pipeline Service Co. visitor center open May to September, 7 days a week. Free literature and information; phone (907) 456-9391. Highway parallels pipeline.

F 9.5 (15.3 km) **C 152.5** (245.4 km) Goldstream Road exit to Old Steese Highway and **Gold Dredge Number 8 National Historic Site.** The dredge, built in 1928, was added to the list of national historic

STEESE HIGHWAY *Fairbanks, AK to Circle, AK*

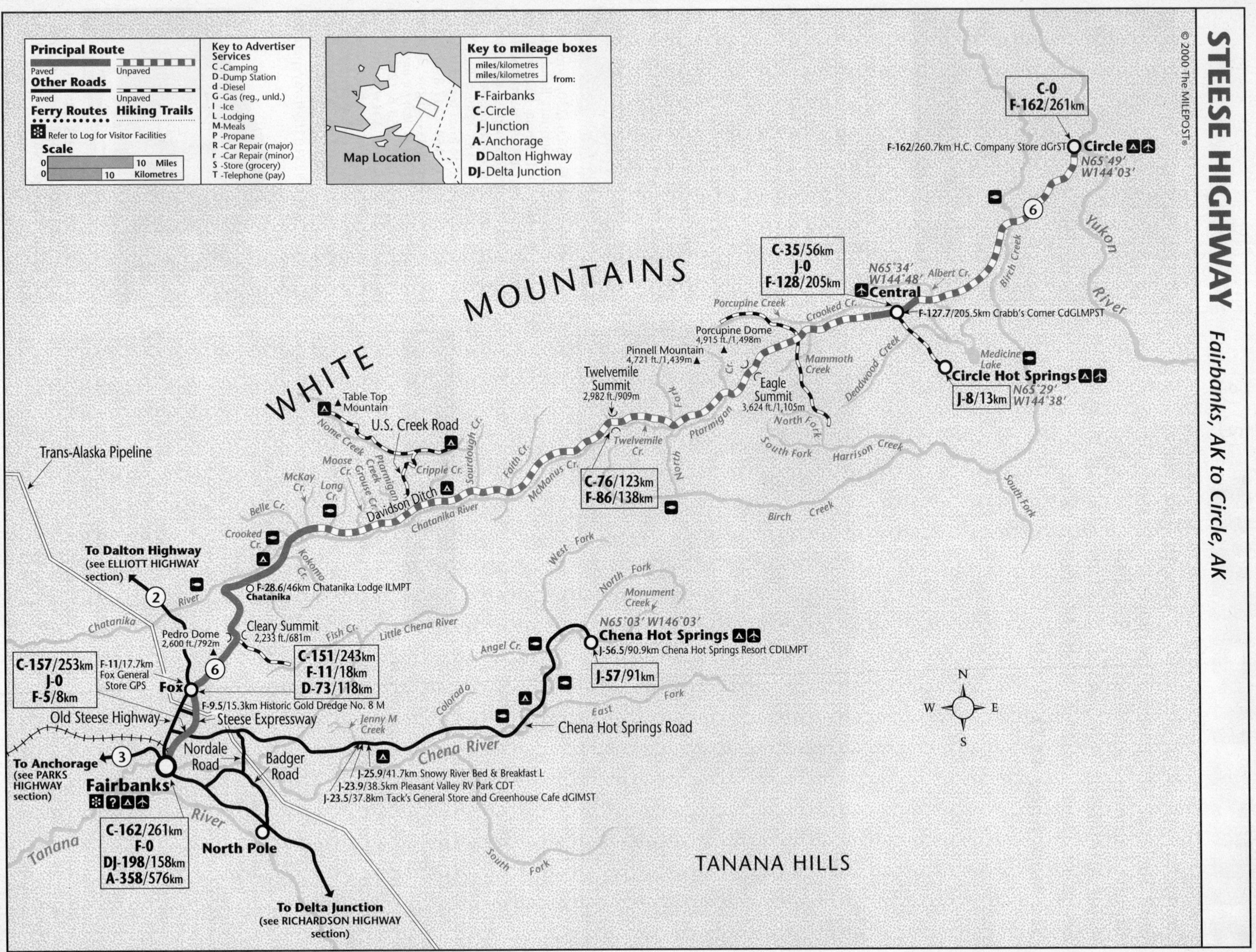
© 2000 The MILEPOST®
Principal Route
Paved
Unpaved
Other Roads
Paved
Unpaved
Ferry Routes
Hiking Trails
Refer to Log for Visitor Facilities
Scale
0 10 Miles
0 10 Kilometres
Key to Advertiser Services
C -Camping
D -Dump Station
d -Diesel
G -Gas (reg., unld.)
I -Ice
L -Lodging
M-Meals
P -Propane
R -Car Repair (major)
r -Car Repair (minor)
S -Store (grocery)
T -Telephone (pay)
Map Location
Key to mileage boxes
miles/kilometres
miles/kilometres
from:
F-Fairbanks
C-Circle
J-Junction
A-Anchorage
D Dalton Highway
DJ-Delta Junction
C-0
F-162/261km
F-162/260.7km H.C. Company Store dGrST
Circle
N65°49′ W144°03′
Yukon River
Birch Creek
Albert Cr.
C-35/56km
J-0
F-128/205km
N65°34′ W144°48′
Central
F-127.7/205.5km Crabb's Corner CdGLMPST
Porcupine Creek
Crooked Cr.
Porcupine Dome 4,915 ft./1,498m
Pinnell Mountain 4,721 ft./1,439m
Mammoth Creek
Deadwood Creek
Medicine Lake
Circle Hot Springs
N65°29′ W144°38′
J-8/13km
Eagle Summit 3,624 ft./1,105m
North Fork
South Fork
Harrison Creek
South Fork
Birch Creek
MOUNTAINS
WHITE
Table Top Mountain
U.S. Creek Road
Nome Creek
Ptarmigan Creek
Cripple Cr.
Sourdough Cr.
Moose Cr.
Grouse Cr.
Long Cr.
McKay Cr.
Belle Cr.
Davidson Ditch
Chatanika River
Faith Cr.
McManus Cr.
Twelvemile Summit 2,982 ft./909m
Twelvemile Cr.
North Fork
Ptarmigan
C-76/123km
F-86/138km
Trans-Alaska Pipeline
Crooked Cr.
Kokomo Cr.
To Dalton Highway (see ELLIOTT HIGHWAY section)
F-28.6/46km Chatanika Lodge ILMPT
Chatanika
Chatanika River
Pedro Dome 2,600 ft./792m
Cleary Summit 2,233 ft./681m
Fish Cr.
Little Chena River
C-151/243km
F-11/18km
D-73/118km
C-157/253km
J-0
F-5/8km
F-11/17.7km Fox General Store GPS
Fox
F-9.5/15.3km Historic Gold Dredge No. 8 M
Old Steese Highway
Steese Expressway
Nordale Road
Badger Road
To Anchorage (see PARKS HIGHWAY section)
Fairbanks
C-162/261km
F-0
DJ-198/158km
A-358/576km
Tanana River
North Pole
To Delta Junction (see RICHARDSON HIGHWAY section)
West Fork
North Fork
Monument Creek
N65°03′ W146°03′
Chena Hot Springs
J-56.5/90.9km Chena Hot Springs Resort CDILMPT
J-57/91km
Angel Cr.
Colorado
Jenny M Creek
East Fork
Chena River
Chena Hot Springs Road
J-25.9/41.7km Snowy River Bed & Breakfast L
J-23.9/38.5km Pleasant Valley RV Park CDT
J-23.5/37.8km Tack's General Store and Greenhouse Cafe dGIMST
South Fork
TANANA HILLS
N E S W

Trans-Alaska Pipeline Viewpoint at Milepost F 8.4 allows for close-up view of the pipeline. (© Kris Graef, staff)

sites in 1984 and designated a National Historical Mechanical Engineering Landmark in 1986. The 5-deck, 250-foot-long dredge operated until 1959; it is now privately owned and open to the public for tours (admission fee).

Historic Gold Dredge No. 8 (Gray Line of Alaska). Gold Dredge No. 8 is a monument to the miners who used the machinery to produce more than 7.5 million ounces of gold and the engineers who built it. Visitors tour the only dredge in Alaska open to the public. Gold panning and a Miner's lunch are also available at this national historic site. See advertisement in FAIRBANKS section. [ADVERTISEMENT]

F 10.4 (16.7 km) **C 151.6** (244 km) Road to Permafrost Tunnel Research Facility to east (not open to public). Excavated in the early 1960s, the tunnel is maintained cooperatively by the University of Alaska–Fairbanks and the U.S. Army Cold Regions Research and Engineering Laboratory.

F 11 (17.7 km) **C 151** (243 km) Steese Expressway from Fairbanks ends at **junction** of Alaska Routes 6 and 2; weigh station with pay phone at northeast corner. Access west to **FOX** (description follows); food, gas, groceries. Dalton Highway information sign. Turn east for continuation of Steese Highway, (now Alaska Route 6); log follows. Distance marker shows Chatanika 17 miles; Central 118 miles; Circle 152 miles. *NOTE: Next gas on Steese Highway is 117 miles from here.*

Fox General Store. See display ad page 455.

Junction with Elliott Highway (Alaska Route 2) which continues northeast to the Dalton Highway and Manley Hot Springs See ELLIOTT HIGHWAY section on page 459 for log.

Fox General Store. Located at the crossroads of Steese Expressway and Elliott Highway; the gateway to fishing, camping, hunting and mining. Last gas for 117 miles when traveling north on Steese, and next to

(Continues on page 455)

Chena Hot Springs Road Log

This good all-weather paved road (45–55 mph speed limit) leads 56.5 miles east to Chena Hot Springs, a private resort open daily year-round. Chena Hot Springs Road passes through the middle of 254,000-acre Chena River Recreation Area, an exceptional year-round recreation area with picnic sites, campgrounds and hiking trails. Easy access to the Chena River, one of the most popular grayling fisheries in the state. *IMPORTANT: Check current ADF&G regulations regarding the taking of any fish.*

Distance is measured from junction with the Steese Highway (J).

J 0 Chena Hot Springs Road exit at **Milepost F 4.9** Steese Expressway.

J 0.5 (0.8 km) Bias Drive; access to bed and breakfast.

J 1.2 (1.9 km) Elementary Drive.

J 4 (6.4 km) Access to Grizzly Lodge.

J 5.3 (8.5 km) Access to A Taste of Alaska Lodge.

J 5.8 (9.3 km) Watch for moose next mile.

J 6.4 (10.3 km) Nordale Road, connects with Badger Road to Richardson Highway.

J 8.3 (13.4 km) Paved double-ended turnout to south.

J 10.4 (16.7 km) Mini-mart.

J 10.5 (16.9 km) Gas station.

J 11.9 (19.2 km) Bridge over Little Chena River. Water gauging station in middle of bridge. This Army Corps of Engineers flood control project, completed in 1979, was designed to prevent floods such as the one which devastated Fairbanks in 1967.

J 15 (24.1 km) *Patched pavement next mile eastbound. Watch for moose.*

J 15.9 (25.6 km) Two Rivers Lodge.

J 16 (25.7 km) Pond.

J 18 (29 km) Trail crossing sign.

J 18.3 (29.5 km) Two Rivers Road; public dumpster and access to firewood cutting access road (permit only; follow signs) and to Two Rivers Elementary School (0.6 mile from highway). Two Rivers Recreation Area (Fairbanks North Star Borough), across from school, has skiing and hiking trail system.

J 20.1 (32.3 km) Jenny M. Creek.

J 20.2 (32.5 km) Parking.

J 20.7 (33.3 km) Watch for horses (sign).

J 21 (33.8 km) Baptist church.

J 23.4 (37.7 km) Valley Center Grocery and gas.

Travelers have a good chance of seeing moose in ponds along Chena Hot Springs Road. (© Rich Reid, Colors of Nature)

J 23.5 (37.8 km) Tacks' General Store; groceries, ice, cafe. Two Rivers post office is in the store. Gas station.

TWO RIVERS (pop. 660) is an unincorporated community, with stores, restaurants and other services located along the road here. The community is home to a number of dog mushers, including 5-time Iditarod champ Rick Swenson. There is an extensive system of mushing trails in the area (motorists will notice the "trail crossing" signs along the road), and the Yukon Quest trail runs through the middle of Two Rivers.

Tacks' General Store and Greenhouse Cafe. See display ad this section.

J 23.8 (38.3 km) Pleasant Valley Plaza; laundry, showers, store, pay phones.

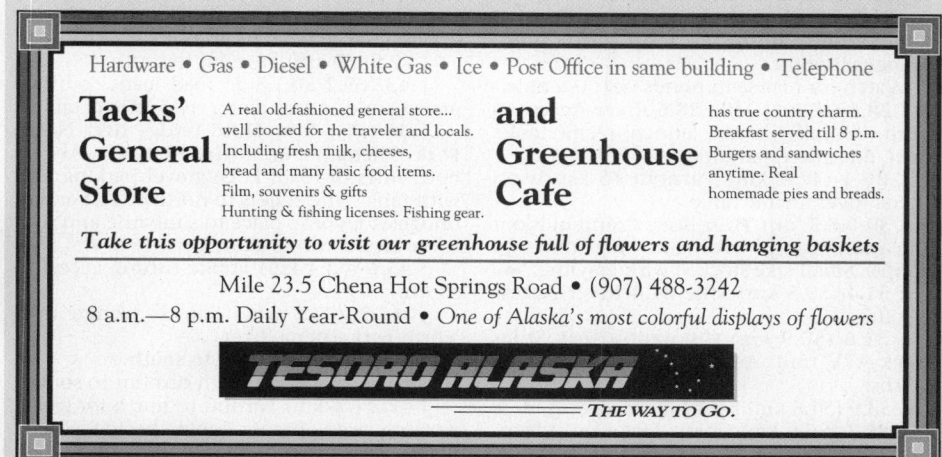

J 23.9 (38.5 km) **Pleasant Valley RV Park** next to Pleasant Valley Plaza. Quiet

Chena Hot Springs Road Log *(continued)*

country setting, gateway to upper Chena Valley. Fishing, hiking, biking, ATV trails, canoe rentals. All pull-throughs. Water and electric hookups, restrooms, dump station, propane and pay phone. Tent sites, firepits, free firewood. Coin-operated laundry and showers available. Convenient to local amenities. P.O. Box 16019, Two Rivers, AK 99716. Phone (907) 488-8198. MasterCard, VISA accepted. [ADVERTISEMENT] ▲

J 25.6 (41.2 km) HIPAS Observatory, UCLA Plasma Physics Lab (Geophysical Institute Chena Radio Facility).

J 25.9 (41.7 km) **Snowy River Bed & Breakfast.** Mile 25.9. Attractive, clean log cabin. 35 minutes from Fairbanks in a private setting on the Chena River. Fishing, guided/unguided, hiking trails, float trips, canoe/raft rentals, wildlife viewing, photography and northern lights viewing. Available year-round. No smoking/pets. B&B in a true Alaskan setting. Full breakfast available. (907) 488-7517. [ADVERTISEMENT]

J 26.1 (42 km) Entering **Chena River Recreation Area.** No shooting except at target range at **Milepost J 36.5.** Grayling fishing (check current regulations).

J 26.7 (43 km) Dog team crossing.

J 27 (43.5 km) Large turnout to south at entrance to Rosehip state campground; 25 level, shaded sites, picnic tables, firepits, toilets, water, water nature trail. $8 nightly fee or resident pass. Large gravel pads and an easy 0.7-mile loop road make this a good campground for large RVs and trailers. Firewood available, $5. Beautifully situated on the Chena River. *CAUTION: Steep, eroded riverbank; supervise small children.* ▲

This is a canoe exit point. The Chena is popular with paddlers, but should not be underestimated: The river is cold and the current very strong. Watch for river-wide logjams and sweepers. Secure your gear in waterproof containers. Local paddlers suggest a float from **Milepost J 39.5** to **J 37.9** for easy paddling; **J 44** to **J 37.9** for a longer float; and **J 52.3** to **J 47.3** for paddlers with more skill. Allow about an hour on the river for each road mile traveled.

J 27.5 (44.3 km) Paved turnout to south.

J 28 (45.1 km) **Mile 28 River Access** to south (0.9 mile); large parking area with picnic tables, dumpster, loop turnaround. Canoe exit point.

Watch for moose in ponds next 0.6 mile.

J 28.6 (46 km) **Mile 28.6 River Access** to south (0.7 mile); canoe launch, picnic table, toilet, dumpster, parking.

J 29.4 (47.3 km) Turnout to south on Chena River; picnic table.

J 30 (48.3 km) Twin Bears Camp outdoor education camp (available for rent by groups). Small lake stocked with grayling.

J 31.4 (50.5 km) **Mile 31.4 River Access** to south.

J 31.6 (50.9 km) Colorado Creek/Stiles Creek ATV trail. Access to Colorado Creek Cabins.

J 33.9 (54.6 km) Four Mile Creek.

J 35.2 (56.6 km) Chena Dog Sled Adventures.

J 35.8 (57.6 km) Paved turnout to south.

J 36.5 (58.7 km) Target shooting range to north. ORV trails, toilets and picnic tables. Cathedral Bluffs view.

J 37.8 (60.8 km) River access to south; informal camping on gravel bar, canoe launch.

J 37.9 (61 km) First bridge over the **North Fork Chena River.** Water gauge in center of bridge (not visible to motorists). There are 3 stream flow meters on the upper Chena. Grayling fishing (check current special regulations).

J 38.2 (61.5 km) River access to north; large parking area on gravel levee.

J 39.2 (63.1 km) Informal camping at turnout to south.

J 39.4 (63.4 km) Second bridge over North Fork Chena River. Loop road through **Tors Trail state campground**; 20 large sites among tall spruce trees, parking area, water, toilets, tables, firepits, $8 nightly fee or resident pass, firewood $5; campground host. Canoe launch. Picnic area on loop road along river. ▲

Trailhead (west side of bridge) for **Granite Tors Trail**; follow dike (levee) on west side upstream 0.3 mile/0.5 km to trail sign. It is a 6-mile/9.7-km hike to the nearest tors, 8 miles/12.9 km to the main grouping. Tors are isolated pinnacles of granite jutting up from the tundra.

J 39.7 (63.9 km) **Mile 39.5 River Access;** 0.2-mile side road leads south to Chena River picnic area with tables, toilets and a riverbank of flat rocks ideal for sunbathing.

J 39.8 (64.1 km) Granite Tors Campground loop road exit.

J 41.6 (66.9 km) Watch for moose in pond.

J 42.1 (67.8 km) Large paved loop turnout south of road. Watch for muskrats and beaver in ponds here.

J 42.8 (68.9 km) **Mile 43 Red Squirrel campground** and picnic area to north, one of the nicest on this road, with covered tables, firepits, toilets, water and dumpster. Located on edge of small lake stocked with grayling. Watch for moose. ▲

J 42.9 (69 km) Turnout to south.

J 43 (69.2 km) Side road leads south to gravel parking area along river; picnic table.

J 44 (70.8 km) Third bridge over North Fork Chena River. **Mile 44 River Access** both sides of road; large gravel parking area with tables and toilets to north at east end of bridge. A favorite place to sunbathe and fish. River access; canoe launch.

J 45.6 (73.4 km) Public fishing access to south.

J 45.7 (73.5 km) Fourth bridge over North Fork Chena River.

J 46 (74 km) Turnout to south.

J 46.8 (75.3 km) Rough turnout to south.

J 47.2 (76 km) Turnoff to north for gravel parking area, picnic table, beside Chena River.

J 47.9 (77.1 km) Public fishing access 0.1 mile south to **48-Mile Pond.** Stocked with grayling; picnic tables, informal campsites.

J 48.9 (78.7 km) Angel Rocks trailhead to south and access to river; table,outhouse, dumpster. Angel Rocks trail is a 3.5-mile loop trail to spectacular rock outcroppings; strenuous hike. Fishing.

J 49 (78.9 km) Fifth bridge over **North Fork Chena River**; access to river via side road to south at west end of bridge.

J 49.1 (79 km) Lower Chena Dome trailhead. Side road leads 0.2 mile/0.3 km north to trailhead, parking, water, dumpster and toilets.

J 49.7 (80 km) Angel Creek Lodge to north.

J 49.9 (80.3 km) **Angel Creek**, grayling 12 to 17 inches.

J 50 (80.5 km) Turnout to north.

J 50.5 (81.3 km) Paved turnout to north. Chena Dome trailhead. This 29-mile/47-km loop trail exits at **Milepost J 49.1.** Angel Creek Cabin ATV trailhead (6 miles/10 km). Parking, toilets. Bring mosquito repellent!

J 52.3 (84.2 km) Bridge over West Fork Chena River. Gravel side road at west end of bridge leads south to parking area along the river.

J 55.3 (89 km) North Fork Chena River bridge. Day-use parking area with outhouses, water pump

J 55.4 (89.2 km) Double-ended parking area to south just east of bridge.

J 56.5 (90.9 km) **CHENA HOT SPRINGS:** food, lodging, camping, bar, swimming pool, trail rides, ATV rentals. There is an airstrip at the lodge. Large parking area at end of road, one-lane wooden bridge. ▲

Chena Hot Springs Resort, Interior Alaska's year-round visitor destination. Relax, refresh and rejuvenate in the natural spring-fed pool and whirlpools. Enjoy the cozy lodge, comfortable hotel rooms, rustic cabins, spacious campground and RV parking (electric hookups, dump station and water available). Each season offers recreational opportunities. Enjoy the scenic 1-hour drive from Fairbanks. Summer solstice brings gold panning, hiking, horseback riding, flightseeing, ATV 4-wheel tours and mountain biking. Plus other activities like basketball, volleyball, horseshoes and picnicking. Fishing and boating areas are conveniently nearby. Massage therapy sessions available all year. Winter activities feature aurora viewing, dogsled rides, cross-country skiing, flightseeing, ice skating, snowshoeing and guided snow machine rides. P.O. Box 73440-MP, Fairbanks, AK 99707; phone (907) 452-7867 or (800) 478-4681. Internet: www.chenahotsprings.com. See display ad in FAIRBANKS section. [ADVERTISEMENT] ▲

Return to Milepost F 4.9 Steese Highway

(Continued from page 453)
last gas for 150 miles when traveling north on Elliott. Gas, propane, grocery, beer, liquor, Alaskana gifts and hunting and fishing licenses. See display ad this section. [ADVERTISEMENT]

FOX (pop. 332), has Fox General Store and gas station and Fox Roadhouse. Fox was established as a mining camp before 1905 and named for nearby Fox Creek.

ALASKA ROUTE 6

F 13.6 (21.9 km) **C 148.4** (238.8 km) Eisele Road; turnoff on right northbound for NOAA/NESDIS Command and Data Acquisition Station at Gilmore Creek. This facility tracks and commands multiple NOAA polar orbiting, environmental satellites. Tours of the satellite tracking station are available 9 A.M. to 4 P.M., Monday through Saturday, from June through August or by appointment September through May. Phone (907) 451-1200 for more information.

F 16.5 (26.6 km) **C 145.5** (234.2 km) Paved parking area to west with monument to Felix Pedro, the prospector who discovered gold on Pedro Creek in July 1902 and started the rush that resulted in the founding of Fairbanks. Informal gravel parking area to east used by recreational gold panners.

F 17.5 (28.2 km) **C 144.5** (232.5 km) Paved parking area to east.

Winding ascent (7 to 8 percent grades) northbound to Cleary Summit area.

F 19.5 (31.4 km) **C 142.5** (229.3 km) Large paved parking area to east.

F 20.5 (33 km) **C 141.5** (227.7 km) **Cleary Summit** (elev. 2,233 feet); Skiland Ski Area 1 mile. Named for early prospector Frank Cleary. View of current mining operation and old buildings from early mining and dredging on Cleary Creek below. On a clear day there are excellent views of the Tanana Valley and Mount McKinley to the south and the White Mountains to the north.

*Highway descends steep winding 7 percent grade northbound. Watch for road improvements under way between **Milepost F 22** and F 35 in summer 2000.*

F 21 (33.8 km) **C 141** (226.9 km) Cleary Summit Ski Area; open weekends in winter.

F 27.6 (44.4 km) **C 134.4** (216.3 km) Tailings (gravel and boulders of dredged streambeds alongside highway) from early mining activity which yielded millions of dollars in gold. There is quite a bit of mining in the Chatanika area now.

Fishing for rainbow at Mile 34.6 Pond. (© Kris Graef, staff)

F 27.9 (44.9 km) **C 134.1** (215.8 km) Sharp right turn up hill for historic Old F.E. Camp (Fairbanks Exploration Co. gold camp) at **CHATANIKA,** built in 1925 to support gold dredging operations in the valley. Between 1926 and 1957 the F.E. Co. removed an estimated $70 million in gold. The gold camp is on the National Register of Historic Places.

F 28.6 (46 km) **C 133.4** (214.7 km) Old gold dredge behind tailing piles to west *(private property, DO NOT TRESPASS).* Lodge to east with meals and lodging.

Chatanika Lodge. Cafe open 9 A.M. daily (year-round). Halibut/catfish fry Friday and Saturday, country-fried chicken on Sunday, served family-style, all you can eat. Diamond Willow Lounge. Rustic atmosphere, Alaska artifacts. Historic Alaska gold dredge across from lodge, plus aurora borealis videos on big-screen TV. Good grayling fishing. Great winter snow machining on groomed trails; snow machine rentals. Dog sled rides. Rooms available. See display ad this section. [ADVERTISEMENT]

F 29.5 (47.5 km) **C 132.5** (213.2 km) Access to **Poker Flat Rocket Facility**; off-limits except to authorized personnel. The Poker Flat rocket range, operated by the Geophysical Institute, University of Alaska, is dedicated to unclassified auroral and upper atmospheric research. It is the only university-owned sounding rocket range in the world and the only high latitude and auroral zone launch facility on U.S. soil. Tours may be arranged; phone (907) 474-7798. Web site: www.pfrr.alaska.edu.

F 30.6 (49.2 km) **C 131.4** (211.5 km) Public fishing access east to **Mile 30.6 Pond.**

F 31.3 (50.4 km) **C 130.7** (210.3 km) **Imaging Riometer Antenna Array** is a joint 10-year study of polar middle and upper atmosphere by CRL of Japan and UAF's Geophysical Institute. "The Aurora Borealis makes the atmospere opaque to radio noise from our galaxy at altitudes of 60–100 km, reducing the intensity of the noise received at the ground. The imaging riometer works like a camera, taking a picture of the radio noise once a second."

F 31.4 (50.5 km) **C 130.6** (210.2 km) Public fishing access to west; pond stocked with grayling.

Upper Chatanika River State Recreation Site at Milepost F 39. (© Kris Graef, staff)

F 32.1 (51.6 km) **C 129.9** (209 km) *CAUTION: Slow down for dips, bumps and patched pavement northbound.*

F 32.3 (52 km) **C 129.7** (208.7 km) Captain Creek bridge.

F 34.6 (55.7 km) **C 127.4** (205 km) **Mile 34.6 Pond** public fishing access; stocked with rainbow. *CAUTION: Steep and abrupt approach to access road.*

F 34.8 (56 km) **C 127.2** (204.7 km) Double-ended paved parking area to west.

F 35.8 (57.6 km) **C 126.2** (203.1 km) **Mile 35.8 Pond** to east; public fishing access.

F 36.4 (58.6 km) **C 125.6** (202.1 km) Weltown.

F 36.6 (58.9 km) **C 125.4** (201.8 km) Gravel turnout alongside **Mile 36.6 Pond** to west; stocked with grayling.

F 36.8 (59.2 km) **C 125.2** (201.5 km) *CAUTION: Patches of rough road northbound to Kokomo Creek. No shoulders.*

F 37.3 (60 km) **C 124.7** (200.7 km) Kokomo Creek bridge.

F 39 (62.8 km) **C 123** (197.9 km) Chatanika River bridge. **Upper Chatanika River State Recreation Site**, just north of the bridge, is a beautiful state campground with river access and rocky beach. There are 25 sites with fireplaces and a gravel parking area with toilets and a water pump at the entrance. Firewood is usually available during the summer. Camping fee $8/night or resident pass. Campground host. Look for wild roses here in June. ▲

Boats can be launched on the gravel bars by the river. Bring your mosquito repellent and suntan lotion. This is an access point to the Chatanika River canoe trail. See **Milepost F 60** for more information on canoeing this river.

Chatanika River, grayling 8 to 20 inches, use flies or spinners, May to September.

F 39.3 (63.2 km) **C 122.7** (197.5 km) **39.3 Mile Pond**, to west, is stocked with grayling.

F 40.2 (64.7 km) **C 121.8** (196 km) *CAUTION: Rough road.*

F 40.4 (65 km) **C 121.6** (195.7 km) Bridge over Crooked Creek.

F 41.5 (66.8 km) **C 120.5** (193.9 km) Bridge over Belle Creek.

F 42.5 (68.4 km) **C 119.5** (192.3 km) Gravel turnout to west; sled dog unloading area. **McKay Creek Trailhead.** McKay Creek Trail is 17.5 miles long. It climbs steeply for 5.5 miles to ridgetop at boundary of White Mountains National Recreation Area. The first 8 miles are suitable for summer use, according to the BLM. Winter use from November to April. This trail intersects with the Lower Nome Creek Trail.

F 42.8 (68.9 km) **C 119.2** (191.8 km) Bridge over McKay Creek..

F 44 (70.8 km) **C 118** (189.9 km) *NOTE: Pavement ends; gravel road begins, northbound.*

Highway parallels the Chatanika River for the next 10 miles northbound.

F 45.4 (73.1 km) **C 116.6** (187.6 km) Long Creek bridge. Long Creek Trading Post to west at north end of bridge; gold panning equipment (and advice), groceries, liquor store, camping. D'nae Bolt at Long Creek suggests amateur gold panners headed to Nome Creek (see **Milepost F 57.3**) use dishwashing detergent (biodegradable) to keep oils off hands and out of the gold pan, because oils cause the gold to float to the surface and out of the pan. Fishing (and gold panning) in **Long Creek**; grayling 8 to 14 inches, use spinners or flies, May to September. ▲

F 49 (78.9 km) **C 113** (181.9 km) Northbound views down Chatanika River valley to east.

F 57.1 (91.9 km) **C 104.9** (168.8 km) Entering **White Mountains National Recreation Area** (BLM) northbound. Access to this area's trails and cabins is from **Milepost F 57.3.**

F 57.3 (92.2 km) **C 104.7** (168.5 km) Turnoff for Nome Creek via U.S. Creek Road to west (description follows). **Davidson Ditch Historical Site** immediately to the west on U.S. Creek. The large pipe was built in 1925 by the Fairbanks Exploration Co. to carry water to float gold dredges. The 83-mile-long ditch, designed and engineered by J.B. Lippincott, begins near **Milepost F 64** on the Steese Highway and ends near Fox. A system of ditches and inverted siphons, the pipeline was capable of carrying 56,100 gallons per minute. After the dredges closed, the water was used for power until 1967, when a flood destroyed a bridge and flattened almost 1,000 feet of pipe.

U.S. Creek Road is a good hard-packed dirt and gravel road (steep, few turnouts) that winds up and over the hills to the northwest 6.9 miles to **Nome Creek Gold Panning Area**; large gravel parking

area, outhouse and signs about White Mountains National Recreation Area and the Nome Creek Gold Panning Area. Continue on Nome Creek Road for Mt. Prindle Campground and Quartz Creek Trail (4 miles) and Ophir Creek Campground and Beaver Creek National Wild River put-in point (12 miles).

F 59 (94.9 km) **C 103** (165.8 km) Wide double-ended parking area to east.

F 60 (96.6 km) **C 102** (164.1 km) Cripple Creek BLM campground and river access to east; 7-day camping limit, 6 tent, 12 level trailer sites; water pumps, firepits, outhouses, bear-proof dumpsters, picnic tables, nature trail. Camping fee $6. Parking for walk-in campers. Firewood is usually available all summer. Recreational gold panning permitted. *Bring mosquito repellent!* ▲

Access to Cripple Creek BLM recreation cabin. Preregister and pay $10 fee at BLM office, 1150 University Ave., Fairbanks, AK 99709; phone (907) 474-2200.

Cripple Creek bridge is the uppermost access point to the Chatanika River canoe trail. Follow 0.2 mile side road near campground entrance to canoe launch site; parking area, outhouses. *CAUTION: This canoe trail may not be navigable at low water.* The Chatanika River is a clear-water Class II stream. The Steese Highway parallels the river for approximately 28 miles/45 km and there are many access points to the highway downstream from the Cripple Creek bridge. No major obstacles on this canoe trail, but watch for overhanging trees. Downstream pullout points are Perhaps Creek, Long Creek and Chatanika Campground.

F 62.3 (100.3 km) **C 99.7** (160.4 km) Scenic viewpoint to east overlooking Chatanika River.

F 63.4 (102 km) **C 98.6** (158.7 km) View of historic Davidson Ditch pipeline to west (see **Milepost F 57.3**).

F 63.8 (102.7 km) **C 98.2** (158 km) Old Steese Highway alignment visible to west.

F 64.8 (104.3 km) **C 9.27** (156.41 km) Side road east to scenic viewpoint. Large parking area.

F 65.6 (105.6 km) **C 96.4** (155.1 km) Sourdough Creek bridge.

F 66 (106.2 km) **C 96** (154.5 km) Davidson Ditch trailhead.

F 69 (111 km) **C 93** (149.7 km) Faith Creek bridge and road. Creek access to east at north end of bridge; large parking area to west.

Highway climbs 7 percent grade northbound.

F 72 (115.9 km) **C 90** (144.8 km) View ahead for northbound travelers of highway route along mountains, McManus Creek below.

F 79.1 (127.3 km) **C 82.9** (133.4 km) Road widens for parking next 500 feet/152m.

F 80.1 (128.9 km) **C 81.9** (131.8 km) Montana Creek state highway maintenance station to west. Long double-ended turnout to east. Montana Creek runs under road and into McManus Creek to the east. McManus Dome (elev. 4,184 feet) to west.

F 81.2 (130.7 km) **C 80.8** (130 km) Turnout to east. Spring water (untested) piped to roadside. *NOTE: Wide gravel highway begins ascent to Twelvemile Summit. Avalanche gates.*

F 83 (133.6 km) **C 79** (127.1 km) *CAUTION: Slow down for sharp turn.*

Watch for snowshoe hares.

F 85.5 (137.6 km) **C 76.5** (123.1 km) Large parking area and viewpoint to east at **Twelvemile Summit** (elev. 3,190 feet) on the divide of the Yukon and Tanana river drainages. Wildflowers carpet the alpine tundra slopes. Entering Game Management Unit 25C, leaving unit 20B, northbound. Fairbanks–North Star Borough limits. Circle to Fairbanks Historic Trial trailhead 0.4 mile. This is caribou country; from here to beyond Eagle Summit (**Milepost F 108**) migrating bands of caribou may be seen from late July through mid-September.

Access to Pinnell Mountain national recreation trail (Twelvemile Summit trailhead). The trail is also accessible from Eagle Summit at **Milepost F 107.1.** Named in honor of Robert Pinnell, who was fatally injured in 1952 while climbing nearby Porcupine Dome. This 27-mile-long hiking trail winds through alpine terrain, along mountain ridges and through high passes. Highest elevation point reached is 4,721 feet. The trail is marked by rock cairns. Shelter cabins at Mile 10.7 and Mile 17.7. Vantage points along the trail with views of the White Mountains, Tanana Hills, Brooks Range and Alaska Range. Watch for willow ptarmigan, hoary marmot, rock pika, moose, wolf and caribou. Mid-May through July is the prime time for wildflowers, with flowers peaking in mid-June. Carry drinking water and insect repellent at all times. Additional information on this trail is available from the Bureau of Land Management, 1150 University Ave., Fairbanks, AK 99708-3844; phone (907) 474-2350.

F 90.5 (145.6 km) **C 71.5** (115.1 km) Double-ended turnout to east.

F 93.4 (150.3 km) **C 68.6** (110.4 km) Bridge over the North Fork Twelve Mile Creek. Nice picnic spot to west below bridge.

F 94 (151.3 km) **C 68** (109.4 km) Birch Creek access. Side road leads 0.2 mile down to north fork of Birch Creek; parking area and canoe launch for Birch Creek canoe trail. This is the main put-in point for canoeing Birch Creek, a Wild and Scenic River. Undeveloped campsite by creek. Extensive mining in area. **Birch Creek,** grayling to 12 inches; use flies, June to October.

F 95.8 (154.2 km) **C 66.2** (106.5 km) Bridge over Willow Creek.

F 97.6 (157.1 km) **C 64.4** (103.6 km) Bridge over Bear Creek. Private land holdings to east.

Circle Hot Springs resort is 8.3 miles from Central. (© Kris Graef, staff)

F 98 (157.7 km) **C 64** (103 km) Much gold mining activity in streams along this part of the highway. These are private mining claims. *IMPORTANT: Do not trespass. Do not approach mining equipment without permission.*

F 99.7 (160.4 km) **C 62.3** (100.3 km) Bridge over Fish Creek. Private land holdings to west.

F 101.5 (163.3 km) **C 60.5** (97.4 km) Bridge over Ptarmigan Creek (elev. 2,398 feet). Alpine meadows carpeted with wildflowers in spring and summer for next 9 miles.

NOTE: Avalanche gates may be closed if road conditions are hazardous over the summit.

F 103 (165.7 km) **C 59** (94.9 km) Highway climbs to summit northbound. Good view to east of mining activity down in valleys.

F 105 (169 km) **C 57** (91.7 km) Snowpoles guide snowplows in winter.

F 107.1 (172.4 km) **C 54.9** (88.4 km) Parking area to west with wheelchair-accessible toilet, trail, bear-proof litter container. Pinnell Mountain trail access (Eagle Summit trailhead); see description at **Milepost F 85.5.**

F 107.5 (173 km) **C 54.5** (87.7 km) **Eagle Summit** (elev. 3,685 feet). This is the third and highest of 3 summits (including Cleary and Twelvemile) along the Steese Highway. Favorite spot for local residents to observe summer solstice (weather permitting) on June 21. Best wildflower viewing on Alaska highway system. Wildflowers found here include: dwarf forget-me-nots, alpine rhododendron or rosebay, rock jasmine, alpine azalea, arctic bell heather, mountain avens, Jacob's ladder, anemones, wallflowers, Labrador tea, lupine, oxytropes, gentians and louseworts. The museum in Central has a photographic display of Eagle Summit alpine flowers to help highway travelers identify the wildflowers of this area.

F 108 (173.8 km) **C 54** (86.9 km) Steep, narrow, rocky side road leads from the highway 0.8 mile to Eagle Summit.

Scalloped waves of soil on hillsides to west are called solifluction lobes. These are formed when meltwater saturates the thawed surface soil, which then flows slowly downhill.

F 109.2 (175.7 km) **C 52.8** (85 km) Large parking area to east; no guardrails. View down into Miller Creek far below.

Highway begins steep descent northbound.

F 111.3 (179.1 km) **C 50.7** (81.6 km) Parking area to east.

F 114.2 (183.8 km) **C 47.8** (76.9 km) Parking area to east looking down onto the Mastodon, Mammoth, Miller and Independence creeks area. Avalanche gates.

F 116.2 (187 km) **C 45.8** (73.7 km) Road east to creek.

F 116.4 (187.3 km) **C 45.6** (73.4 km) Bridge over Mammoth Creek. Near here fossil remains of many species of preglacial Alaskan mammals have been excavated and may be seen at the University of Alaska museum in Fairbanks and at the museum in Central.

F 117 (188.3 km) **C 45** (72.4 km) Highway crosses over Stack Pup Creek. From here the highway gradually descends to Central.

F 117.5 (189.1 km) **C 44.5** (71.6 km) Parking area to west.

F 119.1 (191.7 km) **C 42.9** (69 km) Bedrock Creek.

F 120 (193.1 km) **C 42** (67.6 km) View northbound through foliage of mining operations to west.

F 121 (194.7 km) **C 41** (66 km) Bridge over Sawpit Creek.

F 122.5 (197.1 km) **C 39.5** (63.6 km) Road west to parking space by pond.

F 125.4 (201.8 km) **C 36.6** (58.9 km) Bridge over Boulder Creek.

F 126.2 (203.1 km) **C 35.8** (57.6 km) *CAUTION: Road narrows; slow down for curves northbound.*

F 126.8 (204.1 km) **C 35.2** (56.6 km) Paved highway begins and continues through Central.

F 127.1 (204.5 km) **C 34.9** (56.2 km) Central elementary school.

F 127.5 (205.2 km) **C 34.5** (55.5 km) **CENTRAL** (pop. 62; elev. 965 feet). This small community has a post office (ZIP code 99730), airstrip and park with picnic area. Gas, bar and restaurant, laundry and showers, rooms and other services. State-owned airstrip at **Milepost F 128.4.**

Formerly called Central House, Central is situated on Crooked Creek along the Steese Highway. Central is the central point in the huge Circle Mining District, one of the oldest and still one of the most active districts in the state. The annual Circle Mining District Picnic for local miners and their families is held in August.

The **Circle District Historical Society Museum** has displays covering the history of the Circle Mining District and its people. Also here are a photo display of wildflowers, fossilized remains of preglacial mammals, a minerals display, library and archives, gift shop and visitor information. Admission is $1 for adults, 50¢ for children under 12; members free. Open daily noon to 5 P.M., Memorial Day through Labor Day.

Yukon River travelers pull up along the bank at Circle. *(© Kris Graef, staff)*

F 127.8 (205.7 km) **C 34.2** (55 km)

Junction with Circle Hot Springs Road; see CIRCLE HOT SPRINGS ROAD log below.

F 127.9 (205.8 km) **C 34.1** (54.9 km) Bridge over Crooked Creek. Site of Central House roadhouse on north side of bridge.

F 128.1 (206.2 km) **C 33.9** (54.6 km) Central DOT/PF highway maintenance station.

F 128.2 (206.3 km) **C 33.8** (54.4 km) *Pavement ends, gravel begins, northbound.*

Watch for ptarmigan and snowshoe hares between Central and Circle.

F 128.4 (206.6 km) **C 33.6** (54.1 km) **Private Aircraft**: Central state-maintained airstrip, adjacent north; elev. 932 feet; length 2,700 feet; gravel; unattended.

F 130.5 (210 km) **C 31.5** (50.7 km) Pond frequented by a variety of ducks.

F 131.1 (211 km) **C 30.9** (49.7 km) Albert Creek bridge.

F 138 (222.1 km) **C 24** (38.6 km) *NOTE: Winding road to Circle. Road narrows northbound.*

F 140.4 (225.9 km) **C 21.6** (34.8 km) Birch Creek access; large turnout with toilets, bear-proof litter containers.

F 147.1 (236.7 km) **C 14.9** (24 km) One-lane bridge over Birch Creek; clearance 13 feet, 11 inches. Spur roads at south and north ends of bridge lead to turnouts on creek; primitive camping. Usual takeout point for the **Birch Creek Canoe Trail**.

F 147.6 (237.5 km) **C 14.4** (23.2 km) Turnout to east.

F 148.7 (239.3 km) **C 13.3** (21.4 km) Gravel pit to west.

F 156.7 (252.2 km) **C 5.3** (8.5 km) Large turnout opposite gravel pit to east. Look for bank swallow nests in cliffs.

F 158.5 (255.1 km) **C 3.5** (5.6 km) *NOTE: Slow for 25 mph speed zone northbound into Circle.*

F 159.5 (256.7 km) **C 2.5** (4 km) Old Indian cemetery to east.

F 161 (259.1 km) **C 1** (1.6 km) Circle post office (ZIP code 99733); airstrip (see **Private Aircraft** in Circle); school.

Circle

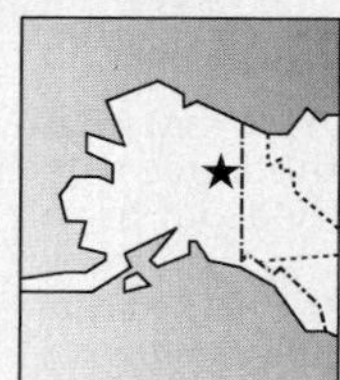

F 162 (260.7 km) **C 0** Located on the banks of the Yukon River, 50 miles/80.5 km south of the Arctic Circle. The Yukon is Alaska's largest river; the 2,000-mile river heads in Canada and flows west into Norton Sound on the Bering Sea. **Population:** 89.

Elevation: 610 feet. **Climate:** Mean monthly temperature in July 61.4°F/16.3°C, in January -10.6°F/-23.7°C. Record high 91°F/32.8°C July 1977, record low -69°F/-56°C in February 1991. Snow from October (8 inches) through April (2 inches). Precipitation in the summer averages 1.45 inches a month.

Private Aircraft: Circle City state-maintained airstrip, adjacent west; elev. 610 feet; length 3,000 feet; gravel; fuel 100LL.

Before the Klondike Gold Rush of 1898, Circle City was the largest gold mining town on the Yukon River. Prospectors discovered gold on Birch Creek in 1893, and the town of Circle City (so named because the early miners thought it was located on the Arctic Circle) grew up as the nearest supply point to the new diggings on the Yukon River.

Today, Circle serves a small local population and visitors coming in by highway or by river. The post office is at **Milepost F 161** just before the airstrip and school. Gas, groceries, snacks and sundries are available at the H.C. Company Store and Yukon Trading Post. The trading post houses the post office, cafe and liquor store. Hunting and fishing licenses are also available at the trading post. A motel is located just beyond the trading post. There's a lot of summer river traffic here: canoeists put in and take out.

The old Pioneer Cemetery, with its markers dating back to the 1800s, is an interesting spot to visit. Walk a short way upriver (past the old machinery) on the gravel road to a barricade: You will have to cross through a private front yard (please be respectful of property) to get to the trail. Walk straight ahead on the short trail, which goes through dense underbrush (many mosquitoes), for about 10 minutes. Watch for a path on your left to the graves, which are scattered among the thick trees.

Camping on the banks of the Yukon at the end of the road; tables, toilets, parking area. In 1989, when the Yukon flooded, water covered the bottom of the welcome sign at the campground entrance. From the campground you are looking at one channel of the mighty Yukon. ▲

H.C. Company Store. See display ad this section.

Circle Hot Springs Road Log

This wide, mostly flat gravel road, leads 8.3 miles to Circle Hot Springs resort.

Distance is measured from junction (J) at Milepost F 127.8 Steese Highway.

J 0 Pavement extends first 0.3 mile/0.5 km of road.

J 0.9 (1.4 km) Cemetery Road.

J 2.8 (4.5 km) Bridge over Deadwood Creek.

J 4.7 (7.6 km;) Ketchem Creek Road (1-lane dirt and gravel) leads to private mining claims and rock formations (keep right at forks in road). Road deteriorates at about Mile 3.4.

J 5.7 (9.2 km) Bridge over Ketchem Creek. Primitive camping at site of former Ketchem Creek BLM campground to south on west side of bridge. *Mosquitoes!*

J 8.3 (13.4 km) **CIRCLE HOT SPRINGS** (pop. 35). This resort offers year-round swimming, lodging, food and RV parking. A popular spot with Alaskans.

According to research done by Patricia Oakes of Central, the hot springs were used as a gathering place by area Athabascans before the gold rush. Local prospectors probably used the springs as early as the 1890s. Cassius Monohan homesteaded the site in 1905, selling out to Frank Leach in 1909. Leach built the airstrip, on which Noel Wien landed in 1924. (Wien pioneered many flight routes between Alaska communities.)

Private Aircraft: Circle Hot Springs state-maintained airstrip; elev. 956 feet; length 3,600 feet; gravel; lighted, unattended.

Return to Milepost F 127.8 Steese Highway

ELLIOTT HIGHWAY ②

Connects: Fox to Manley Hot Springs, AK **Length:** 152 miles
Road Surface: 20 % paved, 80 % gravel **Season:** Open all year
Major Attraction: Minto Lakes, Manley Hot Springs

(See map, page 460)

	Dalton Hwy	Fairbanks	Manley	Minto
Dalton Hwy		84	79	48
Fairbanks	84		163	132
Manley	79	163		53
Minto	48	132	53	

The Elliott Highway travels the ridges and hills to Manley. (© Laurent Dick)

The Elliott Highway leads 152 miles from its junction with the Steese Highway at Fox (11 miles north of Fairbanks) to Manley Hot Springs, a small settlement with a natural hot springs near the Tanana River. The first 73.1 miles of the Elliott Highway provide access to the Dalton Highway to Prudhoe Bay. The highway was named for Malcolm Elliott, president of the Alaska Road Commission from 1927 to 1932.

This is a great drive to a pocket of pioneer Alaska. The road travels the ridges and hills, providing a "top of the world" view of hundreds of square miles in all directions.

The first 30.4 miles of the Elliott Highway are paved; the remaining 121.6 miles are gravel. The highway is wide, hard-based gravel to the Dalton Highway junction. (The road is treated with calcium chloride for dust control; wash your vehicle after travel to prevent corrosion.) From the Dalton Highway junction to Manley, the road is narrow and winding and the surface is rougher. Gas is available on the Elliott Highway at **Milepost F 5.5, F 66** and at Manley. If you are headed up the Dalton Highway, the first gas stop on that highway is at the Yukon River crossing, **Milepost J 56** (56 miles north of junction with the Elliott).

Watch for heavy truck traffic. Drivers pulling trailers should be especially cautious when the road is wet. The highway is open year-round; check with the Dept. of Transportation in Fairbanks regarding winter road conditions by phoning (907) 456-7623.

The Elliott Highway also provides access to 4 trailheads in the White Mountains National Recreation Area. These hiking trails lead to recreation cabins; the trails and cabins are managed by the BLM in Fairbanks. For more information and cabin registration, stop by the BLM office at 1150 University Avenue in Fairbanks (phone 474-2350) or the Alaska Public Lands Information Center (APLIC), 250 N. Cushman (phone 456-0527).

Emergency medical services: Between Fox and Manley Hot Springs, phone the state troopers at 911 or (907) 452-1313. Use CB channels 9, 14, 19.

Elliott Highway Log

Distance from Fox (F) is followed by distance from Manley Hot Springs (M).

ALASKA ROUTE 2

F 0 M 152 (244.6 km) Steese Expressway from Fairbanks ends at **junction** of Alaska Routes 2 (Elliott Highway) and 6 (Steese Highway); weigh station with pay phone at northeast corner. Access west to Fox (description follows); food, gas, groceries. Dalton Highway information sign. Turn east for Steese Highway; continue north for Elliott Highway.

Junction with Steese Highway (Alaska Route 6) to Circle. Turn to **Milepost F 11** in the STEESE HIGHWAY section on page 453 for log of that route.

FOX (pop. 332), west side of intersection, has Fox General Store and gas station and

Fox Roadhouse. Fox was established as a mining camp before 1905 and named for nearby Fox Creek.

F 0.2 (0.3 km) **M 151.8** (244.3 km) Private RV park. ▲

F 0.4 (0.6 km) **M 151.6** (244 km) Fox Spring picnic area; 2 tables, spring water.

F 1.2 (1.9 km) **M 150.8** (242.7 km) Turnoff for **El Dorado Gold Mine**, a commercial gold mine offering tours and gold panning to the public; admission charged.

F 1.7 (2.9 km) **M 150.3** (241.9 km) Fort Knox gold mine access.

F 3.2 (5.1 km) **M 148.8** (239.5 km) Old Murphy Dome Road, very rough but passable, leads southwest around Murphy Dome to Murphy Dome Road.

F 5.5 (8.9 km) **M 146.5** (235.8 km) Hilltop 24-hour gas, diesel, phone and food.

F 6.8 (10.9 km) **M 145.2** (233.7 km) *NOTE: Slow for hills, dips and winding road westbound.*

F 7.5 (12.1 km) **M 144.5** (232.5 km) Views to the east of Pedro Dome and Dome Creek. Buildings of Dome and Eldorado camps are in the valley below to the east (best view is southbound).

F 8.6 (13.8 km) **M 143.4** (230.8 km) Dome Creek Road to east.

F 9.2 (14.8 km) **M 142.8** (229.8 km) Sign reads "Olnes City (pop. 1)." Olnes was a railroad station on the Tanana Valley Railroad and a mining camp. Old tailings and abandoned cabins.

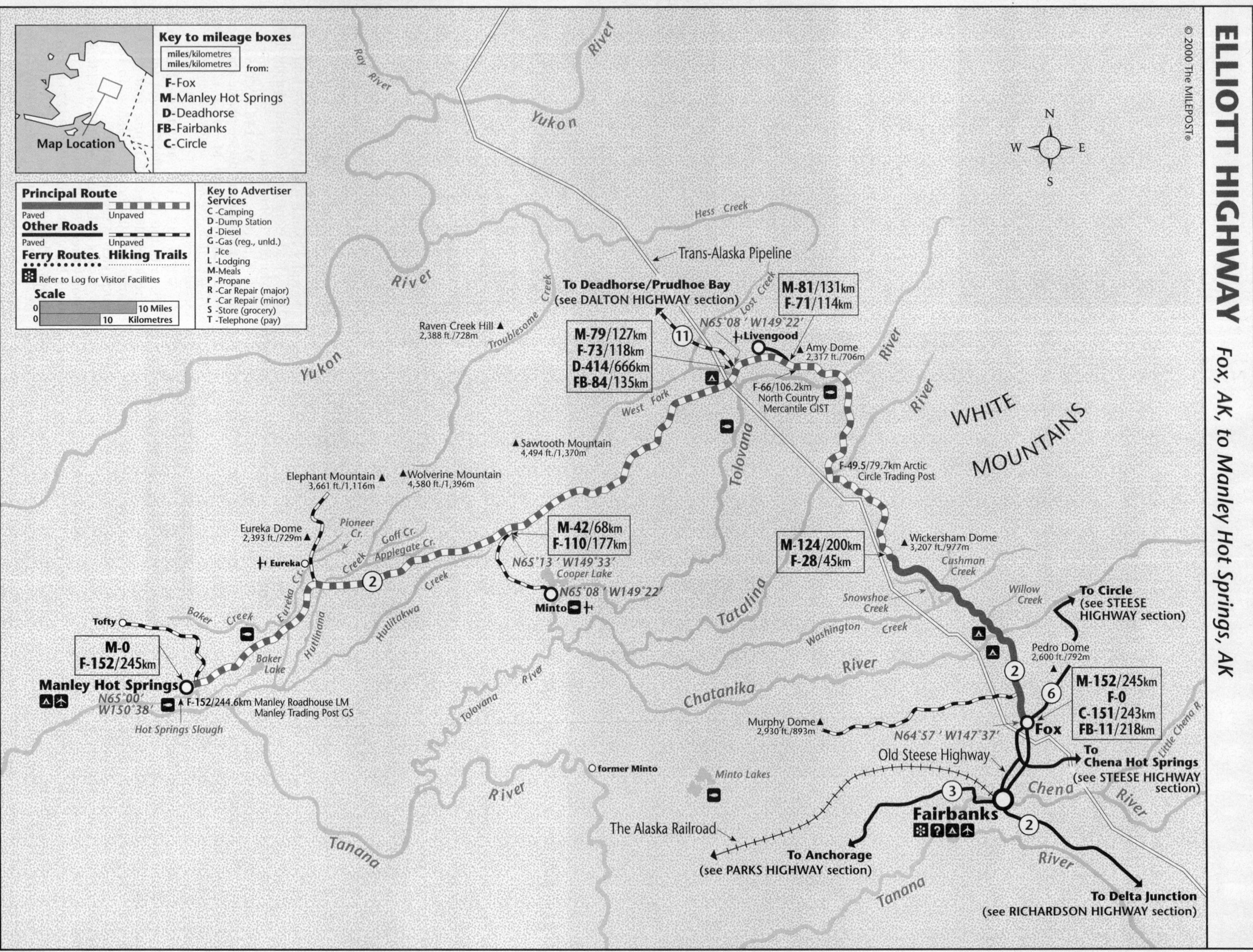
ELLIOTT HIGHWAY
Fox, AK, to Manley Hot Springs, AK
© 2000 The MILEPOST®
Key to mileage boxes
miles/kilometres
miles/kilometres
from:
F-Fox
M-Manley Hot Springs
D-Deadhorse
FB-Fairbanks
C-Circle
Map Location
Principal Route
Paved
Unpaved
Other Roads
Paved
Unpaved
Ferry Routes
Hiking Trails
Refer to Log for Visitor Facilities
Scale
0 10 Miles
0 10 Kilometres
Key to Advertiser Services
C -Camping
D -Dump Station
d -Diesel
G -Gas (reg., unld.)
I -Ice
L -Lodging
M -Meals
P -Propane
R -Car Repair (major)
r -Car Repair (minor)
S -Store (grocery)
T -Telephone (pay)
Trans-Alaska Pipeline
To Deadhorse/Prudhoe Bay (see DALTON HIGHWAY section)
M-81/131km
F-71/114km
N65°08' W149°22'
Livengood
Amy Dome 2,317 ft./706m
M-79/127km
F-73/118km
D-414/666km
FB-84/135km
F-66/106.2km North Country Mercantile GIST
Raven Creek Hill 2,388 ft./728m
Sawtooth Mountain 4,494 ft./1,370m
WHITE MOUNTAINS
F-49.5/79.7km Arctic Circle Trading Post
Elephant Mountain 3,661 ft./1,116m
Wolverine Mountain 4,580 ft./1,396m
Eureka Dome 2,393 ft./729m
Eureka
M-42/68km
F-110/177km
N65°13' W149°33'
Cooper Lake
N65°08' W149°22'
Minto
M-124/200km
F-28/45km
Wickersham Dome 3,207 ft./977m
To Circle (see STEESE HIGHWAY section)
Pedro Dome 2,600 ft./792m
Tofty
M-0
F-152/245km
Manley Hot Springs
N65°00' W150°38'
F-152/244.6km Manley Roadhouse LM Manley Trading Post GS
Hot Springs Slough
M-152/245km
F-0
C-151/243km
FB-11/218km
Fox
Murphy Dome 2,930 ft./893m
N64°57' W147°37'
Old Steese Highway
To Chena Hot Springs (see STEESE HIGHWAY section)
former Minto
Minto Lakes
Fairbanks
The Alaska Railroad
To Anchorage (see PARKS HIGHWAY section)
To Delta Junction (see RICHARDSON HIGHWAY section)

F 10.6 (17.1 km) **M 141.4** (227.6 km) Lower Chatanika River State Recreation Area **Olnes Pond Campground**, 1 mile west of highway on side road (watch for potholes and slow down for creek crossing). Open camping area around pond (good swimming); 50 campsites, toilets, water, tables, group area with campfire ring and benches. Camping fee $8/night or resident pass. Campground host. ▲

F 11 (17.7 km) **M 141** (226.9 km) Chatanika River bridge. Lower Chatanika River State Recreation Area **Whitefish Campground** to west at north end of bridge. Picnic area (wheelchair accessible) with covered picnic tables and campsites along the Lower Chatanika River; toilets, firepits, water, litter barrels, river access and boat launch. Camping fee $8/night or resident pass. Campground host. ♿▲

F 11.3 (18.2 km) **M 140.7** (226.4 km) 11 1/4 Mile Grocery uphill to northeast.

F 13.1 (21.1 km) **M 138.9** (223.5 km) Willow Creek bridge.

F 13.4 (21.6 km) **M 138.6** (223 km) Landmark old cabin to west.

F 15 (24.1 km) **M 137** (220.5 km) Himalya Street.

F 15.8 (25.4 km) **M 136.2** (219.2 km) Perennial summer garage sale.

F 18.3 (29.5 km) **M 133.7** (215.2 km) Parking area to west.

F 18.5 (29.8 km) **M 133.5** (214.8 km) Washington Creek.

F 20.1 (32.3 km) **M 131.9** (212.3 km) Paved double-ended parking area to east on curve.

F 23.5 (37.8 km) **M 128.5** (206.8 km) Large double-ended parking area with view of forested valley to west.

F 24.2 (38.9 km) **M 127.8** (205.7 km) Long double-ended dirt alignment at curve.

F 24.7 (39.7 km) **M 127.3** (204.9 km) Long double-ended turnout to east on curve.

F 25 (40.2 km) **M 127** (204.4 km) Long double-ended alignment at 35 mph curve.

F 27.7 (44.6 km) **M 124.3** (200 km) Large double-ended paved turnout to west. Highway winds around the base of Wickersham Dome (elev. 3,207 feet). Views of the White Mountains, a range of white limestone mountains (elev. 5,000 feet). Entering Livengood/Tolovana Mining District northbound, Fairbanks Mining District southbound.

Wickersham Dome Trailhead (White Mountains National Recreation Area). The Wickersham Creek Trail (winter-use) is 20 miles long; ATVs are permitted. Summit Trail (year-round) is 20 miles long and accesses Borealis–LeFevre BLM cabin.

CAUTION: Slow down for rough road.

F 28.9 (46.5 km) **M 123.1** (198.1 km) Sled Dog Rocks on horizon for northbound travelers. Double-ended gravel parking area to west.

F 29.5 (47.5 km) **M 122.5** (197.1 km) Long double-ended gravel alignment to east.

F 29.8 (48 km) **M 122.2** (196.7 km) Turnout to west. Spring water piped to road.

F 30.4 (48.9 km) **M 121.6** (195.7 km) Large rough double-ended parking area to west; scenic view. Fairbanks–North Star Borough boundary.

NOTE: Pavement ends, gravel begins, northbound.

F 31 (49.9 km) **M 121** (194.7 km) Long double-ended gravel alignment to east.

F 31.8 (51.2 km) **M 120.2** (193.4 km) Large turnout to west; scenic view.

F 32.7 (52.6 km) **M 119.3** (192 km) Steep downgrade and first good view northbound of trans-Alaska pipeline.

F 34 (54.7 km) **M 118** (189.9 km) Good view of pipeline going underground. Highway crosses creek.

F 36.4 (58.6 km) **M 115.6** (186 km) Large double-ended turnout to east.

F 36.9 (59.4 km) **M 115.1** (185.2 km) Turnout to east; creek.

F 37 (59.5 km) **M 115** (185.1 km) Globe Creek bridge. Steep and narrow access west down to single-vehicle parking spot below bridge.

Grapefruit Rocks—2 large outcrops on either side of the highway—are visible ahead, northbound. Grapefruit Rocks is a popular rock-climbing spot; hike in from turnout at **Milepost F 39** or **39.2**.

F 38 (61.2 km) **M 114** (183.5 km) Highway climbs northbound, descends southbound. View of Globe Creek canyon.

F 39 (62.8 km) **M 113** (181.9 km) Double-ended turnout to east. According to APLIC, access to Upper Grapefruit Rocks is from the end of the parking area: follow trail leading up above road. Beautiful views. Trail is steep and exposed to hot sun; bring water, insect repellent and sunscreen.

F 39.2 (63.1 km) **M 112.8** (181.5 km) Double-ended turnout to west. According to APLIC, Lower Grapefruit Rocks is accessible from this turnout by following the 4-wheel drive trail leading east from the turnout to a clearing with a firepit. Hike is an easy 1/4 mile. Trail can be muddy and mosquitos are bad

F 40.6 (65.3 km) **M 111.4** (179.3 km) Double-ended turnout to east.

F 40.7 (65.5 km) **M 111.3** (179.1 km) Scenic view from unmaintained turnout to east at top of hill.

F 41.2 (66.3 km) **M 110.8** (178.3 km) Double-ended parking area on old alignment to east.

F 42.8 (68.9 km) **M 109.2** (175.7 km) Pipeline pump station No. 7 to west (not visible from road).

F 44.8 (72.1 km) **M 107.2** (172.5 km) **Tatalina River** bridge. Large gravel parking area to east at south end of bridge. Nice stop, but no facilities and lots of mosquitoes. Walk to old bridge upstream. The Tatalina is a tributary of the Chatanika.

F 47.3 (76.1 km) **M 104.7** (168.5 km) Turnout at gravel cut to west.

F 49.5 (79.7 km) **M 102.5** (165 km) "Welcome to Joy, AK" (sign). Trading post.

Turnoff at Milepost F 10.6 for Olnes Pond at Lower Chatanika River SRS.
(© Kris Graef, staff)

The Arctic Circle Trading Post. See display ad this section.

F 49.9 (80.3 km) **M 102.1** (164.3 km) Northern Lights School. This 2-room public school has an enrollment of 22 students.

F 51.9 (83.5 km) **M 100.1** (161.1 km) Double-ended parking area, water. View of White Mountains to northeast and the

View from village of Minto of the Tolovana River. (© Kris Graef, staff)

Elliott Highway descending slopes of Bridge Creek valley ahead. Bridge Creek flows into the Tolovana River.

Steep downgrades (signed) northbound to Milepost F 54.

F 57 (91.7 km) **M 95** (152.9) **Colorado Creek Trailhead** to east at south end of Tolovana River Bridge; parking, wheelchair-accessible outhouse, litter container. Colorado Creek trail (recommended for winter-use) leads eastward 15 miles to Colorado Creek Cabin and connects with Windy Creek Trail.

F 57.1 (91.9 km) **M 94.9** (152.7 km) **Tolovana River** bridge. Fishing for grayling to 11 inches; whitefish 12 to 18 inches; northern pike.

F 58 (93.3 km) **M 94** (151.3 km) Highway climbs northbound as it winds around Amy Dome (elev. 2,317 feet) to east. The Tolovana River flows in the valley to the southwest, paralleling the road.

F 59.3 (95.4 km) **M 92.7** (149.2 km) Parking area to west by stream; informal camping.

F 59.7 (96.1 km) **M 92.3** (148.5 km) Parking area to west.

F 62.3 (100.3 km) **M 89.7** (144.4 km) Watch for narrow driveway east side of highway to access **Fred Blixt BLM cabin** (preregister at BLM office in Fairbanks). The original cabin was built in 1935 by Swedish trapper and prospector Fred Blixt.

F 66 (106.2 km) **M 86** (138.4 km) **North Country Mercantile.** Located in the beautiful historic Livengood, Tolovana Mining District. Cigarettes, groceries, hunting and fishing licenses. Ice, gas and tire repair. Notary public and pay phone available. Soft ice cream and espresso with Kaladi Brothers coffee coming soon. Watch for our signs. 11 A.M.–11 P.M. summer; 9 A.M.–9 P.M. winter. Phone (907) 295-6500. [ADVERTISEMENT]

F 70.1 (112.8 km) **M 81.9** (131.8 km) Livengood Creek, 2-lane bridge. Money Knob to northeast.

F 70.8 (113.9 km) **M 81.2** (130.7 km) Double-ended turnout at **junction** with Livengood access road. Drive 2 miles/3.2 km to former mining camp of **LIVENGOOD** (area pop. about 100); state highway maintenance station. No visitor services

The settlement of Livengood began in July 1914 with the discovery of gold by Nathaniel R. Hudson and Jay Livengood. A lively mining camp until 1920, it yielded some $9.5 million in gold. Large-scale mining was attempted in the late 1930s and again in the 1940s, but both operations were eventually shut down and Livengood became a ghost town. A mining corporation acquired much of the gold-rich Livengood Bench. *NO TRESPASSING* on mining claims.

F 71 (114.e km) **M 81** (130.3 km) Large double-ended turnout to south. Overnight parking allowed. ▲

F 73.1 (117.6 km) **M 78.9** (127 km)

Junction with the Dalton Highway (Alaska Route 11). See DALTON HIGHWAY section for log.

TURN SOUTHWEST to continue on Elliott Highway to Minto and Manley Hot Springs.

NOTE: Road narrows (no shoulders) and becomes noticeably rougher westbound.

F 74.3 (119.6 km) **M 77.7** (125 km) Site of old Livengood pipeline camp to north.

F 74.7 (120.2 km) **M 77.3** (124.4 km) River access and informal campsite to south at west end of **Tolovana River** bridge; grayling to 15 inches, use spinners or flies. ▲

Travelers may notice the abundance of dragonflies seen along the Elliott Highway: their main food is mosquitoes.

F 76.3 (122.8 km) **M 75.7** (121.8 km) Cascaden Ridge (low hills to north).

F 86.3 (138.9 km) **M 65.7** (105.7 km) Highway climbs westbound (no guard rails). Looking south toward the Tolovana River valley, travelers should be able to see Tolovana Hot Springs Dome (elev. 2,386 feet).

Tolovana Hot Springs itself is about 11 miles southeast of the highway. The hot springs has 2 wood tubs and 2 cabins. Phone (907) 455-6707 for reservations (required) and directions (necessary).

F 92.4 (148.7 km) **M 59.6** (95.9 km) Sweeping views to southeast and northwest as highway climbs westbound.

F 94.5 (152.1 km) **M 57.5** (92.5 km) Ptarmigan Pass. Long double-ended turnout to south. Good vantage point to view Minto Flats, Tanana River and foothills of the Alaska Range to south. The White Mountains are to the northeast and Sawtooth Mountain is to the northwest.

F 97 (156.1 km) **M 55** (88.5 km) The mountains to the north are (from east to west): Sawtooth (elev. 4,494 feet); Wolverine (4,580 feet); and Elephant (3,661 feet). To the south are Tolovana River flats and Cooper Lake.

F 98.3 (158.2 km) **M 53.7** (86.4 km) Turnout to southwest with view of Minto Lakes.

F 106.8 (171.9 km) **M 45.2** (72.7 km) Turnout with view of Sawtooth Mountains to north.

F 110 (177 km) **M 42** (67.6 km) **Junction** with Minto Road which leads south 11 miles/17.7 km to the Indian village of **MINTO** (pop. 251). The village was moved to its present location on the Tolovana River from the east bank of the Tanana River in 1971 because of flooding.

Minto has a gas station and the Village End Cafe (798-7373). Inquire at Minto Lakeview Lodge about accommodations (798-7448). Minto residents make their living working at the school, clinic or village council, or firefighting for the BLM in summer. Subsistence hunting (moose, bear, waterfowl and small game), fishing (salmon, whitefish) and berry pickking are an important part of this community's lifestyle. Some local people also work in the arts and crafts center, making birch-bark baskets, beaded skin and fur items. Temperatures here range from 55°F to 90°F in summer, and from 32°F to -50°F in winter. Minto Flats is one of the most popular duck hunting spots in Alaska, according to the ADF&G.

Private Aircraft: Minto airstrip 1 mile east; elev. 460 feet; length 2,000 feet; gravel; unattended.

Minto Lakes, name refers to all lakes in this lowland area. Accessible only by plane or boat; best to fly in. Pike to 36 inches; use wobblers, bait, red-and-white spoons, good all summer. Also grayling, sheefish and whitefish.

F 113 (181.9 km) **M 39** (62.8 km) Evidence of 1983 burn.

F 114 (183.5 km) **M 38** (61.1 km) *CAUTION: Narrow, winding, roller-coaster road westbound.*

F 119.5 (192.3 km) **M 32.5** (52.3 km) Eureka Dome (elev. 2,393 feet/729m) to north.

F 123.2 (198.3 km) **M 28.8** (46.3 km) Large parking area to west, scenic view.

F 129.3 (208.1 km) **M 22.7** (36.5 km) Hutlinana Creek bridge. *CAUTION: One-lane bridge.*

F 130.3 (209.7 km) **M 21.7** (34.9 km) Good wide gravel road next 7 miles westbound. *NOTE: New alignment (1998); actual driving distances will vary from log.*

F 131.3 (211.3 km) **M 20.7** (33.3 km) Eureka Road turnoff. Active mining is taking place in this area. *NO TRESPASSING* on private claims. A trail leads to the former mining camp of Eureka, at the junction of Pioneer and Eureka creeks, 3 miles south of Eureka Dome.

F 136.5 (219.7 km) **M 15.5** (24.9 km) Bridge over **Baker Creek.** Fishing for grayling 5 to 20 inches, use flies, black gnats, mosquitoes, May 15 to Sept. 30.

F 137.3 (221 km) **M 14.7** (23.6 km)

CAUTION: Narrow winding road to Manley Hot Springs. Parts of the road can be extremely slick after heavy rains. Drive carefully.

F 150 (241.4 km) **M 2** (3.2 km) Walter Woods Park to west.

F 150.1 (241.5 km) **M 1.9** (3 km) Sanitary landfill.

F 150.4 (242 km) **M 1.6** (2.6 km) Washeteria to north; laundromat, restrooms, showers and RV dump station.

F 151 (243 km) **M 1** (1.6 km) "Welcome to Manley Hot Springs" sign. Community wellhouse to north (turn switch to activate water). Manley DOT Station to south.

F 151.2 (243.3 km) **M 0.8** (1.3 km) Tofty Road leads 16 miles to gold mining area of Tofty, founded in 1908 by pioneer prospector A.F. Tofty. Active placer mining in area; do not trespass.

F 151.7 (244.1 km) **M 0.3** (0.5 km) Turn uphill for private hot springs, which are contained in 3 concrete baths inside a

greenhouse. Check in at the house on the hill (phone 907/672-3171) for reservations; $5/ person.

F 151.9 (244.5 km) **M 0.1** (0.2 km) One-lane bridge over Hot Springs Slough.

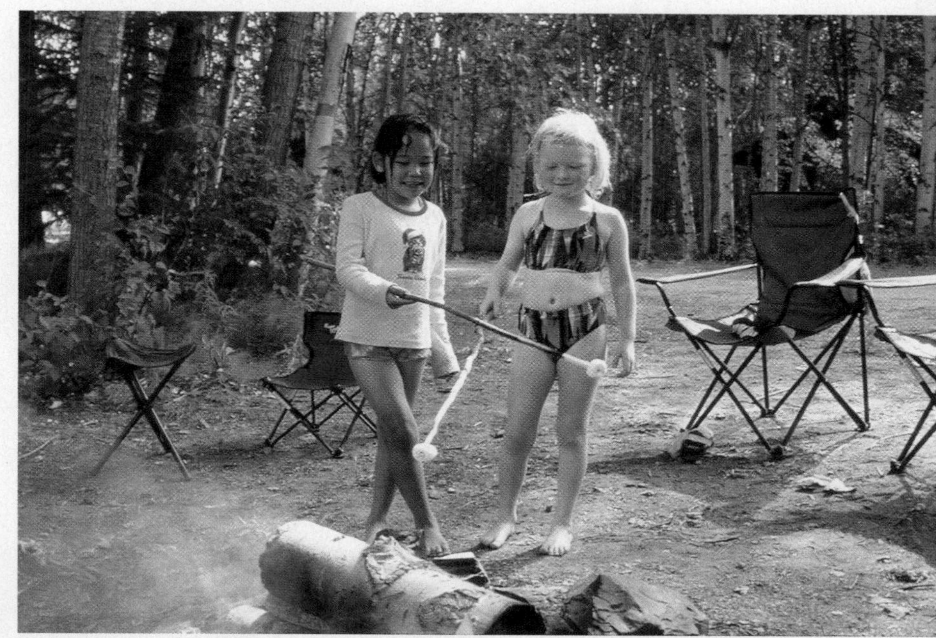

New friends roast marshmallows over 4th of July holiday at Manley. (© Kris Graef, staff)

Manley Hot Springs

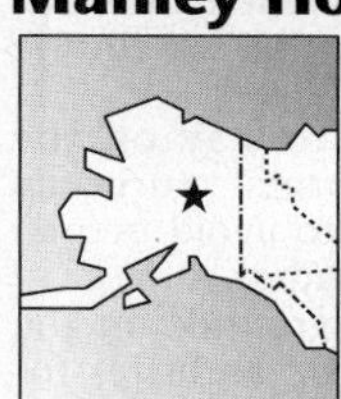

F 152 (244.6 km) **M 0** Located at the end of the Elliott Highway on Hot Springs Slough. **Population:** 94. **Emergency Services:** Volunteer Rescue Squad (EMTs and ETTs). **Elevation:** 330 feet. **Climate:** Mean temperature in July is 59°F, in January -10.4°F. Record high 93°F in June 1969, record low -70°F in January 1934. Precipitation in summer averages 2.53 inches a month. Snow from October through April, with traces in September and May. Greatest mean monthly snowfall in January (11.1 inches). Record snowfall 49 inches in January 1937. **Transportation:** Air taxi service.

Private Aircraft: Manley Hot Springs civil airstrip (open year-round), adjacent southwest; elev. 270 feet; length 2,900 feet; gravel; fuel avgas.

A pocket of "Pioneer Alaska." J.F. Karshner homesteaded here in 1902, about the same time the U.S. Army Signal Corps established a telegraph station nearby. The location soon became known as Baker Hot Springs, after nearby Baker Creek, and later was known simply as Hot Springs. Frank Manley built the 4-story Resort Hotel here in 1907. The population peaked at 101 in 1910, as the village became a trading center for nearby Eureka and Tofty mining districts. In 1913, the hotel burned down. By 1950, the population was down to 29 as mining waned. The settlement's name was changed to Manley Hot Springs in 1957.

Today, Manley Hot Springs is a quiet settlement of small business, with gardening, hunting and fishing helping to sustain many residents.

There is a big annual 4th of July celebration here, featuring a community feed and boat races on the slough. Manley Hot Springs hosts the Stanley Dayo Championship Sled Dog Race in winter. Dog musher Joee Redington Jr. offers sled dog kennel tours by appointment (phone 672-3412). Iditarod musher Charlie Boulding also lives in Manley.

Meals, a bar and overnight accommodations are available at the Manley Roadhouse. The post office, gas station and grocery are at the trading post. Manley Hot Springs Crafters' Guild features local artists in their shop, located down the road from the roadhouse.

Picnic area, playground and tent camping at park on the slough across from Manley Roadhouse. Tent and vehicle camping and boat launch on slough west of bridge. pay camping fee ($5) at Manley Roadhouse. Showers are available at the roadhouse for $3. The new (1999) washeteria just outside town has showers and a laundry (see **Milepost F 150.4**). ▲

Manley Trading Post. See display ad this section.

Manley Roadhouse. Come visit one of Alaska's oldest original roadhouses from the gold rush era. See the many prehistoric and Alaskana artifacts on display. New rooms with private baths added 1997. Private cabins. The Manley Roadhouse is a great place to meet local miners, dog mushers, trappers or fishermen. We specialize in traditional Alaska home-style hospitality, fresh-baked pies, giant cinnamon rolls and good food. Largest liquor selection in Alaska. Stop by and see us. See display ad this section. [ADVERTISEMENT]

Hot Springs Slough flows into the Tanana River. Fishing for pike 18 to 36 inches, use spinning and trolling lures, May through September. Follow the dirt road from the old Northern Commercial Co. store out of town for 2.5 miles to reach the

Tanana River; king, silver and chum salmon from 7 to 40 lbs., June 15 to Sept. 30. Fish wheels and nets are used. Fishing charter services are available locally.

Drive with headlights on at all times!

DALTON HIGHWAY (11)

Connects: Elliott Hwy. to Deadhorse, AK **Length:** 414 miles
Road Surface: Gravel **Season:** Open all year
Steepest Grade: 12 percent
Highest Summit: Atigun Pass 4,800 feet
Major Attraction: Trans-Alaska Pipeline

	Coldfoot	Deadhorse	Fairbanks
Coldfoot		239	259
Deadhorse	239		498
Fairbanks	259	498	

Dalton Highway and pipeline in Atigun Valley. *(© Rich Reid, Colors of Nature)*

The 414-mile Dalton Highway (often still referred to as the "Haul Road") begins at **Milepost F 73.1** on the Elliott Highway, 84 miles from Fairbanks, and ends—for the general public—at Deadhorse, a few miles from Prudhoe Bay and the Arctic Ocean. (Access to the Arctic Ocean is available only through commercial tour operators; private vehicles are not permitted on the oil field.) Permits are no longer required to drive the highway to Deadhorse.

The Dalton Highway is unique in its scenic beauty, wildlife and recreational opportunities, but it is also one of Alaska's most remote and challenging roads.

Road conditions vary depending on weather, maintenance and time of year, but in general the road surface ranges from acceptable to rough. Watch for ruts, rocks, dust, soft shoulders, trucks and rock maintenance equipment. Calcium chloride is used on the road to control dust; it is corrosive to vehicles and slippery when wet. There are several steep (10 to 12 percent) grades. Drive with your headlights on at all times. Slow down and pull over to the side of the road when meeting oncoming trucks. *CAUTION: Soft shoulders and abrupt drop-offs from gravel roadway to tundra; pull over with care!* Stop only at turnouts. Carry spare tires; flat tires are a common occurrence on this road.

Road construction projects will be under way summer 2000. Check project status by phoning (907) 456-7623 or on the web at www.dot.state.ak.us for Summer Construction Advisories.

Services along the Dalton Highway are limited. Shop for groceries before departing Fairbanks. There are no convenience stores or grocery stores along the highway. Gas, diesel fuel, tire repair, restaurant, motel, phone and emergency communications are available at **Milepost J 56**, just past the Yukon River bridge, and at Coldfoot, **Milepost J 175.** The last dump station northbound is also located at Coldfoot. (Please do NOT dump holding tanks along the road.) Phones at both locations are for credit card and collect calls only. Public phone at Wiseman. Alyeska pump stations do not provide any public services. Although noted on the map, former pipeline camps have been removed.

The highway is named for James William Dalton, an arctic engineer involved in early oil exploration efforts on the North Slope. It was built as a haul road between the Yukon River and Prudhoe Bay during construction of the trans-Alaska pipeline, and was originally called the North Slope Haul Road. Construction of the road began April 29, 1974, and was completed 5 months later. The road is 28 feet/9m wide with 3 to 6 feet/1 to 2m of gravel surfacing. Some sections of road are underlain with plastic foam insulation to prevent thawing of the permafrost.

Construction of the 800-mile-/1,287-km-long pipeline between Prudhoe Bay and Valdez took place between 1974 and 1977. The 48-inch-diameter pipeline, of which slightly more than half is above ground, has 10 operating pump stations. The control center is in Valdez. Design, construction and operation of the pipeline are managed by Alyeska Pipeline Service Company, a consortium of 7 oil companies (BP, ARCO, Exxon, Mobil, Amerada Hess, Phillips and Unocal). For more information, contact Public Affairs Dept., Alyeska Pipeline Service Co., 1835 S. Bragaw St., Anchorage, AK 99512.

The Bureau of Land Management (BLM) manages 2.1 million acres of public land along the Dalton Highway between the Yukon and Pump Station No. 3. For information on BLM lands, stop by their office at 1150 University Ave. in Fairbanks; phone (907) 474-2301.

Travelers are requested to stay on the road and to use the formal turnouts and campgrounds provided to avoid permanently scarring the fragile tundra.

There are 4 formal campgrounds on the Dalton, and several informal campsites for self-contained RVs. All are noted in the log. There is overnight parking at the Tesoro in Deadhorse. ▲

For emergency services contact the Alaska State Troopers via CB radio, Channel 19, or contact any state highway maintenance camp along the highway. Highway maintenance camps can provide help only in the event of an accident or medical emergency; they cannot fix flat tires nor do they provide gas. Keep in mind that towing fees by private wrecker service can be costly. For example, last summer a small camper with a fuel pump problem was towed from the Yukon River crossing to Fairbanks—a distance of 140 miles— at a cost of $450.

Report wildlife violations to Fish and Game at Coldfoot.

All waters between the Yukon River bridge and Dietrich River are part of the Yukon River system, and most are tributaries of the Koyukuk River. Fishing for arctic grayling is especially good in rivers accessible by foot from the highway. The large rivers also support burbot, salmon, pike and whitefish. Small Dolly Varden are at higher elevations in streams north of Coldfoot. Fishing for salmon is closed within the trans-Alaska pipeline corridor. According to the Dept. of Fish and Game, anglers should expect high, turbid water

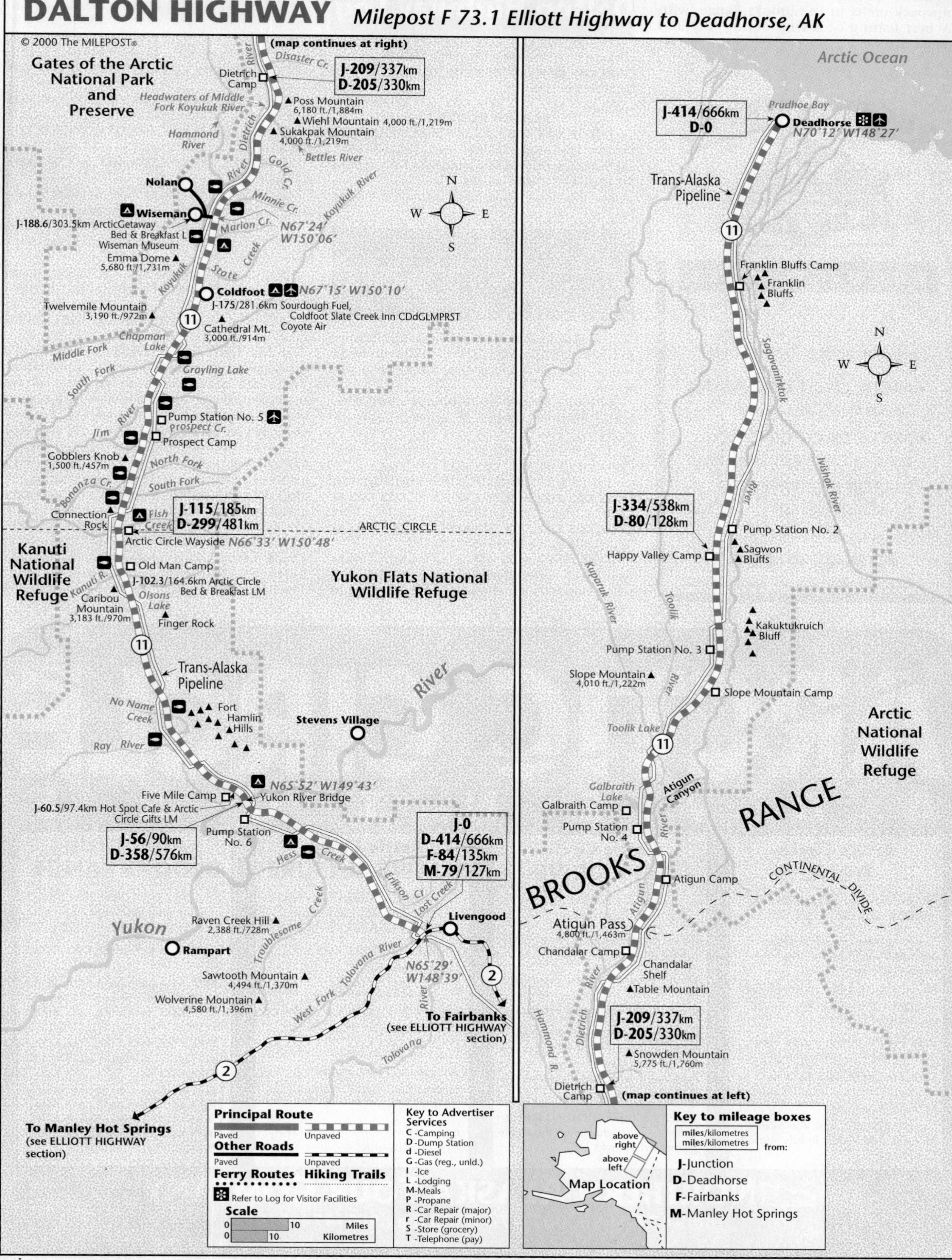
DALTON HIGHWAY
Milepost F 73.1 Elliott Highway to Deadhorse, AK
© 2000 The MILEPOST®
(map continues at right)
Gates of the Arctic National Park and Preserve
Disaster Cr.
Dietrich Camp
J-209/337km
D-205/330km
Headwaters of Middle Fork Koyukuk River
Poss Mountain
6,180 ft./1,884m
Wiehl Mountain 4,000 ft./1,219m
Sukakpak Mountain
4,000 ft./1,219m
Hammond River
Dietrich River
Bettles River
Gold Cr.
Nolan
Minnie Cr.
Koyukuk River
Wiseman
J-188.6/303.5km ArcticGetaway Bed & Breakfast L
Wiseman Museum
Marion Cr.
N67°24' W150°06'
Emma Dome
5,680 ft./1,731m
State Creek
Koyukuk
Coldfoot
N67°15' W150°10'
J-175/281.6km Sourdough Fuel, Coldfoot Slate Creek Inn CDdGLMPRST
Coyote Air
Twelvemile Mountain
3,190 ft./972m
Cathedral Mt.
3,000 ft./914m
11
Chapman Lake
Middle Fork
Grayling Lake
South Fork
Jim River
Pump Station No. 5
Prospect Cr.
Prospect Camp
Gobblers Knob
1,500 ft./457m
North Fork
South Fork
Bonanza Cr.
Connection Rock
Fish Creek
J-115/185km
D-299/481km
ARCTIC CIRCLE
Arctic Circle Wayside N66°33' W150°48'
Kanuti National Wildlife Refuge
Old Man Camp
J-102.3/164.6km Arctic Circle Bed & Breakfast LM
Kanuti R.
Caribou Mountain
3,183 ft./970m
Olsons Lake
Finger Rock
Yukon Flats National Wildlife Refuge
Trans-Alaska Pipeline
No Name Creek
Fort Hamlin Hills
Ray River
Stevens Village
River
N65°52' W149°43'
Five Mile Camp
Yukon River Bridge
J-60.5/97.4km Hot Spot Cafe & Arctic Circle Gifts LM
Pump Station No. 6
J-56/90km
D-358/576km
Hess Creek
J-0
D-414/666km
F-84/135km
M-79/127km
Erikson Cr
Lost Creek
Livengood
Yukon
Raven Creek Hill
2,388 ft./728m
Troublesome Creek
Rampart
Sawtooth Mountain
4,494 ft./1,370m
Wolverine Mountain
4,580 ft./1,396m
West Fork Tolovana River
N65°29' W148°39'
2
To Fairbanks (see ELLIOTT HIGHWAY section)
Tolovana
To Manley Hot Springs (see ELLIOTT HIGHWAY section)
N W E S
Arctic Ocean
Prudhoe Bay
J-414/666km
D-0
Deadhorse
N70°12' W148°27'
Trans-Alaska Pipeline
Franklin Bluffs Camp
Franklin Bluffs
Sagavanirktok River
Ivishak River
J-334/538km
D-80/128km
Pump Station No. 2
Happy Valley Camp
Sagwon Bluffs
Kuparuk River
Toolik River
Kakuktukruich Bluff
Pump Station No. 3
Slope Mountain
4,010 ft./1,222m
Slope Mountain Camp
Toolik Lake
Arctic National Wildlife Refuge
Galbraith Lake
Galbraith Camp
Atigun Canyon
Pump Station No. 4
BROOKS RANGE
Atigun River
Atigun Camp
CONTINENTAL DIVIDE
Atigun Pass
4,800 ft./1,463m
Chandalar Camp
Chandalar Shelf
Table Mountain
Hammond R.
Dietrich River
J-209/337km
D-205/330km
Snowden Mountain
5,775 ft./1,760m
Dietrich Camp
(map continues at left)
Principal Route
Paved
Unpaved
Other Roads
Paved
Unpaved
Ferry Routes
Hiking Trails
Refer to Log for Visitor Facilities
Scale
0 10 Miles
0 10 Kilometres
Key to Advertiser Services
C -Camping
D -Dump Station
d -Diesel
G -Gas (reg., unld.)
I -Ice
L -Lodging
M -Meals
P -Propane
R -Car Repair (major)
r -Car Repair (minor)
S -Store (grocery)
T -Telephone (pay)
above right
above left
Map Location
Key to mileage boxes
miles/kilometres
miles/kilometres
from:
J-Junction
D-Deadhorse
F-Fairbanks
M-Manley Hot Springs

conditions throughout much of June as the snowpack melts in the Brooks Range, with the best fishing occurring during July and August.

Dalton Highway Log

Distance from junction with Elliott Highway (J) is followed by distance from Deadhorse (D).

ALASKA ROUTE 11

J 0 D 414 (666.3 km) Sign at start of Dalton Highway: "Heavy Industrial Traffic. All vehicles drive with headlights on. Speed 50 mph next 416 miles." *CAUTION: Steep grades and narrow road northbound. Watch for trucks!*

Junction with Elliott Highway to Fairbanks and Manley Hot Springs. Turn to **Milepost F 73.1** on page 459 in the ELLIOTT HIGHWAY section for log of that route.

J 1 (1.6 km) **D 413** (664.6 km) Distance marker northbound shows Yukon River 56 miles, Coldfoot 175 miles, Deadhorse 414 miles.

Distance marker southbound shows Fairbanks 81 miles, Minto 48 miles, Manley 80 miles.

J 2.9 (4.7 km) **D 411.1** (661.6 km) Turnout to west.

J 4 (6.4 km) **D 410** (659.8 km) Highway descends steeply into the Lost Creek valley. Lost Creek flows into the West Fork Tolovana River. Pipeline is visible stretching across the ridge of the distant hill.

J 5.5 (8.8 km) **D 408.5** (657.4 km) Yellow numbered signs mark oil spill containment site. Materials are stockpiled here for use in case of an oil spill.

J 7.8 (12.5 km) **D 406.2** (653.7 km) *NOTE: Road narrows northbound; muddy in wet weather.*

J 8.4 (13.5 km) **D 405.6** (652.7 km) Entering Game Management Unit 20F northbound.

J 9.2 (14.8 km) **D 404.8** (651.4 km) *Steep and winding grades northbound.*

J 10.6 (17.1 km) **D 403.4** (649.2 km) Rough dirt turnout to east.

J 12 (19.3 km) **D 402** (646.9 km) Turnout to west.

J 18.5 (29.8 km) **D 395.5** (636.5 km) Highway curves past old alignment.

J 20.7 (33.3 km) **D 393.3** (632.9 km) Long parking area west side of road with sweeping view.

J 21.3 (34.3 km) **D 392.7** (632 km) Begin long (3 miles) descent northbound to Hess Creek.

J 21.5 (34.6 km) **D 392.5** (631.7 km) Large turnout to west.

J 23.7 (38.1 km) **D 390.3** (628.1 km) APL pipeline access road; no public admittance. There are many of these pipeline access roads along the highway; most are signed with the milepost on the pipeline. Because they are so numerous, most APL pipeline access roads are not included in *The MILEPOST®* log unless they occur along with another feature. All these access roads are closed to the public for security and safety concerns. Do not block road access.

*Rough road surface north to **Milepost J 28**.*

J 23.8 (38.3 km) **D 390.2** (627.9 km) **Hess Creek** bridge. Dirt access road to west at north end of bridge to campsite in trees. Track can be muddy; an easy place to get stuck. Bring your mosquito repellent. Whitefish and grayling fishing. Hess Creek, known for its colorful mining history, is the largest stream between the junction and the Yukon River bridge.

J 23.9 (38.5 km) **D 390.1** (627.8 km) Side road to west 0.2 mile to pond with parking space adequate for camping.

J 25 (40.2 km) **D 389** (626 km) Double-ended rough turnout to east. Good view of pipeline and remote-operated valve site as the highway crosses Hess Creek and valley.

Highway climbs northbound; steep curve.

J 25.5 (41 km) **D 388.5** (625.2 km) Small turnout at distance marker northbound: Yukon River 31 miles, Coldfoot 150 miles, Deadhorse 389 miles.

J 26.5 (42.6 km) **D 387.5** (623.6 km) APL access. Pipeline parallels highway about 250 feet/76m away.

J 27 (43.4 km) **D 387** (622.8 km) Evidence of lightning-caused forest fires.

J 28.2 (45.4 km) **D 385.8** (620.9 km) Large turnout opposite APL access.

CAUTION: Downgrade northbound, slow for 35 mph curves next 1.5 miles.

J 29.8 (48 km) **D 384.2** (618.3 km) APL access road at MP 373.2 on the pipeline.

J 32.7 (52.6 km) **D 381.3** (613.6 km) Rough turnout to east. Rough road next mile northbound.

J 33.7 (54.2 km) **D 380.3** (612 km) Turnout at tributary of Hess Creek. Chiming bells bloom in June.

J 33.9 (54.6 km) **D 380.1** (611.7 km) APL pipeline access road. Goalpost-like structures, called "headache bars," guard against vehicles large enough to run into and damage the pipeline.

J 35.5 (57.1 km) **D 378.5** (609.1 km) Turnout to east.

J 38.1 (61.3 km) **D 375.9** (604.9 km) Mile 38 Dalton Highway Crossing: pipeline goes under road. APL access road.

J 39.5 (63.5 km) **D 374.5** (602.7 km) *Steep grades and 35 mph curves next mile northbound.*

J 40.7 (65.5 km) **D 373.3** (600.7 km) Double-ended turnout. Overview of Troublesome and Hess creeks area. Brush obscures sweeping views.

Watch for oncoming trucks on the Dalton Highway. (© Kris Graef, staff)

J 42 (67.6 km) **D 372** (598.7 km) Large turnout. Outcrop of dark gabbroic rock.

Begin steep descent with 30 to 35 mph curves northbound. Rough road

J 43.1 (69.4 km) **D 370.9** (596.9 km) Isom Creek culvert.

J 44 (70.8 km) **D 370** (595.4 km) *Steep upgrades northbound to **Milepost J 47** with 30 mph curves.*

J 47.3 (76.1 km) **D 366.7** (590.1 km) Summit; sweeping view of mountains to north.

J 47.5 (76.4 km) **D 366.5** (589.8 km) Side road east to Yukon radio repeater tower.

J 47.9 (77.1 km) **D 366.1** (589.2 km) Highway begins descent to Yukon River.

J 48.5 (78.1 km) **D 365.5** (588.2 km) APL pipeline access road.

J 50.4 (81.1 km) **D 363.6** (585.1 km) Turnout at pond to east.

J 51.1 (82.2 km) **D 362.9** (584 km) Rough side road leads east 5.4 miles to Yukon River.

Highway climbs northbound.

J 53 (85.6 km) **D 360.8** (580.6 km) First view northbound of the Yukon River. As road drops, you can see the pipeline crossing the river. Fort Hamlin Hills are beyond the river.

J 53.8 (86.6 km) **D 360.2** (579.7 km) **Pump Station No. 6** to west. Alyeska pump stations monitor the pipeline's oil flow on its journey from Prudhoe Bay to Valdez. No public facilities.

J 54.3 (87.4 km) **D 359.7** (578.9 km) Highway passes over pipeline.

J 54.5 (87.7 km) **D 359.5** (578.5 km) APL access road to east; Milepost 354.2 on the pipeline.

J 54.8 (88.2 km) **D 359.2** (578 km) Distance marker northbound shows Arctic Circle 60 miles, Coldfoot 120 miles, Deadhorse 360 miles.

J 55.6 (89.5 km) **D 358.4** (576.8 km) **Yukon River Bridge** (formally the E.L. Patton Bridge, named for the president of the Alyeska Pipeline Service Co. after his death in 1982). This wood-decked bridge, completed in 1975, is 2,290 feet long and has a 6 percent grade. The deck was replaced in 1993.

J 56 (90.1 km) **D 358** (576.1 km) Gas, diesel, tire repair, restaurant, motel, phone and emergency communications available. Next gas stop northbound at Coldfoot, 120 miles.

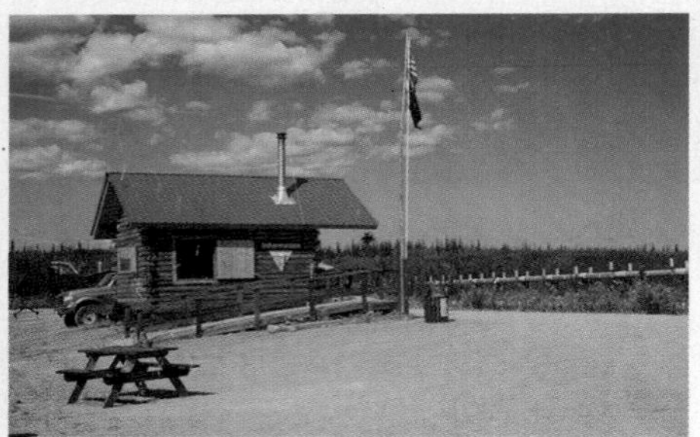

This is the southern boundary of BLM-managed lands. BLM Yukon Crossing Visitor Contact Station here is open daily, June through August. **Alyeska Pipeline Interpretive Display** here with information on the Yukon River, pipeline construction and related subjects. There is also a visitor center at Coldfoot. A hunter check station trailer is located here in season.

East of the highway is a parking area that is used as an informal camping area; litter barrels. ▲

J 60.2 (96.8 km) **D 353.8** (569.3 km) Turnoff to west for loop road to Hot Spot Cafe, Mile 60 BLM dump station, RV camping and water pump. Former Five Mile pipeline construction camp.

J 60.4 (97.2 km) **D 353.6** (569 km) North end of loop road to BLM Mile 60 dump station, RV camping, water pump and Hot Spot Cafe.

J 60.8 (97.8 km) **D 353.2** (568.4 km) Five Mile airstrip (length 3,500 feet); controlled by Alyeska Security. *CAUTION: Be prepared to stop at control gates at both ends of airstrip.*

J 61.3 (98.7 km) **D 352.7** (567.6 km) Airstrip control tower.

J 61.6 (99.1 km) **D 352.4** (567.1 km) View of Fort Hamlin Hills to north, pump station No. 6 to south.

J 61.8 (99.5 km) **D 352.2** (566.8 km) Seven Mile Station (DOT/PF highway maintenance) to east; no services. APL access to west.

J 66.8 (107.5 km) **D 347.2** (558.7 km) Long double-ended turnout to west at bottom of hill. Highway climbs northbound and southbound.

Travelers may note the change in vegetation as they pass through boreal forests, boggy lowlands and tundra. Tall, dense forests of white spruce and birch are found in well-drained soil without permafrost, usually on south-facing slopes. Stunted, low-growing black spruce indicates permafrost (permanently frozen soil) near the surface, or poorly drained soil. The BLM pamphlet, *Utility Corridor Plant Communities*, is helpful in identifying vegetation along the Dalton Highway.

J 67.6 (108.8 km) **D 346.4** (557.5 km) Turnouts both sides of road. *Highway descends steeply northbound; slow for sharp curve.*

J 69 (111 km) **D 345** (555.2 km) Turnout at crest of hill overlooking the Ray River to the north. Pipeline goes underground.

J 70 (112.7 km) **D 344** (553.6 km) View of Ray River and Ray Mountains to the west.

J 70.4 (113.3 km) **D 343.6** (553 km) Turnout to west.

J 72.5 (116.7 km) **D 341.5** (549.6 km) Fort Hamlin Hills Creek bridge. Rough tracks down to creek both ends of bridge.

J 73.5 (118.3 km) **D 340.5** (548 km) *Begin steep 0.5-mile ascent of Sand Hill northbound.*

J 74.8 (120.4 km) **D 339.2** (545.9 km) Turnout. *Steep descent northbound followed by steep ascent; dubbed the "Roller Coaster."*

J 75.7 (121.8 km) **D 338.3** (544.4 km) *"Roller Coaster" begins southbound.*

J 79.1 (127.3 km) **D 334.9** (539 km) **No Name Creek** bridge (narrow). Fishing for burbot, grayling and whitefish.

Sign: Bow hunting only area.

J 81.6 (131.3 km) **D 332.4** (534.9 km) Fort Hamlin Hills are visible to the southeast. Tree line on surrounding hills is about 2,000 feet.

J 86.5 (139.2 km) **D 327.5** (527 km) Side road leads west 1 mile to scenic overlook. Access is steep with rough, rocky spots; no turnaround until you reach the top. Nice view of tors to northeast, Yukon Flats Wildlife Refuge to east and Fort Hamlin Hills to southeast. Tors are high, isolated pinnacles of jointed granite jutting up from the tundra and are a residual feature of erosion.

J 87.2 (140.3 km) **D 326.8** (525.9 km) *Long, steep ascent of Mackey Hill next 1.5 miles northbound; slippery in wet weather.*

J 88.5 (142.4 km) **D 325.5** (523.8 km) Road descends Mackey Hill northbound.

Entering Game Management Unit 25D northbound, Unit 20F southbound.

J 90.2 (145.2 km) **D 323.8** (521.1 km) Parking areas on both sides of highway at crest of hill. A good photo opportunity of the road and pipeline to the north. The zig-zag design allows the pipeline to flex and accommodate temperature changes. The small green structure over the buried pipe is a radio-controlled valve, allowing the pipeline oil flow to be shut down when necessary.

Highway descends northbound to Dall Creek.

J 91.1 (146.6 km) **D 322.9** (519.6 km) Dall Creek. Highway climbs steeply next mile northbound.

J 94.1 (151.4 km) **D 319.9** (514.8 km) Turnout at former gravel pit road to west.

J 95 (152.9 km) **D 319** (513.4 km) The vegetation changes noticeably northbound as the highway crosses an area of moist tundra and alpine tundra for about the next 5 miles. Lichens and white mountain avens dominate the well-drained rocky ridges, while the more saturated soils alongside the road are covered by dense stands of dwarf shrubs.

J 97.5 (156.9 km) **D 316.5** (509.3 km) Good view northbound of **Finger Rock**, a tor, east of the road. Tors are visible for the next 2 miles. Prehistoric hunting sites are numerous in this region. Please do not collect or disturb artifacts.

J 98.1 (157.9 km) **D 315.9** (508.4 km) **Finger Mountain BLM Wayside** at crest of hill; outhouse, parking, interpretive trail. Good opportunities for photos, berry picking (blueberries, lowbush cranberries), wildflower viewing and hiking.

Caribou Mountain is in the distance to the northwest. Olsens Lake, Kanuti Flats, Kanuti River drainage and site of former Old Man Camp are visible ahead northbound as the road descends and passes through several miles of valley bottom. Excellent mountain views.

J 98.4 (158.3 km) **D 315.6** (507.9 km) Distance marker northbound shows Arctic Circle 17 miles, Coldfoot 76 miles, Deadhorse 316 miles.

J 99 (159.3 km) **D 315** (516.9 km) Tors to east.

J 102.3 (164.6 km) **D 311.7** (501.6 km) Arctic Circle Bed and Breakfast on west side of highway.

Arctic Circle Bed & Breakfast. See display ad this section.

J 104.1 (167.5 km) **D 309.9** (498.7 km) Distance marker northbound shows Coldfoot 71 miles, Deadhorse 311 miles.

J 105.8 (170.3 km) **D 308.2** (496 km) Large parking area to east at south end of **Kanuti River** bridge; cement ramp to river, informal camping (no facilities), fishing for burbot and grayling.

J 107 (172.2 km) **D 307** (494.1 km) Site of Old Man Camp, a former pipeline construction camp; no structures remain.

J 109.8 (176.7 km) **D 304.2** (489.5 km) Turnout at Beaver Slide.

CAUTION: Road descends 9 percent grade northbound. Watch for soft spots. Slippery when wet.

J 112.2 (180.6 km) **D 301.8** (485.7 km) Turnout at pipeline access road. Moose and bear frequent willow thickets here.

NOTE: Road surface deteriorates northbound.

J 113.9 (183.3 km) **D 300.1** (483 km) Evidence of old winter trail to Bettles is visible here.

Fishing at the Kanuti River, Milepost J 105.8, at 10 P.M. in June. (© Kris Graef, staff)

J 114 (183.5 km) **D 300** (482.8 km) Turnouts at both ends of **Fish Creek** bridge. Bumpy, sandy access down to creek to west at north end of bridge; informal campsite in trees (no facilities). Fishing for grayling 12 to 18 inches. Nice spot.

J 115.3 (185.5 km) **D 298.7** (480.7 km) Loop road east to **Arctic Circle BLM Wayside** with tables, grills, outhouses and interpretive display. Stop and have your picture taken with the sign showing you are at N 66°33' W 150°48'. At this latitude, the sun does not set on summer solstice (June 20 or 21) and it does not rise on winter solstice (December 21 or 22). A third of Alaska lies within the Arctic Circle, the only true polar region in the state. Good photo point, with views to the south and to the west.

Follow road (tent sign) east from turnoff 0.6 mile for unmaintained camping area on dirt loop road on the hill behind the wayside. If you reach the Alyeska access gate you've gone too far. ▲

J 115.5 (185.9 km) **D 298.5** (480.3 km) Long double-ended turnout to east (can be soft) at APL access road at MP 294 on the pipeline.

J 116 (186.7 km) **D 298** (479.5 km) *Begin steep and winding descent next 2 miles northbound.*

J 120.7 (194.2 km) **D 293.3** (472 km) Connection Rock (signed); north and south road-building crews linked up here.

Steep descent northbound (9 percent grade).

J 122.5 (197.1 km) **D 291.5** (469.1 km) Long doublel-ended turnout at APL access road to east.

J 124.7 (200.7 km) **D 289.3** (465.6 km) Turnout to east at **South Fork Bonanza Creek**; burbot, grayling, whitefish. Gold dredging may be under way here.

J 125.7 (202.3 km) **D 288.3** (464 km) Turnout to east at south end of **North Fork Bonanza Creek** bridge (narrow). Historic gold mining area. Fishing for burbot, grayling, whitefish.

J 126.5 (203.6 km) **D 287.5** (462.7 km) Steep uphill curve northbound as highway climbs Paradise Hill. Blueberries and lowbush cranberries in season.

J 129 (207.6 km) **D 285** (458.6 km) *Begin long, steep, ascent next 2 miles northbound.*

J 131.3 (211.3 km) **D 282.7** (454.9 km) Solar-powered communications tower to west.

J 131.5 (211.6 km) **D 282.5** (454.6 km) View of Pump Station No. 5 to north.

J 132 (212.4 km) **D 282** (453.8 km) Large turnout with litter barrels and outhouse at **Gobblers Knob** (elev. 1,500 feet) overlooking the Jack White Range, Pope Creek Dome (the dominant peak to the northwest), Prospect Creek drainage, Pump Station No. 5, Jim River drainage, South Fork Koyukuk drainage and the Brooks Range on the northern horizon.

Begin long, steep descents northbound and southbound.

J 135.1 (217.4 km) **D 278.9** (448.8 km) Narrow bridge over **Prospect Creek**; grayling, whitefish and pike. Active gold mining area.

CAUTION: Steep uphill grade northbound; watch for trucks on blind hill.

J 135.7 (218.4 km) **D 278.3** (447.9 km) Turnout. Old winter road goes up creek to mines. Turn left for site of **PROSPECT CAMP**, which holds the record for lowest recorded temperature in Alaska (-80°F/-62°C, Jan. 23, 1971). Rough road leads 0.5 mile to Claja Pond; beaver, ducks. Undeveloped campsite on Jim River. Old winter road to Bettles crosses river here. ▲

J 137.1 (220.6 km) **D 276.9** (445.6 km) APL access road at Milepost 274.7 on the pipeline at **Pump Station No. 5** to east. Pump station No. 5 is not actually a pump station, but a "drain down" or pressure relief station to slow the gravity-fed flow of oil descending from Atigun Pass in the Brooks Range. Glacial moraine marks the southern boundary of Brooks Range glaciers during the most recent ice age.

Private Aircraft: Airstrip; length 5,000 feet; lighted runway. This airstrip is used as a BLM fire fighting staging area.

J 138.1 (222.2 km) **D 275.9** (444 km) Jim River Station (DOT/PF highway maintenance) to west; no services.

J 140.1 (225.5 km) **D 273.9** (440.8 km) Small turnout to east at south end of **Jim River No. 1** bridge; informal campsite. Fishing for burbot, chum and king salmon, grayling, pike, whitefish. *CAUTION: Bears here for fall salmon run.*

J 141 (226.9 km) **D 273** (439.3 km) Small turnout to west at south end of **Jim River No. 2** bridge; fishing.

J 141.7 (228.1 km) **D 272.3** (438.2 km) Douglas Creek crossing.

J 144.1 (231.9 km) **D 269.9** (434.4 km) Large parking area at APL access road to east at south end of **Jim River No. 3** bridge crossing the river's main channel. Fishing.

*NOTE: Road construction was under way between **Mileposts 144** and **175** in 1999 and will continue in 2000. The project consists of restoration, widening and resurfacing of the road.*

J 145.6 (234.3 km) **D 268.4** (431.9 km) Pipeline passes under road. First views northbound of Brooks Range foothills to the north.

J 150.3 (241.9 km) **D 263.7** (424.4 km) Large new (1999) turnout with outhouse to east overlooking Grayling Lake.

J 156 (251.1 km) **D 258** (415.2 km) Large parking area with outhouse and litter barrels to east at south end of **South Fork Koyukuk River** bridge. Self-contained RV camping in turnout. Fishing for grayling, whitefish, chum and king salmon. ▲

This large river flows past the villages of Bettles, Allakaket, Hughes and Huslia before draining into the Yukon River near Koyukuk.

The road is passing through the foothills of the Brooks Range. There is an active gold mining area behind the hills to the west. Many side roads off the Dalton Highway lead to private mining claims.

J 159.1 (256 km) **D 254.9** (410.2 km) Bridge over pipeline; large animal crossing over pipeline.

J 160 (257.5 km) **D 254** (408.8 km) Good view of Chapman Lake west of road as highway descends steeply northbound. Old mine trail is visible from the road.

The 2 mountains visible to the north are Twelvemile Mountain (elev. 3,190 feet), left, and Cathedral Mountain (3,000 feet), on right.

J 166.7 (268.3 km) **D 247.3** (398 km) Example of sag bend: short section of buried pipeline that allows large animals to cross.

Bicyclist on the Dalton Highway stops in Coldfoot. (© Kris Graef, staff)

J 175 (281.6 km) **D 239** (384.6 km) Turnoff to east for Soughdough Services, Coldfoot (DOT) Station and visitor center at **COLDFOOT**, a former mining camp at the mouth of Slate Creek on the east bank of the Middle Fork Koyukuk River.

According to the *Dictionary of Alaska Place Names*, Robert Marshall, a forester who made a reconnaissance map of the northern Koyukuk Region, first reported the name Coldfoot in 1933. "As early as 1899 the town of Slate Creek was started at the mouth of the creek which bears that name. In the summer of 1900, one of the waves of green stampeders got as far up the Koyukuk as this point, then got cold feet, turned around, and departed. This incident was enough to change the first, unromantic appellation of the settlement to Coldfoot." A post office was established here in 1902, when Coldfoot consisted of "one gambling hole, 2 roadhouses, 2 stores and 7 saloons." Mining activity later moved upstream to Nolan and Wiseman Creeks. The post office was discontinued in 1912.

Today, Coldfoot Services (phone 907/678-5201) offers motel lodging and 24-hour restaurant. The "trucker's table" at the restaurant is a good place to get news on the highway. There is also a gift shop, general store, trading post, laundromat, fuel facility with gas, diesel and avgas; tire repair, minor vehicle repair; RV park with hookups and dump station; post office, phone and emergency medical service. It is also home of the "farthest North saloon in North America" with "readable walls." Area tours and guided hunting and fishing trips available. ▲

There is a 3,500-foot runway to west, maintained by the state. An Alaska State Trooper, a Fish and Wildlife officer and BLM field station are located at Coldfoot. A visitor center here, operated by the BLM, USF&WS and National Park Service, offers travel information and nightly presentations on the natural and cultural history of the Arctic. It is open from June 1 through Labor Day. Topographic maps for sale.

Sourdough Fuel, Coldfoot Slate Creek Inn. See display ad this section. ▲

Coyote Air. Experience the vast wilderness beauty of the Brooks Range the only way possible, by aircraft with Coyote Air. We offer a full range of flightseeing trips throughout the Gates of the Arctic National Park and the Arctic National Wildlife Refuge, along with remote access to the wilderness of the Brooks Range. Phone (800) 252-0603. [ADVERTISEMENT]

NOTE: Next services northbound are 244 miles from here.

J 175.1 (281.8 km) **D 238.9** (384.5 km) Narrow bridge over Slate Creek.

J 175.7 (282.8 km) **D 238.3** (383.5 km) Radio repeater site on mountains to east.

J 179.7 (289.2 km) **D 234.3** (377.1 km) Turnoff to east for **Marion Creek Campground** (BLM); 27 sites on gravel loop road,

$6 to $8 camping fee, tables, grills, firepits, water, toilets, bear-proof litter containers, resident campground host, information kiosk, RV parking. Good berry picking (blueberries, lowbrush cranberries) in season. Marion Creek trailhead. ▲

J 179.9 (289.5 km) **D 234.1** (376.7 km) Marion Creek.

J 186.7 (300.5 km) **D 227.3** (365.7 km) Parking areas both sides of highway.

J 187.3 (301.4 km) **D 226.7** (364.8 km) Parking area to west at south end of **Minnie Creek** bridge; fishing for burbot, grayling, whitefish.

J 188.4 (303.3 km) **D 225.6** (363 km) Distance marker northbound shows Dietrich 22 miles, Deadhorse 227 miles.

J 188.5 (303.4 km) **D 225.5** (362.9 km) **Middle Fork Koyukuk River No. 1** crossing (narrow bridge); turnout. Dolly Varden, grayling, whitefish.

J 188.6 (303.5 km) **D 225.4** (362.7 km) Turnoff on improved access road which leads 1.6 miles south to **junction** with road

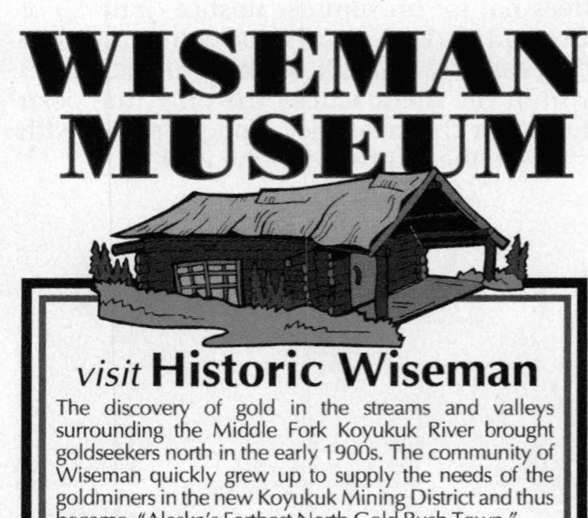

to Nolan and 3 miles south to Wiseman (description follows). This side road also provides good views of the Koyukuk River and the pipeline as it goes under the river.

The road to **NOLAN** is narrow dirt and gravel, ranging from good to very poor, and leads 5.5 miles west to private mining claims.

WISEMAN (pop. 25), 3 miles south of the highway, is a historic mining town on the Koyukuk River established in 1908. The heyday of Wiseman came in about 1910, after gold seekers abandoned Coldfoot. This is still an active mining area.

View of the Koyukuk River from Wiseman access road. (© Kris Graef, staff)

Several interesting historic buildings (all privately owned) are found in Wiseman. The post office is located in an original log cabin. The Historic Pioneer Hall Igloo No. 8 is a bed and breakfast. The **Wiseman Historical Museum** is located in the historic Carl Frank Cabin. The museum contains old miner's journals, hotel registers and historical photos; limited gift items are for sale. Well worth a stop; watch for signs as you enter town. Follow the road south across the river for Wiseman Trading Co. Inquire locally about camping. ▲

Arctic Getaway Bed & Breakfast. See display ad this section.

Wiseman Museum. See display ad this section.

J 189 (304.2 km) **D 225** (362.1 km) Spur (finger) dikes keep river away from highway and pipeline.

J 190.5 (306.6 km) **D 223.5** (359.7 km) Narrow bridge over Hammond River; gold mining area upstream.

J 190.8 (307.1 km) **D 223.2** (359.2 km) **Middle Fork Koyukuk River No. 2** crossing (narrow bridge). "Guide banks," another example of river training structures.

J 192.8 (310.3 km) **D 221.2** (356 km) Link Up (not signed), where 2 sections of road constructed by different crews were joined.

J 193.6 (311.5 km) **D 220.4** (354.7 km) Pavement next 1.2 miles northbound.

J 194 (312.2 km) **D 220** (354 km) First view northbound of **Sukakpak Mountain** (elev. 4,000 feet) to north. Sukakpak Mountain is sometimes said to mark a traditional boundary between Eskimo and Athabascan Indian territories. Wiehl Mountain (4,000 feet) is east of Sukakpak. The high mountain just to the west of the road is unnamed.

J 195 (313.8 km) **D 219** (352.4 km) Pipeline close to road is mounted on sliding shoes to allow flexing.

J 197 (317 km) **D 217** (349.2 km) Gold Creek bridge (narrow).

J 197.2 (317.3 km) **D 216.8** (348.9 km) Turnout to east.

J 197.3 (317.5 km) **D 216.7** (348.7 km) Cat trail to gold mining area.

J 197.5 (317.8 km) **D 216.5** (348.4 km) Linda Creek in culvert.

J 197.7 (318.2 km) **D 216.3** (348.1 km) Turnout east and view of Wiehl Mountain.

J 200 (321.9 km) **D 214** (344.4 km) View of the Middle Fork Koyukuk River, a typical braided river exhibiting frequent changes of the streambed during high water.

J 203.5 (327.5 km) **D 210.5** (338.7 km) Park on shoulder for 0.5-mile footpath to Sukakpak Mountain. The short mounds of earth between the road and Sukakpak are palsas, formed by ice beneath the soil pushing the vegetative mat and soil upward.

J 203.8 (328 km) **D 210.2** (338.3 km) Turnouts next 0.6 mile northbound.

J 204.3 (328.8 km) **D 209.7** (337.5 km) **Middle Fork Koyukuk River No. 3** bridge. Large turnout with toilet (last public outhouse northbound to Deadhorse) and litter barrels to east at north end of bridge. Self-contained RV camping in turnout. ▲

J 204.5 (329.1 km) **D 209.5** (337.1 km) **Middle Fork Koyukuk River No. 4** crossing (narrow bridge).

J 205.3 (330.4 km) **D 208.7** (335.9 km) Turnout to west. Good view of north side of Sukakpak Mountain.

J 206 (331.5 km) **D 208** (334.7 km) View of Wiehl Mountain.

J 207 (333.1 km) **D 207** (333.1 km) **Dietrich River** bridge. Half-way mark on the Dalton highway. Turnout to west at south end of bridge. Access to river to west at north end. Fishing for burbot, grayling, whitefish and Dolly Varden.

J 209.1 (336.5 km) **D 204.9** (329.7 km) **Dietrich** 1 mile/1.6 km west, a former pipeline construction camp.

J 210.9 (339.4 km) **D 203.1** (326.8 km) Large turnout with bear-proof litter container to east.

J 211 (339.6 km) **D 203** (326.7 km) Disaster Creek.

J 216.2 (347.9 km) **D 197.8** (318.3 km) Snowden Creek culvert. Panorama of Dietrich River valley and Brooks Range north and west of the road.

J 217.1 (349.4 km) **D 196.9** (316.9 km) Rock spire to east is Snowden Mountain (elev. 5,775 feet). Cirque above highway was carved by a glacier; hike up to waterfall.

J 218.3 (351.3 km) **D 195.7** (314.9 km) Turnout to west.

J 221.6 (356.6 km) **D 192.4** (309.6 km) Quarry of black marble with white calcite veins to east.

J 224 (360.5 km) **D 190** (305.8 km) Turnout at gravel pit to east.

J 225.9 (363.5 km) **D 188.1** (302.7 km) Pipeline remote valve just west of road. The arch-shaped concrete "saddle weights" keep pipeline buried in areas of possible flooding.

J 228 (366.9 km) **D 186** (299.3 km) Highway parallels Dietrich River.

J 229.5 (369.3 km) **D 184.5** (296.9 km) Turnout to east next to stream in rock culvert.

J 231.4 (372.4 km) **D 182.6** (293.9 km) Small turnouts both sides of highway. Pipeline is buried under river.

J 232.8 (374.6 km) **D 181.2** (291.6 km) Turnout to west.

J 234.6 (377.5 km) **D 179.4** (288.7 km) Pipeline emerges from under river.

J 234.9 (378 km) **D 179.1** (288.2 km) Entering North Slope Borough—"the world's largest municipality"—northbound. North Slope Borough offices are located in Barrow.

J 235.3 (378.7 km) **D 178.7** (287.6 km) Large turnout with litter barrel at foot of Chandalar Shelf. Truck chain-up area.

Begin long, steep (10 percent) grade northbound. Give trucks plenty of room. Do not stop on road. Dirt road surface can be slippery in wet weather. Watch for soft spots.

J 237.1 (381.6 km) **D 176.9** (284.7 km) Narrow turnout to west at top of Chandalar Shelf; former checkpoint when a permit was required to drive beyond this point.

Headwaters of the Chandalar River are to the east. Table Mountain (elev. 6,425 feet) is to the southeast. Dietrich River valley to south.

J 239.2 (384.9 km) **D 174.8** (281.3 km) Site of Chandalar Camp, a former pipeline construction camp, now used as a BLM field station.

Picturesque peaks along northern half of Dalton Highway. (© Harry M. Walker Photo)

J 239.4 (385.3 km) **D 174.6** (281 km) Chandalar Station (DOT/PF highway maintenance) to west; no visitor services.

J 242.1 (389.6 km) **D 171.9** (276.6 km) Avalanche gun emplacement.

J 242.2 (389.8 km) **D 171.8** (276.5 km) West Fork of the North Fork Chandalar River bridge.

Begin long, steep (12 percent) grade northbound toward Atigun Pass. Winter avalanche area. Slide area next 5 miles northbound.

J 243.4 (391.7 km) **D 170.6** (274.5 km) Turnout with spectacular view south of valley and pipeline.

J 244 (392.6 km) **D 170** (273.6 km) Turnout.

J 244.7 (393.8 km) **D 169.3** (272.5 km) Turnout at top of **Atigun Pass** (elev. 4,800 feet) in the Brooks Range, highest highway pass in Alaska; Continental Divide. A Wyoming Gauge to measure moisture is located here. Nice example of a cirque, an amphitheater-shaped bowl or depression caused by glacier erosion, in mountain east of road. Endicott Mountains are to the west, Philip Smith Mountains to the east. James Dalton Mountain is to the left ahead northbound.

J 245 (394.3 km) **D 169** (272 km) Turnout.

J 245.3 (394.8 km) **D 168.7** (271.5 km) Avalanche gun emplacement. Large turnouts. Look for Dall sheep alongside road.

J 245.5 (395.1 km) **D 168.5** (271.2 km) Highway descends steeply toward the North Slope. Many mountains in the area exceed 7,000 feet in elevation. The pipeline is in a buried, insulated concrete cribbing to the east to protect it from rock slides and avalanches, and to keep the ground frozen. Construction in this area was extremely complex, difficult and dangerous.

J 248.4 (399.8 km) **D 165.6** (266.5 km) Turnouts both sides of highway. Good spot to view Dall sheep.

J 250 (402.3 km) **D 164** (263.9 km) Bridge over Spike Camp Creek. Highway follows Atigun River.

J 250.2 (402.6 km) **D 163.8** (263.6 km) Site of Atigun Camp, a former pipeline construction camp. Turnouts both sides of highway. View of Atigun River valley.

J 251.5 (404.7 km) **D 162.5** (261.5 km) Turnouts; wide shoulder next 1.5 miles northbound.

J 253.1 (407.3 km) **D 160.9** (258.9 km) Atigun River Bridge No. 1.

NOTE: Atigun bridge replacement and reconstruction of bridge approaches under way in fall of 1999.

J 254 (408.8 km) **D 160** (257.5 km) Mountains to north exhibit extreme folding of sedimentary rock layers.

J 257.6 (414.6 km) **D 156.4** (251.7 km) Check valves on the pipeline keep oil from flowing backwards in the event of a leak.

J 258.4 (415.8 km) **D 155.6** (250.4 km) Trevor Creek bridge.

J 258.6 (416.2 km) **D 155.4** (250.1 km) Turnout to west. Good spot to hike up to rocks. *CAUTION: Grizzly bears in area.*

J 261.4 (420.7 km) **D 152.6** (245.6 km) Turnout.

J 265 (426.5 km) **D 149** (239.8 km) Roche Mountonee Creek bridge; turnout.

J 266.9 (429.5 km) **D 147.1** (236.7 km) Turnout.

J 267.5 (430.5 km) **D 146.5** (235.8 km) Bridge over Holden Creek.

J 268 (431.3 km) **D 146** (235 km) Good view of Pump Station No. 4.

J 269.3 (433.4 km) **D 144.7** (232.9 km) **Pump Station No. 4.** This station has the highest elevation of all the pipeline stations (2,760 feet), and is also a launching and receiving station for special measuring and cleaning devices called "pigs." A scraper pig consists of spring-mounted scraper blades and/or brushes on a central body which moves through the pipe, cleaning accumulated wax from interior walls and monitoring conditions inside the pipe. There are "dumb" pigs and "smart" pigs. Dumb pigs clean out wax deposits in the line. Smart pigs scan the pipeline to check welds, wall thickness and other properties to help insure the integrity of the piping and identify maintenance needs.

J 269.5 (433.7 km) **D 144.5** (232.5 km) Highway bridge passes over pipeline.

J 270.9 (436 km) **D 143.1** (230.3 km) Atigun River Bridge No. 2.

NOTE: Atigun bridge replacement and reconstruction of bridge approaches under way in fall of 1999. Work includes a wayside parking area.

The Arctic National Wildlife Refuge boundary is located 3 miles east along the Atigun gorge. Galbraith Lake may be seen to the west. There are a large number of archaeological sites in this vicinity.

J 274 (440.9 km) **D 140** (225.3 km) View of Galbraith Lake and Galbraith camp.

J 274.7 (442.1 km) **D 139.3** (224.2 km) Road access leads southwest 1 miles to **GALBRAITH CAMP**; airstrip. Self-contained RV camping available at the public campsite. USF&WS field station. Nice wildflowers in season. ▲

J 276.5 (445 km) **D 137.5** (221.3 km) Island Lake.

J 283 (455.4 km) **D 131** (210.8 km) View of Toolik Camp (see next milepost). Watch for caribou.

J 284.3 (457.5 km) **D 129.7** (208.7 km) Toolik Lake west of road. A former construction camp, it is now the site of **Toolik Lake Research Camp**, run by the Institute of Arctic Biology of the University of Alaska–Fairbanks. The field station conducts global warming studies and has no public facilities or services.

J 286.2 (460.6 km) **D 127.8** (205.7 km) Turnout to east at high point in road. View of Brooks Range south and east. Philip Smith Mountains to west. Panoramic views of incredible beauty.

J 288.8 (464.8 km) **D 125.2** (201.5 km) Highway descends northbound to Kuparuk River bridge. Informal camping at turnout.

J 289.3 (465.6 km) **D 124.7** (200.7 km) Pipeline crossing. Short buried section of pipeline to west is called a sag bend and is to allow for wildlife crossing. Watch for caribou northbound.

J 290.4 (467.3 km) **D 123.6** (198.9 km) Turnout to east; road to materials site.

J 290.6 (467.7 km) **D 123.4** (198.6 km) Toolik Creek.

J 295 (474.7 km) **D 119** (191.5 km) *CAUTION: Watch for caribou crossing the highway.*

J 297 (478 km) **D 117** (188.3 km) Pullout used by hunters in caribou season.

J 297.8 (479.2 km) **D 116.2** (187 km) Oksrukukuyik Creek culvert. Small turnout to east.

J 298.2 (479.9 km) **D 115.8** (186.4 km) Turnout to west. First view northbound of Sagavanirktok River valley.

J 301 (484.4 km) **D 113** (181.8 km) "Lucan Rock" (sign). APL access road. Slope Mountain (elev. 4,010 feet) to west. Watch for Dall sheep. This is the northern boundary of BLM-managed land. Land north of here is managed by the state.

J 303 (487.6 km) **D 111** (178.6 km) *CAUTION: Slow for blind hill northbound. Watch for soft spots in road.*

J 305.7 (492 km) **D 108.3** (174.3 km) Sag River Station (DOT/PF highway maintenance). Slope Mountain Camp, a former pipeline construction camp, 1 mile east.

J 309 (497.3 km) **D 105** (169 km) Highway parallels Sagavanirktok River northbound.

J 311.8 (501.8 km) **D 102.2** (164.5 km) **Pump Station No. 3**; mobile construction camp facility.

J 313.7 (504.8 km) **D 100.3** (161.4 km) Oksrukukuyik Creek in culvert.

J 319.8 (514.7 km) **D 94.2** (151.6 km) Turnout to east at Oil Spill Hill.

J 320 (515 km) **D 94** (151.3 km) The long range of hills east of the road is the Kakuk-

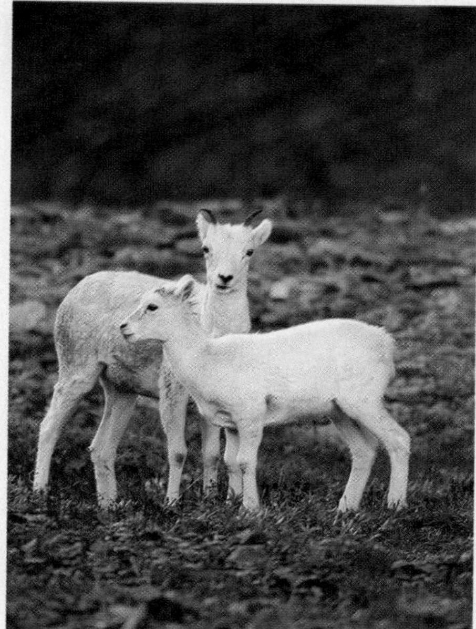
Watch for Dall sheep along the highway in the mountains.

(© Harry M. Walker Photo)

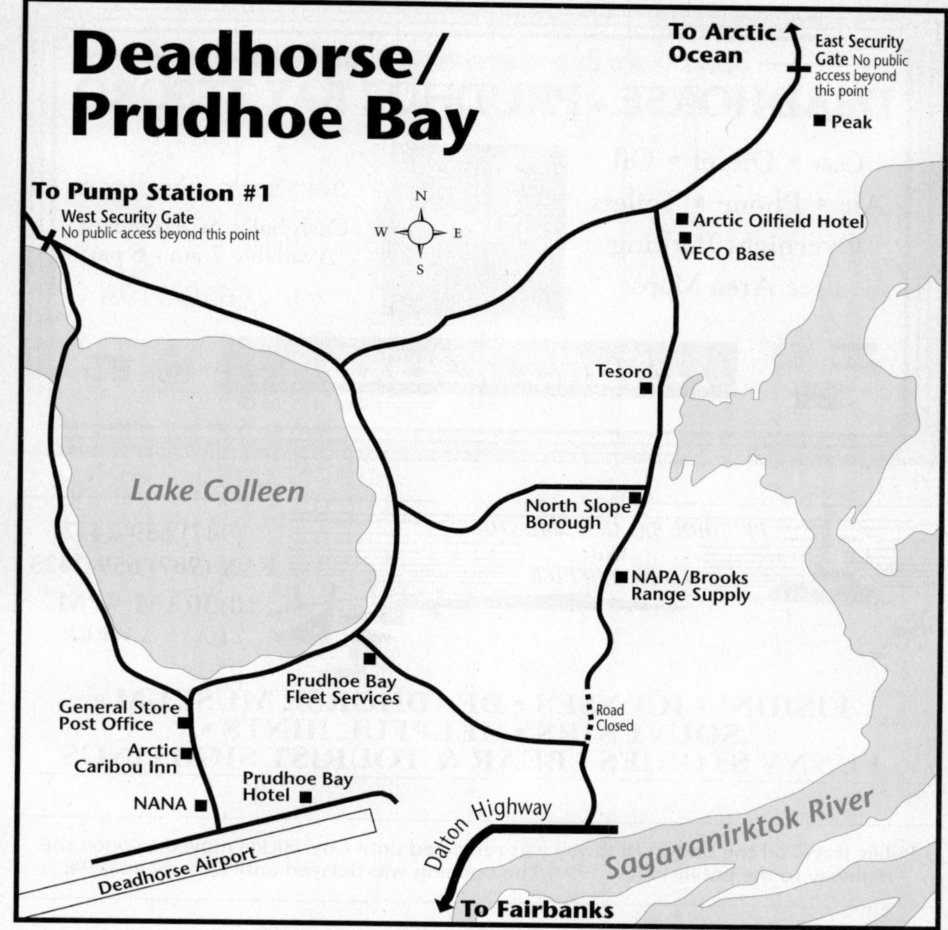

tukruich Bluff. Nice views northbound of Sagavanirktok River.

J 325.3 (523.5 km) **D 88.7** (142.7 km) Turnout to east at the top of a steep and rocky grade called Ice Cut.

J 326.2 (525 km) **D 87.8** (141.3 km) Pipeline crossing on bridge.

CAUTION: Blind hills. Rocky road surface northbound to ***Milepost J 338.***

J 327.7 (527.4 km) **D 86.3** (138.9 km) Watch for grizzly bear digging for food around the pipeline supports.

J 330.7 (532.2 km) **D 83.3** (134.1 km) Dan Creek bridge. *Bump!*

J 334.4 (538.1 km) **D 79.6** (128.1 km) Site of **Happy Valley**, a former pipeline construction camp; Arctic Wilderness Lodge. Airstrip

J 350.5 (564.1 km) **D 63.5** (102.2 km) View of Sagwon Bluffs to the east.

J 355.1 (571.5 km) **D 58.9** (94.8 km) Turnout with litter barrel to east at crest of hill. Panoramic view..

J 358.8 (577.4 km) **D 55.2** (88.8 km) **Pump Station No. 2** to the east.

J 363 (584.2 km) **D 51** (82.1 km) Snow poles mark highway for motorists. *The worst winter weather conditions on the Dalton Highway are experienced the next 38 miles northbound. Blowing snow may obscure visibility and block road.*

J 364 (585.8 km) **D 50** (80.5 km) Low hills to the north are the Franklin Bluffs. East of the road, the Ivishak River empties into the Sagavanirktok River on its journey to the Arctic Ocean.

J 365.1 (587.6 km) **D 48.9** (78.7 km) Turnout to west. Watch for nesting waterfowl in ponds to west northbound along highway.

J 376 (605.1 km) **D 38** (61.2 km) The small hill that rises abruptly on the horizon about 5 miles west of the road is called a pingo. Pingos often form from the bed of a spring-fed lake that has been covered by vegetation. Freezing of the water can raise the surface several hundred feet above the surrounding terrain.

J 377.3 (607.2 km) **D 36.7** (59.1 km) Large turnout to east at Franklin Bluffs, a former pipeline construction camp where winter equipment is stored in summer.

J 383 (616.4 km) **D 31** (49.9 km) Franklin Bluffs to the east and a pingo to the west.

J 389 (626 km) **D 25** (40.2 km) Dalton Highway snakes across the flat coastal plain northbound.

J 398.7 (641.6 km) **D 15.3** (24.6 km) Underground pipeline crossing.

J 411 (661.4 km) **D 3** (4.8 km) Pavement to **Milepost J 413.3.** Oil field activity and equipment become visible along the horizon.

J 414 (666.3 km) **D 0** Northern end of Dalton Highway. About 2 miles ahead is the Deadhorse Airport and the public-access portion of the Prudhoe Bay oil field. Beyond there, travel is on oil company roads and restricted.

Deadhorse

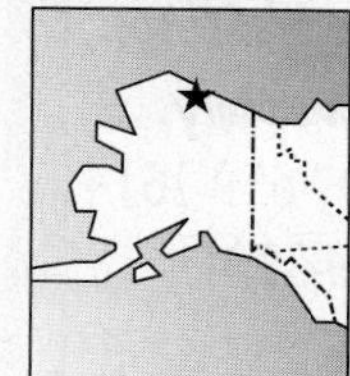

End of the Dalton Highway. **Population:** 25 permanent; 3,500 to 5,000 or more part-time depending on oil production. **Visitor Information:** Try the Prudhoe Bay General Store and the hotels. **Climate:** Arctic, with temperatures ranging from -56°F/-49°C in winter to 78°F/26°C in summer. Precipitation averages 5 inches; snowfall 20 inches. **Transportation:** Scheduled jet service to Deadhorse/Prudhoe Bay from Anchorage (flying time from Anchorage is 1 hour, 35 minutes), Fairbanks and Barrow. Packaged tours of the North Slope area are available from Anchorage and Fairbanks. Air taxi service is available at Deadhorse Airport. Cape Smythe Air and Frontier Flying Service provide air taxi service.

Deadhorse is not a town in the traditional sense. It was established to support oil development in the surrounding area. A number of oil fields make up the Prudhoe Bay industrial area: Kuparuk, Milne Point, Point McIntyre, Prudhoe Bay, Niakuk and Endicott.

Most buildings are modular, pre-fab-type construction, situated on gravel pads on tundra bog. Virtually all the businesses here are engaged in oil field or pipeline support activities, such as drilling, construction,

Public travel on the Dalton Highway was restricted until Gov. Hickel moved to open the highway to the public in July 1991. The opening was delayed until December 1994.

Welcome sign on Prudhoe Bay General Store. (© Deborah M. Bernard)

maintenance, telecommunications, warehousing and transportation. Oil field employees work a rotation, such as 2 weeks on the job, then 2 weeks off. While on rotation, workers typically work 7 days a week, 10 to 12 hours each day. The largest employers are Arco, BP Exploration and Alyeska Pipeline Services.

According to Deborah Bernard in an article in the *Prudhoe Bay Journal*, there is more than one version of how Deadhorse got its name, but basically it was named after Deadhorse Haulers, a company hired to do the gravel work at the Prudhoe Bay airstrip. (How the company came to be called Deadhorse Haulers is another story.) Everybody began calling the airstrip "Deadhorse" and the name stuck—too well for those who prefer the name Prudhoe Bay. Some people were surprised when Prudhoe Bay got its own ZIP code on June 3, 1982, and was listed as "Deadhorse AK 99734," not Prudhoe Bay. It was later changed to Prudhoe Bay, AK 99734.

Visitor accommodations are available at the Arctic Caribou Inn and Arctic Oilfield Hotel. Buffet-style meals are available. Prudhoe Bay Hotel accommodates both oil field workers and visitors. The cafeteria serves breakfast from 5:30 to 8 A.M., lunch from noon to 1 P.M., and dinner from 5 to 8 P.M., with self-serve snacks available inbetween.

Prudhoe Bay General Store carries everything from postcards and snacks to Arctic survival gear. About the only exceptions are alcohol, ammunition and weapons, which are not available in Deadhorse. The store houses the post office and issues fishing and hunting licenses. (You can also get "Dalton Highway Survivor" certificates here.)

There is no bank and no ATM in Deadhorse. Credit cards and traveler's checks are generally accepted, but fish and game licenses and postage must be paid for in cash.

Regular unleaded gasoline and No. 1 diesel are available at NANA (Chevron) or the local Tesoro station. Tesoro is a 24-hour self-serve station; an attendant is available and cash accepted from 7 A.M. until 6 P.M. There are a public phone, toilet and overnight parking with limited services available at Tesoro.

Tire and vehicle repairs are available at Prudhoe Bay Fleet Service, Veco Base Fleet Services and NANA. Local auto parts and hardware store has an assortment of supplies.

Public access beyond Deadhorse is restricted. For security reasons, travel north of Deadhorse, including visits to the Arctic Ocean, is limited to commercial tours. Tour information is available at the hotels.

CAUTION: Beware of bears in the area.

A few of the Porcupine caribou herd grazing at Prudhoe Bay.

(© Rich Reid, Colors of Nature)

Arctic Caribou Inn invites you to tour Prudhoe Bay, May 25–Sept. 8. Providing guided tours since 1975. Tour includes Milepost 0 at Pump Station 1. See oil rigs and Oilfield Visitor Center, and oil field informative video presentation and exhibits. Walk on the beach at the Arctic Ocean. Arctic Caribou Inn. Clean comfortable rooms. Buffet service, laundry and shower facilities. Summer phone (907) 659-2368. Winter phone (907) 659-2449. Tour Arctic/Arctic Caribou Inn, fax (907) 659-2289. Mailing address: P.O. Box 340112, Prudhoe Bay, AK 99734. [ADVERTISEMENT]

Drive with your headlights on at all times.

RICHARDSON HIGHWAY 

Connects: Valdez to Fairbanks, AK **Length:** 368 miles
Road Surface: Paved **Season:** Open all year
Highest Summit: Isabel Pass 3,000 feet
Major Attractions: Trans-Alaska Pipeline, Worthington Glacier

(See maps, pages 477–478)

	Delta Jct.	Fairbanks	Glennallen	Paxson	Valdez
Delta Jct.		98	151	80	270
Fairbanks	98		249	179	368
Glennallen	151	249		71	119
Paxson	80	179	71		190
Valdez	270	368	119	190	

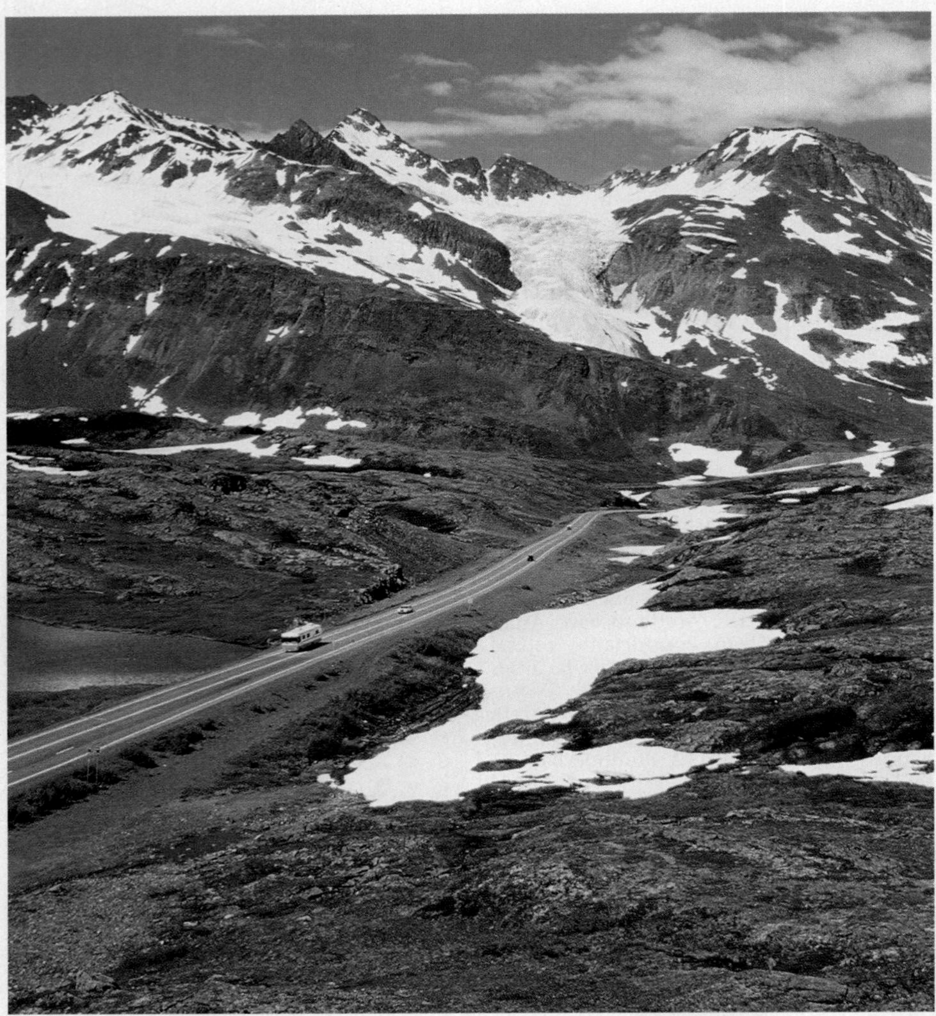

Richardson Highway at Thompson Pass in summer. (© Bruce M. Herman)

The Richardson Highway (Alaska Route 4) extends 368 miles from Valdez to Fairbanks. It was Alaska's first road, known to gold seekers in 1898 as the Valdez to Eagle trail. Gold stampeders started up the trail again in 1902, this time headed for Fairbanks, site of a big gold strike. The Valdez to Fairbanks trail became an important route to the Interior, and in 1910 the trail was upgraded to a wagon road under the direction of Gen. Wilds P. Richardson, first president of the Alaska Road Commission. The ARC updated the road to automobile standards in the 1920s. The Richardson Highway was hard-surfaced in 1957.

Today, the Richardson is a wide paved highway in good condition except for sporadic frost heaving. A scenic route through the magnificent scenery of the Chugach Mountains and Alaska Range, the Richardson passes many fine king salmon streams, including the Gulkana and Tonsina rivers.

The Richardson Highway also offers good views of the Trans-Alaska pipeline. Completed in 1977, the 48-inch-diameter pipe carries oil 800 miles—from Prudhoe Bay on the Arctic Ocean to the pipeline terminus at Port Valdez. Along the Richardson Highway, the pipeline crests the Alaska Range at 3,420 foot at Isabel Pass, before descending into the Copper River basin. It crosses the Chugach Mountains at Thompson Pass and descends through the Keystone Canyon to Valdez, where it is fed by gravity into tanks or directly into waiting oil tankers at the marine terminal.

Because of varying soil conditions along its route, the pipeline is both above and below ground. Where the warm oil would cause icy soil to thaw and erode, the pipeline goes above ground to avoid thawing. Where the frozen ground is mostly well-drained gravel or solid rock, and thawing is not a problem, the line is underground.

The line was designed with 12 pump stations (although Pump Station 11 was never built). Public tours are available of Pump Station No. 9, located at **Milepost V 258.3** on the Richardson Highway. There are several pipeline interpretive viewpoints on the Richardson Highway.

Emergency medical services: Phone 911 anywhere along the highway.

Richardson Highway Log

Distance from New Valdez (NV) is followed by distance from Old Valdez (OV).

Mileposts on the Richardson Highway were erected before the 1964 Good Friday earthquake and therefore begin 4 miles from present-day downtown Valdez near the Old Valdez townsite (destroyed during the earthquake).

ALASKA ROUTE 4

NV 0 OV 4 (6.4 km) Intersection of Meals Avenue and the Richardson Highway.

NV 0.4 (0.6 km) **OV 3.6** (5.8 km) Paved double-ended turnout to north with Valdez information kiosk, maps, brochures, pay phones.

NV 0.5 (0.8 km) **OV 3.5** (5.6 km) DOT/PF district office.

NV 0.6 (1 km) **OV 3.4** (5.5 km) Valdez highway maintenance station.

NV 0.9 (1.4 km) **OV 3.1** (5 km) Double-ended turnout to north at **Crooked Creek** salmon spawning area. Viewing platform offers close-up look at salmon spawning in midsummer and fall. U.S. Forest Service information station is staffed Memorial Day through Labor Day; interpretive displays and educational programs Migrating birds such as Canada geese and various ducks are often here. It is a game sanctuary; no shooting is allowed. Good spot for pictures.

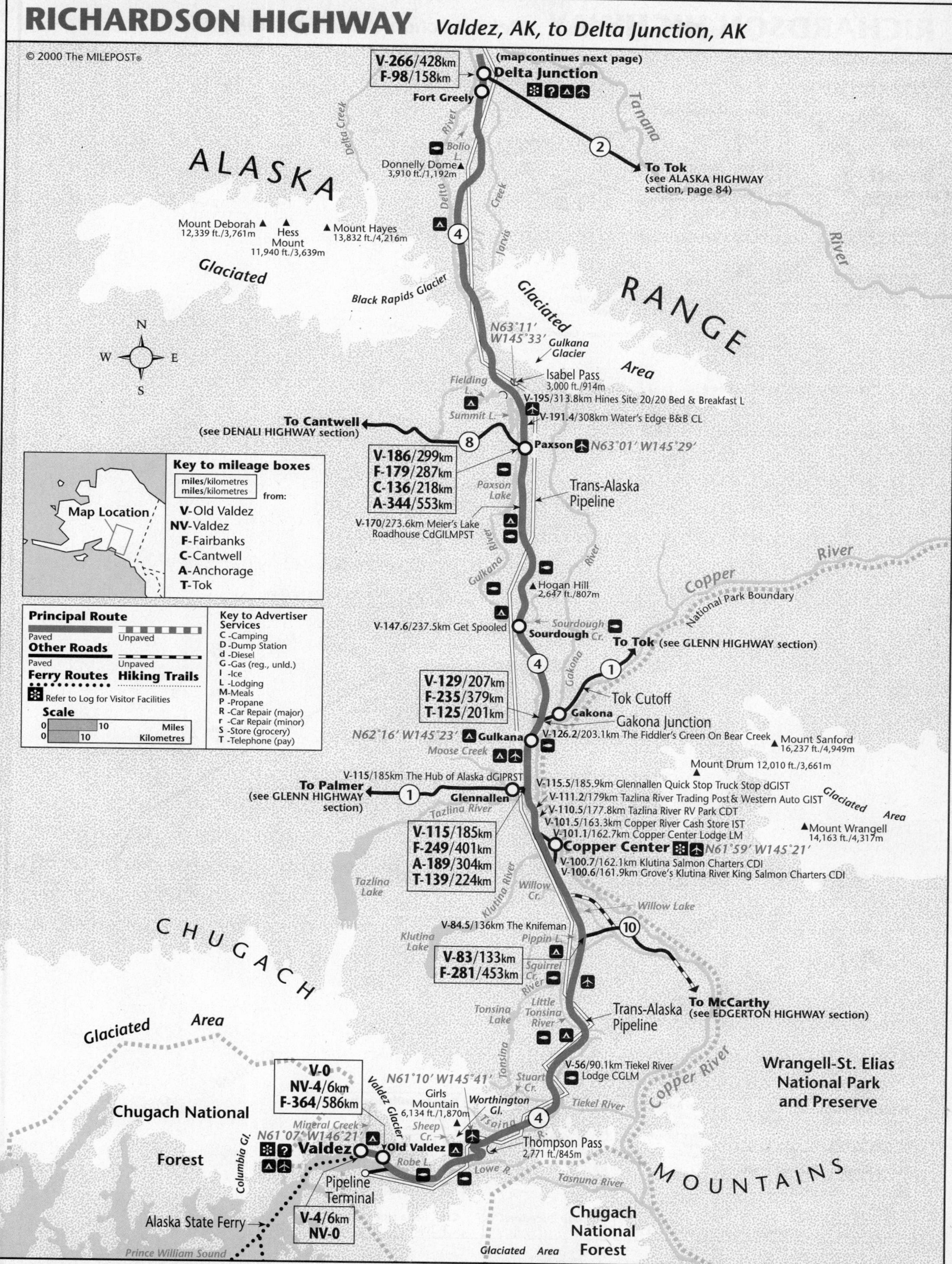

RICHARDSON HIGHWAY
Valdez, AK, to Delta Junction, AK
© 2000 The MILEPOST®
V-266/428km
F-98/158km
(map continues next page)
Delta Junction
Fort Greely
Delta Creek
Delta River
Tanana
Bolio L.
Donnelly Dome 3,910 ft./1,192m
To Tok (see ALASKA HIGHWAY section, page 84)
ALASKA
RANGE
Mount Deborah 12,339 ft./3,761m
Hess Mount 11,940 ft./3,639m
Mount Hayes 13,832 ft./4,216m
Jarvis Creek
River
Glaciated
Black Rapids Glacier
Glaciated Area
N63°11′ W145°33′
Gulkana Glacier
Isabel Pass 3,000 ft./914m
Fielding L.
Summit L.
V-195/313.8km Hines Site 20/20 Bed & Breakfast L
V-191.4/308km Water's Edge B&B CL
To Cantwell (see DENALI HIGHWAY section)
Paxson N63°01′ W145°29′
V-186/299km
F-179/287km
C-136/218km
A-344/553km
Paxson Lake
Trans-Alaska Pipeline
V-170/273.6km Meier's Lake Roadhouse CdGILMPST
Gulkana River
Hogan Hill 2,647 ft./807m
Copper River
National Park Boundary
Key to mileage boxes
miles/kilometres
miles/kilometres
from:
Map Location
V-Old Valdez
NV-Valdez
F-Fairbanks
C-Cantwell
A-Anchorage
T-Tok
Principal Route
Paved
Unpaved
Other Roads
Paved
Unpaved
Ferry Routes
Hiking Trails
Refer to Log for Visitor Facilities
Scale
0 10 Miles
0 10 Kilometres
Key to Advertiser Services
C -Camping
D -Dump Station
d -Diesel
G -Gas (reg., unld.)
I -Ice
L -Lodging
M-Meals
P -Propane
R -Car Repair (major)
r -Car Repair (minor)
S -Store (grocery)
T -Telephone (pay)
V-147.6/237.5km Get Spooled
Sourdough
Sourdough Cr.
To Tok (see GLENN HIGHWAY section)
Gakona
V-129/207km
F-235/379km
T-125/201km
Tok Cutoff
Gakona
Gakona Junction
N62°16′ W145°23′
Gulkana
V-126.2/203.1km The Fiddler's Green On Bear Creek
Mount Sanford 16,237 ft./4,949m
Moose Creek
Mount Drum 12,010 ft./3,661m
V-115/185km The Hub of Alaska dGIPRST
To Palmer (see GLENN HIGHWAY section)
Glennallen
V-115.5/185.9km Glennallen Quick Stop Truck Stop dGIST
V-111.2/179km Tazlina River Trading Post & Western Auto GIST
V-110.5/177.8km Tazlina River RV Park CDT
V-101.5/163.3km Copper River Cash Store IST
V-101.1/162.7km Copper Center Lodge LM
Glaciated Area
Tazlina River
V-115/185km
F-249/401km
A-189/304km
T-139/224km
Mount Wrangell 14,163 ft./4,317m
Copper Center N61°59′ W145°21′
V-100.7/162.1km Klutina Salmon Charters CDI
V-100.6/161.9km Grove's Klutina River King Salmon Charters CDI
Tazlina Lake
Klutina River
Willow Cr.
Willow Lake
CHUGACH
V-84.5/136km The Knifeman
Klutina Lake
Pippin L.
V-83/133km
F-281/453km
Squirrel Cr.
River
To McCarthy (see EDGERTON HIGHWAY section)
Tonsina Lake
Little Tonsina River
Trans-Alaska Pipeline
Glaciated Area
Tonsina
V-56/90.1km Tiekel River Lodge CGLM
Wrangell-St. Elias National Park and Preserve
V-0
NV-4/6km
F-364/586km
Valdez Glacier
N61°10′ W145°41′
Stuart Cr.
Girls Mountain 6,134 ft./1,870m
Worthington Gl.
Tiekel River
Copper River
Chugach National Forest
Mineral Creek
N61°07′ W146°21′
Sheep Cr.
Tsaina R.
Valdez
Old Valdez
Thompson Pass 2,771 ft./845m
Columbia Gl.
Robe L.
Lowe R.
Tasnuna River
MOUNTAINS
Pipeline Terminal
Alaska State Ferry
V-4/6km
NV-0
Chugach National Forest
Prince William Sound
Glaciated Area

RICHARDSON HIGHWAY *Delta Junction, AK to Fairbanks, AK*

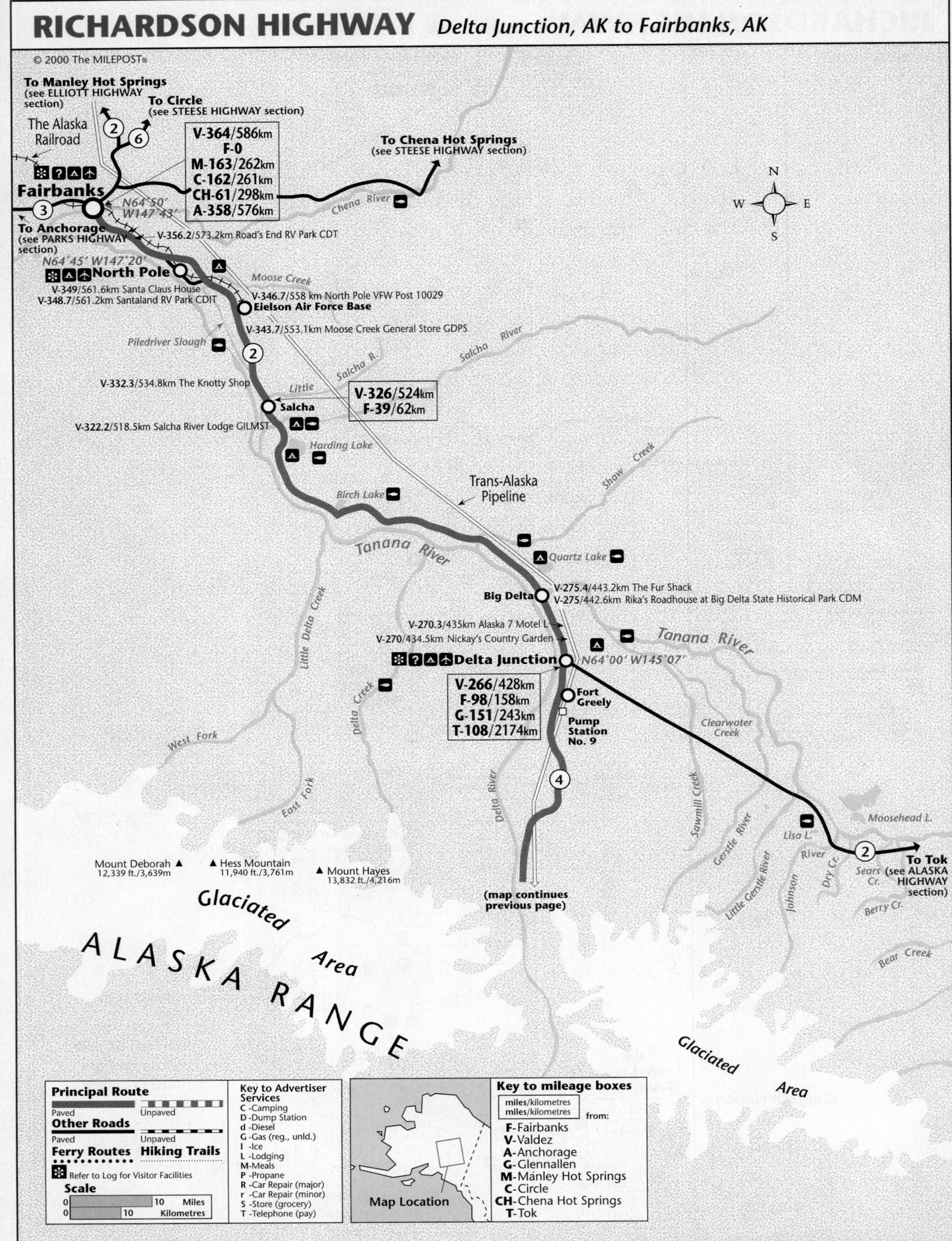

NV 1.3 (2.1 km) **OV 2.7** (4.3 km) Paved turnout to south.

NV 2 (3.2 km) **OV 2** (3.2 km) Paved turnout to south.

NV 2.1 (3.4 km) **OV 1.9** (3.1 km) Mineral Creek Loop Road through business and residential area on outskirts of Old Valdez comes out at **Milepost NV 3.4**. Access to Port of Valdez container terminal and grain elevators.

NV 3.4 (5.5 km) **OV 0.6** (1 km) Gas station at Airport Road turnoff; deli, market, liquor store, laundromat. Turn off to north for **Valdez Airport** (0.7 mile), Valdez Glacier campground (2.4 miles), rifle firing range (2.8 miles) and **Valdez Glacier** (3.9 miles; drive to end of pavement and take left fork). Parking area next to glacial moraine; good views of the glacier area are *not* available from this spot, nor is Valdez Glacier a very spectacular glacier. **Valdez Glacier Campground** has 101 sites in a nicely wooded area, tent camping, covered picnic area, litter barrels, water, toilets and fireplaces; 15-day limit, camping fee. *CAUTION: Beware of bears.* ▲

Mineral Creek Loop Road leads south to the original townsite of Valdez, destroyed during the Good Friday earthquake on March 27, 1964. A few homes and businesses are here now; there is little evidence of the earthquake's destruction.

NV 4 (6.4 km) **OV 0** Former access road to Old Valdez, remains of the old dock and memorial for 1964 earthquake. **Milepost 0** of the Richardson Highway is located here.

Distance from Old Valdez (V) is followed by distance from Fairbanks (F).
Physical mileposts begin northbound showing distance from Old Valdez. (Southbound travelers note: Physical mileposts end here; it is 4 miles to downtown Valdez.)

V 0 F 364 (585.8 km) **Milepost 0** of the Richardson Highway is located here at the former access road to Old Valdez.

V 0.9 (1.4 km) **F 363.1** (584.4 km) The highway passes over the terminal moraine of the Valdez Glacier, bridging several channels and streams flowing from the melting ice.

V 1.4 (2.3 km) **F 362.6** (583.5 km) Valdez Sportsmans Trap Club.

V 1.5 (2.4 km) **F 362.5** (583.4 km) City of Valdez Goldfields Recreation Area; trails, ponds, swimming, picnic sites, baseball field.

V 2.2 (3.5 km) **F 361.8** (582.2 km) Dylen Drive.

V 2.4 (3.9 km) **F 361.6** (581.9 km) Paved turnout to west.

V 2.7 (4.3 km) **F 361.3** (581.5 km) River Road. Large paved double-ended turnout to west beside Robe River. During August and early September watch for pink and silver salmon spawning in roadside creeks and sloughs. *DO NOT* attempt to catch or otherwise disturb spawning salmon. *CAUTION: Beware of bears.*

V 2.9 (4.7 km) **F 361.1** (581.1 km) Turnoff for Old Dayville Road to **Trans-Alaska Pipeline Valdez Marine Terminal** and access to Allison Point fishery. This 5.4-mile paved road (open to the public) crosses the Lowe River 4 times. At Mile 2.4 the road parallels the bay, and there is excellent fishing in season at Allison Point, especially for pink and silver salmon; also watch for sea otters and bald eagles along here. Overnight RV parking $10. At Mile 4.1 is the Solomon Gulch water project and a spectacular view of Solomon Gulch Falls; a fish hatchery is located across from the water project. Entrance to the pipeline terminal is at the end of the road. Supertankers load oil pumped from the North Slope to this facility via the trans-Alaska pipeline. Bus tours of the terminal are available from Valdez Tours in Valdez; phone (907) 835-2686. ▲

V 3 (4.8 km) **F 361** (581 km) Weigh station.

V 3.4 (5.5 km) **F 360.6** (580.3 km) A 0.5-mile gravel road to Robe Lake and floatplane base. *Watch for bears!*

V 4.7 (7.5 km) **F 359.3** (578.2 km) Turnout to east. Access to **Robe River**; Dolly Varden, red salmon (fly-fishing only, mid-May to mid-June).

V 9.7 (15.6 km) **F 354.3** (570.2 km) Fire station.

V 11.6 (18.7 km) **F 352.4** (567.1 km) Large paved turnout to east.

V 12.8 (20.6 km) **F 351.2** (565.2 km) Here the Lowe River emerges from **Keystone Canyon.** The canyon was named by Captain William Ralph Abercrombie, presumably for Pennsylvania, the Keystone State. In 1884, Abercrombie had been selected to lead an exploring expedition up the Copper River to the Yukon River. Although unsuccessful in his attempt to ascend the Copper River, he did survey the Copper River Delta and a route to Port Valdez. He returned in 1898 and again in 1899, carrying out further explorations of the area (see **Milepost V 13.7**). The Lowe River is named for Lt. Percival Lowe, a member of his expedition. Glacier melt imparts the slate-gray color to the river.

V 13.5 (21.7 km) **F 350.5** (564.1 km) Horsetail Falls; large paved turnout to west.

CAUTION: Watch for pedestrians.

V 13.7 (22 km) **F 350.3** (563.7 km) Large turnout across from Bridal Veil Falls is the trailhead for the **Valdez Goat Trail**; scenic overlook 1/4 mile, trail end 2 miles. Gold Rush Centennial interpretive sign at turnout. This is a restored section of the Trans-Alaska Military Packtrain Trail through Keystone Canyon that led to the first glacier-free land route from Valdez to the Interior. The first gold rush trail led over the treacherous Valdez Glacier, then northeast to Eagle and the Yukon River route to the Klondike goldfields. Captain W.R. Abercrombie and the U.S. Army Copper River Exploring Expedition of 1899 rerouted the trail through Keystone Canyon and over Thompson Pass, thus avoiding the glacier. As the Klondike Gold Rush waned, the military kept the trail open to connect Fort Liscum in Valdez with Fort Egbert in Eagle. In 1903, the U.S. Army Signal Corps laid the trans-Alaska telegraph line along this route.

V 13.8 (22.2 km) **F 350.2** (563.6 km) **Bridal Veil Falls**; large paved turnout to west.

V 14.9 (24 km) **F 349.1** (561.8 km) Lowe River bridge (first of 3 bridges northbound); view of Riddleston Falls. About 175 yards east of this bridge and adjacent to the highway is an abandoned hand-drilled tunnel. Large paved turnout with historical marker. Sign reads: "This tunnel was hand cut into the solid rock of Keystone Canyon and is all that is left of the railroad era when 9 companies fought to take advantage of the short route from the coast to the copper country. However, a feud interrupted progress. A gun battle was fought and the tunnel was never finished."

V 15.2 (24.5 km) **F 348.8** (561.3 km) Gravel turnout to east just south of bridge.

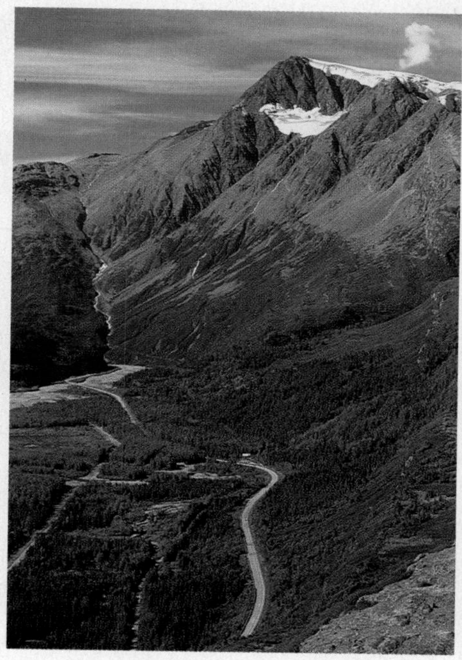

View from Thompson Pass of Richardson Highway and the Lowe River. (© Michael DeYoung)

Horse and Sled Trail (sign) reads: "On the far side just above the water are the remains of the old sled trail used in the early days. This trail was cut out of the rock just wide enough for 2 horses abreast. 200 feet above, the old goat trail can be seen. This road was used until 1945."

V 15.3 (24.6 km) **F 348.7** (561.2 km) Lowe River bridge No. 2, built in 1980, replaced previous highway route through the long tunnel visible beside highway. Turnout at south end of bridge. Spectacular waterfalls.

V 15.9 (25.6 km) **F 348.1** (560.2 km) Leaving Keystone Canyon northbound, entering Keystone Canyon southbound.

V 16.2 (26.1 km) **F 347.8** (559.7 km) Avalanche gun emplacement.

V 16.3 (26.2 km) **F 347.7** (559.6 km) Lowe River bridge No. 3.

V 16.4 (26.4 km) **F 347.6** (559.4 km) Rafting outfitter cabin.

V 18 (29 km) **F 346** (556.8 km) Large paved turnouts both sides of highway; pay phone to west.

V 18.7 (30.1 km) **F 345.3** (555.7 km) Sheep Creek bridge.

Truck lane begins northbound as highway ascends 7.5 miles to Thompson Pass. This was one of the most difficult sections of pipeline construction, requiring heavy blasting of solid rock for several miles. The pipeline runs under the cleared strip beside the road. Low-flying helicopters often seen along the Richardson Highway are usually monitoring the pipeline.

V 21.6 (34.8 km) **F 342.4** (551 km) Paved turnout to east.

V 22.2 (35.7 km) **F 341.8** (550.1 km) Snow poles along highway guide snow plows in winter.

V 23 (37 km) **F 341** (548.8 km) Large gravel turnout to east.

V 23.4 (37.7 km) **F 340.6** (548.1 km) Large paved turnout to east with view.

Two cyclists in front of Worthington Glacier. (© Rich Reid, Colors of Nature)

V 23.6 (38 km) **F 340.4** (547.8 km) Loop road past Thompson Lake to Blueberry Lake and state recreation site; see **Milepost V 24.1.**

V 23.8 (38.3 km) **F 340.2** (547.5 km) Small paved turnout to east.

V 24.1 (38.8 km) **F 339.9** (547 km) Loop road to **Blueberry Lake State Recreation Site**; drive in 1 mile. Tucked into an alpine setting between tall mountain peaks, this is one of Alaska's most beautifully situated campgrounds; 10 campsites, 4 covered picnic tables, toilets, firepits and water. Camping fee $12/night or resident pass. ▲

Blueberry Lake and **Thompson Lake** (formerly Summit No. 1 Lake). Good grayling and rainbow fishing all summer.

V 24.4 (39.3 km) **F 339.6** (546.5 km) Large paved turnout to west. Bare bone peaks of the Chugach Mountains rise above the highway. Thompson Pass ahead; Marshall Pass is to the east.

During the winter of 1907, the A.J. Meals Co. freighted the 70-ton river steamer *Chitina* (or *Chittyna*) from Valdez over Marshall Pass and down the Tasnuna River to the Copper River. The ship was moved piece by piece on huge horse-drawn freight sleds and assembled at the mouth of the Tasnuna. The 110-foot-long ship navigated 170 miles of the Copper and Chitina rivers above Abercrombie Rapids, moving supplies for construction crews of the Copper River & Northwestern Railway. Much of the equipment for the Kennicott mill and tram was moved by this vessel.

V 25.5 (41 km) **F 338.5** (544.7 km) Large paved turnout to west. Entering Game Management Unit 13D, leaving unit 6D, northbound.

V 25.7 (41.4 km) **F 338.3** (544.4 km) Large paved turnout to west with view; Keystone Glacier to the south.

V 26 (41.8 km) **F 338** (543.9 km) **Thompson Pass** (elev. 2,678 feet) at head of Ptarmigan Creek. Truck lane ends northbound; begin 7.5-mile descent southbound.

Thompson Pass, named by Captain Abercrombie in 1899, is comparatively low elevation but above timberline. Wildflower lovers will be well repaid for rambling over the rocks in this area: tiny alpine plants may be in bloom, such as Aleutian heather and mountain harebell.

The National Climatic Center credits snowfall extremes in Alaska to the Thompson Pass station, where record measurements are: 974.5 inches for season (1952–53); 298 inches for month (February 1953); and 62 inches for 24-hour period (December 1955). Snow poles along the highway mark the road edge for snow plows.

Private Aircraft: Thompson Pass airstrip; elev. 2,080 feet; length 2,500 feet; turf, gravel; unattended.

V 27 (43.5 km) **F 337** (542.3 km) Thompson Pass highway maintenance station.

V 27.5 (44.3 km) **F 336.5** (541.5 km) Steep turnout to east by **Worthington Lake**; rainbow fishing.

V 27.7 (44.6 km) **F 336.3** (541.2 km) Good viewpoint of 27 Mile Glacier.

V 28 (45.1 km) **F 336** (540.7 km) Paved turnout to east. Entering winter avalanche area southbound.

V 28.6 (46 km) **F 335.4** (539.8 km) Paved turnout to west.

V 28.7 (46.2 km) **F 335.3** (539.6 km) **Worthington Glacier State Recreation Site**; viewpoints with telescopres, interpretive displays, toilets, parking and pay phone. According to state park rangers, this is the most visited site in the Copper River Basin. The glacier, which heads on Girls Mountain (elev. 6,134 feet), is accessible via a short road (upgraded in 1999) to the west. It is possible to drive almost to the face of the glacier. Care should be exercised when walking on ice because of numerous crevasses.

V 30.2 (48.6 km) **F 333.8** (537.2 km) Large paved turnout both sides of highway. Excellent spot for photos of Worthington Glacier. Gold Rush Centennial interpretive sign about freighting gold over Thompson Pass.

V 29.1 (46.8 km) **F 334.9** (539 km) Turnout to west.

V 32 (51.5 km) **F 332** (534.3 km) Highway parallels Tsaina River northbound. Long climb up to Thompson Pass for southbound motorists.

V 34.7 (55.8 km) **F 329.3** (529.9 km) Tsaina Lodge.

V 36.5 (58.7 km) **F 327.5** (527 km) Pipeline runs under highway.

V 37 (59.5 km) **F 327** (526.2 km) Entering BLM public lands northbound.

V 37.3 (60 km) **F 326.7** (525.8 km) Tsaina River bridge at Devil's Elbow. Large paved turnout at south end of bridge.

V 39 (62.8 km) **F 325** (523 km) Crest of hill; beautiful mountain views.

Highway descends northbound.

V 40.8 (65.7 km) **F 323.2** (520.1 km) Large gravel turnout to west.

V 42 (67.6 km) **F 322** (518.2 km) Gravel turnout to west side. Spruce bark beetles have killed many of the trees in the forest here. Buried pipeline. View of waterbars (ridges on slope designed to slow runoff and control erosion).

V 43.3 (69.7 km) **F 320.7** (516.1 km) Long double-ended turnout.

V 45.6 (73.4 km) **F 318.4** (512.4 km) Large paved turnout to east at north end of Stuart Creek bridge.

V 45.8 (73.7 km) **F 318.2** (512.1 km) Copper River Valley welcome sign. Watch for moose next 20 miles northbound.

V 46.9 (75.5 km) **F 317.1** (510.3 km) **Tiekel River** bridge; small Dolly Varden. Small turnout at north end of bridge.

V 47.8 (76.9 km) **F 316.2** (508.9 km) Large paved rest area to west by Tiekel River; covered picnic sites, outhouses, no drinking water. Viewpoint and historical sign for **Mount Billy Mitchell**.

Lieutenant William "Billy" Mitchell was a member of the U.S. Army Signal Corps, which in 1903 was completing the trans-Alaska telegraph line (Washington–Alaska Military Cable and Telegraph System) to connect all the military posts in Alaska. The 2,000 miles/3,200 km of telegraph wire included the main line between Fort Egbert in Eagle and Fort Liscum at Valdez, and a branch line down the Tanana River to Fort Gibson and on to Fort St. Michael near the mouth of the Yukon and then to Nome. Mitchell was years later to become the "prophet of American military air power."

V 50.7 (81.6 km) **F 313.3** (504.1 km) Bridge over Tiekel River. Dead spruce trees in this area were killed by beetles.

V 53.8 (86.6 km) **F 310.2** (499.2 km) Squaw Creek culvert.

V 54.1 (87.1 km) **F 309.9** (498.7 km) Large paved turnout to east. Look for lupine in June, dwarf fireweed along the Tiekel River in July.

V 54.5 (87.7 km) **F 309.5** (498.1 km) Moose often seen here in the evenings.

CAUTION: Watch for moose.

V 55.1 (88.7 km) **F 308.9** (497.1 km) Large paved turnout to east.

V 56 (90.1 km) **F 308** (495.7 km) Tiekel River Lodge; food, gas, lodging.

Tiekel River Lodge. See display ad this section.

V 56.3 (90.6 km) **F 307.7** (495.2 km) Large paved turnout to east.

V 57 (91.7 km) **F 307** (494.1 km) Old beaver lodge and dams in pond to east. Old beaver lodge. Beaver may inhabit the same site for generations.

Tireless and skillful dam builders, beavers construct their houses in the pond created by the dam. Older beaver dams can reach 15 feet in height and may be hundreds of feet long. The largest rodent in North America, beavers range south from the Brooks Range. They eat a variety of vegetation, including aspen, willow, birch and poplar.

V 58.1 (93.5 km) **F 305.9** (492.3 km) Wagon Point Creek culvert.

V 60 (96.6 km) **F 304** (489.2 km) Large paved turnout to east. Highway parallels **Tiekel River**; fishing for small Dolly Varden.

V 62 (99.7 km) **F 302** (486 km) Ernestine Station (DOT/PF highway maintenance).

V 62.4 (100.4 km) **F 301.6** (485.4 km) Boundary for Sport Fish Management areas. Entering Upper Susitna/Copper River Area N northbound, Prince William Sound southbound.

V 64.7 (104.1 km) **F 299.3** (481.7 km) **Pump Station No. 12 Interpretive Viewpoint** to west, Pump Station 12 to east. Gravel drive leads west to parking area; short boardwalk trail to the viewpoint with interpretive signs about the station and the pipeline.

V 65 (104.6 km) **F 299** (481.2 km) Little Tonsina River.

V 65.1 (104.8 km) **F 298.9** (481 km) **Little Tonsina River State Recreation Site** to west on loop road; 10 campsites, firepits, water pump, litter barrels and toilets. Camping fee $10/night or resident pass. Dolly Varden fishing. Good berry picking in fall. *CAUTION: Beware of bears!* ▲

V 66.2 (106.5 km) **F 297.8** (479.2 km) Double-ended gravel turnout to west.

Watch for moose next 20 miles southbound. Slow for frost heaves northbound.

V 71.2 (114.6 km) **F 292.8** (471.2 km) Long double-ended paved turnout to east.

V 72 (115.9 km) **F 292** (469.9 km) Double-ended paved turnout to west with view across valley of Trans-Alaska pipeline following base of mountains.

Leaving BLM public lands northbound.

V 74.4 (119.7 km) **F 289.6** (466.1 km) Paved double-ended turnout to west.

V 78.6 (126.5 km) **F 285.4** (459.3 km) Tonsina Controlled Use Area (sign); closed to vehicles and pack animals August and September.

V 79 (127.1 km) **F 285** (458.7 km) Tonsina Lodge (closed in 1999; current status unknown).

V 79.2 (127.5 km) **F 284.8** (458.3 km) Bridge over Tonsina River, which rises in Tonsina Lake to the southwest.

V 79.6 (128.1 km) **F 284.4** (457.7 km) Bridge and **Squirrel Creek State Recreation Site**. Pleasant campsites on the bank of Squirrel Creek, some pull-through spaces; $10/night or resident pass; dumpster, boat launch, water, outhouses and firepits. Rough access road through campground; limited turnaround on back loop road. ▲

Mouth of **Squirrel Creek** at Tonsina River. Some grayling and salmon; grayling, small, use flies or eggs, all season; salmon, average size, egg clusters and spoons, all season. Also try the gravel pit beside the campground; according to state park rangers, some fishermen have good luck catching rainbow and grayling here using flies, eggs and spinners.

V 79.7 (128.3 km) **F 284.3** (457.5 km) Begin 1.3-mile truck lane northbound up Tonsina Hill. *CAUTION: Steep hill, watch for bumps; road can be slippery in winter.*

V 81 (130.4 km) **F 283** (455.4 km) Gas station (diesel), coffee shop, gold nuggets.

CAUTION: Begin steep descent southbound; watch for bumps.

V 82.6 (132.9 km) **F 281.4** (452.9 km)

Junction with the Edgerton Highway east to Chitina and McCarthy Road to McCarthy in Wrangell–St. Elias National Park and Preserve. See EDGERTON HIGHWAY section for log of that route.

V 83 (133.6 km) **F 281** (452.2 km) Small paved turnout to west beside Pippin Lake.

"Hill"; highway descends next 3 miles northbound.

V 84.5 (136 km) **F 279.5** (449.8 km) **The Knifeman.** See display ad this section.

V 87.7 (141.1 km) **F 276.3** (444.6 km) Paved double-ended scenic viewpoint to east at **Willow Lake.** On a clear day this lake mirrors the Wrangell Mountains to the east, which lie within Wrangell–St. Elias National Park and Preserve. Gold Rush Centennial interpretive sign about copper mining on the Bonanza Ridge in the Wrangell Mountains.

V 88.5 (142.4 km) **F 275.5** (443.4 km) APL pipeline access road leads west to **Pipeline Interpretive Viewpoint**, 1 of 3 Alyeska pipeline displays along the Richardson Highway. Gravel loop turnout; pedestrian access.

V 90.8 (146.1 km) **F 273.2** (439.7 km) Large paved turnout to west by Willow Creek culvert; thick patches of diamond willow in woods off highway (and thick clouds of mosquitoes!).

V 91.1 (146.6 km) **F 272.9** (439.2 km) Turnoff to east is an 8-mile gravel cutoff that intersects Edgerton Highway at **Milepost J 7.3.** This is a drive through the rolling hills of homestead country and heavy thickets of birch and spruce.

V 91.3 (146.9 km) **F 272.7** (438.8 km) Grizzly Pizza.

V 100.2 (161.2 km) **F 263.8** (424.5 km) *IMPORTANT: South **junction** with Copper Center Bypass (New Richardson Highway). Northbound travelers TURN OFF onto Old Richardson Highway for scenic route through historic Copper Center (log and description follow). The MILEPOST® does not log the bypass route (New Richardson Highway), which is the same distance as the old highway (6.5 miles) with no notable features. The old highway rejoins the bypass route at **Milepost V 106.***

By September, the Richardson Highway has great fall color displays.
(© Alan D. Musy/ADM PhotoGraphics)

Located in the continental climate zone, Copper Center has long, cold winters and relatively warm summers. Snowfall averages 39 inches.

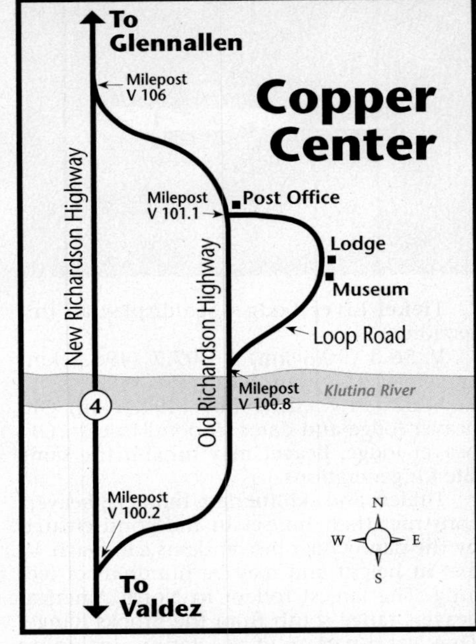

V 100.6 (161.9 km) **F 263.4** (423.9 km) **Grove's Klutina River King Salmon Charters.** See display ad this section.

V 100.7 (162.1 km) **F 263.3** (423.7 km) Klutina River bridges. Excellent fishing in the **Klutina River** for red (sockeye) and king (chinook) salmon. Also grayling and Dolly Varden. Kings to 50 lbs., average 30 lbs.; from June 15 to Aug. 10, peaking in mid-July. Red's peak run is from late June to early August; fish from either bank downstream from the new bridge to the mouth of the Copper River. *NOTE: Most riverfront property is privately owned. Inquire at the tackle shop about river access.* Two campgrounds and fishing charter services are located here. ▲

Klutina Salmon Charters. See display ad this section. ▲

V 100.8 (162.2 km) **F 263.2** (423.6 km) Copper Center (description follows). Turn on loop road opposite gas station for access to Copper Center Lodge, George I. Ashby Memorial Museum. Gas and liquor store.

Copper Center

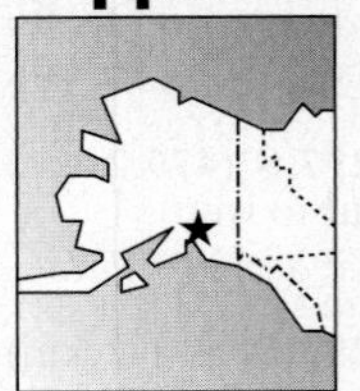

V 100.8 (162.2 km) **F 263.2** (423.6 km) Located on the Klutina River, 1 mile/1.6 km west of its junction with the Copper River; 104.8 miles north of Valdez via Alaska Route 4. An inner loop road leads through Copper Center and rejoins the Richardson Highway at **Milepost V 101.1. Population:** 553. **Emergency Services:** Phone 911. **Ambulance** in Glennallen, phone 911. **Elevation:** 1,000 feet.

Private Aircraft: Copper Center NR 2 airstrip, 1 S; elev. 1,150 feet; length 2,200 feet; gravel; unattended.

Facilities include lodging, private campgrounds, meals, groceries, liquor store, gas station, general store, post office, laundromat and gift shops. Fishing charters, tackle, riverboat services and guides available.

With the influx of gold seekers following the trail from Valdez to the Klondike, a trading post was established in Copper Center in 1898. Gold Rush Centennial interpretive signs here recount the difficulty

Chapel on the Hill at Copper Center was built in 1942.

(© Barb Willard)

of the journey over the Valdez Glacier Trail and the ordeal of the several hundred stampeders who overwintered in Copper Center in 1898-99. A telegraph station and post office were established in 1901, and Copper Center became the principal settlement and supply center in the Nelchina–Susitna region.

Copper Center Lodge on the inner loop road, selected by the Alaska Centennial Commission as a site of historic importance (a plaque is mounted to the right of the lodge's entrance), had its beginning as the Holman Hotel and was known as the Blix Roadhouse during the gold rush days of 1897–98. It was the first lodging place in the Copper River valley and was replaced by the Copper Center Lodge in 1932.

The **George I. Ashby Memorial Museum**, operated by the Copper Valley Historical Society, is housed in the bunkhouse annex at the Copper Center Lodge. It contains early Russian religious articles, Athabascan baskets, telegraph and mineral displays, copper and gold mining memorabilia, and trapping articles from early-day Copper Valley. Hours vary. Donations appreciated.

Historic buildings in Copper Center are located on private property. *Please do not trespass.*

The Copper River reportedly carries the highest sediment load of all Alaskan rivers. The river cuts through the Chugach Mountains and connects the interior of southcentral Alaska with the sea; it is the only corridor of its kind between Cook Inlet and the Canadian border.

Richardson Highway Log

(continued)

V 101 (162.5 km) **F 263** (423.3 km) A visitor attraction in Copper Center is the log **Chapel on the Hill** built in 1942 by Rev. Vince Joy with the assistance of U.S. Army volunteers stationed in the area. The chapel is open daily and there is no admission charge. A short slide show on the Copper River area is usually shown to visitors in the chapel during the summer. A highway-level parking lot is connected by stairs to the Chapel on the Hill.

V 101.1 (162.7 km) **F 262.9** (423 km) Inner loop road to historic Copper Center Lodge, George I. Ashley Memorial Museum and other businesses.

Copper Center Lodge. Beautifully rustic historic landmark, serving the public since 1898; 21 rooms, private or shared baths. Century-old sourdough starter hotcakes, homemade pies. Restaurant serving breakfast, lunch, dinner. Wine and beer served. Located near the base of the Wrangell–St. Elias National Park and next to the Copper and Klutina rivers. See display ad. [ADVERTISEMENT]

V 101.4 (163.2 km) **F 262.6** (422.6 km) Post office to east; outside mailbox. Wild River Gallery.

V 101.5 (163.3 km) **F 262.5** (422.4 km) **Copper River Cash Store**, established in 1896, sits on part of the first farm started in Alaska. The center of the building is the original structure. Behind the store is the old jail, bars still on windows. Open 6 days a week, all year. Complete line of groceries, general merchandise, RV supplies, video rentals. [ADVERTISEMENT]

V 101.9 (164 km) **F 262.1** (421.8 km) Parking area. Historical marker about Copper Center reads: "Founded in 1896 as a government agriculture experiment station, Copper Center was the first white settlement in this area. The Trail of '98 from Valdez over the glaciers came down from the mountains and joined here with the Eagle Trail to Forty Mile and Dawson. 300 miners, destitute and lonely, spent the winter here. Many suffered with scurvy and died. Soon after the turn of the century, the Washington–Alaska Military Cable and Telegraph System, known as WAMCATS, the forerunner of the Alaska communications system, operated telegraph service here between Valdez and Fairbanks."

V 102 (164.1 km) **F 262** (421.6 km) Brenwick–Craig Road.

V 102.2 (164.5 km) **F 261.8** (421.3 km) Copper Center Community Chapel and Indian graveyard.

V 102.5 (165 km) **F 261.5** (420.8 km) Fish wheel may sometimes be seen here operating in Copper River to east. The old school is a local landmark.

V 103.4 (166.4 km) **F 260.6** (419.4 km) Klutikaah Memorial park to east; community ball field.

V 104 (167.4 km) **F 260** (418.4 km) Ahtna building houses Copper River Native Assoc.

V 104.3 (167.8 km) **F 259.7** (417.9 km) Laundromat, showers.

V 104.5 (168.2 km) **F 259.5** (417.6 km) Silver Springs Road. Copper Center school.

V 104.8 (168.7 km) **F 259.2** (417.1 km) Paved turnout to east. Watch for horses.

V 105.1 (169.1 km) **F 258.9** (416.6 km) **Wrangell–St. Elias National Park and Preserve Visitor Center** and National Park Service headquarters to west. Ranger on duty, general information available. A 10-minute video is shown; additional video programs shown on request. Copper ore samples on display. Maps and publications for sale. Open 8 A.M. to 6 P.M. daily, Memorial Day through Labor Day. Winter hours are 8 A.M. to 5 P.M. weekdays. For more information write P.O. Box 439, Copper Center, AK 99573; or phone (907) 822-5234. A new visitor center is under construction near **Milepost V 106.5**.

Access to Wrangell–St. Elias National Park and Preserve is via the Edgerton Highway and McCarthy Road and the Nabesna Road off the Tok Cutoff.

V 106 (170.6 km) **F 258** (415.2 km) *IMPORTANT: North **junction** with Copper Center Bypass (New Richardson Highway). Southbound travelers TURN OFF on to Old Richardson Highway for scenic route through historic Copper Center (see description this section). The MILEPOST® does not log the bypass route (New Richardson Highway), which is the same distance as the old highway (6.5 miles) but without notable features. The old highway rejoins the bypass route at **Milepost V 100.2**.*

V 106.5 (171.4 km) **F 257.5** (414.4 km) New Wrangell-St. Elias National Park and Preserve Visitor Center under construction in 1999.

V 110 (177 km) **F 254** (408.8 km) Dept. of Highways Tazlina station and Dept. of Natural Resources office. Report forest fires here or phone (907) 822-5533.

V 110.5 (177.8 km) **F 253.5** (408 km) Pipeline storage area. Turn west on pipeline storage area road and take second right for private RV park.

V 110.5 (177.8 km) **F 253.5** (408 km) **Tazlina River RV Park.** See display ad this section. ▲

V 110.6 (178 km) **F 253.4** (407.8 km) Rest area to east on banks of Tazlina River; large paved surface, 2 covered picnic tables, water, toilets.

V 110.7 (178.2 km) **F 253.3** (407.6 km) Tazlina River bridge. *Tazlina* is Indian for "swift water." The river flows east from Tazlina Glacier into the Copper River.

V 111 (178.6 km) **F 253** (407.2 km) Trading post; groceries and gas.

Tazlina River Trading Post & Western Auto. See display ad this section.

V 111.7 (179.8 km) **F 252.3** (406 km)

Copperville access road. Developed during pipeline construction, this area has a church and private homes. Glennallen fire station.

V 112.3 (180.7 km) **F 251.7** (405 km) Steep grade southbound from Tazlina River to the top of the Copper River bluffs.

V 112.6 (181.2 km) **F 251.4** (404.6 km) Scenic viewpoint to east; paved parking area, with historical information sign on the development of transportation in Alaska. Short walk to good viewpoint on bluff with schematic diagram of Wrangell Mountains: Mount Sanford (elev. 16,237 feet); Mount Drum (12,010 feet); Mount Wrangell (14,163 feet); and Mount Blackburn (16,390 feet).

Sign at viewpoint reads: "Across the Copper River rise the peaks of the Wrangell Mountains. The 4 major peaks of the range can be seen from this point, with Mount Drum directly in front of you. The Wrangell Mountains, along with the St. Elias Mountains to the east, contain the most spectacular array of glaciers and ice fields outside polar regions. The Wrangell Mountains are part of Wrangell–St. Elias National Park and Preserve, the nation's largest national park. Together with Kluane National Park of Canada, the park has been designated a World Heritage site by the United Nations."

Visitor information for Wrangell–St. Elias National Park is available at **Milepost V 105.1** Old Richardson Highway.

V 114.1 (183.6 km) **F 249.9** (402.2 km) Double-ended turnout to west.

V 115 (185 km) **F 249** (400.7 km) **South junction** of Richardson and Glenn highways at **GLENNALLEN**; pay phone, gas and groceries at Hub of Alaska. **Greater Copper Valley Visitor Information Center** at junction is open daily in summer. The town of Glennallen extends west along the Glenn Highway from here.

The Hub of Alaska and Maxi Mart. See display ad this section.

Junction of the Richardson Highway (Alaska Route 4) and the Glenn Highway (Alaska Route 1). Anchorage- or Tok-bound travelers turn to **Milepost A 189** on page 278 in the GLENN HIGHWAY section for log.

Valdez- or Fairbanks-bound travelers continue with this log. For the next 14 miles/22.5 km northbound the Richardson and Glenn highways share a common alignment. They separate at **Milepost V 128.6.**

V 115.5 (185.9 km) **F 248.5** (399.9 km) Cafe and Glennallen Quick Stop Truck Stop with gas, diesel and convenience store.

V 118 (189.9 km) **F 246** (395.9 km) **Dry Creek State Recreation Site**; 58 campsites, 15-day limit, $10 nightly fee or resident pass, 4 picnic sites, toilets, picnic shelter. Bring mosquito repellent! ▲

V 118.1 (190.1 km) **F 245.9** (395.7 km) **Private Aircraft**: Gulkana airport; elev. 1,579 feet; length 5,000 feet; asphalt; fuel 100LL. Flying service located here.

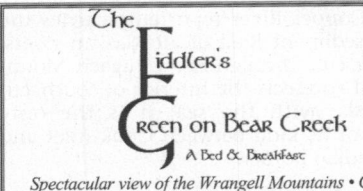

V 123.2 (198.3 km) **F 240.8** (387.5 km) Large paved turnout to east.

V 126 (202.8 km) **F 238** (383 km) Paved double-ended turnout to west.

V 126.2 (203.1 km) **F 237.8** (382.7 km) **The Fiddler's Green on Bear Creek.** See display ad this section.

V 126.8 (204.1 km) **F 237.2** (381.7 km) **Gulkana River** bridge. Large gravel parking areas at both ends of bridge provide access to river. Camping permitted. Excellent fishing mid-June to mid-July for king salmon to 50 lbs. (average is 30 lbs.), and red salmon to 6 lbs. Use bright colored yarn or flies, half-inch hook. Heavy tackle with 25- to 30-lb.-test line recommended for kings. The Gulkana River flows 60 miles from the Gulkana Glacier in the Alaska Range to the Copper River. ▲

Entering Game Management Unit 13B eastbound, 13A westbound.

V 126.9 (204.2 km) **F 237.1** (381.6 km) Access road to **GULKANA** (pop. 90) on the east bank of the Gulkana River at its confluence with the Copper River. Established as a telegraph station in 1903 and named "Kulkana" after the river. Most of the Gulkana River frontage in this area is owned by Gulkana village and managed by Ahtna, Inc. Ahtna lands are closed to the public for hunting, fishing and trapping. The sale, importation and possession of alcohol are prohibited.

V 128.6 (206.9 km) **F 235.4** (378.8 km) **Gakona Junction**; food, gas, lodging, fishing guides. Junction of Richardson Highway (Alaska Route 4) and Tok Cutoff (Alaska Route 1 . The 2 roads share a common alignment for the next 14 miles southbound.

Distance marker shows Paxson 56 miles, Delta Junction 137 miles, Fairbanks 235 miles.

Junction of the Richardson Highway and Tok Cutoff. Tok-bound travelers turn to **Milepost A 203** on page 278 in the GLENN HIGHWAY section for log.

Valdez- or Fairbanks-bound travelers continue with this log.

V 129 (207.6 km) **F 235** (378.2 km) *Watch for road construction next 19 miles northbound in spring 2000.*

V 129.4 (208.2 km) **F 234.6** (377.5 km)

Paved turnout to west. Sailor's Pit (gravel pit opposite lake to west); BLM trail across to **Gulkana River.** Fishing for rainbow trout, grayling, king and red salmon. Highway follows the Gulkana River.

V 132.1 (212.6 km) **F 231.9** (373.2 km) Paved turnout to west.

V 134.6 (216.6 km) **F 229.4** (369.2 km) Paved double-ended turnout with view of Gulkana River to west.

V 135.5 (218.1 km) **F 228.5** (367.7 km) Watch for caribou.

V 135.8 (218.5 km) **F 228.2** (367.2 km) Paved turnout to east. Old beaver pond; 1 mile winter trail to Gulkana River.

V 136.4 (219.5 km) **F 227.6** (366.3 km) Coleman Creek bridge.

V 136.7 (220 km) **F 227.3** (365.8 km) Side road west to **Gulkana River** fishing access: Poplar Grove/Gulkana River BLM-marked vehicle trail, 1 mile. Informal campsites along river.

V 138.1 (222.2 km) **F 225.9** (363.5 km) **Poplar Grove Creek** bridge; spring grayling fishing. Paved turnout to west at north end of bridge.

V 139.3 (224.2 km) **F 224.7** (361.6 km) Paved turnout to west with view of Gulkana River.

V 140.6 (226.3 km) **F 223.4** (359.5 km) Paved turnout to east.

V 141.2 (227.2 km) **F 222.8** (358.6 km) Side road west to Gulkana River fishing access. Informal campsites along river.

V 141.4 (227.6 km) **F 222.6** (358.2 km) Paved double-ended scenic viewpoint to west. One-mile trail to Gulkana River.

V 146 (234.9 km) **F 218** (350.8 km) Lakes and potholes next 9 miles/14.5 km northbound; watch for waterfowl and water lilies. Views of Chugach Mountains southbound.

V 146.4 (235.6 km) **F 217.6** (350.2 km) Entering BLM public lands northbound.

V 147.1 (236.7 km) **F 216.9** (349.1 km) Double-ended paved scenic viewpoint. Fishing trail to Gulkana River.

V 147.6 (237.5 km) **F 216.4** (348.3 km) **SOURDOUGH.** BLM Sourdough Creek Campground; 60 sites, good king salmon fishing. Access to **Gulkana River**, marked trail to Sourdough Creek. Across the bridge (load limit 8 tons) and to the right a road leads to parking, toilets and boat launch on river. Guided fishing trips available. Watch for potholes in access roads. Native lands; check for restrictions.

Get Spooled. See display ad this section.

The Sourdough Roadhouse, destroyed by fire in December 1992, stood next to the creek. It was established in 1903. The old Valdez trail runs 150 yards behind the few buildings left standing.

The Gulkana River is part of the National Wild and Scenic Rivers System managed by the BLM. A popular float trip for experienced canoeists begins at Paxson Lake and ends at Sourdough Campground. See description at **Milepost V 175.**

Gulkana River above Sourdough Creek, grayling 9 to 21 inches (same as Sourdough Creek below), rainbow 10 to 24 inches, spinners, June through September; red salmon 8 to 25 lbs. and king salmon up to 62 lbs., use streamer flies or spinners, mid-June through mid-July. **Sourdough Creek**, grayling 10 to 20 inches, use single yellow eggs or corn, fish deep early May through first week in June, use spinners or flies mid-June until freezeup.

V 148 (238.2 km) **F 216** (347.6 km) *Watch for road construction next 19 miles southbound in spring 2000.*

Alaska Cotton, common along the road, is a member of the sedge family.
(© Barb Willard)

V 150.7 (242.5 km) **F 213.3** (343.3 km) Large gravel turnout to east.

V 151 (243 km) **F 213** (342.8 km) Private gravel driveway to west by large pond; please do not trespass.

V 153.8 (247.5 km) **F 210.2** (338.3 km) Highway passes through boggy terrain; watch for caribou.

CAUTION: No turnouts, little shoulder. Watch for dips and rough patches in highway next 10 miles northbound.

V 154.2 (248.2 km) **F 209.8** (337.6 km) Double-ended gravel turnout to east.

V 156.4 (251.7 km) **F 207.6** (334.1 km) As the highway winds through the foothills of the Alaska Range, over a crest called Hogan Hill (elev. 2,647 feet), there are magnificent views of 3 mountain ranges: the Alaska Range through which the highway leads, the Wrangell Mountains to the southeast and the Chugach Mountains to the southwest. To the west is a vast wilderness plateau where the headwaters of the Susitna River converge to flow west and south into Cook Inlet, west of Anchorage.

V 156.7 (252.2 km) **F 207.3** (333.6 km) Good view of pothole lakes to west.

V 157 (252.7 km) **F 207** (333.1 km) Good long-range viewpoints from highway. Moose and other game may be spotted from here (use binoculars).

V 158.9 (255.7 km) **F 205.1** (330.1 km) Sweeping view of the Glennallen area to the south.

V 160.7 (258.6 km) **F 203.3** (327.2 km) **Haggard Creek** BLM-marked trailhead; grayling fishing. Access to Gulkana River 7 miles to west.

V 162.2 (261 km) **F 201.8** (324.8 km) Double-ended gravel turnout to east.

V 166.5 (267.9 km) **F 197.5** (317.8 km) June Lake trail; 1 mile to west. Fishing access 1/4 mile to west.

V 168.1 (270.5 km) **F 195.9** (315.3 km) **Gillespie Lake** trailhead and parking to west. Walk up creek 0.3 mile to lake; grayling fishing.

V 169.3 (272.5 km) **F 194.7** (313.3 km) Large gravel pit. Turnout to west.

V 169.4 (272.6 km) **F 194.6** (313.2 km) Middle Fork BLM-marked trail to Meier's Lake and Middle Fork Gulkana River.

V 170 (273.6 km) **F 194** (312.2 km) Roadhouse with gas, food, lodging and camping. **Meier's Lake**; parking area, good grayling fishing.

Meier's Lake Roadhouse. See display ad this section.

V 171.6 (276.2 km) **F 192.4** (309.6 km) Gravel turnout by river to west. Long upgrade begins northbound.

Trumpeter swans stop at Summit Lake during their fall migration. (© Tom Culkin)

V 172.7 (277.9 km) **F 191.3** (307.9 km) Small turnout to west, view of pipeline to east.

V 173.3 (278.9 km) **F 190.7** (306.9 km) **Dick Lake** to the east via narrow side road (easy to miss); no turnaround space. Good grayling fishing in summer. View of trans-Alaska oil pipeline across the lake. Good spot for photos.

V 175 (281.6 km) **F 189** (304.2 km) BLM **Paxson Lake Campground** turnoff. Wide gravel road (full of potholes if not recently graded) leads 1.5 miles to large camping area near lakeshore; 50 campsites, some pull-throughs, spaces for all sizes of vehicles but some sites on slope (RVs may need leveling boards); toilets, water, tables, firepits, dump station and concrete boat launch. Parking for 80 vehicles. Bring mosquito repellent. Fishing in Paxson Lake for lake trout, grayling and red salmon.

CAUTION: Watch for bears.

This is the launch site for floating the Gulkana River to Sourdough Campground at **Milepost V 147.6.** Total distance is about 50 miles and 4 days travel, according to the BLM, which manages this national wild river. While portions of the river are placid, the Gulkana does have Class II and III rapids, with a gradient of 38 feet/mile in one section. Canyon Rapids may be Class IV depending on water levels (there is a portage). Recommended for experienced boaters only. For further information on floating the Gulkana, contact the BLM at Box 147, Glennallen, AK 99588, or phone (907) 822-3217.

V 177.1 (285 km) **F 186.9** (300.8 km) Small gravel turnout to west with view of Paxson Lake.

V 178.7 (287.6 km) **F 185.3** (298.2 km) Small gravel turnout to east.

V 179 (288.1 km) **F 185** (297.7 km) Gravel turnout overlooking Paxson Lake. The lake was named for the former owner of the roadhouse (still Paxson Lodge) about 1906. (See interpretive sign at **Milepost V 188.3.**)

V 179.2 (288.4 km) **F 184.8** (297.4 km) Gravel turnout to west overlooking Paxson Lake.

V 179.4 (288.7 km) **F 184.6** (297.1 km) Turnout to east overlooking Paxson Lake.

V 180.1 (289.8 km) **F 183.9** (296 km) Large double-ended gravel turnout to west.

V 180.2 (290 km) **F 183.8** (295.8 km) Small gravel turnout to west.

V 182.1 (293 km) **F 181.9** (292.7 km) Large gravel turnout at head of Paxson Lake. Rough gravel trail to lake.

V 183.2 (294.8 km) **F 180.8** (291 km) Entering Paxson Closed Area northbound (closed to taking of all big game).

V 183 (294.5 km) **F 181** (291.3 km) Small gravel turnout to west.

V 184.3 (296.6 km) **F 179.5** (288.9 km) Large gravel turnout to west.

V 184.7 (297.2 km) **F 179.3** (288.6 km) One Mile Creek bridge.

V 185.5 (298.5 km) **F 178.5** (287.3 km) **PAXSON** (pop. 30; elev. 2,650 feet), at the junction with the Denali Highway, began in 1906 when Alvin Paxson established a roadhouse at Mile 192. He later built a larger roadhouse at Mile 191. Today, services here include lodging at Paxson Inn & Lodge (with restaurant) and Paxson Alpine Cabins, a gas station and post office.

Private Aircraft: Paxson airstrip, adjacent south; elev. 2,653 feet; length 2,800 feet; gravel; emergency fuel; attended.

Junction with Denali Highway (Alaska Route 8) to Cantwell and the Parks Highway. See DENALI HIGHWAY section for log.

V 185.7 (298.9 km) **F 178.3** (286.9 km) Site of original Paxson Lodge. Access west to Paxson Alpine Cabins and Alpine Tours.

V 185.8 (299 km) **F 178.2** (286.8 km) Paxson Station highway maintenance camp.

V 186.4 (300 km) **F 177.6** (285.8 km) Leaving BLM public lands northbound, entering BLM lands southbound.

V 188.3 (303 km) **F 175.7** (282.8 km) Large paved double-ended rest area to east across from Gulkana River; tables, fireplaces, toilets, dumpster and water. The Gulkana River flows south to the Copper River.

Gold Rush Centennial interpretive sign about Alvin J. Paxson's Timberline Tent Roadhouse established near here in 1906.

V 189.5 (305 km) **F 174.5** (280.8 km) Long paved double-ended turnout to west.

V 190.4 (306.4 km) **F 173.6** (279.4 km) Paved parking area by Gulkana River to west with picnic table and interpretive sign about spawning red salmon. Fishing for salmon prohibited. Public fishing access to **Fish Creek** across highway from turnout; grayling fishing.

V 191 (307.4 km) **F 173** (278.4 km) Summit Lake to west; rough, narrow drive to head of stream.

V 192.2 (309.3 km) **F 171.8** (276.5 km) Gravel turnout with public access boat launch on **Summit Lake;** lake trout, grayling, burbot and red salmon.

V 192.6 (310 km) **F 171.4** (275.8 km) Large gravel turnout on Summit Lake. Highway winds along shore of Summit Lake northbound.

V 193.3 (311.1 km) **F 170.7** (274.7 km) Gravel turnout to west on Summit Lake.

V 194.1 (312.4 km) **F 169.9** (273.4 km) Gravel turnout on Summit Lake.

V 195 (313.8 km) **F 169** (271.9 km) Large gravel turnout at **Summit Lake** (elev. 3,210 feet). There are a number of homes in the area and a bed and breakfast. Summit Lake, 7 miles long, is named for its location near the water divide between the Delta and Gulkana rivers. The Gulkana River flows into the Copper River, which flows into Prince William Sound. The Delta River is part of the Yukon River drainage. Fishing for lake trout, grayling, red salmon and burbot.

V 196.8 (316.7 km) **F 167.2** (269.1 km) Gunn Creek bridge. View of Gulkana Glacier to the northeast. This glacier, perched on 8,000-foot Icefall Peak, feeds streams that drain into both Prince William Sound and the Yukon River.

V 197.6 (318 km) **F 166.4** (267.8 km) Summit of **Isabel Pass** (elev. 3,000 feet). Large gravel turnout to east. Gold Rush Centennial interpretive sign about women in the gold rush, including Isabelle Barnette for whom Isabel Pass is named.

Memorial monument honoring Gen. Wilds P. Richardson, for whom the highway is named. Sign here reads: "Captain Wilds P. Richardson presented the need for roads to Congress in 1903. His familiarity with Alaska impressed Congress with his knowledge of the country and his ability as an engineer. When the Act of 1905 became a law, he was placed at the head of the Alaska Road Commission in which position he served for more than a decade. The Richardson Highway, from Valdez to Fairbanks, is a fitting monument to the first great road builder of Alaska."

Entering Sport Fish Management Area C southbound.

V 198.4 (319.3 km) **F 165.6** (266.5 km) Rough gravel turnout to west.

V 200.4 (322.5 km) **F 163.6** (263.3 km) Gravel side road leads west 1.5 miles/2.4 km to **Fielding Lake** Campground. Pleasant area above tree line; 7 campsites, no water, no camping fee, picnic tables, pit toilets, large parking areas and boat ramp. Good fishing for lake trout, grayling and burbot.

Snow poles along highway guide snowplows in winter.

V 201.5 (324.3 km) **F 162.5** (261.5 km) Phelan Creek bridge. Phelan Creek heads near Gulkana Glacier and flows 16 miles to the Delta River.

V 202 (325.1 km) **F 162** (260.7 km) Entering BLM public lands northbound, leaving BLM lands southbound.

V 202.5 (325.9 km) **F 161.5** (259.9 km) McCallum Creek bridge, highway follows Phelan Creek northbound. This stream heads in Gulkana Glacier and flows northwest to the Delta River.

V 203.5 (327.5 km) **F 160.5** (258.3 km) Watch for beaver ponds (and beaver); lupine in June.

V 204 (328.3 km) **F 160** (257.5 km) Springwater piped to east side of highway; paved turnout.

V 204.7 (329.4 km) **F 159.3** (256.4 km) Large gravel turnouts both sides of highway.

V 205.3 (330.4 km) **F 158.7** (255.4 km) Small gravel turnout by stream. Good place for pictures of the pipeline climbing a steep hill.

V 205.6 (330.9 km) **F 158.4** (254.9 km) Snow poles along highway. Gravel turnout.

CAUTION: Slow down for sharp curve.

V 206.4 (332.2 km) **F 157.6** (253.6 km) Double-ended parking area to west with picnic table and view of mineralized **Rainbow Ridge** to northeast. Wildflowers include yellow arnica and sweet pea.

V 207 (333.1 km) **F 157** (252.7 km) Good gravel turnout to west.

V 207.8 (334.4 km) **F 156.2** (251.4 km) Turnout. Rock slide and avalanche area next mile northbound; watch for rocks on road.

V 208.1 (334.9 km) **F 155.9** (250.9 km) Turnout to west.

V 208 4 (335.4 km) **F 155.6** (250.4 km) Large gravel turnout to west.

V 209.5 (337.1 km) **F 154.5** (248.6 km) Wide gravel shoulder along Phelan Creek.

V 211.7 (340.7 km) **F 152.3** (245.1 km) Wide gravel shoulders and turnouts to west beside Phelan Creek next 0.5 mile northbound. Traditional take-out point for Delta River float from Tangle Lakes Campground on the Denali Highway.

V 213.6 (343.7 km) **F 150.4** (242 km) Gravel turnout and road to gravel pit to east. Avalanche area ends northbound.

V 214 (344.4 km) **F 150** (241.4 km) Double-ended paved turnout to east with picnic tables and litter barrels. Highway follows Delta River northbound, Phelan Creek southbound.

V 215.1 (346.2 km) **F 148.9** (239.6 km) Miller Creek bridge; parking at both ends. Pipeline crosses creek next to bridge.

V 215.9 (347.4 km) **F 148.1** (238.3 km) Pipeline interpretive viewpoint with information sign to west.

V 216.7 (348.7 km) **F 147.3** (237 km) Lower Miller Creek bridge. Turnouts at both ends of bridge.

View of Rainbow Ridge near Milepost V 206.4 Richardson Highway. (© Craig Brandt)

V 217.2 (349.5 km) **F 146.8** (236.2 km) Castner Creek; parking at both ends of bridge, west side of road.

V 218.2 (351.1 km) **F 145.8** (234.6 km) Trims Station (DOT/PF highway maintenance).

V 218.8 (352.1 km) **F 145.2** (233.7 km) Bridge over Trims Creek, parking. Wildflowers in the area include lupine, sweet pea and fireweed. Watch for caribou on slopes.

V 219.2 (352.8 km) **F 144.8** (233 km) Access road west to Pump Station No. 10.

V 219.9 (353.9 km) **F 144.1** (231.9 km) Michael Creek bridge; shoulder parking at both ends of bridge.

V 220.9 (355.5 km) **F 143.1** (230.3 km) Flood Creek bridge; parking.

Southbound drivers have a spectacular view of Pump Station No. 10 and the surrounding mountains.

V 223 (358.9 km) **F 141** (226.9 km) Whistler Creek bridge; parking.

V 223.8 (360.2 km) **F 140.2** (225.6 km) Boulder Creek bridge.

V 224.5 (361.3 km) **F 139.5** (224.5 km) Lower Suzy Q Creek bridge; parking.

V 224.8 (361.8 km) **F 139.2** (224 km) Suzy Q Creek bridge; parking area.

V 225.2 (362.4 km) **F 138.8** (223.4 km) Large gravel turnout to east.

V 225.4 (362.7 km) **F 138.6** (223.1 km) Double-ended paved scenic viewpoint with picnic table and litter barrels to west. Historical marker here identifies the terminal moraine of Black Rapids Glacier to the west. Currently a retreating glacier with little ice visible, this glacier was nicknamed the Galloping Glacier when it advanced more than 3 miles during the winter of 1936–37.

Black Rapids Lake trail begins across from historical sign (0.3 mile to lake). Look for river beauty and wild sweet pea blooming in June.

V 226 (363.7 km) **F 138** (222.1 km) Large gravel turnouts to west above Delta River. The Delta River heads at Tangle Lakes and flows 80 miles north to the Tanana River.

V 226.3 (364.2 km) **F 137.7** (221.6 km) Falls Creek bridge.

View of Black Rapids Glacier to west.

V 226.7 (364.8 km) **F 137.3** (221 km) Black Rapids U.S. Army training site at Fall Creek.

Boundary between Game Management Units 20D and 13.

V 227 (365.3 km) **F 137** (220.5 km) Gunnysack Creek.

V 227.4 (366 km) **F 136.6** (219.8 km) Ruins of old Black Rapids Lodge, once the "farthest north of the old-time Richardson trail hostelries."

V 228.4 (367.6 km) **F 135.6** (218.2 km) One Mile Creek bridge; large gravel parking areas.

V 229.8 (369.8 km) **F 134.2** (216 km) Wide shoulder pull-offs west side of highway.

V 230.4 (370.8 km) **F 133.6** (215 km) Large paved turnout to west overlooks Delta River.

V 231 (371.7 km) **F 133** (214 km) Darling Creek; gravel turnout to east at south end.

V 232.2 (373.7 km) **F 131.8** (212.1 km) Gravel turnout to west. Highway climbs southbound.

V 233.3 (375.5 km) **F 130.7** (210.3 km) Bear Creek bridge; gravel turnout with access to creek. Wildflowers include pale oxytrope, yellow arnica, fireweed, wild rhubarb and cow parsnip.

V 234.2 (376.9 km) **F 129.8** (208.9 km) Double-ended gravel turnout to east.

V 234.5 (377.4 km) **F 129.5** (208.4 km) Paved turnout to west.

V 234.8 (377.9 km) **F 129.2** (207.9 km) Ruby Creek bridge; parking area to west at north end.

Distance marker shows Paxson 53 miles, Glennallen 127 miles.

V 237.9 (382.9 km) **F 126.1** (202.9 km) Loop road (watch for potholes) to east through **Donnelly Creek State Recreation Site**; 12 campsites, tables, firepits, toilets and water. Camping fee $8/night or resident pass.

V 239.1 (384.8 km) **F 124.9** (201 km) Small gravel turnout to east.

V 241.3 (388.3 km) **F 122.7** (197.5 km) Large paved turnout to west at top of hill with view of Delta River.

V 242.1 (389.6 km) **F 121.9** (196.2 km) Coal Mine Road (4-wheel-drive vehicles only) leads east to fishing lakes; **Last Lake**, arctic char; **Coal Mine No. 5 Lake**, lake

Watch for bison near Delta Junction on the Richardson Highway. (© Robin Brandt)

trout; **Brodie Lake** and **Pauls Pond,** grayling and lake trout. Check with the ADF&G for details.

V 243.1 (391.2 km) **F 120.9** (194.6 km) Weasel Lake trail (not signed) to west.

V 243.4 (391.7 km) **F 120.6** (194.1 km) Pipeline viewpoint to east with interpretive signs. Good photo stop. The trans-Alaska oil pipeline snakes along the ground and over the horizon. Zigzag design of pipeline converts pipe thermal expansion, as well as movement from other forces (like earthquakes), into a controlled sideways movement.

V 243.9 (392.5 km) **F 120.1** (193.3 km) Paved double-ended scenic viewpoint to east. A spectacular view to the southwest of 3 of the highest peaks of the Alaska Range. From west to south they are: Mount Deborah (elev. 12,339 feet); Hess Mountain (11,940 feet), center foreground; and Mount Hayes (13,832 feet).

V 244.3 (393.2 km) **F 119.7** (192.6 km) Public fishing access to **Donnelly Lake;** king and silver salmon, rainbow trout.

Donnelly Dome ahead northbound.

V 246 (395.9 km) **F 118** (189.9 km) **Donnelly Dome** immediately to the west (elev. 3,910 feet), was first named Delta Dome. For years the mountain has been used to predict the weather: "The first snow on the top of the Donnelly Dome means snow in Delta Junction within 2 weeks."

Great view southbound of peaks in the Alaska Range.

V 247 (397.5 km) **F 117** (188.3 km) Cutoff to Old Richardson Highway loop (dirt road) to west; access to fishing lakes.

V 247.3 (398 km) **F 116.7** (187.8 km) From here northbound the road extends straight as an arrow for 4.8 miles.

Distance marker southbound shows Paxson 65 miles, Glennallen 139 miles.

V 249.3 (401.2 km) **F 114.7** (184.6 km) Bear Drop Zone. Military games area. Controlled access road: No trespassing.

V 252.8 (406.8 km) **F 111.2** (179 km) Paved, double-ended rest area to west with picnic tables and litter barrels.

V 257.6 (414.6 km) **F 106.4** (171.2 km) Entrance to U.S. Army Cold Regions Test Center at Fort Greely.

Meadows Road (4-wheel-drive vehicles only) leads west to fishing lakes. Access to **Bolio Lake;** grayling, rainbow, lake trout. Rainbow-producing **Mark Lake** is 4.5 miles/7.2 km along this road. Meadows Road junctions with the Old Richardson Highway loop. Check with the ADF&G for details on fishing lakes.

V 258.3 (415.7 km) **F 105.7** (170.1 km) **Alyeska Pipeline Pump Station No. 9** to east. Tours of Pump Station 9 are offered daily, except Sundays, from June through August. Limited to 10 people per tour; children must be at least 9 years old. Reservations recommended. For tour times and reservations, phone (907) 869-3270 or 456-9391.

V 261.2 (420.3 km) **F 102.8** (165.4 km) **FORT GREELY** (restricted area) main gate to east. Fort Greely was named for A.W. Greely, arctic explorer and author of *Three Years of Arctic Service*. Fort Greely is scheduled for phased reduction and closure by 2001.

V 262.6 (422.6 km) **F 101.4** (163.2 km) Double-ended paved rest area to west with scenic view. Watch for bison.

CAUTION: Wind area northbound.

V 264.9 (426.3 km) **F 99.1** (159.5 km) Jarvis Creek. "Welcome to Delta Junction" sign northbound. Bike trail begins northbound.

CAUTION: Wind area southbound.

V 265 (426.5 km) **F 99** (159.3 km) Alaskan Steak House & Motel.

V 265.2 (426.8 km) **F 98.8** (159 km) **V 266** (428 km) **F 98** (157.7 km) Delta Fire Department to east.

ALASKA ROUTE 2

V 266 (428 km) **F 98** (157.7 km) Stop sign at intersection of the Richardson and Alaska highways in **DELTA JUNCTION** (see description beginning on page 196). **Delta Junction Visitor Information Center** to east; End of Alaska Highway monument, pipeline display, water, brochures, restrooms.

Junction of the Richardson Highway (Alaska Route 4) and Alaska Highway (Alaska Route 2). Turn to **Milepost DC 1422** (page 196) in the ALASKA HIGHWAY section for log of that route to Tok and the Canadian border (read log back to front).

The Richardson Highway continues north to Fairbanks as Alaska Route 2, and south to Valdez as Alaska Route 4.

V 266.3 (428.6 km) **F 97.7** (157.2 km) Delta Junction post office.

V 266.5 (428.9 km) **F 97.5** (156.9 km) Delta Junction library and city hall. Library hours are 11 A.M. to 6 P.M. Monday through Thursday and 11 A.M. to 4 P.M. Friday and Saturday; free paperback book and magazine exchange, Alaska videos, public fax and copier service. City Hall is open 9 A.M. to 5 P.M. weekdays; pay phone and public restrooms.

V 266.8 (429.4 km) **F 97.2** (156.4 km) Alaska Dept. of Fish and Game office.

V 267 (429.7 km) **F 97** (156.1 km) Airstrip.

V 267.1 (429.8 km) **F 96.9** (155.9 km) **Delta state campground** to east; 24 sites, water, tables, shelter with covered tables, toilets, $8 nightly fee or resident pass. Large turnout at campground entrance. Turnout on west side of highway on bank of the Delta River offers excellent views of the Alaska Range. ▲

V 267.2 (430 km) **F 96.8** (155.7 km) Alaska Division of Forestry office.

V 267.3 (430.2 km) **F 96.7** (155.6 km) Medical clinic.

V 267.6 (430.6 km) **F 96.4** (155.1 km) Delta laundry and fuel.

V 268 (431.3 km) **F 96** (154.5 km) Smith's Green Acres RV Park. ▲

V 268.3 (431.7 km) **F 95.7** (154 km) **Junction** with Jack Warren Road (paved); see Delta Vicinity map this section. Turn here for access to **Clearwater state campground** (10.5 miles). Clearwater campground has toilets, tables, water and boat launch; pleasant campsites on bank of river. Camping fee $8/night or resident pass. ▲

Driving this loop is a good opportunity to see local homesteads. Note that mileposts on these paved side roads run backward from Mile 13 at this junction to Mile 0 at the junction of Clearwater Road and the Alaska Highway.

V 270 (434.5 km) **F 94** (151.3 km) **Nickay's Country Garden.** 2-1/2 acre produce farm and stand. Well-maintained yard, garden and greenhouses. Hydroponic tomatoes, cucumbers, peppers, strawberries and lettuce. Garden crops include broccoli, cauliflower, cabbage, onions, radishes, carrots, beets, potatoes, spinach, peas, beans, collards, etc. Open mid-May through mid-September. Call Nick or Kay, (907) 895-4557. [ADVERTISEMENT]

V 270.3 (435 km) **F 93.7** (150.8 km) **Alaska 7 Motel,** 16 large, clean, comfortable rooms with full bath and showers. Satellite TV and courtesy coffee in each room. Kitchenettes and phone available. Comfort at a comfortable price. Open year-round. Major credit cards accepted. **Milepost 270.3** Richardson Highway. Phone (907) 895-4848. E-mail: akmotel@alaskan.com. Internet: www.alaskan.com/ak7motel See display ad in Delta Junction section. [ADVERTISEMENT]

V 270.6 (435.5 km) **F 93.4** (150.3 km) Welcome to Delta Junction sign for southbound travelers.

V 271.7 (437.2 km) **F 92.3** (148.5 km) Tanana Loop Road (gravel). Turn here to make a loop drive through Delta Junction farmlands. Follow Tanana Loop Road 1.3 miles east; turn south on Tanana Loop Extension and drive 7.8 miles to Jack Warren Road (unsigned). Go west on Jack

Warren Road (paved) for 2.9 miles to junction with Alaska Highway north of Delta Junction (see Delta Vicinity map this section).

V 272.1 (437.9 km) **F 92** (148 km) Big D Fire station.

V 275 (442.6 km) **F 89** (143.2 km) Tanana Trading Post (Tesoro) gas station on west side of highway, turnoff to east for Rika's Roadhouse (a worthwhile stop). Gold Rush Centennial interpretive sign on Big Delta's beginning as a trading post and roadhouse known first as Bates Landing and later as Rika's Landing, then McCarty.

Rika's Roadhouse was built in 1910 by John Hajdukovich. In 1923, Hajdukovich sold it to Rika Wallen, a Swedish immigrant who had managed the roadhouse since 1917. Rika ran the roadhouse into the late 1940s and lived there until her death in 1969. Rika's Roadhouse is now part of **Big Delta State Historical Park.** Drive in on gravel access road to large parking area; it is a short walk through trees to Rika's Roadhouse complex. The parking area also accommodates overnight RV parking; camping fee $8/vehicle, dump station ($3), toilets and phone. ▲

V 275.4 (443.2 km) **F 88.6** (142.6 km) Big Delta Bridge; **Tanana River/Pipeline Crossing.** Spectacular view of pipeline suspended across river. Slow down for parking area to east at south end of bridge with litter barrels and interpretive sign about pipeline.

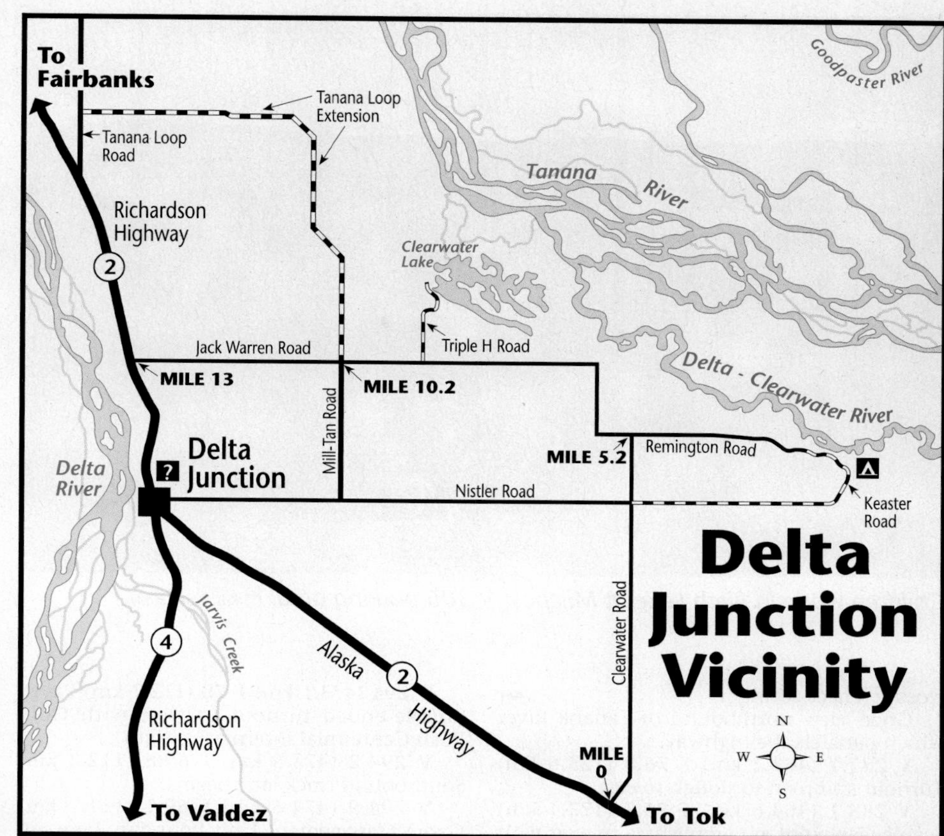

BIG DELTA (pop. 511, unincorporated), at the junction of the Delta and Tanana Rivers, was originally a stop on the Valdez to Fairbanks overland trail, first known as Bates Landing, then Rick'a Landing, McCarty, and finally Big Delta. It was the site of a military telegraph station (part of WAMCATS). Big Delta was also a work camp in 1919 during construction of the Richardson Highway. The Fur Shack is located here.

The Fur Shack. See display ad in the ALASKA HIGHWAY section.

V 277.9 (447.2 km) **F 86.1** (138.6 km) Turnoff to east for **Quartz Lake Recreation Area.** Drive in 2.5 miles on gravel road to intersection: turn left for Lost Lake, continue straight ahead for Quartz Lake (another 0.3 mile). Lost Lake, 0.2 mile from intersection, has 8 campsites with picnic tables, toilet, and a large parking area with tables and litter barrels. A shallow, picturesque lake with no fish. Quartz Lake has more developed campsites on good loop road, firepits, water, tables, toilet and 2 boat launches. Boat launch fee $3 or boat launch pass. Camping fees at both campgrounds: $8/night or resident pass. A trail connects Lost Lake and Quartz Lake camping areas. ▲

Private cabins are scattered along the northern and eastern shorelines of Quartz Lake. About half the land along the lake is undeveloped and there is no road access beyond the campground. The lake covers 1,500 acres, more than 80 percent of which are less than 15 feet deep. Maximum depth is 40 feet. Aquatic vegetation covers most of the lake surface, hampering swimmers and waterskiers. Boat and motor rentals available from Black Spruce Lodge. **Quartz Lake** offers excellent fishing for stocked rainbow to 18 inches, silver salmon to 13 inches and Arctic char; use spinners, plugs and artificial flies. Ice fishing in winter. For more information phone the ADF&G office in Delta at (907) 895-4632.

V 278.9 (448.8 km) **F 85.1** (137 km) Former U.S. Army petroleum station, now closed.

V 280.3 (451.1 km) **F 83.7** (134.7 km) Gravel turnout to east.

V 286.6 (461.2 km) **F 77.4** (124.6 km) Shaw Creek bridge; boat launch and snack shop. Excellent wildflower displays of sweet peas blooming in June.

V 286.7 (461.4 km) **F 77.3** (124.4 km) **Shaw Creek** road. Good to excellent early spring and fall grayling fishing; subject to

Children wade in Birch Lake at Milepost V 306 parking area. (© Kris Graef, staff)

closure (check locally).

Good view northbound of Tanana River which parallels the highway.

V 287.2 (462.2 km) **F 76.8** (123.6 km) Turnout and road to slough to east.

V 288.1 (463.6 km) **F 75.9** (122.1 km) Scenic viewpoint at parking area to west with panoramic view to the south of 3 great peaks of the Alaska Range: Mount Hayes (elev. 13,832 feet) almost due south; Hess Mountain (11,940 feet) to the west or right of Mount Hayes; and Mount Deborah (12,339 feet) to the west or right of Hess Mountain. Mount Hayes is named for Charles Hayes, an early member of the U.S. Geological Survey. Mount Deborah was named in 1907 by the famous Alaskan Judge Wickersham for his wife.

V 289.8 (466.4 km) **F 74.2** (119.4 km) Long paved double-ended turnout to east in trees.

V 291.8 (469.6 km) **F 72.2** (116.2 km) Northbound truck lane begins.

V 292.8 (471.2 km) **F 71.2** (114.6 km) Northbound truck lane ends. Southbound truck lane ends.

V 294 (473.1 km) **F 70** (112.7 km) Paved double-ended turnout to west with Gold Rush Centennial interpretive signs.

V 294.2 (473.5 km) **F 69.8** (112.3 km) Southbound truck lane begins.

V 294.9 (474.6 km) **F 69.1** (111.2 km) Game Management Unit boundary between 20B and 20D. Fairbanks North Star Borough boundary.

V 295.4 (475.4 km) **F 68.6** (110.4 km) Banner Creek bridge; historic placer gold stream.

V 296.4 (477 km) **F 67.6** (108.8 km) Paved parking area to west; view of Alaska Range and Tanana River to south.

CAUTION: Rough road, watch for frost heaves northbound.

V 297.7 (479.1 km) **F 66.3** (106.7 km) Sharp turn downhill to west for scenic viewpoint of Tanana River.

V 298.2 (479.9 km) **F 65.8** (105.9 km) Paved parking area to west.

V 301.6 (485.4 km) **F 62.4** (100.4 km) South end of long double-ended turnout east side of highway.

V 304.3 (489.7 km) **F 59.7** (96.1 km) Parking area to east.

V 305.2 (491.2 km) **F 58.8** (94.6 km) Birch Lake Road to east; access to military recreation area (restricted).

V 306 (492.4 km) **F 58** (93.3 km) Large parking area east side of highway overlooks **Birch Lake**; unimproved gravel boat launch and beach; fish from shore in spring, from boat in summer, for rainbow and silver salmon. Many Fairbanks residents have summer homes at Birch Lake.

V 307.2 (494.3 km) **F 56.8** (91.4 km) Birch Lake highway maintenance station.

V 308 (495.7 km) **F 56** (90.1 km) *CAUTION: Watch for moose. Watch for road construction next 3 miles northbound in spring 2000.*

V 313.1 (503.9 km) **F 50.9** (81.9 km) Paved double-ended turnout to west on Tanana River. Gold Rush Centennial interpretive sign about gold strikes in the Tanana Valley.

V 314.8 (506.6 km) **F 49.2** (79.2 km) Midway Lodge.

V 317.9 (511.6 km) **F 45.4** (73.1 km) Double-ended gravel parking area to west.

V 319.3 (513.8 km) **F 44.7** (71.9 km) Salcha Drive; access east to Harding Lake.

V 319.8 (514.7 km) **F 44.2** (71.1 km) Access road east to Harding Lake summer homes.

V 321.5 (517.4 km) **F 42.5** (68.4 km) Turnoff to east for **Harding Lake State Recreation Area**; drive east 1.4 miles on paved road. Park headquarters, campground

host, drinking water fill-up and dump station ($3) at entrance. Picnic tables on grassy area at lakeshore; boat ramp ($5 launch fee or boat launch pass), ball fields and about 80 campsites. Camping fee $8/night or resident pass. Fishing for lake trout, arctic char, burbot, northern pike and salmon. Lake is reported to be "hard to fish." Worth the drive! *Bring your insect repellent. You may need it!*

V 322.2 (518.5 km) **F 41.8** (67.3 km) **SALCHA** (pop. 387, unincorporated) extends along the highway for several miles. Post office (ZIP code 99714) and Salcha River Lodge with food, gas and lodging on east side of highway. The village was first reported in 1898 as "Salchaket," meaning "mouth of the Salcha."

V 323.1 (520 km) **F 40.9** (65.8 km) Salcha Marine and access to **Salcha River State Recreation Site** to east, a popular boat

launch with a large parking area (75 sites), boat ramp ($3 launch fee or boat launch pass), picnic area, toilets and water. Camping fee $8/night per vehicle or resident pass. Fishing for king and chum salmon, grayling, sheefish, northern pike and burbot.

V 323.4 (520.4 km) **F 40.6** (65.3 km) Salcha River bridge.

V 323.9 (521.2 km) **F 40.1** (64.5 km) Salcha River Trading Post.

V 324.1 (521.6 km) **F 39.9** (64.2 km) Clear Creek bridge.

V 324.6 (522.4 km) **F 39.4** (63.4 km) Double-ended gravel turnout to east.

V 324.8 (522.7 km) **F 39.2** (63.1 km) **Munsons Slough** bridge; fishing.

V 325.6 (523.7 km) **F 38.6** (62.1 km)

Salcha Elementary School.

V 326.4 (525.3 km) **F 37.6** (60.5 km) Salcha Baptist log church to west.

V 326.8 (525.9 km) **F 37.2** (59.9 km) Waste transfer site.

V 327.7 (527.4 km) **F 36.3** (58.4 km) Little Salcha River bridge.

V 328.3 (528.3 km) **F 35.7** (57.4 km) Salcha Store and gas station to east.

V 330.6 (532 km) **F 33.4** (53.7 km) Salcha Rescue; phone (907) 488-5274.

V 331.7 (533.8 km) **F 32.3** (52 km) Salcha Fairgrounds. Salcha Fair is held in late June.

V 332.2 (534.6 km) **F 31.8** (51.2 km) Access east to **31-Mile Pond**; stocked with arctic char.

V 332.3 (534.8 km) **F 31.7** (51 km) The Knotty Shop to west; gifts and wildlife museum.

V 334.5 (538.3 km) **F 29.5** (47.5 km) Waste transfer site.

V 334.7 (538.6 km) **F 29.3** (47.2 km) South boundary of Eielson AFB.

V 335.1 (539.3 km) **F 28.9** (46.5 km) Access east to **28-Mile Pond;** stocked with rainbow and silver salmon.

V 338 (543.9 km) **F 26** (41.8 km) View of Eielson AFB airstrip to northeast. Watch for various military aircraft taking off and landing to the east. Aircraft include Air Force F-16s, F-15s, KC-135s, C-130s, C-141s, OA-10s, Navy A-6s, F-14s and others.

V 340.7 (548.3 km) **F 23.3** (37.5 km) Divided 4-lane highway begins northbound, 2-lane undivided highway begins southbound.

CAUTION: Watch for heavy traffic southbound turning east into the base, 7–8 A.M., and merging northbound traffic, 3:45–5:30 P.M., weekdays.

V 341 (548.8 km) **F 23** (37 km) Entrance to east to **EIELSON AIR FORCE BASE** (pop. 4,751). Built in 1943 as a satellite base to Ladd Field (now Fort Wainwright) in Fairbanks, and called Mile 26 because of its location 26 miles from Fairbanks, Eielson served as a storage site for aircraft on their way to the Soviet Union under the WWII Lend–Lease program. Closed after WWII, the base was reactivated in 1946 and renamed Eielson AFB, after Carl Ben Eielson, the first man to fly from Alaska over the North Pole to Greenland. A tour of the base is offered every Friday during the summer months from 10:30 A.M. to noo ; phone the public affairs office at (907) 377-2116 or 377-1410 for reservations and more information.

V 342.3 (550.9 km) **F 21.7** (34.9 km) North boundary of Eielson AFB.

V 343.7 (553.1 km) **F 20.3** (32.7 km) Moose Creek Road and general store; diesel, gas, propane.

Moose Creek General Store. See display ad this section.

Piledriver Slough parallels the highway from here north, flowing into the Tanana River. It is stocked with rainbow trout. Check with general store for access and fishing information. **Bathing Beauty Pond**, stocked with rainbow, arctic char and grayling, is accessible via Eielson Farm Road off Moose Creek Road.

V 344.7 (554.7 km) **F 19.3** (31.1 km) Moose Creek bridge.

V 345.5 (556 km) **F 18.5** (29.8 km)

View of the Tanana River from the Richardson Highway. (© Kris Graef, staff)

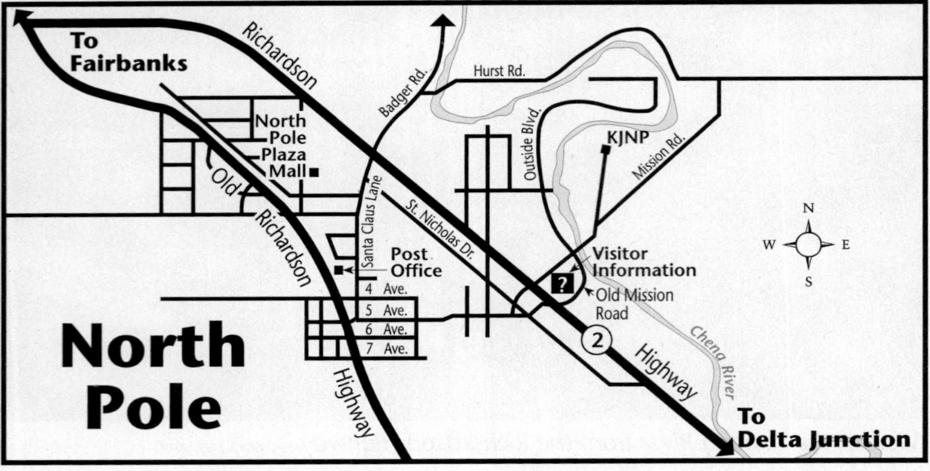

CAUTION: Highway crosses Alaska Railroad tracks.

V 346 (556.8 km) **DC 1502** (2417.2 km) **F 17.9** (28.8 km) Chena Flood Channel bridge. Upstream dam is part of flood control project initiated after the Chena River left its banks and flooded Fairbanks in 1967.

V 346.7 (558 km) **F 17.3** (27.8 km) Laurance Road; park-and-ride. Exit for VFW Post, Moose Creek Dam Bikeway and Chena Lake Recreation Area (descriptions follow).

North Pole VFW Post. See display ad this section.

The 5-mile-long **Moose Creek Dam Bikeway** extends from the park-and-ride lot at Laurence and Nelson Roads (0.8 mile from the highway) to the damsite on the Chena River.

Entrance to **Chena Lake Recreation Area**, 2.5 miles from highway; day-use fee $3, RV/tent camping $10, bikes $1. It is 5.5 miles from the highway to the visitor kisok below the damsite on the Chena River at the end of Main Road (pictured here).

Constructed by the Army Corps of Engineers and run by Fairbanks North Star Borough, the recreation area has 80 campsites, 92 picnic sites (some with wheelchair access), pump water, volleyball courts and a 250-acre lake with swimming beach. Chena Lake Bike Trail begins at Chena Lake swim beach and intersects with the Moose Creek Dam Bikeway. **Chena Lake** is stocked with silver salmon, arctic char, grayling and rainbow trout. Nonmotorized boats may be rented from a concessionaire. The **Chena River** flows through part of the recreation area and offers good grayling fishing and also northern pike, whitefish and burbot. Hiking and self-guiding nature trails. Open year-round. Fees are charged from Memorial Day to Labor Day.

V 347.1 (558.6 km) **F 16.9** (27.2 km) Newby Road.

V 347.7 (559.6 km) **F 16.3** (26.2 km) Exit west for St. Nicholas Drive, east for Dawson Road.

V 348.7 (561.2 km) **F 15.3** (24.6 km) Exit for 5th Avenue/Mission Road. Access to St. Nicholas Drive. Exit to northeast for **North Pole Visitor Information Center** (open 8 A.M. to 7 P.M. daily, Memorial Day to mid-September) and for Mission Road to radio station KJNP.

Exit southwest for 5th Avenue businesses, RV park and Santa Claus House.

Santaland RV Park. Good Sampark. Center of North Pole, next to Santa Claus House, home of Comet and Cupid, North Pole's resident reindeer. City water, full service pull-throughs, car wash. Free private showers, laundry, pay phones. Cable TV. 50-amp available. E-mail access. Handicapped accessible. Tour sales and reservations. Daily shuttle bus to Fairbanks points of interest. See display ad, or call (888)488-9123 or (907) 488-9123. E-mail: npole@ptialaska.net. www.pitalaska.net/~npole. [ADVERTISEMENT]

V 349 (561.6 km) **F 15** (24.1 km) **Santa Claus House.** In 1949, Con Miller began wearing a Santa Claus suit on business trips throughout the territory, bringing the spirit of St. Nicholas to hundreds of children for the first time. Here, the Miller family continues this tradition. Ask about ordering a letter. Mail your cards and letters here for authentic North Pole postmark. Enjoy the unique gift shop and exhibits. Open all year, Extended summer hours, Memorial Day through Labor Day. Visit with Santa Claus and his reindeer. Complimentary shuttle service available. Santa Claus House features exclusive gifts and souvenirs. [ADVERTISEMENT]

V 349.5 (562.3 km) **F 14.5** (23.3 km) North Pole and North Pole Plaza to southwest via Santa Claus Lane; access to Santa Claus House. Badger Road to the northeast.

Santa Claus Lane has several businesses along it, and connects with 5th Avenue, which loops back to the highway at **Milepost V 348.6.**

Truck stop with diesel, 2 small shopping malls, motel and other businesses are located on **Badger Road.** Badger Road is a loop road leading 12 miles along Badger Slough and providing access to an RV park, salmon bake, convenience store with gas, and several bed and breakfasts. It also junctions with Nordale Road to Chena Hot Springs Road. It re-enters the Alaska Highway 7 miles outside of Fairbanks at **Milepost V 357.1.**

North Pole

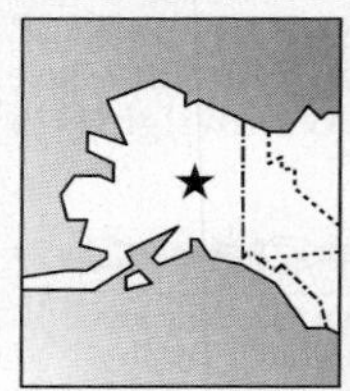

V 349.5 (562.3 km) **F 14.5** (23.3 km) The home of Santa Claus. **Population:** 1,616. **Emergency Services:** Emergencies only phone 911. **Police,** phone (907) 488-6902. **Alaska State Troopers,** phone (907) 452-2114. **Fire**

NORTH POLE ADVERTISERS

Austin Enterprises RV Service ....2828 Badger Rd.
Beaver Lake Resort Motel ....Ph. (970) 488-9600
Bo's Logos ....301 N. Santa Claus Lane
Elf's Den, The ....Ph. (907) 488-3268
Jolly Acres Motel ....Ph. (907) 488-9339
KJNP ....Mission Rd.
North Pole Chamber of Commerce ....Ph. (907) 488-2242
Riverview RV Park ....Ph. (907) 488-6392
Santa Claus House ....Ph. (907) 488-2200
Santaland RV Park & Campground ....125 St. Nicholas Dr

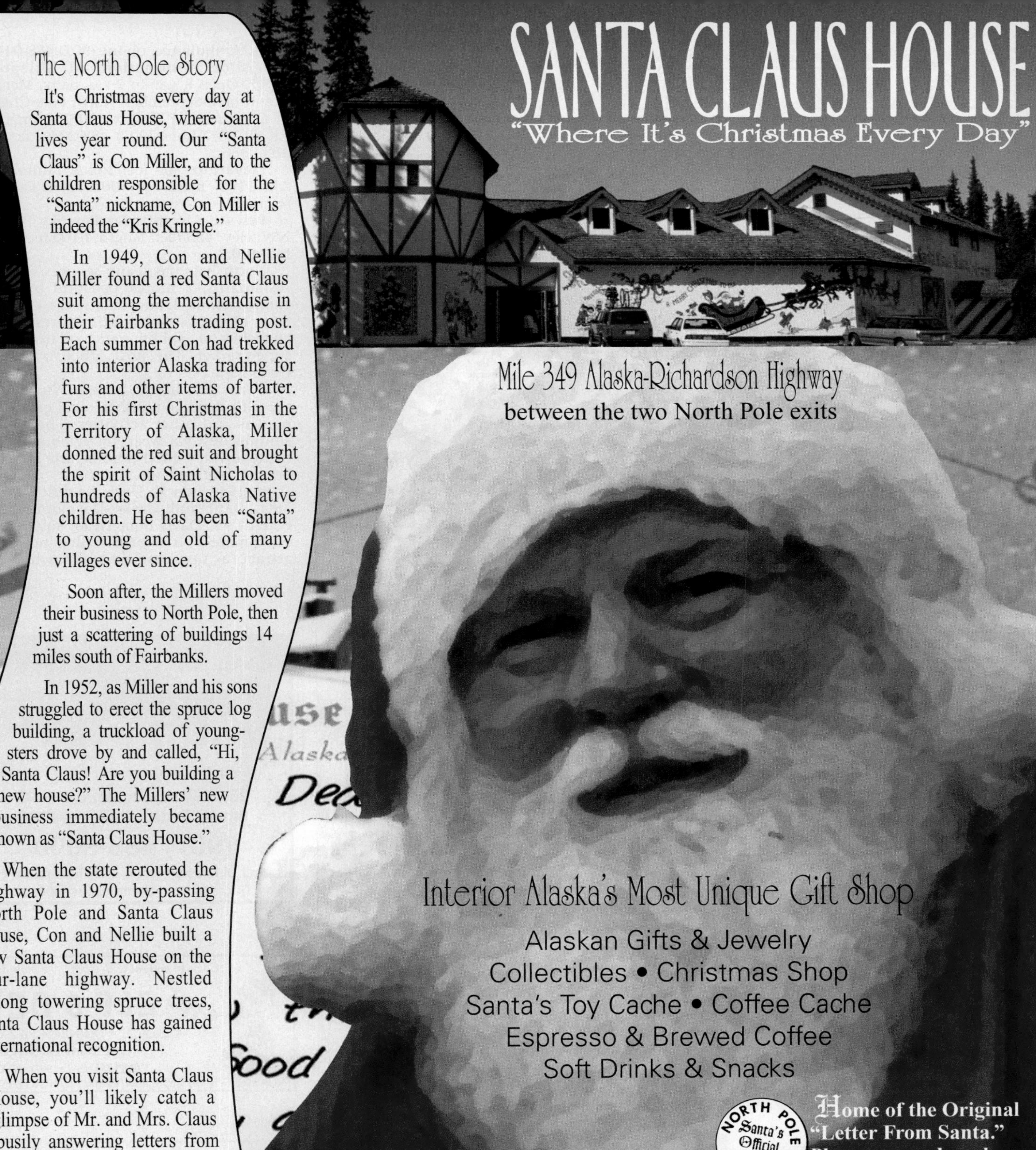

SANTA CLAUS HOUSE
"Where It's Christmas Every Day"
Mile 349 Alaska-Richardson Highway
between the two North Pole exits
Interior Alaska's Most Unique Gift Shop
Alaskan Gifts & Jewelry
Collectibles • Christmas Shop
Santa's Toy Cache • Coffee Cache
Espresso & Brewed Coffee
Soft Drinks & Snacks
NORTH POLE Santa's Official Mail ALASKA
Home of the Original "Letter From Santa." Place your order when you visit or write us.
Mail your cards & letters from Santa Claus House for an authentic North Pole postmark

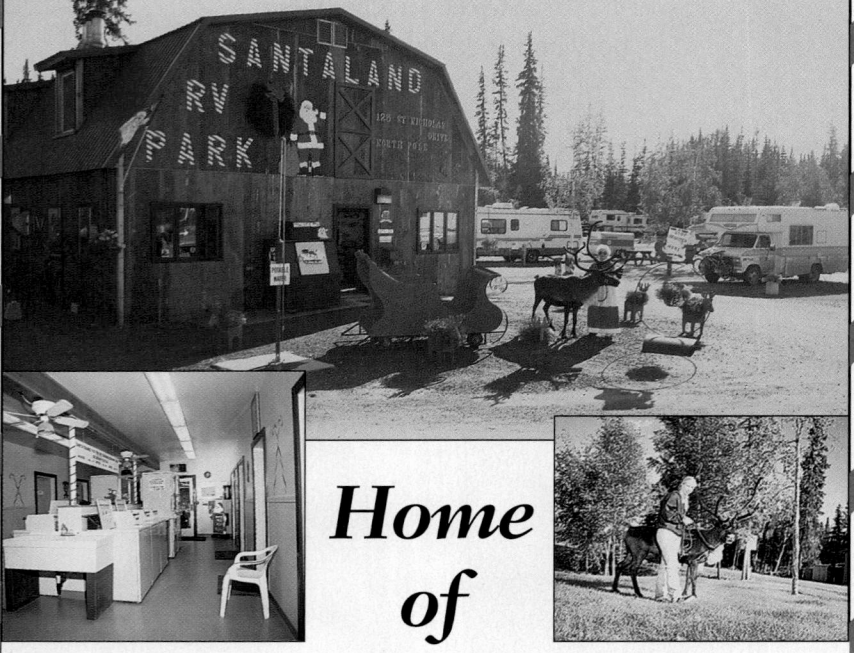

Dept./Ambulance, phone (907) 488-0444.

Visitor Information: At **Milepost V 348.7**. Open 8 A.M. to 7 P.M. daily, Memorial Day to mid-September. North Pole Chamber of Commerce, P.O. Box 55071, North Pole, AK 99705; phone (907) 488-2242, fax (907) 488-0366.

Elevation: 500 feet/152m. **Radio**: KJNP-AM 1170, KJNP-FM 100.3; also Fairbanks stations.

Private Aircraft: Bradley Sky Ranch, 1 NW; elev. 483 feet; length 4,100 feet; gravel; fuel 100.

North Pole has many services, including restaurants, a motel, bed and breakfasts, campgrounds, laundromats, car wash, grocery and gas stops, gift stores, library, churches, a public park, pharmacy and supermarket. The post office is on Santa Claus Lane.

North Pole has an annual Winter Carnival with sled dog races, carnival games, food booths and other activities. There's a big summer festival weekend celebration with carnival rides, food booths, arts and crafts booths, and a parade.

In 1944 Bon V. Davis homesteaded this area. Dahl and Gaske Development Co. bought the Davis homestead, subdivided it and named it North Pole, hoping to attract a toy manufacturer who could advertise products as being made in North Pole.

North Pole is the home of many Fairbanks commuters. It has an oil refinery that produces heating fuel, jet fuel and other products. Eielson and Wainwright military bases are nearby.

Radio station KJNP, operated by Calvary's Northern Lights Mission, broadcasts music and religious programs on 1170 AM and 100.3 FM. They also operate television station KJNP Channel 4. Visitors are welcome between 8 A.M. and 10 P.M.; tours may be arranged. KJNP is located on Mission Road about 0.6 mile/1 km northeast of the Alaska Highway. The missionary project includes a dozen hand-hewn, sod-roofed homes and other buildings constructed of spruce logs.

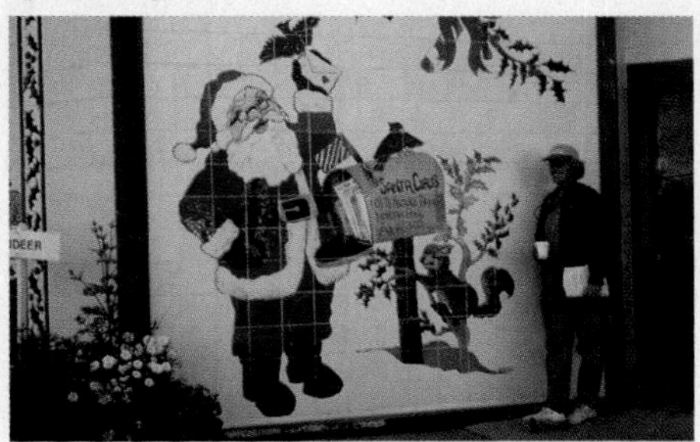

Santa Claus House is a North Pole landmark and favorite stop with travelers, who can shop for Christmas ornaments in July while their children tell Santa what they want in December.

Full-service campgrounds at Santaland RV Park downtown, Road's End RV Park at **Milepost V 356.2** and Riverview RV Park at **Milepost V 357.1** Richardson Highway. North Pole Public Park, on 5th Avenue, has tent sites in the trees along a narrow dirt road; no camping fee. Dump station available at North Pole Plaza. ▲

Richardson Highway Log
(continued)

V 350.2 (563.6 km) **F 13.8** (22.2 km) Peridot Street.

V 350.6 (564.2 km) **F 13.4** (21.6 km) *CAUTION: Highway crosses Alaska Railroad tracks.*

V 351 (564.9 km) **F 13** (20.9 km) Twelvemile Village exit to south; airport

V 356.2 (573.2 km) **F 7.8** (12.6 km) **Road's End RV Park.** See display ad this section. ▲

V 357.1 (574.7 km) **F 6.9** (11.1 km) Badger Road exit; access to Riverview RV Park and other businesses. Badger Road also junctions with Nordale Road to Chena Hot Springs Road and access to the Chena River.

V 357.6 (575.5 km) **F 6.4** (10.3 km) Weigh stations both sides of highway.

V 358.6 (577.1 km) **F 5.4** (8.7 km) Entrance to U.S. Army Fort Wainwright.

V 364 (585.8 km) **F 0 FAIRBANKS.** College Road exit to University of Alaska, Bentley Mall and city center (turn left). For details see FAIRBANKS section.

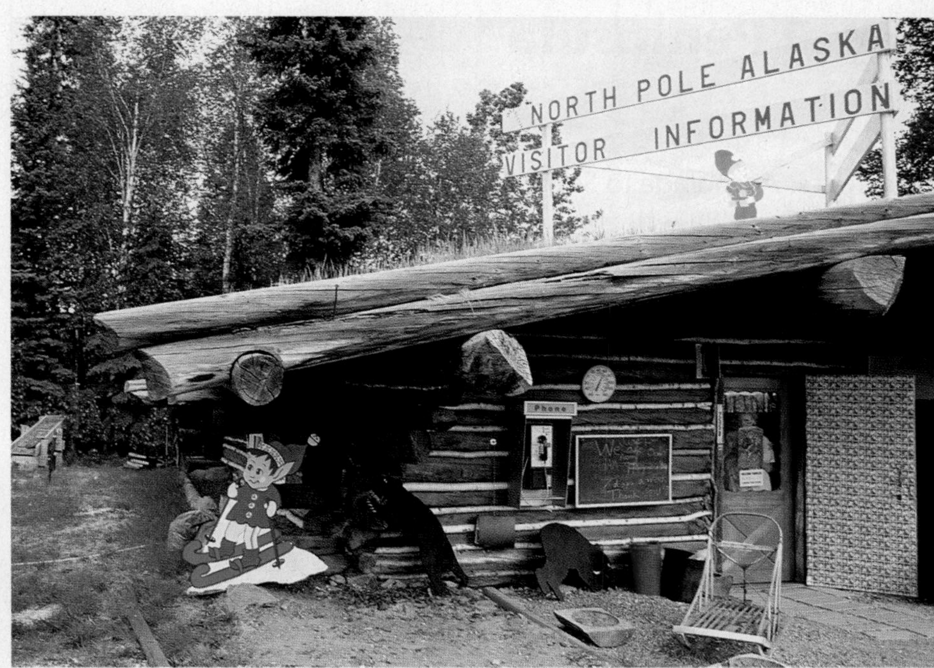

North Pole's visitor information cabin. (© Ralph & Leonor Barrett, Four Corners Imaging)

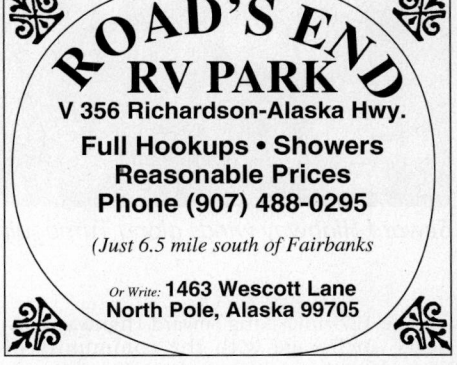

Watch for moose along the Richardson Highway. There is a particularly high incidence of moose–vehicle collisions between North Pole and Fairbanks.

Kenai Peninsula

SEWARD HIGHWAY ① ⑨

Connects: Anchorage to Seward, AK **Length:** 127 miles
Road Surface: Paved **Season:** Open all year
Highest Summit: Turnagain Pass 988 feet
Major Attractions: Mount Alyeska; Portage Glacier; Kenai Fjords National Park

	Alyeska	Anchorage	Hope	Portage Glacier	Seward
Alyeska		42	56	22	95
Anchorage	42		88	54	127
Hope	56	88		46	75
Portage Glacier	22	54	46		85
Seward	95	127	75	85	

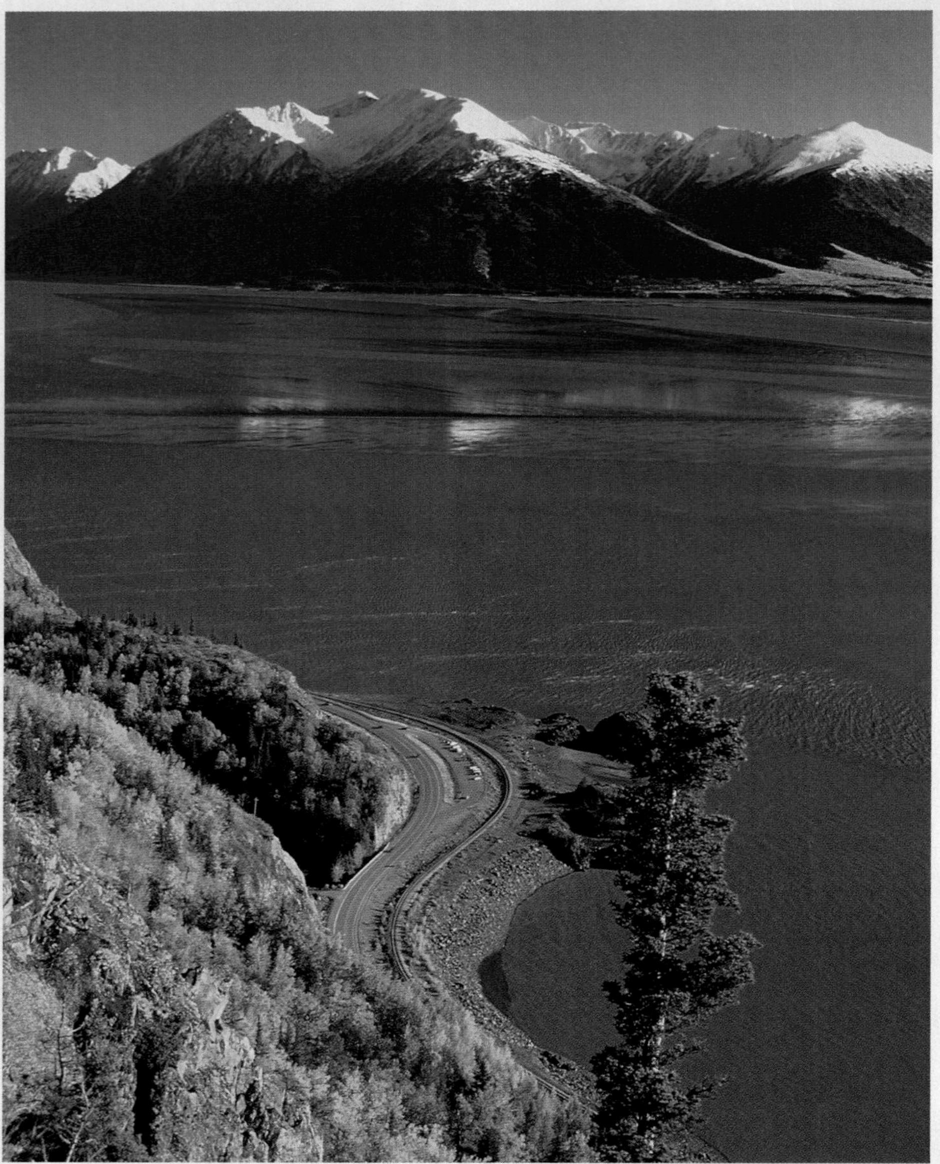

Seward Highway winds along Turnagain Arm south from Anchorage. (© Mike Jones)

The 127-mile--long Seward Highway connects Anchorage with the community of Seward on the east coast of the Kenai Peninsula. It has been called one of the most scenic highways in the country and has been designated a National Forest Scenic Byway. Leaving Anchorage, the Seward Highway follows the north shore of Turnagain Arm through Chugach State Park and Chugach National Forest, permitting a panoramic view of the south shore and the Kenai Mountains.

The Seward Highway provides access to Girdwood and Alyeska ski resort; the Hope Highway; the new Whittier cutoff and Portage Glacier; and Kenai Fjords National Park. The Seward Highway also junctions with the other major Kenai Peninsula route, the Sterling Highway (see STERLING HIGHWAY section).

The first 9 miles of the New Seward Highway are a major Anchorage thoroughfare (4-lane divided freeway), connecting South Anchorage with downtown. South of Anchorage, the Seward Highway is a paved, 2-lane highway with passing lanes. There are no gas stations on the Seward Highway between **Milepost S 90** (Girdwood turnoff) and **Milepost S 6.6**, just outside Seward.

The highway is open all year. Some sections of the highway are subject to avalanches in winter. Check locally for winter road conditions and avalanche road closures.

Bike trails along the Seward Highway include a 3-mile trail between Indian and Bird; a 6-mile trail between Girdwood and Bird Point; and an 8-mile bike trail (the Sixmile Trail) between the Hope Highway junction and the Johnson Pass Trailhead.

There are also a number of trailheads along the Seward Highway for both Chugach State Park and USFS hiking trails.

CAUTION: The Seward Highway from Anchorage to just past Girdwood statistically has one of the highest number of traffic accidents in the state. DRIVE CAREFULLY! Motorists must drive with headlights on at all times.

Delay of 5 vehicles or more is illegal; use slow vehicle turnouts. Pass with care!

Emergency medical services: Phone 911 or use CB channels 9, 11 or 19. Cellular phone service is available as far south as Girdwood and is also available in Seward. Emergency call boxes are located at Turnagain Pass (**Milepost S 68.5**), Hope Highway junction (**S 56.3**), Summit Lake Lodge (**S 45.8**) and at the Sterling Highway junction.

Seward Highway Log

Distance from Seward (S) is followed by distance from Anchorage (A).
Physical mileposts show distance from Seward. Many mileposts were missing in summer 1999.

ALASKA ROUTE 1

S 127 (204.4 km) **A 0** Gambell Street and 10th Avenue in Anchorage. The New Seward Highway (Gambell Street southbound, Ingra northbound)) connects with the Glenn Highway in Anchorage via 5th Avenue (westbound) and 6th Avenue (eastbound).

SEWARD HIGHWAY *Anchorage, AK, to Seward, AK*

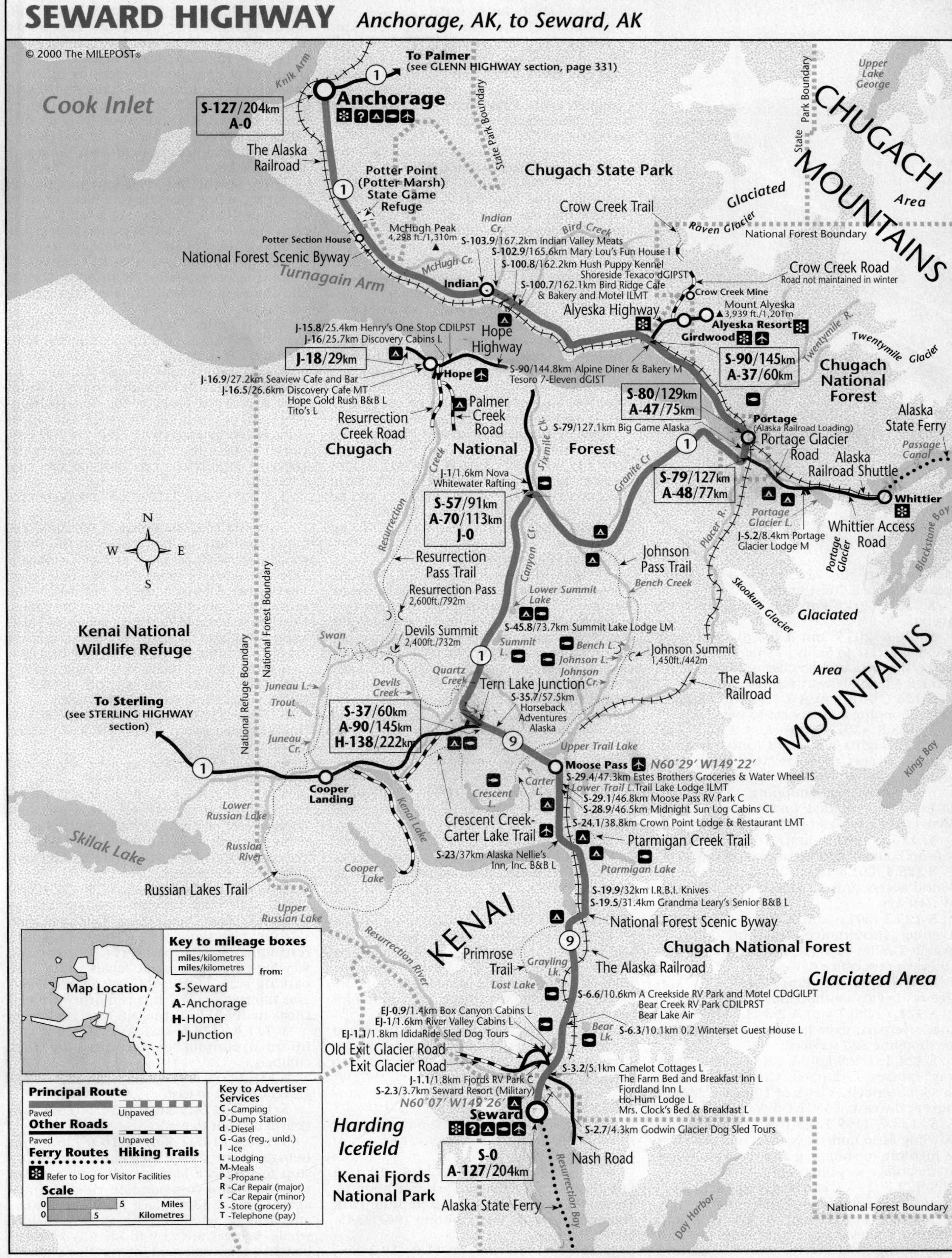
© 2000 The MILEPOST®
To Palmer
(see GLENN HIGHWAY section, page 331)
Cook Inlet
Anchorage
S-127/204km
A-0
The Alaska Railroad
Potter Point (Potter Marsh) State Game Refuge
Chugach State Park
Potter Section House
McHugh Peak 4,298 ft./1,310m
National Forest Scenic Byway
Turnagain Arm
Indian
S-103.9/167.2km Indian Valley Meats
S-102.9/165.6km Mary Lou's Fun House I
S-100.8/162.2km Hush Puppy Kennel
Shoreside Texaco dGIPST
S-100.7/162.1km Bird Ridge Cafe & Bakery and Motel ILMT
Crow Creek Trail
Crow Creek Road
Road not maintained in winter
Crow Creek Mine
Mount Alyeska 3,939 ft./1,201m
Alyeska Highway
Alyeska Resort
Girdwood
National Forest Boundary
CHUGACH MOUNTAINS
Glaciated Area
Raven Glacier
Upper Lake George
J-15.8/25.4km Henry's One Stop CDILPST
J-16/25.7km Discovery Cabins L
Hope Highway
J-18/29km
Hope
J-16.9/27.2km Seaview Cafe and Bar
J-16.5/26.6km Discovery Cafe MT
Hope Gold Rush B&B L
Tito's L
S-90/144.8km Alpine Diner & Bakery M
Tesoro 7-Eleven dGIST
S-90/145km
A-37/60km
Twentymile Glacier
Chugach National Forest
S-80/129km
A-47/75km
Portage
(Alaska Railroad Loading)
Portage Glacier Road
Alaska Railroad Shuttle
Alaska State Ferry
Passage Canal
Whittier
S-79/127.1km Big Game Alaska
Resurrection Creek Road
Palmer Creek Road
Chugach National Forest
J-1/1.6km Nova Whitewater Rafting
S-57/91km
A-70/113km
J-0
S-79/127km
A-48/77km
Portage Glacier L.
J-5.2/8.4km Portage Glacier Lodge M
Whittier Access Road
Resurrection Pass Trail
Resurrection Pass 2,600ft./792m
Johnson Pass Trail
Bench Creek
Lower Summit Lake
S-45.8/73.7km Summit Lake Lodge LM
Devils Summit 2,400ft./732m
Johnson Summit 1,450ft./442m
Kenai National Wildlife Refuge
Glaciated Area
MOUNTAINS
The Alaska Railroad
Tern Lake Junction
S-35.7/57.5km Horseback Adventures Alaska
To Sterling
(see STERLING HIGHWAY section)
S-37/60km
A-90/145km
H-138/222km
Upper Trail Lake
Moose Pass N60°29' W149°22'
S-29.4/47.3km Estes Brothers Groceries & Water Wheel IS
Lower Trail L. Trail Lake Lodge ILMT
S-29.1/46.8km Moose Pass RV Park C
S-28.9/46.5km Midnight Sun Log Cabins CL
S-24.1/38.8km Crown Point Lodge & Restaurant LMT
Cooper Landing
Crescent Creek-Carter Lake Trail
Ptarmigan Creek Trail
Ptarmigan Lake
S-23/37km Alaska Nellie's Inn, Inc. B&B L
Skilak Lake
Russian Lakes Trail
S-19.9/32km I.R.B.I. Knives
S-19.5/31.4km Grandma Leary's Senior B&B L
National Forest Scenic Byway
KENAI
Chugach National Forest
Primrose Trail
The Alaska Railroad
Glaciated Area
S-6.6/10.6km A Creekside RV Park and Motel CDdGILPT
Bear Creek RV Park CDILPRST
Bear Lake Air
EJ-0.9/1.4km Box Canyon Cabins L
EJ-1/1.6km River Valley Cabins L
EJ-1.1/1.8km IdidaRide Sled Dog Tours
S-6.3/10.1km 0.2 Winterset Guest House L
Old Exit Glacier Road
Exit Glacier Road
J-1.1/1.8km Fjords RV Park C
S-2.3/3.7km Seward Resort (Military)
S-3.2/5.1km Camelot Cottages L
The Farm Bed and Breakfast Inn L
Fjordland Inn L
Ho-Hum Lodge L
Mrs. Clock's Bed & Breakfast L
N60°07' W149°26'
Seward
S-2.7/4.3km Godwin Glacier Dog Sled Tours
Harding Icefield
Kenai Fjords National Park
S-0
A-127/204km
Nash Road
Alaska State Ferry
Resurrection Bay
National Forest Boundary
Key to mileage boxes
miles/kilometres
miles/kilometres
from:
S-Seward
A-Anchorage
H-Homer
J-Junction
Map Location
Principal Route
Paved
Unpaved
Other Roads
Paved
Unpaved
Ferry Routes
Hiking Trails
Refer to Log for Visitor Facilities
Scale
Miles
Kilometres
Key to Advertiser Services
C -Camping
D -Dump Station
d -Diesel
G -Gas (reg., unld.)
I -Ice
L -Lodging
M -Meals
P -Propane
R -Car Repair (major)
r -Car Repair (minor)
S -Store (grocery)
T -Telephone (pay)

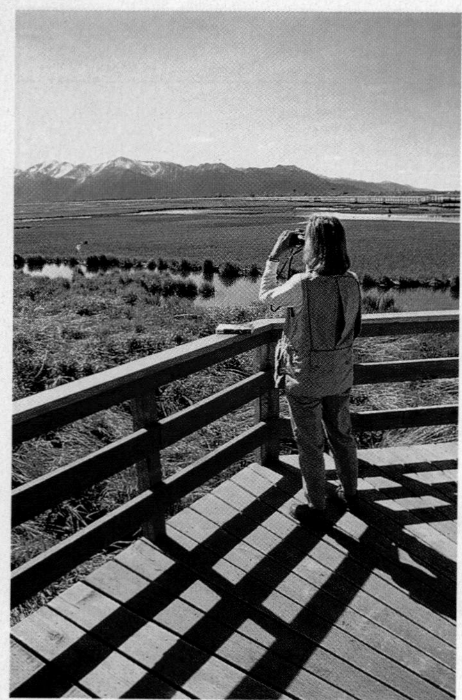

Bird watching at Potter Marsh. Exit at Milepost S 117.4 for Potter Point.

(© Lee Foster)

(See map in the ANCHORAGE section.) Follow Gambell Street south.

S 126.7 (203.9 km) **A 0.3** (0.5 km) 15th Avenue.

S 126.6 (203.7 km) **A 0.4** (0.6 km) 16th Avenue; access to Sullivan sports arena, Ben Boeke ice rinks and baseball stadium. Begin divided 4-lane highway southbound.

S 126 (202.8 km) **A 1** (1.6 km) Fireweed Lane. Shopping and services to west.

S 125.8 (202.4 km) **A 1.2** (1.9 km) Northern Lights Boulevard (one-way westbound). Access to **Sears Mall** from New Seward Highway. This was the first shopping mall in Anchorage. Shopping, services and 24-hour supermarket on Northern Lights Blvd. Fred Meyers east side of highway.

S 125.7 (202.3 km) **A 1.3** (2.1 km) Benson Boulevard (one-way eastbound).

S 125.4 (201.8 km) **A 1.6** (2.6 km) Southbound access only to Old Seward Highway to 36th Ave..

S 125.3 (201.6 km) **A 1.7** (2.7 km) 36th Avenue; **Providence Hospital** approximately 2 miles east. Z.J. Loussac library and Midtown post office to west.

S 125.2 (201.5 km) **A 1.8** (2.9 km) Freeway begins southbound.

S 124.7 (200.7 km) **A 2.3** (3.7 km) Tudor Road overpass; exits both sides of highway for shopping and services.

S 124.2 (199.8 km) **A 2.8** (4.5 km) Highway crosses Campbell Creek; Campbell Creek Greenbelt. Views of Chugach Mountains to the east. *CAUTION: Watch for moose.*

S 123.7 (199.1 km) **A 3.3** (5.3 km) Dowling Road underpass; exits on both sides of highway to shopping and services. Access to Anchorage recycling center to west.

S 122.7 (197.5 km) **A 4.3** (6.9 km) 76th Avenue exit, southbound traffic only.

S 122.2 (196.7 km) **A 4.8** (7.7 km) Dimond Boulevard overpass; exits on both sides of highway. Access west to **Dimond Mall**, gas stations, fast-food and major shopping area. Gas station to east.

S 120.8 (194.4 km) **A 6.2** (10 km) O'Malley Road underpass; exits on both sides of highway. Turn east on O'Malley Road and drive 2 miles to reach the **Alaska Zoo**. Continue east on O'Malley for **Chugach State Park** Upper Hillside hiking trails (follow signs), which include the popular Flattop trail.

Turn west for access to Minnesota Drive to **Anchorage International Airport**.

S 119.7 (192.6 km) **A 7.3** (11.7 km) Huffman Road underpass; exits on both sides of highway. Exit west for gas station, 24-hour supermarket and other services. Exit east for South Anchorage subdivisions.

S 118.5 (190.7 km) **A 8.5** (13.7 km) De Armoun Road overpass, exits both sides of highway.

S 117.8 (189.6 km) **A 9.2** (14.8 km) Overpass: Exits both sides of highway for Old Seward Highway (west); access to Rabbit Creek Road (east) to South Anchorage subdivisions. The picturesque Chapel by the Sea overlooks Turnagain Arm. The church is often photographed because of its unique setting and its display of flowers.

View of Turnagain Arm and Mount Spurr southbound.

S 117.4 (188.9 km) **A 9.6** (15.4 km) Turnoff to west for **Rabbit Creek Rifle Range** (ADF&G); open to the public Feb.–Nov. (closed Dec.–Jan.). Phone (907) 566-0130 for hours and fees. Covered firing positions on handgun and rifle ranges. Shotgun range (shot shells only).

Turnoff to east at Boardwalk Wildlife Viewing exit for **Potter Point State Game Refuge**. This is a very popular spot for bird watching. From the parking lot, an extensive boardwalk crosses Potter Marsh, a refuge and nesting area for waterfowl. The marsh was created when railroad construction dammed a small creek in the area. Today, the marsh is visited by arctic terns, Canada geese, trumpeter swans, many species of ducks and other water birds. Bring binoculars.

S 117.3 (188.8 km) **A 9.7** (15.6 km) *CAUTION: Highway narrows to 2 lanes southbound. Pass with care!*

S 117.2 (188.6 km) **A 9.8** (15.8 km) Small paved turnout east side of road at end of boardwalk.

S 116.1 (186.8 km) **A 10.9** (17.5 km) Paved double-ended turnout to east. Highway parallels Alaska Railroad southbound to **Milepost S 90.8.**

S 115.4 (185.7 km) **A 11.6** (18.7 km) **Junction** with Old Seward Highway; access to Potter Valley Road east to subdivision. Old Johnson trail begins 0.5 mile up Potter Valley Road; parking at trailhead. Only the first 10 miles of this state park trail are cleared. Moderate to difficult hike; watch for bears.

The natural gas pipeline from the Kenai Peninsula emerges from beneath Turnagain Arm here and follows the roadway to Anchorage.

WARNING: When the tide is out, the sand in Turnagain Arm might look inviting. DO NOT go out on it. Some of it is quicksand. You could become trapped in the mud and not be rescued before the tide comes in.

S 115.2 (185.4 km) **A 11.8** (19 km) Entering Chugach State Park southbound. **Potter Section House, Chugach State Park Headquarters** to west; phone (907) 345-5014).

S 115.1 (185.2 km) **A 11.9** (19.2 km) Turnoff to east for **Potter Creek Viewpoint and Trail** (Chugach State Park). Small parking area overlooking marsh with interpretive signs about wetlands and the railroad's role in creating these accidental marshes. Also an interpretive sign about the feeding habits of moose, who eat in marshes like these as well as in the backyards of Anchorage residents. Moose can eat the equivalent in twigs of a 50-lb. sack of dog food a day. Moose munch twigs and strip bark from willow, birch and aspen trees.

Drive up the hill via 2-lane paved road for large parking area, viewing platform with telescopes, interpretive signs and hiking trails. The 0.4-mile nature trail examines the natural history of the surrounding forest, a blending of 2 climates: the continental climate (the boreal forest of Interior Alaska) and the wetter coastal climate (Sitka spruce, hemlock).

This is Potter Creek Trailhead to Turnagain Arm trail, which connects with McHugh Creek Picnic Area (3.3 miles), Rainbow (7.5 miles) and Windy Corner (9.4 miles); see trail information signs. **Turnagain Arm Trail** parallels the Seward Highway and offers good views of Turnagain Arm. Rated as easy, with 250- to 700-foot elevation gains from the parking areas to the generally level trail on the hillside above he 4 trailheads.

S 115 (185 km) **A 12** (19.3 km) Watch for rockfalls.

From here to **Milepost S 90** there are many turnouts on both sides of the highway, some with scenic views of Turnagain Arm. An easterly extension of Cook Inlet, **Turnagain Arm** was called Return by the Russians. Captain Cook, seeking the fabled Northwest Passage in 1778, called it Turnagain River, and Captain Vancouver, doing a more thorough job of surveying in 1794, gave it the present name of Turnagain Arm.

S 114.7 (184.6 km) **A 12.3** (19.8 km) Weigh station and pay phone to east.

S 114.5 (184.3 km) **A 12.5** (20.1 km) Double-ended gravel turnout to east (posted no camping).

S 113.3 (182.3 km) **A 13.7** (22.1 km) Slow vehicle turnout southbound.

S 113.1 (182 km) **A 13.9** (22.4 km) Informal gravel turnout to east at McHugh boulder area. Watch for rock climbers practicing on rock walls alongside the highway. The cliffs are part of the base of McHugh Peak (elev. 4,298 feet).

S 111.9 (180.1 km) **A 15.1** (24.3 km) Paved side road to east goes up hill to **McHugh Creek Picnic Area.** This state wayside on the flank of McHugh Peak has restrooms, paved pathways, boardwalks, viewing platforms, picnic tables and a large parking area. McHugh Creek Scenic Overlook offers views of Turnagain Arm. McHugh Creek trailhead to Turnagain Arm Trail. ♿

S 111.6 (179.6 km) **A 15.4** (24.8 km) Informal turnout to east used by rock climbers.

S 111.2 (179 km) **A 15.8** (25.4 km) Rough gravel turnout to east.

S 110.9 (178.5 km) **A 16.1** (25.9 km) Gravel turnout to east.

S 110.4 (177.7 km) **A 16.6** (26.7 km) **Beluga Point** scenic viewpoint and photo stop to west is a large paved double-ended turnout with a commanding view of Turnagain Arm. A good place to see bore tides and beluga whales. (The only all-white whale, belugas are easy to identify.) Tables, benches, telescopes and interpretive signs on orcas, bore tides, mountain goats, Captain Cook, etc.

Turnagain Arm is known for having one of the world's remarkably high tides, with a diurnal range of more than 33 feet. A bore tide is an abrupt rise of tidal water just after low tide, moving rapidly landward, formed by a flood tide surging into a constricted inlet such as Turnagain Arm. This foaming wall of water may reach a height of 6 feet and is very dangerous to small craft. To see a bore tide, check the Anchorage-area tide tables for low tide, then add approximately 2 hours and 15 minutes to the Anchorage low tide for the bore to reach points between 32 miles and 37 miles south of Anchorage on the Seward Highway. Visitors should watch for bore tides from Beluga Point south to Girdwood.

WARNING: Do not go out on the mud flats at low tide. The glacial silt and water can create a dangerous quicksand.

S 109.9 (176.9 km) **A 17.1** (27.5 km) Slow vehicle turnout southbound.

S 109.2 (175.7 km) **A 17.8** (28.6 km) Paved turnout to west.

S 109 (175.4 km) **A 18** (29 km) Gravel turnout to east.

S 108.7 (174.9 km) **A 18.3** (29.5 km) Paved double-ended viewpoint to west.

S 108.4 (174.4 km) **A 18.6** (29.9 km) Rainbow Trailhead to Turnagain Arm Trail east side of highway.

S 108.3 (174.3 km) **A 18.7** (30.1 km) Trailhead parking to west.

S 108.1 (174 km) **A 18.9** (30.4 km) Slow vehicle turnout southbound.

S 107.9 (173.6 km) **A 19.1** (30.7 km) Turnout to west.

S 107.3 (172.7 km) **A 19.7** (31.7 km) Rough gravel turnout to east is used by rock climbers practicing on the cliffs here.

S 106.9 (172 km) **A 20.1** (32.3 km) Scenic viewpoint to west; double-ended paved turnout. Watch for Dall sheep near road. *NOTE: DO NOT FEED WILDLIFE.*

S 106.7 (171.7 km) **A 20.3** (32.7 km) Windy Corner trailhead to Turnagain Arm Trail east side of highway.

S 106.6 (171.5 km) **A 20.4** (32.8 km) Trailhead parking area to west.

S 106.2 (170.9 km) **A 20.8** (33.5 km) Slow vehicle turnout southbound.

S 105.9 (170.4 km) **A 21.1** (34 km) Slow vehicle turnout southbound.

S 105.7 (170.1 km) **A 21.3** (34.3 km) Falls Creek trailhead and parking east side of highway. Moderate 1.5-mile hike along creek.

S 104.9 (168.8 km) **A 22.1** (35.6 km) Single-vehicle turnout to east under rock overhang by small waterfall.

S 104.4 (168 km) **A 22.6** (36.4 km) Slow vehicle turnout northbound.

S 104.3 (167.8 km) **A 22.7** (36.5 km) Slow vehicle turnout southbound.

S 104 (167.4 km) **A 23** (37 km) Indian Valley Mine National Historic Site.

Silver salmon fishing at Bird Creek, Milepost S 101.5. (© Tom Culkin)

S 103.9 (167.2 km) **A 23.1** (37.2 km) Indian Road to Indian Valley Meats.

Indian Valley Meats. Reindeer sausage and much more from this federally inspected processor of exotic game and fish. Fish boxes ready for shipping, gift packs with game jerky, smoked salmon and much more. Newly expanded retail area in 1999. Great buys! In business 23 years. Please stop in, meet our pet reindeer and tour the stunning grounds, featuring flowers, rock walls, B&B, log conference hall and trophy animal mounts. Just 1/2 mile up Indian Road. See display ad. [ADVERTISEMENT]

S 103.6 (166.7 km) **A 23.4** (37.7 km) **INDIAN.** Indian House motel, restaurant, gift shop (closed in 1999; current status unknown). Begin 3-mile-long Indian to Bird bike trail south to Bird Creek campground.

S 103.1 (165.9 km) **A 23.9** (38.5 km) Bore Tide Road, also called Ocean View Road. Access to Indian Valley trailhead (1.4 miles), a 6-mile moderately steep hike to Indian Pass. Turnagain House restaurant.

S 103 (165.8 km) **A 24** (38.6 km) Bridge over Indian Creek; rest area to west at south end of bridge. Bar and liquor store to east. Pay phone.

Mary Lou's Fun House. See display ad this section.

Indian Creek is heavily fished for pink salmon, sea-run Dolly Varden, few coho (silver) salmon and rainbow, June to September; pink salmon run from latter part of July to mid-August in even-numbered years.

S 102.1 (164.3 km) **A 24.9** (40.1 km) Bird Ridge trailhead and parking east side of highway. This steep 1.5-mile hike (moderate dificulty) is the first snow-free spring hike in Chugach State Park, according to rangers. Hike offers good views of Turnagain Arm.

S 101.5 (163.3 km) **A 25.5** (41 km) Bridge over **Bird Creek**; parking. This is a very popular fishing spot and it is *very* busy during salmon runs. Bird Creek has a tremendous silver salmon run in summer. Check current regulations for daily bag and possession limits and also for king salmon closures.

CAUTION: Watch for pedestrians next mile southbound. Anglers are urged not to trespass on private property or park illegally along the highway. Use Bird Ridge trailhead parking to north, or Bird Creek parking to south.

S 101.2 (162.9 km) **A 25.8** (41.5 km) Bird

Creek fishing access to east; campground to west. **Bird Creek State Recreation Site** has 28 campsites, firepits, pay phone, covered picnic tables, toilets and water. Firewood is sometimes available. Camping fee $10/night or resident pass. A pleasant campground densely wooded but cleared along the high banks of Turnagain Arm. Great spot for sunbathing. This campground is full most weekends in the summer. Paved 3-mile Indian to Bird bike trail goes through campground. ▲

WARNING: Do not go out on the mud flats at low tide. The glacial silt and water can create a dangerous quicksand.

S 100.8 (162.2 km) **A 26.2** (42.2 km) Gas station with diesel and grocery to east. Sled dog rides at kennel.

Shoreside Texaco. See display ad this section.

S 100.7 (162.1 km) **A 26.3** (42.3 km) The 16-foot fibreglass eagle sculpture in front of Bird Ridge Cafe & Bakery and Motel was made by the late Bob James of Whiskey Gulch taxidermy in Anchor Point.

Bird Ridge Cafe & Bakery and Motel. See display ad this section.

S 99.8 (160.6 km) **A 27.2** (43.8 km) Paved turnout to west. Southbound traffic entering avalanche area. "Avalanche alley" is a 9-mile corridor from here south to the Girdwood turnoff that is prone to avalanches.

S 99.4 (160 km) **A 27.6** (44.4 km) Large turnout to west with view across Bird Flats on Turnagain Arm to the cut in the mountains where Sixmile Creek drains into the arm; the old mining settlement of Sunrise was located here. The town of Hope is to the southwest. The peak visible across Turnagain Arm between here and Girdwood is Mount Alpenglow in the Kenai mountain range. Avalanche gates.

Watch for Dall sheep along the Seward Highway. (© Tom Bol)

S 99.2 (159.6 km) **A 27.8** (44.7 km) Avalanche gun emplacement (motorists will notice several of these along the highway).

The guns fire 105mm shells at Penguin Ridge above the highway south from Bird Hill to knock down potential slides and stabilize the slopes in winter.

S 96.7 (155.6 km) **A 30.3** (48.8 km) Improved highway begins southbound. The new "Bird to Gird" segment of the Seward Highway was completed in 1998, replacing the narrow, winding road over Bird Hill. The approximately 7 miles of new alignment lie on the water side of the railroad tracks along the shore of Turnagain Arm. The old Bird Hill road is now part of the Girdwood to Bird Point bike trail.

S 96.5 (155.3 km) **A 30.5** (49.1 km) Southbound-only turnoff follows old alignment to **Bird Point Scenic Overlook**; large paved parking area overlooking Turnagain Arm. Planned access (summer 2000) for Bird Point to Girdwood Trail. This 6-mile bike trail goes over Bird Hill on the old Seward Highway alignment. The trail has information displays, viewpoints and telescopes.

S 95.7 (154 km) **A 31.3** (50.4 km) Passing lane begins southbound.

S 95.3 (153.4 km) **A 31.7** (51 km) Turnout No. 5; large paved parking area to west overlooking Turnagain Arm.

S 95.2 (153.2 km) **A 31.8** (51.2 km) Watch for waterfalls cascading down the huge rock cuts blasted out of the mountainside during construction of this new stretch of highway.

S 93.7 (150.8 km) **A 33.3** (53.6 km) End passing lane southbound.

S 93.3 (150.1 km) **A 33.7** (54.2 km) Turnout No. 3; large paved parking area to west overlooking Turnagain Arm.

S 92.5 (148.9 km) **A 34.5** (55.5 km) Turnout No. 2; large paved parking area to west overlooking Turnagain Arm.

S 92.3 (148.5 km) **A 34.7** (55.8 km) Turnout No. 1A; large paved parking area to east.

S 92.1 (148.2 km) **A 34.9** (56.2 km) Slow vehicle turnout to east.

S 91.5 (147.3 km) **A 35.5** (57.1 km) Turnout No. 1; large paved parking area to west overlooking Turnagain Arm.

S 90.5 (145.6 km) **A 36.5** (58.7 km) Bridge crosses Tidewater Slough.

S 90.4 (145.5 km) **A 36.6** (58.9 km) Single-vehicle turnout to east. Leaving Chugach State Park southbound.

The 1964 Good Friday earthquake caused land to sink in the Turnagain Arm area, particularly apparent from here to **Milepost S 74.** As a result, many trees had their root systems invaded by salt water, as seen by the stands of dead spruce trees along here. Good

bird watching, including bald eagles, arctic terns and sandhill cranes.

S 90.2 (145.2 km) **A 36.8** (59.2 km) Girdwood highway maintenance station. End avalanche area southbound..

S 90 (144.8 km) **A 37** (59.5 km) **Girdwood Junction.** This intersection of the Seward Highway and Alyeska Highway is "old" Girdwood. After the 1964 earthquake, Girdwood moved up the access road 2.1 miles (see ALYESKA HIGHWAY log this section). Girdwood Station Mall here has a 24-hour Tesoro 2Go Mart gas station and Alpine Diner & Bakery (breakfast, lunch, dinner).

Tesoro 2Go Mart. See display ad this section.

Alpine Diner & Bakery. See display ad this section.

Junction with 3-mile Alyeska Highway to Crow Creek road and mine, Girdwood and Alyeska (pronounced al-ee-ES-ka) Recreation Area. Worth the drive! See ALYESKA HIGHWAY log beginning on page 502.

*NOTE: Next gas available southbound on the Seward Highway is at **Milepost S 6.6**; next gas available westbound on Sterling Highway is at **Milepost S 45** (Sunrise).*

S 89.8 (144.5 km) **A 37.2** (59.9 km) Glacier Creek bridge.

S 89.2 (143.5 km) **A 37.8** (60.8 km) Virgin Creek bridge. View of 3 glaciers to east.

S 86.1 (138.6 km) **A 40.9** (65.8 km) Parking area. Chugach National Forest boundary sign.

S 84.1 (135.3 km) **A 42.9** (69 km) Peterson Creek. View of Blueberry Mountain.

S 82.3 (132.4 km) **A 44.7** (71.9 km) Turnout to east.

S 81 (130.4 km) **A 46** (74 km) BLM observation platform with informative plaques on Twentymile River wetlands and wildlife. Watch for dip-netters in the spring fishing for hooligan (also known as eulachon or candlefish), a species of smelt. Road access east to Twentymile River.

Twentymile River, good hooligan fishing in May. These smelt are taken with long-handled dip nets. Pink, red and silver (coho) salmon 4 to 10 lbs., use attraction lures, best in August. Dolly Varden 4 to 10 lbs., eggs best, good all summer in clear-water tributaries.

S 80.7 (129.9 km) **A 46.3** (74.5 km) Bridge over Twentymile River, which flows out of the Twentymile Glacier and other glaciers through a long green valley at the edge of the highway. Twentymile Glacier can be seen at the end of the valley to the northeast. Twentymile River is a popular windsurfing area in summer. Gravel turnout west side of highway.

S 80.3 (129.2 km) **A 46.7** (75.2 km) First of 3 turnoffs southbound for the **Alaska Railroad Whittier Shuttle**. Turn here for the vehicle loading area if you have tickets. Check in at the blue and yellow trailer before getting in line.

The Portage–Whittier shuttle train carries passengers and vehicles from here to Whittier on Prince William Sound. See Railroads in the TRAVEL PLANNING section for details on train travel. See also WHITTIER ACCESS ROAD on page 507 this section for more on Whittier.

S 80.1 (128.9 km) **A 46.9** (75.5 km) **PORTAGE.** No facilities here. A few deteriorating old buildings and a rusting truck are visible on the west side of the highway among the dead trees killed by the invading salt water. The 1964 earthquake caused the land to drop between 6 and 12 feet along Turnagain Arm. High tides then flooded the area, forcing the estimated 50 to 100 residents of Portage to move.

Leaving Game Management Unit 14C, entering unit 7, southbound.

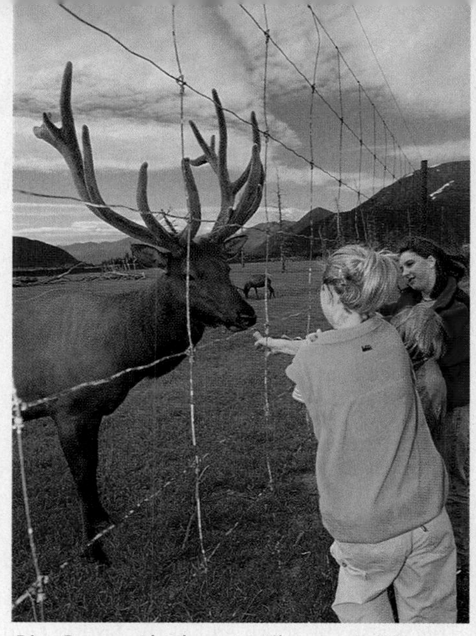

Big Game Alaska at Milepost S 79 features elk, moose, caribou, bison and other animals. (© Mike Jones)

S 80 (128.7 km) **A 47** (75.6 km) Second turnoff southbound to Alaska Railroad Whittier Shuttle. Turn here for the ticket office, parking and pay phone. Small visitor information center, gift shop and tour boat office.

S 79.8 (128.4 km) **A 47.2** (76 km) Third turnoff southbound, first turnoff northbound, to Alaska Railroad Whittier Shuttle; ticket office and parking.

S 79.4 (127.8 km) **A 47.6** (76.6 km) Portage Creek No. 2 bridge. Parking and interpretive sign to west at south end of bridge. This gray-colored creek carries the silt-laden glacial meltwater from Portage Glacier and Portage Lake to Turnagain Arm. Mud flats in Turnagain Arm are created by silt from the creek settling close to shore.

(Continues on page 505)

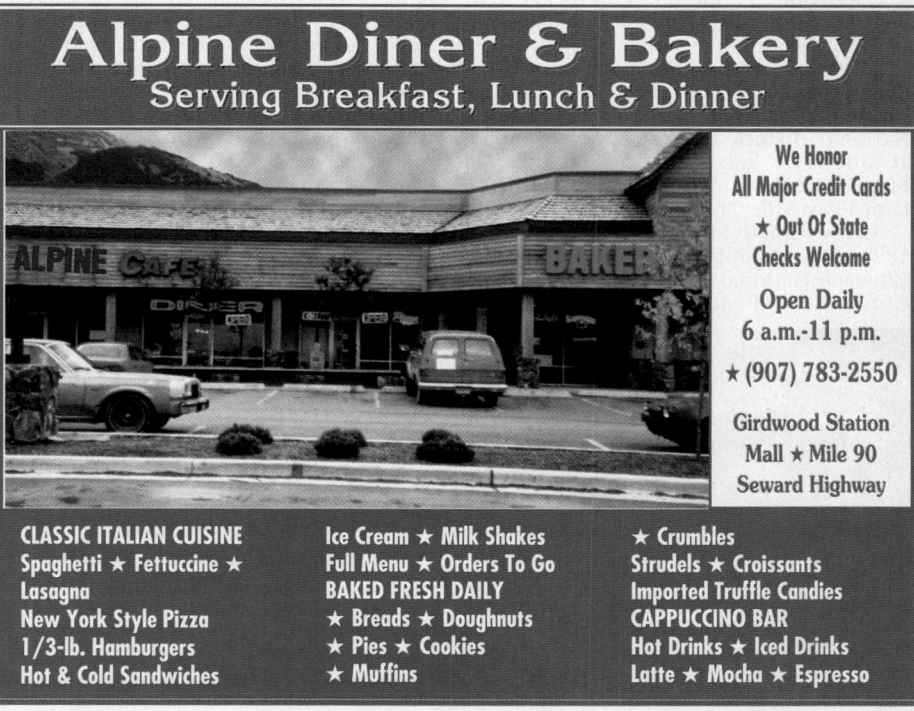

Alyeska Highway Log

The 3-mile Alyeska Highway provides access to Crow Creek Road, Girdwood, Mount Alyeska ski area and Alyeska Resort. There are many restaurants, gift shops and accommodations in the Girdwood/Alyeska area. Major attractions include the Alyeska Aerial Tramway and rainforest hiking trails. Well worth the drive.

There is also a bike trail along this highway. **Distance is measured from junction with Seward Highway (J).**

J 0 Junction with Seward Highway at **Milepost S 90.** Girdwood Station Mall: 24-hour convenience store and gas station, medical clinic with emergency services, restaurant and a bakery.

J 0.2 (0.3 km) Bridge over Alaska Railroad tracks.

Paved bike trail to Alyeska Resort begins. This is also the south end of the Bird to Gird bike trail from Bird Point at **Milepost S 96.5** on the Seward Highway.

J 0.4 (0.6 km) Forest Station Road. **Chugach National Forest Glacier Ranger District** office (P.O. Box 129, Girdwood, AK 99587; phone 907/783-3242). Open 7:30 A.M. to 5 P.M. weekdays in summer; closed holidays. Maps and information available here.

J 0.5 (0.8 km) **Alaska Candle Factory.** One-half mile off Seward Highway on Alyeska Highway. Home of handcrafted

candles made in the form of Alaska wild animals. Hand-dipped tapers and molded candles made daily. All candles have unique individual designs. Open 7 days a week, 10 A.M. to 6 P.M., in summer until 7 P.M. Visitors welcome. Phone (907) 783-2354. P.O. Box 786, Girdwood, AK 99587. [ADVERTISEMENT]

J 1.5 (2.4 km) Bike rentals.

J 1.9 (3.1 km) **Junction** with Crow Creek Road (1-lane dirt and gravel). The Carriage House B&B at Mile 0.2; **Crow Creek Mine National Historic Site** (description follows) at Mile 3.1/5 km; Crow Pass Trailhead at Mile 7/11.3. In winter, the road is not maintained past Mile 0.6.

Crow Creek Mine. Visit this historic 1898 mining camp located in the heart of Chugach National Forest. Drive 3 miles up Crow Creek Road (Old Iditarod trail).

Eight original buildings. Pan for gold. Visit our gift shop. Enjoy beautiful grounds, ponds, flowers. Animals and friendly people. Campground for tents and self-contained vehicles. Open May 15 to September 15, 9 A.M. to 6 P.M. daily. Phone (907) 278-8060 (messages). [ADVERTISEMENT] ▲

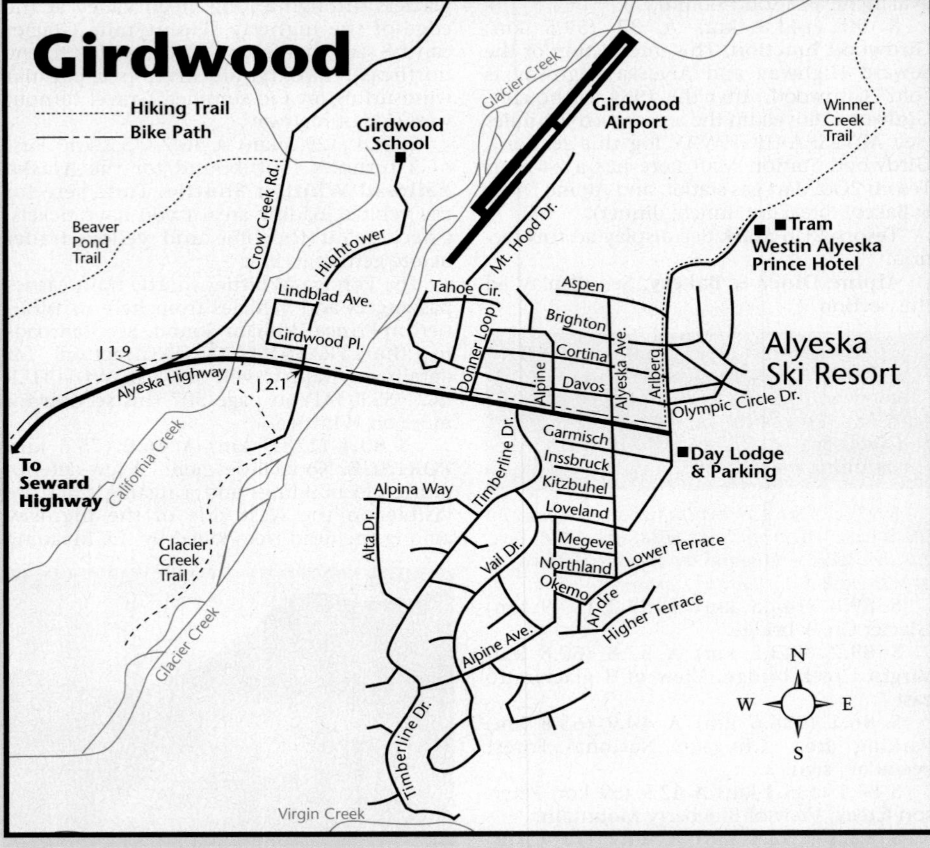

Crow Pass and Old Iditarod trailhead at Mile 7 Crow Creek Road. Crow Pass trail climbs steeply 3 miles to ruins of an old gold mine and a USFS public-use cabin at Crow Pass near Raven Glacier; hiking time approximately 2 1/2 hours. The Old Iditarod trail extends 22.5 miles north from Crow Pass down Raven Creek drainage to the Chugach State Park Visitor Center on Eagle River Road. All of the hiking trail, from Crow Creek Road trailhead to the state park visitor center, is part of the Iditarod National Historic Trail used in the early 1900s. Trail is usually free of snow by mid-June. Closed to motorized vehicles; horses prohibited during early spring due to soft trail conditions.

J 2 (3.2 km) California Creek bridge.

Girdwood

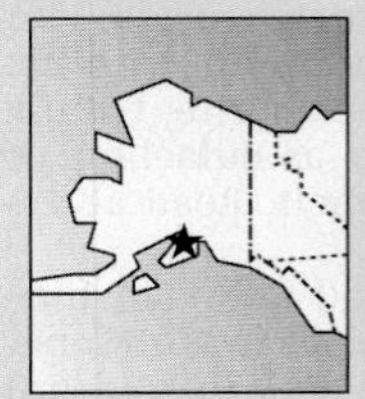

J 2.1 (3.4 km) At the junction of Alyeska Highway and Hightower Road. **Population:** 1,935. **Emergency Services: Alaska State Troopers, EMS** and **Fire Department,** phone 911 or (907) 783-2704 (message only) or (907) 269-5711.

The town was named after Col. James

GIRDWOOD / ALYESKA ADVERTISERS

A Cross Country Meadows B&B..........Timberline & Alta Dr.
Alaska Candle Factory......................Mile 0.5 Alyeska Hwy.
Alaskana Haus..................Ph. (907) 783-2481
Alpina Inn Bed & Breakfast.....................Ph. (907) 783-2482
Alpine Air Inc........................Girdwood Airport
Alyeska Accommodations.................................Mile 3 Alyeska Hwy.
Alyeska Resort..................Ph. (800) 880-3880
Bake Shop, The........Alyeska Resort/Boardwalk
Bud & Carol's B&B...........Ph. (907) 783-3182
Chair 5 Restaurant.......................Linblad Ave.
Crow Creek B&B...............Ph. (888) 783-2001
Crow Creek Mine....................Crow Creek Rd.
Girdwood Bed & Breakfast Assoc............Ph. (907) 783-2747
Girdwood Resort Assoc...........................See ad
Kobuk Valley Jade Co.........Ph. (907) 783-2764
Northern Composure.......Ph. (888) 854-0633

Girdwood, who established a mining operation near here in 1901. Today, Girdwood has a substantial year-round community and a flourishing seasonal population, thanks to its appeal as both a winter and summer resort destination.

Located here are a post office, restaurants, vacation rental offices, grocery store with gas, a rafting business, small shops and fire hall. Flightseeing services located at Girdwood airport.

Girdwood Community Center offers tennis courts, pay phone, Kinder Park daycare center and picnic area. This is site of the Girdwood **Forest Fair**, a midsummer (July) crafts fair.

Area hiking trails include Glacier Creek, Alyeska Basin, Iditarod, Beaver Pond and Winner Creek trails. The Winner Creek trail is a good one to experience Girdwood's rainforest. The trail starts near the Alyeska Aerial Tramway ticket office. Girdwood averages 67 inches of rainfall a year. Inquire at Ranger Station at **Milepost J 0.4** Alyeska Highway for more information on area hiking trails.

Chair Five Restaurant. Favorite of locals and travelers since 1983. This is a must stop fun place to dine and drink. Daily offerings include fresh Alaskan halibut and salmon, the famous tundra steak (reindeer and buffalo) or try the gourmet fresh dough pizza that gets rave reviews. One of Alaska's largest single malt scotch selections and over 60 microbrews round out the menu. House rules are strictly enforced: 1) Use the little fork for the salad and 2) No fist, gun or food fights allowed. Open daily 11 A.M.–midnight. AX/MC/Visa. Phone (907) 783-2500. www.chairfive.com. [ADVERTISEMENT]

Alyeska Highway Log

(continued)

J 2.3 (3.7 km) Glacier Creek bridge.

J 2.5 (4 km) Donner access to Girdwood airstrip (follow signs); flightseeing.

Private Aircraft: Girdwood airstrip; elev. 150 feet; length 2,100 feet; gravel; unattended.

Alpine Air Inc. Home of ZIP the wonder dog! Scenic flights in spacious, intercom-equipped wheel/ski planes and floatplanes into Prince William Sound, the Chugach Mountains and Mount McKinley area. Glacier and floatplane landings are our specialty. Guided and unguided fishing trips. Statewide charters available. Federally licensed and fully insured. Visitors welcome year-round to stop in at our hangar/office at

the Girdwood airport, last blue hangar on the airport road. Phone (907) 783-2360. Internet address: www.alaska.net/~alpinair; e-mail: alpinair@alaska.net. [ADVERTISEMENT]

J 2.6 (4.2 km) Timberline Drive. Access to bed and breakfasts.

A Cross Country Meadows B&B located in Alyeska Basin (1/2 mile down Timberline; turn right onto Alta Drive) caters to those who seek quiet, deluxe accommodations with a private bath/Jacuzzi and spectacular glacier and mountains views. Reservations phone (907) 783-3333 or write to P.O. Box 123, Girdwood, AK 99587. E-mail: XCountryBB@aol.com or www.AlaskaOne.com/crosscountry. [ADVERTISEMENT]

J 2.9 (4.7 km) Alyeska Highway ends at **junction** with Arlberg Avenue, road forks; Welcome to Alyeska Resort sign. Turn west for Alyeska day lodge (ski school, rentals). Turn east for Alyeska Prince Hotel and tram. Bike and walking path continues to hotel.

Alyeska Resort is Alaska's largest ski area and Alaska's premier year-round resort destination. Owned and operated by Seibu Alaska Inc. since 1980. Ski season is generally from mid-November through mid-April. Facilities include the 60-passenger aerial tramway (departs from Alyeska Prince Hotel), a high-speed detachable bubble quad, 2 fixed-grip quads, 3 double chair lifts and 2 pony tows. Night skiing available during holiday periods in December, and Friday through Saturday from January through March. Ski school, ski rental shop and sports shops are available. Phone (907) 754-7669 for snow conditions and mountain information. Other activities include heli and snowcat skiing, Nordic skiing, dog sledding, snowshoeing and snowmobiling.

J 3 (4.8 km) Olympic Circle; Kobuk Valley Jade shop, The Bake Shop and other businesses.

The Bake Shop at Alyeska Resort is a MUST stop for food and flower lovers alike! Turn off the Seward Highway onto Alyeska Highway. Follow the road until you come to the "T" at Alyeska Resort. Turn left onto Arlberg and take the first right onto Olympic Circle. Don't be confused by a sign for another bakery and coffee shop at the bottom of the road! Continue to drive to the very top of the gravel road, use the parking lot to your right and walk up to the front of the condo building and the boardwalk. Here you'll find the annual display of summer flowers such as dazzling begonias, giant ferns and many all-time favorites. Then step inside the Bake Shop to enjoy the heartwarming

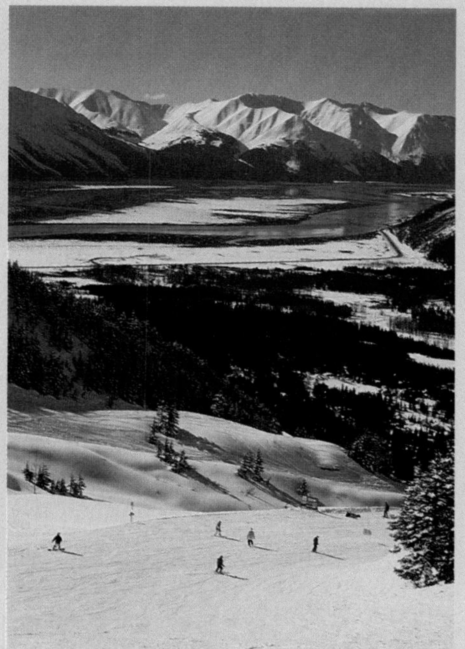

Alyeska in winter. The resort also offers summer views and activities.

(© Tom Bol)

Alyeska Highway Log *(continued)*

aroma of freshly baked breads and buns. The Bake Shop creates these with the original sourdough starter which was once the "prized" possession of a fortune-seeking gold miner in this valley over 80 years ago. Now look at the large menu board and you will find a variety of egg dishes and pancakes for breakfast. For lunch choose between a great selection of sandwiches made with sourdough buns; pizzas and homemade soups. Don't forget to leave room for our "famous" sweet rolls. Bring your breakfast or lunch outside for a garden picnic, enjoy the beauty of the flowers and the valley and remember to take some of our bread and handcrafted preserves for the road! [ADVERTISEMENT]

J 3.2 (5.1 km) Alyeska Field and Moose Meadow Park (Stumpy Faulkner Early Winter Trail).

J 3.9 (6.3 km) Entrance to Alyeska Prince Hotel; follow signs for parking and shuttle bus to hotel and tram.

J 4.1 (6.6 km) The Westin Alyeska Prince Hotel and Aerial Tramway Glacier Terminal; no parking. The 307-room deluxe chateau-style hotel has a cafe, Japanese steakhouse, 2 lounges, 2 retail shops and a fitness center with indoor swimming pool, sauna, whirlpool and exercise room.. For information phone (907) 754-1111 or (800) 880-3880; www.alyeskaresort.com.

Crowd enjoys the entertainment at Girdwood's Forest Fair. (© David Ranta, staff)

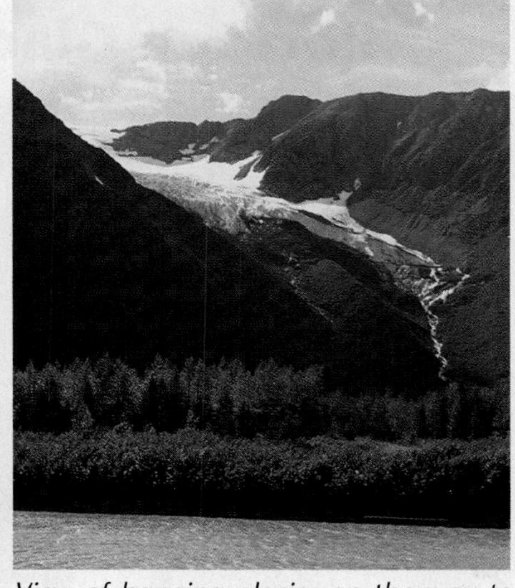

View of hanging glacier on the way to Whittier. (© David Ranta, staff)

The **Alyeska Aerial Tramway** is a state-of-the-art 60-passenger aerial tramway that transports skiers in winter and visitors in summer up to the top of Mount Alyeska (elev. 3,939 feet) and a mountaintop complex featuring fine dining at Seven Glaciers Restaurant and the Glacier Express cafeteria.

Winner Creek Trail (foot travel only) trailhead behind tram ticket office. Follow gravel path 1/4 mile for easy walk through rainforest. Continue on the Access Trail (easy 1.5 miles) to Winner Creek and trailhead junction with the Gorge Trail and the Upper Winner Creek Basin trail. Check bulletin board at trailhead for bear alerts.

Return to Milepost S 90 Seward Highway

(Continued from page 501)

S 79 (127.1 km) **A 48** (77.2 km) Portage Creek No. 1 bridge.

Turnoff to west for **Big Game Alaska**, a drive-through wildlife park and gift shop. The park features bison, caribou, Sitka black-tailed deer, elk, musk ox and moose. Big Game Alaska receives a number of orphaned wild animals to care for each year. Two of its best known orphans are Seymour and Mattie. Both moose have appeared in commercials and films. Mattie

Portage Glacier Road Log

View of Portage Lake from Begich, Boggs Visitor Center. (© Chuck Dell)

Distance is measured from junction with the Seward Highway (J).

J 0 Junction with Seward Highway at **Milepost S 78.9.**

CAUTION: Alaska Railroad tracks, rough crossing.

J 2.4 (3.8 km) Paved turnout. Explorer Glacier viewpoint on right.

J 3.1 (5 km) Bridge. Beaver dam visible from road.

J 3.7 (5.9 km) Black Bear USFS campground; 12 sites (2 will accommodate medium-sized trailers), toilets, water, firepits, dumpsters, tables, $10 fee. Pleasant wooded area. ▲

J 4.1 (6.6 km) Bridge over Williwaw Creek. USFS campground, south of road below Middle Glacier; 60 campsites, toilets, dumpsters, water, firepits, tables, $12 single, $16 double (reservations available, phone 1-877-444-NRRS). Beautiful campground. Campfire programs in the amphitheater; check bulletin board for schedule. Spawning red salmon and dog salmon can be viewed (from late July to mid-September) from Williwaw Creek observation deck near campground entrance. Self-guided Williwaw nature trail off the campground loop road goes through moose and beaver habitat. ▲

J 5.2 (8.4 km) Paved road forks at Portage Glacier Lodge (description follows); left fork leads to visitor center (see **Milepost J 5.5**). Take right fork 0.8 mile to parking lot; 1.2 miles to Byron Glacier overlook; and 1.5 miles to MV *Ptarmigan* sightseeing boat cruise dock and passenger waiting facility.

J 5.5 (8.8 km) **Begich, Boggs Visitor Center** at Portage Glacier and Portage Lake. Open daily in summer (9 A.M.–6 P.M.); weekends in winter (10 A.M.–4 P.M.). Phone the visitor center at (907) 783-2326 or the U.S. Forest Service district office at (907) 783-3242 for current schedule.

Forest Service naturalists are available to answer questions and provide information about Chugach National Forest resources. There are displays on glaciers and on the natural history of the area. The award-winning film *Voices from the Ice* is shown in the theater hourly. Schedules of hikes and programs led by naturalists are posted at the center. One of the most popular activities is the iceworm safari. (Often regarded as a hoax, iceworms actually exist; the small, black worms thrive at temperatures just above freezing.) A self-guided interpretive trail about glacial landforms begins just south of the visitor center.

Large paved parking area provides views of Portage Lake. There are several excellent spots in the area to observe salmon spawning (August and September) in Portage Creek and its tributaries.

Whittier access road branches off Portage Glacier Road. See WHITTIER ACCESS ROAD description opposite page.

Return to Milepost S 78.9 Seward Highway

is fond of bananas.

Big Game Alaska. See display ad this section.

S 78.9 (127 km) **A 48.1** (77.4 km)

Junction with Portage Glacier access road. Portage Glacier is one of Alaska's most popular attractions. Portage Glacier access road also connects with new Whittier Access Road. See PORTAGE GLACIER ROAD log this page.

S 78.7 (126.6 km) **A 48.3** (77.7 km) Large gravel turnout.

S 78.4 (126.1 km) **A 48.6** (78.2 km) **Placer River** bridge; parking and access at south end of bridge. The Placer River has good hooligan fishing in May. These smelt are taken with long-handled dip nets. Silver salmon may be taken in August and September.

Between Placer River and Ingram Creek, there is an excellent view on clear days of Skookum Glacier to the northeast. To the north across Turnagain Arm is Twentymile Glacier. Arctic terns and waterfowl are often seen in the slough here.

S 77.9 (125.4 km) **A 49.1** (79 km) Placer River overflow bridge. Paved turnout to west at south end of bridge.

S 77.4 (124.5 km) **A 49.6** (79.8 km) Distance marker southbound shows Seward 76 miles, Homer 171 miles.

S 77 (123.9 km) **A 50** (80.5 km) Boundary of Chugach National Forest.

S 75.5 (121.5 km) **A 51.5** (82.9 km) Paved double-ended Scenic Byway turnouts both sides of highway.

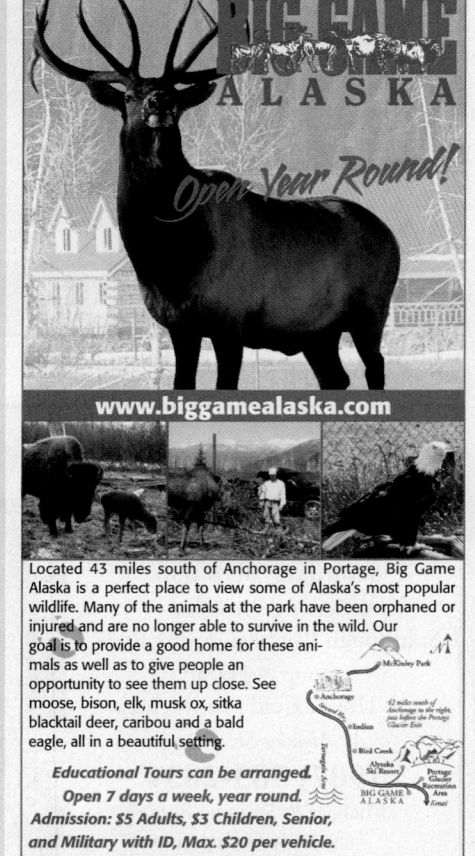

S 75.2 (121 km) **A 51.8** (83.4 km) Bridge over **Ingram Creek**; pink salmon fishing (even years).

S 75 (120.7 km) **A 52** (83.7 km) Paved turnout to west; Welcome to the Kenai Peninsula sign. *Highway begins ascent to Turnagain Pass southbound.*

S 74.9 (120.5 km) **A 52.1** (83.8 km) Passing lane begins southbound and extends 5.7 miles.

S 74.5 (119.9 km) **A 52.5** (84.5 km) Long paved double-ended turnout to east.

S 72.5 (116.7 km) **A 54.5** (87.7 km) Double-ended paved turnout to east.

S 71.5 (115.1 km) **A 55.5** (89.3 km) Long paved double-ended turnout to west.

S 71.2 (114.6 km) **A 55.8** (89.8 km) Double-ended paved turnout to west.

S 71 (114.3 km) **A 56** (90.1 km) Slow vehicle turnout for northbound traffic.

S 69.9 (112.5 km) **A 57.1** (91.9 km) Scenic viewpoint with double-ended parking area to west. The highway traverses an area of mountain meadows and parklike stands of spruce, hemlock, birch and aspen interlaced with glacier-fed streams. The many flowers seen in surrounding alpine meadows here include lupine, wild geranium, yellow and purple violets, mountain heliotrope, lousewort and paintbrush.

S 69.2 (111.4 km) **A 57.8** (93 km) Passing lane ends southbound.

S 69 (111 km) **A 58** (93.3 km) Slow vehicle turnout for northbound traffic.

S 68.9 (110.9 km) **A 58.1** (93.5 km) Divided highway begins southbound, ends northbound.

S 68.5 (110.2 km) **A 58.5** (94.1 km) **Turnagain Pass Recreation Area** (elev. 988 feet). Parking area, restrooms and dumpster (southbound lane). ***Emergency phone***. U-turn lane.

Turnagain Pass Recreation Area is a favorite winter recreation area for snowmobilers (west side of highway) and cross-country skiers (east side of highway). Snow depths here frequently exceed 12 feet.

S 68.1 (109.6 km) **A 58.9** (94.8 km) Parking area, restrooms and dumpster for northbound traffic. U-turn.

S 67.8 (109.1 km) **A 59.2** (95.3 km) Bridge over Lyon Creek.

S 67.6 (108.8 km) **A 59.4** (95.6 km) Divided highway ends southbound, begins northbound.

S 66.8 (107.5 km) **A 60.2** (96.9 km) Paved double-ended turnout to east.

S 65.5 (105.4 km) **A 61.5** (99 km) Bridge over Bertha Creek. Bertha Creek USFS campground; 12 sites, water, toilets, firepits, table, dumpsters and $10 fee.

S 65.4 (105.2 km) **A 61.6** (99.1 km) Parking area to west.

S 65.2 (104.9 km) **A 61.8** (99.4 km) Passing lane begins southbound.

S 64.8 (104.3 km) **A 62.2** (100.1 km) Bridge over Spokane Creek.

S 64.1 (103.1 km) **A 62.9** (101.2 km) Pete's Creek. Passing lane ends southbound.

S 63.7 (102.5 km) **A 63.3** (101.9 km) Johnson Pass (Chugach National Forest) north trailhead. This 23-mile-long trail is a good, fairly level family trail, which follows a portion of the Old Iditarod trail which went from Seward to Nome (see **Milepost S 32.6**). Johnson Pass trail leads to **Bench Lake,** which has arctic grayling, and **Johnson Lake,** which has rainbow trout. Both lakes are about halfway in on trail.

North end of Sixmile Trail, an 8-mile-long bike trail along Sixmile Creek's east fork

Whittier Access Road

Scheduled to open in June 2000, the Whittier access road is the culmination of the 3-year Whittier Access Project to improve the overland connection between the southcentral Alaska road network and the Prince William Sound port of Whittier. Prior to construction of this access road, Whittier was accessible only by train overland. The Alaska Railroad will continue to operate passenger service between the Seward Highway and Whittier, sharing the right-of-way with vehicle traffic.

The Whittier access road begins near the Begich, Boggs Visitor Center on Portage Glacier Road. It goes through a new 430-foot-long tunnel under Begich Peak to a staging area at Bear Valley, where several hundred cars can wait to go through the Anton Anderson Memorial Tunnel that vehicle traffic will share with the railroad. This Alaska Railroad tunnel—the longer of the 2 used by the railroad—is 2.5 miles in length. It was modified to allow both vehicles and trains to pass.

At our press time, tolls, hours of operation and vehicle width restrictions through the tunnel were undecided. Also contact the Alaska Railroad directly for passenger service schedule for Whittier; phone (907) 265-2494.

New access road to Whittier will replace vehicle shuttle train.

(© Kris Graef, staff)

Whittier (pop. 290), located at the head of Passage Canal on Prince William Sound, is the port for the state ferry MV *Bartlett,* which provides ferry service to Cordova and Valdez, and it is also home port for a number of tour boats and charters cruising Prince William Sound.

Whittier has 2 inns providing accommodations, a bed and breakfast, several restaurants, 2 bars, gift shops, laundry facilities, 2 general stores, video rental, gas station, post office, library and a school (preschool through grade 12), and a camper park for tents and self-contained RVs ($5 nightly fee). Fishing licenses may be purchased locally. There is no bank in Whittier.

Whittier also has a harbor office, marine services and repairs, marine supply store, boat launch and lift, freight services, dry storage and self-storage units.

See the PRINCE WILLIAM SOUND section for more on Whittier.

Alaska Sea Kayakers and Honey Charters. See display ad this section.

Bread N' Butter Charters and June's Vacation Condo Suites. See display ad this section.

Soundview Getaway. See display ad this section.

Picturesque Lower Summit Lake is a favorite photo stop. (© Kris Graef, staff)

to the Hope Highway Cutoff at **Milepost S 56.7**.

S 63.3 (101.9 km) **A 63.7** (102.5 km) Bridge over Granite Creek. Traditional halfway point on highway between Anchorage and Seward.

S 63 (101.4 km) **A 64** (103 km) Granite Creek USFS campground, 0.8 mile east of highway; 26 sites (most beside creek), water, toilets, dumpsters, tables, firepits and $10 camping fee. Fishing for small Dolly Varden.

S 62.8 (101.1 km) **A 64.2** (103.3 km) Passing lane next mile southbound.

S 62 (99.8 km) **A 65** (104.6 km) Bridge over East Fork Sixmile Creek.

CAUTION: Watch for moose next 4 miles southbound.

S 61.5 (99 km) **A 65.5** (105.4 km) Passing lane next 0.7 mile southbound.

S 61 (98.2 km) **A 66** (106.2 km) Bridge over Silvertip Creek.

S 59 (94.9 km) **A 68** (109.4 km) Paved parking area to west overlooking **Granite Creek**. Staging area for raft trips. Excellent place to photograph this glacial stream.

The Sixmile bike trail and walking path leads south to the Hope Highway junction and north to Johnson Pass trailhead.

S 58.5 (94.1 km) **A 68.5** (110.2 km) Double-ended parking area to west.

S 57.8 (93 km) **A 69.2** (111.4 km) Rest area and access to bike trail.

S 56.8 (91.4 km) **A 70.2** (113 km) Rest area and access to bike trail.

S 56.7 (91.2 km) **A 70.3** (113.1 km) Turnout to west overlooking Old Canyon Creek bridge.

S 56.5 (90.9 km) **A 70.5** (113.4 km) Canyon Creek bridge.

S 56.3 (90.6 km) **A 70.7** (113.8 km) **Hope Cutoff.** Southbound turn lane for Hope Highway. Rest area and access to bike trail at Mile 0.1 Hope Highway. *Emergency phone at Mile 0.2 Hope Highway.*

Junction with Hope Highway to historic mining community of Hope. See HOPE HIGHWAY log opposite page.

S 56.2 (90.4 km) **A 70.8** (113.9 km) Passing lane begins southbound as highway climbs.

S 54.8 (88.2 km) **A 72.2** (116.2 km) Paved parking area to east.

S 53.5 (86.1 km) **A 73.5** (118.3 km) Turnout to east.

S 53.4 (85.9 km) **A 73.6** (118.4 km) Passing lane ends southbound.

S 52.7 (84.8 km) **A 74.3** (119.6 km) Scenic Byway turnout.

S 52.4 (84.3 km) **A 74.6** (120.1 km) Passing lane begins southbound as highway climbs toward Summit Lake.

S 52 (83.7 km) **A 75** (120.7 km) Scenic viewpoint to east.

S 48 (77.2 km) **A 79** (127.1 km) Fresno Creek bridge; paved double-ended turnout to east at south end of bridge.

S 47.6 (76.6 km) **A 79.4** (127.8 km) Double-ended paved turnout to east on lake.

S 47.2 (76 km) **A 79.8** (128.4 km) Paved double-ended turnout to east next to Lower Summit Lake; a favorite photo stop. Extremely picturesque with lush growth of wildflowers in summer.

Upper and Lower Summit lakes, good spring and fall fishing for landlocked Dolly Varden (goldenfins), ranging in size from 6 to 11 inches, flies and single salmon eggs.

S 46 (74 km) **A 81** (130.4 km) Colorado Creek bridge. Tenderfoot Creek USFS campground 0.6 mile from highway; 28 sites, water, toilets (wheelchair accessible), dumpsters, tables, firepits, boat launch, $10 fee.

S 45.8 (73.7 km) **A 81.2** (130.7 km) Summit Lake Lodge; open year-round. *Emergency call box.* Winter avalanche area begins southbound.

Summit Lake Lodge. Genuine hospitality on the north shore of Summit Lake in Alaska's most beautiful log lodge. Located in the heart of Chugach National Forest, it is a landmark for many. The view is spectacular and the food excellent. Complete menu

from eye-opening omelettes to mouthwatering steaks. Enjoy our cozy motel and relaxing lounge. Open year-round. Fishing, hiking, photography, cross-country skiing, snowmobiling. It's a must stop for every visitor in the last frontier. See display ad this section. [ADVERTISEMENT]

S 45.5 (73.2 km) **A 81.5** (131.2 km) Upper Summit Lake. Paved turnout to east.

S 44.5 (71.6 km) **A 82.5** (132.7 km) Large paved double-ended turnout with interpretive sign to east at end of Upper Summit Lake.

Hope Highway Log

Hope (pop. 130) is located at the end of the Hope Highway on Turnagain Arm.

(© Kris Graef, staff)

The paved 17.7-mile Hope Highway leads northwest from **Milepost S 56.7** on the Seward Highway to the historic community of Hope on the south side of Turnagain Arm and provides access to the Resurrection Creek area. This is a good 2-lane road with 35–40 mph curves.

Distance is measured from junction with the Seward Highway (J).

J 0 **Junction** with Seward Highway at **Milepost S 56.7.**

J 0.1 (0.2 km) Rest area with outhouse, parking and access to Canyon Creek pedestrian bridge. This is the south end of the Sixmile Trail, an 8-mile-long bike trail along Sixmile Creek's east fork to the Johnson Pass trailhead at **Milepost S 63.7** Seward Highway.

J 0.2 (0.4 km) Silvertip highway maintenance station. *Emergency phone.*

J 0.7 (1.1 km) Double-ended turnout to east.

J 1 (1.6 km) **Nova River Runners.** See display ad this section.

J 2.3 (3.7 km) Turnout to east.

J 3.4 (5.5 km) Turnout to east.

J 3.9 (6.3 km) Turnout to east.

J 10 (16.1 km) Double-ended turnout to east with view of Turnagain Arm.

J 11.1 (17.9 km) Large paved turnout to east with view of Turnagain Arm.

J 11.8 (19 km) Double-ended turnout to east overlooking Turnagain Arm.

J 15 (24.1 km) *CAUTION: 35 mph speed limit; watch for pedestrians.*

J 15.8 (25.4 km) **Henry's One Stop.** See display ad this section. ▲

J 16 (25.7 km) Hope School.

CAUTION: 25 mph speed zone.

J 16.2 (26 km) Turnoff to south for Discovery Cabins; Hope airport; USFS Resurrection Pass trailhead (4 miles) on Resurrection Creek Road; and Coeur d'Alene Campground (6.4 miles) on Palmer Creek Road. ▲

Discovery Cabins. See display ad this section.

The 38-mile-long **Resurrection Pass Trail** climbs from an elevation of 400 feet at the trailhead to Resurrection Pass (elev. 2,600 feet) and down to the south trailhead at **Milepost S 53.1** on the Sterling Highway. There are 8 cabins on the trail. Parking area at the trailhead.

Coeur d'Alene USFS campground has 5 sites (not recommended for large RVs or trailers); toilets, tables, firepits; no water, no garbage service, no camping fee. Palmer Creek Road continues past the campground to alpine country above 1,500 feet eleva-

Hope Highway Log (continued)

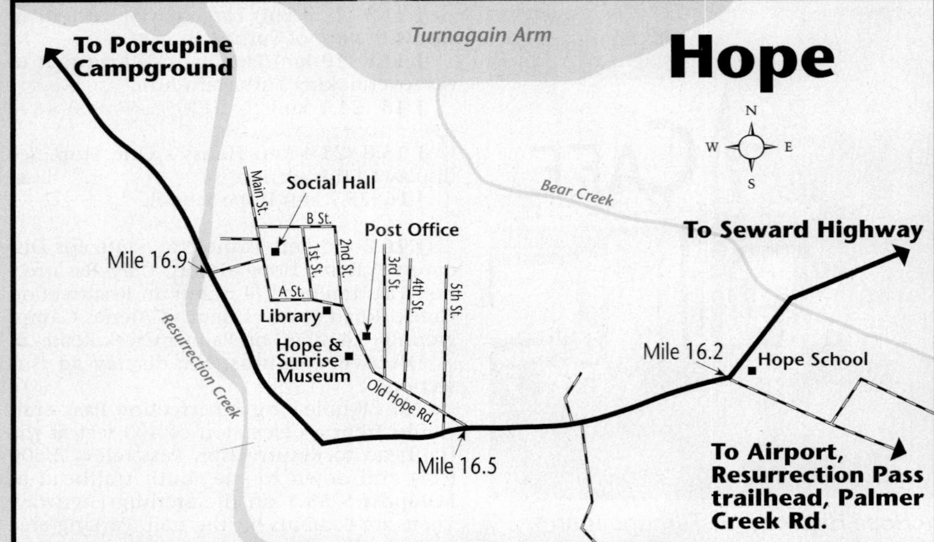

tion, and views of Turnagain Arm and Resurrection Creek valley. The road past the campground is rough and narrow and not recommended for low-clearance vehicles. ▲

J 16.5 (26.6 km) First turnoff northbound for Hope via gravel loop road (description follows). Rebuilt Tito's Discovery Cafe on the highway at turnoff.

Tito's Discovery Cafe. See display ad this section.

HOPE (pop. 130) has a post office, motel, rental cabins, laundry with showers, bed and breakfast, cafe, grocery store, gas station, gift shops, library and museum. **Visitor Information:** Hope Chamber of Commerce, P.O. Box 89, Hope, AK 99605, www.advenalaska.com/hope.

Private aircraft: State-owned airstrip 1 SE; elev. 200 feet; length 2,000 feet; gravel.

This small community at the end of the Hope Highway on Turnagain Arm was a frenzy of gold rush activity in 1896. Miners named their mining camp on Resurrection Creek Hope City, after 17-year-old prospector Percy Hope. But the gold rush here was short-lived. By 1899, many of the miners had joined the gold rush to the Klondike. Hope City persisted, and it is now the best preserved gold rush community in south-central Alaska. Hope's historic district, just off the paved highway, includes the 1896 store (now a cafe) and the 1902 log Social Hall, which still hosts community events.

Today, Hope is a quiet oasis popular with hikers, campers, bicyclists, fishermen, bird watchers and recreational gold miners.

J 16.9 (27.3 km) Second turnoff northbound for Hope via gravel loop road.

Seaview Cafe and Bar. See display ad on page 509.

J 17 (27.5 km) Resurrection Creek bridge.

J 17.7 (28.4 km) Gas station.

J 17.8 (28.6 km) Hope Highway ends, 0.8-mile loop road through **Porcupine USFS Campground** begins. This is a very pleasant campground set in lush vegetation with a few sites overlooking Turnagain Arm. There are 24 sites, tables, tent spaces, campground host, outhouses, firepits, dumpster, drinking water and $10 camping fee. Trailhead for 5-mile **Gull Rock Trail** is located at the campground. ▲

**Return to Milepost S 56.7
Seward Highway**

S 44.3 (71.3 km) **A 82.7** (133.1 km) Beaver dams.

S 44 (70.8 km) **A 83** (133.6 km) Gravel turnout to east. Avalanche gun emplacement.

S 43.8 (70.5 km) **A 83.2** (133.9 km) Winter avalanche area begins northbound. Avalanche gates.

S 43.7 (70.3 km) **A 83.3** (134.1 km) Paved double-ended turnout to east.

S 42.6 (68.6 km) **A 84.4** (135.8 km) Summit Creek bridge.

S 42.2 (67.9 km) **A 84.8** (136.5 km) Quartz Creek bridge.

S 41.4 (66.6 km) **A 85.6** (137.8 km) Passing lane next 1 mile northbound.

S 39.6 (63.7 km) **A 87.4** (140.7 km) Avalanche gates.

S 39.4 (63.4 km) **A 87.6** (141 km) Devils Pass trailhead; parking area and toilets to west. This USFS trail starts at an elevation of 1,000 feet and follows Devils Creek to Devils Pass (elev. 2,400 feet), continuing on to Devils Pass Lake and Resurrection Pass trail. Hiking time to Devils Pass is about 5½ hours.

S 39 (62.8 km) **A 88** (141.6 km) Truck lane extends northbound to **Milepost S 39.3.**

S 38.6 (62.1 km) **A 88.4** (142.3 km) Paved turnout to west adjacent **Jerome Lake,** rainbow and Dolly Varden to 22 inches, use salmon egg clusters, year-round, still fish.

S 38.4 (61.6 km) **A 88.6** (142.6 km) Paved double-ended Scenic Byway turnout to west overlooking Jerome Lake.

S 38.2 (61.5 km) **A 88.8** (142.9 km) Truck lane ends northbound.

S 37.7 (60.7 km) **A 89.3** (143.7 km) Southbound-only exit for Sterling Highway (Alaska Route 1) to west. Continue straight ahead on Alaska Route 9 for Seward.

First **junction** southbound with Sterling Highway to Soldotna, Homer and other Sterling Highway communities. Turn to **Milepost S 38.3** on page 534 in the STERLING HIGHWAY for log.

ALASKA ROUTE 9

S 37.2 (59.9 km) **A 89.8** (144.5 km) Paved turnout to west overlooking Tern Lake for Seward-bound travelers.

S 37 (59.5 km) **A 90** (144.8 km) **Tern Lake Junction.** Turnoff to west (2-way road) on Sterling Highway for access to Tern Lake and **Tern Lake USFS Wildlife Viewing Platform.** Interpretive signs and ranger talks in summer. This is a good spot to see nesting birds, mountain goats, sheep and occasionally moose and bear. Continue around the lake to the Tern Lake picnic area; walk-in picnic sites with water, tables, toilets and fire grates. Salmon-spawning channel with a viewing platform and interpretive signs. Tern Lake is a prime bird-watching area in summer. ▲

Second turnoff southbound and first **junction** northbound of the Seward Highway with the Sterling Highway (Alaska Route 1) to Soldotna, Kenai and Homer. Turn to **Milepost S 37** o page 534 in the STERLING HIGHWAY section for log.

Continue straight ahead on Alaska Route 9 for Seward.

S 36.7 (59.1 km) **A 90.3** (145.3 km) Truck lane begins northbound.

S 36.4 (58.6 km) **A 90.6** (145.8 km) Avalanche gates.

S 35.7 (57.5 km) **A 91.3** (146.9 km) Outfitter for guided horse pack trips.

Tak Outfitters Horseback Adventures Alaska. See display ad this section.

S 35.3 (56.8 km) **A 91.7** (147.6 km) End avalanche area southbound.

S 35 (56.3 km) **A 92** (148 km) For the next 3 miles/4.8 km, many small waterfalls tumble down the brushy slopes. Winter avalanche area between **Milepost S 35.3** and **34.6.** You are driving through the Kenai mountain range.

S 34.1 (54.9 km) **A 92.9** (149.5 km) Turnout to west; large beaver dam.

S 33.1 (53.3 km) **A 93.9** (151.1 km) Carter Lake USFS trailhead No. 4 to west; parking and toilets. Trail starts at an elevation of 500 feet and climbs 986 feet to **Carter Lake** (stocked with rainbow trout). Trail is good, but steep; hiking time about 1½ hours. Good access to sheep and mountain goat country. Excellent snowmobiling area in winter.

S 32.6 (52.5 km) **A 94.4** (151.9 km) Johnson Pass USFS south trailhead with parking area, toilet. North trailhead at **Milepost S 63.7.**

S 32.5 (52.3 km) **A 94.5** (152.1 km) Large paved double-ended turnout; USFS information sign on life cycle of salmon; short trail to observation deck on stream where spawning salmon may be seen in August.

S 32.4 (52.1 km) **A 94.6** (152.2 km) Cook Inlet Aquaculture Association. **Trail Lake Fish Hatchery** on Moose Creek; display room. Open 8 A.M. to 5 P.M. daily; phone (907) 288-3688.

S 31.8 (51.1 km) **A 95.2** (153.2 km) Paved double-ended rest area to east on Upper Trail Lake; toilets.

S 30 (48.3 km) **A 97** (156.1 km) Short side road to large undeveloped gravel parking area on Upper Trail Lake; boat launch.

S 29.9 (48.1 km) **A 97.1** (156.3 km) Gravel turnout by Trail Lake.

S 29.7 (47.8 km) **A 97.3** (156.6 km) Highway maintenance station.

S 29.4 (47.3 km) **A 97.6** (157.1 km) *NOTE: Slow down. "Please slow up and let our children grow up" (sign).*

Entering Moose Pass southbound (description follows).

The large working waterwheel on the west side of the road was built by the late Ed Estes. It is a replica of the peltonwheel hydroelectric plant built by the Estes family in 1927 to power their sawmill. Rebuilt in 1976 by Ed Estes using an 18-inch pipeline from a lake up on the hillside, the peltonwheel generator still generates power to the grocery store in town. There is a parking area at the waterwheel replica and a sign which reads: "Moose Pass is a peaceful little town. If you have an ax to grind, do it here."

MOOSE PASS (pop. 118) has food, lodging, camping, a general store, post office and highway maintenance station. Pay phone outside GTE building. Alaska State Troopers, emergency only phone 911.

This mountain village on Upper Trail Lake was a construction camp on the Alaska Railroad in 1912. Local resident Ed Estes attributed the name Moose Pass to a 1904 observation by Nate White of the first moose recorded in this area. Another version holds that "in 1903, a mail carrier driving a team of dogs had considerable trouble gaining the right-of-way from a giant moose." A post office was established in 1928 and first postmistress Leora (Estes) Roycroft officially named the town Moose Pass.

Moose Pass has a 1.3-mile-long paved bike trail which winds along Trail Lake from the Moose Pass ball diamond to the McFadden house on the south. Gravel turnout by lake.

The main street of town is the site of the Annual Moose Pass Summer Festival, a community-sponsored event which takes place the weekend nearest summer solstice (June 21). The festival features a triathlon, arts and crafts booths, a barbecue, auction and other events.

Estes Brothers Groceries & Water Wheel. See display ad this section.

S 29.1 (46.8 km) **A 97.9** (157.6 km) **Moose Pass RV Park.** 30 spaces. Electric hookups. Scenic campground-like setting. Close to restaurant, post office, small store, telephone. Planned for 2000: laundry and showers. Rural area in beautiful surroundings. Convenient to Seward, but away from the crowds. Just off main highway. E-mail access in office. (907) 288-5624. E-mail: 4m@yahoo.com. [ADVERTISEMENT]

S 28.9 (46.5 km) **A 98.1** (157.9 km) **Midnight Sun Log Cabins.** See display ad this section.

S 26 (41.8 km) **A 101** (162.5 km) Lower Trail Lake. Timbered slopes of Madson Mountain (elev. 5,269 feet/1,605m) to the west. Crescent Lake lies just west of Madson.

S 25.8 (41.5 km) **A 101.2** (162.9 km) Gravel turnout to west.

S 25.4 (40.9 km) **A 101.6** (163.5 km) Bridge over Trail River. Floatplane base.

S 25 (40.2 km) **A 102** (164.1 km) Bridge over Falls Creek.

S 24.2 (38.9 km) **A 102.8** (165.4 km) Side road leads 1.2 miles to Trail River USFS Campground; 64 sites, picnic tables, firepits, dumpsters, toilets, and volleyball and horseshoe area. Group camping area (12 sites) with pavilion; reservations available. Group day-use picnic area. Spacious, wooded campsites in tall spruce on shore of Kenai Lake and Lower Trail River. Pull-through sites available. Fee $10 single, $18 double, reservations available; phone 1-877-444-NRRS. Campground host may be in residence during summer, providing fishing and hiking information. Good spot for mushrooming and berry picking in August.

Lower Trail River, lake trout, rainbow and Dolly Varden, July, August and September, small spinners. Access via Lower Trail River campground road. **Trail River**, Dolly Varden and rainbow. Closed to fishing mid-April to mid-June; use of bait prohibited year-round.

Kenai Lake serves as the headwaters of the Kenai River Special Management Area established in 1984. (© Rich Reid, Colors of Nature)

S 24.1 (38.8 km) **A 102.9** (165.6 km) **Crown Point Lodge & Restaurant.** Special: All lodging includes full breakfast! Homemade breads, soups, desserts and more for breakfast, lunch and dinner. Affordable packages for lodging, meals, charters. Clean comfortable rooms at moderate cost. Dormitory-style room sleeps 8. Circular drive, plenty of parking for big rigs. Phone (907) 288-3136. Fax (907) 288-3641). [ADVERTISEMENT]

S 23.4 (37.7 km) **A 103.6** (166.7 km) *CAUTION: Railroad crossing.* USFS Kenai Lake work center (no information services available). Report forest fires here.

Private Aircraft: Lawing landing strip; elev. 475 feet/144m; length 2,200 feet/671m; gravel; unattended.

S 23.1 (37.1 km) **A 103.9** (167.2 km) **Ptarmigan Creek** bridge and USFS picnic area and campground with 16 sites, water, toilets, tables, firepits and dumpsters, $10 fee (reservations phone 1-877-444-NRRS). Fair to good fishing in creek and in lake outlets at **Ptarmigan Lake** (hike in) for Dolly Varden. Watch for spawning salmon in Ptarmigan Creek in August.

Ptarmigan Creek USFS trail No. 14 begins at campground (elev. 500 feet) and leads 3.5 miles to Ptarmigan Lake (elev. 755 feet). Trail is steep in spots; round-trip hiking time 5 hours. Good chance of seeing sheep, goats, moose and bears. Carry insect repellent. Trail is poor for winter use due to avalanche hazard.

S 23 (37 km) **A 104** (167.3 km) Turnoff for Alaska Nellie's Homestead. The late Nellie Neal–Lawing arrived in Alaska in 1915. Her colorful life included cooking for the railroad workers and big game hunting and guiding.

Alaska Nellie's Inn, Inc. B&B. See display ad this section.

S 22.9 (36.9 km) **A 104.1** (167.5 km) Paved viewpoint to west overlooking Kenai Lake. This lake (elev. 436 feet/132m) extends 24 miles/39 km from the head of the Kenai River on the west to the mouth of Snow River on the east. A sign here explains how glacier meltwater gives the lake its distinctive color.

Winter avalanche area next 3 miles southbound.

S 22.5 (36.2 km) **A 104.5** (168.2 km) Rough gravel double-ended turnout to east.

S 21.3 (34.3 km) **A 105.7** (170.1 km) Gravel turnout to east overlooking lake.

S 20.2 (32.5 km) **A 106.8** (171.9 km) Avalanche gun emplacement.

S 20.1 (32.3 km) **A 106.9** (172 km) Gravel turnout. Avalanche area ends southbound.

S 19.9 (32 km) **A 107.1** (172.4 km) I.R.B.I. Knife Shop; open year-round.

I.R.B.I. Knives. See display ad this section.

S 19.5 (31.4 km) **A 107.5** (173 km) Victor Creek bridge. Access to bed and breakfast south of bridge. Victor Creek USFS trail No. 23; a 2-mile hike with good view of mountains.

Grandma Leary's Senior B&B, located just south of the Victor Creek Bridge at Milepost 19.5 (27066 Seward Highway), in our 3 generation rustic hand-built home. Quiet country setting between Moose Pass and Seward. Ground-level enrance to private bedroom and bath. Home-baked continental breakfast. (Limited smoking area.) $50/night. (907) 288-3168. [ADVERTISEMENT]

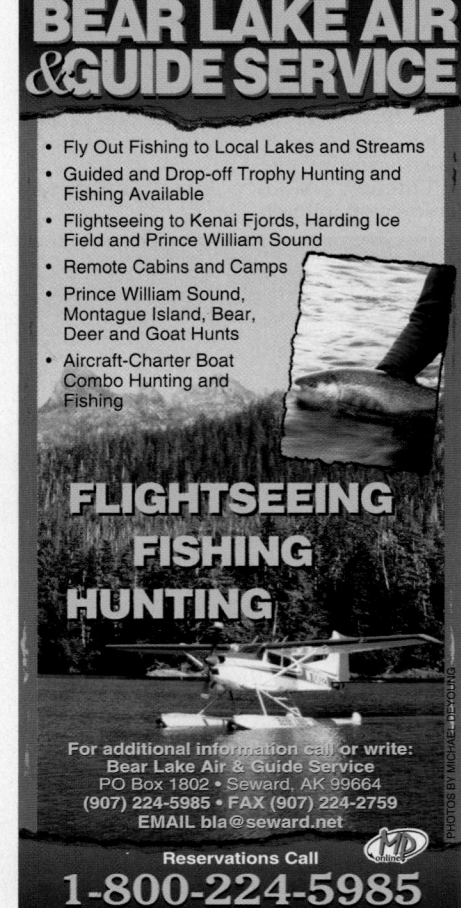

S 17.7 (28.5 km) **A 109.3** (175.9 km) Bridge over center channel of Snow River. This river has 2 forks that flow into Kenai Lake.

S 17 (27 km) **A 110** (177 km) Primrose Road. Access to bed and breakfast. Turn west for **Primrose USFS campground**, 1 mile from the highway. (Campground access road leads past private homes. Drive carefully!) The campground, overlooking Kenai Lake, has 10 sites, toilets, dumpsters, tables, firepits, boat ramp, water, $10 fee. Jetskis are permitted in limited areas of Kenai Lake. Primrose trail (6.5 miles) starts from the campground and connects with Lost Creek trail (7 miles). High alpine hike to **Lost Lake**, rainbow fishing (stocked); trail is posted. ▲

Bridge over south channel of Snow River.

S 16.2 (26.1 km) **A 110.8** (178.3 km) Gravel turnout to east.

S 15 (24.1 km) **A 112** (180.2 km) Watch for moose in ponds and meadows.

S 14.9 (24 km) **A 112.1** (180.4 km) Gravel turnout to east.

S 14 (22.5 km) **A 113** (181.9 km) *CAUTION: Railroad crossing.*

S 13.3 (21.4 km) **A 113.7** (183 km) Grayling Lake USFS trailhead to west, large paved parking area to east. Grayling Lake trail No. 20, 1.6 miles/2.6 km, connects with trails to Meridian and Leech lakes. Good spot for photos of Snow River valley. Watch for moose. **Grayling Lake**, 6- to 12-inch grayling, use flies, May to October.

S 12 (19.3 km) **A 115** (185.1 km) Alaska Railroad crosses under highway.

S 11.6 (18.6 km) **A 115.4** (185.7 km) Gravel parking area to west and trail to **Golden Fin Lake,** Dolly Varden averaging 8 inches. This is a 0.6-mile/1-km hike on a very wet trail: wear rubber footwear. Ski trails in winter.

S 10.8 (17.4 km) **A 116.2** (187 km) Large gravel turnout to east.

S 8.5 (13.6 km) **A 118.5** (190.7 km) Gravel turnout to west.

S 8.3 (13.4 km) **A 118.7** (191 km) Paved turnout by creek to east. Leaving Chugach National Forest land southbound.

S 8 (12.9 km) **A 119** (191.5 km) **Grouse Creek** bridge. Dolly Varden fishing.

S 7.4 (11.9 km) **A 119.6** (192.5 km) **Grouse Lake** access road. Good ice fishing for Dolly Varden in winter.

S 7.1 (11.4 km) **A 119.9** (193 km) Old Mill subdivision.

S 6.6 (10.6 km) **A 120.4** (193.7 km) **Bear Lake Road**; access to gas station. Turnoff on Bear Lake Road for RV parks, bed and breakfast, and a flying service. Drive in 0.7 mile on Bear Lake Road to see a state-operated fish weir. Silver and red (sockeye) salmon are trapped to provide life-cycle data and also eggs for the state's salmon stocking program.

Bear Lake Air & Guide Service. See display ad this section.

A Creekside RV Park & Motel. See display ad this section. ▲

Bear Creek RV Park, drive 1/2 mile on Bear Lake Road. Family-owned and operated Good Sam Park has full and partial hookups, dump station, private restrooms with showers, cable TV, travelers lounge, propane, laundry, convenience store, ice, video rentals. Free showers included with your stay. Pay phone inside. Excellent water. (907) 224-5725. Fax/e-mail service available. Free shuttle when reservations are booked through our office for Kenai Fjords Tours. Fishing charter bookings available. RV and boat storage. Short walk to fish weir. Bear Creek RV Park is not to be mistaken for A Creekside RV Park located at the gas station on the corner of the Seward Highway and Bear Lake Road. E-mail: hettick@alaska.net. See display ad. [ADVERTISEMENT] ▲

S 6.5 (10.5 km) **A 120.5** (193.9 km) Bear Creek bridge.

S 6.3 (10.1 km) **A 120.7** (194.2 km) Stoney Creek Avenue; access to bed and breakfasts.

0.2 Winterset Guest House. First-class accommodations at $85/DO. Land's End down comforters on all our beds and quality mattresses for a good night's sleep. Hearty continental breakfast buffet. All rooms have private baths, cable TV. Laundry facilities, refrigerator, microwave, phone, coffee maker available to guests. Open year-round. (Discounted winter rates.) Smoke-free environment, wooded area with great mountain view. We will assist you with all your activity plans and book Fjord tours, fishing charters at discounted prices. Long-time Alaskan hosts. (907) 224-5185. [ADVERTISEMENT]

S 5.9 (9.4 km) **A 121.1** (194.8 km) **Salmon Creek** bridge. Good fishing in stream begins Aug. 1st for sea-run Dolly Varden averaging 10 inches; use of bait prohibited Sept. 16–Dec. 31.

S 5.2 (8.4 km) **A 121.8** (196 km) Bear Creek volunteer fire department. ***Emergency phone.***

S 3.8 (6.1 km) **A 123.2** (198.3 km) Clear Creek bridge.

Drive with headlights on at all times.

S 3.7 (6 km) **A 123.3** (198.4 km) Access to Exit Glacier.

Junction with Exit Glacier Road. See EXIT GLACIER ROAD LOG opposite page.

S 3.2 (5.1 km) **A 123.8** (199.2 km) **Nash Road**, access to bed and breakfasts. It is a scenic 5-mile drive out Nash Road to Seward's Marine Industrial Center in the Fourth of July Creek valley. Fine views along the way and from Kertulla Point of Resurrection Bay and the city of Seward. At Mile 2.1 Nash Road is the trailhead for the Iditarod Trail, which begins at the ferry terminal in downtown Seward. Hike to Bear Lake; from north end of lake, trail continues to Mile 12 on the Seward Highway..

The Farm Bed & Breakfast Inn. Turn off Seward Highway onto Nash Road, cross the railroad tracks, turn left immediately onto Salmon Creek Road, follow signs to "The Farm." Tranquil country setting on acres of trees and lawn. Choose from our Main House ...Cottages ...Economy Bungalow ...or Kitchenette Units. Enjoy cable TV, decks, barbecue, private baths. Freezer space, laundry facilities. Families welcome. Continental breakfast. Open year-round. VISA, MasterCard, Discover. Long-time Alaskan host Jack Hoogland, Box 305, Seward,AK 99664. Reservations suggested.(907) 224-5691. Fax (907) 224-5698. E-mail: thefarm@ptialaska.net. Internet: www.alaskan.com/thefarm/. See display ad this section. [ADVERTISEMENT]

Camelot Cottages. See display ad this section.

Mrs. Clock's B&B. See display ad this section.

Ho-Hum Lodge B&B. See display ad this section.

Fjordland Inn is nestled in a mountain panorama. Country charm, smoke free, mostly private baths. Private entrance to guest area. Families/groups welcome. Open year-round. Winter rates. Alaskana originals–prints by owner/artist displayed. (907) 224-36315 or 1-800-785-3614. Fax (907) 224-3615. Hosts Lee and Mary George. Mile 1.7 Nash Road. [ADVERTISEMENT]

S 3 (4.8 km) **A 124** (199.6 km) Resurrection River; 3 channels, 3 bridges. This river flows from the Harding Icefield into Resurrection Bay just northeast of Seward. Seward city limits.

S 2.7 (4.3 km) **A 124.3** (200 km) Turnoff for Seward airport.

Godwin Glacier Dog Sled Tours. See display ad this section.

View of Exit Glacier from Exit Glacier Road. (© Mike Jones)

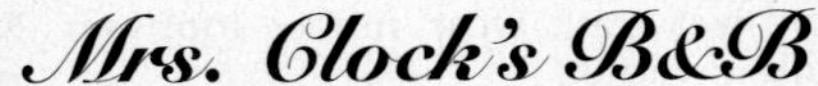

Mrs. Clock's B&B
• Private Baths • Clean As A Whistle
• Hearty Full Breakfast
• Wooded Setting/Salmon Stream
SEMAKA CHARTERS
• Halibut - Cod - Rockfish - Salmon
(907) 224-3195
e-mail: clocksbb@seward.net

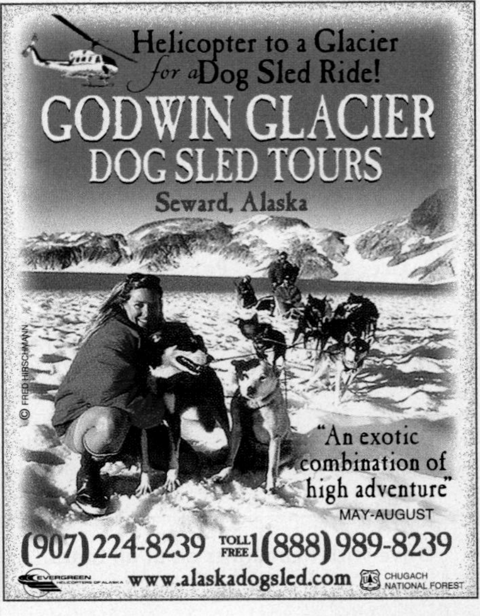

Exit Glacier Road

Exit Glacier Road junctions with the Seward Highway at **Milepost S 3.7** and leads west 9 miles to Exit Glacier in Kenai Fjords National Park. Worth the drive to see an active glacier up close. Lodges, cabins, campgrounds and attractions are located on Exit Glacier Road and on Old Exit Glacier Road, which loops off the main road (logs for both roads follow).

The first 4 miles of Exit Glacier Road are paved (40 mph speed limit), and the remainder is gravel. The road travels through the flat Resurrection River valley with few curves. The 1.5-mile Old Exit Glacier Road is gravel.

Exit Glacier Road is maintained from May to September. In winter, the road is closed to vehicle traffic beyond Mile 1.4 for use by skiers, snow machines and mushers.

EXIT GLACIER ROAD

Distance from junction (J) with the Seward Highway is shown.

J 0 Junction with the Seward Highway at **Milepost S 3.7.**

J 0.1 Junction with Old Exit Glacier Road loop (see log following).

J 0.7 Windsong Lodge.

J 1.1 Fjords RV Park. Nestled in towering trees at Mile 1 of Exit Glacier Road, Gateway to Kenai Fjords National Park. Large open sites with water and electric hookups. Easy access. Caravans, large groups and tenters welcome. Visitor and local activity information and service. Glacier tour boats, sightseeing and fishing trips booked for you. Call today (907) 224-9134. [ADVERTISEMENT] ▲

J 1.2 Large parking area to south.

J 1.3 Junction with Old Exit Glacier Road loop (see log following).

J 1.4 Kenai Fjords National Park (sign). Box Canyon bridge. Winter gates.

J 1.5 Informal campsite on gravel river bar.

J 2.3 Informal gravel turnout and campsite.

J 3.2 Informal campsite at access to river.

J 3.7 Chugach National Forest (sign).

J 3.8 Large turnouts both sides of road.

J 3.9 *Pavement ends, gravel begins, westbound.*

J 6.5 First view from road of Exit Glacier.

J 6.8 Scenic viewpoint of Exit Glacier.

J 7.1 Trailhead for **Resurrection River Trail** (Chugach National Forest). The 16-mile trail ties in with the Russian Lakes trail. It is part of the 75-mile Hope-to-Seward route. *CAUTION: Black and brown bears also use this trail.*

J 7.2 Resurrection River bridge.

J 7.3 *NOTE: Road narrows, 25 mph speed limit.*

J 7.5 Welcome to Kenai Fjords National Park's Exit Glacier (sign).

J 8.3 Turnoff for walk-in tent campgroundwith 9 sites (no fee, reservations). ▲

J 8.6 Entrance station to **Exit Glacier**. Entrance fees are: $5 vehicle; $2 individual; $15 annual pass. The road ends at a parking lot with restrooms and a picnic area next to the ranger station. National Park Service visitor center at the ranger station (seasonal). Summer activities include daily ranger-led nature walks; phone (907) 224-3175. A public-use cabin is available in winter

From the parking lot, it is a flat, easy half-mile walk on a path through alder forest to the glacier's terminus. First 0.3 mile of path is paved and wheelchair accessible to the interpretive shelter. At the glacier's outwash plain, the longer half-mile Upper Loop trail offers excellent views of the glacier. The strenuous 3-mile-long Harding Icefield trail branches off this trail. Return to the parking lot by way of the easy 0.8 mile nature trail loop with its 10 interpretive signs on forest succession. *CAUTION: Falling ice at face of glacier, stay behind warning signs.*

Exit Glacier is 3 miles long and descends some 2,500 feet from the Harding Icefield. Watch for bears on surrounding hillsides.

OLD EXIT GLACIER ROAD

Distance is measured from the east junction (EJ) and west junction (WJ) with Exit Galcier Road.

EJ 0 (WJ 1.5) Junction with Exit Glacier Road at Mile J 0.1.

EJ 0.3 (WJ 1.2) Clear Creek

EJ 0.9 (WJ 0.6) Box Canyon Cabins. See display ad this section.

EJ 1 (WJ 0.5) River Valley Cabins. See display ad this section.

EJ 1.1 (WJ 0.4) IdidaRide Sled Dog Tours. See display ad this section.

EJ 1.5 (WJ 0) Junction with Exit Glacier Road at Mile J 1.3.

Return to Milepost S 3.7
Seward Highway

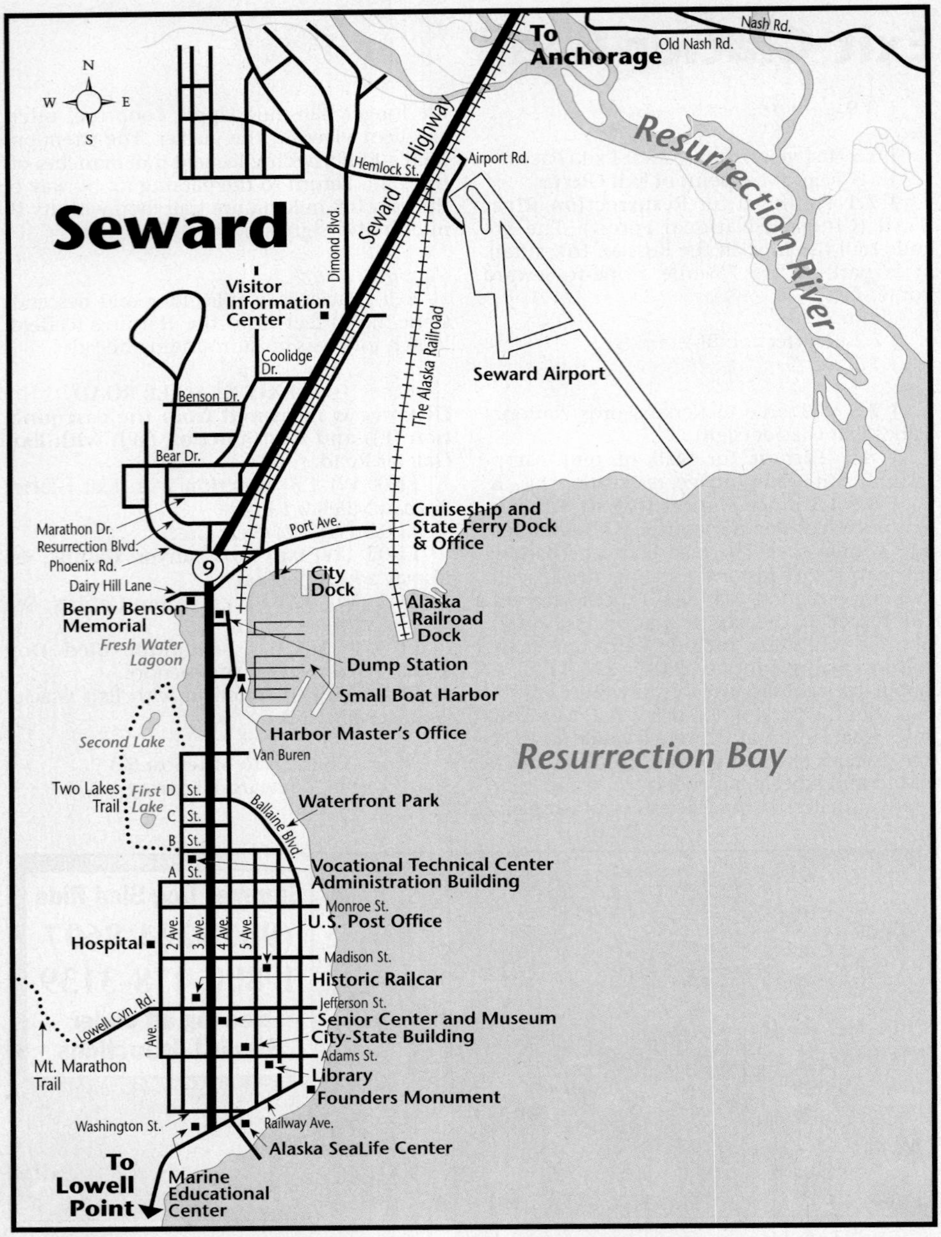

Seward

To Anchorage
Nash Rd.
Old Nash Rd.
Resurrection River
Hemlock St.
Seward Highway
Airport Rd.
Dimond Blvd.
Visitor Information Center
Coolidge Dr.
The Alaska Railroad
Seward Airport
Benson Dr.
Bear Dr.
Marathon Dr.
Resurrection Blvd.
Phoenix Rd.
Dairy Hill Lane
Port Ave.
Cruiseship and State Ferry Dock & Office
City Dock
Alaska Railroad Dock
Benny Benson Memorial
Fresh Water Lagoon
Dump Station
Small Boat Harbor
Harbor Master's Office
Second Lake
Van Buren
Resurrection Bay
Two Lakes Trail
First Lake
D St.
C St.
B St.
A St.
Ballaine Blvd.
Waterfront Park
Vocational Technical Center Administration Building
Monroe St.
U.S. Post Office
Hospital
2 Ave.
3 Ave.
4 Ave.
5 Ave.
Madison St.
Historic Railcar
Jefferson St.
Lowell Cyn. Rd.
Senior Center and Museum
City-State Building
1 Ave.
Mt. Marathon Trail
Adams St.
Library
Founders Monument
Washington St.
Railway Ave.
Alaska SeaLife Center
To Lowell Point
Marine Educational Center

S 2.5 (4 km) **A 124.5** (200.4 km) Hemlock Street; turnoff for public camping at Forest Acres municipal campground; water, flush toilets, 14-day limit. No tables. ▲

S 2.3 (3.7 km) **A 124.7** (200.7 km) Sea Lion Drive. U.S. Air Force and U.S. Army Seward Recreation Area.

Seward Resort (Military). See display ad this section.

S 2.1 (3.4 km) **A 124.9** (201 km) Dimond Boulevard.

S 2 (3.2 km) **A 125** (201.1 km) Seward Chamber of Commerce–Convention and Visitors Bureau visitor center.

S 1.8 (2.9 km) **A 125.2** (201.5 km) Gas station.

S 1.7 (2.7 km) **A 125.3** (201.6 km) Bear Drive; access to bed and breakfasts.

S 1.5 (2.4 km) **A 125.5** (202 km) Resurrection Blvd., Seward High School.

S 1.2 (1.9 km) **A 125.8** (202.4 km) Dairy Hill Lane to west. Large parking area to west with memorial to Benny Benson, who designed the Alaska state flag. Port Avenue to east, access to cruise ship and ferry dock.

S 1 (1.6 km) **A 126** (202.8 km) South Harbor Street and main entrance to boat harbor.

S 0.4 (0.6 km) **A 126.6** (203.7 km) Madison Street. Post office one block east.

S 0.3 (0.5 km) **A 126.7** (203.9 km) Intersection of 3rd Avenue (Seward Highway) and Jefferson. Hospital 2 blocks west. Information Cache railcar at intersection.

S 0 A 127 (204.4 km) Alaska SeaLife Center/Seward Marine Education Center.

Seward

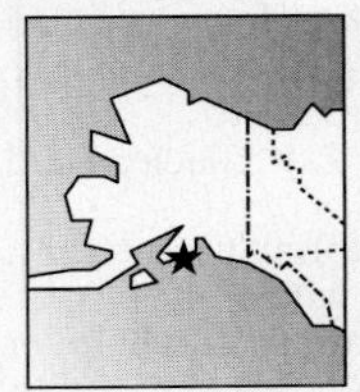

S 0 A 127 (204.4 km) Located on Resurrection Bay, east coast of Kenai Peninsula; 127 miles/204.4 km south of Anchorage by road, or 35 minutes by air. **Population:** 3,010. **Emergency Services: Police, Fire Department** and **Ambulance**, emergency only, phone 911. **State Troopers**, phone (907) 224-3346. **Hospital**, Providence Seward Medical Center, 1st Avenue and Jefferson Street, phone (907) 224-5205. **Maritime Search and Rescue**, phone (800) 478-5555.

Visitor Information: Available at 2 locations, operated by the Seward Chamber of

View of Seward on Resurrection Bay. (© Niebrugge)

Commerce–Convention & Visitors Bureau. The visitor center at **Milepost S 2** Seward Highway (2001 Seward Highway) is open 7 days a week from Memorial Day through Labor Day, weekdays the rest of the year; phone (907) 224-8051. The Information Cache, located in the historic railroad car *Seward* at 3rd and Jefferson Street, is open daily from 9 A.M. to 5 P.M., June through August; write Box 749, Seward, AK 99664.

Kenai Fjords National Park Visitor Center, 1212 4th Ave. (in the Small Boat Harbor), is open 8 A.M. to 7 P.M. daily, Memorial Day to Labor Day; 8:30 A.M. to 5 P.M. weekdays the remainder of the year. Information on the park, slide show, interpretive programs and bookstore. Phone (907) 224-3175 or the Park Information Line (907) 224-2132. Or write P.O. Box 1727, Seward, AK 99664.

Chugach National Forest, Seward Ranger

SEWARD ADVERTISERS

A Cabin On The Cliff.........Ph. (907) 224-8001
Alaska Catamaran Cruises Ph. (888) 305-2515
Alaska Renown Charters & Tours.......................Ph. (907) 224-3806
Alaska Saltwater Lodge ....Ph. (907) 224-5271
Alaska Sealife Center........Ph. (907) 224-6300
Alaska Sunrise Fishing Adventures.................Ph. (800) 818-1250
Aurora Charters...............Ph. (907) 224-3968
Backlash Charters............Ph. (800) 295-4396
Bardarson Studio.............Ph. (907) 224-5448
Bay Vista Bed & Breakfast..............................Phoenix Dr.
Beach House, The............Ph. (907) 224-7000
Bear Creek RV Park..........Ph. (907) 224-5725
Bear's Den Bed & Breakfast.....................Ph. (907) 224-3788
Best Western Hotel Seward........................Ph. (907) 224-2378
Breeze Inn..........................Small Boat Harbor
Brown & Hawkins..............................4th Ave.
Camelot Cottages............Ph. (907) 224-3039
Capt. Bob's Charters.........Ph. (907) 242-4102
Captain's Choice B&B.......Ph. (907) 224-8438
Charter Option, The.........Ph. (800) 224-2026
Chinooks Waterfront Grill............................Ph. (907) 224-2207
Chugach Heritage Center.....`Alaska RR Depot
Clear Creek Cottage.........Ph. (907) 224-3968
Crab Pot, The..........................303 Adams St.
Crow's Nest Cottage........Ph. (907) 224-3979
Eagle Eye Photo...............Ph. (907) 224-2022
Fish House, The..................Small Boat Harbor
Harborview Inn................Ph. (907) 224-3217
Helly Hansen.....................Small Boat Harbor
Hertz Car Rental..............Ph. (907) 224-4378
Hotel Edgewater..............Ph. (907) 224-2700
IdidaRide Sled Dog Tours..Ph. (907) 224-8607
Kayak & Custom Adventures Worldwide..................Ph. (907) 224-3960
Kenai Fjords Tours...........Ph. (800) 478-8068
Kenai Fjords Wilderness Lodge.........................Ph. 1-800-478-8068
Major Marine Tours..........Ph. (907) 224-8030
Mariah Tours...................Ph. (800) 270-1238
Marina Motel....................Ph. (907) 224-5518
Miller's Landing........Mile 2.5 Lowell Point Rd.
Murphy's Motel...............Ph. (907) 224-8090
New Seward Hotel & Saloon.....................Ph. (907) 224-8001
Northern Nights Bed & Breakfast.....................Ph. (907) 224-5688
Northland Book & Charts...........234 4th Ave.
Ranting Raven Bakery & Gifts..........................Ph. (907) 224-2228
Ray's Waterfront................Small Boat Harbor
Resurrect Art Coffee House Gallery................320 3rd Ave.
Sablefish Charters..............Small Boat Harbor
Sauerdough Lodging..................225 4th Ave.
Sea Treasures Inn.............Ph. (907) 224-7667
Seward Chamber of Commerce..................Ph. (907) 224-8051
Seward Laundry........................806 4th Ave.
Seward Reservation Information Line.............................Ph. (800) 844-2424
Seward Resort (Military)..Ph. (907) 224-2659
Seward RV Park...............Ph. (907) 224-2723
Seward Waterfront Lodging......................Ph. (907) 224-5563
Seward Windsong Lodge..........................Ph.1-888-959-9590
Seward's Downtown Lodging.......................Ph. (907) 224-3939
Sweet Darlings..................Ph. (907) 224-7313
Taroka Inn.........................Ph. (907) 224-8975
Terry's Tire & Lube...........Ph. (907) 224-5505
Tim Berg's Alaskan Fishing.........................Ph. (800) 548-3474
Topsail Sailing Adventures......................Small Boat Harbor
Van Gilder Hotel, the........Ph. (800) 204-6835
Victorian Serenity By The Sea.........................Ph. (907) 224-3637
Wildlife Quest..................Ph. (907) 224-2282

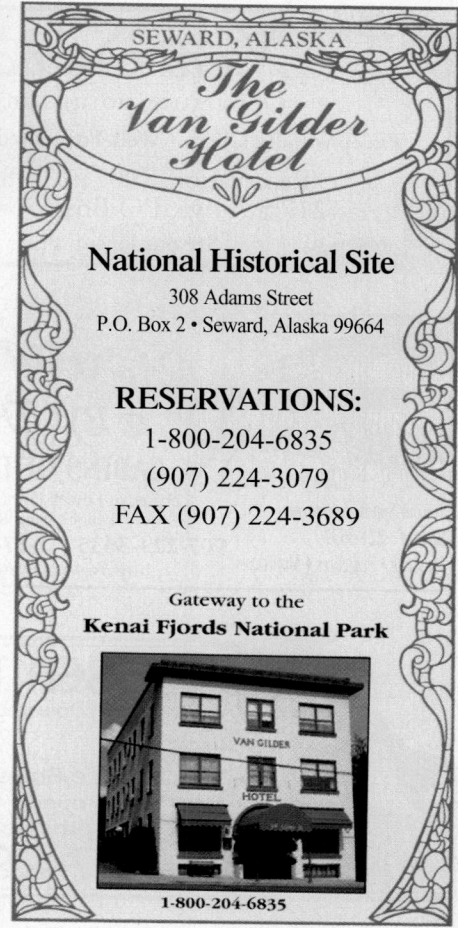

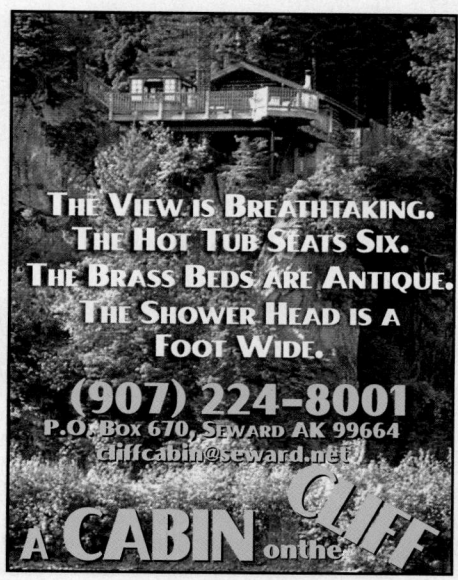

District office, is located at 334 4th Ave. USFS personnel can provide information on hiking, camping and fishing opportunities on national forest lands. Open weekdays, 8 A.M. to 5 P.M. Mailing address: P.O. Box 390, Seward, AK 99664. Phone (907) 224-3374.

Elevation: Sea level. **Climate:** Average daily maximum temperature in July, 62°F /17°C; average daily minimum in January, 18°F/-7°C. Average annual precipitation, 67 inches; average snowfall, 80 inches. **Radio:** KSKA-FM 92, KWAVE 104.9, KPEN 102.3. **Television:** Several channels by cable. **Newspaper:** *Seward Phoenix Log* (weekly).

Private Aircraft: Seward airport, 2 NE; elev. 22 feet; length 4,200 feet; asphalt; fuel 100LL, jet.

Seward—known as the "Gateway to Kenai Fjords National Park"—is a picturesque community nestled between high mountain ranges on a small rise stretching from Resurrection Bay to the foot of Mount Marathon. Thick groves of cottonwood and scattered spruce groves are found in the immediate vicinity of the city, with stands of spruce and alder growing on the surrounding mountainsides.

Downtown Seward (the main street is 4th Avenue) has a frontier-town atmosphere with some homes and buildings dating back to the early 1900s. The town was established in 1903 by railroad surveyors as an ocean terminal and supply center. The 470-mile/756-km railway connecting Fairbanks in the Interior with Seward was completed in 1923.

The city was named for U.S. Secretary of State William H. Seward, who was instrumental in arranging the purchase of Alaska from Russia in 1867. Resurrection Bay was named in 1791 by Russian fur trader and explorer Alexander Baranof. While sailing from Kodiak to Yakutat he found unexpected shelter in this bay from a storm and named the bay Resurrection because it was the Russian Sunday of the Resurrection.

Resurrection Bay is a year-round ice-free harbor, and Seward is an important cargo and fishing port. The Alaska state ferry MV *Tustumena* calls at Seward.

Seward's economic base includes tourism, a coal terminal, marine research, fisheries and government offices. The Alaska Vocational Technical Center is located here. The new (1998) marine educational center—the Alaska SeaLife Center—is located here; see Attractions this section for more details.

Lodging & Services

All visitor facilities, including hotels, motels, a hostel, bed and breakfasts, cafes and restaurants, post office, grocery store,

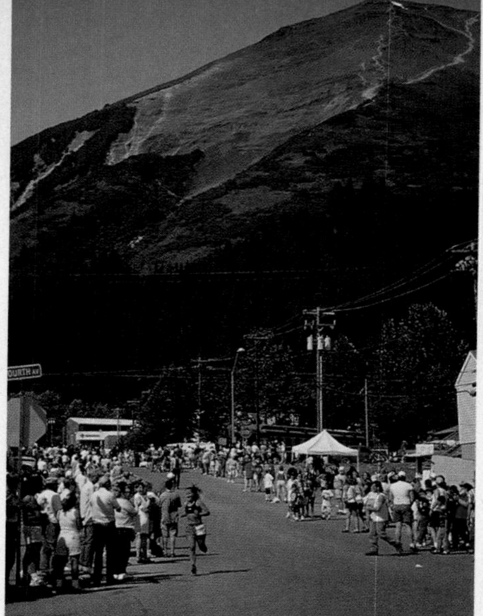

Runners finish the Mount Marathon Race, held the 4th of July.

(© Barb Willard)

drugstore, travel agencies, gift shops, gas stations, bars, laundromats, churches, bowling alley and theater.

The Harbormaster Building has public restrooms, pay showers, drinking water fill-up, mailbox and pay phones. Weather information is available here during the summer. Public restrooms and pay showers on Ballaine Boule vard along the ocean between the boat harbor and town. Dump station at the Small Boat Harbor at the end of 4th Avenue (see city map). There are picnic areas with covered tables along Ballaine Blvd., just south of the harbor, and at Adams Street.

Alaska Saltwater Lodge. Seward's only drive-to oceanfront lodge. Experience sea otters, sea lions, seals, eagles and whale viewing. Scenic mountain and glacier setting. Enjoy beachcombing and fishing, coastal nature trail, on-site kayaking, guided salt-water fishing and daily small group Kenai Fjords National Park wildlife and glacier tours. private baths. (907) 224-5271. www.alaskasaltwaterlodge.com. See display ad. [ADVERTISEMENT]

Bay Vista Bed & Breakfast, is nestled at the bottom of Mount Marathon in Seward, with a spectacular panoramic view of Resurrection Bay. Quiet, peaceful, wooded setting.

We serve a healthy and hearty continental breakfast. Our 2 beautifully appointed private, spacious suites offer private baths, phone, TV/VCR, refrigerator, microwave and private entrances to suites. Smoke-free environment. Close to all Seward attractions. Host: Life-long Seward resident. P.O. Box 1232, Seward, AK 99664. (907) 224-5880. www.seward.net/bayvista. E-mail: bayvista@arctic.net. [ADVERTISEMENT]

Best Western Hotel Seward. Enjoy being in the center of activity, yet in a quiet setting overlooking Resurrection Bay. Our rooms

William Henry Seward negotiated the purchase of Alaska from Russia in 1867. An unpopular deal, Alaska was called "Seward's Icebox" and "Seward's Folly."

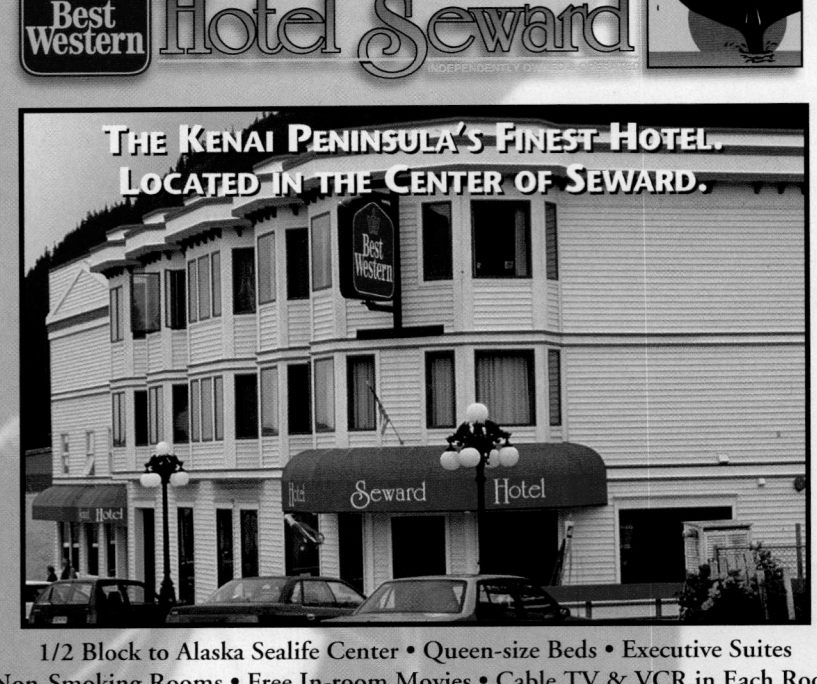

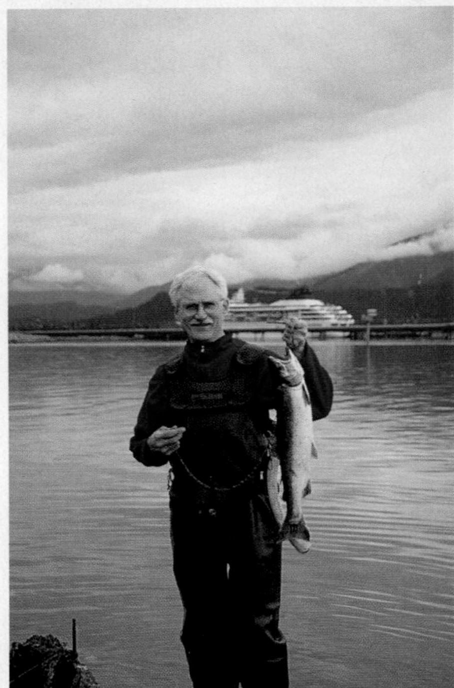

Fishing in Seward when the silvers are in. (© Kris Graef, staff)

include breathtaking views with in-room coffee and your own refrigerator. One floor all nonsmoking rooms. And check this out! For your in-room entertainment, all rooms include data ports, remote control TVs with cable vision and remote control VCRs with videotape rental. Complimentary scheduled shuttle bus service for our guests to boat harbor, train depot and airport. Half-block to the Alaska SeaLife Center. We accept all major credit cards. Reservations (907) 224-2378 or (800) 811-1191 inside Alaska. Fax (907) 224-3112. www.bestwesternseward.com. See display ad this section. [ADVERTISEMENT]

Camelot Cottages. (800) 739-3039. Clean, cozy, affordable cabins in a natural woodland setting. Chalet available for families or groups. All units are furnished, heated, with private baths, fully equipped kitchens, linens and cable TV Relax in our guest-only open air hot tub. Laundry and fish freezer also available. Family-owned and operated by longtime Alaskans. We can also make your reservations for Kenai Fjords Park tours and fishing charters on the world-famous Kenai Peninsula. See display ad at Mile 3.2 Seward Highway. Phone (907) 224-3039 Seward; (907) 346-3039 Anchorage. akcabins@alaska.net and www. alaska.net/~akcabins. [ADVERTISEMENT]

Clear Creek Cottage. Fully furnished smoke-free 2-bedroom cabin, full kitchen. Sleeps up to 8. Clean, comfortable, affordable rates. Perfect hideaway for couples, families, small groups. On the banks of Clear Creek, on Old Exit Glacier Road to Exit Glacier, Mile 3.7 Seward Highway. 7 minutes to downtown Seward. (907) 224-3968. Fax (907) 224-7230. P.O. Box 241, Seward, AK 99664. [ADVERTISEMENT]

Harborview Inn. 804 Third Avenue. New: 37 rooms with private entrances, private baths, cable TV in room, telephone, fine art. Just 10-minute walk to tour boats, fishing charters, downtown and Alaska Sea Life Center. Also "Seaview," our newly remodeled 2-bedroom apartments on the beachfront, breathtaking view of snow-capped mountains and bay. All nonsmoking. $119. Early reservations advised. Alaska Native hostess. Phone (907) 224-3217; fax (907) 224-3218. P.O. Box 1305MP, Seward, AK 99664. E-mail: info@sewardhotel.com. Internet: www.sewardhotel.com. See display ad. [ADVERTISEMENT]

Hotel Edgewater. A waterfront hotel on Resurrection Bay, located in the heart of downtown Seward, the gateway to Kenai Fjords National Park and Exit Glacier. The Hotel Edgewater features comfortable rooms and suites, a conference center, a gift and fine art shop, a spa room with exercise equipment, hot tub and sauna. The lobby is 3 stories tall with a waterfall and fireplace. Most rooms overlook Resurrection Bay or the Kenai Mountains Amenities include valet parking, coffee bar, TV and VCR, hair dryers. The hotel is one block from the Alaska Sea Life Center and Chugach Heritage Center and offers concierge services. A continental breakfast is available for purchase and complimentary transportation to and from the railroad station is available. Open year-round. [ADVERTISEMENT]

Murphy's Motel. Centrally located on Main Street, 2 blocks to Fjords tour departure/fishing charters at the Small Boat Harbor. 3 minutes to SeaLife Center. Quiet, private baths, cable TV, queen beds, free local calls, coffee maker, fridge, microwave, data ports, parking in front of room. Smoking/nonsmoking rooms. New in 2000: 12 n/s deluxe rooms. Bay view. (907) 224-8090. Fax (907) 224-5650. murphys@seward.net. www.alaskan.com/murphysmotel. See display ad. [ADVERTISEMENT]

New Seward Hotel & Saloon. Rooms $40–$96. Centrally located in downtown Seward, half-block to Alaska SeaLife Center, within walking distance of shops, beach, boat harbor; 35 rooms featuring cable TV and phones. Some kitchenettes. Salmon and halibut fishing charters or Kenai Fjords tours available. Year-round service. Brochure. All major credit cards accepted. Reservations (907) 224-8001. Fax (907) 224-3112. See display ad this section. [ADVERTISEMENT]

Ray's Waterfront. Innovative Alaskan cuisine in a spectacular waterfront setting featuring fresh local seafood, steaks and vegetarian selections. Specialties include macadamia nut crusted halibut with Thai curry sauce, cioppino, brandied pepper steak, oven-roasted Tuscan vegetables, king crab and daily specials. Serving lunch and dinner daily. Full bar service with excellent wine selections. Group reservations in advance are welcome. Gourmet box lunches available. Phone (907) 224-5606, fax (907) 224-5631. E-mail: janaska@msn.com. [ADVERTISEMENT]

Seward Resort (Military). hotel, townhouses, RV and tent sites. Charter fishing,

Resurrection Bay wildlife boat tours. Winter snowmachine rentals and discount tour a nd ticket sales. Open year-round. Authorized patrons: active duty military; retirees; National Guard and Reserves; DOD/NAF civilians, families and guests; federal governmental agencies. Phone (800) 770-1858; (907) 224-2659; (907) 224-2654. Internet: www.usarak.army.mil/framwr/seward.htm. See display ad, **Mile 2.3** Seward Highway. [ADVERTISEMENT] ▲

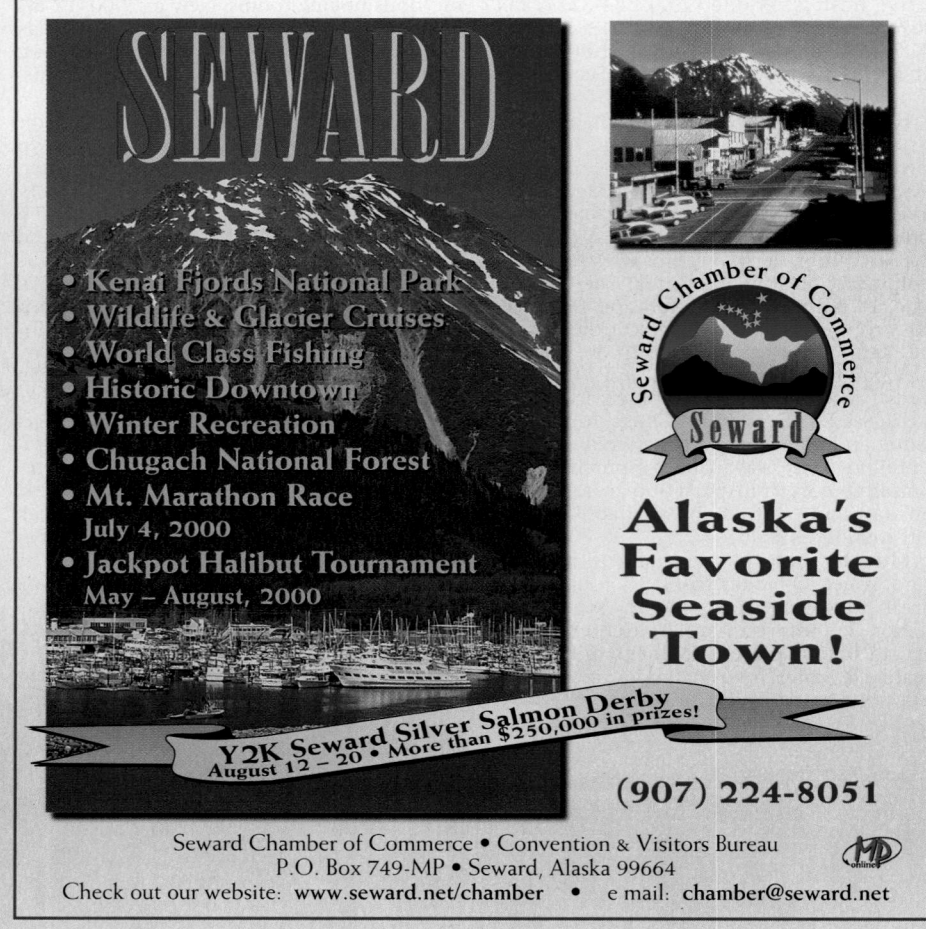

Sauerdough Lodging is located in downtown Seward in William Sauers' historic Seward Commercial Co. Building at 225 4th Avenue and open year-round. The Alaska SeaLife and Native Heritage Centers are nearby, as are most restaurants and shopping. Our private catered suites, located on the second floor, are restored to original 1908 decor. Each hosts a living/dining room, kitchen and bath. They may accommodate from 1 to 7 guests. Breakfast served to your suite. For the budget-minded, new rooms available on first floor with shared bath. Serve-yourself continental breakfast provided. Toll-free (877) 224-8946. E-mail: suites@ptialaska.net. www.alaskan.com/sauerdoughsuites/. [ADVERTISEMENT]

Seward Windsong Lodge. Conveniently located at Mile 0.7 Exit Glacier Road, just 2 miles north of the Seward Small Boat Harbor, the Seward Windsong Lodge offers 72 beautiful rooms in a forested setting. The on-site restaurant, Resurrection Roadhouse, serves delicious Alaskan cuisine offering guests a panoramic view of the Resurrection River Valley as they dine. For hiking or outdoor enthusiast, the lodge is located just 6 miles from Exit Glacier, the only glacier in Kenai Fjords National Park accessible by road. For reservations, call 888-959-9590; in Seward (907) 224-7116; or visit us on the web at www.sewardwindsong.com. [ADVERTISEMENT]

Taroka Inn. We don't pretend to be fancy. We're not. We're just clean, comfortable, convenient and affordable. Family-owned, operated and oriented. We offer kitchen units with private bathroom, cable TV, in-room phone, data ports. Couples traveling together have a little more privacy. One queen bed in the bedroom and another

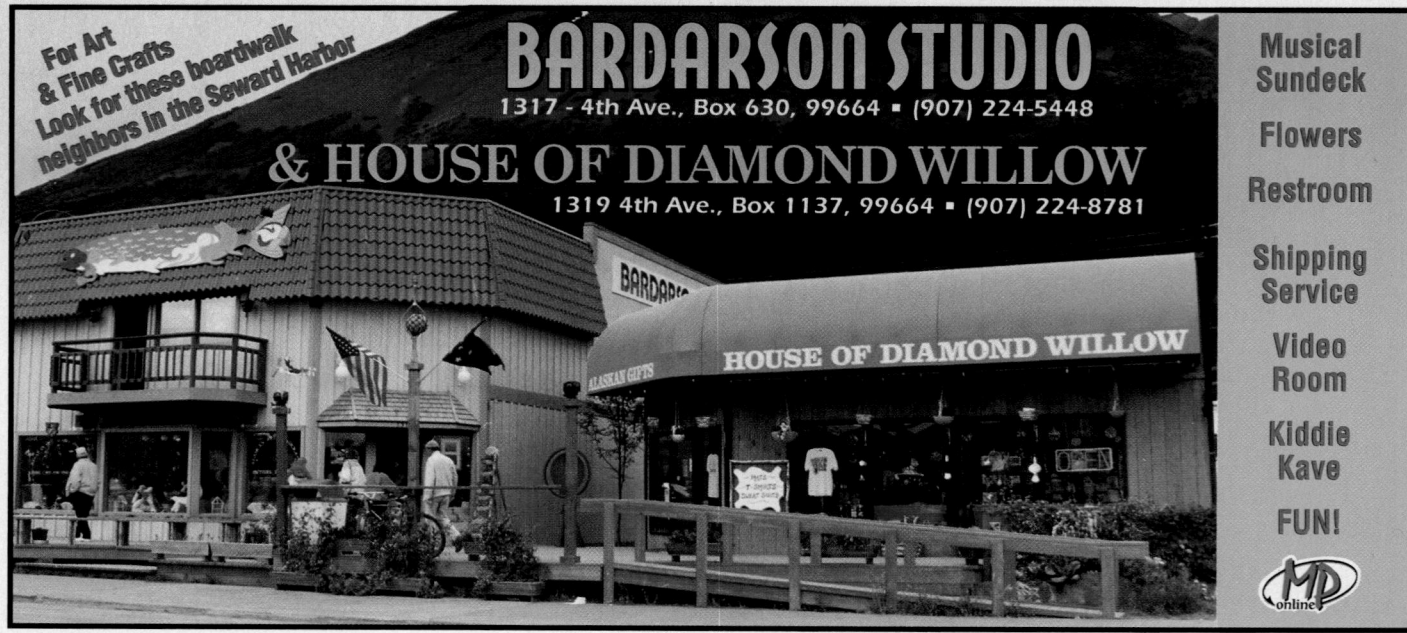

in the living room (not a fold-out). Our larger units accommodate up to 9 persons. Great for family on a budget! Two blocks from Alaska SeaLife Center. One block to restaurants, shops, museum. 3/4 mile to Small Boat Harbor. Nonsmoking available. Pets upon approval only. Phone (907) 224-8975. E-mail: taroka@arctic.net. Internet: www.alaskaone.com/taroka. See display ad.
[ADVERTISEMENT]

Van Gilder Hotel. Seward's favorite small hotel, built in 1916 and completely renovated for the 1990s. Now a National Historic Site, it retains its original Edwardian charm. Centrally located downtown, 308 Adams Street, within easy walking distance to shopping, restaurants and SeaLife Center. For hotel reservations phone (800) 204-6835. P.O. Box 2, Seward, AK, 99664. Fax (907) 224-3689. See display ad this section.
[ADVERTISEMENT]

Camping

Seward has made a good effort to provide overnight parking for self-contained RVs. There are designated tent and RV camping areas along the shore south of Van Buren; camping fee charged. Restrooms with coin-operated showers; water and electric hookups available at some sites. (Caravans: Contact the City Parks and Recreation Dept. for reservations, phone 907/224-4045.) Forest Acres municipal campground is at **Milepost S 2.4** Seward Highway. Private RV parks at Small Boat Harbor, at **Milepost S 6.6** (Nash Road), on Lowell Point Road and on Exit Glacier Road. (See ads this section.) Walk-in tent camping is available at Exit Glacier (turnoff at **Milepost S 3.7** Seward Highway). ▲

Bear Creek RV Park. Good Sam Park. Full and partial hookups, dump station, 4 private restrooms with showers, cable TV, traveler's lounge, propane, laundry, convenience store, ice, video rentals, pay phone. Fax service available. Shuttle service available for Kenai Fjords Tour booking guests. Caravans and large groups welcome. E-mail: hettick@alaska.net. Phone (907) 224-5725.
[ADVERTISEMENT] ▲

Miller's Landing is a campground with down-home Alaskan atmosphere, neighboring Caines Head State Park and hiking trail. Services include: fishing charters, water taxi service, kayak/skiff rentals and boat launching. Owned and operated by the Miller family on their Resurrection Bay homestead, this scenic campground offers beach and forested sites. Electric RV sites, 20/30 amp ($25), large tent sites ($20), cozy cabins

Visitor gets to hold a puppy at IditaRide kennel, just outside Seward on Old Glacier Road. (© Kris Graef, staff)

($30–up), hot showers and flush restrooms centrally located and included. Laundry planned for spring of 2000. Free launch access for our campers. Book a fishing charter for halibut or salmon (full and half-day) on heated cabin boats with gear and bait provided. Our water taxi service takes you to remote camping, kayaking, fishing and hunting sites throughout Kenai Fjords National Park and Resurrection Bay. Those without sea legs can rent a rod and reel to fish from our beaches while watching sea life, birds and the occasional whale. The country store sells bait, tackle, ice, fishing licenses, gifts, wood for campfires and farm fresh eggs. The coffee's always free. Mike Miller, who homesteaded here and survived the 1964 earthquake, is an expert on fishing and visitor information. Fishing advice 5¢. Guaranteed effective or your nickel back! Reservations encouraged for guaranteed site. Mile 3 Lowell Point Road. Look for the blue road sign near the SeaLife Center. Phone (907) 224-5739. Fax (907) 224-5975. E-mail: miland@ptialaska.net. Box 81, Seward, AK 99664. [ADVERTISEMENT] ▲

Transportation

Air: Seward airport is reached by turning east on Airport Road at **Milepost S 2.7** on the Seward Highway. Scheduled daily service to Anchorage; charters also available.

Ferry: Alaska Marine Highway office on Cruise Ship Dock; phone (907) 224-5485. The Alaska ferry MV *Tustumena* departs Seward for Kodiak and Valdez.

Railroad: The Alaska Railroad connects Seward to Anchorage and Fairbanks.

Bus: Scheduled service to Anchorage.

Taxi: Service available.

Highway: Seward is reached via the 127-mile/203.2-km Seward Highway from Anchorage.

Tours: Seward Trolley offers city tours 10

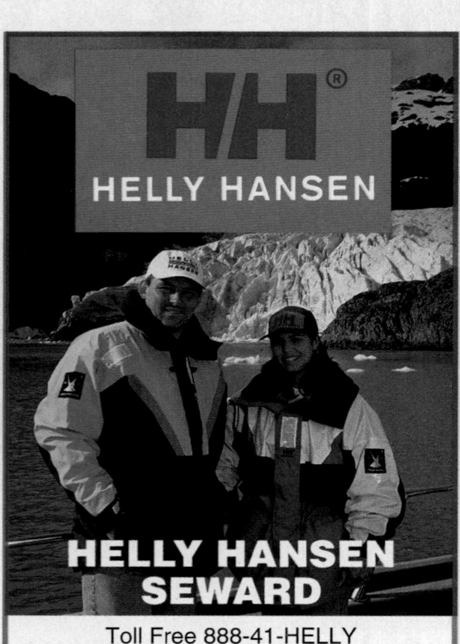

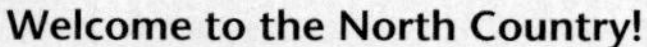

A.M. to 7 P.M. daily, Memorial Day through Labor Day.

Attractions

The Railcar *Seward* houses the chamber of commerce information center. Located at 3rd and Jefferson Street, this railcar was the Seward observation car on the Alaska Railroad from 1936 until the early 1960s. Information and detailed map of the city are available. Phone (907) 224-3094.

Walking Tour of Seward encompasses more than 30 attractions including homes and businesses that date back to the early 1900s; some are still being used, while others have been restored as historic sites. A brochure containing details on all the attractions of the tour is available at the railcar information center. The complete tour covers about 2 miles/3.2 km and takes about 1 to 2 hours, depending upon how much time you wish to spend browsing.

Seward Marine Science Education Center, across from the Alaska SeaLife Center, has laboratories, aquaculture ponds and the research vessel *Alpha Helix*. In 1999, the Pratt Museum's *Darkened Waters* exhibit—which chronicles the impact of the Exxon *Valdez* grounding 10 years ago—will be featured here. Open daily in summer, 10 A.M. to 5 P.M. Admission is $3 adults, $1 for children. For group rates and tours, phone (907) 224-5261.

Alaska SeaLife Center. This 7-acre waterfront site combines research facilities with wildlife rehabilitation and public education. Construction of the SeaLife Center was funded by the Exxon Valdez Oil Spill Restoration fund and private donations.

The Center allows you to come face-to-face with Alaska's exciting marine wildlife, explore their undersea world and experience the wonder of nature in a one-of-a-kind marine science and visitor facility. This $50 million, 115,000-square-foot center opens windows to the sea—above and below the surface. Indoors, view the distinct habitats of marine birds, Steller sea lions, seals, fish and otters. Outdoors, step right to the edge of Resurrection Bay, teeming with Alaska marine wildlife. Open daily. Admission $12.50 adults, $10 youth.

In Seward on June 21, 2000, sunrise will be 4:32 A.M. and sunset at 11:27 P.M.

Fishing at Seward's Small Boat Harbor. (© Kay McElrath Johnson)

Visit the Small Boat Harbor. This municipal harbor, built after the 1964 earthquake, is home port to fishing boats, charter boats and sightseeing boats. The harbor is also home to sea otters—watch for them! Visitors may notice the great number of sailboats moored here: many are members of the William H. Seward Yacht Club, which sponsors an annual sailboat and yacht show.

Seward Museum, at Jefferson and 3rd Avenue, is operated by the Resurrection Bay Historical Society (Box 55, Seward 99664). The museum features artifacts and photographs from the 1964 earthquake, WWII, the founding days of Seward and other highlights of Seward's history. Also on display is a collection of Native baskets and ivory carvings. The museum is open daily, 9 A.M. to 5 P.M., May 1 to Sept. 30. Open reduced hours remainder of year; check locally, or phone (907) 224-3902. A modest admission fee is charged.

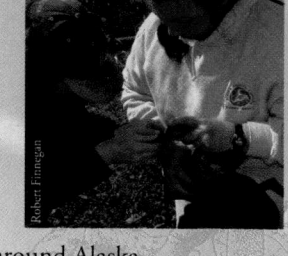

Seward Community Library, across from the City–State Building, presents (on request) short slide/sound shows on a vari-

Steller sea lions hauled out on Resurrection Bay's rocky coastline. (© Kay McElrath Johnson)

ety of subjects and has some informative displays. A program on the 1964 earthquake is shown daily at 2 P.M. (except Sunday) from June 15 through the first Saturday in September. Library hours are 1–8 P.M. Monday through Friday, 1–6 P.M. Saturday.

St. Peter's Episcopal Church is 3 blocks west of the museum at the corner of 2nd Avenue and Adams Street. It was built in 1906 and is considered the oldest Protestant church on the Kenai Peninsula. One feature is the unique painting of the Resurrection, for which Alaskans were used as models and Resurrection Bay as the background. Well-known Dutch artist Jan Van Emple was commissioned to paint the picture in 1925 when he was living in Seward. Obtain key to church from the Seward Museum in season.

Hiking Trails. Two Lakes trail is an easy mile-long loop trail along the base of Mount Marathon. The trail passes through a wooded area and follows what used to be Hemlock Street. Beautiful view of marina below and north end of Resurrection Bay. Start at First Lake, behind the Alaska Vocational and Technical Center Administration Building at 2nd Avenue and B Street.

The **National Historic Iditarod Trail** begins at the Alaska SeaLife Center and follows a marked course through town, then north on the Seward Highway. At Mile 2.1 Nash Road (turn off at **Milepost S 3.2** Seward Highway), the trail continues from a gravel parking area on the east side of Sawmill Creek north to Bear Lake. The trail eventually rejoins the Seward Highway at **Milepost S 12.**

Caines Head State Recreation Area, 6 miles/9.6 km south of Seward, is accessible by boat or via a 4.5-mile/7.2-km beach trail (low tide only). The trailhead/parking is located about Mile 2 Lowell Point Road. The Caines Head area has bunkers and gun emplacements that were used to guard the entrance to Resurrection Bay during WWII.

Mount Marathon Race™, Seward's annual Fourth of July endurance race to the top of Mount Marathon (elev. 3,022 feet/921m) and back down, is a grueling test for athletes. The race is said to have begun in 1909 with a wager between 2 sourdoughs as to how long it would take to run up and down Mount Marathon. The first year of the official race is uncertain: records indicate either 1912 or 1915. Fastest recorded time is 43 minutes, 23 seconds set in 1981 by Bill Spencer, who broke his own 1974 record. The descent is so steep that it's part run, part jump and part slide. The race attracts competitors from all over, and thousands of spectators line the route each year.

Annual Seward Silver Salmon Derby™ in August is one of the largest sporting events in Alaska. It is held over 9 days, starting the second Saturday in August and continuing through Sunday of the following weekend. 2000 will be the derby's 45th year. Record derby catch to date is a 20.59-lb. salmon caught off Twin Rocks by John Westlund of Anchorage.

There are more than $250,000 in prizes for the derby, including $10,000 in cash for the largest fish. Also part of the derby are the sought-after tagged silvers worth as much as $100,000. Prizes are sponsored by various merchants and the Chamber of Commerce.

The town fills up fast during the derby: Make reservations! For more information contact the Seward Chamber of Commerce; phone (907) 224-8051.

Chugach Heritage Center. Situated on picturesque Resurrection Bay in Seward, Alaska. The Center is located in the historic Alaska Railroad depot built in 1917. It has been fully restored to its original condition. The center features a production of the legends of the Chugach Peoples. The 25-minute performance can be seen 6 times daily. Visitors can browse in the gallery of Alaskan Native Art, where they can purchase distinctive pieces and specialy gifts. Open Tuesday through Sunday, mid-May to mid-September. [ADVERTISEMENT]

Bardarson Studio. In Seward find Bardarson Studio on the prettiest boardwalk in the

boat harbor area, with the best selection of Alaska art and fine crafts set to music. Bardarson Studio recognizes that shopping is entertainment for travelers, providing a Kiddie-Kave for children, and a video room for your non-shopper. Public restroom and postal service available. 1317 4th Avenue. Phone (800) 354-0141. E-mail: bardarson

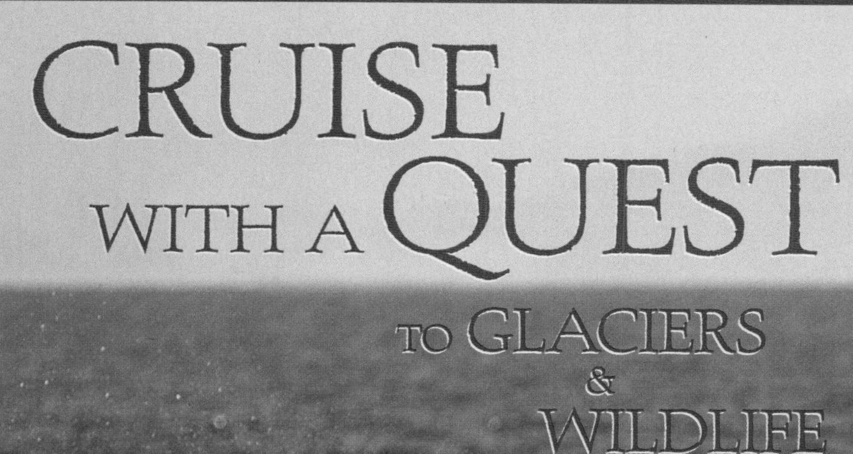

Seward's Alaska SeaLife Center downtown on the waterfront. (© Barb Willard)

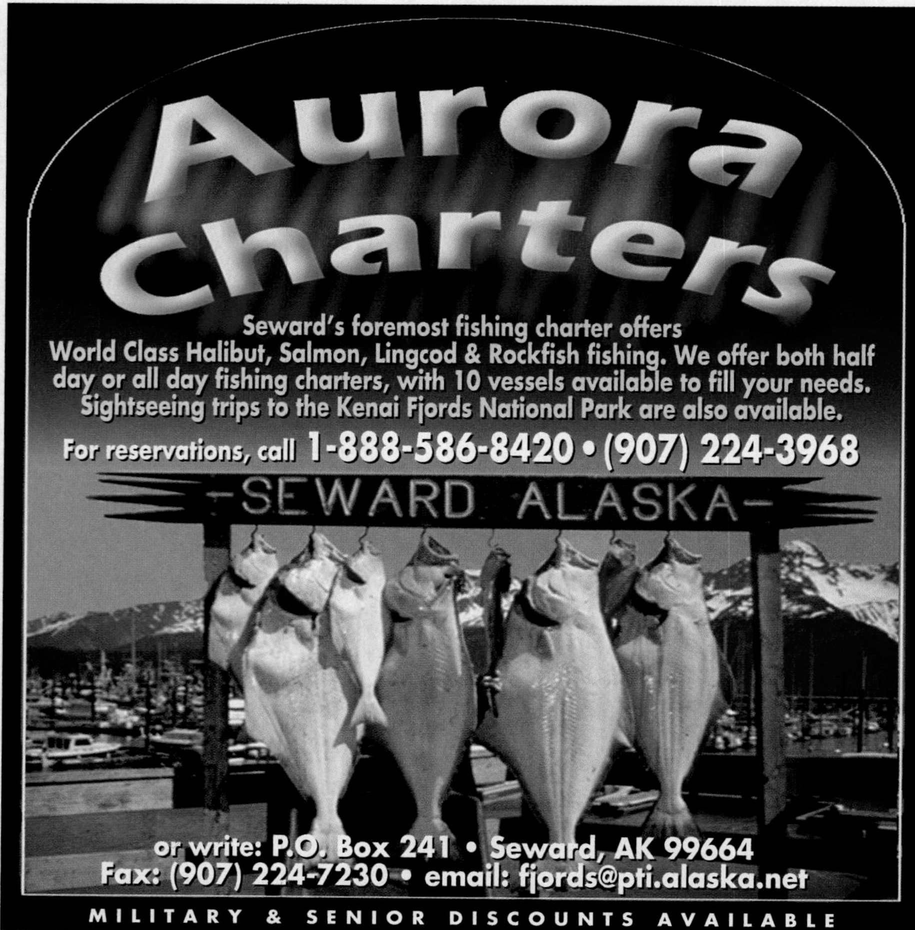

@seward.net. Internet: www.seward.net /bar darson. [ADVERTISEMENT]

The Fish House. First and finest fishing charter service in Seward! Record-class halibut and silver salmon fishing charters available now. While fishing, enjoy the scenic beauty of the Kenai Fjords National Park—glaciers, mountains, puffins, whales, sea otters and seals. The Fish House also supplies a complete line of fishing tackle, bait, ice and outboard motor repairs. Call now for reservations or information on fishing the scenic waters surrounding Seward, Alaska. 1-800-257-7760 or (907) 224-3674. E-mail: fishhous@ptialaska.net. Internet: ptialaska.net/~fishhous/. Halibut charters: April 1–Oct. 1. Salmon charters: June 1–Sept. 20. P.O. Box 1209, Seward, AK 99664. www.alaskan.com/fishhous. See display ad this section. [ADVERTISEMENT]

IdidaRide Sled Dog Tours. Experience dog mushing, summer style, on a 2-mile wilderness dog sled ride at 4th Place Iditarod racer Mitch Seavey's training location. Informative tour includes 60-husky kennel, cuddly puppies, arctic equipment demonstration. 5 tours daily. Reservations recommended. P.O. Box 2906, Seward, AK 99664. (907) 224-8607, fax (907) 224-8608. Internet: www.alaskaone.com/ididaride. Off Exit Glacier Road. See display ad Mile 3.7 Seward Highway. [ADVERTISEMENT]

Kayak & Custom Adventures Worldwide Sea Kayking with Alaska's most experienced outfitter. Day trips on the bay and wilderness expeditions into Kenai Fjords. Take home unforgettably wonderful memories that you can't find standing on the shore. Let us show you the real Alaska by sea kayak! Van-camping road trips also. E-mail: kayak@arctic.net. Web site: www.alaskan.com/kayak/. Seward (907) 224-3960. Reservations: toll-free (800) 288-3134 or (907) 258-FUNN. [ADVERTISEMENT]

Northland Books & Charts is "Alaska's foremost nautical boutique." Chart your Alaska cruise memories on Northland's NOAA and Alaska specialty maps, including USGS topographical, national park and recreational guides. The latest bestsellers, children's books, Alaska historical editions, cookbooks, outdoor guides and one-of-a-kind Alaska-made clocks and barometers await you in this maritime specialty gift shop. Located at the corner of 4th and

Adams. E-mail: northland bks@attmail.com. Web page: www.northlandbooks.com. Open daily from 9 A.M. to 6 P.M. Phone (907) 224-3102. [ADVERTISEMENT]

Kenai Fjords Tours. The excitement begins the moment you pull away from the Seward boat harbor! You'll be greeted by playful sea otters, view boisterous Steller sea lions, look for whales and porpoises, photograph colorful puffins and bald eagles, and watch a calving glacier. Cruising since 1974, Kenai Fjords Tours is the original Kenai

Fjords National Park tour and continues to be the most popular. Our new, custom sightseeing vessels have walk-around decks so you can easily watch and photograph the magnificent scenery. Our captains are experienced naturalists averaging more than 12 years in Kenai Fjords National Park, so you'll learn about this coastal wilderness from guides who really know the area. All cruises include a meal and many include a special stop at Fox Island for our delicious all-you-can-eat salmon bake at Kenai Fjords Wilderness Lodge. Don't miss it! Call today for reservations. Toll free (800) 478-8068 or (907) 224-8068. Located at the Seward Small Boat Harbor. See display ad this section. [ADVERTISEMENT]

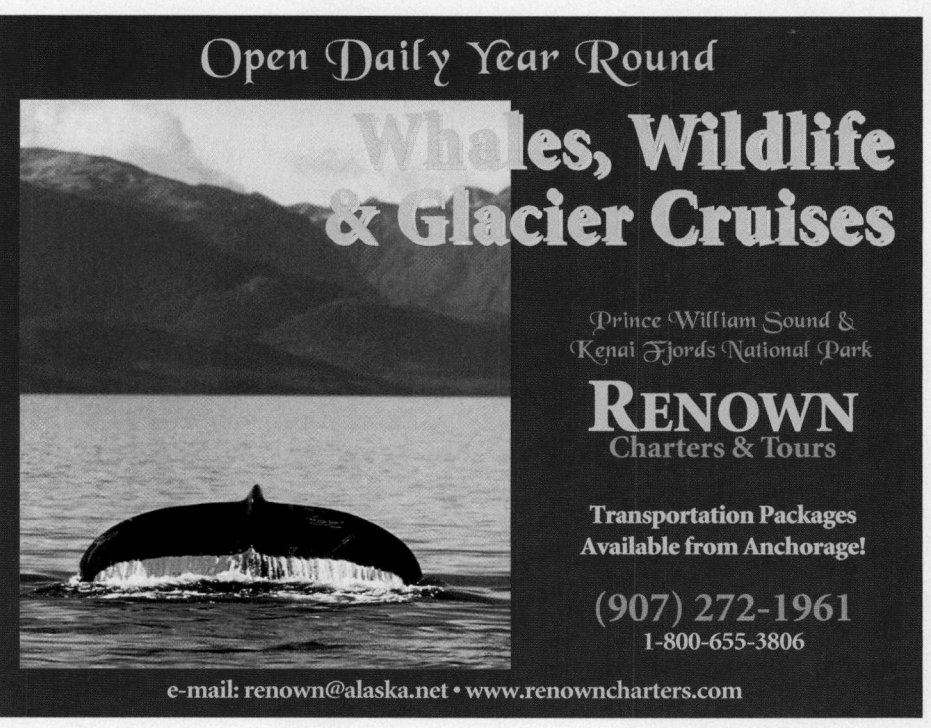

Major Marine Kenai Fjords National Park Tours. Join us for Seward's world-class wildlife and glacier cruises of the Kenai Fjords. Only Major Marine Tours' cruises are hosted by a uniformed National Park ranger. We offer 2 wonderful cruise options: 1) a half-day wildlife cruise of the Kenai Fjords, and 2) a full-day wildlife and glacier cruise of the Kenai Fjords National Park and Chiswell Islands National Wildlife Refuge. During the cruise you'll generally see otters, sea lions, puffins, eagles, porpoises, whales,

Kenai Fjords National Park

The fjords of Kenai Fjords National Park were formed when glaciers flowed down to the sea from the ice field and then retreated, leaving behind the deep inlets that characterize the park's coastline and give it its name.

Substantial populations of marine mammals inhabit or migrate through the park's coastal waters, including sea otters, Steller sea lions, dolphins and whales. Icebergs from calving glaciers provide ideal refuge for harbor seals, and the rugged coastline provides habitat for more than 100,000 nesting birds.

The park's scenic coastline and coastal wildlife is most commonly viewed by private tour and charter boats that depart from Seward's Small Boat Harbor daily in summer (see advertisements this section).

For independent wilderness travelers, 4 public-use cabins along the coast are available in summer by reservation. The cabins are located at Holgate Arm, Aialik Bay and North Arm. Kayakers and boaters can also camp on beaches but must be aware ahead of time of land status; 45,000 acres of coastline are owned by Native corporations and are *not* available for public camping. Maps indicating land ownership are available from the park visitor center. *NOTE: Private boaters should consult with local outfitters and charter operators for detailed information on boating conditions.*

Another dominant feature of the 605,000-acre Kenai Fjords National Park is the Harding Icefield, a 300-square-mile vestige of the last ice age. Harding Icefield can be reached by a strenuous all-day hike from the base of Exit Glacier or by a charter flightseeing trip out of Seward.

Exit Glacier is the most accessible of the park's glaciers. Turn at **Milepost S 3.7** on the Seward Highway and follow Exit Glacier Road to the visitor center parking area. There are several trails through the outwash plain of Exit Glacier that afford excellent views of the ice and surrounding mountains. A half-mile trail leads from the parking lot to the glacier. Ranger-led nature walks are available in summer at Exit Glacier, where there is a picnic area and walk-in campground. Visitor information is available at the Exit Glacier ranger station and visitor center; open summer only. Exit Glacier is accessible in winter by skis, dogsled or snow machine. A public-use cabin is available in winter by permit.

Slide programs, videos, exhibits and information on Kenai Fjords National Park and organized activities at the park are available at the park visitor center on 4th Avenue in the Small Boat Harbor area next to the Harbormaster's office. The center is open daily from Memorial Day to Labor Day; hours are 9 A.M. to 6 P.M. The remainder of the year hours are 8 A.M. to 5 P.M. (subject to change) weekdays. Contact the park superintendent, Box 1727, Seward, AK 99664. For more information, phone the park office at (907) 224-3175 or the Park Information Line at (907) 224-2132. On the Internet, visit www.nps.gov/kefj.

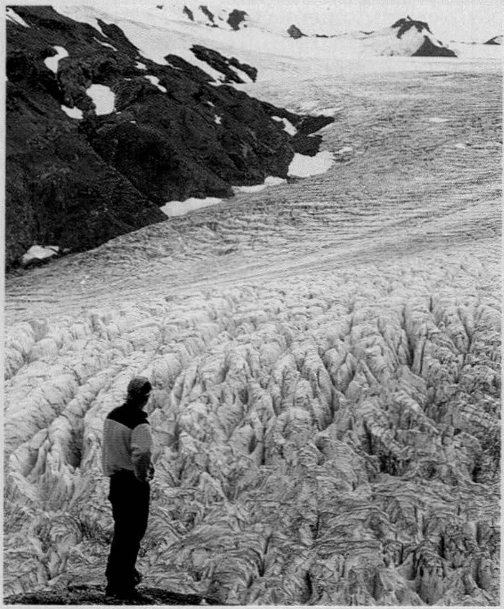

Exit Glacier is about a 12-mile drive from Seward, then a half-mile walk to the face. (© Mike Jones)

bird colonies and more. You'll also pull up close to some of Alaska's most awe-inspiring glaciers. The large tour boats feature reserved table seating, inside heated cabins and multiple outside decks. A freshly prepared all-you-can-eat salmon and prime rib buffet is available on both cruises for only $10. The food is consistently rated the best of any day-cruise company. Both cruises sail from Seward's boat harbor May to late September. The full-day cruise departs at 11:45 A.M. and costs $99. The half-day cruise departs at 12:45 P.M. and costs $64, and at 6 P.M. and costs $49. For reservations or a free brochure, call: (800) 764-7300 or (907) 274-7300. Major Marine Tours, 411 West 4th, Anchorage, AK 99501. Ticket office also located on Seward boardwalk: (907) 224-8030 (May to September). Internet: www.majormarine.com. [ADVERTISEMENT]

Mariah Tours. Join us for a memorable day to the Chiswell Islands and Kenai Fjords National Park on the small ship alternative. You'll enjoy close-up viewing of whales, sea lions and seabirds. You'll appreciate the personalized attention on our 43-foot vessel, with a limit of only 16 passengers on board. Featuring tours to spectacular Northwestern Glacier via Granite Passage, the most scenic area within Kenai Fjords National Park. Popular exclusive tours for birding and naturalist groups. Operating mid-May–September. For reservations: (800) 270-1238. In Seward: (907) 224-8623. [ADVERTISEMENT]

Wildlife Quest in Kenai Fjords. Cruise to the wild side of Kenai Fjords National Park on the only catamaran cruise—the Wildlife Quest. Travel to the park's famous sea lion rookeries, seabird colonies, whale-watching waters, and tidewater glaciers—in total comfort. Departs daily from Seward. $99/person plus tax, lunch and beverages included. Alaska Catamaran Cruises, 1321 4th Ave., Seward, AK 99664. (907) 224-2282 or 1-888-305-2515 . [ADVERTISEMENT]

AREA FISHING: Resurrection Bay, coho (silver) salmon to 22 lbs., use herring, troll or cast, July to October; king salmon to 45 lbs., May to August; also bottom fish, flounder, halibut to 300 lbs. and cod, use weighted spoons and large red spinners by jigging, year-round. Charter and rental boats are available.

Kenai Peninsula

STERLING HIGHWAY ①

Connects: Seward Highway to Homer, AK **Length:** 143 miles
Road Surface: Paved **Season:** Open all year
Major Attractions: Kenai National Wildlife Refuge, Russian Orthodox Churches, Homer Spit

(See maps, pages 535–536)

View of Kenai Lake from Milepost S 47.8 Sterling Highway. (© Kris Graef, staff)

	Anchorage	Homer	Kenai	Seward	Soldotna
Anchorage		233	158	127	147
Homer	233		96	180	85
Kenai	158	96		105	11
Seward	127	180	105		94
Soldotna	147	85	11	94	

The Sterling Highway (Alaska Route 1) begins 90 miles south of Anchorage at its junction with the Seward Highway and travels 143 miles west and south to the community of Homer. Several major Kenai Peninsula side roads junction with the Sterling Highway, including Skilak Lake Loop Road, Swanson River Road, Kenai Spur Highway, Kalifornsky Beach Road, Cohoe Loop Road and Anchor River Beach Road.

From its junction with the Seward Highway at Tern Lake, the Sterling Highway passes through Chugach National Forest and Kenai National Wildlife Refuge. The Kenai Mountains are home to Dall sheep, mountain goats, black and brown bears, and caribou. The many lakes, rivers and streams of the Kenai Peninsula are famous for their sportfishing. The highway also provides access to the Resurrection Pass Trail System.

From Soldotna south, the Sterling Highway follows the west coast of the peninsula along Cook Inlet. There are beautiful views of peaks on the Alaska Peninsula.

Physical mileposts on the Sterling Highway show distance from Seward. The Sterling Highway is a paved, mostly 2-lane highway, with few passing lanes and some short sections of 4-lane highway. The Sterling Highway is open year-round.

Emergency medical services: phone 911 or use CB channels 9, 11 or 19.

Sterling Highway Log

Distance from Seward (S) is followed by distance from Anchorage (A) and distance from Homer (H).
Physical mileposts show distance from Seward.

ALASKA ROUTE 1

S 37 (59.5 km) **A 90** (144.8 km) **H 142.5** (229.3 km) **Tern Lake Junction.** Tern Lake day-use area (see description next milepost). Gravel turnout beside Tern Lake with interpretive boardwalk and viewing platforms. Information signs on area birds and wildlife.

Junction with Seward Highway (Alaska Route 9) to Seward and Anchorage. Turn to **Milepost S 37** on page 510 in the SEWARD HIGHWAY section for log.

NOTE: Reconstruction of the first 8 miles of the Sterling Highway is scheduled for completion in June 2000. Driving distances and facilities may vary from log.

S 37.4 (60.2 km) **A 90.4** (145.5 km) **H 142.1** (228.7 km) USFS Tern Lake day-use picnic area; toilets, water, picnic tables. USFS spawning channel for king salmon on Daves Creek at outlet of Tern Lake. Short viewing trail with information signs illustrating use of log weirs and stream protection techniques.

S 38 (61.1 km) **A 91** (146.4 km) **H 141.5** (227.7 km) Avalanche gates.

S 38.3 (61.6 km) **A 91.3** (146.9 km) **H 141.2** (227.2 km) *Emergency call box.*

S 39 (62.8 km) **A 92** (148 km) **H 140.5** (226.1 km) **Daves Creek** beside highway flows west into Quartz Creek.

S 40.9 (65.8 km) **A 93.9** (151.1 km) **H 138.6** (223 km) Bridge over Quartz Creek. Highway follows Quartz Creek west. This stream empties into Kenai Lake.

S 44.9 (72.3 km) **A 97.9** (157.5 km) **H 134.6** (216.6 km) Sunrise Inn (open year-round); food, gas and lodging. Trail rides. **Junction** with Quartz Creek Road to Quartz Creek and Crescent Creek campgrounds. (Descriptions follow.)

STERLING HIGHWAY *Tern Lake Junction to Soldotna, AK*

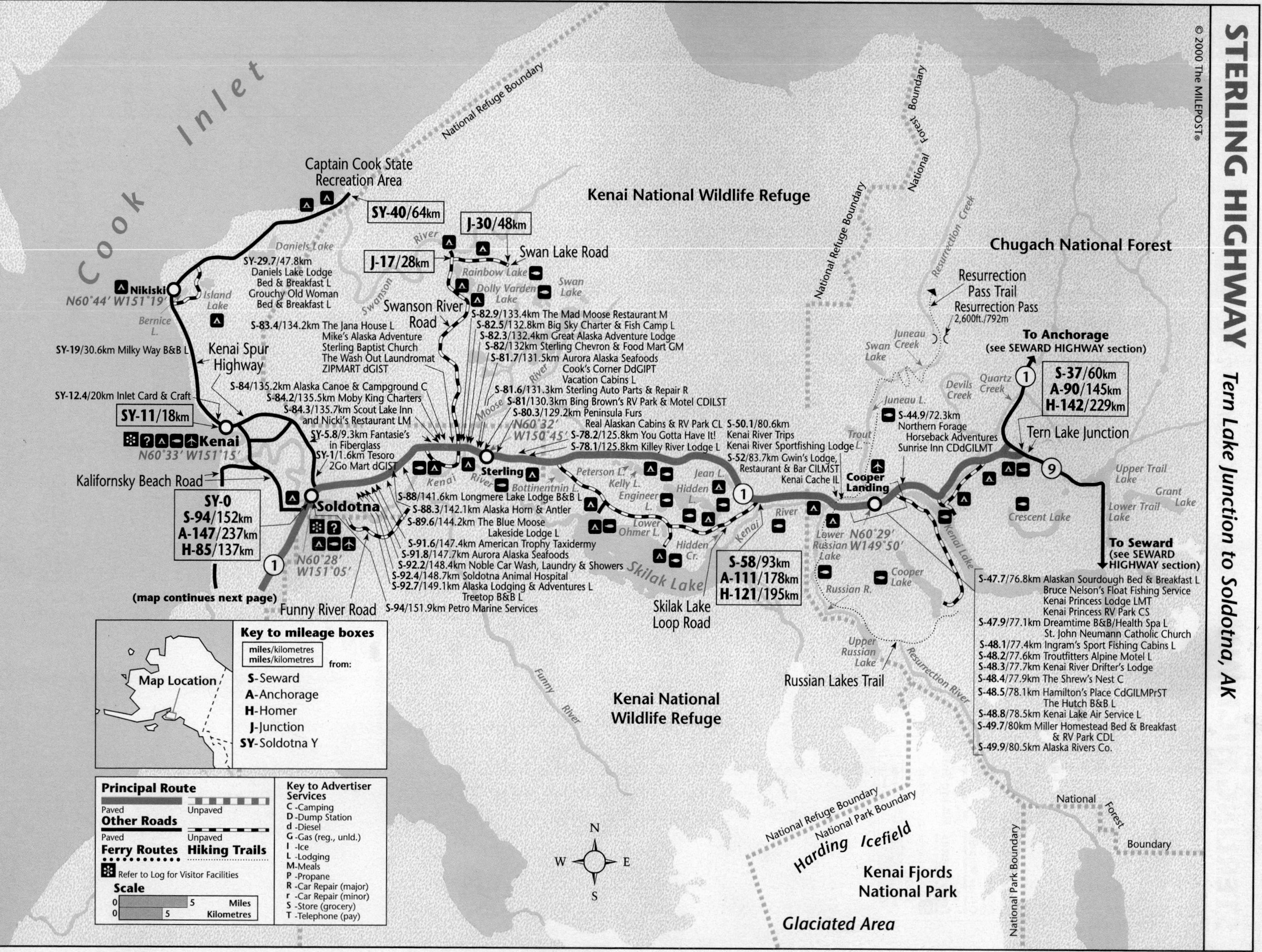

STERLING HIGHWAY *Soldotna, AK, to Homer, AK*

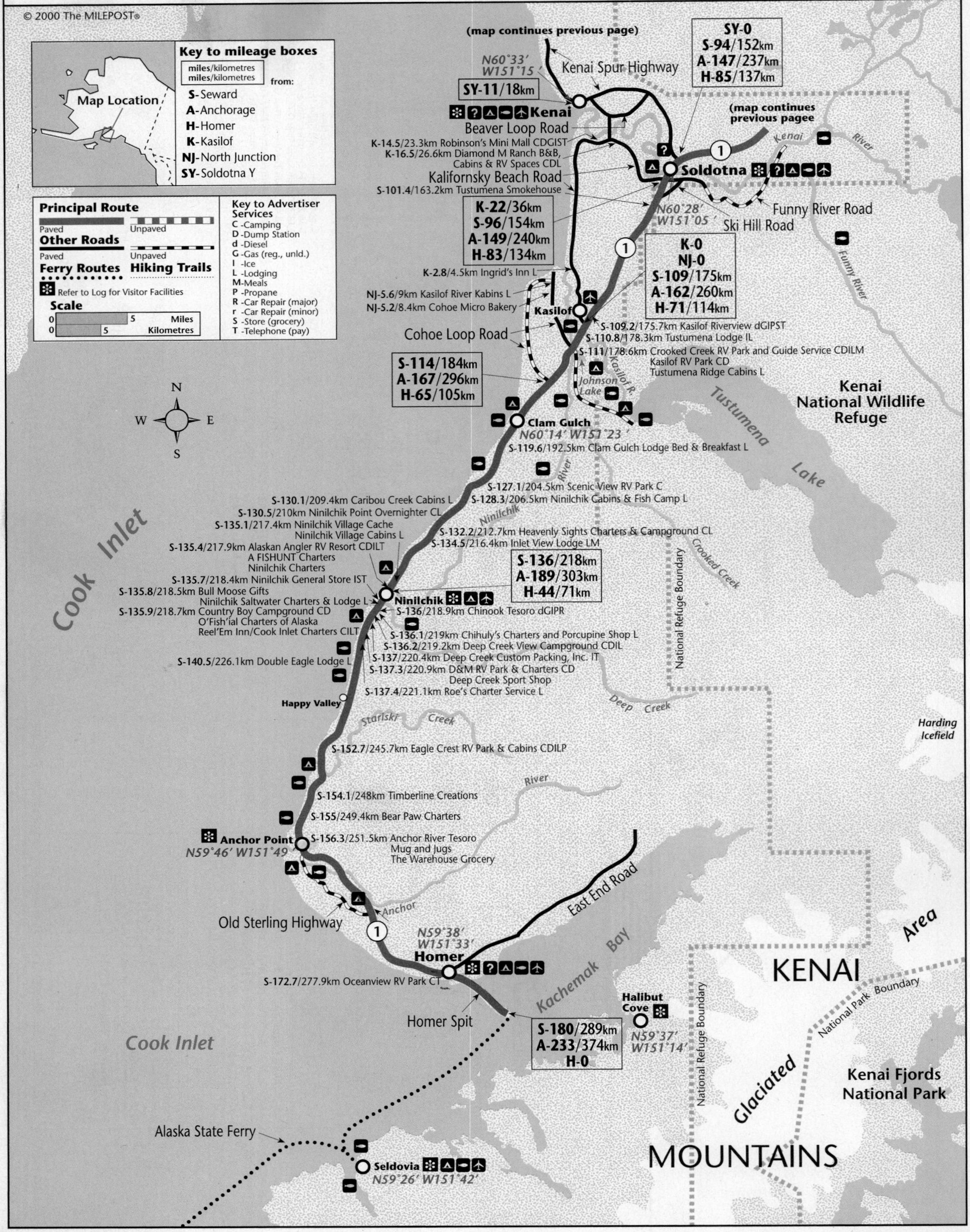

Map Location

Key to mileage boxes

miles/kilometres
miles/kilometres
from:

- **S**-Seward
- **A**-Anchorage
- **H**-Homer
- **K**-Kasilof
- **NJ**-North Junction
- **SY**-Soldotna Y

Principal Route
Paved
Unpaved
Other Roads
Paved
Unpaved
Ferry Routes
Hiking Trails
Refer to Log for Visitor Facilities
Scale
0 5 Miles
0 5 Kilometres

Key to Advertiser Services

- C -Camping
- D -Dump Station
- d -Diesel
- G -Gas (reg., unld.)
- I -Ice
- L -Lodging
- M-Meals
- P -Propane
- R -Car Repair (major)
- r -Car Repair (minor)
- S -Store (grocery)
- T -Telephone (pay)

(map continues previous page)

N60°33′ W151°15′
Kenai Spur Highway
SY-11/18km
Kenai
Beaver Loop Road
K-14.5/23.3km Robinson's Mini Mall CDGIST
K-16.5/26.6km Diamond M Ranch B&B, Cabins & RV Spaces CDL
Kalifornsky Beach Road
S-101.4/163.2km Tustumena Smokehouse

SY-0
S-94/152km
A-147/237km
H-85/137km

(map continues previous pagee)

Kenai River
Soldotna
N60°28′ W151°05′
Funny River Road
Ski Hill Road
Funny River

K-22/36km
S-96/154km
A-149/240km
H-83/134km

K-0
NJ-0
S-109/175km
A-162/260km
H-71/114km

K-2.8/4.5km Ingrid's Inn L
NJ-5.6/9km Kasilof River Kabins L
NJ-5.2/8.4km Cohoe Micro Bakery
Kasilof
Cohoe Loop Road
S-109.2/175.7km Kasilof Riverview dGIPST
S-110.8/178.3km Tustumena Lodge IL
S-111/178.6km Crooked Creek RV Park and Guide Service CDILM
Kasilof RV Park CD
Tustumena Ridge Cabins L

S-114/184km
A-167/296km
H-65/105km

Johnson Lake
Kasilof R.
Tustumena Lake
Kenai National Wildlife Refuge

N
W E
S

Clam Gulch
N60°14′ W151°23′
S-119.6/192.5km Clam Gulch Lodge Bed & Breakfast L
River
S-127.1/204.5km Scenic View RV Park C
S-128.3/206.5km Ninilchik Cabins & Fish Camp L
S-130.1/209.4km Caribou Creek Cabins L
S-130.5/210km Ninilchik Point Overnighter CL
S-135.1/217.4km Ninilchik Village Cache
Ninilchik Village Cabins L
Ninilchik
S-132.2/212.7km Heavenly Sights Charters & Campground CL
S-134.5/216.4km Inlet View Lodge LM
S-135.4/217.9km Alaskan Angler RV Resort CDILT
A FISHUNT Charters
Ninilchik Charters
Crooked Creek

Cook Inlet

S-136/218km
A-189/303km
H-44/71km

S-135.7/218.4km Ninilchik General Store IST
S-135.8/218.5km Bull Moose Gifts
Ninilchik Saltwater Charters & Lodge L
Ninilchik
S-135.9/218.7km Country Boy Campground CD
O'Fish'ial Charters of Alaska
Reel'Em Inn/Cook Inlet Charters CILT
S-136/218.9km Chinook Tesoro dGIPR
S-136.1/219km Chihuly's Charters and Porcupine Shop L
S-136.2/219.2km Deep Creek View Campground CDIL
S-137/220.4km Deep Creek Custom Packing, Inc. IT
S-140.5/226.1km Double Eagle Lodge L
S-137.3/220.9km D&M RV Park & Charters CD
Deep Creek Sport Shop
S-137.4/221.1km Roe's Charter Service L
National Refuge Boundary
Happy Valley
Deep Creek
Starlski Creek
Harding Icefield
S-152.7/245.7km Eagle Crest RV Park & Cabins CDILP
River
S-154.1/248km Timberline Creations
S-155/249.4km Bear Paw Charters
Anchor Point
N59°46′ W151°49′
S-156.3/251.5km Anchor River Tesoro
Mug and Jugs
The Warehouse Grocery
East End Road
Anchor
Old Sterling Highway
N59°38′ W151°33′
Homer
S-172.7/277.9km Oceanview RV Park CT
Kachemak Bay
Homer Spit
Area
KENAI
National Park Boundary
Halibut Cove
N59°37′ W151°14′

S-180/289km
A-233/374km
H-0

Cook Inlet
National Refuge Boundary
Glaciated
Kenai Fjords National Park
Alaska State Ferry
MOUNTAINS
Seldovia
N59°26′ W151°42′

Sunrise Inn. See display ad this section.

Northern Forage Horseback Adventures. Horseback riding year-round. Many of our customers tell us this was their finest trail ride! Two and 4-hour trips on Alaskan horses with fantastic scenery and wildlife viewing. Visit our Pioneer Cabin Gift Shop featuring local arts and crafts. Located on Quartz Creek Road behind Sunrise Inn. Phone (907) 595-1806. E-mail: horses@arctic.net. [ADVERTISEMENT]

Quartz Creek Road leads south to **Quartz Creek Recreation Area.** Quartz Creek Campground, at Mile 0.3, has 45 sites, boat launch and parking lot, flush toilets, water system, firepits, camping fee $13 single, $20 double. **Quartz Creek**, rainbow, midsummer; Dolly Varden to 25 inches, late May through June.

Crescent Creek Campground, at Mile 3, has 9 sites, toilets, firepits, water, $10 camping fee. Crescent Creek Trail (USFS), trailhead parking at Mile 3.4 Quartz Creek Road, is a popular trail with mountain bikers. Nice 6.2-mile/10-km hike through hemlock forest to subalpine **Crescent Lake**; stocked with grayling. *Watch for bears.* A public-use cabin is located at the lake; permit required for use; accessible in summer only.

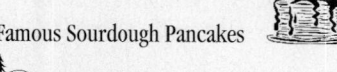

S 45 (72.4 km) **A 98** (157.7 km) **H 134.5** (216.5 km) Beautiful views of Kenai Lake next 3 miles westbound. The lake's unusual color is caused by glacial silt.

Westbound travelers are entering one of Alaska's best-known lake and river fishing regions. *NOTE: The diversity of fishing conditions and frequent regulation changes on all Kenai waters make it advisable to consult locally for fishing news and regulations.*

Kenai Lake, lake trout, May 15 to Sept. 30; trout, May to September; Dolly Varden, May to September. Kenai Lake and tributaries are closed to salmon fishing.

S 46.3 (74.5 km) **A 99.3** (159.8 km) **H 133.2** (214.4 km) Small gravel turnout to south.

S 47 (75.6 km) **A 100** (160.9 km) **H 132.5** (213.2 km) Turnout to south.

S 47.6 (76.6 km) **A 100.6** (161.9 km) **H 131.9** (212.3 km) Laundromat and showers; towing.

S 47.7 (76.8 km) **A 100.7** (162 km) **H 131.8** (212.1 km) **Bean Creek Road**, access to Bruce Nelson's fishing guide service (0.3 mile), Alaskan Sourdough Bed and Breakfast (0.7 mile) and the Kenai Princess Lodge and RV Park on the Kenai River (2 miles). The lodge's lobby has an interesting chandelier made from antlers.

Alaskan Sourdough Bed & Breakfast. See display ad this section.

Bruce Nelson's Float Fishing Service. See display ad on page 538.

Kenai Princess Lodge. A wilderness retreat overlooking the salmon-rich Kenai River featuring cozy bungalow-style rooms with sun porches, wood stoves, televisions and telephones. Spacious view deck, fine restaurant, lounge, gift shop, tour desk, hot tubs, exercise room. Meeting facilities. Open year-round. Call (800) 426-0500. [ADVERTISEMENT]

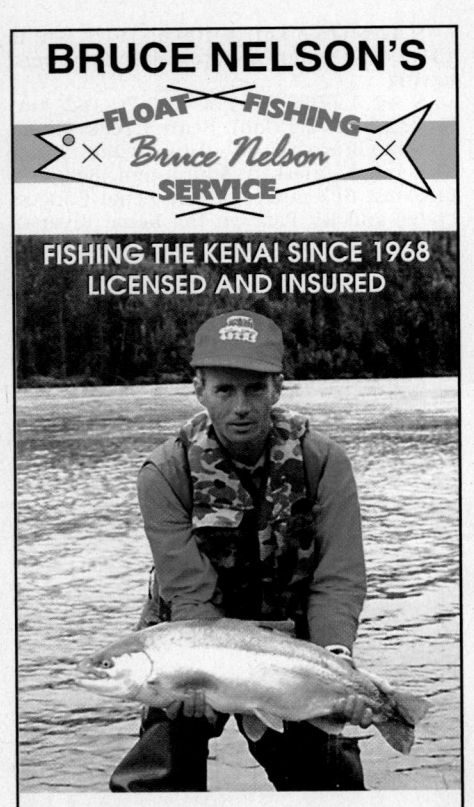

Kenai Princess RV Park. At Cooper Landing on the salmon-rich Kenai River. Featuring 35 sites with water and power, general store, showers, laundry, septic. Use of facilities at adjacent Kenai Princess Lodge. Open mid-May to mid-Septeber. $20 per night. Phone (907) 595-1425 for reservations. [ADVERTISEMENT] ▲

S 47.8 (76.9 km) **A 100.8** (162.2 km) **H 131.7** (211.9 km) Bridge over Kenai River at mouth of Kenai Lake. Kenai Lake serves as the headwaters of the Kenai River Special Management Area, established in 1984 to protect this unique resource. The 105-mile-long KRSMA stretches from Kenai Lake to almost to the city of Kenai. The Kenai River flows directly alongside the highway for the next 10 miles westbound.

S 48 (77.2 km) **A 101** (162.5 km) **H 131.5** (211.6 km) Turnoff to north for access road to **Cooper Landing State Recreation Site Boat Launch Facility,** adjacent to the Kenai River Bridge, contains a concrete boat launch, day-use parking, restrooms, viewing decks, informational panels and telescopes. $5 launching fee or $5 parking fee for vehicles not launching boats.

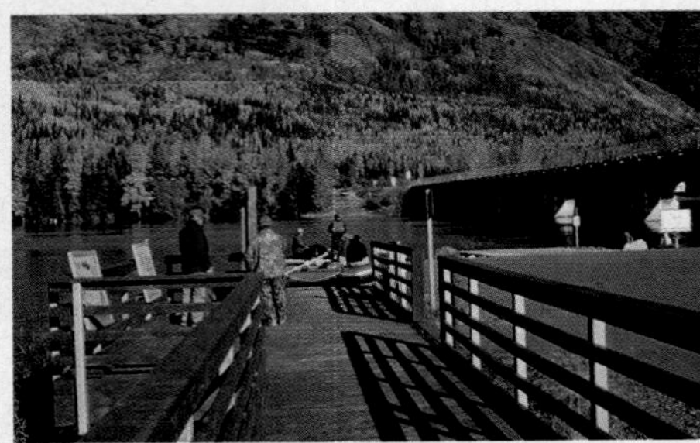

Upper Kenai River, from **Kenai Lake** to **Skilak Lake,** including Skilak Lake within a half mile of the Kenai River inlet, special regulations apply. For current recorded fishing forecast, phone (907) 267-2502. Silver salmon 5 to 15 lbs., August through October; pink salmon 3 to 7 lbs., July and August; red salmon 3 to 12 lbs., June 11 through mid-August; rainbow and Dolly Varden, June 11 through October. *IMPORTANT: Be familiar with current regulations and closures. Dates given here are subject to change!*

NOTE: The Kenai River Special Management Area is managed by the Alaska Division of Parks and Outdoor Recreation (DPOR), and includes the waters of Kenai and Skilak lakes and the Kenai River. Motors are limited to maximum 35 horsepower on the river, and prohibited on some sections. For more information, contact DPOR at P.O. Box 1247, Soldotna, AK 99669, phone (907) 262-5581.

S 47.9 (77.1 km) **A 100.9** (162.4 km) **H 131.6** (211.8 km) Snug Harbor Road. This side road leads 1 mile to picturesque St. John Neumann Catholic Church, named after one of the first American saints, which features a unique log shrine (pictured here).

Also access to bed and breakfast (1 mile) and to Cooper Lake (12 miles) and trailhead for 23-mile USFS trail to Russian River Campground (see **Milepost S 52.6**).

St. John Neumann Catholic Church. See display ad this section.

Dreamtime B&B/Health Spa. Artfully appointed rooms with private/shared bath. View wildlife from our lakeside hot tub. Enjoy organic foods. During your stay, receive massage, polarity or an essential oil bath. Ask about our special healing retreats! We are 1 mile off the Sterling Highway. Call Catherine and Kent (907) 595-1756. www.arctic.net/~dreamtim. [ADVERTISEMENT]

S 48.1 (77.4 km) **A 101.1** (162.7 km) **H 131.4** (211.7 km) **Ingram's Sport Fishing Cabins.** See display ad this section.

S 48.2 (77.6 km) **A 101.2** (162.9 km)

Heading down the Kenai River from Cooper Landing boat launch. (© Kris Graef, staff)

The Shrew's Nest, Last Resort RV Park and Landing Latté. See display ad this section. ▲

S 48.5 (78.1 km) **A 101.5** (163.3 km) **H 131** (210.8 km) **The Hutch B&B.** 12 clean smoke-free rooms with private baths at very reasonable rates. Continental breakfast served until 10 A.M. Common area TVs. View mountain goats, Dall sheep and Kenai River from our covered decks. Our parking area accommodates boat trailers and large vehicles. Also, new self-contained cabin

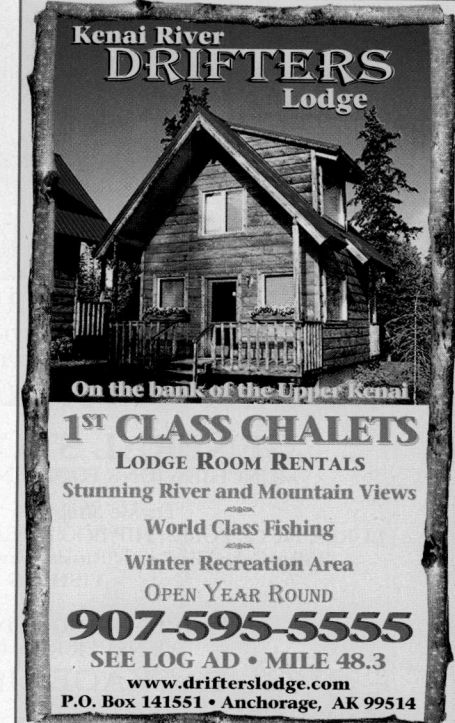

H 131.3 (211.3 km) **Troutfitters Alpine Motel.** See display ad this section.

S 48.3 (77.7 km) **A 101.3** (163 km) **H 131.2 (211.1 km) Kenai River Drifter's Lodge.** When life offers you the best, take it! On the bank of the Kenai River, enjoy comfortable, first-class, tastefully furnished new chalets which include your own large private bath, fridge, microwave, coffee/tea, or your own lodge room. Mesmerizing views of the world-class Kenai River or Chugach Mountains can be seen from every window of your accommodations. Join in on the Alaskan tales during the evening campfires after a day of activities such as: fishing, hiking, rafting, cross-country skiing, snowmobiling or just plain relaxing. Chalets accommodate 5 people or the entire lodge can host 35 plus. Reservations encouraged, all seasons. (907) 595-5555. Web site: Drifterslodge.com. See display ad this section. [ADVERTISEMENT]

S 48.4 (77.9 km) **A 101.4** (163.2 km) **H 131.1** (211 km) **COOPER LANDING** (pop. 285) stretches along several miles of the Sterling Highway at the west end of Kenai Lake. All visitor facilities available. **Emergency services:** Cooper Landing ambulance, phone 911.

Private Aircraft: State-owend Quartz Creek airstrip, 3 W; elev. 450 feet; length 2,200 feet; gravel; unattended. Floatplanes land at Cooper Lake.

Cooper Landing was named for Joseph Cooper, a miner who discovered gold here in 1894. A school and post office opened in the 1920s to serve the miners and their families living in the area. Cooper Landing was connected to Kenai by road in 1948, and to Anchorage in 1951. According to the Alaska Dept. of Community and Regional Affairs, the population of the area nearly doubles each summer to support tourism businesses and activities.

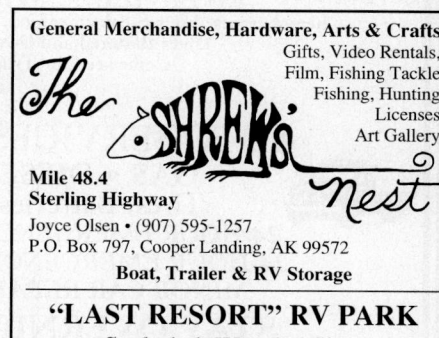

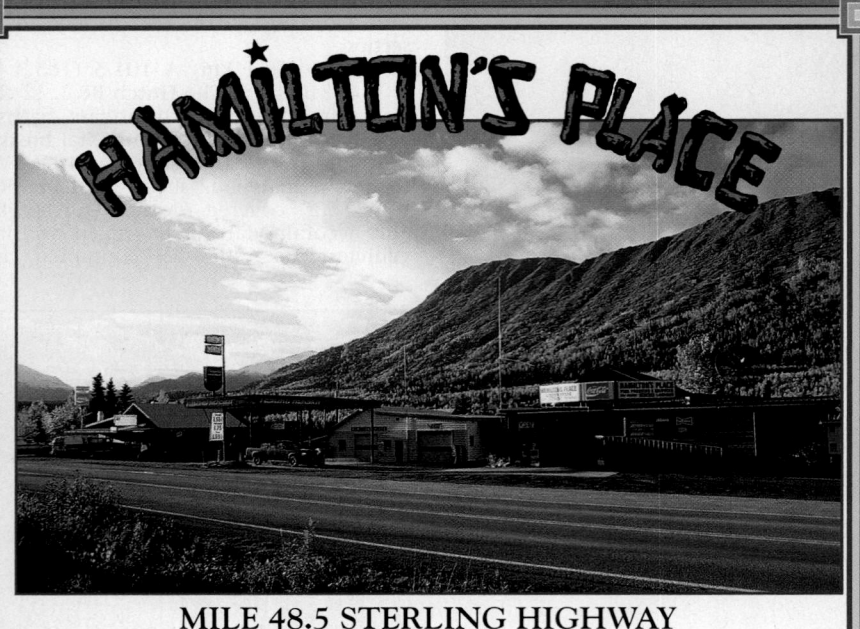

Watch for moose along the Sterling Highway, especially at dusk.
(© Michael DeYoung)

with cooking facilities accommodates families/groups. Look for the "Bunny Trail" sign. Phone (907) 595-1270, fax (907) 595-1829. See display ad this section. [ADVERTISEMENT]

Hamilton's Place river resort, only complete stop on the upper Kenai River. Information center for the famous Russian River and surrounding area. Centrally located for day trips to Seward, Soldotna/Kenai, Homer. Make us your Kenai Peninsula headquarters. Tesoro services, 24-hour recovery and transport (flatbed) service, 24-hour locksmith, propane. All-emergency road service

providers.) General store, groceries, licenses, tackle, ice, liquor store. Restaurant, lounge. RV hookups, modern B&B cabins with cooking facilities, laundromat, phone. Fish freezing, storage, Federal Express shipping. Hamilton's Place, serving the public since 1952, hopes to make your stay enjoyable. Phone (907) 595-1260; fax (907) 595-1530. E-mail: hamspl@arctic.net. See display ad this section. [ADVERTISEMENT] ▲

S 48.7 (78.4 km) **A 101.7** (163.7 km) **H 130.8** (210.5 km) Cooper Landing post office, located in resort; open 9 A.M. to 5 P.M. weekdays and Saturday morning. Pay phone.

S 49.4 (79.5 km) **A 102.4** (164.8 km) **H 130.1** (209.4 km) Large paved turnout to north by Kenai River. The highway winds along the Kenai River.

S 49.7 (80 km) **A 102.7** (165.3 km) **H 129.8** (208.9 km) **The Miller Homestead Bed & Breakfast RV Park.** Make us your vacation headquarters for Kenai Peninsula adventures. We can arrange fishing for trophy rainbow trout, Russian River red salmon, Dolly Varden, Kenai River kings, sil-

vers and halibut. Bank fishing. River-viewing platform. See display ad this section. [ADVERTISEMENT] ▲

S 49.9 (80.4 km) **A 102.9** (165.7 km) **H 129.6** (208.6 km) **Alaska Rivers Co.**, right side westbound. Rafting daily on the beautiful Kenai River. Half-day scenic float, or full-day canyon trip with exhilarating rapids.

Both trips include homemade picnic lunch, excellent viewing of wildlife, professional guides, all equipment provided. All ages welcome. Personalized guided drift boat fishing for all species of fish. Overnight accommodations available. Family-owned and operated by Cooper Landing residents. Gary Galbraith, owner. (907) 595-1226 for reservations or just stop by. E-mail: lrg@arctic.net. [ADVERTISEMENT]

Rafting the Kenai River is a popular activity. (© Kris Graef, staff)

S 50.1 (80.6 km) **A 103.1** (165.9 km) **H 129.4** (208.2 km) **Kenai River Sportfishing Lodge**. See display ad on page 541.

Kenai River Trips with Alaska Wildland Adventures. Don't pass up taking a rafting or fishing trip with Alaska Wildland Adventures. You'll enjoy this facility's unique and scenic setting on the Kenai River. They offer daily guided raft trips along with a delicious Alaskan picnic lunch. You can expect to see wildlife and enjoy the scenery of one of the world's most beautiful rivers. If you're seeking a quality fishing experience, ask about their guided fishing trips for salmon and rainbow trout. This company is well known for its professional guides and deluxe boats. All tackle, rods and reels are furnished. Operating since 1977. Phone toll free (800) 478-4100 for more information or reservations. See "Kenai River Trips" display ad on page 541. Internet address: www.alaskawildland.com/mp. [ADVERTISEMENT]

S 50.4 (81.1 km) **A 103.4** (166.4 km) **H 129.1** (207.8 km) **Juneau Creek**, Dolly Varden and rainbow, mid-June through July.

S 50.5 (81.3 km) **A 103.5** (166.6 km) **H 129** (207.6 km) Bridge over Cooper Creek. USFS **Cooper Creek Campground.** Camping area on the river side of highway (second entrance westbound) has 7 sites, several on the riverbank. Camping area on the other side of the highway has 23 sites. Both have tables, water and firepits. Fee is $10 single, $18 double. Reservations available, phone 1-877-444-NRRS. ▲

S 52 (83.7 km) **A 105** (169 km) **H 127.5** (205.2 km) **Gwin's Lodge, Restaurant and Bar**, left side southbound. One of Alaska's few remaining traditionally built log roadhouses where Alaskans and visitors alike always stop for homemade "Alaska"-sized portions and fast courteous service. Selected by the "Best of Alaska" tour guide as the top restaurant in the northern Kenai Peninsula area. Gwin's specialties include delicious homemade chili, soups, chowders, quiches, pies and cheesecakes as well as steaks, seafood and our world-famous burger line-up. Gwin's Store & Tackle Shop features a full-array of fishing gear and tackle, licenses, rental gear and boots, groceries, Alaska cards/gifts, pizzeria, ice cream shop, espresso/latte, fish freezing and "Trapper's Creek Smoking Company" fish processing/

smoking/shipping drop-off service site. Gwin's exclusive line of "Kenai River," "Russian River," and "Alaska" embroidered shirts, hats, jackets and polar fleece are the Peninsula's finest. Gwin's charter booking service's wide array of excursions include Upper Kenai River rainbow trout; Lower Kenai River king and silver salmon; Cook Inlet Pacific halibut; fly-in trips to remote lakes and streams for rainbow trout and/or arctic grayling; Upper Kenai River scenic and wildlife viewing raft trips; and scenic flightseeing. VISA, MasterCard and Discover accepted. (907) 595-1266 (voice); (907) 595-1681 (fax). See display ad. [ADVERTISEMENT] ▲

Kenai Cache. See display ad this section.

S 52.6 (84.6 km) **A 105.6** (169.9 km) **H 126.9** (204.2 km) Kenaitze Indian Tribe Heritage Site north side of highway; USFS **Russian River Campground** to south (description follows).

Follow paved 2-mile road south for Russian River USFS camping units, parking areas and trailheads. Phones and overflow parking

Skilak Lake Loop Road Log

Originally part of the first Kenai Peninsula highway built in 1947, the 19.1-mile Skilak Lake Loop Road (good gravel) loops south through the Skilak Wildlife Recreation Area to campgrounds, trails and fishing spots. *CAUTION: Do not leave valuables in unattended boats or vehicles.*

Distance from east junction (EJ) with Sterling Highway at Milepost S 58 is followed by distance from west junction (WJ) with Sterling Highway at Milepost S 75.2.

EJ 0 WJ 19.1 (30.7 km) **Junction** with Sterling Highway at **Milepost S 58.**

EJ 0.1 (0.2 km) **WJ 19** (30.5 km) **Jim's Landing** day-use area on Kenai River, 0.2 mile from road; toilets, tables, firepits, water, boat launch, parking area.

NOTE: The Kenai River downstream from Jim's Landing is considered Class II and Class III white water and for experienced boaters only. Wear a personal flotation device. The Kenai River is non-motorized to Skilak Lake. Motors may be used on Skilak Lake to travel to Upper Skilak Lake Campground boat ramp. There is no road access to the Kenai River between Jim's Landing and Upper Skilak Lake Campground: be prepared to travel the entire distance by boat. Use caution when crosssing Skilak Lake, as winds from Skilak Glacier frequently create dangerous boating conditions. Be prepared to wait overnight at river mouth until winds abate.

Kenai River from Skilak Lake to Soldotna. Consult regulations for legal tackle, limits and seasons. King salmon 20 to 80 lbs., use spinners, excellent fishing June to August; red salmon 6 to 12 lbs., many, but hard to catch, use flies, best from July 15 to Aug. 10; pink salmon 4 to 8 lbs., abundant fish on even years Aug. 1 to Sept. 1, spoons; silver salmon 6 to 15 lbs., use spoons, Aug. 15 to Nov. 1; rainbow, Dolly Varden 15 to 20 inches, June through September, use spinners, winged bobber, small-weighted spoon.

EJ 0.6 (1 km) **WJ 18.5** (29.7 km) East entrance parking area for Kenai River Trail; map and trail chart. Hike in 0.5 mile for scenic view of Kenai Canyon. Oversized vehicle parking.

EJ 2.3 (3.7 km) **WJ 16.8** (27 km) West entrance parking area for Kenai River Trail. Hike in 0.3 mile to see regrowth from 1991 Pothole Lake Fire.

EJ 2.4 (3.9 km) **WJ 16.7** (26.9 km) **Pothole Lake Overlook**; gravel parking area overlooks scene of Pothole Lake forest fire of 1991. Interpretive sign on fire.

EJ 3.6 (5.8 km) **WJ 15.5** (24.9 km) **Hidden Lake Campground** 0.5 mile from road is an exceptionally nice lakeshore camping area with 44 sites on paved loop roads. It has picnic pavilions, a dump station, wheelchair-accessible toilets, tables, water, firepits and boat launch. Campfire programs Friday and Saturday evenings in summer at the amphitheater. Observation deck for viewing wildlife. Campground hosts in residence. Camping fee $10 for vehicles. Trailer parking area, interpretive exhibits and kitchen shelter with barbecue.

Hidden Lake, lake trout average 16 inches and kokanee 9 inches, year-round, best from May 15 to July 1, use spoon, red-and-white or weighted, by trolling, casting and jigging. This lake is a favorite among local ice fishermen from late December through March.

EJ 4.6 (7.4 km) **WJ 14.5** (23.3 km) Parking area and information sign at Hidden Creek trailhead; 3 mile round-trip hike to beach on Skilak Lake.

EJ 5.1 (8.2 km) **WJ 14** (22.5 km) Scenic overlook with sweeping view of one arm of Skilak Lake.

Evidence of 1996 Hidden Creek Fire is visible.

EJ 5.4 (8.7 km) **WJ 13.7** (22 km) Parking area at Skilak Lookout trailhead; 5 mile round-trip hike.

EJ 6.4 (10.3 km) **WJ 12.7** (20.4 km) Parking area at Bear Mountain trailhead; 2 mile round-trip hike (moderate, steep) to scenic view of Skilak Lake.

EJ 6.9 (11.1 km) **WJ 12.2** (19.6 km) Scenic viewpoint of Skilak Lake.

EJ 8.5 (13.6 km) **WJ 10.6** (17 km) **Upper Skilak Lake Campground**, drive 2 miles along Lower Ohmer Lake; 0.2-mile loop road through campground. There are 25 campsites (some sites on lakeshore), boat launch, toilets and tables; similar facilities to Hidden Lake Campground (**Milepost EJ 3.6**). Camping fee $10/vehicle, $5/tent site (walk-in).

Lower Ohmer Lake, rainbow 14 to 16 inches, year-round. **Skilak Lake** offers rainbow and Dolly Varden. Red (sockeye) salmon enter lake in mid-July.

EJ 8.6 (13.8 km) **WJ 10.5** (16.9 km) **Lower Ohmer Lake Campground** via short side road to parking area on lake; 3 campsites, toilet, boat launch, firepits, tables.

EJ 9.4 (15 km) **WJ 9.7** (15.6 km) Turnout overlooking Engineer Lake.

EJ 9.5 (15.2 km) **WJ 9.6** (15.4 km) Short side road to **Engineer Lake** boat launch and Seven Lakes trailhead; turnaround and parking area with firepits at lake. Stocked silver salmon to 15 inches, best in July.

EJ 11.7 (18.8 km) **WJ 7.4** (11.9 km) Dump station on paved double-ended turnout to east.

EJ 13.8 (22.2 km) **WJ 5.3** (8.5 km) Well-marked 1-mile side road to **Lower Skilak Lake Campground**; 14 sites, tables, toilets, firepits, and boat launch for Skilak Lake and Kenai River fishing.

CAUTION: Skilak Lake is cold; winds are fierce and unpredictable. Wear life jackets!

EJ 14.2 (22.8 km) **WJ 4.9** (7.8 km) Fire guard station.

EJ 18.7 (30.1 km) **WJ 0.4** (0.6 km) Bottinentnin Lake; well-marked side road leads 0.3 mile/0.5 km to parking area on lakeshore. Shallow lake: No sport fish, but nice area for recreational canoeing. Watch for loons and grebes.

EJ 19.1 (30.7 km) **WJ 0 Junction** with Sterling Highway at **Milepost S 75.2.**

Return to Milepost S 58 or S 75.2 Sterling Highway

at exit to highway. Dump station at Mile 1.3 on the access road. Campground host at Mile 1.7. The Russian River Campground is often full during the summer, particularly during the Russian River red salmon runs. Arrive early! There are 84 sites, toilets, water, tables and firepits. Fish cleaning stations. Fees: $13 single RV occupancy, $20 double RV occupancy, $5 12-hour day-use parking, $6 dump station. Concessionaire-operated. For reservations phone 1-877-444-NRRS.

CAUTION: Bears attracted by the salmon are frequent visitors to this campground.

Upper Russian Lake USFS trailhead parking at Mile 1 on campground road. Lower Russian Lake trailhead parking at Mile 2.6. Lower Russian Lakes Trail: elev. 500 feet; hiking time 1½ hours; good trail first 3 miles; spur trail to Russian River Falls viewing platform. A good place to view jumping salmon, and a nice family hike. Upper Russian Lake: elev. 690 feet, 12 miles. Trail continues to Cooper Lake at end of Snug Harbor Road (see **Milepost S 47.9**). Public-use cabins along trail. Winter use: good snowmobiling to lower lake only, avalanche danger beyond.

The **Russian River:** Closed to all fishing April 15 through June 10. Bait prohibited at all times in Russian River drainage. Check regulations for limits and other restrictions. Red (sockeye) salmon run starts mid-June. Second run begins July 20–25 and lasts about 3 weeks. Must use flies prior to Aug. 21. Silver (coho) salmon to 15 lbs., run begins mid-August. Catch-and-release only for rainbow trout in lower part of river at all times that season is open.

S 53 (85.3 km) **A 106** (170.6 km) **H 126.5** (203.6 km) Bridge over Kenai River.

Resurrection Pass Trailhead USFS just west of bridge; large parking area to north at trailhead. This 38-mile-long trail climbs to Resurrection Pass (elev. 2,600 feet) and descends to north trailhead near Hope on Turnagain Arm.

S 53.7 (86.4 km) **A 106.7** (171.7 km) **H 125.8** (202.5 km) Kenaitze Indian Interpretive Site to south has a walking trail along the Kenai River; fishing, parking (no RVs or trailers).

S 54.7 (88 km) **A 107.7** (173.3 km) **H 124.8** (200.8 km) Leaving Chugach National Forest lands westbound. Many turnouts with recreation access signs on the Kenai River between here and **Milepost S 58.**

S 55 (88.5 km) **A 108** (173.8 km) **H 124.5** (200.4 km) Leaving Game Management Unit 7, entering Unit 15 westbound. Entering **Kenai National Wildlife Refuge** westbound, administered by the USF&WS; contains more than 1.97 million acres of land set aside to preserve the moose, bear, sheep and other wildlife found here.

Russian River Ferry entrance to southeast. 60-space outer parking lot, boat launch, toilets and gatehouse. Tent sites available. During salmon season this recreation area and campground are heavily used. Fees charged for boat launch, parking and camping. Privately operated 28-person ferry crosses the Kenai River to opposite bank and to the mouth of the Russian River. Ferry fee is $5 adults round-trip, $4 children. Parking is $6 a day ($7 for vehicles over 20 feet).

S 56.4 (90.8 km) **A 109.4** (176.1 km) **H 123.1** (198.1 km) Gravel turnout to southeast.

S 57.1 (91.9 km) **A 110.1** (177.2 km) **H 122.4** (197 km) Double-ended turnout to southeast. Fuller Lake trailhead (well marked), parking. **Lower Fuller Lake**, arctic grayling; **Upper Fuller Lake,** Dolly Varden.

S 58 (93.3 km) **A 111** (178.6 km) **H 121.5** (195.5 km) **East junction** with Skilak Lake Road to south; Kenai National Wildlife Refuge visitor contact station to north. The information cabin is open Memorial Day through Labor Day; brochures and information on Kenai National Wildlife Refuge recreation opportunities. Large gravel parking area, water pump, toilets, trailer parking (no camping).

Junction with Skilak Lake Loop Road. See SKILAK LAKE LOOP ROAD log on opposite page.

CAUTION: Moose Danger Zone next 22 miles westbound. Watch for moose!

S 59 (94.9 km) **A 112** (180.2 km) **H 120.5** (193.9 km) **Milepost S 59.** Actual driving distance between here and **Milepost S 61** is 2.6 miles or 0.6 mile more than the posts indicate.

S 60 (96.5 km) **A 113** (181.9 km) **H 119.5** (192.3 km) Large gravel turnout to north.

S 60.6 (97.5 km) **A 113.6** (182.8 km) **H 118.9** (191.3 km) Large gravel turnout to north and easy-to-miss turnoff to south down hill to **Jean Lake Campground**; 3 sites, picnic area; boat launch, rainbow fishing.

S 60.8 (97.8 km) **A 113.8** (183.1 km) **H 118.7** (191 km) **Skyline Trail** to north; double-ended gravel parking area to south.

S 62.3 (100.3 km) **A 115.3** (185.6 km) **H 117.2** (188.6 km) Large gravel turnout to north. Mystery Hills to the north and Hideout Hill to the south.

S 64.5 (103.8 km) **A 117.5** (189.1 km) **H 115** (185.1 km) Highway straightens westbound. *CAUTION: Winding road eastbound.*

S 68.3 (109.9 km) **A 121.3** (195.2 km) **H 111.2** (179 km) Turnoff to south for Peterson Lake (0.5 mile) and Kelly Lake (1 mile) public campgrounds. Both have tables and firepits for 3 camping parties, water and boat launch, and parking space for self-contained RVs. **Kelly** and **Peterson lakes** have rainbow population. Access to Seven Lakes trail.

Calm waters of Jean Lake reflect fall foliage. (© Kris Graef, staff)

S 70.4 (113.3 km) **A 123.4** (198.6 km) **H 109.1** (175.6 km) Egumen Lake gravel parking area to southeast. East Fork Moose River trailhead. Half-mile marshy trail to **Egumen Lake** (lake not visible from highway); good rainbow population.

S 71.3 (114.7 km) **A 124.3** (200 km) **H 108.2** (174.1 km) Parking area at entrance to Watson Lake public campground; 0.4-mile drive from highway to small campground with 3 sites, toilets, picnic tables, fire grates, water, dumpsters and steep boat launch (suitable for canoes or hand-carried boats). **Watson Lake**, rainbow.

S 72.8 (117.2 km) **A 125.8** (202.4 km) **H 106.7** (171.7 km) Paved double-ended turnout to south, lake to north.

S 75.2 (121 km) **A 128.2** (206.3 km) **H 104.3** (167.8 km) **West junction** with Skilak Lake Road.

See SKILAK LAKE LOOP ROAD log on on opposite page.

S 78.1 (125.7 km) **A 131.1** (211 km) **H 101.4** (163.2 km) Fueding Lane.

S 78.2 (125.8 km) **A 131.2** (211.1 km) **H 101.3** (163 km)

S 79.5 (127.9 km) **A 132.5** (213.2 km) **H 100** (160.9 km) Kenai Keys Road.

Begin 4-lane divided highway westbound.

Begin 2-lane undivided highway eastbound. *CAUTION: Moose Danger Zone next 22 miles eastbound.*

S 80.3 (129.2 km) **A 133.3** (214.5 km) **H 99.2** (159.6 km) Turnoff for Peninsula Furs, Real Alaskan Cabins and RV Park, and Bing's Landing State Recreation Site.

Bing's Landing State Recreation Site has 36 RV and tent campsites, picnic area, water, boat launch, toilets (wheelchair accessible), dumpster; access to Kenai River; camping fee $10/night or resident pass; boat launch fee $5; day-use parking fee $5.

Peninsula Furs. See display ad this

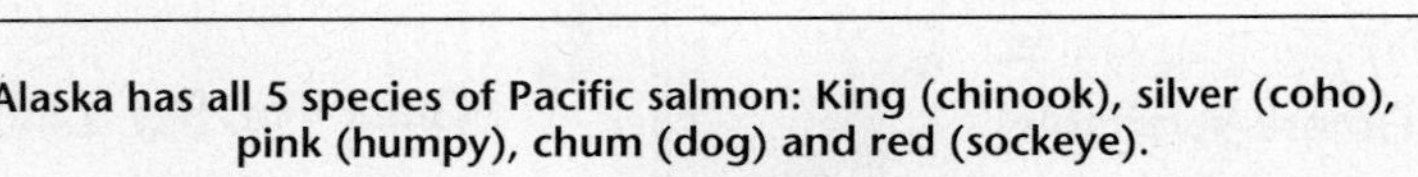

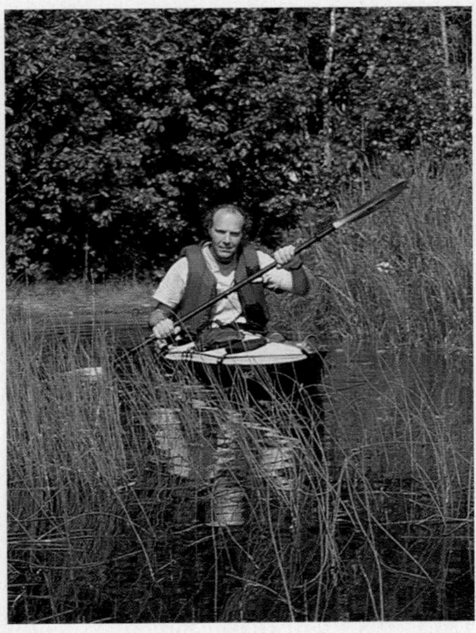

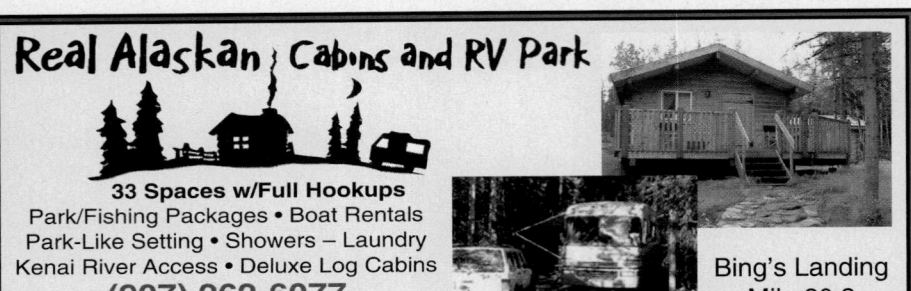

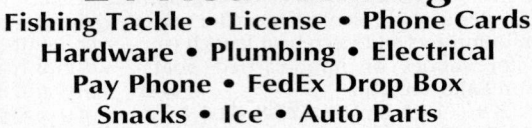

Kenai National Wildlife Refuge has 2 canoe trails: the Swanson River route and Swan Lake route. (©Corinne Smith/RKI)

section.

Real Alaskan Cabins & RV Park. See display ad this section.

S 80.6 (129.7 km) **A 133.6** (215 km) **H 98.9** (159.2 km) Paved parking area to south.

NOTE: 45 mph speed zone.

S 81 (130.3 km) **A 134** (215.6 km) **H 98.5** (158.5 km) **STERLING** (pop. 6,138; elev. 150 feet). This unincorporated community, located on the Sterling Highway at the confluence of the Moose and Kenai Rivers, serves the summer influx of sportfishermen, campers and others. The name was formalized in 1954 when a post office was established. Sterling has one school.

Traveler services include 2 gas stations, 2 motels, a hostel, several restaurants and cafes; gift, grocery, hardware, antique, fur and furniture stores, laundromat and several campgrounds. Post office at **Milepost S 81.6.** (Businesses with a Sterling mailing address extend west to **Milepost S 85.**) Nearby recreational opportunities include fishing and the extensive canoe trail system (see description at **Milepost S 82**). Moose River Raft Race and Sterling Days held in July.

Bing Brown's RV Park & Motel. See display ad this section. ▲

S 81.6 (131.3 km) **A 134.6** (216.6 km) **H 97.9** (157.6 km) Sterling post office (ZIP code 99672).

Sterling Auto Parts & Repair. See display ad this section.

S 81.7 (131.5 km) **A 134.7** (216.8 km) **H 97.8** (157.4 km) Tesoro gas station; cabins, seafood .

Cook's Corner. See display ad this section. ▲

Vacation Cabins. See display ad this section.

Aurora Alaska Seafoods. See display ad this section.

S 82 (132 km) **A 135** (217.3 km) **H 97.5** (156.9 km) Pay phone on highway just before turnoff for **Izaak Walton State Recreation Site**, located at the confluence of the Kenai and Moose rivers. Paved access road, 25 campsites, parking, tables, toilets, water and dumpster. Camping fee $10/night or resident pass; day-use parking $5; boat launch $5 fee. Good access to Kenai River. A small log cabin, totem pole and an information sign about Moose River archaeological site. ▲

Sterling Chevron & Food Mart. See display ad this section.

Bridge over **Moose River**; 0.3 mile of fishing down to confluence with Kenai River. Sockeyes here in June. Big summer run of reds follows into August; silvers into October. **Kenai** and **Moose rivers** (confluence), Dolly Varden and rainbow trout, salmon (king, red, pink, silver). June 15 through October for trout; year-round for Dolly Varden. King salmon from May through July, pink salmon in August and silver salmon from August through October. This is a fly-fishing-only area from May 15 through Aug. 15; closed to fishing from boats, May 15 until the end of the king salmon season or July 31, whichever is later.

This is one terminus of the Swan Lake canoe trail (see SWANSON RIVER ROAD log on page 548).

CAUTION: Drive carefully during fishing season when fishermen walk along bridge and highway.

S 82.3 (132.4 km) **A 135.3** (217.7 km) **H 97.2** (156.4 km) **Great Alaska Adventure Lodge.** Charters, fly-ins, bear-viewing camp; 5 or 7 days. Canoe outfitting. Budget camp and fish trips; salmon, halibut and trout. Budget camping trips. We do it all! Phone (800) 544-2261; fax (907) 262-8797; web page: www.greatalaska.com; e-mail: greatalaska@greatalaska.com. See display ad this section. [ADVERTISEMENT]

S 82.5 (132.8 km) **A 135.5** (218.1 km) **H 97** (156.1 km) Keystone Road. Big Sky Charter & Fish Camp 0.5 mile north.

Big Sky Charter & Fish Camp. See display ad this section.

S 82.8 (133.3 km) **A 135.8** (218.5 km) **H 96.7** (155.6 km) Truck weigh station; senior center across highway.

Highway narrows to 2 lanes westbound. Begin divided 4-lane highway eastbound.

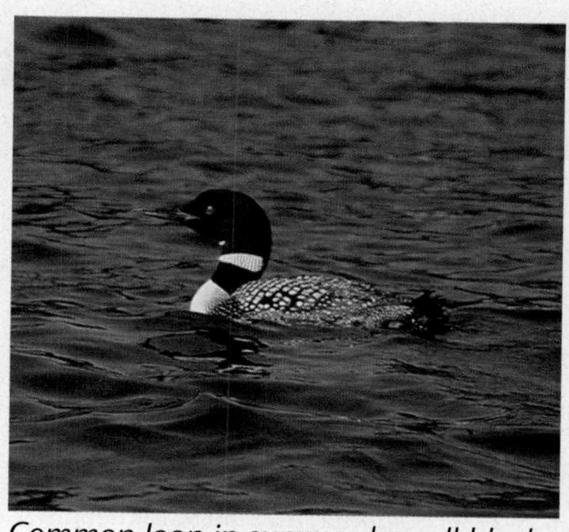

Common loon in summer has all black head with broken white collar.

(© Barb Willard)

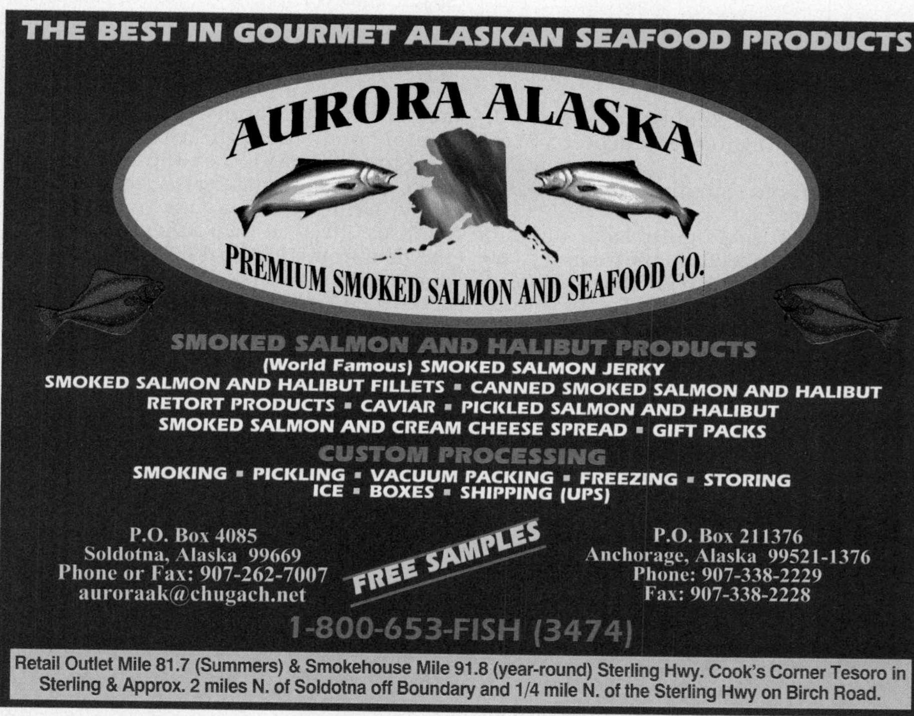

Swanson River Road Log

Swanson River Road is a fairly wide and level winding gravel road which leads north 17.9 miles to Swanson River Landing. It also junctions with Swan Lake Road, which leads east 12 miles and dead ends at Paddle Lake. Both roads provide access to fishing, hiking trails and the 2 canoe trails in Kenai National Wildlife Refuge: the 60-mile Swan Lake route, connecting 30 lakes; and the 80-mile Swanson River route, linking 40 lakes. Portions of the canoe trail system may be traveled, taking anywhere from 1 to 4 days. Contact Kenai National Wildlife Refuge, Box 2139, Soldotna, AK 99669, for details.

CAUTION: Do not leave valuables in vehicles at canoe trailheads.

Distance from junction with the Sterling Highway (J) is shown.

J 0 Junction with Sterling Highway at **Milepost S 83.4.**

J 0.1 (0.2 km) Gas station and grocery; laundromat.

J 0.7 (1.1 km) Robinson Loop Road; rejoins Sterling Highway at **Milepost S 87.5.**

Pavement ends, gravel begins, northbound.

J 4.5 (7.3 km) Entering Kenai National Wildlife Refuge.

J 7.9 (12.7 km) **Mosquito Lake,** turnout; 0.5-mile trail to lake. Rainbow trout.

J 9.2 (14.8 km) **Silver Lake** trailhead parking; 1-mile hike to lake. Rainbow trout and arctic char. Arctic char are most easily caught in spring when the surface water is still cool. Once summer temperatures warm the surface, the char descend to deeper waters and are much harder to catch.

J 10.7 (17.2 km) **Forest Lakes** parking; 0.3-mile trail to lake. Rainbow trout; best fished from canoe or raft.

J 13 (20.9 km) Small turnout by **Weed Lake**; rainbow trout.

J 13.3 (21.4 km) **Drake** and **Skookum lakes** trailhead parking; 2-mile trail. Rainbow trout and arctic char (spring).

J 14 (22.5 km) Parking and access to **Breeze Lake.**

J 14.2 (22.9 km) **Dolly Varden Lake Campground**; 15 sites, water, toilets, boat launch. Large RVs and trailers note: 0.5-mile loop road to campground is narrow and very bumpy; check turnaround space before driving in. Some campsites overlook the lake. Fishing for Dolly Varden and rainbow; best in late August and September.

J 14.9 (24 km) Continue straight ahead northbound for Swanson River Landing. Southbound stop sign at oil field access road to west (gated; closed to private vehicles). The Swanson River Road was originally built as an access road to the Swanson River oil field. Chevron operated the field from 1958 to 1986. It is currently operated by Unocal.

J 15.7 (25.2 km) **Rainbow Lake Campground;** small 3-unit camping area on lakeshore with outhouse, water pump and boat launch. Pack out garbage. Fishing for Dolly Varden and rainbow trout. *CAUTION: Steep road; difficult turnaround. Large RVs check visually before driving in.*

J 17.4 (28 km) **Junction** with **Swan Lake Road,** which leads east to: Fish Lake Campground, 3 miles; Canoe Lake (west entrance to Swan Lake Canoe Route), 4 miles; Merganser Lakes, 6 miles; Nest Lake, 8 miles; Portage Lake (east entrance to Swan Lake Canoe Route), 9.5 miles; and Paddle Lake (entrance to Swanson River Canoe Route), 12 miles.

J 17.9 (28.8 km) **Swanson River Landing** at end of Swanson River Road; gravel parking area with picnic tables, firepits, water, outhouse, boat launch, fishing. This is the terminus of the Swanson River canoe route, which begins at Paddle Lake at the end of Swan Lake Road.

Return to Milepost S 83.4 Sterling Highway

S 82.9 (133.4 km) **A 135.9** (218.7 km) **H 96.6** (155.4 km) **The Mad Moose Restaurant**. See display ad this section.

S 83.4 (134.2 km) **A 136.4** (219.5 km) **H 96.1** (154.7 km) Turnoff for **Swanson River Road** to north. Scout Lake Loop Road to south (see **Milepost S 85** for description).

Junction with Swanson River Road. See SWANSON RIVER ROAD log this section.

ZIPMART. See display ad this section.

The Wash Out Laundromat. See display ad this section.

Sterling Baptist Church. See display ad this section.

Mike's Alaska Adventure. See display ad this section.

Jana House Hostel & RV Park. New! Opening June 1, 2000. Full-service 60 amp pull-through RV and tent sites. Fish cleaning station. Private or dorm-style rooms. Bathroom/shower and kitchen privileges. Satellite TV. Large parties welcome. Easy access to Moose and Kenai Rivers. Turn north on Swanson River Road, Mile 83.4 Sterling Highway (0.4 mile west of weigh station), then drive 0.4 mile further. Reservations phone (907) 260-4151 or e-mail janamae@hotmail.com. [ADVERTISEMENT] ▲

S 84 (135.2 km) **A 137** (220.5 km) **H 95.5** (153.7 km) **Alaska Canoe & Campground.** See display ad this section. ▲

S 84.2 (135.5 km) **A 137.2** (220.8 km) **H 95.1** (153 km) **Moby King Charters.** See display ad this section.

S 84.3 (135.7 km) **A 137.3** (221 km) **H 95.2** (153.2 km) **Scout Lake Inn and Nicki's Restaurant**, located near the Kenai and Moose rivers. Good fishing May to September 30. Clean, modern rooms with phones, satellite TV, and in-room coffee. Guaranteed lower rates than Soldotna. Nicki's specializes in homemade cinnamon rolls, breads and pies. Phone (907) 262-5898, 1-888-829-5898. E-mail: akmunnzo@gci.net. Check out our web site at www.nickis.com. [ADVERTISEMENT]

S 84.9 (136.6 km) **A 137.9** (221.9 km) **H 94.6** (152.2 km) **Scout Lake Loop Road** (paved) leads south to **Scout Lake State Recreation Site** (day-use only); parking (5 fee), water, toilets and a covered picnic shelter. Drive down Scout Lake Loop Road 1.6 miles and turn on Lou Morgan Road (paved) and drive 2.4 miles for **Morgan's Landing State Recreation Area**; 42 campsites, 10 pull-through sites, some double sites, toilets and water; $10 camping fee or resident pass, $5 day-use fee. Good access from Morgan's Landing to bank fishing on the **Kenai River**, king salmon from mid-June through July, average 30 lbs. Red (sockeye) salmon average 8 lbs., use flies in July and August; silver (coho) salmon to 15 lbs., August and September, use lure; pink salmon average 4 lbs. with lure, best in July, even-numbered years only; rainbow and Dolly Varden, use lure, June through August. ▲

Alaska State Parks area headquarters is located at Morgans Landing. Scout Lake Loop Road loops south of the Sterling Highway for 7 miles and rejoins the Sterling Highway at **Milepost S 83.4.**

S 85.9 (138.2 km) **A 138.9** (223.5 km) **H 93.6** (150.6 km) First turnoff westbound for Lakewood subdivision to south.

S 87.5 (140.8 km) **A 140.5** (226.1 km) **H 92** (148.1 km) Robinson Loop Road to northwest. Tustumena Loop Road to southeast.

S 88 (141.6 km) **A 141** (226.9 km) **H 91.5** (147.3 km) St. Theresa Drive. Access to Longmere Lake Lodge B&B to south.

Longmere Lake Lodge B&B. AAA-approved. Look for blue highway sign. Follow St. Theresa's/Edgington to Ryan. Beautiful lakeside setting. Comfortable, spacious accommodations. Large stone fireplace, Alaskan artifacts. Enjoy a hearty

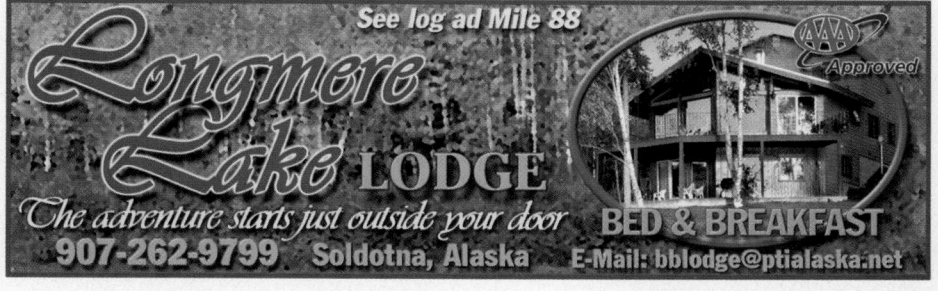

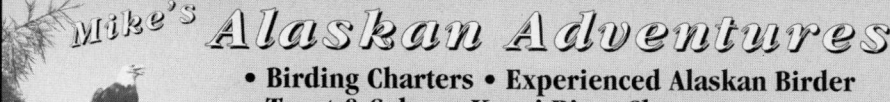

Salmon are anadromous, spawning in fresh water and maturing in the sea.

Boat on the Kenai River near The Pillars. (© Kris Graef, staff)

breakfast. Master bedrooms with full private baths, or large apartment with kitchen. Guided salmon, halibut, hiking, bird watching, flightseeing arranged. Longtime Alaskan hosts. P.O. Box 1707, Soldotna, AK 99669. Phone (907) 262-9799. www.longmere-lakelodge.com. E-mail: bblodge@ptialaska.net. [ADVERTISEMENT]

S 88.3 (142.1 km) **A 141.3** (227.4 km) **H 91.2** (146.8 km) **Alaska Horn & Antler.** Tom Cooper specializes in ram horn/antler carvings; Russ Western scrims fossil walrus and mammoth ivory. See them at work, tour their work areas. Also, purchase quality handmade-in-Alaska souvenirs: Alaskan back-scratchers, Eskimo skinning knives, fire-starters, mammoth ivory necklaces, rocks and antlers. Look for the antler sign. Pack/ship anywhere within U.S. Custom orders. (907) 262-9759. [ADVERTISEMENT]

S 88.6 (142.6 km) **A 141.6** (227.9 km) **H 90.9** (146.3 km) Tesoro gas station.

CAUTION: Moose Danger Zone next 6 miles westbound.

S 89.6 (144.2 km) **A 142.6** (229.5 km) **H 89.9** (144.7 km) **The Blue Moose Lakeside Lodge**, just outside Soldotna, is a picturesque lodge in a wilderness setting overlooking Longmere Lake. Guests are provided with enchanting lodging and various outdoor activities to participate in. Enjoy coffee and a homemade breakfast before you head off with one of the specialty guides for a day of adventure—it's a must on your Alaskan itinerary! Bedroom/bath suite, private rooms and cabin available. Call today. (877) BL-MOOSE. blue–moose.com. [ADVERTISEMENT]

S 91.3 (146.9 km) **A 144.3** (232.2 km) **H 88.2** (141.9 km) Tesoro gas station and grocery to south.

S 91.6 (147.4 km) **A 144.6** (232.7 km) **H 87.9** (141.4 km) Taxidermy shop to south.

American Trophy Taxidermy. See display ad this section.

S 91.8 (147.7 km) **A 144.8** (233 km) **H 87.7** (141.1 km) Boundary Street. Access to smokehouse.

Aurora Alaska Premium Smoked Salmon and Seafood Company. Home of the best gourmet Alaskan smoked salmon and halibut products in the world. We offer a wide variety of products, from refrigerated to non-refrigerated (shelf stable). All our products are low in salt and contain no artificial colors, flavors, or preservatives (no nitrites). They are all-natural. Got your own fish to smoke? We will custom smoke (kipper) or pickle your sport-caught salmon or halibut for you. We will also vacuum pack, freeze, store, box and ship your fish. No luck fishing? Come in and choose from our own specially prepared smoked products. Choose from our world-famous smoked salmon jerky, which is available in 4 delicious flavors, smoked salmon or halibut fillets, canned smoked salmon and halibut, salmon caviar, pickled salmon and halibut, smoked salmon and cream cheese spread, Alaskabits, or our assorted retort products. Gift packs also available in our choosing or you can mix and match your own. Remember, whether it is a gift of appreciation or for something grand, we can help in selecting the right gift for that special someone or important client, even if that someone is you. Come in to try our free samples. Two locations to choose from. Box 4085, Soldotna, AK 99669. Phone or fax (907) 262-7007, or dial toll free at 1-800-653-FISH (3474). See display ad this section. [ADVERTISEMENT]

S 92 (148 km) **A 145** (233.3 km) **H 87.5** (140.8 km) **Birch Ridge public golf course;** 9 holes, driving range, rental clubs, carts, pro shop. Phone (907) 262-5270.

S 92.2 (148.4 km) **A 145.2** (233.7 km) **H 87.3** (140.5 km) **Noble Car Wash, Laundry and Showers.** The friendly one-stop, clean-up spot. RV-sized bays, huge parking lot and powerful vaccums make Nobles Alaska's favorite self-serve car wash. Fully attended laundry facility features roomy, clean showers (accessible), new washers/dryers and affordable drop-off laundry rates. 1.9 miles east of Soldotna Y. (907) 262-5726. [ADVERTISEMENT]

S 92.4 (148.7 km) **A 145.4** (234 km) **H 87.1** (140.2 km) State Division of Forest, Land and Water Management. Fire danger indicator sign. Veterinary hospital; phone (907) 260-7851.

Soldotna Animal Hospital. See display ad this section.

S 92.7 (149.1 km) **A 145.7** (234.5 km) **H 86.8** (139.7 km) Mackey Lake Road. Private lodging is available on this side road.

Alaska Lodging & Adventures. See display ad this section.

Treetop B&B. See display ad this section.

S 93.7 (150.8 km) **A 146.7** (236.1 km) **H 85.8** (138.1 km) Four-lane highway begins southbound and continues through Soldotna; speed zone.

S 94.1 (151.4 km) **A 147.1** (236.7 km) **H 85.4** (137.4 km) East Redoubt Street. Fred Meyers to south; overnight RV parking permitted in parking lot. Access to fast food. Also access to **Swiftwater Park Municipal Campground;** follow signs 0.8 mile south on gravel road. This municipal campground has 20 spaces (some pull-throughs) on loop road above the Kenai River; tables, firepits, firewood ($4), phone, dump station($10), 2-week limit, litter barrels, toilets, boat launch ($6). Camping fee $8; day-use fee $3. No camping Sept. 30–May 1. Steep stairway down to Kenai River. ▲

S 94.2 (151.6 km) **A 147.2** (236.9 km) **H 85.3** (137.3 km) **Soldotna Y.** Turn right southbound on Kenai Spur Highway for more Soldotna businesses and for Kenai.

Junction with Kenai Spur Highway to city of Kenai. See KENAI SPUR HIGHWAY log beginning on page 562.

CAUTION: Moose Danger Zone next 6 miles eastbound.

S 94.4 (151.9 km) **A 147.4** (237.2 km) **H 85.1** (137 km) Soldotna DOT/PF highway maintenance station, gas station. Access to **Soldotna Creek Park** (day use only). Follow road behind Mexican restaurant.

Petro Marine Services. See display ad this section.

S 95.3 (153.4 km) **A 148.3** (238.7 km) **H 84.2** (135.5 km) Binkley Street; access to fire station, police station and post office. Peninsula Center Mall, 24-hour supermarket. Soldotna city center. *See description of Soldotna beginning on page 552.*

S 95.6 (153.8 km) **A 148.6** (239.1 km) **H 83.9** (135 km) Kobuk Street; access to Soldotna High School.

S 95.9 (154.3 km) **A 148.9** (239.6 km) **H 83.6** (134.5 km) Kenai River bridge. *NOTE: Watch for construction at bridge in summer 2000.*

S 96 (154.5 km) **A 149** (239.8 km) **H 83.5** (134.4 km) **Soldotna Visitor Center** at south end of Kenai River bridge.

S 96.1 (154.7 km) **A 149.1** (239.9 KM) **H 83.4** (134.2 km) Intersection of Funny River Road and Kalifornsky Beach Road. *For log of Kalifornsky Beach Road, see page 570. For descriptions of Funny River Road and continuation of Sterling Highway log to Homer, turn to page 571.*

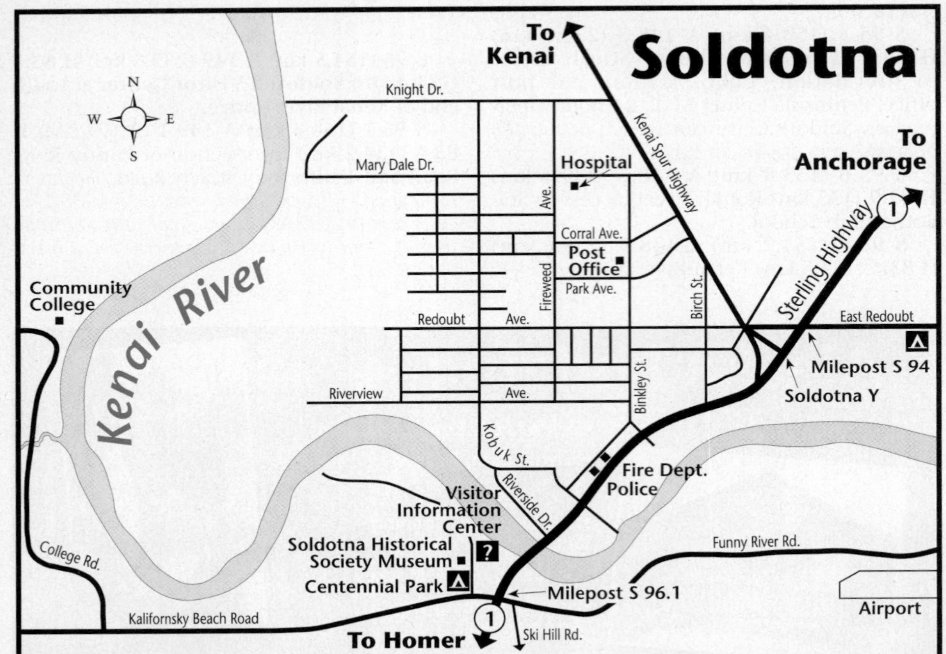

Soldotna

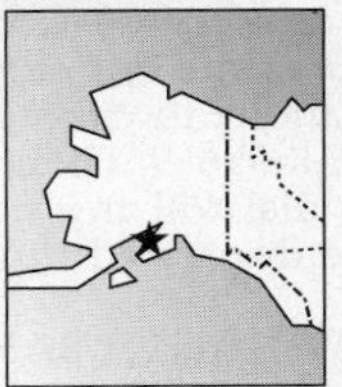

S 95.2 (153.2 km) **A 148.2** (238.5 km) **H 84.3** (135.7 km) On the western Kenai Peninsula, the city stretches over a mile southwest along the Sterling Highway and northwest along the Kenai Spur Highway. **Population:** 4,134; Kenai Peninsula Borough 44,411. **Emergency Services:** Phone 911 for all emergency services. **Alaska State Troopers** at Mile 22 Kalifornsky Beach Road just off Sterling Highway, phone (907) 262-4453. **City Police**, phone (907) 262-4455. **Fire Department**, phone (907) 262-4792. **Ambulance**, phone (907) 262-4500. **Hospital**, Central Peninsula General on Marydale Drive, phone (907) 262-4404. **Veterinarian:** Soldotna Animal Hospital, **Milepost S 92.4** Sterling Highway, phone (907) 260-7851.

Visitor Information: The Soldotna Visitor Information Center is located in downtown Soldotna on the Sterling Highway south of the Kenai River bridge. Fishwalk access to Kenai River. The center is open 9 A.M. to 7 P.M. daily, May through September; weekdays from 9 A.M. to 5 P.M. remainder of the year. Write: Greater Soldotna Chamber of Commerce, 44790 Sterling Highway, Soldotna, AK 99669; phone (907) 262-1337 or 262-9814, fax (907) 262-3566. For a free Soldotna recreation guide, phone (907) 262-9814; e-mail info@soldotnachamber.com; or visit www.SoldotnaChamber.com.

Elevation: 115 feet. **Climate:** Average daily temperature in July, 63°F to 68°F/17°C to 20°C; January, 19°F to 23°F/ -7°C to -5°C. Annual precipitation, approximately 18 inches. **Radio:** KGTL 620, KFQD 750, KSRM 920, KZXX 980, KSLP 1140, KDLL-FM 91.9 (Pickle Hill Public Radio) KGTL-FM 100.9/103.5, MBN-FM 95.3/97.7, KWHQ-FM 1001, KPEN-FM 101.7. **Television:** Channels 2, 4, 9, 12 and 13 via booster

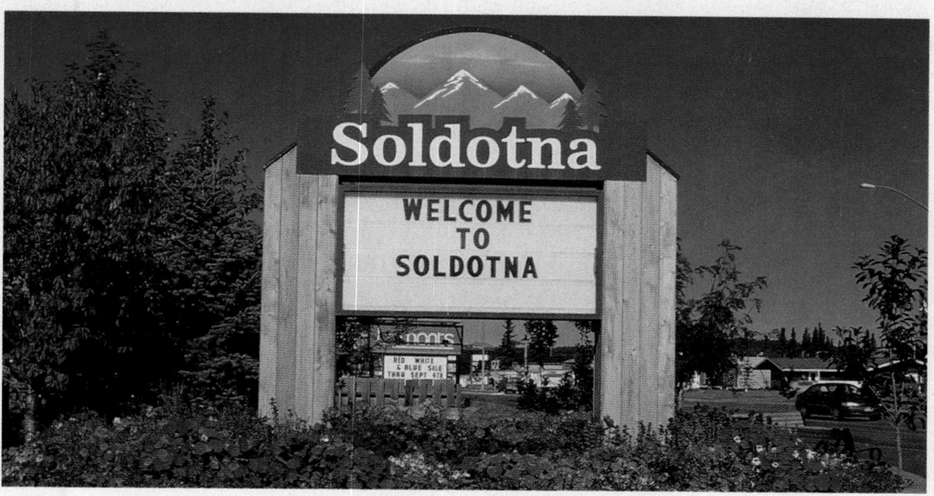

Soldotna is headquarters for the Kenai Peninsula Borough. (© Kris Graef, staff)

line from Anchorage, cable and KANG public education channel. **Newspapers:** *Peninsula Clarion* (daily), *The Dispatch* (weekly).

Private Aircraft: Soldotna airstrip 1 SE on Funny River Road; elev. 107 feet; length 5,000 feet; asphalt; fuel 100LL; unattended.

The town of Soldotna was established in the 1940s because of its strategic location at the Sterling–Kenai Spur Highway junction. (Visitors may see the homestead cabin, which became Soldotna's first post office in

SOLDOTNA ADVERTISERS

Accommodations

Alaska Creative Vacations .... Ph. (907) 283-0599
Alaskan Holiday Suites .... Fireweed & Kobuk
Alaskan Hospitality Bed and Breakfast .... Ph. (907) 260-5388
Best Western King Salmon Motel .... Ph. (907) 262-5857
Diamond M Ranch .... Ph. (907) 283-9424
Gull's Landing .... Ph. (907) 262-6668
High Crest B&B .... Ph. (907) 262-7038
Kenai River Lodge .... Ph. (907) 262-4292
Moose Creek Lodge .... Ph. (907) 260-3380
Moose Hollow Bed & Breakfast .... Mile 2.3 E. Redoubt
Poppy Ridge B&B Cabins .... Ph. (907) 262-4265
Posey's Kenai River Hideaway .... Ph. (907) 262-7430
Riverside House Hotel .... Ph. (907) 262-0500
Salmon Haus .... Ph. (907) 262-2400
Silver Salmon Creek Lodge .... Ph. (888) 872-5666
Soldotna Bed & Breakfast Lodge .... Ph. (907) 262-4779
Soldotna Inn .... Ph. (907) 262-9169

Auto & RV Rentals, Service, Supplies & Gas

Alaska Recreational Rentals .... Ph. (907) 262-2700
Alaska Tire Warehouse .... Ph. (907) 262-2326
Petro Marine Services Mile 94.4 Sterling Hwy.

Campgrounds

Best Western King Salmon RV Park .... Ph. (907) 262-5857
Big Eddy Campground .... Ph. (907) 262-7888
Centennial Campground .... Ph. (907) 262-5299
Diamond M Ranch .... Ph. (907) 283-9424
Edgewater RV Park .... Ph. (907) 262-7733
Kenai Riverbend Campground .... Ph. (800) 625-2324
River Quest RV Park .... Ph. (907) 283-4991
River Terrace RV Park .... Ph. (907) 262-5593
Riverside House RV Park .... Ph. (907) 262-0500
Swiftwater Campground .... Ph. (907) 262-5299

Churches

First Baptist Church .... 159 Binkley St.

Dining

Best Western King Salmon Restaurant .... Ph. (907) 262-5857
Jersey Subs .... Ph. (907) 260-3343
Mykel's Restaurant & Lounge .... Ph. (907) 262-4305
Odie's Cafe .... Ph. (907) 262-5807
River City Books & Espresso Cafe .... Ph. (907) 260-7722
Sal's Klondike Diner .... Ph. (907) 262-9065

Fishing Guides & Charters

Alaska Fishing Charters .... Ph. (907) 262-4779
Dan's Alaskan Sport-fishing Ventures .... Ph. (907) 262-6515
EZ Limit Guide Service .... Ph. (907) 262-6169
Fenton Bros. Guided Sportfishing .... Ph. (907) 262-2502
Harry Gaines Kenai River Fishing Guide .... Ph. (907) 262-5097
Irish Lord Charters .... Ph. (800) 575-2055
Jeff King's Budget Charters .... Ph. (907) 262-4564
Johnson Bros. Guides & Outfitters .... Ph. (800) 918-7233
Riverside House Fishing Guide Service .... Ph. (907) 262-0500
Rod 'N Real Charters .... Ph. (907) 262-6064
Tim Berg's Alaskan Fishing .... Ph. (800) 548-3474
Tom's Cabins & Guide Service .... Ph. (907) 262-3107

Shopping & Services

Beemun's Variety Store .... 35277 Kenai Spur Hwy.
Craftsman Hobbies .... Ph. (907) 262-2839
Custom Seafood Processors .... Ph. (907) 262-9691
Deep Creek Custom Packing .... Ph. (907) 262-2667
Donna's Country & Victorian Gifts .... Blazy's Soldotna Mall
Klondike City .... Ph. (907) 262-9065
Northland Gallery & Wildlife Studio .... At the 'Y'
Peninsula Center Mall .... 44332 Sterling Hwy.
River City Books & Espresso Cafe .... Ph. (907) 260-7722
Robin Place Fabrics .... Ph. (907) 262-5438
Soldotna Wash & Dry .... At the 'Y'
Sweeney Clothing .... Ph. (907) 262-5916

Visitor Information

Soldotna Chamber of Commerce .... Ph. (907) 262-9814

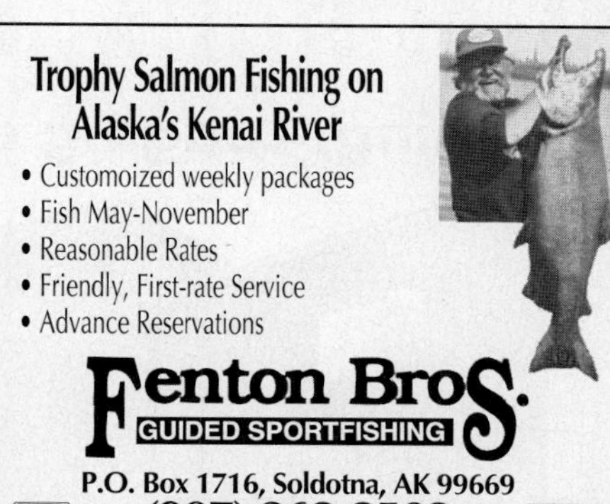

1949, at its original location on the Kenai Spur Highway at Corral Street.) Soldotna was named for a nearby stream; it is a Russian word meaning "soldier," although some believe the name came from an Indian word meaning the "stream fork."

Soldotna was incorporated as a first-class city in 1967. It has a council–manager form of government. Kenai Peninsula Borough headquarters and state offices of the Departments of Highways, Public Safety, Fish and Game, and Forest, Land and Water Management are located here. Soldotna is also headquarters for the Kenai Peninsula Borough school district. There are 3 elementary schools, a junior high school and 2 high schools. University of Alaska–Kenai Peninsula College is also located in Soldotna.

View from Kenai River bridge of Soldotna fishwalk. (© Kris Graef, staff)

Area terrain is level and forested, with many streams and lakes nearby. Large rivers of the area are the Swanson River, the Moose River and the Kenai River, which empties into Cook Inlet just south of Kenai. The area affords a majestic view of volcanic mountains across Cook Inlet. Always snow-covered, they are Mount Spurr (elev. 11,100 feet/3,383m), which erupted in 1992; Mount Iliamna (elev. 10,016 feet/3,053m), which has 3 smaller peaks to the left of the larger one; and Mount Redoubt (elev. 10,197 feet/3,108m), which was identified by its very regular cone shape until it erupted in December 1989.

Lodging & Services

All modern conveniences and facilities are available, including supermarkets, banks, hotels/motels, restaurants and drive-ins, medical and dental clinics, bowling alley, golf course, veterinarians, churches and a library. Two shopping malls are located on the Sterling Highway near the center of town. There are also numerous area bed-and-breakfasts, cabin rentals and lodges offering accommodations.

Alaskan Holiday Suites. Two-bedroom, 2-bath suites with fully equipped kitchens. Suites accommodate up to 6. Convenient location, close to all services and just a short walk to the famous Kenai River. Continental breakfast. Free local calls. Cable TV. Guide reservations available. VISA/MasterCard accepted. Reservations: (907) 242-2387 or (907) 262-9635. See display ad. [ADVERTISEMENT]

Best Western King Salmon Motel, Restaurant and RV Park, downtown Soldotna on Kenai Spur Highway. Large rooms, queen beds, some kitchenettes, cable TV, phones. Free in-room coffee. Restaurant serves early fisherman's breakfast, lunch, dinner. Steaks, seafood, salad bar. Beer and wine available. Fishing licenses, ice. Fish processing close by. RV park with 39 pull-through spaces, full hookups, restrooms, coin-operated showers and laundry. Phone (907) 262-5857; fax (907) 262-9441. See display ad this section. [ADVERTISEMENT] ▲

Riverside House Hotel, RV Park and Fishing Guide Service on the Kenai River in Soldotna. RV spaces with electricity and water $10. Recreational itineraries for fishing, sightseeing, etc., arranged. Walking distance to stores, churches, entertainment. Fine dining in the restaurant and lounge. Spacious newly remodeled rooms. 446111 Sterling Highway, Soldotna, AK 99669. Toll-free 1-877-262-0500. Internet: bob@river side~house.com. [ADVERTISEMENT]

Soldotna B&B Lodge/Alaska Fishing Charter, on the Kenai River. Nicely decorated and very clean. Enjoy fruit-filled pancakes for breakfast in the riverfront sunroom. Quiet location and within walking distance to community services/restaurants. Bank fishing for our guests. We arrange bear-viewing, fishing fly-outs, canoeing, hiking, snowmobile tours. Open year-round. Value seaosn rates. Toll-free 877-262-4779. Local (907) 262-4779. See display ad this section. [ADVERTISEMENT]

Camping

There are several private campgrounds located in and near Soldotna; see ads this section.

For Swiftwater Campground, turn on East Redoubt Street at **Milepost S 94.1** Sterling Highway. Centennial Park Campground is 0.1 mile from the Sterling Highway just south of the Kenai River bridge on Kalifornsky Beach Road; turn west at **Milepost S 96.1**. Both campgrounds are owned by the City of Soldotna. Register for camping at either park; camping fees charged. Wheelchair accessible. Dump station available at Centennial Park Campground. Campsites for both tents and RVs (no hookups). These campgrounds are heavily used; good idea to check in early. ♿▲

Edgewater RV Park on the banks of world famous Kenai River, across from Soldotna visitors' center. Full and partial hookups, laundry, showers, grassy sites, picnic tables, local guide service and fish cleaning facilities. Bank fishing. Walk to stores, restaurants. Reservations and information: (907) 262-7733. ridgerv@ctaz.com. P.O. Box 976, Soldotna, AK 99669. [ADVERTISEMENT] ▲

River Terrace RV Park features a prime Kenai River location near the Soldotna bridge. Easy, comfortable, riverfront access on the 1000-ft. boardwalk with steps right into the river. Handicapped accessible with fishing platform. A great place to fish or view

the exciting action. 28-ft. spaces, full hookups, riverfront sites, 20-30-50 amp, heated restrooms, free showers, unlimited hot water, laundry. Ice, fish processing and taxidermy available on premises. Local guides provide custom king and silver salmon charters. For a true Alaskan experience book remote fly-out fishing or spectacular bear watching. Remember, early and late season dates are easier to get and very enjoyable. (907) 262-5593; Fax (907) 262-8873. P.O. Box 322, Soldotna, AK 99669. [ADVERTISEMENT] ♿▲

Transportation

Air: Charters available. Soldotna airport is south of Soldotna at Mile 2 Funny River Road. Turn off the Sterling Highway at **Milepost S 96.1**, just after crossing Kenai River bridge.

Local: Taxi service, car rentals, vehicle leasing, boat rentals and charters.

Highway: Accessible via the Sterling Highway (Alaska Route 1), 148 miles from Anchorage.

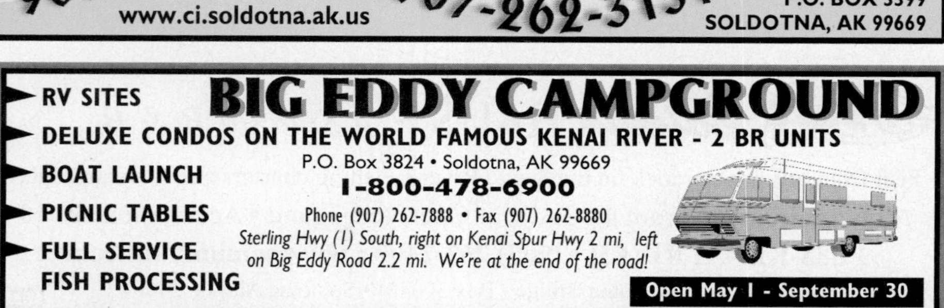

Attractions

Fishwalks. Several public fishwalks have been constructed in the Soldotna area in order to make the popular Kenai River more accessible to the public. Although this beautiful stream cuts right through the center of town, public access is limited by private land ownership along the riverbank, as well as the nature of the river itself. The wide, swift Kenai River does not have an easily accessible, gently sloping riverbank. Try the fishwalks at the Soldotna Visitor Center, right below the Kenai River bridge, and at Soldotna Creek Park, located off the Sterling Highway in the center of town (access road is behind the Mexican restaurant). The park has covered picnic tables, grills, playground and trails.

Join in Local Celebrations. Soldotna's big summer event is the annual Progress Days, held during the 4th of July weekend. Started in 1960 to commemorate the completion of the natural gas line, Progress Days has grown into one of the peninsula's biggest annual attractions. The main event is the parade down Binkley Street, which begins 11 A.M. Saturday morning. Other activities include a rodeo, community barbecues, quilt displays, and other events.

In February, the Peninsula Winter Games take place in Soldotna. Activities include an ice sculpture contest, cross-country ski race, ice bowling and snow volleyball. Games, booths, concessions and demonstrations are held throughout the weekend. The Alaska State Championship Sled Dog Races and Dog Weight Pull Contest take place during the Winter Games.

Donna's Country & Victorian Gifts at Blazy's Soldotna Mall. A shopper's delight, a

fisherman's wife's revenge. This is the perfect place to spend an afternoon while your husband goes fishing. Roomfuls of wonderful things, constantly changing. Enjoy our cozy, relaxing atmosphere. Don't miss our Santa room! You'll find things in our shoppe

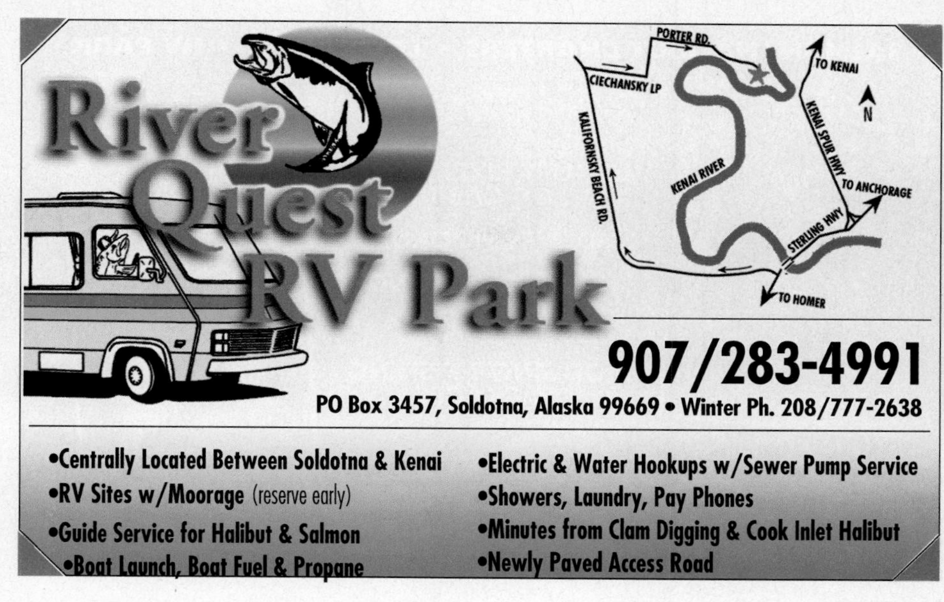

you never thought you'd find in Alaska! [ADVERTISEMENT]

River City Books & Espresso Cafe is a charming bookstore in the heart of Soldotna. Listed in *Alaska's Best Places*, this cheerful oasis serves up a delightful concoction of mysteries, novels, adventures, nonfiction, children's books and a top-notch Alaska selection along with espresso drinks, fabulous quiches, salads, sandwiches and a surprise "Chocolate of the Day!" On the left, at the second stoplight. 43977 Sterling Highway. (907) 260-7722. [ADVERTISEMENT]

Fish the Kenai River. Soldotna is one of Alaska's best-known sportfishing headquarters, and many claim that some of the world's best fishing is here at the Kenai River, which flows next to town. Many charter boats and fishing guides for Kenai River fishing are located in the Soldotna area. In May 1985, Les Anderson of Soldotna landed a 97-lb., 4-oz. king salmon, a new world's record. The mounted fish is on display at the visitor center.

Soldotna gets very busy during fishing season, and for those fishermen who want a more remote fishing spot—or for visitors who want to see wildlife and glaciers—there are fly-in fishing trips for rainbow, grayling, salmon and Dolly Varden, and flightseeing trips to see Tustumena Lake, the Harding Icefield and wildlife, through local outfitters.

In Soldotna, the early run of kings begins about May 15, with the peak of the run occurring between June 12 and 20. The late run enters the river about July 1, peaking between July 23 and 31; season closes July 31. The first run of red salmon enters the river during early June and is present in small numbers through the month; the second run enters about July 15 and is present through early August. In even years pink salmon are present from early through mid-August. The early silver salmon run arrives in early August, peaks in mid-August, and is over by the end of the month. Late run silver salmon enter the Kenai in early September, peak in mid- to late-September, and continue to enter the river through October. Dolly Varden and rainbow trout can be caught all summer.

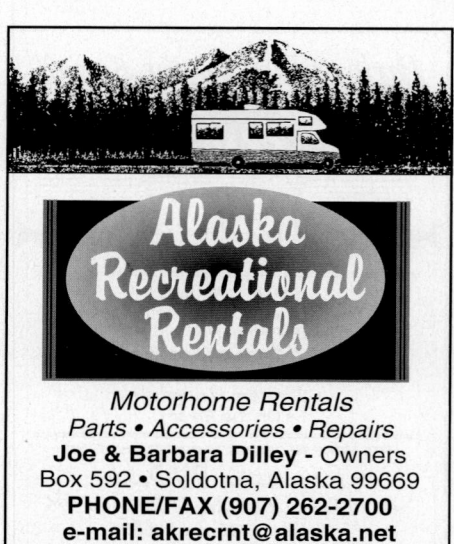

Central Peninsula Sports Center, on Kalifornsky Beach (K-Beach) Road, has an Olympic-sized hockey rink, a jogging track, 2 racquetball/volleyball courts, a weight and exercise room, dressing rooms and showers. The Sports Center also has convention facilities and meeting rooms. Phone (907) 262-3150 for more information.

Soldotna Historical Society Museum, located on Centennial Park Road, features a wildlife museum and the Historic Homestead Village. The Slikok Valley School, the last of the Alaska Territory log schools, built in 1958, is one of the attractions at the museum's log village. Soldotna was settled in 1947. How the homesteaders lived is revealed in a collection of pioneer artifacts and photos in the former Soldotna Chamber of Commerce log tourist center. Damon Hall, a large building constructed for the Alaska Centennial, features an outstanding display of wildlife mounts with a background mural of these species' natural habitat. Open 10 A.M. to 5 P.M., Tuesday through Sunday; closed Monday.

Joyce Carver Memorial Library offers temporary cards for visitors; large sunlit reading areas for both adults and children; Alaska videos on summer Saturday afternoons at 2 P.M. Open 9 A.M. to 8 P.M. Monday through Thursday, noon to 6 P.M. Friday, and 9 A.M. to 6 P.M. Saturdays. 235 Binkley St., Soldotna, phone (907) 262-4227.

Kenai National Wildlife Refuge Visitor Center, located at the top of Ski Hill Road (turnoff at **Milepost S 97.9**) and also accessible from Funny River Road, hosts some 25,000 visitors annually. This modern center has dioramas containing lifelike mounts of area wildlife in simulated natural settings. Free wildlife films are shown on the hour daily from noon to 4 P.M. Information available here on canoeing, hiking and camping. There is a 1-mile-long nature trail with an observation platform and spotting scope on Headquarters Lake. In winter, the refuge visitor centre are hosts 8 miles of cross-country ski trails. The Alaska Natural History Assoc. has a sales outlet here with books, posters

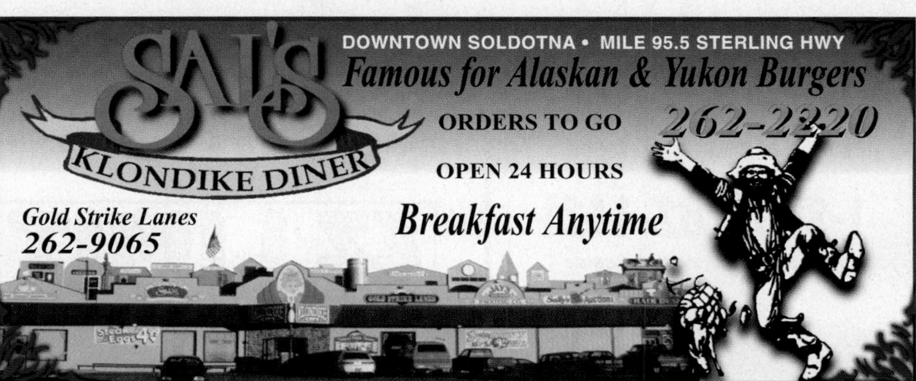

and videos. Pay phone located in center. Open weekdays 8 A.M. to 4:30 P.M., and weekends 10 A.M. to 6 P.M. No admission fee.

The refuge was created in 1941 when President Franklin D. Roosevelt set aside 1,730,000 acres of land (then designated the Kenai National Moose Range) to assure that the large numbers of moose, Dall sheep and other wild game would remain for people to enjoy. With the passage of the Alaska National Interest Lands Conservation Act in 1980, the acreage was increased to 1.97 million acres and redesignated Kenai National Wildlife Refuge. The area is managed by the U.S. Dept. of the Interior's Fish and Wildlife Service. Write: Refuge Manager, Kenai National Wildlife Refuge, P.O. Box 2139, Soldotna, AK 99669-2139; phone (907) 262-7021.

Take a Canoe Trip on one of several routes available in Kenai National Wildlife Refuge. Enjoyment of wildlife in their natural habitat, true wilderness scenery, camping, and fishing for trout and salmon are a few highlights of a canoe trip.

Established canoe trails include the Swanson River route (80 miles) and Swan Lake route (60 miles). Complete information on Kenai Peninsula canoe trails is available at the Kenai National Wildlife Refuge visitor contact station at Mile 58 Sterling Highway, the Kenai NWR visitor center in Soldotna and at chamber of commerce visitor centers in Kenai and Soldotna.

Log of the Sterling Highway continues on page 571.

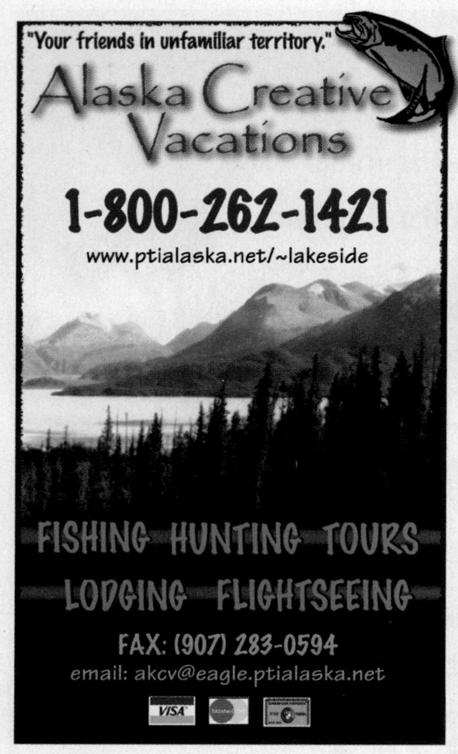

Pacific halibut, the largest sportfish in Alaska, can weigh more than 300 lbs.

Kenai Spur Highway Log

The Kenai Spur Highway junctions with the Sterling Highway at the Soldotna Y and leads north through Soldotna 10 miles to the city of Kenai. It ends at Captain Cook State Recreation Area, 39 miles north of Soldotna.

Distance from Soldotna Y (SY) is shown.

SY 0 Junction with Sterling Highway at **Milepost S 94.2.**

SY 0.6 (1 km) Soldotna City Hall.

SY 0.7 (1.1 km) Soldotna elementary school east on Park; playground. Post office is on N. Binkley.

SY 1 (1.6 km) Marydale Avenue. Central Peninsula General Hospital 0.4 mile west. 24-hour gas station east side of highway.

Tesoro 2Go Mart. See display ad this section.

SY 1.8 (2.8 km) Big Eddy Road to west. Winding paved road to Mile 1.4 (12-hour public parking); potholed gravel to road end at Mile 1.8, crosses private property. Access to fishing guides, private camping and boat launches. ▲

SY 4.2 (6.7 km) Silver Salmon Drive (paved and gravel) leads 0.5 mile west to **The Pillars Boat Launch** (Alaska State Park) on the Kenai River; large gravel parking area, toilets, boat ramp, fee station. Bank angling is not permitted. Fees: $10/launch, $5/day-use.

SY 5.6 (9 km) Gas station (diesel), grocery.

SY 5.9 (9.5 km) **Fantasies in Fiberglass.** See display ad this section.

SY 6.1 (9.8 km) Beaver Creek Park, a small neighborhood day-use park to west.

SY 6.3 (10.1 km) Twin City Raceway to east. South **junction** with **Beaver Loop Road**: Drive 2.7 miles on Beaver Loop Road for **Cunningham Park** public access to Kenai River. The park, which has a trail, fishwalk and restrooms, is one of the more popular area bank fishing spots during peak salmon runs. From here it is 3.9 miles to the Bridge Access Road via Beaver Loop Road.

Kenai Flats viewpoint on the Bridge Access Road. (© Kris Graef, staff)

SY 8.2 (13.2 km) Begin divided 4-lane highway, 35-mph. Paved bike trails both sides of highway to Kenai.

SY 8.8 (14.2 km) Gas station (diesel)

SY 9.4 (15.1 km) Tinker Lane. Access to Peninsula Oilers baseball park, municipal golf course

SY 9.7 (15.6 km) Kenai Central High School.

SY 10.1 (16.2 km) Welcome to Kenai sign and turnoff for City of Kenai tent campground to east; $8 camping fee. ▲

SY 10.2 (16.4 km) Motel and fast-food at intersection with Airport Road and Walker Lane.

SY 10.4 (16.7 km) Kenai Plaza shopping.

SY 10.5 (16.9 km) Carr's/K-Mart shopping.

SY 10.6 (17.1 km) **Junction.** Main Street Loop to east; Bridge Access Road to west.

The **Bridge Access Road** leads west to Port of Kenai (1 mile); junction with Beaver Loop Road (1.3 miles); City of Kenai public dock and boat ramp (1.6 miles); Kenai Flats boardwalk viewing telescope (2.2 miles); Warren Ames Bridge (2.8 miles); Kenai Flats State Recreation Site (3 miles); and junctions with Kalifornsky Road (3.4 miles).

Kenai

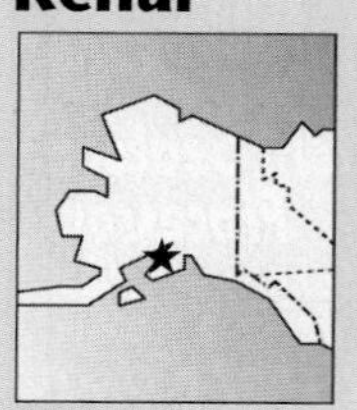

SY 10.6 (17.1 km) Intersection of Main Street Loop and Bridge Access Road in Kenai; 159 miles from Anchorage, 89 miles from Homer. **Population:** 7,058. **Emergency Services:** Phone 911 for all emergency services. **Alaska State Troopers** (in Soldotna), phone (907) 262-4453. **Kenai City Police**, phone (907) 283-7879. **Fire Department** and **Ambulance**, phone 911. **Hospital** (in Soldotna), phone (907) 262-4404. **Maritime Search and Rescue**, dial 0 for Zenith 5555, toll free.

Visitor Information: The Kenai Visitors

and Cultural Center, located at Main Street and Kenai Spur Highway, provides brochures and other visitor information. Very nice restrooms. The center features an excellent cultural museum, wildlife displays and movies. Write the Kenai Visitors and Cultural Center, 11471 Kenai Spur Highway, Kenai, AK 99611; phone (907) 283-1991, fax 283-2230. E-mail: kvcb@alaska.net. Web site: www.visitkenai.com.

Elevation: 93 feet/28m. **Climate:** Average daily maximum temperature in July, 61°F/16°C; January temperatures range from 11° to -19°F/-12° to -28°C. Lowest recorded temperature in Kenai was -48°F/-44°C. Average annual precipitation, 19.9 inches (68.7 inches of snowfall). **Radio:** KCSY 1140, KENI 550, KGTL 620, KSRM 920, KWVV 105, KGTL 100.9/103.5, KDLL-FM 91.9, MBN-FM 95.3/97.7, KENY 980, KWHQ-FM 100.1, KPEN-FM 101.7. **Television:** Several channels and cable. **Newspaper:** *Peninsula Clarion* (daily).

Private Aircraft: Kenai Municipal Airport is the principal airport on the Kenai Peninsula. It is accessible from Willow Street or Airport Way. There is a terminal building with ticket counter and baggage handling for commuter airlines, and a large parking lot. Elev. 92 feet; length 7,575 feet; asphalt; fuel 100LL; attended. A 2,000-foot gravel runway is also available. There is an adjacent 3,500-foot floatplane facility.

Kenai is situated on a low rise overlooking the mouth of the Kenai River where it empties into Cook Inlet. It is the largest city on the Kenai Peninsula. Prior to Russian Alaska, Kenai was a Dena'ina Native community. The Dena'ina people fished, hunted, trapped, farmed and traded with neighboring tribes here. In 1791 it became the second permanent settlement established by the Russians in Alaska, when a fortified post called Fort St. Nicholas, or St. Nicholas Redoubt, was built near here by Russian fur traders. In 1848, the first Alaska gold discovery was made on the Russian River. In 1869 the U.S. Army established Fort Kenai (Kenay); in 1899 a post office was authorized.

Oil exploration began in the mid-1950s, with the first major discovery in this area, the Swanson River oil reserves, 20 miles/32.2 km northeast of Kenai in 1957. Two years

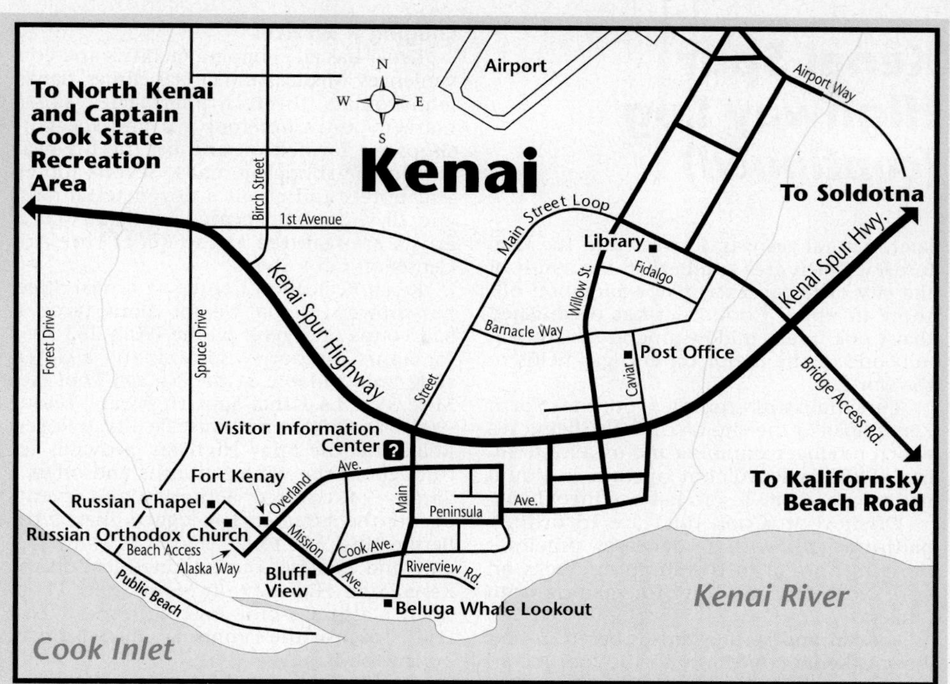

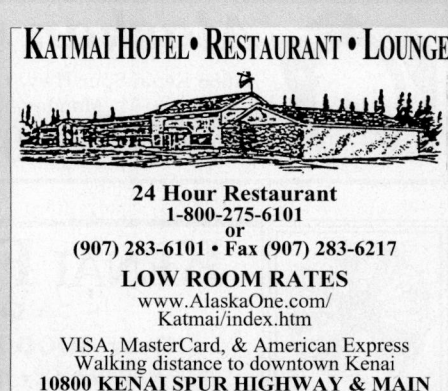

Kenai Spur Highway Log (continued)

later, natural gas was discovered in the Kalifornsky Beach area 6 miles/9.6 km south of the city of Kenai. Extensive exploration offshore in upper Cook Inlet has established that Cook Inlet's middle-ground shoals contain one of the major oil and gas fields in the world.

The industrial complex on the North Kenai Road is the site of Unocal Chemicals, which produces ammonia and urea for fertilizer. Phillips Petroleum operates a liquid natural gas plant. Tesoro has a refinery here.

Offshore in Cook Inlet are 15 drilling platforms, all with underwater pipelines bringing the oil to the shipping docks on both sides of Cook Inlet for loading onto tankers.

Federal and state agencies based in and around Kenai contribute to the local economy. Next to oil, tourism, fishing and fish processing are the leading industries.

Kenai is the home of the Kenai Peninsula Oilers, one of 3 teams that make up the Alaska Central Baseball League.

Kenai is also the home of Challenger Learning Center of Alaska, a science, math and techonology space center for Alaskan youth, grades 4–12.

Lodging & Services

Kenai has all shopping facilities and conveniences. Medical and dental clinics, banks, laundromats, theaters, pharmacies, supermarkets, and numerous gift and specialty shops are located on and off the highway and in the shopping malls. Several motels and hotels and about a dozen restaurants and drive-ins are located in Kenai. Local artists are featured at the Kenai Fine Arts Center on Cook Street.

Kenai Recreation Center on Caviar Street has showers, sauna, weight room, racquetball courts and gym; phone (907) 283-3855 for hours. Indoor swimming and a waterslide are available at the Nikiski Pool (see **Mile SY 23.4** Kenai Spur Highway); phone (907) 776-8800. A multi-use facility at Rogers Road and the Spur Highway provides ice throughout the winter months and offers a variety of covered activities and events during the summer. For joggers there's the Bernie Huss Memorial Trail, a 0.5-mile jogging and exercise course located just off the Kenai Spur Highway on Main Street Loop. There's also a 1-mile jogging track at East End Park near the Peninsula Oilers Ballpark on Lawton Drive.

City of Kenai public boat ramp off the Bridge Access Road has 24-hour parking, restrooms and pay phone.

Drive north of town on the Kenai Spur Highway for more lodging and camping.

Kenai's Old Town Village. Dine in the beautifully refurbished 1918 cannery building, featuring Alaska seafood, steaks, home cooking, beer and wine. Banquet space available for 150. Fantastic view of Kenai River, Cook Inlet and mountains. Visit log shops as they might have been in the early 1900s, featuring local artists and craftspersons. Book charters and sightseeing. Located 2 blocks from visitor center. Phone (907) 283-4515. E-mail:oldtown@ptialaska.net. See display ad. [ADVERTISEMENT]

Tanglewood Bed & Breakfast. Fish king salmon from our backyard, on lower Kenai River. View moose, caribou, bears, wolves, eagles, ducks, seals, beluga whales on regular basis. Rooms $75. Common room with fireplace. Fully equipped private suite with Jacuzzi, $125. Full breakfast. Laundry facilities. (907) 283-6771. Open year-round. Lifelong Alaskans. See display ad. [ADVERTISEMENT]

Toyon Villa. Suites at motel rates; $85 to $125. Studios and one- and 2-bedroom suites. Fully-equipped kitchens, cable TV, private phones, maid service. Located at Kenai River and Cook Inlet, in historic Old Town, across from Old Town Village Restaurant and gift shops. Phone (907) 283-4221. E-mail: tva@alaska.net. See display ad. [ADVERTISEMENT]

Camping

Arrangements for caravan camping may be made in advance through the Kenai Visitors and Cultural Center. Tent camping at **Milepost SY 10.1** Kenai Spur Highway. Private RV parks are available in Kenai; see ads this section or ask at the visitors center for directions. Public campgrounds are also available north of Kenai on the Kenai Spur Highway in Captain Cook State Recreation Area (see highway log). ▲

Dump stations located at several local service stations and city dock.

Beluga Lookout RV Park, 2 blocks from Kenai Visitors Center in historic Old Town, downtown Kenai. Overlooking bluff with fantastic view of beluga whales, Kenai River, Cook Inlet, Mount Redoubt. Historic Russian Orthodox Church, Fort Kenay next door. Log

Kenai Spur Highway Log *(continued)*

lodge office, private bathrooms, hot showers, laundry. 75 full-hookup spaces, cable TV, picnic tables, instant private phone hookups, pull-throughs, 30–50 amp power. Caravans welcome. VISA, MasterCard. Reservations (800) 745-5999 or (907) 283-5999. E-mail: beluga@ptialaska.net. See display ad. [ADVERTISEMENT] ▲

Transportation

Air: Kenai Municipal Airport is served by Era Aviation (scheduled passenger service) and Southcentral Air (charter and cargo service) as well as other charter services.

Local: Limousine and taxi service is available as well as car rentals, vehicle leasing, boat rentals and charters.

Highway: On the Kenai Spur Highway, 11 miles/17.7 km north of Soldotna.

Attractions

Get Acquainted. Kenai Visitors and Cultural Center has an abundance of brochures on attractions, activities and accommodations, as well as showing films on Alaska and hosting art shows. On display are historic and regional artifacts and wildlife mounts.

Kenai River Festival. This annual event is held the second weekend in June on the park strip next to the City of Kenai ball fields on Main Street. The festival features activities for children and adults alike, from fish-hat making and puppet shows to how-to-fish demonstrations and educational exhibits on birds, commercial fishing and water conservation. A parade starts each festival day, led by the famous 29-foot Festival Salmon and the Kenaitze Tribal Drum group. Live music, food and crafts booths. For more information, phone (907) 260-5449.

Old Town Kenai self-guided walking tour takes in Fort Kenay, the Russian Parish House Rectory, Russian Orthodox church and chapel (see descriptions following). Pick up a walking tour brochure at Kenai Visitors and Cultural Center and walk down Overland Street toward Cook Inlet.

Fort Kenay was the first American military installation in the area, established in 1868. More than 100 men were stationed here in the $1^1/_2$ years it officially served to protect American citizens in the area. A replica of the fort's barracks building was built as an Alaskan Purchase Centennial project by Kenai residents in 1967. This was the site of the original Russian schoolhouse which was torn down in 1956.

Parish House Rectory, constructed in 1881, directly east of Fort Kenay, is considered to be the oldest building on the Kenai Peninsula. Of the 4 rectories contracted by the Russian Orthodox Church in Alaska it is the only one still remaining. Restored in 1998–99, the rectory continues to be the residence of priests who serve the church. Hand-hewn logs, joined with square-notched corners, are covered by wood shingle siding and painted the original colors.

Holy Assumption of the Virgin Mary Russian Orthodox Church, across from the rectory, is one of the oldest Russian Orthodox churches in Alaska and the only National Historic Landmark on the Kenai Peninsula. The original church was founded in 1845 by a Russian monk, Father Nicholai. The present church was built with a $400 grant from the Russian Synod some 50 years after the original, and with its 3 onion-shaped domes is considered one of the finest examples of a Russian Orthodox church built on a vessel or quadrilateral floor plan. Icons from Russia and an 1847 Russian edition of the Holy Gospel—with enameled icons of Matthew, Mark, Luke and John on the cover—are displayed. Regular church services are held here. Tours are available during the summer from 11 A.M. to 4 P.M. daily except Sunday. Donations are welcomed.

St. Nicholas Chapel was built in 1906 as a memorial to Father Nicholai and his helper, Makary Ivanov, on the site of the

Kenai Spur Highway Log *(continued)*

original church, which was inside the northwest corner of the Russian trading post of Fort St. Nicholas. The 2 men were honored for their distribution of the first small pox vaccine in the territory.

Kenai River Flats is a must stop for birdwatchers. Great numbers of Siberian snow geese and other waterfowl stop to feed on this saltwater marsh in the spring. Kenai Flats State Recreation Site on the Bridge Access Road at the west end of Warren Ames Bridge; parking and interpretive signs. A boardwalk and viewing telescope for wildlife-watchers is located on the Bridge Access Road east of the Warren Ames Bridge.

Watch Baseball or Play Golf. Some fine semipro baseball is played at the Peninsula Oilers ball park on Tinker Lane. Golfers may try the 18-hole Kenai golf course on Lawton Drive.

Parks. Kenai Parks and Recreation maintains a total of 10 parks, 9 sports fields and the tent campground. Most visitors driving through town will notice the Lief Hansen Memorial Park in downtown Kenai on the Spur highway: it is perhaps the premier location in town for viewing flowers. The park also has a gazebo, water fountain, benches and drinking fountain.

Erick Hansen Scout Park, at the end of Upland Street in Old Towne Kenai, features benches and a great view of Cook Inlet.

Beluga Whale Watching. Good spots are the Kenai River beach at the west end of Spruce Street and Erick Hansen Scout Park at the end of Upland Street. Beluga whales are the only all-white whale. The beach also offers a good view of Kenai's fish-processing industry and volcanoes.

Kenai Spur Highway Log

(Continued)

SY 11.8 (19 km) Spruce Drive; access to beach, parking area; restrooms.

SY 12.1 (19.5 km) Forest Drive. Municipal day-use park with playground, picnic tables and trails to west. Scenic viewpoint overlooking Cook Inlet 0.4 mile west.

SY 12.4 (20 km) C Plaza; shopping.

Inlet Card & Craft. See display ad this section.

SY 13 (20.9 km) Mount Spurr is directly ahead northbound.

SY 15 (24.1 km) Kenai city limits.

SY 19 (30.6 km) Views through trees of Mount Redoubt to west and Mount Spurr to north.

Milky Way B&B. See display ad this section.

SY 20.4 (32.8 km) Gas station.

SY 21 (33.8 km) Unocal Manufacturing Facility (Agricultural Products).

SY 21.4 (34.6 km) Kenai Plant Phillips 66 LNG Plant.

SY 22.1 (35.5 km) Texaco Refinery.

SY 23.4 (37.6 km) **North Peninsula Recreation/Nikiski Pool**. Dome-shaped building in trees near highway is the Nikiski recreational swimming pool, with lap lanes, kiddie swim area and a great indoor slide;

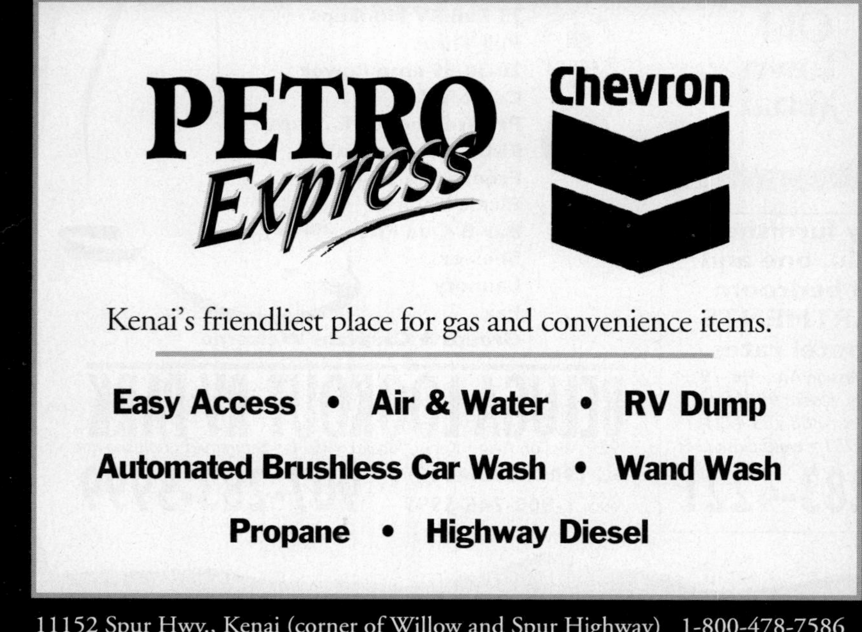

Distinctive dome-shaped building houses Nikiski Pool and Waterslide. (© Kris Graef, staff)

hot tub; visitor observation area; wheelchair-access. Phone (907) 776-8800 for hours. ♿

SY 25.8 (41.5 km) Island Lake Road.

SY 26.6 (42.8 km) Shopping, restaurant, grocery, gas station and post office at **NIKISKI** (pop. 3,060). **Emergency Services**, phone 911 for fire and paramedics.

Nikiski, also known as Port Nikiski and Nikishka, was homesteaded in the 1940s and grew with the discovery of oil on the Kenai Peninsula in 1957. By 1964, oil-related industries here included Unocal Chemical, Phillips LNG, Chevron and Tesoro. Oil docks serving offshore drilling platforms today include Rig-tenders, Standard Oil, Phillips 66 and Unocal Chemical. Commercial fishing is still a source of income for some residents.

SY 26.7 (43 km) Nikiski Fire Station No. 2 at turnoff for Nikiski Beach Road. Access west to Nikiski High School (0.3 mile) and OSK Heliport (0.5 mile). Drive to road end (0.8 mile, limited parking) for good view of Nikishka Bay and oil platforms in Cook Inlet; Arness Dock, built on a base of WWII Liberty ships (still visible); and scenic view of Mount Spurr and Alaska Range.

SY 29.7 (47.8 km) Hal Bouty Road.

Daniels Lake Lodge Bed & Breakfast. See display ad this section.

Grouchy Old Woman B&B. See display ad this section.

SY 30 (48.2 km) Daniels Lake.

SY 32.5 (52.3 km) Turnout west opposite Twin Lakes.

SY 35.5 (57.1 km) Entering **Captain Cook State Recreation Area.**

SY 35.9 (57.8 km) **Bishop Creek** (Captain Cook SRA); 15 tent campsites, parking, toilets, water, picnic area and trail to beach. Camping fee $8/night or resident pass. Watch for spawning red salmon in creek in July and August, silvers August to September. Closed to salmon fishing. ▲

SY 36.5 (58.7 km) Access to **Stormy Lake** (Captain Cook SRA) day-use area; parking, swimming area, change house, toilet, water, and fishing for rainbow and arctic char.

SY 36.7 (59.1 km) Stormy Lake Overlook, a large paved turnout to east, offers a panoramic view.

SY 36.9 (59.4 km) Stormy Lake picnic area (not on lake); water, toilets, covered tables.

SY 37.8 (60.8 km) Stormy Lake boat launch; water, toilets, parking.

SY 38.6 (62.1 km) Swanson River canoe landing area; drive 0.6 mile east to parking and toilets, river access. End of the Swanson River canoe trail system.

SY 38.7 (62.3 km) Clint Starnes Memorial Bridge crosses **Swanson River**; parking next to bridge. *Watch for fishermen on bridge.* View of Mount Spurr. Fishing for silver and red salmon, and rainbow.

SY 39 (62.8 km) Highway ends. Turn left for **Discovery Campground** (0.4 mile) and picnic area (0.5 mile) via bumpy gravel access road. Campground has 53 campsites, Maggie Yurick Memorial hiking trail, water, scheduled fireside programs in season. Camping fee $10/night or resident pass. ▲

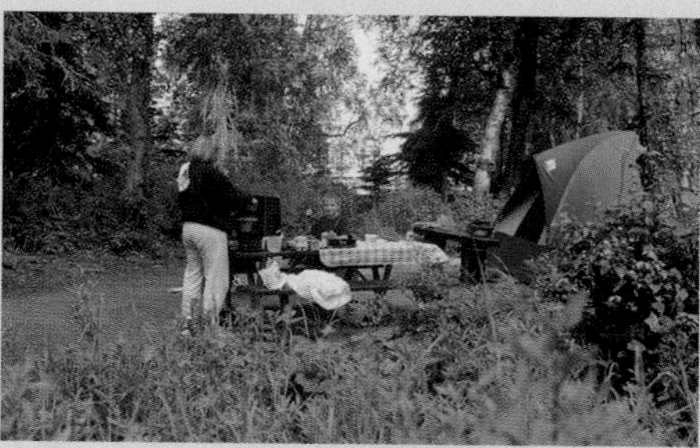

Day-use picnic area (keep to right at second fork) has tables and toilets on bluff overlooking ocean. *CAUTION: Steep cliffs; supervise children!*

Spur access road to beach (4-wheel drive vehicles only); signed as "unsafe due to high tides and loose sand". Parking area. ATVs are allowed in designated areas only.

Return to Milepost S 94.2
Sterling Highway

Kalifornsky Beach Road Log

Also called K–Beach Road, Kalifornsky Beach Road is a paved 45 mph road which leads west from the Sterling Highway at Soldotna, following the shore of Cook Inlet south to Kasilof. K-Beach Road also provides access to Kenai via the Bridge Access Road. *Mileposts run south to north and reflect mileage from Kasilof.*

Distance from the Sterling Highway junction at Milepost S 96.1 at Soldotna (S) is followed by distance from Sterling Highway junction at Milepost S 108.8 at Kasilof (K).

Ciechanski State Recreation Site on the Kenai River at River Mile 15.5. (© Kris Graef, staff)

S 0 K 22.2 (35.7 km) **Junction** with Sterling Highway at **Milepost S 96.1.**

S 0.1 (0.2 km) **K 22.1** (35.6 km) Soldotna Alaska Purchase Centennial Park Campground. Kenai River access for bank fishing, boat launch (fee charged).

S 0.2 (0.3 km) **K 22** (35.4 km) Alaska State Troopers.

S 0.3 (0.5 km) **K 21.9** (35.3 km) Rodeo grounds.

S 0.6 (1 km) **K 21.6** (34.8 km) Central Peninsula Sports Center; hockey, ice skating, jogging track and other sports available; phone (907) 262-3150.

S 1.7 (2.7 km) **K 20.5** (33 km) College Road to Kenai Peninsula Community College (1.3 miles north).

S 2.9 (4.7 km) **K 19.3** (31.1 km) K–Beach center. ADF&G office; stop in here for current sportfishing information.

S 3.1 (5 km) **K 19.1** (30.7 km) East Poppy Lane intersection; Tesoro gas station.

Access to **Kenai Peninsula Community College** (0.9 mile north).

S 3.5 (5.6 km) **K 18.7** (30.1 km) Shopping center, motel, restaurant and gas station. Motor Vehicle Dept. and Fish and Wildlife offices.

S 4.6 (7.4 km) **K 17.6** (28.3 km) Firehouse.

S 4.7 (7.6 km) **K 17.5** (28.2 km) Ciechanski Road leads 2.4 miles to private RV parks and **Ciechanski State Recreation Site** on the Kenai River (River Mile 15.5). This small state recreation site is easy to overlook, as it's tucked in the corner across from Kenai River Quest RV Park. Its primary purpose is to provide restroom access for boaters. There is 12-hour public parking (no camping), a picnic table, outhouse and dock walk.

Kenai Riverbend Campground is 0.2 mile beyond the Ciechanski state recreation site. Road ends at private properpty; no public river access. a day-use only picnic area with tables, toilets, dumpster and Kenai River access. Also access to private campgrounds with RV hookups on the Kenai River. ▲

S 5.7 (9.2 km) **K 16.5** (26.6 km) **Diamond M Ranch B&B, Cabins & RV Spaces.** Hosts: Longtime Alaskans, JoAnne and Carrol Martin family. Nestled in the trees. Full hookups, central shower, dump station. Fish cleaning facility. Magnificent view, wildlife, hiking trails and Kenai River access. Secluded, yet minutes from airport, shopping, restaurants, churches. Credit cards. (907) 283-9424. P.O. Box 1776, Soldotna, AK 99669. Internet: www.diamondmranch.com. See display ad in the Soldotna section. [ADVERTISEMENT] ▲

S 6 (9.7 km) **K 16.2** (26.1 km) Turnoff for city of Kenai via Bridge Access Road. Access to Kenai River Flats state recreation site and boardwalk viewpoint via Bridge Access Road.

S 7.6 (12.2 km) **K 14.6** (23.5 km) **Robinsons Mini Mall**. See display ad this section.

S 7.8 (12.5 km) **K 14.4** (23.2 km) VIP Drive; Kenai Custom Seafoods.

S 8 (12.9 km) **K 14.2** (22.9 km) Cafe.

S 8.8 (14.2 km) **K 13.4** (21.6 km) K-Beach Fire Station.

S 13 (20.9 km) **K 9.2** (14.8 km) Scenic viewpoint overlooking Cook Inlet.

S 17.4 (28 km) **K 4.8** (7.7 km) Kasilof Beach Road; access to beach, harbor, river.

S 19.4 (31.2 km) **K 2.8** (4.5 km) **Ingrid's Inn Bed & Breakfast**. See display ad this section.

S 20.1 (32.3 km) **K 2.1** (3.4 km) Kasilof Airfield Road.

S 22.1 (35.6 km) **K 0.1** (0.2 km) Kasilof post office.

S 22.2 (35.7 km) **K 0 Junction** with Sterling Highway at Kasilof, **Milepost S 108.8.**

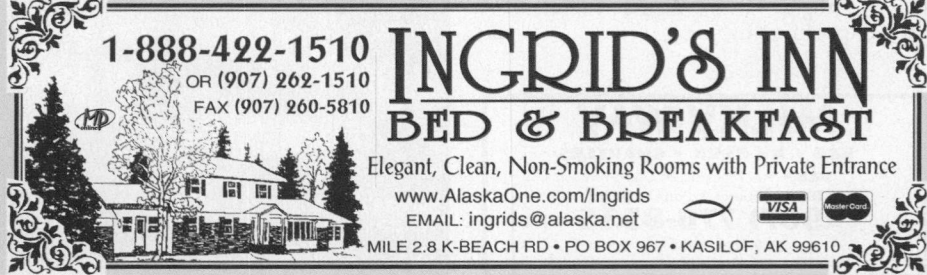

Return to Milepost S 96.1 or S 108.8 Sterling Highway

Sterling Highway Log

(continued from page 551)

S 95.9 (154.3 km) **A 148.9** (239.6 km) **H 83.6** (134.5 km) Kenai River bridge.

NOTE: Watch for road construction at the bridge in summer 2000.

S 96 (154.5 km) **A 149** (239.8 km) **H 83.5** (134.4 km) Soldotna visitor center to west at south end of Kenai River bridge. Entering Game Management Unit 15A northbound.

S 96.1 (154.7 km) **A 149.1** (239.9 km) **H 83.4** (134.2 km) Funny River Road to east; access to Soldotna businesses, airport and state recreation site (description follows). Kalifornsky Beach Road to west; access to Centennial Park campground (description follows).

Junction with Kalifornsky Beach Road. See KALIFORNSKY BEACH ROAD log this section.

A day's catch of Kenai River kings. (© Barb Willard)

Centennial Park Municipal Campground, 0.1 mile west, on the banks of the Kenai River; 126 campsites (some on river), tables, firepits, firewood provided, water, restrooms, dump station, pay phone, 2-week limit. Register at entrance. Boat launch and favorite fishing site on fishwalk.

Funny River Road (paved) leads east to Soldotna airport (2 miles) and **Funny River State Recreation Site** (12 miles). The recreation site has 16 campsites, tent sites, $8 camping fee or resident pass, picnic tables, water, toilets, river access. Salmon and trout fishing at the confluence of the **Kenai** and **Funny rivers** at the recreation area (check for bank closures). Turn on Funny River Road and take first right (Ski Hill Loop Road) for USF&WS visitor center (see description at **Milepost S 97.9**). Funny River Road dead ends 17.2 miles from the highway.

S 97.9 (157.6 km) **A 150.9** (242.8 km) **H 81.6** (131.3 km) Begin southbound turn lane for Sky View High School to west, and abrupt turnoff to east for Ski Hill Road and access to **Kenai National Wildlife Refuge Visitor Center** (description follows). Turnoff is easy to miss and was not signed in 1999. (Sign pictured below is at the visitor center entrance on Ski Hill Road.)

Sky View High School has the popular **Tsalteshi Trails System** (built by volunteers), with 7 miles of loop trails for walking, running and mountain biking in summer, and cross-country skiing in winter. Trails start behind the school.

Drive east 1 mile on on Ski Hill Road for Kenai National Wildlife Refgue Visitor Center.

This popular center has dioramas of area wildlife, free wildlife films, and rangers on hand to answer questions on canoeing, hiking and camping in the refuge. There is a nature trail down to an observation platform and spotting scope on Headquarters Lake. The center is open 8 A.M. to 4:30 P.M. on weekdays, 10 A.M. to 6 P.M. weekends.

Ski Hill Road loops back to Funny River Road (see preceding milepost).

S 98.5 (158.5 km) **A 151.5** (243.8 km) **H 85** (136.8 km) *CAUTION: Moose Danger Zone next 10 miles southbound.*

S 101.4 (163.2 km) **A 154.4** (248.5 km) **H 82.1** (132.1 km) **Tustumena Smokehouse Retail & Gifts.** Free samples! Want to experience a taste of Alaska? Stop in and try our

excellent, savory smoked salmon and buffalo sausages. We specialize in custom processing of your fish or wild game and will ship anywhere. Motorhome friendly access. Family owned. (907) 260-3401. www.tustumenasmokehouse.com. E-mail: fred@tustumenasmokehouse.com. [ADVERTISEMENT]

S 108.8 (175 km) **A 161.8** (260.4 km) **H 70.7** (113.8 km) **South junction** with Kalifornsky Beach Road. Drive west 4.8 miles to Beach Road for access to beach, Kasilof small-boat harbor and Kasilof River. This loop road rejoins Sterling Highway at **Milepost S 96.1.**

Junction with Kalifornsky Beach Road. See KALIFORNSKY BEACH ROAD log this section.

KASILOF (kuh-SEE-lawf; pop. 548; elev. 75 feet) was originally a settlement established in 1786 by the Russians as St. George. A Kenaitze Indian village grew up around the site, but no longer exists. The current population is spread out over the general area which is called Kasilof. The area's income is derived from fishing and fish processing.

Kasilof River. The red salmon dip-net fishery here is open by special announcement for Alaska residents only. Check with the ADF&G for current regulations.

Private Aircraft: Kasilof airstrip, 1.7 miles north; elev. 125 feet; length 2,100 feet; gravel; unattended.

S 109.2 (175.7 km) **A 162.2** (261 km) **H 70.3** (113.1 km) **Kasilof Riverview.** See display ad this section.

S 109.4 (176.1 km) **A 162.4** (261.3 km) **H 70.1** (112.8 km) Bridge over Kasilof River, which drains Tustumena Lake, one of the largest lakes on the Kenai Peninsula. **Kasilof River State Recreation Site**; 10 campsites, $10 nightly fee or resident pass, $5 day-use fee, 5 picnic sites on riverbank, picnic tables, toilets and water are on the south side of the bridge. This is a popular boat launch for drift boaters fishing for king salmon late May to early July. Boat launch $5 fee.

Entering Game Management Subunit 15C southbound, 15B northbound.

S 110 (177 km) **A 163** (262.3 km) **H 69.5** (111.8 km) Tustumena Elementary School and **junction** with north end of Johnson Lake Loop Road. See description and access to Johnson Lake at **Milepost S 111.**

S 110.5 (177.8 km) **A 163.5** (263.1 km) **H 69** (111 km) Double-ended paved parking by Crooked Creek.

S 110.8 (178.3 km) **A 163.8** (263.6 km) **H 68.7** (110.6 km) **Tustumena Lodge.** Phone (907) 262-4216. E-mail:

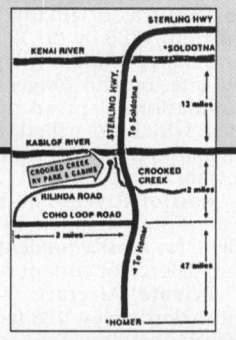

suzieq@ptialaska.net. Motel, cocktail lounge, outdoor patio, volleyball, horseshoes, fishing guides. Clean, affordable rooms at half the price of town. Some kitchenettes. Friendly Alaskan atmosphere where a cold drink, light snack and good fish stories are always available. Home of the $8 dinner: Monday—prime rib; Friday—New York Steak. See the world's largest razor clam and look for a hat from your hometown among the over 17,000 hats in our pending Guinness record collection. [ADVERTISEMENT]

S 111 (178.6 km) **A 164** (263.9 km) **H 68.5** (110.2 km) **Junction** with south end of Johnson Lake Loop Road to east and access to Kasilof RV Park and public campgrounds at Johnson and Tustumena lakes (descriptions follow). **North junction** with Cohoe Loop Road to west and access to Crooked Creek Station Recreation Site (see COHOE LOOP ROAD log for details).

Crooked Creek RV Park & Guide Service. See display ad this section. ▲

Junction with Cohoe Loop Road. See COHOE LOOP ROAD log this section.

Turnoff to east on Johnson Lake Loop Road for access to Crooked Creek Road and Tustumena Lake Road. Entrance to **Johnson Lake State Recreation Area** is 0.4 east (turn at metal T on Tustumena Road). Johnson

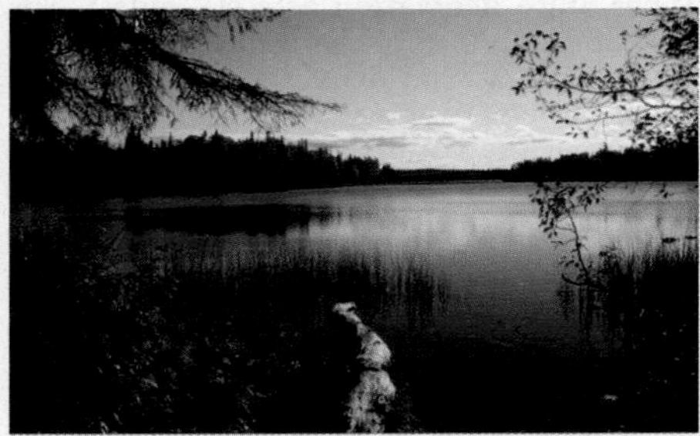

Lake (non-motorized) is a popular spot for family camping and canoeing. The recreation area has a large day-use area with parking, wheelchair accessible restrooms, water, dumpster, picnic tables and firepits in the trees next to the lake. Johnson Lake campground has 50 sites (some double and some pull-throughs), $10 nightly fee or resident pass, water, toilets, boat launch and firewood. Lake is stocked with rainbow. ♿ ▲

Tustumena Lake is 6.4 miles from the highway. A state campground on the Kasilof River near the lake has 10 sites, toilets and boat launch. Fishing for lake trout and salmon. Tustumena Lake is closed to king and sockeye salmon fishing. *CAUTION: Tustumena Lake is 6 miles wide and 25 miles long and subject to severe winds.* ▲

Kasilof RV Park. Modern, clean facilities in a park-like setting make this one of the Kenai Peninsula's favorite RV parks. The traveler is offered a great alternative from the parking lot-style RV parks and a peaceful retreat from the combat fishing campgrounds. The peaceful setting boasts wildflowers, beavers, moose, eagles and a variety of small birds. Enjoy walking, fishing for trout in Johnson Lake, salmon in the nearby Kasilof and Kenai rivers, halibut in Cook Inlet, or clamming on Alaska's famous razor-clam beaches. Level gravel sites, picnic tables, full/partial hookups, spotless restrooms, free showers and friendly owners make for "two thumbs up." Open Memorial weekend to Labor Day. See display ad. [ADVERTISEMENT] ▲

Cohoe Loop Road Log

The Cohoe Loop Road loops loops west and south 15.3 miles from **Milepost S 111** to **Milepost S 114.3** on the Sterling Highway. The popular Crooked Creek fishing and camping area is at the top or north end of the loop.

Distance from north junction with the Sterling Highway (NJ) at Milepost S 111 is followed by distance from south junction (SJ) at Milepost S 114.3.

Mileposts run south to north.

NJ 0 SJ 15.3 (24.6 km) **North junction** with Sterling Highway at **Milepost S 111.**

NJ 1.8 (2.9 km) **SJ 13.5** (21.7 km) Crooked Creek/Rilinda Drive; access to Crooked Creek RV Park & Guide Service and to **Crooked Creek State Recreation Site** at the confluence of Crooked Creek and the Kasilof River. The recreation site has 83 campsites, 36 day-use sites, toilets and water trails to Kasilof River for fishermen. Camping fee $10/ night or resident pass, day-use fee $5/vehicle. ▲

This is one of the most popular and productive sites in the area for bank angling for king salmon. Fishing in **Crooked Creek** closed to king salmon fishing and closed to all fishing near hatchery. Fishing access to confluence of Crooked Creek and Kasilof River is through the state recreation site. *NOTE: Fishing access to Crooked Creek frontage above confluence is through a private RV park; fee charged.* Fishing in the **Kasilof River** for king salmon, 20–30 lbs., late May through early July, best in mid-June; coho salmon, mid-August to September, use salmon egg clusters, wet flies, assorted spoons and spinners. Steelhead available in late fall and early spring for catch-and-release.

NJ 2.4 (3.9 km) **SJ 12.9** (20.7 km) Webb–Ramsell Road. Kasilof River access across private property, fee charged.

NJ 5.2 (8.4 km) **SY 10.1** (16.3 km) **Cohoe Micro Bakery.** See display ad this section.

NJ 5.3 (8.5 km) **SJ 10** (16 km) Cohoe Spur Road **junction.** A post office was established in 1950 at **COHOE** (area pop. 508), originally an agricultural settlement.

NJ 5.6 (9 km) **SJ 9.7** (15.6 km) T intersection; go west 0.8 mile for beach and boat launch. Private campground on Madsen Road. Cabins for rent on St. Elias Road to right. Cohoe Loop Road continues north. Pavement begins northbound. ▲

Kasilof River Cabins. See display ad this section.

NJ 15.3 (24.6 km) **SJ 0 South junction** with Sterling Highway at **Milepost S 114.3.**

Return to Milepost S 114.3 or Milepost S 111 Sterling Highway

A sunny summer day fishing the Kasilof River. (© Barb Willard)

Tustumena Ridge Cabins. See display ad this section.

S 114.3 (183.9 km) **A 167.3** (269.2 km) **H 65.2** (104.9 km) Cohoe Loop Road loops 13 miles/21 km north to **Milepost S 111.**

South **junction** with Cohoe Loop Road. See COHOE LOOP ROAD log this section.

S 117.4 (188.9 km) **A 170.4** (274.2 km) **H 62.1** (99.9 km) **Clam Gulch State Recre-**

Red salmon, also called sockeye salmon, are taken in freshwater streams.

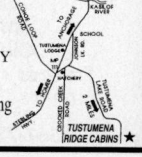

ation Area, 0.5 mile from highway; picnic tables, picnic shelter, toilets, water, 116 campsites, $10 nightly fee or resident pass. $5 day-use fee. *CAUTION: High ocean bluffs are dangerous.* Short access road to beach (recommended for 4-wheel-drive vehicles only, limited turnaround space). ▲

Clam digging for razor clams on most of the sandy beaches of the western Kenai Peninsula from Kasilof to Anchor Point can be rewarding. Many thousands of clams are dug each year at Clam Gulch. You must have a sportfishing license to dig, and these are available at most sporting goods stores. The bag limit is 60 clams regardless of size (always check current regulations). There is no legally closed season, but quality of the clams varies with month; check locally. Good clamming and fewer people in March and April, although there may still be ice on the beach. Any tide lower than minus 1-foot is enough to dig clams; minus 4- to 5-foot tides are best. The panoramic view of Mount Redoubt, Mount Iliamna and Mount Spurr across Cook Inlet and the expanse of beach are well worth the short side trip even during the off-season.

Charter boat fishing for Cook Inlet halibut. (© Bill Sherwonit)

S 118.2 (190.2 km) **A 171.2** (275.5 km) **H 61.3** (98.7 km) **CLAM GULCH** (pop. 108) consists of the lodge and the post office, which was established in 1950.

S 119.6 (192.5 km) **A 172.6** (277.8 km) **H 59.9** (96.4 km) **Clam Gulch Lodge B&B**, home of Captain J Charters. Continental breakfast buffet with mountain view from our fireplace lounge. We guide for salmon and halibut on fresh and saltwater and offer guided clam trips on the best clam beaches in Alaska. Call for tides. We offer a smoke-free environment, large rooms, twin and king-size beds with shared baths. Four RV sites with full hookups. Box 499, Clam Gulch, AK 99568. 1-800-700-9555. Phone/fax (907) 260-3778. Internet: www.clamgulch.com. E-mail: eviej@ptialaska.net. See display ad. [ADVERTISEMENT] ▲

S 122.8 (197.6 km) **A 175.8** (282.9 km) **H 56.7** (91.2 km) Paved, double-ended turnout oceanside (no view).

S 124.8 (200.8 km) **A 177.8** (286.1 km) **H 54.7** (88 km) Paved, double-ended turnout oceanside with view of Cook Inlet.

S 126.8 (204.1 km) **A 179.8** (289.4 km) **H 52.7** (84.8 km) Double-ended paved scenic wayside overlooking upper Cook Inlet. Polly Creek, due west across Cook Inlet, is a popular area for clam diggers (fly in). Across the inlet is Mount Iliamna; north of Iliamna is Mount Redoubt.

S 127.1 (204.5 km) **A 180.1** (289.8 km) **H 52.4** (84.3 km) Double-ended paved scenic viewpoint to west with interpretive display on Mount Redoubt and Mount Spurr volcanoes. Private RV park. ▲

Scenic View RV Park. Easy access off highway. Full hookups with electric, water, dump station. Low monthly/weekly rates. Located between Soldotna and Homer overlooking Cook Inlet and Mt. Redoubt. Fish halibut/king salmon with Elby Charters, dig razor clams on nearby beaches. E-mail: scenicrv@alaska.net. Phone (907) 567-3909.

Landlocked red salmon are commonly called "kokanee."

www.pubcenter.com/scenicviewrv. See display ad. [ADVERTISEMENT] ▲

S 128.3 (206.5 km) **A 181.3** (291.8 km) **H 51.2** (82.4 km) **Ninilchik Cabins & Fish Camp.** See display ad this section.

S 130.1 (209.4 km) **A 183.1** (294.7 km) **H 49.4** (79.5 km) **Caribou Creek Cabins.** See display ad this section.

S 130.5 (210 km) **A 183.5** (295.3 km) **H 49** (78.9 km) **Ninilchik Point Overnighter.** Spacious, comfortable home-grown log cabins. Scenic getaway. Cook Inlet view. Economy camping, with showers. One cabin self-contained with kitchen. 3-cabins served by shower house. 2-burner electric units. Bedding, linens provided. Outdoor grill. Close to famous fishing, clam beaches. Local charters. (907) 567-3423. http://members.tripod.com/Yukon/727/ (comes up on Netscape). See display ad. [ADVERTISEMENT]. ▲

S 132.2 (212.7 km) **A 185.2** (298 km) **H 47.3** (76.1 km) **Heavenly Sights Charters & Camping.** See display ad this section. ▲

S 134.5 (216.4 km) **A 187.5** (301.7 km) **H 45** (72.4 km) Inlet View Lodge and Ninilchik State Recreation Area. **Ninilchik River Scenic Overlook**; $10 camping fee or resident pass, $5 day-use fee. **Ninilchik River Campground**; $10 camping fee, 43 sites, water, toilets, tables. Trail to Ninilchik River; fishing for king and silver salmon, steelhead and Dolly Varden. **Ninilchik Beach Campground**; 35 campsites, toilets, water, $5 camping fee or resident pass. Popular beach for razor clamming. *CAUTION: Drownings have occurred here. Be aware of tide changes when clam digging. Incoming tides can quickly cut you off from the beach.* Access to the clamming beds adjacent to the campgrounds during minus tides. ▲

Inlet View Lodge. See display ad this section.

S 134.7 (216.8 km) **A 187.7** (302 km) **H 44.8** (72.1 km) Coal Street; access west to Ninilchik's historic **Russian Orthodox Church** at top of hill; plenty of parking and turnaround space; scenic overlook.

S 134.8 (216.9 km) **A 187.8** (302.2 km) **H 44.7** (71.9 km) Large double-ended gravel turnout; scenic overlook.

S 135.1 (217.4 km) **A 188.1** (302.7 km) **H 44.4** (71.4 km) Double-ended gravel turnout and dumpsters at north end of Ninilchik River bridge. Side road leads to **NINILCHIK VILLAGE**, the original village of Ninilchik, and to the beach. Access to mouth of **Ninilchik River**; fishing. A short road branches off this side road and leads into the old village of Ninilchik. Continue straight on side road for motel, beach, overnight RV parking, camping and toilets (follow signs). Sea breezes here keep the beach free of mosquitoes. Historic signs near beach and at village entrance tell about Ninilchik Village, which includes several old dovetailed log buildings. A walking tour brochure is available from businesses in the village and along the highway. Present-day Ninilchik is located at **Milepost S 135.5.** ▲

A beautiful white Russian Orthodox church sits on a hill overlooking the sea above the historic old village. Trail leads up to it from the road into town (watch for sign just past the old village store). The church and cemetery are still in use. You are welcome to walk up to it, but use the well-defined path behind the store (please do not walk through private property), or drive up using the Coal Street access at **Milepost S 134.7.**

Ninilchik Village Cache and **Cabins.** See display ad this section.

S 135.3 (217.7 km) **A 188.3** (303 km) **H 44.2** (71.1 km) Gravel turnout to west.

S 135.4 (217.9 km) **A 188.4** (303.2 km) **H 44.1** (71 km) Kingsley Road; access to Ninilchik post office, Alaskan Angler RV Resort and charter services to west. DOT/PF road maintenance station.

Turnoff for **Ninilchik View State Campground** east side of highway; 12 campsites on narrow gravel loop road, view of Ninilchik Village, tables, water, toilets, litter disposal, 2 dump stations ($5 fee), drinking water fill-up. Camping fee $10/night or resident pass. Foot trail from campground down to beach and village. ▲

Alaskan Angler RV Resort (formerly Hylen's) and **AFISHUNT Charters.** Newly remodeled park and cabins at great central Ninilchik location on the corner of Kingsley Road and highway. Walk to old village, downtown, clamming beaches, salmon fishing, post office. Fifty new 50-, 30-, 20-amp

View of Ninilchik Village from the Sterling Highway. (© Kris Graef, staff)

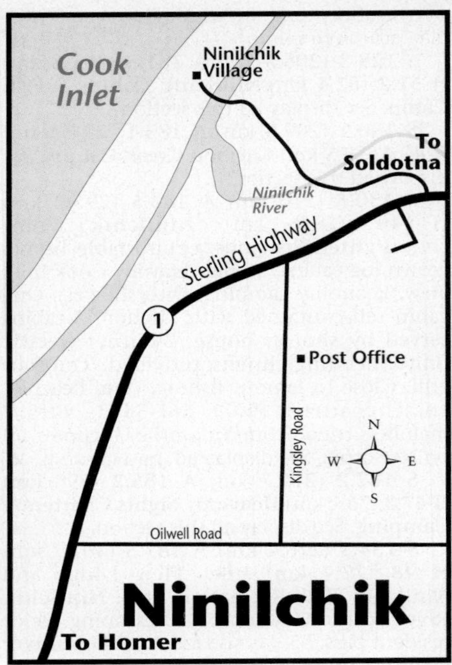

full hookups; 10 partial; cable TV with HBO, telephone lines, tenting. One-, 2- and 3-bedroom furnished cabins. New public showers/laundry. Propane in 2000. We specialize in local fishing and clamming, with licenses, cleaning tables, smoker, vacpak, freezing, shipping and tackle. Experience Alaska's best fishing for succulent halibut and king salmon with on-site AFISHUNT Charters, departing from the park. Good Sam discounts. Owners on-site. Reservations (800) 347-4114, (907) 567-3393. E-mail: info @afishunt.com. www.afishunt.com. See display ad in Ninilchik section. [ADVERTISEMENT] ▲

Ninilchik Charters. Just past Ninilchik post office on Kingsley Road. Fishing, cabins, full-service RV sites. We are committed to providing your group with an exciting and bountiful Alaskan fishing adventure. Package trips available. New cabins feature comfortable rooms, private baths. Vacpac/freezing area, laundry, picnic area. Conveniently located near the abundant razor clam beds of Ninilchik. Close proximity to restaurants/stores. See ad this section. 1-888-290-3507. [ADVERTISEMENT]

Ninilchik

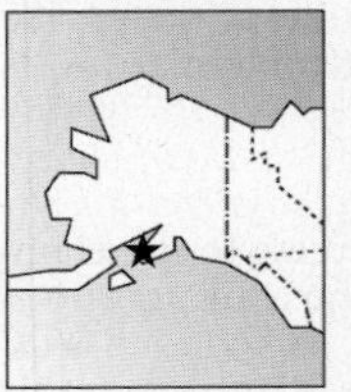

S 135.5 (218 km) **A 188.5** (303.4 km) **H 44** (70.8 km) Pronounced Nin-ILL-chick. **Population:** 687. **Emergency services:** Phone 911. **Visitor Information:** At Kiosk, **Milepost S 136.1.** Local businesses are also very helpful. **Private Aircraft:** Ninilchik airstrip, 3 SE; elev. 276 feet; length 2,400 feet; dirt and gravel; unattended.

Restaurant, lodging and charter service east side of road are part of the community of Ninilchik. Ninilchik extends roughly from Ninilchik State Recreation Area on the north to Deep Creek on the south, with services (grocery stores, gas stations, campgrounds, etc.) located at intervals along the highway. The original village of Ninilchik (signed Ninilchik Village) is reached by a side road from **Milepost S 135.1.**

NINILCHIK ADVERTISERS

Afishunt Charters............Ph. (800) 347-4114
Alaskan Angler RV Resort.........................Ph. (800) 347-4114
Bull Moose Gifts........Mile 135.8 Sterling Hwy.
Chihuly's...................Mile 136.1 Sterling Hwy.
Chinook Tesoro...........Mile 136 Sterling Hwy.
Country Boy Campground..............Ph. (907) 567-3396
Deep Creek Custom Packing, Inc................Ph. (907) 567-3395
Ninilchik Chamber of Commerce...........Mile 136.3 Sterling Hwy.
Ninilchik Charters............Ph. (907) 567-7321
Ninilchik General Store..................Mile 135.7 Sterling Hwy.
Ninilchik Saltwater Charters & Lodge.......................Ph. (800) 382-3611
O'Fish'ial Charters of Alaska, The.....................66670 Oilwell Rd.
Reel'Em Inn and Cook Inlet Charters.........................Mile 1 Oilwell Rd.
Roe's Charter Service........Ph. (907) 567-3496

BULL MOOSE GIFTS

Mile 135.8 Sterling Highway • 567-3415

"One of the Finest Gift Shops on the Kenai Peninsula"

- Alaskan Dolls
- Framed Art Prints
- Native Arts & Crafts
- Alaskan Gold Nuggets
- Russian Arts & Crafts
- Ivory Carvings and Scrimshaw

- Wide Selection of Jewelry
- Over 50 Shirt Designs
- Souvenirs
- Books
- Beanie Babies
- Stuffed Animals
- Postcards and Notecards

Easy access for large RVs
Open 7 days a week
See log ad at Mile 135.8

AMERICAN EXPRESS • VISA • MasterCard • DISCOVER

Duane & Judith Giarratana, Owners
P.O. Box 39434, Ninilchik, AK 99639
(907) 567-3415

NINILCHIK GENERAL STORE

Mile 135.7 Sterling Highway • (907) 567-3378

See log ad at Mile 135.7

DISCOVER • VISA • MasterCard • AMERICAN EXPRESS

All your Fishing & Clamming needs

Licenses • Bait • Tackle • Public Phone • Groceries • Sweatshirts • T-shirts
Gifts • Souvenirs • Postcards • Books • Film • Ice • Hardware • Alaskan Gold Nuggets
Sandwiches • Fountain Soda • Hot Coffee • Espresso

Open Year-round – Easy access for large RVs – Extended Summer Hours

Fax Service Available – Fax 567-1091

Duane & Judith Giarratana, Owners • P.O. Box 39434, Ninilchik, AK 99639

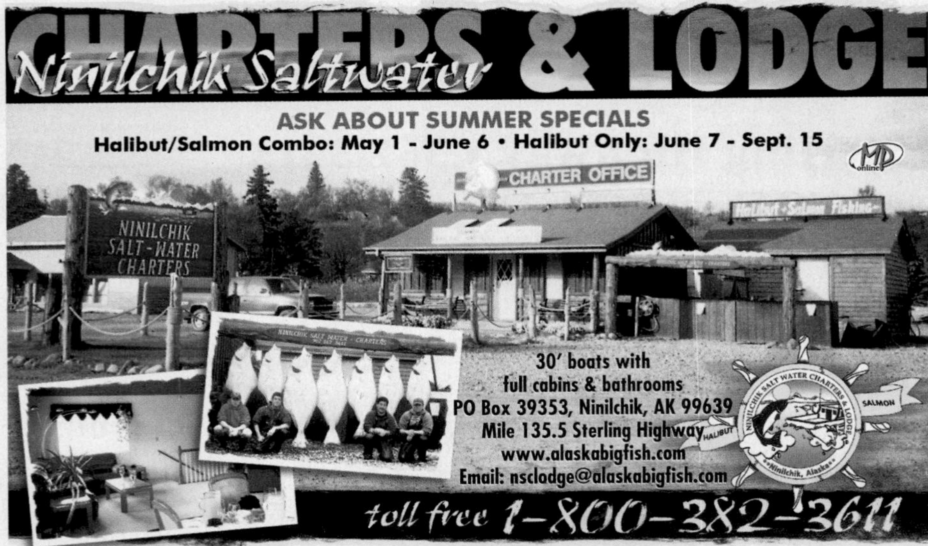

On Memorial Day weekend, Ninilchik is referred to as the third biggest city in Alaska, as thousands of Alaskans arrive for the fishing (see Area Fishing following). The Kenai Peninsula Fair is held at Ninilchik the third weekend in August. Dubbed the "biggest little fair in Alaska," it features a parade, horse show, livestock competition and exhibits ranging from produce to arts and crafts. Pancake breakfasts, bingo and other events, such as the derby fish fry, are held at the fairgrounds throughout the year. The king salmon derby is held from May to June 15. A halibut derby, sponsored by the Ninilchik Chamber of Commerce, runs from Father's Day through Labor Day. There is an active senior center offering meals and events. Swimming pool at the high school.

AREA FISHING: Well-known area for saltwater king salmon fishing and record halibut fishing. Charter services available. (Combination king salmon and halibut charters are available and popular.) Salt water south of the mouth of **Deep Creek** has produced top king salmon fishing in late May, June and July. Kings 50 lbs. and over

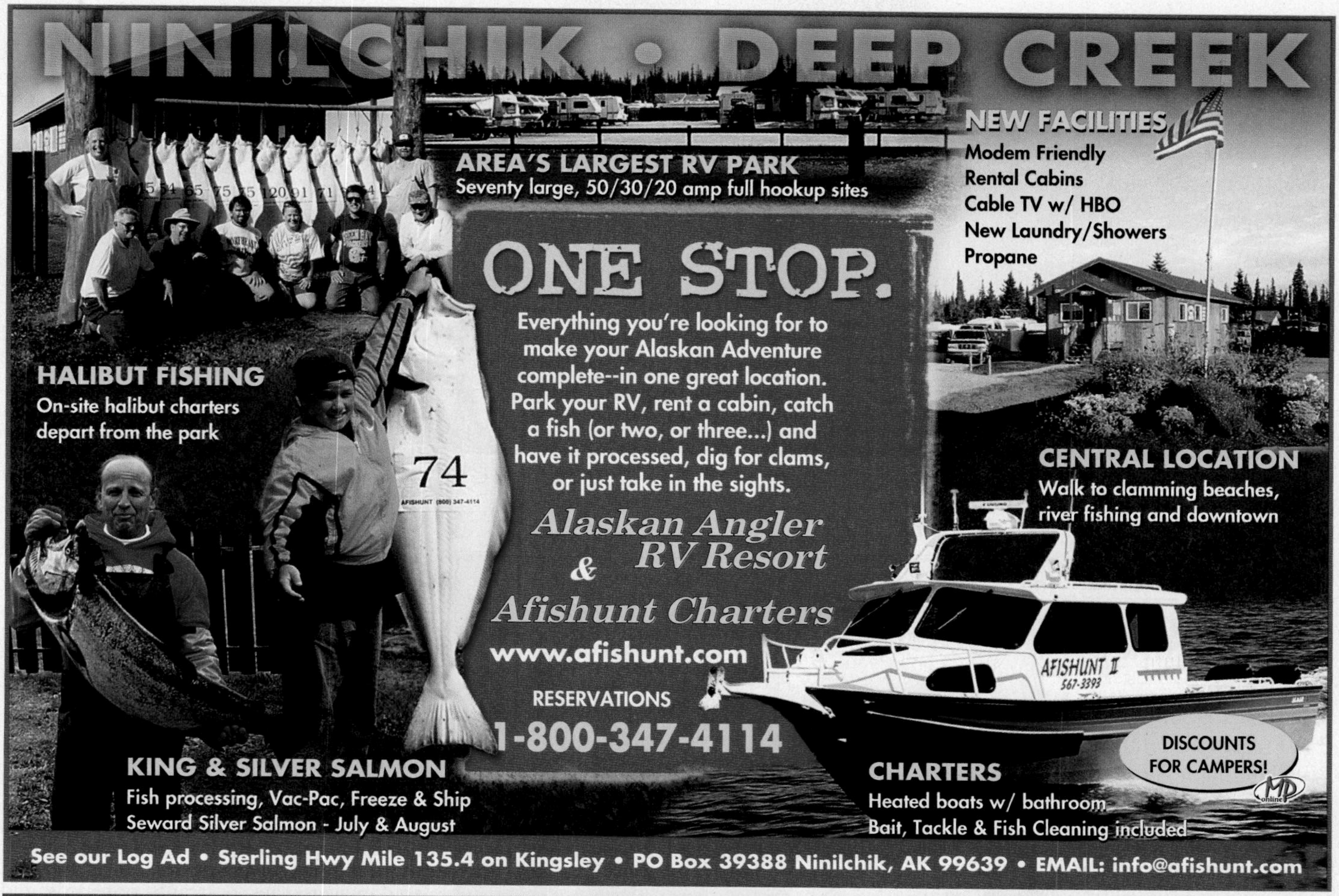

Deserted Deep Creek State Recreation Area, Milepost S 137.3, on a sunny weekend in September. (© Kris Graef, staff)

are frequently caught. "Lunker" king salmon are available 1 mile south of Deep Creek in **Cook Inlet** from late May through July. Trolling a spinner or a spoon from a boat is the preferred method. Silver, red and pink salmon are available in salt water between Deep Creek and the Ninilchik River during July. A major halibut fishery off Ninilchik has produced some of the largest trophy halibut found in Cook Inlet, including a 466-lb. unofficial world record sport-caught halibut.

Sterling Highway Log

(continued)

S 135.6 (218.2 km) **A 188.6** (303.5 km) **H 43.9** (70.6 km) Ninilchik High School. Ninilchik Library, open 10 A.M. to 4 P.M. daily in the summer.

S 135.7 (218.4 km) **A 188.7** (303.7 km) **H 43.8** (70.5 km) **Ninilchik General Store.** Open every day for all your travel needs. Offering groceries, bait, tackle, licenses, rain gear, ice, film, gifts, Beanie Babies, books, T-shirts, gold nugget jewelry, hardware and a snack bar. Try our Fisherman's Bag Lunch. Stop in for free information packet on the Ninilchik area. You'll like our prices and service. Ask your friends who have met us. We compete for your business, we don't just wait for it to happen. See display ad this section. [ADVERTISEMENT]

S 135.8 (218.5 km) **A 188.8** (303.7 km) **H 43.7** (70.3 km) Ninilchik Saltwater Charters & Lodge; Bull Moose Gifts.

Bull Moose Gifts. One of the nicest gift shops on the Kenai Peninsula, offering a wide selection of gifts, souvenirs and Beanie Babies. Alaskan and Russian arts and crafts, fine art prints, jewelry, including Alaskan gold nuggets, caps, postcards, notecards, and over 50 Alaskan designs of T-shirts and sweatshirts. Easy access for large RVs, lots of parking and clean restroom. See display ad this section. [ADVERTISEMENT]

S 135.9 (218.7 km) **A 188.9** (304 km) **H 43.6** (70.2 km) **Junction** with **Oilwell Road**; post office, airstrip, camping and charter services east on Oilwell Road; Tesoro gas station on Sterling Highway south side of junction. Oilwell Road provides acces to Reel'Em Inn/Cook Inlet Charters, O'Fish'ial Charters and Country Boy Campground.

Reel'Em Inn/Cook Inlet Charters. East 1 mile on Oilwell Road from the Chinook Tesoro. Owned and operated by Alaskan family with the knowledge to show you how to experience the area's attractions. Full-service facility. Check us out, you will not be sorry! Reservations welcome. Phone (907) 567-7335. See display ad. [ADVERTISEMENT]

Country Boy Campground, just 3.1 miles down paved Oilwell Road. Turn at Chinook Tesoro. 44 full hookups, immaculate shower/laundry facility. Fish cleaning table, clam shovels. Fishing charters arranged and shuttle service. Potlucks every Sunday. At Country Boy, friends are family and family are friends. We want you to enjoy Alaska. "If you miss us, you miss the party!" (907) 567-3396. See display ad. ▲

S 136 (218.9 km) **A 189** (304.1 km) **H 43.5** (70 km) **Chinook Tesoro.** Ninilchik. 24-hour card lock. Open year-round. Self-serve gasoline, propane, on-road and off-road diesel. We install quality NAPA Auto Parts. Auto/RV mechanics, tire sales and repair, water/air for RVs. Bait, ice, market items. Free tide books, visitor information on clamming and guided fishing. Tesoro, VISA, MasterCard, Discover. All major oil company cards welcome. See display ad this section. [ADVERTISEMENT]

S 136.1 (219 km) **A 189.1** (304.3 km) **H 43.4** (69.8 km) Chihuly's Charters, gift shop and cabins.

S 136.2 (219.2 km) **A 189.2** (304.5 km) **H 43.3** (69.7 km) Private campground; Peninsula Fairgrounds. Ninilchik Chamber of Commerce Visitor Information Kiosk opposite the fairgrounds.

Deep Creek View Campground. See display ad this section. ▲

S 136.7 (219.9 km) **A 189.7** (305.3 km) **H 42.8** (68.9 km) Bridge over Deep Creek. Developed recreation sites on both sides of creek: **Deep Creek North Scenic Overlook** and **Deep Creek South Scenic Overlook**. Deep Creek South offers camping May and June only, day-use only rest of summer. Both have restrooms, water, interpretive kiosks, tables and fireplaces. $10 camping fee or resident pass; $5 day-use fee. ▲

Freshwater fishing in **Deep Creek** for king salmon up to 40 lbs., use spinners with red bead lures, Memorial Day weekend and the 4 weekends following; Dolly Varden in July and August; silver salmon to 15 lbs., August and September; steelhead to 15 lbs., late September through October. No bait fishing permitted after Aug. 31. Mouth of Deep Creek access from Deep Creek State Recreation Area turnoff at **Milepost S 137.3.**

S 137 (220.4 km) **A 190** (305.8 km) **H 42.5** (68.4 km) Cannery and sports shop with tackle and clam shovel rentals west side of road.

Deep Creek Sport Shop. See display ad this section.

Deep Creek Custom Packing, Inc., is a family-owned business overlooking the Deep Creek basin, Mount Redoubt and Mount Iliamna. From this picturesque location, we produce the world's finest smoked salmon and halibut. Stop in for free samples. Convenient double-ended highway access with plenty of parking for big rigs/RVs. Deep Creek prides itself on offering the finest Alaskan Seafood available, including halibut, salmon, scallops, clams, crab, cod, rockfish and more. Our great customer service, quality products and 2 convenient locations (see our New Store at the "Y" in Soldotna) are reasons sport fishermen choose to bring their catch to Deep Creek for custom processing, vacuum packing, freezing, canning and smoking. Fish dropped off in Ninilchik can be picked up in Soldotna. We offer overnight door-to-door shipping for your catch or seafood choices. Deep Creek's canned and smoked gift packs are great holiday choices. World-class halibut and king fishing charters are available through our Sport Shop. For more information, check out our web page at www.deepcreekcustompacking.com or e-mail us at dccp@ptialaksa.net. See display ad this section. [ADVERTISEMENT]

S 137.3 (220.9 km) **A 190.3** (306.2 km) **H 42.2** (67.9 km) Drive 0.5 mile west down paved road for **Deep Creek State Recreation Area** on the beach at the mouth of Deep Creek. Gravel parking area for 300 vehicles, overnight camping, water, tables, dumpsters, restrooms, pay phones and fireplaces. Camping fee $10/night per vehicle or resident pass, day-use fee $5, boat launch $5 fee. Anglers try to intercept king salmon in the saltwater before the salmon reach their spawning rivers. Private boat launch service here uses tractors to launch boats from beach into Cook Inlet. Seasonal checks by U.S. Coast Guard for personal flotation devices, boating safety. Good bird watching in wetlands behind beach; watch for eagles. Good clamming at low tide. The beaches here are lined with coal, which falls from the exposed seams of high cliffs. ▲

CAUTION: Extreme tides, cold water and bad weather can make boating here hazardous. Carry all required and recommended USCG safety equipment. Although the mouth of Deep Creek affords boaters good protection, low tides may prevent return; check tide tables.

D&M RV Park & Charters. Our park site on the bluff overlooking Cook Inlet has a million dollar view. We have 38 sites, 24 with water and electric hookups. Laundry, showers, dump station, storage and fish cleaning facilities on site. Heated cabins that sleep 4 each and daily charters to fish halibut/salmon are conveniently available. Hosts Debbie and Marc encourage you to book early for the best fishing, clamming dates and to reserve your spot. Year-round: phone 1-800-479-7357, (907) 567-4368. Fax (907) 349-3996. **Milepost 127.3.** Sterling Highway. E-mail: dmrvparkcharters@gci.net. [ADVERTISEMENT] ▲

S 137.4 (221.1 km) **A 190.4** (306.4 km) **H 42.1** (67.8 km) **Roe's Charter Service.** Family owned, operated by year-round residents. Halibut, salmon combo charters, April–September. Friendly, personalized ser-

Deep Creek State Recreation Area in summer. The gravel parking area accommodates 300 vehicles. (© Harry M. Walker)

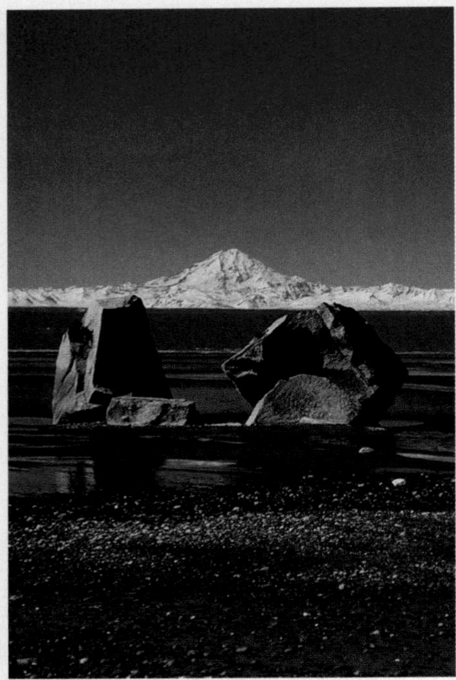

Volcanoes in the Aleutian Range are visible from the Sterling Highway.

(© Barb Willard)

vice at our quiet location. Circle drive for RV convenience. Fish from our custom-built 28- and 30-foot offshore boats, both with heated cabins and enclosed marine bathrooms. Comfortable seating, state- of-the-art electronics, custom made rods, top quality gear. Free filleting. Further processing, shipping services nearby. Lodging, etc. available. Phone (888) 567-3496, (907) 567-3496. Internet: www.alaskafishingcharter.com. E-mail: roe@alaskafishingcharter.com. See display ad. [ADVERTISEMENT]

S 140.3 (225.8 km) **A 193.3** (311.1 km) **H 39.2** (63.1 km) Double-ended turnout with scenic view to west.

S 140.5 (226.1 km) **A 193.5** (311.4 km) **H 39** (62.8 km) **Double Eagle Lodge.** Modern, deluxe cabins, adult setting, with spectacular Inlet view. Each has coffee, microwave, refrigerator and private bathrooms, one with kitchen and laundry. Centrally located on Kenai Peninsula within minutes to charters, rivers, clamming and stores. Full hearty breakfast at your convenience in Alaska-style cook shack included. Phone (907) 567-3492. [ADVERTISEMENT]

S 142.7 (229.6 km) **A 195.7** (314.9 km) **H 36.8** (59.2 km) Double-ended paved turnout with dumpster, view of Mount Iliamna across the inlet.

S 143.8 (231.4 km) **A 196.8** (316.7 km) **H 35.7** (57.4 km) Happy Valley Creek. The area surrounding this creek is known locally as the Happy Valley community.

S 148 (238.1 km) **A 201** (323.5 km) **H 31.5** (50.7 km) Scenic viewpoint to west (sign): "Looking westerly across Cook Inlet, Mt. Iliamna and Mt. Redoubt in the Chigmit Mountains of the Aleutian Range can be seen rising over 10,000 feet above sea level. This begins a chain of mountains and islands known as the Aleutian Chain extending west over 1,700 miles to Attu beyond the International Date Line to the Bering Sea, separating the Pacific and Arctic oceans. Mt. Redoubt on the right, and Iliamna on the left, were recorded as active volcanoes in the mid-18th century. Mt. Redoubt had a minor eruption in 1966."

Mount Redoubt had a major eruption in December 1989. The eruptions continued through April 1990, then subsided to steam plumes. Mount Redoubt is still considered active.

S 150.9 (242.8 km) **A 203.9** (328.1 km) **H 28.6** (46 km) Bridge over Stariski Creek.

S 151.9 (244.4 km) **A 204.9** (329.7 km) **H 27.6** (44.4 km) Sharp turn west down steep access road to **Stariski State Recreation Site;** 16 campsites in trees on narrow and bumpy dirt loop road; $10 nightly fee or resident pass; toilets (wheelchair accessible) and well water. This small campground has outstanding views across the inlet of Iliamna and Redoubt. No beach access. *CAUTION: Steep bluff.* ♿▲

S 152.7 (245.7 km) **A 205.7** (331 km) **H 26.8** (43.1 km) **Eagle Crest RV Park & Cabins.** See display ad this section. ▲

S 154.1 (248 km) **A 207.1** (333.3 km) **H 25.4** (40.9 km) **Timberline Creations Gift Shop** specializes in unique antler, fossil ivory and schrimshaw gifts and jewelry created by the Lettis family in their workshop. They also sell Eskimo artifacts and mammoth fossils. Alaskan antiques decorate the log cabin shop. A must-stop for the traveler that enjoys quality craftsmanship. Call (907) 235-8288. E-mail: tcalaska@xyz.net. See display ad. [ADVERTISEMENT]

S 155 (249.4 km) **A 208** (334.7 km) **H 24.5** (39.4 km) **Bear Paw Charters.** This Anchor Point location is only minutes from trophy halibut/salmon fishing. All equipment provided plus free filleting. Small groups and personalized service are the focus of this family-owned and operated business. Private and unique log cabins feature circular log staircase, wood inlaid mural, and Alaska big game trophies. Sleeps 4–8. Phone (907) 235-5399. See display ad. E-mail bearpaw@xyz.net; web address www.xyz.net/~bearpaw. [ADVERTISEMENT]

S 156.3 (251.5 km) **A 209.3** (336.8 km) **H 23.2** (37.3 km) **Anchor River Tesoro.** See display ad this section.

Mugs and Jugs. See display ad this section.

The Warehouse Grocery. See display ad this section.

S 156.7 (249.4 km) **A 208** (334.7 km) **H 24.5** (39.4 km) Intersection with Milo Fritz Avenue to west and North Fork Road to east. Access to Iliamna Mt. View B&B via Milo Fritz Avenue to Sand Beach Road. Access to Anchor Point Seafood (Mile 3.2) and Dersham's Outlook Lodge (9 miles) via North Fork Road.

S 156.9 (252.5 km) **A 209.9** (337.8 km) **H 22.6** (36.4 km) Anchor Point "Y" **junction** with Old Sterling Highway; access to Anchor Point businesses, Visitor Information Center, Anchor River Inn and Anchor River (Beach) Road. Description of Anchor Point follows.

Junction with Old Sterling Highway and access to Anchor River (Beach) Road. See ANCHOR RIVER (BEACH) ROAD log on page 585.

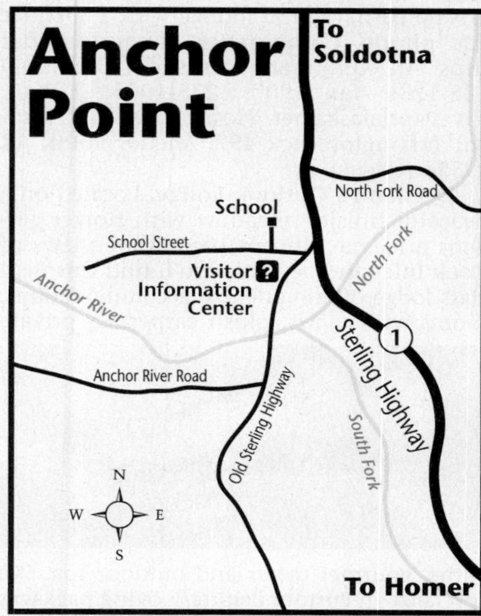

Anchor Point

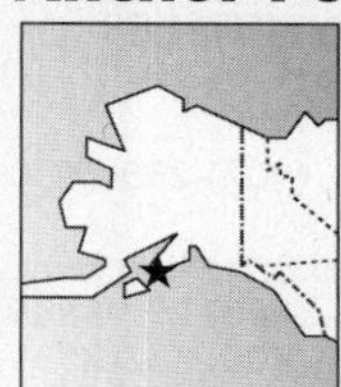

S 156.9 (252.5 km) **A 209.9** (337.8 km) **H 22.6** (36.4 km) **Junction** of the Sterling Highway and Old Sterling Highway. **Population:** 1,227. **Emergency services:** Phone 911. **Visitor Information:** Anchor Point Chamber of Commerce, P.O. Box 610, Anchor Point, AK 99556; phone (907) 235-2600, fax (907) 235-2600. Located in the small cabin at the "Y".

Anchor Point is a full-service community with a variety of businesses, including lodging, restaurants, gas stations, fishing charters, tackle shops, auto repair, RV parks, groceries, laundries and gift shops.

Anchor Point was originally named "Laida" by Captain James Cook in the summer of 1778, when the *Resolution* and *Discovery* sailed into Cook Inlet looking for the Northwest Passage. It was later renamed Anchor Point, commemorating Cook's loss of an anchor to the tidal currents of the inlet. A post office was established here in 1949.

The Anchor Point area is noted for seasonal king and silver salmon, steelhead and rainbow fishing. Saltwater trolling for king salmon to 80 lbs., halibut to 200 lbs., spring through fall. **Anchor River**, king salmon fishing permitted only on 5 consecutive weekends, beginning Memorial Day weekend; trout and steelhead from July to October; closed to all fishing Dec. 31 to June 30, except for king salmon weekends. Excellent fishing for 12- to 24-inch sea-run Dollies in July and late summer. During August silver runs, fish high tides.

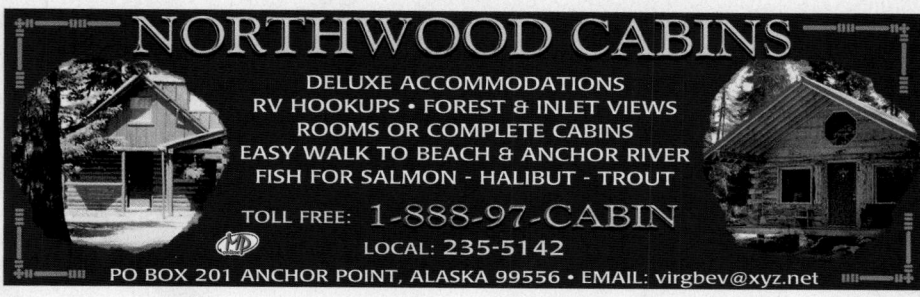

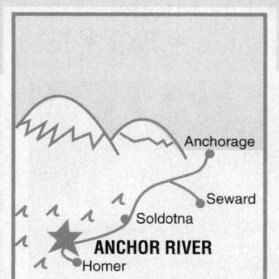

Anchor Point Lodging, Clive's Fishing Guide Service. Just off highway. Walking trails to river and beach. Large rooms with private bath. Central lounge with TV, coffee and phone. Combination salmon/halibut trips. All equipment furnished. Call (907) 235-1236 fax (907) 235-1905. E-mail: clives@ptialaska.net. Hosts: Clive and Marilyn Talkington, Box 497, Anchor Point, AK 99556. [ADVERTISEMENT]

Dersham's Outlook Lodge. Located on a peaceful hillside meadow with flower gardens and magnificent panoramic views of Cook Inlet and beyond, you'll find this first-class lodge offering deluxe accommodations, rooms with views, plush carpeting, private

baths, gourmet meals and outdoor spa. We specialize in custom fishing/lodging packages with world-class fishing for salmon and

ANCHOR POINT ADVERTISERS

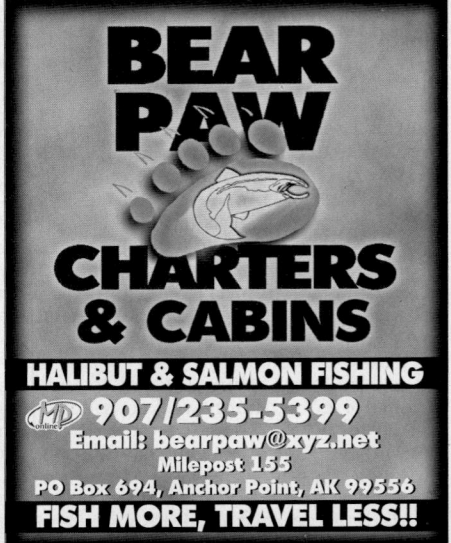

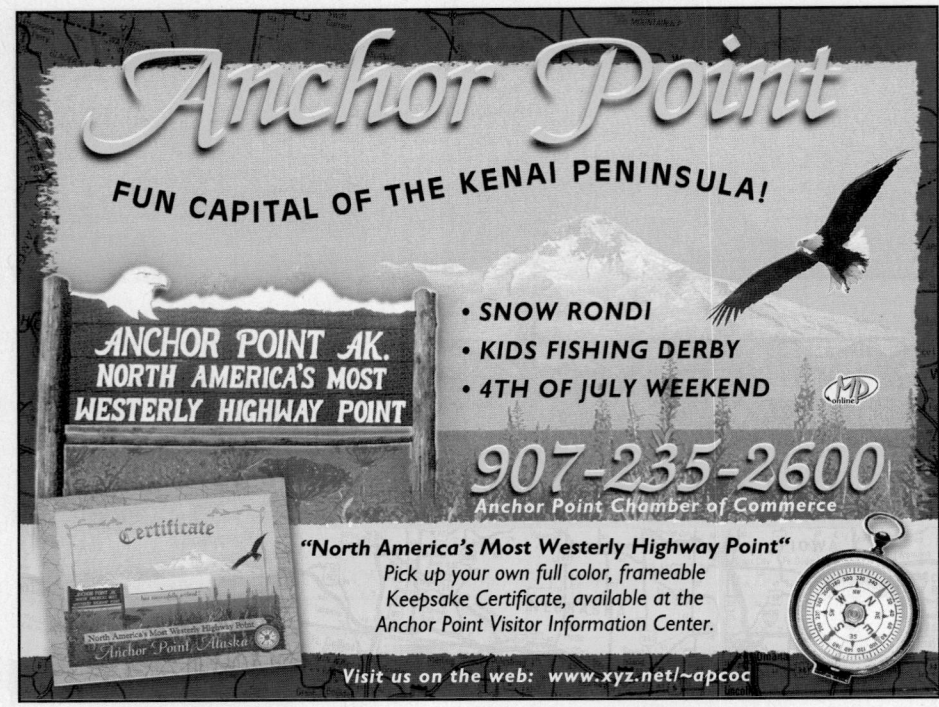

Advertiser	Contact
Anchor Point Chamber of Commerce	Ph. (907) 235-2600
Anchor Point Lodging	Mile 156.8 Sterling Hwy.
Anchor Point Seafoods	Ph. (800) 277-8885
Anchor River Inn	Ph. (800) 435-8531
Anchor River Tesoro	Mile 156.3 Sterling Hwy.
Bear Paw Charters	Ph. (907) 235-5399
Blue Bus	Ph. (907) 235-6285
Clive's Fishing Guide Service & Lodging	Ph. (907) 235-1236
Dersham's Outlook Lodge	Ph. (800) 233-4665
FishTale Charters	(907) 235-6944
Good Time Charters	Ph. (907) 235-8579
Iliamna Mt. View B&B	Ph. (907) 235-6331
Kyllonnen's Park	Ph. (907) 235-7762
Mugs and Jugs	Ph. (907) 235-8457
Northwood Cabins	Ph. (888) 972-2246
Our Front Porch Bed & Breakfast	Ph. (907) 235-8885
The Warehouse Grocery	Ph. (907) 235-7999
Thurmond's Auto & Expresso	Ph. (907) 235-5601

Anchor River (Beach) Road Log

Turn off the Sterling Highway at **Milepost S 156.9** on to the Old Sterling Highway and continue past the Anchor River Inn over the Anchor River. Just beyond the bridge, turn for Anchor River (Beach) Road, a 1.2-mile spur road providing access to Anchor River recreation area.
Distance from junction (J) is shown.

J 0 Junction of Old Sterling Highway and Sterling Highway in Anchor Point at **Milepost S 156.9.**

J 0.1 (0.2 km) School Road. Anchor Point visitor information center.

Anchor River Inn, overlooking beautiful Anchor River and in business for 35 years, has the finest family restaurant on the peninsula, where you can see one of the largest displays of collectible plates in Alaska. Serving breakfast, lunch and dinner. Large cocktail lounge has a wide-screen TV, pool tables, dance floor and video games. 20 modern motel units with phones; 10 spacious units with color TV and 2 queen-sized beds, and 10 smaller units overlooking the river. Our fully stocked liquor, grocery store and gift shop serve the Anchor Point area year-round. Write: Box 154, Anchor Point, AK 99556; phone 1-800-435-8531 in USA, or (907) 235-8531; fax (907) 235-2296. Your hosts: Bob and Simonne Clutts. [ADVERTISEMENT]

J 0.3 (0.5 km) Anchor River bridge, also known as "the erector set bridge."

J 0.4 (0.6 km) Road forks: Old Sterling Highway (gravel) continues south through rural residential area and rejoins Sterling Highway at **Milepost S 164.8.** Turn right for Anchor River (Beach) Road. Tackle shop at intersection across from **Silverking Campground** (Anchor River State Recreation Area); parking area, toilets, dumpster, $10 nightly fee or resident pass.

J 0.6 (1 km) **Coho Campground** (Anchor River SRA); parking, toilets, $10 camping fee or resident pass.

J 0.7 (1.1 km) Tackle shop.

J 0.8 (1.3 km) **Steelhead Campground** (Anchor River SRA); parking, toilets, $10 camping or resident pass.

J 1.1 (1.8 km) **Slidehole Campground** (Anchor River SRA); 30 campsites on loop road, day-use parking area, $10 camping fee or resident pass, tables, water, special senior/wheelchair camping area, large day-use parking lot, trail access to river.

J 1.3 (2.1 km) **Kyllonen's RV Park**, a few steps from famous Anchor River and picturesque Cook Inlet. Providing spring water, electricity and sewer. Additional amenities include fish cleaning station, BBQ pits, free firewood and picnic tables. Showers, restrooms and laundry. Gift shop and Espresso Bar. Fishing licenses. We book fishing charters. May through September. Year-round area information center, phone/fax (907) 235-7762, fax (907) 235-6435. E-mail: susank@xyz.net.www.xyz/~susank/. See display ad this section. [ADVERTISEMENT]

J 1.5 (2.4 km) **Halibut Campground** (Anchor River SRA); day-use parking area and picnic sites, 20 campsites on gravel loop, toilets, water. $10 camping fee or resident pass; $5 day-use fee. Access to beach through meadow. Beautiful view of Aleutian Range from parking area.

J 1.6 (2.6 km) Road dead ends on shore of Cook Inlet; viewing deck, telescopes, beach access, 12-hour parking. Private tractor boat launch service. Tractor assistance has revolutionized sportfish access to Cook Inlet by allowing boats to launch at just about any tide, rather than having to wait for high tide. Sign here marks the most westerly point on the North American continent accessible by continuous road system. N 59°46' W 151°52'. Display depicts outlines of Cook Inlet volcanoes.

Fishing the Anchor River for steelhead in the fall. (© Kris Graef, staff)

Return to Milepost S 156.9 Sterling Highway

halibut with licensed, insured, experienced guides. Family owned and operated. Reservations required. Check our web site at www.salmonfishingalaska.com and call 1-800-233-4665, (907) 235-5555. Located 9 miles out North Fork Road, turn right on Holly Lane to lodge. [ADVERTISEMENT]

Anchor Point Seafoods. Quality and taste are the goal of our family-owned businss. Bring your fresh catch to us for cleaning, vacuum-packing, freezing, smoking and shipping. Or try some of our world-class smoked products, such as fresh Alaska smoked salmon, salmon jerky or smoked halibut. Our unique processing and smoking operation is located just out of Anchor Point at Mile 3.2 North Fork Road. We work with our local charters to ensure that your fish gets home to you in excellent condition. Let us help make your Alaska trip the best it can be. Phone 1-800-277-8885. Fax (907) 235-2788. E-mail: apsf@ptialaska.net or write P.O. Box 1133, Anchor Point, AK 99556. [ADVERTISEMENT]

FishTale Charters. Stop at Mile 157 of the Sterling Highway in Anchor Point at Thurmond's Auto to see pictures of the most recent catch or to book your charter. Offering salmon and halibut trips with a personal touch. Owned and operated by lifetime residents of Anchor Point with more than 20 years experience in the fishing business. We supply all the gear! (907) 235-6944 or e-mail griner@ptialaska.net. [ADVERTISEMENT]

Iliamna Mt. View B&B. New, large, beautiful log home on bluffs overlooking Anchor River and inlet. Rooms, patio, lounge area have views. Private entrance, smoke-free environment. Full Alaskan breakfast. In Anchor Point, take Milo Fritz Avenue west 0.6 mile to Sand Beach Road; turn right 0.2 mile. Hosts: John and Ruhiyyih Baker. (907) 235-6331. [ADVERTISEMENT]

Sterling Highway Log
(continued)

S 157.1 (252.8 km) **A 210.1** (338.1 km) **H 22.4** (36 km) Anchor River bridge.

S 160.9 (258.9 km) **A 213.9** (344.2 km) **H 18.6** (29.9 km) Side road to artist Norman Lowell's studio and KWLS radio station.

S 161 (259.1 km) **A 214** (344.4 km) **H 18.5** (29.8 km) Anchor River bridge.

S 162.4 (261.4 km) **A 215.4** (346.6 km) **H 17.1** (27.5 km) Gravel turnout to east by Anchor River.

S 164.3 (264.4 km) **A 217.3** (349.7 km) **H 15.2** (24.5 km) North Fork Loop Road.

S 164.8 (265.2 km) **A 217.8** (350.5 km) **H 14.7** (23.7 km) **Junction** with Old Sterling Highway which leads 9.4 miles northwest to connect with Anchor River (Beach) Road.

View of Homer and Homer Spit. (© Joanne McCubrey)

S 167.1 (268.9 km) **A 220.1** (354.2 km) **H 12.4** (20 km) Diamond Ridge Road.

S 168.5 (271.2 km) **A 221.5** (356.5 km) **H 11** (17.7 km) Alaska State Parks' South District ranger station is located on the bluff here. A small parking lot is adjacent to the log office where visitors may obtain information on Kachemak Bay state park, as well as other southern Kenai Peninsula state park lands.

S 169.2 (272.3 km) **A 222.2** (357.5 km) **H 10.3** (16.5 km) Gas station/food mart.

S 169.3 (272.5 km) **A 222.3** (357.7 km) **H 10.2** (16.4 km) Homer DOT/PF highway maintenance station.

S 169.6 (272.9 km) **A 222.6** (358.2 km) **H 9.9** (15.9 km) Large viewpoint to west overlooking Kachemak Bay with view of

Homer Spit; large parking area. Good photo stop.

S 170 (273.6 km) **A 223** (358.9 km) **H 9.5** (15.3 km) Bay View Inn.

S 171.9 (276.6 km) **A 224.9** (361.9 km) **H 7.6** (12.2 km) West Hill Road; connects to Skyline Drive and East Hill Road for scenic drive along Homer Bluff.

S 172.5 (277.6 km) **A 225.5** (362.9 km) **H 7** (11.3 km) Bidarka Inn.

S 172.6 (277.8 km) **A 225.6** (363 km) **H 6.9** (11.1 km) Homer Junior High School.

S 172.7 (277.9 km) **A 225.7** (363.2 km) **H 6.8** (10.9 km) **Oceanview RV Park** past Best Western Bidarka Inn on your right coming into Homer. Spectacular view of Kachemak Bay, beachfront setting. 85 large pull-through spaces in terraced park. Full/partial hookups, heated restrooms, free showers, laundry, pay phone, free cable TV, picnic area. Walking distance to downtown Homer. Special halibut charter rates for park guests. Phone (907) 235-3951. E-mail service available. See display ad. [ADVERTISEMENT] ▲

S 172.8 (278.1 km) **A 225.8** (363.4 km) **H 6.7** (10.8 km) Pioneer Avenue; turn here for downtown **HOMER** (description follows). Drive 0.2 mile on Pioneer Avenue and turn left on Bartlett Avenue for the **Pratt Museum** (see Attractions in the Homer section) and **Karen Hornaday Memorial Park** campground (see map). Pioneer Avenue connects with East Hill Road. ▲

S 173.1 (278.6 km) **A 226.1** (363.9 km) **H 6.4** (10.3 km) **Homer Chamber of Commerce Visitor Center** on right side of highway going into Homer. Turn up Main Street for Pioneer Avenue.

For **Bishop's Beach Park,** turn down Main Street (towards water), then left on E. Bunnell Avenue and right on Beluga Avenue; public beach access, parking, picnic tables and Beluga Slough trailhead.

S 173.5 (279.2 km) **A 226.5** (364.5 km) **H 6** (9.7 km) Eagle Quality Center; 24-hour supermarket.

S 173.7 (279.5 km) **A 226.7** (364.8 km) **H 5.8** (9.3 km) Heath Street. Post office (ZIP code 99603).

S 173.9 (279.9 km) **A 226.9** (365.2 km) **H 5.6** (9 km) Lake Street. Access to downtown Homer and Lakeside Center.

S 174 (280 km) **A 227** (365.3 km) **H 5.5** (8.9 km) Beluga Lake; floatplane bases.

S 174.7 (281.1 km) **A 227.7** (366.4 km) **H 4.8** (7.7 km) Alaska Dept. of Fish and Game office. Stop by for a current copy of the Kenai Peninsula–Cook Inlet Salt Water–Susitna–West Cook Inlet regulations.

S 174.8 (281.3 km) **A 227.8** (366.6 km) **H 4.7** (7.6 km) Homer Tesoro. Airport Road to Homer Airport terminal

S 175 (281.6 km) **A 228** (366.9 km) **H 4.5** (7.2 km) Sterling Highway crosses onto Homer Spit (see description in Homer Attractions). Parking for spit bike/walking trail. Katchemak Drive; access to air charter services.

S 179.5 (288.9 km) **A 232.5** (374.2 km) **H 0** Sterling Highway ends at Land's End Resort at the tip of Homer Spit.

Homer

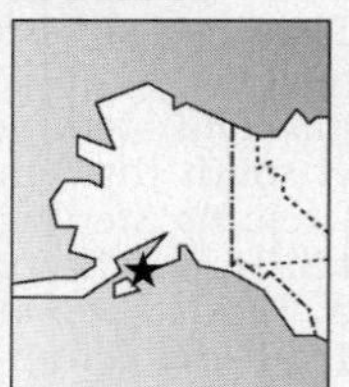

Located on the southwestern Kenai Peninsula on the north shore of Kachemak Bay at the easterly side of the mouth of Cook Inlet; 226 miles by highway or 40 minutes by jet aircraft from Anchorage. **Population:** 4,154. **Emergency Services:** Phone 911 for all emergency services. **City Police,** phone (907) 235-3150. **Alaska State Troopers,** in the Public Safety Bldg., phone (907) 235-8239. **Fire Department** and **Ambulance,** phone (907) 235-3155. **Coast Guard,** phone Zenith 5555. (Coast Guard Auxiliary, phone (907/235-7277.) **Hospital,** South Peninsula Hospital, phone (907) 235-8101. **Veterinary Clinic,** phone (907) 235-8960.

Visitor Information: Chamber of Commerce Visitor Center is located on the Sterling Highway (Homer Bypass) at Main Street. Open year-round. Contact the Homer Chamber of Commerce, Box 541, Homer 99603; phone during business hours (907) 235-7740 or 235-5300.

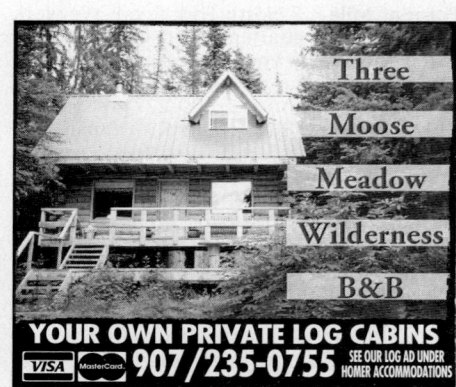

The Pratt Museum is open daily 10 A.M. to 6 P.M. from May through September; open noon to 5 P.M. Tuesday through Sunday from October through April; closed in January. Contact the Pratt Museum, 3779 Bartlett St., Homer 99603. Phone (907) 235-8635.

Elevation: Sea level to 800 feet. **Climate:** Winter temperatures occasionally fall below zero, but seldom colder. The Kenai Mountains north and east protect Homer from severe cold, and Cook Inlet provides warming air currents. The highest temperature recorded is 81°F/27°C. Average annual precipitation is 27.9 inches. Prevailing winds are from the northeast, averaging 6.5 mph/10.5 kmph. **Radio:** KGTL 620, KWAV 103.5/104.9/106.3, MBN-FM 107.1/96.7/95.3, KBBI 890, KPEN-FM 99.3/100.9/102.3, KWHQ-FM 98.3. **Television:** KTUU, KTBY, KTVA, KAKM, KIMO. **Newspaper:** *Homer News* (weekly), *Homer Tribune* (weekly).

Private Aircraft: Homer airport on Airport Road; elev. 78 feet; length 7,400 feet/2,255m; asphalt; fuel 100LL, Jet A; attended. Terminal building.

In the late 1800s, a coal mine was operating at Homer's Bluff Point, and a railroad carried the coal out to the end of Homer Spit. (The railroad was abandoned in 1907.) Gold seekers debarked at Homer, bound for the goldfields at Hope and Sunrise. The community of Homer was established about 1896 and named for Homer Pennock.

Coal mining operations ceased around the time of WWI, but settlers continued to trickle into the area, some to homestead, others to work in the canneries built to process Cook Inlet fish.

Today, Homer's picturesque setting, mild climate and great fishing (especially for halibut) attract thousands of visitors each year. In addition to its tourist industry and role as a trade center, Homer's commercial fishing industry is an important part of its economy. Homer calls itself the "Halibut Fishing Capital of the World." Manufacturing and seafood processing, government offices, trades and construction are other key industries.

Homer is host to a large artist community. Potters, sculptors, painters and jewelers practice their craft and sell their goods in local shops and galleries. The local theater group provides live performances year-

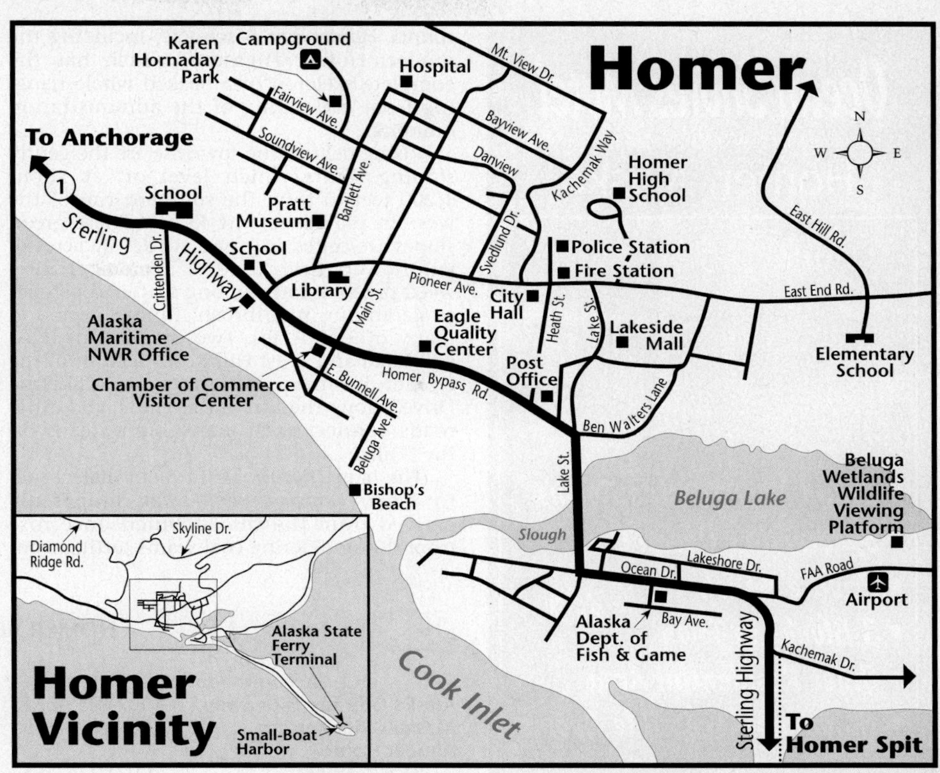

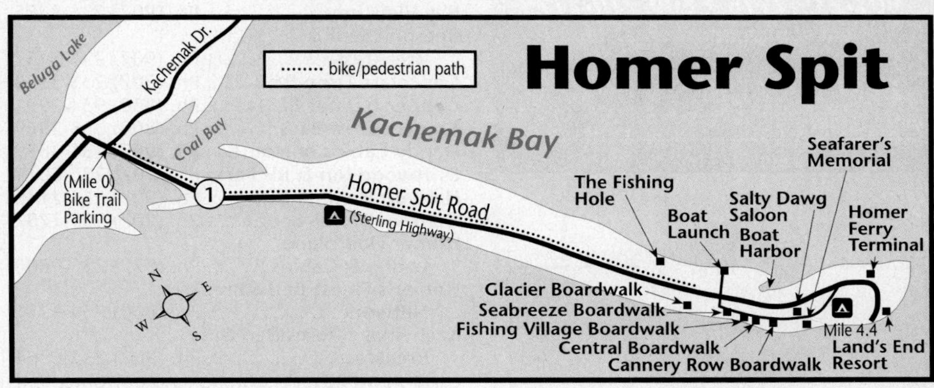

The Russian-American Co. was the only governing power in Alaska from 1799 until 1867.

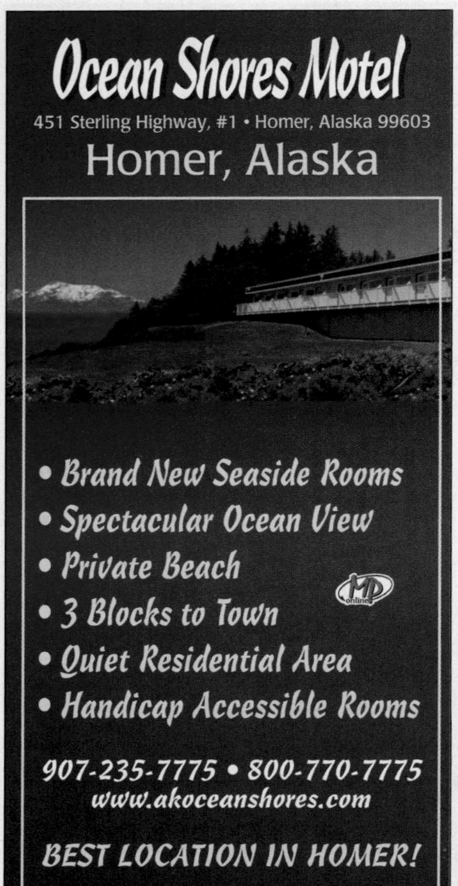

358 Lee Dr. • Homer, AK 99603

— Very Affordable —

Quiet, Convenient, Intown Location

Pvt. Suite to Bunk Rooms

Light to Full Breakfast

Also Secluded Chalet-Sleeps 8

www.sunspin.com

1-800-391-6677

info@sunspin.com

round. Homer has 8 schools, including the modern Homer Highway, which has the complete skeleton of a beaked whale hanging from the ceiling of the administration building.

Rising behind the townsite are the gently sloping bluffs which level off at about 1,200 feet to form the southern rim of the western plateau of the Kenai. These green slopes are tinted in pastel shades by acres of wildflowers from June to September; fireweed predominates among scattered patches of geranium, paintbrush, lupine, rose and many other species. Two main roads (East Hill Road and West Hill Road) lead from the Homer business section to the "Skyline Drive" along the rim of the bluffs, and other roads connect with many homesteads on the "Hill."

The name *Kachemak* (in Aleut dialect said to mean "smoky bay") was supposedly derived from the smoke which once rose from the smoldering coal seams jutting from the clay bluffs of the upper north shore of Kachemak Bay and the cliffs near Anchor Point. In the early days many of the exposed coal seams were slowly burning from causes unknown. Today the erosion of these bluffs drops huge fragments of lignite and bituminous coal on the beaches, creating a plentiful supply of winter fuel for the residents. There are an estimated 400,000,000 tons of coal deposit in the immediate vicinity of Homer.

Kachemak is a magnificent deep-water bay that reaches inland from Cook Inlet for 30 miles, with an average width of 7 miles. The bay is rich in marine life. The wild timbered coastline of the south shore, across from Homer, is indented with many fjords and inlets, reaching far into the rugged glacier-capped peaks of the Kenai Mountains.

Jutting out for nearly 5 miles from the Homer shore is the Homer Spit, a long, narrow bar of gravel. The road along the

HOMER ADVERTISERS

Accommodations

Alaska Cottage Hideaway ... Ph. (907) 235-0755
Alaska's Pioneer Inn ... Ph. (800) 782-9655
Almost Home B&B/Cabins ... Ph. (907) 235-2553
Bay View Inn ... Ph. (907) 235-8485
Beeson's Bed & Breakfast ... Ph. (907) 235-3757
Chocolate Drop B&B ... Ph. (907) 235-3668
Copper Helmet B&B ... Ph. (800) 964-2991
Crane's Crest B&B ... Ph. (800) 338-2969
Dandy Cabins of Homer ... Ph. (907) 235-3839
Driftwood Inn & RV Park ... Ph. (907) 235-8019
Halcyon Heights B&B ... Ph. (907) 235-2148
Heritage Hotel–Lodge ... Ph. (907) 235-7787
Homer Floatplane Lodge & Cabins ... Ph. (877) 235-9600
Homer's Finest Bed &Breakfast Network ... Ph. (800) 764-3211
Kachemak Shores Bed & Breakfast ... Ph. (907) 235-6864
Land's End Resort ... End of Homer Spit
Morning Glory Bed & Breakfast/Charters ... Ph. (907) 235-8084
Ocean Shores Motel ... Ph. (800) 770-7775
Skyline Bed & Breakfast ... Ph. (907) 235-3832
SunSpin Guest House ... Ph. (907) 235-6677
3 Moose Meadow Wilderness B&B ... Ph. (907) 235-0755
Wild Rose Cottages ... 5010 East Hill Rd.
Windjammer Suites ... Ph. (907) 235-9761

Attractions & Entertainment

Pier One Theatre ... Homer Spit
Pratt Museum ... Ph. (907) 235-8635
Salty Dawg Saloon ... Homer Spit

Auto & RV Gas, Services, Supplies

Homer Tesoro Service and Quality Lube ... Ph. (907) 235-5610
Petro Marine Services ... Ph. (907) 276-4262

Campgrounds

Driftwood Inn & RV Park ... Ph. (907) 235-8019
Homer Spit Campground ... Ph. (907) 235-8206
Oceanview RV Park ... Mile 172.7 Sterling Hwy.

Churches

Faith Lutheran Church ... Ph. (907) 235-7600

Fishing Charters

Bob's Trophy Charters ... Ph. (800) 770-6400
Bookie, The ... Ph. (888) 335-1581
Cap'n George's Charters ... Ph. (800) 593-8110
Central Charters Booking Agency, Inc. ... Ph. (907) 235-7847
Inlet Charters ... Ph. (907) 235-6126
Lucky Pierre Charters ... Ph. (907) 235-8903
North Country Halibut Charters ... Ph. (800) 770-7620
Puffin Lady Charters ... Ph. (888) 278-3346
R&D Charters ... Ph. (907) 235-6592
Silver Fox Charters ... Ph. (800) 478-8792
Tacklebuster Charters ... Ph. (800) 789-5155

Guides & Outfitters

Alaska Canoe Base ... Ph. (907) 235-2090
Trails End Horse Adventures ... Ph. (907) 235-6393

Shopping and Services

Alaska Wild Berry Products ... 528 W. Pioneer Ave.
Art Shop Gallery ... Ph. (907) 235-7076
Better Sweater ... Ph. (888) 842-4140
Blackberry Bog ... Ph. (907) 235-5668
Bunnell Street Gallery ... Ph. (907) 235-2662
Coal Point Seafood Co. ... Homer Spit Rd.
Fireweed Gallery ... Ph. (907) 235-7040
Fish Connection Gifts ... Ph. (907) 235-3838
Homer's Jeans ... Ph. (907) 235-6234
Jars of Clay ... Ph. (907) 235-8533
NOMAR (Northern Marine Canvas Products) ... Ph. (907) 235-8363
Picture Alaska ... Ph. (907) 235-2300
Ptarmigan Arts ... Ph. (907) 235-5345
Sea Lion Fine Art Gallery, The ... Ph. (907) 235-3400
Ridge Runners ... Ph. (907) 235-4806
The Washboard ... Ph. (907) 235-6781

Tours and Transportation

Bald Mountain Air Service ... Ph. (907) 235-7969
Coastal Outfitters ... Ph. (907) 235-8492
Homer–Alaska Referral Agency ... Ph. (907) 235-8996
Kachemak Air Service, Inc. ... Ph. (907) 235-8924

Visitor Information

Homer Chamber of Commerce ... 135 Sterling Highway

backbone of the Spit connects with the main road through Homer (all the Sterling Highway). The Spit has had quite a history, and it continues to be a center of activity for the town. In 1964, after the earthquake, the Spit sank 4 to 6 feet, requiring several buildings to be moved to higher ground. Today, the Spit is the site of a major dock facility for boat loading, unloading, servicing and refrigerating. The deep-water dock can accommodate 340-foot vessels and 30-foot drafts, making it accessible to cruise and cargo ships. It is also home port to the Alaska Marine Highway ferry MV *Tustumena*. The small-boat harbor on the Spit has a 5-lane load/launch ramp. Also in the small-boat harbor area are the harbormaster's office, canneries, parking/camping areas, charter services, small shops, live theatre, galleries, restaurants, motels and bed and breakfasts.

Lodging & Services

Homer has hundreds of small businesses offering a wide variety of goods and services. There are many hotels, motels, bed and breakfasts, a hostel and private campgrounds (reservations advised in summer). Dozens of restaurants offer everything from fast food to fine dining.

Homer has a post office, library, museum, laundromats, gas stations with propane and dump stations, banks, a hospital and airport terminal. There are many fishing charter services, boat repair and storage facilities, marine fuel at Homer marina; bait, tackle and sporting goods stores; and also art galleries, gift shops and groceries.

Homer Spit has both long-term parking and camping. Camping and parking areas are well-marked.

Alaska Cottage Hideaways—Where only the moose will find you! Your private log cabin is completely secluded and features vaulted ceilings, hardwood floors, kitchen and bath, fireplace, Jacuzzi, covered porch and a large deck complete with gas grill and porch swing. Great view, hiking trails nearby, 2 nights free with a week's stay! Reservations: (907) 235-0755; e-mail 3moose@xyz.net. [ADVERTISEMENT]

Alaska's Pioneer Inn. 244 Pioneer Ave., in downtown Homer. Clean, comfortable 1-bedroom suites with private baths and furnished kitchens. Sleeps up to 4. Complimentary coffee. Single guest rooms available. Year-round. Homer's best value. Credit cards accepted. Brochure: P.O. Box 1430, Homer,

AK 99603. Phone (907) 235-5670; toll free 1-800-782-9655. Fax (907) 235-7596. E-mail abc@xyz.net. URL: www.xyz.net/~abc. [ADVERTISEMENT]

Almost Home B&B/Cabins. Panoramic view of the mountains and the bay. B&B room has private entrance, mini-kitchen, private bath and continental breakfast. Or, choose our cabin with complete kitchen, living room, bath and 2 bedrooms. Clean, comfortable, affordable and friendly! Halibut fishing packages with hosts, Sorry

Charlie Charters. Clean boat with heated cabin and enclosed bathroom. For great fish pictures, see our website. Advance reservations recommended. West Hill Road, 1½ miles to Highland, then follow the signs. Phone (907) 235-2553, fax (907) 235-0553. In Alaska: 1-800-478-2352; 1269 Upland Court, Homer, AK 99603. http://www.alaskaexcursion.com. E-mail: coates@xyz.net. [ADVERTISEMENT]

Bay View Inn. Spectacular panoramic view, next to the scenic overlook at the top of the hill as you enter Homer. Every room overlooks the shimmering waters of Kachemak Bay and the Kenai Mountains. Immaculately clean rooms, non-smoking, firm comfortable beds, telephone, TV with HBO, private bathrooms, outside entrances and freshly brewed morning coffee. Options include kitchenettes, suite with fireplace and separate honeymoon cottage. Espresso bar, serene setting, picnic tables and Adirondack chairs on the lawn. Friendly staff with local activity recommendations. Phone: (907) 235-8485, Fax (907) 235-8716. In Alaska: 1-800-478-8485. P.O. Box 804, Homer, AK 99603. E-mail: bayview@alaska.net Internet: www.bayviewalaska.com [ADVERTISEMENT]

The Bookie: For all your vacation activities. All fishing (ocean and river), kayaking, water, land and air sightseeing, bear watching, lodging, hunting and winter activities too! Let us help you "catch your Alaskan Dream Vacation"! Look for our office at Mile 5.25 on the Homer Spit or call: (907) 235-1581 or (888) 335-1581. E-mail: bookie@xyz.net. www.alaskabookie.com. [ADVERTISEMENT]

Cranes' Crest B&B. Crandall the Crane and I welcome you to our home. Panoramic view of Kachemak Bay, from 1,200-foot elevation. Sandhill cranes, moose, coyotes visit regularly. Private and shared bath with twin to king beds. Continental breakfast. Ask about wheelchair access. Open year-round. Phone (907) 235-2969, (800) 338-2969. E-mail: crnscrst@xyz.net. See display ad. [ADVERTISEMENT] ♿

Driftwood Inn and RV Park. Charming, historic beachfront inn with 21 rooms and full-hookup RV park. Both have spectacular view overlooking beautiful Kachemak Bay, mountains, glaciers. Quiet in-town location. Immaculately clean, charming rooms. Free coffee, tea, local information. Comfortable common areas with TV, fireplace, library, microwave, refrigerator, barbecue, shellfish cooker, fish cleaning area, freezer, picnic and laundry facilities. Continental breakfast available. We are a smoke-free facility. The RV park has 20-/30-/50-amp electric, water, sewer, clean and comfortable laundry and shower room for RV guests. Phone and cable available. Friendly, knowledgeable staff, specializing in helping make your stay in Homer the best possible. Reasonable, seasonal rates. Open year-round. Write, call for brochure. 135 W. Bunnell Ave., MP, Homer, AK 99603. (907) 235-8019. (800) 478-8019. E-mail: driftinn@xyz.net. Web site: www.thedriftwoodinn.com. See our display ad this section. [ADVERTISEMENT] ▲

Windjammer Suites, "Homer's all suite hotel." Every room has a Kachemak Bay view. Convenient downtown location within walking distance to shops, the Pratt museum, restaurants and beaches. Each

suite has a bedroom with a queen-size bed, full bath, queen sofa sleeper, kitchen with microwave, refrigerator and microwave, coffee maker, cable TV and telephone with free local calls. Reasonable rates. Credit cards accepted. Half-block off the Sterling Highway at 320 W. Pioneer Ave., Homer, AK 99603. (907) 235-9761. Ask us about our free giant cinnamon rolls. [ADVERTISEMENT]

Kachemak Shores Bed and Breakfast. 7 minutes from downtown Homer, we're overlooking the absolute beauty of Kachemak Bay and the Kenai mountains. Bald eagles soar past your window, which frames the bay and icy-blue glaciers. Our spacious suite includes a beautifully appointed sitting room, a generous main living area and a kitchen that comes fully stocked with all the fixins of a do-it-your-way breakfast. Comfortably sleeps 1 to 7. For reservations, call (907) 235-8234 or e-mail kshores@ptialaska.net. www.netalaska.com/kachemakshores. [ADVERTISEMENT]

Heritage Hotel-Lodge. One of Alaska's finest log hotels, conveniently located in the heart of Homer. Walking distance to beach, shops, museum. Accommodations: 36 rooms including suite with 2-person Jacuzzi. Reasonable rates. Color TV, movie channels. Phones, free local calls. Courtesy coffee. Restaurants adjacent. Alaskan hospitality. Open year-round. 147 E. Pioneer Ave., phone (907) 235-7787. Reservations 1-800-380-7787. Fax (907) 235-2804. heritage@xyz.net. See display ad this section. [ADVERTISEMENT]

Homer Alaska Referral Agency. We do it all with one phone call. Your reservation specialists for bed and breakfasts, lodging, halibut and salmon fishing, wildlife viewing, kayaking, bay excursions and adventures, and Kenai Fjords glacier trips. Bookings made at no expense to client for Anchorage, Seward, Homer and all the Kenai Peninsula. For free information, reservations (907) 235-8996 or fax (907) 235-2625. Box 1264, Homer, AK 99603. Established by Seekins, Alaskan residents since 1969. Your reliable source for making Alaskan dreams come true. Call today. E-mail: hara@alaska.net. Internet: www.homer-referral.com. See display ad. [ADVERTISEMENT]

Land's End Resort. 60 hotel rooms. Open year-round on the shores of Kachemak Bay. Beachfront spa and fitness center. Enjoy lunch or cocktails on the deck while the eagles soar overhead and the otters and seals play at your feet. Dine in the famous Chartroom restaurant and lounge. (907) 235-2500. 4786 Homer Spit Rd., Homer, AK 99603. Landsend@alaska.net or visit our web site at http://www.alaskan.com/landsendresort. [ADVERTISEMENT]

Ocean Shores Motel. 28 new, spacious seaside rooms located above our beautiful private beach. Each unit has a balcony and 7-foot picture window with spectacular views of the ocean, mountains and glaciers. Cable TV, phones, 5-star queen

FAITH LUTHERAN CHURCH
On the Sterling Highway as you come into Homer
Summer Service Schedule
Saturday 7:00 pm • Sunday 9:30 am
907-235-7600 • 3634 Soundview Ave. (at Sterling Hwy)

O•C•E•A•N•V•I•E•W R•V P•A•R•K

Spectacular View of Kachemak Bay with Beach Front Setting

Full and Partial Hookups • Pull-thru Spaces
Level • Gift Shop • Visitor Information
Picnic Area • Restrooms • Free Showers
Laundry • Cable TV • Pay Phone
Walking distance to Downtown

See log ad under Visitor Services

Special Halibut Charter Rates for RV Park Guests
• Caravans Welcome •

Phone (907) 235-3951
MILE 172.7 Sterling Highway
P.O. Box 891
Homer, Alaska 99603

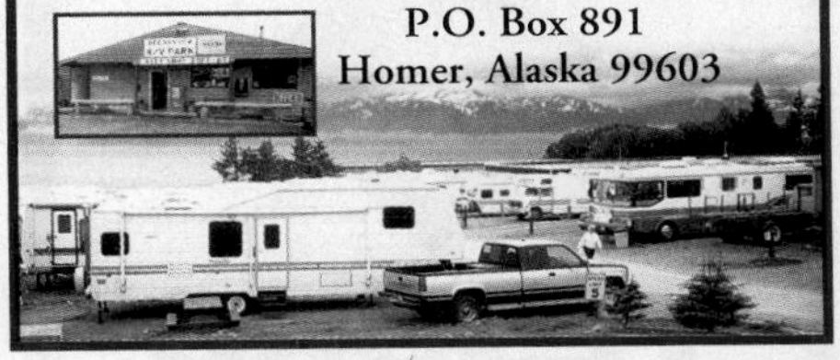

HOMER SPIT CAMPGROUND
~ AT THE END OF THE SCENIC SPIT ~

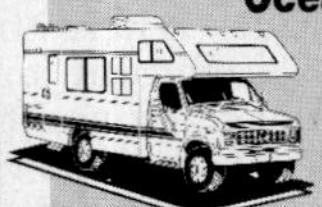

Ocean Front Camping • Trailer Rentals (onsite) • Electric Hook-ups
Dumpstation • Showers • Laundry • Gift Shop
Bookings for Halibut Charters & all recreational activities
(907) 235-8206

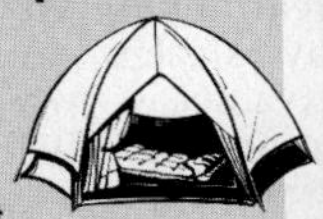

POBox 1196 Homer AK 99603 e-mail:chapple@xyz.net

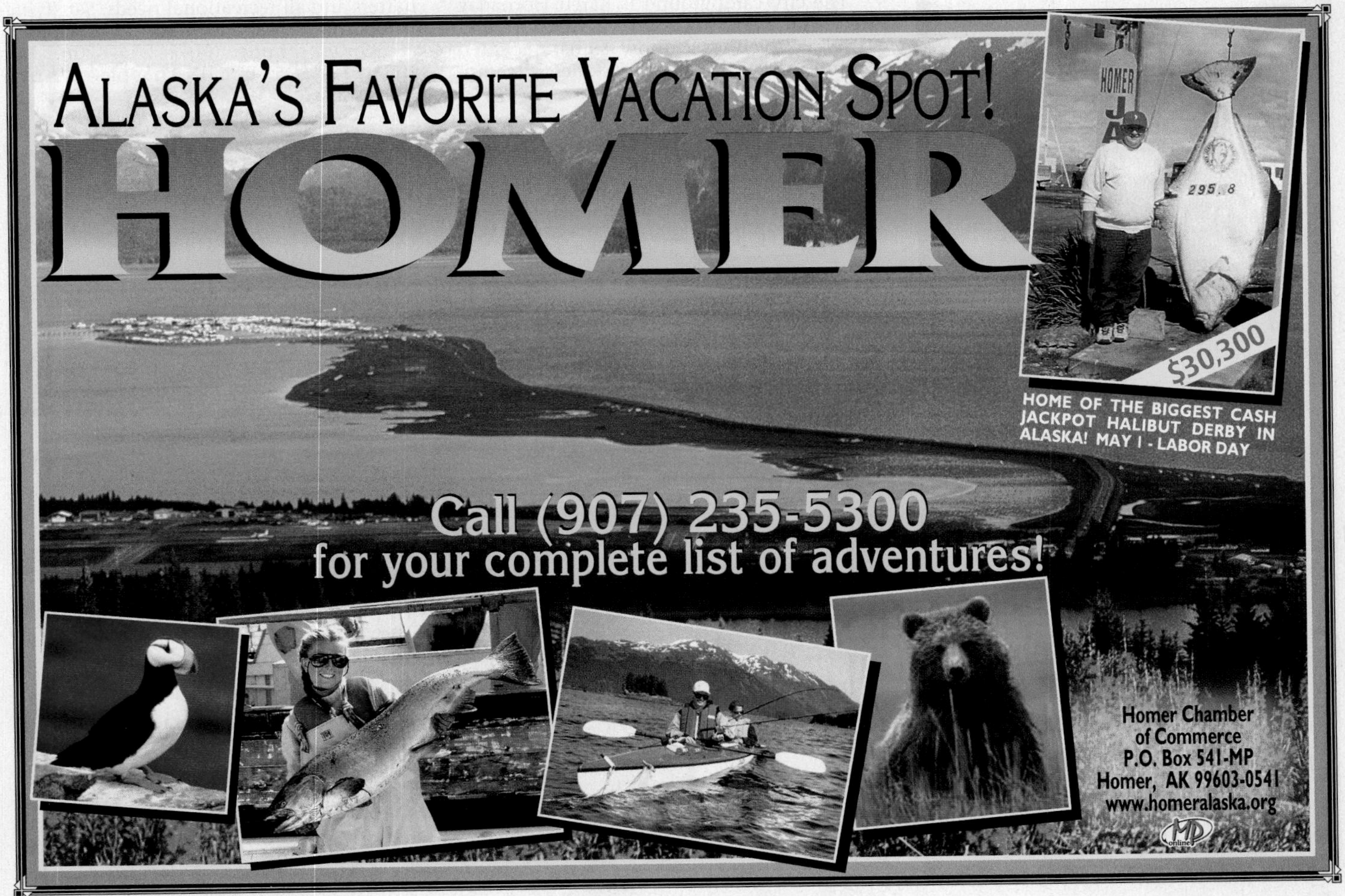

beds, kitchenette and handicap-accessible rooms. Three blocks to downtown Homer, adjacent to restaurants, quiet location and reasonable rates, all make this the best location in Homer. #451, #1 Sterling Highway, Homer, AK 99603. (907) 235-7775 or (800) 770-7775. www. akoceanshores.com. See display ad this section. [ADVERTISEMENT]

3 Moose Meadow Wilderness B&B understands that travelers to Alaska want to experience Alaska. We offer newly constructed log cabins in a wilderness setting. Your cozy cottage is nestled in the woods and overlooks a meadow with snow-capped mountains beyond. It's very private, with a kitchen and bath, fireplace, large deck and even a porch swing. 2 days free with a week's stay. Brochure or reservations call (907) 235-0755. E-mail: 3moose@ xyz.net; webpage: www.xyz.net/~3moose. See display ad this section. [ADVERTISEMENT]

Homer boat harbor on Homer Spit has a 5-lane load/launch ramp. (© Kris Graef, staff)

Wild Rose Cottages. Enjoy your own space in one of our 4 cozy cottages. Each different to accommodate your party. Charmingly furnished, bath with showers and well stocked kitchens. Slip into a complimentary pair of slippers and enjoy our breathtaking view while your catch of the day sizzles on the barbecue. wildrose @xyz.net. www.wildrose.com. P.O. Box 665, Homer, AK 99603. Phone (907) 235-8780. [ADVERTISEMENT]

Camping

The city campground is Karen Hornaday memorial Park, accessed via Bartlett and Fairview Avenues (follow signs). Located behind the ballfields, the park has 33 campsites.

Homer Spit camping fees are $7–10 per night for RVs and $3–5 per night for tents. There is a 14-day limit; restrooms, water and garbage available. Check with the Visitor Center on the Sterling Highway at Main Street, or the Fee Collection Office on Freight Dock Road, for information on rules and regulations pertaining to camping.

Homer Spit Campground. "Where the land ends and sea begins." Beachfront and ocean-view campsites surrounded by beautiful mountains and bay. Walk to harbor, restaurants and shops. Showers. Laundry. Dump station, electric, pull-throughs, overnight rentals, gifts. Bookings for halibut charters and all recreational needs. Satisfying visitors for 26 years. P.O. Box 1196, Homer, AK 99603. Phone (907) 235-8206. Fax (907) 235-2595. E-mail: chapple@xyz.net. [ADVERTISEMENT] ▲

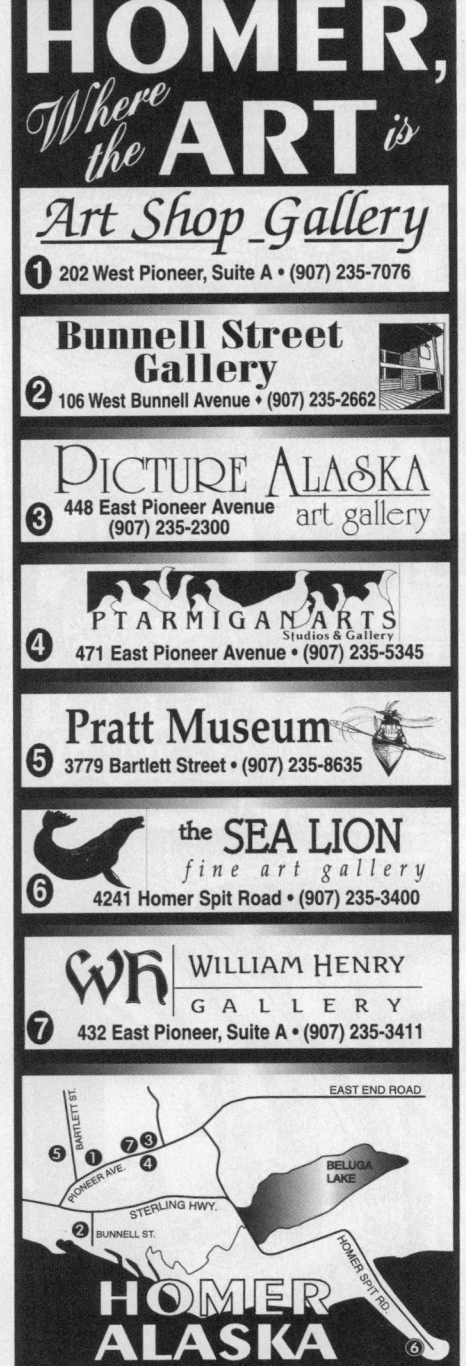

Welcome to the North Country!

Transportation

Air: Regularly scheduled air service to Anchorage. Several charter services also operate out of Homer.

Ferry: The Alaska State ferry *Tustumena* serves Seldovia, Kodiak, Seward, Port Lions, Valdez and Cordova from Homer with a limited schedule to Sand Point, King Cove and Dutch Harbor. Natural history programs offered on ferry in summer by Alaska Maritime National Wildlife Refuge naturalists. Contact the offices of the Alaska Marine Highway System at the City Dock, phone (907) 235-8449 for details. Tour boats offer passenger service to Seldovia and Halibut Cove.

Local: 3 rental car agencies and several taxi services.

Attractions

Pratt Museum, located at 3779 Bartlett St., features the natural and cultural history of southcentral Alaska. Exhibits range from artifacts of the area's first Native people, thousands of years ago, to those of homesteaders of the 1930s and 1940s. Excellent aquariums and a tide pool tank feature live Kachemak Bay sea creatures. Also exhibited are Alaskan birds and land and sea mammals, including the complete skeletons of a Bering Sea beaked whale and a beluga whale. Displays also feature local fish industry ves-

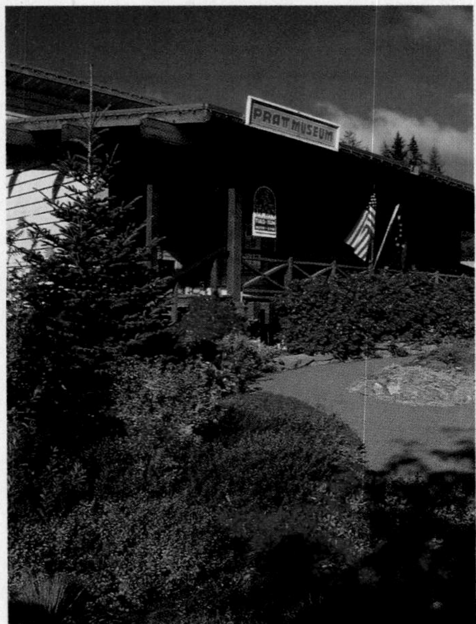

Pratt Museum on Bartlett Street features natural and cultural history displays. (© Kris Graef, staff)

sels and the restored Harrington homesteader cabin.

A popular attraction at the museum are the remote cams, which transmit live images from wildlife refuges like Gull Island—located 8 miles away in Kachemak Bay. Between May and September, visitors can observe wildlife through these remote cameras, as well as manipulate the remote cameras, located on Gull Island, in the Barren Islands and at McNeil River.

Summer visitors may take a self-guided tour through the botanical garden. This forest trail includes interpretive panels on local wild plants and the homesteader's cabin in the museum yard. The Museum Store features books and Alaskan collectibles. On display around the museum are hanging exhibits featuring the work of Alaskan artists in a variety of media.

The Pratt Museum is sponsored by the

R&D Charters & Lodge

PRIVATE • OCEAN VIEW • BEACH ACCESS • FIREPLACE

HALIBUT & KING FISHING • KAYAK & ECO-TOURS

WALKING DISTANCE TO ART GALLERIES, SHOPPING, MUSEUM

ALSO: KASILOF RIVER CABINS & FISHING PACKAGES — FRESH/SALT WATER FISHING SEE COHOE LOOP SECTION

907-235-6592

R&D CHARTERS & LODGE: BOX 1972 SOLDOTNA AK 99669 e-mail: rumiko@alaska.net

Homer Society of Natural History. All facilities are wheelchair accessible. $5 admission charged. Summer hours (May through September), 10 A.M. to 6 P.M. daily. Winter hours (October through April), noon to 5 P.M., Tuesday through Sunday. Closed January. Phone (907) 235-8635.

Homer Spit. Visitors and residents naturally gravitate toward this bustling strip of land jutting out into Kachemak Bay. Highlights include a 3-mile biking/walking trail from the parking area at Kachemak Drive out past the Fishing Hole. Watch for eagles on the mud flats from the trail's viewing platforms.

Fishing charter services and a variety of shops are housed in the Spit's 5 unique boardwalk structures.

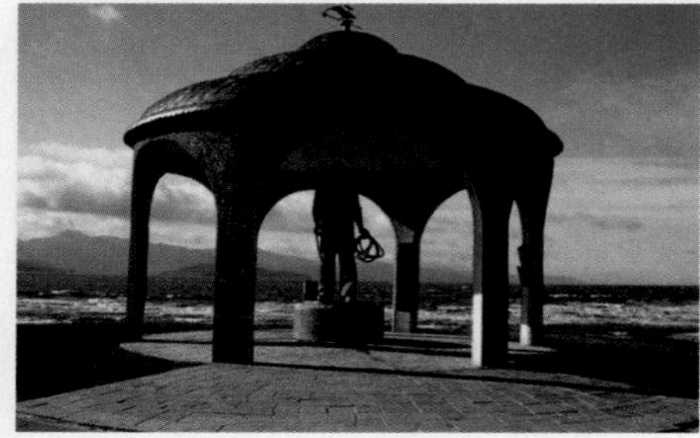

A Spit landmark is the **Seafarer's Memorial**, dedicated to those who have lost their lives at sea. There is a parking area adjacent the memorial.

Bishops Beach. is accessible from the Sterling Highway (Homer Bypass) at Main Street. It offers parking, public access to the beach, picnic tables and the trailhead for the award-winning Beluga Slough Pedestrian Trail. It is possible to walk several miles along the coastline in either direction from Bishops Beach. *CAUTION: Check tide tables.*

The U.S. Fish and Wildlife Alaska Maritime National Wildlife Refuge protects the habitats of seabirds and marine mammals on 3,500 islands and rocks along the coastline from Ketchikan to Barrow. The visitor center is open in summer from 9 A.M. to 6 P.M. daily. The center has displays focusing on the marine environment, videos and a small shop selling books and pamphlets. Wildlife programs include guided bird walks and beach walks and special slide presentations. Join the naturalists at the visitor center for an informative day. Naturalists are also on board the state ferry runs to Seldovia, Dutch Harbor and Kodiak. Information on the latest bird sightings can be obtained by calling the Bird Hotline at (907) 235-PEEP (7337). The visitor center is located at 451 Sterling Highway, Homer, AK 99603; phone (907) 235-6961.

The Kachemak Bay Shorebird Festival celebrates the arrival of 100,000 migrating shorebirds to the tidal flats of Kachemak Bay. The 7th annual festival is scheduled for May 4–7, 2000. The event promotes awareness of this critical shorebird habitat that provides a feeding and resting place for at least 20 species of shorebirds on the last leg

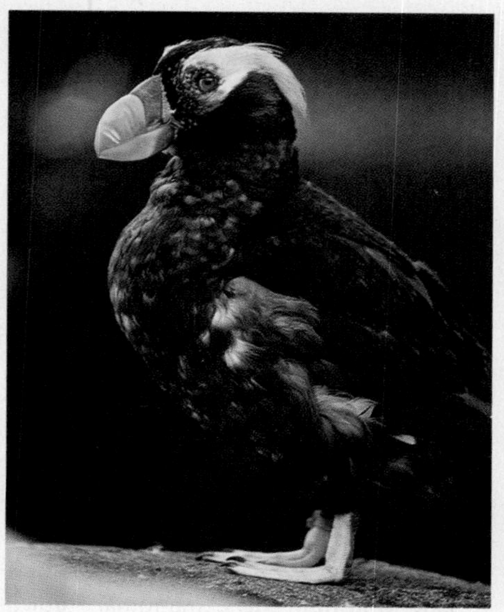

Tufted puffin in winter plumage. These birds may be observed through remote cams at Pratt Museum. (© George Wuerthner)

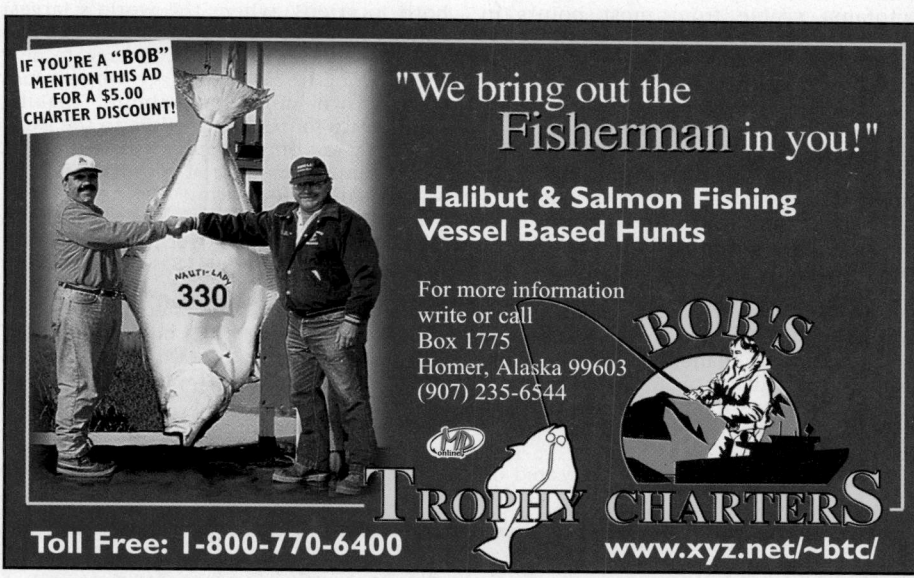

of their journey from Central and South America to breeding grounds in western and northern Alaska. Festival highlights include guided bird walks, classes for beginning and advanced birders, children's activities and more. Sponsored by the Homer Chamber of Commerce and U.S. Fish & Wildlife Service; phone (907) 235-7740 for more details.

Fish the Homer Halibut Derby. The annual Jackpot Halibut Derby, sponsored by the Homer Chamber of Commerce, runs from May 1 through Labor Day. The state's largest cash halibut derby ($85,000) provides 4 monthly cash prizes, tagged fish and final jackpot prize. Tickets are available at the Jackpot Halibut Derby headquarters on Homer Spit, at the visitor center or from local charter service offices. Phone (907) 235-7740 for more information.

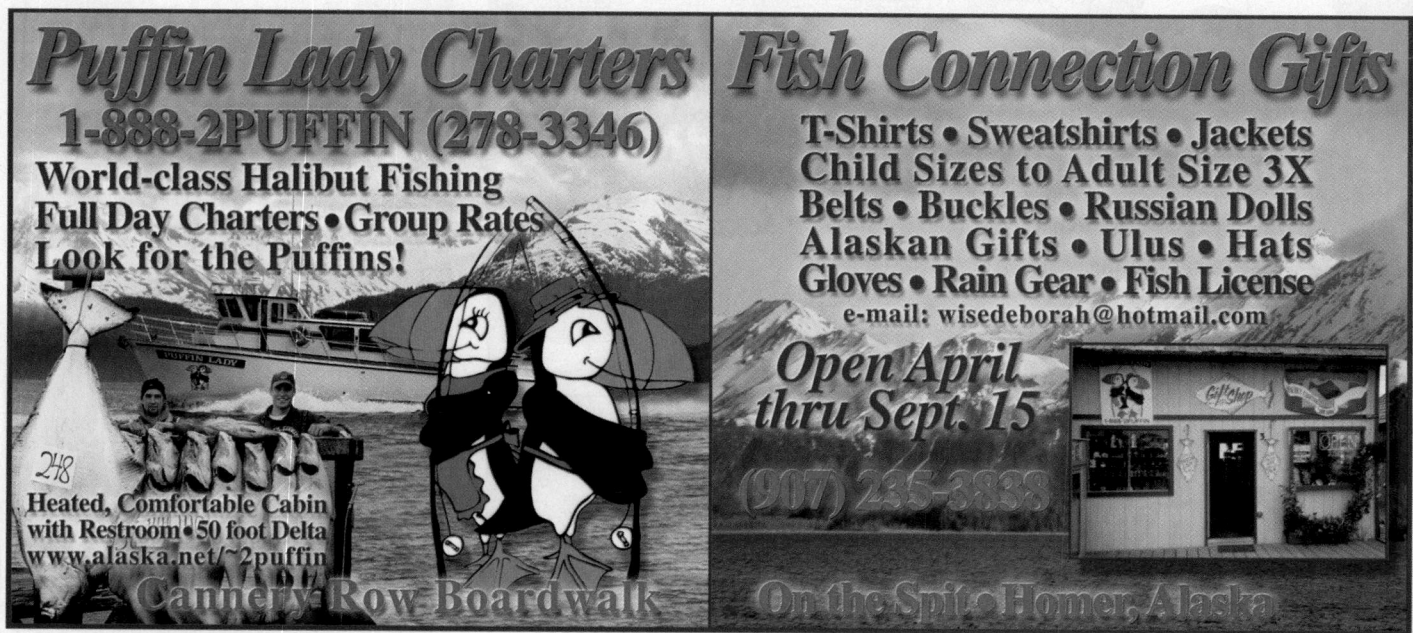

Charter Boats, operating out of the boat harbor on Homer Spit, offer sightseeing and halibut fishing trips. (Charter salmon fishing trips, clamming, crabbing, and sightseeing charters are also available.) These charter operators provide gear, bait and expert knowledge of the area. Homer is one of Alaska's largest charter fishing areas (most charters are for halibut fishing). Charter boats for halibut fishermen cost about $120 to $155 a day. Several sightseeing boats operate off the Homer Spit, taking visitors to view the bird rookery on Gull Island, to Halibut Cove and to Seldovia. (Most sightseeing trips are available Memorial Day to Labor Day). Watch for whales, puffins, sea otters, seals and other marine wildlife.

Take a Scenic Drive. A 13-mile drive out East Road offers beautiful views of Kachemak Bay. Or turn off East Road on to East Hill Road and drive up the bluffs to Skyline Drive; beautiful views of the bay and glaciers. Return to town via West Hill Road, which intersects the Sterling Highway at **Milepost S 167.1**.

The glaciers that spill down from the Harding Icefield straddling the Kenai Mountains across the bay create an ever-changing panorama visible from most points in Homer, particularly from the Skyline Drive. The most spectacular and largest of these glaciers is Grewingk Glacier in Kachemak Bay State Park, visible to the east directly across Kachemak Bay from Homer. The glacier was named by Alaska explorer William H. Dall in 1880 for Constantin Grewingk, a German geologist who had published a work on the geology and volcanism of Alaska. The Grewingk Glacier has a long gravel bar at its terminal moraine, behind which the water draining from the ice flows into the bay. This gravel bar, called Glacier Spit, is a popular excursion spot, and may be visited by charter plane or boat. (There are several charter plane operators and charter helicopter services in Homer.) Portlock and Dixon glaciers are also visible directly across from the spit.

Kachemak Bay State Park is located on the south shore of the bay and accessible by private water taxis from Homer. It is one of Alaska's most popular parks for sea kayaking, hiking, fishing and beachcombing. The park's coves, bay, valleys and mountains provide a great variety of recreational opportunities, including: a 75-mile trail system with hiking from Glacier Spit to China Poot Peak; campsites at Glacier Spit, Halibut Cove Lagoon, China Poot Lake and additional backcountry locations; 5 public-use cabins; and excellent kayaking, clamming, tide pooling and beachcombing opportunities. For cabin reservations, phone (907) 262-5581. For more information, phone the district office at (907) 235-7024, or stop by the state park office at **Milepost S 168.5** Sterling Highway.

Visit Halibut Cove and Seldovia. These 2 communities on Kachemak Bay accessible by ferry from Homer boat harbor. See descriptions of these charming seaside villages on pages 600–601.

McNeil River State Game Sanctuary/Katmai National Park. Homer is the main base for visitors flying across Cook Inlet to both locations, where the world's largest concentration of bears in a natural area this size is found. Brown bears congregate near the mouth of the McNeil River, where a falls slows down migrating salmon, making fishing easy for the bears. Visits to the game sanctuary are on a permit basis; a drawing for the limited number of permits is held in March each year. Permit applications are available from the Alaska Dept. of Fish and Game, Attn: McNeil River, 333 Raspberry Road, Anchorage 99518. Phone (907) 267-2100.

Katmai National Park offers viewing platforms for close (and safe!) brown bear viewing. Several area outfitters provide service, including overnight stays and access to remote areas of the park.

Study Marine Environment. The Center for Alaskan Coastal Studies is located across Kachemak Bay from Homer. Volunteer naturalists lead a day tour which includes Gull Island bird rookery, coastal forest and intertidal areas. Write the Center for Alaskan Coastal Studies, P.O. Box 2225-MP, Homer 99603; phone (907) 235-6667. Reservations, phone (907) 235-7272.

Coastal Outfitters: Experience the best wilderness adventure and photographic opportunity for all that Alaska has to offer. Choose from the following custom marine tours aboard our 66-foot vessel. April, May and June—Thrill to the whale migration through the Gulf of Alaska, along with seeing glaciers, volcanoes, a multitude of seabirds and sea mammals. June through September—World-class bear viewing along the coast of Katmai National Park. Stay on our 66-foot vessel with all the comforts of home while watching the magnificent

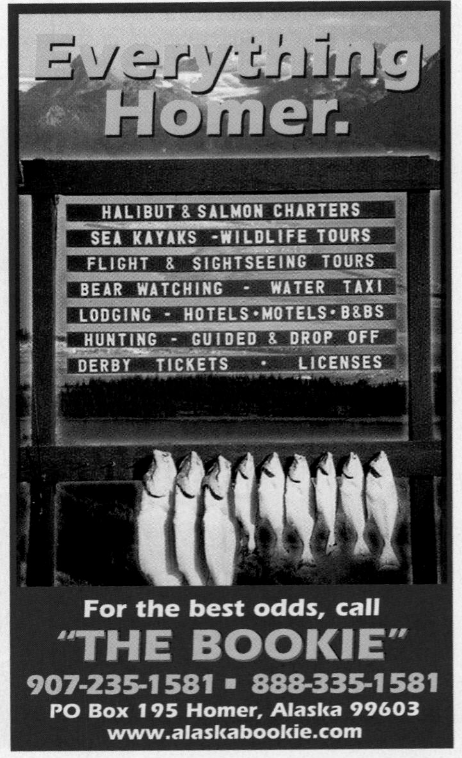

Alaskan brown bears. All tours include unparalleled opportunities for halibut fishing. See display ad. Phone (907) 235-8492; 1-888-235-8492; fax (907) 235-2967. E-mail: bear@xyz.net. Internet: http://www.xyz.net/~bear. [ADVERTISEMENT]

Kachemak Air Service, Inc. offers 2 unique opportunities: Fly over the glaciers across Kachemak Bay with Bill deCreeft in his 1929 Travel Air S6000B floatplane "Limousine of the Air," large, mahogany-framed windows for each passenger; or fly out for the day in Kachemak Air Service, Inc.'s deHavilland Otter floatplane with Chris Day for a Day Trip viewing brown bears since 1967. P.O. Box 1769, Homer, AK 99603. (907) 235-8924. Internet: www.alaskaseaplanes.com. [ADVERTISEMENT]

NOMAR® (Northern Marine Canvas Products) began business the summer of 1978 in a yellow school bus! Today, visit our manufacturing facility and retail store at 104 E. Pioneer Ave., downtown Homer. NOMAR® manufactures a wide variety of products for our Alaskan lifestyles. Warm NOMAR® fleece clothing to keep you warm, no matter what the adventure. Soft-sided 'Laska Luggage that's stuffable and floatplane friendly. Watertight bags and camp gear for kayak tours or whitewater expeditions. Plus, well-made, Homer-made, packable, mailable, useful gifts, for everyone on the "list." Park in our spacious, paved parking lot and walk around our town, it's a nice stroll. We'll gladly ship your purchases for you. See display ad this section. [ADVERTISEMENT]

North Country Charters, on the Homer Spit. Sean and Gerri Martin, original owners since 1979. We have an excellent catch record with prize-winning derby fish, bringing in some of the largest halibut in Homer. Three 6-passenger and one 16-passenger boat for halibut fishing along with a saltwater salmon trolling boat. All vessels are Coast Guard equipped, heated cabins, full restrooms. 1-800-770-7620. E-mail: norco@alaska.net. www.northcountrycharters.com. See display ad. [ADVERTISEMENT]

Pier One Theatre. Local talent lights up an intimate stage in an Alaskan-friendly waterfront atmosphere halfway out the Homer Spit. Plays, new productions, readings, dance theatre, musicals. Offered summer weekends, some midweek shows. Season information available locally. Phone (907) 235-7333. lance@xyz.net. [ADVERTISEMENT]

Trails End Horse Adventures. Horses and Alaska are my life. Join me in my 15th season offering trail rides in the Homer area. Featuring half-day rides and pack adventures to the head of Kachemak Bay. View mountains, glaciers, Fox River flats. Gentle Alaskan horses. Located at **Mile 11.2** East End Road. Write Mark Marette, Box 1771, Homer, AK 99603. Phone (907) 235-6393. [ADVERTISEMENT]

AREA FISHING: The Kachemak Bay and Cook Inlet area is one of Alaska's most popular spots for halibut fishing, with catches often weighing 100 to 200 lbs. Guides and charters are available locally. Halibut up to 350 lbs. are fished from June through September; fish the bottom with herring. Year-round trolling for king salmon is popular; use small herring. King salmon may also be taken during late May and June in area streams. Pink salmon (4 to 5 lbs.) may be caught in July and August; use winged bobbers, small weighted spoons and spinners. Similar tackle or fresh roe will catch silver salmon weighing 6 to 8 lbs. in August and September. Dolly Varden are taken throughout the area April to October; try single eggs or wet flies. Steelhead/rainbow are available in local streams, but for conservation purposes must be immediately released unharmed.

The Fishing Hole on Homer Spit is a favorite spot for salmon. (© Kris Graef, staff)

Fishermen have had great success in recent years casting from the shore of Homer Spit for king salmon. **The Fishing Hole** (also referred to as the Fishing Lagoon or Spit Lagoon) on the Homer Spit supports a large run of hatchery-produced kings and silvers beginning in late May and continuing to September. Kings range from 20 to 40 lbs. The fishery is open 7 days a week in season.

Regulations vary depending on species and area fished, and anglers are cautioned to consult nearby tackle shops or Fish and Game before fishing.

Seldovia

Located on the southwestern Kenai Peninsula on Seldovia Bay, an arm of Kachemak Bay, 16 miles southwest of Homer. **Population:** 284. **Emergency Services: City Police, Ambulance, Fire** and **Rescue**, emergency only, phone 911, monitor CB Channel 9. **Seldovia Medical Clinic**, phone (907) 234-7825. Seldovia has a resident doctor and visiting dentists.

Visitor Information: Seldovia Chamber of Commerce, Drawer F, Seldovia, AK 99663. Phone (970) 234-7612; fax (907) 234-7637; e-mail seldcity@xyz.net; web www.xyz.net/~seldovia. Information cache at Synergy Art Works on Main Street. Most Main Street businesses also provide visitor information.

Transportation: Air—Scheduled and charter service available. **Ferry**—Alaska's Southwestern Marine Highway system serves Seldovia, with connections to and from Homer, Port Lions, Kodiak, Valdez, Cordova and Seward. **Charter and Tour Boats**—Available for passenger service; inquire locally and in Homer.

Private Aircraft: Seldovia airport, 1 E; elev. 29 feet; length 1,845 feet; gravel; unattended.

Seldovia is a small community connected to Homer by the Alaska Marine Highway Southwest ferry system. Because it is removed from Kenai Peninsula highways, Seldovia has retained much of its old Alaska charm and traditions (its historic boardwalk dates from 1931).

The name Seldovia is derived from Russian *Seldevoy,* meaning "herring bay." Between 1869 and 1882, a trading station was located here. The St. Nicholas Russian Orthodox Church was built in 1891. It is now a national historic site. A post office was established in Nov. 1898.

The SOS (Save Our Seas) Response Team is located at 258 Seldovia Street. This one-of-a-kind community group, first organized after the *Exxon Valdez* oil spill, has the ability to respond to local emergencies in southern Cook Inlet and Kachemak Bay using local fishing boats and crews. SOS also serves as a community information center with phone, fax and e-mail access. Visitors are welcome, 8 A.M. to 5 P.M. weekdays.

Lodging & Services

Seldovia has most visitor facilities, including 2 hotels, several bed and breakfasts, a lodge, general store, grocery/deli, restaurants and a variety of shops. The post office is in the center of town. Public restrooms, showers and pay phone in front of the boat harbor near town center. Pay phones are also located at the ferry dock outside ferry office, at the airport, and library.

Gerry's Place B&B. Bed and breakfast one block from harbor. Convenient for fishermen and families. Freshly-baked continental breakfast. Three bedrooms accommodate 6 people with shared bath. Free airport pickup. Close to shops, hiking trails, bike rentals, beachcombing. Open year-round. Box 33, Seldovia, AK 99663. Phone (907) 234-7471. E-mail: rolpat@xyz.net. [ADVERTISEMENT]

Sea Breeze Charters. Excellent fishing, wildlife and bear viewing/photography. Experience remote Alaska with amenities! Accommodations: Home-style B&B accommodations in the Aleutiq village of Port Graham or beautiful Dogfish Bay Sportsman Lodge at the tip of the Kenai Peninsula. Visits to working commercial fishing set-net sites and subsistence activities can be arranged. Coast Guard licensed captain for your safety. (907) 234-7641 or sos@xyz.net. [ADVERTISEMENT]

Seldovia Boardwalk Hotel. Waterfront view. 14 lovely rooms with private baths. Large harbor-view deck. In-room phones. Near bike rental and Otterbahn Trail. Free airport or harbor pickup. Friendly service. Romantic getaway. Package prices from Homer. P.O. Box 72, Seldovia, AK 99663. (907) 234-7816. E-mail: bbutler@alaska.net. [ADVERTISEMENT]

The Mad Fish Restaurant. Dine on fine gourmet cuisine by Chef Kate Fitzgerald-Haralson, as you overlook the picturesque Seldovia waterfront. We specialize in unique and delightful seafood specialties. "It's worth the trip just to eat here." Alaskan beers and fine wines available. Summer: 7 days a week. Winter: Limited hours. Reservations recommended. VISA/MasterCard. (907) 234-7676. E-mail: madfish@alaska.net. [ADVERTISEMENT]

Camping

RV camping at the city-owned Seldovia Wilderness Park located just outside the city. From downtown, drive 1 mile out via Anderson Way to fork in road; turn left and drive 0.9 mile to beach. ▲

Attractions

Visitors can learn about Seldovia's cultural and natural history from a series of interpretive signs placed about the town. Seldovia's sheltered bay is ideal for kayaking. The Otterbaun, a 1.2-mile hiking trail, is a popular way to get from town to Outside Beach, a beautiful spot with beachcombing, surf fishing and a view of Kachemak Bay and the volcanoes St. Augustine, Mount Iliamna and Mount Redoubt. The trailhead is behind the school. Check the tidal charts before you go; access to the Outside Beach is cut off at high tide.

Continue past the Outside Beach turnoff to hilly and unpaved Jakolof Bay Road, which offers panoramic views of Kachemak Bay, McDonald Spit, Jakolof Bay and Kasitsna Bay. At Mile 7.5, steps lead down to 1.5-mile-long McDonald Spit, a favorite spot for seabirds and marine life. Spend an afternoon exploring the spit, or continue out to Jakolof Bay, where the road offers many opportunities to get onto the beach. The road becomes impassable to vehicles at Mile 13.

Stairway Art Gallery meanders up the stairways of the Seldovia Rowing Club B&B on the original boardwalk to professional artist Susan Mumma's colorful studio. She specializes in water colors along with lovely remembrances of Seldovia and vintage glass. Enjoy the spectacular view from her studio windows. Gallery/studio hours: 1:30–5 P.M. daily. (907) 234-7614. www.ptialaska.net/~rowing. E-mail: rowing@ptialaska.net. [ADVERTISEMENT]

Herring Bay Mercantile. Fine Alaskan and natural history gifts on the Seldovia waterfront. Colorful kitchenwares, housewares, Alaskan books, elegant jewelry, creative toys, clothing, Alaska bath products, Christmas ornaments, original art. Many locally designed gifts. Featuring work by local artist and author Susan Woodward Springer, including the Seldovia History Book. Open daily. VISA/Mastercard. Phone (907) 234-7410. www.AlaskaHerringBay.com. [ADVERTISEMENT]

Special Events. Just about the whole town participates in Seldovia's old-fashioned Fourth of July celebration. The holiday includes food booths, parade, games and contests. Check with the chamber of commerce for details.

Fishing: Kachemak Bay, king salmon Jan.–Aug.; halibut May–Oct.; Dolly Varden June–Sept.; silver salmon in August and Sept.; red salmon July–Aug. **Seldovia Bay,** king, silver and red salmon, also halibut, May–Sept. Excellent bottom fishing.

SELDOVIA ADVERTISERS

Gerry's Place B&B	Ph. (907) 234-7471
Herring Bay Mercantile	275 Main St.
Mad Fish Restaurant, The	Ph. (907) 234-7676
Sea Breeze Charters	Ph. (907) 234-7641
Seldovia Boardwalk Hotel	Ph. (907) 234-7816
Seldovia Seaport Cottages	Ph. (907) 234-7483
Stairway Art Gallery	Old Boardwalk

Halibut Cove

Located 7 miles southeast of Homer on the east shore of Kachemak Bay. **Population:** 741. **Emergency Services:** In Homer. **Elevation:** 10 feet. **Climate**: Summer temperatures from 45° to 65°F; winter temperatures from 14° to 27°F; average annual precipitation, 24 inches.

Visitor Information: Welcome and information shack at the top of the ramp at the main dock. www.halibutcove.com.

The community of Halibut Cove is nestled along a 3-mile-wide bay on the east shore of Kachemak Bay. The bay was named Halibut Cove by W.H. Dall of the U.S. Coast & Geodetic Survey in 1880. The entrance to Halibut Cove is sheltered by 1.4-mile-long Ismailof Island, named in 1880 by Dall for Gerassiim Grigorovich Ismailov, IRN, who made explorations in Alaska in the late 18th century.

Between 1911 and 1928, Halibut Cove had 42 herring salteries and a population of about 1,000.

Today, the community of Halibut Cove is made up of self-employed artists, commercial fishermen and craftsmen. There are no state schools in the community.

Lodging & Services

Overnight guests in Halibut Cove can stay in cabins or bed and breakfasts located on Ismailof Island (Halibut Cove Cabins); or on the mainland (Quiet Place Lodge). There is one restaurant (the Saltry). There is a post office. Banks, groceries and similar services are not available in Halibut Cove.

Quiet Place Lodge. Enjoy a memorable wilderness experience in one of 5 beautifully appointed private cabins with shared baths on the waterfront of Quiet Place Lodge. As you arrive, have a homemade cookie from the "Bottomless Cookie Jar." The newly renovated Lodge and cabins house eclectic collections of art, antiques and quilts. Spend

your days hiking, kayaking, charter fishing and art gallery shopping. Relax on your deck viewing beautiful Halibut Cove or curl up with a book on the couch next to the woodstove in the oceanside library. You need 3–5 days to "take it all in." Don't forget a sauna before snuggling into your flannel sheets. Wake to fresh coffee and full hearty breakfast served in our guest dining area. Delightful Alaskan cuisine dinners offered 4 nights weekly. P.O. Box 6474 Halibut Cove, AK 99603. (907) 296-2212. [ADVERTISEMENT]

Transportation

Air: Floatplane. **Boat:** The private Kachemak Bay Ferry, M/V *Danny J*, departs Homer at noon and 5 P.M. daily in summer; reservations and tickets through Central Charters. Group charters through Narrows Charters & Tours. Board at the bottom of Ramp A at Homer boat harbor. The 45-minute ferry ride includes Gull Island bird sanctuary.

Attractions

There are no roads in Halibut Cove, but some 12 blocks of boardwalk run along the water's edge and provide a scenic and relaxing way to explore this charming community. Stroll the boardwalks for spectacular views of Kachemak Bay, access to the Saltry restaurant and to galleries displaying the work of local artists. Well-known artist Diana Tillion, who is famous for her octopus ink and watercolor paintings, has a gallery here.

Visitors can also walk down to the floats to see several historic wooden boats.

Bird watching in the area is excellent and there are good hiking trails. Kachemak Bay State Park hiking trails are accessible from Halibut Cove. China Poot Lake Trail begins at Halibut Cove Lagoon. The Lagoon Trail winds along Halibut Cove to intersect with the China Poot Lake trail. The bay shoreline offers excellent kayaking, clamming, tide pooling and beach combing opportunities. Keep in mind that Kachemak Bay's tides are among the largest in the world and tidal currents can be substantial. A tide book is essential. Phone the district Alaska State Parks office at (907) 235-7024 for more information, or stop by the state park office outside Homer for more information on hiking Kachemak Bay State Park.

Walk to the end of the main boardwalk in Halibut Cove to reach the beach. Beachcomb, look at tide pools or have a picnic lunch at the tables provided. During salmon season, visitors may see seiners set out their nets.

Kachemak Bay is one of Alaska's most popular spots for halibut fishing, with catches often weighing 100 to 200 lbs. Halibut up to 350 lbs. are fished from June through September.

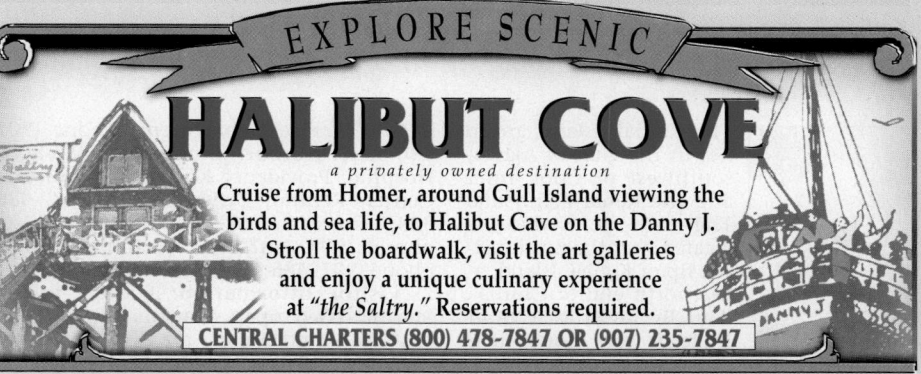

HALIBUT COVE ADVERTISERS

Central Charters	Ph. (800) 478-7847
Diana Tillion's Cove Gallery	Ph. (907) 296-2207
Halibut Cove Cabins	Ph. (907) 296-2214
Quiet Place Lodge	Ph. (907) 296-2212
The Saltry Restaurant	Ph. (907) 296-2223

Commercial fishing is one of Alaska's oldest industries.

KODIAK

(See map, page 606)

Kodiak is one of the largest commercial fishing ports in the U.S. (© Tom Culkin)

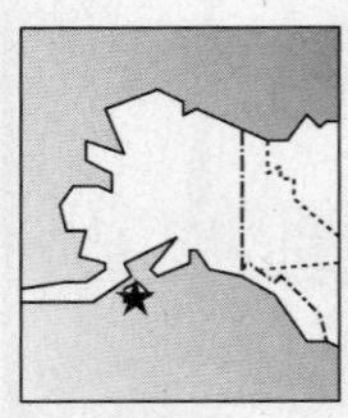

The Kodiak Island group lies in the Gulf of Alaska, southwest of Cook Inlet and the Kenai Peninsula. The city of Kodiak is located near the northeastern tip of Kodiak Island, at the north end of Chiniak Bay. By air it is 1 hour from Anchorage. By ferry from Homer it is 9½ hours.

Population: 13,848 Kodiak Island Borough. **Emergency Services in Kodiak:** Dial 911 for emergencies. **Alaska State Troopers**, phone (907) 486-4121. **Police**, phone (907) 486-8000. **Fire Department**, phone (907) 486-8040. **Harbor:** phone (907) 486-8080. **Hospital**, Providence Kodiak Island Medical Center, Rezanof Drive, phone (907) 486-3281. **Coast Guard**, Public Affairs Officer, phone (907) 487-5542. **Crime Stoppers**, phone (907) 486-3113.

Visitor Information: Located at 100 Marine Way; open year-round. Hours in June, July and August are 8 A.M. to 5 P.M. weekdays, 10 A.M. to 4 P.M. Saturday, 10-4 P.M. Sunday (and later for arriving ferries). Knowledgeable local staff will answer your questions and help arrange tours and charters. Free maps, brochures, hunting and fishing information. For information, contact the Kodiak Island Convention & Visitors Bureau, Dept. MP, 100 Marine Way, Kodiak 99615; (907) 486-4782 or 1-800-789-4782.

Elevation: Sea level. **Climate:** Average daily temperature in July is 58°F/15°C; in January 30°F/-1°C. September, October and January are the wettest months in Kodiak, with each month averaging more than 7 inches/17.8 cm of precipitation. **Radio:** KVOK 560, KMXT-FM 100.1, KRXX-FM 101. **Television:** Via cable and satellite. **Newspapers:** *The Kodiak Daily Mirror* (daily except Saturday and Sunday).

Private Aircraft: Kodiak state airport, 4.8 miles southwest; elev. 73 feet; length 7,500 feet; asphalt; fuel 100LL, Jet A-1. Kodiak Municipal Airport, 2 miles northeast; elev. 139 feet; length 2,500 feet; paved; unattended. Trident Basin seaplane base, on east side of Near Island, unattended, floats for 14 aircraft; fuel. Trident Basin has AVgas, (credit card or pre-pay).

Gravel airstrips at Akhiok, length 3,000 feet; Karluk, length 1,900 feet; Larsen Bay, length 2,400 feet; Old Harbor, length 2,000 feet; Ouzinkie, length 2,500 feet; and Port Lions, length 2,600 feet.

Kodiak Island, home of the oldest permanent European settlement in Alaska, is about 100 miles long. Known as "Alaska's Emerald Isle," Kodiak is the largest island in Alaska and the second largest island in the United States (after Hawaii), with an area of 3,588 square miles and about 87 miles of road (see logs this section). The Kodiak Island Borough includes some 200 islands, the largest being Kodiak, followed in size by Afognak, Sitkalidak, Sitkinak, Raspberry, Tugidak, Shuyak, Uganik, Chirikof, Marmot and Spruce islands. The borough has two unincorporated townsites, **KARLUK** (pop. 48), located on the west coast of Kodiak Island, 75 air miles from Kodiak, and **ALENEVA** (pop. 35) on Afognak Island.

The 6 incorporated cities in the Kodiak Island Borough are: **KODIAK** (pop. 6,859) on Chiniak Bay, with all visitor services (see Visitor Services, Transportation and Attractions this section); **AKHIOK** (pop.109) at Alitak Bay on the south side of Kodiak Island, 80 miles southwest of Kodiak; **LARSEN BAY** (pop. 127) on the northwest coast of Kodiak Island, 62 miles southwest of Kodiak; **OLD HARBOR** (pop. 297) on the southeast side of Kodiak Island, 54 miles from Kodiak; **OUZINKIE** (pop. 252) on the west coast of Spruce Island; and **PORT LIONS** (pop. 242) on Settler Cove on the northeast coast of Kodiak Island.

Kodiak Island was originally inhabited by the Alutiiq people, who were maritime hunters and fishermen. More than 7,000 years later, the Alutiiq still call Kodiak home.

In 1763, the island was discovered by Stephen Glotov, a Russian explorer. The name Kodiak, of which there are several variations, was first used in English by Captain Cook in 1778. Kodiak was Russian Alaska's first capital city, until the capital was moved to Sitka in 1804.

Kodiak's turbulent past includes the 1912 eruption of Novarupta Volcano, on the nearby Alaska Peninsula, and the tidal wave of 1964. The Novarupta eruption covered the island with a black cloud of ash. When the cloud finally dissipated, Kodiak was buried under 18 inches of drifting pumice.

On Good Friday in 1964 the greatest earthquake ever recorded in North America (9.2 on the Richter scale) shook the Kodiak area. The tidal wave that followed virtually leveled downtown Kodiak, destroying the fishing fleet, processing plants, canneries and 158 homes.

Because of Kodiak's strategic location for defense, military facilities were constructed on the island in 1939. Fort Abercrombie, now a state park and a national historic landmark, was one of the first secret radar installations in Alaska. Cement bunkers still remain for exploration by the curious.

The Coast Guard occupies the old Kodiak Naval Station. Kodiak is the base for the Coast Guard's North Pacific operations; the U.S. Coast Guard cutters *Storis, Ironwood* and *Firebush* patrol from Kodiak to seize foreign vessels illegally fishing U.S. waters. (The 200-mile fishing limit went into effect in March 1977.) A 12-foot star, situated halfway up the side of Old Woman Mountain overlooking the base, was rebuilt and rededicated in 1981 in memory of military personnel who have lost their lives while engaged in operations from Kodiak. Originally erected in the 1950s, the star is lit every year between Thanksgiving and Christmas.

Kodiak's St. Paul and St. Herman harbors are home port to 800 local fishing boats and serve several hundred outside vessels each year.

The MV Tustumena *serves Kodiak from Homer and Seward.* (© Rich Reid)

Commercial fishing is the backbone of Kodiak's economy. Kodiak is one of the largest commercial fishing ports in the U.S. Some 1,000 commercial fishing vessels use the harbor each year, delivering salmon, shrimp, herring, halibut and whitefish, plus king, tanner and Dungeness crab to the 9 seafood processing companies in Kodiak. Cannery tours are not available. Kodiak's famous seafood is premarketed, with almost all the commercially caught seafood exported. You can celebrate Kodiak's main industry at the Kodiak Crab Festival, May 25-29, 2000.

Kodiak is also an important cargo port and transshipment center. Container ships stop twice weekly.

Lodging & Services

There are 4 hotels/motels in Kodiak and more than 20 bed and breakfasts. A variety of restaurants offers a wide range of menus and prices. Shopping is readily available for gifts, general merchandise and sporting goods. There is a movie theater and 750-seat performing arts center.

Dump stations are located at the Petro Express station on Mill Bay Road, at the Union 76 service station in downtown Kodiak, and at Buskin River state recreation site at Mile 4.4 Chiniak Road.

There are 37 remote fly-in hunting and fishing lodges in the Kodiak area; several roadhouses on the island road system; public-use cabins available within Kodiak National Wildlife Refuge, Shuyak Island and Afognak Island state parks; and private wilderness camps and cabin rentals available throughout the Kodiak area.

Camping

There are 3 state campgrounds: Fort Abercrombie, north of town (see Rezanof–Monashka Bay Road log); Buskin River state recreation site, south of town (see Chiniak Road log); and Pasagshak River state recreation site at the end of Pasagshak Bay Road (see log). ▲

Transportation

Air: Scheduled service via Era Aviation and Alaska Airlines.

Ferry: The Alaska state ferry MV *Tustumena* serves Kodiak from Homer ($9^1/_2$-hour ferry ride) and Seward (13 hours). It also

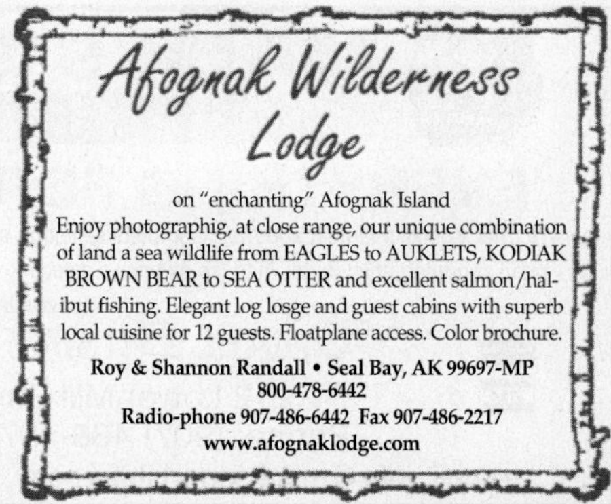

Alutiiq dancers perform daily in summer at the Barabara Sod House.

(© Michael DeYoung)

stops at Port Lions. During the summer season the MV *Tustumena* connects monthly with the 382-foot MV *Kennicott*, coming across the Gulf of Alaska from southeast Alaska. (The MV *Kennicott* is the newest vessel of the Marine Highway fleet.) Ferry terminal is downtown; phone (907) 486-3800 or toll free in the U.S. (800) 526-6731.

Highways: There are 4 roads on Kodiak Island (see logs this section). The 11.3-mile Rezanof–Monashka Bay Road leads from downtown Kodiak north to Fort Abercrombie and Monashka Bay. Chiniak Road leads 42.8 miles south from Kodiak along the island's eastern shore to Chiniak Point and Chiniak Creek. Anton Larsen Bay Road leads 11.8 miles from junction with Chiniak Road near Kodiak airport to Anton Larsen Bay. Pasagshak Bay Road branches off Chiniak Road and leads 16.5 miles to Fossil Beach at Pasagshak Point.

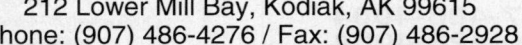

IMPORTANT: Most of the land along the road system is privately owned. Using land owned by Leisnoi, Inc. requires a non-fee user permit, available at the Leisnoi office in Kodiak at 3248 Mill Bay Rd.; phone (907) 486-8191.

Car Rental and Taxi: Available.

Attractions

State Fair and Rodeo held Labor Day weekend, Sept. 2-4, 2000, at the fairgrounds in Womens Bay, includes all-state competitions in crafts, gardening, 4-H livestock raising and home products. Stock car races are held at the fairgrounds on weekends during the summer.

St. Herman's Day, Aug. 7–9, 2000, is of particular significance to the Kodiak community as Father Herman, the first saint of the Russian Orthodox Church in North America, was canonized in Kodiak in 1970. Father Herman arrived in Kodiak in 1794. An annual pilgrimage takes place to his home on Spruce Island. Schedule of service available upon request; contact Father Gerasim, 410 Mission Road, or phone (907) 486-3854.

The Baranov Museum (Erskine House), maintained by the Kodiak Historical Society (101 Marine Way, Kodiak 99615; phone 907/486-5920), is open in summer, 10 A.M. to 4 P.M. Monday through Saturday; 12 noon to 4 P.M. Sunday. (Winter hours 10 A.M. to 3 P.M. weekdays, except Thursday and Sunday. Closed in February.) The building was originally a fur warehouse built in the early 1800s by Alexsandr Baranov. It is one of just 4 Russian-built structures in the United States today. Purchased by the Alaska Commercial Co. around 1867, the building was sold to W.J. Erskine in 1911, who converted it into a residence; it was then referred to as the Erskine House. In 1962 it was declared a national historic landmark. Many items from the Koniag and Russian era are on display. In the gift shop, Russian samovars, Russian Easter eggs, Alaska Native baskets and other items are for sale. Donations accepted, $2 per adult, children under 12 free.

Picnic on the Beach. There are some outstandingly beautiful beaches along Chiniak Road (see log this section). These unpopulated beaches are also good for beachcombing. Watch for Sitka deer and foxes.

Go for a Hike. Hiking trails around the Kodiak area provide access to alpine areas, lakes, coastal rainforests and beaches. Trail guide available for $5 at the visitors center, (907) 486-4782. Pay attention to notes regarding footwear and clothing, tides, bears, trailhead access and weather conditions.

Go Mountain Biking. Kodiak is fast becoming known for its premier mountain biking, attracting racers and enthusiasts from around the country.

Kodiak Bear Country Music Festival. An annual music festival (July 14-16, 2000) features bluegrass, folk, soft rock, country and Alaska music. More than 50 bands from around the state perform during this musical extravaganza. Contact (907) 486-6117.

Kodiak Kids' Pink Salmon Jamboree. August 12-14, 2000, features sportfishing fun and prizes for kids. Contact Kodiak National Wildlife Refuge Visitor Center, (907) 487-2600 for more information.

Kodiak Tribal Council's Barabara Sod House is an authentic Alutiiq dwelling that features presentations of Alutiiq dancing. The Kodiak Alutiiq Dancers form the only Alutiiq dance group in Alaska. The dances have been re-created from stories passed down through generations of the Alutiiq people, who have inhabited Kodiak Island for more than 7,000 years. Dance performances are held in summer, 7 days a week at 3:30 P.M., at the barabara located at 713 Rezanof Drive. Phone (907) 486-4449 to confirm performance times.

Kodiak Whale Festival—A Migration Celebration. From April 14-23, 2000, whale watchers will be celebrating the return of migrating whales. Whale sightings are reported daily, with special art, literature and performances scheduled throughout the festival. Contact (907) 486-4782.

Kodiak King Crab Festival. May 25-29, 2000, is a spring celebration featuring parades, carnival booths and midway, races and tournaments, blessing of the fleet, concerts and more. Contact Kodiak Chamber of Commerce (907) 486-5557 for details.

City Parks and Recreation Department maintains a swimming pool year-round, and the school gyms are available on a year-round basis for community use. The town has 8 parks and playgrounds including the 7-acre Baranof Park with 4 tennis courts, baseball field, track, playgrounds and picnic areas. North End Park on Near Island has a scenic 1-mile improved trail. For more information phone (907) 486-8665.

Bear Valley Golf Course. The 9-hole Bear Valley Golf Course is located on the Anton Larsen Bay Road. Owned and operated by the U.S. Coast Guard, the course has a driving range, putting green and pro shack. The course is open to the public from approximately June until October, depending on weather. The pro shack carries golf clothing, items and rental equipment, and serves food and beer. Hours of operation vary according to weather and daylight hours. Call (907) 486-7561 or 487-5108.

Pillar Mountain Golf Classic. March 31-April 2, 2000, is an irreverent, fun, par-70, one-hole golf tournament up the side of 1400-foot Pillar Mountain. For information phone (907) 486-6445.

Fort Abercrombie State Historic Park. Site of a WWII coastal fortification, bunkers and other evidence of the Aleutian campaign. The park is located north of Kodiak on scenic Miller Point. Picnicking and camping in a setting of lush rain forest, wildflowers, seabirds and eagles.

The U.S. Coast Guard Winter Recreation Area is located on the Anton Larsen Bay Road and has a lighted downhill ski slope with rope-tow lift, a separate sledding area and a ski chalet that serves refreshments. Open to the public, depending on weather and snow conditions. Call (907) 487-5108.

Kodiak is the base for the U.S. Coast Guard's North Pacific operations. (© Tom Culkin)

Alutiiq Museum Archaeological Repository Center in downtown Kodiak houses artifacts from coastal sites around Kodiak Island. The Alutiiq are descendants of the Pacific Eskimos, whom Russian explorers encountered and referred to as the Koniag people, many of whom lived in the Karluk area on Kodiak's west coast around 1200 A.D. However, some of the items found date to 3,000 and even 7,000 years ago. The Karluk area is billed as one of the most amazing archaeological finds in Alaska because of the level of preservation of the artifacts and because of the abundance of items used in daily life. Located at 215 Mission Road; phone (907) 486-7004.

Shuyak Island State Park encompasses 47,000 acres and is located 54 air miles north of Kodiak. Access is by boat or float plane only. Hunting, fishing and kayaking are the major recreational activities. Four public-use cabins are available, at $50 per night. Cabins are 12 feet by 20 feet and sleep up to 8 people. Reservations accepted up to 6 months in advance with a full nonrefundable payment. Call (907) 486-6339 or 269-8400.

Holy Resurrection Russian Orthodox Church. Orthodox priests, following Russian fur traders from Siberia, arrived in Kodiak and established the first Russian Orthodox Church in North America in September 1794. The original church was built on a bluff overlooking St. Paul Harbor in 1796. A second church was built on the same location. The bluff was leveled during reconstruction following the earthquake and tsunami in 1964.

Three churches have been built on the present site. The first appears on an 1869 map of Fort Kodiak. Another church was begun in 1874 and survived until destroyed by fire in 1943. The present church was built in 1945 and is listed on the National Register of Historic Places.

The church interior provides a visual feast, and the public is invited to attend services. The public may visit Thursday and Saturday at 6:30 P.M.; Sunday service at 8:30 A.M. Phone (907) 486-3854. A $1 donation is encouraged.

A scale replica of the original (1796) church building was completed in May 1994 and is located on the grounds of St. Herman's Theological Seminary on Mission Road.

Arrange a Boat or air charter, or guide for fishing and hunting trips, adventure tours, sightseeing and photography. There are several charter services in Kodiak.

See Kodiak by Kayak. One of the best ways to experience Kodiak's beautiful coastline, and view marine mammals and seabirds, is from a kayak. Day tours around the nearby islands are available for all skill levels, or schedule an extended tour. Kayak rentals available.

Kodiak National Wildlife Refuge encompasses 2,812 square miles on Kodiak Island, Uganik Island, Afognak Island and Ban Island. The refuge was established in 1941 to preserve the natural habitat of the famed Kodiak bear and other wildlife. Biologists estimate that more than 3,000 bears inhabit Kodiak Island. Most bears enter dens by October and remain there until April. Bears are readily observable on the refuge in July and August when they congregate along streams to feed on salmon. At other times they feed on grasses or berries.

Native wildlife within the refuge includes the red fox, river otter, short-tailed weasel, little brown bat and tundra vole. Introduced mammals include the Sitka black-tailed deer, beaver, snowshoe hare and mountain goat. On Afognak Island, an introduced herd of elk share the island with the bears. The coastline of Kodiak refuge shelters a large population of waterfowl and marine mammals. Bald eagles are common nesting birds on the refuge.

Visitors to the refuge typically go to fish, observe and photograph wildlife, backpack, kayak, camp and hunt.

NOTE: The refuge is accessible only by floatplane or boat. There are primitive public-use cabins available; applications must be made in advance to the refuge manager. For more information contact the Kodiak National Wildlife Refuge Manager, 1390 Buskin River Road, Kodiak, AK 99615; phone (907) 487-2600. You may also stop by the U.S. Fish and Wildlife Service Visitor Center on Rezanof Road, a half-mile from the state airport. The center features exhibits and films on Kodiak wildlife and is open weekdays year-round, and also Saturdays April through September; hours are variable.

Wildlife/Bird Watching. The best time to observe animals is when they are most active: at daybreak. At least 215 species of birds have been sighted around Kodiak Island archipelago. Kodiak is one of the best places in North America to view seaducks in the winter season. Bald eagles can be seen near the city of Kodiak from January through March, and nesting near water in the summer. Peregrine falcons are spotted frequently from the road in October. In the summer, puffins can be seen at Miller Point on calm days. Narrow Cape, Spruce Cape and Miller Point are good stakeout points in the spring for those in search of gray whales; summer for humpback whales. Womens Bay is home to a variety of migrating geese in April.

Kodiak is a gateway to Katmai National Park and Preserve, well-known for its bear-viewing and sportfishing, as well as for an abundance of other wildlife and activities. There is a National Park Service information office in Kodiak, and local air taxi operators offer direct flights to King Salmon and also to the remote Katmai coast.

Bear-viewing Trips. To see brown bears, it's best to leave the road system and travel to the Bush by plane or boat. Almost all the air charter services offer some sort of bear-viewing excursion, ranging from half-day trips to multiple-day visits in cabins or tent-camps. Many lodge operations and licensed guides/outfitters also provide bear-viewing trips.

AREA FISHING: Kodiak Island is in the center of a fine marine and freshwater fishery and possesses some excellent fishing for rainbow, halibut, Dolly Varden and 5 species of Pacific salmon. Visiting fishermen will have to charter a boat or aircraft to reach remote lakes, rivers and bays, but the island road system offers many good salmon streams in season. Roads access red salmon fisheries in the Buskin and Pasagshak rivers. Pink and silver salmon are also found in the **Buskin** and **Pasagshak rivers**, and **Monashka, Pillar, Russian, Salonie, American, Olds, Roslyn** and **Chiniak creeks.**

Afognak and Raspberry islands, both approximately 30 air miles northeast of Kodiak, have lodges and offer excellent remote hunting and fishing. Both islands are brown bear country. Hikers and fishermen should make noise as they travel and carry a .30–06 or larger rifle. Stay clear of bears. If you take a dog, make sure he is under control. Dogs can create dangerous situations with bears.

CAUTION: A paralytic-shellfish-poisoning alert is in effect for all Kodiak Island beaches. This toxin is extremely poisonous. There are no approved beaches for clamming on Kodiak Island. For more current information, call the Dept. of Environmental Conservation in Anchorage at (907) 349-7343.

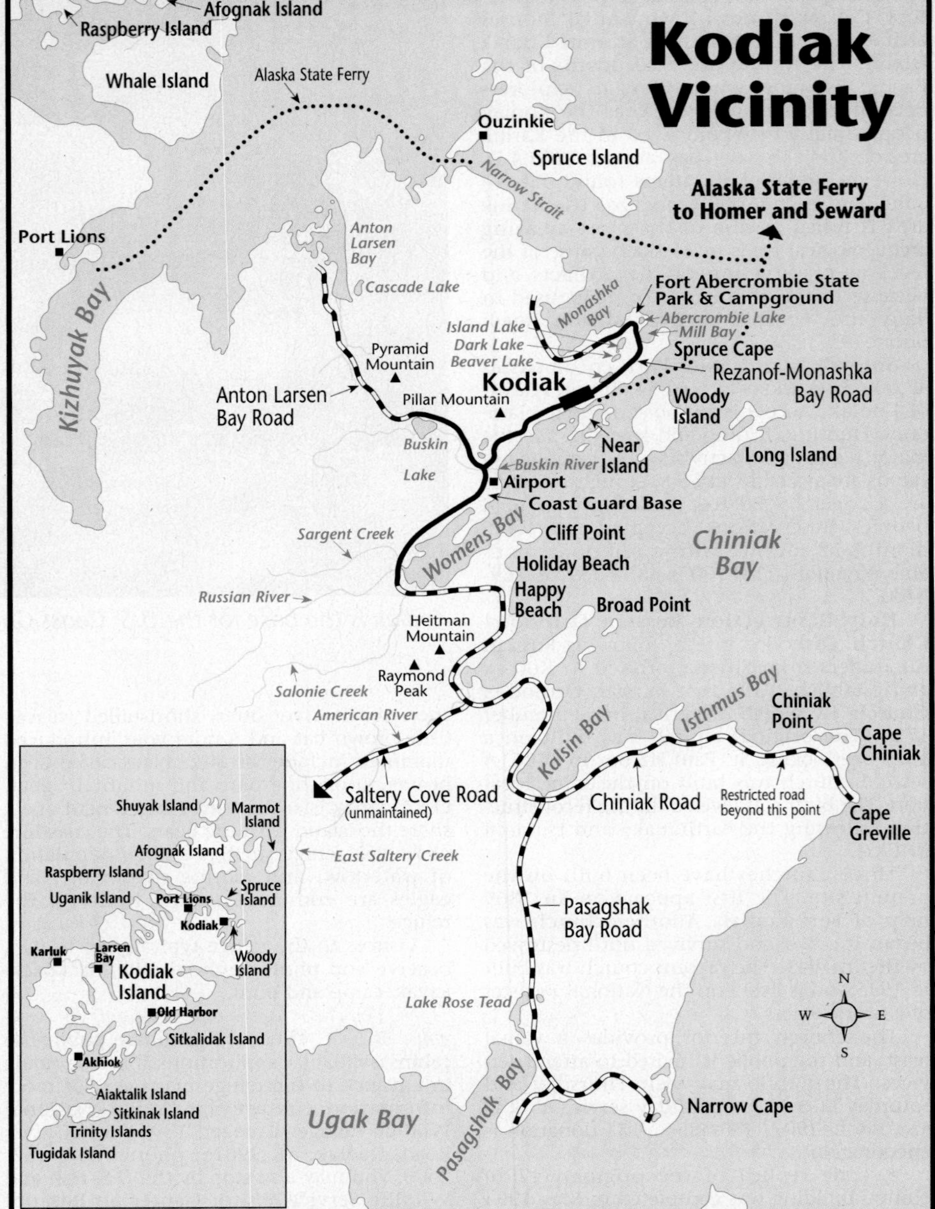

Rezanof–Monashka Bay Road Log

Distance is measured from the junction of Rezanof Drive and Marine Way in downtown Kodiak (K).

K 0.1 (0.2 km) Mill Bay Road access to library, post office and Kodiak businesses.

K 0.4 (0.6 km) Entrance to Near Island bridge to North End Park, a city park with trails and picnic areas; St. Herman Harbor, boat launch ramp, fish-cleaning station; and Fishery Industrial Technology Center (FITC), phone (907) 486-1500 for tours. Kodiak Fisheries Research Center, phone (907) 481-1800 for tours and information. Also access to Trident Basin seaplane base, located beyond FITC on Trident Way.

K 0.7 (1.13 km) Kodiak Auditorium

K 1.5 (2.4 km) Providence Kodiak Island Medical Center on left.

K 2 (3.2 km) Benny Benson Drive. Turnoff left to Kodiak College and beginning of paved bicycle trail, which parallels main road to Fort Abercrombie State Historic Park. Excellent for walking, jogging and bicycling.

K 3.4 (5.5 km) Turnout and gravel parking area to right for Mill Bay Park. Scenic picnic spot with picnic tables, barbecue grates. Good ocean fishing from beach.

K 3.8 (6.12 km) Bayside Fire Department

K 3.9 (6.3 km) Road right to **Fort Abercrombie State Historic Park.** Drive in 0.2 mile to campground; 13 campsites with 7-night limit at $10 per night, water, toilets, fishing, swimming and picnic shelter. Extensive system of scenic hiking trails. No off-road biking. View of bay and beach, WWII fortifications. Miller Point Bunker open Tuesday, Friday and Sunday at 2:30 P.M. for public viewing. Saturday evening naturalist programs June 1 to Aug. 30. Just beyond the campground entrance is the Alaska State Parks ranger station, open weekdays 8 A.M. to 5 P.M.; pay phone, public restrooms, park information.

K 4.6 (7.4 km) Monashka Bay Park left at junction with Otmeloi Way. Playground equipment, covered picnic area, barbecue grates.

K 6.4 (10.3 km) Kodiak Island Borough baler/landfill facility. Recycling center. Pavement ends. Excellent gravel road.

K 6.8 (10.9 km) Gravel turnout to right.

K 6.9 (11.1 km) Good view of Three Sisters mountains.

K 7.2 (11.6 km) Road on right leads to VFW RV park with camping facilities, scenic views, restaurant and lounge, (907) 486-3195; Kodiak Island Sportsman Association indoor shooting range, (907) 486-8566.

K 7.6 (12.2 km) Pillar Creek bridge and Pillar Creek Hatchery to left.

K 8.3 (13.3 km) Road to right leads to Pillar Beach. Beautiful black-sand beach at mouth of creek. Scenic picnic area. Dolly Varden fishing.

K 8.5 (13.7 km) Pullout to right.

K 9.3 (14.9 km) Pullout to right. Scenic overlook and panoramic views of Monashka Bay and Monashka Mountain.

K 10.1 (16.3 km) Gravel pullout and parking to right. Access to North Sister trailhead directly across road.

K 11.2 (18 km) Bridge over Monashka Creek.

K 11.3 (18.2 km) Road ends. Large turnaround parking area. Paths to right lead through narrow band of trees to secluded Monashka Bay beach. Large, sweeping sandy beach. Excellent for picnics. Picnic tables, restrooms, improved beach access. Fishing off beach for Dolly Varden, pink salmon and silvers. To north of parking area is trailhead for Termination Point hike, a beautiful 6-mile loop trail along meadows, ocean bluffs and dense Sitka spruce forest. *NOTE: Leisnoi user-permit required to hike this trail.*

Chiniak Road Log

Distance from Kodiak's U.S. post office building (K).

K 0 Kodiak U.S. post office building.

K 2.4 (3.9 km) Gravel turnout to left with panoramic view of Kodiak, Chiniak Bay and nearby islands.

K 3.8 (6.1 km) **Boy Scout Lake**, stocked; gravel turnout and parking to left.

K 4.4 (7.1 km) U.S. Fish and Wildlife Service Visitor Center and Kodiak National Wildlife Refuge headquarters. Exhibits and films on Kodiak wildlife. Open weekdays year-round, 8 A.M. to 4:30 P.M., in summer; weekends, noon to 4:30 P.M. Closed in off-season except for special events. Phone: (907) 487-2600. Road on left to **Buskin River State Recreation Site**; 15 RV campsites with a 14-night limit at $10/night, picnic tables and shelter, water, pit toilets, trails, beach access and dump station. Fishing along Buskin River and on beach area at river's mouth for red, silver and pink salmon and trout. Wheelchair-accessible fishing platform. Parking for fishermen.

K 5 (8 km) Unmarked turnoff on right for Anton Larsen Bay Road (see log this section).

K 5.1 (8.2 km) Kodiak airport.

K 5.5 (8.9 km) *CAUTION: Jet blast area at end of runway. Stop here and wait if you see a jet preparing for takeoff. Do not enter or stay in this area if you see a jet.*

K 5.7 (9.2 km) Gravel turnout and limited parking to access Barometer Mountain. Steep, straight, well-trodden trail to 2,500-foot peak. Beautiful panoramic views. To access trailhead, cross paved road and walk halfway back to jet blast area.

K 6.6 (10.6 km) Entrance to U.S. Coast Guard station.

K 7.2 (11.6 km) Road continues around Womens Bay. The drive out to Chiniak affords excellent views of the extremely rugged coastline of the island.

K 9.3 (15 km) Turnoff to right to Kodiak Island Fairgrounds. Excellent bird watching on tideflats to Salonie Creek.

K 10.1 (16.3 km) **Sargent Creek** bridge. Good fishing for pink salmon in August.

K 10.3 (16.6 km) Russian River and Bell Flats Road.

K 10.6 (17.1 km) Pavement ends; gravel begins. *NOTE: Be sure you have a spare tire. It is the law in Alaska to drive with headlights on at all times on all posted roads.*

K 10.7 (17.2 km) Grocery and liquor store, diesel and unleaded gas.

K 10.9 (17.5 km) Video store; tire repair.

K 12 (19.3 km) Salonie Creek. Pinks (early August), chums, silvers, Dolly Varden.

K 12.4 (20 km) Salonie Creek Rifle Range turnoff to right.

K 12.8 (20.6 km) Beach access. Remnants on beach of WWII submarine dock. Begin climb up Marine Hill. *NOTE: Very hazardous in winter when icy.*

K 13.6 (21.9 km) Good turnout to left with panoramic view of Mary Island, Womens Bay, Bell Flats, Kodiak. Mountain goats visible with binoculars in spring and fall in mountains behind Bell Flats.

K 14.4 (23.2 km) Pullout to right and limited parking at **Heitman Lake** trailhead. Beautiful views. Lake is stocked with rainbow trout.

K 15 (24.1 km) View of Long Island and Cliff Point.

Icons adorn the interior of St. Herman's Russian Orthodox chapel.

(© Michael DeYoung)

K 16.2 (26 km) Turnout to left.

K 16.7 (26.9 km) Road east to Holiday Beach. Closed to public. Permission by USCG required for access.

K 17.0 (27.4 km) USCG communication facility; emergency phone.

K 17.7 (28.5 km) View of Middle Bay.

K 19 (30.6 km) Undeveloped picnic area in grove of trees along beach of Middle Bay; easy access to beach. Watch for livestock.

K 19.6 (31.5 km) Small Creek bridge.

K 20 (32.2 km) Salt Creek bridge. Excellent bird watching on tideflats to left.

K 20.8 (33.5 km) American River bridge. River empties into Middle Bay.

K 20.9 (33.6 km) Unimproved road on right, marginal for 4-wheel-drive vehicles, leads toward Saltery Cove. *NOTE: Road is barely passable even for 4-wheel drive vehicles.*

K 21 (33.8 km) Felton Creek Bridge.

K 23.1 (37.2 km) Foot access to gravel beach; nice picnic site.

K 24.1 (38.8 km) *CAUTION: Steep switchbacks. Slow to 10 mph.*

K 24.5 (39.4 km) Pullout to right, limited parking. Access to Mayflower Lake. Stocked with landlocked silver salmon.

K 24.6 (39.6 km) Mayflower Beach.

K 25.3 (40.7 km) View of Kalsin Bay.

K 27.7 (44.6 km) Turnout to left. Great views.

K 28.1 (45.2 km) Improved pullout to left.

K 28.2 (45.4 km) Improved pullout to left. Steep road drops down to head of Kalsin Bay; sheer cliffs on both sides of road.

K 28.5 (45.9 km) Improved pullout to left

K 28.9 (46.5 km) Kalsin Bay Inn; food, bar, laundromat, showers, tire repair; open year-round.

K 29.2 (47 km) Deadman Creek Bridge.

K 29.9 (48.1 km) Improved pullout to left. Olds River.

K 30.2 (48.6 km) Kalsin River (creek) bridge.

K 30.6 (49.2 km) Road forks: Turn left for Chiniak, right for Pasagshak Bay. See Pasagshak Bay Road log this section.

K 30.9 (49.7 km) **Kalsin Pond** on right; excellent silver salmon fishing in fall.

K 31.1 (50 km) Turnoff to left; access to mouth of Olds River and beach.

K 31.5 (50.7 km) Highway maintenance station.

K 32 (51.5 km) Picnic area to left beside Kalsin Bay. Nice beach.

K 32.4 (52.1 km) Road to unimproved picnic area. Gravel beach. Fishing for pinks.

K 33.2 (53.4 km) Turnoff. Myrtle Creek, picnic site. Beach access.

K 34.9 (56.2 km) Thumbs Up Cove. Unimproved boat launch ramp.

K 35.1 (56.5 km) Chiniak post office. Window hours Tuesday and Thursday 4 to 6 P.M., Saturday noon to 2 P.M.

K 35.9 (57.8 km) Brookers Lagoon. Access to gravel beach.

K 36.4 (58.6 km) Chiniak Bakery to left.

K 36.9 (59.4 km) Roslyn River. Access to Roslyn Bay beach, a beautiful picnic area.

K 37.2 (59.9 km) Roslyn River Bridge.

K 37.6 (60.5 km) Access to mouth of Roslyn River.

K 39.5 (63.6 km) Access to a beautiful point overlooking the sea; site of WWII installations. Good place for photos. Sea otters in kelp beds year-round.

K 39.9 (64.2 km) Twin Creeks Beach, beautiful dark sand and rolling breakers. Park in pullout area. Do not drive onto soft beach sand.

K 40.4 (65 km) Twin Creek.

K 40.7 (65.5 km) Silver Beach.

K 40.8 (65.7 km) **Pony Lake** (stocked).

K 41.3 (66.4 km) Chiniak wayside, a borough park; benches, beautiful setting.

K 41.5 (66.8 km) Chiniak school, public library, playground and ballfield. Baseball diamond, play area, picnic tables.

K 41.6 (66.9 km) Turnoff to right onto King Crab Way. Location of Tsunami Evacuation Center.

K 42.4 (68.2 km) Road's End lounge and restaurant. Excellent whalewatching for gray whales in April, across road from restaurant.

Beyond this point the cliff is eroded right to the edge of the road. Exercise extreme caution while driving this stretch.

K 42.5 (68.4 km) **Chiniak Point**, also known as Cape Chiniak, is the south point of land at the entrance to Chiniak Bay. Capt. Cook named the point Cape Greville in 1778, but the name is now applied to that point of land 2 miles southeast of here. State road maintenance ends here. Unmaintained road continues as public easement across Leisnoi Native Corp. land. Public access discouraged beyond Chiniak Creek.

K 42.8 (68.9 km) Public road ends at **Chiniak Creek.** Pink salmon fishing in midsummer. View of Chiniak Point. Turnaround point.

Cape Chiniak trail overlooks sandy beaches of this rugged shoreline. (© Rich Reid)

Pasagshak Bay Road Log

Distance is measured from junction with Chiniak Road (J).

J 0 Turn right at **Milepost K 30.6** Chiniak Road for Pasagshak Bay. Road leads up the valley of Kalsin Creek past a private ranch.

J 0.1 (0.2 km) Northland Ranch Resort; lodging, food, lounge.

J 1.2 (1.9 km) Turnout to right to access Kalsin River; good, unimproved picnic area.

J 3.4 (5.47 km) Turnout to unimproved picnic area by beautiful stream.

J 4.7 (7.6 km) Top of Pasagshak Pass; scenic views.

J 5.3 (8.5 km) Turnout to left.

J 6.8 (10.9 km) Road crosses Lake Rose Tead on causeway. Good fishing in river from here to ocean. Good place to view spawning salmon and eagles late summer through fall.

J 7.1 (11.4 km) Combined barn and single aircraft hangar to right. Remnant of Joe Zentner Ranch, established in the 1940s.

J 8.3 (13.4 km) Derelict wooden bridge once connected old road to Portage Bay, now an easy hiking trail. Trailhead begins across the river.

J 8.9 (14.2 km) **Pasagshak River State Recreation Site**: 7 campsites with a 14-night limit (no fee), toilets, water, picnic sites, fishing and beach access.

J 9.3 (15 km) Mouth of Pasagshak River, view of Pasagshak Bay.

J 9.5 (15.3 km) Turnout at Boat Bay, traditional gravel boat launch ramp and mooring area. Four-wheel drive vehicles required to use launch ramp.

J 10.3 (16.6 km) Turnoff to right takes you to Pasagshak Point, 2 trout lakes, nice vistas.

J 11.0 (17.7 km) Entrance to Kodiak Cattle Co. grazing lease. Public land—hunting, fishing, hiking, but keep vehicle on road.

J 11.3 (18.2 km) Turnout to right provides panoramas of Narrow Cape, Ugak Island, Pasagshak Point, Sitkalidik Island. Good beachcombing on sandy beaches.

J 12.0 (19.3 km) Bear Paw Ranch Youth Camp.

J 12.2 (19.6 km) Beach access to the right. *CAUTION: Free-ranging buffalo sometimes block the road. Stop and wait; they will eventually move. Sounding your horn is not advised. Do not approach free-ranging buffalo on foot. They can be dangerous.*

J 14.4 (23.2 km) Entrance to Kodiak Cattle Co. Ranch; guided horseback riding, fishing, camping, hunting.

J 14.8 (23.8 km) Entrance at right to USCG Narrow Cape Loran Station. Emergency phone. No public access.

NOTE: Minimal road maintenance from here to end of road. Drive with caution and have a good spare tire.

J 15.7 (25.3 km) Kodiak Launch Complex, a 3,100-acre, low-earth-orbit launch complex developed by the Alaska Aerospace Development Corporation (AADC). Site includes support, payload and processing facilities and launch pad.

J 15.8 (25.4 km) Road splits; go to right for Fossil Beach.

J15.9 (25.6 km) Turnout to left. *NOTE: 4WD vehicles only beyond this point. Rental cars should park here and continue on foot.*

J 16.2 (26.1 km) **Twin Lakes** to the left and right of road. Trout in lake to the left.

J 16.5 (26.6 km) Road ends at Fossil Cliffs. Fossils imbedded in cliffs are visible along Fossil Beach to left and right (low tide only). *CAUTION: The road leading down to Fossil Beach is very steep and deeply rutted by rain and vehicle wear. Be certain of your ability to drive back up before descending the hill. Cliffs are extremely unstable. Do not approach cliff face, and watch for falling rocks at all times.* Beautiful vistas and views of WWII observation bunkers on Narrow Cape to the left.

Anton Larsen Bay Road Log

Distance is measured from the turnoff (T) at Milepost K 5 Chiniak Road.

T 0 Unmarked turnoff for Anton Larsen Bay Road at **Milepost K 5** on Chiniak Road immediately before crossing the Buskin River bridge.

T 0.6 (1 km) **Buskin River** bridge No. 6. Parking area to left accessing fishing along river. Road to the right leads to good fishing holes.

T 0.7 (1.1 km) Pavement ends.

T 0.9 (1.4 km) Enter posted restricted-access area in USCG antenna field. Do not leave road for approximately next 1.5 miles.

T 1.4 (2.3 km) **Buskin River** bridge No. 7. Turnoff to left before crossing bridge accesses river and outlet of Buskin Lake. Good fishing for Dolly Varden, salmon.

T 1.6 (2.6 km) Immediately after crossing bridge, paved road to right leads to USCG communications site. Turn on gravel road to left to Anton Larsen Bay. Beautiful drive, berry picking, mountain views, wildflowers, boat launch ramp. Excellent kayaking in bay and around outer islands.

T 2 (3.2 km) High hill on right is Pyramid Mountain (elev. 2,420 feet/738m).

T 2.3 (3.7 km) End restricted access area.

T 2.9 (4.7 km) Bear Valley Golf Course. Pyramid Mountain in backdrop. Driving range, parking on left. Nine-hole course operated by USCG. Open to the public April to October, weather permitting. Phone (907) 486-7561 or 486-4782.

T 3.2 (5.1 km) Turnout to left to unimproved trailhead of Buskin Lake. *Watch for bears.*

T 4.1 (6.6 km) Steep switchback.

T 5.7 (9.2 km) Buskin Valley Winter Recreation Area; phone (907) 487-5274 or 486-4782. To right is large parking area and trailhead to top of 2,400-foot/731.5m Pyramid Mountain. Trail follows ridgeline. Great vistas from top.

T 7.5 (12.1 km) Red Cloud River bridge. Small, unimproved campsite is adjacent to river on right.

T 8.9 (14.3 km) **Cascade Lake** trail to right. Approximately 5 miles round-trip. Rubber boots recommended to cross tidal areas. Watch for bears. Lake is stocked.

T 9.3 (15 km) Head of Anton Larsen Bay. Fox, land otters and deer can be seen in this area. Good bird watching along tidal flats.

T 10.3 (16.6 km) Public small-boat launch adjacent to road. Road continues on left side of bay for about 1.5 miles.

T 10.4 (16.7 km) Anton Larsen Bay public dock. Departure point for excellent sea kayaking.

T 11.7 (18.8 km) Road ends at turnaround. A foot-path continues beyond this point. Parking area to right.

PRINCE WILLIAM SOUND

Passengers on the MV Bartlett *view Columbia Glacier.* (© Rich Reid)

Southcentral Alaska's Prince William Sound lies at the northern extent of the Gulf of Alaska. In addition to its spectacular scenery, comparable to that of southeastern Alaska's Inside Passage, the area is also rich in wildlife. Visitors may see Dall sheep, mountain goats, sea lions, sea otters, whales, harbor seals, bald eagles and other birds. The waters contain all species of Pacific salmon; king, Dungeness and tanner crab; halibut; and rockfish.

This section includes: Columbia Glacier; Whittier; Valdez, start of the Richardson Highway; and Cordova, start of the Copper River Highway.

There are several ways to explore Prince William Sound. From Anchorage, drive south on the Seward Highway 47 miles to Portage and either take the Alaska Railroad shuttle train to Whittier or drive the new Whittier Access Road scheduled to open in June 2000 (see description on page 507). You may also start your trip across Prince William Sound from Valdez, by driving 304 miles from Anchorage to Valdez via the Glenn and Richardson highways (see GLENN HIGHWAY and RICHARDSON HIGHWAY sections).

From Whittier, Valdez or Cordova, board the ferry or one of the privately operated excursion boats to tour Prince William Sound. Flightseeing trips are also available. Depending on your itinerary and type of transportation, you may see Columbia Glacier and return to Anchorage the same day or have to stay overnight along the way. All-inclusive tours of Prince William Sound are available out of Anchorage.

Plan your trip in advance. Reservations for the ferry or cruise boats are necessary. The Alaska Railroad does not take reservations, although passengers with confirmed ferry reservations are given first priority when loading.

Columbia Glacier

Star attraction of Prince William Sound is Columbia Glacier, one of the largest and most magnificent of the tidewater glaciers along the Alaska coast.

The Columbia Glacier has an area of about 440 square miles. The glacier is more than 40 miles long. Visitors to Prince William Sound see its tidewater terminus, which is about 3 miles across. Columbia Glacier has receded more than 6 miles since the early 1980s and is expected to leave behind a 26-mile-long fjord. A bay has formed between its face and terminal moraine (where it rested prior to retreat). How close you get to the glacier's face depends on iceberg production: the more icebergs, the less chance boats have to get close.

The face of the glacier varies in height above sea level from 25 to 200 feet, and reaches 1,000 feet or more below sea level. An abundance of plankton thrives here, attracting great numbers of fish which in turn attract bald eagles, kittiwakes, gulls and harbor seals. Seals can usually be seen resting on ice floes or swimming in the icy waters.

The glacier was named by the Harriman Alaska expedition in 1899 for Columbia University in New York City. The glacier's source is Mount Einstein (elev. 11,552 feet) in the Chugach Mountains.

There are daily and weekly charters by yacht or sailboat and flightseeing trips over the glacier. (See the ads in Whittier, Valdez and Cordova in this section for charter boats offering sightseeing trips and flying services offering flightseeing trips.)

Whittier

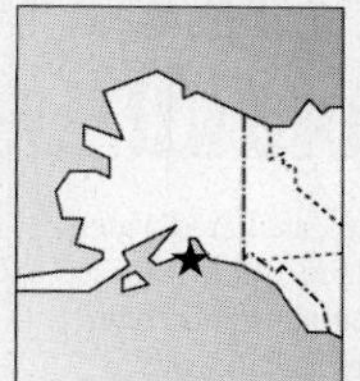

Located at the head of Passage Canal on Prince William Sound, 75 miles southeast of Anchorage. **Population:** 280. **Emergency Services: Police, Fire** and **Medical**, phone (907) 472-2340. **Visitor Information:** Information kiosk at the Harbor Triangle.

Elevation: 30 feet. **Climate:** Normal daily temperature for July is 56°F/13°C; for January, 25°F/-4°C. Maximum temperature is 84°F/29°C and minimum is -29°F/-2°C. Mean annual precipitation is 174 inches, including 260 inches of snow. Winter winds can reach 60 mph.

Private Aircraft: Airstrip adjacent northwest; elev. 30 feet; length 1,100 feet; gravel; no fuel; unattended; emergency only.

Named after the poet John Greenleaf Whittier, the community of Whittier is nestled at the base of mountains that line Passage Canal, a fjord that extends eastward into Prince William Sound. Formerly accessible from the state highway system only by shuttle train, Whittier is now connected to the Seward Highway both by railroad and by a new access road (scheduled completion June 2000). Whittier is connected to other Prince William Sound communities by ferry and charter air service.

Whittier was created by the U.S. Army during WWII as a port and petroleum delivery center tied to bases farther north by the Alaska Railroad and later a pipeline. The railroad spur from Portage was completed in 1943, and Whittier became the primary debarkation point for cargo, troops and dependents of the Alaska Command. Construction of the huge buildings that dominate Whittier began in 1948, and the Port of Whittier, strategically valuable for its ice-free deep-water port, remained activated until 1960, at which time the population was 1,200. The city of Whittier was incorporated in 1969. The government tank farm is still located here.

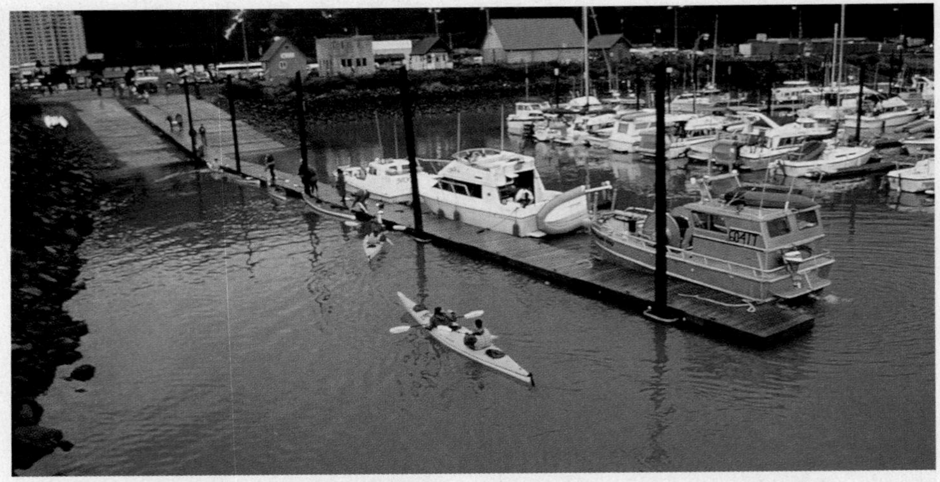

Kayaks are a common sight in Whittier and all of Prince William Sound. (© Lee Foster)

The 14-story Begich Towers, formerly the Hodge Building, houses more than half of Whittier's population. Now a condominium, the building was used by the U.S. Army for family housing and civilian bachelor quarters. The building was renamed in honor of U.S. Rep. Nick Begich of Alaska, who, along with Rep. Hale Boggs of Louisiana, disappeared in a small plane in this area in 1972 while on a campaign tour.

The Buckner Building, completed in 1953, once the largest building in Alaska, was called the "city under one roof." It is now privately owned and is to be renovated.

Whittier Manor was built in the early 1950s by private developers as rental units for civilian employees and soldiers who were ineligible for family housing elsewhere. In early 1964, the building was bought by another group of developers and became a condominium, which now houses the remainder of Whittier's population.

Since military and government activities ceased, the economy of Whittier rests largely on the fishing industry, the port and increasingly on tourism.

Annual events in Whittier include a Fourth of July parade, barbecue and fireworks; a Fish Derby, held Memorial Day weekend to Labor Day weekend; and Regatta, at the end of April or beginning of May, when residents boat to Valdez for Game Night and then bus or fly back to Whittier.

Whittier has 2 inns providing accommodations, a bed and breakfast, several restaurants, 2 bars, gift shops, laundry facilities, 2 general stores, video rental, gas station, post office, a school (preschool through grade 12), and a camper park for tents and self-contained RVs ($5 nightly fee). Fishing licenses may be purchased locally. There is no bank in Whittier. ▲

Whittier also has a harbor office, marine services and repairs, marine supply store, boat launch and lift, freight services, dry storage and self-storage units.

Prince William Sound Cruises & Tours.

Join Prince William Sound Cruises & Tours in Whittier—the Gateway to Prince William Sound. Explore glacier-carved fjords draped with cascading waterfalls and spectacular alpine glaciers. Watch for sea otters, sea lions, seals, porpoise, orcas and giant humpback whales, plus a wide variety of birds. Our experienced, knowledgeable captains and crew are your guides as you travel aboard our custom sightseeing vessels through spectacular Esther Passage. All cruises are fully narrated and include a delicious meal. Daily departures from Pier 1 in Whittier. Toll free 800-468-8068 or (907) 277-2131, or visit us on the web at www.princewilliamsound.com. [ADVERTISEMENT]

26 Glacier Cruise. Cruise the calm, protected waters of Prince William Sound and come face to face with tidewater glaciers plus

an amazing array of wildlife on the fastest, largest and most luxurious high-speed catamaran in Alaska. See our full-page ad in the Anchorage section. Our year-round sales office is located at 519 West 4th Avenue, Anchorage, AK 99501. Toll free from USA and Canada 1-800-544-0529, (907) 276-8023 or phillips@alaskanet.com. [ADVERTISEMENT]

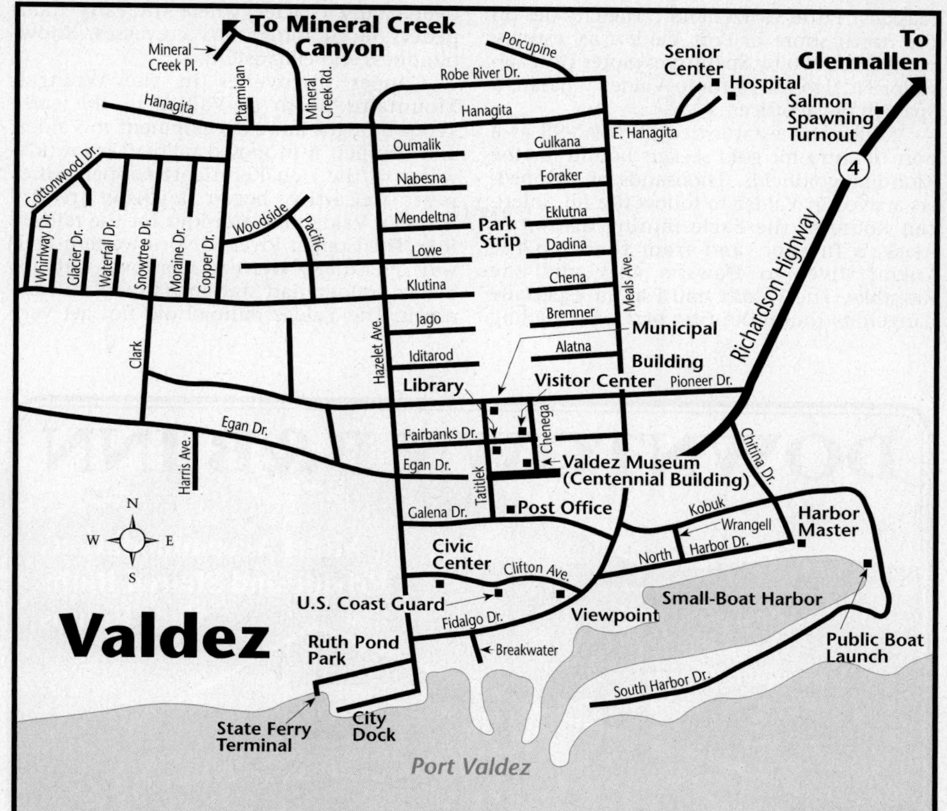

Valdez

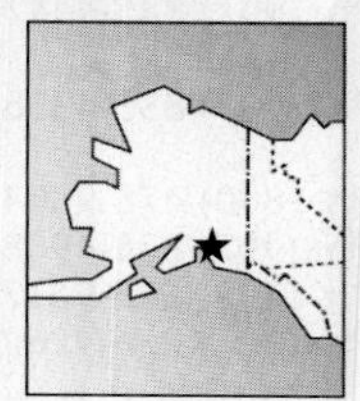

Located on Port Valdez (pronounced val-DEEZ), an estuary off Valdez Arm in Prince William Sound. Valdez is 115 air miles and 304 highway miles from Anchorage, 368 highway miles from Fairbanks. Valdez is the southern terminus of the Richardson Highway and the trans-Alaska pipeline. **Population:** 4,164.

Emergency Services: Alaska State Troopers, phone (907) 822-3263. **City Police, Fire Department** and **Ambulance**, emergency only phone 911. **Hospital**, Valdez Community, phone (907) 835-2249. **Maritime Search and Rescue**, dial 0 for Zenith 5555, toll free. Report oil spills to Dept. of Environmental Conservation, dial 0 and ask for Zenith 9300. **Fish and Wildlife Protection**, (907) 835-4307.

Visitor Information: The visitor information center, located opposite city hall at 200 Chenega St., is open 7 days a week from 8 A.M. to 8 P.M. mid-May through mid-September. The visitor center offers a self-guided tour map of homes moved from Old Valdez. Write: Valdez Convention and Visitors Bureau, Box 1603-MP, Valdez 99686; or phone toll free 800-770-5954 or (907) 835-2984 or (907) 835-4636; fax 835-4845. E-mail: valdezak@alaska.net. Visitors may also check the community calendar at the Valdez Civic Center by phoning the hotline at (907) 835-3200.

Elevation: Sea level. **Climate:** Record high was 86°F/30°C in June 1997; record low -20°F/-29°C in January 1972. Normal daily maximum in January, 30°F/-1°C; daily minimum 21°F/-6°C. Normal daily maximum in July, 61°F/16°C; daily minimum 46°F/8°C. Average snowfall in Valdez from October to May is 329.7 inches, or about 25 feet. (By comparison, Anchorage averages about 6 feet in that period.) New snowfall records were set in January 1990, with snowfall for one day at 47½ inches. Record monthly snowfall is 180 inches in February 1996. Windy (40 mph/64 kmph) in late fall. **Radio:** KCHU 770, am, KVAK 1230 am and KVAK 93.3 fm. **Television:** Many channels via cable and satellite. **Newspapers:** *Valdez Vanguard* (weekly) and *Valdez Star* (weekly).

Private Aircraft: Valdez, 3 miles east; elev. 120 feet; length 6,500 feet; asphalt; fuel 100LL, Jet B; attended.

Situated in a majestic fjord, where the 5,000-foot-tall Chugach Mountains rise from Prince William Sound, Valdez is often called

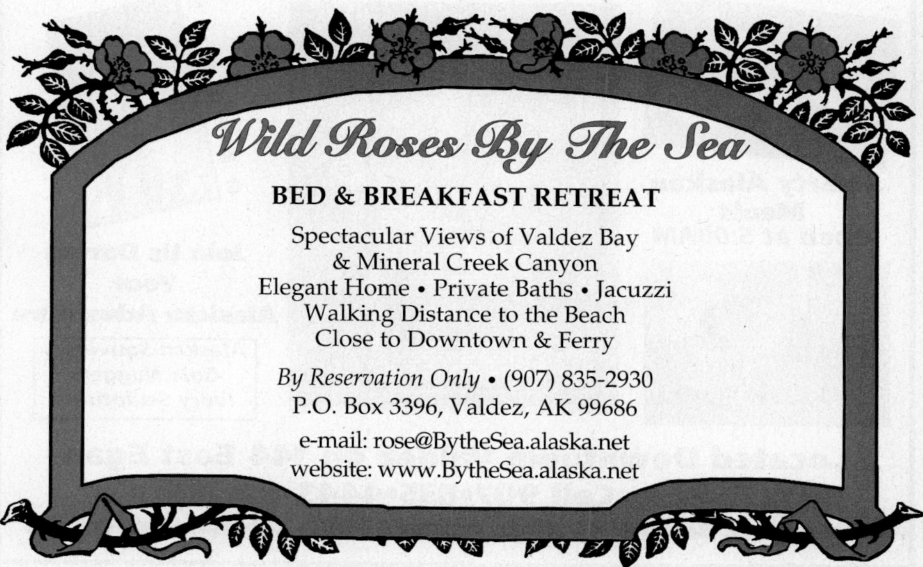

Alaska's "Little Switzerland." The city lies on the north shore of Port Valdez, an estuary named in 1790 by Spanish explorer Don Salvador Fidalgo for Antonio Valdes y Basan, a Spanish naval officer.

Valdez was established in 1897–98 as a port of entry for gold seekers bound for the Klondike goldfields. Thousands of stampeders arrived in Valdez to follow the All American Route to the Eagle mining district in Alaska's Interior, and from there up the Yukon River to Dawson City and the Klondike. The Valdez trail was an especially dangerous route, the first part of it leading over Valdez Glacier, where the early stampeders faced dangerous crevasses, snowblindness and exhaustion.

Copper discoveries in the Wrangell Mountains north of Valdez in the early 1900s brought more development to Valdez, and conflict. A proposed railroad from tidewater to the rich Kennicott copper mines near McCarthy began a bitter rivalry between Valdez and Cordova for the railway line. The Copper River & Northwestern Railway eventually went to Cordova, but not before Valdez had started its own railroad north. The Valdez railroad did not get very far: The only trace of its existence is an old hand-drilled railway tunnel at **Milepost V 14.9** on the Richardson Highway.

The old gold rush trail out of Valdez was developed into a sled and wagon road in the early 1900s. It was routed through Thomp-

VALDEZ ADVERTISERS

ABC Liquor........................Ph. (907) 835-2579
Acres Kwick Trip...............Ph. (907) 835-3278
Alaska Artistry
Bed & Breakfast...........Ph. (907) 835-2542
Alaska River &
Sea Charters................Ph. (907) 455-4041
Anadyr Adventures..........Ph. (800) TO-KAYAK
Anna's Bed & Breakfast....Ph. (907) 835-2202
Bayside RV Park................Ph. (888) 835-4425
Bear Paw R.V. Park..............Small Boat Harbor
Bear Paw Trading Post........Small Boat Harbor
Blessing House B&B..........Ph. (888) 853-5333
Capt'n Joe's Tesoro..........Ph. 1-800-553-7275
Cedar Chalet......................Ph. (907) 835-2769
Chapel of the Sea.............Ph. (907) 835-5141
Downtown B & B Inn........Ph. (800) 478-2791
Eagle B&B..........................Ph. (907) 835-3831
Eagle's Rest
RV Park.......Richardson Hwy. & Pioneer Dr.
Era Helicopters Flightseeing
Tours..........................Ph. (800) 843-1947
Glacier Wildlife Cruises/
Lu-Lu Belle...................... Behind Totem Inn
Harbor Landing
General Store.............Kobuk & Meals Ave.
Ketchum Air Service, Inc. .Ph. (800) 433-9114
Keystone Hotel.................Ph. (888) 835-0665
L&L's B&B........................Ph. (907) 835-4447
Luck of the Irish
Charters.......................Ph. (907) 835-4338
Northern Comfort
Charters.......................Ph. (800) 478-9884
One Call Does It All...........Ph. (907) 835-4988
Pangaea Adventures.........Ph. (800) 660-9637
Petro Marine Services.......Ph. (907) 276-4262
Prince William Sound
Community College....Ph. (907) 834-1625
Prince William Sound
Cruises & Tours...........Ph. (907) 835-4731
Prospector Apparel &
Sporting Goods..................141 Galena St.
Totem Inn.........................Ph. (907) 835-4443
Valdez Convention &
Visitors Bureau............Ph. (907) 835-2984
Valdez Drug & Photo...........321 Fairbanks Dr.
Valdez Museum, The........Ph. (907) 835-2764
Valdez Tesoro..............Meals Ave. & Egan Dr.
Valdez Tours......................Ph. (907) 835-2686
Westmark Valdez.............Ph. (800) 544-0970
Wild Roses By The Sea
Bed & Breakfast..........Ph. (907) 835-2930

son Pass (rather than over the Valdez Glacier) by Captain Abercrombie of the U.S. Army, who was commissioned to connect Fort Liscum (a military post established in 1900 near the present-day location of the pipeline terminal) with Fort Egbert in Eagle. Colonel Wilds P. Richardson of the Alaska Road Commission further developed the wagon road, building the first automobile road from Valdez to Fairbanks which was completed in the early 1920s.

Old photos of Valdez show Valdez Glacier directly behind the town. This is because until 1964 Valdez was located about 4 miles east of its present location, closer to the glacier. The 1964 Good Friday earthquake, the most destructive earthquake ever to hit southcentral Alaska, virtually destroyed Valdez. The quake measured between 8.4 and 8.6 on the Richter scale (since revised to 9.2) and was centered in Prince William Sound. A series of local waves caused by massive underwater landslides swept over and engulfed the Valdez wharf, taking 33 people with it. Seismic action shook the downtown and residential areas with overwhelming power. Though much damage was sustained, only the waterfront was destroyed. After the quake the Army Corps of Engineers determined the town should be relocated as it was situated on unstable glacial remains. By late August 1964, reconstruction projects had been approved and relocation was under way. The last residents remaining at "old" Valdez moved to the new town in 1968.

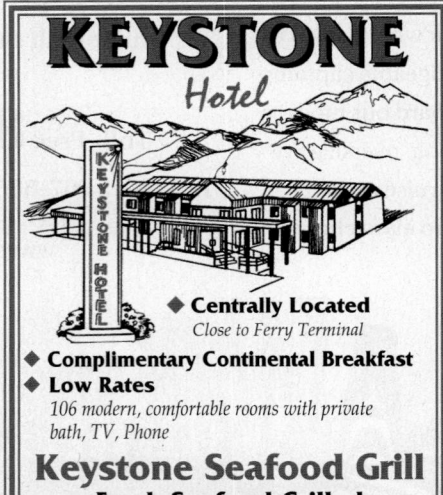

Since its days as a port of entry for gold seekers, Valdez has been an important gateway to Interior Alaska. As the most northerly ice-free port in the Western Hemisphere,

Waterfall along Mineral Creek, accessible by road from Valdez.

(© George Wuerthner)

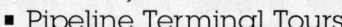

and connected by the Richardson Highway to the Alaska highway system, Valdez has evolved into a shipping center, offering the shortest link to much of interior Alaska for seaborne cargo.

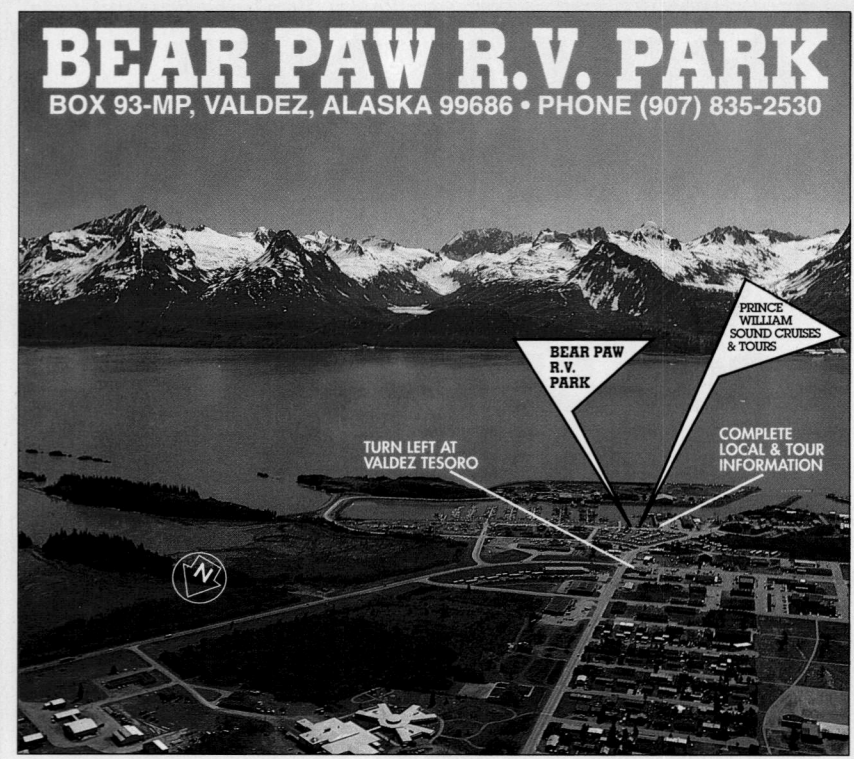

Construction of the trans-Alaska pipeline was begun in 1974 and completed in 1977 (the first tanker load of oil shipped out of Valdez on Aug. 1, 1977). The 1,000-acre site at Port Valdez was chosen as the pipeline terminus; tours of the marine terminal are available (see Attractions).

The 48-inch-diameter, 800-mile-long pipeline begins at Prudhoe Bay on the Arctic Ocean and follows the Sagavanirktok River and Atigun Valley south, crossing the Brooks Mountain Range at 4,739-foot Atigun Pass. South of the Brooks Range it passes through Dietrich and Koyukuk valleys and crosses the hills and muskeg of the Yukon–Tanana uplands to the Yukon River. South of the Yukon, the line passes through more rolling hills 10 miles east of Fairbanks, then goes south from Delta Junction to the Alaska Range, where it reaches an elevation of 3,420 feet at Isabel Pass before descending into the Copper River basin. It crests the Chugach Mountains at Thompson Pass (elev. 2,812 feet) and descends through the Keystone Canyon to Valdez, where it is fed by gravity into tanks or directly into waiting oil tankers at the marine terminal.

Because of varying soil conditions along its route, the pipeline is both above and below ground. Where the warm oil would cause ice to thaw and erode, the pipeline goes above ground to avoid thawing. Where the frozen ground is mostly well-drained gravel or solid rock, and thawing is not a problem, the line is underground.

The line was designed with 12 pump stations (although Pump Station 11 was never built) and numerous large valves to control the flow of oil. Since 1996, 4 pump stations have been placed on standby due to declining North Slope oil production. The entire system can operate on central computer control from Valdez or independent local control at each pump station.

National attention was focused on Valdez and the pipeline when the oil tanker *Exxon Valdez* ran aground on Bligh Reef (some 30 miles from Valdez) in March 1989, causing an 11-million-gallon oil spill.

Valdez's economy depends on the oil industry, the Prince William Sound fishery, government and tourism. The city limits of Valdez comprise an area of 274 square miles and include all surrounding mountains to timberline. Valdez has long been known for its beautiful setting, with the Chugach Mountains rising behind the city, and the small-boat harbor in front. The town has wide streets and open spaces, with the central residential district built around a park strip which runs from the business district almost to the base of the mountains behind the town.

Lodging & Services

Valdez has 7 motel/hotel facilities and numerous bed and breakfasts. You are advised to make reservations well in advance. Summer tourist season is also the peak work season, and accommodations fill up quickly.

Services in Valdez include several restaurants and bars, grocery store, sporting goods stores, gift shops, gas stations, hardware, hair stylists, drugstore, pharmacy, and numerous churches.

Blessing House B & B. Home-away-from-home. Walk to harbor, museum and shopping. Mountain views! See unique locking caribou horns; play piano or cook. Rates $55–$85. King beds, continental breakfast. Reservations phone (888) 853-5333; (907) 835-5333, (907) 835-2259; Address: 616 Meals/Dadina, P.O. Box 233, Valdez, AK 99686. Living units also available throughout year; Hursh Realtors, Diann Hursh, Broker. E-mail: bhousebb @alaska.net. Web site: www.valdezlink. com/bhousebb. [ADVERTISEMENT]

Downtown B & B Inn. Motel accommodations, 113 Galena Dr. Centrally located near small boat harbor, museum, ferry terminal, downtown shopping. View rooms, private and shared baths, coin-op laundry, TV and phones in rooms. Wheelchair accessible. Complimentary breakfast. Reasonable rates. Single, double, family rooms. Phone (800) 478-2791 or (907) 835-2791. E-mail: onen2rs@alaska.net. Internet: www. alaskaone.com/downinn/index.htm. See display ad this section. [ADVERTISEMENT] ♿

Keystone Hotel. Located downtown (corner of Egan and Hazelet) within walking distance to ferry terminal and shops. 106 rooms with private baths, cable TV, phones, nonsmoking or smoking, wheelchair access, coin-op laundry. Complimentary continental breakfast. Enjoy our casual seafood grill for dinner. Comfortable, clean rooms at reasonable rates. (888) 835-0665. E-mail: keyston@alaska.net. [ADVERTISEMENT] ♿

One Call Does It All. Whether it is a place to stay, a chance to catch the big one, something to do, or the means to get there, let us handle the logistics for your Alaskan adventure. VISA, MasterCard accepted. For the spectacular Prince William Sound, One Call Does It All (907) 835-4988. [ADVERTISEMENT]

Totem Inn. Motel and restaurant. Open for breakfast at 5 A.M. Famous for chicken fried steak and reindeer sausage. Lunches include burgers, salad bar and more. Fresh seafood specialties and family favorite diners affordably priced make our restaurant the "locals' choice." Remodeled rooms include private baths, queen beds, TV, phone, fridge and microwave. Reservations suggested. Located downtown Valdez. Close to harbor where the Richardson meets Egan Drive. Open year round. RV parking avail-

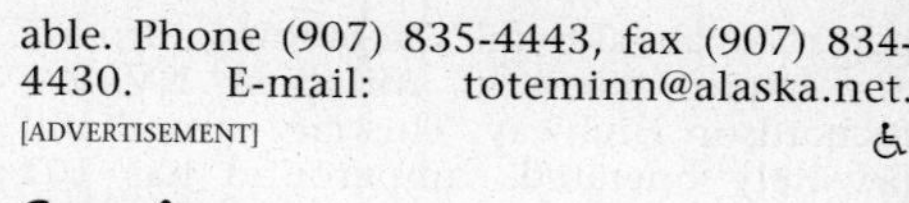

able. Phone (907) 835-4443, fax (907) 834-4430. E-mail: toteminn@alaska.net. [ADVERTISEMENT] ♿

Camping

There are 6 private RV parks with hookups near the small-boat harbor. Dump station and diesel at Valdez Tesoro and Capt'n Joe's Tesoro. Dump station at Bear Paw R.V. Park, Bayside RV Park and Eagle's Rest RV Park for registered guests.

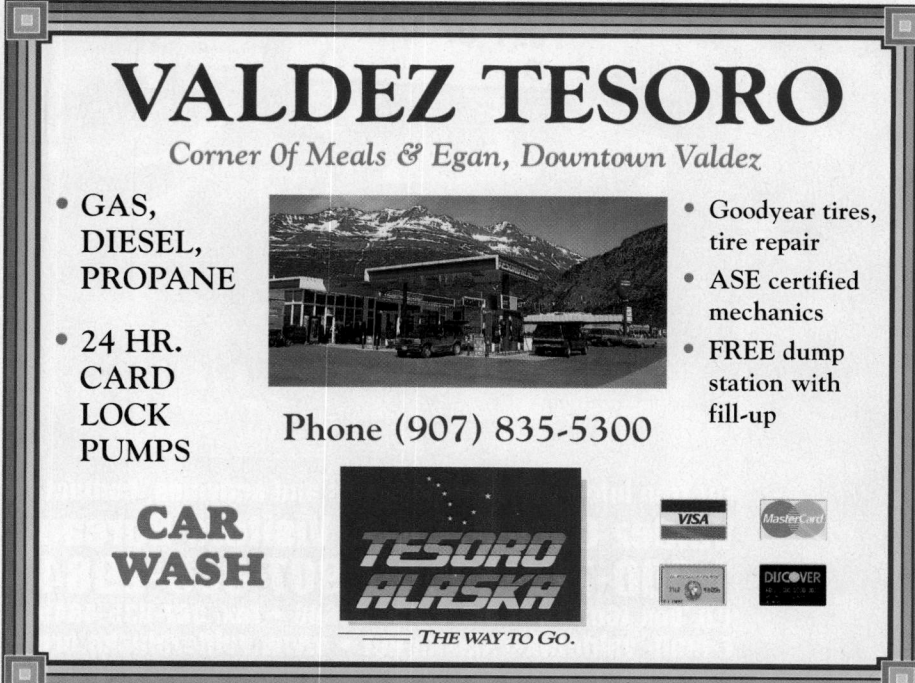

The nearest public campground is Valdez Glacier campground, at the end of the airport road, about 6 miles from town; turn left on Airport Road at **Milepost NV 3.4** Richardson Highway. This city-owned and privately operated campground has 101 sites, tent-camping areas, picnic areas, firepits, tables, litter barrels, water and toilets; 15-day limit, $10 fee charged. ▲

Bear Paw R.V. Park, centrally located on scenic North Harbor Drive overlooking the boat harbor, puts you within easy walking distance of museum, shops, restaurants, entertainment, charter boats—no need to unhook and drive to grocery stores or

points of interest. Full, partial or no hookups; immaculate private restrooms with hot, unmetered showers. Dump station and coin-operated launderette with irons and ironing boards available for guests. Also available, for adults only: waterfront full-hookup RV sites with cable TV, guest lounge, computer modem access line. Very nice, quiet wooded tent sites, some platforms, among the salmonberries on Porcupine Hill. Tables, fire pots and freezer available. Campfire wood for sale. Fuel discount coupons available. Let us book your glacier tour with Prince William Sound Cruises & Tours at the reservations desk in our spacious office lounge. We also book raft trips, flightseeing and pipeline terminal tours. Don't miss the Bear Paw Trading Post Gift Shop. Advance reservations recommended: (907) 835-2530. (Bear Paw does fill up!) The coffee pot is always on at Bear Paw. Let us know if you're coming in on the evening ferry and we'll be there to help you get parked. E-mail: bpawcamp@alaska.net. Internet: www.alaska.net/~bpawcamp/. See our large display ad this section. [ADVERTISEMENT] ▲

Eagle's Rest RV Park, the friendliest RV park in downtown Valdez, offers you Good Sam Park service with a smile. Let our helpful staff take care of all your bookings on

cruises, tours and charters. Enjoy the beautiful panoramic view of our mountains and glaciers right off our front porch! We also can let you know where the hottest fishing spots are or the quietest walking trails! Fish-cleaning table and freezer available. 10-bay golf driving range. Capt'n Joe's Tesoro next door offers gas, diesel, propane; potable water, sewer dump. Parking with us puts you within walking distance of our museum, gift shops, banks and even the largest grocery store on our same block. Shuttle service for glacier cruises. No charge to wash your RV at your site. Phone us for reservations, 1-800-553-7275 or (907) 835-2373. Fax (907) 835-KAMP (835-5267). E-mail: rvpark@alaska.net. Internet: www.alaskaoutdoors.com/eagle/. Stay with us and leave feeling like family. See display ad this section. [ADVERTISEMENT] ▲

Transportation

Air: Daily scheduled service via Alaska Airlines and Era Aviation. Air taxi and helicopter services available.

Ferry: Scheduled state ferry service to Cordova, Whittier and Seward. Phone (907) 835-4436. Reservations are a must!

Bus: Regularly scheduled service to Anchorage and Fairbanks, summer only.

Taxi: One local taxi service.

Car Rental: Two companies offer car rentals; available at airport terminal.

Highway: The Richardson Highway extends north from Valdez to the Glenn Highway and the Alaska Highway. See the RICHARDSON HIGHWAY section.

Attractions

Celebrate Gold Rush Days. Held August 2–6, 2000, this celebration includes a kick-off fashion show and luncheon, a parade, contests, game night and town fish fry. During the celebration cancan girls peruse local establishments and a jail is pulled through town by "deputies" who arrest citizens without beards, and other suspects.

Visit Valdez Museum, located at 217 Egan Dr. Exhibits depict lifestyles and workplaces from 1898 to present. Displays include a beautifully restored 1907 Ahrens steam fire engine, the original Cape Hinchinbrook lighthouse lens, a Civil War-era field cannon and an illuminated model of the Alyeska Pipeline Marine Terminal. Interpretive exhibits explain the impact of the gold rush, the 1964 earthquake, the construction of the trans-Alaska oil pipeline and the 1989 *Exxon Valdez* oil spill cleanup. Visitors can touch Columbia Glacier ice and feel the luxurious softness of a sea otter pelt. The museum's William A. Egan Commons provides a showcase setting for the Ahrens steam fire engine, models of antique aircraft, and the lighthouse lens. Local quilts are on exhibit all summer (June–August) in the Egan Commons. Outdoor exhibits include an oil pipeline "pig" and a unique snow tractor. Valdez Museum is open year-round: daily 9 A.M. to 6 P.M. during summer months (May to September); Monday through Saturday during off-season (October to April). Children free; $3 for adults (18 and older); $2.50 for seniors, $2 for youth 14-18. Phone (907) 835-2764 for more information.

Visit the Valdez Museum Annex Warehouse. Open 9-4 daily June 1 through August 31. The centerpiece of the new facility is the Historic Old Town Model, a 1:20 scale model showing Valdez as it appeared in 1963, just prior to the earthquake. The model is surrounded by exhibits interpreting this period of time and an interactive Earthquake Exhibit. Admission $1.50 for adults over 18. Located at 436 South Hazelet Street, across from Ruth Pond.

The busy small-boat harbor at Valdez. (© Tom Culkin)

Tour the oil pipeline terminus. The marine terminal of the trans-Alaska pipeline is across the bay from the city of Valdez. Two-hour bus tours of the pipeline terminal are available several times daily, from May to September, from Valdez Tours; fee charged, reservations suggested, cameras welcome. Phone (907) 835-2686 for details.

While entry to the terminal is restricted to authorized bus tours only, the drive out to the terminal is worthwhile. From Meals Avenue drive 6.8 miles out the Richardson Highway and turn right on the terminal access road (Dayville exit). The 5.4-mile road leading to the terminal passes Solomon Gulch dam and a spectacular view of Solomon Gulch Falls. There is also excellent fishing in season at Allison Point for pink and silver salmon. Entrance to the pipeline terminal is at the end of the road.

Outside the marine terminal gate is a bronze sculpture commemorating the efforts of men and women who built the trans-Alaska oil pipeline. Dedicated in September 1980, the sculpture was created by Californian Malcolm Alexander. It is composed of 5 figures representing various crafts and skills employed in the construction project. The work is the focal point of a small park from which visitors can watch tankers loading Alaska crude oil at the terminal. A small parking lot accommodates about 30 cars, and a series of signs explains the pipeline and terminal operations.

Take a boat tour to see Columbia Glacier, second largest tidewater glacier in North America, Shoup Glacier and other Prince William Sound attractions. Columbia Glacier, in Columbia Bay 28 miles southwest of Valdez, has become one of Alaska's best-known attractions. See ads in this section.

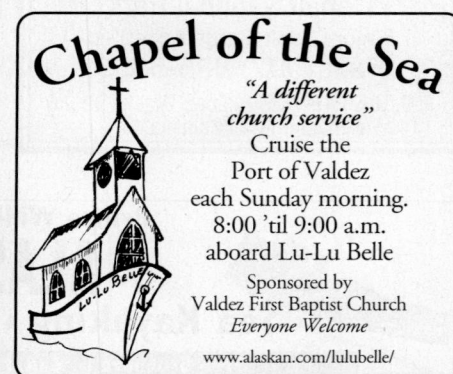

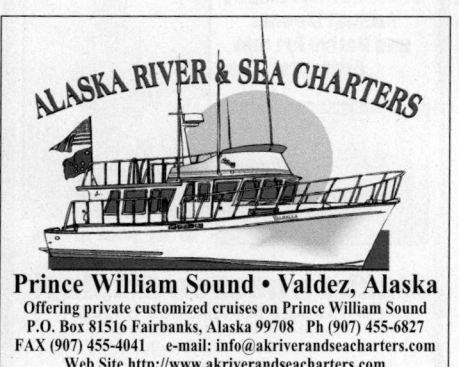

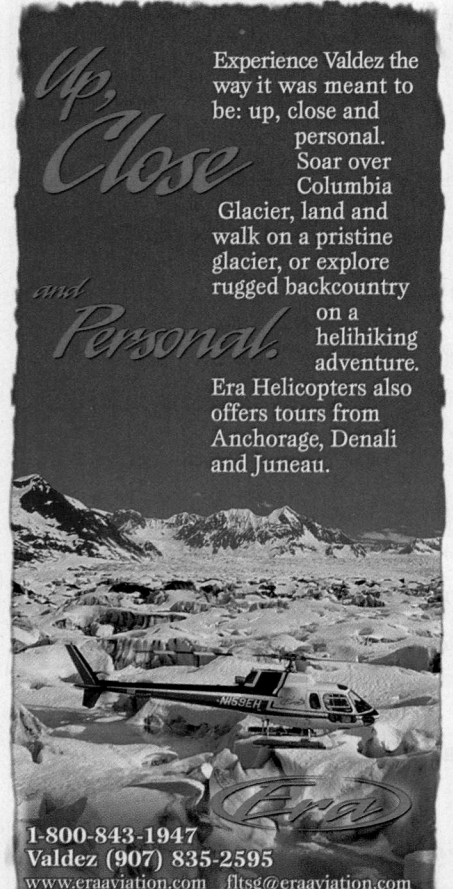

Sail, raft and kayak trips of Prince William Sound, Keystone Canyon and surrounding rivers are available. State marine parks in the Valdez area include Shoup Bay, Jack Bay and Sawmill Bay. Accessible mainly or only by water, these parks offer camping on tent platforms, fire rings and latrines. They are popular with fishermen and sea kayakers. For details on the marine parks, kayaking and public-use cabins, contact the Alaska State Parks office in Soldotna at (907) 262-5581.

Go flightseeing and see Columbia Glacier, spectacular Prince William Sound and the surrounding Chugach Mountains from the air. There are 3 flightseeing charter services in Valdez: 1 fixed-wing, 1 floatplane, and 1 helicopter; see ads in this section.

Our Point of View, an observation platform offering views of the original Valdez townsite, pipeline terminal and the town, is located by the Coast Guard office.

Valdez Consortium Library, located on Fairbanks Street, has an extensive Alaska Historical & Archive section, as well as many Alaska videos which can be viewed at the library. It also features a magazine and paperback exchange for travelers; a trade is appreciated but not required. The library has music listening booths, public computers, typewriters and a photocopier. Wheelchair accessible. Open Monday and Friday 10 A.M. to 6 P.M., Tuesday through Thursday 10 A.M. to 8 P.M., Saturday noon to 5 P.M. and Sunday 1–5 P.M. when school is in session. ♿

Visit Prince William Sound Community College, located at 303 Lowe St. Two huge wooden carvings on campus (1 located in front of the dorms on Pioneer Street), by artist Peter Toth, are dedicated to the Indians of America. Three Elderhostel programs are held at Prince William Sound Community College in July and August. This educational program (college credit given) is available for people over age 55. Subjects include Alaska history, wildlife and fisheries of Prince William Sound, and Alaska literature. Contact Elderhostel, 75 Federal St., Boston, MA 02110-1941, for more information on its Alaska programs. The College is also home to an extensive display of Old Town Valdez and Gold Rush-era photographs. The 7th annual **Edward Albee Theatre Conference**, sponsored by the college, will be held June 24–30, 2000, at the Valdez Convention and Civic Center. Expected guests for the conference include Edward Albee, event founder, and Horton Foote. Past visiting playwrights at the conference have included Edward Albee, Arthur Miller and August Wilson. For more information contact PWSCC, P.O. Box 97, Valdez, AK 99686.

View salmon spawning at Crooked Creek. From Meals Avenue drive 0.9 mileout the Richardson Highway to the Crooked Creek salmon spawning area and hatchery. A U.S. Forest Service information station, open Memorial Day to Labor Day, has interpretive displays and information on cultural history and recreation. An observation platform gives a close-up look at salmon spawning in midsummer and fall. This is also a waterfowl sanctuary and an excellent spot for watching various migrating birds.

Fish a Derby. The Valdez Chamber of Commerce holds a halibut, silver salmon and pink salmon derby every year, with cash prizes awarded to the first through third place winners for all 3 derbies daily, weekly and overall. (Halibut derby: May 13–September 3; pink salmon derby, June 25–July 29; silver salmon derby, July 30–September 3). For further information contact the Valdez Chamber of Commerce at (907) 835-2330.

See Boom Town, the historical comedy/musical review about Valdez. Evenings Tuesday–Saturday 8 P.M. at the Sugarloaf Saloon. Phone (907) 835-4988 for

An aerial view of Shoup Bay and Glacier, Prince William Sound.

(© Michael DeYoung)

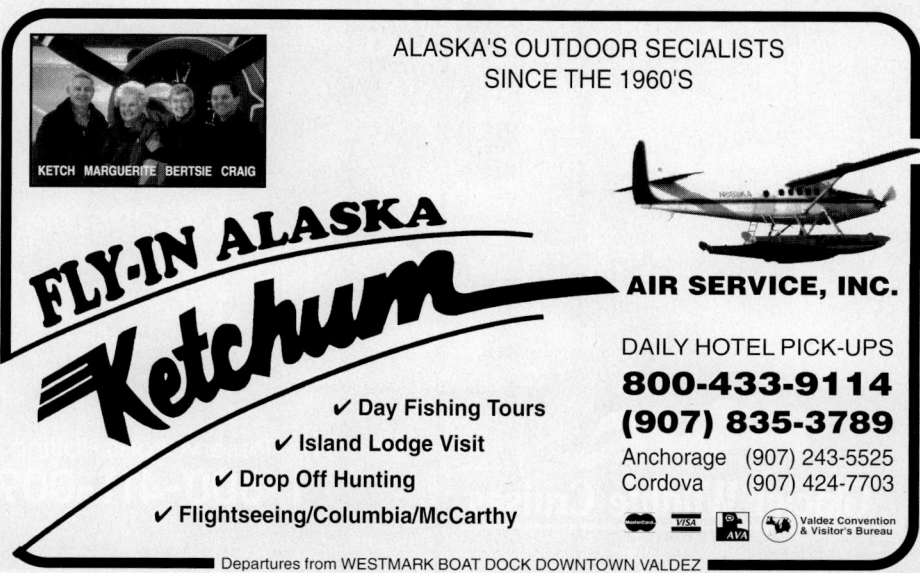

tickets.

Drive Mineral Creek Road. A 5.5-mile drive behind town leading northwest through the breathtaking alpine scenery along Mineral Creek. *Drive carefully!* This is a narrow road; conditions depend on weather and how recently the road has been graded. Bears are frequently sighted here. To reach Mineral Creek Road drive to the end of Hazelet Street toward the mountains and turn left on Hanagita then right on Mineral Creek Road. Excellent view of the city from the water tower hill just to the right at the start of Mineral Creek Road.

Visit the Alaska Cultural Center, home of the Jesse and Maxine Whitney Eskimo Museum. Visitors can see a magnificent collection of Alaskan trophy animal mounts, ivory carvings, Alaska Native artifacts, a film about the 1964 earthquake and much more. Small admission fee. Located at Valdez Airport. Phone (907) 834-1690 for details.

Go Hiking. Hiking for every level is available in the Valdez area. Stop by the Visitor Information Center for maps and descriptions.

The Alaska Division of Parks and Outdoor Recreation suggests hiking to one of the state marine parks in the Valdez area. From the Mineral Creek Trailhead in town to Shoup Bay State Marine Park, it is a 10-mile hike along spectacular Valdez Arm. Public-use cabins are available at Shoup Bay (permit required), which is noted for its views of Shoup Glacier and its large kittiwake colony. A popular short day hike is to Gold Creek, 3.5 miles from Valdez.

Bear Paw Trading Post Gift Shop, next to Bear Paw RV Park on Harbor Drive, features fine Alaska Native arts and crafts. Carved walrus ivory, scrimshaw, soapstone carvings, Native masks, fur items. Gold nugget jewelry, jade, hematite. Prints and books by Doug Lindstrand. Film, postcards, souvenirs, Alaska books. VISA, MasterCard accepted. Phone (907) 835-2530. [ADVERTISEMENT]

Era Helicopters Flightseeing Tours. One hour tours of Prince William Sound and the Columbia Glacier. Highlight your tour by landing at the face of Shoup Glacier. Personally guided Heli-hiking tours by local naturalist guides also available. Try our new Pilot's Choice tour available with glacier landing. Phone (907) 835-2595 locally or 1-800-843-1947. [ADVERTISEMENT]

Ketchum Air Service, Inc. Alaska's outdoor specialists. Floatplane tours/charters into Prince William Sound, Wrangell–St. Elias park. Day fishing/fully equipped. Columbia Glacier tour. Drop-off cabins. Kennecott Mine visit! Floatplane tour office located small-boat harbor, Valdez. Call or write for brochure. VISA, MasterCard. Phone (907) 835-3789 or (800) 433-9114. Box 670, Valdez, AK 99686. [ADVERTISEMENT]

Glacier Wildlife Cruises/*Lu-Lu Belle*. The motor yacht *Lu-Lu Belle* is probably the cleanest, plushest tour vessel you will ever see! We cater to adult travelers. When you come aboard and see all the teak, mahogany and oriental rugs, you will understand why Captain Rodolf asks you to wipe your shoes before boarding. The *Lu-Lu Belle* has wide walk-around decks, thus assuring everyone ample opportunity for unobstructed viewing and photography, and is equipped with 110-volt outlets for your battery chargers. Captain Rodolf has logged over 3,100 Columbia Glacier cruises since 1979; he will personally guide and narrate every cruise. The Columbia Glacier wildlife cruise of Prince William Sound is awesome. The wildlife that is seen on the cruises will vary, depending upon the time of year and time of day, as the *Lu-Lu Belle* cruises from Valdez to Columbia Glacier on the calm, protected waters of the Sound. We guarantee no seasickness. Boarding time is 1:45 P.M. each day from Memorial Day through mid-August. This "5 hour" cruise will vary in duration as much as an hour, because Captain Rodolf will run offshore, in search of whales and other wildlife. Cost is $75 per person (with a cash discount price of $70). During the busier part of the season, an 8 A.M. cruise, boarding at 7:45, is added, each day except Sunday. On Sunday morning the *Lu-Lu Belle* becomes the "Chapel of the Sea" from 8 to 9 A.M. Everyone is welcome. On the trip the crew prepares fresh-baked goods in the galley. Friendliness and gracious hospitality on a beautiful yacht with small intimate groups is the reason why people refer to the *Lu-Lu Belle* as "the limousine of Prince William Sound." Our best advertisement is our happy guests. Join us for an extra-special day and find out why Captain Rodolf refers to Switzerland as the "Valdez of Europe!" Phone (800) 411-0090 or (907) 835-5141. [ADVERTISEMENT]

Harbor Reservations serves as the ticket office for all Prince William Sound glacier tours (*Lu-Lu Belle* too!) in Valdez. Information can be obtained on fishing, helicopter tours and other attractions. Find them at the Valdez Harbor, on the corner of Harbor Drive and Wrangell; hours are from 7 A.M. to 11 P.M. Call toll free (800) 830-4302 or visit them on the web at http://www.valdezalaska.com. [ADVERTISEMENT]

Northern Comfort Charters operates 3 boats designed for your fishing comfort and pleasure. For halibut (and a wide variety of other bottom-feeding fish) the 43-foot *Lady Luck* features a comfortable, warm, cabin, full restroom and a 360 degree all-around fishing deck. The 44-foot *Northern Comfort* is more suitable for 2-day overnight charters and is an excellent boat for silver salmon fishing, featuring a full fishing deck cover, large comfortable cabin and full restroom. Enjoy the excellent fishing and scenery of the Prince William Sound. Phone (800) 478-9884 or (907) 835-3070. See our display ad this section. [ADVERTISEMENT]

Prince William Sound Cruises & Tour. Join Prince William Sound Cruises & Tours as we explore the wonders of Prince William Sound. Experience the famous Columbia Glacier, the largest tidewater glacier in Southcentral Alaska. Explore glacier-carved

fjords draped with cascading waterfalls and spectacular alpine glaciers. Watch for sea otters, sea lions, seals, porpoise, orca and giant humpback whales, plus a wide variety of birds. Our experienced, knowledgeable captains and crew are your guides as you travel aboard our custom sightseeing vessels complete with heated indoor seating, oversized windows, and outside viewing decks. All cruises are fully narrated and include a delicious meal. Only with Prince William Sound Cruises and Tours do you have the option to stop at a wilderness island for a delicious Alaskan buffet. Travelers looking for a true wilderness adventure are invited to stay overnight to relax, hike, canoe, or kayak around this amazing landscape. Daily departures from Valdez and Whittier. Toll free 800-992-1297 or 907-835-4731 or visit us on the web at www.princewilliamsound.com. [ADVERTISEMENT] ♿

Visit Dock Point Park. Located at the east end of the Valdez boat harbor, off North Harbor Drive, this park includes picnic tables, a restroom and a beautiful 1-mile hiking/walking trail with scenic overlooks of the Port of Valdez. The combination gravel and boardwalk trail provides easy access for people of all ability levels.

Valdez Arm supports the largest sport fishery in Prince William Sound. Important species include pink salmon, coho (silver) salmon, halibut, rockfish and Dolly Varden. Charter boats are available in Valdez.

A hot fishing spot near Valdez and accessible by road is the **Allison Point** fishery (or "Winnebago Point" as it is known locally) created by the Solomon Gulch Hatchery, which produces major pink and silver salmon returns annually. Turn off the Richardson Highway at **Milepost V 2.9.** It is one of the largest pink salmon fisheries in the state. Pink salmon returns are best in odd years, but with hatchery production good pink runs are anticipated every year. Pinks average 3–5 lbs., from late June to early August. Silvers from 6–10 lbs., late July into September.

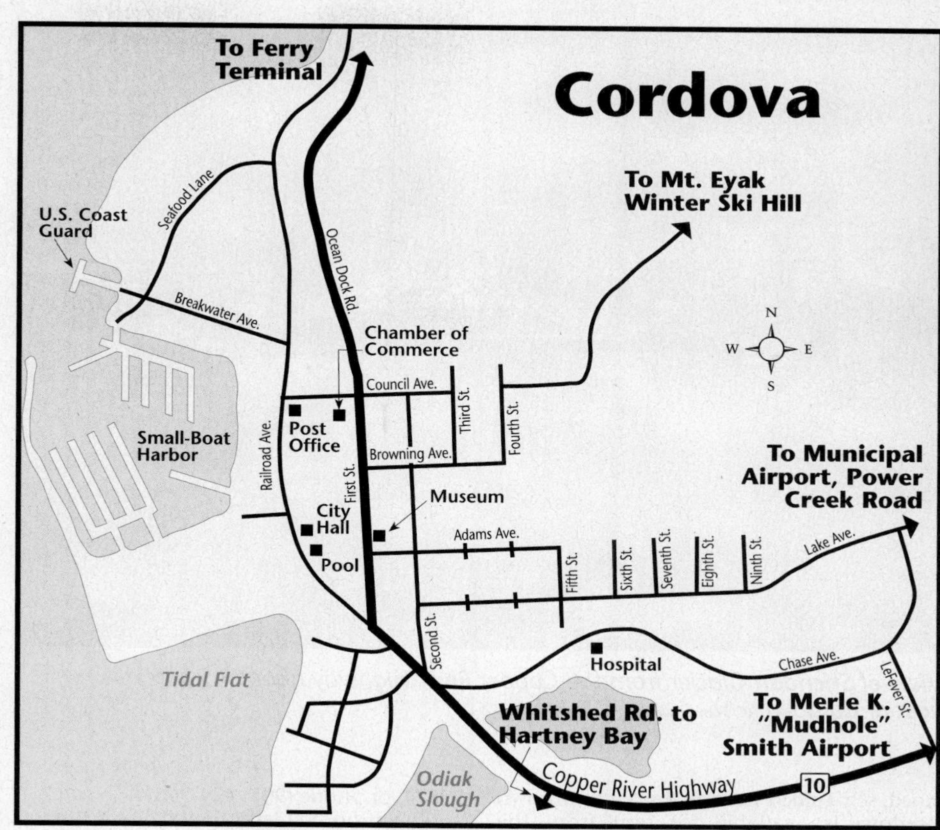

Cordova

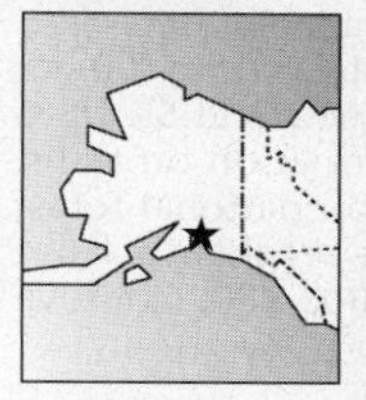

Located on the east side of Prince William Sound on Orca Inlet. **Population:** 2,435. **Emergency Services: Alaska State Troopers**, phone (907) 424-7331, emergency phone 911. **Police, Fire Department, Ambulance**, phone (907) 424-6100, emergency phone 911. **Hospital**, phone (907) 424-8000.

Visitor Information: Chamber of Commerce, 404 1st Street; phone (907) 424-7260 or write Box 99, Cordova, AK 99574. E-mail: cchamber@ptialaska.net. Web site: www.ptialaska.net/~cchamber. A one-hour audio-

CORDOVA ADVERTISERS

Cordova Air Service, Inc. ..Ph. (907) 424-3289
Cordova Chamber of Commerce ....Ph. (907) 424-7260
Cordova Outboard, Inc.....Ph. (907) 424-3220
Powder House Bar and Restaurant ....Ph. (907) 424-3529
Prince William Motel ....Ph. (907) 424-3201

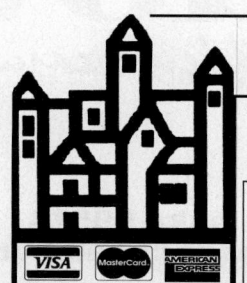

View of Sheridan Glacier from the Copper River Highway about 15 miles east of Cordova. (© Tom Culkin)

taped, self-guided walking tour of downtown Cordova is available for rent from the Chamber of Commerce and museum. A self-guided walking tour map of Cordova historic sites, prepared by the Cordova Historical Society, is also available.

Chugach National Forest Cordova Ranger District office is located at 612 2nd St. USFS personnel can provide information on trails, cabins and other activities on national forest lands. The office is open weekdays from 8 A.M. to 5 P.M. Write P.O. Box 280, Cordova 99574, or phone (907) 424-7661.

Elevation: Sea level to 400 feet. **Climate:** Average temperature in July is 65°F/18°C, in January 21°F/-6°C. Average annual precipitation is 167 inches. During the winter of 1998-99, Cordova had almost 200 inches of snow, the largest amount since the record-breaking winter of 1971-72, when 275 inches fell. Prevailing winds are easterly at about 4 knots. **Radio:** KLAM-AM, KCHU-FM (National Public Radio), KCDV-FM. **Television:** Cable. **Newspaper:** *Cordova Times* (weekly).

Private Aircraft: Merle K. "Mudhole" Smith Airport, 11.3 miles southeast; elev. 42 feet; length 7,500 feet; asphalt; attended. Cordova Municipal (city airfield), 0.9 mile east; elev. 12 feet; length 1,900 feet; gravel; fuel 100, 100LL; unattended. Eyak Lake seaplane base, 0.9 mile east.

It was the Spanish explorer Don Salvador Fidalgo who named the adjacent water Puerto Cordoba in 1790. The town was named Cordova by Michael J. Heney, builder of the Copper River & Northwestern Railway. By 1889, the town had grown into a fish camp and cannery site. A post office was established in 1906. Cordova was incorporated in 1909.

One of the first producing oil fields in Alaska was located at Katalla, 47 miles/76 km southeast of Cordova on the Gulf of Alaska. The discovery was made in 1902 and the field produced until 1933.

The town was chosen as the railroad terminus and ocean shipping port for copper ore shipped by rail from the Kennecott mines near Kennicott and McCarthy. The railroad and town prospered until 1938 when the mine closed.

Commercial fishing has now supplanted mining as the basis of the town's economy. The fishing fleet can be seen at Cordova harbor, home port of the MV *Bartlett* and the USCG cutter *Sweetbrier.* Also at the harbor is the Cordova Fishermen's Memorial, *The Southeasterly*.

The fishing and canning season for salmon runs from about May to September, with red, king and silver (coho) salmon taken from the Copper River area, chum, red and pink salmon from Prince William Sound. Black cod, crab and shrimp season runs during winter. Dungeness crab season runs during the summer and early fall months. Halibut and herring are also processed.

Lodging & Services

Cordova has 2 motels and 2 hotels, 11 bed and breakfasts, 6 restaurants, 2 laundromats and a variety of shopping facilities.

The historic Skater's Cabin on Eyak Lake is available for rent from the city. The rustic cabin has a woodstove and outhouse. The fee is $25 per night. Contact Bidarki Recreation Center, phone (907) 424-7282.

The U.S. Forest Service maintains 17 cabins in the Cordova district. Three are accessible by trail, the rest by boat or plane. Phone 1-877-444-6777 for current fees, reservations and information.

Camping

Cordova has one campground, Odiak Camper Park, located on Whitshed Road and operated by the city. The camper park has 24 RV sites and a tenting area. Free shower tokens are available for paying campers. Contact Cordova's city hall at (907) 424-6200. ▲

Transportation

Cordova is accessible only by plane or boat.

Air: Scheduled service via Alaska Airlines and Era Aviation. Five air taxi services based at the municipal airport, Mile 13 airport and Eyak Lake offer charter and flightseeing service.

Ferry: The Alaska Marine Highway system ferries connect Cordova with Valdez, Whittier and Seward. Phone (907) 424-7333.

Taxi: Local service available.

Car Rental: Available locally.

Highways: The Alaska state highway system does not connect to Cordova. The Copper River Highway leads 48 miles east and north of Cordova, ending at the Million Dollar Bridge and Childs Glacier. (See the COPPER RIVER HIGHWAY section.)

Private Boats: Cordova has an 850-slip boat harbor serving recreational boaters as well as the commercial fishing fleet. Berth arrangements may be made by contacting the harbormaster's office at (907) 424-6400 or on VHF Channel 16.

Attractions

Cordova's Museum and Library, at 622 1st St., are connected by a central entryway. "Where Cultures Meet" is the theme of the museum. Native artifacts such as stone implements, a dugout canoe and skin bidarka (kayak) represent the rich Native culture. One display tells of early explorers to the area, including Vitus Bering, who claimed Alaska for Russia in 1741. Exhibits of the later mining and railroad era explain the development of the copper mines and of the town. Exhibits include a diorama of a vintage fishing vessel. The museum displays original work by Alaskan artists Sydney Laurence, Eustace Ziegler and Jules Dahlager, who all worked in Cordova. The Cordova Historical Society operates a small gift shop at the museum, featuring books of local interest and Alaskan crafts.

Admission to the museum is $1. Open Memorial Day to Labor Day, 10 A.M.–6 P.M. Monday through Saturday, 2–4 P.M. on Sunday; Tuesday–Friday, 1–5 P.M. and Saturday 2–4 P.M. the rest of the year. Tours can be arranged. Write P.O. Box 391 or phone (907) 424-6665 for more information. Library hours are 1–8 P.M. Tuesday through Saturday.

Swim in the Bob Korn Memorial Swimming Pool, Cordova's Olympic-sized pool, located on Railroad Avenue below Main Street. Open year-round to the public. Check locally for hours.

Mount Eyak Ski Area. Ski Hill is usually open for skiing mid-December to the end of April, depending on weather. Winter schedule is Wednesday, Saturday, Sunday and holidays, 9 A.M. to dusk. Phone (907) 424-7766 for further information. To reach the chair lift from 4th Avenue, take Council Avenue 1 block, then follow Ski Hill Road to top (about 1 mile from Main Street).

The single chair lift rises 880 feet/268m up Mount Eyak and overlooks the town and harbor from 1,600 feet. Walk up, take a cab, take the tour bus or drive your own vehicle. A hiking trail from the base of the mountain to top of the chair lift and beyond connects with Forest Service Crater Lake trail.

Visit the USFS office at 612 2nd St. Erected in 1925, it is the original federal building for the town of Cordova. Natural history display in 2nd floor Interpretive Center. The USFS office is next to the old courtroom and jail. Open weekdays 8 A.M. to 5 P.M.

Copper River Delta Shorebird Festival, May 10-14, 2000, offers 5 days of birding along the tidal mudflats and wetlands of the Copper River Delta and the rocky shoreline of Prince William Sound. The festival includes workshops, community activities and numerous field trip opportunities. Contact the Chamber of Commerce, Box 99, Cordova 99574, for details; or phone (907) 424-7260.

Attend the Iceworm Festival: Held the first full weekend of February, this festival offers a parade, art show, variety show, dances, craft show, ski events, survival suit race, beard judging and a King and Queen of Iceworm contest. Highlight is the 100-foot-long "iceworm" that winds its way through the streets of Cordova. Contact Darrel Olsen, P.O. Box 768, Cordova, AK 99574; phone (907) 424-5756 for more information.

Whitshed Road leads out past the miniature lighthouse (Mile 0.4) to a large mudflat at Hartney Bay (Mile 5.5). The lighthouse is privately owned and maintained by the McDowells, who also operate a bed and breakfast in their home: a converted barge. Hartney Bay is part of the 300,000-acre Copper River Delta mudflats. The delta is one of the most important stopover places in the Western Hemisphere for the largest shorebird migration in the world. Birders can view up to 31 different species as millions of shorebirds pass through the delta each spring.

Power Creek Road, from the corner of Lake and Chase avenues, leads out past the municipal airport to Crater Lake trailhead and Skaters Cabin picnic area (Mile 1.2), continues to Hatchery Creek salmon spawning channel (Mile 5.7), and ends at the Power Creek trailhead (Mile 6.9). The Crater Lake trailhead is directly northwest of the Eyak Lake Skaters Cabin. The 2.4-mile trail climbs to 1,500 feet. Excellent views, alpine lake with fishing for stocked rainbow trout. Watch for bears. Visitors may view spawning salmon at the Hatchery Creek channel in July and August. Power Creek trail, 4.2 miles long, accesses both the USFS public-use cabin in Power Creek Basin and a ridge that connects with the Crater Lake trail creating a 12-mile loop. Power Creek trail offers spectacular scenery, with waterfalls, hanging glaciers and views of Power Creek Basin (called "surprise valley" by locals), the Chugach Range and Prince William Sound. Excellent berry picking. Watch for bears.

Drive the Copper River Highway to see the Million Dollar Bridge, Childs Glacier and the Copper River Delta. The 48-mile highway leads east from Cordova through the Delta to the historic Million Dollar Bridge, built in 1909–10, and Childs Glacier. Viewing platform and picnic area at Childs Glacier. Wildlife seen along the highway includes brown and black bear, moose, beaver, mountain goats, trumpeter swans and numerous other species of birds. See COPPER RIVER HIGHWAY section for log of road.

AREA FISHING: According to the ADF&G, "Saltwater fishing in **Orca Inlet** and adjacent eastern Prince William Sound is accessible from Cordova. Species include halibut, rockfish and 5 species of salmon. Trolling for salmon is best for kings in the winter and spring, and silvers in the summer and fall. Boat charters are available locally. Road-accessible fishing opportunities exist for salmon in salt water at **Fleming Spit/Lagoon**, near the ferry terminal off Orca Bay Road. Strong runs of hatchery-enhanced kings (in the spring) and silvers (August and September) return to this terminal fishery.

"Road-accessible freshwater fishing is also good in the Cordova Area. **Eyak River** supports strong returns of sockeye during June and July and silvers in August and September. The area at the outlet of the lake, where the road crosses, is fly-fishing only. Several streams along the **Copper River** Highway between Eyak Lake and the Million Dollar Bridge also support runs of sockeye and coho. These streams include **Clear Creek**, **Alaganik Slough**, **Eighteen-mile Creek** and **Twenty-mile Creek**. In addition, cutthroat trout and Dolly Varden are present in most of these streams. Lake fishing for sockeye salmon, Dolly Varden and cutthroat trout is available in **McKinley Lake** and the **Pipeline Lake** system. Fly-out fishing from Cordova is also popular for salmon, Dolly Varden and cutthroat trout. Charter operators are available locally." See also the COPPER RIVER HIGHWAY section for area fishing.

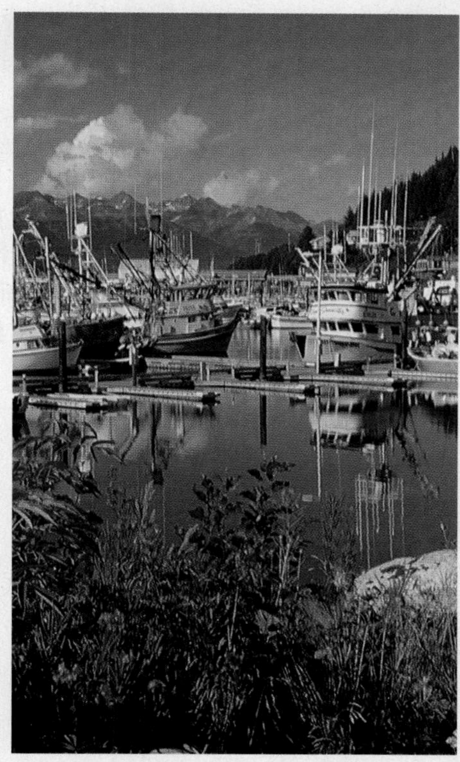

Cordova's boat harbor serves recreational boaters as well as the commercial fishing fleet. (© Susan Cole Kelly)

EDGERTON HIGHWAY/ McCARTHY ROAD

(10)

Connects: Richardson Highway Junction to McCarthy, AK
Length: 93 miles **Road Surface:** 40% paved, 60% gravel
Season: McCarthy Road not maintained in winter
Major Attraction: Wrangell–St. Elias National Park & Preserve

	Chitina	McCarthy	Richardson Hwy.
Chitina		60	33
McCarthy	60		93
Richardson Hwy.	33	93	

The 1,378-foot Copper River bridge provides access to McCarthy and Kennicott.

(© Mike Jones)

The Edgerton Highway, known locally as the Edgerton Cutoff, is a scenic paved road leading 35 miles east from its junction with the Richardson Highway to Chitina, then across the Copper River bridge to the start of the McCarthy Road. Total driving distance from the Richardson Highway turnoff to the end of the McCarthy Road is 93.4 miles. The Edgerton Highway is named for U.S. Army Maj. Glenn Edgerton of the Alaska Territorial Road Commission.

The gravel McCarthy Road leads 58.3 miles east from Chitina and dead ends at the Kennicott River, about 1 mile west of the settlement of McCarthy. The Kennicott River crossing is by 2 foot bridges. There is no vehicle access across the river.

The McCarthy Road follows the right-of-way of the old Copper River & Northwestern Railway. Begun in 1907, the CR&NW (also referred to as the "can't run and never will") was built to carry copper ore from the Kennecott Mines to Cordova. It took 4 years to complete the railway. The railway and mine ceased operation in 1938.

The McCarthy Road is recommended for the adventurous traveler and only in the summer. Maximum speed is about 25 mph. Motorists with large vehicles or trailers should exercise caution, especially in wet weather. Watch for old railroad spikes in the roadbed. Unless recently graded, watch for potholes, soft spots and severe washboard. Tire repair and mechanical light-towing service are available at Silver Lake Campground, **Milepost J 9.3**.

Most land along the McCarthy Road is either privately or publicly held. Local residents have asked that visitors please help protect water sources from contamination.

The solitude and scenery of McCarthy, along with the historic Kennecott Mine and surrounding wilderness of Wrangell–St. Elias National Park and Preserve, have drawn increasing numbers of visitors to this area. It is a 126-mile drive from Glennallen to McCarthy, 315 miles from Anchorage.

The National Park Service ranger station in Chitina has information on current road conditions and also on backcountry travel in Wrangell–St. Elias National Park and Preserve.

Emergency medical services: Between the junction of the Richardson and Edgerton highways and McCarthy, contact the Copper River EMS in Glennallen, phone 911 or (907) 822-3203.

Edgerton Highway Log

Distance from junction with Richardson Highway (R) is followed by distance from junction with McCarthy Road (M).

ALASKA ROUTE 10

R 0 M 35.1 (56.5 km) The Edgerton Highway leads east from the Richardson Highway.

Junction of the Edgerton Highway (Alaska Route 10) and the Richardson Highway (Alaska Route 4). Turn to **Milepost V 82.6** in the Richardson HIGHWAY for log of that route

Edgerton Highway begins long downgrade eastbound. Excellent view of Mount Drum (to the northeast), a 12,010-foot peak of the Wrangell Mountains. Mount Wrangell (elev. 14,163 feet) and Mount Blackburn (elev. 16,390 feet) are visible straight ahead.

R 5.1 (8.2 km) **M 30** (48.3 km) Kenny Lake Fire Station.

R 5.2 (8.4 km) **M 29.9** (48.1 km) Kenny Lake School to the south. **KENNY LAKE** (pop. 507) is an unincorporated agricultural community located along the Edgerton Highway between mile 1 and Mile 17. There are 2 schools.

R 5.3 (8.5 km) **M 29.8** (48 km) Paved turnout to north.

R 7.2 (11.6 km) **M 27.9** (44.9 km) Kenny Lake Mercantile & RV Park to north with grocery store, cafe, gas, laundromat, showers, camping and pay phone.

Kenny Lake Mercantile & RV Park. See display ad this section. ▲

R 7.3 (11.7 km) **M 27.8** (44.7 km) Old Edgerton Loop Road (gravel) leads from here 8 miles through homestead and farm country to the Richardson Highway at **Milepost V 91.1**.

R 7.5 (12.1 km) **M 27.6** (44.4 km) Kenny Lake community hall, fairgrounds.

R 7.7 (12.4 km) **M 27.4** (44.1 km) Long double-ended paved rest area to south with picnic table on shore of Kenny Lake.

R 9.5 (15.3 km) **M 25.6** (41.2 km) Golden Spruce Cabins; lodging.

R 12.3 (19.8 km) **M 22.8** (36.7 km) Paved turnout to south. Tonsina River BLM trailhead, 2 miles.

R 12.5 (20.1 km) **M 22.6** (36.4 km) Paved turnout to north. Copper River BLM trail-

EDGERTON HIGHWAY/McCARTHY ROAD

Richardson Highway to McCarthy, AK

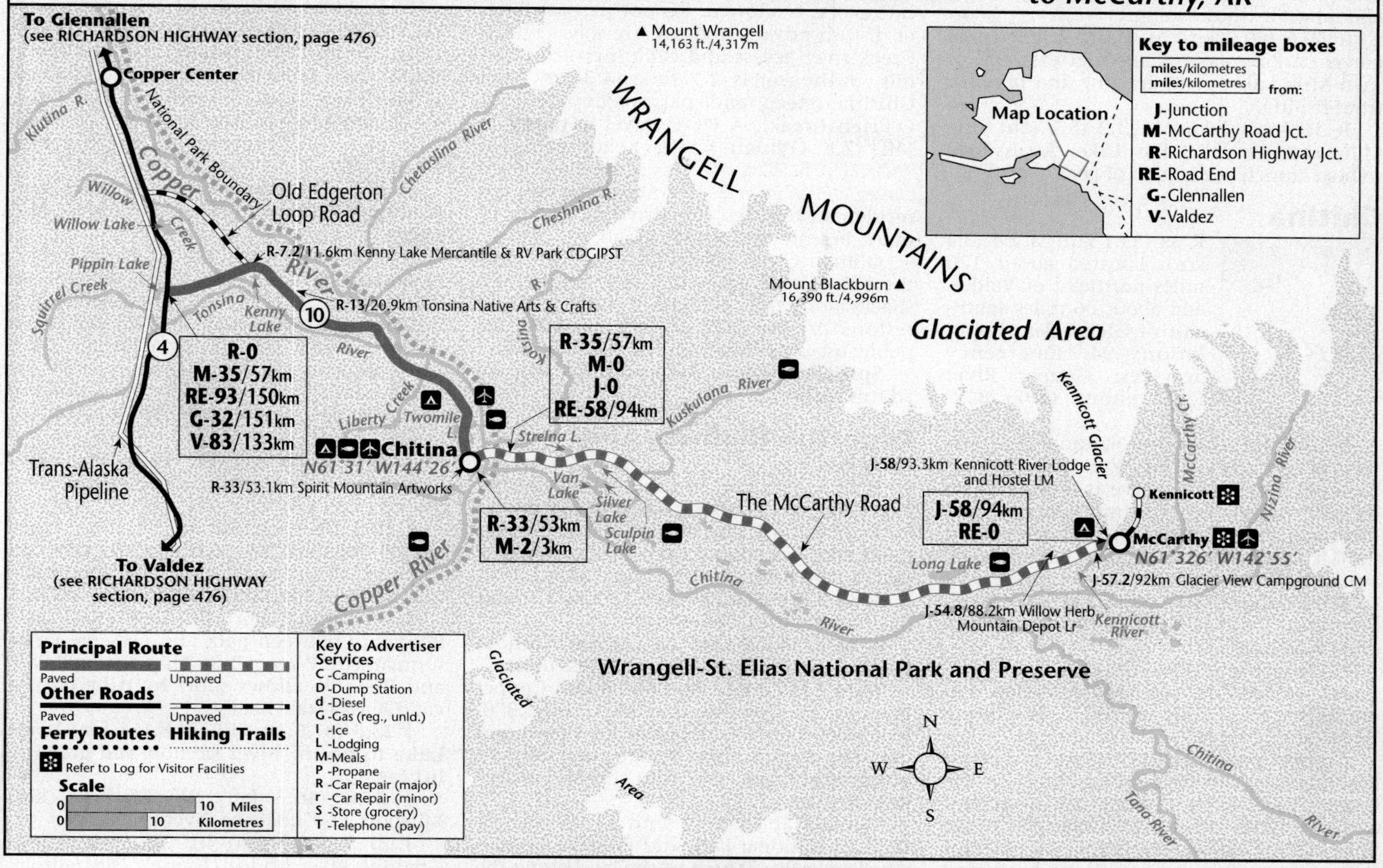

To Glennallen (see RICHARDSON HIGHWAY section, page 476)

Copper Center
National Park Boundary
Klutina R.
Copper River
Willow Creek
Willow Lake
Old Edgerton Loop Road
Chetaslina River
Cheshnina R.
Mount Wrangell 14,163 ft./4,317m
WRANGELL MOUNTAINS
Mount Blackburn 16,390 ft./4,996m
Glaciated Area
R-7.2/11.6km Kenny Lake Mercantile & RV Park CDGIPST
Pippin Lake
Squirrel Creek
Tonsina River
Kenny Lake
R-13/20.9km Tonsina Native Arts & Crafts
Kotsina R.
Kuskulana River
Kennicott Glacier
McCarthy Cr.
Nizina River

R-0
M-35/57km
RE-93/150km
G-32/151km
V-83/133km

R-35/57km
M-0
J-0
RE-58/94km

Liberty Creek
Twomile L.
Strelna L.
Trans-Alaska Pipeline
Chitina N61°31' W144°26'
R-33/53.1km Spirit Mountain Artworks
Van Lake
Silver Lake
Sculpin Lake

R-33/53km
M-2/3km

The McCarthy Road
J-58/93.3km Kennicott River Lodge and Hostel LM
Kennicott

J-58/94km
RE-0

McCarthy N61°326' W142°55'
Long Lake
J-57.2/92km Glacier View Campground CM
J-54.8/88.2km Willow Herb Mountain Depot Lr
Kennicott River
Chitina River
To Valdez (see RICHARDSON HIGHWAY section, page 476)
Copper River
Glaciated Area
Wrangell-St. Elias National Park and Preserve
Tana River
Chitina River

Key to mileage boxes
miles/kilometres
miles/kilometres from:
J-Junction
M-McCarthy Road Jct.
R-Richardson Highway Jct.
RE-Road End
G-Glennallen
V-Valdez

Map Location

Principal Route — Paved / Unpaved
Other Roads — Paved / Unpaved
Ferry Routes
Hiking Trails
Refer to Log for Visitor Facilities
Scale 0 — 10 Miles; 0 — 10 Kilometres

Key to Advertiser Services
C -Camping
D -Dump Station
d -Diesel
G -Gas (reg., unld.)
I -Ice
L -Lodging
M-Meals
P -Propane
R -Car Repair (major)
r -Car Repair (minor)
S -Store (grocery)
T -Telephone (pay)

head, 5 miles.

R 13 (20.9 km) **M 22.2** (35.7 km) **Tonsina Native Arts & Crafts.** See display ad this section.

R 18 (29 km) **M 17.1** (27.5 km) Steep downhill grade eastbound. Views of the Copper River and bluffs to north.

R 19.4 (31.2 km) **M 15.7** (25.3 km) Tonsina River bridge. Highway climbs eastbound; winding road.

R 19.5 (31.4 km) **M 15.6** (25.1 km) Turnout to north.

R 19.6 (31.5 km) **M 15.5** (24.9 km) Double-ended turnout at lake to north.

R 21.6 (34.8 km) **M 13.5** (21.7 km) Paved viewpoint to north above Copper River.

R 22 (35.4 km) **M 13.1** (21.1 km) Top of hill. Steep winding descents both directions.

R 23.5 (37.8 km) **M 11.6** (18.7 km) Liberty Falls Creek BLM trailhead to south.

R 23.7 (38.1 km) **M 11.4** (18.3 km) Liberty Creek bridge (8-ton load limit) and **Liberty Falls State Recreation Site**. The campground is just south of the highway on the banks of Liberty Creek, near the foot of the thundering falls. Scenic spot. Loop road through campground (large RVs and trailers check road before driving in); 5 sites, no water, no camping fee. Berry picking; watch for bears. ▲

R 28.5 (45.9 km) **M 6.6** (10.6 km) Side road north to Chitina DOT/PF maintenance station and Chitina Airport. ADF&G office (dip net permits).

Private Aircraft: Chitina Airport; elev. 556 feet; length 2,800 feet; gravel; unattended.

R 29.5 (47.5 km) **M 5.7** (9.2 km) Small

gravel turnout by Three Mile Lake.

R 29.7 (47.8 km) **M 5.4** (8.7 km) Paved turnout by **Three Mile Lake**; good grayling and rainbow trout fishing.

R 30.6 (49.2 km) **M 4.5** (7.2 km) Large gravel parking area to south at east end of **Two Mile Lake**; good grayling and rainbow trout fishing.

R 31.9 (51.3 km) **M 3.2** (5.1 km) One Mile Lake (also called First Lake). Access road to boat launch at east end of lake.

Chitina

R 33 (53.1 km) **M 2.1** (3.4 km). Located about 120 miles northeast of Valdez, and about 66 miles southeast of Glennallen. **Population:** 94. **Emergency Services:** Copper River EMS, phone (907) 822-3203.

Visitor Information: National Park Service ranger station for Wrangell–St. Elias National Park and Preserve is housed in an historic cabin in Chitina. Open daily, Memorial Day to Labor Day. A slide show on the McCarthy Road and video programs are available. Write Box 439, Copper Center, AK 99573, or phone (907) 822-5234 (park headquarters); Chitina ranger station, phone (907) 823-2205.

Chitina has a post office, grocery, gas, motel, restaurant, tire repair service and phone service. Public restrooms at Chitina Wayside.

Chitina (pronounced CHIT-na) was established about 1908 as a railroad stop on the Copper River & Northwestern Railway and as a supply town for the Kennecott Copper Mines at McCarthy. A surveying engineer for the mines, Otto Adrian Nelson, owned much of the town in 1914, which consisted of 5 hotels, a general store, movie theater and several bars, restaurants and dance halls. When the mine and railroad were abandoned in 1938, Chitna became a ghost town. Pioneer bush pilot "Mudhole" Smith bought the Nelson estate in 1963 and sold off the townsite and buildings.

Today, few of the original buildings remain except for the tinsmith, now on the National Register of Historic Places, which houses Spirit Mountain Artworks.

Most residents are involved in subsistance activities, and a big attraction is the seasonal salmon run (reds, kings or silvers) on the **Copper River**, which draws hundreds of dip-netters (and spectators) from around the state. The dip-net fishery for salmon runs June through September (depending on harvest levels), and it's worth the trip to see fish wheels and dip nets in action. This fishery is open only to Alaska residents with a personal-use or subsistence permit. Check with the Chitina ADF&G office for details and current regulations.

O'Brien Creek Road provides a state right-of-way access to popular fishing areas on large sandbars along the Copper River. Access to the Copper River is not permitted across private land. Access is permitted only at O'Brien Creek and Haley Creek and prohibited elsewhere unless official signs indicate access is allowed. Do not trespass, litter or disturb private lands in any way. O'Brien Creek river access and camping (litter barrels, outhouse) is 2.7 miles/4.3 km from Chitina (steep and narrow downhill to O'Brien Creek). A DOT travel advisory at Mile 2.8 O'Brien Creek Road warns of *"narrow road, rock slides, creek crossings, sharp curves and steep dropoffs."* According to local residents, vehicles can drive in about 17 miles, but the road is very rough.

O'Brien Creek Road follows a portion of the old railroad grade to Cordova. The line shacks along this old right-of-way have been restored by the DOT and are available for public use on a first-come, first-served basis.

Spirit Mountain Artworks. See display ad this section.

Edgerton Highway Log
(continued)

R 33.5 (53.9 km) **M 1.7** (2.7 km) **Chitina Wayside**; paved parking area and restrooms.

R 33.6 (54.1 km) **M 1.6** (2.6 km) Pavement ends eastbound. No road maintenance east of here between Oct. 15 and May 15.

R 33.8 (54.4 km) **M 1.4** (2.3 km) Turnout overlooking the Copper River.

R 34.1 (54.9 km) **M 1.1** (1.8 km) Turnout overlooking the Copper River. Access to river.

R 34.7 (55.8 km) **M 0.5** (0.8 km) Copper River bridge. Completed in 1971, this 1,378-foot steel span was designed for year-round use. The $3.5 million bridge reestablished access across the river into the McCarthy–Kennicott area.

Game Management Unit 11. Wrangell–St. Elias National Park and Preserve boundary. Sign reads: "Much of the land along the road is private owned. For land ownership information, contact Chitina Village Corp. (907/823-2223), Ahtna Inc. (907/822-3476) or the National Park Service (907/822-5234)."

R 35.1 (56.5 km) **M 0 Junction** with McCarthy Road (log follows). Access to fishing and camping on the **Copper River**; red and king salmon.

McCarthy Road Log

Distance from junction with the Edgerton Highway (J) is followed by distance from road end (RE).

Traditional mileposts used by local residents are indicated in the log.

ALASKA ROUTE 10

J 0 RE 58.3 (93.8 km) **Junction** with the Edgerton Highway.

J 3.4 (5.5 km) **RE 54.9** (88.4 km) Turnouts overlooking the Chitina River next 0.1 mile eastbound.

J 8.3 (13.4 km) **RE 50** (80.5 km) **Milepost 10.** Physical mileposts indicate distance from Chitina. Trail opposite homestead leads 0.3 mile/0.5 km north to **Strelna Lake**; rainbow trout and silver salmon. (Private property adjacent trail.)

J 9.2 (14.8 km) **RE 49.1** (79 km) **Milepost 11.** Private campground on **Silver Lake** to south; rainbow trout fishing, boat and canoe rentals, boat launch, tire repair. Trail access to **Van Lake,** located south of Silver Lake; good rainbow trout fishing.

J 14.4 (23.2 km) **RE 43.9** (70.6 km) Milepost 16.

J 15.5 (24.9 km) **RE 42.8** (68.9 km) Turnout with view of Kuskulana River and bridge.

J 15.6 (25.1 km) **RE 42.7** (68.7 km) **Kuskulana Bridge** (1-lane). This old railroad bridge (built in 1910) is approximately 525 feet long and 385 feet above the river. It is a narrow 3-span steel railway bridge with wood decking. Rehabilitated in 1988 for vehicle traffic. People were bungee jumping off the bridge in summer 1999. Road access to river at west end.

J 17.1 (27.5 km) **RE 41.2** (66.3 km) *CAUTION: Very narrow road next mile eastbound.*

J 22.3 (35.9 km) **RE 36** (57.9 km) Large gravel turnout to south with view of Wrangell Mountains. There are several turnouts between here and the Kennicott River.

J 22.5 (36.2 km) **RE 35.8** (57.6 km) Boundary between park and preserve lands (unmarked). Wrangell–St. Elias National Park and Preserve allows sport hunting with a valid Alaska state license.

J 23.5 (37.8 km) **RE 34.8** (56 km) **Lou's Lake** to north; silver salmon and grayling fishing.

J 25.3 (40.7 km) **RE 33** (53.1 km) Milepost 27. Chokosna River bridge.

J 27.5 (44.3 km) **RE 30.8** (49.6 km) Gilahina River bridge (1-lane). Old railroad trestle and parking.

J 28 (45 km) **RE 30.3** (48.8 km) Turnout to south.

J 34 (54.7 km) **RE 24.3** (39.1 km) Turnout by lake.)

J 34.5 (55.5 km) **RE 23.8** (38.3 km) *CAUTION: Road narrows eastbound; heavy brush along both sides. Watch for bears.*

J 36.5 (58.7 km) **RE 21.8** (35.1 km) Milepost 38.

J 40 (64.4 km) **RE 18.3** (29.4 km) Milepost 42.

J 42.4 (68.2 km) **RE 15.9** (25.6 km) Turnout to south.

J 42.6 (68.5 km) **RE 15.7** (25.3 km) One-lane wood-plank bridge (max. height 13′2″) over Lakina River. Access to river at east end.

Long Lake Wildlife Refuge sign; shooting prohibited eastbound.

J 43.2 (69.5 km) **RE 15.1** (24.3 km) Long Lake Wildlife Refuge sign; shooting prohibited westbound.

J 43.7 (70.3 km) **RE 14.6** (23.5 km) Small turnout to south.

J 44.3 (71.3 km) **RE 14** (22.5 km) Watch for salmon spawning in Long Lake outlet (no fishing at outlet within 300 feet of weir).

J 44.7 (71.9 km) **RE 13.6** (21.9 km) Turnout on **Long Lake**; a beautiful spot. Fishing for lake trout, silver salmon, grayling, Dolly Varden, burbot.

J 51.9 (83.5 km) **RE 6.4** (10.3 km) *CAUTION: Slow for downhill curve and dips next 3.8 miles eastbound.*

J 54.8 (88.2 km) **RE 3.5** (5.6 km) **Willow Herb Mountain Depot.** Experience Alaskan hospitality at our arts and crafts gallery or stay in our handscribed log cabin. Stop and chat about log building or winter life with year-round McCarthy residents. Our private cabin contains a woodstove with breakfast provided. Full service tire repair. Terry and Dee Frady. MasterCard, VISA. (907) 554-4420. WilHerbMtn@aol.com. [ADVERTISEMENT]

J 57 (91.7 km) **RE 1.3** (2.1 km) National Park Information cabin to north; airstrip to south.

J 57.2 (92 km) **RE 1.1** (1.8 km) **Glacier View Campground.** Just 1/2 mile from the footbridge, our scenic and private campsites offer breath-taking views of the Root Glacier and surrounding Wrangell Mountains. Rent a mountain bike and hit the trails or just soak up the sun at our outdoor cafe featuring home-style barbecue cooking. At Glacier View we strive to make your ultimate road trip unforgettable. Phone (907) 554-4490 summer, (907) 345-7121 winter, e-mail glacierview@gci.net. [ADVERTISEMENT] ▲

J 58 (93.3 km) **RE 0.3** (0.5 km) **Kennicott River Lodge and Hostel.** Road accessible. Your choice of accommodations include dormitory-style cabins, wall tents or lodge bunkroom. A 2-story log building provides common area for kitchen and dining. The upstairs sitting lounge with large deck offers views of the Kennicott Glacier. $25 per person. Phone (907) 554-4441. Open May 20–September 20. Internet: www2.polarnet.com/~grosswlr. [ADVERTISEMENT]

J 58.2 (93.7 km) **RE 0.1** (0.2 km) Parking lot for visitors crossing Kennicott River; 2 pedestrian-only footbridges cross the channels of the Kennicott River. There is no vehicle access across the river. Until the state constructed the new footbridge across the Kennicott River in 1997, travelers had to haul themselves across the river using a hand-pulled, open-platform cable tram.

CAUTION: Do not attempt to wade across this glacial river; strong currents and cold water make it extremely treacherous. ▲

Parking lot at the Tram Station, which houses a tour booking service, snack shop and gift shop. Telephones are located near the Tram Station and have instructions for calling businesses in McCarthy and Kennicott.

Parking on the riverbank is not recommended in July or early August because of sudden flooding when an ice-dammed lake breaks free upstream.

J 58.3 (93.8 km) **RE 0** McCarthy Road dead ends at Kennicott River. On the east side of the river, follow the road for about 1/2 mile to a fork, where there's a public restroom. The right fork leads to McCarthy, about another 1/2 mile, and the left fork goes to Kennicott, about 5 miles (shuttle bus service available in McCarthy).

Ruins of the Kennecott Copper Mine. (© Susan Cole Kelly)

McCarthy

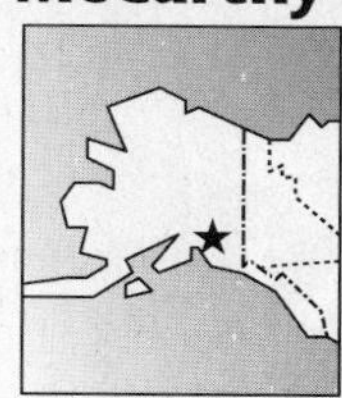

Located across the Kennicott River and about 1 mile by road from the end of the McCarthy Road; within Wrangell–St. Elias National Park and Preserve; approximately 60 miles east of Chitina. **Population:** 27. **Transportation:** Air—Charter service between Chitina, McCarthy and Kennicott. **Van**—Scheduled service between Glennallen and McCarthy via Backcountry Connection; phone (907) 822-5292. Shuttle service between McCarthy and Kennicott via Wrangell Mountain Bus from Wrangell Mountain Air office; 1-way fare $5/adults, $2/dogs; phone (907) 554-4411.

Climate: Temperature extremes from -58° F/-50° C to 91° F/33° C; average snowfall 52 inches; annual precipitation 12 inches. **Radio:** KCAM (Glennallen).

Private Aircraft: McCarthy NR 2, 1 NE; elev. 1,531 feet; length 3,500 feet; gravel; unattended, unmaintained.

Lodging is available in McCarthy at the McCarthy Lodge, which also offers food service and a bar. The McCarthy area has flightseeing services, a bed and breakfast, a pizza restaurant and an operating gold

McCARTHY/KENNICOTT ADVERTISERS

Advertiser	Contact
Backcountry Connection	Ph. (907) 822-5292
Historic Kennicott Bed & Breakfast	Ph. (907) 554-4469
Kennicott Cottage	Ph. (907) 242-1392
Kennicott Glacier Lodge	Ph. (800) 582-5128
McCarthy B&B	Ph. (907) 554-4433
McCarthy Gift Shop & Nugget Liquor Store	Downtown
McCarthy Lodge	Ph. (907) 554-4402
Wrangell Mountain Air	Ph. (800) 478-1160

mine. Check with lodges about activities in the area. Two wilderness guide services operate here. McCarthy has cellular phone service and some businesses can send and receive e-mail and faxes. McCarthy does not have a post office, school or television.

The town of McCarthy is in a beautiful area of glaciers and mountains. The Kennicott River flows by the west side of town and joins the Nizina River which flows into the Chitina River. The local museum, located in the railway depot, has historical artifacts and photos from the early mining days.

McCarthy lies within **WRANGELL–ST. ELIAS NATIONAL PARK AND PRESERVE.** This 13.2 million acre park encompasses the southeast corner of the Alaska mainland, stretching from the Gulf of Alaska to the Copper River basin. Access to the park is by way of the McCarthy Road, the Nabesna Road (off the Tok Cutoff) and out of Yakutat. This vast unspoiled wilderness offers backpacking, mountaineering, river running, hunting and sportfishing. For more information, contact: Superintendent, Wrangell–St. Elias National Park and Preserve, P.O. Box 439, Copper Center, AK 99573; phone (907) 822-5234.

Wrangell Mountain Air provides twice daily, scheduled air service to McCarthy/Kennicott as a time saving alternative to driving the McCarthy Road. Park your car or RV in Chitina at the end of the paved road and enjoy a spectacular flight through the Wrangell–St. Elias Mountains. Affordable fly–drive day trips to Kennicott are also available from Chitina. Wrangell Mountain Air specializes in world-class flightseeing, fly-in alpine hiking, river rafting, glacier trekking. Aircraft are high wing for great viewing and equipped with intercom and headsets for each passenger. Phone free for reservations and information, (800) 478-1160 or (907) 554-4411. E-mail: flywma@aol.com. Internet: www.WrangellMountainAir.com. See display ad.
[ADVERTISEMENT]

It is about 5 miles from McCarthy to the old mining town of **KENNICOTT**. Perched on the side of a mountain next to Kennicott Glacier, the town was built by Kennecott Copper Corp. between 1910 and 1920. (An early-day misspelling made the mining company Kennecott, while the region and settlement are Kennicott.) The richest copper mine in the world until its closure in 1938, Kennecott processed more than 591,535 tons of copper ore and employed some 800 workers in its heyday. Today, a lodge is located here. The 3 dozen barn-red mine buildings are on private land. Kennecott Copper Mine is a National Historic Site. Businesses include the Kennicott Glacier Lodge (ask about their special barbecues), a bed and breakfast and flightseeing service in Kennicott.

Kennicott Cottage, 16 Silk Stocking Row. Stay in the National Historic District of a scenic wilderness community within the Wrangell–St. Elias National Park. Charming 3-bedroom cottage sleeps 6 to 8. For complete privacy, whole cottage rental available. Room rental includes shared kitchen, shower and outhouse. Reservations: phone (907) 345-7961, 554-4460 or 554-1616 (cell). E-mail: kenncott@alaska.net. Web page: www.alaska.net/~kenncott/kcc.htm.
[ADVERTISEMENT]

Kennicott Glacier Lodge, located in the ghost town of Kennicott, offers the area's finest accommodations and dining. Built in 1987, this new lodge has 25 clean, delightful guest rooms, 2 living rooms, a spacious dining room, and a 180-foot front porch with a spectacular panoramic view of the Wrangell Mountains, Chugach Mountains and Kennicott Glacier. The homemade food, served family-style, has been called "wilderness gourmet dining." Guest activities at this destination resort include glacier trekking, flightseeing, photography, alpine hiking, historical and nature tours, rafting. May 15 to Sept. 20. (800) 582-5128. See display ad.
[ADVERTISEMENT]

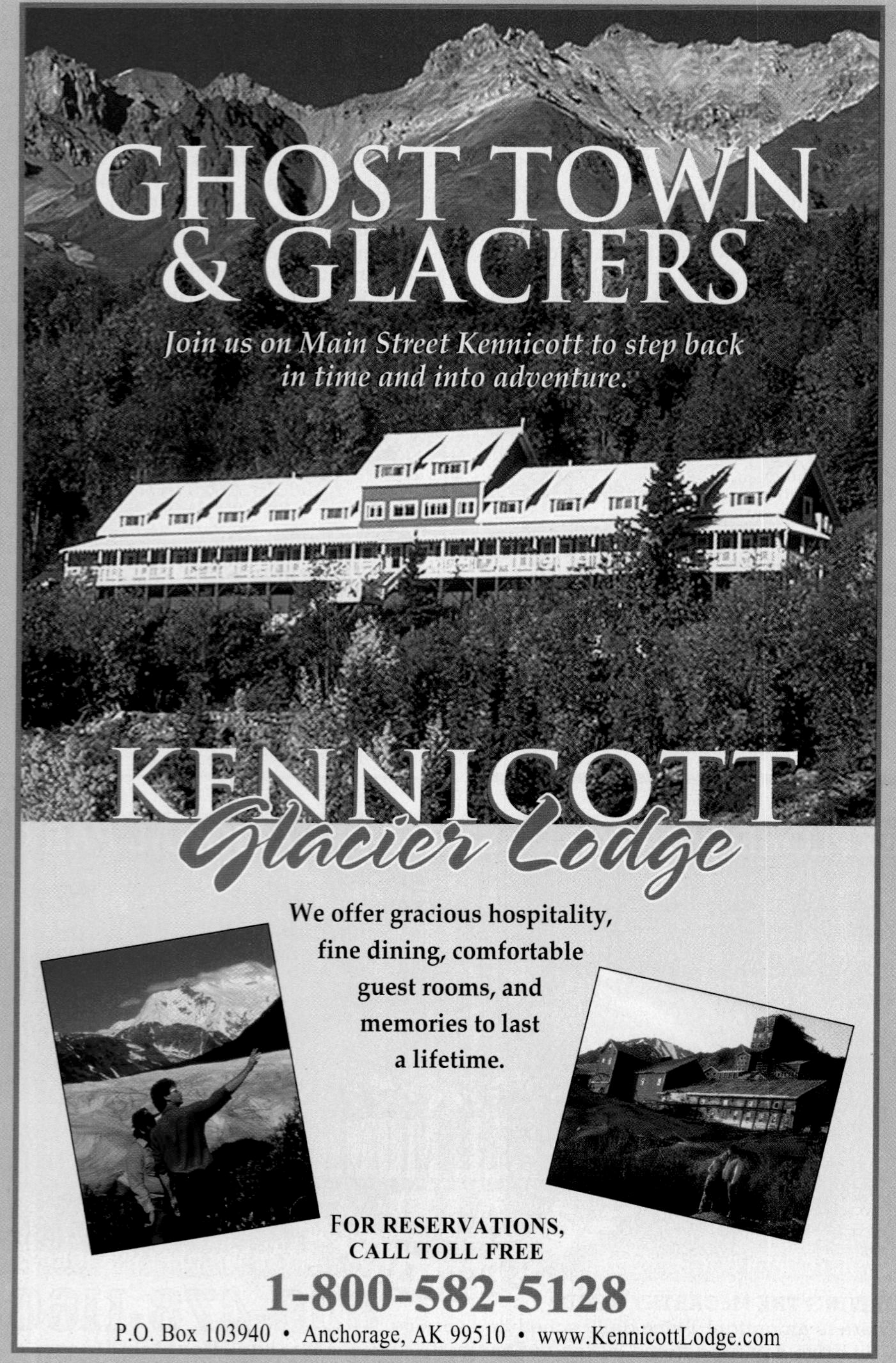

COPPER RIVER HIGHWAY (10)

Connects: Cordova to Million Dollar Bridge, AK **Length:** 48 miles
Road Surface: 25% paved, 75% gravel
Season: Not maintained in winter
Major Attraction: Childs Glacier
(See map, page 632)

	Cordova	Alaganik Slough	Million Dollar Bridge
Cordova		17	48
Alaganik Slough	17		31
Million Dollar Bridge	48	31	

The Million Dollar Bridge at the end of Copper River Highway. (© Kay McElrath Johnson)

The Copper River Highway leads 48.1 miles northeast from Cordova to the Million Dollar Bridge at the Copper River.

Construction of the Copper River Highway began in 1945. Built along the abandoned railbed of the Copper River & Northwestern Railway, the highway was to extend to Chitina (on the Edgerton Highway), thereby linking Cordova to the Richardson Highway.

Construction was halted by the 1964 Good Friday earthquake, which severely damaged the highway's roadbed and bridges. The quake also knocked the north span of the Million Dollar Bridge into the Copper River and distorted the remaining spans. The 48 miles of existing highway have been repaired and upgraded since the earthquake, with temporary repairs to the Million Dollar Bridge. Road work between the Million Dollar Bridge and the Allen River is planned as part of the development of the proposed Copper River hiking and biking trail connecting Cordova, Chitina and Valdez.

Copper River Highway Log

Distance is measured from Cordova (C).

C **0 CORDOVA.** See description on page 623.

C **1.3** (2.1 km) Whitshed Road on right leads 0.5 mile to Odiak municipal camper park (24 sites, tenting area; obtain shower tokens at City Hall), 5.5 miles to **Hartney Bay.** Fishing from Hartney Bay bridge for Dolly Varden from May; pink and chum salmon, mid-July–August; closed for salmon upstream of bridge. Use small weighted spoons, spinners and eggs. Clam digging at low tide (license required). Shorebird migration in early spring.

C **2.1** (3.4 km) Powder House Bar and Liquor Store (restaurant) overlooking Eyak Lake. Site of CR&NW railway powder house.

C **2.3** (3.7 km) Paved turnout to north by Eyak Lake. Heney Range to the south. Mount Eccles (elev. 2,357 feet) is the first large peak. Pointed peak beyond is Heney Peak (elev. 3,151 feet).

C **3.5** (5.6 km) Large paved turnout; Eyak Lake.

C **4.0** (6.4 km) Historical marker on left gives a brief history of the CR&NW railway. Also here is a monument erected by the railroad builder M.J. Heney in memory of those men who lost their lives during construction of the CR&NW. Begun in 1907 and completed in 1911, the CR&NW railway connected the port of Cordova with the Kennecott Copper Mines near Kennicott and McCarthy. The mine and railway ceased operation in 1938.

For the next 2 miles, watch for bears during early morning and late evening (most often seen in June). *CAUTION: Avalanche area.*

C **5.1** (8.2 km) Paved turnout at lake to north.

C **5.5** (8.8 km) Paved turnout at lake to north.

C **5.6** (9.0 km) Bridge over Eyak River; access to **Eyak River trail**. This is a good spot to see waterfowl feeding near the outlet of Eyak Lake. An estimated 100 trumpeter swans winter on Eyak Lake.

Eyak River trailhead is on the west bank of the river. The 2.2-mile trail, much of which is boardwalk over muskeg, is popular with fishermen.

C **5.9** (9.5 km) **Eyak River**. Toilet and boat launch. Dolly Varden; red salmon, June–July; silvers, August–September. Also pinks and chums. Use Vibrax spoon, spinner or salmon eggs. Fly-fishing only for salmon within 200 yards of weir.

C **6.5** (10.5 km) No shoulder on road.

C **7.0** (11.3 km) Small unpaved turnouts on either side of road.

C **7.3** (11.7 km) Paved turnout. *CAUTION: High winds for next 4 miles. In January and February, these winds sweep across this flat with such velocity it is safer to pull off and stop.*

C **7.4** (11.9 km) Bridge over slough.

C **7.5** (12.1 km) First bridge across Scott River.

C **8.0** (12.8 km) Bridge over slough waters. Gravel turnout; access to slough.

C **8.3** (13.4 km) Scott River bridge.

C **9.3** (14.9 km) Between **Mileposts 9** and **10** there are 4 bridges across the Scott River and the slough. Sloughs along here are from the runoff of the Scott Glacier, visible to the northeast. Bear and moose are often seen, especially in July and August. In May and August, thousands of dusky Canada geese nest here. This is the only known nesting area of the dusky geese, which winter in Oregon's Willamette Valley. Also watch for swans.

Moose feed in the willow groves on either side of the highway. Moose are not native to Cordova; the mountains and glaciers prevent them from entering the delta country. Today's herd stems from a transplant of 26 animals made between 1949 and 1959.

C **10.2** (16.4 km) Scott River bridge. Watch for old and new beaver dams and lodges beside the highway.

C **10.5** (16.9 km) U.S. Forest Service information pavilion (8 interpretive plaques about Copper River Delta/Chugach National Forest areas) and large paved turnout with litter barrel to south. Game management area, 330,000 acres. Trumpeter swans and Canada geese. Look for arctic terns.

C **10.6** (17.0 km) Bridge, beaver lodge.

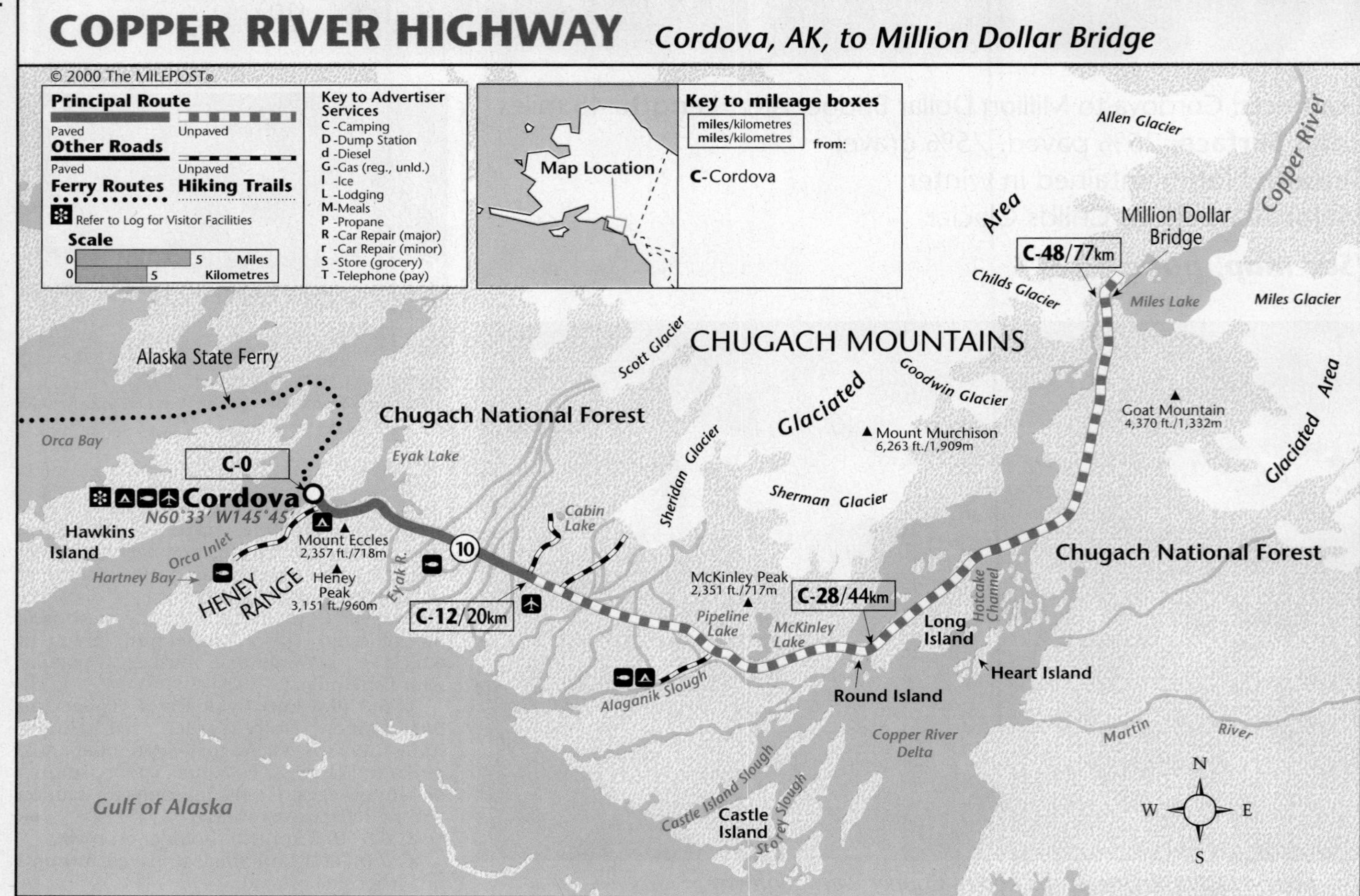

C 10.9 (17.5 km) Elsner River bridge.

C 11.5 (18.5 km) Look for brown bears feeding in the outwash plains of Scott Glacier. Thousands of salmon swim up nearby rivers to spawn. There are numerous beaver lodges on both sides of the highway.

C 11.6 (18.7 km) State of Alaska Cordova highway maintenance station to northeast. U.S. Coast Guard station.

C 11.9 (19.2 km) Cordova airport and access to **Cabin Lake Recreation Area**. Drive north 2.5 miles for recreation area (gravel access road forks 0.3 mile in; right fork leads to gravel pit, continue straight ahead for recreation area). *CAUTION: Narrow road, no directional signs, active logging and logging trucks.* Picnic tables, toilet, litter barrel and firepits at Cabin Lake; cutthroat fishing.

C 12.2 (19.6 km) Pavement ends, gravel begins. Watch for potholes.

C 13.5 (21.7 km) **Sheridan Glacier** access road leads 4 miles to the terminus of Sheridan Glacier. At Mile 1.8 road forks to the left; keep to RIGHT. The left fork connects to the Cabin Lake Access road. *CAUTION: Narrow road, watch for logging trucks.* The glacier was named by U.S. Army explorer Capt. Abercrombie for Gen. Philip H. Sheridan of Civil War fame. Sheridan Mountain trailhead, several picnic tables, litter barrels and a partial view of the glacier are available at the end of the access road. It is about a 0.5-mile/0.8-km hike to the dirt-covered glacial moraine.

C 14.6 (23.5 km) Bridge over Sheridan River. Raft takeout point. View of Sheridan Glacier. To the east of Sheridan Glacier is Sherman Glacier.

Winter moose range next 8 miles eastbound.

C 14.8 (23.8 km) Silver salmon spawn during September and October in the stream beside the highway.

C 15.7 (25.3 km) Beautiful view of Sheridan Glacier to the northeast.

C 16 (25.7 km) Second bridge over Sheridan River. Large unpaved turnout.

C 16.7 (26.9 km) Turnoff for **Alaganik Slough Chugach National Forest Recreation Area**. Drive south 3 miles via gravel road; picnic tables, firepits, wheelchair-accessible toilets, litter barrel, information kiosk and boat launch. Wheel-chair-accessible interpretive boardwalk with viewing blind for watching birds and other wildlife. No water, informal camping. Fishing for Dolly Varden, sockeye (July) and silver salmon (Aug.–Sept.).

Interpretive plaque on side road reads: "Why are Delta moose the largest and healthiest? This moose herd, first introduced in 1949, maintains its vitality primarily due to its abundant willow supply. As part of a normal cycle, accelerated by the 1964 earthquake, much of the willow is becoming unavailable to moose. As the willow grows tall, the moose can no longer reach the tender new shoots. In the future this could cause a decrease in the numbers of moose on the delta. To slow the cycle down, the Forest Service is experimenting in this area, cutting back the shrubs. This should increase the amount of available willow browse. Biologists will evaluate the response of moose to new willow growth."

C 17.2 (27.7 km) Trumpeter swans may be seen in pond beside highway. One of the largest of all North American waterfowl (6- to 8-foot wingspan), it has been almost completely eliminated in the Lower 48 and Canada. Alaska harbors more than 80 percent of breeding trumpeters, and more than 7 percent of the world's trumpeter population breeds in the Copper River Delta.

C 17.8 (28.6 km) For the next mile look for silver salmon spawning in streams during September. To the left and on the slopes above timberline mountain goats may be seen. The mountain to the left of the road ahead eastbound is McKinley Peak (elev. 2,351 feet).

C 17.9 (28.8 km) Entering Chugach National Forest eastbound.

C 18.3 (29.5 km) Road narrows. *NOTE: Road not maintained in winter (after Nov. 1) beyond this point.*

C 18.5 (29.7 km) Turnout to north access to Muskeg Meander cross-country ski trailhead; length 2.5 miles. According to the USFS district office, this trail offers a beautiful view of the Copper River Delta.

C 18.8 (30.2 km) **Haystack Trail** trailhead to south. Easy 0.8-mile trail leads to delta overlook with interpretive signs. Excellent place to see moose and bear, according to the USFS district office in Cordova.

Several small turnouts next mile.

C 19.9 (32.0 km) Large gravel turnout to south; beaver dam, fishing. "Pay to park" area.

C 21.2 (34.1 km) **Pipeline Lakes Trail** trailhead to north, parking to south. The 1.8-mile trail was originally built as a water pipeline route to supply locomotives on the CR&NW railway. Segments of the pipeline are still visible. Fishing for cutthroat, fly or bait. Trail joins McKinley Lake trail. Rubber boots are necessary.

C **21.4** (34.4 km) **McKinley Lake Trail** to north; easy 2.1-mile hike with excellent fishing for sockeye, Dolly Varden and cutthroat. Access to USFS public-use cabins: McKinley Trail cabin (100 yards from highway) and McKinley Lake cabin (45-minute walk in from highway; also accessible by boat via Alaganik Slough).

C **21.9** (35.2 km) **Alaganik Slough.** Boat ramp, picnic tables, firepits, toilets, litter barrel, wildflowers, interpretive signs on local cultural history and fishing access to south at west side of Alaganik Slough river bridge. Sockeye (red) and coho (silver) salmon, July to September. Also boat access to McKinley Lake.

C **22.3** (35.8 km) Salmon Creek bridge, parking; creek access.

C **22.6** (36.4 km) Small turnout.

C **24.6** (39.6 km) Side road leads north 1 mile to Saddlebag Glacier trailhead and parking area; access to canoe route. According to the USFS office in Cordova, this is an easy 3-mile trail to Saddlebag Lake. View of Saddlebag Glacier and icebergs; look for goats on surrounding mountains. *CAUTION: Watch for bears.*

C **24.8** (39.9 km) Channel to beaver pond for spawning salmon. A plaque here reads: "Pathway to salmon rearing grounds. Channel provided access to beaver pond (north side of road) for coho fry. Beaver pond can support up to 25,400 young salmon. Fallen trees and brush provide cover from predators."

C **25.4** (40.9 km) Small gravel turnout by 2 spawning channels with weirs. Interpretive signs along a short trail here explain the project: "Channel built by USDA Forest Service to provide high quality spawning habitat for coho and sockeye salmon. Before construction, the streambed was muddy and the stream dried up during low flow periods. Fish spawned in the streams but few eggs survived. Improved channel is deeper and ensures a consistent flow. Adjustable weirs control water depth. Clean gravels placed in the channel make better spawning conditions while large rip-rap on streambanks prevent erosion.

"Can you see small circles of gravel which appear to have been turned over? These are salmon 'redds,' or nests in which female salmon lay their eggs. Female salmon create the redds by digging with their tails. Environmental conditions and predators take a heavy toll on salmon eggs and small fry. Of the 2,800 eggs which the average female coho salmon lays, only about 14 will survive to adulthood. Most of these will then be caught by commercial, sport or subsistence fishermen. Only 2 salmon from each redd will actually return to spawn and complete their life cycle."

Near here was the cabin of Rex Beach, author of *The Iron Trail,* a classic novel about the building of the CR&NW railway.

C **26.2** (42.2 km) **Flag Point**. Turnout with view of the Copper River which empties into the Gulf of Alaska. Downriver to the southwest is Castle Island Slough. Storey Slough is visible a little more to the south. Castle Island and a number of small islands lie at the mouth of the Copper River. Monument on the riverbank is dedicated to the men who built these bridges and "especially to the crane crew who lost their lives on July 21, 1971."

CAUTION: Extreme high winds next 10 miles in fall and winter. Stay in your vehicle.

Childs Glacier viewing area at end of Copper River Highway. (© Susan Cole Kelly)

C **26.4** (42.5 km) Two bridges cross the Copper River to Round Island, a small island with sand dunes and a good place to picnic.

In midsummer the Copper River has half a million or more red (sockeye) and king salmon migrating 300 miles upstream to spawn in the river's clear tributaries. There is no sportfishing in this stretch of the Copper River because of glacial silt.

Candlefish (eulachon) also spawn in the Copper River. Candlefish oil was once a significant trade item of the Coastal Indians. These fish are so oily that when dried they can be burned like candles.

C **27.3** (43.9 km) Copper River Bridge No. 3 from Round Island to Long Island. The 6.2 miles/10 km of road on Long Island pass through a sandy landscape dotted with dunes. Long Island is in the middle of the Copper River.

C **30.8** (49.5 km) Watch for nesting swans, other birds and beaver in slough to south of road. *NOTE: Use extreme caution if you drive off road: sandy terrain.*

C **31** (49.9 km) Lakes to south.

C **33** (53.1 km) View of 2 glaciers to the northwest; nearest is Goodwin, the other is Childs.

C **33.2** (53.4 km) First bridge leaving Long Island. View to south down Hotcake Channel to Heart Island. Road built on top of a long dike which stretches across the Copper River Delta. From here to **Milepost** C **37.7** there are 7 more bridges across the delta. The Copper River channels have changed and many bridges now cross almost dry gulches. *NOTE: Watch for large potholes before and after bridges through this section.*

C **34.1** (54.8 km) Large gravel turnout to north.

C **34.2** (55.0 km) Copper River bridge.

C **35.6** (57.3 km) Large gravel turnout to north.

C **36.6** (58.9 km) Bridge crossing main flow of the Copper River (this is the 5th bridge after leaving Long Island eastbound). Access to river at east end of bridge.

C **37.2** (59.8 km) Bridge, river access.

C **37.4** (60.2 km) Bridge, river access, large gravel turnout to north.

C **37.6** (60.5 km) Large gravel turnout.

C **38.8** (62.4 km) Childs Glacier directly ahead.

C **39.8** (64.0 km) Milky glacial waters of Sheep Creek pass through large culvert under road.

C **40.4** (65.0 km) **Clear Creek**. Dolly Varden, cutthroat, red salmon (July) and silvers (Aug.–Sept.). Use flies, lures, spinners or eggs. Watch for bears.

C **40.9** (65.8 km) Park on old railroad grade to south for access to Clear Creek.

C **41.7** (67.1 km) Goat Mountain (elev. 4,370 feet) rises to the east of the highway. To the west, parts of the Sherman and Goodwin glaciers flow down the sides of Mount Murchison (elev. 6,263 feet).

C **42.1** (67.7 km) Side road to gravel pit, pond, informal camping and picnic site by Goat Mountain.

C **48** (77.2 km) Access to **Childs Glacier Recreation Area** with 2 covered, wheelchair-accessible viewing areas, one at the bridge, the other 0.7 mile down access road. Picnic sites, covered tables, toilets and trails. No water. Limited RV parking. U.S. Forest Service hosts on site in summer. Childs Glacier was named by Capt. W.R. Abercrombie (1884 expedition) for George Washington Childs of Philadelphia. The glacier face is approximately 350 feet high and very active. In 1993 falling ice caused a 30-foot wave that crashed onto the viewing area. Car-sized icebergs were tossed onto the beach and viewing area. *CAUTION: Calving ice may cause waves to break over the beach and into the viewing area. Be prepared to run to higher ground!*

C **48.1** (77.4 km) **The Million Dollar Bridge.** Sign posted: Weight limit on bridge: 6,600 lbs. Viewing platform. The north span of the bridge collapsed during the 1964 earthquake. Temporary repairs were made and people have been driving across it, but driving across the bridge and beyond is definitely a "drive at your own risk" venture. Primitive road extends only about 10 miles/16 km beyond the bridge to the Allen River. Heavy snow blocks road in winter; road may not be open until June. Proposed extension of the Copper River Highway to Chitina is currently under debate.

From here there is a view of Miles Glacier to the east. This glacier was named by Lieutenant Allen (1885 expedition) for Maj. Gen. Nelson A. Miles.

C **48.2** (77.6 km) End of bridge.

C **48.8** (78.5 km) A 4X4 or 4-wheel-drive vehicle with very high clearance is a must to go any farther!

INSIDE PASSAGE

Southeastern Alaska communities from Ketchikan to Skagway

(See maps, pages 635–639)

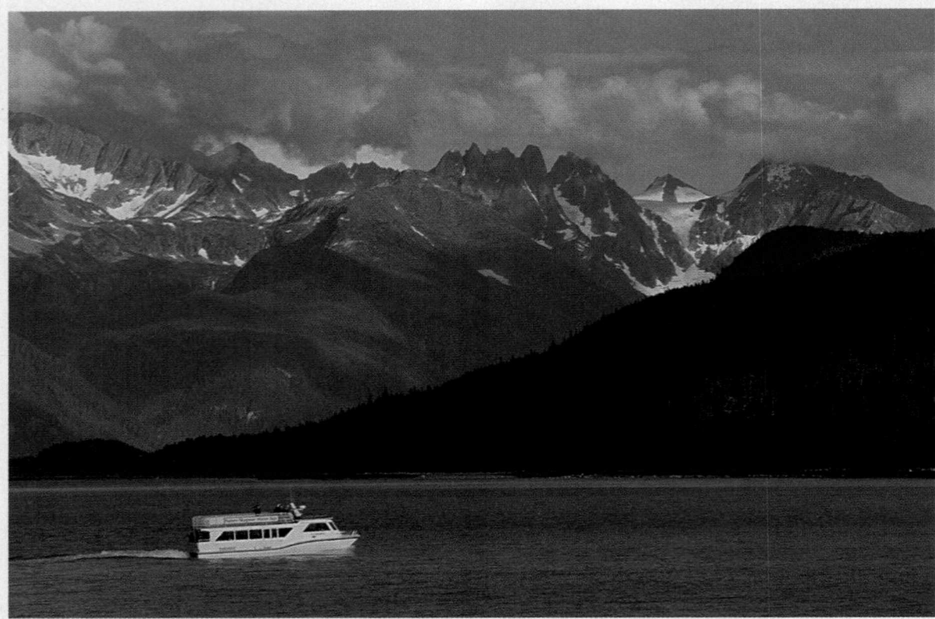

Water taxis, ferries and boats provide transportation between Southeast communities. (© Paul Souders)

Alaska's Inside Passage, located in the southeastern section of the state, is known by many residents simply as "Southeast." It is a unique region where industry, transportation, recreation and community planning are dictated by spectacular topography.

The region is accessible by air, land or sea. Jet service is available to Juneau, Ketchikan, Wrangell, Petersburg, Sitka and Gustavus. Smaller communities are served by local commuter aircraft. The port communities of Haines and Skagway offer road connections to the Alaska Highway system via the Haines Highway and Klondike Highway 2. The Alaska Marine Highway moves people and vehicles between ports, and connects the Inside Passage with Prince Rupert, BC, and Bellingham, WA. Several cruise ship lines ply the waterways of the Inside Passage and offer a variety of cruising opportunities.

Measuring about 125 by 400 miles, 60 percent of the region consists of thousands of islands covered with dense forests of spruce, hemlock and cedar, a result of the mild, moist coastal climate. These islands make up the Alexander Archipelago, and include Prince of Wales Island, the third largest island in the United States (the Big Island of Hawaii is first, followed by Kodiak). The Coast Mountains form the mainland portion of southeastern Alaska.

Southeastern Alaska lies between 54°40' and 60° north latitude, the same as Scotland, Denmark and southern Sweden. The latitude of Scotland's Loch Ness is slightly north of the latitude at Wrangell Narrows. Stockholm and Skagway share the same latitude, and Ketchikan's latitude is a little south of Copenhagen's.

Warmed by ocean currents, this region experiences mild, warm summers, with July temperatures averaging around 60°F. An occasional heat wave may reach the high 80s. Winters are cool, alternating snow, rain and sunshine; January temperatures average 20° to 40°F. Sub-zero winter temperatures are uncommon. The region receives considerable annual rainfall, from 27 inches (Skagway) to more than 200 inches (heaviest in late fall, lightest in summer). Populated areas receive 30 to 200 inches of snow annually; the high mountains more than 400 inches a year.

The majority of southeastern Alaska lies within Tongass National Forest, the largest national forest in the United States. Information web site for Tongass National Forest: www.fs.fed.us/r10/tongass/. (Southeastern Alaska has over 5.6 million acres of wilderness lands.) The forests historically have provided one of the region's major industries; timber harvesting primarily supplies area sawmills.

Commercial fishing and fish processing is another major industry here. Numerous rivers and streams, mountains, valleys, melting glaciers and heavy rainfall create ideal spawning grounds for salmon. Local waters harbor abundant life, including crab, shrimp, halibut, herring and black cod.

Juneau is the state capital, and federal, state and local governments provide the majority of jobs throughout Southeast. Tourism, with its jobs and revenue, is another major contributor to the region's economy.

About 69,000 people live along the Inside Passage, according to 1990 U.S. Census figures. About 70 percent live in the 5 major communities of Juneau (29,755), Ketchikan (15,082), Sitka (9,194), Petersburg (3,350) and Wrangell (2,400). More than 20 percent are Native, mostly Tlingit (KLINK it) Indian, plus Haida (HI duh) and Tsimshian (SHIM shian).

Alaska's Natives, famous for their totem poles, weaving, beading, basketry and dancing, occupied the region long before Vitus Bering discovered Alaska in 1741.

Russia controlled Alaska from the turn of the 19th century until 1867, centering its extensive fur-trading empire in Sitka, the Russian capital of Alaska. Sitka was a port of international trade, controlling trading posts from California to the Aleutians, and was considered cultured because of European influence. At a time when San Francisco was a crude new boom town, Sitka was called the "Paris of the Pacific."

Commercial interest in southeastern Alaska declined with the fur trade, following Alaska's purchase by the United States. Interest in Southeast was rekindled by the salmon industry as canneries were established, the first at Klawock in 1878. Salmon canning peaked in the late 1930s and then declined from overfishing.

But the first significant white populations arrived because of gold. By the time thousands of gold seekers traveled through the Inside Passage in 1898 to Skagway and on to Canada's Klondike (sparking interest in the rest of Alaska), the largest gold ore mine of its day, the Treadwell near Juneau, had been in operation since 1884.

Juneau became Alaska's capital in 1906, and Southeast remained Alaska's dominant region until WWII, when military activity and the Alaska Highway shifted emphasis to Anchorage and Fairbanks.

Additional population growth came to Southeast with new timber harvesting in the 1950s. Increased government activities, as a result of Alaska statehood in 1959, brought

(Continues on page 640)

INSIDE PASSAGE *Prince Rupert, BC to Ketchikan, AK*

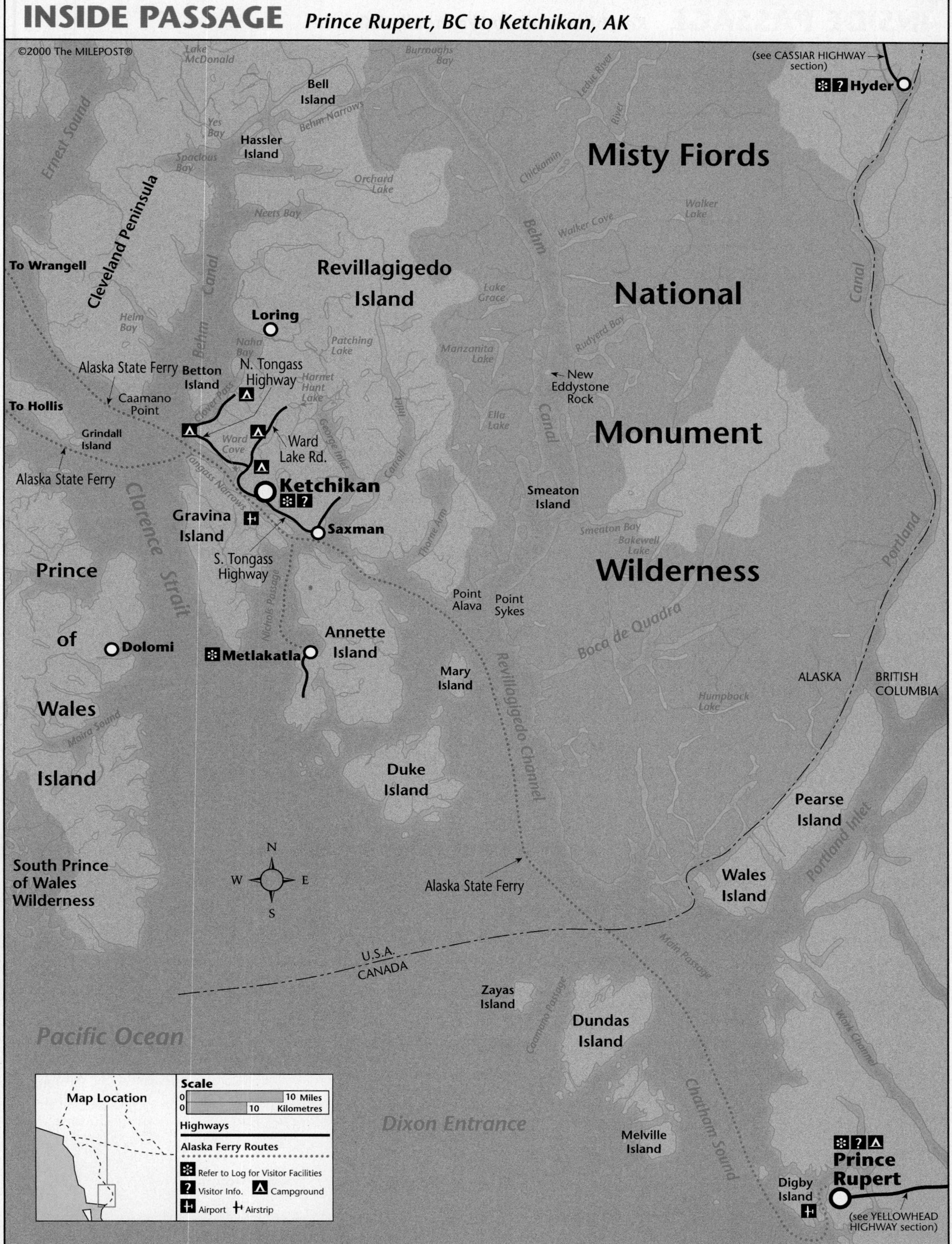
©2000 The MILEPOST®
(see CASSIAR HIGHWAY section)
Hyder
Bell Island
Hassler Island
Misty Fiords
National
Monument
Wilderness
Cleveland Peninsula
Revillagigedo Island
Loring
To Wrangell
To Hollis
Alaska State Ferry
Betton Island
N. Tongass Highway
Caamano Point
Grindall Island
Ward Lake Rd.
Ketchikan
Saxman
Gravina Island
S. Tongass Highway
New Eddystone Rock
Smeaton Island
Point Alava
Point Sykes
Prince of Wales Island
Dolomi
Metlakatla
Annette Island
Mary Island
Duke Island
ALASKA
BRITISH COLUMBIA
Pearse Island
Wales Island
South Prince of Wales Wilderness
Alaska State Ferry
U.S.A.
CANADA
Zayas Island
Dundas Island
Pacific Ocean
Dixon Entrance
Melville Island
Digby Island
Prince Rupert
(see YELLOWHEAD HIGHWAY section)
Map Location
Scale
10 Miles
10 Kilometres
Highways
Alaska Ferry Routes
Refer to Log for Visitor Facilities
Visitor Info.
Campground
Airport
Airstrip

INSIDE PASSAGE *Ketchikan, AK to Wrangell, AK*

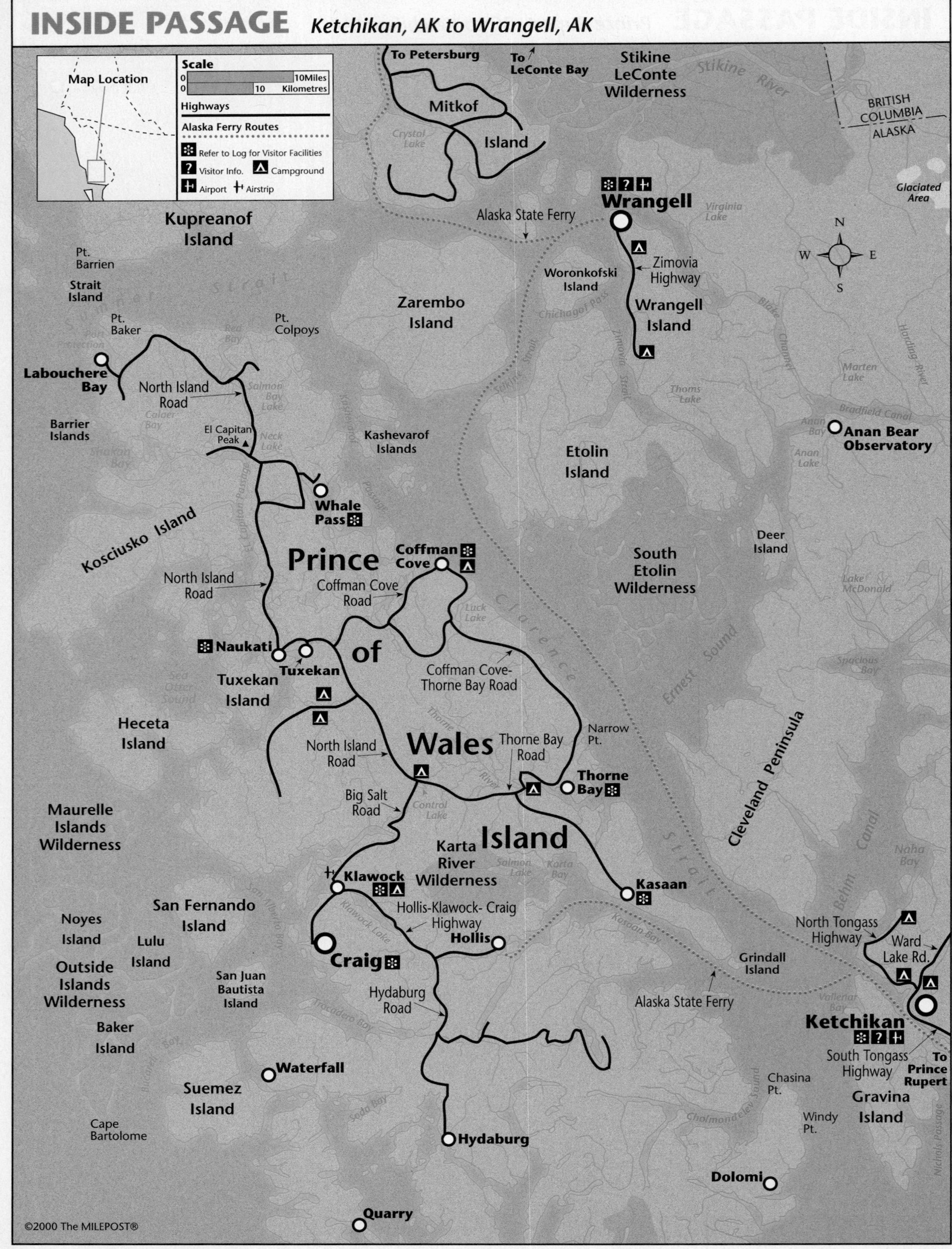
Map Location
Scale
0 10 Miles
0 10 Kilometres
Highways
Alaska Ferry Routes
Refer to Log for Visitor Facilities
Visitor Info.
Campground
Airport
Airstrip
To Petersburg
To LeConte Bay
Stikine LeConte Wilderness
Stikine River
BRITISH COLUMBIA
ALASKA
Mitkof Island
Crystal Lake
Wrangell
Alaska State Ferry
Virginia Lake
Glaciated Area
Kupreanof Island
Pt. Barrien
Strait Island
Sumner Strait
Zarembo Island
Woronkofski Island
Zimovia Highway
Wrangell Island
Chichagof Pass
Pt. Baker
Pt. Colpoys
Labouchere Bay
North Island Road
El Capitan Peak
Barrier Islands
Kashevarof Islands
Etolin Island
Anan Bear Observatory
Whale Pass
Kosciusko Island
Prince of Wales Island
Coffman Cove
Coffman Cove Road
Deer Island
South Etolin Wilderness
Naukati
Tuxekan
Tuxekan Island
Coffman Cove-Thorne Bay Road
Heceta Island
Narrow Pt.
Thorne Bay Road
Thorne Bay
Clarence Strait
Ernest Sound
Cleveland Peninsula
Big Salt Road
Maurelle Islands Wilderness
Karta River Wilderness
Klawock
Kasaan
Hollis-Klawock- Craig Highway
Hollis
Noyes Island
San Fernando Island
Lulu Island
Craig
Outside Islands Wilderness
San Juan Bautista Island
Hydaburg Road
North Tongass Highway
Ward Lake Rd.
Grindall Island
Alaska State Ferry
Ketchikan
South Tongass Highway
To Prince Rupert
Baker Island
Waterfall
Suemez Island
Chasina Pt.
Windy Pt.
Gravina Island
Cape Bartolome
Hydaburg
Dolomi
Quarry
N
S
E
W
©2000 The MILEPOST®

INSIDE PASSAGE *Coffman Cove, AK to Sitka, AK*

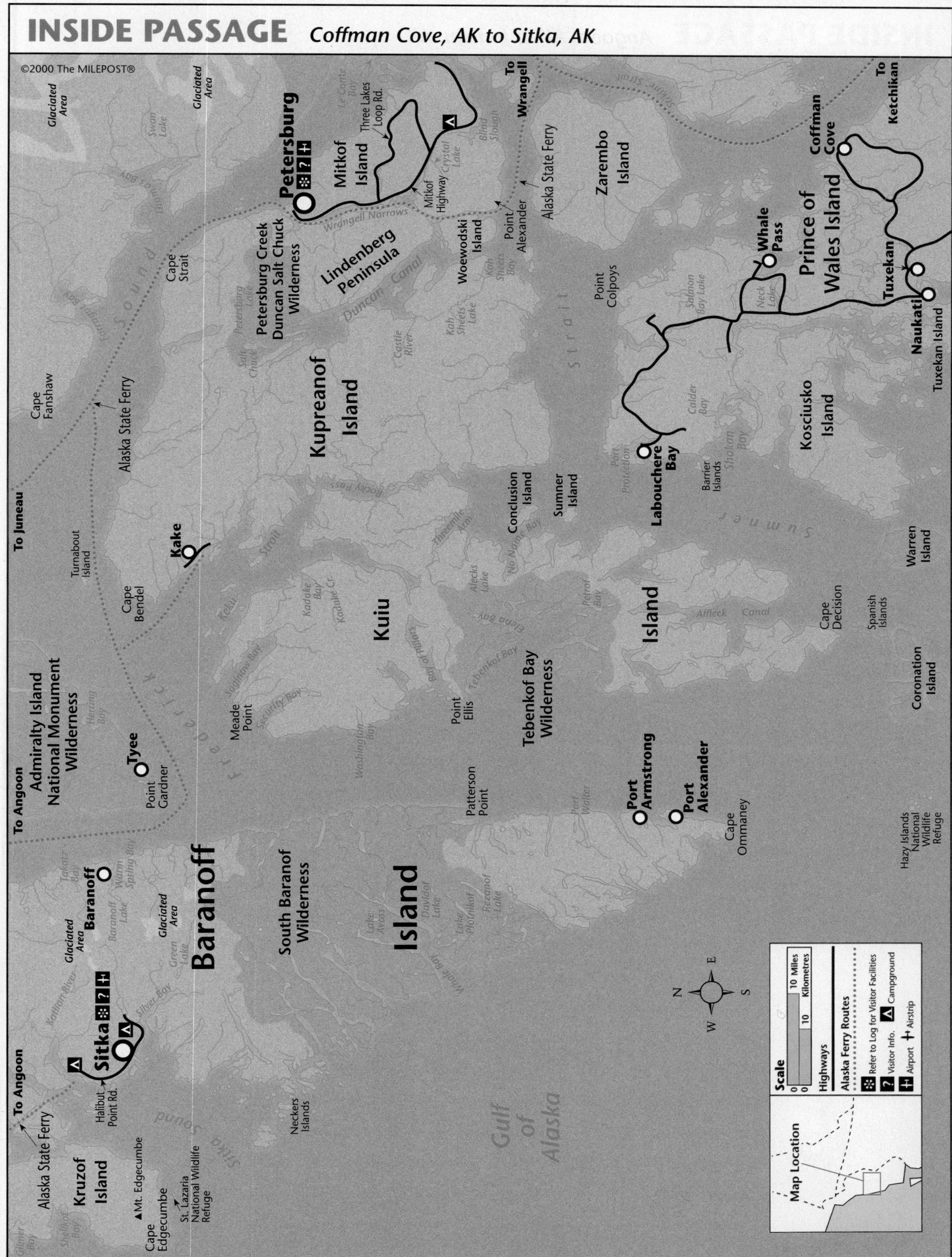

INSIDE PASSAGE *Angoon, AK to Juneau, AK*

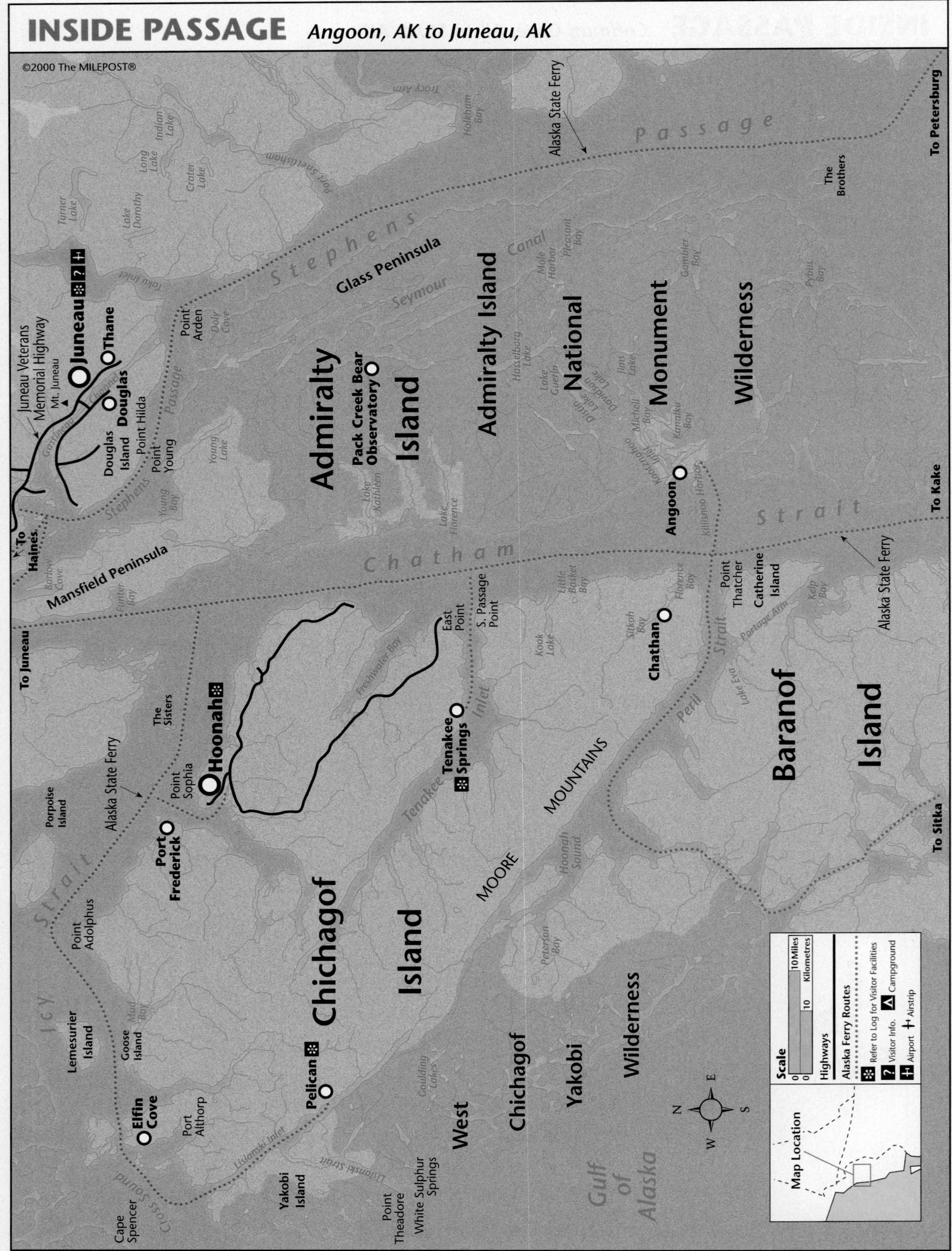
©2000 The MILEPOST®
Juneau
Thane
Douglas
Douglas Island
Point Hilda
Point Young
Juneau Veterans Memorial Highway
Mt. Juneau
To Haines
To Juneau
Stephens Passage
Point Arden
Glass Peninsula
Seymour Canal
Admiralty Island
Pack Creek Bear Observatory
Admiralty Island National Monument Wilderness
Angoon
Chatham Strait
Mansfield Peninsula
To Kake
To Petersburg
Alaska State Ferry
The Brothers
Hoonah
The Sisters
Point Sophia
Port Frederick
Porpoise Island
Icy Strait
Point Adolphus
Tenakee Springs
Tenakee Inlet
East Point
S. Passage Point
Chathan
Point Thatcher
Catherine Island
Peril Strait
Baranof Island
To Sitka
MOORE MOUNTAINS
Chichagof Island
Pelican
Elfin Cove
Port Althorp
Goose Island
Lemesurier Island
Yakobi Island
Cape Spencer
Point Theadore
White Sulphur Springs
West Chichagof Yakobi Wilderness
Gulf of Alaska
N
E
S
W
Map Location
Scale
0 10 Miles
0 10 Kilometres
Highways
Alaska Ferry Routes
Refer to Log for Visitor Facilities
Visitor Info.
Campground
Airport
Airstrip

INSIDE PASSAGE *Juneau, AK to Skagway, AK*

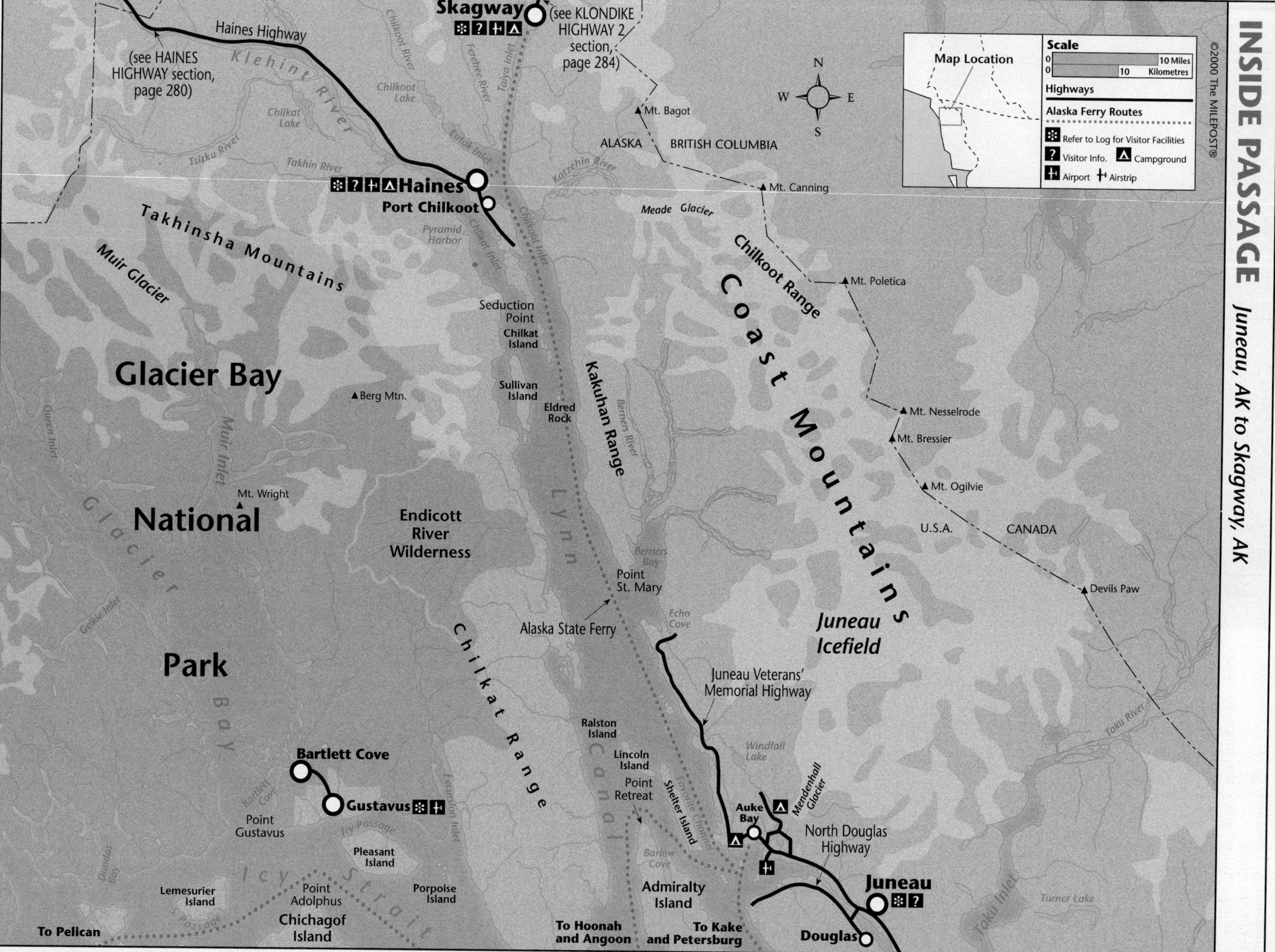

©2000 The MILEPOST®
Map Location
Scale
0 10 Miles
0 10 Kilometres
Highways
Alaska Ferry Routes
Refer to Log for Visitor Facilities
Visitor Info.
Campground
Airport
Airstrip
N
W
E
S
Skagway
(see KLONDIKE HIGHWAY 2 section, page 284)
Haines Highway
(see HAINES HIGHWAY section, page 280)
Klehini River
Chilkoot River
Chilkoot Lake
Chilkat Lake
Ferebee River
Taiya Inlet
Tsirku River
Takhin River
Lutak Inlet
Katzehin River
Haines
Port Chilkoot
Pyramid Harbor
Chilkat Inlet
Chilkoot Inlet
Mt. Bagot
ALASKA
BRITISH COLUMBIA
Mt. Canning
Meade Glacier
Takhinsha Mountains
Muir Glacier
Chilkoot Range
Mt. Poletica
Coast Mountains
Seduction Point
Chilkat Island
Sullivan Island
Eldred Rock
Kakuhan Range
Berners River
Glacier Bay
Berg Mtn.
Mt. Nesselrode
Mt. Bressier
Mt. Ogilvie
Queen Inlet
Muir Inlet
Mt. Wright
National
Glacier
Endicott River Wilderness
Lynn
U.S.A.
CANADA
Berners Bay
Point St. Mary
Devils Paw
Geikie Inlet
Alaska State Ferry
Echo Cove
Juneau Icefield
Park
Chilkat Range
Juneau Veterans' Memorial Highway
Taku River
Bay
Ralston Island
Windfall Lake
Bartlett Cove
Lincoln Island
Canal
Point Retreat
Shelter Island
Favorite Channel
Mendenhall Glacier
Auke Bay
Gustavus
Bartlett Cove
Excursion Inlet
Point Gustavus
Icy Passage
North Douglas Highway
Pleasant Island
Barlow Cove
Dundas Bay
Icy Strait
Lemesurier Island
Point Adolphus
Porpoise Island
Admiralty Island
Juneau
Turner Lake
Taku Inlet
S Passage
Chichagof Island
To Pelican
To Hoonah and Angoon
To Kake and Petersburg
Douglas

(Continued from page 634)
even more people.

Today, visitors enjoy the many wonders the area offers. Spectacular scenery greets the eye at every turn. Glacier Bay National Park and Preserve, Misty Fiords and Admiralty Island national monuments, Mendenhall Glacier at Juneau, LeConte Glacier near Petersburg and the Stikine River near Wrangell are just a few of the attractions.

The Inside Passage is the last stronghold of the American bald eagle. More than 20,000 eagles reside in the region, and sightings are frequent. Humpback and killer whales, porpoises, sea lions and seals are often observed from ferries, cruise ships and charter boats. Bear viewing opportunities are offered at Pack Creek on Admiralty Island and Anan Creek near Wrangell.

Activities and attractions include Russian and Tlingit dance performances; salmon bakes; historical melodramas; festivals; glaciers and icefield flightseeing; sportfishing and wilderness adventure tours by kayak, canoe and raft. Among other attractions are museums, totem poles, hiking trails, colorful saloons and fine dining.

Exploring Tracy Arm by tour boat out of Juneau. (© Paul Souders)

INSIDE PASSAGE ADVERTISERS

The following sections describe the communities and attractions of Southeast with the exception of Hyder, which is accessible by highway from British Columbia and is included in the CASSIAR HIGHWAY section.

Ketchikan

(See map, pages 635-636)

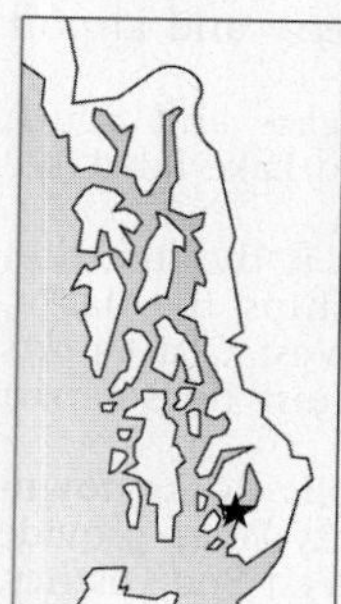

Located on Revillagigedo Island, 235 miles south of Juneau, 90 miles north of Prince Rupert, BC. **Population:** Ketchikan Gateway Borough and city, 15,082. **Emergency Services: Alaska State Troopers**, phone (907) 225-5118. **City Police**, phone (907) 225-6631, or 911 for all emergency services. **Fire Department**, **Ambulance** and **Ketchikan Volunteer Rescue Squad**, phone (907) 225-9616. **Hospital**, Ketchikan General at 3100 Tongass Ave., phone (907) 225-5171. **Maritime Search and Rescue**, call the Coast Guard at (907) 225-5666.

Visitor Information: Ketchikan Visitors Bureau office is located on the downtown dock, open during daily business hours and weekends May through September. Write them at 131M Front St., Ketchikan 99901; phone (907) 225-6166 or (800) 770-2200; fax (907) 225-4250. U.S. Forest Service office for Misty Fiords National Monument and Ketchikan Ranger District is located at 3031 Tongass Ave.; open 8 A.M. to 4:30 P.M. weekdays; phone (907) 225-2148. The Southeast Alaska Visitor Center, located at 50 Main St., is open May 1 to Sept. 30, 8 A.M to 5 P.M. daily; Oct. 1 to April 30, 8:30 A.M. to 4:30 P.M., Tuesday through Saturday; phone (907) 228-6214, fax 228-6234.

Elevation: Sea level. **Climate:** Rainy. Yearly average rainfall is 162 inches and snowfall is 32 inches. Average daily maximum temperature in July 65°F/18°C; daily minimum 51°F/11°C. Daily maximum in January 39°F/4°C; daily minimum 29°F/-2°C. **Radio:** KTKN 930, KRBD-FM 105.9, KGTW-FM 106.7, KFMJ-FM 99.9. **Television:** CFTK (Prince Rupert, BC) and 27 cable channels. **Newspapers:** *Ketchikan Daily News* (daily); *Southeastern Log* (monthly); *New Alaskan* (monthly); *The Local Paper* (weekly).

Private Aircraft: Ketchikan International Airport on Gravina Island; elev. 88 feet; length 7,500 feet; asphalt; fuel 100LL, A. Ketchikan Harbor seaplane base downtown; fuel 80, 100, A.

Ketchikan is located on the southwest side of Revillagigedo (ruh-vee-uh-guh-GAY-doh) Island, on Tongass Narrows opposite Gravina Island. The name Ketchikan is derived from a Tlingit name, Kitschk-Hin, meaning the creek of the "thundering wings of an eagle." The creek flows through the town, emptying into Tongass Narrows. Before Ketchikan was settled, the area at the mouth of Ketchikan Creek was a Tlingit Indian fish camp. Settlement began with interest in both mining and fishing. The first salmon cannery moved here in 1886, operating under the name of Tongass Packing Co. It burned down in August 1889. Gold was discovered nearby in 1898. This, plus residual effects of the gold, silver and copper mines, caused Ketchikan to become a booming little mining town. It was incorporated in 1901.

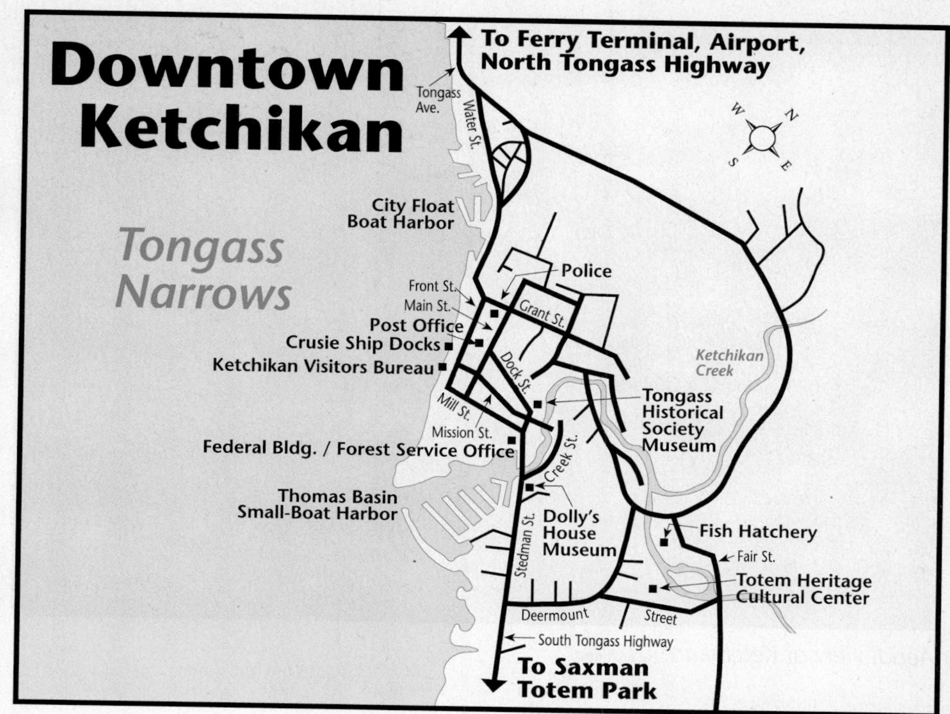

As mining waned, the fishing industry began to grow. By the 1930s more than a dozen salmon canneries had been built; during the peak years of the canned salmon industry, Ketchikan earned the title of "Salmon Capital of the World." Overfishing caused a drastic decline in salmon by the 1940s, and today only 4 canneries and a cold storage plant operate. Trident Seafoods Corp., owner of Ketchikan's oldest and largest cannery, provides lodging for 200-plus salmon processors in a floating bunkhouse. An industry under development is the commercial harvest of abalone near Ketchikan.

As fishing reached a low point, the timber industry expanded. The first sawmill was originally built in 1898 at Dolomi on Prince of Wales Island to cut timber for the Dolomi Mine. It was dismantled and moved to Ketchikan and rebuilt in 1903. A large pulp mill was constructed in 1953 at Ward Cove, a few miles northwest of town. It closed in 1997.

Tourism is an extremely important industry here; Ketchikan is Alaska's first port of call for cruise ships and Alaska Marine Highway vessels.

Ketchikan is Alaska's southernmost major city and the state's fourth largest (after Anchorage, Fairbanks and Juneau). The closest city in British Columbia is Prince Rupert. Ketchikan is a linear waterfront city, with much of its 3-mile/5-km-long business district suspended above water on pilings driven into the bottom of Tongass Narrows. It clings to the steep wooded hillside and has many homes perched on cliffs that are reached by climbing long wooden staircases or narrow winding streets.

The area supports 4 public grade schools, 4 parochial grade schools, a junior high school, 2 high schools and the University of Alaska Southeast campus.

Lodging & Services

Accommodations in Ketchikan include bed and breakfasts (see ads following) and several motels/hotels. The major shopping areas are downtown and the west end.

Ketchikan AYH hostel is located at the First United Methodist Church, Grant and Main streets; write Box 8515, Ketchikan, AK 99901; phone (907) 225-3319 (summer only). Open June 1 to Aug. 31, the hostel has showers, sleeping pads (bring sleeping bag) and kitchen facilities. Check-in time is

Aerial view of Ketchikan. (© Rich Reid)

6 to 11 P.M. Reservations strongly recommended. Cost is $10 per night for members (AYH membership passes may be purchased at the hostel), $13 for nonmembers.

Camping

There are 5 campgrounds (4 public campgrounds and a private resort) north of the city on North Tongass Highway and Ward Lake Road. See highway logs in this section. Dump station located at Ketchikan Public Works office, 2 blocks north of state ferry terminal. Contact the visitors bureau for brochure on RV use and parking. ▲

Transportation

Air: Daily scheduled jet service is provided from the Ketchikan International Airport by Alaska Airlines to other Southeast cities, Anchorage and Seattle, WA. Commuter and charter service to other Southeast communities is available via LAB Flying Service and Promech Air.

Airport terminal, across Tongass Narrows on Gravina Island, is reached via shuttle ferry (10-minute ride, $2.50 per person, $5 per vehicle, one way) departing from the ferry terminal on North Tongass Avenue at half-hour intervals. Airport ferry terminal on Revillagigedo Island is 2.7 miles from downtown. Airporter service between downtown and airport is $11 to $12 (includes ferry fare). Shuttle and taxi service is also available between downtown and the airport.

Ferry: Alaska Marine Highway vessels connect Ketchikan with all mainline southeastern Alaska port cities, Prince Rupert, BC, and Bellingham, WA. There are also daily state ferry connections via the MV *Aurora* between Ketchikan and Metlakatla (1 hr. 15 min.), and Ketchikan and Hollis (2 hrs. 45 min.).

Terminal building with waiting room, ticket counter and loading area is on North Tongass Avenue (Highway), 2 miles/3.2 km north of downtown. Phone (907) 225-6181. Foot passengers can walk from the ferry to a post office, restaurant and grocery store if stopover time permits. Taxi service available.

Bus: Daily municipal bus service, stops at every stop within the city limits at half-hour intervals; schedules available at visitors bureau. Fare is $1/one way.

Car Rental: Available at airport and downtown locations from Alaska Car Rental (907) 225-5000 and Payless Car Rental (907) 225-6004.

Taxi: Taxi cabs meet ferry and airport arrivals.

Highways: North Tongass and South Tongass highways and Ward Lake Road (see logs this section).

Cruise Ships: Ketchikan is the first port of call for many cruise ships to Alaska. Cruises depart from U.S. West Coast ports and Vancouver, BC. Two cruise lines depart from Ketchikan.

Private Boats: Two public docks downtown, Thomas Basin and City Float, provide transient moorage. In the West End District, 1 mile from downtown, Bar Harbor has moorage, showers. No gas available. Permits required. Moorage space in Ketchikan is limited; all private boats should contact the harbormaster's office at (907) 225-3610 prior to arrival to secure a spot.

Attractions

Ketchikan's waterfront is the center of the city. A narrow city on a mountainside, Ketchikan has a waterfront that runs for several miles and consists of docks, stores on pilings, seaplane floats, 3 picturesque boat harbors, a seaplane base and ferry terminal. There is constant activity here as seaplanes take off and vessels move in and out of the harbor. Walking-tour maps are available at the visitors bureau and at the ferry terminal.

The Plaza. Southeast Alaska's premier shopping center. Two comfort-controlled levels feature a variety of national and local retail shops and services for complete one-stop shopping. Plenty of free parking. Less than a mile south of the ferry terminal. Open every day except major holidays. [ADVERTISEMENT]

Fish Pirate's Daughter, a well-done local musical-comedy melodrama, portrays Ketchikan's early fishing days, with some of the city's spicier history included. Performed 7 P.M. and 8:45 P.M. Fridays in July. Contact First City Players, 338 Main St., phone (907) 225-4792 or 225-2211, for more information. Admission fee.

Tongass Historical Museum, located on Dock Street, in central downtown, explores the rich culture of the Tlingit, Haida and Tsimshian people, as well as the early history and development of Ketchikan, Alaska's feisty "First City." Open in summer from 8 A.M. to 5 P.M. daily. Winter (October to mid-May) hours are 1-5 P.M. Wednesday through Friday, 1-4 P.M. Saturday and Sunday. The Raven Stealing the Sun totem stands just outside the entrance. Salmon viewing platforms. Admission fee is $3 for adults; free admission in off-season. Phone (907) 225-5600 for more information.

Creek Street is Ketchikan's famous "red-light district," where Black Mary, Dolly, Frenchie and others plied their trade for over half a century until 1954. Nearly 20 houses lined the far side of Ketchikan Creek; many have been restored. There are also several art and gift shops. Dolly's House, a former brothel, is open during the summer. Admission charged. Creek Street is a wooden street on pilings that begins just past the bridge on Stedman (South Tongass Highway). Watch for salmon in the creek below the bridge in late August. Also look for the metal sculpture paying tribute to the salmon; it's a local landmark.

Totem Heritage Center, at 601 Deermount St., houses 33 totem poles and fragments retrieved from deserted Tlingit and Haida Indian villages. This national landmark collection comprises the largest exhibit of original totems in the United States. Facilities include craft exhibits, craft classes for children and reference library. Gift shop, craft demonstrations and guided tours during summer months. Summer admission fee $4. No admission charged off-season. Summer hours are 8 A.M. to 5 P.M. daily. Winter hours (October through mid-May) are 1–5 P.M. Tuesday through Friday. Phone (907) 225-5900.

Deer Mountain Hatchery and Eagle Center is located in the city park within walking distance of downtown (take the bridge across Ketchikan Creek from the Totem Heritage Center). The hatchery produces about 100,000 king, 150,000 coho, 30,000 rainbow trout and 6,500 steelhead fingerlings annually. Observation platforms and information signs provide education on the life cycles of salmon. Also an opportunity to photograph eagles up close at the Eagle Center. Open from 8 A.M. to 4:30 P.M. daily late May to late September.

The Ketchikan Mural on Stedman Street was created by 21 Native artists in 1978. The 125-by-18-foot design is collectively entitled *The Return of the Eagle.*

Fourth of July is a major celebration in Ketchikan. The Timber Carnival takes place over the Fourth of July with events such as ax throwing and chopping, power saw bucking and a tug-of-war. There are also fireworks, the Calamity Race (by canoe and kayak, bicycle and on foot), a parade and other events.

The Blueberry Arts Festival, in August, features arts and crafts, the performing arts and plenty of homemade blueberry pies, blueberry crepes, blueberry cheesecakes and other culinary delights. Events include a slug race, bed race, pie-eating contest, trivia contest and spelling bee. A juried art show, fun-run and dance are also part of the festival. Sponsored and coordinated by the Ketchikan Area Arts and Humanities Council, Inc. (338 Main St., Ketchikan 99901; 907/225-2211).

Saxman Totem Park, Milepost 2.5 South Tongass Highway, is included in local sightseeing tours. Open year-round. There is no admission charge, but there is a fee for guided tour (offered May through September). The totem park has 30 totems. The tour includes demonstrations at the Carving Center and performances by the Cape Fox Dancers at the Beaver Tribal House. For more information on hours, tours and events, phone the Cape Fox Tours office at (907) 225-4846, ext. 310.

Totem Bight community house and totem park, Milepost 9.9 North Tongass Highway, contains an excellent model of a Tlingit community house and a park with 13 totems.

Misty Fiords National Monument/ Ketchikan Ranger District, Tongass National Forest. 3.2 million acres surrounding Ketchikan and nearby communities. Pristine coastal rain forest, glacially carved fjords, waterfalls, wildlife, fishing, spectacular geologic features. Includes 2.3 million acres of the National Monument Wilderness. Forest Service maintains approximately 60 miles of trails. 30 cabins available for public rental. Most are accessible by floatplane or boat and can be reserved by calling toll free 1-877-444-6777 up to 180 days in advance. Other recreational attractions include Ward Lake Recreation Area (3 campgrounds, day-use area, trails), Naha Dock and Trail, Margaret Bay fish pass and bear viewing. Sea kayaking is a popular means of exploring the coastlines and venturing into remote areas. Cabin reservations, maps, brochures and trip planning assistance available from the Southeast Alaska Visitors Center, 50 Main St., Ketchikan, AK 99901. Phone (907) 228-6214, fax (907) 228-6234. Internet: www.fs.fed.us/r10/ketchikan.

Charter boats: About 120 vessels operate out of Ketchikan for half-day, all-day or overnight sightseeing or fishing trips and transport to USFS public-use cabins and outlying communities. See advertisements this section and check with the visitors bureau or at the marinas.

Fishing lodges and resorts in the area offer sportfishing for steelhead, salmon, halibut, trout, lingcod and red snapper. Resorts near Ketchikan include Misty Fiords Lodge, Salmon Falls Resort and Yes Bay Lodge. There are several fishing lodges on Prince of Wales Island, including Waterfall Resort, which is housed in a renovated fish cannery.

Charter planes operate from the airport and from the waterfront on floats and are available for fly-in fishing, flightseeing or service to lodges and smaller communities.

Picnic areas include Settlers Cove by Settlers Cove Campground, **Milepost 18.2** North Tongass Highway; Refuge Cove, **Milepost 8.7** North Tongass Highway; Rotary Beach at **Milepost 3.5** South Tongass Highway; and Grassy Point and Ward Lake, **Milepost 1.1** Ward Lake Road.

Hiking trails include Deer Mountain trail, which begins at the corner of Fair and Deermount streets. The 3-mile, 3,001-foot ascent gives trekkers an excellent vantage of downtown Ketchikan and Tongass Narrows. Good but steep trail. Access to Deer Mountain cabin, the only USFS public-use cabin accessible by trail from Ketchikan. Cabin reservations are required. Perseverance Lake trail, 2.4 miles from Ward Lake to Perseverance Lake. Connell Lake trail, about 2 miles along north shore of Connell Lake, is in good condition. Silvis Lakes trail, about 2 miles up to Lower Silvis Lake and picnic area. Trail continues to Upper Silvis Lake and Deer Mountain trail, but is very difficult. An easy and informative 1-mile nature trail circles Ward Lake.

Southeast Alaska Visitor Center, 50 Main St., features exhibits on Native cultures, ecosystems, resources and the rain forest in Southeast Alaska. Also 13-minute, award-winning "Mystical Southeast Alaska" audio visual program and Alaska Public Lands trip planning room. Admission charged May–Sept. Open 8 A.M. to 5 P.M. daily in summer, Tuesday through Saturday in winter.

AREA FISHING: Check with the Alaska Dept. of Fish and Game at 2030 Sea Level Dr., Suite 215, or phone (907) 225-2859 for details on fishing in the Ketchikan area. Good fishing spots range from Mountain Point, a 5-mile drive from Ketchikan on South Tongass Highway, to streams, lakes, bays, and inlets 50 miles away by boat or by air. Half-day and longer charters and skiff rentals available out of Ketchikan. There are fishing resorts at Yes Bay, Clover Pass and at the entrance to Behm Canal (Salmon Falls Resort); and 13 fishing resorts on Prince of Wales Island. Fish include salmon, halibut, steelhead, Dolly Varden, cutthroat and rainbow, arctic grayling, eastern brook trout, lingcod and rockfish; shellfish include Dungeness crab and shrimp. Ketchikan has 2 king salmon derbies, a silver salmon derby and a halibut derby in summer.

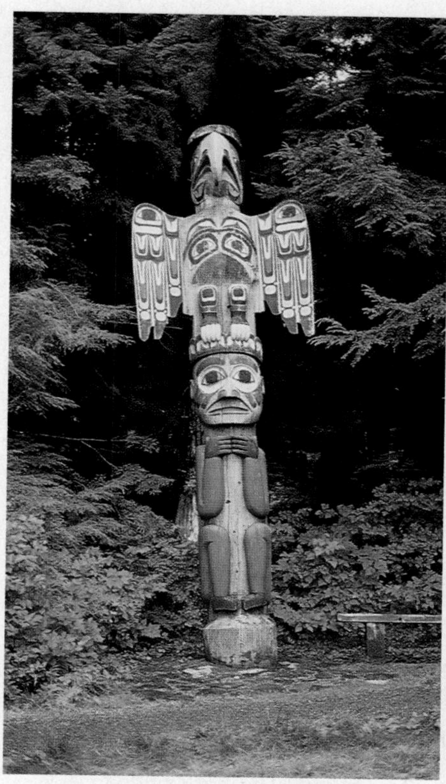

Totems are found at Totem Bight Saxman totem parks. (© Lee Foster)

North Tongass Highway Log

The North Tongass Highway is 18.4 miles long with 15.2 miles paved. It begins at the corner of Mill Street and Stedman (at the Federal Bldg.) and proceeds north to Totem Bight, Clover Pass and Settlers Cove Campground.

0 Federal Building on left with area information display. Proceeding on Mill Street.

0.1 Southeast Alaska Visitor Center with information on federal lands in Alaska.

0.2 Turning right onto Front Street, cruise ship dock on left where passengers disembark from major ships. Ketchikan Visitors Bureau.

0.3 Tunnel. North of this, Front Street becomes Water Street.

0.5 City Float on left. Note older vessels.

0.7 Highway turns left, then right, and becomes Tongass Avenue.

1.2 West end shopping area begins.

1.7 Bar Harbor boat basin on left.

2 Ketchikan General Hospital on right, Ketchikan Ranger Station and Misty Fiords National Monument on left, northbound.

2.3 Ferry terminals for Alaska Marine Highway.

2.4 Main branch post office.

2.6 Carlanna Creek and bridge.

2.7 Airport shuttle ferry.

3.2 Almer Wolfe Memorial viewpoint of Tongass Narrows. Airport terminal is visible across the narrows on Gravina Island.

4 Hillside on right is a logged area, an example of clear-cut logging method and regrowth.

4.4 Alaska State Troopers and Highway Dept.

5.5 Small paved viewpoint overlooking Tongass Narrows and floatplane dock.

6 Ward Cove Cannery next to road. Cannery Creek and bridge.

6.8 Ward Lake Road (see log this section); open to hikers and bikers only.

7 Ward Creek and bridge; Ketchikan sawmill, owned by Ketchikan Pulp Co.; see **Mile 7.8**.

7.1 Junction with Revilla Road (see log this section).

7.3 WARD COVE. Post office, gas station and grocery.

7.8 Ketchikan Pulp Co. pulp mill was built in 1953; it closed in 1997.

8.7 Refuge Cove State Recreation Site with 14 picnic sites.

9.4 Mud Bight; "float houses" rest on mud at low tide and float during high tide.

9.9 Totem Bight State Historical Park; parking area, restrooms and phones. A short trail leads through the woods to Totem Bight community house and totem park. A striking setting. Don't miss this!

10.8 Grocery store and gas station.

12.9 Scenic viewpoint overlooking **Guard Island Lighthouse** built in 1903 and manned until 1969 when finally automated.

14.2 Clover Pass Resort turnoff. Left, North Point Higgins Road leads 0.6 mile to turnoff to resort; food, lodging, camping.

Left, then immediately right, is Knudson Cove Road, leading 0.4 mile to Knudson Cove Marina with public float, boat launch and boat rentals. Road rejoins North Tongass Highway at **Milepost 14.8.** ▲

14.8 Knudson Cove Marina to left 0.5 mile.

15.2 Pavement ends.

16.6 Salmon Falls Resort; private fishing lodge with restaurant and boat rentals.

18.2 Settlers Cove state campground, parking area and picnic area; 13 tent/trailer campsites; 2 covered picnic pavilions flanked by 12 picnic units are along the beach on either side of the campground. Camping fee $6/night. Tables, water, pit toilets. Open year-round. Good gravel beach for kids and boats. To right of beach is **Lunch Creek** (pink salmon in August), falls and trail. ▲

18.4 Road end.

Revilla Road Log

This 7.7-mile paved road off the North Tongass Highway provides access to Ward Lake Recreation Area, Harriet Hunt Lake (via Harriet Hunt Road at **Milepost 6.5**), Brown Mountains Logging Road and Council Lake. Motorists and hikers should be aware of private property boundaries, posted by Cape Fox Corp. (CFC), and logging and trucking activities.

Campers should be aware of USFS regulations in the Ward Lake Recreation Area: Camping is restricted to developed campgrounds and limited to 14 days.

0 Right turn northbound from North Tongass Highway at **Milepost 7.1**.

1.4 Junction with Ward Lake Road (see log this section).

2.3 Last Chance Campground on right; 19 spaces, paved road, gravel sites, tables, pit toilets, water. Camping fee charged. Open end of May to Sept. 30. Situated along Ward Creek among large old-growth trees. Stream fishing access from some sites along creek. Campsites can be reserved; phone 1-877-444-6777; internet: http://www.reserveusa.com.

2.4 Connell Lake Road, on right, a narrow gravel road extending 0.6 mile to Connell Lake Reservoir. At Mile 0.4 Connell Lake Road, a bridge passes over large pipe which once carried water from the reservoir to the pulpmill (closed) at Ward Cove. Connell Lake Trail at reservoir.

2.7 Turnout.

2.8 Ward Creek Salvage Sale Interpretive Thinning Area on left. A 1.5-mile interpretive trail.

6.5 Junction with 2.4-mile Harriet Hunt Lake Road, which dead-ends at **Harriet Hunt Lake Recreation Area**; parking, pit toilets, fishing (rainbow trout to 20 inches, May to November). Road is on Cape Fox Corp. lands. Watch for logging trucks.

7.6 Brown Mountain Logging Road, on right, a narrow gravel logging road 4.2 miles/6.8 km. Open to the public for dispersed camping. No services.

7.7 End public highway. Private logging road begins.

Ward Lake Road Log

The Ward Lake Road turnoff at **Milepost 6.8** North Tongass Highway is open for bikers and hikers only. Motorists take Revilla Road turnoff from North Tongass Highway to **Milepost 1.4** for Ward Lake Road and access to Ward Lake Recreation Area. This log starts at that junction.

0 Junction with Revilla Road at **Milepost 1.4.**

0.5 Ward Lake USFS picnic area on right; beach, parking area, picnic shelters and water. One end of nature trail around Ward Lake.

0.7 Ward Creek bridge. **Grassy Point picnic area** on right. Several walk-in picnic sites with tables and shelters near road. Pit toilet at parking area. Footbridge across Ward Creek to **Ward Lake Nature Trail.** Good fly fishing for steelhead, salmon and Dolly Varden.

0.8 3C's Campground (site of Civilian Conservation Corps camp and WWII Aleut relocation camp) entrance on left; 4 campsites, camping fee, open April to October. (Proposed group camping site.) ▲

0.9 Beginning of **Perseverance Lake Trail** on left. Trailhead is within 100 feet of 3C's Campground with parking across road. The 2.2 mile/3.5 km gravel and boardwalk trail leads to Perseverance Lake (elev. 518 ft/158 m); brook trout fishing.

1.1 Signal Creek USFS campground on right; paved road, 24 gravel sites with tables, water and pit toilets. Open mid-May to Sept. 30. Camping fee charged. Situated among large trees on the shore of Ward Lake. The Ward Lake Nature Trail passes through the campground. The trail loops around Ward Lake, a 30–50-minute, 1.3-mile easy walk on a well-graveled path. Campsites can be reserved; phone 1-877-444-6777; internet: http://www.reserveusa.com. ▲

End of old Ward Lake Road, now open only for foot or bike traffic.

Ward Creek and **Ward Lake**, cutthroat and Dolly Varden year-round, best March to June; steelhead to 16 lbs.; silver salmon to 18 lbs. and pink salmon to 5 lbs., August to October. (Hatchery-raised coho salmon; bring head of tagged fish to ADF&G.)

South Tongass Highway Log

The 12.9-mile South Tongass Highway leads from the corner of Mill and Stedman streets south to Saxman Totem Park. First 8.5 miles/13.7 km are paved.

0 Federal Building on right.

0.1 Ketchikan Creek and bridge. Beginning of Creek Street boardwalk on left next to bridge.

0.2 Thomas Street begins on right, a boardwalk street where old-time businesses are located. Thomas Basin boat harbor.

0.5 Cannery and cold storage plant.

0.9 U.S. Coast Guard base.

2.5 SAXMAN (pop. 389) was founded in 1896 by Tlingit Alaska Natives and named after a Presbyterian missionary who served the Tlingit people. The Native village of Saxman has a gas station and convenience store and is the site of **Saxman Totem Park**. Developed by Cape Fox Corp., this popular attraction includes a carving center and tribal house. Guided tours available from Cape Fox Tours.

2.7 Gas station.

3.5 Rotary Beach, public recreation area, contains a shelter and table.

5 Mountain Point, suburb of Ketchikan. Parking area and access to good salmon fishing from shore in July and August.

5.6 Boat ramp on right.

8.2 Herring Cove bridge and sawmill. Private hatchery for chum, king and coho salmon on short road to left; no tours.

8.5 Pavement ends.

8.8 Whitman Creek and bridge.

9 Scenic turnout on right. Note different shades of green on trees across the water. Light green are cedar; medium, hemlock; and the darker are spruce. Species grow intermixed.

10.3 Left, scenic waterfall.

11 Scenic turnout.

11.8 Lodge.

12.9 Road ends, view of power plant, an experimental sockeye salmon hatchery (no tours) and an abandoned cannery. Two-mile walk up gravel road leads to Lower Silvis Lake picnic area. Trail continues to Upper Silvis Lake and joins Deer Mountain trail, which connects to John Mountain National Recreation trail. Trail between Upper and Lower Silvis lakes is very difficult.

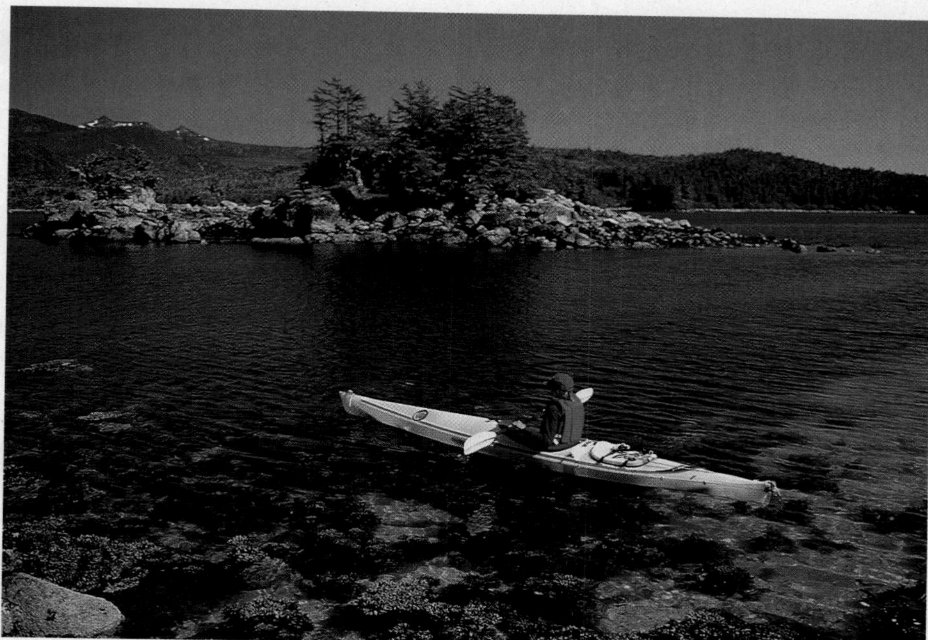

The west coast of Prince of Wales Island offers sea kayaking opportunities.
(© David Job)

Metlakatla

(See map, page 635)

Located on the west coast of Annette Island, 15 miles south of Ketchikan, Southeastern Alaska's southernmost community. **Population:** 1,673. **Emergency Services: Police, fire** and **ambulance,** emergency only, phone 911. **Visitor Information:** Tours to Metlakatla depart daily from Ketchikan; reservations are required. Contact the Community Tour Office at (877) 886-8687 for scheduling information. The Metlakatla tour and salmon bake operates from early-May to September. A permit from Metlakatla Indian Community is required for long-term visits to Annette Island.

Elevation: Sea level. **Climate:** Mild and moist. Summer temperatures range from 36°F/12°C to 65°F/18°C; winter temperatures from 28°F/-2°C to 44°F/7°C. Average annual precipitation is 115 inches: October is the wettest month with a maximum of 35 inches of rainfall. Annual snowfall averages 61 inches. **Radio:** KTKN 930 (Ketchikan). **Television:** 20 channels via cable.

Private Aircraft: Floatplane services.

Transportation: Air—Charter and scheduled floatplane service. **Ferry**—Scheduled state ferry service year-round via MV *Aurora* from Ketchikan; crossing time 1 hour 15 minutes.

Overnight accommodations, restaurant, groceries and banking services available.

Metlakatla was founded in 1887 by William Duncan, a Scottish-born lay minister, who moved here with several hundred Tsimshian Indians from a settlement in British Columbia after a falling-out with church authorities. Congress granted reservation status and title to the entire island in 1891, and the new settlement prospered under Duncan, who built a salmon cannery and sawmill.

Today, fishing and lumber continue to be the main economic base of Metlakatla. The community and island also retain the status of a federal Indian reservation, which is why Metlakatla has the only salmon fish traps in Alaska. (Floating fish traps were outlawed by the state shortly after statehood.)

The well-planned community has a town hall, a recreation center with an Olympic-sized swimming pool, a post office, 2 lumber mills and cold storage. The Metlakatla Indian Community is the largest employer in town, with retail and service trades the second largest. Many residents also are commercial fishermen. Subsistence activities remain an important source of food for residents, who harvest seaweed, salmon, halibut, cod, clams, dungeness crab and waterfowl.

There is a replica of the William Duncan Memorial Church here; the original was destroyed by fire in 1948. The Duncan Museum is located in the original cottage occupied by the Rev. William Duncan until his death in 1918.

Prince of Wales Island

(See map, page 636)

Includes Coffman Cove, Craig, Hollis, Hydaburg, Kasaan, Klawock, Naukati, Thorne Bay and Whale Pass

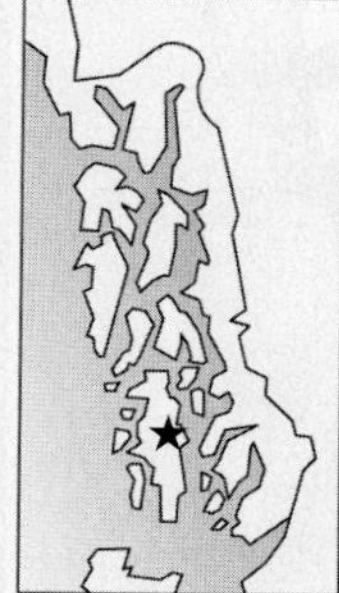

About 15 miles west of Ketchikan. **Population:** Approximately 5,200. **Emergency Services: Alaska State Troopers,** in Klawock, phone (907) 755-2918. **Police,** in Craig, phone (907) 826-3330; in Klawock, phone (907) 755-2777; emergencies only, phone 911; **Village Public Safety Officers** in Thorne Bay, phone (907) 828-3905; in Hydaburg, phone (907) 285-3321; in Klawock, phone (907) 755-2906. **Ambulance,** Hydaburg emergency response team, phone 911. **Health Clinics** for all emergencies, phone 911; in Craig, phone (907) 826-3257; in Klawock, phone (907) 755-4800; in Thorne Bay, phone 911 for emergency medical service; in Hydaburg, phone (907) 285-3462. **Maritime Search and Rescue,** call the Coast Guard at (800) 478-5555.

Visitor Information: Prince of Wales Island Chamber of Commerce, P.O. Box 497, Craig, AK 99921; phone (907) 826-3870, fax (907) 826-5467. E-mail: powcc@ptialaska.net. Web site: www.princeofwalescoc.org.

Elevation: Sea level to 4,000 feet. **Climate:** Mild and moist, but variable due to the island's size and topography. Rainfall in excess of 100 inches per year, with modest snowfall in winter at lower elevations. **Radio:** KRSA 580 (Petersburg), KTKN 930 (Ketchikan), KRBD-FM 90.1 (Ketchikan). **Television:** Via satellite. **Newspaper:** *Island News* (Thorne Bay, weekly).

Private Aircraft: Klawock airstrip, 2 miles northeast; elev. 50 feet; length 5,000 feet; lighted and paved. Seaplane bases adjacent to all the largest communities and in several bays.

Heavily forested with low mountains, Prince of Wales Island measures roughly 135 miles north to south by 45 miles east to west. The third largest island under the American flag (Kodiak is second, the Big Island of Hawaii is first), it is 2,231 square miles. The 6 communities with city status on the island—Craig (the largest with 2,145 residents), Klawock, Thorne Bay, Hydaburg, Coffman Cove and Kasaan are connected by road, as are the other 3 smaller communities of Hollis, Naukati and Whale Pass. Not connected by road are **PORT PROTECTION** and **POINT BAKER,** both at the northwest tip of the island (see *The ALASKA WILDERNESS GUIDE* for details on these communities).

Prince of Wales Island has been the site of several lumbermills and mining camps since the 1800s. But it was salmon that led to permanent settlement on the island. Klawock was the site of one of Alaska's first canneries, built in 1878. In the following years, some 25 canneries were built on the island to process salmon. Today, logging is prevalent on the island.

Prince of Wales Island offers uncrowded

Prince of Wales
Chamber of Commerce
Alaska
Progress Through Unity

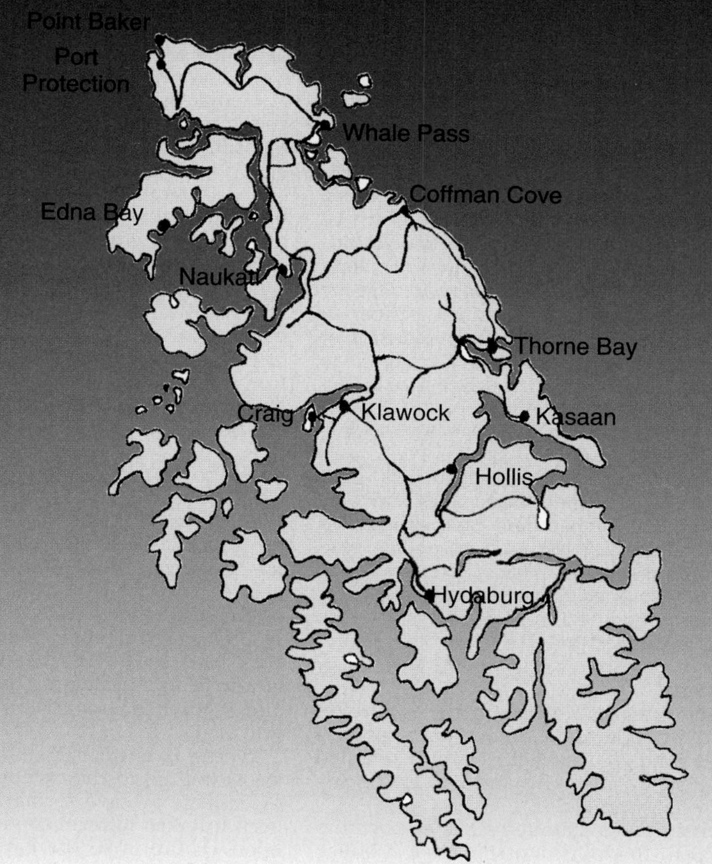
Point Baker
Port Protection
Whale Pass
Coffman Cove
Edna Bay
Naukati
Thorne Bay
Craig
Klawock
Kasaan
Hollis
Hydaburg

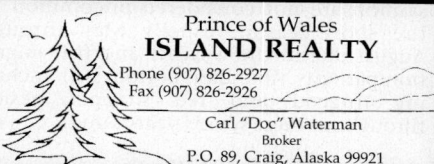

Craig is the largest community on Prince of Wales Island. (© David Job)

backcountry, fishing for salmon and trout, kayaking and canoeing waters, opportunities for viewing wildlife (black bears, Sitka black-tailed deer, bald eagles), adequate visitor facilities and some historical attractions. Most of the island is national forest land. The Forest Service manages 5 large, designated wilderness areas on Prince of Wales Island. There are also some Native corporation and private land holdings. Respect No Trespassing signs.

There are several roadside fishing spots on Prince of Wales Island. See the road logs in this section for details. Lakes and streams support red, pink and silver salmon, cutthroat, rainbow trout and Dolly Varden.

Lodging & Services

Prince of Wales Island has several hotels, lodges, rental cabins and bed and breakfasts. See community descriptions this section.

There are also more than 20 USFS cabins (accessible by plane, boat or on foot) available for public use; reservations and a fee are required. Contact the USFS office in Ketchikan or the local ranger districts at Craig (907/826-3271) and Thorne Bay (907/828-3304), or call toll free 1-877-444-6777.

Camping

There are private campgrounds with hookups at Coffman Cove and Klawock. There are 2 developed USFS campgrounds on the island—Eagle's Nest on Thorne Bay Road ($8 camping fee), and Harris River—and several undeveloped dispersed camping sites accessible via the island road system. See road logs this section. ▲

Transportation

Air: All communities on the island are served by floatplane, most daily. Wheel planes land at Klawock. Daily scheduled service by Pro–Mech Air and LAB Flying Service from Ketchikan.

Ferry: Alaska state ferry MV *Aurora* from Ketchikan to Hollis; crossing time 2 hours, 45 minutes. Phone Craig office at (907) 826-3432, Hollis terminal at (907) 530-7115.

Vehicle rental: Car rentals available in Craig at Wilderness Rent-A-Car (phone 800/949-2205); in Klawock from Log Cabin RV Park & Resort (800/544-2205).

Highways: Prince of Wales Island has the most extensive road network in Southeast Alaska. Over 1,000 miles of road allow access to most areas of the island. The island's 8 main roads are logged in this section. *DRIVER CAUTION: Watch for heavily loaded logging trucks while driving; they have the right-of-way.* CB radios are helpful. Carry a spare tire and spare gas. (Gas is available in Coffman Cove, Hydaburg, Craig, Klawock, Whale Pass, Thorne Bay and Naukati.) Use turnouts and approach hills and corners on your side of the road. Spur roads are *NOT* recommended for large RVs or cars with trailers. Some side roads may be closed intermittently during logging operations or highway construction. Watch for signs posted when roads are closed and expect delays.

Taxi: No free public transport meets the ferry at Hollis, but arrangements can be made with taxis. According to the chamber of commerce (phone 826-3870), fares range from about $25 per person to $50–$60 to charter a taxi (which is usually a van for several people).

Attractions

El Capitan Cave, located just north of Whale Pass off the North Island Road. People have been visiting El Capitan Cave for many years. El Capitan's pit is one of the deepest known in the U.S. Northern Prince of Wales has extensive limestone cave systems. Significant scientific discoveries have been found in these caves, including grizzly bear bones dating back 12,295 years, and black bear bones dating back 11,565 years.

There is a steep trail (more than 365 steps) leading to the cave entrance. Because of damage to cave formations, a gate has been installed to regulate visitation. There is open visitation to the gate some distance within the cave; guided tours beyond the gate. *Call or write for information and reservations; this may not be available in 2000.* schedule. Thorne Bay Ranger District, Box 19001, Thorne Bay 99919; phone (907) 828-3304. There are vault toilets, a government dock and a floatplane and boat tie-up at this U.S. Forest Service-administrated site.

AREA FISHING: Most fish in streams on the island are anadromous (travel upstream to spawn). Try **Klawock Lake** for trout and salmon; **Klawock River** downstream from the hatchery is good for trout, steelhead and salmon; **Thorne River** for Dolly Varden, trout and salmon; and **Sarkar River** for trout, steelhead and salmon. Fresh and saltwater guiding services are available.

World-class saltwater sportfishing abounds immediately offshore and throughout the many smaller islands surrounding Prince of Wales Island. Most communities have boat ramps. For those traveling without a boat, quality half-, full- and multi-day fishing trips are available through many of the local charter operators. Ocean fishing for salmon is best in July and early August for kings (chinook), August and September for coho, July, August and September for pinks, and August and September for chum. 100-lb. halibut, 50-lb. king salmon and 15-lb. coho salmon are not considered uncommon in the sport season, usually May through August due to the weather and fish migration patterns. Abundant bottom fish, including lingcod and red snapper, reside throughout these waters year-round.

Community Descriptions

COFFMAN COVE (pop. 254), 53 miles north of Klawock, a 2½-hour drive from Hollis. Formerly one of the largest independent logging camps in Southeast, Coffman Cove is now a small hamlet. Recreation includes hunting (deer and bear), good freshwater and saltwater fishing, boating, hiking. Charters for fishing and whalewatching available. Canoe Lagoon Oyster Co. here is the state's oldest and largest oyster producer; fresh oysters available locally.

Coffman Cove has a general store, liquor and gift shop (both open daily), gas pump, playground and ballfield, showers and laundry facilities, and an RV park. Tire repair is available. There is a dock and a small beach with access to salt water for canoes and cartop boats. Oceanview RV Park (907/329-2015) has 14 full-hookup sites on the beach. Accommodations at Coffman Cove Cabins (907/329-2251).. EMTs dispatch from Riggin' Shack. ▲

CRAIG (pop. 2,145), 31 miles from Hollis, is on the western shore of Prince of Wales Island. The original townsite, on Craig Island, is now connected to Prince of Wales by a short causeway. **Emergency Services:** Phone 911. **Police**, phone (907) 826-3330. **Clinic**, Seaview Medical Clinic, physician, public health nurses and the Craig Native health aide. Craig also has a chiropractic office and 2 dental clinics.

Visitor information: Craig City Hall, phone (907) 826-3275, open weekdays 8 A.M. to 5 P.M.; U.S. Forest Service office, open weekdays 8 A.M. to 5 P.M., phone (907) 826-3271; Prince of Wales Chamber of Commerce, phone (907) 826-3870.

Craig has several hotels and lodges, including Haida Way Lodge downtown (800/347-4625); Sunnahae Lodge (907/826-4000) and Shelter Cove Lodge (888/826-FISH), as well as Craig's Finest Oceanview B&B (907/826-3851). Sporting goods, fishing, hunting and camping supplies at Log

Cabin Sporting Goods. Gift, seafood, grocery and health food stores are also available. There are a laundromat and showers, liquor stores, bars, beauty and barber shops, a library and 2 banks (one with automatic teller machine). Craig has a school, grades K through 12, and an indoor community swimming pool.

RV camping with full hookups at Rain Country RV & Recreation. Gas, propane, RV supplies, towing and auto repair available. Free RV dump facilities on Cold Storage Road. Contact City Public Works at (907) 826-3405 during business hours for key. Evenings and weekends, contact the police department at (907) 826-3330.

Craig has 2 modern boat harbors, North Cove and South Cove, located on either side of the causeway, a seaplane float, fuel dock, city dock and float, 2 fish-buying docks and an old cannery dock. The Craig harbormaster's office, with public showers and restrooms, is located on the corner close to South Cove; phone (907) 826-3404, VHF Channel 16.

Craig was once a temporary fish camp for the Tlingit and Haida Natives of the area. In 1907, with the help of local Natives, William D. Craig Millar established a mildcure station known as Fish Egg for nearby Fish Egg Island. The Tlingit name for Fish Egg Island is "Sheenda" and the townsite was "Sheensit," which is now used by the Native Shaan-Seet Corp. Between 1908 and 1911, a permanent saltery and cold storage facility, along with about 2 dozen homes, were built on the city's present location and named for founder Craig Millar. In 1912, the post office was established, E.M. Streeter opened a sawmill and Craig constructed a salmon cannery. Both businesses peaked during WWI. Craig was incorporated in 1922, and grew throughout the 1930s, with some families relocating from the Dust Bowl.

Craig is the home port of many commercial fishing and charter sportfishing boats. Halibut, coho and chinook salmon, lingcod and red snapper (yelloweye) are the primary target species.

Fshing and fish processing, logging and timber processing, provide jobs. The Viking Lumber Co. mill, located between Craig and Klawock, produces moulding, window and door stock for the domestic market, and high-grade cants for export. Mining, transportation, tourism, construction and government jobs also contribute to the local economy.

Craig and Klawock host the annual Craig–Klawock King Salmon Derby from April to July 3, followed by a big Fourth of July parade and celebration. In late July the P.O.W. Chamber of Commerce sponsors its annual fair and logging show with booths, fair entrants and a logging competition in Thorne Bay.

In 1996 the Healing Heart totem pole was raised in Craig. The totem was carved by Tsimshian master carver Stan Marsden in memory of his son. The totem is 46 1/2 feet/14m tall and is carved from a red cedar tree more than 500 years old.

Black bears range throughout much of Southeastern Alaska. (© Four Corners Imaging)

HOLLIS (pop. 196), 25 road miles from Klawock, 35 nautical miles west of Ketchikan. Hollis was a mining town with a population of 1,000 from about 1900 to 1915. In the 1950s, Hollis became the site of Ketchikan Pulp Co.'s logging camp and served as the base for timber operations on Prince of Wales Island until 1962, when the camp was moved to Thorne Bay. Recent state land sales have spurred the growth of a small residential community here.

NOTE: Although Hollis is identified in the state ferry schedules as the port of call on Prince of Wales Island for the MV *Aurora* from Ketchikan, the ferry actually docks at Clark Bay, about 2 miles from Hollis.

HYDABURG (pop. 406), 36 miles from Hollis, 45 miles from Craig. Hydaburg was founded in 1911, and combined the populations of 3 Haida villages: Sukkwan, Howkan and Klinkwan. President William Howard Taft established an Indian reservation on the surrounding land in 1912, but, at the residents' request, most of the land was restored to its former status as part of Tongass National Forest in 1926. Hydaburg was incorporated in 1927, 3 years after its people became citizens of the United States.

Most of the residents are commercial fishermen, although there are some jobs in construction and the timber industry. Subsistence is also a traditional and necessary part of life here. Hydaburg has an excellent collection of restored Haida totems. The totem park was developed in the 1930s by the Civilian Conservation Corps, which brought in poles from the three abandoned Haida villages. There is also good salmon fishing here in the fall.

Four boardinghouses provide rooms and meals for visitors. Groceries, hardware and sundry items available locally. There are a gift shop, gas station, public telephones, video store and cafe. Cable television is available.

KASAAN (pop. 41), a small city located at the head of Kasaan Bay, was connected to the road system in 1996. It is approximately 16 miles south of Thorne Bay. There are a bed and breakfast, a post office, a school and boat docks.

KLAWOCK (pop. 659), 24 miles from Hollis. Klawock originally was a Tlingit Indian summer fishing village; a trading post and salmon saltery were established here in 1868. Ten years later a salmon cannery was built—the first cannery in Alaska and the first of several cannery operations in the area. Over the years the population of Klawock, like other Southeast communities, grew and then declined with the salmon harvest. The local economy is still dependent on fishing, along with timber cutting and sawmilling. A fish hatchery operated by Prince of Wales Hatchery Assoc. is located on Klawock Lake, very near the site of a salmon hatchery that operated from 1897 until 1917. Visitors are welcome. Klawock Lake offers good canoeing and boating.

Recreation here includes good fishing for salmon and steelhead in Klawock River, saltwater halibut fishing, and deer and bear hunting. Klawock's totem park contains 21 totems—both replicas and originals—from the abandoned Indian village of Tuxekan (developed by the Civilian Conservation Corps in 1938–40). A 5-year restoration project to restore and replace totems in the park was begun in 1995.

Groceries and gas are available in Klawock. Automatic teller machine located in Klawock Market. Accommodations available at Log Cabin Resort (800/544-2205). Log Cabin Resort also offers full-hookup RV sites on the beach.

NAUKATI (pop. 168). Located 61 miles north of Hollis, Naukati was established as a mining camp, and is currently a logging camp for Ketchikan Pulp Co. Naukati West is privately owned. The Naukati Connection has groceries, gas, propane, liquor, diesel, boat rentals, and tire repair; open daily (phone 907/629-4104). There is a school and a floatplane dock. The EMS squad can be reached on CB channel 16, VHF Channel 16 or phone (907) 629-4283 or 629-4234.

THORNE BAY (pop. 597), 59 miles from Hollis. Thorne Bay was incorporated in 1982, making it one of Alaska's newest cities. The settlement began as a logging camp in 1962, when Ketchikan Pulp Co. (a subsidiary of Louisiana Pacific Corp.) moved its operations from Hollis. Thorne Bay was connected to the island road system in 1974. Camp residents created the community—

and gained city status from the state—as private ownership of the land was made possible under the Alaska Statehood Act. Employment here depends mainly on the lumber company and the U.S. Forest Service, with assorted jobs in municipal government and in local trades and services. Thorne Bay is centrally located between 2 popular Forest Service recreation areas: Eagle's Nest Campground and Sandy Beach picnic area. The Thorne River offers excellent canoeing and kayaking, and the bay offers excellent sailing and waterskiing (wet suit advised).

Accommodations are available. Call City Hall for listings, (907) 828-3380. Groceries available from Thorne Bay Market. General merchandise and fishing and hunting supplies at the Thorne Bay Company (907/828-3330). Boat rentals available. Fuel for boats may be purchased at the Thorne Bay Co. float (unleaded) and JC's float (diesel, unleaded). Aviation fuel available through Petro Alaska. City-operated RV dump station. Facilities include boat dock (with potable water, power, sewer pumpout station and fish cleaning facilities), cement boat-launch ramp, helicopter landing pad, floatplane float, liquor store and parking facility. ▲

WHALE PASS (pop. 92), accessible by 7-mile loop road from **Milepost 39.7** North Island Road, was the site of a floating logging camp on Whale Passage. The camp moved out in the early 1980s, but new residents moved in with a state land sale. The community has a small grocery store and gas pump; cabins and freezer space available. There is also a school, post office and floatplane dock. Accommodations available. Good fishing on the loop road into Whale Pass.

Klawock is located on the west coast of Prince of Wales Island. (© David Job)

Hollis–Klawock–Craig Highway Log

This highway, 31.5 miles long, begins at the ferry landing at Hollis and heads west through Klawock then south to Craig, taking motorists through the temperate rainforest environment typical of Southeast Alaska. It is a wide, paved road. Posted speed is 35 to 50 mph. Many roads and trails off highway lead to private property; please respect barricades and No Trespassing signs. *CAUTION: Watch for logging trucks.*

Distance from Hollis (H) is followed by distance from Craig (C). Physical mileposts show distance from Craig.

H 0 (C 31.5) Alaska Marine Highway, **Hollis ferry terminal** at Clark Bay, open during ferry arrivals and departures only (phone 907/530-7115, or in Craig 826-3432). Pay phone; no other services.

H 0.2 (C 31.3) Clark Bay subdivision access to right.

H 1.4 (C 30.1) Left 0.3 mile to Hollis townsite. School and USFS office, city harbor and float, floatplane dock, post office, telephone; no other services.

H 2 (C 29.5) Alaska Power and Telephone power plant and Alascom satellite station to left. Hollis Fire Department and EMS garage to right.

H 2.4 (C 29.1) **Maybeso Creek**, cutthroat; Dolly Varden; pink and silver salmon; steelhead run begins in mid-April. Pools offer the best fishing. Walking good along streambed but poor along bank. Watch for bears.

H 4.2 (C 27.3) Turnout left, view of mouth of the Harris River.

H 4.8 (C 26.7) Head left for lower Harris subdivision.

H 5.2 (C 26.3) Turnout.

H 6.4 (C 25.1) Entering Tongass National Forest.

H 6.5 (C 25) Head left for upper Harris subdivision.

H 7.7 (C 23.8) Turnout.

H 8.4 (C 23.1) USFS hiking trail to **Harris River** fishing: cutthroat; steelhead run mid-April; salmon and Dolly Varden run beginning in mid-July. Easy walking on the gravel bars in the middle of 1.3-mile-long river.

H 8.5 (C 23) Turnout.

H 10.5 (C 21) **Junction** with Hydaburg Road; see log this section.

H 11.2 (C 20.3) USFS trailhead for 20 Mile Spur Trail (approximately 3 miles long).

H 11.3 (C 20.2) Harris River bridge and Harris River Campground (USFS).

H 12.4 (C 19.1) End of Harris River valley. Island divide is here at 500 feet elev.; streams now flow west. Turnout state DOT gravel storage area.

H 12.6 (C 18.9) Leaving Tongass National Forest.

H 13.6 (C 17.9) East end of Klawock Lake, about 7 miles long and up to 1 mile wide. Lake borders the road on the left at several places. Private property; contact Klawock–Heenya Corp. in Klawock.

H 16.1 (C 15.4) Turnout left, boat launch for Klawock Lake.

H 16.2 (C 15.3) 35 mph curve; believe the sign.

H 17.6 (C 13.9) Turnout left, view of Klawock Lake.

H 20.1 (C 11.4) Turnout right, view of Klawock Lake.

H 22 (C 9.5) **Prince of Wales Hatchery**, operated by the Prince of Wales Assoc. The hatchery produces sockeye, coho and steelhead. Visitors welcome; Daily tours, phone (907) 755-2231.

H 22.1 (C 9.4) Klawock-Heenya Trailer Court to right; turnout left for trail access to Klawock River sportfishing.

H 22.2 (C 9.3) Turnout left, access to Klawock River fishing.

H 22.3 (C 9.2) Turnout left, access to Klawock River fishing.

H 22.4 (C 9.1) Turnout left, access to Klawock River fishing.

H 23.3 (C 8.2) Mall; grocery store, liquor store, gift shop and pizza.

H 23.4 (C 8.1) **Junction** with **Big Salt Road**; access to Thorne Bay, Kasaan, Coffman Cove, Naukati, Whale Pass and the north end of the island.

H 23.5 (C 8) Turnoff right, services available.

H 23.7 (C 7.8) Lodge to left, **St. John's by the Sea Catholic Church** to right. St. John's was designed and built with local lumber and materials by the local church community. The stained-glass designs, representing all known Native tribes, were designed and built by local artists. This is a "must-see" structure. Father Ed Matthews and Sister Tish welcome the opportunity to show the church. Good eagle viewing in Klawock River estuary during salmon season.

H 23.8 (C 7.7) Loop road with 21 totem poles.

H 23.9 (C 7.6) Klawock-Heenya Corp. offices.

H 24.2 (C 7.3) **Klawock River** bridge spans tidal estuary where river meets salt water.

H 24.3 (C 7.2) Klawock Fuels (gas and diesel), Alaska State Troopers and Alaska Dept. of Fish and Game to left. Alesha Roberts Center.

H 24.5 (C 7) Leaving village of **KLAWOCK.** State troopers in building on left.

H 24.6 (C 6.9) Turnoff right to Viking Lumber log sort and shop and Klawock Indian Corp. dock. Ocean-going vessels load locally harvested logs for worldwide transport.

H 25 (C 6.5) Viking Lumber Co. mill; produces moulding, window and door stock for the domestic market and high-grade cants for export.

H 26.6 (C 4.9) Turnout right, scenic view of Klawock Inlet and San Alberto Bay.

H 27.9 (C 3.6) On left is landfill operated by city of Klawock. Bears can usually be seen here.

H 29.1 (C 2.4) Crab Creek subdivision.

H 29.3 (C 2.2) Crab Creek bridge.

H 29.8 (C 1.7) Shaan-Seet Trailer Court and St. Nicholas Road to left. St. Nicholas Road, which extends 14 miles around Port St. Nicholas, is scenic but in very poor condition.

H 30.1 (C 1.4) **P.O.W. Chamber of Commerce** on right.

H 30.2 (C 1.3) Craig schools to left, post office, bank and Thompson House supermarket on right.

H 30.3 (C 1.2) Cold Storage Road. Dump station on right, behind supermarket.

H 30.4 (C 1.1) North and South Cove harbors operated by the city of Craig. Turn left for Cemetery Island, ballpark and archaeological dig.

H 30.7 (C 0.8) Stop sign, downtown **CRAIG.** Turn left 1 block for Craig municipal offices and city gym. Craig clinic is on left, half block past city office. End of highway is 3 blocks right.

H 31 (C 0.5) Road dead ends.

Big Salt Road Log

Big Salt Road begins at **Milepost C 8.1** on the Hollis–Klawock–Craig Highway and extends 17.1 miles, ending at its junction with Thorne Bay Road. It is a gravel road with much logging traffic; under construction in late 1999: straightening and scheduled for seal coating. Top speed for much of the road is 25 mph. Good berry picking for blueberries and huckleberries along the road.
Distance is measured from Klawock.

0 Grocery store, laundromat and gas station. Diner/restaurant.

0.1 Klawock city trailer park on right with some overnight sites; obtain permits from the city clerk. A camping fee is charged. ▲

0.4 Log Cabin R.V. Park & Resort: tackle store, skiff rentals, lodging, campground. ▲

0.9 Airport turnoff. Pavement ends.

8.7 Big Salt Lake, actually a saltwater body protected by small islands but permitting tidal flow in and out, is visible to the left from several spots along road. Waterfowl and bald eagles are often observed here. Wreckage of a military aircraft can be seen across lake. The plane crashed in 1969 en route to Vietnam; all on board survived.

8.9 Boat ramp and canoe launching area on Big Salt Lake. If boating on this tidal lake, be aware of strong currents.

9.7 Black Bear Creek, cutthroat; Dolly Varden; red, pink, dog and silver salmon, run mid-July to mid-September. Except for the lower 2 miles, creek can be fished from the bank. Best at the mouth of stream, 200 yards/183m upstream from the bridge or in large meadow, 1.5 miles from the mouth. Road on right leads to Black Lake. Watch for heavy equipment.

12.6 (20.3 km) **Steelhead Creek**, cutthroat; Dolly Varden; steelhead; pink, dog and silver salmon. Creek can be reached by boat through south entrance to Big Salt Lake. Lake should only be entered during high and low slack tides due to the strong tidal currents. High tide in lake is delayed 2 hours from outside waters. Bank fishing restricted by undergrowth.

15 Muskeg on right.

16.6 Short boardwalk on right leads to **Control Lake**, cutthroat; Dolly Varden; pink and silver salmon; good red salmon stream in August. USFS cabin on other side is available for public use. Skiff docked at end of boardwalk is for registered cabin users. Wolf population in area.

17.1 Control Lake Junction. Junction of Big Salt Road (SR 929) with Thorne Bay Road and North Island Road (FR 20). Road to Thorne Bay (log follows) to east. Road to Labouchere Bay, with access to Whale Pass and Coffman Cove, to north; see North Island Road log this section. Turn right for Eagle's Nest Campground. Last 3 miles to Control Lake is paved. ▲

Thorne Bay Road Log

Thorne Bay Road extends 18 miles to City of Thorne Bay.
Physical mileposts show distance from Thorne Bay post office.

18 Control Lake Junction. Junction with Big Salt Road and North Island Road.

16.6 Eagle's Nest USFS campground; 12 sites, tables, water, hand pump, toilet and canoe launch. Camping fee $8. Balls Lake, picnic area; cutthroat; Dolly Varden; red, pink and silver salmon. ▲

13 Bridge. Rio Roberts and Rio Beaver creeks, cutthroat; pink and silver salmon. A 0.7-mile cedar-chip and double-plank boardwalk leads to a viewing deck overlooking falls and Rio Roberts Fish Pass.

10.7 Rio Beaver Creek bridge.

6.7 Goose Creek, cutthroat; pink and silver salmon. Excellent spawning stream. Good run of pink salmon in mid-August. Lake Ellen Road on right leads 4.5 miles south to **Lake No. 3 USFS campsite**; space to accommodate up to 2 RVs, pit toilet, 2 fire rings and 2 picnic tables. No water or garbage. Road continues beyond campsite to lake and hiking trail to Salt Chuck. Abandoned Salt Chuck Mine is located here. ▲

6.5 Thorne River runs beside road for the next 0.5 mile. Cutthroat; Dolly Varden; steelhead; rainbow; red, pink, dog and silver salmon. Excellent fishing reported from **Milepost 4.9** to **2.1.**

4.9 Thorne River bridge. Thorne River now follows road on right.

4.1 Falls Creek.

4 (6.4 km) **Gravelly Creek USFS picnic area**; walk in to picnic area on the bank of Thorne River at the mouth of Gravelly Creek; 3 tables, fire rings, vault toilet and open-sided shelter. This site was logged in 1918. Note the large stumps with notches. Notches were used by old-time loggers for spring boards to stand on while sawing or chopping.

3.7 Gravelly Creek.

2.1 Right, mouth of Thorne River.

1.3 Log sorting area. Here different species of logs are sorted for rafting and transporting to mills or for export.

1.2 Log raft holding area. After logs are sorted and tied into bundles, the bundles are chained together into a raft suitable for towing by tugboat.

0.7 Dump station on Shoreline Drive just past Bayview Tire; $5 charge.

0 THORNE BAY. The road extends about 10 miles beyond the community to Sandy Beach day-use area with picnic shelter, 6 tables, fire rings, vault toilet and RV parking. Good view of Clarence Strait. Road then continues north to Coffman Cove.

Kasaan Road Log

This narrow road runs southeast 17.1 miles from Thorne Bay Road to Kasaan. Turnouts, occurring every 0.1 mile, are only noted if some other feature is present. A warning sign says to monitor CB channel 3.
Distance is measured from Thorne Bay Road Mile 6.7.

0 Turn off Thorne Bay Road just past Goose Creek. South to Kasaan.

0.4 Road splits. Veer north for Kasaan, south for Forest Service campsite. Speed limit 20 mph. ▲

0.5 Private drive next 1 mile. No hunting. Shake mill to south.

0.6 Thorne Bay solid waste facility to north.

0.8 Sawmill to south.

1.2 Turnout north. Unnamed lake to north. Informal picnic site.

1.4 Gravel pit to north.

2.1 15 mph curve. Turnout to north at the end of the curve. Slide area.

3.0 Turnout to north. First view of the waters of Thorne Bay.

4.1 Road was built around a huge rock. Keep to the right. Note tree growing on top of the rock and splitting it in half.

4.4 Water hose to the right.

4.6 Turnout to south. Informal campsite in old gravel pit.

5.3 Muskeg to north. Turnout to south.

5.4 15 mph curve. No Hunting sign. Road splits; keep north for Kasaan.

5.5 Turnout to south. Road changes to packed shot-rock. Observe sign—"One lane road with pullouts."

5.6 Turnouts to north and south. Informal campsite.

6.1 Turnouts to north and south. Informal tent site.

6.5 Turnout to north. Setter Lake to east.

6.7 Turnout to north. View of small lake for next 0.2 mile.

6.9 Turnout to south. Informal campsite.

7.1 Turnout to north. Informal picnic site.

8.8 Bridge over creek. Turnout to south.

9.2 Turnout to north. Glimpse of Loon Lake to west.

10.2 Beaver dam to south. Road crosses over a culvert.

10.5 Informal picnic site to south.

10.8 Good view of Tolstoi Bay. Beach access, boat portage. Informal picnic site. 10 mph, one-lane road for next 0.5 mile. Packed shot-rock ends and gravel begins.

11.6 Bridges with stop signs over creek.

11.7 Informal campsite to north in the old rock pit.

11.9 Informal campsite to north in the old rock pit.

12.5 Turnout to north. Informal campsite in the old rock pit.

12.8 Turnout to north. Sign announces that surrounding forest was harvested in 1973 by Sealaska and thinned in 1993.

13 Sign on a stump notes trap line 1993–94.

13.1 Road splits. Veer south over the bridge for Kasaan. 2000 Road to north.

13.2 Beaver dams can be seen along creek.

13.9 Road crosses both north and south.

14.3 2300 Road to north.

14.5 First view of Kasaan Bay and up Twelvemile Arm. Please remember this land is privately owned. Contact Sealaska for permission to camp.

15 Turnout to south. Road to north.

15.2 Road to north.

15.7 Beautiful viewpoint of Kasaan Bay.

16.1 Road to south. Note alpine ridge lines.

16.5 Road to south.

16.9 Wide turnout to south.

17.1 Stop sign. Turn south for Kasaan and totem park, go straight for Dexter Wallace Harbor. To get to the totem park, turn south and head towards the waterfront, driving all the way to the end of the road. At the bed and breakfast ask Annette Thompson for permission to walk down the path and for a personal tour of the totem park.

Hydaburg Road Log

The Hydaburg Road is 24 miles long and begins 11 miles west of the Hollis main ferry terminal on the Hollis–Klawock–Craig Highway. Road is chip-sealed/hard surface. Some sections of the road are heavily used by logging trucks.

0 Junction with Hollis–Klawock–Craig Highway at **Milepost H 10.5.**

1.1 Harris River bridge.

2.6 Trailhead for One Duck 1.3-mile-long trail to alpine area and shelter. Contact the USFS office for more information on all trails along the Hydaburg Road.

4.6 Bridge over Trocadero Creek.

8.9 Cable Creek fish pass. Boardwalk to viewing area overlooking stream.

9.3 Trocadero trailhead, gravel pullout.

9.5 Trocadero picnic area; tables, fire grills; no toilets, trash service or water. Good view of Trocadero Valley.

9.9 Road on left leads to Twelvemile Arm. This logging road leads to Polk Inlet. Watch for logging and construction activity.

12.3 Trailhead for Soda Springs trail, 2.5 miles long.

13.9 North Pass.

15.6 Natzuhini logging camp.

15.9 Natzuhini River bridge.

16.8 Road winds along Natzuhini Bay.

21.9 Hydaburg River bridge.

22.3 Quarry Road to right.

23.6 T-junction: right to Hydaburg, left to Saltery Point. Private land. No trespassing.

24 HYDABURG.

North Island Road Log

Signed as USFS Road No. 20, this narrow 2-lane road leads north 79.5 miles from its junction with Big Salt and Thorne Bay roads near Control Lake to Labouchere Bay on the northwest corner of the island. The road has a fair to excellent gravel surfacing and some steep grades. Slow down for approaching vehicles. Posted speed is 25 mph. Gas is available at Whale Pass and Coffman Cove.

0 Control Lake Junction, junction with Big Salt and Thorne Bay roads near Control Lake.

3.1 Drinking water on right (from hose).

4.8 USFS Road No. 2050 leads west to upper Staney Creek/Horseshoe Hole and loops back to Road No. 20. Access to Staney

Humpback whales are present in Southeast Alaska waterways in spring, summer and fall. *(© Michael DeYoung)*

Bridge campsite. ▲

7.4 Rock quarry to east.

10.9 USFS Road No. 2054 leads west to Staney Creek campsite, Staney Creek cabin and access to salt water. ▲

15.5 Junction with Coffman Cove Road (see log this section).

18.4 Naukati Creek.

19.2 View to west of Tuxekan Island and Passage.

21 Logging road leads west to Naukati Bay.

21.4 Yatuk Creek bridge.

23.3 NAUKATI, established and operating as a mining camp, is 3 miles west. The population has grown due to a state land sale. Liquor, grocery, gas, boat rentals and boat repair available.

CAUTION: Road narrows northbound.

26.5 Sarkar Lake to east. Fishing and boat launch. USFS public-use cabin at east end of lake. Public toilets. Skiff docked at end of dock for registered cabin users only.

27.9 Bridge over Sarkar Lake outlet to salt water. Good spot to see eagles and sea lions during salmon season.

39.7 USFS Road No. 25 leads east 7 miles past Neck Lake to small settlement of **WHALE PASS**; groceries and gas available, 4 cabins, floatplane dock, post office and school (1 teacher, 13 grades). Whale Pass Road loops back to the main North Island Road at **Milepost 48.6.**

40 View of Neck Lake to east.

48.6 Whale Pass loop road to east. Whale Pass is 8 miles from here; Exchange Cove is 16 miles from here.

50.3 View of El Capitan Passage and Kosciusko Island to west.

51 Side road leads west 1 mile to USFS El Cap Work Center; access to El Capitan Cave. Public toilets.

55.6 Summit of the North Island Road (elev. 907 feet). Keep an eye out for highbush cranberries.

59.5 Rough road, heavy truck traffic and 1-lane bridges north from here.

60.6 Red Creek 1-lane bridge.

61.7 Big Creek 1-lane bridge.

63.9 View of Red Bay to north; Red Lake is to the south.

67.6 Buster Creek 1-lane bridge.

68.3 Shine Creek 1-lane bridge.

72 Flicker Creek 1-lane bridge.

72.1 Memorial Beach picnic area 1.7 miles north; follow signs to parking area. A short trail leads to picnic tables, pit toilet, memorial plaque and beach. Good view of Sumner Strait and Kupreanof Island. This site is a memorial to 12 victims of a 1978 air crash.

79.5 Labouchere Bay. The road continues several miles and dead ends at the base of Mount Calder.

Coffman Cove Road Log

Coffman Cove Road branches off the North Island Road (No. 20) at **Milepost 15.5** and leads east and north 20.5 miles to the logging camp of Coffman Cove. Watch for heavy truck traffic; 25 mph. Slow down for approaching vehicles.

0 Junction with North Island Road.

4.4 Side road on left (USFS Road No. 30) leads 5 miles through clear-cut and dead ends.

4.5 Logjam Creek bridge; cutthroat and steelhead; Dolly Varden; pink, silver and sockeye salmon.

9.1 Hatchery Creek bridge; fishing same as Logjam Creek. Trailhead for canoe route to Thorne Bay.

9.4 Bumpy road on right leads 13 miles to USFS parking area and canoe launch (no trailers) on Luck Lake, and junctions with the 3030 Road between Coffman Cove and Thorne Bay.

12.1 View of Sweetwater Lake to left. USFS access site: parking area for Sweetwater public-use cabin, located 0.5 mile along west shore of lake.

17 Coffman Creek bridge.

19.5 Chum Creek bridge.

20.2 Junction with Luck Lake loop road.

20.3 Chum Creek bridge.

20.5 COFFMAN COVE, a logging and fishing community; groceries, gas, cafe, rental cabins, gifts and local fresh oysters.

Coffman Cove–Thorne Bay Road Log

The 3030 Road travels 36.1 miles between Coffman Cove and Thorne Bay. Leaving Coffman Cove southbound, cross Dog Creek and begin on the 3030 Road. Turnouts are frequent but are noted here only if some other feature is present. A warning sign says to monitor CB channel 20.

Distance from Coffman Cove (C) is followed by distance from Thorne Bay (T).

C 0.6 (T 35.5) End of Muskeg Subdivision. Boardwalk to west is a private residence.

C 1.1 (T 35) Road crosses over a small creek.

C 1.7 (T 34.4) Rock pit to west. Grassy pullout to east; nice area for a picnic.

C 2.5 (T 33.6) Milepost 6. Road crosses over a small creek.

C 3.3 (T 32.8) Turnout to west. View of Clarence Strait, to the east, begins for next 0.6 mile.

C 3.6 (T 32.5) Turnout to east. Nice informal campsite.

C 3.9 (T 32.2) Turnout to east. Rock pit to west. Good view of Clarence Strait.

C 4.5 (T 31.6) Turnout to east. Room for a small camp. Last View of Clarence Strait for 10 miles.

C 5 (T 31.1) Turnout to east. Road veers to west.

C 7 (T 29.1) Turnout to east. Beginning of Luck Lake trailhead.

C 7.3 (T 28.8) Turnout to east. View of Luck Lake to east.

C 7.8 (T 28.3) Turnout to east. Good view of Luck Lake to east.

C 8.5 (T 27.6) Intersection. Turn east to Thorne Bay and Lick Creek. Turn west to Naukati (29 miles) and Hollis (74 miles). Southbound Forest Service Road 30 continues. Good informal campsite to west.

C 8.9 (T 27.2) Road crosses over Luck Creek. Turnouts both east and west. Good salmon-watching stream late August/early September.

C 9.2 (T 26.9) Milepost 45. Road crosses over creek. Road off to east.

C 9.5 (T 26.6) Steep, narrow climb begins for next 1.2 miles.

C 9.7 (T 26.4) Turnout to west. View to east of alder forest, view to west of alpine forest.

C 10.6 (T 25.5) Turnout to west. Heed warning sign of 15 mph curves for next 0.3 mile.

C 11.4 (T 24.7) Steep, narrow road continues to climb up mountainside. Good view to west of alpine forest.

C 11.6 (T 24.5) Turnout to west. Good informal campsite. Excellent view of mountainside.

C 12.2 (T 23.9) Turnout to west. Heed 15 mph curves warning.

C 12.5 (T 23.6) Turnout to west. Big gravel pit to east. Good view overlooking muskeg and alpine.

C 13.2 (T 22.9) Milepost 41. Road crosses over a little creek. Good berry picking next 0.5 mile in season.

C 13.8 (T 22.3) Turnout to west. View of Little Lake to the east, next 0.5 mile.

C 14.2 (T 21.) Turnout to east. Milepost 40.

C 14.5 (T 21.6) Turnout to west. Road leads to gravel pit and through muskeg. Southbound intersection sign: veer west on FS 30 for Sandy Beach (16 miles) and Thorne Bay (22 miles). East is FS 3026.

C 14.6 (T 21.5) Northbound intersection sign indicates Luck Lake (10 miles), Coffman Cove (15 miles) and Hollis (80 miles). West is FS 3026. First view of Clarence Strait.

C 15.3 (T 20.8) Turnout to east. View of Clarence strait.

C 15.6 (T 20.5) Turnout to east. Descent for next 0.3 mile.

C 16.3 (T 19.8) Turnouts both east and west. Bridge over small stream. Good salmon viewing in late August and early September.

C 16.4 (T 19.7) Turnout to east. Bridge over Big Ratz Creek.

C 17.5 (T 18.6) Turnout to the east. Road to the west.

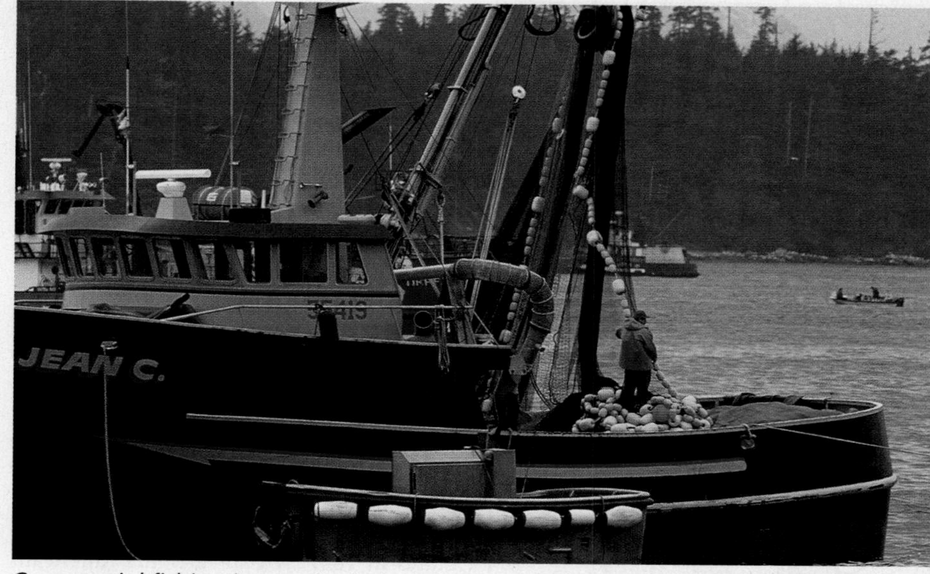

Commercial fishing is a major industry in most southeastern communities.
(© Loren Taft, Alaskan Images)

C 17.6 (T 18.5) Turnout to west. Road to west.

C 18.2 (T 17.9) Turnout to west. First view of Clarence Strait at sea level, continues for next 0.3 mile. Ratz Harbor and beach to east. Road construction 2 miles.

C 18.5 (T 17.6) Road crosses over culvert. Turnout to east, with beach access. Road to west. Good informal campsite.

C 18.7 (T 17.4) Road runs through salt marsh estuary next 0.1 mile. Turnout to west.

C 20.3 (T 15.8) Truck crossing.

C 20.7 (T 15.4) Bridge over small creek. Good salmon-viewing stream in early September.

C 21 (T 15.1) Road to west. Road narrows next 1 mile.

C 21.6 (T 14.5) Road to east.

C 21.8 (T 14.3) Turnout to west. Curves for 2 miles. View of Clarence Strait.

C 22 (T 14.1) Viewpoint east. Possible to see humpback and orca whales and Dall porpoise. Road runs along steep mountainside for next 2 miles.

C 22.4 (T 13.7) Viewpoint. In kelp beds otters may be visible.

C 24.8 (T 11.3) Turnouts to east and west. Road narrows next 0.3 mile.

C 25.5 (T 10.6) Road to west.

C 25.6 (T 10.5) 3020 Road intersects.

C 26.9 (T 9.2) Road crosses over a culvert. Turnout to east. Beach and view of Clarence Strait next 0.4 mile/0.6 km.

C 27.3 (T 8.8) Turnout to east. Beach access.

C 28.2 (T 7.9) Turnout to east. View of cove and beach access next 0.2 mile.

C 30.2 (T 5.9) Bridge over Barren Creek. Salmon viewing. Turnout to west after bridge.

C 30.3 (T 5.8) Turnout to west. Sandy Beach access. Firepit, outhouse, beach access, covered picnic area and trash cans. Parking to east.

C 30.9 (T 5.2) Bridge over Slide Creek. Salmon viewing. Turnout to east. Informal campsite.

C 32.7 (T 3.4) Milepost 22. Turnout to east. Informal campsite. Road to west.

C 35.4 (T 0.7) FS 3018 road to west.

C 35.6 (T 0.5) Road crosses over culvert and runs along marsh to the east for next 0.5 mile/0.8 km. Milepost 19. Turnout to east.

C 35.7 (T 0.4) Creek with natural dams to east. Turnout to west.

C 36 (T 0.1) No hunting begins southbound. Turnout to east.

C 36.1 (T 0) Turnout to west. Veer east for Thorne Bay. Private land and city limits begin here.

Wrangell

(See map, page 636)

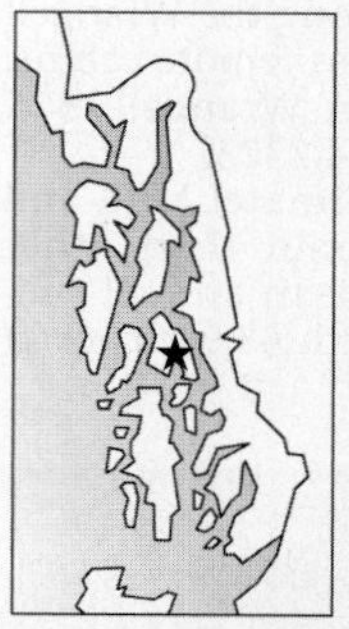

Located at northwest tip of Wrangell Island on Zimovia Strait; 6 miles southwest of the mouth of the Stikine River delta; 3 hours by ferry or 32 air miles southeast of Petersburg, the closest major community; and 6 hours by ferry or 85 air miles north of Ketchikan. **Population:** 2,400. **Emergency Services:** Phone 911 for all emergencies. **Police,** phone (907) 874-3304. **Fire Department** and **Ambulance**, phone (907) 874-2000. **Hospital**, Wrangell General, 310 Bennett St. just off Zimovia Highway, phone (907) 874-7000. **Maritime Search and Rescue**, contact the Coast Guard at (800) 478-5555.

Visitor Information: Center located in the Stikine Inn Building at 107 Stikine Ave., near the cruise ship dock; phone (800)

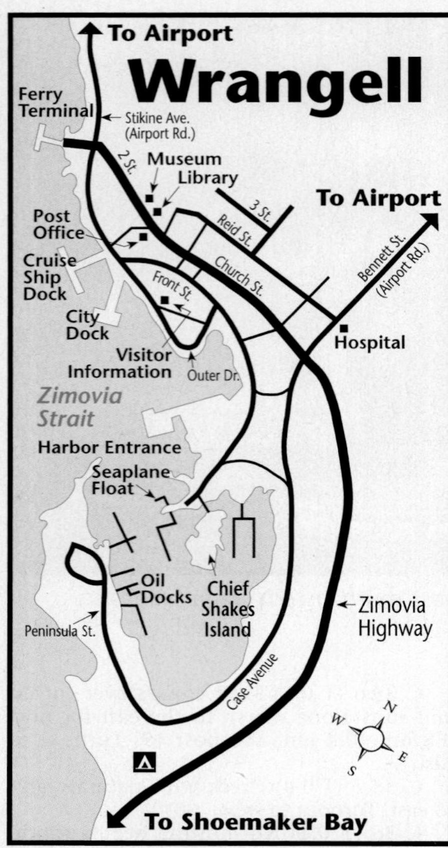

367-9745 or (907) 874-3901, fax (907) 874-3905, Internet: www.wrangell.com, e-mail: wrangell@wrangell.com. Write: Chamber of Commerce, Box 49MP, Wrangell, AK 99929. Information is also available at the Wrangell Museum, 318 Church St.; phone (907) 874-3770.

The U.S. Forest Service maintains several recreation sites and trails along the Wrangell Island road system, as well as remote cabins. Contact the USFS office in Wrangell, 525 Bennett St., phone (907) 874-2323.

Elevation: Sea level. **Climate:** Mild and moist with slightly less rain than other Southeast communities. Mean annual precipitation is 79.2 inches, with 63.9 inches of snow. Record monthly precipitation, 20.43 inches in October 1961. Average daily maximum temperature in June is 61°F/16°C; in July 64°F/18°C. Daily minimum in January is 21°F/-6°C. **Radio:** KSTK-FM 101.7. **Television:** Cable and satellite. **Newspaper:** *Wrangell Sentinel* (weekly).

Private Aircraft: Wrangell airport, adjacent northeast; elev. 44 feet; length 6,000 feet; paved; fuel 100LL, A.

Wrangell is the only Alaskan city to have existed under 4 nations and 3 flags—the Stikine Tlingits, the Russians, Great Britain and the United States. Wrangell began in 1834 as a Russian stockade called Redoubt St. Dionysius, built to prevent the Hudson's Bay Co. from fur trading up the rich Stikine River to the northeast. The Russians, in a change of policy, leased the mainland of southeastern Alaska to Hudson's Bay Co. in 1840. Under the British the stockade was called Fort Stikine.

The post remained under the British flag until Alaska was purchased by the United States in 1867. A year later the Americans established a military post here, naming it Fort Wrangell after the island, which was named by the Russians after Baron von Wrangel, a governor of the Russian–American Co.

Its strategic location near the mouth of the Stikine River, the fastest free-flowing navigable river in North America, made Wrangell an important supply point not only for fur traders but also for gold seekers following the river route to the goldfields. Today, the Stikine River is a popular hunting and recreation area. Currently, there is an active hard rock mine on the largest tributary of the Stikine, the Iskut. They are extracting gold, silver, copper and traces of other minerals from the site.

Wrangell serves as a hub for goods, services and transportation for outlying fishing villages, and logging and mining camps. The town depended largely on fishing until Japanese interests arrived in the mid-1950s and established a mill now operated by Silver Bay Logging Inc. A small, locally owned mill is now in operation 2 miles beyond the end of Zimovia Highway, off Forest 6265. Fishing is one of Wrangell's largest industries, with salmon the major catch.

Lodging & Services

Wrangell has several motels and bed and breakfasts. The Wrangell Hostel is located in the Presbyterian church, about 1/4 mile from the ferry terminal, next to the Wrangell Museum. Open from June 9 to Labor Day, 5 P.M. to 9 A.M.; $10/night; phone (907) 874-3534.

There are 4 restaurants downtown, as well as service stations, hardware and appliance stores, banks, drugstore, laundromat, grocery stores (1 with a bakery and deli), a fish market and gift shops. Bed-and-breakfasts are available. Lodges with restaurants are located on Peninsula Street and at **Milepost 4.4** Zimovia Highway.

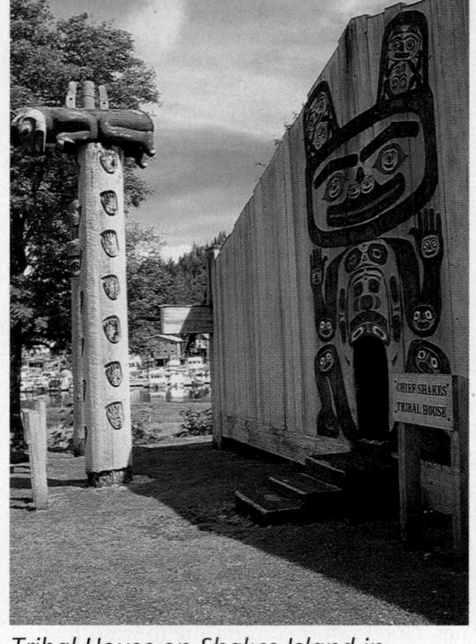

Tribal House on Shakes Island in Wrangell Harbor. (© Four Corners Imaging)

Camping

RV camping at RV park on Berger street. Camping and picnic area at Shoemaker Bay, **Milepost 4.9** Zimovia Highway. Dump stations located at Shoemaker Bay and downtown. City Park, at **Milepost 1.9** Zimovia Highway, has tent sites, camping, picnic area with tables, flush toilets, shelters and playground. ▲

Transportation

Air: Daily scheduled jet service is provided by Alaska Airlines to other Southeast cities with through service to Seattle and Anchorage. Scheduled commuter air service to Petersburg, Kake and Ketchikan. Charter service available.

Airport terminal is 1.1 miles from ferry terminal or 1.1 miles from Zimovia Highway on Bennett Street. Hotel courtesy vans are available from the airport to downtown. Taxi service is also available for about $5.

Ferry: Alaska Marine Highway vessels connect Wrangell with all Southeastern Alaska ports plus Prince Rupert, BC, and Bellingham, WA. Ferry terminal is at the north end of town at the end of Zimovia Highway (also named Church or 2nd Street at this point). Walk or take a taxi from terminal to town for approximately $4. Tours for independent travelers are available downtown. Terminal facilities include ticket office, waiting room and vehicle waiting area. Phone (907) 874-3711.

Car Rental: Available from Practical Rent-A-Car (907) 874-3975.

Taxi: Available to/from airport and ferry terminal. Approximate cost is $4 and $5.

Highways: Zimovia Highway (see log this section). Logging roads have opened up most of Wrangell Island to motorists. Check

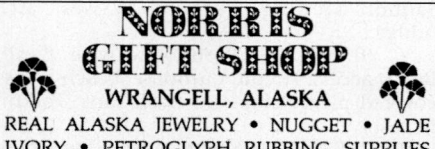

In Southeastern Alaska, most Native villages are Tlingit settlements. — *Alaska A to Z*

with the USFS office at 525 Bennett St. for a copy of the Wrangell Island Road Guide map. (Write USDA Forest Service, Wrangell Ranger District, Box 51, Wrangell, AK 99929; phone 907/874-2323.) City maps are also available at the Chamber of Commerce Visitor Center downtown.

Cruise Ships: Wrangell is a regular port of call in summer for several cruise lines.

Private Boats: Transient floats are located downtown and 4.5 miles south of Wrangell on Zimovia Highway at Shoemaker Bay Harbor. Reliance Float is located near Shakes Tribal House. If you are traveling to Wrangell by boat, radio ahead to the harbor master for tie-up space. Or phone (907) 874-3736 or 874-3051.

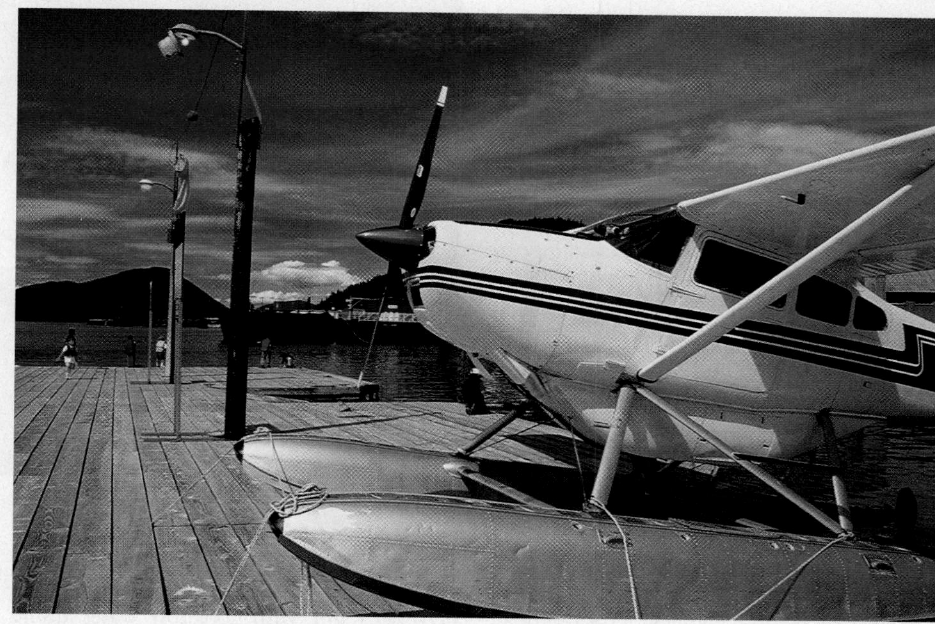

Floatplane docked at Wrangell Harbor. *(© Four Corners Imaging)*

Attractions

Shakes Island and Tribal House, in Wrangell Harbor, is reached by boardwalk. It is the site of several excellent totem poles. The replica tribal house contains Indian working tools, an original Chilkat blanket design carved on a house panel and other cultural items. It is listed on the National Register of Historic Places. Open irregular hours when cruise ships are in port during summer (May to September) or by appointment; phone (907) 874-3747 or 874-2023. Admission $1.50.

Totem Poles. The last original totems standing in Wrangell were cut down in November 1981 and removed for preservation. A totem restoration project funded by both state and federal agencies was initiated, and replicas of original totems can be found at Kiksadi Totem Park at the corner of Front and Episcopal streets.

Wrangell Museum, at 318 Church St., features local history and includes displays representing Tlingit, Russian, British, Chinese, Japanese and American influences in Wrangell. The oldest known Tlingit houseposts in Southeast Alaska are on exhibit, as is a rare "spruce canoe," and spruce root and cedar bark basket collection. Gold rush, trapping, logging, and fishing industry exhibits depict Wrangell's boom and bust economy. May to September hours are Monday through Friday 10-5; Saturdays and Sundays 1-4 as staffing is available. October through April Tuesday through Friday 10-4; closed for lunch 11:30-12:30. Phone (907) 874-3770; Fax (907) 874-3785, E-mail: museum@wrangell.com. Admission $3; children 16 and under free.

Our Collections Museum, located on Evergreen Avenue, is a private collection of antiques and Alaska memorabilia. Open when cruise ships and ferries are in port and by special request. Phone (907) 874-3646. Donations accepted.

Sightseeing tours of attractions and fish bakes are available upon request. Sightseeing buses meet some ferries and cruise ships. Inquire at the visitor center or Wrangell Museum. Flightseeing and jetboat excursions available to Stikine River, Stikine Icefield, Anan Wildlife Observatory and other remote locations.

Special events in Wrangell include a big Fourth of July celebration which begins with a salmon bake. The annual Tent City Festival, celebrated the first weekend in February, commemorates Wrangell's gold rush days. The Garnet Festival, celebrated the third week of April, marks the arrival of spring and the annual bald eagle migration on the Stikine River. The festival celebrates the arts with family activities, and includes a golf tournament at Muskeg Meadows. A tree-lighting and Christmas celebration takes place in December.

Petroglyphs are ancient designs carved into rock faces, usually found between low and high tide marks on beaches. Petroglyph Beach is located 0.7 mile from the ferry terminal; a boardwalk trail leads to the head of the beach from the left of the road. Turn right as you reach the beach and look for petroglyphs between there and a rock outcrop several hundred feet away. This beach has the largest number of petroglyphs found anywhere in southeastern Alaska; at times as many as 40 can be seen. Petroglyphs are also located on the library lawn and are on display in the museum.

Muskeg Meadows is a 9-hole, 36-acre regulation golf course and driving range. Contact the Wrangell Golf Assoc., Box 2199, Wrangell, AK 99929, or association president Lloyd Hartshorn, phone (907) 874-3989.

Anan Wildlife Observatory, managed by the U.S. Forest Service, is located 35 miles southeast of Wrangell; accessible by boat or plane only. During July and August, visitors can watch bears catch pink salmon headed for the salmon spawning grounds. Bald eagles, ravens, crows and seals are frequently seen feeding on the fish. Contact the visitor center. (800) 367-9745, or the Forest Service office, (907) 874-2323, for list of guides permitted to transport visitors to Anan.

Wrangell Salmon Derby runs from mid-May to Memorial Day weekend. Kings weighing more than 50 lbs. are not unusual.

Garnet Ledge, a rocky outcrop on the right bank of the Stikine River delta at Garnet Creek, is 7.5 miles from Wrangell Harbor, reached at high tide by small boat. Garnet, a semiprecious stone, can be found embedded in the ledge here. The garnet ledge is on land deeded to the Southeast Council of the Boy Scouts of America and the children of Wrangell by the late Fred Hanford (former mayor of Wrangell). The bequest states that the land shall be used for scouting purposes and the children of Wrangell may take garnets in reasonable quantities (garnets are sold by children at the docks when ships and ferries are in port). Contact the Wrangell Museum (Box 1050, Wrangell 99929; phone 907/874-3770) for information on digging for garnets.

The Stikine River delta lies north of Wrangell within the Stikine–LeConte Wilderness and is accessible only by boat or plane. The delta is habitat for migrating waterfowl, eagles, bears and moose. During the spring run, the second largest concentration of bald eagles in the world can be seen in the Stikine River delta.

Also watch for seals resting on ice floes from LeConte Glacier. The glacier is at the head of LeConte Bay, just north of the delta. It is the southernmost tidewater glacier in North America. It is also an actively calving glacier, known for its prodigious iceberg production.

The Stikine River is the fastest navigable river on North America, and can be rafted, canoed or run by skiff or jet boat from Telegraph Creek, BC, to Wrangell, AK, 165 miles one way.

USFS trails, cabins and recreation sites on Wrangell Island and in the surrounding area are a major attraction here. Nemo Campsites, for example, only 14 miles south of Wrangell, provides spectacular views of Zimovia Strait and north Etolin Island. No reservations or fees required. Parking areas, picnic tables, fire grills and outhouses at each campsite.

USFS public-use cabins in the Wrangell district are accessible by air or by boat. The 22 USFS cabins are scattered throughout the region.

For details on these sites and others, contact the Forest Service district office at (907) 874-2323, or stop by the USFS office at 525 Bennett St. You may also write the Wrangell Ranger District at Box 51, Wrangell, AK 99929. White courtesy phone located in the ferry terminal building. Reservations for all Forest Service cabins can be made through a national reservation system called ReserveAmerica; web address: ReserveAmerica.co. This service is available 7 days/week, but business hours vary by season. ▲

AREA FISHING: The Wrangell Island

forest road system provides access to several recreation sites and trails with fishing. For more information contact the USFS office in Wrangell at (907) 874-2323.

Fly in to **Thoms Lake, Long Lake, Marten Lake, Salmon Bay, Virginia Lake** and **Eagle Lake.** Thoms Lake and Long Lake are also accessible via road and trail. **Stikine River** near Wrangell (closed to king salmon fishing), Dolly Varden to 22 inches, and cutthroat to 18 inches, best in midsummer to fall; steelhead to 12 lbs., use bait or lures; coho salmon 10 to 15 lbs., use lures, September and October. Saltwater fishing near Wrangell for king salmon, 20 to 40 lbs., best in May and June. Stop by the Dept. of Fish and Game at 215 Front St. for details.

Sons of Norway Hall in Petersburg. (© James D. Ronan, Jr.)

Zimovia Highway Log

Zimovia Highway leads south from the ferry terminal to Mile 14.2, where it connects with island's Forest Development roads.

0 Alaska Marine Highway ferry terminal, ticket office and waiting area. There is a bike path to Mile 4.4.

0.3 St. Rose of Lima Catholic Church, the oldest Roman Catholic parish in Alaska, founded May 2, 1879.

0.4 First Presbyterian Church has a red neon cross, 1 of 2 in the world that serve as navigational aids. This was the first church in Wrangell and is one of the oldest Protestant churches in Alaska (founded in 1877 and built in 1879).

Wrangell Museum interim location situated between the church and Wrangell High School.

0.6 Bennett Street (Airport Road) loops north 2.2 miles to the airport and back to the ferry terminal.

0.7 Public Safety Bldg.

1.9 City park. Picnic area with shelters, firepits, restrooms, litter barrels. Tent camping only; 24-hour limit. ▲

3.6 Turnout with beach access. Several turnouts along the highway here offer beach access and good spots for bird watching.

4.4 Lodge on left with restaurant and lounge. End of bike path.

4.9 Shoemaker Bay small-boat harbor, boat launch, picnic, camping and parking area. Camping area has tent sites, 29 RV sites ($10 per night, with hookups), water, dump station and restrooms. Tennis court, horseshoe pits and children's playground nearby. Rainbow Falls trailhead; 0.7-mile trail to scenic waterfall. Institute Creek trail intersects with Rainbow Falls trail at Mile 0.6 and leads 2.7 miles/4.3 km to viewpoint and shelter overlooking Shoemaker Bay and Zimovia Strait. ▲

6.5 Sawmill owned by Silver Bay Logging Inc. is operating.

7.3 Milepost 7, scenic turnout.

8 Turnout.

8.5 Turnout, beach access (8 Mile Beach undeveloped recreation area).

10.8 Access road west to Pat Creek Log Transfer Facility and small boat launch. Road east (Pat Creek Road) is a 1-lane, maintained, crushed rock road with turnouts. It leads 0.3 mil to Pat's Lake, and continues approximately 6 miles northeast through both old and active logging areas.

Pat Creek and **Pat's Lake**, cutthroat, Dolly Varden, pink and silver salmon, spinning gear or flies.

11 Pat Creek camping area (unmaintained, no facilities); parking for self-contained vehicles.

13.4 McCormack Creek crossing on new concrete bridge. Trout and salmon fishing (in season) downstream at mouth of creek.

13.6 Junction with Nemo Road, single-lane gravel FS Road 6267, which leads to the Nemo Campsites. Spectacular views of Zimovia Strait and north Etolin Island; parking areas, picnic tables, fire grills and outhouses each site. Campground Host during summer. No reservations, no fees.

14.2 Two-lane paved road ends at National Forest boundary; begin single-lane FS road with turnouts. Road 6265 connects with other FS roads. (A map showing island roads with recreation sites and trails is available from the USFS office in Wrangell.) Watch for log trucks and other heavy equipment. ▲

Petersburg

(See map, page 637)

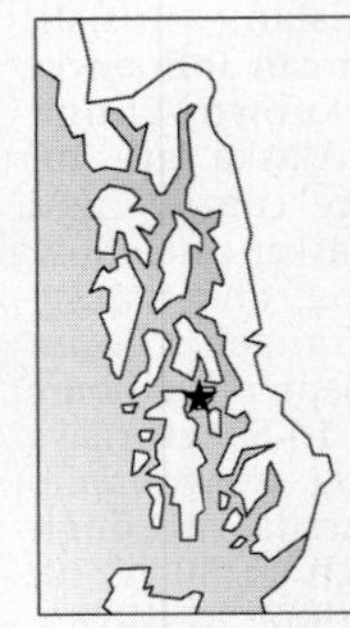

Located on the northwest tip of Mitkof Island at the northern end of Wrangell Narrows, midway between Juneau and Ketchikan. **Population:** 3,350. **Emergency Services:** Phone 911. **Alaska State Troopers**, phone (907) 772-3100. **City Police, Poison Center, Fire Department** and **Ambulance**, phone (907) 772-3838. **Hospital,** Petersburg Medical Center, 2nd and Fram St., phone (907) 772-4291. **Maritime Search and Rescue:** contact the Coast Guard at (800) 478-5555. Harbormaster, phone (907) 772-4688, CB Channel 9, or VHF Channel 16.

Visitor Information: Petersburg Visitor Information Center located at 1st and Fram streets; open Monday–Saturday from 9 A.M.

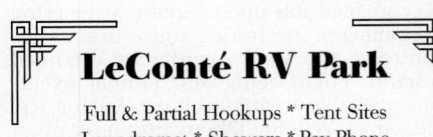

to 5 P.M., noon to 4 P.M. Sundays, spring and summer; 10 A.M. to 2 P.M. fall and winter. Write Petersburg Visitor Information Center, Box 649, Petersburg 99833. Clausen Memorial Museum, 2nd and Fram streets, open daily in summer, limited winter hours; phone (907) 772-3598. Alaska Dept. of Fish and Game, State Office Building, Sing Lee Alley; open 8 A.M. to 4:30 P.M., Monday through Friday, phone (907) 772-3801.

Elevation: Sea level. **Climate:** Average daily maximum temperature in July, 64°F/18°C; daily minimum in January, 20°F/-7°C. All-time high, 84°F/29°C in 1933; record low, -19°F/-28°C in 1947. Mean annual precipitation, 110 inches; mostly as rain. **Radio:** KRSA-AM 580, KFSK-FM 100.9. **Television:** Alaska Rural Communication Service, Channel 15; KTOO (PBS) Channel 9 and cable channels. **Newspaper:** *Petersburg Pilot* (weekly).

Private Aircraft: James A. Johnson Airport, 1 mile southeast; elev. 107 feet; length 6,000 feet; asphalt; fuel 100, A. Seaplane base 0.5 mile from downtown.

Petersburg was named for Peter Buschmann, who selected the present townsite for a salmon cannery and sawmill in 1897. The sawmill and dock were built in 1899, and the cannery was completed in 1900. He was followed by other Norwegian immigrants who came to fish and work in the cannery and sawmill. Since then the cannery has operated continuously (with rebuilding, expansion and different owners) and is now known as Petersburg Fisheries Inc., a division of Icicle Seafoods Inc. Petersburg Fisheries shares the waterfront with two other canneries, two other cold storage plants and several other fish processing facilities.

Today, Petersburg boasts the largest home-based halibut fleet in Alaska and is also well known for its shrimp, crab, salmon, herring and other fish products. Most families depend on the fishing industry for livelihood. Sportfishing questions should be directed to the Alaska Dept. of Fish and Game's Division of Sportfishing in Petersburg. phone (907) 772-3801

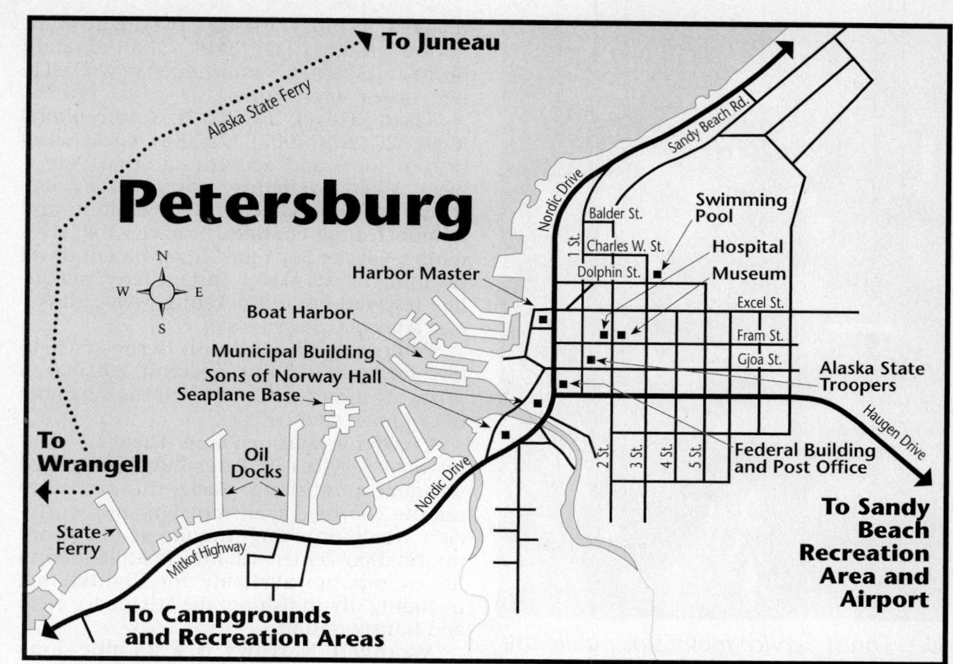

Lodging & Services

Petersburg has 3 hotels, including Scandia House (1-800-772-5006) and Tides Inn (1-800-665-8433). There are also numerous bed and breakfasts and guest houses, several restaurants and fast-food outlets located downtown. The 5-block-long commercial area on Main Street (Nordic Drive) has grocery stores, marine and fishing supply stores, hardware, a drugstore, travel agency, public showers, banks, gift and variety stores specializing in both Alaskan and Scandinavian items, city hall, post office and cocktail bars. A community gym with racquetball courts and a public swimming pool are located a couple of blocks off Nordic Drive. Petersburg has 13 churches.

Camping

There are 2 RV parks: LeConte RV Park and Twin Creek RV Park. The city maintains an RV staging area downtown at 2nd & Haugen St. Parking $6 for up to 12 hours. The tent campground (known locally as Tent City) on Haugen Drive is often filled to capacity in summer with young cannery workers. Public campgrounds (1 developed, several undeveloped) are located on Mitkof Highway some distance south of town. ▲

Transportation

Air: Twice daily scheduled jet service by Alaska Airlines to major Southeast cities and Seattle, WA, with connections to Anchorage and Fairbanks. A scheduled regional carrier and several local carrier and charter services also serve the area.

The airport is located 1 mile from the Federal Building on Haugen Drive. It has a ticket counter and waiting room. There is no shuttle service to town; hotel courtesy vans and taxis are available for a fee.

Ferry: Alaska Marine Highway vessels connect Petersburg with all Southeastern Alaska cities plus Prince Rupert, BC, and Bellingham, WA. Terminal at Milepost 0.8 Mitkof Highway, includes dock, ticket office with waiting room, and parking area. Phone (907) 772-3855.

Car Rental: Available.

Taxi: There are 2 taxi companies. Cab service to and from the airport and ferry terminal.

Highways: Mitkof Highway, Sandy Beach Road and Three Lakes Loop Road (see logs this section).

Cruise Ships: Smaller cruise ships dock $^{1}/_{4}$ mile from town. Vans take passengers to town.

Private Boats: Boaters must check with harbormaster for moorage assignment.

Attractions

Little Norway Festival is scheduled for May 18-21, 2000, as a celebration for Norwegian Independence Day. Pageantry, old-country dress, contests, Vikings, a Viking ship, dancing and a Norwegian "fish feed" for locals and visitors are featured.

Clausen Memorial Museum, 203 Fram St., features Petersburg area history. On display are artifacts representing the cannery

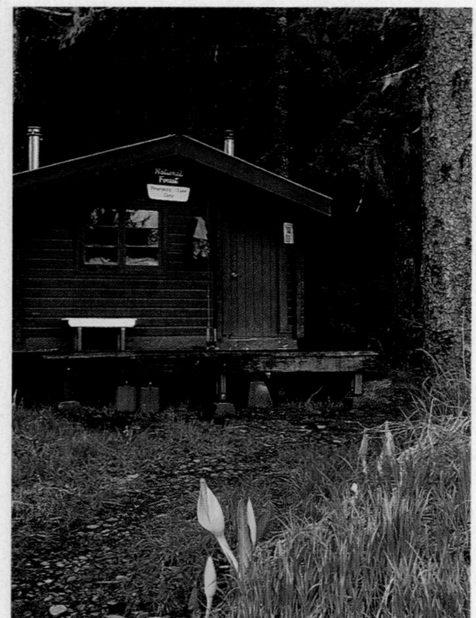

U.S. Forest Service maintains public-use cabins in Tongass National Forest.
(© Michael DeYoung)

and fisheries, a world-record 126.5-lb. king salmon, the Cape Decision light station lens, a Tlingit canoe and the wall piece "Land, Sea, Sky." Open Wednesday and Saturday, 12:30–4:30 P.M., Oct. 1 to April 30. Open daily, 9:30 A.M. to 4:30 P.M., May 1 to Sept. 21. Phone (907) 772-3598 for programs, updated visitor information and to leave messages. Wheelchair accessible.

The Fisk (Norwegian for fish), a 10-foot bronze sculpture commemorating Petersburg's fishing tradition, stands in a working fountain in front of the museum. It was completed during the Alaska centennial year of 1967 by sculptor Carson Boysen.

Sons of Norway Hall, on the National Register of Historic Places, was built in 1912. Situated on pilings over Hammer Slough (a favorite photography subject), its window shutters are decorated with rosemaling (Norwegian tole painting).

Fisherman's Memorial Park, next to the Sons of Norway Hall. Newly constructed in 1998, this park commemorates those townspeople lost at sea.

LeConte Glacier, in LeConte Bay, 25 miles east of Petersburg, is the continent's southernmost tidewater glacier. Fast-moving, the glacier continually "calves," creating icefalls from its face into the bay. Seals and porpoises are common; whales are often seen. Helicopters, small aircraft and boats may be chartered in Petersburg or Wrangell to see LeConte Glacier.

Whale Research and Whale-Watching. Petersburg has become the center for humpback whale research in Southeast Alaska. Three feature documentaries have been filmed in adjacent waters in the past five years. The area attracts professional photographers from around the world.

Petersburg King Salmon Derby is scheduled for Memorial Day weekend. $30,000 in prizes are awarded. Check with the Chamber of Commerce for details.

Charter a Boat or Plane. There are charter boat services in Petersburg for guided saltwater sportfishing, glacier trips, access to remote cabins, kayak transfers and world-class whale watching. Inquire at the visitor information center. Charter floatplanes and helicopters are available for flightseeing, including fly-in fishing, the Stikine Ice Field and transportation.

Wrangell Narrows is a 23-mile--long channel between Mitkof and Kupreanof islands. The channel was dredged in the 1940s to a depth of 26 feet/7.8m. Extremely narrow in places and filled with rocky reefs, islands and strong currents, the narrows is navigated by ships and ferries with the aid of dozens of markers and flashing lights. The 1½-hour run through Wrangell Narrows begins immediately on ferries departing Petersburg southbound, or about 1½ hours after departing Wrangell northbound.

Cabins, canoe/kayaking routes and hiking trails managed by the U.S. Forest Service are all within reach of Petersburg, which is the administrative center for the Stikine Area of Tongass National Forest. Stop by the USFS office in the Federal Building, or phone (907) 772-3871 for detailed information on cabins and trails or contact the Petersburg Visitor Information Center, (907) 772-4636. Information for canoers and kayakers interested in the Stikine River delta or Tebenkof Bay and Kuiu wilderness areas is also available here or at the USFS office in Wrangell.

Salmon migration and spawning are best observed in the Petersburg area July though September. Falls Creek bridge and fish ladder, at **Milepost 10.8** Mitkof Highway, is a good location. The ladder helps migrating salmon bypass difficult falls on the way to spawning grounds in Falls Creek. It can be observed from the creek bank just off the roadside. Other viewing areas include Blind Slough and the Blind River Rapids area, Petersburg Creek and Ohmer Creek.

Crystal Lake Fish Hatchery is at **Milepost 17.5** Mitkof Highway. This hatchery for coho, king and steelhead is operated by the state and used for fish-stocking projects in southeastern Alaska. It is open for visits, and hatchery personnel will explain the operation, though formal guided tours are not available. Best time to visit is between 8 A.M. and 4 P.M., Monday through Friday.

AREA FISHING: Salmon, steelhead, cutthroat and Dolly Varden at **Falls Creek, Blind Slough** and **Blind River Rapids**; see log of Mitkof Highway this section. Salmon can be caught in the harbor area and **Scow Bay** area. (Rapid tidal currents in front of the town necessitate the use of an outboard motor.) **Petersburg Creek,** directly across Wrangell Narrows from downtown within Petersburg Creek–Duncan Salt Chuck Wilderness Area, also offers good fishing. Blind Slough, located 15 miles/24 km south of the ferry terminal, offers good fishing for king salmon. Dolly Varden can be caught from the beach north of town and from downtown docks. Sportfishing opportunities for halibut, crab and shrimp. Harvest of mussels, clams and other shellfish is not recommended because of the possibility of paralytic shellfish poisoning. Contact the Sport Fish Division of the Alaska Dept. of Fish and Game (907) 772-3801 for information.

Sandy Beach Road Log

From Federal Building, drive north through town; road leads to Sandy Beach Recreation Area.

0 Federal Building and post office.

0.1 Petersburg boat harbor 1 block to left, contains one of Alaska's finest fishing fleets.

0.2 Downtown Petersburg.

0.3 Petersburg Fisheries Inc., the city's largest processing plant.

Eagles Roost Park. Eagles feed on beach at low tide; best viewing in early summer.

1.2 Eagle observation point. Eagles can be seen resting nearby and fishing in Wrangell Narrows. To the northeast is Frederick Sound and the mainland.

2 Bed and breakfast, sightseeing cruises.

2.8 Sandy Beach Recreation Area on left; picnic tables, playground, volleyball court, shelter, toilets, limited parking, no camping. Junction with Haugen Drive, which loops to airport and back to town.

Just past Sandy Beach Recreation Area is Sound Drive, a 7.5-mile road completed in 1998 which links Petersburg to the USFS road system and the Three Lakes Loop Road. This is a 1½-lane gravel road recommended for 4-wheel drive or mountain biking.

Mitkof Highway Log

The major road on the island, Mitkof Highway leads 33.8 miles south from the Federal Building to the Stikine River delta at the south end of Mitkof Island. The highway is paved to **Milepost 17.5**; good wide gravel to road end.

0 Federal Building and post office.

0.1 Bridge over Hammer Slough, an intertidal estuary.

0.5 Harbor parking.

0.6 Pier and floatplane base.

0.8 Alaska Marine Highway ferry terminal, office and waiting area on right.

2.9 Scow Bay, a wide portion of Wrangell Narrows with king salmon fishing in spring. Scow Bay Loop Road rejoins highway at **Milepost 3.1**.

7.5 Twin Creek RV Park, private campground, small store and phone.

10.7 North turnoff to Three Lakes Loop Road (see log this section).

10.8 Falls Creek and fish ladder. Steelhead, April and May; pink salmon below falls in August; coho, August and September; Dolly Varden and cutthroat late summer and fall. No fishing within 300 feet of fish ladder.

11 Road on right leads 0.5 mile to

Papke's Landing; transient boat moorage and boat ramp. USFS Log Transportation Facility.

14.3 Entering Tongass National Forest.

14.5 Blind River Rapids parking area and trail; outhouse; 2,600-ft. wheelchair-accessible boardwalk loop added in 1999. 0.3-mile boardwalk trail through muskeg meadow to Blind River Rapids, hatchery steelhead, mid-April to mid-May; king salmon, June to late July; coho, mid-August to October. Also Dolly Varden and cutthroat trout.

16.3 Blind Slough waterfowl viewing area on right. Covered platform with interpretive sign on area waterfowl. Trumpeter swans winter in this area.

17.5 Pavement ends; wide, hard-packed gravel to end of road. Short road leads to Crystal Lake Fish Hatchery and **Blind Slough Recreation Area** with picnic tables, shelter and pit toilets; no overnight camping. Hatchery is open for visiting, though no scheduled tours are available. Fishing for cutthroat and Dolly Varden in summer; coho salmon, mid-August to mid-September; king salmon in June and July. Fishing in this area may be regulated. Check with ADF&G, (907) 772-3801.

20 Manmade Hole picnic area with tables, firepits, swimming and short trail. Ice skating in winter. Fishing for cutthroat and Dolly Varden year-round; best in summer and fall.

20.6 Three Lakes Loop Road begins on left leading to Three Lakes on other side of Mitkof Island, looping back to Mitkof Highway at **Milepost 10.7** near Falls Creek bridge.

21.4 Woodpecker Cove Road (1-lane) leads about 15 miles along south Mitkof Island to Woodpecker Cove and beyond. Good views of Sumner Strait. Watch for logging trucks.

21.5 Ohmer Creek nature trail, 1.5 mile loop; first 0.3 mile is barrier-free.

21.7 Ohmer Creek Campground, 10 sites (2 are wheelchair accessible), toilets, parking area, picnic tables, drinking water and firepits. Set in meadow area among trees. Open spring to fall; small fee; accommodates RVs to 32 feet.

24 Blind Slough USFS Log Transportation Facility. Fishing from skiff for coho salmon, mid-August to mid-September. *NOTE: Kings have not returned to this system for several years.*

26.1 Narrow 0.7-mile road on right to Sumner Strait Campground, locally called Green's Camp (undeveloped); must walk in, no facilities. May be inaccessible at high tide.

27 View of city of Wrangell.

28 Wilson Creek state recreation area (undeveloped); picnic tables, parking. Good view of Sumner Strait.

28.6 Banana Point, boat ramp, outhouse.

31 Stikine River mud flats, visible on right at low tide. Part of the Stikine River delta, this is the area where Dry Strait meets Sumner Strait.

33.8 Road ends with turnaround.

Three Lakes Loop Road Log

Access to this 21.4-mile-long, 1-lane loop road is from **Mileposts 10.7** and **20.6** on the Mitkof Highway. *CAUTION: No services; use turnouts.*

0 Junction at **Milepost 10.7** Mitkof Highway; turn east.

1.4 View of Wrangell Narrows to west. Older clear-cuts; this area was logged between 1964 and 1968.

4.4 Falls Creek bridge.

7 Second-growth stand of spruce–hemlock. First growth was destroyed by fire or wind throw more than 180 years ago. This second-growth stand serves as an example of what a logging unit could look like a century or two after clear-cutting.

9.7 Directly south is a 384-acre clear-cut logged in 1973 under a contract predating the current policy, which usually limits clear-cut tracts to 100 acres.

10.2 Bear Creek; steelhead in April and May; coho late August and September; cutthroat and Dolly Varden, best late summer and fall.

12.3 Muskeg; view of Frederick Sound.

12.8 Turnoff on right to **LeConte Glacier Overlook**, a picnic site with spectacular view of the mainland. Limited turnaround space.

14.2 Sand Lake trail. Short boardwalk trail leads to each of the Three Lakes. Tennis shoes are ideal for these short walks, but for areas around the lakes it is advisable to wear rubber boots. A 0.7-mile connecting trail to Hill Lake.

14.7 Hill Lake trail.

15.1 Crane Lake trail, 1.3 miles to lake; connecting trail to Hill Lake. USFS skiffs and picnic platforms are located at Sand, Hill and Crane lakes; cutthroat from May through September.

16.4 Dry Straits Road.

21.4 Second **junction** with Mitkof Highway, at **Milepost 20.6**.

Sitka

(See map, page 637)

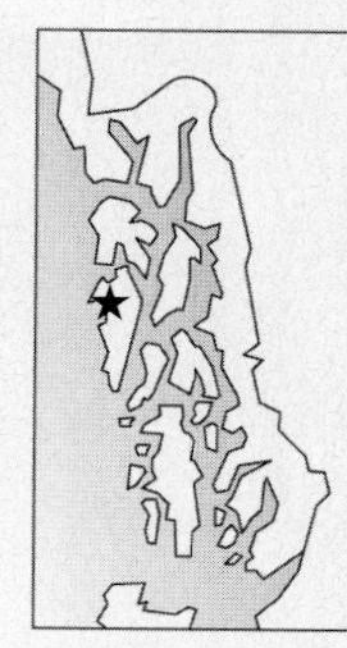

Located on west side of Baranof Island, 95 air miles southwest of Juneau, 185 air miles northwest of Ketchikan; 2 hours flying time from Seattle, WA. **Population:** City and Borough, 9,194. **Emergency Services: Alaska State Troopers, City Police, Fire Department**, and **Ambulance**, phone 911. **Hospital**, Sitka Community, 209 Moller Ave., phone (907) 747-3241; Mount Edgecumbe, 222 Tongass Dr., phone (907) 966-2411. **Maritime Search and Rescue**, phone the Coast Guard at (800) 478-5555.

Visitor Information: Contact the Sitka Convention and Visitors Bureau at Box 1226-MP, Sitka, AK 99835; phone (907) 747-5940. An information desk in Harrigan Centennial Hall, 330 Harbor Drive, is staffed by volunteers during summer . For USDA Forest Service information write the Sitka Ranger District, 201 Katlian, Suite 109, Sitka, AK 99835; phone (907) 747-4220. For information on Sitka National Historical Park, write 106 Metlakatla St., Sitka, AK 99835; phone (907) 747-6281.

Elevation: Sea level. **Climate:** Average daily temperature in July, 55°F/13°C; in January, 33°F/1°C. Annual precipitation, 95

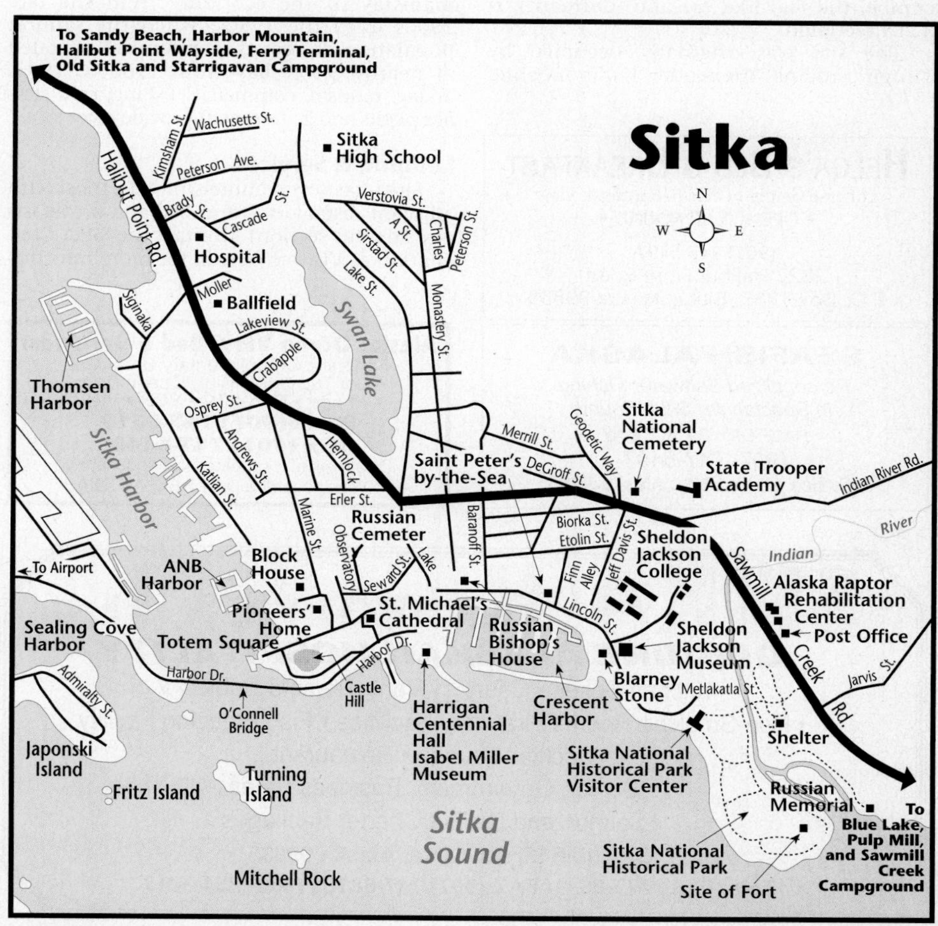

View of Mount Edgecumbe from Sandy Beach. (© Four Corners Imaging)

inches. **Radio:** KIFW 1230, KRSA-FM 94.9, KSBZ-FM 103.1, KCAW-FM 104.7. **Television:** Cable channels. **Newspaper:** *Daily Sitka Sentinel.*

Private Aircraft: Sitka airport on Japonski Island; elev. 21 feet; length 6,500 feet; asphalt; fuel 100, A1. Sitka seaplane base adjacent west; fuel 80, 100.

One of the most scenic of southeastern Alaska cities, Sitka rests on the ocean shore protected at the west by myriad small islands and Cape Edgecumbe. Mount Edgecumbe, the Fuji-like volcano (dormant), is 3,201 feet high.

The site was originally occupied by Tlingit Indians. Alexander Baranof, chief manager of the Russian–American Co. with headquarters in Kodiak, built a trading post and fort (St. Michael's Redoubt) north of Sitka in 1799. Indians burned down the fort and looted the warehouses. Baranof returned in 1804, and by 1808 Sitka was capital of Russian Alaska. Baranof was governor from 1790 to 1818. A statue of the Russian governor was unveiled in 1989; it is located outside of Centennial Hall. Castle Hill in Sitka is where Alaska changed hands from Russia to the United States in 1867. Salmon was the mainstay of the economy from the late 1800s until the 1950s, when the salmon population decreased. A pulp mill operated at nearby Silver Bay from 1960 to 1993. Today, tourism, commercial fishing, cold storage plants and government provide most jobs.

Lodging & Services

Sitka has several hotels/motels, most with adjacent restaurants, and bed-and-breakfasts (see ads this section). Contact the Sitka Convention & Visitors Bureau for more information; phone (907) 747-5940.

Sitka Youth Hostel is located in the United Methodist Church, 303 Kimsham St. (1½ blocks north of McDonald's on Halibut Point Road). Send correspondence to Box 2645, Sitka, AK 99835. Open June 1 to Aug. 31; 20 beds, showers, kitchen facilities, sleeping pads required; $9 plus tax/member; $12 plus tax/nonmembers. Phone (907) 747-8661.

An array of businesses cluster in the downtown area, which saw its first traffic light installed in 1992. Services in Sitka's downtown area include restaurants, a laundromat, drugstore, clothing and grocery stores, and gift shops. Shopping and services are also available along Sawmill and Halibut Point roads. Dump stations are located at the Wastewater Treatment Plant on Japonski Island.

Alaska Ocean View Bed & Breakfast. You'll enjoy casual elegance at affordable rates at this superior B&B, where guests experience a high degree of personal comfort, privacy and friendly hosts. Open your day with the tantalizing aroma of fresh bread, fresh ground coffee and a delicious breakfast; and close your day with a refreshing soak in the bubbling patio spa. Open year-round, smoke-free, on airport/ferry shuttle route. "Delighted beyond our expectations!" Brochure and reservations: 1101 Edgecumbe Drive, Sitka, AK 99835; phone (907) 747-8310. E-mail: alaskaocean view@gci.net. See display ad this section. [ADVERTISEMENT]

Camping

Four campgrounds are available in the Sitka area. From the ferry terminal north they are Starrigavan, Sitka Sportsman's, Sealing Cove and Sawmill Creek. Starrigavan and Sawmill Creek campgrounds are both operated by the USDA Forest Service; phone (907) 747-4216 for more information, or contact them by e-mail: sitka.rd/r10_chatham@fs.fed.us.

Starrigavan Campground (USFS), at **Milepost 7.8** Halibut Point Road, has 32 sites, 2 picnic sites, water, tables, vault toilets, 14-day limit, $8 fee, available first-come, first-served only. Sitka Sportsman's Assoc. RV Park, located 1 block south of the ferry terminal on Halibut Point Road, has 16 RV sites, water and electrical hookups, $18 fee, reservations accepted; phone (907) 747-6033. Sealing Cove, operated by the City and Borough of Sitka, is located adjacent Sealing Cove Boat Harbor on Japonski Island; overnight parking for 26 RVs, water and electrical hookups, 15-night limit, $16 fee. Sawmill Creek Campground (USFS) is located on Blue Lake Road, which is accessible at **Milepost 5.4** Sawmill Creek Road; 11

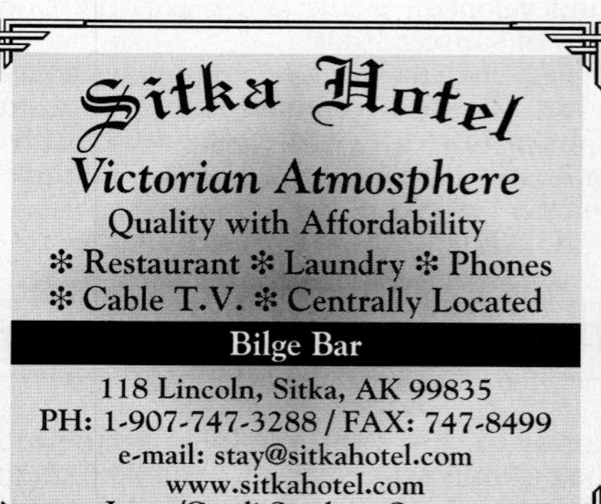

tent sites, vault toilet, boil water, no garbage service, no fee, 14-day limit. ▲

Transportation

Air: Scheduled jet service by Alaska Airlines. Charter and commuter service also available. The airport is on Japonski Island, across O'Connell Bridge, 1.7 miles from downtown. Airport facilities include ticket counters, rental cars, small gift shop, restaurant and lounge. Airport Shuttle (May–Sept.); van and taxi service available to downtown hotels and accommodations .

Ferry: Alaska Marine Highway ferry terminal is located at **Milepost 7** Halibut Point Road; phone (907) 747-8737. The Ferry Shuttle meets all ferries; taxi service also available. Sitka is connected via the Marine Highway to other Southeast ports, Prince Rupert, BC, and Bellingham, WA.

Bus: Shuttle available to accommodations and downtown area. Visitor Transit to attractions 12:30–4:30 with extended hours on large tour ship days.

Car Rental: Available.

Taxi: Available.

Highways: Halibut Point Road, 7.9 miles, and Sawmill Creek Road, 7.4 miles; see logs this section.

Cruise Ships: Sitka is a popular port of call for several cruise lines.

Private Boats: Transient moorage available at Thomsen Harbor, Katlian Street, 0.6 mile from city center. Contact Harbor Master (907) 747-3439 or Channel 16 VHS.

Attractions

St. Michael's Cathedral is the focal point of Sitka's history as the capital of Russian Alaska. Built in 1844–48 under the direction of Bishop Innocent (Ioann Veniaminov) of the Russian Orthodox Church, one of the finest examples of rural Russian church architecture for 118 years. It was destroyed by fire on Jan. 2, 1966. Priceless icons, some predating 1800, were saved by townspeople and are now back in place in the rebuilt cathedral (an exact replica).

St. Michael's is located in the center of Lincoln Street downtown; a donation is requested when entering to view icons. Open daily June 1 to Sept. 30, 11 A.M. to 3 P.M. St. Michael's currently serves a Russian Orthodox congregation of about 100 families. Visitors are reminded that this is an active parish conducting weekly services.

Castle Hill (Baranof Castle Hill Historic Site) is where Alaska changed hands from Russia to the United States on Oct. 18, 1867. Castle Hill was the site of Baranof's castle. Walkway to site is located on the south side by the bridge (look for sign) or on the north side off of Lincoln Street..

Sitka Pioneers' Home, near the waterfront at Lincoln and Katlian streets, was built in 1934. Pioneers welcome visitors, and handicrafts made by the residents are sold in the gift shop located on the first floor of the west wing.

Totem Square is across Katlian Street from the Pioneers' Home and contains a totem, petroglyphs, Russian cannon and 3 large anchors found in Sitka Harbor and believed to be 18th century English.

Russian Blockhouse beside Pioneers' Home is a replica of the blockhouse that separated Russian and Tlingit sections of Sitka after the Tlingits moved back to the area 20 years after the 1804 battle. (See model of early Sitka in Isabel Miller Museum located in Harrigan Centennial Hall.)

Historic buildings from Sitka's Russian days dot the downtown area.
(© Four Corners Imaging)

New Archangel Russian Dancers, a group of local women, perform authentic Russian dances in authentic costumes. Performances are scheduled to coincide with the arrival of cruise ships. Fee charged. Check the dance schedule board for summer performances at Harrigan Centennial Hall or Russian Dance Hotline (907) 747-5516.

Old Russian Cemetery is located behind Pioneers' Home and includes graves of such notables as St. Iahov Netsvetov, a recently canonized saint of the Russian Orthodox Church, who was a priest in Russian Alaska for over 40 years.

The Finnish Lutheran Cemetery, dedicated in 1841, is located on Princess Way next to the Russian cemetery. Just a few steps up the hill from Sitka Lutheran Church, it holds the graves of Princess Maskutov, wife of Alaska's last Russian governor, and other important personages.

Sitka National Cemetery, Milepost 0.5 Sawmill Creek Road, is open 8 A.M. to 5 P.M. daily (maintained by the Veterans Administration). It was known locally as Military Cemetery. In 1924 Pres. Calvin Coolidge designated the site as Sitka National Cemetery, and until WWII it was the only national cemetery west of the Rockies. Civil War veterans, veterans of the Aleutian Campaign in WWII and many notable Alaskans are buried here. One gravestone is dated December 1867, 2 months after the U.S. purchase of Alaska from Russia.

Whale Watching. During the summer, whales are often found in Sitka Sound. During the winter, up to 80 whales are near Sitka shares from mid-September to mid-January. Whale Park, 4.4 miles from town on Sawmill Creek Road, has stationary binoculars for whale viewing.

Alaska Day Celebration, Oct. 14–18, 2000, celebrates the transfer of Alaska from Russia to the United States with a reenactment of the event, complete with Sitka's own 9th (Manchu) Infantry, authentic uniforms and working muskets of the period. Period costumes and beards are the order of the day. Events ranging from pageant to costume ball and parade highlight the affair.

Annual Sitka Summer Music Festival (June 2–23, 2000). Concerts on Tuesday, Friday and some Saturday evenings in Harrigan Centennial Hall, praised for its excellent acoustics. Emphasizing chamber music, an international group of professional musicians give evening concerts during the festival, plus open rehearsals. Advance tickets are a good idea; the concerts are popular. Dress is informal and concert-goers may have the opportunity to talk with the musicians. Children under 6 years not admitted.

Harrigan Centennial Hall, by Crescent Harbor, is used for Russian dance performances, music festivals, banquets and conventions. Its glass-fronted main hall overlooks Sitka Sound. The Isabel Miller Museum is located here. Nearby is a large hand-carved Tlingit canoe made from a single log.

Sheet'ka Kwaan Naa Kahidi (Sitka's Community House) is a northwest coast tribal clan house constructed in traditional Naa Kahidi design and aimed at preserving the Tlingit culture. The Community House is a performing arts center offering Tlingit story telling and dance performances. Exhibits on Native culture are also on display. 200 Katlian St., Sitka, AK 99835; phone (907) 747-7290.

Isabel Miller Museum, located in the Harrigan Centennial Hall, has permanent exhibits highlighting the history of Sitka and its people. Russian tools, paintings from all eras, fishing, forestry, tourism, and Alaska Purchase exhibits, and an 8-foot-square scale model of Sitka in 1867 are among the displays. Operated by the Sitka Historical Society; hosts are available to answer questions. Open year-round; free admission. Hours are 9 A.M. to 5 P.M. daily in summer; 10 A.M. to 4 P.M. Tuesday through Saturday during the winter. Phone (907) 747-6455.

Saint Peter's-by-the-Sea Episcopal Church, at 611 Lincoln Street, was consecrated as "The Cathedral of Alaska" on Easter Sunday, 1900. The church building and See House are listed on the National Historic Register. The Rt. Rev. Peter Trimble Rowe, first Episcopal bishop of Alaska (1895-1942) is buried in the churchyard. Third clipping from the Holy Thorn of Glastonbury was planted in the church garden in

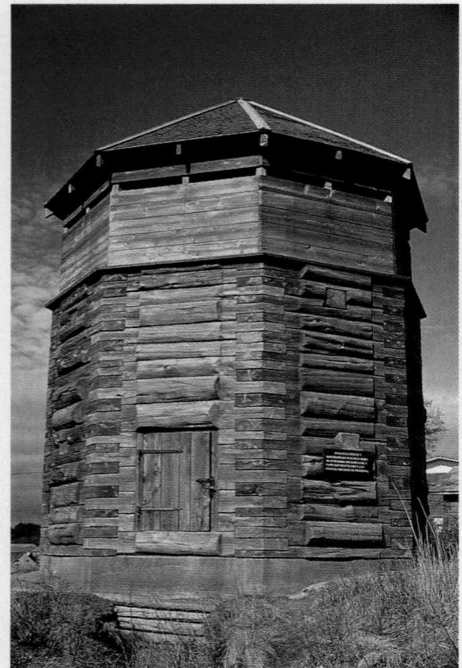

Replica of Russian Blockhouse in Sitka.
(© Harry M. Walker)

1999.

Sitka Lutheran Church, downtown on Lincoln Street, has a small historical display. Established in 1840, it was the first Protestant church organized on the west coast of North America. Free summer tours hosted by volunteers.

Sitka National Historical Park reflects both the community's rich Tlingit Indian heritage and its Russian-ruled past. The park consists of 2 units—the Fort Site, located at the end of Lincoln Street, 0.5 mile from town, and the Russian Bishop's House, located on Lincoln Street near Crescent Harbor.

At the Fort Site stood the Tlingit fort, burned to the ground by Russians after the 1804 Battle of Sitka; this was the last major stand by the Tlingits against Russian settlement. For Alexander Baranof, leader of the Russians, the battle was revenge for the 1802 destruction of Redoubt St. Michael by the Tlingits. There is a visitor center here with audiovisual programs and exhibits of Indian artifacts. The Southeast Alaska Indian Cultural Center has contemporary Tlingit artists demonstrate and interpret various traditional arts for visitors.

There is a self-guiding trail through the park to the fort site and battleground of 1804. The National Park Service conducts guided walks; check for schedule. The park's totem pole collection stands near the visitor center and along the trail. The collection includes original pieces collected in 1901–03, and copies of originals lost to time and the elements. The pieces, primarily from Prince of Wales Island, were collected by Alaska Gov. John Brady (now buried in Sitka National Cemetery). The originals were exhibited at the 1904 St. Louis Exposition.

The Russian Bishop's House was built by the Russian–American Co. in 1842 for the first Russian Orthodox Bishop to serve Alaska. It was occupied by the church until 1969, and was added to Sitka National Historical Park in 1972. The house is 1 of 2 Russian log structures remaining in Sitka, and 1 of 4 remaining in North America.

The park's visitor center is open daily, 8 A.M. to 5 P.M., June through September; weekdays, 8 A.M. to 5 P.M., October through May. The park grounds and trails are open daily, 6 A.M. to 10 P.M. in summer; shorter hours in winter. Russian Bishop's House open 9 A.M. to 5 P.M. daily, closed from 1–2 P.M. for lunch; other times by appointment; hours subject to change. The visitor center is closed Thanksgiving, Christmas and New Year's. Admission fee $3 per person/$6 per immediate family. Tours are $3 per person. Students under 18 free with student identification. Phone (907) 747-6281 for more information.

Sheldon Jackson Museum, 104 College Dr., on the Sheldon Jackson College campus, contains some of the finest Native arts and crafts found in Alaska. Much of it was collected by missionary Sheldon Jackson and is now owned by the state of Alaska. Museum shop specializes in Alaska Native arts and crafts: ivory, dolls, masks, silver jewelry, baskets and beadwork. Admission $3, students 18 and under free, annual pass $10. Open in summer 9 A.M. to 5 P.M. daily. Winter hours: Tuesday through Saturday, 10 A.M. to 4 P.M. Phone (907) 747-8981. Web site: www.eed.state.ak.us/1am/museum/home.html.

The Prospector is a 13½-foot clay and bronze statue in front of the Pioneers' Home. Sculpted by Alonzo Victor Lewis, the statue was dedicated on Alaska Day in 1949. Lewis's model was a genuine pioneer, William "Skagway Bill" Fonda.

Blarney Stone, across from Sheldon Jackson College. Believed to originally have been called Baranof's stone and used as a resting stop by Russian–American Co. chief manager Alexander Baranof.

O'Connell Bridge, 1,225 feet long, connecting Sitka with Japonski Island, was the first cable-stayed, girder-span bridge in the United States. It was dedicated Aug. 19, 1972. You'll get a good view of Sitka and the harbors by walking across this bridge.

Old Sitka, at **Milepost 7.5** Halibut Point Road, is a registered national historic landmark and the site of the first Russian settlement in the area in 1799, known then as Fort Archangel Michael. In 1802, in a surprise attack, the Tlingit Indians of the area destroyed the fort and killed most of its occupants, driving the Russians out until Baranof's successful return in 1804.

Visit the Alaska Raptor Center, located at 1101 Sawmill Creek Road (**Milepost 0.9**) just across Indian River, within walking distance of downtown Sitka. This unique facility treats injured eagles, hawks, owls and other birds. Visitors will have the opportunity to see American bald eagles and other raptors close up, review case histories of birds treated at the center and observe medical care being administered to current patients. From May 15 through September the facility is open daily for tours and educational programs; limited hours October to May 15. Phone (907) 747-8662 for times. Admission charged.

St. Lazaria Island (officially known as Alaska Maritime National Wildlife Refuge) is host to one of the largest seabird colonies in Southeast Alaska. This 65-acre volcanic island was set aside as a wildlife refuge in 1909. A half-million seabirds representing 11 different species breed here. Landing on the island or exploring the island is not advisable because foot traffic damages nesting burrows. Boat charters are available in Sitka for viewing from the water. The best time to visit is May–June. For more information, contact the Refuge Manager, Alaska Maritime National Wildlife Refuge, 2355 Kachemak Bay Dr., Suite 101, Homer, AK 99603; phone (907) 235-6546.

Hiking Trails. Sitka Ranger District office at 201 Katlian, provides information sheets and maps for area trails and remote cabins. Trails accessible from the road include Harbor Mountain Ridge trail; Mount Verstovia trail; the easy 5-mile Indian River trail; and the short Beaver Lake trail off Sawmill Creek Road on Blue Lake Road.

AREA FISHING: Sitka holds an annual salmon derby Memorial Day weekend and the weekend following. Contact the Sitka Sportsmen's Association, P.O. Box 3030, Sitka, AK 99835 or phone (907) 747-6790. Saltwater fishing charters available locally. For a listing contact Sitka Convention & Visitors Bureau at (907) 747-5940. There are also many lakes and rivers on Baranof Island with good fishing; these range from **Katlian River**, 11 miles northeast of Sitka by boat, to more remote waters such as **Rezanof Lake,** which is 40 air miles southeast of Sitka. USFS public-use cabins at some lakes. Stop by the Dept. of Fish and Game office at 304 Lake St. for details; phone (907) 747-5355..

Sawmill Creek Road Log

Sawmill Creek Road is a 7.4-mile road, paved for the first 5.4 miles, which begins at Lake Street and ends beyond the pulp mill (closed) at Silver Bay.

0 Intersection of Lake Street (Halibut Point Road) and Sawmill Creek Road.

0.5 Sitka National Cemetery.

0.6 Sheldon Jackson College entrance.

0.7 Indian River bridge. Beginning of Indian River trail on left.

0.9 Alaska Raptor Rehabilitation Center.

1 Post office.

1.7 Mount Verstovia trail on left next to supper club. The trail extends 2.5 miles/4 km to summit of Mount Verstovia; strenuous hike, great views.

3.6 Thimbleberry Creek bridge.

3.7 On left past bridge is start of Thimbleberry Lake and Heart Lake trail. Hike in 0.5 mile to **Thimbleberry Lake**, brook trout to 12 inches, May–September. *NOTE: It is illegal to use bait in fresh water, except from Sept. 15–Nov. 15.* Trail continues 1 mile past Thimbleberry Lake to **Heart Lake**, brook trout.

4.4 Scenic Whale Park viewpoint turnout; stationary binoculars for whale watching.

5.3 Alaska Pulp Corp. (closed).

5.4 Blue Lake Road on left. Pavement ends on Sawmill Creek Road. Blue Lake Road (narrow dirt) leads 2.2 miles to small parking area and short downhill trail to Blue Lake (no recreational facilities; check with city for information). At Mile 1.5 on right is Sawmill Creek USFS campground. **Blue Lake**, rainbow, May–September; use flies or lure, do not use bait. Lightweight skiff or rubber boat recommended.

5.7 Sawmill Creek and bridge. Pavement ends; gravel begins.

7.2 Public road ends at Herring Cove near mouth of Silver Bay (boat tours of the bay available in Sitka). City road to hydroelectric

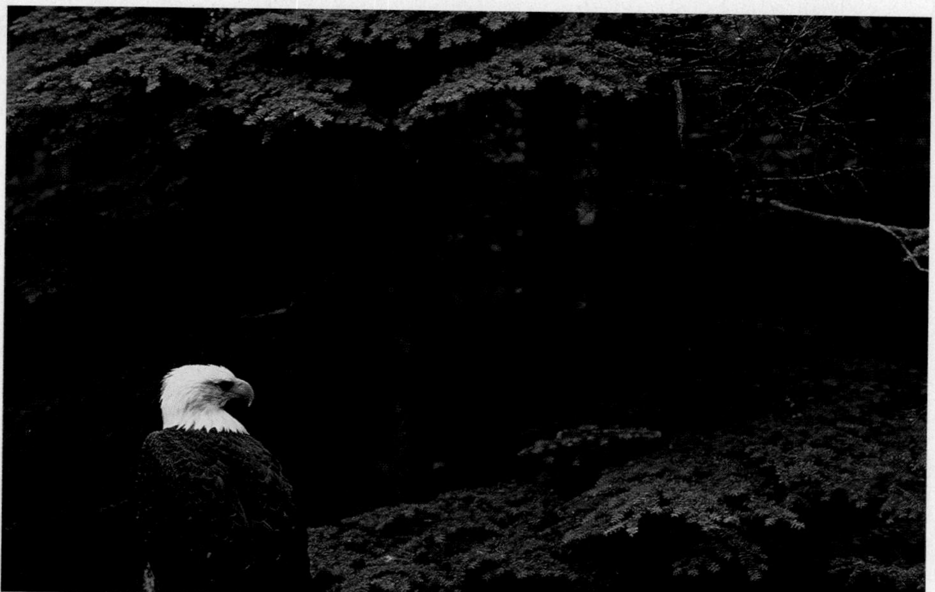

Bald eagle at the Alaska Raptor Rehabilitation Center in Sitka. (© David Job)

power plant continues.

7.4 Gate marking boundary of city road. No vehicles beyond this point; access for hikers and bicyclists only. No guardrails or road signs to road end.

10.5 Fish hatchery and gate.

13.7 Road end. Green Lake Power Plant.

Halibut Point Road Log

Halibut Point Road (paved) leads northwest from the intersection of Harbor Drive and Lincoln Street past Old Sitka to Starrigavan Campground.

0 Harbor Drive and Lincoln Street. Proceed northwest (road is now Lake Street).

0.1 Fire station. Intersection with Sawmill Creek Road; keep left.

0.3 Swan Lake to right of road, rainbow from 12 to 14 inches.

0.6 Katlian Street on left leads to boat ramp and then to downtown. Hospital to the right.

1.8 Pioneer Park picnic and day-use area with beach access; parking available.

2.2 Cascade Creek bridge.

2.3 Tongass National Forest work center.

2.4 Sandy Beach; good swimming beach, ample parking, view of Mount Edgecumbe. Whales are sometimes sighted.

3.8 Viewpoint. On a clear day you can see for 50 miles.

4.2 Harbor Mountain Road; steep gravel, accessible to cars. Road leads 5 miles to road end and Harbor Mountain Ridge trail to lookout at 2,300 feet. Great view of Sitka Sound.

4.4 Granite Creek bridge. Just beyond the bridge on left is Halibut Point state recreation site with swimming beach, shelters, tables, fireplaces and toilets.

7 Alaska Marine Highway ferry terminal on left.

7.3 Boat ramp, litter barrel and pit toilet to left.

7.5 Old Sitka State Historical Site at left, and Starrigavan Creek bridge just ahead. Old Sitka was the site of the Russian Fort Archangel Michael, established in 1799. Commemorative plaque and historical markers. The site is a registered national historic landmark.

7.6 Narrow road on right runs along the bank of Starrigavan Creek, where pink salmon spawn in August and September, and continues several miles through Starrigavan River valley. Off-road vehicles permitted on ATV trail only.

7.7 USFS estuary life trail, Starrigavan Recreation Area; bird watching. Wheelchair access, vault toilets, trails, parking adjacent.

7.8 Turnoff for **Starrigavan USFS campground** and picnic area; artesian well with excellent drinking water. Forest and muskeg nature trail, across from boat ramp, connects with Estuary life trail. Access to beach. Starrigavan Bay, Dolly Varden; pink and silver salmon, May to October.

7.9 (12.7 km) Road ends.

Kake

(See map, page 637)

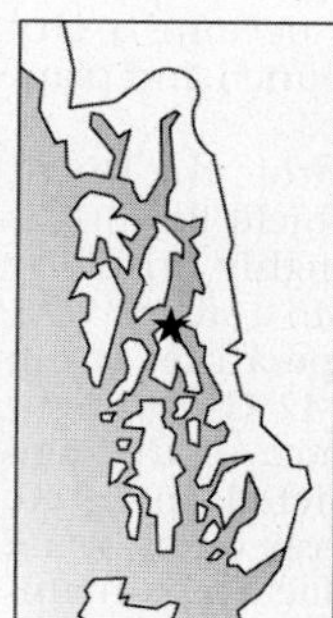

Located on the northwest coast of Kupreanof Island; Petersburg is 40 air miles or 65 miles by boat; Juneau is 95 air miles northeast. **Population:** 820 (approximately 85 percent Native). **Emergency Services:** for all emergencies, 911. **Police**, phone (907) 785-3393. **Public Health Center**, phone (907) 785-3333. **Maritime Search and Rescue**, phone the Coast Guard at (800) 478-5555 or (907) 785-3500.

Visitor Information: City of Kake, Box 500, Kake 99830.

Elevation: Sea level. **Climate:** Less than average rainfall for southeastern Alaska, approximately 50 inches annually. Mild temperatures. January average temperatures are around freezing. Slightly warmer than nearby Petersburg, Kake is noted for being in the "banana belt" of Southeast.

Private Aircraft: Kake seaplane base, located adjacent southeast; fuel 100. Airstrip 1 mile west; elev. 148 feet; length 4,000 feet; asphalt; unattended.

Transportation: Air—Scheduled service from Petersburg (15-minute flight), Juneau (45 minutes), Wrangell and Sitka. Scheduled daily charter service. **Ferry**—Alaska Marine Highway vessel from Petersburg and Sitka.

Accommodations at local inns and bed and breakfasts. There are general, variety and video stores, a cafe and other services. Church groups include Baptist, Salvation Army, Presbyterian and Assembly of God. Kake has an accredited high school, junior high school and elementary.

The town is a permanent village of the Kake (pronounced cake) tribe of the Tlingit Indians. In a series of incidents in the late 1860s, several white men were killed by Kake warriors in reprisal for the deaths of their clansmen. United States gunboats retaliated by shelling and destroying 3 Kake villages.

The tribe eventually settled at the present-day site of Kake, where the government established a school in 1891. Residents have historically drawn ample subsistence from the sea. However, with the advent of a cash economy, the community has come to depend on commercial fishing, fish processing (there is a cold storage) and logging. In recent years, the fish processing has expanded to include the production of value-added products such as smoked and dried fish, and pet treats made from dried salmon skins. The post office was established in 1904, and the city was incorporated in 1952. The city's claim to fame is its totem, reputedly the world's tallest one-piece pole at 132 feet, 6 inches. It was carved for the 1967 Alaska Purchase Centennial Celebration.

The annual Kake Dog Salmon Festival, held in July, celebrates Tlingit culture and the return of dog salmon, also known as chum salmon. Over 700 people joined the festivities in recent years, which included events such as a Tlingit canoe race called "The Challenge of the Chums," the Chum Run foot race and a dog salmon toss. Contact Kake Tribal Corp. for more information, phone (907) 785-3221.

Other area activities include a guided tour of the local salmon hatchery (907/785-6460) and watching black bear fish for salmon in Gunnuk Creek, which flows through the center of the village.

Angoon

(See map, page 638)

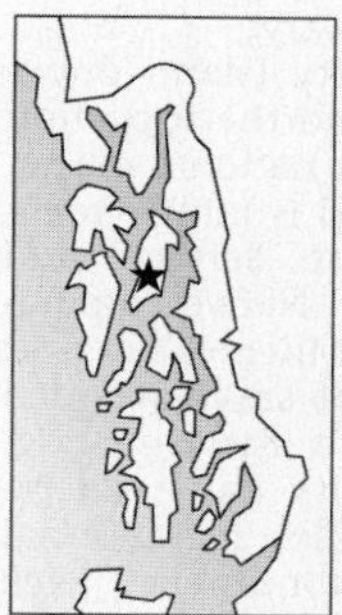

Located on the west coast of Admiralty Island on Chatham Strait, at the mouth of Kootznahoo Inlet. Peril Strait is across Chatham Strait from Angoon. Juneau is 60 air miles northeast. Sitka is 41 miles southwest. **Population:** 587. **Emergency Services: Police**, phone (907) 788-3631. **Clinic**, phone (907) 788-3633.

Visitor Information: Local people are happy to help. You may also contact the USFS Admiralty Island

Decorative clothing reflects traditions of the Tlingit.

(© Lee Foster)

National Monument office in Angoon (phone 907/788-3166) or the city of Angoon (phone 907/788-3653).

Elevation: Sea level. **Climate:** Moderate weather with about 40 inches of annual rainfall and mild temperatures.

Private Aircraft: Angoon seaplane base; 0.9 mile southeast; unattended.

Transportation: Air—Scheduled seaplane service from Juneau. **Ferry**—Alaska Marine Highway service.

Accommodations available at a motel and 2 bed and breakfasts. There are 2 general stores. Fuel service available. There are no RV facilities. Canoes and 12 charter boats available. Transient moorage for private boats also available.

Angoon is a long-established Tlingit Indian settlement at the entrance to Kootznahoo Inlet. It is the only permanent community on Admiralty Island. On Killisnoo Island, across the harbor from the state ferry landing, a community of mostly summer homes has grown up along the island beaches. The lifestyle of this primarily Tlingit community is heavily subsistence: fish, clams, seaweed, berries and venison. Fishing, mostly hand trolling for king and coho salmon, is the principal industry.

The scenery of Admiralty Island draws many visitors. All but the northern portion of the island was declared a national monument in December 1980 and is jointly managed by the U.S. Forest Service and Kootznoowoo Inc., the local Native corporation. Kootznahoo Inlet and Mitchell Bay near Angoon offer a network of small wooded islands, reefs and channels for kayaking. Mitchell Bay and Admiralty Lakes Recreational Area are the 2 major recreational attractions within the monument. Pack Creek, on the east coast of the island, is a well-known bear viewing spot (best mid-July to late August); permit required. Admiralty Island's Indian name, *Kootznoowoo,* means "Fortress of Bears." There are 12 USFS cabins available for public use in the monument; contact the U.S. Forest Service in Angoon.

Local residents can provide directions to the interesting old Killisnoo graveyards, located both on the island and on the Angoon shore of the old Killisnoo settlement, which once was one of the larger communities in southeastern Alaska.

Fishing for salmon is excellent in the Angoon area. (Record kings have been caught in nearby Kelp Bay and in Angoon harbor.) There is also excellent halibut and other bottom fish fishing. Trout (cutthroat and Dolly Varden) fishing in the lakes and streams on Admiralty Island; fair but scattered.

Tenakee Springs

(See map, page 638)

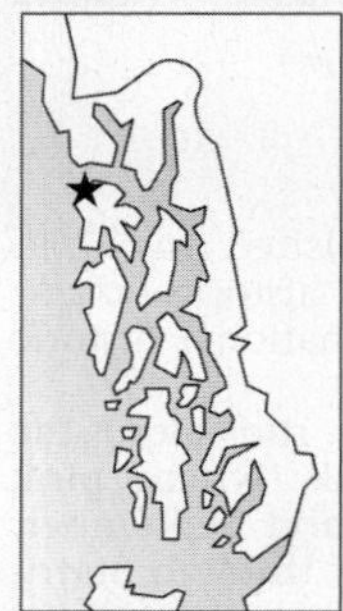

Located on the north shore of Tenakee Inlet on Chichagof Island, 50 miles northeast of Sitka. **Population:** 116. **Visitor Information:** Can be obtained from city hall, phone (907) 736-2207, or from the town's store, phone (907) 736-2205. **Elevation:** Sea level. **Climate:** Average rainfall 63.2 inches annually, with moderate snowfall. **Private Aircraft:** Seaplane base.

Transportation: Air—Scheduled and charter service available through Wings of Alaska out of Juneau. **Ferry**—Alaska Marine Highway service from Sitka and Juneau.

Tenakee Springs has 1 street—Tenakee Avenue—which is about 1.7 miles long and 4 to 12 feet wide. At each end of town is a foot trail that runs 3 miles west and 5 miles east on which no motorized vehicles are allowed. Many residents ride bicycles, some use 3-or 4-wheeled vehicles, but most walk the short distances between buildings. There is a store, cafe, bakery, clinic, post office, art co-op, library and city hall. Accommodations at 7 rental cabins (bring your sleeping bag) are available at Snyder Mercantile, and Tenakee Hot Springs Lodge offers guided sportfishing and sightseeing; phone (907) 736-2400. Tenakee Springs became a city in 1971 and has a mayor, council and planning commission.

The word Tenakee comes from the Tlingit word *tinaghu,* or "Coppery Shield Bay." This refers to 3 copper shields, highly prized by the Tlingits, which were lost in a storm.

The hot springs (temperatures from 106°F to 108°F/41°C to 42°C) brought people to Tenakee at the turn of the century. A bathhouse, completed in 1940, located on the waterfront posts times of use for men and women. The facility is maintained by contributions from residents and visitors.

The major industry at Tenakee might be described as relaxation, as many retirees have chosen to live here, away from the bustle of other Southeast cities. There are many summer homes along Tenakee Avenue. During the summer, watch for whales in Tenakee Inlet, which are sometimes spotted from town.

Some logging is under way in the area around Tenakee. Tenakee Inlet produces salmon, halibut, prawns, Dungeness and king crab, red snapper and cod. A small fleet of fishing vessels is home-ported in Tenakee's harbor, located about 0.5 mile east of the center of town. Although many visitors come to Tenakee to hunt and fish, there are no hunting guides or rental boats available locally. Fishing or sightseeing charters are available locally.

Pelican

(See map, page 638)

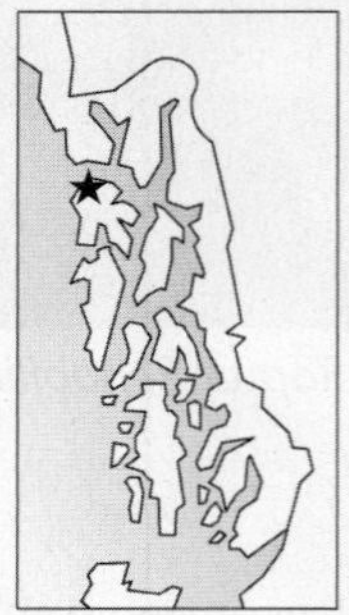

Located on the east shore of Lisianski Inlet on the northwest coast of Chichagof Island; 70 air miles north of Sitka and 70 air miles west of Juneau. **Population:** 149. **Emergency Services: Public Safety Officer** and **Fire Department,** phone 911. **Clinic,** phone (907) 735-2250. **Elevation:** Sea level. **Climate:** Average winter temperatures from 21°F/-6°C to 39°F/4°C; summer temperatures from 51°F/11°C to 62°F/17°C. Total average annual precipitation is 127 inches, with 120 inches of snow.

Visitor Information: Contact the Pelican Visitor Assoc., Box 737, Pelican, AK 99832; phone (907) 735-2282 or 735-2259.

Private Aircraft: Seaplane base; fuel 80, 100. **Transportation: Air**—Scheduled air service from Juneau via Alaska Seaplane Services. Also scheduled service from Sitka. Seaplanes land within walking distance to downtown. **Ferry**—Alaska Marine Highway serves Pelican; terminal is approximately 1/4 mile from downtown boardwalk. There are no cars or taxis in Pelican; they are not necessary, as the town is not very big. Bring good walking shoes. Four-wheelers are available.

Pelican has 2 bar-and-grills (1 with 4 rooms for rent) and a cafe. Accommodations available at a lodge, 2 seasonal lodges, and bed and breakfast. There are a grocery and dry goods store, laundromat and 2 liquor stores. There are a small-boat harbor, marine repair and a fuel dock.

Established in 1938 by Kalle (Charley) Raataikainen, and named for Raataikainen's fish packer *The Pelican,* Pelican relies on commercial fishing and seafood processing. Pelican Seafoods processes salmon, halibut, crab, herring, black cod, rockfish, sea urchin and sea cucumber, and is the primary year-round employer. Pelican has dubbed itself "closest to the fish," a reference to its close proximity to the rich Fairweather salmon grounds. Salmon trolling season is from about June to mid-September, and the king salmon winter season is from October through April. Pelican's population increases greatly when nonresident fishers work during the salmon seasons. Pelican was incorporated in 1943. Most of Pelican is built on pilings over tidelands. A wooden boardwalk extends the length of the community, and there are about 2 miles/3.2 km of gravel road.

Local recreation includes kayaking, hiking, fishing, and watching birds and marine mammals.

Hoonah

(See map, page 638)

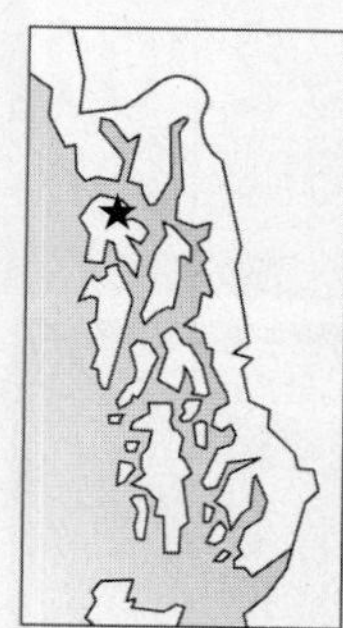

Located on the northeast shore of Chichagof Island, about 40 miles west of Juneau and 20 miles south across Icy Strait from the entrance to Glacier Bay. **Population:** 896. **Emergency Services: Alaska State Troopers** and **Hoonah City Police,** phone (907) 945-3655; emergency only phone 911. **Maritime Search and Rescue,** call the Coast Guard at (800) 478-5555.

Visitor Information: Local business people, city office staff (907/945-3663, weekdays 8 A.M. to 4:30 P.M.) and the postmaster are happy to help. The U.S. Forest Service office in Hoonah (Box 135, Hoonah, AK 99829, phone 907/945-3631) also has visitor information, including an area road guide ($4) showing forest roads on Chichagof Island and a Tongass National Forest map ($4). Hoonah is the starting point for an extensive logging and forest road system for northwest Chichagof Island.

Elevation: Sea level. **Climate:** Typical Southeastern Alaska climate, with average annual precipitation of 70 inches. Average daily temperature in July, 57°F/13°C; in January, 35°F/1°C. Prevailing winds are southeasterly.

Private Aircraft: Hoonah airport, adjacent southeast; elev. 30 feet; length 3,000 feet; paved. Seaplane base adjacent.

Transportation: Air–Scheduled and charter service from Juneau. Airport is located about 3 miles from town. **Ferry**–Alaska Marine Highway vessel serves Hoonah.

Accommodations available at Hoonah Lodge and local bed and breakfasts. Hoonah has 2 restaurants, 2 grocery stores, a hardware store, a gift shop, a variety store, a fishing tackle supply store, a bank, marine fuel docks, a gas pump and 3 flying services. The marina, with showers and a laundromat, is a popular layover for boaters awaiting permits to enter Glacier Bay.

Hoonah is a small coastal community with a quiet harbor for the seining and trolling fleets. The most prominent structures are a cold storage facility, the lodge, bank, post office and the public school. The village has been occupied since prehistory by the Tlingit people. In the late 1800s, missionaries settled here. Canneries established in the area in the early 1900s spurred the growth of commercial fishing, which remains the mainstay of Hoonah's economy. During the summer fishing season, residents work for nearby Excursion Inlet Packing Co. or Hoonah Cold Storage in town. Halibut season begins in May, and salmon season opens in mid-summer and runs through September. Logging also contributes to the economy, with employment loading log ships and other industry-related jobs. Subsistence hunting and fishing remain an important lifestyle here, and many families gather food in the traditional way: catching salmon and halibut in summer, shellfish and bottom fish year-round; hunting deer, geese and ducks; berry picking in summer and fall.

Photograhing Juneau from Mount Jumbo on Douglas Island. (© David Job)

Kayaking, sightseeing, hunting and fishing are the main attractions for visitors. Charter fishing is available locally, with good seasonal king and coho (silver) salmon and halibut fishing as well as crabbing. Guide services are available.

Juneau

(See map, page 638–639)

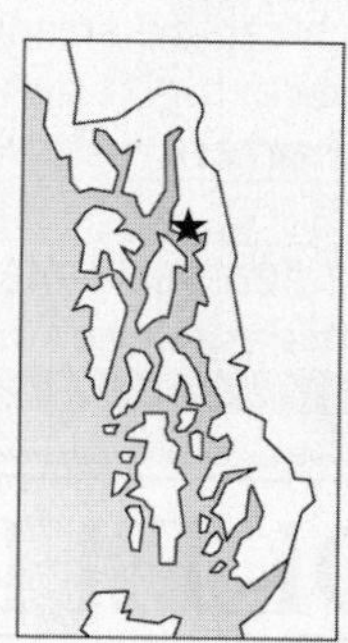

Located on Gastineau Channel; 900 air miles (2 hours, 10 minutes flying time) from Seattle, WA, 650 air miles (1 hour, 25 minutes by jet) from Anchorage. **Population:** Borough 29,755. **Emergency Services:** Phone 911 for all emergencies. **Police,** phone (907) 586-2780. **Fire Department,** phone (907) 586-5245. **Alaska State Troopers,** phone (907) 465-4000. **Poison Center** and **Hospital,** Bartlett Regional, 3260 Hospital Dr., phone (907) 586-2611. **Maritime Search and Rescue,** Coast Guard, phone (907) 463-2000 or (800) 478-5555.

Visitor Information: Juneau Convention & Visitors Bureau, Davis Log Cabin Information Center, 134 3rd St., phone (907) 586-2201 or (888) 581-2201; Internet: www.traveljuneau.com; e-mail: info@traveljuneau.com. Open year-round 8:30 A.M. to 5 P.M. Monday through Friday; additional hours during the summer, 9 A.M. to 5 P.M. Saturday and Sunday. Visitor information kiosk located in Marine Park on waterfront near Merchants Wharf, usually open daily 8:30 A.M. to 6 P.M., from about mid-May to mid-September. Information booth at the airport terminal. Visitor information is also available at the cruise ship terminal on S. Franklin Street when cruise ships are in port, and at the Auke Bay ferry terminal. Large groups contact the Davis Log Cabin Information Center in advance for special assistance.

USFS Information Center at Centennial Hall, 101 Egan Dr.; open 8 A.M. to 5 P.M. weekdays all year. Additional hours during the summer. Phone (907) 586-8751. E-mail: fsic/r10@fs.fed.us. The center has year-round displays and natural history films and seasonal Glacier Bay National Park slide show. Information on camping, trails and USFS cabins is available. The center issues permits for visiting Pack Creek, the bear viewing site

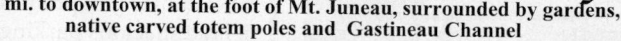

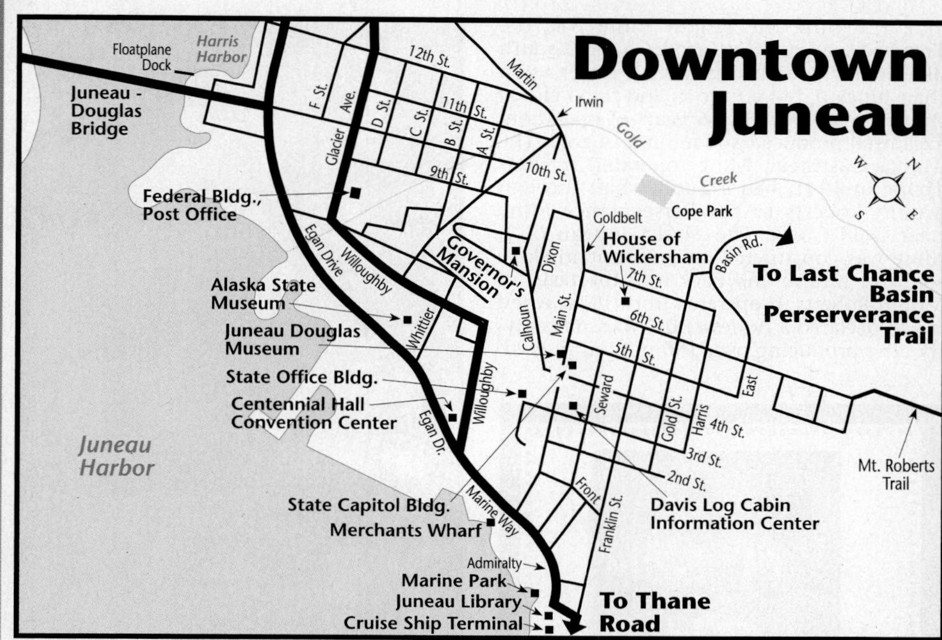

on Admiralty Island. Juneau Ranger District (USFS), **Milepost 9.4** Glacier Highway (airport area), phone (907) 586-8800; open 8 A.M. to 5 P.M. weekdays.

Mendenhall Glacier Visitor Center (USFS) includes an observatory for viewing the glacier and lake, an exhibit gallery, a theater, a merchandise sales area and restrooms. Open 8 A.M. to 6 P.M. daily May through September, 9 A.M. to 4 P.M. Wed.–Sun. the rest of the year. Phone (907) 789-0097.

Elevation: Sea level. **Climate**: Mild and wet. Average daily maximum temperature in July, 63°F/17°C; daily minimum in January, 20°F/-7°C. Highest recorded temperature, 90°F/32°C in July 1975; the lowest -22°F/-30°C in January 1972. Average annual precipitation, 56.5 inches (airport), 92 inches (downtown); 103 inches of snow annually. Snow on ground intermittently from mid-November to mid-April. Prevailing winds are east-southeasterly. **Radio:** KJNO 630, KINY 800, KTOO-FM 104.3, KTKU-FM 105.1, KSUP-FM 106. **Television:** KJUD Channel 8; JATV cable; KTOO (public television). **Newspapers:** *Juneau Empire* (Sunday through Friday) and *Capital City Weekly*.

Private Aircraft: Juneau International Airport, 9 miles northwest; elev. 18 feet; length 8,456 feet; asphalt; fuel 100LL, Jet A. Juneau harbor seaplane base, due east; restricted use, no fuel. International seaplane base, 7 miles northwest; 5,000 feet by 450 feet, avgas, Jet A. For more information, phone the Juneau Flight Service Station at (907) 789-6124.

History and Economy

In 1880, nearly 20 years before the great gold rushes to the Klondike and to Nome, 2 prospectors named Joe Juneau and Dick Harris found "color" in what is now called Gold Creek, a small, clear stream that runs through the center of present-day Juneau. (Local history states that a Tlingit, Chief Kowee, showed Joe Juneau where to find gold in Gold Creek.) . What the prospectors found led to the discovery of one of the largest lodes of gold quartz in the world. Juneau (called Harrisburg the first year) quickly boomed into a gold rush town as claims and mines sprang up in the area.

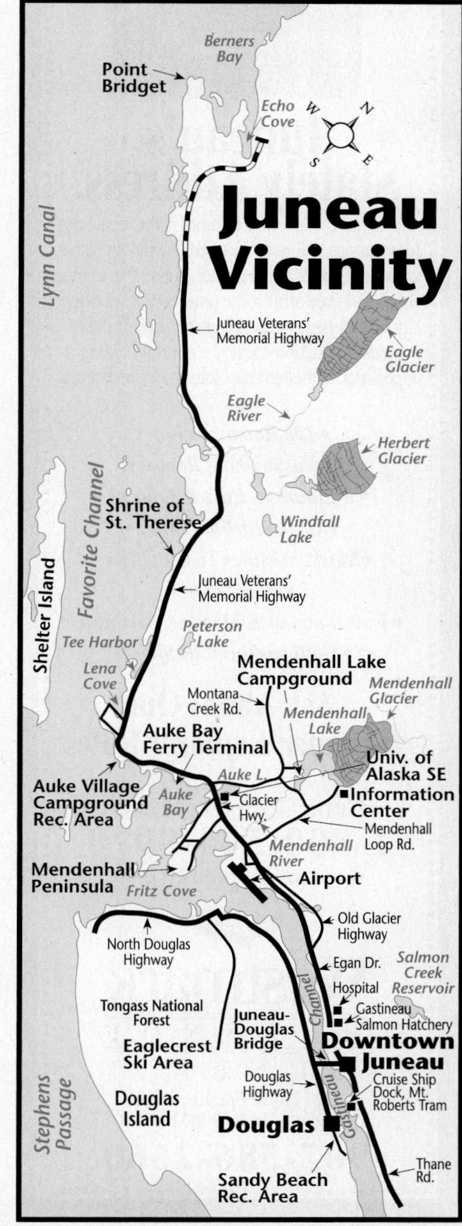

For a time the largest mine was the Treadwell, across Gastineau Channel south of Douglas (which was once a larger town than Juneau), but a cave-in and flood closed the mine in 1917. In 36 years of operation, Treadwell produced $66 million in gold. The Alaska–Gastineau Mine, operated by Bart Thane in 1911, had a 2-mile shaft through Mount Roberts to the Perseverance Mine near Gold Creek. The Alaska–Juneau (A–J) Mine was constructed on a mountain slope south of Juneau and back into the heart of Mount Roberts. It operated until 1944, when it was declared a nonessential wartime activity after producing over $80 million in gold.

Shrine of St. Therese at Mile 23.1 on Juneau Veterans' Memorial Highway.

(© Four Corners Imaging)

Post–WWII wage and price inflation and the fixed price of gold prevented its reopening.

In 1900, the decision to move Alaska's capital to Juneau was made because of the city's growth, mining activity and location on the water route to Skagway and the Klondike; the decline of post-Russian Sitka, as whale and fur trading slackened, secured Juneau's new status as Alaska's preeminent city.

Congress first provided civil government for Alaska in 1884. Until statehood in 1959 Alaska was governed by a succession of presidential appointees, first as the District of Alaska, then as the Territory of Alaska. Between 1867 (when the United States purchased Alaska from Russia) and 1884, the military had jurisdiction over the District of Alaska, except for a 3-year period (1877–79) when Alaska was put under control of the U.S. Treasury Dept. and governed by U.S. Collectors of Customs.

With the arrival of Alaska statehood in 1959, Juneau's governmental role increased even further. In 1974, Alaskans voted to move the capital from Juneau to a site between Anchorage and Fairbanks, closer to the state's population center. In 1976, Alaska voters selected a new capital site near Willow, 65 road miles/105 km north of Anchorage on the Parks Highway. However, in November 1982, voters defeated funding for the capital move.

Today, government (federal, state and local) comprises an estimated half of the total basic industry. Tourism is the largest employer in the private sector.

Description

Juneau, often called "a little San Francisco," is nestled at the foot of Mount Juneau (elev. 3,576 feet) with Mount Roberts (elev. 3,819 feet) rising immediately to the east on the approach up Gastineau Channel. The residential community of Douglas, on Douglas Island, is south of Juneau and connected by a bridge. Neighboring residential areas around the airport, Mendenhall Valley and Auke Bay lie north of Juneau on the mainland.

Shopping is in the downtown area and at suburban malls in the airport and Mendenhall Valley areas.

Juneau's skyline is dominated by several government buildings, including the Federal Building (1962), the massive State Office Building (1974), the State Court Building (1975) and the older brick, and marble-columned Capitol Building (1931). The modern Sealaska Plaza is headquarters for

Sealaska Corp., 1 of the 13 regional Native corporations formed after congressional passage of the Alaska Native Claims Settlement Act in 1971.

To explore downtown Juneau, it is best to park and walk; distances are not great. The streets are narrow and congested with pedestrians and traffic (especially rush hours), and on-street parking is scarce. Visitors should check at the Davis Log Cabin and at the police station to see whether parking permits are available. Public parking lots are located across from Merchants Wharf Mall at Main Street and Egan Drive and south of Marine Park at the Marine Park parking garage; fee required.

The Juneau area supports 35 churches, a high school, 2 middle schools, several elementary schools and a University of Alaska Southeast campus at Auke Lake. There are 3 municipal libraries and the state library. The Perseverance Theatre, which was established in 1978, provides Juneau with classical and original works, September through May.

The area is governed by the unified city and borough of Juneau, which encompasses 3,108 square miles. It is the first unified government in the state, combining the former separate and overlapping jurisdictions of the city of Douglas, city of Juneau and greater Juneau borough.

Lodging & Services

Juneau has several hotels and motels, most of them downtown. There are also numerous bed and breakfasts as well as wilderness lodges; see ads this section.

The Juneau International Hostel is located at 614 Harris St. (Juneau 99801), 4 blocks northeast of the Capitol Bldg. All ages are welcome. Check-in time is 5–11 P.M. during summer, 5–10:30 P.M. the rest of the year. Showers, cooking, laundry and storage facilities are available. Cost for members is $7, nonmembers $10, children accompanied by parent $5. Groups welcome. Open year-round. Phone (907) 586-9559.

More than 60 restaurants offer a wide variety of dining. Also watch for sidewalk food vendors downtown in summer. Juneau also has 2 microbreweries. The Alaskan Brewing Co., located at 5429 Shaune Dr. in the Lemon Creek area, offers tours, phone (907) 780-5866.

AAA Fireweed House Bed & Breakfast. If you are seeking the finest in private, plush accommodations and breakfast dining in the Juneau area, look no further than AAA Fireweed House Bed & Breakfast. This fabulous 4-acre location on Douglas Island is just a few minutes from downtown Juneau; but when you are a guest at Fireweed House, you'll feel like you've stepped into a pampered world away from the vacation hustle and bustle. *What a find!* Although this is a destination by itself, a more ideal base for your Southeast Alaska experience would be difficult to locate. The accommodations are all first class and the breakfast dining experience is a *must!* The Thomas Glacier and the surrounding mountains are prominent from many of the windows. The 2-bedroom, cedar guest house on its own adjoining, 2-acre site is unsurpassed in its beauty, seclusion and spaciousness. In addition, the private Fireweed Apartment and guest rooms in the Main House are also extraordinarily appointed and comfortable. Many amenities. Several accommodations include King-size beds and Jacuzzi baths. Birds and other forms of wildlife grace the grounds surrounding this establishment. Complimentary arrangements for personalized tours and charters. Non-smoking. Children welcome. AAA 3-diamond approved. Toll free (800) 586-3885; phone (907) 586-3885; fax (907) 586-3385. 8530 North Douglas Highway, Juneau, AK 99801; website with e-mail: http://fireweedhouse.com. Reserve early to assure space at this B&B! [ADVERTISEMENT]

Pearson's Pond Luxury Inn and Garden Spa. This spectacular, peaceful retreat on idyllic pond nestled in rainforest by Mendenhall Glacier excels for romance, adventure, business. Their extended-stay property, Alaskan Suites Juneau, near downtown, enjoys privileges here too. Enjoy private baths, kitchens, electric fireplaces,

Flower baskets adorn downtown Juneau lampposts.

(© Stephanie Sater)

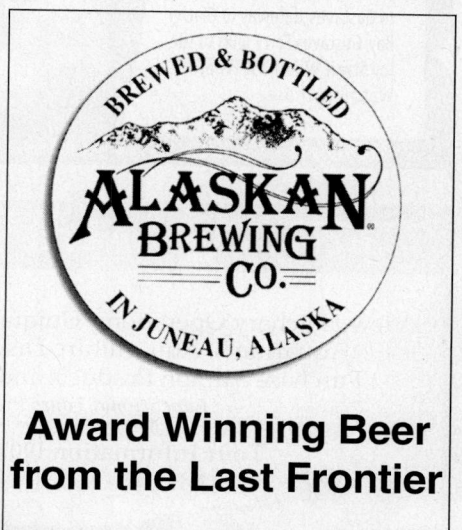

laptops, dock, water-bikes, hot tubs, bicycles, trails, firepit and lush gardens. Explore trails, kayaking, rafting, fishing, glacier trekking and native culture nearby. Ski, spa, fishing, honeymoon packages. Voted a **"Best B&B"** in America and Alaska. AAA Excellence Awards. Book far ahead; plan around their availability. Reservations: (907) 789-3772 or toll free 888-658-6328; E-mail: pearsons.pond@juneau.com. Web site: www.juneau.com/pearsons.pond. [ADVERTISEMENT]

Camping

The city and borough of Juneau offers limited, free, RV overnight parking spaces at Savikko Park/Sandy Beach (**Milepost 2.5** Douglas Highway); sign in at the harbor-master's office (across from high school on Egan Drive). Contact the visitor information center, (907) 586-2201 for a brochure on RV facilities. Dump stations are located at Mendenhall Lake campground, Valley Tesoro at Mendenhall Center shopping mall in the Mendenhall Valley, and Savikko Park in Douglas.

There are 2 USFS campgrounds and 1 private RV park north of Juneau via the Glacier Highway. The USFS campgrounds are Mendenhall Lake (turn off Glacier Highway at **Milepost 9.4** or **12.2** and continue to Montana Creek Road) and Auke Village (**Milepost 15.4** Glacier Highway). Both campgrounds are first come, first served. Auke Village Campground, 1.5 miles west of the ferry terminal, has 12 campsites, flush and pit toilets, water and firewood: first-come, first-served. The private RV park, with hookups, is located at **Milepost 12.3** Glacier Highway; phone (907) 789-9467. RV camping at Eagle Beach State Recreation Area, **Milepost 28** Glacier Highway. ▲

Spruce Meadow RV Park. (Opening spring 2000) 64 private, unique, full-service spaces located on 12.5 acres of virgin wetlands in spruce, alder and meadows. Services available: 30-amp electric, water, sewer, garbage, phone, cable TV, laundromat, showers, restrooms, gazebos, dump station, on-site management, tourist information and brochures. Only 5 minutes from Mendenhall Glacier and Auke Bay boat harbor. Reservations strongly recommended. Visit us at 10200 Mendenhall Loop Rd. E-mail: juneauRVer@aol.com. Phone (907) 789-1990. [ADVERTISEMENT] ▲

Transportation

Air: Juneau Municipal Airport turnoff is at **Milepost 8.8** Egan Drive (Glacier Highway). Airport terminal contains ticket counters, waiting area, gift shop, rental cars, restaurant, lounge and information booth.

The city express bus stops at the airport weekdays from 8 A.M. to 5 P.M. A shuttle and taxi and van service to downtown are also available. Shuttle service $8 1-way per person, $5 each for groups of 3 or more. Taxi service approximately $15 to $20. Courtesy vans to some hotels.

Alaska Airlines serves Juneau daily from Seattle, WA, Anchorage, Fairbanks, Ketchikan, Sitka, Yakutat, Cordova, Petersburg and Wrangell. Scheduled commuter service to Haines, Skagway, Sitka, Angoon and other points via several air services. Scheduled service between Juneau and Whitehorse, YT, available.

Charter air service (wheel and floatplanes and helicopters) is available for hunting, fishing, sightseeing and transportation to other communities (see ads in this section).

Alaska Seaplane Service provides experienced floatplane service to wilderness cabins, villages, and fishing lodges in Southeast Alaska. Over 30 years of flying experience guarantees personalized, professional sightseeing and wildlife tours. Visit our ticket counter in the Juneau International Airport or phone (907) 789-3331 for further information. [ADVERTISEMENT]

Ferry: Juneau is served by Alaska Marine Highway ferries. See ALASKA STATE FERRY SCHEDULES section.

Alaska state ferries dock at the Auke Bay terminal at **Milepost 13.9** Glacier Highway; phone (907) 465-3941 or 789-7453. Taxi service and private shuttle bus is available from Auke Bay terminal to downtown Juneau. Shuttle service runs mid-May to mid-October; $5 each way. There is also a bus stop 1.5 miles toward town from the ferry terminal (see following).

Bus: Capital Transit city bus system runs from the cruise ship terminal downtown and includes Juneau, Douglas, Lemon Creek, Mendenhall Valley and airport area, Auke Bay (the community, which is about 1.5 miles south of the ferry terminal). Hourly service Monday through Saturday, year-round; limited service on Sundays. Route map and schedule available at the visitor information center. Flag buses at any corner except in downtown Juneau, where bus uses marked stops only. Fare: $1.25 anywhere.

Highways: Longest road is Glacier Highway, which begins in downtown Juneau and leads 40.5 miles north to Echo Cove. Other major roads are Mendenhall Loop Road and Douglas and North Douglas highways. See logs this section.

Taxi: Five companies.

Cruise Ships: Juneau is southeastern

Stained-glass window at Juneau Library. (© Harry M. Walker)

Alaska's most frequent port of call. There were approximately 565 port calls by cruise ships in 1999.

Car Rental: Several car rental agencies are available at the airport and vicinity. There are no car rental agencies downtown, but most rental agencies will take you to their offices (sometimes at an extra charge). Best to reserve ahead of time because of the great demand for cars.

Private Boats: Transient moorage is available downtown at Harris and Douglas floats and at Auke Bay. Most boaters use Auke Bay. For more information call the Juneau harbormaster at (907) 586-5255 or hail on Channel 74 and Channel 16 UHF.

Attractions

Juneau walking-tour map (in English, French, Spanish, German, Chinese or Japanese) is available from the Davis Log Cabin Information Center at 134 3rd St. and from other visitor information sites and hotels. See Juneau's many attractions—the St. Nicholas Orthodox Church, totems, Capitol Building, Governor's Mansion, historic graves, monuments, state museum, city museum, hatchery and others.

Marine Park, located at foot of Seward Street, has tables, benches, information kiosk and lighterage facilities for cruise ship launches. The Ed Way bronze sculpture, "Hard Rock Miner," is located at Marine Park. Free concerts on Friday evenings in summer.

Mount Roberts Tramway. A 60-passenger aerial tramway takes you from Juneau's downtown waterfront to a modern mountain complex at the 1800-foot level of Mount Roberts, offering a panoramic view of the town, harbor and surrounding mountains. The mountaintop complex houses a theater, restaurant, bar, gift shop and Native artists. Access to a nature center and alpine walking trails.

Mount Roberts Trail Observation Point offers an elevated view of Juneau. Though the trail extends to the 3,819-foot summit, an excellent observation point above Juneau is reached by a 20-minute hike from the start of Mount Roberts trail at the top of Starr Hill (6th Street).

Visit the Juneau Library. Built on top of the 4-story public parking garage in downtown Juneau, this award-winning library designed by Minch Ritter Voelckers Architects is well worth a visit. Take the elevator to the 5th floor and spend a morning or afternoon reading in this well-lit and comfortable space with a wonderful view of Juneau, Douglas and Gastineau Channel. Located at South Franklin and Admiralty Way, between Marine Park and the cruise ship terminal.

Juneau–Douglas City Museum, located in the Veteran's Memorial Building across from the State Capitol Building at 4th and Main streets, offers exhibits and audiovisual presentations on the Juneau–Douglas area, featuring gold mining and local cultural history. Displays include a turn-of-the-century store and kitchen, a large relief map, a hands-on history room that's fun for kids of all ages and a special summer exhibit. Free historical walking-tour maps of Juneau are available. Museum gift shop. Summer hours are 9 A.M. to 5 P.M. weekdays, 10 A.M. to 5 P.M. weekends, mid-May to mid-September Limited hours in winter. Admission $3 summer rate; $2 in winter. Students free. Phone (907) 586-3572 or write Parks and Recreation, Attn: Juneau–Douglas City Museum, 155 S. Seward St., Juneau, AK 99801, for more information.

State Capitol Building, at 4th and Main streets, contains the legislative chambers and the governor's office. Free tours available from capitol lobby; most days in summer on the half-hour from 9 A.M. to 5 P.M. The **State Office Building**, one block west, houses the State Historical Library and Kimball theater organ (free organ concerts at noon Fridays).

Alaska State Museum is a major highlight of Juneau located downtown at 395 Whittier St. Exhibits include dioramas and contain materials from Alaska's Native groups; icons and other artifacts from Russian–America days; and a popular life-size eagle nesting tree surrounded by a mural of a Southeast Alaska scene. A replica of Capt. George Vancouver's ship, *Discovery*, is located in the children's room for kids to explore.

During the summer of 2000, the museum celebrates its 100th birthday with an exhibition that looks at a century of collecting

Eagle Beach trail is about 28 miles north of Juneau by highway. (© David Job)

Alaska's treasures. From the beautiful to the bizarre; the sublime to the surreal, this landmark exhibition highlights objects from the museum's collection that mark the human and natural history of "the Last Frontier." There is also an exhibition entitled, *Drawing Shadows to Stone: Photographing North Pacific Peoples (1897-1902)*, drawn from some 3000 photographic scenes and portraits produced by the Jesup North Pacific Expedition between 1897 and 1902. It documents the peoples of America's northwest coast and northeastern Siberia and reveals how early anthropologists saw both their photographic task and their science.

The museum store carries Alaska Native crafts and Alaska books and gifts for all ages. Summer hours are 9 A.M. to 6 P.M. Monday through Friday and 10 A.M. to 6 P.M. weekends. Winter hours are 10 A.M. to 4 P.M. Tuesday through Saturday. General admission is $4. Visitors 18 and under and members of the Friends of the Alaska State Museum are admitted free. A $10 museum pass is also available. Phone (907) 465-2901; Internet: http://www.eed.state.ak.us/lam/museum/home.html. E-mail: bruce_kato@eed.state.ak.us.

St. Nicholas Orthodox Church, 5th and Gold streets, a tiny structure built in 1894, is now the oldest original Russian Orthodox church in southeastern Alaska. Visitors are welcome to Sunday services; open daily for summer tours. Phone (907) 586-1023.

The House of Wickersham, 213 7th St., has an important historical collection dating to the days of the late Judge James Wickersham, one of Alaska's first federal judges, who collected Native artifacts and baskets, as well as many photographs and historical documents concerning Native culture, during his extensive travels throughout the territory early in the century. Visiting hours in summer. Phone (907) 586-9001 for more information. (Steep climb up to Seventh Street.)

The Governor's Mansion at 716 Calhoun Ave. has been home to Alaska's chief executives since it was completed in 1913. The $2^1/_2$-story structure, containing 12,900 square feet of floor space, took nearly a year to build. Tours may be possible by advance arrangement. Phone (907) 465-3500.

Take a Tour. Tours of Juneau and area attractions—by boat, bus, plane and helicopter—can be arranged. These tours range from sightseeing trips out to Mendenhall Glacier to river trips on the Mendenhall River.

The Gastineau Salmon Hatchery, operated by Douglas Island Pink and Chum, Inc., is located on Channel Drive 3 miles from downtown. The hatchery offers visitors a chance to see adult salmon, over 100 species of Southeast Alaska sea-life in saltwater aquariums, aquaculture displays, and other seasonal activities. A variety of salmon products is also available for purchase. Fishing available near the hatchery; buy licenses and rent gear at kiosk. Visitor center open in summer 10 A.M. to 6 P.M. Monday through Friday; 10 A.M. to 5 P.M. Saturday and Sunday. Incubation-room tours available May 15 through June 30; spawning salmon sights and hatchery operations tour approximately July 1–Sept. 15. Tours by appointment rest of year. Educational tours provided; $3 adult; $1 child. Group: 5 adults, $12; 12 children, $12. Phone (907) 463-4810.

See Old Mine Ruins. Remnants from the Treadwell Mine may be seen from a marked trail that starts just south of Sandy Beach on Douglas Island. The impressive remains of the A–J Mine mill are located on the hillside along Gastineau Channel just south of downtown Juneau; good views from Douglas Island and from the water. Evidence of the Alaska–Gastineau Mine can be seen south of town along Thane Road. Walking-tour maps of the Treadwell area are available from the city museum.

Thane Road begins just south of downtown Juneau and extends 5.5 miles along Gastineau Channel. Good views of the channel and old mines. Excellent viewpoint for spawning salmon at Sheep Creek bridge and falls, Mile 4.3, in summer.

Mount Juneau Waterfall, scenic but difficult to photograph, descends 3,576 feet from Mount Juneau to Gold Creek behind the city. Best view is from Basin Road. The waterfall is also visible from Marine Park.

Mendenhall Glacier is about 13 miles from downtown Juneau at the end of Mendenhall Glacier Spur Road. Turn right northbound at **Milepost 9.4** Egan Drive (Glacier Highway), and then drive straight for 3.6 miles to the glacier and visitor center. There is a large parking area, and trails lead down to the edge of the lake (a sign warns visitors to stay back; falling ice can create huge waves). A 0.5-mile nature trail starts behind the visitor center. Trailheads for 2 longer trails—East Glacier and Nugget Creek—are a short walk from the visitor center. Programs and guided hikes with Forest Service interpreters are offered in summer. The center features an exhibit area with a model of a glacier and displays on glacial processes. There is also a 100-seat theatre. Phone (907) 586-8751 for more information. There is a $3 entrance fee for the visitor center only; no charge for access to the lake, trail and parking lot.

Bike Paths. There are designated bike routes to Douglas, to Mendenhall Valley and Glacier, and to Auke Bay. The Mendenhall Glacier route starts at the intersection of 12th Street and Glacier Avenue; total biking distance is 15 miles. Bikes can be rented downtown and in the vicinity of the airport. Bike-route map and hiking information are available at the Davis Log Cabin.

Tracy Arm. Located 50 miles southeast of Juneau, Tracy Arm and adjoining Endicott Arm are the major features of the Tracy Arm–Fords Terror Wilderness Area. Both Tracy and Endicott arms are long, deep and narrow fjords that extend more than 30 miles into the heavily glaciated Coast Mountain Range. Active tidewater glaciers at the head of these fjords calve icebergs into the fjords.

Fords Terror, off of Endicott Arm, is an area of sheer rock walls enclosing a narrow entrance into a small fjord. The fjord was named in 1889 for a crew member of a naval vessel who rowed into the narrow canyon at slack tide and was caught in turbulent icy currents for 6 terrifying hours when the tide changed.

Access to this wilderness area is primarily by boat or floatplane from Juneau. Large cruise ships and small cruise ships and charter boats include Tracy Arm and Endicott Arm in their itineraries. It is also a popular destination for sea kayakers.

enclosed and heated cabin, restroom, big windows and plenty of deck space for viewing the majestic scenery and wildlife. For reservations and information, phone (800) 770-3422. 2 Marine Way, Suite 115, Juneau, AK 99801. Phone (907) 463-3422, fax (907) 463-3421. [ADVERTISEMENT]

Charter a Boat for salmon and halibut fishing or sightseeing. The visitor information center can provide a list of charter operators; also see ads in this section.

Charter a Plane for fly-in fishing, hunting, transportation to remote lodges and longer flightseeing trips.

Glacier Bay National Park contains some of the most impressive tidewater glaciers in the world. Juneau is located about 50 miles east of the bay and is the main jumping-off point for many Glacier Bay visitors. There are several local businesses offering 1- and 2-day or longer boat and air packages to the park. The state ferries do not service Glacier Bay. See GLACIER BAY NATIONAL PARK and GUSTAVUS sections for more information.

Juneau Icefield, immediately to the east of Juneau, is a 1,500-square-mile expanse of glaciated mountains that is the source of all the glaciers in the area, including Mendenhall, Taku, Eagle and Herbert. Best way to experience and photograph it is via charter flightseeing. Flights usually take 30 to 60 minutes. Helicopter tours, which land on the glacier, are also available. Helicopter tours last from about 45 minutes to 1½ hours.

Ski Eaglecrest, Juneau's downhill and cross-country ski area on Douglas Island. Built and maintained by the city of Juneau, the area features a day-lodge, cafeteria, ski school, ski patrol, ski rental shop, 2 chair lifts, a surface lift and runs for experienced, intermediate and beginning skiers. Three miles/5 km of maintained cross-country trails available. Open 5 days a week, Dec. to mid-April. The view from the top of the chair lift (operating during ski season only) is worth the visit—Mendenhall Glacier, Juneau Icefield, Lynn Canal, Stephens Passage and more. Drive North Douglas Highway to turnoff left at Eaglecrest sign, then 5.3 miles/8.5 km up the Eaglecrest access road to the lodge. For more information, write Eaglecrest Ski Area, 155 S. Seward St., Juneau, AK 99801; phone (907) 586-5284 (790-2000 during ski season), or phone (907) 586-5330 for a recorded message about ski conditions. Internet: www.juneau.lib.ak.us/eaglecrest/eaglcrst.htm.

Chapel-by-the-Lake (Presbyterian), **Milepost 11.6** Glacier Highway, is a log structure perched above Auke Lake. Its front, made entirely of glass, frames the scenic lake, Mendenhall Glacier and mountains. Popular marriage chapel.

Shrine of St. Therese (Roman Catholic), **Milepost 23.1** Memorial Highway, is a natural stone chapel on its own island, connected to shore by a gravel causeway. A 1 P.M. Sunday mass takes place in summer.

Golden North Salmon Derby is a 3-day derby in late August.

Hiking Trails. *Juneau Trails,* a guidebook of 20-plus area hikes, can be purchased for $4 at the USFS Information Center in Centennial Hall or local bookstores. Juneau Parks and Recreation Dept. offers free organized hikes Wednesday and Saturday, April through October; phone (907) 586-5226 for information.

AREA FISHING: (Several special sportfishing regulations are in effect in the Juneau area; consult current regulations booklet.) Good Dolly Varden fishing available along most saltwater shorelines in Juneau area; king salmon best from mid-May to mid-June, pink salmon available about mid-July through August, silver salmon best August to mid-September. Good fishing by boat from Juneau, Auke Bay or Tee Harbor in **Favorite** and **Saginaw channels, Chatham Strait** and near mouth of **Taku Inlet** for salmon, Dolly Varden and halibut. USFS public-use cabins available.

For up-to-date angling data in the Juneau area, phone (907) 465-4116 for recorded Alaska Dept. of Fish and Game message (April through Oct.). For specific angling information or for a copy of the local sportfishing guide, contact the ADF&G, Division of Sport Fish, Area Management Biologist, P.O. Box 20, Douglas 99824; phone (907) 465-4320. A list of charter boats is available from the Juneau Convention and Visitors Bureau (phone 907/586-2201 or toll free 888-581-2201). Also see ads this section.

Mendenhall Glacier is 13 miles from downtown Juneau. (© Susan Cole Kelly)

Juneau Veterans' Memorial Highway

Egan Drive from downtown Juneau proceeds north to **Milepost 9.4,** then becomes Glacier Highway. Egan Drive is named for William A. Egan (1914–84), first governor of the state of Alaska. From **Milepost 12.2** to road end, Glacier Highway has been renamed the Juneau Veterans' Memorial Highway. The highway ends 40.5 miles north of Juneau near Echo Cove on Berners Bay. It is a scenic drive northward along Favorite Channel.

0 Cruise ship terminal.

0.3 Parking garage, 3-hour limit. Free parking on weekends and holidays.

0.5 Stoplight. Marine Way and Main Street. Egan Drive begins here.

0.7 Alaska State Museum, exit east onto Whittier Street.

1.2 Stoplight. Tenth Street exit east. For access to Douglas Highway and North Douglas Highway, turn west across Juneau–Douglas bridge (see logs this section).

1.3 Turn west (left northbound) for Harris Harbor for small boats.

1.5 Juneau–Douglas High School to east (right northbound).

1.7 Aurora Basin small-boat harbor to west (left northbound). Access to Juneau Yacht Club on Harbor Way Road.

3.9 Stoplight. Picnic tables at Twin Lakes to east. Fish for landlocked, stocked salmon. Also exit east for Bartlett Memorial Hospital and Alaska Native Health Center; access to Old Glacier Highway and residential area. Gastineau Salmon Hatchery to west.

5.5 Stoplight. Lemon Creek area.

6.1 Mendenhall Wetlands viewing area; great place to see eagles and waterfowl.

6.7 Access to Old Glacier Highway and Switzer Creek; exit east. Department store; service station with gas, propane.

8.1 Airport access road.

8.2 Fred Meyer shopping center. Access to Glacier Gardens Rainforest Adventures; guided and self-guided tours, admission charged.

8.8 Stoplight; McDonald's. Airport turnoff and access to Nugget Mall and Airport Shopping Center to west. A 0.3-mile loop road (Old Glacier Highway) provides access to malls and to Juneau International Airport. Access to Mendenhall Wetlands State Game Refuge dike trail (good bird watching) via Berners Avenue and Radcliff Rd. Loop road rejoins Egan Drive at **Milepost 9.4.**

9.4 Stoplight. South **junction** with **Mendenhall Loop Road**. Turn west for airport. Turn east for Mendenhall Center shopping mall and post office (just east of junction), and Mendenhall Glacier and visitor center (3.6 miles from junction).

Mendenhall Loop Road is a paved 6.8-mile loop that rejoins Glacier Highway at **Milepost 12.2.** To reach Mendenhall Glacier from here, drive east 2.2 miles and take spur road another 1.4 miles to the glacier and visitor center. The visitor center is open daily in summer from 8 A.M. to 6 P.M.; Wed.-Sun. in winter, 9 A.M. to 4 P.M.

Continue on Mendenhall Loop Road past glacier spur road turnoff for Montana Creek Road (3.7 miles from junction) and access to Mendenhall Lake USFS campground, at Mile 0.4 Montana Creek Road. The campground has 60 sites, tables, firepits, water, pit toilets and dump station. Sites range from basic ($10) to full service with water, sewer and electric ($20). Shower buildings and a pay phone. *Construction may close all or part of the campground through June of 2000.* 8 sites reservable through National Recreation Reservation Service (NRRS), phone toll free (877) 444-6777; outside the US phone (518)

885-3639. Call (907) 586-8751 for information. ▲

9.7 Airport area access for southbound travelers via Old Glacier Highway.

9.9 Mendenhall River and Brotherhood Bridge. The bridge was named in honor of the Alaska Native Brotherhood and is lined by bronze plaques symbolizing the Raven and Eagle clans.

10 Mendenhall Glacier viewpoint to east; parking area with sign about Brotherhood Bridge and paved walking trail. Trail extends to River Road in Mendenhall Valley. Popular for biking, rollerblading and fishing; access at Montana Creek.

10.5 State troopers office.

10.8 The 2.1-mile is Engineer's Cutoff and continues to Fritz Cove Road. Mendenhall Peninsula road branches off (south) of Engineer's Cutoff and has 2 trailhead markers to access the Mendenhall wetlands (easiest access is at dead-end of Mendenhall Peninsula Road). Both Engineer's Cutoff and Mendenhall Peninsula Road are now paved. Engineer's Cutoff at the Fritz Cove junction is very steep and is closed in the winter.

11.4 Auke Lake scenic wayside to east. Good view of Mendenhall Glacier reflected in the lake. This is one of the most photographed spots in Alaska. Red, pink and coho salmon spawn in Auke Lake system July to September (only limited fishing, for coho in September). Chum salmon are primarily from Auke Creek hatchery program.

11.5 Fritz Cove Road (paved) leads 2.6 miles west and dead ends at Smuggler's Cove; excellent small-boat anchorage. Scenic viewpoint on Fritz Cove Road at Mile 1.2; Engineer's Cutoff at Mile 1.9 branches off at .3 mi. to Mendenhall Peninsula Road and extends to Glacier Highway.

11.6 Turnoff to east for Chapel-by-the-Lake and to southeastern branch of University of Alaska.

11.8 Short road west to National Marine Fisheries Service biological laboratory (self-guided walking tours between 8 A.M. and 4:30 P.M. Monday through Friday).

12.2 North junction with Mendenhall Loop Road to west. Glacier Highway becomes Juneau Veterans' Memorial Highway and curves around Auke Bay to west. A small-boat harbor with snack shop, skiff and tackle rentals, and boat launch located at the head of the bay. Private ferry service (AUK NU) to Glacier Bay departs from here.

The 6.8-mile Mendenhall Loop Road rejoins Glacier Highway at **Milepost 9.4.** Motorists may turn east here and follow loop road 3.1 miles to Montana Creek Road and access to Mendenhall Lake USFS campground, or drive 4.6 miles and turn off on Mendenhall Glacier spur road, which leads another 1.4 miles to the glacier and visitor center. Parking area at Mendenhall Glacier; short, steep path to visitor center. The center is open daily in summer from 8:30 A.M. to 5:30 P.M. ▲

12.3 Private RV park.

12.4 AUKE BAY post office to west. Name derives from Auk Indians.

12.6 Spaulding trailhead to east; 3.5 miles long. Access to John Muir USFS cabin.

12.8 Waydelich Creek and bridge.

13.8 Auke Bay ferry terminal vehicle exit.

13.9 Auke Bay ferry terminal entrance. Visitor information counter staffed in summer; open only for ferry arrivals and departures.

15.1 Auke Village Recreation Area begins northbound; 5 beachside picnic shelters accessible to west of highway (park on highway shoulder). New spur road under construction here (1999).

15.3 Auke Village totem pole to east.

15.4 Auke Village USFS campground; 14 picnic units, 12 campsites, tables, fireplaces, water, flush and pit toilets. $8 fee. Open May 1 to Sept. 30. ▲

16.5 Lena Point Road, south entrance to loop road.

17 Lena Point Road, north entrance to loop road.

17.4 Lena Beach picnic area.

18.4 Tee Harbor–Point Stevens Paved road leads 0.3 mile west to public parking area and a private marina.

19.2 Inspiration Point turnout to west with view of the Chilkat Range, and over Tee Harbor and Shelter Island across Favorite Channel. Once a bread-and-butter commercial fishing area, hence the name "The Breadline" for this stretch of shoreline, it is now a popular sportfishing area.

23.1 Short road west to Roman Catholic **Shrine of St. Therese**, located on a small island reached by a causeway.

23.3 Turnout to west and view of island on which Shrine of St. Therese is situated.

23.9 Peterson Lake trailhead to east; 4 miles long. Access to Peterson Lake USFS cabin. This trail connects with the Spaulding trail (see **Milepost 12.6**).

24.2 Peterson Creek bridge. View spawning salmon here in late summer and early fall. Trout fishing. Black and brown bears in area.

24.8 Gravel road leads 0.6 mile west to Amalga Harbor; dock, boat launch, bait-casting area. Fireplace and chimney near end of road are remains of an old trapper's cabin.

27.1 Windfall Lake trailhead to east; 3 miles long.

27.2 Herbert River bridge.

27.4 Herbert Glacier trailhead to east; 4.5 miles long.

27.7 Eagle River bridge. **Amalga trailhead** just across bridge to east; 5.5 miles long.

28 Eagle Beach State Recreation Area; parking, RV campground (facilities unknown), trails, picnicking.

28.4 Eagle Beach picnic area with beachside picnic shelter and 8 picnic sites. View of Chilkat Range across Lynn Canal. Duck hunting on flats in low tide during open season. Good bird watching.

28.7 Scenic viewpoint to west.

29.3 Scenic viewpoint to west.

32.7 Turnout to west with view of Benjamin Island to southwest; just beyond it is Sentinel Island lighthouse. Visible to the northwest is North Island and northwest of it is **Vanderbilt Reef**, site of a great sea disaster. The SS *Princess Sophia,* carrying 288 passengers and 61 crew, ran aground on Vanderbilt Reef early in the morning of Oct. 24, 1918. All aboard perished when a combination of stormy seas and a high tide forced the *Princess Sophia* off the reef and she sank early in the evening of Oct. 25. Walter Harper, in 1913 the first person to stand on the summit of Mount McKinley, was among the *Princess Sophia*'s casualties. Vanderbilt Reef is now marked by a navigation light.

32.8 Pavement ends northbound; 2-lane gravel extension of the Glacier Highway begins.

33 Scenic viewpoint to west. Yankee Cove and beach below this point.

35.4 Sunshine Cove public beach access.

37.6 North Bridget Cove beach access. The 2,850-acre park offers meadows, forests, rocky beaches, salmon streams and a trail system. Area is popular for cross-country skiing. Fires allowed on beach if fire ring is made.

39 Point Bridget State Park trailhead; 3.5-mile hike to Point Bridget (7 hours round-trip); panoramic view of Lynn Canal and Chilkat Mountains from point.

39.4 Cowee Creek bridge. Large parking area to west. Good fishing.

40.4 City-owned/operated boat launch ramp. Permit required.

40.5 Road dead ends near Echo Cove on Berners Bay. Berners Bay is a popular destination for Juneau paddlers. It is 3 miles across and 34 miles northwest of Juneau.

Douglas Highway

Douglas Highway is a 3-mile paved road beginning on the Juneau side of the Douglas Bridge, crossing to Douglas Island, turning southeast, passing through the city of Douglas to road end and beginning of Treadwell Mine area.

0 Intersection of Egan Drive and Douglas Bridge.

0.5 Right, Cordova Street leads to Dan Moller trail.

1.5 Lawson Creek bridge.

2 Tlingit Indian cemetery and grave houses.

2.5 Turn left to boat harbor; dump station and **Savikko Park** with 4 overnight RV parking spaces without hookups. $5 per night, 3-day limit; obtain permit from Harbormaster's office at 1600 Harbor Way. Short gravel road leads to Juneau Island U.S. Bureau of Mines headquarters. Sandy Beach Recreation Area with water, toilets, play area, tennis courts, track, 2 ball fields, picnic tables, shelters and children's playground. Aptly named, this is one of the few sandy beaches in southeastern Alaska. Highway becomes St. Ann's Avenue.

3 Road end.

North Douglas Highway

North Douglas Highway begins after crossing Douglas Bridge from Juneau and immediately turning right, northwest. **Milepost 1** appears at small bridge on this turn.

0 Douglas Bridge.

0.3 Junction of Douglas Highway and North Douglas Highway.

4.4 Heliport to right.

6.9 Eaglecrest Ski Area turnoff on left; drive 5.3 miles on paved road to ski area. Good blueberry picking in August.

8.3 Fish Creek bridge. Large parking area on right of bridge. This is a popular roadside fishing spot.

8.6 Ninemile trail on right; small parking area.

9.5 Scenic turnout and parking area with excellent view of Mendenhall Glacier; litter barrel. Boat ramp; launch permit required (contact harbormaster before arrival).

10.3 Small waterfall on left.

11.4 False Outer Point public beach access. Scenic view of Favorite Channel and Lynn Canal; parking area on right. Near the northern tip of Douglas Island, this is an excellent spot to observe marine activity and eagles.

12.3 Outer Point trailhead on right.

13.1 Road end.

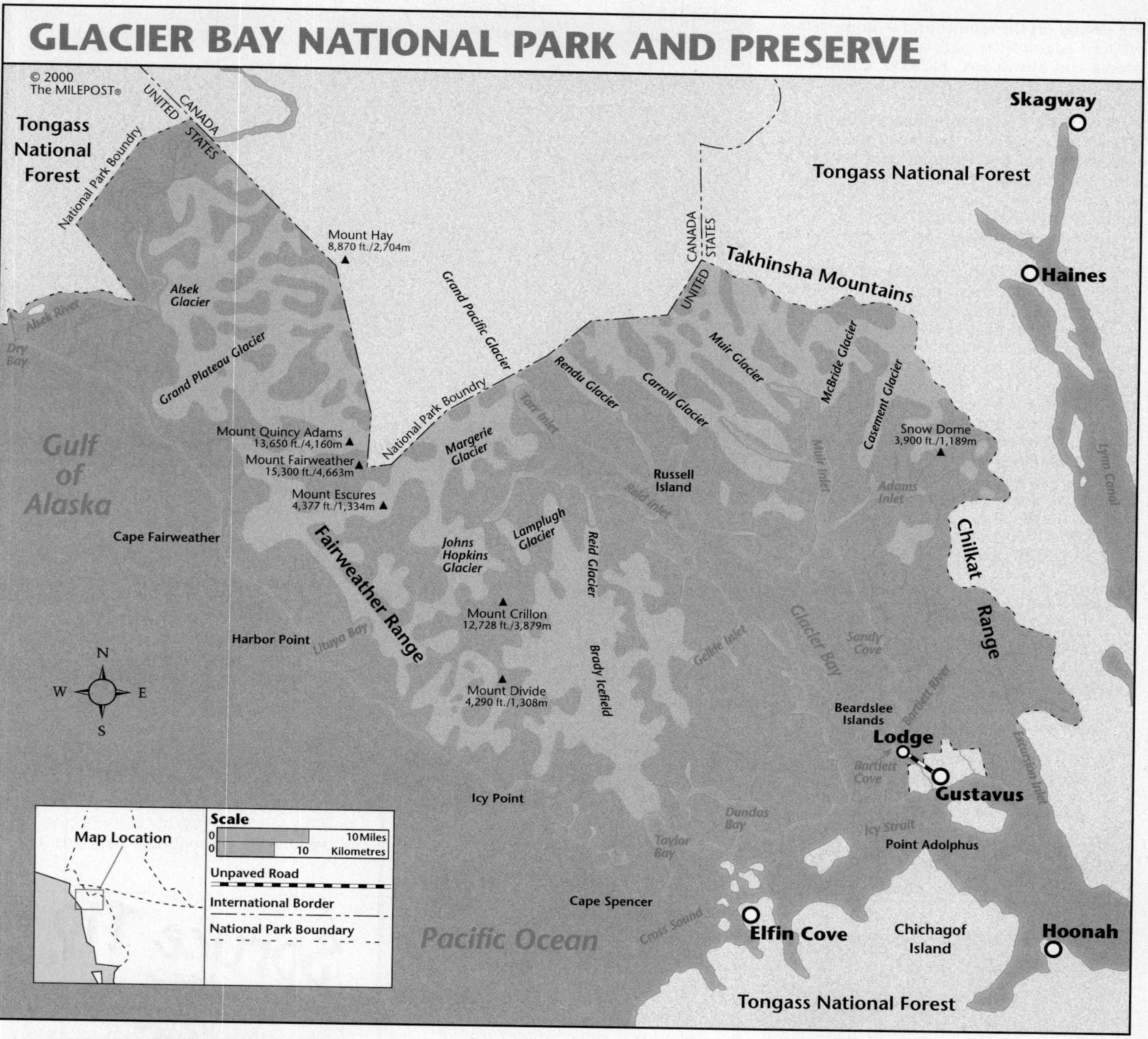

GLACIER BAY NATIONAL PARK AND PRESERVE

Glacier Bay National Park and Preserve

What Tlingit Indians called "Big Ice-Mountain Bay" in naturalist John Muir's day (1879) is today one of southeastern Alaska's most dramatic attractions, Glacier Bay National Park and Preserve. Muir described Glacier Bay as "a picture of icy wildness unspeakably pure and sublime."

There are no roads to Glacier Bay National Park, except for a 10-mile stretch of road connecting Bartlett Cove with Gustavus airport. Bartlett Cove is the site of a ranger station and Glacier Bay Lodge. Park naturalists conduct daily hikes and other activities from the visitor center at the lodge, and the excursion boat departs from there. Airlines service Gustavus airport. See Accommodations/Visitor Services and Transportation under Gustavus this section.

Visitors should contact the Superintendent, Glacier Bay National Park and Preserve, Gustavus, AK 99826-0140, for more information, or check with Glacier Bay tour operators. The national park's headquarters is at Bartlett Cove; phone (907) 697-2230.

Glacier Bay National Park, at the northwest end of Alexander Archipelago, includes not only tidewater glaciers but also Mount Fairweather in the Fairweather Range of the St. Elias Mountains, the highest peak in southeastern Alaska, and also the U.S. portion of the Alsek River.

With passage of the Alaska National Interest Lands Conservation Act in December 1980, Glacier Bay National Monument, established in 1925 by Pres. Calvin Coolidge, became a national park. Approximately 585,000 acres were added to the park/preserve to protect fish and wildlife habitat and migration routes in Dry Bay and along the lower Alsek River, and to include the northwest slope of Mount Fairweather. Total acreage is 3,328,000 (3,271,000 in park, 57,000 in preserve) with 2,770,000 acres designated wilderness.

When the English naval explorer Capt. George Vancouver sailed through the ice-choked waters of Icy Strait in 1794, Glacier Bay was little more than a dent in the coastline. Across the head of this seemingly minor inlet stood a towering wall of ice marking the seaward terminus of an immense glacier that completely filled the broad, deep basin of what is now Glacier Bay. To the north, ice extended more than 100 miles into the St. Elias Mountains, covering the intervening valleys with a 4,000-foot-deep mantle of ice.

During the century following Vancouver's explorations, the glacier retreated some 40 miles back into the bay, permitting a spruce–hemlock forest to gradually fill the land. By 1916, the Grand Pacific Glacier, which once occupied the entire bay, had receded some 65 miles from the position observed by Vancouver in 1794. Nowhere else in the world have glaciers been observed to recede at such a rapid pace.

Today, few of the many tributary glaciers that once supplied the huge ice sheet extend to the sea. Glacier Bay National Park encloses 12 active tidewater glaciers, including several on the remote and seldom-visited western edge of the park along the Gulf of Alaska and Lituya Bay. Icebergs, cracked off from near-vertical ice cliffs, dot the waters of Glacier Bay.

A decline in the number of humpback whales using Glacier Bay for feeding and calf-rearing led the National Park Service to limit the number of boats visiting Glacier Bay from June to August. These regulations affect all motorized vessels. Check with the National Park Service for current regulations.

Glacier Bay National Park is approximately 100 miles from Juneau by boat. Park rangers at Bartlett Cove are available to assist in advising visitors who wish to tour Glacier Bay in private boats or by kayak. Guided kayak trips are available through park concessionaire, Alaska Discovery. Permits are required for motorized pleasure boats between June 1 and Aug. 31. The permits are free. A limited number are available. Permits must be obtained prior to entry into Glacier Bay and Bartlett Cove. Request permits no more than 2 months in advance by writing the National Park Service, Gustavus, AK 99826-0140. For more information, phone (907) 697-2627 (May 1–Sept. 7).

Kaykers explore Muir Inlet in Glacier Bay National Park. (© George Wuerthner)

Glacier Bay Lodge is the only accommodation within the national park, although nearby Gustavus (see description this section) has a number of lodges, inns, bed and breakfasts and rental cabins. Contact Glacier Bay Lodge Inc., (800) 451-5952, for more information on the concessionaire-operated Glacier Bay Lodge and excursion boat cruises offered from the lodge.

Gasoline and diesel fuel may be purchased at Bartlett Cove, where a good anchorage is available. There are no other public facilities for boats within park boundaries; Sandy Cove, about 20 miles/32 km from Bartlett Cove, is a popular anchorage. Gustavus has a dock and small-boat harbor.

CAUTION BOATERS: No attempt should be made to navigate Glacier Bay without appropriate charts, tide tables and local knowledge. Floating ice is a special hazard. Because of the danger from waves caused by falling ice, small craft should not approach closer than 0.5 mile/0.8 km from tidewater glacier fronts.

Wildlife in the national park area is protected and hunting is not allowed. Firearms are illegal. *CAUTION: Brown and black bears are present.*

Fishing for silver and pink salmon, Dolly Varden and halibut is excellent. A valid Alaska fishing license is required. Charter fishing trips are available.

There is an established campground at Bartlett Cove with 25 sites. Wilderness camping is also available throughout the park.

Gustavus

(See maps, pages 639, 675)

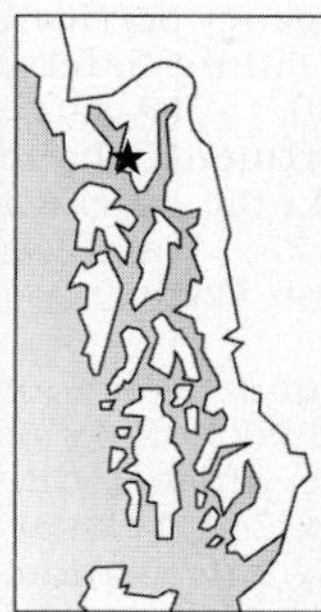

Gateway to Glacier Bay National Park and Preserve, the small community of Gustavus is located just outside the park boundary at the mouth of the Salmon River on the north shore of Icy Passage, 48 miles northwest of Juneau. It is 10 miles/16 km by road from Gustavus to Bartlett Cove within the park. **Population:** 380. **Emergency Services:** Phone 911. **Visitor Information:** Gustavus Visitors Assoc., Box 167, Gustavus 99826.

Private Aircraft: Gustavus airport, adjacent northeast; elev. 36 feet; length 6,700 feet; asphalt. Landing within the park is restricted to salt water. All wilderness/nonmotorized waters are closed to aircraft landing between May 1–Sept. 15.

Surrounded on 3 sides by the snow-covered peaks of the Chilkat Range and the Fairweather Mountains, Gustavus offers miles of level land with expansive sandy beaches, open land and forest. Homesteaded in 1914 as a small agricultural community, the area was once named Strawberry Point because of its abundant wild strawberries. Today, most residents maintain gardens and make their living by fishing (commercial and subsistence), fish processing, tourism, arts and crafts, and working for the National Park Service and in various local trades.

Besides its proximity to the national park, Gustavus offers a number of attractions. Local charter boats—sometimes called "6 packs" because they carry about 6 passengers—are available for sportfishing (salmon, halibut), sightseeing Icy Strait and Glacier Bay, and whale watching. Whale sightings are almost guaranteed at Point Adolphous, where their food source is rich. A paved road in town is great for bike riding.

There are extensive beaches in Gustavus which are great for beachwalking. Flat land walking is possible in the fern wetland environment, which also offers good bird watching. Be sure to bring rubber boots.

Lodging & Services

Accommodations in Gustavus include several inns, lodges, bed and breakfasts, and self-sufficient cabins. There is 1 restaurant. The lodges and inns serve meals for guests; drop-in customers check for space-available meal reservations.

Businesses in Gustavus include a grocery store, art gallery, cafe, gift shop, golf course, hardware/ building supply store, gas station, and fish-processing facilities. Fishing supplies and licenses may be purchased locally.

Mt. Fairweather Golf Course is a 9-hole, par 36, 3,000-yard facility in an amphitheater of mountains and inland waterways. Club and handcart rentals available. Box 51, Gustavus, AK 99826. (907) 697-3080 or (907) 697-2214. , Box 51, Gustavus, AK 99826.

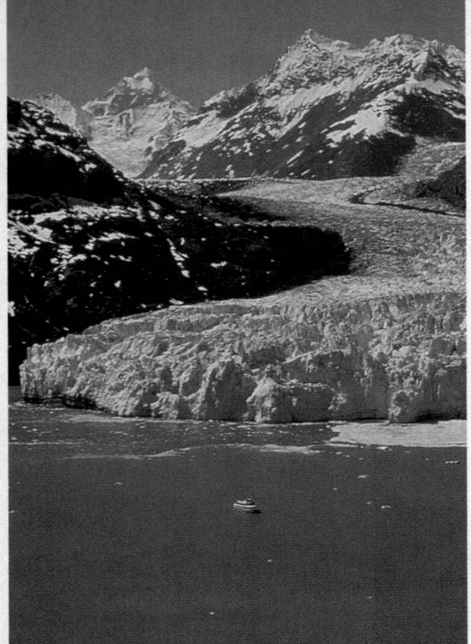

Glacier Bay encloses 12 active tidewater glaciers.

(© Glacier Bay Tours & Cruises)

watching; renowned deep sea fishing for halibut and/or salmon. Many excellent angling and fly fishing opportunities in remote areas. P.O. Box 5, Gustavus, AK 99826. Phone (800) 628-0912. E-mail: gbci@thor.he.net. [ADVERTISEMENT]

Gustavus Inn. Country living, family-style gourmet local seafood meals, cozy bar, kitchen garden, bikes, trout fishing poles, courtesy van, afternoon park naturalist trip. Family-run since 1965. Custom fishing and Glacier Bay sightseeing packages arranged. For map, brochures, please write: Gustavus Inn, Box 60-MP, Gustavus, AK 99826 or call (800) 649-5220. [ADVERTISEMENT]

The Puffin. See nearby Glacier Bay and Icy Strait. Stay in your own modern, comfortable, attractively decorated cabin with electricity on quiet wooded homestead. Picturesque central lodge. Complete breakfast. Bicycles, children, pets welcome. Reservations for all charters, Glacier Bay tours. Qualified captains guide fishing, sightseeing charters. Friendly, personal attention. (907) 697-2260; fax (907) 697-2258; e-mail: puffin@compuserve.com. Homepage: http://www.puffintravel.com. [ADVERTISEMENT]

Spruce Tip Lodge. Stay in our handcrafted log lodge and experience this part of Southeast Alaska in comfort and style. Included in our rates are three home-cooked meals daily, rooms with bath and local ground transportation. We can arrange all activities in Gustavus/Glacier Bay. Phone (907) 697-2215, fax (907) 697-2236 or write Box 299-MP, Gustavus, AK 99826. [ADVERTISEMENT]

TRI Bed and Breakfast of Glacier Bay. Experience restful rainforest wilderness in a modern cottage with insuite bath. Centrally located from Glacier Bay National Park and restaurants/store. Full breakfast available. Agents for Glacier Bay day boat tour and ferry/whale watch. Airflights, kayaking arranged. P.O. Box 214, Gustavus, AK 99826. (907) 697-2425, Fax (907) 697-2450. E-mail: trigbay@pluto.he.net. Web site: www.glacierbaylodging.com. [ADVERTISEMENT]

Whalesong Lodge. Full-service lodge close to the beach and amenities. B&B accommodation with optional American plan. Also, condominium rental with full meal packages available. Unforgettable day or overnight tours of Glacier Bay, whale watching, sport fishing, kayaking, hiking. Airport transfers. Complimentary bicycles. Box 5-MP, Gustavus, AK 99826. Phone (800) 628-0912, fax (907) 697-2289. [ADVERTISEMENT]

Transportation

Ferry: *NOTE: There is no state ferry service to Glacier Bay.* Closest port of call for state ferries is Hoonah. (Kayakers getting off at Hoonah can expect a 2-day paddle across Icy Strait.)

Air: Glacier Bay may be reached by Alaska Airlines daily jet flights from Juneau; summer service begins early June. Air taxi and charter service available from Juneau, Sitka, Haines and Skagway to Gustavus airport; there are many scheduled air taxi flights daily. Bus service between the airport and Bartlett Cove is available for arriving jet flights. Taxi service to local facilities and courtesy van service for some lodges are also available.

Many Gustavus bed and breakfasts will make transportation arrangements for guests from Juneau, Haines and Skagway.

Rental Cars: There is one car rental company in Gustavus.

Boat Service: Excursion boats operated by the park concession depart daily from Bartlett Cove. You may also charter a boat in Gustavus for sightseeing or fishing. Overnight cruise tours are available from Juneau.

Cruise Ships: Several cruise ships include Glacier Bay cruising in their itineraries.

Yakutat

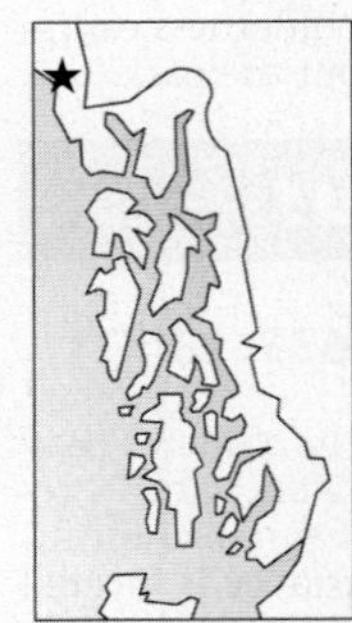

Located on the Gulf of Alaska coast where Southeastern Alaska joins the major body of Alaska to the west; 225 miles northwest of Juneau, 220 miles southeast of Cordova and 380 miles southeast of Anchorage. **Population:** 801. **Emergency Services: Dept. of Public Safety,** phone (907) 784-3206. **Fire Department**, phone 911. **Yakutat Health Center**, phone (907) 784-3275. **Maritime Search and Rescue**, contact the Coast Guard at (800) 478-5555.

Visitor Information: Inquire at one of the lodges, at the USFS and NPS office, or the chamber of commerce office (write Chamber of Commerce, Box 234, Yakutat, AK 99689). For sportfishing information, stop by the ADF&G office, 1/4 mile west of the airport, or write Sport Fish Division, Box 49, Yakutat 99689, phone (907) 784-3222. For information about the National Park Service, contact the visitor center at Box 137, Yakutat, AK 99689; phone (907) 748-3295. Interpretive programs are offered daily at 2 P.M. from June through August. City and Borough of Yakutat offices, (907) 784-3323.; fax (907) 784-3281.

Elevation: Sea level. **Climate:** Similar to the rest of coastal southeastern Alaska; mild in summer, winters are moderate. Average annual snowfall is 201 inches. Total annual precipitation is about 151 inches. Normal daily maximum in August, 60°F/16°C; minimum in January, 17°F/-8°C. Prevailing winds are southeasterly.

Private Aircraft: Yakutat airport, 5 miles southeast; elev. 33 feet; length 7,700 feet; asphalt; fuel 100, A1.

Transportation: Air—Daily jet service from Seattle, Juneau, Anchorage and Cordova. Charter air service available. **Ferry**—The MV *Kennicott* makes a whistle stop at Yakutat. See the ALASKA STATE FERRY SCHEDULES section.

Yakutat has 4 lodges, 1 inn, 7 bed and breakfasts, a restaurant, cafe, 2 gift shops, bank, 2 grocery stores, 1 pizza parlor, 1 hardware store, ATM, post office, clinic and 2 gas stations. Boat rentals, car rentals and cab service are available.

Yakutat Bay is one of the few refuges for vessels along this long stretch of coast in the Gulf of Alaska. The site was originally the principal winter village of the local Tlingit Indian tribe. Sea otter pelts brought Russians to the area in the 19th century. Fur traders were followed by gold seekers, who came to work the black sand beaches. Commercial salmon fishing developed in this century, and the first cannery was built here in 1904. Today's economy is based primarily on fishing and fish processing. Salmon, halibut, crab and black cod make up the fishery. Government and local businesses employ most residents. Subsistence activities are primarily fishing (salmon and shellfish), hunting (moose, bear, goats, ducks and small game), and gathering seaweed and berries. The soil is not suitable for agriculture, and a vegetable garden requires a great deal of preparation to produce small quantities.

Yakutat is considered a world-class sportfishing destination. Steelhead fishing is among the finest anywhere. King and silver (coho) salmon run in abundance in Yakutat area, rivers and streams June through September. The area also boasts red and pink salmon and smelt in season. USFS cabins available on some rivers; check with the Forest Service (907/784-3359).

While hunting and fishing in particular draw visitors to Yakutat, the surge of Hubbard Glacier in June 1986, which sealed off the mouth of Russell Fiord, drew national attention. Malaspina Glacier, largest on the North American continent, is northwest of town. Nearer to town, Cannon Beach has good beachcombing and a picnic area.

AREA FISHING: Lost River and **Tawah Creek**, 10 miles south of Yakutat on Lost River Road, silver (coho) salmon to 20 lbs., mid-August through September. **Situk River**, 12 miles south of Yakutat on the Lost River Road (also accessible by Forest Highway 10), is one of Alaska's top fishing spots spring and fall for steelhead and silver salmon and has one of the best sockeye (red) salmon runs in the state, late June through August; steelhead averaging 10 lbs., April 1–May 30 for spring run, October and November for fall run; king salmon to 45 lbs., mid-June through July; silver salmon to 23 lbs., mid-August through September; pink salmon run in August, yields Dolly Varden also. **Yakutat Bay**, king salmon 30–50 lbs., May through June; silver salmon to 20 lbs., August through September.

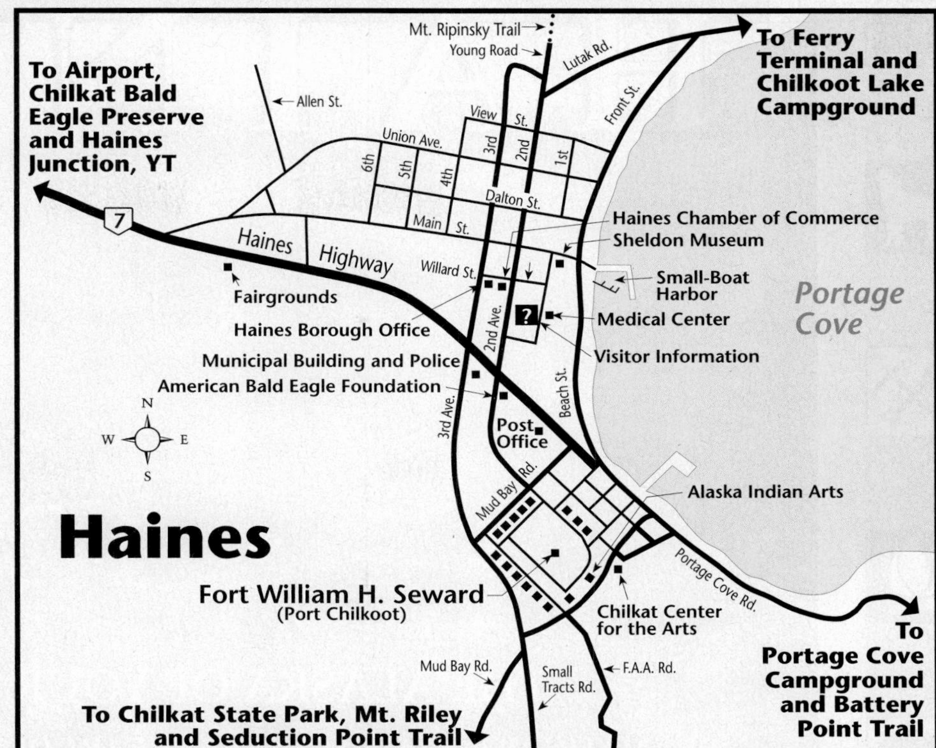

Haines

(See map, page 639)

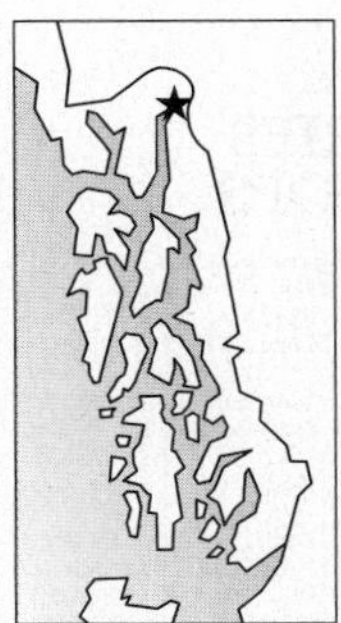

Located on Portage Cove, Chilkoot Inlet, on the upper arm of Lynn Canal, 80 air miles northwest of Juneau; 151 road miles southeast of Haines Junction, YT. Southern terminus of the Haines Highway. *NOTE: Haines is only 13 miles by water from Skagway, but it is 359 miles by road!* **Population:** 2,300. **Emergency Services: Alaska State Troopers**, phone (907) 766-2552. **City Police**, phone (907) 766-2121. **Fire Department** and **Ambulance**, emergency only phone 911; business phone: (907) 766-2115.. **Doctor**, phone (907) 766-2521. **Maritime Search and Rescue**, contact the Coast Guard at 1-800-478-5555.

Visitor Information: At 2nd and Willard streets. There are free brochures for all of Alaska and the Yukon. Open daily, 8 A.M. to 8 P.M., June through August; 8 A.M. to 5 P.M. weekdays, September through May. Phone (907) 766-2234; toll free 1-800-458-3579; Internet: www.haines.ak.us; e-mail: hainesak@wwa.com. Write the Haines Convention and Visitors Bureau at Box 530, Haines, AK 99827. Phone the Alaska Dept. of Transportation at (907) 766-2340.

Elevation: Sea level. **Climate:** Average daily maximum temperature in July, 66°F/19°C; average daily minimum in January, 17°F/-8°C. Extreme high summer temperature, 90°F/32°C; extreme winter low, -16°F/-27°C; average annual precipitation, 59 inches. **Radio:** KHNS-FM 102.3. **Television:** 24 cable channels. **Newspaper:** *Chilkat*

HAINES
THE ALASKA OF YOUR DREAMS
DRAMATIC MOUNTAIN SCENERY • HEART OF THE TLINGIT CULTURE
HISTORIC FORT WILLIAM H. SEWARD • VALLEY OF THE EAGLES

Sponsored by: Haines Chamber of Commerce 907-766-2202
email: chamber@haineschamber.org • website: haineschamber.org

ATTRACTIONS & TOURS

1. **ALASKA BALD EAGLE FESTIVAL** November 9-12, 2000. Celebrate the world's largest gathering of bald eagles. Speakers, art exhibit, family events, eagle release and more. 907-766-2202, FAX 907-766-2271, P.O. Box 1449, Haines, AK 99827-1449
E-mail:chamber@haineschamber.org
http://www.haineschamber.org

2. **ALASKA4YOU** by the TRAVEL CONNECTION Glacier Bay Headquarters, customized tours of Alaska including Denali, the Arctic, Pribilofs, and more. Ferry reservations. Local Haines sightseeing. 907-766-2681, FAX 907-766-2585, 115 2nd Ave. S., P.O. Box 645, Haines, AK 99827-0645
E-mail:randa@alaska4you.com
http://www.alaska4you.com

3. **ALASKA INDIAN ARTS INC./CHILKAT DANCERS** Traditional Northwest Coast totem carvers, silversmiths & print makers. Home of the Chilkat Dancers performing several times weekly during the summer. Phone/FAX907-766-2160, Historic Building #13 Fort Seward Dr., P.O. Box 271, Haines, AK 99827-0271
E-mail:aiaio@seaknet.alaska.edu

4. **ALASKA NATURE TOURS** Wildlife viewing in and around the Chilkat Bald Eagle Preserve by experienced local naturalists. Photography. Bus and walking tours & hiking adventures. 907-766-2876, FAX 907-766-2844, 123 2nd Ave. S., P.O. Box 491, Haines, AK 99827-0491
E-mail:aknature@kcd.com
http://kcd.com/aknature

5. **AMERICAN BALD EAGLE FOUNDATION** Exquisite natural history museum. See over 160 wildlife specimens-eagles, bears, wolverine, mountaingoats, wolves, moose, owls, foxes, otter, waterfowl. 907-766-3094, FAX 907-766-3095, 2nd Avenue & Haines Hwy, P.O. Box 49, Haines, AK 99827-0049.
E-mail:eagleone@wytbear.com
http://www.gauntletllc.com/abef

6. **CHILKAT CRUISES & TOURS** High speed Haines-Skagway Shuttle Ferry. Only 40 minutes between ports, up to 14 crossings per day! Glacier Bay and local tours sold at our Haines Terminal. 888-766-2103 or 907-766-2100, FAX 907-766-2101, 142 Beach Road, P.O. Box 509, Haines, AK 99827-0509
E-mail: chilkat@klukwan.com
http://www.chilkatcruises.com

7. **CHILKAT GUIDES, LTD** Daily scenic raft trips through the Chilkat Bald Eagle Preserve. Multi-day adventures on the Tatshenshini and Alsek Rivers. 907-766-2491, FAX 907-766-2409, 39 Beach Road, P.O. Box 170, Haines, AK 99827-0170
E-mail:raftalaska@aol.com
http://www.raftalaska.com

8. **DEVIL'S CLUB DRIVING RANGE** Balls, clubs, and fees available through 33 Mile Roadhouse across the road from the range. 907-766-2458, 33 Mile Haines Hwy., P.O. Box 858, Haines, AK 99827-0858

9. **GLACIER BAY TRAVEL** Local expertise for your vacation. Specializing in tours, cruises, lodging, sea-kayaking, whale watching, charter fishing, flightseeing packages. Family-owned. Phone/FAX 907-697-2475, 4 Dungeness Way, P.O. Box 103, Gustavus, AK 99826-0103
E-mail: resinfo@glacierbaytravel.com
http://www.glacierbaytravel.com

10. **HAINES AIRWAYS INC.** Travel in style. Haines Airways offers glacier tours and scheduled service in the newest fleet in Southeast Alaska. 800-359-2467 or 907-766-2646, FAX 907-766-2780, 108 Main St., P.O. Box 470, Haines, AK 99827-0470
E-mail: hainesair1@wytbear.com
http://www.hainesairways.com

11. **HAINES-SKAGWAY WATER TAXI** The Sea Venture through Lynn Canal! See eagles, seals, and waterfalls aboard the Sea Venture II. $35 round-trip, $22 one-way. 888-766-3395 or 907-766-3395, FAX 907-766-2393, Small Boat Harbor, P.O. Box 246, Haines, AK 99827-0246
E-mail: h2otaxi@kcd.com
http://kcd.com/watertaxi

12. **KEET GOOSHI TOURS** Exclusive tour thru Bald Eagle Preserve to Native Village of Klukwan. Learn history and culture. View Tribal Houses, totems, screens. 907-766-2168, FAX 907-766-2513, 32 Helms Loop, P.O. Box 997, Haines, AK 99827-0997

13. **L.A.B. FLYING SERVICE INC.** Offering year-round daily scheduled flights, Flightseeing tours and charters. Cities served: Haines, Juneau, Skagway, Gustavus, Hoonah, Kake and Petersburg. Earn Alaska Airlines Miles! 800-426-0543 or 907-766-2222, FAX 907-766-2734, 4th & Main St., P.O. Box 272, Haines, AK 99827
E-mail:labflying@aol.com
http://www.haines.ak.us/lab

14. **RIVER ADVENTURES** Breathtaking scenery and wildlife encounters abound as you explore the world famous Chilkat Bald Eagle Preserve by safe comfortable jetboat! 800-478-9827 (US and Canada), 907-766-2050, FAX 907-766-2051, 1-1/2 Mile Haines Hwy., P.O. Box 556, Haines, AK 99827-0556
E-mail: k.hess@eudoramail.wytbear.com
http://www.AlaskaRiverTours.wytbear.com

15. **SHELDON MUSEUM & CULTURAL CENTER** Features Native Tlingit Art & Culture, Pioneer History (Fort William Seward, Haines Mission, lighthouse lens, etc.). Store: Alaska books & gifts. 907-766-2366, FAX 766-2368, 11 Main St., P.O. Box 269, Haines, AK 99827-0269.
E-mail:curator@sheldonmuseum.org
http://www.sheldonmuseum.org

16. **SOCKEYE CYCLE CO.** Daily 1-3 hour guided and multi day fully supported Mountain Bike Tours. Two full service bike shops in Haines & Skagway. Rentals. Phone/FAX 907-766-2869, 24 Portage St., P.O. Box 829, Haines, AK 99827-0829
E-mail:cycleak@ibm.net
http://www.haines.ak.us/sockeye/

17. **SOUTHEAST ALASKA STATE FAIR, INC.** August 9-13, 2000. Great Music, Parade, Horse Show, Logging Show, Exhibits, Kids Events, Food/Trade booths. For Information call 907-766-2476, FAX 907-766-2478, 296 Fair Drive, P.O. Box 385, Haines, AK 99827-0385
Email:seasfair@seaknet.alaska.edu
http://seaknet.alaska.edu/~seasfair

18. **TSIRKU CANNING COMPANY** Tour a working replica of an old salmon cannery while you learn the fascinating history of salmon canning in Alaska. 800-572-8006, 5th and Main, P.O. Box 645, Haines, AK 99827-0645

19. **WEEPING TROUT SPORTS RESORT** Day tours & overnight accommodations for people seeking paradise. Trout & salmon fishing, Par 29 golf, fine food, spectacular scenery. 907-766-2827, FAX 907-766-2824, Chilkat Lake, P.O. Box 129, Haines, AK 99827-0129
E-Mail: weepingt@kcd.com
http://kcd.com/weepingt

GALLERIES GIFT SHOPS

20. **ALASKAN LIQUOR STORE** Micro Brew and Fine Wine Headquarters of Haines. Located on Main Street Across From Howsers IGA- Local Information 907-766-3131, FAX 907-766-3132, 208 Main Street, P.O. Box 1309, Haines, AK 99827-1309

21. **ALASKAN SPIRIT SHOP** Alcoholic and non-alcoholic beverages, tobacco and snacks. Great location, friendly service. Free ice with purchase! 907-766-3006 FAX 907-766-2182, 842 Main Street, PO Box 1689, Haines, AK 99827-1689

22. **BELL'S STORE** Alaskan Seafood at it's Best. Alaskan Gifts - Fresh Flowers. Clothing. OPEN ALL YEAR. A unique shopping experience. 907-766-2950, FAX 766-2958 18 Second Ave. N., P.O. Box 1189, Haines, AK 99827-1189

23. **CAROLINE'S CLOSET** Not just another gift store! Women's Clothing, Shoes, CD's & Tapes, Joe Boxer, T-Shirts & Lots of other groovy stuff! 907-766-3223, FAX 907-766-2787, 209 Main Street, P.O. Box 1309, Haines, AK 99827-1309

24. **OUTFITTER LIQUOR STORE** Best Deals In Town - Free Ice with Purchase. Widest Variety & Best Selection. Located next to Post Office. 907-766-3220, FAX 907-766-2787, Mile 0 Haines Hwy. P.O. Box 1709, Haines, AK 99827-1709

25. **OUTFITTER SPORTING GOODS** Fishing, Hunting, Camping & Hiking Products. Fishing & Hunting Licenses, Bait. We carry Nike, Woolrich, Helly Hansen, Xtratuf Rubber Boots, & Rocky Brand Boots. 907-766-3221, FAX 907-766-2787, Mile 0 Haines Hwy., P.O. Box 1709, Haines, AK 99827-1709

LODGING

26. **ALASKAN EAGLE RV PARK** Full service RV sites with cable TV. Good Sam. Restaurant on site featuring a salmon bake. 907-766-2335. 755 Union Street., P.O. Box 43, Haines,

AK 99827-0043
E-mail:akeaglerv@aol.com.
http://haines.ak.us/akeaglerv

27. **BEAR CREEK CABINS** Family Cabins ~ $40+. Clean, modern kitchen and bath facilities. Campsites, laundry, bike rentals. Phone/FAX 907-766-2259, 1 Mile Small Tracts Road, P.O. Box 908, Haines, AK 99827-0908
E-mail:hostel@kcd.com
http://kcd.com/hostel

28. **CAPTAIN'S CHOICE INC. MOTEL** Haines finest and most comfortable lodging. Car rentals. Courtesy transfers. Centrally located at corner 2nd & Dalton. Tour Desk. Bus Terminal. 800-478-2345, 907-766-3111, FAX 907-766-3332, 108 2nd Ave. N., P.O. Box 392, Haines, AK 99827-0392
E-mail:capchoice@usa.net
http://www.capchoice.com

29. **CHILKAT EAGLE BED & BREAKFAST** Lovely historic residence, waterfront & mountain views, walk to local services, full breakfast, kitchen facilities, TV lounge. Open Year Round. 907-766-2763, FAX 907-766-3651, #69 Soap Suds Alley, P.O. Box 387, Haines, AK 99827-0387
E-mail:eaglebb@kcd.com
http://www. kcd.com/eaglebb

30. **EAGLES NEST MOTEL** Beautiful rooms, queen size beds, private baths, car rental. Featuring Chilkoot Lake Tours. Winter rates, packages available. See color ad. 907-766-2891, FAX 907-766-2848,1069 Haines Hwy. P.O. Box 250, Haines, AK 99827-0250
E-mail:Eagles_Nest@kcd.com
http://www.EaglesNest.wytbear.com

31. **FORT SEWARD CONDOS** Completely furnish 1 & 2 bedroom suites, full kitchen, bath & laundry. 2 day minimum---no pets. Reasonable. Phone/FAX 907-766-2425, #3 Fort Seward Drive, P.O. Box 75, Haines, AK 99827-0027
http://www.haines.ak.us/condos

32. **FORT SEWARD LODGE & RESTAURANT** Affordable lodging, oceanview kitchenettes, restaurant, cocktail lounge. Full dinner menu, courtesy transfer, military & senior discounts. See our display ad. 800-478-7772, 907-766-2009, FAX 907-766-2006, Mile 0 Haines Highway, P.O. Box 307, Haines, AK 99827-0307
E-mail:ftsewardlodge@wytbear.com
http://www.ftsewardlodge.com

33. **HAINES HITCH-UP RV PARK** 92 Spacious Sites. 20 Pull Thrus. Cable TV Sites Available. Gift Shop. Showers & Laundromat (Guests Only). Tour Information & Ticket Sales. Phone/FAX 907-766-2882, 851 Main Street, P.O. Box 383, Haines, AK 99827-0383
E-mail: HitchupRV@aol.com

34. **RIVER HOUSE BED & BREAKFAST** Private, luxury cottage on Chilkat River. Mountain, waterfront views. Accomodations for five. Gourmet-equipped kitchen. Third-floor tower bedroom. Open year round. 888-747-RHBB (US), Phone/FAX 907-766-3215, #3 River Road, P.O. Box 1173, Haines, AK 99827-1173
E-mail:info@rhbb.com
http://www.rhbb.com

35. **SUMMER INN BED & BREAKFAST** Charming, historical house. Open year round. Full homemade breakfast, centrally located, mountain & ocean views. Recommended by Alaska Best Places Guidebook. Phone/FAX 907-766-2970, 117 Second Ave., P.O. Box 1198, Haines, AK 99827-1198
E-mail:positive@alaska.net
http://www.summerinn.wytbear.com

RESTAURANTS GROCERIES

36. **ALASKAN & PROUD** Bagged ice and finest selection of groceries, freshest meats, produce, dairy products, sandwiches. Enjoy our Alaskan Hospitality! 907-766-2181, FAX 766-2182, 3rd & Dalton, P.O. Box 1689, Haines, AK 99827

37. **ALASKAN SOURDOUGH CAFE** A unique Alaskan dining experience, featuring a salmon bake. Located at the Alaskan Eagle RV Park Phone/FAX 907-766-2335, 755 Union St., P.O. Box 43, Haines, AK 99827-0043

38. **BAMBOO ROOM RESTAURANT** Downtown. Famous Halibut Fish & Chips. Breakfast, Lunch, Dinner. Espresso. Senior & Kid's Menu. Pool, Pull Tabs, Sports Bar. 907-766-2800 FAX 766-3374 11-13 2nd Ave. N., P.O. Box 190, Haines, AK 99827-0190
E-mail:bamboo@kcd.com
http://kcd.com/bamboo

39. **CHILKAT RESTAURANT & BAKERY** Full meals, extensive salad bar (June-August), wide selection of bakery sweets and breads. Corner of 5th & Dalton Street. 907-766-2920 or 907-766-2921, FAX 766-2992, P.O. Box 591, Haines, AK 99827-0591

40. **GRIZZLY GREG'S PIZZERIA & DELI** Homemade pizza and sandwiches • Halibut, chips and homemade chowder • Fresh fudge • Ice cream and more. "Where families come to have fun!" Corner of 2nd and Main Street, 907-766-3622, P.O. Box 970, Haines, AK 99827-0970

41. **HAINES QUICK SHOP** Convenience Store-Snack Headquarters of Haines, Cold Pop-Ice-ATM-Pay Phones OPEN 7 AM - MIDNIGHT Local Information. Near Fort Seward 907-766-2330 FAX 907-766-2787 Mile 0 Haines Hwy., P.O. Box 709, Haines, AK 99827-0709

42. **HOWSERS IGA SUPERMARKET** Your one stop shopping supermarket. We have a variety of travelers needs: ATM cash machine, Block Ice, Coolers, Fresh Produce & Meats. 907-766-2040 FAX 766-2787, 209 Main Street, P.O. Box 1309, Haines, AK 99827-1309

43. **"JUST FOR THE HALIBUT" FISH & CHIPS CAFE** Affordable and delicious waterfront dining on our private pier! Enjoy Fish & Chips, Halibut Kabobs, Burgers, Espresso! At Chilkat Cruises Dock. Toll Free 888-766-2103, 907-766-3800, FAX 907-766-2101, 142 Beach Road, P.O. Box 509, Haines, AK 99827-0509
E-mail:chilkat@klukwan.com
http://www.chilkatcruises.com

44. **KLONDIKE SALOON/ RESTAURANT** May-October Located in Dalton City - Set of Walt Disney's "White Fang" - Outdoor Seating/Horseshoe Pits. For Information - 907-766-2477, FAX 766-2478, 296 Fair Drive, P.O. Box 385, Haines, AK 99827-0385

45. **MOUNTAIN MARKET** Serving the finest in Espresso, Deli Sandwiches, Tortilla Wraps, Baked Goods, Natural and Organic Groceries and Haines first Cyber Cafe. 907-766-3340, FAX 907-766-3339, 151 3rd Ave. S., P.O. Box 863, Haines, AK 99827-0863
E-mail:MtnMarket@wytbear.com

46. **WILD STRAWBERRY** Finest Grilled Alaskan Seafood from Family-Owned Boats, Gourmet Breakfast, Lunch and Dinners, Espresso, Fine Chocolates, Dreyer's Ice Cream. 907-766-3608, 138 Second Ave.S., P.O. Box 770, Haines, AK 99827-0770

47. **VIDEO 144** Not just video rentals--Fast Hot Food Too! Nachos, Burgers, Pizza, Espresso, Popcorn & Frozen Yogurt. Out of Town Welcome! 907-766-3171, 214 Main Street, P.O. Box 1489, Haines, AK 99827-1489

SERVICES

48. **BIGFOOT AUTO SERVICE INC** Full service - cars, pickups, RVs, motorhomes - welding - 24 hour towing - Unleaded & Diesel - NAPA Parts - Tires 800-766-5406 907-766-2458 FAX 907-766-2460 987 Haines Hwy., P.O. Box 150, Haines, AK 99827
E-mail:bigfootautoser@wytbear.com

49. **BUSHMASTER AUTO SERVICE** Alignment/Brakes/ Engines/Transmissions/Electronic Controls. Cars, Light Trucks, RVs. Factory Warranty Service. Professional Workmanship 907-766-3217 FAX 766-2415 Fourth St. North, P.O. Box 1355, Haines, AK 99827
E-mail:Bushmasters@webtv.net

50. **HAINES QUICK LAUNDRY** OPEN 7 AM-MIDNIGHT DAILY Large Washers & Dryers. Pay Phone. Located next to the Post Office. 907-766-2330 FAX 907-766-2787 Mile 0 Haines Hwy. P.O. Box 1709, Haines, AK 99827

51. **PARTS PLACE** Auto-RV-Marine. If you need it and we don't have it we will get it! 907-766-2940 104 3rd Avenue S., P.O. Box 9, Haines, AK 99827-0009

52. **PETRO EXPRESS** 24-Hour Credit Card Fueling, RV Dump, Water, Lube, Oils, Free Ice, Popcorn and Coffee. Marine Fuels, AV Gas. Friendly Service. 907-766-2338, Fax 907-766-2871, Mile 0 Haines Hwy., P.O. Box 590, Haines, AK 99827-0590

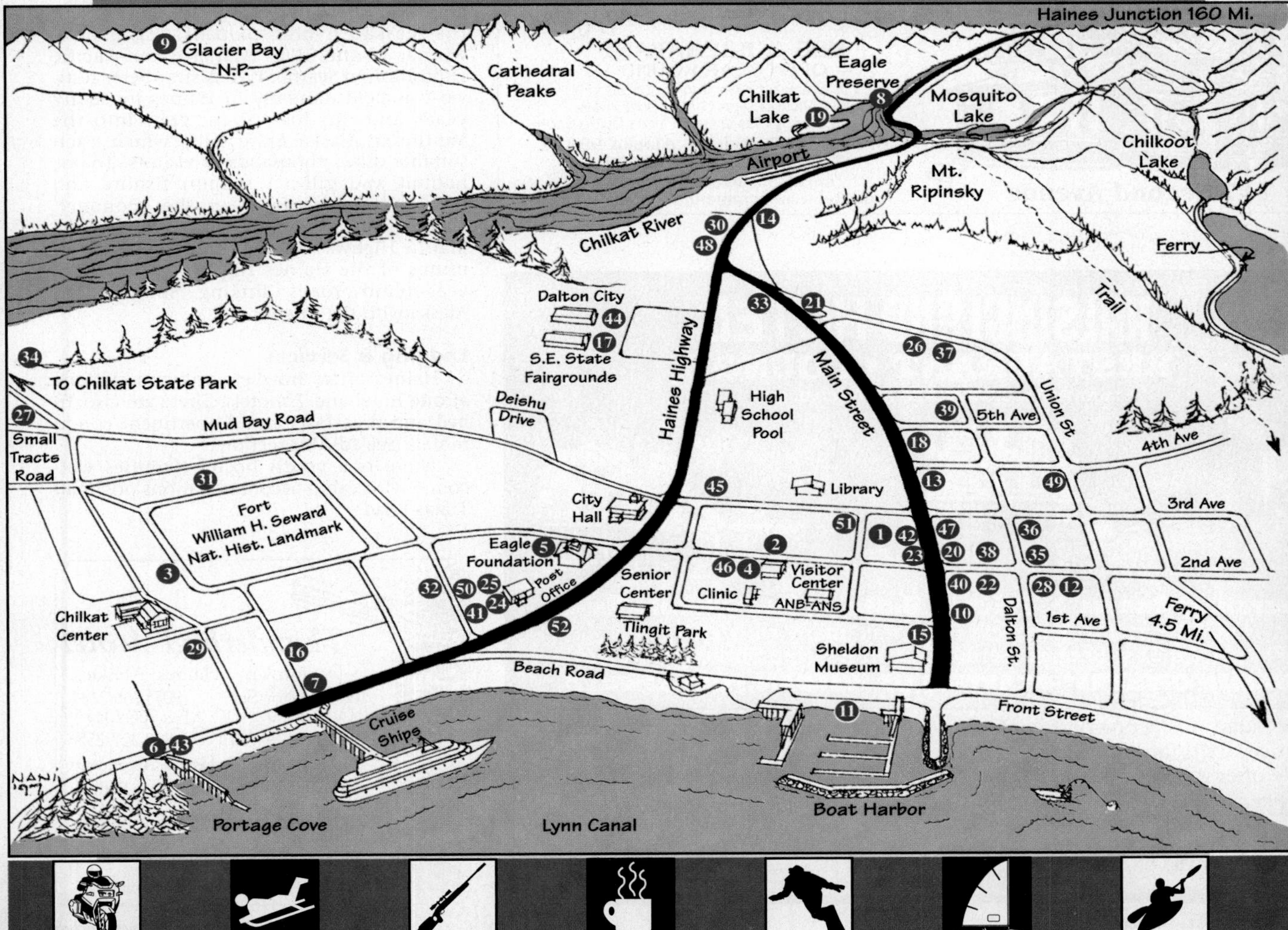

Valley News (weekly), *Eagle Eye*.

Private Aircraft: Haines airport, 4 miles west; elev. 16 feet; length 3,000 feet; asphalt; fuel 100; unattended.

The original Indian name for Haines was *Dei Shu,* meaning "end of the trail." It was an area where Chilkat and Chilkoot Indians met and traded with Russian and American ships. It was also their portage route for transporting canoes from the Chilkat River to Portage Cove and Lynn Canal. The first white man to settle here was George Dickinson, who came as an agent for the North West Trading Co.

In 1879 missionary S. Hall Young and naturalist John Muir came to the village of Yen Dustucky (near today's airport) to determine the location of a Presbyterian mission and school. The site chosen, Dei Shu, was on the narrow portage between the Chilkat River and Lynn Canal. The following year, George Dickinson established a trading post for the Northwest Trading Company, next to the mission site. His wife Sarah began a school for Tlingit children. By 1881, Eugene and Caroline Willard arrived to establish Chilkat Mission. Later, the mission and eventually the town were named for Francina E. Haines, secretary of the Presbyterian Women's Executive Society of Home Missions, who raised funds for the new mission.

In 1882 the Haines post office was established. The town became an important outlet for the Porcupine Mining District, producing thousands of dollars' worth of placer gold at the turn of the century. The Dalton Trail, which crossed the Chilkat mountain pass to the Klondike goldfields in the Yukon, started at Pyramid Harbor Cannery across the Chilkat River from Haines.

Just to the south of Haines city center is Fort Seward on Portage Cove. Named Fort William H. Seward, in honor of the secretary of state who negotiated the purchase of Alaska from Russia in 1867, this was established as the first permanent Army post in the territory. The first troops arrived in 1904 from Camp Skagway. In 1922, the fort was renamed Chilkoot Barracks, after the mountain pass and the Indian tribe on the Chilkoot River. (There are 2 tribes in this area: the Chilkat and the Chilkoot.)

Until WWII this was the only U.S. Army post in Alaska. Chilkoot Barracks was deactivated in 1946 and sold in 1947 to a group of enterprising U.S. veterans who had designs of creating a business cooperative on the site. Their original plans were never fully realized, but a few stayed on, creating the city of Port Chilkoot and converting some of the houses on Officers' Row into permanent homes.

In 1970, Port Chilkoot merged with Haines to become a single municipality, the city of Haines. Two years later, the post was designated a national historic site and became officially known, again, as Fort William H. Seward (although many people still call it Port Chilkoot).

Fishing and gold mining were the initial industries of the Haines area. Haines is also remembered for its famous strawberries, developed by Charles Anway about 1900. His Alaskan hybrid, *Burbank,* was a prize winner at the 1909 Alaska–Yukon–Pacific Exposition in Seattle, WA. A strawberry festival was held annually in Haines for many years, and this local event grew into the Southeast Alaska State Fair, which each summer draws thousands of visitors. Today, halibut and gill-net salmon fishing and tourism are the basis of the economy. Haines is an important port on the Alaska Marine Highway System as the southern terminus of the Haines Highway, 1 of the 2 year-round roads linking southeastern Alaska with the Interior.

Lodging & Services

Haines offers travelers accommodations at one hotel and 7 motels. There are also 10 bed and breakfasts and 2 apartment/condo rentals. See ads this section.

There is a youth hostel (families welcome) with cabin accommodations on Small Tracts Road.

Haines has all traveler facilities, including hardware and grocery stores, gift shops and art galleries, automotive repair, laundry, post office and bank. Gift shops and galleries feature the work of local artisans. There are several restaurants, cafes and taverns. First National Bank of Anchorage and Howser's Supermarket, both on Main Street, have ATMs.

Camping

State campgrounds in the area include Portage Cove, Chilkat State Park, Chilkoot Lake and Mosquito Lake. ▲

Portage Cove State Recreation Site offers 9 tent sites, half-mile past Fort Seward on Portage Cove. Water and toilets available. Campers enjoy view of the Coast Range and Lynn Canal. Watch for cruise ships, ferries, eagles, whales and porpoises. *NOTE: This site is for walk-in and bicyclist camping only.* ▲

Chilkat State Park, with 32 RV sites and 3 tent sites, is about 8 miles from Haines on Mud Bay Road (from the Haines Highway: bear right at the Y by the Welcome to Haines sign; continue straight past the high school and up the hill; turn right on 3rd Ave., which becomes Mud Bay Road at the top of the Hill; then, where the road bends to the right, follow signs from hill to Chilkat State Park). See Mud Bay Road log this section.

Chilkoot Lake Campground (32 sites) is approximately 10 miles from Haines on Lutak Road (6 miles past the ferry terminal; turn right when exiting the ferry for Chilkoot Lake); see Lutak Road log this section. There are 8 private campgrounds in Haines. ▲

Mosquito Lake State Recreation Site is located on Mosquito Lake Road, 3 miles north of Mile 27 Haines Highway. It has 6

Coast Range provides a spectacular backdrop for city of Haines. (© Paul Souders)

campsites nestled in a wooded setting around Mosquito Lake. Toilets, drinking water, a picnic shelter, fishing and boat launch are available. Small store and softball diamond at Mile 27. See the HAINES HIGHWAY section. ▲

A Sheltered Harbor Bed & Breakfast. Waterfront accommodation in Haines, located in historic Fort Seward across from the cruise ship dock providing a panoramic view of the Lynn Canal. Five spacious rooms, each with a private bath, color cable TV with remote, phone and generous hot home-style breakfast. Charter fishing and sightseeing tours available, along with vacuum-packing and freezing of your catch. Browse our gift shop featuring Alaska-made and local arts and crafts. Open year-round. VISA/MasterCard accepted. Reservations: (907) 766-2741. [ADVERTISEMENT]

Haines Hitch-Up RV Park offers easy access to 92 full hookups (30 amps), spacious, grassy, level sites. 20 pull-throughs. Cable TV sites available. Immaculate restrooms and laundromat for registered guests only. Gift shop. Located at the junction of Haines Highway and Main Street. See map in ad this section. P.O. Box 383, Haines, AK 99827. Phone (907) 766-2882. HitchupRV@aol.com. [ADVERTISEMENT] ▲

Salmon Run Adventures RV Campground, Cabins and Charters. "A true Alaska experience." Beautiful forested property overlooking Lutak Inlet with superb mountain and water vistas. Depending on season, watch for whales, porpoises, sea lions or eagles. Fish from the beach or book a fishing expedition on the owner's charter boat; guests have preference, but advance bookings are recommended. The facility has attractive private sites appointed with picnic tables, fire rings and firewood. Hot showers and restrooms. On Lutak Road, 1.8 miles north of ferry terminal. P.O. Box 1122, Haines, AK 99827. Phone (907) 723-4229. E-mail: salmon.run@wytbear.com. Recommended by U.S. News Travel Guide. [ADVERTISEMENT]

Transportation

Air: L.A.B. Flying Service, Haines Airways and Wings of Alaska offer several flights daily to and from Juneau, Skagway and other southeast Alaska communities. Haines airport is 3.5 miles from downtown. Commercial airlines provide transportation to and from motels, and some motels offer courtesy car pickup.

Bus: Local bus service to ferry terminal and guided sightseeing tours are available. Gray Line of Alaska serves Haines to and from the Alaska interior. Alaska Direct bus line connects the interior with Whitehorse, but does not come down to Haines.

Car Rental: Available at Avis Rent-A-Car, Halsingland Hotel (907/766-2733). Rental Car Service also available at Captain's Choice Motel (907/766-3111), and Eagle's Nest Motel (907/766-2891).

Taxi: 24-hour service to ferry terminal and airport.

Highways: The Haines Highway connects Haines, AK, with Haines Junction, YT. It is maintained year-round. See HAINES HIGHWAY section for details.

Ferry: Alaska Marine Highway vessels

serve Haines from southeastern Alaska, Prince Rupert, BC, and Bellingham, WA. There's also daily Juneau–Haines–Skagway service in summer. Alaska state ferries run year-round; phone (907) 766-2111. Ferries unload at the terminal on Lutak Road, 4.5 miles from downtown Haines. Bus/van service meets all ferries in summer.

Water-taxi: The Haines/Skagway Water Taxi (907) 766-3395 and Chilkat Cruises (907) 766-2100 provide daily water-taxi service to Skagway twice daily during the summer.

Cruise Ships: Several cruise ships call in Haines.

Private Boats: Transient moorage is available at Letnikof Cove and at the small-boat harbor downtown. Contact the harbormaster, phone (907) 766-2448.

Attractions

Take the walking tour of historic Fort William H. Seward; details and map are available at the visitor information center and at other businesses. Historic buildings of the post include the former cable office; warehouses and barracks; "Soapsuds Alley," the housing for noncommissioned officers whose wives did washing for the soldiers; the former headquarters building, now a residence, fronted by a cannon and a totem depicting a bear and an eagle; Officers' Row at the "Top O' the Hill," restored homes and apartments; the commanding officers' quarters, now the Halsingland Hotel, where Elinor Dusenbury (who later wrote the music for "Alaska's Flag," which became the state song) once lived; the fire hall; the guard house (jail); the former contractor's office, the plumber's quarters; the post exchange (now a lodge), gymnasium, movie house and the mule stables. Look for historic and interpretive signs.

Visit the Chilkat Center for the Arts. Here, the Chilkat Dancers interpret ancient Tlingit legends. Check with the visitor information center or Alaska Indian Arts Inc. for performance schedule.

Totem Village, on the former post parade ground, includes a replica of a tribal ceremonial house. There is a salmon bake, the Port Chilkoot Potlatch, held nightly in summer next to the tribal house; reservations recommended.

See the Welcome Totems located at the Y on the Haines Highway. These poles were created by carvers of Alaska Indian Arts Inc. *The Raven* pole is symbolic of Raven, as founder of the world and all his great powers. The second figure is *The Whale,* representing Alaska and its great size. The bottom figure is the head of *The Bear,* which shows great strength. *The Eagle* pole tells of its feeding grounds (the Haines area is noted for eagles). Top figure is *The Salmon Chief,* who provides the late run of salmon to the feeding grounds. *The Eagle Chief,* head of the Eagle clan, is the third figure, and the bottom figure is *The Brown Bear,* which also feeds on salmon and is a symbol of strength. Inquire at the visitor information center and museum about location of poles.

The Sheldon Museum and Cultural Center is located on the old Haines Mission property at the end of Main Street by the boat harbor. Exhibits present the pioneer history of the Chilkat Valley and the story and culture of the Tlingit Native people. Chilkat blankets, Russian trunks, the Eldred Rock Lighthouse lens, blue dishes, mounted eagles, Jack Dalton's sawed-off shotgun, photographs and a video on eagles make a fascinating history lesson. Children's "discovery" sheet available. Open daily 1–5 P.M. in summer, plus most mornings and evenings; winter, 1–4 P.M Sunday, Monday and Wednesday, 3–5 P.M. Tuesday, Thursday and Friday. Admission fee $3; children free. Phone (907) 766-2366.

Mountain Flying & Travel. Glacier Bay Flightseeing, Tours and Cruises. Exclusive Ski-Plane operation with the most experienced pilots in the best maintained airplanes in town. Every flight is with the owner of the company in his personal aircraft. Alaska ferry reservations plus Inside Passage tour sales. (907) 766-3007, 800-954-8747; E-mail: mtnfly@yahoo.com. Web site: www.haines.ak.us/mtnfly/ [ADVERTISEMENT]

Enjoy the Fourth of July celebration, which includes canoe and kayak races on Chilkoot Lake, logging events, bicycle and foot races, pie-eating and other contests, parades and performances at the Chilkat Center for the Arts.

The Southeast Alaska State Fair, held at the fairgrounds in Haines (Aug. 9–13, 2000), features agriculture, home arts, and fine arts and crafts. A big event at the fair is the Bald Eagle Music Festival. There are exhibits of flowers, livestock, baked goods, beer and wine, needlework, quilting, woodworking and over a dozen other categories. There are also a parade, horse show and other events. Brochures available from the Fair offices or the visitor information center. Write to Box 385, Haines 99827, or (907) 766-2476.

Summer Solstice Celebration, sponsored by the Southeast Alaska State Fair, takes place on the Saturday closest to the June 21 summer solstice and features bands, dances, games, a beer garden and special activities. All (907) 766-2476 for more information.

American Bald Eagle Foundation is Haines' newest attraction. Interpretive center shows visitors how the bald eagle interacts with its environment through exhibits; mounted eagles, a wide variety of mammals, and fish and undersea life. Admission fee $2 for adults; $5 for families. Children under 12 are free. Open daily 10 A.M. to 6 P.M. in summer. Located at the Haines Highway and 2nd Street, just across 2nd Street from the city/municipal building.

Alaska Bald Eagle Festival. The festival includes release of wild rehabilitated eagles, live bird presentations, art exhibits, naturalist-guided tours to bald eagle preserve, exhibits and more. The events take place in November, and coincide with "the gathering," when eagles congregate to feed on late fall run salmon (see following). Contact the chamber of commerce at (907) 766-2202 for more information.

Alaska Chilkat Bald Eagle Preserve, where the world's greatest concentration of American bald eagles takes place late October through December on Chilkat River flats below Klukwan. The eagle viewing area begins at **Milepost H 17** on the Haines Highway. The 48,000-acre Alaska Chilkat Bald Eagle Preserve was established in 1982. The Chilkat Valley at Haines is the annual gathering site of more than 3,000 bald eagles, which gather to feed on the late run of chum and coho salmon in the Chilkat River. For information contact Alaska State Parks, (907) 465-4563.

Haines King Salmon Derby, May 27, 29, 29–June 3, 4, 2000. Annual king salmon derby sponsored by the Haines Sportsmens Association. King salmon are entered in at the derby station located at the Letnikof boat dock. Large (30–40 lb.) kings can be viewed at the derby station.

Dalton City is housed in the "White Fang" Disney film set. It is located at the fairgrounds. The former movie set houses a few businesses and a Klondike restaurant open in summer.

Visit the small-boat harbor at the foot of Main Street for an interesting afternoon outing. Watch gill-net and crab fishermen setting out from here. Good views from Lookout Park and also from the shoreline between Haines and Portage Cove Campground. Land otters may sometimes be seen cavorting on the floating dock at the northeast corner of the harbor where commercial fishing nets are set out to dry.

Visit State Parks. Chilkoot Lake, at the end of Lutak Road, is worth a visit. Beautiful setting with a picnic area, campground and boat launch. (Private boat tours of Chilkoot Lake are available; check in town.) Chilkat State Park on Mud Bay Road is also a scenic spot with hiking trails, beach access, views of glaciers (Rainbow and Davidson), saltwater fishing (boat required), camping and picnicking. Both parks are within 10 miles of downtown Haines.

Go Flightseeing. Local air charter operators offer flightseeing trips for spectacular close-up views of glaciers, ice fields, mountain peaks and bald eagles. The heart of Glacier Bay is just west of Haines.

Charter boat operators in Haines offer fishing, sightseeing and photography trips.

Watch totem carvers at the Alaska Indian Arts Inc. workshop, located in the restored hospital at Fort Seward. This nonprofit organization is dedicated to the revival of Tlingit Indian art. Craftsmen also work in silver and stone, and sew blankets. Visitor hours 9 A.M. to noon and 1–5 P.M. weekdays year-round.

Hike Area Trails. Hikers should stop at the visitor information center for updates on wildlife sightings and to pick up a free copy of the pamphlet *Haines is for Hikers,* which contains trail descriptions and maps.

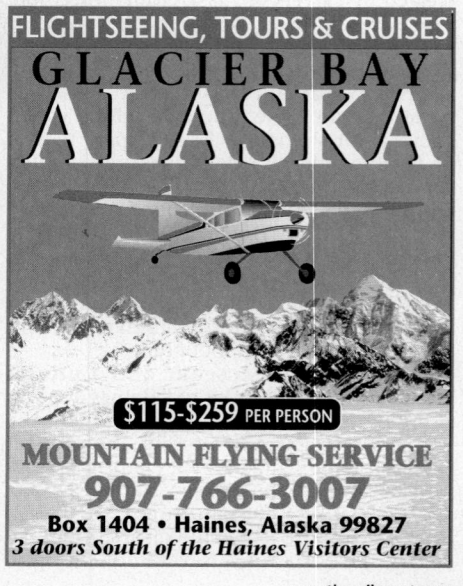

Mount Ripinsky trail is a strenuous all-day hike, with spectacular views from the summit of mountains and tidal waters. Start at the north end of Young Road angling right at the top of the hill. Follow the upper road, then turn left at the water tower. Follow the pipeline right-of-way for 0.5 mile to the chain across the road. Turn left onto the trail which climbs 3.5 miles to the 3,610 foot summit. *CAUTION: This is an unmaintained trail, recommended for experienced hikers only.*

Battery Point trail starts 1 mile/1.6 km beyond Portage Cove Campground and leads about 1.2 miles to Kelgaya Point overlooking Lynn Canal.

Mount Riley (elev. 1,760 feet) has 3 routes to the summit. The steepest and most widely used trail starts at Mile 3 Mud Bay Road and climbs 2.8 miles to the summit. A second route starts at the end of F.A.A. Road and leads 1.9 miles along the city water-supply route to connect with the trail from Mud Bay Road to the summit. A third route follows the Battery Point trail for approximately 0.9 mile, then forks right for a fairly steep climb 3.1 miles to the summit of Mount Riley.

Seduction Point, at the southern tip of the Chilkat Peninsula, is accessible from Chilkat State Park via a 6.9-mile trail; a rolling forest and beach walk. Views of Davidson and Rainbow glaciers.

AREA FISHING: Local charter boat operators and freshwater fishing guides offer fishing trips. Sportfishing lodges at Chilkat Lake offer good fishing in a semi-remote setting. Good fishing in the spring for king salmon in **Chilkat Inlet**. See item above re King Salmon Derby. Halibut best in summer in **Chilkat**, **Lutak** and **Chilkoot inlets**. Dolly Varden fishing good in all lakes and rivers, and along marine shorelines from early spring to late fall. Great pink salmon fishing every other year in August along the marine shoreline of **Lutak Inlet** and in the **Chilkoot River**. Sockeye salmon in the **Chilkoot River**, late June through August. Coho salmon in the **Chilkoot** and **Chilkat rivers**, mid-September through October. Cutthroat trout year-round at **Chilkat** and **Mosquito lakes**. For more information, contact the Alaska Dept. of Fish and Game at (907) 766-2625..

Mud Bay Road Log

Mileposts on Mud Bay Road measure distance from its junction with the Haines Highway near Front Street to road end at Mud Bay, a distance of 8 miles. This road, first paved, then wide gravel, leads to Chilkat State Park, following the shoreline of Chilkat Inlet to Mud Bay on Chilkoot Inlet.
Distance is measured from junction with Haines Highway.

0.1 Hotel on left, motel and private camper park on right. ▲

0.2 Junction with 3rd Street, which leads back to town.

0.5 Small Tracts Road on left, a 1.9-mile loop road which rejoins Mud Bay Road at **Milepost 2.3.** Small Tracts Road leads to private residences and to Bear Creek Camp and Youth Hostel (dorms, cabins and tent camping).

Mud Bay Road leads to the right, down Cemetery Hill (the old military cemetery was located here), then follows the shoreline of Chilkat Inlet, with views of Pyramid Island. Excellent area for eagle pictures.

In winter, the Chilkat River outside Haines draws the world's greatest concentration of bald eagles. (© Loren Taft, Alaskan Images)

2.3 Stop sign at T intersection: go right for state park, left to return to town via Small Tracts Road.

3 Mount Riley trail on left, parking area on right.

3.9 View of Pyramid Island and Rainbow Glacier across Chilkat Inlet. Rainbow Glacier, is a hanging glacier. The ice field moved out over a cliff rather than moving down a valley to the sea. Davidson Glacier is about 2 miles south of Rainbow Glacier.

4.9 Boat dock on right for small boats (summer tie-off only), boat ramp.

5.3 Private road on right to cannery on Letnikof Cove.

6.7 Pavement ends, gravel begins. Turn right and drive in 1.2 miles to entrance of **Chilkat State Park** (camping area 0.5 mile beyond entrance): 32 campsites, 3 tent sites on beach, $6 nightly fee or annual pass, picnic sites, pit toilets and boat launch. Access road paved and graveled, grades to 11 percent. Drive carefully. Beach access, view of glaciers and hiking trail to Seduction Point at southern tip of Chilkat Peninsula. ▲

8 Mud Bay Road turns east and crosses Chilkat Peninsula to Flat Bay (commonly called Mud Bay) off Lynn Canal. Road ends at Mud Bay; short walk to rocky beach. These are private lands. No camping.

Lutak Road Log

Lutak Road begins at Front Street, and leads north along Chilkoot and Lutak inlets past the Alaska Marine Highway ferry terminal. Pavement ends at a fork in the road: the left fork leads straight along the Chilkoot River to Chilkoot Lake campground; the right crosses the the Chilkoot River and serves a residential area at the end of Lutak Inlet (no outlet or turnaround).
Distance is measured from the junction of Front Street with Lutak Road.

0 Junction, Front Street and Lutak Road.

0.1 Turnout on right with view of Fort Seward and Lynn Canal.

1.6 Turnouts along road from here to Mile 7 allow good view of gill-net fleet, July through September.

2.4 Government tank farm, petroleum distribution terminal and beginning of an oil pipeline to Fairbanks. No entry.

3.2 Dock for oil tankers on right.

3.6 Alaska Marine Highway ferry terminal on right.

3.8 City dock on right is used for shipping lumber and also for docking barges.

4.4 Closed and partly dismantled sawmill. A small building for fish processing is also here.

8.3 Road on left follows a wide stretch of the Chilkoot River for 1 mile to Chilkoot Lake picnic area and boat launch; state campground with 32 sites just beyond picnic area, 7-day limit, $10 nightly fee or annual pass. ▲

8.4 Bridge over the mouth of the Chilkoot River. Good salmon fishing June through October. Watch for bears.

In 1983, the Chilkoot tribe dedicated Deer Rock here as a historic reminder of the original location of their village.

Road continues to private homes and dead ends; no turnaround.

Skagway

(See map, page 639)

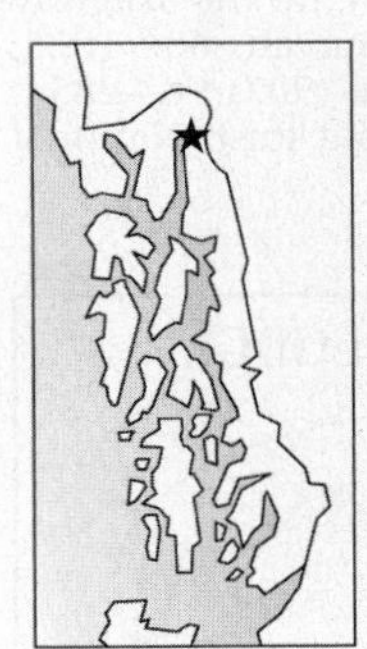

Located on the north end of Taiya Inlet on Lynn Canal, 90 air miles northwest of Juneau; 108 road miles south of Whitehorse, YT. The northern terminus of the Alaska Marine Highway Southeast ferry system and southern terminus of Klondike Highway 2 which connects with the Alaska Highway. *NOTE: Although Skagway is only 13 miles by water from Haines, it is 359 miles by road!* **Population:** 816. **Emergency Services: Skagway Police Department,** phone (907) 983-2232. **Fire Department** and

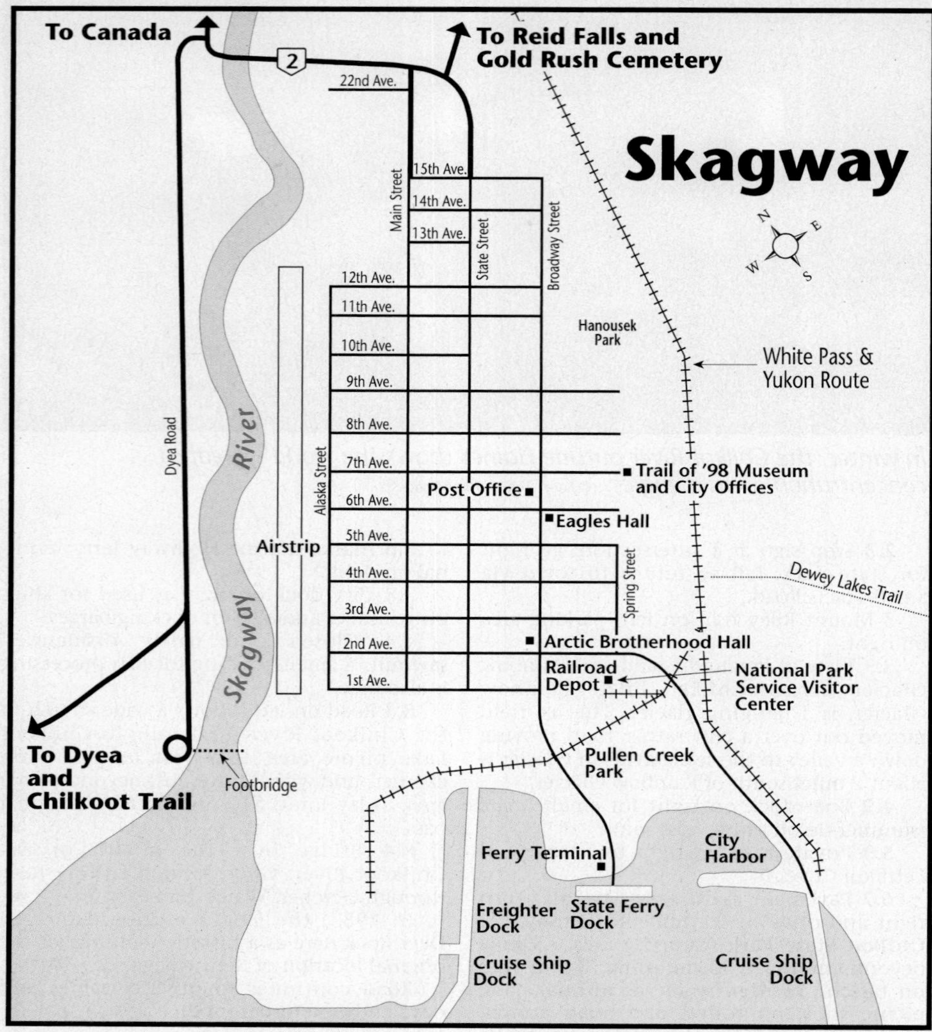

Ambulance, phone 911. **Clinic**, phone (907) 983-2255. **Maritime Search and Rescue**, contact the Coast Guard at (800) 478-5555.

Visitor Information: Write the Skagway Convention and Visitors Bureau, Box 1025, Skagway, AK 99840. Phone (907) 983-2854, fax 983-3854. Klondike Gold Rush National Historical Park Visitor Center has exhibits and films on the history of the area and information on hiking the Chilkoot Trail; write Box 517, Skagway, AK 99840; phone (907) 983-2921, fax (907) 983-9249. Located in the restored railroad depot on 2nd Avenue and Broadway, it is open daily in summer.

Elevation: Sea level. **Climate:** Average daily temperature in summer, 57°F/14°C; in winter, 23°F/-5°C. Average annual precipitation is 29.9 inches. **Radio:** KHNS-FM 91.9; KINY-AM 69.0. **Newspaper:** *Skagway News* (biweekly).

Private Aircraft: Skagway airport, adjacent west; elev. 44 feet; length 3,700 feet; asphalt; fuel 100LL; attended.

The name Skagway (originally spelled Skaguay) is said to mean "home of the north wind" in the local Tlingit dialect. It is the oldest incorporated city in Alaska (incorporated in 1900). Skagway is also a year-round port and 1 of the 2 gateway cities to the Alaska Highway in Southeast Alaska: Klondike Highway 2 connects Skagway with the Alaska Highway. (The other gateway city is Haines, connected to the Alaska Highway via the Haines Highway.)

The first white residents were Capt. William Moore and his son, J. Bernard, who settled in 1887 on the east side of the Skagway River valley (a small part of the Moore homesite was sold for construction of a Methodist college, now the city hall).

But Skagway owes its birth to the Klondike Gold Rush. Skagway, and the once-thriving town of Dyea, sprang up as thousands of gold seekers arrived to follow the White Pass and Chilkoot trails to the Yukon goldfields.

In July 1897, the first boatloads of stampeders bound for the Klondike landed at Skagway and Dyea. By October 1897, according to a North West Mounted Police report, Skagway had grown "from a concourse of tents to a fair-sized town, with well-laid-out streets and numerous frame buildings, stores, saloons, gambling houses, dance houses and a population of about 20,000." Less than a year later it was reported that "Skagway was little better than a hell on earth." Customs office records for 1898 show that in the month of February alone 5,000 people landed at Skagway and Dyea.

By the summer of 1899 the stampede was all but over. The newly built White Pass & Yukon Route railway reached Lake Bennett, supplanting the Chilkoot Trail from Dyea. Dyea became a ghost town. Its post office closed in 1902, and by 1903 its population consisted of one settler. Skagway's population dwindled to 500. But Skagway persisted, both as a port and as terminus of the White Pass & Yukon Route railway, which connected the town to Whitehorse, YT, in 1900. Cruise ships, and later the Alaska State Ferry System, brought tourism and business to Skagway. Scheduled state ferry service to southeastern Alaska began in 1963.

Today, tourism is Skagway's main economic base, with Klondike Gold Rush

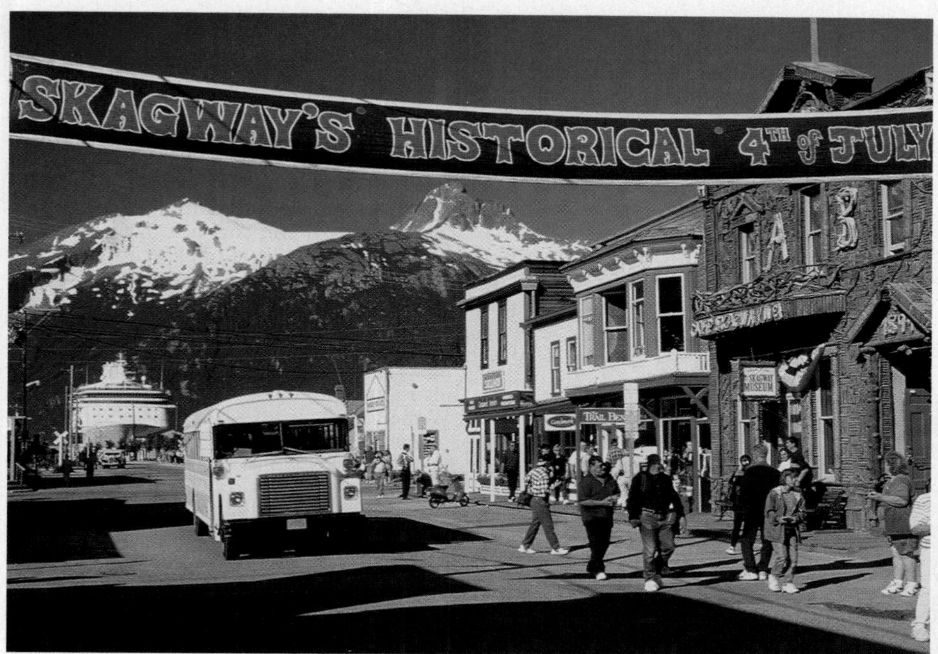

Much of downtown Skagway is part of Klondike Gold Rush National Historical Park. (© Susan Cole Kelly)

National Historical Park Skagway's major visitor attraction. Within Skagway's downtown historical district, false-fronted buildings and boardwalks dating from gold rush times line the streets. The National Park Service, the city of Skagway and local residents have succeeded in retaining Skagway's Klondike atmosphere.

Lodging & Services

Skagway offers a variety of accommodations; see ads this section. Reservations are advised in summer.

There are several restaurants, cafes and bars, grocery, hardware and clothing stores; many gift and novelty shops offering Alaska and gold rush souvenirs, photos, books, records, gold nugget jewelry, furs and ivory; a post office; gas stations (with diesel); a hostel; and several churches.

There is 1 bank in town (National Bank of Alaska), located at 6th and Broadway; open 9:30 A.M. to 5 P.M. Monday through Friday in summer. Automatic teller machines at bank and next to the Trail Bench gift shop on Broadway between 2nd and 3rd avenues., also in the White Pass & Yukon Route lobby.

U.S. customs office is located at Mile 6.8 Klondike Highway 2; phone or fax (907) 983-2325.

The White House. You'll find historic accommodations reminiscent of days past with our family antiques, hardwood floors and restored woodwork. Clean comfortable bedrooms feature many personal touches in addition to the private baths, handcrafted

quilts, ceiling fans, telephones and TVs. Wake to the aroma of homemade breakfast and complete your evening with tea and treats from our cookie jar. Year-round. 475 8th Avenue, Post Office Box 41-MP, Skagway, AK 99840-0041. Phone (907) 983-9000, Fax (907) 983-9010. www.skagway.com/whitehouse. [ADVERTISEMENT]

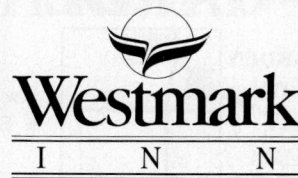

Historic Skagway Inn, established 1897, located at 7th and Broadway in historic district. Once a gold rush brothel, now a historic frontier country Inn filled with antiques. Full hot breakfast served the following morning. Walking distance to all services and attractions. Travel desk for railroad, and tour tickets. Courtesy van. Home of Olivia's restaurant, locally known for fresh Alaska seafood creatively prepared with local produce and the Alaska Garden Gourmet Cooks Tour. Special Chilkoot Trail services. Phone (907) 983-2289, (800) 752-4929. <info@skagwayinn.com>. [ADVERTISEMENT]

Camping

There are several private campgrounds in Skagway offering hookups, tent sites, restrooms and showers, dump stations and laundromats. A campground is located at the Chilkoot Trail trailhead near Dyea. ▲

Transportation

Air: Daily scheduled service between Skagway and Haines and Juneau via L.A.B. Flying Service, Skagway Air and Wings of Alaska. Charter service also available between towns and for flightseeing via Skagway Air. Temsco provides helicopter tours. Transportation to and from the airport is provided by the flight services and local hotels in the summer.

Bus: Bus/van service to Anchorage, Fairbanks, Haines and Whitehorse, YT.

Car Rental: Available from Avis Rent-A-Car (907/983-2247) and Sourdough Car & Van Rental (907/983-2523). Motorhomes available from ABC Motor Home Rentals (800/421-7456 or 907/983-3222).

Highway: Klondike Highway 2 was completed in 1978 and connects Skagway to the Alaska Highway. It is open year-round. See KLONDIKE HIGHWAY 2 section.

Railroad: White Pass & Yukon Route offers 3-hour excursions from Skagway to White Pass Summit and return. Phone 800-343-7373. Through rail/bus connections are also available daily between Skagway and Whitehorse.

Ferry: Alaska Marine Highway vessels call regularly year-round, as Skagway is the northern terminus of the Southeast ferry system. The ferry terminal is in the large building on the waterfront (see city map this section); restrooms, pay phone and lockers inside. Ferry terminal office hours vary: opening hours are usually posted at the front door. Phone (907) 983-2941 or 983-2229. It's an easy walk into town, but hotel and motel vans do meet ferries.

Water-taxi: Service is available between Haines and Skagway. For schedules and rates, phone 888-766-2103 or 888-766-3395.

Cruise Ships: Skagway is a regular port of call for cruise ships and the 17th most visited port in the world. Downtown is not far from the dock. Tours can be purchased dockside and at downtown offices.

Private Boats: Transient moorage is available at the Skagway small-boat harbor. Contact the harbormaster at (907) 983-2628. The boat harbor has space for cruisers up to 100 feet. Gas, diesel fuel and water are available.

Attractions

The Skagway Visitor Center is located in the Arctic Brotherhood Hall on Broadway between 2nd and 3rd avenues. The Arctic Brotherhood Hall's facade has almost 10,000 pieces of driftwood sticks arranged in a mosaic pattern, with the Brotherhood's AB letters and symbols, a gold pan with nuggets.

Trail of '98 Museum moves back to its old location in the McCabe College Building (also City Hall), one block east of Broadway on 7th Avenue; May 1 of 2000 is the scheduled re-opening. The museum's primary interest is to help preserve Alaskan historical material and to display Alaskan pioneer life. The museum is open daily May through the end of September, 9 a.m. to 5 p.m.; contact the museum for winter hours. Phone (907) 983-2420.

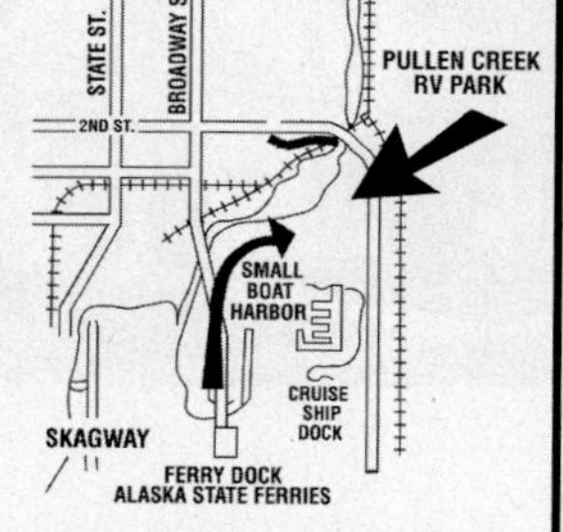

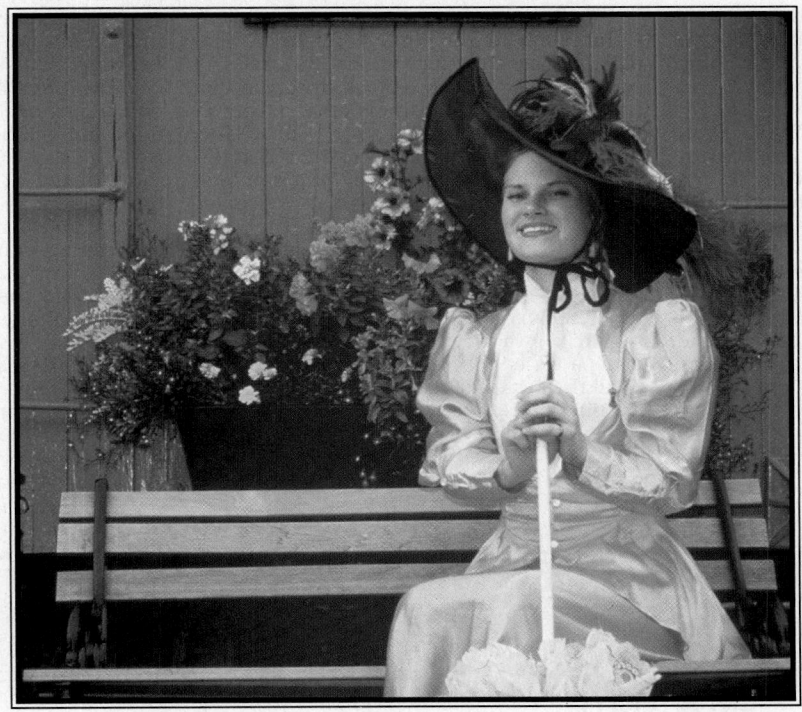

McCabe College Building/City Hall is the first granite building constructed in Alaska. It was built by the Methodist Church as a school in 1899–1900 to be known as McCabe College, but public-school laws were passed that made the enterprise impractical, and it was sold to the federal government. For decades it was used as U.S. District Court No. 1 of Alaska, but as the population of the town declined, the court was abandoned, and in 1956 the building was purchased by the city. The main floor is occupied by City of Skagway offices. From the waterfront, walk up Broadway and turn right on 7th Avenue.

See the show *The Days of 1898 Show With Soapy Smith*. This show, produced by Gold Rush Productions, is put on several times a day; summer evening performances (subject to cruise ship arrivals) in Eagles Hall. Check the billboard in front of the hall for show times. The show relates the history of Skagway, from the days of the notorious Soapy Smith. Phone (907) 983-2545.

This show is good family entertainment; bring your camera, gamble with funny money (during evening show only), and enjoy this well-done historical musical comedy. Admission fee charged.

Alaska Wildlife Adventure displays Alaska wildlife mounts and has an extensive and eclectic collection of Alaskana memorabilia. Gift shop and donut shop. Admission fee charged.

Klondike Gold Rush National Historical Park was authorized in 1976 to preserve and interpret the history of the Klondike Gold Rush of 1897–98. In 1998 this became the nation's only International Historical Park, with units in Seattle, Skagway, British Columbia and the Yukon Territory. The park, managed by the National Park Service, consists of 4 units: a 6-block historical district in Skagway's business area; a 1-mile-wide,17-mile-long corridor of land comprising the Chilkoot Trail; a 1-mile-wide, 5-mile-long corridor of land comprising the White Pass Trail; and a visitor center at 117 S. Main St. in Seattle, WA. The Skagway unit is the most visited national park in Alaska. For more information, phone (907) 983-2921; fax: (907) 983-9249; website: http://www. nps.gov/klgo.

In Skagway, the National Park Service offers a variety of free programs in summer. Visit the restored Mascot Saloon at Third Avenue and Broadway. There are daily, guided walking tours of the downtown Skagway historic district and ranger talks on a variety of topics. Films are also shown. Check with the Park Service's visitor center in the restored railroad depot on 2nd Avenue and Broadway. Summer (May through Sept.) hours are 8 A.M. to 6 P.M. The original Moore cabin and the restored J. Bernard Moore House at 5th Avenue and Spring Street provide insights into the Alaska pioneer lifestyle during Skagway's early years. Entrance to the Moore House and interpretation by National Park Service Rangers .

Hike the Chilkoot Trail. This 33-mile trail begins on Dyea Road (see log this section) and climbs Chilkoot Pass (elev. 3,739 feet) to Lake Bennett, following the historic route of the gold seekers of 1897–98. The trail is arduous but offers both spectacular scenery and historical relics. There are several campgrounds and shelters along the route. Hikers planning to take the Chilkoot Trail should check with the Trail Center in Skagway, phone (907) 983-3655. Permits are required and reservations recommended for travel on the Canadian portion of the trail. Call (867) 667-3910, or from Canada and the U.S. mainland call 1-800-661-0486. The Trail Center is open daily from 7:30 A.M. to 4:30 P.M., May through mid-September. Trail maps, local natural and cultural history guides, bear precaution and safety information, and other materials are available free or for sale.

The ALASKA WILDERNESS GUIDE also

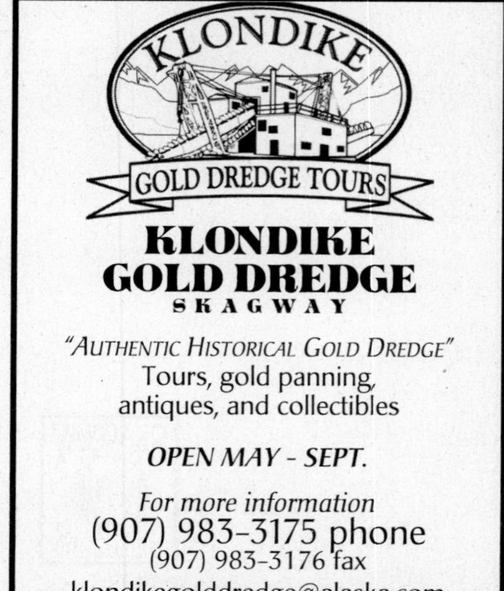

has details on the Chilkoot Trail, and "Chilkoot Pass" by Archie Satterfield is a good hiking and history guide to the trail.

Corrington Museum of Alaska History, located at 5th and Broadway, offers a unique record of events from prehistory to the present. Each of the 40 exhibits at the museum features a scene from Alaska history hand-engraved (scrimshawed) on a walrus tusk. The museum is open in summer. Free admission.

Picnic at Pullen Creek Park. This attractive waterfront park has a covered picnic shelter, 2 footbridges and 2 small docks. It is located between the cruise ship and ferry docks, behind the White Pass & Yukon Route depot. Watch for pink salmon in the intertidal waters in August, silver salmon in September.

Helicopter and airplane tours of Skagway and White Pass are available in summer.

Gold Rush Cemetery is 1.5 miles from downtown and makes a nice walk. Go north on State Street to a sign pointing to the cemetery. Follow dirt road across tracks into railroad yard, follow posted direction signs, then continue about 0.4 mile/0.6 km farther to the cemetery. If you drive in, a circular road around the cemetery eliminates having to back up to get out. A path on left at the end of the road leads to the cemetery where the graves of both "bad guy" Soapy Smith and "good guy" Frank Reid are located (both men died in a gunfight in July 1898). Smith's original gravestone was whittled away by souvenir hunters, and the resting place of the feared boss of Skagway is now marked by a metal marker.

Reid Falls are located near Gold Rush Cemetery, and it is only a short hike from Frank Reid's grave to view them.

AREA FISHING: Local charter boat operators offer fishing trips. The ADF&G Sport Fish Division recommends the following areas and species. Dolly Varden: Fish the shore of **Skagway Harbor, Long Bay** and **Taiya Inlet**, May through June. Try the **Taiya River** by the steel bridge in Dyea in early spring or fall; use red and white spoons or salmon eggs. Hatchery-produced king salmon have been returning to the area in good numbers in recent years. Try fishing in salt water during June and July and in **Pullen Creek** in August. Pink salmon are also plentiful at Pullen Creek in August. Coho and chum salmon near the steel bridge on the **Taiya River**, mid-September through October. Trolling in the marine areas is good but often dangerous for small boats. A steep trail near town will take you to Dewey lakes, which were stocked with Colorado brook trout in the 1920s. **Lower Dewey Lake**, 1/2-hour to 1-hour hike; heavily wooded shoreline, use raft. The brook trout are plentiful and grow to 16 inches but are well fed, so fishing can be frustrating. **Upper Dewey Lake**, a steep 2 1/2-hour to 4-hour hike to above tree line, is full of hungry brook trout to 11 inches. Use salmon eggs or size #10 or #12 artificial flies. **Lost Lake** is reached via a rough trail near Dyea (ask locals for directions). The lake lies at about elev. 1,300 feet and has a good population of rainbow trout. Use small spinners or spoons.

For more information on area fishing, contact the ADF&G office in Haines; phone (907) 766-2625.

Dyea Road Log

The Dyea Road begins at **Milepost S 2.3** on Klondike Highway 2. It leads southwest toward Yakutania Point, then northwest past Long Bay and the Taiya River to the beginning of the Chilkoot Trail and to a side road leading to the old Dyea townsite and Slide Cemetery. The Dyea Road is a narrow winding gravel road. **Distance is from the junction with Klondike Highway 2.**

0 Junction.

0.1 Old cemetery on right.

0.4 View of Reid Falls east across the Skagway River.

1.4 A scenic wayside with platform on left southbound affords view of Skagway, Taiya Inlet and the Skagway River.

1.7 A steep, primitive road on left southbound descends 0.4 mile toward bank of the Skagway River, with a view of the Skagway waterfront and Taiya Inlet.

Drive to parking area and walk 0.2 mile to Yakutania Point; horse trail beyond parking area. Bridge at base of hill leads to a short trail back to town. Dyea Road turns northwest along Long Bay at this point.

1.9 Skyline trailhead (poorly signed). This trail leads to top of AB Mountain (elev. 5,000 feet).

2.1 Head of Long Bay.

4 City dump.

4.3 Taiya Inlet comes into view on left northbound as the road curves away from Long Bay.

5.1 View of the old pilings in Taiya Inlet. The docks of Dyea used to stretch from the trees to beyond the pilings, which are still visible. These long docks were needed to reach deep water because of the great tidal range in this inlet.

5.7 Hooligan (smelt) run here in the Taiya River in May and early June. Local swimming hole across the road.

6.5 Dyea information display.

6.7 Chilkoot Trail trailhead campground, parking area and ranger station.

7.2 The Chilkoot Trail begins on right northbound. Bridge over Taiya River.

7.4 A primitive road on left leads to the

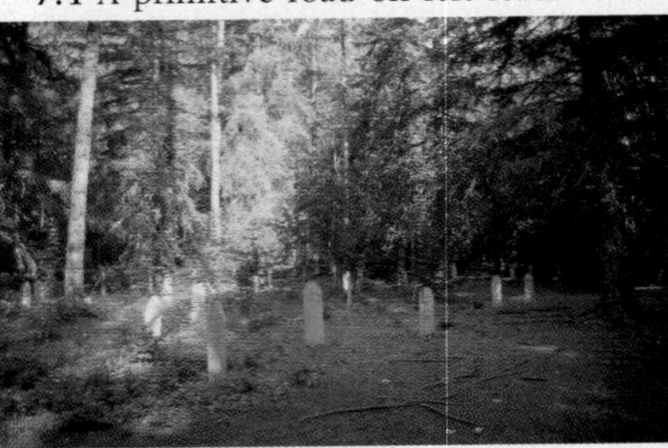

Slide Cemetery (follow signs) and old Dyea townsite (keep left at forks in road). The cemetery, reached by a short unmarked path through the woods, contains the graves of men killed in the Palm Sunday avalanche, April 3, 1898, on the Chilkoot Trail. At Dyea townsite, covered with fireweed and lupine in summer, hardly a trace remains of the buildings that housed 8,000 people here during the gold rush. About 30 people live in the valley today.

8.4 Steel bridge across West Creek. Four-wheel drive recommended beyond this point.

HAINES HIGHWAY

Connects: Haines, AK, to Haines Junction, YT **Length:** 152 miles
Road Surface: Paved **Season:** Open all year
Highest Summit: Chilkat Pass 3,493 feet
Major Attraction: Chilkat Bald Eagle Preserve

(See map, page 696)

	Alaska Hwy. Jct.	Atlin	Carcross	Skagway	Whitehorse
Alaska Hwy. Jct.		125	33	99	10
Atlin	125		92	158	81
Carcross	33	92		66	43
Skagway	99	158	66		109
Whitehorse	10	81	43	109	

Haines Highway heads up Three Guardsmen Pass. (© Earl L. Brown, staff)

The paved 151.6-mile-/244-km-long Haines Highway connects Haines, AK (on the state ferry route), at the head of Lynn Canal with the Alaska Highway at Haines Junction, YT. Allow about 4 hours driving time. The highway is open year-round. The highway is usually snow-free by May.

Noted for the grandeur and variety of its alpine scenery, the highway leads from coastal forests near Haines through the Chilkat Eagle Preserve up over the backbone of the St. Elias Mountains, skirting Tatshenshini–Alsek Wilderness Provincial Park, and running along the eastern border of Kluane National Park Reserve from approximately **Milepost S 111.6** to Haines Junction. Watch for signs for hiking trails, which are posted 3.1 miles/5 km before trailheads. For more information on the park, contact Kluane National Park Reserve, Parks Canada, Box 5495, Haines Junction, YT Y0B 1L0, phone (867) 634-7209, fax (867) 634-7208. Also visit the park information centre in Haines Junction. Open daily, May to September, the centre has excellent interpretive displays.

Part of what is now the Haines Highway was originally a "grease trail" used by the coastal Chilkat Indians trading eulachon oil for furs from the Interior. In the late 1880s, Jack Dalton developed a packhorse trail to the Klondike goldfields along the old trading route. This historic corridor is celebrated each year during Dalton Trail Days, July 1–4. The present road was built in 1943 as a military access highway during WWII to provide an alternative route from the Pacific tidewater into Yukon Territory.

Watch for bikes on the highway during the annual Kluane/Chilkat International Bike Race (June 17, 2000).

U.S. customs is open from 7 A.M. to 11 P.M. (Alaska time); Canada customs is open from 8 A.M. to midnight (Pacific time). There are no facilities or accommodations at the border. All travelers must stop.

A valid Alaska fishing license is required for fishing along the highway between Haines and the international border at **Milepost H 40.7.** The highway then crosses the northern tip of British Columbia into Yukon Territory. You must have valid fishing licenses for both British Columbia and Yukon Territory if you fish these areas, and a national park fishing license if you fish waters in Kluane National Park.

In summer, gas is available along the highway only at 33 Mile Roadhouse and at Kathleen Lake Lodge, **Milepost H 135.2.**

If you plan to drive the Haines Highway in winter, check road conditions before starting out by phoning (867) 667-8215 for the daily recorded road condition report. Note that flashing lights at the Haines Junction weigh scales indicate hazardous winter road conditions; travel not recommended. In Haines Junction, the maintenance garage (867/634-2227) or weigh scale station (867/634-2228) may also have details on driving conditions..

Emergency medical services: Between Haines and the U.S.–Canada border at **Milepost H 40.7,** phone 911. Between the U.S.–Canada border and Haines Junction, phone the RCMP at (867) 634-5555.

In the following highway log, driving distance is measured in miles from Haines, AK. Mileposts are up along the Alaska portion of the highway. The kilometre figures on the Canadian portion of the highway reflect the physical kilometreposts and are not an accurate metric conversion of the mileage figure.

Haines Highway Log

Distance from Haines (H) is followed by distance from Haines Junction (HJ).

ALASKA ROUTE 7

H 0 HJ 151.6 (244 km) **HAINES.** See HAINES section for description.

H 0.2 (0.3 km) **HJ 151.4** (243.7 km) Front Street.

H 0.4 (0.6 km) **HJ 151.2** (243.4 km) Second Street. Turn right northbound (left southbound) for visitor information center and downtown Haines.

H 0.5 (0.8 km) **HJ 151.1** (243.2 km) Third Street. Turn right northbound (left southbound) for downtown Haines.

H 1 (1.6 km) **HJ 150.6** (242.4 km) Haines Hitch-Up RV Park. ▲

H 1.2 (1.9 km) **HJ 150.4** (242.1 km) Main Street Y. If southbound, turn right to Fort William H. Seward, left to downtown Haines.

H 1.3 (2.1 km) **HJ 150.3** (241.9 km) Eagle's Nest Motel.

H 3 (4.8 km) **HJ 148.6** (239.1 km) Sign indicates Customs 38 miles/61 km.

H 3.5 (5.6 km) **HJ 148.1** (238.3 km) **Private Aircraft:** Haines airport; elev. 16 feet; length 4,000 feet; asphalt; fuel 100; unattended.

H 4 (6.4 km) **HJ 147.6** (237.5 km) Takhinsha Mountains to the southwest form a backdrop to the Chilkat River. Haines Highway (2-lanes, 50 mph) winds through the Chilkat River Valley. The Chilkat River flows into Chilkat Inlet of Lynn Canal, a massive fjord about 60 miles/96.5 km long. Lynn Canal was named by English explorer Captain Vancouver for his birthplace (King's Lynn) in England.

H 4.3 (6.9 km) **HJ 147.3** (237 km) Turnout along river.

H 6 (9.6 km) **HJ 145.6** (234.3 km) Picnic spot next to Chilkat River.

H 6.6 (10.6 km) **HJ 145** (233.3 km) Mount Ripinski trailhead (not signed).

HAINES HIGHWAY *Haines, AK, to Haines Junction, YT*

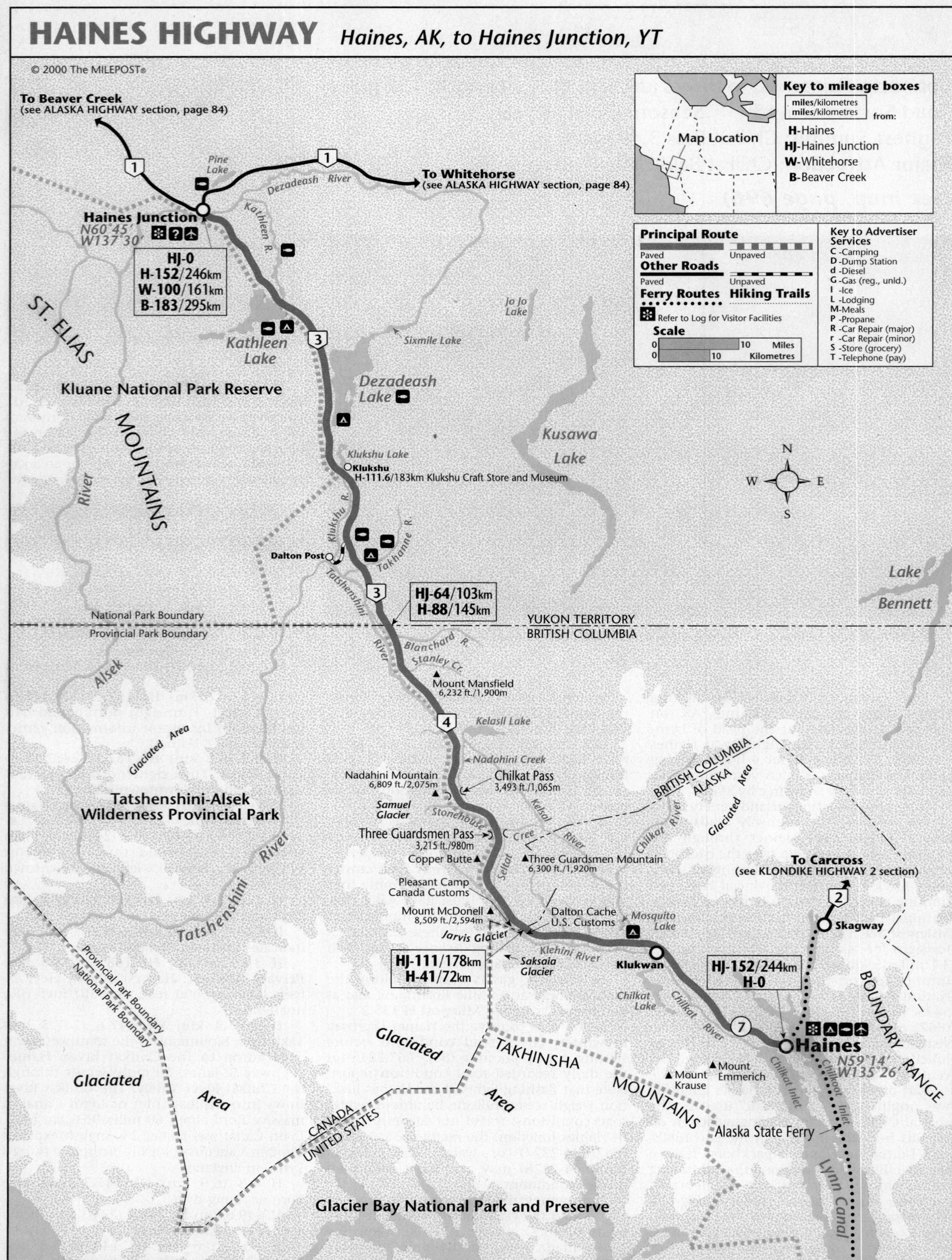

© 2000 The MILEPOST®
To Beaver Creek
(see ALASKA HIGHWAY section, page 84)
To Whitehorse
(see ALASKA HIGHWAY section, page 84)
Map Location
Key to mileage boxes
miles/kilometres
miles/kilometres
from:
H-Haines
HJ-Haines Junction
W-Whitehorse
B-Beaver Creek
Principal Route
Paved
Unpaved
Other Roads
Paved
Unpaved
Ferry Routes
Hiking Trails
Refer to Log for Visitor Facilities
Scale
0 10 Miles
0 10 Kilometres
Key to Advertiser Services
C -Camping
D -Dump Station
d -Diesel
G -Gas (reg., unld.)
I -Ice
L -Lodging
M -Meals
P -Propane
R -Car Repair (major)
r -Car Repair (minor)
S -Store (grocery)
T -Telephone (pay)
Pine Lake
Dezadeash River
Haines Junction
N60°45′
W137°30′
HJ-0
H-152/246km
W-100/161km
B-183/295km
Kathleen R.
Jo Jo Lake
Sixmile Lake
ST. ELIAS
MOUNTAINS
Kathleen Lake
Kluane National Park Reserve
Dezadeash Lake
Kusawa Lake
N
W
E
S
Klukshu Lake
Klukshu
H-111.6/183km Klukshu Craft Store and Museum
River
Klukshu R.
Takhanne R.
Dalton Post
Tatshenshini
HJ-64/103km
H-88/145km
Lake Bennett
National Park Boundary
Provincial Park Boundary
YUKON TERRITORY
BRITISH COLUMBIA
Alsek
River
Blanchard R.
Stanley Cr.
Mount Mansfield
6,232 ft./1,900m
Kelasll Lake
Glaciated Area
Nadahini Creek
Nadahini Mountain
6,809 ft./2,075m
Chilkat Pass
3,493 ft./1,065m
BRITISH COLUMBIA
ALASKA
Tatshenshini-Alsek
Wilderness Provincial Park
Samuel Glacier
Stonehouse Cree
Kelsal River
Chilkat River
Glaciated Area
Three Guardsmen Pass
3,215 ft./980m
Copper Butte
Three Guardsmen Mountain
6,300 ft./1,920m
Seltat
River
Tatshenshini
To Carcross
(see KLONDIKE HIGHWAY 2 section)
Pleasant Camp
Canada Customs
Mount McDonell
8,509 ft./2,594m
Dalton Cache
U.S. Customs
Mosquito Lake
Jarvis Glacier
Skagway
Klehini River
Klukwan
HJ-111/178km
H-41/72km
Saksaia Glacier
HJ-152/244km
H-0
Provincial Park Boundary
National Park Boundary
Chilkat Lake
Chilkat River
BOUNDARY RANGE
Glaciated
Area
Glaciated
Area
TAKHINSHA
MOUNTAINS
Haines
N59°14′
W135°26′
Mount Krause
Mount Emmerich
Chilkat Inlet
Chilkoot Inlet
CANADA
UNITED STATES
Alaska State Ferry
Lynn Canal
Glacier Bay National Park and Preserve

H 9.2 (14.8 km) **HJ 142.4** (229.2 km) Entering **Alaska Chilkat Bald Eagle Preserve** northbound. *NOTE: Please use pullouts.* Established in 1982, the 48,000-acre preserve is the seasonal home to more than 3,000 bald eagles, which gather each year to feed on the late run of chum salmon. Eagle-viewing area begins at **Milepost H 19**; best viewing is mid-October to January.

Of the 40,000 bald eagles in Alaska, most are found in Southeast. Eagles build nests in trees along the shoreline. Nests are added to each year and can be up to 7 feet across. (Nests the size of pickup trucks have fallen out of trees.) Nesting eagles have a second backup nest. Eagles lay their eggs in April; the eaglets fledge in August.

H 9.6 (15.4 km) **HJ 142** (228.5 km) Magnificent view of Takhinsha Mountains across Chilkat River. This range extends north from the Chilkat Range; Glacier Bay is on the other side. Prominent peaks are Mount Krause and Mount Emmerich (elev. 6,405 feet/1,952m) in the Chilkat Range.

H 10 (16 km) **HJ 141.6** (227.8 km) Watch for subsistence fish camps along the highway in June. Also watch for fish wheels on the river.

H 14.7 (23.6 km) **HJ 136.9** (220.3 km) Watch for mountain goats on the ridges.

H 15 (24.1 km) **HJ 136.6** (219.8 km) Milepost 17 (yellow sign) is one of several along the highway that indicate mileages on the U.S. Army oil pipeline. The pipeline formerly pumped oil from Haines over the St. Elias Mountains to the Alaska Highway at Haines Junction, YT. These signs were used for aerial checking and monitoring of the line.

H 17.6 (28.3 km) **HJ 134** (215.6 km) Decaying barn and cabins.

H 18.8 (30.3 km) **HJ 132.8** (213.7 km) Slide area.

H 19 (30.6 km) **HJ 132.6** (213.4 km) Turnout with parking, interpretive panels and restrooms; Chilkat Bald Eagle Preserve. Begin eagle viewing area (northbound) on Chilkat River flats. Best viewing is mid-October to January. Paved and gravel biking and walking trail along river. *CAUTION: Eagle watchers, use turnouts and park well off highway!*

H 20.5 (33 km) **HJ 131.1** (211 km) Turnout with parking area and interpretive panel; Chilkat Bald Eagle Preserve.

H 21.4 (34.4 km) **HJ 130.2** (209.5 km) Turnoff via paved access road to Indian village of **KLUKWAN.**

H 23.8 (38.3 km) **HJ 127.8** (205.6 km) Chilkat River bridge. Highway now follows Klehini River. Watch for eagles beginning in late summer. *CAUTION: Watch for moose.*

H 26.3 (42.3 km) **HJ 125.3** (201.6 km) Porcupine Road west leads across Klehini River; turn off here for jet boat landing on Tsirku River for Birch Island Lodge on Chilkat Lake.

H 27.3 (43.9 km) **HJ 124.3** (200 km) Turnoff for **Mosquito Lake State Recreation Site**; 10 campsites, tables, water, toilets, $8/night or resident. Mosquito Lake general store. Access to private RV park. ▲

H 28.8 (46.3 km) **HJ 122.8** (197.6 km) Muncaster Creek bridge.

H 31 (49.8 km) **HJ 120.6** (194.1 km) Leaving Alaska Chilkat Bald Eagle Preserve northbound.

H 31.6 (50.9 km) **HJ 120** (193.1 km) Bridge over Little Boulder Creek.

H 33.2 (53.4 km) **HJ 118.4** (190.5 km) 33 Mile Roadhouse; gas and phone. RV campground. Store. *NOTE: Last available gas northbound until Kathleen Lake Lodge. Check your gas tank.*

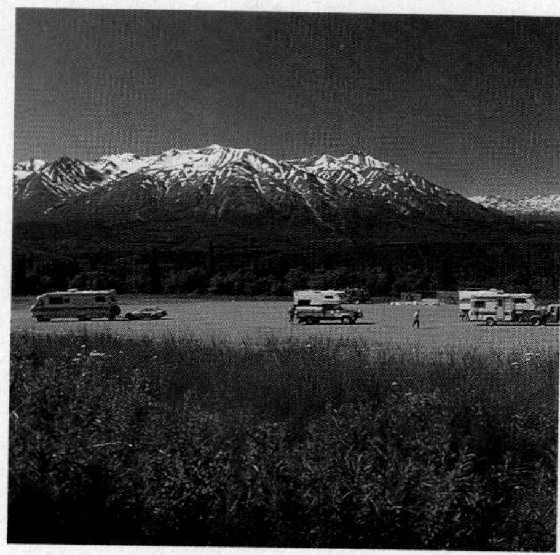

Viewpoint at Milepost H 98.3 Haines Highway. (© Earl L. Brown, staff)

H 33.8 (54.4 km) **HJ 117.8** (189.6 km) Bridge over Big Boulder Creek. Watch for salmon swimming upstream during spawning season. Closed to salmon fishing.

H 36.2 (58.3 km) **HJ 115.4** (185.7 km) View of Saksaia Glacier.

H 40.4 (65 km) **HJ 111.2** (179 km) **U.S. Customs, Dalton Cache station**. All travelers entering United States MUST STOP. Open year-round 7 A.M. to 11 P.M., Alaska time. Phone (907) 767-5511. Restrooms, large parking area. Jarvis Glacier moraine is visible from the old Dalton Cache (on the National Register of Historic Places), located behind the customs building.

H 40.7 (65.5 km) **HJ 110.9** (178.5 km) U.S.–Canada border. Last milepost marker is Mile 40, first kilometrepost marker is Kilometrepost 74, northbound.

TIME ZONE CHANGE: Alaska observes Alaska time, Canada observes Pacific time.

BC HIGHWAY 4

H 40.8 (71.8 km) **HJ 110.8** (178.3 km) **Pleasant Camp Canada Customs and Immigration office**. All travelers entering Canada MUST STOP. Office is open daily year-round, 8 A.M. to midnight, Pacific time. Phone (907) 767-5540. No public facilities.

H 43.4 (76 km) **HJ 108.1** (174.1 km) Granite Creek bridge.

H 44.9 (78.5 km) **HJ 106.7** (171.7 km) Fivemile Creek bridge.

H 49.7 (87 km) **HJ 101.9** (164 km) Highway crosses Seltat Creek. This is eagle country; watch for them soaring over the uplands. Three Guardsmen Mountain (elev. 6,300 feet/1,920m) to the east.

H 53.9 (92 km) **HJ 97.7** (157.2 km) Three Guardsmen Lake to the east. Glave Peak, part of Three Guardsmen Mountain, rises directly behind the lake.

H 55.1 (94.6 km) **HJ 96.5** (155.3 km) Three Guardsmen Pass to the northeast, hidden by low hummocks along the road. Stonehouse Creek meanders through a pass at the base of Seltat Peak to join the Kelsall River about 6 miles/10 km to the east. To the north is the Kusawak Range; to the south is Three Guardsmen Mountain. The tall poles along the highway indicate the edge of the road for snowplows.

H 55.8 (95.8 km) **HJ 95.8** (154.2 km) Stonehouse Creek culvert.

H 56.2 (96.3 km) **HJ 95.4** (153.5 km) Clear Creek culvert.

H 59.8 (102.1 km) **HJ 91.8** (147.7 km) Double-ended paved turnout on west side of highway at **Chilkat Pass**, highest summit on this highway (elev. 3,493 feet/1,065m). White Pass Summit on Klondike Highway 2 is 3,290 feet/1,003m. The wind blows almost constantly on the summit and causes drifting snow and road closures in winter. The summit area is a favorite with snow machine and cross-country ski enthusiasts in winter. Snow until late May.

The Chilkat Pass was one of the few mountain passes offering access into the Yukon from the coast. The Chilkat and the Chilkoot passes were tenaciously guarded by Tlingit Indians. These southern Yukon Indians did not want their lucrative fur-trading business with the coastal Indians and Russians jeopardized by white strangers. But the gold rush of 1898, which brought thousands of white people inland, finally opened Chilkat Pass, forever altering the lifestyle of the Interior Natives.

From the Chilkat Pass over Glacier Flats to Stanley Creek, the highway crosses silt-laden streams flowing from the Crestline Glacier. Nadahini Mountain (elev. 6,809 feet/2,075m) to the northwest. Three Guardsmen Mountain to the southeast.

H 63 (107 km) **HJ 88.6** (142.6 km) Chuck Creek culvert.

H 64.4 (109.3 km) **HJ 87.2** (140.3 km) Nadahini River culvert.

H 67.8 (114.7 km) **HJ 83.8** (134.8 km) **Private Aircraft:** Mule Creek airstrip; elev. 2,900 feet/884m; length 4,000 feet/1,219m; gravel. No services.

H 68.9 (116.4 km) **HJ 82.7** (133 km) Mule Creek. **Historic Milepost 75.**

H 73.6 (124.2 km) **HJ 78** (125.5 km) Goat Creek bridge. Watch for horses on road.

H 75.7 (127.3 km) **HJ 75.9** (122.1 km) Holum Creek.

H 77.6 (130.5 km) **HJ 74** (119 km) Twin Lakes.

H 79.8 (134 km) **HJ 71.8** (115.5 km) Viewpoint to west for Tatshenshini–Alsek Wilderness Provincial Park. This park encompasses the northwest corner of British Columbia and is dominated by the St. Elias Mountains. It is also habitat for grizzly bears, Dall sheep, the rare "glacier" bear and also rare birds such as the king eider and Steller's eider. The Tatshenshini and Alsek rivers are famous for their river rafting opportunities.

H 80 (134.3 km) **HJ 71.6** (115.2 km) Mansfield Creek.

H 86.5 (144.3 km) **HJ 65.1** (104.8 km) Blanchard River bridge. The Blanchard River crosses the Yukon–BC boundary and joins the Tatshenshini River near Dalton Post. It was originally called the Kleheela River by local Native tribes. It was re-named in 1915 after G. Blanchard Dodge, DLS, who was in charge of survey parties which delineated much of the Yukon–BC boundary.

H 87.1 (144.5 km) **HJ 64.5** (103.8 km) Welcome to Kluane Country and Welcome to Yukon signs.

H 87.4 (145 km) **HJ 64.2** (103.3 km) Entering Kluane Game Sanctuary northbound.

H 87.5 (145.2 km) **HJ 64.1** (103.1 km) **BC–YT border**. Former U.S. Army Alaska–Blanchard River Petroleum pump station, now a highway maintenance camp.

YUKON HIGHWAY 3

H 96.2 (159.5 km) **HJ 55.4** (89.1 km) Turnoff for Yukon government **Million Dollar Falls Campground** on south side of Takhanne River bridge. Follow access road

0.7 mile/1.1 km west. Boardwalk trail and viewing platform of scenic falls. View of the St. Elias Mountains. Two kitchen shelters, tenting and group firepit, 33 campsites, camping permit ($8), playground and drinking water (boil water). Hiking trails in area. ▲

Good fishing below **Takhanne Falls** for grayling, Dolly Varden, rainbow and salmon. **Takhanne River**, excellent king salmon fishing in early July.

CAUTION: The Takhanne, Blanchard, Tatshenshini and Klukshu rivers are grizzly feeding areas. Exercise extreme caution when fishing or exploring in these areas.

H 96.4 (159.7 km) **HJ 55.2** (88.8 km) Parking area at Million Dollar Falls trailhead to west.

H 98.3 (162 km) **HJ 53.3** (85.8 km) Large paved photo viewpoint with view of Kluane Range; viewing platform, litter barrels, outhouse.

H 99.5 (164.5 km) **HJ 52.1** (83.8 km) Turnoff to historic **Dalton Post**, a way point on the Dalton Trail. Steep, narrow, winding access road; four-wheel drive recommended in wet weather. Road not recommended for large RVs or trailers at any time. Several old abandoned log cabins and buildings are located here. Indians once formed a human barricade at Dalton Post to harvest the Klukshu River's run of coho salmon. The river system here hosts seasonal runs of chinook, sockeye and coho salmon. Chinook are most visible in July, coho in late September and October, and sockeye from August to October. In fall, grizzly bears come here to feast on the fish.

Fishing for chinook, coho, sockeye salmon in **Village Creek**. Grayling, Dolly Varden and salmon in **Klukshu River**. Fishing restrictions posted. *CAUTION: Watch for bears.*

H 103.4 (169.7 km) **HJ 48.2** (77.5 km) Viewpoint with information sign to west. Alsek Range and Tatshenshini River to southwest.

H 104 (171 km) **HJ 47.6** (76.6 km) Motheral Creek.

H 105 (172 km) **HJ 46.6** (75 km) Klukshu wetland overlook to west; watch for trumpeter swans.

H 106.1 (174 km) **HJ 45.5** (73.2 km) Vand Creek.

H 107 (172 km) **HJ 45.5** (73.2 km) Vand Creek.

H 110.8 (181.6 km) **HJ 40.8** (65.6 km) Klukshu Creek. This area is frequented by grizzly bears.

H 111.6 (183 km) **HJ 40** (64.4 km) **Historic Milepost 118** at turnoff for **KLUKSHU**, an Indian village, located 0.5 mile/0.8 km off the highway via a gravel road. This summer fish camp and village on

the banks of the Klukshu River is a handful of log cabins, meat caches and traditional fish traps. Steelhead, king, sockeye and coho salmon are taken here. Each autumn, families return for the annual catch. The site is on the old Dalton Trail and offers good photo possibilities. Museum, picnic spot, souvenirs for sale. Information panels on First Nations heritage and traditional fishing techniques.

H 112.8 (185 km) **HJ 38.8** (62.4 km) Gribbles Gulch.

H 114 (187 km) **HJ 37.6** (60.5 km) Parking area at **St. Elias Lake trailhead** (4.5-mile/7.2-km round-trip). Novice and intermediate hiking trail winds through subalpine meadow. Watch for mountain goats.

H 117.8 (193 km) **HJ 33.8** (54.4 km) Dezadeash Lodge (closed in 1999, current status unknown). Historically, this spot was known as Beloud Post and is still noted as such on some maps. Mush Lake trail (13.4 miles/21.6 km long) begins behind lodge. It is an old mining road.

NOTE: Watch for horses on highway.

H 119.3 (195 km) **HJ 32.3** (52 km) Turnout along **Dezadeash Lake**, one of the earliest known features in the Yukon, which parallels the highway for 9 miles/14.5 km northbound, and Dezadeash mountain range. Dezadeash (pronounced DEZ-dee-ash) is said to be the Indian word describing their fishing method. In the spring, the Indians built small fires around the bases of large birch trees, peeled the heat-loosened bark and placed it, shiny white side up, on the bottom of the lake near shore, weighted with stones. From log wharfs built over the white bark, Indians waited with spears for lake trout to cross the light area. Another interpretation of Dezadeash relates that Chilkat Indians referred to it as *Dasar-ee-ASH*, meaning "Lake of the Big Winds." Entire tribes were annihilated during mid-19th century Indian wars here.

Dezadeash Lake offers good trolling, also fly-fishing along the shore where feeder streams flow into the lake. There are northern pike, lake trout and grayling in Dezadeash Lake. *CAUTION: This is a mountain lake and storms come up quickly.*

H 119.7 (195.7 km) **HJ 31.9** (51.3 km) Entrance to Yukon government **Dezadeash Lake Campground**, a very scenic spot on the lake; 20 campsites, camping permit ($8), kitchen shelter, picnic area, boat launch, no drinking water, pit toilets. ▲

H 123.9 (202.3 km) **HJ 27.7** (44.6 km) **Rock Glacier Trail** to west; short 0.5-mile/0.8-km self-guiding trail, partially boardwalk. Interesting walk, some steep sections. Parking area and viewpoint.

H 126.2 (206.9 km) **HJ 25.4** (40.8 km) Dalton Trail Lodge to east.

H 134.4 (219 km) **HJ 17.2** (27.6 km) The Cabin Bed and Breakfast.

H 134.8 (219.6 km) **HJ 16.8** (27 km) Access road leads west less than a mile to **Kathleen Lake Campground**, the only established campground within Kluane National Park; 42 campsites and a kitchen area; day-use area with picnic tables, restrooms; boat launch at lake; campfire programs by park staff. Fees charged for camping ($10). Campfire talks and backcountry registration. The 53-mile/85-km Cottonwood loop trail begins here. ▲

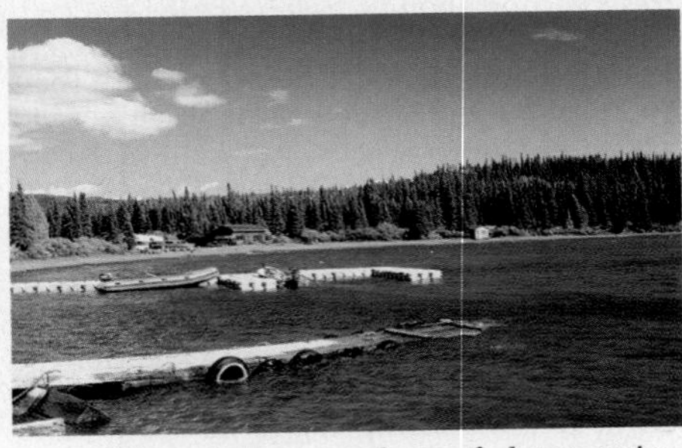

Kathleen Lake is a glacier-fed turquoise-blue lake, nearly 400 feet/122m deep. The lake offers fishing for lake trout averaging 10 lbs., use lures, June and July; kokanee averaging 2 lbs., June best; and grayling to 18 inches, use flies, June to September. **Kathleen River** rainbow to 17 inches, June to September; grayling to 18 inches, July and August; lake trout average 2 lbs., best in September. *NOTE: National parks fishing license required.*

H 135.2 (220.3 km) **HJ 16.4** (26.4 km) Kathleen Lake Lodge; food, gas and lodging.

NOTE: Last available gas southbound for next 102 miles. Check your gas tank.

H 135.8 (221 km) **HJ 15.8** (25.4 km) **Kathleen River bridge**; a popular spot for rainbow, lake trout and grayling fishing. Some kokanee. A turnout on the east side of the road provides access to Kathleen River. From here, you can canoe to Lower Kathleen Lake and Rainbow Lake. This is an easy half-day paddle, but do not attempt to go farther on Kathleen River, as there are many falls. Bird watching in this area includes harlequins, northern pintails, American wigeon, lesser yellowlegs, and spotted sandpipers.

H 139.2 (226.5 km) **HJ 12.4** (20 km) Turnout to west. Good view of Kathleen Lake. Information plaque on Kluane and Wrangell–St. Elias national parks. (World Heritage Site).

H 143.4 (233.5 km) **HJ 8.2** (13.2 km) Quill Creek. **Quill Creek trailhead**; 7-mile/11-km trail.

H 147.1 (239.1 km) **HJ 4.5** (7.2 km) Parking area to west at **Auriol trailhead** (9.3-mile/15-km loop trail); skiing and hiking.

H 148.8 (242 km) **HJ 2.8** (4.5 km) Rest stop to east with litter barrels and pit toilets. View of community of Haines Junction and Shakwak Valley.

H 151 (245 km) **HJ 0.6** (1 km) Dezadeash River Bridge. **Dezadeash River Trail** (2.2 miles/3.5 km); easy walk along river's edge. This river is part of the headwaters system of the Alsek River, which flows into the Pacific near Yakutat, AK.

H 151.6 (246 km) **HJ 0 HAINES JUNCTION** (see description on page 164); turn for Alaska, go straight for Whitehorse.

Junction of the Haines Highway (Yukon Highway 3) and Alaska Highway (Yukon Highway 1) at Haines Junction. Turn to **Milepost DC 985** on page 169 in the ALASKA HIGHWAY section for highway log. Whitehorse-bound travelers read log back to front, Alaska-bound travelers read log front to back.

Approximate driving distances from Haines Junction are: Whitehorse 100 miles/161 km; Tok 297 miles/475 km; Fairbanks 503 miles/805 km; and Anchorage 625 miles/1000 km.

KLONDIKE HIGHWAY 2

Connects: Skagway, AK, to Alaska Hwy., YT **Length:** 99 miles
Road Surface: Paved **Season:** Open all year
Highest Summit: White Pass 3,290 feet
Major Attraction: Klondike Gold Rush National Historical Park

(See map, page 700)

	Alaska Hwy. Jct.	Atlin	Carcross	Skagway	Whitehorse
Alaska Hwy. Jct.		125	33	99	10
Atlin	125		92	158	81
Carcross	33	92		66	43
Skagway	99	158	66		109
Whitehorse	10	81	43	109	

Klondike Highway 2 passes remnant of old Venus Mine. (© Earl L. Brown, staff)

The 98.8-mile-/159-km-long Klondike Highway 2 (also known as the Skagway–Carcross Road and South Klondike Highway) connects Skagway, AK, with the Alaska Highway at **Milepost 874.4** south of Whitehorse. The highway between Skagway and Carcross (referred to locally as the Skagway Road) was built in 1978 and formally dedicated on May 23, 1981. The highway connecting Carcross with the Alaska Highway (referred to locally as the Carcross Road) was built by the U.S. Army in late 1942 to lay the gas pipeline from Skagway to Whitehorse.

Klondike Highway 2 is a 2-lane, asphalt-surfaced road, open year-round. For the daily recorded road condition report, phone (867) 667-8215. The road has been improved in recent years and is fairly wide. There is a steep 11.5-mile/18.5-km grade between Skagway and White Pass.

IMPORTANT: If you plan to cross the border between midnight and 8 A.M., inquire locally regarding customs stations' hours of operation or phone (907) 983-3144.

Klondike Highway 2 is one of the two highways connecting ferry travelers with the Alaska Highway; the other is the Haines Highway out of Haines. Klondike Highway 2 offers some spectacular scenery and adds only about 55 miles/89 km to the trip for Alaska-bound motorists, as compared to the Haines Highway. (The distance from Haines to Tok, AK, is approximately 445 miles/716 km; the distance from Skagway to Tok is 500 miles/805 km.) Klondike Highway 2, like the Haines Highway, crosses from Alaska into British Columbia, then into Yukon Territory.

Klondike Highway 2 continues north of Whitehorse, turning off the Alaska Highway to Dawson City. See KLONDIKE LOOP section for log of Klondike Highway 2 between the Alaska Highway and Dawson City.

Emergency medical services: Between Skagway and Log Cabin at **Milepost S 27.3**, phone 911 or the Skagway Fire Department at (907) 983-2300. Between Log Cabin and Annie Lake Road at **Milepost S 87.5**, phone the RCMP at (403) 821-5555 or the Carcross Ambulance at (403) 821-4444. Between Annie Lake Road and the junction with the Alaska Highway, phone 911 for the Whitehorse ambulance.

Klondike Highway 2 Log

In the following highway log, Mileposts in Alaska and kilometreposts in Canada reflect distance from Skagway. The kilometre distance from Skagway in *The MILEPOST®* log reflects the location of the physical kilometreposts, and is not necessarily an accurate conversion of the mileage figure.
Distance from Skagway (S) is followed by distance from Alaska Highway (AH).

S 0 AH 98.8 (159 km) Ferry terminal in **SKAGWAY**. See description of Skagway beginning on page 687.

S 1.6 (2.6 km) **AH 97.2** (156.4 km) Skagway River bridge.

S 2.3 (3.7 km) **AH 96.5** (155.3 km) **Junction** with Dyea Road. This narrow, winding gravel side road leads 7.4 miles southwest from the highway to the old **Dyea Townsite** and **Slide Cemetery**. During the Klondike Gold Rush, some 8,000 people lived at Dyea. The cemetery contains the graves of men killed in the Palm Sunday avalanche (April 3, 1898) on the Chilkoot Trail. See log of Dyea Road on page 694.

S 2.6 (4.2 km) **AH 96.2** (154.8 km) Highway maintenance camp.

S 2.8 (4.5 km) **AH 96** (154.5 km) Plaque to east honoring men and women of the Klondike Gold Rush, and access to parklike area along Skagway River.

S 2.9 (4.7 km) **AH 95.9** (154.3 km) Access road east to Skagway River. Highway begins steep 11.5-mile/18.5-km ascent northbound from sea level to 3,290 feet/1,003m at White Pass.

S 4.7 (7.6 km) **AH 94.1** (151.4 km) Turnout to west.

S 5 (8 km) **AH 93.8** (151 km) Turnout to east with view across canyon of White Pass & Yukon Route railway tracks and bridge. The narrow-gauge WP&YR railway was completed in 1900.

S 5.5 (8.8 km) **AH 93.3** (150.1 km) Turnout to west with historical information signs.

S 6 (9.6 km) **AH 92.8** (149.3 km) Turnout to east.

S 6.8 (10.9 km) **AH 92** (148 km) **U.S. Customs station**; open 24 hours in summer (manned 8 A.M. to midnight, video camera reporting midnight to 8 A.M.). Phone (907) 983-3144 for border crossing (immigration); phone (907) 983-2325 for customs in Skagway. All travelers entering the United States must stop. Have identification ready. Residents of North America must present birth certificate, driver's license or voter registration. All other foreign visitors must have a passport. ID is also required for children.

S 7.4 (11.9 km) **AH 91.4** (147.1 km) View to east of WP&YR railway line.

KLONDIKE HIGHWAY 2 *Skagway, AK, to Junction with Alaska Highway (includes Tagish and Atlin Roads)*

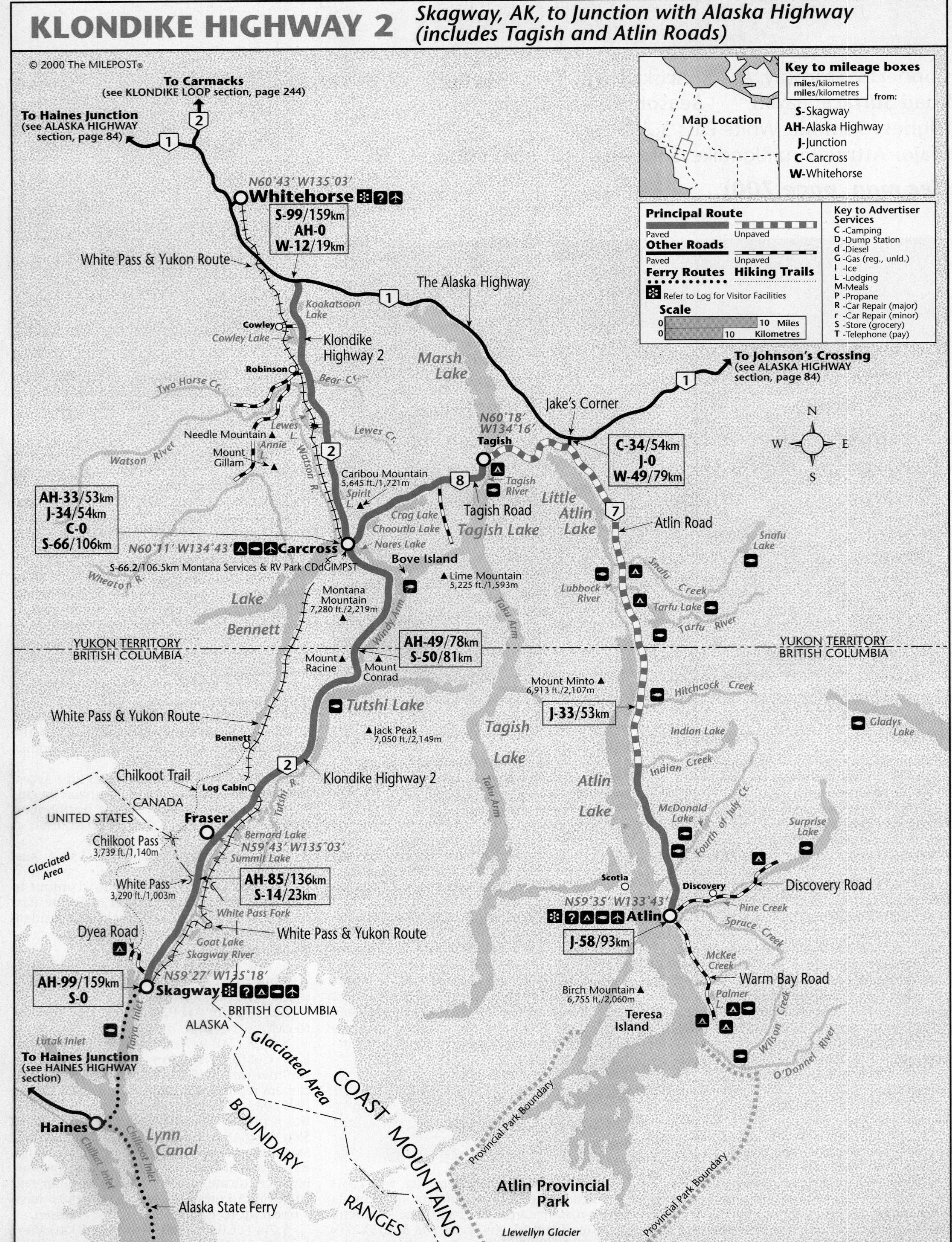
© 2000 The MILEPOST®
To Carmacks (see KLONDIKE LOOP section, page 244)
To Haines Junction (see ALASKA HIGHWAY section, page 84)
N60°43′ W135°03′
Whitehorse
S-99/159km
AH-0
W-12/19km
White Pass & Yukon Route
The Alaska Highway
Kookatsoon Lake
Cowley
Cowley Lake
Klondike Highway 2
Marsh Lake
Robinson
Bear Cr.
Two Horse Cr.
To Johnson's Crossing (see ALASKA HIGHWAY section, page 84)
Jake's Corner
N60°18′ W134°16′
Tagish
C-34/54km
J-0
W-49/79km
Needle Mountain
Lewes L.
Annie L.
Lewes Cr.
Watson River
Mount Gillam
Watson R.
Caribou Mountain 5,645 ft./1,721m
Spirit L.
Tagish River
Tagish Road
Little Atlin Lake
Atlin Road
AH-33/53km
J-34/54km
C-0
S-66/106km
Crag Lake
Chooutla Lake
Tagish Lake
Nares Lake
N60°11′ W134°43′
Carcross
Snafu Lake
Bove Island
S-66.2/106.5km Montana Services & RV Park CDdGIMPST
Lime Mountain 5,225 ft./1,593m
Snafu Creek
Wheaton R.
Montana Mountain 7,280 ft./2,219m
Lubbock River
Lake Bennett
Windy Arm
Taku Arm
Tarfu Lake
Tarfu River
AH-49/78km
S-50/81km
YUKON TERRITORY
BRITISH COLUMBIA
Mount Racine
Mount Conrad
Mount Minto 6,913 ft./2,107m
Hitchcock Creek
Tutshi Lake
J-33/53km
White Pass & Yukon Route
Jack Peak 7,050 ft./2,149m
Tagish Lake
Indian Lake
Gladys Lake
Bennett
Indian Creek
Chilkoot Trail
Log Cabin
Klondike Highway 2
Atlin Lake
CANADA
UNITED STATES
Fraser
Tutshi R.
McDonald Lake
Fourth of July Cr.
Surprise Lake
Bernard Lake
N59°43′ W135°03′
Chilkoot Pass 3,739 ft./1,140m
Summit Lake
Glaciated Area
White Pass 3,290 ft./1,003m
AH-85/136km
S-14/23km
Scotia
Discovery
Discovery Road
N59°35′ W133°43′
Atlin
Pine Creek
White Pass Fork
Dyea Road
White Pass & Yukon Route
Spruce Creek
J-58/93km
Goat Lake
Skagway River
McKee Creek
Warm Bay Road
N59°27′ W135°18′
AH-99/159km
S-0
Skagway
Birch Mountain 6,755 ft./2,060m
Palmer L.
BRITISH COLUMBIA
ALASKA
Teresa Island
Glaciated Area
Wilson Creek
Lutak Inlet
Taiya Inlet
O'Donnel River
To Haines Junction (see HAINES HIGHWAY section)
COAST MOUNTAINS
Haines
Lynn Canal
Chilkoot Inlet
Chilkat Inlet
BOUNDARY RANGES
Provincial Park Boundary
Provincial Park Boundary
Atlin Provincial Park
Alaska State Ferry
Llewellyn Glacier
Map Location
Key to mileage boxes
miles/kilometres
miles/kilometres
from:
S-Skagway
AH-Alaska Highway
J-Junction
C-Carcross
W-Whitehorse
Principal Route
Paved
Unpaved
Other Roads
Paved
Unpaved
Ferry Routes
Hiking Trails
Refer to Log for Visitor Facilities
Scale
0 10 Miles
0 10 Kilometres
Key to Advertiser Services
C -Camping
D -Dump Station
d -Diesel
G -Gas (reg., unld.)
I -Ice
L -Lodging
M -Meals
P -Propane
R -Car Repair (major)
r -Car Repair (minor)
S -Store (grocery)
T -Telephone (pay)
N
E
S
W

S 7.7 (12.4 km) **AH 91.1** (146.6 km) Good photo stop for **Pitchfork Falls**, visible across the canyon.

S 8.1 (13 km) **AH 90.7** (146 km) Turnout to east.

S 9.1 (14.6 km) **AH 89.7** (144.4 km) Paved turnout to east with historical interest signs about the Klondike Gold Rush trail. Viewpoint looks across the gorge to the WP&YR railway tracks.

S 9.9 (15.9 km) **AH 88.9** (143.1 km) Truck runout ramp to west for large transport units that may lose air brakes on steep descent southbound.

S 11.1 (17.9 km) **AH 87.7** (141.1 km) **Captain William Moore Bridge**. This unique cantilever bridge over Moore Creek spans a 110-foot-/34-m-wide gorge. Just north of the bridge to the west is a large waterfall. The bridge is named for Capt. Billy Moore, a riverboat captain and pilot, prospector, packer and trader, who played an important role in settling the town of Skagway. Moore helped pioneer this route over White Pass into the Yukon and was among the first to realize the potential of a railroad across the pass.

S 11.6 (18.7 km) **AH 87.2** (140.3 km) Large paved turnouts to east with view of Skagway River gorge, Captain William Moore Bridge and waterfalls, next 0.1 mile/0.2 km northbound.

S 12 (19.3 km) **AH 86.8** (139.7 km) Truck runout ramp to west.

S 12.6 (20.3 km) **AH 86.2** (138.7 km) Posts on east side of road mark highway shoulders and guide rails for snowplows.

S 14.4 (23.2 km) **AH 84.4** (135.8 km) **White Pass Summit** (elev. 3,292 feet/1,003m). Turnout to west.

CAUTION: Southbound traffic begins steep 11.5-mile/18.5-km descent to Skagway.

Many stampeders on their way to the Klondike goldfields in 1898 chose the White Pass route because it was lower in elevation than the famous Chilkoot Pass trail, and the grade was not as steep. But the White Pass route was longer and the final ascent to the summit treacherous. Dead Horse Gulch (visible from the railway line) was named for the thousands of pack animals that died on this route during the gold rush.

Thousands of gold seekers poured into Canada over the Chilkoot and White Passes on their way to Dawson City. An initial contingent of North West Mounted Police, led by Inspector Charles Constantine, had come over the Chilkoot Pass in 1894—well before the gold rush—to establish law among the miners at Dawson City. But in 1898, the Canadian government sent reinforcements, led by Superintendent Samuel Steele.

Upon his arrival at the foot of Chilkoot Pass in February of 1898, Steele found thousands of men waiting to pack their supplies over the pass. He immediately stationed permanent detachments at the summits of Chilkoot and White passes, both to maintain law and order and to assert Canadian sovereignty at these 2 international borders

After witnessing the desperate condition of many men arriving in the Klondike, Steele was also responsible for setting a minimumum requirement of a year's supply of food and equipment for any miner entering Canada, which translated roughly into "one ton of goods."

S 14.5 (23.3 km) **AH 84.3** (135.7 km) Paved turnout to west.

S 14.9 (24 km) **AH 84** (135.2 km) **U.S.–Canada (AK–BC) border.** Turnout to west. Monument to east.

TIME ZONE CHANGE: Alaska observes Alaska time; British Columbia and Yukon Territory observe Pacific time.

S 16.2 (26.1 km) **AH 82.6** (133 km) Highway winds through rocky valley of Summit Lake (visible to east). Several small gravel turnouts next 6 miles/9.6 km northbound.

S 18.1 (29.1 km) **AH 80.7** (129.9 km) Summit Creek bridge.

S 18.4 (29.6 km) **AH 80.4** (129.4 km) Summit Lake to east.

S 19.3 (31.1 km) **AH 79.5** (128 km) North end of Summit Lake.

S 21.4 (34.4 km) **AH 77.4** (124.5 km) Creek and railroad bridge to east. Railroad parallels highway next 6 miles.

S 22.5 (36.2 km) **AH 76.3** (122.8 km) **Canada Customs** at **FRASER** (elev. 2,400 feet/732m). Open daily, 24 hours in summer. Phone (867) 667-3943 or 3944 for winter hours. Pay phone. All travelers entering Canada must stop. *Reminder: Have proper ID for all travellers, including children.*

Old railroad water tower to east, highway maintenance camp to west.

S 22.6 (36.4 km) **AH 76.2** (122.7 km) Beautiful deep-green Bernard Lake to east.

S 22.8 (36.7 km) **AH 76** (122.3 km) Large double-ended turnout with 2 interpretive panels on area attractions and the WP&YR.

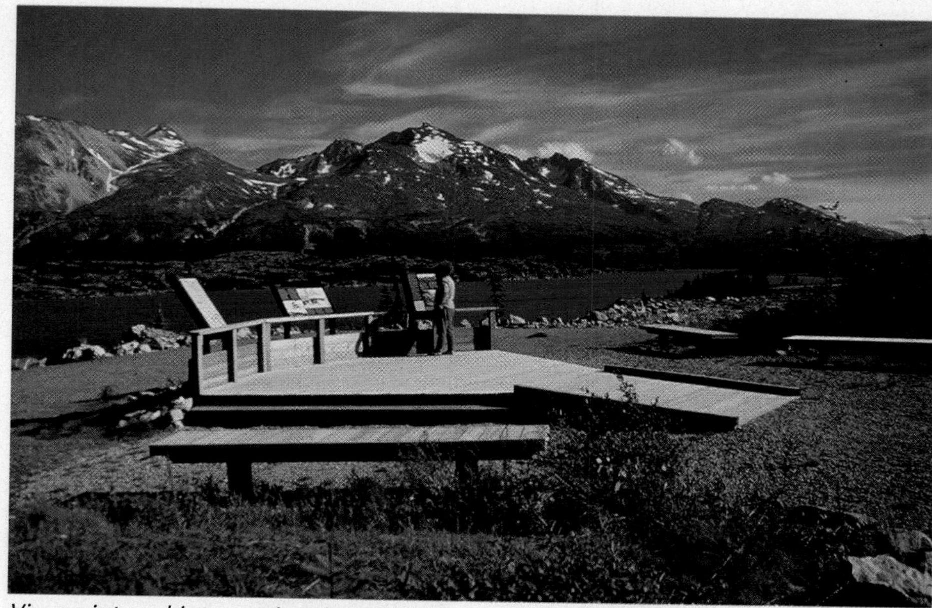

Viewpoint and interpretive signs at Milepost S 22.8 Klondike Highway 2.
(© Earl L. Brown, staff)

S 24.2 (38.9 km) **AH 74.6** (120.1 km) Turnout to east.

S 25.1 (40.4 km) **AH 73.7** (118.6 km) Shallow Lake to east.

S 25.5 (41 km) **AH 73.3** (118 km) Old cabins and buildings to east.

S 26.6 (42.8 km) **AH 72.2** (116.2 km) Turnout to east. Beautiful view of Tormented Valley, a rocky desolate "moonscape" of stunted trees and small lakes east of the highway.

S 27.3 (43.9 km) **AH 71.5** (115 km) Highway crosses tracks of the White Pass & Yukon Route at **LOG CABIN**; Chilkoot Trail Naitonal Historic Site. With completion of the railway in 1900, the North West Mounted Police moved their customs checkpoint from the summit to Log Cabin. There is nothing here today.

There are numerous turnouts along the highway between here and Carcross. Turnouts may be designated for either commercial ore trucks or passenger vehicles.

S 30.7 (49.4 km) **AH 68.1** (109.6 km) Tutshi (too-shy) River visible to east.

S 31.1 (50 km) **AH 67.7** (108.9 km) Highway parallels **Tutshi Lake** for several miles northbound. Excellent fishing for lake trout and grayling early in season. Be sure you have a British Columbia fishing license.

S 40.1 (64.5 km) **AH 58.7** (94.5 km) Short, narrow gravel access road to picnic area with pit toilet on Tutshi Lake. Large vehicles check turnaround space before driving in.

S 40.7 (65.5 km) **AH 58.1** (93.5 km) Good views of Tutshi Lake along here.

S 43.7 (70.5 km) **AH 55.1** (88.7 km) Turnout to east with view of Tutshi Lake.

S 46.4 (75.1 km) **AH 52.4** (84.3 km) To the east is the **Venus Mines concentrator**, with a capacity of 150 tons per day. A drop in silver prices caused the Venus mill's closure in October 1981.

S 48.5 (78.1 km) **AH 50.3** (81 km) South end of Windy Arm, an extension of Tagish Lake.

S 49.2 (79.2 km) **AH 49.6** (79.9 km) Viewpoint to east.

S 49.9 (80.5 km) **AH 48.9** (78.7 km) Dall Creek.

S 50.2 (81 km) **AH 48.6** (78.2 km) **BC–YT border.** Turnout with picnic table and litter barrel to east overlooking Windy Arm.

Yukon Resources wildlife viewing guide suggests searching the slopes of Montana

Mountain to the northwest and Racine Mountain to the southwest for signs of mountain goats and Dall sheep in the summer.

S 51.9 (83.5 km) **AH 46.9** (75.5 km) Large turnout to east with litter barrel, picnic table and historical information sign about Venus Mines.

The first claim on Montana Mountain was staked by W.R. Young in 1899. By 1904 all of the mountain's gold veins had been claimed. In 1905, New York financier Col. Joseph H. Conrad acquired most of the Montana Mountain claims, formed Conrad Consolidated Mines, and began exploration and mining. A town of about 300 people sprang up along Windy Arm and an aerial tramway was built from the Conrad townsite up the side of Montana Mountain to the Mountain Hero adit. (This tramline, visible from the highway, was completed in 1906 but was never used to ship ore because the Mountain Hero tunnel did not find a vein.) More tramways and a mill were constructed, but by 1911 Conrad was forced into bankruptcy: The ore was not as rich as estimated and only a small quantity of ore was milled before operations ceased.

Small mining operations continued over the years, with unsuccessful startups by various mining interests. United Keno Hill Mines (Venus Division) acquired the mining claims in 1979, constructed a 100-ton-per-day mill and rehabilitated the old mine workings in 1980.

S 52.9 (85.1 km) **AH 45.9** (73.8 km) Pooly Creek and canyon, named for J.M. Pooly, who staked the first Venus claims in 1901.

Access road east to Pooly Point and Venus Mines maintenance garage, trailers and security station. No services, facilities or admittance.

S 54.2 (87.2 km) **AH 44.6** (71.8 km) Venus Mines ore storage bin and foundation of old mill to east. The mill was built in the late 1960s, then disassembled and sold about 1970. A sign here warns of arsenic being present: Do not pick or eat berries.

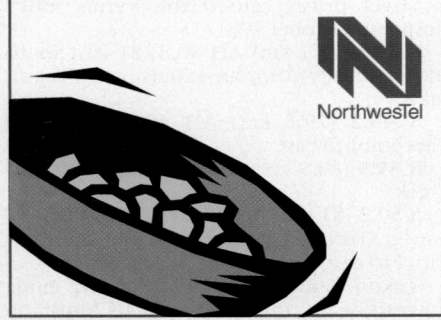

Downtown Carcross, YT. *(© Ralph & Leonor Barrett, Four Corners Imaging)*

S 55.7 (89.6 km) **AH 43.1** (69.4 km) Tramline support just east of highway.

S 59.5 (95.8 km) **AH 39.3** (63.3 km) Turnout with historic information sign. Lt. F. Schwatka, US Army, renamed Tagish Lake in 1883 after Lt. Bove of the Italian navy, who had served with the Austro-Hungarian Expedition of 1872-74. Dr. G.M. Dawson, GSC, gave Tagish Lake its original name in 1887 and left Bove's name on the island. Magnificent views along here of Windy Arm and its islands (Bove is the larger island). Windy Arm is an extension of Tagish Lake. Lime Mountain (elev. 5,225 feet/1,593m) rises to the east beyond Bove Island.

S 63.5 (102.2 km) **AH 35.3** (56.8 km) Sections of the old government wagon roads that once linked Carcross, Conrad and other mining claims, visible on either side of the highway.

S 65.3 (105.1 km) **AH 33.5** (53.9 km) Private road west to homes, Carcross Tagish First Nation's Band office.

S 65.8 (104.3 km) **AH 33** (53.6 km) Small Native-operated convenience store.

S 65.9 (106 km) **AH 32.9** (52.9 km) Access road west to Montana Mountain.

S 66 (106.2 km) **AH 32.8** (52.7 km) Nares Bridge crosses the narrows between Lake Bennett to the west and Tagish Lake to the east. The larger lakes freeze to an ice depth of more than 3 feet/1m.

Nares Lake, on the east side of the highway at Carcross, remains open most winters, despite air temperatures that drop well below -40°F/-40°C. In spring and fall look for swans, teal, pintail, goldeneye and wigeon. This is one of the few areas in the Yukon that waterfowl may be seen in winter.

Caribou Mountain (elev. 5,645 feet/1,721m) is visible to the east.

S 66.2 (106.5 km) **AH 32.6** (52.4 km) Turnoff west for Carcross (description follows).

Carcross

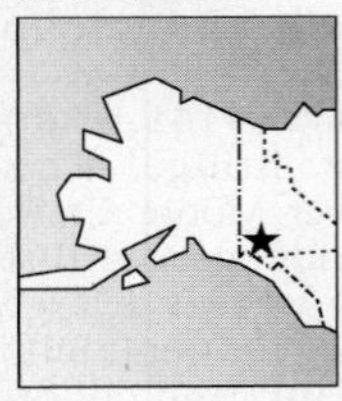

On the shore of Lake Bennett, 44 miles/71 km southeast of Whitehorse. **Population:** 431. **Emergency Services: RCMP,** phone (867) 821-5555. **Fire Department,** phone (867) 821-2222. **Ambulance,** phone (867) 821-4444. **Health Centre,** phone (867) 821-4444.

Visitor Information: Carcross Visitor Reception Centre, operated by Tourism Yukon, is located in the old White Pass & Yukon Route train station. Lifeboat display. The centre operates daily from 8 A.M. to 8 P.M., mid-May to mid-September; phone (867) 821-4431. Ferry schedules, maps and information on Yukon, British Columbia and Alaska available.

Elevation: 2,175 feet/663m. **Climate:** Average temperature in January, -4.2°F/-20.1°C; in July, 55.4°F/13°C. Annual rainfall 11 inches, snowfall 2 to 3 feet. Driest month is April, wettest month August. **Radio:** 590-AM, CHON-FM 90.5, CKRW. **Television:** CBC. **Transportation: Bus**—Scheduled bus service by Atlin Express Service, between Atlin and Whitehorse via Tagish and Carcross, 3 times weekly. Chilkoot Trail hikers should check with visitor centre for boat and bus connections.

Private Aircraft: Carcross airstrip, 0.3 mile/0.5 km north of town via highway; elev. 2,161 feet/659m; length 2,000 feet/610m.

Carcross has a general store and a gift shop. Camping at Montana Services RV Park and Carcross government campground. Gas station with gifts, groceries, laundromat, showers, RV park and cafe located on the highway by the airstrip. ▲

Carcross was formerly known as Caribou Crossing because of the large numbers of caribou that traversed the narrows here between Bennett and Nares lakes. In 1903 Bishop Bompas, who had established a school here for Native children in 1901, petitioned the government to change the name of the community to Carcross because of confusion in mail services due to duplicate names in Alaska, British Columbia and the Klondike. The post office made the change official the following year, but it took the WP&YR until 1916 to change the name of its station.

Carcross became a stopping place for gold stampeders on their way to the Klondike goldfields. It was a major stop on the White Pass & Yukon Route railroad from 1900 until 1982, when the railroad ceased operation. Passengers and freight transferred from rail to stern-wheelers at Carcross. One of these stern-wheelers, the SS *Tutshi* (too-shy), was a historic site here in town until it burned down in July 1990.

A cairn beside the railroad station marks the site where construction crews laying track for the White Pass & Yukon Route from Skagway met the crew from Whitehorse. The golden spike was set in place when the last rail was laid at Carcross on July 29, 1900. The construction project had begun May 27, 1898, during the height of the Klondike Gold Rush.

Other visitor attractions include St. Saviour's Anglican Church, built in 1902; the Royal Mail Carriage; and the little locomotive *Duchess,* which once hauled coal on Vancouver Island. Frontierland, 2 miles/3.2 km north of town on the highway, is also a popular attraction. Ask at the Visitor Reception Centre for the brochure "101 Great Things to Do in the Carcross Tagish Loop."

On sunny days you may sunbathe and picnic at Sandy Beach on Lake Bennett. Or swim at Carcross Pool; for information call (867) 821-3211. Isabelle Pringle Public Library presents programs and displays; phone (867) 821-3801.

Behind the post office there is a foot-bridge across Natasaheenie River. This small body of water joins Lake Bennett and Nares Lake. Check locally for boat tours and boat service on Bennett Lake. Fishing in **Lake Bennett** for lake trout, northern pike, arctic grayling, whitefish and cisco.

Montana Services & RV Park. See display ad this section. ▲

Emerald Lake at Milepost S 73.5 is a favorite photo subject. (© Earl L. Brown, staff)

Klondike Highway 2 Log

(continued)

S 66.4 (106.9 km) **AH 32.4** (52.1 km) Airstrip to east. Turn on access road directly north of airstrip for Yukon government **Carcross Campground**; 12 campsites, picnic tables, firewood, drinking water, outhouses, camping permit ($8). ▲

S 66.5 (107 km) **AH 32.3** (52 km)

Junction with Yukon Highway 8, which leads east to Tagish, Atlin Road and the Alaska Highway at Jake's Corner (see TAGISH ROAD section).

Turn east here for alternate access to Alaska Highway and for Yukon government campground on Tagish Road.

S 67.3 (108.3 km) **AH 31.5** (50.7 km) Turnout with point of interest sign about **Carcross Desert**. This unusual desert area of sand dunes, east of the highway between Kilometreposts 108 and 110, is the world's smallest desert and an International Biophysical Programme site for ecological studies. The desert is composed of sandy lake-bottom material left behind by a large glacial lake. Strong winds off Lake Bennett make it difficult for vegetation to take hold here; only lodgepole pine, spruce and kinnikinnick survive. (Kinnikinnick is a low trailing evergreen with small leathery leaves; used for tea.)

S 67.9 (108.6 km) **AH 30.9** (49.7 km) Frontierland (formerly the Museum of Yukon Natural History). Displays include a saber-toothed tiger and the world's largest mounted bear—a polar bear.

S 70.3 (112.3 km) **AH 28.5** (45.9 km) Dry Creek.

S 71.2 (113.8 km) **AH 27.6** (44.4 km) Carl's Creek.

S 71.9 (115.7 km) **AH 26.9** (43.3 km) Cinnamon Cache Bakery Coffee Shop.

S 72.1 (115 km) **AH 26.7** (43 km) Spirit Lake Wilderness Resort east side of road with food, gas, propane, repairs, lodging, camping and ice cream. ▲

S 73.2 (116.8 km) **AH 25.6** (41.2 km) Spirit Lake is visible to the east.

S 73.5 (117.3 km) **AH 25.3** (40.7 km) Large turnout with point of interest sign to west overlooking beautiful **Emerald Lake**, also called **Rainbow Lake** by Yukoners. (Good view of lake by climbing the hill across from the turnout.) The rainbowlike colors of the lake result from blue-green light waves reflecting off the white sediment of the lake bottom. This white sediment, called marl, consists of fragments of decomposed shell mixed with clay; it is usually found in shallow, freshwater lakes that have low oxygen levels during the summer months.

S 75.4 (120.3 km) **AH 23.4** (37.7 km) Highway follows base of Caribou Mountain (elev. 5,645 feet/1,721m). View of Montana Mountain to south, Caribou Mountain to east and Gray Ridge Range to the west between Kilometreposts 122 and 128. Flora consists of jack and lodgepole pine.

S 79.8 (127.1 km) **AH 19** (30.6 km) Highway crosses Lewes Creek.

S 85.4 (136.3 km) **AH 13.4** (21.6 km) Access road west leads 1 mile/1.6 km to Lewes Lake.

S 85.6 (136.5 km) **AH 13.2** (21.2 km) Rat Lake to west.

S 86.7 (138.2 km) **AH 12.1** (19.4 km) Bear Creek.

S 87 (140 km) **AH 11.8** (19 km) Access to bed and breakfast and Bear Creek Dog Sled Kennels.

S 87.3 (139.1 km) **AH 11.5** (18.5 km) Access road west to large gravel pull-through with historic information sign about Robinson and view of Robinson. In 1899, the White Pass & Yukon Route built a railroad siding at Robinson (named for Stikine Bill Robinson). Gold was discovered nearby in the early 1900s and a townsite was surveyed. A few buildings were constructed and a post office, manned by Charlie McConnell, operated from 1909 to 1915. Low mineral yields caused Robinson to be abandoned, but postmaster McConnell stayed and established one of the first ranches in the Yukon. Robinson is accessible from Annie Lake Road (see next milepost).

S 87.5 (139.4 km) **AH 11.3** (18.2 km) **Annie Lake Road** leads 0.8 mile/1.4 km to Annie Lake golf course (18 holes, wilderness setting), 1.9 miles/3.1 km to McConnell Lake and 11 miles/17.7 km to Annie Lake.

Yukon Resources wildlife viewing guide suggests a side trip on Annie Lake Road. Look for Dall sheep on cliffs on west side of road. There are many hiking routes along old mining roads into the interior of the coastal mountains. Birdwatching for gyrfalcons, golden eagles and ptarmigan (willow, rock and white-tailed). The Southern Lakes caribou herd resides here year-round; found in alpine terrain in summer.

Beyond Annie Lake this side road crosses the Wheaton River, entering the Wheaton Valley–Mount Skukum area. For the adventuresome, this is beautiful and interesting country. There are no facilities along Annie Lake Road. *CAUTION: Road can be very muddy during spring breakup or during rain.*

S 93 (148.5 km) **AH 5.8** (9.4 km) Turnoff west for Cowley and for access to Cowley Lake (1.6 miles/2.6 km).

S 95.5 (154.2 km) **AH 3.3** (5.3 km) Turnoff to east for Yukon government **Kookatsoon Lake Recreation Site** (day use only); picnic tables, firepits, pit toilets, canoe launch. Kookatsoon Lake is shallow and usually warm enough for swimming in summer. Look for Bonaparte's gulls and arctic terns nesting at the south end of the lake.

S 98.4 (156.5 km) **AH 0.4** (0.7 km) Rock shop on east side of road.

S 98.8 (157.1 km) **AH 0** Turn left (north) for Whitehorse, right (south) for Watson Lake.

Junction with the Alaska Highway. Turn to **Milepost DC 874.4** on page 141 in the ALASKA HIGHWAY section: Whitehorse-bound travelers continue with that log; travelers heading south down the Alaska Highway read that log back to front.

ATLIN ROAD

Connects: Tagish Road Jct. to Atlin, BC
Road Surface: 60% gravel, 40% paved
Major Attraction: Atlin Lake
Length: 58 miles
Season: Open all year

(See map, page 700)

	Atlin	Carcross	Jake's Corner	Skagway	Whitehorse
Atlin		92	59	158	106
Carcross	92		35	66	43
Jake's Corner	59	35		101	47
Skagway	158	66	101		109
Whitehorse	106	43	47	109	

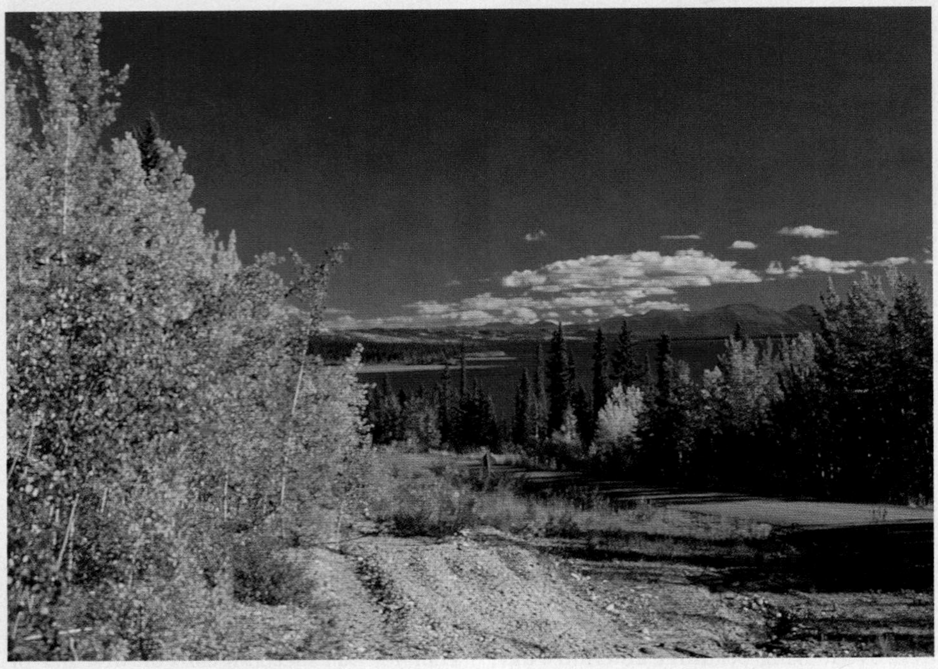

Fall colours make for a beautiful drive along Atlin Road. *(© Earl L. Brown, staff)*

This 58-mile/93.3-km all-weather road leads south to the pioneer gold mining town of Atlin. Built in 1949 by the Canadian Army Engineers, Atlin Road is a good road, usually in excellent condition, with some winding sections. The first 40 miles/64.4 km are gravel, with the remaining 18 miles/29 km into Atlin paved. Watch for slippery spots in wet weather.

To reach Atlin Road, turn south at Jake's Corner, **Milepost DC 836.8** on the Alaska Highway; drive 1.1 miles/1.8 km to the junction of Atlin Road (Highway 7) and Tagish Road (Highway 8); turn left (south) for Atlin.

It is about a 2½-hour drive to Atlin from Whitehorse, and the lake scenery from the village is well worth the trip. For more information contact the Atlin Visitors Assoc., Box 365-M, Atlin, BC V0W 1A0. Or phone the Atlin museum at (250) 651-7522 for visitor information.

Atlin Road Log

Distance from Tagish Road junction (J) is shown.
Physical kilometreposts in Yukon Territory and mileposts in British Columbia show distance from Tagish Road junction.

J 0 Junction of Tagish and Atlin roads.

J 1.4 (2.3 km) Fish Creek crossing. The road is bordered by many low-lying, boggy areas brilliant green with horsetail *(equisetium).*

J 1.8 (2.9 km) Side road west to Little Atlin Lake. Atlin Road descends along east shoreline of Little Atlin Lake approximately 7.6 miles/12.2 km southbound. During midsummer, the roadsides are ablaze with fireweed and wild roses.

J 2.4 (3.9 km) Large turnout to west on Little Atlin Lake; informal boat launch, dumpster, outhouse and camping area. Mount Minto (elev. 6,913 feet/2,107m) can be seen to the southwest. Road climbs southbound.

J 2.8 (4.5 km) Turnout to west. Watch for bald eagles.

J 5 (8 km) Information sign to east about 1983–84 mountain goat transplant. The 12 goats were brought from Kluane National Park. They may be observed on the mountainsides.

J 7.8 (12.6 km) Private campground, cabins and boat rentals. ▲

J 8.1 (13 km) Greenhouse and farm, roadside vegetable stand in season. Haunka Creek. Turnout to west.

J 8.9 (14.3 km) Good view of Mount Minto ahead southbound.

J 13.8 (22.2 km) Unmarked side road leads 2.4 miles/3.9 km to **Lubbock River**, which connects Little Atlin Lake with Atlin Lake. Excellent for grayling from breakup to mid-September.

J 15.5 (24.9 km) Snafu Creek. Turnout to west, north of bridge. According to R. Coutts, author of "Yukon Places & Names," the creek name is an acronym bestowed by army crews who built the road. It stands for Situation Normal—All Fouled Up. (Mr. Coutts resides in Atlin.)

J 16.4 (26 km) Access road leads 0.7 mile/1.1 km to **Snafu Lake** Yukon government campground; 4 sites, camping permit ($8), pit toilets, tables, gravel boat ramp, good fishing. ▲

J 18.6 (29.9 km) Tarfu Creek. Small turnout to east, north of bridge. Creek name is another army acronym. This one stands for Things Are Really Fouled Up.

J 18.7 (30 km) Abandoned cabin and turnout to west.

J 20.4 (32.8 km) Turnoff to east for **Tarfu Lake** Yukon government campground via 2.4-mile/3.8-km side road; 6 sites, camping permit ($8), pit toilets, fishing. Steep grade near campground; not recommended for large RVs or trailers. ▲

J 20.5 (33 km) Short narrow side road leads east to Marcella Lake; good lake for canoeing.

J 21.8 (35.1 km) Turnout to west with view of Atlin Lake, which covers 307 square miles/798 square km and is the largest natural lake in British Columbia. Coast Mountains to the southwest.

J 25.8 (41.5 km) BC–YT border. Road follows east shoreline of Atlin Lake into Atlin.

J 27 (43.5 km) Mount Minto to west, Black Mountain to east, and Halcro Peak (elev. 5,856 feet/1,785m) to the southeast.

J 28.5 (45.8 km) Slow down for sharp curve.

J 32 (51.5 km) Excellent views of Coast Mountains, southwest across Atlin Lake, next 6 miles/9.7 km southbound.

J 32.7 (52.6 km) **Hitchcock Creek**, grayling to 2 lbs.

J 32.8 (52.7 km) Campground on Atlin Lake; 6 sites, pit toilets, tables, ramp for small boats. ▲

J 36.3 (58.4 km) Turnout with litter barrel to west. Base Camp Creek.

J 36.8 (59.2 km) **Historic Milepost 38.**

J 40 (64.4 km) Indian River. Pull-through turnout south of creek. Highway is paved from here to Atlin.

J 40.2 (64.7 km) Big-game outfitter/guest ranch to east. Watch for horses.

J 45.3 (72.9 km) Turnout to west.

J 49.8 (80.1 km) Burnt Creek.

J 49.9 (80.3 km) Davie Hall Lake and

turnout to west. Waterfowl are plentiful on lake.

J 51.6 (83 km) Ruffner Mine Road leads east 40 miles/64.4 km. Access to **MacDonald Lake**, 2 miles/3.2 km east; bird watching and lake trout fishing from spit.

J 52.8 (85 km) Fourth of July Creek.

J 53.4 (85.9 km) Spruce Mountain (elev. 5,141 feet/1,567m) to west.

J 55.1 (88.7 km) Road skirts east shore of Como Lake next 0.6 mile/1 km southbound.

J 55.2 (88.8 km) Turnout with litter barrel to west on **Como Lake**; good lake for canoeing, also used by floatplanes. Stocked with rainbow.

J 55.7 (89.6 km) South end of Como Lake; boat ramp.

J 57.1 (91.9 km) Atlin city limits.

J 58 (93.3 km) **Junction** of Atlin Road with Discovery Road. Turn right (west) on Discovery Avenue for town of Atlin; description follows. Turn left (east) for Discovery Road and Warm Bay Road (see description of these side roads in Atlin Attractions).

Atlin

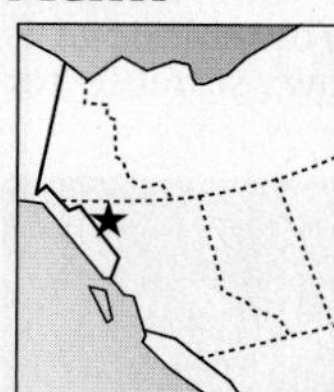

The most northwesterly town in British Columbia, located about 112 miles/180 km southeast of Whitehorse, YT. **Population**: 500. **Emergency Services: Police**, phone (250) 651-7511. **Fire Department**, phone (250) 651-7666. **Ambulance**, phone (250) 651-7700. Red Cross outpost clinic, phone (250) 651-7677.

Visitor Information: Contact the Atlin Visitors Assoc., P.O. Box 365-M, Atlin, BC V0W 1A0, phone (250) 651-7522, (250) 651-7522.

Elevation: 2,240 feet/683m. **Radio**: CBC on FM-band. **Television**: 3 channels (CBC, BCTV and the Knowledge Network).

Private Aircraft: Peterson Field, 1 mile/1.6 km northeast; elev. 2,348 feet/716m; length 3,950 feet/1,204m; gravel.

Transportation: **Air**—Charter service from Juneau. **Bus**—Service from Whitehorse 3 times a week.

Referred to by some visitors as Shangri-la, the village of Atlin overlooks the crystal clear water of 90-mile/145-km-long Atlin Lake and is surrounded by spectacular mountains. On Teresa Island in Atlin Lake is Birch Mountain (elev. 6,755 feet/2,060m), the highest point in fresh water in the world.

Atlin was founded in 1898. The name was taken from the Indian dialect and means Big Water. The Atlin Lake area was one of the richest gold strikes made during the great rush to the Klondike in 1897–98. The first claims were registered here on July 30, 1898, by Fritz Miller and Kenneth McLaren.

Steam shovel from Atlin's gold mining era. (© Ralph & Leonor Barrett, Four Corners Imaging)

Lodging & Services

The village has a hotel, inns, cottages, bed and breakfasts, laundromat (with showers), restaurants, gas station (propane, diesel and unleaded available), grocery, government liquor store and general stores, and a post office. Boarding kennels available. Atlin branch of Bank of Montreal located at Government Agents Office on 3rd Street; open weekdays 10 A.M. to noon and 1–3 P.M. Dump station at Mile 2.3 Discovery Road. The museum and several shops feature local gold nugget jewelry, arts and crafts, and other souvenirs. Air charter service for glacier tours and fly-in fishing trips. Charter boats and fishing charters available. Bus tours are welcome, but phone ahead so this small community can accommodate you.

Camping

RV park with electric and water hookups; showers at laundromat; pay phone and boat moorage downtown on lake. There are also several camping areas on Atlin Road, Discovery Road and Warm Bay Road. Atlin community operates the Pine Creek campground at Mile 1.6 Warm Bay Road; pay camping fee at any downtown business or at the museum).

Attractions

Atlin Historical Museum, open weekends during June and September, daily July through August. Located in Atlin's original 1-room schoolhouse, the museum has mining artifacts and photo exhibits of the Atlin gold rush. Gift shop features northern and Atlin books and the work of local artisans. Admission fee; phone (250) 651-7522.

The MV *Tarahne* (Tah-ron) sits on the lakeshore in the middle of town. Tours daily in summer at 3 P.M.; admission by donation. Built at Atlin in 1916 by White Pass & Yukon Route, she carried passengers and freight from Atlin to Scotia Bay until 1936. (Scotia Bay is across the lake from Atlin and slightly north.) A 2-mile/3.2-km railway connected Scotia Bay on Atlin Lake to Taku Landing on Tagish Lake, where passengers arrived by boat from Carcross, YT. The

MV Tarahne *sits on the lakeshore in the middle of Atlin.*

(© Earl L. Brown, staff)

Tarahne was the first gas-driven boat in the White Pass fleet. After she was lengthened by 30 feet in 1927, she could carry up to 198 passengers. In recent years, Atlin residents have launched a drive to restore the boat; they hope to eventually refloat the vessel and offer tours of Atlin Lake.

The Globe Theatre, built in 1917, was restored by the Atlin Historical Society and re-opened in 1998. Information is available from the Atlin Museum, (250) 651-7522. A Coffee House is held at the Globe Theatre every month, featuring local talent doing skits, songs, readings, story telling, etc.

Visit the mineral springs at the north end of town, where you may have a drink of sparkling cold mineral water. The gazebo-like structure over the springs was built by White Pass in 1922. Picnic area nearby.

The Pioneer Cemetery, located at Mile 1.1 Discovery Road, contains the weathered grave markers of early gold seekers, including Fritz Miller and Kenneth McLaren, who made the first gold discovery in the Atlin area in July 1898. Also buried here is Walter Gladstone Sweet, reputed to have been a card dealer for Soapy Smith in Skagway.

Public Gold Panning Area has been set aside on Spruce Creek. Turn off Discovery Road at Mile 3.6. Check at the museum for details. Gold pans available locally for rent or purchase.

Take a Hike. At Mile 2.3 Warm Bay Road are 2 trails: the 3-mile/4.8-km Monarch trail and the short, easy Beach trail. The Monarch trail is a moderately strenuous hike with a steep climb at the end to a bird's-eye view of the area.

Weekend guided nature walks are available at Warm Bay and Warm Springs, late May to early September. Fee charged. Inquire locally for details.

Tours and Rentals. Motorbike rentals; houseboat rentals; kayak, canoe and boat rentals; boat tours of Atlin and Tagish lakes, guided fishing trips and marine gas are available. Helicopter service, floatplanes for charter hunting and fishing trips and flightseeing trips of Llewellyn Glacier and the Atlin area are also available.

Atlin Provincial Park, accessible by boat or plane only (charters available in Atlin). Spectacular wilderness area; varied topography; exceptional wildlife habitat.

Take a Drive. 13-mile/21-km Discovery Road and 16.5-mile/26.5-km Warm Bay Road are both suitable for passenger cars and RVs, and both offer sightseeing and recreation (mile-by-mile descriptions of both roads follow).

Discovery Road is a good, wide gravel road, bumpy in spots. At Mile 1.1, across from Atlin airport, is the pioneer cemetery, which contains grave markers and monuments to many of Atlin's historical figures. At Mile 3.5 is a turnout with view of Pine Creek and falls. At Mile 3.6 turnoff on to Spruce Creek Road, which leads south 0.9 mile/1.4 km to a designated public recreational gold panning area and 1.5 miles/2.4 km to active gold mining on Spruce Creek (no tours but operations can be photographed from the road). This side road is signed as rough and narrow; suitable for cars, vans and pickups.

Continue on Discovery Road to Mile 5.4 for former townsite of **Discovery**, originally called Pine Creek, now a ghost town. In its boom days, the town supplied miners working in the area.

Beyond Surprise Lake Dam bridge at Mile 11.8, Discovery Road become steep and winding for 1.2 miles/1.9 km until the road dead ends along Boulder Creek. **Surprise Lake** recreation site has some campsites, pit toilets, picnic tables, firepits, and a boat launch for cartop boats and canoes. A gold mining operation is visible across the lake.

Warm Bay Road begins at Mile 0.3 on Discovery Road and leads south 16.5 miles/26.5 km to numerous points of interest and 5 camping areas. At Mile 1.6 is Pine Creek Campground and picnic area, and a short trail to Pine Creek and Pine Creek Falls. At Mile 2 is Atlin Art Centre (see description this section). At Mile 2.3 is the trailhead for the easy Beach trail and for the more strenuous Monarch trail to the 4,723-foot/1,439-m summit of Monarch Mountain (scenic vista of Atlin area).

At Mile 7 on Warm Bay Road is a viewpoint of Llewellyn Glacier and Atlin Lake that is a good photo spot. At Mile 9.5 you'll cross McKee Creek 1-lane bridge. The McKee Creek area has been mined since the 1890s. In July 1981, 2 area miners found what has been dubbed the "Atlin nugget," a 36.86-troy-ounce, hand-sized piece of gold.

Continue on to Mile 11.9 for Palmer Lake recreation site (camping, fishing, picnicking) or Mile 13.9 for Warm Bay recreation site on Atlin Lake; camping, fishing, picnicking and boat launch for small boats. At Mile 14.4 is **Warm Spring**, a small and shallow spring,

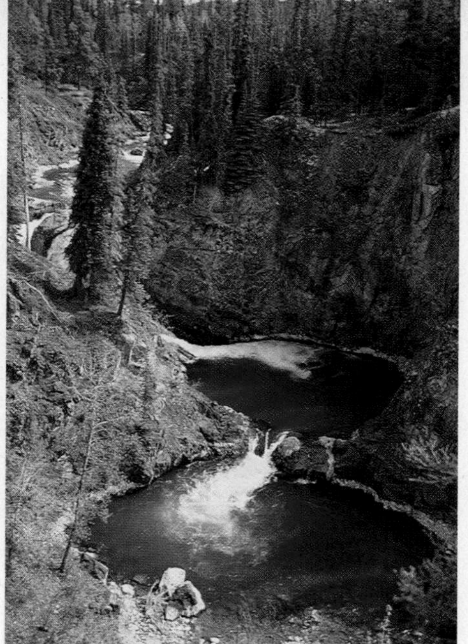

Pine Creek Falls at Mile 1.6 Warm Bay Road.

(© Ralph & Leonor Barrett, Four Corners Imaging)

good for soaking road-weary bones. There's also a large grassy camping area and pit toilet. The meadow streams are lined with watercress.

At Mile 16.3 is Grotto recreation site (camping and picnicking). And just beyond is **"The Grotto"**, where water flows through a hole in the rocks from an underground stream. Locals report this is a good place to obtain drinking water.

Atlin Art Centre, located at Mile 2 Warm Bay Road, offers alpine hiking, boating and canoeing adventures to the general public from June to September. The centre is also a summer school and retreat for artists and students, run by Gernot Dick. The centre is designed to allow participants to distance themselves from urban distractions and focus on the creative process. Contact Atlin Art Centre, Monarch Mountain, Atlin, BC V0W 1A0; (800) 651-8882 for more information. A number of artists, authors and other talented and creative people make their home in Atlin.

AREA FISHING: The Atlin area is well known for its good fishing. Fly-in fishing for salmon, steelhead and rainbow, or troll locally for lake trout. Grayling can be caught at the mouths of most creeks and streams or off Atlin docks. Public boat launch on Atlin Lake, south of the MV *Tarahne*. Boat charters available. British Columbia fishing licenses are available from the government agent and local outlets. Fresh and smoked salmon may be available for purchase locally in the summer.

TAGISH ROAD

Connects: Alaska Hwy. to Carcross, YT
Length: 34 miles
Road Surface: 40% gravel, 60% paved
Season: Open all year

(See map, page 700)

This 33.8-mile/54.4-km road connects the Alaska Highway with Klondike Highway 2. It leads south from the Alaska Highway junction at Jake's Corner (**Milepost DC 836.8**) through the settlement of Tagish to Carcross. It is good gravel road from the Alaska Highway junction to Tagish, asphalt-surfaced between Tagish and Carcross.

Tagish Road was built in 1942 to lay a gas pipeline during construction of the Alaska Highway.

If you are traveling Klondike Highway 2 between Skagway and Whitehorse, Tagish Road provides access to Atlin Road and also makes a pleasant side trip. This is also a very beautiful drive in the fall; good photo opportunities.

Emergency medical services: Phone the RCMP, (867) 667-5555; ambulance, phone (867) 667-3333.

Tagish Road Log

Kilometreposts measure east to west from Alaska Highway junction to Carcross turnoff; posts are up about every 2 kilometres. **Distance from the junction (J) is followed by distance from Carcross (C).**

J 0 C 33.8 (54.4 km) **Jake's Corner.**

Junction with the Alaska Highway. Turn to **Milepost DC 836.8** in the ALASKA HIGHWAY section.

Drive south 1.1 miles/1.8 km from the Alaska Highway to the junction of Tagish Road and Atlin Road (Highway 7).

J 1.1 (1.8 km) **C 32.7** (52.6 km) **Junction** of Tagish and Atlin roads. Head west on Tagish Road.

Turn southeast for Atlin, BC. See ATLIN ROAD log on page 704.

J 8.8 (14.2 km) **C 25** (40.2 km) For several miles, travelers may see the NorthwesTel microwave tower on Jubilee Mountain (elev. 5,950 feet/ 1,814m) to the south between Little Atlin Lake and Tagish River. Jubilee Mountain was named by Dr. G.M. Dawson in 1887 in honor of Queen Victoria's Jubilee.

J 12.8 (20.6 km) **C 21** (33.8 km) *Gravel ends, pavement begins, westbound.* Tagish Yukon government campground, on **Six Mile River** between Marsh Lake to the north and Tagish Lake to the south. Good fishing, boatlaunch, picnic area, playground, kitchen shelter, 28 campsites with firepits and tables, drinking water and toilets. Camping permit ($8). *CAUTION: Watch for black bears.*

J 13 (20.9 km) **C 20.8** (33.5 km) Gas, oil, minor repairs, snacks and post office. Pay phone on road. Marina on north side of road at east end of Tagish bridge has bait, tackle, fishing licenses, boat rental.

J 13.1 (21 km) **C 20.7** (33.3 km) **Tagish Bridge.** Good fishing is a tradition here; Tagish bridge has an anglers' walkway on the north side. Tagish River, lake trout, arctic grayling, northern pike, whitefish and cisco.

West end of bridge has a day-use area with parking, 4 picnic sites and water pump.

J 13.5 (21.7 km) **C 20.3** (32.6 km) Improved gravel road leads through parklike area to settlement of **TAGISH** (pop. about 134) on Tagish River between Marsh and Tagish lakes. Express bus service between Atlin and Whitehorse stops here and in Carcross 3 times weekly. Tagish means "fish trap" in the local Indian dialect. It was traditionally an Indian meeting place in the spring on the way to set up fish camps and again in the fall to celebrate the catch. Post office at Tagish Service at east end of Tagish bridge. Wilderness lodge on Taku Arm of Tagish Lake.

Two miles/3.2 km south of Tagish on the Tagish River is **TAGISH POST**, originally named Fort Sifton, the Canadian customs post established in 1897. Two of the original 5 buildings still stand. The North West Mounted Police and Canadian customs collected duties on thousands of tons of freight carried by stampeders on their way to the Klondike goldfields between September 1897 and February 1898.

J 13.7 (22 km) **C 20.1** (32.3 km) Store, cafe, motel, RV park.

J 16.3 (26.2 km) **C 17.5** (28.1 km) Side road leads 1.2 miles/2 km to homes and **Tagish Lake**; fishing for trout, pike and grayling.

J 23 (37 km) **C 10.8** (17.4 km) Bryden Creek.

J 23.8 (38.3 km) **C 10** (16 km) Tagish Lake wilderness resort.

J 24.7 (39.7 km) **C 9.1** (14.6 km) Eagles Landing Bed & Breakfast.

J 24.8 (39.9 km) **C 9** (14.4 km) Crag Lake. Road now enters more mountainous region westbound. Caribou Mountain (elev. 5,645 feet/1,721m) on right.

J 27.2 (43.8 km) **C 6.6** (10.6 km) Porcupine Creek.

J 27.5 (44.3 km) **C 6.3** (10.1 km) **Historic Milepost 7.**

J 28.4 (45.7 km) **C 5.4** (8.7 km) Pain Creek.

J 30.2 (48.6 km) **C 3.6** (5.8 km) Side road to Chooutla Lake.

J 31 (49.9 km) **C 2.8** (4.5 km) First glimpse westbound of Montana Mountain (elev. 7,230 feet/2,204m) across narrows at Carcross.

J 33.8 (54.4 km) **C 0** Tagish Road ends westbound; turn left for Carcross, right for Whitehorse.

Junction with Klondike Highway 2. See **Milepost S 66.5** on page 703 in the KLONDIKE HIGHWAY 2 section for log.

CAMPBELL HIGHWAY (4)

Connects: Watson Lake, YT, to Klondike Hwy. **Length:** 373 miles
Road Surface: 85% gravel, 15% paved **Season:** Open all year
Major Attraction: Pelly River, Wildlife

	Carmacks	Dawson City	Faro	Ross River	Watson Lake
Carmacks		225	115	150	375
Dawson City	225		338	373	598
Faro	115	338		32	271
Ross River	150	373	32		239
Watson Lake	375	598	271	239	

Summer sunset over Frances Lake on the Campbell Highway. (© Paul Souders)

Named for Robert Campbell, the first white man to penetrate what is now known as Yukon Territory, this all-weather, mostly gravel road leads 373 miles/600.2 km northwest from the Alaska Highway at Watson Lake, to junction with the Klondike Highway 2 miles/3.2 km north of Carmacks (see the KLONDIKE LOOP section). Gas is available at Watson Lake, Ross River, Faro and Carmacks.

The highway is gravel with the exception of stretches of pavement at Watson Lake, Ross River and the Klondike Highway junction (see map). *NOTE: Drive with your headlights on at all times.*

The Campbell Highway is an alternative route to Dawson City. It is about 20 miles/32 km shorter than driving the Alaska Highway through to Whitehorse, then driving up the Klondike Highway to Dawson City.

The Robert Campbell Highway was completed in 1968 and closely follows sections of the fur trade route established by Robert Campbell. Campbell was a Hudson's Bay Co. trader who was sent into the region in the 1840s to find a route west into the unexplored regions of central Yukon. Traveling from the southeast, he followed the Liard and Frances rivers, building a chain of posts along the way. His major discovery came in 1843, when he reached the Yukon River, which was to become the major transportation route within the Yukon.

Emergency medical services: Phone the RCMP or ambulance in Watson Lake, Ross River or Carmacks. Or phone toll free, Yukon-wide, the RCMP at (867) 667-5555, or the ambulance at (867) 667-3333.

Campbell Highway Log

Distance from Watson Lake (WL) is followed by distance from junction with the Klondike Highway just north of Carmacks (J).
Mileages reflect the location of physical kilometreposts; driving distance may vary from log.

YUKON HIGHWAY 4

WL 0 J 373 (600.2 km) **Watson Lake.**

Junction of the Campbell Highway with the Alaska Highway. Turn to description of Watson Lake on page 126 in the ALASKA HIGHWAY section.

The famous sign forest is located at this junction. In the parking area off the Campbell Highway (also called Airport Road) is a point of interest sign relating the highway's history. Also located at this junction is the Alaska Highway Interpretive Centre and visitor information.

WL 0.6 (1 km) **J 372.4** (599.3 km) Hospital on right northbound.

WL 4.3 (6.9 km) **J 368.7** (593.3 km) Access road on right northbound to Mount Maichen ski hill.

WL 6.3 (10.1 km) **J 366.7** (590.1 km) Airport Road left to Watson Lake airport.

WL 6.7 (10.8 km) **J 366.3** (589.5 km) Watson Creek. The highway begins to climb to a heavily timbered plateau and then heads north following the east bank of the Frances River. Tamarack is rare in Yukon, but this northern type of larch can be seen along here. Although a member of the pine family, it sheds its needles in the fall.

WL 10.4 (16.7 km) **J 362.6** (583.5 km) MacDonald Creek.

WL 22.5 (36.2 km) **J 350.5** (564.1 km) Tom Creek, named after an Indian trapper whose cabin is at the mouth of the stream.

WL 27.3 (44 km) **J 345.7** (556.3 km) Sa Dena Hes Mine access.

WL 36.1 (58.1 km) **J 336.9** (542.2 km) **Frances River** bridge. Turnout at north end of bridge; picnic spot. The highway crosses to west bank and follows the river northward. Named by Robert Campbell for the wife of Sir George Simpson, governor of the Hudson's Bay Co. for 40 years, the Frances River is a tributary of the Liard River. Robert Campbell ascended the Liard River to the Frances River and then went on to Frances Lake and the Pelly River. The Frances River was part of Hudson's Bay Co.'s route into central Yukon for many years before being abandoned because of its dangerous rapids and canyons.

WL 47.2 (76 km) **J 325.8** (524.3 km) Lucky Creek.

WL 49.6 (79.8 km) **J 323.4** (520.4 km) Simpson Creek.

WL 51.8 (83.4 km) **J 321.2** (516.9 km) Access road leads west 1 mile/1.6 km to **Simpson Lake** Yukon government campground: 10 campsites, camping permit ($8), boat launch, dock, swimming beach, playground, kitchen shelter and drinking water (boil water). Excellent fishing for lake trout, arctic grayling and northern pike.

WL 58.5 (94.2 km) **J 314.5** (506.1 km) Large turnout with litter barrels.

WL 58.7 (94.5 km) **J 314.3** (505.8 km) Access road west to Simpson Lake.

WL 68.5 (110.2 km) **J 304.5** (490 km) **Miner's Junction**, formerly known as Cantung Junction; no services. **Junction** with Nahanni Range Road to Tungsten (description follows).

The **Nahanni Range Road** leads 125 miles/201.2 km northeast to the former

CAMPBELL HIGHWAY *Watson Lake, YT, to Junction with Klondike Loop*

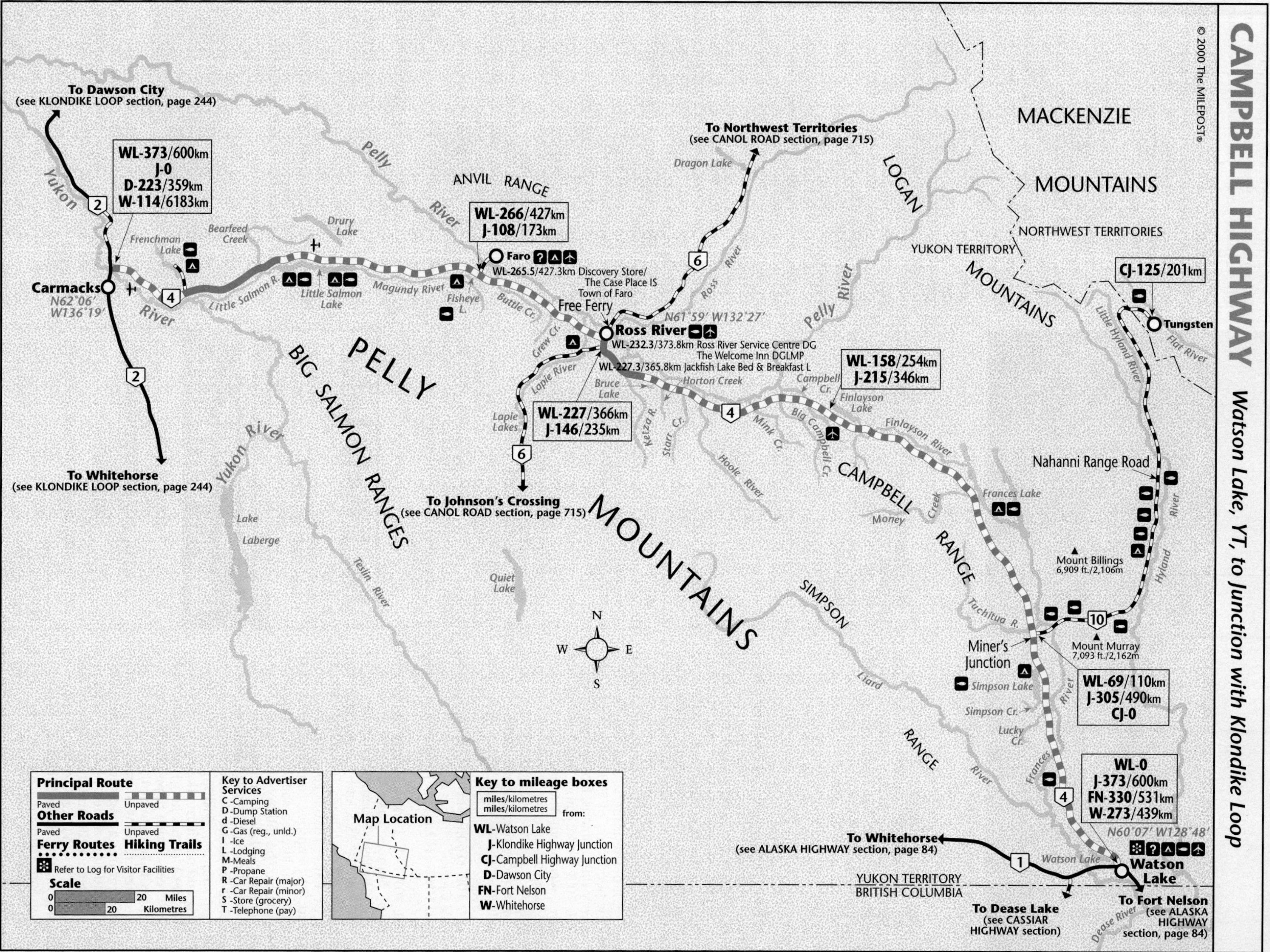

© 2000 The MILEPOST®
To Dawson City (see KLONDIKE LOOP section, page 244)
WL-373/600km
J-0
D-223/359km
W-114/6183km
Yukon
Carmacks
N62°06' W136°19'
River
To Whitehorse (see KLONDIKE LOOP section, page 244)
Frenchman Lake
Bearfeed Creek
Drury Lake
Little Salmon R.
Little Salmon Lake
Magundy River
Fisheye L.
Pelly
River
ANVIL RANGE
WL-266/427km
J-108/173km
Faro
WL-265.5/427.3km Discovery Store/
The Case Place IS
Town of Faro
Buttle Cr.
Free Ferry
Grew Cr.
Ross River
WL-232.3/373.8km Ross River Service Centre DG
The Welcome Inn DGLMP
WL-227.3/365.8km Jackfish Lake Bed & Breakfast L
N61°59' W132°27'
To Northwest Territories (see CANOL ROAD section, page 715)
Dragon Lake
Ross River
Pelly River
LOGAN
Lapie River
Lapie Lakes
WL-227/366km
J-146/235km
Bruce Lake
Horton Creek
Ketza R.
Starr Cr.
To Johnson's Crossing (see CANOL ROAD section, page 715)
PELLY
BIG SALMON RANGES
Yukon River
Lake Laberge
Teslin River
Quiet Lake
MOUNTAINS
N
W
E
S
Hoole River
Mink Cr.
Big Campbell Cr.
Campbell Cr.
WL-158/254km
J-215/346km
Finlayson Lake
Finlayson River
CAMPBELL RANGE
Money Creek
Frances Lake
SIMPSON RANGE
Liard River
MACKENZIE
MOUNTAINS
NORTHWEST TERRITORIES
YUKON TERRITORY
MOUNTAINS
CJ-125/201km
Tungsten
Flat River
Little Hyland River
Nahanni Range Road
Hyland River
Mount Billings 6,909 ft./2,106m
Mount Murray 7,093 ft./2,162m
Tuchitua R.
Miner's Junction
Simpson Lake
Simpson Cr.
Lucky Cr.
Frances River
WL-69/110km
J-305/490km
CJ-0
WL-0
J-373/600km
FN-330/531km
W-273/439km
N60°07' W128°48'
Watson Lake
Watson Lake
To Whitehorse (see ALASKA HIGHWAY section, page 84)
YUKON TERRITORY
BRITISH COLUMBIA
To Dease Lake (see CASSIAR HIGHWAY section)
To Fort Nelson (see ALASKA HIGHWAY section, page 84)
Dease River
Principal Route
Paved
Unpaved
Other Roads
Paved
Unpaved
Ferry Routes
Hiking Trails
Refer to Log for Visitor Facilities
Scale
0 20 Miles
0 20 Kilometres
Key to Advertiser Services
C-Camping
D-Dump Station
d-Diesel
G-Gas (reg., unld.)
I-Ice
L-Lodging
M-Meals
P-Propane
R-Car Repair (major)
r-Car Repair (minor)
S-Store (grocery)
T-Telephone (pay)
Map Location
Key to mileage boxes
miles/kilometres
miles/kilometres
from:
WL-Watson Lake
J-Klondike Highway Junction
CJ-Campbell Highway Junction
D-Dawson City
FN-Fort Nelson
W-Whitehorse

Floatplane on Jackfish Lake outside Ross River. (© Earl L. Brown, staff)

mining town of Tungsten, NWT. Construction of the Nahanni Range Road was begun in 1961 to provide access to the mining property. The road was completed in 1963 with the bridging of the Frances and Hyland rivers. The road is gravel surfaced with some washouts and soft steep shoulders. *CAUTION: The Yukon government does not recommend Nahanni Range Road for tourist travel due to lack of services and maintenance.*

TUNGSTEN, which was the company town for one of the richest mines in the world and Canada's only tungsten producer, was originally called Cantung (Canada Tungsten Mining Corp. Ltd.). Open-pit mining began here in the early 1960s with the discovery of scheelite in the Flat River area. Scheelite is an ore of tungsten, an oxide used for hardening steel and making white gold. The mine shut down in 1986, and the population of 500 moved out. Only a security staff remains. Hot springs in area.

WL 70.3 (113.2 km) **J 302.7** (487.1 km) Yukon government Tuchitua River maintenance camp to east.

WL 70.5 (113.4 km) **J 302.5** (486.8 km) One-lane bridge over Tuchitua River.

WL 91.7 (147.6 km) **J 281.3** (452.7 km) Jules Creek.

WL 100 (160.9 km) **J 273** (439.3 km) 99 Mile Creek.

WL 106.6 (171.6 km) **J 266.4** (428.7 km) Caesar Creek.

WL 107.1 (172.4 km) **J 265.9** (427.9 km) View of Frances Lake to east, Campbell Range of the Pelly Mountains to west.

WL 108.9 (175.3 km) **J 264.1** (425 km) Access road east leads 0.6 mile/1 km to **Frances Lake** Yukon government campground: 24 campsites, camping permit ($8), boat launch, kitchen shelter, drinking water (boil water). The solitary peak between the 2 arms of Frances Lake is Simpson Tower (elev. 5,500 feet/1,676m). It was named by Robert Campbell for Hudson's Bay Co. Governor Sir George Simpson. Fishing for lake trout, grayling and northern pike.

WL 109.1 (175.5 km) **J 263.9** (424.7 km) Money Creek, which flows into the west arm of Frances Lake, one of the Yukon's largest lakes. The creek was named for Anton Money, a mining engineer and prospector who found and mined placer gold in this area between 1929 and 1946. Money later operated "The Village" service station at Mile 442 on the Alaska Highway. He died in 1993, in Santa Barbara, CA.

WL 109.4 (176 km) **J 263.6** (424.2 km) Gravel turnout. View southbound of Frances Lake.

WL 113.8 (183.2 km) **J 259.2** (417.1 km) Dick Creek.

WL 123.8 (199.2 km) **J 249.2** (401 km) Highway descends Finlayson River valley northbound, swinging west away from Frances Lake and following the Finlayson River that may be seen occasionally to the east for about the next 20 miles/32 km. Mountains to the west are part of the Campbell Range.

WL 126.4 (203.5 km) **J 246.6** (396.9 km) Light Creek.

WL 129.1 (207.7 km) **J 243.9** (392.5 km) Van Bibber Creek.

WL 134.1 (215.8 km) **J 238.9** (384.5 km) Wolverine Creek.

WL 147.5 (237.4 km) **J 225.5** (362.9 km) **Finlayson Creek**, which flows into the river of the same name, drains Finlayson Lake into Frances Lake. Named by Robert Campbell in 1840 for Chief Factor Duncan Finlayson, who later became director of the Hudson's Bay Co. Placer gold mined at the mouth of Finlayson River in 1875 is believed to be some of the first gold mined in the territory. Finlayson Lake (elev. 3,100 feet/945m), on the Continental Divide, separates watersheds of Mackenzie and Yukon rivers.

WL 148.1 (238.4 km) **J 224.9** (361.9 km) Access road north to Finlayson Lake picnic area; litter barrels. To the southwest are the Pelly Mountains.

WL 149 (239.8 km) **J 224** (360.5 km) Turnout with observation platform and information panel on Finlayson caribou herd.

WL 158.1 (254.5 km) **J 214.9** (345.8 km) **Private Aircraft**: Finlayson Lake airstrip to south; elev. 3,300 feet/1,006m; length 2,100 feet/640m; gravel. No services.

WL 163.7 (263.5 km) **J 209.3** (336.8 km) Nancy J. Creek.

WL 164.4 (264.5 km) **J 208.6** (335.7 km) Little Campbell Creek. Robert Campbell followed this creek to the Pelly River in 1840.

WL 170.4 (274.2 km) **J 202.6** (326 km) Bridge over Big Campbell Creek, which flows into Pelly River at Pelly Banks. Robert Campbell named the river and banks after Hudson's Bay Co. Governor Sir John Henry Pelly. Campbell built a trading post here in 1846; never successful, it burned down in 1849. Isaac Taylor and William S. Drury later operated a trading post at Pelly Banks, one of a string of successful posts established by their firm in remote spots throughout the Yukon from 1899 on.

The highway follows the Pelly River for the next 90 miles/145 km.

WL 179 (288.1 km) **J 194** (312.2 km) Mink Creek culvert.

WL 193.9 (312 km) **J 179.1** (288.2 km) Bridge over **Hoole Canyon**; turnout to north. Confluence of the Hoole and Pelly rivers. Campbell named the Hoole River after his interpreter, Francis Hoole, a half-Iroquois and half-French Canadian employed by the Hudson's Bay Co. Dig out your gold pan—this river once yielded gold.

WL 199.8 (321.6 km) **J 173.2** (278.7 km) Starr Creek culvert.

WL 206.5 (332.3 km) **J 166.5** (267.9 km) Horton Creek.

WL 210.7 (339 km) **J 162.3** (261.2 km) Bruce Lake to south.

WL 211.8 (340.8 km) **J 161.2** (259.4 km) Bruce Creek.

WL 215.4 (346.6 km) **J 157.6** (253.6 km) Private side road leads south 27.3 miles/44 km to Ketza River Project. The first gold bar was poured at Ketza River mine in 1988. The Ketza River hard-rock gold deposit was first discovered in 1947. No visitor facilities.

WL 217.9 (350.7 km) **J 155.1** (249.6 km) Ketza River. St. Cyr Range to southwest.

WL 219.4 (353 km) **J 153.6** (247.2 km) Ketza Creek.

WL 221.4 (356.3 km) **J 151.6** (244 km) Beautiful Creek culvert.

WL 224.8 (361.8 km) **J 148.2** (238.5 km) **Coffee Lake** to south; local swimming hole, picnic tables, trout fishing (stocked).

WL 227.3 (365.8 km) **J 145.7** (234.5 km) Ross River Flying Service; floatplane base on **Jackfish Lake** here.

Jackfish Lake Bed and Breakfast. See display ad this section.

Junction with South Canol Road, which leads south 129 miles/207 km to Johnson's Crossing and the Alaska Highway. See **Milepost J 136.8** in the CANOL ROAD section.

WL 227.5 (366.1 km) **J 145.5** (234.1 km) Unmaintained side road on right westbound is continuation of Canol Road to Ross River. Use the main Ross River access road next milepost.

WL 232.3 (373.8 km) **J 140.7** (226.4 km) Access road leads 7 miles/11.2 km to Ross River (description follows). Rest area with toilets on highway just north of this turnoff.

Ross River

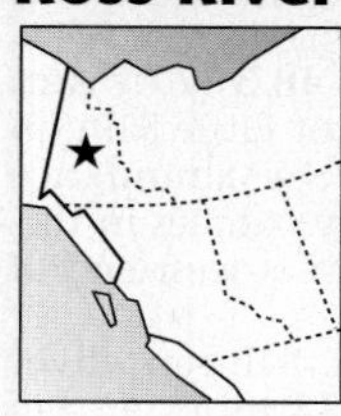

Located on the southwest bank of the Pelly River. **Population:** about 352. **Emergency Services: RCMP**, phone (867) 969-5555. **Hospital,** phone (867) 969-2222. **Radio:** CBC 990, local FM station. **Transportation:** Scheduled air service via Trans North Air.

Private Aircraft: Ross River airstrip; elev. 2,408 feet/734m; length 5,500 feet/1,676m; gravel; fuel 40.

A point of interest sign on the way into Ross River relates that in 1843, Robert Campbell named Ross River for Chief Trader Donald Ross of the Hudson's Bay Co. From 1903, a trading post called Nahanni House (established by Tom Smith and later owned by the Whitehorse firm of Taylor and Drury) located at the confluence of the Ross and Pelly rivers supplied the Indians of the area for nearly 50 years. With the building of the Canol pipeline service road in WWII and the completion of the Robert Campbell Highway in 1968, the community was linked to the rest of the territory by road. Originally situated on the north side of the Pelly River, the town has been in its present location since 1964. Today, Ross River is a supply and communication base for prospectors testing and mining mineral bodies in this region.

Ross River has gas stations with diesel, mechanical and tire repair, grocery stores, 2 motels with dining, and a bed and breakfast. The nearest campground is Lapie Canyon (see **Milepost WL 233.5**). Self-contained RVs may overnight at the gravel parking lot at the end of the pedestrian suspension bridge on the Ross River side.

Ross River is also a jumping-off point for big game hunters and canoeists. There are 2 registered hunting outfitters here. Canoeists traveling the Pelly River can launch just downriver from the ferry crossing. Experienced canoeists recommend camping on the Pelly's many gravel bars and islets to avoid bears, bugs and the danger of accidentally setting tundra fires. The Pelly has many sweepers, sleepers and gravel shallows, some gravel shoals, and extensive channeling. There are 2 sets of rapids between Ross River and the mouth of the Pelly: Fish Hook and Granite Canyon. Water is potable (boil), firewood available and wildlife plentiful. Inquire locally about river conditions before setting out.

Rock hounds check Pelly River gravels for jaspers and the occasional agate.

The suspension footbridge at Ross River leads across the Pelly River to the site of an abandoned Indian village 1 mile/1.6 km upstream at the mouth of the Ross River.

A government ferry crosses the Pelly River daily in summer, from 8 A.M. to noon and 1–5 P.M. Across the river, the North Canol Road leads 144 miles/232 km to Macmillan Pass at the Northwest Territories border. See the CANOL ROAD section for details.

Ross River Service Centre Ltd. See display ad this section.

The Welcome Inn. See display ad this section.

Campbell Highway Log

(continued)

WL 232.3 (373.8 km) **J 140.7** (226.4 km) Access road leads 7 miles/11.2 km to Ross River (see preceding description).

WL 232.5 (374.2 km) **J 140.5** (226.1 km) Rest area with toilets.

WL 233.4 (375.6 km) **J 139.6** (224.6 km) **Lapie River** bridge crosses deep gorge of Lapie River, which flows into the Pelly River from Lapie Lakes on the South Canol Road. Highway continues to follow the Pelly River and Pelly Mountains.

WL 233.5 (375.8 km) **J 139.5** (224.5 km) Turnoff to left (south) to **Lapie Canyon** Yukon government campground adjacent Lapie River: short scenic trails, viewpoint, picturesque canyon; kitchen shelters, firewood, group picnic area; walk-in tent sites, 18 campsites, camping permit ($8), drinking water (boil water); boat launch. ▲

WL 236.3 (380.3 km) **J 136.7** (220 km) Danger Creek. In 1905, naturalist Charles Sheldon named this creek after his horse, Danger.

WL 239.9 (386 km) **J 133.1** (214.2 km) Panoramic view of the Pelly River valley just ahead westbound.

WL 243.6 (392 km) **J 129.4** (208.2 km) *CAUTION: Hill and bad corner.*

WL 244.2 (393 km) **J 128.8** (207.3 km) Highway narrows over Grew Creek, no guide rails. This creek was named for Hudson's Bay Co. trader Jim Grew, who trapped this area for many years before his death in 1906.

WL 251 (404 km) **J 122** (196.3 km) Turnout to north.

WL 260.4 (419 km) **J 112.6** (181.2 km) Buttle Creek, named for Roy Buttle, a trapper, prospector and trader who lived here in the early 1900s and at one time owned a trading post at Ross River.

WL 264.7 (426 km) **J 108.3** (174.3 km) Across the wide Pelly River valley to the north is a view of the mining community of Faro.

WL 265.5 (427.3 km) **J 107.5** (173 km) Access road on right westbound leads 5.6 miles/9 km to Faro. Point of interest sign about Faro at intersection. Rest area with toilets and litter barrels to south just west of this junction.

Faro

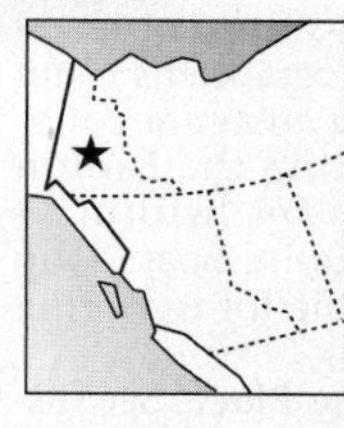

Located in east-central Yukon Territory, 220 road miles/354 km from Whitehorse. **Population:** 500.. **Emergency Services: RCMP,** phone (867) 994-5555. **Fire Department,** phone (867) 994-2222. **Hospital,** phone (867) 994-4444.

Visitor Information: Centre at the municipal-operated John Connelly RV Park, open June through August. For information on wildlife viewing, hiking, biking, horseback trails, town facilities and services, special events and individual businesses, phone (867) 994-2288 (seasonal). Or contact the Faro Town Office, phone (867) 994-2728, fax (867) 994-3154; web site faro.yk.net; e-mail townof@yknet.yk.ca.

The **Campbell Region Interpretive Tourist Information Centre,** located directly across from John Connelly RV Park, has historical displays on the Yukon centennial; phone (867) 994-2728.

Climate: Temperatures range from -51°F/-46°C in winter to a summer maximum of 84°F/29°C. **Radio:** CBC-FM 105.1, CKRW-FM 98.7. **Television:** CBC and 7 cable channels. **Transportation:** Floatplane service from Horizons North.

Private Aircraft: Faro airstrip; 1.5 miles/2.4 km south; elev. 2,351 feet/717m; length 3,000 feet/914m; gravel; fuel 100.

The town of Faro lies on a series of benches or terraces on the northern escarpment of the Tintina Trench. Many places in town offer a commanding view of the Pelly River.

There are 2 restaurants in town: Redmond's (known locally as Cranky Frank's) and Sally's Road House. Both Redmond's and Sally's Road House offer motel accommodations. RV camping and dump station at municipal and private campgrounds. The service station has gas, diesel, propane and full garage services. The area offers excellent fly-in fishing. Other services in town include a large grocery, liquor store, video rental, post office, public library, movie theatre and recreation centre with indoor swimming pool, squash courts and outdoor tennis courts. Catholic and Protestant Sunday services are available. ▲

Attractions include an all-season observation cabin and isolated photographer's blind for wildlife viewing. Viewing areas are accessible via a gravel road skirting the Fannin sheep grazing area and are within 4 miles/6.4 km of town. A public boat ramp and canoe rentals are available for exploring the Pelly River.

Discovery Store/The Case Place. See display ad this section.

Town of Faro. See display ad this section.

Campbell Highway Log

(continued)

WL 268.4 (432 km) **J 104.6** (168.3 km) **Johnson Lake** Yukon government campground; 15 sites (7 pull-throughs), $8 fee, toilets, water pump, firewood, picnic shelter, boat launch. ▲

Westbound, the Campbell Highway follows the Magundy River. There are several turnouts.

WL 285.8 (460 km) **J 87.2** (140.3 km) Magundy River airstrip to north; summer use only. Watch for livestock.

WL 288.1 (463.7 km) **J 84.9** (136.6 km) First glimpse of 22-mile-/35-km-long Little Salmon Lake westbound.

WL 299.3 (481.7 km) **J 73.7** (118.6 km) East end of **Little Salmon Lake**. Highway follows north shore. Lodge with meals, groceries, fishing licenses, guided fishing charters and boat rentals. Fishing for northern pike, grayling, lake trout.

WL 300.1 (483 km) **J 72.9** (117.3 km) Short access road south to Drury Creek Yukon government campground, situated on the creek at the east end of **Little Salmon Lake:** boat launch, fish filleting table, kitchen shelter, group firepit, 6 campsites, $8 fee, drinking water. Good fishing for northern pike, grayling, whitefish, lake trout 2 to 5 lbs., June 15 through July. ▲

WL 300.4 (483.5 km) **J 72.6** (116.8 km) Turnout at east end Drury Creek bridge. Yukon government maintenance camp to north.

WL 308.2 (496 km) **J 64.8** (104.3 km) Turnout overlooking lake.

WL 311.3 (501 km) **J 61.7** (99.3 km) *CAUTION: Slow down for curves.* Highway follows lakeshore; no guide rails. Turnouts overlooking Little Salmon Lake next 8.5 miles/13.6 km westbound.

WL 316.9 (510 km) **J 56.1** (90.3 km) **Private Aircraft**: Little Salmon airstrip; elev. 2,200 feet/671m; length 1,800 feet/549m; sand and silt.

WL 321.4 (517.3 km) **J 51.6** (83 km) Steep, narrow, winding road south leads to Yukon government **Little Salmon Lake** campground; boat launch, fishing, 15 campsites, $8 fee, drinking water, picnic tables, outhouses, firepits and kitchen shelter. ▲

WL 324.7 (522.6 km) **J 48.3** (77.7 km) **Bearfeed Creek**, a tributary of Little Salmon River, named because of the abundance of bears attracted to the berry patches in this area. Access to creek to north at west end of bridge.

Highway follows Little Salmon River (seen to south) for about 25 miles/40 km westbound.

WL 341 (548.7 km) **J 32** (51.5 km) *CAUTION: Slow down for hill.*

WL 343.8 (553.2 km) **J 29.2** (47 km) Picnic spot on Little Salmon River, which flows into the Yukon River.

WL 347.3 (559 km) **J 25.7** (41.4 km) Access road leads 4.9 miles/8 km north to **Frenchman Lake** Yukon government campground (10 sites), 5.6 miles/9 km to photo viewpoint of lake, and 9.3 miles/15 km to Nunatak Yukon government campground (10 sites, $8 fee). Access road narrows and surface deteriorates beyond Frenchman Lake Campground. South end of this 12-mile/19-km-long lake offers good fishing for trout, pike and grayling. ▲

WL 349.5 (562.4 km) **J 23.5** (37.8 km) Turnoff to south for 0.9-mile/1.4-km gravel road to Little Salmon Indian village near confluence of Little Salmon River and Yukon River. There are some inhabited cabins in the area and some subsistence fishing. Private lands, no trespassing.

WL 356.2 (573.2 km) **J 16.8** (27 km) Turnout with point of interest sign overlooking **Eagles Nest Bluff** (formerly called Eagle Rock), well-known marker for river travelers. One of the worst steamboat disasters on the Yukon River occurred near here when the paddle-wheeler *Columbian* blew up and burned after a crew member accidentally fired a shot into a cargo of gunpowder. The accident, in which 6 men died, took place Sept. 25, 1906.

WL 356.7 (574 km) **J 16.3** (26.2 km) View of the Yukon River. At this point Whitehorse is about 160 miles/258 km upstream and Dawson City is about 300 miles/483 km downriver.

WL 360.4 (580 km) **J 12.6** (20.3 km) Northern Canada Power Commission's transmission poles and lines can be seen along highway. Power is transmitted from Aishihik dam site via Whitehorse dam and on to Cyprus Anvil mine and Faro. Orange balls mark lines where they cross river as a hazard to aircraft.

WL 370 (595.4 km) **J 3** (4.8 km) **Private Aircraft**: Carmacks airstrip to south; elev. 1,770 feet/539m; length 5,200 feet/1,585m; gravel.

WL 370.7 (596.5 km) **J 2.3** (3.7 km) Tantalus Butte coal mine on hill to north overlooking junction of Campbell and Klondike highways. The butte was named by U.S. Army Lt. Frederick Schwatka in 1883 because of the tantalizing appearance of the formation around many bends of the river before it is reached.

WL 373 (600.2 km) **J 0** Turn south on the Klondike Highway for Carmacks (2 miles/3.2 km) and Whitehorse (115 miles/184 km); turn north for Dawson City (223 miles/357 km).

Junction with the Klondike Highway (Yukon Highway 2). Turn to **Milepost J 104.4** on page 249 in the KLONDIKE LOOP section for highway log.

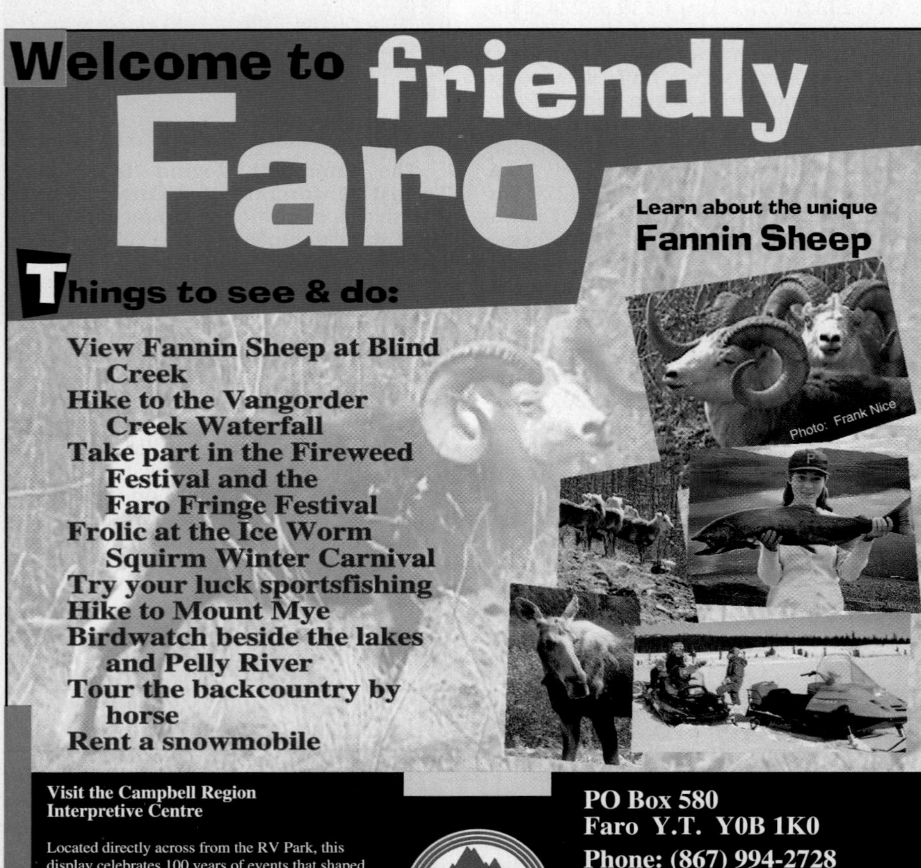

SILVER TRAIL HIGHWAY (11)

Connects: Klondike Hwy. to Keno City, YT **Length:** 69 miles
Road Surface: 50% paved, 50% gravel
Season: Open all year to Mayo and Keno City
Major Attraction: Keno City Mining Museum

(See map page 245)

	Keno City	Klondike Hwy. Jct.	Mayo
Keno City		69	37
Klondike Hwy. Jct.	69		32
Mayo	37	32	

MILEPOST® field editor Earl Brown atop Keno Hill. (© Alisha Brown)

The Silver Trail leads northeast from the Klondike Highway (see **Milepost J 214.4** in the KLONDIKE LOOP section) to Mayo, Elsa and Keno City. From its junction with the Klondike Highway (Yukon Highway 2), the Silver Trail (Yukon Highway 11) leads 31.9 miles/51.3 km to Mayo; 60.3 miles/97 km to Elsa; and 69.1 miles/111.2 km to Keno City. The Silver Trail also provides access to Duncan Creek Road, the original Silver Trail. It is approximately 140 miles/225 km round-trip to Keno City and an easy day trip for motorists. The road is asphalt-surfaced to Mayo, hard-packed gravel from Mayo to Keno. Watch for soft shoulders, especially in wet weather. The highway is open all year to Mayo; maintained winter road to Keno City. Gas is available only at Mayo and at Stewart Crossing.

There is an information kiosk on the Klondike Highway at the south end of Stewart River bridge. Stop at the kiosk for information on the Silver Trail, or visit Binet House in Mayo. Or write Silver Trail Tourism, Box 268, Mayo, YT Y0B 1M0; phone (in summer) (867) 996-2926, fax (867) 995-2409, winter phone (867) 996-2290.

If you have a Yukon Explorer's Passport, the Binet House and Keno Mining Museum are considered the 2 most exclusive passport stamps.

The Silver Trail to Mayo follows the Stewart River through what has been one of the richest silver mining regions in Canada. The Silver Trail region encompasses the traditional lands of the Na Cho N'y'ak Dun First Nations.

Emergency medical services: In Mayo, phone (867) 996-4444; or phone the RCMP toll free, Yukon-wide, at (867) 667-5555.

Silver Trail Log

Distance is measured from the junction with the Klondike Highway (K).

K 0 **Silver Trail (Stewart Crossing).** The Silver Trail leads northeast from **Milepost J 214.4** on the Klondike Highway.

Junction of Silver Trail (Yukon Highway 11) and Klondike Highway (Yukon Highway 2). Turn to **Milepost J 214.4** on page 251 in the KLONDIKE LOOP section for log of Klondike Highway.

K 0.2 (0.3 km) Marker shows distance to Mayo 51 km, Elsa 97 km, Keno 110 km.

K 1.2 (2 km) Stewart River to the south.

K 3 (4.8 km) Bad curve. Turnout to south.

K 9.6 (15.4 km) Large gravel pit turnout to south.

K 12 (19.2 km) Large double-ended turnout with litter barrels overlooking the Stewart River.

K 27.4 (44.1 km) Pull-through rest area; outhouses, litter barrel, picnic tables.

K 30.7 (49.5 km) Winding descent for northeast-bound traffic; good view of valley.

K 31.2 (50.2 km) McIntyre Park picnic area to south on banks of the Mayo River; 9 picnic sites and a shelter.

K 31.3 (50.3 km) **Mayo River** bridge. Good fishing from bridge for grayling.

K 31.9 (51.3 km) **Junction** with access road to Mayo (description follows). Turn right (south) for Mayo, keep left (north) for road to Elsa and Keno City.

Mayo

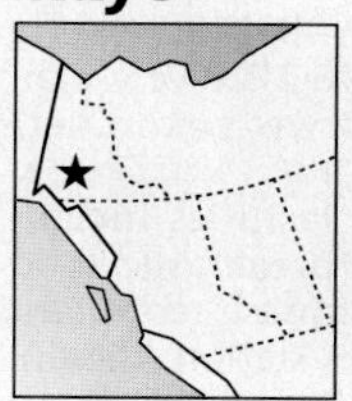

Located on the bank of the Stewart River near its confluence with the Mayo River. **Population:** 500. **Emergency Services: RCMP**, phone (867) 996-5555. **Fire Dept.**, phone (867) 996-2222. **Nursing Station**, phone (867) 996-2345. **Ambulance**, phone (867) 996-4444.

Visitor Information: At **Binet House Interpretive Centre**, open 10 A.M. to 6 P.M. daily from late June through first week in September; phone (867) 996-2926. Exhibits include floral and mineral displays, silver and galena samples, and information panels on mining and geology. Get your Yukon Explorer's Passport stamped here.

Elevation: 1,650 feet/503m. **Climate:** Residents claim it's the coldest and hottest spot in Yukon. Record low, -80°F/-62.2°C (February 1947); record high, 97°F/36.1°C (June 1969). **Radio:** CBC 1230, CHON-FM 98.5, CKRN 98-FM. **Television:** CBC Anik, Channel 7, BCTV, TVNC, ITV, WDIV. **Transportation:** Charter floatplane and helicopter service available. Scheduled bus service.

Private Aircraft: Mayo airstrip, 4 miles/6.5 km north; elev. 1,653 feet/504m; length 4,850 feet/1,478m; gravel; fuel 100, Jet B.

Mayo began as a river settlement and port in 1902–03 after gold was discovered in the area. It was also known as Mayo Landing. River traffic increased with silver ore shipments from Keno Hill silver mines to Whitehorse. A walking tour brochure of Mayo's historic sites is available.

Today, Mayo is a service centre for mineral exploration in the area. Yukon Electrical Co. Ltd. operates a hydroelectric project here. Canoeists can put in at Mayo on the Stewart River for a paddle to Stewart Crossing or Dawson City.

Bedrock Motel. Located 1 mile north of Mayo on the Silver Trail. New facility containing 12 spacious rooms and lounge. Full baths, continental breakfast, home-cooked meals, laundry facilities, air conditioning, wheelchair-accessible suite. Major credit cards accepted. Rates from $75 up. Automotive and bottle propane available, dump station, shower, camping, grassed RV sites (power available). Darren and Joyce Ronaghan, Box 69, Mayo, YT Y0B 1M0. Phone (867) 996-2290, fax (867) 996-2728 or e-mail bedrock@yknet.yk.ca. www.yukon.net/bedrock. [ADVERTISEMENT]

Mayo has most traveler facilities including 2 motels and bed and breakfasts; food service at Bedrock Motel, Chinese restaurant and a cafe; laundromat; 2 gas station (diesel); fishing licenses and snack bar at Heartland Services–Mayo Chevron; hardware, grocery and variety stores (closed Sunday). Tire repair and minor vehicle repair are available. Post office, liquor store and library located in the Territorial Building. Bank service available 10 A.M. to 2 P.M., Tuesday, Thursday and Friday.

The Mayo Midnight Marathon is scheduled for June 24, 2000. The race includes a half marathon, half marathon walk and 10K races. Phone (867) 996-2368 or fax (867) 996-2378 for details.

Heartland Services. See display ad this section.

Silver Trail Log

(continued)

K 32.8 (52.8 km) Mayo airport, built in 1928 by the Treadwell Mining Co.

K 34.9 (56.2 km) Side road to Mayo hydro dam, built in 1951 and completed in 1952.

K 35.8 (57.6 km) Turnoff to west for Five Mile Lake Yukon government campground; 20 sites, boat launch, picnic tables, firepits.

K 36.1 (58.1 km) Five Mile Lake day-use area. Pavement ends, gravel begins, northbound.

K 37.6 (60.5 km) Wareham Lake to east, created by the Mayo River power project.

K 38.2 (61.4 km) Survival shelter to east.

K 42.9 (69 km) **Junction** of Yukon Highway 11 with Minto Lake Road and Duncan Creek Road. Turn west and drive 12 miles/19 km for **Minto Lake**; good fishing for lake trout and grayling. Also access to Highet Creek.

Turn east at junction for 25-mile/40-km **Duncan Creek Road**, which leads to Keno City. The original Silver Trail, Duncan Creek Road was used by Treadwell Yukon during the 1930s to haul silver ore from Keno into Mayo, where it was loaded onto riverboats.

The road is mostly good hard-packed gravel. Motorists note, however, that the last 10 miles/16 km into Keno City via Duncan Creek Road are narrow and winding, slippery when wet and not recommended for large vehicles or trailers. At Mile 14 Duncan Creek Road junctions with a 6-mile/10-km side road which leads to **Mayo Lake**. The lake was named for Alfred S. Mayo, a steamboat captain and a prospecting and trading post partner of Harper and McQuesten in the late 1800s. There is good fishing along the **Mayo River** to the dam at the west end of Mayo Lake. At Mile 14.2 there is a private gold mine (gold panning and guided placer mine tour). At Mile 25 Duncan Creek Road junctions with Highway 11 at Keno City.

K 47.1 (77 km) Watch for turnoff for Mount Haldane trail; follow gravel road 2 miles/3.2 km to trailhead. This 4-mile-/6.4-km-long walking trail leads to the summit of **Mount Haldane**, elev. 6,023 feet/1,836m, and offers sweeping views of the McQuesten River valley and the towns of Elsa and Mayo. A brochure on the trail suggests anyone in average physical condition can make the round-trip in 6 hours (including an hour for lunch at the top). But a couple of *MILEPOST®* readers said they found the trail was poorly marked and a *strenuous* 6-hour (minimum) hike, with slippery sections and a huge scree at the end.The switch-backed trail is visible on the south face of Mount Haldane. The trail was cut by a mining company in the 1970s.

K 48 (77.2 km) **Halfway Lakes;** fishing for northern pike. Silver Trail Inn; food and lodging in summer.

K 49 (78.8 km) Mount Haldane Lions survival shelter.

K 54.9 (88.3 km) South McQuesten River Road.

K 60.3 (97 km) **ELSA** (pop. 10) was a company town for United Keno Hill Mines, formerly one of the largest silver mines in North America and one of the Yukon's oldest continuously operating hardrock mines until its closure in 1989. The Elsa claim is a well-mineralized silver vein, located on Galena Hill and named for the sister of prospector Charlie Brefalt, who received $250,000 for Treadwell Yukon's richest mine. A plaque here commemorates American engineer Livingston Wernecke, who came to the Keno Hill area in 1919 to investigate the silver–lead ore discoveries for Treadwell–Yukon Mining Co.

K 63.8 (102.6 km) Side road leads north to Hanson Lakes and McQuesten Lake. Galena Mountains to east. An information sign marks the Wind River trail, a former winter road to oil and mining exploration sites, which leads 300 miles/483 km north to the Bell River. The twin towers are abandoned telephone relays.

Keno City

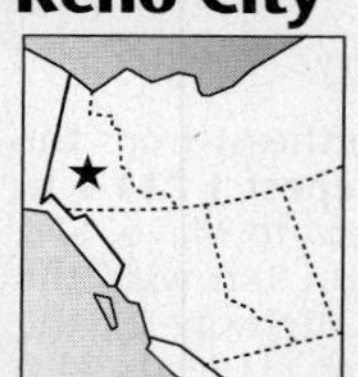

K 69.1 (111.2 km) End of the Silver Trail. **Population:** about 25. Originally called Sheep Hill by the early miners, Keno City was renamed Keno—a gambling game—after the Keno mining claim that was staked by Louis Bouvette in July 1919. This enormously rich discovery of silver and galena sparked the interest of 2 large mining companies, the Guggenheims and Treadwell Yukon, who set up camps in the area. During the 1920s, Keno City was a boom town.

Keno has the Keno City Hotel, with a unique bar (no food service available), and a snack bar. Washers, dryers and showers available for the public at the recreation hall. There is a city campground on Lightning Creek; 17 sites, water, firewood and firepits.

Well worth a visit here is the Keno Mining Museum, phone (867) 995-2792, fax (867) 395-2730. Photographs and tools recall the mining history of the area. It is open 10 A.M. to 6 P.M. in summer. Get your Yukon Explorer's Passport stamped here.

There are a number of hiking trails in the Keno area; inquire at the museum. The Summit trail (can be driven) leads 6.5 miles/10.5 km to the milepost sign on top of **Keno Hill**, elev. 6,065 feet/1,849m. *NOTE: Before driving up to the summit, check at the Keno City Museum or the Keno City Snack Bar for current road conditions.*

CANOL ROAD ⑥

Connects: Alaska Hwy. to NWT Border **Length:** 286 miles
Road Surface: Gravel **Season:** Closed in winter
Highest Summit: Macmillan Pass 4,480 feet
Major Attraction: Canol Heritage Trail

(See map page 716)

	Alaska Hwy. Jct.	Ross River	NWT Border
Alaska Hwy. Jct.		142	286
Ross River	142		144
NWT Border	286	144	

Canol Road winds through mountains near Macmillan Pass. (© Lyn Hancock)

The 513-mile-/825-km-long Canol Road (Yukon Highway 6) was built to provide access to oil fields at Norman Wells, NWT, on the Mackenzie River. Conceived by the U.S. War Dept. to help fuel Alaska and protect it from a Japanese invasion, the Canol (Canadian Oil) Road and a 4-inch-diameter pipeline were constructed from Norman Wells, NWT, through Macmillan Pass, past Ross River, to Johnson's Crossing on the Alaska Highway. From there the pipeline carried oil to a refinery at Whitehorse.

Begun in 1942 and completed in 1944, the Canol Project included the road, pipeline, a telephone line, the refinery, airfields, pumping stations, tank farms, wells and camps. Only about 1 million barrels of oil were pumped to Whitehorse before the war ended in 1945 and the $134 million Canol Project was abandoned. (Today, Norman Wells, pop. 757, is still a major supplier of oil with a pipeline to Zama, AB, built in 1985.) The Canol Road was declared a National Historic Site in 1990.

Since 1958, the Canol Road between Johnson's Crossing on the Alaska Highway and Ross River on the Campbell Highway (referred to as the South Canol Road) and between Ross River and the YT–NWT border (referred to as the North Canol Road) has been rebuilt and is open to summer traffic. It is maintained to minimum standards.

The 136.8-mile/220.2-km South Canol Road is a narrow winding road which crests the Big Salmon Range and threads its way above Lapie Canyon via a difficult but scenic stretch of road. Reconstruction on the South Canol has replaced many old bridges with culverts, but there are still a few 1-lane wooden bridges. Driving time is about 4 hours one way. Watch for steep hills and bad corners. There are no facilities along the South Canol Road, and it is definitely not recommended for large RVs or trailers. Not recommended for any size vehicle in wet weather. Inquiries on current road conditions should be made locally or with the Yukon Dept. of Highways in Whitehorse (867/667-8215) before driving this road.

The 144.2-mile/232-km North Canol Road is also a narrow, winding road which some motorists have compared to a roller coaster. All bridges on the North Canol are 1-lane, and the road surface can be very slippery when wet. Not recommended during wet weather and not recommended for large RVs or trailers. If mining is under way along the North Canol, watch for large transport trucks. *NOTE: Drive with headlights on at all times!*

Our log of the North Canol ends at the YT–NWT border, where vehicles may turn around. Road washouts prohibit travel beyond this point. From the border to Norman Wells it is 230 miles/372 km of unusable road that has been designated the Canol Heritage Trail by the NWT government. Northwest Territories Tourism recommends contacting the Norman Wells Historical Centre (phone 867/587-2415, fax 867/587-2469) for current description of trail conditions and recommended precautions.

WARNING: The only facilities on the Canol Road are at Ross River and at Johnson's Crossing on the Alaska Highway.

Emergency medical services: In Ross River, phone (867) 969-2222; or phone the RCMP, (867) 969-5555, or (867) 667-5555.

South Canol Road Log

Distance from the junction with the Alaska Highway (J) is followed by distance from the Campbell Highway junction (C). *Kilometre figures in the log from the Alaska Highway junction reflect the location of physical kilometreposts when they occur.*

YUKON HIGHWAY 6

J 0 C 136.8 (220.2 km) **Johnson's Crossing**, 0.7 mile/1.1 km from Canol Road turnoff, has food, gas and camping.

Junction of the Canol Road (Yukon Highway 6) with the Alaska Highway (Yukon Highway 1). Turn to **Milepost DC 808.2** in the ALASKA HIGHWAY section for log.

J 0.2 (0.3 km) **C 136.6** (219.8 km) Information panel on the history and construction of Canol Road. Short, dirt road west to auto "boneyard" that includes several WWII Canol Project trucks (all have been significantly cannibalized). Limited turnaround area, not suitable for trailers. Not recommended for any vehicle in wet weather.

J 3.9 (6.2 km) **C 132.9** (213.8 km) Fourmile Creek. Road begins ascent across the Big Salmon Range to the summit (elev. about 4,000 feet/1,219m). Snow possible at summit early October to late spring.

J 13.9 (22.4 km) **C 122.9** (197.8 km) Moose Creek. Small gravel turnout with litter barrels.

J 27 (43.4 km) **C 109.8** (176.7 km) Evelyn Creek 1-lane wooden bridge.

J 28.7 (46.2 km) **C 108.1** (174 km) Sidney Creek 2-lane bridge.

J 30.6 (49.2 km) **C 106.2** (170.9 km) Access road east to **Sidney Lake**. Nice little lake and good place to camp.

From here northbound the South Canol follows the Nisutlin River, which is to the east and can be seen from the road the next 30 miles/48 km until the road crosses the Rose River beyond Quiet Lake.

J 30.9 (49.7 km) **C 105.9** (170.4 km) Turnout with litter barrel to east.

J 39.1 (62.9 km) **C 97.7** (157.2 km) Good view of Pelly Mountains ahead. Road crosses Cottonwood Creek.

CANOL ROAD *Alaska Highway Junction, YT, to NWT Border*

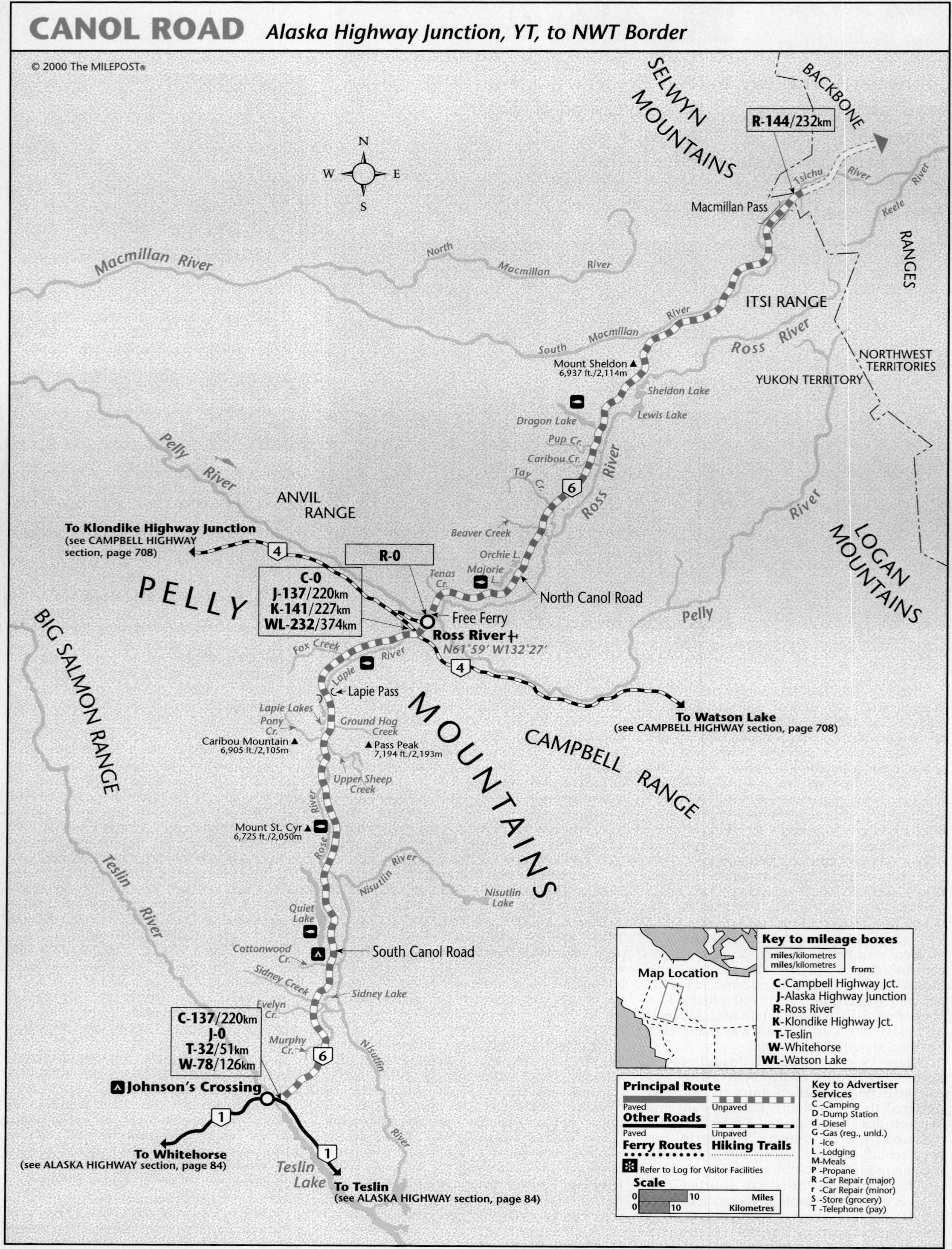

© 2000 The MILEPOST®
SELWYN MOUNTAINS
BACKBONE RANGES
R-144/232km
Tsichu River
Keele River
Macmillan Pass
Macmillan River
North Macmillan River
South Macmillan River
ITSI RANGE
Ross River
NORTHWEST TERRITORIES
YUKON TERRITORY
Mount Sheldon
6,937 ft./2,114m
Sheldon Lake
Lewis Lake
Dragon Lake
Pup Cr.
Caribou Cr.
Tay Cr.
Pelly River
ANVIL RANGE
To Klondike Highway Junction
(see CAMPBELL HIGHWAY section, page 708)
R-0
Beaver Creek
Orchie L.
Majorie L.
Tenas Cr.
North Canol Road
LOGAN MOUNTAINS
C-0
J-137/220km
K-141/227km
WL-232/374km
Free Ferry
Ross River
N61°59' W132°27'
PELLY MOUNTAINS
BIG SALMON RANGE
Fox Creek
Lapie River
Lapie Pass
Lapie Lakes
Pony Cr.
Ground Hog Creek
Caribou Mountain
6,905 ft./2,105m
Pass Peak
7,194 ft./2,193m
To Watson Lake
(see CAMPBELL HIGHWAY section, page 708)
CAMPBELL RANGE
Upper Sheep Creek
Mount St. Cyr
6,725 ft./2,050m
Rose River
Nisutlin River
Nisutlin Lake
Teslin River
Quiet Lake
Cottonwood Cr.
South Canol Road
Sidney Creek
Sidney Lake
Evelyn Cr.
Murphy Cr.
C-137/220km
J-0
T-32/51km
W-78/126km
Johnson's Crossing
To Whitehorse
(see ALASKA HIGHWAY section, page 84)
Teslin Lake
To Teslin
(see ALASKA HIGHWAY section, page 84)
Map Location
Key to mileage boxes
miles/kilometres
miles/kilometres
from:
C-Campbell Highway Jct.
J-Alaska Highway Junction
R-Ross River
K-Klondike Highway Jct.
T-Teslin
W-Whitehorse
WL-Watson Lake
Principal Route
Paved
Unpaved
Other Roads
Paved
Unpaved
Ferry Routes
Hiking Trails
Refer to Log for Visitor Facilities
Scale
0 10 Miles
0 10 Kilometres
Key to Advertiser Services
C -Camping
D -Dump Station
d -Diesel
G -Gas (reg., unld.)
I -Ice
L -Lodging
M -Meals
P -Propane
R -Car Repair (major)
r -Car Repair (minor)
S -Store (grocery)
T -Telephone (pay)

J 42 (67.6 km) **C 94.8** (152.5 km) Access road east 0.4 mile/0.6 km to **Nisutlin River**. Good place to camp with tables and outhouse. ▲

J 47.8 (76.9 km) **C 89** (143.2 km) Quiet Lake Yukon government campground; 20 sites, camping permit ($8), boat launch, picnic tables, kitchen shelter, firewood. Steep hills northbound to Quiet Lake. ▲

J 54.7 (88 km) **C 82.1** (132.1 km) Lake Creek. Road now follows Quiet Lake to west; good fishing for lake trout, northern pike and arctic grayling.

J 56 (90.1 km) **C 80.8** (130 km) Turnout with litter barrels and point of interest sign overlooking **Quiet Lake**. This is the largest of 3 lakes that form the headwaters of the Big Salmon River system. The 17-mile-/28-km-long lake was named in 1887 by John McCormack, 1 of 4 miners who prospected the Big Salmon River from its mouth on the Yukon River to its source. Although they did find some gold, the river and lakes have become better known for their good fishing and fine scenery. Until the completion of the South Canol Road in the 1940s, this area was reached mainly by boating and portaging hundreds of miles up the Teslin and Nisutlin rivers.

J 61.2 (98.5 km) **C 75.6** (121.6 km) Turnoff west for Quiet Lake, day-use area with picnic sites, water, boat launch and fishing. Entry point for canoeists on the Big Salmon River.

J 61.5 (99 km) **C 75.3** (121.2 km) Yukon government Quiet Lake maintenance camp on left northbound. A vintage Canol Project dump truck and pull grader is on display in front of the camp.

J 62.6 (100.7 km) **C 74.2** (119.4 km) Distance marker indicates Ross River 126 km.

J 63.7 (102 km) **C 73.1** (117.6 km) Steep hill and panoramic view of mountains and valley.

J 65.5 (105.4 km) **C 71.3** (114.7 km) One-lane Bailey bridge across **Rose River No. 1**. The road now follows the valley of the Rose River into Lapie Pass northbound. According to R.C. Coutts in *Yukon Places and Names,"* Oliver Rose prospected extensively in this area in the early 1900s. He came to the Yukon from Quebec.

J 94.1 (151.4 km) **C 42.7** (68.7 km) Distance marker indicates Ross River 76 km.

J 95.1 (153 km) **C 41.7** (67.1 km) Upper Sheep Creek joins the Rose River here. To the east is **Pass Peak** (elev. 7,194 feet/2,193m).

J 96.4 (155.1 km) **C 40.4** (65 km) Rose River No. 6.

J 97.1 (156.2 km) **C 39.7** (63.9 km) Rose Lake to east.

J 97.5 (156.9 km) **C 39.3** (63.2 km) Pony Creek. **Caribou Mountain** (elev. 6,905 feet/2,105m) to west.

J 101.1 (162.7 km) **C 35.7** (57.4 km) Lakes to west are part of **Lapie Lakes** chain, headwaters of the Lapie River. These features were named by Dr. George M. Dawson of the Geological Survey of Canada in 1887 for Lapie, an Iroquois Indian companion and canoeman of Robert Campbell, who was the first to explore the Pelly River area in 1843 for the Hudson's Bay Co.

A short dirt road provides access to the lake shore. Watch for grazing moose. Unmaintained camping area and boat launch. ▲

J 102.5 (165 km) **C 34.3** (55.2 km) Access road west to Lapie Lakes. Good place to camp.

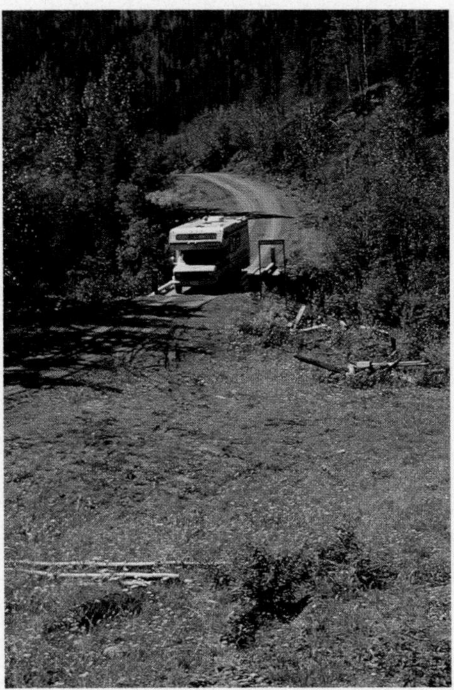

Crossing a 1-lane bridge on the Canol Road. *(© Earl L. Brown, staff)*

J 107.4 (172.8 km) **C 29.4** (47.3 km) Lapie River No. 1 culverts. Ponds reported good for grayling fishing. *NOTE: Watch for horses on the road.*

J 107.5 (173 km) **C 29.3** (47.1 km) Ahead northbound is Barite Mountain (elev. about 6,500 feet/1,981m).

J 120.7 (194.2 km) **C 16.1** (25.9 km) The road follows the Lapie River Canyon for about the next 11 miles/18 km, climbing to an elevation of about 500 feet/152m above the river. *CAUTION: Narrow road, watch for rocks.*

J 123.3 (198.4 km) **C 13.5** (21.7 km) Kilometrepost 200. Distance marker indicates Ross River 26 km. Lapie River runs to east.

J 126.3 (203.2 km) **C 10.5** (16.9 km) Turnouts on right side of road northbound overlooking Lapie River Canyon.

J 132.3 (212.9 km) **C 4.5** (7.2 km) Narrow 1-lane bridge over **Lapie River No. 2**. Point of interest sign on north end of bridge about the **Lapie River Canyon**.

J 133 (214 km) **C 3.8** (6.1 km) Erosional features called hoodoos can be seen in the clay banks rising above the road.

J 133.3 (214.5 km) **C 3.5** (5.6 km) Ash layer can be seen in clay bank on right side of road.

J 135.6 (218.2 km) **C 1.2** (1.9 km) Jackfish Lake to west; floatplane dock.

J 136.8 (220 km) **C 0** Campbell Highway **junction**.

Junction of South Canol Road with the Campbell Highway. Turn to **Milepost WL 227.3** in the CAMPBELL HIGHWAY section for log.

Approximately straight ahead northbound, across the Campbell Highway, a poorly maintained section of the Canol Road continues to Ross River. Motorists bound for Ross River or the North Canol Road are advised to turn left (west) on the Campbell Highway from the South Canol and drive about 5 miles/8 km to the main Ross River access road (see map).

North Canol Road Log

The North Canol Road leads 144.2 miles/232 km to the NWT border. Physical kilometreposts along the North Canol Road reflect distance from the Alaska Highway junction. *WARNING: There are no services along this road.*

Distance from Ross River (R) is shown.

R 0 ROSS RIVER. Yukon government Ross River ferry (free) crosses the Pelly River. Ferry operates from 8 A.M. to noon and 1–5 P.M. daily from late May to mid-October. Those who miss the last ferry crossing of the day may leave their vehicles on the opposite side of the river and use the footbridge to walk into Ross River; vehicles can be brought over in the morning.

R 0.4 (0.6 km) Stockpile to west is barite from the Yukon Barite Mine.

R 0.6 (1 km) Road to east leads to original site of Ross River and Indian village.

R 0.9 (1.4 km) Second access road east to old Ross River and Indian village. Canol Road follows the Ross River.

R 2.1 (3.4 km) *CAUTION: Slide area, watch for falling rocks.*

R 4.7 (7.6 km) Raspberry patch. Good pickings.

R 6.8 (10.9 km) Tenas Creek 1-lane bridge.

R 20.9 (33.6 km) **Marjorie Creek.** Locals report good grayling fishing.

R 21 (33.8 km) Access road to west leads to Marjorie Lake. Access road not recommended for large RVs.

R 28.1 (45.2 km) Boat launch on Orchie Lake to west.

R 29.8 (48 km) Distance marker indicates NWT border 195 km, Ross River 50 km.

R 31.9 (51.3 km) Gravel Creek 1-lane bridge. The next 15 miles/24 km are excellent moose country.

R 33.4 (53.7 km) Flat Creek 1-lane bridge.

R 37 (59.5 km) Beaver Creek 1-lane bridge.

R 41.8 (67.2 km) 180 Mile Creek 1-lane bridge.

R 43.9 (70.6 km) Tay Creek 1-lane bridge.

R 46.3 (74.5 km) Blue Creek 1-lane bridge.

R 48.1 (77.4 km) Kilometrepost 306.

R 57.6 (92.7 km) Clifford's Slough to the east.

R 58.6 (94.3 km) Steep hill to 1-lane bridge over Caribou Creek.

R 61.1 (98.3 km) Distance marker indicates NWT border 145 km, Ross River 100 km.

R 61.8 (99.4 km) **B 82.4** (132.6 km) Pup Creek 1-lane bridge.

R 64.8 (104.3 km) Turnout to west. Steep hill.

R 65.1 (104.7 km) Turnout to **Dragon Lake**; overnight parking, litter barrels. Locals report that early spring is an excellent time for pike and trout in the inlet. Rock hounds check roadsides and borrow pits for colorful chert, which can be worked into jewelry.

R 65.4 (105.2 km) Kilometrepost 334. Large, level gravel turnout to west overlook-

North Canol Road along the Macmillan River. (© Earl L. Brown, staff)

ing Dragon Lake; boat launch.

R 69.6 (112 km) Wreckage of Twin Pioneer aircraft to west. WWII remnants can be found in this area.

R 69.9 (112.5 km) Road to Twin Creek.

R 70.8 (113.9 km) Airstrip.

R 71 (114.2 km) One-lane bridge over Twin Creek No. 1. Yukon government maintenance camp.

R 71.1 (114.4 km) One-lane bridge over Twin Creek No. 2. Good views of Mount Sheldon.

R 75.1 (120.8 km) Kilometrepost 350. **Mount Sheldon** (elev. 6,937 feet/2,114m) ahead northbound, located 3 miles/4.8 km north of Sheldon Lake; a very beautiful and distinguishable feature on the Canol Road. In 1900, Poole Field and Clement Lewis, who were fans of writer Rudyard Kipling, named this peak Kipling Mountain and the lake at its base Rudyard. In 1907, Joseph Keele of the Geological Survey of Canada renamed them after Charles Sheldon, a well-known sheep hunter and naturalist who came to the area to collect Stone sheep specimens for the Chicago Natural History Museum in 1905.

R 76.4 (123 km) Kilometrepost 352. Of the 3-lake chain, Sheldon Lake is farthest north, then Field Lake and Lewis Lake, which is just visible from here. Lewis Lake is closest to the confluence of the Ross and Prevost rivers.

Field Lake and Lewis Lake were named in 1907 by Joseph Keele of the Geological Survey of Canada after Poole Field and Clement Lewis. The 2 partners, who had prospected this country, ran a trading post called Nahanni House at the mouth of the Ross River in 1905.

R 77.6 (124.9 km) Kilometrepost 354. Riddell Creek 1-lane bridge. Tip of **Mount Riddell** (elev. 6,101 feet/1,859m) can be seen to the west.

R 78.8 (126.8 km) View of Sheldon Lake ahead, Field Lake to east.

R 79.8 (128.4 km) Access road east to Sheldon Lake.

R 82.7 (133.1 km) Sheldon Creek 1-lane bridge. Road climbs, leaving Ross River valley and entering Macmillan Valley northbound.

R 89.3 (143.7 km) Height of land before starting descent northbound into South Macmillan River system.

R 89.7 (144.3 km) *Steep hill*. Road may wash out during heavy rains. Deep ditches along roadside help channel water.

R 91.4 (147.1 km) Moose Creek 1-lane bridge.

R 91.6 (147.4 km) **B 52.6** (84.6 km) Milepost 230.

R 92.3 (148.5 km) Kilometrepost 378. Peaks of the Itsi Range ahead. Rugged, spectacular scenery northbound.

R 92.7 (149.1 km) Distance marker indicates NWT border 95 km, Ross River 150 km.

R 93.8 (151 km) First of several WWII vehicle dumps to west. To the east is a wannigan, or skid shack, used as living quarters by Canol Road workers during construction of the road. It was too far to return to base camp; these small buildings were strategically located along the route so the workers had a place to eat and sleep at night.

R 94 (151.3 km) To east are remains of a maintenance depot where heavy equipment was repaired. Concrete foundations to west. First glimpse of the South Macmillan River northbound.

R 94.7 (152.4 km) Kilometrepost 382. Another Canol project equipment dump to explore. Watch ditches for old pieces of pipeline.

R 97.8 (157.4 km) Boulder Creek 1-lane bridge.

R 98.5 (158.5 km) Access road west to **South Macmillan River** where boats can be launched. Locals advise launching boats here rather than from the bridge at **Milepost R 113.6**, which washes out periodically and leaves dangerous debris in the river.

R 100.8 (162.5 km) Kilometrepost 392. **Itsi Range** comes into view ahead northbound. Itsi is said to be an Indian word meaning "wind" and was first given as a name to Itsi Lakes, headwaters of the Ross River. The road dips down and crosses an unnamed creek.

R 104.5 (168.2 km) Kilometrepost 398. View of the South Macmillan River from here.

R 105.3 (169.4 km) View of **Selwyn Mountains**, named in 1901 by Joseph Keele of the Geological Survey of Canada for Dr. Alfred Richard Selwyn (1824–1902), a distinguished geologist in England. Dr. Selwyn later became director of the Geological Survey of Australia and then director of the Geological Survey of Canada from 1869 until his retirement in 1895.

R 111 (178.6 km) Itsi Creek 1-lane bridge.

R 112.2 (180.5 km) Wagon Creek 1-lane bridge.

R 113.6 (182.8 km) Turnout to east on South Macmillan River. Good place for a picnic but not recommended as a boat launch. One-lane Bailey bridge over South Macmillan River No. 1.

Robert Campbell, a Hudson's Bay Co. explorer on a journey down the Pelly River in 1843, named this major tributary of the Pelly after Chief Factor James McMillan, who had sponsored Campbell's employment with the company.

R 115.1 (185.2 km) Access road on left northbound leads about 7 miles/11 km to Yukon Barite Mine. Barite is a soft mineral that requires only crushing and bagging before being shipped over the Dempster Highway to the Beaufort Sea oil and gas wells, where it is used as a lubricant known as drilling mud.

R 118.9 (191.3 km) Jeff Creek 1-lane bridge.

R 121.2 (195 km) Hess Creek 1-lane bridge. Bears in area.

R 123.2 (198.3 km) Gravel turnout to west. Distance marker indicates NWT border 45 km, Ross River 200 km. One-lane bridge over Dewhurst Creek.

R 127.5 (205.2 km) Entering **Macmillan Pass**, "Mac Pass" (elev. 4,480 feet/1,366m).

R 129.4 (208.2 km) One-lane bridge over Macmillan River No. 2.

R 129.5 (208.4 km) Abandoned Army vehicles from the Canol Project to west and east.

R 133.6 (215 km) To the west is Cordilleran Engineering camp, managers of the mining development of Ogilvie Joint Venture's Jason Project. The Jason deposit is a zinc, lead, silver, barite property.

One-lane bridge over Sekie Creek No. 1.

R 136.4 (219.5 km) Access to Macmillan airstrip on left northbound. Access road east to Hudson Bay Mining & Smelting's Tom lead–zinc mineral claims.

R 137.7 (221.6 km) One-lane bridge over Macmillan River No. 3.

R 141.8 (228.2 km) One-lane bridge over Macmillan River No. 4.

R 142.9 (230 km) One-lane bridge over Macmillan River No. 5.

R 144.1 (231.9 km) One-lane bridge over Macmillan River No. 6.

R 144.2 (232 km) **YT–NWT Border.** Sign cautions motorists to proceed at their own risk. The road is not maintained and bridges are not safe beyond this point. Vehicles turn around here.

Ahead is the Tsichu River valley and the Selwyn Mountains. The abandoned North Canol Road continues another 230 miles/372 km from the YT–NWT border to Norman Wells, NWT. Designated the Canol Heritage Trail, and set aside as a territorial park reserve, the trail is under development. Some river crossings required; large stretches deemed dangerous and arduous. It passes through mountains, tundra and forest, and past many relics of the Canol Project. The Historical Centre museum in Norman Wells features the history of the Canol Project and has outdoor displays of Canol vehicles. Phone (867) 587-2415; fax (867) 587-2469.

DEMPSTER HIGHWAY (5) (8)

Connects: Klondike Hwy. to Inuvik, NWT **Length:** 456 miles
Road Surface: Gravel **Season:** Open all year
Highest Summit: North Fork Pass 4,265 feet
Major Attractions: Lost Patrol Gravesite, Mackenzie River Delta

(See map page 720)

	Dawson City	Ft. McPherson	Inuvik	Klondike Hwy.
Dawson City		367	481	25
Ft. McPherson	367		114	342
Inuvik	481	114		456
Klondike Hwy.	25	342	456	

The Dempster Highway climbs above treeline. (© Earl L. Brown, staff)

The Dempster Highway (Yukon Highway 5, NWT Highway 8) begins 25 miles/40.2 km east of Dawson City, YT, at its junction with Klondike Highway 2 and leads 456.3 miles/734.3 km northeast to Inuvik, NWT. The highway can be driven in 12 to 16 hours, but allow extra time to enjoy the wilderness. The Dempster offers hiking, camping, fishing and spectacular photo opportunities. It also has a reputation as a birder's paradise.

Construction of the Dempster Highway began in 1959, under the Road to Resources program. It was completed in 1978. A 5-year major reconstruction program on the highway was completed in 1988.

The Dempster is a mostly gravel road. The first 5 miles/8 km are seal coated, and the last 6 miles/10 km are paved. There are stretches of clay surface that can be slippery in wet weather. Summer driving conditions on the Dempster vary depending on weather and maintenance. Generally, road conditions range from fair to excellent, with highway speeds attainable on some sections. But freezing winter weather and heavy truck traffic can erode both road base and surfacing, resulting in areas of rough road. Calcium chloride is used to reduce dust and as a bonding agent; wash your vehicle as soon as practical.

It is strongly recommended motorists carry at least 2 spare tires while traveling the Dempster. *Drive with your headlights on.*

Facilities are still few and far between on the Dempster. Full auto services are available at Klondike River Lodge at the Dempster Highway turnoff on Klondike Highway 2. Gas, propane, food and lodging, and car repair are also available at Eagle Plains Hotel, located at about the halfway point on the Dempster. Gas, food and lodging are also available in Fort McPherson. Gas up whenever possible.

The Dempster is open year-round, but summer travel gives visitors long hours of daylight for recreation. The highway is fairly well-traveled in summer: A driver may not see another car for an hour, and then pass 4 cars in a row. Locals say the highway is smoother and easier to drive in winter, but precautions should be taken against cold weather, high winds and poor visibility; check road conditions before proceeding in winter. Watch for herds of caribou mid-September to late October and in March and April.

There are 2 ferry crossings on the Dempster, at **Milepost J 334.9** (Peel River crossing) and **J 377.9** (Mackenzie River and

DEMPSTER HIGHWAY *Klondike Highway Junction to Inuvik, NWT*

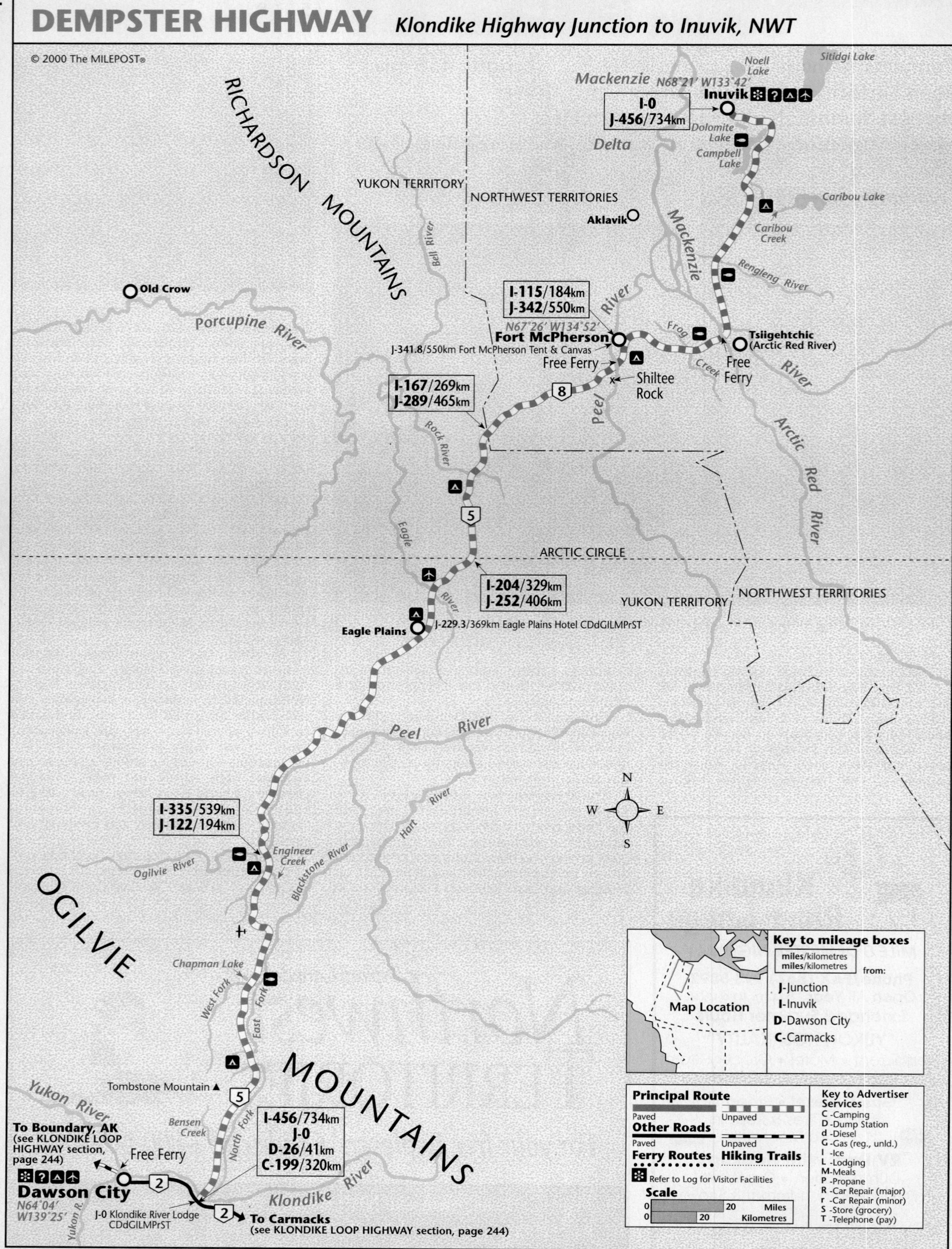

© 2000 The MILEPOST®
RICHARDSON MOUNTAINS
OGILVIE MOUNTAINS
YUKON TERRITORY
NORTHWEST TERRITORIES
ARCTIC CIRCLE
Mackenzie Delta
N68°21' W133°42'
Inuvik
I-0
J-456/734km
Noell Lake
Sitidgi Lake
Dolomite Lake
Campbell Lake
Caribou Lake
Caribou Creek
Aklavik
Mackenzie River
Rengleng River
Bell River
Old Crow
Porcupine River
I-115/184km
J-342/550km
N67°26' W134°52'
Fort McPherson
J-341.8/550km Fort McPherson Tent & Canvas
Free Ferry
Frog Creek
Tsiigehtchic (Arctic Red River)
Free Ferry
Shiltee Rock
Peel River
Arctic Red River
I-167/269km
J-289/465km
Rock River
Eagle River
I-204/329km
J-252/406km
Eagle Plains
J-229.3/369km Eagle Plains Hotel CDdGILMPrST
Peel River
Hart River
N
W
E
S
I-335/539km
J-122/194km
Engineer Creek
Ogilvie River
Blackstone River
Chapman Lake
West Fork
East Fork
North Fork
Tombstone Mountain
Yukon River
Bensen Creek
To Boundary, AK (see KLONDIKE LOOP HIGHWAY section, page 244)
Free Ferry
Dawson City
N64°04' W139°25'
Yukon R.
J-0 Klondike River Lodge CDdGILMPrST
I-456/734km
J-0
D-26/41km
C-199/320km
Klondike River
To Carmacks (see KLONDIKE LOOP HIGHWAY section, page 244)
Map Location
Key to mileage boxes
miles/kilometres
miles/kilometres
from:
J-Junction
I-Inuvik
D-Dawson City
C-Carmacks
Principal Route
Paved
Unpaved
Other Roads
Paved
Unpaved
Ferry Routes
Hiking Trails
Refer to Log for Visitor Facilities
Scale
0 20 Miles
0 20 Kilometres
Key to Advertiser Services
C -Camping
D -Dump Station
d -Diesel
G -Gas (reg., unld.)
I -Ice
L -Lodging
M -Meals
P -Propane
R -Car Repair (major)
r -Car Repair (minor)
S -Store (grocery)
T -Telephone (pay)

Arctic Red River crossings). Free government ferry service is available 15 hours a day (9 A.M. to 12:45 A.M. Northwest Territories time) during summer (from about early June to late October. Cross by ice bridge in winter. For recorded messages on ferry service, road and weather conditions, phone (800) 661-0752.

General information on Northwest Territories is available by calling the Arctic Hotline at (800) 661-0788. If you are in Dawson City, we recommend visiting the Western Arctic Visitor Centre for information on Northwest Territories and the Dempster Highway. Located in the B.Y.N. Building on Front Street, across from the Yukon Visitor Centre, it is open 9 A.M. to 9 P.M., June to September; phone (867) 993-6167. Or write Western Arctic Trade & Tourism, Box 2600MP, Inuvik, NT X0E 0T0; phone (867) 777-4321, fax (867) 777-2434 for more information.

The MILEPOST® expresses its appreciation to the Yukon Dept. of Renewable Resources, Parks and Recreation for its assistance with information in this highway log.

View of North Fork Pass and river from turnout at Milepost J 46. (© Earl L. Brown, staff)

Dempster Highway Log

Distance from junction with Klondike Highway 2 (J) is followed by distance from Inuvik (I).

Driving distance is measured in miles. The kilometre figure on the Yukon portion of the highway reflects the physical kilometreposts and is not necessarily an accurate metric conversion of the mileage figure. Kilometreposts are green with white lettering and are located on the right-hand side of the highway, northbound.

YUKON HIGHWAY 5

J 0 I 456.3 (734.3 km) **Dempster Corner**, 25 miles/40.2 km east of Dawson City. Klondike River Lodge (open all year); food, gas, propane, lodging, camping, and tire repair and sales. ▲

NOTE: Next available gas northbound is at Eagle Plains, 229 miles/369 km from here.

Klondike River Lodge. See display ad on page 719.

Junction of Klondike Highway (Yukon Highway 2) and Dempster Highway (Yukon Highway 5). Turn to **Milepost J 301.6** in the KLONDIKE LOOP section for log of Klondike Highway to Dawson City.

J 0.1 (0.2 km) **I 456.2** (734.2 km) Dempster Highway monument with information panels on history and culture, wildlife, ecology and driving tips.

J 0.2 (0.3 km) **I 456.1** (734 km) One-lane wood-planked bridge over Klondike River. The road follows the wooded (spruce and poplar) North Klondike River valley.

J 0.9 (1.4 km) **I 455.4** (732.9 km) Distance marker shows Eagle Plains 363 km (226 miles), Inuvik 735 km (457 miles).

J 3 (5 km) **I 453.3** (729.5 km) Burn area from 1991 fire that burned 5,189 acres/2,100 hectares.

J 4 (6.4 km) **I 452.3** (727.9 km) The North Fork Ditch channeled water from the North Klondike River to a power plant 15.5 miles/25 km farther west for nearly 60 years, until the 1960s, and it helped to provide electricity and water for huge gold-dredging operations farther down the valley. Watch for salmon migrating upstream from late July through August.

J 4.8 (7.7 km) **I 451.5** (726.6 km) Turnoff for Viceroy Brewery Creek Gold Mine (private road).

J 6.5 (10.5 km) **I 449.8** (723.9 km) Antimony Mountain (elev. 6,693 feet/2,040m) about 18.5 miles/30 km away, is one peak of the Ogilvie Mountains and part of the Snowy Range.

J 12.4 (20 km) **I 443.9** (714.4 km) North Klondike Range, Ogilvie Mountains to the west of the highway lead toward the rugged, interior Tombstone Range. These mountains were glaciated during the Ice Age.

J 15.4 (24.5 km) **I 440.9** (709.5 km) Glacier Creek.

J 16.6 (26.7 km) **I 439.7** (707.6 km) Pullout to west.

J 18.1 (29 km) **I 438.2** (705.2 km) Bensen Creek.

J 25.6 (41 km) **I 430.7** (693.1 km) Pea Soup Creek.

J 29.8 (48 km) **I 426.5** (686.4 km) Scout Car Creek.

J 31.7 (51 km) **I 424.6** (683.3 km) Wolf Creek. Private cabin beside creek.

J 34.7 (55.8 km) **I 421.6** (678.5 km) Highway follows North Fork Klondike River.

J 36.6 (58.9 km) **I 419.7** (675.4 km) Grizzly Creek. Mount Robert Service to right northbound.

J 39.6 (63.7 km) **I 416.7** (670.6 km) Mike and Art Creek.

J 40.4 (65 km) **I 415.9** (669.3 km) Klondike Camp Yukon government highway maintenance station. No visitor services but may provide help in an emergency.

J 41.8 (67.3 km) **I 414.5** (667.1 km) First crossing of the **North Fork Klondike River**. The highway now moves above tree line and on to tundra northbound. At an elevation of approximately 4,003 feet/1,220m, you'll cross the watershed between the Yukon and Mackenzie basins.

J 43 (69.2 km) **I 413.3** (665.2 km) Spectacular first view of Tombstone Range northbound.

J 44.4 (71.5 km) **I 411.9** (662.9 km) Yukon government **Tombstone Mountain Campground** (elev. 3,392 feet/1,034m); 31 sites, camping permit ($8), shelter, fireplaces, water from the river, tables, pit toilets. Designated cyclist camping area. Stop in at the Dempster Interpretive Centre located at the campground; fossil displays, resource library, handouts with area information, campfire talks and nature walks. Open daily from mid-June to early September. Good hiking trail begins past the outhouses and leads toward the headwaters of the North Fork Klondike River. *CAUTION: Hikers should inquire about recent bear activity in the area before setting off.* ▲

J 46 (74 km) **I 410.3** (660.3 km) Large double-ended viewpoint. Good views of North Fork Pass and river. To the southwest is the needle-like peak of **Tombstone Mountain** (elev. 7,195 feet/2,193m), which forms the centrepoint in a panorama of ragged ridges and lush green tundra slopes. To the north is the East Fork Blackstone River valley; on each side are the Ogilvie Mountains, which rise to elevations of 6,890 feet/2,100m. Watch for Dall sheep, grizzlies, hoary marmots and ptarmigan. The Tombstone, Cloudy and Blackstone mountain ranges are identified as a Special Management Area by the Yukon government and will eventually become a Yukon Territorial Park.

Day hikes up the North Klondike River valley and 4-day wilderness hikes to Tombstone Mountain are popular. Heli-hiking is also growing in popularity; inquire at Trans North Helicopters in Dawson City about fly-in/hike-out packages. There are no established trails. The staff at the Dempster Interpretive Centre at Tombstone Campground can provide maps and suggest itineraries. Hikers should be well prepared for rough terrain, drastic weather changes and potential wildlife encounters, as well as practicing "leave-no-trace" camping. For more information on the Tombstone region, call Yukon Dept. of Renewable Resources, Parks & Outdoor Recreation Branch at (867) 667-8299 or e-mail <jack.schick@gov.yk.ca>.

Outstanding aerial view of the mountain available through flightseeing trip out of Dawson City.

J 48.4 (77.9 km) **I 407.9** (656.4 km) Blackstone River culvert. Tundra in the region indicates permafrost.

J 51 (82 km) **I 405.3** (652.2 km) **North Fork Pass Summit**, elev. 4,265 feet/1,300m, is the highest point on the Dempster Highway. Wildflowers abundant late June–early

Sapper Hill and erosion pillars at about Milepost J 120. (© Earl L. Brown, staff)

July. Descent to the Blackstone River. Good bird-watching area. A hike up to the lower knoll to the right of the main mountain increases chances of seeing pika and marmots.

J 52.2 (84 km) **I 404.1** (650.3 km) Anglecomb Peak (also called Sheep Mountain) is a lambing and nursery habitat for Dall sheep during May and June. A 1994 census showed 250 sheep in the area. This is also a frequent nesting area for a pair of golden eagles.

J 54.2 (87.2 km) **I 402.1** (647.1 km) First crossing of East Fork Blackstone River.

J 54.6 (87.9 km) **I 401.7** (646.4 km) White fireweed in summer.

J 56.5 (91 km) **I 399.8** (643.4 km) Guide and outfitters camp to east. *CAUTION: Watch for horses on road.*

The Blackstone Uplands, stretching from North Fork Pass to Chapman Lake, are a rich area for birdlife (long-tailed jaegers, gyrfalcons, peregrine falcons, red-throated loons, whimbrels, upland sandpipers and oldsquaw ducks) and big game hunting for Dall sheep and grizzly bear.

J 63.4 (102 km) **I 392.9** (632.3 km) Distance marker shows Eagle Plains 261 km (162 miles), Inuvik 633 km (393 miles), Dawson 142 km (88 miles), Whitehorse 600 km (373 miles).

J 64.4 (103.6 km) **I 391.9** (630.7 km) **Two Moose Lake**; turnout with information panels and viewing platform.

J 66.9 (107.6 km) **I 389.4** (626.7 km) Large gravel pullout with dumpster. Access to Blackstone River.

J 71.5 (115 km) **I 384.8** (619.3 km) First crossing of **West Fork Blackstone River**. Watch for arctic terns. Good fishing for Dolly Varden and grayling a short distance downstream where the west and east forks of the Blackstone join to form the Blackstone River, which the road now follows. After the river crossing, 2 low, cone-shaped mounds called pingos are visible upriver about 5 miles/8 km.

J 72.1 (116 km) **I 384.2** (618.3 km) Turnout to west. View over **Chapman Lake**, one of the few lakes close to the highway that is large enough to permit floatplane operations. Common loons nest on island. Commemorative road sign about sled dog patrols of the Royal North West Mounted Police.

Porcupine caribou herd sometimes crosses the highway in this area in mid-October.

J 77.3 (124.4 km) **I 379** (609.9 km) **Private Aircraft:** Government airstrip (road is part of the strip); elev. 3,100 feet/945m; length 3,000 feet/914m.

J 96 (154.5 km) **I 360.3** (579.8 km) Northbound, highway passes through barren gray hills of Windy Pass. The mountain ridges are the breeding habitat for some species of butterflies and moths not known to exist anywhere else.

J 98.2 (158 km) **I 358.1** (576.3 km) Gyrfalcon nest on ledge on side of cliff.

J 106 (169.7 km) **I 350.3** (563.7 km) Creek culvert is red from iron oxide. Sulfurous smell is from nearby sulfur springs. Watch for interesting geological features in hills along road.

J 108.1 (173 km) **I 348.2** (560.4 km) Views of red-coloured **Engineer Creek**, and also erosion pillars and red rock of nearby hills between here and Kilometrepost 182.

J 121.7 (194 km) **I 334.6** (538.5 km) **Sapper Hill**, named in 1971 in honour of the 3rd Royal Canadian Engineers who built the Ogilvie River bridge. "Sapper" is a nickname for an army engineer. Yukon government **Engineer Creek Campground**; 15 sites, camping permit ($8), fireplaces, water, tables, pit toilets. Grayling fishing.

J 122.9 (195.7 km) **I 333.4** (536.5 km) The 360-foot/110-m Jeckell Bridge spans the **Ogilvie River** here. Built by the Canadian Armed Forces Engineers as a training exercise, it is named in honour of Allan Jeckell, controller of the Yukon from 1932 to 1946. Fossil coral may be visible in limestone outcrops to the northeast of the bridge.

The Ogilvie River and Ogilvie Mountains were named in honour of William Ogilvie, a highly respected Dominion land surveyor and commissioner of the Yukon during the Klondike Gold Rush.

J 123 (195.8 km) **I 333.3** (536.4 km) Ogilvie grader station, Yukon government maintenance camp is on north side of the river.

For the next 25 miles/40 km, the highway follows the narrow valley of the Ogilvie River. For the first 12 miles/20 km, talus slopes edge the road, and game trails are evident along their precipitous sides.

J 124.3 (197.7 km) **I 332** (534.3 km) View of castlelike outcroppings of rock, known as **tors**, on mountaintops to north.

J 131.9 (209.5 km) **I 324.4** (522.1 km) Between here and Kilometrepost 216, watch for bird nests in the shale embankments along the highway and unusual rock outcroppings and erosion pillars in surrounding hills. Highway crosses rolling plateau country near Kilometrepost 218.

J 137.5 (221.2 km) **I 318.8** (513 km) Small turnout with litter barrels. Easy access to **Ogilvie River**. Good grayling fishing. Elephant Rock may be viewed from right side of road northbound. Fascinating mountain of broken rock and shale near Kilometrepost 224.

J 137.6 (221.5 km) **I 318.7** (512.9 km) Davies Creek.

J 149.1 (235.8 km) **I 307.2** (494.4 km) Ogilvie airstrip. The great gray owl, one of Canada's largest, is known to nest as far north as this area.

J 154.4 (244 km) **I 301.9** (485.8 km) Highway climbs away from the Ogilvie River, following a high ridge to the Eagle Plains plateau. One of the few unglaciated areas in Canada, this country is shaped by wind and water erosion rather than by ice. Views of Mount Cronkhite and Mount McCullum to the east.

Overgrown seismic lines next 62 miles/100 km are a reminder that this was the major area of oil and gas exploration activity for which the road was originally built. In season, fields of cotton grass and varieties of tundra plants make good photo subjects. The road continues to follow a high ridge (elev. 1,969 feet/600m) with broad sweeps and easy grades.

J 160.9 (259 km) **I 295.4** (475.4 km) Panoramic **Ogilvie Ridge** viewpoint is a large double-ended turnout with interpretive panels on the geology of the area; outhouse, litter barrels. Lowbush cranberries in August.

J 169.4 (272.6 km) **I 286.9** (461.7 km) Highway begins descent northbound and crosses fabulous high rolling country above tree line.

J 202 (325 km) **I 254.3** (409.2 km) Road widens to become part of an airstrip.

J 206.9 (325 km) **I 249.4** (401.3 km) Double-ended turnout with litter barrels.

J 215.6 (347 km) **I 240.7** (387.4 km) Richardson Mountains to the northeast. The

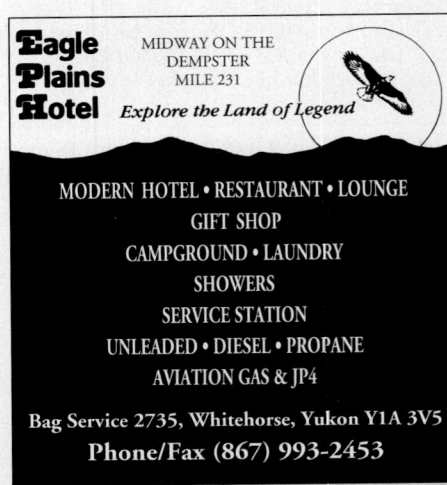

thick blanket of rock and gravel that makes up the roadbed ahead is designed to prevent the underlying permafrost from melting. The roadbed conducts heat more than the surrounding vegetation does and must be extra thick to compensate. Much of the highway was built in winter.

J 229.3 (369 km) **I 227** (365.3 km) **Milepost 231. EAGLE PLAINS;** hotel, phone (867) 993-2453; food, gas, propane, aviation fuel, diesel, tire repair, lodging and camping. Open year-round. ▲

Built in 1978, just before completion of the Dempster Highway, the hotel here was an engineering challenge. Engineers considered the permafrost in the area and found a place where the bedrock was at the surface. The hotel was built on this natural pad, thus avoiding the costly process of building on pilings as was done at Inuvik.

J 234.8 (377.8 km) **I 221.5** (356.5 km) Short side road to picnic site with information sign about Albert Johnson, "The Mad Trapper of Rat River." Something of a mystery man, Johnson killed one mounted policeman and wounded another in 2 separate incidents involving complaints that Johnson was tampering with Native trap lines. The ensuing manhunt became famous in the North, as Johnson eluded Mounties for 48 days during the winter of 1931–32. Johnson was killed in a shoot-out on Feb. 17, 1932. He was buried at Aklavik, a community located 36 miles/58 km west of Inuvik by air.

Dick North, author of 2 books on Johnson (and also author of *The Lost Patrol*), was quoted in the *New York Times* (June 3, 1990) as being 95 percent certain that Johnson, whose true identity has not been known, was a Norwegian–American bank robber named Johnny Johnson.

J 234.9 (378 km) **I 221.4** (356.3 km) **Eagle River Bridge**. Like the Ogilvie bridge, it was built by the Dept. of National Defense as a training exercise. In contrast to the other rivers seen from the Dempster, the Eagle is a more sluggish, silt-laden stream with unstable banks. It is the main drainage channel for the western slopes of the Richardson Mountains. It and its tributaries provide good grayling fishing. Canoeists leave here bound for Alaska via the Porcupine and Yukon rivers.

J 239.4 (385.3 km) **I 216.9** (349.1 km) Views of the Richardson Mountains (elev. 3,937 feet/1,200m) ahead. Named for Sir John Richardson, surgeon and naturalist on both of Sir John Franklin's overland expeditions to the Arctic Ocean.

J 241.7 (389 km) **I 214.6** (345.4 km) **Private Aircraft:** Emergency airstrip; elev. 2,365 feet/721m; length 2,500 feet/762m; gravel. Used regularly by aircraft hauling freight to Old Crow, a Kutchin Indian settlement on the Porcupine River and Yukon's most northerly community.

J 252 (405.5 km) **I 204.3** (328.8 km) Large double-ended turnout at **Arctic Circle Crossing**, 66°33'N; picnic tables, litter barrels, outhouses. On June 21, the sun does not fall below the horizon for 24 hours at this latitude.

Vehicles cross the Mackenzie River at Arctic Red River by ferry. (© Roger Pickenpaugh)

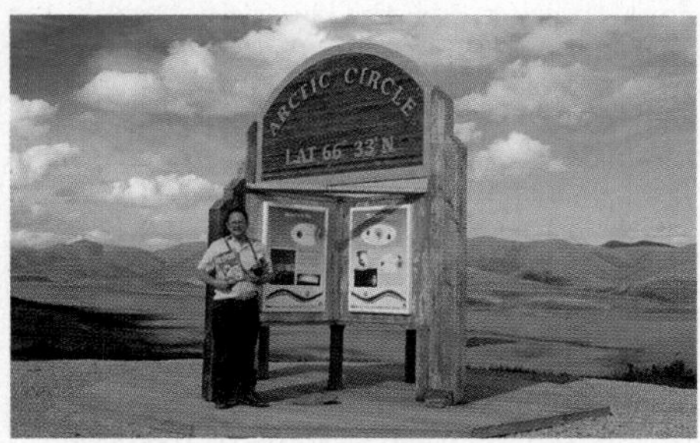

Highway crosses arctic tundra on an elevated berm beside the Richardson Mountains; sweeping views.

J 269 (432.9 km) **I 187.3** (301.4 km) Rock River.

J 277 (445.8 km) **I 179.3** (288.5 km) Yukon government **Cornwall River Campground**; 18 sites, camping permit ($8), tables, kitchen shelter, water, firepits, outhouses. Black flies; bring repellent. ▲

J 280.1 (450.8 km) **I 176.2** (283.6 km) Turnout. Northbound, the highway winds toward the Richardson Mountains, crossing them at George's Gap near the YT–NWT border. Good hiking area and excellent photo possibilities.

J 288 (463.5 km) **I 168.3** (270.8 km) Turnout; good overnight spot for self-contained vehicles.

J 288.5 (464.3 km) **I 167.8** (270 km) Plaque about Wright Pass, named for Al Wright, a highway engineer with Public Works Canada who was responsible for the routing of the Dempster Highway.

J 288.9 (465 km) **I 167.4** (269.4 km) **YT-NWT Border**. Historical marker. *TIME ZONE CHANGE: Yukon Territory observes Pacific standard time; Northwest Territories is on Mountain time.* Continental Divide in the Richardson Mountains: West of here, water flows to the Pacific Ocean. East of here, water flows to the Arctic Ocean. Good photo spot.

NWT HIGHWAY 8

IMPORTANT: Kilometreposts northbound (with white letters on a blue background) indicate distance from YT–NWT border and are indicated at intervals in our log. Highway descends, road narrows, northbound.

J 297.6 (479 km) **I 158.7** (255.4 km) Kilometrepost 14. **James Creek;** good grayling fishing. Highway maintenance camp. Good spot to park overnight.

J 299 (481.2 km) **I 157.3** (253.1 km) Sign advises no passing next 4.3 miles/7 km; climb to Wright Pass summit.

J 303.7 (488.7 km) **I 152.6** (245.6 km) **Wright Pass Summit**. From here northbound, the Dempster Highway descends 2,300 feet/853m to the Peel River crossing, 32 miles/51 km away.

J 316.3 (509 km) **I 140** (225.3 km) Kilometrepost 44. Side road leads down to **Midway Lake**.

J 319.4 (514 km) **I 136.9** (220.3 km) **Private Aircraft:** Highway widens to form Midway airstrip; length 3,000 feet/914m.

J 329.3 (530 km) **I 127** (204.4 km) View of Peel River Valley and Fort McPherson to north. Litter barrels.

J 332.4 (535 km) **I 123.9** (199.4 km) Kilometrepost 70. Highway begins descent northbound to Peel River.

J 334.9 (539 km) **I 121.4** (195.4 km) **Peel River Crossing**, locally called Eightmile because it is situated 8 miles/12.8 km south of Fort McPherson. Free government ferry (CF *Abraham Francis*) operates 15 hours a day during summer from early June to late October. Double-ended cable ferry: Drive on, drive off. Light vehicles cross by ice bridge in late November; heavier vehicles cross as ice thickens. *No crossing possible during freezeup or breakup.* Phone toll free (800) 661-0752 for information on ferry crossings, road conditions and weather.

The level of the Peel River changes rapidly in spring and summer in response to meltwater from the mountains and ice jams on the Mackenzie River. Extreme high and low water level fluctuations may cause delays in ferry service. The alluvial flood plain is covered by muskeg on the flats, and scrubby alder and stunted black spruce on the valley sides.

Indians from Fort McPherson have summer tent camps on the Peel River. The

Indians net whitefish and sheefish (inconnu) then dry them on racks or in smokehouses for the winter.

About 4 miles/6.4 km south upstream is a trail leading to Shiltee Rock, which gives excellent views of the Peel River and the southern end of the Mackenzie.

J 335.9 (540.6 km) **I 120.4** (193.8 km) Nitainilaii territorial campground with 20 sites. (Campground name is from the Gwich'in term *Noo-til-ee,* meaning "fast flowing waters.") Information centre open daily June to September. Camping permits, potable water, firewood, pit toilets and kitchen shelter available. ▲

J 337.4 (543 km) **I 118.9** (191.3 km) Kilometrepost 78.

J 340.4 (547.8 km) **I 115.9** (186.5 km) Access road right to Fort McPherson airport.

J 341.8 (550 km) **I 114.5** (184.3 km) Side road on left to Fort McPherson (Tetlin Zheh); description follows.

Fort McPherson

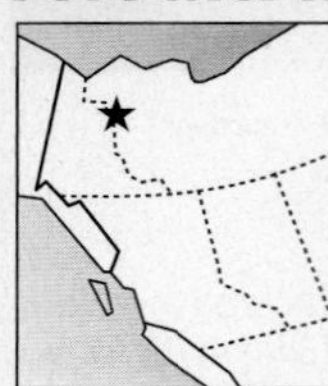

Located on a flat-topped hill about 100 feet/30m above the Peel River, 24 miles/38 km from its junction with the Mackenzie River; 100 miles/160 km southwest of Aklavik by boat along Peel Channel, 31 miles/50 km directly east of the Richardson Mountains. **Population**: 632. **Emergency Services: RCMP**, phone (867) 952-2551. **Health Center**, phone (867) 952-2586.

Visitor Information: Located in a restored log house, the former home of elder Annie G. Robert; open daily, early June through mid-September, 9 A.M. to 9 P.M. **Radio**: CBC 680.

Transportation: Air—Aklak Air provides scheduled air service from Inuvik.

Private Aircraft: Fort McPherson airstrip; 67°24'N 134°51'W; elev. 142 feet/43m; length 3,500 feet/1,067m; gravel.

This Déné Indian settlement has a public phone, cafe, bed and breakfast, 2 general stores and 2 service stations (1 with tire repair). A co-op hotel here offers 8 rooms. Arts and crafts include beadwork and hide garments. Wildlife watching, adventure tours and canoe trips are popular along the Peel River.

Fort McPherson was named in 1848 for Murdoch McPherson, chief trader of the Hudson's Bay Co., which had established its first posts in the area 8 years before. Between 1849 and 1859 there were frequent feuds with neighboring Inuit, who later moved farther north to the Aklavik area, where they established a fur-trading post.

In addition to subsistence fishing and hunting, income is earned from trapping (mostly muskrat and mink), handicrafts, government employment, and commercial enterprises such as Fort McPherson Tent and Canvas factory, which specializes in travel bags, tents and tepees. Tours during business hours, 9 A.M. to 5 P.M. weekdays; (867) 952-2179, fax (867) 952-2718.

Photos and artifacts depicting the history and way of life of the community are displayed in the Chief Julius School. Buried in the cemetery outside the Anglican church are Inspector Francis J. Fitzgerald and 3 men from the ill-fated North West Mounted Police patrol of 1910–1911 between Fort McPherson and Dawson.

Inspector Fitzgerald and the men had left Fort McPherson on Dec. 21, 1910, carrying mail and dispatches to Dawson City. By Feb. 20, 1911, the men had not yet arrived in Dawson, nearly a month overdue. A search party led by Corporal W.J.D. Dempster was sent to look for the missing patrol. On March 22, 1911, Dempster discovered their frozen bodies only 26 miles from where they had started. Lack of knowledge of the trail, coupled with too few rations, had doomed the 4-man patrol. One of the last entries in Fitzgerald's diary, quoted in Dick North's *The Lost Patrol*, an account of their journey, read: "We have now only 10 pounds of flour and 8 pounds of bacon and some dried fish. My last hope is gone. ... We have been a week looking for a river to take us over the divide, but there are dozens of rivers, and I am at a loss."

Lost Patrol gravesite at Fort McPherson.
(© Carol Murdock)

Dempster Highway Log
(continued)

J 342.4 (551 km) **I 113.9** (183.3 km) Kilometrepost 86.

J 365.1 (587.6 km) **I 91.2** (146.8 km) **Frog Creek.** Grayling and pike. Road on right northbound leads to picnic area.

J 377.1 (606.8 km) **I 79.2** (127.5 km) Mackenzie River wayside area.

J 377.9 (608.2 km) **I 78.4** (126.2 km) **Mackenzie River Crossing**. Free government ferry (MV *Louis Cardinal*) operates 15 hours a day during summer from early June to late October. Double-ended ferry: Drive on, drive off. Light vehicles may cross by ice bridge in late November; heavier vehicles can cross as ice thickens. *No crossing possible during freezeup and breakup.*

The ferry travels between landings on either side of the Mackenzie River and also provides access to **TSIIGEHTCHIC (formerly ARCTIC RED RIVER)**, a small Athapaskan community (pop. 140) located at the confluence of the Mackenzie and Arctic Red rivers. Tsiigehtchic has a community-owned grocery store and cafe. The Sunshine Inn provides accommodations for up to 8 people. Boat tours are available through the Band Store or local operators. For more information on lodging or tours call (867) 953-3003 or fax (867) 953-3906.

The Arctic Red River (Tsiigehnjik) was declared a Canadian Heritage River in 1993. Tsiigehnjik, the Gwich'in name for the river, winds its way out of the Mackenzie Mountains and flows into the Mackenzie River at Tsiigehtchic. The Gwichya Gwich'in have long used and traveled the river for fishing, hunting and trapping.

J 399.6 (643 km) **I 56.7** (91.2 km) **Rengling River**, grayling fishing.

J 404.4 (650.8 km) **I 51.9** (83.5 km) Beginning of 13-mile/21-km straight stretch.

J 409.7 (659.3 km) **I 46.6** (75 km) Distance marker shows Inuvik 75 km.

J 426.3 (686 km) **I 30** (48.3 km) Vadzaih Van Tshik picnic and camping area. ▲

J 431.4 (694.3 km) **I 24.9** (40.1 km) Campbell Lake and Campbell escarpment ahead northbound. Good place to glass for peregrine falcons.

J 440.6 (709 km) **I 15.7** (25.3 km) Ehjuu Njik picnic spot; pit toilets.

J 442.4 (712 km) **I 13.9** (22.4 km) Nihtak campground picnic area; pit toilets. Good fishing for pike and whitefish, some sheefish (inconnu). Creek leads a short distance to Campbell Lake. Boat launch. Bring mosquito repellent.

J 449.9 (724 km) **I 6.4** (10.3 km) Airport Road turnoff; pavement begins.

J 451.7 (727 km) **I 4.6** (7.4 km) Kilometrepost 262.

J 454 (730.6 km) **I 2.3** (3.7 km) Chuk Park territorial campground; 38 campsites,

20 pull-through, electric hookups, firewood, water, showers, $15 fee. Lookout tower. Interpretive information available. ▲

J 456.3 (734.3 km) **I 0** Turn left northbound for Inuvik town centre (description follows).

Inuvik

Situated on a flat wooded plateau on the east channel of the Mackenzie River, some 60 air miles/96 km south of the Beaufort Sea, 36 air miles/58 km and 70 water miles/113 km from Aklavik on the western edge of the delta. **Population:** 3,206, Déné, White and Inuvialuit.

Emergency Services: RCMP, phone (867) 777-2935. **Hospital**, Inuvik General, phone (867) 777-2955.

Visitor Information: Western Arctic Regional Visitors Centre is located on Mackenzie Road across from the hospital. The centre is open mid-May to mid-September and features interactive displays, excellent wildlife displays, clean restrooms and knowledgeable staff. A must visit in Inuvik. A green and white Cessna 170 is mounted as a weather vane at the centre and rotates to face into the wind. Phone (867) 777-4727. Or contact Town of Inuvik, Box 1160, Inuvik, NT X0E 0T0, phone (867) 777-4321, fax (867) 777-2434. Or on the internet: http://www.inuvik.net. Visitors are also welcome to stop by the Ingamo Hall Friendship Centre.

Visitors are encouraged to stop by the town office (2 First St.) to sign the guest book and pick up an "Order of the Arctic" adventures certificate. Phone (867) 777-2607 for more information.

Elevation: 224 feet/68m. **Climate:** Weather information available by calling (867) 979-4381. May 24 marks 57 days of midnight sun. The sun begins to set on July 19; on Dec. 6, the sun sets and does not rise until Jan. 6. Average annual precipitation 4 inches rainfall, 69 inches snowfall. July mean high 67°F/19°C, mean low 45°F/7°C. January mean high -11°F/-24°C, mean low is -30°F/-35°C. **Radio** and **Television:** CBC and local. **Newspaper:** *The Drum* (weekly).

Private Aircraft: Inuvik airstrip; elev. 224 feet/68m; length 6,000 feet/1,829m; asphalt; fuel 80, 100. Townsite airstrip; elev. 10 feet/3m; length 1,800 feet/549m; gravel; fuel 80, 100, Jet B, F40. High pressure refueling.

Inuvik, meaning "The Place of Man," is the largest Canadian community north of the Arctic Circle, and the major government, transportation and communication centre for Canada's western arctic. Construction of the town began in 1955 and was completed in 1961. It was the main supply base for the petrochemical exploration of the delta until Tuktoyaktuk took over that role as activity centered in the Beaufort Sea. In Inuvik some hunting, fishing and trapping is done, but most people earn wages in government and private enterprises, particularly in transportation and construction. As the delta is one of the richest muskrat areas in the world, Inuvik is the western centre for shipping furs south.

The town's official monument says, in part, that Inuvik was "the first community north of the Arctic Circle built to provide the normal facilities of a Canadian town."

Transportation

Air: Aklak Air provides scheduled service between Inuvik and Tuktoyaktuk, Sachs Harbour, Holman and Paulatuk. Scheduled service is also available to Aklavik; Whitehorse and Old Crow, YT; Edmonton, AB; and Yellowknife, NWT. Several air charter services operate out of Inuvik, offering flights to delta communities and charter service for hunting, fishing and camping trips.

Highways: Dempster Highway from Dawson City. Winter roads (December into April) to Aklavik and Tuktoyaktuk.

Bus: Service from Dawson City to Inuvik by charter service via Arctic Tour Co., phone (867) 777-4100.

Taxi and **rental cars:** Available.

Lodging & Services

Visitors will find most facilities available, although accommodations should be reserved in advance. Inuvik has 3 hotels, all with dining lounges, and bed and breakfasts. There are also a laundry, post office, territorial liquor store, banks and churches. There are 3 gas stations and a car wash; propane, auto repair and towing are available. Hardware, grocery and general stores, and gift shops are here.

Arctic Chalet B&B. Lakeside country setting on edge of town. 7 rooms and private cabins with private or shared bath. Clean, comfortable, non-smoking rooms with single, double and queen beds. Laundry facility. Complimentary canoes. A hearty breakfast included in rates. $80–$100. VISA, MasterCard accepted. Phone (867) 777-3535; fax (867) 777-4443. [ADVERTISEMENT]

Camping

Happy Valley territorial campground; 38 RV sites, electrical hookups, 10 tent pads, hot showers, firewood, water, dump station, fee. Chuk Park territorial campground; 36

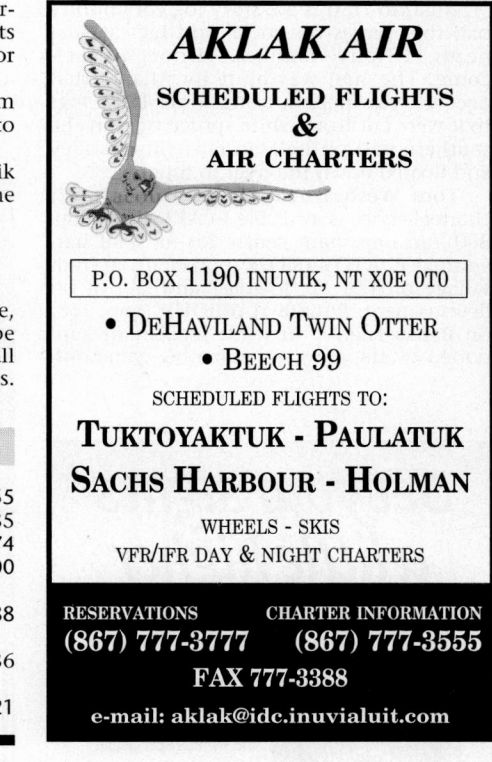

INUVIK ADVERTISERS

Aklak Air	Ph. (867) 777-3555
Arctic Chalet B&B	Ph. (867) 777-3535
Arctic Esso Service	Ph. (867) 777-3974
Arctic Nature Tours	Ph. (867) 777-3300
Government of Northwest Territories	Ph. (800) 661-0788
Great Northern Arts Festival, The	Ph. (867) 777-3536
Town of Inuvik Tourism	Ph. (867) 777-4321

sites, electrical hookups, firewood, water, showers, $10 fee. ▲

Attractions

Igloo Church, painted white with lines

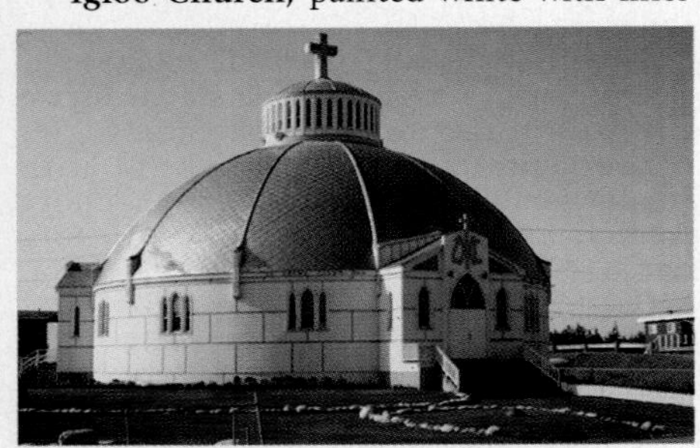

to simulate snow blocks, is on Mackenzie Road as you drive into Inuvik. Inside the church is Inuit painter Mona Thrasher's interpretation of the Stations of the Cross. Visitors are welcome.

Ingamo Hall is a 2-story log community hall that serves the social and recreational needs of Native families. Visitors are welcome. The hall was built by Allan Crich over a 3-year period, using some 1,020 logs that were cut from white spruce trees in the southern part of the Mackenzie River valley and floated down the river to Inuvik.

Tour Western Arctic Communities: Air charter service is available to **AKLAVIK** (pop. 800), an important centre for muskrat harvesting; **TUKTOYAKTUK** (pop. 950), an Inuit village on the Arctic coast and site of oil development; **SACHS HARBOUR** (pop. 158) on Banks Island, an Inuit settlement supported by trapping and some big game outfitters; **PAULATUK** (pop. 255), an Inuit settlement supported by hunting, fishing, sealing and trapping; and **HOLMAN** (pop. 360), an Inuit community on the west coast of Victoria Island, famous for its print-making. Scheduled air service is also available to **OLD CROW** (pop. 267), an Indian settlement on the Porcupine River in Yukon Territory.

The **Mackenzie River delta**, one of the largest deltas in North America and an important wildlife corridor to the Arctic, is 40 miles/64 km wide and 60 miles/97 km long. A maze of lakes, channels and islands, the delta supports a variety of bird life, fish and muskrats. Boat tours of the Mackenzie River are available.

Boreal Books carries a full range of northern books on history, Native studies, exploration and wildlife. Full selection of area postcards, northern posters and local music. Authorized agent for topo maps, marine charts and air charts. Heritage books. Catalogue available. Mail orders welcome. Open year-round. Phone (867) 777-3748, fax (867) 777-4429. [ADVERTISEMENT]

Special Events. The annual Northern Games are held in Inuvik or other western Arctic communities in summer. Visitors are welcome to watch participants compete in traditional Inuit and Déné sports; dances, and crafts are also part of the festival. For information, write Northern Games Assoc., Box 1184, Inuvik, NT X0E 0T0.

The 12th annual **Great Northern Arts Festival** is scheduled for July 21–30, 2000. Over 80 artists and 40 performers from across the North—Inuit, Inuvialuit, Gwich'in, Dene, Metis and non-Native—gather for 10 days every summer for a festival under the midnight sun. Soapstone carvers, print-makers, painters, jewellers and sewers create works of art as visitors look on. Meet the artists, take art workshops or choose from more than 1,500 works of art in the gallery. Evenings are full of music, dance, story-telling and fashion shows showcasing the diverse cultures of the North. A remarkable cultural event.

For more information on this annual event, contact the Great Northern Arts Festival, Box 2921, Inuvik, NT X0E 0T0; phone (867) 777-3536, fax (867) 777-4445. Or check out their web site at www.greatart.nt.ca for current information on participating artists and a schedule of events.

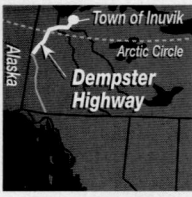

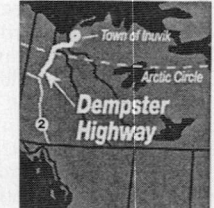

LIARD HIGHWAY 

Connects: Alaska Hwy. to Mackenzie Hwy. **Length:** 244 miles
Road Surface: Gravel **Season:** Open all year
Steepest Grade: 10 percent
Major Attraction: Nahanni National Park

(See map, page 728)

	Fort Liard	Fort Nelson	Fort Simpson
Fort Liard		126	176
Fort Nelson	126		302
Fort Simpson	176	302	

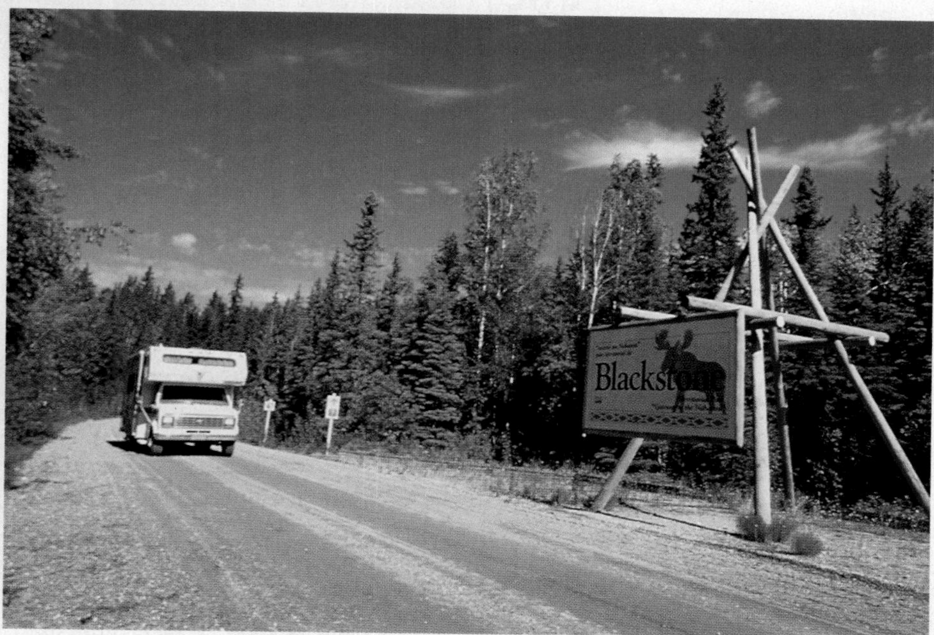

Liard Highway travelers pass through Blackstone Territorial Park. (© Leslie Leong)

The Liard Highway, also called the Liard Trail or "Moose Highway" (after the road sign logo), is named for the Liard River Valley through which it runs for most of its length. The Liard Highway begins about 17 miles/27 km north of Fort Nelson on the Alaska Highway and leads northeast through British Columbia and Northwest Territories for 243 miles/391.3 km to junction with the Mackenzie Highway (NWT Highway 1).

The Liard is a relatively straight 2-lane gravel road through boreal forest and muskeg. In French, Liard means "black poplar," and this wilderness highway (officially opened in June 1984) is a corridor through a forest of white and black spruce, trembling aspen and balsam poplar.

The road can be dusty when dry and very muddy when wet. "Dust-free zones" are treated with calcium chloride. Poor road conditions (potholes, lack of grading) have been reported on the BC portion of the Liard Highway. The NWT portion of the highway is well-maintained. Check current road conditions on the BC section of the highway (first 85 miles/136.8 km of road) by inquiring at the Visitor Infocentre in Fort Nelson, BC. Travel information for the Northwest Territories is available from Northwest Territories Tourism; phone toll free weekdays (800) 661-0788.

Food, lodging, gas and diesel are available at Fort Liard. Gas, food and lodging are also available at the Mackenzie Highway junction. It is a good idea to fill up your gas tank in Fort Nelson.

Although the Northwest Territories portion of the Liard Highway parallels the Liard River, there is limited access to the river. The Liard Highway does offer good views of the Liard River Valley and the Mackenzie Mountain Range. Travelers may enhance their trip by visiting Blackstone Territorial Park (accessible by road) and exploring Nahanni National Park by air charter out of Fort Liard, Fort Simpson or Fort Nelson.

Fishing the highway streams is only fair, but watch for wildlife such as moose, black bear, wood bison and grouse. Remember to bring along lots of insect repellent!

Liard Highway Log

Distance from the junction with the Alaska Highway (A) is followed by distance from the Mackenzie Highway junction (M).

NOTE: Physical kilometreposts are up on the British Columbia portion of the highway about every 5 kilometres, starting here with Km 0 at the Alaska Highway junction and ending at the BC–NWT border.

BC HIGHWAY 77

A 0 M 243 (391.3 km) **Junction** with the Alaska Highway.

A 6.2 (10.1 km) **M 236.8** (381.2 km) Beaver Creek.

A 6.4 (10.3 km) **M 236.6** (381 km) Short side road east to Beaver Lake recreation site; 2 picnic tables, litter barrels, pit toilets, firewood, turnaround space. Short hike downhill through brush to floating dock; limited lake access.

A 14.3 (23.1 km) **M 228.7** (368.2 km) Stanolind Creek. Beaver dams to west.

A 17.5 (28.2 km) **M 225.5** (363.1 km) Pond to west and cut line through trees shows Cat access in summer, ice road in winter.

A 21.1 (34 km) **M 221.9** (357.3 km) Westcoast Transmission Pipeline crossing. Pipeline transports natural gas from Pointed Mountain near Fort Liard to the company's gas plant on the Alaska Highway just south of Fort Nelson.

A 24.2 (38.9 km) **M 218.8** (352.4 km) Road begins descent northbound to Fort Nelson River.

A 26.4 (42.5 km) **M 216.6** (348.8 km) **Fort Nelson River bridge** (elev. 978 feet/298m), single lane, reduce speed. The Nelson bridge is the longest Acrow bridge in the world at 1,410 feet/430m. It is 14 feet/4m wide, with a span of 230 feet/70m from pier to pier. The Acrow bridge, formerly called the Bailey bridge after its designer Sir Donald Bailey, is designed of interchangeable steel panels coupled with pins for rapid construction.

A 26.6 (42.9 km) **M 216.4** (348.4 km) Turnout at north end of bridge with pit toilet, table and garbage container.

A 39.7 (63.9 km) **M 203.3** (327.4 km) **Tsinhia Creek,** grayling run for about 2 weeks in spring.

A 43.4 (69.8 km) **M 199.6** (321.5 km) Trapper's cabin to east.

A 51.8 (83.3 km) **M 191.2** (308 km) Side road leads west 1.9 miles/3 km to Tsinhia Lake and dead-ends in soft sandy track. A recreation site is planned at Tsinhia Lake.

A 59.2 (95.3 km) **M 183.8** (296 km) There are several winter roads in this area used by the forest, oil and gas industries. To most summer travelers these roads look like long cut lines or corridors through the Bush.

The Liard Highway replaced the old Fort Simpson winter road that joined Fort Nelson and Fort Simpson. The original Simpson Trail was first blazed in November 1942 by Alaska Highway engineers, including the 648th, Company A detachment.

LIARD HIGHWAY

Alaska Highway Junction to Mackenzie Route Junction

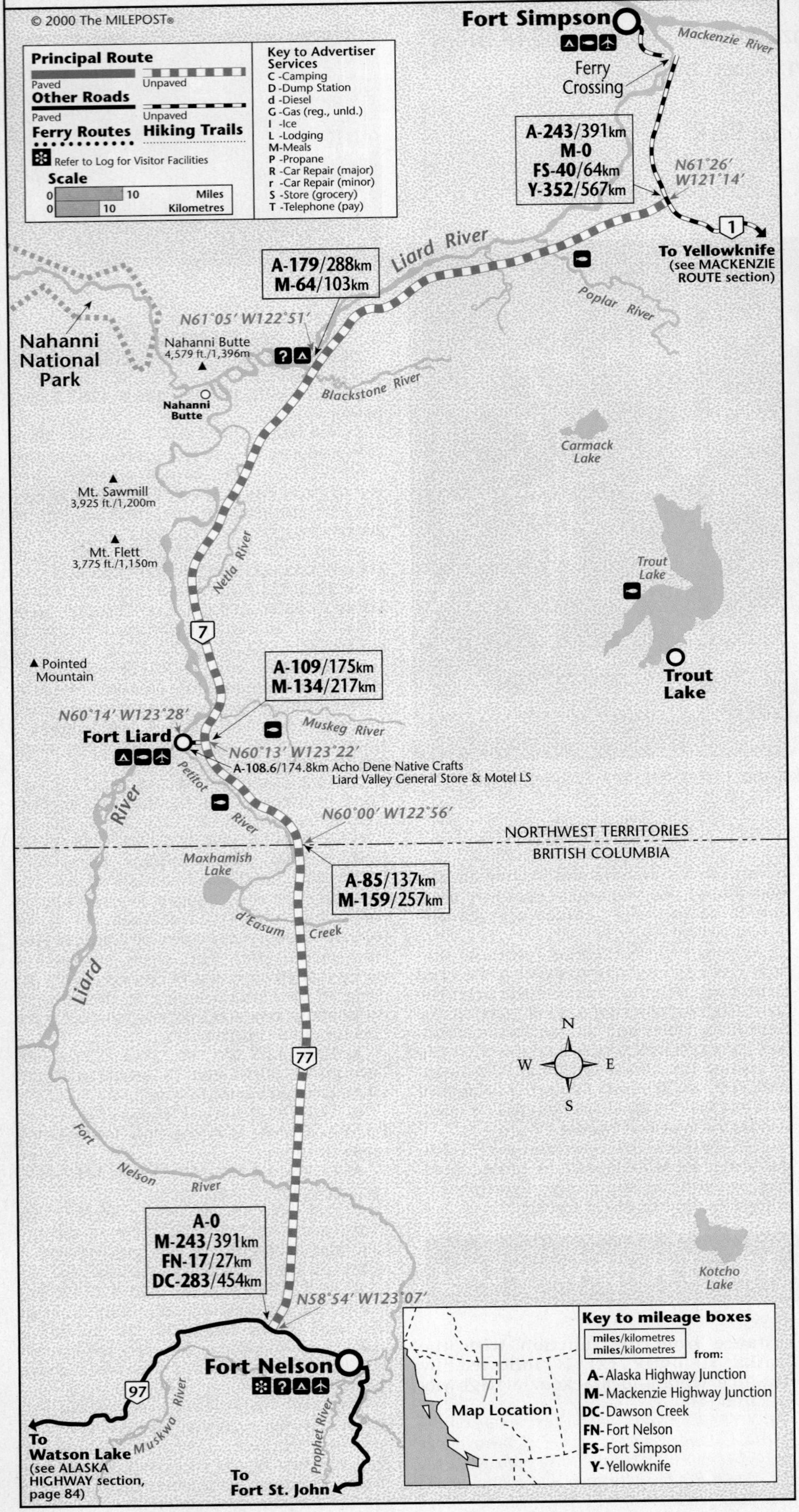

Principal Route
Paved
Unpaved
Other Roads
Paved
Unpaved
Ferry Routes **Hiking Trails**
Refer to Log for Visitor Facilities
Scale
0 10 Miles
0 10 Kilometres

Key to Advertiser Services
C -Camping
D -Dump Station
d -Diesel
G -Gas (reg., unld.)
I -Ice
L -Lodging
M-Meals
P -Propane
R -Car Repair (major)
r -Car Repair (minor)
S -Store (grocery)
T -Telephone (pay)

Fort Simpson
Mackenzie River
Ferry Crossing
A-243/391km
M-0
FS-40/64km
Y-352/567km
N61°26′ W121°14′
1
To Yellowknife (see MACKENZIE ROUTE section)
Liard River
Poplar River
A-179/288km
M-64/103km
N61°05′ W122°51′
Nahanni National Park
Nahanni Butte 4,579 ft./1,396m
Nahanni Butte
Blackstone River
Carmack Lake
Mt. Sawmill 3,925 ft./1,200m
Mt. Flett 3,775 ft./1,150m
Netla River
Trout Lake
7
Pointed Mountain
A-109/175km
M-134/217km
Trout Lake
N60°14′ W123°28′
Fort Liard
Muskeg River
N60°13′ W123°22′
A-108.6/174.8km Acho Dene Native Crafts
Liard Valley General Store & Motel LS
Liard River
Petitot River
N60°00′ W122°56′
NORTHWEST TERRITORIES
BRITISH COLUMBIA
Maxhamish Lake
A-85/137km
M-159/257km
d'Easum Creek
Liard
77
N
W E
S
Fort Nelson River
A-0
M-243/391km
FN-17/27km
DC-283/454km
N58°54′ W123°07′
Kotcho Lake
Fort Nelson
97
Muskwa River
Prophet River
To Watson Lake (see ALASKA HIGHWAY section, page 84)
To Fort St. John
Map Location

Key to mileage boxes
miles/kilometres
miles/kilometres
from:
A- Alaska Highway Junction
M- Mackenzie Highway Junction
DC- Dawson Creek
FN- Fort Nelson
FS- Fort Simpson
Y- Yellowknife

Watch for signs in Northwest Territories warning of buffalo on the road.
(© Lyn Hancock)

A 69.4 (111.7 km) **M 173.6** (279.6 km) Bridge over d'Easum Creek (elev. 1,608 feet/490m). Good bird-watching area.

A 71.4 (115 km) **M 171.6** (276.3 km) Access to Maxhamish Lake via 8-mile/13-km winter road accessible in summer by all-terrain vehicles only. A recreation site is planned for Maxhamish Lake.

A 74 (119.1 km) **M 169** (272.2 km) Wide unnamed creek flows into Emile Creek to east. Good bird-watching area, beaver pond.

A 75.4 (121.4 km) **M 167.6** (269.9 km) Highway emerges from trees northbound; view west of Mount Martin (elev. 4,460 feet/1,360m) and the Kotaneelee Range.

A 80.6 (129.7 km) **M 162.4** (261.6 km) View northwest of mountain ranges in Northwest Territories.

A 81.2 (130.7 km) **M 161.8** (260.6 km) *Highway begins 7 percent downgrade northbound to Petitot River.*

A 82.8 (133.2 km) **M 160.2** (258.1 km) Petitot River bridge. The **Petitot River** is reputed to have the warmest swimming water in British Columbia (70°F/21°C). A 9-hour canoe trip to Fort Liard is possible from here (some sheer rock canyons and rapids en route). Good bird-watching area. Also freshwater clams, pike and pickerel; short grayling run in spring.

The Petitot River was named for Father Petitot, an Oblate missionary who came to this area from France in the 1860s.

The Petitot River bridge was the site of the official opening of the Liard Highway on June 23, 1984. The ceremony was marked by an unusual ribbon-cutting: A 1926 Model T Ford, carrying dignitaries, was driven through the ribbon (which stretched for about 20 feet before snapping) while a guard of kilted pipers from Yellowknife played. The Model T, driven by Marl Brown of Fort Nelson, had been across this route in March 1975 just weeks after the bush road had been punched through by Cats and seismic equipment. This earlier trip, in which Mr. Brown was accompanied by Mickey Hempler, took 44 hours from Fort Nelson to Fort Simpson.

A 84.1 (135.4 km) **M 158.9** (255.9 km) Crest of Petitot River hill. *Highway begins 10 percent downgrade northbound.*

NWT HIGHWAY 7

A 85 (136.8 km) **M 158** (254.5 km) **BC–NWT border.** TIME ZONE CHANGE: British Columbia observes Pacific time, Northwest Territories observes Mountain time.

Northwest Territories restricts liquor importation as follows: 1 40-oz. hard liquor, 1 40-oz. wine or 1 dozen bottles of beer per person.

NOTE: Kilometreposts are up about every 2 kilometres on the Northwest Territories portion of the highway, starting here with Km 0 at the BC–NWT border and ending at the junction with the Mackenzie Highway.

A 85.2 (137.1 km) **M 157.8** (254.2 km) Turnout to east with litter barrels.

A 107 (172.2 km) **M 136** (219.1 km) Vehicle inspection station and weigh scales to east.

A 108.6 (174.8 km) **M 134.4** (216.5 km) **Junction** with dust-free side road that leads 4 miles/6.4 km to Fort Liard (description follows). Double-ended turnout with interpretive signs north of junction.

Views from road into Fort Liard across the Liard River of Mount Coty (elev. 2,715 feet/830m) and Pointed Mountain (elev. 4,610 feet/1,405m) at the southern tip of the Liard Range.

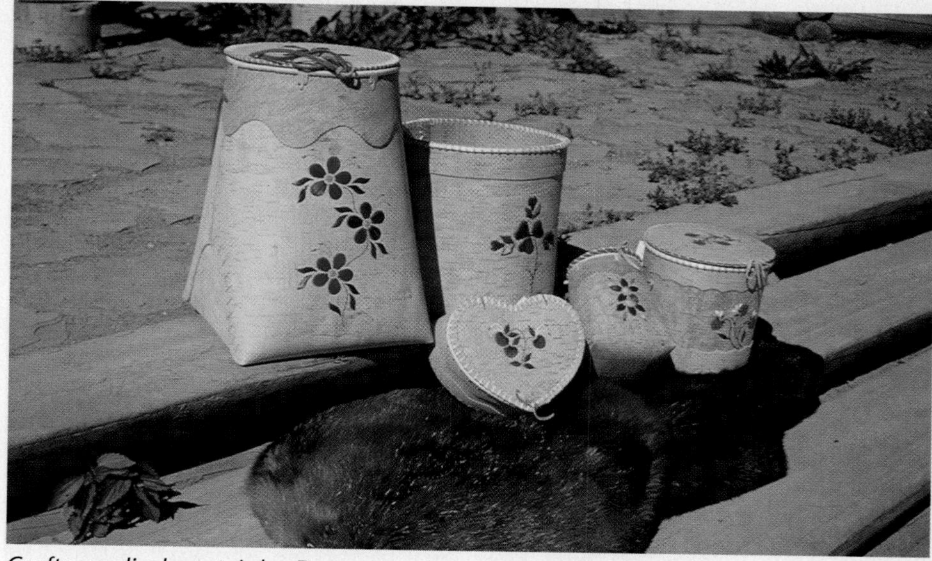

Crafts on display at Acho Dene store in Fort Liard. (© Leslie Leong)

Fort Liard

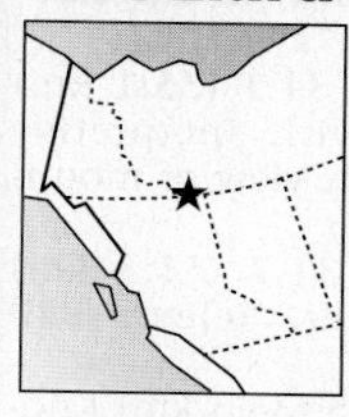

Located on the south bank of the Liard River near its confluence with the Petitot River (known locally as Black River because of its colour), about 50 miles/80 km south of Nahanni Butte. **Population:** 500. **Emergency Services:** **RCMP**, phone (867) 770-4221. **Fire Department**, phone (867) 770-2222. **Health Centre**, phone (867) 770-4301.

Visitor Information: Acho Dene Native Crafts, phone (867) 770-4161; e-mail achoart@internet.com.

Elevation: 686 feet/209m. **Climate:** There is no permafrost here. Good soil and water, a long summer season with long hours of daylight, and comparatively mild climate considering Fort Liard's geographical location. Several luxuriant local gardens. The Liard River here is approximately 1,500 feet/450m wide, fairly swift and subject to occasional flooding. **Radio and Television:** CBC radio (microwave), a Native language station from Yellowknife and a community radio station; 4 channels plus CBC Television (Anik), TVNC and private satellite receivers. Canadian Aerodrome Radio Station (CARS) operates Monday through Friday 8 A.M. to 7 P.M.

Private Aircraft: Fort Liard airstrip; elev. 700 feet/213m; length 2,950 feet/899m; gravel; fuel 100/130 (obtain from Deh Cho Air Ltd.).

Transportation: Air—Charter service year-round via Deh Cho Air. **Barge**—Nonscheduled barge service in summer. Scheduled and charter taxi service available.

This small, well-laid-out settlement of traditional log homes and new modern housing is located among tall poplar, spruce and birch trees on the south bank of the Liard River. Many residents live a comparatively traditional life of hunting, trapping, fishing and making handicrafts. Recently, oil, gas and forestry have created a rise in the local economy. Construction and highway maintenance also provide employment opportunities.

Fort Liard residents are well known for the high quality of their birch-bark baskets and porcupine quill workmanship. Local arts and crafts are featured at Acho Dene Native Crafts shop.

Recreation and sightseeing in the area include fishing (for pike, pickerel, goldeye and spring grayling) at the confluence of the Liard and Petitot rivers and Liard River interpretive boat tours (Hope's Adventures). Air charters and self-guided canoe trips to Trout Lake, Virginia Falls in Nahanni National Park, Nahanni Butte and other destinations are available from Deh Cho Air Ltd. The traditional Dene settlement of **TROUT LAKE** (pop. less than 100) is also accessible by air from Fort Liard.

The North West Co. established a trading post near here at the confluence of the Liard and Petitot rivers called Riviere aux Liards in 1805. The post was abandoned after the massacre of more than a dozen residents by Indians. It was re-established in 1820, then taken over by the Hudson's Bay Co. in 1821 when the 2 companies merged. The well-known geologist Charles Camsell was born at Fort Liard in 1876.

Food and lodging are available at Liard Valley General Store and Motel. Gas, diesel and propane fuel available. Food and general merchandise at the Northern Store, which also houses the Canada Post outlet. There are also a cafe/take-out, the modern Acho Dene School and a Roman Catholic mission. There is no bank in Fort Liard.

Acho Dene Native Crafts. See display ad this section.

Liard Valley General Store & Motel Ltd. See display ad this section.

Community-run Hay Lake Campground located just off the access road into Fort Liard; 6 campsites, picnic tables, toilets,

Picnicking at Blackstone Territorial Park on the Liard Highway. (© Leslie Leong)

floating dock and a hiking trail around the lake. Bring insect repellent. Campground road may be slippery when wet. ▲

Liard Highway Log

(continued)

A 108.6 (174.8 km) **M 134.4** (216.5 km) **Fort Liard junction**. Dust-free zone next 12 miles/20 km northbound.

A 114.2 (183.8 km) **M 128.8** (207.5 km) **Muskeg River** bridge (elev. 814 feet/248m); turnout with interpretive sign at north end. Gravel bars on the river make a good rest area. Trapper's cabin. Fishing for pike, pickerel and freshwater clams. The Muskeg River is the local swimming hole for Fort Liard residents.

A 122.5 (197.2 km) **M 120.5** (194.1 km) Rabbit Creek.

A 123.4 (198.6 km) **M 119.6** (192.7 km) Kilometrepost 62.

A 125.4 (201.9 km) **M 117.6** (189.4 km) Big Island Creek bridge (elev. 827 feet/252m). Highway now runs close to the Liard River with good views of Liard Range to the west and northwest for the next 13 miles/21 km northbound.

A 125.8 (202.5 km) **M 117.2** (188.8 km) Kilometrepost 66.

A 126.2 (203.2 km) **M 116.8** (188.1 km) Views of Mackenzie Mountains to northwest.

A 126.8 (204.1 km) **M 116.2** (187.2 km) Highway maintenance site to west with gravel stockpile.

A 127 (204.4 km) **M 116** (186.9 km) Kilometreost 68. Views of Mackenzie Mountains next mile northbound.

A 128.3 (206.6 km) **M 114.7** (184.7 km) Kilometrepost 70.

A 131.5 (211.8 km) **M 111.5** (179.5 km) Microwave tower to west.

A 132 (212.4 km) **M 111** (178.9 km) Kilometrepost 76.

A 133.2 (214.5 km) **M109.8** (176.8 km) Double-ended turnout to west with litter barrels and interpretive signs.

A 137.3 (221.1 km) **M 105.7** (170.2 km) Kilometrepost 84.

A 142.5 (229.4 km) **M 100.5** (161.9 km) Kilometrepost 92.

A 146.8 (236.3 km) **M 96.2** (155 km) Short road west to locally named Whissel Landing on the Liard River, where road construction materials were brought in by barge during construction of the Liard Highway. This Liard River access site is a fall hunting camp for Fort Liard residents. *Please respect private property*.

A 147.3 (237.1 km) **M 95.7** (154.2 km) Road widens for an emergency airstrip; elev. 981 feet/299m.

A 155.3 (250 km) **M 87.7** (141.3 km) Views of Mackenzie Mountains next 11 miles/17 km southbound .

A 157.4 (253.4 km) **M 85.6** (137.9 km) Netla River bridge. The Netla River Delta is an important waterfowl breeding habitat, and Indian fishing and hunting area.

A 157.5 (253.5 km) **M 85.5** (137.8 km) Kilometrepost 116.

A 162.8 (262 km) **M 80.2** (129.3 km) Road widens for an emergency airstrip; elev. 512 feet/156m.

A 165 (265.5 km) **M 78** (125.8 km) Kilometrepost 128.

A 165.5 (266.5 km) **M 77.5** (124.8 km) *CAUTION: Rough dip in highway.*

A 165.8 (266.9 km) **M 77.2** (124.4 km) Turnoff to west for winter ice road that leads 13.8 miles/22.3 km to the Dene settlement of **NAHANNI BUTTE** (pop. 87), at the confluence of the South Nahanni and Liard rivers. Summer access by boat or floatplane.

A 168.6 (271.4 km) **M 74.4** (119.9 km) Kilometrepost 134.

A 171.7 (276.3 km) **M 71.3** (115 km) Creek Bridge, once called Scotty's Creek after an old trapper who had a cabin upstream. There are many such cabins in this area that once belonged (and still belong) to prospectors and trappers, but they are not visible to the motorist. Stands of white spruce, white birch and balsam poplar along highway.

A 174.6 (281 km) **M 68.4** (110.3 km) Highway passes through stands of mature aspen next mile northbound.

A 175 (281.7 km) **M 68** (109.6 km) Microwave tower.

A 176 (283.2 km) **M 67** (108.1 km) Bridge over Upper Blackstone River (elev. 666 feet/203m). Picnic day-use area on riverbank with tables, firewood, firepits and garbage containers.

A 176.1 (283.4 km) **M 66.9** (107.9 km) Kilometrepost 146.

A 176.2 (283.7 km) **M 66.8** (107.6 km) Blackstone River bridge.

A 178.5 (287.4 km) **M 64.5** (103.9 km) Kilometrepost 150.

A 179 (287.9 km) **M 64** (103.4 km) Entrance to **Blackstone Territorial Park**; 19 campsites with tables and firepits; firewood, water and garbage containers, boat dock and state-of-the-art restroom and shower facility. The boat launch is usable only in high water early in the season; use boat launch at Cadillac Landing, **Milepost A 182.9,** during low water. The visitor information building, built with local logs, is located on the bank of the Liard River with superb views of Nahanni Butte (elev. 4,579 feet/1,396m). The centre is open mid-May to mid-September. ▲

A 180.6 (290.7 km) **M 62.4** (100.6 km) Entrance to Lindberg Landing, the homestead of Liard River pioneers Edwin and Sue Lindberg. The Lindbergs offer a bed and breakfast; rustic accommodations, bring your own sleeping bag. By appointment only. Contact Mobile Telephone JR36644 Arrowhead Channel, or write Sue and Edwin Lindberg, Box 28, Fort Simpson, NWT X0E 0N0.

A 182.5 (293.7 km) **M 60.5** (97.6 km) Barge landing once used to service Cadillac Mine and bring in construction materials. Access to river via 0.6-mile/0.9-km road (muddy when wet).

A 192.4 (309.7 km) **M 50.6** (81.6 km) Road widens northbound (old emergency airstrip).

A 195.6 (314.9 km) **M 47.4** (76.4 km) Kilometrepost 178.

A 198.4 (319.3 km) **M 44.6** (72 km) Kilometrepost 182.

A 208.9 (336.2 km) **M 34.1** (55.1 km) Doubled-ended turnout with inerpretive signs. Hike up gravel pile for view of mountains and Liard River valley.

A 211.3 (340 km) **M 31.7** (51.3 km) Bridge over Birch River (elev. 840 feet/256m).

A 220.5 (355 km) **M 22.5** (36.3 km) Kilometrepost 218.

A 221.5 (356.5 km) **M 21.5** (34.8 km) Good grayling and pike fishing in **Poplar River** culverts.

A 221.7 (356.8 km) **M 21.3** (34.5 km) Dirt road on left northbound leads 4 miles/6.4 km to Liard River; 4-wheel drive recommended. Wide beach, good spot for viewing wildlife.

A 225.5 (362.9 km) **M 17.5** (28.4 km) Kilometrepost 226.

A 226.7 (364.9 km) **M 16.3** (26.4 km) Microwave tower to east. Vegetation changes northbound to muskeg with black spruce, tamarack and jackpine.

A 230.4 (370.8 km) **M 12.6** (20.5 km) Kilometrepost 234.

A 240.2 (386.7 km) **M 2.8** (4.6 km) Kilometrepost 250.

A 242.2 (389.9 km) **M 0.8** (1.4 km) Double-ended turnout with interpretive signs about the Liard Highway.

A 243 (391.3 km) **M 0 "Checkpoint."** Gas, diesel, propane, licensed restaurant and motel; phone (867) 695-2953. Turn right (south) for Hay River and Yellowknife; turn left (north) for Fort Simpson.

Junction with the Mackenzie Highway (NWT 1). Turn to **Milepost B 255.3** on page 738 in the MACKENZIE ROUTE section following for log.

MACKENZIE ROUTE 35 1 2 3 4 5 6

Connects: Grimshaw, AB to Western NWT **Length:** 1,231 miles
Road Surface: 47% paved, 53% gravel **Season:** Open all year
Major Attractions: Nahanni National Park; Wood Buffalo National Park

(See maps, pages 732–733)

	Ft. Resolution	Ft. Simpson	Ft. Smith	Valleyview	Yellowknife
Ft. Resolution		358	185	560	391
Ft. Simpson	358		431	692	393
Ft. Smith	185	431		633	464
Valleyview	560	692	633		725
Yellowknife	391	393	464	725	

Mackenzie Highway extension to Wrigley is still gravel, but Northwest Territories has an ambitious paving program under way for its highways. (© Leslie Leong)

Named for explorer Alexander Mackenzie, who in 1779 navigated Great Slave Lake and sailed to the mouth of the Mackenzie River seeking a trade route for the Hudson's Bay Co., the Mackenzie Route is an adventure for modern explorers. It is not a trip for the impulsive. While there are accommodations, gas stations and other services in cities and settlements along the highways, long distances require that motorists plan in advance.

The Mackenzie Route covers the following highways: Alberta Highway 35 and NWT Highway 1 to Fort Simpson (Mackenzie Highway) and the extension to Wrigley; Highway 2 to Hay River; Highway 3 to Yellowknife; Highway 4 (Ingraham Trail); Highway 5 to Fort Smith; and Highway 6 to Fort Resolution. NWT Highway 7, the Liard Highway, connecting the Mackenzie Highway with the Alaska Highway north of Fort Nelson, is covered in the LIARD HIGHWAY section. The Dempster Highway (NWT Highway 8) to Inuvik is covered in the DEMPSTER HIGHWAY section.

Allow at least 2 weeks to travel the entire route. For general information on travel in the Northwest Territories, phone Northwest Territories Tourism toll free at (800) 661-0788 during business hours on weekdays.

Northwest Territories highways are both paved and gravel. Asphalt chip seal surfacing is under way on the remaining gravel portions of Highways 1 (Mackenzie Highway) and 3 (Yellowknife Highway). Gravel road is treated with calcium chloride to control the dust; wash your vehicle when possible. For road conditions, phone (800) 661-0750.

In summer, the Northwest Territories government provides free ferry service for cars and passengers across the Mackenzie River to Fort Providence, across the Liard River to Fort Simpson and across the Mackenzie River to Wrigley. In winter, traffic crosses on the ice. For current ferry information call (800) 661-0751.

The Mackenzie Highway begins at Grimshaw, AB. There are several routes to Grimshaw to choose from (see map). *The MILEPOST®* logs the Valleyview–Peace River route to the Mackenzie Highway via Highways 49 and 2.

Log of the Valleyview–Peace River Route to the Mackenzie Highway

Distance from Valleyview (V) is followed by distance from Mackenzie Highway (MH).

ALBERTA HIGHWAY 49

V 0 MH 101.1 (162.7 km) **Junction** of Highways 43 and 49. Follow Highway 49 north.

V 0.6 (1 km) **MH 100.5** (161.6 km) Turnoff to west for downtown Valleyview (see description of Valleyview in the EAST ACCESS ROUTE section).

V 2.2 (3.5 km) **MH 98.9** (159.3 km) **Junction** with Secondary Road 669 which leads

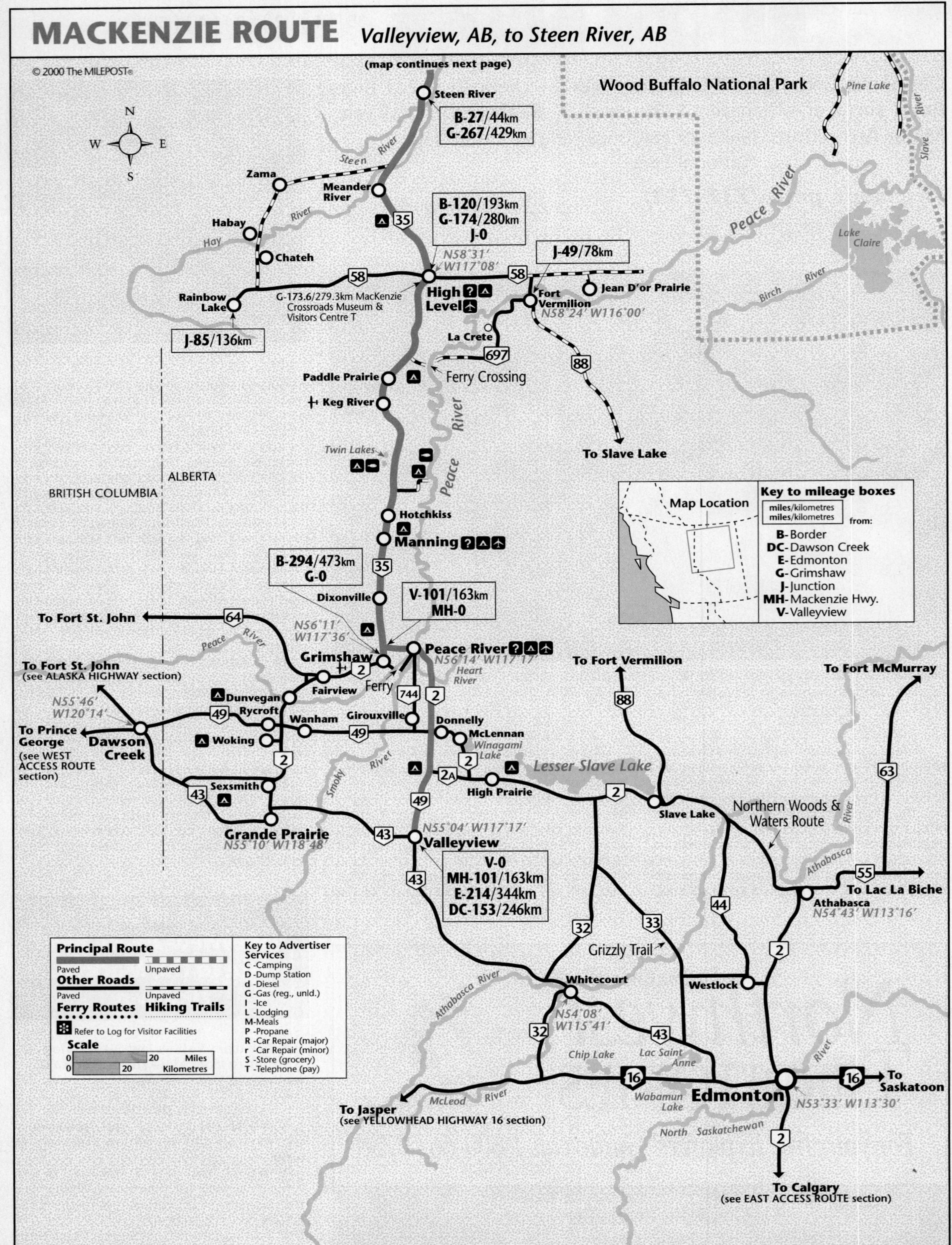
MACKENZIE ROUTE Valleyview, AB, to Steen River, AB
© 2000 The MILEPOST®
(map continues next page)
N
W
E
S
Wood Buffalo National Park
Pine Lake
Steen River
B-27/44km
G-267/429km
Steen River
Zama
Meander River
Habay
Hay River
Chateh
35
B-120/193km
G-174/280km
J-0
N58°31′ W117°08′
J-49/78km
58
58
Rainbow Lake
G-173.6/279.3km MacKenzie Crossroads Museum & Visitors Centre T
High Level
Fort Vermilion
N58°24′ W116°00′
Jean D'or Prairie
J-85/136km
La Crete
697
88
Peace River
Lake Claire
Birch River
Slave River
Ferry Crossing
Paddle Prairie
Keg River
Twin Lakes
Peace River
To Slave Lake
ALBERTA
BRITISH COLUMBIA
Hotchkiss
Manning
35
B-294/473km
G-0
V-101/163km
MH-0
Dixonville
To Fort St. John
64
Peace River
N56°11′ W117°36′
Grimshaw
2
Peace River
N56°14′ W117°17′
Heart River
Ferry
744
2
To Fort Vermilion
88
To Fort McMurray
To Fort St. John (see ALASKA HIGHWAY section)
Fairview
Dunvegan
N55°46′ W120°14′
49
Rycroft
Wanham
Girouxville
49
Donnelly
McLennan
Winagami Lake
To Prince George (see WEST ACCESS ROUTE section)
Dawson Creek
Woking
2
Smoky River
2
2A
High Prairie
Lesser Slave Lake
63
Sexsmith
43
49
2
Slave Lake
Northern Woods & Waters Route
Athabasca River
Grande Prairie
N55°10′ W118°48′
43
N55°04′ W117°17′
Valleyview
V-0
MH-101/163km
E-214/344km
DC-153/246km
43
55
To Lac La Biche
Athabasca
N54°43′ W113°16′
44
33
32
Grizzly Trail
2
Whitecourt
Westlock
Athabasca River
N54°08′ W115°41′
32
43
Chip Lake
Lac Saint Anne
River
16
16
To Saskatoon
To Jasper (see YELLOWHEAD HIGHWAY 16 section)
McLeod River
Wabamun Lake
Edmonton
N53°33′ W113°30′
North Saskatchewan
2
To Calgary (see EAST ACCESS ROUTE section)
Map Location
Key to mileage boxes
miles/kilometres
miles/kilometres
from:
B-Border
DC-Dawson Creek
E-Edmonton
G-Grimshaw
J-Junction
MH-Mackenzie Hwy.
V-Valleyview
Principal Route
Paved
Unpaved
Other Roads
Paved
Unpaved
Ferry Routes
Hiking Trails
Refer to Log for Visitor Facilities
Scale
0 20 Miles
0 20 Kilometres
Key to Advertiser Services
C -Camping
D -Dump Station
d -Diesel
G -Gas (reg., unld.)
I -Ice
L -Lodging
M-Meals
P -Propane
R -Car Repair (major)
r -Car Repair (minor)
S -Store (grocery)
T -Telephone (pay)

MACKENZIE ROUTE *Steen River, AB, to Yellowknife, NWT*

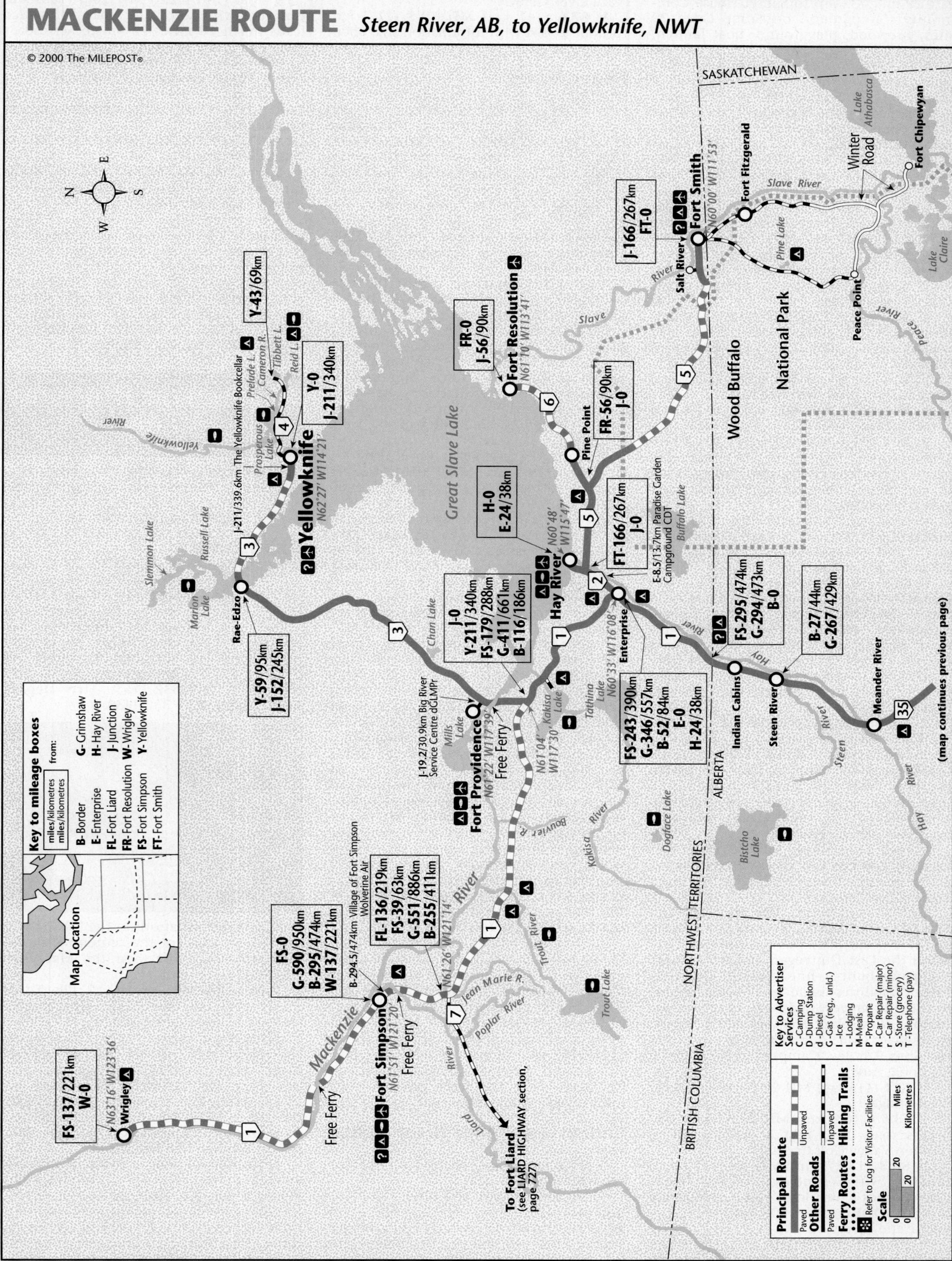

east 20 miles/32 km to Sunset House Community Campground on Snipe Lake; 20 sites, firewood, playground, boat launch, camping fee. ▲

V 18 (29 km) **MH 83.1** (133.7 km) East Dollar Lake to west.

V 23.1 (37.2 km) **MH 78** (125.6 km) Entering Midnight Twilight Tourist Zone northbound, entering Game Country Tourist Zone southbound.

V 25.1 (40.4 km) **MH 76** (122.3 km) **Junction** with Secondary Road 676 to Whitemud Creek, 14 miles/22 km west.

V 28.3 (45.6 km) **MH 72.8** (117.3 km) Entering Grande Prairie Forest southbound.

V 29.1 (46.8 km) **MH 72** (115.8 km) Little Smokey River bridge. Little Smokey River provincial recreation area to west on south bank of river; 12 sites, shelters, picnic tables, camping fee. ▲

V 30.3 (48.8 km) **MH 70.8** (114 km) **Junction** with Highway 2A east, a spur road which leads 17 miles/27 km to junction with Highway 2.

V 31.3 (50.4 km) **MH 69.8** (112.3 km) Turnout with litter barrels to east.

V 32.4 (52.1 km) **MH 68.7** (110.6 km) Entering Peace River Forest northbound.

V 36.4 (58.6 km) **MH 64.7** (104.2 km) Community of **GUY** (pop. 57) to east; pay phone. Access road leads west 7 miles/11 km to Five Star Golf Course; 9 holes, grass greens, pro shop.

V 40.5 (65.2 km) **MH 60.6** (97.5 km) **Junction** with Secondary Road 679 to Highway 2 and Winigami Lake Provincial Park (19 miles/30.5 km east).

V 48.7 (78.4 km) **MH 52.4** (84.4 km) **Donnelly Corners, junction** of Highways 2 and 49. **DONNELLY** (pop. 450) has a hotel, restaurants, stores, service stations with repair facilities and a library. Historic site 3 miles/5 km south of town features a fully operational 1904 Case Steam Engine. Highway 49 ends northbound. Continue on Highway 2 North.

ALBERTA HIGHWAY 2

V 61 (98.1 km) **MH 40.1** (64.5 km) Access leads west 7 miles/11 km to **JEAN COTE** (pop. 65), and 18 miles/28 km to Rainbow Trout Park and Campground; 55 sites, hookups, picnic tables, shelter, firewood, playground, rental cabins, mini-golf, horseshoe pits. Camping fee $9. ▲

V 66.1 (106.5 km) **MH 35** (56.3 km) Entering Land of the Mighty Peace Tourist Zone northbound, Midnight Twilight Tourist Zone southbound.

V 70.7 (113.8 km) **MH 30.4** (49 km) Nampa visitor centre and museum to west. **NAMPA** (pop. 500) was founded in 1917 when the East Dunvegan and BC Railway Company built a line through the area. Visitor facilities include a hotel, motel, restaurants, grocery and retail stores, service stations with repair facilities and a library. Heart River Golf Club, 5 miles/8 km northeast, has 9 holes. Camping at Mill Brown Memorial Park. ▲

V 72.1 (116 km) **MH 29** (46.6 km) Heart River bridge.

V 73.5 (118.3 km) **MH 27.6** (44.4 km) Access road leads east 3 miles/5 km to Harmon Valley Golf Course.

V 84.3 (135.7 km) **MH 16.8** (27 km) **Junction** with Secondary Road 688 (Three Creeks Road) which leads east 5 miles/8 km to **ST. ISIDORE** (pop. 180); gas station, pay phone and library.

V 85 (136.8 km) **MH 16.1** (25.9 km) Highway begins descent northbound into Peace River Valley.

V 87.6 (141 km) **MH 13.5** (21.7 km) Turnout to east with information sign about Peace River.

Peace River

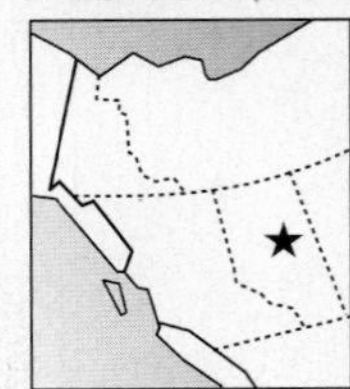

V 88.4 (142.3 km) **MH 12.7** (20.5 km). Located on the banks of the Peace River, 15 miles/24 km northeast of Grimshaw (Mile 0 of the Mackenzie Highway). **Population:** 6,700. **Emergency Services: RCMP**, phone (780) 624-6611. **Hospital**, phone (780) 624-7500. **Ambulance** and **Fire Department**, phone (780) 624-3911.

Visitor Information: Tourist Information located in the NAR station at the first right after the railway trestle at the east entrance to downtown; phone (780) 624-2044. Open mid-May to mid-September, 9 A.M. to 9 P.M. The Mighty Peace Tourist Association, at the north end of Main Street in the restored railway station, also has information on northern Alberta destinations; phone (780) 624-4042. **Elevation:** 1,066 feet/325m.

Private Aircraft: Peace River airport, 7 miles/11.2 km west; elev. 1,873 feet/571m; length 5,000 feet/1,524m; asphalt; fuel 80, 100, Jet B.

An important transportation centre on the Peace River, the town of Peace River was incorporated in 1919, 3 years after the railroad reached Peace River Crossing. Today, Peace River is a centre for government services in the region. Area industry includes Peace River Pulp, Shell Canada and farming.

Visitor facilities include 3 hotels, a motel and many restaurants. Camping at Lions Club Campground on the west side of the river; 85 sites, hookups, restrooms, dump station and laundry. There are 9 campgrounds along the Peace River. For details, contact the Peace Valley Conservation, Recreation and Tourism Society, phone (867) 835-2616 or fax 835-3131. ▲

The **Centennial Museum** (on the south side of town along the river) houses archives and exhibits on Sir Alexander Mackenzie, the fur trade and local history. Historical reenactments in summer. Open 9 A.M. to 5 P.M. Monday to Wednesday, noon to 8 P.M. Thursday to Saturday (May 1 to Aug. 31); 9 A.M. to 5 P.M. weekdays Sept. 1 to April 31. Rail transportation exhibit at restored NAR railway station. Phone (780) 624-4261.

Visitors can take the Historic Mackenzie Moose Walking Trail by following the moose tracks from the Centennial Museum. The tour includes the statue of Twelve-Foot Davis, a gold miner who struck it rich on a 12-foot strip of land between 2 larger claims in the Cariboo gold fields. He invested his $15,000 in gold in a string of trading posts along the Peace. He is buried on Grouard Hill overlooking the Peace River Valley; a stone memorial marks the spot.

Valleyview–Peace River Route
(continued)

V 89.2 (143.5 km) **MH 11.9** (19.1 km) Peace River bridge.

V 90 (144.8 km) **MH 11.1** (17.9 km) **Junction** with Secondary Road 684 which leads southwest 15 miles/24 km to Secondary Road 740 and the Shaftsbury Ferry Crossing of the Peace River.

V 90.8 (146.1 km) **MH 10.3** (16.5 km) **Junction** with Secondary Road 743 which leads north 10 miles/16 km to Secondary Road 686 to the Mackenzie Highway. Access to Peace View golf course, 2.5 miles/4 km north; 9 holes, sand greens, pro shop.

V 91.6 (147.4 km) **MH 9.5** (15.3 km) Turnout to south with information sign about Peace River.

V 94.7 (152.4 km) **MH 6.4** (10.3 km) Peace River airport to south.

V 96 (154.5 km) **MH 5.1** (8.2 km) **Roma Junction** with Highway 2A to Grimshaw (7 miles/12 km southwest).

V 97.1 (156.3 km) **MH 4** (6.5 km) Access road leads 1.2 miles/2 km to Mighty Peace golf course; 18 holes, licensed dining room, pro shop, camping.

V 99.1 (159.5 km) **MH 2** (3.2 km) Access road leads south 0.6 mile/1 km to Wilderness Park; picnic tables, outhouses, hiking.

V 101.1 (162.7 km) **MH 0 Junction** with Highway 35 (Mackenzie Highway).

Mackenzie Highway Log

Distance from Grimshaw (G) is followed by distance from Alberta–NWT border (B).

ALBERTA HIGHWAY 35

Grimshaw

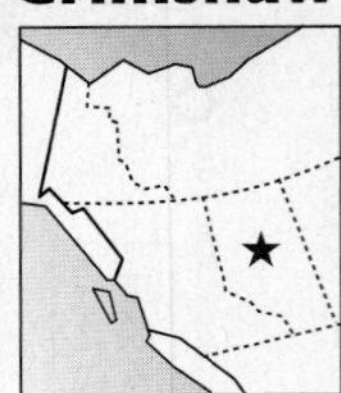

G 0 B 293.7 (472.7 km) Mile 0 of the Mackenzie Highway (Alberta Highway 35). **Population:** 2,812. **Emergency Services: RCMP**, phone (780) 332-4666. **Hospital** and **Ambulance**, phone (780) 332-1155. **Fire Department**, phone (870) 332-4430.

Visitor Information: In the NAR railway car located adjacent the centennial monument marking Mile 0 of the Mackenzie Highway.

Private Aircraft: Airstrip 0.2 mile/0.4 km north; elev. 2,050 feet/625m; length, 3,000 feet/914m; turf; fuel 80, 100.

Named for pioneer doctor M.E. Grimshaw, who established a practice at Peace River Crossing in 1914, Grimshaw developed as a community centre for area farmers and as a shipping point with the arrival of the railroad in 1921. Scheduled air service from Edmonton and High Level to Peace River airport, 8 miles/12.8 km east.

Grimshaw became a town in February 1953. Local resources are wheat and grains, livestock, gravel, lumber, gas and oil.

Grimshaw has a motel with restaurant (Mile 0 Motor Inn), 2 hotels, 6 service stations, 2 car washes, a laundromat and all other visitor facilities. RV dump station and drinking water located south of the Mile 0 marker and 2 blocks east. Camping just north of town (see **Milepost G 1.9**). There are also an outdoor swimming pool, tennis courts, golf course and seasonal market garden located here.

Mackenzie Highway Log

(continued)

G 1.9 (3 km) **B 291.8** 469.6 km) Grimshaw provincial campsite; 20 sites, picnic shelter, firepits, firewood, tables, outhouses, water pump and no camping fee.

Queen Elizabeth Provincial Park, 3 miles/5 km west on Lac Cardinal; 56 campsites, picnic shelter, firewood, firepits, toilets, playground and swimming. ▲

G 2.8 (4.6 km) **B 290.9** (468.1 km) **Junction** of Highways 35 and 2 East.

G 3.4 (5.5 km) **B 290.3** (467.2 km) Signs about construction of the Mackenzie Highway and historic Pine Bluff post office.

G 4.1 (6.6 km) **B 289.6** (466.1 km) Turnout to east with litter barrels.

G 7.8 (12.5 km) **B 285.9** (460.1 km) Bear Creek Drive and Bear Creek golf course to west; 9 holes, sand greens, clubhouse. Campground.

G 8.6 (13.8 km) **B 285.1** (458.8 km) **Junction** with Secondary Road 737 (Warrensville) to west.

G 12.3 (19.8 km) **B 281.4** (452.9 km) Road widens to 4 lanes northbound.

G 12.6 (20.3 km) **B 281.1** (452.4 km) **Junction** with Secondary Road 986 to east.

G 13 (20.9 km) **B 280.7** (451.7 km) Road narrows to 2 lanes northbound.

G 19 (30.6 km) **B 274.7** (442.1 km) Entering Manning Ranger District northbound.

G 23 (37 km) **B 270.7** (435.6 km) Whitemud River.

G 25.1 (40.4 km) **B 268.6** (432.3 km) **DIXONVILLE** (pop. 200) has a post office, gas station, souvenir shop, museum, store and cafe. Sulphur Lake provincial campground is located 34 miles/55 km west via Highway 689 (the first 14 miles/22.5 km are paved, the remainder is gravel to the campground).

G 26.9 (43.3 km) **B 266.8** (429.4 km) Sulphur Lake Road leads west to junction with Highway 689 from Dixonville.

G 38.4 (61.8 km) **B 255.3** (410.9 km) **Junction** with Secondary Road 690 east to Deadwood (6.8 miles/11 km). There is a private exotic bird farm located 2 miles/3.2 km east then 1 mile/1.6 km south. The Bradshaws have geese, peacocks, turkeys, pheasants and other birds; visitors welcome.

G 46.8 (75.4 km) **B 246.9** (397.3 km) Community of **NORTH STAR** (pop. 52) to east.

Manning

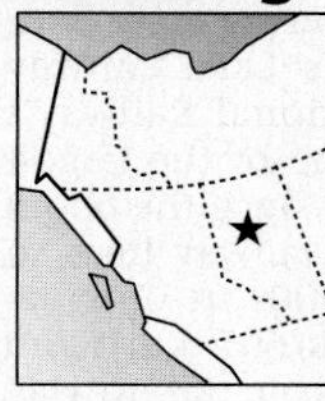

G 50.7 (81.6 km) **B 243** (391.1 km) Located on the Notikewin River at the junction of Highways 35 and 691. **Population:** 1,260. **Emergency Services: RCMP**, phone (780) 836-3007. **Hospital** and **Ambulance**, phone (780) 836-3391. **Fire Department**, phone (780) 836-3000.

Private Aircraft: Manning airstrip to west; elev. 1,611 feet/491m; length 5,577 feet/ 1,700m; asphalt; fuel 100/130, Jet B.

Named for an Alberta premier, Manning was established in 1947. The railway from Roma, AB, to Pine Point, NWT, reached Manning in September 1962. Today, Manning is a service centre and jumping-off point for hunters and fishers.

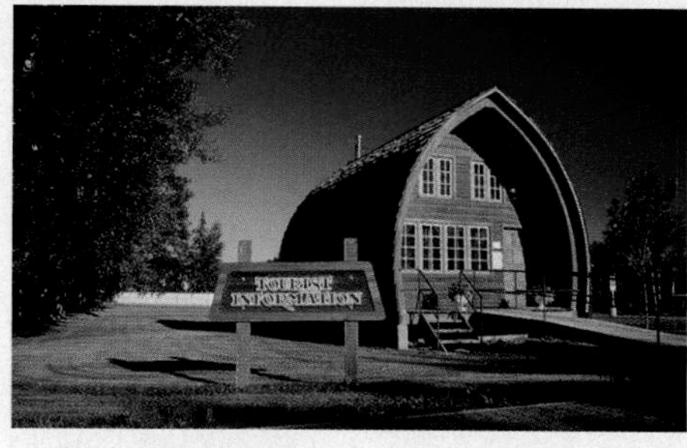

Visitor Information: In the information centre. There is a playground adjacent the centre and a dump station across the street.

Manning has 5 restaurants, 3 hotel/motels, a pharmacy, food market, golf course, swimming pool and ice rink. Attractions here include the Battle River Pioneer Museum, located on the grounds of the Battle River Agricultural Society, 0.6 mile/1 km east via Highway 691. The museum, which features tools and machinery from the pioneer days, is open daily 1–5 P.M., from June 1 to mid-September. A small ski hill is located 12.5 miles/20 km northeast of town via Highways 691 and 741; 1 T-lift and 3 runs.

Turn east at the information centre for Manning municipal campground; 19 sites on the banks of the Notikewin River, fireplaces, tables, water and flush toilets. ▲

Mackenzie Highway Log

(continued)

G 53.2 (85.6 km) **B 240.5** (387 km) Truck stop with 24-hour food and gas; lodging.

G 54.6 (87.8 km) **B 239.1** (384.8 km) Community of Notikewin to west.

G 60.6 (97.6 km) **B 233.1** (375.1 km) Hotchkiss River bridge.

G 60.8 (97.8 km) **B 232.9** (374.8 km) Hotchkiss Provincial Park to east; 10 sites, no fee, picnic shelter, tables, firepits, fishing, outhouses and water pump. ▲

G 61.3 (98.6 km) **B 232.4** (374 km) Community of **HOTCHKISS** to east, golf course to west. Hotchkiss has a post office, service station, pay phone, coffee bar, grocery, and fuel and propane available. Condy Meadow golf course; 9 holes, grass greens, pro shop.

G 66.9 (107.6 km) **B 226.8** (365 km) Meikle River bridge.

G 71.2 (114.6 km) **B 222.5** (358.1 km) Turnout with litter barrel to west.

G 74.3 (119.5 km) **B 219.4** (353.1 km) **Junction** with Highway 692 and access to **Notikewin Provincial Park** (18.6 miles/30 km) on the Notikewin and Peace rivers. Highway 692 is fairly straight with pavement for the first 8 miles/13 km followed by good gravel surface to the park, although the road narrows and the surfacing may be muddy in wet weather as you approach the park. Just past the entrance to the park is the Top of Hill trailer drop-off site; 10 campsites with tables, toilets, water pump and garbage container. The park road then winds down the hill for 1.4 miles/2.2 km (not recommended for trailers, slippery when wet) to the riverside campground and day-use area; 19 campsites on the **Notikewin River** and 6 picnic sites on the **Peace River**; facilities include tables, water pump, pit toilets, garbage containers, firepits, boat launch and fishing. *CAUTION: Bears in area.* ▲

G 88.4 (142.3 km) **B 205.3** (330.4 km) Twin Lakes Lodge to east; gas, food, lodging, pay phone and fishing supplies.

G 88.9 (143 km) **B 204.8** (329.6 km) **Twin Lakes Campground** to west; 48 shaded sites, picnic shelter, fireplaces, firewood, tables, outhouses, water; beach, boat launch (no gas motors). Camping fee $9. Twin Lakes is stocked with rainbow; good fishing June to September. ▲

G 95.8 (154.1 km) **B 197.9** (318.5 km) Turnout to west.

G 111.2 (179 km) **B 182.5** (293.7 km) **Junction** with Highway 695 East which leads 24 miles/38 km to community of **CARCAJOU** (pop. 50). Access to Keg River airstrip 0.4 mile/0.6 km east.

Private Aircraft: Keg River airstrip; elev. 1,350 feet/410m; approximate length 2,700 feet/ 832m; turf; emergency only.

G 112.3 (180.8 km) **B 181.4** (291.9 km) Keg River bridge. The community of **KEG RIVER** (area pop. 400) just north of the bridge has a gas station, post office, grocery, cafe, motel, pay phone and airstrip.

G 115.6 (186 km) **B 178.1** (286.6 km) **Junction** with Secondary Road 695 West. This paved road leads 9 miles/14.5 km to Keg River Post.

G 124 (199.6 km) **B 169.7** (273.1 km) Boyer River bridge.

G 129.5 (208.4 km) **B 164.2** (264.2 km) **PADDLE PRAIRIE** (pop. 164) has a gas station, grocery store and cafe. Paddle Prairie is a Metis settlement. The Metis culture, a combination of French and Amerindian, played a key role in the fur trade and development of northwestern Canada.

G 134.2 (216 km) **B 159.5** (256.7 km) Turnout to west with litter barrels.

G 136.2 (219.2 km) **B 157.5** (253.5 km) **Junction** with Secondary Road 697, which leads northeast 75 miles/121 km to junction with Highway 88 near Fort Vermilion. This is a 2-lane, mostly paved road with a ferry crossing of the Peace River at Tompkin's Landing, 11 miles/18 km east from here. The ferry operates 24 hours a day, except in heavy fog, and carries 6 cars or 4 trucks.

Highway 697 provides access to **BUFFALO HEAD PRAIRIE** (pop. 453), 43.6 miles/70.2 km east, which has a small store and gas. Highway 697 also accesses **LA CRETE** (pop. 902), 53.8 miles/86.6 km east and north, Canada's most northerly agricultural community. La Crete has a motel, 3 restaurants, service stations with repair facilities, car wash, grocery, hardware and retail stores, a laundromat and bank. Recreation facilities include a golf course and a sports complex with hockey, curling and bowling.

G 141 (226.9 km) **B 152.7** (245.7 km) Entering High Level Ranger District northbound.

G 153.5 (247 km) **B 140.2** (225.6 km) Turnout with litter barrel to west. Watch for waterfowl in small lakes along highway.

G 161.2 (259.4 km) **B 132.5** (213.2 km) Bede Creek.

G 161.9 (260.5 km) **B 131.8** (212.1 km) Parma Creek.

G 165.5 (266.3 km) **B 128.2** (206.3 km) Melito Creek.

G 170.6 (274.6 km) **B 123.1** (198.1 km) Turnout with litter barrel to west.

G 171.9 (276.7 km) **B 121.8** (196 km) Private campground. ▲

G 173.3 (278.9 km) **B 120.4** (193.8 km) **Junction** with Highway 58 West, which leads 84.5 miles/136 km to **RAINBOW LAKE**

Display at Mackenzie Crossroads Museum in High Level. (© Brian Stein)

(pop. 1,146), a service community for oil and natural gas development in the region. Food, gas and lodging available.

High Level

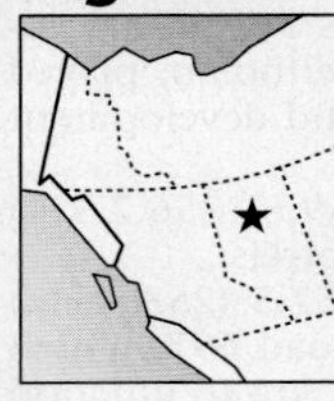

G 173.6 (279.3 km) **B 120.1** (193.3 km) Located at the junction of Highways 35 and 58. **Population:** 3,093. **Emergency Services:** Phone 911. **RCMP**, phone (780) 926-2226. **Hospital,** phone (780) 926-3791. **Ambulance,** phone (780) 926-2545. **Fire Department,** phone (780) 926-3141.

Visitor Information: The visitors centre and Mackenzie Crossroads Museum are located at the south end of town; displays, souvenirs and rest area. Open year-round; 9 A.M. to 9 P.M. daily in summer. Internet address is www.town.highlevel.ab.ca.

Private Aircraft: High Level airport, 7.5 miles/12 km north; elev. 1,110 feet/338m; length 5,000 feet/1,524m; asphalt; fuel 80, 100, Jet B. Floatplane base at Footner Lake, 0.6 mile/1 km west.

Begun as a small settlement on the Mackenzie Highway after WWII, High Level grew with the oil boom of the 1960s and completion of the railroad to Pine Point. High Level has a strong agricultural economy and boasts the most northerly grain elevators in Canada. The community is also supported by a sawmill complex and serves as a transportation centre for the northwestern Peace River region. There is scheduled air service to Edmonton daily.

Visitor facilities include 8 motels, restaurants and service stations with major repair. RV dump located at the Shell station. There are also an ice arena and curling rink, golf course, swimming pool, playgrounds, banks, schools and churches. Recreation includes hunting (moose, caribou, deer) and fishing for northern pike, perch, walleye, whitefish, goldeye and grayling.

There is a private campground at the south edge of town. A campground operated by the local Lions Club is located just east of town on Highway 58. ▲

Mackenzie Crossroads Museum & Visitors Centre. See display ad this section.

Mackenzie Highway Log

(continued)

G 174 (280 km) **B 119.7** (192.6 km) **Junction** with Highway 58 East to Jean D'Or Prairie and **junction** with Highway 88 (77.4 miles/124.5 km, gravel). Highway 88 (the Bicenntennial Highway) leads 48.5 miles/78 km (paved) to **FORT VERMILION** (pop. 850) on the Peace River, established as a trading post by the North West Co. in 1786. Visitor services in Fort Vermilion include food, gas and lodging. Highway 88 continues 255 imles/410 km to Slave Lake; no services on highway south of Fort Vermilion.

G 176.2 (283.5 km) **B 117.5** (189.1km) High Level golf and country club to east. Open daily, May 1 to first snow, until midnight. Clubhouse, grass greens and 9 holes.

G 193.4 (311.2 km) **B 100.3** (161.4 km) Turnoff to west for **Hutch Lake Recreation Area**; parking, 8 picnic sites with tables and firepits, toilets. Short path leads down to lake. Bring mosquito repellent.

G 196 (315.5 km) **B 97.7** (157.2 km) Hutch Lake provincial campground, 2.9 miles/4.6 km west; 12 sites, firepits, firewood, tables, toilets. Beach and boat launch on Hutch Lake. Hiking trails. Good spot for bird watchers. Camping fee $7.50. ▲

G 196.8 (316.7 km) **B 96.9** (155.9 km) Turnouts with litter barrels both sides of highway.

G 207.3 (333.6 km) **B 86.4** (139 km) Wooden railway bridge to east.

G 219.3 (352.9 km) **B 74.4** (119.7 km) **MEANDER RIVER** (pop. 340) has a post office, gas, grocery store and confectionary with pay phone. *NOTE: Last gas northbound until Enterprise at **Milepost G 345.8,** 126.5 miles/203.6 km from here.*

G 221.5 (356.4 km) **B 72.2** (116.2 km) Mission Creek.

G 223.8 (360.1 km) **B 69.9** (112.5 km) The Mackenzie Highway crosses the Hay River here and follows it north into Northwest Territories.

G 227.5 (366.2 km) **B 66.2** (106.5 km) Railway bridge over Hay River to east. Construction of the Great Slave Lake Railway (now part of Canadian National Railway's Peace River Division) was one of the largest railway construction projects since the boom of the first transcontinental railway lines in the late 1800s and early 1900s in Canada. The line extends 377 miles/607 km from Roma Junction near Peace River, AB, to Hay River, NWT, on the shore of Great Slave Lake. (A 54-mile/87-km branch line extended the line to the now-defunct lead–zinc mine at Pine Point, NWT.) Opened for traffic in 1964, the line carries mining shipments south and supplies north to Hay River.

G 228.1 (367.1 km) **B 65.6** (105.6 km) Gravel road leads west 39 miles/63 km to

ZAMA (pop. 200), an oil field community. Drilling and related operations take place at Zama in winter. Zama is the southern terminal of the interprovincial pipeline, carrying Norman Wells crude to Edmonton refineries.

G 231.5 (372.5 km) **B 62.2** (100.1 km) Slavey Creek.

G 243.5 (391.9 km) **B 50.2** (80.8 km) Paved turnout with litter barrels to west.

G 250.2 (402.6 km) **B 43.5** (70 km) Lutose Creek.

G 263.3 (423.7 km) **B 30.4** (48.9 km) Steen River bridge.

G 266.7 (429.2 km) **B 27** (43.5 km) **STEEN RIVER** (pop. 25) to east; no services.

G 266.9 (429.5 km) **B 26.8** (43.1 km) Steen River Forestry Tanker Base to west. Grass airstrip.

G 268.1 (431.5 km) **B 25.6** (41.2 km) Sam's Creek.

G 270.1 (434.7 km) **B 23.6** (38 km) Jackpot Creek.

G 276.2 (444.5 km) **B 17.5** (28.2 km) Bannock Creek.

G 283.3 (455.9 km) **B 10.4** (16.7 km) Indian Cabins Creek.

G 284 (457 km) **B 9.7** (15.6 km) **INDIAN CABINS** (pop. 10); gas, diesel, cafe and native crafts. The old Indian cabins that gave this settlement its name are gone, but nearby is an Indian cemetery with spirit houses. Historic log church.

G 285.3 (459.1 km) **B 8.4** (13.5 km) Delphin Creek.

G 293.7 (472.7 km) **B 0** 60th parallel.

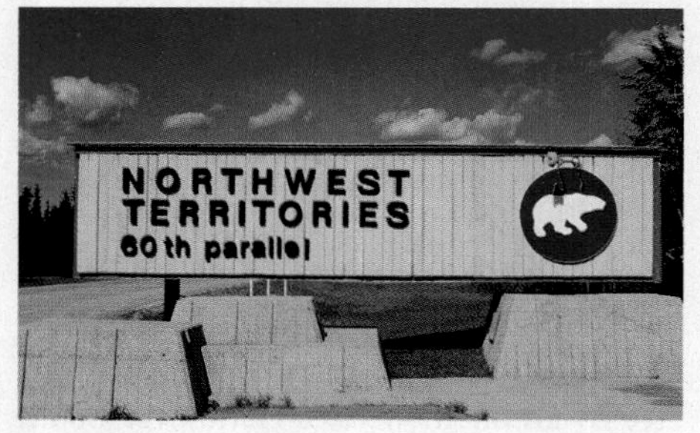

Border between Alberta and Northwest Territories. The Mackenzie Highway now changes from Alberta Highway 35 to NWT Highway 1.

Distance from AB–NWT border (B) is followed by distance from Fort Simpson (FS).

Highway 1 begins its own series of kilometre markers, starting with Kilometre 0 at the border, which appear about every 2 kilometres.

NWT HIGHWAY 1

B 0 FS 294.5 (474 km) **AB–NWT border, 60th Parallel.** Visitor information centre with brochures, maps, fishing licenses, camping permits, a dump station, pay phone and drinking water. Dene (Indian) arts and crafts are on display. Check here on road and ferry conditions before proceeding. The visitor centre is open early May to early September from 8:30 A.M. to 8:30 P.M.

A short walking trail around a pond leads to the 60th Parallel Monument. A mock Trapper's cabin and a commemorative monument for the railway into the north can also be found along this trail.

60th Parallel Campground and picnic area adjacent visitor centre. Facilities include 10 campsites, 2 picnic sites and kitchen shelter. The park overlooks the Hay River and canoeists may launch here. Information on canoeing the river can be obtained at the visitor centre. ▲

Driving distances from the border to destinations in Northwest Territories are as follows (see highway logs this section for details): Hay River 75 miles/121 km; Fort Simpson 295 miles/474 km; Wrigley 432 miles/695 km; Fort Providence 138 miles/222 km; Yellowknife 326 miles/525 km; Fort Smith 238 miles/382 km.

B 1.8 (2.9 km) **FS 292.7** (471.1 km) Reindeer Creek; pike and pickerel fishing.

B 24.8 (39.9 km) **FS 269.7** (434.1 km) Swede Creek.

B 25.1 (40.4 km) **FS 269.4** (433.6) Grumbler Rapids, just off highway, is audible during low water periods in late summer.

B 26.1 (42 km) **FS 268.4** (432 km) Large turnout and gravel stockpile to west.

B 40.5 (65.1 km) **FS 254.1** (408.9 km) Mink Creek.

B 45 (72.4 km) **FS 249.5** (401.6 km) Turnoff to east for **Twin Falls Gorge Territorial Park, Alexandra Falls** picnic area; toilets, picnic shelters and interpretive program. Paved parking area and gravel walkway to falls viewpoint, overlooking the Hay River, which plunges 109 feet/33m to form **Alexandra Falls**. Excellent photo opportunities; walk down stairs to top of falls. A 1.9-mile/3-km trail through mixed boreal forest (with good canyon views) connects with Louise Falls.

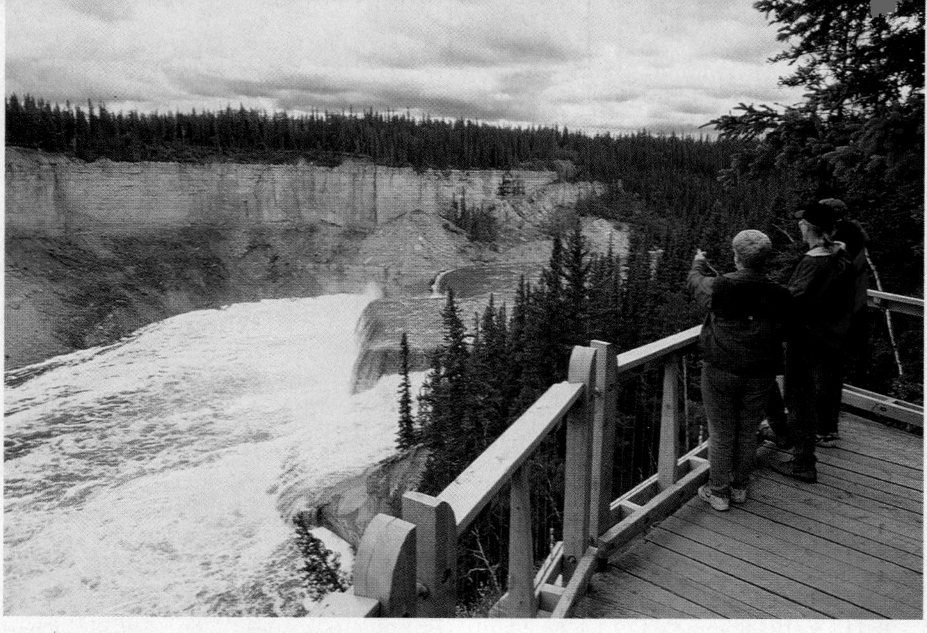
Viewpoint at Twin Falls Gorge Territorial Park, Milepost B 45. (© Leslie Leong)

B 46.4 (74.6 km) **FS 248.2** (399.4 km) Turnoff to east for **Twin Falls Gorge Territorial Park, Louise Falls** picnic area and campground; 18 campsites, 6 picnic sites, kitchen shelter, playground, electric hookups, tables, toilets, firepits, firewood, water. Hiking trails to viewpoint overlooking 3-tiered Louise Falls, which drops 50 feet/15m. Walk down spiral stairs to top of falls. Look for fossils at edge of falls. A 1.9-mile/3-km walking trails connects with Alexandra Falls. ▲

B 47.9 (77.1 km) **FS 246.6** (396.9 km) **Escarpment Creek** picnic area; tables, shelter, toilets, firepits, garbage container, water. Spectacular series of waterfalls on Escarpment Creek; access from north side of creek.

B 48.1 (77.4 km) **FS 246.4** (396.6 km) Highway crosses Escarpment Creek.

B 51.4 (82.8 km) **FS 243.1** (391.2 km) Service station, restaurant and craft shop to west. Entering Enterprise northbound.

B 51.7 (83.3 km) **FS 242.8** (390.1 km) Weigh station.

Junction of Highway 1 with Highway 2 to Hay River. See HAY RIVER HIGHWAY log on page 740.

Continue on Highway 1 for Enterprise (description follows) and Fort Simpson.

ENTERPRISE (pop. 80), a highway community with food, gas, diesel, lodging, grocery store, pay phone. Excellent native craft shop. View of Hay River Gorge just east of the highway. View of historic transportation equipment from road just behind Winnie's (private property, but the glimpses from the road are worthwhile).

B 74.4 (119.8 km) **FS 220.1** (354.2 km) Large paved double-ended turnout to north with outhouses, picnic area, viewing platform and trail with bridge to view falls from north side of canyon..

Highway crosses McNally Creek northbound.

B 76.4 (122.9 km) **FS 218.2** (351.1 km) Large paved turnout to north with picnic site, litter barrels and scenic view from escarpment.

B 80.5 (129.5 km) **FS 214** (344.5 km) Easy-to-miss **Hart Lake Fire Tower** access road turnoff leads 0.6 mile/1 km to picnic area and forest fire lookout tower. Panoramic view over more than 100 square miles/259 square km of forest to Great Slave Lake and Mackenzie River. (On a clear day, sharp eyes can spot Yellowknife highrises on the skyline.) Path to ancient coral reef. *CAUTION: Keep the fly repellent handy and stay away from the edge of escarpment.*

B 84.5 (136 km) **FS 210** (338 km) Crooked Creek.

B 85 (136.8 km) **FS 209.5** (337.2 km) Trapper's cabin to north.

B 92.2 (148.3 km) **FS 202.4** (325.7 km) Side road to gravel pits.

B 103.8 (167.1 km) **FS 190.7** (306.9 km) Access road leads south 4.2 miles/6.8 km to **Lady Evelyn Falls** where the Kakisa River drops 49 feet/15m over an escarpment. Staircase down to viewing platform. Hiking trail to base of falls; swimming and wading. Ample parking, interpretive display, territorial campground with 13 campsites, 7 picnic sites; a group picnic site, showers, toilets, tables, firepits, firewood, garbage containers, water pump, kitchen shelters, visitor centre. At end of road, 3 miles/5 km past campground, is Slavey Indian village and **Kakisa Lake;** fair fishing for walleye, pike and grayling.

B 104.2 (167.7 km) **FS 190.3** (306.3 km) Kilometrepost 168.

B 104.7 (168.5 km) **FS 190.8** (305.5 km) Kakisa River bridge.

B 106.1 (170.7 km) **FS 190.6** (306.8 km) Kakisa River bridge picnic area with 10 sites, tables, fireplaces and firewood. Hiking trails along river lead upstream to Lady Evelyn Falls. Fair fishing in **Kakisa River** for grayling.

B 115.4 (185.7 km) **FS 179.1** (288.3 km) Turnout with litter barrels, log cabin, outhouse, picnic tables and map display on Highways 1 and 3.

B 115.5 (185.8 km) **FS 179.1** (288.2 km)

Junction of Highway 1 and Highway 3. See YELLOWKNIFE HIGHWAY log on page 741.

Highway 3 (paved and gravel) leads 211 miles/339.6 km north to Yellowknife, capital of Northwest Territories .

B 128.3 (206.5 km) **FS 166.2** (267.5 km) Kilometrepost 208.

B 143.5 (230.9 km) **FS 151** (243.1 km) Emergency survival cabin and turnout with litter barrels and outhouse to south.

B 157.9 (254.1 km) **FS 136.6** (219.9 km) Turnout to north with parking and scenic view.

B 160.8 (258.8 km) **FS 133.7** (215.2 km) Kilometrepost 260.

B 161.3 (259.6 km) **FS 133.2** (214.4 km) Axehandle Creek (no sign); good fishing.

B 169.4 (272.7 km) **FS 125.1** (201.3 km) Turnout to south.

B 171.7 (276.3 km)**FS 122.8** (197.7 km) Bouvier River.

B 172.6 (277.8 km) **FS 121.9** (196.2 km) Emergency survival cabin and turnout with litter barrels to south.

B 178.5 (287.3 km) **FS 116** (186.7 km) Turnout to north.

B 179.2 (288.4 km) **FS 115.3** (185.6 km) Wallace Creek. Scenic canyon to north; trail access on west side of creek; 15-minute walk to canyon and waterfall.

B 182.3 (293.4 km) **FS 112.2** (180.6 km) Highway maintenance camp to south.

B 182.9 (294.3 km) **FS 111.7** (179.7 km) Redknife River.

B 194 (312.2 km) **FS 100.5** (161.8 km) Morrissey Creek.

B 199.2 (320.5 km) **FS 95.4** (153.5 km) Winter ice road leads south 78 miles/126 km to **TROUT LAKE** (pop. 66), a Dene settlement.

B 201 (323.5 km) **FS 93.5** (150.5 km) Trout River bridge just east of turnoff to **Sambaa Deh (Whittaker Falls) Territorial Park**; 5 picnic sites, 13 campsites, tables, litter barrels, showers, kitchen shelter, firepits, firewood, water, emergency phone, visitor centre.

Whittaker Falls is under highway bridge. From the campground, hike 0.6 mile/1 km south to **Coral Falls**. Hike 0.6 mile/1 km north on west side of river to third falls and access to **Trout River Canyon.** Fossils are embedded in the rocks along the Trout

Example of beadwork in the Mackenzie River valley region. (© Lyn Hancock)

River.

B 202.2 (325.4 km) **FS 92.3** (148.6 km) Turnout with litter barrels to south.

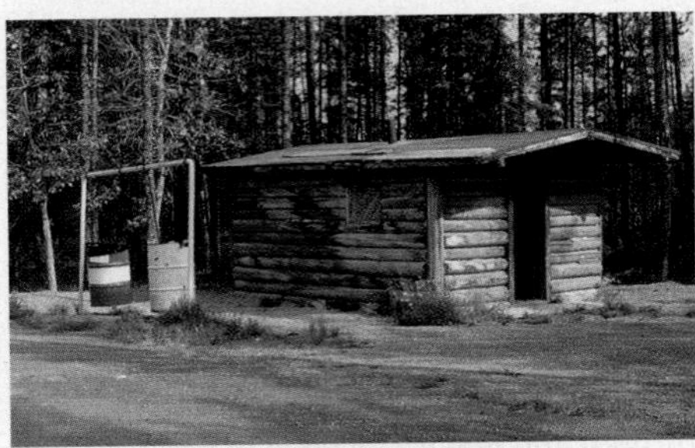

B 205.5 (330.7 km) **FS 89** (143.3 km) Emergency survival cabin and turnout with litter barrels to north.

B 208.2 (335 km) **FS 86.4** (139 km) Kilometrepost 336.

B 226.9 (365.2 km) **FS 67.6** (108.8 km) Kilometrepost 366.

B 229.9 (370 km) **FS 64.6** (104 km) **Ekali Lake** access; pike and pickerel.

B 233 (374.9 km) **FS 61.5** (99.1 km) **Junction** with Jean Marie River extension, an all-weather road leading 17 miles/27 km to community of Jean Marie River (description follows). Travellers are welcome to visit traditional camps along the road. Please respect private property while visiting. History and information sign on the community and culture of Jean Marie River at Km 0.1.

JEAN MARIE RIVER (pop. 53), located on the south shore of the Mackenzie River at the confluence with the Jean Marie River, is a very traditional community well known for its native crafts.

Visitor Information: Available from friendly staff at the Band Office in the large brown building in front of the central playground. If the office is closed, ask anyone you see in the community. Residents are happy to help.

Services here include a campground (located near airport); picnic site on the river; general store, open 10 a.m. to noon and 5–7 P.M.; and gas, available 9 A.M. to 5 P.M. and by call-out after hours. Arts & crafts available; inquire at the Band Office. Boat tours and fishing on the Mackenzie River. Boat launch with dock on the Mackenzie River. The historic Jean Marie River Tugboat rests up shore, retired from shipping lumber down the Mackenzie to Arctic communities.

B 235.5 (379 km) **FS 59** (95 km) Emergency survival cabin and turnout to north with outhouse and litter barrels.

B 240.5 (387.1 km) **FS 54** (86.9 km) I.P.L. pipeline camp and pump station to north. Highway crosses pipeline.

B 241.2 (388.2 km) **FS 53.3** (85.8 km) Microwave tower to south.

B 255.2 (410.7 km) **FS 39.3** (63.3 km) Jean Marie Creek bridge.

B 255.3 (410.8 km) **FS 39.2** (63.2 km) "Checkpoint"; open 8 a.m. to midnight. Gas, diesel, propane, emergency repairs, crafts, licensed restaurant and accommodations. Phone (403) 695-2953. Open year-round.

B 255.3 (410.9 km) **FS 39.2** (63.1 km) Liard Highway leads south to Fort Liard and junctions with the Alaska Highway near Fort Nelson.

Junction with the Liard Highway (NWT Highway 7). See the LIARD HIGHWAY section on page 727 for details.

B 256.4 (412.6km) **FS 38.2** (61.4 km) Turnout to east.

B 268.2 (431.6 km) **FS 26.3** (42.4 km) Emergency survival cabin and turnout with litter barrels and outhouse to west.

B 269.2 (433.3 km) **FS 25.3** (40.7 km) Kilometrepost 434.

B 282.6 (454.8 km) **FS 11.9** (19.2 km) Highway crests hill; view of Liard River ahead. Ferry landing 3,280 feet/1,000m.

B 283 (455.5 km) **FS 11.5** (18.5 km) Liard River Campground to accommodate travelers who miss the last ferry at night, has 5 sites, tables, firepits, water, outhouse and garbage container.

B 283.2 (455.8 km) **FS 11.3** (18.2 km) Free government-operated Liard River (South Mackenzie) ferry service operates daily late May through October from 8 A.M. to 11:45 P.M., 7 days a week; once an hour on the half-hour for westbound traffic, on the hour for eastbound traffic. Crossing time is 6 minutes. Capacity is 8 cars or 2 trucks, with a maximum total weight of 130,000 lbs./59,090 kg. An ice bridge opens for light vehicles in late November and heavier vehicles as ice thickens. *NOTE: This crossing is subject to extreme high and low water level fluctuations which may cause delays. No crossing possible during breakup (about mid-April to mid-May) and freezeup (mid-October to mid-November).* For ferry information phone (867) 695-2018 or (800) 661-0751.

B 284.6 (458 km) **FS 9.9** (15.9 km) Fort Simpson airport. See Private Aircraft information in Fort Simpson.

B 286.6 (461.2 km) **FS 7.9** (12.8 km) Kilometrepost 462.

B 289.1 (465.2 km) **FS 5.5** (8.8 km) Kilometrepost 466.

B 290.5 (467.6 km) **FS 4** (6.4 km) Gravel ends, pavement begins northbound.

B 292.4 (470.5 km) **FS 2.2** (3.5 km) **Junction** with Fort Simpson access road which leads 2.3 miles/3.8 km to Fort Simpson (description follows). The extension of NWT Highway 1 to Wrigley was completed in 1994; see WRIGLEY EXTENSION log on page 740 this section.

Northwest Territories offers great lake trout fishing. (© Leslie Leong)

B 294 (473.2 km) **FS 0.5** (0.8 km) Causeway to Fort Simpson Island.

B 294.4 (473.9 km) **FS 0.1** (0.1 km) Turnoff for village campground; 30 campsites, 4 picnic sites, kitchen shelter; shower planned. ▲

Fort Simpson

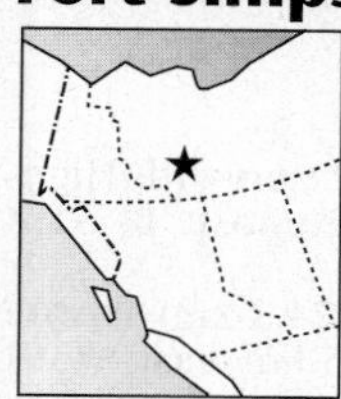

B 294.5 (474 km) **FS 0** Located on an island at the confluence of the Mackenzie and Liard rivers. **Population:** 1,200. **Emergency Services: RCMP**, phone (867) 695-3111. **Hospital** (12 beds), for medical emergency phone (867) 695-2291. **Fire Department** (volunteer), phone (867) 695-2222.

Visitor Information: Village office operates a visitor booth June through August and has a photo exhibit and films. The visitor information centre is open 9 A.M. to 9 P.M., daily in summer; 9 A.M. to 5 P.M. weekdays in winter. Nahanni National Park information centre is open 8:30 A.M. to 5 P.M., 7 days a week in July and August, weekdays the rest of the year.

Transportation: Scheduled service to Yellowknife and Whitehorse, YT. Fixed wing and helicopter charters available. **Rental cars**—Available. **Taxi service**—Available.

Private Aircraft: Fort Simpson airport; elev. 554 feet/169m; length 6,000 feet/1,829m; asphalt; fuel 100, Jet B. Fort Simpson Island; elev. 405 feet/123m; length 3,000 feet/914m; gravel; fuel 100, Jet B.

Fort Simpson is a full-service community. There is a motel with kitchenettes and a hotel with licensed dining; 2 gas stations with repair service (unleaded, diesel and propane available); 2 grocery stores, department store, hardware store, a bank, laundromat, post office, 2 crafts shops and sports shop. Small engine repair shop and mechanics available. Recreational facilities include an arena, curling rink, gym, ball diamond, tennis, small indoor pool, golf course and a boat launch at government wharf.

Public campground at edge of town in wooded area has 30 campsites and 4 picnic sites. ▲

Fort Simpson is the oldest continuously occupied site on the Mackenzie River, dating from 1804 when the North West Co. established its Fort of the Forks. There is a historical marker on the bank of the Mackenzie. The Hudson's Bay Co. began its post here in 1821. At that time the fort was renamed after Sir George Simpson, one of the first governors of the combined North West Co. and Hudson's Bay Co. Fort Simpson served as the Mackenzie District headquarters for the Hudson's Bay Co. fur-trading operation. Its key location on the Mackenzie River also made Fort Simpson an important transportation centre. Anglican and Catholic missions were established here in 1858 and 1894.

Fort Simpson continues to be an important centre for the Northwest Territories water transport system. Visitors may walk along the high banks of the Mackenzie River and watch the boat traffic and floatplanes.

One of the easiest places to get down to the water is by Alfred Faille's cabin on Mackenzie Drive. Faille was a well-known Fort Simpson pioneer and prospector.

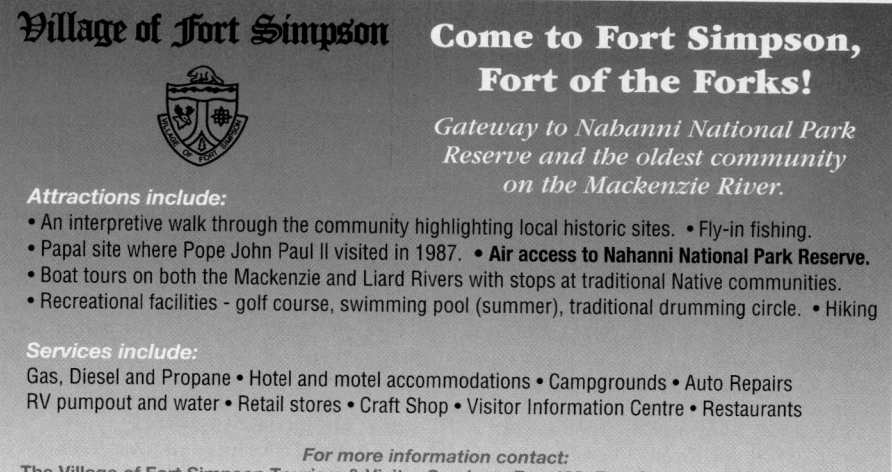

For visitors, Fort Simpson has Slavey crafts, such as birch-bark baskets and beadwork. Aboriginal Dene fashion designer Darcy Moses teaches at the Nats'enelu outlet in Fort Simpson. Nats'enelu is an outlet for Dene dolls as well as other native crafts.

Fort Simpson is also the jumping-off point for jet boat trips on the North Nahanni River; Mackenzie River traffic; and fly-in trips to Nahanni National Park.

Nahanni National Park, listed as a unique geological area on the UNESCO world heritage site list, is accessible only by nonpowered boat or aircraft. Located southwest of Fort Simpson near the Yukon border, the park has day-trip flightseeing tours that may be arranged in Fort Simpson, Fort Liard and Yellowknife, and from Fort Nelson, BC, and Watson Lake, YT. Highlights include the

spectacular **Virginia Falls** (300 feet/90m, twice as high as Niagara Falls). North of the park boundary is the world renowned Cirque of the Unclimbables and Glacier Lake.

One of the most popular attractions in the park is running the South Nahanni River or its tributary, the Flat River. Charter air service for canoe drop-offs is available in Fort Simpson.

The park has a mandatory reservation system for overnight use and charges user fees. For details contact Nahanni National Park Reserve, Box 348, Fort Simpson, NT X0E 0N0; phone (867) 695-3151, fax 695-2446.

Willow, Dogface and Trout lakes are accessible by air. Good fishing for trout and grayling. Inquire locally.

Village of Fort Simpson. See display ad on page 739.

Wolverine Air. See display ad on page 739.

Mackenzie Highway Log

(continued)

Distance from Fort Simpson (FS) is shown.
Kilometreposts reflect distance from Alberta border. Distance to Wrigley is 137 miles/220.5 km; driving time is approximately 3 hours. Allow at least 2 hours from Wrigley to the Camsell ferry crossing.

WRIGLEY EXTENSION

FS 0 Junction with Fort Simpson access road.

FS 9.3 (15 km) Kilometrepost 486.

FS 10..9 (17.5 km) Single-lane bridge over **Martin River**. Turnout at north end of bridge. Good fishing. *CAUTION: Slow down for steep descent to bridge.*

FS 17.9 (28.8 km) Creek crossing. *CAUTION: Slow down, steep drop-offs and no guardrails.*

FS 35.5 (57.1 km) Single-lane bridge over Shale Creek.

FS 35.8 (57.7 km) Kilometrepost 528.

FS 36 (58 km) Turnout to east.

FS 47.8 (76. 9 km) Northbound vista of Mackenzie River from crest of hill.

FS 48.3 (77.8 km) Ferry crossing of the Mackenzie River at Camsell Bend (Ndulee Crossing). Ferry operates daily, late May through October, 9 to 11 A.M. and 2 to 8 P.M.. Capacity is 6 cars or 4 trucks. *NOTE: There are no overnight facilities for anyone missing the ferry. Ferry does not operate in fog. Be prepared to wait.*

FS 53.9 (86.7 km) Kilometrepost 558.

FS 75.1 (120.9 km) Highway maintenance camp to east.

FS 96.2 (154.8 km) Willowlake River bridge, longest bridge in the Northwest Territories.

FS 96.5 (155.3 km) Kilometrepost 626. Road east down to Willowlake River.

FS 97.2 (157 km) Highway climbs steep hill northbound; views to west.

FS 99.8 (160.7 km) Turnout to west at top of hill with litter barrels and scenic view of the Mackenzie River and Mackenzie Mountains.

FS 100.2 (161.3 km) Kilometrepost 632.

FS 112.8 (181.6 km) Single-lane wooden bridge over the "River Between Two Mountains."

FS 117.9 (189.8 km) Kilometrepost 660.

FS 121.8 (196 km) Kilometrepost 666.

FS 123 (197.9 km) Kilometrepost 668.

FS 123.9 (199.4 km) **W 15.5** (25.1 km) Wrigley interprovincial pipeline pump station and radio tower to east.

FS 130.7 (210.4 km) Road east to gravel yard; great views of Pine Phen Mountain and other peaks.

FS 131.2 (211.1 km) Single-lane bridge over Smith's Creek.

FS 133 (214.1 km) Southbound views of Cap Mountains to east.

FS 133.3 (214.5 km) Highway maintenance camp to west.

FS 134.4 (216.3 km) **Airport Lake**, Pehdzeh Ki campground; 12 sites, firepits and outhouses. Suitable for RVs; located on high, dry ground in mostly birch and white spruce trees. ▲

FS 134.6 (216.6 km) **Junction** with winter ice road to east which leads north to Fort Norman, Norman Wells, Fort Franklin and Fort Good Hope. Winter road mileages are as follows: Wrigley to Fort Norman, 148 miles/238 km; Fort Norman to Norman Wells, 50 miles/80 km; Norman Wells to Fort Good Hope, 91 miles/147 km; Norman Wells to Franklin, 68 miles/110 km.

FS 134.8 (216.9 km) Turnoff to west for Wrigley airport. **Private Aircraft**: Wrigley airport, 4 miles/7 km south of town; elev. 493 feet/142m; length 3,500 feet/1,148m; gravel; fuel 80.

FS 137 (220.5 km) **W 0 WRIGLEY** (pop. 200; 90 percent Dene ancestry). **Emergency Services: RCMP**, station manned intermittently. **Nursing Station,** with full-time nurse, phone (867) 587-3441.

Visitor Information: Available at the Youth Centre (open daily in summer). The Pehdzeh Ki Dene Band Complex can also be a source of information.

The Hudson's Bay Co. built a trading post here in 1870 called Fort Wrigley. The fort was abandoned in 1910 due to disease and famine, and the inhabitants moved down river. Although a church and school were built at that site in 1957, the community decided to move to higher ground in 1965. 15 homes were built at the "new" townsite of present-day Wrigley. The church, school and other buildings were moved from the old townsite by boat. Wrigley is the home of the Pehdzeh Ki First Nation.

Visitor facilities here include the Petanea Hotel and restaurant; co-op store; Ed's Mobile Mechanical Service; a convenience store; and a government gas station operating 9 A.M. to 6 P.M. weekdays and 1 to 6 P.M. weekends. Local native crafts are available.

There are hiking trails into the mountains to the east of the community. Inquire locally.

A community-built, walk-in campground with washrooms and fireplaces along the bank of the Mackenzie River, with picturesque, bug-free views of the Mackenzie Mountains. ▲

Hay River Highway Log

Distance from Enterprise (E) is followed by distance from hay River.
Highway 2 is paved from Enterprise to Hay River. Kilometreposts along the highway reflect distance from Enterprise.

NWT HIGHWAY 2

E 0 H 23.6 (38 km) **Junction** with Highways 1 at Enterprise, **Milepost B 51.7** Mackenzie Highway.

E 8.5 (13.7 km) **H 15.1** (24.3 km) Private campground, 0.7 mile/1.1 km east, with large organic gardens. ▲

Paradise Garden Campground. See display ad this section. ▲

E 11.3 (18.2 km) **H 12.3** (19.8 km) Sawmill Road to east.

E 15.7 (25.3 km) **H 7.9** (12.7 km) Gravel road leads east 0.6 mile/1 km to Hay River golf course; large log clubhouse, driving range, 9 holes (par 36), artificial greens.

E 19.8 (31.9 km) **H 3.8** (6.1 km)

Junction with Highway 5 to Fort Smith. See FORT SMITH HIGHWAY log on page 744 this section.

E 20.4 (32.8 km) **H 3.2** (5.1 km) Motel and restaurant north of junction.

E 22 (35.4 km) **H 1.6** (2.6 km) Chamber of Commerce Welcome to Hay River sign.

Parking area to east.

E 22.1 (35.6 km) **H 1.5** (2.4 km) Turnoff to east for parking area and picnic site.

E 22.7 (36.6 km) **H 0.9** (1.4 km) Gas, motel, groceries to east.

E 23.2 (37.4 km) **H 0.4** (0.6 km) Chamber of Commerce tourist information sign.

Hay River

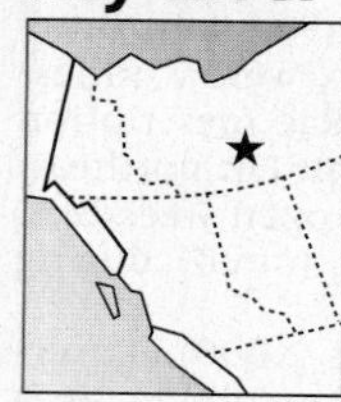

E 23.6 (38 km) **H 0** Located on the south shore of Great Slave Lake at the mouth of the Hay River, on both the mainland and Vale Island. **Population:** 3,600 **Emergency Services: RCMP**, phone (867) 874-6555. **Fire Department**, phone (867) 874-2222. **Ambulance**, phone (867) 874-9333. **Hospital**, phone (867) 874-6512.

Visitor Information: Visitor information centre, just east of the highway, is housed in a 2-story brown structure; phone (867) 874-3180. The centre is open daily, late May to early September; 9 A.M. to 9 P.M. There is a dump station located here. Write the Town of Hay River, 73 Woodland Dr., Hay River, NWT X0E 1G1. Or the Chamber of Commerce at 10K Gagnler St., Hay River, NWT X0E 1G1; phone (867) 874-2565, fax (867) 874-3255.

Transportation: Air—Schedule service. **Bus**—Frontier Coachlines. **Rental cars**—Available.

Private Aircraft: Hay River airport; elev. 543 feet/165m; length 6,000 feet/1,830m, paved; 4,000 feet/1,219m, gravel; fuel 100, Jet B.

Hay River was established in 1868 with the building of a Hudson's Bay Co. post. Today's economy combines transportation, communications, commercial fishing and service industries. Hay River also has Paradise Gardens, the largest market-gardening operation in Northwest Territories, and Perron's Funny Farm, one of the few livestock producers in the territories.

The community is the transfer point from highway and rail to barges on Great Slave Lake bound for arctic and subarctic communities. Hay River harbour is also home port of the Mackenzie River barge fleet that plies the river in summer.

The airstrip was built in 1942 on Vale Island by the U.S. Army Corps of Engineers. Vale Island was the townsite until floods in 1951 and 1963 forced evacuation of the population to the mainland townsite, where most of the community is now concentrated. Vale Island, referred to as "Old Town," is bounded by Great Slave Lake and the west and east channels of the Hay River.

Hay River has schools, churches, a civic centre with a swimming pool (1 of only 2 year-round swimming pools in Northwest Territories), bowling alley, Hay River Golf Club (9-hole), curling sheets, hockey arena and dance hall. The Hay River Speedway has car racing. Northwest Territories Centennial Library headquarters is located here. There is a public boat launch at Porritt Landing on Vale Island.

Visitor services include restaurants, fast-food outlets; 4 hotels and 3 motels; gas stations with unleaded gas, propane and repair service, and supermarkets. There is also a bed and breakfast. Other facilities include 2 banks, 2 laundromats, and a variety of gift and arts and crafts shops.

Just across the river is the **Hay River Reserve**, where the Dene Cultural Institute hosts a Dene cultural afternoon every Friday. Here's also a visitor centre and craft shop. One-hour tours of the reserve are available by reservation; phone (867) 874-8480.

Hay River Territorial Campground and Beach Park is on **Vale Island** on Great Slave Lake (follow signs; it's about 6 miles/10 km past the information centre); 26 sites, some pull-throughs, hookups, showers, firewood and firepits, camping fee $12–$18 per night, open mid-May to mid-Septemer. The beach park has an excellent playground and offers picnic sites, volleyball, swimming and a water slide. Paradise Garden Campground, 14.9 miles/24 km south of Hay River on Highway 2, is a private campground on the Hay River; dry campsites, hookups (electrical and water), dump station, playground and organic gardens. ▲

Great sportfishing area with fly-in fishing camps (check with the visitor centre). Boat rentals on nearby **Great Slave Lake**, where northern pike up to 40 lbs. are not unusual. Inconnu (sheefish), pickerel and grayling also found here.

Yellowknife Highway Log

Distance from the junction of Highways 1 and 3 (J) is followed by distance from Yellowknife (Y).

NWT HIGHWAY 3

J 0 Y 211 (339.6 km) Highway 3 leads north from **Milepost B 115.5** on Highway 1.

Junction of Highways 1 and 3. See **Milepost B 115.5** on page 738 in the MACKENZIE HIGHWAY log this section for log of Highway 1 to Fort Simpson and the Alberta border.

The first 152.3 miles/245.1 km of Highway 3 are paved. There is one remaining stretch of gravel—56.2 miles/90.4 km—between Edzo and Yellowknife. *NOTE: Watch for road construction between Rae and Yellowknife.*

J 4.8 (7.7 km) **Y 206.2** (331.8 km) Chikilee Creek.

J 4.9 (7.9 km) **Y 206.1** (331.6 km) Wolf Skull Creek.

J 9.1 (14.7 km) **Y 201.9** (324.9 km) Dory Point maintenance camp to west.

J 10.6 (17 km) **Y 200.4** (322.5 km) Turnoff for winter ice crossing to east.

J 12.5 (20.2 km) **Y 198.5** (319.4 km) Dory Point picnic area to east with 5 sites and kitchen shelter, no drinking water; overlooking Mackenzie River with view of passing riverboats.

J 14.2 (22.9 km) **Y 196.8** (316.7 km) Dory Point marine services camp to west.

J 14.7 (23.6 km) **Y 196.3** (316 km) Free government-operated **Mackenzie River Ferry;** operates daily 6 A.M. to midnight, from mid- or late May through October or until ice conditions prevent operation. Crossing time is 8 minutes. Capacity is 10 cars or 4 trucks, with a maximum total weight of 220,000 lbs./100,000 kg. Ferry information phone (800) 661-0751. An ice bridge opens for light vehicles in December and heavier vehicles as ice thickens. *NOTE: No crossing possible during breakup (about April to mid-May).* Ice-breaking procedures now keep the channel open for the ferry during freezeup while an ice bridge is being constructed.

Map display of Highway 3 points of interest.

J 15.6 (25.2 km) **Y 195.4** (314.4 km) Ice bridge access road to east. Good fishing in the Mackenzie River.

J 15.9 (25.6 km) **Y 195.1** (314 km) Sign indicates Mackenzie Wood Bison Sanctuary. *NOTE: Use EXTREME CAUTION driving in this area; slow down and watch for bison on highway!*

J 19.2 (30.9 km) **Y 191.8** (308.7 km) Motel, restaurant, lounge; Native crafts; gas station with unleaded, diesel, propane, tire repair and pay phone.

Big River Service Centre. See display ad this section.

J 19.5 (31.4 km) **Y 191.5** (308.2 km) **Junction** with access road which leads 3.1 miles/5 km west to Fort Providence (description follows). There is an airstrip located 0.4 mile/0.6 km west on the access road.

NOTE: Next gas available northbound is in Rae–Edzo.

Fort Providence territorial campground is located 1.3 miles/2 km west of the highway on the access road; 30 sites, tables, firewood,

Beautifully restored church in Fort Providence is a favorite photo subject. (© Leslie Leong)

kitchen shelter, garbage container, water and dump station. Situated on the banks of the Mackenzie River. Rental boats, boat launch and fishing nearby. ▲

Fort Providence

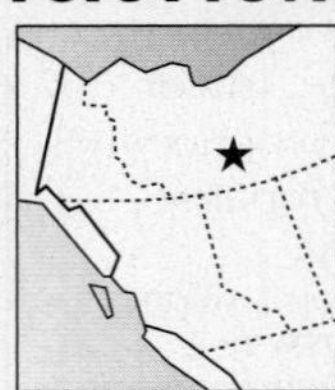

Located on the Mackenzie River, 3.1 miles/5 km northwest of Highway 3. **Population:** 745. **Emergency Services: Police**, phone (867) 699-3291. **Fire Department**, phone (867) 699-4222. **Nursing station**, phone (867) 699-4311. **Elevation:** 627 feet/191m. **Radio:** 1230. **Television:** Channels 6 and 13 (CBC). **Transportation: Air**—Air Providence and charter service. **Bus**—Coachways.

Private Aircraft: Fort Providence airstrip; elev. 530 feet/162m; length 3,000 feet/915m; gravel; fuel emergency only.

Facilities include 2 motels, 2 bed and breakfasts, 2 restaurants; gas stations; grocery and general stores; and crafts shops. Car repair available at C&A Holdings and Snowstar Mechanical Ltd.

A Roman Catholic mission was established here in 1861. Although noted for its early agricultural endeavors, Fort Providence is traditionally a trapping community. Three historical markers in the community commemorate the roles of the church and explorer Alexander Mackenzie in settling the area.

At the far end of the town is the historical monument overlooking the river and boat launch. Follow the road north to 3 picnic sites; good bird watching for eagles, sandhill cranes and other birds.

Unique and popular with northern collectors is the moose hair embroidery found in local gift shops. Local craftswomen are also noted for their porcupine quill work. Along with seeing the crafts, visitors may cruise the Mackenzie River. Spectacular photo opportunities here for sunsets on the Mackenzie. Fort Providence is also the gateway to the Mackenzie Wood Bison Sanctuary, where the bison herd is flourishing.

Good to excellent fishing in **Mackenzie River**; guides and cabins available, also boats and air charter trips. Northern pike to 30 lbs., May 30 to September, use large Red Devils; grayling and pickerel from 1 to 6 lbs., June to September, use anything (small Red Devils will do).

Yellowknife Highway Log

(continued)

J 27.5 (44.3 km) **Y 183.5** (295.3 km) Bluefish Creek.

J 37 (59.5 km) **Y 174** (280 km) Large turnout to east at sand and gravel stockpiles.

J 38.7 (62.3 km) **Y 172.3** (277.3 km) Small gravel turnout to east.

J 42.3 (68.1 km) **Y 168.7** (271.5 km) Turnout to east with litter barrels and interpretive sign.

NOTE: Use EXTREME CAUTION driving in this area; slow down and watch for bison on highway!

J 51.5 (82.8 km) **Y 19.5** (256.8 km) Turnout to west with litter barrels.

J 54.1 (87 km) **Y 156.9** (252.6 km) Telecommunications building to west and access to Caen Lake firetower to east.

J 54.4 (87.6 km) **Y 156.6** (252 km) Kilometrepost 90. Good access road to Caen Lake (0.6 km) with large turnaround.

J 77 (123.8 km) **Y 134** (215.8 km) Turnout with litter barrels to east.

J 99.8 (160.6 km) **Y 111.2** (179 km) Turnout with litter barrels, outhouse and highway map sign to east. Watch for buffalo.

J 124.7 (200.7 km) **Y 86.3** (138.9 km) Entering Yellowknife District northbound.

J 129.7 (208.8 km) **Y 81.3** (130.8 km) Turnout with litter barrels to east. Northbound travelers may notice the trees are getting shorter as you move farther north.

J 140.2 (225.7 km) **Y 70.8** (113.9 km) Turnout to east. Highway descends northbound to Mosquito Creek.

J 141.2 (227.3 km) **Y 69.8** (112.3 km) Highway crosses **Mosquito Creek**. Fishing for pickerel and whitefish, May and June.

J 144.1 (231.9 km) **Y 66.9** (107.7 km) Access road north to telecommunications tower. Good views of Great Slave Lake; great berry picking.

J 144.2 (232.1 km) **Y 66.8** (107.5 km) **North Arm Territorial Park** on the shores of Great Slave Lake to south; picnic area with kitchen shelter, tables, toilets, firewood and firepits. Lowbush cranberries and other berries in area. *Beware of bears.*

J 148.3 (238.6 km) **Y 62.7** (100.9 km) **Junction** with winter ice road north to communities of Lac La Marte and Rae Lakes.

J 148.5 (239 km) **Y 62.5** (100.6 km) **Junction** with access road west to community of Edzo (see description at **Milepost J 152.2**).

J 148.8 (239.5 km) **Y 62,2** (100.1 km) Picnic area to west. Pickerel fishing in **West Channel** in spring.

J 149.3 (240.2 km) **Y 61.7** (99.3 km) West Channel.

J 151.5 (243.8 km) **Y 59.5** (95.8 km) Bridge over **Frank Channel**, which extends from the head of the North Arm of Great Slave Lake to the Indian village of Rae. Watch for turnoff to Rabesca's Bear Healing Rock; lodging, mud baths, boating and fishing for whitefish.

J 152.2 (245 km) **Y 58.8** (94.6 km) **Junction** with road which leads west 7 miles/11.2 km to community of Rae (description follows). **Visitor Information:** On northeast corner at highway junction; open weekdays, 9 A.M. to 5 P.M. (closed at lunch) during summer.

RAE–EDZO (pop. about 2,000). **Emergency Services: RCMP**, in Rae, phone (867) 392-6181. **Nursing station** in Rae, phone (867) 371-3551.

The 2 hamlets of Rae–Edzo contain the territories' largest Dene (Indian) community. The Rae area, where most of the community resides, is an old Dene hunting spot and was the site of 2 early trading posts. The Edzo site was developed in 1965 by the government to provide schools and an adequate sanitation system. Rae has grocery stores, a post office, several pay phones, 2 hotels, food service and gas stations with regular, unleaded and diesel.

J 152.3 (245.1 km) **Y 58.7** (94.5 km) *Pavement ends, gravel begins, eastbound. Watch for road construction.*

J 159.8 (257.2 km) **Y 51.2** (82.4 km) Stagg River bridge. After crossing the North Arm of Great Slave Lake, the highway swings southeast toward Yellowknife. Winding road to Yellowknife, good opportunities to see waterfowl in the many small lakes.

J 160.4 (258.1 km) **Y 50.6** (81.4 km) Turnout with litter barrels and interpretive signs to south.

J 173.5 (279.2 km) **Y 37.5** (60.3 km) Turnout to north, trapper's cabin to south.

J 189.2 (304.5 km) **Y 21.8** (35.1 km) Turnout with litter barrels to north.

J 189.5 (304.9 km) **Y 21.5** (34.6 km) Boundary Creek.

J 192.7 (310.1 km) **Y 18.3** (29.5 km) Kilometrepost 308.

J 205.5 (330.7 km) **Y 5.5** (8.9 km) Yellowknife city limits.

J 206 (331.5 km) **Y 5** (8 km) Yellowknife Golf Club to north; 9 holes, sand greens, pro shop, licensed clubhouse. Built on the Canadian Shield, the course is mostly sand and bedrock. Each player gets a small piece of carpet to take along on the round as their own portable turf. Site of the June 21 Midnight Tournament. Some modified rules have been adopted by this Far North golf course, among them: "No penalty assessed when ball carried off by raven."

J 207.2 (333.5 km) **Y 3.8** (6.1 km) Gravel ends, pavement begins, eastbound.

J 208.5 (335.6 km) **Y 2.5** (4 km) Yellowknife airport to south.

J 208.8 (336 km) **Y 2.2** (3.5 km) **Fred Henne Territorial Park** on Long Lake. Attractive public campground with 82 sites, water, firewood, firepits, picnic area, boat launch, snack bar, showers and pay phone. Daily and seasonal rates available; open from mid-May to mid-September. Sandy beach and swimming in Long Lake. Interpretive trail. ▲

J 209.3 (336.8 km) **Y 1.7** (2.7 km) Old Airport Road access to Yellowknife. Just past the turnoff is the Welcome to Yellowknife sign and the hard-to-miss Wardair Bristol

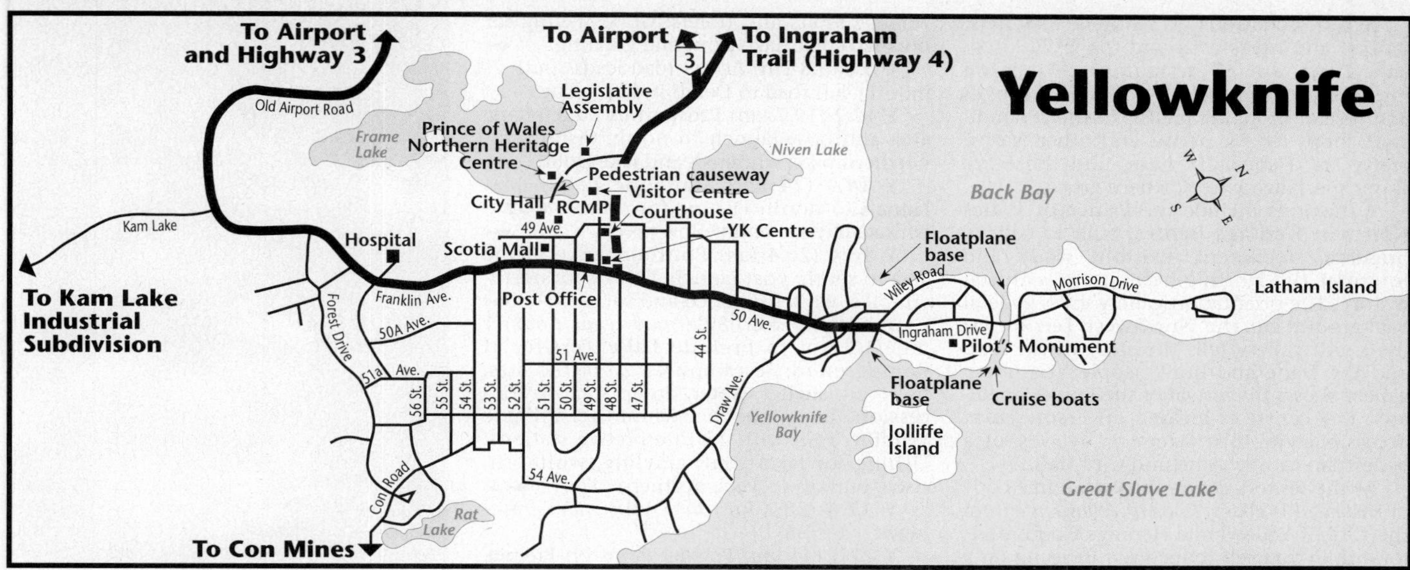

freighter to the south. A historical plaque commemorates the Bristol freighter, which was the first wheel-equipped aircraft to land at the North Pole. Picnic sites nearby.

J 210 (338 km) **Y 1** (1.6 km) Stock Lake to south; turnout with litter barrels and picnic site.

J 210.5 (338.8 km) **Y 0.5** (0.8 km)

Junction with Highway 4 (Ingraham Trail). See INGRAHAM TRAIL log on page 744 this section.

J 210.9 (339.4 km) **Y 0.1** (0.4 km) Access road to museum and Legislative Assembly.

J 211 (339.6 km) **Y 0** Yellowknife; Northern Frontier Regional Visitors Centre (descriptions follows).

Yellowknife

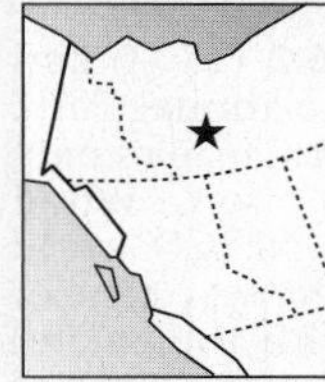

On the north shore of Great Slave Lake, approximately 940 miles/1,513 km from Edmonton, AB. **Population:** 18.000. **Emergency Services: RCMP,** phone (867) 920-8311. **Fire Department** and **Ambulance,** phone (867) 873-3434 or 873-2222. **Hospital,** Stanton Yellowknife, phone (867) 920-4111.

Visitor Information: Northern Frontier Regional Visitors Centre, showcasing the culture and crafts of the area, is located at 4807 49th St. Experienced and friendly staff ready to assist all visitors. Open daily year-round. Summer hours are 8:30 A.M. to 6 P.M. weekdays and 9 A.M. to 5 P.M. weekends, June through August. Winter hours are 8:30 A.M. to 5:30 P.M. weekdays, noon to 4 P.M. weekends, September through May. Phone (867) 873-4262, fax 873-3654.

Information also available from Northwest Territories Tourism Association, P.O. Box 610, Yellowknife, NT X1A 2N5. Phone (800) 661-0788; e-mail arctic@nwttravel.nt.ca; internet www.nwttravel.nt.ca.

Private Aircraft: Yellowknife airport; elev. 674 feet/205m; length 7,500 feet/2,286m; asphalt; fuel 100/130, Jet B. Floatplane bases located at East Bay and West Bay of Latham Island.

Transportation: Air—Scheduled air service to Edmonton. Several carriers serve Yellowknife and Arctic communities. Charter service available. **Bus**—Available. **Rentals**—Several major car rental agencies; boat, canoe and houseboat rentals.

Yellowknife is capital of Northwest Territories. **Northwest Territories Legislative Assembly** building is located on Frame Lake.

Tours of the legislative building are available by calling the Coordinator of Public Information at (867) 669-2230.

Yellowknife is a relatively new community. White settlers arrived in the 1930s with the discovery of gold in the area and radium at Great Bear Lake.

Cominco poured its first gold brick in 1938. WWII intervened and gold mining was halted until Giant Yellowknife Mines began milling on May 12, 1948. It was not until 1960 that the road connecting the city with the provinces was completed. Yellowknife became capital of the Northwest Territories in 1967.

The most recent mining boom in Yellowknife was the discovery of diamonds north of Yellowknife at Lac de Gras in 1992. The find set off a rush of claim stakers. An estimated 150 companies have staked claims in an area stretching from north of Yellowknife to the Arctic coast, and east from the North Arm of Great Slave Lake to Hudson Bay. In winter, the Ingraham Trail (NWT Highway 4) is used as part of the 380-mile/612-km ice road to Lupin gold mine. The winter road also serves Lac de Gras, heart of the diamond rush.

For 2 to 6 weeks each spring, vehicle traffic to Yellowknife is cut off during breakup on the Mackenzie River crossing near Fort Providence. All fresh meat, produce and urgent supplies must be airlifted during this period, resulting in higher prices.

Yellowknife has continued to develop as a mining, transportation and government administrative centre for the territories.

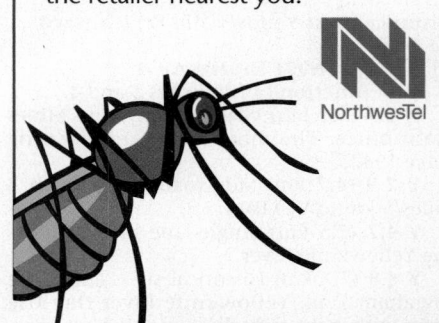

Accommodations at 3 hotels, 3 motels, 14 bed and breakfasts, and the YWCA (co-ed). There are 47 restaurants, 7 dining lounges (no minors), 18 cocktail lounges and several shopping malls. Northern handicraft shops for fur parkas and other Native crafts are a specialty here, and there are shops specializing in Northern art.

Attractions include the **Prince of Wales Northern Heritage Centre,** built to collect, preserve, document, exhibit, study and interpret the North's natural and cultural history. The orientation gallery gives general background on the Northwest Territories; the south gallery tells the story of the land and the Dene and Inuit people; the north gallery shows the arrival of the Euro–Canadians. The centre is located on Frame Lake, accessible via 48th Street or by way of a pedestrian causeway behind City Hall.

At the visitors centre, pick up a free copy of *Historical Walking Tours of Yellowknife* from the City of Yellowknife Heritage Committee, for 4 do-it-yourself tours, each focusing on a district of Yellowknife. **The Rock**, where the original town sprang up on Yellowknife Bay and where there are now barges, fishing boats and a large floatplane base, is included.

Walk through **Old Town** on **Latham Island** to see structures dating back to the 1930s and to see some of the creative solutions modern builders have found to the problem of building on solid rock.

Walk along the popular Frame Lake Trail with its views of Yellowknife's skyline, including the Armed Forces Northern Headquarters and Legislative Assembly buildings.

Visitors may take a 2-hour cruise on Great Slave Lake. Local tour operators also offer tours out to Ingraham Trail (NWT Highway 4) and to a traditional Dene Camp in Ndilo's Rainbow Valley.

The Yellowknife Book Cellar. See display ad this section.

Ingraham Trail Log

NWT Highway 4 begins in Yellowknife and extends 43 miles/69 km to Tibbett Lake. A day-use pass is required for all parking areas. *NOTE: Watch for rough road.*
Distance from Yellowknife (Y) is shown.

NWT HIGHWAY 4

Y 0 Junction of Highways 3 and 4.

Y 1.9 (3.1 km) Giant Yellowknife Mines main office. The mine has been operating since 1947.

Y 2.9 (4.7 km) Side road leads north 3 miles/5 km to Vee Lake.

Y 4.7 (7.5 km) Single-lane bridge across the Yellowknife River.

Y 4.8 (7.7 km) Historical sign about the Ingraham Trail. **Yellowknife River Day Use Area** with boat lannch, 6 picnic sites, firewood, firepits and tiolets. Good fishing for northern pike, lake trout and grayling.

Y 6.1 (9.8 km) Access road leads south 7-mile/11-km road to Detah Indian village.

Y 12.2 (19.7 km) **Prosperous Lake** picnic area and boat launch to north. Fishing for northern pike, whitefish and lake trout.

Y 14.9 (24 km) **Madeline Lake**. Boat launch to north. Fishing for northern pike, whitefish, cisco and yellow perch.

Y 16.4 (26.4 km) **Pontoon Lake** picnic area to south; boat launch, fishing for northern pike, whitefish, cisco and suckers.

Y 17.4 (28 km) Side road leads north 1 mile/1.6 km to **Prelude Lake Territorial Campground**; 38 campsites, 20 picnic sites, firewood, shelter, water, dump station, concession, boat launch, swimming. Prelude Wildlife Trail with 15 interpretive stations. Fishing for lake trout, grayling, whitefish, cisco, burbot, suckers, northern pike.

Y 17.5 (28.2 km) *Pavement ends, gravel begins, eastbound.*

Y 27.3 (44 km) Powder Point on Prelude Lake to north; parking area. Boat launch for canoeists doing the route into Hidden Lake Territorial Park, Lower Cameron River, or 4-day trip to Yellowknife River bridge.

Y 28.4 (45.8 km) **Hidden Lake Day-use Area** and Cameron River Falls trailhead to north; parking. This 0.6-mile/1-km trail leads to cliffs overlooking Cameron River Falls.

Y 33.5 (53.9 km) Bridge across Cameron River; parking area, picnicking, canoeing, hiking and swimming.

Y 34.4 (55.3 km) Informal campsites on sand esker overlooking Cameron River next 0.3 km eastbound.

Y 36.7 (59 km) **Reid Lake Territorial Campground** with 50 campsites, 10 picnic sites, kitchen shelter, swimming, hiking trail, boat launch and fishing. Canoe launch point for Upper Cameron River and Jennejohn Lake routes. *CAUTION: Watch for bears.*

Y 42.8 (68.9 km)**Tibbett Lake**. End of road. Launch point for Pensive Lakes canoe route (advanced canoeists only).

Fort Smith Highway Log

Highway 5 leads leads 166 miles/267.2 km from its junction with Highway 2 to the community of Fort Smith. *Kilometreposts on Highway 5 reflect distance from this junction.*
Distance from Highway 2 junction (J) is followed by distance from Fort Smith (FT).

NWT HIGHWAY 5

J 0 FT 166 (267.2 km) No services or gas available until Fort Smith.

Junction with Highway 2 to Hay River. Turn to **Milepost E 19.8** in the HAY RIVER HIGHWAY log on page 740.

J 1.3 (2.2 km) **FT 164.7** (265 km) Railroad and auto bridge crosses Hay River.

J 1.5 (2.5 km) **FT 164.5** (264.7 km) Access road leads north 3.7 miles/5.9 km to Hay River Reserve.

J 30 (48.4 km) **FT 136** (218.8 km) Good gravel road leads 1 mile/1.6 km north to **Polar Lake**; stocked with rainbow; no motorboats allowed. Good bird watching.

J 34.4 (55.3 km) **FT 131.6** (211.8 km) Buffalo River bridge.

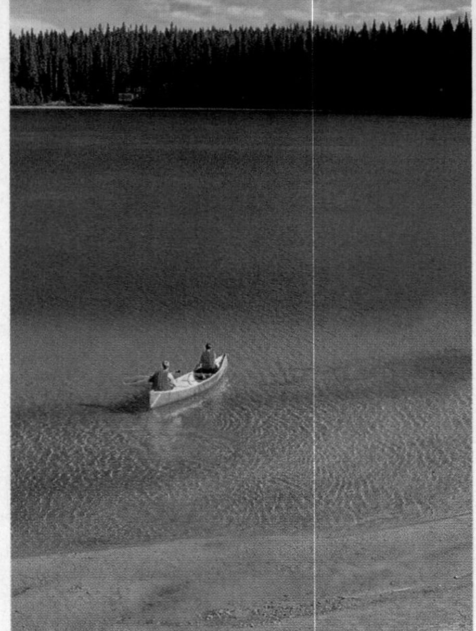

Scenic Pine Lake is located 38 miles/ 61 km south of Fort Smith.
(© Leslie Leong)

J 34.7 (55.9 km) **FT 131.3** (211.3 km) Turnout to north with litter barrel and map.

J 37.8 (60.9 km) **FT 128.2** (206.3 km) Highway 5 turns south for Fort Smith (continue with this log). Highway maintenance camp.

Junction with Highway 6. See FORT RESOLUTION HIGHWAY log on page 745 this section.

J 54.4 (87.6 km) **FT 111.6** (179.6 km) Turnoff for **Sandy Lake,** 8 miles/13 km south; swimming, sandy beach, fishing for northern pike.

J 54.8 (88.2 km) **FT 111.2** (179 km) *Pavement ends, gravel begins, southbound.*

J 59.8 (96.3 km) **FT 106.2** (170.9 km) Entrance to Wood Buffalo National Park. Established in 1922 to protect Canada's only remaining herd of wood bison, **Wood Buffalo National Park** (a UNESCO world heritage site) is a vast wilderness area of 44,800 square kilometres with the greater portion located in the northeast corner of Alberta. Park headquarters and Visitor Reception Centre are located in Fort Smith and Fort Chipewyan. The park is open all year. For more information, contact Wood Buffalo National Park, Box 750, Fort Smith, NT X0E 0P0; phone (867) 872-7900.

The wood bison, a slightly larger and darker northern relative of the Plains bison, numbered about 1,500 in the area at the time the park was established, representing the largest free-roaming herd in Canada. Soon after this, more than 6,600 Plains bison were moved from southern Alberta to the park. Today's herd of about 3,500 bison is considered to be mostly hybrids.

Also found within the park is the world's only remaining natural nesting grounds of the endangered whooping crane.

J 66 (106.2 km) **FT 100** (160.9 km) Picnic area with tables to north at Angus Fire Tower.

J 74.2 (119.4 km) **FT 91.8** (147.7 km) Turnout to south with litter barrel, toilets and interpretive signs on bison and the Nyarling River.

J 110.8 (178.4 km) **FT 55.2** (88.8 km)

Highway crosses Sass River. Shallow lakes from here south to Preble Creek provide nesting areas for whooping cranes.

J 116.2 (187 km) **FT 49.8** (80.1 km) Highway crosses Preble Creek.

J 124.5 (200.3 km) **FT 41.5** (66.8 km) Turnout with litter barrel, walking trail and interpretive signs on Wetlands habitat.

J 130.5 (210 km) **FT 35.5** (57.1 km) The highway leaves and reenters Wood Buffalo National Park several times southbound.

J 131 (211 km) **FT 34.9** (56.1 km) Little Buffalo River bridge.

J 131.7 (212 km) **FT 34.3** (55.2 km) Access road leads 0.6 mile/1 km to **Little Buffalo Falls Day Use Area** with picnic sites, shelter, firewood, firepits and interpretive trail.

J 143.6 (231.1 km) **FT 22.4** (36 km) Turnoff for Parsons Lake Road (narrow gravel) which leads south 8 miles/13 km to **Salt Plains Overlook**. Interpretive exhibit and viewing telescope. Gravel parking area with tables, firepits and toilets at overlook; hiking trail down to Salt Plains (bring boots).

Springs at the edge of a high escarpment bring salt to the surface and spread it across the huge flat plain; only plants adapted to high salinity can grow here. Fine view of a unique environment. *CAUTION: Parsons Lake Road beyond the overlook may be impassable in wet weather.*

J 144.7 (232.8 km) **FT 21.4** (34.4 km) Turnouts to south and north. *Gravel ends, pavement begins, eastbound to Fort Smith.* Access road north to gravel stockpile yard also leads to Salt Mountain Lookout (undeveloped)..

J 147.6 (237.6 km) **FT 18.4** (29.6 km) Salt River bridge.

J 151.6 (244 km) **FT 14.4** (23.2 km) Good gravel side road leads 10 miles/16 km north to settlement of **SALT RIVER**; gas, campground, small-boat launch, and fishing for pike, walleye, inconnu and goldeye. ▲

J 157.1 (252.8 km) **FT 8.9** (14.3 km) Access toad north to old Bell Rock, where goods portaged from Fort Fitzgerald were loaded on boats bound for Great Slave Lake and the Mackenzie River.

J 162.1 (260.8 km) **FT 3.9** (6.2 km) Turnoff to north for Fort Smith airport and **Queen Elizabeth Park** campground with 19

campsites, 15 picnic sites, electrical hookups, toilets, water, kitchen shelter, showers, dump station, firewood, firepits and playground. ▲

Short hike from campground to bluff overlooking Rapids of the Drowned on the Slave River; look for pelicans feeding here.

Fort Smith

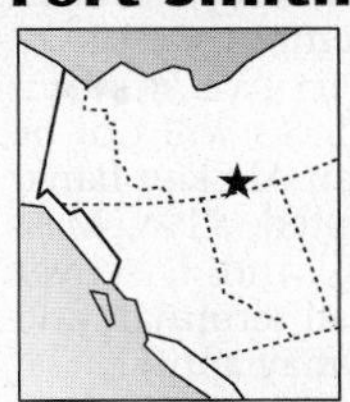

J 166 (267.2 km) **FT 0** Located on the Slave River. **Population:** 2,420. **Emergency Services: RCMP**, phone (867) 872-2107. **Fire Department**, phone (867) 872-6111. **Health Centre**, phone (867) 872-2713. **Visitor Information:** Visitor Information Centre in Conibear Park, open June to September, phone (867) 872-2515. Pick up *A Walking Tour Guide to Historic Trails* brochure here. Or contact the Town of Fort Smith, P.O. Box 147, Fort Smith, NT X0E 0P0; phone (867) 872-2014.

Transportation: Air—Scheduled and charter service available. **Bus**—Available. **Rental cars**—Available.

Private Aircraft: Fort Smith airport; elev. 666 feet/203m; length, 6,000 feet/1,829m; asphalt; fuel 80, 100.

Fort Smith began as a trading post at a favorite campsite of the portagers traveling the 1,600-mile/2575-km water passage from Fort McMurray to the Arctic Ocean. The 4 sets of rapids, named (south to north) Cassette, Pelican, Mountain and the Rapids of the Drowned, separate the Northwest Territories from Alberta. In 1874, Hudson's Bay Co. established a permanent post, and the Roman Catholic mission was transferred here in 1876. By 1911 the settlement had become a major trading post for the area.

There are 2 hotels, a motel, several bed and breakfast establishments, 2 grocery stores, post office, a bookstore/gift shop, a takeout outlet, 4 restaurants, 3 bars, 2 convenience stores, and 3 gas stations with unleaded gas and repair service.

Attractions include the multi-image presentation at Wood Buffalo National Park visitor reception centre and the drive out to Peace Point. There are several hiking trails off the road, as well as good opportunities to see bison. There is a 36-site campground at **Pine Lake**, 38 miles/61 km south of Fort Smith. For details, contact the park office at (867) 872-7900.

A lookout with viewing telescope is located at the north edge of town. River Bank Park has a network of walking trails; walk down to see **pelicans** feeding.

Other attractions in Fort Smith include **The Northern Life Museum**, which features a comprehensive view of the area's Native culture and life of the white settlers since the mid-19th century. Open 1-5 P.M. daily and Tuesday and Thursday evenings in summer. At the museum, you can book tours of the historic Fort Smith Mission Park.

Fort Resolution Highway Log

Distance from junction with Highway 5 (J) is followed by distance from Fort Resolution (FR).

NWT HIGHWAY 6

J 0 FR 55.9 (90 km) Highway 6 begins at **Milepost J 37.8** on Highway 5.

Junction of Highway 6 to Fort Resolution with Highway 5 to Fort Smith. See FORT SMITH HIGHWAY log on page 744 this section.

J 13.2 (21.3 km) **FR 42.7** (68.7 km) Main access road north to **PINE POINT**; no services. Pine Point was built in the 1960s by Cominco Ltd. The open-pit lead–zinc mine shut down in 1987. Once a community of almost 2,000 residents, most people moved out in 1988, and houses and structures have been moved or destroyed. The Great Slave Lake Railway (now CNR) was constructed in 1961 from Roma, AB, to Pine Point to transport the lead–zinc ore to market.

J 14.6 (23.6 km) **FR 41.3** (66.4 km) Secondary access road to Pine Point.

J 14.7 (23.7 km) **FR 41.2** (66.3 km) *Pavement ends, gravel begins, eastbound.*

J 24.6 (39.6 km) **FR 31.3** (50.3 km) Tailing piles from open-pit mining to south.

J 32.3 (52 km) **FR 23.6** (38 km) Turnoff to north for Dawson Landing viewpoint on Great Slave Lake, accessible via a 25-mile/40-km bush road (not recommended in wet weather).

J 34.4 (55.4 km) **FR 21.5** (34.6 km) Paulette Creek.

J 36.5 (58.8 km) **FR 19.4** (31.2 km) Turnout to north with litter barrel.

J 40.5 (65.1 km) **FR 15.4** (24.8 km) Access road north to bison ranch.

J 41.8 (67.3 km) **FR 14.1** (22.7 km) **Little Buffalo Day Use Area** to south; picnic tables, toilets, litter barrels, boat launch. Tourist camp located across highway with cabins, lodge and confectionery.

J 41.9 (67.5 km) **FR 14** (22.5 km) Bridge over **Little Buffalo River.** Good fishing for northern pike and walleye.

J 42.6 (68.5 km) **FR 13.3** (21.4 km) Access road leads 0.6 mile/1 km to Little Buffalo River Indian village.

J 54.4 (87.6 km) **FR 1.5** (2.4 km) Campground to west; 5 gravel sites, outhouses, tables and firepits. ▲

J 55.9 (90 km) **FR 0 FORT RESOLUTION** (pop. 447), located on the south shore of Great Slave Lake on Resolution Bay. **Emergency Services: RCMP**, phone (867) 394-4111. **Visitor Information:** Stop in at the Dene Noo Community Council.

A Hudson's Bay Co. post was established here in 1786. Missionaries settled in the area in 1852, establishing a school and hospital to serve the largely Chipewyan population. The road connecting Fort Resolution with Pine Point was built in the 1960s.

Today's economy is based on trapping, fishing, and a logging and sawmill operation. There are 2 bison ranches in the area.

Visitor services include 2 bed and breakfasts, a small motel, 2 general stores, a gas station and cafe. Meals are also available at the community hall. Canada Post outlet located in Northern Store.

ALASKA STATE FERRY SCHEDULES

On the following pages are summer schedules and rates—effective May 1 through September 30, 2000—provided by the Alaska Marine Highway office. NOTE: The state reserves the right to revise or cancel schedules and rates without prior notice and assumes no responsibility for delays and/or expenses due to such modifications. On-line updates on the Alaska state ferry system are available on the Internet at: http://www.dot.state.ak.us/amhs home.html. Or phone 1-800-642-0066 for more information. Copies of the Alaska Marine Highway summer schedules are available at all state ferry terminals or from the Alaska Marine Highway, 1591 Glacier Ave., Juneau, AK 99801-1427.

For additional information on Alaska State ferry travel, see "Ferry Travel" in the TRAVEL PLANNING section.

How to Determine Fares

Fares for passengers, vehicles and staterooms are all calculated separately and must be added together to determine the total cost of your travel. See the Tariff sections on pages 758-759 and 761-762.

One-way fares for passage, vehicles and alternate means of conveyance (bicycles, kayaks, and inflatable boats) are charged from the port of embarkation to the port of debarkation.

Stateroom fares are calculated according to the route taken, and may vary from the rates printed here depending on the ship and schedules.

Payments and Cancellations

Payment may be made by mail with certified or cashier's check, or money order in U.S. dollars. Mail payments to: Alaska Marine Highway, 1591 Glacier Ave., Juneau, AK 99801-1427. Personal checks will not be accepted unless written on an Alaskan bank. No counter checks are accepted. VISA, MasterCard, American Express and Discover credit cards are accepted at all terminals and by phone (some restrictions may apply).

Cancellation charges apply for changes made within 14 days of sailing. Unless other arrangements are made and noted in your itinerary, full payment is required on or before the due date.

Payment Due Date

If reservation is made 55 days or more before sailing, payment is due 30 days after booking.

If reservation is made less than 55 days before sailing, payment is due within 10 days of making the reservation.

If reservation is made 10 days or less before sailing, payment is due at time of booking

Bookings will be canceled if reservations are not paid for by the payment due date.

Call or Fax Reservations

Reservations are required on all vessels for passengers, vehicles and cabins. For reservations write the Alaska Marine Highway, 1591 Glacier Ave., Juneau, AK 99801-1427; phone toll free 1-800-642-0066, or fax (907) 277-4829; TDD 1-800-764-3779. Phone local reservation numbers in Juneau (907/465-3941) and Anchorage (907/272-7116).

To make a reservation, you will need to provide the following information: ports of embarkation/debarkation; full names of all travelers, and ages of those under 12 years; width, height and overall length of vehicles (including extensions such as trailer hitches, bike racks, and storage containers); mailing address and phone number; alternate travel dates (cabin or vehicle space may not be available on your first choice of travel dates); and approximate date you will be leaving your home.

Getting on our Waitlist

If the desired space is not available, reservation personnel may offer to place your request on a waitlist. A limited number of requests will be added to a waitlist, which is checked on a regular basis. If cancellations occur you will be notified of confirmation of space. If your cabin has not been confirmed, you must sign-up on the purser's "STANDBY" list on board. If your vehicle's waitlist space has not been confirmed, you must sign up on the "STANDBY" list at your boarding terminal. DO NOT SEND PAYMENT FOR WAITLISTED SPACE UNTIL CONFIRMED.

Ferry Office Phone #s

Anchorage, phone (907) 272-4482; fax

(907) 277-4829. Counter at the Public Lands Information Center downtown.

Bellingham, (360) 676-8445 or (360) 676-0212 (24-hour recorded information).

Cordova, phone (907) 424-7333.

Juneau, phone (907) 465-3940.

Haines, phone (907) 766-2113.

Homer, phone (907) 235-8449.

Ketchikan, phone (907) 225-6181.

Kodiak, phone (907) 486-3800

Petersburg, phone (907) 772-3855.

Prince Rupert, phone (250) 627-1744.

Seldovia, phone (907) 234-7868

Seward, phone (907) 224-5485

Sitka, phone (907) 747-3300.

Skagway, phone (907) 983-2229

Valdez, phone (907) 835-4436.

Wrangell, phone (907) 874-3711.

How To Estimate Arrival Times

Arrival times are not generally listed for interport stops. In-port times vary from 30 minutes to 6 hours. To calculate an approximate unlisted arrival time, add the running time listed in the table to the departure time from the port preceding your arrival city.

Please note that these running times are approximate and are listed for the convenience of those meeting passengers, and for travelers planning stopovers. For more accurate arrival times, please contact the local Marine Highway office on the day of arrival.

Due to traffic demands and tidal conditions, most Marine Highway vessels run continuously, docking at all hours of the day for brief transfers of passengers and vehicles. Passengers wishing to explore a particular community should consider a stopover and continuation on another Marine Highway vessel.

Running Time Table

Inside Passage Routes	
Bellingham–Ketchikan	37 hrs.
Prince Rupert–Ketchikan	6 hrs.
Ketchikan–Wrangell	6 hrs.
Wrangell–Petersburg	3 hrs.
Petersburg–Juneau	8 hrs.
Petersburg–Sitka	10 hrs.
Sitka–Juneau/Auke Bay	8 hrs. 45 min.
Juneau/Auke Bay–Haines	4 hrs. 30 min.
Haines–Skagway	1 hr.
Southcentral Routes	
Whittier–Valdez	6 hrs. 45 min.
Valdez–Cordova	5 hrs. 30 min.
Cordova–Whittier	7 hrs.
Cordova–Seward	11 hrs.
Valdez–Seward	11 hrs.
Homer–Seldovia	1 hr. 30 min.
Gulf Crossing Routes	
Juneau to Valdez	32 hrs.
Valdez to Seward	10 hrs.
Southcentral/Southwest Routes	
Homer–Kodiak	9 hrs. 30 min.
Homer–Port Lions	10 hrs.
Seward–Kodiak	13 hrs. 15 min.
Southwest Routes	
Kodiak–Port Lions	2 hrs. 30 min.
Kodiak–Chignik	18 hrs. 30 min.
Chignik–Sand Point	9 hrs. 15 min.
Sand Point–King Cove	6 hrs. 30 min.
King Cove–Cold Bay	2 hrs.
Cold Bay–False Pass	4 hrs. 15 min.
False Pass–Akutan	10 hrs. 30 min.
Akutan–Unalaska	3 hrs. 30 min.

MAY 2000 NORTHBOUND - INSIDE PASSAGE/SOUTHEAST ALASKA 1-800-642-0066

LEAVE BELLINGHAM	LEAVE PRINCE RUPERT	LEAVE METLAKATLA	KETCHIKAN	HOLLIS	WRANGELL	PETERSBURG	KAKE	ARRIVE SITKA	ANGOON	TENAKEE	HOONAH	JUNEAU	HAINES	ARRIVE SKAGWAY
		T2 6:45P	T2 9:00P	T2 11:45P										
	T2 8:00A		T2 2:00P		T2 8:30P	T2 11:55P						W3 9:45A	W3 3:15P	W3 4:15P
		W3 6:30A	W3 8:45A	W3 11:30A										
			W3 4:15P			TH4 12:30A	TH4 5:30A	TH4 1:30P	TH4 10:15P		F5 3:15A	F5 7:30A	F5 1:00P	F5 2:00P
	F5 10:45A		F5 4:45P	F5 8:30P	S6 3:15A	S6 7:00A	S6 11:55A	S6 9:30P				SU7 10:45A	SU7 4:15P	SU7 5:15P
							Lv. Sitka	S6 5:45P	S6 11:55P	SU7 3:15A	SU7 7:30A	SU7 10:45A		
F5 6:00P			SU7 10:00A		SU7 4:45P	SU7 8:30P						M8 7:30A	M8 1:00P	M8 2:00P
		T9 12:15P	T9 2:30P	T9 5:15P										
	T9 10:00A		T9 5:00P		T9 11:45P	W10 3:30A						W10 1:00P	W10 6:30P	W10 7:30P
		T9 11:55P	W10 2:15A	W10 5:00A										
												TH11 7:00A	TH11 12:45P	TH11 1:45P
			W10 10:45A			W10 7:00P	W10 11:55P	TH11 8:00A	TH11 4:30P		TH11 9:30P	F12 12:45A		
												F12 7:00A	F12 12:45P	F12 1:45P
												S13 7:00A	S13 12:45P	S13 1:45P
	F12 11:30A		F12 7:00P		S13 2:00A	S13 5:45A		S13 4:30P				SU14 4:45A		
							Lv. Sitka	S13 1:00P	S13 7:15P	S13 10:30P	SU14 4:00A	SU14 7:15A		
												SU14 7:00A	SU14 12:45P	SU14 1:45P
F12 6:00P			SU14 10:00A		SU14 4:45P	SU14 8:30P						M15 7:30A	M15 1:00P	M15 2:00P
		T16 1:30P	T16 3:45P	T16 6:30P										
	T16 8:00A		T16 2:00P		T16 8:45P	W17 12:30A	W17 5:30A					W17 2:00P	W17 7:30P	W17 8:30P
		W17 1:15A	W17 3:30A	W17 6:15A										
												TH18 7:00A	TH18 12:45P	TH18 1:45P
												F19 7:00A	F19 12:45P	F19 1:45P
		W17 1:00P	W17 3:15P	W17 8:00P		TH18 5:15A	TH18 10:15A	TH18 8:15P	F19 4:45A		F19 9:45A	F19 1:00P		
												S20 7:00A	S20 12:45P	S20 1:45P
	F19 11:15A		F19 6:00P		S20 12:45A	S20 4:30A		S20 3:15P				SU21 4:30A		
												SU21 7:00A	SU21 12:45P	SU21 1:45P
							Lv. Sitka	S20 11:15A	S20 5:30P	S20 8:45P	SU21 4:00A	SU21 7:15A		
									Lv. Pelican	SU21 4:15P		SU21 10:45P		
F19 6:00P			SU21 10:00A		SU21 4:45P	SU21 8:30P						M22 7:30A	M22 1:00P	M22 2:00P
		T23 11:15P	W24 1:30A	W24 4:15A										
	T23 9:00A		T23 3:00P		T23 9:45P	W24 1:15A	W24 6:30A					W24 2:00P		
		W24 11:15A	W24 1:30P	W24 4:15P										
												TH25 7:00A	TH25 12:45P	TH25 1:45P
		W24 11:00P	TH25 2:15A	TH25 6:00A		TH25 3:15P	TH25 9:15P	F26 6:45A	F26 4:15P		F26 9:15P	S27 12:30A		
	W24 10:30P		TH25 4:45A		TH25 11:30A	TH25 4:15P						F26 12:15A		
												F26 7:00A	F26 12:45P	F26 1:45P
	TH25 8:15P		F26 2:15A		F26 9:15A	F26 1:15P						F26 10:00P	S27 3:30A	S27 4:30A
												S27 7:00A	S27 12:45P	S27 1:45P
												SU28 7:00A	SU28 12:45P	SU28 1:45P
							Lv. Sitka	S27 11:15P	SU28 5:30A	SU28 8:45A	SU28 1:00P	SU28 4:15P		
												M29 7:00A	M29 12:45P	M29 1:45P
	S27 10:15A		S27 5:15P		SU28 12:15A	SU28 4:15A		SU28 3:45P				M29 8:45A		
F26 6:00P			SU28 9:30A		SU28 5:00P	SU28 9:00P						M29 8:45A	M29 3:30P	M29 4:30P
												T30 7:00A	T30 12:45P	T30 1:45P
	SU28 7:30P		M29 1:30A		M29 8:15A	M29 11:55A		M29 10:45P			T30 2:15P	T30 5:15P		
		T30 5:45P	T30 8:00P	T30 10:45P										
		W31 2:15P	W31 6:15P	W31 9:00P										
												W31 7:00A	W31 12:45P	W31 1:45P
	W31 8:00A		W31 3:15P		W31 10:00P	TH1 1:45A						TH1 9:45A		

ALL TIMES SHOWN ARE LOCAL TIMES

HOW TO READ YOUR SCHEDULE

1. Reading across the top of each page, find the month you wish to travel, and refer to either the Northbound or Southbound schedule. (Using the example of traveling from Bellingham to Ketchikan, you would read the Northbound schedule on the left hand page.)

2. Reading across the top of the schedule, find the city from which you wish to depart. (e.g., Leave Bellingham)

3. Read down the column to locate your desired departure date. For example: Leave Bellingham F5 (Friday, the 5th) 6:00 P.M.

4. Beginning with the departure date, read horizontally from left to right for dates and times of departure from various ports. For Example: After departing Bellingham, the ferry will dock in Ketchikan, and after a short time in port will depart Ketchikan on SU7, (Sunday the 7th) at 10:00 A.M. for Wrangell.

5. The color of the horizontal bars indicate the vessel on which you will travel.

MAY 2000 SOUTHBOUND - INSIDE PASSAGE/SOUTHEAST ALASKA

LEAVE SKAGWAY	HAINES	JUNEAU	HOONAH	TENAKEE	ANGOON	ARRIVE SITKA	KAKE	PETERSBURG	WRANGELL	HOLLIS	KETCHIKAN	ARRIVE METLAKATLA	ARRIVE PRINCE RUPERT	ARRIVE BELLINGHAM
		SU30 7:30P	SU3011:45P	M1 3:45A	M1 6:45A	M1 11:45A	M1 11:00P	T2 3:30A		T2 1:00P	T2 4:45P	T2 6:00P		
M1 5:30P	M1 7:30P	T2 2:45A				T2 12:30P		W3 3:00A	W3 9:15A		W3 6:15P			F5 9:15A
										W3 12:45A	W3 4:30A	W3 5:45A		
W3 7:15P	W3 9:15P	TH4 2:45A						TH4 11:15A	TH4 3:00P	TH4 10:00P	F5 1:45A		F5 8:45A	
										W3 12:30P	W3 3:15P			
F5 3:30P	F5 5:30P	F5 11:00P	S6 3:15A	S6 7:15A	S6 10:30A	S6 3:30P								
SU7 8:15P	SU7 10:15P	M8 5:45A						M8 2:15P	M8 6:00P		T9 1:00A		T9 8:00A	
		SU7 11:45A	SU7 4:00P	SU7 8:00P	SU7 11:15P	M8 4:15A	M8 4:15P	M8 9:00P		T9 6:30A	T9 10:15A	T9 11:30A		
M8 5:00P	M8 7:00P	T9 2:00A				T9 11:45A		W10 2:30A	W10 6:30A		W10 4:00P			F12 8:00A
										T9 6:15P	T9 10:00P	T9 11:15P		
W10 9:30P	W10 11:30P	TH11 5:15A						TH11 3:45P	TH11 7:30P		F12 2:30A		F12 9:30A	
										W10 6:00A	W10 8:45A			
TH11 4:15P	TH11 6:30P	TH1111:00P												
		F12 11:45A	F12 4:00P	F12 8:00P	F12 11:15P	S13 4:15A								
F12 4:15P	F12 6:30P	F12 11:00P												
S13 4:15P	S13 6:30P	S13 11:00P												
		SU14 7:45A				SU14 5:30P		M15 8:30A	M1512:15P		M1511:00P		T16 6:00A	
		SU14 1:30P	SU14 5:45P	SU14 9:45P	M15 1:00A	M15 6:00A	M15 5:30P	M1510:15P		T16 7:45A	T16 11:30A	T16 12:45P		
SU14 4:15P	SU14 6:30P	SU1411:00P												
M15 5:00P	M15 7:00P	T16 3:00A				T16 12:45P		W17 3:30A	W17 9:30A		W17 5:30P			F19 8:30A
										T16 7:30P	T16 11:15P	W1712:30A		
W17 11:30P	TH18 1:30A	TH18 7:00A						TH18 3:30P	TH18 7:15P		F19 2:15A		F19 9:15A	
										W17 7:15A	W1711:00A	W1712:15P		
TH18 4:15P	TH18 6:30P	TH1811:00P												
F19 4:15P	F19 6:30P	F19 11:00P												
		F19 4:30P	F19 8:45P	S20 12:45A	S20 4:00A	S20 9:00A								
S20 4:15P	S20 6:30P	S20 11:00P												
		SU21 9:30A				SU21 9:45P		M22 1:15P	M22 5:00P		M2211:55P		T23 7:00A	
SU21 4:15P	SU21 6:30P	SU2111:00P												
		SU21 8:15A	Ar. Pelican	SU21 2:45P										
		SU2111:45P	M22 4:00A	M22 8:00A	M22 11:00A	M22 4:00P	T23 3:15A	T23 8:00A		T23 5:30P	T23 9:15P	T23 10:30P		
M22 5:00P	M22 7:00P	T23 1:00A				T23 10:45A		W24 2:00A	W24 6:00A		W24 1:00P		W24 8:30P	
										W24 5:15A	W24 9:00A	W2410:15A		
		W24 4:00P						TH2512:30A	TH25 4:15A		TH2511:15A		TH25 6:15P	
										W24 5:15P	W24 9:00P	W2410:15P		
											W24 5:00P			F26 8:00A
TH25 4:15P	TH25 6:30P	TH2511:00P												
		S27 4:30A	S27 8:45A	S27 12:45P	S27 4:00P	S27 9:00P								
		F26 3:15A						F26 12:15P	F26 4:15P		F26 11:45P		S27 7:15A	
F26 4:15P	F26 6:30P	F26 11:00P												
S27 7:30A	S27 9:30A	S27 3:00P						S27 11:30P	SU28 3:30A		SU2810:30A		SU28 5:30P	
S27 4:15P	S27 6:30P	S27 11:00P												
SU28 4:15P	SU28 6:30P	SU2811:00P												
		SU28 6:00P	SU2810:15P	M29 2:15A	M29 5:30A	M29 10:30A	M29 9:45P	T30 2:30A		T30 11:55A	T30 3:45P	T30 5:00P		
M29 4:15P	M29 6:30P	M29 11:00P												
		M29 2:45P						M2911:45P	T30 3:45A		T30 12:15P		T30 7:30P	
M29 7:00P	M29 9:30P	T30 3:00A				T30 11:30A		W31 1:15A	W31 8:15A		W31 5:15P			F2 8:15A
T30 4:15P	T30 6:30P	T30 11:00P												
		W31 2:00A						W3110:45A	W31 2:45P		W3111:00P		TH1 6:00A	
										W31 6:15A	W3112:15P	W31 1:30P		
W31 4:15P	W31 6:30P	W31 11:00P												

ALL TIMES SHOWN ARE LOCAL TIMES

LEAVE BELLINGHAM	LEAVE PRINCE RUPERT	LEAVE METLAKATLA	KETCHIKAN	HOLLIS	WRANGELL	PETERSBURG	KAKE	ARRIVE SITKA	ANGOON	TENAKEE	HOONAH	JUNEAU	HAINES	ARRIVE SKAGWAY
			W3 4:15P			TH4 12:30A	TH4 5:30A	TH4 1:30P	TH4 10:15P		F5 3:15A	F5 7:30A	F5 1:00P	F5 2:00P
	F5 10:45A		F5 4:45P	F5 8:30P	S6 3:15A	S6 7:00A	S6 11:55A	S6 9:30P				SU7 10:45A	SU7 4:15P	SU7 5:15P
							Lv. Sitka	S6 5:45P	S6 11:55P	SU7 3:15A	SU7 7:30A	SU7 10:45A		
F5 6:00P			SU7 10:00A		SU7 4:45P	SU7 8:30P						M8 7:30A	M8 1:00P	M8 2:00P

EXAMPLE

Day of Week
Day of Month
AM or PM
Time

VESSEL COLOR CODES Aurora Columbia Le Conte Malaspina Matanuska Taku Kennicott

JUNE 2000 NORTHBOUND - INSIDE PASSAGE/SOUTHEAST ALASKA 1-800-642-0066

LEAVE BELLINGHAM	LEAVE PRINCE RUPERT	LEAVE METLAKATLA	KETCHIKAN	HOLLIS	WRANGELL	PETERSBURG	KAKE	ARRIVE SITKA	ANGOON	TENAKEE	HOONAH	JUNEAU	HAINES	ARRIVE SKAGWAY
	W31 8:00A		W31 3:15P		W31 10:00P	TH1 1:45A						TH1 9:45A		
	TH1 9:00A		TH1 6:15P		F2 1:15A	F2 5:00A						F2 3:00P	F2 9:00P	F2 10:00P
	F2 9:00A		F2 3:30P		F2 10:15P	S3 2:00A						S3 11:15A	S3 5:15P	S3 6:15P
							Lv. Sitka	S3 10:30A	S3 4:45P	S3 8:00P	SU4 2:30A	SU4 5:45A		
									Lv. Pelican	SU4 3:30P		SU4 10:00P		
	S3 1:15P		S3 7:30P		SU4 2:30A	SU4 6:30A		SU4 9:15P				M5 9:45A		
F2 6:00P			SU4 12:15P		SU4 8:45P	M5 1:15A						M5 2:00P	M5 8:00P	M5 9:00P
	SU4 6:15P		M5 2:45A		M5 11:00A	M5 2:45P		T6 4:00A			T6 5:45P	T6 8:45P		
						T6 8:30A	T6 1:30P	T6 11:00P	W7 7:30A		W7 12:30P	W7 3:45P		
	M5 9:00P		T6 6:30A		T6 1:15P	T6 5:15P		W7 5:15A				W7 6:30P	TH8 12:30A	TH8 1:30A
	W7 8:00A		W7 3:15P		W7 10:00P	TH8 1:45A						TH8 9:45A		
						TH8 2:45P	TH8 7:45P		F9 12:45A	F9 4:00A	F9 8:15A	F9 11:30A		
	TH8 2:15P		TH8 9:15P		F9 4:15A	F9 8:15A						F9 6:15P	S10 12:15A	S10 1:15A
	F9 6:45P		S10 1:15A		S10 8:00A	S10 11:45A						S10 9:00P	SU11 3:00A	SU11 4:00A
							Lv. Sitka	S10 5:15P	S10 11:30P	SU11 2:45A	SU11 7:00A	SU1110:15A		
	S10 1:45P		S10 10:00P		SU11 6:15A	SU1110:15A		SU1110:00P				M1210:45A		
F9 6:00P			SU11 9:30A		SU11 5:00P	SU11 9:00P						M12 9:15A	M12 3:15P	M12 4:30P
	SU11 7:30P		M12 1:30A		M12 8:30A	M12 12:15P		M1211:00P			T13 2:15P	T13 5:15P		
						T13 3:45A	T13 8:45A	T13 5:45P	W14 2:15A		W14 7:15A	W1410:30A		
	M12 9:15P		T13 4:45A		T13 11:30A	T13 3:30P		W14 6:00A				W14 7:15P	TH15 1:15A	TH15 2:15A
	W14 8:00A		W14 3:15P		W14 10:00P	TH15 1:45A						TH15 9:45A		
						TH1510:45A	TH15 3:45P		TH15 8:45P	TH1511:55P	F16 4:15A	F16 7:30A		
	TH15 9:15A		TH15 6:15P		F16 1:15A	F16 5:15A						F16 6:15P	S17 12:15A	S17 1:15A
	F16 7:30P		S17 2:00A		S17 9:45A	S17 1:30P						S17 10:45P	SU18 4:45A	SU18 5:45A
							Lv. Sitka	S17 10:15A	S17 4:30P	S17 7:45P	S17 11:55P	SU18 3:15A		
									Lv. Pelican	SU18 3:30P		SU1810:00P		
	S17 1:45P		S17 8:00P		SU18 2:45A	SU18 6:30A		SU18 8:45P				M19 9:15A		
F16 6:00P			SU18 9:00A		SU18 5:00P	SU18 9:45P						M19 9:15A	M19 3:15P	M19 4:30P
	SU18 8:30P		M19 5:30A		M19 12:30P	M19 4:30P		T20 3:15A			T20 5:00P	T20 8:00P		
	M19 11:30P		T20 7:30A									W21 5:15A	*TO SE/SW	INTER-TIE*
						T20 7:45A	T20 12:45P	T20 10:00P	W21 6:30A		W2111:30A	W21 2:45P		
	W21 8:00A		W21 3:15P		W21 10:00P	TH22 1:45A						TH22 9:45A		
						TH22 3:00P	TH22 8:00P		F23 1:00A	F23 4:15A	F23 8:30A	F23 11:45A		
	TH2210:45A		TH22 6:45P		F23 1:45A	F23 6:15A						F23 6:15P	S24 12:15A	S24 1:15A
							Lv. Sitka	S24 2:45P	S24 9:00P	SU2512:15A	SU25 4:30A	SU25 7:45A		
	S24 11:45A		S24 8:00P		SU25 3:00A	SU25 7:00A		SU25 8:00P				M26 8:45A		
F23 6:00P			SU25 9:00A		SU25 3:45P	SU25 7:30P						M26 9:45A	M26 3:45P	M26 4:45P
	SU25 5:00P		SU2511:00P		M26 6:00A	M26 10:00A		M26 8:45P			T27 1:15P	T27 4:15P		
						T27 2:15A	T27 7:15A	T27 3:45P	W2812:15A		W28 5:15A	W28 8:30A		
	T27 1:15A		T27 7:15A		T27 4:00P	T27 7:45P		W2810:45A				W2811:45P	TH29 5:45A	TH29 6:45A
	W28 8:00A		W28 3:15P		W28 10:00P	TH29 2:00A						TH2910:00A		
						TH2910:00A	TH29 3:00P		TH29 8:00P	TH2911:15P	F30 3:30A	F30 6:45A		
	TH29 9:00A		TH29 5:15P		F30 12:15A	F30 4:15A						F30 6:15P	S1 12:15A	S1 1:15A
	F30 8:30P		S1 2:30A		S1 9:15A	S1 12:45P						S1 9:30P	SU2 3:00A	SU2 4:00A
F30 6:00P			SU2 10:00A		SU2 8:15P	M3 12:15A						M3 10:45A	M3 4:45P	M3 5:45P

Metlakatla and Hollis columns: SEE M/V AURORA SCHEDULE BELOW

Haines and Skagway columns: SEE DAILY SCHEDULE BELOW

ALL TIMES SHOWN ARE LOCAL TIMES

M/V KENNICOTT **SOUTHEAST/SOUTHWEST INTER-TIE TRIPS**

The M/V Kennicott for the month of June will depart from Juneau as indicated in the following table. To determine the best connection for your trip, use this schedule. Please allow enough time to make appropriate connections with the sailings listed above. (See tables above).

Leave Juneau Wednesday	JUN 21	5:15AM
Arrive Valdez Thursday	JUN 22	5:45PM
Leave Valdez Thursday	JUN 22	9:45PM
Arrive Seward Friday	JUN 23	7:45AM
Leave Seward Friday	JUN 23	2:45PM
Arrive Valdez Saturday	JUN 24	12:45AM
Leave Valdez Saturday	JUN 24	4:45AM
Arrive Juneau Sunday	JUN 25	5:15PM

Whistle Stop service is provided to Yakutat on inter-tie trips in both directions between Juneau and Valdez. The vessel will stop ONLY if there are vehicle reservations.

JUNEAU ~ HAINES ~ SKAGWAY DAILY SCHEDULE

The M/V Malaspina operates on a daily schedule as indicated in the following table. To determine the best connection for your trip, use these schedules. Please allow enough time to make appropriate connections with the sailings listed above. (See tables above)

DAILY SCHEDULEJUNE 1- SEPTEMBER 10, 2000

Leave Juneau	7:00AM
Arrive Haines	11:30AM
Leave Haines	12:45PM
Arrive Skagway	1:45PM
Leave Skagway	4:15PM
Arrive Haines	5:15PM
Leave Haines	6:30PM
Arrive Juneau	11:00PM

www.dot.state.ak.us/amhshome.html

JUNE 2000 SOUTHBOUND - INSIDE PASSAGE/SOUTHEAST ALASKA

LEAVE SKAGWAY	HAINES	JUNEAU	HOONAH	TENAKEE	ANGOON	ARRIVE SITKA	KAKE	PETERSBURG	WRANGELL	HOLLIS	KETCHIKAN	ARRIVE METLAKATLA	ARRIVE PRINCE RUPERT	ARRIVE BELLINGHAM
										SEE M/V AURORA SCHEDULE BELOW	TH1 11:00P	SEE M/V AURORA SCHEDULE BELOW	F2 6:00A	
		TH1 3:00P				F2 12:45A		F2 3:45P	F2 7:45P		S3 2:45A		S3 10:15A	
		F2 3:45P	F2 8:00P	F2 11:55P	S3 3:15A	S3 8:15A								
S3 1:00A	S3 3:30A	S3 9:30A						S3 6:15P	S3 10:15P		SU4 6:15A		SU4 1:15P	
S3 9:15P	S3 11:45P	SU4 5:45A						SU4 2:15P	SU4 6:15P		M5 6:15A		M5 1:15P	
SEE		SU4 7:00A	Ar. Pelican	SU4 1:30P										
		SU4 11:30P	M5 3:45A	M5 7:45A	M5 11:00A	M5 4:00P	T6 3:30A	T6 7:30A						
		M5 4:00P						T6 1:15A	T6 6:15A		T6 1:30P		T6 9:00P	
M5 11:55P	T6 2:30A	T6 8:30A				T6 5:00P		W7 6:15A	W7 10:15A		W7 5:45P			F9 8:45A
		W7 4:30A						W7 3:15P	W7 7:15P		TH8 4:15A		TH8 11:15A	
		W7 4:45P	W7 9:00P		TH8 2:00A		TH8 7:00A	TH8 11:00A						
TH8 4:30A	TH8 7:00A	TH8 1:00P						TH8 9:30P	F9 1:15A		F9 8:45A		F9 3:45P	
		TH8 3:30P				F9 1:15A		F9 4:15P	F9 8:15P		S10 3:15A		S10 10:45A	
		F9 4:30P	F9 8:45P	S10 12:45A	S10 4:00A	S10 9:00A								
S10 4:15A	S10 6:15A	S10 12:15P						S10 9:00P	SU11 2:30A		SU1110:30A		SU11 5:30P	
SU11 7:00A	SU11 9:30A	SU11 3:30P						SU1111:55P	M12 3:45A		M1211:15A		M12 6:15P	
DAILY		SU11 6:15P	SU1110:30P	M12 2:30A	M12 5:45A	M1210:45A	M12 10:15P	T13 2:15A						
		M12 4:45P						T13 2:00A	T13 6:15A		T13 1:30P		T13 9:00P	
M12 7:00P	M12 9:30P	T13 3:15A				T13 11:45A		W14 1:30A	W14 8:30A		W14 5:30P			F16 8:30A
		W14 1:30A						W1410:15A	W14 2:15P		W1411:15P		TH15 6:15A	
		W14 2:30P	W14 6:45P		W1411:45P		TH15 5:15A	TH15 9:15A						
TH15 5:15A	TH15 7:45A	TH15 1:45P						TH1510:15P	F16 2:00A		F16 9:30A		F16 4:30P	
		TH15 2:45P				F16 1:00A		F16 3:45P	F16 7:45P		S17 3:15A		S17 10:45A	
		F16 3:30P	F16 7:45P	F16 11:45P	S17 3:00A	S17 8:00A								
S17 4:15A	S17 6:15A	S17 12:15P						S17 9:00P	SU18 2:00A		SU1810:30A		SU18 5:30P	
SU18 8:00A	SU1810:45A	SU18 5:15P						M19 1:45A	M19 5:30A		M19 1:30P		M19 8:30P	
		SU18 7:00A	Ar. Pelican	SU18 1:30P										
SCHEDULE		SU1811:00P	M19 3:15A	M19 7:15A	M1910:30A	M19 3:30P	T20 3:00A	T20 7:00A						
		M19 3:00P						T20 12:15A	T20 5:00A		T20 1:30P		T20 9:00P	
M19 7:30P	M1910:00P	T20 6:15A				T20 3:45P		W21 6:00A	W2110:00A		W21 5:30P			F23 8:30A
		W21 2:00A						W21 1:45P	W21 6:15P		TH22 1:45A		TH22 8:45A	
		W21 6:45P	W2111:00P		TH22 4:00A		TH22 9:00A	TH22 1:00P						
		TH22 1:45P				TH2211:30P		F23 2:15P	F23 6:15P		S24 1:15A		S24 8:45A	
		F23 2:00P	F23 6:15P	F23 10:15P	S24 1:30A	S24 6:30A								
S24 4:15A	S24 6:15A	S24 11:45A						S24 8:15P	S24 11:55P		SU25 7:00A		SU25 2:00P	
		SU25 4:15P	SU25 8:30P	M26 12:30A	M26 3:45A	M26 8:45A	M26 8:15P	T27 12:15A						
FROM SE/SW INTER-TIE		SU25 9:15P									M26 3:15P		M2610:15P	
		M26 3:00P						T27 12:15A	T27 5:00A		T27 1:30P		T27 9:00P	
M26 7:45P	M2610:15P	T27 7:15A				T27 3:45P		W28 7:30A	W2811:15A		W28 7:00P			F30 10:00A
		W28 2:00A						W2810:45A	W28 2:45P		W2811:00P		TH29 6:00A	
BELOW		W28 1:45P	W28 6:00P		W28 11:00P		TH29 4:00A	TH29 8:00A						
TH29 8:45A	TH2911:15A	TH29 5:15P									F30 10:45A		F30 5:45P	
		TH29 2:00P				TH2911:45P		F30 2:30P	F30 6:30P		S1 1:30A		S1 9:00A	
		F30 2:30P	F30 6:45P	F30 10:45P	S1 2:00A	S1 7:00A								

ALL TIMES SHOWN ARE LOCAL TIMES

M/V AURORA - SOUTHERN PANHANDLE SUMMER 2000
EFFECTIVE JUNE 1, 2000 THROUGH SEPTEMBER 30, 2000

SUN	Lv Hollis	6:15AM
	Ar Ketchikan	9:00AM
	Lv Ketchikan	12:15PM
	Ar Metlakatla	1:30PM
	Lv Metlakatla	2:15PM
	Ar Ketchikan	3:30PM
	Lv Ketchikan	6:15PM
	Ar Hollis	9:00PM
MON	Lv Hollis	6:15AM
	Ar Ketchikan	9:00AM
	Lv Ketchikan	11:00AM
	Ar Metlakatla	12:15PM
	Lv Metlakatla	2:45PM
	Ar Ketchikan	4:00PM
	Lv Ketchikan	6:15PM
	Ar Hollis	9:00PM
MON	Lv Hollis	10:00PM
TUE	Ar Ketchikan	12:45AM
	Lv Ketchikan	1:45AM
	Ar Pr. Rupert	9:15AM
	Lv Pr. Rupert	11:15AM
	Ar Ketchikan	4:45PM
	Lv Ketchikan	6:15PM
	Ar Hollis	9:00PM
WED	Lv Hollis	6:15AM
	Ar Ketchikan	9:00AM
	Lv Ketchikan	12:15PM
	Ar Metlakatla	1:30PM
	Lv Metlakatla	2:15PM
	Ar Ketchikan	3:30PM
	Lv Ketchikan	6:15PM
	Ar Hollis	9:00PM
THU	Lv Hollis	9:15AM
	Ar Ketchikan	11:55AM
	Lv Ketchikan	6:15PM
	Ar Hollis	9:00PM
FRI	Lv Hollis	6:15AM
	Ar Ketchikan	9:00AM
	Lv Ketchikan	12:15PM
	Ar Metlakatla	1:30PM
	Lv Metlakatla	2:15PM
	Ar Ketchikan	3:30PM
FRI	Lv Ketchikan	6:15PM
	Ar Hollis	9:00PM
	Lv Hollis	10:00PM
SAT	Ar Ketchikan	12:45AM
SAT	Lv Ketchikan	6:15AM
	Ar Metlakatla	7:30AM
	Lv Metlakatla	8:15AM
	Ar Ketchikan	9:30AM
	Lv Ketchikan	10:30AM
	Ar Hollis	1:15PM
	Lv Hollis	2:15PM
	Ar Ketchikan	5:00PM
	Lv Ketchikan	6:45PM
	Ar Metlakatla	8:00PM
	Lv Metlakatla	8:45PM
	Ar Ketchikan	10:00PM
	Lv Ketchikan	11:00PM
SUN	Ar Hollis	1:45AM

Aurora Columbia Le Conte Malaspina Matanuska Taku Kennicott

1-800-642-0066

JULY 2000 NORTHBOUND - INSIDE PASSAGE/SOUTHEAST ALASKA 1-800-642-0066

LEAVE BELLINGHAM	LEAVE PRINCE RUPERT	LEAVE METLAKATLA	KETCHIKAN	HOLLIS	WRANGELL	PETERSBURG	KAKE	ARRIVE SITKA	ANGOON	TENAKEE	HOONAH	JUNEAU	HAINES	ARRIVE SKAGWAY
	F30 8:30P	SEE M/V AURORA SCHEDULE BELOW	S1 2:30A	SEE M/V AURORA SCHEDULE BELOW	S1 9:15A	S1 12:45P						S1 9:30P	SU2 3:00A	SU2 4:00A
							Lv. Sitka	S1 9:15A	S1 3:30P	S1 6:45P	S1 11:00P	SU2 2:15A		
	S1 11:55A		S1 6:15P		SU2 1:00A	SU2 5:30A		SU2 8:15P				M3 8:45A		
									Lv. Pelican	SU2 3:30P		SU2 10:00P		
F30 6:00P			SU2 10:00A		SU2 8:15P	M3 12:15A						M3 10:45A	M3 4:45P	M3 5:45P
	SU2 8:30P		M3 5:30A		M3 12:30P	M3 4:30P		T4 3:15A			T4 4:30P	T4 7:30P		
						T4 7:15A	T4 12:15P	T4 10:00P	W5 6:30A		W5 11:30A	W5 2:45P	SEE	
	M3 11:15P		T4 7:15A		T4 2:00P	T4 6:00P		W5 4:00A				W5 5:15P	W5 11:15P	TH6 12:15A
	W5 8:00A		W5 3:15P		W5 10:00P	TH6 1:45A						TH6 9:45A		
						TH6 2:45P	TH6 7:45P		F7 12:45A	F7 4:00A	F7 8:15A	F7 11:30A		
	TH6 10:15A		TH6 6:15P		F7 1:15A	F7 6:15A						F7 6:15P	S8 12:15A	S8 1:15A
	F7 5:30P		F7 11:55P		S8 6:45A	S8 10:30A						S8 7:45P	SU9 1:45A	SU9 2:45A
							Lv. Sitka	S8 3:30P	S8 9:45P	SU9 1:00A	SU9 5:15A	SU9 8:30A		
F7 6:00P			SU9 9:00A		SU9 5:00P	SU9 9:00P						M10 9:15A	M10 3:15P	M10 4:30P
	S8 12:30P		S8 8:45P		SU9 3:45A	SU9 7:45A		SU9 8:30P				M10 9:15A		
	SU9 8:30P		M10 6:15A		M10 1:15P	M10 5:15P		T11 4:00A			T11 5:15P	T11 8:15P		
						T11 2:45A	T11 7:45A	T11 4:15P	W1212:45A		W12 5:45A	W12 9:00A	DAILY	
	M10 9:00P		T11 4:00A		T11 10:45A	T11 2:45P		W12 4:45A				W12 6:00P	W1211:55P	TH13 1:00A
	W12 8:00A		W12 3:15P		W12 10:00P	TH13 1:45A						TH13 9:45A		
						TH1310:00A	TH13 3:00P		TH13 8:00P	TH1311:15P	F14 3:30A	F14 6:45A		
	TH1311:00A		TH13 6:15P		F14 1:00A	F14 4:45A						F14 6:15P	S15 12:15A	S15 1:15A
	F14 6:15P		S15 12:45A		S15 8:45A	S15 12:30P						S15 9:45P	SU16 3:45A	SU16 4:45A
							Lv. Sitka	S15 9:30A	S15 3:45P	S15 7:00P	S15 11:15P	SU16 2:30A		
	S15 12:15P		S15 6:30P		SU16 1:45A	SU16 5:30A		SU16 8:00P				M17 8:15A	SCHEDULE	
									Lv. Pelican	SU16 3:30P		SU1610:00P		
F14 6:00P			SU16 9:00A		SU16 4:00P	SU16 9:00P						M17 9:15A	M17 3:15P	M17 4:30P
	SU16 8:30P		M17 4:45A		M17 11:45A	M17 3:45P		T18 2:30A			T18 4:15P	T18 7:15P		
	M17 11:00P		T18 7:00A									W19 5:15A	* TO SE/SE	INTER-TIE *
						T18 2:00P	T18 7:00P	W19 3:00A	W1911:45A		W19 4:45P	W19 8:00P		
	W19 8:00A		W19 3:00P		W19 10:00P	TH20 1:45A						TH20 9:45A		
						TH20 5:15P	TH2010:15P		F21 3:15A	F21 6:30A	F21 10:45A	F21 2:00P		
	TH2011:00A		TH20 6:15P		F21 1:15A	F21 6:15A						F21 6:15P	S22 12:15A	S22 1:15A
							S22 8:00P		SU23 1:00A	SU23 4:15A	SU23 8:30A	SU2311:45A		
	S22 4:15P		S22 11:55P		SU23 7:00A	SU2311:00A		M2412:15A				M2412:45P		
F21 6:00P			SU23 9:00A		SU23 5:00P	SU23 9:00P						M24 9:15A	M24 3:15P	M24 4:30P
	SU23 8:30P		M24 6:15A		M24 1:15P	M24 6:15P	M24 11:15P	T25 8:00A			T25 9:30P	W2612:30A		
						T25 12:15A	T25 5:15A	T25 2:15P	T25 10:45P		W26 3:45A	W26 7:00A	BELOW	
	M24 11:15P		T25 8:15A		T25 4:00P	T25 8:00P		W26 9:00A				W2610:00P	TH27 4:00A	TH27 5:00A
	W26 7:00A		W26 1:45P		W26 8:30P	TH2712:15A						TH27 8:15A		
						TH27 8:30A	TH27 1:30P		TH27 6:30P	TH27 9:45P	F28 2:00A	F28 5:15A		
	TH27 8:45A		TH27 5:15P		F28 12:15A	F28 7:30A						F28 6:15P	S29 12:15A	S29 1:15A
	F28 10:15P		S29 4:15A		S29 11:00A	S29 2:45P						SU30 1:30A	SU30 7:30A	SU30 8:30A
							Lv. Sitka	S29 8:30A	S29 2:45P	S29 6:00P	S29 10:15P	SU30 1:30A		
									Lv. Pelican	SU30 3:30P		SU3010:00P		
	S29 11:00A		S29 5:15P		S29 11:55P	SU30 4:30A		SU30 7:15P				M31 9:00A		
F28 6:00P			SU30 9:00A		SU30 7:15P	SU3011:15P						M3111:15A	M31 5:15P	M31 6:15P
	SU30 8:30P		M31 4:30A		M31 11:30A	M31 3:30P		T1 2:15A			T1 3:30P	T1 6:30P		

ALL TIMES SHOWN ARE LOCAL TIMES

M/V KENNICOTT **SOUTHEAST/SOUTHWEST INTER-TIE TRIPS**

The M/V Kennicott for the month of July will depart from Juneau as indicated in the following table. To determine the best connection for your trip, use this schedule. Please allow enough time to make appropriate connections with the sailings listed above. (See tables above).

Leave Juneau Wednesday	JUL 19	5:15AM
Arrive Valdez Thursday	JUL 20	5:45PM
Leave Valdez Thursday	JUL 20	9:45PM
Arrive Seward Friday	JUL 21	7:45AM
Leave Seward Friday	JUL 21	2:45PM
Arrive Valdez Saturday	JUL 22	12:45AM
Leave Valdez Saturday	JUL 22	4:45AM
Arrive Juneau Sunday	JUL 23	5:15PM

Whistle Stop service is provided to Yakutat on inter-tie trips in both directions between Juneau and Valdez. The vessel will stop ONLY if there are vehicle reservations.

JUNEAU ~ HAINES ~ SKAGWAY DAILY SCHEDULE

The M/V Malaspina operates on a daily schedule as indicated in the following table. To determine the best connection for your trip, use these schedules. Please allow enough time to make appropriate connections with the sailings listed above. (See tables above)

DAILY SCHEDULEJUNE 1- SEPTEMBER 10, 2000

Leave Juneau	7:00AM
Arrive Haines	11:30AM
Leave Haines	12:45PM
Arrive Skagway	1:45PM
Leave Skagway	4:15PM
Arrive Haines	5:15PM
Leave Haines	6:30PM
Arrive Juneau	11:00PM

www.dot.state.ak.us/amhshome.html

JULY 2000 SOUTHBOUND - INSIDE PASSAGE/SOUTHEAST ALASKA

Hollis and Arrive Metlakatla: SEE M/V AURORA SCHEDULE BELOW

LEAVE SKAGWAY	HAINES	JUNEAU	HOONAH	TENAKEE	ANGOON	ARRIVE SITKA	KAKE	PETERSBURG	WRANGELL	HOLLIS	KETCHIKAN	ARRIVE METLAKATLA	ARRIVE PRINCE RUPERT	ARRIVE BELLINGHAM
S1 4:15A	S1 6:15A	S1 12:15P						S1 10:00P	SU2 3:00A		SU2 11:30A		SU2 6:30P	
SU2 6:30A	SU2 10:30A	SU2 5:00P						M3 1:30A	M3 5:15A		M3 1:15P		M3 8:15P	
		SU2 7:00A	Ar. Pelican	SU2 1:30P										
		M3 3:00P						T4 12:15A	T4 5:00A		T4 1:30P		T4 9:00P	
		SU2 11:00P	M3 3:15A	M3 7:15A	M3 10:15A	M3 3:15P	T4 2:30A	T4 6:30A						
M3 8:45P	M3 11:15P	T4 7:30A				T4 4:00P		W5 5:45A	W5 9:30A		W5 5:00P			F7 8:00A
		W5 3:30A						W5 2:15P	W5 6:15P		TH6 1:15A		TH6 8:15A	
SEE		W5 7:30P	W5 11:45P		TH6 4:45A		TH6 9:45A	TH6 1:45P						
TH6 3:15A	TH6 5:45A	TH6 11:45A						TH6 8:15P	TH6 11:55P		F7 7:30A		F7 2:30P	
		TH6 2:00P				TH6 11:45P		F7 3:00P	F7 7:00P		S8 2:00A		S8 9:30A	
		F7 2:30P	F7 6:45P	F7 10:45P	S8 2:00A	S8 7:00A								
S8 4:15A	S8 6:15A	S8 12:15P						S8 9:00P	SU9 2:00A		SU9 10:00A		SU9 5:00P	
SU9 5:45A	SU9 8:15A	SU9 2:45P						SU9 11:15P	M10 3:00A		M10 11:00A		M10 6:00P	
		SU9 4:45P	SU9 9:00P	M10 1:00A	M10 4:15A	M10 9:15A	M10 8:45P	T11 12:45A						
M10 7:30P	M10 10:00P	T11 7:00A				T11 4:30P		W12 8:00A	W12 11:45A		W12 7:00P			F14 10:00A
		M10 3:00P						T11 12:15A	T11 5:00A		T11 1:30P		T11 9:00P	
DAILY		W12 2:00A						W12 10:45A	W12 2:45P		TH13 1:00A		TH13 8:00A	
		W12 1:45P	W12 6:00P		W12 11:00P		TH13 4:00A	TH13 8:00A						
TH13 4:00A	TH13 6:30A	TH13 11:55A						TH13 8:30P	F14 12:15A		F14 8:15A		F14 3:15P	
		TH13 2:30P				F14 12:15A		F14 2:45P	F14 6:45P		S15 1:45A		S15 9:15A	
		F14 2:45P	F14 7:00P	F14 11:00P	S15 2:15A	S15 7:15A								
S15 4:15A	S15 6:15A	S15 12:15P						S15 9:00P	SU16 1:00A		SU16 10:30A		SU16 5:30P	
SU16 7:30A	SU16 10:00A	SU16 4:45P						M17 1:15A	M17 5:00A		M17 1:00P		M17 8:00P	
		SU16 7:00A	Ar. Pelican	SU16 1:30P										
SCHEDULE		M17 3:00P						T18 12:15A	T18 5:00A		T18 1:30P		T18 9:00P	
		M17 4:00A	M17 8:15A	M17 12:15P	M17 3:30P	M17 8:30P	T18 8:00A	T18 11:55A						
M17 7:30P	M17 10:00P	T18 6:15A				T18 2:45P		W19 5:00A	W19 9:00A		W19 5:00P			F21 8:00A
		W19 2:00A						W19 12:45P	W19 4:45P		TH20 1:15A		TH20 8:15A	
		W19 10:00P	TH20 2:15A		TH20 7:15A		TH20 12:15P	TH20 4:15P						
		TH20 3:15P				F21 4:00A		F21 6:45P	F21 10:45P		S22 5:45A		S22 1:15P	
		*F21 4:15P	F21 8:30P	S22 12:45A	S22 4:00A		S22 8:00A							
S22 4:15A	S22 6:15A	S22 12:15P						S22 9:00P	SU23 2:00A		SU23 10:30A		SU23 5:30P	
		SU23 2:15P	SU23 6:30P	SU23 10:30P	M24 1:45A	M24 6:45A	M24 6:15P	M24 10:15P						
FROM SE/SW INTER-TIE		SU23 7:15P									M24 1:15P		M24 8:15P	
		M24 4:45P						T25 2:00A	T25 6:15A		T25 1:30P		T25 9:00P	
M24 7:30P	M24 10:00P	T25 5:45A				T25 2:15P		W26 5:45A	W26 9:30A		W26 5:00P			F28 8:00A
		W26 2:00A						W26 10:45A	W26 2:45P		W26 11:00P		TH27 6:00A	
BELOW		W26 11:45A	W26 4:00P		W26 9:15P		TH27 2:30A	TH27 6:30A						
TH27 8:00A	TH27 10:30A	TH27 4:30P						F28 1:00A	F28 4:45A		F28 12:15P		F28 7:15P	
		TH27 12:15P				TH27 10:30P		F28 1:30P	F28 5:30P		S29 12:30A		S29 8:00A	
		F28 1:45P	F28 6:00P	F28 10:00P	S29 1:15A	S29 6:15A								
S29 4:15A	S29 6:15A	S29 12:15P						S29 9:00P	SU30 2:00A		SU30 10:30A		SU30 5:30P	
SU30 9:30A	SU30 11:30A	SU30 6:30P						M31 3:00A	M31 6:45A		M31 2:30P		M31 9:30P	
		SU30 7:00A	Ar. Pelican	SU30 1:30P										
		M31 3:30A	M31 7:45A	M31 11:45A	M31 3:00P	M31 8:00P	T1 7:30A	T1 11:30A						
		M31 3:00P						T1 12:15A	T1 5:00A		T1 1:30P		T1 9:00P	
M31 9:15P	M31 11:45P	T1 6:15A				T1 2:45P		W2 4:45A	W2 8:45A		W2 5:00P			F4 8:00A

ALL TIMES SHOWN ARE LOCAL TIMES

M/V AURORA - SOUTHERN PANHANDLE SUMMER 2000
EFFECTIVE JUNE 1, 2000 THROUGH SEPTEMBER 30, 2000

SUN Lv Hollis 6:15AM
Ar Ketchikan 9:00AM
Lv Ketchikan 12:15PM
Ar Metlakatla 1:30PM
Lv Metlakatla 2:15PM
Ar Ketchikan 3:30PM
Lv Ketchikan 6:15PM
Ar Hollis 9:00PM

MON Lv Hollis 6:15AM
Ar Ketchikan 9:00AM
Lv Ketchikan 11:00AM
Ar Metlakatla 12:15PM
Lv Metlakatla 2:45PM
Ar Ketchikan 4:00PM
Lv Ketchikan 6:15PM
Ar Hollis 9:00PM

MON Lv Hollis 10:00PM
TUE Ar Ketchikan 12:45AM
Lv Ketchikan 1:45AM
Ar Pr. Rupert 9:15AM
Lv Pr. Rupert 11:15AM
Ar Ketchikan 4:45PM
Lv Ketchikan 6:15PM
Ar Hollis 9:00PM

WED Lv Hollis 6:15AM
Ar Ketchikan 9:00AM
Lv Ketchikan 12:15PM
Ar Metlakatla 1:30PM
Lv Metlakatla 2:15PM
Ar Ketchikan 3:30PM
Lv Ketchikan 6:15PM
Ar Hollis 9:00PM

THU Lv Hollis 9:15AM
Ar Ketchikan 11:55AM
Lv Ketchikan 6:15PM
Ar Hollis 9:00PM

FRI Lv Hollis 6:15AM
Ar Ketchikan 9:00AM
Lv Ketchikan 12:15PM
Ar Metlakatla 1:30PM
Lv Metlakatla 2:15PM
Ar Ketchikan 3:30PM

FRI Lv Ketchikan 6:15PM
Ar Hollis 9:00PM
Lv Hollis 10:00PM
SAT Ar Ketchikan 12:45AM

SAT Lv Ketchikan 6:15AM
Ar Metlakatla 7:30AM
Lv Metlakatla 8:15AM
Ar Ketchikan 9:30AM
Lv Ketchikan 10:30AM
Ar Hollis 1:15PM
Lv Hollis 2:15PM
Ar Ketchikan 5:00PM
Lv Ketchikan 6:45PM
Ar Metlakatla 8:00PM
Lv Metlakatla 8:45PM
Ar Ketchikan 10:00PM
Lv Ketchikan 11:00PM
SUN Ar Hollis 1:45AM

Aurora | Columbia | Le Conte | Malaspina | Matanuska | Taku | Kennicott

1-800-642-0066

AUGUST 2000 NORTHBOUND - INSIDE PASSAGE/SOUTHEAST ALASKA 1-800-642-0066

LEAVE BELLINGHAM	LEAVE PRINCE RUPERT	LEAVE METLAKATLA	KETCHIKAN	HOLLIS	WRANGELL	PETERSBURG	KAKE	ARRIVE SITKA	ANGOON	TENAKEE	HOONAH	JUNEAU	HAINES	ARRIVE SKAGWAY
	SU30 8:30P	SEE M/V AURORA SCHEDULE BELOW	M31 4:30A	SEE M/V AURORA SCHEDULE BELOW	M31 11:30A	M31 3:30P		T1 2:15A			T1 3:30P	T1 6:30P		
	T1 12:30A		T1 6:30A		T1 1:15P	T1 5:00P		W2 3:00A				W2 3:45P	W2 9:30P	W2 10:30P
						T1 1:30P	T1 6:30P	W2 3:00A	W2 11:30A		W2 4:30P	W2 7:45P		
	W2 7:00A		W2 2:15P		W2 9:00P	TH3 12:45A						TH3 8:45A	SEE	
						TH3 4:00P	TH3 9:00P		F4 1:45A	F4 5:00A	F4 9:15A	F4 12:30P		
	TH3 10:15A		TH3 6:15P		F4 1:15A	F4 6:15A						F4 6:15P	S5 12:15A	S5 1:15A
	F4 3:45P		F4 9:45P		S5 4:30A	S5 8:15A						S5 5:30P	S5 11:30P	SU6 12:30A
							Lv. Sitka	S5 2:00P	S5 8:15P	S5 11:30P	SU6 3:45A	SU6 7:00A		
	S5 11:00A		S5 5:15P		S5 11:55P	SU6 5:15A		SU6 6:45P				M7 9:30A		
F4 6:00P			SU6 9:00A		SU6 5:00P	SU6 8:45P						M7 9:15A	M7 3:15P	M7 4:30P
	SU6 8:30P		M7 4:30A		M7 11:30A	M7 3:30P		T8 2:15A			T8 4:00P	T8 7:00P		
						T8 1:00A	T8 6:00A	T8 2:30P	T8 11:00P		W9 4:00A	W9 7:15A		
	M7 7:45P		T8 2:15A		T8 9:00A	T8 12:45P		W9 3:30A				W9 4:30P	W9 10:30P	W9 11:30P
	W9 8:00A		W9 2:45P		W9 9:30P	TH10 1:15A						TH10 9:15A	DAILY	
						TH10 8:00A	TH10 1:00P		TH10 6:00P	TH10 9:15P	F11 1:30A	F11 4:45A		
	TH10 8:30A		TH10 5:45P		F11 12:30A	F11 4:15A						F11 6:15P	S12 12:15A	S12 1:15A
	F11 4:45P		F11 11:30P		S12 7:45A	S12 11:30A						S12 8:45P	SU13 2:45A	SU13 3:45A
							Lv. Sitka	S12 8:00A	S12 2:15P	S12 5:30P	S12 9:45P	SU13 9:30A	SU13 2:00P	
	S12 11:00A		S12 5:15P		S12 11:55P	SU13 5:00A		SU13 6:45P				M14 9:00A		
F11 6:00P			SU1310:00A		SU13 6:15P	SU1310:30P						M1410:45A	M14 4:45P	M14 5:45P
	SU13 8:30P		M14 4:00A		M14 11:00A	M14 3:00P		T15 1:45A			T15 4:00P	T15 7:00P		
	M14 11:00P		T15 5:30A		T15 12:15P	T15 4:15P		W16 2:15A				W16 3:00P	W16 8:45P	W16 9:45P
						T15 1:00P	T15 6:00P	W16 2:00A	W1611:00A		W16 4:00P	W16 7:15P		
	W16 7:00A		W16 1:45P		W16 8:30P	TH1712:15A						TH17 8:15A	SCHEDULE	
						TH17 3:30P	TH17 8:30P		F18 1:30A	F18 4:45A	F18 9:00A	F18 12:15P		
	TH1710:15A		TH17 6:15P		F18 1:15A	F18 6:15A						F18 6:15P	F18 11:45P	S19 12:45A
	F18 3:00P		F18 9:00P		S19 3:45A	S19 7:30A						S19 4:30P	S19 10:15P	S19 11:15P
							Lv. Sitka	S19 11:55A	S19 6:15P	S19 9:30P	SU20 1:45A	SU20 5:00A		
	S19 10:00A		S19 6:15P		SU20 1:15A	SU20 5:15A		SU20 4:30P				M21 9:15A		
F18 6:00P			SU20 9:15A		SU20 5:00P	SU20 9:00P						M21 9:15A	M21 3:15P	M21 4:30P
	SU20 7:45P		M21 2:15A		M21 9:15A	M21 1:15P		M2111:55P			T22 3:15P	T22 6:15P		
	M21 8:15P		T22 6:15A									W23 5:15A	* TO SE/SW	INTER-TIE*
						M21 11:00P	T22 4:00A	T22 11:55A	T22 8:30P		W23 4:00A	W23 7:15A		
	W23 8:00A		W23 3:00P		W23 9:45P	TH24 1:30A						TH24 9:30A		
						TH24 8:00A	TH24 1:00P		TH24 6:00P	TH24 9:15P	F25 1:30A	F25 4:45A		
	TH2410:00A		TH24 4:30P		TH2411:30P	F25 5:45A						F25 6:15P	S26 12:15A	S26 1:15A
							Lv. Sitka	S26 7:00A	S26 1:15P	S26 4:30P	S26 8:45P	S26 11:55P		
									Lv. Pelican	SU27 3:30P		SU2710:00P		
	S26 4:00P		SU2712:15A		SU27 7:15A	SU2711:15A		M2812:15A				M28 1:00P	BELOW	
F25 6:00P			SU2710:00A		SU27 6:15P	SU2710:15P						M28 9:15A	M28 3:15P	M28 4:30P
	SU27 8:30P		M28 3:30A		M28 10:30A	M28 2:30P		T29 1:15A			T29 3:15P	T29 6:15P		
	M28 11:15P		T29 5:15A		T29 11:55A	T29 4:00P		W30 2:00A				W30 2:45P	W30 8:30P	W30 9:30P
						T29 12:30P	T29 5:30P	W30 1:30A	W3010:30A		W30 3:30P	W30 6:45P		
	W30 8:00A		W30 3:15P		W30 10:00P	TH31 1:45A						TH31 9:45A		
						TH31 3:00P	TH31 8:00P		F1 1:00A	F1 4:15A	F1 8:30A	F1 11:45A		
	TH3110:45A		TH31 6:15P		F1 1:15A	F1 6:15A						F1 6:15P	F1 11:45P	S2 12:45A

ALL TIMES SHOWN ARE LOCAL TIMES

M/V KENNICOTT **SOUTHEAST/SOUTHWEST INTER-TIE TRIPS**

The M/V Kennicott for the month of August will depart from Juneau as indicated in the following table. To determine the best connection for your trip, use this schedule. Please allow enough time to make appropriate connections with the sailings listed above. (See tables above).

Leave Juneau Wednesday	AUG 23	5:15AM
Arrive Valdez Thursday	AUG 24	5:45PM
Leave Valdez Thursday	AUG 24	9:45PM
Arrive Seward Friday	AUG 25	7:45AM
Leave Seward Friday	AUG 25	2:45PM
Arrive Valdez Saturday	AUG 26	12:45AM
Leave Valdez Saturday	AUG 26	4:45AM
Arrive Juneau Sunday	AUG 27	5:15PM

Whistle Stop service is provided to Yakutat on inter-tie trips in both directions between Juneau and Valdez. The vessel will stop ONLY if there are vehicle reservations.

JUNEAU ~ HAINES ~ SKAGWAY DAILY SCHEDULE

The M/V Malaspina operates on a daily schedule as indicated in the following table. To determine the best connection for your trip, use these schedules. Please allow enough time to make appropriate connections with the sailings listed above. (See tables above)

DAILY SCHEDULEJUNE 1 - SEPTEMBER 10, 2000

Leave Juneau	7:00AM
Arrive Haines	11:30AM
Leave Haines	12:45PM
Arrive Skagway	1:45PM
Leave Skagway	4:15PM
Arrive Haines	5:15PM
Leave Haines	6:30PM
Arrive Juneau	11:00PM

www.dot.state.ak.us/amhshome.html

LEAVE SKAGWAY	HAINES	JUNEAU	HOONAH	TENAKEE	ANGOON	ARRIVE SITKA	KAKE	PETERSBURG	WRANGELL	HOLLIS	KETCHIKAN	ARRIVE METLAKATLA	ARRIVE PRINCE RUPERT	ARRIVE BELLINGHAM
M31 9:15P	M31 11:45P	T1 6:15A				T1 2:45P		W2 4:45A	W2 8:45A		W2 5:00P			F4 8:00A
		M31 3:30A	M31 7:45A	M31 11:45A	M31 3:00P	M31 8:00P	T1 7:30A	T1 11:30A						
		M31 3:00P						T1 12:15A	T1 5:00A		T1 1:30P		T1 9:00P	
		W2 2:30A						W2 1:15P	W2 5:15P		TH3 12:15A		TH3 7:15A	
TH3 1:30A	TH3 4:00A	TH3 10:00A						TH3 6:30P	TH3 10:15P		F4 5:45A		F4 12:45P	
		W2 8:45P	TH3 1:00A		TH3 6:00A		TH3 11:00A	TH3 3:00P						
SEE		TH3 12:45P				TH3 10:30P		F4 1:45P	F4 5:45P		S5 12:45A		S5 8:15A	
		F4 7:30P	F4 11:45P	S5 3:45A	S5 6:45A	S5 11:45A				SEE M/V AURORA SCHEDULE BELOW		SEE M/V AURORA SCHEDULE BELOW		
S5 4:15A	S5 6:15A	S5 12:15P						S5 9:00P	SU6 2:00A		SU6 10:30A		SU6 5:30P	
SU6 3:30A	SU6 6:00A	SU6 1:00P						SU6 9:30P	M7 1:15A		M7 9:45A		M7 4:45P	
		SU6 3:00P	SU6 7:15P	SU6 11:15P	M7 2:30A	M7 7:30A	M7 8:00P	T8 12:15A						
		M7 3:00P						T8 12:15A	T8 5:00A		T8 1:30P		T8 9:00P	
M7 7:30P	M7 10:00P	T8 6:15A				T8 2:45P		W9 6:15A	W9 10:00A		W9 5:30P			F11 8:30A
		W9 2:00A						W9 10:45A	W9 2:45P		W9 11:00P		TH10 6:00A	
		W9 11:45A	W9 4:00P		W9 9:00P		TH10 2:00A	TH10 6:00A						
TH10 2:30A	TH10 5:00A	TH10 11:00A						TH10 7:30P	TH10 11:15P		F11 6:45A		F11 1:45P	
DAILY		TH10 1:15P				TH10 11:00P		F11 1:30P	F11 5:30P		S12 12:30A		S12 8:00A	
		F11 1:15P	F11 5:30P	F11 9:30P	S12 12:45A	S12 5:45A								
S12 4:15A	S12 6:15A	S12 12:15P						S12 9:00P	SU13 2:30A		SU13 11:30A		SU13 6:30P	
SU13 6:45A	SU13 10:15A	SU13 4:45P						M14 1:15A	M14 5:00A		M14 1:00P		M14 8:00P	
	SU13 3:30P	M14 3:00A	M14 7:15A	M14 11:15A	M14 2:30P	M14 7:30P	T15 7:00A	T15 11:00A						
		M14 3:00P						T15 12:15A	T15 5:00A		T15 1:30P		T15 9:00P	
M14 8:45P	M14 11:15P	T15 5:45A				T15 2:15P		W16 3:00A	W16 7:00A		W16 4:00P			F18 8:00A
		W16 3:00A						W16 11:45A	W16 3:45P		TH17 12:15A		TH17 7:15A	
TH17 12:45A	TH17 3:15A	TH17 9:15A						TH17 5:45P	TH17 9:30P		F18 5:00A		F18 11:55A	
		W16 8:15P	TH17 12:30A		TH17 5:30A		TH17 10:30A	TH17 2:30P						
SCHEDULE		TH17 11:45A				TH17 9:30P		F18 12:30P	F18 4:30P		F18 11:30P		S19 7:00A	
		F18 5:15P	F18 9:30P	S19 1:30A	S19 4:45A	S19 9:45A								
S19 3:45A	S19 5:45A	S19 11:45A						S19 8:15P	SU20 12:15A		SU20 10:45A		SU20 5:45P	
SU20 2:00A	SU20 4:30A	SU20 11:00A						SU20 7:30P	SU20 11:15P		M21 9:15A		M21 4:15P	
		SU20 1:00P	SU20 5:15P	SU20 9:15P	M21 12:30A	M21 5:30A	M21 6:00P	M21 10:15P						
		M21 3:15P						T22 1:30A	T22 6:15A		T22 1:30P		T22 9:00P	
M21 7:30P	M21 10:00P	T22 3:45A				T22 12:15P		W23 4:15A	W23 8:00A		W23 5:00P			F25 8:00A
		W23 2:00A						W23 10:45A	W23 2:45P		W23 11:55P		TH24 7:00A	
		W23 11:45A	W23 4:00P		W23 9:00P		TH24 2:00A	TH24 6:00A						
		TH24 3:45P				F25 3:45A		F25 6:30P	F25 10:30P		S26 5:30A		S26 1:00P	
		F25 12:15P	F25 4:30P	F25 8:30P	F25 11:45P	S26 4:45A								
S26 4:15A	S26 6:15A	S26 12:15P						S26 9:00P	SU27 2:30A		SU27 11:30A		SU27 6:30P	
		SU27 7:00A	Ar. Pelican	SU27 1:30P										
FROM SE/SW INTER-TIE		SU27 6:45P									M28 1:15P		M28 8:15P	
		M28 2:30A	M28 6:45A	M28 10:45A	M28 2:00P	M28 7:00P	T29 6:30A	T29 10:30A						
BELOW		M28 5:45P						T29 3:00A	T29 7:00A		T29 2:00P		T29 9:30P	
M28 7:30P	M28 10:00P	T29 5:15A				T29 1:45P		W30 3:45A	W30 8:15A		W30 5:00P			F1 8:00A
		W30 2:00A						W30 11:45A	W30 3:45P		TH31 12:45A		TH31 7:45A	
TH31 12:30A	TH31 3:00A	TH31 9:00A						TH31 5:30P	TH31 9:15P		F1 4:45A		F1 11:45A	
		W30 7:45P	W30 11:55P		TH31 5:00A		TH31 10:00A	TH31 2:00P						
		TH31 3:30P				F1 3:15A		F1 6:00P	F1 10:00P		S2 5:00A		S2 12:30P	

ALL TIMES SHOWN ARE LOCAL TIMES

M/V AURORA - SOUTHERN PANHANDLE SUMMER 2000
EFFECTIVE JUNE 1, 2000 THROUGH SEPTEMBER 30, 2000

SUN
- Lv Hollis 6:15AM
- Ar Ketchikan 9:00AM
- Lv Ketchikan 12:15PM
- Ar Metlakatla 1:30PM
- Lv Metlakatla 2:15PM
- Ar Ketchikan 3:30PM
- Lv Ketchikan 6:15PM
- Ar Hollis 9:00PM

MON
- Lv Hollis 6:15AM
- Ar Ketchikan 9:00AM
- Lv Ketchikan 11:00AM
- Ar Metlakatla 12:15PM
- Lv Metlakatla 2:45PM
- Ar Ketchikan 4:00PM
- Lv Ketchikan 6:15PM
- Ar Hollis 9:00PM

MON Lv Hollis 10:00PM
TUE
- Ar Ketchikan 12:45AM
- Lv Ketchikan 1:45AM
- Ar Pr. Rupert 9:15AM
- Lv Pr. Rupert 11:15AM
- Ar Ketchikan 4:45PM
- Lv Ketchikan 6:15PM
- Ar Hollis 9:00PM

WED
- Lv Hollis 6:15AM
- Ar Ketchikan 9:00AM
- Lv Ketchikan 12:15PM
- Ar Metlakatla 1:30PM
- Lv Metlakatla 2:15PM
- Ar Ketchikan 3:30PM
- Lv Ketchikan 6:15PM
- Ar Hollis 9:00PM

THU
- Lv Hollis 9:15AM
- Ar Ketchikan 11:55AM
- Lv Ketchikan 6:15PM
- Ar Hollis 9:00PM

FRI
- Lv Hollis 6:15AM
- Ar Ketchikan 9:00AM
- Lv Ketchikan 12:15PM
- Ar Metlakatla 1:30PM
- Lv Metlakatla 2:15PM
- Ar Ketchikan 3:30PM

FRI
- Lv Ketchikan 6:15PM
- Ar Hollis 9:00PM
- Lv Hollis 10:00PM

SAT Ar Ketchikan 12:45AM

SAT
- Lv Ketchikan 6:15AM
- Ar Metlakatla 7:30AM
- Lv Metlakatla 8:15AM
- Ar Ketchikan 9:30AM
- Lv Ketchikan 10:30AM
- Ar Hollis 1:15PM
- Lv Hollis 2:15PM
- Ar Ketchikan 5:00PM
- Lv Ketchikan 6:45PM
- Ar Metlakatla 8:00PM
- Lv Metlakatla 8:45PM
- Ar Ketchikan 10:00PM
- Lv Ketchikan 11:00PM

SUN Ar Hollis 1:45AM

Aurora | Columbia | Le Conte | Malaspina | Matanuska | Taku | Kennicott

1-800-642-0066

SEPTEMBER 2000 NORTHBOUND - INSIDE PASSAGE/SOUTHEAST ALASKA 1-800-642-0066

LEAVE BELLINGHAM	LEAVE PRINCE RUPERT	LEAVE METLAKATLA	KETCHIKAN	HOLLIS	WRANGELL	PETERSBURG	KAKE	ARRIVE SITKA	ANGOON	TENAKEE	HOONAH	JUNEAU	HAINES	ARRIVE SKAGWAY
		SEE M/V AURORA SCHEDULE BELOW		SEE M/V AURORA SCHEDULE BELOW		TH31 3:00P	TH31 8:00P		F1 1:00A	F1 4:15A	F1 8:30A	F1 11:45A	SEE DAILY SCHEDULE BELOW	
	TH3110:45A		TH31 6:15P		F1 1:15A	F1 6:15A						F1 6:15P	F1 11:45P	S2 12:45A
	F1 2:45P		F1 8:45P		S2 3:30A	S2 7:15A						S2 4:30P	S2 10:15P	S2 11:15P
							Lv. Sitka	S2 7:00P	SU3 1:15A	SU3 4:30A	SU3 8:45A	SU3 11:55A		
	S2 3:30P		S2 10:45P		SU3 5:45A	SU3 9:45A		SU3 11:30P				M4 11:55A		
F1 6:00P			SU3 10:00A		SU3 5:00P	SU3 9:00P						M4 9:15A	M4 3:15P	M4 4:30P
	SU3 6:15P		M4 2:30A		M4 9:30A	M4 1:30P		T5 12:15A			T5 3:15P	T5 6:15P		
						M4 11:30P	T5 4:30A	T5 1:00P	T5 9:30P		W6 4:00A	W6 7:15A		
	M4 4:00P		M4 10:15P		T5 5:00A	T5 8:45A		T5 6:45P				W6 2:00P	W6 7:45P	W6 8:45P
	W6 7:00A		W6 1:45P		W6 8:30P	TH7 12:15A						TH7 8:15A		
						TH7 6:00A	TH7 11:00A		TH7 4:00P	TH7 7:15P	TH7 11:30P	F8 2:45A		
	TH7 8:00A		TH7 2:30P		TH7 9:15P	F8 1:00A						F8 10:00A	F8 3:30P	F8 4:30P
	F8 3:00P		F8 10:00P		S9 6:15A	S9 10:00A						SU1012:15A	SU10 5:45A	SU10 6:45A
							Lv. Sitka	S9 1:00P	S9 7:15P	S9 10:30P	SU10 2:45A	SU10 6:00A		
									Lv. Pelican	SU10 3:30P		SU1010:00P		
	S9 9:45A		S9 5:45P		SU1012:45A	SU10 4:30A		SU10 6:00P				M11 8:30A		
F8 6:00P			SU1010:00A		SU10 5:00P	SU10 9:00P						M11 9:15A	M11 3:15P	M11 4:15P
	SU10 9:45A		SU10 2:45P											
	M11 11:00P		T12 5:00A		T12 11:30A	T12 3:15P		W13 1:15A				W13 1:45P	W13 7:15P	W13 8:15P
						T12 11:55A	T12 5:00P	W13 1:00A	W13 9:45A		W13 2:45P	W13 6:00P		
	W13 8:00A		W13 3:15P		W13 10:00P	TH14 1:45A						TH1412:15P	TH14 6:15P	TH14 7:15P
						TH14 2:15P	TH14 7:15P		F15 12:15A	F15 3:30A	F15 7:45A	F15 11:00A		
	F15 1:15P		F15 7:45P		S16 2:30A	S16 6:15A						S16 3:00P	S16 8:30P	S16 9:30P
							Lv. Sitka	S16 5:15P	S16 11:30P	SU17 2:45A	SU17 7:00A	SU1710:15A		
	S16 2:30P		S16 9:15P		SU17 4:15A	SU17 8:15A		SU1710:00P				M1810:30A		
F15 6:00P			SU17 9:00A		SU17 4:00P	SU17 7:45P						M18 8:15A	M18 2:15P	M18 3:15P
	M18 6:15P		T19 6:15A									W20 5:15A	* TO SE/SW	INTER-TIE*
						T19 2:45A	T19 7:45A	T19 5:15P	W20 1:45A		W20 6:45A	W2010:00A		
	W20 7:00A		W20 1:30P		W20 8:15P	TH2112:15A						TH2112:15P	TH21 6:15P	TH21 7:15P
						TH21 7:00A	TH2111:55A		TH21 5:00P	TH21 8:15P	F22 12:30A	F22 3:45A		
							Lv. Sitka	S23 11:55A	S23 6:15P	S23 9:30P	SU24 1:45A	SU24 5:00A		
									Lv. Pelican	SU243:30P		SU2410:00P		
	S23 2:30P		S23 10:45P		SU24 5:45A	SU24 9:45A		SU2411:00P				M2511:45A		
F22 6:00P			SU2410:00A		SU24 5:00P	SU24 9:00P						M25 9:15A	M25 3:15P	M25 4:15P
	M25 9:45P		T26 4:15A		T26 11:00A	T26 3:00P		W27 1:00A				W27 2:00P	W27 7:30P	W27 8:30P
						T26 11:30A	T26 4:30P	W2712:30A	W27 9:15A		W27 2:15P	W27 5:30P		
	W27 8:00A		W27 3:15P		W27 10:00P	TH28 1:45A						TH2812:15P	TH28 6:15P	TH28 7:15P
						TH28 1:45P	TH28 6:45P		TH2811:45P	F29 3:00A	F29 7:15A	F29 10:30A		
	F29 1:15P		F29 7:45P		S30 2:30A	S30 6:15A						S30 3:30P	S30 9:30P	S30 10:30P
							Lv. Sitka	S30 5:30P	S30 11:45P	SU1 3:00A	SU1 7:15A	SU1 10:30A		

ALL TIMES SHOWN ARE LOCAL TIMES

M/V KENNICOTT **SOUTHEAST/SOUTHWEST INTER-TIE TRIPS**

The M/V Kennicott for the month of September will depart from Juneau as indicated in the following table. To determine the best connection for your trip, use this schedule. Please allow enough time to make appropriate connections with the sailings listed above. (See tables above).

Leave Juneau Wednesday	SEP 20	5:15AM
Arrive Valdez Thursday	SEP 21	5:45PM
Leave Valdez Thursday	SEP 21	9:15PM
Arrive Seward Friday	SEP 22	7:15AM
Leave Seward Friday	SEP 22	2:15PM
Arrive Valdez Saturday	SEP 23	12:15AM
Leave Valdez Saturday	SEP 23	3:45AM
Arrive Juneau Sunday	SEP 24	4:15PM

Whistle Stop service is provided to Yakutat on inter-tie trips in both directions between Juneau and Valdez. The vessel will stop ONLY if there are vehicle reservations.

JUNEAU ~ HAINES ~ SKAGWAY DAILY SCHEDULE

The M/V Malaspina operates on a daily schedule as indicated in the following table. To determine the best connection for your trip, use these schedules. Please allow enough time to make appropriate connections with the sailings listed above. (See tables above)

DAILY SCHEDULEJUNE 1- SEPTEMBER 10, 2000

Leave Juneau	7:00AM
Arrive Haines	11:30AM
Leave Haines	12:45PM
Arrive Skagway	1:45PM
Leave Skagway	4:15PM
Arrive Haines	5:15PM
Leave Haines	6:30PM
Arrive Juneau	11:00PM

www.dot.state.ak.us/amhshome.html

1-800-642-0066 SEPTEMBER 2000 SOUTHBOUND - INSIDE PASSAGE/SOUTHEAST ALASKA

LEAVE SKAGWAY	HAINES	JUNEAU	HOONAH	TENAKEE	ANGOON	ARRIVE SITKA	KAKE	PETERSBURG	WRANGELL	HOLLIS	KETCHIKAN	ARRIVE METLAKATLA	ARRIVE PRINCE RUPERT	ARRIVE BELLINGHAM
SEE DAILY SCHEDULE BELOW		TH31 3:30P				F1 3:15A		F1 6:00P	F1 10:00P	SEE M/V AURORA SCHEDULE BELOW	S2 5:00A	SEE M/V AURORA SCHEDULE BELOW	S2 12:30P	
		F1 5:45P	F1 10:00P	S2 2:00A	S2 5:15A	S2 10:15A								
S2 3:45A	S2 5:45A	S2 11:15A						S2 8:00P	S2 11:55P		SU3 7:00A		SU3 2:00P	
SU3 2:15A	SU3 4:45A	SU3 10:45A						SU3 7:15P	SU3 11:00P		M4 6:30A		M4 1:30P	
		SU3 1:30P	SU3 5:45P	SU3 9:45P	M4 1:00A	M4 6:00A	M4 5:30P	M4 9:30P						
		M4 5:00P						T5 2:15A	T5 6:15A		T5 1:30P		T5 9:00P	
M4 7:30P	M4 10:00P	T5 4:30A				T5 1:00P		W6 4:00A	W6 8:00A		W6 5:00P			F8 8:00A
		W6 2:00A						W6 10:45A	W6 2:45P		W6 11:00P		TH7 6:00A	
		W6 9:45A	W6 2:00P		W6 7:00P		W6 11:55P	TH7 4:00A						
W6 11:45P	TH7 2:15A	TH7 8:15A						TH7 4:45P	TH7 8:30P		F8 5:00A		F8 11:55A	
		TH7 11:45A				TH7 9:30P		F8 12:15P	F8 4:15P		F8 11:15P		S9 6:45A	
		F8 12:15P	F8 4:30P	F8 8:30P	F8 11:45P	S9 4:45A								
F8 7:30P	F8 9:30P	S9 3:30A						S9 12:15P	S9 4:15P		S9 11:45P		SU10 6:45A	
SU10 9:30A	SU1011:30A	SU10 6:00P						M11 2:30A	M11 6:15A		M11 1:45P		M11 8:45P	
		SU10 7:00A	Ar. Pelican	SU10 1:30P										
		M11 2:00A	M11 6:15A	M11 10:15A	M11 1:30P	M11 6:30P	T12 6:00A	T12 10:00A						
		M11 3:15P						T12 12:30A	T12 5:15A		T12 1:30P		T12 9:00P	
M11 7:15P	M11 9:45P	T12 4:30A				T12 1:00P		W13 3:15A	W13 8:15A		W13 5:15P			F15 8:15A
W13 11:15P	TH14 1:30A	TH14 7:30A						TH14 4:00P	TH14 7:45P		F15 3:15A		F15 10:15A	
		W13 7:00P	W1311:15P		TH14 4:15A		TH14 9:15A	TH14 1:15P						
TH14 1015P	F15 12:45A	F15 8:00A						F15 5:00P	F15 9:00P		S16 4:00A		S16 11:30A	
		F15 4:30P	F15 8:45P	S16 12:45A	S16 4:00A	S16 9:00A								
SU1712:30A	SU17 3:00A	SU17 9:30A						SU17 6:00P	SU17 9:45P		M18 6:15A		M18 1:15P	
		SU17 5:45P	SU1710:00P	M18 2:00A	M18 5:15A	M18 10:15A	M18 9:45P	T19 1:45A						
		M18 4:45P						T19 1:45A	T19 6:00A		T19 1:30P		T19 9:00P	
M18 6:00P	M18 8:30P	T19 2:30A				T19 11:00A		W20 2:45A	W20 6:45A		W20 4:00P			F22 8:00A
		W20 11:45A	W20 4:00P		W20 9:00P		TH21 2:00A	TH21 6:00A						
TH2110:15P	F22 12:45A	F22 8:00A						F22 5:00P	F22 9:00P		S23 4:00A		S23 11:30A	
		F22 11:15A	F22 3:30P	F22 7:30P	F22 10:45P	S23 3:45A								
		SU24 7:00A	Ar. Pelican	SU24 1:30P										
FROM SE/SW INTER-TIE		SU24 6:45P									M2512:15P		M25 7:15P	
		M25 1:30A	M25 5:45A	M25 9:45A	M25 1:00P	M25 6:00P	T26 5:30A	T26 9:30A						
		M25 5:45P						T26 3:00A	T26 7:00A		T26 2:00P		T26 9:30P	
M25 7:15P	M25 9:45P	T26 4:15A				T26 12:45P		W27 2:30A	W27 8:15A		W27 5:15P			F29 8:15A
W27 11:30P	TH28 1:30A	TH28 7:30A						TH28 4:00P	TH28 7:45P		F29 3:15A		F29 10:15A	
		W27 6:30P	W2710:45P		TH28 3:45A		TH28 8:45A	TH2812:45P						
TH2810:15P	F29 12:45A	F29 8:00A						F29 5:00P	F29 9:00P		S30 4:00A		S30 11:30A	
		F29 4:30P	F29 8:45P	S30 12:45A	S30 4:00A	S30 9:00A								

ALL TIMES SHOWN ARE LOCAL TIMES

M/V AURORA - SOUTHERN PANHANDLE SUMMER 2000
EFFECTIVE JUNE 1, 2000 THROUGH SEPTEMBER 30, 2000

SUN	Lv Hollis	6:15AM
	Ar Ketchikan	9:00AM
	Lv Ketchikan	12:15PM
	Ar Metlakatla	1:30PM
	Lv Metlakatla	2:15PM
	Ar Ketchikan	3:30PM
	Lv Ketchikan	6:15PM
	Ar Hollis	9:00PM
MON	Lv Hollis	6:15AM
	Ar Ketchikan	9:00AM
	Lv Ketchikan	11:00AM
	Ar Metlakatla	12:15PM
	Lv Metlakatla	2:45PM
	Ar Ketchikan	4:00PM
	Lv Ketchikan	6:15PM
	Ar Hollis	9:00PM
MON	Lv Hollis	10:00PM
TUE	Ar Ketchikan	12:45AM
	Lv Ketchikan	1:45AM
	Ar Pr. Rupert	9:15AM
	Lv Pr. Rupert	11:15AM
	Ar Ketchikan	4:45PM
	Lv Ketchikan	6:15PM
	Ar Hollis	9:00PM
WED	Lv Hollis	6:15AM
	Ar Ketchikan	9:00AM
	Lv Ketchikan	12:15PM
	Ar Metlakatla	1:30PM
	Lv Metlakatla	2:15PM
	Ar Ketchikan	3:30PM
	Lv Ketchikan	6:15PM
	Ar Hollis	9:00PM
THU	Lv Hollis	9:15AM
	Ar Ketchikan	11:55AM
	Lv Ketchikan	6:15PM
	Ar Hollis	9:00PM
FRI	Lv Hollis	6:15AM
	Ar Ketchikan	9:00AM
	Lv Ketchikan	12:15PM
	Ar Metlakatla	1:30PM
	Lv Metlakatla	2:15PM
	Ar Ketchikan	3:30PM
FRI	Lv Ketchikan	6:15PM
	Ar Hollis	9:00PM
	Lv Hollis	10:00PM
SAT	Ar Ketchikan	12:45AM
SAT	Lv Ketchikan	6:15AM
	Ar Metlakatla	7:30AM
	Lv Metlakatla	8:15AM
	Ar Ketchikan	9:30AM
	Lv Ketchikan	10:30AM
	Ar Hollis	1:15PM
	Lv Hollis	2:15PM
	Ar Ketchikan	5:00PM
	Lv Ketchikan	6:45PM
	Ar Metlakatla	8:00PM
	Lv Metlakatla	8:45PM
	Ar Ketchikan	10:00PM
	Lv Ketchikan	11:00PM
SUN	Ar Hollis	1:45AM

Aurora Columbia Le Conte Malaspina Matanuska Taku Kennicott **1-800-642-0066**

INSIDE PASSAGE/SOUTHEAST ALASKA CABIN TARIFFS

FOUR BERTH CABIN/SITTING ROOM - OUTSIDE/COMPLETE FACILITIES — ITEM 4BS
M/V COLUMBIA - M/V MALASPINA

BETWEEN AND	BELLINGHAM	PRINCE RUPERT	KETCHIKAN	HOLLIS	WRANGELL	PETERSBURG	KAKE	SITKA	JUNEAU	HAINES
KETCHIKAN	272	63		N			N			
WRANGELL	300	89	58	O			O			
PETERSBURG	318	103	71		47					
SITKA	351	128	91	S	71	60	S			
JUNEAU	371	145	107	T	91	78	T	54		
HAINES	405	177	142	O	121	110	O	87	64	
SKAGWAY	405	177	142	P	121	110	P	87	64	39

THREE BERTH CABIN - OUTSIDE/COMPLETE FACILITIES — ITEM 3BF
M/V COLUMBIA - M/V MATANUSKA

BETWEEN AND	BELLINGHAM	PRINCE RUPERT	KETCHIKAN	HOLLIS	WRANGELL	PETERSBURG	KAKE	SITKA	JUNEAU	HAINES
KETCHIKAN	202	45		N			N			
WRANGELL	222	63	44	O			O			
PETERSBURG	232	72	52		35					
SITKA	254	90	67	S	52	45	S			
JUNEAU	271	102	77	T	62	55	T	40		
HAINES	304	129	101	O	84	77	O	63	47	
SKAGWAY	304	129	101	P	84	77	P	63	47	38

FOUR BERTH CABIN - OUTSIDE/COMPLETE FACILITIES — ITEM 4BF
M/V COLUMBIA - M/V MALASPINA - M/V MATANUSKA - M/V TAKU - M/V KENNICOTT

BETWEEN AND	BELLINGHAM	PRINCE RUPERT	KETCHIKAN	HOLLIS	WRANGELL	PETERSBURG	KAKE	SITKA	JUNEAU	HAINES
KETCHIKAN	248	58								
HOLLIS	266	71	48							
WRANGELL	274	80	53	50						
PETERSBURG	289	92	65	56	41					
KAKE	304	104	75	65	53	48				
SITKA	319	114	84	74	64	53	50			
JUNEAU	337	128	100	90	80	69	63	48		
HAINES	373	163	132	121	111	101	88	78	56	
SKAGWAY	373	163	132	121	111	101	88	78	56	44

TWO BERTH - OUTSIDE/COMPLETE FACILITIES — ITEM 2BF
M/V COLUMBIA - M/V MALASPINA - M/V MATANUSKA - M/V TAKU - M/V KENNICOTT

BETWEEN AND	BELLINGHAM	PRINCE RUPERT	KETCHIKAN	HOLLIS	WRANGELL	PETERSBURG	KAKE	SITKA	JUNEAU	HAINES
KETCHIKAN	177	43								
HOLLIS	188	50	35							
WRANGELL	193	58	37	36						
PETERSBURG	204	67	46	44	33					
KAKE	216	76	54	46	40	34				
SITKA	227	84	61	58	47	40	36			
JUNEAU	243	97	72	70	58	50	45	37		
HAINES	271	121	92	90	77	70	68	56	42	
SKAGWAY	271	121	92	90	77	70	68	56	42	33

FOUR BERTH CABIN - INSIDE/COMPLETE FACILITIES — ITEM 4BI
M/V COLUMBIA - M/V MALASPINA - M/V MATANUSKA - M/V TAKU - M/V KENNICOTT

BETWEEN AND	BELLINGHAM	PRINCE RUPERT	KETCHIKAN	HOLLIS	WRANGELL	PETERSBURG	KAKE	SITKA	JUNEAU	HAINES
KETCHIKAN	210	50								
HOLLIS	229	57	42							
WRANGELL	233	69	48	43						
PETERSBURG	250	80	57	49	39					
KAKE	262	90	64	56	46	40				
SITKA	275	100	75	65	56	48	42			
JUNEAU	292	112	88	78	69	60	55	42		
HAINES	321	141	116	106	98	89	79	69	49	
SKAGWAY	321	141	116	106	98	89	79	69	49	39

TWO BERTH CABIN - INSIDE/COMPLETE FACILITIES — ITEM 2BI
M/V COLUMBIA - M/V MALASPINA - M/V MATANUSKA - M/V TAKU

BETWEEN AND	BELLINGHAM	PRINCE RUPERT	KETCHIKAN	HOLLIS	WRANGELL	PETERSBURG	KAKE	SITKA	JUNEAU	HAINES
KETCHIKAN	156	38								
HOLLIS	164	44	27							
WRANGELL	174	53	34	28						
PETERSBURG	180	60	41	36	29					
KAKE	189	68	48	42	36	30				
SITKA	199	74	53	47	41	35	32			
JUNEAU	211	83	63	60	51	44	40	33		
HAINES	234	105	83	80	70	64	63	51	38	
SKAGWAY	234	105	83	80	70	64	63	51	38	31

TWO BERTH CABIN - OUTSIDE/NO FACILITIES — ITEM 2NO
M/V KENNICOTT

BETWEEN AND	BELLINGHAM	PRINCE RUPERT	KETCHIKAN	HOLLIS	WRANGELL	PETERSBURG	KAKE	SITKA	JUNEAU	HAINES
KETCHIKAN	142	33		N			N			
WRANGELL	157	46	30	O			O			
PETERSBURG	165	53	37		23					
SITKA	182	65	48	S	37	31	S			
JUNEAU	193	73	57	T	46	39	T	27		
HAINES	213	93	75	O	63	57	O	44	31	
SKAGWAY	213	93	75	P	63	57	P	44	31	25

TWO BERTH ROOMETTE - OUTSIDE/NO FACILITIES/*NO LINEN — ITEM 2RO
M/V KENNICOTT

BETWEEN AND	BELLINGHAM	PRINCE RUPERT	KETCHIKAN	HOLLIS	WRANGELL	PETERSBURG	KAKE	SITKA	JUNEAU	HAINES
KETCHIKAN	85	20		N			N			
WRANGELL	94	27	18	O			O			
PETERSBURG	99	32	22		14					
SITKA	109	39	29	S	22	19	S			
JUNEAU	116	44	34	T	27	24	T	16		
HAINES	128	56	45	O	38	35	O	27	19	
SKAGWAY	128	56	45	P	38	35	P	27	19	15

TWO BERTH - INSIDE/NO FACILITIES — ITEM 2NI
M/V KENNICOTT

BETWEEN AND	BELLINGHAM	PRINCE RUPERT	KETCHIKAN	HOLLIS	WRANGELL	PETERSBURG	KAKE	SITKA	JUNEAU	HAINES
KETCHIKAN	128	30		N			N			
WRANGELL	141	41	27	O			O			
PETERSBURG	149	47	33		21					
SITKA	164	59	43	S	33	28	S			
JUNEAU	173	66	51	T	41	35	T	25		
HAINES	192	84	68	O	57	52	O	40	29	
SKAGWAY	192	84	68	P	57	52	P	40	29	23

TWO BERTH ROOMETTE - INSIDE/NO FACILITIES/*NO LINEN — ITEM 2RI
M/V KENNICOTT

BETWEEN AND	BELLINGHAM	PRINCE RUPERT	KETCHIKAN	HOLLIS	WRANGELL	PETERSBURG	KAKE	SITKA	JUNEAU	HAINES
KETCHIKAN	71	17		N			N			
WRANGELL	78	23	15	O			O			
PETERSBURG	83	26	19		12					
SITKA	91	33	24	S	18	16	S			
JUNEAU	96	37	29	T	23	20	T	14		
HAINES	106	46	38	O	32	29	O	22	16	
SKAGWAY	106	46	38	P	32	29	P	22	16	13

SOUTHEAST/SOUTHWEST INTER-TIE TARIFFS

	PR. RUPERT VALDEZ	KETCHIKAN VALDEZ	JUNEAU VALDEZ
Passengers (12 yrs & older)	202	164	90
Child (2 yrs through 11 yrs)	100	82	44
AMC (Bicycles-Kayaks-Inflatables)	38	28	12
2 Wheeled Motorcycles	161	133	72
Vehicles up to 10 feet	263	218	119
Vehicles up to 15 feet	449	374	206
Vehicles up to 19 feet	535	445	245
Vehicles up to 21 feet	669	557	300
Vehicles up to 23 feet	838	698	376
Vehicles up to 25 feet	995	829	447
CABINS			
4 Berth - Outside/complete facilities	306	248	148
4 Berth -Inside/complete facilities	260	210	122
2 Berth Outside/no facilities	175	142	85
2 Berth - Inside/no facilities	158	128	76
2 Berth Roomette - Outside/no facilities*	105	85	51
2 Berth Roomette - Inside/no facilities*	88	71	42

*No linen - Linen may be rented separately.

	PR. RUPERT YAKUTAT	KETCHIKAN YAKUTAT	JUNEAU YAKUTAT
Passengers (12 yrs & older)	166	128	54
Child (2 yrs through 11 yrs)	82	64	26
AMC (Bicycles-Kayaks-Inflatables)	33	23	7
2 Wheeled Motorcycles	132	104	43
Vehicles up to 10 feet	215	170	71
Vehicles up to 15 feet	367	292	124
Vehicles up to 19 feet	437	347	147
Vehicles up to 21 feet	549	437	180
Vehicles up to 23 feet	688	548	226
Vehicles up to 25 feet	816	650	268
CABINS			
4 Berth - Outside/complete facilities	247	189	89
4 Berth -Inside/complete facilities	211	161	73
2 Berth Outside/no facilities	141	108	51
2 Berth - Inside/no facilities	127	97	46
2 Berth Roomette - Outside/no facilities*	85	65	31
2 Berth Roomette - Inside/no facilities*	71	54	25

*No linen - Linen may be rented separately.

	PR. RUPERT SEWARD	KETCHIKAN SEWARD	JUNEAU SEWARD
Passengers (12 yrs & older)	260	222	148
Child (2 yrs through 11 yrs)	130	112	74
AMC (Bicycles-Kayaks-Inflatables)	48	38	22
2 Wheeled Motorcycles	201	173	112
Vehicles up to 10 feet	331	286	187
Vehicles up to 15 feet	561	486	318
Vehicles up to 19 feet	669	579	379
Vehicles up to 21 feet	841	729	472
Vehicles up to 23 feet	1054	914	592
Vehicles up to 25 feet	1251	1085	703
CABINS			
4 Berth - Outside/complete facilities	397	339	239
4 Berth -Inside/complete facilities	336	286	198
2 Berth Outside/no facilities	229	196	139
2 Berth - Inside/no facilities	206	176	125
2 Berth Roomette - Outside/no facilities*	137	117	83
2 Berth Roomette - Inside/no facilities*	115	98	69

*No linen - Linen may be rented separately.

INSIDE PASSAGE/SOUTHEAST ALASKA PASSENGER & VEHICLE TARIFFS

ADULT 12 YEARS OR OVER (Meals and Berth NOT included)

BETWEEN AND	BELLINGHAM	PRINCE RUPERT	KETCHIKAN	METLAKATLA	HOLLIS	WRANGELL	PETERSBURG	KAKE	SITKA	ANGOON	HOONAH	JUNEAU	HAINES	SKAGWAY	PELICAN
KETCHIKAN	164	38													
METLAKATLA	168	42	14												
HOLLIS	178	52	20	22											
WRANGELL	180	56	24	28	24										
PETERSBURG	192	68	38	42	38	18									
KAKE	202	80	48	52	48	34	22								
SITKA	208	86	54	58	54	38	26	24							
ANGOON	222	100	68	72	68	52	40	28	22						
HOONAH	226	104	74	78	74	56	44	38	24	20					
JUNEAU	226	104	74	78	74	56	44	44	26	24	20				
HAINES	244	122	92	96	92	74	62	62	44	42	38	24			
SKAGWAY	252	130	98	102	98	82	70	70	50	48	46	32	17		
PELICAN	248	126	96	100	96	78	66	52	40	38	22	32	50	60	
TENAKEE	226	104	74	78	74	56	44	32	22	16	16	22	38	46	32

CHILD 2 THROUGH 11 YEARS (Under 2 Transported Free)

BETWEEN AND	BELLINGHAM	PRINCE RUPERT	KETCHIKAN	METLAKATLA	HOLLIS	WRANGELL	PETERSBURG	KAKE	SITKA	ANGOON	HOONAH	JUNEAU	HAINES	SKAGWAY	PELICAN
KETCHIKAN	82	18													
METLAKATLA	84	20	8												
HOLLIS	88	26	12	14											
WRANGELL	90	28	12	14	12										
PETERSBURG	96	34	20	22	20	10									
KAKE	102	40	24	26	24	18	12								
SITKA	104	42	26	28	26	20	14	12							
ANGOON	110	50	34	36	34	26	20	14	12						
HOONAH	114	52	38	40	38	28	22	20	12	10					
JUNEAU	114	52	38	40	38	28	22	22	12	12	10				
HAINES	122	62	46	48	46	38	32	32	22	22	20	12			
SKAGWAY	127	65	49	51	49	41	35	35	25	25	23	17	9		
PELICAN	126	64	48	50	48	40	34	26	20	20	12	16	26	31	
TENAKEE	114	52	38	40	38	28	22	16	12	8	8	12	20	23	16

ALTERNATE MEANS OF CONVEYANCE (Bicycles-Small Boats-Inflatables)

BETWEEN AND	BELLINGHAM	PRINCE RUPERT	KETCHIKAN	METLAKATLA	HOLLIS	WRANGELL	PETERSBURG	KAKE	SITKA	ANGOON	HOONAH	JUNEAU	HAINES	SKAGWAY	PELICAN
KETCHIKAN	28	10													
METLAKATLA	29	11	7												
HOLLIS	30	12	8	9											
WRANGELL	31	13	9	10	9										
PETERSBURG	32	14	11	12	11	8									
KAKE	34	16	12	13	12	10	8								
SITKA	35	17	13	14	13	11	9	8							
ANGOON	37	19	15	16	15	13	11	9	7						
HOONAH	38	20	16	17	16	14	12	11	8	8					
JUNEAU	38	20	16	17	16	14	12	12	9	9	8				
HAINES	41	24	20	21	20	18	16	16	13	12	12	10			
SKAGWAY	42	25	21	22	21	19	17	17	14	13	13	11	8		
PELICAN	41	23	19	20	19	17	15	13	11	10	8	10	14	15	
TENAKEE	38	20	16	17	16	14	12	10	8	7	7	9	12	13	10

TWO WHEELED MOTORCYCLES (No Trailers - Driver NOT included)

BETWEEN AND	BELLINGHAM	PRINCE RUPERT	KETCHIKAN	METLAKATLA	HOLLIS	WRANGELL	PETERSBURG	KAKE	SITKA	ANGOON	HOONAH	JUNEAU	HAINES	SKAGWAY	PELICAN
KETCHIKAN	133	28													
METLAKATLA	140	32	8												
HOLLIS	146	40	16	17											
WRANGELL	150	45	20	23	20										
PETERSBURG	160	54	30	33	30	14									
KAKE	169	66	40	44	40	26	17								
SITKA	174	70	45	48	45	30	20	18							
ANGOON	186	82	56	60	56	43	32	22	16						
HOONAH	191	86	61	64	61	46	36	30	18	15					
JUNEAU	191	86	61	64	61	46	36	36	20	18	15				
HAINES	208	102	76	80	76	62	51	51	35	34	30	19			
SKAGWAY	213	109	82	86	82	67	58	58	41	40	36	25	10		
PELICAN	210	106	79	83	79	64	53	41	32	30	17	26	42	49	
TENAKEE	191	86	61	64	61	46	36	25	17	13	13	17	32	37	26

All motorcycles must be fully secured on the car deck with tie-downs. It is the responsibility of the owner to ensure this is completed properly. Rope may be obtained from car deck personnel for lashing purposes.

VEHICLES UP TO 10 FEET (Driver NOT Included)

BETWEEN AND	BELLINGHAM	PRINCE RUPERT	KETCHIKAN	METLAKATLA	HOLLIS	WRANGELL	PETERSBURG	KAKE	SITKA	ANGOON	HOONAH	JUNEAU	HAINES	SKAGWAY	PELICAN
KETCHIKAN	218	45													
METLAKATLA	223	53	14												
HOLLIS	238	66	26	29											
WRANGELL	243	73	31	38	31										
PETERSBURG	259	89	49	54	49	23									
KAKE	275	105	65	71	65	43	28								
SITKA	284	114	73	79	73	49	33	30							
ANGOON	303	133	91	98	91	69	53	36	26						
HOONAH	310	140	99	105	99	75	59	49	30	25					
JUNEAU	310	140	99	105	99	75	59	59	33	30	24				
HAINES	336	166	124	130	124	100	82	82	57	55	49	31			
SKAGWAY	346	176	133	139	133	109	93	93	67	64	59	41	18		
PELICAN	341	171	129	134	129	104	86	68	53	49	29	43	69	79	
TENAKEE	310	140	99	105	99	75	59	41	28	20	20	28	51	61	43

ALL TARIFFS AND RATES ARE QUOTED IN U.S. DOLLARS

VEHICLES UP TO 15 FEET (Driver NOT Included)

BETWEEN AND	BELLINGHAM	PRINCE RUPERT	KETCHIKAN	METLAKATLA	HOLLIS	WRANGELL	PETERSBURG	KAKE	SITKA	ANGOON	HOONAH	JUNEAU	HAINES	SKAGWAY
KETCHIKAN	374	75												
METLAKATLA	372	84	21											
HOLLIS	394	107	41	46										
WRANGELL	405	117	51	61	51									
PETERSBURG	433	145	80	90	80	35								
KAKE	460	174	109	119	109	70	44							
SITKA	473	187	122	132	122	80	52	49						
ANGOON	505	220	155	164	155	116	86	60	41					
HOONAH	534	240	168	177	168	126	98	82	49	39				
JUNEAU	534	240	168	177	168	126	98	98	52	47	38			
HAINES	578	283	210	220	210	168	139	139	95	90	81	49		
SKAGWAY	594	299	226	237	226	185	156	156	112	107	98	66	26	
PELICAN	570	285	220	228	220	176	147	114	86	80	47	70	114	132
TENAKEE	(Unable to off-load vehicles longer than ten feet)													

VEHICLES UP TO 19 FEET (Driver NOT Included)

BETWEEN AND	BELLINGHAM	PRINCE RUPERT	KETCHIKAN	METLAKATLA	HOLLIS	WRANGELL	PETERSBURG	KAKE	SITKA	ANGOON	HOONAH	JUNEAU	HAINES	SKAGWAY
KETCHIKAN	445	90												
METLAKATLA	443	100	25											
HOLLIS	470	128	49	55										
WRANGELL	482	139	61	73	61									
PETERSBURG	515	172	95	107	95	42								
KAKE	548	207	130	141	130	83	52							
SITKA	563	223	145	157	145	96	63	58						
ANGOON	602	261	184	196	184	138	103	71	49					
HOONAH	636	285	200	211	200	150	117	97	58	47				
JUNEAU	636	285	200	211	200	150	117	117	62	56	45			
HAINES	687	336	249	261	249	199	165	165	112	106	95	57		
SKAGWAY	707	356	269	282	269	220	186	186	132	127	116	78	31	
PELICAN	679	339	261	271	261	210	175	136	103	95	56	83	135	156
TENAKEE	(Unable to off-load vehicles longer than ten feet)													

VEHICLES UP TO 21 FEET (Driver NOT Included)

BETWEEN AND	BELLINGHAM	PRINCE RUPERT	KETCHIKAN	METLAKATLA	HOLLIS	WRANGELL	PETERSBURG	KAKE	SITKA	ANGOON	HOONAH	JUNEAU	HAINES	SKAGWAY
KETCHIKAN	557	112												
METLAKATLA	572	129	31											
HOLLIS	606	164	62	70										
WRANGELL	622	179	78	93	78									
PETERSBURG	665	222	122	137	122	53								
KAKE	707	267	167	182	167	107	67							
SITKA	727	287	187	202	187	123	80	74						
ANGOON	777	337	237	252	237	177	132	91	63					
HOONAH	821	368	257	272	257	193	150	125	74	60				
JUNEAU	821	368	257	272	257	193	150	150	79	72	57			
HAINES	887	434	322	337	322	257	213	213	145	137	123	74		
SKAGWAY	913	460	347	364	347	284	240	240	171	164	150	101	39	
PELICAN	877	437	337	350	337	270	225	175	132	122	71	107	174	202
TENAKEE	(Unable to off-load vehicles longer than ten feet)													

TARIFFS — All fares are one-way. Fares for passengers, vehicles and cabins are all calculated separately and must be added together to determine the total cost of your travel. Passage and vehicle fares are charged from the port of embarkation to the port of debarkation. Cabin fares are calculated according to the route taken, and may vary from the printed rates depending on the ship and schedules. ***Note: Selected tariff adjustments may be made prior to or during the Summer 2000 season***

PETS — Dogs, cats, and other household pets are charged $25 to/from Bellingham, and $10 to/from Prince Rupert. There is no charge for a certified service animal traveling with a disabled person.

VEHICLE FARES — Vehicle fares are determined by the vehicle's overall length and width. Vehicles 8-1/2 to 9 feet wide will be charged approximately 125% of the listed fare. Vehicles over 9 feet wide will be charged approximately 150% of the listed fare. If you are towing a vehicle, the overall connected length is used to determine fares. Vehicles may be measured at check-in prior to boarding and adjustments will be made to quoted fares based on actual vehicle length.

VEHICLES OVER 21 FEET — Contact any Marine Highway office for fares. Vessels in Southeast Alaska can load vehicles up to 70 feet long with special arrangements. Fares for towed vehicles or trailers are calculated at their combined connected length. Vehicles may not be disconnected for travel at separate rates on the same sailing.

MINIMUM 25' RATE — Vehicles with high centers of gravity (commercial highway vans, loaded flat bed trailers) are charged at the 25 ft. rate unless the vehicle is over 25 ft. in which case the appropriate rate for the vehicle length applies. Contact the commerical booking desk (907) 465-8816 for information and reservations.

SOUTHCENTRAL/SOUTHWEST ALASKA M/V TUSTUMENA

MAY EASTBOUND

Leave SELDOVIA	Leave HOMER	PORT LIONS	Arrive KODIAK	Leave SEWARD	Arrive VALDEZ
SU30 6:00A	SU30 9:30A		SU30 7:00P		
	M1 9:30A		M1 7:00P		
T2 4:00P	T2 7:55P	W3 6:30A	Lv. W3 4:00P	Ar. TH4 5:15A	
SU7 6:00A	SU7 9:30A		SU7 7:00P		
	M8 9:30A		M8 7:00P		
T9 4:00P	T9 11:30P		W10 9:00A		
FROM ALEUTIAN CHAIN TRIP			M15 8:15P		
T16 4:00P	T16 7:55P	W17 6:30A	Lv. W17 4:00P	TH18 9:45A	TH18 11:00P
SU21 6:00A	SU21 9:30A		SU21 7:00P		
	M22 9:30A		M22 7:00P		
*T23 4:00P	W24 12:30A		Lv. W24 4:00P	TH25 9:45A	TH25 11:00P
SU28 6:00A	SU28 9:30A		SU28 7:00P		
	M29 9:30A		M29 7:00P		
T30 5:00P	T30 7:55P	W31 6:30A	Lv. W31 4:00P	TH1 9:45A	TH1 11:00P

* Kodiak King Crab Festival May 23 - 29

MAY WESTBOUND

Leave VALDEZ	Leave SEWARD	Leave KODIAK	PORT LIONS	Leave HOMER	Arrive SELDOVIA
		SU30 10:30P		Ar. M1 8:00A	
		M1 10:30P		T2 12:30P	T2 2:00P
	F5 9:30P	S6 12:45P	S6 3:45P	SU7 3:30A	SU7 4:55A
		SU7 10:30P		Ar. M8 8:00A	
		M8 10:30P		T9 12:30P	T9 2:00P
		W10 4:55P	***TO ALEUTIAN CHAIN TRIP***		
		M15 10:30P		T16 12:30P	T16 2:00P
F19 6:30A	F19 9:30P	S20 12:45P	S20 3:45P	SU21 3:30A	SU21 4:55A
		SU21 10:30P		Ar. M22 8:00A	
		M22 10:30P		T23 12:30P	T23 2:00P
F26 6:30A	F26 9:30P	S27 12:45P	S27 3:45P	SU28 3:30A	SU28 4:55A
		SU28 10:30P		Ar. M29 8:00A	
		*M29 11:55P		T30 2:00P	T30 3:30P

JUNE EASTBOUND

Leave SELDOVIA	Leave HOMER	PORT LIONS	Arrive KODIAK	Leave SEWARD	Arrive VALDEZ
SU4 6:00A	SU4 9:30A		SU4 7:00P		
	M5 9:30A		M5 7:00P		
T6 4:00P	T6 11:30P		W7 9:00A		
FROM ALEUTIAN CHAIN TRIP			M12 8:15P		
T13 4:00P	T13 7:55P	W14 6:30A	Lv. W14 4:00P	TH15 9:45A	TH15 11:00P
SU18 6:00A	SU18 9:30A		SU18 7:00P		
	M19 9:30A		M19 7:00P		
T20 4:00P	T20 7:55P	W21 6:30A	Lv. W21 4:00P	TH22 9:45A	TH22 11:00P
SU25 6:00A	SU25 9:30A		SU25 7:00P		
	M26 9:30A		M26 7:00P		
T27 4:00P	T27 7:55P	W28 6:30A	Lv. W28 4:00P	TH29 9:45A	TH29 11:00P

JUNE WESTBOUND

Leave VALDEZ	Leave SEWARD	Leave KODIAK	PORT LIONS	Leave HOMER	Arrive SELDOVIA
F2 6:30A	F2 9:30P	S3 12:45P	S3 3:45P	SU4 3:30A	SU4 4:55A
		SU4 10:30P		Ar. M5 8:00A	
		M5 10:30P		T6 12:30P	T6 2:00P
		W7 4:55P	***TO ALEUTIAN CHAIN TRIP***		
		M12 10:30P		T13 12:30P	T13 2:00P
F16 6:30A	F16 9:30P	S17 12:45P	S17 3:45P	SU18 3:30A	SU18 4:55A
		SU18 10:30P		Ar. M19 8:00A	
		M19 10:30P		T20 12:30P	T20 2:00P
F23 6:30A	F23 9:30P	S24 12:45P	S24 3:45P	SU25 3:30A	SU25 4:55A
		SU25 10:30P		Ar. M26 8:00A	
		M26 10:30P		T27 12:30P	T27 2:00P
F30 6:30A	F30 9:30P	S1 12:45P	S1 3:45P	SU2 3:30A	SU2 4:55A

JULY EASTBOUND

Leave SELDOVIA	Leave HOMER	PORT LIONS	Arrive KODIAK	Leave SEWARD	Arrive VALDEZ
SU2 6:00A	SU2 9:30A		SU2 7:00P		
	M3 9:30A		M3 7:00P		
T4 4:00P	T4 7:55P	W5 6:30A	Lv. W5 4:00P	TH6 9:45A	TH6 11:00P
SU9 6:00A	SU9 9:30A		SU9 7:00P		
	M10 9:30A		M10 7:00P		
T11 4:00P	T11 7:55P	W12 6:30A	W12 4:00P	TH13 9:45A	TH13 11:00P
SU16 6:00A	SU16 9:30A		SU16 7:00P		
	M17 9:30A		M17 7:00P		
T18 4:00P	T18 11:30P		W19 9:00A		
FROM ALEUTIAN CHAIN TRIP			M24 8:15P		
T25 4:00P	T25 7:55P	W26 6:30A	Lv. W26 4:00P	TH27 9:45A	TH27 11:00P
SU30 6:00A	SU30 9:30A		SU30 7:00P		

JULY WESTBOUND

Leave VALDEZ	Leave SEWARD	Leave KODIAK	PORT LIONS	Leave HOMER	Arrive SELDOVIA
		SU2 10:30P		Ar. M3 8:00A	
		M3 10:30P		T4 12:30P	T4 2:00P
F7 6:30A	F7 9:30P	S8 12:45P	S8 3:45P	SU9 3:30A	SU9 4:55A
		SU9 10:30P		Ar. M10 8:00A	
		M10 10:30P		T11 12:30P	T11 2:00P
F14 6:30A	F14 9:30P	S15 12:45P	S15 3:45P	SU16 3:30A	SU16 4:55A
		SU16 10:30P		Ar. M17 8:00A	
		M17 10:30P		T18 12:30P	T18 2:00P
		W19 4:55P	***TO ALEUTIAN CHAIN TRIP***		
		M24 10:30P		T25 12:30P	T25 2:00P
F28 6:30A	F28 9:30P	S29 12:45P	S29 3:45P	SU30 3:30A	SU30 4:55A
		SU30 10:30P		Ar. M31 8:00A	

AUGUST EASTBOUND

Leave SELDOVIA	Leave HOMER	PORT LIONS	Arrive KODIAK	Leave SEWARD	Arrive VALDEZ
	M31 9:30A		M31 7:00P		
T1 4:00P	T1 7:55P	W2 6:30A	Lv. W2 4:00P	TH3 9:45A	TH3 11:00P
SU6 6:00A	SU6 9:30A		SU6 7:00P		
	M7 9:30A		M7 7:00P		
T8 4:00P	T8 11:30P		W9 9:00A		
FROM ALEUTIAN CHAIIN TRIP			M14 8:15P		
T15 4:00P	T15 7:55P	W16 6:30A	Lv. W16 4:00P	TH17 9:45A	TH17 11:00P
SU20 6:00A	SU20 9:30A		SU20 7:00P		
	M21 9:30A		M21 7:00P		
T22 4:00P	T22 7:55P	W23 6:30A	Lv. W23 4:00P	TH24 9:45A	TH24 11:00P
SU27 6:00A	SU27 9:30A		SU27 7:00P		
	M28 9:30A		M28 7:00P		
T29 4:00P	T29 7:55P	Lv. W306:30A	Lv. W30 4:00P	TH31 9:45A	TH31 11:00P

AUGUST WESTBOUND

Leave VALDEZ	Leave SEWARD	Leave KODIAK	PORT LIONS	Leave HOMER	Arrive SELDOVIA
		M31 10:30P		T1 12:30P	T1 2:00P
F4 6:30A	F4 9:30P	S5 12:45P	S5 3:45P	SU6 3:30A	SU6 4:55A
		SU6 10:30P		Ar. M7 8:00A	
		M7 10:30P		T8 12:30P	T8 2:00P
		W9 4:55P	***TO ALEUTIAN CHAIN TRIP***		
		M14 10:30P		T15 12:30P	T15 2:00P
F18 6:30A	F18 9:30P	S19 12:45P	S19 3:45P	SU20 3:30A	SU20 4:55A
		SU20 10:30P		Ar. M21 8:00A	
		M21 10:30P		T22 12:30P	T22 2:00P
F25 6:30A	F25 9:30P	S26 12:45P	S26 3:45P	SU27 3:30A	SU27 4:55A
		SU27 10:30P		Ar. M28 8:00A	
		M28 10:30P		T29 12:30P	T29 2:00P

SEPTEMBER EASTBOUND

Leave SELDOVIA	Leave HOMER	PORT LIONS	Arrive KODIAK	Leave SEWARD	Leave CORDOVA	Arrive VALDEZ
SU3 6:00A	SU3 9:30A		SU3 7:00P			
	M4 9:30A		M4 7:00P			
T5 4:00P	T5 11:30P		W6 9:00A			
FROM ALEUTIAN CHAIN TRIP			M11 8:15P			
T12 4:00P	T12 7:55P	W13 6:30A	Lv. W134:00P	TH14 9:45A		TH14 11:00P
SU17 6:00A	SU17 9:30A		SU17 7:00P			
	M18 9:30A		M18 7:30P			
T19 4:00P	T19 7:55P	W20 6:30A	Lv. W204:55P	TH21 9:45A	TH21 11:45P	*F22 7:15A
					S23 9:55P	SU24 3:30A
T26 1:00P	T26 7:55P	W27 6:30A	Lv. W274:55P	TH28 9:45A	TH28 11:45P	F29 5:15A
					S30 9:55P	SU1 3:30A

Whistle stops at Chenega Bay are on Thursdays Between Seward and Valdez arriving Chenega Bay at 2:15PM. Vessel will not stop if there are no reservations.

SEPTEMBER WESTBOUND

Leave VALDEZ	Arrive CORDOVA	Leave SEWARD	Leave KODIAK	PORT LIONS	Leave HOMER	Arrive SELDOVIA
F1 6:30A		F1 9:30P	S2 12:45P	S2 3:45P	SU3 3:30A	SU3 4:55A
			SU3 10:30P		Ar. M4 8:00A	
			M4 10:30P		T5 12:30P	T5 2:00P
			W6 4:55P	***TO ALEUTIAN CHAIN TRIP***		
			M11 10:30P		T12 12:30P	T12 2:00P
F15 6:30A		F15 9:30P	S16 12:45P	S16 3:45P	SU17 3:30A	SU17 4:55A
			SU17 10:30P		Ar. M18 8:00A	
			M18 10:30P		T19 12:30P	T19 2:00P
F22 8:45A	F22 2:15P					
SU24 4:30A	LV *SU241:45P	M25 2:15A	M25 6:00P	M25 9:00P	T26 9:00A	T26 10:30A
F29 8:45A	F29 2:15P					

* SEPTEMBER ONLY - Whistle stops at Tatitlek. Vessel will not stop if there are no reservations.

SOUTHCENTRAL/SOUTHWEST ALASKA PASSENGER & VEHICLE TARIFFS

PASSENGER 12 YEARS & OVER (Meals and Berths NOT included)

BETWEEN / AND	UNALASKA	AKUTAN	FALSE PASS	COLD BAY	KING COVE	SAND POINT	CHIGNIK	KODIAK	PORT LIONS	SELDOVIA	HOMER	SEWARD	WHITTIER	VALDEZ	TATITLEK
AKUTAN	16														
FALSE PASS	46	34													
COLD BAY	62	50	18												
KING COVE	74	66	34	18											
SAND POINT	98	90	58	42	32										
CHIGNIK	132	124	92	76	66	42									
KODIAK	202	194	162	146	136	112	76								
PORT LIONS	202	194	162	146	136	112	76	20							
SELDOVIA	246	240	208	192	180	156	122	52	52						
HOMER	242	236	204	188	176	152	118	48	48	18					
SEWARD	250	242	210	194	184	160	124	54	54	100	96				
WHITTIER	316	308	276	260	250	226	190	120	120	166	162				
VALDEZ	292	286	254	238	226	202	168	98	98	142	138	58	58		
TATITLEK	292	286	254	238	226	202	168	98	98	142	138	58	58	30	
CORDOVA	292	286	254	238	226	202	168	98	98	142	138	58	58	30	30

CHILDREN 2 THROUGH 11 YEARS OLD (Under 2 Transported Free)

BETWEEN / AND	UNALASKA	AKUTAN	FALSE PASS	COLD BAY	KING COVE	SAND POINT	CHIGNIK	KODIAK	PORT LIONS	SELDOVIA	HOMER	SEWARD	WHITTIER	VALDEZ	TATITLEK
AKUTAN	8														
FALSE PASS	24	18													
COLD BAY	32	26	10												
KING COVE	38	34	18	10											
SAND POINT	50	46	30	22	16										
CHIGNIK	66	62	46	38	34	22									
KODIAK	102	98	82	74	68	56	38								
PORT LIONS	102	98	82	74	68	56	38	10							
SELDOVIA	124	120	104	96	90	78	62	26	26						
HOMER	122	118	102	94	88	76	60	24	24	10					
SEWARD	126	122	106	98	92	80	62	28	28	50	48				
WHITTIER	158	154	138	130	126	114	96	60	60	84	82				
VALDEZ	146	144	128	120	114	102	84	50	50	70	70	30	30		
TATITLEK	146	144	128	120	114	102	84	50	50	70	70	30	30	16	
CORDOVA	146	144	128	120	114	102	84	50	50	70	70	30	30	16	16

ALTERNATE MEANS OF CONVEYANCE (Bicycles-Kyaks-Inflatables)

BETWEEN / AND	UNALASKA	AKUTAN	FALSE PASS	COLD BAY	KING COVE	SAND POINT	CHIGNIK	KODIAK	PORT LIONS	SELDOVIA	HOMER	SEWARD	WHITTIER	VALDEZ	TATITLEK
AKUTAN	6														
FALSE PASS	10	8													
COLD BAY	12	10	8												
KING COVE	14	12	10	6											
SAND POINT	18	16	12	9	8										
CHIGNIK	23	18	14	15	13	9									
KODIAK	33	23	18	25	23	20	15								
PORT LIONS	33	23	23	25	23	20	15	6							
SELDOVIA	40	33	23	32	30	26	21	11	11						
HOMER	39	40	33	31	29	26	21	10	10	5					
SEWARD	40	39	40	32	30	27	22	11	11	18	17				
WHITTIER	50	44	42	42	40	37	31	21	21	28	27				
VALDEZ	47	54	52	38	37	33	28	18	18	24	24	10	8		
TATITLEK	47	54	52	38	37	33	28	18	18	24	24	10	8	8	
CORDOVA	47	54	52	38	37	33	28	18	18	24	24	10	8	8	8

TWO-WHEELED MOTORCYCLES (No trailers-Driver not included)

BETWEEN / AND	UNALASKA	AKUTAN	FALSE PASS	COLD BAY	KING COVE	SAND POINT	CHIGNIK	KODIAK	PORT LIONS	SELDOVIA	HOMER	SEWARD	WHITTIER	VALDEZ	TATITLEK
FALSE PASS	38	N													
COLD BAY	52	O	14												
KING COVE	61		28	14											
SAND POINT	197	V	48	35	25										
CHIGNIK	227	E	78	64	55	35									
KODIAK	171	H	139	125	115	209	64								
PORT LIONS	171	I	139	125	115	209	64	15							
SELDOVIA	210	C	176	162	153	132	102	43	43						
HOMER	207	L	174	160	151	130	99	39	39	12					
SEWARD	213	E	178	164	155	135	105	45	45	84	81				
WHITTIER	265	S	232	219	209	189	160	100	100	139	135				
VALDEZ	246		213	199	190	169	139	82	82	121	118	40	29		
TATITLEK	246		213	199	190	169	139	82	82	121	118	40	29	24	
CORDOVA	246		213	199	190	169	139	82	82	121	118	40	29	24	24

All motorcycles must be fully secured on the car deck with tie-downs. It is the responsibility of the owner to ensure this is completed properly. Rope may be obtained from car deck personnel for lashing purposes.

VEHICLES UP TO 10 FEET (Driver NOT included)

BETWEEN / AND	UNALASKA	AKUTAN	FALSE PASS	COLD BAY	KING COVE	SAND POINT	CHIGNIK	KODIAK	PORT LIONS	SELDOVIA	HOMER	SEWARD	WHITTIER	VALDEZ	TATITLEK
FALSE PASS	61	N													
COLD BAY	84	O	23												
KING COVE	99		45	23											
SAND POINT	133	V	79	56	41										
CHIGNIK	181	E	128	105	90	56									
KODIAK	279	H	225	203	188	154	105								
PORT LIONS	279	I	225	203	188	154	105	25							
SELDOVIA	341	C	286	264	249	215	166	69	69						
HOMER	335	L	281	259	214	210	161	64	64	19					
SEWARD	345	E	290	268	253	219	170	73	76	136	131				
WHITTIER	436	S	383	360	345	311	263	165	165	229	223				
VALDEZ	405		350	328	313	279	230	133	133	196	191	68	49		
TATITLEK	405		350	328	313	279	230	133	133	196	191	68	49	39	
CORDOVA	405		350	328	313	279	230	133	133	196	191	68	49	39	39

VEHICLES UP TO 15 FEET (Driver NOT included)

BETWEEN / AND	UNALASKA	AKUTAN	FALSE PASS	COLD BAY	KING COVE	SAND POINT	CHIGNIK	KODIAK	PORT LIONS	SELDOVIA	HOMER	SEWARD	WHITTIER	VALDEZ	TATITLEK
FALSE PASS	104	N													
COLD BAY	142	O	38												
KING COVE	168		72	34											
SAND POINT	226	V	131	93	67										
CHIGNIK	311	E	215	177	151	93									
KODIAK	480	H	384	346	320	262	177								
PORT LIONS	480	I	384	346	320	262	177	39							
SELDOVIA	587	C	492	454	428	369	285	116	116						
HOMER	577	L	482	444	418	359	275	106	106	29					
SEWARD	593	E	498	460	434	376	291	122	122	233	223				
WHITTIER	753	S	657	619	593	535	450	281	281	392	382				
VALDEZ	697		602	564	538	480	395	226	226	337	327	112	72		
TATITLEK	697		602	564	538	480	395	226	226	337	327	112	72	64	
CORDOVA	697		602	564	538	480	395	226	226	337	327	112	72	64	64

VEHICLES UP TO 19 FEET (Driver NOT included)

BETWEEN / AND	UNALASKA	AKUTAN	FALSE PASS	COLD BAY	KING COVE	SAND POINT	CHIGNIK	KODIAK	PORT LIONS	SELDOVIA	HOMER	SEWARD	WHITTIER	VALDEZ	TATITLEK
FALSE PASS	123	N													
COLD BAY	169	O	46												
KING COVE	200		87	41											
SAND POINT	269	V	156	110	80										
CHIGNIK	370	E	257	211	180	110									
KODIAK	571	H	458	412	381	312	211								
PORT LIONS	571	I	458	412	381	312	211	46							
SELDOVIA	699	C	586	540	509	439	339	138	138						
HOMER	687	L	574	528	497	428	327	126	126	35					
SEWARD	706	E	594	548	517	447	347	145	145	277	265				
WHITTIER	896	S	783	737	706	637	536	335	335	467	455				
VALDEZ	830		718	672	641	571	470	269	269	401	389	134	85		
TATITLEK	830		718	672	641	571	470	269	269	401	389	134	85	76	
CORDOVA	830		718	672	641	571	470	269	269	401	389	134	85	76	76

VEHICLES UP TO 21 FEET (Driver NOT included)

BETWEEN / AND	UNALASKA	AKUTAN	FALSE PASS	COLD BAY	KING COVE	SAND POINT	CHIGNIK	KODIAK	PORT LIONS	SELDOVIA	HOMER	SEWARD	WHITTIER	VALDEZ	TATITLEK
FALSE PASS	158	N													
COLD BAY	217	O	59												
KING COVE	257		111	52											
SAND POINT	347	V	201	142	102										
CHIGNIK	477	E	331	272	232	142									
KODIAK	737	H	591	532	492	402	272								
PORT LIONS	737	I	591	532	492	402	272	59							
SELDOVIA	902	C	756	697	657	567	437	177	177						
HOMER	887	L	741	682	642	552	422	162	162	44					
SEWARD	912	E	766	707	667	577	447	187	187	357	342				
WHITTIER	1157	S	1011	952	912	822	692	432	432	602	587				
VALDEZ	1072		926	867	827	737	607	347	347	517	502	172	110		
TATITLEK	1072		926	867	827	737	607	347	347	517	502	172	110	97	
CORDOVA	1072		926	867	827	737	607	347	347	517	502	172	110	97	97

TARIFFS — All fares are one-way. Fares for passengers, vehicles and cabins are all calculated separately and must be added together to determine the total cost of your travel.

Passage and vehicle fares are charged from the port of embarkation to the port of debarkation. Cabin fares are calculated according to the route taken, and may vary from the printed rates depending on the ship and schedules. ***Note: Selected tariff adjustments may be made prior to or during the Summer 2000 season.***

VEHICLE FARES — Vehicle fares are determined by the vehicle's overall length and width. Vehicles 8-1/2 to 9 feet wide will be charged approximately 125% of the listed fare. Vehicles over 9 feet wide will be charged approximately 150% of the listed fare. If you are towing a vehicle, the overall connected length is used to determine fares.

ALL TARIFFS AND RATES ARE QUOTED IN U.S. DOLLARS

VEHICLES OVER 21 FEET — Contact any Marine Highway office for fares. The M/V TUSTUMENA can load vehicles to a maximum length of 40 feet. The M/V BARTLETT will accept vehicles up to 60 feet in length. Please notify your reservation agent at the time of booking if your vehicle is over 6 foot 6 inches in height. Fares for towed vehicles or trailers are calculated at their combined connected length. Vehicles may not be disconnected for travel at separate rates on the same sailing.

MINIMUM 25' RATE — Vehicles with high centers of gravity (commercial highway vans, loaded flat bed trailers) are charged at the 25 ft. rate unless the vehicle is over 25 ft. in which case the appropriate rate for the vehicle length applies. Contact the commerical booking desk (907) 465-8816 for information and reservations.

M/V TUSTUMENA CABIN TARIFFS

FOUR BERTH CABIN - OUTSIDE/COMPLETE FACILITIES

BETWEEN AND	UNALASKA	AKUTAN	FALSE PASS	COLD BAY	KING COVE	SAND POINT	CHIGNIK	KODIAK	PORT LIONS	SELDOVIA	HOMER	SEWARD
AKUTAN	23											
FALSE PASS	80	57										
COLD BAY	109	86	29									
KING COVE	122	129	72	43								
SAND POINT	152	165	108	79	68							
CHIGNIK	194	210	153	124	113	80						
KODIAK	282	295	238	209	194	166	124					
PORT LIONS	282	295	238	209	194	166	124	43				
SELDOVIA	337	350	293	264	250	216	182	96	96			
HOMER	328	342	285	256	242	209	175	88	88	43		
SEWARD	349	362	305	276	262	228	194	98	98	163	155	
VALDEZ	(NO DIRECT SAILINGS)							164	164	216	209	91

FOUR BERTH CABIN - INSIDE/NO FACILITIES

BETWEEN AND	UNALASKA	AKUTAN	FALSE PASS	COLD BAY	KING COVE	SAND POINT	CHIGNIK	KODIAK	PORT LIONS	SELDOVIA	HOMER	SEWARD
AKUTAN	19											
FALSE PASS	66	47										
COLD BAY	91	72	25									
KING COVE	102	108	61	36								
SAND POINT	127	138	91	66	57							
CHIGNIK	162	175	128	103	94	67						
KODIAK	235	246	199	174	162	138	103					
PORT LIONS	235	246	199	174	162	138	103	36				
SELDOVIA	281	292	245	220	208	180	152	80	80			
HOMER	274	285	238	213	202	174	146	73	73	36		
SEWARD	291	302	255	230	218	190	162	82	82	136	129	
VALDEZ	(NO DIRECT SAILINGS)							137	137	180	174	76

TWO BERTH CABIN - OUTSIDE/NO FACILITIES

BETWEEN AND	UNALASKA	AKUTAN	FALSE PASS	COLD BAY	KING COVE	SAND POINT	CHIGNIK	KODIAK	PORT LIONS	SELDOVIA	HOMER	SEWARD
AKUTAN	13											
FALSE PASS	47	33										
COLD BAY	64	51	17									
KING COVE	75	79	45	28								
SAND POINT	100	97	63	46	40							
CHIGNIK	129	129	95	78	68	43						
KODIAK	179	192	158	141	130	110	76					
PORT LIONS	179	192	158	141	130	110	76	28				
SELDOVIA	213	226	192	175	164	140	115	56	56			
HOMER	208	221	187	170	159	136	111	52	52	28		
SEWARD	218	230	196	179	168	144	119	60	60	101	96	
VALDEZ	(NO DIRECT SAILINGS)							103	103	144	140	54

M/V TUSTUMENA ALEUTIAN CHAIN TRIPS

LV	KODIAK	WED	4:55 PM
LV	CHIGNIK	THU	1:00 PM
LV	SAND POINT	FRI	12:30 AM
LV	KING COVE	FRI	9:00 AM
LV	COLD BAY	FRI	11:55 AM
LV	FALSE PASS	FRI	5:30 PM
AR	UNALASKA	SAT	6:30 AM
LV	UNALASKA	SAT	11:45 AM
LV	AKUTAN	SAT	4:00 PM
LV	COLD BAY	SUN	4:45 AM
LV	KING COVE	SUN	7:15 AM
LV	SAND POINT	SUN	3:00 PM
LV	CHIGNIK	MON	1:45 AM
AR	KODIAK	MON	8:15 PM

REFER TO COLOR CODED BARS ON M/V TUSTUMENA SCHEDULE BEGINNING AND ENDING AT KODIAK

M/V BARTLETT / AK RAILROAD SCHEDULE

Effective May 1, 2000

The M/V BARTLETT serves the port of Whittier using the Alaska Railroad shuttle between Portage and Whittier. In Portage, passengers and their vehicles load on an Alaska Railroad flatcar for a 40 minute sight-filled trip through mountain tunnels to Whittier, a former military town. Ferry service from Whittier is available to Cordova and Valdez.

Mid-May 2000, a vehicle tunnel from Portage to Whittier is scheduled to open. Transporting vehicles via the Alaska Railroad between Portage and Whittier will be suspended at that time.

PORTAGE TO WHITTIER*

LV	PORTAGE	1:20 PM
AR	WHITTIER	2:00 PM

WHITTIER TO PORTAGE

LV	WHITTIER	3:30 PM
AR	PORTAGE	4:10 PM

*Check-in time in Portage is one hour earlier than departure.

THE STATE OF ALASKA RESERVES THE RIGHT TO ALTER, REVISE OR CANCEL SCHEDULES AND RATES WITHOUT PRIOR NOTICE AND ASSUMES NO RESPONSIBILITY FOR DELAYS AND/OR EXPENSES DUE TO SUCH MODIFICATIONS.

1-800-642-0066

www.dot.state.ak.us/amhshome.html

SOUTHCENTRAL/SOUTHWEST ALASKA - M/V BARTLETT SCHEDULE

EFFECTIVE MAY 1 - MAY 25 AND SEPTEMBER 3 - SEPTEMBER 22, 2000

*MON	LV CORDOVA	7:00 AM
	AR WHITTIER	2:00 PM
	LV WHITTIER	2:45 PM
	AR CORDOVA	9:45 PM
TUE	LV CORDOVA	12:30 AM
	AR VALDEZ	6:15 AM
	LV VALDEZ	7:15 AM
	AR WHITTIER	2:00 PM
	LV WHITTIER	2:45 PM
	AR VALDEZ	9:30 PM
WED	LV VALDEZ	6:45 AM **
	AR CORDOVA	2:30 PM
	LV CORDOVA	6:30 PM **
THU	AR VALDEZ	2:15 AM
THU	LV VALDEZ	7:15 AM
	AR WHITTIER	2:00 PM
	LV WHITTIER	2:45 PM
	AR VALDEZ	9:30 PM
FRI	LV VALDEZ	12:15 AM
	AR CORDOVA	6:00 AM
	LV CORDOVA	7:00 AM
	AR WHITTIER	2:00 PM
	LV WHITTIER	2:45 PM
	AR CORDOVA	9:45PM
SAT	LV CORDOVA	12:30 AM
	AR VALDEZ	6:15 AM
	LV VALDEZ	7:15 AM
	AR WHITTIER	2:00 PM
	LV WHITTIER	2:45 PM
	AR VALDEZ	9:30 PM
SUN	LV VALDEZ	7:15 AM
	AR WHITTIER	2:00 PM
	LV WHITTIER	2:45 PM
	AR VALDEZ	9:30 PM
	LV VALDEZ	11:45 PM ###
MON	AR CORDOVA	5:30 AM

EFFECTIVE MAY 25 — SEPTEMBER 3, 2000

MON	LV VALDEZ	7:15 AM
	AR WHITTIER	2:00 PM
	LV WHITTIER	2:45 PM
	AR CORDOVA	9:45 PM
MON	LV CORDOVA	10:45 PM **
TUE	AR VALDEZ	6:15 AM
	LV VALDEZ	7:15 AM
	AR WHITTIER	2:00 PM
TUE	LV WHITTIER	2:45 PM
	AR VALDEZ	9:30 PM
	LV VALDEZ	11:45 PM
WED	AR CORDOVA	5:30 AM
WED	LV CORDOVA	7:00 AM
	AR WHITTIER	2:00 PM
	LV WHITTIER	2:45 PM
	AR VALDEZ	9:30PM
THU	LV VALDEZ	7:15 AM
	AR WHITTIER	2:00 PM
	LV WHITTIER	2:45 PM +++
	AR VALDEZ	9:30 PM
FRI	LV VALDEZ	5:00 AM **
	AR CORDOVA	12:45 PM
	LV CORDOVA	6:30 PM
SAT	AR VALDEZ	12:15 AM
SAT	LV VALDEZ	7:15 AM
	AR WHITTIER	2:00 PM
	LV WHITTIER	2:45 PM
	AR VALDEZ	9:30 PM
SUN	LV VALDEZ	7:15 AM
	AR WHITTIER	2:00 PM
	LV WHITTIER	2:45 PM
	AR VALDEZ	9:30 PM

* Schedule begins here May 1, 2000.
** Tatitlek Whistle Stops available by notifying Valdez or Cordova Terminal
+++ Switch to this schedule at Whittier, Thursday May 25.
Switch to this schedule at Valdez, Sunday September 3.

GENERAL INFORMATION

Arctic Circle

The Arctic Circle is the latitude at which the sun never sets on the day of the summer solstice (June 20 or 21) and never rises on the day of the winter solstice (December 21 or 22). In Barrow, the sun shines continually for about 2 months during summer; during winter there are 2 months of darkness. The only light is that of the moon and the aurora borealis (northern lights).

The northern third of Alaska lies within the Arctic Circle—the only true polar region in the state. The Brooks Range separates the Arctic region from the Interior of Alaska and, surprisingly, the temperature in the Interior is often more severe, as the Arctic Ocean has an ameliorating effect on temperatures in the Far North.

Motorists will cross the Arctic Circle in Alaska at **Milepost J 115.3** on the Dalton Highway, where there is a BLM Wayside and interpretive display about the Arctic Circle. In Canada, motorists cross the Arctic Circle at **Milepost J 252** on the Dempster Highway in Yukon Territory. A sign and turnout mark this crossing.

Aurora Borealis

The aurora borealis, or northern lights, are one of the North's greatest attractions. They range from simple arcs to drapery-like forms of light in green, red, blue and purple hues in northern night skies.

The auroras are natural phenomena caused by the presence of charged particles in the earth's magnetic field. For more on auroras, turn to page 409 in the FAIRBANKS section.

Bicycling

Every summer, a number of intrepid travelers decide to explore Alaska by bicycle, whether its a long-distance tour by bike, or just bringing a bike along in the car to ride around the campground. Alaska offers opportunities for both.

If you are planning on doing long-distance bike touring, read the highway logs in *The MILEPOST*® for details on road conditions, grades and highway shoulders.

According to the Alaska Dept. of Transportation, of the more than 1,500 miles of paved highway in the state, a little over 1,000 miles have 4 foot or wider paved shoulders suitable for bicyclists. (Paved routes used by bicyclists in Alaska are the Alaska, Glenn/Tok Cutoff, Haines, Klondike, Parks, Richardson, Seward and Sterling highways.)

Gravel roads don't seem to deter bicycle tourers either. The Denali Highway is a particularly popular route with cyclists. And the Dalton Highway always draws its share of adventurers in summer; those who don't mind cycling about 500 miles of gravel or sharing the road with very large trucks.

Both long-distance bike tourers and those looking for a short bicycle ride can use the more than 100 miles of bike trails in the state. Officially designated "shared-use pathways," these trails are intended for use by pedestrians, bicyclists, joggers, in-line skaters, etc., in summer, and cross-country skiers, dog sledders and others in winter. These paths are particularly well developed along the Parks Highway, including Big Lake Road and Palmer-Wasilla Highway; the Seward Highway (Six-Mile Creek, Bird to Indian, and Bird Point to Girdwood trails); and the Glenn Highway (from Anchorage to Eagle River). With the TRAAK initiative—Trails and Recreation Access for Alaska—more shared-use paths along Alaska's highways and byways are planned. For current information on this program, look at the TRAAK homepage at www.dot.state.ak.us/external/state_wide/planning/traakhome.html

Cities and communities offer plenty of opportunities for bicyclists. Tok, for example, has a couple of miles of shared-use pathways along the Tok Cutoff and the Alaska Highway. Anchorage, Fairbanks and Juneau have extensive bike trail systems. Anchorage, in particular, offers visiting bicyclists miles of scenic trails. Especially popular is the 11-mile-long Tony Knowles Coastal Trail from downtown to Kincaid Park along Knik Arm.

Read the community descriptions and highway logs throughout *The MILEPOST*® for ideas on where to go on a day bike trip. For example, just outside Anchorage at Eklutna Lake State Park, bicyclists can ride the wide, flat trail around the lake. Last summer, a concessionaire at the lake was offering rental bikes to ride 1-way around the lake and a barge trip the other way.

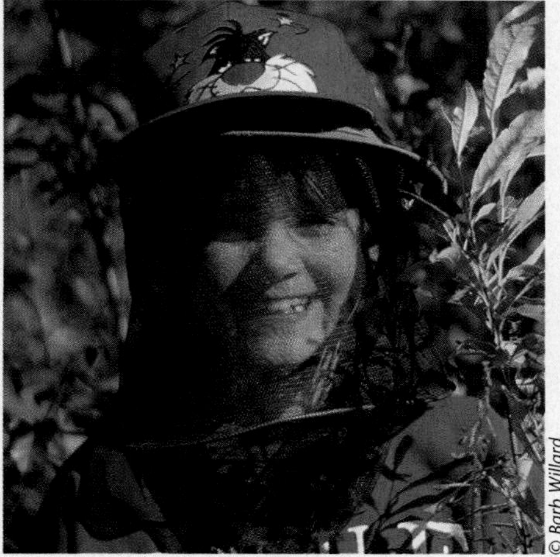

© Barb Willard

Bugs

The North has its share of pesky insects. Black flies are present from May until freeze-up; snipe flies are found during the summer months north to the Alaska Range. No-see-ums swarm in coastal areas from June to August. Mosquitoes are perhaps the most widespread and persistent of insects in the North.

Mosquitoes emerge from hibernation in early spring and are present through the fall. They hatch their eggs in water, so the North—with its marshy tundra and many lakes—is a good breeding ground.

Mosquitoes are especially active in the early morning and at dusk. They are attracted to warmth, moisture, carbon dioxide and dark colors, among other things.

Mosquito repellents containing diethyl-meta-toluamide (DEET) are recommended by the USDA. Apply to all exposed skin. Mosquitoes can bite through thin material, such as a cotton shirt, so wear heavier protection when and where mosquitoes are active. The USDA also recommends a liightweight parka, tight fitting at the wrists, with a drawstring hood to fit snugly around the face, and trousers tucked securely into socks, to reduce mosquito bites.

Choose a campsite away from mosquito-breeding areas. A 5-mph wind grounds most mosquitoes, so position your camp where it may get a breeze.

Fishing

The biggest challenge for fishermen visiting Alaska and northwestern Canada is the sheer number and variety of fishing opportunities available. The following information is designed to help figure out the what, when, where and how of your fishing trip.

Fishermen are advised to first identify whether they want to fish fresh water or salt water and their desired species. Salmon are the most popular sport fish in Alaska, with all 5 species of Pacific salmon found here: King (chinook), silver (coho), pink (humpy), chum (dog) and red (sockeye). Salmon are anadromous, spawning in fresh water and maturing in the sea. King salmon fishing in Southeast is restricted to salt water. Silver and pink salmon can be taken in fresh water and salt water. Reds are taken in freshwater streams. Large landlocked lakes have populations of kokanee (landlocked red salmon).

Other sport fish include halibut, rainbow trout and steelhead, Dolly Varden and Arctic char, cutthroat and brook trout, northern pike, and lake trout.

Halibut, a saltwater fish that can weigh more than 300 pounds, is the largest fish in Alaska that a fisherman is likely to catch. The Pacific halibut is also the best known member of the "bottomfish" family, a catch-all term for non-salmon fish that includes lingcod, rockfish and a variety of other species.

Rainbows are a freshwater trout, the sea-run of which is the steelhead. Cutthroat are common on the mainland and every major island in Southeastern Alaska, occurring in both fresh water (non-seagoing) and salt water (sea-going). Dolly Varden and Arctic char also both have populations that go to sea and do not, which spawn in streams and migrate to sea in the spring to feed, and may be either a saltwater or freshwater sportfish. Eastern brook trout is an introduced species to freshwater lakes.

Northern pike (also called pike, jack fish and pickerel) are widely distributed throughout most of Alaska except southeastern. The northern pike is the most sought-after indigenous sport fish in Interior Alaska after the Arctic grayling. Alaska's Interior also has the largest Arctic grayling fishery in North America. These popular game fish are the main sport fish species in the Tanana River drainage.

If you know what kind of fish you want, that may also determine when to go. Although most fishing enthusiasts focus their trips between April and October, when the weather is generally more mild, the fish have something to say about timing. The Alaska Dept. of Fish and Game Sportfish Division gives a run timing for all fisheries by region.

Where to fish is probably the most difficult choice, with the number of fishing destinations available well beyond the capability of most anglers to visit. The list of possible fishing spots is also beyond our capability to list here. Throughout *The MILEPOST®* you will find this friendly little symbol. Wherever you see one, you will find a description of the fishing at that point. Fishing spots are also listed under Area Fishing in the Attractions section of each community covered in *The MILEPOST®*.

The Alaska Dept. of Fish and Game has literally hundreds of pamphlets on fishing regional waters. Particularly helpful is their "Sportfishing Alaska" brochure, which shows run times and also lists area office phone numbers. Or write the Sport Fish Division, Box 25526, Juneau, AK 99802-5526; phone (907) 465-4180. Information is also posted on their web site at www.state.ak.us/local/akpages/FISH.GAME/adfghome.htm. Online licensing is available as well.

While you may fish any body of water with fish in it, local knowledge greatly increases your chances of success. Many fishing guides and charter operators advertise in *The MILEPOST®*.

Glaciers

Alaska-bound travelers interested in seeing glaciers are certainly headed in the right direction. Although these rivers of ice exist in other areas of the United States, chiefly in the Pacific Northwest, one typical valley glacier system in Alaska is larger than those of all the other states combined. Changes in the appearance of a particular glacier may be imperceptible to the human eye, but constant motion is occurring within, the downhill flow dictated by gravity, and advances, retreats and surges triggered by complex factors such as water pressure, earthquakes, snow accumulation, avalanches, plasticity and temperature changes.

Glaciers are visible along almost every highway in the state. Motorists can enjoy close encounters with Mendenhall, Matanuska, Portage and Worthington glaciers as well as countless others, while travelers on cruise ships and airliners are rewarded with views of the mind-boggling icefields of Columbia, Bering and Malaspina glaciers and the wonders of Glacier Bay.

Portage Glacier, 48 miles south of Anchorage, has a fine visitor center and boat tour. Exit Glacier, 132 miles south of Anchorage, can be approached by paved trail. Matanuska Glacier, about 100 miles northeast of Anchorage, has several excellent vantage points for viewing. Worthington, 29 miles north of Valdez, looms right over the Richardson Highway. Highly accessible Mendenhall Glacier is just a short drive out of Juneau.

Many summer sightseeing cruises offer opportunities to view Alaska's glaciated coastline in Prince William Sound, Glacier Bay and Kenai Fjords National Park. See ads in Inside Passage, Glacier Bay, Seward Highway and Prince William Sound sections for information on glacier cruises. Also see Scheduled Day Cruises on page 11 in the TRAVEL PLANNING section.

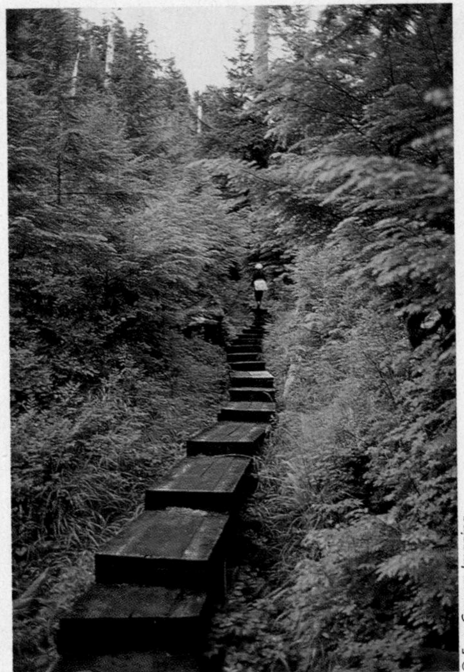

© Four Corners Imaging

Hiking

Alaska State Parks, the U.S. Forest Service, and Bureau of Land Management maintain most of the established trails within Alaska. *The MILEPOST®* notes all trailheads along roads and highways in the highway logs, and popular hiking trails accessible from a major city are usually noted under Attractions in that community. Check trail conditions locally before hiking.

Within the Alaska state park system, Chugach State Park outside of Anchorage has the most extensive trail system, with more than 200 miles of hiking trails (see page XXX in the ANCHORAGE section). Kachemak Bay State Park, across the water from Homer, also has a fairly extensive trail system.

Tongass National Forest in Southeast Alaska has almost 600 miles of trails.

Chugach National Forest offers some 200 miles of trail, including an extensive system of hiking trails on the Kenai Peninsula, maintained by the Glacier and Seward Ranger districts. The most popular trail is the Resurrection Pass trail, a 38.6-mile/62.1-km trail that follows Resurrection Creek from Hope up Resurrection Pass then down Juneau Creek to the Sterling Highway.

Other popular Kenai Peninsula trails are Johnson Pass USFS Trail (which follows a portion of the Iditarod National Historic Trail), Crow Pass (a Chugach State Park trail that also follows a portion of the Iditarod National Historic Trail), Russian Lakes and Ptarmigan Creek USFS trails. There are USFS public-use cabins along many of the trails; these must be reserved in advance. See the STERLING HIGHWAY and SEWARD HIGHWAY for trailhead locations.

The Alaska Public Lands Information Center, 605 W. 4th, Anchorage, AK 99501, has general information on hiking in all public lands in Alaska. The USDA Forest Service Supervisor and District Ranger offices have trail maps and detailed information on hiking trails in Tongass and Chugach national forests.

Most national parklands in Alaska have no established trail systems, instead offering cross-country hiking or—depending on the terrain—bushwacking. An exception is the 33-mile Chilkoot Trail out of Skagway, managed by the National Park Service. See "National Parks" this section.

The BLM's White Mountains National Recreation Area north of Fairbanks has more than 200 miles of winter trails and 20 miles of summer hiking trails. The BLM also manages the 27-mile Pinnell Mountain National Recreation Trail—the first national recreation trail established in the state—located within Steese National Conservation Area outside Fairbanks. See both the ELLIOTT HIGHWAY and STEESE HIGHWAY sections.

Yukon Territory has established wilderness trails, too. Information about hiking in Kluane National Park Reserve is available from Parks Canada, Canadian Heritage, 300 Main St., Room 105, Whitehorse, YT Y1A 2B5. For other hiking trails in the Yukon, contact Tourism Yukon, Box 2703, Whitehorse, YT Y1A 2C6, phone (867) 667-5340.

Holidays

The following list of observed holidays for 2000 in Alaska and Canada can help you plan your trip. Keep in mind that banks and other agencies may be closed on these holidays and traffic may be heavier.

Alaska

New Year's Day	Jan. 1
Martin Luther King Day	Jan. 17
Presidents' Day	Feb. 21
Seward's Day	March 29
Easter Sunday	April 23
Memorial Day	May 28
Independence Day	July 4
Labor Day	Sept. 4
Columbus Day	Oct. 9
Alaska Day	Oct. 18
Veterans Day	Nov. 11
Thanksgiving Day	Nov. 23
Christmas Day	Dec. 25

Canada

New Year's Day	Jan. 1
Good Friday	April 21
Easter Monday	April 24
Victoria Day	May 22
Canada Day	July 1
Civic Holiday	Aug. 7
Labour Day	Sept. 4
Thanksgiving Day	Oct. 9
Remembrance Day	Nov. 11
Christmas Day	Dec. 25
Boxing Day	Dec. 26

Internet

The MILEPOST® includes Internet addresses when available. You may also visit our website at www.themilepost.com.

All of our print advertisers are listed on our web site. Many of those who also advertise on our web site—or link to it—feature this icon in their print ad.

Metric System

Canada is on the metric system. Equivalent metric measurements follow miles, feet, yards and temperatures in *The MILEPOST®*. Equivalents are: 1 mile=1.609 kilometers; 1 kilometre=0.62 miles; 1 yard=0.9144 meters; 1 metre=39.37 inches.

National Parks

Denali National Park and Preserve is one of 15 national park units in Alaska. Parklands range from the remote Bering Land

Bridge National Preserve on the Bering Sea to Skagway's Klondike Gold Rush National Historical Park, one of the state's most visited attractions.

The MILEPOST® has detailed information on Denali National Park and Glacier Bay National Park. Other national parks in Alaska covered in *The MILEPOST®* (see the index) are: Wrangell-St. Elias National Park, Kenai Fjords National Park; Sitka National Historical Park and Klondike Gold Rush National Historial Park; and Yukon–Charley Rivers National Park.

On-line information is available on the National Park Service's World Wide Web pages (www.nps.gov) for the following national parks in Alaska: Aniakchak (/ania); Bering Land Bridge (/bela); Cape Krusenstern (/cakr); Denali (/dena); Gates of the Arctic (/gaar); Glacier Bay (/glba); Katmai (/katm); Kenai Fjords (/kefj)/ Klondike Gold Rush (/klgo); Kobuk Valley (/kobu); Lake Clark (/lacl); Noatak (/noat); Sitka (/sitk); Wrangell-St. Elias (/wrst) and Yukon–Charley Rivers (/yuch).

Or contact the Alaska Public Lands Information Centers in Anchorage, AK at 605 W. 4th Ave., Suite 105, Anchorage 99510, phone (907) 271-2737; Fairbanks, AK at 250 Cushman St., Suite 1A, Fairbanks 99701, phone (907) 456-0527; or Ketchikan at 50 Main St., Ketchikan, AK 99901, phone (907) 228-6214.

Rules of the Road

Regulations common to Alaska, Alberta, British Columbia, Northwest Territories and Yukon Territory include: Right turn on red permitted after complete stop, unless prohibited by sign; transporting open alcoholic beverage containers within a motor vehicle is prohibited.

Following are rules and regulations in effect in Alaska and northwestern Canada at our presstime:

ALASKA

Headlight use: One-half hour after sunset to one-half hour before sunrise. Driving with headlights on during all hours of the day is permitted. Headlights required at all times on designated roadways where speed is in excess of 45 mph.

Minimum driver's age: 16 years; 14 with driver's permit if accompanied by a licensed driver 19 years or older.

Rest area camping: Permitted as posted.

Seat belts: Seat belts are mandatory for all drivers and passengers. Child restraints are mandatory for children under 7 years. Applies to out-of-state drivers also.

Studded tires: Permitted from Sept. 15 to May 1 (Sept. 30 to April 15 south of 60°N).

Motorcycles: Protective glasses, goggles or windscreen required. Reflectorized helmet required if under 19 and for passenger.

CB Radio: The following channels may be monitored: 2,9,11,14,19, 21 and 22.

Firearms: Permitted. Unlawful to discharge firearm on, from or across the driveable portion of any roadway including roadway shoulders.

Trailers: Independent braking system not required for trailers where gross weight is less than 3,000 lbs. Riding in trailer is prohibited, but riding in pickup/camper is permitted.

ALBERTA

Headlight use: When light conditions restrict visibility to 500 feet/150m or less. Driving with headlights on during all hours of the day is permitted.

Minimum driver's age: 16 years; 14 to receive learner's permit.

Rest area camping: Prohibited unless otherwise designated.

Seat belts: Seat belts are mandatory for all drivers. Child restraints are mandatory for children under 6 years or 18kg (40 lbs.). Applies to out-of-province drivers also.

Studded tires: Permitted year-round but only where marked or posted within federal parks.

Motorcycles: Safety helmet required.

CB Radio: Channel 9 is monitored for emergencies.

Firearms: Rifles must be unloaded and safely stored in trunk. Pistols must be carried in a secure storage box, unloaded, trigger locked and safely stored in trunk.

Trailers: Independent braking system not required for trailers where gross weight is less than 909 kg (2,000 lbs.) and is less than half that of towing vehicle. Riding in trailer prohibited.

BRITISH COLUMBIA

Minimum driver's age: Driver's license divided into 6 classes—age 19 for class 1, 2 and 4; 18 for class 3; 16 for classes 5 and 6.

Rest area camping: Prohibited.

Seat belts: Seat belts are mandatory for driver and all passengers. Child restraints are mandatory for children under 6 years. Applies to out-of-province drivers also.

Studded tires: Permitted from Oct. 1 to April 30.

Motorcycles: Safety helmet required.

CB Radio: Not monitored for emergencies.

Firearms: All rifles and shotguns must be declared at the border. Pistols are prohibited; strictly enforced.

Trailers: Independent braking system not required for trailers where gross weight is less than 2,000 kg (4,400 lbs.) and is less than 40 percent of licensed weight of towing vehicle. Riding in trailer prohibited.

NORTHWEST TERRITORIES

Minimum driver's age: 16 years, 15 with learner's permit.

Rest area camping: Prohibited.

Seat belts: Seat belts are mandatory for driver and all passengers. Child restraints are mandatory for children less than 18 kg (40 lbs.). Applies to out-of-territory drivers also.

Studded tires: Tires that are manufactured as studded tires are permitted year-round for passenger vehicles.

Motorcycles: Safety helmet required for driver and passenger.

CB Radio: Channel 9 or 19 is monitored for emergencies.

Firearms: Contact the Canadian Firearms Centre, phone 1-800-731-4000.

Trailers: Independent braking system not required for trailers where gross weight is less than 1,360 kg (2,992 lbs.) and is less than half of licensed weight of towing vehicle. Riding in trailer prohibited, but riding in pickup/camper is permitted.

YUKON TERRITORY

Minimum driver's age: 16 years, 15 with learner's permit.

Rest area camping: Prohibited.

Seat belts: Seat belts are mandatory for driver and all passengers. Child restraints are mandatory for children 6 and under weighing less than 18 kg (40 lbs.). Applies to out-of-territory drivers also.

Studded Tires: No restrictions.

Motorcycles: Safety helmet required.

CB Radio: Channel 9 may be monitored for emergencies.

Firearms: No regulations on firearms in vehicles.

Trailers: Independent braking system not required for trailers where gross weight is less than 910 kg (2002 lbs.) and is less than half of licensed weight of towing vehicle. Riding in trailer prohibited.

Wildlife

The MILEPOST® road logs point out wildlife viewing spots along the highways where travelers have a good chance of seeing Dall sheep, moose, caribou, mountain goats, and other mammals and birds.

Besides the chance encounter with wildlife along the roads or in the parks, Alaska offers several opportunities for planned wildlife viewing.

Formal bear viewing areas include: Pack Creek bear observatory on Admiralty Island (permit required, fly-in or boat-in from Sitka or Juneau); Anan Bear Observatory (fly-in or boat-in from Wrangell); McNeil River State Game Sanctuary (permit required, fly-in from Homer or Anchorage); and Brooks Falls/Katmai National Park (fly-in from Homer and Anchorage). Visitors are most likely to see brown/grizzly bears in Denali National Park and on Kodiak Island.

Bird watching events are held in Cordova (Copper River Delta Shorebird Festival) and Homer (Kachemak Bay Shorebird Festival), in May; and in Haines (Bald Eagle Festival) in November).

Eagles and other birds may also be seen at the Raptor Rehabilitation Center in Sitka.

Summer sightseeing cruises and ferry trips along Alaska's coastline provide a great opportunity to see marine mammals and birds.

Visitors may not see North America's largest rodent while traveling in Alaska, but they probably will see its work: Beaver dams reaching 15 feet in height and hundreds of feet in length are not uncommon.

Much more visible are 2 members of the squirrel familiy: the arctic ground squirrel and the hoary marmot. There's also a good chance of seeing snowshoe hare, especially during cyclical population highs.

Moose and caribou are commonly spotted from the road.

Bears may be encountered anywhere in Alaska, from a remote campground to a city park in Anchorage. Pay attention to bear alerts posted at trailheads and in campgrounds. Keep a clean campsite. When hiking, make a lot of noise and avoid dense brush.

For a close-up look at large Alaska mammals, try the Alaska Zoo in Anchorage; the Musk Ox Farm in Palmer; and Big Game Alaska on the Seward Highway.

Best rules for observing all wildlife, especially the larger mammals: Keep your distance and do not feed them. Contact the Alaska Dept. of Fish and Game for more information on wildlife watching.

Communities, Highways, National Parks (NP), National Recreation Areas (NRA), National Wildlife Refuges (NWR), State Parks (SP), State Historic Parks (SHP), State Recreation Areas (SRA), State Recreation Sites (SRS), other attractions.

(*Detailed map.)